P9-CEB-624

S. Pub.112-12

2011-2012

OFFICIAL CONGRESSIONAL DIRECTORY

112TH CONGRESS

CONVENED JANUARY 5, 2011

JOINT COMMITTEE ON PRINTING
UNITED STATES CONGRESS

UNITED STATES GOVERNMENT PRINTING OFFICE
WASHINGTON, DC

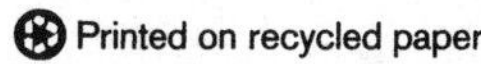

Printed on recycled paper

Front Cover

Birdseye View of the City of Washington, with the Capitol in the Foreground

Drawn by George Henry Andrews and published in *The Illustrated London News* on May 25, 1861, this detail of his wood engraving shows the partially constructed cast-iron Capitol Dome with the unfinished Washington Monument in the distance at the beginning of the Civil War.

U.S. GOVERNMENT OFFICIAL EDITION NOTICE

Use of ISBN Prefix

This is the Official U.S. Government edition of this publication and is herein identified to certify its authenticity. Use of the 0-16 ISBN prefix is for U.S. Government Printing Office Official Editions only. The Superintendent of Documents of the U.S. Government Printing Office requests that any reprinted edition clearly be labeled as a copy of the authentic work with a new ISBN.

ISBN 13: 978-1-60175-860-6 (paperback)

ISBN 13: 978-1-60175-859-0 (cloth)

NOTES

Closing date for compilation of the Congressional Directory was September 15, 2011.

[Democrats in roman, Republicans in *italic*.]

The following changes have occurred in the membership of the 112th Congress since the election of November 2, 2010:

Name	Resigned or [Died]	Successor	Elected or [Appointed]	Sworn in
SENATOR				
John Ensign, NV	May 3, 2011	*Dean Heller*	[May 3, 2011]	May 9, 2011
REPRESENTATIVES				
Christopher John Lee, 26th NY	Feb. 9, 2011	Kathleen C. Hochul	May 24, 2011	June 1, 2011
Jane Harman, 36th CA	Feb. 28, 2011	Janice Hahn	July 12, 2011	July 19, 2011
Dean Heller, 2nd NV [1]	May 9, 2011	*Mark E. Amodei*	Sept. 13, 2011	Sept. 15, 2011
Anthony D. Weiner, 9th NY	June 21, 2011	*Robert L. Turner*	Sept. 13, 2011	Sept. 15, 2011
David Wu, 1st OR	Aug. 3, 2011			

[1] Resigned having been appointed to the United States Senate.

[Democrats in roman, Republicans in *italic*.]

The following changes occurred in the membership of the 111th Congress since the election of November 4, 2008:

Name	Resigned, [Died] or {Term Ended}	Successor	Elected or [Appointed]	Sworn in
SENATORS				
Roland Burris, IL [1]			[Dec. 31, 2008]	Jan. 15, 2009
Joseph R. Biden, Jr., DE [2]	Jan. 15, 2009	Edward E. Kaufman	[Jan. 15, 2009]	Jan. 16, 2009
Hillary Rodham Clinton, NY [3]	Jan. 21, 2009	Kirsten E. Gillibrand	[Jan. 26, 2009]	Jan. 27, 2009
Ken Salazar, CO [4]	Jan. 21, 2009	Michael F. Bennet	[Jan. 21, 2009]	Jan. 22, 2009
Arlen Specter, PA [5]				
Al Franken, MN			Nov. 4, 2008 [6]	July 7, 2009
Edward M. Kennedy, MA	[Aug. 25, 2009]	Paul G. Kirk, Jr. [7]	[Sept. 24, 2009]	Sept. 25, 2009
Mel Martinez, FL	Sept. 9, 2009	*George S. LeMieux*	[Sept. 9, 2009]	Sept. 10, 2009
Paul G. Kirk, Jr., MA [8]	{Feb. 4, 2010}	*Scott P. Brown*	Jan. 19, 2010	Feb. 4, 2010
Robert C. Byrd, WV	[June 28, 2010]	Carte P. Goodwin	[July 16, 2010]	July 20, 2010
Carte P. Goodwin, WV [9]	{Nov. 15, 2010}	Joe Manchin III	Nov. 2, 2010	Nov. 15, 2010
Edward E. Kaufman, DE [10]	{Nov. 15, 2010}	Christopher A. Coons	Nov. 2, 2010	Nov. 15, 2020
Roland Burris, IL [11]	{Nov. 29, 2010}	*Mark Steven Kirk* [11]	Nov. 2, 2010	Nov. 29, 2010
REPRESENTATIVES				
Rahm Emanuel, 5th IL [12]	Jan. 2, 2009	Mike Quigley	Apr. 7, 2009	Apr. 21, 2009
Kirsten E. Gillibrand, 20th NY [13]	Jan. 26, 2009	Scott Murphy	Mar. 31, 2009	Apr. 29, 2009
Hilda Solis, 32d CA [14]	Feb. 24, 2009	Judy Chu	July 14, 2009	July 16, 2009
Ellen O. Tauscher, 10th CA [15]	June 26, 2009	John Garamendi	Nov. 3, 2009	Nov. 5, 2009
John M. McHugh, 23d NY [16]	Sept. 21, 2009	William L. Owens	Nov. 3, 2009	Nov. 6, 2009
Parker Griffith, 5th AL [17]				
Robert Wexler, 19th FL	Jan. 4, 2010	Theodore E. Deutch	Apr. 13, 2010	Apr. 15, 2010

Name	Resigned, [Died] or {Term Ended}	Successor	Elected or [Appointed]	Sworn in
John P. Murtha, 12th PA	[Feb. 8, 2010]	Mark S. Critz	May 18, 2010	May 20, 2010
Neil Abercrombie, 1st HI	Feb. 28, 2010	*Charles K. Djou*	May 22, 2010	May 25, 2010
Eric J. J. Massa, 29th NY	Mar. 8, 2010	*Tom Reed*	Nov. 2, 2010	Nov. 18, 2010
Nathan Deal, 9th GA	Mar. 21, 2010	*Tom Graves*	June 8, 2010	June 14, 2010
Mark E. Souder, 3rd IN	May 21, 2010	*Marlin A. Stutzman*	Nov. 2, 2010	Nov. 16, 2010
Mark Steven Kirk, 10th IL[18]	Nov. 29, 2010			

[1] Appointed to this seat after Senator Barack Obama resigned on November 16, 2008, Senator Burris was appointed before the end of the 110th Congress; however, because his credentials were not immediately accepted by the Senate, he was not sworn-in until after the 111th Congress had begun.

[2] Resigned having been elected Vice President of the United States.

[3] Resigned to become Secretary of State.

[4] Resigned to become Secretary of the Interior.

[5] Changed party affiliation from Republican to Democrat on April 30, 2009.

[6] Contested election resolved June 30, 2009.

[7] Following the death of Senator Kennedy, Massachusetts enacted legislation that revised the state's election-only policy; the law authorized the Governor to make a temporary appointment to serve until the special election of January 19, 2010.

[8] The term of Senator Kirk, appointed to this seat after Senator Kennedy died, ended when Senator Brown took the oath of office. Senator Brown was elected in special election to complete the term ending January 3, 2013.

[9] The term of Senator Goodwin, appointed to this seat after Senator Byrd died, ended when Senator Manchin took the oath of office. Senator Manchin was elected in special election to complete the term ending January 3, 2013.

[10] The term of Senator Kaufman, appointed to this seat after Senator Biden resigned, ended when Senator Coons took the oath of office. Senator Coons was elected in special election to complete the term ending January 3, 2015.

[11] The term of Senator Burris, appointed to this seat after Senator Obama resigned, ended when Senator Kirk took the oath of office. Senator Kirk was elected in special election to complete the term ending January 3, 2011.

[12] Representative Emanuel resigned on January 2, 2009, the last full day of the 110th Congress. At that time, he was also a representative-elect for the 111th Congress (which began at noon on January 3, 2009), but he did not take the oath on January 6, 2009, when the 111th Congress was sworn-in, in anticipation of becoming White House Chief of Staff on January 20, 2009.

[13] Resigned having been appointed to the United States Senate.

[14] Resigned to become Secretary of Labor.

[15] Resigned to become Under Secretary of State for Arms Control and International Security.

[16] Resigned to become Secretary of the Army.

[17] Changed party affiliation from Democrat to Republican on December 22, 2009.

[18] Resigned having been elected to the United States Senate.

FOREWORD

The *Congressional Directory* is one of the oldest working handbooks within the United States Government. While there were unofficial directories for Congress in one form or another beginning with the 1st Congress in 1789, the Congressional Directory published in 1847 for the 30th Congress is considered by scholars and historians to be the first official edition because it was the first to be ordered and paid for by Congress. With the addition of biographical sketches of legislators in 1867, the Congressional Directory attained its modern format.

The Congressional Directory is published by the United States Congress in partnership with the Government Printing Office, at the direction of the Joint Committee on Printing under the authority of Title 44, Section 721 of the U.S. Code.

JOINT COMMITTEE ON PRINTING

Gregg Harper, Representative from Mississippi, *Chair*

Charles E. Schumer, Senator from New York, *Vice Chair*

House

Daniel E. Lungren, of California.
Aaron Schock, of Illinois.
Robert A. Brady, of Pennsylvania.
Charles A. Gonzalez, of Texas.

Senate

Patty Murray, of Washington.
Tom Udall, of New Mexico.
Lamar Alexander, of Tennessee.
Saxby Chambliss, of Georgia.

The 2011–2012 Congressional Directory was compiled by the Government Printing Office, under the direction of the Joint Committee on Printing by:

Project Manager.—Evangeline R. Brown.

Editors: Farnsworth Alston; Mary Ann Carter; Regina G. Mitchell.

Typographers: Michael E. Colbert; Margaret Oliver.

Proofreader.—Margaret Ross-Smith.

Special Assistance.—Peter Byrd, former Congressional Staff.

State District Maps.—Election Data Services, Inc.

Representatives' Zip Codes.—House Office of Mailing Services / U.S. Postal Service.

CONTENTS

Name Index on page 1135

	Page
The Vice President	1
Members of Congress, biographies, office listings, district descriptions—arranged by State	
Alabama	2
Alaska	7
Arizona	9
Arkansas	14
California	18
Colorado	46
Connecticut	51
Delaware	55
Florida	57
Georgia	72
Hawaii	80
Idaho	82
Illinois	84
Indiana	95
Iowa	101
Kansas	105
Kentucky	109
Louisiana	114
Maine	119
Maryland	122
Massachusetts	127
Michigan	133
Minnesota	142
Mississippi	148
Missouri	152
Montana	158
Nebraska	160
Nevada	163
New Hampshire	166
New Jersey	168
New Mexico	176
New York	179
North Carolina	195
North Dakota	203
Ohio	205
Oklahoma	215
Oregon	219
Pennsylvania	223
Rhode Island	235
South Carolina	237
South Dakota	242
Tennessee	244
Texas	250
Utah	269
Vermont	272
Virginia	274
Washington	281
Members of Congress, biographies, office listings, district descriptions—arranged by State—Continued	
West Virginia	287
Wisconsin	290
Wyoming	295
American Samoa	297
District of Columbia	297
Guam	298
Northern Mariana Islands	299
Puerto Rico	299
Virgin Islands	300
State Delegations	301
Alphabetical List of Members—Senate	311
Alphabetical List of Members—House	312
Senate, House—Nine-Digit Postal Zip Codes	317
Terms of Service	321
Standing Committees of the Senate	339
Agriculture, Nutrition, and Forestry	339
Subcommittees:	
Commodities, Markets, Trade and Risk Management	339
Conservation, Forestry and Natural Resources	339
Jobs, Rural Economic Growth and Energy Innovation	340
Livestock, Dairy, Poultry, Marketing and Agriculture Security	340
Nutrition, Specialty Crops, Food and Agricultural Research	340
Appropriations	341
Subcommittees:	
Agriculture, Rural Development, Food and Drug Administration, and Related Agencies	341
Commerce, Justice, Science, and Related Agencies	341
Department of Defense	342
Department of Homeland Security	342
Department of the Interior, Environment, and Related Agencies	342
Departments of Labor, Health and Human Services, and Education, and Related Agencies	342
Energy and Water Development	342

	Page
Appropriations—Continued	
Subcommittees—Continued	
Financial Service and General Government	343
Legislative Branch	343
Military Construction and Veterans Affairs, and Related Agencies	343
State, Foreign Operations, and Related Programs	343
Transportation and Housing and Urban Development, and Related Agencies	343
Armed Services	346
Subcommittees:	
Airland	346
Emerging Threats and Capabilities	346
Personnel	346
Readiness and Management Support	347
Seapower	347
Strategic Forces	347
Banking, Housing, and Urban Affairs	351
Subcommittees:	
Economic Policy	351
Financial Institutions and Consumer Protection	351
Housing, Transportation, and Community Development	351
Securities, Insurance, and Investment	352
Security and International Trade and Finance	352
Budget	354
No Subcommittees.	
Commerce, Science, and Transportation	356
Subcommittees:	
Aviation Operations, Safety, and Security	356
Communications and Technology, and the Internet	356
Competitiveness, Innovation, and Export Promotion	356
Consumer Protection, Product Safety, and Insurance	357
Oceans, Atmosphere, Fisheries, and Coast Guard	357
Science and Space	357
Surface Transportation and Merchant Marine Infrastructure, Safety, and Security	357
Energy and Natural Resources	359
Subcommittees:	
Energy	359
National Parks	359
Public Lands and Forests	359
Water and Power	360
Environment and Public Works	361
Subcommittees:	
Children's Health and Environmental Responsibility	361
Clean Air and Nuclear Safety	361
Green Jobs and the New Economy	361
Oversight	361
Superfund, Toxics and Environmental Health	361
Transportation and Infrastructure	362
Water and Wildlife	362
Finance	363
Finance—Continued	
Subcommittees:	
Energy, Natural Resources, and Infrastructure	363
Fiscal Responsibility and Economic Growth	363
Health Care	363
International Trade, Customs, and Global Competitiveness	364
Social Security, Pensions, and Family Policy	364
Taxation and IRS Oversight	364
Foreign Relations	366
Subcommittees:	
African Affairs	366
East Asian and Pacific Affairs	366
European Affairs	366
International Development and Foreign Assistance, Economic Affairs, and International Environmental Protection	366
International Operations and Organizations, Human Rights, Democracy. and Global Women's Issues	367
Near Eastern and South and Central Asian Affairs	367
Western Hemisphere, Peace Corps, and Global Narcotics Affairs	367
Health, Education, Labor, and Pensions	368
Subcommittees:	
Children and Families	368
Employment and Workplace Safety	368
Primary Health and Aging	368
Homeland Security and Governmental Affairs	371
Subcommittees:	
Permanent Subcommittee on Investigations (PSI)	371
Oversight of Government Management, the Federal Workforce, and the District of Columbia (OGM)	371
Federal Financial Management, Government Information, Federal Services, and International Security (FFM)	371
Ad Hoc Disaster Recovery and Intergovernmental Affairs (DRIA)	371
Ad Hoc Contracting Oversight (SCO)	372
Judiciary	374
Subcommittees:	
Administrative Oversight and the Courts	374
Antitrust, Competition Policy and Consumer Rights	374
The Constitution, Civil Rights and Human Rights	374
Crime and Terrorism	374
Immigration, Refugees and Border Security	374
Privacy, Technology and the Law	375
Rules and Administration	377
No Subcommittees.	
Small Business and Entrepreneurship	378

	Page
Small Business and Entrepreneurship—Continued	
No Subcommittees.	
Veterans' Affairs	379
No Subcommittees.	
Select and Special Committees of the Senate	381
Committee on Indian Affairs	381
Select Committee on Ethics	381
Select Committee on Intelligence	382
Special Committee on Aging	382
Democratic Senatorial Campaign Committee	383
Democratic Policy and Communications Center	383
Steering and Outreach Committee	384
Senate Democratic Conference	384
Senate Democratic Media Center	385
National Republican Senatorial Committee	385
Senate Republican Policy Committee	385
Senate Republican Conference	386
Officers and Officials of the Senate	387
President of the Senate	387
President Pro Tempore	387
Majority Leader	387
Assistant Majority Leader	388
Republican Leader	388
Republican Communications Center	388
Office of the Republican Whip	388
Office of the Secretary	389
Office of the Chaplain	390
Office of the Sergeant at Arms	390
Office of the Secretary for the Majority	392
Office of the Secretary for the Minority	392
Office of the Legislative Counsel	392
Office of Senate Legal Counsel	393
Standing Committees of the House	395
Agriculture	395
Subcommittees:	
Conservation, Energy, and Forestry	396
Nutrition and Horticulture	396
General Farm Commodities and Risk Management	396
Livestock, Dairy, and Poultry	396
Rural Development, Research, Biotechnology, and Foreign Agriculture	397
Department Operations, Oversight, and Credit	397
Appropriations	398
Subcommittees:	
Agriculture, Rural Development, Food and Drug Administration, and Related Agencies	398
Commerce, Justice, Science, and Related Agencies	399
Defense	399
Energy and Water Development, and Related Agencies	399
Financial Services and General Government	399
Homeland Security	399
Interior, Environment, and Related Agencies	399
Appropriations—Continued	
Subcommittees—Continued	
Labor, Health and Human Services, Education, and Related Agencies	400
Legislative Branch	400
Military Construction, Veterans' Affairs, and Related Agencies	400
State, Foreign Operations, and Related Programs	400
Transportation, Housing and Urban Development, and Related Agencies	400
Armed Services	402
Subcommittees:	
Emerging Threats and Capabilities	402
Military Personnel	403
Oversight and Investigations	403
Readiness	403
Seapower and Projection Forces	403
Strategic Forces	403
Tactical Air and Land Forces	404
Budget	405
No Subcommittees.	
Education and the Workforce	406
Subcommittees:	
Early Childhood, Elementary and Secondary Education	406
Higher Education and Workforce Training	406
Health, Employment, Labor, and Pensions	407
Workforce Protections	407
Energy and Commerce	409
Subcommittees:	
Commerce, Manufacturing, and Trade	409
Communications and Technology	410
Energy and Power	410
Environment and the Economy	410
Health	411
Oversight and Investigations	411
Ethics	413
No Subcommittees.	
Financial Services	414
Subcommittees:	
Capital Markets and Government Sponsored Enterprises	415
Domestic Monetary Policy and Technology	415
Financial Institutions and Consumer Credit	415
Insurance, Housing and Community Opportunity	416
International Monetary Policy and Trade	416
Oversight and Investigations	416
Foreign Affairs	418
Subcommittees:	
Africa, Global Health, and Human Rights	418
Asia and the Pacific	418
Europe and Eurasia	419
The Middle East and South Asia	419
Oversight and Investigations	419
Terrorism, Nonproliferation, and Trade	419
The Western Hemisphere	419
Homeland Security	421

Page

Homeland Security—Continued
Subcommittees:
Border and Maritime Security ... 421
Counterterrorism and Intelligence ... 421
Cybersecurity, Infrastructure Protection, and Security Technologies ... 421
Emergency Preparedness, Response and Communications ... 422
Oversight, Investigations, and Management ... 422
Transportation Security ... 422
House Administration ... 424
Subcommittees:
Elections ... 424
Oversight ... 424
Judiciary ... 425
Subcommittees:
The Constitution ... 425
Courts, Commercial and Administrative Law ... 425
Crime, Terrorism, and Homeland Security ... 426
Immigration Policy and Enforcement ... 426
Intellectual Property, Competition, and the Internet ... 426
Natural Resources ... 428
Subcommittees:
Energy and Mineral Resources ... 428
Fisheries, Wildlife, Oceans and Insular Affairs ... 429
Indian and Alaska Native Affairs ... 429
National Parks, Forests and Public Lands ... 429
Water and Power ... 429
Oversight and Government Reform ... 431
Subcommittees:
Federal Workforce, U.S. Postal Service and Labor Policy ... 431
Government Organization, Efficiency and Financial Management ... 431
Health Care, District of Columbia, Census and the National Archives ... 432
National Security, Homeland Defense and Foreign Operations ... 432
Regulatory Affairs, Stimulus Oversight and Government Spending ... 432
Tarp, Financial Services and Bailouts of Public and Private Programs ... 432
Technology, Information Policy, Intergovernmental Relations and Procurement Reform ... 432
Rules ... 434
Subcommittees:
Legislative and Budget Process ... 434
Rules and Organization of the House ... 434
Science, Space, and Technology ... 435
Subcommittees:
Energy and Environment ... 435
Investigations and Oversight ... 435
Research and Science Education ... 436
Space and Aeronautics ... 436
Technology and Innovation ... 436
Small Business ... 438
Subcommittees:
Agriculture, Energy and Trade ... 438
Contracting and Workforce ... 438

Page

Small Business—Continued
Subcommittees—Continued
Economic Growth, Tax and Capital Access ... 438
Healthcare and Technology ... 439
Investigations, Oversight and Regulations ... 439
Transportation and Infrastructure ... 440
Subcommittees:
Aviation ... 441
Coast Guard and Maritime Transportation ... 441
Economic Development, Public Buildings, and Emergency Management ... 441
Highways and Transit ... 442
Railroads, Pipelines, and Hazardous Materials ... 442
Water Resources and Environment ... 443
Veterans' Affairs ... 445
Subcommittees:
Disability Assistance and Memorial Affairs ... 445
Economic Opportunity ... 445
Health ... 445
Oversight and Investigations ... 445
Ways and Means ... 447
Subcommittees:
Health ... 447
Human Resources ... 447
Oversight ... 448
Select Revenue Measures ... 448
Social Security ... 448
Trade ... 448

Select and Special Committees of the House ... 451
Permanent Select Committee on Intelligence ... 451
Subcommittees:
Terrorism, Human Intelligence, Analysis and Counterintelligence ... 451
Technical and Tactical Intelligence ... 451
Oversight and Investigations ... 451
House Republican Policy Committee ... 452
House Republican Conference ... 452
Democratic Congressional Campaign Committee ... 453
Democratic Steering and Policy Committee ... 453
Democratic Caucus ... 454

Officers and Officials of the House ... 455
Office of the Speaker ... 455
Office of the Majority Leader ... 455
Office of the Majority Whip ... 456
Office of the Chief Deputy Republican Whip ... 456
Office of the Democratic Leader ... 457
Democratic Leader's Press Office ... 457
Democratic Leader's Floor Office ... 457
Office of the Democratic Whip ... 457
Office of the Assistant Democratic Leader ... 458
Office of the Clerk ... 458
Chief Administrative Officer ... 459
Chaplain ... 459
Office of the House Historian ... 459
Office of Interparliamentary Affairs ... 459
House Information Resources ... 460
Office of the Attending Physician ... 460

	Page
Office of Inspector General	460
Office of the Law Revision Counsel	460
Office of the Legislative Counsel	460
Office of the Parliamentarian	461
Office of the Sergeant at Arms	461
Joint Committees	463
Joint Economic Committee	463
Joint Committee on the Library of Congress	463
Joint Committee on Printing	463
Joint Committee on Taxation	463
Joint Select Committee on Deficit Reduction	466
Assignments of Senators to Committees	467
Assignments of Representatives to Committees	475
Congressional Advisory Boards, Commissions, and Groups	493
United States Air Force Academy Board of Visitors	493
United States Military Academy Board of Visitors	493
United States Naval Academy Board of Visitors	493
United States Coast Guard Academy Board of Visitors	494
British-American Parliamentary Group	494
Canada-United States Interparliamentary Group	494
China-United States Interparliamentary Group	494
Japan-Interparliamentary Group	495
Korea-United States Interparliamentary Group	495
Mexico-United States Interparliamentary Group	495
NATO Parliamentary Assembly	495
Russia-United States Interparliamentary Group	495
Commission on Congressional Mailing Standards	495
Commission on Security and Cooperation in Europe	496
Congressional Award Foundation	497
Congressional Club	497
Executive Board	498
Congressional Executive Commission on China	498
House Democracy Partnership	499
House Office Building Commission	499
Japan-United States Friendship Commission	499
Migratory Bird Conservation Commission	500
Permanent Committee for the Oliver Wendell Holmes Devise Fund	500
United States-China Economic and Security Review Commission	500
Senate National Security Working Group	501
U.S. Association of Former Members of Congress	501
U.S. Capitol Historical Society	502
U.S. Capitol Preservation Commission	502
U.S. House of Representatives Fine Arts Board	503
U.S. Senate Commission on Art	503
Other Congressional Officials and Services	505
Architect of the Capitol	505
Capitol Telephone Exchange	506
Child Care Centers	506
House of Representatives Child Care Center	506
Senate Employees' Child Care Center	506
Combined Airlines Ticket Offices (CATO)	506
Congressional Record Daily Digest	506
Congressional Record Index Office	507
Office of Congressional Accessibility Services	507
Liaison Offices:	
Air Force	507
Army	507
Coast Guard	508
Navy/Marine Corps	508
Government Accountability Office	508
Office of Personnel Management	509
Social Security Administration	509
State Department Liaison Office	509
Veterans' Affairs	509
United States Senate Page School	509
U.S. Capitol Police	510
Statistical Information	513
Votes Cast for Senators	513
Votes Cast for Representatives, Resident Commissioner, and Delegates	514
Sessions of Congress	522
Joint Sessions and Meetings, Addresses to the Senate or the House, and Inaugurations	540
Representatives Under Each Apportionment	556
Impeachment Proceedings	558
Representatives, Senators, Delegates, and Resident Commissioners Serving in the 1st–112th Congresses	560
Political Divisions of the Senate and House from 1855 to 2011	562
Governors of the States, Commonwealth, and Territories—2010	563
Presidents and Vice Presidents and the Congresses Coincident With Their Terms	564
Capitol Buildings and Grounds	565
Legislative Branch Agencies	575
Congressional Budget Office	575
Government Accountability Office	575
U.S. Government Printing Office	576
Library of Congress	580
U.S. Copyright Office, LM 403	582
United States Botanic Garden	583
The Cabinet	585
Executive Branch	587
The President	587
Executive Office of the President	587
Office of the Vice President	587
Council of Economic Advisers	587
Council on Environmental Quality	588
President's Intelligence Advisory Board	589
National Security Council	589
Office of Administration	589
Office of Management and Budget	589
Office of National Drug Control Policy	590
Office of Science and Technology Policy	590

	Page
Executive Office of the President—Continued	
Office of the United States Trade Representative	590
The White House Office	591
Cabinet Affairs	591
Chief of Staff	591
Communications	591
Office of Digital Strategy	591
Domestic Policy Council	591
Office of the First Lady	592
Office of Legislative Affairs	592
Office of Management and Administration	592
National Economic Council	592
Office of the National Security Advisor	592
Office of Presidential Personnel	592
Office of Public Engagement and Intergovernmental Affairs	593
Office of Scheduling and Advance	593
Office of the Staff Secretary	593
White House Counsel	593
President's Commission on White House Fellowships	593
White House Military Office	593
Department of State	595
Office of the Secretary	595
Ambassador-At-Large for War Crimes Issues	595
Office of the Chief of Protocol	595
Office of Civil Rights	595
Office of Coordinator for Counterterrorism	595
Coordinator for Reconstruction and Stabilization	595
Executive Secretariat	595
Office of the Inspector General	596
Bureau of Intelligence and Research	596
Office of Legal Adviser	596
Bureau of Legislative Affairs	596
Policy Planning Staff	596
Bureau of Resource Management	596
Office of the U.S. Global Aids Coordinator	596
Under Secretary for Political Affairs	596
African Affairs	596
East Asian and Pacific Affairs	596
European and Eurasian Affairs	597
Near Eastern Affairs	597
South and Central Asian Affairs	597
Western Hemisphere Affairs	597
International Narcotics and Law Enforcement Affairs	597
International Organization Affairs	597
Under Secretary for Economic, Energy, and Agricultural Affairs	597
Economic, Energy, and Business Affairs	597
Under Secretary for Arms Control and International Security	597
International Security and Nonproliferation	597
Political-Military Affairs	598
Arms Control, Verification and Compliance	598
Department of State—Continued	
Under Secretary for Public Diplomacy and Public Affairs	598
Educational and Cultural Affairs	598
International Information Programs	598
Public Affairs	598
Under Secretary for Management	598
Administration	598
Consular Affairs	598
Diplomatic Security and Office of Foreign Missions	598
Director General of the Foreign Service and Director of Human Resources	599
Foreign Service Institute	599
Information Resource Management	599
Medical Services	599
Overseas Building Operations	599
Under Secretary for Democracy and Global Affairs	599
Democracy, Human Rights and Labor	599
Oceans and International Environmental and Scientific Affairs	599
Population, Refugees and Migration	599
United States Permanent Representative to the United Nations	599
Director of Foreign Assistance	600
United States Diplomatic Offices—Foreign Service	600
List of Chiefs of Mission	600
United States Permanent Diplomatic Missions to International Organizations	603
Department of the Treasury	605
Office of the Secretary	605
Office of the Deputy Secretary	605
Office of the Chief of Staff	605
Office of the General Counsel	605
Office of the Inspector General	606
Office of the Under Secretary for Domestic Finance	606
Office of the Assistant Secretary for Financial Institutions	606
Office of the Assistant Secretary for Financial Markets	606
Office of the Fiscal Assistant Secretary	606
Office of Research and Quantitative Studies	607
Office of the Assistant Secretary for Financial Stability	607
Financial Management Service	607
Bureau of the Public Debt	607
Office of the Under Secretary for International Affairs	607
Office of the Assistant Secretary for International Affairs	608
U.S. Banks	608
Overseas	608
Under Secretary for Terrorism and Financial Intelligence	608
Assistant Secretary for Terrorist Financing	609
Assistant Secretary for Intelligence and Analysis	609
Office of Foreign Assets Control	609
Executive Office for Asset Forfeiture	609

	Page
Department of the Treasury—Continued	
Under Secretary for Terrorism and Financial Intelligence—Continued	
Financial Crimes Enforcement Network (FINCEN)	609
Office of the Assistant Secretary for Economic Policy	609
Office of the Assistant Secretary for Legislative Affairs	609
Office of the Assistant Secretary for Management/Chief Financial Officer	610
Office of the Assistant Secretary for Public Affairs	610
Office of the Assistant Secretary for Tax Policy	610
Bureau of Engraving and Printing	611
Office of the Comptroller of the Currency	611
Internal Revenue Service	611
Office of Thrift Supervision	612
Inspector General for Tax Administration (TIGTA)	612
Office of the Treasurer of the United States	612
United States Mint	613
Department of Defense	615
Office of the Secretary	615
Office of the Deputy Secretary	615
Executive Secretariat	615
General Counsel	615
Operational Test and Evaluation	615
Inspector General	616
Under Secretary of Defense for Acquisition, Technology and Logistics	616
Joint Strike Fighter Program Office	616
Under Secretary of Defense (Comptroller) and Chief Financial Officer	616
Under Secretary of Defense for Personnel and Readiness	616
Under Secretary of Defense for Policy	616
Assistant Secretary for Networks and Information Integration/Chief Information Officer	617
Assistant Secretary for Legislative Affairs	617
Assistant to the Secretary of Defense for Intelligence Oversight	617
Assistant Secretary for Public Affairs	617
Administration and Management	617
Department of Defense Field Activities	617
Defense Media Activity	617
Department of Defense Education Activity	617
Department of Defense Human Resources Activity	618
TRICARE Management Activity	618
Defense Prisoner of War/Missing Personnel Office	618
Office of Economic Adjustment	618
Washington Headquarters Services	618
Joint Chiefs of Staff	618
Office of the Chairman	618
Joint Staff	618
Defense Agencies	619
Ballistic Missile Defense Agency	619
Defense Advanced Research Projects Agency	619
Department of Defense—Continued	
Defense Agencies—Continued	
Defense Commissary Agency	619
Washington Office	619
Defense Contract Audit Agency	619
Defense Finance and Accounting Service	619
Defense Information Systems Agency	620
Defense Intelligence Agency	620
Defense Legal Services Agency	620
Defense Logistics Agency	620
Defense Security Cooperation Agency	620
Defense Security Service	620
Defense Threat Reduction Agency	620
National Geospatial-Intelligence Agency	620
National Security Agency/Central Security Service	620
Joint Service Schools	621
Defense Acquisition University	621
National Defense Intelligence College	621
National Defense University	621
Information Resources Management College	621
Joint Forces Staff College	621
Industrial College of the Armed Forces	621
National War College	621
Uniformed Services University of the Health Sciences	621
Department of the Air Force	623
Secretary of the Air Force	623
SECAF/CSAF Executive Action Group	623
Under Secretary of the Air Force	623
Chief of Staff	623
Deputy Under Secretary for International Affairs	623
Assistant Secretary for Acquisition	624
Deputy Assistant Secretary for Acquisition Integration	624
Deputy Assistant Secretary for Contracting	624
Deputy Assistant Secretary for Science, Technology and Engineering	624
Capability Directorate for Global Power Programs	624
Capability Directorate for Global Reach Programs	624
Capability Directorate for Information Dominance	624
Capability Directorate for Space Programs	624
Directorate for Special Programs	625
Directorate for Air Force Rapid Capabilities	625
Assistant Secretary for Financial Management and Comptroller of the Air Force	625
Principal Deputy Assistant Secretary for Financial Management	625
Deputy Assistant Secretary for Budget	625
Deputy Assistant Secretary for Cost and Economics	625
Deputy Assistant Secretary for Financial Operations	625
Assistant Secretary for Installations, Environment and Logistics	626

Page

Department of Defense—Continued
Department of the Air Force—Continued
Deputy Assistant Secretary for Installations (SAF/IEI) 626
Brac Program Management Office (SAF/IEI–PMO) 626
Air Force Real Property Agency 626
Deputy Assistant Secretary for Environment, Safety and Occupational Health (SAF/IEE) 626
Deputy Assistant Secretary for Logistics (SAF/IEL) 627
Deputy Assistant Secretary for Energy (SAF/IEN) 627
Assistant Secretary for Manpower and Reserve Affairs 627
Deputy Assistant Secretary for Force Management Integration 627
Deputy Assistant Secretary for Reserve Affairs 627
Deputy Assistant Secretary for Strategic Diversity Integration 628
Air Force Review Boards Agency (SAF/MRB) 628
Air Force Board for Correction of Military Records (AFBCMR), SAF/MRBC 628
Air Force Civilian Appellate Review Office (AFCARO), SAF/MRBA 628
Secretary of the Air Force Personnel Council (SAFPC), SAF/MRBP 628
Air Force Personnel Security Appeal Board (PSAB), SAF/MRBS 628
DoD Physical Disability Board of Review (PDBR), SAF/MRBD 628
Chief of Warfighting Integration and Chief Information Officer 628
Deputy Chief of Staff for Intelligence, Surveillance and Reconnaissance (ISR) 629
Deputy Chief of Staff for Logistics, Installations and Mission Support 629
Deputy Chief of Staff for Manpower, Personnel and Services 629
Deputy Chief of Staff for Operations, Plans and Requirements 629
Deputy Chief of Staff for Strategic Plans and Programs 630
Directorate of Studies and Analysis, Assessments and Lessons Learned 630
Strategic Deterrence and Nuclear Integration (A10) 630
Administrative Assistant to the Secretary 630
Auditor General 631
Air Force Audit Agency 631
Chief of Chaplains 631
Air Force Chief of Safety 631
General Counsel 631
Air Force Historian 631
Inspector General 632
Judge Advocate General 632
Legal Operations 632
Directorate of Legislative Liaison 632
National Guard Bureau 633
Office of Public Affairs 633

Page

Department of Defense—Continued
Department of the Air Force—Continued
Air Force Reserve 633
Scientific Advisory Board 633
Air Force Scientist 633
Air Force Office of Small Business Programs 633
Surgeon General 633
Directorate of Test and Evaluation 634
Army and Air Force Exchange Service 634
Washington Office/Office of the Board of Directors 634
Department of the Army 635
Office of the Secretary 635
Office of the Under Secretary 635
Chief of Staff 635
Deputy Under Secretary of the Army 635
Assistant Secretary for Acquisition, Logistics and Technology 635
Assistant Secretary for Civil Works 636
Assistant Secretary for Financial Management and Comptroller 636
Assistant Secretary for Installations, Energy and Environment 636
Assistant Secretary of the Army (Manpower and Reserve Affairs) 636
Assistant Chief of Staff for Installation Management 637
Office of the Administrative Assistant to the Secretary of the Army (OAA) 637
Army Reserve 637
Auditor General 637
Chief Information Officer/G–6 638
Chief of Chaplains 638
Chief of Engineers 638
General Counsel 638
Inspector General 638
Intelligence/G–2 638
The Judge Advocate General 639
Legislative Liaison 639
Liaison Offices 639
Logistics/G–4 639
National Guard Bureau 640
Operations and Plans/G–3/5/7 640
Personnel/G–1 640
Programs/G–8 640
Public Affairs 640
Small Business Programs 641
Major Army Commands 641
U.S. Army Criminal Investigation Command (USACIDC) 641
U.S. Army Forces Command (FORSCOM) 641
U.S. Army Materiel Command (AMC) 641
U.S. Army Special Forces Command 641
U.S. Army Special Operations Command 642
U.S. Army Training and Doctrine Command (TRADOC) 642
Joint Force Headquarters—National Capital Region and Military District of Washington (JFHQ–NCR/MDW) 642
Surgeon General / U.S. Army Medical Command (MEDCOM) 642
Department of the Navy 643

	Page
Department of Defense—Continued	
Department of the Navy—Continued	
Office of the Secretary of the Navy	643
Office of the Under Secretary of the Navy	643
General Counsel	643
Naval Inspector General	643
Office of Information	643
Judge Advocate General	644
Legislative Affairs	644
Assistant Secretary for Financial Management and Comptroller	645
Assistant Secretary for Energy, Installations and Environment	645
Assistant Secretary for Manpower and Reserve Affairs	645
Secretary of the Navy Council of Review Boards	645
Assistant Secretary for Research, Development and Acquisition	645
Chief Information Officer	646
Chief of Naval Operations	646
Bureau of Medicine and Surgery	646
Military Sealift Command	646
Walter Reed National Military Medical Center	646
Naval Air Systems Command	647
Naval Criminal Investigative Service Command	647
Naval District of Washington	647
Naval Facilities Engineering Command	647
Office of Naval Intelligence	647
Naval Sea Systems Command	647
Naval Supply Systems Command	647
Space and Naval Warfare Systems Command Space Field Activity	647
U.S. Naval Academy	647
U.S. Marine Corps Headquarters	647
Marine Barracks	648
Training and Education Command	648
Department of Justice	649
Office of the Attorney General	649
Office of the Deputy Attorney General	649
Office of the Associate Attorney General	650
Office of the Solicitor General	650
Antitrust Division	650
Field Offices	650
Civil Division	651
Appellate Staff	651
Commercial Litigation Branch	651
Consumer Litigation	651
Federal Programs Branch	651
Immigration Litigation	651
Management Programs	652
Torts Branch	652
Civil Rights Division	652
Office of Community Oriented Policing Services	652
Director's Office	652
Administrative Division	653
External Affairs	653
Audit Division	653
Grants Administration Division	653
Grant Monitoring Division	653
Legal Division	653
Department of Justice—Continued	
Office of Community Oriented Policing Services—Continued	
Program/Policy Support and Evaluation	653
Technical Assistance and Training Division	653
Community Relations Service	653
Regional Directors	654
Criminal Division	654
Office of Dispute Resolution	655
Drug Enforcement Administration	655
Financial Management Division	655
Human Resources Division	655
Inspections Division	656
Intelligence Division	656
Operations Division	656
Operational Support Division	656
Field Offices	657
Other DEA Offices	658
Foreign Offices	658
Environment and Natural Resources Division	660
Field Offices	661
Executive Office for Immigration Review (EOIR)	662
Executive Office for United States Attorneys (EOUSA)	662
Executive Office for United States Trustees	663
U.S. Trustees	663
Bureau of Alcohol, Tobacco, Firearms, and Explosives (ATF)	665
Office of the Director	665
Office of Chief Counsel	665
Office of Enforcement Programs and Services	665
Office of Equal Opportunity	665
Office of Field Operations	666
Office of Management/CFO	666
Office of Ombudsman	666
Office of Professional Responsibility and Security Operations	666
Office of Public and Governmental Affairs	666
Office of Science and Technology/CIO	666
Office of Strategic Intelligence and Information	666
Office of Human Resources and Professional Development	666
Federal Bureau of Investigation	666
Office of the Director/Deputy Director/ Associate Deputy Director	667
Office of the Chief Information Officer	667
Criminal Investigations Branch	667
Human Resources Branch	667
National Security Branch	667
Science and Technology Branch	667
Field Divisions	668
Federal Bureau of Prisons (BOP)	669
Office of the Federal Detention Trustee	669
Foreign Claims Settlement Commission	669
Office of Information Policy	669
Office of the Inspector General	670
Regional Audit Offices	670
Regional Investigations Offices	671
INTERPOL-U.S. National Central Bureau	671

	Page
Department of Justice—Continued	
Office of Intergovernmental and Public Liaison	671
Justice Management Division	671
Office of Justice Programs (OJP)	672
Office of the Assistant Attorney General	672
Bureau of Justice Assistance	672
Bureau of Justice Statistics	672
National Institute of Justice	672
Office of Juvenile Justice and Delinquency Prevention	672
Office for Victims of Crime	672
Community Capacity Development Office	673
Office of Administration	673
Office of the Chief Financial Officer	673
Office of the Chief Information Officer	673
Office for Civil Rights	673
Office of Communication	673
Office of the General Counsel	673
Office of Sex Offender Sentencing, Monitoring, Apprehending, Registering, and Tracking	673
Office of Legal Counsel	673
Office of Legal Policy	673
Office of Legislative Affairs	674
National Drug Intelligence Center (NDIC)	674
National Security Division	674
Counterespionage Section	674
Counterterrorism Section	674
Office of Intelligence	674
Office of Justice for Victims of Overseas Terrorism	675
Office of the Pardon Attorney	675
Office of Professional Responsibility	675
Professional Responsibility Advisory Office	675
Office of Public Affairs	675
Tax Division	675
United States Marshals Service (USMS)	676
Equal Employment Opportunity (EEO)	676
Office of the General Counsel (OGC)	676
Office of Inspection (OI)	676
Asset Forfeiture Division (AFD)	676
Financial Services Division (FSD)	676
Human Resources Division (HRD)	676
Information Technology Division (ITD)	676
Management Support Division (MSD)	677
Training Division	677
Investigative Operations Division (IOD)	677
Justice Prisoner and Alien Transportation System (JPATS)	677
Judicial Security Division (JSD)	677
Prisoner Operations Division (POD)	677
Tactical Operations Division (TOD)	677
Witness Security Division (WSD)	677
U.S. Parole Commission	677
Office on Violence Against Women	677
Department of the Interior	679
Office of the Secretary	679
Executive Secretariat	679
Congressional and Legislative Affairs	679
Office of Communications	679
Office of the Deputy Secretary	679

	Page
Department of the Interior—Continued	
Assistant Secretary for Fish and Wildlife and Parks	680
U.S. Fish and Wildlife Service	680
National Park Service	680
Assistant Secretary for Indian Affairs	681
Bureau of Indian Affairs	681
Bureau of Indian Education	681
Assistant Secretary for Land and Minerals Management	681
Bureau of Land Management	681
Bureau of Ocean Energy Management, Regulation and Enforcement	682
Office of Surface Mining Reclamation and Enforcement	682
Assistant Secretary for Policy, Management and Budget	682
Assistant Secretary for Water and Science	682
U.S. Geological Survey	683
Bureau of Reclamation	683
Office of Inspector General	684
Office of the Solicitor	684
Office of the Special Trustee for American Indians	684
Department of Agriculture	685
Office of the Secretary	685
Assistant Secretary for Administration	685
Office of Administrative Law Judges	685
Office of Human Resources Management	685
Office of the Judicial Officer	685
Office of Management Services	685
Office of Operations	686
Office of Procurement and Property Management	686
Office of Homeland Security	686
Office of Small and Disadvantaged Business Utilization	686
Assistant Secretary for Civil Rights	686
Office of Budget and Program Analysis	686
Office of the Chief Economist	687
Office of the Chief Financial Officer	687
Office of the Chief Information Officer	687
Office of Communications	687
Office of Congressional Relations	688
External and Intergovernmental Affairs	688
Office of Tribal Affairs	688
Office of the Executive Secretariat	688
General Counsel	688
Inspector General	689
National Appeals Division	689
Under Secretary for Natural Resources and Environment	689
Forest Service	689
Business Operations	689
National Forest System	689
Research and Development	690
State and Private Forestry	690
Natural Resources Conservation Service	690
Deputy Chief for Financial Management	690
Deputy Chief of Management	690
Deputy Chief of Programs	691
Deputy Chief of Science and Technology	691

	Page
Department of Agriculture—Continued	
Natural Resources Conservation Service—Continued	
Deputy Chief of Soil Survey and Resource Assessment	691
Deputy Chief of Strategic Planning and Accountability	691
Under Secretary for Farm and Foreign Agricultural Services	691
Farm Service Agency	691
Foreign Agricultural Service	692
Office of Administrative Operations	692
Office of Capacity Building and Development	692
Office of Country and Regional Affairs	692
Office of Foreign Service Operations	692
Office of Global Analysis	693
Office of Agreements and Scientific Affairs	693
Office of Trade Programs	693
Risk Management Agency	693
Under Secretary for Rural Development	693
Business and Cooperative Programs	694
Rural Housing Service	694
Rural Utilities Service	694
Food, Nutrition, and Consumer Services	695
Food and Nutrition Service	695
Office of the Administrator	695
Office of Research and Analysis	695
Office of Communications and Governmental Affairs	695
Office of Management Technology and Finance	695
Management	695
Financial Management	695
Information Technology	696
Regional Operations and Support	696
Office of Supplemental Nutrition Assistance Program	696
Office of Special Nutrition Programs	696
Center for Nutrition Policy and Promotion	696
Under Secretary for Food Safety	696
Food Safety and Inspection Service	696
Office of Field Operations (OFO)	696
Office of Data Integration and Food Protection (ODIFP)	697
Office of International Affairs (OIA)	697
Office of Management (OM)	697
Office of Policy, Program Development (OPPD)	697
Office of Program Evaluation, Enforcement and Review (OPEER)	697
Office of Public Affairs and Consumer Education (OPACE)	697
Office of Public Health Science (OPHS)	697
Office of Outreach, Employee Education and Training (OOEET)	697
Under Secretary for Research, Education, and Economics	698
Agricultural Research Service	698
Area Offices	698
Cooperative State Research, Education and Extension Service	698
Department of Agriculture—Continued	
Economic Research Service	699
National Agricultural Statistics Service	699
Under Secretary for Marketing and Regulatory Programs	699
Agricultural Marketing Service	699
Animal and Plant Health Inspection Service (APHIS)	699
Office of the Administrator	699
Animal Care	700
Biotechnology Regulatory Services	700
International Services	700
Legislative and Public Affairs	700
Marketing and Regulatory Programs Business Services	700
Plant Protection and Quarantine	700
Policy and Program Development	700
Veterinary Services	701
Wildlife Services	701
Grain Inspection, Packers and Stockyards Administration	701
Department of Commerce	703
Office of the Secretary	703
General Counsel	703
Assistant Secretary for Legislative and Intergovernmental Affairs	703
Chief Financial Officer (CFO) and Assistant Secretary for Administration	703
Chief Information Officer	704
Inspector General	704
Economics and Statistics Administration	704
Bureau of Economic Analysis	704
The Bureau of the Census	705
Bureau of Industry and Security	706
Economic Development Administration	706
International Trade Administration	707
Administration	707
Trade Promotion and U.S. and Foreign Commercial Service	707
Assistant Secretary for Import Administration	707
Assistant Secretary for Market Access and Compliance	707
Assistant Secretary for Manufacturing and Services	708
President's Export Council	708
Minority Business Development Agency	708
National Oceanic and Atmospheric Administration	708
National Marine Fisheries Service	709
National Ocean Service	709
National Environmental Satellite, Data and Information Service	710
National Weather Service	710
Oceanic and Atmospheric Research	710
Program, Planning and Integration	711
United States Patent and Trademark Office	711
Commissioner for Patents	711
Commissioner for Trademarks	712
Policy and External Affairs	712
Chief Financial Officer	712
Chief Administrative Officer	712

	Page
Department of Commerce—Continued	
United States Patent and Trademark Office—Continued	
Office of General Counsel	713
Chief Information Officer	713
Chief Performance Improvement Officer	713
National Institute of Standards and Technology	713
National Technical Information Service	715
National Telecommunications and Information Administration	715
Department of Labor	717
Office of the Secretary	717
Office of Public Engagement	717
Administrative Law Judges	717
Administrative Review Board	717
Assistant Secretary for Administration and Management	717
Business Operations Center	718
Center for Program Planning and Results	718
Civil Rights Center	718
Departmental Budget Center	718
Emergency Management Center	718
Govbenefits.gov	718
Human Resources Center	718
Information Technology Center	719
Security Center	719
Assistant Secretary for Policy	719
Benefits Review Board	719
Bureau of Labor Statistics	719
Bureau of International Labor Affairs	720
Office of Trade and Labor Affairs	720
Office of Child Labor, Forced Labor, and Human Trafficking	720
Office of International Relations	720
Office of the Chief Financial Officer	720
Office of Fiscal Integrity	720
Office of Financial Systems	720
Office of Congressional and Intergovernmental Affairs	720
Regional Offices	721
Office of Disability Employment Policy	721
Employee Benefits Security Administration	721
Employees' Compensation Appeals Board	722
Employment and Training Administration	722
DOL Center for Faith-Based and Neighborhood Partnerships	722
Office of the Inspector General	722
Mine Safety and Health Administration	722
Coal Mine Safety and Health	722
Metal and Nonmetal Mine Safety and Health	723
Educational Policy and Development	723
Occupational Safety and Health Administration	723
Office of Public Affairs	723
Regional Offices	723
Office of Small and Disadvantaged Business Utilization	724
Office of the Solicitor	724
Division of Black Lung and Longshore Legal Services	724
Department of Labor—Continued	
Office of the Solicitor—Continued	
Division of Civil Rights and Labor-Management	724
Division of Employment and Training Legal Services	724
Division of Fair Labor Standards	724
Division of Federal Employee and Energy Workers Compensation	724
Division of Mine Safety and Health	725
Division of Occupational Safety and Health	725
Division of Plan Benefits Security	725
Honors Program	725
Office of Legal Counsel	725
Management and Administrative Legal Services	725
Veterans' Employment and Training Service	725
Regional Offices	726
Women's Bureau	726
Department of Health and Human Services	727
Office of the Secretary	727
Office of the Deputy Secretary	727
Assistant Secretary for Administration and Management	727
Program Support Center	727
Assistant Secretary for Legislation	727
Assistant Secretary for Planning and Evaluation	728
Assistant Secretary for Public Affairs	728
Assistant Secretary for Preparedness and Response	728
Assistant Secretary for Financial Resources	728
Office for Civil Rights	728
Office of the General Counsel	728
Office of Global Health Affairs	729
Office of the Inspector General	729
Office of Medicare Hearings and Appeals	729
Office of the National Coordinator for Health Information Technology	729
Office of Public Health and Science	729
Administration on Aging	730
Administration for Children and Families	730
Agency for Healthcare Research and Quality (AHRQ)	730
Agency for Toxic Substances and Disease Registry	730
Center for Disease Control and Prevention	730
Center for Faith Based and Community Initiatives	731
Centers for Medicare and Medicaid Services	731
Food and Drug Administration	732
Health Resources and Services Administration	732
Indian Health Service	733
National Institutes of Health	733
Substance Abuse and Mental Health Services Administration	734
Department of Housing and Urban Development	737

	Page
Department of Housing and Urban Development—Continued	
Office of the Secretary	737
Office of the Deputy Secretary	737
Assistant Secretary for Community Planning and Development	737
Assistant Secretary for Congressional and Intergovernmental Relations	737
Assistant Secretary for Fair Housing and Equal Opportunity	737
Assistant Secretary for Housing	738
Assistant Secretary for Policy Development and Research	738
Assistant Secretary for Public Affairs	738
Assistant Secretary for Public and Indian Housing	738
Office of Field Policy and Management	738
Government National Mortgage Association	738
Chief Financial Officer	738
Chief Information Officer	739
Chief Procurement Officer	739
General Counsel	739
Inspector General	739
Office of Departmental Equal Employment Opportunity	739
Office of the Human Capital Officer	739
Office of Departmental Operations and Coordination	740
Office of Healthy Homes and Lead Hazard Control	740
Small and Disadvantaged Business Utilization	740
HUD Regional Directors	740
Department of Transportation	741
Office of the Secretary	741
Assistant Secretary for Administration	741
Assistant Secretary for Aviation and International Affairs	741
Assistant Secretary for Budget and Programs	742
Assistant Secretary for Governmental Affairs	742
Assistant Secretary for Transportation Policy	742
General Counsel	742
Inspector General	742
Regional Audit Offices	742
Regional Investigations Offices	743
Office of Public Affairs	743
Federal Aviation Administration	743
Federal Highway Administration	745
Field Services	745
Federal Motor Carrier Safety Administration	745
Field Offices	746
Federal Railroad Administration	746
Regional Offices (Railroad Safety)	746
Federal Transit Administration	747
Maritime Administration	747
Field Activities	748
U.S. Merchant Marine Academy	748
National Highway Traffic Safety Administration	748
Regional Offices	748
Department of Transportation—Continued	
Pipeline and Hazardous Materials Safety Administration	749
Hazardous Materials Safety Offices	749
Pipeline Safety Offices	749
Research and Innovative Technology Administration (RITA)	750
Saint Lawrence Seaway Development Corporation	750
Seaway Operations	750
Surface Transportation Board	750
Department of Energy	751
Office of the Secretary	751
Under Secretary of Energy	751
Under Secretary for Science	751
National Nuclear Security Administration	752
Major Field Organizations	752
Operations Offices	752
Integrated Support/Business Centers	752
Power Marketing Administrations	752
Petroleum Reserves	752
Federal Energy Regulatory Commission	752
Department of Education	755
Office of the Secretary	755
Office of the Deputy Secretary	755
Office of the Under Secretary	755
Office of the Chief Financial Officer	755
Office of the Chief Information Officer	756
Office of Management	756
Office for Civil Rights	756
Office of Communications and Outreach	756
Office of Elementary and Secondary Education	757
Office of English Language Acquisition	757
Office of Federal Student Aid	757
Office of the General Counsel	757
Office of Innovation and Improvement	757
Office of Inspector General	758
International Affairs Office	758
Institute of Education Sciences	758
Office of Legislation and Congressional Affairs	758
Office of Planning, Evaluation and Policy Development	758
Office of Postsecondary Education	758
Office of Safe and Drug-Free Schools	759
Office of Special Education and Rehabilitative Services	759
Office of Vocational and Adult Education	759
Department of Veterans Affairs	761
Office of the Secretary	761
Board of Veterans' Appeals	761
Office of General Counsel	761
Office of Inspector General	761
Office of Acquisitions, Logistics, and Construction	761
Assistant Secretary for Congressional and Legislative Affairs	762
Assistant Secretary for Public and Intergovernmental Affairs	762
Assistant Secretary for Policy and Planning	762
Assistant Secretary for Operations, Security and Preparedness	762

	Page
Department of Veterans Affairs—Continued	
Assistant Secretary for Management	762
Assistant Secretary for Information and Technology	762
Assistant Secretary for Human Resources and Administration	762
National Cemetery Administration	763
Veterans Benefits Administration	763
Veterans Health Administration	763
Department of Homeland Security	765
Office of the Secretary	765
Citizenship and Immigration Services Ombudsman	765
Office for Civil Rights and Civil Liberties	765
Office of Counternarcotics Enforcement	765
Executive Secretariat	765
Office of the General Counsel	765
Office of Inspector General	765
Office of Intelligence and Analysis	766
Office of Intergovernmental Affairs	766
Office of Legislative Affairs	766
Military Advisor's Office	766
Privacy Office	766
Office of Public Affairs	766
National Protection and Programs Directorate	766
Science and Technology Directorate	767
Management Directorate	767
Office of Policy Directorate	767
Federal Emergency Management (FEMA) Directorate	767
Office of Operations Coordination and Planning	768
Domestic Nuclear Detection Office	768
Transportation Security Administration (TSA)	768
United States Customs and Border Protection (CBP)	769
United States Immigration and Customs Enforcement (ICE)	769
Federal Law Enforcement Training Center	770
United States Citizenship and Immigration Services	770
United States Coast Guard	770
United States Secret Service	771
Independent Agencies, Commissions, Boards	773
Advisory Council on Historic Preservation	773
American Battle Monuments Commission	773
American National Red Cross	774
Honorary Officers	774
Corporate Officers	774
Board of Governors	774
Administrative Officers	774
Governmental Relations and Strategic Partnerships	774
Appalachian Regional Commission	775
Armed Forces Retirement Home	775
Armed Forces Retirement Home/Washington	775
Armed Forces Retirement Home/Gulfport	775
Board of Governors of the Federal Reserve System	775
Board of Governors of the Federal Reserve System—Continued	
Division of Banking Supervision and Regulation	775
Division of Consumer and Community Affairs	775
Division of Federal Reserve Bank Operations and Payment Systems	776
Division of Information Technology	776
Division of International Finance	776
Division of Monetary Affairs	776
Division of Research and Statistics	776
Inspector General	777
Legal Division	777
Management Division	777
Office of the Secretary	777
Office of Staff Director	777
Office of Financial Stability Policy and Research	777
Broadcasting Board of Governors	777
International Broadcasting Bureau	777
Governors	778
Central Intelligence Agency	778
Commission of Fine Arts	778
Board of Architectural Consultants for the Old Georgetown Act	778
Committee for Purchase from People Who are Blind or Severely Disabled	779
Commodity Futures Trading Commission	779
Regional Offices	779
Consumer Product Safety Commission	780
Corporation for National and Community Service	780
Defense Nuclear Facilities Safety Board	780
Delaware River Basin Commission	780
Federal Representatives	781
Delaware Representatives	781
New Jersey Representatives	781
New York Representatives	781
Pennsylvania Representatives	781
Environmental Protection Agency	781
Administration and Resources Management	782
Air and Radiation	782
Enforcement and Compliance Assurance	782
Office of Environmental Information	782
Chief Financial Officer	782
General Counsel	782
Inspector General	782
International Affairs	782
Chemical Safety and Pollution Prevention	782
Research and Development	782
Solid Waste and Emergency Response	783
Water	783
Regional Administration	783
Equal Employment Opportunity Commission	783
Commissioners	783
Export-Import Bank of the United States	784
Farm Credit Administration	785
Federal Communications Commission	785
Office of Administrative Law Judges	785
Office of Communications Business Opportunities	785
Consumer and Governmental Affairs Bureau	785
Enforcement Bureau	786

	Page
Federal Communications Commission—Continued	
Office of Engineering and Technology	786
Office of General Counsel	786
Office of Inspector General	786
International Bureau	786
Office of Legislative Affairs	786
Office of Managing Director	787
Media Bureau	787
Office of Media Relations	787
Office of Strategic Planning and Policy Analysis	787
Wireless Telecommunications Bureau	787
Wireline Competition Bureau	787
Office of Workplace Diversity	787
Regional and Field Offices	788
Northeast Region	788
Field Offices—Northeast Region	788
South Central Region	788
Field Offices—South Central Region	788
Western Region	788
Field Offices—Western Region	788
Federal Deposit Insurance Corporation	789
Federal Election Commission	789
Federal Housing Finance Agency	789
Office of Congressional Affairs and Communications	790
Federal Labor Relations Authority	790
Authority	790
General Counsel of the FLRA	790
Office of Administrative Law Judges	790
Federal Service Impasses Panel (FSIP)	791
Regional Offices	791
Federal Maritime Commission	791
Office of the Chairman	791
Office of the Secretary	791
Office of Equal Employment Opportunity	791
Office of the General Counsel	791
Office of Consumer Affairs and Dispute Resolution	791
Office of Administrative Law Judges	792
Office of the Inspector General	792
Office of the Managing Director	792
Area Representatives	792
Bureau of Certification and Licensing	792
Bureau of Enforcement	792
Bureau of Trade Analysis	792
Federal Mediation and Conciliation Service	792
Federal Mine Safety and Health Review Commission	793
Federal Retirement Thrift Investment Board	793
Federal Trade Commission	793
Regional Directors	794
Foreign-Trade Zones Board	794
General Services Administration	794
Office of the Administrator	794
Central Office	794
Office of Congressional and Intergovernmental Affairs	794
Office of the Chief Financial Officer	794
Office of the Chief People Officer	795
Office of the General Counsel	795
Office of the Chief Information Officer	795
Office of Governmentwide Policy	795
Office of Citizen Services and Innovative Technologies	795
General Services Administration—Continued	
Central Office—Continued	
Office of Civil Rights	795
Office of Small Business Utilization	795
Office of the Inspector General	795
Civilian Board of Contract Appeals	795
National Services	796
Federal Acquisition Service	796
Public Buildings Service	796
Regional Offices	796
Harry S. Truman Scholarship Foundation	797
Board of Trustees	797
James Madison Memorial Fellowship Foundation	798
Board of Trustees	798
Inter-American Foundation	798
John F. Kennedy Center for the Performing Arts	798
Board of Trustees	798
Legal Services Corporation	799
Board of Directors	799
National Aeronautics and Space Administration	799
Office of the Administrator	799
Aeronautics Research Mission Directorate	800
Office of the Chief Financial Officer (CFO)	800
Office of Diversity and Equal Opportunity Programs	800
Office of International and Interagency Relations	800
Office of the General Counsel	800
Office of Human Capital Management	800
Mission Support Directorate	800
Office of Inspector General	800
Office of Legislative Affairs	800
Office of Procurement	800
Office of Communications	801
Safety and Mission Assurance	801
Science Mission Directorate	801
Office of Protective Services	801
Office of Small Business Programs	801
Human Exploration and Operations Mission Directorate	801
NASA National Offices	801
NASA Overseas Representatives	802
National Archives and Records Administration	802
Administrative Committee of the Federal Register	803
National Archives Trust Fund Board	803
National Historical Publications and Records Commission	803
Regional Liaisons	803
Presidential Libraries	804
National Capital Planning Commission	804
Appointive Members	804
Executive Staff	805
National Council on Disability	805
National Credit Union Administration	805
Regional Offices	806
National Foundation on the Arts and the Humanities	806
National Endowment for the Arts	806
The National Council on the Arts	806
National Endowment for the Humanities	806

	Page
National Foundation on the Arts and the Humanities—Continued	
National Council on the Humanities	807
Federal Council on the Arts and Humanities	807
Institute of Museum and Library Services	807
National Museum and Library Services Board	808
National Gallery of Art	808
Board of Trustees	808
National Labor Relations Board	808
Division of Judges	809
Division of Operations Management	809
Division of Advice	809
Division of Enforcement Litigation	809
National Mediation Board	810
National Research Council—National Academy of Sciences—National Academy of Engineering—Institute of Medicine	810
National Research Council	810
National Academy of Sciences	810
National Academy of Engineering	810
Institute of Medicine	810
National Science Foundation	810
National Science Board	811
National Transportation Safety Board	811
Neighborhood Reinvestment Corporation	812
Board of Directors	812
Nuclear Regulatory Commission	812
Office of the Chairman	812
Commissioners	812
Staff Offices of the Commission	812
Advisory Committee on Medical Uses of Isotopes	813
Advisory Committee on Reactor Safeguards	813
Atomic Safety and Licensing Board Panel	813
Office of the Executive Director for Operations	813
Regional Offices	813
Occupational Safety and Health Review Commission	813
Office of Government Ethics	814
Office of Personnel Management	814
Office of the Director	814
Chief Financial Officer	815
Communications and Public Liaison	815
Congressional and Legislative Affairs	815
Federal Investigative Services	815
Merit System Audit and Compliance	815
Chief Information Officer	815
Human Resources Solutions	816
Retirement Services	816
Office of the General Counsel	816
Office of the Inspector General	816
Facilities, Security, and Contracting	816
Equal Employment Opportunity	816
Diversity and Inclusion	817
Internal Oversight and Compliance	817
Executive Secretariat and Ombudsman	817
Healthcare and Insurance	817
Employee Services	817
Office of the Special Counsel	817
The Peace Corps	817
Office of the Director	817
The Peace Corps—Continued	
Regional Offices	818
Pension Benefit Guaranty Corporation	819
Board of Directors	819
Officials	819
Postal Regulatory Commission	820
Securities and Exchange Commission	820
The Commission	820
Office of the Secretary	820
Office of Legislative and Intergovernmental Affairs	820
Office of the Chief Operating Officer	820
Office of Investor Education and Advocacy	820
Office of FOIA, Records Management and Security	820
Office of Equal Employment Opportunity	821
Office of the Chief Accountant	821
Office of Compliance Inspections and Examinations	821
Division of Risk, Strategy, and Financial Innovation	821
Office of the General Counsel	821
Division of Investment Management	822
Division of Corporation Finance	822
Division of Enforcement	823
Division of Trading and Markets	823
Office of Administrative Law Judges	824
Office of International Affairs	824
Office of the Inspector General	824
Office of Public Affairs	824
Office of Financial Management	824
Office of Information Technology	824
Office of Administrative Services	824
Office of Human Resources	824
Regional Offices	824
Selective Service System	826
Small Business Administration	827
Smithsonian Institution	827
The Board of Regents	827
Office of the Secretary	828
Office of the Under Secretary for Finance and Administration	828
Office of the Under Secretary for History, Art, and Culture	828
Office of the Under Secretary for Science	829
Smithsonian Enterprises	829
Social Security Administration	829
Office of the Commissioner	829
Office of the Chief Actuary	830
Office of Communications	830
Office of Disability Adjudication and Review	830
Office of Retirement and Disability Policy	831
Office of Budget, Finance and Management	831
Office of the General Counsel	831
Office of Human Resources	832
Office of the Inspector General	832
Office of Legislation and Congressional Affairs	832
Office of Operations	832
Office of Systems/Office of the Chief Information Officer	833
Office of Quality Performance	834
State Justice Institute	834

	Page
Susquehanna River Basin Commission	834
Tennessee Valley Authority	834
Board of Directors	834
Executive Officers	834
Washington Office	835
U.S. Advisory Commission on Public Diplomacy	835
U.S. Agency for International Development	835
U.S. Commission on Civil Rights	835
U.S. Election Assistance Commission	836
Office of the Executive Director	836
Office of Communications and Congressional Affairs	836
Office of the General Counsel	836
Office of the Inspector General	836
U.S. Holocaust Memorial Council	836
U.S. Institute of Peace	837
Board of Directors	837
U.S. International Trade Commission	838
Commissioners	838
U.S. Merit Systems Protection Board	838
Regional Offices	839
U.S. Overseas Private Investment Corporation	839
Board of Directors	839
U.S. Postal Service	840
Board of Governors	840
Officers of the Board of Governors	840
Officers of the Postal Service	840
U.S. Railroad Retirement Board	841
U.S. Sentencing Commission	841
U.S. Trade and Development Agency	842
Washington Metropolitan Area Transit Authority	842
Washington National Monument Society	842
Woodrow Wilson International Center for Scholars	843
Judiciary	845
Supreme Court of the United States	845
United States Courts of Appeals	849
United States Court of Appeals/District of Columbia Circuit	851
United States Court of Appeals/Federal Circuit	855
United States District Court for the District of Columbia	860
United States Court of International Trade	867
United States Court of Federal Claims	872
United States Tax Court	878
United States Court of Appeals for the Armed Forces	885
United States Court of Appeals for Veterans Claims	889
United States Judicial Panel on Multidistrict Litigation	891
Administrative Office of the United States Courts	893
Federal Judicial Center	894
District of Columbia Courts	894
District of Columbia Court of Appeals	894
Superior Court of the District of Columbia	895
Government of the District of Columbia	897
Council of the District of Columbia	897
Executive Office of the Mayor	897
Office of the City Administrator	898
Government of the District of Columbia—Continued	
Office of the City Administrator—Continued	
Commissions	898
Departments	898
Offices	899
Independent Agencies	900
Other	902
Post Office Locations	902
Classified Stations	902
International Organizations	905
European Space Agency (E.S.A.)	905
Inter-American Defense Board	905
Chiefs of Delegation	905
Inter-American Defense College	906
Inter-American Development Bank	906
Officers	906
Board of Executive Directors	907
Inter-American Tropical Tuna Commission	907
International Boundary and Water Commission, United States and Mexico	911
United States Section	911
Mexican Section	911
International Boundary Commission, United States and Canada	911
United States Section	911
Canadian Section	912
International Cotton Advisory Committee	912
Member Countries	912
International Joint Commission, United States and Canada	912
United States Section	912
Canadian Section	912
Great Lakes Regional Office	913
International Labor Organization	913
International Monetary Fund	913
Management and Senior Officers	913
Executive Directors and Alternates	914
International Organization for Migration	915
Headquarters	915
Member States	915
States With Observer Status	916
IOM Overseas Liaison and Operational Offices	916
International Pacific Halibut Commission, United States and Canada	917
Organization of American States	917
Permanent Missions to the OAS	917
General Secretariat	918
Organization for Economic Co-Operation and Development	919
OECD Washington Center	919
Pan American Health Organization (PAHO)	
Regional Office of the World Health Organization	919
PAHO/WHO Field Offices/OPS/Oficinas De Los Representantes En Los Paises	919
Centers	921
Permanent Joint Board on Defense, Canada–United States	921
Canadian Section	921
United States Section	922

Page

Pan American Health Organization (PAHO) Regional Office of the World Health Organization—Continued

Secretariat of the Pacific Community 922
Secretariat of the Pacific Regional Environmental Programme 923
United Nations 923
General Assembly 923
Security Council 923
Economic and Social Council 924
Trusteeship Council 924
International Court of Justice 924
United Nations Secretariat 924
Executive Office of the Secretary-General 925
Office of Internal Oversight Services 925
Office of Legal Affairs 925
Department of Political Affairs 925
Department for Disarmament Affairs 925
Department of Peace-Keeping Operations 925
Office for the Coordination of Humanitarian Affairs 925
Department of Economic and Social Affairs 925
Department of General Assembly and Conference Management 925
Department of Public Information 925
Department of Management 925
Office of the Special Representative of the Secretary-General for Children and Armed Conflict 926
United Nations Fund for International Partnerships 926
United Nations at Geneva (UNOG) 926
United Nations at Vienna (UNOV) 926
United Nations Information Centre 926
Regional Economic Commissions 926
Funds, Programmes, and Bodies of the United Nations 926
Specialized Agencies 928
Related Body 929
Special and Personal Representatives and Envoys of the Secretary-General 929
Africa 929
The Americas 930
Asia and the Pacific 930
Europe 931
Middle East 931
Other High Level Appointments 931
World Bank Group 932
International Bank for Reconstruction and Development 932
Other World Bank Offices 933

Page

Pan American Health Organization (PAHO) Regional Office of the World Health Organization—Continued

World Bank Group—Continued
Board of Executive Directors 933
International Development Association .. 935
International Finance Corporation 935
Multilateral Investment Guarantee Agency 935

Foreign Diplomatic Offices in the United States 937

Press Galleries 969
Senate Press Gallery 969
House Press Gallery 969
Standing Committee of Correspondents 969
Rules Governing Press Galleries 969
Members Entitled to Admission 971
Newspapers Represented in Press Galleries 987
Press Photographers Gallery 999
Standing Committee of Press Photographers 999
Rules Governing Press Photographers' Gallery 999
Members Entitled for Admission 1001
Services Represented 1004
White House News Photographers' Association 1007
Officers 1007
Executive Board 1007
Members Represented 1007
Radio and Television Correspondents' Galleries 1013
Senate Radio and Television Gallery 1013
House Radio and Television Gallery 1013
Executive Committee of the Radio and Television Correspondents' Galleries .. 1013
Rules Governing Radio and Television Correspondents' Galleries 1013
Members Entitled to Admission 1015
Networks, Stations, and Services Represented 1042
Periodical Press Galleries 1057
House Periodical Press Gallery 1057
Senate Periodical Press Gallery 1057
Executive Committee of Correspondents ... 1057
Rules Governing Periodical Press Galleries 1057
Members Entitled to Admission 1059
Periodicals Represented in Press Galleries . 1071

Congressional District Maps 1079

Name Index 1135

112th Congress*

THE VICE PRESIDENT

JOSEPH R. BIDEN, Jr., Democrat, of Wilmington, DE; born in Scranton, PA, November 20, 1942; education: St. Helena's School, Wilmington, DE; Archmere Academy, Claymont, DE; A.B., history and political science, University of Delaware; J.D., Syracuse University College of Law; married: Jill Tracy Biden; children: Joseph R. Biden III, Robert Hunter Biden, and Ashley Blazer Biden; admitted to the bar, December 1968, Wilmington, DE; engaged in private practice until 1972; served on New Castle County Council, 1970–72; elected to the U.S. Senate on November 7, 1972; reelected to each succeeding Senate term; served on committees: chair, Foreign Relations; Judiciary; elected as 47th Vice President of the United States on November 4, 2008; took the oath of office on January 20, 2009.

The Ceremonial Office of the Vice President is S–212 in the Capitol. The Vice President has offices in the Dirksen Senate Office Building, the Eisenhower Executive Office Building (EEOB) and the White House (West Wing).

Chief of Staff to the Vice President.—Bruce Reed, EEOB, room 202, 456–9000.
Deputy Chief of Staff to the Vice President.—Alan Hoffman, EEOB, room 202, 456–9000.
Counsel to the Vice President.—Cynthia Hogan, EEOB, room 246, 456–3241.
Director of Communications to the Vice President.—Shailagh Murray, EEOB, room 284, 456–5249.
Press Secretary to the Vice President.—Kendra Barkoff, EEOB, room 284, 456–5249.
Assistant to the Vice President for—
  Domestic Policy.—Terrell McSweeny, EEOB, room 222, 456–3071.
  Economic Policy.—Sarah Bianchi, EEOB, room 222, 456–3071.
  National Security Advisor.—Tony Blinken, EEOB, room 246, 456–2646.
Chief of Staff to Dr. Jill Biden.—Cathy Russell, EEOB, room 200, 456–6773.
Director of Scheduling to the Vice President.—Elisabeth Hire, EEOB, room 239, 456–6773.
Director of Advance to the Vice President.—Sam Myers, EEOB, room 241, 456–6773.
Executive Assistants to the Vice President: Michele Smith, Kellen Suber, West Wing.
Director of Correspondence.—Jillian Doody, EEOB, room 233, 456–6770.

---

*Biographies are based on information furnished or authorized by the respective Senators and Representatives.

ALABAMA

(Population 2010, 4,779,736)

SENATORS

RICHARD C. SHELBY, Republican, of Tuscaloosa, AL; born in Birmingham, AL, May 6, 1934; education: attended the public schools; B.A., University of Alabama, 1957; LL.B., University of Alabama School of Law, 1963; professional: attorney; admitted to the Alabama bar in 1961 and commenced practice in Tuscaloosa; member, Alabama State Senate, 1970–78; law clerk, Supreme Court of Alabama, 1961–62; city prosecutor, Tuscaloosa, 1963–71; U.S. Magistrate, Northern District of Alabama, 1966–70; special assistant Attorney General, State of Alabama, 1969–71; chairman, legislative council of the Alabama Legislature, 1977–78; former president, Tuscaloosa County Mental Health Association; member of Alabama Code Revision Committee, 1971–75; member: Phi Alpha Delta legal fraternity, Tuscaloosa County; Alabama and American bar associations; First Presbyterian Church of Tuscaloosa; Exchange Club; American Judicature Society; Alabama Law Institute; married: the former Annette Nevin in 1960; children: Richard C., Jr., and Claude Nevin; committees: ranking member, Banking, Housing, and Urban Affairs; Appropriations; Rules and Administration; Special Committee on Aging; elected to the 96th Congress on November 7, 1978; reelected to the three succeeding Congresses; elected to the U.S. Senate on November 4, 1986; reelected to each succeeding Senate term.

Office Listings

http://shelby.senate.gov

304 Russell Senate Office Building, Washington, DC 20510 .... (202) 224–5744
FAX: 224–3416
Chief of Staff.—Alan Hanson.
Personal Secretary / Appointments.—Anne Caldwell.
Press Secretary.—Jonathan Graffeo.
The Federal Building, 1118 Greensboro Avenue #240, Tuscaloosa, AL 35401 .... (205) 759–5047
Vance Federal Building, Room 321, 1800 5th Avenue North, Birmingham, AL 35203 .... (205) 731–1384
John A. Campbell Federal Courthouse, Suite 445, 113 St. Joseph Street, Mobile, AL 36602 .... (251) 694–4164
Frank M. Johnson Federal Courthouse, Suite 208, 15 Lee Street, Montgomery, AL 36104 .... (334) 223–7303
Huntsville International Airport, 1000 Glenn Hearn Boulevard, Box 20127, Huntsville, AL 35824 .... (256) 772–0460

* * *

JEFF SESSIONS, Republican, of Mobile, AL; born in Selma, AL, December 24, 1946; education: graduated Wilcox County High School, Camden, AL; B.A., Huntingdon College, Montgomery, AL, 1969; J.D., University of Alabama, Tuscaloosa, 1973; professional: U.S. Army Reserves, captain, 1973–86; attorney; admitted to the Alabama bar in 1973 and commenced practice for Guin, Bouldin and Porch in Russellville, 1973–75; Assistant U.S. Attorney, South District of Alabama, 1975–77; attorney for Stockman & Bedsole, 1977–81; U.S. Attorney, South District of Alabama, 1981–93; attorney for Stockman, Bedsole and Sessions, 1993–94; Attorney General, State of Alabama, 1994–96; member: Huntingdon College Board of Trustees; Samford University, Board of Overseers; delegate, General Conference, United Methodist Church; Montgomery Lions Club; Mobile United Methodist Inner City Mission; American Bar Association; Ashland Place United Methodist Church; married: the former Mary Blackshear, 1969; children: Ruth, Mary Abigail, and Samuel; International Narcotics Control Caucus; committees: Armed Services; Budget; Environment and Public Works; Judiciary; elected to the U.S. Senate on November 5, 1996; reelected to each succeeding Senate term.

Office Listings

http://sessions.senate.gov

326 Russell Senate Office Building, Washington, DC 20510 .... (202) 224–4124
FAX: 224–3149
Chief of Staff.—Rick Dearborn.
Scheduler.—Kate Hollis.
Executive Assistant.—Peggi Hanrahan.
Press Secretary.—Sarah Haley.
341 Vance Federal Building, 1800 Fifth Avenue North, Birmingham, AL 35203 .... (205) 731–1500
Field Representative.—Lindsay Davis.
Colonial Bank Centre, Suite 2300–A, 41 West I–65 Service Road North, Mobile, AL 36608 .... (251) 414–3083

Field Representative.—Valerie Day.
200 Clinton Avenue, NW., Suite 802, Huntsville, AL 35801 .... (256) 533–0979
Field Representative.—Lisa Montgomery.
7550 Halcyon Summit Drive, Suite 150, Montgomery, AL 36117 .... (334) 244–7017
State Director.—Chuck Spurlock.

REPRESENTATIVES

FIRST DISTRICT

JO BONNER, Republican, of Mobile, AL; born in Selma, AL, November 19, 1959; education: B.A., in Journalism, University of Alabama, 1982; organizations: Rotary Club; Mobile Area Chamber of Commerce; University of Alabama Alumni Association; Leadership Mobile; Junior League of Mobile; International Committee for the Mobile Tricentennial; professional: congressional aide to Representative Sonny Callahan, serving as Press Secretary, 1985–89, and Chief of Staff, 1989–2002; married: Janee; children: Jennifer Lee and Josiah Robins III; committees: chair, Ethics; Appropriations; elected to the 108th Congress on November 5, 2002; reelected to each succeeding Congress.

Office Listings

http://bonner.house.gov

2236 Rayburn House Office Building, Washington, DC 20515 .... (202) 225–4931
Chief of Staff.—Alan Spencer. FAX: 225–0562
Legislative Director.—Kelle Strickland.
Scheduler.—Errical Bryant.
11 North Water Street, Suite 15290, Mobile, AL 36602 .... (251) 690–2811
(800) 288–8721
1302 North McKenzie Street, Foley, AL 36535 .... (251) 943–2073

Counties: BALDWIN, CLARKE (part), ESCAMBIA, MOBILE, MONROE, WASHINGTON. Population (2000), 635,300.

ZIP Codes: 36420, 36425–27, 36432, 36436, 36439, 36441, 36444–46, 36451, 36456–58, 36460–62, 36470–71, 36475, 36480–83, 36502–05, 36507, 36509, 36511–13, 36515, 36518, 36521–30, 36532–33, 36535–36, 36538–39, 36541–45, 36547–51, 36553, 36555–56, 36558–62, 36564, 36567–69, 36571–72, 36575–85, 36587, 36590, 36601–13, 36615–19, 36621–22, 36628, 36633, 36640, 36652, 36660, 36663, 36670–71, 36685, 36688–89, 36691, 36693, 36695, 36720–23, 36726, 36728, 36741, 36751, 36762, 36768–69, 36784

* * *

SECOND DISTRICT

MARTHA ROBY, Republican, of Montgomery, AL; born in Montgomery, July 26, 1976; education: B.M., New York University, New York, NY, 1998; J.D., Cumberland School of Law at Samford University, Birmingham, AL, 2001; professional: attorney, Copeland, Franco, Screws, and Gill, P.A.; Councilor, District Seven, City of Montgomery; religion: Christian (Presbyterian); family: husband, Riley; children: Margaret and George; committees: Agriculture; Armed Services; Education and the Workforce; elected to the 112th Congress on November 2, 2010.

Office Listings

http://roby.house.gov

414 Cannon House Office Building, Washington, DC 20515 .... (202) 225–2901
Chief of Staff.—Stephen Boyd. FAX: 225–8913
Legislative Director.—Jennifer Warren.
Communications Director.—Brecke Popelka.
Director of Scheduling.—Jessica Fuller.
22 Monroe Street, Suite 1B, Montgomery, AL 36104 .... (334) 277–9113
188 North Foster Street, Suite 105, Dothan, AL 36303 .... (334) 794–9680
505 East Three Notch Street, Andalusia City Hall, Room 322, Andalusia, AL 36420 .... (334) 428–1129

Counties: AUTAUGA, BARBOUR, BULLOCK, BUTLER, COFFEE, CONECUH, COVINGTON, CRENSHAW, DALE, ELMORE, GENEVA, HENRY, HOUSTON, LOWNDES, MONTGOMERY (part), PIKE. Population (2000), 635,300.

ZIP Codes: 35010, 36003, 36005–06, 36008–10, 36015–17, 36020, 36022, 36024–43, 36046–49, 36051–54, 36061–62, 36064–69, 36071–72, 36078–82, 36089, 36091–93, 36101–18, 36120–21, 36123–25, 36130, 36132, 36135, 36140–42, 36177, 36191, 36301–05, 36310–14, 36316–23, 36330–31, 36340, 36343–46, 36349–53, 36360–62, 36370–71, 36373–76, 36401, 36420, 36426, 36429, 36432, 36442, 36449, 36453–56, 36467, 36471, 36473–77, 36483, 36502, 36524, 36703, 36749, 36752, 36758, 36761, 36775, 36785

* * *

THIRD DISTRICT

MIKE ROGERS, Republican, of Saks, AL; born in Hammond, IN, July 16, 1958; education: B.A., Jacksonville State University, 1981; M.P.A., Jacksonville State University, 1984; J.D., Birmingham School of Law, 1991; professional: attorney; awards: Anniston Star Citizen of the Year, 1998; public service: Calhoun County Commissioner, 1987–91; Alabama House of Representatives, 1994–2002; family: married to Beth; children: Emily, Evan, and Elliot; committees: Armed Services; Homeland Security; elected to the 108th Congress on November 5, 2002; reelected to each succeeding Congress.

Office Listings

http://www/house.gov/mike-rogers

324 Cannon House Office Building, Washington, DC 20515 .... (202) 225–3261
Chief of Staff.—Marshall Macomber. FAX: 226–8485
Deputy Chief of Staff.—Chris Brinson.
Legislative Director.—Whitney Verett.
Press Secretary.—Shea Snider.
Scheduler.—Cameron Bishop.
1129 Noble Street, 104 Federal Building, Anniston, AL 36201 .... (256) 236–5655
District Director.—Sheri Rollins.
1819 Pepperell Parkway, Suite 203, Opelika, AL 36801 .... (334) 745–6221
Field Representative.—Cheryl Cunningham.
7550 Halcyon Summit Drive, Montgomery, AL 36117 .... (334) 277–4210
Field Representative.—Alvin Lewis.

Counties: CALHOUN, CHAMBERS, CHEROKEE, CLAY, CLEBURNE, COOSA (part), LEE, MACON, MONTGOMERY (part), RANDOLPH, RUSSELL, TALLADEGA, TALLAPOOSA. Population (2000), 635,300.

ZIP Codes: 35010, 35014, 35032, 35044, 35078, 35082, 35089, 35096, 35136, 35160, 35183, 35960, 35973, 35983, 36013, 36023, 36026, 36036, 36039, 36043, 36046–47, 36052, 36057–58, 36064–65, 36069–70, 36075, 36088, 36101–21, 36123–25, 36201, 36215, 36252–63, 36265–76, 36278–80, 36766, 36801–04, 36825, 36830, 36850, 36853–55, 36858–65, 36867–79, 36959

* * *

FOURTH DISTRICT

ROBERT B. ADERHOLT, Republican, of Haleyville, AL; born in Haleyville, July 22, 1965; education: graduate, Birmingham Southern University; J.D., Cumberland School of Law, Samford University; professional: attorney; assistant legal advisor to Governor Fob James, 1995–96; Haleyville municipal judge, 1992–96; George Bush delegate, Republican National Convention, 1992; Republican nominee for the 17th District, Alabama House of Representatives, 1990; married: Caroline McDonald; children: Mary Elliott and Robert Hayes; committees: Appropriations; elected to the 105th Congress; reelected to each succeeding Congress.

Office Listings

http://www.aderholt.house.gov

2264 Rayburn House Office Building, Washington, DC 20515 .... (202) 225–4876
Chief of Staff.—Mark Busching. FAX: 225–5587
Legislative Director.—Mark Dawson.
Communications Director/Press Secretary.—Darrell Jordan.
Executive Assistant.—Tiffany Noel.
Carl Elliott Building, 1710 Alabama Avenue, Room 247, Jasper, AL 35501 .... (205) 221–2310
District Field Director.—Paul Housel.
205 Fourth Avenue, NE., Suite 104, Cullman, AL 35055 .... (256) 734–6043
Director of Constituent Services.—Jennifer Taylor.
107 Federal Building, 600 Broad Street, Gadsden, AL 35901 .... (256) 546–0201
Field Representative.—Jason Harper.
Morgan County Courthouse, P.O. Box 668, Decatur, AL 35602 .... (256) 350–4093
Field Representative.—Daniel Tidwell.

Counties: BLOUNT, CULLMAN, DEKALB, ETOWAH, FAYETTE, FRANKLIN, LAMAR, MARION, MARSHALL, MORGAN (part), PICKENS (part), ST. CLAIR (part), WALKER, WINSTON. Population (2000), 635,300.

ZIP Codes: 35006, 35013, 35016, 35019, 35031, 35033, 35038, 35049, 35053, 35055–58, 35062–63, 35070, 35077, 35079, 35083, 35087, 35097–98, 35121, 35126, 35130–31, 35133, 35146, 35148, 35172, 35175, 35179–80, 35205–07, 35212–13, 35215, 35441, 35447, 35461, 35466, 35481, 35501–04, 35540–46, 35548–55, 35559–60, 35563–65, 35570–82, 35584–87, 35592–94, 35601, 35603, 35619, 35621–22, 35640, 35651, 35653–54, 35670, 35672–73, 35747,

35754–55, 35760, 35765, 35769, 35771, 35775–76, 35901–07, 35950–54, 35956–57, 35959–64, 35966–68, 35971–76, 35978–81, 35983–84, 35986–90, 36064, 36117, 36271–72, 36275

* * *

FIFTH DISTRICT

MO BROOKS, Republican, of Huntsville, AL; born in Charleston, SC, April 29, 1954; education: B.A., Duke University, Durham, NC, 1975; J.D., University of Alabama School of Law, Tuscaloosa, AL, 1978; professional: lawyer, private practice, partner in Leo and Brooks law firm; prosecutor, Office of the District Attorney, Tuscaloosa County, AL, 1978–80; clerk, Circuit Court Judge John Snodgrass, 1980–82; member of the Alabama State House of Representatives, 1983–91; district attorney, Office of the District Attorney, Madison County, AL, 1991–93; special assistant attorney general, state of Alabama, 1995–2002; commissioner, Madison County, AL, board of commissions, 1996–2010; religion: Christian; married: Martha; four children; committees: Armed Services; Science, Space, and Technology; elected to the 112th Congress on November 2, 2010.

Office Listings

http://brooks.house.gov

1641 Longworth House Office Building, Washington, DC 20515 .... (202) 225–4801
Chief of Staff.—Mark Pettitt. FAX: 225–4392
Legislative Director.—Vacant.
Scheduler.—Stephanie Campbell.
2101 West Clinton Avenue, Suite 302, Huntsville, AL 35805 .... (256) 551–0190
District Director.—Tiffany Noel.
Field Representative.—Kathy Murray.
Special Projects Coordinator and Caseworker.—Sandy Garvey.
Caseworkers: Debi Echols, Timothy Jackson.
302 Lee Street, Room 86, Decatur, AL 35601 .... (256) 355–9400
District Field Representative and Caseworker.—Johnny Turner.
1011 George Wallace Boulevard, Tuscumbia, AL 35674 .... (256) 381–3450
District Field Representative and Caseworker.—Laura Webb.

Counties: COLBERT, JACKSON, LAUDERDALE, LAWRENCE, LIMESTONE, MADISON, MORGAN (part). Population (2000), 635,300.

ZIP Codes: 35016, 35205–06, 35209–10, 35212, 35215, 35540, 35582, 35601–03, 35609–20, 35630–34, 35640, 35643, 35645–54, 35660–62, 35671–74, 35677, 35699, 35739–42, 35744–46, 35748–52, 35755–69, 35771–74, 35776, 35801–16, 35824, 35893–96, 35898–99, 35958, 35966, 35978–79, 36104

* * *

SIXTH DISTRICT

SPENCER BACHUS, Republican, of Vestavia Hills, AL; born in Birmingham, AL, December 28, 1947; education: B.A., Auburn University, 1969; J.D., University of Alabama, 1972; professional: law firm, Bachus, Dempsey, Carson, and Steed, senior partner; member: Hunter Street Baptist Church; Alabama State Representative and Senator; school board; Republican Party Chair; children: Warren, Stuart, Elliott, Candace, and Lisa; committees: chair, Financial Services; elected to the 103rd Congress, November 3, 1992; reelected to each succeeding Congress.

Office Listings

http://www.house.gov/bachus

2246 Rayburn House Office Building, Washington, DC 20515 .... (202) 225–4921
Chief of Staff.—Michael Staley. FAX: 225–2082
Press Secretary.—Tim Johnson.
Legislative Director.—Philip Swartzfager.
1900 International Park Drive, Suite 107, Birmingham, AL 35243 .... (205) 969–2296
703 Second Avenue North, P.O. Box 502, Clanton, AL 35046 .... (205) 280–0704
Scheduler.—Brett Williams.

Counties: BIBB, CHILTON, COOSA (part), JEFFERSON (part), SHELBY, ST. CLAIR (part), TUSCALOOSA (part). CITIES AND TOWNSHIPS: Adamsville, Alabaster, Argo, Brookside, Brookwood, Calera, Cardiff, Clanton, Columbiana, County Line, Fultondale, Gardendale, Graysville, Harpersville, Helena, Homewood, Hoover, Hueytown, Irondale, Jemison, Kimberly, Leeds, Maytown, Montevallo, Morris, Mountain Brook, Mulga, North Johns, Northport, Pelham, Pell City, Pleasant Grove, Ragland, Sumiton, Sylvan Springs, Thorsby, Trafford, Trussville, Vestavia Hills, Vincent, Warrior, West Jefferson, Wilsonville, Wilton, and portions of Bessemer, Birmingham, Tarrant, Tuscaloosa, and West Blocton. Population (2000), 635,300.

ZIP Codes: 35004–07, 35015, 35022–23, 35035, 35040, 35043, 35046, 35048, 35051–52, 35054, 35060, 35062–63, 35068, 35071, 35073–74, 35078–80, 35085, 35091, 35094, 35096, 35111–12, 35114–20, 35123–28, 35130–31, 35133, 35135, 35137, 35139, 35142–44, 35146–48, 35151, 35171–73, 35175–76, 35178, 35180–88, 35201–03, 35205–07, 35209–10, 35212–17, 35219, 35222–26, 35230, 35233, 35235–37, 35240, 35242–46, 35249, 35253–55, 35259–61, 35266, 35277–83, 35285, 35287–99, 35402–03, 35406–07, 35444, 35446, 35452, 35456–58, 35466, 35468, 35473, 35475–76, 35480, 35482, 35490, 35546, 35579, 35953, 35987, 36006, 36051, 36064, 36091, 36750, 36758, 36790, 36792–93

* * *

SEVENTH DISTRICT

TERRI A. SEWELL, Democrat, of Birmingham, AL; born in Selma, AL, January 1, 1965; education: graduated from Selma High School, Selma, AL; B.A., *cum laude,* Princeton University, Princeton, NJ, 1986; Masters degree with first class Honors from Oxford University, Oxford, UK, 1988; J.D., Harvard Law School, Cambridge, MA, 1992; professional: Attorney; judicial law clerk to the Honorable Chief Judge U.W. Clemon, U.S. District Court, Northern District of Alabama, in Birmingham; memberships and boards: Treasurer of the Board and Chair of the Finance Committee, St. Vincent's Foundation, Girl Scouts of Cahaba Council, Community Advisory Board for the DAB Minority Health and Research Center, Governing Board of the Alabama Council on Economic Education, Corporate Partners Council for the Birmingham Art Museum, Alpha Kappa Alpha Sorority, Incorporated, The Links, Incorporated; professional affiliations: American Bar Association, National Bar Association, Alabama Bar Association; religion: Methodist; committees: Agriculture; Science, Space and Technology; Senior Whip; elected to the 112th Congress on November 2, 2010.

Office Listings

http://sewell.house.gov/

1133 Longworth House Office Building, Washington, DC 20515 .... (202) 225–2665
Chief of Staff.—Nichole Francis Reynolds. FAX: 226–9567
Legislative Director / Deputy Chief of Staff.—Matt Reel.
Deputy Press Secretary / Legislative Assistant.—Allison Abney.
Deputy Press Secretary.—Janna Pea.
Legislative Assistant.—Cachavious English.
Legislative Correspondent.—John Scott Vowell.
Scheduler.—Sophie Cooper.
Staff Assistant.—Kendra Key.

Two 20th Street North, Suite 1130, Birmingham, AL 35203 .... (205) 254–1960
District Director.—Terri Sharpley. FAX: 254–1974

186 Field of Dreams Drive, Demopolis, AL 36732 .... (334) 287–0860
FAX: 877–4489

UWA Station 40 Webb Hall 236–237, 205 North Washington Street, Livingston, AL 35470 .... (205) 652–5834
FAX: 652–5935

300 Washington Street, Marion, AL 36756 .... (334) 683–2157
FAX: 683–2201

Federal Building, Suite 112, 908 Alabama Avenue, Selma, AL 36701 .... (334) 877–4414
FAX: 877–4489

Federal Building, Suite 336, 1118 Greensboro Avenue, Tuscaloosa, AL 35401 .... (205) 752–5380
FAX: 752–5899

Counties: CHOCTAW, CLARKE (part), DALLAS, GREENE, HALE, JEFFERSON (part), MARENGO, PERRY, PICKENS (part), SUMTER, TUSCALOOSA (part), WILCOX. Population (2000), 635,300.

ZIP Codes: 35005–06, 35020–23, 35034, 35036, 35041–42, 35061, 35064, 35068, 35071, 35073–74, 35079, 35111, 35117, 35126–27, 35173, 35175, 35184, 35188, 35203–15, 35217–18, 35221–22, 35224, 35228–29, 35233–35, 35238, 35243, 35401, 35404–06, 35440–44, 35446–49, 35452–53, 35456, 35459–60, 35462–64, 35466, 35469–71, 35473–78, 35480–81, 35485–87, 35490–91, 35546, 35601, 35603, 35640, 35754, 36030, 36032, 36040, 36064, 36105, 36435–36, 36451, 36482, 36524, 36540, 36545, 36558, 36701–03, 36720, 36722–23, 36726–28, 36732, 36736, 36738, 36740–42, 36744–45, 36748–54, 36756, 36758–59, 36761–69, 36773, 36775–76, 36782–86, 36790, 36792–93, 36901, 36904, 36906–08, 36910, 36912–13, 36915–16, 36919, 36921–22, 36925

ALASKA

(Population 2010, 710,231)

SENATORS

LISA MURKOWSKI, Republican, of Anchorage, AK; born in Ketchikan, AK, May 22, 1957; education: Willamette University, 1975–77; Georgetown University, 1978–80, B.A., economics; Willamette College of Law, 1982–85, J.D.; professional: attorney; private law practice; Alaska and Anchorage Bar Associations: public service: Anchorage Equal Rights Commission; Anchorage District Court Attorney, 1987–89; Task Force on the Homeless, 1990–91; Alaska State Representative, 1998–2002; family: married to Verne Martell; children: Nicholas and Matthew; committees: Appropriations; Energy and Natural Resources; Health, Education, Labor and Pensions; Indian Affairs; appointed to the U.S. Senate on December 20, 2002; elected to the 109th Congress for a full Senate term on November 2, 2004; reelected as a write-in candidate to the 112th Congress on November 2, 2010.

Office Listings

http://murkowski.senate.gov

709 Hart Senate Office Building, Washington, DC 20510 .... (202) 224–6665
Chief of Staff.—Karen Y. Knutson. FAX: 224–5301
Legislative Director.—Edward Hild.
Scheduler.—Kristen Daimler-Nothdurft.
510 L Street, #550, Anchorage, AK 99501 .... (907) 271–3735
101 12th Avenue, Room 329, Fairbanks, AK 99701 .... (907) 456–0233
4079 Tongass Avenue; Suite 204, Ketchikan, AK 99901 .... (907) 225–6880
851 East Westpoint Drive, Wasilla, AK 99654 .... (907) 376–7665
805 Frontage Road, Suite 105, Kenai, AK 99611 .... (907) 283–5808

* * *

MARK BEGICH, Democrat, of Anchorage, AK; born in Anchorage, March 31, 1962; education: Stellar High School, 1981; professional: Small Business Owner; Real Estate and Property Management; Alaska Student Loan Corporation 1995–02, chair 1996–02; Alaska Commission of Post-Secondary Education 1995–02, chair 1996–98; University of Alaska Board of Regents 2001–02; public service: Anchorage Assembly Member, 1988–98; Mayor of Anchorage, 2003–09; member: Boys & Girls Club; Association of the United States Army; Air Force Association; family: married to Deborah Bonito; children: Jacob Begich; committees: Armed Services; Budget; Commerce, Science, and Transportation; Homeland Security and Governmental Affairs; Veterans' Affairs; elected to U.S. Senate on November 4, 2008.

Office Listings

http://begich.senate.gov

144 Russell Senate Office Building, Washington, DC 20510 .... (202) 224–3004
Chief of Staff.—David Ramseur. FAX: 228–3205
Legislative Director.—John Richards.
Scheduling Director.—Maya Ashwal.
Communications Director.—Rachel Barinbaum.
222 West Seventh Avenue, No. 2, Anchorage, AK 99513 .... (907) 271–5915
101 12th Avenue, Room 328, Fairbanks, AK 99701 .... (907) 456–0261
851 East Westpoint Drive, Suite 309, Wasilla, AK 99654 .... (907) 357–9956
One Sealaska Plaza, Suite 308, Juneau, AK 99802 .... (907) 586–7700
805 Frontage Road, Suite 101, Kenai, AK 99611 .... (907) 283–4000
Whitecliff Building, Suite 230, 1900 First Avenue, Ketchikan, AK 99901 .... (907) 225–3000

REPRESENTATIVE

AT LARGE

DON YOUNG, Republican, of Fort Yukon, AK; born in Meridian, CA, June 9, 1933; education: A.A., Yuba Junior College; B.A., Chico State College, Chico, CA; Honorary Doctorate of Laws, University of Alaska, Fairbanks; State House of Representatives, 1966–70; U.S. Army, 41st Tank Battalion, 1955–57; elected member of the State Senate, 1970–73; served on the Fort Yukon City Council for six years, serving four years as mayor; educator for nine years; river boat captain; member: National Education Association, Elks, Lions, Jaycees; married: Lula Fredson of Fort Yukon; children: Joni and Dawn; committees: Natural Resources; Transportation and Infrastructure; elected to the 93rd Congress in a special election, March 6, 1973, to fill the vacancy created by the death of Congressman Nick Begich; reelected to each succeeding Congress.

Office Listings

http://www.house.gov/donyoung

2314 Rayburn House Office Building, Washington, DC 20515 .... (202) 225–5765
Administrative Assistant.—Pamela Day. FAX: 225–0425
Executive Assistant / Office Manager.—Mary Hiratsuka.
Legislative Director.—Erik Elam.
510 L Street, Suite 580, Anchorage, AK 99501 .... (907) 271–5978
FAX: 271–5950
101 12th Avenue, Suite 10, Fairbanks, AK 99701 .... (907) 456–0210
FAX: 456–0279
612 West Willoughby Avenue, Suite B, P.O. Box 21247, Juneau, AK 99802 .... (907) 586–7400
FAX: 586–8922
805 Frontage Road, Suite 110, Kenai, AK 99611 .... (907) 283–7701

Population (2000), 626,932.

ZIP Codes: 99501–24, 99540, 99546–59, 99561, 99563–69, 99571–81, 99583–91, 99599, 99602–15, 99619–22, 99624–41, 99643–45, 99647–72, 99674–95, 99697, 99701–12, 99714, 99716, 99720–27, 99729–30, 99732–34, 99736–86, 99788–89, 99791, 99801–03, 99811, 99820–21, 99824–27, 99829–30, 99832–33, 99835–36, 99840–41, 99850, 99901, 99903, 99918–19, 99921–23, 99925–29, 99950

ARIZONA

(Population 2010, 6,392,017)

SENATORS

JOHN McCAIN, Republican, of Phoenix, AZ; born in the Panama Canal Zone, August 29, 1936; education: graduated Episcopal High School, Alexandria, VA, 1954; graduated, U.S. Naval Academy, Annapolis, MD, 1958; National War College, Washington, DC, 1973; retired captain (pilot), U.S. Navy, 1958–81; military awards: Silver Star, Bronze Star, Legion of Merit, Purple Heart, and Distinguished Flying Cross; chair, International Republican Institute; married to the former Cindy Hensley; seven children: Doug, Andy, Sidney, Meghan, Jack, Jim, and Bridget; committees: ranking member, Armed Services; Health, Education, Labor and Pensions; Homeland Security and Governmental Affairs; Indian Affairs; elected to the 98th Congress in November, 1982; reelected to the 99th Congress in November, 1984; elected to the U.S. Senate in November, 1986; reelected to each succeeding Senate term.

Office Listings

http://mccain.senate.gov

241 Russell Senate Office Building, Washington, DC 20510 .... (202) 224–2235
Chief of Staff.—Mark Buse. TDD: 224–7132
Legislative Director.—Joseph Donoghue.
Communications Director.—Brooke Buchanan.
Scheduler.—Ellen Cahill.
5353 North 16th Street, Suite 105, Phoenix, AZ 85016 .... (602) 952–2410
TDD: 952–0170
4703 South Lakeshore Drive, Suite 1, Tempe, AZ 85282 .... (480) 897–6289
407 West Congress Street, Suite 103, Tucson, AZ 85701 .... (602) 670–6334

* * *

JON KYL, Republican, of Phoenix, AZ; born in Oakland, NE, April 25, 1942; education: graduated Bloomfield High School, Bloomfield, IA, 1960; B.A., University of Arizona, Tucson, 1964 (Phi Beta Kappa, Phi Kappa Phi); LL.B., University of Arizona, 1966; professional: editor-in-chief, *Arizona Law Review*; attorney, admitted to the Arizona State bar, 1966; former partner in Phoenix law firm of Jennings, Strouss and Salmon, 1966–86; chairman, Phoenix Chamber of Commerce (1984–85); married: the former Caryll Louise Collins; children: Kristine and John; committees: Finance; Judiciary; elected to the 100th Congress on November 4, 1986; reelected to the three succeeding Congresses; elected to the U.S. Senate in November, 1994; reelected to each succeeding Senate term.

Office Listings

http://kyl.senate.gov

730 Hart Senate Office Building, Washington, DC 20515 .... (202) 224–4521
Chief of Staff.—Tim Glazewski. FAX: 224–2207
Legislative Director.—Elizabeth Maier.
Office Director.—Celeste Gold.
Scheduler.—Kelicia Rice.
Suite 120, 2200 East Camelback Road, Phoenix, AZ 85016 .... (602) 840–1891
Suite 150, 6840 North Oracle Road, Tucson, AZ 85704 .... (520) 575–8633

REPRESENTATIVES

FIRST DISTRICT

PAUL GOSAR, Republican, of Flagstaff, AZ; born in Rock Springs, WY, November 27, 1958; education: graduated, Pinedale High School, Pinedale, WY; B.S., Creighton University, Omaha, NE, 1981; D.D.S., Creighton University, Omaha, NE, 1985; professional: served as the President of the Northern Arizona Dental Society; Vice-Chair of the American Dental Association's Council on Governmental Affairs; awards: Arizona Dental Association's ''Dentist of the Year''; inducted into the Arizona Dental Association Hall of Fame; religion: Catholic; family: wife, Maude; children: Elle, Gaston, and Isabelle; caucuses: GOP Doctor's caucus, Immigration Reform caucus, and Coal caucus; committees: Natural Resources; Oversight and Government Reform; elected to the 112th Congress on November 2, 2010.

Office Listings

http://www.gosar.house.gov

504 Cannon House Office Building, Washington, DC 20515 .... (202) 225–2315
Chief of Staff.—Rob Robinson. FAX: 226–9739
Legislative Director.—Tom Van Flein.
Communications Director.—Stefani Zimmerman.
Scheduler / Office Manager.—Tiffany Dinneen.
240 South Montezuma Street, #101, Prescott, AZ 86303 .... (928) 445–1683
District Legislative Assistant.—Anthony Smith. FAX: 445–3414
1515 East Cedar Avenue, #A6, Flagstaff, AZ 86004 .... (928) 214–6055
District Constituent Services Director.—Penny Pew. FAX: 214–6124
211 North Florence Street, Suite 3, Casa Grande, AZ 85122 .... (520) 836–5289
Office Manager.—Rachel Aja. FAX: 836–8417

Counties: APACHE, COCONINO, GILA, GRAHAM, GREENLEE, NAVAJO (part), PINAL (part), YAVAPAI. CITIES AND TOWNSHIPS: Flagstaff, Prescott, Casa Grande, Sedona, Show Low, Payson, Florence, Coolidge, Eloy, Kearny, Hayden, San Manuel, Mammoth, Oracle, Winkelman, Superior, Globe, Miami, Bylas, Safford, Thatcher, Clifton, Morenci, Duncan, Window Rock, St. Johns, Springerville, Pinetop-Lakeside, McNary, Winslow, Holbrook, Page, Tuba City, Prescott Valley, Chino Valley, Skull Valley, Williams, Seligman, Mayer, Dewey-Humboldt, Cottonwood, Verde Valley. Population (2000), 641,329.

ZIP Codes: 85218, 85221–23, 85228, 85230–32, 85235, 85237–38, 85241, 85245, 85272–73, 85291–94, 85324, 85332, 85362, 85390, 85501–02, 85530–36, 85539–48, 85550–54, 85618, 85623, 85631, 85643, 85653, 85658, 85739, 85901–02, 85911–12, 85920, 85922–42, 86001–04, 86011, 86015–18, 86020, 86022–25, 86028–29, 86031–33, 86035–36, 86038, 86040, 86045–47, 86052–54, 86301–05, 86312–15, 86320–27, 86329–43, 86351, 86502–08, 86510–12, 86514–15, 86520, 86535, 86538, 86540, 86544–45, 86547, 86556

* * *

SECOND DISTRICT

TRENT FRANKS, Republican, of Phoenix, AZ; born in Uravan, CO, June 19, 1957; education: attended Ottawa University; graduate of the Center for Constitutional Studies; professional: small business owner; oil field and drilling engineer; Executive Director, Arizona Family Research Institute; conservative writer, and former radio commentator, with Family Life Radio and NBC affiliate KTKP 1280 AM; public service: Arizona House of Representatives, 1985–87; appointed in 1987 to head the Arizona Governor's Office for Children; awards: True Blue award, Family Research Council; Spirit of Enterprise award, U.S. Chamber of Commerce; Taxpayer Hero, Council for Citizens Against Government Waste; Friend of Education award, Education Freedom Coalition; religion: Baptist; member, North Phoenix Baptist Church; married: Josephine; committees: Armed Services; Judiciary; elected to the 108th Congress on November 5, 2002; reelected to each succeeding Congress.

Office Listings

http://www.house.gov/franks

2435 Rayburn House Office Building, Washington, DC 20515 .... (202) 225–4576
Chief of Staff.—Randy Kutz. FAX: 225–6328
Executive Assistant.—Lisa Teschler.
Scheduler.—Anna Hurley.
Communications Director.—Ben Carnes.
Press Assistant.—Kate Middleton.
Speech Writer.—Bethany Haley.
Legislative Director.—Bobby Cornett.
MLA.—Drew Nishiyama.
Judiciary Counsel.—Jacki Pick.
Legislative Assistant.—Stephanie Hammond.
Legislative Correspondent.—Catherine Kutz.
DoD Fellow.—Sanjit Singh.
7121 West Bell Road, Suite 200, Glendale, AZ 85308 .... (623) 776–7911
District Director.—Dan Hay.
District Representatives: Lloyd Bostrom, Denise Diehl, Steve Montenegro, Brian Van Hovel, Doyle Scott.
Field Representative.—Shari Farrington.
Business / Commerce Liaison.—Michael Jameson.
Legal Counsel.—David Sheasby.
Staff Assistant.—Daniel Stefanski.

Counties: COCONINO (part), LAPAZ (part), MARICOPA (part), MOHAVE, NAVAJO (part), YAVAPAI (part). Population (2000), 641,329.

ZIP Codes: 85029, 85037, 85051, 85098, 85301–10, 85312, 85318, 85320, 85326, 85335, 85338, 85340, 85342, 85345, 85351, 85355, 85358, 85360–61, 85363, 85372–76, 85378–83, 85385, 85387, 85390, 86021, 86030, 86034, 86039, 86042–43, 86401–06, 86411–13, 86426–27, 86429–46

* * *

THIRD DISTRICT

BENJAMIN QUAYLE, Republican, of Phoenix, AZ; born in Fort Wayne, IN, November 5, 1976; education: B.A., Duke University, 1998; J.D., Vanderbilt University, 2002; professional: former associate, Real Estate Transactional Department, Snell and Wilmer; founder, Tynwald Capital; religion: Christian; married: Tiffany; committees: Homeland Security; Judiciary; Science, Space, and Technology; elected to the 112th Congress on November 2, 2010.

Office Listings

http://quayle.house.gov

1419 Longworth House Office Building, Washington, DC 20515 .... (202) 225–3361
Chief of Staff.—Renee Hudson. FAX: 225–3462
Legislative Director.—Rachel Dresen.
Scheduler.—Alison Babb.
Press Secretary.—Richard Cullen.
2400 East Arizona Biltmore Circle, Suite 1290, Phoenix, AZ 85016 .... (602) 263–5300
Deputy Chief of Staff.—James Ashley.

Counties: MARICOPA (part). CITIES AND TOWNSHIPS: Carefree, Cave Creek, Paradise Valley, and Phoenix (part). Population (2000), 641,329.

ZIP Codes: 85012–24, 85027–29, 85032, 85046, 85050–51, 85053–54, 85060, 85071, 85075, 85078–80, 85082, 85098–99, 85250–51, 85253–54, 85262, 85308, 85310, 85327, 85331, 85377

* * *

FOURTH DISTRICT

ED PASTOR, Democrat, of Phoenix, AZ; born in Claypool, AZ, June 28, 1943; education: attended public schools in Miami, AZ; graduate of Arizona State University; B.A., chemistry, 1966; J.D., Arizona University, 1974; professional: member, Governor Raul Castro's staff; taught chemistry, North High School; former deputy director of Guadalupe Organization, Inc.; elected supervisor, board of supervisors, Maricopa County; served board of directors for the National Association of Counties; vice chairman, Employment Steering Committee; president, Arizona County Supervisors Association; member, executive committee of the Arizona Association of Counties; resigned, May, 1991; board of directors, Neighborhood Housing Services of America; National Association of Latino Elected Officials; served as director at large, ASU Alumni Association; founding board member, ASU Los Diablos Alumni Association; served on board of directors of the National Council of La Raza; Arizona Joint Partnership Training Council; National Conference of Christians and Jews; Friendly House; Chicanos Por La Causa; Phoenix Economic Growth Corporation; Sun Angel Foundation; vice president, Valley of the Sun United Way; advisory member, Boys Club of Metropolitan Phoenix; married: Verma; two daughters: Yvonne and Laura; appointed a Chief Deputy Minority Whip; committees: Appropriations; elected by special election on September 24, 1991, to fill the vacancy caused by the resignation of Morris K. Udall; elected in November, 1992, to the 103rd Congress; reelected to each succeeding Congress.

Office Listings

http://www.house.gov/pastor

2465 Rayburn House Office Building, Washington, DC 20515 .... (202) 225–4065
Executive Assistant.—Laura Campos. FAX: 225–1655
411 North Central Avenue, Suite 150, Phoenix, AZ 85004 .... (602) 256–0551
District Director.—Elisa de la Vara.

Counties: MARICOPA (part). Population (2000), 641,329.

ZIP Codes: 85001–09, 85012–19, 85025–26, 85030–31, 85033–36, 85038, 85040–44, 85051. 85061–64, 85066–69, 85072–74, 85076, 85082, 85099, 85283, 85301, 85303, 85309, 85311, 85339, 86045, 86329, 86337

* * *

FIFTH DISTRICT

DAVID SCHWEIKERT, Republican, of Fountain Hills, AZ; born March 3, 1962; education: B.A., Arizona State University, Tempe, AZ, 1988; M.B.A., Arizona State University, Tempe,

AZ, 2005; professional: business owner of a real estate company; realtor; financial consultant; member of the Arizona state house of representatives, 1989–94; member of the Arizona state board of equalization, 1995–2003; former treasurer, Maricopa County, AZ, 2004–06; religion: Catholic; married: Joyce Schweikert; committees: Financial Services; elected to 112th Congress on November 2, 2010.

Office Listings

http://schweikert.house.gov

1205 Longworth House Office Building, Washington, DC 20515 .... (202) 225–2190
Chief of Staff.—Oliver Schwab. FAX: 225–0096
Scheduler.—Susan Marshall.
Legislative Director.—Matthew Tully.
Communications Director.—Rachel Semmel.
10603 North Hayden Road, Suite 108, Scottsdale, AZ 85260 .... (480) 946–2411
FAX: 946–2446

Counties: MARICOPA (part). CITIES AND TOWNSHIPS: Chandler, Fountain Hills, Mesa, Phoenix, Rio Verde, Scottsdale, Tempe. Ahwatukee, the Salt River Pima Indian Reservation, and the Fort McDowell Yavapai Apache Indian Reservation. Population (2000), 641,329.

ZIP Codes: 85008, 85018, 85044–45, 05048, 85070, 85076, 85201–03, 85210, 85215, 85224–26, 85250–64, 85267–69, 85274, 85287, 85331, 85281, 85283

* * *

SIXTH DISTRICT

JEFF FLAKE, Republican, of Mesa, AZ; born in Snowflake, AZ, December 31, 1962; education: Brigham Young University; B.A., International Relations; M.A., Political Science; religion: Mormon; served a mission in South Africa and Zimbabwe; professional: businessman; Shipley, Smoak & Henry (public affairs firm); Executive Director, Foundation for Democracy; Executive Director, Goldwater Institute; married: Cheryl; children: Ryan, Alexis, Austin, Tanner, and Dallin; committees: Appropriations; elected to the 107th Congress on November 7, 2000; reelected to each succeeding Congress.

Office Listings

http://www.house.gov/flake

240 Cannon House Office Building, Washington, DC 20515 .... (202) 225–2635
Chief of Staff.—Matthew Specht. FAX: 226–4386
Scheduler.—Nikki Olave.
Press Secretary.—Genevieve Rozansky.
1640 South Stapley, Suite 215, Mesa, AZ 85204 .... (480) 833–0092

Counties: MARICOPA (part), PINAL (part). CITIES AND TOWNSHIPS: Apache Junction, Chandler, Gilbert, Mesa, and Queen Creek. Population (2000), 641,329.

ZIP Codes: 85201, 85203–08, 85210–20, 85224–25, 85227, 85233–34, 85236, 85242, 85244, 85246, 85248–49, 85254, 85275, 85277–78, 85290, 85296–97, 85299

* * *

SEVENTH DISTRICT

RAÚL M. GRIJALVA, Democrat, of Tucson, AZ; born in Tucson, February 19, 1948; education: Sunnyside High School, Tucson, AZ; B.A., University of Arizona; professional: former Assistant Dean for Hispanic Student Affairs, University of Arizona; former Director of the El Pueblo Neighborhood Center; public service: Tucson Unified School District Governing Board, 1974–86; Pima County Board of Supervisors, 1989–2002; family: married to Ramona; three daughters; committees: Education and the Workforce; Natural Resources; elected to the 108th Congress on November 5, 2002; reelected to each succeeding Congress.

Office Listings

http://www.house.gov/grijalva

1511 Longworth House Office Building, Washington, DC 20515 .... (202) 225–2435
Chief of Staff.—Amy Emerick. FAX: 225–1541
Legislative Director.—Chris Kaumo.
Press Liaison.—Adam Sarvana.
Scheduler.—Anna Maldonado.
810 East 22nd Street, Suite 102, Tucson, AZ 85713 .... (520) 622–6788

1455 South 4th Avenue, Suite 4, Yuma, AZ 85364 .... (928) 343–7933

Counties: LA PAZ (part), MARICOPA (part), PIMA (part), PINAL (part), SANTA CRUZ (part), YUMA. Population (2000), 641,329.

ZIP Codes: 85033, 85035, 85037, 85043, 85221–22, 85226, 85228, 85232, 85239, 85242, 85248–49, 85273, 85321–23, 85325–26, 85328–29, 85333–34, 85336–37, 85339–41, 85343–44, 85346–50, 85352–54, 85356–57, 85359, 85364–67, 85369, 85371, 85601, 85621, 85628, 85631, 85633–34, 85639–40, 85648, 85653, 85662, 85701–03, 85705–06, 85711, 85713–14, 85716–17, 85719, 85721–26, 85733–36, 85743, 85745–46, 85754

* * *

EIGHTH DISTRICT

GABRIELLE GIFFORDS, Democrat, of Tucson, AZ; born in Tucson, June 8, 1970; education: B.A., Scripps College, Claremont, CA, 1993; William Fulbright Scholarship, study abroad Chihuahua, Mexico; M.A. in regional planning, Cornell University, NY, 1996; selected for the inaugural two-year class of the Aspen-Rodel Fellowships in Public Leadership, 2005; Arizona State House of Representatives, 2001–03; Arizona State Senator, 2003–05; religion: Jewish; married: Mark Kelly, Captain United States Navy; committees: Armed Services; Science, Space, and Technology; elected to the 110th Congress on November 7, 2006; reelected to each succeeding Congress.

Office Listings

http://giffords.house.gov/

1030 Longworth House Office Building, Washington, DC 20515 .... (202) 225–2542
Chief of Staff.—Pia Carusone. FAX: 225–0378
Scheduler.—Jennifer Cox.
3945 East Fort Lowell, Suite 211, Tucson, AZ 85712 .... (520) 881–3588
District Director.—Ron Barber.
77 Calle Portal, Suite B–160, Sierra Vista, AZ 85635 .... (520) 459–3115

Counties: COCHISE, PIMA (part), PINAL (part), SANTA CRUZ (part). Population (2000), 641,329.

ZIP Codes: 85602–03, 85605–11, 85613–17, 85619–20, 85622, 85624–27, 85629–30, 85632, 85635–38, 85641, 85643–46, 85650, 85652–55, 85670, 85704–16, 85718–19, 85728, 85730–32, 85736–45, 85747–52

ARKANSAS

(Population 2010, 2,915,918)

SENATORS

MARK L. PRYOR, Democrat, of Little Rock, AR; born in Fayetteville, AR, January 10, 1963; education: B.A., University of Arkansas, 1985; J.D., University of Arkansas, 1988; professional: attorney; Wright, Lindsey & Jennings (law firm); public service: elected, Arkansas House of Representatives, 1990; elected, Arkansas Attorney General, 1998; family: married to Jill; children: Adams and Porter; his father, David Pryor, was a former Governor and U.S. Senator from Arkansas; committees: Appropriations; Commerce, Science, and Transportation; Homeland Security and Governmental Affairs; Rules and Administration; Small Business and Entrepreneurship; Select Committee on Ethics; elected to the U.S. Senate on November 5, 2002; reelected to each succeeding Senate term.

Office Listings

http://pryor.senate.gov

255 Dirksen Senate Office Building, Washington, DC 20510 .... (202) 224–2353
Chief of Staff.—Andy York. FAX: 228–0908
Legislative Director.—Kristen Sharp.
Communications Director.—Michael Teague.
Office Manager.—Patrice Bolling.
500 Clinton Avenue, Suite 401, Little Rock, AR 72201 .... (501) 324–6336

* * *

JOHN NICHOLS BOOZMAN, Republican, of Rogers, AR; born in Shreveport, LA, December 10, 1950; education: Southern College of Optometry, Memphis, TN, 1977; also attended University of Arkansas, Fayetteville, AR; professional: doctor of optometry; business owner; rancher; religion: Southern Baptist; married: Mrs. Cathy Boozman; children: three daughters; committees: Agriculture, Nutrition, and Forestry; Environment and Public Works; Commerce, Science, and Transportation; Veterans' Affairs; elected to the U.S. House of Representatives 2001–11; elected to the U.S. Senate on November 2, 2010.

Office Listings

http://boozman.senate.gov

SRC–1 Russell Senate Office Building, Washington, DC 20510 .... (202) 224–4843
Chief of Staff.—C. Matthew Sagely. FAX: 228–1371
Legislative Director.—Kathee Facchiano.
Communications Director.—Sara Lasure.
Scheduler.—Lesley Parker.
1401 West Capitol Avenue, Plaza Suite F, Little Rock, AR 72201.
213 West Monroe, Suite N, Lowell, AR 72745 .... (479) 725–0400
1120 Garrison Avenue, Fort Smith, AR 72901 .... (479) 573–0189
1001 Highway 62 East, Suite 11, Mountain Home, AR 72653 .... (870) 424–0129
300 South Church Street, Suite 400, Jonesboro, AR 72401.
620 East 22nd Street, Suite 204, Stuttgart, AR 72160.
106 West Main Street, Suite 104, El Dorado, AR 71730.

REPRESENTATIVES

FIRST DISTRICT

RICK CRAWFORD, Republican, of Jonesboro, AR; born in Homestead AFB, FL, January 22, 1966; education: graduated, Alvirne High School; B.A., Agricultural Business and Economics, Arkansas State University, 1996; professional: U.S. Army—Bomb Disposal Technician, 1985–89, Professional Rodeo Announcer; KAIT–TV Jonesboro—News Anchor; KFIN–FM—Farm Director; Delta Farm Roundup TV Show—Producer and Anchor; Agwatch—Owner and Operator; member: National Association of Farm Broadcasting; 4-H Foundation Board of Arkansas; recipient of the NAFB Newscast Award, 2006 and 2008; married: Stacy; children: Will and Delaney; Republican Study Committee; committees: Agriculture; Transportation and Infrastructure; elected to the 112th Congress on November 2, 2010.

Office Listings

http://crawford.house.gov

1408 Longworth House Office Building, Washington, DC 20515 .... (202) 225–4076
Chief of Staff.—Jonah Shumate. FAX: 225–5602
Press Secretary.—Anna Nix.
Legislative Director.—Ted Verrill.
112 South First Street, Cabot, AR 72023 .... (501) 843–3043
2400 East Highland Drive, Suite 300, Jonesboro, AR 72401 .... (870) 203–0540

Counties: ARKANSAS, BAXTER, CLAY, CLEBURNE, CRAIGHEAD, CRITTENDEN, CROSS, FULTON, GREENE, INDEPENDENCE, IZARD, JACKSON, LAWRENCE, LEE, LONOKE, MISSISSIPPI, MONROE, PHILLIPS, POINSETT, PRAIRIE, RANDOLPH, ST. FRANCIS, SEARCY, SHARP, STONE, WOODRUFF. Population (2000), 668,360.

ZIP Codes: 72003, 72005–07, 72014, 72017, 72020–21, 72023–24, 72026, 72029, 72031, 72036–38, 72040–44, 72046, 72048, 72051, 72055, 72059–60, 72064, 72067, 72069, 72072–76, 72083, 72086, 72101–02, 72108, 72112, 72121, 72123, 72130–31, 72134, 72137, 72139–40, 72142–43, 72153, 72160, 72165–66, 72169–70, 72175–76, 72179, 72189, 72301, 72303, 72310–13, 72315–16, 72319–22, 72324–33, 72335–36, 72338–42, 72346–48, 72350–55, 72358–60, 72364–70, 72372–74, 72376–77, 72383–84, 72386–87, 72389–92, 72394–96, 72401–04, 72410–17, 72419, 72421–22, 72424–45, 72447, 72449–51, 72453–62, 72464–67, 72469–76, 72478–79, 72482, 72501, 72503, 72512–13, 72515, 72517, 72519–34, 72536–40, 72542–46, 72550, 72553–56, 72560–62, 72564–69, 72571–73, 72575–79, 72581, 72583–85, 72587, 72610, 72613, 72617, 72623, 72626, 72629, 72631, 72633, 72635–36, 72639, 72642, 72645, 72650–51, 72653–54, 72658, 72663, 72669, 72675, 72679–80, 72685–86

* * *

SECOND DISTRICT

TIM GRIFFIN, Republican, of Little Rock, AR; born in Charlotte, NC, August 21, 1968; education: B.A., Hendrix College, Conway, AR, 1990; attended Pembroke College, Oxford University, 1991; J.D., Tulane Law School, New Orleans, LA, 1994; professional: United States Army Reserve; Judge Advocate General's (JAG) Corps, 1996–present; business owner; lawyer, private practice; U.S. Attorney for the Eastern District of Arkansas, 2006–07; deputy director and special assistant to the President, White House Office of Political Affairs, 2005; religion: Baptist; married, two children; caucuses: National Guard and Reserve Components Caucus (NGRCC); General Aviation Caucus; Congressional Natural Gas Caucus; Congressional Sportsmen's Caucus; Congressional Military Family Caucus; Congressional Health Care Caucus; Air Force Caucus; Army Caucus; Congressional Motorcycle Safety Caucus; Congressional C–130 Modernization Caucus; Congressional Caucus for Competitiveness in Entertainment Technology (E-TECH); Balanced Budget Amendment Caucus; International Anti-Piracy Caucus; Wounded to Work Caucus; Multiple Sclerosis Caucus; Congressional Mississippi River Delta Caucus; Congressional Arthritis Caucus; Congressional Modeling and Simulation Caucus; Congressional Prayer Caucus; Congressional Cancer Caucus; Republican Israel Caucus; Congressional Nuclear Issues Working Group; Congressional Waterways Caucus; Congressional Diabetes Caucus; Congressional Turkey Caucus; Majority Assistant Whip; committees: Armed Services; Foreign Affairs; Judiciary; elected to the 112th Congress on November 2, 2010.

Office Listings

http://www.griffin.house.gov

1232 Longworth House Office Building, Washington, DC 20515 .... (202) 225–2506
Chief of Staff.—Clayton Hall. FAX: 225–5903
Communications Director.—Jonathan Samford.
Legislative Director.—A. Brooke Bennett.
1501 North University, Suite 150, Little Rock, AR 72207 .... (501) 324–5941
District Director.—Carl Vogelphol.

Counties: CONWAY, FAULKNER, PERRY, PULASKI, SALINE, VAN BUREN, WHITE, YELL. Population (2010), 751,377.

ZIP Codes: 71772, 71909, 72001–02, 72010–13, 72015–18, 72020, 72022–23, 72025, 72027–28, 72030–35, 72039, 72045–47, 72052–53, 72057–61, 72063, 72065–68, 72070, 72076, 72078–82, 72085, 72087–89, 72099, 72102–04, 72106–08, 72110–11, 72113–22, 72124–27, 72131, 72135–37, 72139, 72141–43, 72145, 72149, 72153, 72156–57, 72164, 72167, 72173, 72178, 72180–81, 72183, 72190, 72199, 72201–07, 72209–12, 72214–17, 72219, 72221–23, 72225, 72227, 72231, 72260, 72295, 72419, 72568, 72629, 72645, 72679, 72823–24, 72827–29, 72833–34, 72838, 72841–42, 72853, 72857, 72860, 72943

* * *

THIRD DISTRICT

STEVE WOMACK, Republican, of Rogers, AR; born in Russellville, AR, February 18, 1957; education: Russellville High School, Russellville, AR; B.A., Arkansas Tech University, 1979;

professional: radio station manager; financial consultant, mayor of Rogers, AR; military: retired colonel, National Guard; awards: Legion of Merit; Meritorious Service Medal; Army Commendation Medal; Army Achievement Medal; Global War on Terror Expeditionary and Service Medals; religion: Southern Baptist; family: married the former Terri Williams of DeWitt, AR; three sons; caucuses: Republican Study Committee, National Guard; committees: Appropriations; elected to the 112th Congress on November 2, 2010.

Office Listings

http://womack.house.gov

1508 Longworth House Office Building, Washington, DC 20515 .... (202) 225–4301
Chief of Staff.—Beau Walker. FAX: 225–5713
Communications Director.—J.R. Davis.
Scheduler.—Stephanie Fontenot.
Legislative Director.—Margo Klosterman.
Legislative Assistants: Adrielle Churchill, Chris Huffaker.
Legislative Correspondents: Chad Hall, Ivy Williams.
Staff Assistant.—Amanda Ladden-Stirling.
3333 Pinnacle Hills, Suite 120, Rogers, AR 72758 .... (479) 464–0446
District Director.—Keri Wilkinson. FAX: 464–0063
Constituent Service Manager.—Janet Foster.
Caseworker.—Pam Forester.
Field Representative.—Jeff Thacker.
Projects Director.—Kyle Weaver.
Military and Veterans Advisor.—Lewis Kaslow.
423 North 6th Street, Fort Smith, AR 72902 .... (479) 424–1146
Field Representative.—Bob Moody. FAX: 424–2737
Caseworker.—Chris Bader.
303 North Main Street, Suite 102, Harrison, AR 72601 .... (870) 741–6900
Field Representative.—Teri Garrett. FAX: 741–7741

Counties: BENTON, BOONE, CARROLL, CRAWFORD, FRANKLIN, JOHNSON, MADISON, MARION, NEWTON, POPE, SEBASTIAN, WASHINGTON. Population (2000), 668,479.

ZIP Codes: 71937, 71944–45, 71953, 71972–73, 72063, 72080, 72601–02, 72611, 72613, 72615–16, 72619, 72624, 72628, 72630–34, 72638–41, 72644–45, 72648, 72653, 72655, 72660–63, 72666, 72668, 72670, 72672, 72675, 72677, 72679, 72682–83, 72685–87, 72701–04, 72711–12, 72714–19, 72721–22, 72727–30, 72732–42, 72744–45, 72747, 72749, 72751–53, 72756–58, 72760–62, 72764–66, 72768–70, 72773–74, 72776, 72801–02, 72811–12, 72820–21, 72823, 72830, 72832, 72837–43, 72845–47, 72852, 72854, 72856–58, 72860, 72901–06, 72908, 72913–14, 72916–19, 72921, 72923, 72927–28, 72930, 72932–38, 72940–41, 72944–49, 72951–52, 72955–57, 72959

* * *

FOURTH DISTRICT

MIKE ROSS, Democrat, of Prescott, AR; born in Texarkana, AR, August 2, 1961; education: Hope High School; B.A., University of Arkansas at Little Rock, 1987; professional: former small business owner; public service: Chief of Staff to Arkansas Lt. Governor Winston Bryant, 1985–89; three term State Senator, 1991–2000; organizations: Executive Director, Arkansas Youth Suicide Prevention Commission, 1985–89; First United Methodist Church in Prescott, AR; awards: Advocates for Community and Rural Education's ''Champion of Rural Arkansas'' award, 2008; Arkansas Hospital Association's ''Statesman of the Year'' award, 2008; Blue Dog Coalition's ''Spirit of Freedom'' award, 2008; NAACP Pine Bluff Chapter's ''Shining Star'' award, 2008; 60 Plus Association's ''Cyber Security Crusader'' award, 2008; U.S. Chamber of Commerce's ''Spirit of Enterprise'' award, 2010; National Association of Manufacturers' ''Award for Manufacturing Legislative Excellence'', 2010; caucus: co-chair/leadership, Blue Dog Coalition; Congressional Sportsmen's Caucus; co-chair, Second Amendment Task Force; married: Holly; children: Alex and Sydney Beth; committees: Energy and Commerce; elected to the 107th Congress on November 7, 2000; reelected to each succeeding Congress.

Office Listings

http://ross.house.gov

2436 Rayburn House Office Building, Washington, DC 20515 .... (202) 225–3772
Chief of Staff.—Jarod Yates. FAX: 225–1314
Legislative Director.—Laura Abshire.
Communications Director.—Brad Howard.
District Director.—Jeff Weaver.
221 West Main Street, Prescott, AR 71857 .... (870) 887–6787
George Howard Jr. Federal Building, 100 East 8th Avenue, Room 2521 Pine Bluff, AR 71601 .... (870) 536–3376

100 Reserve Street, Suite 307, Hot Springs National Park, AR 71901 .... (501) 520–5892
Union County Courthouse, Suite 406, 101 North Washington Street, El Dorado, AR 71730 .... (870) 881–0681

Counties: ASHLEY, BRADLEY, CALHOUN, CHICOT, CLARK, CLEVELAND, COLUMBIA, DALLAS, DESHA, DREW, GARLAND, GRANT, HEMPSTEAD, HOT SPRING, HOWARD, JEFFERSON, LAFAYETTE, LINCOLN, LITTLE RIVER, LOGAN, MILLER, MONTGOMERY, NEVADA, OUACHITA, PIKE, POLK, SCOTT, SEVIER, UNION. Population (2000), 668,385.

ZIP Codes: 71601–03, 71611–13, 71630–31, 71635, 71638–40, 71642–44, 71646–47, 71651–63, 71665–67, 71670–71, 71674–78, 71701, 71711, 71720–22, 71724–26, 71728, 71730–31, 71740, 71742–45, 71747–54, 71758–59, 71762–66, 71768, 71770, 71772, 71801–02, 71820, 71822–23, 71825–28, 71831–42, 71844–47, 71851–55, 71857–62, 71864–66, 71901–03, 71909–10, 71913–14, 71920–23, 71929, 71932–33, 71935, 71937, 71940–45, 71949–50, 71952–53, 71956–62, 71964–65, 71968–73, 71998–99, 72004, 72015, 72046, 72055, 72057, 72065, 72072–73, 72079, 72084, 72087, 72104–05, 72128–29, 72132–33, 72150, 72152, 72160, 72167–68, 72175, 72182, 72379, 72826–27, 72833–35, 72838, 72841–42, 72851, 72855, 72863, 72865, 72924, 72926–28, 72933, 72943–44, 72949–51, 72958

CALIFORNIA

(Population 2010, 37,253,956)

SENATORS

DIANNE FEINSTEIN, Democrat, of San Francisco, CA; born in San Francisco, June 22, 1933; education: B.A., Stanford University, 1955; elected to San Francisco Board of Supervisors, 1970–78; president of Board of Supervisors: 1970–71, 1974–75, 1978; mayor of San Francisco, 1978–88; candidate for governor of California, 1990; recipient: Distinguished Woman Award, *San Francisco Examiner;* Achievement Award, Business and Professional Women's Club, 1970; Golden Gate University, California, LL.D. (hon.), 1979; SCOPUS Award for Outstanding Public Service, American Friends of the Hebrew University of Jerusalem; University of Santa Clara, D.P.S. (hon.); University of Manila, D.P.A. (hon.), 1981; Antioch University, LL.D. (hon.), 1983; Los Angeles Anti-Defamation League of B'nai B'rith's Distinguished Service Award, 1984; French Legion d'Honneur from President Mitterand, 1984; Mills College, LL.D. (hon.), 1985; U.S. Army's Commander's Award for Public Service, 1986; Brotherhood/Sisterhood Award, National Conference of Christians and Jews, 1986; Paulist Fathers Award, 1987; Episcopal Church Award for Service, 1987; U.S. Navy Distinguished Civilian Award, 1987; Silver Spur Award for Outstanding Public Service, San Francisco Planning and Urban Renewal Association, 1987; All Pro Management Team Award for No. 1 Mayor, *City and State* Magazine, 1987; Community Service Award Honoree for Public Service, 1987; American Jewish Congress, 1987; President's Award, St. Ignatius High School, San Francisco, 1988; Coro Investment in Leadership Award, 1988; President's Medal, University of California at San Francisco, 1988; University of San Francisco, D.H.L. (hon.), 1988; member: Coro Foundation, Fellowship, 1955–56; California Women's Board of Terms and Parole, 1960–66, executive committee; U.S. Conference of Mayors, 1983–88; Mayor's Commission on Crime, San Francisco; Bank of California, director, 1988–89; San Francisco Education Fund's Permanent Fund, 1988–89; Japan Society of Northern California, 1988–89; Inter-American Dialogue, 1988–present; Publius Award from the Center for the Study of the Presidency and Congress, 2009; chair, U.S. Senate Caucus on International Narcotics Control; married: Dr. Bertram Feinstein (dec.); married on January 20, 1980, to Richard C. Blum; children: one child; three stepchildren; religion: Jewish; committees: chair, Select Committee on Intelligence; Appropriations; Judiciary; Rules and Administration; elected to the U.S. Senate, by special election, on November 3, 1992, to fill the vacancy caused by the resignation of Senator Pete Wilson; reelected to each succeeding Senate term.

Office Listings

http://feinstein.senate.gov

331 Hart Senate Office Building, Washington, DC 20510 .... (202) 224–3841
Chief of Staff.—Chris Thompson. FAX: 228–3954
Legislative Director.—John Watts.
Director of Communications.—Gil Duran.
750 B Street, Suite 1030, San Diego, CA 92101 .... (619) 231–9712
2500 Tulare Street, Suite 4290, Fresno, CA 93721 .... (559) 485–7430
One Post Street, Suite 2450, San Francisco, CA 94104 .... (415) 393–0707
11111 San Monica Boulevard, Suite 915, Los Angeles, CA 90025 .... (310) 914–7300

* * *

BARBARA BOXER, Democrat, of Rancho Mirage, CA; born in Brooklyn, NY, November 11, 1940; education: B.A. in economics, Brooklyn College, 1962; professional: stockbroker and economic researcher with securities firms on Wall Street, 1962–65; journalist and associate editor, *Pacific Sun* newspaper, 1972–74; congressional aide, Fifth Congressional District, California, 1974–76; elected Marin County Board of Supervisors, 1976–82; first woman president, Marin County Board of Supervisors; awards: Human Rights for Vietnam Award, Vietnamese Community of Southern California, 1994; Legislator of the Year Award, Southern California Public Health Association, 1996; Lifetime Consumer Hero, Consumer Federation of America, 1997; Edgar Wayburn Award, Sierra Club, 1997; President's Award, California State Conference of the NAACP, 2001; Phillip Burton Wilderness Award, California Wilderness Coalition (CWC), 2003; Children's Champion Award, California Head Start Association, 2003; Circle of Courage Award, Afghan Women's Association International, 2003; National End Family Violence Achievement Award, Family Violence Law Center, 2003; Leadership Award, National Foundation for Women Legislators, 2005; Champion of Affordability Award, Housing Trust of Santa Clara County, 2005; Friend of the National Parks, National Parks Conservation Association, 2005; Impossible Dream Award, Planned Parenthood Action Council, 2005; Champion for

Children Award, California Children's Hospital, 2006; Woman of the Year, Women's Image Network, 2006; Visionary Leadership Award, San Francisco Democratic Party, 2006; Award, Native American Heritage Association, 2007; Champion Award for Public Service, Endangered Species Coalition, 2007; Lifetime Achievement Award, City Year San Jose / Silicon Valley, 2008; Breakfast of Champions, Afterschool Alliance, 2008; Transportation Leader's Award, National Stone, Sand, and Gravel Association, 2008; John H. Chafee Congressional Environmental Award, Association of American Railroads, 2008; Legislative Leadership Award, National Association of Clean Water Agencies, 2008; Legislator of the Year Award, American Planning Association, 2008; Humane Champion, Humane Society of the United States, 2008; Legislator of the Year Award, Information and Technology Industry Council, 2008; Vera Shultz Visionary Leadership Award, Marin Women's Commission, 2009; 25th Annual Leadership Conference Award, Cyprus and Hellenic Leadership, 2009; Aviation Safety Award, National Air Traffic Controllers Association, 2009; Legislator of the Year Award, California Primary Care Association, 2009; Children's Champion Award, Global Action for Children, 2009; Award, Oxfam America, 2009; Legislator of the Year Award, Air Quality Management District, 2009; National Transportation Leadership Award for the 21st Century, American Association of State Highway and Transportation Officials, 2009; Defender of Children Award, First Focus Campaign for Children, 2010; Golden Triangle Award, National Farmers Union, 2010; Safety Leadership Award, Advocates for Highway and Auto Safety, 2010; Award National Association of Community Health Centers, 2010; Safety Net Award, National Association of Public Hospitals and Health Systems, 2010; President's Leadership Award, American Burn Association, 2010; Phil Burton Badge of Courage Award, The Sierra Club—San Francisco Bay Chapter, 2010; Service Award, Entertainment Leadership Initiative / Grammy Foundation, 2010; Champion for the National Parent Helpline Award, Parents Anonymous, 2011; married: Stewart Boxer, 1962; children: Doug and Nicole; committees: chair, Environment and Public Works; chair, Select Committee on Ethics; Commerce, Science, and Transportation; Foreign Relations; elected November 2, 1982 to the 98th Congress; reelected to the 99th–102nd Congresses; elected to the U.S. Senate on November 3, 1992; reelected to each succeeding Senate term.

Office Listings

http://boxer.senate.gov

112 Hart Senate Office Building, Washington, DC 20510	(202) 224–3553
Chief of Staff.—Laura Schiller.	FAX: 228–2382
Legislative Director.—Sean Moore.	
Director of Scheduling.—Kelly Boyer.	
Communications Director.—Zachary Coile.	
1700 Montgomery Street, Suite 240, San Francisco, CA 94111	(415) 403–0100
312 North Spring Street, Suite 1748, Los Angeles, CA 90012	(213) 894–5000
501 I Street, Suite 7–600, Sacramento, CA 95814	(916) 448–2787
600 B Street, Suite 2240, San Diego, CA 92101	(619) 239–3884
2500 Tulare Street, Suite 5290, Fresno, CA 93721	(559) 497–5109
3403 10th Street, Suite 704, Riverside, CA 92501	(951) 684–4849

REPRESENTATIVES

FIRST DISTRICT

MIKE THOMPSON, Democrat, of Napa Valley, CA; born in St. Helena, CA, January 24, 1951; education: graduated, St. Helena High School, St. Helena, CA; U.S. Army, 1969–72; Purple Heart; B.A., Chico State University, 1982; M.A., Chico State University, 1996; teacher at San Francisco State University, and Chico State University; elected to the California State Senate, 2nd District, 1990–98; former chairman of the California State Senate Budget Committee; married to Janet; two children: Christopher and Jon; committees: Ways and Means; Permanent Select Committee on Intelligence; elected to the 106th Congress; reelected to each succeeding Congress.

Office Listings

http://mikethompson.house.gov http://www.house.gov/writerep

231 Cannon House Office Building, Washington, DC 20515	(202) 225–3311
Chief of Staff.—Anne Steckel.	FAX: 225–4335
Legislative Directors: Melanie Rhinehart, Van Tassell.	
Communications Director.—Caroline Hogan.	
1040 Main Street, Suite 101, Napa, CA 94559	(707) 226–9898
317 Third Street, Suite 1, Eureka, CA 95501	(707) 269–9595
Post Office Box 2208, Fort Bragg, CA 95437	(707) 962–0933
712 Main Street, Suite 1, Woodland, CA 95695	(530) 662–5272

Counties: DEL NORTE COUNTY. CITIES AND TOWNSHIPS: Crescent City, Fortdeck, Gasquet, Klamath, Prison, Smith River. HUMBOLDT COUNTY. CITIES AND TOWNSHIPS: Alderpoint, Areata, Bayside, Blocksburg, Blue Lake, Burcka, Carlotta, Eureka, Ferndale, Fortuna, Garberville, Hoopa, Hydseville, Kneeland, Korbel, Loleta, McKinlayville, Myers Flat, Orick, Petrolia, Redcrest, Redway, Rio Del, Scotia, Trinidad, Whitehorn, Willow Creek. LAKE COUNTY. CITIES AND TOWNSHIPS: Clearlake, Clearlake Oaks, Clearlake Park, Cobb, Glenhaven, Kelseyville, Lakeport, Lower Lake, Lucerne, Middletown, Nice, Upper Lake. MENDOCINO COUNTY. CITIES AND TOWNSHIPS: Albion, Boonville, Calpella, Compiche, Covelo, Elk, Finley, Fort Bragg, Gualala, Hopland, Laytonville, Little River, Manchester, Mendocino, Philo, Piercy, Point Arena, Potter Valley, Redwood Valley, Talmage, Ukiah, Willits, Yorkville. NAPA COUNTY. CITIES AND TOWNSHIPS: American Canyon, Angwin, Aetna Springs, Calistoga, Deer Park, Oakville, Pope Valley, Rutherford, St. Helena. SONOMA COUNTY (part). CITIES AND TOWNSHIPS: Alexander Valley, Cloverdale, Geyserville, Healdsburg, Mark West, Santa Rosa, Sonoma, Windsor. YOLO COUNTY (part). CITIES AND TOWNSHIPS: Davis, West Sacramento, Winters, and Woodland. Population (2000), 639,087.

ZIP Codes: 94503, 94508, 94515, 94558–59, 94562, 94567, 94573–74, 94576, 94581, 94589–90, 94599, 95403–04, 95409–10, 95415–18, 95420, 95422–29, 95432–33, 95435, 95437, 95441–43, 95445, 95448–49, 95451–54, 95456–61, 95463–64, 95466, 95468–70, 95476, 95481–82, 95485, 95487–88, 95490, 95492–94, 95501–03, 95511, 95514, 95518–19, 95521, 95524–26, 95528, 95531–32, 95534, 95536–38, 95540, 95542–43, 95545–51, 95553–56, 95558–60, 95562, 95564–65, 95567, 95569–71, 95573, 95585, 95587, 95589, 95605, 95612, 95615–16, 95618, 95691, 95694–95, 95776, 95798–99, 95899

* * *

SECOND DISTRICT

WALLY HERGER, Republican, of Marysville, CA; born in Sutter County, CA, May 20, 1945; education: graduated East Nicolaus High School; attended California State University, Sacramento, CA; professional: cattle rancher; small businessman; East Nicolaus High School Board of Trustees, 1977–80; California State Assemblyman, 1980–86; member: National Federation of Independent Business; Sutter County Taxpayers Association; Yuba-Sutter Farm Bureau; California Cattlemen's Association; California Chamber of Commerce; Big Brothers/ Big Sisters Board of Directors; South Yuba Rotary Club; married: Pamela; children: nine; committees: Ways and Means; Joint Committee on Taxation; elected to the 100th Congress, November 4, 1986; reelected to each succeeding Congress.

Office Listings

242 Cannon House Office Building, Washington, DC 20515 .... (202) 225–3076
Administrative Assistant.—Derek Harley. FAX: 226–0852
Legislative Director.—Darin Thacker.
Press Secretary.—Matt Lavoie.
Executive Assistant / Scheduler.—Kate Barlow.
2635 Forest Avenue, Suite 100, Chico, CA 95928 .... (530) 893–8363
District Director.—Fran Peace.
280 Hemsted Drive, Suite 105, Redding, CA 96002 .... (530) 223–5898

Counties: BUTTE (part), COLUSA, GLENN, SHASTA, SISKIYOU, SUTTER, TEHAMA, TRINITY, YOLO (part), YUBA. Population (2000), 639,087.

ZIP Codes: 95526–27, 95552, 95563, 95568, 95595, 95606–07, 95627, 95637, 95645, 95653, 95659, 95668, 95674, 95676, 95679, 95692, 95697–98, 95837, 95901, 95903, 95912–14, 95917–20, 95922, 95925–29, 95932, 95935–39, 95941–43, 95947–48, 95950–51, 95953–55, 95957–58, 95960–63, 95967, 95969–74, 95976–79, 95981–82, 95987–88, 95991–93, 96001–03, 96007–08, 96010–11, 96013–14, 96016–17, 96019, 96021–25, 96027–29, 96031–35, 96037–41, 96044, 96046–52, 96055–59, 96061–65, 96067, 96069–71, 96073–76, 96078–80, 96084–97, 96099, 96101, 96103–04, 96114, 96118, 96122, 96124, 96134, 96137, 96161

* * *

THIRD DISTRICT

DANIEL E. LUNGREN, Republican, of Gold River, CA; born in Long Beach, CA, September 22, 1946; education: St. Anthony's High School, Long Beach, CA, 1964; B.A., english, University of Notre Dame, 1968 (with honors); attended University of Southern California Law Center, 1968–69; J.D., Georgetown University Law Center, 1971; professional: attorney, associate and partner, Ball, Hunt, Brown & Baerwitz (law firm), 1973–78; U.S. House of Representatives, 1979–89; elected California Attorney General, 1990, served two terms; Republican nominee for Governor of California, 1998; radio talk show host; consultant; private law practice, 1999–2004; religion: Catholic; married: the former Barbara (Bobbi) Knolls, 1969; children: Jeff, Kelly, and Kathleen; committees: chair, House Administration; Homeland Security; Judiciary; Joint Committee on the Library; Joint Committee on Printing; elected to the 109th Congress on November 2, 2004; reelected to each succeeding Congress.

Office Listings

http://www.house.gov/lungren

2313 Rayburn House Office Building, Washington, DC 20515 .... (202) 225–5716
Chief of Staff.—Peter Tateishi. FAX: 226–1298
Communications Director.—Brian Kaveney.
Scheduler.—Yelena Alaverdian.
2339 Gold Medal Way, Suite 220, Gold River, CA 95670 .... (916) 859–9906

Counties: ALPINE, AMADOR, CALAVERAS, SACRAMENTO (part), SOLANO (part). CITIES AND TOWNSHIPS: Amador, Arden-Arcade, Carmichael, Citrus Heights, Elk Grove, Fair Oaks, Folsom, Foothill Farms, Galt, Gold River, Ione, Jackson, Laguna, Laguna West, LaRiviera, North Highland, Rancho Cordova, Rancho Murieta, Rio Linda, Rio Vista, Roseville, Sacramento, Vineyard, and Wilton. Population (2000), 639,088.

ZIP Codes: 94571, 94585, 95221–26, 95228–30, 95232–33, 95236, 95245–52, 95254–55, 95257, 95601, 95608, 95610–11, 95615, 95620–21, 95624, 95626, 95628–30, 95632, 95638–40, 95642, 95646, 95652, 95654–55, 95660, 95662, 95665–66, 95668–71, 95673, 95675, 95683, 95685, 95688–90, 95693–94, 95699, 95742, 95758–59, 95763, 95821, 95825–30, 95832, 95835–37, 95841–43, 95864, 96021–22, 96029, 96035, 96055, 96061, 96080, 96120

* * *

FOURTH DISTRICT

TOM McCLINTOCK, Republican, of Granite Bay, CA; born in Bronxville, NY, July 10, 1956; education: B.A., *cum laude* political science, UCLA, Los Angeles, CA; 1978; married: Lori; two children; committees: Budget; Natural Resources; elected to the 111th Congress on November 4, 2008; reelected to the 112th Congress.

Office Listings

http://www.mcclintock.house.gov

428 Cannon House Office Building, Washington, DC 20515 .... (202) 225–2511
Chief of Staff.—Igor Birman. FAX: 225–5444
Scheduler.—Chris Tudor.
Legislative Director.—Kristen Glenn.
Legislative Aide.—Brittan Specht.
Legislative Assistant.—Will Dunham.
8700 Auburn Folsom Road, Suite 100, Granite Bay, CA 95746 .... (916) 786–5560
District Director.—Rocky Deal.

Counties: BUTTE (part), EL DORADO, LASSEN, MODOC, NEVADA, PLACER, PLUMAS, SACRAMENTO (part), SIERRA. Population (2000), 639,088.

ZIP Codes: 95602–04, 95609, 95613–14, 95617, 95619, 95623, 95626, 95628–31, 95633–36, 95648, 95650–51, 95656, 95658, 95661–64, 95667–68, 95672, 95677–78, 95681–82, 95684, 95701, 95703, 95709, 95712–15, 95717, 95720–22, 95724, 95726, 95728, 95735–36, 95741, 95746–47, 95762, 95765, 95816, 95910, 95915–16, 95922–24, 95930, 95934, 95940–41, 95944–47, 95949, 95956, 95959–60, 95965–66, 95968, 95971, 95975, 95977, 95980, 95983–84, 95986, 96006, 96009, 96015, 96020, 96054, 96056, 96068, 96101, 96103–30, 96132–33, 96135–37, 96140–43, 96145–46, 96148, 96150–52, 96154–56, 96158, 96160–62

* * *

FIFTH DISTRICT

DORIS OKADA MATSUI, Democrat, of Sacramento, CA; born in Posten, AZ, September 25, 1944; education: B.A., University of California, Berkeley, CA, 1966; professional: staff, White House, 1992–98; private advocate; organizations: Meridian International Center Board of Trustees; Woodrow Wilson Center Board of Trustees; California Institute Board of Directors; married: Robert Matsui, 1966; children: Brian Robert; committees: Energy and Commerce; elected by special election on March 8, 2005 to the 109th Congress, to fill the vacancy caused by the death of her husband, Representative Robert Matsui; reelected to each succeeding Congress.

Office Listings

http://www.house.gov/matsui

222 Cannon House Office Building, Washington, DC 20515 .... (202) 225–7163
Chief of Staff.—Julie Eddy. FAX: 225–0566
Executive Assistant.—Erin Robbins.
Legislative Director.—Kyle Victor.
Deputy Chief of Staff / Communications Director.—Mara Lee.
501 I Street, 12–600, Sacramento, CA 95814 .... (916) 498–5600

District Director.—Nathan Dietrich.

County: SACRAMENTO COUNTY (part). CITY: Sacramento. Population (2000), 639,088.

ZIP Codes: 94204–09, 94211, 94229–30, 94232, 94234–37, 94239–40, 94244, 94246–49, 94252, 94254, 94256–59, 94261–63, 94267–69, 94271, 94273–74, 94277–80, 94282, 94284–91, 94293–99, 95660, 95670, 95758, 95812–20, 95822–29, 95831–35, 95838, 95840–43, 95851–53, 95860, 95864–67, 95887, 95894

* * *

SIXTH DISTRICT

LYNN C. WOOLSEY, Democrat, of Petaluma, CA; born in Seattle, WA, November 3, 1937; education: graduated from Lincoln High School, Seattle; B.S., University of San Francisco, 1981; professional: president and founder, Woolsey Personnel Service, 1980–92; human resources manager, Harris Digital Telephone Systems, 1969–80; elected member, Petaluma City Council, 1984–92; vice mayor, 1989 and 1992; family: four children, and five grandchildren; caucuses: member and chair, Sonoma County National Women's Political Caucus; chair, Sonoma County Commission on the Status of Women; Business and Professional Women; National Organization for Women; Sierra Club; chair, Sonoma County Hazardous Materials Management Commission; Association of Bay Area Governments, Regional Hazardous Materials Representative; advisory committee, CAL Energy Commission; African Great Lakes Caucus, Armenian Caucus, Bicameral Congressional Caucus on Parkinson's Disease, Bipartisan Congressional Refugee Caucus, Bipartisan Task Force on Nonproliferation, Community College Caucus, Congressional Animal Protection Caucus, Congressional Arts Caucus, Congressional Asthma and Allergy Caucus, Congressional Bike Congress, Congressional Buy American Caucus, Congressional Caucus for Women's Issues, Congressional Caucus to Fight and Control Methamphetamine, Congressional Caucus on Hellenic Issues, Congressional Caucus on Homelessness, Congressional Caucus on Missing, Exploited, and Runaway Children, Congressional Caucus on Wild Salmon, Congressional Entertainment Industries Caucus, Congressional Fire Services Caucus, Congressional Hazards Caucus, Congressional Humanities Caucus, Congressional Labor and Working Families Caucus, Congressional Lesbian, Gay, Bisexual, Transgender (LGBT) Equality Caucus, Congressional Mental Health Caucus, Congressional Neuroscience Caucus, Congressional Pro-Choice Caucus, Congressional Shellfish Caucus, Congressional Wildlife Refuge Caucus, Croatia Caucus, Freedom of the Press Caucus, Green Schools Caucus, House Hunger Caucus, House International Conservation Caucus, House Renewable Energy and Energy Efficiency Caucus, House Trade Working Group, Tom Lantos Commission on Human Rights, Intelligent Transportation Systems Caucus, International Workers Rights Caucus, Malaria Caucus, National Marine Sanctuary Caucus, Neuroscience Caucus, Oceans Caucus, Out of Afghanistan Caucus, U.S.-Philippines Friendship Caucus, Small Brewers Caucus, Sudan Caucus, Sustainable Energy and Environmental Coalition (SEEC), Wine Caucus, former co-chair of the Congressional Progressive Caucus; president, Americans for Democratic Action; committees: Education and the Workforce; Science, Space, and Technology; elected on November 3, 1992 to the 103rd Congress; reelected to each succeeding Congress.

Office Listings

http://www.house.gov/woolsey

2263 Rayburn House Office Building, Washington, DC 20515 .... (202) 225–5161
Chief of Staff.—Nora Matus. FAX: 225–5163
Communications Director / Press Secretary.—Bart Acocella.
1101 College Avenue, Suite 200, Santa Rosa, CA 95404 .... (707) 542–7182
District Director.—Wendy Friefeld.
1050 Northgate Drive, Suite 354, San Rafael, CA 94903 .... (415) 507–9554

Counties: MARIN, SONOMA (part). CITIES AND TOWNSHIPS: Santa Rosa, Sebastapol, Cotati, Petaluma, and Sonoma to Golden Gate Bridge. Population (2000), 639,087.

ZIP Codes: 94901, 94903–04, 94912–15, 94920, 94922–31, 94933, 94937–42, 94945–57, 94960, 94963–66, 94970–79, 94998–99, 95401–07, 95409, 95412, 95419, 95421, 95430–31, 95436, 95439, 95441–42, 95444, 95446, 95448, 95450, 95452, 95462, 95465, 95471–73, 95476, 95480, 95486, 95492, 95497

* * *

SEVENTH DISTRICT

GEORGE MILLER, Democrat, of Martinez, CA; born in Richmond, CA, May 17, 1945; education: attended Martinez public schools; Diablo Valley College; graduated, San Francisco State

College, 1968; J.D., University of California at Davis School of Law, 1972; member: California State bar; Davis Law School Alumni Association; served five years as legislative aide to Senate majority leader, California State Legislature; past chairman and member of Contra Costa County Democratic Central Committee; past president of Martinez Democratic Club; married: the former Cynthia Caccavo; children: George and Stephen; six grandchildren; committees: Education and the Workforce; elected to the 94th Congress, November 5, 1974; reelected to each succeeding Congress.

Office Listings

http://www.georgemiller.house.gov George.Miller@mail.house.gov

2205 Rayburn House Office Building, Washington, DC 20515 .... (202) 225–2095
Chief of Staff.—Daniel Weiss. FAX: 225–5609
Executive Assistant / Scheduler.—Courtney Rochelle.
1333 Willow Pass Road, Suite 203, Concord, CA 94520 .... (925) 602–1880
District Director.—Barbara Johnson.
3220 Blume Drive, Suite 160, Richmond, CA 94806 .... (510) 262–6500
Field Representative.—Latressa Alford.
375 G Street, Suite 1, Vallejo, CA 94592 .... (707) 645–1888
Field Representative.—Kathy Hoffman.

Counties: CONTRA COSTA (part), SOLANO (part). CITIES AND TOWNSHIPS: Benicia, Clayton, Concord, Crockett, El Sobrante, Green Valley, Hercules, Martinez, Pinole, Pittsburgh, Port Costa, Richmond, Rodeo, San Pablo, Sulsun Valley, Vacaville, and Vallejo. Population (2000), 639,088.

ZIP Codes: 94503, 94510, 94517, 94519–25, 94527, 94529, 94533–34, 94547, 94553, 94564–65, 94569, 94572, 94585, 94589–92, 94801–08, 94820, 94875, 95687–88, 95696

* * *

EIGHTH DISTRICT

NANCY PELOSI, Democrat, of San Francisco, CA; born in Baltimore, MD, March 26, 1940; daughter of the late Representative Thomas D'Alesandro, Jr., of MD; education: graduated, Institute of Notre Dame High School, 1958; B.A., Trinity College, Washington, DC (major, political science; minor, history), 1962; northern chair, California Democratic Party, 1977–81; state chair, California Democratic Party, 1981–83; chair, 1984 Democratic National Convention Host Committee; finance chair, Democratic Senatorial Campaign Committee, 1985–86; member: Democratic National Committee; California Democratic Party Executive Committee; San Francisco Library Commission; Board of Trustees, LSB Leakey Foundation; married: Paul F. Pelosi, 1963; children: Nancy Corinne, Christine, Jacqueline, Paul, Jr., and Alexandra; 8 grandchildren; elected by special election, June 2, 1987, to the 100th Congress to fill the vacancy caused by the death of Representative Sala Burton; reelected to each succeeding Congress; elected Democratic Whip in the 107th Congress; Democratic Leader in the 108th and 109th Congresses; elected Speaker of the House in the 110th and 111th Congresses; elected Democratic Leader in the 112th Congress.

Office Listings

http://www.house.gov/pelosi sf.nancy@mail.house.gov

235 Cannon House Office Building, Washington, DC 20515 .... (202) 225–4965
Chief of Staff.—Vacant. FAX: 225–8259
90 7th Street, Suite 2–800, San Francisco, CA 94103 .... (415) 556–4862
District Director.—Dan Bernal.

County: SAN FRANCISCO COUNTY (part). CITY: San Francisco. Population (2000), 639,088.

ZIP Codes: 94101–12, 94114–15, 94117–26, 94128–47, 94150–52, 94155–56, 94158–66, 94168, 94170, 94172, 94175, 94177, 94188, 94199

* * *

NINTH DISTRICT

BARBARA LEE, Democrat, of Oakland, CA; born in El Paso, TX, July 16, 1946; education: graduated, San Fernando High School; B.A., Mills College, 1973; MSW, University of California, Berkeley, 1975; congressional aide and public servant; senior advisor and chief of staff to Congressman Ronald V. Dellums in Washington, DC, and Oakland, CA, 1975–87; California State Assembly, 1990–96; California State Senate, 1996–98; Assembly committees: Housing and Land Use; Appropriations; Business and Professions; Industrial Relations; Judiciary; Revenue and Taxation; board member, California State Coastal Conservancy, District Export Council, and California Defense Conversion Council; committees: Appropriations; elected to the 105th Congress on April 7, 1998, by special election, to fill the remaining term of retiring Representative Ronald V. Dellums; reelected to each succeeding Congress.

Office Listings

http://lee.house.gov

2267 Rayburn House Office Building, Washington, DC 20515 .... (202) 225–2661
Chief of Staff.—Julie Nickson. FAX: 225–9817
Scheduler.—Tatyana Kalinga.
Communications Director.—Joel Payne.
Legislative Director.—Julie Nickson.
1301 Clay Street, Suite 1000–N, Oakland, CA 94612 .... (510) 763–0370

Counties: ALAMEDA COUNTY. CITIES: Alameda, Albany, Berkeley, Emeryville, Kensington, Piedmont. OAKLAND COUNTY (part). Population (2000), 639,088.

ZIP Codes: 94541–42, 94546, 94552, 94577–80, 94588, 94601–13, 94615, 94617–26, 94643, 94649, 94659–62, 94666, 94701–10, 94712, 94720

* * *

TENTH DISTRICT

JOHN GARAMENDI, Democrat, of Walnut Grove, CA; born in Mokelumne Hill, CA, January 24, 1945; education: B.A., business, University of California-Berkeley, Berkeley, CA, 1966; M.B.A., Harvard University, Cambridge, MA, 1974; professional: small business owner; Peace Corps volunteer, 1966–68; California State Assembly member, 1974–76; member of the California State Senator, 1976–90; California Insurance Commissioner, 1991–94, and 2002–06; Deputy Secretary of the U.S. Interior Department, 1995–98; previously California Lieutenant Governor, 2007–09; regent, University of California; trustee, California State University; member of Make It In America Working Group; religion: Christian; family: married to Patricia Garamendi; six children; ten grandchildren; Deputy Whip; committees: Armed Services; Natural Resources; elected by special election on November 3, 2009, to fill the vacancy caused by the resignation of U.S. Representative Ellen Tauscher; elected to the 112th Congress on November 2, 2010.

Office Listings

http://garamendi.house.gov

228 Cannon House Office Building, Washington, DC 20515 .... (202) 225–1880
Chief of Staff.—Charles "Chic" Dambach. FAX: 225–5914
Scheduler.—Mayra Chavez.
Communications Director.—Donald Lathbury.
Legislative Director.—Chris Austin.
1981 North Broadway, Suite 220, Walnut Creek, CA 94596 .... (925) 932–8899
FAX: 932–8159
420 West 3rd Street, Antioch, CA 94509 .... (925) 757–7187
FAX: 757–7056
609 Jefferson Street, Fairfield, CA 94533 .... (707) 438–1822
FAX: 438–0523

Counties: ALAMEDA (part), CONTRA COSTA (part), SACRAMENTO (part), SOLANO (part). CITIES AND TOWNSHIPS: Alamo, Antioch, Bethel Island, Concord, Dixon, El Cerrito, Elmira, Fairfield, Isleton, Kensington, Knightsen, Lafayette, Livermore, Moraga, Oakley, Orinda, Pleasant Hill, Suisun City, Waldon, Walnut Creek and Walnut Grove. Population (2000), 639,088.

ZIP Codes: 94506–07, 94509–14, 94517–18, 94520–21, 94523, 94526, 94530, 94533, 94535, 94547, 94549–50, 94553, 94556, 94561, 94563, 94565, 94569, 94571, 94583, 94585, 94595–96, 94598, 94707–08, 95376, 95620, 95625, 95641, 95687–90, 94707–08

* * *

ELEVENTH DISTRICT

JERRY MCNERNEY, Democrat, of Pleasanton, CA; born in Albuquerque, NM, June 18, 1951; attended the U.S. Military Academy, West Point, NY, 1969–71; A.S., University of New

Mexico, Albuquerque, NM, 1973; M.S., University of New Mexico, NM, 1975; Ph.D. in Mathematics, University of New Mexico, 1981; professional: wind engineer; entrepreneur; business owner; married: Mary; children: Michael, Windy and Greg; committees: Science, Space, and Technology; Veterans' Affairs; elected to the 110th Congress on November 7, 2006; reelected to each succeeding Congress.

Office Listings

http://www.house.gov

1210 Longworth House Office Building, Washington, DC 20515 .... (202) 225–1947
Chief of Staff.—Nick Holder. FAX: 225–4060
Executive Assistant.—Teresa Frison.
Communications Director.—Sarah Hersh.
Legislative Director.—Andrew Horowitz.
5776 Stoneridge Mall Road, #175, Pleasanton, CA 94588 .... (925) 737–0727
District Director.—Nicole Damasco Alioto.
2222 Grand Canal Boulevard, #7, Stockton, CA 95207 .... (209) 476–8552

Counties: ALAMEDA (part), CONTRA COSTA (part), SAN JOAQUIN (part), SANTA CLARA (part). CITIES AND TOWNSHIPS: Blackhawk, Brentwood, Byron, Clements, Danville, Diablo, Discovery Bay, Dublin, Escalon, Farmington, Linden, Lockeford, Lodi, Manteca, Morada, Morgan Hill, Pleasanton, Ripon, San Ramon, Stockton, Sunol, Tracy, and Woodbridge. Population (2000), 639,088.

ZIP Codes: 94506–07, 94509, 94513–14, 94526, 94528, 94539, 94550, 94566, 94568, 94583, 94586, 94588, 95020, 95023, 95037–38, 95046, 95127, 95132, 95135, 95138, 95140, 95204, 95207, 95209–12, 95215, 95219–20, 95227, 95230, 95234, 95236–37, 95240–42, 95253, 95258, 95267, 95297, 95304, 95320, 95336–37, 95361, 95366, 95376–77, 95391, 95686

* * *

TWELFTH DISTRICT

JACKIE SPEIER, Democrat, of Hillsborough, CA; born in San Francisco, CA, May 14, 1950; education: B.A., University of California at Davis; J.D., University of California, Hastings College of the Law, 1976; legislative council, Congressman Leo J. Ryan; member, San Mateo County Board of Supervisors; member, California State Assembly; senator, California State Senate; married: Barry Dennis; two children: Jackson Sierra and Stephanie Sierra; committees: Financial Services, Homeland Security; Oversight and Government Reform; elected in a special election, April 8, 2008, to fill the vacancy caused by the death of Representative Thomas P. Lantos; elected to the 111th Congress on November 4, 2008; reelected to the 112th Congress on November 2, 2010.

Office Listings

http://speier.house.gov

211 Cannon House Office Building, Washington, DC 20515 .... (202) 225–3531
Chief of Staff.—Cookab Hashemi. FAX: 226–4183
Legislative Director.—Erin Ryan.
400 South El Camino Real, Suite 410, San Mateo, CA 94402 .... (650) 342–0300
District Representative.—Richard Steffan. FAX: 375–8270

Counties: SAN MATEO COUNTY (part). CITIES: Brisbane, Burlingame, Colma, Daly City, Foster City, Hillsborough, Millbrae, Montara, Moss Beach, Pacifica, Redwood City, San Bruno, San Carlos, San Mateo, South San Francisco. SAN FRANCISCO COUNTY (part). CITIES: San Francisco. Population (2000), 639,088.

ZIP Codes: 94005, 94010–11, 94013–17, 94021, 94030, 94037–38, 94044, 94061–63, 94065–66, 94070, 94080, 94083, 94099, 94112, 94116–17, 94122, 94127–28, 94131–32, 94143, 94401–09, 94497

* * *

THIRTEENTH DISTRICT

FORTNEY PETE STARK, Democrat, of Fremont, CA; born in Milwaukee, WI, November 11, 1931; education: graduated, Wauwatosa, WI, High School, 1949; B.S., Massachusetts Institute of Technology, 1953; M.B.A., University of California, Berkeley, 1960; G.E.D., East Bay Skills Center, Oakland, 1972 (honorary); served in U.S. Air Force, 1955–57, first lieutenant; banker, founder, and president, Security National Bank, Walnut Creek, CA, 1963–72; trustee, California Democratic Council; chairman, board of trustees, Starr King School of Ministry,

Berkeley; trustee, Graduate Theological Union, Berkeley; sponsor, Northern California American Civil Liberties Union; board member, Housing Development Corporation and Council for Civic Unity; director, Common Cause, 1971–72; married: Deborah Roderick; children: Jeffrey Peter, Beatrice Stark Winslow, Thekla Stark Wainwright, Sarah Stark Ramirez, Fortney Stark III, Hannah and Andrew; committees: Ways and Means; elected to the 93rd Congress, November 7, 1972; reelected to each succeeding Congress.

Office Listings

239 Cannon House Office Building, Washington, DC 20515 .... (202) 225–5065
Chief of Staff.—Debbie Curtis. FAX: 226–3805
Personal Assistant.—Rebecca Slater.
39300 Civic Center Drive, Fremont, CA 94538 .... (510) 494–1388
District Administrator.—Jo Cazenave.

Counties: ALAMEDA COUNTY (part). CITIES AND TOWNSHIPS: Alameda, Castro Valley, Fremont, Hayward, Newark, Oakland, San Leandro, San Lorenzo, Sunol, and Union City. Population (2000), 639,088.

ZIP Codes: 94501–02, 94536, 94538–39, 94541–42, 94544–06, 94552, 94560, 94566, 94588, 94577–80, 94586–87, 94603, 94614, 94557

* * *

FOURTEENTH DISTRICT

ANNA G. ESHOO, Democrat, of Menlo Park, CA; born in New Britain, CT, December 13, 1942; education: attended Canada College; San Mateo supervisor, 1983–92; served on the House Committees on Science, Space, and Technology, and Merchant Marine and Fisheries; selected to co-chair the House Medical Technology Caucus, 1994; committees: Energy and Commerce; elected on November 3, 1992, to the 103rd Congress; reelected to each succeeding Congress.

Office Listings

http://www.eshoo.house.gov

205 Cannon House Office Building, Washington, DC 20515 .... (202) 225–8104
Chief of Staff.—Mieke Eoyang. FAX: 225–8890
Executive Assistant.—Jena Gross.
698 Emerson Street, Palo Alto, CA 94301 .... (650) 323–2984
Chief of Staff.—Karen Chapman.

Counties: SAN MATEO (part), SANTA CLARA (part), SANTA CRUZ (part). CITIES AND TOWNSHIPS: Amesti, Aptos, Atherton, Belmont, Ben Lomond, Bonny Doon, Boulder Creek, Brookdale, Corralitos, Davenport, East Palo Alto, Felton, Half Moon Bay, Interlaken, La Honda, Los Altos, Los Altos Hills, Menlo Park, Monte Sereno, Mountain View, Palo Alto, Portola Valley, Redwood City, San Carlos, Scotts Valley, Stanford, Sunnyvale, and Woodside. Population (2000), 639,088.

ZIP Codes: 94002, 94018–28, 94035, 94039–43, 94060–64, 94074, 94085–89, 94301–06, 94309, 95003, 95005–08, 95014, 95017–18, 95030, 95033, 95041, 95051, 95060, 95065–67, 95070–71, 95073, 95076, 95130

* * *

FIFTEENTH DISTRICT

MICHAEL M. HONDA, Democrat, of San Jose, CA; born in Walnut Creek, CA, June 27, 1941; education: San Jose State University, received degrees in Biological Sciences and Spanish, and a Masters Degree in Education; awards: California Federation of Teachers Legislator of the Year; Outreach Paratransit Services Humanitarian Award; AEA Legislator of the Year; Service Employees International Union Home Care Champion Award; Asian Law Alliance Community Impact Award; AFL–CIO Distinguished Friend of Labor Award; chair emeritus, Congressional Asian Pacific American Caucus; chair, Ethiopia and Ethiopian American Caucus; public service: Peace Corps; San Jose Planning Commission; San Jose Unified School Board; Santa Clara County Board of Supervisors; California State Assemblyman; family: widower; children: Mark and Michelle; committees: Appropriations; Budget; vice chair, Democratic National Committee; Democratic Senior Whip; elected to the 107th Congress on November 7, 2000; reelected to each succeeding Congress.

Office Listings

http://www.house.gov/honda

1713 Longworth House Office Building, Washington, DC 20515 .... (202) 225–2631

Chief of Staff.—Jennifer Van der Heide. FAX: 225–2699
Legislative Director.—Eric Werwa.
Communications Director.—Michael Shank.
1999 South Bascom Avenue, Suite 815, Campbell, CA 95008 .... (408) 558–8085
District Director.—Meri Maben.

Counties: SANTA CLARA COUNTY (part). CITIES AND TOWNSHIPS: Campbell, Cambrian Park, Cupertino, Fruitdale, Gilroy, Lexington Hill, Los Gatos, Milpitas, San Jose, and Santa Clara. Population (2000), 639,088.

ZIP Codes: 94024, 94087, 95002, 95008–09, 95011, 95014–15, 95020–21, 95026, 95030–33, 95035–37, 95044, 95050–56, 95070, 95101, 95112, 95117–18, 95120, 95123–34, 95150, 95153–55, 95157, 95160–61, 95170

* * *

SIXTEENTH DISTRICT

ZOE LOFGREN, Democrat, of San Jose, CA; born in San Mateo, CA, December 21, 1947; education: graduated Gunn High School, 1966; B.A., Stanford University, Stanford, CA, 1970; J.D., Santa Clara Law School, Santa Clara, CA, 1975; admitted to the California bar, 1975; District of Columbia bar, 1981; Supreme Court, 1986; member: board of trustees, San Jose Evergreen Community College District, 1979–81; board of supervisors, Santa Clara County, CA, 1981–94; married: John Marshall Collins, 1978; children: Sheila and John; committees: House Administration; Judiciary; Science, Space, and Technology; Joint Committee on the Library; elected to the 104th Congress; reelected to each succeeding Congress.

Office Listings

http://www.house.gov/lofgren

1401 Longworth House Office Building, Washington, DC 20515 .... (202) 225–3072
Chief of Staff.—Stacey Leavandosky. FAX: 225–3336
Communications Director.—Pedro Ribeiro.
Executive Assistant / Scheduler.—Monica Swintz.
635 North First Street, Suite B, San Jose, CA 95112 .... (408) 271–8700
Chief of Staff.—Sandra Soto.

Counties: SANTA CLARA COUNTY (part). CITIES AND TOWNSHIPS: San Jose, San Martin, and unincorporated portions of southern Santa Clara County. Population (2000), 639,088.

ZIP Codes: 95008, 95013, 95020, 95035, 95037, 95042, 95046, 95103, 95106, 95108–13, 95115–16, 95118–28, 95131–36, 95138–40, 95148, 95151–52, 95156, 95158–59, 95164, 95172–73, 95190–94, 95196

* * *

SEVENTEENTH DISTRICT

SAM FARR, Democrat, of Carmel, CA; born in San Francisco, CA, July 4, 1941; education: attended Carmel, CA, public schools; B.S., biology, Willamette University, Salem, OR; studied at the Monterey Institute of International Studies; served in the Peace Corps for two years in Colombia, South America; worked as a consultant and employee of the California Assembly; elected to the California Assembly, 1980–93; former member of California Assembly's Committees on Education, Insurance, and Natural Resources; married to Shary Baldwin; one daughter: Jessica; committees: Appropriations; elected on June 8, 1993, by special election, to fill the vacancy caused by the resignation of Representative Leon Panetta; reelected to each succeeding Congress.

Office Listings

http://www.farr.house.gov

1126 Longworth House Office Building, Washington, DC 20515 .... (202) 225–2861
Chief of Staff.—Rochelle Dornatt.
Legislative Director.—Debbie Merrill.
Press Secretary.—David Beltran.
701 Ocean Avenue, Santa Cruz, CA 95060 .... (831) 429–1976
100 West Alisal Street, Salinas, CA 93901 .... (831) 424–2229

Counties: MONTEREY, SAN BENITO, SANTA CRUZ (southern half). Population (2000), 639,088.

ZIP Codes: 93426, 93450–51, 93901–02, 93905–08, 93912, 93915, 93920–28, 93930, 93932–33, 93940, 93942–44, 93950, 93953–55, 93960, 93962, 95001, 95003–04, 95010, 95012, 95019, 95023–24, 95039, 95043, 95045, 95060–65, 95073, 95075–77

* * *

EIGHTEENTH DISTRICT

DENNIS A. CARDOZA, Democrat, of Atwater, CA; born in Merced, CA, March 31, 1959; education: B.A., University of Maryland, 1982; professional: businessman; public service: Atwater City Council, 1984–87; California State Assembly, 1996–2002; awards: California State Sheriff's Association Legislator of the Year; Small Business Roundtable Legislator of the Year; Small Business Association Legislator of the Year; and University of California Legislator of the Year, for his work on behalf of U.C. Merced; religion: Catholic; family: married to Dr. Kathleen McLoughlin; children: Joey, Brittany, and Elaina; committees: Agriculture; Foreign Affairs; elected to the 108th Congress on November 5, 2002; reelected to each succeeding Congress.

Office Listings

http://www.house.gov/cardoza

2437 Rayburn House Office Building, Washington, DC 20515 .... (202) 225–6131
FAX: 225–0819
Chief of Staff.—Jennifer Walsh.
1010 10th Street, Suite 5800, Modesto, CA 95354 .... (209) 527–1914
District Director.—Lisa Mantarro Moore.

Counties: FRESNO (part), MADERA (part), MERCED, SAN JOAQUIN (part), STANISLAUS (part). CITIES AND TOWNSHIPS: Atwater, Ceres, Dos Palos, Gustine, Lathrop, Livingston, Los Banos. Modesto, Newman, Patterson, and Stockton. Population (2000), 639,088.

ZIP Codes: 93606, 93610, 93620, 93622, 93630, 93635, 93637, 93661, 93665, 93706, 93722, 95201–08, 95210, 95213, 95215, 95231, 95269, 95296, 95301, 95303–04, 95307, 95312–13, 95315, 95317, 95319, 95322, 95324, 95326, 95330, 95333–34, 95336–37, 95340–41, 95344, 95348, 95350–54, 95357–58, 95360, 95363, 95365, 95369, 95374, 95380, 95385, 95387–88, 95397

* * *

NINETEENTH DISTRICT

JEFF DENHAM, Republican, of Atwater, CA; born in Hawthorne, CA, July 29, 1967; education: A.A., Victor Valley Junior College, Victorville, CA, 1989; B.A., California Polytechnic State University, San Luis Obispo, CA, 1992; military: United States Air Force, 1984–88; United States Air Force Reserve, 1988–2000; professional: business owner; served in the California State senate, 2002–10; religion: Christian; family: wife-Sonia, two children; committees: Natural Resources; Transportation and Infrastructure; Veterans' Affairs; elected to the 112th Congress on November 2, 2010.

Office Listings

http://www.denham.house.gov

1605 Longworth House Office Building, Washington, DC 20515 .... (202) 225–4540
FAX: 225–3402
Chief of Staff.—Jason Larrabee.
Scheduler.—Carol Kresse.
1040 East Herndon, Suite 201, Fresno, CA 93720 .... (559) 449–2490
District Director.—Bob Rucker.
3509 Coffee Road, Suite D3, Madesto, CA 95355 .... (209) 579–5438

Counties: FRESNO (part), MADERA (part), MARIPOSA (part), STANISLAUS (part), TUOLUMNE. CITIES AND TOWNSHIPS: Ahwahnee, Auberry, Bass Lake, Big Oak Flat, Cathey's Valley, Ceres, Chinese Camp, Chowchilla, Coarsegold, Columbia, Coleville, Coulterville, Crows Landing, Dardanelle, Denair, El Portal, Farmington, Firebaugh, Fish Camp, Fresno, Groveland, Hickman, Hornitos, Hughson, Kerman, Keyes, La Grange, Long Barn, Madera, Mariposa, Mendota, Midpines, Mi Wuk Village, Moccasin, Modesto, North Fork, Oakdale, Oakhurst, O'Neals, Pinecrest, Raymond, Riverbank, Salida, San Joaquin, Snelling, Sonora, Soulsbyville, Standard, Strawberry, Tranquillity, Tuolumne, Turlock, Twain Harte, Vernalis, Waterford, Wishon, and Yosemite National Park. Population (2000), 639,088.

ZIP Codes: 93601–02, 93604, 93610, 93614, 93622–23, 93626, 93630, 93637–40, 93643–45, 93650, 93653, 93660, 93668–69, 93703–06, 93710–11, 93720, 93722, 93726, 93728–29, 93741, 93755, 93765, 93780, 93784, 93790–94, 95230, 95305–07, 95309–11, 95313–14, 95316, 95318, 95321, 95323, 95325–29, 95335, 95338, 95345–47, 95350, 95355–58, 95361, 95364, 95367–69, 95370, 95372–73, 95375, 95379–83, 95385–86, 95389–90, 96107

* * *

TWENTIETH DISTRICT

JIM COSTA, Democrat, of Fresno, CA; born in Fresno, April 13, 1952; education: B.A., California State University, Fresno, CA, 1974; professional: employee, Costa Brothers Dairy,

1959–74; special assistant, Congressman John Krebs, 1975–76; administrative assistant, California Assemblyman Richard Lehman, 1976–78; California State Assembly, 1978–94; California State Senate, 1994–2002; chief executive officer, Costa Group, 2002–present; religion: Catholic; committees: Agriculture; Foreign Affairs; Natural Resources; elected to the 109th Congress on November 2, 2004; reelected to each succeeding Congress.

Office Listings

http://www.costa.house.gov

1314 Longworth House Office Building, Washington, DC 20515 .... (202) 225–3341
Chief of Staff.—Scott Nishioki. FAX: 225–9308
Deputy Chief of Staff / Scheduler.—Juan Lopez.
855 M Street, Suite 940, Fresno, CA 93721 .... (559) 495–1620
2700 N Street, Suite 225, Bakersfield, CA 93301 .... (661) 869–1620
District Director.—Kathy Eide.

Counties: FRESNO (part), KERN (part), KINGS. Population (2000), 639,088.

ZIP Codes: 93202–04, 93206, 93210, 93212, 93215–16, 93220, 93230, 93232, 93234, 93239, 93241–42, 93245–46, 93249–50, 93263, 93266, 93280, 93282, 93301, 93305, 93307, 93383, 93387, 93518, 93607–09, 93616, 93620, 93622, 93624–25, 93627, 93631, 93640, 93648, 93652, 93656–57, 93660, 93662, 93668, 93701–09, 93712, 93714–18, 93721–22, 93724–25, 93727–28, 93744–45, 93750, 93760–62, 93764, 93771–79, 93786, 93844, 93888

* * *

TWENTY-FIRST DISTRICT

DEVIN NUNES, Republican, of Tulare, CA; born in Tulare County, CA, October 1, 1973; education: A.A., College of the Sequoias; B.S., Agricultural Business, and a Masters Degree in Agriculture, from California Polytechnic State University, San Luis Obispo; graduate, California Agriculture Leadership Fellowship Program; professional: farmer and businessman; elected, College of the Sequoias Board of Trustees, 1996; reelected, 2000; appointed by President George W. Bush to serve as California State Director of the U.S. Department of Agriculture Rural Development Office, 2001; religion: Catholic; married: the former Elizabeth Tamariz, 2003; two children; committees: Ways and Means; Permanent Select Committee on Intelligence; elected to the 108th Congress on November 5, 2002; reelected to each succeeding Congress.

Office Listings

http://www.nunes.house.gov

1013 Longworth House Office Building, Washington, DC 20515 .... (202) 225–2523
Chief of Staff.—Johnny Amaral. FAX: 225–3404
Legislative Director.—Damon Nelson.
Communications Director.—Andrew House.
Executive Assistant.—Jennifer Morrow.
113 North Church Street, Suite 208, Visalia, CA 93291 .... (559) 733–3861
264 Clovis Avenue, Suite 206, Clovis, CA 93612 .... (559) 323–5235

Counties: TULARE, FRESNO (part). Population (2000), 639,088.

ZIP Codes: 93201, 93207–08, 93212, 93215, 93218–19, 93221, 93223, 93227, 93235, 93237, 93242, 93244, 93247, 93256–58, 93260–62, 93265, 93267, 93270–72, 93274–75, 93277–79, 93286, 93290–92, 93602–03, 93605, 93609, 93611–13, 93615–16, 93618, 93621, 93625–26, 93628, 93631, 93633–34, 93641–42, 93646–49, 93651, 93654, 93656–57, 93662, 93664, 93666–67, 93670, 93673, 93675, 93703, 93710, 93720, 93726–27, 93740, 93747

* * *

TWENTY-SECOND DISTRICT

KEVIN McCARTHY, Republican, of Bakersfield, CA; born in Bakersfield, January 26, 1965; education: graduated, Bakersfield High School, 1983; B.S., business administration, CSU–Bakersfield, 1989; M.B.A., CSU–Bakersfield, 1994; professional: intern, worked up to District Director for U.S. Congressman Bill Thomas, 1987–2002; served as Trustee, Kern Community College District, 2000–02; served in the California State Assembly, 2002–06; elected, California Assembly Republican Leader, 2003–06; married to the former Judy Wages, 1992; two children: Connor and Meghan; committees: Financial Services; elected to the 110th Congress on November 7, 2006; reelected to each succeeding Congress.

Office Listings

http://www.kevinmccarthy.house.gov

326 Cannon House Office Building, Washington, DC 20515 .... (202) 225–2915
Chief of Staff.—James Min. FAX: 225–2908
Scheduler.—Kristin Thomson.
Legislative Director.—Kyle Lombardi.
Press Secretary.—Andrea McCarthy.
4100 Empire Drive, Suite 150, Bakersfield, CA 93309 .... (661) 327–3611
District Administrator.—Robin Lake Foster.
5805 Capistrano Avenue, Suite C, Atascadero, CA 93422 .... (805) 461–1034

Counties: KERN COUNTY (part). CITIES AND TOWNSHIPS: Arvin, Bakersfield, Bodfish, Boron, Caliente, California City, Cantil, China Lake, Edison, Edwards, Fellows, Frazier Park, Glennville, Havilah, Inyokern, Keene, Kernville, Lake Isabella, Lebec, Maricopa, McKittrick, Mojave, Monolith, North Edwards, Onyx, Randsberg, Ridgecrest, Rosamond, Taft, Tehachapi, Tupman, Weldon, Willow Springs, Wofford Heights, Woody. SAN LUIS OBISPO COUNTY (part). CITIES AND TOWNSHIPS: Arroyo Grande, Paso Robles, San Miguel, Atascadero, Shandon, Templeton, San Luis Obispo, Nipomo. LOS ANGELES COUNTY (part). CITIES AND TOWNSHIPS: Lancaster. Population (2000) 639,088.

ZIP Codes: 91390, 92832, 92834, 93203, 93205–06, 93215, 93222, 93224–26, 93238, 93240–41, 93243, 93249–52, 93255, 93263, 93268, 93276, 93283, 93285, 93287, 93301–09, 93311–14, 93380, 93384–86, 93388–90, 93401–02, 93405, 93407, 93409–10, 93420, 93422–23, 93426, 93428, 93430, 93432, 93442, 93444, 93446–47, 93451, 93453–54, 93461, 93465, 93501–02, 93504–05, 93516, 93518–19, 93522–24, 93527–28, 93531–32, 93534–36, 93539, 93554–56, 93558, 93560–61, 93581, 93584, 93596

* * *

TWENTY-THIRD DISTRICT

LOIS CAPPS, Democrat, of Santa Barbara, CA; born in Ladysmith, WI, January 10, 1938; education: graduated Flathead County High School, Kalispell, MT, 1955; B.S. in Nursing, Pacific Lutheran University, 1959; M.A. in Religion, Yale University, 1964; M.A. in Education, University of California at Santa Barbara, 1990; professional: head nurse, Yale New Haven Hospital; staff nurse, Visiting Nurses Association, Hamden, CT; elementary district nurse, Santa Barbara School District; director, Teenage Pregnancy and Parenting Project, Santa Barbara County; director, Santa Barbara School District Parent and Child Education Center; instructor of early childhood education, Santa Barbara City College; board member: American Red Cross, American Heart Association, Family Service Agency, Santa Barbara Women's Political Committee; married: Walter Capps, 1960; children: Lisa, Todd, and Laura; committees: Energy and Commerce; elected by special election on March 10, 1998, to the 105th Congress, to fill the vacancy caused by the death of her husband Rep. Walter Capps; reelected to each succeeding Congress.

Office Listings

http://www.house.gov/capps

2231 Rayburn House Office Building, Washington, DC 20515 .... (202) 225–3601
Chief of Staff.—Randolph Harrison. FAX: 225–5632
Legislative Director.—Jonathan Levenshus.
Press Secretary.—Ashley Schapitl.
Executive Assistant.—Sarah Rubinfield.
1411 Marsh Street, Suite 205, San Luis Obispo, CA 93401 .... (805) 546–8348
District Representatives: Betsy Umhofer, Greg Haas.
301 East Carrillo Street, Suite A, Santa Barbara, CA 93101 .... (805) 730–1710
District Director.—Sharon Siegel.
District Representative.—Rachel Kondor.
2675 North Ventura Road, Suite 104, Port Hueneme, CA 93041 .... (805) 985–6807
District Representatives: Carla Castilla, Vanessa Hernandez.

Counties: SAN LUIS OBISPO COUNTY (part). CITIES AND TOWNSHIPS: Baywood-Los Osos, Cambria, Cayucos, Grover Beach, Morro Bay, Nipomo, Oceano, Pismo Beach, San Luis Obispo. SANTA BARBARA COUNTY (part). CITIES AND TOWNSHIPS: Carpinteria, Goleta, Guadalupe, Isla Vista, Mission Canyon, Montecito, Santa Barbara, Santa Maria, Summerland, Toro Canyon. VENTURA COUNTY (part). CITIES AND TOWNSHIPS: Channel Island, El Rio, Oxnard, Port Hueneme, and San Buenaventura. Population (2000), 639,088.

ZIP Codes: 92832, 93001, 93003, 93013–14, 93030–36, 93041, 93043–44, 93067, 93101–03, 93105–11, 93116–18, 93120–21, 93130, 93140, 93150, 93160, 93190, 93199, 93401–03, 93405–06, 93408, 93412, 93420–21, 93424, 93428, 93430, 93433–35, 93442–45, 93448–49, 93452, 93454–56, 93458, 93483

* * *

TWENTY-FOURTH DISTRICT

ELTON GALLEGLY, Republican, of Simi Valley, CA; born in Huntington Park, CA, March 7, 1944; education: graduated Huntington Park High School, 1962; attended Los Angeles State College; businessman; member, Simi Valley City Council, 1979; mayor, city of Simi Valley, 1980–86; former vice-chairman and chairman, Ventura County Association of Governments; former member, board of directors, Moorpark College Foundation; delegate to 1988 Republican National Convention; married: the former Janice L. Shrader, 1974; children: Shawn G., Shawn P., Kevin, and Shannon; committees: Foreign Affairs; Judiciary; elected to the 100th Congress on November 4, 1986; reelected to each succeeding Congress.

Office Listings

2309 Rayburn House Office Building, Washington, DC 20515 .... (202) 225–5811
Chief of Staff.—Joel D. Kassiday. FAX: 225–1100
Executive Assistant.—Marianne Brant.
Press Secretary.—Tom Pfeifer.
5051 Verdugo Way, Suite 120, Camarillo, CA 93012 .... (805) 497–2224
District Chief of Staff.—Brian Miller. (800) 423–0023

Counties: VENTURA COUNTY (part). CITIES AND TOWNSHIPS: Bell Canyon, Camarillo, Fillmore, Moorpark, Newbury Park, Oak Park, Oak View, Ojai, Piru, Santa Paula, Simi Valley, Somis, Thousand Oaks, Ventura, Westlake Village. SANTA BARBARA COUNTY (part). CITIES AND TOWNSHIPS: Buellton, Lompoc, Los Alamos, Los Olivos, Orcutt, Santa Barbara, Santa Ynez, and Solvang. Population (2000), 639,088.

ZIP Codes: 91301, 91304, 91307, 91311, 91319–20, 91358–62, 91377, 91406, 91413, 93001, 93003–07, 93009–13, 93015–16, 93020–24, 93030, 93033, 93036, 93040–42, 93060–66, 93094, 93099, 93105, 93111, 93117, 93225, 93252, 93254, 93427, 93429, 93436–38, 93440–41, 93454–55, 93457–58, 93460, 93463–64

* * *

TWENTY-FIFTH DISTRICT

HOWARD P. ''BUCK'' McKEON, Republican, of Santa Clarita, CA; born in Los Angeles, CA, September 9, 1938; education: graduated, Verdugo Hills High School, Tujunga, CA; B.S., Brigham Young University; mayor and city councilman, Santa Clarita, 1987–92; former member: board of directors, Canyon Country Chamber of Commerce; California Republican State Central Committee; advisory council, Boy Scouts of America; president and trustee, William S. Hart School District, 1979–87; former chairman and director, Henry Mayo Newhall Memorial Hospital, 1983–87; former chairman and founding director, Valencia National Bank, 1987–92; honorary chairman, Red Cross Community Support Campaign, 1992; honorary chairman, Leukemia Society Celebrity Program, 1990 and 1994; president, Republican Freshman Class of the 103rd Congress; married: to the former Patricia Kunz, 1962; children: Tamara, Howard D., John Matthew, Kimberly, David Owen, and Tricia; committees: chair, Armed Services; Education and the Workforce; elected on November 3, 1992, to the 103rd Congress; reelected to each succeeding Congress.

Office Listings

http://www.house.gov/mckeon

2184 Rayburn House Office Building, Washington, DC 20515 .... (202) 225–1956
Chief of Staff.—Bob Cochran. FAX: 226–0683
Executive Assistant/Appointments.—Candace Dodge.
District Director.—Bob Haueter.
26650 The Old Road, Suite 203, Santa Clarita, CA 91355 .... (661) 254–2111
1008 West Avenue, M–14, Suite E1, Palmdale, CA 93551 .... (661) 274–9688

Counties: INYO, LOS ANGELES (part), MONO, SAN BERNARDINO (part). CITIES AND TOWNSHIPS: Acton, Adelanto, Baker, Barstow, Benton, Big Pine, Bishop, Bridgeport, Castaic, Canyon Country, Coleville, Death Valley, Edwards, Ft. Irwin, Helendale, Hesperia, Hinkley, Independence, Inyokern, June Lake, Keeler, La Crescenta, Lancaster, Littlerock, Little Lake, Little Vinning, Llano, Lone Pine, Mammoth Lakes, Newberry Springs, Newhall, Nipton, Olancha, Oro Grande, Palmdale, Pearblossom, Phelan, Pinon Hills, Ridgecrest, Santa Clarita, Shoshone, Stevenson Ranch, Sunland, Sylmar, Tecopa, Topaz, Trona, Tujunga, Valencia, Valyerno, Victorville, and Yermo. Population (2000), 639,087.

ZIP Codes: 91042, 91214, 91310, 91321–22, 91350–51, 91354–55, 91380–81, 91383–87, 91390, 92301, 92309–12, 92328, 92342, 92345, 92347, 92364–65, 92368, 92371–72, 92384, 92389, 92392–94, 92398, 92832, 93510, 93512–17, 93524, 93526–27, 93529–30, 93534–35, 93541–46, 93549–53, 93560, 93562, 93586, 93590–92, 93599, 96107, 96133

* * *

TWENTY-SIXTH DISTRICT

DAVID DREIER, Republican, of San Dimas, CA; born in Kansas City, MO, July 5, 1952; education: B.A. (*cum laude*) in political science, Claremont McKenna College, 1975; M.A., American Government, Claremont Graduate School, 1976; Winston S. Churchill Fellow; Phi Sigma Alpha; professional: director, corporate relations, Claremont McKenna College, 1975–78; member: board of governors, James Madison Society; Republican State Central Committee of California; Los Angeles Town Hall; named Outstanding Young Man of America and Outstanding Young Californian, 1976 and 1978; director, marketing and government affairs, Industrial Hydrocarbons, 1979–80; vice president, Dreier Development, 1985–present; author of congressional reform package incorporated into the House Rules; committees: chair, Rules; elected to the 97th Congress on November 4, 1980; reelected to each succeeding Congress.

Office Listings

http://www.house.gov/dreier

233 Cannon House Office Building, Washington, DC 20515 .... (202) 225–2305
Chief of Staff.—Bradley W. Smith. FAX: 225–7018
Executive Assistant.—Erin Wall.
Legislative Director.—Alisa Do.
510 East Foothill Boulevard, Suite 201, San Dimas, CA 91773 .... (909) 575–6226

Counties: LOS ANGELES (part). CITIES: Altadena, Arcadia, Bradbury, Claremont, Covina, Glendora, La Canada Flintridge, La Crescenta, La Verne, Monrovia, Montrose, Pasadena, San Antonio Heights, San Dimas, San Gabriel, San Marino, Sierra Madre, Walnut. SAN BERNARDINO (part). CITIES: Montclair, Rancho Cucamonga, Upland, and Wrightwood. Population (2000), 639,088.

ZIP Codes: 91001, 91006–07, 91010–12, 91016–17, 91020–21, 91023–25, 91066, 91077, 91104, 91107–08, 91118, 91131, 91185, 91187, 91191, 91214, 91390, 91410, 91701, 91711, 91730, 91737, 91739–41, 91750, 91759, 91763, 91773, 91775, 91784, 91786, 91789, 92329, 92336, 92345, 92358, 92371–72, 92397, 92407

* * *

TWENTY-SEVENTH DISTRICT

BRAD SHERMAN, Democrat, of Sherman Oaks, CA; born in Los Angeles, CA, October 24, 1954; education: B.A., *summa cum laude,* UCLA, 1974; J.D., *magna cum laude,* Harvard Law School, 1979; professional: admitted to the California bar in 1979 and began practice in Los Angeles; attorney, CPA, certified tax law specialist; elected to the California State Board of Equalization, 1990, serving as chairman, 1991–95; committees: Financial Services; Foreign Affairs; elected to the 105th Congress; reelected to each succeeding Congress.

Office Listings

2242 Rayburn House Office Building, Washington, DC 20515 .... (202) 225–5911
Chief of Staff.—Don MacDonald. FAX: 225–5879
Legislative Director.—Rebecca Korman.
Communications Director.—Matt Farrauto.
Legislative Correspondent.—Lauren Wolman.
5000 Van Nuys Boulevard, Suite 420, Sherman Oaks, CA 91403 .... (818) 501–9200
District Director.—Matthew Dababneh.

Counties: LOS ANGELES COUNTY (part). Population (2000), 639,088.

ZIP Codes: 91040–41, 91043, 91303–06, 91309, 91311–12, 91316, 91324–30, 91335, 91337, 91342–46, 91352, 91356–57, 91364, 91367, 91371, 91394–96, 91401, 91403, 91405–06, 91409, 91411, 91416, 91423, 91426, 91436, 91470, 91482, 91495–96, 91504–07, 91510, 91601, 91605–06

* * *

TWENTY-EIGHTH DISTRICT

HOWARD L. BERMAN, Democrat, of Van Nuys, CA; born in Los Angeles, CA, April 15, 1941; education: B.A. in international relations, UCLA, 1962; LL.B., UCLA School of Law, 1965; California Assembly Fellowship Program, 1965–70; Vista volunteer, 1966–67; admitted to the California bar, 1966; practiced law until election to California Assembly in

1972; named assembly majority leader in first term; served as chair of the Assembly Democratic Caucus and policy research management committee; member: regional board of the Anti-Defamation League; past president, California Federation of Young Democrats; married: Janis; children: Brinley and Lindsey; committees: ranking member, Foreign Affairs; Judiciary; elected to the 98th Congress on November 2, 1982; reelected to each succeeding Congress.

Office Listings

http://www.house.gov/berman

2221 Rayburn House Office Building, Washington, DC 20515 .... (202) 225–4695
Chief of Staff.—Julia Massimino. FAX: 225–3196
Executive Assistant / Appointments.—Deanne Samuels.
Communications Director.—Gabby Adler.
14546 Hamlin Street, Suite 202, Van Nuys, CA 91411 .... (818) 994–7200
District Director.—Gene Smith.

Counties: LOS ANGELES COUNTY (part). Portions of the city of Los Angeles, including all or part of the communities of Arleta, Encino, North Hollywood, North Hills, Pacoima, Panorama City, San Fernando, Sherman Oaks, Studio City, Valley Village, and Van Nuys. Population (2000), 639,087.

ZIP Codes: 90028, 90046, 90049, 90068, 91316, 91331, 91333–34, 91340–43, 91345, 91352–53, 91356, 91388, 91392–93, 91401–08, 91411–12, 91423, 91436, 91497, 91499, 91505, 91601–12, 91614–18

* * *

TWENTY-NINTH DISTRICT

ADAM B. SCHIFF, Democrat, of Burbank, CA; born in Framingham, MA, June 20, 1960; education: B.A., Stanford University, 1982; J.D., Harvard University, 1985; professional: Attorney; U.S. Attorney's Office, served as a criminal prosecutor; chosen by the Dept. of Justice to assist the Czechoslovakian Government in reforming their criminal justice system; public service: elected to the California State Senate, 1996; involved in numerous community service activities; awards: Dept. of Justice Special Achievement Award; Council of State Governments Toll Fellowship; California League of High Schools Legislator of the Year; family: married: Eve; children: Alexa and Elijah; committees: Appropriations; Permanent Select Committee on Intelligence; elected to the 107th Congress on November 7, 2000; reelected to each succeeding Congress.

Office Listings

http://www.house.gov/schiff

2411 Rayburn House Office Building, Washington, DC 20515 .... (202) 225–4176
Chief of Staff.—Timothy Bergreen. FAX: 225–5828
Communications Director.—Maureen Shanahan.
Executive Assistant.—Christopher Hoven.
87 North Raymond Avenue, Suite 800, Pasadena, CA 91103 .... (626) 304–2727
District Director.—Ann Peifer.

Counties: LOS ANGELES COUNTY (part). CITIES: Alhambra, Altadena, Burbank, Glendale, Griffith Park, Monterey Park, Pasadena, San Gabriel, South Pasadena, and Temple City. Population (2000), 639,088.

ZIP Codes: 90004–06, 90010, 90020, 90026–27, 90029, 90035–36, 90038–39, 90046, 90048, 90064, 90068, 91001, 91003, 91007, 91011, 91030–31, 91046, 91101–10, 91114–17, 91121, 91123–26, 91129, 91175, 91182, 91184, 91186, 91188–89, 91201–10, 91214, 91221–22, 91224–26, 91501–06, 91508, 91521–23, 91775–76, 91780, 91801, 91803–04

* * *

THIRTIETH DISTRICT

HENRY A. WAXMAN, Democrat, of Los Angeles, CA; born in Los Angeles, September 12, 1939; education: B.A., political science, UCLA, 1961; J.D., School of Law; admitted to the California State bar, 1965; served three terms as California State Assemblyman; former chairman, California Assembly Health Committee; Select Committee on Medical Malpractice; and Committee on Elections and Reapportionment; president, California Federation of Young Democrats, 1965–67; member: Guardians of the Jewish Home for the Aged; American Jewish Congress; Sierra Club; married: the former Janet Kessler, 1971; children: Carol Lynn and Michael David; committees: Energy and Commerce; elected to the 94th Congress on November 5, 1974; reelected to each succeeding Congress.

Office Listings

http://www.house.gov/waxman

2204 Rayburn House Office Building, Washington, DC 20515 .... (202) 225–3976
Chief of Staff.—Pat Delgado. FAX: 225–4099
8436 West Third Street, Suite 600, Los Angeles, CA 90048 .... (323) 651–1040
District Director.—Lisa Pinto.

Counties: LOS ANGELES COUNTY (part). CITIES AND TOWNSHIPS: Agoura Hills, Bel-Air, Beverly Hills, Brentwood, Calabasas, Canoga Park, Century City, Chatsworth, Hidden Hills, Malibu, Northridge, Pacific Palisades, Pico-Robertson, Santa Monica, Tarzana, Topanga, West Hills, West Hollywood, Westlake Village, West Los Angeles, Westwood, and Woodland Hills. Population (2000), 639,088.

ZIP Codes: 90024–25, 90027–29, 90032, 90034–36, 90038–39, 90046, 90048–49, 90057, 90063–64, 90067–69, 90072–73, 90075–77, 90095, 90209–13, 90263–65, 90272, 90290–91, 90401–11, 91301–04, 91307–08, 91311, 91313, 91324, 91356, 91361–65, 91367, 91372, 91376, 91399

* * *

THIRTY-FIRST DISTRICT

XAVIER BECERRA, Democrat, of Los Angeles, CA; born in Sacramento, CA, January 26, 1958; education: graduated, McClatchy High School, Sacramento, 1976; B.A., Stanford University, 1980; J.D., Stanford Law School, 1984; admitted to California bar, 1985; attended Universidad de Salamanca, 1978–79; staff attorney, "Reggie Fellow," Legal Assistance Corporation of Central Massachusetts, 1984–85; administrative assistant for State Senator Art Torres, California State Legislature, 1986; Deputy Attorney General, Office of the Attorney General, State of California, 1987–90; Assemblyman, California State Legislature, 1990–92; member: Mexican American State Legislators Policy Institute; Mexican American Bar Association; chairperson: Hispanic Employee Advisory Committee to the State Attorney General, 1989; honorary member: Association of California State Attorneys and Administrative Law Judges; former member: steering committee, Greater Eastside Voter Registration Project; Construction and General Laborers Union, Local 185 (Sacramento); Pitzer College Board of Trustees; National Association of Latino's Electoral and appointed to the Official Board of Directors; vice chair, Democratic Caucus of the 111th Congress; reelected vice chair, Democratic Caucus of the 112th Congress; married to Dr. Carolina Reyes; children: Clarisa, Olivia, Natalia; committees: Ways and Means; appointed Assistant to the Speaker of the House for the 110th Congress; elected on November 3, 1992, to the 103rd Congress; reelected to each succeeding Congress.

Office Listings

http://www.house.gov/becerra

1226 Longworth House Office Building, Washington, DC 20515 .... (202) 225–6235
Chief of Staff.—Debra Dixon. FAX: 225–2202
Legislative Director.—Sean McCluskie.
Scheduler.—Stephanie Venegas.
1910 Sunset Boulevard, Suite 810, Los Angeles, CA 90026 .... (213) 483–1425
District Director.—Liz Saldivar.

Counties: LOS ANGELES COUNTY (part). CITIES: Los Angeles. Population (2000), 639,088.

ZIP Codes: 90004–07, 90011–12, 90015, 90018, 90020–22, 90026, 90028–29, 90031–32, 90037–39, 90041–42, 90048, 90057–58, 90065, 90072

* * *

THIRTY-SECOND DISTRICT

JUDY M. CHU, Democrat, of El Monte, CA; born in Los Angeles, CA, July 7, 1953; education: B.A. in math from UCLA, Los Angeles, CA, 1974; Ph.D. in psychology from the California School of Professional Psychology, 1979; professional: Garvey School District Board member, 1985–88; Monterey Park City Council and Mayor, 1988–2001; California State Assembly, 2001–2006; California State Board of Equalization, 2006–2009; first Chinese American woman elected to Congress; family: married to Assemblymember Mike Eng in 1978; committees: Judiciary; Small Business; elected to the 111th Congress on July 14, 2009, by special election to fill the vacancy caused by the resignation of United States Representative Hilda Solis; reelected to the 112th Congress on November 2, 2010.

Office Listings

http://www.chu.house.gov

1520 Longworth House Office Building, Washington, DC 20515 .... (202) 225–5464
Chief of Staff.—Amelia Wang. FAX: 225–5467
Legislative Director.—Allison Rose.
Congressional Asian Pacific American Caucus (CAPAC) Executive Director.—Gene Kim.
Legislative Assistant.—Lelaine Bigelow.
Legislative Correspondent / System Administrator.—Eric Stecklow.
Legislative Counsel.—Vacant.
Press Secretary.—Austin Vevurka.
Scheduler.—Cyndy Hernandez.
Staff Assistant.—Vacant.
4401 Santa Anita Avenue, Suite 211, El Monte, CA 91731 .... (626) 448–1271
District Director.—Fred Ortega. FAX: 448–8062
Field Deputy / Case Workers: Becky Cheng, Anthony Duarte, Bryan Urias.
Caseworker / VITA Site Coordinator.—Lena Ng.
Caseworker.—Rita Medina.
District Scheduler.—Lindsay Plake.
Staff Assistant.—Vacant.

Counties: LOS ANGELES COUNTY (part). CITIES: Azusa, Baldwin Park, Covina, Duarte, El Monte, South El Monte, Irwindale, Monterey Park, Rosemead, San Gabriel, South San Gabriel, and portions of East Los Angeles, Citrus CDP, Glendora, Industry City, Los Angeles, Temple City, Vincent CDP, and West Covina. Population (2000), 639,087.

ZIP Codes: 90022, 90032, 90034–36, 90044–45, 90047–48, 90063–64, 90066–67, 90089, 91009–10, 91016, 91702, 91706, 91722–24, 91731–33, 91740, 91754–55, 91770, 91790–93

* * *

THIRTY-THIRD DISTRICT

KAREN R. BASS, Democrat, of Los Angeles, CA; born in Los Angeles, October 3, 1953; education: B.S., health sciences, California State University, Dominguez Hills, CA, 1990; P.A., University of Southern California School of Medicine, Los Angeles; professional: elected first Democratic woman Speaker of the California Assembly; founded and served as Executive Director of the non-profit organization Community Coalition, Los Angeles; physician assistant, Los Angeles County General Hospital; religion: Baptist; family: daughter Emilia Bass-Lechuga, son-in-law Michael Wright; step children: Scythia, Omar, Yvette, and Jesse Lechuga; awards: JFK profiles in Courage Award; Congressional Black Caucus Phoenix Award; committees: Budget; Foreign Affairs; elected to the 112th Congress on November 2, 2010.

Office Listings

http://karenbass.house.gov

408 Cannon Office Building, Washington, DC 20515 .... (202) 225–7084
Chief of Staff.—Marilyn Davis. FAX: 225–2422
Senior Legislative Assistant.—Kemi Jemilohun.
Scheduler / Executive Assistant.—MacKenzie Smith.
Communications Director.—Adam Sharon.
4322 Wilshire Boulevard, Suite 302, Los Angeles, CA 90010 .... (323) 965–1422
District Director.—Sylvia Castillo.

Counties: LOS ANGELES COUNTY (part). CITIES: Culver City, Los Angeles City, communities of Ladera Heights and View Park-Windsor Hills. Population (2000), 639,088.

ZIP Codes: 90004–08, 90010–11, 90016, 90018–20, 90022, 90026–29, 90033–39, 90043–45, 90047–48, 90053, 90056–58, 90062–64, 90066, 90068, 90070, 90078, 90083, 90093, 90099, 90103, 90230–33

* * *

THIRTY-FOURTH DISTRICT

LUCILLE ROYBAL-ALLARD, Democrat, of Los Angeles, CA; born in Los Angeles, June 12, 1941; education: B.A., California State University, Los Angeles, 1965; served in the California State Assembly, 1987–92; the first woman to serve as the chair of the California Democratic Congressional Delegation in the 105th Congress; in the 106th Congress, she became the first woman to chair the Congressional Hispanic Caucus, and the first Latina in history to be appointed to the House Appropriations Committee; married: Edward T. Allard III; two children:

Lisa Marie and Ricardo; two stepchildren: Angela and Guy Mark; committees: Appropriations; the first Mexican-American woman elected to Congress on November 3, 1992 to the 103rd Congress; reelected to each succeeding Congress.

Office Listings

http://www.house.gov/roybal-allard

2330 Rayburn House Office Building, Washington, DC 20515–0534 .... (202) 225–1766
Chief of Staff.—Paul Cunningham. FAX: 226–0350
Legislative Director.—Victor G. Castillo.
Executive Assistant.—Christine C. Ochoa.
255 East Temple Street, Suite 1860, Los Angeles, CA 90012–3334 .... (213) 628–9230
District Director.—Ana Figueroa.

Counties: LOS ANGELES COUNTY (part). CITIES: Bell, Belflower, Bell Gardens, Boyle Heights, Chinatown, Commerce, Cudahy, Downey, Downtown Los Angeles, East Los Angeles, Florence, Huntington Park, Little Tokyo, Maywood, Pico Union, South Park, Vernon, and Westlake. Population (2000), 639,088.

ZIP Codes: 90001, 90005–7, 90011–15, 90017, 90020–23, 90026, 90033, 90040, 90057–58, 90063, 90071, 90201, 90240, 90255, 90270, 90241–42, 90706

* * *

THIRTY-FIFTH DISTRICT

MAXINE WATERS, Democrat, of Los Angeles, CA; born in St. Louis, MO, August 15, 1938; education: B.A., California State University; honorary degrees: Harris-Stowe State College, St. Louis, MO, and Central State University, Wilberforce, OH, Spelman College, Atlanta, GA, North Carolina A&T State University, Howard University, Central State University, Bishop College, Morgan State University; elected to California State Assembly, 1976; reelected every two years thereafter; member: Assembly Democratic Caucus, Board of TransAfrica Foundation, National Women's Political Caucus; chair, Democratic Caucus Special Committee on Election Reform; chair, Ways and Means Subcommittee on State Administration; chair, Joint Committee on Public Pension Fund Investments; founding member, National Commission for Economic Conversion and Disarmament; member of the board, Center for National Policy; Clara Elizabeth Jackson Carter Foundation (Spelman College); Minority AIDS Project; married to Sidney Williams, former U.S. Ambassador to the Commonwealth of the Bahamas; two children: Karen and Edward; committees: Financial Services; Judiciary; Chief Deputy Whip; elected to the 102nd Congress on November 6, 1990; reelected to each succeeding Congress.

Office Listings

2344 Rayburn House Office Building, Washington, DC 20515 .... (202) 225–2201
Chief of Staff.—Mikael Moore. FAX: 225–7854
Deputy Chief of Staff.—Charla Ouertatani.
10124 South Broadway, Suite 1, Los Angeles, CA 90003 .... (323) 757–8900
District Director.—Blanca Jimenez.

Counties: LOS ANGELES COUNTY (part). CITIES: Gardena, Hawthorne, Inglewood, Lawndale, Los Angeles, Playa Del Ray, and Torrance. Population (2000), 639,088.

ZIP Codes: 90001–03, 90007, 90009, 90037, 90044–45, 90047, 90052, 90056, 90059, 90061, 90066, 90082, 90094, 90189, 90247–51, 90260–61, 90293, 90301–13, 90397–98, 90504, 90506

* * *

THIRTY-SIXTH DISTRICT

JANICE HAHN, Democrat, of San Pedro, CA; born in Los Angeles, CA, March 30, 1952; education: B.S. in education, Abilene Christian University, Abilene, TX, 1974; professional: teacher, Good News Academy, 1974–78; stay-at-home mother, 1978–88; Director of Marketing, Alexander Haagan Company, 1988–90; Director of Community Outreach, Western Waste Industries, 1990–92; Vice President of Public Finance, Prudential Securities, 1993–95; Public Affairs Regional Manager, Southern California Edison, Co., 1995–2000; elected to the Charter Reform Commission, 1997–99; Los Angeles City Council, 15th District, 2001–11; family: children Danny, Mark, and Katy; grandchildren, McKenna, Brooklyn, Isabela, Josiah, and Luke; committees: Homeland Security; Small Business; elected to the 112th Congress by special election, July 12, 2011, to fill the vacancy caused by the resignation of United States Representative Jane Harman, and took the oath of office July 19, 2011.

Office Listings

http://www.house.gov/hahn

2400 Rayburn House Office Building, Washington, DC 20515 .... (202) 225–8220
Chief of Staff.—Jason Linde. FAX: 226–7290
Legislative Director.—Vacant.
Scheduler.—Dana Sandman.
2321 East Rosecrans Boulevard, Suite 3270, El Segundo, CA 90245 .... (310) 643–3636
544 North Avalon Boulevard, Suite 307, Wilmington, CA 90744 .... (310) 549–8282

Counties: LOS ANGELES COUNTY (part). CITIES: El Segundo, Harbor City, Hermosa Beach, Lawndale, Lennox, Los Angeles, Manhattan Beach, Marina Del Rey, Playa Del Rey, Redondo Beach, San Pedro, Torrance, Venice, Westchester, West Carson, and Wilmington. Population (2000), 639,087.

ZIP Codes: 90009, 90025, 90034, 90039, 90045, 90064, 90066, 90080, 90245, 90248, 90254, 90266–67, 90277–78, 90291–92, 90294–96, 90304, 90404–05, 90501–10, 90710, 90717, 90731–34, 90744, 90748

* * *

THIRTY-SEVENTH DISTRICT

LAURA RICHARDSON, Democrat of Long Beach, CA; born in Los Angeles, CA, April 14, 1962; education: B.A., political science, University of California, Los Angeles, 1984; M.B.A., University of Southern California, Los Angeles, 1996; professional: businesswoman, Xerox Corporation; member, Long Beach City Council, 2000–06; member, California State Assembly, 2006–07; commissions and caucuses: founding member and co-chair, California High Speed Rail; regional whip, Democratic Caucus; Congressional Black Caucus; New Democrat Caucus; Progressive Caucus; committees: Homeland Security; Transportation and Infrastructure; elected to the 110th Congress, by special election on August 21, 2007, to fill the vacancy caused by the death of United States Representative Juanita Millender-McDonald; elected to a full term in the 111th Congress on November 4, 2008; reelected to the 112th Congress.

Office Listings

http://www.richardson.house.gov

1130 Longworth House Office Building, Washington, DC 20515 .... (202) 225–7924
Chief of Staff.—Shirley Cooks.
Legislative Director.—Gregory Berry.
Communications Director.—Ray Zaccaro.
Scheduler.—Jakki Dennis.
100 West Broadway, West Tower, Suite 600, Long Beach, CA 90802 .... (562) 436–3828
District Director.—Eric Boyd.
Scheduler.—Daysha Austin.

Counties: LOS ANGELES COUNTY (part). CITIES: Carson, Compton, and Long Beach, Signal Hill, South Los Angeles, Watts and Willowbrook. Population (2000), 639,088.

ZIP Codes: 90002–03, 90044, 90059, 90061, 90220–24, 90247, 90501–02, 90713, 90723, 90745–47, 90749, 90755, 90801–10, 90813–15, 90822, 90842, 90844–48, 90888, 90899

* * *

THIRTY-EIGHTH DISTRICT

GRACE F. NAPOLITANO, Democrat, of Los Angeles, CA; born in Brownsville, TX, December 4, 1936; education: Brownsville High School, Brownsville, TX; Cerritos College, Norwalk, CA; Texas Southmost College, Brownsville, TX; professional: Transportation Coordinator, Ford Motor Company; elected to Norwalk, CA, City Council, 1986; became mayor of Norwalk, CA, 1989; elected to the California Assembly, 58th District, 1992–98; organizations: Norwalk Lions Club; Veterans of Foreign Wars (auxiliary); American Legion (auxiliary); Soroptimist International; past director, Cerritos College Foundation; director, Community Family Guidance Center; League of United Latin American Citizens; director, Los Angeles County Sanitation District; director, Los Angeles County Vector Control (Southeast District); director, Southeast Los Angeles Private Industry Council; director, Los Angeles County Sheriff's Authority; National Women's Political Caucus; past national board secretary, United States-Mexico Sister Cities Association; member, Congressional Hispanic Caucus; co-chair, Congressional Mental Health Caucus; maiden name: Flores; married: Frank Napolitano; children: Yolanda Dyer, Fred Musquiz, Edward Musquiz, Michael Musquiz, and Cynthia Dowling; committees:

Natural Resources; Transportation and Infrastructure; elected to the 106th Congress; reelected to each succeeding Congress.

Office Listings

http://www.house.gov/napolitano

1610 Longworth House Office Building, Washington, DC 20515 .... (202) 225–5256
Chief of Staff.—Daniel Chao. FAX: 225–0027
Legislative Director.—Joe Sheehy.
Press Secretary.—Nathan Landers.
Scheduler.—Elizabeth Decker.
11627 East Telegraph Road, Suite 100, Santa Fe Springs, CA 90670 .... (562) 801–2134
District Director.—Ben Cardenas.

Counties: LOS ANGELES COUNTY (part). Population (2000), 639,088.

ZIP Codes: 90601, 90605–06, 90640, 90650–52, 90659–62, 90665, 90670, 90703, 90731, 90806, 91715–16, 91744–47, 91766–70, 91789–90, 91792, 91795

* * *

THIRTY-NINTH DISTRICT

LINDA T. SÁNCHEZ, Democrat, of Lakewood, CA; born in Orange, CA, January 28, 1969; education: B.A., University of California, Berkeley; J.D., U.C.L.A. Law School; passed bar exam in 1995; professional: attorney; has practiced in the areas of appellate, civil rights, and employment law; International Brotherhood of Electrical Workers Local 441; National Electrical Contractors Association; and Orange County Central Labor Council Executive Secretary, AFL–CIO; organizations: National Women's Political Caucus; Women in Leadership; religion: Catholic; committees: ranking member, Ethics; Judiciary; Veterans' Affairs; elected to the 108th Congress on November 5, 2002; reelected to each succeeding Congress.

Office Listings

http://www.house.gov/lindasanchez

2423 Rayburn House Office Building, Washington, DC 20515 .... (202) 225–6676
Chief of Staff.—Adam Brand. FAX: 226–1012
Legislative Director.—Celeste Drake.
Communications Director.—Adam Hudson.
Senior Adviser.—Ruth Carnegie.
17906 Crusader Avenue, Suite 100, Cerritos, CA 90703 .... (562) 860–5050
District Director.—José Delgado.

Counties: LOS ANGELES COUNTY (part). Population (2000), 639,088.

ZIP Codes: 90001–02, 90059, 90255, 90262, 90280, 90601–06, 90608–10, 90637–39, 90670, 90701–03, 90706, 90711–16, 90723, 90805, 90807–08

* * *

FORTIETH DISTRICT

EDWARD R. ROYCE, Republican, of Fullerton, CA; born in Los Angeles, CA, October 12, 1951; education: B.A., California State University, Fullerton, 1977; professional: small business owner; controller; corporate tax manager; California State Senate, 1982–92; member: Fullerton Chamber of Commerce; board member, Literacy Volunteers of America; California Interscholastic Athletic Foundation board of advisers; married: Marie Therese Porter, 1985; committees: Financial Services; Foreign Affairs; elected on November 3, 1992 to the 103rd Congress; reelected to each succeeding Congress.

Office Listings

http://www.royce.house.gov

2185 Rayburn House Office Building, Washington, DC 20515 .... (202) 225–4111
Chief of Staff.—Amy Porter. FAX: 226–0335
Legislative Director.—Michael Ahern.
Communications Director.—Audra McGeorge.
1110 East Chapman Avenue, Suite 207, Orange, CA 92866 .... (714) 744–4130

District Director.—Sara Catalan. FAX: 744–4056

Counties: ORANGE COUNTY. The north and west part including the cities of Anaheim, Buena Park, Cypress, Fullerton, Garden Grove, La Palma, Los Alamitos, Orange, Placentia, Rossmoor, Stanton, Villa Park, and Westminster. Population (2000), 639,088.

ZIP Codes: 90620–24, 90630–31, 90638, 90680, 90720–21, 90740, 90808, 92647, 92683–84, 92705–06, 92801–02, 92804–07, 92821, 92831–38, 92840–41, 92844–46, 92856–57, 92859, 92861, 92863, 92865–71

* * *

FORTY-FIRST DISTRICT

JERRY LEWIS, Republican, of Redlands, CA; born in Seattle, WA, October 21, 1934; education: graduated, San Bernardino High School, 1952; B.A., UCLA, 1956; graduate intern in public affairs, Coro Foundation; life underwriter; former member, San Bernardino School Board; served in California State Assembly, 1968–78; insurance executive, 1959–78; married to Arlene Willis; seven children; committees: Appropriations; elected to the 96th Congress, November 7, 1978; reelected to each succeeding Congress.

Office Listings

http://www.house.gov/jerrylewis

2112 Rayburn House Office Building, Washington, DC 20515 .... (202) 225–5861
Administrative Assistant.—Arlene Willis. FAX: 225–6498
Deputy Chief of Staff / Communications Director.—Jim Specht.
1150 Brookside Avenue, No. J5, Redlands, CA 92373 .... (909) 862–6030
District Representative.—Tara Clarke.

Counties: RIVERSIDE (part), SAN BERNARDINO (part). CITIES AND TOWNSHIPS: Adelanto, Amboy, Angelus Oaks, Apple Valley, Argus, Arrowbear Lake, Banning, Beaumont, Big Bear City, Big Bear Lake, Blue Jay, Bryn Mawr, Big River, Cabazon, Cadiz, Calimesa, Cedar Glen, Cedar Pines Park, Cherry Valley, Cima, Colton, Crestline, Crest Park, Daggett, Desert Hot Springs, Earp, East Highlands, Essex, Fawnskin, Forest Falls, Grand Terrace, Green Valley Lake, Havasu Lake, Hesperia, Highland, Joshua Tree, Kelso, Lake Arrowhead, Landers, Loma Linda, Lucerne Valley, Ludlow, Mentone, Morongo Valley, Mountain Pass, Needles, Newberry Springs, Nipton, Oro Grande, Parker Dam, Redlands, Rim Forest, Running Springs, San Bernardino, San Jacinto, Sky Forest, Spring Valley Lake, Sugarloaf, Twentynine Palms, Twin Peaks, Valle Vista, Vidal, Yucaipa, and Yucca Valley. Population (2000), 639,088.

ZIP Codes: 92220, 92223, 92230, 92240–42, 92252, 92256, 92258, 92267–68, 92277–78, 92280, 92282, 92284–86, 92304–05, 92307–08, 92311, 92313–15, 92317–18, 92320–27, 92332–33, 92338–42, 92345–46, 92350, 92352, 92354, 92356–57, 92359, 92363–66, 92368–69, 92371, 92373–75, 92378, 92382, 92385–86, 92391–92, 92399, 92404–05, 92407–08, 92410, 92424, 92427, 92544, 92555, 92557, 92581–83

* * *

FORTY-SECOND DISTRICT

GARY G. MILLER, Republican, of Diamond Bar, CA; born in Huntsville, AR, October 16, 1948; education: Loma Vista Elementary School, Whittier, CA; California High School, Whittier, CA; Lowell High School, LaHabra, CA; Mount San Antonio College, Walnut, CA; military service: private, U.S. Army, 1967; professional: developer; owner, G. Miller Development Company; public service: Diamond Bar, CA, City Council, 1989–95; Mayor, 1992; California State Assembly, 1995–98; married: Cathy Miller; children: Brian, Elizabeth, Loren, and Matthew; committees: Financial Services; Transportation and Infrastructure; elected to the 106th Congress; reelected to each succeeding Congress.

Office Listings

http://www.house.gov/garymiller

2349 Rayburn House Office Building, Washington, DC 20515 .... (202) 225–3201
Chief of Staff.—John Rothrock. FAX: 226–6962
Legislative Director / Senior Policy Advisor.—Sandra Bitter.
Executive Director.—Kevin McKee.
1800 East Lambert Road, Suite 150, Brea, CA 92821 .... (714) 257–1142
District Director.—Steven Thornton.

Counties: LOS ANGELES (part), ORANGE (part), and SAN BERNARDINO (part). CITIES AND TOWNSHIPS: Anaheim, Brea, Chino, Chino Hills, Diamond Bar, La Habra, La Habra Heights, Las Flores, Mission Viejo, Placentia, Rancho Santa Margarita, Rowland Heights, Yorba Linda and Whittier. Population (2000), 639,088.

ZIP Codes: 90601–05, 90607, 90631–33, 91708–10, 91729, 91743, 91748, 91758, 91765, 92676, 92679, 92688, 92691–92, 92807–08, 92821–23, 92833, 92885–87

* * *

FORTY-THIRD DISTRICT

JOE BACA, Democrat, of San Bernardino County, CA; born in Belen, NM, January 23, 1947; education: graduated from California State University, Los Angeles, with a bachelor's degree in Sociology; professional: GTE Corp. (community relations); Interstate World Travel (owner); military service: Army; public service: elected to the California State Assembly, 1992, and served as Assistant Speaker Pro Tempore, and the Speaker's Federal Government Liaison, 1997–98; elected to the California State Senate, 1998; awards: American Legion California Legislator of the Year; VFW Outstanding Legislator; League of Women Voters Citizen of Distinction; San Bernardino Kiwanis Club Kiwanian of the Year; Boy Scouts of America Distinguished Citizen; 2004 National Farmers Union Presidential Award; U.S. Department of Agriculture Coalition of Minority Employees Award of Excellence; U.S. Hispanic Chamber of Commerce President's Achievement Award; married: Barbara; four children: Joe Jr., Jeremy, Natalie, and Jennifer; caucuses: Democratic Caucus Task Force on Homeland Security; Democratic Caucus Task Force on Immigration; past chair, Congressional Hispanic Caucus; co-chair, Congressional Sex and Violence in the Media Caucus; House Army Caucus; Congressional Diabetes Caucus; Cancer Caucus; Military / Veterans Caucus; U.S.-Mexico Caucus; Blue Dog Coalition, the Nursing Caucus, Native American Caucus; Armenian Caucus; Good Movement Caucus and Out of Poverty Caucus; chair, CHC Corporate America Task Force; committees: Agriculture; Financial Services; elected to the 106th Congress on November 16, 1999, by special election; reelected to each succeeding Congress.

Office Listings

2366 Rayburn House Office Building, Washington, DC 20515 .... (202) 225–6161
Chief of Staff.—Linda Macias. FAX: 225–8671
Executive Assistant.—Sadaf Khan.
Press Secretary.—John Lowrey.
201 North E Street, Suite 102, San Bernardino, CA 92401 .... (909) 885–2222
District Director.—Sam Garcia.

Counties: SAN BERNARDINO COUNTY (part). CITIES: Colton, Fontana, Ontario, Redlands, Rialto, and San Bernardino. Population (2000), 639,087.

ZIP Codes: 91758, 91761–62, 91764, 92316, 92324, 92334–37, 92346, 92376–77, 92401–08, 92410–13, 92415, 92418, 92423

* * *

FORTY-FOURTH DISTRICT

KEN CALVERT, Republican, of Corona, CA; born in Corona, June 8, 1953; education: A.A., Chaffey College, CA, 1973; B.A. in economics, San Diego State University, 1975; professional: congressional aide to Rep. Victor V. Veysey, CA; general manager, Jolly Fox Restaurant, Corona, 1975–79; Marcus W. Meairs Co., Corona, 1979–81; president and general manager, Ken Calvert Real Properties, 1981–92; County Youth Chairman, Rep. Veysey's District, 1970, then 43rd District, 1972; Corona / Norco Youth Chairman for Nixon, 1968 and 1972; Reagan-Bush campaign worker, 1980; co-chair, Wilson for Senate Campaign, 1982; chairman, Riverside Republican Party, 1984–88; co-chairman, George Deukmejian election, 1978, 1982 and 1986; co-chairman, George Bush election, 1988; co-chairman, Pete Wilson Senate elections, 1982 and 1988; co-chairman, Pete Wilson for Governor election, 1990; charter member, Riverside County Republican Winners Circle; former vice president, Corona / Norco Republican Assembly; chairman and charter member, Lincoln Club of Riverside County, 1986–90; president, Corona Rotary Club, 1991; past president, Corona Elks; Navy League of Corona / Norco; Corona Chamber of Commerce, 1990; past chairman, Norco Chamber of Commerce; County of Riverside Asset Leasing; past chairman, Corona / Norco Board of Realtors; Monday Morning Group; Corona Group; executive board, Economic Development Partnership; charter member, Corona Community Hospital Corporate 200 Club; Silver Eagles (March AFB Support Group); Corona Airport Advisory Commission; House Republican Steering Committee; Baltic Caucus; Caucus on India and Indian Americans; Coalition for Autism Research and Education; Congressional Caucus on Hellenic Issues; Congressional Caucus on Intellectual Property Promotion and Piracy Prevention; Congressional Caucus to Fight and Control Methamphetamine, co-chair; Congressional Coastal Caucus; Congressional Diabetes Caucus; Congressional Fire Services Caucus; Congressional Manufactured Housing Caucus, co-chair; Congressional Missing and Exploited Children's Caucus; Congressional Modeling and Simulation Training Caucus; Congressional Morocco Caucus; Congressional Native American Caucus; Congressional Sportsmen's Caucus; Congressional Travel and Tourism Caucus; Congressional Wine Caucus; Defense Study Group; Generic Drug Equity Caucus, co-chair; Law Enforcement Caucus; Medical Technology Caucus; National Guard and Reserve Caucus; Navy-Marine Corps Caucus; Real Estate Caucus; Renewable Energy and Energy Efficiency Caucus; Tests and Evaluation Caucus; Western Caucus; Zero Capital Gains Tax Caucus; Tom Lantos Human Rights Commission; Friends of Australia Caucus; Congressional Animal Protection Caucus; Congressional Caucus on Korea; committees: Appropriations; Permanent Select Committee on Intelligence; elected on November 3, 1992 to the 103rd Congress; reelected to each succeeding Congress.

Office Listings

http://www.house.gov/calvert

2201 Rayburn House Office Building, Washington, DC 20515 .... (202) 225–1986
Chief of Staff.—Dave Ramey. FAX: 225–2004
Legislative Director.—Maria Bowie.
Press Secretary.—Rebecca Rudman.
3400 Central Avenue, Suite 200, Riverside, CA 92506 .... (951) 784–4300
District Director.—Jolyn Murphy.
Deputy District Director.—Jason Gagnon.

Counties: ORANGE COUNTY (part). CITIES AND TOWNSHIPS: Coto d'Casa, Ledera Ranch, San Clemente, San Juan Capistrano. RIVERSIDE COUNTY (part). CITIES AND TOWNSHIPS: Corona, March AFB, Mira Loma, Norco, and Riverside. Population (2000), 639,088.

ZIP Codes: 92501–09, 92513–18, 92521–22, 92532, 92557, 92570, 92672–75, 92679, 92694, 92860, 92879–83

* * *

FORTY-FIFTH DISTRICT

MARY BONO MACK, Republican, of Palm Springs, CA; born in Cleveland, OH, October 24, 1961; daughter of Clay Whitaker, retired physician and surgeon, and Karen, retired chemist; Bachelor of Fine Arts in Art History, University of Southern California, 1984; Woman of the Year, 1993, San Gorgonio Chapter of the Girl Scouts of America for her assistance to victims of a tragic Girl Scout bus crash in Palm Springs; board member: Palm Springs International Film Festival; first lady of Palm Springs and active in a wide range of community charities and service organizations; leadership role in support of the D.A.R.E. program, Olive Crest Home for Abused Children, Tiempos de Los Ninos; certified personal fitness instructor in martial arts (Karate, Tae Kwan Do); accomplished gymnast with Gymnastics Olympica; appointed chair, Congressional Salton Sea Task Force; married Sonny Bono, 1986; two children: Chesare Elan and Chianna Maria; married U.S. Representative Connie Mack, 2007; committees: Energy and Commerce; elected by special election on April 7, 1998 to the 105th Congress, to fill the vacancy caused by the death of her husband Rep. Sonny Bono; reelected to each succeeding Congress.

Office Listings

http://www.house.gov/bono

104 Cannon House Office Building, Washington, DC 20515 .... (202) 225–5330
Chief of Staff.—Frank Cullen. FAX: 225–2961
Legislative Director.—Paul Cancienne.
Communications Director.—Anjulen Anderson.
Scheduler/Executive Assistant.—Sarah Tippit.
36–953 Cook Street, Suite 104, Palm Desert, CA 92211 .... (760) 320–1076
District Director.—Marc Troast.
1600 East Florida Avenue, Suite 301, Hemet, CA 92544 .... (951) 658–2312

Counties: RIVERSIDE COUNTY (part). CITIES AND TOWNSHIPS: Bermuda Dunes, Blythe, Cathedral City, Coachella, East Blythe, East Hemet, Hemet, Idyllwild-Pine, Indian Wells, Indio, La Quinta, Mecca, Moreno Valley, Murrieta, Palm Desert, Palm Springs, Rancho Mirage, Thousand Palms, and Winchester. Population (2000), 639,088.

ZIP Codes: 92201, 92203, 92210–11, 92220, 92225–26, 92234–36, 92239–41, 92253–55, 92260–64, 92270, 92274, 92276, 92282, 92536, 92539, 92543–46, 92548–49, 92551–57, 92561–64, 92567, 92571, 92584–86, 92590–92, 92595–96

* * *

FORTY-SIXTH DISTRICT

DANA T. ROHRABACHER, Republican, of Huntington Beach, CA; born in Coronado, CA, June 21, 1947; education: graduated Palos Verdes High School, CA, 1965; attended Los Angeles Harbor College, Wilmington, CA, 1965–67; B.A., Long Beach State College, CA, 1969; M.A., University of Southern California, Los Angeles, 1975; professional: writer / journalist; speechwriter and special assistant to the President, The White House, Washington, DC, 1981–88; assistant press secretary, Reagan/Bush Committee, 1980; reporter, City News Service/Radio News West, and editorial writer, *Orange County Register*, 1972–80; family: wife and triplets; committees: Foreign Affairs; Science, Space, and Technology; elected on November 8, 1988, to the 101st Congress; reelected to each succeeding Congress.

Office Listings

http://www.house.gov/rohrabacher

2300 Rayburn House Office Building, Washington, DC 20515 .... (202) 225–2415
Chief of Staff.—Rick Dykema. FAX: 225–0145
Legislative Director.—Jeff Vanderslice.
Communications Director.—Tara Setmayer.
Legislative Assistant.—Kip Payne.
Legislative Correspondent.—Ray Gennawey.
Executive Assistant / Scheduler.—Fess Cassels.
Staff Assistant.—Justin Ahn.
101 Main Street, Suite 380, Huntington Beach, CA 92648 .... (714) 960–6483
District Director.—Kathleen Staunton.
District Executive Assistant / Scheduler.—Alexandra Peterson.

Counties: ORANGE COUNTY (part). Communities of Fountain Valley, Huntington Beach, Costa Mesa, Westminster, Seal Beach, Santa Ana, Midway City, Garden Grove, Newport Beach, Sunset Beach, Surfside. LOS ANGELES COUNTY (part). COMMUNITIES OF: Avalon, Long Beach, Palos Verdes, Palos Verdes Estates, Rancho Palos Verdes, Rolling Hills, Rolling Hills Estates, and San Pedro. Population (2000), 639,088.

ZIP Codes: 90274–75, 90704, 90731–32, 90740, 90742–44, 90802–04, 90808, 90813–15, 90822, 90831–35, 90840, 90853, 92626–28, 92646–49, 92655, 92683, 92702, 92708, 92711–12, 92725, 92735, 92799, 92841, 92843–44

* * *

FORTY-SEVENTH DISTRICT

LORETTA SANCHEZ, Democrat, of Anaheim, CA; born in Lynwood, CA, January 7, 1960; education: graduate of Chapman University; M.B.A., American University; specializes in assisting public agencies with finance matters; member, Blue Dog Coalition; Law Enforcement Caucus; Congressional Women's Caucus; New Democratic Coalition; committees: Armed Services; Homeland Security; Joint Economic Committee; elected to the 105th Congress; reelected to each succeeding Congress.

Office Listings

http://www.house.gov/sanchez

1114 Longworth House Office Building, Washington, DC 20515 .... (202) 225–2965
Chief of Staff.—Adrienne Elrod. FAX: 225–5859
Deputy Chief of Staff / Scheduler.—Shane Moore.
Legislative Director.—Eduardo Lerma.
Legislative Assistants: Jessica Fernendez, Annie Yea.
Communications Director.—Adrienne Watson.
12397 Lewis Street, Suite 101, Garden Grove, CA 92840 .... (714) 621–0102
District Director.—Paula Negrete.

Counties: ORANGE COUNTY (part). CITIES: Anaheim (west and north-south of the Anaheim Stadium-Disneyland corridor), Fullerton, Garden Grove, Orange, and Santa Ana. Population (2000), 639,087.

ZIP Codes: 90680, 92609, 92616, 92619, 92623, 92650, 92652, 92654, 92658, 92679, 92697–98, 92701–04, 92706–07, 92735, 92781, 92801–02, 92804–05, 92812, 92815–17, 92825, 92832–33, 92840–41, 92843–44, 92850, 92868

* * *

FORTY-EIGHTH DISTRICT

JOHN CAMPBELL, Republican, of Irvine, CA; born in Los Angeles, CA, July 19, 1955; education: B.A., University of California, Los Angeles, CA; M.A., University of Southern California, Los Angeles, CA; professional: certified public accountant; member of the California State Senate; married: Catherine; children: two sons; committees: Budget; Financial Services; Joint Economic Committee; elected to the 109th Congress by special election to fill the vacancy caused by the resignation of United States Representative Christopher Cox; elected to the 110th Congress; reelected to each succeeding Congress.

Office Listings

http://www.house.gov/campbell

1507 Longworth House Office Building, Washington, DC 20515 .... (202) 225–5611
Chief of Staff.—Muffy Lewis. FAX: 225–9177
Executive Assistant.—Carolyn Noble.
Legislative Director.—David Malech.
Communications Director.—Chris Bognanno.
610 Newport Center Drive, Suite 330, Newport Beach, CA 92660 .... (949) 756–2244

Counties: ORANGE COUNTY (part). CITIES: Aliso Viejo, Corona del Mar, Dana Point, Foothill Ranch, Irvine, Laguna Beach, Laguna Hills, Laguna Niguel, Laguna Woods, Lake Forest, Newport Beach, Orange, San Juan Capistrano, Santa Ana, and Tustin. Population (2010), 727,833.

ZIP Codes: 92602–04, 92606–07, 92610, 92612, 92614, 92618, 92620, 92624–25, 92629–30, 92651, 92653, 92656–57, 92660–63, 92674–75, 92677–79, 92690, 92693, 92705, 92780, 92782

* * *

FORTY-NINTH DISTRICT

DARRELL E. ISSA, Republican, of Vista, CA; born in Cleveland, OH, November 1, 1953; education: Siena Heights College; military service: U.S. Army; attended college on an ROTC scholarship; professional: Businessman; founder and CEO of Directed Electronics, Inc.; past Chairman, Consumer Electronics Association; Board of Directors, Electronics Industry Association; public service: Co-Chairman of the campaign to pass the California Civil Rights Initiative (Proposition 209); Chairman of the Volunteer Committee for the 1996 Republican National Convention; Chairman of the San Diego County Lincoln Club; candidate for the U.S. Senate in 1998; architect of 2003 California recall campaign of former Governor Gray Davis; married: Kathy; children: William; committees: chair, Oversight and Government Reform; Judiciary; elected to the 107th Congress on November 7, 2000; reelected to each succeeding Congress.

Office Listings

http://www.house.gov/issa

2347 Rayburn House Office Building, Washington, DC 20515 .... (202) 225–3906
Chief of Staff.—Dale Neugebauer. FAX: 225–3303
Legislative Director.—Laurent Crenshaw.
Press Secretary.—Ray Zaccaro.
Scheduler.—Mary Pritschau.
1800 Thibodo Road, #310, Vista, CA 92081 .... (760) 599–5000

Counties: RIVERSIDE (part), SAN DIEGO (part). Population (2000), 639,087

ZIP Codes: 92003, 92025–28, 92036, 92049, 92051–52, 92054–61, 92065–66, 92068–70, 92081–86, 92088, 92128, 92530, 92532, 92548, 92562–63, 92567, 92570–72, 92584–87, 92589–93, 92595–96, 92599

* * *

FIFTIETH DISTRICT

BRIAN P. BILBRAY, Republican, of San Diego, CA; born in Coronado, CA, January 28, 1951; education: graduated Mar Vista High School; attended South Western College; professional: tax consultant; city council; Imperial Beach, CA; 1976–78; mayor, Imperial Beach, CA, 1978–85; San Diego County Board of Supervisors, 1985–95; married: Karen; five children; committees: Energy and Commerce; elected to the 104th Congress and to the two succeeding Congresses (January 3, 1995–2001); unsuccessful candidate for reelection to the 107th Congress; elected by special election, June 6, 2006, to fill the vacancy caused by the resignation of United States Representative Randall ''Duke'' Cunningham and reelected to each succeeding Congress.

Office Listings

http://www.house.gov/bilbray

2410 Rayburn House Office Building, Washington, DC 20515 .... (202) 225–0508
Chief of Staff.—Steve Danon. FAX: 225–2558
Legislative Director.—Lorissa Bounds.
Scheduler.—Jennifer Polk.
Press Secretary.—Travis Considine.
380 Stevens Avenue, Suite 212, Solana Beach, CA 92075 .... (858) 350–1150

Counties: SAN DIEGO COUNTY (part). Population (2000), 639,087.

ZIP Codes: 92007–09, 92013–14, 92018, 92023–27, 92029–30, 92033, 92037, 92046, 92067, 92069, 92075, 92078–79, 92081–84, 92091, 92096, 92109–11, 92117, 92121–22, 92126–30, 92145, 92172, 92177, 92191, 92196, 92198

* * *

FIFTY-FIRST DISTRICT

BOB FILNER, Democrat, of San Diego, CA; born in Pittsburgh, PA, September 4, 1942; education: B.A., Cornell University, Ithaca, NY, 1963; M.A., University of Delaware, 1969; Ph.D., Cornell University, 1973; professor, San Diego State University, 1970–92; San Diego Board of Education, 1979–83 (president, 1982); San Diego City Council, 1987–92 (deputy mayor, 1990); member: Sierra Club, NAACP, Navy League, Gray Panthers, Economic Conversion Council, Common Cause, ACLU, ADL, NWPC, MAPA; married: Jane Merrill Filner, 1985; children: Erin and Adam; committees: ranking minority member, Veterans' Affairs; Transportation and Infrastructure; elected on November 3, 1992 to the 103rd Congress; reelected to each succeeding Congress.

Office Listings

http://www.house.gov/filner

2428 Rayburn House Office Building, Washington, DC 20515 .... (202) 225–8045
Chief of Staff.—Tony Buckles. FAX: 225–9073
Executive Assistant.—Kim Messineo.
Legislative Director.—Sharon Wagener.
333 F Street, Suite A, Chula Vista, CA 91910 .... (619) 422–5963
1101 Airport Road, Suite D, Imperial, CA 92251 .... (760) 355–8800

Counties: SAN DIEGO COUNTY (part), IMPERIAL COUNTY. CITIES: Brawley, Calexico, Calipatria, Chula Vista, El Centro, Holtville, Imperial, National City, San Diego, San Ysidro, and Westmorland. Population (2000), 639,087.

ZIP Codes: 91902, 91905–06, 91908–15, 91917, 91921, 91934, 91945, 91947, 91950, 91963, 91977, 91980, 92102, 92105, 92113–15, 92136, 92139, 92143, 92149, 92153–54, 92173, 92179, 92222, 92227, 92231–33, 92243–44, 92249–51, 92257, 92259, 92266, 92273–75, 92281, 92283

* * *

FIFTY-SECOND DISTRICT

DUNCAN HUNTER, Republican, of Lakeside, CA; born in San Diego, CA, December 7, 1976; education: graduated from Granite Hills High School; B.S., Business Administration, San Diego State University, San Diego, CA, 2001; professional: business analyst; military: captain, United States Marine Corps, 2002–05; United States Marine Corps Reserves, 2005–08; religion: Protestant; married: Margaret; children: Duncan, Elizabeth, and Sarah; committees: Armed Services; Education and the Workforce; Transportation and Infrastructure; elected to the 111th Congress on November 4, 2008, reelected to the 112th Congress.

Office Listings

http://www.hunter.house.gov

223 Cannon House Office Building, Washington, DC 20515 .... (202) 225–5672
Chief of Staff.—Victoria Middleton. FAX: 225–0235
Scheduler/Office Manager.—Allison Sadoian.
Communications Director.—Joe Kasper.
1870 Cordell Court, Suite 206, El Cajon, CA 92020 .... (619) 448–5201

Counties: SAN DIEGO COUNTY (part). CITIES AND TOWNSHIPS: Alpine, Barona I.R., Borrego Springs, Boulder Park, Boulevard, Campo, Descanso, Dulzura, El Cajon, Guatay, Indian Res., Jacumba, Jamul, Lakeside, La Mesa, Lemon Grove, Mount

Laguna, Pine Valley, Potrero, Poway, Ramona, San Diego, Santee, Spring Valley, Tecate, and Palo Verde. Population (2000), 639,087.

ZIP Codes: 91901, 91903, 91905–06, 91915–17, 91931, 91935, 91941–45, 91948, 91962, 91976–79, 92004, 92019–22, 92025, 92036, 92040, 92064–66, 92071–72, 92074, 92090, 92108, 92111, 92115, 92119–20, 92123–24, 92126, 92128–29, 92131, 92142, 92145, 92150, 92158–60, 92190, 92193–94, 92199

* * *

FIFTY-THIRD DISTRICT

SUSAN A. DAVIS, Democrat, of San Diego, CA; born in Cambridge, MA, April 13, 1944; education: B.S., University of California at Berkeley; M.A., University of North Carolina; public service: served three terms in the California State Assembly; served nine years on the San Diego City School Board; former President of the League of Women Voters of San Diego; awards: California School Boards Association Legislator of the Year; League of Middle Schools Legislator of the Year; family: married to Steve; children: Jeffrey and Benjamin; grandsons: Henry and Theo; granddaughter: Jane; committees: Armed Services; Education and the Workforce; elected to the 107th Congress on November 7, 2000; reelected to each succeeding Congress.

Office Listings

http://www.house.gov/susandavis

1526 Longworth House Office Building, Washington DC 20515 .... (202) 225–2040
Chief of Staff.—Lisa Sherman. FAX: 225–2948
Press Secretary.—Aaron Hunter.
Scheduler.—Cynthia Patton.
2700 Adams Avenue, Suite 102, San Diego, CA 92116 .... (619) 280–5353
District Director.—Jessica Poole. FAX: 280–5311

Counties: SAN DIEGO COUNTY (part). Population (2000), 639,087.

ZIP Codes: 91932–33, 91945–46, 91977, 92037–39, 92092–93, 92101–18, 92120–23, 92132–38, 92140, 92147, 92152, 92155, 92161, 92163–71, 92175–76, 92178, 92182, 92184, 92186–87, 92192, 92195

COLORADO

(Population 2010, 5,029,196)

SENATORS

MARK UDALL, Democrat, of Eldorado Springs, CO; born in Tucson, AZ, July 18, 1950; B.A., Williams College, Williamstown, MA, 1972; field coordinator, Morris K. Udall for President, 1974; executive director, Colorado Outward Bound School, 1985–95; member of the Colorado State House of Representatives, 1996–98; member of the U.S. House of Representatives, 1999–2008; married: Maggie Fox; two children; committees: Armed Services; Energy and Natural Resources; Select Committee on Intelligence; Special Committee on Aging; elected to the U.S. Senate on November 4, 2008.

Office Listings

http://markudall.senate.gov

SH–317 Hart Senate Office Building, Washington, DC 20510 .... (202) 224–5941
Chief of Staff.—Michael Sozan. FAX: 224–6471
Administrative Director.—John Fossum.
Legislative Director.—Joseph Britton.
Communications Director.—Tara Trujillo.
Director of Scheduling.—Kathy Chung.
999 18th Street, Suite 1525, North Tower, Denver, CO 80202 .... (303) 650–7820
State Director.—Jennifer Rokala.
107 West B Street, Pueblo, CO 81003 .... (719) 542–1701
954 East 2nd Avenue, Suite 106, Durango, CO 81301 .... (970) 247–1047
2880 International Circle, Suite 107, Colorado Springs, CO 80910 .... (719) 471–3993
609 Main Street, Suite 205, Alamosa, CO 81101 .... (719) 589–2101
801 8th Street, Suite 140A, Greeley, CO 80631 .... (970) 356–5586
400 Rood Avenue, Suite 215, Grand Junction, CO 81501 .... (970) 245–9553
P.O. Box 866, Clark, CO 80428 .... (303) 650–7820
P.O. Box 743, Tabernash, CO 80478 .... (303) 650–7820

* * *

MICHAEL F. BENNET, Democrat, of Denver, CO; born in New Delhi, India, November 28, 1964; education: B.A., Wesleyan University, 1987; J.D., Yale Law School, 1993; editor-in-chief of the *Yale Law Journal;* counsel to U.S. Deputy Attorney General, 1995–97; special assistant, U.S. Attorney, CT, 1997; managing director, Anschutz Investment Co., 1997–2003; chief of staff to mayor of Denver, CO, 2003–05; superintendent, Denver Public Schools, 2005–09; married: Susan D. Dagget; children: Caroline, Halina, and Anne; committees: Agriculture, Nutrition, and Forestry; Banking, Housing, and Urban Affairs; Health, Education, Labor and Pensions; Special Committee on Aging; appointed January 21, 2009, to the 111th United States Senate for the term ending January 3, 2011; elected to the 112th Congress for a full Senate term on November 2, 2010.

Office Listings

http://bennet.senate.gov

702 Hart Senate Office Building, Washington, DC 20510–0606 .... (202) 224–5852
Chief of Staff.—Jonathan Davidson. FAX: 228–5036
Legislative Director.—Layth Elhassani.
Communications Director.—Adam Bozzi.
Scheduler.—Karin Ballman.
2300 15th Street, Suite 450, Denver, CO 80202 .... (303) 455–3358
FAX: 455–8851
129 West B Street, Pueblo, CO 81003 .... (719) 542–7550
FAX: 542–7555
609 Main Street, Suite 110, Alamosa, CO 81101 .... (719) 587–0096
FAX: 587–0098
409 North Tejon, Suite 107, Colorado Springs, CO 80903 .... (719) 328–1100
FAX: 328–1129
1200 South College Avenue, Suite 211, Fort Collins, CO 80524 .... (970) 224–2200
FAX: 224–2205
225 North 5th Street, Suite 511, Grand Junction, CO 81501 .... (970) 241–6631
FAX: 241–8313
835 East 2nd Avenue, Suite 203, Durango, CO 81301 .... (970) 259–1710
FAX: 259–9789

REPRESENTATIVES

FIRST DISTRICT

DIANA DEGETTE, Democrat, of Denver, CO; born in Tachikowa, Japan, July 29, 1957; education: B.A., political science, *magna cum laude*, The Colorado College, 1979; J.D., New York University School of Law, 1982 (Root Tilden Scholar); professional: attorney with McDermott, Hansen, and Reilly; Colorado Deputy State Public Defender, Appellate Division, 1982–84; Colorado House of Representatives, 1992–96; board of directors, Planned Parenthood, Rocky Mountain Chapter; member and formerly on board of governors, Colorado Bar Association; member, Colorado Women's Bar Association; past memberships: board of trustees, The Colorado College; Denver Women's Commission; board of directors, Colorado Trial Lawyers Association; former editor, *Trial Talk* magazine; listed in 1994–96 edition of *Who's Who in America*; Chief Deputy Whip; committees: Energy and Commerce; elected to the 105th Congress; reelected to each succeeding Congress.

Office Listings

http://degette.house.gov

2335 Rayburn House Office Building, Washington, DC 20515 .... (202) 225–4431
Chief of Staff.—Lisa B. Cohen. FAX: 225–5657
Scheduler.—Tish Mills.
Communications Director.—Juliet Johnson.
600 Grant Street, Suite 202, Denver, CO 80203 .... (303) 844–4988
District Administrator.—Morris Price.

Counties: ADAMS (part), ARAPAHOE (part), DENVER, JEFFERSON (part). Population (2010), 718,457.

ZIP Codes: 80110–11, 80113, 80121, 80123, 80127, 80150–51, 80155, 80201–12, 80214–24, 80226–32, 80235–39, 80243–44, 80246–52, 80255–57, 80259, 80261–62, 80264–66, 80270–71, 80273–75, 80279, 80281, 80285, 80290–95, 80299

* * *

SECOND DISTRICT

JARED POLIS, Democrat, of Boulder, CO; born in Boulder, CO, May 12, 1975; education: B.A., political science, Princeton University, Princeton, NJ, 1996; professional: internet entrepreneur; founder of New America Schools; chair, Colorado State Board of Education; House Democratic Steering and Policy Committee; religion: Jewish; committees: Rules; elected to the 111th Congress on November 4, 2008; reelected to the 112th Congress.

Office Listings

http://www.polis.house.gov

501 Cannon House Office Building, Washington, DC 20515 .... (202) 225–2161
Chief of Staff.—Brian Branton.
Legislative Director.—Rosalyn Kumar.
Press Secretary.—Lara Cottingham.
Scheduler.—Danielle Oliveto.
4770 Baseline Road, Suite 220, Boulder, CO 80303 .... (303) 484–9596
1200 East 78th Avenue, Suite 105, Thornton, CO 80229 .... (303) 287–4159
101 West Main Street, P.O. Box 1453, Suite 101G, Frisco, CO 80443 .... (970) 668–3240

Counties: ADAMS (part), BOULDER (part), BROOMFIELD, CLEAR CREEK, EAGLE, GILPIN, GRAND, JEFFERSON (part), SUMMIT, WELD (part). Population (2000), 614,465.

ZIP Codes: 80003, 80005, 80007, 80020–21, 80025–28, 80030–31, 80035–36, 80038, 80212, 80221, 80229, 80233–34, 80241, 80260, 80263, 80301–10, 80314, 80321–23, 80328–29, 80403, 80422–24, 80426–28, 80435–36, 80438–39, 80442–44, 80446–47, 80451–52, 80455, 80459, 80463, 80466, 80468, 80471, 80474, 80476–78, 80481–82, 80497–98, 80503–04, 80510, 80514, 80516, 80520, 80530, 80540, 80544, 80602, 80614, 80640, 81620–21, 81623, 81631–32, 81637, 81645, 81649, 81655, 81657–58

* * *

THIRD DISTRICT

SCOTT TIPTON, Republican, of Cortez, CO; born in Espanola, NM, November 9, 1956; education: graduated, B.S., political science, Ft. Lewis College, Durango, CO, 1978; professional: Owner/President of Mesa Verde Pottery, Cortez, CO; public service: elected to Colorado House of Representatives, 2008–10; religion: Anglican; married: Jean Marie Tipton; children: Liesl (married to Chris Ross) and Elizabeth Tipton; caucuses: Coal; Natural Gas; Western; Sportsman; Israel; Taiwan; Beef; Dairy; Down Syndrome; Balanced Budget; committees: Agriculture; Natural Resources; Small Business; elected to the 112th Congress on November 2, 2010.

Office Listings

http://tipton.house.gov

218 Cannon House Office Building, Washington, DC 20515 .... (202) 225–4761
Chief of Staff.—Mike Hesse. FAX: 226–9669
Legislative Director.—Nicholas Zupancic.
Executive Assistant.—Jen Bailey.
225 North 5th Street, Suite 702, Grand Junction, CO 81501 .... (970) 241–2499
District Director.—Scott Streit.
503 North Main Street, Suite 658, Pueblo, CO 81003 .... (719) 542–1073
2 West Main Street, Cortez, CO 81321 .... (970) 739–5586
609 Main Street, Suite 105, Box 11, Alamosa, CO 81101 .... (719) 587–5105

Counties: ALAMOSA, ARCHULETA, CONEJOS, COSTILLA, CUSTER, DELTA, DOLORES, GARFIELD, GUNNISON, HINSDALE, HUERFANO, JACKSON, LA PLATA, LAS ANIMAS, MESA, MINERAL, MOFFAT, MONTEZUMA, MONTROSE, OTERO (part), OURAY, PITKIN, PUEBLO, RIO BLANCO, RIO GRANDE, ROUTT, SAGUACHE, SAN JUAN, SAN MIGUEL. Population (2000), 614,467.

ZIP Codes: 80423–24, 80428, 80430, 80434–35, 80443, 80446–47, 80456, 80459, 80463, 80467, 80469, 80473, 80479–80, 80483, 80487–88, 80498, 81001–12, 81019–20, 81022–25, 81027, 81029, 81033, 81039–41, 81043–44, 81046, 81049–50, 81054–55, 81058–59, 81062, 81064, 81067, 81069, 81077, 81081–82, 81089, 81091, 81101–02, 81120–38, 81140–41, 81143–44, 81146–49, 81151–55, 81157, 81201, 81210–12, 81215, 81220–26, 81228, 81230–33, 81235–37, 81239–41, 81243, 81248, 81251–53, 81301–03, 81320–21, 81323–32, 81334–35, 81401–02, 81410–11, 81413–16, 81418–20, 81422–35, 81501–06, 81520–27, 81601–02, 81610–12, 81615, 81621, 81623–26, 81630, 81633, 81635–36, 81638–43, 81646–48, 81650, 81652–56

* * *

FOURTH DISTRICT

CORY GARDNER, Republican, of Yuma, CO; born in Yuma, CO, August 22, 1976; education: B.S., political science, Colorado State University, Fort Collins, CO, 1997; J.D., University of Colorado, Boulder, CO, 2001; professional: agricultural advocate; staff, United States Senator Wayne Allard of Colorado, 2002–05; member of the Colorado State House of Representatives, 2005–10; committees: Energy and Commerce; elected to the 112th Congress on November 2, 2010.

Office Listings

http://www.gardner.house.gov

213 Cannon House Office Building, Washington, DC 20515 .... (202) 225–4676
Chief of Staff.—Chris Hansen.
Legislative Director.—Natalie Farr.
Communications Director.—Rachel Boxer.
Director of Scheduling.—Juliet Kroll.
123 North College Avenue, Suite 220, Ft. Collins, CO 80524 .... (970) 221–7110
822 7th Street, #9, Greeley, CO 80631 .... (970) 351–6007
301 South 5th Street, Lamar, CO 81052 .... (719) 931–4003
109½ South Third Street, Sterling, CO 80721 .... (970) 522–0203

Counties: BACA, BOULDER (part), BENT, CHEYENNE, CROWLEY, KIOWA, KIT CARSON, LARIMER, LINCOLN, LOGAN, MORGAN, PHILLIPS, PROWERS, OTERO (part), SEDGEWICK, WASHINGTON, WELD (part), YUMA. Population (2000), 614,466.

ZIP Codes: 80501–04, 80510–13, 80515, 80517, 80521–28, 80530, 80532–43, 80545–47, 80549–51, 80553, 80603, 80610–12, 80615, 80620–24, 80631–34, 80638–39, 80642–46, 80648–54, 80701, 80705, 80720–23, 80726–29, 80731–37, 80740–47, 80749–51, 80754–55, 80757–59, 80801–02, 80804–05, 80807, 80810, 80812, 80815, 80818, 80821–26, 80828, 80830, 80832–34, 80836, 80861–62, 81021, 81024, 81027, 81029–30, 81033–34, 81036, 81038, 81041, 81043–47, 81049–50, 81052, 81054, 81057, 81059, 81062–64, 81071, 81073, 81076, 81084, 81087, 81090, 81092

* * *

FIFTH DISTRICT

DOUG LAMBORN, Republican, of Colorado Springs, CO; born in Leavenworth, KS, May 24, 1954; education: B.S., University of Kansas, Lawrence, 1978; J.D., University of Kansas,

Lawrence, 1985; lawyer, private practice (business and real estate); Colorado State House of Representatives, 1995–98; Colorado State Senate, 1998–2006; married: Jeanie; five children; committees: Armed Services; Natural Resources; Veterans' Affairs; elected to the 110th Congress on November 7, 2006; reelected to each succeeding Congress.

Office Listings

http://www.lamborn.house.gov

437 Cannon House Office Building, Washington, DC 20515 .... (202) 225–4422
Chief of Staff.—Chris Phelen. FAX: 226–2638
Legislative Director.—Leslie Bolz.
Director of Communications.—Catherine Mortensen.
Scheduler / Executive Assistant.—Erin Newton.
1271 Kelly Johnson Boulevard, Suite 110, Colorado Springs, CO 80920 .... (719) 520–0055

Counties: CHAFFEE, EL PASO, FREMONT, LAKE, PARK (part), TELLER. Population (2000), 614,467.

ZIP Codes: 80104, 80106, 80132–33, 80135, 80420, 80432, 80438, 80440, 80443, 80448–49, 80456, 80461, 80475, 80808–09, 80813–14, 80816–17, 80819–20, 80827, 80829–33, 80835, 80840–41, 80860, 80863–64, 80866, 80901, 80903–22, 80925–26, 80928–37, 80940–47, 80949–50, 80960, 80962, 80970, 80977, 80995, 80997, 81008, 81154, 81201, 81211–12, 81221, 81223, 81226–28, 81233, 81236, 81240–42, 81244, 81251, 81253

* * *

SIXTH DISTRICT

MIKE COFFMAN, Republican, of Aurora, CO; born in Fort Leonard Wood, MO, March 19, 1955; education: attended, Aurora Central High School; B.A., University of Colorado, Boulder, CO, 1979; military: United States Army, 1972–74; United States Army Reserve, 1975–78; United States Marine Corps, 1979–82; United States Marine Corps Reserve, 1983–94, and 2005–06; professional: business owner; elected to the Colorado State House of Representatives, 1989–94; elected to the Colorado State Senate, 1994–98; Colorado State Treasurer, 1999–2007; Colorado Secretary of State, 2007–08; religion: Methodist; married: Cynthia; committees: Armed Service; Natural Resources; Small Business; elected to the 111th Congress on November 4, 2008; reelected to the 112th Congress.

Office Listings

http://www.coffman.house.gov

1222 Longworth House Office Building, Washington, DC 20515 .... (202) 225–7882
Chief of Staff.—Jacque Ponder. FAX: 226–4623
Scheduler.—Ashling Thurmond.
9220 Kimmer Drive, Suite 200, Lone Tree, CO 80124 .... (720) 283–9772

Counties: ARAPAHOE (part), DOUGLAS, ELBERT, JEFFERSON (part), PARK (part). Population (2000), 614,466.

ZIP Codes: 80013–16, 80018, 80046, 80101–09, 80111–12, 80116–18, 80120–31, 80134–38, 80160–63, 80165–66, 80225, 80231, 80235–36, 80247, 80401, 80403, 80421, 80425, 80433, 80437, 80439, 80453–54, 80457, 80465, 80470, 80808, 80828, 80830–33, 80835

* * *

SEVENTH DISTRICT

ED PERLMUTTER, Democrat, of Golden, CO; born in Denver, CO, May 1, 1953; education: B.A., University of Colorado, 1975; J.D., University of Colorado, 1978; professional: served as a member of the Board of Governors of the Colorado Bar Association; served on the Board of Trustees and Judicial Performance Commission for the First Judicial District; Trustee, Midwest Research Institute, the primary operator of the National Renewable Energy Laboratory; board member, National Jewish Medical and Research Center; elected to two four-year terms to represent central Jefferson County as a Colorado State Senator, 1995–2003; served on numerous committees in the State Senate, including Water, Finance, Judiciary, Child Welfare, Telecommunication, Transportation, Legal Services, and Oil and Gas; also served as chair of the Public Policy and Planning Committee, chair of the Bi-Partisan Renewable Energy Caucus, and President Pro Tem (2001–02 session); married; three children; committees: Financial Services; elected to the 110th Congress on November 7, 2006; reelected to each succeeding Congress.

Office Listings

http://perlmutter.house.gov/

1221 Longworth House Office Building, Washington, DC 20515 .... (202) 225–2645
Chief of Staff.—Danielle Radovich Piper. FAX: 225–5278
Legislative Director.—Matt Henken.
Scheduler / Executive Assistant.—Alison Inderforth.
Staff Assistant.—Daniel J. Dingmann.
12600 West Colfax Avenue, Suite B400, Lakewood, CO 80215 .... (303) 274–7944

Counties: ADAMS (part), ARAPAHOE (part), JEFFERSON (part). CITIES AND TOWNSHIPS: Arvada, Aurora, Bennett, Brighton, Commerce City, Edgewater, Golden, Lakewood, and Wheat Ridge. Population (2000), 614,465.

ZIP Codes: 80001–07, 80010–14, 80017–19, 80021–22. 80030, 80033–34, 80040–42, 80044–45, 80047, 80102–03, 80105, 80123, 80127, 80136–37, 80212, 80214–16, 80221, 80226–35, 80241, 80247, 80401–03, 80419, 80465, 80601–03, 80640, 80642–43, 80654

CONNECTICUT

(Population 2010, 3,574,097)

SENATORS

JOSEPH I. LIEBERMAN, Independent Democrat, of Stamford, CT; born in Stamford, February 24, 1942; education: attended Stamford public schools; B.A., Yale University, 1964; law degree, Yale Law School, 1967; Connecticut State Senate, 1970–80; majority leader, 1974–80; honorary degrees: Yeshiva University, University of Hartford; Connecticut's 21st attorney general, 1983; reelected in 1986; author of ''The Power-Broker'' (Houghton Mifflin Company, 1966), a biography of late Democratic Party chairman John M. Bailey; ''The Scorpion and the Tarantula'' (Houghton Mifflin Company, 1970), a study of early efforts to control nuclear proliferation; ''The Legacy'' (Spoonwood Press, 1981), a history of Connecticut politics from 1930–80; ''Child Support in America'' (Yale University Press, 1986); ''In Praise of Public Life'' (Simon and Schuster, 2000); and ''An Amazing Adventure'' (Simon and Schuster, 2003); married: Hadassah Lieberman; children: Matthew, Rebecca, Ethan, and Hana; member, Democratic Leadership Council; Democratic candidate for Vice President, 2000; committees: chair, Homeland Security and Governmental Affairs; Armed Services; Small Business and Entrepreneurship; elected on November 8, 1988, to the U.S. Senate; reelected to each succeeding Senate term.

Office Listings

http://lieberman.senate.gov

706 Hart Senate Office Building, Washington, DC 20510 .... (202) 224–4041
Chief of Staff.—Clarine Nardi Riddle. FAX: 224–9750
Executive Assistant.—Rayanne Bostick.
Legislative Director.—Todd Stein.
One Constitution Plaza, 7th Floor, Hartford, CT 06103 .... (860) 549–8463
State Director.—Sherry Brown.

* * *

RICHARD BLUMENTHAL, Democrat, of Greenwich, CT; born in Brooklyn, NY, February 13, 1946; son of Martin and Jane Rosenstock Blumenthal; education: graduated, Riverdale Country School, Riverdale, NY, 1963; B.A., government, Harvard College, Cambridge, MA, 1967; J.D., Yale Law School, New Haven, CT, 1973; admitted to Connecticut Bar, 1976; admitted to District of Columbia Bar, 1977; appointed United States Attorney for the District of Connecticut, 1977–81; Connecticut State House of Representatives, 1984–87; Connecticut State Senate, 1987–90; elected Attorney General for the State of Connecticut, 1990, reelected in 1994, 1998, 2002, and 2006; military: served in the United States Marine Corps Reserves, 1970–76, honorably discharged as Sergeant; married: Cynthia M. Blumenthal; four children: Matthew, Michael, David, and Claire; committees: Armed Services; Health, Education, Labor, and Pensions; Judiciary; Special Committee on Aging; elected to the U.S. Senate on November 2, 2010.

Office Listings

http://blumenthal.senate.gov

G55 Dirksen Senate Office Building, Washington, DC 20510 .... (202) 224–2823
Chief of Staff.—Laurie Rubiner. FAX: 224–9673
Legislative Director.—Jeremy Bratt.
Scheduling Director.—Meghan Goodman.
Communications Director.—Ty Matsdorf.
30 Lewis Street, Suite 101, Hartford, CT 06103 .... (860) 258–6940
FAX: 258–6958

REPRESENTATIVES

FIRST DISTRICT

JOHN B. LARSON, Democrat, of East Hartford, CT; born in Hartford, CT, July 22, 1948; education: Mayberry Elementary School, East Hartford, CT; East Hartford High School; B.A., Central Connecticut State University; Senior Fellow, Yale University, Bush Center for Child Development and Social Policy; professional: high school teacher, 1972–77; insurance broker,

1978–98; president, Larson and Lyork; public service: Connecticut State Senate, 12 years, President Pro Tempore, 8 years; married: Leslie Larson; children: Carolyn, Laura, and Raymond; committees: Ways and Means; elected to the 106th Congress; reelected to each succeeding Congress.

Office Listings

http://www.house.gov/larson

1501 Longworth House Office Building, Washington, DC 20515 .... (202) 225–2265
Chief of Staff.—Shelley Rubino. FAX: 225–1031
Legislative Director.—Lee Slater.
Director of Scheduling.—Marvene Resendez.
Communications Director.—Ellis Brachman.
221 Main Street, Hartford, CT 06106–1864 .... (860) 278–8888

Counties: HARTFORD (part), LITCHFIELD (part), MIDDLESEX (part). Population (2000), 681,113.

ZIP Codes: 06002, 06006, 06010–11, 06016, 06021, 06023, 06025–28, 06033, 06035, 06037, 06040–41, 06045, 06057, 06060–61, 06063–65, 06067, 06073–74, 06088, 06090–91, 06094–96, 06098, 06101–12, 06114–15, 06117–20, 06123, 06126–29, 06131–34, 06137–38, 06140–47, 06150–56, 06160–61, 06176, 06180, 06183, 06199, 06416, 06422, 06444, 06457, 06467, 06479–80, 06489, 06759, 06790

* * *

SECOND DISTRICT

JOE COURTNEY, Democrat, of Vernon, CT; born in Hartford, CT, April 6, 1953; education: B.A., Tufts University, 1971–75; University of Connecticut Law School, 1975–78; public service: Connecticut State Representative, 1987–94; Vernon Town Attorney, 2003–06; professional: attorney, Courtney, Boyan, and Foran, LLC, 1978–2006; religion: Roman Catholic; married: Audrey Courtney; children: Robert and Elizabeth; committees: Agriculture; Armed Services; Ethics; elected to the 110th Congress on November 7, 2006; reelected to each succeeding Congress.

Office Listings

http://www.house.gov/courtney

215 Cannon House Office Building, Washington, DC 20515 .... (202) 225–2076
Chief of Staff.—Jason Gross. FAX: 225–4977
Deputy Chief of Staff/Communications Director.—Josh Zembik.
Scheduler.—Tracey Roberts.
Legislative Director.—Neil McKiernan.
2 Courthouse Square, Norwich, CT 06360 .... (860) 886–0139
District Director.—Jenny Contois.
77 Hazard Avenue, Unit J, Enfield, CT 06082 .... (860) 741–6011
FAX: 741–6036
101 Water Street, Suite 301, Norwich, CT 06360 .... (860) 886–0139
FAX: 886–2974

Counties: HARTFORD (part), MIDDLESEX (part), NEW LONDON, TOLLAND, WINDHAM. Population (2000), 681,113.

ZIP Codes: 06029, 06033, 06040, 06043, 06066, 06071–73, 06075–78, 06080, 06082–84, 06093, 06226, 06230–35, 06237–39, 06241–51, 06254–56, 06258–60, 06262–69, 06277–82, 06320, 06330–40, 06349–51, 06353–55, 06357, 06359–60, 06365, 06370–80, 06382–85, 06387–89, 06409, 06412–15, 06417, 06419–20, 06422–24, 06426, 06438–39, 06441–43, 06447, 06456–57, 06459, 06469, 06474–75, 06498

* * *

THIRD DISTRICT

ROSA L. DELAURO, Democrat, of New Haven, CT; born in New Haven, March 2, 1943; education: graduated, Lauralton Hall High School; attended London School of Economics, Queen Mary College, London, 1962–63; B.A., *cum laude*, history and political science, Marymount College, NY, 1964; M.A., international politics, Columbia University, NY, 1966; professional: executive assistant to Mayor Frank Logue, city of New Haven, 1976–77; executive assistant/development administrator, city of New Haven, 1977–78; chief of staff, Senator Christopher Dodd, 1980–87; executive director, Countdown '87, 1987–88; executive director, Emily's List, 1989–90; religion: Catholic; family: married, Stanley Greenberg; children: Anna,

Kathryn, and Jonathan; co-chair, Democratic Steering and Policy Committee; committees: Appropriations; elected to the 102nd Congress on November 6, 1990; reelected to each succeeding Congress.

Office Listings

http://www.delauro.house.gov

2413 Rayburn House Office Building, Washington, DC 20515 .... (202) 225–3661
Chief of Staff.—Leticia Mederos. FAX: 225–4890
Executive Assistant.—Elyse Schoenfeld.
59 Elm Street, New Haven, CT 06510 .... (203) 562–3718
District Director.—Jennifer Lamb.

Counties: FAIRFIELD (part), MIDDLESEX (part), NEW HAVEN (part). CITIES AND TOWNSHIPS: Ansonia, Beacon Falls, Bethany, Branford, Derby, Durham, East Haven, Guilford, Hamden, Middlefield, Middletown, Milford, Naugatuck, New Haven, North Branford, North Haven, Orange, Prospect, Seymour, Shelton, Stratford, Wallingford, Waterbury, West Haven, and Woodbridge. Population (2000), 681,113.

ZIP Codes: 06401, 06403, 06405, 06410, 06418, 06422, 06437, 06450, 06455, 06457, 06460, 06471–73, 06477, 06481, 06483–84, 06492–94, 06501–21, 06524–25, 06530–38, 06540, 06607, 06614–15, 06706, 06708, 06712, 06762, 06770

* * *

FOURTH DISTRICT

JAMES A. HIMES, Democrat, of Cos Cob, CT; born in Lima, Peru to American parents, July 5, 1966; education: B.A., Harvard University, Cambridge, MA, 1988; M.Phil, Oxford University, Oxford, England, 1990; professional: vice president, Goldman Sachs & Co., 1990–2002; vice president, Enterprise Community Partners, 2002–07; Commissioner, Greenwich Housing Authority; chair, Greenwich Democratic Town Committee; religion: Presbyterian; married: Mary Himes, 1994; children: Emma and Linley; committees: Financial Services; elected to the 111th Congress on November 4, 2008; reelected to the 112th Congress.

Office Listings

http://www.himes.house.gov

119 Cannon House Office Building, Washington, DC 20515 .... (202) 225–5541
Chief of Staff.—Jason Cole. FAX: 225–9629
Executive Assistant.—Caitlin Donohue.
888 Washington Boulevard, Stamford, CT 06901–2927 .... (866) 453–0028
211 State Street, 2nd Floor, Bridgeport, CT 06604–4223 .... (866) 453–0028
District Director.—Kathleen Warner.

Counties: FAIRFIELD (part), NEW HAVEN (part). CITIES AND TOWNSHIPS: Bridgeport, Darien, Easton, Fairfield, Greenwich, Monroe, New Canaan, Norwalk, Oxford, Redding, Ridgefield, Shelton, Stamford, Trumbull Weston, Westport, and Wilton. Population (2000), 681,113.

ZIP Codes: 06468, 06478, 06483–84, 06491, 06601–02, 06604–08, 06610–12, 06673, 06699, 06807, 06820, 06824–25, 06828–31, 06836, 06838, 06840, 06850–58, 06860, 06870, 06875–81, 06883, 06888–90, 06896–97, 06901–07, 06910–14, 06920–22, 06925–28

* * *

FIFTH DISTRICT

CHRISTOPHER S. MURPHY, Democrat, of Cheshire, CT; born August 3, 1973; grew up in Connecticut; graduated with honors, double major in history and political science, Williams College, MA; graduated, University of Connecticut Law School, Hartford, CT, 2002; former member, Southington Planning and Zoning Commission; served for eight years in the Connecticut General Assembly; in 2005, succeeding in passing Connecticut's landmark Stem Cell Investment Act; committees: Foreign Affairs; Oversight and Government Reform; elected to the 110th Congress on November 7, 2006; reelected to each succeeding Congress.

Office Listings

http://www.chrismurphy.house.gov

412 Cannon House Office Building, Washington, DC 20515 .... (202) 225–4476
Chief of Staff.—Francis Creighton. FAX: 225–5933
Communications Director.—Kristen Bossi.
Scheduler / Executive Assistant.—Jessica Elledge.
114 West Main Street, Suite 206, New Britain, CT 06053 .... (860) 223–8412

District Director.—Robert Michalik.

Counties: FAIRFIELD (part), HARTFORD (part), LITCHFIELD, NEW HAVEN (part). CITIES: Danbury, Meriden, New Britain, Torrington, and Waterbury. Population (2000), 681,113.

ZIP Codes: 06001, 06013, 06018–20, 06022, 06024, 06030–32, 06034, 06039, 06050–53, 06058–59, 06062, 06068–70, 06079, 06081, 06085, 06087, 06089, 06092, 06107, 06404, 06408, 06410–11, 06440, 06450–51, 06454, 06470, 06482, 06487–88, 06701–06, 06708, 06710, 06716, 06720–26, 06749–59, 06762–63, 06776–79, 06781–87, 06790–91, 06793–96, 06798, 06801, 06804, 06810–14, 06816–17

DELAWARE

(Population 2010, 897,934)

SENATORS

THOMAS R. CARPER, Democrat, of Wilmington, DE; born in Beckley, WV, January 23, 1947; education: B.A., Ohio State University, 1968; M.B.A., University of Delaware, 1975; military service: U.S. Navy, served during Vietnam War; public service: Delaware State Treasurer, 1977–83; U.S. House of Representatives, 1983–93; Governor of Delaware, 1993–2001; organizations: National Governors' Association; Democratic Leadership Council; religion: Presbyterian; family: married to the former Martha Ann Stacy; children: Ben and Christopher; committees: Environment and Public Works; Finance; Homeland Security and Governmental Affairs; elected to the U.S. Senate on November 7, 2000; reelected to each succeeding Senate term.

Office Listings

http://carper.senate.gov

513 Hart Senate Office Building, Washington, DC 20510 .... (202) 224–2441
Chief of Staff.—Jim Reilly. FAX: 228–2190
Legislative Director.—Bill Ghent.
Administrative Director.—Madge Farooq.
2215 Federal Building, 300 South New Street, Dover, DE 19904 .... (302) 674–3308
301 North Walnut Street, Suite 102 L–1, Wilmington, DE 19801 .... (302) 573–6291
12 The Circle, Georgetown, DE 19947 .... (302) 856–7690

* * *

CHRISTOPHER A. COONS, Democrat, of Wilmington, DE; born in Greenwich, CT, September 9, 1963; education: B.A., Amherst College, 1985; M.A.R., Yale University, 1992; J.D., Yale University, 1992; professional: associate (legal counsel), W.L. Gore & Associates, 1996–2004; president of New Castle County Council, 2000–04; county executive, New Castle County, 2005–10; religion: Presbyterian; married: Annie; children: Michael, Jack, and Maggie; committees: Budget; Energy and Natural Resources; Foreign Relations; Judiciary; elected on November 2, 2010 to the United States Senate to fill the remainder of the vacancy caused by the unfinished term of Joseph R. Biden, Jr. and took the oath of office on November 15, 2010.

Office Listings

http://coons.senate.gov

127A Russell Senate Office Building, Washington, DC 20510 .... (202) 224–5042
Chief of Staff.—Todd Webster. FAX: 228–3075
Legislative Director.—Jonathan Stahler.
Communications Director.—Ian Koski.
Office Manager.—Trinity Hall.
1105 North Market Street, Suite 2000, Wilmington, DE 19801–1233 .... (302) 573–6345
State Director.—Christy Gleason (acting).
500 West Loockerman Street, Suite 450, Dover, DE 19904 .... (302) 736–5601

REPRESENTATIVE

AT LARGE

JOHN CARNEY, JR., Democrat, of Wilmington, DE; born in Wilmington, May 20, 1956; education: B.A., english, Dartmouth College, Hanover, NH, 1978; M.P.A., University of Delaware, Newark, DE, 1987; professional: staff assistant, United States Senator Joseph Biden, Jr., Delaware, 1986–89; deputy chief administrative officer, New Castle County Executive Dennis Greenhouse, Delaware, 1989–94; deputy chief of staff, Governor Tom Carper, 1994–97; secretary of finance, Delaware, 1997–2000; lieutenant governor, Delaware, 2001–2009; awards: Order of the First State; Outstanding Alumni, University of Delaware; Recipient of the Outstanding Public Service Award, National Association of Community Health Centers, 2004; Recipient of the James Ewing Layman Award, Society of Surgical Oncology, 2008; City of Wilmington Public Service Award; religion: Roman Catholic; family: wife, Tracey, two sons; caucuses: New Democrats Caucus; National Guard Caucus; committees: Financial Services; elected to the 112th Congress on November 2, 2010.

Office Listings

http://www.johncarney.house.gov

1429 Longworth House Office Building, Washington, DC 20515 .... (202) 225–4165
Chief of Staff.—Elizabeth Hart. FAX: 225–2291
Communications Director.—James Allen.
Legislative Director.—Sam Hodas.
DC Scheduler.—Katie Paisley.
201 North Walnut Street, Suite 107, Wilmington, DE 19801 .... (302) 428–1902
State Director.—Doug Gramiak. FAX: 428–1905
DE Scheduler.—Kristy Huxhold.

Counties: KENT, NEW CASTLE, SUSSEX. CITIES AND TOWNSHIPS: Bethany Beach, Bethel, Bellefonte, Blades, Bowers, Bridgeville, Camden, Cheswold, Dagsboro, Delmar, Delaware City, Dewey Beach, Dover, Ellendale, Elsmere, Farmington, Felton, Fenwick Island, Frankford, Frederica, Georgetown, Greenwood, Harrington, Hartly, Henlopen Acres, Houston, Kenton, Laurel, Lewes, Little Creek, Leipsic, Magnolia, Middletown, Milford, Millsboro, Millville, Milton, New Castle, Newark, Newport, Ocean View, Odessa, Rehoboth Beach, Seaford, Selbyville, Slaughter Beach, South Bethany, Smyrna, Townsend, Viola, Wilmington, Woodside, and Wyoming. Population (2010), 897,934.

ZIP Codes: 19701–03, 19706–18, 19720–21, 19725–26, 19730–36, 19801–10, 19850, 19880, 19884–87, 19890–99, 19901–06, 19930–31, 19933–34, 19936, 19938–41, 19943–47, 19950–56, 19958, 19960–64, 19966–71, 19973, 19975, 19977, 19979–80

FLORIDA

(Population 2010, 18,801,310)

SENATORS

BILL NELSON, Democrat, of Orlando, FL, born in Miami, FL, September 29, 1942; education: Melbourne High School, 1960; B.A., Yale University, 1965; J.D. University of Virginia School of Law, 1968; professional: attorney; admitted to the Florida Bar, 1968; captain, U.S. Army Reserve, 1965–71; active duty, 1968–70; public service: Florida State House of Representatives, 1973–79; U.S. House of Representatives, 1979–91; Florida Treasurer, Insurance Commissioner, and State Fire Marshal, 1995–2001; Astronaut: payload specialist on the space shuttle *Columbia*, January, 1986; married: the former Grace Cavert; children: Bill Jr. and Nan Ellen; committees: Armed Services; Budget; Commerce, Science, and Transportation; Finance; Select Committee on Intelligence; Special Committee on Aging; elected to the U.S. Senate on November 7, 2000; reelected to each succeeding Senate term.

Office Listings

http://billnelson.senate.gov

716 Hart Senate Office Building, Washington, DC 20510 .... (202) 224–5274
Chief of Staff.—Pete Mitchell. FAX: 228–2183
Deputy Chief of Staff, Communications.—Dan McLaughlin.
Deputy Chief of Staff, Administration.—Brenda Strickland.
Legislative Director.—Susie Perez Quinn.
U.S. Courthouse Annex, 111 North Adams Street, Tallahassee, FL 32301 .... (850) 942–8415
Chief of Staff.—Pete Mitchell.
801 North Florida Avenue, 4th Floor, Tampa, FL 33602 .... (813) 225–7040
2925 Salzedo Street, Coral Gables, FL 33134 .... (305) 536–5999
3416 University Drive, Ft. Lauderdale, FL 33328 .... (954) 693–4851
413 Clematis Street, Suite 210, West Palm Beach, FL 33401 .... (561) 514–0189
225 East Robinson Street, Suite 410, Orlando, FL 32801 .... (407) 872–7161
1301 Riverplace Boulevard, Suite 2010, Jacksonville, FL 32207 .... (904) 346–4500
2000 Main Street, Suite 801, Ft. Myers, FL 33901 .... (239) 334–7760

* * *

MARCO A. RUBIO, Republican, of West Miami, FL; born in Miami, FL, May 28, 1971; education: South Miami Senior High School, 1989; B.S., political science, University of Florida, 1993; J.D., *cum laude,* University of Miami, 1996; professional: Florida House of Representatives, 2000–08; served as Majority Whip, Majority Leader and Speaker of the House; attorney, Broad and Cassel; Marco Rubio, P.A.; lecturer at Florida International University's Metropolitan Center, 2009–10; Bob Dole for President, 1996, Miami-Dade County Director; religion: Roman Catholic; married: Jeanette; children: Amanda, Daniella, Anthony, and Dominick; committees: Commerce, Science, and Transportation; Foreign Relations; Small Business and Entrepreneurship; Select Committee on Intelligence; elected to the U.S. Senate on November 2, 2010.

Office Listings

http://rubio.senate.gov

SDB–40A Dirksen Building, Washington, DC 20510 .... (202) 224–3041
Chief of Staff.—Cesar Conda FAX: 228–0285
Legislative Director.—Sally Canfield.
201 South Orange Avenue, Suite 350, Orlando, FL 32801 .... (407) 254–2573
1650 Prudential Drive, Suite 220, Jacksonville, FL 32207 .... (904) 398–8586
1 North Palafox Street, Suite 159, Pensacola, FL 32502 .... (850) 433–2603
3802 Spectrum Boulevard, Suite 106, Tampa, FL 33612 .... (813) 977–6450
8669 Northwest 36th Street, Suite 110, Miami, FL 33166 .... (305) 444–8332

REPRESENTATIVES

FIRST DISTRICT

JEFF MILLER, Republican, of Chumuckla, FL; born in St. Petersburg, FL, June 27, 1959; education: B.A., University of Florida, 1984; professional: real estate broker; public service: Executive Assistant to the Commissioner of Agriculture, 1984–88; Environmental Land

Management Study Commission, 1992; Santa Rosa County Planning Board Vice Chairman, 1996–98; elected to the Florida House of Representatives in 1998; reelected in 2000; served as House Majority Whip: organizations: Kiwanis Club of Milton; Florida Historical Society; Santa Rosa County United Way; Milton Pregnancy Resource Center Advisory Board; Gulf Coast Council of Boy Scouts; Florida FFA Foundation; religion: Methodist; married: Vicki Griswold; children: Scott and Clint; committees: chair, Veterans' Affairs; Armed Services; Permanent Select Committee on Intelligence; elected to the 107th Congress, by special election, on October 16, 2001; reelected to each succeeding Congress.

Office Listings

2416 Rayburn House Office Building, Washington, DC 20515 .... (202) 225–4136
Chief of Staff.—Dan McFaul. FAX: 225–3414
Legislative Director.—Pete Giambastiani.
Scheduler.—Diane Cihota.
4300 Bayou Boulevard, Suite 13, Pensacola, FL 32503 .... (850) 479–1183
District Director.—Sheilah Bowman.
348 Southwest Miracle Strip Parkway, Unit 24, Ft. Walton Beach, FL 32548 .... (850) 664–1266

Counties: ESCAMBIA, HOLMES, OKALOOSA (part), SANTA ROSA, WALTON (part), WASHINGTON. CITIES AND TOWNSHIPS: Bonifay, Carryville, Crestview, DeFuniak Springs, Destin, Fountain, Freeport, Ft. Walton Beach, Gulf Breeze, Jay, Laurel Hill, Lynn Haven, Milton, Noma, Pace, Paxton, Pensacola, Sunnyside, Westville, and Youngstown. Population (2000), 639,295.

ZIP Codes: 32501–09, 32511–14, 32516, 32520–24, 32526, 32530–31, 32533–42, 32544, 32547–49, 32559–72, 32577–79, 32580, 32583, 32588, 32591, 32598

* * *

SECOND DISTRICT

STEVE SOUTHERLAND II, Republican, of Panama City, FL; born in Nashville, TN, October 10, 1965; education: graduated, A. Crawford Mosley High School, Panama City, FL, 1983; B.S., Troy State University, 1987; A.A., Jefferson State Community College, 1989; professional: owner / president, Southerland Family Funeral Homes; former chairman, Florida Board of Funeral Directors; former chairman, Early Learning Coalition of Northwest Florida; former member: Bay County Economic Development Alliance; Bay Defense Alliance; Covenant Hospice Foundation Board; religion: Baptist; charter member and former trustee, Northstar Church; married: Susan Southerland; children: daughters, Samantha, Stephanie, Ally, and Abby; committees: Agriculture; Natural Resources; Transportation and Infrastructure; elected to the 112th Congress on November 2, 2010.

Office Listings

http:/southerland.house.gov

1229 Longworth House Office Building, Washington, DC 20515 .... (202) 225–5235
Chief of Staff.—Tom Stallings. FAX: 225–5615
Legislative Director.—Karen Williams.
Communications Director.—Matt McCullough.
Legislative Assistant.—Blair Mixon.
Scheduler.—Kara Schoeffling.
840 West 11th Street, Suite 2250, Panama City, FL 32401 .... (850) 785–0812
District Director.—Jonathan Hayes.
Deputy District Director (West) / District Scheduler.—Melissa Thompson.
3116 Capital Circle Northeast, Suite 9, Tallahassee, FL 32308 .... (850) 561–3979
Deputy District Director (East).—Lori Hutto.

Counties: BAY, CALHOUN, DIXIE, FRANKLIN, GADSDEN, GULF, JACKSON, JEFFERSON (part), LAFEYETTE, LEON (part), LIBERTY, OKALOOSA (part), SUWANNE, TAYLOR, WALKULLA, WALTON (part). Population (2000), 639,295.

ZIP Codes: 32008, 32013, 32024, 32038, 32055, 32060, 32062, 32064, 32066, 32071, 32094, 32096, 32126, 32140, 32170, 32175, 32267, 32301–18, 32320–24, 32326–34, 32336, 32343–44, 32346–48, 32351–53, 32355–62, 32395, 32399, 32401–13, 32417, 32420–21, 32423–24, 32426, 32428, 32430–32, 32437–38, 32440, 32442–49, 32454, 32456–57, 32459–61, 32465–66, 32541, 32550, 32578, 32628, 32648, 32680, 32692

* * *

THIRD DISTRICT

CORRINE BROWN, Democrat, of Jacksonville, FL; born in Jacksonville, November 11, 1946; education: B.S., Florida A&M University, 1969; master's degree, Florida A&M University, 1971; education specialist degree, University of Florida; honorary doctor of law, Edward Waters College; faculty member: Florida Community College in Jacksonville; University of Florida; and Edward Waters College; served in the Florida House of Representatives for 10 years; first woman elected chairperson of the Duval County Legislative Delegation; served as a consultant to the Governor's Committee on Aging; member: Congressional Black Caucus; Women's Caucus; and Progressive Caucus; Human Rights Caucus; Missing and Exploited Children's Caucus; Diabetes Caucus; Duma Study Group; Community College Caucus; Older Americans Caucus; one child: Shantrel; committees: Transportation and Infrastructure; Veterans' Affairs; elected on November 3, 1992, to the 103rd Congress; reelected to each succeeding Congress.

Office Listings

http://www.house.gov/corrinebrown

2336 Rayburn House Office Building, Washington, DC 20515 .... (202) 225–0123
Chief of Staff.—E. Ronnie Simmons. FAX: 225–2256
Executive Assistant/Scheduler.—Cathy Gass.
Legislative Director.—Nick Martinelli.
Communications Director.—David Simon.
101 East Union Street, Suite 202, Jacksonville, FL 32202 .... (904) 354–1652
805 South Kirkman Road, Suite 202, Orlando, FL 32811 .... (407) 290–9031

Counties: ALACHUA (part), CLAY (part), DUVAL (part), LAKE (part), MARION (part), ORANGE (part), PUTNAM (part), SEMINOLE (part), VOLUSIA (part). Population (2000), 639,295.

ZIP Codes: 32003, 32007, 32043, 32066, 32073, 32102, 32105, 32112–13, 32130–31, 32134, 32138, 32140, 32147–49, 32160, 32177, 32179–80, 32182, 32185, 32190, 32201–11, 32215–16, 32218–19, 32231–32, 32234, 32236, 32238–39, 32244, 32247, 32254, 32277, 32601–04, 32627, 32631, 32640–41, 32653–54, 32662, 32666–67, 32681, 32702–03, 32712–13, 32720–24, 32736, 32751, 32757, 32763, 32767–68, 32771–73, 32776, 32789, 32798, 32801, 32804–05, 32808–11, 32818–19, 32835, 32839, 32855, 32858, 32861, 32868, 33142, 33160–61, 33179, 34488, 34761

* * *

FOURTH DISTRICT

ANDER CRENSHAW, Republican, of Jacksonville, FL; born in Jacksonville, September 1, 1944; education: B.A., University of Georgia, 1966; J.D., University of Florida, 1969; professional: investment banker; religion: Episcopal; public service: former member of the Florida House of Representatives and the Florida State Senate; served as President of the Florida State Senate; married: Kitty; children: Sarah and Alex; committees: Appropriations; Joint Committee on the Library; elected to the 107th Congress on November 7, 2000; reelected to each succeeding Congress.

Office Listings

http://www.crenshaw.house.gov

440 Cannon House Office Building, Washington, DC 20515 .... (202) 225–2501
Chief of Staff.—John Ariale. FAX: 225–2504
Legislative Director.—Erica Striebel.
Communications Director.—Barbara Riley.
1061 Riverside Avenue, Suite 100, Jacksonville, FL 32204 .... (904) 598–0481
District Director.—Jacqueline Smith.
Mobile Office .... (386) 365–3316

Counties: BAKER, COLUMBIA, DUVAL (part), HAMILTON, JEFFERSON (part), LEON (part), MADISON, NASSAU, UNION. CITIES AND TOWNSHIPS: Greenville, Hilliard, Jacksonville, Jacksonville Beach, Jasper, Jennings, Lake Butler, Lake City, Lee, Macclenny, Madison, Monticello, Nassau Village-Ratliff, Palm Valley, Tallahassee, White Springs, and Yulee. Population (2000), 639,295.

ZIP Codes: 32009, 32011, 32024–26, 32034–35, 32038, 32040–41, 32046, 32052–56, 32058–59, 32061, 32063, 32072, 32083, 32087, 32094, 32096–97, 32204–05, 32207, 32210–12, 32214, 32216–18, 32223–29, 32233–35, 32237, 32240–41, 32244–46, 32250, 32255–58, 32266, 32277, 32301, 32311, 32317, 32331, 32336–37, 32340–41, 32344–45, 32350, 32643, 32697, 33142

* * *

FIFTH DISTRICT

RICHARD NUGENT, Republican, of Spring Hill, FL; born in Evergreen Park, IL, May 26, 1951; education: B.A. in criminology, Saint Leo College, Saint Leo, FL, 1990; FBI National

Academy graduate, FBI Academy, Quantico, VA, 1991; M.P.A., public administration, Troy State University, MacDill Air Force Base, FL, 1995; executive leadership training, National Sheriff's Institute, Longmount, CO, 2002; professional: Illinois Air National Guard, 1969–75; 38+ years in law enforcement; Deputy County Sheriff, Hernando County, FL; elected Sheriff, Hernando County, FL, 2001–10; military: law enforcement; family: wife, Wendy; children: three sons; committees: House Administration; Rules; elected to the 112th Congress on November 2, 2010.

Office Listings

http://nugent.house.gov

1517 Longworth House Office Building, Washington, DC 20515 .... (202) 225–1002
Chief of Staff.—Justin Grabelle. FAX: 226–6559
Legislative Director.—Katharine Troller.
Scheduler.—Cate Minichino.
Communications Director.—Harrison Lewis.
16224 Spring Hill Drive, Brooksville, FL 34605 .... (352) 799–8354
FAX: 799–8776

Counties: CITRUS, HERNANDO, LAKE (part), LEVY (part), MARION (part), PASCO (part), POLK (part), SUMTER. CITIES AND TOWNSHIPS: Brooksville, Dade City, and Clermont. Population (2010), 829,029.

ZIP Codes: 32159, 32162, 32621, 32625–26, 32635, 32639, 32644, 32658, 32668, 32683, 32696, 32778, 32825, 33513–14, 33521, 33523–26, 33537–38, 33540–44, 33548–49, 33556, 33558–59, 33574, 33576, 33585, 33593, 33597, 33809–10, 33849, 33868, 34218, 34220, 34423, 34428–34, 34436, 34442, 34445–53, 34460–61, 34464–65, 34481–82, 34484, 34487, 34498, 34601–11, 34613–14, 34636, 34639, 34653–55, 34661, 34667, 34669, 34711–13, 34731, 34736–37, 34748, 34753, 34755, 34762, 34785, 34787–89, 34797

* * *

SIXTH DISTRICT

CLIFF STEARNS, Republican, of Ocala, FL; born in Washington, DC, April 16, 1941; education: graduated, Woodrow Wilson High, Washington, DC, 1959; B.S., electrical engineering, George Washington University, Washington, DC, 1963; Air Force ROTC Distinguished Military Graduate; graduate work, University of California, Los Angeles, 1965; served, U.S. Air Force (captain), 1963–67; businessman; past president: Silver Springs Kiwanis; member: Marion County/Ocala Energy Task Force, Tourist Development Council, Ocala Board of Realtors, American Hotel/Motel Association in Florida, American Hotel/Motel Association of the United States, Grace Presbyterian Church; board of directors, Boys Club of Ocala; trustee: Munroe Regional Hospital; married: the former Joan Moore; children: Douglas, Bundy, and Scott; committees: Energy and Commerce; Veterans' Affairs; elected November 8, 1988, to the 101st Congress; reelected to each succeeding Congress.

Office Listings

http://www.house.gov/stearns

2306 Rayburn House Office Building, Washington, DC 20515 .... (202) 225–5744
Chief of Staff.—Jack Seum. FAX: 225–3973
Legislative Director.—Matt Mandel.
Scheduler / Office Manager.—Sara Shafer.
115 Southeast 25th Avenue, Ocala, FL 34471 .... (352) 351–8777
District Manager.—John Konkus.
1900 SW. 34th Street, Suite 207, Gainesville, FL 32608 .... (352) 337–0003
1726 Kinglsey Avenue SE., Suite 8, Orange Park, FL 32073 .... (904) 269–3203

Counties: ALACHUA (part), BRADFORD, CLAY (part), DUVAL (part), GILCHREST, LAKE (part), LEVY (part), MARION (part). CITIES AND TOWNSHIPS: Ocala, Gainesville, Leesburg, Orange Park, Middleburg, and Jacksonville. Population (2000), 639,295.

ZIP Codes: 32003, 32006, 32008, 32030, 32042–44, 32050, 32054, 32058, 32065, 32067–68, 32073, 32079, 32083, 32091, 32099, 32111, 32113, 32133, 32140, 32158–59, 32162, 32179, 32183, 32195, 32205, 32210, 32215, 32219–22, 32234, 32244, 32254, 32276, 32601, 32603, 32605–12, 32614–16, 32618–19, 32621–22, 32631, 32633–34, 32643, 32653, 32655–56, 32658, 32663–64, 32666–69, 32681, 32686, 32693–94, 32696, 33142, 33160–61, 34420–21, 34432, 34436, 34470–76, 34478, 34480–83, 34491–92, 34731, 34748–49

* * *

SEVENTH DISTRICT

JOHN L. MICA, Republican, of Winter Park, FL; born in Binghamton, NY, January 27, 1943; education: graduated, Miami-Edison High School, Miami, FL; B.A., University of

Florida, 1967; professional: president, MK Development; managing general partner, Cellular Communications; former government affairs consultant, Mica, Dudinsky and Associates; executive director, Local Government Study Commissions, Palm Beach County, 1970–72; executive director, Orange County Local Government Study Commission, 1972–74; Florida State House of Representatives, 1976–80; administrative assistant, U.S. Senator Paula Hawkins, 1980–85; Florida State Good Government Award, 1973; one of five Florida Jaycees Outstanding Young Men of America, 1978; member: Kiwanis, U.S. Capitol Preservation Commission, Tiger Bay Club, co-chairman, Speaker's Task Force for a Drug Free America, Florida Blue Key; U.S. Capitol Preservation Commission; brother of former Congressman Daniel A. Mica; married: the former Patricia Szymanek, 1972; children: D'Anne Leigh and John Clark; committees: chair, Transportation and Infrastructure; Oversight and Government Reform; elected on November 3, 1992 to the 103rd Congress; reelected to each succeeding Congress.

Office Listings

http://www.house.gov/mica

2187 Rayburn House Office Building, Washington, DC 20515 .... (202) 225–4035
Chief of Staff.—Wiley Deck. FAX: 226–0821
Legislative Director.—Brian Waldrip.
Scheduler.—Mary Klappa.
100 East Sybelia Avenue, Suite 340, Maitland, FL 32751 .... (407) 657–8080
840 Deltona Boulevard, Suite G, Deltona, FL 32725 .... (386) 860–1499
770 West Granada Boulevard, Suite 315, Ormond Beach, FL 32174 .... (386) 676–7750
3000 North Ponce de Leon Boulevard, Suite 1, St. Augustine, FL 32084 .... (904) 810–5048
2509 Crill Avenue, Suite 200, Palatka, FL 32177 .... (386) 328–1622
1 Florida Park Drive South, Suite 100, Palm Coast, FL 32137 .... (386) 246–6042

Counties: ORANGE COUNTY (part). CITIES AND TOWNSHIPS: Maitland, Winter Park. SEMINOLE COUNTY. CITIES AND TOWNSHIPS: Altamonte Springs, Casselberry, Heathrow, Lake Mary, Longwood, Sanford, Winter Springs. VOLUSIA COUNTY (part). CITIES AND TOWNSHIPS: Daytona Beach, Debary, Deland, Deltona, Holly Hill, Lake Helen, Orange City, Ormond Beach, Pierson. FLAGLER COUNTY. CITIES AND TOWNSHIPS: Beverly Beach, Bunnell, Flagler Beach, Marineland, Palm Coast. ST. JOHNS COUNTY. CITIES AND TOWNSHIPS: Hastings, Ponte Vedra Beach, St. Augustine, St. Augustine Beach. PUTNAM COUNTY (part). CITIES AND TOWNSHIPS: Crescent City, Palatka, Pomona Park, and Welaka. Population, (2000), 639,295.

ZIP Codes: 32004, 32033, 32080, 32082, 32084–86, 32092, 32095, 32110, 32112, 32114–22, 32125, 32130–31, 32135–37, 32139, 32142, 32145, 32151, 32157, 32164, 32173–78, 32180–81, 32187, 32189, 32193, 32198, 32259–60, 32701, 32706–08, 32713–15, 32718, 32720, 32724–25, 32728, 32730, 32738, 32744, 32746–47, 32750–53, 32763–64, 32771, 32773–74, 32779, 32789, 32791–92, 32795, 32799

* * *

EIGHTH DISTRICT

DANIEL WEBSTER, Republican, of Winter Garden, FL; born in Charleston, WV, April 27, 1949; education: graduated from Evans High School, Orlando, FL; B.S., Georgia Institute of Technology, Atlanta, GA, 1971; professional: owner, Webster Air Conditioning & Heating, Inc., Orlando, FL; married: Sandy Jordan; father of six children and grandfather of seven; committees: Rules; elected to the 112th Congress on November 2, 2010.

Office Listings

http://www.webster.house.gov

1039 Longworth House Office Building, Washington, DC 20515 .... (202) 225–2176
Chief of Staff.—Pepper Pennington. FAX: 225–0999
District Director.—Nathan Dunn.
300 West Plant Street, Winter Garden, FL 34787 .... (407) 654–5705
FAX: 654–5814

Counties: ORANGE (part), OSCEOLA (part), MARION (part), LAKE (part). CITIES AND TOWNSHIPS: Astatula, Azalea, Bay Hill, Bay Lake, Belle Isle, Belleview, Celebration, Conway, Doctor Phillips, Edgewood, Eustis, Fairview Shores, Howey-in-the-Hills, Holden Heights, Leesburg, Meadow Wood, Mid Florida Lakes, Montverde, Oakland, Ocala Part, Ocoee, Orlando, Silver Springs Shores, Sky Lakes, Tavares, Umatilla, Union Park, Williamsburg, Windermere, Winter Garden, and Winter Park. Population (2000), 639,295.

ZIP Codes: 32113, 32179, 32192, 32617, 32702–03, 32710, 32726–27, 32735–36, 32756–57, 32777–78, 32784, 32789, 32792, 32801–07, 32809–12, 32814, 32817–19, 32821–22, 32824–25, 32827, 32829–30, 32835–37, 32839, 32853–54, 32856–57, 32859–60, 32862, 32867, 32869, 32872, 32877, 32885–87, 32890–91, 32893, 32896–98, 33030, 33032–33, 33161, 33186, 34470–72, 34475, 34479–80, 34488–89, 34705, 34711, 34729, 34734, 34740, 34746–47, 34756, 34760–61, 34777–78, 34786–88

* * *

NINTH DISTRICT

GUS M. BILIRAKIS, Republican, of Palm Harbor, FL; born in Gainesville, FL, February 8, 1963; raised in Tarpon Springs, FL; education: B.A., University of Florida, 1986; J.D., Stetson University, 1989; son of former Representative Michael Bilirakis (1983–2006); volunteered on his father's congressional campaigns; interned for President Ronald Reagan and the National Republican Congressional Committee; worked for former Representative Don Sundquist (R–TN); ran the Bilirakis Law Group, specializing in wills, trusts, and estate planning, Holiday, FL; taught government classes, St. Petersburg College; member of the Florida House of Representatives, 1998–2006; chaired several prominent panels in the State House, including Crime Prevention, Public Safety Appropriations, and the Economic Development, Trade, and Banking Committee; married: Eva; children: Michael, Teddy, Manuel, and Nicholas; Senior Republican Freshman Whip; committees: Foreign Affairs; Homeland Security; Veterans' Affairs; elected to the 110th Congress on November 7, 2006; reelected to each succeeding Congress.

Office Listings

http://bilirakis.house.gov

407 Cannon House Office Building, Washington, DC 20515 .... (202) 225–5755
Chief of Staff.—David Peluso. FAX: 225–4085
Press Secretary.—Creighton Welch.
Executive Assistant.—Brian Prokes.
Palm Harbor Professional Center, 35111 U.S. Highway 19 North, Suite 301, Palm Harbor, FL 34684 .... (727) 773–2871
District Director.—Shawn Foster.
10941 North 56th Street, Temple Terrace, FL 33617 .... (813) 985–8541

Counties: HILLSBOROUGH (part), PASCO (part), PINELLAS (part). CITIES AND TOWNSHIPS: Bearss, Bloomingdale, Brandon, Carrollwood Village, Citrus Park, Clearwater, Countryside, Crystal Springs, Dale Mabry, Eastlake Woodlands, Elfers, Fishhawk, Holiday, Hudson, Hunters Green, Lutz, New Port Richey, Odessa, Oldsmar, Palm Harbor, Plant City, Safety Harbor, Seffner, Seven Springs, Tarpon Springs, Temple Terrace, Thonotosassa, Trinity, Valrico, and Veterans Village. Population (2000), 639,296.

ZIP Codes: 33511, 33527, 33530, 33539–40, 33542, 33547–49, 33556, 33558–59, 33563, 33565–67, 33569, 33583–84, 33587, 33592, 33594–95, 33598, 33612–13, 33617–18, 33624–26, 33637, 33647, 33688, 33755–59, 33761, 33763–66, 33769, 33810, 34652–56, 34667–69, 34673–74, 34677, 34679–80, 34683–85, 34688–91, 34695

* * *

TENTH DISTRICT

C. W. BILL YOUNG, Republican, of Indian Shores, FL; born in Harmarville, PA, December 16, 1930; elected Florida's only Republican State Senator in 1960; reelected 1964, 1966, 1967 (special election), and 1968, serving as minority leader from 1963 to 1970; national committeeman, Florida Young Republicans, 1957–59; state chairman, Florida Young Republicans, 1959–61; member, Florida Constitution Revision Commission, 1965–67; dean of the Florida Republican delegation; the senior Republican in the Congress; married: Beverly; children: three sons; committees: Appropriations; elected to the 92nd Congress, November 3, 1970; reelected to each succeeding Congress.

Office Listings

2407 Rayburn House Office Building, Washington, DC 20515 .... (202) 225–5961
Chief of Staff.—Harry Glenn. FAX: 225–9764
Legislative Director.—Brad Stine.
Defense Appropriations.—Kent Clark.
9210 113th Street, Seminole, FL 33772 .... (727) 394–6950

Counties: PINELLAS COUNTY (part). Population (2000), 639,295.

ZIP Codes: 33701–16, 33729, 33731–32, 33734, 33736–38, 33740–44, 33755–56, 33760–65, 33767, 33770–82, 33784–86, 34660, 34681–84, 34697–98

* * *

ELEVENTH DISTRICT

KATHY CASTOR, Democrat, of Tampa, FL; born in Miami, FL, August 20, 1966; education: B.A., political science, Emory University, 1988; J.D., Florida State University, 1991; professional: Assistant General Counsel, State of Florida, Department of Community Affairs, 1991–94; attorney, Icard Merrill, 1994–95; partner, Broad and Cassel, 1995–2000; ran for Florida State Senate, 2000; Hillsborough County Commissioner, 2002–06; religion: member of Palma Ceia Presbyterian Church; married: William Lewis; children: two; committees: Budget; Energy and Commerce; elected to the 110th Congress on November 7, 2006; reelected to each succeeding Congress.

Office Listings

http://castor.house.gov

137 Cannon House Office Building, Washington, DC 20515 .... (202) 225–3376
Chief of Staff.—Clay Phillips. FAX: 225–5652
Legislative Director.—Rene Munoz.
Scheduler.—Lara Hopkins.
4144 North Armenia Avenue, Suite 300, Tampa, FL 33607 .... (813) 871–2817
District Director.—Chloe Coney.
Press Secretary.—Ellen Gedalius.

Counties: HILLSBOROUGH (part), MANATEE (part), PINELLAS (part). CITIES: Apollo Beach, Bradenton, Carrollwood, Carrollwood Village, Citrus Park, Ellenton, Gibsonton, Gulfport, Lutz, Northdale, Oldsmar, Palmetto, Riverview, Ruskin, St. Petersburg, Tampa, Temple Terrace, and Town 'N' Country, Ybor City. Population (2000), 639,295.

ZIP Codes: 33534, 33549, 33559, 33569–70, 33572, 33586, 33601–19, 33621–26, 33629–31, 33634–35, 33637, 33647, 33650–51, 33655, 33663–64, 33672–75, 33677, 33679–82, 33684–87, 33690, 33694, 33697, 33701, 33705, 33707, 33710–13, 33730, 33733, 33747, 33784, 34205, 34208, 34221–22, 34677

* * *

TWELFTH DISTRICT

DENNIS A. ROSS, Republican, of Lakeland, FL; born in Lakeland, October 18, 1959; education: Lakeland Senior High School; B.S., organizational management, Auburn University, Auburn, AL, 1981; J.D., Cumberland School of Law at Samford University, Birmingham, AL, 1987; professional: attorney, Holland & Knight; attorney, Walt Disney World; founder and attorney, Ross Vecchio, PA, 1989–2010; awards: Workers Compensation Section, Appreciation Award, 2001; Florida Building Material Association, Legislator of the Year Award, 2001 and 2003; Florida Workers Advocate, Outstanding Freshman Representative Award, 2001; The Trust for Public Land, Legislative Leadership Award, 2001; Polk Community College, Outstanding Legislator, 2001; Florida Crane Owners Council, Representative of the Year, 2003; Florida Association of Roofing Professionals, Legislative Achievement Award, 2003; Florida Automotive Dealer Association, Legislator of the Year, 2003; Florida Retail Federation, Legislator of the Year, 2003; Florida Bankers Association, Outstanding Leadership Award, 2004; ARC Florida, Representative of the Year, 2004; YMCA of Florida, Outstanding Leadership Award, 2005; Florida League of Cities, Legislative Appreciation Award, 2005, 2006 and 2007; Florida Insurance Council, Harry G. Landrum Outstanding Legislative Leadership, 2005 and 2008; Florida Association of Counties, Champion Award, 2005; Florida Trucking Association, Legislator of the Year, 2005 and 2006; Associated Industries of Florida, Champion for Business Award, 2005; Florida Association of Insurance and Financial Advisors, Representative of the Year, 2005; Florida Association of Mortgage Brokers, Grateful Recognition Award, 2005; Florida Association of Insurance Agents, Legislator of the Year, 2006; Florida Chamber, Most Valuable Legislator, 2008; Governor's Hurricane Conference, Legislative Award, 2008; Associated Industries of Florida Financial Securities Council, Legislator of the Year, 2008; Florida Chamber Honor Roll 2001, 2002, 2003, 2004, 2005, 2007 and 2008; religion: member, First Presbyterian Church, Lakeland; married: Cindy; children: Shane and Travis; committees: Oversight and Government Reform, Judiciary, Education and the Workforce; elected to the 112th Congress on November 2, 2010.

Office Listings

http://www.house.gov/dennisross

404 Cannon House Office Building, Washington, DC 20515 .... (202) 225–1252
Chief of Staff.—Fred Piccolo. FAX: 226–0585
Legislative Director.—Omar Raschid.
Office Coordinator.—Lisa Griffin.
170 Fitzgerald Road, Suite 1, Lakeland, FL 33813 .... (863) 644–8215

District Director.—Blaine Gravitt. FAX: 648–0749
Director of Administration / Scheduler.—Shelee Meeker.
Community Outreach Director.—Kristin Collis.

Counties: HILLSBOROUGH (part), OSCEOLA (part), POLK (part). CITIES AND TOWNSHIPS: Apollo Beach, Auburndale, Babson Park, Bartow, Brandon, Davenport, Dundee, Eagle Lake, Fort Meade, Frostproof, Gibsonton, Haines City, Highland City, Hillcrest Heights, Indian Lake Estates, Lakeland, Lake Alfred, Lake Hamilton, Lake Wales, Mulberry, Plant City, Poinciana, Polk City, Riverview, Ruskin, Seffner, Sun City Center, Tampa, Temple Terrace, Thonotosassa, Wimauma, and Winter Haven. Population (2000), 639,296.

ZIP Codes: 33030, 33033, 33170, 33183, 33186, 33503, 33508–11, 33527, 33534, 33547, 33550, 33563–64, 33566–73, 33575, 33584, 33592, 33594, 33598, 33610, 33617, 33619, 33637, 33689, 33801–07, 33809–11, 33813, 33815, 33820, 33823, 33825, 33827, 33830–31, 33834–41, 33843–47, 33850–51, 33853–56, 33859–60, 33863, 33867–68, 33877, 33880–85, 33888, 33896–98, 34758–59

* * *

THIRTEENTH DISTRICT

VERN BUCHANAN, Republican, of Longboat Key, FL; born in Detroit, MI, May 8, 1951; education: B.B.A., business administration, Cleary University; M.B.A., University of Detroit; honorary degree: Doctorate of Science in Business Administration, Cleary University; professional: founder and chairman, Buchanan Enterprises; founder and chairman, Buchanan Automotive Group, 1992; operations include Sarasota Ford and 18 auto franchises in the southeastern United States; experience in real estate including home building and property development and management; awards: One of America's Ten Outstanding Young Men, U.S. Jaycees; Entrepreneur of the Year, Inc. Magazine and Arthur Young; Entrepreneur of the Year, Harvard Business School, Club of Detroit; One of Michigan's Five Outstanding Young Men, Michigan Jaycees; President's Award, Ford Motor Company; Certified Retailer Award, J.D. Power and Associates; Outstanding Citizen Award, United Negro College Fund; Outstanding Philanthropic Corporation Award, National Society of Fund Raising Executives; Freedom Award for Business and Industry, NAACP; The American Jewish Committee Civic Achievement Award; Tampa Bay Business Hall of Fame Award; married: Sandy Buchanan; children: James and Matt; committee: Ways and Means; elected to the 110th Congress on November 7, 2006; reelected to each succeeding Congress.

Office Listings

http://www.buchanan.house.gov

221 Cannon House Office Building, Washington, DC 20515 .... (202) 225–5015
Chief of Staff.—Dave Karvelas. FAX: 226–0828
Deputy Chief of Staff.—Don Green.
Legislative Director.—Shane Lieberman.
Communications Director.—Max Goodman.
Scheduler.—Margo Keeler.
111 South Orange Avenue, Suite 200W, Sarasota, FL 34236 .... (941) 951–6643
District Director.—Sally Tibbetts.
Scheduler.—Sydney Gruters.
2424 Manatee Avenue West, Suite 104, Bradenton, FL 34205 .... (941) 747–9081

Counties: CHARLOTTE (part), DESOTO, HARDEE, MANATEE (part), SARASOTA. Population (2000), 639,295.

ZIP Codes: 33138, 33160–61, 33598, 33834, 33865, 33873, 33890, 33946–47, 34201–12, 34215–19, 34221–24, 34228–43, 34250–51, 34260, 34264–70, 34272, 34274–78, 34280–82, 34284–89, 34292–93, 34295

* * *

FOURTEENTH DISTRICT

CONNIE MACK, Republican, of Fort Myers, FL; born in Fort Myers, August 12, 1967; education: B.S., University of Florida, Gainesville, FL, 1993; professional: marketing executive; member, Florida state House of Representatives, 2000–03; son of U.S. Senator Connie Mack III, step-great-grandson of Senator Tom Connally, great-grandson of Senator Morris Sheppard, and great-great-grandson of Congressman John Levi Sheppard; married: U.S. Representative Mary Bono Mack; children: Addison and Connie; committees: Foreign Affairs; Oversight and Government Reform; elected to the 109th Congress on November 2, 2004; reelected to each succeeding Congress.

Office Listings

http://mack.house.gov

115 Cannon House Office Building, Washington, DC 20515 .... (202) 225–2536
Chief of Staff.—Hans Klingler. FAX: 226–0439
Legislative Director.—Vacant.
Press Secretary.—David James.
Executive Assistant.—Vacant.
804 Nicholas Parkway East, Suite 1, Cape Coral, FL 33990 .... (239) 573–5837
3299 Tamiami Trail E, Suite 105, Naples, FL 34112 .... (239) 252–6225

Counties: CHARLOTTE (part), COLLIER (part), LEE. Population (2000), 639,295.

ZIP Codes: 33030, 33033, 33160, 33186, 33189, 33901–22, 33924, 33927–28, 33931–32, 33936, 33945–46, 33948, 33953–57, 33965, 33970–72, 33981, 33990–91, 33993–94, 34101–10, 34112–14, 34116, 34119, 34133–36, 34140, 34142, 34145–46, 34224

* * *

FIFTEENTH DISTRICT

BILL POSEY, Republican, of Rockledge, FL; born in Washington, DC, December 18, 1947; education: graduated Cocoa High School, 1966; A.A., Brevard Community College, Cocoa, FL; National Legislator of the Year by the American Legislative Exchange Council; married: Katie Posey; children: Pamela and Catherine; member, House Aerospace Caucus, Republican Study Committee; committees: Financial Services; elected to the 111th Congress on November 4, 2008; reelected to the 112th Congress.

Office Listings

http://www.posey.house.gov

120 Cannon House Office Building, Washington, DC 20515 .... (202) 225–3671
Chief of Staff.—Stuart Burns. FAX: 225–3516
Legislative Director.—Marcus Brubaker.
Scheduler.—Catherine Eng.
2725 Judge Fran Jamieson Way Building C, Melbourne, FL 32940 .... (321) 632–1776
Directors of Community Relations: Patrick Gavin, Pam Gillespie, David Jackson, Rob Medina.

Counties: BREVARD (part), INDIAN RIVER, OSCEOLA (part), POLK (part). Population (2000), 639,295.

ZIP Codes: 32815, 32899, 32901–12, 32919–20, 32922–26, 32931–32, 32934–37, 32940–41, 32948–53, 32955–58, 32960–71, 32976, 32978, 33837, 33848, 33858, 33868, 33896–98, 34739, 34741–47, 34758–59, 34769–73, 34972

* * *

SIXTEENTH DISTRICT

THOMAS J. ROONEY, Republican, of Tequesta, FL; born in Philadelphia, PA, November 21, 1970; education: B.A., Washington and Jefferson, Washington, PA; M.A., University of Florida, Gainesville, FL; J.D., University of Miami, Coral Gables, FL; member, Roman Catholic Church; married: Tara; children: Tommy, Sean, and Seamus; committees: Agriculture; Armed Services; Permanent Select Committee on Intelligence; elected to the 111th Congress on November 4, 2008; reelected to the 112th Congress on November 2, 2010.

Office Listings

http://www.rooney.house.gov

1529 Longworth House Office Building, Washington, DC 20515 .... (202) 225–5792
Chief of Staff.—Brian Crawford. FAX: 225–3132
Communications Director.—Michael Mahaffey.
171 Southwest Flagler Avenue, Stuart, FL 34994 .... (772) 288–4668
226 Taylor Street, Suite 200, Punta Gorda, FL 33950 .... (941) 575–9101

Counties: CHARLOTTE (part), GLADES, HENDRY (part), HIGHLANDS, MARTIN (part), OKEECHOBEE, PALM BEACH (part), ST. LUCIE (part). Population (2000), 639,295.

ZIP Codes: 33138, 33160–61, 33170, 33186, 33410–12, 33414, 33418, 33421, 33440, 33455, 33458, 33467, 33469–71, 33475, 33477–78, 33825–26, 33852, 33857, 33862, 33870–72, 33875–76, 33917, 33920, 33930, 33935, 33938, 33944,

33948–55, 33960, 33972, 33975, 33980, 33982–83, 34142, 34945–47, 34949–53, 34956–58, 34972–74, 34981–88, 34990–92, 34994–97

* * *

SEVENTEENTH DISTRICT

FREDERICA S. WILSON, Democrat, of Miami, FL; born in Miami, November 5, 1942; education: B.S., Fisk University, 1963; M.S., University of Miami, 1972; professional: executive director, Office of Alternative Education and Dropout Prevention, Miami-Dade County Schools; member, Miami-Dade County School Board, 1992–98; Florida State House of Representatives, 1998–2002; Democratic Whip, Florida State Senate, 2002–04; Florida State Senate, 2002–10; Minority Whip, Florida State Senate, 2008–11; members: regional director, Alpha Kappa Alpha Sorority Incorporated, 1986-present; founder/member, 5000 Role Models of Excellence Incorporated, 1993–present; member, National Association of Black School Educators, present; member, the Links Incorporated, present; founder, Stop Day Enough is Enough, 1996-present; Miami Delegate, President's Summit for America's Future, 1997; board member, Women's Action for New Directions Educational Fund, 2004; honors and awards: State of Florida ''STOP DAY'', Enough is Enough, founder, 1996; President's Summit for America's Future, Philadelphia, Pennsylvania, Miami Delegate, 1997; founder, Miami-Dade County ''Keep Me Safe'' summit, march, and candlelight vigil, 1997; American Red Cross, Spectrum Award, 1998; African-American Achiever Award for Education, 1998; NAACP, Florida Chapter, Morris Milton Memorial Award, 2001; Community Action Agency, Citizen of the Year Award, 2004; American Cancer Society, Florida Chapter, Legislative Leadership Award, 2004; Florida Education Association, Educator of the Year, 2004; Association of Black Health-System Pharmacists, Legislator Achievement Award, 2004; Easter Seals of Miami-Dade, Legislator of the Year Award, 2004; Northside Seventh Day Adventist Church (Miami), Distinguished Community Leader Award, 2004; The Black Archives, History and Research Foundation of South Florida, Inc., Chairman's Award, 2004; Sierra Club, Florida Chapter, Legislative Recognition Award, 2004; Alpha Kappa Alpha Sorority, Ft. Pierce, Florida Chapter, Soror of the Year, 2005; Alpha Kappa Alpha Sorority, Ft. Walton Beach, Florida Chapter, Soror of the Year, 2005; Alpha Kappa Alpha Sorority, Thomasville, GA Chapter, Soror of the Year, 2005; Carrie P. Meek Education Leadership Achievement Award, 2005; Miami Gardens Jaycees, Distinguished Service Award, 2005; Alpha Kappa Alpha, Inc., Emerald Service Award, 2005; The Links, Inc., Links of Gold Award, 2005; SEIU Florida Healthcare Union, Legislative Hero Award, 2006; Barry University, SGA Acknowledgement of Florida's Residents Access Grant Award, 2006; City of Miami, Women Builders of Community Dreams Award, 2006; Florida Memorial University, SGA Leadership Character and Service Award, 2006; Holy Faith Missionary Baptist Church, Participation Award, 2006; Miami-Dade Police Department, Appreciation Award, 2006; The Historic St. Agnes Episcopal Church, 108th Anniversary Appreciation Award, 2006; FAU, Small Business Development Appreciation Award, 2006; Day of the Child, Mentoring Award, 2006; Project H.O.P.E., Katrina Humanitarian Award, 2006; South Florida Chapter of the Coalition of Black Trade Unionists, Audrey McCollum Scholarship Award, 2006; CEO Magazine, Legislative Action Recognition, 2006; Community Action Agency, Youth Leadership Award, 2006; I.B.P.O.E. of W., Antlers Temple #39, Legislative Excellence Award, 2006; Community Health of South Dade, Inc., Health Hero Award, 2006; Health Council of South Florida, Inc., Health Leadership Award, 2006; National Coalition of 100 Black Women, Inc., Greater Miami Chapter, Candace Award, 2006; Kiwanis Club of Miami Shores, North Dade Exemplary Service Award, 2006; Academy of Florida Trial Lawyers, Rosemary Barkett Award, 2006; NAACP Milton Morris Award, 2007; Jessie C. Trice Humanitarian Award, 2007; Liberty City's Community Action Agency, Community Service Award, 2007; Miami Dade College, Pathway to Opportunity Appreciation Award, 2007; Florida Association of School Administrators, Legislator of the Year, 2007; Florida Association of Women Lawyers, Legislative Recognition Award, 2007; The National Medical Association, Scroll of Merit for Public Education Advocacy, 2008; American School Health Association, Legislator of the Year, 2008; Alpha Kappa Alpha Sorority International, Rosa Parks Coretta Scott King Award, 2008; Florida Association of Counties (FAC), County Partner Award, 2008; Florida Cable Telecommunications Association, Leaders in Learning Award, 2008; committees: Foreign Affairs; Science, Space, and Technology; elected to the 112th Congress on November 2, 2010.

Office Listings

http://wilson.house.gov

208 Cannon House Office Building, Washington, DC 20515 .... (202) 225–4506
Chief of Staff.—Tasha Cole. FAX: 226–0777
Senior Advisor.—Keenan Austin.
Legislative Director.—James Williams.
Legislative Correspondent.—Michael T. Ashley.
Legislative Assistant.—David Bagby.
Communications Director.—Mahen Gunaratna.
Scheduler.—Toby Watkins.
10100 Pines Boulevard, 3rd Floor, Building B, Pembroke Pines, FL 33026 .... (954) 450–6767
District Office Director.—Joyce Postell.
18425 Northwest 2nd Avenue, Suite 355, Miami, FL 33169 .... (305) 690–5905

Counties: DADE (part), BROWARD (part). Population (2000), 639,296.

ZIP Codes: 33008–09, 33013, 33020–25, 33054–56, 33081, 33083, 33090, 33092, 33101, 33110, 33127, 33136–38, 33142, 33147, 33150–51, 33156, 33160–62, 33164, 33167–69, 33179–81, 33197, 33238, 33242, 33247, 33256, 33261

* * *

EIGHTEENTH DISTRICT

ILEANA ROS-LEHTINEN, Republican, of Miami, FL; born in Havana, Cuba, July 15, 1952; education: B.A., English, Florida International University; M.S., educational leadership, Florida International University; Ed.D, University of Miami, 2004; certified Florida school teacher; founder and former owner, Eastern Academy; elected to Florida House of Representatives, 1982; elected to Florida State Senate, 1986; former president, Bilingual Private School Association; regular contributor to leading Spanish-language newspaper; during House tenure, married then-State Representative Dexter Lehtinen; two children and two step-children; committees: chair, Foreign Affairs; elected on August 29, 1989 to the 101st Congress; reelected to each succeeding Congress.

Office Listings

2206 Rayburn House Office Building, Washington, DC 20515 .... (202) 225–3931
Chief of Staff.—Arthur Estopinan. FAX: 225–5620
Deputy Director.—Christine del Portillo.
Legislative Director.—Joshua H. Salpeter.
Press Secretary.—Alex Cruz.
4960 Southwest 72nd Avenue, Suite 208, Miami, FL 33155 .... (305) 668–2285

Counties: DADE (part), MONROE (part). CITIES AND TOWNSHIPS: Coral Gables, Florida City, Homestead, Key Biscayne, Miami, Miami Beach, South Miami, and West Miami. Population (2000), 639,295.

ZIP Codes: 33001, 33030, 33032–34, 33036–37, 33039–45, 33050–52, 33070, 33109, 33111–12, 33114, 33119, 33121, 33124–36, 33139–46, 33149, 33154–59, 33165, 33170, 33174, 33176, 33186, 33189–90, 33195, 33197, 33199, 33231, 33233–34, 33239, 33243, 33245, 33255, 33257, 33265, 33296, 33299

* * *

NINETEENTH DISTRICT

THEODORE DEUTCH, Democrat, of Boca Raton, FL; born in Bethlehem, PA, May 7, 1966; education: graduate of Liberty High School; B.A., University of Michigan, Ann Arbor, MI, 1988; J.D., University of Michigan Law School, Ann Arbor, MI, 1990; admitted to the Florida bar, 1991; attorney: Florida State Senator, 2006–10; member: Florida Bar Association; Jewish Federation of South Palm Beach County; League of Women Voters; married to the former Jill Weinstock, three children; committees: Foreign Affairs; Judiciary; elected to the 111th Congress on April 13, 2010, by special election to fill the vacancy caused by the resignation of United States Representative Robert Wexler; reelected to the 112th Congress on November 2, 2010.

Office Listings

http://deutch.house.gov

1024 Longworth House Office Building, Washington, DC 20515 .... (202) 225–3001
Chief of Staff.—Joshua Rogin. FAX: 225–5974
Legislative Director.—Ellen McLaren.
Communications Director.—Ashley Mushnick.
2500 North Military Trail, Suite 490, Boca Raton, FL 33431 .... (561) 988–6302

District Director.—Wendi Lipsich. FAX: 988–6423
5790 Margate Boulevard, Margate, FL 33063 .... (954) 972–6454

Counties: BROWARD (part), PALM BEACH (part). CITIES AND TOWNSHIPS: Atlantis, Boca Raton, Boynton Beach, Coconut Creek, Coral Springs, Deerfield Beach, Delray Beach, Greenacres, Lake Worth, Lantana, Margate, Pompano Beach, and Tamarac. Population (2000) 639,295.

ZIP Codes: 33063–66, 33068–69, 33071, 33073, 33075–77, 33093, 33321, 33406, 33411, 33413–15, 33417, 33426, 33428, 33431, 33433–34, 33436–37, 33441–42, 33445–46, 33448, 33454, 33461–63, 33466–67, 33481–82, 33484, 33486–88, 33496–99

* * *

TWENTIETH DISTRICT

DEBBIE WASSERMAN SCHULTZ, Democrat, of Weston, FL; born in Forest Hills, Queens County, NY, September 27, 1966; education: B.A., University of Florida, Gainesville, FL, 1988; M.A., University of Florida, FL, 1990; professional: Public Policy Curriculum Specialist, Nova Southeastern University; Adjunct Instructor, Political Science, Broward Community College; aide to United States Representative Peter Deutsch, 1989–92; member, Florida State House of Representatives, 1992–2000; member, Florida State Senate, 2000–04; organizations: Board of Trustees, Westside Regional Medical Center; Outstanding Freshman Legislator, Florida Women's Political Caucus; Secretary; Board of Directors, American Jewish Congress; Member, Broward National Organization for Women; Board of Directors, National Safety Council, South Florida Chapter; religion: Jewish; married: Steve; children: Rebecca, Jake, Shelby; Senior Democratic Whip; elected chair, Democratic National Committee, 2011; committees: Budget; elected to the 109th Congress on November 2, 2004; reelected to each succeeding Congress.

Office Listings

http://www.house.gov/wassermanschultz

118 Cannon House Office Building, Washington, DC 20515 .... (202) 225–7931
Chief of Staff.—Tracie Pough. FAX: 226–2052
Communications Director.—Jonathon Beeton.
Legislative Director.—Coby Dolan.
Office Manager.—Irena Vidulovic.
10100 Pines Boulevard, Pembroke Pines, FL 33026 .... (954) 437–3926
19200 West Country Club Drive, Third Floor, Aventura, FL 33180 .... (305) 936–5724

Counties: BROWARD COUNTY (PART). CITIES: Dania Beach, Davie, Lazy Lake, Plantation, Wilton Manors, Weston. DADE COUNTY (part). CITIES: Bay Harbor Island, North Bay Village, and Sunny Isles. MIAMI-DADE COUNTY (part). CITIES: Davie, Fort Lauderdale, Hollywood, Miami Beach, North Miami, Sunrise. Population (2000), 639,295.

ZIP Codes: 33004, 33009, 33019–21, 33024, 33026, 33030, 33033, 33084, 33137, 33139–41, 33147, 33154, 33156, 33160–61, 33170, 33180–81, 33301, 33304–05, 33309, 33311–15, 33317–19, 33321–32, 33334, 33336, 33338, 33345, 33351, 33355, 33394

* * *

TWENTY-FIRST DISTRICT

MARIO DIAZ-BALART, Republican, of Miami, FL; born in Ft. Lauderdale, FL, September 25, 1961; education: University of South Florida; professional: president, Gordon Diaz-Balart and Partners (public relations and marketing business); religion: Catholic; public service: administrative assistant to the Mayor of Miami, 1985–88; Florida House of Representatives, 1988–92, and 2000–02; Florida State Senate, 1992–2000; committees: Appropriations; elected to the 25th District in the 108th Congress on November 5, 2002, reelected to each succeeding Congress. In 2010 ran unopposed and was elected to the 21st District in the 112th Congress on November 2, 2010.

Office Listings

http://www.house.gov/mariodiaz-balart

436 Cannon House Office Building, Washington, DC 20515 .... (202) 225–4211
Chief of Staff.—Cesar A. Gonzalez. FAX: 226–8576
Legislative Director.—Miguel Mendoza.
8669 Northwest 36th Street, Suite 100, Doral, FL 33166 .... (305) 470–8555
District Director.—Miguel Otero. FAX: 470–8575

Counties: BROWARD COUNTY (part), DADE COUNTY (part). CITIES AND TOWNSHIPS: Central Kendall, Doral, Fontainebleau, Hialeah, Miami Lakes, Miami Springs, Miramar, Pembroke Pines, Richmond Heights, Sweetwater, Virginia Gardens, and Westchester. Population (2000), 639,295.

ZIP Codes: 33002, 33010–17, 33027–29, 33054–55, 33082, 33102, 33107, 33116, 33122, 33126, 33143, 33148, 33152, 33155–58, 33165–66, 33172–74, 33176, 33178, 33186, 33188, 33266, 33283

* * *

TWENTY-SECOND DISTRICT

ALLEN B. WEST, Republican, of Plantation, FL; born in Atlanta, GA; February 7, 1961; education: graduated, Grady High School, 1979; B.A., University of Tennessee, 1983; M.A., Kansas State University, 1996, both in political science; M.M.A.S., U.S. Army Command and General Staff Officer College, political theory and military operations, 1996; professional: United States Army, 1982–2004; teacher, Deerfield Beach High School, 2004–05; Department of Defense Contractor, 2005–10; married: Angela Graham West, 1989; children: Aubrey and Austen; committees: Armed Services; Small Business; elected to the 112th Congress on November 2, 2010.

Office Listings

http://www.west.house.gov

1708 Longworth House Office Building, Washington, DC 20515 .... (202) 225–3026
Chief of Staff.—Jonathan Blyth. FAX: 225–8398
Deputy Chief of Staff / Legislative Director.—Josh Grodin.
Legislative Assistant.—Reginald Darby.
Communications Director.—Angela Sachitano.
Scheduler.—JoBeth Banas.
Legislative Correspondent.—Taryn Dorfman.
Staff Assistant.—Ari Zimmerman.
6300 Northeast 1st Avenue, Suite 100, Ft. Lauderdale, FL 33334 .... (954) 202–6211
District Director.—Steve Martino. FAX: 202–6212
Deputy District Director.—Kate Wesner.
3111 South Dixie Highway, Suite 308, West Palm Beach, FL 33405 .... (561) 655–1943
FAX: 655–8018

Counties: BROWARD (part), PALM BEACH (part). CITIES: Aventura, Bal Harbour, Bay Harbor Islands, Biscayne Park, Boca Raton, Boynton Beach, Bring Breezes, Cloud Lake, Dania, Deerfield Beach, Delray Beach, Fort Lauderdale, Glen Ridge, Golden Beach, Gulf Stream, Hallandale, Highland Beach, Hillsboro Beach, Hollywood, Hypoluxo, Indian Creek, Juno Beach, Lake Park, Lake Worth, Lantana, Lauderdale by the Sea, Lazy Lake, Lighthouse Point, Manalapan, North Bay Village, North Palm Beach, Oakland Park, Ocean Ridge, Palm Beach, Palm Beach Gardens, Palm Beach Shores, Pembroke Park, Pompano Beach, Rivera Beach, Sea Ranch Lakes, South Palm Beach, Surfside, West Palm Beach, and Wilton Manors. Population (2000), 639,295.

ZIP Codes: 33004, 33009, 33015, 33033, 33060–62, 33064–65, 33067, 33071–74, 33076, 33097, 33128, 33153, 33155–56, 33161, 33163, 33165, 33179, 33186, 33189, 33280, 33301, 33303–09, 33312, 33314–17, 33324, 33328, 33334–35, 33339, 33346, 33348, 33401, 33403–08, 33410–12, 33415, 33418–20, 33424, 33426–27, 33429, 33431–36, 33441–45, 33458, 33460–64, 33468, 33477–78, 33480, 33483, 33486–87

* * *

TWENTY-THIRD DISTRICT

ALCEE L. HASTINGS, Democrat, of Miramar, FL; born in Altamonte Springs, FL, September 5, 1936; education: graduated, Crooms Academy, Sanford, FL, 1954; B.A., Fisk University, Nashville, TN, 1958; Howard University, Washington, DC; J.D., Florida A&M University, Tallahassee, 1963; attorney; admitted to the Florida bar, 1963; circuit judge, U.S. District Court for the Southern District of Florida; member: African Methodist Episcopal Church, NAACP, Miami-Dade Chamber of Commerce, Family Christian Association, ACLU, Southern Poverty Law Center, National Organization for Women, Planned Parenthood, Women and Children First, Inc., Sierra Club, Cousteau Society, Broward County Democratic Executive Committee, Dade County Democratic Executive Committee, Lauderhill Democratic Club, Hollywood Hills Democratic Club, Pembroke Pines Democratic Club, Urban League, National Bar Association, Florida Chapter of the National Bar Association, T.J. Reddick Bar Association, National Conference of Black Lawyers, Simon Wiesenthal Center, The Furtivist Society; Progressive Black Police Officers Club, International Black Firefighters Association; co-chair, Florida Delegation; co-chair, Helsinki Commission; three children: Alcee Lamar II, Chelsea, and Leigh; Senior Democratic Whip; committees: Rules; elected on November 3, 1992, to the 103rd Congress; reelected to each succeeding Congress.

Office Listings

http://www.house.gov/alceehastings

2353 Rayburn House Office Building, Washington, DC 20515 .... (202) 225–1313
Chief of Staff / Press Secretary.—Lale Mamaux. FAX: 225–1171
Legislative Director.—Jason Harris.
Legislative Assistants: Laure Fabrega, Anna Gonzalez, Oneshia Herring, Erin Moffet, Christian Sy, Ian Wolf.
Office Manager / Scheduler.—Barbara Harper.
2701 West Oakland Park Boulevard, Suite 200, Ft. Lauderdale, FL 33311 .... (954) 733–2800
Chief of Staff.—Arthur W. Kennedy.
Mangonia Park Town Hall, 1755 East Tiffany Drive, West Palm Beach, FL 33407 (561) 881–9618

Counties: BROWARD (part), HENDRY (part), MARTIN (part), PALM BEACH (part), ST. LUCIE (part). Population (2000), 639,295.

ZIP Codes: 33025, 33027–28, 33033, 33060, 33064, 33066, 33068–69, 33142, 33155–56, 33158, 33160–61, 33179, 33269, 33301–02, 33304–05, 33309–13, 33315, 33317, 33319–22, 33330–32, 33334, 33340, 33349, 33351, 33359, 33401–09, 33411, 33413–17, 33425, 33430, 33435, 33437–41, 33444–45, 33447, 33459–62, 33465, 33467, 33470, 33476, 33483, 33493, 34945–48, 34950–51, 34954, 34956, 34972, 34974, 34979, 34981, 34986–87

* * *

TWENTY-FOURTH DISTRICT

SANDRA ''SANDY'' ADAMS, Republican of Orlando, FL; born in Wyandotte, MI, December 14, 1956; education: B.A., Columbia College, Orlando, FL, 2000; public service: Orange County Sheriff's Office, 1985–2002; member of Florida House of Representatives, 2002–10; military: United States Air Force; religion: Episcopalian; married: Judge John Adams; children: Sonya, John, Jr. and Kathryn; committees: Judiciary; Science, Space, and Technology; elected to the 112th Congress on November 2, 2010.

Office Listings

http://www.adams.house.gov

216 Cannon House Office Building, Washington, DC 20515 .... (202) 225–2706
Chief of Staff.—Charlie Keller. FAX: 226–6299
Legislative Director.—Theresa Wang.
Scheduler.—Courtney Cannon.
Communications Director.—Lisa Boothe.
2461 West SR 426, Suite 1041, Oviedo, FL 32765 .... (407) 977–7601
1000 City Center Circle, 2nd Floor, Port Orange, FL 32129 .... (386) 756–9798

Counties: BREVARD (part), ORANGE (part), SEMINOLE (part), VOLUSIA (part). Population (2000), 639,295.

ZIP Codes: 32114, 32118–19, 32123–24, 32127–29, 32132, 32141, 32168–70, 32701, 32703–04, 32707–09, 32712, 32714, 32716, 32719, 32732–33, 32738–39, 32751, 32754, 32757, 32759, 32762, 32764–66, 32775, 32779–83, 32789–90, 32792–94, 32796, 32798, 32810, 32816–17, 32820, 32824–29, 32831–33, 32878, 32922, 32926–27, 32953–54, 32959, 33313, 33319, 33337, 33388

* * *

TWENTY-FIFTH DISTRICT

DAVID RIVERA, Republican, of Miami, FL; born in New York, NY, September 16, 1965; education: B.A., political science, Florida International University, Miami, FL, 1986; M.P.A., Florida International University, Miami, FL, 1994; professional: public affairs consultant; legislative assistant to Florida Senator Connie Mack, 1989; special assistant to the director at the Office of Cuba Broadcasting, 1991–99; member of Florida House of Representatives, 2002–10; religion: Catholic; committees: Foreign Affairs; Natural Resources; elected to the 112th Congress on November 2, 2010.

Office Listings

http://www.rivera.house.gov

417 Cannon House Office Building, Washington, DC 20515 .... (202) 225–2778

Chief of Staff.—Stephen Vermillion. FAX: 226–0646
Deputy Chief of Staff.—Javier Correoso.
Legislative Assistant.—Hector Arguello.
DC Scheduler.—Barbara Lopez.
Legislative Correspondent.—Kevin Neumann.
Staff Assistants: Carlos Fleites, Adelana Lopez.

12851 Southwest 42nd Street, Suite 131, Miami, FL 33175 .... (305) 222–0160
District Director.—Alina Garcia.
Deputy District Director.—Ariel Fernandez.
Communications Director.—Leslie Veiga.
Miami Scheduler.—Marilu Armenteros.
Congressional Community Liaison.—Alfred Santamaria.
Congressional Aide.—Ileana Garcia.
Staff Assistant.—Marisela Valladares.

4715 Golden Gate Parkway, Suite 1, Naples, FL 34116 .... (239) 348–1620
District Representative.—Monica Aranegui.
Congressional Aide.—Karen Harmon.

Counties: COLLIER (part), DADE (part). Population (2010), 807,176.

ZIP Codes: 33015–16, 33018, 33030–35, 33157, 33166, 33170, 33175–78, 33182–87, 33189–90, 33193–94, 33196, 34113–14, 34116–17, 34120, 34137–39, 34141–43

GEORGIA

(Population 2010, 9,687,653)

SENATORS

SAXBY CHAMBLISS, Republican, of Moultrie, GA; born in Warrenton, NC, November 10, 1943; education: graduated, C.E. Byrd High School, Shreveport, LA, 1962; B.B.A., University of Georgia, 1966; J.D., University of Tennessee College of Law, 1968; professional: served on the state bar of Georgia's Disciplinary Review Panel, 1969; member: Moultrie-Colquitt County Economic Development Authority; Colquitt County Economic Development Corporation; married: the former Julianne Frohbert, 1966; children: Lia Chambliss Baker, and C. Saxby (Bo), Jr.; committees: vice-chair, Select Committee on Intelligence; Agriculture, Nutrition, and Forestry; Armed Services; Rules and Administration; Joint Committee on Printing; Special Committee on Aging; elected to the 104th Congress; reelected to each succeeding Congress; elected to the U.S. Senate on November 5, 2002; reelected to the U.S. Senate on November 4, 2008.

Office Listings

http://chambliss.senate.gov

416 Russell Senate Office Building, Washington, DC 20510 .... (202) 224–3521
Chief of Staff.—Charlie Harman. FAX: 224–0103
Deputy Chief of Staff.—Teresa Ervin.
Office Manager.—Kate Vickers.
Legislative Director.—Hugh Gamble.
Communications Director.—Bronwyn Lance Chester.
100 Galleria Parkway, Suite 1340, Atlanta, GA 30339 .... (770) 763–9090
State Director.—Camila Knowles.
585 South Main Street, P.O. Box 3217, Moultrie, GA 31776 .... (229) 985–2112
Field Representative.—Debbie Cannon.
P.O. Box 13832, Savannah, GA 31416 .... (800) 234–4208
Field Representative.—Kathryn Murph.
3633 Wheeler Road, Suite 270, Augusta, GA 30909 .... (706) 650–1555
Field Representative.—Jim Hussey.
300 Mulberry Street, Suite 502, Macon, GA 31201 .... (478) 741–1417
FAX: 471–1437

* * *

JOHNNY ISAKSON, Republican, of Marietta GA; born in Fulton County, GA, December 28, 1944; education: University of Georgia; professional: real estate executive; president, Northside Realty; public service: Georgia State House of Representatives, 1977–90; Georgia State Senate, 1993–96; appointed chairman of the Georgia Board of Election, 1996–97; awards: Republican National Committee ''Best Legislator in America,'' 1989; organizations: chairman of the board, Georgian Club; trustee, Kennesaw State University; board of directors, Metro Atlanta and Georgia Chambers of Commerce; past president, Cobb Chamber of Commerce; executive committee, National Association of Realtors; president, Realty Alliance; advisory board, Federal National Mortgage Association; married: Dianne; children: John, Kevin, and Julie; religion: Methodist; elected to the 106th Congress on February 23, 1999, by special election; reelected to each succeeding Congress; committees: vice chair, Select Committee on Ethics; Commerce, Science, and Transportation; Foreign Relations; Health, Education, Labor, and Pensions; Veterans' Affairs; elected to the U.S. Senate on November 2, 2004; reelected to the U.S. Senate on November 2, 2010.

Office Listings

http://isakson.senate.gov

131 Russell Senate Office Building, Washington, DC 20510 .... (202) 224–3643
Chief of Staff.—Chris Carr. FAX: 228–0724
Deputy Chief of Staff/Communications Director.—Joan Kirchner.
Scheduler.—Stefanie Higgins.
One Overton Park, 3625 Cumberland Boulevard, Suite 970, Atlanta, GA 30339 ..... (770) 661–0999

REPRESENTATIVES

FIRST DISTRICT

JACK KINGSTON, Republican, of Savannah, GA; born in Bryan, TX, April, 24, 1955; education: Michigan State University, 1973–74; University of Georgia, 1974–78; insurance salesman; vice president, Palmer and Cay/Carswell; Georgia State Legislature, 1984–92; member: Savannah Health Mission, Isle of Hope Community Association, Christ Church; married: Elizabeth Morris Kingston, 1979; children: Betsy, John, Ann, and Jim; committees: Appropriations; elected on November 3, 1992 to the 103rd Congress; reelected to each succeeding Congress.

Office Listings

http://www.house.gov/kingston

2372 Rayburn House Office Building, Washington, DC 20515 .... (202) 225–5831
Chief of Staff.—Adam Sullivan. FAX: 226–2269
Deputy Chief of Staff / Communications Director.—Chris Crawford.
Legislative Director.—Allison Thigpen.
Legislative Assistant.—Mike Donnal.
Military Legislative Assistant.—Tom Lamb.
Constituent Services Director.—Monya Baldwin.
Legislative Correspondent.—Whitney Jacobs.
Outreach Coordinator.—Alexandra Kendrick.
1 Diamond Causeway, Suite 7, Savannah, GA 31406 .... (912) 352–0101
Casework Manager.—Trish DePriest.
Caseworker.—Bruce Bazemore.
Scheduler / Executive Assistant.—Brianna Foran.
P.O. Box 40, Baxley, GA 31515 .... (912) 367–7403
District Director.—Shiela Elliott.
Field Representative.—Brooke Floyd.
Brunswick Federal Building, 805 Gloucester Street, Room 304, Brunswick, GA 31520 .... (912) 265–9010
Field Representative.—Charles Wilson.
District Press Secretary.—Tim Wessinger.
3670 North Valdosta Road, Suite C, Valdosta, GA 31602 .... (229) 247–9188
Field Representative.—Shae Walden.
District Representative / Agriculture Liaison.—Merritt Myers.

Counties: APPLING, ATKINSON, BACON, BERRIEN, BRANTLEY, BRYAN, CAMDEN, CHARLTON, CHATHAM (part), CLINCH, COFFEE, COOK, ECHOLS, GLYNN, JEFF DAVIS, LANIER, LIBERTY, LONG, LOWNDES (part), MCINTOSH, PIERCE, TELFAIR, WARE, WAYNE, WHEELER. POPULATION (2005), 629,727.

ZIP Codes: 30411, 30427–28, 31037, 31055, 31060, 31077, 31083, 31300–01, 31305, 31308–09, 31313–16, 31319–21, 31323–24, 31327–28, 31331–33, 31404, 31406, 31410–11, 31419, 31500–31602, 31605–24, 31627, 31630–32, 31634–36, 31637, 31639–42, 31645–99, 31749, 31794, 31798

* * *

SECOND DISTRICT

SANFORD D. BISHOP, JR., Democrat, of Albany, GA; born in Mobile, AL, February 4, 1947; education: attended Mobile County public schools; B.A., Morehouse College, 1968; J.D., Emory University, 1971; professional: attorney; admitted to the Georgia and Alabama Bars; Georgia House of Representatives, 1977–91; Georgia Senate, 1991–93; former member: Executive Board, Boy Scouts of America; YMCA; Sigma Pi Phi Fraternity; Kappa Alpha Psi Fraternity; 32nd Degree Mason, Shriner; member: Mt. Zion Baptist Church, Albany, GA; married: Vivian Creighton Bishop; child: Aeysha Reese; committees: Appropriations; elected to the 103rd Congress; reelected to each succeeding Congress.

Office Listings

http://www.bishop.house.gov

2429 Rayburn House Office Building, Washington, DC 20515 .... (202) 225–3631
Chief of Staff.—Tracey Thornton. FAX: 225–2203
Deputy Chief of Staff.—Michael Reed.
Office Manager / Scheduler.—Julian Johnson.
Legislative Director.—Jonathan Halpern.
Senior Legislative Assistant.—Jonathan Black.
Communications Director.—Adam Hodge.
Albany Towers, 235 West Roosevelt Avenue, Suite 114, Albany, GA 31701 .... (229) 439–8067

Deputy District Director / Ag Advisor.—James Crozier.
Constituent Services Director.—Sharon Richter.
Office Manager / Constituent Services.—Toni Pickel.
Staff Assistant / District Scheduler.—Kelli Hand.
18 Ninth Street, Suite 201, Columbus, GA 31901 .... (706) 320–9477
Office Manager / Constituent Services.—Harry Crawford.
Constituent Services.—Patricia Ashley.
Staff Assistant.—Peggy Sagul.
210 South Broad Street, Thomasville, GA 31792 .... (229) 226–7789
Staff Assistant / Constituent Services.—Rusty Wetherington.

Counties: BAKER, BROOKS, CALHOUN, CHATTAHOOCHEE, CLAY, CRAWFORD, CRISP, DECATUR, DOOLY, DOUGHERTY, EARLY, GRADY, LEE, LOWNDES, MACON, MARION, MILLER, MITCHELL, MUSCOGEE, PEACH, QUITMAN, RANDOLPH, SCHLEY, SEMINOLE, STEWART, SUMTER, TALBOT, TAYLOR, TERRELL, THOMAS, WEBSTER, WORTH. Population (2000), 629,735.

ZIP Codes: 30150, 30290, 31010, 31015, 31039, 31068–69, 31072, 31092, 31201, 31204, 31211, 31217, 31328, 31601–03, 31605–06, 31625–26, 31629, 31636–38, 31641, 31643, 31698, 31701–12, 31714, 31716, 31719–22, 31727, 31730, 31733, 31735, 31738–39, 31743–44, 31747, 31749, 31753, 31756–58, 31763–65, 31768, 31771–72, 31775–76, 31778–84, 31787–96, 31799, 31803, 31805, 31814–15, 31821, 31824–25, 31832, 31901–07, 31914, 31995, 31997–99, 39813, 39815, 39817–19, 39823–29, 39832, 39834, 39836–37, 39840–42, 39845–46, 39851–52, 39854, 39859, 39861–62, 39866–67, 39870, 39877, 39885–86, 39897

* * *

THIRD DISTRICT

LYNN A. WESTMORELAND, Republican, of Grantville, GA; born in Atlanta, GA, April 2, 1950; education: graduated from Therrell High School, Atlanta, GA; attended Georgia State University, Atlanta, GA, 1969–71; professional: real estate developer; public service: Minority Leader, Georgia State House, 2000–04; Representative, Georgia State House, 1992–2004; religion: Baptist; organizations: National Rifle Association; married: Joan; children: Heather, Marcy, and Trae; committees: Financial Services; Permanent Select Committee on Intelligence; elected to the 109th Congress on November 2, 2004; reelected to each succeeding Congress.

Office Listings

http://www.westmoreland.house.gov

2433 Rayburn House Office Building, Washington, DC 20515 .... (202) 225–5901
Chief of Staff.—Chip Lake. FAX: 225–2515
Communications Director.—Leslie Shedd.
Legislative Director.—Kevin Doran.
Office Manager.—Claire Ouiment.
1601–B East Highway 34, Suite 3, Newnan, GA 30265 .... (770) 683–2033

Counties: BIBB COUNTY (part). CITIES AND TOWNSHIPS: Macon, Payne. BUTTS COUNTY (part). CITIES AND TOWNSHIPS: Flovilla, Jackson, Jenkinsburg. CARROLL COUNTY (part). CITIES AND TOWNSHIPS: Bowdon, Carrollton, Mount Zion, Roopville, Temple, Villa Rica, Whitesburg. COWETA COUNTY (part). CITIES AND TOWNSHIPS: Grantville, Haralson, Lone Oak (also Meriwether), Luthersville, Moreland, Newnan, Palmetto, Senoia, Sharpsburg, Turin. DOUGLAS COUNTY (part). CITIES AND TOWNSHIPS: Austell, Douglasville, Lithia Springs, Winston. FAYETTE COUNTY. CITIES AND TOWNSHIPS: Brooks, Fayetteville, Peachtree City, Tyrone, Woolsey. HARRIS COUNTY (part). CITIES AND TOWNSHIPS: Cataula, Ellerslie, Fortson, Hamilton, Midland, Pine Mountain, Pine Mountain Valley, Shiloh, Waverly Hall, West Point. HENRY COUNTY (part). CITIES AND TOWNSHIPS: Hampton, Locust Grove, McDonough, Stockbridge. JASPER COUNTY (part). CITIES AND TOWNSHIPS: Monticello, Shady Dale. JONES COUNTY (part). CITIES AND TOWNSHIPS: Gray, Haddcock. LAMAR COUNTY. CITIES AND TOWNSHIPS: Aldora, Barnesville, Milner. MUSCOGEE COUNTY (part). CITIES AND TOWNSHIPS: Bibb City, Columbus. NEWTON COUNTY (part). CITIES AND TOWNSHIPS: Covington, Mansfield, Newborn, Oxford, Porterdale. PIKE COUNTY. CITIES AND TOWNSHIPS: Concord, Meansville, Molena, Williamson, Zebulon. ROCKDALE COUNTY (part). CITIES AND TOWNSHIPS: Conyers. SPALDING COUNTY (part). CITIES AND TOWNSHIPS: Griffin, Orchard Hill, Sunny Side. TROUP COUNTY (part). CITIES AND TOWNSHIPS: Hogansville, LaGrange. UPSON COUNTY (part). CITIES AND TOWNSHIPS: Thomaston, and Yatesville. Population (2000), 629,700.

ZIP Codes: 30013–14, 30016, 30055–56, 30094, 30108, 30110, 30116–17, 30122, 30133–35, 30154, 30170, 30179–80, 30185, 30187, 30204–06, 30213–17, 30220, 30223–24, 30228–30, 30233–34, 30236, 30238, 30240–41, 30248, 30252–53, 30256–59, 30263–66, 30268–69, 30271, 30273, 30275–77, 30281, 30284–86, 30289–90, 30292, 30295, 30904, 31002, 31004, 31016, 31024, 31029, 31032, 31038, 31046, 31064, 31066, 31085, 31097, 31204, 31210–11, 31220–21, 31602, 31632, 31801, 31804, 31807–08, 31811, 31820, 31822–23, 31826, 31829–31, 31833, 31904, 31907–09, 31993

* * *

FOURTH DISTRICT

HENRY C. ''HANK'' JOHNSON, JR., Democrat, of Lithonia, GA; born in Washington, DC, October 2, 1954; B.A., Clark College (Clark Atlanta University), Atlanta, GA, 1976; J.D.,

Thurgood Marshall School of Law, Texas Southern University, Houston, TX, 1979; professional: partner, Johnson & Johnson Law Group LLC, 1980–2007; judge, Magistrate Court, 1989–2001; associate, Dekalb County Commissioner, 2001–06; married: Mereda, 1979; two children: Randi and Alex; committees: Armed Services; Judiciary; elected to the 110th Congress on November 7, 2006; reelected to each succeeding Congress.

Office Listings

http://www.hankjohnson.house.gov

1427 Longworth House Office Building, Washington, DC 20515 .... (202) 225–1605
Chief of Staff.—Arthur D. Sidney. FAX: 226–0691
Legislative Director.—Scott Goldstein.
Office Manager / Scheduler.—Ebony Y. Simpson.
5700 Hillandale Drive, Suite 12D, Lithonia, GA 30058 .... (770) 987–2291
District Director.—Kathy Register.

Counties: DEKALB (part), GWINNETT (part). CITIES: Avondale Estates, Chamblee, Conyers, Clarkston, Decatur, Doraville, Lilburn, Lithonia, Pine Lake, Norcross and Stone Mountain. Population (2000), 629,726.

ZIP Codes: 30002–03, 30012–13, 30021, 30030–38, 30039, 30047, 30052, 30058, 30071, 30079, 30083–88, 30093–94, 30096, 30316–17, 30319, 30329, 30340–41, 30345

* * *

FIFTH DISTRICT

JOHN LEWIS, Democrat, of Atlanta, GA; born in Pike County, AL, February 21, 1940; education: graduated Pike County Training School, Brundidge, AL, 1957; B.A., American Baptist Theological Seminary, Nashville, TN, 1961; B.A., Fisk University, Nashville, TN, 1963; civil rights leader; Atlanta City Council, 1982–86; member: Martin Luther King Center for Social Change, African American Institute, Robert F. Kennedy Memorial; married the former Lillian Miles in 1968; one child, John Miles Lewis; appointed Senior Chief Deputy Democratic Whip for the 109th Congress; committees: Ways and Means; elected to the 100th Congress on November 4, 1986; reelected to each succeeding Congress.

Office Listings

http://www.house.gov/johnlewis

343 Cannon House Office Building, Washington, DC 20515 .... (202) 225–3801
Chief of Staff.—Michael Collins. FAX: 225–0351
Officer Manager / Scheduler.—Jacob Gillison.
Director of Communications.—Brenda Jones.
Legislative Director.—Michaeleen Crowell.
100 Peachtree Street, NW., Suite 1920, Atlanta, GA 30303 .... (404) 659–0116
District Director.—Aaron Ward.

Counties: CLAYTON (part), COBB (part), DEKALB (part), FULTON (part). Population (2000), 629,727.

ZIP Codes: 30030, 30032–34, 30297, 30303–19, 30322, 30324, 30326–29, 30331, 30336–39, 30342, 30344–45, 30349, 30354

* * *

SIXTH DISTRICT

TOM PRICE, Republican, of Roswell, GA; born in Lansing, MI, October 8, 1954; education: B.A., University of Michigan, 1976; M.D., University of Michigan, 1979; professional: physician; member of the Georgia state senate, 1997–2004; member: Cobb Chamber of Commerce; Civil Air Patrol; Advisory Board, Georgia Partnership for Excellence in Education; chair, Republican Policy Committee; religion: Presbyterian; married: Elizabeth; one child, Robert; committees: Budget; Ways and Means; elected to the 109th Congress on November 2, 2004; reelected to each succeeding Congress.

Office Listings

http://www.house.gov/tomprice

403 Cannon House Office Building, Washington, DC 20515 .... (202) 225–4501

Chief of Staff.—Matt McGinley. FAX: 225–4656
District Director.—Jeff Hamling.
3710 Roswell Road, Suite 50, Marietta, GA 30062 .... (770) 565–4990
100 North Street, Suite 150, Canton, GA 30114 .... (678) 493–6176

Counties: CHEROKEE (part), COBB (part), FULTON (part). CITIES AND TOWNSHIPS: Dunwoody, Marietta, Roswell, Sandy Springs, and Smyrna. Population (2000), 629,725.

ZIP Codes: 30004–07, 30009–10, 30022–24, 30041, 30060, 30062, 30064–68, 30075–77, 30092, 30096–97, 30101–02, 30106, 30115, 30127, 30141, 30144, 30152, 30156, 30160, 30168, 30188–89, 30327–28, 30339, 30342, 30350, 31032, 31146, 31150, 31156, 31602, 31632

* * *

SEVENTH DISTRICT

W. ROBERT WOODALL, Republican, of Lawrenceville, GA; born in Athens, GA, February 11, 1970; education: undergraduate, B.A., Furman University, Greenville, SC, 1992; graduate, J.D., University of Georgia, Athens, GA, 1997; awards: co-author of the New York Times bestsellling book *Fair Tax: The Truth*; religion: Methodist; committees: Budget; Rules; elected to the 112th Congress on November 2, 2010.

Office Listings

http://woodall.house.gov

1725 Longworth House Office Building, Washington, DC 20515 .... (202) 225–4272
Legislative Director.—Janet Rossi. FAX: 225–4696
75 Langley Drive, Lawrenceville, GA 30046 .... (770) 232–3005
FAX: 232–2909

Counties: BARROW, FORSYTH (part), GWINNETT (part), NEWTON, WALTON. Population (2000), 629,725.

ZIP Codes: 30004–05, 30012, 30017, 30019, 30024, 30039–47, 30049, 30052, 30071, 30078, 30087, 30092, 30095–97, 30101–03, 30107, 30114–15, 30120–21, 30123, 30127, 30132, 30134, 30137, 30141–43, 30145–46, 30153, 30157, 30168–69, 30178–80, 30183–84, 30188–89, 30515, 30518–19, 31139

* * *

EIGHTH DISTRICT

AUSTIN SCOTT, Republican, of Ashburn, GA; born in Augusta, GA, December 10, 1969; B.B.A., University of Georgia, 1993; professional: business owner; member of the Georgia State House of Representatives, 1997–2010; religion: Baptist; married: wife, Vivien; one son, Wells; member, National Association of Insurance and Financial Advisors; Coastal Plains Chapter of the American Red Cross; awards: American Cancer Society's Outstanding Legislative Leadership Award, 2003 and 2004; Georgia Association of Emergency Medical Services Star of Life Legislative Award, 2007 and 2008; Republican Freshman Class President; committees: Agriculture; Armed Services; elected to the 112th Congress on November 2, 2010.

Office Listings

http://austinscott.house.gov

516 Cannon House Office Building, Washington, DC 20515 .... (202) 225–6531
Chief of Staff.—Joby Young. FAX: 225–3013
Legislative Director.—Jim Dolbow.
Communications Director.—Cassie Smedile.
Scheduler.—Bart Reising.
127–B North Central Avenue, Tifton, GA 31794 .... (229) 396–5175
FAX: 396–5179
230 Margie Drive, Suite 500, Warner Robins, GA 31088 .... (478) 971–1776
FAX: 971–1778
Laurens County Courthouse, 101 North Jefferson Street, 2nd Floor, Dublin, GA 31021 .... (478) 971–1776

Counties: BALDWIN (part), BEN HILL, BIBB, BLECKLEY, BUTTS, COLQUITT, DODGE, HOUSTON, JASPER, JONES, IRWIN, LAURENS, MONROE, NEWTON (part), PULASKI, TIFT, TURNER, TWIGGS, WILCOX, WILKINSON, WORTH (part). Population (2000), 629,748.

ZIP Codes: 30013–16, 30025, 30052, 30054–56, 30070, 30094, 30204, 30216, 30223–24, 30233–34, 30248, 30252, 30411, 30428, 30454, 30457, 31001–05, 31008–09, 31011–15, 31017, 31019–25, 31027–34, 31036–38, 31040, 31042, 31044,

31046–47, 31052, 31054, 31059–62, 31064–66, 31069, 31071–72, 31075, 31077, 31079, 31084–88, 31090–93, 31095–99, 31201–13, 31216–17, 31220–21, 31295–97, 31622, 31637, 31705, 31712, 31714, 31722, 31727, 31733–34, 31738, 31744, 31747, 31753, 31756, 31765, 31768–69, 31771–73, 31775–76, 31778, 31781, 31783–84, 31788–91, 31793–96, 31798

* * *

NINTH DISTRICT

TOM GRAVES, Republican, of Ranger, GA; born in St. Petersburg, FL, February 3, 1970; education: B.A.A., finance, University of Georgia, Athens, GA, 1993; professional: business owner; Georgia State House of Representatives, 2003–10; religion: Baptist: married: Julie Howard Graves; children: JoAnn, John and Janey; committees: Appropriations; elected by special election to the 111th Congress on June 8, 2010, to fill the vacancy caused by the resignation of United States Representative John Nathan Deal; elected to the 112th Congress on November 2, 2010.

Office Listings

http://www.tomgraves.house.gov

1113 Longworth House Office Building, Washington, DC 20515 .... (202) 225–5211
Chief of Staff.—Tim Baker. FAX: 225–8272
Communications Director.—John Donnelly.
Legislative Director.—Josh Finestone.
Scheduler.—Kate Parker.
702 South Thornton Avenue, Dalton, GA 30720 .... (706) 226–5320
311 Green Street, NW., Suite 302, Gainesville, GA 30501 .... (770) 535–2592

Counties: CATOOSA, DADE, DAWSON, FANNIN, FORSYTH (part), GILMER, GORDON, HALL, LUMPKIN, MURRAY, PICKENS, UNION, WALKER, WHITE, AND WHITFIELD. CITIES AND TOWNSHIPS: Blairsville, Blue Ridge, Calhoun, Chatsworth, Chickamauga, Cisco, Clermont, Cleveland, Cohutta, Conyers, Cumming, Dacula, Dahlonega, Dalton, Dawsonville, East Ellijay, Ellijay, Eton, Fairmount, Flowery Branch, Fort Oglethorpe, Gainesville, Gillsville, Grayson, Helen, Jasper, LaFayette, Lawrenceville, Loganville, Lookout Mountain, Lula, McCaysville, Morgantown, Oakwood, Plainville, Ranger, Rest Haven, Resaca, Ringgold, Rossville, Sautee Nacoochee, Talking Rock, Trenton, Tunnel Hill, and Varnell. Population (2000), 629,702.

ZIP Codes: 30004–05, 30024, 30028, 30040–41, 30097, 30103, 30107, 30139, 30143, 30148, 30171, 30175, 30177, 30501–07, 30510, 30512–14, 30517–19, 30522, 30527–28, 30533–34, 30536, 30539, 30541–43, 30545, 30548, 30554–55, 30559–60, 30564, 30566–67, 30571–72, 30575, 30582, 30597, 30635, 30641, 30701, 30703, 30707–08, 30710–11, 30719–22, 30724–28, 30731–42, 30747, 30750–51, 30753, 30755–57

* * *

TENTH DISTRICT

PAUL C. BROUN, Republican, of Athens, GA; born in Clarke County, GA, May 14, 1946; education: B.S. in chemistry, University of Georgia, Athens, GA, 1967; M.D., Medical College of Georgia, Augusta, GA, 1971; professional: physician; served, U.S. Marine Corps Reserves, 1964–67; member: Rotary Club; Athens-Clarke County Chamber of Commerce; Prince Avenue Baptist Church; religion: Southern Baptist; married: Nancy ''Niki'' Bronson Broun; children: Carly, Collins, Lucy; grandchildren: Lucile, Tillman; committees: Homeland Security; Natural Resources; Science, Space, and Technology; elected by special election to the 110th Congress on July 17, 2007; reelected to the 112th Congress on November 2, 2010.

Office Listings

http://www.house.gov/broun

325 Cannon House Office Building, Washington, DC 20515 .... (202) 225–4101
Chief of Staff.—David Bowser. FAX: 226–0776
Office Manager / Scheduler.—Teddie Norton.

Counties: BANKS, COLUMBIA, CLARKE, ELBERT, FRANKLIN, GREENE, HABERSHAM, HART, JACKSON, LINCOLN, MCDUFFIE, MADISON, MORGAN, OCONEE, OGLETHORPE, PUTNAM, RABUN, RICHMOND (part), STEPHENS, TOWNS, WILKES. Population (2000), 629,762.

ZIP Codes: 30025, 30055–56, 30510–11, 30516–17, 30520–21, 30523, 30525, 30529–31, 30535, 30537–38, 30543–44, 30546–49, 30552–54, 30557–58, 30562–63, 30565, 30567–68, 30571, 30573, 30575–77, 30580–82, 30596, 30598–99, 30601–09, 30612, 30619, 30621–31, 30633–35, 30638–39, 30641–43, 30645–50, 30660, 30662–69, 30671, 30673, 30677–78, 30683, 30802, 30805–06, 30808–09, 30813–14, 30817, 30824, 30901, 30903–07, 30909, 30911–14, 30916–17, 30919, 31024, 31026, 31061

* * *

ELEVENTH DISTRICT

PHIL GINGREY, Republican, of Marietta, GA; born in Augusta, GA, July 10, 1942; education: B.S., Georgia Tech, 1965; M.D., Medical College of Georgia, 1969; professional: Physician; set up a pro-life OB-GYN practice; organizations: Cobb County Medical Society; Medical Association of Georgia; American Medical Association; Georgia OB-GYN Society; public service: Marietta School Board, 1993–97; Georgia State Senate, 1999–2002; House Policy Committee; married: Billie Ayers; children: Billy, Gannon, Phyllis, and Laura; committees: Energy and Commerce; House Administration; elected to the 108th Congress on November 5, 2002; reelected to each succeeding Congress.

Office Listings

http://www.house.gov/gingrey

442 Cannon House Office Building, Washington, DC 20515 .... (202) 225–2931
Chief of Staff.—David Sours. FAX: 225–2944
Legislative Director.—Michael Calvo.
Executive Assistant / Director of Operations.—Elizabeth Ezzell.
219 Roswell Street, Marietta, GA 30060 .... (770) 429–1776
600 East 1st Street, Suite 301, Rome, GA 30161 .... (706) 290–1776

Counties: BARTOW, CARROLL (part), CHATTOOGA, COBB (part), FLOYD, HARALSON, GORDON (part), PAULDING, POLK. Population (2010) 794,969.

ZIP Codes: 30008, 30060–64, 30066–67, 30069, 30080–81, 30090, 30101–05, 30108–13, 30116–27, 30129, 30132, 30134, 30137–41, 30144–45, 30147, 30149–50, 30152–53, 30161–65, 30176, 30178–80, 30182

* * *

TWELFTH DISTRICT

JOHN BARROW, Democrat, of Savannah, GA; born in Athens, October 31, 1955; education: graduated from Clarke Central High School, Athens-Clarke County, GA, 1973; B.A., University of Georgia, Athens, GA, 1976; J.D., Harvard University, Cambridge, MA, 1979; professional: law clerk for Judge, Savannah, GA; law clerk for Judge, Fiftieth Circuit Court of Appeals; founding member, Wilburn, Lewis, Barrow and Stotz, PC.; county commissioner; lawyer, private practice; Athens-Clarke, GA, city-county commissioner, 1990–2004; religion: Baptist; children: James and Ruth; committees: Energy and Commerce; Veterans' Affairs; elected to the 109th Congress on November 2, 2004; reelected to each succeeding Congress.

Office Listings

http://www.barrow.house.gov

2202 Rayburn House Office Building, Washington, DC 20515 .... (202) 225–2823
Chief of Staff.—Ashley Jones. FAX: 225–3377
Legislative Director.—Hill Thomas.
Communications Director.—Christopher Cashman.
925 Laney Walker Boulevard, Suite 300, Augusta, GA 30901 .... (706) 722–4494
450 Mall Boulevard, Suite A, Savannah, GA 31406 .... (912) 354–7282
127 East Hancock Street, Milledgeville, GA 31061 .... (478) 452–4611
City Hall, 141 West Haynes Street, P.O. Box 1017, Sandersville, GA 31082 .... (478) 553–1923
Vidalia Community Center, 107 Old Airport Road, Suite A, Vidalia, GA .... (912) 537–9301

Counties: BALDWIN (part), BULLOCH, BURKE, CANDLER, CHATHAM (part), EFFINGHAM, EMANUEL, EVANS, GLASCOCK, HANCOCK, JEFFERSON, JENKINS, JOHNSON, MONTGOMERY, RICHMOND (part), SCREVEN, TALIAFERRO, TATTNALL, TOOMBS, TREUTLEN, WARREN, WASHINGTON. CITIES AND TOWNSHIPS: Augusta, Milledgeville, Savannah, Statesboro, Vidalia. Population (2000) 629,727.

ZIP Codes: 30400–01, 30410, 30412–15, 30417, 30420–21, 30423, 30425–27, 30429, 30436, 30438–39, 30441–42, 30445–48, 30456, 30452–53, 30455–58, 30461, 30464, 30467, 30470–71, 30473–74, 30477, 30631, 30664, 30669, 30678, 30803, 30805, 30807, 30810, 30815–16, 30818, 30820–24, 30828, 30830, 30833, 30901, 30904, 30906, 30909, 30934, 31002, 31018, 31033–35, 31045, 31049, 31061, 31067, 31082, 31087, 31089, 31094, 31096, 31302–03, 31307–08, 31312, 31318, 31321–22, 31326, 31329, 31401, 31404–08, 31410, 31415, 31419

* * *

THIRTEENTH DISTRICT

DAVID SCOTT, Democrat, of Atlanta, GA; born in Aynor, SC, June 27, 1945; education: Florida A&M University, graduated with honors, 1967; M.B.A., graduated with honors, University of Pennsylvania Wharton School of Finance, 1969; professional: businessman; owner and CEO, Dayn-Mark Advertising; public service: Georgia House of Representatives, 1974–82; Georgia State Senate, 1983–2002; married: Alfredia Aaron, 1969; children: Dayna and Marcye; committees: Agriculture; Financial Services; elected to the 108th Congress on November 5, 2002; reelected to each succeeding Congress.

Office Listings

http://davidscott.house.gov

225 Cannon House Office Building, Washington, DC 20515 .... (202) 225–2939
Chief of Staff.—Michael Andel. FAX: 225–4628
Deputy Chief of Staff for Administration.—Angie Borja.
Legislative Director.—Gary Woodward.
173 North Main Street, Jonesboro, GA 30236 .... (770) 210–5073
888 Concord Road, Suite 100, Smyra, GA 30080 .... (770) 432–5405

Counties: CLAYTON, COBB, DEKALB, DOUGLAS, FULTON, HENRY. POPULATION (2000) 629,732.

ZIP Codes: 30008, 30034, 30060, 30064, 30067, 30080, 30081–82, 30106, 30111, 30122, 30126–27, 30133–35, 30141, 30154, 30168, 30187, 30213, 30215, 30228, 30236–38, 30250, 30253, 30260, 30268, 30272–74, 30281, 30287–88, 30291, 30294, 30296–97, 30331, 30337, 30339, 30344, 30349, 31192

HAWAII

(Population 2010, 1,360,301)

SENATORS

DANIEL K. INOUYE, Democrat, of Honolulu, HI; born in Honolulu, September 7, 1924; education: A.B., government and economics, University of Hawaii, 1950; J.D., George Washington University Law School, 1952; majority leader, Territorial House of Representatives, 1954–58; Territorial Senate, 1958–59; enlisted as private, 442nd Infantry Regimental Combat Team, 1943; second lieutenant, battlefield commission, 1944; served in France and Italy; retired captain, U.S. Army; Senate Democratic Steering and Coordination; religion: Methodist; married: Irene Hirano, first wife the former Margaret Shinobu Awamura of Honolulu died in 2006; one son: Daniel Ken Inouye, Jr.; committees: chair, Appropriations; Commerce, Science, and Transportation; Indian Affairs; Rules and Administration; elected on July 28, 1959, to the 86th Congress; reelected to the 87th Congress; elected to the U.S. Senate on November 6, 1962; reelected to each succeeding Senate term.

Office Listings

http://inouye.senate.gov

722 Hart Senate Office Building, Washington, DC 20510 .... (202) 224–3934
Chief of Staff.—Patrick H. DeLeon. FAX: 224–6747
Office Manager.—Beverly MacDonald. TDD: 224–1233
Personal Secretary.—Jessica Lee.
Administrative Manager.—Marie Blanco.
300 Ala Moana Boulevard, Suite 7–212, Honolulu, HI 96850 .... (808) 541–2542
Hilo Auxiliary Office, 101 Aupuni Street, No. 205, Hilo, HI 96720 .... (808) 935–0844

* * *

DANIEL K. AKAKA, Democrat, of Honolulu, HI; born in Honolulu, September 11, 1924; education: graduated, Kamehameha High School, 1942; University of Hawaii, 1948–66, bachelor of education, professional certificate, master of education; served in the U.S. Army, 1945–47; teacher, 1953–60; vice principal, 1960; principal, 1963–71; program specialist, 1968–71; director, 1971–74; director and special assistant in human resources, 1975–76; board of directors, Hanahauoli School; Act 4 Educational Advisory Commission; Library Advisory Council; Na Hookama O Pauahi Scholarship Committee, Kamehameha Schools; commissioner, Manpower and Full Employment Commission; member and Minister of Music, Kawaiahao Church; married: Mary Mildred Chong; children: Millannie, Daniel, Jr., Gerard, Alan, and Nicholas; committees: chair, Indian Affairs; Armed Services; Banking, Housing and Urban Affairs; Homeland Security and Government Affairs; Veterans' Affairs; elected to the 95th Congress in November, 1976; reelected to each succeeding Congress; appointed to the U.S. Senate in April, 1990, to fill the vacancy caused by the death of Senator Spark Matsunaga; elected to complete the unexpired term in November, 1990; reelected to each succeeding Senate term.

Office Listings

http://akaka.senate.gov

141 Hart Senate Office Building, Washington, DC 20510 .... (202) 224–6361
Legislative Director/Counsel.—Jennifer L. Tyree. FAX: 224–6747
Fiscal Office Secretary.—Patricia L. Hill.
Prince Kuhio Federal Building, 300 Ala Moana Boulevard, Room 3–106, P.O. Box 50144, Honolulu, HI 96850 .... (808) 522–8970
Chief of Staff.—Joan Ohashi Akai.
101 Aupuni Street, Suite 213, Hilo, HI 96720 .... (808) 935–1114

REPRESENTATIVES

FIRST DISTRICT

COLLEEN HANABUSA, Democrat, of Waianae, HI; born in Honolulu, HI, May 4, 1951; education: graduated from St. Andrews Priory School, Honolulu, HI, 1969; B.A., University of Hawaii, Honolulu, HI, 1973; M.A., University of Hawaii, Honolulu, HI, 1975; J.D., University of Hawaii, Honolulu, HI, 1977; professional: attorney, 1977–2010; Hawaii State Senate,

1998–2010; Hawaii State Senate President, 2006–10; religion: Buddhism; married: John Souza; caucuses: Congressional Asian Pacific American Caucus (CAPAC); Seniors Caucus; Native American Caucus; National Guard Caucus, Navy / Marine Corp Caucus; Coast Guard Caucus; Air Force Caucus; Congressional Army Caucus, USO Caucus; Sustainable Energy and Environment Coalition; committees: Armed Services; Natural Resources; elected to the 112th Congress on November 2, 2010.

Office Listings

http://www.hanabusa.house.gov

238 Cannon House Office Building, Washington, DC 20515 .... (202) 225–2726
Chief of Staff.—Julie Tippens FAX: 225–0688
Legislative Director.—Christopher Raymond.
Communications Director.—Ashley Nagaoka.
300 Ala Moana Boulevard, Room 4–104, Honolulu, HI 96850 .... (808) 541–2570
District Director.—Rod Tanonaka.

Counties: HONOLULU COUNTY (part). CITIES AND TOWNSHIPS: Aiea Pearl City, Ewa Beach, Honolulu, Mililani, and Waipahu. Population (2000), 606,718.

ZIP Codes: 96701, 96706, 96782, 96789, 96797, 96801–28, 96830, 96835–44, 96846–50, 96853, 96858–61

* * *

SECOND DISTRICT

MAZIE K. HIRONO, Democrat, of Hawaii; born in Fukushima, Japan, November 3, 1947; naturalized U.S. citizen in 1959; education: Kaimuki High School, 1966; Phi Beta Kappa, University of Hawaii at Manoa, 1970; Georgetown University Law Center, 1978; Deputy Attorney General, Anti-Trust Division, State of Hawaii, 1978–80; Shim, Tam, Kirimitsu, Kitamura and Chang (law firm), 1984–88; State Representative, Hawaii State Legislature, 1980–94; Lt. Governor, State of Hawaii, 1994–2002; candidate for Governor, State of Hawaii, 2002; married to Leighton Kim Oshima; committees: Education and the Workforce; Transportation and Infrastructure; elected to the 110th Congress on November 7, 2006; reelected to each succeeding Congress.

Office Listings

http://hirono.house.gov

1410 Longworth House Office Building, Washington, DC 20515 .... (202) 225–4906
Chief of Staff (DC).—Anne Stewart. FAX: 225–4987
Prince Kuhio Federal Building, Room 5104, Honolulu, HI 96850 .... (808) 541–1986
District Director.—Susan Kodani.

Counties: HAWAI'I COUNTY. CITIES: Hawi, Hilo, Honoka'a, Kailua-Kona, Na'alehu, Kealakekua, Pahoa, Ocean View, Volcano, Waimea, Waikoloa. MAUI COUNTY. CITIES: Hana, Kahului, Kaunakakai, Lahaina, Lana'i City, Makawao, Wailuku. KALAWAO COUNTY. CITY: Kalaupapa. HONOLULU COUNTY (part). CITIES: Hale'iwa, Honolulu, Kailua, Kane'ohe, Kapolei, La'ie, Makakilo, Nanakuli, Wahiawa, Waialua, Wai'anae, Waimanalo. KAUA'I COUNTY. CITIES: Hanalei, Hanapepe, Kalaheo, Kapa'a, Kekaha, Kilauea, Koloa, Lihue, Waimea. NORTHWESTERN HAWAIIAN ISLANDS. ISLANDS OF: Becker, French Frigate Shoals, Gardener Pinnacles, Hermes and Kure Atolls, Laysan, Lisianski, Maro Reef, Nihoa, and Pearl. Population (2000), 604,819.

ZIP Codes: 96703–05, 96707–10, 96712–22, 96725–34, 96737–57, 96759–74, 96776–81, 96783–86, 96788–93, 96795–97, 96854, 96857, 96862–63

IDAHO

(Population 2010, 1,567,582)

SENATORS

MIKE CRAPO, Republican, of Idaho Falls, ID; born in Idaho Falls, May 20, 1951; education: graduated, Idaho Falls High School, 1969; B.A., Brigham Young University, Provo, UT, 1973; J.D., Harvard University Law School, Cambridge, MA, 1977; professional: attorney; admitted to the California bar, 1977; admitted to the Idaho bar, 1979; law clerk, Hon. James M. Carter, Judge of the U.S. Court of Appeals for the Ninth Circuit, San Diego, CA, 1977–78; associate attorney, Gibson, Dunn, and Crutcher, San Diego, 1978–79; attorney, Holden, Kidwell, Hahn and Crapo, 1979–92; partner, 1983–92; Idaho State Senate, 1984–92, assistant majority leader, 1987–89, president pro tempore, 1989–92; member: American Bar Association, Boy Scouts of America, Idaho Falls Rotary Club, 1984–88; married: the former Susan Diane Hasleton, 1974; children: Michelle, Brian, Stephanie, Lara, and Paul; co-chair, Western Water Caucus; co-chair, Sportsman Caucus; co-chair, COPD Caucus; committees: Banking, Housing, and Urban Affairs; Budget; Environment and Public Works; Finance; Indian Affairs; elected on November 3, 1992, to the 103rd Congress; reelected to each succeeding Congress; elected to the U.S. Senate on November 3, 1998; reelected to each succeeding Senate term.

Office Listings

http://crapo.senate.gov

239 Dirksen Senate Office Building, Washington, DC 20510 .... (202) 224–6142
Chief of Staff.—Peter Fischer. FAX: 228–1375
Communications Director.—Susan Wheeler.
Legislative Director.—Ken Flanz.
251 East Front Street, Suite 205, Boise, ID 83702 .... (208) 334–1776
Chief of Staff.—John Hoehne.
610 Hubbard Street, Suite 209, Coeur d'Alene, ID 83814 .... (208) 664–5490
Director.—Karen Roetter.
313 D Street, Suite 105, Lewiston, ID 83501 .... (208) 743–1492
Director.—Peter Stegner.
275 South 5th Avenue, Suite 225, Pocatello, ID 83201 .... (208) 236–9635
Director.—Farhanna Hibbert.
410 Memorial Drive, Suite 204, Idaho Falls, ID 83402 .... (208) 522–9779
Director.—Leslie Huddleston.
202 Falls Avenue, Suite 2, Twin Falls, ID 83301 .... (208) 734–2515
Director.—A.J. Church.

* * *

JAMES E. RISCH, Republican, of Boise, ID; born in Milwaukee, WI, May 3, 1943; education: St. Johns Cathedral High School, Milwaukee, WI; B.S., forestry, University of Idaho, Moscow, ID, 1965; J.D., University of Idaho, Moscow, ID, 1968, Law Review, College of Law Advisory Committee; professional: Ada County Prosecuting Attorney, 1970–74; president, Idaho Prosecuting Attorneys Association, 1973; Idaho State Senate, 1974–88, 1995–2003; Assistant Majority Leader, 1996; Majority Leader, 1997–82, 1997–2002; President Pro Tempore, 1983–1988; Lieutenant Governor of Idaho, 2003–06, 2007–09; Governor of Idaho, 2006; small business owner; ranch / farmer; former partner Risch, Goss, Insinger, Gustavel law firm; member, National Cattle Association; Idaho Cattle Association; American, Idaho and Boise Valley Angus Association; National Rifle Association; Ducks Unlimited; Rocky Mountain Elk Foundation; married: Vicki; children: James, Jason, and Jordan, 2 daughters-in-law; 6 grandchildren; Congressional Youth Leadership Council; Impact Aid Coalition; Senate Rural Health Caucus; Rural Education Caucus; WMD / Terrorism Caucus; National Guard Caucus; Western Caucus, Sportsman Caucus, Recycling Caucus, Republican High Tech Task Force; committees: Energy and Natural Resources; Foreign Relations; Small Business and Entrepreneurship; Joint Economic Committee; Select Committee on Ethics; Select Committee on Intelligence; elected to the U.S. Senate on November 4, 2008.

Office Listings

http://risch.senate.gov

483 Russell Senate Office Building, Washington, DC 20510 .... (202) 224–2752
Chief of Staff.—John Sandy. FAX: 224–2573
Communications Director.—Brad Hoaglun.
Executive Assistant / Scheduler.—Vanessa Kermick.
Legislative Director.—Chris Socha.
350 North Ninth Street, Suite 302, Boise, ID 83702 .... (208) 342–7985

610 Hubbard, Harbor Plaza, Suite 213, Coeur d'Alene, ID 83814	(208) 667–6130
901 Pier View Drive, Suite 202A, Idaho Falls, ID 83402	(208) 523–5541
313 D Street, Suite 106, Lewiston, ID 83501	(208) 743–0792
275 South Fifth Avenue, Suite 290, Pocatello, ID 83201	(208) 236–6817
1411 Falls Avenue East, Suite 201, Twin Falls, ID 83301	(208) 734–6780

REPRESENTATIVES

FIRST DISTRICT

RAÚL R. LABRADOR, Republican, of Eagle, ID; born in Carolina, PR, December 8, 1967; education: B.A., Brigham Young University, Provo, UT, 1992, J.D., University of Washington, Seattle, WA, 1995; professional: attorney; religion: The Church of Jesus Christ of Latter-Day Saints; married: Becca Labrador; five children; committees: Natural Resources; Oversight and Government Reform; elected to the 112th Congress on November 2, 2010.

Office Listings

http://labrador.house.gov/

1523 Longworth House Office Building, Washington, DC 20515	(202) 225–6611
Chief of Staff.—John Goodwin.	FAX: 225–3029
Legislative Director.—Jason Bohrer.	
Scheduler.—Mike Cunnington.	
33 East Broadway Avenue, Suite 251, Meridian, ID 83642	(208) 888–3188
1250 Ironwood Drive, Suite 243, Coeur d'Alene, ID 83814	(208) 667–0127
310 Main Street, Lewiston, ID 83501	(208) 743–1388

Counties: ADA (part), ADAMS, BENEWAH, BOISE, BONNER, BOUNDARY, CANYON, CLEARWATER, GEM, IDAHO, KOOTENAI, LATAH, LEWIS, NEZ PERCE, OWYHEE, PAYETTE, SHOSHONE, VALLEY, WASHINGTON. Population (2000), 648,774.

ZIP Codes: 83501, 83520, 83522–26, 83530–31, 83533, 83535–37, 83539–49, 83552–55, 83602, 83604–07, 83610–12, 83615–17, 83619, 83622, 83624, 83626–32, 83634–39, 83641–45, 83647, 83650–57, 83660–61, 83666, 83669–72, 83676–77, 83680, 83686–87, 83702, 83704–06, 83708–09, 83711, 83713–14, 83716, 83719, 83799, 83801–06, 83808–16, 83821–27, 83830, 83832–37, 83839–58, 83860–61, 83864–74, 83876–77

* * *

SECOND DISTRICT

MICHAEL K. SIMPSON, Republican, of Blackfoot, ID; born in Burley, ID, September 8, 1950; education: graduated, Blackfoot High School, 1968; Utah State University, 1972; Washington University School of Dental Medicine, 1977; professional: dentist, private practice; Blackfoot, ID, City Council, 1981–85; Idaho State Legislature, 1985–98; Idaho Speaker of the House 1992–98; married: Kathy Simpson; committees: Appropriations; Budget; elected to the 106th Congress; reelected to each succeeding Congress.

Office Listings

http://simpson.house.gov

2312 Rayburn House Office Building, Washington, DC 20515	(202) 225–5531
Chief of Staff.—Lindsay Slater.	FAX: 225–8216
Scheduler.—Kaylyn Bessey.	
Legislative Director.—Malisah Small.	
Press Secretary.—Nikki Watts.	
802 West Bannock, Suite 600, Boise, ID 83702	(208) 334–1953
1341 Fillmore, #202, Twin Falls, ID 83301	(208) 734–7219
410 Memorial Drive, Suite 203, Idaho Falls, ID 83402	(208) 523–6701
275 South Fifth Avenue, #275, Pocatello, ID 83201	(208) 233–2222

Counties: ADA (part), BANNOCK, BEAR LAKE, BINGHAM, BLAINE, BONNEVILLE, BUTTE, CAMAS, CARIBOU, CASSIA, CLARK, CUSTER, ELMORE, FRANKLIN, FREMONT, GOODING, JEFFERSON, JEROME, LEMHI, LINCOLN, MADISON, MINIDOKA, ONEIDA, POWER, TETON, TWIN FALLS. Population (2000), 645,179.

ZIP Codes: 83201–06, 83209–15, 83217–18, 83220–21, 83223, 83226–30, 83232–39, 83241, 83243–46, 83250–56, 83261–63, 83271–72, 83274, 83276–78, 83281, 83283, 83285–87, 83301–03, 83311–14, 83316, 83318, 83320–25, 83327–28, 83330, 83332–38, 83340–44, 83346–50, 83352–55, 83401–06, 83415, 83420–25, 83427–29, 83431, 83433–36, 83438, 83440–46, 83448–52, 83454–55, 83460, 83462–69, 83601–02, 83604, 83623–24, 83627, 83633–34, 83647–48, 83701–09, 83712, 83714–17, 83720–33, 83735, 83744, 83756

ILLINOIS

(Population, 2010 12,830,632)

SENATORS

RICHARD DURBIN, Democrat, of Springfield, IL; born in East St. Louis, IL, November 21, 1944; son of William and Ann Durbin; education: graduated, Assumption High School, East St. Louis; B.S., foreign service and economics, Georgetown University, Washington, DC, 1966; J.D., Georgetown University Law Center, 1969; professional: attorney, admitted to the Illinois bar in 1969; began practice in Springfield; legal counsel to Lieutenant Governor Paul Simon, 1969–72; legal counsel to Illinois Senate Judiciary Committee, 1972–82; parliamentarian, Illinois Senate, 1969–82; president, New Members Democratic Caucus, 98th Congress; associate professor of medical humanities, Southern Illinois University School of Medicine; elected as Assistant Democratic Leader, 2004; elected as Assistant Majority Leader, 2006; married: the former Loretta Schaefer, 1967; children: Christine, Paul, and Jennifer; committees: Appropriations; Foreign Relations; Judiciary; Rules and Administration; Joint Committee on the Library; elected to the 98th Congress, November 2, 1982; reelected to each succeeding Congress; elected to the U.S. Senate on November 5, 1996; reelected to each succeeding Senate term.

Office Listings

http://durbin.senate.gov

711 Hart Senate Office Building, Washington, DC 20510 .... (202) 224–2152
Chief of Staff.—Patrick Souders. FAX: 228–0400
Legislative Director.—Dena Morris. TTY: 224–8180
Director of Scheduling.—Claire Dickhut.
230 South Dearborn, Kluczynski Building 38th Floor, Chicago, IL 60604 .... (312) 353–4952
Chief of Staff.—Mike Daly.
525 South Eighth Street, Springfield, IL 62703 .... (217) 492–4062
Director.—Bill Houlihan.
701 North Court Street, Marion, IL 62959 .... (618) 998–8812

* * *

MARK KIRK, Republican, of Highland Park, IL; born in Champaign, IL, September 15, 1959; education: B.A., Cornell University, Ithaca, NY, 1981; M.S., London School of Economics, London, UK, 1982; J.D., Georgetown University, Washington, DC, 1992; professional: United States Naval Reserve, 1989–present; staff member, U.S. Representative John Porter, 1984–90; served, World Bank, 1990–91; special assistant, U.S. State Department, 1991–93; attorney, Baker & McKenzie, 1993–95; counsel, House International Relations Committee, 1995–99, elected to the U.S. House of Representatives, 2001–10; awards: Navy and Marine Corps Commendation Medal; Navy Achievement Medal; National Defense Service Medal; Global War on Terror Service Medal; and other various decorations; married: no; children: none; committees: Appropriations; Banking, Housing, and Urban Affairs; Health, Education, Labor, and Pensions; Special Committee on Aging; elected in a special election on November 2, 2010 and sworn-in on November 29, 2010 to the United States Senate to serve the remainder of former Senator Barack Obama's unexpired term; concurrently elected in a general election on November 2, 2010 to the United States Senate for a full six-year term.

Office Listings

http://kirk.senate.gov

524 Hart Senate Office Building, Washington, DC 20510 .... (202) 224–2854
Chief of Staff.—Lester Munson. FAX: 228–4611
Deputy Chief of Staff.—Richard Goldberg.
Legislative Director.—Patrick Magnuson.
Policy and Communications Director.—Kate Dickens.
Executive Assistant.—Lisa Radogno.
230 South Dearborn Street, Suite 3900, Chicago, IL 60604 .... (312) 886–3506
607 East Adams Street, Suite 1520, Springfield, IL 62701 .... (217) 492–5089

REPRESENTATIVES

FIRST DISTRICT

BOBBY L. RUSH, Democrat, of Chicago, IL; born in Albany, GA; November 23, 1946; education: attended Marshall High School, Marshall, IL; B.A., Roosevelt University, Chicago,

IL, 1974; M.A., University of Illinois, Chicago, IL, 1994; M.A., McCormick Theological Seminary, Chicago, IL, 1998; professional: United States Army, 1963–68; insurance agent; alderman, Chicago, Illinois, city council, 1983–93; deputy chairman, Illinois Democratic Party, 1990; unsuccessful candidate for mayor of Chicago, IL, 1999; minister; married: Carolyn; five children; committees: Energy and Commerce; elected on November 3, 1992 to the 103rd Congress; reelected to each succeeding Congress.

Office Listings

http://www.house.gov/rush

2268 Rayburn House Office Building, Washington, DC 20515 .... (202) 225–4372
Chief of Staff.—Rev. Stanley Watkins. FAX: 226–0333
Senior Policy Counsel and Legislative Director.—Timothy Robinson.
Director of Administration, Operations and Scheduler.—N. Lenette Myers.
Communications Director.—Sharon Jenkins.
700–706 East 79th Street, Chicago, IL 60619 .... (773) 224–6500
Deputy Chief of Staff and District Director.—Louanner Peters.
3235 West 147th Street, Midlothian, IL 60445 .... (708) 385–9550
Deputy District Director.—Younus Suleman. FAX: 385–3860

Counties: COOK COUNTY (part). CITIES AND TOWNSHIPS: Alsip, Blue Island, Chicago, Crestwood, Dixmoor, Evergreen Park, Markham, Midlothian, Oak Forest, Orland Hills, Orland Park, Palos Heights, Palos Park, Posen, Robbins, Tinley Park and Worth. Population (2000), 653,647.

ZIP Codes: 60406, 60445, 60452, 60456, 60462–63, 60469, 60472, 60477–78, 60482, 60615–17, 60619–21, 60628–29, 60636–37, 60643, 60649, 60652–53, 606555, 60803, 60805, 60827

* * *

SECOND DISTRICT

JESSE L. JACKSON, JR., Democrat, of Chicago, IL; born in Greenville, SC, March 11, 1965; education: B.S. in business management, *magna cum laude,* North Carolina A&T State University, 1987; M.A., Chicago Theological Seminary, 1989; J.D., University of Illinois College of Law, 1993; member, Congressional Black Caucus, Congressional Progressive Caucus; elected Secretary of the Democratic National Committee's Black Caucus; national field director, National Rainbow Coalition, 1993–95; member, Rainbow/Push Action Network; married: Sandi; two children; committees: Appropriations; elected to the 104th Congress (special election); reelected to each succeeding Congress.

Office Listings

http://www.house.gov/jackson

2419 Rayburn House Office Building, Washington, DC 20515 .... (202) 225–0773
Chief of Staff.—Rick Bryant. FAX: 225–0899
Legislative Director.—Charles Dujon.
Legislative Assistant.—Kathleen Hall.
Legislative Correspondent.—Terri E. Jones.
Director of Operations / Scheduler.—DeBorah Posey.
17926 South Halsted, Homewood, IL 60430 .... (708) 798–6000
District Director.—Rick Bryant.
7121 South Yates Boulevard, Chicago, IL 60649 .... (773) 734–9660

Counties: COOK (part), WILL (part). CITIES AND TOWNSHIPS: Blue Island, Burnham, Calumet City, Calumet Park, Chicago, Chicago Heights, Country Club Hills Crestwood, Dixmoor, Dolton, East Hazel Crest, Flossmoor, Ford Heights, Glenwood, Harvey, Hazel Crest, Homewood, Lansing, Lynwood, Markham, Matteson, Midlothian, Monee, Oak Forest, Olympia Fields, Park Forest, Phoenix, Posen, Richton Park, Riverdale, Robbins, Sauk Village, South Chicago Heights, South Holland, Steger, Tinley Park, Thornton, and University Park. Population (2000), 653,647.

ZIP Codes: 60406, 60409, 60411–12, 60417, 60419, 60422–23, 60425–26, 60429–30, 60438, 60443, 60445, 60449, 60452, 60461, 60466, 60471, 60473, 60475–78, 60615, 60617, 60620, 60628, 60633, 60636–37, 60643, 60649, 60827

* * *

THIRD DISTRICT

DANIEL LIPINSKI, Democrat, of Chicago, IL; born in Chicago, July 15, 1966; son of former Congressman William Lipinski, 1983–2004; education: B.S., mechanical engineering, *magna cum laude,* Northwestern University, 1988; M.S., engineering-economic systems, Stanford University, 1989; Ph.D., political science, Duke University, 1998; professional: aide to United States Representative George Sangmeister, 1993–94; aide to United States Representative Jerry Costello, 1995–96; aide to United States Representative Rod Blagojevich, 1999–2000; professor, James Madison University Washington Program, Washington, DC, 2000; professor, University of Notre Dame, South Bend, IN, 2000–01; professor, University of Tennessee, Knoxville, TN, 2001–04; married: Judy; committees: Science, Space, and Technology; Transportation and Infrastructure; elected to the 109th Congress on November 2, 2004; reelected to each succeeding Congress.

Office Listings

http://www.lipinski.house.gov

1717 Longworth House Office Building, Washington, DC 20515 .... (202) 225–5701
Deputy Chief of Staff / Legislative Director.—Eric Lausten. FAX: 225–1012
Office Administrative.—Jennifer Sypolt.
Senior Legislative Assistant.—John Veysey.
6245 South Archer Avenue, Chicago, IL 60638 .... (312) 886–0481
Chief of Staff.—Michael McLaughlin.
26 South LaGrange Road, Suite 204, LaGrange, IL 60525 .... (708) 352–0524
5309 West 95th Street, Oak Lawn, IL 60453 .... (708) 424–0853

Counties: Cook County (part). Cities and townships: Alsip, Argo, Bedford Park, Berwyn, Bridgeview, Burr Ridge, Chicago, Chicago Ridge, Cicero, Countryside, Hickory Hills, Hinsdale, Hometown, Hodgkins, Indian Head Park, Justice Burbank, LaGrange, Lyons, McCook, North Riverside, Oak Lawn, Oak Park, Palos Hills, Palos Park, Proviso, Riverside, Stickney, Summit Brookfield, Western Springs, Willow Springs, and Worth. Population (2000), 653,647

ZIP Codes: 60126, 60130, 60154, 60162, 60402, 60415, 60426, 60430, 60453–59, 60463–65, 60477, 60480, 60482, 60499, 60501, 60513, 60521, 60525–27, 60534, 60546, 60558, 60570, 60608–09, 60616, 60620, 60623, 60629, 60632, 60636, 60638, 60643, 60652, 60655, 60803–05

* * *

FOURTH DISTRICT

LUIS V. GUTIERREZ, Democrat, of Chicago, IL; born in Chicago, December 10, 1953; education: B.A., Northeastern Illinois University, DeKalb, IL, 1974; professional: teacher; social worker, Illinois; state department of children and family services; administrative assistant, Chicago, IL, mayor's office subcommittee on infrastructure, 1984–85; co-founder, West Town-26th Ward Independent Political Organization, 1985; alderman, Chicago, IL, city council, 1986–93, president pro tem, 1989–92; Democratic National Committee, 1984; married: Soraida Arocho; children: Omaira and Jessica; committees: Financial Services; Permanent Select Committee on Intelligence; elected on November 3, 1992, to the 103rd Congress; reelected to each succeeding Congress.

Office Listings

http://www.house.gov/gutierrez

2266 Rayburn House Office Building, Washington, DC 20515 .... (202) 225–8203
Chief of Staff.—Jennice Fuentes. FAX: 225–7810
Legislative Director.—Susan Collins.
Communications Director.—Scott Frotman.
2201 West North Avenue, Chicago, IL 60647 .... (773) 342–0774
FAX: 342–0776

Counties: Cook County (part). Cities: Berkeley, Brookfield, Chicago, Ciero, Elmwood Park, Forest Park, Hillside, Maywood, Melrose Park, Northlake, Oak Park, Stickney, Stone Park, and Westchester. Population (2000), 653,647.

ZIP Codes: 60130, 60141, 60153–55, 60160, 60162–65, 60304–05, 60402, 60443, 60446, 60473, 60513, 60526, 60542, 60546, 60608–09, 60612, 60614, 60616, 60618, 60622–23, 60625, 60629, 60632, 60639, 60641, 60644, 60647, 60651, 60707, 60804

* * *

FIFTH DISTRICT

MIKE QUIGLEY, Democrat, of Chicago, IL; born in Indianapolis, October 17, 1958; education: B.A., political science, Roosevelt University, 1981; M.P.P., University of Chicago, 1985; J.D., Loyola University, 1989; professional: Cook County aldermanic aide, 1983–89; practicing attorney, 1990–present; Cook County Commissioner, 1998–2009; adjunct professor, Roosevelt University, 2006–07; adjunct professor, Loyola University, 2002–09; married: Barbara; children:

Meghan and Alyson; committees: Oversight and Government Reform, Judiciary; elected to the 111th Congress on April 7, 2009, by special election, to fill the vacancy caused by the resignation of United States Representative Rahm Emanuel; reelected to the 112th Congress on November 2, 2010.

Office Listings

http://www.quigley.house.gov

1124 Longworth House Office Building, Washington, DC 20515 .... (202) 225–4061
Chief of Staff.—Sean O'Brien. FAX: 225–5603
Communications Director.—Aviva Gibbs.
Scheduler.—Monica Foskett.
Legislative Director.—Lindsey Matese.
3742 West Irving Park Road, Chicago, IL 60618 .... (773) 267–5926
1057 West Belmont Chicago, IL 60657.

Counties: COOK COUNTY (part). Population (2007), 652,430.

ZIP Codes: 60018, 60106, 60131, 60153, 60160–61, 60164–65, 60171, 60176, 60504, 60525, 60613–14, 60618, 60625, 60630–31, 60634, 60639–41, 60646, 60656–57, 60659–60, 60677, 60706–07, 60712, 60714

* * *

SIXTH DISTRICT

PETER J. ROSKAM, Republican, of Wheaton, IL; born in Hinsdale, IL, September 13, 1961; education: B.A., University of Illinois, Urbana-Champaign, IL, 1983; J.D., Illinois Institute of Technology Chicago-Kent College of Law, Chicago, IL, 1989; professional: lawyer, private practice; staff, United States Representative Tom DeLay of Texas, 1985–86; United States Representative Henry Hyde of Illinois, 1986–87; teacher; businessman; member, Illinois house of representatives, 1993–99; member, Illinois senate, 2000–06; married: Elizabeth; children: four; committees: Ways and Means; elected to the 110th Congress on November 7, 2006; reelected to each succeeding Congress.

Office Listings

http://www.house.gov/roskam

227 Cannon House Office Building, Washington, DC 20515 .... (202) 225–4561
Chief of Staff.—Steven Moore. FAX: 225–1166
Scheduler.—Mike Dankler.
Legislative Director.—David Mork.
Press Secretaries: Dan Conston, Garret Lansing.
150 South Bloomingdale Road, Suite 200, Bloomingdale, IL 60108 .... (630) 893–9670

Counties: COOK (part), DUPAGE (part). CITIES AND TOWNSHIPS: Addison, Arlington Heights, Bensenville, Bloomingdale, Carol Stream, Des Plaines, Elk Grove, Elk Grove Village, Elmhurst, Glen Ellyn, Glendale Heights, Hanover Park Streamwood, Itasca, Leyden Proviso, Lombard, Maine, Milton, Oak Brook, Oak Brook Terrace, Roselle, Villa Park, Wayne, Westchester, Westmont, Wheaton, Winfield, and York. Population (2000), 615,419.

ZIP Codes: 60005, 60007–09, 60016–18, 60056, 60067, 60101, 60103, 60105–08, 60116–17, 60120, 60125–26, 60128, 60131–33, 60137–39, 60143, 60148, 60157, 60172–73, 60176, 60181, 60185, 60187–95, 60197, 60199, 60399, 60515, 60523, 60532, 60559, 60563, 60666, 60688, 60701

* * *

SEVENTH DISTRICT

DANNY K. DAVIS, Democrat, of Chicago, IL; born in Parkdale, AR, September 6, 1941; education: B.A., Arkansas AM&N College, 1961; M.A., Chicago State University; Ph.D., Union Institute, Cincinnati, OH; educator and health planner-administrator; board of directors, National Housing Partnership; Cook County Board of Commissioners, 1990–96; former alderman of the Chicago City Council's 29th ward, receiving the Independent Voters of Illinois "Best Alderman Award" for 1980–81, 1981–82, and 1989–90; co-chair, Clinton-Gore-Braun '92; founder and past president, Westside Association for Community Action; past president, National Association of Community Health Centers; 1987 recipient of the Leon M. Despres Award; married to Vera G. Davis; two sons: Jonathan and Stacey; committees: Homeland Security; Oversight and Government Reform; elected to the 105th Congress; reelected to each succeeding Congress.

Office Listings

http://www.davis.house.gov

2159 Rayburn House Office Building, Washington, DC 20515 .... (202) 225–5006
Chief of Staff.—Yul Edwards. FAX: 225–5641
Legislative Director.—Jill Hunter-Williams.
Director of Issues and Communications.—Ira Cohen.
3333 West Arthington Street, Suite 130, Chicago, IL 60624 .... (773) 533–7520
2301 Roosevelt Road, Broadview, IL 60155 .... (708) 345–6857

Counties: COOK COUNTY (part). CITIES AND TOWNSHIPS: Bellwood, Berkley, Broadview, Chicago, Forest Park, Hillside, Maywood, Oak Park, River Forest, and Westchester. Population (2000), 653,647.

ZIP Codes: 60104, 60130, 60141, 60153–55, 60160, 60162–63, 60301–05, 60546, 60601–12, 60614–16, 60621–24, 60636–37, 60639, 60644, 60651, 60653–54, 60661, 60663–65, 60667–75, 60678–81, 60683–88, 60690–91, 60693–97, 60707, 60804

* * *

EIGHTH DISTRICT

JOE WALSH, Republican, of McHenry, IL, born in Chicago, IL, December 27, 1961; education: B.A., english, University of Iowa, IA, 1985; M.P.P., University of Chicago, IL, 1991; professional: business executive; religion: Catholic; married: Helene Miller; committees: Homeland Security; Oversight and Government Reform; Small Business; elected to the 112th Congress on November 2, 2010.

Office Listings

http://walsh.house.gov

432 Cannon House Office Building, Washington, DC 20515 .... (202) 225–3711
Chief of Staff.—Justin Roth. FAX: 225–7830
50 East Grand Avenue, Fox Lake, IL 60073 .... (847) 973–9341
District Director.—David Carlin.

Counties: COOK COUNTY (part). TOWNSHIPS: Barrington, Hanover, Palatine, and Schaumburg. LAKE COUNTY (part). TOWNSHIPS: Antioch, Avon, Bentor, Cuba, Ela, Fremont, Grant, Lake Villa, Libertyville, Newport, Warren, Wauconda, and Zion. MCHENRY COUNTY (part). CITIES: Burton, Dorr, Greenwood, Hebron, McHenry, Nunda, and Richmond. Population (2000), 653,647.

ZIP Codes: 60002, 60004–05, 60007–08, 60010–14, 60020–21, 60030–31, 60033–34, 60038, 60041–42, 60046–51, 60060–61, 60067, 60071–75, 60081, 60083–85, 60087, 60095–99, 60103, 60107, 60120, 60133, 60159, 60168, 60172–73, 60179, 60192–96

* * *

NINTH DISTRICT

JANICE D. SCHAKOWSKY, Democrat, of Evanston, IL; born in Chicago, IL, May 26, 1944; education: B.A., University of Illinois, 1965; consumer advocate; program director, Illinois Public Action; executive director, Illinois State Council of Senior Citizens, 1985–90; State Representative, 18th District, Illinois General Assembly, 1991–99; served on Labor and Commerce, Human Service Appropriations, Health Care, and Electric Deregulation Committees; religion: Jewish; married: Robert Creamer; children: Ian, Mary, and Lauren; committees: Energy and Commerce; Permanent Select Committee on Intelligence; elected to the 106th Congress; reelected to each succeeding Congress.

Office Listings

http://www.house.gov/schakowsky

2367 Rayburn House Office Building, Washington, DC 20515 .... (202) 225–2111
Chief of Staff.—Cathy Hurwit. FAX: 226–6890
Communications Director.—Sarah Baldauf.
Legislative Director.—Isaac Brown.
Appointments Secretary.—Kim Muzeroll.
5533 Broadway, Chicago, IL 60640 .... (773) 506–7100
District Director.—Leslie Combs.
820 Davis Street, Suite 105, Evanston, IL 60201 .... (847) 328–3409

Counties: COOK COUNTY (part). CITIES: Chicago, Evanston, Glenview, Golf, Lincolnwood, Morton Grove, Niles, and Skokie. Population (2000), 653,647.

ZIP Codes: 60016, 60018–19, 60025, 60029, 60053, 60056, 60068, 60076–77, 60091, 60176, 60201–04, 60208, 60611, 60613, 60626, 60630–31, 60640, 60645–46, 60656–57, 60659–60, 60706, 60712, 60714

* * *

TENTH DISTRICT

ROBERT J. DOLD, Republican, of Winnetka, IL; born in Evanston, IL, June 23, 1969; education: New Trier High School, Winnetka, IL, 1987; B.A., Denison University, Granville, OH, 1991; J.D., Indiana University, Bloomington, IN, 1996; M.B.A., Kellogg School of Management, Evanston, IL, 2000; professional: small business owner; attorney; investigative counsel, United States House Government Reform and Oversight Committee; judicial clerk, New York State Judge; committees: Financial Services; elected to the 112th Congress on November 2, 2010.

Office Listings

http://dold.house.gov

212 Cannon House Office Building, Washington, DC 20515 .... (202) 225–4835
Chief of Staff.—Eric Burgeson. FAX: 225–0837
650 Dundee Road, Suite 380, Northbrook, IL 60062 .... (847) 940–0202
District Director.—Kelley Folino.

Counties: COOK (part), LAKE (part). Population (2000), 653,647.

ZIP Codes: 60004–06, 60008, 60010, 60015–16, 60022, 60025–26, 60030–31, 60035, 60037, 60040, 60043–45, 60047–48, 60056, 60060–62, 60064–65, 60067, 60069–70, 60074, 60078–79, 60082–83, 60085–93, 60173, 60195, 60201

* * *

ELEVENTH DISTRICT

ADAM KINZINGER, Republican, of Manteno, IL; born in Kankakee, IL, February 27, 1978; education: graduated, Normal Community West High School, 1996; B.S., Illinois State University, 2000; professional: McLean County Board, 1998–2003; Sales Representative, STL Technologies, 2000–03; United States Air National Guard, 2003–present, current rank: Captain; religion: Protestant; single; House Majority Transition Team; Deputy Republican Whip; committee: Energy and Commerce; elected to the 112th Congress on November 2, 2010.

Office Listings

http://www.kinzinger.house.gov

1218 Longworth House Office Building, Washington, DC 20515 .... (202) 225–3635
Chief of Staff.—Erik Rayman. FAX: 225–3521
Deputy Chief of Staff.—Pamela Mattox.
2701 Black Road, Suite 201, Joliet, IL 60435 .... (815) 729–2308
District Manager.—Bonnie Walsh.
Director of Communications.—Brook Hougesen.

Counties: BUREAU (part), GRUNDY, KANKAKEE, LA SALLE, LIVINGSTON (part), MCLEAN (part), WILL (part), and WOODFORD (part). Population (2000), 653,658.

ZIP Codes: 60401, 60407–11, 60416–17, 60420–21, 60423–24, 60430–37, 60442, 60444–45, 60447–51, 60466, 60468, 60470, 60474–75, 60477, 60479, 60481, 60504, 60518, 60531, 60541, 60544, 60548–49, 60551–52, 60557, 60625, 60640, 60646, 60660, 60901–02, 60910, 60912–15, 60917, 60919, 60922, 60935, 60940–41, 60944, 60950, 60954, 60961, 60964, 61238, 61240–41, 61254, 61262, 61273, 61301, 61312, 61314–17, 61320–23, 61325–26, 61328–30, 61332, 61334, 61337–38, 61341–42, 61344–45, 61348–50, 61354, 61356, 61358–62, 61364, 61368, 61370–74, 61376–77, 61379, 61701–02, 61704, 61725, 61732, 61736, 61744–45, 61748, 61752, 61754, 61760–61, 61772, 61774, 61790

* * *

TWELFTH DISTRICT

JERRY F. COSTELLO, Democrat, of Belleville, IL; born in East St. Louis, IL, September 25, 1949; education: graduated, Assumption High, East St. Louis, IL, 1968; A.A., Belleville Area College, IL, 1970; B.A., Maryville College of the Sacred Heart, St. Louis, MO, 1973; professional: county bailiff, Illinois 20th judicial circuit; deputy sheriff, St. Clair County,

IL; director of court services and probation, Illinois 20th judicial district; chief investigator, Illinois state attorney's office, St. Clair County, IL; elected board chair, St. Clair County, IL, 1980–88; married: the former Georgia Jean Cockrum, 1968; children: Jerry II, Gina Costello, and John; committees: Science, Space, and Technology; Transportation and Infrastructure; elected to the 100th Congress by special election to fill the vacancy caused by the death of United States Representative Charles Melvin Price; reelected to each succeeding Congress.

Office Listings

http://www.house.gov/costello

2408 Rayburn House Office Building, Washington, DC 20515 ... (202) 225–5661
Chief of Staff.—David Gillies. FAX: 225–0285
Scheduler.—Karl Britton.
Legislative Director.—Sarah Blackwood.
Press Secretary.—David Gillies.
2060 Delmar Avenue, Suite B, Granite City, IL 62040 ... (618) 451–7065
8787 State Street, Suite 102, East Saint Louis, IL 62203 ... (618) 397–8833
144 Lincoln Place Court, Suite 4, Belleville, IL 62221 ... (618) 233–8026
201 East Nolen Street, West Frankfort, IL 62896 ... (618) 937–6402
250 West Cherry Street, Carbondale, IL 62901 ... (618) 529–3791
1330 Swanwick Street, Chester, IL 62233 ... (618) 826–3043

Counties: Alexander, Franklin, Jackson, Madison (part), Monroe, Perry, Pulaski, Randolph, St. Clair, Union, Williamson (part). Population (2000), 653,647.

ZIP Codes: 62002, 62010, 62018, 62024–25, 62035, 62040, 62048, 62059–60, 62071, 62084, 62087, 62090, 62095, 62201–08, 62217, 62220–26, 62232–34, 62236–44, 62246, 62248, 62254–61, 62263–65, 62268–69, 62272, 62274, 62277–80, 62282, 62284–86, 62288–89, 62292–95, 62297–98, 62812, 62819, 62822, 62831–32, 62836, 62840, 62846, 62859–60, 62865, 62883–84, 62888, 62890, 62896–97, 62901–03, 62905–07, 62912, 62914–18, 62920, 62922–24, 62926–27, 62932–33, 62939–42, 62948–52, 62956–59, 62961–64, 62966, 62969–71, 62973–76, 62983, 62987–88, 62990, 62992–94, 62996–99

* * *

THIRTEENTH DISTRICT

JUDY BIGGERT, Republican, of Hinsdale, IL; born in Chicago, IL, August 15, 1937; education: graduated from New Trier High School, 1955; B.A., Stanford University, 1959; J.D., Northwestern University School of Law, 1963; professional: attorney, 1975–99; Illinois House of Representatives (81st District), 1993–98; Assistant House Republican Leader, 1995–99; has served on numerous local civic and community organizations and groups; religion: Episcopalian; married: Rody P. Biggert; children: Courtney, Alison, Rody, and Adrienne; committees: Education and the Workforce; Financial Services; Science, Space, and Technology; elected to the 106th Congress; reelected to each succeeding Congress.

Office Listings

http://www.judybiggert.house.gov

2113 Rayburn House Office Building, Washington, DC 20515 ... (202) 225–3515
Chief of Staff.—Kathy Lydon. FAX: 225–9420
Press Secretary.—Zachary Cikanek.
Legislative Director.—Cade Clurman.
Scheduler.—Matt Leighton.
6262 South Route 83, Suite 305, Willowbrook, IL 60527 ... (630) 655–2052

Counties: Cook (part), DuPage (part), Will (part). Population (2000), 653,647.

ZIP Codes: 60181, 60403, 60432, 60435, 60439, 60440–41, 60446, 60448, 60462–64, 60467, 60477, 60483, 60487, 60490–91, 60502–04, 60514–17, 60519, 60521–23, 60527, 60532, 60540, 60543–44, 60555, 60559, 60561, 60563–67, 60572, 60585–86, 60597, 60599

* * *

FOURTEENTH DISTRICT

RANDY HULTGREN, Republican, of Winfield, IL; born in Park Ridge, IL, March 1, 1966; education: graduated, B.A., Bethel College, 1988; J.D., Chicago-Kent College of Law, 1993; professional: elected to the DuPage County Board and county Forest Preserve Board, 1994; elected to the Illinois House of Representatives, 1999, elected to the Illinois State Senate, 2007;

married: wife, Christy; four children; committees: Agriculture; Science, Space, and Technology; Transportation and Infrastructure; elected to the 112th Congress on November 2, 2010.

Office Listings

http://hultgren.house.gov

427 Cannon House Office Building, Washington, DC 20515 .... (202) 225–2976
FAX: 225–0697
Chief of Staff.—Jerry Clarke.
Senior Legislative Aide.—Mischa Fisher.
Scheduler.—Laura Finch.
Legislative Aides: Scott Luginbill, Gill Stevens, John Weber.
Staff Assistant.—Katie Brookens.
1797 State Street, Suite A, Geneva, IL 60134 .... (630) 232–7104
District Director.—Jeremy Cirks.
Communications Director.—Andrew Flach.
Deputy District Director.—Kevin Smith.
119 West First Street, P.O. Box 343, Dixon, IL 61021 .... (815) 288–0680
100 West Main, Geneseo, IL 61254 .... Hours by Appointment

Counties: BUREAU (part), DEKALB (part), DUPAGE (part), HENRY (part), KANE, KENDALL, LEE, WHITESIDE (part). CITIES AND TOWNSHIPS: Amboy, Ashton, Aurora, Barrington Hills, Bartlett, Batavia, Big Rock, Bristol, Burlington, Carol Stream, Carpentersville, Clare, Compton, Cornell, Cortland, DeKalb, Dixon, Dundee, East and West, Earlville, Elburn, Elgin, Esmond, Forreston, Franklin Grove, Geneva, Genoa, Gilberts, Hampshire, Harmon, Hinckley, Kaneville, Kingston, Kirkland, Lee, Leland, Malta, Maple Park, Mendota, Millbrook, Millington, Minooka, Montgomery, Mooseheart, Nelson, Newark, North Aurora, Oswego, Paw Paw, Plano, Plato Center, St. Charles, Sandwich, Shabbona, Sleepy Hollow, Somonauk, South Elgin, Steward, Sublette, Sugar Grove, Sycamore, Virgil, Warrenville, Wasco, Waterman, Wayne, West Brooklyn, West Chicago, Wheaton, Winfield, and Yorkville. Population (2000), 653,647.

ZIP Codes: 60010, 60102–03, 60109–10, 60112, 60115, 60118–23, 60134, 60136, 60140, 60142, 60144, 60147, 60150–52, 60170, 60174–75, 60177–78, 60183–87, 60190, 60431, 60447, 60450, 60504–06, 60510–12, 60518, 60520, 60530–31, 60536–39, 60541–45, 60548, 60550, 60552–56, 60560, 60563, 60568, 60640, 60660, 61006, 61021, 61031, 61042, 61057–58, 61068, 61071, 61081, 61234–35, 61238, 61240–41, 61243, 61250, 61254, 61258, 61270, 61273–74, 61277, 61283, 61310, 61318, 61324, 61330–31, 61342, 61344, 61346, 61349, 61353, 61367, 61376, 61378, 61434, 61443

* * *

FIFTEENTH DISTRICT

TIMOTHY V. JOHNSON, Republican, of Sidney, IL; born in Champaign, IL, July 23, 1946; education: B.A., University of Illinois, Phi Beta Kappa; J.D., University of Illinois College of Law, graduated with high honors; professional: attorney; public service: Urbana, IL, City Council, 1971–75; Illinois House of Representatives, 1976–2000; Deputy Majority Leader; Champaign County, IL, Republican Party Chair, 1990–96; committees: Agriculture; Transportation and Infrastructure; elected to the 107th Congress on November 7, 2000; reelected to each succeeding Congress.

Office Listings

http://www.timjohnson.house.gov

1207 Longworth House Office Building, Washington, DC 20515 .... (202) 225–2371
FAX: 226–0791
Chief of Staff.—Mark Sheldon.
Legislative Director.—Stephen Borg.
2004 Fox Drive, Champaign, IL 61820 .... (217) 403–4690

Counties: CHAMPAIGN, CLARK, COLES, CRAWFORD, CUMBERLAND, DEWITT, DOUGLAS, EDGAR, EDWARDS (part), FORD, GALLATIN (part), IROQUOIS, LAWRENCE (part), LIVINGSTON (part), MACON (part), MCLEAN (part), MOULTRIE, PIATT, SALINE (part), VERMILION, WABASH (part), WHITE (part). CITIES AND TOWNSHIPS: Bloomington-Normal, Champaign-Urbana, Charleston-Mattoon, Danville, Decatur, Mount Carmel, and Pontiac. Population (2000), 653,647.

ZIP Codes: 60420, 60423, 60437, 60449, 60460, 60518, 60531, 60551–52, 60901–02, 60911–14, 60917–22, 60924, 60926–34, 60936, 60938–42, 60945–46, 60948–49, 60951–53, 60955–57, 60959–64, 60966–70, 60973–74, 61252, 61270, 61311, 61313, 61319, 61321, 61333, 61364, 61401, 61434, 61448–49, 61530, 61701–02, 61704, 61709–10, 61720, 61722, 61724, 61726–28, 61730–31, 61735, 61737, 61739–41, 61743, 61748–50, 61752–53, 61758, 61761, 61764, 61769–70, 61772–73, 61775–78, 61791, 61799, 61801–03, 61810–18, 61820–22, 61824–26, 61830–34, 61839–59, 61862–66, 61870–78, 61880, 61882–84, 61910–14, 61917, 61919–20, 61924–25, 61928–33, 61936–38, 61940–44, 61949, 61951, 61953, 61955–56, 62401, 62410, 62413, 62420–21, 62423, 62427–28, 62432–33, 62435–36, 62439–42, 62445, 62447, 62449, 62451, 62454, 62460, 62462, 62466–69, 62474, 62477–78, 62481, 62521–22, 62526, 62532, 62544, 62549–50, 62701–03, 62821, 62827, 62844, 62863, 62867, 62869, 62871, 62930, 62934, 62946, 62984

* * *

SIXTEENTH DISTRICT

DONALD A. MANZULLO, Republican, of Egan, IL; born in Rockford, IL, March 24, 1944; education: B.A., American University, Washington, DC, 1987; J.D., Marquette University Law School, Milwaukee, WI, 1970; admitted to Illinois bar, 1970; president, Ogle County Bar Association, 1971, 1973; advisor, Oregon Ambulance Corporation; founder, Oregon Youth, Inc.; member: State of Illinois and City of Oregon chambers of commerce; Friends of Severson Dells; Natural Land Institute; Ogle County Historic Society; Northern Illinois Alliance for the Arts; Aircraft Owners and Pilots Association; Ogle County Pilots Association; Kiwanis International; Illinois Farm Bureau; Ogle County Farm Bureau; National Federation of Independent Business; Citizens Against Government Waste; married: Freda Teslik, 1982; children: Niel, Noel, and Katherine; committees: Financial Services; Foreign Affairs; elected on November 3, 1992, to the 103rd Congress; reelected to each succeeding Congress.

Office Listings

http://www.manzullo.house.gov

2228 Rayburn House Office Building, Washington, DC 20515 .... (202) 225–5676
Chief of Staff.—Adam Magary. FAX: 225–5284
Legislative Director.—Phil Eskeland.
Scheduler.—Elaine Wilson.
Communications Director (Rockford).—Rich Carter.
415 South Mulford Road, Rockford, IL 61108 .... (815) 394–1231
District Director.—Pam Sexton.
101 North Virginia Street, Suite 170, Crystal Lake, IL 60014 .... (815) 356–9800
Caseworker.—Kathleen Davis.

Counties: BOONE, CARROLL, DEKALB (part), JO DAVIESS, MCHENRY (part), OGLE, STEPHENSON, WHITESIDE (part), WINNEBAGO. Population (2000), 653,647.

ZIP Codes: 60001, 60010, 60012–14, 60021, 60033–34, 60039, 60042, 60050–51, 60098, 60102, 60111, 60113, 60115, 60129, 60135, 60140, 60142, 60145–46, 60150, 60152, 60156, 60178, 60180, 60530, 61001, 61006–08, 61010–16, 61018–21, 61024–25, 61027–28, 61030–32, 61036, 61038–39, 61041, 61043–44, 61046–54, 61059–65, 61067–68, 61070–75, 61077–81, 61084–85, 61087–89, 61091, 61101–12, 61114–15, 61125–26, 61130–32, 61230, 61250–52, 61261, 61266, 61270, 61285

* * *

SEVENTEENTH DISTRICT

BOBBY SCHILLING, Republican, of Moline, IL; born in Rock Island, IL, January 23, 1964; education: graduated, Alleman High School; attended Black Hawk Community College, Moline, IL; professional: owner, Saint Giuseppe's Heavenly Pizzeria, Moline, IL; religion: Roman Catholic; married: Christie; children: Terry, Aaron, Levi, Joseph, Isabel, Rachel, Olivia, Sam, Sophia, and Anthony; committees: Agriculture; Armed Services; Small Business; elected to the 112th Congress on November 2, 2010.

Office Listings

http://schilling.house.gov

507 Cannon House Office Building, Washington, DC 20515 .... (202) 225–5905
Chief of Staff.—Mike Roman. FAX: 225–5396
Scheduler.—Claire Repass.
Legislative Director.—Robert Frederick.
Press Secretary.—Scott Tranter.
3000 41st Street, Suite 2, Moline, IL 61265 .... (309) 757–7630
District Director.—Adrian Madunic.
Office Manager.—Mitch Heckenkamp.
185 South Kellogg Street, Galesburg, IL 61401 .... (309) 343–1194
Field Representative.—Devin Wilcoxen.

Counties: ADAMS (part), CALHOUN, CHRISTIAN (part), FAYETTE (part), FULTON, GREENE (part), HANCOCK, HENDERSON, HENRY (part), JERSEY (part), KNOX (part), MACON (part), MACOUPIN, MADISON (part), MCDONOUGH, MERCER, MONTGOMERY (part), PIKE (part), ROCK ISLAND, SANGAMON (part), SHELBY (part), WARREN, WHITESIDE (part). Population (2000), 653,647.

ZIP Codes: 61037, 61071, 61081, 61201, 61204, 61230–33, 61236–37, 61239–42, 61244, 61251, 61256–57, 61259–65, 61272, 61275–76, 61278–79, 61281–82, 61284, 61299, 61318, 61342, 61364, 61401–02, 61410–20, 61422–23, 61425,

61427, 61430–43, 61447–48, 61450, 61452–55, 61458–60, 61462, 61465–78, 61480, 61482, 61484, 61486, 61488–90, 61501, 61519–20, 61524, 61531, 61533, 61542–44, 61553, 61560, 61563, 61569, 61572, 61611, 61701, 61761, 62001–02, 62006, 62009, 62011–14, 62017, 62019, 62021, 62023, 62027, 62031–33, 62036–37, 62044–45, 62047, 62049–53, 62056, 62058, 62063, 62065, 62069–70, 62074–75, 62077–79, 62082, 62085–86, 62088–89, 62091–94, 62097–98, 62262, 62301, 62305–06, 62311, 62313, 62316, 62320–21, 62326, 62329–30, 62334, 62336, 62338, 62341, 62343, 62345, 62348, 62351, 62354–56, 62358, 62360–61, 62366–67, 62370, 62373–74, 62376, 62379–80, 62431, 62513–15, 62520–23, 62525–26, 62537, 62539, 62544, 62549–51, 62557, 62560–61, 62572, 62615, 62624, 62626, 62629–30, 62640, 62644, 62649, 62661, 62667, 62670, 62672, 62674, 62683, 62685, 62690, 62692, 62701–05, 62707–08, 62713, 62781, 62794, 62796

* * *

EIGHTEENTH DISTRICT

AARON SCHOCK, Republican, of Peoria, IL; born in Morris, MN, May 28, 1981; B.S. in Finance, Bradley University, Peoria, IL, 2002; professional: President of Peoria Board of Education, youngest school board president in history; Illinois House of Representatives 2005–09, Director of Development for Petersen Companies of Peoria, 2007; awards: named one of Peoria's *40 Leaders Under 40*, 2004; Peoria Jaycees Good Government Award, 2004; Richard Mautino Excellence in Government Award, 2005; Community Workshop and Training Center Advocacy Award, 2005; Guardian Angels Arc-Angel Award, 2005; Illinois Healthcare Association's Legislator of the Year, 2005–07; Illinois Long Term Care Association's Legislator of the Year Award, 2006; Life Services Network Legislator of the Year, 2006; Illinois Committee for Honest Government Outstanding Legislative and Constituent Service Award, 2007; religion: Christian; Deputy Republican Whip; Animal Protection Caucus; Community College Caucus; House Diversity and Innovation Caucus; House Rural Education Caucus; Congressional Hunger Caucus; Congressional Fire Services Caucus; Congressional Services Caucus; House Recycling Caucus; Republican Study Group, Tuesday Group; chair, Franking Commission (otherwise known as the Commission on Congressional Mailing Standards); committees: Ways and Means; House Administration; Joint Committee on Printing; elected to the 111th Congress on November 4, 2008; reelected to the 112th Congress.

Office Listings

http://www.schock.house.gov

328 Cannon House Office Building, Washington, DC 20515 .... (202) 225–6201 FAX: 225–9249
Chief of Staff.—Steven Shearer.
Executive Assistant.—Jeannie Etchart.
Legislative Director.—Mark Roman.
Communications Director.—Steve Dutton.
Legislative Assistants: Margie Almanza, Mike Pasko.
Legislative Correspondent.—Kelli Ripp.
Staff Assistant.—Ben Jarrett.

100 Northeast Monroe Street, Room 100, Peoria, IL 61602 .... (309) 671–7027 FAX: 671–7309

209 West State Street, Jacksonville, IL 62650 .... (217) 245–1431 FAX: 243–6852

235 South 6th Street, Springfield, IL 62701 .... (217) 670–1653 FAX: 670–1806

Counties: ADAMS (part), BROWN, BUREAU (part), CASS, KNOX (part), LOGAN, MACON (part), MARSHALL, MASON, MCLEAN, MENARD, MORGAN, PEORIA, PIKE (part), PUTNAM, SANGAMON (part), SCHUYLER, SCOTT, STARK, TAZEWELL, WOODFORD (part). Population (2000), 653,647.

ZIP Codes: 61314, 61320–21, 61326–27, 61330, 61334–36, 61340, 61345, 61349, 61362–63, 61369–70, 61375, 61377, 61401, 61410, 61414, 61421, 61424, 61426, 61428, 61434, 61436, 61440, 61443, 61448–49, 61451–52, 61455, 61458, 61467, 61472, 61479, 61483–85, 61488–89, 61491, 61501, 61516–17, 61523, 61525–26, 61528–37, 61539–42, 61545–48, 61550, 61552, 61554–55, 61558–62, 61564–65, 61567–72, 61601–07, 61610–12, 61614–16, 61625, 61628–30, 61632–41, 61643–44, 61650–56, 61704, 61721, 61723, 61729, 61733–34, 61738, 61742, 61747, 61749, 61751, 61755–56, 61759–61, 61771, 61774, 61778, 61830, 62305, 62311–12, 62314, 62319–20, 62323–25, 62338–40, 62344, 62346–47, 62349, 62352–53, 62357, 62359–60, 62362–63, 62365, 62367, 62375, 62378, 62501, 62512, 62515, 62518–22, 62524, 62526, 62535, 62539, 62541, 62543, 62548, 62551, 62554, 62561, 62573, 62601, 62610–13, 62615, 62617–18, 62621–22, 62624–25, 62627–29, 62631, 62633–35, 62638–39, 62642–44, 62650–51, 62655–56, 62660–68, 62670–71, 62673, 62675, 62677, 62681–82, 62684, 62688, 62690–95, 62701–07, 62713, 62715, 62719, 62721–22, 62726, 62736, 62739, 62746, 62756–57, 62761, 62765, 62767, 62769, 62776–77, 62781, 62786, 62791, 62796

* * *

NINETEENTH DISTRICT

JOHN SHIMKUS, Republican, of Collinsville, IL; born in Collinsville, February 21, 1958; education: graduated from Collinsville High School; B.S., West Point Military Academy, West

Point, NY, 1980; teaching certificate, Christ College, Irvine, CA, 1990; M.B.A., Southern Illinois University, Edwardsville, 1997; U.S. Army Reserves, 1980–85; government and history teacher, Metro East Lutheran High School, Edwardsville, IL; Collinsville township trustee, 1989; Madison county treasurer, 1990–96; married: the former Karen Muth, 1987; children: David, Daniel, and Joshua; committees: Energy and Commerce; elected to the 105th Congress; reelected to each succeeding Congress.

Office Listings

http://www.shimkus.house.gov

2452 Rayburn House Office Building, Washington, DC 20515 .... (202) 225–5271
Chief of Staff.—Craig Roberts. FAX: 225–5880
Legislative Director.—Ryan Tracy.
240 Regency Centre, Collinsville, IL 62234 .... (618) 344–3065
3130 Chatham Road, Suite C, Springfield, IL 62704 .... (217) 492–5090
District Director.—Deb Detmers.
221 East Broadway, Suite 102, Centralia, IL 62801 .... (618) 532–9676
120 South Fair, Olney, IL 62450 .... (618) 392–7737
110 East Locust Street, Room 12, Harrisburg, IL 62946 .... (618) 252–8271

Counties: BOND, CHRISTIAN (part), CLAY, CLINTON, EDWARDS (part), EFFINGHAM, FAYETTE (part), GALLATIN (part), GREENE (part), HAMILTON, HARDIN, JASPER, JEFFERSON, JERSEY (part), JOHNSON, LAWRENCE (part), MADISON (part), MARION, MASSAC, MONTGOMERY (part), POPE, RICHLAND, SALINE (part), SANGAMON (part), SHELBY (part), WABASH (part), WASHINGTON, WAYNE, WHITE (part), WILLIAMSON (part). Population (2000), 653,647.

ZIP Codes: 61957, 62001–02, 62010, 62012, 62015–17, 62019, 62021–22, 62024–26, 62028, 62030, 62034–35, 62040, 62044, 62046, 62049, 62051–52, 62054, 62056, 62061–62, 62067, 62074–76, 62080–81, 62083, 62086, 62088, 62094, 62097, 62214–16, 62218–19, 62230–31, 62234, 62237, 62245–47, 62249–50, 62252–55, 62257–58, 62262–63, 62265–66, 62268–69, 62271, 62273, 62275, 62281, 62284, 62293–94, 62338, 62401, 62410–11, 62413–14, 62417–28, 62431–36, 62438–52, 62454, 62458–69, 62471, 62473–81, 62510, 62513, 62515, 62517, 62520–22, 62526, 62530–31, 62533–34, 62536, 62538–40, 62545–48, 62550, 62553, 62555–58, 62560, 62563, 62565, 62567–68, 62570–72, 62615, 62629, 62689–90, 62703–04, 62707, 62716, 62723, 62762–64, 62766, 62791, 62801, 62803, 62805–12, 62814–25, 62827–31, 62833–44, 62846, 62848–72, 62874–87, 62889–99, 62908–10, 62912, 62917, 62919, 62921–23, 62926, 62928, 62930–31, 62934–35, 62938–39, 62941, 62943, 62946–47, 62953–56, 62959–60, 62965, 62967, 62972, 62977, 62979, 62982–85, 62987, 62991, 62995

INDIANA

(Population 2010, 6,483,802)

SENATORS

RICHARD G. LUGAR, Republican, of Indianapolis, IN; born in Indianapolis, April 4, 1932; education: graduated, Shortridge High School, valedictorian, 1950; B.A., Denison University, Granville, OH, valedictorian, 1954; Rhodes Scholar, B.A., M.A., Pembroke College, Oxford, England, 1956; professional: served in the U.S. Navy, 1957–60; businessman; president and treasurer, Lugar Stock Farms, Inc., a grain operation and tree farm; vice president and treasurer, Thomas L. Green and Co., manufacturers of food production machinery, 1960–67; member, Indianapolis Board of School Commissioners, 1964–67; mayor of Indianapolis, 1968–75; member, advisory board, U.S. Conference of Mayors, 1969–75; National League of Cities, advisory council, 1972–75, president, 1971; Advisory Commission on Intergovernmental Relations, 1969–75, vice chairman, 1971–75; board of trustees, Denison University; Phi Beta Kappa; 44 honorary degrees; member, St. Luke's Methodist Church; married the former Charlene Smeltzer, 1956; four sons and thirteen grandchildren; committees: Agriculture, Nutrition, and Forestry; Foreign Relations; elected to the U.S. Senate on November 2, 1976, sworn in on January 3, 1977 as the 1,705th Senator; reelected to each succeeding Senate term.

Office Listings

http://lugar.senate.gov

306 Hart Senate Office Building, Washington, DC 20510 .... (202) 224–4814
FAX: 228–0360
Administrative Assistant.—Martin W. Morris.
Legislative Director.—Chris Geeslin.
Press Secretary.—Mark Helmke.
Scheduler.—Liz Bartlett.
10 West Market Street, Room 1180, Indianapolis, IN 46204 .... (317) 226–5555
Federal Building, Room 122, 101 Northwest Martin Luther King Boulevard, Evansville, IN 47708 .... (812) 465–6313
6384–A West Jefferson Boulevard, Fort Wayne, IN 46804 .... (260) 422–1505
175 West Lincolnway, Suite G–1, Valparaiso, IN 46383 .... (219) 548–8035

* * *

DANIEL COATS, Republican, of Indianapolis, IN; born in Jackson, MI, May 16, 1943; education: B.A., Wheaton College, Wheaton, IL, 1965; J.D., Indiana University, Indianapolis, IN, 1971; professional: served in the United States Army, 1966–68; U.S. House of Representatives, 1981–89; U.S. Senate, 1989–98; U.S. Ambassador to the Federal Republic of Germany, 2001–05; religion: Presbyterian (P.C.A.); married: Marsha Crawford, 1965; three children; eight grandchildren; committees: Appropriations; Energy and Natural Resources; Joint Economic Committee; Select Committee on Intelligence; elected to the U.S. Senate on November 2, 2010.

Office Listings

http://coats.senate.gov

SR–493 Russell Senate Office Building, Washington, DC 20510 .... (202) 224–5623
FAX: 228–1820
Chief of Staff.—Dean Hingson.
Legislative Director.—Viraj Mirani.
Communications Director.—Tara DiJulio.
Scheduler.—Katie Maloy.
11035 Broadway, Suite A, Crown Point, IN 46307 .... (219) 663–2595
FAX: 663–4586
101 Martin Luther King, Jr. Boulevard, Evansville, IN 47708 .... (812) 465–6500
FAX: 465–6503
1300 South Harrison Street, Suite 3161, Ft. Wayne, IN 46802 .... (260) 426–3151
FAX: 420–0060
1650 Market Tower, 10 West Market Street, Indianapolis, IN 46204 .... (317) 554–0750
FAX: 554–0760
2 East McClain Avenue, Suite 2–A, Scottsburg, IN 47170 .... (812) 754–0520
FAX: 754–0539

REPRESENTATIVES

FIRST DISTRICT

PETER J. VISCLOSKY, Democrat, of Merrillville, IN; born in Gary, IN, August 13, 1949; education: graduated, Andrean High School, Merrillville, 1967; B.S., accounting, Indiana University Northwest, Gary, 1970; J.D., University of Notre Dame Law School, Notre Dame, IN, 1973; LL.M., international and comparative law, Georgetown University Law Center, Washington, DC, 1982; professional: attorney; admitted to the Indiana state bar, 1974, the District of Columbia bar, 1978, and the U.S. Supreme Court bar, 1980; associate staff, U.S. House of Representatives, Committee on Appropriations, 1977–80, Committee on the Budget, 1980–82; practicing attorney, Merrillville law firm, 1983–84; wife: Joanne Royce; children: John Daniel and Timothy Patrick; committees: Appropriations; elected to the 99th Congress on November 6, 1984; reelected to each succeeding Congress.

Office Listings

http://www.house.gov/visclosky

2256 Rayburn House Office Building, Washington, DC 20515 .... (202) 225–2461
Chief of Staff.—Mark Lopez. FAX: 225–2493
Appropriations Director.—Joe DeVooght.
Executive Assistant.—Korry Baack.
Communications Director.—Katie Mounts.
7895 Broadway, Suite A, Merrillville, IN 46410 .... (219) 795–1844
District Director.—Te-Reika Chambers. FAX: 795–1850
(888) 423–7383

Counties: BENTON, JASPER, LAKE, NEWTON, PORTER (part). Population (2000), 675,767.

ZIP Codes: 46301–04, 46307–08, 46310–12, 46319–25, 46327, 46341–42, 46345, 46347–49, 46355–56, 46360, 46366, 46368, 46372–73, 46375–77, 46379–85, 46390, 46392–94, 46401–11, 47917, 47921–22, 47942–44, 47948, 47951, 47963–64, 47970–71, 47977–78, 47984, 47986, 47995

* * *

SECOND DISTRICT

JOE DONNELLY, Democrat, of Granger, IN; born in Massapequa, NY, September 29, 1955; education: B.A., major: government, the University of Notre Dame, 1977; J.D., the University of Notre Dame, 1981; member: Law Firm of Nemeth, Feeny and Masters, in South Bend, IN; small business owner in Mishawaka; served on Indiana State Election Board, 1988–89; member of the Mishawaka Marian High School Board, 1997–2001, served as president; 2000–01; married to Jill; children: Molly and Joseph Jr.; committees: Financial Services; Veterans' Affairs; elected to the 110th Congress on November 7, 2006; reelected to each succeeding Congress.

Office Listings

http://donnelly.house.gov

1530 Longworth House Office Building, Washington, DC 20515 .... (202) 225–3915
Chief of Staff.—Joel Elliott. FAX: 225–6798
Legislative Director.—Nathan Fenstermacher.
Scheduler.—Audrey Porter.
Communications Director.—Elizabeth Shappell.
207 West Colfax Avenue, South Bend, IN 46601–1601 .... (574) 288–2780

Counties: CARROLL, CASS, ELKHART (part), FULTON, LAPORTE, MARSHALL, PORTER (part), PULASKI, ST. JOSEPH, STARKE, WHITE (part). CITIES: Elkhart, Kokomo, LaPorte, Logansport, Monticello, Mishawaka, Plymouth, Rochester, South Bend, and Westville. Population (2000), 675,767.

ZIP Codes: 46041, 46051, 46056, 46065, 46143, 46301, 46304, 46340–42, 46345–46, 46348, 46350, 46352, 46360–61, 46365–66, 46371, 46374, 46382–83, 46390–91, 46501, 46504, 46506, 46511, 46513–17, 46524, 46526, 46528, 46530–32, 46534, 46536–37, 46539, 46544–46, 46550, 46552, 46554, 46556, 46561, 46563, 46570, 46572, 46574, 46595, 46601, 46604, 46613–17, 46619–20, 46624, 46626, 46628–29, 46634–35, 46637, 46660, 46680, 46699, 46901–02, 46910, 46912–13, 46915–17, 46920, 46922–23, 46926, 46929, 46931–32, 46939, 46942, 46945, 46947, 46950–51, 46960–61, 46967–68, 46970, 46975, 46977–79, 46982, 46985, 46988, 46994, 46996, 46998, 47920, 47923, 47925–26, 47946, 47950, 47957, 47959, 47960, 47997

* * *

THIRD DISTRICT

MARLIN A. STUTZMAN, Republican, of Howe, IN; born in Sturgis, MI, August 31, 1976; education: graduated from Lake Area Christian High School, 1994; studied business at Glen Oaks Community College, Centreville, MI and Trine State University, Angola, IN; professional: co-owner and runs family's 4,000-acre farm in northeast Indiana; owner, Stutzman Farms Trucking; religion: Baptist; elected to the Indiana House as the youngest member of the Legislature, 2002–08; elected to the State Senate, 2008–10; caucus and member: Indiana Senate Conservative Caucus, 2009; served on the Commerce, Public Policy and Interstate Cooperation Committee; Pensions and Labor Committee; Natural Resources Committee; ranking member, Utilities and Technology Committee; Association for Retarded Children (ARC); Howe Community Association; Indiana Farm Bureau; LaGrange County Farm Bureau; National Federation for Independent Businesses (NFIB); National Rifle Association (NRA); Young Republicans of LaGrange County; married: the former Christy Chavers, 2000; children: Payton and Preston; chair, assistant Republican Whip; committees: Agriculture; Budget; Veterans' Affairs; elected to the 111th Congress, by special election to fill the vacancy caused by the resignation of United States Representative Mark Souder and simultaneously elected to the 112th Congress on November 2, 2010.

Office Listings

http://stutzman.house.gov

1728 Longworth House Office Building, Washington, DC 20515 .... (202) 225–4436
Chief of Staff.—Timothy ''Tim'' Harris. FAX: 226–9870
Legislative Director.—John Hammond IV.
Scheduler.—Emily Adams.
1300 South Harrison, Room 3105, Fort Wayne, IN 46802 .... (260) 424–3041
District Director.—Daniel ''Dan'' Harman. FAX: 424–4042
Press Secretary.—Christopher ''Chris'' Sanders.
320 North Chicago Avenue, Suite 9B, Goshen, IN 46528 .... (574) 533–5802
700 Park Avenue, Suite D, Winona Lake, IN 46590 .... (574) 269–1940
874 North Lima Road, Suite B, Kendallville, IN 46755 .... (260) 599–0554

Counties: ALLEN (part), DEKALB, ELKHART (part), KOSCIUSKO, LAGRANGE, NOBLE, STEUBEN, WHITELY. Population (2010), 723,633.

ZIP Codes: 46502, 46504, 46506–08, 46510, 46516, 46524, 46526–28, 46538–40, 46542–43, 46550, 46553, 46555, 46562, 46565–67, 46571, 46573, 46580–82, 46590, 46701, 46703–06, 46710, 46721, 46723, 46725, 46730, 46732, 46737–38, 46741–43, 46746–48, 46750, 46755, 46760–61, 46763–65, 46767, 46771, 46773–74, 46776–77, 46779, 46783–89, 46793–99, 46801–09, 46814–16, 46818–19, 46825, 46835, 46845, 46850–69, 46885, 46895–99, 46910, 46962, 46975, 46982

* * *

FOURTH DISTRICT

TODD ROKITA, Republican, of Indianapolis, IN; born in Munster, IN, February 9, 1970; education: graduated with a B.A., Wabash College, Crawfordsville, IN, 1992; J.D., Indiana University School of Law, Indianapolis, IN, 1995; professional: practicing attorney, 1995–97; general counsel at the Indiana Secretary of State's office, 1997–2000; deputy Secretary of State, 2000–2002; Secretary of State, 2002–2010; President of the Association of Secretaries of State (NASS), 2007–08; awards: Indianapolis Choice Award, by the Indianapolis Chapter of the Association of Women Business Owners, 2008; ''Award of Merit'', by the International Association of Commercial Administrators (IACA), 2008 and 2010; Friend of Foreign Service Medal, by the Taiwanese Government, 2010; religion: Roman Catholic; married: Kathy Rokita; children: Teddy and Ryan; committees: Budget; Education and the Workforce; House Administration; elected to the 112th Congress on November 2, 2010.

Office Listings

http://www.rokita.house.gov

236 Cannon House Office Building, Washington, DC 20515 .... (202) 225–5037
Chief of Staff.—Mike Ward. FAX: 226–0544
Legislative Director.—Lindley Kratovil.
Press Secretary.—Ericka Andersen.
Scheduler.—Nancy Deckard.
355 South Washington Street, Danville, IN 46122 .... (317) 718–0404
District Director.—Liz Keele.
337 Columbia Street, Lafayette, IN 47901 .... (765) 838–3930

407 South 6th Street, Mitchell, IN 47446 .... (812) 849–9378

Counties: BOONE, CLINTON, FOUNTAIN (part), HENDRICKS, JOHNSON (part), LAWRENCE (part), MARION (part), MONROE (part), MONTGOMERY, MORGAN, TIPPECANOE, WHITE (part). Population (2000), 675,617.

ZIP Codes: 46035, 46039, 46041, 46049–50, 46052, 46057–58, 46060, 46065, 46067, 46069, 46071, 46075, 46077, 46102–03, 46106, 46111–13, 46118, 46120–23, 46125, 46131, 46142–43, 46147, 46149, 46151, 46157–58, 46160, 46165–68, 46172, 46175, 46180–81, 46183–84, 46214, 46221, 46224, 46231, 46234, 46241, 46254, 46268, 46278, 46920, 46923, 46979, 47108, 47260, 47264, 47403–04, 47420–21, 47429–30, 47433, 47436–37, 47446, 47451, 47456, 47460, 47462–64, 47467, 47470, 47901–07, 47909, 47916, 47918, 47920, 47923–24, 47929–30, 47932–41, 47944, 47949, 47952, 47954–55, 47958–60, 47962, 47965, 47967–68, 47970–71, 47978, 47980–81, 47983, 47987–90, 47992, 47994–96

* * *

FIFTH DISTRICT

DAN BURTON, Republican, of Indianapolis, IN; born in Indianapolis, June 21, 1938; education: graduated, Shortridge High School, 1956; Indiana University, 1956–57; Cincinnati Bible Seminary, 1958–60; served in the U.S. Army, 1957–58; U.S. Army Reserves, 1958–64; businessman, insurance and real estate firm owner since 1968; served, Indiana House of Representatives, 1967–68 and 1977–80; Indiana State Senate, 1969–70 and 1981–82; president: Volunteers of America, Indiana Christian Benevolent Association, Committee for Constitutional Government, and Family Support Center; member, Jaycees; 33rd degree Mason, Scottish rite division; married the former Barbara Jean Logan, 1959 (deceased, 2002); three children: Kelly, Danielle Lee, and Danny Lee II; remarried: Dr. Samia Tawil, 2006; committees: Foreign Affairs; Oversight and Government Reform; elected on November 2, 1982, to the 98th Congress; reelected to each succeeding Congress.

Office Listings

http://www.burton.house.gov

2308 Rayburn House Office Building, Washington, DC 20515 .... (202) 225–2276
Chief of Staff.—Mark Walker. FAX: 225–0016
Scheduler / Office Manager.—Diane Menorca.
Press Secretary.—Josh Gillespie.
8900 Keystone at the Crossing, Suite 1050, Indianapolis, IN 46240 .... (317) 848–0201
District Director.—Rick Wilson.
209 South Washington Street, Marion, IN 46952 .... (765) 662–6770

Counties: GRANT, HAMILTON, HANCOCK, HOWARD (part), HUNTINGTON, JOHNSON (part), MARION (part), MIAMI, SHELBY, TIPTON, WABASH. Population (2000), 675,794.

ZIP Codes: 46030–34, 46036, 46038, 46040, 46045, 46047, 46049, 46055, 46060–61, 46064, 46068–70, 46072, 46074, 46076–77, 46082, 46110, 46115, 46117, 46124, 46126, 46129–31, 46140, 46143, 46148, 46150, 46154, 46161–63, 46176, 46182, 46184, 46186, 46217, 46220, 46226–27, 46229, 46236–37, 46239–40, 46250, 46256, 46259–60, 46280, 46290, 46307, 46347, 46355, 46379–80, 46702, 46713–14, 46725, 46750, 46766, 46770, 46783, 46787, 46792, 46901–04, 46910–11, 46914, 46919, 46921, 46926, 46928–30, 46932–33, 46936–38, 46940–41, 46943, 46946, 46951–53, 46957–59, 46962, 46965, 46970–71, 46974–75, 46979–80, 46982, 46984, 46986–87, 46989–92, 46995, 47234, 47246, 47272, 47342, 47384

* * *

SIXTH DISTRICT

MIKE PENCE, Republican, of Columbus, IN; born in Columbus, June 7, 1959; education: Hanover College, 1981; J.D., Indiana University School of Law, 1986; professional: former Republican nominee for the U.S. House of Representatives in the 2nd District in 1988 and 1990; President, Indiana Policy Review Foundation, 1991–93; radio broadcaster: the Mike Pence Show, syndicated statewide in Indiana; married: Karen; children: Michael, Charlotte, and Audrey; committees: Foreign Affairs; Judiciary; elected to the 107th Congress on November 7, 2000; reelected to each succeeding Congress.

Office Listings

http://mikepence.house.gov

100 Cannon House Office Building, Washington, DC 20515 .... (202) 225–3021
Chief of Staff.—Bill Smith. FAX: 225–3382
Deputy Chief of Staff.—Joshua Pitcock.
Legislative Director.—Brian Neale.
Press Secretary.—Matt Lloyd.
Executive Assistant.—Jennifer Pavlik.
1134 Meridian Street, Anderson, IN 46016 .... (765) 640–2919

District Director.—Lani Czarniecki.

Counties: ALLEN (part), ADAMS, BARTHOLOMEW (part), BLACKFORD, DEARBORN (part), DECATUR, DELAWARE, FAYETTE, FRANKLIN, HENRY, JAY, JOHNSON (part), MADISON, RANDOLPH, RUSH, SHELBY (part), UNION, WAYNE, WELLS. Population (2000), 675,669.

ZIP Codes: 46001, 46011–18, 46036, 46040, 46044, 46048, 46051, 46056, 46063–64, 46070, 46104, 46110, 46115, 46124, 46126–27, 46131, 46133, 46140, 46142, 46144, 46146, 46148, 46150–51, 46155–56, 46160–62, 46164, 46173, 46176, 46181–82, 46186, 46711, 46714, 46731, 46733, 46740, 46745, 46750, 46759, 46766, 46769–70, 46772–73, 46777–78, 46780–83, 46791–92, 46797–98, 46809, 46816, 46819, 46928, 46952–53, 46989, 46991, 47003, 47006, 47010, 47012, 47016, 47022, 47024–25, 47030, 47035–37, 47060, 47201, 47203, 47225–26, 47234, 47240, 47244, 47246, 47261, 47263, 47265, 47272, 47280, 47283, 47302–08, 47320, 47322, 47324–27, 47330–31, 47334–42, 47344–46, 47348, 47351–62, 47366–71, 47373–75, 47380–88, 47390, 47392–94, 47396, 47448

* * *

SEVENTH DISTRICT

ANDRÉ CARSON, Democrat, of Indianapolis, IN; born in Indianapolis, October 16, 1974; graduated Arsenal Technical High School, Indianapolis, IN; education: B.A. in Criminal Justice Management, Concordia University Wisconsin, Mequon, WI; M.B.A, Indiana Wesleyan University, Marion, IN; professional: Investigative Officer for the Indiana State Excise Police, 1997–2006; Indiana Department of Homeland Security's Intelligence Fusion Center, 2006; City County Councilor, Marion County, 2007; religion: Muslim; married: Mariama; children: Salimah; caucuses: Whip, Congressional Black Caucus; Progressive Caucus; New Democrat Coalition; committees: Financial Services; elected to the 110th Congress on March 11, 2008, by special election, to fill the vacancy caused by the death of United States Representative Julia Carson; reelected to each succeeding Congress.

Office Listings

http://www.carson.house.gov

425 Cannon House Office Building, Washington, DC 20515 .... (202) 225–4011
Chief of Staff.—Kim Rudolph. FAX: 225–5633
Legislative Director.—Tammy McAthey.
Legislative Assistants: Nathan Bennett, Erica Powell, Nida Zaman.
Scheduler.—Kasey Kendrick.
300 East Fall Creek Parkway North Drive, Suite 300, Indianapolis, IN 46205 .... (317) 283–6516
District Director.—Chris Worden. FAX: 283–6567
Press Secretary.—Jason Tomcsi.

Counties: MARION. City of Indianapolis, township of Center, parts of the townships of Decatur, Lawrence, Perry, Pike, Warren, Washington, and Wayne, included are the cities of Beech Grove and Lawrence. Population (2000), 675,456.

ZIP Codes: 46107, 46160, 46201–09, 46211, 46214, 46216–22, 46224–31, 46234–35, 46237, 46239–42, 46244, 46247, 46249, 46251, 46253–55, 46260, 46266, 46268, 46274–75, 46277–78, 46282–83, 46285, 46291, 46295–96, 46298

* * *

EIGHTH DISTRICT

LARRY BUCSHON, Republican, of Newburgh, IN; born in Kincaid, IL, May 31, 1962; graduated from South Fork High School, Kincaid, IL, 1980; B.S., with a concentration in chemistry, University of Illinois, Urbana-Champaign, IL, 1984; M.D., University of Illinois, Chicago, 1988; residency, Medical College of Wisconsin in Milwaukee, 1988–95; cardiothoracic surgeon, 1995–2010; commissioned lieutenant, U.S. Navy Reserves, 1989; promoted, lieutenant commander, 1994; honorable discharge, 1998; married: Kathryn; children: Luke, Alec, Blair, and Zoe; committees: Education and the Workforce; Science, Space, and Technology; Transportation and Infrastructure; elected to the 112th Congress on November 2, 2010.

Office Listings

http://www.bucshon.house.gov

1123 Longworth House Office Building, Washington, DC 20515 .... (202) 225–4636
Chief of Staff.—Jon Causey. FAX: 225–3284
Communications Director.—Matthew Ballard.
Legislative Director.—Sarah Whiting.
Executive Assistant.—Whitney Gehlhausen.
101 Northwest Martin Luther King, Jr. Boulevard, Room 124, Evansville, IN 47708 .... (812) 465–6484

District Director.—Justin Groenert.
901 Wabash Avenue, Suite 140, Terre Haute, IN 47807 .... (812) 232–0523

Counties: CLAY, DAVIESS, FOUNTAIN (part), GIBSON, GREENE, KNOX, MARTIN, OWEN, PARKE, PIKE, POSEY, PUTNAM, SULLIVAN, VANDERBURGH, VERMILLION, VIGO, WARREN, WARRICK. Population (2010), 694,398.

ZIP Codes: 46105, 46120–21, 46128, 46135, 46165–66, 46170–72, 46175, 47403–04, 47424, 47427, 47429, 47431–33, 47438–39, 47441, 47443, 47445–46, 47449, 47453, 47455–57, 47459–60, 47462, 47465, 47469–71, 47501, 47512, 47516, 47519, 47522–24, 47527–29, 47535, 47537, 47541–42, 47553, 47557–58, 47561–62, 47564, 47567–68, 47573, 47578, 47581, 47584–85, 47590–91, 47596–98, 47601, 47610–14, 47616, 47618–20, 47629–31, 47633, 47637–40, 47647–49, 47654, 47660, 47665–66, 47670, 47683, 47701–06, 47708, 47710–16, 47719–22, 47724–25, 47727–28, 47730–37, 47739–41, 47744, 47747, 47750, 47801–05, 47807–09, 47811–12, 47830–34, 47836–38, 47840–42, 47845–66, 47868–72, 47874–76, 47878–82, 47884–85, 47917–18, 47921, 47928, 47932, 47952, 47966, 47969–70, 47974–75, 47982, 47987, 47989, 47991–93

* * *

NINTH DISTRICT

TODD C. YOUNG, Republican, of Bloomington, IN; born in Indianapolis, IN, August 24, 1972; education: B.S., political science, United States Naval Academy, Annapolis, MD, 1995; M.B.A., University of Chicago, Chicago, IL, 2000; M.A., american history, School of Advanced Study, University of London, UK, 2001; J.D., Indiana University, Bloomington, IN, 2005; professional: legislative assistant, United States Senate, 2002–03; management consultant, Crowe Chizek, 2003–05; attorney, Tucker and Tucker, PC in Paoli, IN, 2005–09; military: United States Navy, 1990–95; United States Marine Corps, 1995–2000; member: Sherwood Oaks Christian Church, Bloomington, IN; married: Jennifer Tucker Hill; children: Tucker, Annalise, Abigal, and Ava; committees: Armed Services; Budget; elected to the 112th Congress on November 2, 2010.

Office Listings

http://toddyoung.house.gov

1721 Longworth House Office Building, Washington, DC 20515 .... (202) 225–5315
Chief of Staff.—John Connell. FAX: 226–6866
Legislative Director.—Tim Welter.
Communications Director.—Trevor Foughty.
Scheduler.—Jodi Richardson.
279 Quartermaster Drive, Jeffersonville, IN 47130 .... (812) 288–3999
320 West 8th Street, Suite 114, Bloomington, IN 47404 .... (812) 335–3355

Counties: BARTHOLOMEW (part), BROWN, CLARK, CRAWFORD, DEARBORN (part), DUBOIS, FLOYD, HARRISON, JACKSON, JEFFERSON, JENNINGS, MONROE (part), OHIO, ORANGE, PERRY, RIPLEY, SCOTT, SPENCER, SWITZERLAND, WASHINGTON. Population (2000), 675,599.

ZIP Codes: 46151, 46160, 46164, 46181, 47001, 47006, 47011, 47017–23, 47025, 47031–34, 47037–43, 47102, 47104, 47106–08, 47110–12, 47114–20, 47122–26, 47129–47, 47150–51, 47160–67, 47170, 47172, 47174, 47177, 47199, 47201–03, 47220, 47223–24, 47227–32, 47235–36, 47240, 47243–45, 47247, 47249–50, 47260, 47264–65, 47270, 47273–74, 47281–83, 47401–08, 47426, 47432, 47434–36, 47448, 47452, 47454, 47458, 47462, 47468–69, 47513–15, 47520–21, 47523, 47525, 47527, 47531–32, 47536–37, 47541–42, 47545–47, 47549–52, 47556, 47564, 47574–77, 47579–81, 47586, 47588, 47590, 47601, 47611, 47615, 47617, 47634–35, 47637

IOWA

(Population 2010, 3,046,355)

SENATORS

CHUCK GRASSLEY, Republican, of Cedar Falls, IA; born in New Hartford, IA, September 17, 1933; education: graduated, New Hartford Community High School, 1951; B.A., University of Northern Iowa, 1955; M.A., University of Northern Iowa, 1956; doctoral studies, University of Iowa, 1957–58; professional: farmer; member: Iowa State Legislature, 1959–74; Farm Bureau; State and County Historical Society; Masons; Baptist Church; and International Association of Machinists, 1962–71; co-chair, International Narcotics Control Caucus; married: the former Barbara Ann Speicher, 1954; children: Lee, Wendy, Robin Lynn, Michele Marie; committees: ranking member, Judiciary; Agriculture, Nutrition, and Forestry; Budget; Finance; Joint Committee on Taxation; elected to the 94th Congress, November 5, 1974; reelected to the 95th and 96th Congresses; elected to the U.S. Senate, November 4, 1980; reelected to each succeeding Senate term.

Office Listings

http://grassley.senate.gov

135 Hart Senate Office Building, Washington, DC 20510 .... (202) 224–3744
Chief of Staff.—David Young. FAX: 224–6020
Director of Communications.—Jill Kozeny.
Legislative Director.—Kolan Davis.
721 Federal Building, 210 Walnut Street, Des Moines, IA 50309 .... (515) 288–1145
State Administrator.—Robert Renaud.
150 1st Avenue, NE., Suite 325, Cedar Rapids, IA 52401 .... (319) 363–6832
120 Federal Courthouse Building, 320 Sixth Street, Sioux City, IA 51101 .... (712) 233–1860
210 Waterloo Building, 531 Commercial Street, Waterloo, IA 50701 .... (319) 232–6657
131 West Third Street, Suite 180, Davenport, IA 52801 .... (563) 322–4331
307 Federal Building, 8 South Sixth Street, Council Bluffs, IA 51501 .... (712) 322–7103

* * *

TOM HARKIN, Democrat, of Cumming, IA; born in Cumming, November 19, 1939; education: graduated, Dowling Catholic High School, Des Moines, IA; B.S., Iowa State University, Ames, 1962; U.S. Navy, 1962–67; military service: LCDR, U.S. Naval Reserves; LL.B., Catholic University of America, Washington, DC, 1972; admitted to the bar, Des Moines, IA, 1972; married: the former Ruth Raduenz, 1968; children: Amy and Jenny; committees: chair, Health, Education, Labor, and Pensions; Agriculture, Nutrition, and Forestry; Appropriations; Small Business and Entrepreneurship; elected to the 94th Congress on November 5, 1974; reelected to four succeeding Congresses; elected to the U.S. Senate on November 6, 1984; reelected to each succeeding Senate term.

Office Listings

http://harkin.senate.gov

731 Hart Senate Office Building, Washington, DC 20510 .... (202) 224–3254
Chief of Staff.—Brian Ahlberg. FAX: 224–9369
Communications Director.—Kate Cyrul.
Federal Building, 210 Walnut Street, Room 733, Des Moines, IA 50309 .... (515) 284–4574
150 First Avenue, NE., Suite 370, Cedar Rapids, IA 52401 .... (319) 365–4504
1606 Brady Street, Suite 323, Davenport, IA 52801 .... (563) 322–1338
Federal Building, 320 Sixth Street, Room 110, Sioux City, IA 51101 .... (712) 252–1550
Federal Building, 350 West Sixth Street, Room 315, Dubuque, IA 52001 .... (563) 582–2130

REPRESENTATIVES

FIRST DISTRICT

BRUCE L. BRALEY, Democrat, of Waterloo, IA; born in Grinnell, IA, October 30, 1957; education: B.A., Iowa State University, Ames, IA, 1980; J.D., University of Iowa Law School, Iowa City, IA, 1983; professional: attorney, Dulton, Braun, Staack & Hellman, 1983–2006; married: Carolyn; children: Lisa, David and Paul; chair, Populist Caucus; committees: Oversight and Government Reform; Veterans' Affairs; elected to the 110th Congress on November 7, 2006; reelected to each succeeding Congress.

Office Listings

http://www.house.gov/braley

1727 Longworth House Office Building, Washington, DC 20515 .... (202) 225–2911
Chief of Staff.—John Davis. FAX: 225–6666
219 East Fourth Street, Waterloo, IA 50703 .... (319) 287–3233
1050 Main Street, Dubuque, IA 52001 .... (563) 557–7789
Deputy District Director.—John Murphy.
209 West Fourth Street, Suite 104, Davenport, IA 52801 .... (563) 323–5988
District Director.—Pete DeKock.

Counties: BLACK HAWK, BREMER, BUCHANAN, BUTLER, CLAYTON, CLINTON, DELAWARE, DUBUQUE, FAYETTE, JACKSON, JONES, SCOTT. Population (2000), 585,302.

ZIP Codes: 50601–02, 50604–08, 50611, 50613–14, 50619, 50622–23, 50625–26, 50629, 50631, 50634, 50636, 50641, 50643–44, 50647–51, 50654–55, 50660, 50662, 50664–68, 50670–71, 50674, 50676–77, 50681–82, 50701–04, 50706–07, 50799, 52001–04, 52030–33, 52035–50, 52052–54, 52056–57, 52060, 52064–66, 52068–79, 52099, 52135, 52141–42, 52147, 52156–59, 52164, 52166, 52169, 52171, 52175, 52205, 52207, 52210, 52212, 52223, 52226, 52237, 52252, 52254, 52305, 52309–10, 52312, 52320–21, 52323, 52326, 52329–30, 52362, 52701, 52722, 52726–33, 52736, 52742, 52745–48, 52750–51, 52753, 52756–58, 52765, 52767–68, 52771, 52773–74, 52777, 52801–09

* * *

SECOND DISTRICT

DAVID LOEBSACK, Democrat, of Mt. Vernon, IA; born in Sioux City, IA, December 23, 1952; education: graduated, East High School, 1970; B.A., Iowa State University, 1974; M.A., Iowa State University, 1976; Ph.D., political science, University of California, Davis, 1985; professional: professor, political science, Cornell College, 1982–2006; married: Teresa Loebsack; four children; committees: Armed Services; Education and the Workforce; elected to the 110th Congress on November 7, 2006; reelected to each succeeding Congress.

Office Listings

http://www.loebsack.house.gov

1527 Longworth House Office Building, Washington, DC 20515 .... (202) 225–6576
Chief of Staff.—Eric Witte.
Office Manager / Scheduler.—Heidi Hotopp.
150 First Avenue, NE., Suite 375, Cedar Rapids, IA 52401 .... (319) 364–2288
District Director.—Rob Sueppel. FAX: 226–0757
125 South Dubuque Street, Iowa City, IA 52240–4003 .... (319) 351–0789

Counties: APPANOOSE, CEDAR, DAVIS, DES MOINES, HENRY, JEFFERSON, JOHNSON, LEE, LINN, LOUISA, MUSCATINE, VAN BUREN, WAPELLO, WASHINGTON, WAYNE. Population (2000), 585,241.

ZIP Codes: 50008, 50052, 50060, 50123, 50147, 50165, 50238, 52201–02, 52213–14, 52216, 52218–19, 52227–28, 52233, 52235, 52240–48, 52253, 52255, 52302, 52305–06, 52314, 52317, 52319–20, 52322–24, 52327–28, 52333, 52336–38, 52340–41, 52344, 52350, 52352–53, 52356, 52358–59, 52401–11, 52497–99, 52501, 52530–31, 52533, 52535–38, 52540, 52542, 52544, 52548–49, 52551, 52553–57, 52560, 52565–67, 52570–74, 52580–81, 52583–84, 52588, 52590, 52593–94, 52601, 52619–21, 52623–27, 52630–32, 52635, 52637–42, 52644–56, 52658–60, 52720–21, 52731, 52737–39, 52747, 52749, 52752, 52754–55, 52759–61, 52766, 52769, 52772, 52776, 52778

* * *

THIRD DISTRICT

LEONARD L. BOSWELL, Democrat, of Des Moines, IA; born in Harrison County, MO, January 10, 1934; education: graduated, Lamoni High School, 1952; B.A., Graceland College, Lamoni, IA, 1969; military service: lieutenant colonel, U.S. Army, 1956–76; awards: two Distinguished Flying Crosses, two Bronze Stars, Soldier's Medal; Iowa State Senate, 1984–96; Iowa State Senate President, 1992–96; lay minister, RLDS Church; member: American Legion, Disabled American Veterans of Foreign Wars, Iowa Farm Bureau, Iowa Cattlemen's Association, Graceland College Board of Trustees; Farmer's Co-op Grain and Seed Board of Directors, 1979–93 (president for 13 years); The Coalition (Blue Dogs); co-chair and member emeritus, Mississippi River Caucus; co-chair, Methamphetamine Caucus; married: Darlene (Dody) Votava Boswell, 1955; children: Cindy, Diana, and Joe; committees: Agriculture; Transportation and Infrastructure; elected to the 105th Congress; reelected to each succeeding Congress.

Office Listings

http://boswell.house.gov

1026 Longworth House Office Building, Washington, DC 20515 .... (202) 225–3806
Chief of Staff.—Sandy Carter. FAX: 225–5608
Deputy Chief of Staff.—Ross Maradian.
Executive Assistant.—Sandy Carter.
300 East Locust Street, Suite 320, Des Moines, IA 50309 .... (515) 282–1909
Chief of Staff.—Julie Stauch.

Counties: BENTON, GRUNDY, IOWA, JASPER, KEOKUK, LUCAS, MAHASKA, MARION, MONROE, POLK, POWESHIEK, TAMA. Population (2000), 585,305.

ZIP Codes: 50007, 50009, 50015, 50021, 50027–28, 50032, 50035, 50044, 50047, 50049, 50054, 50057, 50061–62, 50068, 50073, 50104, 50109, 50111–12, 50116, 50119, 50127, 50131, 50135–39, 50143, 50148, 50150–51, 50153, 50156–58, 50163, 50168–71, 50173, 50206–08, 50214, 50219, 50222, 50225–26, 50228, 50232, 50237–38, 50240, 50242–43, 50251–52, 50255–58, 50265–66, 50268, 50272, 50301–23, 50325, 50327–36, 50338–40, 50347, 50350, 50359–64, 50367–69, 50380–81, 50391–96, 50398, 50601, 50604, 50609, 50612–13, 50621, 50624, 50627, 50632, 50635, 50638, 50642–43, 50651–52, 50657, 50660, 50665, 50669, 50672–73, 50675, 50680, 50936, 50940, 50947, 50950, 50980–81, 52203–04, 52206, 52208–09, 52211, 52213, 52215, 52217, 52220–22, 52224–25, 52228–29, 52231–32, 52236, 52248–49, 52251, 52257, 52301, 52307–08, 52313, 52315–16, 52318, 52322, 52324–25, 52332, 52334–35, 52339, 52342, 52345–49, 52351, 52354–55, 52361, 52404, 52531, 52534, 52543, 52550, 52552, 52561–63, 52568–69, 52576–77, 52585–86, 52591, 52595

* * *

FOURTH DISTRICT

TOM LATHAM, Republican, of Ames, IA; born in Hampton, IA, July 14, 1948; education: attended Alexander Community School; graduated Cal (Latimer) Community College, 1966; attended Wartburg College, 1966–67; Iowa State University, 1967–70; agriculture business major; professional: marketing representative, independent insurance agent, bank teller and bookkeeper; member and past president, Nazareth Lutheran Church; past chairman, Franklin County Extension Council; secretary, Republican Party of Iowa; 5th District representative, Republican State Central Committee; co-chairman, Franklin County Republican Central Committee; Iowa delegation whip; member: 1992 Republican National Convention, Iowa Farm Bureau Federation, Iowa Soybean Association, American Seed Trade Association, Iowa Corn Growers Association, Iowa Seed Association, Agribusiness Association of Iowa, I.S.U. Extension Citizens Advisory Council; married: Mary Katherine (Kathy), 1975; children: Justin, Jennifer, and Jill; committees: Appropriations; elected to the 104th Congress; reelected to each succeeding Congress.

Office Listings

http://www.house.gov/latham

2217 Rayburn House Office Building, Washington, DC 20515 .... (202) 225–5476
Chief of Staff.—James Carstensen. FAX: 225–3301
Press Secretary.—Fred Love.
Scheduler.—Amanda McDonnell.
1421 South Bell Avenue, Ames, IA 50010 .... (515) 232–2885
District Director.—Clarke Scanlon.
812 Highway 18 East, P.O. Box 532, Clear Lake, IA 50428 .... (641) 357–5225
Regional Representative.—Ben Hammes.
1426 Central Avenue, Suite A, Fort Dodge, IA 50501 .... (515) 573–2738
Regional Representative.—Jim Oberhelman.

Counties: ALLAMAKEE, BOONE, CALHOUN, CERRO GORDO, CHICKASAW, DALLAS, EMMET, FLOYD, FRANKLIN, GREENE, HAMILTON, HANCOCK, HARDIN, HOWARD, HUMBOLDT, KOSSUTH, MADISON, MARSHALL, MITCHELL, PALO ALTO, POCAHONTAS, STORY, WARREN, WEBSTER, WINNEBAGO, WINNESHIEK, WORTH, WRIGHT. Population (2000), 585,305.

ZIP Codes: 50001, 50003, 50005–06, 50010–14, 50028, 50031, 50033–34, 50036–41, 50046–47, 50050–51, 50055–56, 50058–59, 50061, 50063–64, 50066, 50069–72, 50075, 50078, 50101–02, 50105–07, 50109, 50118, 50120, 50122, 50124–26, 50129–30, 50132, 50134, 50139, 50141–42, 50145–46, 50148–49, 50151–52, 50154–56, 50158, 50160–62, 50166–67, 50201, 50206, 50210–13, 50217–18, 50220, 50222–23, 50225, 50227, 50229–31, 50233–36, 50239–41, 50244, 50246–49, 50252, 50257–59, 50261, 50263, 50266, 50269, 50271, 50273, 50276, 50278, 50320, 50323, 50325, 50401–02, 50420–21, 50423–24, 50426–28, 50430–36, 50438–41, 50444, 50446–61, 50464–73, 50475–84, 50501, 50510–11, 50514–33, 50536, 50538–46, 50548, 50551–52, 50554, 50556–63, 50566, 50568–71, 50573–75, 50577–79, 50581–83, 50586, 50590–91, 50593–95, 50597–99, 50601, 50603, 50605, 50609, 50616, 50619–21, 50625, 50627–28, 50630, 50632–33, 50635–36, 50645, 50653, 50658–59, 50661, 50672, 50674, 50680, 51334, 51342, 51344, 51358, 51364–65, 51433, 51443, 51449, 51453, 51462, 51510, 52101, 52132–34, 52136, 52140, 52144, 52146, 52149, 52151, 52154–56, 52159–63, 52165, 52168, 52170–72

* * *

FIFTH DISTRICT

STEVE KING, Republican, of Odebolt, IA; born in Storm Lake, IA, May 28, 1949; education: graduated, Denison Community High School; attended Northwest Missouri State University, Maryville, MO, 1967–70; professional: agri-businessman; owner and operator of King Construction Company; public service: Iowa State Senate, 1996–2002; religion: Catholic; family: married to Marilyn; children: David, Michael, and Jeff; committees: Agriculture; Judiciary; Small Business; elected to the 108th Congress on November 5, 2002; reelected to each succeeding Congress.

Office Listings

http://www.steveking.house.gov

1131 Longworth House Office Building, Washington, DC 20515 .... (202) 225–4426
Chief of Staff.—Bentley Graves. FAX: 225–3193
Legislative Director.—Casaday Nguyen.
Scheduler / Executive Assistant.—Leah Scott.
Communications Director.—John Kennedy.
Press Secretary.—Eden Gordon.
526 Nebraska Street, Sioux City, IA 51101 .... (712) 224–4692
40 Pearl Street, Council Bluffs, IA 51503 .... (712) 325–1404
208 West Taylor Street, Creston, IA 50801 .... (641) 782–2495
306 North Grand Avenue, Spencer, IA 51301 .... (712) 580–7754
800 Oneida Street, Suite A, Storm Lake, IA 50588 .... (712) 732–4197

Counties: ADAIR, ADAMS, AUDUBON, BUENA VISTA, CARROLL, CASS, CHEROKEE, CLARKE, CLAY, CRAWFORD, DECATUR, DICKINSON, FREMONT, GUTHRIE, HARRISON, IDA, LYON, MILLS, MONONA, MONTGOMERY, O'BRIEN, OSCEOLA, PAGE, PLYMOUTH, POTTAWATTAMIE, RINGGOLD, SAC, SHELBY, SIOUX, TAYLOR, UNION, WOODBURY. Population (2000), 584,967.

ZIP Codes: 50002, 50020, 50022, 50025–26, 50029, 50042, 50048, 50058, 50065, 50067, 50070, 50074, 50076, 50103, 50108, 50110, 50115, 50117, 50119, 50123, 50128, 50133, 50140, 50144, 50146, 50149, 50151, 50155, 50164, 50174, 50210, 50213, 50216, 50222, 50233, 50250, 50254, 50257, 50262, 50264, 50273–77, 50510, 50535, 50565, 50567–68, 50576, 50583, 50585, 50588, 50592, 50801, 50830–31, 50833, 50835–37, 50839–43, 50845–49, 50851, 50853–54, 50857–64, 51001–12, 51014–16, 51018–20, 51022–31, 51033–41, 51044–56, 51058–63, 51101–06, 51108–09, 51111, 51201, 51230–32, 51234–35, 51237–50, 51301, 51331, 51333, 51338, 51340–41, 51343, 51345–47, 51350–51, 51354–55, 51357, 51360, 51363–64, 51366, 51401, 51430–33, 51436, 51439–52, 51454–55, 51458–61, 51463, 51465–67, 51501–03, 51510, 51520–21, 51523, 51525–37, 51540–46, 51548–49, 51551–66, 51570–73, 51575–79, 51591, 51593, 51601–03, 51630–32, 51636–40, 51645–54, 51656

KANSAS

(Population 2010, 2,853,118)

SENATORS

PAT ROBERTS, Republican, of Dodge City, KS; born in Topeka, KS, April 20, 1936; education: graduated, Holton High School, Holton, KS, 1954; B.S., journalism, Kansas State University, Manhattan, KS, 1958; professional: captain, U.S. Marine Corps, 1958–62; editor and reporter, Arizona newspapers, 1962–67; aide to Senator Frank Carlson, 1967–68; aide to Representative Keith Sebelius, 1969–80; U.S. House of Representatives, 1980–96; founding member: bipartisan Caucus on Unfunded Mandates, House Rural Health Care Coalition; shepherded the 1996 Freedom to Farm Act through the House and Senate; awards: honorary American Farmer, Future Farmers of America; 1993 Wheat Man of the Year, Kansas Association of Wheat Growers; Golden Carrot Award, Public Voice; Golden Bulldog Award, Watchdogs of the Treasury; numerous Guardian of Small Business awards, National Federation of Independent Business; 1995 Dwight D. Eisenhower Medal, Eisenhower Exchange Fellowship; 2001 U.S. Marine Corps Semper Fidelis Award; married: the former Franki Fann, 1969; children: David, Ashleigh, and Anne-Wesley; committees: ranking member, Agriculture, Nutrition, and Forestry; Finance; Health, Education, Labor, and Pensions; Rules and Administration; Select Committee on Ethics; elected to the U.S. Senate in November, 1996; reelected to each succeeding Senate term.

Office Listings

http://roberts.senate.gov

109 Hart Senate Office Building, Washington, DC 20510 .... (202) 224–4774
    Chief of Staff.—Jackie Cottrell. FAX: 224–3514
    Legislative Director.—Amber Sechrist.
    Scheduler.—Jensine Moyer.
    Communications Director.—Sarah Little.
100 Military Plaza, P.O. Box 550, Dodge City, KS 67801 .... (620) 227–2244
    District Director.—Debbie Pugh.
155 North Market Street, Suite 120, Wichita, KS 67202 .... (316) 263–0416
    District Director.—Karin Wisdom.
Frank Carlson Federal Building, 444 SE Quincy, Room 392, Topeka, KS 66683 .... (785) 295–2745
    District Director.—Gilda Lintz.
11900 College Boulevard, Suite 203, Overland Park, KS 66210 .... (913) 451–9343
    State Director.—Chad Tenpenny.

* * *

JERRY MORAN, Republican, of Hays, Kansas; born in Plainville, Kansas, May 29, 1954; education: B.S., University of Kansas, Lawrence, KS, 1976; J.D., University of Kansas School of Law, Lawrence, KS, 1981; M.B.A., candidate, Fort Hays State University, Hays, KS; professional: bank officer; instructor; U.S. House of Representatives, 1997–2010; Kansas State Senate, 1989–97, serving as vice president, 1993–95, majority leader, 1995–97; Kansas State Special Assistant Attorney General, 1982–85; deputy attorney, Rooks County, KS, 1987–95; University of Kansas School of Law Board of Governors, served as vice president, 1993–94, president, 1994–95; Board of Directors, Kansas Chamber of Commerce and Industry, 1996–97; religion: Christian; family: married Robba; two daughters, Kelsey and Alex; caucuses: The Senate Hunger Caucus, The Senate Western Caucus, Senate Rural Health Caucus, co-chair of Community Pharmacy Caucus; committees: Appropriations; Banking, Housing, and Urban Affairs; Homeland Security and Governmental Affairs; Veterans' Affairs; Small Business and Entrepreneurship; Special Committee on Aging; elected to the U.S. Senate on November 2, 2010.

Office Listings

http://moran.senate.gov

354 Russell Senate Office Building, Washington, DC 20510 .... (202) 224–6521
    Chief of Staff.—Todd Novascone. FAX: 228–6966
    Legislative Director.—Alex Richard.
    Scheduler.—Emily Whitfield.
    Communications Director.—Garrette Silverman.
1200 Main Street, Suite 402, Hays, KS 67601 .... (785) 628–6401
    State Casework Director.—Rachel Robben.
    Constituent Services Representative.—Chelsey Gillogly.
23600 College Boulevard, Suite 201, Olathe, KS 66061 .... (913) 393–0711
    Kansas State Scheduler.—Lisa Dethloff.
800 Southwest Jackson, Suite 1108, Topeka, KS 66612 .... (785) 232–2605

State Director / Deputy Chief of Staff.—Riley Scott.
3450 North Rock Road, Building 200, Suite 209, Wichita, KS 67226 .... (316) 631–1410
Deputy State Director.—Mike Zamrzia.

REPRESENTATIVES

FIRST DISTRICT

TIM HUELSKAMP, Republican, of Fowler, KS; born in Fowler, November 11, 1968; education: attended seminary of Santa Fe, NM; B.S., social science, College of Santa Fe, Santa Fe, NM, 1991; Ph.D., political science, American University of Washington, DC, 1995; professional: farmer; rancher; budget and legislative analyst for the State of New Mexico; served in the Kansas State Senate, 1996–2010; married: Angela Huelskamp; children: Natasha, Rebecca, Athan, and Alexander; committees: Agriculture; Budget; Veterans' Affairs; elected to the 112th Congress on November 2, 2010.

Office Listings

http://huelskamp.house.gov

126 Cannon House Office Building, Washington, DC 20515 .... (202) 225–2715
Chief of Staff.—Jim Pfaff. FAX: 225–5124
Legislative Director.—Mark Kelly.
Press Secretary.—Karen Steward.
Office Manager—Nichole Kotschwar.
100 Military Avenue, Suite 204, Dodge City, KS 67801–0249 .... (620) 225–0172
1 North Main, Suite 525, P.O. Box 1128, Hutchinson, KS 67504–1128 .... (620) 665–6138
119 West Iron Avenue, Suite 403, P.O. Box 766, Salina, KS 67401 .... (785) 309–0572

Counties: BARBER, BARTON, CHASE, CHEYENNE, CLARK, CLAY, CLOUD, COMANCHE, DECATUR, DICKINSON, EDWARDS, ELLIS, ELLSWORTH, FINNEY, FORD, GEARY (part), GOVE, GRAHAM, GRANT, GRAY, GREELEY, GREENWOOD (part), HAMILTON, HASKELL, HODGEMAN, JEWELL, KEARNY, KIOWA, LANE, LINCOLN, LOGAN, LYON, MCPHERSON, MARION (part), MARSHALL, MEADE, MITCHELL, MORRIS, MORTON, NEMAHA (part), NESS, NORTON, OSBORNE, OTTAWA, PAWNEE, PHILLIPS, PRATT, RAWLINS, RENO, REPUBLIC, RICE, ROOKS, RUSH, RUSSELL, SALINE, SCOTT, SEWARD, SHERIDAN, SHERMAN, SMITH, STAFFORD, STANTON, STEVENS, THOMAS, TREGO, WABAUNSEE, WALLACE, WASHINGTON, WICHITA. Population (2000), 672,105.

ZIP Codes: 66401, 66403–04, 66406–08, 66411–13, 66423, 66427, 66431, 66438, 66441, 66501–02, 66507–08, 66514, 66518, 66523, 66526, 66534, 66536, 66538, 66541, 66544, 66547–48, 66610, 66614–15, 66801, 66830, 66833–35, 66838, 66840, 66843, 66845–46, 66849–51, 66853–54, 66858–62, 66864–66, 66868–70, 66872–73, 66901, 66930, 66932–33, 66935–46, 66948–49, 66951–53, 66955–56, 66958–64, 66966–68, 66970, 67009, 67020–21, 67028–29, 67035, 67053–54, 67057, 67059, 67061–63, 67065–66, 67068, 67070, 67073, 67104, 67107–09, 67112, 67114, 67124, 67127, 67134, 67138, 67143, 67151, 67155, 67335, 67401–02, 67410, 67416–18, 67420, 67422–23, 67425, 67427–28, 67430–32, 67436–39, 67441–52, 67454–60, 67464, 67466–68, 67470, 67473–76, 67478, 67480–85, 67487, 67490–92, 67501–02, 67504–05, 67510–16, 67518–26, 67529–30, 67543–48, 67550, 67552–54, 67556–57, 67559–61, 67563–68, 67570, 67572–76, 67578–79, 67581, 67583–85, 67601, 67621–23, 67625–29, 67631–32, 67634–35, 67637–40, 67642–51, 67653–61, 67663–65, 67667, 67669, 67671–75, 67701, 67730–41, 67743–45, 67748–49, 67751–53, 67756–58, 67761–62, 67764, 67801, 67831, 67834–42, 67844, 67846, 67849–51, 67853–55, 67857, 67859–65, 67867, 67869–71, 67876–80, 67882, 67901, 67905, 67950–54

* * *

SECOND DISTRICT

LYNN JENKINS, Republican, of Topeka, KS; born in Topeka, KS, June 10, 1963; education: A.A., Kansas State University, Manhattan, KS, 1985; B.S., accounting / economics, Weber State College, Ogden, UT, 1985; professional: certified public accountant; accountant, Braunsdorf, Carson, and Clinkinbeard; accountant, Baird, Kurtz and Dobson; certified public accountant, Public Accounting / Specialty Taxation, 1985–present; Representative, Kansas State House of Representatives, 1999–2000; Senator, Kansas State Senate, 2001–02; Treasurer, State of Kansas, 2003–08; children: Hayley and Hayden; Community Pharmacy Caucus; House Army Caucus; Military Veterans Caucus; Nuclear Issues Working Group; Cystic Fibrosis Caucus; committees: Ways and Means; elected to the 111th Congress on November 4, 2008; reelected to the 112th Congress.

Office Listings

http://lynnjenkins.house.gov

1122 Longworth House Office Building, Washington, DC 20515 .... (202) 225–6601
Chief of Staff.—Pat Leopold. FAX: 225–7986
Legislative Director.—Eric Schmutz.
Scheduler.—Kathy Calderon.
Press Aide.—Sean Fitzpatrick.
510 Southwest 10th Avenue, Topeka, KS 66612 .... (785) 234–5966

1001 North Broadway, Suite C, Pittsburgh, KS 66762 .... (620) 231–5966

Counties: ALLEN, ANDERSON, ATCHISON, BOURBON, BROWN, CHEROKEE, COFFEY, CRAWFORD, DONIPHAN, DOUGLAS (part), FRANKLIN, GEARY, JACKSON, JEFFERSON, LABETE, LEAVENWORTH, LINN, MIAMI, NEMAHA (part), NEOSHO, OSAGE, POTTAWATOMIE, RILEY, SHAWNEE, WILSON, WOODSON. Population (2000), 672,102.

ZIP Codes: 66002, 66006–08, 66010, 66012–17, 66020–21, 66023–27, 66032–33, 66035–36, 66039–50, 66052–54, 66056, 66058, 66060, 66064, 66066–67, 66070–73, 66075–80, 66083, 66086–88, 66090–91, 66093–95, 66097, 66109, 66112, 66401–04, 66407, 66409, 66413–20, 66422, 66424–29, 66431–32, 66434, 66436, 66439–40, 66442, 66449, 66451, 66502–03, 66505–06, 66509–10, 66512, 66515–17, 66520–24, 66527–28, 66531–40, 66542–44, 66546–50, 66552, 66554, 66601, 66603–12, 66614–22, 66624–26, 66628–29, 66636–37, 66642, 66647, 66652–53, 66667, 66675, 66683, 66692, 66699, 66701, 66710–14, 66716–17, 66720, 66724–25, 66728, 66732–36, 66738–43, 66746, 66748–49, 66751, 66753–63, 66767, 66769–73, 66775–83, 66834, 66839, 66849, 66852, 66854, 66856–57, 66864, 66868, 66870–71, 66933, 67047, 67330, 67332, 67335–37, 67341–42, 67351, 67354, 67356–57

* * *

THIRD DISTRICT

KEVIN YODER, Republican, of Overland Park; born in Hutchison, KS, January 8, 1976; education: B.A., University of Kansas, Lawrence, KS, 1999; J.D., University of Kansas College of Law, Lawrence, KS, 2002; professional: attorney; admitted to the Kansas Bar, 2002; State Representative, Kansas House of Representatives, 20th District; 2003–11; chairman, House Appropriations Committee; chairman, General Government Budget Committee; serves on the Board of Directors of the Johnson County Bar Association; married: Brooke Robinson Yoder; members: member of the Kansas Sentencing Commission; Kansas City Chamber's Congressional Forum; Overland Park Rotary Club; Johnson County Bar Association; Greater Kansas City Area University of Kansas Alumni Association Board of Directors; Overland Park Republican Precinct Committeeman; committees: Appropriations; elected to the 112th Congress on November 2, 2010.

Office Listings

http://www.yoder.house.gov

214 Cannon House Office Building, Washington, DC 20515 .... (202) 225–2865
Chief of Staff.—Travis Smith. FAX: 225–2807
Scheduler.—Cate Stark.
Communications Director.—Alissa McCurley.
500 State Avenue, Room 176, Kansas City, KS 66101 .... (913) 621–0832
District Director.—Molly Haase.
Constituent Services Director.—Cheyne Worley.

Counties: DOUGLAS (part), JOHNSON, WYANDOTTE. Population (2000), 672,124.

ZIP Codes: 66006–07, 66012–13, 66018–19, 66026, 66030–31, 66035–36, 66044–47, 66049–51, 66053, 66061–64, 66071, 66077, 66083, 66085, 66092, 66101–06, 66109–13, 66115, 66117–19, 66160, 66201–27, 66250–51, 66276, 66282–83, 66285–86

* * *

FOURTH DISTRICT

MIKE POMPEO, Republican, of Wichita, KS; born in Orange, CA, December 30, 1963; education: B.S., mechanical engineering, United States Military Academy at West Point, NY, 1986, graduated first in his class; J.D., Harvard Law School, Cambridge, MA, 1994; professional: owned/founder, Thayer Aerospace; president, Sentry International; editor of Harvard Law Review; religion: Presbyterian; married: Susan Pompeo of Wichita, KS; children: Nick; caucus: Republican Study Committee; committees: Energy and Commerce; elected to the 112th Congress on November 2, 2010.

Office Listings

http://www.pompeo.house.gov

107 Cannon House Office Building, Washington, DC 20515 .... (202) 225–6216
Chief of Staff.—Mark Chenoweth. FAX: 225–3489
Legislative Director.—Jim Richardson.
Legislative Assistants: Keith Dater, Chris Parinello.
Legislative Aide.—Caitlin Poling.
Communications Director.—Rachel Bauer Taylor.
Scheduler/Office Manager.—Lauren O'Reilly.
Staff Assistant.—Paige Sutherland.
7701 East Kellogg, Suite 510, Wichita, KS 67207 .... (316) 262–8992

District Director.—Lea Stueve.

Counties: BUTLER, CHAUTAUQUA, COWLEY, ELK, GRENWOOD (part), HARPER, HARVEY, KINGMAN, MONTGOMERY, SEDGWICK, SUMNER. Population (2010), 720,192.

ZIP Codes: 66840, 66842, 66853, 66863, 66866, 66870, 67001–05, 67008–10, 67012–13, 67016–20, 67022–26, 67030–31, 67035–39, 67041–42, 67045, 67047, 67049–52, 67055–56, 67058, 67060–62, 67067–68, 67070, 67072, 67074, 67101, 67103, 67105–08, 67110–12, 67114, 67117–20, 67122–23, 67131–33, 67135, 67137–38, 67140, 67142, 67144, 67146–47, 67149–52, 67154, 67156, 67159, 67201–21, 67226, 67230, 67235, 67260, 67275–78, 67301, 67333–35, 67337, 67340, 67344–47, 67349, 67351–53, 67355, 67360–61, 67363–64, 67522, 67543

KENTUCKY

(Population 2010, 4,339,367)

SENATORS

MITCH McCONNELL, Republican, of Louisville, KY; born in Colbert County, AL, February 20, 1942; education: graduated Manual High School, Louisville, 1960, president of the student body; B.A. with honors, University of Louisville, 1964, president of the student council, president of the student body of the College of Arts and Sciences; J.D., University of Kentucky Law School, 1967, president of student bar association, outstanding oral advocate; professional: attorney, admitted to the Kentucky bar, 1967; chief legislative assistant to U.S. Senator Marlow Cook, 1968–70; Deputy Assistant U.S. Attorney General, 1974–75; Judge/Executive of Jefferson County, KY, 1978–84; chairman, National Republican Senatorial Committee, 1997–2000; chairman, Joint Congressional Committee on Inaugural Ceremonies, 1999–2001; Senate Majority Whip, 2002–06; Senate Republican Leader, 2007–present; married to Elaine Chao on February 6, 1993; children: Elly, Claire and Porter; committees: Agriculture, Nutrition, and Forestry; Appropriations; Rules and Administration; elected to the U.S. Senate on November 6, 1984; reelected to each succeeding Senate term.

Office Listings

http://mcconnell.senate.gov

317 Russell Senate Office Building, Washington, DC 20510 .... (202) 224–2541
Chief of Staff.—Josh Holmes. FAX: 224–2499
Scheduler.—Stefanie Hagar.
Legislative Director.—Reb Brownell.
Press Secretary.—Robert Steurer.
601 West Broadway, Suite 630, Louisville, KY 40202 .... (502) 582–6304
State Director.—Terry Carmack.
1885 Dixie Highway, Suite 345, Fort Wright, KY 41011 .... (606) 578–0188
300 South Main Street, Suite 310, London, KY 40741 .... (606) 864–2026
Professional Arts Building, Suite 100, 2320 Broadway, Paducah, KY 42001 .... (270) 442–4554
771 Corporate Drive, Suite 108, Lexington, KY 40503 .... (606) 224–8286
Federal Building, Room 102, 241 Main Street, Bowling Green, KY 42101 .... (270) 781–1673

* * *

RAND PAUL, Republican, of Bowling Green, KY; born in Pittsburgh, PA, January 7, 1963; education: undergraduate, Baylor University, Waco, Texas, 1981–84; M.D., Duke University School of Medicine, 1988; religion: Presbyterian; family: married to the former Kelley Ashby; three sons, William, Duncan, and Robert; committees: Energy and Natural Resources; Health, Education, Labor, and Pensions; Homeland Security and Government Affairs; Small Business and Entrepreneurship; elected to the U.S. Senate on November 2, 2010.

Office Listings

http://paul.senate.gov

208 Russell Senate Office Building, Washington, DC 20510 .... (202) 224–4343
Chief of Staff.—Doug Stafford. FAX: 228–6917
Deputy Chief of Staff / Legislative Director.—William Henderson.
Communications Director.—Moira Bagley.
Scheduler.—Jessica Jelgerhuis.
600 Dr. Martin Luther King, Jr. Place, Suite 1072B, Louisville, KY 40202 .... (502) 582–5341
State Director.—Jim Milliman.
1029 State Street, Bowling Green, KY 42101 .... (270) 782–8303
1100 South Main Street, Suite 12, Hopkinsville, KY 42240 .... (270) 885–1212
423 Frederica Street, Room 305, Owensboro, KY 42301 .... (270) 689–9085
541 Buttermilk Pike, Suite 102, Crescent Springs, KY 41017 .... (859) 426–0165
601 Mail Street, Suite 2, Hazard, KY 41701 .... (606) 435–2390
771 Corporate Drive, Suite 105, Lexington, KY 40503 .... (859) 219–2269

REPRESENTATIVES

FIRST DISTRICT

ED WHITFIELD, Republican, of Hopkinsville, KY; born in Hopkinsville, May 25, 1943; education: graduated, Madisonville High School, Madisonville, KY; B.S., University of Kentucky, Lexington, 1965; J.D., University of Kentucky, 1969; attended American University's Wesley Theological Seminary, Washington, DC; military service: first lieutenant, U.S. Army Reserves, 1967–73; professional: attorney, private practice, 1970–79; vice president, CSX Corporation, 1979–90; admitted to bar: Kentucky, 1970, and Florida, 1993; began practice in 1970 in Hopkinsville, KY; member, Kentucky House, 1973, one term; married: Constance Harriman Whitfield; children: Kate; committees: Energy and Commerce; elected to the 104th Congress; reelected to each succeeding Congress.

Office Listings

http://www.whitfield.house.gov

2368 Rayburn House Office Building, Washington, DC 20515 .... (202) 225–3115
Chief of Staff.—John Sparkman. FAX: 225–3547
Scheduler / Office Manager.—Melissa Buchanan.
Legislative Director.—Cory Hicks.
1403 South Main Street, Hopkinsville, KY 42240 .... (270) 885–8079
District Director.—Michael Pape.
200 North Main, Suite F, Tompkinsville, KY 42167 .... (270) 487–9509
Field Representative.—Sandy Simpson.
222 First Street, Suite 224, Henderson, KY 42420 .... (270) 826–4180
Field Representative.—Ed West.
100 Fountain Avenue, Room 104, Paducah, KY 42001 .... (270) 442–6901
Field Representative.—Janece Everett.

Counties: ADAIR, ALLEN, BALLARD, BUTLER, CALDWELL, CALLOWAY, CARLISLE, CASEY, CHRISTIAN, CLINTON, CRITTENDEN, CUMBERLAND, FULTON, GRAVES, HENDERSON, HICKMAN, HOPKINS, LINCOLN (part), LIVINGSTON, LOGAN, LYON, MARSHALL, MCCRACKEN, MCLEAN, METCALF, MONROE, MUHLENBERG, OHIO (part), RUSSELL, SIMPSON, TODD, TRIGG, UNION, WEBSTER. Population (2000), 673,629.

ZIP Codes: 40009, 40328, 40437, 40442, 40448, 40464, 40484, 40489, 42001–03, 42020–25, 42027–29, 42031–33, 42035–41, 42044–45, 42047–51, 42053–56, 42058, 42060–61, 42063–64, 42066, 42069–71, 42076, 42078–79, 42081–88, 42101, 42104, 42120, 42122–24, 42129, 42133–35, 42140–41, 42150–51, 42153–54, 42164, 42166–67, 42170, 42201–04, 42206, 42209–211, 42214–17, 42219–21, 42223, 42232, 42234, 42236, 42240–41, 42251–52, 42254, 42256, 42261–62, 42265–67, 42273–74, 42276, 42280, 42283, 42286–88, 42301, 42320–28, 42330, 42332–34, 42337, 42339, 42344–45, 42347, 42349–50, 42352, 42354, 42356, 42367–69, 42371–72, 42374–76, 42402–04, 42406, 42408–11, 42413, 42419–20, 42431, 42436–37, 42440–42, 42444–45, 42450–53, 42455–64, 42516, 42528, 42539, 42541, 42544, 42565–67, 42602–03, 42629, 42642, 42711, 42715, 42717, 42720–21, 42728, 42731, 42733, 42735, 42740–43, 42746, 42749, 42753, 42759, 42786

* * *

SECOND DISTRICT

BRETT GUTHRIE, Republican, of Bowling Green, KY; born in Florence, AL, February 18, 1964; education: B.S., United States Military Academy, West Point, NY, 1987; M.P.M., Yale University, New Haven, CT, 1997; military service: U.S. Army, Field Artillery Office, 101st Airborne Division, 1987–90; professional: Vice President, Trace Die Cast, 1991–2009; member: Kentucky Senate, 1998–2009; married: Beth; children: Caroline, Robby, and Elizabeth; committees: Energy and Commerce; elected to the 111th Congress on November 4, 2008; reelected to the 112th Congress.

Office Listings

http://www.guthrie.house.gov

308 Cannon House Office Building, Washington, DC 20515 .... (202) 225–3501
Chief of Staff.—Eric Bergren.
Legislative Director.—Megan Spindel.
Communications Director.—Courtney Yopp Norris.
Scheduler.—Jennifer Beil.
1001 Center Street, Suite 300, Bowling Green, KY 42101 .... (270) 842–9896
District Director.—Mark Lord.

Counties: BARREN, BRECKINRIDGE, BULLITT, DAVIESS, EDMONSON, GRAYSON, GREEN, HANCOCK, HARDIN, HART, JEFFERSON (part), LARUE, MARION, MEADE, NELSON, OHIO (part), SHELBY, SPENCER, TAYLOR, WARREN, WASHINGTON. Population (2000), 673,244.

ZIP Codes: 40003–04, 40008–09, 40012–13, 40018–20, 40022–23, 40033, 40037, 40040, 40046–49, 40051–52, 40057, 40060–63, 40065–69, 40071, 40076, 40078, 40104, 40107–11, 40115, 40117–19, 40121, 40129, 40140, 40142–46, 40150, 40152–53, 40155, 40157, 40159–62, 40164–65, 40170–71, 40175–78, 40219, 40229, 40245, 40272, 40291, 40299, 40328, 40330, 40342, 40448, 40468, 40601, 42101–04, 42122–23, 42127–31, 42133, 42141–42, 42152, 42156–57, 42159–60, 42163, 42166, 42170–71, 42201, 42206–07, 42210, 42251, 42257, 42259, 42270, 42274–75, 42283, 42285, 42301–04, 42320, 42327, 42333–34, 42338, 42343, 42347–49, 42351–52, 42355–56, 42361, 42364, 42366, 42368, 42370, 42375–78, 42701–02, 42712–13, 42716, 42718–19, 42721–22, 42724, 42726, 42728–29, 42732–33, 42740, 42743, 42746, 42748–49, 42754–55, 42757–58, 42762, 42764–65, 42776, 42782–84, 42788

* * *

THIRD DISTRICT

JOHN A. YARMUTH, Democrat, of Louisville, KY; born in Louisville, November 4, 1947; education: graduated, Atherton High School, Louisville, 1965; graduated, Yale University, New Haven, CT, 1969; professional: Legislative Aide for Kentucky Senator Marlow Cook 1971–74; publisher, *Louisville Today Magazine*, 1976–82; Associate Vice President of University Relations at the University of Louisville, 1983–86; Vice President of a local healthcare firm 1986–90; founder, editor and writer *LEO Newsweekly*, 1990–2005; Television host and commentator, 2003–05; awards: 2007 Spirit of Enterprise Award; Louisville Alzheimer's Association Person of the Year; named Outstanding New Member of Congress by the Committee for Education and Funding; 16 Metro Louisville Journalism Awards for editorial and column writing; married: Cathy Yarmuth, 1981; child: Aaron; committees: Budget; Ethics; Oversight and Government Reform; elected to the 110th Congress on November 7, 2006; reelected to each succeeding Congress.

Office Listings

http://www.yarmuth.house.gov

435 Cannon House Office Building, Washington, DC 20515 .... (202) 225–5401
Chief of Staff.—Julie Carr. FAX: 225–5776
Legislative Director.—Ashley Bromagen.
Press Secretary.—Trey Pollard.
Scheduler.—Keidra King.
600 Martin Luther King, Jr. Place, Suite 216, Louisville, KY 40202 .... (502) 582–5129
District Director.—Carolyn Tandy.

Counties: JEFFERSON COUNTY. Population (2000), 674,032.

ZIP Codes: 40018, 40023, 40025, 40027, 40041, 40059, 40109, 40118, 40201–25, 40228–29, 40231–33, 40241–43, 40245, 40250–53, 40255–59, 40261, 40266, 40268–70, 40272, 40280–83, 40285, 40287, 40289–99

* * *

FOURTH DISTRICT

GEOFF DAVIS, Republican, of Hebron, KY; born October 26, 1958; education: attended public schools, West Pittsburgh, PA; B.S., U.S. Military Academy, West Point, NY, 1981; professional: U.S. Army, 1976–87; Assault Helicopter Flight Commander, 82nd Airborne Division; Army Ranger and Senior Parachutist; manufacturing consultant; founder, Republic Consulting, formerly known as Capstone, Incorporated, 1992–present; organizations: 82nd Airborne Association; American Legion volunteer chaplain; National Rifle Association; Northern Kentucky Chamber of Commerce; married: Pat; six children; committees: Ways and Means; elected to the 109th Congress on November 2, 2004; reelected to each succeeding Congress.

Office Listings

http://www.geoffdavis.house.gov

1119 Longworth House Office Building, Washington, DC 20515 .... (202) 225–3465
Chief of Staff.—Armstrong Robinson. FAX: 225–0003
Legislative Director.—Lauren O'Brien.
Scheduler / Office Manager.—Rebecca Hobbs.
Press Secretary.—Rick VanMeter.
300 Buttermilk Pike, Suite 101, KY 41017 .... (859) 426–0080
1405 Greenup Avenue, Suite 236, Ashland, KY 41101 .... (606) 324–9898
108 West Jefferson Street, La Grange, KY 40031 .... (502) 222–2233
201 Government Street, Suite 102, Maysville, KY 41056 .... (606) 564–6004
400 North Main Street, Suite 145, Williamstown, KY 41097 .... (859) 824–3320

Counties: BATH (part), BOONE, BOYD, BRACKEN, CAMPBELL, CARROLL, CARTER, ELLIOTT, FLEMING, GALLATIN, GRANT, GREENUP, HARRISON, HENRY, KENTON, LEWIS, MASON, NICHOLAS, OLDHAM, OWEN, PENDLETON, ROBERTSON, SCOTT (part), TRIMBLE. Population (2000), 673,588.

ZIP Codes: 40006–07, 40010–11, 40014, 40019, 40026, 40031–32, 40036, 40045, 40050, 40055–59, 40068, 40070, 40075, 40077, 40241, 40245, 40311, 40324, 40346, 40350–51, 40353, 40355, 40358–61, 40363, 40366, 40370–71, 40374, 40379, 40601, 41001–08, 41010–12, 41014–19, 41022, 41030–31, 41033–35, 41037, 41039–46, 41048–49, 41051–56, 41059, 41061–65, 41071–76, 41080–81, 41083, 41085–86, 41091–99, 41101–02, 41105, 41121, 41128–29, 41132, 41135, 41139, 41141–44, 41146, 41149, 41164, 41166, 41168–69, 41171, 41173–75, 41179–81, 41183, 41189, 41472, 45275, 45277, 45298, 45999

* * *

FIFTH DISTRICT

HAROLD ROGERS, Republican, of Somerset, KY; born in Barrier, KY, December 31, 1937; education: graduated, Wayne County High School, 1955; attended Western Kentucky University, 1956–57; A.B., University of Kentucky, 1962; LL.B., University of Kentucky Law School, 1964; professional: lawyer, admitted to the Kentucky State bar, 1964; commenced practice in Somerset; member, North Carolina and Kentucky National Guard, 1957–64; associate, Smith and Blackburn, 1964–67; private practice, 1967–69; Commonwealth Attorney, Pulaski and Rockcastle Counties, KY, 1969–80; delegate, Republican National Convention, 1972, 1976, 1980, 1984, and 1988; Republican nominee for Lieutenant Governor, KY, 1979; past president, Kentucky Commonwealth Attorneys Association; member and past president, Somerset-Pulaski County Chamber of Commerce and Pulaski County Industrial Foundation; founder, Southern Kentucky Economic Development Council, 1986; member, Chowder and Marching Society, 1981–present; member, Republican Steering Committee; married the former Shirley McDowell, 1957; three children: Anthony, Allison, and John Marshall; committees: chair, Appropriations; elected to the 97th Congress, November 4, 1980; reelected to each succeeding Congress.

Office Listings

http://halrogers.house.gov

2406 Rayburn House Office Building, Washington, DC 20515	(202) 225–4601
Chief of Staff.—Michael Higdon.	FAX: 225–0940
Office Manager.—Vacant.	
Communications Director.—Vacant.	
551 Clifty Street, Somerset, KY 42503	(606) 679–8346
District Administrator.—Robert L. Mitchell.	
601 Main Street, Hazard, KY 41701	(606) 439–0794
100 Resource Drive, Suite A, Prestonsburg, KY 41653	(606) 886–0844

Counties: BATH (part), BELL, BREATHITT, CLAY, FLOYD, HARLAN, JACKSON, JOHNSON, KNOTT, KNOX, LAUREL, LAWRENCE, LEE, LESLIE, LETCHER, MAGOFFIN, MARTIN, MCCREARY, MENIFEE, MORGAN, OWSLEY, PERRY, PIKE, PULASKI, ROCKCASTLE, ROWAN, WAYNE, WHITLEY, WOLFE. Population (2000), 673,670.

ZIP Codes: 40313, 40316–17, 40319, 40322, 40329, 40336–37, 40346, 40351, 40358, 40360, 40371, 40387, 40402–03, 40409, 40419, 40421, 40434, 40445, 40447, 40456, 40460, 40467, 40481, 40486, 40488, 40492, 40701–02, 40724, 40729–30, 40734, 40737, 40740–45, 40751, 40754–55, 40759, 40763, 40769, 40771, 40801, 40803, 40806–08, 40810, 40813, 40815–16, 40818–20, 40823–24, 40826–31, 40840, 40843–45, 40847, 40849, 40854–56, 40858, 40862–63, 40865, 40868, 40870, 40873–74, 40902–03, 40906, 40913–15, 40921, 40923, 40927, 40930, 40932, 40935, 40939–41, 40943–44, 40946, 40949, 40951, 40953, 40955, 40958, 40962, 40964–65, 40972, 40977, 40979, 40981–83, 40988, 40995, 40997, 40999, 41124, 41129, 41132, 41159–60, 41164, 41168, 41180, 41201, 41203–04, 41214, 41216, 41219, 41222, 41224, 41226, 41230–32, 41234, 41238, 41240, 41250, 41254–57, 41260, 41262–65, 41267–68, 41271, 41274, 41301, 41307, 41310–11, 41313–14, 41317, 41332–33, 41338–39, 41342, 41344, 41347–48, 41351–52, 41360, 41362, 41364–68, 41385–86, 41390, 41397, 41408, 41410, 41413, 41419, 41421–22, 41425–26, 41433, 41451, 41459, 41464–65, 41472, 41477, 41501–03, 41512–14, 41517, 41519–20, 41522, 41524, 41526–28, 41531, 41534–35, 41537–40, 41542–44, 41546–49, 41553–55, 41557–64, 41566–68, 41571–72, 41601–07, 41612, 41615–16, 41619, 41621–22, 41630–32, 41635–36, 41640, 41642–43, 41645, 41647, 41649–51, 41653, 41655, 41659–60, 41663, 41666–67, 41669, 41701–02, 41712–14, 41719, 41721–23, 41725, 41727, 41729, 41731, 41735–36, 41739–40, 41743, 41745–47, 41749, 41751, 41754, 41759–60, 41762–64, 41766, 41772–78, 41804, 41810, 41812, 41815, 41817, 41819, 41821–22, 41824–26, 41828, 41831–40, 41843–45, 41847–49, 41855, 41858–59, 41861–62, 42501–03, 42518–19, 42533, 42544, 42553, 42558, 42564, 42567, 42603, 42631, 42633–35, 42638, 42642, 42647, 42649, 42653

* * *

SIXTH DISTRICT

BEN CHANDLER, Democrat, of Woodford County, KY; born in Versailles, KY, September 12, 1959; education: B.A., history, University of Kentucky; J.D., University of Kentucky College of Law; public service: elected Kentucky State Auditor, 1991; elected Kentucky Attorney General, 1995; reelected in 1999; Democratic nominee for Governor, 2003; religion: member of Pisgah Presbyterian Church; family: married to Jennifer; children: Lucie, Albert IV, and Branham; committees: Foreign Affairs; Permanent Select Committee on Intelligence; elected to the 108th Congress, by special election, on February 17, 2004; reelected to each succeeding Congress.

Office Listings

http://www.chandler.house.gov

1504 Longworth House Office Building, Washington, DC 20515	(202) 225–4706
Chief of Staff.—Denis Fleming, Jr.	FAX: 225–2122
Legislative Director.—Sarah Curtis.	
Communications Director.—Jennifer Krimm.	
1010 Monarch Street, Suite 310, Lexington, KY 40503	(859) 219–1366

Counties: ANDERSON, BOURBON, BOYLE, CLARK, ESTILL, FAYETTE, FRANKLIN, GARRARD, JESSAMINE, LINCOLN (part), MADISON, MERCER, MONTGOMERY, POWELL, SCOTT (part), WOODFORD. Population (2000), 673,626.

ZIP Codes: 40003, 40046, 40076, 40078, 40310–12, 40320, 40324, 40328, 40330, 40334, 40336–37, 40339–40, 40342, 40346–48, 40353, 40355–57, 40361–62, 40370, 40372, 40374, 40376, 40379–80, 40383–86, 40390–92, 40403–05, 40409–10, 40419, 40422–23, 40437, 40440, 40444–47, 40452, 40461, 40464, 40468, 40472–73, 40475–76, 40484, 40489, 40495, 40502–17, 40522–24, 40526, 40533, 40536, 40544, 40546, 40550, 40555, 40574–83, 40588, 40591, 40598, 40601–04, 40618–22, 41031, 41901–06, 42567

LOUISIANA

(Population 2010, 4,553,762)

SENATORS

MARY L. LANDRIEU, Democrat, of New Orleans, LA; born in Alexandria, VA, November 23, 1955; education: B.A., Louisiana State University, 1977; real estate broker, specializing in townhouse development; represented New Orleans House District 90 in Louisiana Legislature, 1979–87; State Treasurer, 1987–95; vice chair, Louisiana Council on Child Abuse; member, Business and Professional Women; majority council member, Emily's List; past national president, Women's Legislative Network; past vice president, Women Executives in State Government; delegate to every Democratic National Convention since 1980; married: E. Frank Snellings; children: Connor, and Mary Shannon; committees: chair, Small Business and Entrepreneurship; Appropriations; Energy and Natural Resources; Homeland Security and Governmental Affairs; elected to the U.S. Senate on November 5, 1996; reelected to each succeeding Senate term.

Office Listings

http://landrieu.senate.gov

431 Dirksen Senate Office Building, Washington, DC 20510 .... (202) 224–5824
Chief of Staff.—Jane Campbell. FAX: 224–9735
Scheduler.—Kim DeLatte.
Communications Director.—Taylor Henry.
Legislative Director.—Tanner Johnson.
Hale Boggs Federal Building, 500 Poydras Street, Room 1005, New Orleans, LA 70130 .... (504) 589–2427
U.S. Courthouse, 300 Fannin Street, Room 2240, Shreveport, LA 71101–3086 .... (318) 676–3085
U.S. Federal Court House, 707 Florida Street, Room 326, Baton Rouge, LA 70801 . (225) 389–0395
Hibernia Tower, One Lakeshore Drive, Suite 1260, Lake Charles, LA 70629 .... (337) 436–6650

* * *

DAVID VITTER, Republican, of Metairie, LA; born in Metairie, May 3, 1961; education: Harvard University; Oxford University Rhodes Scholar; Tulane University School of Law; professional: attorney; adjunct law professor, Tulane and Loyola Universities; religion: Catholic; public service: Louisiana House of Representatives, 1992–99; U.S. House of Representatives, 1999–2005; awards: Alliance for Good Government ''Legislator of the Year''; Victims and Citizens Against Crime ''Outstanding Legislator'' and ''Lifetime Achievement Award''; married: Wendy Baldwin Vitter; children: Sophie, Lise, Airey, and Jack; committees: Armed Services; Banking, Housing, and Urban Affairs; Environment and Public Works; Small Business and Entrepreneurship; elected to the U.S. Senate on November 2, 2004; reelected to the U.S. Senate on November 2, 2010.

Office Listings

http://vitter.senate.gov

516 Hart Senate Office Building, Washington, DC 20510 .... (202) 224–4623
Chief of Staff.—Kyle Ruckert. FAX: 228–5061
2800 Veterans Boulevard, Suite 201, Metairie, LA 70002 .... (504) 589–2753
858 Convention Street, Baton Rouge, LA 70802 .... (225) 383–0331
1217 North 19th Street, Monroe, LA 71201 .... (318) 325–8120
2230 South MacArthur Street, Suite 4, Alexandria, LA 71301 .... (318) 448–0169
920 Pierremont Road, Suite 113, Shreveport, LA 71106 .... (318) 861–0437
3221 Ryan Street, Suite E, Lake Charles, LA 70601 .... (337) 436–0453
800 Lafayette Street, Suite 1200, Lafayette, LA 70501 .... (337) 262–6898

REPRESENTATIVES

FIRST DISTRICT

STEVE SCALISE, Republican, of Jefferson, LA; born in New Orleans, LA, October 6, 1965; education: B.S., Louisiana State University, Baton Rouge, LA, 1983; professional: computer programmer for technology company; Louisiana House of Representatives, 1995–2007, Louisiana Senate, 2007–2008; awards: Spirit of Enterprise, U.S. Chamber of Commerce; religion: Catholic; married: former Jennifer LeTulle; children: Madison; committees: Energy and Commerce; elected to 110th Congress on May 4, 2008 in special election; elected to the 111th Congress on November 4, 2008; reelected to the 112th Congress.

Office Listings

http://www.scalise.house.gov

429 Cannon House Office Building, Washington, DC 20515 .... (202) 225–3015
Chief of Staff.—Lynnel Ruckert. FAX: 226–0386
Legislative Director.—Megan Bel.
Scheduler.—Rebecca Heilig.
Communications Director.—Stephen Bell.
110 Veterans Memorial Boulevard, Suite 500, Metaire, LA 70005 .... (504) 837–1259
District Director.—Charles Henry.
21454 Koop Drive, Suite 1E, Mandeville, LA 70471 .... (985) 893–9064
112 South Cypress Street, Hammond, LA 70403 .... (985) 340–2185

Parishes: JEFFERSON (part), ORLEANS (part), ST. CHARLES (part), ST. TAMMANY, TANGIPAHOA, WASHINGTON. Population (2000), 638,355.

ZIP Codes: 70001–06, 70009–11, 70033, 70047, 70053, 70055–56, 70058, 70060, 70062, 70064–65, 70072, 70087, 70094, 70115, 70118–19, 70121–24, 70160, 70181, 70183–84, 70401–04, 70420, 70422, 70426–27, 70429, 70431, 70433–38, 70442–48, 70450–52, 70454–67, 70469–71

* * *

SECOND DISTRICT

CEDRIC L. RICHMOND, Democrat, of New Orleans; born in New Orleans, LA, September 13, 1973; education: B.A., Morehouse College, Atlanta, GA, 1995; J.D., Tulane School of Law, New Orleans, LA, 1998; Harvard University Executive Education Program at the John F. Kennedy School of Government, Cambridge, MA; professional: military; member of the Louisiana State House of Representatives, 1999–2008; awards: *Time* Magazine's 2010 40 Under 40, Innocence Project Legislative Champion Award; religion: Baptist; commissions, caucuses; New Democrat Coalition; Congressional Black Caucus; Gulf Coast Caucus; committees: Homeland Security; Small Business; elected to the 112th Congress on November 2, 2010.

Office Listings

http://www.richmond.house.gov

415 Cannon House Office Building, Washington, DC 20515 .... (202) 225–6636
Chief of Staff.—Virgil Miller. FAX: 225–1988
Office Manager / Scheduler.—Kelsey Smith.
Legislative Director.—Fabrice Coles.
Communications Director.—Aketa Marie Simmons.
2021 Lakeshore Drive, Suite 309, New Orleans, LA 70122 .... (504) 288–3777
Deputy District Director.—Karen Domino.
200 Derbigny Street, Suite 3200, Gretna, LA 70053 .... (504) 365–0390

Parishes: JEFFERSON, ORLEANS. Population (2000), 638,562.

ZIP Codes: 70001, 70003, 70053, 70056, 70058, 70062, 70065, 70094, 70112–19, 70121–23, 70125–31, 70163

* * *

THIRD DISTRICT

JEFF LANDRY, Republican, of New Iberia, LA; born in St. Martinville, LA, December 23, 1970; education: B.S., environmental and sustainable resources, University of Southwestern Louisiana, Lafayette, LA, 1998, J.D., Loyola University, New Orleans, LA, 2004; professional: Louisiana Army National Guard, 1987–98; Veteran of Desert Storm, small business owner; attorney; religion: Catholic; married: Sharon; child: Jeffrey Thomas; medals: Army Achievement Medal; Army Commendation Medal; National Defense Ribbon; Overseas Training Ribbon; Louisiana War Cross; caucuses: Republican Study Committee, Congressional Sportsmen's Caucus, National Guard and Reserve Components Caucus, Coast Guard Caucus, and Tea Party Caucus; committees: Natural Resources; Small Business; Transportation and Infrastructure; elected to the 112th Congress on November 2, 2010.

Office Listings

http://landry.house.gov

206 Cannon House Office Building, Washington, DC 20515 .... (202) 225–4031

Chief of Staff.—Philip Joffrion. FAX: 226–3944
Legislative Director.—Aaron Smith.
Communications Director.— Millard Mule.
Scheduler.— Leilani Hardee.
423 Lafayette Street, Suite 107, Houma, LA 70360 .... (985) 879–2300
301 East St. Peter Street, Suite 102, New Iberia, LA 70560 .... (337) 359–9080
District Director.—Wilbur Stiles. FAX: 359–9090

Parishes: ASCENSION (part), ASSUMPTION, IBERIA, JEFFERSON (part), LAFOURCHE, PLAQUEMINES, ST. BERNARD, ST. CHARLES (part), ST. JAMES, ST. JOHN THE BAPTIST, ST. MARTIN, ST. MARY, TERREBONNE. Population (2000), 638,322.

ZIP Codes: 70030–32, 70036–41, 70043–44, 70047, 70049–52, 70056–58, 70067–72, 70075–76, 70078–87, 70090–92, 70301–02, 70310, 70339–46, 70353–54, 70356–61, 70363–64, 70371–75, 70377, 70380–81, 70390–95, 70397, 70512–14, 70517–19, 70521–23, 70528, 70538, 70540, 70544, 70552, 70560, 70562–63, 70569, 70582, 70592, 70723, 70725, 70734, 70737, 70743, 70763, 70778, 70792

* * *

FOURTH DISTRICT

JOHN FLEMING, Republican, of Minden, LA; born in Meridian, MS, July 5, 1951; education: B.S., University of Mississippi, Oxford, MS, 1973; M.D., University of Mississippi, Oxford, MS, 1976; professional: family physician and businessman; military: Lieutenant Commander, U.S. Navy; awards: Louisiana Family Doctor of the Year, 2007; religion: Southern Baptist; married: Cindy; four children; committees: Armed Services; Natural Resources; elected to the 111th Congress on November 4, 2008; reelected to the 112th Congress.

Office Listings

http://www.fleming.house.gov

416 Cannon House Office Building, Washington, DC 20515 .... (202) 225–2777
Chief of Staff.—Lee Fletcher. FAX: 225–8039
Legislative Director.—Ben Schultz.
Scheduler.—Ariana Raveica.
Communications.—Michael Tadeo.
6425 Youree Drive, Suite 350, Shreveport, LA 71105 .... (318) 798–2254
District Director.—Stephanie McKenzie.
103 North Third Street, Leesville, LA 71446 .... (337) 238–0778
District Director.—Lee Turner.
700 Benton Road, Bossier City, LA 71111 .... (318) 549–1712

Parishes: ALLEN, BEAUREGARD, BIENVILLE, BOSSIER, CADDO, CLAIBORNE, DESOTO, GRANT, NATCHITOCHES, RED RIVER, SABINE, VERNON, WEBSTER. Population (2000), 638,466.

ZIP Codes: 70633–34, 70637–39, 70644, 70648, 70651–57, 70659–60, 70662, 71001–04, 71006–09, 71016, 71018–19, 71021, 71023–25, 71027–34, 71036–40, 71043–52, 71055, 71058, 71060–61, 71063–73, 71075, 71078–80, 71082, 71101–13, 71115, 71118–20, 71129–30, 71133–38, 71148–49, 71151–54, 71156, 71161–66, 71171–72, 71222, 71235, 71251, 71256, 71268, 71275, 71360, 71403–04, 71406–07, 71411, 71414, 71416–17, 71419, 71423, 71426–29, 71432, 71434, 71438–39, 71443, 71446–47, 71449–50, 71452, 71454–63, 71467–69, 71474–75, 71486, 71496–97

* * *

FIFTH DISTRICT

RODNEY ALEXANDER, Republican, of Quitman, LA; born in Bienville, LA, December 5, 1946; education: graduated, University of Louisiana-Monroe; professional: businessman, with a background in the insurance and construction industries; organizations: member, Louisiana Farm Bureau and the National Rifle Association; public service: Jackson Parish Police Jury, 1970–85; served as President during the last seven years of his tenure; Louisiana House of Representatives, 1987–2002; U.S. Air Force Reserves, 1965–71; religion: Baptist; married: Nancy; three children; committees: Appropriations; elected to the 108th Congress on December 7, 2002; reelected to each succeeding Congress.

Office Listings

http://www.house.gov/alexander

316 Cannon House Office Building, Washington, DC 20515 .... (202) 225–8490
Chief of Staff.—Adam Terry. FAX: 225–5639
Press Secretary.—Jamie Hanks.
Scheduler.—Virginia Stewart.
1900 Stubbs Avenue, Suite B, Monroe, LA 71201 .... (318) 322–3500

1412 Centre Court, Suite 402, Alexandria, LA 71301 .... (318) 445–0818

Parishes: ALLEN (part), AVOYELLES, CALDWELL, CATAHOULA, CONCORDIA, EVANGELINE (part), EAST CARROLL, FRANKLIN, IBERVILLE (part), JACKSON, LASALLE, LINCOLN, MADISON, MOREHOUSE, OUACHITA, POINT COUPEE (part), RAPIDES, RICHLAND, TENSAS, UNION, WEST CARROLL, WINN. Population (2000), 638,517.

ZIP Codes: 70532, 70554, 70576, 70585–86, 70655–57, 70759–60, 70764–65, 70772, 70781, 70783, 71001, 71031, 71201–03, 71207–13, 71218–23, 71225–27, 71229–30, 71232–35, 71237–38, 71240–43, 71245, 71247, 71249–51, 71253–54, 71256, 71259–61, 71263–64, 71266, 71268–70, 71272–73, 71275–77, 71279–82, 71284, 71286, 71291–92, 71294–95, 71301–03, 71306–07, 71309, 71315–16, 71320, 71322–31, 71333–34, 71336, 71339–43, 71346, 71348, 71350–51, 71354–57, 71360–63, 71365–69, 71371, 71373, 71375, 71377–78, 71401, 71404–05, 71407, 71409–10, 71415, 71417–18, 71422–25, 71427, 71430–33, 71435, 71438, 71440–41, 71447–48, 71454–55, 71457, 71463, 71465–67, 71471–73, 71477, 71479–80, 71483, 71485

* * *

SIXTH DISTRICT

BILL CASSIDY, Republican, of Baton Rouge, LA; born in Highland Park, IL, September 28, 1957; education: graduated, Tara High School; B.S., Louisiana State University, Baton Rouge, LA, 1979; M.D., Louisiana State University medical school, New Orleans, LA, 1983; professional: medical doctor; Associate Professor, Baton Rouge; medical doctor, founder, Associate Professor of Medicine with LSU Health Science Center; member of the Louisiana State Senate; married: Laura Layden Cassidy, M.D.; children: Will, Meg, and Kate; committees: Energy and Commerce; elected to the 111th Congress on November 4, 2008; reelected to the 112th Congress.

Office Listings

http//:www.cassidy.house.gov

1535 Longworth House Office Building, Washington, DC 20515 .... (202) 225–3901
Chief of Staff.—James Quinn. FAX: 225–7313
Press Secretary.—John Cummins.
Executive Assistant.—Cristin Buckels Prosser.
5555 Hilton Avenue, Suite 100, Baton Rouge, LA 70808 .... (225) 929–7711
29261 Frost Road, Livingston, LA 70753 .... (225) 686–4413

Parishes: ASCENSION, EAST BATON ROUGE, EAST FELICIANA, IBERVILLE, Livingston, Pointe Coupee, St. Helena, West Baton Rouge, West Feliciana. Population (2000), 638,324.

ZIP Codes: 70403, 70422, 70436, 70441, 70443–44, 70449, 70453, 70462, 70466, 70586, 70704, 70706–07, 70710–12, 70714–15, 70718–19, 70721–22, 70726–30, 70732–34, 70736–40, 70744, 70747–49, 70752–57, 70759–62, 70764, 70767, 70769–70, 70772–78, 70780, 70782–89, 70791, 70801–23, 70826, 70831, 70833, 70835–37, 70874, 70879, 70883–84, 70892–96, 70898

* * *

SEVENTH DISTRICT

CHARLES W. BOUSTANY, JR., Republican, of Lafayette, LA; born in New Orleans, LA, February 21, 1956; education: graduated Cathedral Carmel High School, Lafayette, LA; B.S., University of Southwestern Louisiana, Lafayette, LA, 1978; M.D., Louisiana State University School of Medicine, New Orleans, LA, 1982; professional: surgeon; public service: served on the Louisiana Organ Procurement Agency Tissue Advisory Board; board of directors for the Greater Lafayette Chamber of Commerce, 2001; Chamber of Commerce as Vice President for Government Affairs, 2002; president of the Lafayette Parish Medical Society; chaired the American Heart Association's Gala; Healthcare Division of the UL-Lafayette Centennial Fundraiser, which provided $75 million of university endowed chairs, professorships and scholarships; member of Leadership Lafayette Class IIIXX, 2002; member, Lafayette Parish Republican Executive Committee, 1996–2001; Republican Policy Committee; vice-chairman of the Bush/Cheney Victory 2000 Campaign for Lafayette Parish; board of directors for Lafayette General Medical Center; married: the former Bridget Edwards; children: Erik and Ashley; committees: Ways and Means; elected to the 109th Congress on December 4, 2004; reelected to each succeeding Congress.

Office Listings

http://www.house.gov/boustany

1431 Longworth House Office Building, Washington, DC 20515 .... (202) 225–2031

Chief of Staff.—Jeff Dobrozsi. FAX: 225–5724
Legislative Director.—Terry Fish.
Scheduler.—Hunter Pickels.
800 Lafayette Street, Suite 1400, Lafayette, LA 70501 .... (337) 235–6322
One Lakeshore Drive, Suite 1775, Lake Charles, LA 70629 .... (337) 433–1747

Parishes: ACADIA, CALCASIEU, CAMERON, EVANGELINE, JEFFERSON DAVIS, LAFAYETTE, ST. LANDRY, VERMILION. Population (2000), 638,430.

ZIP Codes: 70501–12, 70515–18, 70520, 70524–29, 70531–35, 70537, 70541–43, 70546, 70548–51, 70554–56, 70558–59, 70570–71, 70575, 70577–78, 70580–81, 70583–84, 70586, 70589, 70591–92, 70596, 70598, 70601–02, 70605–07, 70609, 70611–12, 70615–16, 70630–33, 70640, 70643, 70645–48, 70650, 70655, 70658, 70661, 70663–65, 70668–69, 70750, 71322, 71345, 71353, 71356, 71358, 71362

MAINE

(Population, 2010 1,328,361)

SENATORS

OLYMPIA J. SNOWE, Republican, of Auburn, ME; born in Augusta, ME, February 21, 1947; education: graduated from Edward Little High School, Auburn, ME, 1965; B.A., University of Maine, Orono, 1969; member, Holy Trinity Greek Orthodox Church of Lewiston-Auburn; active member of civic and community organizations; elected to the Maine House of Representatives, 1973, to the seat vacated by the death of her first husband, the late Peter Snowe; reelected for a full two-year term in 1974; elected to the Maine Senate, 1976; chaired the Joint Standing Committee on Health and Institutional Services; elected to the 96th Congress on November 7, 1978—the youngest Republican woman, and first Greek-American woman elected; reelected to the 97th through 103rd Congresses; past member: House Budget Committee; House Foreign Affairs Committee; leading member of the former House Select Committee on Aging, ranking Republican on its Subcommittee on Human Services; married to former Maine Governor John R. McKernan, Jr.; committees: ranking member, Small Business and Entrepreneurship; Commerce, Science, and Transportation; Finance; Select Committee on Intelligence; elected to the U.S. Senate on November 8, 1994; reelected to each succeeding Senate term.

Office Listings

http://snowe.senate.gov

154 Russell Senate Office Building, Washington, DC 20510 .... (202) 224–5344
Chief of Staff.—John Richter. FAX: 224–1946
Executive Assistant.—Anna Levin.
Communications Director.—Ken Lundberg.
2 Great Falls Plaza, Suite 7B, Auburn, ME 04210 .... (207) 786–2451
Regional Representative.—Diane Jackson.
40 Western Avenue, Suite 408C, Augusta, ME 04330 .... (207) 622–8292
Regional Representative.—Brian Whitney.
202 Harlow Street, Suite 214, Bangor, ME 04401 .... (207) 945–0432
State Director.—Gail Kelly.
227 Main Street, P.O. Box 215, Biddeford, ME 04005 .... (207) 282–4144
Regional Representative.—Peter Morin.
3 Canal Plaza, Suite 601, P.O. Box 188, Portland, ME 04112 .... (207) 874–0883
Regional Representative.—Cheryl Leeman.
169 Academy Street, Suite A, Presque Isle, ME 04769 .... (207) 764–5124
Regional Representative.—Sharon Campbell.

* * *

SUSAN M. COLLINS, Republican, of Bangor, ME; born in Caribou, ME, December 7, 1952; education: graduated, Caribou High School, 1971; B.A., *magna cum laude,* Phi Beta Kappa, St. Lawrence University, Canton, NY; Outstanding Alumni Award, St. Lawrence University, 1992; staff director, Senate Subcommittee on the Oversight of Government Management, 1981–87; for 12 years, principal advisor on business issues to former Senator William S. Cohen; Commissioner of Professional and Financial Regulation for Maine Governor John R. McKernan, Jr., 1987; New England administrator, Small Business Administration, 1992–93; appointed Deputy Treasurer of Massachusetts, 1993; executive director, Husson College Center for Family Business, 1994–96; committees: ranking member, Homeland Security and Governmental Affairs; Appropriations; Armed Services; Special Committee on Aging; elected to the U.S. Senate on November 5, 1996; reelected to each succeeding Senate term.

Office Listings

http://collins.senate.gov

413 Dirksen Senate Office Building, Washington, DC 20510 .... (202) 224–2523
Chief of Staff.—Mary Dietrich. FAX: 224–2693
Communications Director.—Kevin Kelley.
Legislative Director.—Rob Epplin.
P.O. Box 655, 202 Harlow Street, Room 204, Bangor, ME 04402 .... (207) 945–0417
State Representative.—Carol Woodcock.
68 Sewall Street, Room 507, Augusta, ME 04330 .... (207) 622–8414
State Representative.—Bobby Reynolds.
160 Main Street, Biddeford, ME 04005 .... (207) 283–1101
State Representative.—Cathy Goodwin.
11 Lisbon Street, Lewiston, ME 04240 .... (207) 784–6969

State Representative.—Carlene Tremblay.
25 Sweden Street, Suite A, Caribou, ME 04736 .... (207) 493–5873
State Representative.—Philip Bosse.
1 Canal Plaza, Suite 802, Portland, ME 04101 .... (207) 780–3575
State Representative.—Alec Porteous.

REPRESENTATIVES

FIRST DISTRICT

CHELLIE PINGREE, Democrat, of North Haven, ME; born in Minneapolis, MN, April 2, 1955; education: B.A., College of the Atlantic, Bar Harbor, ME, 1979; professional: farmer; businesswoman; religion: Lutheran; divorced: three children; House Oceans Caucus; Progressive Caucus, Women's Caucus; Sustainable Energy and Environment Coalition; National Guard and Reserve Component Caucus; Humanities Caucus; Bicycle Caucus; Philanthropy Caucus; House Trade Working Group; committees: Armed Services; Agriculture; elected to the 111th Congress on November 4, 2008; reelected to each succeeding Congress.

Office Listings

http://pingree.house.gov

1318 Longworth House Office Building, Washington, DC 20515 .... (202) 225–6116
Chief of Staff.—Lisa Prosienski. FAX: 225–5590
Legislative Director.—Claire Benjamin.
Scheduler.—Elizabeth Frazier.
2 Portland Fish Pier, Suite 304, Portland, ME 04101 .... (207) 774–5019

Counties: CUMBERLAND, KENNEBEC (part), KNOX, LINCOLN, SAGADAHOC, YORK. Population (2000), 637,461.

ZIP Codes: 03901–11, 04001–11, 04013–15, 04017, 04019–21, 04024, 04027–30, 04032–34, 04038–40, 04042–43, 04046–50, 04053–57, 04061–64, 04066, 04069–79, 04082–87, 04090–98, 04101–10, 04112, 04116, 04122–24, 04259–60, 04265, 04284, 04287, 04330, 04332–33, 04336, 04338, 04341–55, 04357–60, 04363–64, 04530, 04535–39, 04541, 04543–44, 04547–48, 04551, 04553–56, 04558, 04562–65, 04567–68, 04570–76, 04578–79, 04841, 04843, 04846–56, 04858–65, 04901, 04910, 04917–18, 04922, 04926–27, 04935, 04937, 04941, 04949, 04952, 04962–63, 04973, 04987–89, 04992

* * *

SECOND DISTRICT

MICHAEL H. MICHAUD, Democrat, of East Millinocket, ME; born on January 18, 1955; grew up in Medway, ME; education: graduate, Harvard University John F. Kennedy School of Government Program for Senior Executives in State and Local Government; professional: mill worker; community service: actively involved in a variety of local, regional, and statewide civic and economic development organizations; public service: Maine House of Representatives, 1980–94; Maine State Senate, 1994–2002; religion: Catholic; committees: Transportation and Infrastructure; Veterans' Affairs; elected to the 108th Congress on November 5, 2002; reelected to each succeeding Congress.

Office Listings

http://www.house.gov/michaud

1724 Longworth House Office Building, Washington, DC 20515 .... (202) 225–6306
Chief of Staff.—Peter Chandler. FAX: 225–2943
Legislative Director.—Nora Todd.
Scheduler.—Diane Smith.
Communications Director.—Ed Gilman.
6 State Street, Suite 101, Bangor, ME 04401 .... (207) 942–6935
179 Lisbon Street, Ground Floor, Lewiston, ME 04240 .... (207) 782–3704
445 Main Street, Presque Isle, ME 04769 .... (207) 764–1036
108 Main Street, Waterville, ME 04901 .... (207) 873–5713

Counties: ANDROSCOGGIN, AROOSTOOK, FRANKLIN, HANCOCK, KENNEBEC (part), OXFORD, PENOBSCOT, PISCATAQUIS, SOMERSET, WALDO, WASHINGTON. Population (2000), 637,461.

ZIP Codes: 04010, 04016, 04022, 04037, 04041, 04051, 04068, 04088, 04210–12, 04216–17, 04219–28, 04230–31, 04234, 04236–41, 04243, 04250, 04252–58, 04261–63, 04266–68, 04270–71, 04274–76, 04278, 04280–83, 04285–86, 04288–92, 04294, 04354, 04401–02, 04406, 04408, 04410–24, 04426–31, 04434–35, 04438, 04441–44, 04448–51, 04453–

57, 04459–64, 04467–69, 04471–76, 04478–79, 04481, 04485, 04487–93, 04495–97, 04549, 04605–07, 04609, 04611–17, 04619, 04622–31, 04634–35, 04637, 04640, 04642–46, 04648–50, 04652–58, 04660, 04662, 04664, 04666–69, 04671–77, 04679–81, 04683–86, 04691, 04693–94, 04730, 04732–47, 04750–51, 04756–66, 04768–70, 04772–77, 04779–81, 04783, 04785–88, 04848–51, 04857, 04903, 04911–12, 04915, 04920–25, 04928–30, 04932–33, 04936–45, 04947, 04949–58, 04961, 04964–67, 04969–76, 04978–79, 04981–88, 04992

MARYLAND

(Population 2010, 5,773,552)

SENATORS

BARBARA A. MIKULSKI, Democrat, of Baltimore, MD; born in Baltimore, July 20, 1936; education: B.A., Mount St. Agnes College, 1958; M.S.W., University of Maryland School of Social Work, 1965; former social worker for Catholic Charities and city of Baltimore; served as an adjunct professor, Department of Sociology, Loyola College; elected to the Baltimore City Council, 1971; Democratic nominee for the U.S. Senate in 1974, winning 43 percent of vote; elected to the U.S. House of Representatives in November, 1976; first woman appointed to the Energy and Commerce Committee; also served on the Merchant Marine and Fisheries Committee; became the first woman representing the Democratic Party to be elected to a Senate seat not previously held by her husband, and the first Democratic woman ever to serve in both houses of Congress; Secretary, Democratic Conference; first woman to be elected to a leadership post; committees: Appropriations; Health, Education, Labor, and Pensions; Select Committee on Intelligence; elected to the U.S. Senate in November, 1986; reelected to each succeeding Senate term.

Office Listings

http://mikulski.senate.gov

503 Hart Senate Office Building, Washington, DC 20510	(202) 224–4654
Chief of Staff.—Julia Frifield.	FAX: 224–8858
Legislative Director.—Jean Doyle.	
901 South Bond Street, Suite 400, Baltimore, MD 21231	(410) 962–4510
State Director.—Jan Gardner.	
60 West Street, Suite 302, Annapolis, MD 21401	(410) 263–1805
6404 Ivy Lane, Suite 406, Greenbelt, MD 20770	(301) 345–5517
32 West Washington Street, Suite 203, Hagerstown, MD 21740	(301) 797–2826
The Gallery Plaza Building, 212 Main Street, Suite 200, Salisbury, MD 21801	(410) 546–7711

* * *

BENJAMIN L. CARDIN, Democrat, of Baltimore, MD; born in Baltimore, October 5, 1943; education: graduated, City College High School, 1961; B.A., *cum laude*, University of Pittsburgh, 1964; L.L.B., 1st in class, University of Maryland School of Law, 1967; professional: attorney, Rosen and Esterson, 1967–78; elected to Maryland House of Delegates in November 1966, served from 1967–87; Speaker of the House of Delegates, youngest Speaker at the time, 1979–87; elected to U.S. House of Representatives in November 1986, Maryland 3rd Congressional District, served from 1987–2007; member: Associated Jewish Charities and Welfare Fund, 1985–89; Trustee, St. Mary's College, 1988–99; Lifetime Member, NAACP, since 1990; Board of Visitors, University of Maryland Law School, 1991–present; President's Board of Visitors, UMBC, 1998–present; Board of Visitors, U.S. Naval Academy, 2007–present; Board of Trustees, The James Madison Memorial Fellowship, 2010–present; awards: Congressional Award, Small Business Council of America, 1993, 1999, 2005; Public Sector Distinguished Award, Tax Foundation, 2003; Congressional Voice for Children Award, National PTA, 2009; Congressional Leadership Award, American College of Emergency Physicians, 2010; Commissioner, Commission for Security and Cooperation in Europe (CSCE), since 1993; co-chair, CSCE, 2007–08; chair, CSCE, 2009–2919; co-chair, CSCE, 2011–present; Vice President, Organization for Security and Cooperation in Europe Parliamentary Assembly, 2006–present; religion: Jewish; married: Myrna Edelman of Baltimore, 1964; two children, (one deceased); two grandchildren; committees: Budget; Environment and Public Works; Finance; Foreign Relations; Small Business and Entrepreneurship; elected to the U.S. Senate on November 7, 2006.

Office Listings

http://cardin.senate.gov

509 Hart Senate Office Building, Washington, DC 20510	(202) 224–4524
Chief of Staff.—Chris Lynch.	FAX: 224–1651
Policy Director.—Priscilla Ross.	TDD: 224–3452
Appointments Secretary.—Debbie Yamada.	
100 South Charles Street, Tower I, Suite 1710, Baltimore, MD 21201	(410) 962–4436
State Director.—Bailey Fine.	FAX: 962–4256
10201 Martin Luther King, Jr. Highway, Suite 210, Bowie, MD 20720	(301) 860–0414
451 Hungerford Drive, Suite 230, Rockville, MD 20850	(301) 762–2974
129 East Main Street, Suite 115, P.O. Box 11, Salisbury, MD 21803	(410) 546–4250
13 Canal Street, Room 305, Cumberland, MD 21502	(301) 777–2957

REPRESENTATIVES

FIRST DISTRICT

ANDY HARRIS, Republican, of Cockeysville, MD; born in Brooklyn, NY, January 25, 1957; education: B.S., Johns Hopkins University, Baltimore, MD, 1977; M.D., Johns Hopkins University, Baltimore, 1980; M.H.S., Johns Hopkins University, Baltimore, 1995; professional: anesthesiologist, as an Associate Professor of Anesthesiology and Critical Care Medicine; member of the Maryland State Senate, 1998–2010; minority whip, Maryland State Senate; military: Commander, Johns Hopkins Medical Naval Reserve Primus Unit P0605C; religion: Catholic; married: M. Sylvia; five children; committees: Natural Resources; Science, Space, and Technology; Transportation and Infrastructure; elected to the 112th Congress on November 2, 2010.

Office Listings

http://harris.house.gov

506 Cannon House Office Building, Washington, DC 20515 .... (202) 225–5311
Chief of Staff.—Kevin Reigrut. FAX: 225–0254
Legislative Director.—John Dutton.
Communications Director.—Dave Schwartz.
Scheduler.—Katharine Tate.
100 Olde Point Village, Suite 101, Chester, MD 21619 .... (410) 643–5425
15 Churchville Road, Suite 102B, Bel Air, MD 21014 .... (410) 588–5670
212 West Main Street, Suite 204B, Salisbury, MD 21801 .... (443) 944–8624

Counties: ANNE ARUNDEL (part), BALTIMORE (part), CAROLINE, CECIL, DORCHESTER, HARFORD (part), KENT, QUEEN ANNE'S, SOMERSET, TALBOT, WICOMICO, WORCESTER. Population (2000), 662,062.

ZIP Codes: 21001, 21009, 21012–15, 21018, 21023, 21028, 21030–32, 21034, 21047, 21050–51, 21054, 21057, 21078, 21082, 21084–85, 21087, 21092–93, 21108, 21111, 21113, 21122, 21128, 21131, 21136, 21144, 21146, 21156, 21162, 21206, 21225–26, 21234, 21236, 21240, 21286, 21401–05, 21411–12, 21601, 21606–07, 21609–10, 21612–13, 21617, 21619–20, 21622–29, 21631–32, 21634–36, 21638–41, 21643–45, 21647–73, 21675–79, 21681–85, 21687, 21690, 21801–04, 21810–11, 21813–14, 21817, 21821–22, 21824, 21826, 21829–30, 21835–38, 21840–43, 21849–53, 21856–57, 21861–67, 21869, 21871–72, 21874–75, 21890, 21901–04, 21911–22, 21930

* * *

SECOND DISTRICT

C.A. DUTCH RUPPERSBERGER, Democrat, of Cockeysville, MD; born in Baltimore, MD, January 31, 1946; education: Baltimore City College; University of Maryland, College Park; J.D., University of Baltimore Law School, 1970; professional: attorney; partner, Ruppersberger, Clark, and Mister (law firm); public service: Baltimore County Assistant State's Attorney; Baltimore County Council; Baltimore County Executive, 1994–2002; married: the former Kay Murphy; children: Cory and Jill; committees: ranking member, Permanent Select Committee on Intelligence; Armed Services; elected to the 108th Congress on November 5, 2002; reelected to each succeeding Congress.

Office Listings

http://dutch.house.gov

2453 Rayburn House Office Building, Washington, DC 20515 .... (202) 225–3061
Chief of Staff.—Tara Oursler. FAX: 225–3094
Deputy Chief of Staff.—Cori Duggins.
Press Secretary.—Jaime Lennon.
Legislative Director.—Ann Jacobs.
Senior Policy Advisor.—Walter Gonzales.
The Atrium, 375 West Padonia Road, Suite 200, Timonium, MD 21093 .... (410) 628–2701
District Director.—Jennifer Riggs.
Casework Supervisor.—Cori Duggins.
Scheduler.—Carol Merkel.

Counties: ANNE ARUNDEL (part), BALTIMORE CITY (part), BALTIMORE COUNTY (part), HARFORD (part). Population (2000), 662,060.

ZIP Codes: 20755, 21001, 21005, 21009–10, 21017, 21022, 21027, 21030–31, 21034, 21040, 21047, 21050–52, 21056–57, 21060–62, 21065, 21071, 21076–78, 21085, 21087, 21090, 21093–94, 21104, 21111, 21113, 21117, 21122–23, 21130, 21133, 21136, 21144, 21162–63, 21204, 21206, 21208, 21212–14, 21219–22, 21224–27, 21230, 21234, 21236–37, 21239, 21244, 21252, 21284–86

* * *

THIRD DISTRICT

JOHN P. SARBANES, Democrat, of Baltimore, MD; born in Baltimore, May 22, 1962; education: A.B., *cum laude*, Woodrow Wilson School of Public and International Affairs, Princeton University, 1984; Fulbright Scholar, Greece, 1985; J.D., Harvard University School of Law, 1988; professional: law clerk to Judge J. Frederick Motz, U.S. District Court for the District of Maryland, 1988–89; admitted to Maryland Bar, 1988; member: American Bar Association; Maryland State Bar Association; attorney, Venable, LLP, 1989–2006 (chair, health care practice); founding member, Board of Trustees, Dunbar Project, 1990–94; Board of Directors, Public Justice Center, 1991–2006 (president, 1994–97); Institute for Christian and Jewish Studies, 1991–present (past chair, membership committee); Special Assistant to State Superintendent of Schools, State Department of Education, 1998–2005; awards: Unsung Hero Award, Maryland Chapter of the Association of Fundraising Professionals, 2006; Arthur W. Machen, Jr., Award, Maryland Legal Services Corp., 2006; married to Dina Sarbanes; three children; committees: Natural Resources; Science, Space, and Technology; elected to the 110th Congress on November 7, 2006; reelected to each succeeding Congress.

Office Listings

http://www.sarbanes.house.gov

2444 Rayburn House Office Building, Washington, DC 20510 .... (202) 225–4016
Chief of Staff.—Jason Gleason. FAX: 225–9219
Deputy Chief of Staff / Legislative Director.—Dvora Lovinger.
Press Assistant / Legislative Correspondent.—Linda Ko.
Scheduler / Staff Assistant.—Lauren Hickey.
Legislative Assistants: Roy Chrobocinski, Jim Notter, Michael Pierce.
Press Secretary.—Brianne Nadeau.
600 Baltimore Avenue, Suite 303, Towson, MD 21204 .... (410) 832–8890

Counties: ANNE ARUNDEL (part), BALTIMORE (part), HOWARD (part), BALTIMORE CITY (part). TOWNS: Arbutus, Crofton, Ellicott City, Elkridge, Glen Burnie, Halethrope, Lansdowne, Linthicum, Maryland City, Odenton, Owings Mills, Parkville, Pikesville, Reisterstown, Russett City, Severn, and Towson. Population (2000), 662,062.

ZIP Codes: 20701, 20723–24, 20755, 20759, 20794, 21022, 21029, 21032, 21035, 21037, 21043–46, 21054, 21060–61, 21071, 21075, 21090, 21093, 21108, 21113–14, 21117, 21122–23, 21136, 21144, 21146, 21153, 21201–02, 21204–06, 21208–15, 21218, 21222, 21227–31, 21234, 21236–37, 21239, 21252, 21281–82, 21285–86, 21401–05, 21411–12

* * *

FOURTH DISTRICT

DONNA F. EDWARDS, Democrat, of Fort Washington, MD; born in Yanceyville, NC, June 28, 1959; education: B.A., Wake Forest University, Winston-Salem, NC, 1980; J.D., Franklin Pierce Law Center, Concord, NH, 1989; professional: executive director, Arca Foundation, 2000–08; founder and executive director, National Network to End Domestic Violence, 1996–99; executive director, Center for New Democracy, 1994–96; member: board of directors, National Network to End Domestic Violence; Citizens for Responsibility and Ethics in Washington; League of Conservation Voters, Common Cause; Tom Lantos Human Rights Commission; committees: Ethics; Science, Space, and Technology; Transportation and Infrastructure; elected by special election on June 17, 2008, to fill the vacancy caused by the resignation of U.S. Representative Albert Russell Wynn, and elected to a full term in the 111th Congress on November 4, 2008; reelected to the 112th Congress.

Office Listings

http://www.donnaedwards.house.gov

318 Cannon House Office Building, Washington, DC 20515 .... (202) 225–8699
Chief of Staff.—Adrienne Christian. FAX: 225–8714
Legislative Director.—Terra Sabag.
Communications Director.—Dan Weber.
5001 Silver Hill Road, Suite 106, Suitland, MD 20746 .... (301) 516–7601
8730 Georgia Avenue, Suite 610, Silver Spring, MD 20910 .... (301) 562–7960

Counties: MONTGOMERY (part), PRINCE GEORGE'S (part). CITIES AND TOWNSHIPS: Bladensburg, Brentwood, Brookeville, Capitol Heights, Cheverly, Colmar Manor, Cottage City, District Heights, Edmonston, Fairmount Heights, Glenarden, Landover Hills, Largo, Laytonsville, Morningside, Mount Rainier, New Carrollton, North Brentwood, Olney, Riverdale, Rockville, Seat Pleasant, University Park, and Upper Marlboro. Population (2000), 662,062.

ZIP Codes: 20703, 20706–07, 20710, 20720–21, 20731, 20735, 20737, 20743–48, 20750, 20752–53, 20757, 20762, 20769, 20772, 20774–75, 20777, 20781–85, 20788, 20790–92, 20797, 20799, 20830, 20832–33, 20841, 20853, 20855, 20860–62, 20866, 20868, 20871–72, 20874, 20876–77, 20879, 20882, 20886, 20901, 20903–06, 20910–12, 21771, 21797

* * *

FIFTH DISTRICT

STENY H. HOYER, Democrat, of Mechanicsville, MD; born in New York, NY, June 14, 1939; education: graduated Suitland High School; B.S., University of Maryland, 1963; J.D., Georgetown University Law Center, 1966; Honorary Doctor of Public Service, University of Maryland, 1988; admitted to the Maryland Bar Association, 1966; professional: practicing attorney, 1966–90; Maryland State Senate, 1967–79; vice chairman, Prince George's County, MD, Senate delegation, 1967–69; chairman, Prince George's County, MD, Senate delegation, 1969–75; president, Maryland State Senate, 1975–79; member, State Board for Higher Education, 1978–81; married: Judith Pickett, deceased, February 6, 1997; children: Susan, Stefany, and Anne; Democratic Steering Committee; Democratic Whip, 108 and 109th Congresses; House Majority Leader, 110th and 111th Congresses; Democratic Whip, 112th Congress; elected to the 97th Congress on May 19, 1981, by special election; reelected to each succeeding Congress.

Office Listings

http://www.hoyer.house.gov

1705 Longworth House Office Building, Washington, DC 20515 .... (202) 225–4131
Chief of Staff.—Terry Lierman. FAX: 226–0663
Administrative Assistant.—Jim Wood.
U.S. Federal Courthouse, Suite 310, 6500 Cherrywood Lane, Greenbelt, MD 20770 .... (301) 474–0119
401 Post Office Road, Suite 202, Waldorf, MD 20602 .... (301) 843–1577

Counties: ANNE ARUNDEL (part), CALVERT, CHARLES, PRINCE GEORGE'S (part), ST. MARY'S. Population (2000), 662,060.

ZIP Codes: 20601–04, 20606–13, 20615–30, 20632, 20634–37, 20639–40, 20643, 20645–46, 20650, 20653, 20656–62, 20664, 20667, 20670, 20674–78, 20680, 20682, 20684–90, 20692–93, 20695, 20697, 20704–09, 20711, 20714–21, 20725–26, 20732–33, 20735–38, 20740–42, 20744, 20748–49, 20751, 20754, 20758, 20764–65, 20768–74, 20776, 20778–79, 20781–84, 20904, 21035, 21037, 21054, 21106, 21113, 21140

* * *

SIXTH DISTRICT

ROSCOE G. BARTLETT, Republican, of Frederick, MD; born in Moreland, KY, June 3, 1926; education: B.A., Columbia Union College, 1947; M.A., 1948, and Ph.D., University of Maryland, 1952; professional: farmer, prior to his election to Congress, retired after owning and operating a small business for 10 years; awards: awarded 20 patents for inventions during his scientific career as a professor and research engineer; Jeffries Aerospace Medicine and Life Sciences Research Award, 1999; held positions at Loma Linda University, the Navy's School of Aviation Medicine, John Hopkins Applied Physics Laboratory, and at IBM; married to Ellen; 10 children; committees: Armed Services; Science, Space, and Technology; Small Business; elected to the 103rd Congress; reelected to each succeeding Congress.

Office Listings

http://www.bartlett.house.gov

2412 Rayburn House Office Building, Washington, DC 20515 .... (202) 225–2721
Chief of Staff / Legislative Director.—Bud Otis. FAX: 225–2193
Office Manager / Scheduler.—Barb Calligan.
1800 Dual Highway, Suite 301, Hagerstown, MD 21742 .... (301) 797–6043
7360 Guilford Drive, Suite 101, Frederick, MD 21704 .... (301) 694–3030
412 Malcolm Drive, Suite 200, Westminster, MD 21157 .... (410) 857–1115
1 Frederick Street, Cumberland, MD 21502 .... (301) 724–3105

Counties: ALLEGANY, BALTIMORE (part), CARROLL, FREDERICK, GARRETT, HARFORD (part), MONTGOMERY (part), WASHINGTON. CITIES AND TOWNSHIPS: Baltimore, Boonsboro, Cumberland, Emmitsburg, Frederick, Frostburg, Funkstown, Hagerstown, Hancock, Middletown, Mount Airy, Oakland, Reisterstown, Sharpsburg, Smithburg, Thurmont, Timonium, Walkersville, Westminster, Williamsport, Woodsboro. Also includes Antietam National Battlefield and Camp David. Population (2000), 662,060.

ZIP Codes: 20842, 20871–72, 20876, 20882, 21014, 21020, 21029–30, 21034, 21036, 21041–43, 21047–48, 21050, 21053, 21074–75, 21084, 21088, 21102, 21104–05, 21111, 21120, 21131–32, 21136, 21152, 21154–55, 21157–58,

21160–61, 21163, 21501–05, 21520–24, 21528–32, 21536, 21538–43, 21545, 21550, 21555–57, 21560–62, 21701–05, 21709–11, 21713–23, 21727, 21733–34, 21740–42, 21746–50, 21754–59, 21762, 21766–67, 21769–71, 21773–84, 21787–88, 21790–91, 21793, 21795, 21797–98

* * *

SEVENTH DISTRICT

ELIJAH E. CUMMINGS, Democrat, of Baltimore, MD; born in Baltimore, January 18, 1951; education: graduated, Baltimore City College High School, 1969; B.S., political science, Phi Beta Kappa, Howard University, Washington, DC, 1973; J.D., University of Maryland Law School, 1976; professional: attorney; admitted to the Maryland Bar in 1976; delegate, Maryland State Legislature, 1982–96; chairman, Maryland Legislative Black Caucus, 1984; speaker pro tempore, Maryland General Assembly, 1995–96; vice chairman, Constitutional and Administrative Law Committee; vice chairman, Economic Matters Committee; president, sophomore class, student government treasurer and student government president at Howard University; member: Governor's Commission on Black Males; New Psalmist Baptist Church, Baltimore, MD; active in civic affairs, and recipient of numerous community awards; co-chair of the House AIDS Working Group; Task Force on Health Care Reform; committees: Oversight and Government Reform; Transportation and Infrastructure; Joint Economic Committee; elected to the 104th Congress by special election in April, 1996; reelected to each succeeding Congress.

Office Listings

http://www.house.gov/cummings

2235 Rayburn House Office Building, Washington, DC 20515 .... (202) 225–4741
Chief of Staff.—Vernon Simms. FAX: 225–3178
Legislative Director.—Nikki Jones.
Legislative Assistants: Kim Johnson, Lucinda Lessley, Martin Levine.
Press Secretary.—Jennifer Kohl.
1010 Park Avenue, Suite 105, Baltimore, MD 21201 .... (410) 685–9199
754 Frederick Road, Catonsville, MD 21228 .... (410) 719–8777
8267 Main Street, Room 102, Ellicott City, MD 21043 .... (410) 465–8259

Counties: BALTIMORE (part), HOWARD (part), BALTIMORE CITY (part). Population (2000), 662,060.

ZIP Codes: 20701, 20723, 20759, 20763, 20777, 20794, 20833, 21029, 21036, 21042–45, 21075, 21104, 21117, 21133, 21163, 21201–03, 21205–18, 21223–24, 21227–31, 21233, 21235, 21239, 21241, 21244, 21250–51, 21263–65, 21268, 21270, 21273–75, 21278–80, 21283, 21287–90, 21297–98, 21723, 21737–38, 21765, 21771, 21784, 21794, 21797

* * *

EIGHTH DISTRICT

CHRIS VAN HOLLEN, Democrat, of Kensington, MD; born in Karachi, Pakistan, January 10, 1959; education: B.A., Swarthmore College, 1982; masters in public policy, Harvard University, 1985; J.D., Georgetown University, 1990; professional: attorney; legislative assistant to former Maryland U.S. Senator Charles McC. Mathias, Jr.; staff member, U.S. Senate Committee on Foreign Relations; senior legislative advisor to former Maryland Governor William Donald Schaefer; public service: elected, Maryland House of Delegates, 1990; elected, Maryland State Senate, 1994; married: Katherine; children: Anna, Nicholas, and Alexander; committees: ranking member, Budget; elected to the 108th Congress on November 5, 2002; reelected to each succeeding Congress.

Office Listings

http://www.vanhollen.house.gov

1707 Longworth House Office Building, Washington, DC 20515 .... (202) 225–5341
Chief of Staff.—C.R. Wooters. FAX: 225–0375
Deputy Chief of Staff / Legislative Director.—Bill Parsons.
Press Secretary.—Bridgett Frey.
51 Monroe Street, Suite 507, Rockville, MD 20850 .... (301) 424–3501
District Director.—Joan Kleinman.

Counties: MONTGOMERY (part), PRINCE GEORGES (part). Population (2000), 662,060.

ZIP Codes: 20712, 20722, 20782–83, 20787, 20810–18, 20824–25, 20827, 20837–39, 20841–42, 20847–55, 20857, 20859, 20871, 20874–80, 20883–86, 20889, 20891–92, 20894–99, 20901–08, 20910, 20912–16, 20918, 20997

MASSACHUSETTS

(Population 2010, 6,547,629)

SENATORS

JOHN F. KERRY, Democrat, of Boston, MA; born in Denver, CO, December 11, 1943; education: graduated, St. Paul's School, Concord, NH, 1962; B.A., Yale University, New Haven, CT, 1966; J.D., Boston College Law School, Boston, MA, 1976; served, U.S. Navy, discharged with rank of lieutenant; decorations: Silver Star, Bronze Star with Combat ''V'', three Purple Hearts, various theatre campaign decorations; attorney, admitted to Massachusetts bar, 1976; appointed first assistant district attorney, Middlesex County, 1977; elected lieutenant governor, Massachusetts, 1982; married: Teresa Heinz; committees: chair, Foreign Relations; Commerce, Science, and Transportation; Finance; Small Business and Entrepreneurship; appointed to Democratic Leadership for 104th and 105th Congresses; elected to the U.S. Senate on November 6, 1984; reelected to each succeeding Senate term.

Office Listings

http://kerry.senate.gov

218 Russell Senate Office Building, Washington, DC 20510 .... (202) 224–2742
Chief of Staff.—David Wade. FAX: 224–8525
Legislative Director.—John Phillips.
Deputy Chief of Staff.—Kaaren Hinck.
One Bowdoin Square, 10th Floor, Boston, MA 02114 .... (617) 565–8519
Suite 311, 222 Milliken Place, Fall River, MA 02722 .... (508) 677–0522
One Financial Plaza, Springfield, MA 01103 .... (413) 747–3942

* * *

SCOTT P. BROWN, Republican, of Wrentham, MA; born in Kittery, ME, September 12, 1959; education: graduated, Wakefield High School, 1977; B.A., Tufts University *cum laude*, Medford, MA, 1981; J.D., Boston College Law School, Newton, MA, 1985; professional: Assessor, Town of Wrentham, 1992–95; Selectman, Town of Wrentham, 1995–98; Massachusetts State House of Representatives, 9th Norfolk District, 1998–2004; Massachusetts State Senate, Norfolk, Bristol and Middlesex District, 2004–10; military: Lt. Colonel, JAG Corps, Army National Guard, 1979–present; married: Gail (Huff) Brown; daughters: Ayla and Arianna; committees: Armed Services; Homeland Security and Governmental Affairs; Small Business and Entrepreneurship; Veterans' Affairs; elected to the U.S. Senate on January 19, 2010 in a special election to fill the term of the late Senator Edward M. Kennedy.

Office Listings

http://scottbrown.senate.gov

359 Dirksen Senate Office Building, Washington, DC 20510 .... (202) 224–4543
Chief of Staff.—Vanessa Sinders. FAX: 228–2646
Deputy Chief of Staff.—Gregory Casey.
Legislative Director.—Nathaniel Hoopes.
2400 John F. Kennedy Federal Building, 15 New Sudbury Street, Boston, MA 02203 .... (617) 565–3170
State Director.—Jerry P. McDermott.

REPRESENTATIVES

FIRST DISTRICT

JOHN W. OLVER, Democrat, of Amherst, MA; born in Honesdale, PA, September 3, 1936; education: B.S., Rensselaer Polytechnic Institute, 1955; M.A., Tufts University, 1956; taught for 2 years at Franklin Technical Institute, Boston, MA; Ph.D., Massachusetts Institute of Technology, 1961; professional: chemistry professor, University of Massachusetts-Amherst; Massachusetts House, 1968–72; Massachusetts Senate, 1972–91; became first Democrat since the Spanish-American War to represent the First Congressional District, 1991; married: Rose Olver; children: Martha; committees: Appropriations; elected on June 4, 1991, to fill the vacancy caused by the death of Silvio Conte, by special election to the 102nd Congress; reelected to each succeeding Congress.

Office Listings

http://www.house.gov/olver

1111 Longworth House Office Building, Washington, DC 20515 .... (202) 225–5335
Chief of Staff.—Hunter Ridgway. FAX: 226–1224
Press Secretary / Scheduler.—Elizabeth Murphy.
Legislative Director.—Lisa Wiehl.
463 Main Street, Fitchburg, MA 01420 .... (978) 342–8722
Office Manager.—Peggy Kane.
57 Suffolk Street, Suite 310, Holyoke, MA 01040 .... (413) 532–7010
District Director.—Jon Niedzielski.
78 Center Street, Pittsfield, MA 01201 .... (413) 442–0946
Office Manager.—Cindy Clark.

Counties: BERKSHIRE, FRANKLIN, HAMPDEN (part), HAMPSHIRE (part), MIDDLESEX (part), WORCESTER (part). Population (2000), 634,479.

ZIP Codes: 01002–05, 01007–08, 01011–12, 01026–27, 01029, 01031–34, 01037–41, 01050, 01054, 01059, 01066, 01068–75, 01077, 01080–82, 01084–86, 01088–90, 01093–94, 01096–98, 01102, 01107, 01201–03, 01220, 01222–27, 01229–30, 01235–38, 01240, 01242–45, 01247, 01252–60, 01262–64, 01266–67, 01270, 01301–02, 01330–31, 01337–44, 01346–47, 01349–51, 01355, 01360, 01364, 01366–68, 01370, 01373, 01375–76, 01378–80, 01420, 01430–31, 01436, 01438, 01440–41, 01452–53, 01462–63, 01468–69, 01473–75, 01477, 01531, 01564, 01585

* * *

SECOND DISTRICT

RICHARD E. NEAL, Democrat, of Springfield, MA; born in Springfield, February 14, 1949; education: graduated, Springfield Technical High School, 1968; B.A., American International College, Springfield, 1972; M.A., University of Hartford Barney School of Business and Public Administration, West Hartford, CT, 1976; instructor and lecturer; assistant to mayor of Springfield, 1973–78; Springfield City Council, 1978–84; mayor, City of Springfield, 1983–89; member: Massachusetts Mayors Association; Adult Education Council; American International College Alumni Association; Boys Club Alumni Association; Emily Bill Athletic Association; Cancer Crusade; John Boyle O'Reilly Club; United States Conference of Mayors; Valley Press Club; Solid Waste Advisory Committee for the State of Massachusetts; Committee on Leadership and Government; Mass Jobs Council; trustee: Springfield Libraries and Museums Association, Springfield Red Cross, Springfield YMCA; married: Maureen; four children: Rory Christopher, Brendan Conway, Maura Katherine, and Sean Richard; committees: Ways and Means; elected on November 8, 1988 to the 101st Congress; reelected to each succeeding Congress.

Office Listings

http://www.house.gov/neal

2208 Rayburn House Office Building, Washington, DC 20515 .... (202) 225–5601
Administrative Assistant.—Ann Jablon. FAX: 225–8112
Executive Assistant.—Tim Ranstrom.
Press Secretary.—William Tranghese.
300 State Street, Suite 200, Springfield, MA 01105 .... (413) 785–0325
District Manager.—James Leydon.
4 Congress Street, Milford, MA 01757 .... (508) 634–8198
Office Manager.—Virginia Purcell.

Counties: HAMPDEN (part), HAMPSHIRE (part), NORFOLK (part), WORCESTER (part). Population (2000), 634,444.

ZIP Codes: 01001, 01009–10, 01013–14, 01020–22, 01027–28, 01030, 01035–36, 01053, 01056–57, 01060–63, 01069, 01075, 01079–81, 01083, 01092, 01095, 01101–09, 01111, 01115–16, 01118–19, 01128–29, 01133, 01138–39, 01144, 01151–52, 01199, 01504, 01506–09, 01515–16, 01518–19, 01521, 01524–27, 01529, 01534–38, 01540, 01542, 01550, 01560, 01562, 01566, 01568–71, 01585–86, 01588, 01590, 01607, 01611, 01747, 01756–57

* * *

THIRD DISTRICT

JAMES P. McGOVERN, Democrat, of Worcester, MA; born in Worcester, November 20, 1959; education: B.A., M.P.A., American University; legislative director and senior aide to Congressman Joe Moakley (D–South Boston); led the 1989 investigation into the murders of six Jesuit priests and two lay women in El Salvador; managed George McGovern's (D–SD) 1984 presidential campaign in Massachusetts and delivered his nomination speech at the Democratic

National Convention; board of directors, Jesuit International Volunteers; former volunteer, Mt. Carmel House, an emergency shelter for battered and abused women; married: Lisa Murray McGovern; committees: Agriculture; Rules; elected to the 105th Congress; reelected to each succeeding Congress.

Office Listings

http://www.house.gov/mcgovern

438 Cannon House Office Building, Washington, DC 20515 .... (202) 225–6101
Chief of Staff.—Christopher Philbin. FAX: 225–5759
Legislative Director.—Cindy Buhl.
Press Secretary.—Michael Mershon.
34 Mechanic Street, Worcester, MA 01608 .... (508) 831–7356
District Director.—Kathleen Polanowicz.
8 North Main Street, Room 200, Attleboro, MA 02703 .... (508) 431–8025
District Representative.—Lisa Nelson.
218 South Main Street, Room 204, Fall River, MA 02721 .... (508) 677–0140
District Representative.—Patrick Norton.
255 Main Street, Room 104, Marlborough, MA 01752 .... (508) 460–9292
District Representative.—Mary Pat Gibbons.

Counties: BRISTOL (part), MIDDLESEX (part), NORFOLK (part), WORCESTER (part). CITIES AND TOWNSHIPS: Ashland, Attleborough, Auburn, Boylston, Clinton, Fall River, Franklin, Holden, Holliston, Hopkinton, Marlborough, Medway, North Attleborough, Northborough, Paxton, Plainville, Princeton, Rehoboth, Rutland, Seekonk, Shrewsbury, Somerset, Southborough, Swansea, West Boylston, Westborough, Worcester, and Wrentham. Population (2000), 634,585.

ZIP Codes: 01501, 01505, 01510, 01517, 01520, 01522, 01527, 01532, 01541, 01543, 01545–46, 01580–83, 01601–15, 01653–55, 01721, 01745–46, 01748–49, 01752, 01772, 01784, 02038, 02053, 02070, 02093, 02703, 02720–21, 02723–26, 02760–63, 02769, 02771, 02777

* * *

FOURTH DISTRICT

BARNEY FRANK, Democrat, of Newton, MA; born in Bayonne, NJ, March 31, 1940; education: graduated, Bayonne High School, 1957; B.A., Harvard College, 1962; graduate student in political science, Harvard University, 1962–67; teaching fellow in government, Harvard College, 1963–66; J.D., Harvard University, 1977; admitted to the Massachusetts bar, 1979; executive assistant to Mayor Kevin White of Boston, 1968–71; administrative assistant to U.S. Congressman Michael F. Harrington, 1971–72; member, Massachusetts Legislature, 1973–80; Senior Whip; co-chair, Democratic Parliamentary Group; committees: ranking member, Financial Services; elected to the 97th Congress, November 4, 1980; reelected to each succeeding Congress.

Office Listings

http://www.house.gov/frank

2252 Rayburn House Office Building, Washington, DC 20515 .... (202) 225–5931
Chief of Staff.—Bruno Freitas. FAX: 225–0182
Deputy Chief of Staff / Staff Director.—Maria Giesta.
29 Crafts Street, Suite 375, Newton, MA 02458 .... (617) 332–3920
Office Manager / District Scheduler.—Alex Wilson.
558 Pleasant Street, Room 309, New Bedford, MA 02740 .... (508) 999–6462
Office Manager.—Ines Goncalves-Drolet.
The Jones Building, Suite 310, 29 Broadway, Taunton, MA 02780 .... (508) 822–4796
District Director.—Garth Patterson.
Office Manager.—Lisa Lowney.

Counties: BRISTOL (part), MIDDLESEX (part), NORFOLK (part), PLYMOUTH (part). CITIES AND TOWNSHIPS: Acushnet, Berkley, Brookline, Dartmouth, Dighton, Dover, Fairhaven, Fall River, Foxboro, Freetown, Halifax, Lakeville, Mansfield, Marion, Mattapoisett, Middleborough, Millis, New Bedford, Newton, Norfolk, Norton, Raynham, Rochester, Sharon, Sherborn, Taunton, Wareham, Wellesley, and Westport. Population (2000), 634,624.

ZIP Codes: 02021, 02030, 02032, 02035, 02048, 02053–54, 02056, 02067, 02130, 02135, 02215, 02330, 02333, 02338, 02344, 02346–47, 02349, 02360, 02367, 02445–47, 02456–62, 02464–68, 02472, 02476, 02481–82, 02492–93, 02495, 02532, 02538, 02558, 02571, 02576, 02702, 02712, 02714–15, 02717–23, 02738–48, 02764, 02766–70, 02779–80, 02783, 02790–91

* * *

FIFTH DISTRICT

NIKI TSONGAS, Democrat, of Lowell, MA; born in Chico, CA, April 26, 1946; graduated from Narimasu American High School, Japan, 1964; B.A., Smith College, Northampton, MA,

1968; J.D., Boston University, Boston, MA, 1988; professional: social worker; lawyer, Middlesex Community College's dean of external affairs; widowed: Paul Tsongas; children: Ashley Tsongas, Katina Tsongas, and Molly Tsongas; committees: Armed Services; Natural Resources; elected to the 110th Congress, by special election, to fill the vacancy caused by the resignation of Representative Martin Meehan; elected to the 111th Congress on November 4, 2008; reelected to the 112th Congress.

Office Listings

http://www.tsongas.house.gov

1607 Longworth House Office Building, Washington, DC 20515 .... (202) 225–3411
Chief of Staff.—Katie Enos. FAX: 226–0771
Legislative Director.—Sarah Christopherson.
Scheduler.—Kristen Hagan.
492 Main Street, Acton, MA 01720 .... (978) 263–1951
District Director.—Jane Adams.
305 Essex Street, 4th Floor, Lawrence, MA 01840 .... (978) 681–6200
District Director.—June Black.
11 Kearney Square, 3rd Floor, Lowell, MA 01852 .... (978) 459–0101
District Director.—Brian Martin.

Counties: Essex County, Middlesex County, Worcester County. Population (2000), 635,326.

ZIP Codes: 01432, 01450–51, 01460, 01464, 01503, 01523, 01718–20, 01740–42, 01749, 01754, 01775–76, 01778, 01810, 01821, 01824, 01826–27, 01830, 01840–44, 01850–54, 01862–63, 01876, 01879, 01886

* * *

SIXTH DISTRICT

JOHN F. TIERNEY, Democrat, of Salem, MA; born in Salem, September 18, 1951; education: graduated, Salem High School; B.A., political science, Salem State College, 1973; J.D., Suffolk University, 1976; professional: attorney, admitted to the Massachusetts bar in 1976; sole practitioner, 1976–80; partner, Tierney, Kalis and Lucas, 1981–96; member: Salem Chamber of Commerce, 1976–96 (president, 1995); trustee, Salem State College, 1992–97; married: Patrice M., 1997; committees: Education and the Workforce; Oversight and Government Reform; elected to the 105th Congress; reelected to each succeeding Congress.

Office Listings

http://www.house.gov/tierney

2238 Rayburn House Office Building, Washington, DC 20515 .... (202) 225–8020
Chief of Staff.—Betsy Arnold Marr. FAX: 225–5915
Legislative Director.—Kevin McDermott.
Executive Assistant.—Bambi Yingst.
17 Peabody Square, Peabody, MA 01960 .... (978) 531–1669
District Director.—Gary Barrett.
Lynn City Hall, Room 412, Lynn, MA 01902 .... (781) 595–7375

Counties: Essex, Middlesex. Cities and townships: Amesbury, Bedford, Beverly, Boxford, Burlington, Danvers, Essex, Georgetown, Gloucester, Groveland, Hamilton, Ipswich, Lynn, Lynnfield, Manchester by the Sea, Marblehead, Merrimac, Middletown, Nahant, Newbury, Newburyport, North Andover, North Reading, Peabody, Reading, Rockport, Rowley, Salem, Salisbury, Saugus, Swampscott, Topsfield, Wenham, West Newbury, Wakefield, and Wilmington. Population (2000), 636,554.

ZIP Codes: 01730–31, 01801, 01803, 01805, 01810, 01821, 01833–34, 01845, 01860, 01864, 01867, 01880, 01885, 01887, 01889, 01901–08, 01910, 01913, 01915, 01921–23, 01929–31, 01936–38, 01940, 01944–45, 01949–52, 01960–61, 01965–66, 01969–71, 01982–85

* * *

SEVENTH DISTRICT

EDWARD J. MARKEY, Democrat, of Malden, MA; born in Malden, July 11, 1946; graduated from Malden Catholic High School, Malden, MA, 1964; B.A., Boston College, Chestnut Hill, MA, 1968; J.D., Boston College Law School, Chestnut Hill, MA, 1972; professional: lawyer, private practice; member, Massachusetts State House of Representatives, 1973–76; military: United States Army Reserve, 1968–73; Commission on Security and Cooperation in Europe; married: Dr. Susan Blumenthal; committees: ranking member, Natural Resources;

Energy and Commerce; elected to the 94th Congress, November 2, 1976, to fill the vacancy caused by the death of Representative Torbert H. Macdonald; at the same time elected to the 95th Congress; reelected to each succeeding Congress.

Office Listings

http://www.house.gov/markey

2108 Rayburn House Office Building, Washington, DC 20515 .... (202) 225–2836
Chief of Staff.—Mark Bayer. FAX: 226–0092
Scheduler.—Nancy Morrissey.
5 High Street, Suite 101, Medford, MA 02155 .... (781) 396–2900
188 Concord Street, Suite 102, Framingham, MA 01701 .... (508) 875–2900

Counties: MIDDLESEX (part), SUFFOLK (part). CITIES AND TOWNSHIPS: Arlington, Belmont, Everett, Framingham, Lexington, Lincoln, Malden, Medford, Melrose, Natick, Revere, Stoneham, Waltham, Watertown, Wayland, Weston, Winchester, Winthrop, and Woburn. Population (2000), 634,287.

ZIP Codes: 01701–02, 01760, 01773, 01778, 01801, 01890, 02148–49, 02151–52, 02155, 02176, 02180, 02420–21, 02451–54, 02472, 02474–76, 02478, 02493

* * *

EIGHTH DISTRICT

MICHAEL E. CAPUANO, Democrat, of Somerville, MA; born in Somerville, January 9, 1952; education: graduated, Somerville High School, 1969; B.A., Dartmouth College, 1973; J.D., Boston College Law School, 1977; professional: admitted to the Massachusetts Bar, 1977; Alderman in Somerville, MA, 1977–79; Alderman-at-Large, 1985–89; elected Mayor for five terms, 1990 to January, 1999, when he resigned to be sworn in as a U.S. Representative; Democratic Regional Whip; chair, Organizational, Study, and Review Committee, Democratic Caucus; married: Barbara Teebagy of Somerville, MA, in 1974; children: Michael and Joseph; committees: Financial Services; Transportation and Infrastructure; elected to the 106th Congress; reelected to each succeeding Congress.

Office Listings

http://www.house.gov/capuano

1414 Longworth House Office Building, Washington, DC 20515 .... (202) 225–5111
Chief of Staff.—Robert Primus. FAX: 225–9322
Office Manager / Scheduler.—Mary Doherty.
Senior Legislative Assistant.—Noelle Melton.
110 First Street, Cambridge, MA 02141 .... (617) 621–6208
District Director.—Jon Lenicheck.

Counties: MIDDLESEX (part), SUFFOLK (part). CITIES AND TOWNSHIPS: Boston, Cambridge, Chelsea, and Somerville. Population (2000), 634,835.

ZIP Codes: 02108–11, 02113–22, 02124–26, 02128–31, 02133–36, 02138–45, 02150–51, 02155, 02163, 02199, 02215–17, 02228, 02238–39, 02295, 02297, 02446, 02458, 02467, 02472, 02478

* * *

NINTH DISTRICT

STEPHEN F. LYNCH, Democrat, of South Boston, MA; born in South Boston, March 31, 1955; education: South Boston High School, 1973; B.S., Wentworth Institute of Technology; J.D., Boston College Law School; master in public administration, JFK School of Government, Harvard University; professional: attorney; former President of Ironworkers Local #7; organizations: South Boston Boys and Girls Club; Colonel Daniel Marr Boys and Girls Club; Friends for Children; public service: elected to the Massachusetts House of Representatives in 1994, and the State Senate in 1996; family: married to Margaret; two children: Victoria and Crystal; committees: Financial Services; Oversight and Government Reform; elected to the 107th Congress, by special election, on October 16, 2001; reelected to each succeeding Congress.

Office Listings

http://www.house.gov/lynch

2348 Rayburn House Office Building, Washington, DC 20515 .... (202) 225–8273
Chief of Staff.—Kevin Ryan. FAX: 225–3984
Legislative Director.—Bruce Fernandez.
Executive Assistant.—Meghan Aldridge.
88 Black Falcon Avenue, Suite 340, Boston, MA 02210 .... (617) 428–2000

Plymouth County Registry Building, 155 West Elm Street, Brockton, MA 02401 ... (508) 586–5555

Counties: BRISTOL (part), NORFOLK (part), PLYMOUTH (part), SUFFOLK (part). Population (2000), 634,062.

ZIP Codes: 02021, 02026–27, 02032, 02052, 02062, 02071–72, 02081, 02090, 02101–10, 02112, 02114, 02116, 02122, 02124–27, 02130–32, 02136–37, 02151, 02169–71, 02184–87, 02196, 02201–12, 02222, 02241, 02266, 02283–84, 02293, 02297, 02301–05, 02322, 02324–25, 02333–34, 02337, 02341, 02343, 02350, 02356–57, 02368, 02375, 02379, 02382, 02467, 02481, 02492, 02494

* * *

TENTH DISTRICT

WILLIAM "BILL" KEATING, Democrat, of Quincy, MA; born in Norwood, MA, September 6, 1952; education: B.A., business administration, Boston College, MA, 1974; M.B.A., business administration, Boston College, MA, 1982; J.D., Suffolk University Law School, MA, 1985; professional: admitted to the Massachusetts bar in 1985 and began practice in Boston; Massachusetts House of Representatives, 1977–84; Massachusetts State Senate, 1985–98; chairman, Judiciary Committee; Committee on Taxation; Committee on Public Safety, Steering and Policy Committee; vice chairman, Committee on Criminal Justice; Norfolk County District Attorney, 1999–2011; religion: Roman Catholic; family: wife, Tevis, two children, Kristen and Patrick; committees: Foreign Affairs; Homeland Security; Small Business; elected to the 112th Congress on November 2, 2010.

Office Listings

http://www.keating.house.gov

315 Cannon House Office Building, Washington, DC 20515 .... (202) 225–3111
Chief of Staff.—Garrett Donovan. FAX: 225–5658
1250 Hancock Street, Suite 802N, Quincy, MA 02169 .... (617) 770–3700
297 North Street, Suite 312, Hyannis, MA 02061 .... (508) 771–0666
District Director.—Michael Jackson.

Counties: BARNSTABLE, DUKES, NANTUCKET, NORFOLK (part), PLYMOUTH (part). Population (2000), 635,901.

ZIP Codes: 02018, 02020, 02025, 02035, 02040–41, 02043–45, 02047, 02050–51, 02055, 02059–61, 02065–66, 02169–71, 02184, 02186, 02188–91, 02269, 02327, 02330–32, 02339–41, 02345, 02351, 02355, 02358–62, 02364, 02366–67, 02370, 02381, 02532, 02534–37, 02539–43, 02552–54, 02556–57, 02559, 02561–65, 02568, 02573–75, 02584, 02601, 02630–35, 02637–39, 02641–53, 02655, 02657, 02659–64, 02666–73, 02675, 02713

MICHIGAN

(Population 2010, 9,883,640)

SENATORS

CARL LEVIN, Democrat, of Detroit, MI; born in Detroit, June 28, 1934; education: graduated, Central High School, Detroit, 1952; Swarthmore College, Swarthmore, PA, 1956; Harvard Law School, Boston, MA, 1959; admitted to the Michigan bar in 1959; professional: lawyer; Grossman, Hyman and Grossman, Detroit, 1959–64; assistant attorney general and general counsel for Michigan Civil Rights Commission, 1964–67; chief appellate defender for city of Detroit, 1968–69; counsel, Schlussel, Lifton, Simon, Rands and Kaufman, 1971–73; counsel, Jaffe, Snider, Raitt, Garratt and Heuer, 1978–79; member, City Council of Detroit, 1969–77 (president, 1974–77); member: Congregation T'Chiyah; American, Michigan and Detroit bar associations; former instructor at Wayne State University and the University of Detroit; married: the former Barbara Halpern, 1961; children: Kate, Laura, and Erica; committees: chair, Armed Services; Homeland Security and Governmental Affairs; Small Business and Entrepreneurship; Select Committee on Intelligence; elected to the U.S. Senate on November 7, 1978; reelected to each succeeding Senate term.

Office Listings

http://levin.senate.gov

269 Russell Senate Office Building, Washington, DC 20510 .... (202) 224–6221
Chief of Staff.—David Lyles. FAX: 224–1388
Legislative Director.—Jack Danielson.
Scheduler.—Alison Warner.
Press Secretary.—Tara Andringa.
477 Michigan Avenue, McNamara Building, Room 1860, Detroit, MI 48226 .... (313) 226–6020
Federal Building, Room 720, 110 Michigan Street, NW., Grand Rapids, MI 49503. (616) 456–2531
1810 Michigan National Tower, 124 West Allegan Street, Suite 1810, Lansing, MI 48933 .... (517) 377–1508
524 Ludington Street, Suite LL103, Escanaba, MI 49829 .... (906) 789–0052
515 North Washington, Suite 402, Saginaw, MI 48607 .... (989) 754–2494
30500 VanDyke, Suite 206, Warren, MI 48093 .... (586) 573–9145
107 Cass Street, Suite E, Traverse City, MI 49684 .... (616) 947–9569

* * *

DEBBIE STABENOW, Democrat, of Lansing, MI; born in Gladwin, MI, April 29, 1950; education: Clare High School; B.A., Michigan State University, 1972; M.S.W., Michigan State University, 1975; public service: Ingham County, MI, Commissioner, 1975–78, chairperson for two years; Michigan State House of Representatives, 1979–90; Michigan State Senate, 1991–94; religion: Methodist; married to Thomas Athans; children: Todd and Michelle; committees: chair, Agriculture, Nutrition, and Forestry; Budget; Finance; Energy and Natural Resources; elected to the U.S. House of Representatives in 1996 and 1998; elected to the U.S. Senate on November 7, 2000; reelected to each succeeding Senate term.

Office Listings

http://stabenow.senate.gov

133 Hart Senate Office Building, Washington, DC 20510 .... (202) 224–4822
Chief of Staff.—Amanda Renteria. FAX: 228–0325
Legislative Director.—Vacant.
Scheduler.—Anne Stanski.
221 West Lake Lansing Road, Suite 100, East Lansing, MI 48823 .... (517) 203–1760
Marquette Building, 243 West Congress, Suite 550, Detroit, MI 48226 .... (313) 961–4330
432 North Saginaw, Suite 301, Flint, MI 48502 .... (810) 720–4172
3335 South Airport Road West, Suite 6B, Traverse City, MI 49684 .... (231) 929–1031
3280 Beltline Court, Suite 400, Grand Rapids, MI 49525 .... (616) 975–0052
1901 West Ridge, Suite 7, Marquette, MI 49855 .... (906) 228–8756

REPRESENTATIVES

FIRST DISTRICT

DAN BENISHEK, Republican, of Crystal Falls, MI; born in Iron Mountain, MI, April 20, 1952; education: graduated from West Iron County High School, 1970; B.S., biology, University of Michigan, 1974; M.D., Wayne State Medical School, Detroit, MI, 1978; completed, family practice internship in Flint at St. Joseph's Hospital; completed, general surgery residency at Wayne State in Detroit; professional: served as a general surgeon in Michigan's Upper Peninsula in a private practice since 1983; worked part-time at Oscar G. Johnson VA Medical Center in Iron Mountain for twenty years; married: wife Judy; five children and two grandchildren; Dr. Benishek, avid hunter and fisherman; proud member of the National Rifle Association (NRA) and Gun Owners of America (GOA); committees: Natural Resources; Veterans' Affairs; Science, Space, and Technology; elected to the 112th Congress on November 2, 2010.

Office Listings

http://www.benishek.house.gov

514 Cannon House Office Building, Washington, DC 20515 .... (202) 225–4735
Chief of Staff.—Lawrence Purpuro. FAX: 225–4710
Press Secretary.—Kyle Bonini.
Legislative Director.—Tad Rupp.
Scheduler / Executive Assistant.—Katie Toskey.
810 South Otsego Avenue, Suite 105, Gaylord, MI 49735 .... (989) 448–8811
District Director.—Lori Latham.
200 Division Street, Suite 178, Petoskey, MI 49770 .... (231) 348–0657
500 South Stephenson Avenue, Suite 500, Iron Mountain, MI 49801 .... (906) 828–1581
307 South Front Street, Suite 120, Marquette, MI 49855 .... (906) 273–1661

Counties: ALCONA, ALGER, ALPENA, ANTRIM, ARENAC, BARAGA, BAY (part), CHARLEVOIX, CHEBOYGAN, CHIPPEWA, CRAWFORD, DELTA, DICKINSON, EMMET, GLADWIN, GOGEBIC, HOUGHTON, IOSEO, IRON, KEWEENAW, LUCE, MACKINAC, MARQUETTE, MENOMINEE, MONTMORENCY, OGEMAW, ONTONAGON, OSCODA, OTSEGO, PRESQUE ISLE, SCHOOLCRAFT. Population (2000), 662,563.

ZIP Codes: 48610–13, 48618–19, 48621, 48623–24, 48628, 48631, 48634–36, 48642, 48647, 48650, 48652–54, 48658–59, 48661, 48703, 48705–06, 48721, 48728, 48730, 48737–40, 48742–43, 48745, 48748–50, 48756, 48761–66, 48770, 49611–12, 49615, 49622, 49627, 49629, 49648, 49659, 49676, 49701, 49705–07, 49709–13, 49715–30, 49733–40, 49743–49, 49751–53, 49755–57, 49759–62, 49764–66, 49768–70, 49774–77, 49779–85, 49788, 49790–93, 49795–97, 49799, 49801–02, 49805–08, 49812, 49814–22, 49825–27, 49829, 49831, 49833–41, 49845, 49847–49, 49852–55, 49858, 49861–64, 49866, 49868, 49870–74, 49876–81, 49883–87, 49891–96, 49901–03, 49905, 49908, 49910–13, 49915–22, 49925, 49927, 49929–31, 49934–35, 49938, 49945–48, 49950, 49952–53, 49955, 49958–65, 49967–71

* * *

SECOND DISTRICT

BILL HUIZENGA, Republican, of Zeeland, MI; born in Zeeland, January 31, 1969; education: graduated, Holland Christian High School; B.A., Calvin College, Grand Rapids, MI, 1987; professional: co-owner, Huizenga Gravel Company, Jenison, MI; formerly licensed realtor and developer; married: the former Natalie Tiesma; children: Garrett, Adrian, Alexandra, Willam, and Sieger; committees: Financial Services; elected to the 112th Congress on November 2, 2010.

Office Listings

http://huizenga.house.gov

1217 Longworth House Office Building, Washington, DC 20515 .... (202) 225–4401
Chief of Staff / Legislative Director.—Jon DeWitte. FAX: 226–0779
Scheduler / Executive Assistant.—Meggie Lyzenga.
District Director of Policy.—Greg Van Woerkom.
184 South River, Holland, MI 49423 .... (616) 395–0030
900 Third Street, Suite 203, Muskegon, MI 49440 .... (231) 722–8386
210½ North Mitchell Street, Cadillac, MI 49601 .... (231) 775–0050

Counties: ALLEGAN (part), BENZIE, KENT (part), LAKE, MANISTEE, MASON, MUSKEGON, NEWAYGO, OCEANA, OTTAWA, WEXFORD. Population (2000), 662,563.

ZIP Codes: 49010, 49078, 49080, 49303–04, 49307, 49309, 49312, 49314–15, 49318–19, 49321, 49323, 49327–30, 49333, 49336–38, 49343, 49345–46, 49348–49, 49401–06, 49408–13, 49415, 49417–31, 49434–37, 49440–46, 49448–49, 49451–61, 49463–64, 49544, 49601, 49613–14, 49616–20, 49623, 49625–26, 49628, 49630, 49633–35, 49638, 49640, 49642–45, 49649–50, 49655–56, 49660, 49663, 49668, 49675, 49677, 49683, 49688–89

* * *

THIRD DISTRICT

JUSTIN A. AMASH, Republican, of Cascade, MI; born in Grand Rapids, MI, April 18, 1980; education: attended Kelloggsville Christian School and Grand Rapids Christian High School;

B.A., economics, *magna cum laude,* University of Michigan, Ann Arbor, MI, 2002; J.D., University of Michigan Law School, Ann Arbor, MI, 2005; professional: small business owner; attorney; member, State Bar of Michigan, Grand Rapids Bar Association; State Representative, Michigan's 72nd district, 2009–10; religion: member, St. Nicholas Antiochian Orthodox Christian Church; married: Kara; three children: Alexander, Anwen, and Evelyn; committees: Budget; Oversight and Government Reform; Joint Economic Committee; elected to the 112th Congress on November 2, 2010.

Office Listings

http://amash.house.gov

facebook.com/repjustinamash

114 Cannon House Office Building, Washington, DC 20515 .... (202) 225–3831
Chief of Staff.—Ben Vanderveen. FAX: 225–5144
Deputy Chief of Staff.—Will Adams.
Executive Assistant / Scheduler.—Hillary DeJong.
Press Secretary.—Emily O'Neill.
110 Michigan Street, NW., Suite 166, Grand Rapids, MI 49503 .... (616) 451–8383
Deputy District Director.—Jordan Bush.

Counties: BARRY, IONIA, KENT (part). CITIES: Belding, Cedar Springs, East Grand Rapids, Grand Rapids, Grandville, Hastings, Ionia, Kentwood, Lowell, Portland, Rockford, Walker, and Wyoming. Population (2000), 662,563.

ZIP Codes: 48809, 48815, 48834, 48837–38, 48845–46, 48849, 48851, 48860–61, 48865, 48870–71, 48873, 48875, 48881, 48887, 48890, 48897, 49017, 49021, 49035, 49046, 49050, 49058, 49060, 49073, 49080, 49083, 49301–02, 49306, 49315–17, 49319, 49321, 49325–26, 49331, 49333, 49341, 49343–45, 49347–48, 49351, 49355–57, 49418, 49468, 49501–10, 49512, 49514–16, 49518, 49523, 49525, 49530, 49544, 49546, 49548, 49550, 49555, 49560, 49588, 49599

* * *

FOURTH DISTRICT

DAVE CAMP, Republican, of Midland, MI; born in Midland, July 9, 1953; education: graduated, H.H. Dow High School, Midland, 1971; B.A., *magna cum laude*, Albion College, Albion, MI, 1975; J.D., University of San Diego, 1978; attorney; member: State Bar of Michigan; State Bar of California; District of Columbia Bar, U.S. Supreme Court; U.S. District Court, Eastern District of Michigan and Southern District of California; Midland County Bar Association; law practice, Midland, 1979–91; Special Assistant Attorney General, 1980–84; administrative assistant to Congressman Bill Schuette, Michigan's 10th Congressional District, 1985–87; State Representative, Michigan's 102nd district, 1989–91; chairman, Corrections Day Advisory Group; Deputy Minority Whip; Executive Committee, National Republican Congressional Committee; Rural Health Care Coalition; 1998 Adoption Hall of Fame Inductee; American Farm Bureau Federation 1998 Golden Plow award recipient; married: attorney Nancy Keil of Midland, 1994; three children; committees: chair, Ways and Means; chair, Joint Committee on Taxation; elected to Congress on November 6, 1990; reelected to each succeeding Congress.

Office Listings

http://www.house.gov/camp

341 Cannon House Office Building, Washington, DC 20515 .... (202) 225–3561
Chief of Staff.—Jim Brandell. FAX: 225–9679
Communications Director.—Megan Piwowar.
Legislative Director.—Rob Guido.
Scheduler.—Allie Judson.
135 Ashman Street, Midland, MI, 48640 .... (989) 631–2552
District Director.—Eric Friedman.
121 East Front Street, Suite 202, Traverse City, MI 49684 .... (231) 929–4711

Counties: CLARE COUNTY. CITIES: Clare, Farwell, Harrison, Lake, Lake George. GRAND TRAVERSE COUNTY. CITIES: Acme, Fife Lake, Grawn, Interlochen, Kingsley, Mayfield, Old Mission, Traverse City, Williamsburg. GRATIOT COUNTY. CITIES: Alma, Ashley, Bannister, Breckenridge, Elm Hall, Elwell, Ithaca, Middleton, North Star, Perrinton, Pompeii, Riverdale, Sumner, St. Louis, Wheeler. ISABELLA COUNTY. CITIES: Blanchard, Millbrook, Mt. Pleasant, Rosebush, Shepherd, Weidman, Winn. KALKASKA COUNTY. CITIES: Kalkaska, Rapid City, South Boardman. LEELANAU COUNTY. CITIES: Cedar, Empire, Glen Arbor, Lake Leelanau, Leland, Maple City, Northport, Omena, Suttons Bay. MECOSTA COUNTY. CITIES: Barryton, Big Rapids, Canadian Lakes, Chippewa Lakes, Mecosta, Morley, Paris, Remus, Stanwood. MIDLAND COUNTY. CITIES: Coleman, Edenville, Hope, Laporte, Midland, North Bradley, Poseyville, Sanford. MISSAUKEE COUNTY. CITIES: Falmouth, Lake City, McBain, Merritt, Moorestown. MONTCALM COUNTY. CITIES: Alger, Butternut, Carson City, Cedar Lake, Coral, Crystal, Edmore, Entrican, Fenwick, Gowen, Greenville, Howard City, Lakeview, Langston, Maple Hill, McBride, Pierson, Sand Lake, Sheridan, Sidney, Six Lakes, Stanton, Trufant, Vestaburg, Vickeryville. OSCEOLA COUNTY. CITIES: Evart, Hersey, LeRoy, Marion, Reed City, Sears, Tustin. ROSCOMMON COUNTY. CITIES: Higgins Lake, Houghton Lake, Houghton Lake Heights, Prudenville, Roscommon, St. Helen. SAGINAW COUNTY (part). CITIES: Birch Run, Brant, Bridgeport, Burt, Carrolton, Chesaning, Fosters, Freeland, Fremont, Hemlock, Merrill, Oakley, Richland, Saginaw, Shields, Spalding, St. Charles, University Center. SHIAWASSEE COUNTY (part). CITIES: Bancroft,

Caledonia, Chapin, Corunna, Henderson, Laingsburg, Morrice, New Haven, New Lothrup, Owosso, Perry, Shaftsburg, Venice, and Vernon. Population (2000), 662,563.

ZIP Codes: 48415, 48417, 48429, 48433, 48436, 48449, 48457, 48460, 48476, 48601–04, 48608–09, 48614–18, 48620, 48622–30, 48632–33, 48637, 48640–42, 48649, 48651–53, 48655–57, 48662, 48667, 48670, 48674, 48686, 48706, 48722, 48724, 48801–02, 48804, 48806–07, 48809, 48811–12, 48817–18, 48829–32, 48834, 48837–38, 48841, 48845, 48847, 48850, 48852–53, 48856, 48858–59, 48862, 48866–67, 48874–75, 48877–80, 48883–86, 48888–89, 48891, 48893, 48896, 49305, 49307, 49310, 49320, 49322–23, 49326, 49328–29, 49332, 49336–40, 49342–43, 49346–47, 49601, 49610, 49612, 49620–21, 49630–33, 49636–37, 49639–40, 49643, 49646, 49649, 49651, 49653–55, 49657, 49659, 49663–67, 49670, 49673–74, 49676–77, 49679–80, 49682–86, 49688, 49690, 49696, 49738

* * *

FIFTH DISTRICT

DALE E. KILDEE, Democrat, of Flint, MI; born in Flint, September 16, 1929; education: graduated, St. Mary High School, 1947; B.A., Sacred Heart Seminary, Detroit, 1952; M.A., University of Michigan, Ann Arbor, 1961; graduate studies in history and political science, University of Peshawar, Pakistan, under Rotary Foundation Fellowship; professional: teacher, University of Detroit High School, 1954–56; Flint Central High School, 1956–64; served as State Representative, 1965–74; State Senator, 1975–77; member: Optimists, Urban League, Knights of Columbus, Phi Delta Kappa national honorary fraternity, American Federation of Teachers; life member, National Association for the Advancement of Colored People; married: the former Gayle Heyn, 1965; children: David, Laura, and Paul; six grandchildren; committees: Education and the Workforce; Natural Resources; elected to the 95th Congress, November 2, 1976; reelected to each succeeding Congress.

Office Listings

2107 Rayburn House Office Building, Washington, DC 20515 .... (202) 225–3611
Chief of Staff.—Callie Coffman. FAX: 225–6393
Legislative Director.—Peter Karafotas.
Executive Assistant.—Evita Mendiola.
432 North Saginaw, Suite 410, Flint, MI 48502 .... (810) 239–1437
District Director, all Districts.—Tiffany Anderson-Flynn. (800) 662–2685
515 North Washington Avenue, Suite 401, Saginaw, MI 48607 .... (989) 755–8904
916 Washington Avenue, Suite 205, Bay City, MI 48708 .... (989) 891–0990

Counties: BAY (part), GENESEE, SAGINAW (part), TUSCOLA. Population (2000), 662,563.

ZIP Codes: 48411, 48415, 48417–18, 48420–21, 48423, 48426, 48429–30, 48433, 48435–39, 48449, 48451, 48453, 48457–58, 48460, 48462–64, 48473, 48501–07, 48509, 48519, 48529, 48531–32, 48550–57, 48601–07, 48623, 48631, 48663, 48701, 48706–08, 48710, 48722–23, 48726–27, 48729, 48732–36, 48741, 48744, 48746–47, 48757–60, 48767–69, 48787

* * *

SIXTH DISTRICT

FRED UPTON, Republican, of St. Joseph, MI; born in St. Joseph, April 23, 1953; education: graduated, Shattuck School, Fairbault, MN, 1971; B.A., journalism, University of Michigan, Ann Arbor, 1975; professional: field manager, Dave Stockman Campaign, 1976; staff member, Congressman Dave Stockman, 1976–80; legislative assistant, Office of Management and Budget, 1981–83; deputy director of Legislative Affairs, 1983–84; director of Legislative Affairs, 1984–85; member: First Congregational Church, Emil Verbin Society; married: the former Amey Rulon-Miller; committees: chair, Energy and Commerce; elected to the 100th Congress on November 4, 1986; reelected to each succeeding Congress.

Office Listings

http://www.upton.house.gov

2183 Rayburn House Office Building, Washington, DC 20515 .... (202) 225–3761
Chief of Staff.—Joan Hillebrands. FAX: 225–4986
Executive Assistant.—Bits Thomas.
800 Centre, Suite 106, 800 Ship Street, St. Joseph, MI 49085 .... (269) 982–1986
157 South Kalamazoo Mall, Suite 180, Kalamazoo, MI 49007 .... (269) 385–0039

Counties: ALLEGAN (part), BERRIEN, CALHOUN (part), CASS, KALAMAZOO, ST. JOSEPH, VAN BUREN. CITIES AND TOWNSHIPS: Allegan, Augusta, Bangor, Baroda, Benton Harbor, Berrien Springs, Berrien Center, Bloomingdale, Breedsville, Bridgman, Buchanan, Burr Oak, Cassopolis, Centreville, Climax, Coloma, Colon, Comstock, Constantine, Covert, Decatur, Delton,

Dowagiac, Eau Claire, Edwardsburg, Fulton, Galesburg, Galien, Gobles, Grand Junction, Hagar Shores, Harbert, Hartford, Hickory Corners, Jones, Kalamazoo, Lakeside, Lawrence, Lawton, Leonidas, Marcellus, Mattawan, Mendon, Nazareth, New Troy, New Buffalo, Niles, Nottawa, Oshtemo, Otsego, Paw Paw, Plainwell, Portage, Pullman, Richland, Riverside, Sawyer, Schoolcraft, Scotts, Sodus, South Haven, St. Joseph, Stevensville, Sturgis, Three Oaks, Three Rivers, Union Pier, Union, Vandalia, Vicksburg, Watervliet, and White Pigeon. Population (2000), 662,563.

ZIP Codes: 48867, 49001–15, 49017, 49019, 49022–24, 49026–27, 49030–32, 49034, 49038–43, 49045, 49047–48, 49051–53, 49055–57, 49060–67, 49070–72, 49074–75, 49077–81, 49083–85, 49087–88, 49090–91, 49093, 49095, 49097–99, 49101–04, 49106–07, 49111–13, 49115–17, 49119–21, 49125–30, 49311, 49315–16, 49323, 49328, 49333, 49335, 49344, 49348, 49408, 49416, 49450

* * *

SEVENTH DISTRICT

TIMOTHY L. WALBERG, Republican, of Tipton, MI; born in Chicago, IL, April 12, 1951; education: studied forestry at Western Illinois University, Macomb, IL; attended Moody Bible Institute, Chicago, IL; B.A., religious education, Fort Wayne Bible College, 1975; M.A., communications, Wheaton College Graduate School, Wheaton, IL, 1978; professional: minister, Union Grace Gospel Church, 1978–82; member of the Michigan House of Representatives, 1983–98; president, Warren Reuther Center for Education and Community Impact; division manager, Moody Bible Institute; elected to the U.S. House of Representatives for the 110th Congress, 2007–09; married: Susan; three children; committees: Education and the Workforce; Homeland Security; Oversight and Government Reform; elected to the 112th Congress on November 2, 2010.

Office Listings

http://www.walberg.house.gov

418 Cannon House Office Building, Washington, DC 20515 .... (202) 225–6276
Chief of Staff.—Joe Wicks. FAX: 225–6281
Legislative Director.—R.J. Laukitis.
Press Secretary.—Kent Sholars.
800 West Ganson Street, Jackson, MI 49202 .... (517) 780–9075

Counties: BRANCH, CALHOUN (part), EATON, HILLSDALE, JACKSON, LENAWEE, WASHTENAW (part). Population (2000), 662,563.

ZIP Codes: 48103, 48105, 48115, 48118, 48130, 48158, 48160, 48167, 48170, 48175–76, 48178, 48189, 48601, 48813, 48821, 48827, 48837, 48849, 48861, 48876, 48890, 48906, 48908, 48911, 48917, 49011, 49014–18, 49020–21, 49028–30, 49033, 49036, 49040, 49051–52, 49058, 49068–69, 49073, 49076, 49082, 49089, 49092, 49094, 49096, 49201–04, 49220–21, 49224, 49227–30, 49232–42, 49245–59, 49261–69, 49271–72, 49274–77, 49279, 49281–89

* * *

EIGHTH DISTRICT

MIKE ROGERS, Republican, of Howell, MI; born in Livingston County, MI, June 2, 1963; education: B.S., Adrian College; also attended the University of Michigan as an Army ROTC member; military service: U.S. Army, Captain, served in a rapid deployment unit as a Company Commander; professional: FBI Special Agent, assigned to public corruption and organized crime units; businessman; co-founder of E.B.I. Builders, Inc.; organizations: American Heart Association; Women's Resource Center; Brighton Rotary Club; Society of Former Special Agents of the FBI; religion: Methodist; married: Kristi; children: Erin and Jonathan; committees: chair, Permanent Select Committee on Intelligence; Energy and Commerce; elected to the 107th Congress on November 7, 2000; reelected to each succeeding Congress.

Office Listings

http://www.house.gov/mikerogers

133 Cannon House Office Building, Washington, DC 20515 .... (202) 225–4872
Chief of Staff.—Andy Keiser. FAX: 225–5820
Legislative Director.—Andrew Hawkins.
Scheduler.—Mary Randolph Carpenter.
Press Secretary.—Dave Yonkman.
1000 West St. Joseph, Lansing, MI 48915 .... (517) 702–8000

Counties: CLINTON, INGHAM, LIVINGSTON, OAKLAND (part), SHIAWASSE (part). Population (2000), 662,563.

ZIP Codes: 48114, 48116, 48137, 48139, 48143, 48169, 48178, 48189, 48329, 48346–48, 48350, 48353, 48356–57, 48359–62, 48366–67, 48370–71, 48380, 48386, 48414, 48418, 48428–30, 48436, 48438–39, 48442, 48451, 48455, 48462,

48504, 48507, 48805, 48807–08, 48816–17, 48819–27, 48831, 48833, 48835–37, 48840, 48842–45, 48848, 48854–55, 48857, 48863–64, 48866–67, 48872–73, 48875, 48879, 48882, 48892, 48894–95, 48901, 48906, 48909–13, 48915–19, 48921–22, 48924, 48929–30, 48933, 48937, 48950–51, 48956, 48980, 49078, 49080, 49251, 49264, 49285

* * *

NINTH DISTRICT

GARY C. PETERS, Democrat, of Bloomfield Township, MI; born in Pontiac, MI, December 1, 1958; education: B.A., Alma College, Alma, MI, 1980; M.B.A., University of Detroit, Detroit, MI, 1984; J.D., Wayne State University, Detroit, MI, 1989; M.A., Michigan State University, East Lansing, MI, 2007; professional: Assistant Vice President, Merrill Lynch, 1980–89; Vice President, UBS / Paine Webber, 1989–2003; City Council, Rochester Hills, MI, 1991–93; Lt. Commander, Navy Reserve, 1993–2005; Michigan Senate, 1995–2002; Chief Administrative Officer for the Bureau of Investments, State of Michigan, 2003; Lottery Commissioner, State of Michigan, 2003–07; Griffin Endowed Chair in American Government, Central Michigan University, 2007–08; religion: Episcopalian; married: Colleen Ochoa Peters; three children: Gary Jr., Madeline, and Alana; Armenian Caucus; Congressional Automotive Caucus; Congressional Caucus on India and Indian Americans; Congressional Fire Services Caucus; Congressional Pakistan Caucus; House Bangladesh Caucus; House Manufacturing Caucus; Law Enforcement Caucus; LGBT Equality Caucus; National Guard and Reserve Component Caucus; New Democrat Coalition; Pro-Choice Caucus; committees: Financial Services; Small Business; elected to the 111th Congress on November 4, 2008; reelected to the 112th Congress.

Office Listings

http://www.peters.house.gov

1609 Longworth House Office Building, Washington, DC 20515 .... (202) 225–5802
Chief of Staff.—Eric Feldman. FAX: 226–2356
Legislative Director.—Jonathan Smith.
Press Secretary.—Clark Pettig.
560 Kirts Boulevard, Suite 105, Troy, MI 48084 .... (248) 273–4227
District Office Director.—Dianna McBroom.

Counties: OAKLAND (part). CITIES AND TOWNSHIPS: Auburn Hills, Berkley, Beverly Hills, Bingham Farms, Birmingham, Bloomfield Hills, Bloomfield, Clawson, Farmington, Farmington Hills, Franklin, Keego Harbor, Lake Angelus, Oakland, Orchard Lake, Orion, Pontiac, Rochester, Rochester Hills, Royal Oak, Southfield, Sylvan Lake, Troy, Waterford, and West Bloomfield. Population (2000), 662,563.

ZIP Codes: 48007, 48009, 48012, 48017, 48025, 48067–68, 48072–73, 48083–85, 48098–99, 48167, 48301–04, 48306–09, 48320–36, 48340–43, 48346, 48359–60, 48362–63, 48367, 48370, 48382, 48387, 48390, 48398

* * *

TENTH DISTRICT

CANDICE S. MILLER, Republican, of Harrison Township, MI; born in St. Clair Shores, MI, May 7, 1954; education: attended Macomb Community College and Northwood University; public service: Harrison Township Board of Trustees, 1979; Harrison Township Supervisor, 1980–92; Macomb County Treasurer, 1992–94; Michigan Secretary of State, 1994–2002; professional: worked in a family-owned marina business before she became involved in public service; religion: Presbyterian; married: Macomb County Circuit Court Judge Donald Miller; children: Wendy; committees: Homeland Security; Transportation and Infrastructure; elected to the 108th Congress on November 5, 2002; reelected to each succeeding Congress.

Office Listings

http://candicemiller.house.gov

1034 Longworth House Office Building, Washington, DC 20515 .... (202) 225–2106
Chief of Staff.—Jamie Roe. FAX: 226–1169
Deputy Chief of Staff.—Sean Moran.
Legislative Director.—Kyle Burleson.
Scheduler.—Christopher Stewart.
Press Secretary.—Erin Sayago.
48653 Van Dyke Avenue, Shelby Township, MI 48317 .... (586) 997–5010

Counties: HURON, LAPEER, MACOMB (part), SAINT CLAIR, SANILAC. Population (2000), 662,562.

ZIP Codes: 48001–06, 48014, 48022–23, 48027–28, 48032, 48039–42, 48044–45, 48047–51, 48054, 48059–65, 48074, 48079, 48094–97, 48306, 48310–18, 48371, 48401, 48410, 48412–13, 48416, 48419, 48421–23, 48426–28, 48432,

48434–35, 48438, 48440–41, 48444–46, 48450, 48453–56, 48461–72, 48475, 48720, 48725–27, 48729, 48731, 48735, 48741, 48744, 48754–55, 48759–60, 48767

* * *

ELEVENTH DISTRICT

THADDEUS G. McCOTTER, Republican, of Livonia, MI; born in Detroit, MI, August 22, 1965; education: B.A., University of Detroit, 1987; J.D., University of Detroit Law School, 1990; professional: attorney; public service: elected to the Schoolcraft Community College Trustees, 1989; elected to the Wayne County Commission, 1992; elected to the Michigan State Senate, 1998; awards: Michigan Jaycees Outstanding Michigander, 2001; Police Officers Association of Michigan Legislator of the Year, 2002; chair, Republican House Policy Committee; religion: Catholic; married: Rita; children: George, Timothy, and Emilia; committees: Financial Services; elected to the 108th Congress on November 5, 2002; reelected to each succeeding Congress.

Office Listings

http://www.mccotter.house.gov

2243 Rayburn House Office Building, Washington, DC 20515 .... (202) 225–8171
Chief of Staff.—Jack Daly.
Scheduler.—Shawn Scott.
Legislative Director.—Artur Suchorzewski.
Communications Director.—Michael Bars.
17197 North Laurel Park Drive, Suite 216, Livonia, MI 48152 .... (734) 632–0314
213 West Huron, Milford, MI 48381 .... (248) 685–9495

Counties: WAYNE COUNTY. CITIES: Livonia, Canton Township, Plymouth City, Plymouth Township, Northville City, Northville Township, Belleville, Van Buren Township, Wayne, Westland, Garden City, Redford Township, Dearborn Heights. OAKLAND COUNTY. CITIES: Novi, South Lyon, Lyon Township, Milford, Wixom, Walled Lake, Commerce Township, White Lake, Highland, and Waterford. Population (2000), 662,563.

ZIP Codes: 48111–12, 48127, 48135–36, 48141, 48150–54, 48165, 48167, 48170, 48174, 48178, 48184–88, 48239–40, 48327, 48329, 48346, 48356–57, 48374–77, 48380–83, 48386–87, 48390–91, 48393

* * *

TWELFTH DISTRICT

SANDER M. LEVIN, Democrat, of Royal Oak, MI; born in Detroit, MI, September 6, 1931; education: graduated, Central High School, Detroit, 1949; B.A., University of Chicago, 1952; M.A., Columbia University, New York, NY, 1954; LL.B., Harvard University, Cambridge, MA, 1957; professional: attorney, admitted to the Michigan Bar in 1958 and commenced practice in Detroit, MI; member: Oakland Board of Supervisors, 1961–64; Michigan Senate, 1965–70; Democratic floor leader in State Senate; served on the Advisory Committee on the Education of Handicapped Children in the Department of Health, Education, and Welfare, 1965–68; chairman, Michigan Democratic Party, 1968–69; Democratic candidate for governor, 1970 and 1974; fellow, Kennedy School of Government, Institute of Politics, Harvard University, 1975; assistant administrator, Agency for International Development, 1977–81; married: the former Victoria Schlafer (deceased); children: Jennifer, Andrew, Madeleine, and Matthew; committees: Ways and Means; Joint Committee on Taxation; elected on November 2, 1982, to the 98th Congress; reelected to each succeeding Congress.

Office Listings

http://www.house.gov/levin

1236 Longworth Office House Building, Washington, DC 20515 .... (202) 225–4961
Chief of Staff.—Hilarie Chambers. FAX: 226–1033
Scheduler.—Monica Chrzaszcz.
27085 Gratiot Avenue, Roseville, MI 48066 .... (586) 498–7122

Counties: MACOMB (part), OAKLAND (part). CITIES: Center Line, Clinton Township, Eastpointe, Ferndale, Fraser, Hazel Park, Huntington Woods, Lake Township, Lathrup Village, Madison Heights, Mt. Clemens, Oak Park, Pleasant Ridge, Roseville, Royal Oak, Royal Oak Township, Southfield, St. Clair Shores, Sterling Heights, and Warren. Population (2000), 662,563.

ZIP Codes: 48015, 48021, 48025–26, 48030, 48034–38, 48043, 48046, 48066–67, 48069–71, 48075–76, 48080–82, 48086, 48088–93, 48220, 48236–37, 48310, 48312, 48397

* * *

THIRTEENTH DISTRICT

HANSEN H. CLARKE, Democrat, of Detroit, MI; born in Detroit, March 2, 1957; education: graduated, B.F.A., in fine arts, Cornell University, 1984; J.D., Georgetown University Law Center, Washington, DC, 1987; professional: served in Michigan House of Representatives, 1991–92 and 1999–2002; served in Michigan State Senate, 2003–11; member, Alpha Phi Alpha Fraternity, Incorporated; former treasurer, Michigan Legislative Black Caucus; minister of service, Sacred Heart Church; former executive assistant, Wayne County Executive; former associate, Wayne County Executive and Administrator; married; committees: Homeland Security; Science, Space, and Technology; elected to the 112th Congress on November 2, 2010.

Office Listings

http://www.hansenclarke.house.gov

1913 Longworth House Office Building, Washington, DC 20515 .... (202) 225–2261
Senior Advisor / Counsel.—Kim Bowman. FAX: 225–5730
Executive Assistant.—Corey Solow.
Policy Advisor.—David Weinreich.
400 Monroe Street, Suite 290, Detroit, MI 48226 .... (313) 962–7700
District Director.—Washington Youson, Jr. FAX: 962–7710
Communications Director.—Kim Bowman.
10600 West Jefferson, Room 203, River Rouge, MI 48218 .... (313) 297–6951

Counties: WAYNE COUNTY. Population (2010), 519,570.

ZIP Codes: 48146, 48192, 48201–02, 48204–18, 48224–26, 48229–30, 48234, 48236

* * *

FOURTEENTH DISTRICT

JOHN CONYERS, JR., Democrat, of Detroit, MI; born in Detroit, May 16, 1929; son of John and Lucille Conyers; education: B.A., Wayne State University, 1957; LL.B., Wayne State Law School, June 1958; served as officer in the U.S. Army Corps of Engineers, one year in Korea; awarded combat and merit citations; engaged in many civil rights and labor activities; legislative assistant to Congressman John D. Dingell, December 1958 to May 1961; appointed Referee for the Workmen's Compensation Department, State of Michigan, by Governor John B. Swainson in October 1961; former vice chairman of Americans for Democratic Action; vice chairman of the National Advisory Council of the ACLU; member: Kappa Alpha Psi; Wolverine Bar; NAACP; Tuskegee Airmen, Inc.; organizations: Congressional Black Caucus; Progressive Caucus; married: Monica Conyers; children: John III, and Carl; committees: ranking member, Judiciary; elected to the 89th Congress on November 3, 1964; reelected to each succeeding Congress.

Office Listings

http://www.house.gov/conyers

2426 Rayburn House Office Building, Washington, DC 20515 .... (202) 225–5126
Chief of Staff.—Cynthia Martin. FAX: 225–0072
Scheduler.—Rinia Shelby.
Federal Courthouse, Suite 669, 231 West Lafayette, Detroit, MI 48226 .... (313) 961–5670
District Director.—Yolanda Lipsey.
2615 West Jefferson, Trenton, MI 48183 .... (734) 675–4084
FAX: 675–4218

Counties: WAYNE COUNTY (part). CITIES AND TOWNSHIPS: Allen Park, Detroit, Dearborn, Gibraltar, Grosse Ile, Hamtramack, Highland Park, Melvindale, Riverview, Southgate, and Trenton. Population (2000), 662,563.

ZIP Codes: 48101–02, 48120–22, 48124, 48126–27, 48138, 48173, 48180, 48183, 48192, 48195, 48203–04, 48206, 48210–12, 48219, 48221, 48223, 48227–28, 48235, 48238–40

* * *

FIFTEENTH DISTRICT

JOHN D. DINGELL, Democrat, of Dearborn, MI; born in Colorado Springs, CO, July 8, 1926; education: B.S., Georgetown University, 1949; J.D., Georgetown University Law School,

1952; professional: World War II veteran; assistant Wayne County prosecutor, 1953–55; member: Migratory Bird Conservation Commission; married: the former Deborah Insley; committees: Energy and Commerce; elected to the 84th Congress in a special election to fill the vacant seat of his late father, the Honorable John D. Dingell, December 13, 1955; reelected to the 85th and each succeeding Congress.

Office Listings

http://www.house.gov/dingell

2328 Rayburn House Office Building, Washington, DC 20515 .... (202) 225–4071
Chief of Staff.—Michael Robbins.
Legislative Director.—Katie Murtha.
Scheduler.—Beth Siniawsky.
Press Secretary.—Betsy Barrett.
19855 West Outer Drive, Suite 103–E, Dearborn, MI 48124 .... (313) 278–2936
District Administrator.—Andy LaBarre.
23 East Front Street, Suite 103, Monroe, MI 48161 .... (734) 243–1849
301 West Michigan Avenue, Ypsilanti, MI 48197 .... (734) 481–1100

Counties: WAYNE COUNTY (part). CITIES AND TOWNSHIPS: Brownstown Township, Dearborn, Dearborn Heights, Flat Rock, Gibraltar, Rockwood, Romulus, Taylor, Woodhaven. MONROE COUNTY. CITIES AND TOWNSHIPS: Azalia, Carleton, Dundee, Erie, Ida, Lambertville, LaSalle, Luna Pier, Maybee, Milan, Monroe, Newport, Ottawa Lake, Petersburg, Samaria, S. Rockwood, Temperance. WASHTENAW COUNTY (part). CITIES AND TOWNSHIPS: Ann Arbor, Pittsfield Township, York Township, Superior Township, Ypsilanti, and Ypsilanti Township. Population (2000), 662,563.

ZIP Codes: 48103–11, 48113, 48117, 48123–28, 48131, 48133–34, 48140–41, 48144–45, 48157, 48159–62, 48164, 48166, 48170, 48173–74, 48176–77, 48179–80, 48182–84, 48186, 48190–92, 48197–98, 48228, 48239, 49228–29, 49238, 49267, 49270, 49276

MINNESOTA

(Population 2010, 5,303,925)

SENATORS

AMY KLOBUCHAR, Democrat, of Minneapolis, MN; born in Plymouth, MN, May 25, 1960; education: B.A., *magna cum laude*, Yale University, 1982; J.D., *magna cum laude*, University of Chicago Law School, 1985; professional: Attorney at law firm Dorsey & Whitney, 1985–93, Partner in 1993; Partner at law firm Gray, Plant, Mooty, Mooty & Bennett, 1993–98; religion: Congregationalist; public service: City of Minneapolis prosecutor, 1988; elected Hennepin County Attorney, 1998, reelected, 2002; married: John; child: Abigail; committees: Agriculture, Nutrition, and Forestry; Commerce, Science, and Transportation, Judiciary; Joint Economic Committee; elected to the U.S. Senate on November 7, 2006.

Office Listings

http://klobuchar.senate.gov

302 Hart Senate Office Building, Washington, DC 20510 .... (202) 224–3244
Chief of Staff.—Jonathan Becker.
Legislative Director.—Rose Baumann.
Deputy Chief of Staff.—Tom Sullivan.
Communications Director.—Linden Zakula.
Scheduler.—Megan Lahr.
1200 Washington Avenue South, Suite 250, Minneapolis, MN 55415 .... (612) 727–5220
State Director.—Allison O'Toole.
1130½ 7th Street Northwest, Suite 208, Rochester, MN 55901 .... (507) 288–5321
121 4th Street South, Moorhead, MN 56560 .... (218) 287–2219
Olcott Plaza, 820 9th Street North, Suite 105, Virginia, MN 55792 .... (218) 741–9690

* * *

AL FRANKEN, Democrat, of Minneapolis, MN; raised in St. Louis Park, MN, born May 21, 1951; education: Harvard, Cambridge, MA, 1973; professional: comedy writer, author, and radio talk show host; has taken part in seven USO tours, visiting our troops overseas in Germany, Bosnia, Kosovo and Uzbekistan—as well as visiting Iraq, Afghanistan, and Kuwait four times; married: Franni Franken for 34 years; two children; committees: Energy and Natural Resources; Health, Education, Labor, and Pension; Judiciary; Indian Affairs; elected to the 111th U.S. Senate on November 4, 2008, the election was contested; following a June 30, 2009, decision in his favor by the Minnesota State Supreme Court, he took the oath of office and began service on July 7, 2009.

Office Listings

www.franken.senate.gov

H309 Hart Senate Office Building, Washington, DC 20510 .... (202) 224–5641
Chief of Staff.—Drew Littman. FAX: 224–0044
State Director.—Alana Petersen.
Legislative Director.—Ben Olinksy.
Scheduler.—Tara Yurgin.
Communications Director.—Casey Aden-Wansbury.
Press Secretary.—Ed Shelleby.
60 East Plato Boulevard, Suite 220, St. Paul, MN 55107 .... (651) 221–1016
FAX: 221–1078
208 South Minnesota Avenue, Suite 6, St. Peter, MN 56082 .... (507) 931–5813
FAX: 931–7345
916 West St. Germain Street, Suite 110, St. Cloud, MN 56301 .... (320) 251–2721
FAX: 251–4164
515 West First Street, Suite 104, Duluth, MN 55802 .... (218) 722–2390
FAX: 622–4131

REPRESENTATIVES

FIRST DISTRICT

TIMOTHY J. WALZ, Democrat, of Mankato, MN; born in West Point, NE, April 6, 1964; education: B.S., Chadron State College, Chadron, NE; M.S., St. Mary's University, Winona, MN; professional: high school teacher; military: Command Sergeant Major, Minnesota's 1st/

34th Division of the Army National Guard, 1981–2005; awards: 2002 Minnesota Ethics in Education award winner, 2003 Mankato Teacher of the Year, and the 2003 Minnesota Teacher of Excellence; married: Gwen Whipple Walz, 1994; children: Hope and Gus; committees: Agriculture; Transportation and Infrastructure; Veterans' Affairs; elected to the 110th Congress on November 7, 2006; reelected to each succeeding Congress.

Office Listings

http://www.walz.house.gov

1722 Longworth House Office Building, Washington, DC 20515 .... (202) 225–2472
Chief of Staff.—Josh Syrjamaki. FAX: 225–3433
Legislative Director.—Elizabeth Glidden.
Scheduler.—Andrea Fetherston.
227 East Main Street, Suite 220, Mankato, MN 56001 .... (507) 388–2149
1134 Seventh Street, NW., Rochester, MN 55901 .... (507) 206–0643

Counties: BLUE EARTH COUNTY. CITIES: Amboy, Eagle Lake, Garden City, Good Thunder, Lake Crystal, Madison Lake, Mankato, Mapleton, Pemberton, St. Clair, Vernon Center. BROWN COUNTY. CITIES: Comfrey, Hanska, New Ulm, Sleepy Eye, Springfield. COTTONWOOD COUNTY. CITIES: Mountain Lake, Storedon, Westbrook. DODGE COUNTY. CITIES: Claremont, Dodge Center, Hayfield, Kasson, Mantorville, West Concord, Windom. FARIBAULT COUNTY. CITIES: Blue Earth, Bricelyn, Delavan, Easton, Elmore, Frost, Huntley, Kiester, Minnesota Lake, Walters, Wells, Winnebago. FILLMORE COUNTY. CITIES: Canton, Chatfield, Fountain, Harmony, Lanesboro, Mabel, Ostrander, Peterson, Preston, Rushford, Spring Valley, Whalan, Wykoff. FREEBORN COUNTY. CITIES: Albert Lea, Alden, Clarks Grove, Conger, Emmons, Freeborn, Geneva, Glenville, Hartland, Hayward, Hollandale, London, Manchester, Myrtle, Oakland, Twin Lakes. HOUSTON COUNTY. CITIES: Brownsville, Caledonia, Eitzen, Hokah, Houston, La Crescent, Spring Grove. JACKSON COUNTY. CITIES: Heron, Jackson, Lake Field. MARTIN COUNTY. CITY: Fairmont. MOWER COUNTY. CITIES: Adams, Austin, Brownsdale, Dexter, Elkton, Grand Meadow, Lansing, LeRoy, Lyle, Rose Creek, Sargeant, Taopi, Waltham. MURRAY COUNTY. CITIES: Fulda, Slayton. NICOLLET COUNTY. CITIES: North Mankato, St. Peter. NOBLES COUNTY. CITIES: Adrian, Worthington. OLMSTED COUNTY. CITIES: Byron, Dover, Eyota, Oronoco, Rochester, Stewartville, Viola. PIPESTONE COUNTY. CITIES: Edgerton, Jasper, Pipestone Ruthton. ROCK COUNTY. CITY: Lurverne. STEELE COUNTY. CITIES: Blooming Prairie, Ellendale, Hope, Medford, Meriden, Owatonna. WABASHA COUNTY. CITIES: Elgin, Hammond, Kellogg, Lake City, Mazeppa, Milleville, Plainview, Reads Landing, Theilman, Wabasha. WASECA COUNTY. CITIES: Janesville, New Richland, Otisco, Waldorf, Waseca. WATONWAN COUNTY. CITIES: Madelia, St. James. WINONA COUNTY. CITIES: Altura, Dakota, Goodview, Homer, Lewiston, Minnesota City, Rollingstone, St. Charles, Stockton, Utica, and Winona. Population (2000), 614,935.

ZIP Codes: 55021, 55027, 55041, 55049, 55052, 55060, 55901–06, 55909–10, 55912, 55917–27, 55929, 55931–36, 55939–47, 55949–57, 55959–65, 55967–77, 55979, 55981–83, 55985, 55987–88, 55990–92, 56001–03, 56006–07, 56009–11, 56013–14, 56016, 56019–21, 56023–29, 56031, 56033–34, 56036–37, 56039, 56041–43, 56045–48, 56050–51, 56054–55, 56058, 56060, 56062–63, 56065, 56068, 56072–74, 56078, 56080–83, 56085, 56087–91, 56093, 56096–98, 56101, 56110–11, 56114–23, 56125, 56127–29, 56131, 56134, 56136–41, 56143–47, 56149–53, 56155–56, 56158–62, 56164–68, 56170–74, 56176–77, 56180–81, 56183, 56185–87, 56266

* * *

SECOND DISTRICT

JOHN KLINE, Republican, of Lakeville, MN; born in Allentown, PA, September 6, 1947; education: B.A., Rice University, 1969; M.P.A., Shippensburg University, 1988; military service: U.S. Marine Corps, 1969–94; retired at the rank of Colonel; organizations: Boy Scouts of America; Marine Corps League; Veterans of Foreign Wars; Marine Corps Association; American Legion; Retired Officers Association; past president, Marine Corps Coordinating Council of Minnesota; religion: Methodist; family: married to Vicky; children: Kathy and Dan; committees: chair, Education and the Workforce; Armed Services; elected to the 108th Congress on November 5, 2002; reelected to each succeeding Congress.

Office Listings

http://www.house.gov/kline

2439 Rayburn House Office Building, Washington, DC 20515 .... (202) 225–2271
Chief of Staff.—Jean Hinz. FAX: 225–2595
Legislative Director.—Yelena Vaynberg.
Communications Director.—Troy Young.
Scheduler.—Janelle Belland.
101 West Burnsville Parkway, Suite 201, Burnsville, MN 55337 .... (952) 808–1213
District Director.—Mike Osskopp.
Deputy District Director.—Brooke Dorobiala.

Counties: CARVER COUNTY. CITIES: Chanhassen, Chaska, Waconia, Victoria. DAKOTA COUNTY (part). CITIES: Apple Valley, Burnsville, Eagan, Farmington, Hastings, Inver Grove Heights. GOODHUE COUNTY. CITIES: Cannon Falls, Pine Island, Red Wing, Zumbrota. LE SUEUR COUNTY. CITIES: Le Sueur, Le Center, Montgomery. RICE COUNTY. CITIES: Faribault, Northfield. SCOTT COUNTY. CITIES: Shakopee, Savage, Prior Lake, New Prague, Jordan, Belle Plaine. WASHINGTON COUNTY (part). CITIES: Woodbury, and Cottage Grove. Population (2000), 614,934.

ZIP Codes: 55001, 55009–10, 55016, 55018–20, 55021, 55024, 55026–27, 55031, 55033, 55041, 55044, 55046, 55049, 55052–55, 55057, 55065–66, 55068, 55071, 55075–77, 55085, 55087–89, 55118, 55121–25, 55129, 55306, 55315,

55317–18, 55322, 55328, 55331, 55337–39, 55346, 55352, 55359–60, 55363, 55367–68, 55372, 55378–79, 55383, 55386–88, 55394–95, 55397, 55399, 55550–55560, 55562, 55564, 55566–55568, 55573, 55583, 55594, 55946, 55956, 55963, 55983, 55985, 55992, 56011, 56017, 56028, 56050, 56052, 56057–58, 56063, 56069, 56071, 56093, 56096

* * *

THIRD DISTRICT

ERIK PAULSEN, Republican, of Eden Prairie, MN; born in Bakersfield, CA, May 14, 1965; education: B.A., St. Olaf College, Northfield, MN, 1987; Med Tech Caucus; National Guard Caucus; Diabetes Caucus; Law Enforcement Caucus; Financial Literacy Caucus; Sportsman's Caucus; Nuclear Issues Working Group; U.S. China Working Group; Renewable Energy Caucus; India Caucus; Zoo Caucus; Land Conservation Caucus; Bike Caucus; Congressional Services Fire Caucus; religion: Lutheran; married: Kelly; children: four daughters; committees: Ways and Means; elected to the 111th Congress on November 4, 2008; reelected to the 112th Congress.

Office Listings

http://www.paulsen.house.gov

127 Cannon House Office Building, Washington, DC 20515 .... (202) 225–2871
Chief of Staff.—Laurie Esau. FAX: 225–6351
Legislative Director.—Noah Jacobson.
Press Secretary.—Philip Minardi.
Scheduler.—Stacy Fuller.
250 Prairie Center Drive, Suite 230, Eden Prairie, MN 55344 .... (952) 405–8510
FAX: 405–8514

Counties: ANOKA (part), HENNEPIN (part). CITIES AND TOWNSHIPS: Bloomington, Brooklyn Center, Brooklyn Park, Champlin, Coon Rapids, Corcoran, Dayton, Deephaven, Eden Prarie, Edina, Excelsior, Greenfield, Greenwood, Hassan, Hopkins, Independence, Long Lake, Loretto, Maple Grove, Maple Plain, Medicine Lake, Medina, Minnetonka Beach, Minnetonka, Minnetrista, Mound, Orono, Osseo, Plymouth, Rogers, Saint Bonifacius, Shorewood, Spring Park, Tonka Bay, Wayzata, and Woodland. Population (2010), 650,185.

ZIP Codes: 55304–05, 55311, 55316, 55323, 55327, 55331, 55340–41, 55343–48, 55356–57, 55359, 55361, 55364, 55369, 55373–75, 55378, 55384, 55387–88, 55391–92, 55410, 55416, 55420, 55422–26, 55428–31, 55433, 55435–39, 55441–48, 55569–72, 55574, 55576–79, 55592–93, 55595–99

* * *

FOURTH DISTRICT

BETTY MCCOLLUM, Democrat-Farmer-Labor, of St. Paul, MN; born in Minneapolis, MN, July 12, 1954; education: A.A., Inver Hills Community College; B.S., College of St. Catherine; professional: teacher and sales manager; public service: North St. Paul City Council, 1986–92; Minnesota House of Representatives, 1992–2000; single; children: Sean and Katie; organizations: Girl Scouts of America; VFW Ladies' Auxiliary; and American Legion Ladies' Auxiliary; awards: Friend of the National Parks Award, National Parks Conservation Association, 2005; Friend of College Access Award, National Association for College Admission Counseling, 2006; Congressional Leadership Award, InterAction, 2006; Congressional Arts Leadership Award, Americans for the Arts, 2007; founder, Congressional Global Health Caucus; Senior Democratic Whip; appointments: National Council on the Arts; single; children: Sean and Katie; committees: Appropriations; Budget; elected to the 107th Congress on November 7, 2000; reelected to each succeeding Congress.

Office Listings

http://www.house.gov/mccollum

1714 Longworth House Office Building, Washington, DC 20515 .... (202) 225–6631
Chief of Staff.—Bill Harper. FAX: 225–1968
Legislative Director.—Peter Frosch.
Office Director.—Melissa Jamrock.
Communications Director.—Maria Reppas.
165 Western Avenue North, Suite 17, St. Paul, MN 55102 .... (651) 224–9191
District Director.—Joshua Straka.

Counties: DAKOTA (part), RAMSEY, WASHINGTON (part). Population (2000), 614,935.

ZIP Codes: 55016, 55042, 55055, 55071, 55075–77, 55090, 55101–10, 55112–20, 55125–29, 55133, 55144, 55146, 55150, 55155, 55161, 55164–66, 55168–70, 55172, 55175, 55177, 55182, 55187–88, 55190–91, 55199, 55421, 55432, 55449

* * *

FIFTH DISTRICT

KEITH ELLISON, Democrat-Farmer-Labor, of Minneapolis, MN; born in Detroit, MI, August 4, 1963; education: University of Detroit Jesuit High School and Academy, 1981; Wayne State University, 1987; University of Minnesota Law School, 1990; professional: The Law Office of Lindquist & Vennum, 1990–93; Executive Director of the nonprofit Legal Rights Center in Minneapolis, 1993–98; Hassan & Reed Ltd., 1998–2001; Ellison Law Offices, 2003–06; served in Minnesota State Legislature District 58B, 2003–06; married, four children; commissions: Center for Strategic and International Studies Commission on Global Health; House Democracy Assistance Commission; Tom Lantos Human Rights Commission; caucuses: founder, Consumer Justice Caucus; co-chair, Progressive Caucus; vice-chair, LBT Caucus; Congressional Black Caucus; Populist Caucus; Pro-Choice Caucus; Green Jobs Caucus; committees: Financial Services; elected to the 110th Congress on November 7, 2006; reelected to each succeeding Congress.

Office Listings

http://ellison.house.gov

1027 Longworth House Office Building, Washington, DC 20515 .... (202) 225–4755
Chief of Staff.—Kari Moe.
Legislative Director.—Minh Ta.
Communications Director.—Jennifer Gore.
2100 Plymouth Avenue, Minneapolis, MN 55411 .... (612) 522–1212
District Director.—Darlynn Benjamin.

Counties: ANOKA (part), HENNEPIN (part), RAMSEY (part). CITIES: Columbia Heights, Crystal, Ft. Snelling, Fridley, Golden Valley, Hilltop, Hopkins, Minneapolis, New Hope, Richfield, Robbinsdale, St. Anthony, St. Louis Park, and Spring Lake Park, Population (2000), 614,935.

ZIP Codes: 55111–12, 55305, 55343, 55401–30, 55432–33, 55440–41, 55450, 55454–55, 55458–60, 55470, 55472, 55474, 55479–80, 55483–88

* * *

SIXTH DISTRICT

MICHELE BACHMANN, Republican, of Stillwater, MN; born in Waterloo, IA, April 6, 1956; education: B.A., Winona State University, Winona, MN, 1978; J.D., Coburn School of Law, Oral Roberts University, Tulsa, OK; LL.M. in tax law at the College of William and Mary, Williamsburg, VA; professional: federal tax litigation attorney; served six years in the Minnesota State Senate; organizations: New Heights Charter School; married: Marcus; children: Lucas, Harrison, Elisa, Caroline, and Sophia; committees: Financial Services; Select Committee on Intelligence; elected to the 110th Congress on November 7, 2006; reelected to each succeeding Congress.

Office Listings

http://www.bachmann.house.gov

103 Cannon House Office Building, Washington, DC 20515 .... (202) 225–2331
Chief of Staff.—Brooke Bialke. FAX: 225–6475
Legislative Director.—Robert Boland.
Scheduler.—Kim Rubin.
Press Secretary.—Becky Rogness.
6043 Hudson Road, Suite 330, Woodbury, MN 55125 .... (651) 731–5400
110 2nd Street South, Suite 232, Waite Park, MN 56387 .... (320) 253–5931
FAX: 240–6905

Counties: ANOKA (part), BENTON, SHERBURNE, STEARNS (part), WASHINGTON (part), WRIGHT. CITIES: Andover, Anoka, Blaine, Elk River, Forest Lake, Lino Lakes, St. Cloud, Stillwater, Ramsey, and Woodbury. Population (2000), 614,935.

ZIP Codes: 55001, 55003, 55005–06, 55011, 55014, 55025, 55031, 55038, 55042–43, 55047, 55070, 55073, 55079, 55082–83, 55092, 55110, 55112, 55115, 55125, 55128–29, 55301–04, 55308–09, 55313, 55319–21, 55328–30, 55341, 55349, 55353, 55358–59, 55362–63, 55365, 55371, 55373–74, 55376, 55380–82, 55388–90, 55395, 55398, 55412–13, 55417–18, 55429–30, 55432, 55434, 55448–49, 56301, 56303–04, 56307, 56310, 56314, 56320, 56329–31, 56340, 56352, 56357, 56362, 56367–68, 56373–75, 56377, 56379, 56387–88, 56393, 56395–99

* * *

SEVENTH DISTRICT

COLLIN C. PETERSON, Democrat, of Detroit Lakes, MN; born in Fargo, ND, June 29, 1944; education: graduated from Glyndon (MN) High School, 1962; B.A. in business administration and accounting, Moorhead State University, 1966; U.S. Army National Guard, 1963–69; CPA, owner and partner; Minnesota State Senator, 1976–86; member: AOPA, Safari Club, Ducks Unlimited, American Legion, Sea Plane Pilots Association, Pheasants Forever, Benevolent Protective Order of Elks, Cormorant Lakes Sportsmen Club; three children: Sean, Jason, and Elliott; committees: ranking member, Agriculture; elected to the 102nd Congress, November 6, 1990; reelected to each succeeding Congress.

Office Listings

http://collinpeterson.house.gov

2211 Rayburn House Office Building, Washington, DC 20515 .... (202) 225–2165
Chief of Staff.—Cherie Slayton.
Legislative Director.—Robin Goracke.
Executive Assistant.—Martha Josephson.
Assistants: Matt Forbes, Chris Iacaruso, Shannon Juhnke, Richard Lee, Rebekah Solem, Brian Werner.
Lake Avenue Plaza Building, Suite 107, 714 Lake Avenue, Detroit Lakes, MN 56501 .... (218) 847–5056
Minnesota Wheat Growers Building, 2603 Wheat Drive, Red Lake, MN 56750 ..... (218) 253–4356
324 3rd Street, SW., Suite 4, Willmar, MN 56201 .... (320) 235–1061

Counties: BECKER, BELTRAMI (part), BIG STONE, CHIPPEWA, CLAY, CLEARWATER, DOUGLAS, GRANT, KANDIYOHI, KITTSON, LAC QUI PARLE, LAKE OF THE WOODS, LINCOLN, LYON, MAHNOMEN, MARSHALL, MCLEOD, MEEKER, NORMAN, OTTER TAIL, PENNINGTON, POLK, POPE, RED LAKE, REDWOOD, RENVILLE, ROSEAU, SIBLEY, STEARNS (part), STEVENS, SWIFT, TODD, TRAVERSE, WILKIN, YELLOW MEDICINE. Population (2000) 614,935.

ZIP Codes: 55307, 55310, 55312, 55314, 55321, 55324–25, 55329, 55332–36, 55338–39, 55342, 55350, 55353–55, 55366, 55368, 55370, 55381–82, 55385, 55389, 55395–96, 55409, 55970, 56011, 56044, 56054, 56058, 56083, 56085, 56087, 56113, 56115, 56129, 56132, 56136, 56142, 56149, 56152, 56157, 56164, 56166, 56169–70, 56175, 56178, 56180, 56201, 56207–12, 56214–16, 56218–32, 56235–37, 56239–41, 56243–45, 56248–49, 56251–53, 56255–58, 56260, 56262–67, 56270–71, 56273–74, 56276–85, 56287–89, 56291–97, 56301–04, 56307–12, 56314–16, 56318–21, 56323–24, 56326–27, 56329, 56331–32, 56334, 56336, 56339–40, 56343, 56345, 56347, 56349, 56352, 56354–55, 56360–62, 56368, 56372–74, 56377–79, 56381–82, 56385, 56387, 56393, 56395–99, 56433–34, 56436–38, 56440, 56443, 56446, 56453, 56458, 56461, 56464, 56466–67, 56470, 56475, 56477–79, 56481–82, 56501–02, 56510–11, 56514–25, 56527–29, 56531, 56533–38, 56540–54, 56556–57, 56560–63, 56565–81, 56583–94, 56601, 56619, 56621, 56623, 56633–34, 56644, 56646–47, 56650–52, 56661, 56663, 56666–67, 56670–71, 56673, 56676, 56678, 56682–87, 56701, 56710–11, 56713–16, 56720–29, 56731–38, 56740–42, 56744, 56748, 56750–51, 56754–63

* * *

EIGHTH DISTRICT

RAYMOND "CHIP" CRAVAACK, Republican, of Lindstrom, MN; born in Charleston, WV, December 29, 1959; B.S., U.S. Naval Academy, Annapolis, MD, 1981; M.Ed., University of West Florida, Pensacola, FL, 1989; U.S. Navy and Navy Reserve-Captain; active duty, 1981–90; Navy Reserve, 1990–2005; pilot, Northwest Airlines, 1990–2007; religion: Roman Catholic; married: Traci Cravaack; two children; committees: Homeland Security; Science, Space, and Technology; Transportation and Infrastructure; elected to the 112th Congress on November 2, 2010.

Office Listings

http://www.cravaack.house.gov

508 Cannon House Office Building, Washington, DC 20515 .... (202) 225–6211
Chief of Staff.—Mike Tomberlin.
Deputy Chief of Staff / Scheduler.—Alisa Rossini.
Legislative Director.—Paul Blocher.
Communications Director.—Shawn Ryan.
6448 Main Street, Suite 6, North Branch, MN 55056 .... (651) 237–8220
(888) 563–7390
Gerald W. Heaney Federal Building, 515 West First Street, Room 235, Duluth, MN 55802 .... (218) 740–7803
FAX: 740–7804
Brainerd City Hall, 501 Laurel Street, Brainerd, MN 56401 .... (218) 454–4078
FAX: 454–4096

Counties: AITKIN, BELTRAMI (part), CARLTON, CASS, CHISAGO, COOK, CROW WING, HUBBARD, ISANTI, ITASCA, KANABEC, KOOCHICHING, LAKE, MILLE LACS, MORRISON, PINE, ST. LOUIS, WADENA. CITIES: Brainerd, Chisholm, Cloquet, Duluth, Grand Rapids, Hibbing, International Falls, and Little Falls. Population (2000), 614,935.

ZIP Codes: 55002, 55005–08, 55012–13, 55017, 55025, 55029–30, 55032, 55036–37, 55040, 55045, 55051, 55056, 55063, 55067, 55069–70, 55072–74, 55078–80, 55084, 55092, 55330–31, 55362, 55371, 55377, 55398, 55408, 55601–07, 55609, 55612–16, 55701–13, 55716–26, 55730–36, 55738, 55741–42, 55744–46, 55748–53, 55756–58, 55760, 55763–69, 55771–72, 55775, 55777, 55779–87, 55790–93, 55795–98, 55801–08, 55810–12, 55814–16, 56028, 56058, 56304, 56307, 56309–11, 56313–15, 56317–19, 56323, 56325–33, 56335–36, 56338–45, 56347, 56350, 56353–61, 56363–64, 56367–69, 56371, 56373, 56376–77, 56381–82, 56384, 56386, 56389, 56401, 56425, 56430–31, 56433–35, 56437, 56441–44, 56446–50, 56452–53, 56455–56, 56458–59, 56461, 56464–70, 56472–75, 56477, 56479, 56481–82, 56484, 56601, 56623, 56626–31, 56633, 56636–37, 56639, 56641, 56647, 56649, 56653–55, 56657–63, 56668–69, 56672, 56678–81, 56683, 56688

MISSISSIPPI

(Population 2010, 2,967,297)

SENATORS

THAD COCHRAN, Republican, of Jackson, MS; born in Pontotoc, MS, December 7, 1937; education: B.A., University of Mississippi, 1959; J.D., University of Mississippi Law School, 1965; received a Rotary Foundation Fellowship and studied international law and jurisprudence at Trinity College, University of Dublin, Ireland, 1963–64; military service: served in U.S. Navy, 1959–61; professional: admitted to Mississippi bar in 1965; board of directors, Jackson Rotary Club, 1970–71; Outstanding Young Man of the Year Award, Junior Chamber of Commerce in Mississippi, 1971; president, young lawyers section of Mississippi State Bar, 1972–73; married: the former Rose Clayton of New Albany, MS, 1964; two children and three grandchildren; committees: ranking member, Appropriations; Agriculture, Nutrition, and Forestry; Rules and Administration; Joint Committee on the Library; elected to the 93rd Congress, November 7, 1972; reelected to 94th and 95th Congresses; chairman of the Senate Republican Conference, 1990–96; elected to the U.S. Senate, November 7, 1978, for the six-year term beginning January 3, 1979; subsequently appointed by the governor, December 27, 1978, to fill the vacancy caused by the resignation of Senator James O. Eastland; reelected to each succeeding Senate term.

Office Listings

http://cochran.senate.gov

113 Dirksen Senate Office Building, Washington, DC 20510 .... (202) 224–5054
Chief of Staff.—T.A. Hawks.
Legislative Director.—Steven Wall.
Press Secretary.—Chris Gallegos.
Scheduler.—Doris Wagley.
190 East Capitol Street, Suite 550, Jackson, MS 39201 .... (601) 965–4459
911 East Jackson Avenue, Suite 249, Oxford, MS 38655 .... (662) 236–1018
2012 15th Street, Suite 451, Gulfport, MS 39501 .... (228) 867–9710

* * *

ROGER F. WICKER, Republican, of Tupelo, MS; born in Pontotoc, MS, July 5, 1951; education: graduated Pontotoc High School; University of Mississippi: B.A., 1973; J.D., 1975; president, Associated Student Body, 1972–73; *Mississippi Law Journal,* 1973–75; Air Force ROTC; U.S. Air Force, 1976–80; U.S. Air Force Reserve, 1980–2004 (retired with rank of lieutenant colonel); U.S. House of Representatives Rules Committee staff for Representative Trent Lott, 1980–82; private law practice, 1982–94; Lee County Public Defender, 1984–87; Tupelo City Judge pro tempore, 1986–87; Mississippi State Senate, 1988–94, chairman: Elections Committee (1992), Public Health and Welfare Committee (1993–94); member: Lions Club, University of Mississippi Hall of Fame, Sigma Nu Fraternity Hall of Fame, Omicron Delta Kappa, Phi Delta Phi; religion: Southern Baptist, deacon, adult choir of First Baptist Church, Tupelo, MS; married: Gayle Long Wicker; children: Margaret (Manning) McPhillips, Caroline (Kirk) Sims, and McDaniel; grandchildren: Caroline McPhillips; committees: Armed Services; Banking, Housing, and Urban Affairs; Commerce, Science and Transportation; Veterans' Affairs; elected to the 104th Congress, November 8, 1994; president, Republican freshman class, 1995; reelected to each succeeding Congress; appointed by the governor, December 31, 2007, to fill the vacancy caused by the resignation of Senator Trent Lott; elected to the U.S. Senate on November 4, 2008.

Office Listings

http://wicker.senate.gov

555 Dirksen Senate Office Building, Washington, DC 20510 .... (202) 224–6253
Chief of Staff.—Michelle Barlow. FAX: 228–0378
Legislative Director.—Bob Foster.
Scheduler.—Hall Carter.
Communications Director.—Rick Curtsinger.
U.S. Federal Courthouse, 501 East Court Street, Suite 3–500, Jackson, MS 39201 (601) 965–4644
FAX: 695–4007
452 Courthouse Road, Suite F, Gulfport, MS 39507 .... (228) 604–2383
FAX: 896–4359
3118 Pascagoula Street, Suite 179, Pascagoula, MS 39567 .... (228) 762–5400
FAX: 762–0137
2801 West Main Street, Tupelo, MS 38801 .... (662) 844–5010

FAX: 844–5030
321 Losher Street, P.O. Box 385, Hernando, MS 38632 .... (662) 429–1002
FAX: 429–6002

REPRESENTATIVES

FIRST DISTRICT

ALAN NUNNELEE, Republican, of Tupelo, MS; born in Columbus, MS, October 9, 1958; education: Clinton High School, Clinton, MS, 1976; B.S., Mississippi State University, Starkville, MS, 1980; professional: Mississippi State Senate, 1994–2010; chairman, Appropriations Committee, 2008–10; religion: Southern Baptist; married: Tori Nunnelee; children: Reed, Emily, and Nathan; caucuses: Congressional Prayer Caucus; Congressional Sportsmen's Caucus; Congressional Constitution Caucus; Congressional Military Family Caucus; National Guard and Reserve Components Caucus; Immigration Reform Caucus; Congressional Coal Caucus; Congressional Nursing Caucus; committees: Appropriations; elected to the 112th Congress on November 2, 2010.

Office Listings

http://nunnelee.house.gov

1432 Longworth House Office Building, Washington, DC 20515 .... (202) 225–4306
Chief of Staff.—Diane Hawks. FAX: 225–3549
Legislative Director.—Meyer Seligman.
Communications Director.—Alexander Finestone.
Scheduler.—Tara Morgan.
133 East Commerce Street, Hernando, MS 38632 .... (662) 449–3090
337 East Main Street, Tupelo, MS 38804 .... (662) 841–8808
FAX: 841–8845
318–D Seventh Street North, Columbus, MS 39701 .... (662) 327–0748
FAX: 328–5982

Counties: ALCORN, BENTON, CALHOUN, CHICKASAW, CHOCTAW, CLAY, DESOTO, GRENADA, ITTAWAMBA, LAFAYETTE, LEE, LOWNDES, MARSHALL, MONROE, PANOLA, PONTOTOC, PRENTISS, TATE, TIPPAH, TISHIMINGO, UNION, WEBSTER (part), WINSTON (part), YALOBUSHA. Population (2000), 711,160.

ZIP Codes: 38601–03, 38606, 38610–11, 38618–21, 38625, 38627, 38629, 38632–35, 38637–38, 38641–42, 38647, 38649–52, 38654–55, 38658–59, 38661, 38663, 38665–66, 38668, 38670–74, 38677, 38679–80, 38683, 38685–86, 38801–04, 38820–21, 38824–29, 38833–35, 38838–39, 38841, 38843–44, 38846–52, 38854–60, 38862–66, 38868–71, 38873–80, 38901–02, 38913–16, 38920, 38922, 38925–27, 38929, 38940, 38948–49, 38951, 38953, 38955, 38960–61, 38965, 39108, 39339, 39701–05, 39710, 39730, 39735–37, 39740–41, 39743–46, 39750–56, 39759, 39766–67, 39769, 39771–73, 39776

* * *

SECOND DISTRICT

BENNIE G. THOMPSON, Democrat, of Bolton, MS; born in Bolton, January 28, 1948; education: graduated, Hinds County Agriculture High School; B.A., Tougaloo College, 1968; M.S., Jackson State University, 1972; professional: teacher; Bolton Board of Aldermen, 1969–73; mayor of Bolton, 1973–79; Hinds County Board of Supervisors, 1980–93; Congressional Black Caucus; Congressional Gaming Caucus; Congressional Sportsmen's Caucus; House Education Caucus; Rural Caucus; Progressive Caucus; Housing Assistance Council; NAACP 100 Black Men of Jackson, MS; Southern Regional Council; Kappa Alpha Psi Fraternity; married to the former London Johnson, Ph.D.; one daughter: BendaLonne; committees: ranking member, Homeland Security; elected to the 103rd Congress in a special election; reelected to each succeeding Congress.

Office Listings

http://www.benniethompson.house.gov

2466 Rayburn House Office Building, Washington, DC 20515 .... (202) 225–5876
Chief of Staff / Communications Director.—Lanier Avant. FAX: 225–5898
Administrative Assistant.—Marsha G. McCraven.
Legislative Director.—Vacant.
Scheduler.—Andrea Lee.
107 West Madison Street, P.O. Box 610, Bolton, MS 39041–0610 .... (601) 866–9003
District Director.—Charlie Horhn.
3607 Medgar Evers Boulevard, Jackson, MS 39213 .... (601) 982–8582

263 East Main Street, Marks, MS 38646 .... (662) 326–9003
Mound Bayou City Hall, Room 134, 106 West Green Street, Mound Bayou, MS 38762 .... (662) 741–9003
509 Highway 82 West, Greenwood, MS 38930 .... (662) 455–9003
910 Courthouse Lane, Greenville, MS 38701 .... (662) 335–9003

Counties: ATTALA, BOLIVAR, CARROLL, CLAIBORNE, COAHOMA, COPIAH, HINDS (part), HOLMES, HUMPHREYS, ISSAQUENA, JEFFERSON, LEAKE (part), LEFLORE, MADISON (part), MONTGOMERY, QUITMAN, SHARKEY, SUNFLOWER, TALLAHATCHIE, TUNICA, WARREN, WASHINGTON, YAZOO. Population (2000), 711,164.

ZIP Codes: 38606, 38609, 38614, 38617, 38621–23, 38626, 38628, 38630–31, 38639, 38643–46, 38664–65, 38669–70, 38676, 38701–04, 38720–23, 38725–26, 38730–33, 38736–40, 38744–46, 38748–49, 38751, 38753–54, 38756, 38758–62, 38764–65, 38767–69, 38771–74, 38776, 38778, 38780–82, 38901, 38912, 38917, 38920–21, 38923–25, 38927–28, 38930, 38935, 38940–41, 38943–48, 38950, 38952–54, 38957–59, 38961–64, 38966–67, 39038–41, 39045–46, 39051, 39054, 39056, 39058–61, 39063, 39066–67, 39069, 39071–72, 39077–79, 39083, 39086, 39088, 39090, 39095–97, 39107–08, 39110, 39113, 39115, 39120, 39144, 39146, 39150, 39154, 39156–57, 39159–60, 39162–63, 39166, 39169–71, 39173–77, 39179–83, 39191–92, 39194, 39201–07, 39209–10, 39212–13, 39215–17, 39225, 39235, 39269, 39271–72, 39282–84, 39286, 39289, 39296, 39653, 39661, 39668, 39745, 39747, 39767

* * *

THIRD DISTRICT

GREGG HARPER, Republican, of Pearl, MS; born in Jackson, MS, June 1, 1956; education: graduated from Pearl High School, Pearl, MS, 1974; B.S., Mississippi College, Clinton, MS, 1978; J.D., University of Mississippi, Oxford, MS, 1981; professional: prosecuting attorney; member, Pearl Chamber of Commerce, Rankin County Chamber of Commerce; Republican Steering Committee; religion: Southern Baptist; married: the former Sidney Carol Hancock; children: Livingston and Maggie; committees: chair, Joint Committee on Printing; vice-chair, Joint Committee on the Library; Energy and Commerce; House Administration; Ethics; elected to the 111th Congress on November 4, 2008; reelected to the 112th Congress.

Office Listings

http://www.harper.house.gov

307 Cannon House Office Building, Washington, DC 20515 .... (202) 225–5031
Chief of Staff.—Michael Cravens. FAX: 225–5797
Policy Director.—Scot Malvaney.
Communications Director.—Adam Buckalew.
Scheduler.—Marcy Scoggins.
2507–A Old Brandon Road, Pearl, MS 39208 .... (601) 932–2410
District Director.—Chip Reynolds.
1901 Front Street, Suite A, Meridian, MS 39301 .... (601) 693–6681
Special Assistant.—Ginny Clair Hitt.
1 Research Boulevard, Suite 206, Starkville, MS 39759 .... (662) 324–0007
Special Assistant.—Henry Moseley.
230 South Whitworth Street, Brookhaven, MS 39601 .... (601) 823–3400
District Field Representative.—Evan Gardner.

Counties: ADANS, AMITE, COVINGTON, FRANKLIN, HINDS (part), JASPER (part), JEFF DAVIS, JONES (part), KEMPER, LAUDERDALE, LAWRENCE, LEAKE (part), LINCOLN, MADISON (part), MARION (part), NESHOBA, NEWTON, NOXUBEE, OKTIBBEHA, PIKE, RANKIN, SCOTT, SIMPSON, SMITH, WALTHALL, WEBSTER (part), WILKINSON, WINSTON. Population (2000), 711,164.

ZIP Codes: 39041–44, 39046–47, 39051, 39057, 39062, 39069, 39071, 39073–74, 39078, 39080, 39082–83, 39087, 39090, 39092, 39094, 39098, 39108–12, 39114, 39116–17, 39119–22, 39130, 39140, 39145, 39148–49, 39151–53, 39157–58, 39161, 39165, 39167–68, 39189–91, 39193, 39202, 39206, 39208–09, 39211, 39213, 39216, 39218, 39232, 39236, 39288, 39298, 39301–05, 39307, 39309, 39320, 39323, 39325–28, 39332, 39335–39, 39341–42, 39345–46, 39350, 39352, 39354, 39358–59, 39361, 39364–65, 39402, 39421–22, 39427–29, 39439, 39443, 39460, 39474, 39478–80, 39482–83, 39601–03, 39629–33, 39635, 39638, 39641, 39643, 39645, 39647–49, 39652–54, 39656–57, 39661–69, 39701, 39735, 39739, 39743, 39750, 39755, 39759–60, 39762, 39769

* * *

FOURTH DISTRICT

STEVEN M. PALAZZO, Republican, of Biloxi, MS; born in Gulfport, MS, February 21, 1970; education: B.S., University of Southern Mississippi, Hattiesburg, MS, 1994; M.P.A., University of Southern Mississippi, Hattiesburg, 1996; professional: accountant; military, United States Marine Corps Reserve, 1988–96; Mississippi Army National Guard, 2007–present; member of Mississippi State House of Representatives, 2007–10; commissions and caucuses: Congressional Sportmen's Caucus; Gulf Coast Caucus; family: spouse, Lisa; children: Barrett, Aubrey, and Bennett; committees: Armed Services; Science, Space, and Technology; elected to the 112th Congress on November 2, 2010.

Office Listings

http://www.palazzo.house.gov

331 Rayburn House Office Building, Washington, DC 20515 .... (202) 225–5772
Chief of Staff.—Vacant. FAX: 225–7074
Deputy Chief of Staff / Legislative Director.—J.T. Jezierski.
Scheduler.—Whitney Donald.
1325 25th Avenue, Gulfport, MS 39501 .... (228) 864–7670
Deputy Chief of Staff.—Jamie M. Miller.
701 Main Street, Suite 215, Hattiesburg, MS 39401 .... (601) 582–3246
3118 Pascagoula Street, Suite 181, Pascagoula, MS 39567 .... (228) 202–8104

Counties: CLARKE, FORREST, GEORGE, GREENE, HANCOCK, HARRISON, JACKSON, JASPER (part), JONES, LAMAR, MARION (part), PEARL RIVER, PERRY, STONE, WAYNE. CITIES AND TOWNSHIPS: Biloxi, Gulfport, Hattiesburg, Laurel, and Pascagoula. Population (2000), 711,170.

ZIP Codes: 39301, 39307, 39322, 39324, 39330, 39332, 39347–48, 39355–56, 39360, 39362–63, 39366–67, 39401–04, 39406, 39422–23, 39425–26, 39429, 39436–37, 39439–43, 39451–52, 39455–57, 39459, 39461–66, 39470, 39475–78, 39480–82, 39501–03, 39505–07, 39520–22, 39525, 39529–35, 39540, 39552–53, 39555–56, 39558, 39560–69, 39571–74, 39576–77, 39581, 39595

MISSOURI

(Population 2010, 5,988,927)

SENATORS

CLAIRE McCASKILL, Democrat, of Kirkwood, MO; born in Rolla, MO, July 24, 1953; raised in Lebanon, MO and Columbia, MO; education: B.A., University of Missouri-Columbia, 1975; J.D., University of Missouri-Columbia School of Law, 1978; professional: clerk with the Missouri Court of Appeals, Western District in Kansas City, 1978; assistant prosecutor, Jackson County prosecutor's office, 1979–83; Missouri State Representative, 1983–88; practiced law in Kansas City, MO, 1983–92; Jackson County Legislator-At-Large, 1991–93; Jackson County Prosecutor, 1993–99; Missouri State Auditor, 1999–2006; married: Joseph Shephard, 2002; together, they have seven children: Benjamin, Carl, Marilyn, Michael, Austin, Maddie, Lily; appointed deputy whip for the majority, 2007; committees: Armed Services; Commerce, Science, and Transportation; Homeland Security and Governmental Affairs; Special Committee on Aging; elected to the U.S. Senate of the 110th Congress on November 7, 2006.

Office Listings

http://mccaskill.senate.gov

506 Hart Senate Office Building, Washington, DC 20510 .... (202) 224–6154
Chief of Staff.—Julie Dwyer. FAX: 228–6326
Deputy Chief of Staff.—Tod Martin.
Legislative Director.—Stephen Hedger.
Communications Director.—Trevor Kincaid.
5850 Delmar Boulevard, Suite A, St. Louis, MO 63112 .... (314) 367–1364
Regional Director.—Michelle Sherod.
4141 Pennsylvania Avenue, Suite 101, Kansas City, MO 64111 .... (816) 421–1639
Regional Director.—Corey Dillon.
555 Independence Avenue, Room 1600, Cape Girardeau, MO 63703 .... (573) 651–0964
District Director.—Christy Mercer.
915 East Ash Street, Columbia, MO 65201 .... (573) 442–7130
Regional Director.—Cindy Hall.
324 Park Central West, Suite 101, Springfield, MO 65806 .... (417) 868–8745
District Director.—David Rauch.

* * *

ROY BLUNT, Republican, of Springfield, MO; born in Niangua, MO, January 10, 1950; education: B.A., Southwest Baptist University, 1970; M.A., Missouri State University, 1972; professional: county clerk and chief election official of Greene County, 1972–84; Secretary of State of Missouri, 1984–92; president of Southwest Baptist University, 1993–96; U.S. House of Representatives for Missouri's 7th District, 1997–2010; married: Abigail Blunt; children: Governor Matthew Blunt, Amy Blunt, Andrew Blunt, Alexander Charles Blunt; committees: Appropriations; Commerce, Science and Transportation; Rules and Administration; Select Committee on Intelligence; elected to the U.S. Senate on November 2, 2010.

Office Listings

http://blunt.senate.gov

260 Russell Senate Office Building, Washington, DC 20510 .... (202) 224–5721
Chief of Staff.—Glen Chambers. FAX: 224–8149
Deputy Chief of Staff.—Burson Snyder.
Legislative Director.—Brian Diffell.
Communications Director.—Amber Marchand.
Director of Scheduling.—Richard Eddings.
2740B East Sunshine, Springfield, MO 65804 .... (417) 877–7814
911 Main Street, Suite 2224, Kansas City, MO 64105 .... (816) 471–7141
7700 Bonhomme, Suite 315, Clayton, MO 63105 .... (314) 725–4484
1001 Cherry Street, Suite 104, Columbia, MO 65201 .... (573) 442–8151
State Director.—Derek Coats.
308 East High, Suite 202, Jefferson City, MO 65101 .... (573) 634–2488
555 Independence Street, Suite 1500, Cape Girardeau, MO 63703 .... (573) 334–7044

REPRESENTATIVES

FIRST DISTRICT

WM. LACY CLAY, Democrat, of St. Louis, MO; born in St. Louis, July 27, 1956; education: Springbrook High School, Silver Spring, MD, 1974; B.S., University of Maryland, 1983, with a degree in government and politics, and a certificate in paralegal studies; public service: Missouri House of Representatives, 1983–91; Missouri State Senate, 1991–2000; nonprofit organizations: St. Louis Gateway Classic Sports Foundation; Mary Ryder Homes; William L. Clay Scholarship and Research Fund; divorced; children: Carol, and William III; committees: Financial Services; Oversight and Government Reform; elected to the 107th Congress on November 7, 2000; reelected to each succeeding Congress.

Office Listings

http://www.lacyclay.house.gov

2418 Rayburn House Office Building, Washington, DC 20515 .... (202) 225–2406
Chief of Staff.—Darryl A. Piggee.
Scheduler.—Karyn Long.
Legislative Assistants: Anthony Clark, Richard Pecantee, Marvin Steele.
625 North Euclid Avenue, Suite 326, St. Louis, MO 63108 .... (314) 367–1970
8021 West Florissant, St. Louis, MO 63136 .... (314) 890–0349
Communications Director.—Steven Engelhardt.

Counties: ST. LOUIS (part). Population (2000), 621,690.

ZIP Codes: 63031–34, 63042–44, 63074, 63101–08, 63110, 63112–15, 63117, 63119–22, 63124, 63130–38, 63141, 63145–47, 63150, 63155–56, 63160, 63164, 63166–67, 63169, 63171, 63177–80, 63182, 63188, 63190, 63195–99

* * *

SECOND DISTRICT

W. TODD AKIN, Republican, of St. Louis, MO; born in New York, NY, July 5, 1947; education: B.S., Worcester Polytechnic Institute, 1971; military service: Officer, U.S. Army Engineers; professional: engineer and businessman; IBM; Laclede Steel; taught International Marketing, undergraduate level; public service: appointed to the Bicentennial Commission of the U.S. Constitution, 1987; Missouri House of Representatives, 1988–2000; organizations: Boy Scouts of America; Missouri Right to Life; Mission Gate Prison Ministry; family: married to Lulli; children: Wynn, Perry, Micah, Ezra, Hannah and Abigail; committees: Armed Services; Budget; Science, Space, and Technology; elected to the 107th Congress on November 7, 2000; reelected to each succeeding Congress.

Office Listings

http://www.house.gov/akin

117 Cannon House Office Building, Washington, DC 20515 .... (202) 225–2561
Chief of Staff.—Lauren Ellis. FAX: 225–2563
Scheduler.—Tressa Merola.
301 Sovereign Court, Suite 201, St. Louis, MO 63011 .... (314) 590–0029
District Director.—Patrick Werner.

Counties: LINCOLN, ST. CHARLES (part), ST. LOUIS (part). Population (2000), 621,690.

ZIP Codes: 63001, 63005–06, 63011, 63017, 63021–22, 63024–26, 63038, 63040, 63043, 63049, 63069, 63088, 63099, 63110, 63114, 63117, 63119, 63122–29, 63131, 63134, 63141, 63144–46, 63301–04, 63333–34, 63338, 63343–44, 63346–49, 63359, 63362, 63366–67, 63369–70, 63373, 63376–77, 63379, 63381, 63383, 63385–87, 63389–90

* * *

THIRD DISTRICT

RUSS CARNAHAN, Democrat, of St. Louis, MO; born in Columbia, MO, July 10, 1958; education: B.S., public administration, University of Missouri-Columbia, 1979; J.D., University of Missouri-Columbia School of Law, 1983; professional: Missouri State Representative, 2001–04; BJC Healthcare, 1995–2004; private law practice; organizations: United Way of Greater St.

Louis; St. Louis Regional Commerce and Growth Association; FOCUS Leadership St. Louis, Class of 1997–98; State Historical Society of Missouri; Landmarks Association of St. Louis; Compton Heights Neighborhood Association; Missouri Bar Association; Bar Association of Metropolitan St. Louis; Boy Scouts, Eagle Scout recipient; Friends of Tower Grove Park, Missouri Botanical Gardens and DeMenil Mansion; awards: St. Louis Regional Chamber of Commerce and Growth Association Lewis and Clark Statesman Award; St. Louis Business Journal 2002 Legislative Award and the Missouri Bar 2002 Legislative Award; married: Debra Carnahan; children: Austin and Andrew; committees: Foreign Affairs; Transportation and Infrastructure; Veterans' Affairs; elected to the 109th Congress on November 2, 2004; reelected to each succeeding Congress.

Office Listings

http://russcarnahan.house.gov

1710 Longworth House Office Building, Washington, DC 20515 .... (202) 225–2671
Chief of Staff.—Caroline Pelot Battles. FAX: 225–7452
Legislative Director.—Ken Reidy.
Communications Director.—Sara Howard.
Scheduler.—Margy Levinson.
8764 Manchester Road, Suite 203, St. Louis, MO 63144 .... (314) 962–1523
Communications Director.—Jim Hubbard.

Counties: JEFFERSON, SAINTE GENEVIEVE, ST. LOUIS, ST. LOUIS CITY. CITIES: St. Louis. Population (2000), 621,690.

ZIP Codes: 63010, 63012, 63015–16, 63019–20, 63023, 63025–26, 63028, 63030, 63036, 63041, 63047–53, 63057, 63060, 63065–66, 63069–72, 63087, 63102, 63104–05, 63109–11, 63116–19, 63122–30, 63132, 63139, 63143–44, 63151, 63157–58, 63163, 63627–28, 63640, 63645, 63661, 63670, 63673

* * *

FOURTH DISTRICT

VICKY HARTZLER, Republican, of Harrisonville, MO; born in Archie, MO, October 13, 1960; education: B.S., in education, *summa cum laude,* University of Missouri-Columbia, Columbia, MO, 1983; M.S., in education, Central Missouri State University (now University of Central Missouri), Warrensburg, MO, 1992; professional: served as State spokesperson for the Coalition to Protect Marriage, 2004; member of the Missouri State House of Representatives, 124th District, 1995–2001; appointed chair, Missouri Women's Council, 2005; teacher of family and consumer sciences for 11 years in Lebanon and Belton, MO; religion: Evangelical Christian; family: married Lowell Hartzler; one child: Tiffany, caucuses: Pro-Life Caucus; Israel Allies Caucus; Republican Study Committee; Tea Party Caucus; Air Force Caucus; Immigration Caucus; Missile Defense Caucus; Human Trafficking Caucus; Small Business Caucus; Prayer Caucus; Military Family Caucus; Job Creators' Caucus; Rural Caucus; committees: Agriculture; Armed Services; elected to the 112th Congress on November 2, 2010.

Office Listings

http://www.hartzler.house.gov

1023 Longworth House Office Building, Washington, DC 20515 .... (202) 225–2876
Chief of Staff.—Jim Hayes. FAX: 225–0148
Legislative Director.—Eric Bohl.
Communications Director.—Steve Walsh.
Scheduler.—Kristin Dowd.
2409 Hyde Park, Jefferson City, MO 65109 .... (573) 634–4884
1909 North Commercial Street, Harrisonville, MO 64701 .... (816) 884–3411
219 North Adams Street, Lebanon, MO 65536 .... (417) 532–5582
415 South Ohio Avenue, Suite 212B, Sedalia, MO 65301 .... (573) 634–4884

Counties: BARTON, BATES, BENTON, CAMDEN (part), CASS (part), CEDAR, COLE, DADE, DALLAS, HENRY, HICKORY, JACKSON (part), JOHNSON, LACLEDE, LAFAYETTE, MONITEAU, MORGAN, PETTIS, POLK (part), PULASKI, RAY, SALINE, ST. CLAIR, VERNON, WEBSTER. Population (2000), 621,690.

ZIP Codes: 64001, 64011, 64013–14, 64016–17, 64019–22, 64024, 64029, 64034–37, 64040, 64058, 64061–62, 64067, 64071, 64074–77, 64080, 64082, 64084–86, 64088, 64090, 64093, 64096–97, 64624, 64637, 64668, 64670–71, 64701, 64720, 64722–26, 64728, 64730, 64733, 64735, 64738–48, 64750, 64752, 64755–56, 64759, 64761–63, 64765, 64767, 64769–72, 64776, 64778–81, 64783–84, 64788, 64790, 64832, 64855, 65011, 65018, 65020, 65023, 65025–26, 65032, 65034, 65037–38, 65040, 65042, 65046, 65049–50, 65052–53, 65055, 65065, 65072, 65074, 65076, 65078–79, 65081, 65084, 65101–11, 65287, 65301–02, 65305, 65320–21, 65323–27, 65329–30, 65332–40, 65344–45, 65347–51, 65354–55, 65360, 65452, 65457, 65459, 65461, 65463, 65470, 65473, 65534, 65536, 65543, 65550, 65552, 65556–67, 65572, 65583–84, 65590–91, 65601, 65603–04, 65607, 65632, 65634–36, 65640, 65644, 65646, 65648–50, 65652, 65661–62, 65668, 65674, 65682, 65685, 65706, 65713, 65722, 65724, 65727, 65732, 65735, 65742, 65746, 65752, 65757, 65764, 65767, 65774, 65779, 65783, 65785–87

* * *

FIFTH DISTRICT

EMANUEL CLEAVER II, Democrat, of Kansas City, MO; born in Waxahachie, TX, October 27, 1944; education: M. Div., Saint Paul School of Theology, MO, 1974; B.S., Prairie View A&M University, TX, 1972; professional: Senior Pastor, St. James United Methodist Church, 1973–2009; City Councilman, Kansas City, MO, 5th District, 1979–91; founder, Harmony in a World of Difference, 1991; founder, Southern Christian Leadership Conference, Kansas City Chapter; Mayor of Kansas City, MO, 1991–99; member, President-elect Bill Clinton's Transitional Team, 1992; host, Under the Clock, KCUR radio, 1999–2004; chairman of the Congressional Black Caucus; married: Dianne; four children; three grandchildren; committees: Financial Services; elected to the 109th Congress on November 2, 2004; reelected to each succeeding Congress.

Office Listings

http://www.house.gov/cleaver

1433 Longworth House Office Building, Washington, DC 20515 .... (202) 225–4535
Chief of Staff.—Leslie Woolley FAX: 225–4403
Legislative Director.—Cassandra Young.
Scheduler.—Brad Benton.
101 West 31st Street, Kansas City, MO 64108 .... (816) 842–4545
District Director.—Geoff Jolley.
Communications Director.—Danny Rotert.
211 Maple Avenue, Independence, MO 64050 .... (816) 833–4545

Counties: CASS COUNTY (part), JACKSON COUNTY (part). CITIES AND TOWNSHIPS: Belton, Grandview, Greenwood, Independence, Kansas City, Lee's Summit, Peculiar, Raymore, Raytown, and Sugar Creek. Population (2000), 621,691.

ZIP Codes: 64012, 64014–15, 64029–30, 64034, 64050–58, 64061, 64063–65, 64070, 64075, 64078, 64080–83, 64086, 64101–02, 64105–06, 64108–14, 64120–21, 64123–34, 64136–39, 64141, 64145–49, 64170–71, 64179–80, 64184–85, 64187–88, 64191–94, 64196–99, 64701, 64734, 64944, 64999

* * *

SIXTH DISTRICT

SAM GRAVES, Republican, of Tarkio, MO; born in Fairfax, MO, November 7, 1963; education: B.S., University of Missouri-Columbia, 1986; professional: farmer; organizations: Missouri Farm Bureau; Northwest Missouri State University Agriculture Advisory Committee; University Extension Council; Rotary Club; awards: Associated Industries Voice of Missouri Business Award; Tom Henderson Award; Tarkio Community Betterment Award; Missouri Physical Therapy Association Award; Outstanding Young Farmer Award, 1997; Hero of the Taxpayer Award; NFIB Guardian of Small Business Award; public service: elected to the Missouri House of Representatives, 1992; and the Missouri State Senate, 1994; religion: Baptist; married: Lesley; children: Megan, Emily, and Sam III; committees: chair, Small Business; Transportation and Infrastructure; elected to the 107th Congress on November 7, 2000; reelected to each succeeding Congress.

Office Listings

http://www.house.gov/graves

1415 Longworth House Office Building, Washington, DC 20515 .... (202) 225–7041
Chief of Staff.—Tom Brown. FAX: 225–8221
Press Secretary.—Jason Klindt.
201 South Eighth Street, Room 330, St. Joseph, MO 64501 .... (816) 233–9818
113 Blue Jay Drive, Suite 100, Liberty, MO 64068 .... (816) 792–3976

Counties: ANDREW, ATCHISON, BUCHANAN, CALDWELL, CARROLL, CHARITON, CLAY, CLINTON, COOPER, DAVIESS, DEKALB, GENTRY, GRUNDY, HARRISON, HOLT, HOWARD, JACKSON (part), LINN, LIVINGSTON, MERCER, NODAWAY, PLATTE, PUTNAM, SCHUYLER, SULLIVAN, WORTH. Population (2000), 621,690.

ZIP Codes: 63535–36, 63541, 63544–46, 63548, 63551, 63556–57, 63560–61, 63565–67, 64013–16, 64018, 64024, 64028–29, 64048, 64056–58, 64060, 64062, 64064, 64066, 64068–69, 64072–75, 64077, 64079, 64085–88, 64092, 64098, 64116–19, 64144, 64150–58, 64161, 64163–68, 64188, 64190, 64193, 64195, 64243, 64401–02, 64420–24, 64426–34, 64436–49, 64451, 64453–59, 64461, 64463, 64465–71, 64473–77, 64479–94, 64496–99, 64501–08, 64601, 64620, 64622–25, 64628, 64630–33, 64635–61, 64664, 64667–68, 64670–74, 64676, 64679, 64681–83, 64686, 64688–89, 65018, 65025, 65046, 65068, 65081, 65230, 65233, 65236–37, 65246, 65248, 65250, 65254, 65256–57, 65261, 65274, 65276, 65279, 65281, 65286–87, 65301, 65322, 65347–48, 65354

* * *

SEVENTH DISTRICT

BILLY LONG, Republican, of Springfield, MO; born in Niangua, MO, August 11, 1955; education: attended, University of Missouri, Columbia, MO, 1973–74; Missouri Auction School, Kansas City, MO, 1979; Certified Auctioneer Institute designation, University of Indiana, Bloomington, IN; professional: owner, Billy Long Auctions, LLC; radio talk show host, KWTO AM 560; member: National Association of Realtors; National Auctioneers Association; National Board of Directors; Springfield Area Chamber of Commerce; former president, Missouri Professional Auctioneers Association; Southeast Rotary Club, Springfield; awards: Missouri Professional Auctioneers' Hall of Fame; Outstanding Young Alumni Award, Greenwood Lab School; religion: Presbyterian; family: wife, Barbara Long; daughters; caucuses: Republican Caucus; committees: Homeland Security; Transportation and Infrastructure; elected to the 112th Congress on November 2, 2010.

Office Listings

http://long.house.gov

1541 Longworth House Office Building, Washington, DC 20515 .... (202) 225–6536
Chief of Staff.—Joe Lillis. FAX: 225–5604
Legislative Director.—Scott Shiller.
Scheduler.—Laura McElwain.
Communications Director.—Bret Funk.
3232 East Ridgeview Street, Springfield, MO 65804 .... (417) 889–1899
FAX: 889–4915
2727 East 32nd Street, Suite 2, Joplin, MO 64804 .... (417) 781–1041
FAX: 781–2832

Counties: BARRY, CHRISTIAN, GREENE, JASPER, LAWRENCE, MCDONALD, NEWTON, POLK (part), STONE, TANEY (part). Population (2000), 621,690.

ZIP Codes: 64748, 64755–56, 64766, 64769, 64801–04, 64830–36, 64840–44, 64847–50, 64853–59, 64861–70, 64873–74, 65603–05, 65608–20, 65622–27, 65629–31, 65633, 65635, 65637–38, 65640–41, 65645–50, 65652–58, 65661, 65663–64, 65666, 65669, 65672–76, 65680–82, 65686, 65702, 65705, 65707–08, 65710, 65712, 65714–15, 65720–21, 65723, 65725–30, 65733–34, 65737–42, 65744–45, 65747, 65752–57, 65759–62, 65765–73, 65781, 65784–85, 65801–10, 65814, 65817, 65890, 65898–99

* * *

EIGHTH DISTRICT

JO ANN EMERSON, Republican, of Cape Girardeau, MO; born in Washington, DC, September 16, 1950; education: B.A., political science, Ohio Wesleyan University, Delaware, OH, 1972; Senior Vice President of Public Affairs, American Insurance Association; director, State Relations and Grassroots Programs, National Restaurant Association; deputy communications director, National Republican Congressional Committee; member: board of directors, Bread for the World; co-chair, board of directors, Congressional Hunger Caucus; PEO Women's Service Group, Cape Girardeau, MO; Copper Dome Society, Southeast Missouri State University; advisory committee, Children's Inn, National Institutes of Health; advisory board, Arneson Institute for Practical Politics and Public Affairs, Ohio Weslyan University; married: Ron Gladney, 2000; children: Victoria and Katharine; six stepchildren: Elizabeth, Abigail, Victoria, Stephanie, Alison, Jessica, and Sam; committees: Appropriations; elected on November 5, 1996, by special election, to the 104th Congress; reelected to each succeeding Congress.

Office Listings

http://www.house.gov/emerson

2230 Rayburn House Office Building, Washington, DC 20515 .... (202) 225–4404
Chief of Staff.—Jeffrey Connor. FAX: 226–0326
Executive Assistant / Scheduler.—Atalie Ebersole.
555 Independence, Suite 1400, Cape Girardeau, MO 63703 .... (573) 335–0101
Chief of Staff.—Josh Haynes.
1301 Kingshighway, Rolla, MO 65401 .... (573) 364–2455
35 Court Square, Suite 300, West Plains, MO 65775 .... (417) 255–1515
22 East Columbia, Farmington, MO 63640 .... (573) 756–9755

Counties: BOLLINGER, BUTLER, CAPE GIRARDEAU, CARTER, DENT, DOUGLAS, DUNKLIN, HOWELL, IRON, MADISON, MISSISSIPPI, NEW MADRID, OREGON, OZARK, PEMISCOT, PERRY, PHELPS, REYNOLDS, RIPLEY, ST. FRANCOIS, SCOTT, SHANNON, STODDARD, TANEY (part), TEXAS, WASHINGTON, WAYNE, WRIGHT. Population (2000), 621,690.

ZIP Codes: 63036, 63071, 63601, 63620–26, 63628–33, 63636–38, 63640, 63648, 63650–51, 63653–56, 63660, 63662–66, 63674–75, 63701–03, 63730, 63732, 63735–40, 63742–48, 63750–52, 63755, 63758, 63760, 63763–64, 63766–67, 63769–72, 63774–76, 63779–85, 63787, 63801, 63820–30, 63833–34, 63837, 63839–41, 63845–53, 63855, 63857, 63860, 63862–63, 63866–70, 63873–82, 63901–02, 63931–45, 63950–57, 63960–67, 65401–02, 65409, 65436, 65438–41, 65444, 65446, 65449, 65453, 65456, 65459, 65461–62, 65464, 65466, 65468, 65479, 65483–84, 65501, 65529, 65532, 65541–42, 65546, 65548, 65550, 65552, 65555, 65557, 65564–66, 65570–71, 65586, 65588–89, 65606, 65608–09, 65614, 65616, 65618, 65620, 65626–27, 65629, 65637–38, 65652–53, 65655, 65660, 65662, 65666–67, 65676, 65679–80, 65688–90, 65692, 65701–02, 65704, 65711, 65713, 65715, 65717, 65720, 65729, 65731, 65733, 65740–41, 65744, 65746, 65753, 65755, 65759–62, 65766, 65768, 65773, 65775, 65777–78, 65784, 65788–91, 65793

* * *

NINTH DISTRICT

BLAINE LUETKEMEYER, Republican, of St. Elizabeth, MO; born in Jefferson City, MO, May 7, 1952; education: graduate of Lincoln University, Jefferson City, MO, 1974; where he earned a degree with distinction in political science and a minor in business administration, 1999–2005; professional: served as Missouri State Representative and after leaving office was appointed by the governor to serve as the Director of the Missouri Division of Tourism; lifelong member of St. Elizabeth Catholic Church; married: Jackie, three children; committees: Financial Services; elected to the 111th Congress on November 4, 2008; reelected to the 112th Congress.

Office Listings

http://luetkemeyer.house.gov

1740 Longworth House Office Building, Washington, DC 20515 .... (202) 225–2956
Chief of Staff.—Seth Appleton. FAX: 225–5712
Legislative Director.—Ali Gabel.
Senior Legislative Assistant.—Chris Brown.
Legislative Assistant.—Chris Mindnich.
Legislative Aide.—Christy Knese.
Deputy Press Secretary.—Keith Beardslee.
Director of Scheduling.—Brittney Loch.

3809 South Providence, Suite A, Columbia, MO 65203 .... (573) 443–1041
District Director.—Gary Marble FAX: 443–1050
Press Secretary.—Paul Sloca.
Special Assistant.—Jeremy Ketterer.
Director of Constituent Affairs.—Keri Stuart.
Caseworker.—Lori Boykin.
Office Manager.—Laura Hardecke.

516 Jefferson Street, Washington, MO 63090 .... (636) 239–2276
Deputy District Director.—Dan Engemann. FAX 239–0478
Staff Assistant.—Mary Tinsley.

201 North Third Street, Suite 120, Hannibal, MO 63401 .... (573) 231–1012
Field Representative.—Tanner Smith. FAX: 231–1014

Counties: Adair, Audrain, Boone, Callaway, Camden (part), Clark, Crawford, Franklin, Gasconade, Knox, Lewis, Macon, Maries, Marion, Miller, Monroe, Montgomery, Osage, Pike, Ralls, Randolph, St. Charles (part), Scotland, Shelby, Warren. Population (2000), 621,690.

ZIP Codes: 63005, 63013–15, 63037, 63039, 63041, 63055–56, 63060, 63068–69, 63072–73, 63077, 63079–80, 63084, 63089–91, 63303–04, 63330, 63332–34, 63336, 63339, 63341–42, 63344–45, 63348–53, 63357, 63359, 63361, 63363, 63365–67, 63376, 63378, 63381–85, 63388, 63390, 63401, 63430–43, 63445–48, 63450–54, 63456–69, 63471–74, 63501, 63530–34, 63536–40, 63543–44, 63546–47, 63549, 63552, 63555, 63557–59, 63563, 64631, 64658, 64856, 65001, 65010, 65013–14, 65016–17, 65024, 65026, 65031–32, 65035–36, 65039–41, 65043, 65047–49, 65051, 65054, 65058–59, 65061–67, 65069, 65072, 65074–77, 65080, 65082–83, 65085, 65101, 65201–03, 65205, 65211–12, 65215–18, 65230–32, 65239–40, 65243–44, 65247, 65251, 65255–60, 65262–65, 65270, 65275, 65278–85, 65299, 65337, 65441, 65443, 65446, 65449, 65452–53, 65456, 65459, 65486, 65535, 65559–60, 65565, 65580, 65582, 65586, 65591

MONTANA

(Population 2010, 989,415)

SENATORS

MAX BAUCUS, Democrat, of Helena, MT; born in Helena, December 11, 1941; education: graduated, Helena High School, 1959; B.A. in economics, Stanford University, 1964; LL.B., Stanford University Law School, 1967; attorney, Civil Aeronautics Board, 1967–71; attorney, George and Baucus law firm, Missoula, MT; member, Montana and District of Columbia Bar Associations; served in Montana House of Representatives, 1973–74; one child, Zeno; committees: chair, Finance; vice chair, Joint Committee on Taxation; Agriculture, Nutrition, and Forestry; Environment and Public Works; elected to the 94th Congress, November 5, 1974; reelected to the 95th Congress; elected to the U.S. Senate, November 7, 1978, for the six-year term beginning January 3, 1979; subsequently appointed on December 15, 1978, to fill the vacancy caused by the resignation of Senator Paul Hatfield; reelected to each succeeding Senate term.

Office Listings

http://baucus.senate.gov

511 Hart Senate Office Building, Washington, DC 20510 .... (202) 224–2651
Chief of Staff.—Jon Selib. FAX: 224–0515
Legislative Director.—Paul Wilkins.
Press Secretary.—Jennifer Donohue.
DC Scheduler.—Nancy Orloff.
222 North 32nd Street, Suite 100, Billings, MT 59101 .... (406) 657–6790
220 West Lamme, Suite 1D, Bozeman, MT 59715 .... (406) 586–6104
27 North Wyoming, Suite A, Butte, MT 59701 .... (406) 782–8700
113 3rd Street North, Great Falls, MT 59401 .... (406) 761–1574
30 West 14th Street, Helena, MT 59601 .... (406) 449–5480
8 Third Street East, Kalispell, MT 59901 .... (406) 756–1150
280 East Front Street, Missoula, MT 59801 .... (406) 329–3123
122 West Towne Street, Glendive, MT 59330 .... (406) 365–7002
State Chief of Staff.—John Lewis.

* * *

JON TESTER, Democrat, of Big Sandy, MT; born in Havre, MT, August 21, 1956; education: graduated, Big Sandy High School, 1974; B.S. in Music, University of Great Falls, 1978; professional: farmer, T-Bone Farms, Big Sandy, 1978–present; teacher, Big Sandy School District, 1978–80; member, Big Sandy Soil Conservation Service Committee, 1980–83; chairman, Big Sandy School Board of Trustees, 1983–92; Past Master, Treasure Lodge #95 of the Masons; member, Chouteau County Agricultural Stabilization and Conservation Service Committee, 1990–95; member, Organic Crop Improvement Association, 1996–97; served in Montana Senate, 1999–2007; Montana Senate Democratic Whip, 2001–03; Montana Senate Democratic Leader, 2003–05; Montana Senate President, 2005–07; vice chair, Congressional Sportsmen's Caucus; married: Sharla Tester; two children: Christine and Shon; committees: Appropriations; Banking, Housing, and Urban Affairs; Homeland Security and Governmental Affairs; Indian Affairs; Veterans' Affairs; elected to the U.S. Senate on November 7, 2006.

Office Listings

http://tester.senate.gov

http://www.facebook.com/senatortester

724 Hart Senate Office Building, Washington, DC 20510 .... (202) 224–2644
Chief of Staff.—Tom Lopach. FAX: 224–8594
Legislative Director.—James Wise
Communications Director.—Aaron Murphy.
Director of Scheduling.—Trecia McEvoy.
State Director.—Bill Lombardi.
Montana Staff Director.—Dayna Swanson.
222 North 32nd Street, Suite 101, Billings, MT 59101 .... (406) 252–0550
1 East Main Street, Suite 202, Bozeman, MT 59715 .... (406) 586–4450
125 West Granite, Suite 200, Butte, MT 59701 .... (406) 723–3277
122 West Towne, Glendive, MT 59330 .... (406) 452–9585
119 First Avenue North, Suite 102, Great Falls, MT 59401 .... (406) 452–9585
208 North Montana Avenue, Suite 202, Helena, MT 59601 .... (406) 449–5401
State Director.—Bill Lombardi.
14 Third Street East, Suite 230, Kalispell, MT 59901 .... (406) 257–3360

130 West Front Street, Missoula, MT 59801 .... (406) 728–3003

REPRESENTATIVE

AT LARGE

DENNY REHBERG, Republican, of Billings, MT; born in Billings, October 5, 1955; education: B.A., Washington State University, 1977; professional: rancher; public service: interned in the Montana State Senate, 1977–79; legislative assistant to Rep. Ron Marlenee (R–MT), 1979–82; elected to the Montana House of Representatives, 1984; appointed Lt. Governor of Montana in 1991; elected Lt. Governor in 1992; chairman, Drought Advisory Committee; Worker's Compensation Task Force; and the Montana Rural Development Council; Republican nominee for the U.S. Senate, 1996; married: Janice; children: A.J., Katie, and Elsie; committees: Appropriations; elected to the 107th Congress on November 7, 2000; reelected to each succeeding Congress.

Office Listings

http://www.rehberg.house.gov

2448 Rayburn House Office Building, Washington, DC 20515 .... (202) 225–3211
Chief of Staff.—Jay Martin. FAX: 225–5687
Communications Director.—Jed Link.
1201 Grand Avenue, Suite 101, Billings, MT 59102 .... (406) 256–1019
District Director.—Randy Vogel.
105 Smelter Avenue, NE., Suite 116, Great Falls, MT 59404 .... (406) 454–1066
950 North Montana Avenue, Helena, MT 59601 .... (406) 443–7878
301 East Broadway, Suite 2, Missoula, MT 59802 .... (406) 543–9550

Counties: Beaverhead, Big Horn, Blaine, Broadwater, Carbon, Carter, Cascade, Chouteau, Custer, Daniels, Dawson, Deer Lodge, Fallon, Fergus, Flathead, Gallatin, Garfield, Glacier, Golden Valley, Granite, Hill, Jefferson, Judith Basin, Lake, Lewis and Clark, Liberty, Lincoln, Madison, McCone, Meagher, Mineral, Missoula, Mussellshell Park, Petroleum, Phillips, Pondera, Powder River, Powell, Prairie, Ravalli, Richland, Roosevelt, Rosebud, Sanders, Sheridan, Silver Bow, Stillwater, Sweet Grass, Teton, Toole, Treasure, Valley, Wheatland, Wibaux, Yellowstone. Population (2000), 902,195.

ZIP Codes: 59001–04, 59006–08, 59010–16, 59018–20, 59022, 59024–39, 59041, 59043–44, 59046–47, 59050, 59052–55, 59057–59, 59061–72, 59074–79, 59081–89, 59101–08, 59201, 59211–15, 59217–19, 59221–23, 59225–26, 59230–31, 59240–44, 59247–48, 59250, 59252–63, 59270, 59273–76, 59301, 59311–19, 59322–24, 59326–27, 59330, 59332–33, 59336–39, 59341, 59343–45, 59347, 59349, 59351, 59353–54, 59401–06, 59410–12, 59414, 59416–22, 59424–25, 59427, 59430, 59432–36, 59440–48, 59450–54, 59456–57, 59460–69, 59471–72, 59474, 59477, 59479–80, 59482–87, 59489, 59501, 59520–32, 59535, 59537–38, 59540, 59542, 59544–47, 59601–02, 59604, 59620, 59623–24, 59626, 59631–36, 59638–45, 59647–48, 59701–03, 59710–11, 59713–22, 59724–25, 59727–33, 59735–36, 59739–41, 59743, 59745–52, 59754–56, 59758–62, 59771–73, 59801–04, 59806–08, 59812, 59820–21, 59823–35, 59837, 59840–48, 59851, 59853–56, 59858–60, 59863–68, 59870–75, 59901, 59903–04, 59910–23, 59925–37

NEBRASKA

(Population 2010, 1,826,341)

SENATORS

BEN NELSON, Democrat, of Omaha, NE; born in McCook, NE, May 17, 1941; education: B.A., 1963, M.A., 1965, J.D., 1970, University of Nebraska, Lincoln, NE; honorary degrees, Creighton University, 1992; Peru State College, 1993; College of Saint Mary, 1995; Midland Lutheran College, 1998; Dana College, 1999; professional: attorney; Director, Nebraska Department of Insurance; President and CEO of the Central National Insurance Group; Executive Vice President and Chief of Staff of the National Association of Insurance Commissioners; Kennedy, Holland, DeLacy, and Svoboda (law firm); Governor of Nebraska, 1991–99; awards: American Legislative Exchange Council, Thomas Jefferson Freedom Award; National Guard, Charles Dick Medal of Merit; American Legion, Nebraska Chapter, Outstanding Service and Assistance to Veterans; Business Industry Political Action Committee, Adam Smith Award; U.S. Chamber of Commerce, Spirit of Enterprise Awards; National Association of Manufacturers, Award for Manufacturing Legislative Excellence; Independent Bankers Association, Hon. Horst G. Denk Congressional Award; Small Business Survival Committee Award; National Association of Mutual Insurance Companies, Benjamin Franklin Public Policy Award; Coalition for Medicare Choices, Leadership Award; American Hospital Association, Appreciation for Distinguished Leadership; National Rural Health Association, Rural Health Champion Award; Nebraska Rural Health Association, President's Award; Madonna Rehabilitation Hospital, Madonna Spirit Award; American Network of Community Options and Resources, Congressional Award; American Association of Community Colleges' Council for Resource Development, Congressional Award; Nebraska Investment Finance Authority, Housing Champion Award; National Council for Adoption, Hall of Fame Award; Indian American Friendship Council, Recognition of Service Award; Pheasants Forever, Conservation Service Award; Renewable Energy Alliance, Renewable Energy Leadership Award; American Farm Bureau, Friend of Farm Bureau Award; National Farmers Union, Presidential Award for Leadership and Golden Triangle Awards; Agricultural Retailers Association, Legislator of the Year; Nebraska Wheat Growers Association; Man of the Year Award; Water Systems Council, Wellcare Leadership Award; University of Nebraska Alumni Association, Founders Medallion Award; George W. Norris Award; Nebraska Broadcasters Association, Friend of Nebraska Broadcasters Award; Governors' Ethanol Coalition Award; Nebraska Groundwater Foundation Achievement Award; National Insurance Regulatory Examiners Society, Schrader-Nelson Award; National Eagle Scout Association, Distinguished Eagle Award; married: Diane; four children; committees: Agriculture, Nutrition, and Forestry; Appropriations; Armed Services; Rules and Administration; elected to the U.S. Senate on November 7, 2000; reelected to each succeeding Senate term.

Office Listings

http://bennelson.senate.gov

720 Hart Senate Office Building, Washington, DC 20510	(202) 224–6551
Chief of Staff.—Tim Becker.	FAX: 228–0012
Communications Director.—Jake Thompson.	
Scheduler.—Melanie Rogge.	
Legislative Director.—Kate Howard.	
440 North Eighth Street, Suite 120, Lincoln, NE 68508	(402) 441–4600
11819 Miracle Hills Drive, Suite 205, Omaha, NE 68154	(402) 391–3411
P.O. Box 1472, Scottsbluff, NE 69363	(308) 631–7614
P.O. Box 2105, Kearney, NE 68848	(308) 293–5818
P.O. Box 791, South Sioux City, NE 68776	(402) 209–3595

* * *

MIKE JOHANNS, Republican, of Omaha, NE; born in Osage, IA, June 18, 1950; education: B.A., St. Mary's College, Winona, MN, 1971; J.D., Creighton University, Omaha, NE, 1974; professional: Lancaster County Board, 1983–87; Lincoln City Council, 1989–91; Mayor of Lincoln, 1991–98; Nebraska Governor, 1999–2005; Secretary of Agriculture, 2005–2007; caucus: Senate Community College Caucus, Senate Impact Aid Coalition, Rural Health Caucus, Congressional Heart and Stroke Coalition, Parkinson's Action Network, Army Caucus, Air Force Caucus, Senate Cultural Caucus; Congressional Vision Caucus; Farmer Cooperative Caucus; Senate Republican Capitol Markets Task Force; Senate Western Caucus; Congressional Sportsmen's Caucus; Multiple Sclerosis Caucus; religion: Catholic; married: Stephanie Johanns; two children, five grandchildren; committees: Agriculture, Nutrition, and Forestry; Banking, Housing, and Urban Affairs; Environment and Public Works; Indian Affairs; Veterans' Affairs; elected to the U.S. Senate on November 4, 2008.

Office Listings

http://johanns.senate.gov

404 Russell Senate Office Building, Washington, DC 20510 .... (202) 224–4224
Chief of Staff.—Terri Moore. FAX: 224–0436
Legislative Director.—Terry Van Doren.
Communications Director.—Steve Wymer.
Administrative Director.—Cherri Carpenter.
294 Federal Building, 100 Centennial Mall, North, Lincoln, NE 68508 .... (402) 476–1400
State Director.—Nancy Johner.
9900 Nicholas Street, Suite 325, Omaha, NE 68114 .... (402) 758–8981
4111 Fourth Avenue, Suite 26, Kearney, NE 68845 .... (308) 236–7473
115 Railway Street, Suite C102, Scottsbluff, NE 69361 .... (308) 632–6032

REPRESENTATIVES

FIRST DISTRICT

JEFF FORTENBERRY, Republican, of Lincoln, NE; born in Baton Rouge, LA, December 27, 1960; education: B.A., Louisiana State University, 1978; M.P.P., Georgetown University, Washington, DC, 1986; M. Div., Franciscan University, Steubenville, Ohio, 1996; professional: Lincoln City Council, 1997–2001; publishing executive; worked as economist; managed a public relations firm; congressional aide for the Senate Subcommittee on Intergovernmental Relations; family: married to Celeste Gregory; children: five; committees: Agriculture; Foreign Affairs; elected to the 109th Congress on November 2, 2004; reelected to each succeeding Congress.

Office Listings

http://www.fortenberry.house.gov

1514 Longworth House Office Building, Washington, DC 20515 .... (202) 225–4806
Chief of Staff.—Patty Sheetz. FAX: 225–5686
Legislative Director.—Alan Feyerherm.
Press Secretary.—Kerri Price.
Scheduler.—Rachel Simonin.
301 South 13th Street, Suite 100, Lincoln, NE 68508 .... (402) 438–1598
629 North Broad Street, P.O. Box 377, Fremont, NE 68025 .... (402) 727–0888
125 South 4th Street, Suite 101, Norfolk, NE 68701 .... (402) 379–2064

Counties: BURT, BUTLER, CASS, CEDAR (part), COLFAX, CUMING, DAKOTA, DIXON, DODGE, GAGE, JOHNSON, LANCASTER, MADISON, NEMAHA, OTOE, PAWNEE, RICHARDSON, SARPY (part), THURSTON, WASHINGTON, WAYNE. Population (2000), 570,421.

ZIP Codes: 68001–04, 68007–09, 68014–20, 68023, 68025–26, 68028–31, 68033–34, 68036–42, 68044–48, 68050, 68055, 68057–59, 68061–68, 68070–73, 68112, 68122–23, 68133, 68136, 68138, 68142, 68144, 68152, 68301, 68304–05, 68307, 68309–10, 68313–14, 68316–21, 68323–24, 68328–33, 68336–37, 68339, 68341–49, 68351, 68355, 68357–60, 68364, 68366–68, 68371–72, 68376, 68378, 68380–82, 68401–05, 68407, 68409–10, 68413–15, 68417–24, 68428, 68430–31, 68433–34, 68437–39, 68441–43, 68445–48, 68450, 68452–58, 68460–67, 68501–10, 68512, 68514, 68516, 68520–24, 68526, 68528–29, 68532, 68542, 68583, 68588, 68601, 68621, 68624, 68626, 68629, 68631–33, 68635, 68641–44, 68648–49, 68658–59, 68661–62, 68666–67, 68669, 68701–02, 68710, 68715–17, 68723–24, 68727–28, 68731–33, 68739–41, 68743, 68745, 68747–49, 68751–52, 68757–58, 68767–68, 68770–71, 68776, 68779, 68781, 68784–85, 68787–88, 68790–92

* * *

SECOND DISTRICT

LEE TERRY, Republican, of Omaha, NE; born in Omaha, January 29, 1962; education: B.A., University of Nebraska, 1984; J.D., Creighton Law School, 1987; attorney; elected to the Omaha, NE, City Council, 1990–98; served as vice president and president, and on the audit, legislative, and cable television committees; religion: Christian; married: Robyn; children: Nolan, Ryan, and Jack; committees: Energy and Commerce; elected to the 106th Congress; reelected to each succeeding Congress.

Office Listings

http://www.leeterry.house.gov

2331 Rayburn House Office Building, Washington, DC 20515 .... (202) 225–4155

Chief of Staff.—Mark Anderson. FAX: 226–5452
Legislative Director.—Brad Schweer.
Executive Assistant.—John McDonald.
Communications Director.—Charles Isom.
11717 Burt Street, Suite 106, Omaha, NE 68154 .... (402) 397–9944
District Director.—Charles Isom.

Counties: DOUGLAS, SARPY (part). CITIES: Bellevue, Bennington, Boys Town, Elkhorn, Gretna, La Vista, Omaha, Offutt AFB, Papillion, Plattsmouth, Ralston, Springfield, Valley, and Waterloo. Population (2007), 620,000.

ZIP Codes: 68005, 68007, 68010, 68022, 68028, 68046, 68056, 68064, 68069, 68101–14, 68116–20, 68122–24, 68127–28, 68130–35, 68137–39, 68142, 68144–45, 68147, 68152, 68154–55, 68157, 68164, 68175–76, 68178–80, 68182–83, 68197–98

* * *

THIRD DISTRICT

ADRIAN SMITH, Republican, of Gering, NE; born in Scotts Bluff, NE, December 19, 1970; education: graduated from Gering High School, Gering, NE, 1989; attended Liberty University, Lynchburg, VA; 1989–90; B.S., University of Nebraska, 1993; professional: business owner; teacher; Gering, NE, city council, 1994–98; member of the Nebraska state legislature, 1999–2007; committees: Ways and Means; elected to the 110th Congress on November 7, 2006; reelected to each succeeding Congress.

Office Listings

http://adriansmith.house.gov

503 Cannon House Office Building, Washington, DC 20515 .... (202) 225–6435
Chief of Staff.—Jeff Shapiro. FAX: 225–0207
Legislative Director.—Monica Jirik.
Press Secretary.—Nate Hodson.
Scheduler.—Jena Hoehne.
416 Valley View Drive, Suite 600, Scottsbluff, NE 69361 .... (308) 633–6333
1811 West Second Street, Suite 105, Grand Island, NE 68803 .... (308) 384–3900

Counties: ADAMS, ANTELOPE, ARTHUR, BANNER, BLAINE, BOONE, BOX BUTTE, BOYD, BROWN, BUFFALO, CEDAR (part), CHASE, CHERRY, CHEYENNE, CLAY, CUSTER, DAWES, DAWSON, DEUEL, DUNDY, FILLMORE, FRANKLIN, FRONTIER, FURNAS, GARDEN, GARFIELD, GOSPER, GRANT, GREELEY, HALL, HAMILTON, HARLAN, HAYES, HITCHCOCK, HOLT, HOOKER, HOWARD, JEFFERSON, KEARNEY, KEITH, KEYA PAHA, KIMBALL, KNOX, LINCOLN, LOGAN, LOUP, MCPHERSON, MERRICK, MORRILL, NANCE, NUCKOLLS, PERKINS, PHELPS, PIERCE, PLATTE, POLK, RED WILLOW, ROCK, SALINE, SCOTTS BLUFF, SHERIDAN, SHERMAN, SIOUX, THAYER, THOMAS, VALLEY, WEBSTER, WHEELER, YORK. Population (2000), 570,421.

ZIP Codes: 68303, 68310, 68313, 68315–16, 68319, 68322, 68325–27, 68333, 68335, 68338–43, 68350–52, 68354, 68359, 68361–62, 68365, 68367, 68370–71, 68375, 68377, 68401, 68405–06, 68416, 68423–24, 68429, 68436, 68440, 68444–45, 68452–53, 68460, 68464–65, 68467, 68601–02, 68620–23, 68627–28, 68631, 68634, 68636–38, 68640, 68642–44, 68647, 68651–55, 68658, 68660, 68662–66, 68701, 68711, 68713–14, 68717–20, 68722–27, 68729–30, 68734–36, 68738–39, 68742, 68746–48, 68752–53, 68755–56, 68758–61, 68763–67, 68769, 68771, 68773–74, 68777–78, 68780–81, 68783, 68786, 68789, 68792, 68801–03, 68810, 68812–18, 68820–28, 68831–38, 68840–50, 68852–56, 68858–66, 68869–76, 68878–79, 68881–83, 68901–02, 68920, 68922–30, 68932–50, 68952, 68954–61, 68964, 68966–67, 68969–82, 69001, 69020–30, 69032–34, 69036–46, 69101, 69103, 69120–23, 69125, 69127–35, 69138, 69140–57, 69160–63, 69165–71, 69190, 69201, 69210–12, 69214, 69216–21, 69301, 69331, 69333–37, 69339–41, 69343, 69345–48, 69350–58, 69360–61, 69363, 69365–67

NEVADA

(Population 2010, 2,700,551)

SENATORS

HARRY REID, Democrat, of Searchlight, NV; born in Searchlight, December 2, 1939; education: graduated, Basic High School, Henderson, NV, 1957; associate degree, College of Southern Utah (now Southern Utah State College), 1959; B.S., Utah State University, Phi Kappa Phi, 1961; J.D., George Washington School of Law, Washington, DC, 1964; admitted to the Nevada State Bar in 1963, a year before graduating from law school; while attending law school, worked as a U.S. Capitol police officer; city attorney, Henderson, 1964–66; member and chairman, South Nevada Memorial Hospital Board of Trustees, 1967–69; elected: Nevada State Assembly, 1969–70; Lieutenant Governor, State of Nevada, 1970–74; served, executive committee, National Conference of Lieutenant Governors; chairman, Nevada Gaming Commission, 1977–81; member: Nevada State, Clark County and American Bar Associations; married the former Landra Gould in 1959; five children: Lana, Rory, Leif, Josh, and Key; elected to the 98th Congress on November 2, 1982, and reelected to the 99th Congress; Assistant Democratic Leader, 1998–2004; elected Democratic leader for the 109th Congress, and Majority leader for the 110th, 111th, and 112th Congress; elected to the U.S. Senate on November 4, 1986; reelected to each succeeding Senate term.

Office Listings

http://reid.senate.gov

522 Hart Senate Office Building, Washington, DC 20510 .... (202) 224–3542
Chief of Staff.—David Krone. FAX: 224–7327
Deputy Chief of Staff: David McCallum.
Executive Assistant.—Janice Shelton.
Legislative Director.—Dayle Cristinzio.
600 East Williams Street, Room 302, Carson City, NV 89701 .... (775) 882–7343
State Director.—Mary Conelly.
333 Las Vegas Boulevard South, Suite 8016, Las Vegas, NV 89101 .... (702) 388–5020
Southern Nevada Director.—Rob Elliott.
400 South Virginia Street, Suite 902, Reno, NV 89501 .... (775) 686–5750
State Director.—Mary Conelly.

* * *

DEAN HELLER, Republican, of Carson City, NV; born in Castro Valley, CA, May 10, 1960; education: B.B.A., specializing in finance and securities analysis, University of Southern California, 1985; professional: institutional stockbroker and broker / trader on the Pacific Stock Exchange; Chief Deputy State Treasurer, Public Funds Representative; Nevada State Assemblyman, 1990–94; Secretary of State, 1994–2002; founding member of the Boys and Girls Club of Western Nevada Community College Foundation; married: Lynne Heller; children: Hillary, Harris, Drew, and Emmy; committees: Energy and Natural Resources; Commerce, Science, and Transportation; Special Committee on Aging; elected to the 110th Congress on November 7, 2006, reelected to two succeeding Congresses, when he resigned to become a U.S. Senator; appointed May 3, 2011, to the U.S. Senate for the term ending January 3, 2013, to fill the vacancy caused by the resignation of John E. Ensign; took the oath of office on May 9, 2011.

Office Listings

http://Heller.Senate.gov

361–A Russell Senate Office Building, Washington, DC 20515 .... (202) 224–6244
Chief of Staff.—Mark Abrams. FAX: 228–6753
Legislative Director.—Sarah Timoney.
Press Secretary.—Chandler Smith.
Scheduler.—Corrine Zakzeski.
Communications Director.—Stewart Bybee.
Lloyd George Federal Building, 333 Las Vegas Boulevard South, Suite 8203, Las Vegas, NV 89101 .... (702) 388–6605
Fax: 388–6501
Bruce Thompson Federal Building, 400 South Virginia Street, Suite 738, Reno, NV 89501 .... (775) 686–5770
Fax: 686–5729
305 North Carson Street, Suite 201, Carson City, NV 89701 .... (775) 885–9111
Fax: 883–5590

REPRESENTATIVES

FIRST DISTRICT

SHELLEY BERKLEY, Democrat, of Las Vegas, NV; born in New York, NY, January 20, 1951; education: graduate of Clark County, NV, public school system; B.A., University of Nevada at Las Vegas, 1972; J.D., University of San Diego School of Law, 1976; professional: attorney; Nevada State Assembly, 1982–84; former deputy director, Nevada State Commerce Department; hotel executive; vice-chair, Nevada University and Community College System Board of Regents, 1990–98; has served on numerous civic, business, and professional organizations; married: Larry Lehrner; children: Max Berkley and Sam Berkley; committees: Ways and Means; elected to the 106th Congress; reelected to each succeeding Congress.

Office Listings

http://www.house.gov/berkley

405 Cannon House Office Building, Washington, DC 20515 .... (202) 225–5965
Chief of Staff.—Richard Urey. FAX: 225–3119
Legislative Director.—Bryan George.
Communications Director.—David Cherry.
Scheduler.—Joanne Rider.
2340 Paseo Del Prado, Suite D–106, Las Vegas, NV 89102 .... (702) 220–9823
District Director.—Tod Story.

Counties: CLARK COUNTY (part). CITIES: Las Vegas, and North Las Vegas. Population (2000), 666,088.

ZIP Codes: 89030–33, 89036, 89084, 89086, 89101–04, 89106–10, 89114–17, 89119, 89121–22, 89125–35, 89137, 89142–46, 89149–56, 89160, 89170, 89177, 89185, 89193

REPRESENTATIVES

SECOND DISTRICT

MARK E. AMODEI, Republican, of Carson City, NV; born in Carson City, June 12, 1958; education: B.A., University of Nevada, Reno, NV, 1980; J.D., University of Pacific, McGeorge School of Law, Sacramento, CA, 1983; professional: lawyer, Allison, MacKenzie et al., 1987–present; lawyer, United States Army Judge Advocate General Corps, 1983–87; Nevada State Assembly, 1996–98; Senator, Nevada State Senate, 1998–2010; President Pro Tempore, Nevada State Senate, 2003–05; member of Carson City Master Plan Advisory Committee; member of Education Commission of the States; vice chair of Governor's Task Force on Access to Public Health Care; member of Nevada Supreme Court's Committee on Court Funding; member of Tahoe Regional Planning Agency Legislative Oversight Committee; committees: Judiciary; Natural Resources; Veterans' Affairs; elected by special election to the 112th Congress on September 13, 2011.

Office Listings

http://www.amodei.house.gov

125 Cannon House Office Building, Washington, DC 20515 .... (202) 225–6155
Chief of Staff.—Rick Goddard. FAX: 225–5679
600 Las Vegas Boulevard South, Suite 680, Las Vegas, NV 89101 .... (702) 255–1651
FAX: 255–1927
405 Idaho Street, Suite 214, Elko, NV 89801 .... (775) 777–7920
FAX: 777–8974
400 South Virginia Street, Suite 502, Reno, NV 89501 .... (775) 686–5760
FAX: 686–5711

Counties: CARSON CITY, CHURCHILL, CLARK (part), DOUGLAS, ELKO, ESMERALDA, EUREKA, HUMBOLDT, LANDER, LINCOLN, LYON, MINERAL, NYE, PERSHING, STOREY, WASHOE, WHITE PINE. Population (2000), 666,087.

ZIP Codes: 89001, 89003, 89008, 89010, 89013, 89017, 89019–24, 89026–27, 89030–31, 89041–43, 89045, 89047–49, 89052, 89060–61, 89115, 89124, 89137, 89139, 89141, 89156, 89191, 89301, 89310–11, 89314–19, 89402–15, 89418–36, 89438–40, 89442, 89444–52, 89460, 89496, 89501–07, 89509–13, 89515, 89520–21, 89523, 89533, 89557, 89570, 89701–06, 89711–14, 89721, 89801–03, 89815, 89820–26, 89828, 89830–32, 89834–35, 89883

* * *

THIRD DISTRICT

JOSEPH HECK, Republican, of Henderson, NV; born in Queens, NY, October 30, 1961; education: B.A., Penn State University, 1984; D.O., Philadelphia College of Osteopathic Medicine, 1988; M.S.S., United States Army War College, Carlisle, PA, 2006; professional: colonel, U.S. Army Reserve; emergency room physician; president of emergency management consulting firm; Nevada State Senate 2004–05; religion: Roman Catholic; married: Lisa Heck; committees: Armed Services; Education and the Workforce; Permanent Select Committee on Intelligence; elected to the 112th Congress on November 2, 2010.

Office Listings

http://www.heck.house.gov

132 Cannon House Office Building, Washington, DC 20515 .... (202) 225–3252
Chief of Staff.—Greg Facchiano. FAX: 225–2185
Legislative Director.—Courtney Temple.
Communications Director.—Darren Littell.
Scheduler.—Caitlin Callahan.
8485 West Sunset Road, Suite 300, Las Vegas, NV 89113 .... (702) 387–4941
District Director.—Grant Hewitt.

Counties: CLARK COUNTY (part). Population (2010), 1,043,855.

ZIP Codes: 89004–05, 89007, 89009, 89011–12, 89014–16, 89018, 89025, 89028–30, 89039–40, 89046, 89052–53, 89070, 89074, 89077, 89101–4, 89108–11, 89113, 89117–24, 89128–29, 89134–36, 89138–39, 89141–42, 89146–49, 89156, 89159, 89162–63, 89170, 89173, 89177, 89180, 89185, 89191, 89193, 89195, 89199

NEW HAMPSHIRE

(Population 2010, 1,316,470)

SENATORS

JEANNE SHAHEEN, Democrat, of Madbury, NH; born in Saint Charles, MO, January 28, 1947; education: graduated, Selinsgrove Area High School, Selinsgrove, PA, 1965; B.A., Shippensburg University, Shippensburg, PA, 1969; M.S.S., University of Mississippi, 1973; professional: high school teacher; co-owner of a small retail business; consultant; New Hampshire State Senator; Governor of New Hampshire; Director of Harvard's Institute of Politics; married: William Shaheen; three children: Stefany, Stacey, and Molly; Commission on Security and Cooperation in Europe; committees: Armed Services; Foreign Relations; Energy and Natural Resources; Small Business and Entrepreneurship; elected to the 111th U.S. Senate on November 4, 2008.

Office Listings

http://shaheen.senate.gov

520 Hart Senate Office Building, Washington, DC 20510 .... (202) 224–2841
Chief of Staff.—Maura Keefe.
Deputy Chief of Staff.—Justin Burkhardt.
Legislative Director.—Judy Reardon.
Communications Director.—Jonathan Lipman.
Scheduler.—Jennifer MacLellan.
Executive Assistant.—Liza Bruno.
1589 Elm Street, Suite 3, Manchester, NH 03101 .... (603) 647–7500
State Director.—Mike Vlacich.
60 Main Street, Nashua, NH 03060 .... (603) 883–0196
340 Central Avenue, Suite 205, Dover, NH 03820 .... (603) 750–3004
50 Opera House Square, Claremont, NH 03743 .... (603) 542–4872
961 Main Street, Berlin, NH 03570 .... (603) 752–6300

* * *

KELLY AYOTTE, Republican, of Nashua, NH; born in Nashua, NH, June 27, 1968; education: graduated Nashua High School, 1986; B.A., Pennsylvania State University, University Park, PA, 1990; J.D., Villanova University School of Law, Villanova, PA, 1993; professional: lawyer; married: Lt. Col. Joseph Daley; two children; committees: Armed Services; Budget; Commerce, Science, and Transportation; Small Business and Entrepreneurship; elected to the 112th U.S. Senate on November 2, 2010.

Office Listings

http://ayotte.senate.gov

144 Russell Senate Office Building, Washington, DC 20510 .... (202) 224–3324
Chief of Staff.—John Easton. FAX: 224–4952
Administrative Director.—Debra Jarrett.
Legislative Director.—Adam Hechavarria.
Communications Director.—Jeff Grappone.
Scheduler.—Katie Horgan.
41 Hooksett Road, Unit 2, Manchester, NH 03104 .... (603) 622–7979
FAX: 622–0422
144 Main Street, Nashua, NH 03060 .... (603) 880–3335
14 Manchester Square, Suite 140, Portsmouth, NH 03801 .... (603) 436–7161

REPRESENTATIVES

FIRST DISTRICT

FRANK GUINTA, Republican, of Manchester, NH; born in Edison, NJ, September, 1970; education: graduated from Canterbury School, New Milford, CT, 1989; B.A., Assumption College, MA, 1993; M.A., Franklin Pierce Law Center, 2000; professional: mayor of Manchester; married: Morgan, two children; committees: Budget; Oversight and Government Reform; Transportation and Infrastructure; elected to the 112th Congress on November 2, 2010.

Office Listings

http://www.guinta.house.gov

1223 Longworth House Office Building, Washington, DC 20515 .... (202) 225–5456
Chief of Staff.—Ethan Zorfas. FAX: 225–5822
Legislative Director.—Austen Jensen.
Communications Director.—J. Mark Powell.
Scheduler.—Kayla Priehs.
33 Lowell Street, Manchester, NH, 03101 .... (603) 641–9536

Counties: BELKNAP (part), CARROLL, HILLSBOROUGH (part), ROCKINGHAM, STAFFORD. CITIES: Bedford, Conway, Derry, Dover, Exeter, Goffstown, Laconia, Londonderry, Manchester, Merrimack, Portsmouth, and Rochester. Population (2000), 617,575.

ZIP Codes: 03032, 03034, 03036–38, 03040–42, 03044–45, 03053–54, 03077, 03101–06, 03108–11, 03218, 03220, 03225–27, 03237, 03246–47, 03249, 03253–54, 03256, 03259, 03261, 03263, 03269, 03290–91, 03298–99, 03307, 03801–05, 03809–10, 03812–22, 03824–27, 03830, 03832–33, 03835–60, 03862, 03864–75, 03878, 03882–87, 03890, 03894, 03896–97

* * *

SECOND DISTRICT

CHARLES F. BASS, Republican, of Peterborough, NH; born in Boston, MA, January 8, 1952; education: B.A., Dartmouth College, Hanover, NH, 1974; professional: served in the New Hampshire State House of Representatives, 1982–88; New Hampshire State Senate, 1988–92; United States House of Representatives, 1995–2007; married: Lisa Bass; children: Jonathan and Lucy; committees: Energy and Commerce; elected to the 112th Congress on November 2, 2010.

Office Listings

http://www.bass.gov

2350 Rayburn House Office Building, Washington, DC 20515 .... (202) 225–5206
Chief of Staff.—John Billings. FAX: 225–2946
Legislative Director.—Grant Erdel.
Scheduler.—Danielle Varallo.
Press Secretary.—Stephanie DuBois.
114 North Main Street, Suite 200, Concord, NH 03301 .... (603) 226–0064
District Director.—Matt Hagerty FAX: 226–0085
221 Main Street, Suite 201, Nashua, NH 03060 .... (603) 595–7701
FAX: 595–7706
32 Main Street, Room 110, Littleton, NH 03561 .... (603) 444–5505

Counties: BELKNAP (part), CHESHIRE, COOS, GRAFTON, HILLSBOROUGH (part), MERRIMACK (part), ROCKINGHAM (part), SULLIVAN. Population (2010), 658,486.

ZIP Codes: 03031, 03033, 03037, 03043, 03045–49, 03051–52, 03055, 03057, 03060–64, 03070–71, 03073, 03076, 03079, 03082, 03084, 03086–87, 03215–17, 03220–24, 03226, 03229–31, 03233–35, 03238, 03240–45, 03251–52, 03255, 03257–58, 03260–64, 03266, 03268–69, 03272–76, 03278–82, 03284, 03287, 03289, 03293, 03301–05, 03307, 03431, 03435, 03440–52, 03455–58, 03461–62, 03464–70, 03561, 03570, 03574–76, 03579–85, 03587–90, 03592–93, 03595, 03597–98, 03601–05, 03607–09, 03740–41, 03743, 03745–46, 03748–56, 03765–66, 03768–71, 03773–74, 03777, 03779–82, 03784–85, 03811

NEW JERSEY

(Population 2010 8,791,894)

SENATORS

FRANK R. LAUTENBERG, Democrat, of Cliffside Park, NJ; born in Paterson, NJ, January 23, 1924; education: Nutley High School, Nutley, NJ, 1941; B.S., economics, Columbia University School of Business, New York, NY, 1949; professional: U.S. Army Signal Corps, 1942–46; ADP data processing firm founder, and CEO, 1952–82; commissioner, Port Authority of New York and New Jersey, 1978–82; commissioner, New Jersey Economic Development Authority; member: U.S. Holocaust Memorial Council; Advisory Council of the Graduate School of Business, Columbia University; appointed by the Governor on December 27, 1982, to complete the unexpired term of Senator Nicholas F. Brady; elected to the U.S. Senate on November 2, 1982; reelected in 1988 and 1994; not a candidate for reelection in 2000; replaced Senator Robert Torricelli as the Democratic candidate for the U.S. Senate in October 2002; spouse: Bonnie Englebardt Lautenberg; four children: Ellen, Nan, Lisa and Joshua; committees: Appropriations; Commerce, Science, and Transportation; Environment and Public Works; elected to the U.S. Senate on November 5, 2002; reelected to the U.S. Senate on November 4, 2008.

Office Listings

http://lautenberg.senate.gov

324 Hart Senate Office Building, Washington, DC 20510 .... (202) 224–3224
    Chief of Staff.—Dan Katz. FAX: 228–4054
    Chief Counsel.—Doug Mehan.
    Legislative Director.—Michelle Schwartz.
    Communications Director.—Caley Gray.
One Gateway Center, 23rd Floor, Newark, NJ 07102 .... (973) 639–8700
    FAX: 639–8723
One Port Center, Suite 505, 2 Riverside Drive, Camden, NJ 08101 .... (856) 338–8922
    FAX: 338–8936

* * *

ROBERT MENENDEZ, Democrat, of North Bergen, NJ; born in New York City, NY, January 1, 1954; education: graduated, Union Hill High School, 1972; B.A., St. Peter's College, Jersey City, NJ, 1976; J.D., Rutgers Law School, Newark, NJ, 1979; professional: attorney; elected to the Union City Board of Education, 1974–78; admitted to the New Jersey Bar, 1980; mayor of Union City, 1986–92; member: New Jersey Assembly, 1987–91; New Jersey State Senate, Alliance Civic Association; U.S. House of Representatives 1993–2006; vice chair, Democratic Caucus, 1998–99; chair, Democratic Caucus, 2003–06; chair, Democratic Senatorial Campaign Committee, 2009–10; children: Alicia and Robert; committees: Banking, Housing and Urban Affairs; Finance; Foreign Relations; elected on November 3, 1992 to the 103rd Congress; reelected to each succeeding Congress; appointed to the U.S. Senate on January 17, 2006 by Governor Jon S. Corzine; elected to the 110th Congress for a full Senate term on November 7, 2006.

Office Listings

http://menendez.senate.gov

528 Hart Senate Office Building, Washington, DC 20510 .... (202) 224–4744
    Chief of Staff.—Danny O'Brien. FAX: 228–2197
    Deputy Chief of Staff.—Karissa Willhite.
    Administrative Director.—Robert Kelly.
One Gateway Center, 11th Floor, Newark, NJ 07102 .... (973) 645–3030
208 Whitehorse Pike, Suite 18, Barrington, NJ 08007–1322 .... (856) 757–5353

REPRESENTATIVES

FIRST DISTRICT

ROBERT E. ANDREWS, Democrat, of Haddon Heights, NJ; born in Camden, NJ, August 4, 1957; education: graduated, Triton High School, Runnemede, NJ, 1975; B.S., political science, Bucknell University, *summa cum laude*, Phi Beta Kappa, Lewisburg, PA, 1979; J.D., *magna cum laude*, Cornell Law School, Cornell Law Review, Ithaca, NY, 1982; Camden

County Freeholder, 1986–90; Camden County Freeholder Director, 1988–90; married: Camille Spinello; children: Jacquelyn and Josi; committees: Armed Services; Education and the Workforce; elected on November 6, 1990, to the 101st Congress, to fill the vacancy caused by the resignation of James Florio; elected at the same time to the 102nd Congress; reelected to each succeeding Congress.

Office Listings

http://www.house.gov/andrews

2265 Rayburn House Office Building, Washington, DC 20515 .... (202) 225–6501
Legislative Director.—Vacant. FAX: 225–6583
515 Grove Street, Suite 3C, Haddon Heights, NJ 08035 .... (856) 546–5100
Chief of Staff.—Fran Tagmire.
Scheduler.—Tim Garvin.
Press Secretary.—Fran Tagmire.
District Director.—Amanda Caruso.
63 North Broad Street, Woodbury, NJ 08096 .... (856) 848–3900

Counties: BURLINGTON COUNTY. CITIES AND TOWNSHIPS: Maple Shade, Palmyra, Riverton. CAMDEN COUNTY. CITIES AND TOWNSHIPS: Audubon, Audubon Park, Barrington, Bellmawr, Berlin, Berlin Township, Brooklawn, Camden, Chesilhurst, Clementon, Collingswood, Gibbsboro, Gloucester City, Gloucester Township, Haddon Heights, Haddon Township, Hi-Nella, Laurel Springs, Lawnside, Lindenwold, Magnolia, Mt. Ephraim, Oaklyn, Pennsauken, Pine Hill, Pine Valley, Runnemede, Somerdale, Stratford, Tavistock, Voorhees, Winslow, Woodlynne. GLOUCESTER COUNTY. CITIES AND TOWNSHIPS: Deptford, E. Greenwich, Greenwich, Logan Township, Mantua, Monroe, National Park, Paulsboro, Washington Township, and Wenonah. Population (2000), 647,258.

ZIP Codes: 08002–04, 08007, 08009, 08012, 08014, 08018, 08020–21, 08026–33, 08035, 08037, 08043, 08045, 08049, 08051–52, 08056, 08059, 08061–63, 08065–66, 08071, 08076–80, 08081, 08083–86, 08089–91, 08093–97, 08099, 08101–10

* * *

SECOND DISTRICT

FRANK A. LoBIONDO, Republican, of Ventnor, NJ; born in Bridgeton, NJ, May 12, 1946; education: graduated, B.S., St. Joseph's University, Philadelphia, PA, 1968; professional: operations manager, LoBiondo Brothers Motor Express, 1968–94; Cumberland County Freeholder, 1985–87; New Jersey General Assembly, 1988–94; awards and honors: honorary Coast Guard Chief Petty Officer; Board of Directors, Young Men's Christian Association; Honorary Rotarian; Taxpayer Hero Award; Watchdog of the Treasury Award; Veterans Foreign Wars ''Outstanding Federal Legislator of the Year'' Award; Humane Society of the United States-Humane Champion Award; National Association of Community Health Centers—Distinguished Community Health Superhero; Super Friend of Seniors Award; two-time winner of the Friend of the National Parks Award; March of Dimes FDR Award for community service; 2001 President's Award, Literacy Volunteers of America, NJ, Inc.; committees: Armed Services; Transportation and Infrastructure; Permanent Select Committee on Intelligence; elected to the 104th Congress; reelected to each succeeding Congress.

Office Listings

http://www.house.gov/lobiondo

2427 Rayburn House Office Building, Washington, DC 20515 .... (202) 225–6572
Chief of Staff.—Mary Annie Harper. FAX: 225–3318
Executive Assistant.—Allison Kersey.
5914 Main Street, Mays Landing, NJ 08330 .... (609) 625–5008
District Director.—Linda Hinckley.

Counties: BURLINGTON (part). CITIES AND TOWNSHIPS: Shamong, Washington. CAMDEN COUNTY (part). ATLANTIC COUNTY. CITIES AND TOWNSHIPS: Absecon, Atlantic City, Brigantine, Buena, Cardiff, Collings Lake, Cologne, Corbin City, Dorothy, Egg Harbor, Estell Manor, Galloway, Hammonton, Landisville, Leeds Point, Linwood, Longport, Margate, Mays Landing, Milmay, Minotola, Mizpah, Newtonville, Northfield, Oceanville, Pleasantville, Pomona, Port Republic, Richland, Somers Point, Ventnor. CAPE MAY COUNTY. CITIES AND TOWNSHIPS: Avalon, Bargaintown, Beesley's, Belleplain, Burleigh, Cape May, Cape May C.H., Cape May Point, Cold Springs, Del Haven, Dennisville, Dias Creek, Eldora, Erma, Fishing Creek, Goshen, Green Creek, Greenfield, Marmora, Ocean City, Ocean View, Rio Grande, Sea Isle, South Dennis, South Seaville, Stone Harbor, Strathmere, Tuckahoe, Villas, Whitesboro, Wildwood, Woodbine. CUMBERLAND COUNTY. CITIES AND TOWNSHIPS: Bridgeton, Cedarville, Centerton, Deerfield, Delmont, Dividing Creek, Dorchester, Elwood, Fairton, Fortescue, Greenwich, Heislerville, Hopewell, Leesburg, Mauricetown, Millville, Newport, Port Elizabeth, Port Norris, Rosenhayn, Shiloh, Vineland. GLOUCESTER COUNTY (part). CITIES AND TOWNSHIPS: Clayton, Ewan, Franklinville, Glassboro, Harrisonville, Malaga, Mantua, Mickleton, Mullica Hill, Newfield, Pitman, Richwood, Sewell, Swedesboro, Williamstown, Woodbury. SALEM COUNTY. CITIES AND TOWNSHIPS: Alloway, Carney's Point, Daretown, Deepwater, Elmer, Elsinboro, Hancocks Bridge, Monroeville, Norma, Pedricktown, Penns Grove, Pennsville, Quinton, Salem, and Woodstown. Population (2000), 647,258.

ZIP Codes: 08001, 08004, 08009, 08019–20, 08023, 08025, 08028, 08037–39, 08051, 08056, 08061–62, 08067, 08069–72, 08074, 08079–80, 08085, 08088–89, 08094, 08098, 08201–05, 08210, 08212–15, 08217–21, 08223, 08225–26,

08230–32, 08234, 08240–48, 08250–52, 08260, 08270, 08302, 08310–24, 08326–30, 08332, 08340–50, 08352–53, 08360–62, 08401–04, 08406

* * *

THIRD DISTRICT

JON RUNYAN, Republican, of Mt. Laurel, NJ; born in Flint, MI, November 27, 1973; education: graduated from Carman-Ainsworth High School, Flint, MI; attended University of Michigan, Ann Arbor, MI, 1992–95; attended University of Pennsylvania, Wharton School of Business; professional: football player, NFL Philadelphia Eagles; television commentator; married: Loretta; committees: Armed Services; Natural Resources; Veterans' Affairs; elected to the 112th Congress on November 2, 2010.

Office Listings

http://www.runyan.house.gov

1239 Longworth House Office Building, Washington, DC 20515 .... (202) 225–4765
Chief of Staff.—Stacy Barton. FAX: 225–0778
4167 Church Road, Mt. Laurel, NJ 08054 .... (856) 780–6436
District Director.—Kristin Antonello. FAX: 780–6440
600 Mule Road, Unit 6, Toms River, NJ 08757 .... (732) 279–6013
FAX: 279–6062

Counties: BURLINGTON (part), CAMDEN (part), OCEAN (part). Population (2000), 647,257.

ZIP Codes: 08002–06, 08008–11, 08015–16, 08019, 08034, 08036, 08043, 08046, 08048, 08050, 08053–55, 08057, 08060, 08064–65, 08068, 08073, 08075, 08077, 08087–88, 08092, 08094, 08109, 08215, 08224, 08352, 08501, 08511, 08562, 08618, 08640–41, 08690, 08721–23, 08731–32, 08734–36, 08739–41, 08751–59

* * *

FOURTH DISTRICT

CHRISTOPHER H. SMITH, Republican, of Robbinsville, NJ; born in Rahway, NJ, March 4, 1953; attended Worcester College, England, 1974; B.A., Trenton State College, 1975; businessman; executive director, New Jersey Right to Life Committee, Inc., 1976–78; religion: Catholic; married to the former Marie Hahn, 1977; four adult children; two grandchildren; chairman, Commission on Security and Cooperation in Europe; co-chair, Congressional Pro-Life Caucus; former chairman, House Veterans' Affairs Committee; commissioner, Congressional-Executive Commission on China; committees: Foreign Affairs; elected to the 97th Congress, November 4, 1980; reelected to each succeeding Congress.

Office Listings

http://www.house.gov/chrissmith

2373 Rayburn House Office Building, Washington, DC 20515 .... (202) 225–3765
Chief of Staff.—Mary McDermott Noonan. FAX: 225–7768
1540 Kuser Road, Suite A9, Hamilton, NJ 08619 .... (609) 585–7878
108 Lacey Road, Suite 38A, Whiting, NJ 08759 .... (732) 350–2300

Counties: BURLINGTON COUNTY. MUNICIPALITIES: Bordentown City, Bordentown Township, Burlington City, Burlington Township, Chesterfield, Fieldsboro, Florence, Mansfield, Springfield. MERCER COUNTY. MUNICIPALITIES: East Windsor, Hamilton, Highstown, Trenton, Washington Township. MONMOUTH COUNTY. MUNICIPALITIES: Allentown, Brielle, Colts Neck, Farmingdale, Freehold, Freehold Borough, Howell, Manasquan, Millstone Township, Roosevelt, Sea Girt, Spring Lake Heights, Upper Freehold, Wall. OCEAN COUNTY. MUNICIPALITIES: Bay Head, Brick, Jackson, Lakehurst, Lakewood, Manchester, Mantoloking, Plumstead, Pt. Pleasant, and Pt. Pleasant Beach. Population (2000), 647,258.

ZIP Codes: 07710, 07715, 07719, 07722, 07726–28, 07731, 07753, 07762, 08010, 08016, 08022, 08041–42, 08060, 08068, 08075, 08501, 08505, 08510, 08512, 08514–15, 08518, 08520, 08526–27, 08533, 08535, 08554–55, 08561, 08601–07, 08609–11, 08619–20, 08625, 08629, 08638, 08645–48, 08650, 08666, 08690–91, 08695, 08701, 08720, 08723–24, 08730, 08733, 08736, 08738, 08742, 08750, 08753, 08757, 08759

* * *

FIFTH DISTRICT

SCOTT GARRETT, Republican, of Wantage Township, NJ; born in Englewood, NJ, July 7, 1959; education: High Point Regional High School, 1977; B.A., Montclair State University,

1981; J.D., Rutgers University Law School, 1984; professional: attorney; counsel attorney with law firm of Sellar Richardson; organizations: Big Brothers, Big Sisters; Sussex County Chamber of Commerce; Sussex County Board of Agriculture; New Jersey State Assemblyman, 1990–2002; family: married to Mary Ellen; children: Jennifer and Brittany; committees: Budget; Financial Services; elected to the 108th Congress on November 5, 2002; reelected to each succeeding Congress.

Office Listings

http://www.house.gov/garrett

2244 Russell House Office Building, Washington, DC 20515 .... (202) 225–4465
Chief of Staff.—Amy Smith. FAX: 225–9048
Legislative Director.—Andrew Shaw.
Communications Director.—Ben Veghte.
266 Harristown Road, Suite 104, Glen Rock, NJ 07452 .... (201)444–5454
District Director.—Gina Diorio.
83 Spring Street, Suite 302A, Newton, NJ 07860 .... (973) 300–2000

Counties: BERGEN (part), PASSAIC (part), SUSSEX, WARREN. Population (2000), 647,257.

ZIP Codes: 07401, 07403, 07416–23, 07428, 07430, 07432, 07435–36, 07438–39, 07446, 07450–52, 07456, 07458, 07460–63, 07465, 07480–81, 07495, 07498, 07620–21, 07624, 07626–28, 07630, 07640–42, 07645–49, 07652–53, 07656, 07661–62, 07670, 07675–77, 07820–23, 07825–27, 07829, 07831–33, 07838–40, 07844, 07846, 07848, 07851, 07855, 07860, 07863, 07865, 07871, 07875, 07877, 07879–82, 07890, 08802, 08804, 08808, 08865–86

* * *

SIXTH DISTRICT

FRANK PALLONE, JR., Democrat, of Long Branch, NJ; born in Long Branch, October 30, 1951; education: B.A., Middlebury College, Middlebury, VT, 1973; M.A., Fletcher School of Law and Diplomacy, 1974; J.D., Rutgers University School of Law, 1978; member of the bar: Florida, New York, Pennsylvania, and New Jersey; attorney, Marine Advisory Service; assistant professor, Cook College, Rutgers University Sea Grant Extension Program; counsel, Monmouth County, NJ, Protective Services for the Elderly; instructor, Monmouth College; Long Branch City Council, 1982–88; New Jersey State Senate, 1983–88; married the former Sarah Hospodor, 1992; committees: Energy and Commerce; Natural Resources; elected to the 100th Congress, by special election, on November 8, 1988, to fill the vacancy caused by the death of James J. Howard; reelected to each succeeding Congress.

Office Listings

http://www.house.gov/pallone

237 Cannon House Office Building, Washington, DC 20515 .... (202) 225–4671
Chief of Staff.—Jeff Carroll. FAX: 225–9665
Legislative Director.—Tiffany Guarascio.
Communications Director.—Rich McGrath.
District Director.—Janice Fuller.
504 Broadway, Long Branch, NJ 07740 .... (732) 571–1140
67/69 Church Street, Kilmer Square, New Brunswick, NJ 08901–1242 .... (732) 249–8892

Counties: MONMOUTH COUNTY. CITIES AND TOWNSHIPS: Aberdeen, Allenhurst, Asbury Park, Atlantic Highlands, Avon-by-the-Sea, Belmar, Bradley Beach, Cliffwood Beach, Deal, Hazlet, Highlands, Interlaken, Keansburg, Keyport, Loch Arbour, Long Branch, Manalapan, Marlboro, Matawan, Middletown, Monmouth Beach, Neptune City, Neptune Twp., Ocean, Red Bank, Sea Bright, South Belmar, Union Beach, West Long Branch. MIDDLESEX COUNTY. CITIES AND TOWNSHIPS: Dunellen, Edison, Highland Park, Metuchen, Middlesex, New Brunswick, Old Bridge, Piscataway, Sayerville, South Amboy. SOMERSET COUNTY. CITIES: Franklin. UNION COUNTY. CITIES: Plainfield. Population (2000), 647,257.

ZIP Codes: 07060–63, 07080, 07701–02, 07704, 07709–12, 07715–21, 07723–24, 07726, 07730, 07732, 07734–35, 07737, 07740, 07746–48, 07750–56, 07758, 07760, 07764, 08812, 08816–18, 08820, 08830–31, 08837, 08840, 08846, 08854–55, 08857, 08859, 08871–73, 08877–79, 08899, 08901, 08903–04, 08906, 08922, 08933, 08988–89

* * *

SEVENTH DISTRICT

LEONARD LANCE, Republican, of Clinton Township, NJ; born in Easton, PA, June 25, 1952; education: B.A., Lehigh University, Bethlehem, PA, 1974; J.D., Vanderbilt University Law School, Memphis, TN, 1977; M.P.A., Woodrow Wilson School of Public and International Affairs at Princeton University, Princeton, NJ, 1982; professional: judicial clerk; lawyer, private practice; member, New Jersey State Assembly, 1991–2002; member, New Jersey State Senate, 2002–09; minority leader, New Jersey State Senate, 2004–08; Congressional Diabetes Caucus; Congressional Wildlife Caucus; co-chair, House Republican Israel Caucus; House Cancer Care Working Group; Passenger Rail Caucus; religion: Roman Catholic; committees: Energy and Commerce; elected to the 111th Congress on November 4, 2008; reelected to the 112th Congress.

Office Listings

http://www.lance.house.gov

426 Cannon House Office Building, Washington, DC 20515 .... (202) 225–5361
Chief of Staff.—Todd Mitchell. FAX: 225–9460
Legislative Director.—Jon Taets.
Scheduler.—Sarah Armstrong.
Communications Director.—Angie Lundberg.
425 North Avenue, East, Westfield, NJ 07090 .... (908) 518–7733
23 Royal Road, Suite 101, Flemington, NJ 08822 .... (908) 789–6900
District Director.—Amanda Woloshen.

Counties: MIDDLESEX COUNTY. MUNICIPALITIES: Edison, South Plainfield, Woodbridge. UNION COUNTY. MUNICIPALITIES: Berkeley Heights, Clark, Cranford, Fanwood, Garwood, Kenilworth, Linden, Mountainside, New Providence, Roselle Park, Scotch Plains, Springfield, Summit, Union, Westfield, Winfield. HUNTERDON COUNTY. MUNICIPALITIES: Alexandria, Bethlehem, Bloomsbury, Califon, Clinton Township, Clinton, Flemington, Glen Gardner, Hampton, High Bridge, Holland, Lebanon, Lebanon Township, Milford, Oldwick, Raritan, Readington, Tewksbury, Union. SOMERSET COUNTY. MUNICIPALITIES: Bedminster, Bernardsville, Bound Brook, Branchburg, Bridgewater, Far Hills, Green Brook, Hillsborough, Manville, Montgomery Township, Millstone, North Plainfield, Peapack-Gladstone, Rocky Hill, South Bound Brook, Warren, and Watchung. Population (2000), 647,257.

ZIP Codes: 07001, 07008, 07016, 07023, 07027, 07033, 07036, 07040, 07059–60, 07062–64, 07066–67, 07069, 07076, 07080–81, 07083, 07090–92, 07095, 07204, 07830, 07901–02, 07921–22, 07924, 07931, 07934, 07974, 07977–79, 08502, 08504, 08540, 08551, 08553, 08558, 08801–02, 08804–05, 08807, 08809, 08812, 08820–22, 08825–27, 08829–30, 08832–37, 08840, 08844, 08848, 08853, 08858, 08863, 08867, 08870, 08876, 08880, 08885, 08887–89

* * *

EIGHTH DISTRICT

BILL PASCRELL, JR., Democrat, of Paterson, NJ; born in Paterson, January 25, 1937; education: B.A., journalism, and M.A., philosophy, Fordham University; veteran, U.S. Army and Army Reserves; professional: educator; elected Minority Leader Pro Tempore, New Jersey General Assembly, 1988–96; mayor of Paterson, 1990–96; named Mayor of the Year by bipartisan NJ Conference of Mayors, 1996; started Paterson's first Economic Development Corporation; married the former Elsie Marie Botto; three children: William III, Glenn, and David; committees: Budget; Ways and Means; elected to the 105th Congress; reelected to each succeeding Congress.

Office Listings

http://www.pascrell.house.gov

2370 Rayburn House Office Building, Washington, DC 20515 .... (202) 225–5751
Chief of Staff.—Ben Rich. FAX: 225–5782
Deputy Chief of Staff.—Assad Akhter.
Senior Legislative Assistant.—Arthur Mandel.
Economic Policy Advisor.—Keith Castaldo.
Health Policy Advisor.—Rose Hacking.
Legislative Correspondent / Scheduler.—Kristen Molloy.
Staff Assistant.—Ian McTiernan.
200 Federal Plaza, Suite 500, Paterson, NJ 07505 .... (201) 523–5152
Communications Director.—Paul Brubaker.

Counties: ESSEX COUNTY. CITIES: Belleville, Bloomfield, Cedar Grove. Glen Ridge, Livingston, Montclair, Nutley, South Orange, Verona, West Orange. PASSAIC COUNTY. CITIES: Clifton, Haledon, Little Falls, North Haledon, Passaic, Paterson, Pompton Lakes, Prospect Park, Totowa, Wayne, and West Paterson. Population (2000), 647,258

ZIP Codes: 07003–04, 07009, 07011–15, 07028, 07039, 07042–44, 07052, 07055, 07079, 07107, 07109–10, 07424, 07442, 07470, 07474, 07477, 07501–14, 07522, 07524, 07533, 07538, 07543–44

* * *

NINTH DISTRICT

STEVEN R. ROTHMAN, Democrat, of Fair Lawn, NJ; born in Englewood, NJ, October 14, 1952; education: graduate, Tenafly High School, 1970; B.A., Syracuse University, Syracuse,

NY, 1974; J.D., Washington University School of Law, St. Louis, MO, 1977; professional: attorney; two-term mayor of Englewood, NJ, spearheaded business growth and installed a fiscally conservative management team, transforming Englewood's bond rating from one of the worst to the best in Bergen County; Judge, Bergen County Surrogate Court, 1993–96; founding member, New Democratic Coalition; authored the Secure Our Schools Act; two children; committees: Appropriations; elected to the 105th Congress; reelected to each succeeding Congress.

Office Listings

http://www.rothman.house.gov

2303 Rayburn House Office Building, Washington, DC 20515 .... (202) 225–5061
Chief of Staff.—Tom O'Donnell. FAX: 225–5851
Executive Assistant / Scheduler.—Caherine Collentine.
Deputy Chief of Staff.—Marc Cevasco.
Communications Director.—Aaron Keyak.
25 Main Street, Court Plaza, Hackensack, NJ 07601–7089 .... (201) 646–0808
District Director.—Michele DiIorgi.
130 Central Avenue, Jersey City, NJ 07306–2118 .... (201) 798–1366
Staff Assistant.—Al Zampella.

Counties: BERGEN COUNTY. CITIES AND TOWNS: Bogota, Carlstadt, Cliffside Park, East Rutherford, Edgewater, Elmwood Park, Englewood, Englewood Cliffs, Fair Lawn, Fairview, Fort Lee, Garfield, Hackensack, Hasbrouck Heights, Leonia, Little Ferry, Lodi, Lyndhurst, Maywood, Moonachie, New Milford, North Arlington, Palisades Park, Ridgefield, Ridgefield Park, Rutherford, Saddle Brook, South Hackensack, Teaneck, Teterboro, Wallington, Wood Ridge. HUDSON COUNTY. CITIES AND TOWNS: Kearny (ward 1: districts 1, 2, and 6; ward 3; and ward 4: districts 5–7), Secaucus, North Bergen, Jersey City. PASSAIC COUNTY (part). BOROUGH: Hawthorne. Population (2000), 647,258.

ZIP Codes: 07010, 07020, 07022, 07024, 07026, 07031–32, 07042, 07047, 07057, 07070–75, 07094, 07096–97, 07099, 07306–08, 07407, 07410, 07601–08, 07631–32, 07643–44, 07646, 07650, 07657, 07660, 07663, 07666, 07670

* * *

TENTH DISTRICT

DONALD M. PAYNE, Democrat, of Newark, NJ; born in Newark, July 16, 1934; education: graduated, Barringer High School, Newark, 1952; B.A., Seton Hall University, South Orange, NJ, 1957; attended graduate school at Springfield College in Massachusetts; professional: executive at Prudential Insurance Company; vice president of Urban Data Systems, Inc; national president, YMCA of the USA, 1970–73; elected to the Essex County Board of Chosen Freeholders, 1972–78; elected to the Newark Municipal Council, 1982–88; chairman, Essex County Democratic Committee, 2003–04; educator, Newark and Passaic Public School Districts; caucus: chairman, Congressional Black Caucus Foundation, Inc; former chair, Congressional Black Caucus; co-chair, Congressional TRIO Caucus; co-chair Congressional Caribbean Caucus; co-founder of the Congressional Malaria Caucus; board of directors: National Endowment for Democracy, Discovery Foundation, Congressional Award Foundation, YMCA of Newark and Vicinity, Newark Day Center; family: widower; three children; committees: Education and the Workforce; Foreign Affairs; elected on November 8, 1988, to the 101st Congress; reelected to each succeeding Congress.

Office Listings

2310 Rayburn House Office Building, Washington, DC 20515 .... (202) 225–3436
Chief of Staff / Legislative Director.—LaVerne Alexander. FAX: 225–4160
Press Secretary.—Amirah Salaam.
60 Nelson Place, 14th Floor, Newark, NJ 07102 .... (973) 645–3213
333 North Broad Street, Elizabeth, NJ 07202 .... (908) 629–0222
253 Martin Luther King Drive, Jersey City, NJ 07305 .... (201) 369–0392

Counties: ESSEX, HUDSON, UNION. CITIES AND TOWNSHIPS: Bayonne, East Orange, Elizabeth, Hillside, Irvington, Jersey City, Linden, Maplewood Millburn, Montclair, Newark, Orange, Rahway, Roselle, South Orange, Union, and West Orange. Population (2000), 647,258.

ZIP Codes: 07002, 07017–19, 07028, 07036, 07040–42, 07044, 07050–52, 07065, 07078–79, 07083, 07088, 07101–03, 07105–08, 07111–12, 07114–75, 07184, 07188–89, 07191–95, 07197–99, 07201–03, 07205–08, 07304–05

* * *

ELEVENTH DISTRICT

RODNEY P. FRELINGHUYSEN, Republican, of Morristown, NJ; born in New York, NY, April 29, 1946; education: graduated Hobart College, NY, 1969; attended graduate school in

Connecticut; served, U.S. Army, 93rd Engineer Battalion; honorably discharged, 1971; Morris County State and Federal aid coordinator and administrative assistant, 1972; member, Morris County Board of Chosen Freeholders, 1974–83 (director, 1980); served on: Welfare and Mental Health boards; Human Services and Private Industry councils; New Jersey General Assembly, 1983–94; chairman, Assembly Appropriations Committee, 1988–89 and 1992–94; member: American Legion, and Veterans of Foreign Wars; named Legislator of the Year by the Veterans of Foreign Wars, the New Jersey Association of Mental Health Agencies, and the New Jersey Association of Retarded Citizens; honored by numerous organizations; married: Virginia Frelinghuysen; children: Louisine and Sarah; committees: Appropriations; elected to the 104th Congress in November, 1994; reelected to each succeeding Congress.

Office Listings

http://www.frelinghuysen.house.gov

2369 Rayburn House Office Building, Washington, DC 20515 .... (202) 225–5034
Chief of Staff.—Nancy Fox. FAX: 225–3186
Press Secretary.—Steve Wilson.
Legislative Director.—Kathleen Hazlett.
Scheduler.—Alexandra Wouters.
30 Schuyler Place, 2nd Floor, Morristown, NJ 07960 .... (973) 984–0711

Counties: ESSEX COUNTY. CITIES AND TOWNSHIPS: Caldwell, Essex Fells, Fairfield Township, Livingston, Millburn, North Caldwell, Roseland, West Caldwell. MORRIS COUNTY. CITIES AND TOWNSHIPS: Bernardsville, municipalities of Boonton Town, Boonton Township, Brookside, Budd Lake, Butler, Califon, Cedar Knolls, Chatham Borough, Chatham Township, Chester Borough, Chester Township, Convent Station, Denville, Dover Town, East Hanover, Flanders, Florham Park, Gillette, Green Pond, Green Village, Hanover, Harding, Hibernia, Ironia, Jefferson, Kenvill, Kinnelon, Lake Hiawatha, Lake Hopatcong, Landing, Ledgewood, Lincoln Park, Long Valley, Madison, Mendham Borough, Mendham Township, Millington, Mine Hill, Montville, Morris Plains, Morris Township, Morristown, Mount Arlington, Mountain Lakes, Mount Olive, Mount Tabor, Netcong, Newfoundland, New Vernon, Oak Ridge, Parsippany-Troy Hills, Passaic Township, Pequannock, Picatinny, Pine Brook, Randolph, Riverdale, Rockaway Borough, Rockaway Township, Roxbury, Schooley's Mountain, Stanhope, Stirling, Succasunna, Towaco, Victory Gardens, Washington Township, Wharton, and Whippany. PASSAIC COUNTY. CITIES: Bloomingdale. SOMERSET COUNTY. CITIES AND TOWNSHIPS: Bernards Township, Bridgewater, Raritan Borough, and Somerville. SUSSEX COUNTY. CITIES AND TOWNSHIPS: Byram, Hopatcong, Sparta, and Stanhope. Population (2000), 647,258.

ZIP Codes: 07004–07, 07021, 07034–35, 07039, 07041, 07045–46, 07054, 07058, 07068, 07078, 07082, 07405, 07438, 07440, 07444, 07457, 07801–03, 07806, 07821, 07828, 07830, 07834, 07836–37, 07840, 07842–43, 07845, 07847, 07849–50, 07852–53, 07856–57, 07866, 07869–71, 07874, 07876, 07878, 07885, 07920, 07926–28, 07930, 07932–36, 07938–40, 07945–46, 07950, 07960–63, 07970, 07976, 07980–81, 07983, 07999, 08807, 08869, 08876, 08896

* * *

TWELFTH DISTRICT

RUSH D. HOLT, Democrat, of Hopewell Township, NJ; born in Weston, WV, October 15, 1948; son of the youngest person ever to be elected to the U.S. Senate; education: B.A., Carleton College, 1970; M.S. and Ph.D., physics, New York University, 1981; physicist; New York City Environmental Protection Administration, 1972–74; teaching fellow, New York University, 1974–80; Congressional Science Fellow, U.S. House of Representatives, Office of Representative Bob Edgar, 1982–83; professor, Swarthmore College, 1980–88; acting chief, Nuclear & Scientific Division, Office of Strategic Forces, U.S. Department of State, 1987–89; assistant director, Princeton Plasma Physics Laboratory, Princeton, NJ, 1989–97; Protestant; married: Margaret Lancefield; children: Michael, Dejan, and Rachel; committees: Education and the Workforce; Natural Resources; elected to the 106th Congress; reelected to each succeeding Congress.

Office Listings

http://holt.house.gov

1214 Longworth House Office Building, Washington, DC 20515 .... (202) 225–5801
Chief of Staff.—Christopher Hartmann. FAX: 225–6025
Legislative Director.—Christopher Gaston.
Communications Director.—Vacant.
Executive Assistant.—Nicole Williams.
50 Washington Road, West Windsor, NJ 08550 .... (609) 750–9365
District Director.—Sarah Steward.

Counties: HUNTERDON COUNTY. CITIES AND TOWNSHIPS: Delaware, East Amwell, Franklin, Frenchtown, Kingwood, Lambertville, Stockton, West Amwell. MERCER COUNTY. CITIES AND TOWNSHIPS: Ewing, Hopewell Borough, Hopewell Township, Lawrence, Pennington, Princeton Borough, Princeton Township, Trenton, West Windsor. MIDDLESEX COUNTY. CITIES AND TOWNSHIPS: Cranbury, East Brunswick, Helmetta, Jamesburg, Milltown, Monroe, North Brunswick, Old Bridge, Plainsboro Township, South River, Spotswood, South Brunswick. MONMOUTH COUNTY. CITIES AND TOWNSHIPS: Eatontown, Englishtown, Fair Haven, Freehold Township, Holmdel, Little Silver, Manalapan, Marlboro, Middletown,

Oceanport, Rumson, Shrewsbury Borough, Shrewsbury Township, Tinton Falls. SOMERSET COUNTY. CITIES AND TOWNSHIPS: Franklin Township. Population (2000), 647,258.

ZIP Codes: 07701–04, 07712, 07724, 07726, 07728, 07733, 07738–39, 07746, 07748, 07751, 07753, 07757, 07760, 07763, 07765, 07777, 07799, 08512, 08525, 08528, 08530, 08534, 08536, 08540–44, 08550–51, 08556–57, 08559–60, 08570, 08608–09, 08611, 08618–19, 08628, 08638, 08648, 08690, 08801, 08803, 08809–10, 08816, 08822–25, 08828, 08831, 08844, 08850, 08852, 08857, 08859, 08867–68, 08873, 08875, 08882, 08884, 08890, 08901–02, 08905, 08922

* * *

THIRTEENTH DISTRICT

ALBIO SIRES, Democrat, of West New York, NJ; born in Bejucal, Provincia de la Habana, Cuba, January 26, 1951; education: graduated, Memorial High School; B.A., St. Peter's College, 1974; M.A., Middlebury College, Middlebury, VT, 1985; studied Spanish in Madrid, Spain; professional: businessman, teacher; part-owner, A.M. Title Agency, Union Township; mayor, West New York, NJ, 1995–2006; member: New Jersey House, 1999–2006; speaker, New Jersey House, 2002–2005; family: wife, Adrienne; stepdaughter, Tara Kole; committees: Foreign Affairs; Transportation and Infrastructure; elected to the 109th Congress by special election to fill the vacancy caused by the resignation of Robert Menendez; elected to the 110th Congress; reelected to the each succeeding Congress.

Office Listings

http://www.sires.house.gov

2342 Rayburn House Office Building, Washington, DC 20515 .... (202) 225–7919
Chief of Staff.—Gene Martorony. FAX: 226–0792
Administrative Director / Scheduler.—Judi Wolford.
Legislative Director.—Hannah Izon.
Communications Director.—Erica Daughtrey.
35 Journal Square, Suite 906, Jersey City, NJ 07306 .... (201) 222–2828
Bayonne City Hall, 630 Avenue C, Room 4, Bayonne, NJ 07002 .... (201) 823–2900
5500 Palisades Avenue, Suite A, West New York, NJ 07093 .... (201) 558–0800
100 Cooke Avenue, Second Floor, Carteret, NJ 07008 .... (732) 969–9160
Perth Amboy City Hall, First Floor, Perth Amboy, NJ 08861 .... (732) 442–0610

Counties: ESSEX (part), HUDSON (part), MIDDLESEX (part), UNION (part). CITIES AND TOWNSHIPS: Bayonne, Carteret, East Newark, Elizabeth, Guttenberg, Harrison Township, Hoboken, Jersey City, Kearny, Linden, Newark, North Bergen, Port Reading, Perth Amboy, Sewaren, Union City, Weehawken, West New York, and Woodbridge. Population (2000), 647,258.

ZIP Codes: 07002–03, 07008, 07029–30, 07036, 07047, 07064, 07077, 07086–87, 07093, 07095, 07102–05, 07107, 07114, 07201–02, 07206, 07302–11, 08861–62

NEW MEXICO

(Population 2010, 2,059,179)

SENATORS

JEFF BINGAMAN, Democrat, of Santa Fe, NM; born in El Paso, TX, October 3, 1943; raised in Silver City, NM; graduate of Western High (now Silver High), 1961; B.A., government, Harvard University, 1965; J.D., Stanford Law School, 1968; U.S. Army Reserves, 1968–74; Assistant New Mexico Attorney General, 1969, as counsel to the State constitutional convention; private practice, 1970–78; New Mexico Attorney General, 1979–83; member: Methodist Church; married: the former Anne Kovacovich; one son, John; committees: chair, Energy and Natural Resources; Finance; Health, Education, Labor, and Pensions; Joint Economic Committee; elected to the U.S. Senate on November 2, 1982; reelected to each succeeding Senate term.

Office Listings

http://bingaman.senate.gov

703 Hart Senate Office Building, Washington, DC 20510 .... (202) 224–5521
Chief of Staff.—Stephen Ward. TDD: 224–1792
Legislative Director.—Trudy Vincent.
Press Secretary.—Jude McCartin.
Personal Assistant.—Virginia White.
Loretto Town Centre, Suite 148, 505 South Main, Las Cruces, NM 88001 .... (505) 523–6561
625 Silver Avenue SW., Suite 130, Albuquerque, NM 87102 .... (505) 346–6601
105 West Third Street, Suite 409, Roswell, NM 88201 .... (505) 622–7113
119 East Marcy, Suite 101, Santa Fe, NM 87501 .... (505) 988–6647
106–B West Main, Farmington, NM 87102 .... (505) 325–5030

* * *

TOM UDALL, Democrat, of Santa Fe, NM; born in Tucson, AZ, May 18, 1948; education: graduate of McLean High School, 1966; B.A., Prescott College, Prescott, AZ, 1970; LL.B., Cambridge University, Cambridge, England, 1975; J.D., University of New Mexico, Albuquerque, NM, 1977; professional: admitted to New Mexico Bar, 1978; served as New Mexico Attorney General, 1990–98; served as U.S. Representative for New Mexico's Third Congressional District, 1998–2008; married: Jill Z. Cooper; children: Amanda; member of the Commission on Security and Cooperation in Europe; committees: Commerce, Science and Transportation; Environment and Public Works, Foreign Relations; Indian Affairs; Rules and Administration; Joint Committee on Printing; elected to the U.S. Senate on November 4, 2008.

Office Listings

http://tomudall.senate.gov

110 Hart Senate Office Building, Washington, DC 20510 .... (202) 224–6621
Chief of Staff.—Tom Nagle. FAX: 228–3261
Legislative Director.—Michael Collins.
Communications Director.—Marissa Padilla.
Executive Assistant.—Donda Morgan.
219 Central Avenue, NW., Suite 210, Albuquerque, NM 87102 .... (505) 346–6791
201 North Church Street, Suite 201B, Las Cruces, NM 88001 .... (575) 526–5475
120 South Federal Place, Suite 302, Santa Fe, NM 87501 .... (505) 988–6511

REPRESENTATIVES

FIRST DISTRICT

MARTIN HEINRICH, Democrat, of Albuquerque, NM; born in Fallon, NV, October 17, 1971; B.S., University of Missouri, 1995; Albuquerque City Council, 2003–07, including one term as president, 2005–06; trustee, New Mexico State Natural Resources; married: Julie Heinrich; children: Carter and Micah Heinrich; committees: Armed Services; Natural Resources; elected to the 111th Congress on November 4, 2008; reelected to the 112th Congress.

Office Listings

http://www.heinrich.house.gov

336 Cannon House Office Building, Washington, DC 20515 .... (202) 225–6316
Chief of Staff.—Steve Haro. FAX: 225–4975
Legislative Director.—John Blair.
Executive Assistant.—Catherine Melsheimer.
505 Marquette Avenue, NW., Suite 1605, Albuquerque, NM 87102 .... (505) 346–6781

Counties: BERNALILLO (part), SANDOVAL (part), SANTA FE (part), TORRANCE, VALENCIA (part). CITIES AND TOWNSHIPS: Albuquerque, Belen, Estancia, Los Lunas, Moriarty, Mountainair, and Rio Rancho. Population (2000), 606,391.

ZIP Codes: 87001–02, 87004, 87008–09, 87015–16, 87031–32, 87035–36, 87042–43, 87047–48, 87059–61, 87063, 87068, 87070, 87101–25, 87131, 87151, 87153–54, 87158, 87176, 87181, 87184–85, 87187, 87190–99, 88301, 88321

* * *

SECOND DISTRICT

STEVAN PEARCE, Republican, of Hobbs, NM; born in Lamesa, TX, August 24, 1947; education: M.B.A., Eastern New Mexico, Las Cruces, NM, 1970; B.B.A., New Mexico State University, Portales, NM, 1991; professional: owner, oil well services company; served in Vietnam as a pilot for the Air Force; member of the New Mexico State House of Representatives, 1997–2000; elected as a Republican to the 108th, 109th, and 110th Congress, January 3, 2003–January 3, 2009; religion: Baptist; married: Cynthia; caucuses: chairman of Western Caucus; member of Sportsmen's Caucus; Tea Party Caucus; China Caucus; Dairy Caucus; Republican Study Committee; committees: Financial Services; elected to the 112th Congress on November 2, 2010.

Office Listings

http://www.pearce.house.gov

2432 Rayburn House Office Building, Washington, DC 20515 .... (202) 225–2365
Chief of Staff.—Todd Willens. FAX: 225–9599
Press Secretary.—Jamie Dickerman.
Legislative Director.—Kate Schmucker.
Executive Assistant / New Media Director.—Allison Cunningham.
Legislative Correspondent.—Michael O'Donnell.
Legislative Aides: Claire Manatt, Jonathan Shuffield.
Staff Assistant.—Jacquelyn Stafford.
1101 New York Avenue, Room 115, Alamogordo, NM 88310 .... (855) 473–2723
200 East Broadway, Suite 200, Hobbs, NM 88240 .... (855) 473–2723
570 North Telshor Boulevard, Las Cruces, NM 88011 .... (575) 522–0771
3445 Lambros Loop Northeast, Los Lunas, NM 87031 .... (855) 473–2723
1717 West 2nd Street, Suite 110, Roswell, NM 88201 .... (575) 622–6200
111 School of Mines Road, Socorro, NM 87801 .... (575) 855–8979

Counties: BERNALILLO (part), CATRON, CHAVES, CIBOLA, DEBACA, DONA ANA, EDDY, GRANT, GUADALUPE, HIDALGO, LEA, LINCOLN, LUNA, MCKINLEY (part), OTERO, SIERRA, SOCORRO, VALENCIA (part). Population (2000), 606,406.

ZIP Codes: 87002, 87005–07, 87011, 87014, 87020–23, 87026, 87028, 87031, 87034, 87038, 87040, 87045, 87049, 87051, 87062, 87068, 87105, 87121, 87315, 87321, 87327, 87357, 87711, 87724, 87801, 87820–21, 87823–25, 87827–32, 87901, 87930–31, 87933, 87935–37, 87939–43, 88001–09, 88011–12, 88020–21, 88023–34, 88036, 88038–49, 88051–56, 88058, 88061–63, 88065, 88072, 88081, 88114, 88116, 88119, 88134, 88136, 88201–03, 88210–11, 88220–21, 88230–32, 88240–42, 88244, 88250, 88252–56, 88260, 88262–65, 88267–68, 88301, 88310–12, 88314, 88316–18, 88323–25, 88330, 88336–55, 88417, 88431, 88435

* * *

THIRD DISTRICT

BEN RAY LUJÁN, Democrat, of Santa Fe, NM; born in Nambe, NM; June 7, 1972; education: New Mexico Highland University; business administration, Highlands University, Las Vegas, NM; professional: elected to the New Mexico Public Regulation Commission, 2005–08; member of the Hispanic Caucus; Native American Caucus; Sustainable Energy and Environment Coalition; co-chair of the Technology Transfer Caucus; committees: Natural Resources; Science, Space, and Technology; elected to the 111th Congress on November 4, 2008; reelected to the 112th Congress.

Office Listings

http://www.lujan.house.gov

330 Cannon House Office Building, Washington, DC 20515 .... (202) 225–6190
Chief of Staff.—Angela Ramirez. FAX: 226–1528
Legislative Director.—Andrew Jones.
Communications Director.—Andrew Stoddard.
Executive Assistant / Scheduler.—Chris Garcia.
811 St. Michaels Drive, Suite 104, Santa Fe, NM 87505 .... (505) 984–8950
District Director.—Jennifer Catechis.
800 Municipal Drive, Farmington, NM 87401 .... (505) 324–1005
Constituent Services Representative / Veterans Liaison.—Pete Valencia.
110 West Aztec, Suite 102, Gallup, NM 87301 .... (505) 863–0582
Constituent and Navajo Liaison.—Mark Freeland.
903 University Avenue, P.O. Box 1368, Las Vegas, NM 87701 .... (505) 454–3038
Constituent Liaison Manager.—Pamela Garcia.
404 West Route 66 Boulevard, Tucumcari, NM 88401 .... (575) 461–3029
Field Representative.—Ron Wilmot.
3200 Civic Center Circle, NE., #330, Rio Rancho, NM 87144 .... (505) 994–0499
Deputy Director.—Chris Neubauer.

Counties: BERNALILLO (part), NAVAJO NATION, COLFAX, CURRY, HARDING; LOS ALAMOS, MCKINLEY (part), MORA, QUAY, RIO, ROOSEVELT, SANDOVAL (part), SAN JUAN, SAN MIGUEL, SANTA FE, TAOS, UNION. Population (2000), 606,249.

ZIP Codes: 87001, 87004, 87010, 87012–13, 87015, 87017–18, 87024–25, 87027, 87029, 87037, 87041, 87044–48, 87052–53, 87056, 87064, 87072, 87083, 87114, 87120, 87123–24, 87144, 87174, 87301–02, 87305, 87310–13, 87316–17, 87319–23, 87325–26, 87328, 87347, 87364–65, 87375, 87401–02, 87410, 87412–13, 87415–21, 87455, 87461, 87499, 87501–25, 87527–33, 87535, 87537–40, 87543–45, 87548–49, 87551–54, 87556–58, 87560, 87562, 87564–67, 87569, 87571, 87573–83, 87592, 87594, 87701, 87710, 87712–15, 87718, 87722–23, 87728–36, 87740, 87742–43, 87745–47, 87749–50, 87752–53, 88101–03, 88112–13, 88115–16, 88118, 88120–26, 88130, 88132–35, 88401, 88410–11, 88414–16, 88418–19, 88421–22, 88424, 88426–27, 88430, 88433–34, 88436–37, 88439

NEW YORK

(Population 2010, 19,378,102)

SENATORS

CHARLES E. SCHUMER, Democrat, of Brooklyn and Queens, NY; born in Brooklyn, November 23, 1950; education: graduated valedictorian, Madison High School; Harvard University, *magna cum laude*, 1971; J.D. with honors, Harvard Law School, 1974; professional: admitted to the New York State Bar in 1975; elected to the New York State Assembly, 1974; served on Judiciary, Health, Education, and Cities committees; chairman, subcommittee on City Management and Governance, 1977; chairman, Committee on Oversight and Investigation, 1979; reelected to each succeeding legislative session until December 1980; married: Iris Weinshall, 1980; children: Jessica Emily and Alison Emma; committees: chair, Rules and Administration; chair, Joint Committee on the Library; vice chair, Joint Committee on Printing; Banking, Housing, and Urban Affairs; Finance; Judiciary; elected to the 97th Congress on November 4, 1980; reelected to each succeeding Congress; elected to the U.S. Senate on November 3, 1998; reelected to each succeeding Senate term.

Office Listings

http://schumer.senate.gov

322 Hart Senate Office Building, Washington, DC 20510 .... (202) 224–6542
Chief of Staff.—Mike Lynch. FAX: 228–3027
Upstate Press Secretary.—Matt House.
Executive Assistant.—Alexandra Victor.
780 Third Avenue, Suite 2301, New York, NY 10017 .... (212) 486–4430
Leo O'Brien Building, 1 Clinton Square, Room 420, Albany, NY 12207 .... (518) 431–4070
130 South Elmwood Avenue, #660, Buffalo, NY 14202 .... (716) 846–4111
100 State Street, Room 3040, Rochester, NY 14614 .... (585) 263–5866
100 South Clinton, Room 841, Syracuse, NY 13261–7318 .... (315) 423–5471
Federal Office Building, 15 Henry Street, #M106, Binghamton, NY 13901 .... (607) 772–8109
Two Greenway Plaza, 145 Pine Lawn Road, #300N, Melville, NY 11747 .... (631) 753–0978
One Park Place, Suite 100, Peekskill, NY 10566 .... (914) 734–1532

* * *

KIRSTEN E. GILLIBRAND, Democrat, of Greenport, NY; born in Albany, NY, December 9, 1966; education: B.A., Dartmouth College, Hanover, NH, 1988; J.D., UCLA, Los Angeles, CA, 1991; professional: attorney; Special Counsel to the U.S. Secretary of Housing and Urban Development Andrew Cuomo; private legal practice; religion: Catholic; married: Jonathan Gillibrand 2001; two sons: Theodore 2004, Henry 2008; committees: Agriculture, Nutrition, and Forestry; Armed Services; Environment and Public Works; Special Committee on Aging; appointed to the 111th Congress on January 23, 2009, to fill the vacancy caused by the resignation of Hillary Clinton, subsequently elected on November 2, 2010, for the remaining two years of the unexpired term.

Office Listings

http://gillibrand.senate.gov

478 Russell Senate Office Building, Washington, DC 20510 .... (202) 224–4451
Chief of Staff.—Jess Fassler. FAX: 228–0282
Legislative Director.—Brooke Jamison.
Communications Director.—Bethany Lesser.
Scheduler.—Carlissia Graham.
780 Third Avenue, Suite 2601, New York, NY 10017 .... (212) 688–6262
Federal Office Building, 1 Clinton Square, Room 821, Albany, NY 12207 .... (518) 431–0120
Larkin at Exchange, 726 Exchange Street, Suite 511, Buffalo, NY 14210 .... (716) 854–9725
155 Pinelawn Road, Suite 250 North, Melville, NY 11747 .... (631) 249–2825
P.O. Box 273, Lowville, NY 13367 .... (315) 376–6118
Federal Office Building, 100 State Street, Room 4195, Rochester, NY 14614 .... (585) 263–6250
Federal Office Building, 100 South Clinton Street, Room 1470, P.O. Box 7378, Syracuse, NY 13261 .... (315) 448–0470
Lower Hudson Valley Office, P.O. Box 893, Mahopac, NY 10541 .... (845) 875–4585
Westchester County Office .... (914) 725–9294

REPRESENTATIVES

FIRST DISTRICT

TIMOTHY H. BISHOP, Democrat, of Southampton, NY; born in Southampton, June 1, 1950; education: Southampton High School, 1968; A.B., in history, from Holy Cross College; M.P.A., Long Island University, 1981; professional: educator; Provost of Southampton College, 1986–2002; community service: Southampton Rotary Club Scholarship Committee; Southampton Town Board of Ethics; Eastern Long Island Coastal Conservation Alliance; Bridgehampton Childcare and Recreation Center; religion: Catholic; married: Kathryn; children: Molly and Meghan; committees: Education and the Workforce; Transportation and Infrastructure; elected to the 108th Congress on November 5, 2002; reelected to each succeeding Congress.

Office Listings

http:/www.house.gov/timbishop

306 Cannon House Office Building, Washington, DC 20515 .... (202) 225–3826
Chief of Staff.—Pete Spiro. FAX: 225–3143
Legislative Director.—Mark Copeland.
Scheduler / Staff Assistant.—Tim Powers.
District Director / Communications Director.—Jon Schneider.
3680 Route 112, Suite C, Coram, NY 11727 .... (631) 696–6500
137 Hampton Road, Southampton, NY 11968 .... (631) 259–8450

Counties: SUFFOLK COUNTY (part). CITIES: Brookhaven, Smithtown, Southampton, and Montauk. Population (2000), 654,360.

ZIP Codes: 00501, 00544, 11713, 11715, 11719–20, 11727, 11733, 11738, 11741–42, 11745, 11754–55, 11763–64, 11766–68, 11772, 11776–80, 11784, 11786–90, 11792, 11794, 11901, 11930–35, 11937, 11939–42, 11944, 11946–65, 11967–73, 11975–78, 11980

* * *

SECOND DISTRICT

STEVE ISRAEL, Democrat, of Huntington, NY; born in Brooklyn, NY, May 30, 1958; education: B.A., George Washington University, 1982; professional: public relations and marketing executive; public service: legislative assistant for Rep. Richard Ottinger (D–NY), 1980–83; Suffolk County Executive for Intergovernmental Relations, 1988–91; elected to the Huntington Town Board, 1993; reelected two times; organizations: Institute on the Holocaust; Touro Law Center; Nature Conservancy; Audubon Society; awards: Child Care Council of Suffolk Leadership Award; Anti-Defamation League and Sons of Italy Purple Aster Award; elected to the 107th Congress on November 7, 2000; reelected to each succeeding Congress.

Office Listings

http://www.house.gov/israel

2457 Rayburn House Office Building, Washington, DC 20515 .... (202) 225–3335
Chief of Staff.—Jack Pratt. FAX: 225–4669
Communications Director.—Lindsay Hamilton.
Legislative Director.—Tricia Russell.
150 Motor Parkway, Suite 108, Hauppauge, NY 11788 .... (631) 951–2210
District Director.—Tracie Holmberg. (516) 505–1448

Counties: NASSAU COUNTY (part), SUFFOLK COUNTY (part). CITIES: Asharoken, Bay Shore, Bayport, Bohemia, Brentwood, Brightwaters, Centerport, Central Islip, Cold Springs Harbor, Commack, Copiague, Deer Park, Dix Hills, East Farmingdale, East Northport, Eaton's Neck, Elwood, Fort Salonga, Great River, Greenlawn, Halesite, Hauppauge, Holbrook, Huntington, Huntington Station, Islandia, Islip, Islip Terrace, Jericho, King's Park, Lindenhurst, Lloyd Harbor, Melville, North Amityville, Northport, Oakdale, Ocean Beach, Old Bethpage, Plainview, Ronkonkoma, Sayville, Smithtown, South Huntington, Syosset, West Babylon, West Hills, West Islip, West Sayville, Wheatley Heights, Woodbury and Wyandanch. Population (2000), 654,360.

ZIP Codes: 11701, 11703–06, 11714–18, 11721–22, 11724–26, 11729–31, 11735, 11737, 11739–43, 11746–47, 11749–54, 11757, 11760, 11767–70, 11772, 11775, 11779, 11782, 11787–88, 11791, 11796–98, 11801, 11803–04

* * *

THIRD DISTRICT

PETER T. KING, Republican, of Seaford, NY; born in Manhattan, NY, April 5, 1944; education: B.A., St. Francis College, NY, 1965; J.D., University of Notre Dame Law School,

IN, 1968; military service: served, U.S. Army Reserve National Guard, specialist 5, 1968–73; admitted to New York bar, 1968; professional: attorney; Deputy Nassau County Attorney, 1972–74, executive assistant to the Nassau County Executive, 1974–76; general counsel, Nassau Off-Track Betting Corporation, 1977; Hempstead Town Councilman, 1978–81; Nassau County Comptroller, 1981–92; member: Ancient Order of Hiberians, Long Island Committee for Soviet Jewry, Sons of Italy, Knights of Columbus, 69th Infantry Veterans Corps, American Legion; married: Rosemary Wiedl King, 1967; children: Sean and Erin; grandson, Jack; committees: chair, Homeland Security; Financial Services; Permanent Select Committee on Intelligence; elected on November 3, 1992 to the 103rd Congress; reelected to each succeeding Congress.

Office Listings

http://www.peteking.house.gov

339 Cannon House Office Building, Washington, DC 20515 .... (202) 225–7896
Chief of Staff / Press Secretary.—Kevin Fogarty. FAX: 226–2279
Legislative Director.—Adam Paulson.
1003 Park Boulevard, Massapequa Park, NY 11762 .... (516) 541–4225
District Director.—Anne Rosenfeld.
Suffolk County .... (631) 541–4225

Counties: NASSAU (part), SUFFOLK (part). CITIES AND TOWNSHIPS: Amityville, Babylon, Baldwin, Bayshore, Bayville, Bellmore, Bethpage, Brightwaters, Brookville, Cedar Beach, Centre Island, Copiague, Cove Neck, East Islip, East Norwich, Farmingdale, Freeport, Gilgo Beach, Glen Cove, Glen Head, Glenwood Landing, Greenvale, Harbor Isle, Hicksville, Island Park, Islip, Jericho, Lattingtown, Laurel Hollow, Levittown, Lido Beach, Lindenhurst, Locust Grove, Locust Valley, Long Beach, Massapequa, Massapequa Park, Matinecock, Merrick, Mill Neck, Muttontown, North Babylon, North Bellmore, North Lindenhurst, Oak Beach, Oceanside, Old Bethpage, Old Brookville, Old Westbury, Oyster Bay, Oyster Bay Cove, Plainview, Point Lookout, Sea Cliff, Seaford, Syosset, Wantagh, West Babylon, West Bayshore, Westbury, West Islip, and Woodbury. Population (2000), 654,361.

ZIP Codes: 11510, 11520, 11542, 11545, 11547–48, 11558, 11560–61, 11566, 11568–69, 11572, 11576, 11579, 11590, 11599, 11701–04, 11706, 11709–10, 11714, 11718, 11724, 11726, 11730, 11732, 11735–37, 11751, 11753, 11756–58, 11762, 11765, 11771, 11773–74, 11783, 11791, 11793, 11795, 11797, 11801–04, 11815, 11819, 11854–55

* * *

FOURTH DISTRICT

CAROLYN McCARTHY, Democrat, of Mineola, NY; born in Brooklyn, NY, January 5, 1944; education: graduated, Mineola High School, 1962; graduated, nursing school, 1964; professional: licensed practical nurse in ICU Section, Glen Cove Hospital; married: Dennis McCarthy, 1967; widowed on December 7, 1993, when her husband was killed and her only son, Kevin, severely wounded in the Long Island Railroad Massacre; turned personal nightmare into a crusade against violence—speaking out with other families of the Long Island tragedy, not just to the victims of the shooting but to crime victims across the country; committees: Education and the Workforce; Financial Services; elected to the 105th Congress; reelected to each succeeding Congress.

Office Listings

http://www.house.gov/carolynmccarthy

2346 Rayburn House Office Building, Washington, DC 20515 .... (202) 225–5516
Chief of Staff.—Stuart Chapman. FAX: 225–5758
District Director.—Christopher Chaffee.
Executive Assistant.—Ellen McNamara.
Communications Director.—Shams Tarek.
300 Garden City Plaza, Suite 200, Garden City, NY 11530 .... (516) 739–3008

Counties: NASSAU (part). CITIES AND TOWNSHIPS: Atlantic Beach, Baldwin, Bellerose, Carle Place, Cedarhurst, East Meadow, East Rockaway, East Williston, Elmont, Floral Park, Franklin Square, Freeport, Garden City, Garden City Park, Hempstead, Hewlett, Inwood, Lakeview, Lawrence, Lynbrook, Malverne, Merrick, Mineola, New Cassel, New Hyde Park, North Bellmore, North New Hyde Park, Oceanside, Rockville Centre, Roosevelt, Salisbury, Stewart Manor, South Floral Park, South Valley Stream, Uniondale, Valley Stream, West Hempstead, Westbury, Williston Park, Woodmere, and Woodsburgh. Population (2000) 654,360.

ZIP Codes: 11001–03, 11010, 11040, 11096, 11501, 11509–10, 11514, 11516, 11518, 11520, 11530, 11540, 11549–57, 11559, 11561, 11563–66, 11568, 11570–72, 11575, 11577, 11580–83, 11588, 11590, 11592–99, 11710, 11793

* * *

FIFTH DISTRICT

GARY L. ACKERMAN, Democrat, of Queens, NY; born in Brooklyn, NY, November 19, 1942; education: graduate, Queens College, Flushing, NY; attended St. John's University, Jamaica, NY; professional: public school teacher; newspaper editor; businessman; New York State Senate, 1979–83; married: the former Rita Tewel; children: Lauren, Corey, and Ari; committees: Financial Services; Foreign Affairs; elected by special election on March 1, 1983, to the 98th Congress, to fill the vacancy caused by the death of Representative Benjamin Rosenthal; reelected to each succeeding Congress.

Office Listings

http://www.house.gov/ackerman

2243 Rayburn House Office Building, Washington, DC 20515 .... (202) 225–2601
Chief of Staff.—Jedd Moskowitz. FAX: 225–1589
Scheduler.—Brenda Connolly.
Legislative Director.—Jared Frost.
Press Secretary.—Jordan Goldes.
218–14 Northern Boulevard, Bayside, NY 11361 .... (718) 423–2154
District Office Administrator.—Moya Berry.

Counties: NASSAU (part), QUEENS (part). CITIES AND TOWNSHIPS: Auburndale, Bay Terrace, Bayside, Bell Park Gardens, Bell Park Manor, Centre Island, Clearview, Corona, Deepdale, Douglaston, Douglaston Manor, East Elmhurst, East Hills, Flushing, Fresh Meadows, Glen Oaks, Great Neck, Great Neck Estates, Great Neck Gardens, Great Neck Plaza, Greenvale, Herricks, Hillcrest, Hollis Court Gardens, Hollis Hills, Jackson Heights, Jamaica Estates, Kensington, Kew Gardens Hills, Kings Point, Lake Success, Lefrak City, Linden Hill, Little Neck, Malba, Manor Haven, North Shore Towers, Oakland Gardens, Pomonok, Port Washington, Port Washington North, Queensboro Hill, Roslyn, Roslyn Estates, Roslyn Harbor, Roslyn Heights, Russell Gardens, Saddle Rock, Saddle Rock Estates, Sands Point, Searington, Thomaston, University Gardens, West Neck, and Windsor Park. Population (2000), 654,361.

ZIP Codes: 11004–05, 11020–24, 11030, 11040, 11042, 11050–55, 11351–52, 11354–58, 11360–66, 11368–69, 11372–73, 11375, 11379, 11423, 11426–27, 11432, 11507, 11542, 11548, 11560, 11568, 11576–77, 11596

* * *

SIXTH DISTRICT

GREGORY W. MEEKS, Democrat, of Southern Queens, NY; born in Harlem, NY, September 25, 1953; education: P.S. 183; Robert F. Wagner Junior High School; Julia Richman High School, New York, NY; B.A., Adelphi University, 1971–75; J.D., Howard University School of Law, 1975–78; professional: lawyer, admitted to bar, 1979; Queens District Attorney's Office, 1978–83, Assistant Specialist Narcotic Prosecutor, 1981–83; Assistant Counsel to State Investigation Commission, 1983–85; serving as Assistant District Attorney; Supervising Judge, New York State Workers' Compensation Board; public service: New York State Assemblyman, 1992–97; organizations: Alpha Phi Alpha Fraternity; Council of Black-Elected Democrats; National Bar Association; Task Force on Financial Services; co-chair of the Congressional Services Caucus; co-chair of the Organizations of American States; active member of the Congressional Black Caucus; married: Simone-Marie Meeks, 1997; children: Aja, Ebony, and Nia-Ayana; committees: Financial Services; Foreign Affairs; elected to the 105th Congress on February 3, 1998; reelected to each succeeding Congress.

Office Listings

http://www.house.gov/meeks

2342 Rayburn House Office Building, Washington, DC 20515 .... (202) 225–3461
Chief of Staff.—Sophia Lafargue. FAX: 226–4169
Legislative Director.—Milan Dalal.
Office Manager / Scheduler.—Kim Fuller.
153–01 Jamaica Avenue, Jamaica, NY 11432 .... (718) 725–6000
Chief of Staff.—Robert Simmons.
1931 Mott Avenue, Room 305, Far Rockaway, NY 11691 .... (718) 327–9791
Community Liaison.—Veronica Beckford.

Counties: QUEENS COUNTY (part). CITIES AND TOWNSHIPS: Arverne, Cambria Heights, Edgemere, Far Rockaway, Floral Park, Glen Oaks, Hammels, Hollis, Howard Beach, Jamaica, Jamaica Estates, Kew Gardens, Laurelton, New Hyde Park, Ozone Park, Queens Village, Richmond Hill, Rosedale, St. Albans, South Jamaica, South Ozone Park, Springfield Gardens, and Woodhaven. Population (2000), 654,361.

ZIP Codes: 11001, 11004, 11040, 11405, 11411–20, 11422–23, 11425–36, 11439, 11451, 11484, 11690–93

* * *

SEVENTH DISTRICT

JOSEPH CROWLEY, Democrat, of Elmhurst, Queens, NY; born in Woodside, NY, March 16, 1962; education: graduated, Power Memorial High School, 1981; B.A., political science communications, Queens College (City University of New York), Flushing, NY, 1985; professional: elected to the New York State Assembly, 1986–98; assembly committees: Racing and Wagering; Banking, Consumer Affairs, and Protection; Election Law; Labor and Housing; serving in the leadership of the U.S. House of Representatives as the Chief Deputy Whip; chair, New Democrats Coalition Caucus; founder and current chair of the Bangladesh Caucus; founder and co-chair of the Congressional Musicians Caucus; religion: Roman Catholic; married: Kasey Nilson; children: Cullen, Kenzie and Liam; committees: Ways and Means; elected to the 106th Congress; reelected to each succeeding Congress.

Office Listings

http://house.gov/crowley

2404 Rayburn House Office Building, Washington, DC 20510 .... (202) 225–3965
Chief of Staff.—Kate Winkler. FAX: 225–1909
Office Manager.—John Sweeney.
Legislative Director.—Jeremy Woodrum.
2800 Bruckner Boulevard, Suite 301, Bronx, NY 10465 .... (718) 931–1400
177 Dreiser Loop, Room 3, Bronx, NY 10475 .... (718) 320–2314
74–09 37th Avenue, Suite 306–B, Jackson Heights, NY 11372 .... (718) 779–1400

Counties: BRONX (part), QUEENS (part). Population (2000), 654,360.

ZIP Codes: 10458, 10460–62, 10464–67, 10469, 10472–75, 10805, 11103–04, 11354, 11356, 11368–73, 11377–78, 11380

* * *

EIGHTH DISTRICT

JERROLD NADLER, Democrat, of New York, NY; born in Brooklyn, NY, June 13, 1947; education: graduated from Stuyvesant High School, 1965; B.A., Columbia University, 1970; J.D., Fordham University, 1978; professional: New York State Assembly, 1977–92; member: ACLU; NARAL Pro-Choice America; AIPAC; National Organization for Women; Assistant Whip; married: 1976; one child; committees: Judiciary; Transportation and Infrastructure; elected to the 102nd Congress on November 3, 1992, to fill the vacancy caused by the death of Representative Ted Weiss; at the same time elected to the 103rd Congress; reelected to each succeeding Congress.

Office Listings

http://www.house.gov/nadler

2334 Rayburn House Office Building, Washington, DC 20515 .... (202) 225–5635
Director.—John Doty. FAX: 225–6923
201 Varick Street, Suite 669, New York, NY 10014 .... (212) 367–7350
Chief of Staff.—Amy Rutkin.
445 Neptune Avenue, Brooklyn, NY 11224 .... (718) 373–3198

Counties: KINGS (part), NEW YORK (part). Population (2000), 654,360.

ZIP Codes: 10001–08, 10010–14, 10016, 10018–20, 10023–24, 10036, 10038, 10041, 10043, 10047–48, 10069, 10072, 10080–81, 10101–02, 10108–09, 10113–14, 10116–17, 10119–24, 10129, 10132–33, 10149, 10199, 10209, 10213, 10242, 10249, 10256, 10260, 10265, 10268–70, 10272–82, 10285–86, 10292, 11204, 11214–15, 11218–20, 11223–24, 11228, 11230–32, 11235

* * *

NINTH DISTRICT

ROBERT L. TURNER, Republican, of Queens, NY; born in Queens, NY, May 2, 1941; education: graduated, Richmond Hill High School; B.A., St. John's University; professional: President and CEO of Pearson PLC's North American television operations; President and CEO of Multimedia Entertainment; founder of Orbis Communications and Orbis Entertainment; President of LBS Communications; Director of Advertising for Bristol-Myers Company; General Manager of CBS Cable; married: Peggy Turner; children: Lee, Matt, Meg, Beth, and CJ; committees: Foreign Affairs; Homeland Security; Veterans' Affairs; elected by special election to the 112th Congress on Tuesday, September 13, 2011 to fill the vacancy in New York's Ninth District.

Office Listings

http://www.bobturner.house.gov

2104 Rayburn House Office Building, Washington, DC 20515 .... (202) 225–6616
Chief of Staff.—Michael Giuliani. FAX: 226–0218
Legislative Director.—Vacant.
Scheduler.—Brittany Belt.
80–02 Kew Gardens Road, Suite 5000, Kew Gardens, NY 11415 .... (718) 520–9001
District Director.—Vacant.

Counties: KINGS COUNTY (part). CITIES AND TOWNSHIPS: Bergen Beach, Brighton Beach, Canasie, Flatbush, Flatlands, Gerritsen Beach, Georgetowne, Kensington, Manhattan Beach, Marine Park, Midwood, Mill Basin, Park Slope, Parkville, Sheepshead Bay, Windsor Terrace. QUEENS COUNTY (part). CITIES AND TOWNSHIPS: Belle Harbor, Breezy Point, Briarwood, Broad Channel, Corona, Elmhurst, Far Rockaway, Forest Hills, Glendale, Hamilton Beach, Howard Beach, Kew Gardens, Lindenwood, Middle Village, Neponsit, Ozone Park, Rego Park, Richmond Hill, Ridgewood, Rockaway Point, Roxbury, West Lawrence, and Woodhaven. Population (2000), 654,360.

ZIP Codes: 111204, 11208, 11210, 11218, 11223, 11229–30, 11234–36, 11358, 11361, 11364–67, 11373–75, 11378–79, 11381, 11385, 11414–18, 11421, 11424, 11427, 11432, 11435, 11693–95, 11697

* * *

TENTH DISTRICT

EDOLPHUS TOWNS, Democrat, of Brooklyn, NY; born in Chadbourn, NC, July 21, 1934; graduated, West Side High School, Chadbourn, 1952; B.S., North Carolina A&T State University, Greensboro, 1956; master's degree in social work, Adelphi University, Garden City, NY, 1973; U.S. Army, 1956–58; teacher, Medgar Evers College, Brookyln, NY, and for the New York City public school system; deputy hospital administrator, 1965–71; deputy president, Borough of Brooklyn, 1976–82; member: Kiwanis, Boy Scouts Advisory Council, Salvation Army, Phi Beta Sigma Fraternity; married the former Gwendolyn Forbes in 1960; two children: Darryl and Deidra; committees: Energy and Commerce; Oversight and Government Reform; elected on November 2, 1982, to the 98th Congress; reelected to each succeeding Congress.

Office Listings

http://www.house.gov/towns

2232 Rayburn House Office Building, Washington, DC 20515 .... (202) 225–5936
Senior Political and Policy Advisor.—Lars Hydle. FAX: 225–1018
Deputy Chief of Staff.—Charles Lewis.
Executive Assistant / Scheduler.—Bill Jusino.
186 Joralemon Street, Suite 1102, Brooklyn, NY 11201 .... (718) 855–8018
Chief of Staff.—Albert Wiltshire.
District Director.—Gail Muhammad.
104–08 Flatlands Avenue, Brooklyn, NY 11236 .... (718) 272–1175

Counties: KINGS COUNTY (part). Population (2000), 654,361.

ZIP Codes: 11201–03, 11205–08, 11210–13, 11216–17, 11221, 11230, 11233–34, 11236, 11238–39, 11245, 11247–48, 11251, 11256

* * *

ELEVENTH DISTRICT

YVETTE D. CLARKE, Democrat, of Brooklyn, NY; born in Brooklyn, November 21, 1964; education: attended Edward R. Murrow High School; attended Oberlin College; professional: legislative aide to New York State Senator Velmanette Montgomery; executive assistant to NY Assemblywoman Barbara Clark; staff assistant, NY Compensation Board Chair Barbara Patton; Director of Youth Programs, Hospital League / Local 1199 Training and Upgrading Fund; Director of Business Development for the Bronx Empowerment Zone (BOEDC); member of City Council of New York, 2001–06; committees: Homeland Security; Small Business; elected to the 110th Congress on November 7, 2006; reelected to each succeeding Congress.

Office Listings

http://clarke.house.gov

1029 Longworth House Office Building, Washington, DC 20515 .... (202) 225–6231
Chief of Staff.—Shelley Davis. FAX: 226–0112
Legislative Director.—Asi Ofosu.
123 Linden Boulevard, 4th Floor, Brooklyn, NY 11226 .... (718) 287–1142

Counties: KINGS COUNTY (part). Population (2000), 654,361.

ZIP Codes: 11201, 11203, 11210, 11212–13, 11215–18, 11225–26, 11230–31, 11233–34, 11236, 11238, 11241–42

* * *

TWELFTH DISTRICT

NYDIA M. VELÁZQUEZ, Democrat, of New York, NY; born in Yabucoa, Puerto Rico, March 28, 1953; education: B.A. in political science, University of Puerto Rico, 1974; M.A. in political science, New York University, 1976; professional: faculty member, University of Puerto Rico, 1976–81; adjunct professor, Hunter College of the City University of New York, 1981–83; special assistant to Congressman Ed Towns, 1983; member, City Council of New York, 1984–86; national director of Migration Division Office, Department of Labor and Human Resources of Puerto Rico, 1986–89; director, Department of Puerto Rican Community Affairs in the United States, 1989–92; committees: Financial Services; Small Business; elected on November 3, 1992, to the 103rd Congress; reelected to each succeeding Congress.

Office Listings

http://www.house.gov/velazquez

2302 Rayburn House Office Building, Washington, DC 20515 .... (202) 225–2361
Chief of Staff.—Michael Day. FAX: 226–0327
Communications Director.—Alex Haurek.
Scheduler.—Maria Elena Juarez.
Legislative Director.—Clarinda Landeros.
266 Broadway, Suite 201, Brooklyn, NY 11211 .... (718) 599–3658
16 Court Street, Suite 1006, Brooklyn, NY 11241 .... (718) 222–5819
173 Avenue B, New York, NY 10009 .... (212) 673–3997

Counties: KINGS (part), NEW YORK (part), QUEENS (part). Population (2000), 654,360.

ZIP Codes: 10002, 10009, 10012–13, 10038, 11104, 11201, 11205–08, 11211, 11215, 11219–22, 11231–32, 11237, 11251, 11377–78, 11385, 11416, 11421

* * *

THIRTEENTH DISTRICT

MICHAEL G. GRIMM, Republican, of Staten Island, NY; born in Brooklyn, NY, February 7, 1970; education: B.B.A., Accounting Baruch College, New York, NY, 1994; J.D., New York Law School, 2002; professional: U.S. Marine Corps and Reserve, 1989–97; FBI special agent, small business owner; religion: Roman Catholic; commissions and caucuses: Assistant Deputy Whip; chairman, House Republican Policy Committee's Task Force on Foreign Policy; co-chair, House Republican Israel Caucus; co-chair, Zoo and Aquarium Caucus; committees: Financial Services; elected to the 112th Congress on November 2, 2010.

Office Listings

http://www.grimm.house.gov

512 Cannon House Office Building, Washington, DC 20515 .... (202) 225–3371
Chief of Staff.—Chris Berardini. FAX: 226–1272
Legislative Director.—Aaron Ringel.
Communications Director.—Carol Danko.
Executive Assistant.—Blaire Bartlett.
265 New Dorp Lane, 2nd Floor, Staten Island, NY 10306 .... (718) 351–1062
District Director.—Bill Smith.
7308 13th Avenue, Brooklyn, NY 11228 .... (718) 630–5277
Brooklyn Director.—Nick Curran.

Counties: KINGS (part), RICHMOND. Population (2000), 654,361.

ZIP Codes: 10301–10, 10312–14, 11204, 11209, 11214, 11219–20, 11223, 11228, 11252

* * *

FOURTEENTH DISTRICT

CAROLYN B. MALONEY, Democrat, of New York City, NY; born in Greensboro, NC, February 19, 1946; education: B.A., Greensboro College, Greensboro, NC, 1968; professional: various positions, New York City Board of Education, 1970–77; legislative aide, New York State Assembly, senior program analyst, 1977–79; executive director of advisory council, 1979–82; director of special projects, New York State Senate Office of the Minority Leader; New York City council member, 1982–93; chairperson, New York City Council Committee on Contracts; member: Council Committee on Aging, National Organization of Women, Common Cause, Sierra Club, Americans for Democratic Action, New York City Council Committee on Housing and Buildings, Citizens Union, Grand Central Business Improvement District, Harlem Urban Development Corporation (1982–91), Commission on Early Childhood Development Programs, Council of Senior Citizen Centers of New York City (1982–87); married: Clifton H.W. Maloney, 1976; children: Virginia Marshall Maloney and Christina Paul Maloney; committees: Financial Services; Oversight and Government Reform; Joint Economic Committee; elected on November 3, 1992, to the 103rd Congress; reelected to each succeeding Congress.

Office Listings

http://www.maloney.house.gov

2332 Rayburn House Office Building, Washington, DC 20515 .... (202) 225–7944
Chief of Staff.—Ben Chevat. FAX: 225–4709
Legislative Director.—Orly Isaacson.
Administrative Assistant.—Lauren Shapiro.
1651 Third Avenue, Suite 311, New York, NY 10128 .... (212) 860–0606
21–77 31st Street, Astoria, NY 11105 .... (718) 932–1804

Counties: NEW YORK (part), QUEENS (part). CITIES AND TOWNSHIPS: Astoria, Manhattan, Queens, Long Island City, Roosevelt Island, Sunnyside, and Woodside. Population (2000), 654,361.

ZIP Codes: 10012, 10016–24, 10026, 10028–29, 10036, 10044, 10055, 10103–07, 10110–12, 10126, 10128, 10138, 10150–60, 10162–79, 11101–06, 11375, 11377

* * *

FIFTEENTH DISTRICT

CHARLES B. RANGEL, Democrat-Liberal, of New York, NY; born in Harlem, NY, June 11, 1930; attended DeWitt Clinton High School; served in U.S. Army, 1948–52; awarded the Purple Heart, Bronze Star for Valor, U.S. and Korean presidential citations, and three battle stars while serving in combat with the Second Infantry Division in Korea; honorably discharged with rank of staff sergeant; after military duty, completed high school, 1953; graduated from New York University School of Commerce, student under the G.I. bill; 1957 dean's list; graduated from St. John's University School of Law, dean's list student under a full 3-year scholarship, 1960; lawyer; admitted to practice in the courts of the State of New York, U.S. Federal Court, Southern District of New York, and U.S. Customs Court; appointed assistant U.S. attorney, Southern District of New York, 1961; legal counsel, New York City Housing and Redevelopment Board, Neighborhood Conservation Bureau; general counsel, National Advisory Commission on Selective Service, 1966; served two terms in the New York State Assembly, 1966–70; active in 369th Veterans Association; Community Education Program; and Martin Luther King, Jr., Democratic Club; married: Alma Carter; two children: Steven and Alicia; committees: Ways and Means; Joint Committee on Taxation; elected to the 92nd Congress, November 3, 1970; reelected to each succeeding Congress.

Office Listings

http://www.house.gov/rangel

2354 Rayburn House Office Building, Washington, DC 20515 .... (202) 225–4365
Counsel/Chief of Staff.—George Henry. FAX: 225–0816
163 West 125th Street, Room 737, New York, NY 10027 .... (212) 663–3900
District Administrator.—Vivian E. Jones.

Counties: BRONX (part), NEW YORK (part), QUEENS (part). Population (2010), 639,873.

ZIP Codes: 10023–27, 10029–35, 10037, 10039–40, 10115–16, 10169, 10463, 11105

* * *

SIXTEENTH DISTRICT

JOSÉ E. SERRANO, Democrat, of Bronx, NY; born in Mayagüez, PR, October 24, 1943; education: Dodge Vocational High School, Bronx, NY; attended Lehman College, City University of New York, NY; served with the U.S. Army Medical Corps, 1964–66; employed by the Manufacturers Hanover Bank, 1961–69; Community School District 7, 1969–74; New York State Assemblyman, 1974–90; chairman, Consumer Affairs Committee, 1979–83; chairman, Education Committee, 1983–90; five children: Lisa, Jose Marco, Justine, Jonathan and Benjamin; committees: Appropriations; elected to the 101st Congress, by special election, March 28, 1990, to fill the vacancy caused by the resignation of Robert Garcia; reelected to each succeeding Congress.

Office Listings

http://serrano.house.gov

2227 Rayburn House Office Building, Washington, DC 20515 .... (202) 225–4361
Chief Administrator.—Idalia Dominguez de Marty. FAX: 225–6001
Legislative Director.—Nadine Berg.
Scheduler.—Carla Coley.
1231 Lafayette Street, 4th Floor, Bronx, NY 10474 .... (718) 620–0084
District Office Chief of Staff.—Angela Fernandez.

Counties: BRONX COUNTY (part). CITIES AND TOWNSHIPS: Bronx. Population (2000), 654,360.

ZIP Codes: 10451–60, 10463, 10468, 10472–74‘

* * *

SEVENTEENTH DISTRICT

ELIOT L. ENGEL, Democrat, of Bronx, NY; born in Bronx, February 18, 1947; education: B.A., Hunter-Lehman College, 1969; M.A., City University of New York, 1973; J.D., New York Law School, 1987; professional: teacher and counselor in the New York City public school system, 1969–77; elected to the New York legislature, 1977–88; chaired the Assembly Committee on Alcoholism and Substance Abuse and subcommittee on Mitchell-Lama Housing (twelve years prior to his election to Congress); member: Congressional Human Rights Caucus; Democratic Study Group on Health; Long Island Sound Caucus; co-chairman, Albanian Issues Caucus; board member, Congressional Ad Hoc Committee on Irish Affairs; married: Patricia Ennis, 1980; children: Julia, Jonathan, and Philip; committees: Energy and Commerce; Foreign Affairs; elected on November 8, 1988, to the 101st Congress; reelected to each succeeding Congress.

Office Listings

http://www.engel.house.gov

2161 Rayburn House Office Building, Washington, DC 20515 .... (202) 225–2464
Administrative Assistant.—E.H. ‘‘Ned’’ Michalek. FAX: 225–5513
Office Manager.—Heather Estler.
3655 Johnson Avenue, Bronx, NY 10463 .... (718) 796–9700
Chief of Staff.—William Weitz.
6 Gramatan Avenue, Suite 205, Mt. Vernon, NY 10550 .... (914) 699–4100
261 West Nyack Road, West Nyack, NY 10994 .... (845) 358–7800

Counties: BRONX (part), WESTCHESTER (part). CITIES AND TOWNSHIPS: Parts of Bronx, Mount Vernon, Yonkers. ROCKLAND COUNTY. TOWNSHIPS: Clarkstown, Orangetown, Ramapo, Population (2000), 654,360.

ZIP Codes: 10458, 10463, 10466–71, 10475, 10522, 10533, 10550–52, 10557–58, 10591, 10701, 10704–06, 10708, 10901, 10913, 10920, 10931, 10952, 10954, 10956, 10960, 10962, 10964–65, 10968, 10970, 10974, 10976–77, 10983, 10989, 10994

* * *

EIGHTEENTH DISTRICT

NITA M. LOWEY, Democrat, of Harrison, NY; born in New York, NY, July 5, 1937; education: graduated, Bronx High School of Science, 1955; B.A., Mount Holyoke College,

1959; assistant to Secretary of State for Economic Development and Neighborhood Preservation, and deputy director, Division of Economic Opportunity, 1975–85; Assistant Secretary of State, 1985–87; member: boards of directors, Close-Up Foundation; Effective Parenting Information for Children; Windward School, Downstate (New York Region); Westchester Jewish Conference; Westchester Opportunity Program; National Committee of the Police Corps; Women's Network of the YWCA; Legal Awareness for Women; National Women's Political Caucus of Westchester; American Jewish Committee of Westchester; married: Stephen Lowey, 1961; children: Dana, Jacqueline, and Douglas; committees: Appropriations; elected on November 8, 1988, to the 101st Congress; reelected to each succeeding Congress.

Office Listings

http://www.house.gov/lowey

2365 Rayburn House Office Building, Washington, DC 20515 .... (202) 225–6506
Chief of Staff.—Elizabeth Stanley. FAX: 225–0546
Executive Assistant.—Kelly Healton.
Legislative Director.—Chris Bigelow.
Communications Director.—Matt Dennis.
222 Mamaroneck Avenue, Suite 310, White Plains, NY 10605 .... (914) 428–1707
District Administrator.—Patricia Keegan.

Counties: Rockland (part), Westchester (part). Cities and townships: Ardsley, Ardsley on the Hudson, Briarcliff Manor; Bronxville, Chappaqua, Congers, Crestwood, Dobbs Ferry, Eastchester, Elmsford, Harrison, Hartsdale, Hasting-on-Hudson, Haverstraw, Hawthorne, Irvington, Larchmont, Mamaroneck, Maryknoll, Millwood, Mt. Kisco, New City, New Rochelle, North Castle, Ossining, Pelham, Pleasantville, Port Chester, Purchase, Rye, Rye Brook, Scarsdale, Sleepy Hollow, Tarrytown, Thornwood, Tuckahoe, Valhalla, Valley Cottage, West Harrison, West Haverstraw, White Plains, and Yonkers. Population (2000), 654,360.

ZIP Codes: 10502, 10504, 10506, 10510, 10514, 10522–23, 10528, 10530, 10532–33, 10538, 10543, 10546, 10549, 10562, 10570, 10573, 10577, 10580, 10583, 10591, 10594–95, 10601–07, 10610, 10650, 10701–10, 10801–05, 10920, 10923, 10927, 10956, 10989, 10993–94

* * *

NINETEENTH DISTRICT

NAN A.S. HAYWORTH, Republican, of Bedford, NY; born in Chicago, IL, December 14, 1959; education: graduated A.B., *summa cum laude*, in biology at Princeton University, Princeton, NJ, 1981; M.D., Cornell University Medical College, New York, NY, 1985; professional: ophthalmologist in her own solo practice; partner in the Mount Kisco Medical Group; attending physician at Sinai School of Medicine, New York; honors: elected to the Alpha Omega Alpha Medical Honors Society; religion: Lutheran; married: Dr. Scott Hayworth; two sons; committees: Financial Services; elected to the 112th Congress on November 2, 2010.

Office Listings

http://www.hayworth.house.gov

1440 Longworth House Office Building, Washington, DC 20515 .... (202) 225–5441
Chief of Staff.—Jonathan Day. FAX: 225–3289
Legislative Director.—Matthew Turkstra.
2 Summit Court, Suite 103, Fishkill, NY 12524 .... (845) 206–4600
225 Main Street, Room 3232G, Goshen, NY 10924 .... (845) 225–3641
Towne Centre at Somers, 268 Route 202, Suite D105, Somers, NY 10589 .... (845) 206–4600
District Director.—Don Scott. EXT: 60737

Counties: Dutchess County (part). Cities and townships: Beacon, Castle Point, Chelsea, Dover Plains, Fishkill, Glenham, Holmes, Hopewell Junction, Hughsonville, Pawling, Poughkeepsie, Poughquag, Stormville, Wappingers Falls, Wingdale. Orange County (part). Cities and townships: Amity, Arden, Bear Mountain, Bellvale, Blooming Grove, Burnside, Campbell Hall, Central Valley, Chester, Cornwall, Cornwall-on-Hudson, Craigville, Cuddebackville, Durlandville, Eagle Valley, Edenville, Finchville, Finnegan's Corner, Firthcliff, Florida, Fort Montgomery, Gardnerville, Goddefroy, Goshen, Greenwood Lake, Guymard, Harriman, Highland Falls, Highland Mills, Huguenot, Johnson, Kiryas Joel, Little Britain, Little York, Maybrook, Middletown, Monroe, Montgomery, Mountainville, New Hampton, New Milford, New Vernon, New Windsor, Newburgh, Otisville, Oxford Depot, Phillipsburg, Pine Island, Port Jervis, Ridgebury, Rock Tavern, Salisbury Mills, Slate Hill, Sloatsburg, Southfields, Sparrowbush, Sterling Forest, Stony Ford, Suffern, Sugarloaf, Tuxedo, Tuxedo Park, Unionville, Vails Gate, Wallkill, Warwick, Washingtonville, West Point, Westbrookville, Westtown, Wickham Village. Putnam County. Cities and townships: Baldwin Place, Brewster, Carmel, Cold Spring, Garrison, Kent, Lake Peekskill, Mahopac, Mahopac Falls, Patterson, Putnam Valley. Rockland County. Cities and townships: Garnerville, Haverstraw, Pomona, Stony Point, Thiells, Tomkins Cove. Westchester County. Cities and townships: Amawalk, Baldwin Place, Bedford, Bedford Hills, Buchanan, Cortlandt Manor, Crompound, Cross River, Croton Falls, Croton-on-Hudson, Golden's Bridge, Jefferson Valley, Katonah, Lincolndale, Mohegan Lake, Montrose, Mt. Kisco, North Salem, Peekskill, Pound Ridge, Purdys, Shenorock, Shrub Oak, Somers, South Salem, Verplanck, Waccabuc, and Yorktown Heights. Population (2000), 654,361.

ZIP Codes: 10501, 10504–07, 10509, 10511–12, 10516–21, 10524, 10526–27, 10530, 10535–37, 10540–42, 10545, 10547–49, 10551, 10558, 10560, 10562, 10566–67, 10571–72, 10576, 10578–79, 10587–90, 10596–98, 10602, 10911, 10916–

18, 10921–26, 10928, 10930, 10940–41, 10943, 10950, 10953, 10958, 10963, 10969–70, 10973, 10975, 10979–80, 10984, 10986–87, 10990, 10992, 10996–98, 11518, 11542, 11568, 11572, 11701–02, 11704, 11706–09, 11721, 11724, 11730–31, 11740, 11757, 11768, 11797, 12508, 12510–12, 12518, 12520, 12522, 12524, 12527, 12531, 12533, 12537–38, 12540, 12543, 12549, 12552–53, 12555, 12563–64, 12570, 12575, 12577–78, 12582, 12584, 12590, 12592, 12594, 12601–04, 12729, 12746, 12771, 12780, 12785

* * *

TWENTIETH DISTRICT

CHRISTOPHER GIBSON, Republican, Kinderhook, NY; born in Rockville Centre; May 13, 1964; education: graduated, B.A., *magna cum laude,* history, ROTC Commission, Siena College, Loudonville, NY, 1986; M.P.A., government, Cornell University, Ithaca, NY, 1995; Ph.D., government, Cornell University, Ithaca, 1998; professional: military, colonel, U.S. Army; Hoover National Security Affairs Fellowship, Stanford University; Congressional Fellow; awards: 2 Legions of Merit, 4 Bronze Star Medals; Purple Heart; Combat Infantryman's Badge with Star; Master Parachutist Badge, Ranger Tab; book: *Securing the State*; religion: Roman Catholic; married: Mary Jo; children: Katie, Maggie, and Connor; committees: Agriculture; Armed Services; elected to the 112th Congress on November 2, 2010.

Office Listings

http://www.gibson.house.gov

502 Cannon House Office Building, Washington, DC 20515 .... (202) 225–5614
Chief of Staff.—Steve Stallmer. FAX: 225–1168
Communications Director.—Stephanie Valle.
Legislative Director.—Brad Gentile.
Scheduler / Executive Assistant.—Kate Better.
513 Broadway, Saratoga Springs, NY 12866 .... (518) 306–5450
District Director.—Steve Bulger.
2 Hudson Street, Kinderhook, NY 12106 .... (518) 610–8133
136 Glen Street, Glens Falls, NY 12801 .... (518) 743–0964
Deputy District Director.—Mark Wescott.
111 Main Street, Delhi, NY 13753 .... (607) 746–9537
7578 North Broadway, Red Hook, NY 12571 .... (845) 514–3790

Counties: COLUMBIA, DELAWARE (part), DUTCHESS (part), ESSEX (part), GREENE, RENSSELAER (part), SARATOGA (part), OTSEGO (part), WARREN, and WASHINGTON. Population (2000), 654,360.

ZIP Codes: 12010, 12015, 12017–20, 12022, 12024–25, 12027–29, 12033, 12037, 12040, 12042, 12046, 12050–52, 12057–60, 12062, 12065, 12074–76, 12083, 12086–87, 12089–90, 12093–94, 12106, 12115, 12118, 12123–25, 12130, 12132–34, 12136, 12138, 12140, 12143, 12148, 12151, 12153–56, 12165, 12167–70, 12172–74, 12176, 12180, 12182, 12184–85, 12192, 12195–96, 12198, 12405–07, 12413–14, 12418, 12421–24, 12427, 12430–31, 12434, 12438–39, 12442, 12444, 12450–51, 12454–55, 12459–60, 12463, 12468–70, 12473–74, 12480, 12482, 12485, 12492, 12496, 12501–03, 12507, 12513–14, 12516–17, 12521–23, 12526, 12529, 12533–34, 12538, 12540, 12545–46, 12565, 12567, 12569–72, 12578, 12580–81, 12583, 12585, 12590, 12592, 12594, 12601, 12603, 12776, 12801, 12803–04, 12808–11, 12814–17, 12819–24, 12827–28, 12831–39, 12841, 12843–46, 12848–50, 12853–56, 12859–63, 12865–66, 12870–74, 12878, 12883–87, 12942–43, 12946, 12977, 12983, 13326, 13450, 13488, 13731, 13739–40, 13750, 13752–53, 13755, 13757, 13775, 13782, 13786, 13788, 13804, 13806–07, 13820, 13838, 13842, 13846, 13849, 13856, 13860

* * *

TWENTY-FIRST DISTRICT

PAUL D. TONKO, Democrat, of Amsterdam, NY; born in Amsterdam, NY, June 18, 1949; education: graduated Amsterdam High School, Amsterdam, NY, in 1967; B.S. degree, mechanical and industrial engineering, Clarkson University, Potsdam, NY, 1971; professional: engineer, NYS Department of Transportation; engineer, NYS Department of Public Service; Montgomery County Board of Supervisors, 1976–83; chairman, Montgomery County Board of Supervisors, 1981–83; NYS Assembly, 1983–2007; chairman, NYS Assembly Standing Committee on Energy, 1992–2007; President & CEO, NYS Energy Research and Development Authority, 2007–08; caucuses: vice-chair, Sustainable Energy and Environment Coalition; committees: Budget, Science, Space, and Technology; elected to the 111th Congress on November 4, 2008; reelected to the 112th Congress on November 2, 2010.

Office Listings

http://www.tonko.house.gov

422 Cannon House Office Building, Washington, DC 20515 .... (202) 225–5076
Chief of Staff.—Dustin Todd. FAX: 225–5077
Communications Director.—Beau Duffy.
Legislative Director.—Joseph Eaves.
61 Columbia Street, 4th Floor, Albany, NY 12210 .... (518) 465–0700

105 Jay Street, (Schenetady City Hall), Room 15, Schenectady, NY 12305 .... (518) 374–4547
61 Church Street, (Amsterdam City Hall), Room 309, Amsterdam, NY 12010 .... (518) 843–3400

Counties: ALBANY, FULTON (part), MONTGOMERY, RENSSELAER (part), SARATOGA (part), SCHOHARIE, and SCHENECTADY. Population (2000), 654,361.

ZIP Codes: 12007–10, 12016, 12019, 12027, 12031, 12033, 12035–36, 12041, 12043, 12045–47, 12053–54, 12056, 12061, 12063–64, 12066–73, 12077–78, 12082–87, 12092–93, 12095, 12107, 12110, 12116, 12120–23, 12128, 12131, 12137, 12141, 12143–44, 12147, 12149–50, 12157–61, 12166–67, 12175, 12177, 12179–83, 12186–89, 12193–94, 12197–98, 12201–12, 12214, 12220, 12222–40, 12242–50, 12252, 12255–57, 12260–61, 12288, 12301–09, 12325, 12345, 12434, 12469, 13317, 13320, 13339, 13410, 13428, 13452, 13459

* * *

TWENTY-SECOND DISTRICT

MAURICE D. HINCHEY, Democrat, of Hurley, NY; born in New York, NY, October 27, 1938; education: graduated, Saugerties High School, 1956; B.S., State College, New Paltz, NY, 1968; M.A., State College, New Paltz, 1969; professional: Seaman First Class, U.S. Navy, 1956–59; teacher; public administrator; elected to the New York State Assembly, 1975–92; member: New York Council of State Governments; National Conference of State Legislatures; married: Allison Lee Hinchey, 2006; three children: Maurice Scott, Josef, and Michelle Rebecca; committees: Appropriations; Joint Economic Committee; elected on November 3, 1992 to the 103rd Congress; reelected to each succeeding Congress.

Office Listings

http://www.house.gov/hinchey

2431 Rayburn House Office Building, Washington, DC 20515 .... (202) 225–6335
Chief of Staff.—Jeff Lieberson. FAX: 226–0774
Legislative Director.—Michael Iger.
Communications Director.—Mike Morosi.
291 Wall Street, Kingston, NY 12401 .... (845) 331–4466
100A Federal Building, Binghamton, NY 13901 .... (607) 773–2768
123 South Cayuga Street, Suite 201, Ithaca, NY 14850 .... (607) 273–1388
City Hall, Third Floor, 16 James Street, Middletown, NY 10940 .... (845) 344–3211

Counties: BROOME COUNTY (part); CITIES AND TOWNS OF: Binghamton, Conklin, Kirkwood, Sanford, Union (includes villages of Endicott and Johnson City), Vestal, and Windsor. DELAWARE COUNTY (part); TOWNS OF: Deposit, Hancock, and Tompkins. DUTCHESS COUNTY (part). CITIES: Poughkeepsie. ORANGE COUNTY (part); CITIES AND TOWNS OF: Crawford, Middletown, Montgomery (includes village of Walden), Newburgh, and Wallkill. SULLIVAN COUNTY; CITIES AND TOWNS OF: Bethel, Callicoon, Cochecton, Delaware, Fallsburg, Forestburgh, Fremont, Highland, Liberty, Lumberland, Mamakating, Neversink, Rockland, Thompson, and Tusten. TIOGA COUNTY (part). CITIES AND TOWNS: Barton, Nichols, Owego, and Spencer. TOMPKINS COUNTY (part). CITIES AND TOWNS: Danby, and Ithaca. ULSTER COUNTY. CITIES AND TOWNS: Denning, Esopus, Gardiner, Hardenburgh, Hurley, Kingston, Lloyd, Marbletown, Marlborough, New Paltz, Olive, Plattekill, Rochester, Rosendale, Saugerties, Shandaken, Shawangunk, Ulster, Wawarsing (includes village of Ellenville), and Woodstock. Population (2000), 654,361.

ZIP Codes: 10915, 10919, 10932, 10940–41, 10985, 12401–02, 12404, 12406, 12409–12, 12416, 12419–20, 12428–29, 12432–33, 12435–36, 12440–41, 12443, 12446, 12448–49, 12451–53, 12455–58, 12461, 12464–66, 12469, 12471–72, 12475, 12477, 12480–81, 12483–84, 12486–87, 12489–91, 12493–95, 12498, 12504, 12506, 12515, 12525, 12528, 12530, 12541–44, 12547–51, 12561, 12566, 12568, 12574–75, 12583, 12586, 12588–89, 12601, 12603, 12701, 12719–27, 12729, 12732–34, 12736–38, 12740–43, 12745, 12747–52, 12754, 12758–60, 12762–70, 12775–84, 12786–92, 12814, 12853, 12857–58, 12879, 12883, 12928, 12983, 13068, 13501, 13730, 13732, 13734, 13737, 13743, 13748–49, 13754, 13756, 13760, 13774, 13783, 13790, 13795, 13811–13, 13820, 13826, 13850, 13856, 13864–65, 13901–05, 14817, 14850–51, 14853, 14859, 14867, 14883, 14889, 14892

* * *

TWENTY-THIRD DISTRICT

WILLIAM L. OWENS, Democrat, of Plattsburgh, NY; born in Brooklyn, NY, January 20, 1949; education: graduated, Chaminade High School; B.B.A., *summa cum laude*, business administration, Manhattan College, Riverdale, NY, 1971; J.D., Fordham University School of Law, New York, NY, 1974; professional: captain, U.S. Air Force active duty, 1975–79; reserves 1979–82; attorney; economic developer; married: Jane Owens; three children: Tara, Jenna, and Brenden; four grandchildren; committees: Agriculture; Armed Services; Small Business; elected by special election on November 3, 2009, to the 111th Congress, to fill the vacancy caused by the resignation of United States Representative John McHugh; elected to the 112th Congress on November 2, 2010.

Office Listings

http://www.owens.house.gov

431 Cannon House Office Building, Washington, DC 20515 .... (202) 225–4611
FAX: 226–0621
Chief of Staff.—Brad Katz
Legislative Director.—Nell Maceda.
Communications Director.—Sean Magers.
Scheduler.—Craig Belden.
120 Washington Street, Suite 200, Watertown, NY 13601 .... (315) 782–3150
14 Durkee Street, Suite 320, Plattsburgh, NY 12901 .... (518) 563–1406
131 Main Street, Suite 106, Oneida, NY 13421 .... (315) 367–0041

Counties: CLINTON, ESSEX (part), FRANKLIN, FULTON (part), HAMILTON, JEFFERSON, LEWIS, MADISON (part), ONEIDA (part), OSWEGO, ST. LAWRENCE. CITIES, TOWNS AND VILLAGES: Watertown, Plattsburgh, Oswego, Oneida, Malone, Potsdam, Canton, Massena, Ogdensburg, Gloversville, Eassex. Population (2000), 654,361.

ZIP Codes: 12010, 12023, 12025, 12032, 12036, 12070, 12078, 12086, 12095, 12108, 12117, 12134, 12139, 12164, 12167, 12190, 12812, 12842, 12847, 12851–52, 12857, 12864, 12883, 12901, 12903, 12910–24, 12926–30, 12932–37, 12939, 12941, 12944–46, 12949–50, 12952–53, 12955–62, 12964–67, 12969–70, 12972–76, 12978–81, 12983, 12985–87, 12989, 12992–93, 12996–98, 13028, 13030, 13032–33, 13035–37, 13042–44, 13052, 13061, 13064, 13069, 13072, 13074, 13076, 13082–83, 13093, 13103–04, 13107, 13111, 13114–15, 13121–23, 13126, 13131–32, 13134–36, 13142, 13144–45, 13156, 13158, 13163, 13167, 13301–04, 13308–10, 13313–16, 13318–19, 13321–23, 13325–29, 13332–35, 13337–43, 13345–46, 13348, 13350, 13352, 13354–55, 13357, 13360–65, 13367–68, 13401–03, 13406–11, 13413, 13415, 13417–18, 13421, 13424–25, 13428, 13431, 13433, 13435–41, 13449–50, 13452, 13455–57, 13460–61, 13465, 13468–69, 13471, 13473, 13475, 13477–80, 13482–86, 13488–95, 13501–05, 13599, 13601–03, 13605–08, 13611–28, 13630–43, 13645–52, 13654–62, 13664–85, 13687–88, 13690–97, 13699

* * *

TWENTY-FOURTH DISTRICT

RICHARD L. HANNA, Republican, of Barneveld, NY; born in Utica, January 25, 1951; education: graduated from Witesboro High School, 1969; B.A., economics and political science with honors, Reed College, Portland, OR; 1976; professional: owner and president of Hanna Construction; married: two children; committees: Education and the Workforce; Small Business; Transportation and Infrastructure; elected to the 112th Congress on November 2, 2010.

Office Listings

http://www.hanna.house.gov

319 Cannon House Office Building, Washington, DC 20515 .... (202) 225–3665
FAX: 225–1891
Chief of Staff.—Justin Stokes.
Executive Assistant.—Carla Virgilio.
258 Genesee Street, First Floor, Utica, NY 13502 .... (315) 724–9740
FAX: 724–9746
18 Tompkins Street, Cortland, NY 13045 .... (607) 756–2470
FAX: 756–2472
110 Genesee Street, Suite 110, Auburn, NY 13021 .... (315) 252–6700
FAX: 252–6709

Counties: BROOME (part), CAYUGA (part), CHENANGO, CORTLAND, HERKIMER (part), ONEIDA (part), ONTARIO (part), OTSEGO (part), SENECA, TIOGA (part), TOMPKINS (part). Population (2000), 654,361.

ZIP Codes: 13021–22, 13024, 13026, 13032–34, 13040, 13042, 13045, 13052–54, 13056, 13062, 13065, 13068, 13071–74, 13077, 13080–81, 13083, 13087, 13092, 13101–02, 13117–18, 13124, 13136, 13139–41, 13147–48, 13152, 13155, 13157–60, 13162, 13165–66, 13302–05, 13308–09, 13312, 13315, 13317–20, 13322–29, 13331–33, 13335, 13337–40, 13342–43, 13345, 13348, 13350, 13353–54, 13357, 13360–61, 13363, 13365, 13367–68, 13403–04, 13406–07, 13411, 13413, 13415–17, 13420–21, 13424–26, 13431, 13433, 13436–42, 13452, 13454, 13456, 13460–61, 13464, 13468–73, 13475–78, 13480, 13485–86, 13489–93, 13495, 13501–02, 13601, 13603, 13605–08, 13611–26, 13628, 13630, 13632–43, 13645–52, 13654–56, 13658–62, 13664–69, 13672–85, 13687, 13690–97, 13699, 13730, 13733–34, 13736, 13738, 13743–47, 13752–54, 13758, 13760, 13776–78, 13780, 13784, 13787, 13790, 13794, 13796–97, 13801–03, 13807–11, 13813–15, 13820, 13825–27, 13830, 13832–33, 13835, 13838, 13840–41, 13843–45, 13848–49, 13856, 13859, 13861–64, 14433, 14443, 14456, 14468–69, 14489, 14504, 14521, 14532, 14541, 14548, 14571, 14588, 14817, 14841, 14847, 14850–52, 14854, 14860, 14867, 14881–83, 14886

* * *

TWENTY-FIFTH DISTRICT

ANN MARIE BUERKLE, Republican, of Syracuse, NY; born in Auburn, NY, May 8, 1951; education: St. Joseph's Hospital School of Nursing, registered nurse, 1972; B.S., science, LeMoyne College, 1977; J.D., Syracuse University College of Law, 1994; professional: nurse; assistant, New York State Attorney General, 1997–2010; member of the Syracuse

Common Council, 1994–95; religion: Catholic; committees: Foreign Affairs; Oversight and Government Reform; Veterans' Affairs; elected to the 112th Congress on November 2, 2010.

Office Listings

http://www.buerkle.house.gov

1630 Longworth House Office Building, Washington, DC 20515 .... (202) 225–3701
Chief of Staff.—John Buttarazzi. FAX: 225–4042
Executive Assistant.—Ann Buttarazzi.
1000 South Clinton Street, Room 1340, P.O. Box 7306, Syracuse, NY 13216 .... (315) 423–5657
District Office Director.—Nancy Lowery. FAX: 423–5669
1280 Titus Avenue, Rochester, NY 14617 .... (585) 336–7291
FAX: 336–7274

Counties: CAYUGA (part), MONROE (part), ONONDAGA, and WAYNE. CITIES AND TOWNSHIPS: Arcadia, Butler, Camillus, Cato, Cicero, Clay, Conquest, DeWitt, Elbridge, Fabius, Galen, Geddes, Huron, Ira, Irondequoit, LaFayette, Lyons, Lysander, Macedon, Manlius, Marcellus, Marion, Onondaga, Ontario, Otisco, Palmyra, Penfield, Pompey, Rose, Salina, Savannah, Skaneateles, Sodus, Spafford, Sterling, Syracuse, Tully, Van Buren, Victory, Walworth, Webster, Williamson, and Wolcott. Population (2000), 654,361.

ZIP Codes: 13020–21, 13027, 13029–31, 13033, 13035, 13037, 13039–41, 13051–53, 13057, 13060, 13063–64, 13066, 13068–69, 13077–78, 13080, 13082, 13084, 13088, 13090, 13104, 13108, 13110–13, 13116–17, 13119–20, 13122, 13126, 13135, 13137–38, 13140–41, 13143, 13146, 13148, 13152–54, 13156, 13159, 13164–66, 13201–12, 13214–15, 13217–21, 13224–25, 13235, 13244, 13250–52, 13261, 13290, 14413, 14432–33, 14449–50, 14489, 14502, 14505, 14513, 14516, 14519–20, 14522, 14526, 14537–38, 14542, 14551, 14555, 14563–64, 14568, 14580, 14589–90, 14609, 14617, 14621–22, 14625

* * *

TWENTY-SIXTH DISTRICT

KATHLEEN C. HOCHUL, Democrat, of Hamburg, NY; born in Buffalo, NY, August 27, 1958; education: B.A., Syracuse University, NY, 1980; J.D., Catholic University, Washington, DC, 1983; professional: clerk, Erie County, 2007–11; deputy clerk, Erie County, NY, 2003–07; board member, Town of Hamburg, 1994–2007; awards: American Planning Association's Public Servant of the Year; Annual Award from Unlimited Possibilities Overcoming Poverty Ministry; Niagara Frontier Recreation and Parks Association Award for Public Service; Town Rejuvenaton Project: Recognition for Founding Blast on the Beach; YWCA Leadership Award; Person of the Year from the Binational Tourism Alliance; co-chairperson of the Great American Clean-Up of Western New York; President's Community Service Award from the Buffalo Niagara Association of Realtors; religion: Catholic; married: William; children: William and Katie; committees: Armed Services; Homeland Security; elected to the 112th Congress, by special election on May 24, 2011.

Office Listings

http://www.hochul.house.gov

1711 Longworth House Office Building, Washington, DC 20515 .... (202) 225–5265
Chief of Staff.—Daniel Krupnick. FAX: 225–1891
325 Essjay Road, Suite 405, Williamsville, NY 14221 .... (716) 634–2324

Counties: ERIE (part), GENESEE, LIVINGSTON, MONROE (part), NIAGARA (part), ORLEANS (part), WYOMING. Population (2000), 654,361.

ZIP Codes: 14001, 14004–05, 14008–09, 14011–13, 14020–21, 14024, 14026, 14030–32, 14036, 14038–39, 14043, 14051, 14054, 14056, 14058–59, 14066–68, 14082–83, 14086, 14094–95, 14098, 14103, 14105, 14113, 14120, 14125, 14130–32, 14139, 14143, 14145, 14167, 14215, 14221, 14224–26, 14228, 14231, 14260, 14304, 14410–11, 14414, 14416, 14420, 14422–23, 14427–30, 14435, 14437, 14452, 14454, 14462, 14464, 14466, 14468, 14470–72, 14476–77, 14479–82, 14485–88, 14510–12, 14514–15, 14517, 14525, 14530, 14533, 14536, 14539, 14545–46, 14549–50, 14556–60, 14569, 14571–72, 14591–92, 14606, 14612, 14615–16, 14624, 14626, 14822, 14836, 14846

* * *

TWENTY-SEVENTH DISTRICT

BRIAN HIGGINS, Democrat, of Buffalo, NY; born in Buffalo, October 6, 1959; education: B.A., Buffalo State College, NY, 1984; M.A., Buffalo State College, 1985; M.P.A., Harvard University, Cambridge, MA, 1996; professional: lecturer, Buffalo State College; member of the Buffalo Common Council, 1988–94; member of the New York State Assembly, 1999–2004; married: Mary Jane Hannon; two children: John and Maeve; committees: Foreign Affairs;

Homeland Security; elected to the 109th Congress on November 2, 2004; reelected to each succeeding Congress.

Office Listings

http://www.higgins.house.gov

2459 Rayburn House Office Building, Washington, DC 20515 .... (202) 225–3306
Chief of Staff.—Andy Tantillo. FAX: 226–0347
Communications Director.—Theresa Kennedy.
Legislative Director.—Andy Tantillo.
Larkin Building, 726 Exchange Street, Suite 601, Buffalo, NY 14210 .... (716) 852–3501
Fenton Building, 2 East 2nd Street, Suite 300, Jamestown, NY 14701 .... (716) 484–0729

Counties: CHAUTAUQUA, ERIE (part). CITIES AND TOWNSHIPS: Boston, Brant, Buffalo, Cheektowaga, Colden, Concord, Collins, East Aurora, Eden, Elma, Evans, Hamburg, Holland, Lackawanna, North Boston, North Collins, Orchard Park, Sardinia, and Seneca. Population (2000), 654,361.

ZIP Codes: 14004, 14006, 14010, 14025–27, 14030, 14033–35, 14037, 14040, 14043, 14047–48, 14052, 14055, 14057, 14059, 14061–63, 14069–70, 14075, 14080–81, 14085–86, 14091, 14102, 14110–12, 14127, 14134–36, 14138–41, 14145, 14166, 14169–70, 14201–03, 14206–16, 14218–22, 14224–27, 14233, 14240–41, 14264–65, 14267, 14269, 14272, 14276, 14280, 14504, 14701–04, 14710, 14712, 14716, 14718, 14720, 14722–24, 14726, 14728, 14732–33, 14736, 14738, 14740, 14742, 14747, 14750, 14752, 14756–58, 14767, 14769, 14775, 14781–82, 14784–85, 14787

* * *

TWENTY-EIGHTH DISTRICT

LOUISE McINTOSH SLAUGHTER, Democrat, of Fairport, NY; born in Harlan County, KY, August 14, 1929; education: B.S. in microbiology (1951) and M.S. in public health (1953), University of Kentucky; elected to Monroe County Legislature, two terms, 1976–79; elected to New York State Assembly, two terms, 1982–86; Distinguished Public Health Legislation Award, American Public Health Association, 1998; married: Robert Slaughter; three daughters; seven grandchildren; committees: ranking member, Rules; elected to the 100th Congress on November 4, 1986; reelected to each succeeding Congress.

Office Listings

http://www.louise.house.gov

2469 Rayburn House Office Building, Washington, DC 20515 .... (202) 225–3615
Chief of Staff.—Greg Regan. FAX: 225–7822
Legislative Director.—John Monsif.
Press Secretary.—Victoria Dillon.
Scheduler.—Tess Troha-Thompson
3120 Federal Building, 100 State Street, Rochester, NY 14614 .... (585) 232–4850
465 Main Street, Suite 105, Buffalo, NY 14203 .... (716) 853–5813
640 Park Place, Niagara Falls, NY 14301 .... (716) 282–1274

Counties: Erie (part), Monroe (part), Niagara (part), Orleans (part). CITIES AND TOWNSHIPS: Appleton, Barker, Brighton, Buffalo, Burt, East Rochester, Fairport, Grand Island, Greece, Hamlin, Hilton, Irondequoit, Kendall, Kent, Lewiston, Lyndonville, Model City, Morton, Newfane, Niagara Falls, Olcott, Penfield, Perinton, Ransomville, Rochester, Sanborn, Stella Niagara, Tonawanda, Waterport, Wilson and Youngstown. Population (2000), 654,361.

ZIP Codes: 14008, 14012, 14028, 14067, 14072, 14092, 14094, 14098, 14107–09, 14126, 14131–32, 14144, 14150–51, 14172, 14174, 14202–12, 14214–17, 14222–23, 14225–26, 14228, 14240, 14263, 14267, 14270, 14273, 14280, 14301–05, 14411, 14420, 14445, 14450, 14464, 14468, 14470, 14476–77, 14508, 14526, 14534, 14571, 14602–25, 14627, 14638–39, 14642–47, 14649–53, 14660, 14664, 14673

* * *

TWENTY-NINTH DISTRICT

THOMAS W. REED II, Republican, of Corning, NY; born in Joliet, IL, November 18, 1971; education: graduated, B.A., Alfred University, Alfred, NY, 1993; J.D., Ohio Northern University College of Law, Ada, OH, 1996; professional: lawyer, private practice, Law Office of Thomas W. Reed II; business owner; mayor of Corning, NY, 2008–09; religion: Catholic; married: wife, Jean, and two children; committees: Ways and Means; elected November 2, 2010, to the 111th Congress by special election to fill the vacancy caused by the resignation of United States Representative Eric J.J. Massa; subsequently elected to a full term in the 112th Congress on November 2, 2010.

Office Listings

http://reed.house.gov

1037 Longworth House Office Building, Washington, DC 20515 .... (202) 225–3161
Chief of Staff.—Jay Dutcher. FAX: 226–6599
Deputy Chief of Staff.—Vicki Hook.
Legislative Director.—Steve Pfrang.
Communications Director.—Tim Kolpien.
District Director.—Joe Sempolinski.
89 West Market Street, Corning, NY 14830 .... (607) 654–7566
One Bluebird Square, Olean, NY 14760 .... (716) 379–8434
672 Pittsford Victor Road, Suite 2, Pittsford, NY 14534 .... (585) 218–0040

Counties: ALLEGANY, CATTARAUGUS, CHEMUNG, MONROE (part), ONTARIO (part), SCHUYLER, STEUBEN, YATES. Population (2000), 654,361.

ZIP Codes: 14009, 14024, 14029–30, 14041–42, 14060, 14065, 14070, 14081, 14101, 14129, 14133, 14138, 14141, 14168, 14171, 14173, 14414–15, 14418, 14423–25, 14428, 14432, 14437, 14441, 14445, 14450, 14453, 14456, 14461, 14463, 14466–67, 14469, 14471–72, 14475, 14478, 14482, 14485, 14487, 14489, 14502, 14504, 14506–07, 14512–14, 14518, 14522, 14526–27, 14529, 14532, 14534, 14536, 14543–44, 14546–48, 14559–61, 14564, 14572, 14585–86, 14606, 14610, 14618, 14620, 14623–25, 14706–09, 14711, 14714–15, 14717, 14719, 14721, 14726–27, 14729–31, 14735, 14737–39, 14741, 14743–45, 14747–48, 14751, 14753–55, 14760, 14766, 14770, 14772, 14774, 14777–79, 14783, 14786, 14788, 14801–10, 14812–16, 14818–27, 14830–31, 14836–46, 14855–59, 14861, 14863–65, 14867, 14869–74, 14876–80, 14884–87, 14889, 14891–95, 14897–98, 14901–05, 14925

NORTH CAROLINA

(Population 2010, 9,535,483)

SENATORS

RICHARD BURR, Republican, of Winston-Salem, NC; born in Charlottesville, VA, November 30, 1955; education: R.J. Reynolds High School, Winston-Salem, NC, 1974; B.A., communications, Wake Forest University, Winston-Salem, NC, 1978; professional: sales manager, Carswell Distributing; member: Reynolds Rotary Club; board member, Brenner Children's Hospital; public service: U.S. House of Representatives, 1995–2005; served as vice-chairman of the Energy and Commerce Committee; married: Brooke Fauth, 1984; children: two sons; committees: ranking member, Veterans' Affairs; Finance; Health, Education, Labor, and Pensions; Select Committee on Intelligence; elected to the U.S. Senate on November 2, 2004; re-elected to the U.S. Senate on November 2, 2010.

Office Listings

http://burr.senate.gov

217 Russell Senate Office Building, Washington, DC 20510	(202) 224–3154
Chief of Staff.—Chris Joyner.	FAX: 228–2981
Legislative Director.—Natasha Hickman.	
2000 West First Street, Suite 508, Winston-Salem, NC 27104	(336) 631–5125
State Director.—Dean Myers.	
100 Coast Line Street, Room 210, Rocky Mount, NC 27804	(252) 977–9522
201 North Front Street, Suite 809, Wilmington, NC 28401	(910) 251–1058

* * *

KAY R. HAGAN, Democrat, of Greensboro, NC; born in Shelby, NC, May 26, 1953; education: B.A., Florida State University, 1975; J.D., Wake Forest University School of Law, 1978; professional: attorney and vice president of the Estate and Trust Division, NCNB, 1978–88; public service: North Carolina State Senator, 1999–2009; religion: Presbyterian; married: Chip Hagan; children: two daughters, one son; committees: Armed Services; Banking, Housing, and Urban Affairs; Health, Education, Labor, and Pensions; Small Business and Entrepreneurship; elected to the U.S. Senate on November 4, 2008.

Office Listings

htttp://hagan.senate.gov

521 Dirksen Senate Office Building, Washington, DC 20510	(202) 224–6342
Chief of Staff.—Thomas P. O'Donnell.	FAX: 228–2563
Deputy Chief of Staff.—Mike Harney.	
Communications Director.—Mary Hanley.	
State Director.—Melissa Midgett.	
701 Green Valley Road, Suite 201, Greensboro, NC 27408	(877) 852–9462
82 Patton Avenue, Suite 635, Asheville, NC 28801	(828) 257–6510
301 South Evans Street, Suite 102, Greenville, NC 27858	(252) 754–0707
310 New Bern Avenue, Suite 122, Raleigh, NC 27601	(919) 856–4630
1520 South Boulevard, Charlotte, NC 28203	(704) 334–2448

REPRESENTATIVES

FIRST DISTRICT

G. K. BUTTERFIELD, Democrat, of Wilson County, NC; born, April 27, 1947; education: North Carolina Central University, graduated in 1971, with degrees in sociology and political science; North Carolina Central University School of Law, graduated in 1974, with a Juris Doctor degree; military service: U.S. Army, 1968–1970; served as a Personnel Specialist; discharged with the rank of Specialist E–4; professional: attorney; private practice, 1974–1988; public service: elected to the North Carolina Superior Court bench in November, 1988; appointed on February 8, 2001, by Governor Michael F. Easley to the North Carolina Supreme Court; after leaving the Supreme Court, following the 2002 election, Governor Easley appointed Justice Butterfield as a Special Superior Court Judge; served until his retirement on May 7, 2004; organizations: North Carolina Bar Association; North Carolina Association of Black Lawyers; Wilson Opportunities Industrialization Center; religion: Baptist; appointed Chief Deputy Whip, 110th Congress; committees: Energy and Commerce; elected to the 108th Congress, by special election, on July 20, 2004; elected to the 109th Congress on November 2, 2004; reelected to each succeeding Congress.

Office Listings

http://www.butterfield.house.gov

2305 Rayburn House Office Building, Washington, DC 20515 .... (202) 225–3101
Chief of Staff.—Tonya Williams. FAX: 225–3354
Communications Director.—Ken Willis.
Scheduler.—Darnise Nelson.
216 West Nash Street, Suite B, Wilson, NC 27893 .... (252) 237–9816
309 West Third Street, Suite 100, Weldon, NC 27890 .... (252) 538–4123

Counties: BEAUFORT (part), BERTIE, CHOWAN, CRAVEN (part), EDGECOMBE, GATES, GRANVILLE VANCE (part), GREENE, HALIFAX, HARTFORD, JONES (part), MARTIN, NORTHAMPTON, PASQUOTANK, PERQUIMANS, PITT (part), WARREN, WASHINGTON, WAYNE (part), WILSON (part). Population (2000), 619,178.

ZIP Codes: 27507, 27530–31, 27533–34, 27536–37, 27551, 27553, 27556, 27563, 27565, 27570, 27584, 27586, 27589, 27594, 27801, 27803–06, 27809, 27811–14, 27817–23, 27825, 27827–29, 27831–35, 27837, 27839–47, 27849–50, 27852–55, 27857–58, 27860–64, 27866–67, 27869–74, 27876–77, 27879, 27881, 27883–84, 27886–95, 27897, 27906–07, 27909–10, 27919, 27922, 27924, 27926, 27928, 27930, 27932, 27935, 27937–38, 27942, 27944, 27946, 27957, 27962, 27967, 27969–70, 27979–80, 27983, 27985–86, 28216, 28226, 28502–04, 28513, 28523, 28526, 28530, 28538, 28551, 28554–55, 28560–63, 28573, 28580, 28585–86, 28590, 28645

* * *

SECOND DISTRICT

RENEE ELLMERS, Republican, of Dunn, NC; born in Ironwood, MI, February 9, 1964; education: B.S., nursing, Oakland University, Auburn Hills, MI, 1990; professional: registered nurse; president elect/vice president, Community Development for the Chamber of Commerce; member of the Betsy Johnson Hospital Foundation, member of the Dunn Planning Board, NC, 2006–10; chair, Dunn Planning Board, NC, 2008–10; member of the Harnett County Nursing Home Committee; religion: Roman Catholic; married: Dr. Brent Ellmers; one child: Ben; committees: Agriculture; Small Business; Foreign Affairs; elected to the 112th Congress on November 2, 2010.

Office Listings

http://www.ellmers.house.gov

1533 Longworth House Office Building, Washington, DC 20515 .... (202) 225–4531
Chief of Staff.—Al Lytton. FAX: 225–5662
Legislative Director.—Elaine Acevedo.
Press Secretary.—Tom Doheny.
Scheduler.—Josie Rundlett.
406 West Broad Street, Dunn, NC 28334 .... (910) 230–1910

Counties: CHATHAM (part), Cumberland (part), Franklin, Harnett, Johnston, Lee, Nash (part), Sampson (part), VANCE (part), and WAKE (part). Population (2000), 619,178.

ZIP Codes: 27207–08, 27213, 27237, 27252, 27256, 27298, 27312, 27325, 27330–32, 27344, 27349, 27355, 27405, 27501, 27504–06, 27508, 27520–21, 27524–26, 27529, 27536–37, 27540, 27542–44, 27546, 27549, 27552, 27555, 27557, 27559, 27562, 27564, 27568–70, 27576–77, 27589, 27591–93, 27596–97, 27601–03, 27605–07, 27610, 27614, 27625, 27698, 27801–04, 27807, 27809, 27816, 27822, 27829, 27850, 27856, 27863, 27878, 27880, 27882, 27891, 27893–94, 27896, 28301, 28303, 28307–08, 28310–11, 28314, 28323, 28326, 28328, 28334–35, 28339, 28341, 28355–56, 28365–66, 28368, 28382, 28385, 28390, 28393, 28441, 28444, 28447, 28453, 28458, 28466, 28478

* * *

THIRD DISTRICT

WALTER B. JONES, Republican, of Farmville, NC; born in Farmville, February 10, 1943; education: graduated Hargrave Military Academy, Chatham, VA, 1961; B.A., Atlantic Christian College, Wilson, NC, 1966; served in North Carolina National Guard; self-employed, sales; member: North Carolina House of Representatives, 1983–92; married: Joe Anne Whitehurst Jones; one child, Ashley Elizabeth Jones; committees: Armed Services; Financial Services; elected to the 104th Congress; reelected to each succeeding Congress.

Office Listings

2333 Rayburn House Office Building, Washington, DC 20515 .... (202) 225–3415
Chief of Staff.—Glen Downs. FAX: 225–3286
Office Manager.—Molly Norton.
Communications Director.—Catherine Fodor.
1105–C Corporate Drive, Greenville, NC 27858 .... (252) 931–1003
District Office Manager.—Millicent A. Lilley.

Counties: BEAUFORT (part), CAMDEN, CARTERET, CRAVEN (part), CURRITUCK, DARE, DUPLIN (part), HYDE, JONES (part), LENOIR (part), MARTIN (part), ONSLOW (part), PAMLICO, PENDER (part), PITT (part), SAMPSON, TYRRELL and WAYNE (part). CITIES: Atlantic Beach, Ayden, Beaufort, Belhaven, Burgaw, Clinton, Emerald Isle, Fremont, Goldsboro, Greenville, Havelock, Jacksonville, Kill Devil Hills, Kinston, Kitty Hawk, Morehead City, Mount Olive, Nags Head, New Bern, Newport, River Bend, Trent Woods, Wallace, Washington, and Winterville. Population (2000), 619,178.

ZIP Codes: 27530–32, 27534, 27542, 27557, 27569, 27803–04, 27807–10, 27814, 27817, 27822, 27824, 27826, 27828–30, 27834, 27836–37, 27851–52, 27856, 27858, 27860, 27863, 27865, 27868, 27871, 27875, 27879, 27880, 27882–83, 27885, 27888–89, 27892–93, 27896, 27909, 27915–17, 27920–21, 27923, 27925, 27927–29, 27936, 27939, 27941, 27943, 27947–50, 27953–54, 27956, 27958–60, 27962, 27964–66, 27968, 27972–74, 27976, 27978, 27981–82, 28333, 28341, 28445, 28454, 28460, 28501, 28504, 28508–13, 28515–16, 28518–22, 28524–29, 28531–33, 28537, 28539–47, 28551–53, 28555–57, 28560, 28562, 28564, 28570–72, 28574–75, 28577–87, 28589–90, 28594

* * *

FOURTH DISTRICT

DAVID E. PRICE, Democrat, of Chapel Hill, NC; born in Erwin, TN, August 17, 1940; education: B.A., Morehead Scholar, University of North Carolina; Bachelor of Divinity, 1964, and Ph.D., political science, 1969, Yale University; professional: professor of political science and public policy, Duke University; author of four books on Congress and the American political system; served North Carolina's Fourth District in the U.S. House of Representatives, 1987–94; in the 102nd Congress, wrote and pushed for passage of the Scientific and Advanced Technology Bill and sponsored the Home Ownership Assistance Act; past chairman and executive director, North Carolina Democratic Party; Hubert Humphrey Public Service Award, American Political Science Association, 1990; member, North Carolina's Transit 2001 Commission; past chairman of the board and Sunday School teacher, Binkley Memorial Baptist Church; married: Lisa Price; children: Karen and Michael; committees: Appropriations; elected to the 100th–103rd Congresses; elected to the 105th Congress; reelected to each succeeding Congress.

Office Listings

http://www.price.house.gov

2162 Rayburn House Office Building, Washington, DC 20515 .... (202) 225–1784
Chief of Staff.—Jean-Louise Beard. FAX: 225–2014
Legislative Director / Deputy Chief of Staff.—Asher Hildebrand.
Executive Assistant.—Teresa Saunders.
Systems Manager.—Jackson Tufts.
5400 Trinity Place, Suite 205, Raleigh, NC 27607 .... (919) 859–5999
District Director.—Beau Mills.
88 Vilcom Center, Suite 140, Chapel Hill, NC 27514 .... (919) 967–7924
411 West Chapel Hill Street, Durham, NC 27701 .... (919) 688–3004

Counties: CHATHAM (part), DURHAM, ORANGE, WAKE (part). Population (2000), 619,178.

ZIP Codes: 27228, 27231, 27243, 27278, 27302, 27312, 27330, 27501–03, 27510–17, 27519, 27523, 27526, 27529, 27539–41, 27560, 27562, 27572, 27583, 27592, 27599, 27603, 27606–07, 27610, 27612–15, 27617, 27623–24, 27656, 27675–76, 27690, 27695, 27699, 27701–05, 27707–13, 27715, 27717, 27722

* * *

FIFTH DISTRICT

VIRGINIA FOXX, Republican, of Banner Elk, NC; born in New York, NY, June 29, 1943; education: A.B., University of North Carolina, Chapel Hill, NC, 1968; M.A.C.T., University of North Carolina, Chapel Hill, NC, 1972; Ed.D., University of North Carolina, Greensboro, NC, 1985; professional: instructor, Caldwell Community College, Hudson, NC; instructor, Appalachian State University, Boone, NC; Assistant Dean, Appalachian State University, Boone, NC; president, Mayland Community College, Spruce Pine, NC, 1987–94; nursery operator; deputy secretary for management, North Carolina Department of Administration; organizations: member, Watauga County Board of Education, 1967–88; member, North Carolina State Senate,

1994–2004; Executive Committee of North Carolina Citizens for Business and Industry; Z. Smith Reynolds Foundation Advisory Panel; National Advisory Council for Women's Educational Programs; Board of Directors of the NC Center for Public Research; UNC–Chapel Hill Board of Visitors; National Conference of State Legislatures' Blue Ribbon Advisory Panel on Child Care; Foscoe-Grandfather Community Center Board; family: married to Tom Foxx; one daughter; committees: Education and the Workforce; Rules; elected to the 109th Congress on November 2, 2004; reelected to each succeeding Congress.

Office Listings

http://www.foxx.house.gov

1230 Longworth House Office Building, Washington, DC 20515 .... (202) 225–2071
Chief of Staff.—Todd Poole. FAX: 225–2995
Legislative Director.—Brandon Renz.
Press Secretary.—Aaron Groen.
6000 Meadowbrook Mall, Suite 3, Clemmons, NC 27012 .... (336) 778–0211
240 Highway 105 Extension, Suite 200, Boone, NC 28607 .... (828) 265–0240

Counties: ALEXANDER COUNTY. CITIES: Bethlehem, Hiddenite, Stony Point, Taylorsville. ALLEGANY COUNTY. CITIES: Ennice, Glade Valley, Laurel Springs, Sparta. ASHE COUNTY. CITIES: Crumpler, Glendale Springs, Grassy Creek, Jefferson, Lansing, Scottville, Todd, Warrensville, West Jefferson. DAVIE COUNTY. CITIES: Advance, Cooleemee, Mocksville. FORSYTH COUNTY (part). CITIES: Bethania, Clemmons, Kernersville, King, Lewisville, Pfafftown, Rural Hall, Tobaccoville, Walkertown, Winston-Salem. IREDELL COUNTY (part). CITIES: Harmony, Love Valley, Mooresville, Olin, Statesville, Turnersburg, Troutman. ROCKINGHAM COUNTY (part). CITIES: Madison, Stokesdale. STOKES COUNTY. CITIES: Danbury, Germanton, Lawsonville, King, Pine Hall, Pinnacle, Sandy Ridge, and Walnut Cove. SURRY COUNTY. CITIES: Ararat, Dobson, Elkin, Flat Rock, Mount Airy, Pilot Mountain, Siloam, Toast, Westfield, White Plains. WATAUGA COUNTY. CITIES: Beech Mountain, Blowing Rock, Boone, Deep Gap, Seven Devils, Sugar Grove, Triplett, Vilas, Zionville. WILKES COUNTY. CITIES: Boomer, Cricket, Hays, Fairplains, Ferguson, Millers Creek, Moravian Falls, Mulberry, N. Wilkesboro, Olin, Pleasant Hill, Roaring River, Ronda, Thurmond, Traphill, Wilkesboro. YADKIN COUNTY. CITIES: Arlington, Booneville, East Bend, Hamptonville, Jonesville, Turnersburg, and Yadkinville. Population (2000), 619,178.

ZIP Codes: 27006–07, 27009–14, 27016–25, 27028, 27030, 27040–43, 27045–47, 27049–53, 27055, 27094, 27098–99, 27101–09, 27111, 27113–17, 27120, 27127, 27130, 27150–51, 27155–57, 27199, 27201–02, 27235, 27244, 27265, 27284–85, 27305, 27314–15, 27320, 27326, 27343, 27357–58, 27360, 27379, 27565, 27582, 27893, 28115, 28125, 28166, 28601, 28604–08, 28615, 28617–18, 28621–27, 28629–31, 28634–36, 28640, 28642–45, 28649, 28651, 28654, 28656, 28659–60, 28663, 28665, 28668–70, 28672, 28675–79, 28681, 28683–85, 28688–89, 28691–94, 28697–99

* * *

SIXTH DISTRICT

HOWARD COBLE, Republican, of Greensboro, NC; born in Greensboro, March 18, 1931; education: Appalachian State University, Boone, NC, 1949–50; A.B., history, Guilford College, Greensboro, NC, 1958; J.D., University of North Carolina School of Law, Chapel Hill, 1962; military service: U.S. Coast Guard as a seaman recruit, 1952; active duty, 1952–56 and 1977–78; reserve duty, 1960–82; retired with rank of captain; last reserve duty assignment, commanding officer, U.S. Coast Guard Reserve Unit, Wilmington, NC; professional: attorney; admitted to North Carolina Bar, 1966; field claim representative and superintendent, auto insurance, 1961–67; elected to North Carolina House of Representatives, 1969; Assistant U.S. Attorney, Middle District of North Carolina, 1969–73; commissioner (secretary), North Carolina Department of Revenue, 1973–77; North Carolina House of Representatives, 1979–83; practiced law with law firm of Turner, Enochs and Sparrow, Greensboro, NC, 1979–84; member: Alamance Presbyterian Church, American Legion, Veterans of Foreign Wars of the United States, Lions Club, Greensboro Bar Association, North Carolina Bar Association, North Carolina State Bar; North Carolina State co-chairman, American Legislative Exchange Council, 1983–84; committees: Judiciary; Transportation and Infrastructure; elected to the 99th Congress on November 6, 1984; reelected to each succeeding Congress.

Office Listings

http://www.house.gov/coble

2188 Rayburn House Office Building, Washington, DC 20515 .... (202) 225–3065
Chief of Staff / Press Secretary.—Ed McDonald. FAX: 225–8611
Executive Assistant.—Betsy Huffine.
2102 North Elm Street, Suite B, Greensboro, NC 27408–5100 .... (336) 333–5005
Office Manager.—Kathy McClellan.
1634 North Main Street, Suite 101, High Point, NC 27262–7723 .... (336) 886–5106
District Representative.—Nancy Mazza.
241 Sunset Avenue, Suite 101, Asheboro, NC 27203–5658 .... (336) 626–3060
District Representative.—Rebecca Briles.
P.O. Box 807, Granite Quarry, NC 28027–0807 .... (704) 209–0426
District Representative.—Terri Welch.
124 West Elm Street, P.O. Box 812, Graham, NC 27253–0812 .... (336) 229–0159
District Representative.—Janine Osborne.

Counties: ALAMANCE (part), DAVIDSON (part), GUILFORD (part), MOORE, RANDOLPH, ROWAN (part). Population (2000), 620,590.

ZIP Codes: 27201–05, 27208–09, 27214–17, 27220, 27230, 27233, 27235, 27239, 27242, 27244, 27248–49, 27252–53, 27258–65, 27281–84, 27288–89, 27292, 27295, 27298–99, 27301–02, 27310, 27312–13, 27316–17, 27325, 27330, 27340–42, 27344, 27349–50, 27355–61, 27370–71, 27373–74, 27376–77, 27401–10, 27415–17, 27419–20, 27425, 27427, 27429, 27435, 27438, 27455, 27495, 27498–99, 27607, 27612–13, 27640, 27803–04, 28023, 28041, 28071–72, 28081, 28083, 28088, 28125, 28127, 28137–38, 28144, 28146–47, 28315, 28326–27, 28347, 28350, 28370, 28373–74, 28387–88, 28394

* * *

SEVENTH DISTRICT

MIKE McINTYRE, Democrat, of Lumberton, NC; born in Robeson County, August 6, 1956; education: B.A., Phi Beta Kappa Morehead Scholar, 1978, and J.D., 1981, University of North Carolina; upon graduation, received the Algernon Sydney Sullivan Award for ''unselfish interest in the welfare of his fellow man''; professional: attorney; past president, Lumberton Economic Advancement for Dowtown; formerly on board of directors of Lumberton Rotary Club, Chamber of Commerce and a local group home for the mentally handicapped; active in the Boy Scouts of America, and Lumberton PTA; married: the former Dee Strickland; two children; committees: Agriculture; Armed Services; elected to the 105th Congress; reelected to each succeeding Congress.

Office Listings

http://www.house.gov/mcintyre

2133 Rayburn House Office Building, Washington, DC 20515 .... (202) 225–2731
Chief of Staff / Press Secretary.—Dean Mitchell. FAX: 225–5773
Deputy Chief of Staff.—Audrey Lesesne.
Chief of Constituent Services.—Vivian Lipford.
Legislative Director.—Blair Miligan.
Federal Building, 301 Green Street, Room 315, Fayetteville, NC 28401 .... (910) 323–0260
201 North Front Street, Suite 410, Wilmington, NC 28401 .... (910) 815–4959
500 North Cedar Street, Lumberton, NC 28358 .... (910) 735–0610
District Chief of Staff.—Marie Thompson.

Counties: BLADEN, BRUNSWICK, COLUMBUS, CUMBERLAND (part), DUPLIN (part), NEW HANOVER, PENDER, ROBESON, SAMPSON (part). Population (2000), 619,178.

ZIP Codes: 28301–06, 28309, 28311–12, 28318–20, 28325, 28328, 28331–32, 28334, 28337, 28340–42, 28344, 28348–49, 28356–60, 28362, 28364–66, 28369, 28371–72, 28375, 28377–78, 28383–86, 28390–93, 28395, 28398–99, 28401–12, 28420–25, 28428–36, 28438–39, 28441–59, 28461–70, 28472, 28478–80, 28513, 28518, 28521, 28572, 28574

* * *

EIGHTH DISTRICT

LARRY KISSELL, Democrat, of Biscoe, NC; born in Biscoe, January 31, 1951; education: B.A. in economics, Wake Forest University, 1973; professional: textile mill worker, 27 years at Russell Hosiery Mill; seven years as a high school teacher at East Montgomery High School; married: Tina; children: Jenny and Aspen; committee: Agriculture, Armed Services; elected to the 111th Congress on November 4, 2008; reelected to the 112th Congress.

Office Listings

http://www.kissell.house.gov

1632 Longworth House Office Building, Washington, DC 20515 .... (202) 225–3715
Chief of Staff.—Leanne Powell. FAX: 225–4036
Communications Director.—Christopher Schuler.
Legislative Director.—Zach Pfister.
Executive Assistant.—Elena DiTraglia.
325 McGill Avenue, Suite 500, Concord, NC 28027 .... (704) 786–1612
Chief of Staff.—Leanne Powell.
230 East Franklin Street, Rockingham, NC 28379 .... (910) 997–2070
Deputy Chief of Staff.—Thomas Thacker.
6257 Raeford Road, Suite 2, Fayetteville, NC 28304 .... (910) 920–2070

Counties: ANSON, CABARRUS (part), CUMBERLAND (part), HOKE, MECKLENBURG (part), MONTGOMERY, RICHMOND, SCOTLAND (part), STANLY, UNION (part). Population (2000), 619,178.

ZIP Codes: 27209, 27215, 27229, 27247, 27253, 27281, 27284, 27306, 27312, 27320, 27341, 27356, 27358, 27371, 27405, 27534, 27803–04, 27893, 28001–02, 28007, 28009, 28025–27, 28036, 28071, 28075, 28081–83, 28091, 28097, 28102–04, 28107–12, 28119, 28124, 28127–29, 28133, 28135, 28137–38, 28159, 28163, 28167, 28170, 28174, 28204–05, 28209–13, 28215, 28217–18, 28220, 28223, 28227, 28229, 28262, 28270, 28278, 28301, 28303–06, 28308, 28311, 28314–15, 28325, 28329–30, 28338, 28343, 28345, 28347, 28349, 28351–53, 28357, 28361, 28363–64, 28367, 28371, 28376–77, 28379–80, 28382, 28386, 28396

* * *

NINTH DISTRICT

SUE WILKINS MYRICK, Republican, of Charlotte, NC; born in Tiffin, OH, August 1, 1941; education: graduated Port Clinton High School, Port Clinton, OH; attended Heidelberg College; professional: former president and CEO, Myrick Advertising and Myrick Enterprises; mayor of Charlotte, NC, 1987–91; Charlotte City Council, 1983–85; active with the National League of Cities and the U.S. Conference of Mayors; served on former President Bush's Affordable Housing Commission; member: Charlotte Chamber of Commerce; Muscular Dystrophy Association; March of Dimes; Elks Auxiliary; PTA; Cub Scout den mother; United Methodist Church; founder, Charitable Outreach Society; married: Ed Myrick, 1977; five children; committees: Energy and Commerce; Permanent Select Committee on Intelligence; elected to the 104th Congress; reelected to each succeeding Congress.

Office Listings

http://www.myrick.house.gov

230 Cannon House Office Building, Washington, DC 20515 .... (202) 225–1976
Chief of Staff.—Sarah Hale. FAX: 225–3389
Executive Assistant.—Emily Lashbrook.
6525 Morrison Boulevard, Suite 100, Charlotte, NC 28211 .... (704) 362–1060
197 West Main Avenue, Gastonia, NC 28052 .... (704) 861–1976

Counties: GASTON (part), MECKLENBURG (part), UNION (part). Population (2000), 619,178.

ZIP Codes: 28006, 28012, 28016–17, 28031–34, 28036, 28042, 28052–56, 28070, 28077–80, 28086, 28092–93, 28098, 28101, 28103–07, 28110, 28112, 28114, 28120, 28126, 28130, 28134, 28136, 28150–52, 28164, 28169, 28173–74, 28201, 28203–04, 28206–11, 28213–17, 28222, 28226–27, 28241, 28247, 28250, 28253, 28261–62, 28269–71, 28273–74, 28277–78, 28287

* * *

TENTH DISTRICT

PATRICK T. MCHENRY, Republican, of Cherryville, NC; born in Gastonia, NC, October 22, 1975; education: graduated Ashbrook High School, Gastonia, NC; attended North Carolina State University, Raleigh, NC; B.A., Belmont Abbey College, Belmont, NC, 1999; professional: realtor; media executive; appointed special assistant to the U.S. Secretary of Labor by President George W. Bush in 2001; member, North Carolina House of Representatives, 2002–04; married: Giulia, 2010; organizations: Gaston Chamber of Commerce, Gastonia Rotary Club, the National Rifle Association, Saint Michael Church; board of directors, United Way's Success by Six Youth Program; committees: Financial Services; Oversight and Government Reform; elected to the 109th Congress on November 2, 2004; reelected to each succeeding Congress.

Office Listings

http://www.house.gov/mchenry

224 Cannon House Office Building, Washington, DC 20515 .... (202) 225–2576
Chief of Staff.—Parker Poling. FAX: 225–0316
Legislative Director.—Jennifer Flitton.
Communications Director.—Michael Babyak.
Scheduler.—Kristen Keen.
87 Fourth Street, NW., Suite A, P.O. Box 1830, Hickory, NC 28603 .... (828) 327–6100

Counties: AVERY, BURKE, CALDWELL, CATAWBA, CLEVELAND, GASTON (part), IREDELL (part), LINCOLN, MITCHELL, and RUTHERFORD (part). CITIES AND TOWNSHIPS: Hickory, Lenoir, Morganton, Shelby, and Mooresville. Population (2000), 619,178.

ZIP Codes: 28006, 28010, 28016–21, 28024, 28033, 28036–38, 28040, 28042–43, 28052, 28073–74, 28076, 28080, 28086, 28089–90, 28092, 28114–15, 28117, 28139, 28150, 28152, 28164, 28166–69, 28601–07, 28609–13, 28616, 28619, 28621–22, 28624–25, 28628–30, 28633, 28635–38, 28641, 28645–47, 28650, 28652–55, 28657–58, 28661–62, 28664, 28666–67, 28671, 28673, 28676–78, 28680–82, 28687, 28690, 28699, 28705, 28720, 28740, 28746, 28752, 28761, 28765, 28777

* * *

ELEVENTH DISTRICT

HEATH SHULER, Democrat, of Waynesville, NC; born in Bryson City, NC, December 31, 1971; graduated from Swain County High School; B.A., University of Tennessee, 2001; entrepreneur; religion: Southern Baptist; married: wife, Nikol Davis; two children: Navy and Island; caucuses: administrative co-chair, Blue Dog Coalition; co-chair, Professional Sports Caucus; co-chair, International Religious Freedom Caucus; co-chair, Restaurant, Resort, and Hospitality; committees: Budget; Transportation and Infrastructure; elected to the 110th Congress on November 7, 2006; reelected to each succeeding Congress.

Office Listings

http://www.shuler.house.gov

229 Cannon House Office Building, Washington, DC 20515 .... (202) 225–6401
Chief of Staff.—Hayden Rogers. FAX: 226–6422
Legislative Director.—Vacant.
Communications Director.—Andrew Whalen.
Scheduler.—Julie Fishman.
205 College Street, Suite 100, Asheville, NC 28801 .... (828) 252–1651

Counties: BUNCOMBE, CHEROKEE, CLAY, GRAHAM, HAYWOOD, HENDERSON, JACKSON, MCDOWELL, MACON, MADISON, POLK, RUTHERFORD (part), SWAIN, TRANSYLVANIA, YANCEY. Population (2000), 619,177.

ZIP Codes: 28043, 28074, 28114, 28139, 28160, 28647, 28655, 28701–02, 28704, 28707–19, 28721–45, 28747–58, 28760–63, 28766, 28768, 28770–79, 28781–93, 28801–06, 28810, 28813–16, 28901–06, 28909

* * *

TWELFTH DISTRICT

MELVIN L. WATT, Democrat, of Charlotte, NC; born in Charlotte, August 26, 1945; education: graduated, York Road High School, Charlotte, 1963; B.S., business administration, University of North Carolina, Chapel Hill, 1967; J.D., Yale University Law School, New Haven, CT, 1970; professional: attorney; admitted to the District of Columbia Bar, 1970, admitted to the North Carolina Bar, 1971; began practice with Chambers, Stein, Ferguson and Becton, 1971–92; North Carolina State Senate, 1985–86; life member, NAACP; member, Mount Olive Presbyterian Church; past president, Mecklenburg County Bar Association, Johnson C. Smith University Board of Visitors; Central Piedmont Community College Foundation; North Carolina Association of Black Lawyers; North Carolina Association of Trial Lawyers; Legal Aid of Southern Piedmont; NationsBank Community Development Corporation; Charlotte Chamber of Commerce; Sports Action Council; Auditorium-Coliseum-Civic Center Authority; United Way; Mint Museum; Inroads, Inc.; Family Housing Services; Public Education Forum; Dilworth Community Development Association; Cities in Schools; West Charlotte Business Incubator; Housing Authority Scholarship Board; Morehead Scholarship Selection Committee, Forsyth Region; married: the former Eulada Paysour, 1968; children: Brian and Jason; committees: Financial Services; Judiciary; elected on November 3, 1992, to the 103rd Congress; reelected to each succeeding Congress.

Office Listings

http://www.house.gov/watt

2304 Rayburn House Office Building, Washington, DC 20515 .... (202) 225–1510
Chief of Staff.—Danielle Owen. FAX: 225–1512
1230 West Morehead Street, Suite 306, Charlotte, NC 28208 .... (704) 344–9950
301 South Greene Street, Suite 210, Greensboro, NC 27401 .... (336) 275–9950
District Director.—Keith Kelly.

Counties: CABARRUS COUNTY (part). DAVIDSON COUNTY (part). CITIES AND TOWNSHIPS: Lexington, and Thomasville. FORSYTH COUNTY (part). CITIES AND TOWNSHIPS: Winston-Salem. GUILFORD COUNTY (part). CITIES AND TOWNSHIPS: High Point, Greensboro. MECKLENBURG COUNTY. CITIES AND TOWNSHIPS: Charlotte. ROWAN COUNTY. CITIES: Salisbury. Population (2000), 619,178.

ZIP Codes: 27010, 27012–13, 27019, 27040, 27045, 27051, 27054, 27101, 27103–07, 27110, 27127, 27214, 27260, 27262–63, 27265, 27282, 27284, 27292–95, 27299, 27310, 27320, 27351, 27360, 27401, 27403, 27405–11, 27534, 27803–04, 27893, 28023, 28027, 28035–36, 28039, 28078, 28081, 28115, 28123, 28125, 28134, 28144–47, 28159, 28202–17, 28219, 28221, 28224, 28226–28, 28230–37, 28240, 28242–43, 28254–56, 28258, 28260, 28262, 28265–66, 28269–70, 28272–73, 28275, 28278, 28280–82, 28284–85, 28289–90, 28296–97

* * *

THIRTEENTH DISTRICT

BRAD MILLER, Democrat, of Raleigh, NC; born in Fayetteville, NC, May 19, 1953; education: B.A., political science, University of North Carolina, 1975; M.A., political science, London School of Economics, 1978; J.D., Columbia University Law School, 1979; professional: attorney; law clerk to Circuit Court of Appeals Judge J. Dickson Phillips, Jr., 1979–80; has practiced law in Raleigh since 1980, and has been in private practice since 1991; public service: North Carolina House of Representatives, 1992–94; North Carolina State Senate, 1996–2002; religion: Episcopal; committees: Financial Services; Science, Space, and Technology; elected to the 108th Congress on November 5, 2002; reelected to each succeeding Congress.

Office Listings

http://www.house.gov/bradmiller

1127 Longworth House Office Building, Washington, DC 20515 .... (202) 225–3032
Chief of Staff.—Ryan Hedgepeth. FAX: 225–0181
Legislative Director.—Heather Parsons.
Communications Director.—LuAnn Canipe.
Scheduler.—Anna Rose.
1300 St. Mary's Street, Suite 504, Raleigh, NC 27605 .... (919) 836–1313
125 South Elm Street, Suite 504, Greensboro, NC 27401 .... (336) 574–2909

Counties: ALAMANCE (part), CASWELL, GRANVILLE (part), GUILFORD (part), PERSON, ROCKINGHAM (part), WAKE (part). Population (2000), 619,178.

ZIP Codes: 27025, 27027, 27048, 27212, 27214–17, 27231, 27244, 27249, 27253, 27258, 27288–89, 27291, 27301–02, 27305, 27311, 27320, 27323, 27326, 27343, 27375, 27379, 27401, 27403, 27403–10, 27412–13, 27415, 27419, 27455, 27495, 27497, 27507, 27509, 27511–12, 27522, 27525, 27541, 27544–45, 27564–65, 27571–74, 27581–83, 27587–88, 27591, 27596–97, 27601, 27603–10, 27612–17, 27619–20, 27622, 27625, 27627–29, 27635–36, 27640, 27658, 27661, 27668, 27690, 27698

NORTH DAKOTA

(Population 2010, 675,591)

SENATORS

KENT CONRAD, Democrat, of Bismarck, ND; born in Bismarck, March 12, 1948; education: graduated from Wheelus High School, Tripoli, Libya, 1966; attended the University of Missouri, Columbia, 1967; B.A., Stanford University, CA, 1971; M.B.A., George Washington University, Washington, DC, 1975; professional: assistant to the Tax Commissioner, Bismarck, 1974–80; director, Management Planning and Personnel, North Dakota Tax Department, March–December 1980; Tax Commissioner, State of North Dakota, 1981–86; married Lucy Calautti, February 1987; one child by former marriage: Jessamyn Abigail; committees: chair, Budget; Agriculture, Nutrition, and Forestry; Finance; Indian Affairs; Joint Committee on Taxation; Select Committee on Intelligence; elected to the U.S. Senate on November 4, 1986; was not a candidate for a second term to Senate seat he had won in 1986; subsequently elected by special election on December 4, 1992, to fill the vacancy caused by the death of Senator Quentin Burdick, whose term would have expired on January 3, 1995; took the oath of office on December 14, 1992; reelected to each succeeding Senate term.

Office Listings

http://conrad.senate.gov

530 Hart Senate Office Building, Washington, DC 20510 .... (202) 224–2043
Chief of Staff.—Sara Garland. FAX: 224–7776
Legislative Director.—Tom Mahr.
220 East Rosser Avenue, Room 228, Bismarck, ND 58501 .... (701) 258–4648
State Director (West Region).—Marty Boeckel.
657 Second Avenue North, Room 306, Fargo, ND 58102 .... (701) 232–8030
State Director (East Region).—Scott Stofferahn. TDD: 232–2139
33 South 3rd Street, Suite B, Grand Forks, ND 58201 .... (701) 775–9601
100 First Street, SW., Room 105, Minot, ND 58701 .... (701) 852–0703

* * *

JOHN HOEVEN, Republican, of Bismarck, ND; born in Bismarck, March 13, 1957; education: B.A., Dartmouth College, Hanover, NH, 1979; M.B.A., Northwestern University, Chicago, IL, 1981; professional: executive vice president, First Western Bank, Minot, 1986–93; president and CEO, Bank of North Dakota, 1993–2000; governor of North Dakota, 2000–10; religion: Catholic; family: married to Mikey; two children; caucuses: Air Force Caucus; Congressional Sportsmen's Caucus; Senate Western Caucus; Norway Caucus; Rural Education Caucus; National Guard Caucus; E–911 Caucus; Rural Health Caucus; General Aviation Caucus; Impact Aid Coalition; committees: Agriculture, Nutrition, and Forestry; Appropriations; Energy and Natural Resources; Indian Affairs; elected to the U.S. Senate on November 2, 2010.

Office Listings

http://hoeven.senate.gov

120 Russell Senate Office Building, Washington, DC 20510 .... (202) 224–2551
Chief of Staff.—Don Larson. FAX: 224–7999
Deputy Chief of Staff.—Ryan Bernstein.
Legislative Director.—Tony Eberhard.
Communications Director.—Don Canton.
U.S. Federal Building, 220 Easter Rosser Avenue, Room 312, Bismarck, ND 58501 .... (701) 250–4618
State Director.—Shane Goettle FAX: 239–5112
1802 32nd Avenue South, Suite B, Fargo, ND 58103 .... (701) 239–5389
Federal Building, 102 North Fourth Street, Room 108, Grand Forks, ND 58203 .... (701) 746–8972
315 Main Street South, Suite 204, Minot, ND 58701 .... (701) 838–1361

REPRESENTATIVE

AT LARGE

RICK BERG, Republican, of Fargo, ND; born in Hettinger, ND, August 16, 1959; education: B.A., agricultural economics, North Dakota State University, Fargo, ND, 1981; professional:

co-founder, Goldmark Schlossman Commercial Real Estate Services, 1981–2011; North Dakota House of Representatives, 1985–2011; board member, Greater Fargo-Moorhead Economic Development Corporation, 1999–2007; married: Tracy Martin; child: Jack; committees: Ways and Means; elected to the 112th Congress on November 2, 2010.

Office Listings

http://berg.house.gov

323 Cannon House Office Building, Washington, DC 20515 .... (202) 225–2611
Chief of Staff.—Lonnie Dietz. FAX: 226–0893
Legislative Director.—Jonathan Casper.
Press Secretary.—Alee Lockman.
Federal Building, 220 East Rosser Avenue, Room 328, Bismarck, ND 58501 .... (701) 224–0355
3170 43rd Street South, Fargo, ND 58104 .... (701) 235–9760
State Director.—Tom Nelson.

Population (2010), 672,591.

ZIP Codes: 58001–02, 58004–09, 58011–13, 58015–18, 58021, 58027, 58029, 58030–33, 58035–36, 58038, 58040–43, 58045–49, 58051–54, 58056–65, 58067–69, 58071–72, 58074–79, 58081, 58102–09, 58121–22,58124–26, 58201–06, 58208, 58210, 58212, 58214, 58216, 58218–20, 58222–25, 58227–31, 58233, 58235–41, 58243–44, 58249–51, 58254–62, 58265–67, 58269–78, 58281–82, 58301, 58310–11, 58313, 58316–19, 58321, 58323–25, 58327, 58329–32, 58335, 58338–39, 58341, 58343–46, 58348, 58351–53, 58355–57, 58359, 58361–63, 58365–70, 58372, 58374, 58377, 58379–82, 58384–86, 58401–02, 58405, 58413, 58415–16, 58418, 58420–26, 58428–31, 58433, 58436, 58438–45, 58448, 58451–52, 58454–56, 58458, 58460–61, 58463–64, 58466–67, 58472, 58474–84, 58486–88, 58490, 58492, 58494–97, 58501–07, 58520–21, 58523–24, 58528–33, 58535, 58538, 58540–42, 58544–45, 58549, 58552, 58554, 58558–66, 58568–73, 58575–77, 58579–81, 58601–02, 58620–23, 58625–27, 58630–32, 58634, 58636, 58638–47, 58649–56, 58701–05, 58707, 58710–13, 58716, 58718, 58721–23, 58725, 58727, 58730–31, 58733–37, 58740–41, 58744, 58746–48, 58750, 58752, 58755–63, 58765, 58768–73, 58775–76, 58778–79, 58781–85, 58787–90, 58792–95, 58801–02, 58830–31, 58833, 58835, 58838, 58843–45, 58847, 58849, 58852–54, 58856

OHIO

(Population 2010, 11,536,504)

SENATORS

SHERROD BROWN, Democrat, of Avon Lake, OH; born in Mansfield, OH, November 9, 1952; education: B.A., Yale University, New Haven, CT, 1974; M.A., education, Ohio State University, Columbus, OH, 1979; M.A., public administration, Ohio State University, Columbus, OH, 1981; professional: Ohio House of Representatives, 1975–83; Ohio Secretary of State, 1983–91; U.S. House of Representatives, 1992–2006; member: Eagle Scouts of America; married: Connie Schultz; children: Emily, Elizabeth, Andrew and Caitlin; committees: Agriculture, Nutrition, and Forestry; Appropriations; Banking, Housing, and Urban Affairs; Veterans' Affairs; Select Committee on Ethics; elected to the 103rd Congress on November 3, 1992; reelected to each succeeding Congress; elected to the U.S. Senate on November 7, 2006.

Office Listings

http://brown.senate.gov

713 Hart Senate Office Building, Washington, DC 20510 .... (202) 224–2315
Chief of Staff.—Mark Powden. FAX: 228–6321
Legislative Director.—Jeremy Hekhuis.
Communications Director.—Meghan Dubyak.
Press Secretaries: Lauren Kulik, Allison Preiss.
1301 East Ninth Street, Suite 1710, Cleveland, OH 44114 .... (216) 522–7272
State Director.—John Ryan.
Deputy State Director.—Beth Thames.
425 Walnut Street, Suite 2310, Cincinnati, OH 45202 .... (513) 684–1021
200 North High Street, Room 614, Columbus, OH 43215 .... (614) 469–2083
205 West 20th Street, Suite M280, Lorain, OH 44052 .... (440) 242–4100

* * *

ROBERT J. PORTMAN, Republican, of Terrace Park, OH; born in Cincinnati, December 19, 1955; education: B.A., Dartmouth College, Hanover, NH, 1979; J.D., University of Michigan Law School, Ann Arbor, MI, 1984; professional: associate counsel to George H.W. Bush, 1989; deputy assistant and director, White House Office of Legislative Affairs, 1989–91; member of the U.S. House of Representatives, 1993–2005; U.S. Trade Representative, 2005–06; Director of the Office of Management and Budget, 2006–07; religion: Methodist; married: Jane Portman; three children: Jed, Will, and Sally; committees: Armed Services; Budget; Energy and Natural Resources; Homeland Security and Governmental Affairs; elected to the U.S. Senate on November 2, 2010.

Office Listings

http://portman.senate.gov

338 Russell Senate Office Building, Washington, DC 20510 .... (202) 224–3353
Chief of Staff.—Rob Lehman.
Communications Director.—Jeff Sadosky.
Legislative Director.—Pam Thiessen.
Director of Operations.—Jim Durrett.
37 West Broad Street, Suite 300, Columbus, OH 43215 .... (614) 469–6774
State Director.—Teri Geiger.
District Director.—John Campbell.
District Representative.—Apps Akpofure.
36 East 7th Street, Room 2615, Cincinnati, OH 45202 .... (513) 684–3265
District Director.—Connie Laug.
District Representative.—Vacant.
1240 East 9th Street, Room 3061, Cleveland, OH 44199 .... (216) 522–7095
District Director.—Caryn Candisky.
District Representative.—George Brown.
420 Madison Avenue, Room 1210, Toledo, OH 43604 .... (419) 259–3895
District Representative.—Wes Fahrbach.

REPRESENTATIVES

FIRST DISTRICT

STEVE CHABOT, Republican, of Cincinnati, OH; born in Cincinnati, January 22, 1953; education: graduated from LaSalle High School in Cincinnati; B.A., College of William and

Mary, Williamsburg, VA, 1975; J.D., Salmon P. Chase College of Law, Highland Heights, KY, 1978; professional: teacher, 1975–76; member of the city council, Cincinnati, OH, 1985–90; commissioner, Hamilton County, OH, 1990–94; elected as a Republican to the 104th–110th Congresses January 3, 1995–January 3, 2009; served as ranking member on the Committee on Small Business, 2007; family: wife, Donna; two children: Erica and Randy; committees: Foreign Affairs; Judiciary; Small Business; elected to the 112th Congress on November 2, 2010.

Office Listings

http://chabot.house.gov

2351 Rayburn House Office Building, Washington, DC 20515 .... (202) 225–2216
Chief of Staff.—Brian Griffith. FAX: 225–3012
Deputy Chief of Staff.—Jamie Schwartz.
Legislative Director.—Steve Denis.
Director of Scheduling / Administration.—Alyssa Polewski.
Carew Tower, 441 Vine Street, Room 3003, Cincinnati, OH 45202 .... (513) 684–2723
District Director.—Mike Cantwell. FAX: 421–8722

Counties: BUTLER (part), HAMILTON (part). Population (2000), 630,730.

ZIP Codes: 45001–02, 45013–14, 45030, 45033, 45040–41, 45051–54, 45056, 45070, 45201–21, 45223–25, 45229, 45231–34, 45236–41, 45246–48, 45250–53, 45258, 45262–64, 45267–71, 45273–74, 45277, 45280, 45296, 45298–99

* * *

SECOND DISTRICT

JEAN SCHMIDT, Republican, of Miami Township; born in Cincinnati, OH, November 29th; education: B.A., University of Cincinnati, 1974; professional: Miami Township Trustee, 1989–2000; Ohio House of Representatives, 2000–04; president, Right to Life of Greater Cincinnati, 2004–05; religion: Catholic; married: Peter; children: Emilie; co-chair, Congressional Pro-Life Women's Caucus; committees: Agriculture; Foreign Affairs; Transportation and Infrastructure; elected to the 109th Congress by special election on August 5, 2005; reelected to each succeeding Congress.

Office Listings

http://www.house.gov/schmidt

2464 Rayburn House Office Building, Washington, DC 20515 .... (202) 225–3164
Chief of Staff.—Joe Jansen. FAX: 225–1992
Legislative Director.—Dee Weghorst.
Communications Director.—Bruce Pfaff.
Scheduler.—Teddy Siegel.
8044 Montgomery Road, Suite 170, Cincinnati, OH 45236 .... (513) 791–0381
District Director.—Gertrud Whitaker.
602 Chillicothe Street, Suite 304, Portsmouth, OH 45662 .... (740) 354–1440

Counties: ADAMS, BROWN, CLERMONT, HAMILTON (part), PIKE, SCIOTO (part), WARREN (part). Population (2000), 630,730.

ZIP Codes: 45034, 45036, 45039–40, 45054, 45065, 45068, 45101–03, 45105–07, 45111–13, 45115, 45118–22, 45130–31, 45133, 45140, 45142, 45144–45, 45147–48, 45150, 45152–54, 45156–58, 45160, 45162, 45167–68, 45171, 45174, 45176, 45202, 45206–09, 45212–13, 45222, 45226–27, 45230, 45235–37, 45241–46, 45249, 45254–55, 45601, 45612–13, 45616, 45618, 45624, 45630, 45642, 45646, 45648, 45650, 45652, 45657, 45660–63, 45671, 45679, 45683–84, 45687, 45690, 45693, 45697

* * *

THIRD DISTRICT

MICHAEL R. TURNER, Republican, of Dayton, OH; born in Dayton, January 11, 1960; education: B.A., Ohio Northern University, 1982; J.D., Case Western Reserve University Law School, 1985; M.B.A., University of Dayton, 1992; professional: attorney; president, JMD Development (real estate company); corporate counsel, MTC International (holding company); organizations: Ohio Bar Association; California Bar Association; public service: Mayor of Dayton, 1994–2002; married to Lori; children: Jessica and Carolyn; committees: Armed Services; Oversight and Government Reform; elected to the 108th Congress on November 5, 2002; reelected to each succeeding Congress.

Office Listings

http://www.turner.house.gov

2454 Rayburn House Office Building, Washington, DC 20515 .... (202) 225–6465
Chief of Staff.—Ryan P. Dwyer. FAX: 225–6754
Legislative Director.—Vacant.
120 West Third Street, Suite 305, Dayton, OH 45402 .... (937) 225–2843
61 East Main Street, Suite 1, Wilmington, OH 45177 .... (937) 383–8931

Counties: CLINTON, HIGHLAND, MONTGOMERY (part), WARREN (part). Population (2000), 630,730.

ZIP Codes: 45005, 45032, 45036, 45040, 45042, 45044, 45054, 45066, 45068, 45107, 45110, 45113–14, 45118, 45123, 45132–33, 45135, 45138, 45140, 45142, 45146, 45148, 45155, 45159, 45164, 45166, 45169, 45177, 45206, 45240–41, 45309, 45315, 45322, 45325, 45327, 45335, 45338, 45342–45, 45354, 45371, 45377, 45381, 45401–10, 45412–20, 45422, 45426–29, 45431–32, 45437, 45439–41, 45448–49, 45454, 45458–59, 45463, 45469–70, 45475, 45479, 45481–82, 45490, 45612, 45660, 45679, 45697

* * *

FOURTH DISTRICT

JAMES D. ''JIM'' JORDAN, Republican, of Urbana, OH; born in Troy, OH, February 17, 1964; education: graduated, Graham High School, St. Paris, OH, 1982; B.S. in economics, University of Wisconsin, Madison, WI, 1986; M.A. in education, The Ohio State University, Columbus, OH, 1991; J.D., Capital University School of Law, Columbus, OH, 2001; professional: assistant wrestling coach, The Ohio State University, 1987–95; State Representative, Ohio House of Representatives, 85th District, 1995–2001; State Senator, Ohio State Senate, 12th District, 2001–07; awards: four-time high school wrestling champion (Ohio), 1979–82; two-time NCAA Division I National Wrestling Champion, 1985–86; three-time All American, 1984–86; Wisconsin Badgers Hall of Fame; third place, Olympic Trials in Wrestling, 1988; Friend of the Taxpayer, Americans for the Tax Reform, 1997; Leadership in Government Award from the Ohio Roundtable and Freedom Forum, 2001; awards from the United Conservatives of Ohio: Outstanding Freshman Legislator Award, 1996; Watchdog of the Treasury, 1996, 2000, 2004; Pro-Life Legislator of the Year, 1998; Outstanding Legislator Award, 2004; activities: Grace Bible Church, Springfield; Local and National Right to Life organizations; Champaign County Republican Executive Committee; married: Polly (Stickley) Jordan; parents: John and Shirley Jordan; children: Rachel, Benjamin, Jessie, and Issac; committees: Oversight and Government Reform; Judiciary; elected to the 110th Congress on November 7, 2006; reelected to each succeeding Congress.

Office Listings

http://www.jordan.house.gov

1524 Longworth House Office Building, Washington, DC 20515 .... (202) 225–2676
Chief of Staff.—Ray Yonkura. FAX: 226–0577
Legislative Director.—George Poulios.
Executive Assistant / Scheduler.—Melissa Evans.
3121 West Elm Plaza, Lima, OH 45805–2516 .... (419) 999–6455
100 East Main Cross Street, Suite 101, Findlay, OH 45840–3311 .... (419) 423–3210
24 West Third Street, Room 314, Mansfield, OH 44902–1299 .... (419) 522–5757
District Director.—Ray Yonkura.

Counties: ALLEN, AUGLAIZE, CHAMPAIGN, HANCOCK, HARDIN, LOGAN, MARION, MORROW, RICHLAND, SHELBY, WYANDOT (part). Population (2000), 630,730.

ZIP Codes: 43003, 43009, 43011, 43019, 43044–45, 43047, 43050, 43060, 43067, 43070, 43072, 43074, 43078, 43083–84, 43301–02, 43306, 43310–11, 43314–26, 43330–38, 43340–51, 43356–60, 43516, 44802, 44804–05, 44813, 44817, 44822, 44827, 44830, 44833, 44837, 44843, 44849, 44862, 44864–65, 44875, 44878, 44901–07, 44999, 45013, 45302, 45306, 45312, 45317, 45326, 45333–34, 45336, 45340, 45344, 45353, 45356, 45360, 45363, 45365, 45380, 45388–89, 45404, 45414, 45420, 45424, 45431–32, 45502, 45801–02, 45804–10, 45812, 45814, 45816–17, 45819–20, 45822, 45830, 45833, 45835–36, 45839–41, 45843–45, 45850, 45854, 45856, 45858–59, 45862, 45865, 45867–72, 45877, 45881, 45884–85, 45887–90, 45894–97

* * *

FIFTH DISTRICT

ROBERT E. ''BOB'' LATTA, Republican, of Bowling Green, OH; born in Bluffton, OH, April 18, 1956; graduated, Bowling Green High School, Bowling Green, OH, 1974; Bowling Green State University, Bowling Green, OH, 1978; B.A., history, University of Toledo School of Law, Toledo, OH, 1981; J.D., legislator, lawyer; awards: Ohio Farm Bureau ''Friend of Farm Bureau'' Award, 2008; the United States Chamber of Commerce ''Spirit of Enterprise'' Award, 2008; and the American Conservative Union ''ACU Conservative'' Award, 2008; United Conservatives of Ohio ''Watchdog of the Treasury'' in 1998, 2000, and 2005; The U.S. Sportsmen's Alliance, ''Patriot Award'', 2002, Ohio National Guard ''Major General Charles Dick Award for Legislative Excellence'', 1999; ''President's Award'', 2006; religion: Roman Catholic; wife, Marcia ''Sloan'' Latta; daughters, Elizabeth and Maria Latta; member, Bowling Green Noon Kiwanis, Bowling Green Chamber of Commerce, Wood County Farm Bureau; committees: Energy and Commerce; elected to the 111th Congress on November 4, 2008; reelected to the 112th Congress on November 2, 2010.

Office Listings

http://latta.house.gov

1323 Longworth House Office Building, Washington, DC 20515 .... (202) 225–6405
Chief of Staff.—Ryan Walker. FAX: 225–1985
Legislative Director.—Allison Witt.
Press Secretary.—Izzy Santa.
Executive Assistant / Scheduler.—Courtney Powell.
1045 North Main Street, Suite 6, Bowling Green, OH 43402 .... (419) 354–8700
101 Clinton Street, Suite 1200, Defiance, OH 43512 .... (419) 782–1996
11 East Main Street, Norwalk, OH 44857 .... (419) 668–0206

Counties: ASHLAND (part), CRAWFORD, DEFIANCE, FULTON, HENRY, HURON, LUCAS (part), MERCER (part), PAULDING, PUTNAM, SANDUSKY, SENECA, VAN WERT, WILLIAMS, WOOD, WYANDOT (part). Population (2000), 630,730.

ZIP Codes: 43302, 43314, 43316, 43323, 43337, 43351, 43402–03, 43406–07, 43410, 43413–14, 43416, 43420, 43430–31, 43435, 43437, 43441–43, 43447, 43449–51, 43457, 43460, 43462–67, 43469, 43501–02, 43504–06, 4351012, 43515–27, 43529–36, 43540–43, 43545, 43547–58, 43565–67, 43569–71, 43605, 43619, 43654, 44035, 44235, 44287, 44802, 44805, 44807, 44809, 44811, 44815, 44817–18, 44820, 44825–28, 44830, 44833, 44836–37, 44841, 44844–51, 44853–57, 44859–61, 44865–67, 44874–75, 44878, 44880–83, 44887–90, 45813, 45815, 45817, 45821–22, 45827–28, 45830–33, 45837–38, 45844, 45846, 45848–49, 45851, 45853, 45855–56, 45858, 45861–64, 45868, 45872–77, 45879–80, 45882, 45886–87, 45889, 45891, 45893–94, 45898–99

* * *

SIXTH DISTRICT

WILLIAM L. ''BILL'' JOHNSON, Republican, of Marietta, OH; born in Roseboro, NC, November 10, 1954; raised in Roseboro, NC; education: B.A., graduated *summa cum laude* at Troy University; Troy, AL, 1979; M.A., computer sciences, Georgia Tech; Atlanta, GA, 1984; professional: co-founder of Johnson-Schley Management Group, Inc; founder of J2 Business Solutions, Inc; chief information officer of a global manufacturer of highly electronic components for the transportation industry; military: retired as Lieutenant Colonel, distinguished graduate from the Air Force Reserve Officer Training Corps, Squadron Officers School, and Air Command and Staff College, religion: Protestant; family: married to LeeAnn Johnson; children: Nathan, Joshua, Julie, and Jessica; awards: recipient of Air Force Meritorious Service Medal; Air Force Commendation Medal; National Defense Service Medal; caucuses: Pro-Life; Coal; Marcellus Shale; Air Force; House Republican Israel; Congressional Sportsmen; Congressional Prayer; Military Veterans; Congressional Anti-Terrorism; Congressional Wounded to Work; Congressional China; Congressional Turkish; United Service Organizations Congressional; Congressional Taiwan; Ohio River Basin; committees: Natural Resources, Veterans' Affairs, Foreign Affairs; elected to the 112th Congress on November 2, 2010.

Office Listings

http://billjohnson.house.gov

317 Cannon House Office Building, Washington, DC 20515 .... (202) 225–5905
Chief of Staff.—Mike Smullen.
Legislative Director.—Patrick Orth.
Communications Director.—Jessica Towhey.
Scheduler.—Angela Weaver.
246 Front Street, Marietta, OH 45750 .... (740) 376–0868
192 East State Street, Salem, OH 44460 .... (330) 337–6951
202 Park Avenue, Suite C, Ironton, OH 45638 .... (740) 534–9431

Counties: ATHENS (part), BELMONT (part), COLUMBIANA, GALLIA, JEFFERSON, LAWRENCE, MAHONING (part), MEIGS, MONROE, NOBLE, SCIOTO (part), WASHINGTON. Population (2000), 630,730.

ZIP Codes: 43711, 43713, 43716–19, 43724, 43728, 43732, 43747, 43752, 43754, 43757, 43759, 43772–73, 43779–80, 43786–88, 43793, 43901–03, 43905–08, 43910, 43912–17, 43920, 43925–26, 43930–35, 43937–48, 43950–53, 43961–

64, 43967–68, 43970–71, 43973, 43977, 43983, 43985, 44401, 44406, 44408, 44412–13, 44415–16, 44422–23, 44427, 44429, 44431–32, 44441–45, 44449, 44451–52, 44454–55, 44460, 44481, 44490, 44492–93, 44502, 44507, 44511–15, 44601, 44609, 44619, 44625, 44634, 44657, 44665, 44672, 45053, 45614, 45619–20, 45623, 45629, 45631, 45636, 45638, 45640, 45643, 45645, 45648, 45653, 45656, 45658–59, 45662, 45669, 45674–75, 45677–78, 45680, 45682, 45685–86, 45688, 45694, 45696, 45699, 45701, 45710–15, 45720–21, 45723–24, 45727, 45729, 45734–35, 45739, 45741–46, 45750, 45760–61, 45766–73, 45775–80, 45783–84, 45786–89

* * *

SEVENTH DISTRICT

STEVE AUSTRIA, Republican, of Beavercreek, OH; born in Xenia, OH, October 12, 1958; education: B.A., Marquette University, Milwaukee, WI, 1982; Freshman Class President, 2008–10; religion: Catholic; committees: Appropriations; elected to the 111th Congress on November 4, 2008; reelected to the 112th Congress.

Office Listings

http://www.austria.house.gov

439 Cannon House Office Building, Washington, DC 20515 .... (202) 225–4324
Chief of Staff.—Ted Maness.
Press Secretary.—Stephanie Sonksen.
Legislative Director.—Tyler Grassmeyer.
Legislative Assistants: Steven Gilleland, Jessica Talbert.
Scheduler.—Erika Luth.
Legislative Correspondent.—Heather Hagerman.
Staff Assistant.—John Drzewicki.
5 West North Street, Suite 200, Springfield, OH 45504 .... (937) 325–0474
District Director.—Bob Clark.
207 South Broad Street, Lancaster, OH 43130 .... (740) 654–5149

Counties: CLARK, FAIRFIELD, FAYETTE, FRANKLIN (part), GREENE, PERRY, PICKAWAY, ROSS (part). Population (2000), 630,730.

ZIP Codes: 43009–10, 43044, 43046, 43062, 43068, 43076, 43078, 43102–03, 43105–07, 43109–10, 43112–13, 43115–17, 43125, 43128, 43130, 43135–38, 43140, 43142–43, 43145–48, 43150, 43153–57, 43160, 43163–64, 43199, 43207, 43213, 43217, 43227, 43232, 43314, 43730–31, 43739, 43748, 43758, 43760–61, 43764, 43766, 43777, 43782–83, 45123, 45135, 45169, 45301, 45305, 45307, 45314, 45316, 45319, 45323–24, 45335, 45341, 45344, 45349, 45368–70, 45372, 45384–85, 45387, 45424, 45430–35, 45440, 45458–59, 45501–06, 45601, 45628, 45644, 45671, 45732

* * *

EIGHTH DISTRICT

JOHN A. BOEHNER, Republican, of West Chester, OH; born in Reading, OH, November 17, 1949; education: graduated, Moeller High School, Cincinnati, OH, 1968; B.S., Xavier University, 1977; president, Nucite Sales, Inc.; Ohio House of Representatives, 1984–90; ranking Republican member, Commerce and Labor Committee; Energy and Environment Committee; Judiciary and Criminal Justice; elected, Union Township Trustees, 1981; elected, president, Union Township Board of Trustees, 1984; member: St. John Catholic Church; Ohio Farm Bureau; Lakota Hills Homeowners Association; Knights of Columbus, Pope John XXIII; Union Chamber of Commerce; American Heart Association Board; Butler County Mental Health Association; YMCA Capital Campaign; Union Elementary School PTA; Middletown Chamber of Commerce; American Legion Post 218 of Middletown Butler County Trustees and Clerks Association; married the former Deborah Gunlack, 1973; two children: Lindsay, Tricia; elected to the 102nd Congress; reelected to each succeeding Congress; elected Republican Leader in the 109th, 110th and 111th Congresses; elected Speaker of the House in the 112th Congress.

Office Listings

http://johnboehner.house.gov

1011 Longworth House Office Building, Washington, DC 20515 .... (202) 225–6205
Chief of Staff.—Mick Krieger. FAX: 225–5117
Press Secretary.—Brittany Bramell.
7969 Cincinnati-Dayton road, Suite B, West Chester, OH 45069 .... (513) 779–5400
12 South Plum Street, Troy, Ohio 45373 .... (937) 339–1524

Counties: BUTLER (part), DARKE, MERCER (part), MIAMI, MONTGOMERY (part), PREBLE. Population (2000), 630,730.

ZIP Codes: 45003–05, 45011–15, 45018, 45025–26, 45036, 45042–44, 45050, 45055–56, 45061–64, 45067, 45069, 45071, 45073, 45099, 45241, 45246, 45303–04, 45308–12, 45317–18, 45320–22, 45325–28, 45330–32, 45337–39, 45344, 45346–

48, 45350–52, 45356, 45358–59, 45361–62, 45365, 45371, 45373–74, 45378, 45380–83, 45388, 45390, 45402–04, 45406, 45414, 45424, 45431–32, 45822, 45826, 45828, 45845–46, 45860, 45865–66, 45869, 45883, 45885

* * *

NINTH DISTRICT

MARCY KAPTUR, Democrat, of Toledo, OH; born in Toledo, June 17, 1946; education: graduated, St. Ursula Academy, Toledo, 1964; B.A., University of Wisconsin, Madison, 1968; Master of Urban Planning, University of Michigan, Ann Arbor, 1974; attended University of Manchester, England, 1974; professional: urban planner; assistant director for urban affairs, domestic policy staff, White House, 1977–79; American Planning Association and American Institute of Certified Planners Fellow; member: National Center for Urban Ethnic Affairs Advisory Committee; University of Michigan Urban Planning Alumni Association; NAACP Urban League; Polish Museum; Polish American Historical Association; Lucas County Democratic Party Executive Committee; Democratic Women's Campaign Association; Little Flower Parish Church; House Auto Parts Task Force; co-chair, Ukrainian and 4–H Caucuses; religion: Roman Catholic; committees: Appropriations; Budget; elected on November 2, 1982, to the 98th Congress; reelected to each succeeding Congress.

Office Listings

http://www.kaptur.house.gov

2186 Rayburn House Office Building, Washington, DC 20515 .... (202) 225–4146
Chief of Staff.—Steve Katich.
Deputy Chief of Staff.—Nathan Facey. FAX: 225–7711
Office Manager / Scheduler.—Norma Olsen.
One Maritime Plaza, Suite 600, Toledo, OH 43604 .... (419) 259–7500

Counties: ERIE COUNTY. CITIES AND TOWNSHIPS: Bellevue, Berlin Heights, Berlinville, Birmingham, Bloomingville, Bronson, Castalia, Chatham, Clarksfield, Collins, East Townsend, Fitchville, Hartland, Huron, Kimball, Litchfield, Milan, Mitiwanga, Monroeville, New London, Norwalk, Nova, Olena, Ridgefield, River Corners, Ruggles, Ruggles Beach, Sandusky, Shinrock, Spencer, Steuben, Sullivan, Wakeman, West Clarksfield. LORAIN COUNTY. CITIES AND TOWNSHIPS: Amherst, Beaver Park, Belden, Beulah Beach, Brownhelm, Columbia Station, Elyria, Grafton, Henrietta, Kipton, Lagrange, Linwood Park, Lorain, North Eaton, Oberlin, Ridgeville, Rochester, South Amherst, Vermilion, Wellington. LUCAS COUNTY (part). CITIES AND TOWNSHIPS: Berkey, Curtice, Gypsum, Harbor View, Holland, Maumee, Monclova, Northwood, Oregon, Swanton, Sylvania, Toledo, Waterville, Whitehouse, Woodville. OTTAWA COUNTY. CITIES AND TOWNSHIPS: Bay Shore, Bono, Catawba Island, Clay Center, Danbury, Eagle Beach, Elliston, Elmore, Gem Beach, Genoa, Graytown, Hessville, Isle St. George, Kelleys Island, Lacarne, Lakeside, Lindsey, Marblehead, Martin, Oak Harbor, Port Clinton, Portage, Put-in-Bay, Rocky Ridge, Springbrook, Vickery, Washington, Wayne, Whites Landing, and Williston. Population (2000), 630,730.

ZIP Codes: 43408, 43412, 43416, 43430, 43432–34, 43436, 43438–40, 43442, 43445–47, 43449, 43452, 43456, 43458, 43464, 43468–69, 43504, 43528, 43537, 43542, 43558, 43560, 43566, 43571, 43601–18, 43620, 43623–24, 43635, 43652, 43656–57, 43659–61, 43666–67, 43681–82, 43697, 43699, 44001, 44028, 44035, 44044, 44049–50, 44053, 44074, 44089–90, 44253, 44256, 44275, 44280, 44811, 44814, 44816, 44824, 44826, 44839, 44846–47, 44851, 44857, 44859, 44870–71, 44880, 44889

* * *

TENTH DISTRICT

DENNIS J. KUCINICH, Democrat, of Cleveland, OH; born in Cleveland, October 8, 1946; B.A., and M.A. in speech and communications, Case Western Reserve University, 1974; editor, professor; Cleveland City Councilman, 1969–75; Clerk of the Municipal Court, 1975–77; Mayor of Cleveland, 1977–79; Ohio State Senate, 1994–96; named Outstanding Ohio Senator by National Association of Social Workers for his work on health and social welfare issues; one child, Jackie; committees: Education and the Workforce; Oversight and Government Reform; elected to the 105th Congress; reelected to each succeeding Congress.

Office Listings

http://kucinich.house.gov

2445 Rayburn House Office Building, Washington, DC 20515 .... (202) 225–5871
Chief of Staff.—Vic Edgerton. FAX: 225–5745
Legislative Director.—Diala Jadallah.
14400 Detroit Avenue, Lakewood, OH 44107 .... (216) 228–8850

Counties: CUYAHOGA COUNTY (part). CITIES AND TOWNSHIPS: Bay Village, Berea, Brooklyn, Brooklyn Heights, Cleveland, Cuyahaga Heights, Fairview Park, Lakewood, Newberg Heights, North Olmsted, Olmsted Falls, Olmsted Township, Parma, Rocky River, Seven Hills, Strongsville, and Westlake. Population (2000), 630,730.

ZIP Codes: 44017, 44070, 44102, 44105, 44107, 44109, 44111, 44113, 44115–16, 44125–27, 44129–31, 44134–42, 44144–46, 44149, 44181

* * *

ELEVENTH DISTRICT

MARCIA L. FUDGE, Democrat, of Cleveland, OH; born in Shaker Heights, OH, October 29, 1952; B.S., Ohio State University, 1975; J.D., Cleveland Marshall College of Law, 1983; professional: Director of Budget and Finance, Cuyahoga County Prosecutor's Office; Chief Administrator for Cuyahoga County Prosecutor Stephanie Tubbs Jones; Mayor of Warrensville Heights, OH; committees: Agriculture; Science, Space, and Technology; elected to the 110th Congress, by special election, to fill the vacancy caused by the death of United States Representative Stephanie Tubbs Jones; elected to the 111th Congress on November 4, 2008; reelected to the 112th Congress on November 2, 2010.

Office Listings

http://www.fudge.house.gov

1019 Longworth House Office Building, Washington, DC 20515 .... (202) 225–7032
Legislative Director.—LaDavia Drane.
Legislative Counsel / Legislative Assistant.—Maheen Siddiqui.
Press Secretary.—Laura Allen.
Legislative Correspondent / Staff Assistant.—Ticora Jones.
Legislative Assistants: Casey Miller, Clifton Williams.
Legislative Fellow.—Greg Tinch.
Scheduler / Office Manager.—Jerica Daniels.
4834 Richmond Road, Suite 150, Warrensville Heights, OH 44128 .... (216) 522–4900
Staff Assistant.—Ariella Brown.
Healthcare / Senior Citizen Liaison.—Beverly R. Charles.
Assistant / Media / Government Liaison.—Vacant.
Scheduler.—Linda R. Matthews.
Faith Based Liaison.—Stephen Caviness.
Jewish Community Liaison and County Government Liaison.—Anita Gray.
Veterans Liaison.—Jessica Norton.
Communications Director.—Belinda Prinz.

Counties: CUYAHOGA COUNTY (part). CITIES: Beachwood, Bedford, Bedford Heights, Brahtenahl Village, Cleveland, Cleveland Heights, East Cleveland, Euclid, Garfield Heights, Highland Hills Village, Lyndhurst, Maple Heights, Mayfield Heights, North Randall Village, Oakwood Village, Orange Village, Pepper Pike, Richmond Heights, Shaker Heights, South Euclid, University Heights, Warrensville Heights, and Woodmere Village. Population (2000), 630,730.

ZIP Codes: 44101–15, 44118–44130, 44132, 44135, 44137, 44143–44, 44146, 44178, 44181, 44185, 44188–95, 44197–99

* * *

TWELFTH DISTRICT

PATRICK J. TIBERI, Republican, of Columbus, OH; born in Columbus, October 21, 1962; education: B.A., Ohio State University, 1985; professional: real estate agent; assistant to U.S. Representative John Kasich (R–OH); public service: served as Majority Leader, Ohio House of Representatives, 1992–2000; organizations: Westerville Chamber of Commerce; Columbus Board of Realtors; Military Veterans and Community Service Commission; Sons of Italy; awards: Fraternal Order of Police Outstanding Legislator; Watchdog of the Treasury Award; American Red Cross Volunteer Service Award; married: Denice; committees: Ways and Means; elected to the 107th Congress on November 7, 2000; reelected to each succeeding Congress.

Office Listings

http://www.house.gov/tiberi

106 Cannon House Office Building, Washington, DC 20515 .... (202) 225–5355
Chief of Staff.—Chris Zeigler. FAX: 226–4523
Legislative Director.—Kelli Briggs.
Communications Director.—Breann Gonzalez.
3000 Corporate Drive, Suite 310, Columbus, OH 43231 .... (614) 523–2555
District Director.—Mark Bell.

Counties: DELAWARE, FRANKLIN (part), LICKING (part). Population (2000), 630,730.

ZIP Codes: 43001–04, 43011, 43013, 43015–18, 43021, 43023, 43025–27, 43031–33, 43035, 43040, 43046, 43054–56, 43061–62, 43064–66, 43068, 43071, 43073–74, 43080–82, 43085–86, 43105, 43147, 43201, 43203, 43205–07, 43209, 43211, 43213–15, 43218–19, 43224, 43226–27, 43229–32, 43235–36, 43240, 43334, 43342, 43344, 43356

* * *

THIRTEENTH DISTRICT

BETTY SUTTON, Democrat, of Copley, OH; born in Barberton, OH, July 31, 1963; education: B.A., Kent State University, Kent, OH, 1985; J.D., University of Akron, Akron, OH, 1990; professional: lawyer, private practice; city council, Barberton, OH, 1991–92; member, Ohio House of Representatives, State of Ohio, 1993–2000; married: Doug Corwon; committees: Armed Services; Natural Resources; elected to the 110th Congress on November 7, 2006; reelected to each succeeding Congress.

Office Listings

http://www.sutton.house.gov

1721 Longworth House Office Building, Washington, DC 20515 .... (202) 225–3401
Chief of Staff.—Angela Kouters. FAX: 225–2266
Legislative Director.—Christine Corcoran.
Scheduler.—Mike Kerrigan.
205 West Twentieth Street, M–230, Lorain, OH 44052 .... (440) 245–5350
John F. Seiberling Federal Building, 2 South Main Street, Suite 380, Akron, OH 44308 .... (330) 865–8450

Counties: CUYAHOGA (part), LORAIN (part), MEDINA (part), SUMMIT (part). CITIES AND TOWNSHIPS: Akron, Lorain, Elyria, N. Ridgeville, Brunswick, Strongsville, and N. Royalton. Population (2000), 630,730.

ZIP Codes: 44001, 44011–12, 44028, 44035–36, 44039, 44044, 44052–55, 44133, 44136, 44141, 44147, 44149, 44203, 44210, 44212, 44216, 44221–24, 44230, 44233, 44253, 44256, 44264, 44280–81, 44286, 44301–04, 44306–14, 44317, 44319–22, 44325–26, 44328, 44333–34, 44372, 44393, 44398–99, 44614, 44645, 44685, 44720

* * *

FOURTEENTH DISTRICT

STEVEN C. LATOURETTE, Republican, of Bainbridge Township, OH; born in Cleveland, OH, July 22, 1954; education: graduated, Cleveland Heights High School, 1972; B.A., University of Michigan, 1976; J.D., Cleveland State University, 1979; professional: assistant public defender, Lake County, OH, Public Defender's Office, 1980–83; associated with Painesville firm of Cannon, Stern, Aveni and Krivok, 1983–86; Baker, Hackenberg and Collins, 1986–88; prosecuting attorney, Lake County, OH, 1988–94; served on the Lake County Budget Commission; executive board of the Lake County Narcotics Agency; chairman, County Task Force on Domestic Violence; trustee, Cleveland Policy Historical Society; director, Regional Forensic Laboratory; member: Lake County Association of Police Chiefs, Ohio Prosecuting Attorneys Association, and National District Attorneys Association; appointed to serve as a fellow of the American College of Prosecuting Attorneys; married: Jennifer; children: Sarah, Sam, Clare, Amy, and Emma; committees: Appropriations; elected to the 104th Congress; reelected to each succeeding Congress.

Office Listings

http://www.latourette.house.gov

2371 Rayburn House Office Building, Washington, DC 20515 .... (202) 225–5731
Chief of Staff.—Dino DiSanto. FAX: 225–3307
Communications Director.—Deborah Setliff.
Executive Assistant / Scheduler.—Kathy Kato.
Legislative Director.—Kate Ostrander.
1 Victoria Place, Room 320, Painesville, OH 44077 .... (440) 352–3939
Twinsburg Government Center, 10075 Ravenna Road, Twinsburg, OH 44087 .... (330) 425–9291

Counties: ASHTABULA, CUYAHOGA (part), GEAUGA LAKE, PORTAGE (part), SUMMIT (part), TRUMBULL (part). Population (2000), 630,730.

ZIP Codes: 44003–05, 44010, 44021–24, 44026, 44030, 44032–33, 44040–41, 44045–48, 44056–57, 44060–62, 44064–65, 44067–68, 44072–73, 44076–77, 44080–82, 44084–88, 44092–97, 44099, 44124, 44139, 44141, 44143, 44202, 44221, 44223–24, 44231, 44234, 44236–37, 44240, 44255, 44262, 44264, 44278, 44404, 44410, 44417–18, 44428, 44439, 44450, 44470, 44491

* * *

FIFTEENTH DISTRICT

STEVE STIVERS, Republican, of Columbus, OH; born in Cincinnati, OH, March 24, 1965; education: B.A., Ohio State University, Columbus, OH, 1989; M.B.A., Ohio State University, 1996; professional: military; lieutenant colonel, Ohio Army National Guard, 1988–present; Ohio Company and Bank One; member of the Ohio State Senate, 2003–08; married: Karen Stivers; children: Sarah; committees: Financial Services; elected to the 112th Congress on November 2, 2010.

Office Listings

http://www.stivers.house.gov

1007 Longworth House Office Building, Washington, DC 20515 .... (202) 225–2015
Chief of Staff.—Mary Beth Carozza. FAX: 225–3529
Scheduler.—Monica Hueckel.
Legislative Director.—Lindsay Vogtsberger.
Communications Director.—Courtney Whetstone.
3790 Municipal Way, Hilliard, OH 43026 .... (614) 771–4968
FAX: 771–3990

Counties: FRANKLIN (part), MADISON, UNION. Population (2000), 630,730.

ZIP Codes: 43016–17, 43026, 43029, 43036, 43040–41, 43045, 43060, 43064–65, 43067, 43077, 43085, 43119, 43123, 43125, 43137, 43140, 43143, 43146, 43151, 43153, 43162, 43201–06, 43207, 43210–12, 43214–15, 43220–21, 43223–24, 43228–29, 43235, 43344, 43358

* * *

SIXTEENTH DISTRICT

JIM RENACCI, Republican, of Wadsworth, OH; born in Monongahela, PA, December 3, 1958; education: B.S., Indiana University of Pennsylvania, 1980; professional: certified public accountant (CPA); owner, nursing home facility; executive, professional arena football team; Wadsworth Board of Zoning Appeals, 1994–95; president, Wadsworth City Council, 1999–2003; mayor of Wadsworth, 2004–2008; business management consultant; religion: Roman Catholic; married: Tina Renacci; 3 children; caucuses: Congressional Coal; Congressional Steel; Northeast-Midwest Coalition; Congressional CPA; General Aviation; Hydrogen and Fuel Cell; committees: Financial Services; elected to the 112th Congress on November 2, 2010.

Office Listings

http://www.renacci.house.gov

130 Cannon House Office Building, Washington, DC 20515 .... (202) 225–3876
Chief of Staff.—James Slepian. FAX: 225–3059
Press Secretary.—Karin Davenport.
DC Scheduler.—Michelle Runk.
Legislative Director.—Brian Werstler.
4150 Belden Village Street, Suite 408, Canton, OH 44718 .... (330) 489–4414
Constituent Service Director.—Heidi Matthews. FAX: 493–9265

Counties: ASHLAND (part), MEDINA (part), STARK, WAYNE. Population (2000), 630,730.

ZIP Codes: 44090, 44201, 44203, 44214–17, 44230, 44233, 44235, 44251, 44253–54, 44256, 44258, 44260, 44270, 44273–76, 44280–82, 44287, 44321, 44333, 44601, 44606, 44608, 44611–14, 44618, 44624, 44626–27, 44630, 44632, 44634, 44636, 44638, 44640–41, 44643, 44645–48, 44650, 44652, 44657, 44659, 44662, 44666–67, 44669–70, 44676–77, 44680, 44685, 44688–89, 44691, 44701–12, 44714, 44718, 44720–21, 44730, 44735, 44750, 44760, 44767, 44799, 44805, 44822, 44838, 44840, 44842–43, 44864, 44866, 44878, 44880, 44903

* * *

SEVENTEENTH DISTRICT

TIM RYAN, Democrat, of Niles, OH; born in Niles, July 16, 1973; education: B.S., Bowling Green University, 1995; J.D., University of New Hampshire School of Law (formerly Franklin Pierce Law Center), 2000; professional: legislative aide, Washington, DC; committees: Armed Services; Budget; elected to the 108th Congress on November 5, 2002; reelected to each succeeding Congress.

Office Listings

http://timryan.house.gov

1421 Longworth House Office Building, Washington, DC 20515 .... (202) 225–5261
Chief of Staff.—Ron Grimes. FAX: 225–3719
Scheduler.—Erin Isenberg.
Legislative Director.—Ryan Keating.
197 West Market Street, Warren, OH 44481 .... (330) 373–0074
241 Federal Plaza West, Youngstown, OH 44503 .... (330) 740–0193

Counties: MAHONING (part), PORTAGE (part), SUMMIT (part), TRUMBULL (part). Population (2000), 630,730.

ZIP Codes: 44201, 44211, 44221, 44223–24, 44231–32, 44236, 44240–43, 44250, 44255, 44260, 44265–66, 44272, 44278, 44285, 44288, 44302–06, 44308, 44310–13, 44315–16, 44319, 44402–06, 44410–12, 44417–18, 44420, 44424–25, 44429–30, 44436–38, 44440, 44444, 44446, 44449–50, 44453, 44470–71, 44473, 44481–86, 44488, 44491, 44501–07, 44509–12, 44514–15, 44555, 44599, 44632, 44685, 44720

* * *

EIGHTEENTH DISTRICT

ROBERT B. GIBBS, Republican, of Lakeville, OH; born in Peru, IN, June 14, 1954; education: graduated from Bay Village Senior High School, Bay Village, OH; A.A.S., Ohio State University Agricultural Technical Institute, Wooster, OH, 1974; professional: technician; farmer; business owner; president, Ohio Farm Bureau Federation; member of the Ohio State House of Representatives, 2003–09; member of the Ohio State Senate, 2009–10; married: Jody Gibbs; children: Adam, Amy, and Andrew; committees: Agriculture; Transportation and Infrastructure; elected to the 112th Congress on November 2, 2010.

Office Listings

http://www.gibbs.house.gov

329 Cannon House Office Building, Washington, DC 20515 .... (202) 225–6265
Chief of Staff.—Ryan Stenger. FAX: 225–3394
Scheduler.—Meghan Keivel.
Senior Policy Advisor.—Emily Pettigrew.
Legislative Aides: Joe Price, Pat Tully.
Communications Director.—Catherine Gatewood.
1166 Military Road, Suite B, Zanesville, OH 43701 .... (740) 452–2279
District Director.—Susan Brinker. FAX: 452–2557

Counties: ATHENS (part), BELMONT (PART), CARROLL, COSHOCTON, GUERNSEY, HARRISON, HOCKING, HOLMES, JACKSON, KNOX, LICKING (part), MORGAN, MUSKINGUM, ROSS (part), TUSCARAWAS, VINTON. Population (2000), 630,730.

ZIP Codes: 43005–06, 43008, 43011, 43014, 43019, 43022–23, 43025, 43028, 43030, 43037, 43048, 43050, 43055–56, 43058, 43071, 43076, 43080, 43093, 43098, 43101–02, 43107, 43111, 43127, 43130, 43135, 43138, 43144, 43149, 43152, 43155, 43158, 43160, 43701–02, 43718, 43720–25, 43727–28, 43730–36, 43738–40, 43746, 43749–50, 43755–56, 43758, 43760, 43762, 43766–68, 43771–73, 43777–78, 43780, 43787, 43791, 43802–05, 43811–12, 43821–22, 43824, 43828, 43830, 43832, 43836–37, 43840, 43842–45, 43901, 43903, 43906–08, 43910, 43927–28, 43933, 43945, 43950, 43972–74, 43976–77, 43981, 43983–84, 43986, 43988, 44427, 44607–08, 44610–12, 44615, 44617, 44620–22, 44624–29, 44631, 44633, 44637–39, 44643–44, 44651, 44653–54, 44656–57, 44660–61, 44663, 44671, 44675–76, 44678–83, 44687–90, 44693, 44695, 44697, 44699, 44730, 44813, 44822, 44842, 45123, 45601, 45612–13, 45617, 45621–22, 45628, 45633–34, 45640, 45644, 45647, 45651, 45653–54, 45656, 45672–73, 45681–82, 45685, 45690, 45692, 45695, 45698, 45701, 45710–11, 45715–16, 45719, 45732, 45740–41, 45761, 45764, 45766, 45780, 45782, 45786

OKLAHOMA

(Population 2010, 3,751,351)

SENATORS

JAMES M. INHOFE, Republican, of Tulsa, OK; born in Des Moines, IA, November 17, 1934; education: graduated Central High School, Tulsa, OK, 1953; B.A., University of Tulsa, OK, 1959; military service: served in the U.S. Army, private first class, 1957–58; professional: businessman; active pilot; president, Quaker Life Insurance Company; Oklahoma House of Representatives, 1967–69; Oklahoma State Senate, 1969–77; Mayor of Tulsa, OK, 1978–84; religion: member, First Presbyterian Church of Tulsa; married: Kay Kirkpatrick; children: Jim, Perry, Molly, and Katy; twelve grandchildren; committees: ranking member, Environment and Public Works; Armed Services; Foreign Relations; elected to the 100th Congress on November 4, 1986; reelected to each succeeding Congress; elected to the U.S. Senate on November 8, 1994, finishing the unexpired term of Senator David Boren; reelected to each succeeding Senate term.

Office Listings

http://inhofe.senate.gov

205 Russell Senate Office Building, Washington, DC 20510 .... (202) 224–4721
Chief of Staff.—Ryan Jackson. FAX: 228–0380
Legislative Director.—Clark Peterson.
Press Secretary.—Jared Young.
Scheduler.—Wendi Price.
1924 South Utica, Suite 530, Tulsa, OK 74104–6511 .... (918) 748–5111
1900 Northwest Expressway, Suite 1210, Oklahoma City, OK 73118 .... (405) 608–4381
302 North Independence, Suite 104, Enid, OK 73701 .... (580) 234–5105
215 East Choctaw, Suite 106, McAlester, OK 74501 .... (918) 426–0933

* * *

TOM COBURN, Republican, of Muskogee, OK; born in Casper, WY, March 14, 1948; education: Central High School, Muskogee, OK, 1966; B.S., Oklahoma State University, 1970; Oklahoma University Medical School, 1983; professional: manufacturing manager, Coburn Ophthalmic Division, Coburn Optical Industries, 1970–78; family physician, 1983–present; member, American Medical Association, Oklahoma State Medical Association, East Central County Medical Society, American Academy of Family Practice; religion: First Baptist Church, ordained deacon; member, Promise Keepers; public service: U.S. House of Representatives, 1995–2001; married: Carolyn Denton Coburn, 1968; children: Callie, Katie, and Sarah; committees: Finance; Homeland Security and Government Affairs; Judiciary; elected to the U.S. Senate on November 2, 2004; reelected to the U.S. Senate on November 2, 2010.

Office Listings

http://coburn.senate.gov

172 Russell Hart Senate Office Building, Washington, DC 20510 .... (202) 224–5754
Chief of Staff.—Michael Schwartz. FAX: 224–6008
Legislative Director.—Roland Foster.
Communications Director.—John Hart.
Scheduler.—Courtney Shadegg.
1800 South Baltimore, Suite 800, Tulsa, OK 74119 .... (918) 581–7651
100 North Broadway, Suite 1820, Oklahoma City, OK 73102 .... (405) 231–4941

REPRESENTATIVES

FIRST DISTRICT

JOHN SULLIVAN, Republican, of Tulsa, OK; born in Tulsa, January 1, 1965; education: B.B.A., Northeastern State University, 1992; professional: fuel sales, Love's Country Stores; Real Estate, McGraw, Davison, Stewart; public service: Oklahoma House of Representatives, 1995–2002; organizations: member, St. Mary's Church; member, National Rifle Association; member, Tulsa County Republican Men's Club; U.S. House of Representatives Assistant Majority Whip; family: married to Judy; children: Thomas, Meredith, Sydney, Daniel; committees: Energy and Commerce; elected to the 107th Congress, by special election, on January 8, 2002; reelected to each succeeding Congress.

Office Listings

http://sullivan.house.gov

434 Cannon House Office Building, Washington, DC 20510 .... (202) 225–2211
Chief of Staff.—Elizabeth Bartheld. FAX: 225–9187
Executive Assistant.—John Senger.
5727 South Lewis, Suite 520, Tulsa, OK 74105 .... (918) 749–0014
District Director.—Richard Hedgecock.

Counties: CREEK (part), ROGERS (part), TULSA, WAGONER, WASHINGTON. Population (2000), 690,131.

ZIP Codes: 74003–06, 74008, 74011–14, 74021–22, 74029, 74033, 74037, 74039, 74041, 74043, 74047–48, 74050–51, 74053, 74055, 74061, 74063, 74066, 74070, 74073, 74080, 74082–83, 74101–08, 74110, 74112, 74114–17, 74119–21, 74126–30, 74132–37, 74141, 74145–50, 74152–53, 74155–59, 74169–72, 74182–84, 74186–87, 74189, 74192–94, 74337, 74352, 74403, 74429, 74434, 74436, 74446, 74454, 74458, 74467, 74477

* * *

SECOND DISTRICT

DAN BOREN, Democrat, of Muskogee, OK; born in Shawnee, OK, August 2, 1973; education: B.S., Texas Christian University, Fort Worth, TX, 1997; M.B.A., University of Oklahoma, 2001; professional: president, Seminole State College Educational Foundation; vice-president, Robbins Energy Corporation; loan processor, Banc First Corporation; staff for United States Representative Wesley Watkins; education administrator; bank teller; aide, Oklahoma Corporation Commission; member of the Oklahoma State House of Representatives, 2002–04; organizations: Big Brothers Big Sisters Board; The Jasmine Moran Children's Museum Board; KIPP Foundation Board Member; married: Andrea; children: Janna; committees: Natural Resources; Permanent Select Committee on Intelligence; elected to the 109th Congress on November 2, 2004; reelected to each succeeding Congress.

Office Listings

http://www.house.gov/boren

2447 Rayburn House Office Building, Washington, DC 20515 .... (202) 225–2701
Chief of Staff.—Jason Buckner. FAX: 225–3038
Legislative Director.—Jaryd Bern.
Press Secretary.—Cole Perryman.
Scheduler.—Erica Rixen.
431 West Broadway, Muskogee, OK 74401 .... (918) 687–2533
District Coordinator.—Ben Robinson.
309 West 1st Street, Claremore, OK 74017 .... (918) 341–9336
25 East Carl Albert Parkway, Suite B, McAlester, OK 74501 .... (918) 423–5951
112 North 12th Avenue, Durant, OK 74701 .... (580) 931–0333

Counties: ADAIR, ATOKA, BRYAN, CANADIAN, CHEROKEE, CHOCTAW, COAL, CRAIG, CREEK, DELAWARE, HASKELL, HUGHES, JOHNSTON, LATIMER, LEFLORE, MAYES, MCCURTAIN, MCINTOSH, MUSKOGEE, NOWATA, OKFUSKEE, OTTAWA, PAWNEE, PITTSBURGH, PUSHMATAHA, ROGERS, SEMINOLE, SEQUOYAH. Population (2000), 690,130.

ZIP Codes: 73014, 73036, 73064, 73078, 73085, 73090, 73447, 73449–50, 73455, 73460–62, 74010, 74015–16, 74018, 74020, 74027–28, 74030–31, 74034, 74036, 74038–39, 74041–42, 74044–45, 74047–49, 74052–53, 74058, 74067–68, 74071–72, 74080–81, 74083, 74085, 74101, 74103, 74301, 74330–33, 74335, 74337–40, 74343–44, 74346–47, 74349–50, 74352, 74355, 74358–63, 74365–67, 74369–70, 74401–02, 74421–23, 74425–26, 74428, 74430–32, 74434–38, 74441–42, 74445, 74447, 74450, 74455, 74459, 74461–64, 74468–70, 74472, 74502, 74521–23, 74525, 74530–31, 74533–34, 74536, 74538, 74546–47, 74552–54, 74556, 74560–63, 74565, 74569–72, 74576, 74578, 74650, 74701, 74720, 74723, 74726–30, 74733, 74735–36, 74740–41, 74743, 74745, 74747–48, 74750, 74756, 74759, 74764, 74766, 74829–30, 74833, 74837, 74839, 74845, 74848–50, 74856, 74859–60, 74867–68, 74880, 74883–85, 74901–02, 74930, 74932, 74935–37, 74940–42, 74944–46, 74948, 74951, 74953–56, 74959–60, 74962, 74964–66

* * *

THIRD DISTRICT

FRANK D. LUCAS, Republican, of Cheyenne, OK; born in Cheyenne, January 6, 1960; education: B.S., agricultural economics, Oklahoma State University, 1982; professional: rancher and farmer; served in Oklahoma State House of Representatives, 1989–94; secretary, Oklahoma House Republican Caucus, 1991–94; member: Oklahoma Farm Bureau, Oklahoma Cattlemen's Association, and Oklahoma Shorthorn Association; married: Lynda Bradshaw Lucas; children: Jessica, Ashlea, and Grant; committees: chair, Agriculture; Financial Services; Science, Space, and Technology; elected to the 103rd Congress, by special election, in May 1994; reelected to each succeeding Congress.

Office Listings

http://www.house.gov/lucas

2311 Rayburn House Office Building, Washington, DC 20515 .... (202) 225–5565
Legislative Director.—Courtney Box. FAX: 225–8698
Communications Director.—Laramie Adams.
Scheduler / Office Manager.—Molly Johnson.
Legislative Assistants: Chelsea Barnett, Larry Calhoun, Jason Grassie.
10952 Northwest Expressway, Suite B, Yukon, OK 73099 .... (405) 373–1958
Chief of Staff.—Stacey Glasscock.
720 South Husband, Suite 7, Stillwater, OK 74075 .... (405) 624–6407
Field Representative.—Brianna Jett.
2728 Williams Avenue, Suite F, Woodward, OK 73801 .... (580) 256–5752
Field Representative.—Garrett King.

Counties: ALFALFA, BEAVER, BECKHAM, BLAINE, CADDO, CANADIAN (part), CIMARRON, CREEK (part), CUSTER, DEWEY, ELLIS, GARFIELD, GRANT, GREER, HARMON, HARPER, JACKSON, KINGFISHER, KAY, KIOWA, LINCOLN, LOGAN, MAJOR, NOBLE, OSAGE, PAWNEE, PAYNE, ROGER MILLS, TEXAS, WASHITA, WOODS, AND WOODWARD. CITIES: Altus, Clinton, El Reno, Elk City, Enid, Guthrie, Guymon, Oklahoma City, Perry, Ponce City, Sapulpa, Stillwater, Tulsa, Weatherford, Woodward and Yukon. Population (2000), 690,131.

ZIP Codes: 73001, 73003, 73005–07, 73009, 73014–17, 73021–22, 73024, 73027–29, 73033–34, 73036, 73038, 73040–45, 73047–48, 73050, 73053–54, 73056, 73058–59, 73061–64, 73073, 73077–79, 73085, 73090, 73092, 73094, 73096–97, 73099, 73127, 73437, 73501, 73521–23, 73526, 73532, 73537, 73539, 73544, 73547, 73549–50, 73554, 73556, 73559–60, 73564, 73566, 73571, 73601, 73620, 73622, 73624–28, 73632, 73638–39, 73641–42, 73644–48, 73650–51, 73654–55, 73658–64, 73666–69, 73673, 73701–03, 73705–06, 73716–20, 73722, 73724, 73726–31, 73733–39, 73741–44, 73746–47, 73749–50, 73753–64, 73766, 73768, 73770–73, 73801–02, 73832, 73834–35, 73838, 73840–44, 73847–48, 73851–53, 73855, 73857–60, 73901, 73931–33, 73937–39, 73942, 73944–47, 73949–51, 74001–03, 74010, 74020, 74022–23, 74026, 74028, 74030, 74032, 74034–35, 74038–39, 74044–47, 74051–52, 74054, 74056, 74058–60, 74062–63, 74066–68, 74070–71, 74073–79, 74081, 74084–85, 74106, 74126–27, 74131–32, 74601–02, 74604, 74630–33, 74636–37, 74640–41, 74643–44, 74646–47, 74650–53, 74824, 74832, 74834, 74851, 74855, 74859, 74864, 74869, 74875, 74881

* * *

FOURTH DISTRICT

TOM COLE, Republican, of Moore, OK; born in Shreveport, LA, April 28, 1949; education: B.A., Grinnell College, 1971; M.A. Yale University, 1974; Ph.D., University of Oklahoma, 1984; Watson Fellow, 1971–72; and a Fulbright Fellow, 1977–78; professional: former college professor of history and politics; President, Cole Hargrave Snodgrass & Associates (political consulting firm); public service: Oklahoma State Senate, 1988–91; Oklahoma Secretary of State, 1995–99; has served as Chairman, and Executive Director, of the Oklahoma Republican Party; former Chairman of the National Republican Congressional Committee; and Chief of Staff of the Republican National Committee; family: married to Ellen; one child: Mason; religion: United Methodist; committees: Appropriations; Budget; elected to the 108th Congress on November 5, 2002; reelected to each succeeding Congress.

Office Listings

http://www.house.gov/cole

2458 Rayburn House Office Building, Washington, DC 20515 .... (202) 225–6165
Chief of Staff.—Sean Murphy. FAX: 225–3512
Deputy Chief of Staff / Legislative Director.—Chris Caron.
Press Secretary.—Jocelyn Rogers.
2424 Springer Drive, Suite 201, Norman, OK 73069 .... (580) 436–5375
711 Southwest, D Avenue, Suite 201, Lawton, OK 73501 .... (580) 357–2131
Sugg Clinic Office Building, 100 East 13th Street, Suite 213, Ada, OK 74820 .... (405) 329–6500

Counties: CANADIAN (part), CARTER, CLEVELAND, COMANCHE, COTTON, GARVIN, GRADY, JEFFERSON, LOVE, MARSHALL, MCCLAIN, MURRAY, OKLAHOMA (part), PONTOTOC, STEPHENS, TILLMAN. Population (2000), 690,131.

ZIP Codes: 73002, 73004, 73006, 73010–11, 73017–20, 73023, 73026, 73030–32, 73036, 73051–52, 73055, 73057, 73059, 73064–65, 73067–72, 73074–75, 73079–80, 73082, 73086, 73089, 73092–93, 73095, 73098–99, 73110, 73115, 73127–30, 73135, 73139–40, 73145, 73149–50, 73153, 73159–60, 73165, 73169–70, 73173, 73179, 73189, 73401–03, 73425, 73430, 73433–44, 73446, 73448, 73453, 73456, 73458–59, 73463, 73476, 73481, 73487–88, 73491, 73501–03, 73505–07, 73520, 73527–31, 73533–34, 73536, 73538, 73540–43, 73546, 73548, 73551–53, 73555, 73557, 73559, 73561–62, 73564–70, 73572–73, 74820–21, 74825, 74831, 74842–44, 74851, 74857, 74865, 74871–72

* * *

FIFTH DISTRICT

JAMES LANKFORD, Republican, of Oklahoma City, OK; professional: director of the Falls Creek Youth Camp, 1996–2009; wife: Cindy; children: Hannah (14), Jordan (11); committees:

Budget; Transportation and Infrastructure; Oversight and Government Reform; elected to the 112th Congress on November 2, 2010.

Office Listings

http://www.lankford.house.gov

509 Cannon House Office Building, Washington, DC 20515 .... (202) 225–2132
Chief of Staff.—Randy Swanson. FAX: 226–1463
Department Chief of Staff / Legislative Director.—Michelle Altman.
Scheduler.—Katie Weiss.
Communications Director.—William Allison.
District Director.—Mona Taylor.
1015 North Broadway Avenue, Suite 310, Oklahoma City, OK 73102 .... (405) 234–9900
20 East 9th Street, Suite 100, Shawnee, OK 74801 .... (405) 273–1733

Counties: OKLAHOMA (part), POTTAWATOMIE, and SEMINOLE. CITIES: Arcadia, Asher, Aydelotte, Bethany, Bethel Acres, Bowlegs, Brooksville, Choctaw, Cromwell, Del City, Earlsboro, Edmond, Forrest Park, Harrah, Johnson, Jones, Konawa, Lake Aluma, Lima, Luther, Macomb, Maud, McLoud, Midwest City, Newalla, Nichols Hills, Nicoma Park, Oklahoma City, Pink, Sasakwa, Seminole, Shawnee, Smith Village, Spencer, St. Louis, Tecumesh, The Village, Tribbey, Valley Brook, Wanette, Warr Acres, Wewoka, and Woodlawn Park. Population (2000), 690,131.

ZIP Codes: 73003, 73007–08, 73013, 73020, 73034, 73045, 73049, 73054, 73066, 73078, 73083–84, 73097, 73099, 73101–32, 73134–37, 73139, 73141–49, 73151–52, 73154–57, 73159–60, 73162, 73164, 73169, 73172–73, 73178–79, 73184–85, 73190, 73194–96, 73198, 74587, 74801–02, 74804, 74818, 74826, 74830, 74837, 74840, 74849, 74851–52, 74854–55, 74857, 74859, 74866–68, 74873, 74878, 74884

OREGON

(Population 2010, 3,831,074)

SENATORS

RON WYDEN, Democrat, of Portland, OR; born in Wichita, KS, May 3, 1949; education: graduated from Palo Alto High School, 1967; B.A. in political science, with distinction, Stanford University, 1971; J.D., University of Oregon Law School, 1974; professional: attorney; member, American Bar Association; former director, Oregon Legal Services for the Elderly; former public member, Oregon State Board of Examiners of Nursing Home Administrators; co-founder and codirector, Oregon Gray Panthers, 1974–80; married: Nancy Bass Wyden; children: Adam David, Lilly Anne, Ava Rose, and William Peter; committees: Budget; Energy and Natural Resources; Finance; Special Committee on Aging; Select Committee on Intelligence; elected to the 97th Congress, November 4, 1980; reelected to each succeeding Congress; elected to the U.S. Senate on February 6, 1996, to fill the unexpired term of Senator Bob Packwood; reelected to each succeeding Senate term.

Office Listings

http://wyden.senate.gov

223 Dirksen Senate Office Building, Washington, DC 20510 .... (202) 224–5244
Chief of Staff.—Jeff Michels. FAX: 228–2717
Legislative Director.—Joshua Sheinkman.
Deputy Chief of Staff and Communications Director.—Jennifer Hoelzer.
Schedulers: Sallie Derr, Wayne Binkley.
911 Northeast 11th Avenue, Suite 630, Portland, OR 97232 .... (503) 326–7525
405 East Eighth Avenue, Suite 2020, Eugene, OR 97401 .... (541) 431–0229
The Federal Courthouse, 310 West Sixth Street, Room 118, Medford, OR 97501 ... (541) 858–5122
The Jamison Building, 131 Northwest Hawthorne Avenue, Suite 107, Bend, OR 97701 .... (541) 330–9142
SAC Annex Building, 105 Fir Street, Suite 201, LaGrande, OR 97850 .... (541) 962–7691
707 Thirteenth Street, SE., Suite 285, Salem, OR 97310 .... (503) 589–4555

* * *

JEFF MERKLEY, Democrat, of East Multnomah County, OR; born in Myrtle Creek, OR; October 24, 1956; education: graduated from David Douglas High School, B.A., international relations, Stanford University, 1979; M.P.P., Woodrow Wilson School, Princeton University, 1982; professional: Presidential Fellow at the Office of the Secretary of Defense, 1982–85; Policy Analyst at the Congressional Budget Office, 1985–89; Executive Director of Portland Habitat for Humanity, 1991–94; Director of Housing Development at Human Solutions, 1995–96; President of World Affairs Council of Oregon, 1996–2003; elected to Oregon House of Representatives, 1999; Democratic Leader of the Oregon House of Representatives, 2003; elected Speaker of the Oregon House of Representatives, 2007; married: Mary Sorteberg; children: Brynne and Jonathan; committees: Banking, Housing, and Urban Affairs; Budget; Environment and Public Works; Health, Education, Labor, and Pensions; elected to U.S. Senate on November 4, 2008.

Office Listings

http://merkley.senate.gov

313 Hart Senate Office Building, Washington, DC 20510 .... (202) 224–3753
Chief of Staff.—Michael Zamore. FAX: 228–3997
Legislative Director.—Jeremiah Baumann.
Director of Administration.—Jennifer Piorkowski.
Communications Director.—Julie Edwards.
1400 One World Trade Center, 121 Southwest Salmon, Portland, OR 97204 .... (503) 326–3386
Jamison Building, 131 Northwest Hawthorne, Suite 208, Bend, OR 97701 .... (541) 318–1298
Wayne Morse Federal Courthouse, 405 East 8th, Suite 2010, Eugene, OR 97401 ... (541) 465–6750
10 South Bartlett Street, Suite 201, Medford, OR 97501 .... (541) 608–9102
495 State Street, Suite 330, Salem, OR 97301 .... (503) 362–8102
310 Southeast Second Street, Suite 105, Pendleton, OR 97801 .... (541) 278–1129

REPRESENTATIVES

FIRST DISTRICT

VACANT

Counties: CLATSOP, COLUMBIA, MULTNOMAH (part), WASHINGTON, YAMHILL. Population (2000), 684,277.

ZIP Codes: 97005–08, 97016, 97018, 97035, 97048, 97051, 97053–54, 97056, 97062, 97064, 97070, 97075–78, 97101–03, 97106, 97109–11, 97113–17, 97119, 97121, 97123–25, 97127–28, 97132–33, 97138, 97140, 97144–46, 97148, 97201, 97204–05, 97207–10, 97219, 97221, 97223–25, 97228–29, 97231, 97239–40, 97251, 97253–55, 97258, 97272, 97280–81, 97291, 97296, 97298, 97378, 97396, 97498

* * *

SECOND DISTRICT

GREG WALDEN, Republican, of Hood River, OR; born in The Dalles, OR, January 10, 1957; education: B.S., journalism, University of Oregon, 1981; member: Associated Oregon Industries; Oregon Health Sciences Foundation; Hood River Rotary Club; Hood River Elk's Club; National Federation of Independent Business; Hood River Chamber of Commerce; Hood River Memorial Hospital; Columbia Bancorp; Oregon State House of Representatives, 1989–95, and majority leader, 1991–93; assistant majority leader, Oregon State Senate, 1995–97; awards: Oregon Jaycees Outstanding Young Oregonian, 1991; National Republican Legislators Association Legislator of the Year, 1993; married: Mylene Walden; one child: Anthony David Walden; committees: Energy and Commerce; elected to the 106th Congress on November 3, 1998; reelected to each succeeding Congress.

Office Listings

http://www.walden.house.gov

2182 Rayburn House Office Building, Washington, DC 20515	(202) 225–6730
Chief of Staff.—Brian MacDonald.	FAX: 225–5774
Senior Policy Advisor.—Ray Baum.	
Executive Assistant.—Wade Foster.	
Press Secretary.—Andrew Whelan.	
14 North Central Avenue, Suite 112, Medford, OR 97504	(541) 776–4646
District Director.—Rob Patridge.	(800) 533–3303
1211 Washington Avenue, LaGrande, OR 97850	(541) 624–2400
	FAX: 624–2402
1051 Northwest Bond Street, Suite 400, Bend, OR 97701	(541) 389–4408
	FAX: 389–4452

Counties: BAKER, CROOK, DESCHUTES, GILLIAM, GRANT, HARNEY, HOOD RIVER, JACKSON, JEFFERSON, JOSEPHINE (part), KLAMATH, LAKE, MALHEUR, MORROW, SHERMAN, UMATILLA, UNION, WALLOWA, WASCO, WHEELER. Population (2000), 684,280.

ZIP Codes: 97001, 97014, 97021, 97029, 97031, 97033, 97037, 97039–41, 97044, 97050, 97057–58, 97063, 97065, 97116, 97425, 97501–04, 97520, 97522, 97524–28, 97530, 97533, 97535–37, 97539–41, 97544, 97601–04, 97620–27, 97630, 97632–41, 97701–02, 97707–12, 97720–22, 97730–39, 97741, 97750–54, 97756, 97758–61, 97801, 97810, 97812–14, 97817–20, 97823–28, 97830, 97833–46, 97848, 97850, 97856–57, 97859, 97861–62, 97864–65, 97867–70, 97873–77, 97880, 97882–86, 97901–11, 97913–14, 97917–18, 97920

* * *

THIRD DISTRICT

EARL BLUMENAUER, Democrat, of Portland, OR; born in Portland, August 16, 1948; education: graduated from Centennial High School; B.A., Lewis and Clark College; J.D., Northwestern School of Law; professional: assistant to the president, Portland State University; served in Oregon State Legislature 1973–78; chaired Revenue and School Finance Committee; Multnomah County Commissioner, 1978–85; Portland City Commissioner 1986–96; served on Governor's Commission on Higher Education; National League of Cities Transportation Committee; National Civic League Board of Directors; Oregon Environmental Council; Oregon Public Broadcasting; married: Margaret Kirkpatrick; children: Jon and Anne; committees: Budget; Ways and Means; elected to the U.S. House of Representatives on May 21, 1996, to fill the vacancy created by Representative Ron Wyden's election to the U.S. Senate; reelected to each succeeding Congress.

Office Listings

http://blumenauer.house.gov

1502 Longworth House Office Building, Washington, DC 20515 .... (202) 225–4811
Deputy Chief of Staff.—James Koski. FAX: 225–8941
Scheduler.—Heidi Black.
Communications Director.—Derek Schlickeisen.
Legislative Director.—Janine Benner.
729 Northeast Oregon Street, Suite 115, Portland, OR 97232 .... (503) 231–2300
District Director.—Julia Pomeroy.

Counties: MULTNOMAH (part), CLAKAMUS (part). Population (2000), 684,279.

ZIP Codes: 97004, 97009, 97011, 97014–15, 97017, 97019, 97022–24, 97028, 97030, 97035, 97045, 97049, 97055, 97060, 97067, 97080, 97124, 97133, 97202–03, 97206, 97210–18, 97220, 97222, 97227, 97229–33, 97236, 97238, 97242, 97256, 97266–67, 97269, 97282–83, 97286, 97290, 97292–94, 97299

* * *

FOURTH DISTRICT

PETER A. DEFAZIO, Democrat, of Springfield, OR; born in Needham, MA, May 27, 1947; B.A., Tufts University, 1969; M.S., University of Oregon, 1977; professional: aide to Representative Jim Weaver, 1977–82; commissioner, Lane County, 1983–86; married: Myrnie Daut; committees: Natural Resources; Transportation and Infrastructure; elected to the 100th Congress, November 4, 1986; reelected to each succeeding Congress.

Office Listings

http://www.house.gov/defazio

2134 Rayburn House Office Building, Washington, DC 20515 .... (202) 225–6416
Chief of Staff.—Penny Dodge. FAX: 225–0032
Legislative Director.—Auke Mahar-Piersma.
Scheduler.—Jamie Harrell.
405 East Eighth Avenue, Suite 2030, Eugene, OR 97401 .... (541) 465–6732
District Director.—Karmen Fore.
125 Central Avenue, Room 350, Coos Bay, OR 97420 .... (541) 269–2609
612 Southeast Jackson Street, Room 9, Roseburg, OR 97470 .... (541) 440–3523

Counties: BENTON (part), COOS, CURRY, DOUGLAS, JOSEPHINE (part), LANE, LINN. CITIES: Eugene, Roseburg, and Coos Bay. Population (2000), 684,280.

ZIP Codes: 97321–22, 97324, 97326–27, 97329–30, 97333, 97335–36, 97345–46, 97348, 97350, 97352, 97355, 97358, 97360–61, 97370, 97374, 97377, 97383, 97386, 97389, 97401–17, 97419–20, 97423–24, 97426–32, 97434–44, 97446–59, 97461–67, 97469–70, 97472–73, 97476–82, 97484, 97486–99, 97523, 97526–27, 97530–34, 97537–38, 97543–44

* * *

FIFTH DISTRICT

KURT SCHRADER, Democrat, of Canby, OR; born in Bridgeport, CT, October 19, 1951; education; B.A., Cornell University, 1973, D.V.M., University, IL, 1977; professional: small business owner, veterinarian; past member; Oregon State Senate, Oregon House of Representatives, Canby Planning Commission; religion: Episcopalian; married: Martha Schrader; children: Clare, Maren, Steven, Travis, and R.J.; committees; Agriculture; Small Business; elected to the 111th Congress on November 4, 2008, reelected to the 112th Congress.

Office Listings

http://schrader.house.gov

314 Cannon House Office Building, Washington, DC 20515 .... (202) 225–5711
Chief of Staff.—Paul Gage. FAX: 225–5699
Legislative Director.—Chris Huckleberry.
Executive Assistant / Scheduler.—Anne Marie Feeney.
494 State Street, Suite 210, Salem, OR 97301 .... (503) 588–9100
621 High Street, Oregon City, OR 97045 .... (503) 557–1324

District Director.—Suzanne Kunse

Counties: BENTON (part); CLACKAMAS (part); LINCOLN; MARION; MULTNOMAH (part); POLK; TILLAMOOK. CITIES: Corvallis, Portland, Salem, and Tillamook. Population (2000), 684,333.

ZIP Codes: 97002, 97004, 97010, 97013, 97015, 97017, 97020, 97023, 97026–27, 97032, 97034–36, 97038, 97042, 97045, 97062, 97068, 97070–71, 97101, 97107–08, 97112, 97118, 97122, 97130–31, 97134–37, 97140–41, 97143, 97147, 97149, 97201, 97219, 97222, 97239, 97267–68, 97301–14, 97321, 97324–25, 97330–31, 97333, 97338–39, 97341–44, 97346–47, 97350–52, 97357–62, 97364–73, 97375–76, 97380–81, 97383–85, 97388, 97390–92, 97394, 97396, 97498

PENNSYLVANIA

(Population 2010, 12,702,379)

SENATORS

ROBERT P. CASEY, JR., Democrat, of Scranton, PA; born in Scranton, April 13, 1960; education: A.B., English, College of the Holy Cross, 1982; J.D., Catholic University of America, 1988; professional: lawyer; Pennsylvania State Auditor General, 1997–2005; Pennsylvania State Treasurer, 2005–07; married: Terese; four daughters: Elyse, Caroline, Julia, and Marena; committees: chair, Joint Economic Committee; Agriculture, Nutrition, and Forestry; Health, Education, Labor, and Pension; Foreign Relations; Special Committee on Aging; elected to the U.S. Senate on November 7, 2006.

Office Listings

http://casey.senate.gov

393 Russell Senate Office Building, Washington, DC 20510 .... (202) 224–6324
(866) 802–2833
Chief of Staff.—James W. Brown. FAX: 228–0604
Deputy Chief of Staff.—Larry Smar.
Legislative Director.—Richard D. Spiegelman.
Communications Director.—April Mellody.
Administrative Director.—Kristen Gentile.
22 South Third Street, Suite 6A, Harrisburg, PA 17101 .... (717) 231–7540
(866) 461–9159
FAX: 231–7542
2000 Market Street, Suite 1870, Philadelphia, PA 19103 .... (215) 405–9660
FAX: 405–9669
Regional Enterprise Tower, 425 Sixth Avenue, Suite 2490, Pittsburgh, PA 15219 .. (412) 803–7370
FAX: 803–7379
409 Lackawanna Avenue, Suite 301, Scranton, PA 18503 .... (570) 941–0930
FAX: 941–0937
817 East Bishop Street, Suite C, Bellefonte, PA 16823 .... (814) 357–0314
FAX: 375–0318
17 South Park Row, Suite B–150, Erie, PA 16501 .... (814) 874–5080
FAX: 874–5084
840 Hamilton Street, Suite 301, Allentown, PA 18101 .... (610) 782–9470
FAX: 782–9474

* * *

PAT TOOMEY, Republican, of Allentown, PA; born in East Providence, RI, November 17, 1961; education: graduated from La Salle Academy as valedictorian in 1980; B.A., political science, *cum laude,* Harvard University, Cambridge, MA, 1984; professional: worked for Chemical Bank and Morgan Grenfell in New York City before spending one year as a financial consultant in Hong Kong, 1990; founded several restaurants in Allentown, PA, with his two brothers, Steve and Michael Toomey, 1990–97; married: Kris Duncan, 1997; children: Bridget, Patrick, and Duncan; member of the Allentown Government Study Commission, 1994; elected to U.S. House of Representatives in 1998, winning two reelections, 2000–02; president, Club for Growth, 2005; co-chairman of the Board of Directors of Team Capital Bank, 2005–09; committees: Banking, Housing, and Urban Affairs; Budget; Commerce, Science, and Transportation, Joint Economic Committee; elected to the U.S. Senate on November 2, 2010.

Office Listings

http://toomey.senate.gov

502 Hart Senate Office Building, Washington, DC 20510 .... (202) 224–4254
Chief of Staff.—Christopher Gahan. FAX: 228–0284
Legislative Director.—James Wallner.
Director of Operations.—Laurel Edmondson.
1628 John F. Kennedy Boulevard, 8 Penn Center, Suite 1702, Philadelphia, PA 19103 .... (215) 241–1090
The Landmarks Building, 100 West Station Square Drive, Suite 225, Pittsburgh, PA 15219 .... (412) 803–3501
Federal Building, 17 South Park Row, Suite B–120, Erie, PA 16501 .... (814) 453–3010
Federal Building, 228 Walnut Street, Room 1104, Harrisburg, PA 17101 .... (717) 782–3951
1150 South Cedar Crest Boulevard, Suite 101, Allentown, PA 18103 .... (610) 434–1444
538 Spruce Street, Suite 302, Scranton, PA 18503 .... (570) 941–3540
Richland Square III, Suite 302, 1397 Eisenhower Boulevard, Johnstown, PA 15904 (814) 266–5970

REPRESENTATIVES

FIRST DISTRICT

ROBERT A. BRADY, Democrat, of Philadelphia, PA; born in Philadelphia, April 7, 1945; education: graduated from St. Thomas More High School; professional: carpenter; union official; assistant Sergeant-At-Arms, Philadelphia City Council, 1975–83; Deputy Mayor for Labor, W. Wilson Goode Administration; consultant to Pennsylvania State Senate; Pennsylvania Turnpike Commissioner; board of directors, Philadelphia Redevelopment Authority; Democratic Party Executive; ward leader; chairman, Philadelphia Democratic Party; member of Pennsylvania Democratic State Committee, and Democratic National Committee; religion: Catholic; married: Debra Brady; children: Robert and Kimberly; committees: ranking member, House Administration; Armed Services; Joint Committee on the Library; Joint Committee on Printing; elected to the 105th Congress on May 21, 1998, to fill the unexpired term of Representative Tom Foglietta; reelected to each succeeding Congress.

Office Listings

http://www.house.gov/robertbrady

102 Cannon House Office Building, Washington, DC 20515 .... (202) 225–4731
Chief of Staff.—Stan White. FAX: 225–0088
Appointments Secretary.—Tierney Houck.
Press Secretary.—Karen Warrington.
1907–09 South Broad Street, Philadelphia, PA 19148 .... (215) 389–4627
417 Avenue of the States Chester, Chester, PA 19103 .... (610) 874–7094
2637 East Clearfield Street, Philadelphia, PA 19134 .... (267) 519–2252
2630 Memphis St. Philadelphia, PA 19121 .... (215) 426–4616

Counties: PHILADELPHIA (part). CITIES AND TOWNSHIPS: Chester City, Chester Township, Eddystone Borough, Colwyn Borough, Ridley Township, Tinicum Township, Darby Township, and Yeadon Borough. Population (2000), 630,730.

ZIP Codes: 19012–16, 19018, 19022–23, 19029, 19032, 19036, 19050, 19078–79, 19086, 19092–93, 19101, 19105–09, 19111–13, 19120, 19122–26, 19130–34, 19137–51, 19153–54, 19160–62, 19170–73, 19175, 19177–78, 19181–82, 19185, 19187–88

* * *

SECOND DISTRICT

CHAKA FATTAH, Democrat, of Philadelphia, PA; born in Philadelphia, November 21, 1956; education: attended Overbrook High School, Community College of Philadelphia, University of Pennsylvania's Wharton School; M.A., University of Pennsylvania's Fels School of State and Local Government, 1986; completed Senior Executive Program for State Officials at Harvard University's John F. Kennedy School of Government; Pennsylvania State House of Representatives, 1988; Pennsylvania State Senate, 1988–94; author, *Gaining Early Awareness and Readiness for Undergraduate Programs* (GEAR-UP), enacted in 1998 offering college readiness preparation and scholarships for low-income students; founded Graduate Opportunity Initiative Conference, 1987; founded Philadelphia College Opportunity Resources for Education (CORE Philly) scholarship program; founded the American Cities Foundation; Chief sponser of the American Opportunity Tax Credit Act; leading advocate for the Energy Efficiency and Conservation Block Grants; Emergency Homeowners' Relief Fund; authored the White House Conference on Children and Youth Act of 2010; former trustee, Temple University, Pennsylvania State University, Lincoln University and Community College of Philadelphia; past chair, Executive Board, Pennsylvania Higher Education Assistance Agency; named one of the 50 most promising leaders in *Time* magazine, and in *Ebony* magazine as one of 50 Future Leaders; member, Mt. Carmel Baptist Church; chair, Congressional Urban Caucus; married: the former Renee' Chenault; four children; committees: Appropriations; elected to the 104th Congress on November 8, 1994; reelected to each succeeding Congress.

Office Listings

http://www.fattah.house.gov

2301 Rayburn House Office Building, Washington, DC 20515 .... (202) 225–4001
Chief of Staff.—Maisha Leek. FAX: 225–5392
Legislative Counsel / Legislative Director.—Nuku Ofori.
Deputy Chief of Staff / Communications Director.—Debra Anderson.
4104 Walnut Street, Philadelphia, PA 19104 .... (215) 387–6404
6632 Germantown Avenue, Philadelphia, PA 19119 .... (215) 848–9386

Counties: MONTGOMERY (part), PHILADELPHIA. Population (2000), 630,730.

ZIP Codes: 19004, 19012, 19027, 19038, 19046, 19093, 19095, 19101–04, 19107, 19109–11, 19118–24, 19126–32, 19138–41, 19143–48, 19150, 19161–62, 19170–71, 19173, 19178, 19184, 19187, 19191–93, 19196–97

* * *

THIRD DISTRICT

MIKE KELLY, Republican, of Butler, PA; born in Pittsburgh, PA, May 10, 1948; education: B.A., sociology with a minor in philosophy and theology, University of Notre Dame, South Bend, IN, 1970; profession: owner and operator of Kelly Automotive Cadillac, Chevrolet, Hyundai, and Kia car dealership; married 37 years: Vicki Kelly; four children; committees: Education and the Workforce; Foreign Affairs; Government Oversight and Reform; elected to the 112th Congress on November 2, 2010.

Office Listings

http://www.kelly.house.gov

515 Cannon House Office Building, Washington, DC 20515 .... (202) 225–5406
Chief of Staff.—Karen Czarnecki. FAX: 225–3103
Legislative Director.—Matthew Stroia.
Legislative Assistants: Tricia Cascio, Isaac Fong.
Press Secretary.—Julia Thornton.
Director of Administration.—Ruth Knouse.
Legislative Correspondent.—John Ray.
Special Assistant.—Samuel Breene.
208 East Bayfront Parkway, Suite 102, Erie, PA 16507 .... (814) 456–8190
District Director.—Brad Moore.
108 East Diamond Street, Butler, PA 16001 .... (724) 282–2557
FAX: 282–3682
182 Main Street, Greenville, PA 16125 .... (724) 885–1113
FAX: 885–1114
908 Diamond Park Meadville, PA 16335 .... (814) 454–8190
Office Hours: Wednesday from 9 a.m. to 4 p.m. FAX: 454–8197

Counties: ARMSTRONG (part), BUTLER (part), CRAWFORD (part), ERIE, MERCER (part), VENANGO (part), WARREN (part). Population (2000), 630,730.

ZIP Codes: 16001–03, 16016–18, 16020, 16022–23, 16025, 16027–30, 16033–35, 16037–41, 16045–46, 16048–53, 16055–57, 16059, 16061, 16110–11, 16113–14, 16124–25, 16127, 16130–31, 16133–34, 16137, 16142–43, 16145–46, 16148, 16150–51, 16153–54, 16156, 16159, 16201, 16210, 16218, 16222–24, 16226, 16229, 16232, 16242, 16244–45, 16249–50, 16253, 16259, 16261–63, 16311–12, 16314, 16316–17, 16319, 16323, 16327, 16329, 16335, 16340, 16342, 16345, 16350–51, 16354, 16360, 16362, 16365–69, 16371–74, 16388, 16401–07, 16410–13, 16415, 16417, 16420–24, 16426–28, 16430, 16432–36, 16438, 16440–44, 16475, 16501–12, 16514–15, 16522, 16530–34, 16538, 16541, 16544, 16546, 16550, 16553–54, 16563, 16565

* * *

FOURTH DISTRICT

JASON ALTMIRE, Democrat, of McCandless, PA; born in Lower Burrell, PA, March 7, 1968; B.S., Florida State University, Tallahassee, FL, 1990; M.H.S.A., George Washington University, Washington, DC, 1998; professional: Acting Vice President for Government Relations and Community Health Services for University of Pittsburgh Medical Center; Director of Federal Government Relations, Federation of American Hospitals; Legislative Assistant to Congressman Pete Peterson (D-FL); married: Kelly Altmire; two children; committees: Education and the Workforce; Transportation and Infrastructure; elected to the 110th Congress on November 7, 2006; reelected to each succeeding Congress.

Office Listings

http://www.altmire.house.gov

332 Cannon House Office Building, Washington, DC 20515 .... (202) 225–2565
Chief of Staff.—Sharon Werner. FAX: 226–2274
Legislative Director.—Cara Toman.
Scheduler.—Mariel Schwartz.
2110 McLean Street, Aliquippa, PA 15001 .... (724) 378–0928
District Director.—Michelle Dorothy.
2124 Freeport Road, Natrona Heights, PA 15065 .... (724) 226–1304

Counties: ALLEGHENY (part), BEAVER, BUTLER (part), LAWRENCE, MERCER (part), WESTMORELAND (part). Population (2000), 630,730.

ZIP Codes: 15001, 15003, 15005–07, 15009–10, 15014–15, 15024, 15026–27, 15030, 15032, 15042–44, 15046, 15049–52, 15056, 15059, 15061, 15065–66, 15068–69, 15074, 15076–77, 15081, 15084–86, 15090–91, 15095–96, 15101,

15108, 15116, 15127, 15139, 15143–44, 15146, 15202, 15209, 15212, 15214–15, 15223, 15229, 15235, 15237–39, 15601, 15626, 15632, 15650, 15668, 16002, 16024–25, 16033, 16037, 16040, 16046, 16051–52, 16055–57, 16059, 16061, 16063, 16066, 16101–03, 16105, 16107–08, 16112, 16115–17, 16120–21, 16123, 16127, 16132, 16136, 16140–43, 16148, 16155–57, 16159–61, 16172, 16229

* * *

FIFTH DISTRICT

GLENN THOMPSON, Republican, of Howard Township, PA; born in Bellefonte, PA, July 27, 1959; education: B.S., therapeutic recreation, Pennsylvania State University, 1981; M.Ed., health science / therapeutic recreation, Temple University, 1998; NHA / L, Nursing Home Administrator, Marywood University, 2006; professional: Rehabilitation Services Manager for Susquehanna Health Services, Adjunct Faculty for Cambria County Community College; Chief, Recreational Therapist for the Williamsport Hospital; Residential Services Aid for Hope Enterprises, Orderly for Centre Crest Nursing Home; Organization / Awards: Past President / Fire Fighter / EMT / Rescue Technician for Howard VFD; former, Howard Boy Scout Master; former, President and Senior VP for Juniata Valley Boy Scout Council; International Advisory Council Member for the Accreditation of Rehabilitation Facilities Commission; board member / vice chair of Private Industry Council of Central Corridors; political career: Centre County Republican chair, Pennsylvania Republican State Committee, alternate delegate for the Republican National Convention; candidate for the Pennsylvania House of Representatives, 1998 and 2000; member, Bald Eagle Area School District Board of Education; religion: Protestant; married to Penny Ammerman-Thompson; three sons, Parker, Logan and Kale; committees: Agriculture; Education and the Workforce; Natural Resources; elected to the 111th Congress on November 4, 2008; reelected to the 112th Congress on November 2, 2010.

Office Listings

http://thompson.house.gov

124 Cannon House Office Building, Washington, DC 20515 .... (202) 225–5121
Chief of Staff.—Jordan Clark. FAX: 225–5796
Legislative Director.—Matthew Brennan.
Scheduler.—Rachel Ross.
Communications Director.—Parish Braden.
127 West Spring Street, Suite C, Titusville, PA 16354 .... (814) 827–3985
District Director.—Peter Winkler.
3555 Benner Pike, Suite 101, Bellefonte, PA 16823 .... (814) 353–0215

Counties: CAMERON, CENTRE, CLARION, CLEARFIELD (part), CLINTON, CRAWFORD (part), ELK, FOREST, JEFFERSON, JUNIATA (part), LYCOMING (part), MCKEAN, MIFFLIN (part), POTTER, TIOGA, VENANGO (part), WARREN (part). Population (2000), 630,730.

ZIP Codes: 15711, 15715, 15730, 15733, 15744, 15753, 15757, 15764, 15767, 15770, 15772, 15776, 15778, 15780–81, 15784, 15801, 15821, 15823–25, 15827–29, 15831–32, 15834, 15840–41, 15845–49, 15851, 15853, 15856–57, 15860–61, 15863–66, 15868, 15870, 16028, 16036, 16049, 16054, 16058, 16153, 16213–14, 16217, 16220–22, 16224–26, 16230, 16232–35, 16239–40, 16242, 16248, 16254–58, 16260, 16301, 16311, 16313–14, 16317, 16319, 16321–23, 16326–29, 16331–34, 16340–47, 16351–54, 16361–62, 16364–65, 16370–71, 16373–75, 16404, 16416, 16434, 16620, 16627, 16645, 16651, 16661, 16663, 16666–77, 16681, 16686, 16701, 16720, 16724–35, 16738, 16740, 16743–46, 16748–50, 16801–05, 16820–23, 16825–30, 16832–41, 16843–45, 16847–56, 16858–61, 16863–66, 16868, 16870–79, 16881–82, 16901, 16911–12, 16914–15, 16917–18, 16920–23, 16927–30, 16932–33, 16935–40, 16942–43, 16946–48, 16950, 17004, 17009, 17029, 17044, 17051, 17063, 17084, 17099, 17701–02, 17720–21, 17723–24, 17726–27, 17729, 17738–40, 17744–45, 17747–48, 17750–52, 17754, 17759–60, 17764–65, 17767, 17769, 17773, 17776–79, 17810, 17841

* * *

SIXTH DISTRICT

JIM GERLACH, Republican, of Chester Springs, PA; born in Ellwood City, PA, February 25, 1955; education: B.A., Dickinson College, 1977; J.D., Dickinson School of Law, 1980; professional: attorney; former special counsel to the regional law firm of Fox, Rothschild, O'Brien & Frankel; community service: board of directors, MECA (Mission for Educating Children with Autism); Dickinson College Board of Trustees; Chester County Agricultural Development Council; public service: Pennsylvania House of Representatives, 1991–94; Pennsylvania State Senate, 1995–2002; children: Katie, Jimmy, and Robby; committees: Ways and Means; elected to the 108th Congress on November 5, 2002; reelected to each succeeding Congress.

Office Listings

http://www.gerlach.house.gov

2442 Rayburn House Office Building, Washington, DC 20515 .... (202) 225–4315

Chief of Staff.—Annie Fultz. FAX: 225–8440
Legislative Director.—Lauryn Schothorst.
Communications Director.—Kori Walter.
111 East Uwchlan Avenue, Exton, PA 19341 .... (610) 594–1415
840 North Park Road, Wyomissing, PA 19610 .... (610) 376–7630
580 Main Street, Suite #4, Trappe, PA 19426 .... (610) 409–2780

Counties: BERKS (part), CHESTER (part), LEHIGH (part), MONTGOMERY (part). Population (2000), 630,730.

ZIP Codes: 17527, 17555, 17569, 18011, 18031, 18041, 18056, 18062, 18070, 18092, 19003–04, 19010, 19025, 19031, 19034–35, 19041, 19066, 19072, 19085, 19087, 19096, 19131, 19151, 19301, 19310, 19312, 19316, 19320, 19333, 19335, 19341, 19343–45, 19353–55, 19358, 19365–67, 19369, 19371–72, 19376, 19380, 19382, 19401, 19403–04, 19409, 19421, 19423, 19425–26, 19428, 19430, 19432, 19438, 19442, 19444, 19446, 19457, 19460, 19462, 19464–65, 19468, 19470, 19473–75, 19480–85, 19490, 19493–96, 19503–05, 19508, 19511–12, 19518–20, 19522–23, 19525, 19530, 19535, 19538–40, 19542–43, 19545, 19547–48, 19562, 19565, 19601–02, 19604–12

* * *

SEVENTH DISTRICT

PATRICK MEEHAN, Republican, of Drexel Hill, PA; born in Cheltenham, PA, October 20, 1955; education: B.S., Bowdoin College, Brunswick, ME, 1978; J.D., Temple University, Philadelphia, PA, 1985; professional: district attorney for Delaware County, 1996–2001; United States Attorney for the Eastern District of Pennsylvania, 2001–08; religion: Roman Catholic; married: Carolyn Meehan; children: Jack, Patrick, and Colin; caucuses: Congressional Hockey, Jordan; committees: Homeland Security; Oversight and Government Reform, Transportation and Infrastructure; elected to the 112th Congress on November 2, 2010.

Office Listings

http://meehan.house.gov

513 Cannon House Office Building, Washington, DC 20515 .... (202) 225–2011
Chief of Staff.—Sarah Beatty. FAX: 226–0280
940 Sproul Road, Springfield, PA 19064 .... (610) 892–8623
District Director.—Caitlin Ganley.

Counties: CHESTER (part), DELAWARE (part), MONTGOMERY (part). Population (2000), 630,730.

ZIP Codes: 19008, 19010, 19014–15, 19017–18, 19022–23, 19026, 19028–29, 19032–33, 19036–37, 19039, 19041, 19043, 19050, 19052, 19061, 19063–65, 19070, 19073–74, 19076, 19078–79, 19081–83, 19085–87, 19094, 19312, 19317, 19319, 19331, 19333, 19339–40, 19342, 19355, 19373, 19380, 19382, 19395, 19403, 19405–06, 19426, 19428, 19468

* * *

EIGHTH DISTRICT

MICHAEL FITZPATRICK, Republican, of Levittown, PA; born in Philadelphia, PA, June 28, 1963; education: B.S., St. Thomas University, Miami Gardens, FL, 1985; J.D., Dickinson School of Law, Carlisle, PA, 1988; professional: Bucks County Board of Commissioners; practiced law at Begley Carlin and Mandio; religion: Roman Catholic; married: Kathleen; three daughters, Katie, Maggie, and Molly; three sons, Jimmy, Mick, and Tommy; committees: Financial Services; elected to the 109th Congress on November 2, 2004; elected to the 112th Congress on November 2, 2010.

Office Listings

http://www.fitzpatrick.house.gov

1224 Longworth House Office Building, Washington, DC 20515 .... (202) 225–4276
Chief of Staff.—Patrick Lyden. FAX: 225–9511
Legislative Director.—Kyle Whatley.
1717 Langhorne Newtown Road, Suite 400, Langhorne, PA 19047 .... (215) 579–8102
District Director.—Rob Mitchell. FAX: 579–8109

Counties: BUCKS, MONTGOMERY (part), PHILADELPHIA (part). Population (2000), 630,730.

ZIP Codes: 18036, 18039, 18041–42, 18054–55, 18073, 18077, 18081, 18901, 18910–17, 18920–23, 18925–35, 18938, 18940, 18942–44, 18946–47, 18949–51, 18953–56, 18960, 18962–64, 18966, 18968–70, 18972, 18974, 18976–77, 18980–81, 18991, 19001–02, 19006–08, 19020–21, 19025, 19030, 19034, 19038, 19040, 19044, 19047–49, 19053–59, 19067, 19075, 19090, 19114, 19116, 19154–55, 19440, 19454

* * *

NINTH DISTRICT

BILL SHUSTER, Republican, of Hollidaysburg, PA; born in McKeesport, PA, January 10, 1961; education: Everett High School, Bedford County, PA; B.A., Dickinson College; M.B.A., American University; professional: businessman; Goodyear Tire & Rubber Corp.; Bandag, Inc.; President and General Manager, Shuster Chrysler; organizations: member, Zion Lutheran Church; National Federation of Independent Business; National Rifle Association; Y.M.C.A.; Precious Life, Inc.; Rotary Club; Board of Directors, Pennsylvania Automotive Association; Board of Trustees, Homewood Home Retirement Community; Sigma Chi Fraternity; family: married to Rebecca; two children: Ali and Garrett; committees: Armed Services; Transportation and Infrastructure; elected to the 107th Congress, by special election, on May 15, 2001; re-elected to each succeeding Congress.

Office Listings

http://www.house.gov/shuster

204 Cannon House Office Building, Washington, DC 20515 .... (202) 225–2431
Chief of Staff.—Rob Simms. FAX: 225–2486
Deputy Chief of Staff / Legislative Director.—Stephen Martinko.
Scheduler.—Kelley Halliwell.
310 Penn Street, Suite 200, Hollidaysburg, PA 16648 .... (814) 696–6318
100 Lincoln Way East, Suite B, Chambersburg, PA 17201 .... (717) 264–8308
827 Water Street, #3, Indiana, PA 15701 .... (724) 463–0516
118 West Main Street, Suite 302, Somerset, PA 15501 .... (814) 443–3918

Counties: BEDFORD, BLAIR, CAMBRIA (part), CLEARFIELD (part), CUMBERLAND (part), FAYETTE (part), FRANKLIN, FULTON, HUNTINGDON, INDIANA (part), JUNIATA, MIFFLIN, PERRY (part), SOMERSET (part), WESTMORELAND (part). Population (2000), 630,730.

ZIP Codes: 15411, 15416, 15421, 15424–25, 15431, 15436–37, 15440, 15445, 15451, 15459, 15462, 15464–65, 15469–70, 15478–79, 15501, 15510, 15521–22, 15530, 15532–42, 15545, 15549–54, 15557–60, 15562–65, 15681, 15701, 15712–14, 15716–17, 15720–25, 15727–29, 15731–32, 15734, 15738–39, 15741–42, 15746–48, 15750, 15752–54, 15756–59, 15763, 15765, 15767, 15771–72, 15774–75, 15777, 15783, 15840, 15920, 15924, 15926, 15929, 15931, 15936, 15940, 15944, 15946, 15949, 15954, 15961, 15963, 16211, 16222, 16246, 16256, 16601–03, 16611, 16613, 16616–17, 16619, 16621–25, 16627, 16629–31, 16633–41, 16644, 16646–48, 16650–52, 16654–57, 16659–62, 16664–65, 16667–75, 16678–80, 16682–86, 16689, 16691–95, 16823, 16833, 16844, 16861, 16865, 16871, 16877, 17002, 17004, 17006, 17013–14, 17021, 17024, 17035, 17037, 17040, 17044–45, 17047, 17049, 17051–54, 17056, 17058–60, 17062, 17065–66, 17068, 17071, 17074–76, 17081–82, 17086, 17090, 17094, 17201, 17210–15, 17217, 17219–25, 17228–29, 17231–33, 17235–41, 17243–44, 17246–47, 17249–57, 17260–68, 17270–72, 17307, 17324

* * *

TENTH DISTRICT

THOMAS A. MARINO, Republican, of Cogan Station, PA; born in Williamsport, PA, August 13, 1952; education: American Institute of Baking, 1982; A.A., general studies, Williamsport Area Community College, 1983; B.A., political science / education, Lycoming College, 1985; J.D., Dickinson School of Law, 1987; United States Army War College, 2005; professional: manufacturing manager; lawyer, private practice; served as a Lycoming County District Attorney, PA, 1992–2002; U.S. Attorney for the Middle District of Pennsylvania, 1992–2002; married: Edith, 1974; two children: Chloe, Victor; committees: Foreign Affairs; Homeland Security; Judiciary; elected to the 112th Congress on November 2, 2010.

Office Listings

http://www.marino.house.gov

410 Cannon House Office Building, Washington, DC 20515 .... (202) 225–3731
Chief of Staff.—Bill Tighe. FAX: 225–9594
Legislative Director.—Drew Kent.
Director of Operations / Scheduler.—Sara Rogers.
Legislative Assistants: Matt Minor, Robert Savino.
Special Assistant.—Philip Pulizzi.
Legislative Correspondent.—Sarah Wolf.
Staff Assistant.—Alec Davis.
1020 Commerce Park Drive, Suite 1A, Williamsport, PA 17701 .... (570) 322–3961
Constituent Services Manager.—Jacqueline Bell.
Executive Assistant.—Colleen Kemp.
District Representative.—Bill McCleary.
181 West Tioga Street, Suite 2, Tunkhannock, PA 18651 .... (570) 836–8020

District Director.—Dave Weber.
Communications Director.—Renita Fennick.
District Representatives: Tom Cahill, Cathy Romaniello.
106 Arch Street, Sunbury, PA 17801 .... (570) 988–7801
District Representative.—Amiee Snyder.

Counties: BRADFORD, LACKAWANNA (part), LUZERNE (part), LYCOMING (part), MONTOUR, NORTHUMBERLAND, PIKE, SNYDER, SULLIVAN, SUSQUEHANNA, TIOGA (part), UNION, WAYNE, WYOMING. Population (2000), 630,730.

ZIP Codes: 16910, 16914, 16925–26, 16930, 16932, 16936, 16945, 16947, 17017, 17045, 17063, 17086, 17701, 17703, 17705, 17724, 17728, 17730, 17731, 17735, 17737, 17742, 17749, 17756, 17758, 17762–63, 17765, 17768, 17771–72, 17774, 17777, 17801, 17810, 17812–15, 17820–24, 17827, 17829–37, 17840–42, 17844–45, 17847, 17850–51, 17853, 17855–57, 17860–62, 17864–68, 17870, 17872, 17876–77, 17880–87, 17889, 18301, 18324–26, 18328, 18336–37, 18340, 18371, 18403, 18405, 18407, 18410–11, 18413–17, 18419–21, 18424–28, 18430–31, 18433–41, 18443–49, 18451–65, 18469–73, 18512, 18612, 18614–16, 18618–19, 18622–23, 18625–30, 18632, 18636, 18640–41, 18653–54, 18656–57, 18704, 18708, 18801, 18810, 18812–18, 18820–34, 18837, 18840, 18842–48, 18850–51, 18853–54

* * *

ELEVENTH DISTRICT

LOU BARLETTA, Republican, of Hazleton, PA; born in Hazleton, January 28, 1956; education: attended Bloomsburg University, Bloomsburg, PA; professional: business owner; member of city council in Hazleton, PA, 1998–2000; mayor of Hazleton, PA, 2000–10; married: Mary Grace; four daughters; committees: Education and the Workforce; Small Business; Transportation and Infrastructure; elected to the 112th Congress on November 2, 2010.

Office Listings

http://www.house.gov/barletta

510 Cannon House Office Building, Washington, DC 20515 .... (202) 225–6511
Chief of Staff.—Patrick Rothwell. FAX: 226–6250
Legislative Director.—Andrea Waldock.
Executive Assistant.—Cherie Homa.
Press Secretary.—Shawn Kelly.
1 South Church Street, Hazleton, PA 18201–5283 .... (570) 751–0050
802 South Main Street, Taylor, PA 18517 .... (570) 562–6240
1112 Route 315, Plaza 315, Wilkes-Barre, PA 18702 .... (570) 235–1420

Counties: CARBON, COLUMBIA, LACKAWANNA (part), LUZERNE (part), MONROE. Population (2000), 630,730.

ZIP Codes: 17814–15, 17820–21, 17824, 17839, 17846, 17858–59, 17878, 17888, 17920, 17985, 18012, 18030, 18058, 18071, 18201–02, 18210–12, 18216, 18219, 18221–25, 18229–30, 18232, 18234–35, 18237, 18239–41, 18244, 18246–47, 18249–51, 18254–56, 18301–02, 18320–23, 18325–27, 18330–35, 18341–42, 18344, 18346–50, 18352–57, 18360, 18370, 18372, 18434, 18447–48, 18452, 18466, 18501–05, 18507–10, 18512, 18514–15, 18517–19, 18601–03, 18610–12, 18617, 18621–22, 18624, 18631, 18634–35, 18640–44, 18651, 18655, 18660–61, 18690, 18701–11, 18761–67, 18769, 18773

* * *

TWELFTH DISTRICT

MARK S. CRITZ, Democrat, of Johnstown, PA; born in Jeannette, PA, January 5, 1962; education: graduated, Norwin High School, North Huntingdon, PA, 1980; B.A., management information systems, Indiana University of Pennsylvania, Indiana, PA, 1987; professional: business manager; aide to United States Representative John Patrick Murtha, Jr., 1998–2010; married: Nancy Jean Knox; twin children, Joseph and Sadonia; awards: recipient of the highest civilian award issued by the National Guard Association of the United States; Patrick Henry Award, the award recognizes local officials and civic leaders, who in a position of great responsibility distinguished themselves with outstanding and exceptional service to the Armed Forces of the United States, the National Guard or NGAUS; committees: Armed Services; Small Business; elected by special election to the 111th Congress, May 18, 2010, to fill the vacancy caused by the death of Representative John P. Murtha; elected to the 112th Congress November 2, 2010.

Office Listings

http://www.critz.house.gov

1022 Longworth House Office Building, Washington, DC 20515 .... (202) 225–2065

Chief of Staff.—Matthew Mazonkey.
Office Manager / Schedule Coordinator.—Jane Phipps.
Legislative Director.—Noel Holmes.
Communications Director.—Matthew Mazonkey.
Armed Services Staff.—Matthew Mazonkey.
Small Business Staff.—Noel Holmes.
647 Main Street, Suite 401, Johnstown, PA 15901 .... (814) 535–2642
District Director.—Jim Penna.

Counties: ALLEGHENY COUNTY (part). CITIES AND TOWNSHIPS: East Deer, and Tarentum; ARMSTRONG COUNTY (part). CITIES AND TOWNSHIPS: Apollo, Bethel, Burrell, Elderton, Ford City, Ford Cliff, Freeport, Gilpin, Kiskiminetas, Kittanning, Leechburg, Manor, Manorville, North Apollo, North Buffalo, Parks, Plumcreek, South Bend, and South Buffalo; CAMBRIA COUNTY (part). CITIES AND TOWNSHIPS: Adams, Barr, Blacklick, Brownstown, Cambria, Carrolltown, Cassandra, Conemaugh, Cresson, Croyle, Daisytown, Dale, East Carroll, East Conemaugh, East Taylor, Ebensburg, Ehrenfeld, Ferndale, Franklin, Geistown, Jackson, Johnstown, Lilly, Lorain, Lower Yoder, Middle Taylor, Munster, Nanty Glo, Portage, Richland, Sankertown, Scalp Level, South Fork, Southmonth, Stonycreek, Summerhill, Susquehanna, Upper Yoder, Vintondale, Washington, Westmont, West Carroll, West Taylor, Wilmore. FAYETTE COUNTY (part). CITIES AND TOWNSHIPS: Belle Vernon, Brownsville, Bullskin, Connellsville, Dawson, Dunbar, Everson, Fayette City, Franklin, Georges, German, Jefferson, Lower Tyrone, Luzerne, Masontown, Menallen, Newell, Nicholson, North Union, Perry, Perryopolis, Point Marion, Redstone, Saltlick, South Union, Springhill, Upper Tyrone, Uniontown, Vanderbilt, Washington. GREENE COUNTY, INDIANA COUNTY (part). CITIES AND TOWNSHIPS: Cherryhill, Clymer, Indiana, Pine, White. SOMERSET COUNTY (part). CITIES AND TOWNSHIPS: Benson, Boswell, Conemaugh, Hooversville, Jefferson, Jenner, Jennerstown, Lincoln, Middlecreek, Paint, Quemahoning, Seven Springs, Stoystown, Windber. WASHINGTON COUNTY (part). CITIES AND TOWNSHIPS: Allenport, Beallsville, Bentleyville, California, Canonsburg, Canton, Carroll, Centerville, Charleroi, Chartier, Coal Center, Cokeburg, Deemston, Donora, Dunlevy, East Bethlehem, East Washington, Elco, Ellsworth, Fallowfield, Finleyville, Houston, Long Branch, Marianna, Monongahela, New Eagle, North Bethlehem, North Charleroi, North Strabane, Roscoe, Somerset, South Strabane, Speers, Stockdale, Twilight, Union, Washington, West Bethlehem, West Brownsville, West Pike Run. WESTMORELAND COUNTY (part). CITIES AND TOWNSHIPS: Allegheny, Arnold, Avonmore, Bell, Bessemer, Bolivar, Bovard, Bridgeport, Crabtree, Derry, Dorothy, Duncan, East Herminie, East Huntingdon, East Vandergrift, Fairfield, Hannastown, Heccla, Hempfield, Hugus, Hyde Park, Jacobs Creek, Latrobe, Laurel Run, Lloydsville, Lowber, Lower Burrell, Loyalhanna, Luxor, Mammoth, Mechlings, Mineral, Monessen, Mount Pleasant, New Alexandria, New Florence, New Kensington, North Belle Vernon, North Washington, Oklahoma, Paulton, Port Royal, Rillton, Rostraver, Salem, Scottdale, Seward, Sewickley, Smithton, South Huntingdon, Spring Garden, St. Clair, United, Unity, Upper Burrell, Vandergrift, Washington, Wayne, Westmoreland, West Herminie, West Leechburg, West Newton, Wyano, and Yukon. Population (2000), 630,730.

ZIP Codes: 15012, 15022, 15030, 15033, 15038, 15062–63, 15067–68, 15072, 15083, 15087, 15089, 15301, 15310, 15313–17, 15320, 15322, 15324–25, 15327, 15329–34, 15336–38, 15341–42, 15344–49, 15351–54, 15357–60, 15362–64, 15366, 15368, 15370, 15377, 15380, 15401, 15410–13, 15415, 15417, 15419–20, 15422–25, 15427–36, 15438, 15442–44, 15446–47, 15449–51, 15454–56, 15458, 15460, 15463, 15466–68, 15472–77, 15479–80, 15482–86, 15488–90, 15492, 15501–02, 15520, 15531, 15541, 15544, 15547–48, 15551, 15555, 15557, 15561, 15563, 15601, 15610, 15613, 15618, 15620–22, 15624–25, 15627, 15629, 15631, 15633, 15635, 15637, 15641–42, 15644, 15646, 15650, 15655–56, 15660–62, 15664, 15666, 15670–71, 15673–74, 15677–78, 15680–90, 15701, 15705, 15710, 15714, 15717, 15722, 15724, 15728, 15732, 15736–37, 15745, 15748, 15760–62, 15765, 15773–74, 15779, 15901–02, 15904–07, 15909, 15921–23, 15925, 15927–28, 15930–31, 15934–38, 15940, 15942–46, 15948, 15951–63, 16055, 16201, 16215, 16226, 16228–29, 16236, 16238, 16240, 16249, 16630, 16641, 16646, 16668–69

* * *

THIRTEENTH DISTRICT

ALLYSON Y. SCHWARTZ, Democrat, of Rydal, PA; born in Queens County, NY, October 3, 1948; education: graduated from the Calhoun School, New York, NY, 1966; B.A., Simmons College, Boston, MA, 1970; M.S.W., Bryn Mawr College, Bryn Mawr, PA, 1972; professional: executive director of the Elizabeth Blackwell Center, 1977–88; Deputy Commissioner of the Philadelphia Department of Human Services, 1988–90; elected to the Pennsylvania State Senate, 1991–2004; member: Pennsylvania State Board of Education; Pennsylvania Council on Higher Education; Education Commission of the States; married: Dr. David Schwartz; children: Daniel and Jordan; committees: Budget; Foreign Affairs; elected to the 109th Congress on November 2, 2004; reelected to each succeeding Congress.

Office Listings

http://www.house.gov/schwartz

1227 Longworth House Office Building, Washington, DC 20515 .... (202) 225–6111
Chief of Staff.—Rachel Magnuson. FAX: 226–0611
Legislative Director.—Aaron Davis.
Communications Director.—Tali Israeli.
706 West Avenue, Jenkintown, PA 19046 .... (215) 517–6572
District Director.—Vacant.
7219 Frankford Avenue, Philadelphia, PA 19135 .... (215) 335–3355

County: MONTGOMERY COUNTY; CITIES AND TOWNSHIPS: Abington Wards, Hatfield, Horsham, Lower Frederick, Lower Gwynedd, Lower Moreland, Lower Salford, Malborough, Montgomery, New Hanover, Plymouth, Springfield, Towamencin, Upper Dublin, Upper Frederick, Upper Gwynedd, Upper Moreland, Upper Salford, Whitemarsh, Whitpain. Boroughs of Ambler, Bryn Athyn, Green Lane, Hatboro, Hatfield, Jenkintown, Lansdale, North Wales, Rockledge, Schwenksville. PHILADELPHIA COUNTY; CITY OF: Philadelphia. Population (2000), 630,730.

ZIP Codes: 18054, 18074, 18914–15, 18932, 18936, 18957–58, 18964, 18969, 18979, 19001–02, 19006, 19009, 19019, 19025, 19027, 19038, 19040, 19044, 19046, 19075, 19090, 19096, 19111, 19114–16, 19118, 19120, 19124, 19128, 19134–37, 19149, 19152, 19154–55, 19244, 19255, 19422, 19424, 19428, 19435–38, 19440–41, 19443–44, 19446, 19450–51, 19454–55, 19462, 19464, 19473, 19477–78, 19486–87, 19489, 19492, 19504, 19512, 19525

* * *

FOURTEENTH DISTRICT

MICHAEL F. DOYLE, Democrat, of Forest Hills, PA; born in Swissvale, PA, August 5, 1953; graduated, Swissvale Area High School, 1971; B.S., Pennsylvania State University, 1975; co-owner, Eastgate Insurance Agency, Inc., 1983; elected and served as finance and recreation chairman, Swissvale Borough Council, 1977–81; member: Leadership Pittsburgh Alumni Association, Lions Club, Ancient Order of the Hibernians, Italian Sons and Daughters of America, and Penn State Alumni Association; member: Democratic Caucus, Democratic Study Group, Pennsylvania Democratic Delegation, Congressional Steel Caucus, Travel and Tourism CMO, Ad Hoc Committee on Irish Affairs, and National Italian-American Foundation; married Susan Beth Doyle, 1975; four children: Michael, David, Kevin, and Alexandra; committees: Energy and Commerce; elected to the 104th Congress, November 8, 1994; reelected to each succeeding Congress.

Office Listings

http://doyle.house.gov

401 Cannon House Office Building, Washington, DC 20515 .... (202) 225–2135
Administrative Assistant.—David Lucas. FAX: 225–3084
Legislative Director.—Jean Roehrenbeck.
Office Manager / Scheduler.—Ellen Young.
2637 East Carson Street, Pittsburgh, PA 15203 .... (412) 390–1499
District Director.—Paul D'Alesandro.
11 Duff Road, Penn Hills, PA 15235 .... (412) 241–6055
627 Lysle Boulevard, McKeesport, PA 15132 .... (412) 664–4049

County: ALLEGHENY COUNTY (part); CITIES AND TOWNSHIPS OF: Avalon, Baldwin Borough, Baldwin Township, Bellvue, Blawnox, Braddock, Braddock Hills, Chalfant, Clairton, Coraopolis, Crafton, Dravosburg, Duquesne, E. McKeesport, E. Pittsburgh, Edgewood, Elizabeth Borough, Elizabeth Township, Etna, Forest Hills, Glassport, Homestead, Ingram, Kennedy, Liberty, Lincoln, McKees Rocks, McKeesport, Millvale, Monroeville, Mt. Oliver, Munhall, Neville, North Braddock, North Versailles, O'Hara Township, Penn Hills, Pitcairn, Pittsburgh, Port Vue, Rankin, Reserve, Robinson, Stowe, Swissvale, Sharpsburg, Turtle Creek, Verona, Versailles, Wall, West Homestead, West Mifflin, Whitaker, Wilkins, Wilkinsburg, and Wilmerding. Population (2000), 630,730.

ZIP Codes: 15025, 15034–35, 15037, 15044–45, 15063, 15104, 15106, 15108, 15110, 15112, 15116, 15120, 15122, 15132–37, 15140, 15145–48, 15201–19, 15221–27, 15230, 15232–36, 15238–40, 15242, 15244, 15250–51, 15253, 15255, 15257–62, 15264–65, 15267–68, 15272, 15274, 15278–79, 15281–83, 15285–86, 15290, 15295

* * *

FIFTEENTH DISTRICT

CHARLES W. DENT, Republican, of Allentown, PA, born in Allentown, May 24, 1960; education: B.A., foreign service and international politics, Pennsylvania State University, 1982; M.A., public administration, Lehigh University, 1993; professional: Legislator Development Officer, Lehigh University, 1986–90; sales representative, P.A. Peters, Inc.; Pennsylvania State House, District 132, 1991–98; Representative, Pennsylvania State Senate, 1998–2004; religion: First Presbyterian Church; married: Pamela Jane Serfass; children: Kathryn Elizabeth, William Reed, and Charles John (Jack); committees: Appropriations; Ethics; elected to the 109th Congress on November 2, 2004; reelected to each succeeding Congress.

Office Listings

http://www.dent.house.gov

1009 Longworth House Office Building, Washington, DC 20515 .... (202) 225–6411
Chief of Staff.—George McElwee. FAX: 226–0778
Legislative Director.—Kristin Dini.
3900 Hamilton Boulevard, Suite 207, Allentown, PA 18103 .... (610) 770–3490
206 Main Street, East Greenville, PA 18041 .... (215) 541–4106

Counties: BERKS (part), LEHIGH, MONTGOMERY (part), NORTHAMPTON. POPULATION (2000), 630,730.

ZIP Codes: 18001–03, 18010–11, 18013–18, 18020, 18025, 18031–32, 18034–38, 18040–46, 18049–55, 18059–60, 18062–70, 18072–74, 18076–80, 18083–88, 18091–92, 18098–99, 18101–06, 18109, 18175, 18195, 18343, 18351, 18918, 18924, 18951, 18960, 18964, 18969, 18971, 19438, 19440, 19464, 19472, 19504–05, 19512, 19525, 19529–30, 19539

* * *

SIXTEENTH DISTRICT

JOSEPH R. PITTS, Republican, of Kennett Square, PA; born in Lexington, KY, October 10, 1939; education: B.A., philosophy and religion, Asbury College, KY; military service: served in U.S. Air Force, 1963–69, rising from second lieutenant to captain; professional: nursery business owner and operator; math and science teacher, Great Valley High School, Malvern, PA, 1969–72; teacher, Mortonsville Elementary School, Versailles, KY; member: Pennsylvania House of Representatives, 1972–96, serving as chairman of Appropriations Committee, 1989–96, and of Labor Relations Committee, 1981–88; married: the former Virginia M. Pratt in 1961; children: Karen, Carol, and Daniel; committees: Energy and Commerce; elected to the 105th Congress; reelected to each succeeding Congress.

Office Listings

http://www.house.gov/pitts

420 Cannon House Office Building, Washington, DC 20515 .... (202) 225–2411
Chief of Staff.—Gabe Neville. FAX: 225–2013
Legislative Director.—Monica Volante.
Press Secretary.—Andrew Wimer.
P.O. Box 837, Unionville, PA 19375 .... (610) 444–4581
150 North Queen Street, Suite 716, Lancaster, PA 17603 .... (717) 393–0667

Counties: LANCASTER, BERK (part). CITIES AND TOWNSHIPS: Reading, Bern, Lower Heidelberg, South Heidelberg, Spring. BOROUGH OF: Wernersville. CHESTER COUNTY (part). CITIES AND TOWNSHIPS: Birmingham, East Bradford, East Fallowfield, East Marlborough, East Nottingham, Elk, Franklin, Highland, Kennett, London Britain, London Grove, Londonderry, Lower Oxford, New Garden, New London, Newlin, Penn, Pennsbury, Upper Oxford, West Fallowfield, West Marlborough, West Nottingham. BOROUGHS OF: Avondale, Kennett Square, Oxford, Parkesburg, West Chester, and West Grove. Population (2000), 630,730.

ZIP Codes: 17501–09, 17512, 17516–22, 17527–29, 17532–38, 17540, 17543, 17545, 17547, 17549–52, 17554–55, 17557, 17560, 17562–70, 17572–73, 17575–76, 17578–85, 17601–08, 19106, 19310–11, 19317–20, 19330, 19342, 19346–48, 19350–52, 19357, 19360, 19362–63, 19365, 19374–75, 19380–83, 19390, 19395, 19464, 19501, 19540, 19543, 19565, 19601–02, 19604–05, 19608–11

* * *

SEVENTEENTH DISTRICT

TIM HOLDEN, Democrat, of St. Clair, PA; born in Pottsville, PA, March 5, 1957; education: attended St. Clair High School, St. Clair; Fork Union Military Academy; University of Richmond, Richmond, VA; B.A., Bloomsburg State College, 1980; professional: sheriff of Schuylkill County, PA, 1985–93; licensed insurance broker and real estate agent, John J. Holden Insurance Agency and Holden Realty Company, St. Clair; member: Pennsylvania Sheriffs Association; Fraternal Order of Police; St. Clair Fish and Game Association; Benevolent and Protective Order of the Elks Lodge 1533; co-chair, Correctional Officers Caucus; co-chair, House Mining Caucus; co-chair, Northeast Agriculture Caucus; Ad-Hoc Committee for Irish Affairs; Alzheimer's Caucus; Appalachian Region Commission Caucus; Arts Caucus; Autism Caucus; Blue Dog Coalition; Congressional 4–H Caucus; Congressional Beef Caucus; Congressional Caucus on Armenian Issues; Congressional Cement Caucus; Congressional Hellenic Caucus; Diabetes Caucus; Firefighter's Caucus; Friends of Ireland; Home Health Care Working Group; Homeland Security Caucus; House Auto Caucus; House Baltic Caucus; House Commuter Caucus; House Nursing Caucus; Iraq Fallen Heroes Caucus; Law Enforcement Caucus; Mental Health Caucus; National Guard and Reserve Components Caucus; Rural Caucus; Rural Health Care Caucus; Special Operations Forces Caucus; Sportsmens Caucus; Steel Caucus; Water Infrastructure Caucus; Wine Caucus; committees: Agriculture; Transportation and Infrastructure; elected to the 103rd Congress; reelected to each succeeding Congress.

Office Listings

2417 Rayburn House Office Building, Washington, DC 20515 .... (202) 225–5546
Chief of Staff.—Trish Reilly. FAX: 226–0996
Legislative Director.—Keith Pemrick.
Projects Director.—Bill Hanley.
Scheduler.—Thomas Kennedy.
1511 North Front Street, 1st Floor, Harrisburg, PA 17102 .... (717) 234–5904
4918 Kutztown Road, Temple, PA 19560 .... (610) 921–3502
758 Cumberland Street, Lebanon, PA 17042 .... (717) 270–1395
101 North Centre Street, Suite 303, Pottsville, PA 17901 .... (570) 622–4212

Counties: BERKS (part), DAUPHIN, LEBANON, PERRY (part), SCHUYLKILL. Population (2000), 630,730.

ZIP Codes: 17003, 17005, 17010, 17016–18, 17020, 17022–24, 17026, 17028, 17030, 17032–34, 17036, 17038–39, 17041–42, 17045–46, 17048, 17053, 17057, 17061–62, 17064, 17067–69, 17073–74, 17077–78, 17080, 17083, 17085, 17087–88, 17097–98, 17101–13, 17120–30, 17140, 17177, 17502, 17830, 17836, 17901, 17921–23, 17925, 17929–36, 17938, 17941–46, 17948–49, 17951–54, 17957, 17959–61, 17963–68, 17970, 17972, 17974, 17976, 17978–83, 17985, 18211, 18214, 18218, 18220, 18231, 18237, 18240–42, 18245, 18248, 18250, 18252, 18255, 19506–07, 19510, 19512, 19516, 19518, 19522, 19526, 19529–30, 19533–34, 19536, 19541, 19544, 19547, 19549–51, 19554–55, 19559–60, 19564–65, 19567, 19601, 19604–06

* * *

EIGHTEENTH DISTRICT

TIM MURPHY, Republican, of Upper St. Clair, PA; born in Cleveland, OH, September 11, 1952; education: B.S., Wheeling Jesuit University, 1974; M.A., Cleveland State University, 1976; Ph.D., University of Pittsburgh, 1979; professional: psychologist; holds two adjunct faculty positions at the University of Pittsburgh; Associate Professor in the Department of Public Health, and in the Department of Pediatrics; public service: Pennsylvania State Senate, 1996–2002; military: Lieutenant Commander, Medical Service Corps, United States Navy Reserve; religion: Catholic; family: married to Nan Missig; children: Bevin; co-chair, 21st Century Healthcare Caucus; Ad Hoc Congressional Committee for Irish Affairs / Friends of Ireland Caucus; Bipartisan Congressional Down Syndrome Caucus; Bipartisan Congressional Pro-Life Caucus; Congressional Caucus on Hellenic Issues; Congressional Caucus on India and Indian Americans; Congressional Cystic Fibrosis Caucus; Congressional Fire Services Caucus; Congressional Manufacturing Caucus; co-chair, Congressional Men's Health Caucus; co-chair, Congressional Mental Health Caucus; Congressional Multiple Sclerosis Caucus; co-chair, Congressional Natural Gas Caucus; Congressional Services Caucus; Congressional Sportsmen's Caucus; Congressional Steel Caucus; Congressional Study Group on Public Health; House Land Conservation Caucus; House Recycling Caucus; Hydrogen Fuel Cell Caucus; National Guard and Reserve Component Caucus; Northeast Midwest Congressional Coalition / Caucus; Medical and Dental Doctors in Congress Caucus; Middle Class Caucus; Military Veteran Caucus; Nuclear Issues Working Group; Renewable Energy and Energy Efficiency Caucus; Robotics Caucus; Suburban Agenda Caucus; USO Congressional Caucus; committees: Energy and Commerce; elected to the 108th Congress on November 5, 2002; reelected to each succeeding Congress.

Office Listings

http://murphy.house.gov

322 Cannon House Office Building, Washington, DC 20515 .... (202) 225–2301
Chief of Staff.—Susan Mosychuk.
Legislative Director.—Brad Grantz.
Scheduler.—Ashleigh Kazmeraski.
Press Secretary.—Demetrios Karoutsos.
504 Washington Road, Pittsburgh, PA 15228 .... (412) 344–5583

Counties: ALLEGHENY (part), WASHINGTON (part), WESTMORELAND (part). CITIES AND TOWNSHIPS: Greensburg, and Jeannette. Population (2000), 630,730.

ZIP Codes: 15001, 15004, 15017–22, 15025–26, 15028, 15031, 15033, 15036–37, 15044, 15046–47, 15053–55, 15057, 15060, 15063–64, 15071, 15075, 15078, 15082–83, 15085, 15088–89, 15102, 15106, 15108, 15126, 15129, 15131, 15136, 15142, 15146, 15205, 15209, 15212, 15215–16, 15220–21, 15226–28, 15231, 15234–36, 15238, 15241, 15243, 15270, 15277, 15301, 15311–12, 15314, 15317, 15321, 15323, 15329–30, 15332, 15339–40, 15342, 15345, 15350, 15361, 15363, 15365, 15367, 15376–79, 15448, 15501, 15601, 15605–06, 15611–12, 15615–17, 15619, 15622–23, 15626, 15628, 15632, 15634, 15636–40, 15642, 15644, 15647, 15650, 15655, 15658, 15663, 15665, 15668, 15672, 15675–76, 15679, 15683, 15687–88, 15691–93, 15695–97

* * *

NINETEENTH DISTRICT

TODD RUSSELL PLATTS, Republican, of York County, PA; born in York County, March 5, 1962; education: York Suburban High School, 1980; B.S. in public administration, Shippensburg University of Pennsylvania, 1984; J.D., Pepperdine University School of Law, 1991; professional: attorney; organizations: York County Transportation Coalition; Statewide Children's Health Insurance Program Advisory Council; York Metropolitan Planning Organization; public service: Pennsylvania House of Representatives, 1992–2000; married: Leslie; children: T.J. and Kelsey; committees: Armed Services; Education and the Workforce; Transportation and Infrastructure; Oversight and Government Reform; elected to the 107th Congress on November 7, 2000; reelected to each succeeding Congress.

Office Listings

http://www.house.gov/platts

2455 Rayburn House Office Building, Washington, DC 20515 .... (202) 225–5836
Chief of Staff.—Scott E. Miller. FAX: 226–1000
2209 East Market Street, York, PA 17402 .... (717) 600–1919
Deputy Chief of Staff.—Bob Reilly.
22 Chambersburg Street, Gettysburg, PA 17325 .... (717) 338–1919
59 West Louther Street, Carlisle, PA 17013 .... (717) 249–0190

Counties: ADAMS COUNTY, CUMBERLAND COUNTY (part), YORK COUNTY. Population (2000), 647,065.

ZIP Codes: 17001, 17007, 17011–13, 17015, 17019, 17025, 17027, 17043, 17050, 17053, 17055, 17065, 17070, 17072, 17089–90, 17093, 17214, 17222, 17257, 17301–04, 17306–07, 17309–25, 17327, 17329, 17331–33, 17337, 17339–40, 17342–45, 17347, 17349–50, 17352–56, 17358, 17360–66, 17368, 17370–72, 17375, 17401–08, 17415

RHODE ISLAND

(Population 2010, 1,052,567)

SENATORS

JACK REED, Democrat, of Jamestown, RI; born in Providence, RI, November 12, 1949; graduated, La Salle Academy, Providence, RI, 1967; B.S., U.S. Military Academy, West Point, NY, 1971; M.P.P., Kennedy School of Government, Harvard University, 1973; J.D., Harvard Law School, 1982; professional: served in the U.S. Army, 1967–79; platoon leader, company commander, battalion staff officer, 1973–77; associate professor, Department of Social Sciences, U.S. Military Academy, West Point, NY, 1978–79; 2nd BN (Abn) 504th Infantry, 82nd Airborne Division, Fort Bragg, NC; lawyer, admitted to the Washington, DC Bar, 1983; military awards: Army commendation medal with Oak Leaf Cluster, ranger, senior parachutist, jumpmaster, expert infantryman's badge; elected to the Rhode Island State Senate, 1985–90; committees: Appropriations; Armed Services; Banking, Housing, and Urban Affairs; elected to the 102nd Congress on November 6, 1990; served three terms in the U.S. House of Representatives; elected to the U.S. Senate, November 5, 1996; reelected to each succeeding Senate term.

Office Listings

http://reed.senate.gov

728 Hart Senate Office Building, Washington, DC 20510 .... (202) 224–4642
Chief of Staff.—Neil Campbell. FAX: 224–4680
Deputy Chief of Staff.—Cathy Nagle.
Press Secretary.—Chip Unruh.
1000 Chapel View Boulevard, Suite 290, Cranston, RI 02920 .... (401) 943–3100
Chief of Staff.—Raymond Simone.
U.S. District Courthouse, One Exchange Terrace, Suite 408, Providence, RI 02903 (401) 528–5200

* * *

SHELDON WHITEHOUSE, Democrat, of Newport, RI; born in New York City, NY, October 20, 1955; education: B.A., Yale University, New Haven, CT, 1978; J.D., University of Virginia, Charlottesville, VA, 1982; director, Rhode Island Department of Business Regulation, 1992–94; United States Attorney, 1994–98; Attorney General, Rhode Island State, 1999–2003; committees: Budget; Environment and Public Works; Health, Education, Labor, and Pensions; Judiciary; Special Committee on Aging; elected to the U.S. Senate on November 7, 2006.

Office Listings

http://whitehouse.senate.gov

717 Hart Senate Office Building, Washington, DC 20510 .... (202) 224–2921
Chief of Staff.—Mindy Myers. FAX: 228–6362
Legislative Director.—Sam Goodstein.
Communications Director.—Matthew Thornton.
170 Westminster Street, Suite 1100, Providence, RI 02903 .... (401) 453–5294
State Director.—George Carvalho.

REPRESENTATIVES

FIRST DISTRICT

DAVID N. CICILLINE, Democrat, of Providence, RI; born in Providence, RI, July 15, 1961; education: graduated, Narragansett High School, Narragansett, RI; B.A., Brown University, Providence, RI, 1983; J.D., Georgetown University Law Center, Washington, DC, 1986; professional: public defender, Washington, DC, 1986–87; lawyer, private practice; lawyer, American Civil Liberties Union; faculty, Roger Williams Law School, Bristol, RI; member of the Rhode Island State House of Representatives, 1995–2003; mayor of Providence, RI, 2002–10; Democrats' Steering and Policy Committee; committees: Foreign Affairs; Small Business; elected to the 112th Congress on November 2, 2010.

Office Listings

http://www.cicilline.house.gov

128 Cannon House Office Building, Washington, DC 20515 .... (202) 225–4911

Chief of Staff.—C. Scott Fay. FAX: 225–3290
Legislative Director.—Jessica Lemos.
Senior Policy Advisor.—Christopher Bizzacco.
Executive Assistant / Scheduler.—Alisa Sarkisian-Tatarian.
Communications Director.—Jessica Kershaw.
1070 Main Street, Suite 300, Pawtucket, RI 02860 .... (401) 729–5600

Counties: BRISTOL, NEWPORT, PROVIDENCE (part). CITIES AND TOWNSHIPS: Barrington, Bristol, Burrillville, Central Falls, Cumberland, East Providence, Jamestown, Lincoln, Little Compton, Middleton, Newport, North Providence, North Smithfield, Providence, Pawtucket, Portsmouth, Smithfield, Tiverton, Warren, and Woonsocket. Population (2000), 524,157.

ZIP Codes: 02801, 02802, 02806, 02809, 02824, 02826, 02828, 02830, 02835, 02837, 02838, 02839, 02840, 02841, 02842, 02858, 02859, 02860, 02861, 02862, 02863, 02864, 02865, 02871, 02872, 02876, 02878, 02885, 02895, 02896, 02903, 02904, 02906, 02908, 02909, 02911, 02912, 02914, 02915, 02916, 02917, 02918, 02940

* * *

SECOND DISTRICT

JAMES R. LANGEVIN, Democrat, of Warwick, RI; born in Providence, RI, April 22, 1964; education: B.A., political science / public administration, Rhode Island College, 1990; M.P.A., Harvard University, 1994; community service: American Red Cross; March of Dimes; Lions Club of Warwick; PARI Independent Living Center; Knights of Columbus; public service: secretary, Rhode Island Constitutional Convention, 1986; Rhode Island State Representative, 1989–95; Rhode Island Secretary of State, 1995–2000; committees: Armed Services; Permanent Select Committee on Intelligence; elected to the 107th Congress; reelected to each succeeding Congress.

Office Listings

http://www.langevin.house.gov

109 Cannon House Office Building, Washington, DC 20515 .... (202) 225–2735
Chief of Staff.—Kristin Nicholson. FAX: 225–5976
Legislative Director.—Rachel Bornstein.
Office Manager.—Stu Rose.
The Summit South, 300 Centerville Road, Suite 200, Warwick, RI 02886 .... (401) 732–9400
District Director.—Ken Wild.

Counties: KENT, PROVIDENCE (part), WASHINGTON. CITIES AND TOWNSHIPS: Charleston, Coventry, Cranston, Exeter, Foster, Glocester, Greenwich (East and West), Hopkinton, Johnston, Kingstown (North and South), Narragansett, New Shoreham, Providence, Richmond, Scituate, Warwick, West Warwick, and Westerly. Population (2000), 538,032.

ZIP Codes: 02804, 02807–08, 02812–18, 02822–23, 02825, 02827–29, 02831–33, 02836, 02852, 02857, 02873–75, 02877, 02879–83, 02886–89, 02891–94, 02898, 02901–05, 02907–11, 02917, 02919–21

SOUTH CAROLINA

(Population 2010, 4,625,364)

SENATORS

LINDSEY GRAHAM, Republican, of Seneca, SC; born in Seneca, July 9, 1955; education: graduated, Daniel High School, Central, SC; B.A., University of South Carolina, 1977; awarded J.D., 1981; military service: joined the U.S. Air Force, 1982; Base Legal Office and Area Defense Counsel, Rhein Main Air Force Base, Germany, 1984; circuit trial counsel, U.S. Air Forces; Base Staff Judge Advocate, McEntire Air National Guard Base, SC, 1989–94; presently a Colonel, Air Force Reserves; award: Meritorious Service Medal for Outstanding Service; Meritorious Service Medal for Active Duty Tour in Europe; professional: established private law practice, 1988; former member, South Carolina House of Representatives; Assistant County Attorney for Oconee County, 1988–92; City Attorney for Central, SC, 1990–94; member: Walhalla Rotary; American Legion Post 120; appointed to the Judicial Arbitration Commission by the Chief Justice of the Supreme Court; religion: attends Corinth Baptist Church; committees: Appropriations; Armed Services; Budget; Judiciary; Special Committee on Aging; elected to the 104th Congress on November 8, 1994; reelected to each succeeding Congress; elected to the U.S. Senate on November 5, 2002, reelected to each succeeding Senate term.

Office Listings

http://lgraham.senate.gov

290 Russell Senate Office Building, Washington, DC 20510 .... (202) 224–5972
Chief of Staff.—Richard Perry. FAX: 224–3808
Legislative Director.—Mathew Rimkunas.
Press Secretary.—Meghan Hughes.
Scheduler.—Alice James.
130 South Main Street, Suite 700, Greenville, SC 29601 .... (864) 250–1417
State Director.—Van Cato.
Upstate Regional Director.—Laura Bauld.
530 Johnnie Dodds Boulevard, Suite 202, Mt. Pleasant, SC 29464 .... (843) 849–3887
Low Country Regional Director.—Bill Tuten.
508 Hampton Street, Suite 202, Columbia, SC 29201 .... (803) 933–0112
Midlands Regional Director.—Yvette Rowland.
John L. McMillan Federal Building, 401 West Evans Street, Suite 111, Florence, SC 29501 .... (843) 669–1505
Pee Dee Regional Director.—Celia Urquhart.
235 East Main Street, Suite 100, Rock Hill, SC 29730 .... (803) 366–2828
124 Exchange Street, Suite A, Pendleton, SC 29670 .... (864) 646–4090
Senior Advisor.—Denise Bauld.

* * *

JIM DEMINT, Republican, of Greenville, SC; born in Greenville, September 2, 1951; education: West Hampton High School, Greenville, SC, 1969; B.S., University of Tennessee, 1973; M.B.A., Clemson University, 1981; certified management consultant and certified quality trainer; advertising and marketing businessman; started his own company, DeMint Marketing; active in Greenville, SC, business and educational organizations; U.S. House of Representatives, 1999–2005; religion: Presbyterian; family: married to Debbie; four children; committees: Banking, Housing, and Urban Affairs; Commerce, Science, and Transportation; Foreign Relations; Joint Economic Committee; elected to the U.S. Senate on November 2, 2004; reelected to each succeeding Senate term.

Office Listings

http://demint.senate.gov

167 Russell Senate Office Building, Washington, DC 20510 .... (202) 224–6121
Chief of Staff.—Bret Bernhardt. FAX: 228–5143
Policy Director.—Kimberly Wallner.
Communications Director.—Wesley Denton.
1901 Main Street, Suite 1475, Columbia, SC 29201 .... (803) 771–6112
State Director.—Ellen Weaver.
40 West Broad Street, Suite 320, Greenville, SC 29601 .... (843) 727–4525
29 Broad Street, Suite 300, Charleston, SC 29401 .... (864) 233–5366

REPRESENTATIVES

FIRST DISTRICT

TIM SCOTT, Republican, of North Charleston, SC; born in North Charleston, September 19, 1965; education: R.B. Stall High School; B.S., Charleston Southern University, Charleston, SC, 1988; professional: former owner of Tim Scott Allstate and partner of Pathway Real Estate Group; served on the Charleston County Council, 1995–2008; four terms as chair of the Charleston County Council; member of the South Carolina State House of Representatives, 2009–10; elected chairman of the Freshman Caucus and House Whip; named ''Friend of the Taxpayer'' commendation from the SC Association of Tax Payers; earned ''A'' rating from Club for Growth in SC State House; committees: Rules; elected to the 112th Congress on November 2, 2010.

Office Listings

http://www.timscott.house.gov

1117 Longworth House Office Building, Washington, DC 20515 .... (202) 225–3176
Chief of Staff.—Nick Muzin. FAX: 225–3407
Legislative Director.—Jennifer DeCasper.
Press Secretary.—Sean Smith.
2000 Sam Rittenberg Boulevard, Suite 3007, Charleston, SC 29407 .... (843) 852–2222
District Toll Free (888) 868–0737
1800 North Oak Street, Suite C, Myrtle Beach, SC 29577 .... (843) 445–6459

Counties: BERKELEY (part), CHARLESTON (part), DORCHESTER (part), GEORGETOWN (part), HORRY. Population (2000), 668,668.

ZIP Codes: 29401–07, 29410, 29412–14, 29416–20, 29422–25, 29429, 29436, 29439–40, 29442, 29445, 29449, 29451, 29455–58, 29461, 29464–66, 29469–70, 29472, 29474–75, 29482–85, 29487, 29511, 29526–28, 29544–45, 29566, 29568–69, 29572, 29575–79, 29581–82, 29585, 29587–88, 29597–98

* * *

SECOND DISTRICT

JOE WILSON, Republican, of Springdale, SC; born in Charleston, SC, July 31, 1947; education: graduated, B.A., Washington & Lee University, Lexington, VA; J.D., University of South Carolina School of Law; professional: attorney; Kirkland, Wilson, Moore, Taylor & Thomas (law firm); served on the staff of Senator Strom Thurmond and Congressman Floyd Spence; former Deputy General Counsel, U.S. Department of Energy; former Judge of the town of Springdale, SC; military service: U.S. Army Reserves, 1972–75; retired Colonel in the South Carolina Army National Guard as a Staff Judge Advocate for the 218th Mechanized Infantry Brigade, 1975–2003; organizations: Cayce-West Columbia Rotary Club; Sheriff's Department Law Enforcement Advisory Council; Reserve Officers Association; Lexington County Historical Society; Columbia Home Builders Association; County Community and Resource Development Committee; American Heart Association; Mid-Carolina Mental Health Association; Cayce-West Columbia Jaycees; Kidney Foundation; South Carolina Lung Association; Alston-Wilkes Society; Cayce-West Metro Chamber of Commerce; Columbia World Affairs Council; Fellowship of Christian Athletes, Sinclair Lodge 154; Jamil Temple; Woodmen of the World; Sons of Confederate Veterans; Military Order of the World Wars; Lexington, Greater Irmo, Chapin, Columbia, West Metro, and Batesburg-Leesville Chambers of Commerce; West Metro and Dutch Fork Women's Republican Clubs; and Executive Council of the Indian Waters Council, Boy Scouts of America; awards: U.S. Chamber of Commerce Spirit of Enterprise Award; Americans for Tax Reform Friend of the Taxpayer Award; National Taxpayers' Union; Taxpayers' Friend Award; Americans for Prosperity; Friend of the American Motorist Award; public service: South Carolina State Senate, 1984–2001; family: married to Roxanne Dusenbury McCrory; four sons; Assistant GOP Whip; member, Republican Policy Committee; committees: Armed Services; Education and the Workforce; Foreign Affairs; elected to the 107th Congress, by special election, on December 18, 2001; reelected to each succeeding Congress.

Office Listings

http://joewilson.house.gov

2229 Rayburn House Office Building, Washington, DC 20515 .... (202) 225–2452
Chief of Staff.—Eric Dell. FAX: 225–2455
Press Secretary.—Neal Patel.
Deputy Chief of Staff / Legislative Director.—Melissa Chandler.
903 Port Republic Street, P.O. Box 1538, Beaufort, SC 29901 .... (843) 521–2530
1700 Sunset Boulevard (U.S. 378), Suite 1, West Columbia, SC 29169 .... (803) 939–0041

Counties: AIKEN (part), ALLENDALE, BARNWELL, BEAUFORT, CALHOUN (part), HAMPTON, JASPER, LEXINGTON, ORANGEBURG (part), RICHLAND (part). CITIES AND TOWNSHIPS: Aiken, Allendale, Ballentine, Barnwell, Batesburg, Beaufort, Blackville, Bluffton, Blythewood, Brunson, Cayce, Chapin, Columbia, Coosawhatchie, Cope, Cordova, Crocketville, Daufuskie Island, Early Branch, Elko, Estill, Fairfax, Furman, Garnett, Gaston, Gifford, Gilbert, Hampton, Hardeeville, Hilda, Hilton Head Island, Irmo, Islandston, Kline, Leesville, Lexington, Livingston, Luray, Martin, Miley, Montmorenci, Neeses, North, Norway, Orangeburg, Pelion, Pineland, Port Royal, Ridgeland, Ruffin, Scotia, Springfield, St. Helena Island, St. Matthews, State Park, Swansea, Sycamore, Tillman, Ulmer, Varnville, West Columbia, White Rock, Williams, Williston, Windsor, and Yemassee. Population (2000), 668,668.

ZIP Codes: 29002, 29006, 29016, 29033, 29036, 29045, 29053–54, 29063, 29070–73, 29075, 29078, 29107, 29112–13, 29115–16, 29118, 29123, 29128, 29130, 29135, 29137, 29142, 29146–47, 29160, 29164, 29169–72, 29177, 29180, 29203–07, 29209–10, 29212, 29219, 29221, 29223–24, 29226–27, 29229, 29260, 29290, 29292, 29405, 29412–13, 29436, 29470, 29472, 29801, 29803, 29805, 29810, 29812–13, 29817, 29826–27, 29836, 29839, 29843, 29846, 29849, 29853, 29901–07, 29909–11, 29913–16, 29918, 29920–28, 29932–36, 29938–41, 29943–45

* * *

THIRD DISTRICT

JEFF DUNCAN, Republican, of Laurens, SC; born in Greenville, SC, January 7, 1966; education: B.A., political science, Clemson University, 1988; professional: small business owner; public service: South Carolina House of Representatives, 2002–10; religion: Southern Baptist, attends Clinton First Baptist Church; married: Melody; children: Graham, John Philip, and Parker; committees: Foreign Affairs; Homeland Security; Natural Resources; elected to the 112th Congress on November 2, 2010.

Office Listings

http://jeffduncan.house.gov

116 Cannon House Office Building, Washington, DC 20515 .... (202) 225–5301
Chief of Staff.—Lance Williams. FAX: 225–3216
Legislative Director.—Joshua Gross.
303 West Beltline Boulevard, Anderson, SC 29625 .... (864) 224–7401
District Director.—Rick Adkins.
200 Courthouse Public Square, P.O. Box 471, Laurens, SC 29360 .... (864) 681–1028
1028 Hayne Avenue, SW., Aiken, SC 29801 .... (803) 649–5571

Counties: ABBEVILLE, AIKEN (part), ANDERSON, EDGEFIELD, GREENWOOD, LAURENS (part), MCCORMICK, OCONEE, PICKENS, SALUDA. Population (2000), 668,669.

ZIP Codes: 29006, 29037, 29070, 29105, 29127–29, 29138, 29166, 29178, 29325, 29332, 29334–35, 29351, 29355, 29360, 29370, 29384, 29388, 29406, 29611, 29620–28, 29630–33, 29635, 29638–49, 29653–59, 29661, 29664–67, 29669–73, 29675–79, 29682, 29684–86, 29689, 29691–93, 29695–97, 29801–05, 29808–09, 29816, 29819, 29821–22, 29824, 29828–29, 29831–32, 29834–35, 29838, 29840–42, 29844–45, 29847–48, 29850–51, 29853, 29856, 29860–61

* * *

FOURTH DISTRICT

TREY GOWDY, Republican, of Spartanburg, SC; born in Greenville, SC, August 22, 1964; native of Spartanburg, SC; education: Spartanburg High School, Spartanburg, SC, 1982; B.A., Baylor University, Waco, TX, 1986; J.D., University of South Carolina Law School, Columbia, SC, 1989; professional: Nelson, Mullins, Riley & Scarborough (law firm), 1992–94; United States Attorney, 1994–2000; South Carolina Solicitor, 7th Circuit, 2001–10; religion: Baptist; member, First Baptist Church of Spartanburg; married: the former Terri Dillard, 1989; two children; committees: Education and the Workforce; Judiciary; Oversight and Government Reform; elected to the 112th Congress on November 2, 2010.

Office Listings

http://www.gowdy.house.gov

1237 Longworth House Office Building, Washington, DC 20515 .... (202) 225–6030
Chief of Staff.—Matthew Van Patton. FAX: 226–1177
Legislative Director.—Ann Woods Hawks.
Legislative Assistants: Anna Ready, Beth Davis Webb.
Executive Assistant.—Mary Ann Lynch.
Communications Director.—Robert Hughes.
104 South Main Street, Greenville, SC 29601 .... (864) 241–0175
District Director.—Cindy Crick.
Constituent Liaison.—George Ramsey.
101 West St. John Street, Spartanburg, SC 29306 .... (864) 583–3264
Administrative Coordinator.—Missy House.
Constituent Liaison.—Hallie Hurst.

Counties: GREENVILLE, LAURENS (part), SPARTANBURG, UNION. Population (2010), 770,226.

ZIP Codes: 29031, 29178, 29301–07, 29316, 29318–24, 29329–31, 29333–36, 29338, 29346, 29348–49, 29353, 29356, 29364–65, 29368–69, 29372–79, 29385–86, 29388, 29390–91, 29395, 29564, 29601–17, 29627, 29635–36, 29644–45, 29650–52, 29654, 29661–62, 29669, 29673, 29680–81, 29683, 29687–88, 29690, 29698

* * *

FIFTH DISTRICT

MICK MULVANEY, Republican, of Indian Land, SC; born in Alexandria, VA, July 21, 1967; education: graduated, Charlotte Catholic High School, 1985; B.S.F.S., international economics, commerce, and finance, Georgetown University, Washington, DC, 1989; J.D., University of North Carolina, Chapel Hill, NC, 1992; professional: Owners and Presidents Management Program, Harvard University Business School, Cambridge, MA, 2006; lawyer, private practice; real estate developer; member of the South Carolina State House of Representatives, 2007–09; member of the South Carolina State Senate, 2009–10 religion: Roman Catholic; committees: Budget; Small Business; Joint Economic Committee; elected to the 112th Congress on November 2, 2010.

Office Listings

http://www.mulvaney.house.gov

1004 Longworth House Office Building, Washington, DC 20515 .... (202) 225–5501
Chief of Staff.—Al Simpson. FAX: 225–0464
Communications Director.—Bryan Patridge.
1456 Ebenezer Road, Rock Hill, SC 29731 .... (803) 327–1114
District Administrator.—Eric Bedingfield.

Counties: CHEROKEE, CHESTER, CHESTERFIELD, DARLINGTON, DILLON, FAIRFIELD, FLORENCE (part), KERSHAW, LANCASTER, LEE, MARLBORO, NEWBERRY, SUMTER (part), YORK. Population (2000), 668,668.

ZIP Codes: 29009–10, 29014–16, 29020, 29031–32, 29036–37, 29040, 29045, 29055, 29058, 29065, 29067, 29069, 29074–75, 29078–79, 29101–02, 29104, 29106, 29108, 29122, 29126–28, 29130, 29132, 29145, 29150–54, 29161, 29163, 29175–76, 29178, 29180, 29203, 29218, 29307, 29323, 29330, 29332, 29340–42, 29355, 29372, 29501, 29506, 29512, 29516, 29520, 29525, 29532, 29536, 29540, 29543, 29547, 29550–51, 29563, 29565, 29567, 29570, 29573–74, 29581, 29584, 29592–94, 29596, 29654, 29702–04, 29706, 29708–10, 29712, 29714–18, 29720–22, 29724, 29726–32, 29734, 29741–45

* * *

SIXTH DISTRICT

JAMES E. CLYBURN, Democrat, of Columbia, SC; born in Sumter, SC, July 21, 1940; education: graduated, Mather Academy, Camden, SC, 1957; B.S., South Carolina State University, Orangeburg, 1962; attended University of South Carolina Law School, Columbia, 1972–74; professional: South Carolina State Human Affairs Commissioner; assistant to the Governor for Human Resource Development; executive director, South Carolina Commission for Farm Workers, Inc.; director, Neighborhood Youth Corps and New Careers; counselor, South Carolina Employment Security Commission; member: lifetime member, NAACP; Southern Regional Council; Omega Psi Phi Fraternity, Inc.; Arabian Temple, No. 139; Nemiah Lodge No. 51 F&AM; married: the former Emily England; children: Mignon, Jennifer and Angela; elected vice chair, Democratic Caucus, 2002; chair, Democratic Caucus 2006; Majority Whip; Assistant Democratic Leader, 2010; elected on November 3, 1992, to the 103rd Congress; reelected to each succeeding Congress.

Office Listings

http://www.clyburn.house.gov

2135 Rayburn House Office Building, Washington, DC 20515 .... (202) 225–3315
Chief of Staff.—Yelberton Watkins. FAX: 225–2313
Deputy Chief of Staff.—Barvetta Singletary.
Scheduler.—Alexandria Russell.
1225 Lady Street, Suite 200, Columbia, SC 29201 .... (803) 799–1100
District Director.—Robert Nance.
181 East Evans Street, Suite 314, Post Office Box 6286, Florence, SC 29502 .... (803) 662–1212
176 Brooks Boulevard, Santee, SC 29142 .... (803) 854–4700

Counties: BAMBERG COUNTY. CITIES AND TOWNSHIPS: Bamberg, Denmark, Erhardt, Olar. BERKELEY COUNTY (part). CITIES AND TOWNSHIPS: Bethera, Cross, Daniel Island, Huger, Jamestown, Pineville, Russellville, Saint Stephen, Wando. CAL-

HOUN COUNTY (part). CITY OF: Cameron, Creston, Fort Motte, St. Matthews. CHARLESTON COUNTY (part). CITIES AND TOWNSHIPS: Adams Run, Charleston, Edisto Island, Hollywood, Johns Island, Ravenel, Wadmalaw Island. CLARENDON COUNTY. CITIES AND TOWNSHIPS: Alcolu, Davis Station, Gable, Manning, New Zion, Rimini, Summerton, Turbeville. COLLETON COUNTY. CITIES AND TOWNSHIPS: Ashton, Cottageville, Green Pond, Hendersonville, Islandton, Jacksonboro, Lodge, Ritter, Round O, Smoaks, Walterboro, Williams. DORCHESTER COUNTY (part). CITIES AND TOWNSHIPS: Dorchester, Harleyville, Reevesville, Ridgeville, Rosinville, Saint George. FLORENCE COUNTY (part). CITIES AND TOWNSHIPS: Coward, Effingham, Florence, Johnsonville, Lake City, Olanta, Pamplico, Quinby, Scranton, Timmonsville. GEORGETOWN COUNTY (part). CITIES AND TOWNSHIPS: Andrews, Outland, Sampit. MARION COUNTY. CITIES AND TOWNSHIPS: Centenary, Gresham, Marion, Mullins, Nichols, Rains, Sellers. LEE COUNTY (part). CITIES AND TOWNSHIPS: Elliott, Lynchburg. ORANGEBURG COUNTY (part). CITIES AND TOWNSHIPS: Bowman, Branchville, Cardova, Cope, Elloree, Eutawville, Holly Hill, Norway, Orangeburg, Rowesville, Santee, Vance. RICHLAND COUNTY (part). CITIES AND TOWNSHIPS: Blythewood, Columbia, Eastover, Gadsden, Hopkins. SUMTER COUNTY (part). CITIES AND TOWNSHIPS: Mayesville, Oswego, Pinewood, Sumter. WILLIAMSBURG COUNTY. CITIES AND TOWNSHIPS: Cades, Greeleyville, Hemingway, Kingstree, Lane, Nesmith, Salters, and Trio. Population (2000), 668,670.

ZIP Codes: 29001, 29003, 29010, 29018, 29030, 29038–42, 29044, 29046–48, 29051–52, 29056, 29059, 29061, 29078, 29080–82, 29102, 29104, 29107, 29111, 29113–15, 29117–18, 29125, 29128, 29133, 29135, 29142–43, 29148, 29150, 29153–54, 29161–63, 29168, 29201–05, 29208–09, 29211, 29214–17, 29220, 29223, 29225, 29228, 29230, 29240, 29250, 29403, 29405–06, 29409, 29415, 29418, 29426, 29431–38, 29440, 29446–50, 29452–53, 29461, 29468, 29470–72, 29474–77, 29479, 29481, 29488, 29492–93, 29501–06, 29510, 29518–19, 29530, 29541, 29546, 29554–56, 29560, 29565, 29571, 29574, 29580–81, 29583, 29589–92, 29817, 29843, 29929, 29945

SOUTH DAKOTA

(Population 2010, 814,180)

SENATORS

TIM JOHNSON, Democrat, of Vermillion, SD, born in Canton, SD, December 28, 1946; education: B.A., Phi Beta Kappa, University of South Dakota, 1969; M.A., political science, University of South Dakota, 1970; post-graduate study in political science, Michigan State University, 1970–71; J.D., University of South Dakota, 1975; budget advisor to the Michigan State Senate Appropriations Committee, 1971–72; admitted to the South Dakota Bar in 1975 and began private law practice in Vermillion; elected to the South Dakota House of Representatives, 1978; reelected, 1980; elected to the South Dakota State Senate, 1982; reelected, 1984; served on the Joint Appropriations Committee and the Senate Judiciary Committee; served as Clay County Deputy State's Attorney, 1985; awards: named Outstanding Citizen of Vermillion, 1983; received South Dakota Education Association's ''Friend of Education'' Award, 1983; Billy Sutton Award for Legislative Achievement, 1984; elected to the U.S. House of Representatives, 1986; reelected to each succeeding Congress; delegate, Democratic National Convention, 1988–92; member: President's Export Council, 1999; religion: Lutheran; married: Barbara Brooks, 1969; children: Brooks, Brendan and Kelsey Marie; committees: chair, Banking, Housing, and Urban Affairs; Appropriations; Energy and Natural Resources; Indian Affairs; elected to the U.S. Senate on November 5, 1996; reelected to each succeeding Senate term.

Office Listings

http://johnson.senate.gov

136 Hart Senate Office Building, Washington, DC 20510 .... (202) 224–5842
Chief of Staff.—Drey Samuelson. FAX: 228–5765
Legislative Director.—Todd Stubbendieck.
Communications Director.—Perry Plumart.
5015 South Bar Oak, Sioux Falls, SD 57108 .... (605) 332–8896
State Director.—Sharon Boysen.
320 South First Street, Suite 103, Aberdeen, SD 57401 .... (605) 226–3440
405 East Omaha Street, Suite B, Rapid City, SD 57701 .... (605) 341–3990

* * *

JOHN THUNE, Republican, of Sioux Falls, SD; born in Pierre, SD, January 7, 1961; education: Jones County High School, 1979; B.S., business administration, Biola University, CA; M.B.A., University of South Dakota, 1984; professional: executive director, South Dakota Municipal League; board of directors, National League of Cities; executive director, South Dakota Republican Party, 1989–91; appointed, State Railroad Director, 1991; former congressional legislative assistant, and deputy staff director; elected, U.S. House of Representatives, 1997–2003; married: Kimberly Weems, 1984; children: Brittany and Larissa; committees: Agriculture, Nutrition, and Forestry; Budget; Commerce, Science, and Transportation; Finance; elected to the U.S. Senate on November 2, 2004; reelected to each succeeding Senate term.

Office Listings

http://thune.senate.gov

511 Dirksen Senate Office Building, Washington, DC 20510 .... (202) 224–2321
Chief of Staff.—Ryan Nelson. FAX: 228–5429
General Counsel.—Summer Mersinger.
Legislative Director.—Dave Schwietert.
Communications Director.—Andi Fouberg.
320 North Main Avenue, Suite B, Sioux Falls, SD 57104 .... (605) 334–9596
1312 West Main Street, Rapid City, SD 57701 .... (605) 348–7551
320 South First Street, Suite 101, Aberdeen, SD 57401 .... (605) 225–8823

REPRESENTATIVE

AT LARGE

KRISTI NOEM, Republican, of Castlewood, SD; born in Watertown, SD, November 30, 1971; professional: farmer; rancher; member of South Dakota State House of Representatives, 2007–10; committees: Agriculture; Education and the Workforce; Natural Resources; elected to the 112th Congress on November 2, 2010.

Office Listings

http://www.noem.house.gov

226 Cannon House Office Building, Washington, DC 20515 .... (202) 225–2801
Chief of Staff.—Jordan Stoick. FAX: 225–5823
Legislative Director.—Andrew Christianson.
Communications Director.—Joshua Shields.
Scheduler.—Jennifer Fierro.
2310 West 41st Street, Suite 101, Sioux Falls, SD 57105 .... (605) 275–2868
Southeast Director.—Suzanne Veenis.
343 Quincy Street, Rapid City, SD 57702 .... (605) 791–4673
Western Director.—Brad Otten.
415 South Main Street, Suite 203, Aberdeen, SD 57401 .... (605) 262–2862
Northeast Director.—Beth Hollatz.
505 12th Street Southeast, Watertown, SD 57201 .... (605) 878–2868
Northeast Director.—Beth Hollatz.

Population (2000), 754,844.

ZIP Codes: 57001–07, 57010, 57012–18, 57020–22, 57024–59, 57061–73, 57075–79, 57101, 57103–10, 57117–18, 57186, 57188–89, 57192–98, 57201, 57212–14, 57216–21, 57223–27, 57231–39, 57241–43, 57245–49, 57251–53, 57255–66, 57268–74, 57276, 57278–79, 57301, 57311–15, 57317, 57319, 57321–26, 57328–32, 57334–35, 57337, 57339–42, 57344–46, 57348–50, 57353–56, 57358–59, 57361–71, 57373–76, 57379–86, 57399, 57401–02, 57420–22, 57424, 57426–30, 57432–42, 57445–46, 57448–52, 57454–57, 57460–61, 57465–77, 57479, 57481, 57501, 57520–23, 57528–29, 57531–34, 57536–38, 57540–44, 57547–48, 57551–53, 57555, 57559–60, 57562–64, 57566–72, 57574, 57576–77, 57579–80, 57584–85, 57601, 57620–23, 57625–26, 57630–34, 57636, 57638–42, 57644–46, 57648–52, 57656–61, 57701–03, 57706, 57709, 57714, 57716–20, 57722, 57724–25, 57730, 57732, 57735, 57737–38, 57741, 57744–45, 57747–48, 57750–52, 57754–56, 57758–64, 57766–67, 57769–70, 57772–73, 57775–77, 57779–80, 57782–83, 57785, 57787–88, 57790–94, 57799

TENNESSEE

(Population 2010, 6,346,105)

SENATORS

LAMAR ALEXANDER, Republican, of Nashville, TN; born in Maryville, TN, July 3, 1940; education: graduated with honors in Latin American history, Phi Beta Kappa, Vanderbilt University; New York University Law School; served as *Law Review* editor; professional: clerk to Judge John Minor Wisdom, U.S. Court of Appeals in New Orleans; legislative assistant to Senator Howard Baker (R–TN), 1967; executive assistant to Bryce Harlow, counselor to President Nixon, 1969; President, University of Tennessee, 1988–91; co-director, Empower America, 1994–95; helped found a company that is now the nation's largest provider of worksite day care, Bright Horizons; public service: Republican nominee for Governor of Tennessee, 1974; Governor of Tennessee, 1979–87; U.S. Secretary of Education, 1991–93; community service: chairman, Salvation Army Red Shield Family Initiative; chairman, Senate Republican Conference; and the Museum of Appalachia in Norris, TN; received Tennessee Conservation League Conservationist of the Year Award; family: married to Honey Alexander; four children; committees: Appropriations; Environment and Public Works; Health, Education, Labor, and Pensions; Rules and Administration; Joint Committee on the Library; Joint Committee on Printing; elected to the U.S. Senate on November 5, 2002; reelected to the U.S. Senate on November 4, 2008.

Office Listings

http://alexander.senate.gov

455 Dirksen Senate Office Building, Washington, DC 20510 .... (202) 224–4944
Chief of Staff.—Ryan Loskarn. FAX: 228–3398
Legislative Director.—David Cleary.
Press Secretary.—Jim Jeffries.
Executive Assistant / Scheduler.—Bonnie Sansonetti.
3322 West End Avenue, Suite 120, Nashville, TN 37203 .... (615) 736–5129
Howard H. Baker, Jr. U.S. Courthouse; 800 Market Street, Suite 112, Knoxville, TN 37902 .... (865) 545–4253
Federal Building, 167 North Main Street, Suite 1068, Memphis, TN 38103 .... (901) 544–4224
Federal Building, 109 South Highland Street, Suite B–9, Jackson, TN 38301 .... (731) 423–9344
Joel E. Solomon Federal Building, 900 Georgia Avenue, Suite 260, Chattanooga, TN 37402 .... (423) 752–5337
Tri-Cities Regional Airport, Terminal Building, P.O. Box 1113, 2525 Highway 75, Suite 101, Blountville, TN 37617 .... (423) 325–6240

* * *

BOB CORKER, Republican, of Chattanooga, TN; born in Orangeburg, SC, August 24, 1952; education: B.S., Industrial Management, University of Tennessee, Knoxville, TN, 1974; professional: founder of Bencor Corporation, a construction company specializing in retail properties which operated in 18 states, 1978–90; founder of the Corker Group, acquisition, development, and operation of commercial real estate, 1982–2006; honors: named to the University of Tennessee at Chattanooga's ''Entrepreneurial Hall of Fame,'' 2005; community service: founding chair, Chattanooga Neighborhood Enterprise, Inc., a non-profit organization that has helped over 10,000 families secure decent, fit and affordable housing, 1986–92; public service: commissioner, State of Tennessee Department of Finance and Administration, 1995–96; mayor, City of Chattanooga, 2001–05; married: Elizabeth Corker, 1987; two children: Julia and Emily; committees: Banking, Housing, and Urban Affairs; Energy and Natural Resources; Foreign Relations; Special Committee on Aging; elected to the U.S. Senate on November 7, 2006.

Office Listings

http://corker.senate.gov

185 Dirksen Senate Office Building, Washington, DC 20510 .... (202) 224–3344
Chief of Staff.—Todd Womack. FAX: 228–0566
Legislative Director.—Ryan Berger.
Executive Assistant / Scheduler.—Ramona Lessen.
Communications Director.—Laura Herzog.
3322 West End Avenue, Suite 610, Nashville, TN 37203 .... (615) 279–8125
100 Peabody Place, Suite 1125, Memphis, TN 38103 .... (901) 683–1910
Howard Baker Federal Building, 800 Market Street, Suite 121, Knoxville, TN 37902 .... (865) 637–4180
Tri-Cities Regional Airport 2525, Highway 75, Suite 126, Blountville, TN 37617 .. (423) 323–1252
10 West Martin Luther King Boulevard, Sixth Floor, Chattanooga, TN 37402 .... (423) 756–2757
Ed Jones Federal Building, 109 South Highland Avenue, Suite B8, Jackson, TN 38301 .... (731) 424–9655

REPRESENTATIVES

FIRST DISTRICT

DAVID ''PHIL'' ROE, Republican, of Johnson City, TN; born in Clarksville, TN; July 21, 1945; education: B.S., Austin Peay State University, Clarksville, TN, 1967; M.D., University of Tennessee, Knoxville, TN, 1970; professional: United States Army Medical Corps, 1970–72; Vice Mayor of Johnson City, 2003–07; Mayor of Johnson City, 2007–09; Physicians' Caucus; Health Caucus; religion: Members of Munsey United Methodist Church; married: Pam; children: David C. Roe, John Roe, and Whitney Larkin: committees: Education and the Workforce; Veterans' Affairs; elected to the 111th Congress; reelected to the 112th Congress.

Office Listings

http://www.roe.house.gov

419 Cannon House Office Building, Washington, DC 20515 .... (202) 225–6356
Chief of Staff.—Matt Meyer. FAX: 225–5714
Communications Director.—Amanda Little.
Scheduler.—Barbie McCarron.
Legislative Director.—John Martin.
Staff Assistant.—Alex Large.
205 Revere Street, Kingsport, TN 37660 .... (423) 247–8161
FAX: 247–0119
Higher Education Building, P.O. Box 1728, Kingsport, TN 37662.
District Director.—Bill Snodgrass
Field Representative.—John Abe Teague.
Administrative Assistant.—Sheila Houser.
Caseworker.—Carolyn Ferguson.
1609 College Park Drive, Suite 4, Morristown, TN 37813 .... (423) 254–1400
Field Representative.—John Abe Teague. FAX: 254–1403
Caseworkers: Cheryl Bennett, Ann Reuschel.

Counties: CARTER, COCKE, GREENE, HAMBLEN, HANCOCK, HAWKINS, JEFFERSON, JOHNSON, SEVIER, SULLIVAN, UNICOI, WASHINGTON. Population (2000), 632,143.

ZIP Codes: 37601–02, 37604–05, 37614–18, 37620–21, 37625, 37640–45, 37650, 37656–60, 37662–65, 37680–84, 37686–88, 37690–92, 37694, 37699, 37711, 37713, 37722, 37725, 37727, 37731, 37738, 37743–45, 37752–53, 37760, 37764–65, 37778, 37809–11, 37813–16, 37818, 37821–22, 37843, 37857, 37860, 37862–65, 37868–69, 37873, 37876–77, 37879, 37881, 37890–91

* * *

SECOND DISTRICT

JOHN J. DUNCAN, JR., Republican, of Knoxville, TN; born in Lebanon, TN, July 21, 1947; education: B.S. in journalism, University of Tennessee, 1969; J.D., National Law Center, George Washington University, 1973; served in both the Army National Guard and the U.S. Army Reserves, retiring with the rank of captain; private law practice, Knoxville, 1973–81; appointed State Trial Judge by Governor Lamar Alexander in 1981 and elected to a full 8-year term in 1982 without opposition, receiving the highest number of votes of any candidate on the ballot that year; member: American Legion 40 and 8, Elks, Sertoma Club, Masons, Scottish Rite and Shrine; present or past board member: Red Cross, Girl's Club, YWCA, Sunshine Center for the Mentally Retarded, Beck Black Heritage Center, Knoxville Union Rescue Mission, Senior Citizens Home Aid Service; religion: active elder at Eastminster Presbyterian Church; married: the former Lynn Hawkins; children: Tara, Whitney, John J. III and Zane; committees: Natural Resources; Transportation and Infrastructure; elected to both the 100th Congress (special election) and the 101st Congress in separate elections held on November 8, 1988; reelected to each succeeding Congress.

Office Listings

http://www.house.gov/duncan

2207 Rayburn House Office Building, Washington, DC 20515 .... (202) 225–5435
Chief of Staff.—Bob Griffitts. FAX: 225–6440
Deputy Chief of Staff.—Don Walker.
Press Secretary.—Patrick Newton.
6 East Madison Avenue, Athens, TN 37303 .... (423) 745–4671
800 Market Street, Suite 100, Knoxville, TN 37902 .... (865) 523–3772
District Director.—Bob Griffitts.
331 Court Street, Blount County Courthouse, Maryville, TN 37804 .... (865) 984–5464

Counties: BLOUNT, KNOX (part), LOUDON, MCMINN, MONROE. CITIES AND TOWNSHIPS: Alcoa, Athens, Englewood, Etowah, Farragut, Halls (Knox Co.), Knoxville, Lenoir City, Loudon, Madisonville, Maryville, Powell, Seymour, and Sweetwater. Population (2000), 632,144.

ZIP Codes: 37303, 37309, 37311–12, 37314, 37322–23, 37325, 37329, 37331, 37353–54, 37369–71, 37385, 37701, 37709, 37721, 37725, 37737, 37742, 37754, 37764, 37771–72, 37774, 37777, 37779, 37801–04, 37806–07, 37820, 37826, 37830, 37846, 37849, 37853, 37865, 37871, 37874, 37876, 37878, 37880, 37882, 37885–86, 37901–02, 37909, 37912, 37914–24, 37927–33, 37938–40, 37950, 37990, 37995–98

* * *

THIRD DISTRICT

CHUCK FLEISCHMANN, Republican, of Ooltewah, TN; born in New York City, NY, October 11, 1962; graduated from Elk Grove High School, Village, IL, 1980; B.A., political science, University of Illinois, Urbana-Champaign, IL, 1983; J.D., University of Tennessee College of Law, Knoxville, TN, 1986; professional: attorney; small business owner; former president of the Chattanooga Bar Association, 1996; former chairman of the Chattanooga Lawyers Pro Bono Committee; religion: Catholic; married: Brenda Fleischmann; three children; committees: Natural Resources; Transportation and Infrastructure; Science, Space, and Technology; elected to the 112th Congress on November 2, 2010.

Office Listings

http://www.fleischmann.house.gov

511 Cannon House Office Building, Washington, DC 20515 .... (202) 225–3271
Chief of Staff.—Chip Saltsman. FAX: 225–3494
Legislative Director.—Jim Hippe.
Scheduler.—Grace Johnson.
900 Georgia Avenue, Suite 126, Chattanooga, TN 37402 .... (423) 756–2342
District Director.—Daphne Kirksey.
Federal Building, 200 Administration Road, Suite 100, Oak Ridge, TN 37830 .... (865) 576–1976
Special Assistant.—Adria Tutton.

Counties: ANDERSON, BRADLEY, CLAIBORNE, GRAINGER, HAMILTON, JEFFERSON (part), MEIGS, POLK, RHEA, ROANE (part), UNION. Population (2000), 632,143.

ZIP Codes: 37302, 37304, 37307–12, 37315–17, 37320–23, 37325–26, 37332–33, 37336–38, 37341, 37343, 37350–51, 37353, 37361–64, 37369, 37373, 37375, 37377, 37379, 37381, 37384, 37391, 37397, 37401–12, 37414–16, 37419, 37421–22, 37424, 37450, 37705, 37707–10, 37715–17, 37719, 37721, 37724–26, 37730, 37752, 37754, 37760, 37763–64, 37769, 37771, 37774, 37779, 37806–07, 37811, 37820–21, 37824–26, 37828, 37830–31, 37840, 37846, 37848–49, 37851, 37861, 37866, 37869–71, 37874, 37876–77, 37879–81, 37888, 37890, 37931, 37938

* * *

FOURTH DISTRICT

SCOTT DESJARLAIS, Republican, of South Pittsburg; TN; born in Sturgis, SD, February 21, 1964; education: B.S., chemistry and psychology, University of South Dakota, 1987; M.D., University of South Dakota School of Medicine, Vermillion, 1991; professional: general practitioner, Grand View Medical Center, Jasper, TN; religion: member, Epiphany Episcopalian Church, Sherwood, TN; married: Amy; children: Tyler, Ryan, and Maggie; committees: Agriculture; Education and the Workforce; Oversight and Government Reform; elected to the 112th Congress on November 2, 2010.

Office Listings

http://www.desjarlais.house.gov

413 Cannon House Office Building, Washington, DC 20515 .... (202) 225–6831
Chief of Staff.—Trent Edwards. FAX: 226–5172
Legislative Director.—Richard Vaughn.
Communications Director.—Robert Jameson.
62 East 2nd Street, Crossville, TN 38555 .... (931) 707–9091
807 South Garden Street, Columbia, TN 38401 .... (931) 381–9920
212 First Avenue Southeast, Winchester, TN 37398 .... (931) 962–3180

Counties: BLEDSOE, CAMPBELL, COFFEE, CUMBERLAND, FENTRESS, FRANKLIN, GILES, GRUNDY, HICKMAN (part), LAWRENCE, LEWIS, LINCOLN, MARION, MAURY, MOORE, MORGAN, PICKETT, ROANE (part), SCOTT, SEQUATCHIE, VAN BUREN, WARREN, WHITE, WILLIAMSON (part). Population (2010), 688, 008.

ZIP Codes: 37018, 37025–26, 37033, 37037, 37047, 37062, 37064, 37078, 37091, 37096, 37098, 37110–11, 37129–33, 37137, 37144, 37160, 37166, 37171, 37174, 37179, 37183, 37190, 37301, 37305–06, 37313, 37318, 37324, 37327–

28, 37330, 37334–35, 37337, 37339–40, 37342, 37345, 37347–49, 37352, 37355–57, 37359–60, 37365–67, 37374–83, 37387–89, 37394, 37396–98, 37419, 37714–15, 37719, 37721, 37723, 37726, 37729, 37732–33, 37748, 37755–57, 37762–63, 37766, 37769–71, 37773, 37778, 37819, 37829, 37840–41, 37845, 37847, 37852, 37854, 37867, 37869–70, 37872, 37880, 37887, 37892, 38370, 38401–02, 38449, 38451, 38453–57, 38459–64, 38468–69, 38472–78, 38481–83, 38486–88, 38504, 38506, 38549–50, 38553, 38555–59, 38565, 38571–72, 38574, 38577–79, 38581, 38583, 38585, 38587, 38589

* * *

FIFTH DISTRICT

JIM COOPER, Democrat, of Nashville, TN; born in Nashville, June 19, 1954; education: B.A., history and economics, University of North Carolina at Chapel Hill, 1975; Rhodes Scholar, Oxford University, 1977; J.D., Harvard Law School, 1980; admitted to Tennessee Bar, 1980; professional: attorney; Waller, Lansden, Dortch, and Davis (law firm), 1980–82; Managing Director, Equitable Securities, 1995–99; Adjunct Professor, Vanderbilt University Owen School of Management, 1995–2002 and 2006–present; partner, Brentwood Capital Advisors LLC, 1999–2002; married: Martha Hays; three children; caucuses: Blue Dog Coalition; New Democrat Coalition; committees: Armed Services; Oversight and Government Reform; elected to the U.S. House of Representatives, 1982–95; elected to the 108th Congress on November 5, 2002; reelected to each succeeding Congress.

Office Listings

http://www.cooper.house.gov

1536 Longworth House Office Building, Washington, DC 20515 .... (202) 225–4311
Chief of Staff.—Lisa Quigley. FAX: 226–1035
Legislative Director/Deputy Chief of Staff.—Jason Lumia.
605 Church Street, Nashville, TN 37219 .... (615) 736–5295

Counties: CHEATHAM (part), DAVIDSON, WILSON (part). Population (2000), 632,143.

ZIP Codes: 37011, 37013, 37015, 37027, 37032, 37034–35, 37064, 37070–72, 37076, 37080, 37082, 37086–88, 37090, 37115–16, 37121–22, 37135, 37138, 37143, 37146, 37189, 37201–22, 37224, 37227–30, 37232, 37234–36, 37238–50

* * *

SIXTH DISTRICT

DIANE BLACK, Republican, of Gallatin, TN; born in Baltimore, MD, January 16, 1951; education: A.S.N., Arundel Community College, Baltimore, MD, 1971; B.S.N., Belmont University, Nashville, TN, 1991; professional: nurse; nonprofit community organization fundraiser; member of the Tennessee State House of Representatives, 1999–2005; member of the Tennessee State Senate, 2005–10; religion: attends Christian Community Church, Hendersonville, married: Dr. David Black; three children; six grandchildren; caucus: member of the Republican Caucus; freshman Representative to Republican Policy Committee; committees: Budget; Ways and Means; elected to the 112th Congress on November 2, 2010.

Office Listings

http://www.black.house.gov

1531 Longworth House Office Building, Washington, DC 20515 .... (202) 225–4231
Chief of Staff.—Annie Palisi. FAX: 225–6887
Scheduler.—Rebecca Schussler.
305 West Main Street, Murfreesboro, TN 37130 .... (615) 896–1986
District Chief of Staff.—Teresa Koeberlein.
321 East Spring Street, Suite 301, Cookeville, TN 38501 .... (931) 854–0069
355 North Belvedere Drive, Suite 308, Gallatin, TN 37066 .... (615) 206–8204

Counties: BEDFORD, CANNON, CLAY, DEKALB, JACKSON, MACON, MARSHALL, OVERTON, PUTNAM, ROBERTSON, RUTHERFORD, SMITH, SUMNER, TROUSDALE, WILSON (part). CITIES AND TOWNSHIPS: Carthage, Celina, Cookeville, Gainesboro, Gallatin, Hartsville, Lafayette, Lewisburg, Livingston, Murfreesboro, Shelbyville, Smithville, Springfield, Watertown, and Woodbury. Population (2000), 632,143.

ZIP Codes: 37010, 37012, 37014, 37016, 37018–20, 37022, 37026, 37030–32, 37034, 37037, 37046–49, 37057, 37059–60, 37063, 37066, 37072–75, 37077, 37080, 37083, 37085–87, 37090–91, 37095, 37110, 37118–19, 37122, 37127–28, 37135–36, 37141, 37144–46, 37148–53, 37160–62, 37166–67, 37172, 37174, 37180, 37183–84, 37186, 37188, 37190, 37357, 37360, 37388, 38451, 38472, 38501–03, 38505–06, 38541–45, 38547–48, 38551–52, 38554, 38560, 38562–64, 38567–70, 38573–75, 38580–83, 38588–89

* * *

SEVENTH DISTRICT

MARSHA BLACKBURN, Republican, of Franklin, TN; born in Laurel, MS, June 6, 1952; education: B.S., Mississippi State University, 1973; professional: retail marketing; public service: American Council of Young Political Leaders; executive director, Tennessee Film, Entertainment, and Music Commission; chairman, Governor's Prayer Breakfast; Tennessee State Senate, 1998–2002; minority whip; community service: Rotary Club; Chamber of Commerce; Arthritis Foundation; Nashville Symphony Guild Board; Tennessee Biotechnology Association; March of Dimes; American Lung Association; awards: Chi Omega Alumnae Greek Woman of the Year, 1999; Middle Tennessee 100 Most Powerful People, 1999–2002; married: Chuck; children: Mary Morgan Ketchel and Chad; committees: Energy and Commerce; elected to the 108th Congress on November 5, 2002; reelected to each succeeding Congress.

Office Listings

http://www.house.gov/blackburn

217 Cannon House Office Building, Washington, DC 20515 .... (202) 225–2811
Chief of Staff.—Anthony Hulen. FAX: 225–3004
Executive Assistant.—Katie Morgan.
7975 Stage Hill Boulevard, Suite 1, Memphis, TN 38133 .... (901) 382–5811
198 East Main Street, Suite 1, Franklin, TN 37064 .... (615) 591–5161
1850 Memorial Drive, Clarksville, TN 37043 .... (931) 503–0391

Counties: CHEATHAM (part), CHESTER, DAVIDSON (part), DECATUR, FAYETTE, HARDEMAN, HARDIN, HENDERSON, HICKMAN (part), MCNAIRY, MONTGOMERY (part), PERRY, SHELBY (part), WAYNE, WILLIAMSON (part). Population (2000), 632,139.

ZIP Codes: 37010, 37014–15, 37024–25, 37027, 37032–33, 37035–36, 37040–43, 37046, 37052, 37055, 37060, 37062, 37064–65, 37067–69, 37079, 37082, 37096–98, 37101, 37135, 37137, 37140, 37155, 37174, 37179, 37187, 37191, 37211, 37215, 37220–21, 38002, 38004, 38008, 38010–11, 38014, 38016–18, 38027–29, 38036, 38039, 38042, 38044–46, 38048–49, 38052–53, 38057, 38060–61, 38066–69, 38075–76, 38088, 38128, 38133–34, 38138–39, 38141, 38163, 38183–84, 38310–11, 38313, 38315, 38321, 38326–29, 38332, 38334, 38339–41, 38345, 38347, 38351–52, 38356–57, 38359, 38361, 38363, 38365–68, 38370–72, 38374–76, 38379–81, 38388, 38390, 38392–93, 38425, 38450, 38452, 38463, 38471, 38475, 38485–86

* * *

EIGHTH DISTRICT

STEPHEN FINCHER, Republican, of Frog Jump, TN; born in Memphis, TN, February 7, 1973; education: Crockett County High School, 1990; professional: managing partner in Fincher Farms; public service: "The Fincher Family" singing ministry; president of Alamo Dixie Youth Baseball and Crockett County Dixie Youth Baseball; chairman of the board of the PPR Committee at Archer's Chapel United Methodist Church; president of United Methodist Men; religion: Archer's Chapel United Methodist Church; married: Lynn; children: John Austin, Noah, and Sarah; committees: Financial Services; elected to the 112th Congress on November 2, 2010.

Office Listings

http://www.fincher.house.gov

1118 Longworth House Office Building, Washington, DC 20515 .... (202) 225–4714
Chief of Staff.—Jessica Carter. FAX: 225–1765
Deputy Chief of Staff.—Scott Golden.
Communications Director.—Sara Sendek.
Federal Building, Room B–7, Jackson, TN 38301 .... (731) 423–4848

Counties: BENTON, CARROLL, CROCKETT, DICKSON, DYER, GIBSON, HAYWOOD, HENRY, HOUSTON, HUMPHREYS, LAKE, LAUDERDALE, MADISON, MONTGOMERY (part), OBION, SHELBY (part), STEWART, TIPTON, WEAKLEY. Population (2000), 632,142.

ZIP Codes: 37015, 37023, 37025, 37028–29, 37036, 37040, 37043–44, 37050–52, 37055–56, 37058, 37061–62, 37078–79, 37097, 37101, 37134, 37142, 37165, 37171, 37175, 37178, 37181, 37185, 37187, 38001, 38004, 38006–07, 38011–12, 38015, 38019, 38021, 38023–25, 38030, 38034, 38037, 38040–41, 38047, 38049–50, 38053–55, 38058–59, 38063, 38069–71, 38075, 38077, 38079–80, 38083, 38127–29, 38135, 38201, 38220–26, 38229–33, 38235–38, 38240–42, 38251, 38253–61, 38271, 38281, 38301–03, 38305, 38308, 38313–14, 38316–18, 38320–21, 38324, 38330–31, 38333, 38336–38, 38341–44, 38346, 38348, 38355–56, 38358, 38362, 38366, 38369, 38378, 38380, 38382, 38387, 38389–92

* * *

NINTH DISTRICT

STEPHEN IRA ''STEVE'' COHEN, Democrat, of Memphis, TN; born in Memphis, May 24, 1949 of Dr. Morris D. Cohen and Genevieve Cohen; B.A., Vanderbilt University in Nashville, TN, 1971; J.D., Cecil C. Humphreys School of Law of Memphis State University (renamed University of Memphis), 1973; legal advisor for the Memphis Police Department, 1974–77; Delegate to and Vice President of Tennessee Constitutional Convention, 1977; Commissioner on the Shelby County Commission, 1978–80; Tennessee State Senator for District 30, 1982–2006; Delegate at the 1980 and 1992 Democratic National Conventions; Regional Whip; Commission on Security and Cooperation in Europe; committees: Judiciary; Transportation and Infrastructure; elected to the 110th Congress on November 7, 2006; reelected to each succeeding Congress.

Office Listings

http://www.cohen.house.gov

1005 Longworth House Office Building, Washington, DC 20515 .... (202) 225–3265
Chief of Staff.—Marilyn Dillihay. FAX: 225–5663
Scheduler.—Craig Dulniak.
Legislative Director.—Reisha Phills.
Communications Director.—Michael Pagan.
167 North Main Street, Suite 369, Memphis, TN 38103 .... (901) 544–4131
FAX: 544–4329

County: SHELBY COUNTY (part). CITY OF: Memphis. Population (2000), 632,143.

ZIP Codes: 37501, 38016–18, 38101, 38103–09, 38111–20, 38122, 38124–28, 38130–37, 38139, 38141–42, 38145–48, 38151–52, 38157, 38159, 38161, 38165–68, 38173–75, 38177, 38181–82, 38186–88, 38190, 38193–95, 38197

TEXAS

(Population 2010, 25,145,561)

SENATORS

KAY BAILEY HUTCHISON, Republican, of Dallas, TX; born in Galveston, TX, July 22, 1943; raised in La Marque, TX; education: graduated, the University of Texas at Austin and the University of Texas School of Law; professional: Texas House of Representatives, 1972–76; appointed vice chair, National Transportation Safety Board, 1976; senior vice president and general counsel, RepublicBank Corporation; co-founded, Fidelity National Bank of Dallas; owned, McCraw Candies, Inc.; political and legal correspondent, KPRC–TV, Houston; member: development boards of SMU and Texas A&M schools of business; trustee, the University of Texas Law School Foundation; elected Texas State Treasurer, 1990; religion: Episcopalian; married: Ray Hutchison; committees: ranking member, Commerce, Science, and Transportation; Appropriations; Rules and Administration; elected to the U.S. Senate, by special election, on June 5, 1993, to fill the vacancy caused by the resignation of Senator Lloyd Bentsen; reelected to each succeeding Senate term.

Office Listings

http://hutchison.senate.gov

284 Russell Senate Office Building, Washington, DC 20510 .... (202) 224–5922
Chief of Staff.—Cliff Shannon.
Legislative Director.—David W. Davis.
Federal Building, 300 East Eighth Street, Suite 961, Austin, TX 78701 .... (512) 916–5834
10440 North Central Expressway, Suite 1160, LB 606, Dallas, TX 75231 .... (214) 361–3500
1919 Smith Street, Suite 800, Houston, TX 77002 .... (713) 653–3456
1906–G Tyler Street, Harlingen, TX 78550 .... (956) 425–2253
500 Chestnut Street, Suite 1570, Abilene, TX 79602 .... (325) 676–2839
3133 General Hudnell Drive, Suite 120, San Antonio, TX 78226 .... (210) 340–2885

* * *

JOHN CORNYN, Republican, of Austin, TX; born in Houston, TX, February 2, 1952; education: graduated, Trinity University, and St. Mary's School of Law, San Antonio, TX; Masters of Law, University of Virginia, Charlottesville, VA; professional: attorney; Bexar County District Court Judge; Presiding Judge, Fourth Administrative Judicial Region; Texas Supreme Court, 1990–97; Texas Attorney General, 1999–2002; community service: Salvation Army Adult Rehabilitation Council; World Affairs Council of San Antonio; Lutheran General Hospital Board; chair, National Republican Senatorial Committee; committees: Armed Services; Budget; Finance; Judiciary; elected to the U.S. Senate on November 5, 2002, for the term beginning January 3, 2003; appointed to the Senate on December 2, 2002, to fill the vacancy caused by the resignation of Senator Phil Gramm; reelected to the U.S. Senate on November 4, 2008.

Office Listings

http://cornyn.senate.gov

517 Hart Senate Office Building, Washington, DC 20510 .... (202) 224–2934
Chief of Staff.—Beth Jafari. FAX: 228–2856
Legislative Director.—Russ Thomasson.
5300 Memorial Drive, Suite 980, Houston, TX 77007 .... (713) 572–3337
Providence Tower, 5001 Spring Valley Road, #1125E, Dallas, TX 75244 .... (972) 239–1310
100 East Ferguson Street, Suite 1004, Tyler, TX 75702 .... (903) 593–0902
221 West Sixth Street, Suite 1530, Austin, TX 78701 .... (512) 469–6034
Wells Fargo Center, 1500 Broadway, #1230, Lubbock, TX 79401 .... (806) 472–7533
222 East Van Buren, Suite 404, Harlingen, TX 78550 .... (956) 423–0162
600 Navarro Street, Suite 210, San Antonio, TX 78205 .... (210) 224–7485

REPRESENTATIVES

FIRST DISTRICT

LOUIE GOHMERT, Republican, of Tyler, TX; born in Pittsburg, TX, August 18, 1953; education: B.A., Texas A&M University, 1975; J.D., Baylor University, Waco, TX, 1977; professional: United States Army, 1978–82; district judge, Smith County, 1992–2002; appointed by Governor Rick Perry to complete an unexpired term as Chief Justice of the 12th Court of

Appeals, 2002–03; Brigade Commander of the Corps of Cadets, Texas A&M; organizations: President of the South Tyler Rotary Club; Boy Scout District Board of Directors; religion: deacon at Green Acres Baptist Church; director of Leadership Tyler; director of Centrepoint Ministries; married: Kathy; children: Katy, Caroline, Sarah; committees: Judiciary; Natural Resources; elected to the 109th Congress on November 2, 2004; reelected to each succeeding Congress.

Office Listings

http://www.gohmert.house.gov

2440 Rayburn House Office Building, Washington, DC 20515 .... (202) 225–3035
Chief of Staff.—Connie Hair. FAX: 226–1230
Legislative Director.—Curtis Philp.
Communications Director.—Kimberly Willingham.
1121 East Southeast Loop 323, Suite 206, Tyler, TX 75701 .... (903) 561–6349

Counties: ANGELINA, CASS (part), GREGG, HARRISON, MARION, NACOGDOCHES, PANOLA, RUSK, SABINE, SAN AUGUSTINE, SHELBY, SMITH, UPSHUR. Population (2000), 651,619.

ZIP Codes: 75551, 75555, 75562, 75564–65, 75601–08, 75615, 75631, 75633, 75637, 75639–45, 75647, 75650–54, 75657–63, 75666–67, 75669–72, 75680, 75682–85, 75687–89, 75691–94, 75701–13, 75750, 75755, 75757, 75760, 75762, 75771, 75788–89, 75791–92, 75797–99, 75901–04, 75915, 75929–31, 75935, 75937, 75941, 75943–44, 75946–49, 75954, 75958–59, 75961–65, 75968–69, 75972–75, 75978, 75980

* * *

SECOND DISTRICT

TED POE, Republican, of Humble, TX; born in Temple, TX, September 10, 1948; education: B.A., political science, Abilene Christian University, Abilene, TX, 1970; J.D., University of Houston, TX, 1973; professional: United States Air Force, 1970–1976; Felony Court Judge, 1981–2004; Trainer, Federal Bureau of Investigations National Academy; Chief Felony Prosecutor, District Attorney, Harris County, TX; United States Air Force Reserves Instructor, University of Houston; organizations: Board of the National Children's Alliance; Child Abuse Prevention Council; Victim's Rights Caucus; family: married to Carol; children: Kim, Kara, Kurt, and Kellee; committees: Foreign Affairs; Judiciary; elected to the 109th Congress on November 2, 2004; reelected to each succeeding Congress.

Office Listings

http://www.poe.house.gov

430 Cannon House Office Building, Washington, DC 20515 .... (202) 225–6565
Chief of Staff.—Gina Santucci. FAX: 225–5547
Press Secretary.—Shaylyn Hynes.
Scheduler.—Allyson Browning.
1801 Kingwood Drive, Suite 240, Kingwood, TX 77339 .... (866) 447–0242
505 Orleans Street, Suite 100, Beaumont, TX 77701 .... (409) 212–1997

Counties: HARRIS (part), JEFFERSON, LIBERTY (part). Population (2000), 651,619.

ZIP Codes: 77066, 77068–69, 77073, 77090, 77327–28, 77336, 77338–39, 77346, 77373, 77379, 77388–89, 77396, 77520–21, 77530, 77532, 77535, 77562, 77575, 77619, 77622, 77627, 77640, 77642, 77651, 77659, 77702–03, 77705–08, 77713

* * *

THIRD DISTRICT

SAM JOHNSON, Republican, of Dallas, TX; born in San Antonio, TX, October 11, 1930; education: B.S., business administration, Southern Methodist University, Dallas, TX, 1951; M.A., international affairs, George Washington University, Washington, DC, 1974; military service: served in Air Force, 29 years; Korea and Vietnam (POW in Vietnam, six years, ten months); director, Air Force Fighter Weapons School; flew with Air Force Thunderbirds Precision Flying Demonstration Team; graduate of Armed Services Staff College and National War College; military awards: two Silver Stars, two Legions of Merit, Distinguished Flying Cross, one Bronze Star with Valor, two Purple Hearts, four Air Medals, and three Outstanding Unit awards; ended career with rank of colonel and Air Division commander; retired, 1979; professional: opened homebuilding company, 1979; served 7 years in Texas House of Representatives; Smithsonian Board of Regents; U.S./Russian Joint Commission on POW/MIA; Texas State

Society; Congressional Medal of Honor Society; National Patriot Award Recipient, 2009; caucus and award: co-chair, Air Force Caucus; Living Legends of Aviation ''Freedom of Flight'' Award recipient, 2011; Rotary International, Paul Harris Fellow; founder, Republican Study Committee (formerly Conservative Action Team); chairman of the Board of Directors, Institute of Basic Life Principles; Deputy Whip; married the former Shirley L. Melton, 1950; three children: Dr. James Robert Johnson, Shirley Virginia (Gini) Mulligan and Beverly Briney; committees: Ways and Means; Joint Committee on Taxation; elected to the 102nd Congress by special election on May 18, 1991, to fill the vacancy caused by the resignation of Steve Bartlett; reelected to each succeeding Congress.

Office Listings

http://www.samjohnson.house.gov

1211 Longworth House Office Building, Washington, DC 20515 .... (202) 225–4201
Chief of Staff.—Dave Heil. FAX: 225–1485
Legislative Director.—Mark Williams.
Executive Assistant.—Lindsey Ray.
2929 North Central Expressway, Suite 240, Richardson, TX 75080 .... (972) 470–0892

Counties: COLLIN (part), DALLAS, (part). CITIES AND TOWNSHIPS: Allen, Dallas, Frisco, Garland, McKinney, Murphy, Parker, Plano, Richardson, Rowlett, and Sachse. Population (2000), 651,620.

ZIP Codes: 75002, 75007, 75009, 75013, 75023–26, 75030, 75034–35, 75040–42, 75044–48, 75069–71, 75074–75, 75078, 75080–82, 75085–86, 75088–89, 75093–94, 75098, 75228, 75238, 75245, 75248, 75252, 75287, 75355, 75367, 75370, 75378, 75382, 75409, 75424, 75442, 75454, 78243

* * *

FOURTH DISTRICT

RALPH M. HALL, Republican, of Rockwall, TX; born in Fate, TX, May 3, 1923; education: graduated, Rockwall High School, 1941; attended, Texas Christian University and the University of Texas; LL.B., Southern Methodist University, 1951; professional: lieutenant, carrier pilot (senior grade), U.S. Navy, 1942–45; lawyer; admitted to the Texas Bar, 1951; practiced law in Rockwall; county judge, Rockwall County, 1950–62; former president and chief executive officer, Texas Aluminum Corporation; past general counsel, Texas Extrusion Company, Inc.; past organizer, chairman, board of directors, now chairman of board, Lakeside National Bank of Rockwall (now Lakeside Bancshares, Inc.); past chairman, board of directors, Lakeside News, Inc.; past vice chairman, board of directors, Bank of Crowley; president, North and East Trading Company; vice president, Crowley Holding Co.; member: Texas State Senate, 1962–72; American Legion Post 117; VFW Post 6796; Rockwall Rotary Club; Rotary Clubs International; member: First Methodist Church; widower: (was married to the former Mary Ellen Murphy, 1944 (deceased); three sons: Hampton, Brett and Blakeley; committees: chair, Science, Space, and Technology; elected to the 97th Congress, November 4, 1980; reelected to each succeeding Congress.

Office Listings

http://www.house.gov/ralphhall

2405 Rayburn House Office Building, Washington, DC 20515 .... (202) 225–6673
Chief of Staff.—Janet Poppleton. FAX: 225–3332
Legislative Director.—Kyle Oliver.
104 North San Jacinto Street, Rockwall, TX 75087–2508 .... (972) 771–9118
District Assistant.—Tom Hughes.
101 East Pecan Street, Suite 114, Sherman, TX 75090–5989 .... (903) 892–1112
District Assistant.—Judy Rowton.
U.S. P.O., 320 Church Street, Suite 132, Sulphur Springs, TX 75482–2606 .... (903) 885–8138
District Assistant.—Martha Glover.
Bowie County Courthouse, 710 James Bowie Drive, New Boston, TX 75570–2328 (903) 628–8309
District Assistant.—Eric Cain.
4303 Texas Boulevard, Suite 2, Texarkana, TX 75503–3094 .... (903) 794–4445
District Assistant.—Marjorie Chandler.
Collin County Courts Facility, 1800 North Graves Street, Suite 101, McKinney, TX 75069–3322 .... (214) 726–9949
District Assistant.—Linda Schenck.

Counties: BOWIE COUNTY. CITIES AND TOWNSHIPS: De Kalb, Hooks, Leary, Maud, Nash, New Boston, Red Lick, Redwater, Texarkana, Wake Village. CAMP COUNTY, CITIES AND TOWNSHIPS: Pittsburg, Rocky Mound. CASS COUNTY. CITIES AND TOWNSHIPS: Atlanta, Avinger, Bloomburg, Domino, Douglassville, Hughes Springs, Linden, Marietta, Queen City. COLLIN COUNTY. CITIES AND TOWNSHIPS: Allen, Anna, Blue Ridge, Celina, Fairview, Farmersville, Frisco, Josephine, Lavon, Lowry Crossing, Lucas, McKinney, Melissa, Nevada, New Hope, Parker, Princeton, Prosper, Royse City, Sachse,

St. Paul, Van Alstyne, Westminster, Weston, Wylie, Winfield. DELTA COUNTY. CITIES AND TOWNSHIPS: Cooper, Pecan Gap. FANNIN COUNTY. CITIES AND TOWNSHIPS: Bailey, Bonham, Dodd City, Ector, Honey Grove, Ladonia, Leonard, Pecan Gap, Ravenna, Savoy, Trenton, Whitewright, Windom. FRANKLIN COUNTY. CITIES AND TOWNSHIPS: Mount Vernon, Winnsboro. GRAYSON COUNTY. CITIES AND TOWNSHIPS: Bells, Collinsville, Denison, Dorchester, Gunter, Howe, Knollwood, Pottsboro, Sadler, Sherman, Southmayd, Tioga, Tom Bean, Van Alstyne, Whitesboro, Whitewright. HOPKINS COUNTY. CITIES AND TOWNSHIPS: Como, Cumby, Sulphur Springs, Tira. HUNT COUNTY. CITIES AND TOWNSHIPS: Caddo Mills, Campbell, Celeste, Commerce, Greenville, Hawk Cove, Josephine, Lone Oak, Neylandville, Quinlan, West Tawakoni, Wolfe City. LAMAR COUNTY. CITIES AND TOWNSHIPS: Blossom, Deport, Paris, Reno, Roxton, Sun Valley, Toco. MORRIS COUNTY. CITIES AND TOWNSHIPS: Daingerfield, Hughes Springs, Lone Star, Naples, Omaha. RAINS COUNTY. CITIES AND TOWNSHIPS: Alba, East Tawakoni, Emory, Point. RED RIVER COUNTY. CITIES AND TOWNSHIPS: Annona, Avery, Bogata, Clarksville, Deport, Detroit. ROCKWALL COUNTY. CITIES AND TOWNSHIPS: Fate, Garland, Heath, McLendon-Chisholm, Mobile City, Rockwall, Rowlett, Royse City, Wylie. TITUS COUNTY. CITIES AND TOWNSHIPS: Miller's Cove, Mount Pleasant, Talco.

ZIP Codes: 75002, 75009, 75013, 75019, 75030, 75032, 75034–35, 75040–41, 75058, 75069, 75071, 75074, 75076, 75078, 75087–88, 75090, 75094, 75097–98, 75132, 75135, 75164, 75166, 75173, 75189, 75407, 75409, 75413–14, 75416–18, 75422–24, 75426, 75428–29, 75431–33, 75435–36, 75438–40, 75442, 75446, 75449, 75452–55, 75457, 75459, 75460, 75462, 75469, 75472–73, 75474, 75476, 75477, 75479, 75482, 75486–87, 75489, 75490–95, 75501, 75550–51, 75554, 75556, 75559–61, 75563, 75566–73, 75572, 75630, 75638, 75656, 75668, 75686, 75855, 76233, 76264, 76268, 76271, 76273

* * *

FIFTH DISTRICT

JEB HENSARLING, Republican, of Dallas, TX; born in Stephenville, TX, May 29, 1957; education: B.A., economics, Texas A&M University, 1979; J.D., University of Texas School of Law, 1982; professional: businessman; vice president, Maverick Capital, 1993–96; owner, San Jacinto Ventures, 1996–2002; vice president, Green Mountain Energy Co., 1999–2001; community service: American Cancer Society for the Dallas Metro Area; Children's Education Fund; Habitat for Humanity; religion: Christian; married: Melissa; children: Claire and Travis; chair, House Republican Conference; committees: Financial Services; elected to the 108th Congress on November 5, 2002; reelected to each succeeding Congress.

Office Listings

http://www.hensarling.house.gov

129 Cannon House Office Building, Washington, DC 20515 .... (202) 225–3484
Chief of Staff.—Andrew Duke. FAX: 226–4888
Legislative Director.—Kirsten Mork.
Press Secretary.—Sarah Rozier.
6510 Abrams Road, Suite 243, Dallas, TX 75238 .... (214) 349–9996
810 East Corsicana Street, Suite C, Athens, TX 77571 .... (903) 675–8288

Counties: ANDERSON, CHEROKEE, DALLAS (part), HENDERSON, KAUFMAN, VAN ZANDT, WOOD. Population (2000), 651,620.

ZIP Codes: 75030, 75032, 75041, 75043, 75047, 75049, 75088, 75103, 75114, 75117–18, 75124, 75126–27, 75140, 75142–43, 75147–50, 75156–61, 75163, 75169, 75180–82, 75185, 75187, 75214, 75218, 75227–28, 75231, 75238, 75243, 75253, 75336, 75355, 75357, 75359, 75374, 75382, 75390, 75393–94, 75410, 75444, 75474, 75480, 75494, 75497, 75751–52, 75754, 75756–59, 75763–66, 75770, 75772–73, 75778–80, 75782–85, 75789–90, 75801–03, 75832, 75839, 75844, 75853, 75861, 75880, 75882, 75884, 75886, 75925, 75976

* * *

SIXTH DISTRICT

JOE BARTON, Republican, of Ennis, TX; born in Waco, TX, September 15, 1949; education: graduated Waco High School, 1968; B.S., industrial engineering, Texas A&M University, College Station, 1972; M.S., industrial administration, Purdue University, West Lafayette, IN, 1973; professional: plant manager, and assistant to the vice president, Ennis Business Forms, Inc., 1973–81; awarded White House Fellowship, 1981–82; served as aide to James B. Edwards, Secretary, Department of Energy; member, Natural Gas Decontrol Task Force in the Office of Planning, Policy and Analysis; worked with the Department of Energy task force in support of the President's Private Sector Survey on Cost Control; natural gas decontrol and project cost control consultant, Atlantic Richfield Company; cofounder, Houston County Volunteer Ambulance Service, 1976; vice president, Houston County Industrial Development Authority, 1980; chairman, Crockett Parks and Recreation Board, 1979–80; vice president, Houston County Chamber of Commerce, 1977–80; member, Dallas Energy Forum; religion: Methodist; married: Terri; son, Jack; children: Brad, Alison and Kristin, from a previous marriage; stepchildren: Lindsay, and Cullen; committees: chair emeritus, Energy and Commerce; elected to the 99th Congress on November 6, 1984; reelected to each succeeding Congress.

Office Listings

http://www.joebarton.house.gov

2109 Rayburn House Office Building, Washington, DC 20515 .... (202) 225–2002
Chief of Staff.—Ryan Thompson. FAX: 225–3052
Communications Director.—Sean Brown.
Legislative Director.—Michael Weems.
Legislative Assistants: Emmanual Guillory, Julicann Martin.
Legislative Correspondent.—Nina Shelat.
Staff Assistant.—Jenny Howell.
6001 West Ronald Reagan Memorial Highway, Suite 200, Arlington, TX 76017 .... (817) 543–1000
Constituent Liaison.—Deborah Rollings. FAX: 548–7029
District Assistant.—Jodi Sacgesser.
Deputy District Director (Tarrant Co).—Michael Taylor.
Casework Director.—Christi Townsend.
2106A West Ennis Avenue, Ennis, TX 75119 (direct phone) .... (972) 875–8488
Deputy Chief of Staff.—Linda Gillespie. (972) 875–1907
Deputy District Director.—Dub Maines.
303 North 6th Street, Crockett, TX 75835 .... (936) 544–8488
District Assistant.—Karla Carr. FAX: 544–1739

Counties: Ellis, Freestone, Houston, Leon, Limestone, Navarro, Tarrant, Trinity. Cities and townships: Arlington, Bardwell, Buffalo, Centerville, Corsicana, Crockett, Crowley, Dawson, Ennis, Fairfield, Ferris, Fort Worth, Frost, Grapeland, Groveton, Italy, Kerens, Lovelady, Mansfield, Maypearl, Mexia, Midlothian, Milford, Oak Leaf, Palmer, Pecan Hill, Red Oak, Rice, Richland, and Waxahachie. Population (2000), 651,620.

ZIP Codes: 75050, 75052, 75054, 75101–02, 75104–06, 75109–10, 75119–20, 75125, 75144, 75146, 75151–55, 75165, 75167–68, 75831, 75833–35, 75838, 75840, 75844–52, 75855–56, 75858–60, 75862, 75865, 75926, 76001–07, 76010–19, 76028, 76036, 76040–41, 76050, 76055, 76060, 76063–65, 76084, 76094, 76096–97, 76119–20, 76123, 76126, 76132–34, 76140, 76155, 76162–63, 76623, 76626, 76635, 76639, 76641–42, 76651, 76667, 76670, 76679, 76681, 76686, 76693, 77850, 77855, 77865, 77871

* * *

SEVENTH DISTRICT

JOHN ABNEY CULBERSON, Republican, of Harris County, TX; born in Houston, TX, August 24, 1956; education: B.A., Southern Methodist University; J.D., South Texas College of Law; professional: attorney; awards: Citizens for a Sound Economy Friend of the Taxpayer Award; Texas Eagle Forum Freedom and Family Award; Houston Jaycees Outstanding Young Houstonian Award; Champion of Border Security; Ancient Coin Collectors Guild; Friend of Numismatics; Club for Growth's Defender of Economic Freedom; Congressional Management Foundation's Silver Mouse Award; Family Research Canals True Blue Award; Water Advocate ''Friend of the Shareholder'' Recognition; U.S. Chamber of Commerce; Spirit of Enterprise Guardian of Small Business by NFIB; Recognition from the 60 Plus Association; NumbersUSA ''A'' for Consistently Voting for American Workers and the Environment through Immigration Reduction; public service: Texas House of Representatives, 1987–2000; married: Belinda Burney, 1989; child: Caroline; committees: Appropriations; elected to the 107th Congress on November 7, 2000; reelected to each succeeding Congress.

Office Listings

http://www.culberson.house.gov

2352 Rayburn House Office Building, Washington, DC 20515 .... (202) 225–2571
Chief of Staff.—Tony Essalih. FAX: 225–4381
Legislative Director.—Ryan Stalnaker.
Deputy Chief of Staff.—Jamie Gahun.
10000 Memorial Drive, Suite 620, Houston, TX 77024–3490 .... (713) 682–8828
District Director.—Brittany Seabury.

County: Harris County (part). Population (2000), 651,620.

ZIP Codes: 77002, 77004–08, 77019, 77024–25, 77027, 77030, 77035–36, 77040–43, 77046, 77055–57, 77063–65, 77070, 77074, 77077, 77079–81, 77084, 77086, 77094–96, 77098, 77215, 77218–19, 77224–25, 77227, 77241–44, 77255–57, 77265–66, 77269, 77277, 77279–82, 77284, 77401–02, 77429, 77433

* * *

EIGHTH DISTRICT

KEVIN BRADY, Republican, of The Woodlands, TX; born in Vermillion, SD, April 11, 1955; education: B.S., business, University of South Dakota; professional: served in Texas

House of Representatives, 1991–96, the first Republican to capture the 15th District seat since the 1800s; chair, Council of Chambers of Greater Houston; president, East Texas Chamber Executive Association; president, South Montgomery County Woodlands Chamber of Commerce, 1985–present; director, Texas Chamber of Commerce Executives; Rotarian; awards: Achievement Award, Texas Conservative Coalition; Outstanding Young Texan (one of five), Texas Jaycees; Ten Best Legislators for Families and Children, State Bar of Texas; Legislative Standout, Dallas Morning News; Scholars Achievement Award for Excellence in Public Service, North Harris Montgomery Community College District; Victims Rights Equalizer Award, Texans for Equal Justice Center; Support for Family Issues Award, Texas Extension Homemakers Association; religion: attends Saints Simon and Jude Catholic Church; married: Cathy Brady; committees: vice chair, Joint Economic Committee; Ways and Means; elected to the 105th Congress; reelected to each succeeding Congress.

Office Listings

http://www.house.gov/brady

301 Cannon House Office Building, Washington, DC 20515 .... (202) 225–4901
Chief of Staff.—Doug Centilli. FAX: 225–5524
Communications Director.—Tracee Evans.
Press Secretary.—Rebecca Mark.
Legislative Director.—Kimberly Ellis.
200 River Pointe Drive, Suite 304, Conroe, TX 77304 .... (936) 441–5700
District Director.—Sarah Stephens.
1202 Sam Houston Avenue, Suite 8, Huntsville, TX 77340 .... (936) 439–9542
420 Green Avenue, Orange, TX 77630 .... (409) 883–4197

COUNTIES: HARDIN, JASPER, LIBERTY (part), MONTGOMERY, NEWTON, ORANGE, POLK, SAN JACINTO, TRINTY (part), TYLER, WALKER. CITIES AND TOWNSHIPS: Bevil Oaks, Bridge City, Browndell, Buna, Chester, Coldspring, Conroe, Colmesneil, Corrigan, Cut and Shoot, Dayton Lakes, Deweyville, Evadale, Goodrich, Hardin, Huntsville, Jasper, Kenefick, Kirbyville, Kountze, Lake Livingston, Lumberton, Magnolia, Mauriceville, Montgomery, New Waverly, Newton, Oak Ridge North, Oakhurst, Onalaska, Orange, Palton Village, Panorama Village, Pine Forest, Pinehurst, Pinewood Estates, Point Blank, Porter Heights, Roman Fores, Rose City, Rose Hill Acres, Seven Oaks, Shenandoah, Shepherd, Silshee, Sour Lake, South Toledo Bend, Splendora, Stagecoach, The Woodlands, Trinity, Vidor, West Livingston, West Orange, Willis, Woodbranch, and Woodville. Population (2000), 651,619.

ZIP Codes: 75931, 75951, 75956, 75966, 77318, 77320, 77340–44, 77348–49, 77350–51, 77355, 77359–60, 77364, 77367, 77371, 77378, 77399, 77561, 77611, 77614, 77630–32, 77656, 77659, 77862, 77939

* * *

NINTH DISTRICT

AL GREEN, Democrat, of Houston, TX; born in New Orleans, LA, September 1, 1947; raised in Florida; education: Florida A&M University, Tallahassee, FL, 1966–71; attended Tuskegee University, Tuskegee, AL; J.D., Texas Southern University, Houston, TX, 1974; professional: co-founded and co-managed the law firm of Green, Wilson, Dewberry and Fitch; Justice of the Peace, Precinct 7, Position 2, 1977–2004; organizations: former president of the Houston NAACP; Houston Citizens Chamber of Commerce; awards: Distinguished Service Award, 1978; Black Heritage Society, Outstanding Leadership Award, 1981; American Federation of Teachers, Citation for Service as a ''Courageous Defender of Due Process for Educators,'' 1983; *Ebony* Magazine's 100 Most Influential Black People, 2006; and the NAACP Fort Bend Branch Mickey Leland Humanitarian Award, 2006; Texas Black Democrats' Profiles of Courage Award, 2007; the AFL-CIO MLK Drum Major Award for Service, 2007; committees: Financial Services; elected to the 109th Congress on November 2, 2004; reelected to each succeeding Congress.

Office Listings

http://www.house.gov/algreen

2201 Rayburn House Office Building, Washington, DC 20515 .... (202) 225–7508
Chief of Staff.—Jacqueline Ellis. FAX: 225–2947
Legislative Director.—Susie Saavedra.
Senior Legislative Assistant.—Gregg Orton.
Press Secretary.—Alvaro Oritz. (713) 383–9234
3003 South Loop West, Suite 460, Houston, TX 77054 .... (713) 383–9234
District Office Policy Manager.—Kevin Dancy. FAX: 383–9202
District Office Administrative Manager.—Crystal Webster.
Press Secretary.—Alvaro Ortiz.

Counties: FORT BEND, HARRIS. Population (2000), 651,619.

ZIP Codes: 77004–05, 77021, 77025, 77030–31, 77033, 77035–36, 77042, 77045, 77047–48, 77051, 77053–54, 77056–57, 77061, 77063, 77071–72, 77074, 77077, 77081–83, 77085, 77087, 77096, 77099, 77230–31, 77233, 77235–37, 77251, 77254, 77263, 77271–72, 77274, 77401, 77411, 77469, 77477–78, 77489

* * *

TENTH DISTRICT

MICHAEL T. MCCAUL, Republican, of Austin, TX; born in Dallas, TX, January 14, 1962; education: B.S., Trinity University, San Antonio, TX, 1984; J.D., St. Mary's University, San Antonio, TX, 1987; professional: lawyer, private practice; deputy attorney general, office of Texas State Attorney General; committees: Ethics; Foreign Affairs; Homeland Security; Science, Space, and Technology; elected to the 109th Congress on November 2, 2004; reelected to each succeeding Congress.

Office Listings

http://www.mccaul.house.gov

131 Cannon House Office Building, Washington, DC 20515 .... (202) 225–2401
Chief of Staff.—Greg Hill. FAX: 225–5955
Legislative Director.—Alex Manning.
Scheduler/Office Manager.—Megan O'Brien.
5929 Balcones Drive, Suite 305, Austin, TX 78731 .... (512) 473–2357
Communications Director.—Mike Rosen.
Rosewood Professional Building, 990 Village Square, Suite B, Tomball, TX 77375 (281) 255–8372
1550 Foxlake, Suite 120, Houston, TX 77084 .... (281) 398–1247
2000 South Market Street, Suite 303, Brenham, TX 77833 .... (979) 830–8497

Counties: AUSTIN, BASTROP, BURLESON, HARRIS, LEE, TRAVIS, WALLER, WASHINGTON. Population (2000), 651,619.

ZIP Codes: 77070, 77084, 77094–95, 77218, 77269, 77284, 77375, 77377, 77379, 77383, 77388–89, 77391, 77410, 77413, 77418, 77423, 77426, 77429, 77433, 77445–47, 77449–50, 77452, 77466, 77473–74, 77476, 77484–85, 77491–94, 77833–36, 77838, 77852–53, 77863, 77868, 77878–80, 78602, 78615, 78621, 78650–51, 78653, 78659–60, 78664, 78682–83, 78691, 78703, 78705, 78708, 78710, 78713, 78716, 78718, 78720, 78724, 78727–31, 78733, 78746, 78751–59, 78761, 78763, 78765–66, 78779–80, 78785, 78788–89, 78931–33, 78940, 78942, 78944, 78946–48, 78950

* * *

ELEVENTH DISTRICT

K. MICHAEL CONAWAY, Republican, of Midland, TX; born in Borger, TX, June 11, 1948; education: B.B.A., Texas A&M–Commerce, 1970; professional: Spec 5 United States Army, 1970–72; tax manager, Price Waterhouse & Company, 1972–80; Chief Financial Officer, Keith D. Graham & Lantern Petroleum Company, 1980–81; Chief Financial Officer, Bush Exploration Company, 1982–84; Chief Financial Officer, Spectrum 7 Energy Corporation, 1984–86; Senior Vice President/Chief Financial Officer, United Bank, 1987–90; Senior Vice President, Texas Commerce Bank, 1990–92; owner, K. Conaway CPA, 1993–present; Deputy Republican Whip; religion: Baptist; married: Suzanne; children: Brian, Erin, Kara, and Stephanie; committees: Agriculture; Armed Services; Ethics; Permanent Select Committee on Intelligence; elected to the 109th Congress on November 2, 2004; reelected to each succeeding Congress.

Office Listings

http://www.house.gov/conaway

2430 Rayburn House Office Building, Washington, DC 20515 .... (202) 225–3605
Chief of Staff.—Richard Hudson. FAX: 225–1783
Legislative Director.—Scott C. Graves.
Scheduler.—Emily Lashbrook.
6 Desta Drive, Suite 2000, Midland, TX 79705 .... (432) 687–2390
District Scheduler.—Patsy Bain.
33 East Twohig, Room 307, San Angelo, TX 76903 .... (325) 659–4010
Regional Director.—Joanne Powell.

Counties: ANDREWS, BROWN, BURNET, COKE, COLEMAN, COMANCHE, CONCHO, CRANE, DAWSON, ECTOR, GILLESPIE, MENARD, MIDLAND, MILLS, GLASSCOCK, IRION, KIMBLE, LAMPASAS, LLANO, LOVING, MARTIN, MASON, MCCULLOCH, SUTTON (part), TOM GREEN, UPTON, MITCHELL, NOLAN (part), REAGAN, RUNNELS, SAN SABA, SCHLEICHER, SCURRY, STERLING, WARD, WINKLER. POPULATION (2000), 651,620.

ZIP Codes: 76246, 76432, 76442, 76444, 76455, 76550, 76801–04, 76821, 76823, 76825, 76834, 76837, 76844, 76853, 76856, 76859, 76861, 76864, 76866, 76872–73, 76877, 76901–04, 76932–33, 76935–36, 76941, 76945, 76950–51,

76957, 77381–82, 77393, 78611, 78624, 78643, 78654–69, 79331, 79512, 79532, 79545, 79549–50, 79556, 79565, 79567, 79605–09, 79714, 79760–69, 79701–13, 79739, 79742, 79745, 79756, 79778, 79789

* * *

TWELFTH DISTRICT

KAY GRANGER, Republican, of Fort Worth, TX; born in Greenville, TX, January 18, 1943; education: B.S., *magna cum laude*, 1965, and Honorary Doctorate of Humane Letters, 1992, Texas Wesleyan University; professional: owner, Kay Granger Insurance Agency, Inc.; former public school teacher; elected Mayor of Fort Worth, 1991, serving three terms; during her tenure, Fort Worth received All-America City Award from the National Civic League; former Fort Worth Councilwoman; past chair, Fort Worth Zoning Commission; past board member: Dallas-Fort Worth International Airport; North Texas Commission; Fort Worth Convention and Visitors Bureau; U.S. Conference of Mayors Advisory Board; Business and Professional Women's Woman of the Year, 1989; three grown children: J.D., Brandon and Chelsea; first woman Republican to represent Texas in the U.S. House; vice chair, Republican Conference; Deputy Republican Whip; committees: Appropriations; elected to the 105th Congress; reelected to each succeeding Congress.

Office Listings

http://www.house.gov/granger

320 Cannon House Office Building, Washington, DC 20515 .... (202) 225–5071
Chief of Staff.—Chelsey Hickman. FAX: 225–5683
Deputy Chief of Staff.—Matt Leffingwell.
Legislative Director.—Shannon Meade.
Staff Assistant.—Robert Ritz.
Scheduler.—Carlie Christensen.
1701 River Run Road, Suite 407, Fort Worth, TX 76107 .... (817) 338–0909
District Director.—Barbara Ragland. (817) 335–5852

Counties: PARKER, TARRANT (part), WISE. Population (2000), 651,619.

ZIP Codes: 76008, 76020, 76023, 76035–36, 76049, 76052, 76066–68, 76071, 76073, 76078, 76082, 76085–88, 76098, 76101–02, 76104, 76106–11, 76113–18, 76121–23, 76126–27, 76129–37, 76147–48, 76161–64, 76177, 76179–82, 76185, 76191–93, 76195–99, 76225, 76234, 76244, 76246, 76248, 76262, 76267, 76270, 76299, 76426, 76431, 76439, 76462, 76485–87, 76490

* * *

THIRTEENTH DISTRICT

MAC THORNBERRY, Republican, of Clarendon, TX; born in Clarendon, July 15, 1958; education: graduate, Clarendon High School; B.A., Texas Tech University; law degree, University of Texas; professional: rancher; attorney; admitted to the Texas Bar, 1983; member: Joint Forces Command Transformation; Republican Study Committee; Proliferation Prevention Forum; Congressional Rural Caucus; Rural Health Care Coalition; Anti-Terrorism Caucus; Interagency Coordination, Western Caucus; married: Sally Adams, 1986; children: Will and Mary Kemp; committees: Armed Services; Permanent Select Committee on Intelligence; elected to the 104th Congress; reelected to each succeeding Congress.

Office Listings

http://www.house.gov/thornberry

2209 Rayburn House Office Building, Washington, DC 20515 .... (202) 225–3706
Administrative Assistant.—Kelly Buck. FAX: 225–3486
Office Manager.—Alexandra Igleheart.
905 South Filmore, Suite 520, Amarillo, TX 79101 .... (806) 371–8844
Chief of Staff.—Josh Martin.
4245 Kemp, Suite 506, Wichita Falls, TX 76308 .... (940) 692–1700

Counties: ARCHER (part), ARMSTRONG, BAYLOR, BRISCOE, CARSON, CHILDRESS, CLAY, COLLINGSWORTH, COOKE (part), COTTLE, CROSBY, DALLAM, DICKENS, DONLEY, FOARD, GRAY, HALL, HANSFORD, HARDEMAN, HARTLEY, HASKELL, HEMPHILL, HUTCHINSON, JACK, JONES, KING, KNOX, LIPSCOMB, MONTAGUE, MOORE, MOTLEY, OCHILTREE, OLDHAM, PALO PINTO, POTTER, RANDALL, ROBERTS, SHERMAN, STONEWALL, SWISHER, THROCKMORTON, WHEELER, WICHITA, WILBARGER. Population (2000), 651,619.

ZIP Codes: 76066, 76067–68, 76228, 76230, 76234, 76238–40, 76250–53, 76255, 76261, 76263, 76265–66, 76270, 76272, 76301–02, 76305–11, 76352, 76354, 76357, 76360, 76363–67, 76369, 76371–73, 76377, 76379–80, 76384–85, 76388–

89, 76427, 76430, 76449–50, 76453, 76458–59, 76462–63, 76472, 76475, 76483–84, 76486–87, 76491, 79001–03, 79005, 79007–08, 79010–16, 79018–19, 79022, 79024, 79029, 79033–34, 79036, 79039–40, 79042, 79044, 79046, 79051–52, 79054, 79056–59, 79061–62, 79065–66, 79068, 79070, 79077–81, 79083–84, 79086–88, 79091–97, 79101–11, 79114, 79116–21, 79124, 79159, 79166, 79168, 79172, 79174, 79178, 79185, 79187, 79189, 79201, 79220, 79223, 79225–27, 79229–30, 79233–34, 79236–37, 79239, 79243–45, 79247–48, 79251–52, 79255–57, 79259, 79261, 79322, 79343, 79357, 79370, 79501–03, 79505, 79520–21, 79525, 79529, 79533, 79536, 79539–40, 79544, 79547–48, 79553, 79560, 79601

* * *

FOURTEENTH DISTRICT

RON PAUL, Republican, of Lake Jackson, TX; born in Pittsburgh, PA, August 20, 1935; education: B.A., Gettysburg College, 1957; M.D., Duke College of Medicine, North Carolina, 1961; professional: captain, U.S. Air Force, 1963–68; obstetrician and gynecologist; represented Texas' 22nd District in the U.S. House of Representatives, 1976–77, and 1979–85; married: the former Carol Wells, 1957; children: Ronnie, Lori Pyeatt, Rand, Robert and Joy LeBlanc; committees: Financial Services; Foreign Affairs; elected to the 105th Congress; reelected to each succeeding Congress.

Office Listings

http://www.house.gov/paul

203 Cannon House Office Building, Washington, DC 20515 .... (202) 225–2831
Chief of Staff.—Jeff Deist.
Legislative Director.—Norman Singleton.
Press Secretary.—Rachel Mills.
1501 East Mockingbird Lane, Suite 229, Victoria, TX 77904 .... (361) 576–1231
122 West Way Street, Suite 301, Lake Jackson, TX 77566 .... (979) 285–0231

Counties: ARANSAS, BRAZORIA (part), CALHOUN, CHAMBERS, FORT BEND (part), GALVESTON (part), JACKSON, MATAGORDA, VICTORIA, WHARTON. Population (2000), 651,619.

ZIP Codes: 77082, 77404, 77414–15, 77417, 77419–20, 77422–23, 77428, 77430–32, 77435–37, 77440–41, 77443–44, 77448, 77450–51, 77453–58, 77461, 77463–65, 77467–69, 77471, 77476, 77480, 77482–83, 77485–86, 77488, 77493–94, 77510–12, 77514–18, 77520–21, 77531, 77534–35, 77539, 77541–42, 77546, 77549–55, 77560, 77563, 77565–66, 77568, 77571, 77573–74, 77577–78, 77580–81, 77583–84, 77590–92, 77597, 77617, 77623, 77650, 77661, 77665, 77901–05, 77951, 77957, 77961–62, 77968–71, 77973, 77976–79, 77982–83, 77988, 77991, 77995, 78336, 78358, 78381–82

* * *

FIFTEENTH DISTRICT

RUBÉN HINOJOSA, Democrat, of Mercedes, TX; born in Edcouch, August 20, 1940; education: B.B.A., 1962, and M.B.A., 1980, University of Texas; professional: president and chief financial officer, H&H Foods, Inc.; elected member, Texas State Board of Education, 1975–84; board of directors, National Livestock and Meat Board and Texas Beef Industry Council, 1989–93; past president and chair of the board of directors, Southwestern Meat Packers Association; chair and member, board of trustees, South Texas Community College, 1993–96; past public member, Texas State Bar Board of Directors; former adjunct professor, Pan American University School of Business; past director, Rio Grande Valley Chamber of Commerce; Knapp Memorial Hospital Board of Trustees; Our Lady of Mercy Church Board of Catholic Advisors; past member, board of trustees, Mercedes Independent School District; former U.S. Jaycee Ambassador to Colombia and Ecuador; married: Martha; children: Ruben, Jr., Laura, Iliana, Kaitlin, and Karén; committees: Education and the Workforce; Financial Services; elected to the 105th Congress; reelected to each succeeding Congress.

Office Listings

http://www.hinojosa.house.gov

2262 Rayburn House Office Building, Washington, DC 20515 .... (202) 225–2531
Chief of Staff.—Connie Humphrey. FAX: 225–5688
Policy Advisor.—Greg Davis.
Communications Director.—Patricia Guillermo.
2864 West Trenton Road, Edinburg, TX 78539 .... (956) 682–5545
District Director.—Salomon Torres.
107 South St. Mary's Street, Beeville, TX 78102 .... (361) 358–8400
District Director.—Sylvia Ramirez.

Counties: BEE, BROOKS, CAMERON (part), DEWITT, DUVALL, GOLIAD, HIDALGO (part), JIM WELLS, KARNES, LIVE OAK, REFUGIO, SAN PATRICIO (part). CITIES AND TOWNSHIPS: Alamo, Alice, Beeville, Donna, Edcouch, Edinburg, Elroy,

Elsa, Goliad, Harlingen, LaVilla, Mathis, McAllen, Mercedes, Mission, Odem, Pharr, San Juan, Sinton, Taft, Three Rivers, and Weslaco. Population: (2000) 651,619.

ZIP Codes: 77905, 77954, 77960, 77963, 77967, 77974, 77989, 77993–94, 78022, 78060, 78071, 78075, 78102, 78104, 78107, 78119, 78125, 78142, 78145–46, 78151, 78162, 78330, 78332, 78335–36, 78343, 78350, 78352–53, 78355, 78359, 78362–64, 78368, 78370, 78372, 78374, 78380, 78383, 78387, 78389–91, 78501–05, 78516, 78537–41, 78543, 78549, 78557–58, 78561–63, 78565, 78569–70, 78572–74, 78577, 78579–80, 78589, 78595–96, 78599

* * *

SIXTEENTH DISTRICT

SILVESTRE REYES, Democrat, of El Paso, TX; born in Canutillo, TX, November 10, 1944; education: graduated, Canutillo High School, 1964; associate degree, El Paso Community College, 1976; attended University of Texas, Austin, 1964–65, and El Paso, 1965–66; served in U.S. Army, 1966–68, Vietnam combat veteran; U.S. Border Patrol, chief patrol agent, 26½ years, retired December 1, 1995; member: Canutillo School Board, 1968–69, 21st Century Democrats, El Paso County Democrats, and Unite El Paso; married: the former Carolina Gaytan, 1968; children: Monica, Rebecca and Silvestre Reyes, Jr.; committees: Armed Services; Veterans' Affairs; elected on November 5, 1996, to the 105th Congress; reelected to each succeeding Congress.

Office Listings

http://www.house.gov/reyes

2210 Rayburn House Office Building, Washington, DC 20515 .... (202) 225–4831
Chief of Staff.—Perry Finney Brody. FAX: 225–2016
Press Secretary.—Vincent Perez.
Scheduler / Office Manager.—Liza Lynch.
Legislative Director.—Luis Torres.
310 North Mesa, Suite 400, El Paso, TX 79901 .... (915) 534–4400
Deputy Chief of Staff.—Sal Payan. FAX: 534–7426

Counties: EL PASO (part). CITIES AND TOWNSHIPS: Anthony, Canutillo, El Paso, Fabens, Horizon City, San Elizario, Socorro, Vinton, and Westway. Population (2000), 651,619.

ZIP Codes: 79821, 79835–36, 79838–39, 79849, 79901–08, 79910, 79912–18, 79920, 79922–27, 79929–32, 79934–38, 79940–55, 79958, 79960–61, 79968, 79976, 79978, 79980, 79995–99, 88510–21, 88523–36, 88538–50, 88553–63, 88565–90, 88595

* * *

SEVENTEENTH DISTRICT

WILLIAM H. ''BILL'' FLORES, Republican, of Bryan, TX; born at Warren Air Force Base, Cheyenne, WY, February 25, 1954; education: graduated, Stratford High School; Stratford, TX, 1972; B.B.A., *cum laude,* Texas A&M University, College Station, TX, 1976; M.B.A., Houston Baptist University, Houston, TX, 1985; Texas Certified Public Accountant (CPA), 1978–present; commissioner, Texas Real Estate Commission (appointed by Governor Perry), 2004–09; CEO and president, Phoenix Exploration Company, 2006–09; Texas A&M University Distinguished Alumnus, 2010; married: the former Gina Bass; children: Will and John; daughter-in-law, Aimee; granddaughter, Britain Grace; committees: Budget; Natural Resources; Veterans' Affairs; elected to the 112th Congress on November 2, 2010.

Office Listings

http://flores.house.gov

1505 Longworth House Office Building, Washington, DC 20515 .... (202) 225–6105
Chief of Staff.—Jeff Morehouse. FAX: 225–0350
Press Secretary.—Genny Carter.
400 Austin Avenue, Suite 302, Waco, TX 76710 .... (254) 732–0748
District Director.—Edward Getterman.
1 North Walnut Street, Suite 145, Cleburne, TX 76033 .... (817) 774–2551
2800 South Texas Avenue, Suite 403, Bryan, TX 77802 .... (979) 703–4037
FAX: 691–8939

Counties: BOSQUE, BRAZOS, BURLESON (part), GRIMES (part), HILL, HOOD, JOHNSON, LIMESTONE (part), MADISON, MCLENNAN, ROBERTSON (part), SOMMERVELL. CITIES OF: Anderson, Bryan, Cleburne, College Station, Glen Rose, Granbury, Groesbeck, Hillsboro, Madisonville, Miami, Valley Mills, and Waco. Population (2005), 651,786.

ZIP Codes: 75846, 75852, 76009, 76028, 76031, 76033, 76035–36, 76043–44, 76048–50, 76055, 76058–59, 76061, 76063, 76070, 76077, 76084, 76087, 76093, 76097, 76433, 76439, 76462, 76465, 76467, 76476, 76524, 76557, 76561, 76596,

76621–22, 76624, 76627–31, 76633–38, 76640, 76642–45, 76648–50, 76652–55, 76657, 76660, 76664–66, 76670–71, 76673, 76676, 76678, 76682, 76684, 76687, 76689–92, 76701–08, 76710–12, 76714–16, 76795, 76797–99, 77333, 77356, 77363, 77801–03, 77805–08, 77830–31, 77836–38, 77840–45, 77852, 77856, 77859, 77861–64, 77866–68, 77870, 77872–73, 77875–76, 77878–79, 77881–82

* * *

EIGHTEENTH DISTRICT

SHEILA JACKSON LEE, Democrat, of Houston, TX; born in Queens, NY, January 12, 1950; education: graduated, Jamaica High School; B.A., Yale University, New Haven, CT, 1972; J.D., University of Virginia Law School, 1975; professional: practicing attorney for twelve years; AKA Sorority; Houston Area Urban League; American Bar Association; staff counsel, U.S. House Select Committee on Assassinations, 1977–78; admitted to the Texas Bar, 1975; city council (at large), Houston, 1990–94; Houston Municipal Judge, 1987–90; married Dr. Elwyn Cornelius Lee, 1973; two children: Erica Shelwyn and Jason Cornelius Bennett; committees: Homeland Security; Judiciary; elected to the 104th Congress; reelected to each succeeding Congress.

Office Listings

http://www.jacksonlee.house.gov

2160 Rayburn House Office Building, Washington, DC 20515 .... (202) 225–3816
Chief of Staff.—Glenn Rushing. FAX: 225–3317
Legislative Director / Chief Counsel.—Janice Bashford.
Legislative Counsel.—Christina Weaver.
Legislative Correspondent.—Sara McGovern.
Executive / Staff Assistant.—Sharef Al Najjar.
1919 Smith Street, Suite 1180, Houston, TX 77002 .... (713) 655–0050
District Director.—Ernest McGowan.
District Administrator.—Michael Halpin.
Caseworker.—Matt Phelan.
Senior Field Representative / Law Enforcement Liaison.—Reginald Williams.
Staff Liaison.—Gerald Womack.
Special Assistant.—Janice Weaver.
Executive Assistant.—Bronson E. Woods.
Caseworkers: Gareth Morgans, Tonya Williams.
420 West 19th Street, Houston, TX 77008 .... (713) 861–4070
6719 West Montgomery, Suite 204, Houston, Texas 77091 .... (713) 691–4882

Counties: HARRIS COUNTY (part). CITY OF: Houston. Population (2000), 651,620.

ZIP Codes: 77001–10, 77013, 77016, 77018–24, 77026, 77028–30, 77033, 77035, 77038, 77040–41, 77045, 77047–48, 77051–52, 77054–55, 77064, 77066–67, 77076, 77078, 77080, 77086–88, 77091–93, 77097–98, 77201–06, 77208, 77210, 77212, 77216, 77219, 77221, 77226, 77230, 77233, 77238, 77240–41, 77251–53, 77255, 77265–66, 77277, 77288, 77291–93, 77297–99

* * *

NINETEENTH DISTRICT

RANDY NEUGEBAUER, Republican, of Lubbock, TX; born in St. Louis, MO, December 24, 1949; education: Texas Tech University, 1972; professional: small businessman (home building industry); organizations: West Texas Home Builders Association; Land Use and Developers Council; Texas Association of Builders; National Association of Home Builders; Campus Crusade for Christ; public service: Lubbock City Council, 1992–98; served as Mayor Pro Tempore, 1994–96; leader, coalition to create the Ports-to-Plains Trade Corridor; awards: Lubbock Chamber of Commerce Distinguished Service Award; Reese Air Force Base Friend of Reese Award; religion: Baptist; married: Dana; two children; committees: Agriculture; Financial Services; Science, Space, and Technology; elected to the 108th Congress, by special election, on June 3, 2003; reelected to each succeeding Congress.

Office Listings

http://www.randy.house.gov

1424 Longworth House Office Building, Washington, DC 20515 .... (202) 225–4005

Chief of Staff.—Jeanette Whitener. FAX: 225–9615
Communications Director.—Matt Crow.
Senior Legislative Assistant.—Andrew Brandt.
Legislative Assistants: Erik Johnson, David Rokeach.
Office Manager / Scheduler / Executive Assistant.—Melissa James.
Legislative Correspondent.—Caitlin Alcala.
Staff Assistant.—Lindsey Shackelford.
Communications Assistant.—Jennabeth Taliaferro.
Federal Building, 611 University Avenue, #220, Lubbock, TX 79401 .... (806) 763–1611
District Director.—Brice Foster.

Counties: ARCHER, BAILEY, BORDEN, CALLAHAN, CASTRO, COCHRAN, DEAF SMITH, EASTLAND, FISHER, FLOYD, GAINES, GARZA, HALE, HOCKLEY, HOWARD, KENT, LAMB, LUBBOCK, LYNN, NOLAN, PARMER, SHACKELFORD, STEPHENS, TAYLOR, TERRY, YOAKUM, YOUNG. Population (2000), 651,619.

ZIP Codes: 76302, 76305, 76308, 76310, 76351, 76360, 76366, 76370, 76372, 76374, 76379, 76389, 76424, 76427, 76429–30, 76435, 76437, 76442–43, 76445, 76448, 76450, 76454, 76459–60, 76462–64, 76466, 76469–70, 76475, 76481, 76491, 79009, 79021, 79025, 79027, 79031–32, 79035, 79041, 79043, 79045, 79053, 79063–64, 79072–73, 79082, 79085, 79221, 79231, 79235, 79241, 79250, 79258, 79311–14, 79316, 79320, 79323–26, 79329–30, 79336, 79338–39, 79342, 79344–47, 79350–51, 79353, 79355–56, 79358–60, 79363–64, 79366–67, 79369–73, 79376, 79378–83, 79401–16, 79423–24, 79430, 79452–53, 79457, 79464, 79490–91, 79493, 79499, 79504, 79506, 79508, 79510–11, 79518–20, 79526, 79528, 79530, 79532–37, 79541, 79543, 79545–46, 79549, 79556, 79560–63, 79566–67, 79601–05, 79720–21, 79733, 79738, 79748

* * *

TWENTIETH DISTRICT

CHARLES A. GONZALEZ, Democrat, of San Antonio, TX; born in San Antonio, May 5, 1945; son of former Representative Henry Gonzalez, who served the 20th District from 1961–99; education: Thomas A. Edison High School, 1965; B.A., University of Texas at Austin, 1969; J.D., St. Mary's School of Law, 1972; professional: elementary school teacher; private attorney, 1972–82; Municipal Court Judge; County Court at Law Judge, 1983–87; District Judge, 1989–97; chair, Congressional Hispanic Caucus; committees: Energy and Commerce; House Administration; Joint Committee on Printing; elected to the 106th Congress; reelected to each succeeding Congress.

Office Listings

http://www.gonzalez.house.gov

1436 Longworth House Office Building, Washington, DC 20515 .... (202) 225–3236
Chief of Staff.—Leo Muñoz. FAX: 225–1915
Scheduler.—Sophie Torres.
Federal Building, B–124, 727 East Durango Boulevard, San Antonio, TX 78206 ... (210) 472–6195

Counties: BEXAR COUNTY (part). CITIES OF: Alamo Heights, Balcones Heights, Converse, Kirby, Lackland AFB, Leon Valley, and San Antonio. Population (2000), 651,619.

ZIP Codes: 78073, 78109, 78201–19, 78225–31, 78233, 78236–46, 78250, 78252, 78254

* * *

TWENTY-FIRST DISTRICT

LAMAR S. SMITH, Republican, of San Antonio, TX; born in San Antonio, November 19, 1947; education: graduated, Texas Military Institute, San Antonio, 1965; B.A., Yale University, New Haven, CT, 1969; management intern, Small Business Administration, Washington, DC, 1969–70; business and financial writer, *The Christian Science Monitor*, Boston, MA, 1970–72; J.D., Southern Methodist University School of Law, Dallas, TX, 1975; admitted to the State Bar of Texas, 1975, and commenced practice in San Antonio with the firm of Maebius and Duncan, Inc.; elected chairman of the Republican Party of Bexar County, TX, 1978 and 1980; elected District 57–F State Representative, 1981; elected Precinct 3 Commissioner of Bexar County, 1982 and 1984; partner, Lamar Seeligson Ranch, Jim Wells County, TX; married: Beth Schaefer; children: Nell Seeligson and Tobin Wells; committees: chair, Judiciary; Homeland Security; Science, Space, and Technology; elected to the 100th Congress on November 4, 1986; reelected to each succeeding Congress.

Office Listings

http://lamarsmith.house.gov

2409 Rayburn House Office Building, Washington, DC 20515 .... (202) 225–4236

Chief of Staff.—Jennifer Brown. FAX: 225–8628
Legislative Director / Scheduler.—Ashlee Vinyard.
Guaranty Federal Building, 1100 North East Loop 410, Suite 640, San Antonio, TX 78209 .... (210) 821–5024
District Director.—Mike Asmus.
3532 Bee Cave Road, Suite 100, Austin, TX 78746 .... (512) 306–0439
301 Junction Highway, Suite 346C, Kerrville, TX 78028 .... (830) 896–0154

Counties: BANDERA, BEXAR (part), BLANCO, COMAL, KENDALL, KERR, REAL, TRAVIS (part). Population (2000), 651,619.

ZIP Codes: 78006, 78015, 78070, 78135, 78148, 78150, 78154, 78163, 78209, 78213, 78216–18, 78239, 78247, 78258–61, 78266, 78270, 78280, 78606, 78610–11, 78613, 78618–20, 78623, 78630–31, 78635–36, 78641, 78645–46, 78652, 78654, 78663, 78666, 78669, 78676, 78726, 78730, 78732–39, 78746, 78749–50, 78759, 78780

* * *

TWENTY-SECOND DISTRICT

PETE OLSON, Republican, of Sugar Land, TX; born in Fort Lewis, WA, December 9, 1962; education: B.A., Rice University, Houston, TX, 1985; Law Degree, University of Texas, Austin, TX, 1988; United States Navy, 1988–98; United States Senate, 1998–2007; Naval Aviator wings, 1991; Naval Liaison United States Senate; religion: United Methodist; married: Nancy Olson; children: Kate and Grant; committees: Energy and Commerce; elected to the 111th Congress on November 4, 2008; reelected each succeeding Congress.

Office Listings

http://olson.house.gov

312 Cannon House Office Building, Washington, DC 20515 .... (202) 225–5951
Chief of Staff.—Steve Ruhlen. FAX: 225–5241
Legislative Director.—Nicole Alexander.
Communications Director.—Melissa Kelly.
Scheduler.—Marjorie Dornette.
1650 Highway 6, Suite 150, Sugarland, TX 77478 .... (281) 494–2690
District Director.—Tyler Nelson.
17225 El Camino Real, Suite 447, Houston, TX 77058 .... (281) 486–1095
Deputy District Director.—Robert Quarles. FAX: 486–1479

Counties: BRAZORIA, FORT BEND, GALVESTON, HARRIS (part), JEFFERSON. CITIES OF: Baytown, Beaumont, Galveston, La Marque, Missouri City, Port Arthur, Pearland, Rosenberg, Stafford, Sugar Land and Texas City. Population (2000), 651,619.

ZIP Codes: 77044, 77049, 77058, 77062, 77089, 77258, 77346, 77362, 77364, 77369, 77435, 77510–11, 77514, 77517–18, 77520–22, 77532, 77535, 77539, 77546, 77549–55, 77560, 77562–63, 77565, 77568, 77573–75, 77580–82, 77590–92, 77597–98, 77613, 77617, 77619, 77622–23, 77625–27, 77629, 77631, 77640–43, 77650–51, 77655, 77659–61, 77663–65, 77701–08, 77710, 77713, 77720, 77725–26

* * *

TWENTY-THIRD DISTRICT

FRANCISCO ''QUICO'' CANSECO, Republican, of San Antonio; born in Laredo, TX, July 30, 1949; attended Culver Military Academy, IN; B.A., history, Saint Louis University, St. Louis, MO, 1972; J.D., Saint Louis University School of Law, St. Louis, 1975; professional: attorney, General Counsel at Union National Bank of Texas, 1987–92, chairman of Texas Heritage Bancshares, 2001–07; president / director of FMC Developers since 1998; director of Hondo National Bank of Texas since 1995; religion: Roman Catholic; spouse: Gloria Canseco; children: Anni, Quico Jr., and Carlos; committees: Financial Services; elected to the 112th Congress on November 2, 2010.

Office Listings

http://www.canseco.house.gov

1339 Longworth House Office Building, Washington, DC 20515 .... (202) 225–4511

Chief of Staff.—Scott Yeldell. FAX: 225–2237
Legislative Director.—Kyle Jackson.
Scheduler.—Amanda Canada.
Communications Director.—Valentina Weis.
Deputy Communications Director.—Spencer Yeldell.
Senior Legislative Assistant.—Brian O'Shea.
Legislative Assistant.—Jason Herbert.
Legislative Correspondent.—Alexandra Franceschi.
Staff Assistant.—Jimmy Milstead.
1313 Southeast Military Drive, Suite 101, San Antonio, TX 78214 .... (210) 922–7826
FAX: 924–3560
6363 DeZavala Road, Suite 105, San Antonio, TX 78249 .... (210) 561–8855
FAX: 877–5835
309 Mills Street, Suite C, 2nd Floor, Del Rio, TX 78840.
100 South Monroe Street, Eagle Pass, TX 78852.
103 West Callaghan, Fort Stockton, TX 79735.

Counties: BEXAR (part), BREWSTER, CROCKETT, CULBERSON, DIMMIT, EDWARDS, EL PASO (part), HUDSPETH, JEFF DAVIS, KINNEY, MAVERICK, MEDINA, PECOS, PRESIDIO, REEVES, SUTTON (part), TERRELL, UVALDE, VAL VERDE, ZAVALA. POPULATION (2000) 651,619.

ZIP Codes: 76943, 76950, 78002, 78006, 78009, 78015–16, 78023, 78039, 78052, 78054, 78056, 78059, 78066, 78069, 78073, 78112, 78163, 78202–03, 78205, 78210–11, 78214, 78216, 78220–26, 78230–32, 78235, 78240, 78242, 78245, 78248–58, 78260, 78263–64, 78269, 78801–02, 78827–30, 78832, 78834, 78836–43, 78847, 78850–53, 78860–61, 78870–72, 78877, 78880–81, 78884, 78886, 79718, 79730, 79734–35, 79740, 79743–44, 79770, 79772, 79780–81, 79785–86, 79830–32, 79834, 79836–37, 79839, 79842–43, 79845–48, 79851–55, 79927–28, 79938

* * *

TWENTY-FOURTH DISTRICT

KENNY MARCHANT, Republican, of Coppell, TX; born in Bonham, TX, February 23, 1951; education: B.A., Southern Nazarene University, Bethany, OK, 1974; attended Nazarene Theological Seminary, Kansas City, MO, 1975–76; professional: real estate developer; member of the Carrollton, TX, city council, 1980–84; mayor of Carrollton, TX, 1984–87; member of the Texas State House of Representatives, 1987–2004; member, Advisory Board of Children's Medical Center; married: Donna; four children; committees: Ways and Means; elected to the 109th Congress on November 2, 2004; reelected to each succeeding Congress.

Office Listings

http://www.house.gov/marchant

1110 Longworth House Office Building, Washington, DC 20515 .... (202) 225–6605
Chief of Staff.—Brian Thomas. FAX: 225–0074
Legislative Director / Scheduler.—Scott Cunningham.
Communications Director.—Ryan Moy.
9901 East Valley Ranch Parkway, Suite 3035, Irving, TX 75063 .... (972) 556–0162

Counties: DALLAS (part), TARRANT (part), DENTON (part). CITIES AND TOWNSHIPS: Bedford, Carrollton, Cedar Hill, Colleyville, Coppell, Dallas, Duncanville, Euless, Farmer's Branch, Fort Worth, Grand Prairie, Grapevine, Hurst, Irving, Lewisville, Plano, and Southlake. Population (2000), 651,619.

ZIP Codes: 75006–07, 75010–11, 75014–17, 75019, 75024, 75027, 75029, 75037, 75038, 75050–54, 75056–57, 75060–63, 75067, 75093, 75099, 75104, 75106, 75116, 75137–38, 75211, 75234, 75236, 75244, 75249, 75261, 75287, 75368, 75370, 75379, 75381, 75387, 75396, 75398, 76005–06, 76011, 76021–22, 76034, 76039, 76040, 76051, 76054, 76092, 76095, 76099, 76155, 76262, 76299

* * *

TWENTY-FIFTH DISTRICT

LLOYD DOGGETT, Democrat, of Austin, TX; born in Austin, October 6, 1946; education: graduated, Austin High School; B.B.A., University of Texas, Austin, 1967; J.D., University of Texas, 1970; president, University of Texas Student Body; associate editor, *Texas Law Review*; Outstanding Young Lawyer, Austin Association of Young Lawyers; president, Texas Consumer Association; religion: member, First United Methodist Church; admitted to the Texas State Bar, 1971; Texas State Senate, 1973–85, elected at age 26; Senate author of 124 state laws and Senate sponsor of 63 House bills enacted into law; elected president pro tempore of Texas Senate; served as acting governor; named Outstanding Young Texan by Texas Jaycees; Arthur B. DeWitty Award for outstanding achievement in human rights, Austin NAACP; honored for work by Austin Rape Crisis Center, Planned Parenthood of Austin; Austin Chapter, American

Institute of Architects; Austin Council on Alcoholism; Disabled American Veterans; justice on Texas Supreme Court, 1989–94; chairman, Supreme Court Task Force on Judicial Ethics, 1992–94; Outstanding Judge (Mexican-American Bar of Texas), 1993; adjunct professor, University of Texas School of Law, 1989–94; James Madison Award, Texas Freedom of Information Foundation, 1990; First Amendment Award, National Society of Professional Journalists, 1990; member: co-founder, House Information Technology Roundtable; Democratic Caucus Task Force on Education; Congressional Task Force on Tobacco and Health; Democratic Caucus Task Force on Child Care; married: Libby Belk Doggett, 1969; children: Lisa and Cathy; committees: Budget; Ways and Means; elected to the 104th Congress; reelected to each succeeding Congress.

Office Listings

http://www.house.gov/doggett

201 Cannon House Office Building, Washington, DC 20515 .... (202) 225–4865
Chief of Staff.—Michael J. Mucchetti. FAX: 225–3073
Systems Administrator.—Andrew Okuyiga.
Press Secretary.—Sarah Dohl.
Staff Assistant.—Doug Molof.
300 East 8th Street, Suite 763, Austin, TX 78701 .... (512) 916–5921
District Director.—Amanda Tyler

Counties: BASTROP, CALDWELL, COLORADO, FAYETTE, GONZALES, HAYS, LAVACA, TRAVIS (part). Population (2000), 651,619.

ZIP Codes: 77434, 77442, 77474, 77954, 77964, 77975, 77984, 77986–87, 77994–95, 78122, 78130, 78140, 78159, 78602, 78604, 78610, 78612, 78614, 78616–17, 78619–23, 78629, 78632, 78638, 78640, 78644, 78648, 78652–53, 78655–56, 78658–59, 78661–63, 78666–67, 78669, 78676–77, 78701–02, 78704–05, 78719, 78721–25, 78734–39, 78741–42, 78744–49, 78751–52, 78760–62, 78932–35, 78938, 78940–43, 78945–46, 78949–54, 78956–57, 78959–63

* * *

TWENTY-SIXTH DISTRICT

MICHAEL C. BURGESS, Republican, of Denton County, TX; born, December 23, 1950; education: Bachelor and Masters degrees in physiology, North Texas State University, M.D., University of Texas medical school in Houston; Masters degree in Medical Management, University of Texas in Dallas; completed medical residency programs, Parkland Hospital in Dallas; professional: founder, Private Practice Specialty Group for Obstetrics and Gynecology; former Chief of Staff and Chief of Obstetrics, Lewisville Medical Center; organizations: former president, Denton County Medical Society; Denton County delegate, Texas Medical Association; alternate delegate, American Medical Association; married: Laura; three children; committees: Energy and Commerce; Joint Economic Committee; elected to the 108th Congress on November 5, 2002; reelected to each succeeding Congress.

Office Listings

http://www.burgess.house.gov

2241 Rayburn House Office Building, Washington, DC 20515 .... (202) 225–7772
Chief of Staff.—Barry Brown. FAX: 225–2919
Legislative Director.—James Paluskiewicz.
Press Secretary.—Whitney Thompson.
Scheduler.—Amanda Stevens.
1660 South Stemmons Freeway, Suite 230, Lewisville, TX 75067 .... (972) 434–9700
1100 Circle Drive, Suite 200, Fort Worth, TX 76119 .... (817) 531–8454

Counties: COOKE (part), DALLAS (part), DENTON (part), TARRANT (part). Population (2000) 651,619.

ZIP Codes: 75009, 75019, 75022, 75028, 75034, 75056–57, 75063, 75067–68, 75077–78, 75261, 76012–13, 76021–22, 76034, 76040, 76051–54, 76092, 76102–05, 7610–12, 76115, 76117–20, 76134, 76140, 76148, 76177, 76180, 76201, 76205, 76207–10, 76226–27, 76233–34, 76240, 76247–49, 76258–59, 76262, 76266, 76272, 76273

* * *

TWENTY-SEVENTH DISTRICT

BLAKE FARENTHOLD, Republican, of Corpus Christi, TX; born in Corpus Christi, December 12, 1961; education: B.S., radio television, and film, University of Texas, Austin, TX, 1985; J.D., St. Mary's University of Law School, San Antonio, TX, 1989; professional: lawyer, private practice; business owner; committees: Homeland Security; Oversight and Government Reform; Transportation and Infrastructure; elected to the 112th Congress on November 2, 2010.

Office Listings

http://www.farenthold.house.gov

2110 Rayburn House Office Building, Washington, DC 20515 .... (202) 225–7742
Chief of Staff.—Scott Graves. FAX: 226–1134
Executive Assistant / Scheduling.—Emily Wilkes.
Legislative Director.—Blake Adami.
Communications Director.—Margarita Valdez.
101 North Shoreline Boulevard, Suite 300, Corpus Christi, TX 78401 .... (361) 884–2222
1805 Ruben Torres, Suite B–27, Brownsville, TX 78521 .... (956) 544–8800

Counties: CAMERON (part), KENNEDY, KLEBERG, NUECES, SAN PATRICO, (part), WILLACY. Population (2000), 651,619.

ZIP Codes: 78330, 78335–36, 78338–39, 78343, 78347, 78351, 78359, 78362–64, 78373–74, 78379–80, 78383, 78385, 78390, 78401–19, 78426–27, 78460, 78463, 78465–78, 78480, 78520–23, 78526, 78550, 78552, 78559, 78561, 78566–67, 78569, 78575, 78578, 78580, 78583, 78586, 78590, 78592, 78594, 78597–98

* * *

TWENTY-EIGHTH DISTRICT

HENRY CUELLAR, Democrat, of Laredo, TX; born in Laredo, September 19, 1955; education: Associate's Degree from Laredo Community College, Laredo, TX, 1976 (then known as Laredo Junior College); B.S., *cum laude*, foreign service from the Edmund A. Walsh School of Foreign Service at Georgetown University, Washington, DC, 1978; J.D., University of Texas, Austin, TX, 1981; M.B.A., international trade, from Texas A&M University, Laredo, TX, 1982; Ph.D., government, University of Texas, Austin, TX, 1998; with a total of five advanced degrees, Congressman Cuellar is the most degreed member of Congress; professional: lawyer, private practice; attorney, Law Office of Henry Cuellar, 1981–present; instructor, Department of Government, Laredo Community College, Laredo, TX, 1982–86; Licensed United States Customs Broker, 1983–present; adjunct professor, International Commercial Law, Texas A&M International, 1984–86; Representative, Texas State House of Representatives, 1986–2001; Secretary of State, State of Texas, 2001; public and civic organizations: board of directors, Kiwanis Club of Laredo, TX, 1982–83; co-founder/president, Laredo Volunteers Lawyers Program, Inc., 1982–83; board of directors, United Way, 1982–83; co-founder/treasurer, Stop Child Abuse and Neglect, 1982–83, and advisory board member, 1984; president, board of directors, Laredo Legal Aid Society, Inc., 1982–84; president, board of directors, Laredo Young Lawyers Association, 1983–84; sustaining member, Texas Democratic Party, 1984; legal advisor, American GI, local chapter, 1986–87; International Trade Association, Laredo State University, 1988; Texas Delegate, National Democratic Convention, 1992; president, board of directors, International Good Neighbor Council; member, The College of the State Bar of Texas, 1994; Texas Lyceum, 1997; policy board of advisors, Texas Hispanic Journal of Law, University of Texas Law School, 2002; member: American Bar Association; Inter-American Bar Association; Texas Bar Association; Webb/Laredo Bar Association; recipient of various awards; vice chairman of the Steering and Policy Committee; Congressional Unmanned Systems Caucus, Senior Whip; member of the Blue Dog Coalition; religion: Catholic; married: wife, Imelda; two daughters, Christina Alexandra and Catherine Ann; committees: Agriculture; Homeland Security; elected to the 109th Congress on November 2, 2004; reelected to each succeeding Congress.

Office Listings

http://www.cuellar.house.gov

2463 Rayburn House Office Building, Washington, DC 20515 .... (202) 225–1640
Chief of Staff.—Terry Stinson. FAX: 225–1641
Legislative Director.—Alastair Rami.
Scheduler.—Amy Travieso.
615 East Houston Street, Suite 451, San Antonio, TX 78205 .... (210) 271–2851
602 East Calton Road, Suite 2, Laredo, TX 78041 .... (956) 725–0639
FAX: 725–2647
117 East Tom Landry, Mission, TX 78572 .... (956) 424–3942
FAX: 424–3936
100 North F.M. 3167, Rio Grande City, Texas 78582 .... (956) 487–5603
FAX: 488–0952
615 East Houston Street, Suite 563, San Antonio, TX 78205 .... (210) 271–2851
FAX: 277–6671
100 South Austin Street, Suite 1, Seguin, TX 78155 .... (830) 401–0457

FAX: 379–0984

Counties: ATASCOSA, BEXAR, FRIO, GUADALUPE, HIDALGO, JIM HOGG, LA SALLE, MCMULLEN, STARR, WEBB, WILSON, ZAPATA. Population (2000), 651,627.

ZIP Codes: 76272, 78005–08, 78011–12, 78014, 78017, 78019, 78021, 78026, 78040–41, 78043, 78045–46, 78050, 78052, 78057, 78061–62, 78064–65, 78067, 78072, 78076, 78108, 78112–14, 78121, 78123–24, 78143, 78147, 78150, 78152, 78154–55, 78160–61, 78263, 78344, 78360–61, 78369, 78371, 78501, 78503–04, 78536, 78545, 78548, 78557, 78560, 78565, 78572–74, 78576–77, 78582, 78584–85, 78588, 78591, 78595, 78638, 78670

* * *

TWENTY-NINTH DISTRICT

GENE GREEN, Democrat, of Houston, TX; born in Houston, October 17, 1947; education: B.A., University of Houston, 1971; J.D., University of Houston Bates College of Law, 1977; admitted, Texas Bar, 1977; professional: business manager; attorney; Texas State Representative, 1973–85; Texas State Senator, 1985–92; member: Houston Bar Association; Texas Bar Association; American Bar Association; Communications Workers of America; Aldine Optimist Club; Gulf Coast Conservation Association; Lindale Lions Club; Texas Historical Society; Texas State Society; co-chair, Democratic Israel Working Group; Traumatic Brain Injury Task Force; Bi-Cameral Congressional Caucus on Parkinson's Disease; Community College Caucus; Congressional Steel Caucus; co-chair, Congressional Urban Healthcare Caucus; Missing and Exploited Children's Caucus; National Marine Sanctuary Caucus; National Wildlife Refuge Caucus; Pell Grant Caucus; Recycling Caucus; Sportsmen's Caucus; Urban Caucus; Victim's Rights Caucus; co-chair, Vision Caucus; Democratic Senior Whip; married: Helen Albers, January 23, 1970; children: Angela and Christopher; committees: Energy and Commerce; elected on November 3, 1992, to the 103rd Congress; reelected to each succeeding Congress.

Office Listings

http://www.house.gov/green

2470 Rayburn House Office Building, Washington, DC 20515 .... (202) 225–1688
Legislative Director.—Abigail Pinkele. FAX: 225–9903
Press Secretary.—Veronica Custer.
Legislative Assistants: Sergio Espinosa, Lindsay Mosshart, Nathaniel Tipton.
Scheduler.—Veronica Custer.
256 North Sam Houston Parkway East, Suite 29, Houston, TX 77060 .... (281) 999–5879
Chief of Staff / Administrative Assistant.—Rhonda Jackson.
11811 Interstate–10 East, Suite 430, Houston, TX 77029 .... (713) 330–0761
909 Decker Drive, Suite 124, Baytown, TX 77520 .... (281) 420–0502

Counties: HARRIS COUNTY (part). CITIES AND TOWNSHIPS: Baytown, Channelview, Galena Park, Houston, Humble, Jacinto City, La Porte, Pasadena, and South Houston. Population (2000), 651,620.

ZIP Codes: 77003, 77009, 77011–13, 77015–18, 77020–23, 77026, 77029, 77032, 77034, 77037, 77039, 77044, 77049–50, 77060–61, 77075–76, 77087, 77091, 77093, 77205–07, 77213, 77216–17, 77220–23, 77226, 77229, 77234, 77249, 77261–62, 77275, 77287, 77291–93, 77315, 77396, 77501–04, 77506, 77520–22, 77530, 77536, 77547, 77562, 77571–72, 77580, 77587

* * *

THIRTIETH DISTRICT

EDDIE BERNICE JOHNSON, Democrat, of Dallas, TX; born in Waco, TX, December 3, 1935; education: nursing diploma, St. Mary's at Notre Dame, 1955; B.S., nursing, Texas Christian, 1967; M.P.A, Southern Methodist, 1976; proprietor, Eddie Bernice Johnson and Associates consulting and airport concession management; Texas House of Representatives, 1972–77; Carter administration appointee, 1977–81; Texas State Senate, 1986–92; NABTP Mickey Leland Award for Excellence in Diversity, 2000; National Association of School Nurses, Inc., Legislative Award, 2000; The State of Texas Honorary Texan issued by the Governor of Texas, 2000; Links, Inc., Co-Founders Award, 2000; 100 Black Men of America, Inc., Woman of the Year, 2001; National Black Caucus of State Legislators Image Award, 2001; National Conference of Black Mayors, Inc. President's Award, 2001; Alpha Kappa Alpha Trailblazer, 2002; Thurgood Marshall Scholarship Community Leader, 2002; Phi Beta Sigma Fraternity Woman of the Year, 2002; CBCF Outstanding Leadership, 2002; congressional caucuses: Asian-Pacific; Airpower; Army; Arts; Biomedical Research; chair (107th Congress), Congressional Black Caucus; Children's Working Group; co-chair, Task Force on International HIV / AIDS; Fire Services; Human

Rights Caucus; Korean Caucus; Livable Communities Task Force; Medical Technology; Oil & Gas Educational Forum; Singapore Caucus; Study Group on Japan; Tex-21 Transportation Caucus; Urban; Womens' Caucus; Women's Issues; member: St. John Baptist Church, Dallas; children: Dawrence Kirk; grandchildren: Kirk, Jr., David and James; committees: ranking member, Science, Space, and Technology; Transportation and Infrastructure; elected on November 3, 1992, to the 103rd Congress; reelected to each succeeding Congress.

Office Listings

http://www.ebjohnson.house.gov

2468 Rayburn House Office Building, Washington, DC 20515 .... (202) 225–8885
Chief of Staff / Legislative Director.—Murat Gokcigdem. FAX: 226–1477
Director of Operations.—Aleysha Proctor.
Scheduler / Executive Assistant.—Nanette Ladell Spencer.
Communications Director.—Dena Craig.
New Media Assistant.—Cameron Trimble.
Senior Legislative Assistant.—Jennifer Stiddard.
Legislative Assistants: Eric Hammond, Jamie Jackson, Chris Kelley.
3102 Maple Avenue, Suite 600, Dallas, TX 75201 .... (214) 922–8885
District Director.—Rod Givens.

Counties: DALLAS (part). CITIES AND TOWNSHIPS: Cedar Hill, Dallas, De Soto, Duncanville, Glenn Heights, Hutchins, Lancaster, Ovilla, and Wilmer. Population (2000), 651,620.

ZIP Codes: 75104, 75115–16, 75125, 75134, 75137, 75141, 75146, 75149, 75154, 75159, 75172, 75201–04, 75206–10, 75212, 75214–20, 75223–24, 75226–28, 75232–33, 75235–37, 75239, 75241, 75246–47, 75253

* * *

THIRTY-FIRST DISTRICT

JOHN R. CARTER, Republican, of Round Rock, TX; born in Houston, TX, November 6, 1941; education: Texas Tech University, 1964; University of Texas Law School, 1969; professional: attorney; private law practice; public service: appointed and elected a Texas District Court Judge, 1981–2001; awards: recipient and namesake of the Williamson County ''John R. Carter Lifetime Achievement Award''; family: married to Erika Carter; children: Gilianne, John, Theodore, and Erika Danielle; committees: Appropriations; elected to 108th Congress on November 5, 2002; reelected to each succeeding Congress.

Office Listings

http://www.carter.house.gov

409 Cannon House Office Building, Washington, DC 20515 .... (202) 225–3864
Leadership Chief of Staff.—John Walker. FAX: 225–5886
Deputy Chief of Staff.—Brendan Belair.
Communications Director.—John Stone.
Scheduler.—Holly Noles.
1717 North IH 35, Suite 303, Round Rock, TX 78664 .... (512) 246–1600
Chief of Staff.—Jonas Miller.
6544B South General Bruce Drive, Temple, TX 76502 .... (254) 933–1392
Regional Director.—Greg Schannep.

Counties: BELL, CORYELL, ERATH, FALLS, HAMILTON, MILIAM, SOUTHERN ROBERTSON, WILLIAMSON. Population (2000), 651,209.

ZIP Codes: 76401, 76436, 76446, 76457, 76501–05, 76508, 76511, 76513, 76518–20, 76522–28, 76530–31, 76533–34, 76537–38, 76540–44, 76547–49, 76554, 76557–59, 76561, 76564–67, 76569–71, 76573–74, 76577–79, 76596–99, 76632, 76656, 76680, 76685, 76689, 77410, 77426, 77466, 77473, 77492, 77805–07, 77834, 77836, 77838, 77841, 77852, 77857, 77862, 77866, 77878–79, 77881, 78363, 78602, 78613, 78615, 78626, 78628, 78634, 78641–42, 78646, 78673–74, 78664, 78681, 78717, 78729, 78931, 78933, 78940, 78942, 78944, 78948, 78950

* * *

THIRTY-SECOND DISTRICT

PETE SESSIONS, Republican, of Dallas, TX; born in Waco, TX, March 22, 1955; education: B.S., in social sciences, political science, Southwestern University, Georgetown, TX, 1978; professional: worked for Southwestern Bell, and Bell Communications Research (formerly Bell Labs), 1978–94; vice president for public policy, National Center for Policy Analysis, 1994–

95; board member, White Rock YMCA; trustee, Southwestern University; member, National Eagle Scout Association's national committee; advisor to president, Special Olympics Texas; past chairman, East Dallas Chamber of Commerce; awards: Honorary Doctorate, Dallas Baptist University; National Distinguished Eagle Scout Award; Boy Scouts of America; Leadership Award, American College of Emergency Physicians; Spirit of Enterprise Award, U.S. Chamber of Commerce; Best and Brightest, American Conservative Union; Guardian of Small Business Award, National Federation of Independent Business; Taxpayers' Friend Award, National Taxpayers Union; National Leadership Award, National Down Syndrome Society; Champion of Healthcare Innovation Award, Healthcare Leadership Council; Wireless Industry Achievement Award, Cellular Telecommunications and Internet Association; religion: Methodist; married: Juanita Sessions; two children: Bill and Alex; chair, National Republican Congressional Committee; co-chairman, Congressional Down Syndrome Caucus; co-chairman, Congressional Missile Defense Caucus; committees: Rules; elected on November 5, 1996, to the 105th Congress; reelected to each succeeding Congress.

Office Listings

http://www.sessions.house.gov

2233 Rayburn House Office Building, Washington, DC 20515–4332 .... (202) 225–2231
Chief of Staff.—Josh Saltzman. FAX: 225–5878
Press Secretary.—Torrie Miller.
Legislative Director.—Keagan Lenihan.
Park Central VII, 12750 Merit Drive, Suite 1434, Dallas, TX 75251 .... (972) 392–0505

County: DALLAS (part). CITIES AND TOWNSHIPS: Addison, Cockrell Hill, Dallas, Grand Prairie, Highland Park, Irving, Richardson, and University Park. Population (2000), 651,619.

ZIP Codes: 75001, 75038–39, 75050–51, 75060–63, 75080–81, 75203–06, 75208–09, 75211–12, 75214, 75219–20, 75222, 75224–25, 75229–31, 75233, 75240, 75244, 75248, 75251, 75254, 75262

UTAH

(Population 2010, 2,763,885)

SENATORS

ORRIN G. HATCH, Republican, of Salt Lake City, UT; born in Pittsburgh, PA, March 22, 1934; education: B.S., Brigham Young University, Provo, UT, 1959; J.D., University of Pittsburgh, 1962; practiced law in Salt Lake City, UT, and Pittsburgh, PA; senior partner, Hatch and Plumb law firm, Salt Lake City; worked his way through high school, college, and law school at the metal lathing building trade; holds ''AV'' rating in Martindale-Hubbell Law Directory; member: AFL-CIO; Salt Lake County Bar Association; Utah Bar Association; American Bar Association; Pennsylvania Bar Association; Allegheny County Bar Association and numerous other professional and fraternal organizations; honorary doctorate, University of Maryland; honorary doctor of laws: Pepperdine University; Southern Utah University; Widener University, University of Pittsburgh; honorary national ski patroller and other honorary degrees; Senate Republican High Tech Task Force; Congressional International Anti-Privacy Caucus; author of numerous national publications; member, Church of Jesus Christ of Latter-Day Saints; married: Elaine Hansen of Newton, UT; children: Brent, Marcia, Scott, Kimberly, Alysa, and Jess; committees: ranking member, Finance; Health, Education, Labor, and Pensions; Judiciary; Joint Committee on Taxation; Special Committee on Aging; elected to the U.S. Senate on November 2, 1976; reelected to each succeeding Senate term.

Office Listings

http://hatch.senate.gov

SR–318 Russell Senate Office Building, Washington, DC 20510 .... (202) 224–5251
Chief of Staff.—Michael Kennedy. FAX: 224–6331
Legislative Director.—Jay Khosla.
Communications Director.—Mark Eddington.
Scheduler.—Ruth Montoya.
Federal Building, Suite 8402, Salt Lake City, UT 84138 .... (801) 524–4380
State Director.—Melanie Bowen.
Federal Building, 324 25th Street, Suite 1006, Ogden, UT 84401 .... (801) 625–5672
51 South University Avenue, Suite 320, Provo, UT 84601 .... (801) 375–7881
196 East Tabernacle, Suite 14, St. George, UT 84770 .... (435) 634–1795
77 North Main Street, Suite 112, Cedar City, UT 84720 .... (435) 586–8435

* * *

MICHAEL S. LEE, Republican, of Alpine, UT; Mesa, AZ, June 4, 1971; education: B.S., Brigham Young University, Provo, UT, 1994; J.D., Brigham Young University, 1997; professional: law clerk to Judge Dee Benson of the U.S. District Court for the District of Utah; law clerk to Judge Samuel A. Alito, Jr. on the U.S. Court of Appeals for the Third Circuit Court; attorney with the law firm Sidley & Austin; Assistant U.S. Attorney in Salt Lake City; general counsel to the Governor of Utah; law clerk to Supreme Court Justice Samuel A. Alito; partner at Howrey law firm; religion: Church of Jesus Christ of Latter-Day Saints; married: Sharon Burr of Provo, UT; children: James, John, and Eliza; committees: Energy and Natural Resources; Foreign Relations; Judiciary; Joint Economic Committee; elected to the U.S. Senate on November 2, 2010.

Office Listings

http://lee.senate.gov
http://youtube.com/senatormikelee
http://facebook.com/senatormikelee
http://twitter.com/SenMikeLee

316 Hart Senate Office Building, Washington, DC 20510 .... (202) 224–5444
Chief of Staff.—Spencer Stokes. FAX: 228–1168
Legislative Director.—Ryan McCoy.
Administrative Director.—Allyson Bell.
Communications Director.—Brian Phillips.
Press Secretary.—Emily Bennion.
Federal Building, 125 South State, Suite 4425, Salt Lake City, UT 84138 .... (801) 524–5933
State Director.—Dan Hauser.
285 West Tabernacle Street, Suite 200, St. George, UT 84770 .... (435) 628–5514

REPRESENTATIVES

FIRST DISTRICT

ROB BISHOP, Republican, of Brigham City, UT; born in Kaysville, UT, July 13, 1951; education: B.A., political science, *magna cum laude,* University of Utah, 1974; professional: high school teacher; public service: Utah House of Representatives, 1979–94, Speaker of the House his last two years; elected, chair, Utah Republican Party, 1997 (served two terms); religion: Church of Jesus Christ of Latter-day Saints; family: married to Jeralynn Hansen; children: Shule, Jarom, Zenock, Maren, and Jashon; committees: Natural Resources; Rules; elected to the 108th Congress on November 5, 2002; reelected to each succeeding Congress.

Office Listings

http://www.house.gov/robbishop

123 Cannon House Office Building, Washington, DC 20515 .... (202) 225–0453
Chief of Staff.—Scott Parker. FAX: 225–5857
Legislative Assistants: Wayne Bradshaw, Steve Petersen, Cody Stewart.
Scheduler.—Jessica Sanford.
6 North Main Street, Brigham City, UT 84302 .... (435) 734–2270
FAX: 734–2290
125 South State Street, Suite 5420, Salt Lake City, UT 84138–1102 .... (801) 532–3244
(801) 532–3583
324 25th Street, 1017 Federal Building, Ogden, UT 94401 .... (801) 625–0107

Counties: BOX ELDER, CACHE, DAVIS, JUAB (part), MORGAN, RICH, SALT LAKE (part), SUMMIT, TOOELE, WEBER. Population (2000), 744,389.

ZIP Codes: 84010–11, 84014–18, 84022, 84024–25, 84028–29, 84033–34, 84036–38, 84040–41, 84044, 84050, 84054–56, 84060–61, 84064, 84067–69, 84071, 84074–75, 84080, 84083, 84086–87, 84089, 84098, 84101–06, 84110–11, 84114–16, 84119–20, 84122, 84125–28, 84130–31, 84133–34, 84136, 84138–39, 84141, 84144–45, 84147, 84150–51, 84180, 84189–90, 84199, 84201, 84244, 84301–02, 84304–41, 84401–05, 84407–09, 84412, 84414–15, 84628

* * *

SECOND DISTRICT

JIM MATHESON, Democrat, of Salt Lake City, UT; born in Salt Lake City, March 21, 1960; education: B.A., Harvard University; M.B.A., University of California at Los Angeles (UCLA); professional: energy businessman; Bonneville Pacific; Energy Strategies, Inc.; The Matheson Group; organizations: Environmental Policy Institute; Salt Lake Public Utilities Board; Scott M. Matheson Leadership Forum; religion: Church of Jesus Christ of Latter-Day Saints; married: Amy; children: William and Harris; committees: Energy and Commerce; elected to the 107th Congress on November 7, 2000; reelected to each succeeding Congress.

Office Listings

http://www.matheson.house.gov

2434 Rayburn House Office Building, Washington, DC 20515 .... (202) 225–3011
Chief of Staff.—Meg Joseph. FAX: 225–5638
Executive Assistant.—Macey Matthews.
240 East Morris Avenue, #235, Salt Lake City, UT 84115 .... (801) 486–1236
District Director.—Mike Reberg.
321 North Mall Drive, #E101B, St. George, UT 84790 .... (435) 627–0880
120 East Main Street-LL, Price, UT 84501 .... (435) 636–3722

Counties: CARBON, DAGGETT, DUCHENSNE, EMERY, GARFIELD, GRAND, IRON, KANE, PIUTE, SALT LAKE (part), SAN JUAN, UNITAH, UTAH (part), WASATCH, WASHINGTON, WAYNE. Population (2000), 744,390.

ZIP Codes: 84001–04, 84007–08, 84020–21, 84023, 84026–27, 84031–32, 84035, 84039, 84043, 84046–47, 84049, 84051–53, 84062–63, 84066, 84070, 84072–73, 84076, 84078–79, 84082, 84085, 84090–94, 84102–03, 84105–09, 84112–13, 84115–17, 84119, 84121, 84123–24, 84132, 84143, 84148, 84152, 84157–58, 84165, 84171, 84501, 84510–13, 84515–16, 84518, 84520–23, 84525–26, 84528–37, 84539, 84540, 84542, 84604, 84710, 84712, 84714–23, 84725–26, 84729, 84732–38, 84740–43, 84745–47, 84749–50, 84753, 84755–65, 84767, 84770–76, 84779–84, 84790–91

* * *

THIRD DISTRICT

JASON CHAFFETZ, Republican, of Alpine, UT; born in Los Gatos, CA; March 26, 1967; education: B.A., communications, Brigham Young University, Provo, UT, 1989; professional:

business executive; chief of staff, Utah governor John Huntsman, 2004; President, Maxtera Utah, 2005–present; trustee, Utah Valley board of trustees; chair, Utah National Guard Adjutant General Review; Commissioner, Highland City Planning Commission; President, BYU Utah County Cougar Club; Cougar Club (BYU) Board of Directors; awards: starting placekicker, BYU Football Team, 1988–89; Best Run Campaign, General Election, Utah 2004, Huntsman for Governor; Western Athletic Conference Champions, 1989; Cougar Club Academic Athlete Award, 1988–89; Academic All-WAC Football Team, 1989; National All-Bowl Football Team, 1988; religion: Church of Jesus Christ of Latter-Day Saints; married: Julie, in 1991; children: Max, Ellis, and Kate; committees: Budget; Judiciary; Oversight and Government Reform; elected to the 111th Congress on November 4, 2008; reelected to the 112th Congress.

Office Listings

http://chaffetz.house.gov

1032 Longworth House Office Building, Washington, DC 20515 .... (202) 225–7751
Chief of Staff.—Justin Harding. FAX: 225–5629
Legislative Director.—Mike Jerman.
Scheduler / Office Manager.—Karilyn Henshaw.
Communications Director / Legislative Aide.—Alisia Essig.
Counsel.—Troy Stock.
Legislative Assistant.—Fred Ferguson.
Staff Assistant.—John Hadlock.
51 South University Avenue, Suite 318, Provo, UT 84601 .... (801) 851–2500
District Director.—Dell Smith. FAX: 851–2509
3895 West 7800 South, Suite 201, West Jordan, UT 84088 .... (801) 282–5502
District Director.—Jennifer Scott. FAX: 282–6081

Counties: BEAVER, JUAB (part), MILLARD, SALT LAKE (part), SANPETE, SEVIER, UTAH (part). Population (2000), 744,390.

ZIP Codes: 84003, 84006, 84013, 84042–44, 84047, 84057–59, 84062, 84065, 84070, 84084, 84088, 84095, 84097, 84107, 84118–20, 84123, 84128, 84170, 84184, 84199, 84601–06, 84620–24, 84626–27, 84629–40, 84642–57, 84660, 84662–65, 84667, 84701, 84711, 84713, 84724, 84728, 84730–31, 84739, 84744, 84751–52, 84754, 84766

VERMONT

(Population 2010, 625,741)

SENATORS

PATRICK J. LEAHY, Democrat, of Middlesex, VT; born in Montpelier, VT, March 31, 1940, son of Howard and Alba Leahy; education: graduate of St. Michael's High School, Montpelier, 1957; B.A., St. Michael's College, 1961; J.D., Georgetown University, 1964; professional: attorney, admitted to the Vermont Bar, 1964; admitted to the District of Columbia Bar, 1979; admitted to practice before: the Vermont Supreme Court, 1964; the Federal District Court of Vermont, 1965; the Second Circuit Court of Appeals in New York, 1966; and the U.S. Supreme Court, 1968; State's Attorney, Chittenden County, 1966–74; vice president, National District Attorneys Association, 1971–74; married: the former Marcelle Pomerleau, 1962; children: Kevin, Alicia, and Mark; first Democrat and youngest person in Vermont to be elected to the U.S. Senate; committees: chair, Judiciary; Agriculture, Nutrition, and Forestry; Appropriations; Rules and Administration; Joint Committee on the Library; elected to the Senate on November 5, 1974; reelected to each succeeding Senate term.

Office Listings

http://leahy.senate.gov

437 Russell Senate Office Building, Washington, DC 20515 .... (202) 224–4242
Chief of Staff.—Ed Pagano. FAX: 224–3479
Administrative Director.—Ann Berry.
Legislative Director.—John P. Dowd.
Communications Director.—David Carle.
Federal Building, Room 338, Montpelier, VT 05602 .... (802) 229–0569
199 Main Street, Courthouse Plaza, Burlington, VT 05401 .... (802) 863–2525
State Director.—John Tracy.

* * *

BERNARD SANDERS, Independent, of Burlington, VT; born in Brooklyn, NY, September 8, 1941; education: graduated, Madison High School, Brooklyn; B.S., political science, University of Chicago, 1964; professional: carpenter; writer; college professor; Mayor of Burlington, VT, 1981–89; married: the former Jane O'Meara, 1988; children: Levi, Heather, Carina and David; committees: Budget; Energy and Natural Resources; Environment and Public Works; Health, Education, Labor, and Pensions; Veterans' Affairs; Joint Economic Committee; elected to the 102nd Congress on November 6, 1990; reelected to each succeeding Congress; elected to the U.S. Senate on November 7, 2006.

Office Listings

http://sanders.senate.gov

332 Dirksen Senate Office Building, Washington, DC 20510 .... (202) 224–5141
Chief of Staff.—Stanley ''Huck'' Gutman. FAX: 228–0776
Legislative Director.—Michael Behan.
Communications Director.—Michael Briggs.
1 Church Street, Second Floor, Burlington, VT 05401 .... (800) 339–9834

REPRESENTATIVE

AT LARGE

PETER WELCH, Democrat, of Hartland, VT; born in Springfield, MA, May 2, 1947; education: Cathedral High School, Springfield, MA, 1969; B.A., *magna cum laude*, College of the Holy Cross, 1969; J.D., University of California at Berkeley, 1973; professional: attorney, admitted to Vermont Bar, 1974; founding partner, Welch, Graham & Manby; served in Vermont State Senate, 1981–89, 2001–07; Minority Leader, 1983–85; President pro tempore, 1985–89, 2003–07; family: wife, Joan Smith (deceased), currently married to Margaret Cheney; five children: Beth, Mary, Bill, John and Michael; three stepchildren; committees: Agriculture; Oversight and Government Reform; elected to the 110th Congress on November 7, 2006; reelected to each succeeding Congress.

Office Listings

http://www.welch.house.gov

1404 Longworth House Office Building, Washington, DC 20515 .... (202) 225–4115

Chief of Staff.—Bob Rogan.
Scheduler / Executive Assistant.—Julia Drost.
Legislative Director.—Jake Oster.
Communications Director.—Scott Coriell.
30 Main Street, Third Floor, Suite 350, Burlington, VT 05401 .... (802) 652–2450
State Director.—Patricia Coates.

Population (2000), 608,827.

ZIP Codes: 05001, 05009, 05030–43, 05045–56, 05058–62, 05065, 05067–77, 05079, 05081, 05083–86, 05088–89, 05091, 05101, 05141–43, 05146, 05148–56, 05158–59, 05161, 05201, 05250–55, 05257, 05260–62, 05301–04, 05340–46, 05350–63, 05401–07, 05439–66, 05468–74, 05476–79, 05481–83, 05485–92, 05494–95, 05601–04, 05609, 05620, 05633, 05640–41, 05647–58, 05660–67, 05669–82, 05701–02, 05730–48, 05750–51, 05753, 05757–70, 05772–78, 05819–30, 05832–33, 05836–43, 05845–51, 05853, 05855, 05857–63, 05866–68, 05871–75, 05901–07

VIRGINIA

(Population 2010, 8,001,024)

SENATORS

JIM WEBB, Democrat, of Arlington County, VA; born in St. Joseph, MO, February 9, 1946; education: B.S., engineering, U.S. Naval Academy, 1968; J.D., Georgetown University Law Center, 1975; professional: Infantry officer, U.S. Marine Corps, 1968–72 (combat service in Vietnam); counsel, House Committee on Veterans' Affairs, 1977–81; Assistant Secretary of Defense, Reserve Affairs, 1984–87; Secretary of the Navy, 1987–88; broad career as a writer and journalist; literature professor, U.S. Naval Academy; Emmy-Award winning TV journalist; author, six best-selling novels, two non-fiction works, including a history of the Scots-Irish people; screenwriter and producer; business consultant; awards: Military awards: Navy Cross; Silver Star Medal; two Bronze Star Medals with combat ''V''; two Purple Heart Medals; campaign and unit citations; numerous civilian awards including Military Order of the Purple Heart's (MOPH) Special Leadership Award; Military Coalition's Award of Merit; Blinded American Veterans Foundation's George ''Buck'' Gillespie Congressional Award for Meritorious Service; Veterans of Foreign Wars, 2008; Gold Medal and Citation of Merit; American Legion's National Commander's Public Relations Award, 2008; Military Officers Association of America (MOAA) Colonel Arthur T. Marix Congressional Leadership Award, 2009; Department of Defense Distinguished Public Service Medal; Medal of Honor Society's Patriot Award; American Legion National Commander's Public Service Award; Veterans of Foreign Wars Media Service Award; Marine Corps League's Military Order of the Iron Mike Award; John H. Russell Leadership Award; Marine Corps Correspondent Association's Robert L. Denig Distinguished Service Award; married: Hong: Hong Le; children: Amy, James Robert, Sarah, Julia, and Georgia; committees: Armed Services; Foreign Relations; Veterans' Affairs; Joint Economic Committee; elected to the U.S. Senate on November 7, 2006.

Office Listings

http://webb.senate.gov

248 Russell Senate Office Building, Washington, DC 20510 .... (202) 224–4024
Chief of Staff.—Paul Reagan. FAX: 228–6363
Communications Director.—Jessica Smith.
Legislative Director.—David Bonine.
Scheduler.—Melissa Bruns.
State Director.—Conaway Haskins.
222 Central Park Avenue, Suite 120, Virginia Beach, VA 23462 .... (757) 518–1674
507 East Franklin Street, Richmond, VA 23219 .... (804) 771–2221
3140 Chaparral Drive, Building C, Suite 101, Roanoke, VA 24018 .... (540) 772–4236
756 Park Avenue, Norton, VA 24273 ....
TBD, Arlington, VA.
7309 Arlington Boulevard, Suite 316, Falls Church, VA 22042 .... (703) 573–7090
FAX: 573–7098
308 Craghead Street, Suite 102A, Danville, VA 24541 .... (434) 792–0976
FAX: 972–0960

* * *

MARK R. WARNER, Democrat, of Alexandria, VA; born in Indianapolis, IN, December 15, 1954; son of Robert and Marge Warner of Vernon, CT; education: B.A., political science, George Washington University, 1977, J.D., Harvard Law School, 1980; Governor, Commonwealth of Virginia, 2002–06; chairman of the National Governor's Association, 2004–05; religion: Presbyterian; wife: Lisa Collis; children: Madison, Gillian, Eliza; committees: Banking, Housing, and Urban Affairs; Budget, Commerce, Science, and Transportation; Rules and Administration; Joint Economic Committee; Select Committee on Intelligence; elected to the U.S. Senate on November 4, 2008.

Office Listings

http://warner.senate.gov

SR–459A Russell Senate Office Building, Washington, DC 20510 .... (202) 224–2023
Chief of Staff.—Luke S. Albee. FAX: 224–2530
Communications Director.—Kevin Hall.
Press Assistant.—Beth Adelson.
Scheduler.—Walker Irving.
Chief Counsel.—Tom Walls.
Projects Coordinator.—Kelly Thomasson.
8000 Towers Crescent Drive, Suite 200, Vienna, VA 22182 .... (703) 442–0670

	FAX: 442–0408
180 West Main Street, Abingdon, VA 24210	(276) 628–8158
	FAX: 628–1036
101 West Main Street, Suite 4900, Norfolk, VA 23510	(757) 441–3079
	FAX: 441–6250
919 East Main Street, Richmond, VA 23219	(804) 775–2314
	FAX: 775–2319
129B Salem Avenue, Southwest, Roanoke, VA 24011	(540) 857–2676
	FAX: 857–2800

REPRESENTATIVES

FIRST DISTRICT

ROBERT J. WITTMAN, Republican, of Montross, VA; born in Washington, DC, February 2, 1959; B.S., biology, Virginia Polytechnic Institute and State University, 1981; M.P.H., health policy and administration, University of North Carolina at Chapel Hill, 1989; Ph.D., Virginia Commonwealth University, Richmond, VA, 2002; professional: field director for the Virginia Health Department's Division of Shellfish Sanitation; public service: Montross Town Council, 1986–96; public policy and administration, 1992; mayor of Montross, 1992–96; Westmoreland County Board of Supervisors, 1995–2003 and chairman, 2003–05; Virginia House of Delegates, 2005–07; religion: Episcopalian; married: Kathryn Wittman; children: Devon and Joshua; committees: Armed Services; Natural Resources; elected to the 110th Congress on December 11, 2007 in a special election; elected to the 111th Congress; reelected to the 112th Congress on November 2, 2010.

Office Listings

http://www.wittman.house.gov

1317 Longworth House Office Building, Washington, DC 20515	(202) 225–4261
Chief of Staff.—Mary Springer.	FAX: 225–4382
Legislative Director.—Jamie Miller.	
Press Secretary.—Abbey Shilling.	
Scheduler / Office Manager.—Leigh Pettis.	
4904–B George Washington Memorial Parkway, Yorktown, VA 23692	(757) 874–6687
District Director.—Joe Schumacher.	
3504 Plank Road, Suite 203 Fredericksburg, VA 22407	(540) 548–1086
508 Church Lane, Tappahannock, VA 22560	(804) 443–0668

Counties: CAROLINE (part), ESSEX, FAUQUIER (part), GLOUCESTER, JAMES CITY, KING AND QUEEN, KING GEORGE, KING WILLIAM, LANCASTER, MATHEWS, MIDDLESEX, NORTHUMBERLAND, PRINCE WILLIAM (part), RICHMOND, SPOTSYLVANIA (part), STAFFORD, WESTMORELAND, YORK. CITIES AND TOWNSHIPS: Bowling Green, Chancellorsville, Cobbs Creek, Colonial Beach, Dumfries, Falmouth, Fredericksburg, Hampton, Kilmarnock, Lightfoot, Montross, Newport News, Poquoson, Quantico, Saluda, Seaford, Tappahannock, Toano, Triangle, Warsaw, West Point, White Stone, Williamsburg, and Yorktown. Population (2000), 643,514.

ZIP Codes: 20106, 20112, 20115, 20119, 20128, 20138–39, 20181, 20186–87, 22026, 22134–35, 22172, 22191, 22193, 22401–08, 22412, 22427, 22430, 22432, 22435–38, 22442–43, 22446, 22448, 22451, 22454, 22456, 22460, 22463, 22469, 22471–73, 22476, 22480–82, 22485, 22488, 22501, 22503–04, 22507–09, 22511, 22513–14, 22517, 22520, 22523–24, 22526, 22528–30, 22535, 22538–39, 22544–48, 22552–56, 22558, 22560, 22570, 22572, 22576–81, 22639, 22712, 22720, 22728, 22734, 22739, 22742, 23001, 23003, 23009, 23011, 23017–18, 23021, 23023–25, 23031–32, 23035, 23043, 23045, 23050, 23056, 23061–62, 23064, 23066, 23068–72, 23076, 23079, 23081, 23085–86, 23089–92, 23106–10, 23115, 23117, 23119, 23125–28, 23130–31, 23138, 23148–49, 2315356, 23161, 23163, 23168–69, 23175–78, 23180–81, 23183–88, 23190–91, 23354, 23601–03, 23605–06, 23608–09, 23612, 23662–63, 23665–67, 23669–70, 23681, 23690–94, 23696

* * *

SECOND DISTRICT

E. SCOTT RIGELL, Republican, of Virginia Beach, VA; born in Titusville, FL, May 28, 1960; education: A.A., Brevard Community College, Cocoa, FL, 1981; B.B.A., Mercer University, Macon, GA, 1983; M.B.A., Regent University, Virginia Beach, VA, 1990; professional: founder and chairman of Freedom Automotive; United States Marine Corps Reserve, 1978–84; married: Teri; children: Lindsey, Mallory, Justus, and Shannon; committees: Armed Services; Homeland Security; Science, Space, and Technology; elected to the 112th Congress on November 2, 2010.

Office Listings

http://www.rigell.house.gov

327 Cannon House Office Building, Washington, DC 20515 .... (202) 225–4215
Chief of Staff.—Chris Connelly. FAX: 225–4218
Communications Director.—Kim Mosser.
Legislative Director.—John Thomas.
4772 Euclid Road, Suite E, Virginia Beach, VA 23462 .... (757) 687–8290
District Director.—Shannon Kendrick.
23386 Front Street, Accomac, VA 23301 .... (757) 789–5172

Counties: ACCOMACK, NORTHAMPTON. CITIES: Hampton, Norfolk, and Virginia Beach. Population (2000), 643,510.

ZIP Codes: 23301–03, 23306–08, 23310, 23313, 23316, 23336–37, 23341, 23345, 23347, 23350, 23354, 23356–59, 23389, 23395, 23398–99, 23401, 23404–05, 23407–10, 23412–23, 23426–27, 23429, 23440–43, 23450–67, 23471, 23479–80, 23482–83, 23486, 23488, 23502–03, 23505–08, 23511–13, 23515, 23518–19, 23521, 23529, 23541, 23551, 23605, 23651, 23661, 23663–66, 23669

* * *

THIRD DISTRICT

ROBERT C. ''BOBBY'' SCOTT, Democrat, of Newport News, VA; born in Washington, DC, April 30, 1947; education: graduated, Groton High School; B.A., Harvard University; J.D., Boston College Law School; professional: served in the Massachusetts National Guard; attorney; admitted to the Virginia Bar; Virginia House of Delegates, 1978–83; Senate of Virginia, 1983–92; member: Alpha Phi Alpha Fraternity; March of Dimes Board of Directors; NAACP; Peninsula Chamber of Commerce; Peninsula Legal Aid Center Board of Directors; Sigma Pi Phi Fraternity; committees: Education and the Workforce; Judiciary; elected on November 3, 1992 to the 103rd Congress; reelected to each succeeding Congress.

Office Listings

http://www.bobbyscott.house.gov

1201 Longworth House Office Building, Washington, DC 20515 .... (202) 225–8351
Chief of Staff.—Joni L. Ivey. FAX: 225–8354
Executive Assistant.—Randi Petty.
Legislative Director.—Ilana Brunner.
Legislative Counsel.—Rashage Green.
Legislative Assistants: David Dailey, Christian Haines, Carolyn Hughes.
2600 Washington Avenue, Suite 1010, Newport News, VA 23607 .... (757) 380–1000
District Director.—Gisele Russell.
400 North 8th Street, Suite 430, Richmond, VA 23219 .... (804) 644–4845
District Scheduler.—Nkechi George-Winkler.

Counties: CHARLES CITY, HENRICO (part), NEW KENT, PRINCE GEORGES, SURRY. CITIES: Hampton (part), Newport News (part), Norfolk (part), Portsmouth and Richmond (part). Population (2000), 643,476.

ZIP Codes: 23011, 23030, 23059–60, 23075, 23089, 23111, 23124, 23140–41, 23147, 23150, 23181, 23185, 23218–25, 23227–28, 23230–32, 23234, 23240–41, 23249–50, 23260–61, 23269–70, 23272, 23274–76, 23278–79, 23282, 23284–86, 23290–93, 23295, 23298, 23501–02, 23504–05, 23507–10, 23513–14, 23517–18, 23520, 23523, 23530, 23601–09, 23628, 23630–31, 23653, 23661, 23663–64, 23666–70, 23701–05, 23707–09, 23839, 23842, 23846, 23860, 23875, 23881, 23883, 23888, 23898–99

* * *

FOURTH DISTRICT

J. RANDY FORBES, Republican, of Chesapeake, VA; born in Chesapeake, February 17, 1952; education: B.A., Randolph-Macon College; J.D., University of Virginia School of Law; professional: attorney; religion: Baptist; public service: Virginia House of Delegates, 1990–97; Virginia State Senate, 1997–2001; Republican House Floor Leader, 1994–97; Republican Senate Floor Leader, 1998–2001; Chairman of the Republican Party of Virginia, 1996–2000; married: Shirley; children: Neil, Jamie, Jordan, and Justin; committees: Armed Services; Judiciary; elected to the 107th Congress, by special election, on June 19, 2001; reelected to each succeeding Congress.

Office Listings

2438 Rayburn House Office Building, Washington, DC 20515 .... (202) 225–6365

Chief of Staff.—Dee Gilmore. FAX: 226–1170
Communications Director.—Jessica Mancari.
Legislative Director.—Vacant.
505 Independence Parkway, Lake Center 2, Suite 104, Chesapeake, VA 23322 ...... (757) 382–0080
District Representative.—Curtis Byrd.
9401 Courthouse Road, Suite 201, Chesterfield, VA 23832 .... (804) 318–1363
District Representative.—Ron White.
425 H. South Main Street, Emporia, VA 23847 .... (434) 634–5575
District Field Representative.—Rick Franklin.

Counties: AMELIA, BRUNSWICK (part), CHESTERFIELD (part), DINWIDDIE, GREENSVILLE, ISLE OF WIGHT (part), NOTTOWAY, POWHATAN, PRINCE GEORGE (part), SOUTHAMPTON, SUSSEX. Population (2000), 643,477.

ZIP Codes: 23002, 23083, 23101, 23105, 23112–14, 23120, 23139, 23234, 23236–37, 23304, 23314–15, 23320–28, 23397, 23424, 23430–39, 23487, 23501, 23801, 23803–06, 23821, 23824, 23827–34, 23836–38, 23840–42, 23844–45, 23847, 23850–51, 23856–57, 23860, 23866–67, 23872–76, 23878–79, 23882, 23884–85, 23887–91, 23894, 23897–98, 23920, 23922, 23930, 23938, 23950, 23955

* * *

FIFTH DISTRICT

ROBERT HURT, Republican, of Chatham, VA; born in New York, NY, June 16, 1969; raised in Chatham, VA; education: B.S., Hampden-Sydney College, Hampden-Sydney, VA, 1991; J.D., Mississippi College School of Law, Clinton, MS, 1995; professional: attorney, Chatham Town Council, 2000–01; member of Virginia State House of Representatives, 2002–08; member of Virginia State Senate, 2008–10; committees: Financial Services; elected to the 112th Congress on November 2, 2010.

Office Listings

http://www.hurt.house.gov

1516 Longworth House Office Building, Washington, DC 20515 .... (202) 225–4711
Chief of Staff.—Jeff Rosenbaum. FAX: 225–5681
Scheduler.—Katie Banks.
Communications Director.—Amanda Henneberg.
Legislative Director.—Kelly Simpson.
308 Craghead Street, Suite 102–D, Danville, VA 24541 .... (434) 791–2596
District Director.—Linda Green.
686 Berkmar Circle, Charlottesville, VA 22901 .... (434) 973–9631
515 South Main Street, P.O. Box 0, Farmville, VA 23901 .... (434) 395–0120

Counties: ALBEMARLE COUNTY. CITIES AND TOWNSHIPS: Charlotteville, Batesville, Covesville, Esmont, Greenwood, Hatton, Ivy, Keene, Keswick, North Garden, Scottsville. APPOMATTOX COUNTY. CITIES AND TOWNSHIPS: Appomattox, Evergreen, Pamplin, Spout Spring. BEDFORD COUNTY. CITIES AND TOWNSHIPS: Bedford, Big Island, Goodview, Coleman Falls, Forest, Goode, Huddleston, Lowry, Thaxton. BRUNSWICK COUNTY. BUCKINGHAM COUNTY. CITIES AND TOWNSHIPS: Andersonville, Arvonia, Buckingham, Dillwyn, Buckingham, New Canton. CAMPBELL COUNTY. CITIES AND TOWNSHIPS: Altavista, Brookneal, Concord, Evington, Gladys, Long Island, Lynch Station, Naruna, Rustburg. CHARLOTTE COUNTY. CITIES AND TOWNSHIPS: Barnesville, Charlotte Court House, Cullen, Drakes Branch, Keysville, Phenix, Randolph, Red House, Red Oak, Saxe, Wylliesburg. CUMBERLAND COUNTY. CITIES AND TOWNSHIPS: Carterville, Cumberland. DANVILLE CITY: Danville. FLUVANNA COUNTY. CITIES AND TOWNSHIPS: Bremo Bluff, Bybee, Carysbrook, Columbia, Fort Union, Kents Store, Palmyra, Troy. FRANKLIN COUNTY. CITIES AND TOWNSHIPS: Boones Mill, Callaway, Ferrum, Glade Hill, Henry, Redwood, Penhook, Rocky Mount, Union Hall, Waidsboro, Wirtz. GREENE COUNTY. HALIFAX COUNTY. CITIES AND TOWNSHIPS: Alton, Clover, Cluster Springs, Crystal Hall, Denniston, Halifax, Ingram, Lennig, Mayo, Nathalie, Republican Grove, Scottsburg, Turbeville, Vernon Hill, Virgilina. HENRY COUNTY. CITIES AND TOWNSHIPS: Axton, Bassett, Collinsville, Fieldale, Ridgeway, Spencer, Stanleytown. LUNENBURG COUNTY. CITIES AND TOWNSHIPS: Tamworth, Dundas, Fort Mitchell, Kenbridge, Lunenburg, Rehoboth, Victoria. MARTINSVILLE CITY: Martinsville. MECKLENBURG COUNTY. CITIES AND TOWNSHIPS: Baskerville, Blackridge, Boydton, Bracey, Chase City, Clarksville, Forksville, LaCross, Palmer Springs, Skipwith, South Hill, Union Level Buffalo Junction, Nelson. NELSON COUNTY. CITIES AND TOWNSHIPS: Afton, Arrington, Faber, Lovingston, Massies Mill, Nellysford, Montebello, Gladstone, Norwood, Piney River, Roseland, Schuyler, Shipman, Tye River, Tyro, Wingina. PITTSYLVANIA COUNTY. CITIES AND TOWNSHIPS: Blairs, Callands, Cascade, Chatham, Pittsville, Sandy Level, Dry Fork, Gretna, Hurt, Java, Keeling, Ringgold, Sutherlin. PRINCE EDWARD COUNTY. CITIES AND TOWNSHIPS: Green Bay, Farmville, Darlington Heights, Green Bay, Hampden-Sydney, Meherrin, Prospect, Rice, and South Boston. Population (2000), 643,497.

ZIP Codes: 22901–11, 22920, 22922–24, 22931–32, 22935–38, 22940, 22942–43, 22945–47, 22949, 22952, 22954, 22958–59, 22963–65, 22967–69, 22971, 22973–74, 22976, 22987, 23004, 23022, 23027, 23038, 23040, 23055, 23084, 23093, 23123, 23139, 23821, 23824, 23843, 23845, 23856–57, 23868, 23887, 23889, 23893, 23901, 23909, 23915, 23917, 23919–24, 23927, 23934, 23936–39, 23941–44, 23947, 23950, 23952, 23954, 23958–60, 23962–64, 23966–68, 23970, 23974, 23976, 24012, 24053–55, 24059, 24064–65, 24067, 24069, 24076, 24078–79, 24082, 24088–89, 24091–92, 24095, 24101–02, 24104, 24112–15, 24120–22, 24133, 24137, 24139, 24146, 24148, 24151, 24153, 24161, 24168, 24171, 24174, 24176–77, 24179, 24184–85, 24312, 24464, 24483, 24501–02, 24504, 24517, 24520, 24522–23, 24527–31, 24534–35, 24538–41, 24543–44, 24549–51, 24553–54, 24556–58, 24562–63, 24565–66, 24569–71, 24574, 24576–77, 24580–81, 24585–86, 24588–90, 24592–94, 24597–99

* * *

SIXTH DISTRICT

BOB GOODLATTE, Republican, of Roanoke, VA; born in Holyoke, MA, September 22, 1952; education: B.A., Bates College, Lewiston, ME, 1974; J.D., Washington and Lee University, 1977; Massachusetts Bar, 1977; Virginia Bar, 1978; professional: began practice in Roanoke, VA, 1979; district director for Congressman M. Caldwell Butler, 1977–79; attorney, sole practitioner, 1979–81; partner, 1981–92; chairman of the sixth district Virginia Republican Committee, 1983–88; member: Civitan Club of Roanoke (president, 1989–90); former member, Building Better Boards Advisory Council; married: Maryellen Flaherty, 1974; children: Jennifer and Robert; Deputy Republican Whip; committees: Agriculture; Education and the Workforce; Judiciary; elected on November 3, 1992, to the 103rd Congress; reelected to each succeeding Congress.

Office Listings

http://www.goodlatte.house.gov

2240 Rayburn House Office Building, Washington, DC 20515 .... (202) 225–5431
Chief of Staff.—Shelley Husband. FAX: 225–9681
Legislative Counsel.—Branden Ritchie.
Press Secretary.—Kathryn Rexrode.
10 Franklin Road, SE, Suite 540, Roanoke, VA 24011 .... (540) 857–2672
District Director.—Pete Larkin.
916 Main Street, Suite 300, Lynchburg, VA 24504 .... (804) 845–8306
117 South Lewis Street, Suite 215, Staunton, VA 24401 .... (540) 885–3861
2 South Main Street, First Floor, Suite A, Harrisonburg, VA 22801 .... (540) 432–2391

Counties: ALLEGHANY (part), AMHERST, AUGUSTA, BATH, BEDFORD (part), BOTETOURT, HIGHLAND, ROANOKE (part), ROCKBRIDGE, ROCKINGHAM , SHENANDOAH. CITIES: Buena Vista, Covington, Harrisonburg, Lexington, Lynchburg, Roanoke, Salem, Staunton, and Waynesboro. Population (2000), 643,504.

ZIP Codes: 22626, 22641, 22644–45, 22652, 22654, 22657, 22660, 22664, 22801–03, 22807, 22810–12, 22815, 22820–21, 22824, 22827, 22830–34, 22840–48, 22850, 22853, 22920, 22922, 22939, 22952, 22967, 22980, 24001–20, 24022–38, 24040, 24042–44, 24048, 24053, 24059, 24064–66, 24070, 24077, 24079, 24083, 24085, 24087, 24090, 24101, 24121–22, 24130, 24153, 24156, 24174–75, 24178–79, 24401–02, 24411–13, 24415–16, 24421–22, 24426, 24430–33, 24435, 24437–42, 24445, 24450, 24458–60, 24463, 24465, 24467–69, 24471–73, 24476–77, 24479, 24482–87, 24501–06, 24512–15, 24521, 24523, 24526, 24533, 24536, 24550–51, 24553, 24555–56, 24572, 24574, 24578–79, 24595

* * *

SEVENTH DISTRICT

ERIC CANTOR, Republican, of Richmond, VA; born in Henrico County, June 6, 1963; education: B.A., George Washington University, 1985; J.D., College of William and Mary, 1988; M.S., Columbia University, 1989; professional: attorney; organizations: Western Henrico Rotary; elected to the Virginia State House of Delegates, 1991; appointed Chief Deputy Majority Whip, December, 2002; elected Republican Whip, December, 2008; elected Majority Leader, November, 2010; married: Diana; three children; elected to the 107th Congress on November 7, 2000; reelected to each succeeding Congress.

Office Listings

http://www.cantor.house.gov

H–329 The Capitol, Washington, DC 20515 .... (202) 225–4000
Chief of Staff.—Steve Stombres.
Policy Director.—Neil Bradley.
303 Cannon House Office Building, Washington, DC 20515 .... (202) 225–2815
Chief of Staff.—Kristi Way. FAX: 225–0011
4201 Dominion Boulevard, Suite 110, Glen Allen, VA 23060 .... (804) 747–4073
763 Madison Road, Suite 207, Culpeper, VA 22701 .... (540) 825–8960

Counties: CAROLINE (part), CHESTERFIELD (part), CULPEPER, GOOCHLAND, HANOVER, HENRICO (part), LOUISA, MADISON, ORANGE, PAGE, RAPPAHANNOCK, SPOTSYLVANIA (part). CITIES: Richmond. Population (2000), 643,499.

ZIP Codes: 20106, 20119, 20186, 22407, 22433, 22508, 22534, 22542, 22546, 22553, 22565, 22567, 22580, 22610, 22623, 22627, 22630, 22640, 22650, 22701, 22709, 22711, 22713–16, 22718–19, 22721–27, 22729–38, 22740–41, 22743, 22746–49, 22827, 22835, 22849, 22851, 22903, 22923, 22942, 22947–48, 22957, 22960, 22972, 22974, 22989, 23005, 23015, 23024, 23038–39, 23047, 23058–60, 23063, 23065, 23067, 23069, 23084, 23093, 23102–03, 23111–14, 23116–17, 23120, 23124, 23129, 23146, 23153, 23160, 23162, 23170, 23173, 23192, 23221–30, 23233–36, 23242, 23255, 23273, 23280, 23288–89, 23294–95

* * *

EIGHTH DISTRICT

JAMES P. MORAN, Democrat, of Alexandria, VA; born in Buffalo, NY, May 16, 1945; education: B.A., College of Holy Cross; Bernard Baruch Graduate School of Finance—City University of New York; M.P.A., University of Pittsburgh Graduate School of Public and International Affairs; served on City Council of Alexandria, 1979–82; Vice Mayor, 1982–84; Mayor, 1985–90; founding member of the New Democrat Coalition; co-chair of Congressional Animal Protection Caucus; Task Force on Sovereign Wealth Funds; named as one of two "High Technology Legislators of the Year" by the Information Technology Industry Council; in 2000 named to the "Legislative Hall of Fame" by the American Electronics Association for his work on technology issues; in 2010 named "Legislator of Year" by the Humane Society of the United States for his work on animal welfare legislation; children: James, Patrick, Mary, and Dorothy; committees: Appropriations; elected to the 102nd Congress on November 6, 1990; reelected to each succeeding Congress.

Office Listings

http://moran.house.gov

2239 Rayburn House Office Building, Washington, DC 20515 .... (202) 225–4376
Chief of Staff.—Austin Durrer. FAX: 225–0017
Legislative Director.—Tim Aiken.
333 North Fairfax Street, Suite 201, Alexandria, VA 22314 .... (703) 971–4700
District Director.—Susie Warner.

Counties: ARLINGTON, FAIRFAX (part). CITIES: Alexandria, and Falls Church. Population (2000), 643,503.

ZIP Codes: 20170–71, 20190–91, 20194–96, 20206, 20231, 20301, 20310, 20330, 20350, 20406, 20453, 22003, 22027, 22031, 22037, 22040–44, 22046–47, 22060, 22079, 22101–03, 22107–09, 22122, 22124, 22150–51, 22159, 22180–82, 22201–07, 22209–17, 22219, 22222, 22225–27, 22229–30, 22234, 22240–45, 22301–07, 22310–15, 22320–21, 22331–34, 22336

* * *

NINTH DISTRICT

H. MORGAN GRIFFITH, Republican, of Salem, VA; born March 15, 1958; education: graduated, Andrew Lewis High School, 1976; B.A., Emory and Henry College, 1980; J.D., Washington and Lee University School of Law, 1983; professional: attorney, private practice, 1983–2011; partner, Albo & Oblon, L.L.P., 2008–11; Virginia House of Delegates, 1994–2011; majority leader, Virginia House of Delegates, 2001–11; married Hilary; children: Abby, Davis, and Starke; committees: Energy and Commerce; elected to the 112th Congress on November 2, 2010.

Office Listings

http://www.morgangriffith.house.gov

1108 Longworth House Office Building, Washington, DC 20515 .... (202) 225–3861
Chief of Staff.—Kelly Lungren McCollum. FAX: 225–0076
Press Secretary.—Beth Breeding.
323 West Main Street, Abingdon, VA 24210 .... (276) 525–1405
District Director.—Michelle Jenkins.
17 West Main Street, Christiansburg, VA 24073 .... (540) 381–5671

Counties: ALLEGHANY (part), BLAND, BUCHANAN, CARROLL, CRAIG, DICKENSON, FLOYD, GILES, GRAYSON, HENRY (part), LEE, MONTGOMERY, PATRICK, PULASKI, ROANOKE (part), RUSSELL, SCOTT, SMYTH, TAZEWELL, WASHINGTON, WISE, WYTHE. CITIES: Bristol, Covington, Galax, Norton, and Radford. Population (2000), 643,514.

ZIP Codes: 24018–19, 24053, 24055, 24058–64, 24068, 24070, 24072–73, 24076, 24079, 24082, 24084, 24086–87, 24089, 24091, 24093–94, 24104–05, 24111–12, 24120–22, 24124, 24126–29, 24131–34, 24136, 24138, 24141–43, 24147–50, 24153, 24162, 24165, 24167, 24171, 24175, 24177, 24185, 24201–03, 24209–12, 24215–21, 24224–26, 24228, 24230, 24236–37, 24239, 24243–46, 24248, 24250–51, 24256, 24258, 24260, 24263, 24265–66, 24269–73, 24277, 24279–83, 24290, 24292–93, 24301, 24311–19, 24322–28, 24330, 24333, 24340, 24343, 24347–48, 24350–52, 24354, 24360–61, 24363, 24366, 24368, 24370, 24374–75, 24377–78, 24380–82, 24422, 24426, 24448, 24457, 24474, 24502, 24526, 24550–51, 24556, 24601–09, 24612–14, 24618–20, 24622, 24624, 24627–28, 24630–31, 24634–35, 24637, 24639–41, 24646–47, 24649, 24651, 24656–58

* * *

TENTH DISTRICT

FRANK R. WOLF, Republican, of Vienna, VA; born in Philadelphia, PA, January 30, 1939; education: B.A., Pennsylvania State University, 1961; LL.B., Georgetown University Law

School, 1965; served in the U.S. Army Signal Corps (Reserves); professional: lawyer, admitted to the Virginia State Bar; legislative assistant for former U.S. Congressman Edward G. Biester, Jr., 1968–71; assistant to Secretary of the Interior Rogers C.B. Morton, 1971–74; Deputy Assistant Secretary for Congressional and Legislative Affairs, Department of the Interior, 1974–75; member, Vienna Presbyterian Church; married: the former Carolyn Stover; children: Frank, Jr., Virginia, Anne, Brenda, and Rebecca; co-chair, Tom Lantos Human Rights Commission; committees: Appropriations; elected to the 97th Congress, November 4, 1980; reelected to each succeeding Congress.

Office Listings

http://www.wolf.house.gov

241 Cannon House Office Building, Washington, DC 20515 .... (202) 225–5136
Chief of Staff / Press Secretary.—Dan Scandling. FAX: 225–0437
Legislative Director.—Janet Shaffron.
13873 Park Center Road, Suite 130, Herndon, VA 20171 .... (703) 709–5800
Director of Constituent Services.—Judy McCary.
110 North Cameron Street, Winchester, VA 22601 .... (540) 667–0900

Counties: CLARKE, FAIRFAX (part), FAUQUIER (part), FREDERICK, LOUDOUN, PRINCE WILLIAM (part), WARREN. CITIES: Manassas, Manassas Park, and Winchester. Population (2000), 643,512.

ZIP Codes: 20101–05, 20107–13, 20115–18, 20120–22, 20129–32, 20134–35, 20137, 20140–44, 20146–49, 20151–53, 20158–60, 20163–67, 20170–72, 20175–78, 20180, 20184–90, 20194, 20197–98, 22026, 22033, 22043–44, 22046, 22066–67, 22101, 22106, 22184–85, 22193, 22207, 22556, 22601–04, 22610–11, 22620, 22622, 22624–25, 22630, 22637, 22639, 22642–43, 22645–46, 22649, 22654–57, 22663

* * *

ELEVENTH DISTRICT

GERALD E. CONNOLLY, Democrat, of Fairfax, VA; born in Boston, MA, March 30, 1950; education: graduated B.A., Maryknoll College; M.A., public administration, Harvard University, 1979; professional: member, Fairfax County Board of Supervisors, 1995–2003, chairman, 2003–07; religion: Roman Catholic; married: Cathy; children: Caitlin; committees: Foreign Affairs; Oversight and Government Reform; elected to the 111th Congress on November 4, 2008; reelected to the 112th Congress.

Office Listings

http://www.geraldconnolly.house.gov

424 Cannon House Office Building, Washington, DC 20515 .... (202) 225–1492
Chief of Staff.—James Walkinshaw. FAX: 225–3071
Legislative Director.—Dominic Bonaiuto.
Communications Director.—George Burke.
4115 Annandale Road, Annandale, VA 22003 .... (703) 256–3071
District Director.—Sharon Stark.
4308 Ridgewood Center Drive, Woodbridge, VA 22192 .... (703) 670–4989
Prince William Director.—Colin Davenport.

Counties: FAIRFAX (part), PRINCE WILLIAM (part). CITIES: Alexandria, Annandale, Burke, Centreville, Clifton, Fairfax, Fairfax Station, Herndon, Lorton, Manassas, Oakton, Occoquan, Springfield, Vienna, and Woodbridge. Population (2000), 643,509.

ZIP Codes: 20069–70, 20109–10, 20112, 20119–22, 20124, 20136–37, 20155–56, 20168–69, 20171, 20181–82, 22003, 22009, 22015, 22027, 22030–33, 22035, 22038–39, 22044, 22060, 22079, 22081–82, 22102, 22116, 22118–21, 22124–25, 22150–53, 22156, 22158–61, 22180–83, 22185, 22191–95, 22199, 22308–09, 22312

WASHINGTON

(Population 2010, 6,724,540)

SENATORS

PATTY MURRAY, Democrat, of Seattle, WA; born in Seattle, October 11, 1950; education: B.A., Washington State University, 1972; professional: teacher; lobbyist; Shoreline Community College; citizen lobbyist for environmental and educational issues, 1983–88; parent education instructor for Crystal Springs, 1984–87; school board member, 1985–89; elected Board of Directors, Shoreline School District, 1985–89; Washington State Senate, 1988–92; Democratic Whip, 1990–92; State Senate committees: Education; Ways and Means; Commerce and Labor; Domestic Timber Processing Select Committee; Open Government Select Committee; chair, School Transportation Safety Task Force; award: Washington State Legislator of the Year, 1990; married: Rob Murray; children: Randy and Sara; committees: chair, Veterans' Affairs; Appropriations; Budget; Health, Education, Labor and Pensions; Rules and Administration; Joint Committee on Printing; elected to the U.S. Senate on November 3, 1992; reelected to each succeeding Senate term.

Office Listings

http://murray.senate.gov

448 Russell Senate Office Building, Washington, DC 20510 .... (202) 224–2621
Chief of Staff.—Mike Spahn. FAX: 224–0238
Deputy Chief of Staff/Legislative Director.—Evan Schatz. TDD: 224–4430
Communications Director.—Matt McAlvanah.
2988 Jackson Federal Building, 915 Second Avenue, Seattle, WA 98174 .... (206) 553–5545
State Director.—Brian Kristjansson.
District Director.—Sergio Cueva-Flores.
The Marshall House, 1323 Officer's Row, Vancouver, WA 98661 .... (360) 696–7797
District Director.—Page Phillips.
10 North Post Road, Suite 600, Spokane, WA 99201 .... (509) 624–9515
District Director.—Erin Vincent.
2930 Wetmore Avenue, Suite 903, Everett, WA 98201 .... (425) 259–6515
District Director.—Uriel Ybarra.
402 East Yakima Avenue, Suite 390, Yakima, WA 98901 .... (509) 453–7462
District Director.—Rebecca Thornton.
950 Pacific Avenue, Room 650, Tacoma, WA 98402 .... (253) 572–3636
District Directors: Sean Murphy, Kristine Reeves.

* * *

MARIA CANTWELL, Democrat, of Edmonds, WA; born in Indianapolis, IN, October 13, 1958; education: B.A., Miami University, Miami, OH, 1980; professional: businesswoman; RealNetworks, Inc.; organizations: South Snohomish County Chamber of Commerce; Alderwood Rotary; Mountlake Terrace Friends of the Library; public service: Washington State House of Representatives, 1987–92; U.S. House of Representatives, 1992–94; religion: Roman Catholic; committees: Commerce, Science, and Transportation; Energy and Natural Resources; Finance; Indian Affairs; Small Business and Entrepreneurship; elected to the U.S. Senate on November 7, 2000; reelected to each succeeding Senate term.

Office Listings

http://cantwell.senate.gov

311 Hart Senate Office Building, Washington, DC 20510 .... (202) 224–3441
Chief of Staff.—Katharine Lister. FAX: 228–0514
Deputy Chief of Staff.—Amit Ronen.
Legislative Director.—Mac Campbell.
Office Manager.—Nancy Hadley.
915 Second Avenue, Suite 3206, Seattle, WA 98174 .... (206) 220–6400
The Marshall House, 1313 Officers Row, Vancouver, WA 98661 .... (360) 696–7838
950 Pacific Avenue, Suite 615, Tacoma, WA 98402 .... (253) 572–2281
U.S. Federal Courthouse, West 920 Riverside, Suite 697, Spokane, WA 99201 ...... (509) 353–2507
825 Jadwin Avenue, 204/204A, Richland, WA 99352 .... (509) 946–8106
2930 Wetmore Avenue, Suite 9B, Everett, WA 98201 .... (425) 303–0114

REPRESENTATIVES

FIRST DISTRICT

JAY INSLEE, Democrat, of Bainbridge Island, WA; born in Seattle, WA, February 9, 1951; education: graduated, Ingraham High School, 1969; B.A., University of Washington, 1973; J.D., Willamette School of Law, 1976; professional: attorney, 1976–92; Washington State House of Representatives, 14th Legislative District, 1988–92; served on Appropriations; Housing; Judiciary; and Financial Institutions and Insurance Committees; attorney, 1995–96; Regional Director, U.S. Department of Health and Human Services, 1997–98; married: Trudi; three children: Jack, Connor, and Joe; committees: Energy and Commerce; elected to the 103rd Congress to represent the 4th District, November 3, 1992; elected to the 106th Congress to represent the 1st District on November 3, 1998; reelected to each succeeding Congress.

Office Listings

http://www.house.gov/inslee

403 Cannon House Office Building, Washington, DC 20515 .... (202) 225–6311
Chief of Staff.—Brian Bonlender. FAX: 226–1606
Legislative Director.—Beth Osborne.
Press Secretary.—Robert Kellar.
Scheduler.—Casey Katims.
Shoreline Center, 18560 First Avenue, NE., Suite E–800, Shoreline, WA 98155–2150 .... (206) 361–0233
17701 Fjord Drive, NE., Suite A–112, Liberty Bay Marina, Poulsbo, WA 98370 ... (360) 598–2342
District Director.—Sharmila K. Swenson.

Counties: KING (part), KITSAP (part), SNOHOMISH (part). CITIES AND TOWNSHIPS: Bainbridge Island, Bothell, Bremerton, Brier, Duvall, Edmonds, Everett, Hansville, Indianola, Kenmore, Keyport, Kingston, Kirkland, Lake Forest, Lynnwood, Mill Creek, Monroe, Mountlake Terrace, Mukilteo, Port Gamble, Poulsbo, Redmond, Rollingbay, Seabeck, Seattle, Shoreline, Silverdale, Snohomish, Suquamish, and Woodinville. Population (2000), 654,904.

ZIP Codes: 98011–12, 98019–20, 98021, 98026, 98028, 98033–34, 98036–37, 98041, 98043, 98046, 98052, 98061, 98072–74, 98077, 98082–83, 98110, 98133, 98155, 98160, 98177, 98204, 98208, 98272, 98275, 98290, 98296, 98311–12, 98315, 98340, 98342, 98345–46, 98364, 98370, 98380, 98383, 98392–93

* * *

SECOND DISTRICT

RICK LARSEN, Democrat, of Everett, WA; born in Arlington, WA, June 15, 1965; education: B.A., Pacific Lutheran University; M.P.A., University of Minnesota; professional: economic development official at the Port of Everett; Director of Public Affairs for a health provider association; public service: Snohomish County Council; religion: Methodist; married: Tiia Karlen; children: Robert and Per; committees: Armed Services; Transportation and Infrastructure; elected to the 107th Congress on November 7, 2000; reelected to each succeeding Congress.

Office Listings

http:/www.house.gov/larsen

108 Cannon House Office Building, Washington, DC 20515 .... (202) 225–2605
Chief of Staff.—Kimberly Johnston. FAX: 225–4420
Legislative Director.—Jasper MacSlarrow.
Communications Director.—Emily Halnon.
2930 Wetmore Avenue, Suite 9F, Everett, WA 98201 .... (425) 252–3188
119 North Commercial Street, Suite 1350, Bellingham, WA 98225 .... (360) 733–5144

Counties: ISLAND, KING (part), SAN JUAN, SKAGIT, SNOHOMISH (part), WHATCOM. CITIES AND TOWNSHIPS: Bellingham, Everett, and Mount Vernon. Population (2000), 654,903.

ZIP Codes: 98201, 98203–08, 98213, 98220–33, 98235–41, 98243–45, 98247–53, 98255–64, 98266–67, 98270–84, 98286–88, 98290–97

* * *

THIRD DISTRICT

JAIME HERRERA BEUTLER, Republican, of Camas, born in Glendale, CA, November 3, 1978; education: communications, University of Washington, Seattle, WA, 2004; religion:

Christian; family: married to Daniel Beutler; caucuses: co-vice chair of the Congressional Congress for Women's Issues / co-chair of the Women and the Economy / Business Task Force; committees: Transportation and Infrastructure; Small Business; elected to the 112th Congress on November 2, 2010.

Office Listings

http://www.herrerabeutler.house.gov

1130 Longworth House Office Building, Washington, DC 20515 .... (202) 225–3536
Chief of Staff.—Afton Swift. FAX: 225–3478
Legislative Assistant.—Chad Ramey.
Legislative Correspondents: Amy Lee, Jessica Wixson.
Communications Director.—Casey Bowman.
Executive Assistant / Scheduler.—Amy Pennington.
Staff Assistant.—Jordon Evich.
750 Anderson Street, Suite B, Vancouver, WA 98661 .... (360) 695–6292
District Director.—Ryan Hart.
Deputy District Directors: Keith Bundy, Shari Hildreth.
Field Representative.—Pam Peiper.
Caseworkers: Ashley Lara, Jordan Meade, Emily Wilson.

Counties: CLARK COUNTY. CITIES AND TOWNSHIPS: Amboy, Ariel, Battle Ground, Brush Prairie, Camas, Heisson, La Center, Ridgefield, Vancouver, Washougal, Woodland, Yacolt. COWLITZ COUNTY. CITIES AND TOWNSHIPS: Carrolls, Castle Rock, Cougar, Kalama, Kelso, Longview, Ryderwood, Silverlake, Toutle. LEWIS COUNTY. CITIES AND TOWNSHIPS: Adna, Centralia, Chehalis, Cinebar, Curtis, Doty, Ethel, Galvin, Glenoma, Mineral, Morton, Mossyrock, Napavine, Onalaska, Packwood, Pe Ell, Randle, Salkum, Silver Creek, Toledo, Vader, Winlock. PACIFIC COUNTY. CITIES AND TOWNSHIPS: Bay Center, Chinook, Ilwaco, Lebam, Long Beach, Menlo, Nahcotta, Naselle, Ocean Park, Oysterville, Raymond, Seaview, South Bend, Tokeland. PIERCE COUNTY. CITIES AND TOWNSHIPS: Elbe. SKAMANIA COUNTY (part). CITIES AND TOWNSHIPS: Carson, North Bonneville, Stevenson, Underwood. THURSTON COUNTY (part). CITIES AND TOWNSHIPS: Buroda, Littlerock, Olympia, Tenino, and Rochester. WAHKIAKUM COUNTY. CITIES AND TOWNSHIPS: Cathlamet, Grays River, Rosburg, and Skamokawa. Population (2000), 654,898.

ZIP Codes: 98304, 98328, 98330, 98336, 98355–56, 98361, 98377, 98501–09, 98511–13, 98522, 98527, 98531–33, 98537–39, 98541–42, 98544, 98547, 98554, 98556–57, 98559, 98561, 98564–65, 98568, 98570, 98572, 98576–77, 98579, 98581–83, 98585–86, 98589–91, 98593, 98595–97, 98601–04, 98606–07, 98609–12, 98614, 98616, 98621–22, 98624–26, 98628–29, 98631–32, 98635, 98637–45, 98647–51, 98660–66, 98668, 98671–72, 98674–75, 98682–87

* * *

FOURTH DISTRICT

DOC HASTINGS, Republican, of Pasco, WA; born in Spokane, WA, February 7, 1941; education: graduated, Pasco High School, 1959; attended Columbia Basin College and Central Washington State University, Ellensburg, WA; military service: U.S. Army Reserves, 1963–69; professional: president, Columbia Basin Paper and Supply; board of directors, Yakima Federal Savings and Loan; member: Washington State House of Representatives, 1979–87; Republican Caucus chairman, assistant majority leader, and National Platform Committee, 1984; president: Pasco Chamber of Commerce; Pasco Downtown Development Association; Pasco Jaycees (chamber president); chairman, Franklin County Republican Central Committee, 1974–78; delegate, Republican National Convention, 1976–84; married: Claire Hastings, 1967; children: Kirsten, Petrina and Colin; committees: chair, Natural Resources; elected to the 104th Congress; reelected to each succeeding Congress.

Office Listings

http://www.house.gov/hastings

1203 Longworth House Office Building, Washington, DC 20515 .... (202) 225–5816
Chief of Staff.—Jessica Gleason. FAX: 225–3251
Scheduler / Office Manager.—Ilene Clauson.
Press Secretary.—Erin Daly.
2715 Saint Andrews Loop, Suite D, Pasco, WA 99302 .... (509) 543–9396
402 East Yakima Avenue, Suite 760, WA 98901 .... (509) 452–3243

Counties: ADAMS COUNTY (part). CITIES: Othello. BENTON COUNTY. CITIES AND TOWNSHIPS: Benton City, Kennewick, Paterson, Plymouth, Prosser, Richland, West Richland. CHELAN COUNTY. CITIES AND TOWNSHIPS: Ardenvoir, Cashmere, Chelan, Chelan Falls, Dryden, Entiat, Leavenworth, Malaga, Manson, Monitor, Peshastin, Stehekin, Wenatchee. DOUGLAS COUNTY. CITIES AND TOWNSHIPS: Bridgeport, East Wenatchee, Leahy, Mansfield, Orondo, Palisades, Rock Island, Waterville. FRANKLIN COUNTY. CITIES AND TOWNSHIPS: Basin City, Connell, Eltopia, Kahlotus, Mesa, Pasco, Windust. GRANT COUNTY. CITIES AND TOWNSHIPS: Beverly, Coulee City, Desert Aire, Electric City, Ephrata, George, Grand Coulee, Hartline, Marlin, Mattawa, Moses Lake, Quincy, Royal City, Soap Lake, Stratford, Warden, Wilson Creek. KITTITAS COUNTY. CITIES AND TOWNSHIPS: Cle Elum, Easton, Ellensburg, Hyak, Kittitas, Ronald, Roslyn, Snoqualmic Pass, South Cle Elum, Thorp, Vantage. KLICKITAT COUNTY. CITIES AND TOWNSHIPS: Alderdale, Appleton, Bickleton, Bingen, Centerville, Cook, Dallesport, Glenwood, Goldendale, Husum, Klickitat, Lyle, Roosevelt, Trout Lake, Wahkiacus, White Salmon, Wishram, Wishram Heights. SKAMANIA COUNTY (part), YAKIMA COUNTY. CITIES AND TOWNSHIPS:

Brownstown, Buena, Carson, Cowiche, Grandview, Granger, Harrah, Mabton, Moxee, Naches, Outlook, Parker, Selah, Sunnyside, Tieton, Toppenish, Underwood, Wapato, White Swan, Yakima, and Zillah. Population (2000), 654,901.

ZIP Codes: 98068, 98602, 98605, 98610, 98613, 98617, 98619–20, 98623, 98628, 98635, 98648, 98650–51, 98670, 98672–73, 98801–02, 98807, 98811–13, 98815–17, 98819, 98821–24, 98826, 98828–32, 98834, 98836–37, 98843, 98845, 98847–48, 98850–53, 98857–58, 98860, 98901–04, 98907–09, 98920–23, 98925–26, 98929–30, 98932–44, 98946–48, 98950–53, 99103, 99115–16, 99123–24, 99133, 99135, 99155, 99301–02, 99320–22, 99326, 99330, 99335–38, 99343–46, 99349–50, 99352–54, 99356–57

* * *

FIFTH DISTRICT

CATHY McMORRIS RODGERS, Republican, of Spokane, WA; born in Salem, OR, May 22, 1969; education: B.A., Pensacola Christian College, Pensacola, FL, 1990; M.B.A., University of Washington, Seattle, WA, 2002; professional: fruit orchard worker; member, Washington State House of Representatives, 1994–2004; minority leader, 2002–03; organizations: member, Grace Evangelical Free Church; married: Brian Rodgers; children: Cole; committees: Energy and Commerce; elected to the 109th Congress on November 2, 2004; reelected to each succeeding Congress.

Office Listings

http://www.house.gov/mcmorris

2421 Rayburn House Office Building, Washington, DC 20515 .... (202) 225–2006
Chief of Staff.—Jeremy Deutsch. FAX: 225–3392
Legislative Director.—Kim Betz.
Scheduler.—Jinyoung Lee.
Communications Director.—Todd Weiner.
10 North Post Street, 6th floor, Spokane, WA 99210 .... (509) 353–2374
District Director.—David Condon.
555 South Main Street, Colville, WA 99114 .... (509) 684–3481
29 South Palouse Street, Walla Walla, WA 99362 .... (509) 529–9358

Counties: ADAMS (part), ASOTIN, COLUMBIA, FERRY, GARFIELD, LINCOLN, PEND OREILLE, OKANAGAN, SPOKANE, STEVENS, WALLA WALLA, WHITMAN. Population (2000), 654,901.

ZIP Codes: 98812, 98814, 98819, 98827, 98829, 98832–34, 98840–41, 98844, 98846, 98849, 98855–57, 98859, 98862, 99001, 99003–06, 99008–09, 99011–14, 99016–23, 99025–27, 99029–34, 99036–37, 99039–40, 99101–05, 99107, 99109–11, 99113–14, 99116–19, 99121–22, 99125–26, 99128–31, 99133–41, 99143–44, 99146–61, 99163–67, 99169–71, 99173–74, 99176, 99179–81, 99185, 99201–20, 99223–24, 99228, 99251–52, 99256, 99258, 99260, 99302, 99323–24, 99326, 99328–29, 99333, 99335, 99341, 99344, 99347–48, 99356, 99359–63, 99371, 99401–03

* * *

SIXTH DISTRICT

NORMAN D. DICKS, Democrat, of Bremerton, WA; born in Bremerton, December 16, 1940; education: graduated, West Bremerton High School, 1959; B.A., political science, University of Washington, 1963; J.D., University of Washington School of Law, 1968; admitted to Washington Bar, 1968; joined the staff of Senator Warren G. Magnuson in 1968 as legislative assistant and appropriations assistant, named administrative assistant in 1973, and held that post until he resigned to campaign for Congress in February 1976; member: Democratic Caucus; Washington State Bar Association; Puget Sound Naval Bases Association; Navy League of the United States; married: the former Suzanne Callison, 1967; children: David and Ryan; committees: ranking member, Appropriations; elected to the 95th Congress; reelected to each succeeding Congress.

Office Listings

2467 Rayburn House Office Building, Washington, DC 20515 .... (202) 225–5916
Chief of Staff / Press Secretary.—George Behan. FAX: 226–1176
Legislative Director.—Pete Modaff.
Scheduler.—Yodit Tewelde.
1019 Pacific Avenue, Suite 806, Tacoma, WA 98402 .... (253) 593–6536
District Director.—Clark Mather.
345 Sixth Street, Suite 500, Bremerton, WA 98337 .... (360) 479–4011
Deputy District Director.—Cheri Williams.
322 East Fifth Street, Port Angeles, WA 98362 .... (360) 452–3370
District Representative.—Judith Morris.

Counties: CLALLAM COUNTY. CITIES AND TOWNSHIPS: Forks, Port Angeles, La Push, Sequim, Sekiu, Neah Bay. GRAYS HARBOR COUNTY. CITIES AND TOWNSHIPS: Aberdeen, Hoquiam, Montesano, Ocean City, Ocean Shores, Moclips, Westport.

JEFFERSON COUNTY. CITIES AND TOWNSHIPS: Port Townsend, Quilcene. KITSAP COUNTY (part). CITIES AND TOWNSHIPS: Bremerton, Port Orchard, Gorst. MASON COUNTY. CITIES AND TOWNSHIPS: Shelton, Belfair, Allyn, Union. PIERCE COUNTY (part). CITIES AND TOWNSHIPS: Tacoma, Gig Harbor, Lakebay, and Lakewood. Population (2000), 654,902.

ZIP Codes: 98305, 98310–12, 98314, 98320, 98322, 98324–26, 98329, 98331–33, 98335, 98337, 98339, 98343, 98349–51, 98353, 98357–59, 98362–63, 98365–68, 98373, 98376, 98378, 98380–82, 98384, 98386, 98394–95, 98401–09, 98411–13, 98415–16, 98418, 98442, 98444–45, 98464–67, 98471, 98477, 98481, 98492, 98497–99, 98502, 98520, 98524, 98526, 98528, 98535–37, 98541, 98546–48, 98550, 98552, 98555, 98557, 98560, 98562–63, 98566, 98568–69, 98571, 98575, 98584, 98587–88, 98592, 98595

* * *

SEVENTH DISTRICT

JIM McDERMOTT, Democrat, of Seattle, WA; born in Chicago, IL, December 28, 1936; education: B.S., Wheaton College, Wheaton, IL, 1958; M.D., University of Illinois Medical School, Chicago, 1963; residency in adult psychiatry, University of Illinois Hospitals, 1964–66; residency in child psychiatry, University of Washington Hospitals, Seattle, 1966–68; served, U.S. Navy Medical Corps, lieutenant commander, 1968–70; psychiatrist; Washington State House of Representatives, 1971–72; Washington State Senate, 1975–87; Democratic nominee for governor, 1980; regional medical officer, Sub-Saharan Africa, U.S. Foreign Service, 1987–88; practicing psychiatrist and assistant clinical professor of psychiatry, University of Washington, Seattle, 1970–83; member: Washington State Medical Association; King County Medical Society; American Psychiatric Association; religion: St. Mark's Episcopal Church, Seattle; married: Therese M. Hansen; grown children: Katherine and James; grandchildren; committees: Ways and Means; elected on November 8, 1988, to the 101st Congress; reelected to each succeeding Congress.

Office Listings

http://www.house.gov/mcdermott

1035 Longworth House Office Building, Washington, DC 20515 .... (202) 225–3106
Chief of Staff.—Diane Shust. FAX: 225–6197
Legislative Director.—Toby Whitney.
Executive Assistant.—Myat Khaing.
Communications Director. Kinsey Kiriakos.
1809 Seventh Avenue, Suite 1212, Seattle, WA 98101–1313 .... (206) 553–7170
District Administrator.—Darcy Nothnagle.

Counties: KING COUNTY (part). CITIES AND TOWNSHIPS: Burien (part), Lake Forest Park, Vashon Island, Shoreline, SeaTac, Seattle, Tukwila. Population (2000), 654,902.

ZIP Codes: 98013, 98055, 98070, 98101–09, 98111–19, 98121–22, 98124–27, 98129, 98131, 98133–34, 98136, 98139, 98141, 98144–46, 98151, 98154–55, 98161, 98164–66, 98168, 98171, 98174–75, 98177–78, 98181, 98184–85, 98190–91, 98194–95, 98199

* * *

EIGHTH DISTRICT

DAVID G. REICHERT, Republican, of Auburn, WA; born in Detroit Lakes, MI, August 29, 1950; education: graduated, Kent Meridian High School, Renton, WA, 1968; A.A., Concordia Lutheran College, Portland, OR, 1970; professional: U.S. Air Force Reserve, 1971–76; U.S. Air Force, 1976; police officer, King County, WA, 1972–97; sheriff, King County, WA, 1997–2004; member: president, Washington State Sheriff's Association; executive board member, Washington Association of Sheriffs and Police Chiefs; co-chair, Washington State Partners in Crisis; awards: recipient of the 2004 National Sheriff's Association's ''Sheriff of the Year''; two-time Medal of Valor Award Recipient from the King County sheriff's office; Washington Policy Center's Champion of Freedom Award; Families Northwest Public Policy Award; married: Julie; children: Angela, Tabitha, and Daniel; committees: Ways and Means; elected to the 109th Congress on November 2, 2004; reelected to each succeeding Congress.

Office Listings

http://www.reichert.house.gov

1730 Longworth House Office Building, Washington, DC 20515 .... (202) 225–7761
Chief of Staff.—Jeff Harvey. FAX: 225–4282
Legislative Director.—Jason Edgar.
Executive Assistant / Scheduler.—Nichole Robison.
2737 Seventh-Eighth Avenue, SE., Suite 202, Mercer Island, WA 98040 .... (206) 275–3438

District Director.—Sue Foy.

Counties: KING COUNTY (part). CITIES AND TOWNSHIPS: Auburn, Baring, Beaux Arts Village, Bellevue, Black Diamond, Carnation, Duvall, Enumclaw, Fall City, Issaquah, Kent, Mercer Island, Maple Valley, New Castle, North Bend, Preston, Redmond, Renton, Skykomish, Snoqualmie, Summit, Woodinville. PIERCE COUNTY. CITIES AND TOWNSHIPS: Ashford, Bonney Lake, Buckley, Carbonado, Eatonville, Elbe, Graham, Orting, Roy, South Prairie, Spanaway, and Wilkeson. Population (2000), 654,905.

ZIP Codes: 98002, 98004–10, 98014–15, 98019, 98022, 98024–25, 98027, 98029–31, 98033, 98035, 98038–40, 98042, 98045, 98050–53, 98055–56, 98058–59, 98064–65, 98068, 98074–75, 98077, 98092, 98304, 98321, 98323, 98328, 98330, 98338, 98344, 98348, 98352, 98360, 98372–75, 98385, 98387, 98390, 98396–98, 98446

* * *

NINTH DISTRICT

ADAM SMITH, Democrat, of Tacoma, WA; born in Washington, DC, June 15, 1965; education: graduated, Tyee High School, 1983; graduated, Fordham University, NY, 1987; law degree, University of Washington, 1990; admitted to the Washington Bar in 1991; professional: prosecutor for the city of Seattle; Washington State Senate, 1990–96; member: Kent Drinking Driver Task Force; board member, Judson Park Retirement Home; married: Sara Smith, 1993; committees: ranking member, Armed Services; elected to the 105th Congress; reelected to each succeeding Congress.

Office Listings

http://www.adamsmith.house.gov

2402 Rayburn House Office Building, Washington, DC 20515 .... (202) 225–8901
Chief of Staff.—Shana Chandler. FAX: 225–5893
Communications Director.—Libby Denkmann.
2209 Pacific Avenue, Suite B, Tacoma, WA 98402 .... (253) 593–6600
District Director.—Linda Danforth.
Office Manager.—Carrie Locken.

Counties: KING (part), PIERCE (part), THURSTON (part). CITIES: Algona, Auburn, Burien, Des Moines, Dupont, Edgewood, Federal Way, Fife, Kent, Lacey, Lakewood, Milton, Muckleshoot Indian Reservation, Nisqually Indian Reservation, Normandy Park, Olympia, Pacific, Puyallup, Puyallup Indian Reservation, Renton, Roy, SeaTac, Spanaway, Steilacoom, Tacoma, Tukwila, and Yelm. Population (2000), 654,902.

ZIP Codes: 98001–03, 98023, 98030–32, 98047, 98054–55, 98057–58, 98062–63, 98071, 98089, 98092–93, 98131–32, 98138, 98148, 98158, 98166, 98168, 98171, 98178, 98188, 98198, 98303, 98327–28, 98338, 98354, 98371–75, 98387–88, 98390–91, 98402, 98404, 98421–22, 98424, 98430–31, 98433, 98438–39, 98443–46, 98467, 98492–93, 98497–99, 98503, 98506, 98509, 98513, 98516, 98558, 98576, 98580, 98597

WEST VIRGINIA

(Population 2010, 1,852,994)

SENATORS

JOHN D. ROCKEFELLER IV, Democrat, of Charleston, WV; born in New York City, NY, June 18, 1937; education: graduated, Phillips Exeter Academy, Exeter, NH, 1954; A.B., Harvard University, Cambridge, MA, 1961; honorary degrees: J.D., West Virginia University; Marshall University; Davis and Elkins College; Dickinson College; University of Alabama; University of Cincinnati; doctor of humanities, West Virginia Institute of Technology; doctor of public service, Salem College; professional service: Vista volunteer, Emmons, WV, 1964; West Virginia House of Delegates, 1966–68; elected Secretary of State of West Virginia, 1968; president, West Virginia Wesleyan College, 1973–76; Governor of West Virginia, 1976–84; married: the former Sharon Percy; children: John, Valerie, Charles and Justin; committees: chair, Commerce, Science, and Transportation, Finance; Veterans' Affairs; Select Committee on Intelligence; Joint Committee on Taxation; elected to the U.S. Senate on November 6, 1984; reelected to each succeeding Senate term.

Office Listings

http://rockefeller.senate.gov

531 Hart Senate Office Building, Washington, DC 20510 .... (202) 224–6472
Chief of Staff.—Kerry Ates. FAX: 224–7665
Legislative Director.—Jocelyn Moore.
Communications Director.—Vincent Morris.
405 Capitol Street, Suite 508, Charleston, WV 25301 .... (304) 347–5372
220 North Kanawha Street, Suite 1, Beckley, WV 25801 .... (304) 253–9704
118 Adams Street, Suite 301, Fairmont, WV 26554 .... (304) 367–0122
217 West King Street, Suite 307, Martinsburg, WV 25401 .... (304) 262–9285

* * *

JOE MANCHIN III, Democrat, of Fairmont, WV; born in Farmington, August 24, 1947; education: graduated, Farmington High School, Farmington, 1965; B.A., West Virginia University, WV, 1970; businessman; member of the West Virginia House of Delegates, 1982–86; member of the West Virginia State Senate, 1986–96; Secretary of State, West Virginia, 2000–04; elected governor of West Virginia in 2004 and reelected in 2008; chairman of the National Governors Association, 2010; religion: Catholic; married: Gayle Conelly; three children, Heather, Joseph IV, and Brooke; seven grandchildren; committees: Armed Services; Energy and Natural Resources; Special Committee on Aging; elected to the 111th U.S. Senate in the November 2, 2010, special election to the term ending January 3, 2013, a seat previously held by Senator Carte Goodwin, and took the oath of office on November 15, 2010.

Office Listings

http://manchin.senate.gov

303 Hart Senate Office Building, Washington, DC 20510 .... (202) 224–3954
Chief of Staff.—Chris Kofinis. FAX: 228–0002
Administrative Assistant.—Molly George.
Communications Director.—Emily Bittner.
300 Virginia Street East, Suite 2630, Charleston, WV 25301 .... (304) 342–5855
State Director.—Kelley Goes.
217 West King Street, Room 238, Martinsburg, WV 25401 .... (304) 264–4626
48 Donley Street, Suite 504, Morgantown, WV 26501 .... (304) 284–8663
FAX: 284–8681

REPRESENTATIVES

FIRST DISTRICT

DAVID B. McKINLEY, P.E., Republican, of Wheeling, WV; born in Wheeling, March 28, 1947; education: B.S.C.E., civil engineering, Purdue University, West Lafayette, IN, 1969; professional: engineer (started McKinley and Associates with offices in Wheeling and Charleston, WV and Washington, PA); member of West Virginia State House of Representatives, 1981–94; chairman, West Virginia Republican Party, 1990–94; religion: Episcopalian; married: Mary

McKinley; children: David, Amy, Elizabeth, and Bennett; committees: Energy and Commerce; elected to the 112th Congress on November 2, 2010.

Office Listings

313 Cannon House Office Building, Washington, DC 20515 .... (202) 225–4172
Chief of Staff.—Andy Seré. FAX: 225–7564
Scheduler.—Sheila Westerfield.
Legislative Director.—J.T. Jezierski.
Press Secretary.—Katie Martin.
709 Beechurst Avenue, Suite 14B, Morgantown, WV 26505 .... (304) 284–8506
The Federal Building, 1125 Chapline Street, Wheeling, WV 26003 .... (304) 232–3801
Federal Building, 425 Juliana Street, Suite 1004, Parkersburg, WV 26101 .... (304) 422–5972

Counties: BARBOUR, BROOKE, DODDRIDGE, GILMER, GRANT, HANCOCK, HARRISON, MARION, MARSHALL, MINERAL, MONONGALIA, OHIO, PLEASANTS, PRESTON, RITCHIE, TAYLOR, TUCKER, TYLER, WETZEL, WOOD. CITIES AND TOWNSHIPS: Albright, Alma, Alvy, Anmoore, Arthur, Arthurdale, Auburn, Aurora, Baldwin, Barrackville, Baxter, Bayard, Beech Bottom, Belington, Belleville, Belleville, Bellview, Belmont, Bens Run, Benwood, Berea, Bethany, Big Run, Blacksville, Blandville, Booth, Brandonville, Bretz, Bridgeport, Bristol, Brownton, Bruceton Mills, Burlington, Burnt House, Burton, Cabins, Cairo, Cameron, Carolina, Cassville, Cedarville, Center Point, Central Station, Century, Chester, Clarksburg, Coburn, Colfax, Colliers, Core, Corinth, Cove, Coxs Mills, Cuzzart, Dallas, Davis, Davisville, Dawmont, Dellslow, Dorcas, Eglon, Elk Garden, Ellenboro, Elm Grove, Enterprise, Eureka, Everettville, Fairmont, Fairview, Farmington, Flemington, Flower, Follansbee, Folsom, Fort Ashby, Fort Neal, Four States, Friendly, Galloway, Gilmer, Glen Dale, Glen Easton, Glenville, Goffs, Gormania, Grafton, Grant Town, Granville, Greenwood, Gypsy, Hambleton, Harrisville, Hastings, Haywood, Hazelton, Hebron, Hendricks, Hepzibah, Highland, Hundred, Idamay, Independence, Industrial, Jacksonburg, Jere, Jordan, Junior, Keyser, Kingmont, Kingwood, Knob Fork, Lahmansville, Letter Gap, Lima, Linn, Littleton, Lockney, Lost Creek, Lumberport, MacFarlan, Mahone, Maidsville, Mannington, Masontown, Maysville, McMechen, McWhorter, Meadowbrook, Medley, Metz, Middlebourne, Mineralwells, Moatsville, Monongah, Montana Mines, Morgantown, Moundsville, Mount Clare, Mount Storm, Mountain, New Creek, New Cumberland, New England, New Manchester, New Martinsville, New Milton, Newberne, Newburg, Newell, Normantown, North Parkersburg, Nutter Fort, Osage, Owings, Paden City, Parkersburg, Parsons, Pennsboro, Pentress, Perkins, Petersburg, Petroleum, Philippi, Piedmont, Pine Grove, Porters Falls, Proctor, Pullman, Pursglove, Rachel, Reader, Red Creek, Reedsville, Reynoldsville, Riegeley, Rivesville, Rocket Center, Rockport, Rosedale, Rosemont, Rowlesburg, Saint George, Saint Marys, Salem, Sand Fork, Shinnston, Shirley, Shocks, Short Creek, Simpson, Sistersville, Smithburg, Smithfield, Smithville, Spelter, Stonewood, Stouts Mill, Stumptown, Tanner, Terra Alta, Thomas, Thornton, Toll Gate, Troy, Triadelphia, Tunnelton, Valley Grove, Vienna, Volga, Wadestown, Walker, Wallace, Wana, Warwood, Washington, Watson, Waverly Weirton, Wellsburg, Wendel, West Liberty, West Milford, West Union, Westover, Wheeling Wick, Wilbur, Wiley Ford, Wileyville, Williamstown, Wilson, Wilsonburg, Windsor Heights, Wolf Summit, Worthington, and Wyatt. Population (2000), 602,543.

ZIP Codes: 25258, 25267, 26003, 26030–41, 26047, 26050, 26055–56, 26058–60, 26062, 26070, 26074–75, 26101–06, 26120–21, 26133–34, 26142–43, 26146–50, 26155, 26159, 26161–62, 26164, 26167, 26169–70, 26175, 26178, 26180–81, 26184, 26186–87, 26201, 26238, 26250, 26254, 26260, 26263, 26269, 26271, 26275–76, 26283, 26287, 26289, 26292, 26301–02, 26306, 26320–21, 26323, 26325, 26327, 26330, 26332, 26334–35, 26337, 26339, 26342, 26346–49, 26351, 26354, 26361–62, 26366, 26369, 26374, 26377–78, 26384–86, 26404–05, 26408, 26410–12, 26415–16, 26419, 26421–22, 26424–26, 26430–31, 26434–38, 26440, 26443–44, 26448, 26451, 26456, 26463, 26501–02, 26504–08, 26519–21, 26524–25, 26527, 26529, 26531, 26534, 26537, 26541–44, 26546–47, 26554–55, 26559–63, 26566, 26568, 26570–72, 26574–76, 26578, 26581–82, 26585–88, 26590–91, 26611, 26623, 26636, 26638, 26705, 26710, 26716–17, 26719–20, 26726, 26731, 26734, 26739, 26743, 26750, 26753, 26764, 26767, 26833, 26847, 26852, 26855

* * *

SECOND DISTRICT

SHELLEY MOORE CAPITO, Republican, of Charleston, WV; born in Glen Dale, WV, November 26, 1953; education: B.S., Duke University; M.Ed., University of Virginia; professional: career counselor; West Virginia State College; West Virginia Board of Regents; organizations: Community Council of Kanawha Valley; YWCA; West Virginia Interagency Council for Early Intervention; Habitat for Humanity; public service: elected to the West Virginia House of Delegates, 1996; reelected in 1998; awards: Coalition for a Tobacco-Free West Virginia Legislator of the Year; religion: Presbyterian; married: to Charles L., Jr.; three children; committees: Financial Services; Transportation and Infrastructure; elected to the 107th Congress on November 7, 2000; reelected to each succeeding Congress.

Office Listings

http://www.house.gov/capito

2443 Rayburn House Office Building, Washington, DC 20515 .... (202) 225–2711
Chief of Staff.—Joel Brubaker. FAX: 225–7856
Office Manager.—Alison Bibbee.
Legislative Director.—Dan Casto.
4815 MacCorkle Avenue, Southeast, Charleston, WV 25304 .... (304) 925–5964
300 Foxcroft Avenue, Suite 102, Martinsburg, WV 25401 .... (304) 264–8810

Counties: BERKELEY, BRAXTON, CALHOUN, CLAY, HAMPSHIRE, HARDY, JACKSON, JEFFERSON, KANAWHA, LEWIS, MASON, MORGAN, PENDLETON, PUTNAM, RANDOLPH, ROANE, UPSHUR, WIRT. Population (2010), 654,275.

ZIP Codes: 25002–03, 25005, 25011, 25015, 25019, 25025–26, 25030, 25033, 25035, 25039, 25043, 25045–46, 25054, 25059, 25061, 25063–64, 25067, 25070–71, 25075, 25079, 25081–83, 25085–86, 25088, 25102–03, 25106–07, 25109–

13, 25123–26, 25132–34, 25136, 25139, 25141, 25143, 25147, 25150, 25156, 25159–60, 25162, 25164, 25168, 25177, 25187, 25201–02, 25211, 25213–14, 25231, 25234–35, 25239, 25241, 25243–45, 25247–48, 25251–53, 25259–62, 25264–68, 25270–71, 25275–76, 25279, 25281, 25285–87, 25301–06, 25309, 25311–15, 25317, 25320–39, 25350, 25356–58, 25360–62, 25364–65, 25375, 25392, 25396, 25401–02, 25410–11, 25413–14, 25419–23, 25425, 25427–32, 25434, 25437–38, 25440–44, 25446, 25502–03, 25510, 25515, 25520, 25523, 25526, 25541, 25550, 25560, 25569, 26133, 26136–38, 26141, 26143, 26147, 26151–52, 26160–61, 26164, 26173, 26180, 26201–02, 26205, 26210, 26215, 26218, 26224, 26228–30, 26234, 26236–38, 26241, 26253–54, 26257, 26259, 26261, 26263, 26267–68, 26270, 26273, 26276, 26278, 26280, 26282–83, 26285, 26293–94, 26296, 26321, 26335, 26338, 26342–43, 26351, 26372, 26376, 26378, 26384–85, 26412, 26430, 26443, 26447, 26452, 26546, 26590, 26601, 26610–11, 26615, 26617, 26619, 26621, 26623–24, 26627, 26629, 26631, 26636, 26638–39, 26641, 26651, 26656, 26660, 26662, 26667, 26671, 26675–76, 26678–79, 26681, 26684, 26690–91, 26704–05, 26707, 26710–11, 26714, 26717, 26722, 26731, 26739, 26743, 26750, 26755, 26757, 26761, 26763–64, 26801–02, 26804, 26807–08, 26810, 26812, 26814–15, 26817–18, 26823–24, 26836, 26838, 26845, 26847, 26851–52, 26865–66, 26884, 26886

* * *

THIRD DISTRICT

NICK J. RAHALL II, Democrat, of Beckley, WV; born in Beckley, May 20, 1949; education: graduated, Woodrow Wilson High School, Beckley, 1967; A.B., Duke University, Durham, NC, 1971; graduate work, George Washington University, Washington, DC; colonel, U.S. Air Force Civil Air Patrol; president, West Virginia Society of Washington, DC; business executive; sales representative, WWNR radio station; president, Mountaineer Tour and Travel Agency, 1974; president, West Virginia Broadcasting; awards: Coal Man of the Year, *Coal Industry News,* 1979; Young Democrat of the Year, Young Democrats, 1980; recipient, West Virginia American Legion Distinguished Service Award, 1984; delegate, Democratic National Conventions, 1972, 1976, 1980, 1984; member: Rotary; Elks; Moose; Eagles; NAACP; National Rifle Association; AF & AM; RAM; Mount Hope Commandery; Shrine Club; Benie Kedeem Temple in Charleston; Beckley Presbyterian Church; chairman and founder, Congressional Coal Group; Democratic Leadership Council; Congressional Arts Caucus; Congressional Black Caucus; Congressional Fitness Caucus; International Workers' Rights Caucus; ITS Caucus; Qatar Caucus; Congressional Rural Caucus; Congressional Steel Caucus; Congressional Textile Caucus; Congressional Travel and Tourism Caucus; Congressional Truck Caucus; Wine Caucus; Automobile Task Force; Democratic Congressional Campaign Committee; Democratic Study Group; Energy and Environment Study Conference; married: the former Melinda Ross; children: Rebecca Ashley, Nick Joe III, and Suzanne Nicole; grandchildren: Madison; committees: ranking member, Transportation and Infrastructure; elected to the 95th Congress, November 2, 1976; reelected to each succeeding Congress.

Office Listings

http://www.house.gov/rahall

2307 Rayburn House Office Building, Washington, DC 20515 .... (202) 225–3452
Administrative Assistant.—David McMaster. FAX: 225–9061
Executive Assistant.—Kate Denmen.
Legislative Director.—Aaron Pritchard.
Press Secretary.—Diane Luensmann.
845 Fifth Avenue, Huntington, WV 25701–2086 .... (304) 522–6425
109 Main Street, Beckley, WV 25801 .... (304) 252–5000
220 Dingess Street, Logan, WV 25601 .... (304) 752–4934
601 Federal Street, Room 1005, Bluefield, WV 24701 .... (304) 325–6222

Counties: BOONE, CABELL, FAYETTE, GREENBRIER, LINCOLN, LOGAN, MCDOWELL, MERCER, MINGO, MONROE, NICHOLAS, POCAHONTAS, RALEIGH, SUMMERS, WAYNE, WEBSTER, WYOMING. Population (2000), 603,556.

ZIP Codes: 24701, 24712, 24714–16, 24719, 24724, 24726, 24729, 24731–33, 24736–40, 24747, 24751, 24801, 24808, 24811, 24813, 24815–18, 24820–31, 24834, 24836, 24839, 24842–57, 24859–62, 24866–74, 24878–82, 24884, 24887–88, 24892, 24894–99, 24901–02, 24910, 24915–18, 24920, 24924–25, 24927, 24931, 24934–36, 24938, 24941, 24943–46, 24950–51, 24954, 24957, 24961–63, 24966, 24970, 24974, 24976–77, 24981, 24983–86, 24991, 24993, 25002–04, 25007–10, 25021–22, 25024, 25028, 25031, 25036, 25040, 25043–44, 25047–49, 25051, 25053, 25057, 25059–60, 25062, 25076, 25081, 25083, 25085, 25090, 25093, 25108, 25114–15, 25118–19, 25121, 25130, 25136, 25139–40, 25142, 25148–49, 25152, 25154, 25161, 25165, 25169, 25173–74, 25180–81, 25183, 25185–86, 25193, 25202–06, 25208–09, 25213, 25501, 25504–08, 25510–12, 25514, 25517, 25520–21, 25523–24, 25526, 25529–30, 25534–35, 25537, 25540–41, 25544–45, 25547, 25555, 25557, 25559, 25562, 25564–65, 25567, 25570–73, 25601, 25606–08, 25611–12, 25614, 25617, 25621, 25624–25, 25628, 25630, 25632, 25634–39, 25644, 25646–47, 25649–54, 25661, 25665–67, 25669–72, 25674, 25676, 25678, 25682, 25685–88, 25690–92, 25694, 25696, 25699, 25701–29, 25755, 25770–79, 25801–02, 25810–13, 25816–18, 25820, 25823, 25825–27, 25831–33, 25836–37, 25839–41, 25843–49, 25851, 25853–57, 25859–60, 25862, 25864–66, 25868, 25870–71, 25873, 25875–76, 25878–80, 25882, 25901–02, 25904, 25906–09, 25911, 25913–22, 25927–28, 25931–32, 25934, 25936, 25938, 25942–43, 25951, 25958, 25961–62, 25965–67, 25969, 25971–72, 25976–79, 25981, 25984–86, 25989, 26202–03, 26205–06, 26208–09, 26217, 26222, 26230, 26234, 26261, 26264, 26266, 26288, 26291, 26294, 26298, 26610, 26617, 26639, 26651, 26656, 26660, 26662, 26674, 26676, 26678–81, 26684, 26690–91

WISCONSIN

(Population 2010, 5,686,986)

SENATORS

HERB KOHL, Democrat, of Milwaukee, WI; born in Milwaukee, February 7, 1935; education: graduated, Washington High School, Milwaukee, 1952; B.A., University of Wisconsin, Madison, 1956; M.B.A., Harvard Graduate School of Business Administration, Cambridge, MA, 1958; LL.D., Cardinal Stritch College, Milwaukee, WI, 1986 (honorary); served, U.S. Army Reserves, 1958–64; businessman; president, Herbert Kohl Investments; owner, Milwaukee Bucks NBA basketball team; past chairman, Milwaukee's United Way Campaign; State Chairman, Democratic Party of Wisconsin, 1975–77; honors and awards: Pen and Mike Club Wisconsin Sports Personality of the Year, 1985; Wisconsin Broadcasters Association Joe Killeen Memorial Sportsman of the Year, 1985; Greater Milwaukee Convention and Visitors Bureau Lamplighter Award, 1986; Wisconsin Parkinson's Association Humanitarian of the Year, 1986; Kiwanis Milwaukee Award, 1987; Madison Magazine's Best Corporate Citizen, 1997; Inducted into the Wisconsin Athletic Hall of Fame, 2007; Working Mothers Magazine Best of Congress Award, 2008; committees: chair, Special Committee on Aging; Appropriations; Banking, Housing and Urban Affairs; Judiciary; elected to the U.S. Senate on November 8, 1988; reelected to each succeeding Senate term.

Office Listings

http://kohl.senate.gov

330 Hart Senate Office Building, Washington, DC 20510 .... (202) 224–5653
Chief of Staff.—Phil Karsting. FAX: 224–9787
Legislative Director.—Chad Metzler.
Communications Director.—Lynn Becker.
Executive Assistant.—Arlene Branca.
310 West Wisconsin Avenue, Suite 950, Milwaukee, WI 53203 .... (414) 297–4451
14 West Mifflin Street, Suite 207, Madison, WI 53703 .... (608) 264–5338
402 Graham Avenue, Suite 206, Eau Claire, WI 54701 .... (715) 832–8424
4321 West College Avenue, Suite 235, Appleton, WI 54914 .... (920) 738–1640
205 5th Avenue, Room 216, LaCrosse, WI 54601 .... (608) 796–0045

* * *

RONALD H. JOHNSON, Republican, of Oshkosh, WI; born in Mankato, MN, April 18, 1955; education: B.A., business administration, University of Minnesota, Twin Cities, MN, 1977; professional: CEO Pacur, LLC.; married: wife, Jane; three children: daughters, Carey and Jeanna; son, Ben; committees: Appropriations; Budget; Homeland Security and Governmental Affairs; Special Committee on Aging; elected to the U.S. Senate on November 2, 2010.

Office Listings

http://ronjohnson.senate.gov

386 Russell Senate Office Building, Washington, DC 20510 .... (202) 224–5323
Chief of Staff.—Don Kent, Jr. FAX: 228–6965
Legislative Director.—Robert Duncan.
Communications Director.—Mary Vought.
517 East Wisconsin Avenue, Room 408, Milwaukee, WI 53202 .... (414) 276–7282
219 Washington Avenue, Suite 100, Oshkosh, WI 54901 .... (920) 230–7250
State Director.—Tony Blando.

REPRESENTATIVES

FIRST DISTRICT

PAUL RYAN, Republican, of Janesville, WI; born in Janesville, January 29, 1970; education: Joseph A. Craig High School; economic and political science degrees, Miami University, Ohio; professional: marketing consultant, Ryan Inc., Central (construction firm); aide to former U.S. Senator Bob Kasten (R–WI); advisor to former Vice Presidential candidate Jack Kemp, and U.S. Drug Czar Bill Bennett; legislative director, U.S. Senate; organizations: Janesville Bowmen, Inc.; Ducks Unlimited; married: Janna Ryan; three children: daughter, Liza; sons, Charlie and Sam; committees: chair, Budget; Ways and Means; elected to the 106th Congress; reelected to each succeeding Congress.

Office Listings

http://paulryan.house.gov

1233 Longworth House Office Building, Washington, DC 20515 .... (202) 225–3031
Administrative Assistant.—Joyce Meyer. FAX: 225–3393
Legislative Director.—Allison Steil.
Scheduler.—Sarah Peer.
20 South Main Street, Suite 10, Janesville, WI 53545 .... (608) 752–4050
5455 Sheridan Road, Suite 125, Kenosha, WI 53140 .... (262) 654–1901
216 Sixth Street, Racine, WI 53403 .... (262) 637–0510

Counties: KENOSHA, MILWAUKEE (part), RACINE, ROCK (part), WALWORTH (part), WAUKESHA (part). Population (2000), 670,458.

ZIP Codes: 53101–05, 53108–09, 53114–15, 53119–21, 53125–26, 53128–30, 53132, 53138–44, 53146–54, 53156–59, 53167–68, 53170–72, 53176–77, 53179, 53181–82, 53184–85, 53189–92, 53194–95, 53207, 53219–21, 53228, 53401–08, 53501, 53505, 53511, 53525, 53534, 53538, 53545–48, 53563, 53585

* * *

SECOND DISTRICT

TAMMY BALDWIN, Democrat, of Madison, WI; born in Madison, February 11, 1962; education: graduated from Madison West High School, 1980; A.B., mathematics and government, Smith College, 1984; J.D., University of Wisconsin Law School, 1989; professional: attorney, 1989–92; elected to the Dane County Board of Supervisors, 1986–94; elected to the State Assembly from the 78th district, 1993–99; committees: Energy and Commerce; elected to the 106th Congress; reelected to each succeeding Congress.

Office Listings

http://tammybaldwin.house.gov

2446 Rayburn House Office Building, Washington, DC 20515 .... (202) 225–2906
Chief of Staff.—Bill Murat. FAX: 225–6942
Legislative Director.—Ken Reidy.
Appointment Secretary.—Maureen Hekmat.
Press Secretary.—Jerilyn Goodman. (608) 258–9800
10 East Doty Street, Suite 405, Madison, WI 53703 .... (608) 258–9800
District Director.—Curt Finkelmeyer.
400 East Grand Avenue, Suite 402, Beloit, WI 53511 .... (608) 362–2800
FAX: 362–2838

Counties: COLUMBIA, DANE, GREEN, JEFFERSON (part), ROCK (part), SAUK (part), WALWORTH (part). Population (2000), 670,457.

ZIP Codes: 53038, 53094, 53098, 53190, 53501–02, 53504, 53508, 53511–12, 53515–17, 53520–23, 53527–29, 53531–32, 53534, 53536–38, 53542, 53544–46, 53548–51, 53555, 53558–63, 53566, 53570–72, 53574–76, 53578, 53581–83, 53589–91, 53593–94, 53596–98, 53701–08, 53711, 53713–19, 53725–26, 53744, 53777–79, 53782–94, 53901, 53911, 53913, 53916, 53923, 53925–26, 53928, 53932–33, 53935, 53951, 53954–57, 53959–60, 53965, 53968–69

* * *

THIRD DISTRICT

RON KIND, Democrat, of La Crosse, WI; born in La Crosse, March 16, 1963; education: B.A., Harvard University, 1985; M.A., London School of Economics, 1986; J.D., University of Minnesota Law School, 1990; admitted to the Wisconsin Bar, 1990; state prosecutor, La Crosse County District Attorney's Office; board of directors, La Crosse Boys and Girls Club; Coulee Council on Alcohol and Drug Abuse; Wisconsin Harvard Club; Wisconsin Bar Association; La Crosse County Bar Association; married: Tawni Zappa in 1994; two sons: Jonathan and Matthew; committees: Ways and Means; elected to the 105th Congress; reelected to each succeeding Congress.

Office Listings

http://www.kind.house.gov

1406 Longworth House Office Building, Washington, DC 20515 .... (202) 225–5506
Chief of Staff.—Erik Olson. FAX: 225–5739
Press Secretary.—Leah Hunter.
Legislative Director.—Travis Robey.
Scheduler.—Elizabeth Stower.
205 Fifth Avenue South, Suite 400, La Crosse, WI 54601 .... (608) 782–2558

District Director.—Loren Kannenberg.
131 South Barstow Street, Suite 301, Eau Claire, WI 54701 .... (715) 831–9214
Staff Assistant / Case Worker.—Mark Aumann.

Counties: BUFFALO, CLARK (part), CRAWFORD, DUNN, EAU CLAIRE, GRANT, IOWA, JACKSON, JUNEAU, LA CROSSE, LAFAYETTE, MONROE, PEPIN, PIERCE, RICHLAND, SAUK (part), ST. CROIX, TREMPEALEAU, VERNON. Population (2000), 670,462.

ZIP Codes: 53503–04, 53506–07, 53510, 53516–18, 53522, 53526, 53530, 53533, 53535, 53540–41, 53543–44, 53553–54, 53556, 53560, 53565, 53569, 53573, 53577–78, 53580–84, 53586–88, 53595, 53599, 53801-13, 53816–18, 53820–21, 53824–27, 53913, 53924, 53929, 53937, 53940–44, 53948, 53950–51, 53958–59, 53961–62, 53965, 53968, 54001–05, 54007, 54009–11, 54013–17, 54020–28, 54082, 54420, 54436–37, 54446, 54449, 54456–57, 54460, 54466, 54479, 54488, 54493, 54601–03, 54610–12, 54614–16, 54618–32, 54634–46, 54648–62, 54664–67, 54669–70, 54701–03, 54720–30, 54733–43, 54746–47, 54749–51, 54754–65, 54767–73

* * *

FOURTH DISTRICT

GWEN MOORE, Democrat, of Milwaukee, WI; born in Racine, WI, April 18, 1951; education: graduated North Division High School, Milwaukee; B.A., political science, Marquette University, Milwaukee, WI, 1978; professional: Program and Planning Analyst for the State of Wisconsin Services; housing officer, Wisconsin Housing and Development Authority; member: Wisconsin State Assembly, 1989–92; Wisconsin State Senate, 1993–2004; president pro tempore, 1997–98; three children; committees: Budget; Financial Services; elected to the 109th Congress on November 2, 2004; reelected to each succeeding Congress.

Office Listings

http://www.house.gov/moore

2245 Rayburn House Office Building, Washington, DC 20515 .... (202) 225–4572
Chief of Staff.—Andrew Stevens (acting). FAX: 225–8135
219 North Milwaukee Street, Suite 3A, Milwaukee, WI 53202 .... (414) 297–1140
District Administrator.—Lois O'Keefe.

Counties: MILWAUKEE (part). CITIES AND TOWNSHIPS: Milwaukee, Cudahy, South Milwaukee, St. Francis, West Allis, and West Milwaukee. Population (2000), 670,458.

ZIP Codes: 53110, 53154, 53172, 53201–28, 53233–35, 53237, 53268, 53270, 53277–78, 53280–81, 53284–85, 53288, 53290, 53293, 53295

* * *

FIFTH DISTRICT

F. JAMES SENSENBRENNER, JR., Republican, of Menomonee Falls, WI; born in Chicago, IL, June 14, 1943; education: graduated, Milwaukee Country Day School, 1961; A.B., Stanford University, 1965; J.D., University of Wisconsin Law School, 1968; admitted to the Wisconsin Bar, 1968; commenced practice in Cedarburg, WI; admitted to practice before the U.S. Supreme Court in 1972; professional: attorney; staff member of former U.S. Congressman J. Arthur Younger of California, 1965; elected to the Wisconsin Assembly, 1968, reelected in 1970, 1972, and 1974; elected to Wisconsin Senate in a special election, 1975, reelected in 1976 (assistant minority leader); member: Waukesha County Republican Party; Wisconsin Bar Association; Friends of Museums; American Philatelic Society; married: the former Cheryl Warren, 1977; children: Frank James III and Robert Alan; committees: Judiciary; Science, Space, and Technology; elected to the 96th Congress, November 7, 1978; reelected to each succeeding Congress.

Office Listings

http://www.sensenbrenner.house.gov

2449 Rayburn House Office Building, Washington, DC 20515 .... (202) 225–5101
Chief of Staff.—Tom Schreibel.
Deputy Chief of Staff.—Mike Lenn.
Press Secretary.—Amanda Infield.
Scheduler / Office Manager.—Todd Washam.
120 Bishops Way, Room 154, Brookfield, WI 53005 .... (262) 784–1111
Chief of Staff.—Tom Schreibel.

Counties: JEFFERSON (part), MILWAUKEE (part), OZAUKEE, WASHINGTON, WAUKESHA (part). Population (2000), 670,458.

ZIP Codes: 53002, 53004–05, 53007–08, 53012–13, 53017–18, 53021–22, 53024, 53027, 53029, 53033, 53037–38, 53040, 53045–46, 53051–52, 53056, 53058, 53060, 53064, 53066, 53069, 53072, 53074, 53076, 53080, 53085–86, 53089–90, 53092, 53095, 53097–98, 53118, 53122, 53127, 53137, 53146, 53151, 53156, 53178, 53183, 53186–90, 53208–14, 53217, 53219, 53222–23, 53225–28, 53263, 53538, 53549

* * *

SIXTH DISTRICT

THOMAS E. PETRI, Republican, of Fond du Lac, WI; born in Marinette, WI, May 28, 1940; education: graduated, Lowell P. Goodrich High School, 1958; B.A., Harvard University, Cambridge, MA, 1962; J.D., Harvard Law School, 1965; professional: admitted to the Wisconsin State and Fond du Lac County Bar Associations, 1965; lawyer; law clerk to Federal Judge James Doyle, 1965; Peace Corps volunteer, 1966–67; White House aide, 1969; commenced law practice in Fond du Lac, 1970; elected to the Wisconsin State Senate in 1972; reelected in 1976, and served until April, 1979; married; one daughter; committees: Education and the Workforce; Transportation and Infrastructure; elected to the 96th Congress, by special election, on April 3, 1979, to fill the vacancy caused by the death of William A. Steiger; reelected to each succeeding Congress.

Office Listings

http://www.petri.house.gov

2462 Rayburn House Office Building, Washington, DC 20515 .... (202) 225–2476
Chief of Staff / Legislative Director.—Debra Gebhardt. FAX: 225–2356
Communications Director.—Niel Wright.
Office Manager.—Linda Towse.
490 West Rolling Meadows Drive, Suite B, Fond du Lac, WI 54937 .... (920) 922–1180
District Director.—Tyler Vorpagel.
2390 State Road 44, Suite B, Oshkosh, WI 54904 .... (920) 231–6333

Counties: Adams, Calumet (part), Dodge, Fond du Lac, Green Lake, Jefferson (part), Manitowoc, Marquette, Outagamie (part), Sheboygan, Waushara, Winnebago. Population (2000), 670,459.

ZIP Codes: 53001, 53003, 53006, 53010–11, 53013–16, 53019–21, 53023, 53026–27, 53031–32, 53034–36, 53039, 53042, 53044, 53047–50, 53057, 53059, 53061–63, 53065–66, 53070, 53073, 53075, 53078–79, 53081–83, 53085, 53088, 53091, 53093–94, 53098–99, 53137, 53205, 53207, 53215, 53221, 53557, 53579, 53594, 53901, 53910, 53916–17, 53919–20, 53922–23, 53925–27, 53930–34, 53936, 53939, 53946–47, 53949–50, 53952–54, 53956, 53963–65, 53968, 54110, 54115, 54123, 54126, 54129–30, 54136, 54140, 54160, 54169, 54207–08, 54214–16, 54220–21, 54227–28, 54230, 54232, 54240–41, 54245, 54247, 54413, 54457, 54486, 54494, 54499, 54613, 54619, 54638, 54648, 54660, 54755, 54901–04, 54906, 54909, 54911, 54913–15, 54921–23, 54927, 54930, 54932–37, 54941, 54943–44, 54947, 54950, 54952, 54956–57, 54960, 54963–68, 54970–71, 54974, 54976, 54979–86

* * *

SEVENTH DISTRICT

SEAN P. DUFFY, Republican, of Ashland, WI; born in Hayward, WI, October 3, 1971; education: B.A., marketing, St. Mary's University, Winona, MN, 1994; J.D., William Mitchell College of Law, St. Paul, MN, 1999; professional: lawyer, private practice; prosecutor, Ashland County, WI; acting assistant district attorney and district attorney, Ashland County, WI, 2002–10; religion: Roman Catholic; married: wife, Rachel Campos-Duffy; six children; committees: Financial Services; Joint Economic Committee; elected to the 112th Congress on November 2, 2010.

Office Listings

http://duffy.house.gov

1208 Longworth House Office Building, Washington, DC 20515 .... (202) 225–3365
Chief of Staff.—Kirt Charles Johnson. FAX: 225–3240
Legislative Director.—Bryan Blom. (855) 585–4251
Communications Director.—Daniel Son.
Scheduler.—Colleen Hodgman.
208 Grand Avenue, Wausau, WI 54403 .... (715) 298–9344
District Director.—David Anderson. FAX: 298–9348
District Scheduler.— Debbie Osowski.
Director of Constituent Services.—Jocelyn Berkhahn.
823 Belknap Street, Suite 102, Superior, WI 54880 .... (715) 392–3984
Regional Representative.—Mary Willett. FAX: 392–3999

Counties: Ashland, Barron, Bayfield, Burnett, Chippewa, Clark (part), Douglas, Iron, Langlade (part), Lincoln, Marathon, Oneida (part), Polk, Portage, Price, Rusk, Sawyer, Taylor, Washburn, Wood. Population (2000), 670,462.

ZIP Codes: 54001, 54004–07, 54009, 54017, 54020, 54024, 54026, 54401–12, 54414–15, 54417–18, 54420–29, 54432–35, 54437, 54439–43, 54447–49, 54451–52, 54454–55, 54457–60, 54462–63, 54466–67, 54469–76, 54479–81, 54484–85, 54487–90, 54492, 54494–95, 54498–99, 54501, 54513–15, 54517, 54524–27, 54529–32, 54534, 54536–38, 54545–47, 54550, 54552, 54555–56, 54559, 54563–65, 54703, 54724, 54726–33, 54739, 54745, 54748, 54757, 54762–63, 54766, 54768, 54771, 54774, 54801, 54805–06, 54810, 54812–14, 54816–22, 54824, 54826–30, 54832, 54834–50, 54853–59, 54861–62, 54864–65, 54867–68, 54870–76, 54880, 54888–91, 54893, 54895–96, 54909, 54921, 54945, 54966, 54977, 54981

* * *

EIGHTH DISTRICT

REID RIBBLE, Republican, of Appleton, WI; born in Neenah, WI, April 05, 1956; education: Appleton East High School, WI, 1974; Grand Rapids School of Bible and Music, MI; professional: business owner; married: DeaNa; committees: Agriculture; Budget; Transportation and Infrastructure; elected to the 112th Congress on November 2, 2010.

Office Listings

http://www.ribble.house.gov

1513 Longworth House Office Building, Washington, DC 20515 .... (202) 225–5665
Chief of Staff.—McKay Daniels. FAX: 225–5729
Legislative Director.—Paul Bleiberg.
Scheduler.—Teri Dorn.
Communications Director.—Brandon Moody.
333 West College Avenue, Appleton, WI 54911 .... (920) 380–0061
District Director.—Rick Sense.
550 North Military Avenue, Suite 4B, Green Bay, WI 54303 .... (920) 471–1950

Counties: BROWN, CALUMET (part), DOOR, FLORENCE, FOREST, KEWAUNEE, LANGLADE (part), MARINETTE, MENOMINEE, OCONTO, ONEIDA (part), OUTAGAMIE (part), SHAWANO, VILAS, WAUPACA. Population (2000), 670,461.

ZIP Codes: 54101–04, 54106–07, 54110–15, 54119–21, 54124–28, 54130–31, 54135, 54137–41, 54143, 54149–57, 54159, 54161–62, 54165–66, 54169–71, 54173–75, 54177, 54180, 54182, 54201–02, 54204–05, 54208–13, 54216–17, 54226–27, 54229–30, 54234–35, 54241, 54246, 54301–08, 54311, 54313, 54324, 54344, 54408–09, 54414, 54416, 54418, 54424, 54427–28, 54430, 54435, 54450, 54452, 54462–65, 54485–87, 54491, 54499, 54501, 54511–12, 54519–21, 54529, 54531, 54538–43, 54545, 54548, 54554, 54557–58, 54560–62, 54564, 54566, 54568, 54911–15, 54919, 54922, 54926, 54928–29, 54931, 54933, 54940, 54942, 54944–50, 54952, 54956, 54961–62, 54965, 54969, 54975, 54977–78, 54981, 54983, 54990

WYOMING

(Population 2010, 563,626)

SENATORS

MICHAEL B. ENZI, Republican, of Gillette, WY; born in Bremerton, WA, February 1, 1944; education: B.A., accounting, George Washington University, 1966; M.B.A., Denver University, 1968; professional: served in Wyoming National Guard, 1967–73; accounting manager and computer programmer, Dunbar Well Service, 1985–97; director, Black Hills Corporation, a New York Stock Exchange company, 1992–96; member, founding board of directors, First Wyoming Bank of Gillette, 1978–88; owner, with wife, of NZ Shoes; served in Wyoming House of Representatives, 1987–91, and in Wyoming State Senate, 1991–96; Mayor of Gillette, 1975–82; commissioner, Western Interstate Commission for Higher Education, 1995–96; served on the Education Commission of the States, 1989–93; president, Wyoming Association of Municipalities, 1980–82; president, Wyoming Jaycees, 1973–74; member: Lions Club; elder, Presbyterian Church; Eagle Scout; married: Diana Buckley, 1969; children: Amy, Brad, and Emily; committees: ranking member, Health, Education, Labor and Pensions; Budget; Finance; Small Business and Entrepreneurship; elected to the U.S. Senate in November, 1996; reelected to each succeeding Senate term.

Office Listings

http://enzi.senate.gov

379–A Russell Senate Office Building, Washington, DC 20510 .... (202) 224–3424
Chief of Staff.—Flip McConnaughey. FAX: 228–0359
Legislative Director.—Randi Reid.
Press Secretary.—Daniel Head.
Office Manager.—Christen Thompson.
Federal Center, Suite 2007, 2120 Capitol Avenue, Cheyenne, WY 82001 .... (307) 772–2477
400 South Kendrick, Suite 303, Gillette, WY 82716 .... (307) 682–6268
100 East B Street, Room 3201, P.O. Box 33201, Casper, WY 82602 .... (307) 261–6572
P.O. Box 12470, Jackson, WY 83002 .... (307) 739–9507

* * *

JOHN BARRASSO, Republican, of Casper, WY; born in Reading, PA, July 21, 1952; education: B.S., Georgetown University, Washington, DC, 1974; M.D., Georgetown University, Washington, DC, 1978; professional: Casper Orthopaedic Associates, 1983–2007; Chief of Staff, Wyoming Medical Center, 2003–05; President, Wyoming Medical Society; President, National Association of Physician Broadcasters, 1988–89; member, Wyoming State Senate, 2002–06; wife: Bobbi; children: Peter, Emma and Hadley; committees: ranking member, Indian Affairs; Energy and Natural Resources; Environment and Public Works; Foreign Relations; appointed to the United States Senate on June 22, 2007, sworn in by Vice President Cheney on June 25, 2007 to the 110th Congress to fill the vacancy caused by the death of Senator Craig Thomas; elected to the U.S. Senate on November 4, 2008.

Office Listings

http://barrasso.senate.gov

307 Dirksen Senate Office Building, Washington, DC 20510 .... (202) 224–6441
Chief of Staff.—Dan Kunsman. FAX: 224–1724
Legislative Director.—Bryn Stewart.
Communications Director.—Emily Lawrimore.
Office Manager.—Amber Moyerman.
100 East B Street, Suite 2201, Casper, WY 82602 .... (307) 261–6413
FAX: 265–6706
2120 Capitol Avenue, Suite 2013, Cheyenne, WY 82001 .... (307) 772–2451
FAX: 638–3512
324 East Washington Avenue, Riverton, WY 82501 .... (307) 856–6642
FAX: 856–5901
1575 Dewar Drive, Suite 218, Rock Springs, WY 82901 .... (307) 362–5012
FAX: 362–5129
2 North Main Street, Suite 206, Sheridan, WY 82801 .... (307) 672–6456
FAX: 672–8227

REPRESENTATIVE

AT LARGE

CYNTHIA M. LUMMIS, Republican, of Cheyenne, WY; born in Cheyenne, WY, September 10, 1954; education: graduated, B.S., animal science, University of Wyoming, 1976; B.S., biology, University of Wyoming, 1978; J.D., University of Wyoming, 1985; professional: Attorney at Law, 1986–present; rancher, 1976–present; Representative, Wyoming State House of Representatives, 1979–82; clerk, Wyoming Supreme Court, 1985; Representative, Wyoming State House of Representatives, 1985–93; Senator, Wyoming State Legislature, 1993–94; Interim Director of State Lands, State of Wyoming, 1997–98; General Counsel, Office of the Governor, 1995–97; State Treasurer, State of Wyoming, 1998–2006; chair, Western State Treasurer's Association; Advisory Board, Center for the Rocky Mountain West at the University of Montana; Board of Member, American Women's Financial Education Foundation; Director, Cheyenne Frontier Days; member, Cheyenne's Vision 2020; member, Laramie Foundation and its Wyoming Women's History House; member, Leadership Wyoming Board; Advisory Board, Ruckelshaus Institute for Environment and Natural Resources at the University of Wyoming; member, Trinity Lutheran Church; member, Wyoming Business Alliance; member, Wyoming Stock Growers Agricultural Land Trust, married: Al Wiederspahn; children: Annaliese; committees: Appropriations; elected to the 111th Congress on November 4, 2008; reelected to the 112th Congress.

Office Listings

http://lummis.house.gov

113 Cannon House Office Building, Washington, DC 20515 .... (202) 225–2311
Chief of Staff.—Tom Wiblemo. FAX: 225–3057
Legislative Director.—Rick Axthelm.
Press Secretary.—Ryan Taylor.
100 East B Street, Suite 4003, Casper, WY 82602 .... (307) 261–6595
District Representatives: Jackie King, Ryan McConnaughey.
8005 Capitol Avenue, Suite 2015, Cheyenne, WY 82001 .... (307) 772–2595
Chief of Staff.—Tucker Fagan. FAX: 772–2597
Scheduler.—Christie Clark.
District Representative.—Johnnie Burton, Barbara Dilts.
45 East Loucks, Suite 300F, Sheridan, WY 82801 .... (307) 673–4608
District Representative.—Matt Jones. FAX: 673–4982
404 N Street, Suite 204, Rock Springs, WY 82901 .... (307) 362–4095
District Representatives: Pat Aullman, Bonnie Cannon. FAX: 362–4097

Population (2000), 493,782.

ZIP Codes: 82001, 82003, 82005–10, 82050–55, 82058–61, 82063, 82070–73, 82081–84, 82190, 82201, 82210, 82212–15, 82217–19, 82221–25, 82227, 82229, 82240, 82242–44, 82301, 82310, 82321–25, 82327, 82329, 82331–32, 82334–36, 82401, 82410–12, 82414, 82420–23, 82426, 82428, 82430–35, 82440–43, 82450, 82501, 82510, 82512–16, 82520, 82523–24, 82601–02, 82604–05, 82609, 82615, 82620, 82630, 82633, 82635–40, 82642–44, 82646, 82648–49, 82701, 82710–12, 82714–18, 82720–21, 82723, 82725, 82727, 82729–32, 82801, 82831–40, 82842, 82844–45, 82901–02, 82922–23, 82925, 82929–39, 82941–45, 83001–02, 83011–14, 83025, 83101, 83110–16, 83118–24, 83126–28

AMERICAN SAMOA

(Population 2010, 67,380)

DELEGATE

ENI F. H. FALEOMAVAEGA, Democrat, of Vailoatai, AS; born in Vailoatai, August 15, 1943; education: graduate of Kahuku High School, Hawaii, 1962; B.A., Brigham Young University, 1966; J.D., University of Houston Law School, 1972; LL.M., University of California, Berkeley, 1973; admitted to U.S. Supreme Court and American Samoa Bars; military service: enlisted, U.S. Army, 1966–69; Vietnam veteran; captain, USAR, Judge Advocate General Corps, 1982–92; professional: administrative assistant to American Samoa's Delegate to Washington, 1973–75; staff counsel, Committee on Interior and Insular Affairs, 1975–81; Deputy Attorney General, American Samoa, 1981–84; elected Lieutenant Governor, American Samoa, 1984–89; member: Democratic Study Group; National American Indian Prayer Breakfast Group; National Association of Secretaries of State; National Conference of Lieutenant Governors; Navy League of the United States; Pago Pago Lions Club; Veterans of Foreign Wars; Congressional Arts Caucus; Congressional Hispanic Caucus; Congressional Human Rights Caucus; Congressional Travel and Tourism Caucus; Central Asia Caucus; married: Hinanui Bambridge Cave of Tahiti; five children; committees: Foreign Affairs; Natural Resources; elected to the 101st Congress on November 8, 1988; reelected to each succeeding Congress.

Office Listings

http://www.house.gov/faleomavaega

2422 Rayburn House Office Building, Washington, DC 20515 .... (202) 225–8577
Chief of Staff.—Lisa Williams. FAX: 225–8757
Scheduler / Office Manager.—Hana Atuatasi.
Legislative Director.—David Richmond.
P.O. Drawer X, Pago Pago, AS 96799 .... (684) 633–1372

ZIP Codes: 96799

* * *

DISTRICT OF COLUMBIA

(Population 2010, 601,723)

DELEGATE

ELEANOR HOLMES NORTON, Democrat, of Washington, DC; born in Washington, DC, June 13, 1937; education: graduated, Dunbar High School, 1955; B.A., Antioch College, 1960; M.A., Yale Graduate School, 1963; J.D., Yale Law School, 1964; honorary degrees: Cedar Crest College, 1969; Bard College, 1971; Princeton University, 1973; Marymount College, 1974; City College of New York, 1975; Georgetown University, 1977; New York University, 1978; Howard University, 1978; Brown University, 1978; Wilberforce University, 1978; Wayne State University, 1980; Gallaudet College, 1980; Denison University, 1980; Syracuse University, 1981; Yeshiva University, 1981; Lawrence University, 1981; Emanuel College, 1981; Spelman College, 1982; University of Massachusetts, 1983; Smith College, 1983; Medical College of Pennsylvania, 1983; Tufts University, 1984; Bowdoin College, 1985; Antioch College, 1985; Haverford College, 1986; Lesley College, 1986; New Haven University, 1986; University of San Diego, 1986; Sojourner-Douglas College, 1987; Salem State College, 1987; Rutgers University, 1988; St. Joseph's College, 1988; University of Lowell, 1988; Colgate University, 1989; Drury College, 1989; Florida International University, 1989; St. Lawrence University, 1989; University of Wisconsin, 1989; University of Hartford, 1990; Ohio Wesleyan University, 1990; Wake Forest University, 1990; Fisk University, 1991; Tougalvo University, 1992; University of Southern Connecticut, 1992; professional: professor of law, Georgetown University, 1982–90; past / present member: chair, New York Commission on Human Rights, 1970–76; chair, Equal Employment Opportunity Commission, 1977–81; Community Foundation of Greater Washington, board; Yale Corporation, 1982–88; trustee, Rockefeller Foundation, 1982–90; executive assistant to the mayor of New York City (concurrent appointment); law clerk, Judge A. Leon Higginbotham, Federal District Court, 3rd Circuit; attorney, admitted to practice by examination in the District of Columbia, Pennsylvania and in the U.S. Supreme Court; Council on Foreign Relations; Overseas Development Council; U.S. Committee to Monitor the Helsinki Accords; Carter Center, Atlanta, Georgia; boards of Martin Luther King, Jr. Center for Social Change and Environmental Law Institute; Workplace Health Fund; honors awards: Harper Fellow, Yale Law School, 1976, (for ''a person . . . who has made a distinguished contribution to the public life of the nation . . .''); Yale Law School Association Citation of Merit Medal to the Outstanding Alumnus of the Law School, 1980; Chancellor's Distinguished Lecturer, University of California Law School (Boalt Hall), Berkeley, 1981; Visiting Fellow, Harvard University, John F. Kennedy School of Government, spring 1984; Visiting Phi Beta Kappa Scholar, 1985; Distinguished Public Service Award, Center for National Policy, 1985; Ralph E. Shikes Bicentennial Fellow, Harvard Law School, 1987; One Hundred Most Important Women (*Ladies Home Journal*, 1988); One Hundred Most Powerful Women in Washington (The *Washingtonian* magazine, September 1989); divorced; two children: John and Katherine; committees: Oversight and Government Reform; Transportation and Infrastructure; elected to the 102nd Congress on November 6, 1990; reelected to each succeeding Congress.

Office Listings

http://www.norton.house.gov

2136 Rayburn House Office Building, Washington, DC 20515 .... (202) 225–8050
Chief of Staff.—Sheila Bunn. FAX: 225–3002
Legislative Director.—Bradley Truding.
Executive Assistant.—Gwen Benson-Walker.
Communications Director.—Kezmiche Atterbury.

ZIP Codes: 20001–13, 20015–20, 20024, 20026–27, 20029–30, 20032–33, 20035–45, 20047, 20049–53, 20055–71, 20073–77, 20080, 20088, 20090–91, 20099, 20201–04, 20206–08, 20210–13, 20215–24, 20226–33, 20235, 20237, 20239–42, 20244–45, 20250, 20254, 20260, 20268, 20270, 20277, 20289, 20301, 20303, 20306–07, 20310, 20314–15, 20317–19, 20330, 20340, 20350, 20370, 20372–76, 20380, 20388–95, 20398, 20401–16, 20418–29, 20431, 20433–37, 20439–42, 20444, 20447, 20451, 20453, 20456, 20460, 20463, 20469, 20472, 20500, 20503–10, 20515, 20520–27, 20530–36, 20538–44, 20546–49, 20551–55, 20557, 20559–60, 20565–66, 20570–73, 20575–77, 20579–81, 20585–86, 20590–91, 20593–94, 20597, 20599

* * *

GUAM

(Population 2000, 154,805)

DELEGATE

MADELEINE Z. BORDALLO, Democrat, of Tamuning, Guam, born on May 31, 1933; education: associate degree in music, St. Catherine's College, St. Paul, MN, 1953; professional: First Lady of Guam, 1975–78, and 1983–86; Guam Senator, 1981–82, and 1987–94 (five terms); Lt. Governor of Guam, 1995–2002 (two terms); National Committee Chair for the National Democratic Party, 1964–2004; family: Ricardo J. Bordallo (deceased); daughter, Deborah; granddaughter, Nicole; committees: Armed Services; Natural Resources; elected to the 108th Congress on November 5, 2002; reelected to each succeeding Congress.

Office Listings

http://www.house.gov/bordallo

2441 Rayburn House Office Building, Washington, DC 20515 .... (202) 225–1188
Chief of Staff.—John Whitt. FAX: 226–0341
Legislative Director.—Matthew Herrmann.
Press Secretary.—Adam Carbullido.
Scheduler.—Rosanne Meno.
120 Father Duenas Avenue, Suite 107, Hagåtña, GU 96910 .... (671) 477–4272

ZIP Codes: 96910, 96912–13, 96915–17, 96919, 96921, 96923, 96926, 96928–29, 96931–32

NORTHERN MARIANA ISLANDS

(Population 2000, 69,221)

DELEGATE

GREGORIO KILILI CAMACHO SABLAN, Democrat, of Saipan, MP; born in Saipan, MP, January 19, 1955; education: University of Hawaii, Manoa Honolulu, HI; 1989–90; professional: member, Northern Mariana Islands Commonwealth Legislature, 1982–86 (2 terms); special assistant to Senator Daniel Inouye; special assistant to Northern Mariana Islands Governor Pedro P. Tenorio; Executive Director of the Commonwealth Election Commission; family: married Andrea C. Sablan, son Jesse, daughter Patricia; caucuses: Congressional Asian Pacific American Caucus; Congressional Hispanic Caucus; American Citizens Abroad Caucus; Bi-Partisan Disabilities Caucus; Democratic Caucus; Community College Caucus; National Marine Sanctuary Caucus; Friends of New Zealand Caucus; International Conservation Caucus; committees: Agriculture; Natural Resources; elected to the 111th Congress on November 4, 2008; reelected to each succeeding Congress.

Office Listings

http://www.sablan.house.gov

423 Cannon House Office Building, Washington, DC 20515 .... (202) 225–2646
Chief of Staff.—Robert J. Schwalbach. FAX: 226–4249
Scheduler.—Chai Cruz.
JCT II Building, Susupe, P.O. Box 504879, Saipan, MP 96950 .... (670) 323–2647
District Officer Director.—Mike Tenorio. FAX: 323–2649

ZIP Codes: 96950, 96951, 96952

* * *

PUERTO RICO

(Population 2010, 3,725,789)

RESIDENT COMMISSIONER

PEDRO R. PIERLUISI, Democratic, of Guaynabo, PR; born in San Juan, PR, April 26, 1959; education: contemporary U.S. history, Tulane University, New Orleans, LA, 1981; Juris Doctor, George Washington University, Washington, DC, 1984; professional: Verner & Lipfert Assoc., Washington, DC, 1984–85; Cole, Corette & Abrutyn, Washington, DC, 1985–88; Pierluisi & Pierluisi, San Juan, PR, 1990–92; Attorney General of Puerto Rico, 1993–96; O'Neill & Borges, San Jaun, PR, 1997–2007; religion: Catholic; married: Maria Elena Carrión; family: four children; committees: Ethics; Judiciary; Natural Resources, elected to the 111th Congress on November 4, 2008, serving a four-year term through the 112th Congress.

Office Listings

http://www.pierluisi.house.gov

1213 Longworth House Office Building, Washington, DC 20515 .... (202) 225–2615
Chief of Staff.—Carmen M. Feliciano. FAX: 225–2154
Communications Director.—Dennise Pérez.
Scheduler.—Frances Agosto.
Legislative Director.—John Laufer.
Senior Legislative Counsel.—Jonathan Thessin.
Senior Legislative Adviser.—Jed Bullock.
Legislative Assistant.—Eduardo Hilera.
Legislative Correspondent.—Luis Miguel Lopez.
Staff Assistant.—Angelique Vélez.
157 Avenida de la Constitución Antiguo Edificio de Medicina Tropical, Ala de la Enfermería 2ndo Piso, San Juan, PR 00901 .... (787) 723–6333

District Office Director.—Rosemarie ''Maí'' Vizcarrondo. FAX: 729–7738
Deputy District Office Director.—Cristina Figueroa.
Office Manager.—Aimée Irlanda.
Constituent Liaison.—Carlos Cátala.
Press Aides: Carla Escoto, Marlena Riccio.
Staff Assistant.—Michelle Manzano.
Senior Case Worker.—Luis Ortiz.
Social Security Case Worker.—Cristina Sierra.
Counsel.—María Teresa Carro.
Veteran's Case Worker.—Jorge Mas.

ZIP Codes: 00601–06, 00610–14, 00616–17, 00622–25, 00627, 00631, 00636–38, 00641, 00646–48, 00650, 00652–62, 00664, 00667, 00669–70, 00674, 00676–78, 00680–83, 00685, 00687–88, 00690, 00692–94, 00698, 00701, 00703–05, 00707, 00714–21, 00723, 00725–42, 00744–45, 00751, 00754, 00757, 00765–69, 00771–73, 00775, 00777–78, 00780, 00782–86, 00791–92, 00794–95, 00901–36, 00938, 00940, 00949–63, 00965–66, 00968–71, 00975–79, 00981–88

* * *

VIRGIN ISLANDS

(Population 2000, 108,612)

DELEGATE

DONNA M. CHRISTENSEN, Democrat, of St. Croix, VI; born in Teaneck, NJ, September 19, 1945; B.S., St. Mary's College, Notre Dame, IN, 1966; M.D., George Washington University School of Medicine, 1970; physician, family medicine; Acting Commissioner of Health, 1994–95; medical director, St. Croix Hospital, 1987–88; founding member and vice president, Virgin Islands Medical Institute; trustee, National Medical Association; past secretary and two-time past president, Virgin Islands Medical Society; founding member and trustee, Caribbean Youth Organization; member: Democratic National Committee; Virgin Islands Democratic Territorial Committee (past vice chair); Substance Abuse Coalition; St. Dunstan's Episcopal School Board of Directors; Caribbean Studies Association; Women's Coalition of St. Croix; St. Croix Environmental Association; past chair, Christian Education Committee; Friedensthal Moravian Church; past member: Virgin Islands Board of Education; Democratic Platform Committee; cohost, Straight Up TV interview program, 1993; married: Chris Christensen; children: two daughters: Rabiah Layla and Karida Yasmeen; member: Congressional Black Caucus; Congressional Women's Caucus; committees: Energy and Commerce; elected to the 105th Congress; reelected to each succeeding Congress.

Office Listings

http://www.donnachristensen.house.gov

1510 Longworth House Office Building, Washington, DC 20515 .... (202) 225–1790
Chief of Staff.—Monique Clendinen Watson. FAX: 225–5517
Executive Assistant / Scheduler.—Shelley Thomas.
Nisky Center, 2nd Floor, Suite 207, St. Thomas, VI 00802 .... (340) 774–4408
Office Manager.—Joyce Jackson.
Sunshine Mall Space 204–205, Frederiksted, P.O. Box 5980, St. Croix, VI 00823 (340) 778–5900
Office Manager.—Luz Belardo-Webster.

ZIP Codes: 00801–05, 00820–24, 00830–31, 00840–41, 00850–51

STATE DELEGATIONS

Number before names designates Congressional district. Senate Democrats in roman; Senate Republicans in *italic*; Independent in SMALL CAPS; Independent Democrat in *SMALL CAPS ITALIC;* House Republicans in roman; House Democrats in *italic*; Resident Commissioner and Delegates in ***boldface italic***.

ALABAMA

SENATORS
Richard C. Shelby
Jeff Sessions

REPRESENTATIVES
[Republicans 6, Democrat 1]

1. Jo Bonner
2. Martha Roby
3. Mike Rogers
4. Robert B. Aderholt
5. Mo Brooks
6. Spencer Bachus
7. *Terri A. Sewell*

ALASKA

SENATORS
Lisa Murkowski
Mark Begich

REPRESENTATIVE
[Republican 1]
At Large - Don Young

ARIZONA

SENATORS
John McCain
Jon Kyl

REPRESENTATIVES
[Republicans 5, Democrats 3]

1. Paul A. Gosar
2. Trent Franks
3. Benjamin Quayle
4. *Ed Pastor*
5. David Schweikert
6. Jeff Flake
7. *Raúl M. Grijalva*
8. *Gabrielle Giffords*

ARKANSAS

SENATORS
Mark L. Pryor
John Boozman

REPRESENTATIVES
[Republicans 3, Democrat 1]

1. Eric A. ''Rick'' Crawford
2. Tim Griffin
3. Steve Womack
4. *Mike Ross*

CALIFORNIA

SENATORS
Dianne Feinstein
Barbara Boxer

REPRESENTATIVES
[Republicans 19, Democrats 34]

1. *Mike Thompson*
2. Wally Herger
3. Daniel E. Lungren
4. Tom McClintock

5. *Doris O. Matsui*
6. *Lynn C. Woolsey*
7. *George Miller*
8. *Nancy Pelosi*
9. *Barbara Lee*
10. *John Garamendi*
11. *Jerry McNerney*
12. *Jackie Speier*
13. *Fortney Pete Stark*
14. *Anna G. Eshoo*
15. *Michael M. Honda*
16. *Zoe Lofgren*
17. *Sam Farr*
18. *Dennis A. Cardoza*
19. Jeff Denham
20. *Jim Costa*
21. Devin Nunes
22. Kevin McCarthy
23. *Lois Capps*
24. Elton Gallegly
25. Howard P. "Buck" McKeon
26. David Dreier
27. *Brad Sherman*
28. *Howard L. Berman*
29. *Adam B. Schiff*
30. *Henry A. Waxman*
31. *Xavier Becerra*
32. *Judy Chu*
33. *Karen Bass*
34. *Lucille Roybal-Allard*
35. *Maxine Waters*
36. *Janice Hahn*
37. *Laura Richardson*
38. *Grace F. Napolitano*
39. *Linda T. Sánchez*
40. Edward R. Royce
41. Jerry Lewis
42. Gary G. Miller
43. *Joe Baca*
44. Ken Calvert
45. Mary Bono Mack
46. Dana Rohrabacher
47. *Loretta Sanchez*
48. John Campbell
49. Darrell E. Issa
50. Brian P. Bilbray
51. *Bob Filner*
52. Duncan Hunter
53. *Susan A. Davis*

COLORADO

SENATORS
Mark Udall
Michael F. Bennet

REPRESENTATIVES
[Republicans 4, Democrats 3]

1. *Diana DeGette*
2. *Jared Polis*
3. Scott R. Tipton
4. Cory Gardner
5. Doug Lamborn
6. Mike Coffman
7. *Ed Perlmutter*

CONNECTICUT

SENATORS
JOSEPH I. LIEBERMAN **
Richard Blumenthal

REPRESENTATIVES
[Democrats 5]

1. *John B. Larson*
2. *Joe Courtney*
3. *Rosa L. DeLauro*
4. *James A. Himes*
5. *Christopher S. Murphy*

DELAWARE

SENATORS
Thomas R. Carper
Christopher A. Coons

REPRESENTATIVE
[Democrat 1]

At Large - *John C. Carney, Jr.*

FLORIDA

SENATORS
Bill Nelson
Marco Rubio

REPRESENTATIVES
[Republicans 19, Democrats 6]

1. Jeff Miller
2. Steve Southerland II
3. *Corrine Brown*
4. Ander Crenshaw
5. Richard B. Nugent
6. Cliff Stearns
7. John L. Mica
8. Daniel Webster
9. Gus M. Bilirakis
10. C. W. Bill Young

11. *Kathy Castor*
12. Dennis A. Ross
13. Vern Buchanan
14. Connie Mack
15. Bill Posey
16. Thomas J. Rooney
17. *Frederica S. Wilson*
18. Ileana Ros-Lehtinen
19. *Theodore E. Deutch*
20. *Debbie Wasserman Schultz*
21. Mario Diaz-Balart
22. Allen B. West
23. *Alcee L. Hastings*
24. Sandy Adams
25. David Rivera

GEORGIA

SENATORS
Saxby Chambliss
Johnny Isakson

REPRESENTATIVES
[Republicans 8, Democrats 5]

1. Jack Kingston
2. *Sanford D. Bishop, Jr.*
3. Lynn A. Westmoreland
4. *Henry C. "Hank" Johnson, Jr.*
5. *John Lewis*
6. Tom Price
7. Rob Woodall
8. Austin Scott
9. Tom Graves
10. Paul C. Broun
11. Phil Gingrey
12. *John Barrow*
13. *David Scott*

HAWAII

SENATORS
Daniel K. Inouye
Daniel K. Akaka

REPRESENTATIVES
[Democrats 2]

1. *Colleen W. Hanabusa*
2. *Mazie K. Hirono*

IDAHO

SENATORS
Mike Crapo
James E. Risch

REPRESENTATIVES
[Republicans 2]

1. Raúl R. Labrador
2. Michael K. Simpson

ILLINOIS

SENATORS
Richard J. Durbin
Mark Kirk

REPRESENTATIVES
[Republicans 11, Democrats 8]

1. *Bobby L. Rush*
2. *Jesse L. Jackson, Jr.*
3. *Daniel Lipinski*
4. *Luis V. Gutierrez*
5. *Mike Quigley*
6. Peter J. Roskam
7. *Danny K. Davis*
8. Joe Walsh
9. *Janice D. Schakowsky*
10. Robert J. Dold
11. Adam Kinzinger
12. *Jerry F. Costello*
13. Judy Biggert
14. Randy Hultgren
15. Timothy V. Johnson
16. Donald A. Manzullo
17. Robert T. Schilling
18. Aaron Schock
19. John Shimkus

INDIANA

SENATORS
Richard G. Lugar
Daniel Coats

REPRESENTATIVES
[Republicans 6, Democrats 3]

1. *Peter J. Visclosky*
2. *Joe Donnelly*
3. Marlin A. Stutzman
4. Todd Rokita
5. Dan Burton
6. Mike Pence
7. *André Carson*
8. Larry Bucshon
9. Todd C. Young

IOWA

SENATORS
Chuck Grassley
Tom Harkin

REPRESENTATIVES
[Republicans 2, Democrats 3]

1. *Bruce L. Braley*
2. *David Loebsack*
3. *Leonard L. Boswell*
4. Tom Latham
5. Steve King

KANSAS

SENATORS
Pat Roberts
Jerry Moran

REPRESENTATIVES
[Republicans 4]

1. Tim Huelskamp
2. Lynn Jenkins
3. Kevin Yoder
4. Mike Pompeo

KENTUCKY

SENATORS
Mitch McConnell
Rand Paul

REPRESENTATIVES
[Republicans 4, Democrats 2]

1. Ed Whitfield
2. Brett Guthrie
3. *John A. Yarmuth*
4. Geoff Davis
5. Harold Rogers
6. *Ben Chandler*

LOUISIANA

SENATORS
Mary L. Landrieu
David Vitter

REPRESENTATIVES
[Republicans 6, Democrat 1]

1. Steve Scalise
2. *Cedric L. Richmond*
3. Jeffrey M. Landry
4. John Fleming
5. Rodney Alexander
6. Bill Cassidy
7. Charles W. Boustany, Jr.

MAINE

SENATORS
Olympia J. Snowe
Susan M. Collins

REPRESENTATIVES
[Democrats 2]

1. *Chellie Pingree*
2. *Michael H. Michaud*

MARYLAND

SENATORS
Barbara A. Mikulski
Benjamin L. Cardin

REPRESENTATIVES
[Republicans 2, Democrats 6]

1. Andy Harris
2. *C.A. Dutch Ruppersberger*
3. *John P. Sarbanes*
4. *Donna F. Edwards*
5. *Steny H. Hoyer*
6. Roscoe G. Bartlett
7. *Elijah E. Cummings*
8. *Chris Van Hollen*

MASSACHUSETTS

SENATORS
John F. Kerry
Scott P. Brown

REPRESENTATIVES
[Democrats 10]

1. *John W. Olver*
2. *Richard E. Neal*
3. *James P. McGovern*
4. *Barney Frank*
5. *Niki Tsongas*
6. *John F. Tierney*
7. *Edward J. Markey*
8. *Michael E. Capuano*
9. *Stephen F. Lynch*
10. *William R. Keating*

MICHIGAN

SENATORS
Carl Levin
Debbie Stabenow

REPRESENTATIVES
[Republicans 9, Democrats 6]

1. Dan Benishek
2. Bill Huizenga
3. Justin Amash
4. Dave Camp
5. *Dale E. Kildee*
6. Fred Upton
7. Tim Walberg
8. Mike Rogers
9. *Gary C. Peters*
10. Candice S. Miller
11. Thaddeus G. McCotter
12. *Sander M. Levin*
13. *Hansen Clarke*
14. *John Conyers, Jr.*
15. *John D. Dingell*

MINNESOTA

SENATORS
Amy Klobuchar
Al Franken

REPRESENTATIVES
[Republicans 4, Democrats 4]

1. *Timothy J. Walz*
2. John Kline
3. Erik Paulsen
4. *Betty McCollum*
5. *Keith Ellison*
6. Michele Bachmann
7. *Collin C. Peterson*
8. Chip Cravaack

MISSISSIPPI

SENATORS
Thad Cochran
Roger F. Wicker

REPRESENTATIVES
[Republicans 3, Democrat 1]

1. Alan Nunnelee
2. *Bennie G. Thompson*
3. Gregg Harper
4. Steven M. Palazzo

MISSOURI

SENATORS
Claire McCaskill
Roy Blunt

REPRESENTATIVES
[Republicans 6, Democrats 3]

1. *Wm. Lacy Clay*
2. W. Todd Akin
3. *Russ Carnahan*
4. Vicky Hartzler
5. *Emanuel Cleaver*
6. Sam Graves
7. Billy Long
8. Jo Ann Emerson
9. Blaine Luetkemeyer

MONTANA

SENATORS
Max Baucus
Jon Tester

REPRESENTATIVE
[Republican 1]

At Large - Denny Rehberg

NEBRASKA

SENATORS
Ben Nelson
Mike Johanns

REPRESENTATIVES
[Republicans 3]

1. Jeff Fortenberry
2. Lee Terry
3. Adrian Smith

NEVADA

SENATORS
Harry Reid
Dean Heller

REPRESENTATIVES
[Republicans 2, Democrat 1]

1. *Shelley Berkley*
2. Mark E. Amodei
3. Joseph J. Heck

NEW HAMPSHIRE

SENATORS
Jeanne Shaheen
Kelly Ayotte

REPRESENTATIVES
[Republicans 2]

1. Frank C. Guinta
2. Charles F. Bass

NEW JERSEY

SENATORS
Frank R. Lautenberg
Robert Menendez

REPRESENTATIVES
[Republicans 6, Democrats 7]

1. *Robert E. Andrews*
2. Frank A. LoBiondo
3. Jon Runyan
4. Christopher H. Smith
5. Scott Garrett
6. *Frank Pallone, Jr.*
7. Leonard Lance
8. *Bill Pascrell, Jr.*
9. *Steven R. Rothman*
10. *Donald M. Payne*
11. Rodney P. Frelinghuysen
12. *Rush D. Holt*
13. *Albio Sires*

NEW MEXICO

SENATORS
Jeff Bingaman
Tom Udall

REPRESENTATIVES
[Republican 1, Democrats 2]

1. *Martin Heinrich*
2. Stevan Pearce
3. *Ben Ray Luján*

NEW YORK

SENATORS
Charles E. Schumer
Kirsten E. Gillibrand

REPRESENTATIVES
[Republicans 8, Democrats 21]

1. *Timothy H. Bishop*
2. *Steve Israel*
3. Peter T. King
4. *Carolyn McCarthy*
5. *Gary L. Ackerman*
6. *Gregory W. Meeks*
7. *Joseph Crowley*
8. *Jerrold Nadler*
9. Robert L. Turner
10. *Edolphus Towns*
11. *Yvette D. Clarke*
12. *Nydia M. Velázquez*

13. Michael G. Grimm
14. *Carolyn B. Maloney*
15. *Charles B. Rangel*
16. *José E. Serrano*
17. *Eliot L. Engel*
18. *Nita M. Lowey*
19. Nan A.S. Hayworth
20. Christopher P. Gibson
21. *Paul Tonko*
22. *Maurice D. Hinchey*
23. *William L. Owens*
24. Richard L. Hanna
25. Ann Marie Buerkle
26. *Kathleen C. Hochul*
27. *Brian Higgins*
28. *Louise McIntosh Slaughter*
29. Tom Reed

NORTH CAROLINA

SENATORS
Richard Burr
Kay R. Hagan

REPRESENTATIVES
[Republicans 6, Democrats 7]

1. *G. K. Butterfield*
2. Renee L. Ellmers
3. Walter B. Jones
4. *David E. Price*
5. Virginia Foxx
6. Howard Coble
7. *Mike McIntyre*
8. *Larry Kissell*
9. Sue Wilkins Myrick
10. Patrick T. McHenry
11. *Heath Shuler*
12. *Melvin L. Watt*
13. *Brad Miller*

NORTH DAKOTA

SENATORS
Kent Conrad
John Hoeven

REPRESENTATIVE
[Republican 1]

At Large - Rick Berg

OHIO

SENATORS
Sherrod Brown
Rob Portman

REPRESENTATIVES
[Republicans 13, Democrats 5]

1. Steve Chabot
2. Jean Schmidt
3. Michael R. Turner
4. Jim Jordan
5. Robert E. Latta
6. Bill Johnson
7. Steve Austria
8. John A. Boehner
9. *Marcy Kaptur*
10. *Dennis J. Kucinich*
11. *Marcia L. Fudge*
12. Patrick J. Tiberi
13. *Betty Sutton*
14. Steven C. LaTourette
15. Steve Stivers
16. James B. Renacci
17. *Tim Ryan*
18. Bob Gibbs

OKLAHOMA

SENATORS
James M. Inhofe
Tom Coburn

REPRESENTATIVES
[Republicans 4, Democrat 1]

1. John Sullivan
2. *Dan Boren*
3. Frank D. Lucas
4. Tom Cole
5. James Lankford

OREGON

SENATORS
Ron Wyden
Jeff Merkley

REPRESENTATIVES
[Republican 1, Democrats 3, Vacant 1]

1. ——[1]

2. Greg Walden
3. *Earl Blumenauer*
4. *Peter A. DeFazio*
5. *Kurt Schrader*

PENNSYLVANIA

SENATORS
Robert P. Casey, Jr.
Patrick J. Toomey

REPRESENTATIVES
[Republicans 12, Democrats 7]

1. *Robert A. Brady*
2. *Chaka Fattah*
3. Mike Kelly
4. *Jason Altmire*
5. Glenn Thompson
6. Jim Gerlach
7. Patrick Meehan
8. Michael G. Fitzpatrick
9. Bill Shuster
10. Tom Marino
11. Lou Barletta
12. *Mark S. Critz*
13. *Allyson Y. Schwartz*
14. *Michael F. Doyle*
15. Charles W. Dent
16. Joseph R. Pitts
17. *Tim Holden*
18. Tim Murphy
19. Todd Russell Platts

RHODE ISLAND

SENATORS
Jack Reed
Sheldon Whitehouse

REPRESENTATIVES
[Democrats 2]

1. *David N. Cicilline*
2. *James R. Langevin*

SOUTH CAROLINA

SENATORS
Lindsey Graham
Jim DeMint

REPRESENTATIVES
[Republicans 5, Democrat 1]

1. Tim Scott
2. Joe Wilson
3. Jeff Duncan
4. Trey Gowdy
5. Mick Mulvaney
6. *James E. Clyburn*

SOUTH DAKOTA

SENATORS
Tim Johnson
John Thune

REPRESENTATIVE
[Republican 1]

At Large - Kristi L. Noem

TENNESSEE

SENATORS
Lamar Alexander
Bob Corker

REPRESENTATIVES
[Republicans 7, Democrats 2]

1. David P. Roe
2. John J. Duncan, Jr.
3. Charles J. "Chuck" Fleischmann
4. Scott DesJarlais
5. *Jim Cooper*
6. Diane Black
7. Marsha Blackburn
8. Stephen Lee Fincher
9. *Steve Cohen*

TEXAS

SENATORS
Kay Bailey Hutchison
John Cornyn

REPRESENTATIVES
[Republicans 23, Democrats 9]

1. Louie Gohmert
2. Ted Poe
3. Sam Johnson
4. Ralph M. Hall
5. Jeb Hensarling
6. Joe Barton
7. John Abney Culberson
8. Kevin Brady
9. *Al Green*
10. Michael T. McCaul
11. K. Michael Conaway
12. Kay Granger
13. Mac Thornberry
14. Ron Paul
15. *Rubén Hinojosa*
16. *Silvestre Reyes*
17. Bill Flores
18. *Sheila Jackson Lee*
19. Randy Neugebauer
20. *Charles A. Gonzalez*
21. Lamar Smith
22. Pete Olson
23. Francisco ''Quico'' Canseco
24. Kenny Marchant
25. *Lloyd Doggett*
26. Michael C. Burgess
27. Blake Farenthold
28. *Henry Cuellar*
29. *Gene Green*
30. *Eddie Bernice Johnson*
31. John R. Carter
32. Pete Sessions

UTAH

SENATORS
Orrin G. Hatch
Mike Lee

REPRESENTATIVES
[Republicans 2, Democrat 1]

1. Rob Bishop
2. *Jim Matheson*
3. Jason Chaffetz

VERMONT

SENATORS
Patrick J. Leahy
BERNARD SANDERS*

REPRESENTATIVE
[Democrat 1]

At Large - *Peter Welch*

VIRGINIA

SENATORS
Jim Webb
Mark R. Warner

REPRESENTATIVES
[Republicans 8, Democrats 3]

1. Robert J. Wittman
2. E. Scott Rigell
3. *Robert C. ''Bobby'' Scott*
4. J. Randy Forbes
5. Robert Hurt
6. Bob Goodlatte
7. Eric Cantor
8. *James P. Moran*
9. H. Morgan Griffith
10. Frank R. Wolf
11. *Gerald E. Connolly*

WASHINGTON

SENATORS
Patty Murray
Maria Cantwell

REPRESENTATIVES
[Republicans 4, Democrats 5]

1. *Jay Inslee*
2. *Rick Larsen*
3. Jaime Herrera Beutler
4. Doc Hastings
5. Cathy McMorris Rodgers
6. *Norman D. Dicks*
7. *Jim McDermott*
8. David G. Reichert
9. *Adam Smith*

WEST VIRGINIA

SENATORS
John D. Rockefeller IV
Joe Manchin III

REPRESENTATIVES
[Republicans 2, Democrats 1]

1. David B. McKinley
2. Shelley Moore Capito
3. *Nick J. Rahall II*

WISCONSIN

SENATORS
Herb Kohl
Ron Johnson

REPRESENTATIVES
[Republicans 5, Democrats 3]

1. Paul Ryan
2. *Tammy Baldwin*
3. *Ron Kind*
4. *Gwen Moore*
5. F. James Sensenbrenner, Jr.
6. Thomas E. Petri
7. Sean P. Duffy
8. Reid J. Ribble

WYOMING

SENATORS
Michael B. Enzi
John Barrasso

REPRESENTATIVE
[Republican 1]
At Large - Cynthia M. Lummis

AMERICAN SAMOA

DELEGATE
[Democrat 1]

Eni F. H. Faleomavaega

DISTRICT OF COLUMBIA

DELEGATE
[Democrat 1]

Eleanor Holmes Norton

GUAM

DELEGATE
[Democrat 1]

Madeleine Z. Bordallo

NORTHERN MARIANA ISLANDS

DELEGATE
[Democrat 1]

Gregorio Kilili Camacho Sablan

PUERTO RICO

RESIDENT COMMISSIONER
[Democrat 1]

Pedro R. Pierluisi

VIRGIN ISLANDS

DELEGATE
[Democrat 1]

Donna M. Christensen

*Independent
**Independent Democrat
[1] Vacancy due to the resignation of David Wu, August 3, 2011.

ALPHABETICAL LIST
SENATORS

Alphabetical list of Senators, Representatives, Delegates, and Resident Commissioner. Democrats in roman (51); Republicans in *italic* (47); Independent in SMALL CAPS (1); Independent Democrat in *SMALL CAPS ITALIC* (1).

Akaka, Daniel K., HI
Alexander, Lamar, TN
Ayotte, Kelly, NH
Barrasso, John, WY
Baucus, Max, MT
Begich, Mark, AK
Bennet, Michael F., CO
Bingaman, Jeff, NM
Blumenthal, Richard, CT
Blunt, Roy, MO
Boozman, John, AR
Boxer, Barbara, CA
Brown, Scott P., MA
Brown, Sherrod, OH
Burr, Richard, NC
Cantwell, Maria, WA
Cardin, Benjamin L., MD
Carper, Thomas R., DE
Casey, Robert P., Jr., PA
Chambliss, Saxby, GA
Coats, Daniel, IN
Coburn, Tom, OK
Cochran, Thad, MS
Collins, Susan M., ME
Conrad, Kent, ND
Coons, Christopher A., DE
Corker, Bob, TN
Cornyn, John, TX
Crapo, Mike, ID
DeMint, Jim, SC
Durbin, Richard J., IL
Enzi, Michael B., WY
Feinstein, Dianne, CA
Franken, Al, MN
Gillibrand, Kirsten E., NY
Graham, Lindsey, SC
Grassley, Chuck, IA
Hagan, Kay R., NC
Harkin, Tom, IA
Hatch, Orrin G., UT
Heller, Dean, NV
Hoeven, John, ND
Hutchison, Kay Bailey, TX
Inhofe, James M., OK
Inouye, Daniel K., HI
Isakson, Johnny, GA
Johanns, Mike, NE
Johnson, Ron, WI
Johnson, Tim, SD
Kerry, John F., MA
Kirk, Mark, IL
Klobuchar, Amy, MN
Kohl, Herb, WI
Kyl, Jon, AZ
Landrieu, Mary L., LA
Lautenberg, Frank R., NJ
Leahy, Patrick J., VT
Lee, Mike, UT
Levin, Carl, MI
LIEBERMAN, JOSEPH I., CT
Lugar, Richard G., IN
McCain, John, AZ
McCaskill, Claire, MO
McConnell, Mitch, KY
Manchin, Joe III, WV
Menendez, Robert, NJ
Merkley, Jeff, OR
Mikulski, Barbara A., MD
Moran, Jerry, KS
Murkowski, Lisa, AK
Murray, Patty, WA
Nelson, Ben, NE
Nelson, Bill, FL
Paul, Rand, KY
Portman, Rob, OH
Pryor, Mark L., AR
Reed, Jack, RI
Reid, Harry, NV
Risch, James E., ID
Roberts, Pat, KS
Rockefeller, John D., IV, WV
Rubio, Marco, FL
SANDERS, BERNARD,VT
Schumer, Charles E., NY
Sessions, Jeff, AL
Shaheen, Jeanne, NH
Shelby, Richard C., AL
Snowe, Olympia J., ME
Stabenow, Debbie, MI
Tester, Jon, MT
Thune, John, SD
Toomey, Patrick J., PA
Udall, Mark, CO
Udall, Tom, NM
Vitter, David, LA
Warner, Mark R., VA
Webb, Jim, VA
Whitehouse, Sheldon, RI
Wicker, Roger F., MS
Wyden, Ron, OR

REPRESENTATIVES, RESIDENT COMMISSIONER, AND DELEGATES

Republicans in roman (242); Democrats in *italic* (192); Vacancy (1); Resident Commissioner and Delegates in ***boldface italic*** (6); total, 441.

Ackerman, Gary L., NY (5th)
Adams, Sandy, FL (24th)
Aderholt, Robert B., AL (4th)
Akin, W. Todd, MO (2d)
Alexander, Rodney, LA (5th)
Altmire, Jason, PA (4th)
Amash, Justin, MI (3d)
Amodei, Mark E., NV (2d)
Andrews, Robert E., NJ (1st)
Austria, Steve, OH (7th)
Baca, Joe, CA (43d)
Bachmann, Michele, MN (6th)
Bachus, Spencer, AL (6th)
Baldwin, Tammy, WI (2d)
Barletta, Lou, PA (11th)
Barrow, John, GA (12th)
Bartlett, Roscoe G., MD (6th)
Barton, Joe, TX (6th)
Bass, Charles F., NH (2d)
Bass, Karen, CA (33d)
Becerra, Xavier, CA (31st)
Benishek, Dan, MI (1st)
Berg, Rick, ND (At Large)
Berkley, Shelley, NV (1st)
Berman, Howard L., CA (28th)
Biggert, Judy, IL (13th)
Bilbray, Brian P., CA (50th)
Bilirakis, Gus M., FL (9th)
Bishop, Rob, UT (1st)
Bishop, Sanford D., Jr., GA (2d)
Bishop, Timothy H., NY (1st)
Black, Diane, TN (6th)
Blackburn, Marsha, TN (7th)
Blumenauer, Earl, OR (3d)
Boehner, John A., OH (8th)
Bonner, Jo, AL (1st)
Bono Mack, Mary, CA (45th)
Boren, Dan, OK (2d)
Boswell, Leonard L., IA (3d)
Boustany, Charles W., Jr., LA (7th)
Brady, Kevin, TX (8th)
Brady, Robert A., PA (1st)
Braley, Bruce L., IA (1st)
Brooks, Mo, AL (5th)
Broun, Paul C., GA (10th)
Brown, Corrine, FL (3d)
Buchanan, Vern, FL (13th)
Bucshon, Larry, IN (8th)
Buerkle, Ann Marie, NY (25th)
Burgess, Michael C., TX (26th)
Burton, Dan, IN (5th)
Butterfield, G. K., NC (1st)
Calvert, Ken, CA (44th)
Camp, Dave, MI (4th)
Campbell, John, CA (48th)
Canseco, Francisco "Quico", TX (23d)
Cantor, Eric, VA (7th)
Capito, Shelley Moore, WV (2d)
Capps, Lois, CA (23d)
Capuano, Michael E., MA (8th)
Cardoza, Dennis A., CA (18th)
Carnahan, Russ, MO (3d)
Carney, John C., Jr., DE, (At Large)
Carson, André, IN (7th)
Carter, John R., TX (31st)
Cassidy, Bill, LA (6th)
Castor, Kathy, FL (11th)
Chabot, Steve, OH (1st)
Chaffetz, Jason, UT (3d)
Chandler, Ben, KY (6th)
Chu, Judy, CA (32d)
Cicilline, David N., RI (1st)
Clarke, Hansen, MI (13th)
Clarke, Yvette D., NY (11th)
Clay, Wm. Lacy, MO (1st)
Cleaver, Emanuel, MO (5th)
Clyburn, James E., SC (6th)
Coble, Howard, NC (6th)
Coffman, Mike, CO (6th)
Cohen, Steve, TN (9th)
Cole, Tom, OK (4th)
Conaway, K. Michael, TX (11th)
Connolly, Gerald E., VA (11th)
Conyers, John, Jr., MI, (14th)
Cooper, Jim, TN (5th)
Costa, Jim, CA (20th)
Costello, Jerry F., IL (12th)
Courtney, Joe, CT (2d)
Cravaack, Chip, MN (8th)
Crawford, Eric A. "Rick", AR (1st)
Crenshaw, Ander, FL (4th)
Critz, Mark S., PA (12th)
Crowley, Joseph, NY (7th)
Cuellar, Henry, TX (28th)
Culberson, John Abney, TX (7th)
Cummings, Elijah E., MD (7th)
Davis, Danny K., IL (7th)
Davis, Geoff, KY (4th)
Davis, Susan A., CA (53d)
DeFazio, Peter A., OR (4th)
DeGette, Diana, CO (1st)
DeLauro, Rosa L., CT (3d)
Denham, Jeff, CA (19th)
Dent, Charles W., PA (15th)
DesJarlais, Scott, TN (4th)
Deutch, Theodore E., FL (19th)
Diaz-Balart, Mario, FL (21st)
Dicks, Norman D., WA (6th)
Dingell, John D., MI (15th)
Doggett, Lloyd, TX (25th)
Dold, Robert J., IL (10th)
Donnelly, Joe, IN (2d)
Doyle, Michael F., PA (14th)
Dreier, David, CA (26th)
Duffy, Sean P., WI (7th)
Duncan, Jeff, SC (3d)
Duncan, John J., Jr., TN, (2d)
Edwards, Donna F., MD (4th)

Ellison, Keith, MN (5th)
Ellmers, Renee L., NC (2d)
Emerson, Jo Ann, MO (8th)
Engel, Eliot L., NY (17th)
Eshoo, Anna G., CA (14th)
Farenthold, Blake, TX (27th)
Farr, Sam, CA (17th)
Fattah, Chaka, PA (2d)
Filner, Bob, CA (51st)
Fincher, Stephen Lee, TN (8th)
Fitzpatrick, Michael G., PA (8th)
Flake, Jeff, AZ (6th)
Fleischmann, Charles J. "Chuck", TN (3d)
Fleming, John, LA (4th)
Flores, Bill, TX (17th)
Forbes, J. Randy, VA (4th)
Fortenberry, Jeff, NE (1st)
Foxx, Virginia, NC (5th)
Frank, Barney, MA (4th)
Franks, Trent, AZ (2d)
Frelinghuysen, Rodney P., NJ (11th)
Fudge, Marcia L., OH (11th)
Gallegly, Elton, CA (24th)
Garamendi, John, CA (10th)
Gardner, Cory, CO (4th)
Garrett, Scott, NJ (5th)
Gerlach, Jim, PA (6th)
Gibbs, Bob, OH (18th)
Gibson, Christopher P., NY (20th)
Giffords, Gabrielle, AZ (8th)
Gingrey, Phil, GA (11th)
Gohmert, Louie, TX (1st)
Gonzalez, Charles A., TX (20th)
Goodlatte, Bob, VA (6th)
Gosar, Paul A., AZ (1st)
Gowdy, Trey, SC (4th)
Granger, Kay, TX (12th)
Graves, Sam, MO (6th)
Graves, Tom, GA (9th)
Green, Al, TX (9th)
Green, Gene, TX (29th)
Griffin, Tim, AR (2d)
Griffith, H. Morgan, VA (9th)
Grijalva, Raúl M., AZ (7th)
Grimm, Michael G., NY (13th)
Guinta, Frank C., NH (1st)
Guthrie, Brett, KY (2d)
Gutierrez, Luis V., IL (4th)
Hahn, Janice, CA (36th)
Hall, Ralph M., TX (4th)
Hanabusa, Colleen W., HI (1st)
Hanna, Richard L., NY (24th)
Harper, Gregg, MS (3d)
Harris, Andy, MD (1st)
Hartzler, Vicky, MO (4th)
Hastings, Alcee L., FL (23d)
Hastings, Doc, WA (4th)
Hayworth, Nan S.A., NY (19th)
Heck, Joseph J., NV (3d)
Heinrich, Martin, NM (1st)
Hensarling, Jeb, TX (5th)
Herger, Wally, CA (2d)
Herrera Beutler, Jaime, WA (3d)
Higgins, Brian, NY (27th)
Himes, James A., CT (4th)
Hinchey, Maurice D., NY (22d)
Hinojosa, Rubén, TX (15th)
Hirono, Mazie K., HI (2d)
Hochul, Kathleen C., NY (26th)
Holden, Tim, PA (17th)
Holt, Rush D., NJ (12th)
Honda, Michael M., CA (15th)
Hoyer, Steny H., MD (5th)
Huelskamp, Tim, KS (1st)
Huizenga, Bill, MI (2d)
Hultgren, Randy, IL (14th)
Hunter, Duncan, CA (52d)
Hurt, Robert, VA (5th)
Inslee, Jay, WA (1st)
Israel, Steve, NY (2d)
Issa, Darrell E., CA (49th)
Jackson, Jesse L., Jr., IL, (2d)
Jackson Lee, Sheila, TX (18th)
Jenkins, Lynn, KS (2d)
Johnson, Bill, OH (6th)
Johnson, Eddie Bernice, TX (30th)
Johnson, Henry C. "Hank", Jr., GA, (4th)
Johnson, Sam, TX (3d)
Johnson, Timothy V., IL (15th)
Jones, Walter B., NC (3d)
Jordan, Jim, OH (4th)
Kaptur, Marcy, OH (9th)
Keating, William R., MA (10th)
Kelly, Mike, PA (3d)
Kildee, Dale E., MI (5th)
Kind, Ron, WI (3d)
King, Peter T., NY (3d)
King, Steve, IA (5th)
Kingston, Jack, GA (1st)
Kinzinger, Adam, IL (11th)
Kissell, Larry, NC (8th)
Kline, John, MN (2d)
Kucinich, Dennis J., OH (10th)
Labrador, Raúl R., ID (1st)
Lamborn, Doug, CO (5th)
Lance, Leonard, NJ (7th)
Landry, Jeffrey M., LA (3d)
Langevin, James R., RI (2d)
Lankford, James, OK (5th)
Larsen, Rick, WA (2d)
Larson, John B., CT (1st)
Latham, Tom, IA (4th)
LaTourette, Steven C., OH (14th)
Latta, Robert E., OH (5th)
Lee, Barbara, CA (9th)
Levin, Sander M., MI (12th)
Lewis, Jerry, CA (41st)
Lewis, John, GA (5th)
Lipinski, Daniel, IL (3d)
LoBiondo, Frank A., NJ (2d)
Loebsack, David, IA (2d)
Lofgren, Zoe, CA (16th)
Long, Billy, MO (7th)
Lowey, Nita M., NY (18th)
Lucas, Frank D., OK (3d)
Luetkemeyer, Blaine, MO (9th)
Luján, Ben Ray, NM (3d)
Lummis, Cynthia M., WY (At Large)
Lungren, Daniel E., CA (3d)
Lynch, Stephen F., MA (9th)
McCarthy, Carolyn, NY (4th)
McCarthy, Kevin, CA (22d)

McCaul, Michael T., TX (10th)
McClintock, Tom, CA (4th)
McCollum, Betty, MN (4th)
McCotter, Thaddeus G., MI (11th)
McDermott, Jim, WA (7th)
McGovern, James P., MA (3d)
McHenry, Patrick T., NC (10th)
McIntyre, Mike, NC (7th)
McKeon, Howard P. "Buck", CA (25th)
McKinley, David B., WV (1st)
McMorris Rodgers, Cathy, WA (5th)
McNerney, Jerry, CA (11th)
Mack, Connie, FL (14th)
Maloney, Carolyn B., NY (14th)
Manzullo, Donald A., IL (16th)
Marchant, Kenny, TX (24th)
Marino, Tom, PA (10th)
Markey, Edward J., MA (7th)
Matheson, Jim, UT (2d)
Matsui, Doris O., CA (5th)
Meehan, Patrick, PA (7th)
Meeks, Gregory W., NY (6th)
Mica, John L., FL (7th)
Michaud, Michael H., ME (2d)
Miller, Brad, NC (13th)
Miller, Candice S., MI (10th)
Miller, Gary G., CA (42d)
Miller, George, CA (7th)
Miller, Jeff, FL (1st)
Moore, Gwen, WI (4th)
Moran, James P., VA (8th)
Mulvaney, Mick, SC (5th)
Murphy, Christopher S., CT (5th)
Murphy, Tim, PA (18th)
Myrick, Sue Wilkins, NC (9th)
Nadler, Jerrold, NY (8th)
Napolitano, Grace F., CA (38th)
Neal, Richard E., MA (2d)
Neugebauer, Randy, TX (19th)
Noem, Kristi L., SD (At Large)
Nugent, Richard B., FL (5th)
Nunes, Devin, CA (21st)
Nunnelee, Alan, MS (1st)
Olson, Pete, TX (22d)
Olver, John W., MA (1st)
Owens, William L., NY (23d)
Palazzo, Steven M., MS (4th)
Pallone, Frank, Jr., NJ, (6th)
Pascrell, Bill, Jr., NJ, (8th)
Pastor, Ed, AZ (4th)
Paul, Ron, TX (14th)
Paulsen, Erik, MN (3d)
Payne, Donald M., NJ (10th)
Pearce, Stevan, NM (2d)
Pelosi, Nancy, CA (8th)
Pence, Mike, IN (6th)
Perlmutter, Ed, CO (7th)
Peters, Gary C., MI (9th)
Peterson, Collin C., MN (7th)
Petri, Thomas E., WI (6th)
Pingree, Chellie, ME (1st)
Pitts, Joseph R., PA (16th)
Platts, Todd Russell, PA (19th)
Poe, Ted, TX (2d)
Polis, Jared, CO (2d)
Pompeo, Mike, KS (4th)
Posey, Bill, FL (15th)
Price, David E., NC (4th)
Price, Tom, GA (6th)
Quayle, Benjamin, AZ (3d)
Quigley, Mike, IL (5th)
Rahall, Nick J., II, WV (3d)
Rangel, Charles B., NY (15th)
Reed, Tom, NY (29th)
Rehberg, Denny, MT (At Large)
Reichert, David G., WA (8th)
Renacci, James B., OH (16th)
Reyes, Silvestre, TX (16th)
Ribble, Reid J., WI (8th)
Richardson, Laura, CA (37th)
Richmond, Cedric L., LA (2d)
Rigell, E. Scott, VA (2d)
Rivera, David, FL (25th)
Roby, Martha, AL (2d)
Roe, David P., TN (1st)
Rogers, Harold, KY (5th)
Rogers, Mike, AL (3d)
Rogers, Mike, MI (8th)
Rohrabacher, Dana, CA (46th)
Rokita, Todd, IN (4th)
Rooney, Thomas J., FL (16th)
Roskam, Peter J., IL (6th)
Ros-Lehtinen, Ileana, FL (18th)
Ross, Dennis A., FL (12th)
Ross, Mike, AR (4th)
Rothman, Steven R., NJ (9th)
Roybal-Allard, Lucille, CA (34th)
Royce, Edward R., CA (40th)
Runyan, Jon, NJ (3d)
Ruppersberger, C.A. Dutch, MD (2d)
Rush, Bobby L., IL (1st)
Ryan, Paul, WI (1st)
Ryan, Tim, OH (17th)
Sánchez, Linda T., CA (39th)
Sanchez, Loretta, CA (47th)
Sarbanes, John P., MD (3d)
Scalise, Steve, LA (1st)
Schakowsky, Janice D., IL (9th)
Schiff, Adam B., CA (29th)
Schilling, Robert T., IL (17th)
Schmidt, Jean, OH (2d)
Schock, Aaron, IL (18th)
Schrader, Kurt, OR (5th)
Schwartz, Allyson Y., PA (13th)
Schweikert, David, AZ (5th)
Scott, Austin, GA (8th)
Scott, David, GA (13th)
Scott, Robert C. "Bobby", VA (3d)
Scott, Tim, SC (1st)
Sensenbrenner, F. James, Jr., WI (5th)
Serrano, José E., NY (16th)
Sessions, Pete, TX (32d)
Sewell, Terri A., AL (7th)
Sherman, Brad, CA (27th)
Shimkus, John, IL (19th)
Shuler, Heath, NC (11th)
Shuster, Bill, PA (9th)
Simpson, Michael K., ID (2d)
Sires, Albio, NJ (13th)
Slaughter, Louise McIntosh, NY (28th)
Smith, Adam, WA (9th)
Smith, Adrian, NE (3d)

Smith, Christopher H., NJ (4th)
Smith, Lamar, TX (21st)
Southerland, Steve, II, FL (2d)
Speier, Jackie, CA (12th)
Stark, Fortney Pete, CA (13th)
Stearns, Cliff, FL (6th)
Stivers, Steve, OH (15th)
Stutzman, Marlin A., IN (3d)
Sullivan, John, OK (1st)
Sutton, Betty, OH (13th)
Terry, Lee, NE (2d)
Thompson, Bennie G., MS (2d)
Thompson, Glenn, PA (5th)
Thompson, Mike, CA (1st)
Thornberry, Mac, TX (13th)
Tiberi, Patrick J., OH (12th)
Tierney, John F., MA (6th)
Tipton, Scott R., CO, (3d)
Tonko, Paul, NY (21st)
Towns, Edolphus, NY (10th)
Tsongas, Niki, MA (5th)
Turner, Michael R., OH (3d)
Turner, Robert L., NY (9th)
Upton, Fred, MI (6th)
Van Hollen, Chris, MD (8th)
Velázquez, Nydia M., NY (12th)
Visclosky, Peter J., IN (1st)
Walberg, Tim, MI (7th)
Walden, Greg, OR (2d)
Walsh, Joe, IL (8th)
Walz, Timothy J., MN (1st)
Wasserman Schultz, Debbie, FL (20th)
Waters, Maxine, CA (35th)
Watt, Melvin L., NC (12th)
Waxman, Henry A., CA (30th)
Webster, Daniel, FL (8th)
Welch, Peter, VT (At Large)
West, Allen B., FL (22d)
Westmoreland, Lynn A., GA (3d)
Whitfield, Ed, KY (1st)
Wilson, Frederica S., FL (17th)
Wilson, Joe, SC (2d)
Wittman, Robert J., VA (1st)
Wolf, Frank R., VA (10th)
Womack, Steve, AR (3d)
Woodall, Rob, GA (7th)
Woolsey, Lynn C., CA (6th)
Yarmuth, John A., KY (3d)
Yoder, Kevin, KS (3d)
Young, C. W. Bill, FL (10th)
Young, Don, AK (At Large)
Young, Todd C., IN (9th)

RESIDENT COMISSIONER
Pierluisi, Pedro R., PR

DELEGATES
Faleomavaega, Eni F. H., AS
Norton, Eleanor Holmes, DC
Bordallo, Madeleine Z., GU
Sablan, Gregorio Kilili Camacho, MP
Christensen, Donna M., VI

112th Congress
Nine-Digit Postal ZIP Codes

Senate Post Office (20510): The four-digit numbers in these tables were assigned by the Senate Committee on Rules and Administration. Mail to all Senate offices is delivered by the main Post Office in the Dirksen Senate Office Building.

Senate Committees

Committee on Agriculture, Nutrition, and Forestry	–6000
Committee on Appropriations	–6025
Committee on Armed Services	–6050
Committee on Banking, Housing, and Urban Affairs	–6075
Committee on the Budget	–6100
Committee on Commerce, Science, and Transportation	–6125
Committee on Energy and Natural Resources	–6150
Committee on Environment and Public Works	–6175
Committee on Finance	–6200
Committee on Foreign Relations	–6225
Committee on Health, Education, Labor and Pensions	–6300
Committee on Homeland Security and Governmental Affairs	–6250
Committee on Indian Affairs	–6450
Committee on the Judiciary	–6275
Committee on Rules and Administration	–6325
Committee on Small Business and Entrepreneurship	–6350
Committee on Veterans' Affairs	–6375
Committee on Aging (Special)	–6400
Committee on Ethics (Select)	–6425
Committee on Intelligence (Select)	–6475

Joint Committee Offices, Senate Side

Joint Economic Committee	–6602
Joint Committee on the Library	–6625
Joint Committee on Printing	–6650
Joint Committee on Taxation	–6675

Senate Leadership Offices

President Pro Tempore	–7000
Chaplain	–7002
Majority Leader	–7010
Assistant Majority Leader	–7012
Secretary for the Majority	–7014
Minority Leader	–7020
Assistant Minority Leader	–7022
Secretary for the Minority	–7024
Democratic Policy Committee	–7050
Republican Conference	–7060
Secretary to the Republican Conference	–7062
Republican Policy Committee	–7064
Republican Steering Committee	–7066
National Security Working Group	–7070

Senate Officers

Secretary of the Senate	–7100
Curator	–7102
Disbursing Office	–7104
Printing and Document Service	–7106
Historical Office	–7108
Human Resources	–7109
Interparliamentary Services	–7110
Senate Library	–7112
Office of Senate Security	–7114
Office of Public Records	–7116
Office of Official Reporters of Debates	–7117
Stationery Room	–7118
U.S. Capitol Preservation Commission	–7122
Office of Conservation and Preservation	–7124
Information Systems	–7125
Web Technology Office	–7126
Legislative Systems	–7127
Senate Gift Shop	–7128
Senate Legal Counsel	–7130
Emergency Terror Response (COOP)	–7131
Chief Counsel for Employment	–7132
Senate Sergeant at Arms	–7200
General Counsel	–7201
Finance Division	–7205
Budget	–7205
Accounting	–7205
Hair Care Services	–7206
Procurement	–7207
Capitol Guide Service	–7209
Employee Assistance Program Office	–7211
Human Resources	–7212
Safety Program	–7212
Health Promotion / Seminars	–7213
Placement Office	–7214
Workman's Compensation	–7214
Joint Office of Education and Training	–7215
Capitol Police	–7218
Congressional Special Services Office	–7228
Office Support Services	–7230
Customer Support	–7231
IT Request Processing	–7232
Chief Information Officer	–7233
State Liaison	–7285
Periodical Press Gallery	–7234
Press Gallery	–7238
Press Photo Gallery	–7242
Radio and TV Gallery	–7246
Webster Hall	–7248
Police Operations, Security and Emergency Preparedness	–7249

Other Offices on the Senate Side

Senate Legal Counsel	–7250
Central Operations—Administration	–7260
Parking / ID	–7262
Printing Graphics and Direct Mail—PSQ	–7264
Printing Graphics and Direct Mail—Capitol Hill	–7266
Facilities	–7204
Furniture Shop	–7204
Framing Shop	–7204
Cabinet Shop	–7204
Photo Studio	–7216
Post Office	–7220
Recording Studio	–7220
Senate Legislative Counsel	–7275
Program Management	–7276
IT Support Services—Administration	–7280
Telecom Support	–7281

Equipment Services -7282
Desktop / Lan Support -7284
IT Research / Deployment -7292
Technology Development-Administration -7290
Systems Architecture -7277
Information Security -7278
Applications Development -7291
Network Engineering and Management -7293
Enterprise IT Systems -7294
Inter / Intranet Services -7296
Architect of the Capitol -8000
Superintendent of Senate Buildings -8002
Restaurant -8050
Amtrak Ticket Office -9010
Airlines Ticket Office (CATO) -9014
Child Care Center -9022
Credit Union -9026
Veterans' Liaison -9054
Social Security Liaison -9064
Caucus of International Narcotics Control -9070
Army Liaison -9082
Air Force Liaison -9083
Coast Guard Liaison -9084
Navy Liaison -9085
Marine Liaison -9087

House Post Office (20515): Mail to all House offices is delivered by the main Post Office in the Longworth House Office Building.

House Committees Leadership

U.S. House of Representatives -0001
Cannon House Office Building -0002
Rayburn House Office Building -0003
Longworth House Office Building -0004
Ford House Office Building -0006
The Capitol -0007
Committee on Agriculture -6001
Committee on Appropriations -6015
Committee on Armed Services -6035
Committee on the Budget -6065
Committee on Education and the Workforce -6100
Committee on Energy and Commerce -6115
Committee on Ethics -6328
Committee on Financial Services -6050
Committee on Foreign Affairs -6128
Committee on Homeland Security -6480
Committee on House Administration -6157
Committee on the Judiciary -6216
Committee on Natural Resources -6201
Committee on Oversight and Government Reform -6143
Committee on Rules -6269
Committee on Science, Space, and Technology -6301
Committee on Small Business -6315
Committee on Transportation and Infrastructure -6256
Committee on Veterans' Affairs -6335
Committee on Ways and Means -6348
Permanent Select Committee on Intelligence -6415

Joint Committee Offices, House Side

Joint Economic Committee -6432
Joint Committee on the Library -6157
Joint Committee on Printing -6157
Joint Committee on Taxation -6453

House Leadership Offices

Office of the Speaker -6501
Office of the Majority Leader -6502
Office of the Majority Whip -6503
Democratic Caucus -6524
Democratic Congressional Campaign Committee -6525
Democratic Steering and Policy Committee -6527
Democratic Cloakroom -6528
Office of the Democratic Leader -6537
Office of the Democratic Whip -6538
House Republican Conference -6544
Republican Congressional Committee, National -6547
Republican Policy Committee -6549
Republican Cloakroom -6650

House Officers

Office of the Clerk -6601
Office of Art and Archives -6612
Office of Employment and Counsel -6622
Legislative Computer Systems -6618
Office of Legislative Operations -6602
Legislative Resource Center -6612
Official Reporters -6615
Office of Communications -6611
Office of Interparliamentary Affairs -6579
Office of the Chaplain -6655
Office of the House Historian -6701
Office of the Parliamentarian -6731
Chief Administrative Officer -6860
First Call -6660
Administrative Counsel -6660
Periodical Press Gallery -6624
Press Gallery -6625
Radio / TV Correspondents' Gallery -6627
HIR Call Center -6165
HIR Information Systems Security -6165
Outplacement Services -9920
Office of Employee Assistance -6619
ADA Services -6860
Personnel and Benefits -9980
Child Care Center -0001
Payroll and Benefits -6604
Financial Counseling -6604
Members' Services -9970
Office Supply Service -6860
House Gift Shop -6860
Mail List / Processing -6860
Mailing Services -6860
Contractor Management -6860
Photography -6623
House Recording Studio -6613
Furniture Support Services -6610
House Office Service Center -6860
Budget -6604
Financial Counseling -6604
Procurement Management -9940
Office of the Sergeant at Arms -6634

House Commissions and Offices

Congressional Executive Commission on China	–6481
Commission on Security and Cooperation in Europe	–6460
Commission on Congressional Mailing Standards	–6461
Office of the Law Revision Counsel	–6711
Office of Emergency Management	–6462
Office of the Legislative Counsel	–6721
General Counsel	–6532
Architect of the Capitol	–6906
Attending Physician	–6907
Congressional Budget Office	–6925

Liaison Offices

Air Force	–6854
Army	–6855
Coast Guard	–6856
Navy	–6857
Office of Personnel Management	–6858
Veterans' Administration	–6859

TERMS OF SERVICE

EXPIRATION OF THE TERMS OF SENATORS

CLASS I.—SENATORS WHOSE TERMS OF SERVICE EXPIRE IN 2013

[33 Senators in this group: Democrats, 21; Republicans, 10; Independent, 1; Independent Democrat, 1]

Name	Party	Residence
Akaka, Daniel K.[1]	D.	Honolulu, HI.
Barrasso, John[2]	R.	Casper, WY.
Bingaman, Jeff	D.	Santa Fe, NM.
Brown, Scott P.[3]	R.	Wrentham, MA.
Brown, Sherrod	D.	Avon, OH.
Cantwell, Maria	D.	Edmonds, WA.
Cardin, Benjamin L.	D.	Baltimore, MD.
Carper, Thomas R.	D.	Wilmington, DE.
Casey, Robert P., Jr.	D.	Scranton, PA.
Conrad, Kent[4]	D.	Bismarck, ND.
Corker, Bob	R.	Chattanooga, TN.
Feinstein, Dianne[5]	D.	San Francisco, CA.
Gillibrand, Kirsten E.[6]	D.	Hudson, NY.
Hatch, Orrin G.	R.	Salt Lake City, UT.
Heller, Dean[7]	R.	Carson City, NV.
Hutchison, Kay Bailey[8]	R.	Dallas, TX.
Klobuchar, Amy	D.	Minneapolis, MN.
Kohl, Herb	D.	Milwaukee, WI.
Kyl, Jon	R.	Phoenix, AZ.
Lieberman, Joseph I.	I.D.	New Haven, CT.
Lugar, Richard G.	R.	Indianapolis, IN.
McCaskill, Claire	D.	Kirkwood, MO.
Manchin, Joe III[9]	D.	Fairmont, WV.
Menendez, Robert[10]	D.	Hoboken, NJ.
Nelson, Ben	D.	Omaha, NE.
Nelson, Bill	D.	Orlando, FL.
Sanders, Bernard	I.	Burlington, VT.
Snowe, Olympia J.	R.	Auburn, ME.
Stabenow, Debbie	D.	Lansing, MI.
Tester, Jon	D.	Big Sandy, MT.
Webb, Jim	D.	Arlington, VA.
Whitehouse, Sheldon	D.	Providence, RI.
Wicker, Roger F.[11]	R.	Tupelo, MS.

[1] Senator Akaka was appointed April 28, 1990, to fill the vacancy caused by the death of Senator Spark M. Matsunaga, and took the oath of office on May 16, 1990; subsequently elected in a special election on November 6, 1990, for the remainder of the unexpired term; subsequently elected to a full term in 1994.

[2] Senator Barrasso was appointed on June 22, 2007, to fill the vacancy caused by the death of Senator Craig Thomas. He took the oath of office on June 25, 2007; subsequently elected in a special election on November 4, 2008.

[3] Senator Brown won a special election on January 19, 2010, to fill the vacancy caused by the death of Senator Edward M. Kennedy. Brown took the oath of office on February 4, 2010, replacing appointed Senator Paul G. Kirk, Jr.

[4] Senator Conrad resigned his term from Class III after winning a special election on December 4, 1992, to fill the vacancy caused by the death of Senator Quentin Burdick. Senator Conrad's seniority in the Senate continues without a break in service. He took the oath of office on December 15, 1992.

[5] Senator Feinstein won the special election held on November 3, 1992, to fill the vacancy caused by the resignation of Senator Pete Wilson. She took the oath of office on November 10, 1992. She won the seat from Senator John Seymour who had been appointed on January 7, 1991. She was elected to a full term in 1994.

[6] Senator Gillibrand was appointed on January 23, 2009, to fill the vacancy caused by the resignation of Hillary Rodham Clinton. She took the oath of office on January 27, 2009; subsequently elected in a special election on November 2, 2010.

[7] Senator Heller was appointed on May 3, 2011, to fill the vacancy caused by the resignation of John Ensign. He took the oath of office on May 9, 2011.

[8] Senator Hutchison won the special election on June 5, 1993, to fill the vacancy caused by the resignation of Senator Lloyd Bentsen. She took the oath of office on June 14, 1993. She won the seat from Senator Bob Krueger, who had been appointed on January 21, 1993. She was elected to a full term in 1994.

[9] Senator Manchin won a special election on November 2, 2010, to fill the vacancy caused by the death of Senator Robert C. Byrd, Manchin took the oath of office on November 15, 2010, replacing appointed Senator Carte P. Goodwin.

[10] Senator Menendez was appointed on January 17, 2006, to fill the vacancy caused by the resignation of Senator Jon S. Corzine; He took the oath of office on January 18, 2006; subsequently elected to a full term in November 2006.

[11] Senator Wicker was appointed on December 31, 2007, to fill the vacancy caused by the resignation of Trent Lott. He took the oath of office on December 31, 2007; subsequently elected in a special election on November 4, 2008.

CLASS II.—SENATORS WHOSE TERMS OF SERVICE EXPIRE IN 2015

[33 Senators in this group: Democrats, 20; Republicans, 13]

Name	Party	Residence
Alexander, Lamar	R.	Nashville, TN.
Baucus, Max	D.	Helena, MT.
Begich, Mark	D.	Anchorage, AK.
Chambliss, Saxby	R.	Moultrie, GA.
Cochran, Thad	R.	Jackson, MS.
Collins, Susan M.	R.	Bangor, ME.
Coons, Christopher A.[1]	D.	Wilmington, DE.
Cornyn, John	R.	San Antonio, TX.
Durbin, Richard J.	D.	Springfield, IL.
Enzi, Michael B.	R.	Gillette, WY.
Franken, Al[2]	D.	Minneapolis, MN.
Graham, Lindsey	R.	Seneca, SC.
Hagan, Kay R.	D.	Greensboro, NC.
Harkin, Tom	D.	Cumming, IA.
Inhofe, James M.[3]	R.	Tulsa, OK.
Johanns, Mike	R.	Omaha, NE.
Johnson, Tim	D.	Vermillion, SD.
Kerry, John F.	D.	Boston, MA.
Landrieu, Mary L.	D.	New Orleans, LA.
Lautenberg, Frank R.	D.	Cliffside Park, NJ.
Levin, Carl	D.	Detroit, MI.
McConnell, Mitch	R.	Louisville, KY.
Merkley, Jeff	D.	Portland, OR.
Pryor, Mark L.	D.	Little Rock, AR.
Reed, Jack	D.	Jamestown, RI.
Risch, James E.	R.	Boise, ID.
Roberts, Pat	R.	Dodge City, KS.
Rockefeller, John D., IV	D.	Charleston, WV.
Sessions, Jeff	R.	Mobile, AL.
Shaheen, Jeanne	D.	Madbury, NH.
Udall, Mark	D.	Eldorado Springs, CO.
Udall, Tom	D.	Santa Fe, NM.
Warner, Mark R.	D.	Alexandria, VA.

[1] Senator Coons won a special election on November 2, 2010 to fill the vacancy caused by the resignation of Joseph R. Biden, Jr. He took the oath of office on November 15, 2010, replacing appointed Senator Ted Kaufman.

[2] Contested election was resolved June 30, 2009; Senator Franken was sworn into office on July 7, 2009.

[3] Senator Inhofe won the special election held on November 8, 1994, to fill the vacancy caused by the resignation of Senator David Boren, and took the oath of office on November 17, 1994. He was elected to a full term in 1996.

CLASS III.—SENATORS WHOSE TERMS OF SERVICE EXPIRE IN 2017

[34 Senators in this group: Democrats, 10; Republicans, 24]

Name	Party	Residence
Ayotte, Kelly	R.	Nashua, NH.
Bennet, Michael F.[1]	D.	Denver, CO.
Blunt, Roy	R.	Strafford, MO.
Blumenthal, Richard	D.	Greenwich, CT.
Boozman, John	R.	Rogers, AR.
Boxer, Barbara	D.	Palm Springs, CA.
Burr, Richard	R.	Winston-Salem, NC.
Coats, Daniel	R.	Fort Wayne, IN.
Coburn, Tom	R.	Muskogee, OK.
Crapo, Mike	R.	Idaho Falls, ID.
DeMint, Jim	R.	Greenville, SC.
Grassley, Chuck	R.	Cedar Falls, IA.
Hoeven, John	R.	Minot, ND.
Inouye, Daniel K.	D.	Honolulu, HI.
Isakson, Johnny	R.	Marietta, GA.
Johnson, Ron	R.	Oshkosh, WI.
Kirk, Mark[2]	R.	Highland Park, IL.
Leahy, Patrick J.	D.	Middlesex, VT.
Lee, Mike	R.	Alpine, UT.
McCain, John	R.	Phoenix, AZ.
Mikulski, Barbara A.	D.	Baltimore, MD.
Moran, Jerry	R.	Hays, KS.
Murkowski, Lisa[3]	R.	Anchorage, AK.
Murray, Patty	D.	Seattle, WA.
Paul, Rand	R.	Bowling Green, KY.
Portman, Rob	R.	Cincinnati, OH.
Reid, Harry	D.	Searchlight, NV.
Rubio, Marco	R.	West Miami, FL.
Schumer, Charles E.	D.	Brooklyn, NY.
Shelby, Richard C.[4]	R.	Tuscaloosa, AL.
Thune, John	R.	Sioux Falls, SD.
Toomey, Patrick J.	R.	Zionsville, PA.
Vitter, David	R.	Metairie, LA.
Wyden, Ron[5]	D.	Portland, OR.

[1] Senator Bennet was appointed on January 21, 2009, to fill the vacancy caused by the resignation of Kenneth L. Salazar. He took the oath of office on January 22, 2009. Elected to a full term on November 2, 2010.

[2] Senator Kirk won a special election on November 2, 2010, to fill the vacancy caused by the resignation of Barack Obama, and at the same time was elected in the general election for the 6-year term edning January 3, 2017. He took the oath of office on November 29, 2010, replacing appointed Senator Roland Burris.

[3] Senator Murkowski was appointed on December 20, 2002, to fill the vacancy caused by the resignation of her father, Senator Frank Murkowski. She was elected to a full term in 2004.

[4] Senator Shelby changed party affiliation from Democrat to Republican on November 5, 1994.

[5] Senator Wyden won a special election on January 30, 1996, to fill the vacancy caused by the resignation of Senator Robert Packwood, and began service on February 6, 1996. He was elected to a full term in 1998.

CONTINUOUS SERVICE OF SENATORS

[Democrats in roman (51); Republicans in *italic* (47); Independent in SMALL CAPS (1); Independent Democrat in *SMALL CAPS ITALIC* (1); total, 100]

Rank	Name	State	Beginning of present service
1	Inouye, Daniel K.†	Hawaii	Jan. 3, 1963.
2	Leahy, Patrick J.	Vermont	Jan. 3, 1975.
3	*Hatch, Orrin G.*	Utah	Jan. 3, 1977.
	Lugar, Richard G.	Indiana	
4	Baucus, Max †[1]	Montana	Dec. 15, 1978.
5	*Cochran, Thad* †[2]	Mississippi	Dec. 27, 1978.
6	Levin, Carl	Michigan	Jan. 3, 1979.
7	*Grassley, Chuck* †	Iowa	Jan. 3, 1981.
8	Bingaman, Jeff	New Mexico	Jan. 3, 1983.
9	Kerry, John F.[3]	Massachusetts	Jan. 2, 1985.
10	Harkin, Tom †	Iowa	Jan. 3, 1985.
	McConnell, Mitch	Kentucky	
11	Rockefeller, John D. IV[4]	West Virginia	Jan. 15, 1985.
12	Conrad, Kent	North Dakota	Jan. 3, 1987.
	McCain, John †	Arizona	
	Mikulski, Barbara A.†	Maryland	
	Reid, Harry †	Nevada	
	Shelby, Richard C.†	Alabama	
13	Kohl, Herb	Wisconsin	Jan. 3, 1989.
	LIEBERMAN, JOSEPH I.	Connecticut	
14	Akaka, Daniel K.†[5]	Hawaii	May 16, 1990.
15	Feinstein, Dianne[6]	California	Nov. 10, 1992.‡
16	Boxer, Barbara †	California	Jan. 3, 1993.
	Murray, Patty	Washington	
17	*Hutchison, Kay Bailey*[7]	Texas	June 14, 1993.
18	*Inhofe, James M.* †[8]	Oklahoma	Nov. 17, 1994. ‡
19	*Kyl, Jon* †	Arizona	Jan. 3, 1995.
	Snowe, Olympia J.†	Maine	
20	Wyden, Ron †[9]	Oregon	Feb. 6, 1996. ‡
21	*Collins, Susan M.*	Maine	Jan. 3, 1997.
	Durbin, Richard J. †	Illinois	
	Enzi, Michael B.	Wyoming	
	Johnson, Tim †	South Dakota	
	Landrieu, Mary L.	Louisiana	
	Reed, Jack †	Rhode Island	
	Roberts, Pat †	Kansas	
	Sessions, Jeff	Alabama	
22	*Crapo, Mike* †	Idaho	Jan. 3, 1999.
	Schumer, Charles E. †	New York	
23	Cantwell, Maria †	Washington	Jan. 3, 2001.
	Carper, Thomas R.†	Delaware	
	Nelson, Bill †	Florida	
	Nelson, Ben	Nebraska	
	Stabenow, Debbie †	Michigan	
24	*Cornyn, John*[10]	Texas	Dec. 2, 2002.
25	*Murkowski, Lisa*[11]	Alaska	Dec. 20, 2002.
26	*Alexander, Lamar*	Tennessee	Jan. 3, 2003.
	Chambliss, Saxby †	Georgia	
	Graham, Lindsey †	South Carolina	
	Lautenberg, Frank R.[12]	New Jersey	
	Pryor, Mark L.	Arkansas	
27	*Burr, Richard* †	North Carolina	Jan. 3, 2005.
	Coburn, Tom †	Oklahoma	

CONTINUOUS SERVICE OF SENATORS—CONTINUED

[Democrats in roman (51); Republicans in *italic* (47); Independent in SMALL CAPS (1); Independent Democrat in *SMALL CAPS ITALIC* (1); total, 100]

Rank	Name	State	Beginning of present service
	DeMint, Jim †	South Carolina	
	Isakson, Johnny †	Georgia	
	Thune, John †	South Dakota	
	Vitter, David †	Louisiana	
28	Menendez, Robert † [13]	New Jersey	Jan. 18, 2006.
29	Brown, Sherrod †	Ohio	Jan. 3, 2007.
	Cardin, Benjamin L. †	Maryland	
	Casey, Robert P., Jr.	Pennsylvania	
	Corker, Bob	Tennessee	
	Klobuchar, Amy	Minnesota	
	McCaskill, Claire	Missouri	
	SANDERS, BERNARD †	Vermont	
	Tester, Jon	Montana	
	Webb, Jim	Vermont	
	Whitehouse, Sheldon	Rhode Island	
30	*Barrasso, John* [14]	Wyoming	June 22, 2007.
31	*Wicker, Roger F.* † [15]	Mississippi	Dec. 31, 2007.
32	Begich, Mark	Alaska	Jan. 3, 2009.
	Hagan, Kay R.	North Carolina	
	Johanns, Mike	Nebraska	
	Merkley, Jeff	Oregon	
	Risch, James E.	Idaho	
	Shaheen, Jeanne	New Hampshire	
	Udall, Mark †	Colorado	
	Udall, Tom †	New Mexico	
	Warner, Mark R.	Virginia	
33	Bennet, Michael F. [16]	Colorado	Jan. 21, 2009.
34	Gillibrand, Kirsten E.† [17]	New York	Jan. 27, 2009.
35	Franken, Al [18]	Minnesota	July 7, 2009.
36	*Brown, Scott P.* [19]	Massachusetts	Feb. 4, 2010.
37	Coons, Christopher A. [20]	Delaware	Nov. 15, 2010.
	Manchin, Joe III [21]	West Virginia	
38	*Kirk, Mark* † [22]	Illinois	Nov. 29, 2010. ‡
39	*Ayotte, Kelly*	New Hampshire	Jan. 3, 2011.
	Blumenthal, Richard	Connecticut	
	Blunt, Roy	Missouri	
	Boozman, John †	Arkansas	
	Coats, Daniel † [23]	Indiana	
	Hoeven, John	North Dakota	
	Johnson, Ron	Wisconsin	
	Lee, Mike	Utah	
	Moran, Jerry	Kansas	
	Paul, Rand	Kentucky	
	Portman, Rob	Ohio	
	Rubio, Marco	Florida	
	Toomey, Patrick J.	Ohio	
40	*Heller, Dean* † [24]	Nevada	May 9, 2011.

† Served in the House of Representatives previous to service in the Senate.

‡ Senators elected to complete unexpired terms typically begin their terms on the day following the election, but individual cases may vary.

[1] Senator Baucus was elected November 7, 1978, for the 6-year term commencing January 3, 1979; subsequently appointed December 15, 1978, to fill the vacancy caused by the resignation of Senator Paul Hatfield. He was elected to a full term in 1984.

[2] Senator Cochran was elected November 6, 1978, for the 6-year term commencing January 3, 1979; subsequently appointed December 27, 1978, to fill the vacancy caused by the resignation of Senator James Eastland. He was elected to a full term in 1984.

[3] Senator Kerry was elected November 6, 1984, for the 6-year term commencing January 3, 1985; subsequently appointed January 2, 1985, to fill the vacancy caused by the resignation of Senator Paul E. Tsongas.

[4] Senator Rockefeller was elected November 6, 1984, for the 6-year term commencing January 3, 1985; did not take his seat until January 15, 1985.

[5] Senator Akaka was appointed April 28, 1990, to fill the vacancy caused by the death of Senator Spark M. Matsunaga, and took the oath of office on May 16, 1990; subsequently elected in a special election on November 6, 1990, for the remainder of the unexpired term. He was elected to a full term in 1994.

[6] Senator Feinstein was elected on November 3, 1992, to fill the vacancy caused by the resignation of Senator Pete Wilson. She replaced appointed Senator John Seymour when she took the oath of office on November 10, 1992. She was elected to a full term in 1994.

[7] Senator Hutchison won a special election on June 5, 1993, to fill the vacancy caused by the resignation of Senator Lloyd Bentsen. She won the seat from Senator Bob Krueger, who had been appointed on January 21, 1993. She was elected to a full term in 1994.

[8] Senator Inhofe won the special election held on November 8, 1994, to fill the vacancy caused by the resignation of Senator David Boren, and took the oath of office on November 17, 1994. He was elected to a full term in 1996.

[9] Senator Wyden won a special election on January 30, 1996, to fill the vacancy caused by the resignation of Senator Bob Packwood. He was elected to a full term in 1998.

[10] Senator Cornyn was elected on November 5, 2002, for a 6-year term commencing January 3, 2003; subsequently appointed on December 2, 2002, to fill the vacancy caused by the resignation of Senator Phil Gramm.

[11] Senator Murkowski was appointed on December 20, 2002, to fill the vacancy caused by the resignation of her father, Senator Frank Murkowski. She was elected to a full term in 2004.

[12] Senator Lautenberg previously served in the Senate from December 27, 1982, until January 3, 2001.

[13] Senator Menendez was appointed on January 17, 2006, to fill the vacancy caused by the resignation of Senator Jon S. Corzine; subsequently elected to a full term in November 2006.

[14] Senator Barrasso was appointed on June 22, 2007, to fill the vacancy caused by the death of Senator Craig Thomas, and took the oath of office on June 25, 2007; subsequently elected in a special election on November 2008.

[15] Senator Wicker was appointed on December 31, 2007, to fill the vacancy caused by the resignation of Trent Lott; subsequently elected in a special election on November 4, 2008.

[16] Senator Bennet was appointed on January 21, 2009, to fill the vacancy caused by the resignation of Ken Salazar, and took the oath of office on January 22, 2009; subsequently elected to a full term on November 2, 2010.

[17] Senator Gillibrand was appointed on January 23, 2009, to fill the vacancy caused by the resignation of Senator Hillary Clinton, and took the oath of office on January 27, 2009; subsequently elected in a special election on November 2, 2010.

[18] The contested election case between Senator Franken and former Senator Coleman was resolved by Minnesota's Supreme Court on June 30, 2009. Franken was sworn into office on July 7, 2009. The Senate seat had remained vacant from January 3 until July 6.

[19] Senator Brown won a special election on January 19, 2010, to fill the vacancy caused by the death of Senator Edward M. Kennedy. He took the oath of office on February 4, 2010, replacing appointed Senator Paul G. Kirk, Jr.

[20] Senator Coons won a special election on November 2, 2010, to fill the vacancy caused by the resignation of Joseph Biden, Jr. Coons took the oath of office on November 15, 2010, replacing appointed Senator Edward E. Kaufman.

[21] Senator Manchin won a special election on November 2, 2010, to fill the vacancy caused by the death of Robert C. Byrd. He took the oath of office on November 15, 2010, replacing appointed Senator Carte P. Goodwin.

[22] Senator Kirk won a special election to the term ending January 3, 2011 on November 2, 2010, to fill the vacancy caused by the resignation of Barack Obama, and at the same time elected in the general election for the 6-year term ending January 3, 2017; took the oath of office on November 29, 2010, replacing appointed Senator Roland Burris.

[23] Senator Coats previously served in the Senate from January 3, 1989, until January 3, 1999.

[24] Senator Heller was appointed on May 3, 2011, to fill the vacancy caused by the resignation of Senator John Ensign, and took the oath of office on May 9, 2011.

CONGRESSES IN WHICH REPRESENTATIVES, RESIDENT COMMISSIONER, AND DELEGATES HAVE SERVED WITH BEGINNING OF PRESENT SERVICE

[* Elected to fill a vacancy; Republicans in roman (242); Democrats in *italic* (192); Vacancy (1); Resident Commissioner and Delegates in ***boldface italic*** (6); total, 441]

Name	State	Congresses (inclusive)	Beginning of present service
29 terms, consecutive			
Dingell, John D.	MI	*84th to 112th	Dec. 13, 1955
24 terms, consecutive			
Conyers, John, Jr.	MI	89th to 112th	Jan. 3, 1965
21 terms, consecutive			
Rangel, Charles B.	NY	92d to 112th	Jan. 3, 1971
Young, C. W. Bill	FL	92d to 112th	Jan. 3, 1971
20 terms, consecutive			
Stark, Fortney Pete	CA	93d to 112th	Jan. 3, 1973
Young, Don	AK	*93d to 112th	Mar. 6, 1973
19 terms, consecutive			
Markey, Edward J.	MA	*94th to 112th	Nov. 2, 1976
Miller, George	CA	94th to 112th	Jan. 3, 1975
Waxman, Henry A.	CA	94th to 112th	Jan. 3, 1975
18 terms, consecutive			
Dicks, Norman D.	WA	95th to 112th	Jan. 3, 1977
Kildee, Dale E.	MI	95th to 112th	Jan. 3, 1977
Rahall, Nick J., II	WV	95th to 112th	Jan. 3, 1977
17 terms, consecutive			
Lewis, Jerry	CA	96th to 112th	Jan. 3, 1979
Petri, Thomas E.	WI	*96th to 112th	Apr. 3, 1979
Sensenbrenner, F. James, Jr.	WI	96th to 112th	Jan. 3, 1979
16 terms, consecutive			
Dreier, David	CA	97th to 112th	Jan. 3, 1981
Frank, Barney	MA	97th to 112th	Jan. 3, 1981
Hall, Ralph M.	TX	97th to 112th	Jan. 3, 1981
Hoyer, Steny H.	MD	*97th to 112th	May 19, 1981
Rogers, Harold	KY	97th to 112th	Jan. 3, 1981
Smith, Christopher H.	NJ	97th to 112th	Jan. 3, 1981
Wolf, Frank R.	VA	97th to 112th	Jan. 3, 1981
15 terms, consecutive			
Ackerman, Gary L.	NY	*98th to 112th	Mar. 1, 1983
Berman, Howard L.	CA	98th to 112th	Jan. 3, 1983
Burton, Dan	IN	98th to 112th	Jan. 3, 1983
Kaptur, Marcy	OH	98th to 112th	Jan. 3, 1983
Levin, Sander M.	MI	98th to 112th	Jan. 3, 1983
14 terms, consecutive			
Barton, Joe	TX	99th to 112th	Jan. 3, 1985
Coble, Howard	NC	99th to 112th	Jan. 3, 1985

CONGRESSES IN WHICH REPRESENTATIVES, RESIDENT COMMISSIONER, AND DELEGATES HAVE SERVED WITH BEGINNING OF PRESENT SERVICE—CONTINUED

[* Elected to fill a vacancy; Republicans in roman (242); Democrats in *italic* (192); Vacancy (1); Resident Commissioner and Delegates in ***boldface italic*** (6); total, 441]

Name	State	Congresses (inclusive)	Beginning of present service
Visclosky, Peter J.	IN	99th to 112th	Jan. 3, 1985
13 terms, consecutive			
Costello, Jerry F.	IL	*100th to 112th	Aug. 9, 1988
DeFazio, Peter A.	OR	100th to 112th	Jan. 3, 1987
Duncan, John J., Jr.	TN	*100th to 112th	Nov. 8, 1988
Gallegly, Elton	CA	100th to 112th	Jan. 3, 1987
Herger, Wally	CA	100th to 112th	Jan. 3, 1987
Lewis, John	GA	100th to 112th	Jan. 3, 1987
Pelosi, Nancy	CA	*100th to 112th	June 2, 1987
Slaughter, Louise McIntosh	NY	100th to 112th	Jan. 3, 1987
Smith, Lamar	TX	100th to 112th	Jan. 3, 1987
Upton, Fred	MI	100th to 112th	Jan. 3, 1987
12 terms, consecutive			
Andrews, Robert E.	NJ	*101st to 112th	Nov. 6, 1990
Engel, Eliot L.	NY	101st to 112th	Jan. 3, 1989
Lowey, Nita M.	NY	101st to 112th	Jan. 3, 1989
McDermott, Jim	WA	101st to 112th	Jan. 3, 1989
Neal, Richard E.	MA	101st to 112th	Jan. 3, 1989
Payne, Donald M.	NJ	101st to 112th	Jan. 3, 1989
Rohrabacher, Dana	CA	101st to 112th	Jan. 3, 1989
Ros-Lehtinen, Ileana	FL	*101st to 112th	Aug. 29, 1989
Serrano, José E.	NY	*101st to 112th	Mar. 20, 1990
Stearns, Cliff	FL	101st to 112th	Jan. 3, 1989
12 terms, not consecutive			
Paul, Ron	TX	*94th, 96th to 98th, 105th to 112th.	Jan. 3, 1997
Price, David E.	NC	100th to 103d, 105th to 112th.	Jan 3. 1997
11 terms, consecutive			
Boehner, John A.	OH	102d to 112th	Jan. 3, 1991
Camp, Dave	MI	102d to 112th	Jan. 3, 1991
DeLauro, Rosa L.	CT	102d to 112th	Jan. 3, 1991
Johnson, Sam	TX	*102d to 112th	May 8, 1991
Moran, James P.	VA	102d to 112th	Jan. 3, 1991
Nadler, Jerrold	NY	*102d to 112th	Nov. 3, 1992
Olver, John W.	MA	*102d to 112th	June 4, 1991
Pastor, Ed	AZ	*102d to 112th	Sep. 24, 1991
Peterson, Collin C.	MN	102d to 112th	Jan. 3, 1991
Waters, Maxine	CA	102d to 112th	Jan. 3, 1991
11 terms, not consecutive			
Cooper, Jim	TN	98th to 103d and 108th to 112th.	Jan. 3, 2003
10 terms, consecutive			
Bachus, Spencer	AL	103d to 112th	Jan. 3, 1993
Bartlett, Roscoe G.	MD	103d to 112th	Jan. 3, 1993

CONGRESSES IN WHICH REPRESENTATIVES, RESIDENT COMMISSIONER, AND DELEGATES HAVE SERVED WITH BEGINNING OF PRESENT SERVICE—CONTINUED

[* Elected to fill a vacancy; Republicans in roman (242); Democrats in *italic* (192); Vacancy (1); Resident Commissioner and Delegates in ***boldface italic*** (6); total, 441]

Name	State	Congresses (inclusive)	Beginning of present service
Becerra, Xavier	CA	103d to 112th	Jan. 3, 1993
Bishop, Sanford D., Jr.	GA	103d to 112th	Jan. 3, 1993
Brown, Corrine	FL	103d to 112th	Jan. 3, 1993
Calvert, Ken	CA	103d to 112th	Jan. 3, 1993
Clyburn, James E.	SC	103d to 112th	Jan. 3, 1993
Eshoo, Anna G.	CA	103d to 112th	Jan. 3, 1993
Farr, Sam	CA	*103d to 112th	June 8, 1993
Filner, Bob	CA	103d to 112th	Jan. 3, 1993
Goodlatte, Bob	VA	103d to 112th	Jan. 3, 1993
Green, Gene	TX	103d to 112th	Jan. 3, 1993
Gutierrez, Luis V.	IL	103d to 112th	Jan. 3, 1993
Hastings, Alcee L.	FL	103d to 112th	Jan. 3, 1993
Hinchey, Maurice D.	NY	103d to 112th	Jan. 3, 1993
Holden, Tim	PA	103d to 112th	Jan. 3, 1993
Johnson, Eddie Bernice	TX	103d to 112th	Jan. 3, 1993
King, Peter T.	NY	103d to 112th	Jan. 3, 1993
Kingston, Jack	GA	103d to 112th	Jan. 3, 1993
Lucas, Frank D.	OK	*103d to 112th	May 10, 1994
McKeon, Howard P. "Buck"	CA	103d to 112th	Jan. 3, 1993
Maloney, Carolyn B.	NY	103d to 112th	Jan. 3, 1993
Manzullo, Donald A.	IL	103d to 112th	Jan. 3, 1993
Mica, John L.	FL	103d to 112th	Jan. 3, 1993
Roybal-Allard, Lucille	CA	103d to 112th	Jan. 3, 1993
Royce, Edward R.	CA	103d to 112th	Jan. 3, 1993
Rush, Bobby L.	IL	103d to 112th	Jan. 3, 1993
Scott, Robert C. "Bobby"	VA	103d to 112th	Jan. 3, 1993
Thompson, Bennie G.	MS	*103d to 112th	Apr. 13, 1993
Velázquez, Nydia M.	NY	103d to 112th	Jan. 3, 1993
Watt, Melvin L.	NC	103d to 112th	Jan. 3, 1993
Woolsey, Lynn C.	CA	103d to 112th	Jan. 3, 1993
9 terms, consecutive			
Blumenauer, Earl	OR	*104th to 112th	May 21, 1996
Cummings, Elijah E.	MD	*104th to 112th	Apr. 16, 1996
Doggett, Lloyd	TX	104th to 112th	Jan. 3, 1995
Doyle, Michael F.	PA	104th to 112th	Jan. 3, 1995
Emerson, Jo Ann	MO	*104th to 112th	Nov. 5, 1996
Fattah, Chaka	PA	104th to 112th	Jan. 3, 1995
Frelinghuysen, Rodney P.	NJ	104th to 112th	Jan. 3, 1995
Hastings, Doc	WA	104th to 112th	Jan. 3, 1995
Jackson Lee, Sheila	TX	104th to 112th	Jan. 3, 1995
Jackson, Jesse L., Jr.	IL	*104th to 112th	Dec. 12, 1995
Jones, Walter B.	NC	104th to 112th	Jan. 3, 1995
Latham, Tom	IA	104th to 112th	Jan. 3, 1995
LaTourette, Steven C.	OH	104th to 112th	Jan. 3, 1995
LoBiondo, Frank A.	NJ	104th to 112th	Jan. 3, 1995
Lofgren, Zoe	CA	104th to 112th	Jan. 3, 1995
Myrick, Sue Wilkins	NC	104th to 112th	Jan. 3, 1995
Thornberry, Mac	TX	104th to 112th	Jan. 3, 1995
Whitfield, Ed	KY	104th to 112th	Jan. 3, 1995

CONGRESSES IN WHICH REPRESENTATIVES, RESIDENT COMMISSIONER, AND DELEGATES HAVE SERVED WITH BEGINNING OF PRESENT SERVICE—CONTINUED

[* Elected to fill a vacancy; Republicans in roman (242); Democrats in *italic* (192); Vacancy (1); Resident Commissioner and Delegates in ***boldface italic*** (6); total, 441]

Name	State	Congresses (inclusive)	Beginning of present service
9 terms, not consecutive			
Lungren, Daniel E.	CA	96th to 100th and 109th to 112th.	Jan. 3, 2005
8 terms			
Aderholt, Robert B.	AL	105th to 112th	Jan. 3, 1997
Bono Mack, Mary	CA	*105th to 112th	Apr. 7, 1998
Boswell, Leonard L.	IA	105th to 112th	Jan. 3, 1997
Brady, Kevin	TX	105th to 112th	Jan. 3, 1997
Brady, Robert A.	PA	*105th to 112th	May 19, 1998
Capps, Lois	CA	*105th to 112th	Mar. 10, 1998
Davis, Danny K.	IL	105th to 112th	Jan. 3, 1997
DeGette, Diana	CO	105th to 112th	Jan. 3, 1997
Granger, Kay	TX	105th to 112th	Jan. 3, 1997
Hinojosa, Rubén	TX	105th to 112th	Jan. 3, 1997
Kind, Ron	WI	105th to 112th	Jan. 3, 1997
Kucinich, Dennis J.	OH	105th to 112th	Jan. 3, 1997
Lee, Barbara	CA	*105th to 112th	Apr. 7, 1998
McCarthy, Carolyn	NY	105th to 112th	Jan. 3, 1997
McGovern, James P.	MA	105th to 112th	Jan. 3, 1997
McIntyre, Mike	NC	105th to 112th	Jan. 3, 1997
Meeks, Gregory W.	NY	*105th to 112th	Feb. 3, 1998
Pascrell, Bill, Jr.	NJ	105th to 112th	Jan. 3, 1997
Pitts, Joseph R.	PA	105th to 112th	Jan. 3, 1997
Reyes, Silvestre	TX	105th to 112th	Jan. 3, 1997
Rothman, Steven R.	NJ	105th to 112th	Jan. 3, 1997
Sanchez, Loretta	CA	105th to 112th	Jan. 3, 1997
Sessions, Pete	TX	105th to 112th	Jan. 3, 1997
Sherman, Brad	CA	105th to 112th	Jan. 3, 1997
Shimkus, John	IL	105th to 112th	Jan. 3, 1997
Smith, Adam	WA	105th to 112th	Jan. 3, 1997
Tierney, John F.	MA	105th to 112th	Jan. 3, 1997
8 terms, not consecutive			
Chabot, Steve	OH	104th to 110th and 112th.	Jan. 3, 2011
Inslee, Jay	WA	103d, 106th to 112th.	Jan. 3, 1999
7 terms			
Baca, Joe	CA	*106th to 112th	Nov. 16, 1999
Baldwin, Tammy	WI	106th to 112th	Jan. 3, 1999
Berkley, Shelley	NV	106th to 112th	Jan. 3, 1999
Biggert, Judy	IL	106th to 112th	Jan. 3, 1999
Capuano, Michael E.	MA	106th to 112th	Jan. 3, 1999
Crowley, Joseph	NY	106th to 112th	Jan. 3, 1999
Gonzalez, Charles A.	TX	106th to 112th	Jan. 3, 1999
Holt, Rush D.	NJ	106th to 112th	Jan. 3, 1999
Larson, John B.	CT	106th to 112th	Jan. 3, 1999
Miller, Gary G.	CA	106th to 112th	Jan. 3, 1999

CONGRESSES IN WHICH REPRESENTATIVES, RESIDENT COMMISSIONER, AND DELEGATES HAVE SERVED WITH BEGINNING OF PRESENT SERVICE—CONTINUED

[* Elected to fill a vacancy; Republicans in roman (242); Democrats in *italic* (192); Vacancy (1); Resident Commissioner and Delegates in ***boldface italic*** (6); total, 441]

Name	State	Congresses (inclusive)	Beginning of present service
Napolitano, Grace F.	CA	106th to 112th	Jan. 3, 1999
Ryan, Paul	WI	106th to 112th	Jan. 3, 1999
Schakowsky, Janice D.	IL	106th to 112th	Jan. 3, 1999
Simpson, Michael K.	ID	106th to 112th	Jan. 3, 1999
Terry, Lee	NE	106th to 112th	Jan. 3, 1999
Thompson, Mike	CA	106th to 112th	Jan. 3, 1999
Walden, Greg	OR	106th to 112th	Jan. 3, 1999
7 terms, not consecutive			
Bass, Charles F.	NH	104th to 109th and 112th.	Jan. 3, 2011
Bilbray, Brian P.	CA	104th to 106th and *109th to 112th.	June 6, 2006
6 terms			
Akin, W. Todd	MO	107th to 112th	Jan. 3, 2001
Cantor, Eric	VA	107th to 112th	Jan. 3, 2001
Capito, Shelley Moore	WV	107th to 112th	Jan. 3, 2001
Clay, Wm. Lacy	MO	107th to 112th	Jan. 3, 2001
Crenshaw, Ander	FL	107th to 112th	Jan. 3, 2001
Culberson, John Abney	TX	107th to 112th	Jan. 3, 2001
Davis, Susan A.	CA	107th to 112th	Jan. 3, 2001
Flake, Jeff	AZ	107th to 112th	Jan. 3, 2001
Forbes, J. Randy	VA	*107th to 112th	June 19, 2001
Graves, Sam	MO	107th to 112th	Jan. 3, 2001
Honda, Michael M.	CA	107th to 112th	Jan. 3, 2001
Israel, Steve	NY	107th to 112th	Jan. 3, 2001
Issa, Darrell E.	CA	107th to 112th	Jan. 3, 2001
Johnson, Timothy V.	IL	107th to 112th	Jan. 3, 2001
Langevin, James R.	RI	107th to 112th	Jan. 3, 2001
Larsen, Rick	WA	107th to 112th	Jan. 3, 2001
Lynch, Stephen F.	MA	*107th to 112th	Oct. 16, 2001
McCollum, Betty	MN	107th to 112th	Jan. 3, 2001
Matheson, Jim	UT	107th to 112th	Jan. 3, 2001
Miller, Jeff	FL	*107th to 112th	Oct. 16, 2001
Pence, Mike	IN	107th to 112th	Jan. 3, 2001
Platts, Todd Russell	PA	107th to 112th	Jan. 3, 2001
Rehberg, Denny	MT	107th to 112th	Jan. 3, 2001
Rogers, Mike	MI	107th to 112th	Jan. 3, 2001
Ross, Mike	AR	107th to 112th	Jan. 3, 2001
Schiff, Adam B.	CA	107th to 112th	Jan. 3, 2001
Shuster, Bill	PA	*107th to 112th	May 15, 2001
Sullivan, John	OK	*107th to 112th	Feb. 15, 2002
Tiberi, Patrick J.	OH	107th to 112th	Jan. 3, 2001
Wilson, Joe	SC	*107th to 112th	Dec. 18, 2001
5 terms			
Alexander, Rodney	LA	108th to 112th	Jan. 3, 2003
Bishop, Rob	UT	108th to 112th	Jan. 3, 2003
Bishop, Timothy H.	NY	108th to 112th	Jan. 3, 2003

CONGRESSES IN WHICH REPRESENTATIVES, RESIDENT COMMISSIONER, AND DELEGATES HAVE SERVED WITH BEGINNING OF PRESENT SERVICE—CONTINUED

[* Elected to fill a vacancy; Republicans in roman (242); Democrats in *italic* (192); Vacancy (1); Resident Commissioner and Delegates in ***boldface italic*** (6); total, 441]

Name	State	Congresses (inclusive)	Beginning of present service
Blackburn, Marsha	TN	108th to 112th	Jan. 3, 2003
Bonner, Jo	AL	108th to 112th	Jan. 3, 2003
Burgess, Michael C.	TX	108th to 112th	Jan. 3, 2003
Butterfield, G. K.	NC	* 108th to 112th	July 20, 2004
Cardoza, Dennis A.	CA	108th to 112th	Jan. 3, 2003
Carter, John R.	TX	108th to 112th	Jan. 3, 2003
Chandler, Ben	KY	* 108th to 112th	Feb. 17, 2004
Diaz-Balart, Mario	FL	108th to 112th	Jan. 3, 2003
Franks, Trent	AZ	108th to 112th	Jan. 3, 2003
Garrett, Scott	NJ	108th to 112th	Jan. 3, 2003
Gerlach, Jim	PA	108th to 112th	Jan. 3, 2003
Gingrey, Phil	GA	108th to 112th	Jan. 3, 2003
Grijalva, Raúl M.	AZ	108th to 112th	Jan. 3, 2003
Hensarling, Jeb	TX	108th to 112th	Jan. 3, 2003
King, Steve	IA	108th to 112th	Jan. 3, 2003
Kline, John	MN	108th to 112th	Jan. 3, 2003
McCotter, Thaddeus G.	MI	108th to 112th	Jan. 3, 2003
Michaud, Michael H.	ME	108th to 112th	Jan. 3, 2003
Miller, Brad	NC	108th to 112th	Jan. 3, 2003
Miller, Candice S.	MI	108th to 112th	Jan. 3, 2003
Murphy, Tim	PA	108th to 112th	Jan. 3, 2003
Neugebauer, Randy	TX	*108th to 112th	June 3, 2003
Nunes, Devin	CA	108th to 112th	Jan. 3, 2003
Rogers, Mike	AL	108th to 112th	Jan. 3, 2003
Ruppersberger, C.A. Dutch	MD	108th to 112th	Jan. 3, 2003
Ryan, Tim	OH	108th to 112th	Jan. 3, 2003
Sánchez, Linda T.	CA	108th to 112th	Jan. 3, 2003
Scott, David	GA	108th to 112th	Jan. 3, 2003
Turner, Michael R.	OH	108th to 112th	Jan. 3, 2003
Van Hollen, Chris	MD	108th to 112th	Jan. 3, 2003
4 terms			
Barrow, John	GA	109th to 112th	Jan. 3, 2005
Boren, Dan	OK	109th to 112th	Jan. 3, 2005
Boustany, Charles W., Jr.	LA	109th to 112th	Jan. 3, 2005
Campbell, John	CA	109th to 112th	Dec. 6, 2005
Carnahan, Russ	MO	109th to 112th	Jan. 3, 2005
Cleaver, Emanuel	MO	109th to 112th	Jan. 3, 2005
Conaway, K. Michael	TX	109th to 112th	Jan. 3, 2005
Costa, Jim	CA	109th to 112th	Jan. 3, 2005
Cuellar, Henry	TX	109th to 112th	Jan. 3, 2005
Davis, Geoff	KY	109th to 112th	Jan. 3, 2005
Dent, Charles W.	PA	109th to 112th	Jan. 3, 2005
Fortenberry, Jeff	NE	109th to 112th	Jan. 3, 2005
Foxx, Virginia	NC	109th to 112th	Jan. 3, 2005
Gohmert, Louie	TX	109th to 112th	Jan. 3, 2005
Green, Al	TX	109th to 112th	Jan. 3, 2005
Higgins, Brian	NY	109th to 112th	Jan. 3, 2005
Lipinski, Daniel	IL	109th to 112th	Jan. 3, 2005
McCaul, Michael T.	TX	109th to 112th	Jan. 3, 2005
McHenry, Patrick T.	NC	109th to 112th	Jan. 3, 2005

CONGRESSES IN WHICH REPRESENTATIVES, RESIDENT COMMISSIONER, AND DELEGATES HAVE SERVED WITH BEGINNING OF PRESENT SERVICE—CONTINUED

[* Elected to fill a vacancy; Republicans in roman (242); Democrats in *italic* (192); Vacancy (1); Resident Commissioner and Delegates in ***boldface italic*** (6); total, 441]

Name	State	Congresses (inclusive)	Beginning of present service
McMorris Rodgers, Cathy	WA	109th to 112th	Jan. 3, 2005
Mack, Connie	FL	109th to 112th	Jan. 3, 2005
Marchant, Kenny	TX	109th to 112th	Jan. 3, 2005
Matsui, Doris O.	CA	109th to 112th	Mar. 8, 2005
Moore, Gwen	WI	109th to 112th	Jan. 3, 2005
Poe, Ted	TX	109th to 112th	Jan. 3, 2005
Price, Tom	GA	109th to 112th	Jan. 3, 2005
Reichert, David G.	WA	109th to 112th	Jan. 3, 2005
Schwartz, Allyson Y.	PA	109th to 112th	Jan. 3, 2005
Schmidt, Jean	OH	109th to 112th	Aug. 2, 2005
Sires, Albio	NJ	109th to 112th	Nov. 13, 2006
Wasserman Schultz, Debbie	FL	109th to 112th	Jan. 3, 2005
Westmoreland, Lynn A.	GA	109th to 112th	Jan. 3, 2005
4 terms, not consecutive			
Pearce, Stevan	NM	108th to 110th and 112th.	Jan. 3. 2011
3 terms			
Altmire, Jason	PA	110th to 112th	Jan. 3, 2007
Bachmann, Michele	MN	110th to 112th	Jan. 3, 2007
Braley, Bruce L.	IA	110th to 112th	Jan. 3, 2007
Broun, Paul C.	GA	*110th to 112th	July 17, 2007
Buchanan, Vern	FL	110th to 112th	Jan. 3, 2007
Carson, André	IN	*110th to 112th	Mar. 11, 2008
Castor, Kathy	FL	110th to 112th	Jan. 3, 2007
Clarke, Yvette D.	NY	110th to 112th	Jan. 3, 2007
Cohen, Steve	TN	110th to 112th	Jan. 3, 2007
Courtney, Joe	CT	110th to 112th	Jan. 3, 2007
Donnelly, Joe	IN	110th to 112th	Jan. 3, 2007
Edwards, Donna F.	MD	*110th to 112th	June 17, 2008
Ellison, Keith	MN	110th to 112th	Jan. 3, 2007
Fudge, Marcia L.	OH	*110th to 112th	Nov. 18, 2008
Giffords, Gabrielle	AZ	110th to 112th	Jan. 3, 2007
Hirono, Mazie K.	HI	110th to 112th	Jan. 3, 2007
Johnson, Henry C. ''Hank'', Jr.	GA	110th to 112th	Jan. 3, 2007
Jordan, Jim	OH	110th to 112th	Jan. 3, 2007
Lamborn, Doug	CO	110th to 112th	Jan. 3, 2007
Latta, Robert E.	OH	*110th to 112th	Dec. 11, 2007
Loebsack, David	IA	110th to 112th	Jan. 3, 2007
McCarthy, Kevin	CA	110th to 112th	Jan. 3, 2007
McNerney, Jerry	CA	110th to 112th	Jan. 3, 2007
Murphy, Christopher S.	CT	110th to 112th	Jan. 3, 2007
Perlmutter, Ed	CO	110th to 112th	Jan. 3, 2007
Richardson, Laura	CA	*110th to 112th	Aug. 21, 2007
Roskam, Peter J.	IL	110th to 112th	Jan. 3, 2007
Sarbanes, John P.	MD	110th to 112th	Jan. 3, 2007

CONGRESSES IN WHICH REPRESENTATIVES, RESIDENT COMMISSIONER, AND DELEGATES HAVE SERVED WITH BEGINNING OF PRESENT SERVICE—CONTINUED

[* Elected to fill a vacancy; Republicans in roman (242); Democrats in *italic* (192); Vacancy (1); Resident Commissioner and Delegates in ***boldface italic*** (6); total, 441]

Name	State	Congresses (inclusive)	Beginning of present service
Scalise, Steve	LA	*110th to 112th	May 3, 2008
Shuler, Heath	NC	110th to 112th	Jan. 3, 2007
Smith, Adrian	NE	110th to 112th	Jan. 3, 2007
Speier, Jackie	CA	*110th to 112th	Apr. 8, 2008
Sutton, Betty	OH	110th to 112th	Jan. 3, 2007
Tsongas, Niki	MA	*110th to 112th	Oct. 16, 2007
Walz, Timothy J.	MN	110th to 112th	Jan. 3, 2007
Welch, Peter	VT	110th to 112th	Jan. 3, 2007
Wittman, Robert J.	VA	*110th to 112th	Dec. 11, 2007
Yarmuth, John A.	KY	110th to 112th	Jan. 3, 2007
2 terms			
Austria, Steve	OH	111th and 112th	Jan. 3, 2009
Cassidy, Bill	LA	111th and 112th	Jan. 3, 2009
Chaffetz, Jason	UT	111th and 112th	Jan. 3, 2009
Chu, Judy	CA	*111th and 112th	July 16, 2009
Coffman, Mike	CO	111th and 112th	Jan. 3, 2009
Connolly, Gerald E.	VA	111th and 112th	Jan. 3, 2009
Critz, Mark S.	PA	*111th and 112th	May 18, 2010
Garamendi, John	CA	*111th and 112th	Nov. 3, 2009
Deutch, Theodore E.	FL	*111th and 112th	Apr. 13, 2010
Fleming, John	LA	111th and 112th	Jan. 3, 2009
Graves, Tom	GA	*111th and 112th	June 8, 2010
Guthrie, Brett	KY	111th and 112th	Jan. 3, 2009
Harper, Gregg	MS	111th and 112th	Jan. 3, 2009
Heinrich, Martin	NM	111th and 112th	Jan. 3, 2009
Himes, James A.	CT	111th and 112th	Jan. 3, 2009
Hunter, Duncan	CA	111th and 112th	Jan. 3, 2009
Jenkins, Lynn	KS	111th and 112th	Jan. 3, 2009
Kissell, Larry	NC	111th and 112th	Jan. 3, 2009
Lance, Leonard	NJ	111th and 112th	Jan. 3, 2009
Luján, Ben Ray	NM	111th and 112th	Jan. 3, 2009
Lummis, Cynthia M.	WY	111th and 112th	Jan. 3, 2009
McClintock, Tom	CA	111th and 112th	Jan. 3, 2009
Olson, Pete	TX	111th and 112th	Jan. 3, 2009
Owens, William L.	NY	*111th and 112th	Nov. 3, 2009
Paulsen, Erik	MN	111th and 112th	Jan. 3, 2009
Peters, Gary C.	MI	111th and 112th	Jan. 3, 2009
Pingree, Chellie	ME	111th and 112th	Jan. 3, 2009
Polis, Jared	CO	111th and 112th	Jan. 3, 2009
Posey, Bill	FL	111th and 112th	Jan. 3, 2009
Quigley, Mike	IL	*111th and 112th	Apr. 7, 2009
Reed, Tom	NY	*111th and 112th	Nov. 2, 2010
Roe, David P.	TN	111th and 112th	Jan. 3, 2009
Rooney, Thomas J.	FL	111th and 112th	Jan. 3, 2009
Schock, Aaron	IL	111th and 112th	Jan. 3, 2009

CONGRESSES IN WHICH REPRESENTATIVES, RESIDENT COMMISSIONER, AND DELEGATES HAVE SERVED WITH BEGINNING OF PRESENT SERVICE—CONTINUED

[* Elected to fill a vacancy; Republicans in roman (242); Democrats in *italic* (192); Vacancy (1); Resident Commissioner and Delegates in ***boldface italic*** (6); total, 441]

Name	State	Congresses (inclusive)	Beginning of present service
Schrader, Kurt	OR	111th and 112th	Jan. 3, 2009
Stutzman, Marlin A.	IN	*111th and 112th	Nov. 2, 2010
Thompson, Glenn	PA	111th and 112th	Jan. 3, 2009
Tonko, Paul	NY	111th and 112th	Jan. 3, 2009
2 terms, not consecutive			
Fitzpatrick, Michael G.	PA	109th and 112th	Jan. 3, 2011
Walberg, Tim	MI	110th and 112th	Jan. 3, 2011
1 term			
Adams, Sandy	FL	112th	Jan. 3, 2011
Amash, Justin	MI	112th	Jan. 3, 2011
Amodei, Mark E.	NV	*112th	Sept. 13, 2011
Barletta, Lou	PA	112th	Jan. 3, 2011
Bass, Karen	CA	112th	Jan. 3, 2011
Benishek, Dan	MI	112th	Jan. 3, 2011
Berg, Rick	ND	112th	Jan. 3, 2011
Black, Diane	TN	112th	Jan. 3, 2011
Brooks, Mo	AL	112th	Jan. 3, 2011
Bucshon, Larry	IN	112th	Jan. 3, 2011
Buerkle, Ann Marie	NY	112th	Jan. 3, 2011
Canseco, Francisco ''Quico''	TX	112th	Jan. 3, 2011
Carney, John C., Jr.	DE	112th	Jan. 3, 2011
Cicilline, David N.	RI	112th	Jan. 3, 2011
Clarke, Hansen	MI	112th	Jan. 3, 2011
Cravaack, Chip	MN	112th	Jan. 3, 2011
Crawford, Eric A. ''Rick''	AR	112th	Jan. 3, 2011
Denham, Jeff	CA	112th	Jan. 3, 2011
DesJarlais, Scott	TN	112th	Jan. 3, 2011
Dold, Robert J.	IL	112th	Jan. 3, 2011
Duffy, Sean P.	WI	112th	Jan. 3, 2011
Duncan, Jeff	SC	112th	Jan. 3, 2011
Ellmers, Renee L.	NC	112th	Jan. 3, 2011
Farenthold, Blake	TN	112th	Jan. 3, 2011
Fincher, Stephen Lee	TN	112th	Jan. 3, 2011
Fleischmann, Charles J. ''Chuck''	TN	112th	Jan. 3, 2011
Flores, Bill	TX	112th	Jan. 3, 2011
Gardner, Cory	CO	112th	Jan. 3, 2011
Gibbs, Bob	OH	112th	Jan. 3, 2011
Gibson, Christopher P.	NY	112th	Jan. 3, 2011
Gosar, Paul A.	AZ	112th	Jan. 3, 2011
Gowdy, Trey	SC	112th	Jan. 3, 2011
Griffin, Tim	AR	112th	Jan. 3, 2011
Griffith, H. Morgan	VA	112th	Jan. 3, 2011
Grimm, Michael G.	NY	112th	Jan. 3, 2011
Guinta, Frank C.	NH	112th	Jan. 3, 2011
Hahn, Janice	CA	*112th	July 12, 2011
Hanabusa, Colleen W.	HI	112th	Jan. 3, 2011
Hanna, Richard L.	NY	112th	Jan. 3, 2011
Harris, Andy	MD	112th	Jan. 3, 2011

CONGRESSES IN WHICH REPRESENTATIVES, RESIDENT COMMISSIONER, AND DELEGATES HAVE SERVED WITH BEGINNING OF PRESENT SERVICE—CONTINUED

[* Elected to fill a vacancy; Republicans in roman (242); Democrats in *italic* (192); Vacancy (1); Resident Commissioner and Delegates in ***boldface italic*** (6); total, 441]

Name	State	Congresses (inclusive)	Beginning of present service
Hartzler, Vicky	MO	112th	Jan. 3, 2011
Hayworth, Nan A.S.	NY	112th	Jan. 3, 2011
Heck, Joseph J.	NV	112th	Jan. 3, 2011
Herrera Beutler, Jaime	WA	112th	Jan. 3, 2011
Hochul, Kathleen C.	NY	*112th	May 24, 2011
Huelskamp, Tim	KS	112th	Jan. 3, 2011
Huizenga, Bill	MI	112th	Jan. 3, 2011
Hultgren, Randy	IL	112th	Jan. 3, 2011
Hurt, Robert	VA	112th	Jan. 3, 2011
Johnson, Bill	OH	112th	Jan. 3, 2011
Keating, William R.	MA	112th	Jan. 3, 2011
Kelly, Mike	PA	112th	Jan. 3, 2011
Kinzinger, Adam	IL	112th	Jan. 3, 2011
Labrador, Raúl R.	ID	112th	Jan. 3, 2011
Landry, Jeffrey M.	LA	112th	Jan. 3, 2011
Lankford, James	OK	112th	Jan. 3, 2011
Long, Billy	MO	112th	Jan. 3, 2011
McKinley, David B.	WV	112th	Jan. 3, 2011
Marino, Tom.	PA	112th	Jan. 3, 2011
Meehan, Patrick	PA	112th	Jan. 3, 2011
Mulvaney, Mick	SC	112th	Jan. 3, 2011
Noem, Kristi L.	SD	112th	Jan. 3, 2011
Nugent, Richard B.	FL	112th	Jan. 3, 2011
Nunnelee, Alan	MS	112th	Jan. 3, 2011
Palazzo, Steven M.	MS	112th	Jan. 3, 2011
Pompeo, Mike	KS	112th	Jan. 3, 2011
Quayle, Benjamin	AZ	112th	Jan. 3, 2011
Renacci, James B.	OH	112th	Jan. 3, 2011
Ribble, Reid J.	WI	112th	Jan. 3, 2011
Richmond, Cedric L.	LA	112th	Jan. 3, 2011
Rigell, E. Scott	VA	112th	Jan. 3, 2011
Rivera, David	FL	112th	Jan. 3, 2011
Roby, Martha	AL	112th	Jan. 3, 2011
Rokita, Todd	IN	112th	Jan. 3, 2011
Ross, Dennis A.	FL	112th	Jan. 3, 2011
Runyan, Jon	NJ	112th	Jan. 3, 2011
Schilling, Robert T.	IL	112th	Jan. 3, 2011
Schweikert, David	AZ	112th	Jan. 3, 2011
Scott, Austin	GA	112th	Jan. 3, 2011
Scott, Tim	SC	112th	Jan. 3, 2011
Sewell, Terri A.	AL	112th	Jan. 3, 2011
Southerland, Steve, II	FL	112th	Jan. 3, 2011
Stivers, Steve	OH	112th	Jan. 3, 2011
Tipton, Scott R.	CO	112th	Jan. 3, 2011
Turner, Robert L.	NY	*112th	Sept. 13, 2011
Walsh, Joe	IL	112th	Jan. 3, 2011
Webster, Daniel	FL	112th	Jan. 3, 2011
West, Allen B.	FL	112th	Jan. 3, 2011
Wilson, Frederica S.	FL	112th	Jan. 3, 2011
Womack, Steve	AR	112th	Jan. 3, 2011
Woodall, Rob	GA	112th	Jan. 3, 2011

CONGRESSES IN WHICH REPRESENTATIVES, RESIDENT COMMISSIONER, AND DELEGATES HAVE SERVED WITH BEGINNING OF PRESENT SERVICE—CONTINUED

[* Elected to fill a vacancy; Republicans in roman (242); Democrats in *italic* (192); Vacancy (1); Resident Commissioner and Delegates in ***boldface italic*** (6); total, 441]

Name	State	Congresses (inclusive)	Beginning of present service
Yoder, Kevin	KS	112th	Jan. 3, 2011
Young, Todd C.	IN	112th	Jan. 3, 2011
RESIDENT COMMISSIONER			
Pierluisi, Pedro R.	PR	111th and 112th	Jan. 3, 2009
DELEGATES			
Faleomavaega, Eni F. H.	AS	101st to 112th	Jan. 3, 1989
Norton, Eleanor Holmes	DC	102d to 112th	Jan. 3, 1991
Bordallo, Madeleine Z.	GU	108th to 112th	Jan. 3, 2003
Sablan, Gregorio Kilili Camacho	MP	111th to 112th	Jan. 3, 2009
Christensen, Donna M.	VI	105th to 112th	Jan. 3, 1997

NOTE: Members elected by special election are considered to begin service on the date of the election, except for those elected after a sine die adjournment. If elected after the Congress has adjourned for the session, Members are considered to begin their service on the day after the election.

STANDING COMMITTEES OF THE SENATE

[Democrats in roman; Republicans in *italic*; Independent in SMALL CAPS; Independent Democrat in *SMALL CAPS ITALIC*]

[Room numbers beginning with SD are in the Dirksen Building, SH in the Hart Building, SR in the Russell Building, and S in The Capitol]

Agriculture, Nutrition, and Forestry

328A Russell Senate Office Building 20510–6000

phone 224–2035, fax 224–1725, TTY / TDD 224–2587

http://agriculture.senate.gov

meets first and third Wednesdays of each month

Debbie Stabenow, of Michigan, *Chair*

Patrick J. Leahy, of Vermont.
Tom Harkin, of Iowa.
Kent Conrad, of North Dakota.
Max Baucus, of Montana.
Ben Nelson, of Nebraska.
Sherrod Brown, of Ohio.
Robert P. Casey, Jr., of Pennsylvania.
Amy Klobuchar, of Minnesota.
Michael F. Bennet, of Colorado.
Kirsten E. Gillibrand, of New York.

Pat Roberts, of Kansas.
Richard G. Lugar, of Indiana.
Thad Cochran, of Mississippi.
Mitch McConnell, of Kentucky.
Saxby Chambliss, of Georgia.
Mike Johanns, of Nebraska.
John Boozman, of Arkansas.
Chuck Grassley, of Iowa.
John Thune, of South Dakota.
John Hoeven, of North Dakota.

SUBCOMMITTEES

[The chairman and ranking minority member are ex officio (non-voting) members of all subcommittees on which they do not serve.]

Commodities, Markets, Trade and Risk Management

Ben Nelson, of Nebraska, *Chair*

Kent Conrad, of North Dakota.
Max Baucus, of Montana.
Sherrod Brown, of Ohio.
Michael F. Bennet, of Colorado.
Kirsten E. Gillibrand, of New York.

Saxby Chambliss, of Georgia.
Thad Cochran, of Mississippi.
Mike Johanns, of Nebraska.
John Boozman, of Arkansas.
Chuck Grassley, of Iowa.

Conservation, Forestry and Natural Resources

Michael F. Bennet, of Colorado, *Chair*

Patrick J. Leahy, of Vermont.
Tom Harkin, of Iowa.
Kent Conrad, of North Dakota.
Max Baucus, of Montana.
Amy Klobuchar, of Minnesota.

John Boozman, of Arkansas.
Richard G. Lugar, of Indiana.
Thad Cochran, of Mississippi.
Mitch McConnell, of Kentucky.
Saxby Chambliss, of Georgia.

Jobs, Rural Economic Growth and Energy Innovation

Sherrod Brown, of Ohio, *Chair*

Tom Harkin, of Iowa.
Kent Conrad, of North Dakota.
Ben Nelson, of Nebraska.
Robert P. Casey, Jr., of Pennsylvania.
Amy Klobuchar, of Minnesota.
John Thune, of South Dakota.
Richard G. Lugar, of Indiana.
Saxby Chambliss, of Georgia.
Chuck Grassley, of Iowa.
John Hoeven, of North Dakota.

Livestock, Dairy, Poultry, Marketing and Agriculture Security

Kirsten E. Gillibrand, of New York, *Chair*

Patrick J. Leahy, of Vermont.
Max Baucus, of Montana.
Ben Nelson, of Nebraska.
Robert P. Casey, Jr., of Pennsylvania.
Amy Klobuchar, of Minnesota.
Mike Johanns, of Nebraska.
Mitch McConnell, of Kentucky.
John Boozman, of Arkansas.
Chuck Grassley, of Iowa.
John Thune, of South Dakota.

Nutrition, Specialty Crops, Food and Agricultural Research

Robert P. Casey, Jr., of Pennsylvania, *Chair*

Patrick J. Leahy, of Vermont.
Tom Harkin, of Iowa.
Sherrod Brown, of Ohio.
Michael F. Bennet, of Colorado.
Kirsten E. Gillibrand, of New York.
Richard G. Lugar, of Indiana.
Thad Cochran, of Mississippi.
Mitch McConnell, of Kentucky.
Mike Johanns, of Nebraska.
John Hoeven, of North Dakota.

STAFF

Committee on Agriculture, Nutrition, and Forestry (SR–328A), 224–2035, fax 224–1725.
Majority Staff Director.—Chris Adamo.
Senior Professional Staff: Bill Imbergamo, Brandon McBride, Tina May, Jacqlyn Schneider.
Senior Counsels: Todd Wooten, Bart Kempf.
Press Secretary.—Ben Becker.
Chief Counsel.—Jonathan Coppess.
Professional Staff: Cory Claussen, David Lloyd, Karla Thieman.
Chief Economist.—Joe Shultz.
Legislative Aide.—Catie Lee.
Executive Assistant.—Hanna Abou El Seoud.
Economic Policy Advisor.—Colleen Briggs.
Minority Staff Director.—Mike Seyfert.
Deputy Republican Staff Director.—Joel Leftwich.
Senior Professional Staff: Greg Doud, Tara Smith, Eric Steiner, Autumn Veazey.
Communications Director.—Sarah Little.
Chief Economist.—Max Fisher.
Professional Staff: Keira Franz, Andrew Vlasaty.
Chief Counsel.—Anne Hazlett.
Counsels: Chris Hicks, Dave Johnson.
Executive Assistant.—Jenae Brady.
Non-designated:
Staff Assistant.—Rachel Silverman, Alvaro Zarco.
IT.—Jacob Chaney.
Archivist.—Katie Salay.
GPO Detailee.—Micah Wortham.
Chief Clerk.—Jessie Williams.
Deputy Chief Clerk.—Kristi Bansemer.

Appropriations

S–128 The Capitol 20510–6025, phone 224–7363

http://appropriations.senate.gov

meets upon call of the chair

Daniel K. Inouye, of Hawaii, *Chair*

Patrick J. Leahy, of Vermont.
Tom Harkin, of Iowa.
Barbara A. Mikulski, of Maryland.
Herb Kohl, of Wisconsin.
Patty Murray, of Washington.
Dianne Feinstein, of California.
Richard J. Durbin, of Illinois.
Tim Johnson, of South Dakota.
Mary L. Landrieu, of Louisiana.
Jack Reed, of Rhode Island.
Frank R. Lautenberg, of New Jersey.
Ben Nelson, of Nebraska.
Mark L. Pryor, of Arkansas.
Jon Tester, of Montana.
Sherrod Brown, of Ohio.

Thad Cochran, of Mississippi.
Mitch McConnell, of Kentucky.
Richard C. Shelby, of Alabama.
Kay Bailey Hutchison, of Texas.
Lamar Alexander, of Tennessee.
Susan M. Collins, of Maine.
Lisa Murkowski, of Alaska.
Lindsey Graham, of South Carolina.
Mark Kirk, of Illinois.
Daniel Coats, of Indiana.
Roy Blunt, of Missouri.
Jerry Moran, of Kansas.
John Hoeven, of North Dakota.
Ron Johnson, of Wisconsin.

SUBCOMMITTEES

[The chairman and ranking minority member are ex officio members of all subcommittees on which they do not serve.]

Agriculture, Rural Development, Food and Drug Administration, and Related Agencies

Herb Kohl, of Wisconsin, *Chair*

Tom Harkin, of Iowa.
Dianne Feinstein, of California.
Tim Johnson, of South Dakota.
Ben Nelson, of Nebraska.
Mark L. Pryor, of Arkansas.
Sherrod Brown, of Ohio.

Roy Blunt, of Missouri.
Thad Cochran, of Mississippi.
Mitch McConnell, of Kentucky.
Susan M. Collins, of Maine.
Jerry Moran, of Kansas.
John Hoeven, of North Dakota.

Commerce, Justice, Science, and Related Agencies

Barbara A. Mikulski, of Maryland, *Chair*

Daniel K. Inouye, of Hawaii.
Patrick J. Leahy, of Vermont.
Herb Kohl, of Wisconsin.
Dianne Feinstein, of California.
Jack Reed, of Rhode Island.
Frank R. Lautenberg, of New Jersey.
Ben Nelson, of Nebraska.
Mark L. Pryor, of Arkansas.
Sherrod Brown, of Ohio.

Kay Bailey Hutchison, of Texas.
Richard C. Shelby, of Alabama.
Mitch McConnell, of Kentucky.
Lamar Alexander, of Tennessee.
Lisa Murkowski, of Alaska.
Ron Johnson, of Wisconsin.
Susan M. Collins, of Maine.
Lindsey Graham, of South Carolina.

Department of Defense

Daniel K. Inouye, of Hawaii, *Chair*

Patrick J. Leahy, of Vermont.
Tom Harkin, of Iowa.
Richard J. Durbin, of Illinois.
Dianne Feinstein, of California.
Barbara A. Mikulski, of Maryland.
Herb Kohl, of Wisconsin.
Patty Murray, of Washington.
Tim Johnson, of South Dakota.
Jack Reed, of Rhode Island.

Thad Cochran, of Mississippi.
Mitch McConnell, of Kentucky.
Richard C. Shelby, of Alabama.
Kay Bailey Hutchison, of Texas.
Lamar Alexander, of Tennessee.
Susan M. Collins, of Maine.
Lisa Murkowski, of Alaska.
Lindsey Graham, of South Carolina.
Daniel Coats, of Indiana.

Department of Homeland Security

Mary L. Landrieu, of Louisiana, *Chair*

Frank R. Lautenberg, of New Jersey.
Daniel K. Inouye, of Hawaii.
Patrick J. Leahy, of Vermont.
Patty Murray, of Washington.
Jon Tester, of Montana.

Daniel Coats, of Indiana.
Thad Cochran, of Mississippi.
Richard C. Shelby, of Alabama.
Lisa Murkowski, of Alaska.
Jerry Moran, of Kansas.

Department of the Interior, Environment, and Related Agencies

Jack Reed, of Rhode Island, *Chair*

Dianne Feinstein, of California.
Patrick J. Leahy, of Vermont.
Barbara A. Mikulski, of Maryland.
Herb Kohl, of Wisconsin.
Tim Johnson, of South Dakota.
Ben Nelson, of Nebraska.
Jon Tester, of Montana.
Mary L. Landrieu, of Louisiana.

Lisa Murkowski, of Alaska.
Lamar Alexander, of Tennessee.
Thad Cochran, of Mississippi.
Susan M. Collins, of Maine.
Ron Johnson, of Wisconsin.
Roy Blunt, of Missouri.
John Hoeven, of North Dakota.

Departments of Labor, Health and Human Services, and Education, and Related Agencies

Tom Harkin, of Iowa, *Chair*

Daniel K. Inouye, of Hawaii.
Herb Kohl, of Wisconsin.
Patty Murray, of Washington.
Mary L. Landrieu, of Louisiana.
Richard J. Durbin, of Illinois.
Jack Reed, of Rhode Island.
Mark L. Pryor, of Arkansas.
Barbara A. Mikulski, of Maryland.
Sherrod Brown, of Ohio.

Richard C. Shelby, of Alabama.
Thad Cochran, of Mississippi.
Kay Bailey Hutchison, of Texas.
Lamar Alexander, of Tennessee.
Ron Johnson, of Wisconsin.
Mark Kirk, of Illinois.
Lindsey Graham, of South Carolina.
Jerry Moran, of Kansas.

Energy and Water Development

Dianne Feinstein, of California, *Chair*

Patty Murray, of Washington.
Tim Johnson, of South Dakota.
Mary L. Landrieu, of Louisiana.
Jack Reed, of Rhode Island.
Frank R. Lautenberg, of New Jersey.
Tom Harkin, of Iowa.
Jon Tester, of Montana.
Richard J. Durbin, of Illinois.

Lamar Alexander, of Tennessee.
Thad Cochran, of Mississippi.
Mitch McConnell, of Kentucky.
Kay Bailey Hutchison, of Texas.
Richard C. Shelby, of Alabama.
Susan M. Collins, of Maine.
Lisa Murkowski, of Alaska.
Lindsey Graham, of South Carolina.

Financial Service and General Government

Richard J. Durbin, of Illinois, *Chair*

Frank R. Lautenberg, of New Jersey.
Ben Nelson, of Nebraska.
Jerry Moran, of Kansas.
Mark Kirk, of Illinois.

Legislative Branch

Ben Nelson, of Nebraska, *Chair*

Jon Tester, of Montana.
Sherrod Brown, of Ohio.
John Hoeven, of North Dakota.
Lindsey Graham, of South Carolina.

Military Construction and Veterans Affairs, and Related Agencies

Tim Johnson, of South Dakota, *Chair*

Daniel K. Inouye, of Hawaii.
Mary L. Landrieu, of Louisiana.
Patty Murray, of Washington.
Jack Reed, of Rhode Island.
Ben Nelson, of Nebraska.
Mark L. Pryor, of Arkansas.
Jon Tester, of Montana.
Mark Kirk, of Illinois.
Kay Bailey Hutchison, of Texas.
Mitch McConnell, of Kentucky.
Lisa Murkowski, of Alaska.
Roy Blunt, of Missouri.
John Hoeven, of North Dakota.
Daniel Coats, of Indiana.

State, Foreign Operations, and Related Programs

Patrick J. Leahy, of Vermont, *Chair*

Daniel K. Inouye, of Hawaii.
Tom Harkin, of Iowa.
Barbara A. Mikulski, of Maryland.
Richard J. Durbin, of Illinois.
Mary L. Landrieu, of Louisiana.
Frank R. Lautenberg, of New Jersey.
Sherrod Brown, of Ohio.
Lindsey Graham, of South Carolina.
Mitch McConnell, of Kentucky.
Mark Kirk, of Illinois.
Roy Blunt, of Missouri.
Daniel Coats, of Indiana.
Ron Johnson, of Wisconsin.
John Hoeven, of North Dakota.

Transportation and Housing and Urban Development, and Related Agencies

Patty Murray, of Washington, *Chair*

Barbara A. Mikulski, of Maryland.
Herb Kohl, of Wisconsin.
Richard J. Durbin, of Illinois.
Patrick J. Leahy, of Vermont.
Tom Harkin, of Iowa.
Dianne Feinstein, of California.
Tim Johnson, of South Dakota.
Frank R. Lautenberg, of New Jersey.
Mark L. Pryor, of Arkansas.
Susan M. Collins, of Maine.
Richard C. Shelby, of Alabama.
Kay Bailey Hutchison, of Texas.
Lamar Alexander, of Tennessee.
Mark Kirk, of Illinois.
Daniel Coats, of Indiana.
Jerry Moran, of Kansas.
Roy Blunt, of Missouri.
Ron Johnson, of Wisconsin.

STAFF

Committee on Appropriations (S–128), 224–7363.
Majority Staff Director.—Charles J. Houy (S–128).
Deputy Staff Director.—Margaret Cummisky (S–128).
Chief Clerk.—Robert W. Putnam (SD–114).
Deputy Chief Clerk.—Bridget Zarate (SD–122).
Communications Director.—Rob Blumenthal (S–128).
Deputy Communications Director.—John Bray (S–128).
Professional Staff: Michael Bain (S–128); John J. Conway (SD–114); Lila Helms (S–128); Fernanda Motta (SD–114).

Assistant to the Chairman.—Ericka Rojas (S–128).
Security Manager.—Hong Nguyen (SD–114).
Minority Staff Director.—Bruce Evans (S–146A), 4–7257.
Communications Director.—Chris Gallegos (SD–113).
Professional Staff.—Katie Batte (S–146A).
Subcommittee on Agriculture, Rural Development, Food and Drug Administration and Related Agencies (SD–129), 4–8090.
Majority Clerk.—Galen Fountain (SD–129).
Professional Staff: Jessica Arden Frederick, Dianne Nellor (SD–129).
Staff Assistant.—Molly Barackman (SD–184).
Minority Clerk.—Stacy McBride (SD–190), 4–5270.
Subcommittee on Commerce, Justice, Science, and Related Agencies (SD–142), 4–5202.
Majority Clerk.—Gabrielle Batkin (SD–142).
Professional Staff: Jessica M. Berry (SD–142); Jean Toal Eisen (SD–142); Jeremy Weirich (SD–142).
Staff Assistant.—Molly O'Rourke (SD–142).
Minority Clerk.—James Christoferson (SH–125), 4–7277.
Professional Staff: Allen Cutler (SH–125); Goodloe Sutton (SH–125).
Staff Assistant.—Courtney Stevens (SH–125).
Subcommittee on Department of Defense (SD–122), 4–6688.
Majority Clerk.—Betsy Schmid (SD–122).
Professional Staff: Nicole Di Resta (SD–122); Kate Fitzpatrick (SD–122); Colleen Gaydos (SD–122); Katy Hagan (SD–122); Kate Kaufer (SD–122), Erik Raven (SD–122); Gary Reese (SD–122); Teri Spoutz (SD–122); Bridget Zarate (SD–122).
Staff Assistant.—Rachel Meyer (SD–122).
Minority Clerk.—Stewart Holmes (SD–117), 4–7255.
Professional Staff: Alycia Farrell (SD–115); Brian Potts (SD–115); Rachelle Schroeder (SD–115).
Subcommittee on Department of Homeland Security (SD–135), 4–8244.
Majority Clerk.—Charles Kieffer (SD–135).
Professional Staff: Drenan A. Dudley (SD–135); Scott Nance (SD–135); Chip Walgren (SD–135).
Staff Assistant.—Michael Bain (SD–142).
Minority Clerk.—Rebecca Davies (SH–125), 4–4319.
Professional Staff.—Carol Cribbs (SH–125).
Staff Assistant.—Courtney Stevens (SH–125).
Subcommittee on Department of the Interior, Environment, and Related Agencies (SD–131), 8–0774.
Majority Clerk.—Peter Keifhaber (SD–131).
Professional Staff: Ryan Hunt (SD–131); Ginny James (SD–131); Rachael Taylor (SD–131).
Staff Assistant.—Teri Curtin (SD–131).
Minority Clerk.—Leif Fonnesbeck (SH–125), 4–7233.
Professional Staff: Rebecca Benn (SH–125); Brent Wiles (SH–125).
Staff Assistant.—Courtney Stevens (SH–125).
Subcommittee on Departments of Labor, Health and Human Services, and Education, and Related Agencies (SD–131), 4–9145.
Majority Clerk.—Erik Fatemi (SD–131).
Professional Staff: Mark Laisch (SD–131); Adrienne Hallett (SD–131); Lisa Bernhardt (SD–131); Michael Gentile (SD–131); Robin Juliana (SD–131).
Staff Assistant.—Teri Curtin (SD–131).
Minority Clerk.—Laura A. Friedel (SD–156), 4–7230.
Professional Staff: Jennifer Castagna (SD–156); Love Rawlings (SD–156).
Staff Assistant.—Jeff Kratz (SD–156).
Subcommittee on Energy and Water, and Development (SD–184), 4–8119.
Majority Clerk.—Doug Clapp (SD–184).
Professional Staff: Roger Cockrell (SD–184); Leland Cogliani (SD–184).
Staff Assistant.—Molly Barackman-Eder (SD–184).
Minority Clerk.—Carolyn E. Apostolou (SD–188), 4–7260.
Professional Staff.—Tom Craig (SD–188); Tyler Owens (SD–188); LaShawnda Smith (SH–125).
Subcommittee on Financial Services and General Government (SD–135), 4–1133.
Majority Clerk.—Marianne Upton (SD–135).
Professional Staff: Diana Gourlay Hamilton (SD–135); Melissa Z. Petersen (SD–135).
Staff Assistant.—Nora Martin (SD–135).
Minority Clerk.—Ellen Beares (SH–125), 4–2104.
Professional Staff.—Rachel Jones (SD–125); LaShawnda Smith (SH–125).

Subcommittee on Legislative Branch (S–128) 4–7271.
Majority Clerk.—Lila Helms (S–128).
Staff Assistant.—Maria Veklich (SD–134).
Minority Clerk.—Rachelle Schroeder (S–146A), 4–9747.
Staff Assistant.—Katie Batte (S–146A).
Subcommittee on Military Construction and Veterans Affairs, and Related Agencies (SD–125), 4–8224.
Majority Clerk.—Christina Evans (SD–125).
Professional Staff: Chad Schulken (SD–125); Andrew Vanlandingham (SD–125).
Staff Assistant.—Rachel Meyer (SD–122).
Minority Clerk.—Dennis Balkham (SH–125), 4–5245.
Professional Staff.—D'Ann Lettieri (SH–125).
Staff Assistant.—Courtney Stevens (SH–125).
Subcommittee on State, Foreign Operations, and Related Programs (SD–127), 4–7284.
Majority Clerk.—Tim Rieser (SD–127).
Professional Staff: Nikole Manatt (SD–127); Janet Stormes (SD–127).
Staff Assistant.—Maria Veklich (SD–134).
Minority Clerk.—Paul Grove (SH–125), 4–2104.
Professional Staff.—LaShawnda Smith (SH–125); Michele Wymer (SH–125).
Subcommittee on Transportation and Housing and Urban Development, and Related Agencies (SD–142), 4–7281.
Majority Clerk.—Alex Keenan (SD–142).
Professional Staff: Dabney Hegg (SD–142); Meaghan L. McCarthy (SD–142); Rachel Milberg (SD–142).
Staff Assistant.—Molly O'Rourke (SD–142).
Minority Clerk.—Heideh Shahmoradi (SD–128), 4–5310.
Professional Staff: Carl Barrick (SD–128); Brooke Hayes Stringer (SD–128).
Editorial and Printing (SD–126): Richard L. Larson, 4–7265; Mark Moore (GPO), 4–7266; Reginald Stewart (GPO), 4–7267; Celina Inman (GPO), 4–7217.
Clerical Assistant.—George Castro (SD–120), 4–5433; Chris Watkins (SD–120), 4–9259.

Armed Services

228 Russell Senate Office Building 20510–6050

phone 224–3871, http://www.senate.gov/~armed_services

meets every Tuesday and Thursday

Carl Levin, of Michigan, *Chair*

JOSEPH I. LIEBERMAN, of Connecticut.
Jack Reed, of Rhode Island.
Daniel K. Akaka, of Hawaii.
Ben Nelson, of Nebraska.
Jim Webb, of Virginia.
Claire McCaskill, of Missouri.
Mark Udall, of Colorado.
Kay R. Hagan, of North Carolina.
Mark Begich, of Alaska.
Joe Manchin III, of West Virginia.
Jeanne Shaheen, of New Hampshire.
Kirsten E. Gillibrand, of New York.
Richard Blumenthal, of Connecticut.

John McCain, of Arizona.
James M. Inhofe, of Oklahoma.
Jeff Sessions, of Alabama.
Saxby Chambliss, of Georgia.
Roger F. Wicker, of Mississippi.
Scott P. Brown, of Massachusetts.
Rob Portman, of Ohio.
Kelly Ayotte, of New Hampshire.
Susan M. Collins, of Maine.
Lindsey Graham, of South Carolina.
John Cornyn, of Texas.
David Vitter, of Louisiana.

SUBCOMMITTEES

[The chairman and the ranking minority member are ex officio (non-voting) members of all subcommittees on which they do not serve.]

Airland

JOSEPH I. LIEBERMAN, of Connecticut, *Chair*

Ben Nelson, of Nebraska.
Claire McCaskill, of Missouri.
Joe Manchin III, of West Virginia.
Kirsten E. Gillibrand, of New York.
Richard Blumenthal, of Connecticut.

Scott P. Brown, of Massachusetts.
James M. Inhofe, of Oklahoma.
Jeff Sessions, of Alabama.
Roger F. Wicker, of Mississippi.
David Vitter, of Louisiana.

Emerging Threats and Capabilities

Kay R. Hagan, of North Carolina, *Chair*

Jack Reed, of Rhode Island.
Mark Udall, of Colorado.
Joe Manchin III, of West Virginia.
Jeanne Shaheen, of New Hampshire.
Kirsten E. Gillibrand, of New York.

Rob Portman, of Ohio.
Saxby Chambliss, of Georgia.
Scott P. Brown, of Massachusetts.
Lindsey Graham, of South Carolina.
John Cornyn, of Texas.

Personnel

Jim Webb, of Virginia, *Chair*

JOSEPH I. LIEBERMAN, of Connecticut.
Daniel K. Akaka, of Hawaii.
Claire McCaskill, of Missouri.
Kay R. Hagan, of North Carolina.
Mark Begich, of Alaska.
Richard Blumenthal, of Connecticut.

Lindsey Graham, of South Carolina.
Saxby Chambliss, of Georgia.
Scott P. Brown, of Massachusetts.
Kelly Ayotte, of New Hampshire.
Susan M. Collins, of Maine.
David Vitter, of Louisiana.

Readiness and Management Support

Claire McCaskill, of Missouri, *Chair*

Daniel K. Akaka, of Hawaii.
Ben Nelson, of Nebraska.
Jim Webb, of Virginia.
Mark Udall, of Colorado.
Mark Begich, of Alaska.
Joe Manchin III, of West Virginia.
Jeanne Shaheen, of New Hampshire.

Kelly Ayotte, of New Hampshire.
James M. Inhofe, of Oklahoma.
Saxby Chambliss, of Georgia.
Rob Portman, of Ohio.
Susan M. Collins, of Maine.
Lindsey Graham, of South Carolina.
John Cornyn, of Texas.

Seapower

Jack Reed, of Rhode Island, *Chair*

Daniel K. Akaka, of Hawaii.
Jim Webb, of Virginia.
Kay R. Hagan, of North Carolina.
Richard Blumenthal, of Connecticut.

Roger F. Wicker, of Mississippi.
Jeff Sessions, of Alabama.
Kelly Ayotte, of New Hampshire.
Susan M. Collins, of Maine.

Strategic Forces

Ben Nelson, of Nebraska, *Chair*

JOSEPH I. LIEBERMAN, of Connecticut.
Jack Reed, of Rhode Island.
Mark Udall, of Colorado.
Mark Begich, of Alaska.
Jeanne Shaheen, of New Hampshire.
Kirsten E. Gillibrand, of New York.

Jeff Sessions, of Alabama.
James M. Inhofe, of Oklahoma.
Roger F. Wicker, of Mississippi.
Rob Portman, of Ohio.
John Cornyn, of Texas.
David Vitter, of Louisiana.

STAFF

Committee on Armed Services (SR–228), 224–3871.
Majority Staff Director.—Richard D. DeBobes.
Chief Clerk.—Christine E. Cowart.
General Counsel.—Peter K. Levine.
Counsels: Johnathan D. Clark, Ilona R. Cohen, Madelyn R. Creedon, Gabriella E. Fahrer, Gerald J. Leeling, Jason W. Maroney, William G.P. Monahan, Russell L. Shaffer.
Professional Staff Members: Joseph M. Bryan, Richard W. Fieldhouse, Creighton Greene, Michael J. Kuiken, Thomas K. McConnell, Michael J. Noblet, John H. Quirk V, Roy F. Phillips, William K. Sutey, Robie I. Samanta Roy.
Research Assistant.—Jessica L. Kingston.
Assistant Chief Clerk and Security Manager.—Cindy Pearson.
Nominations and Hearings Clerk.—Leah C. Brewer.
Systems Administrator.—Gary J. Howard.
Printing and Documents Clerk.—June M. Borawski.
Security Clerk.—Jennifer L. Stoker.
Legislative Clerk.—Mary J. Kyle.
Special Assistant.—Travis E. Smith.
Staff Assistants.—Jennifer R. Knowles, Kathleen A. Kulenkampff, Christine G. Lang, Hannah I. Lloyd, Brian F. Sebold, Bradley S. Watson, Breon N. Wells.
Minority Staff Director.—David M. Morriss.
Executive Assistant for the Minority.—Greg R. Lilly.
Minority Counsels: Jay Heath, Richard F. Walsh.
Investigative Counsels: Pablo E. Carrillo, Bryan D. Parker.
Professional Staff Members: Adam J. Barker, Christian D. Brose, Daniel A. Lerner, Lucian L. Niemeyer, Christopher J. Paul, Diana G. Tabler.
Research Assistant.—Michael J. Sistak.
Subcommittee on Airland:
Majority Professional Staff Members: William K. Sutey (Lead), Creighton Greene, Michael J. Kuiken.
Minority Professional Staff Members: Christopher J. Paul (Lead), Pablo E. Carrillo.

Staff Assistants: David M. Morriss, Brian F. Sebold.

Subcommittee on Emerging Threats and Capabilities:

Majority Professional Staff Members: Richard W. Fieldhouse (Lead), Madelyn R. Creedon, Michael J. Noblet, Russell L. Shaffer, Michael J. Kuiken, William G.P. Monahan, Robie I. Samanta Roy.

Minority Professional staff Members: Jay Heath (Lead), Adam J. Barker, Christian D. Brose, Michael J. Sistak.

Staff Assistant.—Kathleen A. Kulenkampff.

Subcommittee on Personnel:

Majority Professional Staff Members: Gerald J. Leeling (Lead), Jonathan D. Clark, Gabriella E. Fahrer.

Minority Professional Staff Members: Diana G. Tabler (Co-lead), Richard F. Walsh (Co-lead).

Staff Assistant.—Jennifer R. Knowles.

Subcommittee on Readiness and Management Support:

Majority Professional Staff Members: Peter K. Levine (Lead), Jason W. Maroney, John H. Quirk V, Russell L. Shatfer.

Minority Professional Staff Members: Lucian L. Niemeyer (Lead), Adam J. Barker, Pablo E. Carrillo, David M. Morriss, Christopher J. Paul.

Staff Assistant.—Breon N. Wells.

Subcommittee on Seapower:

Majority Professional Staff Members: Creighton Greene (Lead), Jason W. Maroney, Thomas K. McConnell.

Minority Professional Staff Members: Christopher J. Paul (Lead), Pablo E. Carrillo, David M. Morriss.

Staff Assistant.—Brian F. Sebold.

Subcommittee on Strategic Forces:

Majority Professional Staff Members: Madelyn R. Creedon (Lead), Richard W. Fieldhouse, Creighton Greene, Thomas K. McConnell.

Minority Professional Staff Members: Daniel A. Lerner (Lead), Christian D. Brose, Jay Heath, Christopher J. Paul.

Staff Assistant.—Hannah I. Lloyd.

Majority Professional Staff Members for:

Acquisition Policy.—Peter K. Levine.

Acquisition Workforce.—Peter K. Levine.

Ammunition.—John H. Quirk V.

Arms Control / Non-proliferation: Richard W. Fieldhouse, Madelyn R. Creedon.

Aviation Systems: Madelyn R. Creedon, Creighton Greene.

Base Realignment and Closure (BRAC).—Jason W. Maroney.

Budget and Reprogramming.—Roy F. Phillips.

Buy America.—Peter K. Levine.

Chemical-Biological Defense.—Richard W. Fieldhouse.

Chemical Demilitarization.—Richard W. Fieldhouse.

Civilian Nominations.—Peter K. Levine .

Civilian Personnel Policy: Gabriella E. Fahrer, Gerald J. Leeling, Peter K. Levine.

Combatant Commands.—

AFRICOM.—Michael J. Kuiken.

CENTCOM: William G.P. Monahan, Michael J. Kuiken, William K. Sutey.

EUCOM.—William G.P. Monahan.

NORTHCOM.—Richard W. Fieldhouse.

PACOM.—Russell L. Shaffer.

SOCOM.—Michael J. Noblet.

SOUTHCOM.—Michael J. Kuiken.

STRATCOM.—Madelyn R. Creedon.

TRANSCOM.—Creighton Greene.

Combating Terrorism: Michael J. Kuiken, Thomas K. McConnell, William G.P. Monahan, Michael J. Noblet, Russell L. Shaffer.

Competition Policy / Mergers and Acquisitions.—Peter K. Levine.

Competitive Sourcing / A–76.—Peter K. Levine.

Contracting (including service contracts).—Peter K. Levine.

Construction, Housing, Global Basing, and Land Use.—Jason W. Maroney.

Cooperative Threat Reduction Programs.—Madelyn R. Creedon.

Counterdrug Programs.—Michael J. Kuiken.

Cybersecurity / Information Assurance: Creighton Greene, Thomas K. McConnell.

Defense Energy Use / Alternative Energy Issues: John H. Quirk V, Robie I. Samanta Roy.

DefenseLaboratory Management: Peter K. Levine, Robie I. Samanta Roy.

Defense Security Assistance: Michael J. Kuiken, William G.P. Monahan, Russell L. Shatter.
Department of Defense Schools: Gabriella E. Fahrer, Gerald J. Leeling.
Department of Energy Issues.—Madelyn R. Creedon.
Depot Maintenance.—John H. Quirk V.
Detainee Policy: Peter K. Levine, William G.P. Monahan.
Domestic Preparedness.—Richard W. Fieldhouse.
Environmental Issues.—Russell L. Shaffer.
Export Controls.—Peter K. Levine.
Financial Management.—Peter K. Levine.
Force Readiness/Training.—John H. Quirk V.
Foreign Language Policy.—Creighton Greene.
Foreign Policy/Geographical Region.—
Afghanistan/Pakistan/Central Asia.—William G.P. Monahan.
Africa.—Michael J. Kuiken.
Asia/Pacific.—Russell L. Shaffer.
Europe/Russia.—Madelyn R. Creedon, William G.P. Monahan.
Iraq.—William K. Sutey.
Middle East.—Michael J. Kuiken.
South and Central Americas.—Michael J. Kuiken.
Ground Systems.—
Army: William K. Sutey, Michael J. Kuiken.
Marine Corps.—Thomas K. McConnell .
Homeland Defense/Security: Richard W. Fieldhouse, Gerald J. Leeling.
Humanitarian, Disaster, and Civic Assistance: Michael J. Kuiken, William G.P. Monahan.
Information Management: Creighton Greene, Peter K. Levine.
Information Operations/Strategic Communications.—Michael J. Kuiken.
Information Technology Systems.—
(IT Acquisition Policy): Peter K. Levine, Jason W. Maroney.
(Business Systems): Michael J. Kuiken, Jason W. Maroney.
(Tactical Systems).—Creighton Greene.
Intelligence Issues: Creighton Green, Thomas K. McConnell.
Interagency Reform: Michael J. Kuiken, Thomas K. McConnell, William G.P. Monahan.
Imernational Defense Cooperation: Michael J. Kuiken, William G.P. Monahan.
Inventory Management: Peter K. Levine, John H. Quirk V.
Investigations: Joseph M. Bryan, Ilona R. Cohen.
Military Personnel Issues: Jonathan D. Clark, Gabriella E. Fahrer, Gerald J. Leeling.
End Strength: Jonathan D. Clark, Gerald J. Leeling.
Military Family Policy: Gabriella E. Fahrer, Gerald J. Leeling.
Health Care: Gabriella E. Fahrer, Gerald J. Leeling.
Homosexual Conduct Policy: Jonathan D. Clark, Gerald J. Leeling.
Military Justice: Gerald J. Leeling, Peter K. Levine, Russell L. Shaffer.
Military Nominations.—Gerald J. Leeling .
POW/MIA Issues.—Johnathan D. Clark.
Pay and Benefits: Jonathan D. Clark, Gerald J. Leeling.
Military Personnel Policy: Jonathan D. Clark, Gerald J. Leeling.
National Guard and Reserves: Jonathan D. Clark, Gerald J. Leeling.
Sexual Harassment I Sexual Assault Policy: Gabriella E. Fahrer, Gerald J. Leeling.
Suicide Prevention and Response: Gabriella E. Fahrer, Gerald J. Leeling.
Women in Combat: Jonathan D. Clark, Gerald J. Leeling.
Wounded Warrior Issues: Gabriella E. Fahrer, Gerald J. Leeling.
Military Space.—Madelyn R. Creedon.
Military Strategy.—William K. Sutey.
Missile Defense.—Richard W. Fieldhouse.
Morale, Welfare and Recreation/Commissaries/Exchanges.—Gabriella E. Fahrer.
National Defense Stockpile.—John H. Quirk V.
Nuclear Weapons Stockpile.—Madelyn R. Creedon.
Peacekeeping: Michael J. Kuiken, William G.P. Monahan.
Personnel Protective Items.—John H. Quirk V.
Quadrennial Defense Review (QDR).—William K. Sutey.
Readiness/O&M.—John H. Quirk V.
Reprogramming.—Roy F. Phillips.
Science and Technology.—Robie I. Samanta Roy.
Shipbuilding Programs: Creighton Greene, Jason W. Maroney.
Small Business.—Peter K. Levine.
Special Operations Forces.—Michael J. Noblet.
Stability Operations: Michael J. Kuiken, William G.P. Monahan.

Strategic Programs.—Madelyn R. Creedon.
Test and Evaluation: Peter K. Levine, Robie I. Samanta Roy.
Transportation and Logistics Policy: Creighton Greene, Jason W. Maroney.
Unmanned Aircraft Systems: Creighton Greene, Thomas K. McConnell.
Working Capital Fund.—John H. Quirk V.

Minority Professional Staff Members for—

Acquisition and Contracting Policy.—Pablo E. Carrillo, Christopher J. Paul.
Air Force Programs, Readiness, and Operations and Maintenance: Pablo E. Carrillo, Christopher J. Paul.
Arms Control and Non-proliferation.—Christian D. Brose.
Army Programs, Readiness, and Operations and Maintenance: Adam J. Barker, Jay Heath.
Budget and Reprogramming.—Lucian L. Niemeyer.
Chemical-Biological Defense.—Adam J. Barker.
Chemical-Demilitarization.—Adam J. Barker.
Civilian Personnel.—Diana G. Tabler.
Combatant Commands.—
AFRICOM: Christian D. Brose (Lead), Adam J. Barker.
CENTCOM: Christian D. Brose (Lead), Adam J. Barker.
EUCOM: Christian D. Brose (Lead), Adam J. Barker.
JFCOM: Adam J. Barker (Lead), Christian D. Brose.
NORTHCOM.—Adam J. Barker (Lead).
PACOM: Christian D. Brose (Lead), Adam J. Barker.
SOCOM.—Adam J. Barker (Lead).
SOUTHCOM: Christian D. Brose (Lead), Adam J. Barker.
STRATCOM.—Daniel A. Lerner (Lead).
TRANSCOM.—Christopher J. Paul (Lead).
Counterdrug Programs.—Adam J. Barker.
Defense Security Assistance.—Christian D. Brose.
Depot Maintenance.—Lucian L. Niemeyer.
Detainees and Military Commissions.—David M. Morriss.
Department of Energy National Security Programs.—Daniel A. Lerner.
Environmental Issues.—David M. Morriss.
Export Controls.—Christian D. Brose.
Health Care.—Diana G. Tabler.
Homeland Defense.—Adam J. Barker.
Information Assurance and Cyber Security.—Daniel A. Lerner.
Information Technology.—Daniel A. Lerner.
Intelligence Programs: Christian D. Brose, Jay Heath.
Joint IED Defeat Organization (JIEDDO).—Jay Heath.
Laboratories.—Daniel A. Lerner.
Marine Corps Programs. Readiness, and Operations and Maintenance.—David M. Morriss.
Military Construction and BRAC.—Lucian Niemeyer.
Military Personnel and Family Benefits: Diana G. Tabler, Richard F. Walsh.
Mine Resistant Ambush Protected (MRAP) Vehicles.—Jay Heath.
Missile Defense.—Daniel A. Lerner.
National Military Strategy.—Christian D. Brose.
National Reconnaissance Office: Jay Heath, Daniel A. Lerner.
Navy Programs, Readiness, and Operations and Maintenance: Pablo E. Carrillo, Christopher J. Paul.
Nominations.—Richard F. Walsh.
Oversight Investigations: Bryan D. Parker (Lead), Pablo E. Carrillo, Christopher J. Paul.
Science and Technology.—Daniel A. Lerner.
Space Programs.—Daniel A. Lerner.
Special Operations Forces.—Adam J. Barker.
Test and Evaluation.—Jay Heath.

Banking, Housing, and Urban Affairs

534 Dirksen Senate Office Building 20510

phone 224–7391, http://banking.senate.gov

Tim Johnson, of South Dakota, *Chair*

Jack Reed, of Rhode Island.
Charles E. Schumer, of New York.
Robert Menendez, of New Jersey.
Daniel K. Akaka, of Hawaii.
Sherrod Brown, of Ohio.
Jon Tester, of Montana.
Herb Kohl, of Wisconsin.
Mark R. Warner, of Virginia.
Jeff Merkley, of Oregon.
Michael F. Bennet, of Colorado.
Kay R. Hagan, of North Carolina.

Richard C. Shelby, of Alabama.
Mike Crapo, of Idaho.
Bob Corker, of Tennessee.
Jim DeMint, of South Carolina.
David Vitter, of Louisiana.
Mike Johanns, of Nebraska.
Patrick J. Toomey, of Pennsylvania.
Mark Kirk, of Illinois.
Jerry Moran, of Kansas.
Roger F. Wicker, of Mississippi.

SUBCOMMITTEES

[The chairman and ranking minority member are ex officio members of all subcommittees.]

Economic Policy

Jon Tester, of Montana, *Chair*

Mark R. Warner, of Virginia.
Kay R. Hagan, of North Carolina.
Tim Johnson, of South Dakota.

David Vitter, of Louisiana.
Roger F. Wicker, of Mississippi.
Mike Johanns, of Nebraska.

Financial Institutions and Consumer Protection

Sherrod Brown, of Ohio, *Chair*

Jack Reed, of Rhode Island.
Charles E. Schumer, of New York.
Robert Menendez, of New Jersey.
Daniel K. Akaka, of Hawaii.
Jon Tester, of Montana.
Herb Kohl, of Wisconsin.
Jeff Merkley, of Oregon.
Kay R. Hagan, of North Carolina.

Bob Corker, of Tennessee.
Jerry Moran, of Kansas.
Mike Crapo, of Idaho.
Mike Johanns, of Nebraska.
Patrick J. Toomey, of Pennsylvania.
Jim DeMint, of South Carolina.
David Vitter, of Louisiana.

Housing, Transportation, and Community Development

Robert Menendez, of New Jersey, *Chair*

Jack Reed, of Rhode Island.
Charles E. Schumer, of New York.
Daniel K. Akaka, of Hawaii.
Sherrod Brown, of Ohio.
Jon Tester, of Montana.
Herb Kohl, of Wisconsin.
Jeff Merkley, of Oregon.
Michael F. Bennet, of Colorado.

Jim DeMint, of South Carolina.
Mike Crapo, of Idaho.
Bob Corker, of Tennessee.
Patrick J. Toomey, of Pennsylvania.
Mark Kirk, of Illinois.
Jerry Moran, of Kansas.
Roger F. Wicker, of Mississippi.

Securities, Insurance, and Investment

Jack Reed, of Rhode Island, *Chair*

Charles E. Schumer, of New York.
Robert Menendez, of New Jersey.
Daniel K. Akaka, of Hawaii.
Herb Kohl, of Wisconsin.
Mark R. Warner, of Virginia.
Jeff Merkley, of Oregon.
Michael F. Bennet, of Colorado.
Kay R. Hagan, of North Carolina.
Tim Johnson, of South Dakota.

Mike Crapo, of Idaho.
Patrick J. Toomey, of Pennsylvania.
Mark Kirk, of Illinois.
Bob Corker, of Tennessee.
Jim DeMint, of South Carolina.
David Vitter, of Louisiana.
Jerry Moran, of Kansas.
Roger F. Wicker, of Mississippi.

Security and International Trade and Finance

Mark R. Warner, of Virginia, *Chair*

Sherrod Brown, of Ohio.
Michael F. Bennet, of Colorado.
Tim Johnson, of South Dakota.

Mike Johanns, of Nebraska.
Mark Kirk, of Illinois.

STAFF

Committee on Banking, Housing, and Urban Affairs (SD–534), 224–7391, fax 224–5137.
Majority Staff Director.—Dwight Fettig.
Deputy Staff Director and Chief Counsel.—Charles Yi.
Senior Policy Advisor.—Glen Sears.
Senior Counsels: Catherine Galicia, Colin McGinnis, Lynsey Graham Rea, Dean V. Shahinian, Jeff Siegel.
Professional Staff Members: Erin Barry, Homer Carlisle, Beth Cooper.
Policy Director.—Laura Swanson.
Communications Director.—Sean Oblack.
Press Secretary.—Sam Gilford.
Chief Economist.—Marc Jarsulic.
Legislative Assistants: Levon Bagramian, Drew Colbert, William Fields, Brian Filipowich, Lisa Frumin.
Research Director.—Peter Bondi.
Staff Assistant.—Brett Hewitt.
Counsel.—Patrick Grant.
Minority Staff Director and Counsel.—Bill Duhnke.
Deputy Staff Director and Chief Counsel.—Andrew Olmem.
Senior Counsel.—Hester Peirce.
Counsels: John O'Hara, Beth Zorc.
Professional Staff Members: Chad Davis, Shannon Hines.
Communications Director.—Jonathan Graffeo.
Chief Economist.—Mike Piwowar.
Legislative Assistant.—Emily Pereira.
Non-Designated Staff:
Chief Clerk.—Dawn Ratliff.
Archivist.—Anu Kasarabada.
IT Director.—Shelvin Simmons.
Editor.—Jim Crowell.
GPO Detailees: Sheryl Arrington, Jason Parker.
Staff Assistant.—Pamela Streeter.
Subcommittee on Economic Policy (SD–534), 224–7391, fax 224–5137.
Majority Staff Director.—Allison O'Donnell (SD–534), 224–2744.
Minority Staff Director.—Travis Johnson (SD–534), 224–4623.
Subcommittee on Financial Institutions and Consumer Protection (SD–534), 224–7391, fax 224–5137.
Majority Staff Director.—Graham Steele (SD–534), 224–2315.
Minority Staff Director.—Michael Bright (SD–534), 224–3344.
Subcommittee on Housing, Transportation, and Community Development (SD–534), 224–7391; fax 224–5137.
Majority Staff Director.—Michael Passante (SD–534), 224–4744.
Minority Staff Director.—Jeff Murray (SD–534), 224–4623.
Subcommittee on Securities, Insurance, and Investment (SD–534), 224–7391; fax 224–5137.

Majority Staff Director.—Kara Stein (SD–534), 224–4642.
Minority Staff Director.—Gregg Richard (SD–534), 224–6142.

Subcommittee on Security and International Trade and Finance (SD–534), 224–7391; fax 224–5137.

Majority Staff Director.—Nathan Steinwald (SD–534), 224–2023.
Minority Staff Director.—Sarah Novascone (SD–534), 224–4224.

Budget

624 Dirksen Senate Office Building 20510–6100

phone 224–0642, http://budget.senate.gov

meets first Thursday of each month

Kent Conrad, of North Dakota, *Chair*

Patty Murray, of Washington.
Ron Wyden, of Oregon.
Bill Nelson, of Florida.
Debbie Stabenow, of Michigan.
Benjamin L. Cardin, of Maryland.
BERNARD SANDERS, of Vermont.
Sheldon Whitehouse, of Rhode Island.
Mark R. Warner, of Virginia.
Jeff Merkley, of Oregon.
Mark Begich, of Alaska.
Christopher A. Coons, of Delaware.

Jeff Sessions, of Alabama.
Chuck Grassley, of Iowa.
Michael B. Enzi, of Wyoming.
Mike Crapo, of Idaho.
John Cornyn, of Texas.
Lindsey Graham, of South Carolina.
John Thune, of South Dakota.
Rob Portman, of Ohio.
Patrick J. Toomey, of Pennsylvania.
Ron Johnson, of Wisconsin.
Kelly Ayotte, of New Hampshire.

(No Subcommittees)

STAFF

Committee on Budget (SD–624), 224–0642.
Majority Staff Director.—Mary Naylor.
Deputy Staff Directors: Joel Friedman, John Righter.
Chief Counsel.—Joe Gaeta.
Chief Economist.—Matt Salomon.
Director of Strategic Planning and Outreach.—Adam Hughes.
Senior Policy Adviser.—Jim Miller.
Senior Analyst for Revenues.—Steve Bailey.
Senior Analyst and Director of Appropriations.—Mike Jones.
Senior Analyst for Social Security and Medicare.—Sarah Kuehl.
Budget Analyst for Income Security, Discretionary and Health.—Jennifer Hanson-Kilbride.
Budget Analyst for Education and Appropriations.—Robyn Hiestand.
Budget Analyst for Transportation and Community Development.—Matthew Mohning.
Budget Analyst.—Miles Patrie.
Analyst for International Affairs and National Security.—Russell Rumbaugh.
Analyst for Energy and Environment.—Michael Obeiter.
Communications Director.—Stu Nagurka.
Deputy Communications Director.—Steve Posner.
Associate Economist.—Jean Biniek.
Performance Budget Specialist.—Amy Edwards.
Graphics Production Coordinator.—Kobye Noel.
Executive Assistant.—Anne Page.
Staff Assistants: Josh Ryan, Ben Soskin, Ronald Storhaug.
Detailees: Emily Ealman, Matt Levy.
Minority Staff Director.—Marcus Peacock.
Chief Counsel.—William Smith.
Deputy Press Secretary.—Andrew Logan.
Press Assistant.—Katie Moses.
Director of Communications.—Stephen Miller.
Communication Advisor.—Garrett Murch.
Director of Revenues.—Daniel Brandt.
Director of Budget Enforcement.—Tori Gorman.
Director for Federal Programs and Budget Process.—Jim Hearn.
Senior Advisor.—Cheri Reidy.
Senior Analyst for Special Projects.—Dan Kowalski.
Budget Analyst for Science and Technology.—Greg McNeill.
Budget Review Analyst.—Gene Emmans.
Executive Assistant.—Kimberly Proctor.
Legislative Correspondent.—Paige Hallen

Professional Staff Members: Gregory D'Angelo, George Everly, Matt Giroux, Jason Knox, Mike Lofgren, Patrick Mullane, Dave Myers.

Staff Non-Designated:

Archivist.—Cathey Dugan.

Publications.—Letitia Fletcher.

Chief Clerk.—Lynne Seymour.

Computer Systems Administrator.—George Woodall.

Staff Assistants: Kathleen Llewellyn-Butts, Dylan Morris.

Commerce, Science, and Transportation

254 Russell Senate Office Building 20510–6125
phone 224–0411, TTY / TDD 224–8418 http://commerce.senate.gov

meets first and third Tuesdays of each month

John D. Rockefeller IV, of West Virginia, *Chair*

Daniel K. Inouye, of Hawaii.
John F. Kerry, of Massachusetts.
Barbara Boxer, of California.
Bill Nelson, of Florida.
Maria Cantwell, of Washington.
Frank R. Lautenberg, of New Jersey.
Mark L. Pryor, of Arkansas.
Claire McCaskill, of Missouri.
Amy Klobuchar, of Minnesota.
Tom Udall, of New Mexico.
Mark R. Warner, of Virginia.
Mark Begich, of Alaska.

Kay Bailey Hutchison, of Texas.
Olympia J. Snowe, of Maine.
Jim DeMint, of South Carolina.
John Thune, of South Dakota.
Roger F. Wicker, of Mississippi.
Johnny Isakson, of Georgia.
Roy Blunt, of Missouri.
John Boozman, of Arkansas.
Patrick J. Toomey, of Pennsylvania.
Marco Rubio, of Florida.
Kelly Ayotte, of New Hampshire.
Dean Heller, of Nevada.

SUBCOMMITTEES

[The chair and the vice chair are ex officio members of all subcommittees.]

Aviation Operations, Safety, and Security

Maria Cantwell, of Washington, *Chair*

Daniel K. Inouye, of Hawaii.
Barbara Boxer, of California.
Bill Nelson, of Florida.
Frank R. Lautenberg, of New Jersey.
Amy Klobuchar, of Minnesota.
Tom Udall, of New Mexico.
Mark R. Warner, of Virginia.
Mark Begich, of Alaska.

John Thune, of South Dakota.
Jim DeMint, of South Carolina.
Roger F. Wicker, of Mississippi.
Johnny Isakson, of Georgia.
Roy Blunt, of Missouri.
John Boozman, of Arkansas.
Patrick J. Toomey, of Pennsylvania.
Dean Heller, of Nevada.

Communications and Technology, and the Internet

John F. Kerry, of Massachusetts, *Chair*

Daniel K. Inouye, of Hawaii.
Barbara Boxer, of California.
Bill Nelson, of Florida.
Maria Cantwell, of Washington.
Frank R. Lautenberg, of New Jersey.
Mark L. Pryor, of Arkansas.
Claire McCaskill, of Missouri.
Amy Klobuchar, of Minnesota.
Tom Udall, of New Mexico.
Mark R. Warner, of Virginia.
Mark Begich, of Alaska.

Jim DeMint, of South Carolina.
Olympia J. Snowe, of Maine.
John Thune, of South Dakota.
Roger F. Wicker, of Mississippi.
Johnny Isakson, of Georgia.
Roy Blunt, of Missouri.
John Boozman, of Arkansas.
Patrick J. Toomey, of Pennsylvania.
Marco Rubio, of Florida.
Kelly Ayotte, of New Hampshire.
Dean Heller, of Nevada.

Competitiveness, Innovation, and Export Promotion

Amy Klobuchar, of Minnesota, *Chair*

John F. Kerry, of Massachusetts.
Maria Cantwell, of Washington.
Mark L. Pryor, of Arkansas.
Tom Udall, of New Mexico.
Mark R. Warner, of Virginia.
Mark Begich, of Alaska.

Roy Blunt, of Missouri.
Jim DeMint, of South Carolina.
John Thune, of South Dakota.
John Boozman, of Arkansas.
Kelly Ayotte, of New Hampshire.
Dean Heller, of Nevada.

Consumer Protection, Product Safety, and Insurance

Mark L. Pryor, of Arkansas, *Chair*

John F. Kerry, of Massachusetts.
Barbara Boxer, of California.
Claire McCaskill, of Missouri.
Amy Klobuchar, of Minnesota.
Tom Udall, of New Mexico.

Patrick J. Toomey, of Pennsylvania.
John Thune, of South Dakota.
John Boozman, of Arkansas.
Roger F. Wicker, of Mississippi.
Dean Heller, of Nevada.

Oceans, Atmosphere, Fisheries, and Coast Guard

Mark Begich, of Alaska, *Chair*

Daniel K. Inouye, of Hawaii.
John F. Kerry, of Massachusetts.
Bill Nelson, of Florida.
Maria Cantwell, of Washington.
Frank R. Lautenberg, of New Jersey.
Amy Klobuchar, of Minnesota.
Mark R. Warner, of Virginia.

Olympia J. Snowe, of Maine.
Roger F. Wicker, of Mississippi.
Johnny Isakson, of Georgia.
John Boozman, of Arkansas.
Marco Rubio, of Florida.
Kelly Ayotte, of New Hampshire.
Dean Heller, of Nevada.

Science and Space

Bill Nelson, of Florida, *Chair*

Daniel K. Inouye, of Hawaii.
John F. Kerry, of Massachusetts.
Maria Cantwell, of Washington.
Mark L. Pryor, of Arkansas.
Mark R. Warner, of Virginia.

John Boozman, of Arkansas.
Roger F. Wicker, of Mississippi.
Marco Rubio, of Florida.
Kelly Ayotte, of New Hampshire.
Dean Heller, of Nevada.

Surface Transportation and Merchant Marine Infrastructure, Safety, and Security

Frank R. Lautenberg, of New Jersey, *Chair*

Daniel K. Inouye, of Hawaii.
John F. Kerry, of Massachusetts.
Barbara Boxer, of California.
Maria Cantwell, of Washington.
Mark L. Pryor, of Arkansas.
Claire McCaskill, of Missouri.
Amy Klobuchar, of Minnesota.
Tom Udall, of New Mexico.
Mark R. Warner, of Virginia.
Mark Begich, of Alaska.

Roger F. Wicker, of Mississippi.
Jim DeMint, of South Carolina.
John Thune, of South Dakota.
Johnny Isakson, of Georgia.
Roy Blunt, of Missouri.
John Boozman, of Arkansas.
Patrick J. Toomey, of Pennsylvania.
Marco Rubio, of Florida.
Kelly Ayotte, of New Hampshire.
Dean Heller, of Nevada.

STAFF

Committee on Commerce, Science, and Transportation (SR–254), 224–0411.
Majority Staff Director.—Ellen Doneski.
Deputy Staff Director.—James Reid.
General Counsel.—Bruce Andrews.
Senior Climate Advisor.—Tom Dower.
Communications Director.—Vincent Morris.
Deputy Communications Director.—Jena Longo.
Press Assistant.—Charles Stewart.
Director of Operations, Special Assistant.—Vanessa Jones.
Staff Assistants: Andrew Clough, Tyler Roth.
Oversight and Investigations Office:
Chief Investigator.—John Williams.
Counsel.—Erik Jones.
Professional Staff.—Jeff Zubricki.
Research Assistant.—Melanie Tiano.
FTC Detailee.—Jim Trilling.
Minority Staff Director.—Todd Bertoson.

Deputy Minority Staff Director.—Jarrod Thompson.
Minority General Counsel/Chief Investigator.—Rebecca Seidel.
Communications Director.—Rebecca Fisher.
Executive Assistant.—Theresa Eugene.
Senior Counsel.—Chris Herndon.
Professional Staff.—Becky Hooks.

Aviation Operations, Safety, and Security Staff
Majority Senior Professional Staff.—Gael Sullivan.
Professional Staff Member.—Rich Swayze.
Staff Assistant.—Adam Duffy.
Minority Senior Professional Staff.—Dan Neumann.

Communications and Technology, and the Internet Staff
Majority Senior Counsel.—Jessica Rosenworcel.
Counsel.—John Branscome.
Staff Assistant.—Dylan Merrill.
Detailee.—David Goldman.
Professional Staff Member.—David Quinalty.

Competitiveness, Innovation, and Export Promotion Staff
Counsel.—Christian Fjeld.
Professional Staff.—Anna Laitin.
Staff Assistants: Jared Bomberg, Natasha Mbabazi.
Minority Professional Staff.—Jack Smedile.

Consumer Protection, Product Safety, and Insurance Staff
Counsel.—Christian Fjeld.
Professional Staff.—Anna Laitin.
Staff Assistants: Jared Bomberg, Natasha Mbabazi.
Minority Professional Staff: Will Carty, Galen Roehl.

Oceans, Atmosphere, Fisheries, and Coast Guard Staff
Majority Professional Staff.—Catherine Hazlewood.
Counsel.—Jeff Lewis.
Staff Assistant.—Sean Houton.
Coast Guard Detailee.—Tim Barelli.
Sea Grant Fellow.—Katie Cramer.
Minority Professional Staff.—Kelly Pennington.
Staff Assistant.—Sara Gibson.
Coast Guard Fellow.—Paul Mehler.
Sea Grant Fellow.—Andy Coleman.

Science and Space Staff
Majority Professional Staff: Jake Olcott, Ann Zulkosky.
Staff Assistant.—Andrew Ruffin.
Minority Senior Advisor.—Jeff Bingham.
Professional Staff.—Maryam Khan.
NASA Detailee.—Trent Smith.

Surface Transportation and Merchant Marine Infrastructure, Safety, and Security Staff
Majority Professional Staff: John Drake, Dan Easley.
Counsels: Ian Jefferies, Melissa Porter.
Staff Assistant.—Taylor Woods.
Minority Professional Staff: Mike Meenan.
Staff Assistant.—Dan Neumann.

Bipartisan Staff:
Chief Clerk.—Anne Willis Hill.
Hearing Clerk.—Collenne Wider.
Director, Information Technology.—Jonathan Bowen.
Editor.—Rebecca Kojm.
GPO Detailee.—Jacqueline Washington.

Bipartisan Staff, Legislative Counsel's Office:
Legislative Counsel.—Jennifer Dorrer.
Staff Assistants: Caitlin Irwin, Stephanie Lieu.

Energy and Natural Resources

304 Dirksen Senate Office Building 20510

phone 224–4971, fax 224–6163, http://energy.senate.gov

meets upon call of the chair

Jeff Bingaman, of New Mexico, *Chair*

Ron Wyden, of Oregon.
Tim Johnson, of South Dakota.
Mary L. Landrieu, of Louisiana.
Maria Cantwell, of Washington.
BERNARD SANDERS, of Vermont.
Debbie Stabenow, of Michigan.
Mark Udall, of Colorado.
Jeanne Shaheen, of New Hampshire.
Al Franken, of Minnesota.
Joe Manchin III, of West Virginia.
Christopher A. Coons, of Delaware.

Lisa Murkowski, of Alaska.
John Barrasso, of Wyoming.
James E. Risch, of Idaho.
Mike Lee, of Utah.
Rand Paul, of Kentucky.
Daniel Coats, of Indiana.
Rob Portman, of Ohio.
John Hoeven, of North Dakota.
Dean Heller, of Nevada.
Bob Corker, of Tennessee.

SUBCOMMITTEES

[The chairman and the ranking minority member are ex officio members of all subcommittees.]

Energy

Maria Cantwell, of Washington, *Chair*

Ron Wyden, of Oregon.
Tim Johnson, of South Dakota.
Mary L. Landrieu, of Louisiana.
BERNARD SANDERS, of Vermont.
Mark Udall, of Colorado.
Jeanne Shaheen, of New Hampshire.
Al Franken, of Minnesota.
Joe Manchin III, of West Virginia.
Christopher A. Coons, of Delaware.

James E. Risch, of Idaho.
John Barrasso, of Wyoming.
Mike Lee, of Utah.
Rand Paul, of Kentucky.
Daniel Coats, of Indiana.
Rob Portman, of Ohio.
John Hoeven, of North Dakota.
Bob Corker, of Tennessee.

National Parks

Mark Udall, of Colorado, *Chair*

Mary L. Landrieu, of Louisiana.
BERNARD SANDERS, of Vermont.
Debbie Stabenow, of Michigan.
Al Franken, of Minnesota.
Joe Manchin III, of West Virginia.
Christopher A. Coons, of Delaware.

Rand Paul, of Kentucky.
John Barrasso, of Wyoming.
Daniel Coats, of Indiana.
Rob Portman, of Ohio.
Dean Heller, of Nevada.
Bob Corker, of Tennessee.

Public Lands and Forests

Ron Wyden, of Oregon, *Chair*

Tim Johnson, of South Dakota.
Mary L. Landrieu, of Louisiana.
Maria Cantwell, of Washington.
Mark Udall, of Colorado.
Jeanne Shaheen, of New Hampshire.
Al Franken, of Minnesota.
Christopher A. Coons, of Delaware.

John Barrasso, of Wyoming.
James E. Risch, of Idaho.
Mike Lee, of Utah.
Rand Paul, of Kentucky.
Rob Portman, of Ohio.
John Hoeven, of North Dakota.
Dean Heller, of Nevada.

Water and Power

Jeanne Shaheen, of New Hampshire, *Chair*

Ron Wyden, of Oregon.
Tim Johnson, of South Dakota.
Maria Cantwell, of Washington.
BERNARD SANDERS, of Vermont.
Debbie Stabenow, of Michigan.
Joe Manchin III, of West Virginia.
Mike Lee, of Utah.
James E. Risch, of Idaho.
Daniel Coats, of Indiana.
John Hoeven, of North Dakota.
Dean Heller, of Nevada.
Bob Corker, of Tennessee.

STAFF

Committee on Energy and Natural Resources (SD–304), 224–4971, fax 224–6163.
Majority Staff Director.—Bob Simon.
Administrator Director.—Yvonne Costello.
Chief Counsel.—Sam Fowler.
Senior Counsels: Patty Beneke, David Brooks, Deborah Estes, Linda Lance.
Counsels: Michael Carr, Scott Miller.
Chief Clerk.—Mia Bennett.
Executive Assistant.—Allison Seyferth.
Systems Administrator.—Dawson Foard.
Communications Director.—Bill Wicker.
Press Secretary.—Rosemarie Calabro.
Professional Staff: Allyson Anderson, Tara Billingsley, Jonathan Black, Leon Lowery, Kevin Rennert, Al Stayman. Sara Tucker.
Legislative Aide.—Jorge Silva-Banuelos.
Staff Assistants: Abigail Campbell, Meagan Gins, Jake McCook.
Calendar Clerk.—Amanda Kelly.
Printer/Editors: Monica Chestnut, Wanda Green.
Receptionist.—Symone Green.
Minority Staff Director.—McKie Campbell.
Chief Counsel.—Karen Billups.
Deputy Chief Counsel.—Kellie Donnelly.
Counsels: Isaac Edwards, Kaleb Froehlich, Kevin Simpson.
Executive Assistant.—Kristin Collins.
Communications Director.—Robert Dillon.
Press Secretary.—Megan Hermann.
Professional Staff Members: Frank Gladics, Colin Hayes, Josh Johnson, Chuck Kleeschulte.
Legislative Assistant.—Chuck Kleeschulte.

Environment and Public Works

410 Dirksen Senate Office Building 20510–6175
phone 224–8832, www.senate.gov/~epw

meets first and third Thursdays of each month

Barbara Boxer, of California, *Chair*

Max Baucus, of Montana.
Thomas R. Carper, of Delaware.
Frank R. Lautenberg, of New Jersey.
Benjamin L. Cardin, of Maryland.
BERNARD SANDERS, of Vermont.
Sheldon Whitehouse, of Rhode Island.
Tom Udall, of New Mexico.
Jeff Merkley, of Oregon.
Kirsten E. Gillibrand, of New York.

James M. Inhofe, of Oklahoma.
David Vitter, of Louisiana.
John Barrasso, of Wyoming.
Jeff Sessions, of Alabama.
Mike Crapo, of Idaho.
Lamar Alexander, of Tennessee.
Mike Johanns, of Nebraska.
John Boozman, of Arkansas.

SUBCOMMITTEES

[The chairman and the ranking minority member are ex officio (non-voting) members of all subcommittees on which they do not serve.]

Children's Health and Environmental Responsibility

Tom Udall, of New Mexico, *Chair*

Sheldon Whitehouse, of Rhode Island.
Kirsten E. Gillibrand, of New York.

Lamar Alexander, of Tennessee.
David Vitter, of Louisiana.

Clean Air and Nuclear Safety

Thomas R. Carper, of Delaware, *Chair*

Max Baucus, of Montana.
Frank R. Lautenberg, of New Jersey.
Benjamin L. Cardin, of Maryland.
BERNARD SANDERS, of Vermont.
Jeff Merkley, of Oregon.

John Barrasso, of Wyoming.
David Vitter, of Louisiana.
Jeff Sessions, of Alabama.
Lamar Alexander, of Tennessee.
Mike Johanns, of Nebraska.

Green Jobs and the New Economy

BERNARD SANDERS, of Vermont, *Chair*

Thomas R. Carper, of Delaware.
Jeff Merkley, of Oregon.

John Boozman, of Arkansas.
Jeff Sessions, of Alabama.

Oversight

Sheldon Whitehouse, of Rhode Island, *Chair*

Benjamin L. Cardin, of Maryland.
BERNARD SANDERS, of Vermont.

Mike Johanns, of Nebraska.
John Boozman, of Arkansas.

Superfund, Toxics and Environmental Health

Frank R. Lautenberg, of New Jersey, *Chair*

Max Baucus, of Montana.
Thomas R. Carper, of Delaware.
Jeff Merkley, of Oregon.
Kirsten E. Gillibrand, of New York.

Mike Crapo, of Idaho.
Lamar Alexander, of Tennessee.
Mike Johanns, of Nebraska.
John Boozman, of Arkansas.

Transportation and Infrastructure

Max Baucus, of Montana, *Chair*

Thomas R. Carper, of Delaware.
Frank R. Lautenberg, of New Jersey.
Benjamin L. Cardin, of Maryland.
BERNARD SANDERS, of Vermont.
Sheldon Whitehouse, of Rhode Island.
Tom Udall, of New Mexico.
David Vitter, of Louisiana.
John Barrasso, of Wyoming.
Jeff Sessions, of Alabama.
Mike Crapo, of Idaho.
Mike Johanns, of Nebraska.
John Boozman, of Arkansas.

Water and Wildlife

Benjamin L. Cardin, of Maryland, *Chair*

Max Baucus, of Montana.
Frank R. Lautenberg, of New Jersey.
Sheldon Whitehouse, of Rhode Island.
Tom Udall, of New Mexico.
Kirsten E. Gillibrand, of New York.
Jeff Sessions, of Alabama.
John Barrasso, of Wyoming.
David Vitter, of Louisiana.
Mike Crapo, of Idaho.
Lamar Alexander, of Tennessee.

STAFF

Committee on Environment and Public Works (SD–410), phone 224–8832; Majority fax (SD–410), 224–1273; (SH–508), 228–0574.
Majority Staff Director/Chief Counsel.—Bettina Poirier.
Majority Senior Counsels: Grant Cope, Thomas Fox, James Wrathall.
Counsels: Alyson Cooke, Ted Illston, Tyler Rushforth.
Majority Senior Policy Advisors: Jason Albritton, David Napoliello.
Majority Senior Policy Director for Transportation.—Katherine Dedrick.
Office Manager.—Carolyn Mack.
Chief Clerk.—Alicia Gordon.
System Administrator.—Rae Ann Phipps.
Communications Director.—Mary Kerr.
Professional Staff Member.—Andrew Dohrmann.
Editorial Director.—Stephen Chapman.
GPO Detailees: LaVern Finks, Brenda Samuels.
Staff Assistants: Jonathan Aronchick, Javier Gamboa, Kathleen Lee.
Majority Press Assistant.—Nathan McCray.
Majority Special Assistant.—Paul Ordal.
Majority Deputy Communications Director/Press Secretary.—Kate Gilman.
Detailee.—Terrance Horner, Jr.
Majority Senior Investigator.—Robert Tanner.
Research Assistant.—Heather Majors.
Minority fax (SD–456), 224–5167; (SH–415), 228–2322.
Minority Staff Director.—Ruth Van Mark.
Deputy Staff Director.—George David Banks.
Communications Director.—Matt Dempsey.
Investigator.—David Lungren.
Chief Counsel.—George Sugiyama.
Counsels: Jonathan Hackett, Matthew Hite, Dimitri Karakitsos, Kyle Miller.
Senior Economist.—James O'Keeffe.
Senior Policy Advisors: Dan Barron, Todd Johnson.
Professional Staff Members: Murphie Barrett, Annie Caputo, Elizabeth Fox.
Deputy Press Secretary.—Katie Brown.
Research Assistants: Anna Burhop, William Henneberg, Alex Renjel.
Staff Assistant.—Andrew Herther.

Finance

219 Dirksen Senate Office Building 20510

phone 224–4515, fax 224–0554, http://finance.senate.gov

meets second and fourth Tuesdays of each month

Max Baucus, of Montana, *Chair*

John D. Rockefeller IV, of West Virginia.
Kent Conrad, of North Dakota.
Jeff Bingaman, of New Mexico.
John F. Kerry, of Massachusetts.
Ron Wyden, of Oregon.
Charles E. Schumer, of New York.
Debbie Stabenow, of Michigan.
Maria Cantwell, of Washington.
Bill Nelson, of Florida.
Robert Menendez, of New Jersey.
Thomas R. Carper, of Delaware.
Benjamin L. Cardin, of Maryland.

Orrin G. Hatch, of Utah.
Chuck Grassley, of Iowa.
Olympia J. Snowe, of Maine.
Jon Kyl, of Arizona.
Mike Crapo, of Idaho.
Pat Roberts, of Kansas.
Michael B. Enzi, of Wyoming.
John Cornyn, of Texas.
Tom Coburn, of Oklahoma.
John Thune, of South Dakota.
Richard Burr, of North Carolina.

SUBCOMMITTEES

[The chairman and the ranking minority member are ex officio (non-voting) members of all subcommittees on which they do not serve.]

Energy, Natural Resources, and Infrastructure

Jeff Bingaman, of New Mexico, *Chair*

John D. Rockefeller IV, of West Virginia.
Kent Conrad, of North Dakota.
John F. Kerry, of Massachusetts.
Maria Cantwell, of Washington.
Bill Nelson, of Florida.
Thomas R. Carper, of Delaware.

John Cornyn, of Texas.
Chuck Grassley, of Iowa.
Pat Roberts, of Kansas.
Michael B. Enzi, of Wyoming.
John Thune, of South Dakota.
Richard Burr, of North Carolina.

Fiscal Responsibility and Economic Growth

Bill Nelson, of Florida, *Chair*

Max Baucus, of Montana.
Kent Conrad, of North Dakota.
Jeff Bingaman, of New Mexico.

Mike Crapo, of Idaho.
Tom Coburn, of Oklahoma.
Richard Burr, of North Carolina.

Health Care

John D. Rockefeller IV, of West Virginia, *Chair*

Jeff Bingaman, of New Mexico.
John F. Kerry, of Massachusetts.
Ron Wyden, of Oregon.
Debbie Stabenow, of Michigan.
Maria Cantwell, of Washington.
Robert Menendez, of New Jersey.
Thomas R. Carper, of Delaware.
Benjamin L. Cardin, of Maryland.

Chuck Grassley, of Iowa.
Jon Kyl, of Arizona.
Pat Roberts, of Kansas.
Michael B. Enzi, of Wyoming.
John Cornyn, of Texas.
Tom Coburn, of Oklahoma.
Richard Burr, of North Carolina.

International Trade, Customs, and Global Competitiveness

Ron Wyden, of Oregon, *Chair*

John D. Rockefeller IV, of West Virginia.
John F. Kerry, of Massachusetts.
Charles E. Schumer, of New York.
Debbie Stabenow, of Michigan.
Bill Nelson, of Florida.
Robert Menendez, of New Jersey.

John Thune, of South Dakota.
Orrin G. Hatch, of Utah.
Chuck Grassley, of Iowa.
Mike Crapo, of Idaho.
Pat Roberts, of Kansas.

Social Security, Pensions, and Family Policy

Debbie Stabenow, of Michigan, *Chair*

John D. Rockefeller IV, of West Virginia.
Charles E. Schumer, of New York.
Benjamin L. Cardin, of Maryland.

Tom Coburn, of Oklahoma.
Orrin G. Hatch, of Utah.
Jon Kyl, of Arizona.

Taxation and IRS Oversight

Kent Conrad, of North Dakota, *Chair*

Max Baucus, of Montana.
John F. Kerry, of Massachusetts.
Charles E. Schumer, of New York.
Ron Wyden, of Oregon.
Maria Cantwell, of Washington.
Bill Nelson, of Florida.
Robert Menendez, of New Jersey.
Thomas R. Carper, of Delaware.
Benjamin L. Cardin, of Maryland.

Jon Kyl, of Arizona.
Olympia J. Snowe, of Maine.
Mike Crapo, of Idaho.
Pat Roberts, of Kansas.
Michael B. Enzi, of Wyoming.
John Cornyn, of Texas.
Tom Coburn, of Oklahoma.
John Thune, of South Dakota.

STAFF

Committee on Finance (SD–219), 224–4515, fax 228–0554.
Majority Staff Director.—Russ Sullivan.
Chief Counsel.—Vacant
Senior Advisor.—John Angell.
Counsel and Senior Advisor for Indian Affairs.—Richard Litsey.
Chief Tax.—Lily Batchelder.
Tax Counsels: Ryan Abraham, David Hughes, Holly Porter, Tom Reeder, Tiffany Smith, Jeff VanderWolk.
Tax Advisors.—Amber Roberts.
Tax Assistants: Blaise Cote, Sean Morrison.
Tax Fellow.—Jessica Kawamura.
Health Counsels: David Schwartz, Tony Clapsis, Diedra Henry-Spires.
Health Advisor.—Matt Kazan, Kelly Whitener.
Health Assistant.—Callan Smith.
Health Fellow.—Laura Jaskierski.
Trade Counsel.—Amber Cottle.
Trade Advisors: Gabriel Adler, Ayesha Khanna, Hun Quach, Mike Smart, Chelsea Thomas.
Trade Assistant.—Rory Murphy.
Trade Fellow.—Danielle Fidler.
Investigator.—Christopher Law.
Social Security Counsels: Alan Cohen, Tom Klouda.
Social Security Fellow.—Claire Green.
Communication Director.—Scott Mulhauser.
Press Secretary.—Meghan Smith.
Press Assistant.—Ryan Carey.
Assistant to the Chief of Staff.—Jim Frisk.
Veterans Advisor.—Michael Grant.
Fellow from Department of State.—Joseph Scovitch.
Budget Fellow.—Sarah Babcock.
Staff Assistants: Kasi Goodwin, Athena Schritz, Challee Stefani.
IT Director.—Joe Carnucci.

Archivist.—Bryan Palmer.

Minority Staff Director and Chief Counsel.—Chris Campbell.

Deputy Staff Director / Chief Tax Counsel.—Mark Prater.

Tax Counsels: Curt Beaulieu, Tony Coughlan, James Lyons.

Senior Tax Policy Advisor.—Christopher Hanna.

Tax and Benefits Counsel.—Preston Rutledge.

Tax and Nomination Professional Staff.—Nick Wyatt.

Research Assistant.—Aaron Taylor.

Special Counsel.—Bryan Hickman.

Special Counsel and Chief Investigator.—Brendan Dunn.

Senior Health Investigative Counsel.—Kim Brandt.

Oversight and Investigative Professional Staff.—Peter Russo.

Health Policy Director and Chief Health Counsel.—Mark Hayes.

Health Policy Advisors: Stephanie Carlton, Becky Shipp, Dan Todd, Kristin Welsh, Paul Williams.

Special Assistant.—Shannon Crowley.

Chief International Trade Counsel.—Everett Eissenstat.

International Trade Counsels: Paul Delaney, David Johanson, Greg Kalbaugh.

Trade Staff Assistant.—Rebecca Nasca.

State Dept Trade Detail.—Ryika Hooshangi.

Chief Economist and Social Security Analyst.—Jeff Wrase.

Communications Director.—Antonia Ferrier.

Press Secretary.—Julia Lawless.

Detailees: Jesse Baker, Jim Bossenmeyer, David Burt, Maureen McLaughlin.

Foreign Relations

450 Dirksen Senate Office Building 20510–6225

phone 224–4651, http://foreign.senate.gov

meets each Tuesday

John F. Kerry, of Massachusetts, *Chair*

Barbara Boxer, of California.
Robert Menendez, of New Jersey.
Benjamin L. Cardin, of Maryland.
Robert P. Casey, Jr., of Pennsylvania.
Jim Webb, of Virginia.
Jeanne Shaheen, of New Hampshire.
Christopher A. Coons, of Delaware.
Richard J. Durbin, of Illinois.
Tom Udall, of New Mexico.

Richard G. Lugar, of Indiana.
Bob Corker, of Tennessee.
James E. Risch, of Idaho.
Marco Rubio, of Florida.
James M. Inhofe, of Oklahoma.
Jim DeMint, of South Carolina.
Johnny Isakson, of Georgia.
John Barrasso, of Wyoming.
Mike Lee, of Utah.

SUBCOMMITTEES

[The chairman and ranking minority member are ex officio (non-voting) members of all subcommittees on which they do not serve.]

African Affairs

Christopher A. Coons, of Delaware, *Chair*

Benjamin L. Cardin, of Maryland.
Jim Webb, of Virginia.
Richard J. Durbin, of Illinois.
Tom Udall, of New Mexico.

Johnny Isakson, of Georgia.
James M. Inhofe, of Oklahoma.
Mike Lee, of Utah.
Bob Corker, of Tennessee.

East Asian and Pacific Affairs

Jim Webb, of Virginia, *Chair*

Barbara Boxer, of California.
Robert P. Casey, Jr., of Pennsylvania.
Jeanne Shaheen, of New Hampshire.
Christopher A. Coons, of Delaware.

James M. Inhofe, of Oklahoma.
James E. Risch, of Idaho.
John Barrasso, of Wyoming.
Marco Rubio, of Florida.

European Affairs

Jeanne Shaheen, of New Hampshire, *Chair*

Benjamin L. Cardin, of Maryland.
Robert P. Casey, Jr., of Pennsylvania.
Jim Webb, of Virginia.
Richard J. Durbin, of Illinois.

John Barrasso, of Wyoming.
James E. Risch, of Idaho.
Bob Corker, of Tennessee.
Jim DeMint, of South Carolina.

International Development and Foreign Assistance, Economic Affairs, and International Environmental Protection

Benjamin L. Cardin, of Maryland, *Chair*

Robert Menendez, of New Jersey.
Christopher A. Coons, of Delaware.
Richard J. Durbin, of Illinois.
Tom Udall, of New Mexico.

Bob Corker, of Tennessee.
Marco Rubio, of Florida.
James E. Risch, of Idaho.
James M. Inhofe, of Oklahoma.

International Operations and Organizations, Human Rights, Democracy, and Global Women's Issues

Barbara Boxer, of California, *Chair*

Robert Menendez, of New Jersey.
Robert P. Casey, Jr., of Pennsylvania.
Jeanne Shaheen, of New Hampshire.
Richard J. Durbin, of Illinois.
Jim DeMint, of South Carolina.
James M. Inhofe, of Oklahoma.
Johnny Isakson, of Georgia.
John Barrasso, of Wyoming.

Near Eastern and South and Central Asian Affairs

Robert P. Casey, Jr., of Pennsylvania, *Chair*

Barbara Boxer, of California.
Robert Menendez, of New Jersey.
Benjamin L. Cardin, of Maryland.
Christopher A. Coons, of Delaware.
Tom Udall, of New Mexico.
James E. Risch, of Idaho.
Bob Corker, of Tennessee.
Mike Lee, of Utah.
Marco Rubio, of Florida.
Johnny Isakson, of Georgia.

Western Hemisphere, Peace Corps, and Global Narcotics Affairs

Robert Menendez, of New Jersey, *Chair*

Barbara Boxer, of California.
Jim Webb, of Virginia.
Jeanne Shaheen, of New Hampshire.
Tom Udall, of New Mexico.
Marco Rubio, of Florida.
Mike Lee, of Utah.
Jim DeMint, of South Carolina.
Johnny Isakson, of Georgia.
John Barrasso, of Wyoming.

STAFF

Committee on Foreign Relations (SD–444), 224–4651.
Majority Staff Director.—Frank Lowenstein.
Deputy Staff Director.—Peter Scoblic.
Chief Counsel.—Andrew Keller.
Counsels: Steven Feldstein, Robin Lerner, Atman Trivedi.
Legislative Assistants: Laura Dean, Royal Kastens.
Legislative Correspondents: Sanaa Khan, Laura Talverdian.
Press Secretary.—Jennifer Berlin.
Professional Staff: Fulton Armstrong, Jonah Blank, Jason Bruder, Perry Cammack, Heidi Crebo-Rediker, Frank Jannuzi, Greg Kausner, Tamara Klajn, Andrew Imbrie, Emily Mendrala, Melanie Nakagawa, Shannon Smith, Fatema Sumar, Anthony Wier.
Minority Staff Director.—Kenneth A. Myers, Jr. 224–6797.
Deputy Staff Director.—Daniel C. Diller.
Press Secretary.—Andrew J. Fisher.
Communications Director.—Mark Helmke.
Minority Chief Counsel.—Michael Mattler.
Professional Staff: Jay Branegan, Shellie Bressler, Neil Brown, Paul Foldi, Patrick Garvey, Keith Luse, Carl Meacham, Thomas Moore, Michael Phelan, Lori Rowley, Marik String, Manisha Singh.
Legislative Assistants: Cory Gill, Katie Lee, Alexandra Utsey.
Staff Assistant.—Nick McCormick.
Non-Designated Committee Staff (SD–446), 224–4651.
Office Manager.—Samantha Hamilton.
Chief Clerk.—Susan Oursler.
Deputy Chief Clerk.—Megan Moyerman.
Executive / Legislative Clerk.—Gail Coppage.
Director of Protocol / Foreign Travel.—Meg Murphy.
Hearing Coordinator.—Bertie H. Bowman.
Systems Administrator.—James Carter.
Staff Assistants: Barbara Allem, Vanessa Jean-Simon, Brittney Opacak.
Archivist Research Assistant.—Lexi Simpson.
Printing Clerks: Betty Acton, Michael W. Bennett.

Health, Education, Labor, and Pensions

428 Dirksen Senate Office Building 20510–6300

phone 224–5375, http://help.senate.gov

meets second and fourth Wednesdays of each month

Tom Harkin, of Iowa, *Chair*

Barbara A. Mikulski, of Maryland.
Jeff Bingaman, of New Mexico.
Patty Murray, of Washington.
BERNARD SANDERS, of Vermont.
Robert P. Casey, Jr., of Pennsylvania.
Kay R. Hagan, of North Carolina.
Jeff Merkley, of Oregon.
Al Franken, of Minnesota.
Michael F. Bennet, of Colorado.
Sheldon Whitehouse, of Rhode Island.
Richard Blumenthal, of Connecticut.

Michael B. Enzi, of Wyoming.
Lamar Alexander, of Tennessee.
Richard Burr, of North Carolina.
Johnny Isakson, of Georgia.
Rand Paul, of Kentucky.
Orrin G. Hatch, of Utah.
John McCain, of Arizona.
Pat Roberts, of Kansas.
Lisa Murkowski, of Alaska.
Mark Kirk, of Illinois.

SUBCOMMITTEES

[The chairman and ranking minority member are ex officio members of all subcommittees on which they do not serve.]

* Children and Families [1]

Barbara A. Mikulski, of Maryland, *Chair*

Patty Murray, of Washington.
BERNARD SANDERS, of Vermont.
Robert P. Casey, Jr., of Pennsylvania.
Kay R. Hagan, of North Carolina.
Jeff Merkley, of Oregon.
Al Franken, of Minnesota.
Michael F. Bennet, of Colorado.
Richard Blumenthal, of Connecticut.

Richard Burr, of North Carolina.
Lamar Alexander, of Tennessee.
Johnny Isakson, of Georgia.
Rand Paul, of Kentucky.
John McCain, of Arizona.
Pat Roberts, of Kansas.
Mark Kirk, of Illinois.

Employment and Workplace Safety

Patty Murray, of Washington, *Chair*

Jeff Bingaman, of New Mexico.
Al Franken, of Minnesota.
Michael F. Bennet, of Colorado.
Sheldon Whitehouse, of Rhode Island.
Richard Blumenthal, of Connecticut.

Johnny Isakson, of Georgia.
Lamar Alexander, of Tennessee.
Orrin G. Hatch, of Utah.
Mark Kirk, of Illinois.

Primary Health and Aging [1]

BERNARD SANDERS, of Vermont, *Chair*

Barbara A. Mikulski, of Maryland.
Jeff Bingaman, of New Mexico.
Robert P. Casey, Jr., of Pennsylvania.
Kay R. Hagan, of North Carolina.
Jeff Merkley, of Oregon.
Sheldon Whitehouse, of Rhode Island.

Rand Paul, of Kentucky.
Richard Burr, of North Carolina.
Johnny Isakson, of Georgia.
Orrin G. Hatch, of Utah.
Lisa Murkowski, of Alaska.

STAFF

Committee on Health, Education, Labor, and Pensions (SD–644), 224–0767, fax 224–6510, TDD 224–1975.

Staff Director.—Daniel Smith, SD–644, 4–0767.
Deputy Staff Director.—Pam Smith, SD–644, 4–0767.
Staff Assistant.—Kale Blessum, SD–644, 4–0767.
Senior Counsel.—Carrie Wofford, SD–644, 4–0767.
Special Assistant.—Molly Click, SD–644, 4–0767.
Press Secretary.—Justine Sessions, SD–644, 4–0767.
Press Assistant.—Elizabeth Donovan, SD–644, 4–0767.
Health Policy Office 4–7675
Health Policy Director.—Jenelle Krishnamoorthy, SH–527, 4–7675.
Health Policy Advisor.—Andrea Harris, SH–527, 4–7675.
Legislative Correspondent.—Brian Massa, SH–527, 4–7675.
Senior Health Policy Advisors: Elizabeth Jungman, Nick Bath, SH–527, 4–7675.
Health Policy Advisor.—Craig Martinez, SH–527, 4–7675.
Detailees: Andi LipsteinFristedt, William McConagha, SH–527, 4–7675.
Staff Assistant.—Kathleen Laird, SH–527, 4–7675.
Education Policy Office 4–5501
Research Assistant.—Thomas Showalter, SH–615, 4–5501.
Staff Assistant.—Ashley Eden, SH–615, 4–5501.
Education Policy Advisor.—Robin Juliano, SH–615, 4–5501.
Chief Education Counsel.—Bethany Little, SH–615, 4–5501.
Senior Education Policy Advisors: David Johns, Luke Swarthout, SH–615, 4–5501.
Senior Education Advisor for K–12.—Michele McLaughlin.
Education Policy Advisors: Soncia Coleman, Spiros Protopsaltis, SH–615, 4–5501.
Detaillee.—Maria Worthen, SH–615, 4–5501.
Kennedy Fellow.—Michael Gamel-McCormick, SH–615, 4–5501.
Oversight and Investigation Office 4–6403
Chief Investigative Counsel.—Beth Stein, SH–404, 4–6403.
Counsel.—Keramin Hamadanchy, SH–404, 4–6403.
Staff Assistant.—Madeline Daniels, SH–404, 4–6403.
Investigation Counsel.—Ryan McCord, SH–404, 4–6403.
Senior Investigator.—Elizabeth Baylor, SH–404, 4–6403.
Disability Office 8–3453
Senior Counsel and Disability Policy Director.—Andrew Imparato, SH–404, 8–3453.
Disability Counsel.—Lee Perselay, SH–404, 8–3453.

Subcommittee on Children and Families 4–9243
Subcommittee Staff Director.—Jessica McNiece, SH–607, 4–9243.
Fellow.—Jeffery Okamoto, SH–607, 4–9243.
Professional Staff Member.—Christine Evans, SH–607, 4–9243.
Legislative Assistant.—Mario Cardona, SH–607, 4–9243.

Subcommittee on Employment and Workplace Safety 8–1455
Subcommittee Staff Director.—Scott Cheney, SH–143, 8–1455.
Professional Staff Member.—Michael Waske, SH–143, 8–1455.
Legislative Assistant.—Jordan Smith, SH–143, 8–1455.
Senior Policy Advisor.—Crystal Bridgeman, SH–143, 8–1455.

Subcommittee on Primary Health and Aging 4–5480
Subcommittee Staff Director.—Ashley Carson Cottingham, SD–648, 4–5480.
Senior Staff Member.—Robert Dempsey, SD–648, 4–5480.
Minority Staff

Committee on Health, Education, Labor, and Pensions (SH–835), 224–6770.
Staff Director.—Frank Macchiarola, SH–833, 4–6770.
Chief Counsel.—Greg Dean, SH–833, 4–6770.
Assistant to the Staff Director.—Alicia Hermann, SH–833, 4–6770.
Staff Director.—Julia Corker, SH–835, 4–6770.
Communications Office SH–132, 4–6770
Communications Director.—Craig Orfield, SH–132, 4–6770.
Senior Communications Advisor.—Ron Hindle, SH–132, 4–6770.
Press Secretary.—Joe Brenckle, SH–132, 4–6770.
Oversight and Investigations Office SH–622B, 4–6770.
Senior Policy Advisor.—Amy Shank, SH–622B, 4–6770.
Oversight and Investigation Counsel.—Nick Geale, SH–622B, 4–6770.
Health Policy Office SH–725, 4–0623
Health Policy Director.—Chuck Clapton, SH–725, 4–0623.
Senior Health Policy Advisor.—Katy Spangler, SH–725, 4–0623.

Health Counsel.—Keith Flanagan, SH–725, 4–0623.
Professional Staff Members: Melissa Pfaff, Todd Spangler, Riley Swinehard, SH–725, 4–0623.
Staff Assistants: Omar De La Rosa, Robert Walton, SH–725, 4–0623.
Research Assistant.—Katie Adams, SH–725, 4–0623.
Education Office SH–828, 4–8484
Education Policy Director.—Beth Buehlmann, SH–828, 4–8484.
Senior Education Policy Advisor.—Lindsay Hunsicker, SH–828, 4–8484.
Professional Staff Members: Kelly Hastings, Christopher Toppings, SH–828, 4–8484.
Counsel.—Christopher Eyler, SH–828, 4–8484.
Labor Policy Office, SH–828, 8–6770.
Labor Policy Director.—Kyle Hicks, SH–828, 8–6770.
Labor Counsel.—Kai Hirabayashi, SH–828, 8–6770.
Staff Assistant.—Laura Hill, SH–828, 8–6770.
Subcommittee on Children and Families SH–440, 4–0121.
Health Policy Assistant.—Walter Zaykowski, SH–440, 4–0121.
Retirement Policy Director.—Steve Perrotta, SH–440, 4–0121.
Health Policy Assistant.—Margaret Coulter, SH–440, 4–0121.
Health Policy Director.—Anna Abram, SH–440, 4–0121.
Subcommittee on Employment and Workplace Safety SH–833, 4–5800.
Staff Director.—Tommy Nguyen, SH–833, 4–5800.
Subcommittee on Primary Health and Aging SH–440, 4–5406.
Staff Director.—Evan Feinberg, SH–440, 4–5406.

---

[1] On January 31, 2007, the Committee was polled and agreed that the name of the Subcommittee on Education and Early Childhood Development would be changed to the Subcommittee on Children and Families, the Subcommittee on Retirement Security and Aging would be changed to the Subcommittee on Retirement and Aging, and that the Committee would discontinue the Subcommittee on Bioterrorism and Public Health Preparedness. On March 15, 2011, the Committee was polled and agreed that the name of the Subcommittee on Retirement Security and Aging would be changed to the Subcommittee on Primary Health and Aging.

* Minority Subcommittee Member order corrected March 2007.

Homeland Security and Governmental Affairs

340 Dirksen Senate Office Building 20510

phone 224–2627, fax 228–3792, http://hsgac.senate.gov

Hearing Room—SD–342 Dirksen Senate Office Building

meets first Wednesday of each month

JOSEPH I. LIEBERMAN, of Connecticut, *Chair*

Carl Levin, of Michigan.
Daniel K. Akaka, of Hawaii.
Thomas R. Carper, of Delaware.
Mark L. Pryor, of Arkansas.
Mary L. Landrieu, of Louisiana.
Claire McCaskill, of Missouri.
Jon Tester, of Montana.
Mark Begich, of Alaska.

Susan M. Collins, of Maine.
Tom Coburn, of Oklahoma.
Scott P. Brown, of Massachusetts.
John McCain, of Arizona.
Ron Johnson, of Wisconsin.
Rob Portman, of Ohio.
Rand Paul, of Kentucky.
Jerry Moran, of Kansas.

SUBCOMMITTEES

[The chairman and the ranking minority member are ex officio members of all subcommittees.]

Permanent Subcommittee on Investigations (PSI)

Carl Levin, of Michigan, *Chair*

Thomas R. Carper, of Delaware.
Mary L. Landrieu, of Louisiana.
Claire McCaskill, of Missouri.
Jon Tester, of Montana.
Mark Begich, of Alaska.

Tom Coburn, of Oklahoma.
Susan M. Collins, of Maine.
Scott P. Brown, of Massachusetts.
John McCain, of Arizona.
Rand Paul, of Kentucky.

Oversight of Government Management, the Federal Workforce, and the District of Columbia (OGM)

Daniel K. Akaka, of Hawaii, *Chair*

Carl Levin, of Michigan.
Mary L. Landrieu, of Louisiana.
Mark Begich, of Alaska.

Ron Johnson, of Wisconsin.
Tom Coburn, of Oklahoma.
Jerry Moran, of Kansas.

Federal Financial Management, Government Information, Federal Services, and International Security (FFM)

Thomas R. Carper, of Delaware, *Chair*

Carl Levin, of Michigan.
Daniel K. Akaka, of Hawaii.
Mark L. Pryor, of Arkansas.
Claire McCaskill, of Missouri.
Mark Begich, of Alaska.

Scott P. Brown, of Massachusetts.
Tom Coburn, of Oklahoma.
John McCain, of Arizona.
Ron Johnson, of Wisconsin.
Rob Portman, of Ohio.

Ad Hoc Disaster Recovery and Intergovernmental Affairs (DRIA)

Mark L. Pryor, of Arkansas, *Chair*

Daniel K. Akaka, of Hawaii.
Mary L. Landrieu, of Louisiana.
Jon Tester, of Montana.

Rand Paul, of Kentucky.
Scott P. Brown, of Massachusetts.
Ron Johnson, of Wisconsin.

Ad Hoc Contracting Oversight (SCO)

Claire McCaskill, of Missouri, *Chair*

Thomas R. Carper, of Delaware.
Mark L. Pryor, of Arkansas.
Jon Tester, of Montana.
Mark Begich, of Alaska.

Rob Portman, of Ohio.
Susan M. Collins, of Maine.
John McCain, of Arizona.
Jerry Moran, of Kansas.

STAFF

Committee on Homeland Security and Governmental Affairs (SD–340), 224–2627.
Majority Staff Director.—Michael Alexander.
Chief Counsel/Deputy Staff Director.—Beth Grossman.
Chief Clerk.—Trina Driessnack Tyrer.
Associate Staff Directors: Christian Beckner, Gordon Lederman, Larry Novey, Mary Beth Schultz.
Senior Counsels: Troy Cribb, Jeff Greene, Holly Idelson.
Counsels: Jonathan Kraden, Jeff Ratner, Kenya Wiley.
Senior Professional Staff.—Jason Yanussi.
Professional Staff: Jason Barnosky, Aaron Firoved, Elyse Greenwald, Matt Grote, Seamus Hughes, Kristine Lam, Jim McGee, Blas Nunez-Neto, Carly Steier.
Senior Investigator.—Al Cumming.
Senior Advisor.—Vance Serchuk.
Communications Director.—Leslie Phillips.
Communications Advisor.—Scott Campbell.
Deputy Press Secretary.—Sara Lonardo.
Executive Assistant/Office Manager.—Janet Burrell.
Legislative Aide.—Nicole Martinez.
Staff Assistants: Robert Bradley, Katrina Calixte, Danielle Gilliam-Moore.
Detailee.—Cheryl Bassett.
Hearing Clerk.—Laura Kilbride.
Publications Clerks: Pat Hogan, Joyce Ward.
Financial Clerk.—Claudette David.
Archivist/Librarian.—Katie Delacenserie.
Systems Administrator/Web Master.—Dan Muchow.
Deputy Systems Administrator.—Scott Langill.
Minority Staff Director.—Nick Rossi (SD–344), 224–4751.
General Counsel.—Molly Wilkinson.
Deputy General Counsel.—Amanda Wood.
Director of Homeland Security Affairs.—Brendan Shields.
Director of Governmental Affairs.—Katy French.
Legislative Counsel.—Mark LeDuc.
Counsels: Lorinda Harris, Jen Tarr.
Senior Defense/Homeland Security Advisor.—Ryan Kaldahl.
Professional Staff: Eric Heighberger, Trey Hicks, Chris Keach, Heather Raiti, Denise Zheng.
Press Secretary.—E.R. Anderson.
Deputy Press Secretary.—Meaghan Cronin.
Office Manager.—Rachel Nitsche.
Staff Assistant.—James Murphy.
Legislative Correspondent.—Kristina Ng.
Research Assistants.—Daniel Jenkins, Chris MacDonald.
Detailees: Rob Graves, Scott Lemasters, Lisa Nieman, Anne Terry, Britton Yee.
Permanent Subcommittee on Investigations (PSI) (SR–199), 224–9505.
Majority Staff Director/Chief Counsel.—Elise Bean.
Clerk.—Mary Robertson.
Counsel/Chief Investigator.—Robert Roach.
Counsels: Daniel Goshorn, David Katz, Alison Murphy, Zachary Schram, Laura Stuber.
Professional Staff Member.—Adam Henderson.
Detailees: Allie Abrams, Michael Martineau.
Fellow.—Mary McKoy.
Minority Staff Director.—Chris Barkley (SR–199), 224–3721.
Counsels: Anthony Cotto, Andrew Dockham.
Chief Investigator.—Keith Ashdown.
Senior Investigator.—Justin Rood.
Professional Staff.—David Cole.

Detailees: John DeDona, Sarah Deutschmann, Candice Wright.

Subcommittee on Oversight of Government Management, the Federal Workforce, and the District of Columbia (OGM) (SH–601), 224–4551.

Majority Staff Director.—Lisa Powell.

Clerk.—Aaron Woolf.

Counsels: Christine Khim, Bryan Polisuk, Eric Tamarkin, Kata Sybenga.

Professional Staff: Evan Cash, Jessica Nagasako.

Fellow.—Ray Ciarcia.

Minority Staff Director.—Rachel Weaver (SH–605), 224–3682.

Professional Staff.—Sean Kennedy.

Subcommittee on Federal Financial Management, Government Information, Federal Services, and International Security (FFM) (SH–432), 224–7155.

Majority Staff Director.—John Kilvington.

Clerk.—Deirdre Armstrong.

Counsel.—Velvet Johnson.

Professional Staff: John Collins, Harlan Geer, Peter Tyler.

Legislative Aide.—Garth Spencer.

Detailee.—Heather Dunahoo.

Minority Staff Director.—Bill Wright (SH–439), 224–2254.

Counsel.—Steven Hutchinson.

Professional Staff.—Justin Stevens.

Research Assistant.—Brandon Aitchison.

Ad Hoc Subcommittee on Disaster Recovery and Intergovernmental Affairs (DRIA) (SH–601), 224–4462.

Majority Staff Director.—Vacant.

Clerk.—Kelsey Stroud.

Professional Staff: Jason Bockenstedt, Amanda Fox, Lauren McClain.

Detailee.—John Vocino.

Minority Staff Director.—Vacant (SH–605), 224–4462.

Research Assistant.—Michael Tyler.

Ad Hoc Subcommittee on Contracting Oversight (SCO) (SH–601), 224–4462.

Majority Staff Director.—Margaret Daum.

Clerk.—Kelsey Stroud.

Senior Counsel.—Alan Kahn.

Counsel.—Sarah Garcia.

Detailee.—Mike Capobianco.

Minority Staff Director.—Brian Callanan (SH–605), 224–4462.

Judiciary

224 Dirksen Senate Office Building 20510–6275

phone 224–7703, fax 224–9516, http://www.senate.gov/~judiciary

meets upon call of the chair

Patrick J. Leahy, of Vermont, *Chair*

Herb Kohl, of Wisconsin.
Dianne Feinstein, of California.
Charles E. Schumer, of New York.
Richard J. Durbin, of Illinois.
Sheldon Whitehouse, of Rhode Island.
Amy Klobuchar, of Minnesota.
Al Franken, of Minnesota.
Christopher A. Coons, of Delaware.
Richard Blumenthal, of Connecticut.

Chuck Grassley, of Iowa.
Orrin G. Hatch, of Utah.
Jon Kyl, of Arizona.
Jeff Sessions, of Alabama.
Lindsey Graham, of South Carolina.
John Cornyn, of Texas.
Mike Lee, of Utah.
Tom Coburn, of Oklahoma.

SUBCOMMITTEES

Administrative Oversight and the Courts

Amy Klobuchar, of Minnesota, *Chair*

Patrick J. Leahy, of Vermont.
Herb Kohl, of Wisconsin.
Sheldon Whitehouse, of Rhode Island.
Christopher A. Coons, of Delaware.

Jeff Sessions, of Alabama.
Chuck Grassley, of Iowa.
Mike Lee, of Utah.
Tom Coburn, of Oklahoma.

Antitrust, Competition Policy and Consumer Rights

Herb Kohl, of Wisconsin, *Chair*

Charles E. Schumer, of New York.
Amy Klobuchar, of Minnesota.
Al Franken, of Minnesota.
Richard Blumenthal, of Connecticut.

Mike Lee, of Utah.
Chuck Grassley, of Iowa.
John Cornyn, of Texas.

The Constitution, Civil Rights and Human Rights

Richard J. Durbin, of Illinois, *Chair*

Patrick J. Leahy, of Vermont.
Sheldon Whitehouse, of Rhode Island.
Al Franken, of Minnesota.
Christopher A. Coons, of Delaware.
Richard Blumenthal, of Connecticut.

Lindsey Graham, of South Carolina.
Jon Kyl, of Arizona.
John Cornyn, of Texas.
Mike Lee, of Utah.
Tom Coburn, of Oklahoma.

Crime and Terrorism

Sheldon Whitehouse, of Rhode Island, *Chair*

Herb Kohl, of Wisconsin.
Dianne Feinstein, of California.
Richard J. Durbin, of Illinois.
Amy Klobuchar, of Minnesota.
Christopher A. Coons, of Delaware.

Jon Kyl, of Arizona.
Orrin G. Hatch, of Utah.
Jeff Sessions, of Alabama.
Lindsey Graham, of South Carolina.

Immigration, Refugees and Border Security

Charles E. Schumer, of New York, *Chair*

Patrick J. Leahy, of Vermont.
Dianne Feinstein, of California.
Richard J. Durbin, of Illinois.
Al Franken, of Minnesota.
Richard Blumenthal, of Connecticut.

John Cornyn, of Texas.
Chuck Grassley, of Iowa.
Orrin G. Hatch, of Utah.
Jon Kyl, of Arizona.
Jeff Sessions, of Alabama.

Privacy, Technology and the Law

Al Franken, of Minnesota, *Chair*

Charles E. Schumer, of New York.	*Tom Coburn,* of Oklahoma.
Sheldon Whitehouse, of Rhode Island.	*Orrin G. Hatch,* of Utah.
Richard Blumenthal, of Connecticut.	*Lindsey Graham,* of South Carolina.

STAFF

Committee on the Judiciary (SD–224), 224–7703, fax 224–9516.
Majority Staff Director/Chief Counsel.—Bruce Cohen.
Legislative Staff Assistant to the Chief Counsel.—Kelsey Kobelt.
Deputy Staff Director/General Counsel.—Kristine Lucius.
Chief Counsel for Nominations and Oversight.—Jeremy Paris.
Chief Counsel for Privacy and Information Policy.—Lydia Griggsby.
Chief Counsel for Criminal Justice.—Noah Bookbinder.
Senior Counsel, I.P. and Antitrust.—Aaron Cooper.
Senior Counsels: Liz Aloi, Curtis LeGeyt, Anya McMurray, Tara Magner, Chan Park, Matthew Virkstis.
Investigative Counsel.—Margaret Whitney.
Nominations Counsel.—Alexandra Givens.
Counsels: John Amaya.
Professional Staff Member.—Adrienne Wojeciechowski.
Detailee.—Ed Chung.
Press Secretary.—Erica Chabot.
Press Assistant.—Dan Taylor.
Chief Clerk.—Roslyne Turner.
Assistant to Chief Clerk.—Theresa Reuss.
Nominations Clerk.—Zach Blau.
Hearings Clerk.—Halley Ross.
Law Librarian.—Charles Papirmeister.
Archivist.—Michael Donaghue.
Legislative Calendar Clerk.—Alberta Easter.
Systems Administrator.—Brian Hockin.
Legislative Staff Assistants: Aaron Kaigle, Rachel Pelham, Patrick Sheahan, Matthew Smith, Joseph Thomas, Scott Wilson.
Staff Assistants: Clark Flynt, Charles Smith.
Court Reporter.—Lisa Dennis.
GPO Printer.—Cecilia Morcombe.
Minority Office (SD–152), 224–5225, fax 224–9102.
Minority Staff Director and Chief Counsel.—Kolan Davis.
Deputy Staff Director and Chief Civil Counsel.—Rita Lari Jochum.
Counsels: Chris Conlin, Dayle Elieson, Nathan Hallford, Ralph Johnson, Ted Lehman, Nick Podsiadly.
Chief Counsel for Nominations.—David Best.
Professional Staff Member for Nominations.—Lauren Pastarnack.
Legislative Counsel.—Kimberly Kilpatrick.
Professional Staff Members: Kevin Courtois, Barbara Ledeen.
Press Secretary.—Beth Levine.
Staff Assistants: Kat Mayne, Emily Tocknell.
Archivist.—Stuart Paine.
Director of Information Systems.—Steve Kirkland.
Staff Member.—Jim Cook.
Voluntary Counsel.—Lake Dishman.
Investigators.—Robert Donovan, Brian Downey, Tristan Leavitt.
Legislative Aide.—Sarah Thompson.
Legislative Assistant.—Kathy Nuebel.
Investigative Counsel.—Chris Lucas.
Chief Investigative Counsel.—Jason Foster.
Subcommittee on Administrative Oversight and the Courts (SH–807), 224–3244.
Majority Chief Counsel and Staff Director.—Craig Kalkut.
Counsel.—Detailee.—Chris McDonough.
Professional Staff Member.—Elizabeth Frosch.
Minority Deputy Chief Counsel.—Danielle Cutrona (SD–G66), 224–7572.
Legislative Counsel.—Katherine Green.
Legislative Correspondent.—Kate Laborde.

Subcommittee on Antitrust, Competition Policy and Consumer Rights (SD–308), 224–3406.
Majority Chief Counsel and Staff Director.—Caroline Holland.
General Counsel.—Seth Bloom.
Counsels: Marni Karlin, Kristen Kreple.
Legislative Aide.—Jennifer Brody.
Subcommittee on the Constitution, Civil Rights, and Human Rights (SH–815), 224–2152.
Majority Chief Counsel and Staff Director.—Joseph Zogby.
Counsels: Albert Sanders, Mara Silver.
Senior Counsel.—Daniel Swanson.
Staff Assistant.—Sergio Alaya.
Minority Chief Counsel.—Walt Kuhn (SD–153), 224–5972.
Legislative Correspondent.—Jason Brown.
Subcommittee on Crime and Terrorism (SH–325), 224–6791.
Majority Chief Counsel.—Stephen Lilley.
Counsels: Justin Florence, Ayo Griffin.
Detailee.—Nicholas Patterson.
Associate Legislative Assistant.—Bill Hoffman.
Minority Chief Counsel.—Stephen Higgins (SH–325), 224–6791.
Counsel.—Joe Matal.
Legislative Correspondent.—Eva Arlia.
Subcommittee on Immigration, Refugees, and Border Security (SD–305), 224–6498.
Majority Chief Counsel.—Stephanie Martz.
Staff Director.—Leon Fresco.
Senior Counsel.—Rebecca Kelly.
Detailee.—Jessica Owens.
Legislative Correspondent.—Daniel Rudolfsky.
Minority Chief Counsel.—Matthew Johnson (SD–141), 224–7840.
Legislative Director.—Russ Thomasson.
Legal Assistant.—Valera Vollor.
Counsel.—Stephen Tausend.
Subcommittee on Privacy, Technology and the Law (SH–223), 228–3177.
Majority Chief Counsel.—Alvaro Bedoya.
Senior Counsel.—Susan Rohol.
Legislative Aides.—Michelle Liszt, Charlotte Slaiman.
Minority Chief Counsel.—Elizabeth Hays (SH–153), 224–5225.
Counsel.—Sarah Beth Groshart.
Legislative Correspondent.—Russ Ferguson.
Senator Feinstein Judiciary Staff (SD–524), 224–4933.
Chief Counsel.—Neil Quinter.
Counsels: Kim Alton, Eric Haren, Tony Orza.
Legislative Correspondent.—Juliana Goldrosen, Estee Sepulveda.
Senator Coons Judiciary Staff (SR–127A), 224–5042.
Chief Counsel.—Ted Shroeder.
Deputy Counsel.—Nhan Nguyen.
Senator Blumenthal Judiciary Staff (SH–702), 224–2823.
Chief Counsel.—Jon Donenberg.
Senator Hatch Judiciary Staff (SH–202), 224–5251.
Staff Members: Jason Bartolomei, Jason Castle, Jordan Cox, Harrison Hawkes, Tom Jipping, Ron Rowe, Matt Sandgreen, Andrea Shattuck.

Rules and Administration

305 Russell Senate Office Building 20510–6325

phone 224–6352, http://rules.senate.gov

[Legislative Reorganization Act of 1946]

meets second and fourth Wednesday of each month

Charles E. Schumer, of New York, *Chair*

Daniel K. Inouye, of Hawaii.
Dianne Feinstein, of California.
Richard J. Durbin, of Illinois.
Ben Nelson, of Nebraska.
Patty Murray, of Washington.
Mark L. Pryor, of Arkansas.
Tom Udall, of New Mexico.
Mark R. Warner, of Virginia.
Patrick J. Leahy, of Vermont.

Lamar Alexander, of Tennessee.
Mitch McConnell, of Kentucky.
Thad Cochran, of Mississippi.
Saxby Chambliss, of Georgia.
Kay Bailey Hutchison, of Texas.
Pat Roberts, of Kansas.
Richard C. Shelby, of Alabama.
Roy Blunt, of Missouri.

(No Subcommittees)

STAFF

Committee on Rules and Administration (SR–305), 224–6352.
Majority Staff Director.—Jean Parvin Bordewich.
Deputy Staff Director.—Joshua Brekenfeld.
Director, Operations Oversight.—Kelly Fado.
Administrative and Legisltaive Counsel.—Adam Ambrogi.
Elections Counsel.—Veronica Gillespie.
Counsels: Sonia Gill, Julia Richardson.
Administrative Assistant to Democratic Staff Director.—Carole Blessington.
Professional Staff.—Nicole Tatz.
Minority Staff Director.—Mary Suit Jones.
Deputy Staff Director.—Shaun Parkin.
Chief Counsel.—Paul Vinovich.
Elections Counsel.—Michael Merrell.
Professional Staff: Rachel Creviston, Trish Kent, Lindsey Ward.
Non-Designated Staff:
Director for Administration and Policy.—Chris Shunk.
Chief Clerk.—Lynden Armstrong.
Professional Staff.—Matthew McGowan, 4–0281.
Staff Assistants: Nicki Dittemore, Jeff Johnson.
Auditors: Leann Alwood, Joanne Yi.

Small Business and Entrepreneurship

428A Russell Senate Office Building 20510

phone 224–5175, fax 224–5619, http://sbc.senate.gov/

[Created pursuant to S. Res. 58, 81st Congress]

meets first Thursday of each month

Mary L. Landrieu, of Louisiana, *Chair*

Carl Levin, of Michigan.
Tom Harkin, of Iowa.
John F. Kerry, of Massachusetts.
JOSEPH I. LIEBERMAN, of Connecticut.
Maria Cantwell, of Washington.
Mark L. Pryor, of Arkansas.
Benjamin L. Cardin, of Maryland.
Jeanne Shaheen, of New Hampshire.
Kay R. Hagan, of North Carolina.

Olympia J. Snowe, of Maine.
David Vitter, of Louisiana.
James E. Risch, of Idaho.
Marco Rubio, of Florida.
Rand Paul, of Kentucky.
Kelly Ayotte, of New Hampshire.
Michael B. Enzi, of Wyoming.
Scott P. Brown, of Massachusetts.
Jerry Moran, of Kansas.

(No Subcommittees)

STAFF

Committee on Small Business and Entrepreneurship (SR–428A), 224–5175, fax 224–6619.
Majority Staff Director.—Donald Cravins, Jr.
Deputy Staff Director.—Kevin Wheeler.
Executive Assistant.—Princess Prince.
Policy Director.—Brian van Hook.
General Counsel.—Caroline Bruckner.
Tax Counsel.—Krystal Brumfield.
Counsels: David Gillers, Ami Sanchez.
Legislative Aide.—Ellen Devine.
Research Analysts: Kathryn Elder, Alex Johnson.
Deputy Press Secretary.—Elle Ourso.
Chief Clerk.—Joan Evans.
Hearing Clerk.—Monisha Smith.
Staff Assistants: Ruda Pollard, Hope Stephens.
Minority Staff Director.—Wallace K. Hsueh.
Deputy Staff Director and Chief Counsel.—Matthew Walker.
Assistant to the Staff Director.—Shelley New.
Senior Counsel.—Jelena McWilliams.
Tax Counsel.—Scott McCandless.
Counsel.—James Gelfland.
Professional Staff Members: Christopher Averill, Diane Dietz, Adam Reece.
Research Analyst.—Steve Keen.
Staff Assistant.—Tara Crumb.

Veterans' Affairs

SR–412 Russell Senate Office Building

phone 224–9126, http://veterans.senate.gov

meets first Wednesday of each month

Patty Murray, of Washington, *Chair*

John D. Rockefeller IV, of West Virginia.
Daniel K. Akaka, of Hawaii.
BERNARD SANDERS, of Vermont.
Sherrod Brown, of Ohio.
Jim Webb, of Virginia.
Jon Tester, of Montana.
Mark Begich, of Alaska.

Richard Burr, of North Carolina.
Johnny Isakson, of Georgia.
Roger F. Wicker, of Mississippi.
Mike Johanns, of Nebraska.
Scott P. Brown, of Massachusetts.
Jerry Moran, of Kansas.
John Boozman, of Arkansas.

(No Subcommittees)

STAFF

Committee on Veterans' Affairs (SR–412), 224–9126, fax 224–9575.
Majority Staff Director.—Kim Lipsky.
Deputy Staff Director.—Joshua Jacobs.
General Counsel.—Dahlia Melendrez.
Counsels: Dave Brown, Travis Murphy.
Special Projects Counsel.—Mary Ellen McCarthy.
Senior Legislative Assistant.—Ryan Pettit.
Issue Director.—Jenny McCarthy.
Legislative Assistants: Kathryn Monet, Elvin Valenzuela.
Legislative Aides: Sam Kussin-Shoptaw, Oriana Parker.
Minority Staff Director.—Lupe Wissel (825–A Hart), 224–2074, fax 224–8908.
Office Manager.—Hilda Harder.
General Counsel.—Amanda Meredith.
Professional Staff Members: John McDonald, Maureen O'Neill.
Legislative Assistant.—Victoria Lee.
Staff Assistant.—Elijah Abram.
Non-Designated: (SR–412), 224–9126.
Chief Clerk/Systems Administrator.—Matt Lawrence.

SELECT AND SPECIAL COMMITTEES OF THE SENATE

Committee on Indian Affairs

838 Hart Senate Office Building 20510–6450

phone 224–2251, http://indian.senate.gov

[Created pursuant to S. Res. 4, 95th Congress; amended by S. Res. 71, 103d Congress]

meets every Thursday of each month

Daniel K. Akaka, of Hawaii, *Chair*

John Barrasso, of Wyoming, *Vice Chair*

Daniel K. Inouye, of Hawaii.
Kent Conrad, of North Dakota.
Tim Johnson, of South Dakota.
Maria Cantwell, of Washington.
Jon Tester, of Montana.
Tom Udall, of New Mexico.
Al Franken, of Minnesota.

John McCain, of Arizona.
Lisa Murkowski, of Alaska.
John Hoeven, of North Dakota.
Mike Crapo, of Idaho.
Mike Johanns, of Nebraska.

(No Subcommittees)

STAFF

Majority Staff Director / Chief Counsel.—Loretta A. Tuell.
General Counsel.—Lenna Aoki.
Senior Counsel.—Denise Desiderio.
Counsel: Wendy Helgemo, Cisco Minthorn, Erik Stegman.
Policy Director.—Jade Danner.
Professional Staff Member.—Josh Pitre.
Staff Assistant.—Christiane Cardoza.
Minority Staff Director / Chief Counsel.—David A. Mullon, Jr.
Deputy Chief Counsel.—Rhonda Harjo.
Legislative Aide.—Ken Degenfelder.
Legislative Counsel.—Justin Memmott.
Clerk.—Marilyn Bruce.
Administrator Director.—Jim Eismeier.
Systems Administrator.—David Stuart.
Receptionist.—Sarah Overton.
GPO Detail.—Jack Fulmer.

Select Committee on Ethics

220 Hart Senate Office Building 20510, phone 224–2981, fax 224–7416

[Created pursuant to S. Res. 338, 88th Congress; amended by S. Res. 110, 95th Congress]

Barbara Boxer, of California, *Chair*

Johnny Isakson, of Georgia, *Vice Chair*

Mark L. Pryor, of Arkansas.
Sherrod Brown, of Ohio.

Pat Roberts, of Kansas.
James E. Risch, of Idaho.

STAFF

Staff Director/Chief Counsel.—John C. Sassaman.
Deputy Staff Director.—Annette Gillis.
Counsel and Director of Education and Training.—Matthew Mesmer.
Counsels: Tremayne Bunaugh, William Corcoran, Rochelle Ford, Tonia Smith, Lynn Tran.
Professional Staff.—John Lewter.
Director of IT.—Danny Remington.
Legal Assistant.—Emily Chucovich.
Staff Assistants: Philip Kibbey, Kathleen Nicholas, Chelsey Simonovich.

Select Committee on Intelligence

211 Hart Senate Office Building 20510–6475, phone 224–1700

http://www.senate.gov/~intelligence

[Created pursuant to S. Res. 400, 94th Congress]

Dianne Feinstein, of California, *Chair*

Saxby Chambliss, of Georgia, *Vice Chair*

John D. Rockefeller IV, of West Virginia.
Ron Wyden, of Oregon.
Barbara A. Mikulski, of Maryland.
Bill Nelson, of Florida.
Kent Conrad, of North Dakota.
Mark Udall, of Colorado.
Mark R. Warner, of Virginia.

Olympia J. Snowe, of Maine.
Richard Burr, of North Carolina.
James E. Risch, of Idaho.
Daniel Coats, of Indiana.
Roy Blunt, of Missouri.
Marco Rubio, of Florida.

Ex Officio

Harry Reid, of Nevada.
Carl Levin, of Michigan.

Mitch McConnell, of Kentucky.
John McCain, of Arizona.

STAFF

Majority Staff Director.—David Grannis.
Minority Staff Director.—Martha Scott Poindexter.
Chief Clerk.—Kathleen P. McGhee.

Special Committee on Aging

G–31 Dirksen Senate Office Building 20510, phone 224–5364

http://aging.senate.gov

[Reauthorized pursuant to S. Res. 4, 95th Congress]

Herb Kohl, of Wisconsin, *Chair*

Ron Wyden, of Oregon.
Bill Nelson, of Florida.
Robert P. Casey, Jr., of Pennsylvania.
Claire McCaskill, of Missouri.
Sheldon Whitehouse, of Rhode Island.
Mark Udall, of Colorado.
Michael F. Bennet, of Colorado.
Kirsten E. Gillibrand, of New York.
Joe Manchin III, of West Virginia.
Richard Blumenthal, of Connecticut.

Bob Corker, of Tennessee.
Susan M. Collins, of Maine.
Orrin G. Hatch, of Utah.
Mark Kirk, of Illinois.
Dean Heller, of Nevada.
Jerry Moran, of Kansas.
Ron Johnson, of Wisconsin.
Richard C. Shelby, of Alabama.
Lindsey Graham, of South Carolina.
Saxby Chambliss, of Georgia.

STAFF

Majority Staff Director.—Debra Whitman.
Senior Policy Advisor.—Cara Goldstein.
Press Secretary.—Ken Willis.
Chief of Oversight and Investigations.—Jack Mitchell.
Senior Policy Advisor.—Anne Montgomery.
Health Policy Advisor.—Sarah Levin.
Associate Investigator.—Sarah Molinoff.
Staff Assistants: Matt Burr, Kristin Rzeczkowski.
Minority Staff (SH–628), 224–5364, fax 224–9926.
Staff Director.—Michael Bassett.
Policy Advisors: Clay Brockman, Alicia Hennie.
Communications Director.—Chuck Harper.
Senior Professional Staff Member.—Darlene Rosenkoetter.
Professional Staff Member.—Martin Schuh.

Democratic Senatorial Campaign Committee

120 Maryland Avenue, NE., 20002, phone 224–2447

Patty Murray, of Washington, *Chair*
Harry Reid, of Nevada, *Democratic Leader*

STAFF

Executive Director.—Guy Cecil.
Communications Director.—Matt Canter.
Political Director.—Crystal King.
Finance Director.—Angelique Cannon.
Legal Counsel.—Mark Elias.

Democratic Policy and Communications Center

419 Hart Senate Office Building, phone 224–3232

Harry Reid, of Nevada, Majority Leader

Charles E. Schumer, of New York, *Chair.*
Debbie Stabenow, of Michigan, *Vice Chair.*
Amy Klobuchar, of Minnesota, *Regional Chair.*
Mary L. Landrieu, of Louisiana, *Regional Chair.*
Patty Murray, of Washington, *Regional Chair.*
JOSEPH I. LIEBERMAN, of Connecticut.
Dianne Feinstein, of California.
Ron Wyden, of Oregon.
Tim Johnson, of South Dakota.
Bill Nelson, of Florida.
Thomas R. Carper, of Delaware.
Barbara A. Mikulski, of Maryland.
Frank R. Lautenberg, of New Jersey.
Sherrod Brown, of Ohio.
Richard J. Durbin, of Illinois, ex officio, (as Assistant Majority Leader).
Patty Murray, of Washington, ex officio, (as Secretary of the Conference).

STAFF

Staff Director.—Katie Beirne, Capitol / S–318, katie_beirne@dpcc.senate.gov (202) 224–2939.
Communications Director.—Adam Jentleson, Capitol / S–318, adam_jentleson@reid.senate.gov, 224–2939.
Chief Spokesman.—Brian Fallon, Capitol / S–318, brian_fallon@dpcc.senate.gov, 224–2939.
Regional Media Director.—Max Young, Capitol / S–318, maxwell_young@dpcc.senate.gov, 224–2939.
Speech Writer.—Phoebe Sweet, Capitol / S–221, phoebe_sweet@reid.senate.gov, 224–2939.
Deputy Communications Director/Director of Hispanic Media.—Jose Parra, Capitol / S–318, jose_parra@reid.senate.gov, 224–2939.

Communication Director for NV/Press Secretary.—Zac Petkanas, Capitol/S–318, zac_petkanas@reid.senate.gov, 224–2939.
Deputy Press Secretary for Hispanic Media.—Nathaly Arriola, Capitol/S–329, nathaly_arriola@dpcc.senate.gov, 224–2939
Deputy Regional Press Secretary.—Colin Milligan, SH419, colin_milligan@dpcc.senate.gov, 224–2939.
Press Assistants.—Kenya James, Capitol/S–318, kenya_james@dpcc.senate.gov, Irma Palmer, irma_palmer@dpcc.senate.gov, 224–2939.
Policy Director.—Judith Wallner, SH419, judith_wallner@dpcc.senate.gov, 224–2939.
Counsel/Policy Advisor.—Pat Collier, SH419, pat_collier@dpcc.senate.gov, 224–2939.
Policy Advisors: Julie Klein, SH419, julie_klein@dpcc.senate.gov, Benjamin Nathanson, benjamin_nathanson@dpcc.senate.gov, 224–2939.
Staff Assistant.—Ashlyn Bilbray, SH419, ashlyn_bilbray@dpcc.senate.gov, 224–2939.
Research Director.—Matt McNally, Capitol/S–318, matt_mcnally@dpcc.senate.gov, 224–2939.
Director of Member Services.—Matt Fuehermeyer, SH419, matt_fuehermeyer@dpcc.senate.gov, 224–2939.
Research Associates: Kati Card, SH419, kati_card@dpcc.senate.gov, Dan Yoken, dan_yoken@dpcc.senate.gov, 224–2939.
Senior Vote Analyst.—Doug Connolly, SH705, doug_connolly@dpcc.senate.gov, 224–2939.
Votes Analyst.—Michael Mozden, SH705, michael_mozden@dpcc.senate.gov, 224–2939.

Steering and Outreach Committee

712 Hart Senate Office Building, phone 224–9048

Mark Begich, of Alaska *Chair*

Daniel K. Akaka, of Hawaii *Vice Chair*

Daniel K. Inouye, of Hawaii.
Patrick J. Leahy, of Vermont.
Tom Harkin, of Iowa.
Max Baucus, of Montana.
Kent Conrad, of North Dakota.
Carl Levin, of Michigan.
John F. Kerry, of Massachusetts.
Herb Kohl, of Wisconsin.
Barbara Boxer, of California.
Jeff Bingaman, of New Mexico.
Harry Reid, of Nevada.
Richard J. Durbin, of Illinois.
Mark L. Pryor, of Arkansas.
John D. Rockefeller IV, of West Virginia.
Kirsten E. Gillibrand, of New York.

STAFF

Staff Director.—Terrence Thompson.
Deputy Director.—Kat Pustay.
Director of Outreach Communications.—LaVenia LaVelle.
Associate Director.—Eloy Martinez.
Associate Director for Business Outreach.—Marcus Fleming.
Associate Director for Rural Outreach.—Blake Kelly.
Outreach Coordinator.—Kate Stallbaumer.

Senate Democratic Conference

448 Russell Senate Office Building, phone 224–2621, fax 224–0238

Secretary.—Patty Murray, of Washington State.
Chief of Staff.—Mike Spahn.
Senior Leadership Advisor and Floor Director.—Stacy Rich.

Senate Democratic Media Center

619 Hart Senate Office Building, phone 224–1430

Harry Reid, of Nevada, *Chair*

STAFF

Staff Director.—Katie Beirne.
Director of Broadcast Operations.—Brian Jones.
Director of New Media.—Aaron Myers.
Deputy Director of New Media.—Sarah Lovenheim.
Editors: Alice Altenburg, Toby Hayman, Kerry Sullivan.
Engineer.—Luis Mattos.
Event Coordinator.—Jason Botelho.
Graphic Design Specialist.—Perisha Gates.
Senior Developer.—Judson Blewett.
Multimedia Specialist.—Ian Shifrin.
Video Producer/Editor.—Ike Blake.
Audio Specialist.—Stephanie Milne.
Videographers: Clare Flood, Kevin Kelleher.

National Republican Senatorial Committee

425 Second Street, NE., 20002, phone 675–6000, fax 675–6058

John Cornyn, of Texas, *Chair*

STAFF

Executive Director.—Rob Jesmer.
Director of:
Administration.—Vacant.
Communications.—Brian Walsh.
Finance.—Dorinda Moss.
Legal Counsel.—Sean Cairncross.
Political Director.—Rich Dunn.
Research.—Mike Reed.

Senate Republican Policy Committee

347 Russell Senate Office Building, phone 224–2946
fax 224–1235, http://rpc.senate.gov

John Thune, of South Dakota, *Chair*

STAFF

Staff Director.—Doug Schwartz.
Communications Director.—Kyle Downey.
Administrative Director.—Craig Cheney.
Analysts:
Budget, Tax Appropriations.—Spencer Wayne.
Health Care.—Chris Jacobs.
Commerce, Transportation, Banking, Housing and Trade.—Charles "Chip" Abernathy.
Defense, Foreign Affairs, Intelligence, Veterans Affairs.—Michael Stransky.
Judiciary/Immigration.—Gregg Nunziata.
Professional Staff:
Editor.—John Mitchell.
System Administrator/RVA Analyst.—Thomas Pulju.
Station Manager/Special Projects.—Carolyn Laird.
Station Operator/Project Assistant.—Shane Scanlon.

Senate Republican Conference

405 Hart Senate Office Building, phone 224–2764
http://src.senate.gov

Chair.—Lamar Alexander, of Tennessee.
Vice Chair.—John Barrasso, of Wyoming.

STAFF

Conference of the Minority (SH–405), 224–2764.
Staff Director.—Ryan Loskarn.
Media Services Director.—Dave Hodgdon.
Office Manager.—Misty Marshall.
Press Secretary.—Nick Simpson.
Senior Writer.—Mary Katherine Ascik.
Deputy Press Secretaries: Emily Kirlin, Ryan Wrasse.
Spanish News Coordinator.—Carlos Gonzalez.
Production Manager.—Cyrus Pearson.
Videographer / Editor.—Lane Marshall.
Senior Graphics Designers: Chris Angrisani, Laura Gill.
Systems Engineer.—Nate Green.
Floor Monitor.—Mitch Relfe.
Member and Guest Relations.—Nick Hecker.

OFFICERS AND OFFICIALS OF THE SENATE

Capitol Telephone Directory, 224–3121

Senate room prefixes:

Capitol—S, Russell Senate Office Building—SR

Dirksen Senate Office Building—SD, Hart Senate Office Building—SH

PRESIDENT OF THE SENATE

Vice President of the United States and President of the Senate.—Joseph R. Biden, Jr.

The Ceremonial Office of the Vice President is S–212 in the Capitol. The Vice President has offices in the Dirksen Senate Office Building, the Eisenhower Executive Office Building (EEOB) and the White House (West Wing).

Chief of Staff to the Vice President and Counsel.—Bruce Reed, EEOB, room 202, 456–9000.
Deputy Chief of Staff.—Alan Hoffman, EEOB, room 204, 456–9000.
Counsel to the Vice President.—Cynthia Hogan, EEOB, room 245, 456–9590.
Assistant to the Vice President for—
Communications.—Shailagh Murray, EEOB, room 288, 456–0373.
Domestic Policy.—Terrell McSweeny, EEOB, room 218, 456–2728.
Legislative Affairs.—Sudafi Henry, EEOB, room 243, 456–1540.
National Security Affairs.—Tony Blinken, EEOB, room 246A, 456–9501.
Executive Assistant to the Vice President.—Michele Smith, West Wing, 456–7000.
Chief of Staff to Dr. Biden.—Cathy Russell, EEOB, room 201, 456–7458.
Deputy Assistant to the Vice President and Director of Scheduling.—Elisabeth Hire, EEOB, room 239, 456–6773.

PRESIDENT PRO TEMPORE

S–126 The Capitol, phone 224–9400

President Pro Tempore of the Senate.—Daniel K. Inouye.
Staff Director.—Diane Miyasato.
Special Assistants: George Greenwell, Maile Zeng.

MAJORITY LEADER

S–221 The Capitol, phone 224–2158, fax 224–7362

Majority Leader.—Harry Reid.
Chief of Staff.—David Krone.
Deputy Chief of Staff.—David McCallum.
Executive Assistant.—Janice Shelton.
Scheduler.—Krysta Juris.
Deputy Chief of Staff for Policy.—Bill Dauster.
Legislative Director.—Dayle Cristinzio.
Communications Director.—Adam Jentleson.
Speechwriter.—Phoebe Sweet.
Legal Counsel.—Serena Hoy.
Executive Assistant to the Chief of Staff.—Danica Daneshforouz.
Assistant Scheduler.—Vaughn Bray.
Staff Assistant.—Precious Rideout.

ASSISTANT MAJORITY LEADER

S–321 The Capitol, phone 224–9447

Assistant Democratic Leader.—Richard J. Durbin.
Chief of Staff.—Pat Souders.
Director of Operations.—Sally Brown-Shaklee.
Director of Scheduling.—Claire Reuschel.
Deputy Scheduler.—Loida Tapia.
Communications Director.—Max Gleischman.
Deputy Communications Director.—Christina Mulka.
Press Secretary-New Media.—Ben Garmisa.
Speechwriter.—Molly Rowley.
Director of Floor Operations / Counsel.—Anne Wall.
Floor Counsel.—Reema Dodin.
Staff Assistant.—Beth Cook.

REPUBLICAN LEADER

S–230 The Capitol, phone 224–3135, fax 228–1264

Republican Leader.—Mitch McConnell.
Chief of Staff.—Sharon Soderstrom.
Deputy Chief of Staff.—Rohit Kumar.
Deputy Chief of Staff for Communications.—Don Stewart.
Scheduler.—Stefanie Hagar.
Assistant Scheduler.—Rebecca Winnett.
Director of Administration.—Julie Adams.
Policy Advisors: Neil Chatterjee, Jon Lieber, Denzel McGuire, Scott Raab, Dan Schneider, Lanier Swann, Brandi Wilson White.
Legal Counsels: John Abegg, Brian Lewis.
National Security Advisor.—Tom Hawkins.
Communications Director.—Michael Brumas.
Deputy Communications Director and Director of Speechwriting.—Brian McGuire.
Press Assistant.—Emily Hesselbrock.
Systems Administrator.—Elmamoun Sulfab.
Staff Assistants: Natalie McIntyre, Katie Mohler, Kara Osborne.

REPUBLICAN COMMUNICATIONS CENTER

S–230 The Capitol, phone 228–6397

Staff Director.—John Ashbrook.
Deputy Press Secretary.—Allison Moore.
Press Assistant.—Stephanie Penn.
Analyst.—Matt Kenney.
Communications Advisor, New Media.—David Hauptmann.
Communications Advisors: Jane Vick, Rich Ward.

OFFICE OF THE REPUBLICAN WHIP

S–208 The Capitol, phone 224–2708, fax 228–1507

Republican Whip.—Jon Kyl.
Chief of Staff.—Lisa Wolski.
Deputy Chief of Staff.—Jon Gans.
Whip Liaison.—Andy Moskowitz.
Floor Assistant.—Conner Collins.
Policy Council.—Michael O'Rielly.
Speech Writer.—Rachel Currie.
Scheduler.—Kelicia Rice.
Office Manager.—Kathleen Lochridge.
Office Director.—Celeste Gold.

OFFICE OF THE SECRETARY

S–312 The Capitol, phone 224–3622

NANCY ERICKSON, Secretary of the Senate; elected and sworn in as the 32nd Secretary of the Senate on January 4, 2007; native of South Dakota; B.A. in government and history from Augustana College, Sioux Falls, SD; M.A. in public policy from American University, Washington, DC; Democratic Representative, Senate Sergeant at Arms (SAA); Deputy Chief of Staff, Senator Tom Daschle; General Accounting Office.

Secretary of the Senate.—Nancy Erickson (S–312), 224–3622.
Chief of Staff.—Robert W. Paxton (S–333), 224–5636.
Deputy Chief of Staff.—Mark S. Tratos (S–312), 224–9461.
Capitol Offices Liaison.—Gerald Thompson (SB–36), 224–1483.
Assistant Secretary of the Senate.—Sheila M. Dwyer (S–414C), 224–2114.
General Counsel.—Adam Bramwell (S–333), 224–8789.
Executive Accounts Administrator.—Zoraida Torres (S–414B), 224–7099.
Director (LIS Project Office).—Marsha Misenhimer (SD–B44A), 224–2500.
Bill Clerk.—Mary Anne Clarkson (S–123), 224–2120.
Director of:
Captioning Services.—JoEllen R. Dicken (ST–54), 224–4321.
Conservation and Preservation.—Carl Fritter, (S–416), 224–4550.
Curator.—Diane Skvarla (S–411), 224–2955.
Daily Digest, Editor.—Elizabeth Brown (S–421 and S–421A), 224–2658.
Assistant Editor.—Joseph Johnston, 224–2658.
Disbursing Office, Financial Clerk.—Chris J. Doby (SH–127), 224–3205.
Assistant Financial Clerk.—Ileana M. Garcia, 224–3208.
Enrolling Clerk.—Margarida Curtis (S–139), 224–8427.
Assistant Enrolling Clerk.—Cassandra Byrd, 224–7108.
Executive Clerk.—Michelle Haynes (S–138), 224–4341.
Assistant Executive Clerk.—Brian Malloy, 224–1918.
Historian.—Donald A. Ritchie (SH–201), 224–6900.
Associate Historian.—Betty K. Koed, 224–0753.
Human Resources, Director.—Roger Brown (SH–231B), 224–3625.
Information Systems, Systems Administrator.—Dan Kulnis (S–422), 224–4883.
Webmaster.—Arin Shapiro, 224–2020.
Interparliamentary Services, Director.—Sally Walsh (SH–808), 224–3047.
Journal Clerk.—Scott Sanborn (S–135), 224–4650.
Legislative Clerk.—Kathleen Alvarez (S–134), 224–4350.
Assistant Legislative Clerk.—John Merlino, 224–3630.
Librarian.—Leona Faust (SR–B15), 224–3313.
Official Reporters of Debates, Chief Reporter.—Jerald D. Linell (S–410A), 224–7525.
Coordinator of the Record.—Petie Gallacher, 224–1238.
Morning Business Editor.—Val Mihalache (S–123), 224–3079.
Parliamentarian.—Alan S. Frumin (S–133), 224–6128.
Senior Assistant Parliamentarians: Leigh Hildebrand, 224–5994; Elizabeth MacDonough, 224–6128.
Printing and Document Services, Director.—Karen Moore (SH–B04), 224–0205.
Assistant to the Director.—Bud Johnson, 224–2555.
Public Records, Superintendent.—Dana McCallum (SH–232), 224–0329.
Assistant Superintendent.—Erica Omorogieva, 224–0794.
Information Specialist for—
Campaign Finance.—Raymond Davis, 224–0761.
Ethics and Disclosure.—Catina Hadijski, 224–5949.
Lobbying and Foreign Travel.—Erica Omorogieva, 224–0758.
Senate Chief Counsel for Employment.—Jean Manning (SH–103), 224–5424.
Senate Gift Shop, Director.—Vacant (SDG–42), 224–7308.
Senate Page School, Principal.—Kathryn S. Weeden, 224–3926.
Senate Security, Director.—Michael P. DiSilvestro (S–407), 224–5632.
Deputy Director.—Margaret Garland, 224–5632.
Stationery, Keeper of the Stationery.—Tony Super, 224–4846.
Joint Office of Education and Training, Director.—Cam Stickley (SH–121), 224–3569.

OFFICE OF THE CHAPLAIN

S–332 The Capitol, phone 224–2510, fax 224–9686

BARRY C. BLACK, Chaplain, U.S. Senate; born in Baltimore, MD, on November 1, 1948; education: Bachelor of Arts, Theology, Oakwood College, 1970; Master of Divinity, Andrews Theological Seminary, 1973; Master of Arts, Counseling, North Carolina Central University, 1978; Doctor of Ministry, Theology, Eastern Baptist Seminary, 1982; Master of Arts, Management, Salve Regina University, 1989; Doctor of Philosophy, Psychology, United States International University, 1996; military service: U.S. Navy, 1976–2003; rising to the rank of Rear Admiral; Chief of Navy Chaplains, 2000–2003; awards: Navy Distinguished Service Medal; Legion of Merit Medal; Defense Meritorious Service Medal; Meritorious Service Medals (two awards); Navy and Marine Corps Commendation Medals (two awards); 1995 NAACP Renowned Service Award; family: married to Brenda; three children: Barry II, Brendan, and Bradford.

Chaplain of the Senate.—Barry C. Black.
Chief of Staff.—Alan N. Keiran, 224–7456.
Communications Director.—Lisa Schultz, 224–3894.
Staff Scheduler/Executive Assistant.—Jody Spraggins-Scott, 224–2048.

OFFICE OF THE SERGEANT AT ARMS

S–151 The Capitol, phone 224–2341, fax 224–7690

TERRANCE W. GAINER, Sergeant at Arms, U.S. Senate; elected and sworn in as the 38th Sergeant at Arms on January 4, 2007; education: B.A., sociology from St. Benedict's College; M.S., management and public service; J.D. from DePaul University of Chicago; Military service: Decorated veteran who served in the Vietnam War and as a Captain in the U.S. Naval Reserve until 2000; professional: Law enforcement career began in Chicago, IL, 1968; rose through the ranks serving as Deputy IG of Illinois, Deputy Director of Illinois State Police and U.S. Department of Transportation; appointed Director of Illinois State Police in March, 1991; Gainer went on to serve as second in command of the Metropolitan Police Department of the District of Columbia beginning in May 1998 and Chief of the U.S. Capitol Police from 2002–06 until his appointment as Sergeant at Arms; Gainer served the private sector focusing on emergency preparedness issues and law enforcement programs supporting Army and Marine operations in Iraq and Afghanistan; family: married, with 6 children and 12 grandchildren.

Sergeant at Arms.—Terrance W. Gainer.
Deputy Sergeant at Arms.—Martina L. Bradford.
Administrative Assistant.—Rick Edwards, SB–8.
Assistant Sergeant at Arms Intelligence and Protective Services, Contingency and Emergency Preparedness.—Michael Stenger, SVC 305, 224–1969.
Assistant Sergeant at Arms for Contingency and Emergency Preparedness.—Richard Majauskas, SVC 305, 224–1404.
Assistant Sergeant at Arms for Operations.—Bret Swanson, SD–150, 224–7052.
Assistant Sergeant at Arms and Chief Information Officer.—Kimball Win, (Postal Square), 224–0459.
Assistant Sergeant at Arms for Security and Emergency Prepardness.—Richard Majauskas, SVC 305, 224–1404.

EXECUTIVE OFFICE

Appointment Desk Manager.—Joy Ogden, North Door Capitol Building, 1st Floor, 224–6304.
Deputy Assistant SAA for Operations.—Laura Parker, SD–G61, 224–1082.
Doorkeeper Supervisor.—Myron J. Fleming, SB–6, 224–1879.
Employee Assistance Program Administrator.—Christy Prietsch, Hart Senate Office Building, 228–3902.
Protocol Officer.—Becky Daugherty, S–151, 224–2341.

CAPITOL FACILITIES

Capitol Facilities Manager.—Skip Rouse, ST–62, 224–4171.

CENTRAL OPERATIONS

Director of Central Operations.—Mike Brown (acting), SD–G61A, 224–4035.
Operations Budget Manager.—Joann Soults, SD–G82, 224–4716.
Hair Care Manager.—Kimberly Johnson, SR–B70, 224–4560.
Parking Manager.—Juanita Rilling, SD–G58, 224–8888.
Photo Studio Manager.—Bill Allen, SD–G85, 224–6000.
Printing, Graphics and Direct Mail Manager.—Dean Lusk, SD–G82, 224–0173.

FINANCIAL MANAGEMENT

Chief Financial Officer.—Christopher Dey (Postal Square), 224–6292.
Accounting and Budget Manager.—Jeanne Burcham, 228–5584.
Accounts Payable Manager.—Roy McElwee, 224–6074.
Financial Analysis Manager.—David Salem, 224–8844.
Procurement Manager.—David Baker, 224–2547.

HUMAN RESOURCES

Director of Human Resources.—Patrick Murphy, SH–142, 224–2889.
SAA Safety Office Officer.—Irvin Queja, 228–0823.
Senate Placement Officer Manager.—Brian Bean, 224–9167.
Workers' Compensation Office Manager.—Catherine Modeste Brooks, 224–3796.

IT SUPPORT SERVICES

Director of IT Support Services.—Vicki Sinnet (Postal Square), 224–0459.
Desktop/LAN Support Manager.—Tim Dean, 224–3564.
Office Equipment Services Manager.—Win Grayson, 224–6779.
Telecom Services Manager.—Rick Kauffman, 224–9293.

MEDIA GALLERIES

Director of the Daily Press Gallery.—S. Joseph Keenan, S–316, 224–0241.
Director of the Periodical Press Gallery.—Edward V. Pesce, S–320, 224–0265.
Director of the Press Photographers Gallery.—Jeff Kent, S–317, 224–6548.
Director of the Radio and Television Gallery.—Michael Mastrian, S–325, 224–7610.

OFFICE OF EDUCATION AND TRAINING

Director of the Office of Education and Training.—Cam Stickley, SH–121, 224–7952.

OFFICE OF POLICE OPERATIONS, SECURITY AND EMERGENCY PREPARDNESS

Deputy Assistant Sergeant at Arms for LESO.—Dick Attridge, SVC–305, 224–3691.
Director for Security Policy and Planning (Postal Square).—Michael Chandler, 228–0635.

OFFICE SUPPORT SERVICES

Administrative Services Executive Manager.—Barbara Graybill (Postal Square), 224–5402.
Customer Support Manager.—Dave Cape, SD–150, 224–0310.
State Office Liaison.—Jeanne Tessieri (Postal Square), 224–5409.

PAGE PROGRAM

Director of the Page Program.—Elizabeth Roach (Webster Hall), 228–1291.

POLICE OPERATIONS

Senior Advisor to the SAA.—Dan O'Sullivan, SVC–305, 224–8794.

PROCESS MANAGEMENT & INNOVATION

Director of Process Management & Innovation.—Ed Jankus (Postal Square), 224–7780.
IT Research & Deployment Manager.—Steve Walker, 224–1768.
Program Management Manager.—Joe Eckert, 224–2982.

RECORDING STUDIO

Recording Studio Manager.—Dave Bass, SVC–160, 224–4979.

SENATE POST OFFICE

Senate Postmaster.—Joe Collins, SD–B23, 224–5675.
Superintendent of Mails.—Anthony Simmons, SD–B23, 224–0070.

TECHNOLOGY DEVELOPMENT

Director of Technology Development.—Tracy Williams (Postal Square), 224–8157.
Enterprise IT Operations Manager.—Karlos Davis, 224–3322.
Information Technology Security Manager.—Paul Grabow, 224–4966.
Research Services Branch.—Tom Meenan, 224–8620.
Network Engineering and Management Manager.—Wes Gardner, 224–9269.
Systems Development Services Manager.—Jay Moore, 224–0092.

OFFICE OF THE SECRETARY FOR THE MAJORITY

S–309 The Capitol, phone 224–3735

Secretary for the Majority.—Gary Myrick.
Assistant Secretary for the Majority.—Tim Mitchell (S–118), 224–5551.
Administrative Assistant to the Secretary.—Nancy Iacomini.
Executive Assistant to the Secretary.—Amber Huus.

S–225 Majority Cloakroom, phone 224–4691

Cloakroom Assistants: Tequia Delgado, Emma Fulkerson, Dan Tinsley, Brad Watt.

OFFICE OF THE SECRETARY FOR THE MINORITY

S–337 The Capitol, phone 224–3835, fax 224–2860

Secretary for the Minority.—David J. Schiappa (S–337).
Assistant Secretary for the Minority.—Laura Dove (S–335).
Administrative Assistant.—Noelle Busk Ringel (S–337).
Floor Assistant.—Ashley Messick (S–335), phone 224–6191.

S–226 Minority Cloakroom, phone 224–6191

Cloakroom Assistants: Megan Mercer, Mary Elizabeth Taylor, Chris Tuck.

S–335 Republican Legislative Scheduling, phone 224–5456

OFFICE OF THE LEGISLATIVE COUNSEL

668 Dirksen Senate Office Building, phone 224–6461, fax 224–0567

Legislative Counsel.—James W. Fransen.
Deputy Legislative Counsel.—William F. Jensen III.
Senior Counsels: Anthony C. Coe, Polly W. Craighill, Gary L. Endicott, Mark J. Mathiesen.
Assistant Counsels: Charles E. Armstrong, Laura M. Ayoud, John W. Baggaley, William R. Baird, Heather L. Burnham, Darcie E. Chan, Kevin M. Davis, Stephanie Easley,

Ruth A. Ernst, Vincent J. Gaiani, Amy E. Gaynor, John A. Goetcheus, Robert A. Grant, John A. Henderson, Michelle L. Johnson-Weider, Stacy E. Kern-Scheerer, Elizabeth Aldridge King, Heather A. Lowell, Kelly J. Malone, Matthew D. McGhie, Mark M. McGunagle, Allison M. Otto, Kristin K. Romero, Margaret A. Roth-Warren, Kimberly A. Tamber, Alison J. Wright.

Staff Attorneys: Margaret A. Bomba, Rachelle E. Celebrezze, Kimberly D. Albrecht-Taylor.

Systems Integrator.—Thomas E. Cole.

Office Manager.—Donna L. Pasqualino.

Senior Staff Assistants: Kimberly Bourne-Goldring, Diane E. Nesmeyer.

Staff Assistants: Lauren M. DeLaCruz, Daniela A. Gonzalez, Rebekah J. Musgrove, Patricia H. Olsavsky.

OFFICE OF SENATE LEGAL COUNSEL

642 Hart Senate Office Building, phone (202) 224–4435, fax 224–3391

Senate Legal Counsel.—Morgan J. Frankel.

Deputy Senate Legal Counsel.—Patricia Mack Bryan.

Assistant Senate Legal Counsels: Thomas E. Caballero, Grant R. Vinik.

Systems Administrator/Legal Assistant.—Sara Fox Jones.

Administrative Assistant.—Kathleen M. Parker.

STANDING COMMITTEES OF THE HOUSE

[Republicans in roman; Democrats in *italic*; Resident Commissioner and Delegates in ***boldface italic***]

[Room numbers beginning with H are in the Capitol, with CHOB in the Cannon House Office Building, with LHOB in the Longworth House Office Building, with RHOB in the Rayburn House Office Building, with H1 in O'Neill House Office Building, and with H2 in the Ford House Office Building]

Agriculture

1301 Longworth House Office Building, phone 225–2171, fax 225–8510

http://agriculture.house.gov

meets first Wednesday of each month

Frank D. Lucas, of Oklahoma, *Chair*

Bob Goodlatte, of Virginia.
Timothy V. Johnson, of Illinois.
Steve King, of Iowa.
Randy Neugebauer, of Texas.
K. Michael Conaway, of Texas.
Jeff Fortenberry, of Nebraska.
Jean Schmidt, of Ohio.
Glenn Thompson, of Pennsylvania.
Thomas J. Rooney, of Florida.
Marlin A. Stutzman, of Indiana.
Bob Gibbs, of Ohio.
Austin Scott, of Georgia.
Scott R. Tipton, of Colorado.
Steve Southerland II, of Florida.
Eric A. ''Rick'' Crawford, of Arkansas.
Martha Roby, of Alabama.
Tim Huelskamp, of Kansas.
Scott DesJarlais, of Tennessee.
Renee L. Ellmers, of North Carolina.
Christopher P. Gibson, of New York.
Randy Hultgren, of Illinois.
Vicky Hartzler, of Missouri.
Robert T. Schilling, of Illinois.
Reid J. Ribble, of Wisconsin.
Kristi L. Noem, of South Dakota.

Collin C. Peterson, of Minnesota.
Tim Holden, of Pennsylvania.
Mike McIntyre, of North Carolina.
Leonard L. Boswell, of Iowa.
Joe Baca, of California.
Dennis A. Cardoza, of California.
David Scott, of Georgia.
Henry Cuellar, of Texas.
Jim Costa, of California.
Timothy J. Walz, of Minnesota.
Kurt Schrader, of Oregon.
Larry Kissell, of North Carolina.
William L. Owens, of New York.
Chellie Pingree, of Maine.
Joe Courtney, of Connecticut.
Peter Welch, of Vermont.
Marcia L. Fudge, of Ohio.
Gregorio Kilili Camacho Sablan, of Northern Mariana Islands.
Terri A. Sewell, of Alabama.
James P. McGovern, of Massachusetts.

SUBCOMMITTEES

[The chairman and ranking minority member are ex officio (voting) members of all subcommittees on which they do not serve.]

Conservation, Energy, and Forestry

Glenn Thompson, of Pennsylvania, *Chair*

Bob Goodlatte, of Virginia.
Marlin A. Stutzman, of Indiana.
Bob Gibbs, of Ohio.
Scott R. Tipton, of Colorado.
Steve Southerland II, of Florida.
Martha Roby, of Alabama.
Tim Huelskamp, of Kansas.
Randy Hultgren, of Illinois.
Reid J. Ribble, of Wisconsin.
Kristi L. Noem, of South Dakota.

Tim Holden, of Pennsylvania.
Kurt Schrader, of Oregon.
William L. Owens, of New York.
Mike McIntyre, of North Carolina.
Jim Costa, of California.
Timothy J. Walz, of Minnesota.
Chellie Pingree, of Maine.
Marcia L. Fudge, of Ohio.
Gregorio Kilili Camacho Sablan, of Northern Mariana Islands.

Nutrition and Horticulture

Jean Schmidt, of Ohio, *Chair*

Steve King, of Iowa.
Thomas J. Rooney, of Florida.
Steve Southerland II, of Florida.
Eric A. ''Rick'' Crawford, of Arkansas.

Joe Baca, of California.
Chellie Pingree, of Maine.
Gregorio Kilili Camacho Sablan, of Northern Mariana Islands.

General Farm Commodities and Risk Management

K. Michael Conaway, of Texas, *Chair*

Steve King, of Iowa.
Randy Neugebauer, of Texas.
Jean Schmidt, of Ohio.
Bob Gibbs, of Ohio.
Austin Scott, of Georgia.
Eric A. ''Rick'' Crawford, of Arkansas.
Martha Roby, of Alabama.
Tim Huelskamp, of Kansas.
Renee L. Ellmers, of North Carolina.
Christopher P. Gibson, of New York.
Randy Hultgren, of Illinois.
Vicky Hartzler, of Missouri.
Robert T. Schilling, of Illinois.

Leonard L. Boswell, of Iowa.
Mike McIntyre, of North Carolina.
Timothy J. Walz, of Minnesota.
Larry Kissell, of North Carolina.
James P. McGovern, of Massachusetts.
Dennis A. Cardoza, of California.
David Scott, of Georgia.
Joe Courtney, of Connecticut.
Peter Welch, of Vermont.
Terri A. Sewell, of Alabama.

Livestock, Dairy, and Poultry

Thomas J. Rooney, of Florida, *Chair*

Bob Goodlatte, of Virginia.
Steve King, of Iowa.
Randy Neugebauer, of Texas.
K. Michael Conaway, of Texas.
Tim Huelskamp, of Kansas.
Scott DesJarlais, of Tennessee.
Christopher P. Gibson, of New York.
Reid J. Ribble, of Wisconsin.
Kristi L. Noem, of South Dakota.

Dennis A. Cardoza, of California.
David Scott, of Georgia.
Joe Courtney, of Connecticut.
Tim Holden, of Pennsylvania.
Leonard L. Boswell, of Iowa.
Joe Baca, of California.
Kurt Schrader, of Oregon.
William L. Owens, of New York.

Rural Development, Research, Biotechnology, and Foreign Agriculture

Timothy V. Johnson, of Illinois, *Chair*

Glenn Thompson, of Pennsylvania.
Marlin A. Stutzman, of Indiana.
Austin Scott, of Georgia.
Randy Hultgren, of Illinois.
Vicky Hartzler, of Missouri.
Robert T. Schilling, of Illinois.

Jim Costa, of California.
Henry Cuellar, of Texas.
Peter Welch, of Vermont.
Terri A. Sewell, of Alabama.
Larry Kissell, of North Carolina.

Department Operations, Oversight, and Credit

Jeff Fortenberry, of Nebraska, *Chair*

Timothy V. Johnson, of Illinois.
Steve King, of Iowa.
Eric A. ''Rick'' Crawford, of Arkansas.
Kristi L. Noem, of South Dakota.

Marcia L. Fudge, of Ohio.
James P. McGovern, of Massachusetts.
Joe Baca, of California.

STAFF

Committee on Agriculture (1301 LHOB), 225–2171.
Majority Staff
Staff Director.—Nicole Scott.
Deputy Counsel.—Patricia Barr.
Subcommittee Staff Director, Conservation, Energy and Forestry.—R. Brent Blevins.
Subcommittee Staff Director, Rural Development, Research, Biotechnology and Foreign Agriculture.—Mike Dunlap.
Chief Economist.—Bart Fisher.
Science Advisor.—John Goldberg.
Communications Director.—Tamara Hinton.
Information Technology Assistant.—John Konya.
Chief Counsel.—Kevin Kramp.
Subcommittee Staff Director, Counsel, Department Operations, Oversight and Credit.—Brandon Lipps.
Deputy Staff Director.—Josh Mathis.
Senior Professional Staff: Pamilyn Miller, Richard G. Thomson.
Professional Staff: Ryan McKee, Josh Maxwell, Heather Vaughan.
Director of Information Technology.—Merrick Munday.
Counsel.—DaNita Murray.
Legislative Assistants: Mary Nowak, John Porter.
Subcommittee Staff Director, Nutrition and Horticulture.—Matt Perin.
Subcommittee Staff Director, General Farm Commodities and Risk Management.—Matt Schertz.
Chief Clerk.—Debbie Smith.
Policy Director.—Pelham Straughn.
Staff Assistant.—Lauren Sturgeon.
Subcommittee Staff Director, Livestock, Dairy and Poultry.—Michelle Weber.
Administrative Director.—Margaret Wetherald.
Hearing Clerk.—Jamie J. Weyer.
Minority Staff 1305 LHOB (202) 225–0317
Staff Director.—Rob Larew.
Chief Counsel.—Andy Baker.
Professional Staff: Nona Darrell, Keith Jones, Mary Knigge, Clark Olgilvie, Lisa Shelton.
Counsel.—Nathan Fretz.
Communications Director.—Liz Friedlander.
Chief Economist.—Craig Jagger.
Senior Policy Advisor.—Anne Simmons.
Office Manager.—Faye Smith.

Appropriations

H–307 The Capitol, phone 225–2771

http://www.house.gov/appropriations

Harold Rogers, of Kentucky, *Chair*

C. W. Bill Young, of Florida.
Jerry Lewis, of California.
Frank R. Wolf, of Virginia.
Jack Kingston, of Georgia.
Rodney P. Frelinghuysen, of New Jersey.
Tom Latham, of Iowa.
Robert B. Aderholt, of Alabama.
Jo Ann Emerson, of Missouri.
Kay Granger, of Texas.
Michael K. Simpson, of Idaho.
John Abney Culberson, of Texas.
Ander Crenshaw, of Florida.
Denny Rehberg, of Montana.
John R. Carter, of Texas.
Rodney Alexander, of Louisiana.
Ken Calvert, of California.
Jo Bonner, of Alabama.
Steven C. LaTourette, of Ohio.
Tom Cole, of Oklahoma.
Jeff Flake, of Arizona.
Mario Diaz-Balart, of Florida.
Charles W. Dent, of Pennsylvania.
Steve Austria, of Ohio.
Cynthia M. Lummis, of Wyoming.
Tom Graves, of Georgia.
Kevin Yoder, of Kansas.
Steve Womack, of Arkansas.
Alan Nunnelee, of Mississippi.

Norman D. Dicks, of Washington.
Marcy Kaptur, of Ohio.
Peter J. Visclosky, of Indiana.
Nita M. Lowey, of New York.
José E. Serrano, of New York.
Rosa L. DeLauro, of Connecticut.
James P. Moran, of Virginia.
John W. Olver, of Massachusetts.
Ed Pastor, of Arizona.
David E. Price, of North Carolina.
Maurice D. Hinchey, of New York.
Lucille Roybal-Allard, of California.
Sam Farr, of California.
Jesse L. Jackson, Jr., of Illinois.
Chaka Fattah, of Pennsylvania.
Steven R. Rothman, of New Jersey.
Sanford D. Bishop, Jr., of Georgia.
Barbara Lee, of California.
Adam B. Schiff, of California.
Michael M. Honda, of California.
Betty McCollum, of Minnesota.

SUBCOMMITTEES

[The chairman and ranking minority member are ex officio (voting) members of all subcommittees on which they do not serve.]

Agriculture, Rural Development, Food and Drug Administration, and Related Agencies

Jack Kingston, of Georgia, *Chair*

Cynthia M. Lummis, of Wyoming, *Vice Chair*

Tom Latham, of Iowa.
Jo Ann Emerson, of Missouri.
Robert B. Aderholt, of Alabama.
Alan Nunnelee, of Mississippi.
Tom Graves, of Georgia.

Sam Farr, of California.
Rosa L. DeLauro, of Connecticut.
Sanford D. Bishop, Jr., of Georgia.
Marcy Kaptur, of Ohio.

Commerce, Justice, Science, and Related Agencies

Frank R. Wolf, of Virginia, *Chair*

Jo Bonner, of Alabama, *Vice Chair*

John Abney Culberson, of Texas.
Robert B. Aderholt, of Alabama.
Steve Austria, of Ohio.
Tom Graves, of Georgia.
Kevin Yoder, of Kansas.

Chaka Fattah, of Pennsylvania.
Adam B. Schiff, of California.
Michael M. Honda, of California.
José E. Serrano, of New York.

Defense

C. W. Bill Young, of Florida, *Chair*

Jerry Lewis, of California, *Vice Chair*

Rodney P. Frelinghuysen, of New Jersey.
Jack Kingston, of Georgia.
Kay Granger, of Texas.
Ander Crenshaw, of Florida.
Ken Calvert, of California.
Jo Bonner, of Alabama.
Tom Cole, of Oklahoma.

Norman D. Dicks, of Washington.
Peter J. Visclosky, of Indiana.
James P. Moran, of Virginia.
Marcy Kaptur, of Ohio.
Steven R. Rothman, of New Jersey.
Maurice D. Hinchey, of New York.

Energy and Water Development, and Related Agencies

Rodney P. Frelinghuysen, of New Jersey, *Chair*

Steve Womack, of Arkansas, *Vice Chair*

Jerry Lewis, of California.
Michael K. Simpson, of Idaho.
Denny Rehberg, of Montana.
Rodney Alexander, of Louisiana.
Alan Nunnelee, of Mississippi.

Peter J. Visclosky, of Indiana.
Ed Pastor, of Arizona.
Chaka Fattah, of Pennsylvania.
John W. Olver, of Massachusetts.

Financial Services and General Government

Jo Ann Emerson, of Missouri, *Chair*

Mario Diaz-Balart, of Florida, *Vice Chair*

Rodney Alexander, of Louisiana.
Jo Bonner, of Alabama.
Tom Graves, of Georgia.
Kevin Yoder, of Kansas.
Steve Womack, of Arkansas.

José E. Serrano, of New York.
Barbara Lee, of California.
Peter J. Visclosky, of Indiana.
Ed Pastor, of Arizona.

Homeland Security

Robert B. Aderholt, of Alabama, *Chair*

John Abney Culberson, of Texas, *Vice Chair*

John R. Carter, of Texas.
Rodney P. Frelinghuysen, of New Jersey.
Tom Latham, of Iowa.
Ander Crenshaw, of Florida.
Charles W. Dent, of Pennsylvania.

David E. Price, of North Carolina.
Lucille Roybal-Allard, of California.
Nita M. Lowey, of New York.
John W. Olver, of Massachusetts.

Interior, Environment, and Related Agencies

Michael K. Simpson, of Idaho, *Chair*

Ken Calvert, of California, *Vice Chair*

Jerry Lewis, of California.
Steven C. LaTourette, of Ohio.
Tom Cole, of Oklahoma.
Jeff Flake, of Arizona.
Cynthia M. Lummis, of Wyoming.

James P. Moran, of Virginia.
Betty McCollum, of Minnesota.
Maurice D. Hinchey, of New York.
José E. Serrano, of New York.

Labor, Health and Human Services, Education, and Related Agencies

Denny Rehberg, of Montana, *Chair*

Rodney Alexander, of Louisiana, *Vice Chair*

Jerry Lewis, of California.
Jack Kingston, of Georgia.
Kay Granger, of Texas.
Michael K. Simpson, of Idaho.
Jeff Flake, of Arizona.
Cynthia M. Lummis, of Wyoming.

Rosa L. DeLauro, of Connecticut.
Nita M. Lowey, of New York.
Jesse L. Jackson, Jr., of Illinois.
Lucille Roybal-Allard, of California.
Barbara Lee, of California.

Legislative Branch

Ander Crenshaw, of Florida, *Chair*

Jo Ann Emerson, of Missouri, *Vice Chair*

Steven C. LaTourette, of Ohio.
Denny Rehberg, of Montana.
Ken Calvert, of California.

Michael M. Honda, of California.
David E. Price, of North Carolina.
Sanford D. Bishop, Jr., of Georgia.

Military Construction, Veterans' Affairs, and Related Agencies

John Abney Culberson, of Texas, *Chair*

John R. Carter, of Texas, *Vice Chair*

C. W. Bill Young, of Florida.
Jeff Flake, of Arizona.
Steve Austria, of Ohio.
Kevin Yoder, of Kansas.
Alan Nunnelee, of Mississippi.

Sanford D. Bishop, Jr., of Georgia.
Sam Farr, of California.
Betty McCollum, of Minnesota.
James P. Moran, of Virginia.

State, Foreign Operations, and Related Programs

Kay Granger, of Texas, *Chair*

Tom Cole, of Oklahoma, *Vice Chair*

Jerry Lewis, of California.
Frank R. Wolf, of Virginia.
Mario Diaz-Balart, of Florida.
Charles W. Dent, of Pennsylvania.
Steve Austria, of Ohio.

Nita M. Lowey, of New York.
Jesse L. Jackson, Jr., of Illinois.
Adam B. Schiff, of California.
Steven R. Rothman, of New Jersey.

Transportation, Housing and Urban Development, and Related Agencies

Tom Latham, of Iowa, *Chair*

Steven C. LaTourette, of Ohio, *Vice Chair*

Frank R. Wolf, of Virginia.
John R. Carter, of Texas.
Mario Diaz-Balart, of Florida.
Charles W. Dent, of Pennsylvania.
Steve Womack, of Arkansas.

John W. Olver, of Massachusetts.
Ed Pastor, of Arizona.
Marcy Kaptur, of Ohio.
David E. Price, of North Carolina.

STAFF

Committee on Appropriations (H–307), 225–2771.
Majority Clerk and Staff Director.—William Inglee.
Deputy Clerk and Staff Director.—Will Smith.
Staff Assistants: Jim Kulikowski, Dale Oak, Stephen Sepp.
Coalitions Director.—Mike Robinson.
Communications Director.—Jennifer Hing.
Press Assistant.—Marta Dehmlow.
Administrative Assistant.—Sandy Farrow.

Assistant to the Chairman.—Julia Casey.
Administrative Aides: Tammy Hughes, Cornell Teague.
Editors: Larry Boarman, Cathy Edwards (B–301A RHOB), 5–2851.
Computer Operations: Cathy Little, Linda Muir, Chauncey Powell, Jay Sivulich (B–305 RHOB), Eric Jackson 5–2718.
Minority Staff Director.—David Pomerantz (1016 LHOB), 5–3481.
Minority Deputy Staff Director.—Lesley Turner.
Minority Press Secretary.—Ryan Nickel.
Minority Staff Assistant.—Rebecca Motley.
Administrative Aide.—Deborah Spriggs.
Subcommittee on Agriculture, Rural Development, Food and Drug Administration, and Related Agencies (2362–A RHOB), 5–2638.
Staff Assistants: Betsy Bina, Martin Delgado, Tom O'Brien.
Administrative Aide.—Andrew Cooper.
Minority Staff Assistants: Martha Foley, Matthew Smith (1016 LHOB), 5–3481.
Subcommittee on Commerce, Justice, Science and Related Agencies (H–309), 5–3351.
Staff Assistants: Leslie Albright, Stephanie Myers, Mike Ringler, Diana Simpson.
Administrative Aide.—Colin Samples.
Minority Staff Assistants: Bob Bonner, Darek Newby (1016 LHOB), 5–3481.
Subcommittee on Defense (H–405), 5–2847.
Staff Assistants: Brooke Boyer, Walter Hearne, Tom McLemore, Jennifer Miller, Tim Prince, Adrienne Ramsay, Ann Reese, Megan Rosenbusch, Paul Terr, B.G. Wright.
Administrative Aide.—Sherry Young.
Minority Staff Assistants: Paul Juola, Rebecca Leggieri (1016 LHOB), 5–3481.
Subcommittee on Energy and Water Development, and Related Agencies (2362–B RHOB), 5–3421.
Staff Assistants: Rob Blair, Angie Giancarlo, Loraine Heckenberg, Joseph Levin.
Administrative Aide.—Perry Yates.
Minority Staff Assistant.—Taunja Berquam (1016 LHOB), 5–3481.
Subcommittee on Financial Services (B–300 RHOB), 5–7245.
Staff Assistants: Winnie Chang, John Martens, Ariana Sarar, Kelly Shea.
Minority Staff Assistants: Laura Hogshead (1016 LHOB), 5–3481.
Subcommittee on Homeland Security (B–307 RHOB), 5–5834.
Staff Assistants: Jeff Ashford, Kathy Kraninger, Kris Mallard, Ben Nicholson.
Administrative Aide.—Miles Taylor.
Minority Staff Assistant.—Stephanie Gupta (1016 LHOB), 5–3481.
Subcommittee on Interior, Environment, and Related Agencies (B–308 RHOB), 5–3081.
Staff Assistants: Darren Benjamin, Jason Gray, Dave LesStrang, Erica Rhoad.
Administrative Aide.—Colin Vickery.
Minority Staff Assistants: Rick Healy, Shalanda Young (1016 LHOB), 5–3481.
Subcommittee on Labor, Health and Human Services, Education, and Related Agencies (2358 RHOB), 5–3508.
Staff Assistants: John Bartrum, Steve Crane, Kevin Jones, Susan Ross, Donna Shahbaz.
Administrative Aide.—Lori Bias.
Minority Staff Assistants: Lisa Molyneux, David Reich (1016 LHOB), 5–3481.
Subcommittee on Legislative Branch (HT–2), 6–7252.
Staff Assistants: Liz Dawson, Jennifer Kisiah.
Minority Staff Assistant.—Shalanda Young.
Subcommittee on Military Construction, Veterans' Affairs, and Related Agencies (HVC–227), 5–3047.
Staff Assistants: Tim Peterson, Sue Quantius, Sarah Young.
Administrative Aide.—Tracey Russell.
Minority Staff Assistants: Danny Cromer, Matt Washington (1016 LHOB), 5–3481.
Subcommittee on State and Foreign Operations (HT–2), 5–2401.
Staff Assistants: Susan Adams, Anne Marie Chotvacs, Craig Higgins, Alice Hogans.
Administrative Aide.—Clelia Alvarado.
Minority Staff Assistants: Erin Kolodjeski, Steve Marchese (1016 LHOB), 5–3481.
Subcommittee on Transportation, HUD and Independent Agencies (2358A RHOB), 5–2141.
Staff Assistants: Dena Baron, Michael Friedberg, Matt McCardle, Sara Peters.
Administrative Aide.—Brian Barnard.
Minority Staff Assistants: Joe Carlile, Kate Hallahan (1016 LHOB), 5–3481.

Armed Services

2120 Rayburn House Office Building, phone 225–4151, fax 225–9077

http://www.armedservices.house.gov

Howard P. ''Buck'' McKeon, of California, *Chair*

Roscoe G. Bartlett, of Maryland.
Mac Thornberry, of Texas.
Walter B. Jones, of North Carolina.
W. Todd Akin, of Missouri.
J. Randy Forbes, of Virginia.
Jeff Miller, of Florida.
Joe Wilson, of South Carolina.
Frank A. LoBiondo, of New Jersey.
Michael R. Turner, of Ohio.
John Kline, of Minnesota.
Mike Rogers, of Alabama.
Trent Franks, of Arizona.
Bill Shuster, of Pennsylvania.
K. Michael Conaway, of Texas.
Doug Lamborn, of Colorado.
Robert J. Wittman, of Virginia.
Duncan Hunter, of California.
John Fleming, of Louisiana.
Mike Coffman, of Colorado.
Thomas J. Rooney, of Florida.
Todd Russell Platts, of Pennsylvania.
E. Scott Rigell, of Virginia.
Christopher P. Gibson, of New York.
Vicky Hartzler, of Missouri.
Joseph J. Heck, of Nevada.
Robert T. Schilling, of Illinois.
Jon Runyan, of New Jersey.
Austin Scott, of Georgia.
Tim Griffin, of Arkansas.
Steven M. Palazzo, of Mississippi.
Allen B. West, of Florida.
Martha Roby, of Alabama.
Mo Brooks, of Alabama.
Todd C. Young, of Indiana.

Adam Smith, of Washington.
Silvestre Reyes, of Texas.
Loretta Sanchez, of California.
Mike McIntyre, of North Carolina.
Robert A. Brady, of Pennsylvania.
Robert E. Andrews, of New Jersey.
Susan A. Davis, of California.
James R. Langevin, of Rhode Island.
Rick Larsen, of Washington.
Jim Cooper, of Tennessee.
Madeleine Z. Bordallo, of Guam.
Joe Courtney, of Connecticut.
David Loebsack, of Iowa.
Gabrielle Giffords, of Arizona.
Niki Tsongas, of Massachusetts.
Chellie Pingree, of Maine.
Larry Kissell, of North Carolina.
Martin Heinrich, of New Mexico.
William L. Owens, of New York.
John Garamendi, of California.
Mark S. Critz, of Pennsylvania.
Tim Ryan, of Ohio.
C.A. Dutch Ruppersberger, of Maryland.
Henry C. ''Hank'' Johnson, Jr., of Georgia.
Betty Sutton, of Ohio.
Colleen W. Hanabusa, of Hawaii.
Kathleen C. Hochul, of New York.

SUBCOMMITTEES

Emerging Threats and Capabilities

Mac Thornberry, of Texas, *Chair*

Jeff Miller, of Florida.
John Kline, of Minnesota.
Bill Shuster, of Pennsylvania.
K. Michael Conaway, of Texas.
Christopher P. Gibson, of New York.
Robert T. Schilling, of Illinois.
Allen B. West, of Florida.
Trent Franks, of Arizona.
Duncan Hunter, of California.

James R. Langevin, of Rhode Island.
Loretta Sanchez, of California.
Robert E. Andrews, of New Jersey.
Susan A. Davis, of California.
Tim Ryan, of Ohio.
C.A. Dutch Ruppersberger, of Maryland.
Henry C. ''Hank'' Johnson, Jr., of Georgia.

Military Personnel

Joe Wilson, of South Carolina, *Chair*

Walter B. Jones, of North Carolina.
Mike Coffman, of Colorado.
Thomas J. Rooney, of Florida.
Joseph J. Heck, of Nevada.
Allen B. West, of Florida.
Austin Scott, of Georgia.
Vicky Hartzler, of Missouri.

Susan A. Davis, of California.
Robert A. Brady, of Pennsylvania.
Madeleine Z. Bordallo, of Guam.
David Loebsack, of Iowa.
Niki Tsongas, of Massachusetts.
Chellie Pingree, of Maine.

Oversight and Investigations

Robert J. Wittman, of Virginia, *Chair*

K. Michael Conaway, of Texas.
Mo Brooks, of Alabama.
Todd C. Young, of Indiana.
Thomas J. Rooney, of Florida.
Mike Coffman, of Colorado.

Jim Cooper, of Tennessee.
Robert E. Andrews, of New Jersey.
Loretta Sanchez, of California.
Colleen W. Hanabusa, of Hawaii.

Readiness

J. Randy Forbes, of Virginia, *Chair*

Mike Rogers, of Alabama.
Joseph J. Heck, of Nevada.
Austin Scott, of Georgia.
Frank A. LoBiondo, of New Jersey.
Christopher P. Gibson, of New York.
Vicky Hartzler, of Missouri.
Robert T. Schilling, of Illinois.
Jon Runyan, of New Jersey.
Tim Griffin, of Arkansas.
Steven M. Palazzo, of Mississippi.
Martha Roby, of Alabama.

Madeleine Z. Bordallo, of Guam.
Silvestre Reyes, of Texas.
Joe Courtney, of Connecticut.
David Loebsack, of Iowa.
Gabrielle Giffords, of Arizona.
Larry Kissell, of North Carolina.
William L. Owens, of New York.
Tim Ryan, of Ohio.
Colleen W. Hanabusa, of Hawaii.

Seapower and Projection Forces

W. Todd Akin, of Missouri, *Chair*

Duncan Hunter, of California.
Mike Coffman, of Colorado.
E. Scott Rigell, of Virginia.
Tim Griffin, of Arkansas.
Steven M. Palazzo, of Mississippi.
Todd C. Young, of Indiana.
Roscoe G. Bartlett, of Maryland.
J. Randy Forbes, of Virginia.
Robert J. Wittman, of Virginia.
Todd Russell Platts, of Pennsylvania.

Mike McIntyre, of North Carolina.
Susan A. Davis, of California.
James R. Langevin, of Rhode Island.
Rick Larsen, of Washington.
Joe Courtney, of Connecticut.
Chellie Pingree, of Maine.
Mark S. Critz, of Pennsylvania.
Henry C. ''Hank'' Johnson, Jr., of Georgia.
Betty Sutton, of Ohio.

Strategic Forces

Michael R. Turner, of Ohio, *Chair*

Trent Franks, of Arizona.
Doug Lamborn, of Colorado.
Mo Brooks, of Alabama.
Mac Thornberry, of Texas.
Mike Rogers, of Alabama.
John Fleming, of Louisiana.
E. Scott Rigell, of Virginia.
Austin Scott, of Georgia.

Loretta Sanchez, of California.
James R. Langevin, of Rhode Island.
Rick Larsen, of Washington.
Martin Heinrich, of New Mexico.
John Garamendi, of California.
C.A. Dutch Ruppersberger, of Maryland.
Betty Sutton, of Ohio.

Tactical Air and Land Forces

Roscoe G. Bartlett, of Maryland, *Chair*

Frank A. LoBiondo, of New Jersey.
John Fleming, of Louisiana.
Thomas J. Rooney, of Florida.
Todd Russell Platts, of Pennsylvania.
Vicky Hartzler, of Missouri.
Jon Runyan, of New Jersey.
Martha Roby, of Alabama.
Walter B. Jones, of North Carolina.
W. Todd Akin, of Missouri.
Joe Wilson, of South Carolina.
Michael R. Turner, of Ohio.
Bill Shuster, of Pennsylvania.
Doug Lamborn, of Colorado.

Silvestre Reyes, of Texas.
Mike McIntyre, of North Carolina.
Jim Cooper, of Tennessee.
Gabrielle Giffords, of Arizona.
Niki Tsongas, of Massachusetts.
Larry Kissell, of North Carolina.
Martin Heinrich, of New Mexico.
William L. Owens, of New York.
John Garamendi, of California.
Mark S. Critz, of Pennsylvania.

STAFF

Committee on Armed Services (2120 RHOB), 225–4151, fax 225–9077.

Staff Director.—Bob Simmons.

Deputy Staff Director/General Counsel.—Roger Zakheim.

Counsels: William S. Johnson, Paul Lewis, Catherine A. McElroy, Michele Pearce, Leonor Tomero.

Director, Legislative Operations.—Zach Steacy.

Professional Staff: Michael Amato, Paul Arcangeli, Kari Bingen, Heath R. Bope, Douglas Bush, Michael Casey, John D. Chapla, Jaime Cheshire, Everett Coleman, Ryan Crumpler, Cathy Garman, Brian Garrett, Kevin Gates, Craig Greene, Michael R. Higgins, Jeanette S. James, Alex Kugajevsky, Mark R. Lewis, Jamie R. Lynch, Timothy McClees, Thomas MacKenzie, Phil MacNaughton, Elizabeth Nathan, Vickie Plunkett, Douglas C. Roach, Rebecca A. Ross, Ben Runkle, Jack Schuler, David Sienicki, Jenness Simler, John F. Sullivan, Jesse D. Tolleson, Jr., Debra S. Wada, Andrew T. Walter, Nancy M. Warner, John Wason, Lynn M. Williams, Peter Villano.

Senior Advisor to the Chairman.—Jaime Cheshire.

Deputy Communications Director.—John Noonan.

Communications Assistant.—Robert J. McAlister.

Security Manager.—Cyndi Howard.

Executive Assistants: Betty B. Gray, Katie Sendak.

Research Assistant.—Lauren Hauhn.

Staff Assistants: Scott Bousum, Jeff Cullen, Mary Kate Cunningham, Megan Howard, John N. Johnson, Elizabeth McWhorter, Nicholas Rodman, Melissa Tuttle, Christine Wagner, Dustin Walker, Jim Weiss, Alejandra Villarreal.

Budget

207 Cannon House Office Building 20515–6065, phone 226–7270, fax 226–7174
http://www.budget.house.gov

Paul Ryan, of Wisconsin, *Chair*

Scott Garrett, of New Jersey.
Michael K. Simpson, of Idaho.
John Campbell, of California.
Ken Calvert, of California.
W. Todd Akin, of Missouri.
Tom Cole, of Oklahoma.
Tom Price, of Georgia.
Tom McClintock, of California.
Jason Chaffetz, of Utah.
Marlin A. Stutzman, of Indiana.
James Lankford, of Oklahoma.
Diane Black, of Tennessee.
Reid J. Ribble, of Wisconsin.
Bill Flores, of Texas.
Mick Mulvaney, of South Carolina.
Tim Huelskamp, of Kansas.
Todd C. Young, of Indiana.
Justin Amash, of Michigan.
Todd Rokita, of Indiana.
Frank C. Guinta, of New Hampshire.
Rob Woodall, of Georgia.

Chris Van Hollen, of Maryland.
Allyson Y. Schwartz, of Pennsylvania.
Marcy Kaptur, of Ohio.
Lloyd Doggett, of Texas.
Earl Blumenauer, of Oregon.
Betty McCollum, of Minnesota.
John A. Yarmuth, of Kentucky.
Bill Pascrell, Jr., of New Jersey.
Michael M. Honda, of California.
Tim Ryan, of Ohio.
Debbie Wasserman Schultz, of Florida.
Gwen Moore, of Wisconsin.
Kathy Castor, of Florida.
Heath Shuler, of North Carolina.
Paul Tonko, of New York.
Karen Bass, of California.

(No Subcommittees)

STAFF

Committee on Budget (207 CHOB), 226–7270, fax 226–7174.
Majority Staff Director.—Austin Smythe
Deputy Staff Director.—Andy Morton.
Executive Assistant to the Staff Director.—Eric Davis.
Chief Counsel.—Paul Restuccia.
Counsel.—Nicole Foltz.
Chief Economist.—Timothy Flynn.
Policy Director.—Pat Knudsen.
Counsels/Budget Analysts: Charlotte Ivancic, Courtney Reinhard, Jon Romito.
Budget Analysts: Jon Burks, Jim Herz, Matt Hoffmann, Jane Lee, Ted McCann, Stephanie Parks.
Communications Director.—Conor Sweeney.
Visual/New Media Director.—Vanessa Day.
Communications Advisor.—Stephen Spruiell.
Press Secretary.—Gerrit Lansing.
Senior Advisor.—Dennis Teti.
Chief Administrator.—Marsha Douglas.
Staff Assistants: Jenna Spealman, Alex Stoddard.
Systems Administrator.—Jose Guillen.
Committee Printer.—Richard E. Magee.
Minority Staff Director.—Tom Kahn (B71 Cannon), 226–7200, fax 225–9905.
Executive Assistant to the Staff Director.—Beth Stephenson.
Chief Counsel.—Karen Robb.
General Counsel.—Gail Millar.
Chief Economist.—Adam Carasso.
Senior Policy Coordinator.—Sarah Abernathy.
Budget Review Director.—Kimberly Overbeek.
Senior Budget Review Specialist.—Ellen J. Balis.
Senior Budget Analyst.—Diana Meredith.
Budget Analysts: Stephen G. Elmore, Scott R. Russell, Greg R. Waring, Andrea R. Weathers.
Communications Director.—Nu Wexler.
Office Manager.—Sheila A. McDowell.
Special Assistant to the Ranking Minority Member.—Brian Brady.

Education and the Workforce

2181 Rayburn House Office Building, phone 225–3725, fax 226–5398

http://edworkforce.house.gov

John Kline, of Minnesota, *Chair*

Thomas E. Petri, of Wisconsin.
Howard P. ''Buck'' McKeon, of California.
Judy Biggert, of Illinois.
Todd Russell Platts, of Pennsylvania.
Joe Wilson, of South Carolina.
Virginia Foxx, of North Carolina.
Bob Goodlatte, of Virginia.
Duncan Hunter, of California.
David P. Roe, of Tennessee.
Glenn Thompson, of Pennsylvania.
Tim Walberg, of Michigan.
Scott DesJarlais, of Tennessee.
Richard L. Hanna, of New York.
Todd Rokita, of Indiana.
Larry Bucshon, of Indiana.
Trey Gowdy, of South Carolina.
Lou Barletta, of Pennsylvania.
Kristi L. Noem, of South Dakota.
Martha Roby, of Alabama.
Joseph J. Heck, of Nevada.
Dennis A. Ross, of Florida.
Mike Kelly, of Pennsylvania.

George Miller, of California.
Dale E. Kildee, of Michigan.
Donald M. Payne, of New Jersey.
Robert E. Andrews, of New Jersey.
Robert C. ''Bobby'' Scott, of Virginia.
Lynn C. Woolsey, of California.
Rubén Hinojosa, of Texas.
Carolyn McCarthy, of New York.
John F. Tierney, of Massachusetts.
Dennis J. Kucinich, of Ohio.
Rush D. Holt, of New Jersey.
Susan A. Davis, of California.
Raúl M. Grijalva, of Arizona.
Timothy H. Bishop, of New York.
David Loebsack, of Iowa.
Mazie K. Hirono, of Hawaii.
Jason Altmire, of Pennsylvania.

SUBCOMMITTEES

[The chairman and ranking minority member are ex officio (non-voting) members of all subcommittees on which they do not serve.]

Early Childhood, Elementary and Secondary Education

Duncan Hunter, of California, *Chair*

John Kline, of Minnesota.
Thomas E. Petri, of Wisconsin.
Judy Biggert, of Illinois.
Todd Russell Platts, of Pennsylvania.
Virginia Foxx, of North Carolina.
Bob Goodlatte, of Virginia.
Richard L. Hanna, of New York.
Lou Barletta, of Pennsylvania.
Kristi L. Noem, of South Dakota.
Martha Roby, of Alabama.
Mike Kelly, of Pennsylvania.

Dale E. Kildee, of Michigan.
Donald M. Payne, of New Jersey.
Robert C. ''Bobby'' Scott, of Virginia.
Carolyn McCarthy, of New York.
Rush D. Holt, of New Jersey.
Susan A. Davis, of California.
Raúl M. Grijalva, of Arizona.
Mazie K. Hirono, of Hawaii.
Lynn C. Woolsey, of California.

Higher Education and Workforce Training

Virginia Foxx, of North Carolina, *Chair*

John Kline, of Minnesota.
Thomas E. Petri, of Wisconsin.
Howard P. ''Buck'' McKeon, of California.
Judy Biggert, of Illinois.
Todd Russell Platts, of Pennsylvania.
David P. Roe, of Tennessee.
Glenn Thompson, of Pennsylvania.
Richard L. Hanna, of New York.
Larry Bucshon, of Indiana.
Lou Barletta, of Pennsylvania.
Joseph J. Heck, of Nevada.

Rubén Hinojosa, of Texas.
John F. Tierney, of Massachusetts.
Timothy H. Bishop, of New York.
Robert E. Andrews, of New Jersey.
Susan A. Davis, of California.
Raúl M. Grijalva, of Arizona.
David Loebsack, of Iowa.
George Miller, of California.
Jason Altmire, of Pennsylvania.

Health, Employment, Labor, and Pensions

David P. Roe, of Tennessee, *Chair*

Joe Wilson, of South Carolina.
Glenn Thompson, of Pennsylvania.
Tim Walberg, of Michigan.
Scott DesJarlais, of Tennessee.
Richard L. Hanna, of New York.
Todd Rokita, of Indiana.
Larry Bucshon, of Indiana.
Lou Barletta, of Pennsylvania.
Kristi L. Noem, of South Dakota.
Martha Roby, of Alabama.
Joseph J. Heck, of Nevada.
Dennis A. Ross, of Florida.

Robert E. Andrews, of New Jersey.
Dennis J. Kucinich, of Ohio.
David Loebsack, of Iowa.
Dale E. Kildee, of Michigan.
Rubén Hinojosa, of Texas.
Carolyn McCarthy, of New York.
John F. Tierney, of Massachusetts.
Rush D. Holt, of New Jersey.
Robert C. ''Bobby'' Scott, of Virginia.
Jason Altmire, of Pennsylvania.

Workforce Protections

Tim Walberg, of Michigan, *Chair*

John Kline, of Minnesota.
Bob Goodlatte, of Virginia.
Todd Rokita, of Indiana.
Larry Bucshon, of Indiana.
Trey Gowdy, of South Carolina.
Kristi L. Noem, of South Dakota.
Dennis A. Ross, of Florida.
Mike Kelly, of Pennsylvania.

Lynn C. Woolsey, of California.
Donald M. Payne, of New Jersey.
Dennis J. Kucinich, of Ohio.
Timothy H. Bishop, of New York.
Mazie K. Hirono, of Hawaii.
George Miller, of California.

STAFF

Committee on Education and Labor (2181 RHOB), 225–4527.
Majority Staff Director.—Barrett Karr.
General Counsel.—Krisann Pearce.
Administrative Director and Senior Advisor.—Angelyn Shapiro.
Director of Education and Human Resources.—James Bergeron.
Director of Workforce Policy.—Ed Gilroy.
Communications Director.—Alex Sollberger.
Coalitions and Member Services Coordinator.—Casey Bulbotz.
Deputy Communications Director.—Brian Newell.
Press Assistant and New Media Coordinator.—Katherine Bathgate.
Deputy Director of Education Policy.—Heather Couri.
Senior Education Policy Advisor.—Brad Thomas.
Education and Human Services Oversight Counsel.—Amanda Schaumburg.
Education Policy Counsel and Senior Advisor.—Amy Jones.
Professional Staff Members: Lindsay Fryer, Daniela Garcia, Rosemary Lahasky.
Legislative Assistants: Brian Melnyk, Dan Shorts.
Deputy Director of Workforce Policy.—Molly Salmi.
Senior Policy Advisor.—Loren Sweatt.
Professional Staff Members: Andrew Banducci, Marvin Kaplan, Donald McIntosh, Joe Wheeler.
Legislative Assistants: Ben Hoog, Ryan Kearney.
Chief Clerk/Assistant to the General Counsel.—Linda Stevens.
Deputy Clerk.—Alissa Strawcutter.
Financial Administrative Officer.—Dianna Ruskowsky.
Systems Administrator.—Benjamin Thomas.
Office Administrator.—Theresa Gambo.
Staff Assistant.—Adam Bennot.
Committee Printer.—Richard ''Dick'' Magee.
Minority Staff Director.—Jody Calemine (2101 RHOB), 5–3725.
General Counsel.—Megan O'Reily.
Clerk Intern Coordinator.—Tylease Alli.
Chief Policy Advisory/Labor Policy Director.—Michele Varnhagen.
Special Assistant to Staff Director.—Liz Hollis.
Deputy Staff Director.—Julie R. Peller.

New Media Press Assistant.—Brian P. Levin.
Staff Assistant.—John D'Elia.
Communications Director for Labor.—Aaron Albright.
Communications Director for Education.—Melissa Salmanowitz.
Executive Assistant.—Courtney Rochelle.
Special Assistant to Chairman.—Daniel Weiss.
Labor Counsel.—Celine McNicholas.
Director of Information Technology.—Dray Thorne.
Labor Policy Advisor.—Livia Lam.
Labor Policy Associate.—Meredith Regine.
Junior Legislative Assistant.—Danny Brown.
Education Policy Advisory.—Helen Pajcic.
Deputy Director of Education Policy.—Jamie P. Fasteau.
Senior Education Policy Advisor.—Kara Ann Marchione.
Investigate Counsel.—Kate Ahlgren.
Senior Education and Disability Advisor.—Laura Schifter.
Senior Labor Policy Advisor.—Richard D. Miller.
Director of Education Policy.—Ruth Friedman.
Legal Intern, Education.—Adam Schaefer.
CBCF Fellow, Labor.—Waverly Gordon.
Legal Intern, Labor.—Greg Meditz.

Energy and Commerce

2125 Rayburn House Office Building, phone 225–2927

http://www.house.gov/commerce

Fred Upton, of Michigan, *Chair*

Joe Barton, of Texas.
Cliff Stearns, of Florida.
Ed Whitfield, of Kentucky.
John Shimkus, of Illinois.
Joseph R. Pitts, of Pennsylvania.
Mary Bono Mack, of California.
Greg Walden, of Oregon.
Lee Terry, of Nebraska.
Mike Rogers, of Michigan.
Sue Wilkins Myrick, of North Carolina.
John Sullivan, of Oklahoma.
Tim Murphy, of Pennsylvania.
Michael C. Burgess, of Texas.
Marsha Blackburn, of Tennessee.
Brian P. Bilbray, of California.
Charles F. Bass, of New Hampshire.
Phil Gingrey, of Georgia.
Steve Scalise, of Louisiana.
Robert E. Latta, of Ohio.
Cathy McMorris Rodgers, of Washington.
Gregg Harper, of Mississippi.
Leonard Lance, of New Jersey.
Bill Cassidy, of Louisiana.
Brett Guthrie, of Kentucky.
Pete Olson, of Texas.
David B. McKinley, of West Virginia.
Cory Gardner, of Colorado.
Mike Pompeo, of Kansas.
Adam Kinzinger, of Illinois.
H. Morgan Griffith, of Virginia.

Henry A. Waxman, of California.
John D. Dingell, of Michigan.
Edward J. Markey, of Massachusetts.
Edolphus Towns, of New York.
Frank Pallone, Jr., of New Jersey.
Bobby L. Rush, of Illinois.
Anna G. Eshoo, of California.
Eliot L. Engel, of New York.
Gene Green, of Texas.
Diana DeGette, of Colorado.
Lois Capps, of California.
Michael F. Doyle, of Pennsylvania.
Janice D. Schakowsky, of Illinois.
Charles A. Gonzalez, of Texas.
Jay Inslee, of Washington.
Tammy Baldwin, of Wisconsin.
Mike Ross, of Arkansas.
Jim Matheson, of Utah.
G. K. Butterfield, of North Carolina.
John Barrow, of Georgia.
Doris O. Matsui, of California.
Donna M. Christensen, of Virgin Islands.
Kathy Castor, of Florida.

SUBCOMMITTEES

[The chairman and ranking minority member are ex officio (voting) members of all subcommittees on which they do not serve.]

Commerce, Manufacturing, and Trade

Mary Bono Mack, of California, *Chair*

Marsha Blackburn, of Tennessee.
Cliff Stearns, of Florida.
Charles F. Bass, of New Hampshire.
Gregg Harper, of Mississippi.
Leonard Lance, of New Jersey.
Bill Cassidy, of Louisiana.
Brett Guthrie, of Kentucky.
Pete Olson, of Texas.
David B. McKinley, of West Virginia.
Mike Pompeo, of Kansas.
Adam Kinzinger, of Illinois.
Joe Barton, of Texas.

G. K. Butterfield, of North Carolina.
Charles A. Gonzalez, of Texas.
Jim Matheson, of Utah.
John D. Dingell, of Michigan.
Edolphus Towns, of New York.
Bobby L. Rush, of Illinois.
Janice D. Schakowsky, of Illinois.
Mike Ross, of Arkansas.

Communications and Technology

Greg Walden, of Oregon, *Chair*

Lee Terry, of Nebraska.
Cliff Stearns, of Florida.
John Shimkus, of Illinois.
Mary Bono Mack, of California.
Mike Rogers, of Michigan.
Brian P. Bilbray, of California.
Charles F. Bass, of New Hampshire.
Marsha Blackburn, of Tennessee.
Phil Gingrey, of Georgia.
Steve Scalise, of Louisiana.
Robert E. Latta, of Ohio.
Brett Guthrie, of Kentucky.
Adam Kinzinger, of Illinois.
Joe Barton, of Texas.

Anna G. Eshoo, of California.
Edward J. Markey, of Massachusetts.
Michael F. Doyle, of Pennsylvania.
Doris O. Matsui, of California.
John Barrow, of Georgia.
Donna M. Christensen, of Virgin Islands.
Edolphus Towns, of New York.
Frank Pallone, Jr., of New Jersey.
Bobby L. Rush, of Illinois.
Diana DeGette, of Colorado.
John D. Dingell, of Michigan.

Energy and Power

Ed Whitfield, of Kentucky, *Chair*

John Sullivan, of Oklahoma.
John Shimkus, of Illinois.
Greg Walden, of Oregon.
Lee Terry, of Nebraska.
Michael C. Burgess, of Texas.
Brian P. Bilbray, of California.
Steve Scalise, of Louisiana.
Cathy McMorris Rodgers, of Washington.
Pete Olson, of Texas.
David B. McKinley, of West Virginia.
Cory Gardner, of Colorado.
Mike Pompeo, of Kansas.
H. Morgan Griffith, of Virginia.
Joe Barton, of Texas.

Bobby L. Rush, of Illinois.
Jay Inslee, of Washington.
Kathy Castor, of Florida.
John D. Dingell, of Michigan.
Edward J. Markey, of Massachusetts.
Eliot L. Engel, of New York.
Gene Green, of Texas.
Lois Capps, of California.
Michael F. Doyle, of Pennsylvania.
Charles A. Gonzalez, of Texas.

Environment and the Economy

John Shimkus, of Illinois, *Chair*

Tim Murphy, of Pennsylvania.
Ed Whitfield, of Kentucky.
Joseph R. Pitts, of Pennsylvania.
Mary Bono Mack, of California.
John Sullivan, of Oklahoma.
Charles F. Bass, of New Hampshire.
Robert E. Latta, of Ohio.
Cathy McMorris Rodgers, of Washington.
Gregg Harper, of Mississippi.
Bill Cassidy, of Louisiana.
Cory Gardner, of Colorado.
Joe Barton, of Texas.

Gene Green, of Texas.
Tammy Baldwin, of Wisconsin.
G. K. Butterfield, of North Carolina.
John Barrow, of Georgia.
Doris O. Matsui, of California.
Frank Pallone, Jr., of New Jersey.
Diana DeGette, of Colorado.
Lois Capps, of California.
John D. Dingell, of Michigan.

Health

Joseph R. Pitts, of Pennsylvania, *Chair*

Michael C. Burgess, of Texas.
Ed Whitfield, of Kentucky.
John Shimkus, of Illinois.
Mike Rogers, of Michigan.
Sue Wilkins Myrick, of North Carolina.
Tim Murphy, of Pennsylvania.
Marsha Blackburn, of Tennessee.
Phil Gingrey, of Georgia.
Robert E. Latta, of Ohio.
Cathy McMorris Rodgers, of Washington.
Leonard Lance, of New Jersey.
Bill Cassidy, of Louisiana.
Brett Guthrie, of Kentucky.
Joe Barton, of Texas.

Frank Pallone, Jr., of New Jersey.
John D. Dingell, of Michigan.
Edolphus Towns, of New York.
Eliot L. Engel, of New York.
Lois Capps, of California.
Janice D. Schakowsky, of Illinois.
Charles A. Gonzalez, of Texas.
Tammy Baldwin, of Wisconsin.
Mike Ross, of Arkansas.
Jim Matheson, of Utah.

Oversight and Investigations

Cliff Stearns, of Florida, *Chair*

Lee Terry, of Nebraska.
John Sullivan, of Oklahoma.
Tim Murphy, of Pennsylvania.
Michael C. Burgess, of Texas.
Marsha Blackburn, of Tennessee.
Sue Wilkins Myrick, of North Carolina.
Brian P. Bilbray, of California.
Phil Gingrey, of Georgia.
Steve Scalise, of Louisiana.
Cory Gardner, of Colorado.
H. Morgan Griffith, of Virginia.
Joe Barton, of Texas.

Diana DeGette, of Colorado.
Janice D. Schakowsky, of Illinois.
Mike Ross, of Arkansas.
Kathy Castor, of Florida.
Edward J. Markey, of Massachusetts.
Gene Green, of Texas.
Donna M. Christensen, of Virgin Islands.
John D. Dingell, of Michigan.

STAFF

Committee on Energy and Commerce (2125 RHOB), 225–2927, fax 225–1919.
Majority Staff Director.—Gary Andres.
Deputy Staff Director.—Michel Beckerman.
General Counsel.—James Barnette.
Deputy Chief Counsel.—Michael Bloomquist.
Director, Communications.—Alexa Marrero.
Deputy Director, Communications.—Sean Bonyun.
Chief Economist.—Heidi King.
Chief Counsel, Energy and Power.—Maryam Brown.
Chief Counsel, Environment and the Economy.—David McCarthy.
Chief Counsel, Oversight.—Todd Harrison.
Deputy Chief Counsel, Oversight.—Alan M. Slobodin.
Chief Counsel, Health.—Ryan Long.
Chief Health Counsel.—Howard Cohen.
Chief Counsel, Communications and Technology.—Neil Fried.
Chief Counsel, Commerce, Manufacturing, and Trade.—John ''Gib'' Mullan.
Deputy Policy Director.—Aaron Cutler.
Counsels: Clayton Alspach, Carl Anderson, Karen E. Christian, Patrick Currier, Sean Hayes, Ben Lieberman, Mary Neumayr, David Redl, Tina Richards, Samuel Spector, Shannon M. Weinberg.
Senior Advisor, Health Policy and Communications.—Marty Dannenfelser.
Counsel to Chairman Emeritus.—Krista Rosenthall.
Senior Policy Advisor to Chairman Emeritus.—Anita Bradley.
Policy Advisor, Health.—Julie Goon.
Senior Policy Advisor and Director of Coalitions.—Ray Baum.
Senior Policy Advisor.—Michael Gruber.
Associate Counsels: Peter Kielty, John Stone.
Senior Professional Staff Member.—Brian McCullough.
Professional Staff: Gerald S. Couri II, Brenda Destro, Paul Edattel, Garrett Golding, Jeffrey Mortier, John O'Shea, Monica Popp, Peter Spencer.

Policy Coordinator, Energy and Power.—Cory Hicks.
Policy Coordinator, Environment and the Economy.—Christopher Sarley.
Policy Coordinator, Communications and Technology.—Paul Cancienne.
Policy Coordinator, Health.—Heidi Stirrup.
Policy Coordinator, Oversight and Investigations.—James Thomas.
Director, Information Technology.—Jean M. Woodrow.
Deputy Director, Information Technology.—Tim Torres.
Administrative and Human Resources Coordinator.—Linda L. Walker.
Office Manager.—Sean Corcoran.
Press Secretaries: Charlotte Baker, Debbee Keller.
New Media Specialist.—Nika Nour.
Press Assistant.—Andrew Powaleny.
Legislative Clerks: Allison Busbee, Brian Howard, Carlyle McWilliams, Kathryn Novaria, Alex Yergin.
Special Assistant to Chairman.—Andrew Duberstein.
Executive Assistant.—Charlotte Savercool.
Staff Assistants: Nicholas Abraham, Caroline Basile, Brett Scott, Tom Wilbur.

Minority Staff Director.—Phil Barnett.
Deputy Committee Staff Director for Health.—Karen Nelson.
Chief Counsel.—Kristin Amerling.
Communications Director, Senior Policy Advisor.—Karen Lightfoot.
Chief Counsel, Commerce, Manufacturing, and Trade.—Michelle Ash.
Energy and Environment.—Greg Dotson.
Chief Public Health Counsel.—Ruth Katz.
Chief Counsel, Communications and Technology.—Roger Sherman.
Investigations Staff Director and Senior Policy Advisor.—Brian Cohen.
Senior Counsels, Energy and Environment: Rachel Sher, Alexandra Teitz.
Senior Counsel.—Jeff Baran, Purvee Kempf.
Counsels: Stacia Cardille, Shawn Chang, Jacqueline Cohen, Felipe Mendoza, Anne Tindall.
Investigative Counsel.—Tiffany Benjamin.
Senior Professional Staff Members: Alison Cassady, Stephen Cha, Tim Gronniger.
Chief Clerk.—Jennifer Berenholz.
Deputy Clerk.—Elizabeth B. Ertel.
Press Secretary.—Lindsay Vidal.
Chief Information Officer.—Zhongrui Deng.
Online Communications Director.—Kathleen J. Skiles.
Assistant Clerk.—Alvin Banks.
Policy Analysts: Allison Corr, Sarah Fisher, Caitlin Haberman, Will Wallace.
Investigator.—Alison Neubauer.
Assistant Clerk.—Mitch Smiley.

Ethics

1015 Longworth House Office Building, phone 225–7103, fax 225–7392

Jo Bonner, of Alabama, *Chair*

Michael T. McCaul, of Texas.
K. Michael Conaway, of Texas.
Charles W. Dent, of Pennsylvania.
Gregg Harper, of Mississippi.

Linda T. Sánchez, of California.
John A. Yarmuth, of Kentucky.
Donna F. Edwards, of Maryland.
Pedro R. Pierluisi, of Puerto Rico.
Joe Courtney, of Connecticut.

(No Subcommittees)

STAFF

Chief Counsel / Staff Director.—Dan Schwager.
Administrative Staff Director.—Joanne White.
Counsel to the Chairman.—Kelle Strickland.
Counsel to the Ranking Member.—Dan Taylor.
Director of:
Advice and Education.—Carol Dixon.
Investigations.—Deborah Mayer.
Senior Counsels: Heather Jones, Tom Rust, Clifford Stoddard, Tiguel Toruño.
Counsels: Sheria Clarke, Karena Dees, Robert Eskridge, Patrick McMullen, Tamar Nedzar, Christopher Tate.
Investigator.—Frank Davies.
Financial Disclosure Advisor.—Deborah Peay.
System Administrator.—Peter Johnson.
Investigative Clerk.—Brittany Bohren.
Staff Assistants: Donna Hayes, Matt Scott, Kaitlin Vogt.

Financial Services

2129 Rayburn House Office Building, phone 225–7502

http://www.house.gov/financialservices

meets first Tuesday of each month

Spencer Bachus, of Alabama, *Chair*

Jeb Hensarling, of Texas, *Vice Chair*

Peter T. King, of New York.
Edward R. Royce, of California.
Frank D. Lucas, of Oklahoma.
Ron Paul, of Texas.
Donald A. Manzullo, of Illinois.
Walter B. Jones, of North Carolina.
Judy Biggert, of Illinois.
Gary G. Miller, of California.
Shelley Moore Capito, of West Virginia.
Scott Garrett, of New Jersey.
Randy Neugebauer, of Texas.
Patrick T. McHenry, of North Carolina.
John Campbell, of California.
Michele Bachmann, of Minnesota.
Thaddeus G. McCotter, of Michigan.
Kevin McCarthy, of California.
Stevan Pearce, of New Mexico.
Bill Posey, of Florida.
Michael G. Fitzpatrick, of Pennsylvania.
Lynn A. Westmoreland, of Georgia.
Blaine Luetkemeyer, of Missouri.
Bill Huizenga, of Michigan.
Sean P. Duffy, of Wisconsin.
Nan A.S. Hayworth, of New York.
James B. Renacci, of Ohio.
Robert Hurt, of Virginia.
Robert J. Dold, of Illinois.
David Schweikert, of Arizona.
Michael G. Grimm, of New York.
Francisco ''Quico'' Canseco, of Texas.
Steve Stivers, of Ohio.
Stephen Lee Fincher, of Tennessee.

Barney Frank, of Massachusetts.
Maxine Waters, of California.
Carolyn B. Maloney, of New York.
Luis V. Gutierrez, of Illinois.
Nydia M. Velázquez, of New York.
Melvin L. Watt, of North Carolina.
Gary L. Ackerman, of New York.
Brad Sherman, of California.
Gregory W. Meeks, of New York.
Michael E. Capuano, of Massachusetts.
Rubén Hinojosa, of Texas.
Wm. Lacy Clay, of Missouri.
Carolyn McCarthy, of New York.
Joe Baca, of California.
Stephen F. Lynch, of Massachusetts.
Brad Miller, of North Carolina.
David Scott, of Georgia.
Al Green, of Texas.
Emanuel Cleaver, of Missouri.
Gwen Moore, of Wisconsin.
Keith Ellison, of Minnesota.
Ed Perlmutter, of Colorado.
Joe Donnelly, of Indiana.
André Carson, of Indiana.
James A. Himes, of Connecticut.
Gary C. Peters, of Michigan.
John C. Carney, Jr., of Delaware.

SUBCOMMITTEES

[The chairman and ranking minority member are ex officio (voting) members of all subcommittees on which they do not serve.]

Capital Markets and Government Sponsored Enterprises

Scott Garrett, of New Jersey, *Chair*

David Schweikert, of Arizona, *Vice Chair*

Peter T. King, of New York.
Edward R. Royce, of California.
Frank D. Lucas, of Oklahoma.
Donald A. Manzullo, of Illinois.
Judy Biggert, of Illinois.
Jeb Hensarling, of Texas.
Randy Neugebauer, of Texas.
John Campbell, of California.
Thaddeus G. McCotter, of Michigan.
Kevin McCarthy, of California.
Stevan Pearce, of New Mexico.
Bill Posey, of Florida.
Michael G. Fitzpatrick, of Pennsylvania.
Nan A.S. Hayworth, of New York.
Robert Hurt, of Virginia.
Michael G. Grimm, of New York.
Steve Stivers, of Ohio.
Robert J. Dold, of Illinois.

Maxine Waters, of California.
Gary L. Ackerman, of New York.
Brad Sherman, of California.
Rubén Hinojosa, of Texas.
Stephen F. Lynch, of Massachusetts.
Brad Miller, of North Carolina.
Carolyn B. Maloney, of New York.
Gwen Moore, of Wisconsin.
Ed Perlmutter, of Colorado.
Joe Donnelly, of Indiana.
André Carson, of Indiana.
James A. Himes, of Connecticut.
Gary C. Peters, of Michigan.
Al Green, of Texas.
Keith Ellison, of Minnesota.

Domestic Monetary Policy and Technology

Ron Paul, of Texas, *Chair*

Walter B. Jones, of North Carolina, *Vice Chair*

Frank D. Lucas, of Oklahoma.
Patrick T. McHenry, of North Carolina.
Blaine Luetkemeyer, of Missouri.
Bill Huizenga, of Michigan.
Nan A.S. Hayworth, of New York.
David Schweikert, of Arizona.

Wm. Lacy Clay, of Missouri.
Carolyn B. Maloney, of New York.
Gregory W. Meeks, of New York.
Al Green, of Texas.
Emanuel Cleaver, of Missouri.
Gary C. Peters, of Michigan.

Financial Institutions and Consumer Credit

Shelley Moore Capito, of West Virginia, *Chair*

James B. Renacci, of Ohio, *Vice Chair*

Edward R. Royce, of California.
Donald A. Manzullo, of Illinois.
Walter B. Jones, of North Carolina.
Jeb Hensarling, of Texas.
Patrick T. McHenry, of North Carolina.
Thaddeus G. McCotter, of Michigan.
Kevin McCarthy, of California.
Stevan Pearce, of New Mexico.
Lynn A. Westmoreland, of Georgia.
Blaine Luetkemeyer, of Missouri.
Bill Huizenga, of Michigan.
Sean P. Duffy, of Wisconsin.
Francisco ''Quico'' Canseco, of Texas.
Michael G. Grimm, of New York.
Stephen Lee Fincher, of Tennessee.

Carolyn B. Maloney, of New York.
Luis V. Gutierrez, of Illinois.
Melvin L. Watt, of North Carolina.
Gary L. Ackerman, of New York.
Rubén Hinojosa, of Texas.
Carolyn McCarthy, of New York.
Joe Baca, of California.
Brad Miller, of North Carolina.
David Scott, of Georgia.
Nydia M. Velázquez, of New York.
Gregory W. Meeks, of New York.
Stephen F. Lynch, of Massachusetts.
John C. Carney, Jr., of Delaware.

Insurance, Housing and Community Opportunity

Judy Biggert, of Illinois, *Chair*

Robert Hurt, of Virginia, *Vice Chair*

Gary G. Miller, of California.
Shelley Moore Capito, of West Virginia.
Scott Garrett, of New Jersey.
Patrick T. McHenry, of North Carolina.
Lynn A. Westmoreland, of Georgia.
Sean P. Duffy, of Wisconsin.
Robert J. Dold, of Illinois.
Steve Stivers, of Ohio.

Luis V. Gutierrez, of Illinois.
Maxine Waters, of California.
Nydia M. Velázquez, of New York.
Emanuel Cleaver, of Missouri.
Wm. Lacy Clay, of Missouri.
Melvin L. Watt, of North Carolina.
Brad Sherman, of California.
Michael E. Capuano, of Massachusetts.

International Monetary Policy and Trade

Gary G. Miller, of California, *Chair*

Robert J. Dold, of Illinois, *Vice Chair*

Ron Paul, of Texas.
Donald A. Manzullo, of Illinois.
John Campbell, of California.
Michele Bachmann, of Minnesota.
Thaddeus G. McCotter, of Michigan.
Bill Huizenga, of Michigan.

Carolyn McCarthy, of New York.
Gwen Moore, of Wisconsin.
André Carson, of Indiana.
David Scott, of Georgia.
Ed Perlmutter, of Colorado.
Joe Donnelly, of Indiana.

Oversight and Investigations

Randy Neugebauer, of Texas, *Chair*

Michael G. Fitzpatrick, of Pennsylvania, *Vice Chair*

Peter T. King, of New York.
Michele Bachmann, of Minnesota.
Stevan Pearce, of New Mexico.
Bill Posey, of Florida.
Nan A.S. Hayworth, of New York.
James B. Renacci, of Ohio.
Francisco ''Quico'' Canseco, of Texas.
Stephen Lee Fincher, of Tennessee.

Michael E. Capuano, of Massachusetts.
Stephen F. Lynch, of Massachusetts.
Maxine Waters, of California.
Joe Baca, of California.
Brad Miller, of North Carolina.
Keith Ellison, of Minnesota.
James A. Himes, of Connecticut.
John C. Carney, Jr., of Delaware.

STAFF

Committee on Financial Services (2129 RHOB), 225–7502.

Majority Chief of Staff.—Larry C. Lavender.

Deputy Chief of Staff.—Warren Tryon.

Chief Counsel.—James H. Clinger.

Deputy Chief of Staff/Communications.—Jeffrey W. Emerson.

Parliamentarian/Senior Counsel.—Natalie N. McGarry.

General Counsel.—Clinton Columbus Jones, III.

Senior Counsels: John R. Bartling, Michael Borden, Kevin R. Edgar, Mark D. Epley, Thomas L. Krebs, Francisco A. Medina.

Counsels: Susan Mitchell Blavin, John W. Cole, Jason M. Goggins, Kenneth G. Leonczyk, W. Walton Liles.

Senior Professional Staff: Anthony J. Cimino, Tallman Johnson, Joe Pinder, Edward G. Skala.

Professional Staff: Nicole C. Austin, Michael Caswell, Andrew Duke, Scott Eckel, Paul-Martin Foss, Lesli Gooch, Kylin B. McCardle, James Kimble V. Ratliff III, Clifford Roberti, Aaron T. Sporck, Alexander H. Teel.

Policy Advisor.—Michael Staley.

Senior Analyst.—Gisele G. Roget.

Communications Director.—Marisol Garibay.

Director/New Media.—Caleb J. Smith.

Press Assistant.—Chara R. Bray.

Administrative Assistant.—Angela S. Gambo.

Executive Assistant.—Anna Bartlett Wright.

Systems Administrator.—Kim Trimble.
Assistant Systems Administrator.—Steve F. Arauz.
Executive Staff Assistant.—Rosemary E. Keech.
Clerk.—Margaret E. Henson.
Editor.—Terisa L. Allison.
Staff Assistants: Norman R. Bishop, E. Chase Burgess, Emily J. Frumberg, Jonathan E. Madison, Samuel C. Mahler, Blake J. Punek.

Minority Staff Director/Chief Counsel.—Jeanne M. Roslanowick (B301C RHOB), 225–4247.
Deputy Staff Director.—Michael T. Beresik.
Deputy Chief Counsels: Gail Laster, Lawranne Stewart.
Chief Economist.—David A. Smith.
Legislative Director.—Kellie Larkin.
Senior Counsels: Erika Jeffers, Kathryn J. Marks, Dominique M. McCoy, Adrianne G. Threatt.
Senior Professional Staff: Kristofor S. Erickson, Daniel McGlinchey.
Professional Staff Members: Meredith Connelly, Bruno Freitas, Maria E. Giesta, Patricia Lord, Kirk Schwarzbach.
Policy Director, Housing.—Scott Olson.
Communications Director.—Harry Gural.
Press Secretary.—Addie Whisenant.
Staff Associate.—Marcos Manosalvas.
Systems Administrator.—Alfred J. Forman, Jr.

Foreign Affairs

2170 Rayburn House Office Building, phone 225–5021

http://www.foreignaffairs.house.gov

meets first Tuesday of each month

Ileana Ros-Lehtinen, of Florida, *Chair*

Christopher H. Smith, of New Jersey.
Dan Burton, of Indiana.
Elton Gallegly, of California.
Dana Rohrabacher, of California.
Donald A. Manzullo, of Illinois.
Edward R. Royce, of California.
Steve Chabot, of Ohio.
Ron Paul, of Texas.
Mike Pence, of Indiana.
Joe Wilson, of South Carolina.
Connie Mack, of Florida.
Jeff Fortenberry, of Nebraska.
Michael T. McCaul, of Texas.
Ted Poe, of Texas.
Gus M. Bilirakis, of Florida.
Jean Schmidt, of Ohio.
Bill Johnson, of Ohio.
David Rivera, of Florida.
Mike Kelly, of Pennsylvania.
Tim Griffin, of Arkansas.
Tom Marino, of Pennsylvania.
Jeff Duncan, of South Carolina.
Ann Marie Buerkle, of New York.
Renee L. Ellmers, of North Carolina.
Robert L. Turner, of New York.

Howard L. Berman, of California.
Gary L. Ackerman, of New York.
Eni F. H. Faleomavaega, of American Samoa.
Donald M. Payne, of New Jersey.
Brad Sherman, of California.
Eliot L. Engel, of New York.
Gregory W. Meeks, of New York.
Russ Carnahan, of Missouri.
Albio Sires, of New Jersey.
Gerald E. Connolly, of Virginia.
Theodore E. Deutch, of Florida.
Dennis A. Cardoza, of California.
Ben Chandler, of Kentucky.
Brian Higgins, of New York.
Allyson Y. Schwartz, of Pennsylvania.
Christopher S. Murphy, of Connecticut.
Frederica S. Wilson, of Florida.
Karen Bass, of California.
William R. Keating, of Massachusetts.
David N. Cicilline, of Rhode Island.

SUBCOMMITTEES

[The chairman and ranking minority member are ex officio (non-voting) members of all subcommittees on which they do not serve.]

Africa, Global Health, and Human Rights

Christopher H. Smith, of New Jersey, *Chair*

Jeff Fortenberry, of Nebraska.
Tim Griffin, of Arkansas.
Tom Marino, of Pennsylvania.
Ann Marie Buerkle, of New York.

Donald M. Payne, of New Jersey.
Karen Bass, of California.
Russ Carnahan, of Missouri.

Asia and the Pacific

Donald A. Manzullo, of Illinois, *Chair*

Ron Paul, of Texas.
Bill Johnson, of Ohio.
Dan Burton, of Indiana.
Edward R. Royce, of California.
Steve Chabot, of Ohio.
Mike Kelly, of Pennsylvania.
Jeff Duncan, of South Carolina.

Eni F. H. Faleomavaega, of American Samoa.
Frederica S. Wilson, of Florida.
Gary L. Ackerman, of New York.
Brad Sherman, of California.
Gregory W. Meeks, of New York.
Dennis A. Cardoza, of California.

Europe and Eurasia

Dan Burton, of Indiana, *Chair*

Elton Gallegly, of California.
Gus M. Bilirakis, of Florida.
Tim Griffin, of Arkansas.
Tom Marino, of Pennsylvania.
Jean Schmidt, of Ohio.
Ted Poe, of Texas.

Gregory W. Meeks, of New York.
Eliot L. Engel, of New York.
Albio Sires, of New Jersey.
Theodore E. Deutch, of Florida.

The Middle East and South Asia

Steve Chabot, of Ohio, *Chair*

Mike Pence, of Indiana.
Joe Wilson, of South Carolina.
Jeff Fortenberry, of Nebraska.
Ann Marie Buerkle, of New York.
Renee L. Ellmers, of North Carolina.
Dana Rohrabacher, of California.
Donald A. Manzullo, of Illinois.
Connie Mack, of Florida.
Michael T. McCaul, of Texas.
Gus M. Bilirakis, of Florida.
Tom Marino, of Pennsylvania.

Gary L. Ackerman, of New York.
Gerald E. Connolly, of Virginia.
Theodore E. Deutch, of Florida.
Dennis A. Cardoza, of California.
Ben Chandler, of Kentucky.
Brian Higgins, of New York.
Allyson Y. Schwartz, of Pennsylvania.
Christopher S. Murphy, of Connecticut.
William R. Keating, of Massachusetts.

Oversight and Investigations

Dana Rohrabacher, of California, *Chair*

Mike Kelly, of Pennsylvania.
Ron Paul, of Texas.
Ted Poe, of Texas.
David Rivera, of Florida.

Russ Carnahan, of Missouri.
David N. Cicilline, of Rhode Island.
Karen Bass, of California.

Terrorism, Nonproliferation, and Trade

Edward R. Royce, of California, *Chair*

Ted Poe, of Texas.
Jeff Duncan, of South Carolina.
Bill Johnson, of Ohio.
Tim Griffin, of Arkansas.
Ann Marie Buerkle, of New York.
Renee L. Ellmers, of North Carolina.

Brad Sherman, of California.
David N. Cicilline, of Rhode Island.
Gerald E. Connolly, of Virginia.
Brian Higgins, of New York.
Allyson Y. Schwartz, of Pennsylvania.

The Western Hemisphere

Connie Mack, of Florida, *Chair*

Michael T. McCaul, of Texas.
Jean Schmidt, of Ohio.
David Rivera, of Florida.
Christopher H. Smith, of New Jersey.
Elton Gallegly, of California.

Eliot L. Engel, of New York.
Albio Sires, of New Jersey.
Eni F. H. Faleomavaega, of American Samoa.
Donald M. Payne, of New Jersey.

STAFF

Committee on Foreign Affairs (2170 RHOB), 225–5021.
Majority Staff Director.—Yleem Poblete, Ph.D.
Senior Professional Staff Member.—Doug Seay.
General Counsel.—Douglas Anderson.
Chief Counsel, Investigations and Oversight.—Harold Rees.
Communications Director.—Brad Goehner.
Deputy Communications Director/Professional Staff Member.—Andeliz Castillo.
Press Secretary.—Alejandro Cruz.
Senior Professional Staff Members: Joan O. Condon, Dennis Halpin, Gregory McCarthy, Robyn Wapner, Matthew Zweig.

Senior Professional Staff Member/Senior Counsel.—James W. "Jamie" McCormick.
Professional Staff Members: Eddy Acevedo, Sarah Blocher, Alan Goldsmith, Christina Jenckes, Sarah Kiko Leiby, Kristal Quarker.
Junior Professional Staff Member.—Riley Moore.
Security Officer/Professional Staff Member.—George Ritchey.
Director of Travel/Junior Professional Staff Member.—Amber Garlock.
Parliamentarian and Administrative Officer.—Layla Calderon.
Director of Committee Operations.—Jean Carroll.
Hearing Coordinator.—Janelle Perez.
Counsel for Oversight and Investigations.—Ari Fridman.
Legislative Correspondence Manager and Documents Clerk.—Jay Henderson.
New Media Director/Press Assistant.—Andrew Lee.
Policy Analyst.—Gabriella Ra'anan.
Staff Associate/Policy Analyst.—Andrew Alonso.
Staff Associate.—Priyanka Desai.
Finance Administrator.—John Gleason.
Information Resource Manager.—Vladimir Cerga.
Assistant Systems Administrator.—Danny Marca.
Printing Manager/Web Assistant.—Shirley Y. Alexander.
Minority Staff Director.—Richard J. Kessler.
Deputy Staff Director.—Douglas J. Campbell.
General Counsel and Senior Policy Advisor.—Shanna A. Winters.
Senior Deputy Chief Counsel.—Daniel Silverberg.
Deputy Chief Counsel.—Janice Kaguyutan.
Communications Director.—Gabby Adler.
Senior Professional Staff Members: David P. Fite, Alan Makovsky, Diana L. Ohlbaum, Peter Quilter, Edmund Rice.
Professional Staff Members: Sajit Gandhi, Daniel Harsha, Robert Marcus, Joo-Jin Ong, Jackie Quinones, Brent Woolfork.
Executive Assistant.—Guillermina Garcia.
Press Assistant.—David Barnes.
Staff Associates: Samantha Goldstein, Mary McVeigh
Subcommittee on Africa, Global Health, and Human Rights (H2–259A FHOB), 226–7812.
Staff Director.—Sheri Rickert.
Professional Staff Member.—Gregory Simpkins.
Staff Associate.—Mark Kearny.
Minority Professional Staff.—Algene Sajery.
Subcommittee on Asia and the Pacific (H2–255 FHOB), 226–7825.
Staff Director.—Nien Su.
Professional Staff Member.—Priscilla Koepke.
Minority Professional Staff.—Lisa Williams.
Staff Associate.—Karl Gutfrucht.
Subcommittee on Europe and Eurasia (H2–256 FHOB), 226–6434.
Staff Director.—Mark Walker.
Professional Staff Member.—Brian Wanko.
Minority Professional Staff.—Jesper Pedersen.
Subcommittee on the Middle East and South Asia (B–358 RHOB), 225–3345.
Staff Director.—Kevin Fitzpatrick.
Professional Staff Member.—Ed Stein.
Staff Associate.—Delia Barr.
Minority Professional Staff.—Howard Diamond.
Subcommittee on Oversight and Investigations (2401A RHOB), 226–5045.
Staff Director.—Paul Berkowitz.
Professional Staff Member.—William Hawkins.
Staff Associate.—Scott Cullinane.
Minority Professional Staff.—Jeremy Haldeman.
Subcommittee on Terrorism, Nonproliferation, and Trade (H2–340 FHOB), 226–1500.
Staff Director.—Tom Sheehy.
Professional Staff Member.—Ed Burrier.
Staff Associate.—Hunter Strupp.
Minority Professional Staff.—Don MacDonald.
Subcommittee on the Western Hemisphere (H2–257 FHOB), 226–9980.
Staff Director.—Kristin Jackson.
Professional Staff Member.—Hubbell Knapp.
Staff Associate.—Nathan Gately.
Minority Professional Staff.—Jason Steinbaum.

Homeland Security

phone 226–8417, fax 226–3399

Peter T. King, of New York, *Chair*

Lamar Smith, of Texas.
Daniel E. Lungren, of California.
Mike Rogers, of Alabama.
Michael T. McCaul, of Texas.
Gus M. Bilirakis, of Florida.
Paul C. Broun, of Georgia.
Candice S. Miller, of Michigan.
Tim Walberg, of Michigan.
Chip Cravaack, of Minnesota.
Joe Walsh, of Illinois.
Patrick Meehan, of Pennsylvania.
Benjamin Quayle, of Arizona.
E. Scott Rigell, of Virginia.
Billy Long, of Missouri.
Jeff Duncan, of South Carolina.
Tom Marino, of Pennsylvania.
Blake Farenthold, of Texas.
Robert L. Turner, of New York.

Bennie G. Thompson, of Mississippi.
Loretta Sanchez, of California.
Sheila Jackson Lee, of Texas.
Henry Cuellar, of Texas.
Yvette D. Clarke, of New York.
Laura Richardson, of California.
Danny K. Davis, of Illinois.
Brian Higgins, of New York.
Jackie Speier, of California.
Cedric L. Richmond, of Louisiana.
Hansen Clarke, of Michigan.
William R. Keating, of Massachusetts.
Kathleen C. Hochul, of New York.
Janice Hahn, of California.

SUBCOMMITTEES

[The chairman and ranking minority member are ex officio members of all subcommittees on which they do not serve.]

Border and Maritime Security

Candice S. Miller, of Michigan, *Chair*

Mike Rogers, of Alabama.
Michael T. McCaul, of Texas.
Paul C. Broun, of Georgia.
Benjamin Quayle, of Arizona.
E. Scott Rigell, of Virginia.
Jeff Duncan, of South Carolina.

Henry Cuellar, of Texas.
Loretta Sanchez, of California.
Sheila Jackson Lee, of Texas.
Brian Higgins, of New York.
Hansen Clarke, of Michigan.

Counterterrorism and Intelligence

Patrick Meehan, of Pennsylvania, *Chair*

Paul C. Broun, of Georgia.
Chip Cravaack, of Minnesota.
Joe Walsh, of Illinois.
Benjamin Quayle, of Arizona.
E. Scott Rigell, of Virginia.
Billy Long, of Missouri.

Jackie Speier, of California.
Loretta Sanchez, of California.
Brian Higgins, of New York.
Kathleen C. Hochul, of New York.
Janice Hahn, of California.

Cybersecurity, Infrastructure Protection, and Security Technologies

Daniel E. Lungren, of California, *Chair*

Michael T. McCaul, of Texas.
Tim Walberg, of Michigan.
Patrick Meehan, of Pennsylvania.
Billy Long, of Missouri.
Tom Marino, of Pennsylvania.

Yvette D. Clarke, of New York.
Laura Richardson, of California.
Cedric L. Richmond, of Louisiana.
William R. Keating, of Massachusetts.

Emergency Preparedness, Response and Communications

Gus M. Bilirakis, of Florida, *Chair*

Joe Walsh, of Illinois.
E. Scott Rigell, of Virginia.
Tom Marino, of Pennsylvania.
Blake Farenthold, of Texas.
Laura Richardson, of California.
Hansen Clarke, of Michigan.
Kathleen C. Hochul, of New York.

Oversight, Investigations, and Management

Michael T. McCaul, of Texas, *Chair*

Gus M. Bilirakis, of Florida.
Billy Long, of Missouri.
Jeff Duncan, of South Carolina.
Tom Marino, of Pennsylvania.
William R. Keating, of Massachusetts.
Yvette D. Clarke, of New York.
Danny K. Davis, of Illinois.

Transportation Security

Mike Rogers, of Alabama, *Chair*

Daniel E. Lungren, of California.
Tim Walberg, of Michigan.
Chip Cravaack, of Minnesota.
Joe Walsh, of Illinois.
Sheila Jackson Lee, of Texas.
Danny K. Davis, of Illinois.
Jackie Speier, of California.
Cedric L. Richmond, of Louisiana.

STAFF

Committee on Homeland Security (H2–176 Ford House Office Building) phone 226–8417, fax 226–3399.

Staff Director / Chief Counsel.—Michael J. Russell, FHOB / H2–176 (202) 226–8417.

Senior Counsel.—Jennifer Arangio, FHOB / H2–176 (202) 226–8417.

Senior Counsel.—Matthew McCabe, FHOB / H2–176 (202) 226–8417.

Senior Counterterrorism Advisor.—Jonathan A. Duecker, FHOB / H2–176 (202) 226–8417.

Communications Director.—Shane Wolfe, FHOB / H2–176 (202) 226–8417.

Staff Director, Border and Maritime Security Subcommittee.—Paul Anstine, FHOB / H2–176 (202) 226–8417.

Staff Director, Counterterrorism and Intelligence Subcommittee.—Kevin Gundersen, FHOB / H2–176 (202) 226–8417.

Staff Director, Transportation Security Subcommittee.—Amanda Halpern, FHOB / H2–176 (202) 226–8417.

Staff Director, Emergency Preparedness, Response, and Communications Subcommittee.—Kerry Kinirons, FHOB / H2–176 (202) 226–8417.

Staff Director, Cyber Security, Infrastructure Protection, and Security Technologies Subcommittee.—Coley O'Brien, FHOB / H2–176 (202) 226–8417.

Staff Director, Oversight, Investigations, and Management Subcommittee.—Nick Palarino, FHOB / H2–176 (202) 226–8417.

Senior Policy Director.—Mandy L. Bowers, FHOB / H2–176 (202) 226–8417.

Senior Professional Staff Member.—Meghann Peterlin, FHOB / H2–176 (202) 226–8417.

Staff Assistant.—Zach Harris, FHOB / H2–176 (202) 226–8417.

Senior Professional Staff Member.—Diane Berry, FHOB / H2–176 (202) 226–8417.

Professional Staff Members: Luke Burke, Ellen Carlin, Brett DeWitt, Jason Miller, Edward Parkinson, Krista Powers, Lauren Wenger, FHOB / H2–176 (202) 226–8417.

Professional Staff Member / Deputy Parliamentarian.—Jerry White, FHOB / H2–176 (202) 226–8417.

Staff Assistant.—Jake Vreeburg, FHOB / H2–176 (202) 226–8417.

Subcommittee Clerks: Diana Bergwin, Alan Carroll, FHOB / H2–176, (202) 226–2616.

Legislative Assistants: Kate Bonvechio, Mary Rose Rooney, Nicole Smith, FHOB / H2–176, (202) 226–2616.

Counsels: Kevin Carroll, Steven Giaier, Monica Sanders, FHOB / H2–176, (202) 226–2616.

Press Assistant.—April Corbett, FHOB / H2–176, (202) 226–2616.

Chief Parliamentarian.—Towner French, FHOB / H2–176, (202) 226–2616.

Chief Operating Officer.—Laura Fullerton, FHOB / H2–176, (202) 226–2616.

Senior Counsel.—Kevin Gronberg, FHOB / H2–176, (202) 226–2616.

Senior Investigator.—James Meek, FHOB / H2–176, (202) 226–2616.

Senior Policy Director.—Kerry Ann Watkins, FHOB / H2–176, (202) 226–2616.
Security Director.—Dennis Wilson, FHOB / H2–176, (202) 226–2616.

Minority (Democratic) Staff Director.—I. Lanier Avant, FHOB / H2–117, (202) 226–2616.
Minority (Democratic) Chief Counsel.—Rosaline Cohen, FHOB / H2–117, (202) 226–2616.
Minority (Democratic) Chief Oversight Counsel.—Cherri L. Branson, FHOB / H2–117, (202) 226–2616.
Minority (Democratic) Communications Director.—Adam Comis, FHOB / H2–117, (202) 226–2616.
Minority (Democratic) Director, Subcommittee on Border and Maritime Security.—Alison Northrop, FHOB / H2–117, (202) 226–2616.
Minority (Democratic) Director, Subcommittee on Counterterrorism and Intelligence.—Stephen Viña, FHOB / H2–117, (202) 226–2616.
Minority (Democratic) Outreach Coordinator.—Pizza Ashby, FHOB / H2–117, (202) 226–2616.
Minority (Democratic) Director, Subcommittee on Oversight, Investigations, and Management.—Tamla Scott, FHOB / H2–117, (202) 226–2616.
Minority (Democratic) Director, Subcommittee on Transportation Security.—Thomas McDaniels, FHOB / H2–117, (202) 226–2616.
Minority (Democratic) Senior Professional Staff Member.—Marisela Salayandia, FHOB / H2–117, (202) 226–2616.
Minority (Democratic) Professional Staff Member, Counsel.—Hope Goins, HVC / 3H2–117, (202) 226–9492.
Minority (Democratic) Professional Staff Members: Curtis Brown, Mario Cantu, Paula Delcambre, Cory Horton, Nicole Tisdale, Brian Turbyfill, Charles Snyder, FHOB / H2–117, (202) 226–2616.
Minority (Democratic) Office Manager.—Nicole Wade Johnson, FHOB / H2–117, (202) 226–2616.
Printer.—Heather Crowell, FHOB / H2–117, (202) 226–8417.
Chief Financial Officer.—Dawn M. Criste, FHOB / H2–117, (202) 226–8417.
Chief Clerk.—Michael S. Twinchek, FHOB / H2–117, (202) 226–8417.
Deputy Chief Clerk.—Natalie Nixon, FHOB / H2–117, (202) 226–8417.

House Administration

1309 Longworth House Office Building, phone 225–8281, fax 225–9957

http://cha.house.gov/

Daniel E. Lungren, of California, *Chair*

Gregg Harper, of Mississippi.
Phil Gingrey, of Georgia.
Aaron Schock, of Illinois.
Todd Rokita, of Indiana.
Richard B. Nugent, of Florida.

Robert A. Brady, of Pennsylvania.
Zoe Lofgren, of California.
Charles A. Gonzalez, of Texas.

SUBCOMMITTEES

Elections

Gregg Harper, of Mississippi, *Chair*

Aaron Schock, of Illinois.
Richard B. Nugent, of Florida.
Todd Rokita, of Indiana.

Charles A. Gonzalez, of Texas.
Robert A. Brady, of Pennsylvania.

Oversight

Phil Gingrey, of Georgia, *Chair*

Aaron Schock, of Illinois.
Richard B. Nugent, of Florida.
Todd Rokita, of Indiana.

Zoe Lofgren, of California.
Charles A. Gonzalez, of Texas.

STAFF

Committee on House Administration (1309 LHOB), 5–2061.
Staff Director and General Counsel.—Philip Kiko.
Deputy Staff Director.—Andi Snow.
Director of Administration.—Mary Sue Englund.
Director of Member and Committee Services.—George Hadijski.
Director of Technology Policy.—Reynold Schweickhardt.
Deputy General Counsel.—Peter Schalestock.
Counsel / Parliamentarian.—Kimani Little.
Senior Legislative Clerk.—Joe Wallace.
Assistant Legislative Clerk.—Yael Barash.
Acquisition Program Manager.—George Bath.
Director of Oversight.—Linda Ulrich.
Director of Communications.—Salley Wood.
Communications Assistant.—Michael Calvo.
Executive Assistant.—Paige Oneto.
Elections Counsel: Karin Moore, Bob Sensenbrenner.
Finance Administrator.—Anne Binsted.
Professional Staff: Richard Cappetto, Sean Evins, Matthew Field, Katie Ryan, Dominic Storelli.
Professional Oversight Staff.—Barry Brinker.
Staff Assistants: Maximilian Engling, Ryan Kelly, Virginia Meyers, John Rich.
Democratic Staff Director.—James Fleet.
Deputy Staff Director.—Teri Morgan.
Chief Counsel.—Michael Harrison.
Democratic Chief Clerk.—Eddie Flaherty.
Deputy Counsel.—Khalil Abboud.
Senior Policy Adviser.—Matt Pinkus.
Senior Elections Counsel.—Thomas Hicks.
Democratic Finance Director.—Kim Stevens.
Professional Staff: Gregory Abbott, Matthew DeFreitas, Robert Henline, Ricky Le, Kristie Muchnok, Richard Subbio.

Commission on Congressional Mailing Standards (1216 LHOB), 5–9337.
Staff Director.—Jack Dail.
Minority Staff Director.—Constance Thomas.

Judiciary

2138 Rayburn House Office Building, phone 225–3951

http://www.house.gov/judiciary

meets every Wednesday

Lamar Smith, of Texas, Chair

F. James Sensenbrenner, Jr., of Wisconsin.
Howard Coble, of North Carolina.
Elton Gallegly, of California.
Bob Goodlatte, of Virginia.
Daniel E. Lungren, of California.
Steve Chabot, of Ohio.
Darrell E. Issa, of California.
Mike Pence, of Indiana.
J. Randy Forbes, of Virginia.
Steve King, of Iowa.
Trent Franks, of Arizona.
Louie Gohmert, of Texas.
Jim Jordan, of Ohio.
Ted Poe, of Texas.
Jason Chaffetz, of Utah.
Tim Griffin, of Arkansas.
Tom Marino, of Pennsylvania.
Trey Gowdy, of South Carolina.
Dennis A. Ross, of Florida.
Sandy Adams, of Florida.
Benjamin Quayle, of Arizona.
Mark E. Amodei, of Nevada.

John Conyers, Jr., of Michigan.
Howard L. Berman, of California.
Jerrold Nadler, of New York.
Robert C. ''Bobby'' Scott, of Virginia.
Melvin L. Watt, of North Carolina.
Zoe Lofgren, of California.
Sheila Jackson Lee, of Texas.
Maxine Waters, of California.
Steve Cohen, of Tennessee.
Henry C. ''Hank'' Johnson, Jr., of Georgia.
Pedro R. Pierluisi, of Puerto Rico.
Mike Quigley, of Illinois.
Judy Chu, of California.
Theodore E. Deutch, of Florida.
Linda T. Sánchez, of California.

SUBCOMMITTEES

[The chairman and the ranking minority member are ex officio (non-voting) members of all subcommittees on which they do not serve.]

The Constitution

Trent Franks, of Arizona, *Chair*

Mike Pence, of Indiana.
Steve Chabot, of Ohio.
J. Randy Forbes, of Virginia.
Steve King, of Iowa.
Jim Jordan, of Ohio.

Jerrold Nadler, of New York.
Mike Quigley, of Illinois.
John Conyers, Jr., of Michigan.
Robert C. ''Bobby'' Scott, of Virginia.

Courts, Commercial and Administrative Law

Howard Coble, of North Carolina, *Chair*

Trey Gowdy, of South Carolina.
Elton Gallegly, of California.
Trent Franks, of Arizona.
Dennis A. Ross, of Florida.

Steve Cohen, of Tennessee.
Henry C. ''Hank'' Johnson, Jr., of Georgia.
Melvin L. Watt, of North Carolina.

Crime, Terrorism, and Homeland Security

F. James Sensenbrenner, Jr., of Wisconsin, *Chair*

Louie Gohmert, of Texas.
Bob Goodlatte, of Virginia.
Daniel E. Lungren, of California.
J. Randy Forbes, of Virginia.
Ted Poe, of Texas.
Jason Chaffetz, of Utah.
Tim Griffin, of Arkansas.
Tom Marino, of Pennsylvania.
Trey Gowdy, of South Carolina.
Sandy Adams, of Florida.
Benjamin Quayle, of Arizona.

Robert C. "Bobby" Scott, of Virginia.
Steve Cohen, of Tennessee.
Henry C. "Hank" Johnson, Jr., of Georgia.
Pedro R. Pierluisi, of Puerto Rico.
Judy Chu, of California.
Theodore E. Deutch, of Florida.
Sheila Jackson Lee, of Texas.
Mike Quigley, of Illinois.

Immigration Policy and Enforcement

Elton Gallegly, of California, *Chair*

Steve King, of Iowa.
Daniel E. Lungren, of California.
Louie Gohmert, of Texas.
Ted Poe, of Texas.
Trey Gowdy, of South Carolina.
Dennis A. Ross, of Florida.

Zoe Lofgren, of California.
Sheila Jackson Lee, of Texas.
Maxine Waters, of California.
Pedro R. Pierluisi, of Puerto Rico.

Intellectual Property, Competition, and the Internet

Bob Goodlatte, of Virginia, *Chair*

F. James Sensenbrenner, Jr., of Wisconsin.
Howard Coble, of North Carolina.
Steve Chabot, of Ohio.
Darrell E. Issa, of California.
Mike Pence, of Indiana.
Jim Jordan, of Ohio.
Ted Poe, of Texas.
Jason Chaffetz, of Utah.
Tim Griffin, of Arkansas.
Tom Marino, of Pennsylvania.
Sandy Adams, of Florida.
Benjamin Quayle, of Arizona.

Melvin L. Watt, of North Carolina.
John Conyers, Jr., of Michigan.
Howard L. Berman, of California.
Judy Chu, of California.
Theodore E. Deutch, of Florida.
Linda T. Sánchez, of California.
Jerrold Nadler, of New York.
Zoe Lofgren, of California.
Sheila Jackson Lee, of Texas.
Maxine Waters, of California.

STAFF

Committee on the Judiciary (2138 RHOB), 225–3951, fax 5–7680.
Staff Director.—Sean McLaughlin.
Press Secretaries: Brittney Bain, Jessica Baker, Charlotte Sellmyer.
Oversight Counsel.—Harold Damelin.
Parliament.—Allison Halataei.
Deputy Parliament.—Karas Pattison.
Deputy.—Richard Hertling.
Chief Oversight.—Crystal Jezierski.
Oversights: Daniel Huff, Kelsey Whitlock.
Executive Assistants: Sarah Kish, Kayla Munro.
Legislative Clerk.—Jennifer Lackey.
Communication Director.—Kim Smith.
Finances.—Gaye Stafford.
Clerk.—Teresa Vest.
Web.—Tricia White.
Crime B–370 Rayburn, phone: 5–5727, fax: 5–3672.
Chief Counsel.—Caroline Lynch.
Counsels: Sarah Allen, Arthur Baker, Sam Ramer.
Clerk.—Lindsay Hamilton.
Immigration B–353 Rayburn, phone: 5–3926, fax: 5–3737.

Chief Counsel.—George Fishman.
Counsels: Andrea Loving, Dimple Shah.
Professional Staff.—Emily Sanders.
Clerk.—Marian White.

Constitution H2–362 Ford, phone: 5–2825, fax: 5–4299.
Chief Counsel.—Paul Taylor.
Counsels: Holt Lackey, Zachary Somers.
Clerk.—Sarah Vance.

Courts 517 Cannon, phone: 6–7680, fax: 5–3746.
Counsel.—Travis Norton.
Clerks: Daniel Flores, Ashley Lewis.
Professional Staff.—Allison Rose.
Committee Printer.—Doug Alexander, 105 Cannon, fax: 6–2362.

Intellectual Property B–352 Rayburn, phone: 5–5741, fax: 5–3673.
Chief Counsel.—Blaine Merritt.
Counsels: Vishal Amin, David Whitney.
Clerk.—Olivia Lee.

Computer Office 2451 Rayburn, fax: 5–1842.
IT: Kerli Philippe, Banyon Vassar.

Committee Publications B–29 Cannon, phone: 5–0408, fax: 5–1842.
Clerk Calendar.—Jennifer Noll.
Document Clerk.—Tim Pearson.

Minority Staff Members
Minority Parliament.—Danielle Brown, B–351 Rayburn, phone: 5–6906, fax: 5–7682.
Minority Counsels: Carol Chodroff, Jason Everett, Joe Graupensperger, Aaron Hiller, Tom Jawetz, Susan Jensen-Lachmann, Keenan Keller, Michelle Millben, Matthew Morgan.
Professional Staff: Rosalind Jackson, Matthew Morgan, Dwight Sullivan.
Minority Chief Counsel and Staff Director.—Perry Apelbaum, 2142 Rayburn, phone: 5–6504, fax: 5–7686.
Professional Staff: Veronica Eligan, Maggie Littlewood, Benjamin Staub.
Minority Counsel.—Liliana Coronado, David Lachmann, Ron LeGrand, Heather Sawyer, Bobby Vassar, B–336 Rayburn, fax: 5–1845.
Minority Counsels: James Park, Norberto Salinas, H2–347 Ford, fax: 6–4940.

Natural Resources

1324 Longworth House Office Building, phone 225–2761

http://naturalresources.house.gov

meets each Wednesday

Doc Hastings, of Washington, *Chair*

Don Young, of Alaska.
John J. Duncan, Jr., of Tennessee.
Louie Gohmert, of Texas.
Rob Bishop, of Utah.
Doug Lamborn, of Colorado.
Robert J. Wittman, of Virginia.
Paul C. Broun, of Georgia.
John Fleming, of Louisiana.
Mike Coffman, of Colorado.
Tom McClintock, of California.
Glenn Thompson, of Pennsylvania.
Jeff Denham, of California.
Dan Benishek, of Michigan.
David Rivera, of Florida.
Jeff Duncan, of South Carolina.
Scott R. Tipton, of Colorado.
Paul A. Gosar, of Arizona.
Raúl R. Labrador, of Idaho.
Kristi L. Noem, of South Dakota.
Steve Southerland II, of Florida.
Bill Flores, of Texas.
Andy Harris, of Maryland.
Jeffrey M. Landry, of Louisiana.
Charles J. ''Chuck'' Fleischmann, Tennessee.
Jon Runyan, of New Jersey.
Bill Johnson, of Ohio.
Mark E. Amodei, of Nevada.

Edward J. Markey, of Massachusetts.
Dale E. Kildee, of Michigan.
Peter A. DeFazio, of Oregon.
Eni F. H. Faleomavaega, of American Samoa.
Frank Pallone, Jr., of New Jersey.
Grace F. Napolitano, of California.
Rush D. Holt, of New Jersey.
Raúl M. Grijalva, of Arizona.
Madeleine Z. Bordallo, of Guam.
Jim Costa, of California.
Dan Boren, of Oklahoma.
Gregorio Kilili Camacho Sablan, of Northern Mariana Islands.
Martin Heinrich, of New Mexico.
Ben Ray Luján, of New Mexico.
John P. Sarbanes, of Maryland.
Betty Sutton, of Ohio.
Niki Tsongas, of Massachusetts.
Pedro R. Pierluisi, of Puerto Rico.
John Garamendi, of California.
Colleen W. Hanabusa, of Hawaii.

SUBCOMMITTEES

[The chairman and ranking minority member are ex officio (non-voting) members of all subcommittees on which they do not serve.]

Energy and Mineral Resources

Doug Lamborn, of Colorado, *Chair*

Louie Gohmert, of Texas.
Paul C. Broun, of Georgia.
John Fleming, of Louisiana.
Mike Coffman, of Colorado.
Glenn Thompson, of Pennsylvania.
Dan Benishek, of Michigan.
David Rivera, of Florida.
Jeff Duncan, of South Carolina.
Paul A. Gosar, of Arizona.
Bill Flores, of Texas.
Jeffrey M. Landry, of Louisiana.
Charles J. ''Chuck'' Fleischmann, Tennessee.
Bill Johnson, of Ohio.
Mark E. Amodei, of Nevada.

Rush D. Holt, of New Jersey.
Peter A. DeFazio, of Oregon.
Madeleine Z. Bordallo, of Guam.
Jim Costa, of California.
Dan Boren, of Oklahoma.
Gregorio Kilili Camacho Sablan, of Northern Mariana Islands.
Martin Heinrich, of New Mexico.
John P. Sarbanes, of Maryland.
Betty Sutton, of Ohio.
Niki Tsongas, of Massachusetts.

Fisheries, Wildlife, Oceans and Insular Affairs

John Fleming, of Louisiana, *Chair*

Don Young, of Alaska.
Robert J. Wittman, of Virginia.
Jeff Duncan, of South Carolina.
Steve Southerland II, of Florida.
Bill Flores, of Texas.
Andy Harris, of Maryland.
Jeffrey M. Landry, of Louisiana.
Jon Runyan, of New Jersey.

Gregorio Kilili Camacho Sablan, of Northern Mariana Islands.
Eni F. H. Faleomavaega, of American Samoa.
Frank Pallone, Jr., of New Jersey.
Madeleine Z. Bordallo, of Guam.
Pedro R. Pierluisi, of Puerto Rico.
Colleen W. Hanabusa, of Hawaii.

Indian and Alaska Native Affairs

Don Young, of Alaska, *Chair*

Tom McClintock, of California.
Jeff Denham, of California.
Dan Benishek, of Michigan.
Paul A. Gosar, of Arizona.
Raúl R. Labrador, of Idaho.
Kristi L. Noem, of South Dakota.

Dan Boren, of Oklahoma.
Dale E. Kildee, of Michigan.
Eni F. H. Faleomavaega, of American Samoa.
Ben Ray Luján, of New Mexico.
Colleen W. Hanabusa, of Hawaii.

National Parks, Forests and Public Lands

Rob Bishop, of Utah, *Chair*

Don Young, of Alaska.
John J. Duncan, Jr., of Tennessee.
Doug Lamborn, of Colorado.
Paul C. Broun, of Georgia.
Mike Coffman, of Colorado.
Tom McClintock, of California.
David Rivera, of Florida.
Scott R. Tipton, of Colorado.
Raúl R. Labrador, of Idaho.
Kristi L. Noem, of South Dakota.
Bill Johnson, of Ohio.
Mark E. Amodei, of Nevada.

Raúl M. Grijalva, of Arizona.
Peter A. DeFazio, of Oregon.
Rush D. Holt, of New Jersey.
Martin Heinrich, of New Mexico.
John P. Sarbanes, of Maryland.
Betty Sutton, of Ohio.
Niki Tsongas, of Massachusetts.
John Garamendi, of California.

Water and Power

Tom McClintock, of California, *Chair*

Louie Gohmert, of Texas.
Jeff Denham, of California.
Scott R. Tipton, of Colorado.
Paul A. Gosar, of Arizona.
Raúl R. Labrador, of Idaho.
Kristi L. Noem, of South Dakota.

Grace F. Napolitano, of California.
Raúl M. Grijalva, of Arizona.
Jim Costa, of California.
Ben Ray Luján, of New Mexico.
John Garamendi, of California.

STAFF

Committee on Natural Resources (1324 LHOB), 5–2761.
Majority Chief of Staff.—Todd Young.
Director of Legislative Operations.—Kathy Loden.
Chief Legislative Counsel.—Lisa Pittman.
Senior Counsel, Office of Oversight and Investigations.—Traci Rodriguez.
Director of NW Energy and Environmental Policy, Senior Counsel.—Todd Ungerecht.
Policy Advisor.—Melissa Burnison.
Director of Member Services and Administration.—Sophia Varnasidis.
Assistant to the Chairman, Member Services Coordinator.—Tim Kovis.
Staff Assistants: Matt Schafle, Bryson Wong.
Communications Director.—Jill Strait (1328 LHOB), 6–9109.

Director of Outreach.—Jamie Hennigan.
Press Secretaries: Crystal Feldman, Spencer Pederson.
Online and New Media Coordinator.—Neal Kirby.
Press Assistant.—Mallory Micetich.
Chief Financial Officer.—Linda Booth (1324 LHOB), 5–2761.
Personnel and Financial Officer.—Meghan Foley.
Chief Legislative Clerk.—Nancy Locke.
Calendar Clerk.—Joycelyn Coleman.
Director, Information Technology.—Matt Vaccaro.
Senior IT Engineer.—Ed Van Scoyoc.
Editor/Printer.—Kathy Miller (H2–550), 6–3529.
Democratic Staff Director.—Jeffrey Duncan (1329 LHOB), 5–6065.
Chief Democratic Counsel.—David Watkins.
Deputy Democratic Staff Director.—Ana Unruh Cohen (H2–186), 5–6065.
Chief Democratic Clerk.—Sarah Butler.
Deputy Staff Director for Communications.—Eben Burnham-Snyder (H2–269), 5–6065.
Senior Communications Advisor and Outreach Coordinator.—Jeffrey Sharp.
New Media Specialist.—Jacqueline Chenault.
Senior Investigator and Policy Coordinator.—Michal Freedhoff (2108 RHOB), 5–2836.
Democratic Professional Staff Member.—Camille Calimlim Touton (H2–186), 5–6065.
Subcommittee on Energy and Mineral Resources (1333 LHOB), 5–9297.
Majority Staff Director.—Tim Charters.
Legislative Staff: Kathy Benedetto, Amanda Tharpe.
Clerk.—Jessica Gregg.
Democratic Senior Policy Advisors: Morgan Gray, Jonathon Phillips (H2–186), 5–6065.
Subcommittee on Fisheries, Wildlife, Oceans and Insular Affairs (140 CHOB), 6–0200.
Majority Staff Director.—Harry Burroughs.
Legislative Staff: Bonnie Bruce, Dave Whaley.
Clerk.—John Hanline.
Democratic Counsel, Insular Affairs.—Brian Modeste (H2–186), 5–6065.
Democratic Professional Staff Member.—Karen Hyun.
Subcommittee on Indian and Alaska Native Affairs (1337 LHOB), 6–9725.
Majority Staff Director.—Chris Fluhr.
Professional Legislative Staff.—Brandon Ashley.
Clerk.—Ana Fonokalafi-McMullen.
Democratic Counsel.—Jennifer Romero (H2–186), 5–6065.
Subcommittee on National Parks, Forests, and Public Lands (1017 LHOB), 6–7736.
Majority Staff Director.—Jim Streeter.
Legislative Staff.—Casey Hammond, Otto Mucklo, Tyler Hamman.
Clerk.—Casey Snider.
Democratic Professional Staff Member.—David Watkins (1329 LHOB), 5–6065.
Subcommittee on Water and Power (1522 LHOB), 5–8331.
Majority Staff Director.—Kiel Weaver.
Legislative Staff.—Ian Lyle.
Clerk.—Matt Gall.

Oversight and Government Reform

2157 Rayburn House Office Building, phone 225–5074, fax 225–3974, TTY 225–6852

http://oversight.house.gov

Darrell E. Issa, of California, *Chair*

Dan Burton, of Indiana.
John L. Mica, of Florida.
Todd Russell Platts, of Pennsylvania.
Michael R. Turner, of Ohio.
Patrick T. McHenry, of North Carolina.
Jim Jordan, of Ohio.
Jason Chaffetz, of Utah.
Connie Mack, of Florida.
Tim Walberg, of Michigan.
James Lankford, of Oklahoma.
Justin Amash, of Michigan.
Ann Marie Buerkle, of New York.
Paul A. Gosar, of Arizona.
Raúl R. Labrador, of Idaho.
Patrick Meehan, of Pennsylvania.
Scott DesJarlais, of Tennessee.
Joe Walsh, of Illinois.
Trey Gowdy, of South Carolina.
Dennis A. Ross, of Florida.
Frank C. Guinta, of New Hampshire.
Blake Farenthold, of Texas.
Mike Kelly, of Pennsylvania.

Elijah E. Cummings, of Maryland.
Edolphus Towns, of New York.
Carolyn B. Maloney, of New York.
Eleanor Holmes Norton, of District of Columbia.
Dennis J. Kucinich, of Ohio.
John F. Tierney, of Massachusetts.
Wm. Lacy Clay, of Missouri.
Stephen F. Lynch, of Massachusetts.
Jim Cooper, of Tennessee.
Gerald E. Connolly, of Virginia.
Mike Quigley, of Illinois.
Danny K. Davis, of Illinois.
Bruce L. Braley, of Iowa.
Peter Welch, of Vermont.
John A. Yarmuth, of Kentucky.
Christopher S. Murphy, of Connecticut.
Jackie Speier, of California.

SUBCOMMITTEES

[The chairman and ranking minority member are ex officio (voting) members of all subcommittees]

Federal Workforce, U.S. Postal Service and Labor Policy

Dennis A. Ross, of Florida, *Chair*

Justin Amash, of Michigan, *Vice Chair*

Jim Jordan, of Ohio.
Jason Chaffetz, of Utah.
Connie Mack, of Florida.
Tim Walberg, of Michigan.
Trey Gowdy, of South Carolina.

Stephen F. Lynch, of Massachusetts.
Eleanor Holmes Norton, of District of Columbia.
Gerald E. Connolly, of Virginia.
Danny K. Davis, of Illinois.

Government Organization, Efficiency and Financial Management

Todd Russell Platts, of Pennsylvania, *Chair*

Connie Mack, of Florida, *Vice Chair*

James Lankford, of Oklahoma.
Justin Amash, of Michigan.
Paul A. Gosar, of Arizona.
Frank C. Guinta, of New Hampshire.
Blake Farenthold, of Texas.

Edolphus Towns, of New York.
Jim Cooper, of Tennessee.
Gerald E. Connolly, of Virginia.
Eleanor Holmes Norton, of District of Columbia.

Health Care, District of Columbia, Census and the National Archives

Trey Gowdy, of South Carolina, *Chair*

Paul A. Gosar, of Arizona, *Vice Chair*

Dan Burton, of Indiana.
John L. Mica, of Florida.
Patrick T. McHenry, of North Carolina.
Scott DesJarlais, of Tennessee.
Joe Walsh, of Illinois.

Danny K. Davis, of Illinois.
Eleanor Holmes Norton, of District of Columbia.
Wm. Lacy Clay, of Missouri.
Christopher S. Murphy, of Connecticut.

National Security, Homeland Defense and Foreign Operations

Jason Chaffetz, of Utah, *Chair*

Raúl R. Labrador, of Idaho, *Vice Chair*

Dan Burton, of Indiana.
John L. Mica, of Florida.
Todd Russell Platts, of Pennsylvania.
Michael R. Turner, of Ohio.
Paul A. Gosar, of Arizona.
Blake Farenthold, of Texas.

John F. Tierney, of Massachusetts.
Bruce L. Braley, of Iowa.
Peter Welch, of Vermont.
John A. Yarmuth, of Kentucky.
Stephen F. Lynch, of Massachusetts.
Mike Quigley, of Illinois.

Regulatory Affairs, Stimulus Oversight and Government Spending

Jim Jordan, of Ohio, *Chair*

Ann Marie Buerkle, of New York, *Vice Chair*

Connie Mack, of Florida.
Raúl R. Labrador, of Idaho.
Scott DesJarlais, of Tennessee.
Frank C. Guinta, of New Hampshire.
Mike Kelly, of Pennsylvania.

Dennis J. Kucinich, of Ohio.
Jim Cooper, of Tennessee.
Jackie Speier, of California.
Bruce L. Braley, of Iowa.

Tarp, Financial Services and Bailouts of Public and Private Programs

Patrick T. McHenry, of North Carolina, *Chair*

Frank C. Guinta, of New Hampshire, *Vice Chair*

Ann Marie Buerkle, of New York.
Justin Amash, of Michigan.
Patrick Meehan, of Pennsylvania.
Joe Walsh, of Illinois.
Trey Gowdy, of South Carolina.
Dennis A. Ross, of Florida.

Mike Quigley, of Illinois.
Carolyn B. Maloney, of New York.
Peter Welch, of Vermont.
John A. Yarmuth, of Kentucky.
Jackie Speier, of California.
Jim Cooper, of Tennessee.

Technology, Information Policy, Intergovernmental Relations and Procurement Reform

James Lankford, of Oklahoma, *Chair*

Mike Kelly, of Pennsylvania, *Vice Chair*

Jason Chaffetz, of Utah.
Tim Walberg, of Michigan.
Raúl R. Labrador, of Idaho.
Patrick Meehan, of Pennsylvania.
Blake Farenthold, of Texas.

Gerald E. Connolly, of Virginia.
Christopher S. Murphy, of Connecticut.
Stephen F. Lynch, of Massachusetts.
Jackie Speier, of California.

STAFF

Oversight and Government Reform (2157 RHOB), 202–225–5074.

Majority Staff Director.—Lawrence J. Brady.

Deputy Staff Director.—John Cuaderes.
General Counsel.—Robert Borden.
Director of Member Services and Committee Operations.—Adam Fromm.
Parliamentarian.—Molly Boyl.
Director of Communications and Senior Policy Advisor.—Frederick Hill.
Senior Communications Advisor.—Jeff Solsby.
Communications Advisor.—Ali Ahmad.
Director of Digital Strategies and Press Secretary.—Seamus Kraft.
Deputy Director of Digital Strategy.—Justin LoFranco.
Press Secretary.—Rebecca Watkins.
Press Assistant.—Cheyenne Steel.
Legislative Policy Director.—Peter Warren.
Senior Counsel.—Richard Beutel.
Counsel.—Hudson Hollister.
Senior Professional Staff Member.—Jennifer Hemingway.
Professional Staff Members: Ryan Little, Jeffrey Post, James Robertson.
Chief Clerk.—Linda Good.
Deputy Chief Clerk.—Laura Rush.
Senior Assistant Clerk.—Sharon Casey.
Assistant Clerks: Michael Bebeau, Gwen D'Luzansky.
Staff Assistants: Alexia Ardolina, Will Boyington, Drew Colliatie, Donna Harkins, Noelle Turbitt, Nadia Zahran.
Executive Assistant.—Kathy Brayton.
Financial Administrator.—Robin Butler.
Deputy Chief Information Officer.—Jeff Wease.

Director of Oversight.—Mark Marin.
Deputy Chief Counsel, Oversight.—Christopher Hixon.
Senior Counsels: Thomas Alexander, Howard Denis, Peter Haller, Kristina Moore.
Counsels: Joseph Brazauskas, David Brewer, Sery Kim, Mitchell Kominsky, Christine Martin.
Senior Policy Advisor.—Jim Lewis.
Professional Staff Members: Brien Beattie, Brian Blase, Tyler Grimm, Ryan Hambleton, Kristin Nelson, Michael Whatley, Sang Yi.
Research Analysts: Katelyn Christ, Tegan Millspaw, Sharon Meredith Utz.

Chief Counsel, Investigations.—Steve Castor.
Deputy Chief Counsel, Investigations.—Ashok Pinto.
Senior Counsels: Henry Kerner, Jonathan Skladany.
Counsels: Ashley Callen, Carlton Davis, Jean Humbrecht, Jessica Laux, Rafael Maryahin, John Zadrozny.
Professional Staff Member.—John Ohly.
Investigator.—Matthew Tallmer.
Legislative Assistant.—Kate Dunbar.

Minority Staff Director.—Dave Rapallo, (2471 RHOB), 202–225–5051.
Minority Chief Counsel.—Susanne Sachsman Grooms.
Minority Chief Oversight Counsel.—Leah Perry.
Minority Legislative Director.—Mark Stephenson.
Minority Policy Director.—Lucinda Lessley.
Minority Administrative Director.—Jaron Bourke.
Minority Communications Director.—Ashley Etienne.
Minority Press Secretary.—Jennifer Hoffman.
Minority Press Secretary.—Paul Kincaid.
Minority Senior Investigator.—Chris Knauer.
Minority Senior Investigative Counsel.—Chris Staszak.
Minority Investigator.—Lisa Cody.
Minority Senior Counsels: Jason Powell, Steven Rangel.
Minority Counsels: Krista Boyd, Beverly Britton Fraser, Claire Coleman, Yvette Cravins, Justin Kim, Scott Lindsay, Brian Quinn, Donald Sherman, Carlos Uriarte, David Walsh.
Minority Professional Staff Members: William Miles, Amy Miller.
Chief Clerk/Office Administrator.—Carla Hultberg.
Deputy Clerk/Counsel.—Cecelia Thomas.
Staff Assistants: Ronald Allen, Kevin Corbin.
Technology Director.—Eddie Walker.

Rules

H–312 The Capitol, phone 225–9191

http://www.rules.house.gov

meets every Tuesday

David Dreier, of California, *Chair*

Pete Sessions, of Texas.
Virginia Foxx, of North Carolina.
Rob Bishop, of Utah.
Rob Woodall, of Georgia.
Richard B. Nugent, of Florida.
Tim Scott, of South Carolina.
Daniel Webster, of Florida.

Louise McIntosh Slaughter, of New York.
James P. McGovern, of Massachusetts.
Alcee L. Hastings, of Florida.
Jared Polis, of Colorado.

SUBCOMMITTEES

Legislative and Budget Process

Pete Sessions, of Texas, *Chair*

Virginia Foxx, of North Carolina.
Rob Woodall, of Georgia.
Daniel Webster, of Florida.
David Dreier, of California.

Alcee L. Hastings, of Florida.
Jared Polis, of Colorado.

Rules and Organization of the House

Richard B. Nugent, of Florida, *Chair*

Rob Bishop, of Utah.
Tim Scott, of South Carolina.
David Dreier, of California.

James P. McGovern, of Massachusetts.
Louise McIntosh Slaughter, of New York.

STAFF

Committee on Rules (H–312 The Capitol), 225–9191.
Majority Staff Director.—Hugh Halpern.
Deputy Staff Director.—Adam Jarvis.
Policy Director.—Rachael Leman.
Communications Director.—Jo Maney.
Professional Staff: Lydia Calio, Stephen Cote, Jenny Gorski, Celeste West.
Director of Information Technology.—Tom Ulrich.
Legislative Clerk.—Kevin Conroy.
Deputy Clerk.—Monica Chinn.
Staff Assistant.—Sarah Minkel.
Associate Staff: Jennifer DeCasper (1117 LHOB); Keagan Lenihan (2233 RHOB); Steve Peterson (123 CHOB); Brandon Renz (1230 LHOB); Janet Rossi (1725 LHOB); Brad Smith (233 CHOB); Katharine Troller (1517 LHOB); Frank Walker (1039 LHOB).
Minority Staff Director.—Miles Lackey.
Associate Counsel: Adam Berg, Liz Pardue.
Legislative Director.—Don Sisson.
Professional Staff: Tony Abate, Tim Sheehan.
Chief Clerk.—Deb Delaney.
Legislative Clerk.—George Agurkis.
Associate Staff: Rosalyn Kumar (Polis 501 CHOB); Lale Mamaux (Hastings 2353 RHOB); Keith Stern (McGovern 438 CHOB).
Subcommittee on Legislative and Budget Process (2233 RHOB), 5–2231.
Majority Staff Director.—Keagan Lenihan (Sessions).
Minority Staff Director.—Lale Mamaux (Hastings).
Subcommittee on Rules and Organization of the House (1517 LHOB), 5–1002.
Majority Staff Director.—Katharine Troller (Nugent).
Minority Staff Director.—Keith Stern (McGovern).

Science, Space, and Technology

2321 Rayburn House Office Building, phone 225–6371, fax 226–0113

http://www.house.gov/science

meets second and fourth Wednesdays of each month

Ralph M. Hall, of Texas, *Chair*

F. James Sensenbrenner, Jr., of Wisconsin, *Vice Chair*

Lamar Smith, of Texas.
Dana Rohrabacher, of California.
Roscoe G. Bartlett, of Maryland.
Frank D. Lucas, of Oklahoma.
Judy Biggert, of Illinois.
W. Todd Akin, of Missouri.
Randy Neugebauer, of Texas.
Michael T. McCaul, of Texas.
Paul C. Broun, of Georgia.
Sandy Adams, of Florida.
Benjamin Quayle, of Arizona.
Charles J. ''Chuck'' Fleischmann, of Tennessee.
E. Scott Rigell, of Virginia.
Steven M. Palazzo, of Mississippi.
Mo Brooks, of Alabama.
Andy Harris, of Maryland.
Randy Hultgren, of Illinois.
Chip Cravaack, of Minnesota.
Larry Bucshon, of Indiana.
Dan Benishek, of Michigan.

Eddie Bernice Johnson, of Texas.
Jerry F. Costello, of Illinois.
Lynn C. Woolsey, of California.
Zoe Lofgren, of California.
Brad Miller, of North Carolina.
Daniel Lipinski, of Illinois.
Gabrielle Giffords, of Arizona.
Donna F. Edwards, of Maryland.
Marcia L. Fudge, of Ohio.
Ben Ray Luján, of New Mexico.
Paul Tonko, of New York.
Jerry McNerney, of California.
John P. Sarbanes, of Maryland.
Terri A. Sewell, of Alabama.
Frederica S. Wilson, of Florida.
Hansen Clarke, of Michigan.

SUBCOMMITTEES

[The chairman and ranking minority member are ex officio (voting) members of all subcommittees on which they do not serve.]

Energy and Environment

Andy Harris, of Maryland, *Chair*

Dana Rohrabacher, of California, *Vice Chair*

Roscoe G. Bartlett, of Maryland.
Frank D. Lucas, of Oklahoma.
Judy Biggert, of Illinois.
W. Todd Akin, of Missouri.
Randy Neugebauer, of Texas.
Paul C. Broun, of Georgia.
Charles J. ''Chuck'' Fleischmann, of Tennessee.

Brad Miller, of North Carolina.
Lynn C. Woolsey, of California.
Ben Ray Luján, of New Mexico.
Paul Tonko, of New York.
Zoe Lofgren, of California.
Jerry McNerney, of California.

Investigations and Oversight

Paul C. Broun, of Georgia, *Chair*

Sandy Adams, of Florida, *Vice Chair*

F. James Sensenbrenner, Jr., of Wisconsin.
Randy Hultgren, of Illinois.
Larry Bucshon, of Indiana.
Dan Benishek, of Michigan.

Donna F. Edwards, of Maryland.
Zoe Lofgren, of California.
Brad Miller, of North Carolina.
Jerry McNerney, of California.

Research and Science Education

Mo Brooks, of Alabama, *Chair*

Roscoe G. Bartlett, of Maryland, *Vice Chair*

Benjamin Quayle, of Arizona.
Steven M. Palazzo, of Mississippi.
Andy Harris, of Maryland.
Randy Hultgren, of Illinois.
Larry Bucshon, of Indiana.
Dan Benishek, of Michigan.
Daniel Lipinski, of Illinois.
Hansen Clarke, of Michigan.
Paul Tonko, of New York.
John P. Sarbanes, of Maryland.
Terri A. Sewell, of Alabama.

Space and Aeronautics

Steven M. Palazzo, of Mississippi, *Chair*

Lamar Smith, of Texas, *Vice Chair*

F. James Sensenbrenner, Jr., of Wisconsin.
Dana Rohrabacher, of California.
Frank D. Lucas, of Oklahoma.
W. Todd Akin, of Missouri.
Michael T. McCaul, of Texas.
Sandy Adams, of Florida.
E. Scott Rigell, of Virginia.
Mo Brooks, of Alabama.
Gabrielle Giffords, of Arizona.
Marcia L. Fudge, of Ohio.
Jerry F. Costello, of Illinois.
Terri A. Sewell, of Alabama.
Donna F. Edwards, of Maryland.
Frederica S. Wilson, of Florida.

Technology and Innovation

Benjamin Quayle, of Arizona, *Chair*

Judy Biggert, of Illinois, *Vice Chair*

Lamar Smith, of Texas.
Randy Neugebauer, of Texas.
Michael T. McCaul, of Texas.
Charles J. ''Chuck'' Fleischmann, of Tennessee.
E. Scott Rigell, of Virginia.
Randy Hultgren, of Illinois.
Chip Cravaack, of Minnesota.
John P. Sarbanes, of Maryland.
Frederica S. Wilson, of Florida.
Daniel Lipinski, of Illinois.
Gabrielle Giffords, of Arizona.
Ben Ray Luján, of New Mexico.

STAFF

Committee on Science, Space, and Technology (2321 RHOB), 225–6371, fax 226–0113.
Chief of Staff.—Janet Poppleton.
Staff Director.—Leslee Gilbert.
Chief Counsel.—Margaret Caravelli.
Deputy Chief Counsel.—Katy Crooks.
Communications Director.—Zachary Kurz.
Administrative Director.—Katie Comer.
Distinguished Professional Staff.—Harlan Watson.
Legislative Clerk.—Deborah Emerson Samantar.
Press Assistant.—Lindsay Meyers.
Legal Assistant.—Lana Frost.
Director of Information Technology.—Larry Whittaker.
Committee Printer.—Sangina Wright.
Financial Administrator.—Leslie Coppler.
Staff Assistant.—Molly Keaton.
Minority Staff (2321 RHOB), 5–6371, fax 6–0113
Chief of Staff.—Dick Obermann.
Chief Counsel.—John Piazza.
Deputy Counsel.—Robert Etter.
Administrative Director/Research Assistant.—Kristin Kopshever.
Administrative and Legal Assistant.—Brystol English.
Subcommittee on Energy and Environment
Majority Staff Director.—Dan Byers.

Senior Professional Staff.—Tara Rothschild.
Professional Staff: Kyle Oliver, Clint Woods, Andy Zach.
Policy Staff.—Alex Matthews.
Minority Staff Director.—Chris King.
Professional Staff: Shimere Williams, Jetta Wong.

Subcommittee on Technology and Innovation
Majority Staff Director.—Julia Jester.
Professional Staff: Jamie Brown, Neil Canfield.
Staff Assistant.—Daniel Rhea.
Minority Staff Director.—Hilary Cain.
Professional Staff.—Marcy Gallo.

Subcommittee on Research and Science Education
Majority Staff Director.—Melé Williams.
Professional Staff.—Kirsten Duncan.
Policy Staff.—Aaricka Aldridge.
Staff Assistant.—Ashley Force.
Minority Staff Director.—Dahlia Sokolov.
Professional Staff.—Bess Caughran.

Subcommittee on Space and Aeronautics
Majority Staff Director.—Ed Feddeman.
Senior Professional Staff.—Ken Monroe.
Professional Staff.—Anne Connor.
NOAA Detailee.—Mike Beavin.
Staff Assistant.—Ben Schell.
Minority Staff Director.—Pam Whitney.
Professional Staff.—Allen Li.

Subcommittee on Investigations and Oversight
Majority Staff Director.—Tom Hammond.
Professional Staff.—Raj Bharwani.
Subcommittee Counsel.—Joe Keeley.
Staff Assistant.—John Serrano.
Minority Staff Director.—Dan Pearson.
Professional Staff.—Doug Pasternak.

Small Business

2361 Rayburn House Office Building, phone 225–4038, fax 226–5276

http://www.house.gov/smbiz

meets second Thursday of each month

Sam Graves, of Missouri, *Chair*

Roscoe G. Bartlett, of Maryland.
Steve Chabot, of Ohio.
Steve King, of Iowa.
Mike Coffman, of Colorado.
Mick Mulvaney, of South Carolina.
Scott R. Tipton, of Colorado.
Jeffrey M. Landry, of Louisiana.
Jaime Herrera Beutler, of Washington.
Allen B. West, of Florida.
Renee L. Ellmers, of North Carolina.
Joe Walsh, of Illinois.
Lou Barletta, of Pennsylvania.
Richard L. Hanna, of New York.
Robert T. Schilling, of Illinois.

Nydia M. Velázquez, of New York.
Kurt Schrader, of Oregon.
Mark S. Critz, of Pennsylvania.
Yvette D. Clarke, of New York.
Judy Chu, of California.
David N. Cicilline, of Rhode Island.
Cedric L. Richmond, of Louisiana.
Janice Hahn, of California.
Gary C. Peters, of Michigan.
William L. Owens, of New York.
William R. Keating, of Massachusetts.

SUBCOMMITTEES

[The chairman and ranking minority member are ex officio (non-voting) members of all subcommittees on which they do not serve.]

Agriculture, Energy and Trade

Scott R. Tipton, of Colorado, *Chair*

Roscoe G. Bartlett, of Maryland.
Steve King, of Iowa.
Renee L. Ellmers, of North Carolina.
Jeffrey M. Landry, of Louisiana.
Lou Barletta, of Pennsylvania.
Robert T. Schilling, of Illinois.

Mark S. Critz, of Pennsylvania.
David N. Cicilline, of Rhode Island.
William R. Keating, of Massachusetts.
Judy Chu, of California.

Contracting and Workforce

Mick Mulvaney, of South Carolina, *Chair*

Steve King, of Iowa.
Mike Coffman, of Colorado.
Allen B. West, of Florida.
Renee L. Ellmers, of North Carolina.
Jeffrey M. Landry, of Louisiana.
Lou Barletta, of Pennsylvania.

Judy Chu, of California.
Kurt Schrader, of Oregon.
Mark S. Critz, of Pennsylvania.
Yvette D. Clarke, of New York.
Cedric L. Richmond, of Louisiana.

Economic Growth, Tax and Capital Access

Joe Walsh, of Illinois, *Chair*

Steve Chabot, of Ohio.
Steve King, of Iowa.
Mike Coffman, of Colorado.
Mick Mulvaney, of South Carolina.
Richard L. Hanna, of New York.
Robert T. Schilling, of Illinois.

Kurt Schrader, of Oregon.
Yvette D. Clarke, of New York.
David N. Cicilline, of Rhode Island.
Judy Chu, of California.
Gary C. Peters, of Michigan.

Healthcare and Technology

Renee L. Ellmers, of North Carolina, *Chair*

Steve King, of Iowa.
Mick Mulvaney, of South Carolina.
Scott R. Tipton, of Colorado.
Jaime Herrera Beutler, of Washington.
Joe Walsh, of Illinois.
Richard L. Hanna, of New York.
Robert T. Schilling, of Illinois.

Cedric L. Richmond, of Louisiana.
Gary C. Peters, of Michigan.

Investigations, Oversight and Regulations

Mike Coffman, of Colorado, *Chair*

Scott R. Tipton, of Colorado.
Jaime Herrera Beutler, of Washington.
Allen B. West, of Florida.
Joe Walsh, of Illinois.
Jeffrey M. Landry, of Louisiana.
Richard L. Hanna, of New York.

Kurt Schrader, of Oregon.

STAFF

Committee on Small Business (B–343 RHOB), 225–4038.
Majority Staff Director.—Lori Salley (B–2361 RHOB) 225–5821.
Deputy Staff Director.—Paul Sass.
Chief Counsel.—Barry Pineles.
Deputy Chief Counsel.—Jan Oliver.
Senior Counsel.—Emily Murphy.
Counsel.—Andy Guggenheim.
Press Secretary.—Wendy Knox.
Press Assistant/New Media.—Cielo Villasenor.
Clerk/Press Assistant.—Caroline Rabbitt.
Professional Staff: Lisa Christian, Joe Hartz, Andy Karellas, Mark Ratto, Brooke Shupe, Mindi Walker.
Staff Assistant/Systems Admnistrator.—Jeff Leieritz.
Staff Assistant.—Hilary Dungan.
Chief of Staff to the Member.—Tom Brown.
Minority Staff Director.—Michael Day.
Deputy Staff Director.—Adam Minehardt.
Banking Counsel.—Andy Jiminez.
Office Manager.—Mory Garcia.
Communications Director.—Alex Haurek.
Professional Staff: Melissa Johnson, Eminence Northcutt.
Oversight Counsel.—Chris Lyons.
Tax Counsel.—Naveeen Parmar.

Transportation and Infrastructure

2165 Rayburn House Office Building, phone 225–4472, fax 225–6782

http://www.house.gov/transportation

meets first Wednesday of each month

Majority (202) 225–9446, room 2165 RHOB

Minority (202) 225–4472, room 2163 RHOB

John L. Mica, of Florida, *Chair*

Don Young, of Alaska.
Thomas E. Petri, of Wisconsin.
Howard Coble, of North Carolina.
John J. Duncan, Jr., of Tennessee.
Frank A. LoBiondo, of New Jersey.
Gary G. Miller, of California.
Timothy V. Johnson, of Illinois.
Sam Graves, of Missouri.
Bill Shuster, of Pennsylvania.
Shelley Moore Capito, of West Virginia.
Jean Schmidt, of Ohio.
Candice S. Miller, of Michigan.
Duncan Hunter, of California.
Andy Harris, of Maryland.
Eric A. ''Rick'' Crawford, of Arkansas.
Jaime Herrera Beutler, of Washington.
Frank C. Guinta, of New Hampshire.
Randy Hultgren, of Illinois.
Lou Barletta, of Pennsylvania.
Chip Cravaack, of Minnesota.
Blake Farenthold, of Texas.
Larry Bucshon, of Indiana.
Billy Long, of Missouri.
Bob Gibbs, of Ohio.
Patrick Meehan, of Pennsylvania.
Richard L. Hanna, of New York.
Jeffrey M. Landry, of Louisiana.
Steve Southerland II, of Florida.
Jeff Denham, of California.
James Lankford, of Oklahoma.
Reid J. Ribble, of Wisconsin.
Charles J. ''Chuck'' Fleischmann, of Tennessee.

Nick J. Rahall II, of West Virginia.
Peter A. DeFazio, of Oregon.
Jerry F. Costello, of Illinois.
Eleanor Holmes Norton, of District of Columbia.
Jerrold Nadler, of New York.
Corrine Brown, of Florida.
Bob Filner, of California.
Eddie Bernice Johnson, of Texas.
Elijah E. Cummings, of Maryland.
Leonard L. Boswell, of Iowa.
Tim Holden, of Pennsylvania.
Rick Larsen, of Washington.
Michael E. Capuano, of Massachusetts.
Timothy H. Bishop, of New York.
Michael H. Michaud, of Maine.
Russ Carnahan, of Missouri.
Grace F. Napolitano, of California.
Daniel Lipinski, of Illinois.
Mazie K. Hirono, of Hawaii.
Jason Altmire, of Pennsylvania.
Timothy J. Walz, of Minnesota.
Heath Shuler, of North Carolina.
Steve Cohen, of Tennessee.
Laura Richardson, of California.
Albio Sires, of New Jersey.
Donna F. Edwards, of Maryland.

SUBCOMMITTEES

[The chairman and ranking minority member are ex officio (voting) members of all subcommittees on which they do not serve.]

Aviation

Thomas E. Petri, of Wisconsin, *Chair*

Howard Coble, of North Carolina.
John J. Duncan, Jr., of Tennessee.
Frank A. LoBiondo, of New Jersey.
Sam Graves, of Missouri.
Jean Schmidt, of Ohio.
Frank C. Guinta, of New Hampshire.
Randy Hultgren, of Illinois.
Chip Cravaack, of Minnesota.
Blake Farenthold, of Texas.
Billy Long, of Missouri.
Patrick Meehan, of Pennsylvania.
Steve Southerland II, of Florida.
James Lankford, of Oklahoma.
Reid J. Ribble, of Wisconsin.
Charles J. ''Chuck'' Fleischmann, of Tennessee.

Jerry F. Costello, of Illinois.
Russ Carnahan, of Missouri.
Daniel Lipinski, of Illinois.
Peter A. DeFazio, of Oregon.
Bob Filner, of California.
Eddie Bernice Johnson, of Texas.
Leonard L. Boswell, of Iowa.
Tim Holden, of Pennsylvania.
Michael E. Capuano, of Massachusetts.
Mazie K. Hirono, of Hawaii.
Steve Cohen, of Tennessee.
Eleanor Holmes Norton, of District of Columbia.

Coast Guard and Maritime Transportation

Frank A. LoBiondo, of New Jersey, *Chair*

Don Young, of Alaska.
Howard Coble, of North Carolina.
Andy Harris, of Maryland.
Frank C. Guinta, of New Hampshire.
Chip Cravaack, of Minnesota.
Blake Farenthold, of Texas.
Jeffrey M. Landry, of Louisiana.

Rick Larsen, of Washington.
Elijah E. Cummings, of Maryland.
Corrine Brown, of Florida.
Timothy H. Bishop, of New York.
Mazie K. Hirono, of Hawaii.
Michael H. Michaud, of Maine.

Economic Development, Public Buildings, and Emergency Management

Jeff Denham, of California, *Chair*

Timothy V. Johnson, of Illinois.
Eric A. ''Rick'' Crawford, of Arkansas.
Randy Hultgren, of Illinois.
Lou Barletta, of Pennsylvania.
Bob Gibbs, of Ohio.
Patrick Meehan, of Pennsylvania.
Richard L. Hanna, of New York.
Charles J. ''Chuck'' Fleischmann, of Tennessee.

Eleanor Holmes Norton, of District of Columbia.
Heath Shuler, of North Carolina.
Michael H. Michaud, of Maine.
Russ Carnahan, of Missouri.
Timothy J. Walz, of Minnesota.
Donna F. Edwards, of Maryland.
Bob Filner, of California.

Highways and Transit

John J. Duncan, Jr., of Tennessee, *Chair*

Don Young, of Alaska.
Thomas E. Petri, of Wisconsin.
Howard Coble, of North Carolina.
Frank A. LoBiondo, of New Jersey.
Gary G. Miller, of California.
Timothy V. Johnson, of Illinois.
Sam Graves, of Missouri.
Bill Shuster, of Pennsylvania.
Shelley Moore Capito, of West Virginia.
Jean Schmidt, of Ohio.
Candice S. Miller, of Michigan.
Andy Harris, of Maryland.
Eric A. "Rick" Crawford, of Arkansas.
Jaime Herrera Beutler, of Washington.
Frank C. Guinta, of New Hampshire.
Lou Barletta, of Pennsylvania.
Blake Farenthold, of Texas.
Larry Bucshon, of Indiana.
Billy Long, of Missouri.
Bob Gibbs, of Ohio.
Richard L. Hanna, of New York.
Steve Southerland II, of Florida.

Peter A. DeFazio, of Oregon.
Jerrold Nadler, of New York.
Bob Filner, of California.
Leonard L. Boswell, of Iowa.
Tim Holden, of Pennsylvania.
Michael E. Capuano, of Massachusetts.
Michael H. Michaud, of Maine.
Grace F. Napolitano, of California.
Mazie K. Hirono, of Hawaii.
Jason Altmire, of Pennsylvania.
Timothy J. Walz, of Minnesota.
Heath Shuler, of North Carolina.
Steve Cohen, of Tennessee.
Laura Richardson, of California.
Albio Sires, of New Jersey.
Donna F. Edwards, of Maryland.
Eddie Bernice Johnson, of Texas.
Elijah E. Cummings, of Maryland.

Railroads, Pipelines, and Hazardous Materials

Bill Shuster, of Pennsylvania, *Chair*

Gary G. Miller, of California.
Sam Graves, of Missouri.
Shelley Moore Capito, of West Virginia.
Jean Schmidt, of Ohio.
Candice S. Miller, of Michigan.
Jaime Herrera Beutler, of Washington.
Randy Hultgren, of Illinois.
Lou Barletta, of Pennsylvania.
Larry Bucshon, of Indiana.
Billy Long, of Missouri.
Patrick Meehan, of Pennsylvania.
Richard L. Hanna, of New York.
Jeffrey M. Landry, of Louisiana.
Jeff Denham, of California.
Reid J. Ribble, of Wisconsin.
Charles J. "Chuck" Fleischmann, of Tennessee.

Corrine Brown, of Florida.
Jerrold Nadler, of New York.
Rick Larsen, of Washington.
Timothy H. Bishop, of New York.
Michael H. Michaud, of Maine.
Grace F. Napolitano, of California.
Daniel Lipinski, of Illinois.
Jason Altmire, of Pennsylvania.
Timothy J. Walz, of Minnesota.
Laura Richardson, of California.
Albio Sires, of New Jersey.
Peter A. DeFazio, of Oregon.
Jerry F. Costello, of Illinois.

Water Resources and Environment

Bob Gibbs, of Ohio, *Chair*

Don Young, of Alaska.
John J. Duncan, Jr., of Tennessee.
Gary G. Miller, of California.
Timothy V. Johnson, of Illinois.
Bill Shuster, of Pennsylvania.
Shelley Moore Capito, of West Virginia.
Candice S. Miller, of Michigan.
Duncan Hunter, of California.
Andy Harris, of Maryland.
Eric A. ''Rick'' Crawford, of Arkansas.
Jaime Herrera Beutler, of Washington.
Chip Cravaack, of Minnesota.
Larry Bucshon, of Indiana.
Jeffrey M. Landry, of Louisiana.
Jeff Denham, of California.
James Lankford, of Oklahoma.
Reid J. Ribble, of Wisconsin.

Timothy H. Bishop, of New York.
Jerry F. Costello, of Illinois.
Eleanor Holmes Norton, of District of Columbia.
Russ Carnahan, of Missouri.
Donna F. Edwards, of Maryland.
Corrine Brown, of Florida.
Bob Filner, of California.
Eddie Bernice Johnson, of Texas.
Michael E. Capuano, of Massachusetts.
Grace F. Napolitano, of California.
Jason Altmire, of Pennsylvania.
Steve Cohen, of Tennessee.
Laura Richardson, of California.
Mazie K. Hirono, of Hawaii.

STAFF

Committee on Transportation and Infrastructure (2165 RHOB) 225–9446, fax 225–6782.
Majority Full Committee Staff
Chief of Staff.—James W. Coon.
Policy Director.—Amy B. Smith.
General Counsel.—Suzanne Mullen.
Senior Professional Staff.—Sharon Barkeloo.
Director of Facilities and Operations.—Jimmy Miller.
Senior Legislative Assistant.—Jason W. Rosa.
Staff Assistants: Clint Hines, Jason Klink, Tracy Zea.
Minority Full Committee Staff (2163 RHOB) 225–4472, fax 226–1270.
Staff Director.—Jim Zoia.
Chief Counsel.—Ward McCarragher.
Deputy Staff Director.—Ann Adler.
Executive Assistant.—Lisa James.
Staff Assistant.—Kim Le.
Information Systems (2165 RHOB) 225–9446, fax 225–6782.
Information Systems Manager.—Keven Sard.
Assistant Systems Administrator.—Scott Putz.
Majority Communications (2165 RHOB) 225–9446, fax 225–6782.
Communications Director.—Justin Harclerode.
Press Secretary.—Caroline Califf.
Press Aide.—Nicholas Bailey.
Minority Communications (2163 RHOB) 225–4472, fax 226–1270.
Communications Director.—Blake Androff.
Clerk's Office (588 Ford HOB) 225–9960, fax 226–3475.
Clerk.—Tracy G. Mosebey.
Printer.—Jean Paffenback.
Oversight and Investigations (586 Ford HOB) 225–9446, fax 226–6012.
Majority Staff
Oversight and Investigations: Shant Boyijian, Sean McMaster.
Subcommittee on Aviation (2251 RHOB) 226–3220, fax 225–4629.
Majority Staff
Staff Director.—Holly E. Woodruff Lyons.
Professional Staff: Bailey Edwards, Simone Perez.
Staff Assistant.—Andrew Rademaker.
Minority Staff (2251 RHOB) 225–9161, fax 225–4629.
Staff Director.—Giles Giovinazzi.
Counsel.—Alex Burkett.
Professional Staff.—Sarah Blackwood.
Staff Assistant.—Julia Rowe.
Subcommittee on Coast Guard and Maritime Transportation (507 Ford HOB) 226–3552, fax 226–2524.

Majority Staff
Staff Director.—John Rayfield.
Professional Staff.—Geoff Gosselin.
Staff Assistant.—Zach Tronti.
Minority Staff (505 Ford HOB) 226–3587, fax 226–1898.
Staff Director.—Ken Kopocis.
Professional Staff.—Dave Jansen.
Staff Assistant.—Dominick Carroll.

Subcommittee on Economic Development, Public Buildings, and Emergency Management (585 Ford HOB) 225–3014, fax 226–0922.
Majority Staff
Staff Director.—Dan Mathews.
Counsel.—Johanna Hardy.
Staff Assistant.—Ben Dudek.
Minority Staff (592 Ford HOB) 225–9961, fax 226–1898.
Counsels: Elliot Doomes, Janet Erickson.
Staff Assistant.—Dominick Carroll.

Subcommittee on Highways and Transit (B–376 RHOB) 225–6715, fax 226–4377.
Majority Staff
Staff Director.—Jim Tymon.
Counsel.—Jennifer Hall.
Professional Staff.—Dan Veoni.
Staff Assistant.—Geoff Strobeck.
Minority Staff (B–375 RHOB) 225–9989, fax 226–5435.
Staff Director.—Jim Kolb.
Senior Professional Staff.—Helena Zyblikewycz.
Staff Assistant.—Katherine Waring.

Subcommittee on Railroads, Pipelines, and Hazardous Materials (B–376 RHOB) 226–0727, fax 226–4377.
Majority Staff
Staff Director.—Joyce Rose.
Professional Staff.—Steve Martinko.
Counsel.—Fred Miller.
Staff Assistant.—Erin Sulla.
Minority Staff (592 Ford HOB) 225–3274, fax 226–1898.
Staff Director.—Jennifer Esposito.
Counsel.—Rachel Carr.
Professional Staff.—Nick Martinelli.
Staff Assistant.—Dominick Carroll.

Subcommittee on Water Resources and Environment (B–370A RHOB) 225–4360.
Majority Staff
Staff Director.—John Anderson.
Professional Staff.—Geoff Bowman.
Counsel.—Jonathan Pawlow.
Legislative Staff Assistant.—Caryn Moore.
Minority Staff (B–375 RHOB) 225–0060, fax 226–5435.
Counsel.—Ryan Seiger.
Professional Staff: Jean Flemma, David Wegner.
Staff Assistant.—Katherine Waring.

Veterans' Affairs

335 Cannon House Office Building, phone 225–3527, fax 225–5486

http://www.veterans.house.gov

Jeff Miller, of Florida, *Chair*

Cliff Stearns, of Florida.
Doug Lamborn, of Colorado.
Gus M. Bilirakis, of Florida.
David P. Roe, of Tennessee.
Marlin A. Stutzman, of Indiana.
Bill Flores, of Texas.
Bill Johnson, of Ohio.
Jeff Denham, of California.
Jon Runyan, of New Jersey.
Dan Benishek, of Michigan.
Ann Marie Buerkle, of New York.
Tim Huelskamp, of Kansas.
Mark E. Amodei, of Nevada.
Robert L. Turner, of New York.

Bob Filner, of California.
Corrine Brown, of Florida.
Silvestre Reyes, of Texas.
Michael H. Michaud, of Maine.
Linda T. Sánchez, of California.
Bruce L. Braley, of Iowa.
Jerry McNerney, of California.
Joe Donnelly, of Indiana.
Timothy J. Walz, of Minnesota.
John Barrow, of Georgia.
Russ Carnahan, of Missouri.

SUBCOMMITTEES

Disability Assistance and Memorial Affairs

Jon Runyan, of New Jersey, *Chair*

Doug Lamborn, of Colorado.
Ann Marie Buerkle, of New York.
Marlin A. Stutzman, of Indiana.

Jerry McNerney, of California.
John Barrow, of Georgia.
Michael H. Michaud, of Maine.
Timothy J. Walz, of Minnesota.

Economic Opportunity

Marlin A. Stutzman, of Indiana, *Chair*

Gus M. Bilirakis, of Florida.
Bill Johnson, of Ohio.
Tim Huelskamp, of Kansas.
Jeff Denham, of California.

Bruce L. Braley, of Iowa.
Linda T. Sánchez, of California.
Timothy J. Walz, of Minnesota.

Health

Ann Marie Buerkle, of New York, *Chair*

Cliff Stearns, of Florida.
Gus M. Bilirakis, of Florida.
David P. Roe, of Tennessee.
Dan Benishek, of Michigan.
Jeff Denham, of California.
Jon Runyan, of New Jersey.

Michael H. Michaud, of Maine.
Corrine Brown, of Florida.
Silvestre Reyes, of Texas.
Russ Carnahan, of Missouri.
Joe Donnelly, of Indiana.

Oversight and Investigations

Bill Johnson, of Ohio, *Chair*

Cliff Stearns, of Florida.
Doug Lamborn, of Colorado.
David P. Roe, of Tennessee.
Dan Benishek, of Michigan.
Bill Flores, of Texas.

Joe Donnelly, of Indiana.
Jerry McNerney, of California.
John Barrow, of Georgia.
Bob Filner, of California.

STAFF

Committee on Veterans' Affairs (335 CHOB), 225–3527, fax 225–5486.
Majority Staff Director and Chief Counsel.—Helen Tolar.
Deputy Staff Director.—Jon Towers.
Legislative Coordinator.—Michael Siegel.
Communications Director.—Amy Mitchell.
Financial Administrator and Chief Clerk.—Bernadine Dotson.
Staff Assistant.—Micah Ketchel.
Professional Staff Member.—Casey Street.
Printing Clerk.—Diane Kirkland.
Minority Staff Director.—Malcom Shorter (333 CHOB), 225–9756, fax 225–2034.
Chief of Staff.—Tony Buckles.
Deputy Staff Director and Chief Counsel.—David Tucker.
Legislative Coordinator.—Debbie Smith.
Office Manager.—Carol Murray.
Subcommittee on Disability Assistance and Memorial Affairs (337 CHOB), 225–9164, fax 226–4691.
Majority Staff Director.—Bill Collins (acting).
Professional Staff Member.—Jon Clark.
Minority Staff Director and Counsel.—Kimberly Ross.
Senior Legislative Assistant.—Jian Zapata.
Subcommittee on Economic Opportunity (335 CHOB), 226–5491, fax 225–5486.
Majority Staff Director.—Mike Brinck.
Professional Staff Member.—Jon Clark.
Minority Staff Director.—Juan Lara.
Senior Legislative Assistant.—Orfa Torres.
Subcommittee on Health (338 CHOB), 225–9154, fax 226–4536.
Majority Staff Director.—Dolores Dunn.
Research Assistant.—Samantha Gonzalez.
Minority Staff Director.—Cathy Wiblemo.
Senior Legislative Assistant.—Jian Zapata.
Subcommittee on Oversight and Investigations (337A CHOB), 225–3569, fax 225–6392.
Majority Staff Director.—Eric Hannel.
Professional Staff Member.—Elby Godwin.
Minority Staff Director.—Marty Herbert.
Senior Legislative Assistant.—Orfa Torres.

Ways and Means

1102 Longworth House Office Building, phone 225–3625

http://waysandmeans.house.gov

Dave Camp, of Michigan, *Chair*

Wally Herger, of California.
Sam Johnson, of Texas.
Kevin Brady, of Texas.
Paul Ryan, of Wisconsin.
Devin Nunes, of California.
Patrick J. Tiberi, of Ohio.
Geoff Davis, of Kentucky.
David G. Reichert, of Washington.
Charles W. Boustany, Jr., of Louisiana.
Peter J. Roskam, of Illinois.
Jim Gerlach, of Pennsylvania.
Tom Price, of Georgia.
Vern Buchanan, of Florida.
Adrian Smith, of Nebraska.
Aaron Schock, of Illinois.
Lynn Jenkins, of Kansas.
Erik Paulsen, of Minnesota.
Kenny Marchant, of Texas.
Rick Berg, of North Dakota.
Diane Black, of Tennessee.
Tom Reed, of New York.

Sander M. Levin, of Michigan.
Charles B. Rangel, of New York.
Fortney Pete Stark, of California.
Jim McDermott, of Washington.
John Lewis, of Georgia.
Richard E. Neal, of Massachusetts.
Xavier Becerra, of California.
Lloyd Doggett, of Texas.
Mike Thompson, of California.
John B. Larson, of Connecticut.
Earl Blumenauer, of Oregon.
Ron Kind, of Wisconsin.
Bill Pascrell, Jr., of New Jersey.
Shelley Berkley, of Nevada.
Joseph Crowley, of New York.

SUBCOMMITTEES

[The chairman and ranking minority member are ex officio (non-voting) members of all subcommittees.]

Health

Wally Herger, of California, *Chair*

Sam Johnson, of Texas.
Paul Ryan, of Wisconsin.
Devin Nunes, of California.
David G. Reichert, of Washington.
Peter J. Roskam, of Illinois.
Jim Gerlach, of Pennsylvania.
Tom Price, of Georgia.
Vern Buchanan, of Florida.

Fortney Pete Stark, of California.
Mike Thompson, of California.
Ron Kind, of Wisconsin.
Earl Blumenauer, of Oregon.
Bill Pascrell, Jr., of New Jersey.

Human Resources

Geoff Davis, of Kentucky, *Chair*

Erik Paulsen, of Minnesota.
Rick Berg, of North Dakota.
Tom Reed, of New York.
Tom Price, of Georgia.
Diane Black, of Tennessee.
Charles W. Boustany, Jr., of Louisiana.

Lloyd Doggett, of Texas.
Jim McDermott, of Washington.
John Lewis, of Georgia.
Joseph Crowley, of New York.

Oversight

Charles W. Boustany, Jr., of Louisiana, *Chair*

Diane Black, of Tennessee.
Aaron Schock, of Illinois.
Lynn Jenkins, of Kansas.
Kenny Marchant, of Texas.
Tom Reed, of New York.
Erik Paulsen, of Minnesota.
John Lewis, of Georgia.
Xavier Becerra, of California.
Ron Kind, of Wisconsin.
Jim McDermott, of Washington.

Select Revenue Measures

Patrick J. Tiberi, of Ohio, *Chair*

Peter J. Roskam, of Illinois.
Erik Paulsen, of Minnesota.
Rick Berg, of North Dakota.
Charles W. Boustany, Jr., of Louisiana.
Kenny Marchant, of Texas.
Jim Gerlach, of Pennsylvania.
Richard E. Neal, of Massachusetts.
Mike Thompson, of California.
John B. Larson, of Connecticut.
Shelley Berkley, of Nevada.

Social Security

Sam Johnson, of Texas, *Chair*

Kevin Brady, of Texas.
Patrick J. Tiberi, of Ohio.
Aaron Schock, of Illinois.
Rick Berg, of North Dakota.
Adrian Smith, of Nebraska.
Kenny Marchant, of Texas.
Xavier Becerra, of California.
Lloyd Doggett, of Texas.
Shelley Berkley, of Nevada.
Fortney Pete Stark, of California.

Trade

Kevin Brady, of Texas, *Chair*

Geoff Davis, of Kentucky.
David G. Reichert, of Washington.
Wally Herger, of California.
Devin Nunes, of California.
Vern Buchanan, of Florida.
Adrian Smith, of Nebraska.
Aaron Schock, of Illinois.
Lynn Jenkins, of Kansas.
Jim McDermott, of Washington.
Richard E. Neal, of Massachusetts.
Lloyd Doggett, of Texas.
Joseph Crowley, of New York.
John B. Larson, of Connecticut.

STAFF

Committee on Ways and Means (1102 LHOB), 225–3625, fax 225–2610.
Majority Chief of Staff.—Jon Traub.
Deputy Staff Director.—Sage Eastman.
Chief Economist.—Warren Payne.
Economic and Media Analyst.—Mike Stober.
Senior Advisor, Public Affairs and Communications.—Michelle Dimarob.
Communications Director.—Jim Billimoria.
Press Secretary.—Sarah Swinehart.
Calendar Clerk.—Carren Turko.
Document Clerk.—Reggie Greene.
Director of Information Technology.—Ted Clark.
Systems Administrator/Web Administrator.—Wuan Perkins.
Assistant Clerks: Michael Baker, Joseph Valent.
Committee Administrator.—Chris Stottmann.
Staff Assistants: Sarah Feagan, Matthew Hittle.
Staff Director, Select Revenue Measures.—George Callas.
Chief Tax Counsel.—Dave Olander.
Tax Counsel: Aharon Friedman, Harold Hancock.
Tax Counsel and Special Advisor on Tax Reform.—Ray Beeman.
Tax Advisor.—Sean Hailey.

Legislative Assistant, Select Revenue Measures.—Zach Rudisill.
General Counsel/Oversight Staff Director.—Jennifer Safavian.
Oversight Counsel: Jennifer Acuna, Chris Armstrong.
Legislative Assistant, Oversight.—Lauren Savory.
Chief Trade Counsel.—Angela Ellard.
Trade Counsel: Geoffrey Antell, Stephen Claeys, Welby Leaman, Neena Shenai.
Legislative Assistant, Trade.—Kristin Isabelli.
Health Staff Director.—Dan Elling.
Senior Professional Staff, Health.—Jill Schmalz.
Professional Staff Health: Brett Baker, Laura Bozell, Brian Sutter.
Legislative Assistant, Health.—Nick Uehlecke.
Staff Director, Social Security.—Kim Hildred.
Professional Staff, Social Security: Margret Hostetler, Amy Shuart.
Staff Assistant, Social Security.—Jessica Cameron.
Staff Director, Human Resources.—Matt Weidinger.
Professional Staff, Human Resources.—Anne DeCesaro, Ryan Martin.
Legislative Assistant, Human Resources.—Tim Ford.

Minority Chief Counsel and Chief Tax Counsel.—Janice Mays.
Staff and Communications Director.—Askia Suruma.
Office Manager.—Jennifer Gould.
Assistant to Janice Mays.—Carrie Breidenbach.
Staff/Research Assistants: Moyer McCoy, John Young.
IT Director.—Antoine Walker.
Press Secretary.—Lauren Bloomberg.
Oversight Staff Director.—Karen McAfee.
Select Revenue Measures Staff Director.—Aruna Kalyanam.
Tax Counsel: Drew Crouch, Michael Hauswirth.
Staff Director, Health.—Cybele Bjorklund.
Professional Staff, Health (Rep. Stark).—Debbie Curtis.
Deputy Staff Director, Health.—Jennifer Friedman.
Staff Director, Human Resources.—Nick Gwyn.
Deputy Staff Director, Human Resources.—Sonja Nesbit.
Staff Director, Social Security.—Kathryn Olson.
Professional Staff, Social Security.—Morna Miller.
Staff Director, Trade.—Viji Rangaswami.
Trade Counsel: Jason Kearns, Behnaz Kibria, Alex Perkins.
ITC Detailee (SML).—Russell Duncan.

SELECT AND SPECIAL COMMITTEES OF THE HOUSE

Permanent Select Committee on Intelligence

HVC–304 The Capitol, phone 225–4121

[Created pursuant to H. Res. 658, 95th Congress]

Mike Rogers, of Michigan, *Chair*

Mac Thornberry, of Texas.
Sue Wilkins Myrick, of North Carolina.
Jeff Miller, of Florida.
K. Michael Conaway, of Texas.
Peter T. King, of New York.
Frank A. LoBiondo, of New Jersey.
Devin Nunes, of California.
Lynn A. Westmoreland, of Georgia.
Michele Bachmann, of Minnesota.
Thomas J. Rooney, of Florida.
Joseph J. Heck, of Nevada.

C.A. Dutch Ruppersberger, of Maryland.
Mike Thompson, of California.
Janice D. Schakowsky, of Illinois.
James R. Langevin, of Rhode Island.
Adam B. Schiff, of California.
Dan Boren, of Oklahoma.
Luis V. Gutierrez, of Illinois.
Ben Chandler, of Kentucky.

SUBCOMMITTEES

[The Speaker and Minority Leader are ex officio (non-voting) members of the committee.]

Terrorism, Human Intelligence, Analysis, and Counterintelligence

Sue Wilkins Myrick, of North Carolina, *Chair*

K. Michael Conaway, of Texas.
Peter T. King, of New York.
Frank A. LoBiondo, of New Jersey.
Thomas J. Rooney, of Florida.

Mike Thompson, of California.
Dan Boren, of Oklahoma.
Luis V. Gutierrez, of Illinois.

Technical and Tactical Intelligence

Joseph J. Heck, of Nevada, Chair

Mac Thornberry, of Texas.
Frank A. LoBiondo, of New Jersey.
Devin Nunes, of California.
Michele Bachmann, of Minnesota.

Adam B. Schiff, of California.
James R. Langevin, of Rhode Island.
Ben Chandler, of Kentucky.

Oversight and Investigations

Lynn A. Westmoreland, of Georgia, Chair

Jeff Miller, of Florida.
Devin Nunes, of California.
Michele Bachmann, of Minnesota.
Thomas J. Rooney, of Florida.

Janice D. Schakowsky, of Illinois.
Mike Thompson, of California.
Dan Boren, of Oklahoma.

STAFF

Majority Staff Director.—Michael Allen.
Deputy Staff Director.—Darren Dick.
Senior Policy Advisor.—Tom Corcoran.
Chief Counsel.—Chris Donesa.
Senior Counsel: Sarah Geffroy, Jamil Jaffer, Katie Wheelbarger.
Budget Director.—Bryan Smith.
Budget Auditor.—Brooke Eisele.
Chief Clerk.—Ashley Lowry.
Executive Assistant.—Leah Scott.
Security Director.—Kristin Jepson.
Deputy Security Director.—Kevin Klein.
System Administrator.—Brandon Smith.
Professional Staff: Chelsey Campbell, Frank Garcia, Sarah Geffroy, Nate Hauser, Will Koella, George Pappas, Katie Wheelbarger.
Minority Staff Director.—TBD.
Deputy Staff Director.—Heather Molino.
Chief Counsel.—Judith Boyd.
Deputy Chief Counsel.—Abbas Ravjani.
Policy Advisor.—Robert Minehart.
Research Assistant.—Khizer Syed.
Professional Staff: Linda Cohen, Amanda Rogers Thorpe, Carly Scott.

House Republican Policy Committee

403 Cannon House Office Building, phone 225–4501

http://policy.house.gov

meets at the call of the Chair or the Speaker

Tom Price, M.D. of Georgia, *Chair*

Republican Leadership:
Speaker of the House.—John A. Boehner, of Ohio.
Majoirty Leader.—Eric Cantor, of Virginia.
Conference Chair.—Jeb Hensarling, of Texas.
Conference Vice Chair.—Cathy McMorris Rogers, of Washington.
Conference Secretary.—John R. Carter, of Texas.
NRCC Chair.—Pete Sessions, of Texas.

Policy Committee Staff.—403 Cannon HOB, 225–4501.
Chief of Staff.—Kris Skrzycki.

House Republican Conference

202A Cannon House Office Building, phone 225–5107, fax 226–0154

Jeb Hensarling, of Texas, *Chair*

Cathy McMorris Rodgers, of Washington, *Vice Chair*

John R. Carter, of Texas, *Secretary*

STAFF

Chief of Staff.—Dee Buchanan.
Director of Operations.—Chelsea Brown.
Staff Assistants: Dylan Colligan, Phillip Pinegar, John Puskar.
Director of Member Services and Events.—Katie Patru.
Deputy Director of Member Services and Events.—Chelsea Brown.
Policy Director and Legislative Counsel.—Daris Meeks.
Deputy Policy Director.—Andy Koenig.

Senior Health Counsel.—David Rosenfeld.
Policy Advisor and Coalitions Liaison.—Sarah Makin.
Policy Advisor.—Jonathan Hiler.
Communications Director.—Shannon McGahn.
Deputy Communications Director.—David Popp.
Deputy Press Secretary.—Rebeccah Propp.
Speechwriter.—Tom Qualtere.
Press Assistant.—Clay Sutton.
Visual Media: David Holley, Ryan Howell, Mike Lurie, Josh Sharp.

Democratic Congressional Campaign Committee

430 South Capitol Street, SE., 20003, phone (202) 863–1500

Executive Committee:
Nancy Pelosi, of California, *Democratic Leader.*
Steve Israel, of New York, *Chair.*
Chairs:
Pedro R. Pierluisi, *Community Mobilization.*
Keith Ellison, *National Community Outreach.*
Allyson Y. Schwartz, *National Recruitment and Candidate Services.*
Joseph Crowley, *Finance.*

STAFF

Executive Director.—Robby Mook, 485–3509.
Deputy Executive Director.—Jennifer Crider, 485–3442.
Chief Operating Officer.—Kristie Mark, 485–3435.
Political Director.—Kelly Ward, 478–9485.
Campaign Director.—Travis Lowe, 485–3513.
Chief Financial Officer.—Jackie Forte-Mackay, 485–3401.
Director of:
Candidate Services.—Amy Strathdee, 485–3420.
Member Services.—Vacant.
Research.—Kevin McKeon, 485–3421.
Managing Director of Finance and New Media Programs.—Taryn Rosenkranz, 485–3527.
National Finance Directors.—Missy Kurek 485–3455; Lindsey Melander, 485–3445.
Press Secretary.—Jesse Ferguson, 485–3456.
National Field Director.—Brynne Craig, 741–1858.
Policy Director.—Mike Ryan, 485–3531.

Democratic Steering and Policy Committee

H–204 The Capitol, phone 225–0100

Chair.—Nancy Pelosi, Democratic Leader from California.
Co-Chairs:
Steering.—Rosa L. DeLauro, Representative from Connecticut.
Policy.—George Miller, Representative from California.

STAFF

Democratic Steering Committee 225–0100, fax 225–4188.
Steering Advisors: George Kundanis, Jonathan Stivers.

Democratic Policy Committee (H–130), 225–0100, fax 226–0938.
Policy Advisors: George Kundanis, John Lawrence, Richard Meltzer.

Democratic Caucus

1420 Longworth House Office Building, phone 225–1400, fax 226–4412

www.dems.gov

John B. Larson, of Connecticut, *Chair*

Xavier Becerra, of California, *Vice Chair*

STAFF

Chief of Staff.—Shelley Rubino.
Executive Director.—George Felix Shevlin IV.
Communications Director.—Ellis Andrew Brachman.
Executive Advisor.—Stephen Dagadakis.
Director of Special Projects.—Kimberly Hazel Jaworski.
Policy and Outreach Director.—Katherine Grady.
Assistant to the Chairman.—Srdan Banjac.
Correspondence Assistant.—Geraldine De Puy.
Research and Technology Assistant.—Andrew Joseph Platt.
Director of Multimedia.—Antonio Peronace.
Press Assistant.—Kyle Andrew McMahon.
Staff Director to the Vice Chair.—Sean Edward McCluskie.
Director of Member Outreach to the Vice Chair.—Melody Star Gonzales.
Press Secretary to the Vice Chair.—James Monroe Gleeson.
Member Outreach Assistants to the Vice Chair: Eric Louis Delaney, Jasmine Mora, Lorenzo Antonio Rodriguez-Olvera.

OFFICERS AND OFFICIALS OF THE HOUSE

OFFICE OF THE SPEAKER

H–232 The Capitol, phone 225–0600, fax 225–5117

Speaker of the House of Representatives.—John A. Boehner.
Chief of Staff.—Barry Jackson.
Deputy Chief of Staff for Leadership Operations.—Mike Sommers.
Deputy Chief of Staff for Communications Operations.—Dave Schnittger.
Director of Administrative Operations.—Amy Lozupone.
Director of Scheduling and Special Events.—Kristen Chaplin.
Deputy Scheduler/Executive Assistant.—Kristene Blake.
Special Events Coordinator.—Kerry Stockwell.
Director of House Operations.—Ed Cassidy.
House Operations Assistant.—Patrick Finnegan.
Press Secretaries: Brendan Buck, Michael Steel.
Deputy Press Secretary.—Rebeccah Propp.
Assistant Press Secretary.—Heather Reed.
Director of Advance.—Betsy Andres.
Communications Director.—Kevin Smith.
Deputy Communications Director.—Don Seymour.
Assistant Communications Director.—Katie Boyd.
Advance and Digital Production.—Bryant Avondoglio.
Director of Speechwriting.—Michael Ricci.
Member Services: Johnny DeStefano, Trevor Kolego.
Member Services Manager.—Grant Saunders.
Outreach Director.—Bill Greene.
Director, Information Technology.—Billy Benjamin.
Systems Administrator.—Mike Sager.
General Counsel/Chief of Legislative Operations.—Jo-Marie St. Martin.
Assistant to the General Counsel.—Kate Lukeman.
Director of Floor Operations.—Anne Thorsen.
Deputy Director of Floor Operations.—Jeff Strunk.
Policy Director.—Brett Loper.
Counsel/Policy Advisors: Will Kinzel, George Rogers.
Policy Advisors: Mike Catanzaro, Katherine Haley, Cindy Herrle, Emily Porter, David Stewart, Jen Stewart.
Research Assistant.—Justin Lampert.
Financial Administrator.—Karen Paulson.
Cloakroom Manager.—Tim Harroun.
Floor Assistants: Jared Eichhorn, Thane Hutcheson, Jay Pierson, Adam Wolf.
Staff Assistants: Tom Andrews, Alex Becker, Erin Boyle, Maura Gillespie, Tim Lolli, Annie Minkler.

OFFICE OF THE MAJORITY LEADER

H–329 The Capitol, phone 225–4000, fax 226–1115

Majority Leader.—Eric Cantor.
Chief of Staff.—Steve Stombres.
Deputy Chiefs of Staff: Neil Bradley, John Murray, Kyle Nevins.
Senior Advisor.—Bill Dolbow.
Senior Policy Advisors: Mike Ference, Nicole Gustafson, Cheryl Jaeger, Rodger Mahan, Shimmy Stein.
Floor Assistants: Matt Bravo, Chris Vieson.

Director of New Media.—Matt Lira.
Deputy Director of New Media.—Steve Johnston.
Communications Director.—Brad Dayspring.
Press Secretary.—Laena Fallon.
Deputy Press Secretary.—Megan Whittemore.
Assistant Press Secretary.—Jessica Straus.
Speechwriter.—Sergio Rodriguera.
Director of Member Services.—Valerie Nelson.
Scheduler.—Amy Barrera.
Assistant Scheduler.—Christine Schaffer.
Special Assistant to the Majority Leader.—Matt Zackon.
Operations Coordinator.—Austin Tuell.
Staff Assistant.—Emily Keech.
Strategic Communications.—Brian Patrick.

OFFICE OF THE MAJORITY WHIP

H–107 The Capitol, phone 225–0197, fax 225–0781

Majority Whip.—Kevin McCarthy.
Chief of Staff.—Tim Berry.
Deputy Chief of Staff.—James Min.
Floor Director.—John Stipicevic.
Coalitions Director.—Brian Worth.
Policy Director and Counsel.—Steve Pinkos.
Communications Director.—Sarah Pompei.
Member Services and Coalitions Deputy Director.—Natalie Buchanan.
Deputy Floor Director.—Kelly Dixon.
Policy Advisors: Wes McClelland, Emily Murry.
Floor Assistants: Freddy Barnes, Ben Howard.
Press Secretary.—Erica Elliott.
New Media Director.—Lauren Pratapas.
Press Aide.—Mike Long.
Scheduler.—Kristin Thomson.
Senior Staff Assistant.—Ashley Mettler.
Staff Assistants: Brittany Carey, Tim Pataki.

OFFICE OF THE CHIEF DEPUTY REPUBLICAN WHIP

H–305 The Capitol, phone 225–0197

Chief of Staff to Chief Deputy Whip.—Steven Moore.
Special Assistant to Chief Deputy Whip.—Dean Thompson.
Chief of Staff.—Tim Berry.
Deputy Chief of Staff.—James Min.
Policy Advisers: Wes McClellan, Emily Murry.
Policy Director and Counsel.—Steve Pinkos.
Press Secretary.—Erica Elliott.
Press Aide.—Mike Long.
Director of New Media.—Lauren Pratapas.
Director of Strategic Communications.—Kris Anderson.
Communications Director.—Sarah Pompei.
Deputy Director of Floor Operations.—Kelly Dixon.
Director of Floor Operations.—John Stipicevic.
Floor Assistants: Freddy Barnes, Ben Howard.
Scheduler.—Kristin Thomson.
Director of Coalitions.—Brian Worth.
Deputy Director of Member Services and Coalitions.—Natalie Buchanan.
Senior Staff Assistant.—Ashley Mettler.
Staff Assistants: Brittany Carey, Tim Pataki.

OFFICE OF THE DEMOCRATIC LEADER

H–204 The Capitol, phone 225–0100, fax 225–4188

www.democraticleader.gov

Office of the Democratic Leader.—Hon. Nancy Pelosi.
Chief of Staff.—John Lawrence, H–204, The Capitol, 225–0100.
Assistant to the Chief of Staff.—Declan Cashman, H–204, The Capitol, 225–0100.
Chief of Staff (CA08 Office).—Catlin W. O'Neill, 235 CHOB, 225–4965.
Deputy Chief of Staff.—George Kundanis, H–204, The Capitol, 225–0100.
Senior Advisors: Diane Dewhirst, Jonathan Stivers, H–204, The Capitol, 225–0100.
Counsel to the Democratic Leader.—Bernie Raimo, H–204, The Capitol, 225–0100.
Special Assistants to the Democratic Leader: Kate Knudson, Bina Surgeon, H–204, The Capitol, 225–0100.
Staff Assistant.—Lydia Wileden, H–204, The Capitol, 225–0100.
Co-Directors of Correspondence: Robyn Lea, David Silverman, 421 Cannon, 225–0100.
Director of Scheduling.—Melinda Medlin, H–204, The Capitol, 225–0100.
Deputy Director of Scheduling.—Tim Merritt, H–204, The Capitol, 225–0100.
Policy Director.—Dick Meltzer, H–204, The Capitol, 225–0100.
Policy Advisor.—Stacey Rolland, H–204, The Capitol, 225–0100.
Senior Policy Advisors: Kenneth DeGraff, Wyndee Parker, Wendell Primus, H–204, The Capitol, 225–0100.
Senior Advance Policy and Communications: Margaret Capron, Kit Judge, H–204, The Capitol.
Counsel.—Michael Tecklenburg, H–204, The Capitol, 225–0100.
Deputy Policy Director.—Michael Bloom, H–204, The Capitol, 225–0100.
Senior Advance and Director of Member Service.—Jaime Lizarraga, H–204, The Capitol, 225–0100.
Deputy Director of Member Services.—Michael Long, H–204, The Capitol.
Director of Protocol and Special Events.—Bridget Fallon Charville, H–204, The Capitol, 225–0100.
Director of Speechwriting.—Alexandra Veitch, H–204, The Capitol, 225–0100.
Deputy Speechwriter.—Jonathan Powell, H–204, The Capitol, 225–0100.
IT Director.—Wil Haynes, HB–13, The Capitol, 225–0100.
Deputy IT Director.—Kamilah Keita, HB–13, The Capitol, 225–0100.
Director of Advance.—Kelly Berens, H–204, The Capitol, 225–0100.
Deputy Director of Advance.—Mary-Kate Barry, H–204, The Capitol, 225–0100.
Advisor to the Leader.—Reva Price, H–204, The Capitol, 225–0100.
Outreach Assistant.—Stephanie Ueng, H–204, The Capitol, 225–0100.

DEMOCRATIC LEADER'S PRESS OFFICE

H–204 The Capitol, phone 225–0100

Communications Director and Senior Advisor.—Nadeam Elshami.
Press Secretary and Deputy Communications Director.—Drew Hammill.
Press Advisors: Stephanie Cherry, Evangeline George.
Deputy Press Secretary and Advisor to the Leader.—Carlos Sanchez.
Researcher Director.—April Greener.
Director of New Media.—Karina Newton.

DEMOCRATIC LEADER'S FLOOR OFFICE

H–204 The Capitol, phone 225–0100

Director of Floor Operations.—Jerry Hartz.
Deputy Director of Floor Operations.—Lori Pepper.

OFFICE OF THE DEMOCRATIC WHIP

H–148 The Capitol, phone 225–3130, fax 226–0663

Democratic Whip.—Steny H. Hoyer.
Chief of Staff.—Terry Lierman.

Deputy Chief of Staff.—Stacey Bernards.
Office Manager/Executive Assistant.—Daniel Shott.
Floor Director.—Alexis Covey-Brandt.
Deputy Floor Director.—Austin Burnes.
Floor Assistant.—Shuwanza Goff.
Whip Coordinator.—Michael Eisenberg.
Director of Member Services.—Chris DeBosier.
Member Services and Outreach Coordinators: Courtney Fry, Lizet Ocampo.
Communications Director.—Katie Grant.
Press Secretary.—Dan Reilly.
Deputy Press Secretary.—Maureen Beach.
Press and Research Assistant.—Mariel Saez.
Speechwriter.—Rob Goodman.
Senior Policy Advisors: Keith Abouchar, John Hughes, James Leuschen, Elizabeth Murray, Mary Frances Repko, Mariah Sixkiller.
Director of Scheduling.—Simone LiTrenta.
Special Assistant.—Apratim Ghosh.
Director of Technology.—Steve Dwyer.
Whip Director and Senior Advisor.—Brian Romick.
Staff Assistants: Danielle Aviles, Elliot Gensemer.

OFFICE OF THE ASSISTANT DEMOCRATIC LEADER

132 The Capitol, phone 226–3210

http://assistantdemocraticleader.house.gov

Assistant Democratic Leader.—James E. Clyburn.
Chief of Staff.—Yelberton R. Watkins.
Director of Policy.—Barvetta Singletary.
Communications Director.—Patrick Devlin.
Legislative Assistant.—Matthew Ellison.
Special Assistant to the Assistant Democratic Leader.—Tamika Day.

OFFICE OF THE CLERK

H–154 The Capitol, phone 225–7000

KAREN L. HAAS, Clerk of the House of Representatives; Karen Lehman Haas, a native of Catonsville, MD, was sworn in as Clerk of the House of Representatives on January 5, 2011. She is the 34th individual to serve as Clerk. This is Ms. Haas' second occupancy of this position—in 2005, Speaker J. Dennis Hastert appointed Ms. Haas as Clerk of the U.S. House of Representatives. As Clerk, Ms. Haas plays a central role in the daily operations and legislative activities of the House. Ms. Haas began her service on Capitol Hill in 1984, when she worked for then-Minority Leader Robert H. Michel. For nearly 11 years, she served as his Executive Legislative Assistant. Following a brief leave to work in the private sector, Ms. Haas returned to Capitol Hill in June 1999 to serve as Floor Assistant to Speaker Hastert. Following her first term as Clerk, she served as Staff Director of the House Republican Conference and Minority Staff Director for the House Small Business Committee. Ms. Haas attended public schools in Maryland and received a bachelor's degree from the University of Maryland, College Park, with a major in political science and a minor in economics.

Clerk.—Karen L. Haas.
Deputy Clerk.—Robert F. Reeves.
Senior Advisor.—Marjorie ''Gigi'' Kelaher.
Chief of—
Legislative Computer Systems.—Goldey Vansant, 2401 RHOB, 225–1182.
Legislative Operations.—Frances Chiappardi, HT–13, 225–7925.
Legislative Resource Center.—Ronald Dale Thomas, B–106 CHOB, 226–5200.
Office of:
Art and Archives.—Farar Elliott, B–53 CHOB, 226–1300.
Communications.—Phillip McGowan, B–28 CHOB, 225–1908.
House Employment Counsel.—Gloria Lett, 1036 LHOB, 225–7075.
Official Reporter.—Joe Strickland, 1718 LHOB, 225–2627.
Service Groups—

Congresswomen's Suite.—225–4196.
Members and Family Committee.—225–0622.
Prayer Room.—225–8070.

CHIEF ADMINISTRATIVE OFFICER

HB–28 The Capitol, phone 225–5555

DANIEL J. STRODEL, Chief Administrative Officer of the House of Representatives; native of Syracuse, NY; B.A., (1984) Hobart College; J.D., (1994), Catholic University of America.

Chief Administrative Officer.—Daniel J. Strodel.
Deputy Chief Administrative Officer.—Stacy Carlson, HB–28 The Capitol.
Administrative Counsel.—Carol Black, H2–217, FHOB.
Chief Financial Officer.—Traci Beaubian, H2–330, FHOB.
Human Resources Director.—Jason Hite, H2–105B, FHOB.
Chief Information Officer.—Louis Magnotti, H2–631, FHOB.
Director of Communications.—Dan Weiser, H2–217, FHOB.
Executive Assistant.—Meagan Pa, HB–28, The Capitol.

CHAPLAIN

HB–25 The Capitol, phone 225–2509, fax 226–4928

PATRICK J. CONROY, S.J., Chaplain, House of Representatives, residence, Portland, OR; a Jesuit of the Oregon Province of the Society of Jesus, graduated from Claremont McKenna College in CA in 1972, attended Gonzaga University Law School for one year before entering the Jesuit Order in 1973. Earned an M.A. in philosophy from Gonzaga University, a J.D. from St. Louis University, an M.Div. from the Jesuit School of Theology at Berkeley (CA), and an STM from Regis College of the University of Toronto in missiology. Practiced law for the Colville Confederated Tribes in Omak, WA and the U.S. Conference of Catholic Bishops representing Salvadoran refugees in San Francisco. Ordained a priest in 1983. From 1984 to 1989, pastored four villages on the Colville and Spokane Indian Reservations. Worked for the national Jesuit Office of Social Ministries in Washington, D.C., then began a career of university chaplaincy at Georgetown University and Seattle University. In 2003 transferred to Jesuit High School in Portland, OR, to teach freshman theology and coach the mighty JV II girls; softball team. Also served as the Oregon Province's Provincial Assistant for Formation and as superior of the Jesuit community at Jesuit High School in Portland. Sworn in as 60th House Chaplain on May 25, 2001.

Chaplain of the House.—Patrick J. Conroy.
Assistant to the Chaplain.—Elisa Aglieco.
Liaison to Staff.—Karen Bronson.

OFFICE OF THE HOUSE HISTORIAN

B–56 Cannon House Office Building, phone 226–5525

http://historian.house.gov; history@mail.house.gov

House Historian.—Mathew Wasniewski.
Associate Historian.—Ken Kato.
Manager of Historical Services.—Erin M. Hromada.
Oral Historian.—Kathleen Johnson.

OFFICE OF INTERPARLIAMENTARY AFFAIRS

HC–4 Capitol, phone 226–1766

Director.—Vacant.

Assistant Director.—Janice Robinson.

HOUSE INFORMATION RESOURCES

H2–631C, phone: 226–9823, facsimile: 226–2433

Assistant CAO/HIR and CIO (Chief Information Officer) and CISO (Chief Information Security Officer) for the House of Representatives.—Brent Conran.
Assistant CAO for Technical Support.—Tina Hanonu.

OFFICE OF THE ATTENDING PHYSICIAN

H–166 The Capitol, phone 225–5421

(After office hours, call Capitol Operator 224–2145)

Attending Physician.—Dr. Brian P. Monahan.
Chief of Staff.—Christopher R. Picaut.
Deputy Chief of Staff.—Keith Pray.

OFFICE OF INSPECTOR GENERAL

H2–386 Ford House Office Building, phone 226–1250

Inspector General.—Theresa M. Grafestine.
Deputy Inspector Generals: Debbie B. Hunter, Michael T. Ptasienski.
Director of Support Services.—Terry Upshur.
Assistant Director of:
Finance and Administration.—Susan Kozubski.
Quality Assurance and Contract Service.—Steven Johnson.
Administrative Assistant.—Deborah E. Jones.
Director, Performance and Financial Audits and Investigations.—Jeffrey Hannahs.
Assistant Director of:
Financial Audits.—Susan Simpson.
Investigations.—Julie Poole.
Auditors: Ronnette Bailey, Joshua Zader.
Director, Information Systems Audit.—Kimberly Figel.
Assistant Director, Information Systems Audits.—Michael Howard.
Auditors: Douglas Carney, Stephen Lockhart, Saad M. Patel.
Director, Management and Advisory Services.—Joseph C. Picolla.
Assistant Directors: Gregory Roberts, Donna Wolfgang.
Management Analysts: Leslie Chaney, Kevin Cornell, Annika Moje.

OFFICE OF THE LAW REVISION COUNSEL

H2–308 Ford House Office Building, 20515–6711, phone 226–2411, fax 225–0010

Law Revision Counsel.—Ralph V. Seep.
Deputy Counsel.—Robert M. Sukol.
Senior Counsels: Kenneth I. Paretzky, Timothy D. Trushel.
Assistant Counsels: Sally-Anne Cleveland, Michelle Evans, Katrina M. Hall, Raymond Kaselonis, Katherine L. Lane, Brian Lindsey, Edward T. Mulligan, Michele K. Skarvelis, John F. Wagner, Jr., Nicholas Weil.
Staff Assistants: Sylvia Tahirkheli, Monica Thompson.
Printing Editors: Robert E. Belcher, James Cahill.
Senior Systems Engineer.—Eric Loach.

OFFICE OF THE LEGISLATIVE COUNSEL

136 Cannon House Office Building, phone 225–6060

Legislative Counsel.—Sandra L. Strokoff.
Deputy Legislative Counsel.—Edward G. Grossman.

Senior Counsels: Wade Ballou, Douglass Bellis, Timothy Brown, Paul Callen, Sherry Chriss, Ira Forstater, Rosemary Gallagher, James Grossman, Curt Haensel, Jean Harmann, Gregory M. Kostka, Lawrence Johnston, Edward Leong, Hank Savage, Robert Weinhagen, Noah Wofsy.

Assistant Counsels: Marshall Barksdale, Philip Bayer, Alison Bell, Hallet Brazelton, Warren Burke, Thomas Cassidy, Henry Christrup, Shawn Conley, Lisa Daly, Thomas Dillon, Mathew Eckstein, Hershel Eisenberger, Susan Fleishman, Ryan Greenlaw, Justin Gross, Kakuti Lin, Molly Lothamer, Christopher Osborne, Scott Probst, Megan Renfrew, Hadley Ross, Anthony Sciascia, Jessica Shapiro, Anna Shpak, Ellen J. Sutherland, Mark Synnes, Michelle Vanek, Sally Walker, Brady Young.

Office Administrator.—Nancy McNeillie.

Assistant Office Administrator.—Debra Birch.

Systems Administrator.—David Topper.

Senior Systems Analyst.—Peter Szwec.

Director, Information Systems.—Willie Blount.

Publications Coordinator.—Craig Sterkx.

Paralegal.—Kristen Amarosa.

Staff Assistants: Ashley Anderson, Elonda Blount, Tomas Contreras, Pamela Griffiths, Miekl Joyner, Kelly Meryweather, Tom Meryweather, Angelina Patton, Perry Rosen, Emily Volberding.

OFFICE OF THE PARLIAMENTARIAN

H–209 The Capitol, phone 225–7373

Parliamentarian.—John V. Sullivan.

Deputy Parliamentarian.—Thomas J. Wickham.

Assistant Parliamentarians: Anne Gooch, Ethan B. Lauer, Jason A. Smith, Carrie E. Wolf.

Clerk to the Parliamentarian.—Brian C. Cooper.

Assistant Clerks to the Parliamentarian: Lloyd A. Jenkins, Monica Rodriguez.

Precedent Consultant.—Charles W. Johnson III.

Precedent Editors: Deborah W. Khalili, Andrew S. Neal, Max A. Spitzer.

Information Technology Manager.—Bryan J. Feldblum.

OFFICE OF THE SERGEANT AT ARMS

H–124 The Capitol, phone 225–2456

WILSON ''BILL'' LIVINGOOD, Sergeant at Arms of the U.S. House of Representatives; born on October 1, 1936 in Philadelphia, PA; B.S., Police Administration, Michigan State University; career record: special agent, U.S. Secret Service's Dallas Field Office, 1961–69; assistant to the special agent in charge of the Presidential Protective Division, 1969; special agent in charge of the Office of Protective Forces, 1970; inspector, Office of Inspection, 1978–82; special agent in charge, Houston Field Office, 1982–86; deputy assistant director, Office of Training, 1986–89; executive assistant to the Director of Secret Service, 1989–95; elected 36th Sergeant at Arms of the U.S. House of Representatives on January 4, 1995, for the 104th Congress; reelected for each succeeding Congress.

Sergeant at Arms.—Wilson ''Bill'' Livingood.

Deputy Sergeant at Arms.—Keni L. Hanley.

Deputy Sergeant at Arms for Police Services and Congressional Relations.—Donald T. Kellaher.

Director, Special Events/Protocol.—Ted Daniel.

Assistant to the Sergeant at Arms, Special Events/Protocol.—Vacant.

Assistants to the Sergeant at Arms, Special Events: Robert Fitzpatrick, Jack Looney.

Assistant Sergeant at Arms for Administration.—Kathleen Joyce.

Assistant to the Sergeant at Arms, Operations.—Stefan J. Bieret.

Assistants to the Sergeant at Arms, Floor Security: Joyce Hamlett, Rick Villa.

Senior Assistant Sergeant at Arms for Emergency Management.—Curt Coughin.

Assistant Sergeant at Arms for Emergency Management.—John E. Veatch.

Systems Administrators: David Cohen, Bernard Hill.

Staff Assistant.—KaSandra Greenhow.

Counsel to the Sergeant at Arms.—Timothy Blodgett.

Chief Information Officer.—Jim Kaelin.

Director, Office of House Security.—William McFarland.

Manager, Appointments Desk.—Teresa Johnson.
Director, Chamber Security.—Bill Sims.
Assistant Director, Chamber Security.—Richard Wilson.
Manager, Chamber Support Services.—Andrew Bums.
Director, Identification Services.—Melissa K. Franger.
Director, Garage and Parking Security.—Rod Myers.
Assistant Director, Garage and Parking Secuirty.—Dorian Coward.
Directors:
Continuity Planning.—W. Lee Trolan.
Operations.—Michael P. Susalla.
Preparedness.—Traci L. Brasher.
SAA Internal Preparedness.—Kevin Brennan.

JOINT COMMITTEES

Joint Economic Committee

G01 Dirksen Senate Office Building 20510–6432, phone 224–5171

[Created pursuant to sec. 5(a) of Public Law 304, 79th Congress]

Robert P. Casey, Jr., Senator, Pennsylvania, *Chair*
Kevin Brady, Representative, Texas, *Vice Chair*

SENATE

Jeff Bingaman, of New Mexico.
Amy Klobuchar, of Minnesota.
Jim Webb, of Virginia.
Mark R. Warner, of Virginia.
BERNARD SANDERS, of Vermont.
Jim DeMint, of South Carolina.
Daniel Coats, of Indiana.
Mike Lee, of Utah.
Patrick J. Toomey, of Pennsylvania.

HOUSE

Michael C. Burgess, of Texas.
John Campbell, of California.
Sean P. Duffy, of Wisconsin.
Justin Amash, of Michigan.
Mick Mulvaney, of South Carolina.
Maurice D. Hinchey, of New York.
Carolyn B. Maloney, of New York.
Loretta Sanchez, of California.
Elijah E. Cummings, of Maryland.

STAFF

Joint Economic Committee (G–01), 224–5171, fax 224–0240.
Democratic Staff:
Executive Director.—Will Hansen.
Senior Economist.—Cary Elliott.
Economist.—Paul Chen.
Chief Macroeconomist.—Matt Salomon.
Financial Director.—Colleen Healy.
Senior Policy Advisor.—Jim Whitney.
Senior Policy Analyst.—Annabelle Tamerjan.
Policy Analysts: Michael Neal, Dan Neumann, Brian Phillips, Ashely Stover.
Press Secretary.—Brenda Arredondo.
Press Assistant.—Madi Joyce.
System Administrator.—Barry Dexter.
Research Assistants: Jessica Knowles, David Michaelson, Justin Ungson, Andrew Wilson.
Staff Assistant.—Jesse Hervitz.
Detail.—Rob Fitzpatrick.
Republican Staff:
Republican Staff Director.—Robert O'Quinn.
Senior Economist and Energy Policy Advisor.—Ted Boll.
Senior Economists: Gordon Brady, Dan Miller.
Economist and Counsel.—Sean Ryan.
Economist.—Christina Forsberg.
Senior Advisor.—Jeff Schlagenhauf.
Senior Policy Advisors.—Doug Branch, Steve Robinson.
Executive Assistant.—Connie Foster.
Research Assistant.—John Trantin.
Republican Staff-Senate Location:

Director of Senate Republican Staff.—Michael Connolly.
Senior Economist.—Rachel Greszler.
Senior Policy Advisors: Tom Jones, Brian Robertson.
Research Assistant.—Emily Jaroma.
Staff Assistant.—Billy Gribbin.

Joint Committee on the Library of Congress

SR–305 Russell Senate Office Building, 20515, phone 224–6352

Charles E. Schumer, Senator from New York, *Chair*
Gregg Harper, Representative from Mississippi, *Vice Chair*

SENATE

Richard J. Durbin, of Illinois.
Patrick J. Leahy, of Vermont.
Lamar Alexander, of Tennessee.
Thad Cochran, of Mississippi.

HOUSE

Daniel E. Lungren, of California.
Ander Crenshaw, of Florida.
Robert A. Brady, of Pennsylvania.
Zoe Lofgren, of California.

Joint Committee on Printing

1309 Longworth House Office Building, 20515, phone 224–6352

[Created by act of August 3, 1846 (9 Stat. 114); U.S. Code 44, Section 101]

Gregg Harper, Representative from Mississippi, *Chair*
Charles E. Schumer, Senator from New York, *Vice Chair*

HOUSE

Daniel E. Lungren, of California.
Aaron Schock, of Illinois.
Robert A. Brady, of Pennsylvania.
Charles A. Gonzalez, of Texas.

SENATE

Patty Murray, of Washington.
Tom Udall, of New Mexico.
Lamar Alexander, of Tennessee.
Saxby Chambliss, of Georgia.

Joint Committee on Taxation

1625 Longworth House Office Building 20515–6453, phone 225–3621

http://www.house.gov/jct

[Created by Public Law 20, 69th Congress]

Dave Camp, Representative from Michigan, *Chair*
Max Baucus, Senator from Montana, *Vice Chair*

HOUSE

Wally Herger, of California.
Sam Johnson, of Texas.
Sander M. Levin, of Michigan.
Charles B. Rangel, of New York.

SENATE

John D. Rockefeller IV, of West Virginia.
Kent Conrad, of North Dakota.
Orrin G. Hatch, of Utah.
Chuck Grassley, of Iowa.

STAFF

Joint Committee on Taxation (1625 LHOB), 225–3621.

Chief of Staff.—Thomas A. Barthold (1625 LHOB).

Deputy Chief of Staff.—Bernard A. Schmitt (594 FHOB), 226–7575.

Administrative Specialist.—Frank J. Shima (1625 LHOB), 225–3621.

Executive Assistant to the Chief of Staff.—Pamela Williams (1625 LHOB), 225–3621.

Chief Clerk.—John H. Bloyer (1620 LHOB), 225–7377.

Senior Legislation Counsels: Laurie A. Coady (1620 LHOB), 225–7377; Harold E. Hirsch (1620 LHOB), 225–7377; Deirdre James (1620 LHOB), 225–7377; Cecily W. Rock (1620 LHOB), 225–7377; Joseph W. Nega (1620 LHOB), 225–7277.

Legislation Counsels: Gordon M. Clay (G–18 SD), 224–5561; Brion D. Graber (1620 LHOB), 225–7377; Adam Gropper (G–18 SD), 224–5561; Marjorie Hoffman (1620 LHOB), 225–7377; David L. Lenter (1620 LHOB), 225–7377; Rachel Levy (G–18 SD), 224–5561; Patrick Nash (1620 LHOB), 225–7377; Alex Reid (1620 LHOB), 225–7377; Kristine Roth (G–18 SD), 224–5561; Kashi Way (1620 LHOB), 225–7377; Kristeen Witt (1604 LHOB), 225–7377.

Senior Economists: Nicholas Bull (579A FHOB), 226–7575; James Cilke (593 FHOB), 226–7575; Patrick Driessen (560A FHOB), 226–7575; Robert P. Harvey (561 FHOB), 226–7575; Pamela H. Moomau (595 FHOB), 226–7575; John F. Navratil (1620 LHOB), 6–7575; "Ned" D.E. Newland (579A FHOB), 6–7575; Christopher J. Overend (574B FHOB), 6–7575; William T. Sutton (560B FHOB), 6–7575.

Economists: Timothy Dowd (578 FHOB), 6–7575; Thomas P. Holtmann (578 FHOB), 6–7575; Sally Kwak (1620 LHOB), 225–7377; Jeff Larrimore (593 FHOB), 6–7575; Julie Marshall (578 FHOB), 6–7575; Jamie McGuire (560 FHOB), 6–7575; Zachary Richards (593 FHOB), 6–7575; Karl E. Russo (1620 LHOB), 5–7377; Lori Stuntz (593 FHOB), 6–7575; Kathleen Toma (561 FHOB), 6–7575; Brent Trigg (561 FHOB), 6–7575.

Legislation Tax Accountants: Mary Duffy (1604 LHOB), 5–7377; Stephanie Jones (1604 LHOB), 5–7377.

Senior Refund Counsel.—Norman J. Brand (3565 IRS), 622–3580.

Refund Counsels: Chase Gibson (3565 IRS), 622–3580; Robert C. Gotwald (3565 IRS), 622–3580.

Chief Statistical Analyst.—Melani M. Houser (596 FHOB), 6–7575.

Statistical Analyst.—Tanya Butler, (596 FHOB), 6–7575.

Document Production Specialist.—Christine J. Simmons (1620 LHOB), 5–7377.

Tax Resource Specialist.—Melissa A. O'Brien (SD–462), 4–0494.

Executive Assistants: B. Jean Best (596 LHOB), 6–7575; Jayne Northern (G–18 SD), 4–5561; Lucia J. Rogers (596 FHOB), 6–7575; Patricia C. Smith (1620 LHOB), 5–7377; Sharon Watts (3565 IRS), 622–3580.

Senior Computer Specialist.—Hal G. Norman (577 FHOB), 6–7575.

Computer Specialists: Mark High (577 FHOB), 6–7575; Jonathan Newton (577 FHOB), 6–7575; Sandeep Yadav (577 FHOB), 6–7575.

Senior Staff Assistant.—Debra L. McMullen (1620 LHOB), 5–2647.

Staff Assistants: Neval E. McMullen (1620 LHOB), 5–2647; Kris Means (1620 LHOB, 5–2647.

Joint Select Committee on Deficit Reduction

2123 Rayburn House Office Building

Patty Murray, Senator from Washington, *Co-Chair*
Jeb Hensarling, Representative from Texas, *Co-Chair*

SENATE

Max Baucus, of Montana.
John F. Kerry, of Massachusetts.

Jon Kyl, of Arizona.
Rob Portman, of Ohio.
Patrick J. Toomey, of Pennsylvania.

HOUSE

Dave Camp, of Michigan.
Fred Upton, of Michigan.

James E. Clyburn, of South Carolina.
Xavier Becerra, of California.
Chris Van Hollen, of Maryland.

ASSIGNMENTS OF SENATORS TO COMMITTEES

[Democrats in roman (51); Republicans in *italic* (47); Independent in SMALL CAPS (1); Independent Democrat in *SMALL CAPS ITALIC* (1); total, 100]

Senator	Committees (Standing, Joint, Special, Select)
Akaka	Indian Affairs, *chair.* Armed Services. Banking, Housing, and Urban Affairs. Homeland Security and Governmental Affairs. Veterans' Affairs.
Alexander	Appropriations. Environment and Public Works. Health, Education, Labor, and Pensions. Rules and Administration. Joint Committee on the Library. Joint Committee on Printing.
Ayotte	Armed Services. Budget. Commerce, Science, and Transportation. Small Business and Entrepreneurship.
Barrasso	Indian Affairs, *vice chair.* Energy and Natural Resources. Environment and Public Works. Foreign Relations.
Baucus	Finance, *chair.* Joint Committee on Taxation, *vice chair.* Agriculture, Nutrition, and Forestry. Environment and Public Works. Joint Select Committee on Deficit Reduction.
Begich	Armed Services. Budget. Commerce, Science, and Transportation. Homeland Security and Governmental Affairs. Veterans' Affairs.
Bennet	Agriculture, Nutrition, and Forestry. Banking, Housing, and Urban Affairs. Health, Education, Labor, and Pensions. Special Committee on Aging.
Bingaman	Energy and Natural Resources, *chair.* Finance. Health, Education, Labor, and Pensions. Joint Economic Committee.
Blumenthal	Armed Services. Health, Education, Labor, and Pensions. Judiciary. Special Committee on Aging.
Blunt	Appropriations. Commerce, Science, and Transportation. Rules and Administration. Select Committee on Intelligence.

Senator	Committees (Standing, Joint, Special, Select)
Boozman	Agriculture, Nutrition, and Forestry. Commerce, Science, and Transportation. Environment and Public Works. Veterans' Affairs.
Boxer	Environment and Public Works, *chair.* Select Committee on Ethics, *chair.* Commerce, Science, and Transportation. Foreign Relations.
Brown, Scott P., of Massachusetts	Armed Services. Homeland Security and governmental Affairs. Small Business and Entrepreneurship. Veterans' Affairs.
Brown, Sherrod, of Ohio	Agriculture, Nutrition, and Forestry. Appropriations. Banking, Housing, and Urban Affairs. Veterans' Affairs. Select Committee on Ethics.
Burr	Finance. Health, Education, Labor, and Pensions. Veterans' Affairs. Select Committee on Intelligence.
Cantwell	Commerce, Science, and Transportation. Energy and Natural Resources. Finance. Indian Affairs. Small Business and Entrepreneurship.
Cardin	Budget. Environment and Public Works. Foreign Relations. Finance. Small Business and Entrepreneurship.
Carper	Environment and Public Works. Finance. Homeland Security and Governmental Affairs.
Casey	Joint Economic Committee, *chair.* Agriculture, Nutrition, and Forestry. Foreign Relations. Health, Education, Labor, and Pensions. Special Committee on Aging.
Chambliss	Agriculture, Nutrition, and Forestry. Armed Services. Rules and Administration. Joint Committee on Printing. Select Committee on Intelligence. Special Committee on Aging.
Coats	Appropriations. Energy and Natural Resources. Joint Economic Committee. Special Committee on Aging.
Coburn	Finance. Homeland Security and Governmental Affairs. Judiciary.
Cochran	Agriculture, Nutrition, and Forestry. Appropriations. Rules and Administration. Joint Committee on the Library.

Senator	Committees (Standing, Joint, Special, Select)
Collins	Appropriations. Armed Services. Homeland Security and Governmental Affairs. Special Committee on Aging.
Conrad	Budget, *chair.* Agriculture, Nutrition, and Forestry. Finance. Indian Affairs. Joint Committee on Taxation. Select Committee on Intelligence.
Coons	Budget. Energy and Natural Resources. Foreign Relations. Judiciary.
Corker	Banking, Housing, and Urban Affairs. Energy and Natural Resources. Foreign Relations. Special Committee on Aging.
Cornyn	Armed Services. Budget. Finance. Judiciary.
Crapo	Indian Affairs. Banking, Housing, and Urban Affairs. Budget. Environment and Public Works. Finance.
DeMint	Banking, Housing, and Urban Affairs. Commerce, Science, and Transportation. Foreign Relations. Joint Economic Committee.
Durbin	Appropriations. Foreign Relations. Judiciary. Rules and Administration. Joint Committee on the Library.
Enzi	Budget. Finance. Health, Education, Labor, and Pensions. Small Business and Entrepreneurship.
Feinstein	Select Committee on Intelligence, *chair.* Appropriations. Judiciary. Rules and Administration.
Franken	Indian Affairs. Energy and Natural Resources. Health, Education, Labor, and Pensions. Judiciary.
Gillibrand	Agriculture, Nutrition, and Forestry. Armed Services. Environment and Public Works. Special Committee on Aging.
Graham	Appropriations. Armed Services. Budget. Judiciary. Special Committee on Aging.

Senator	Committees (Standing, Joint, Special, Select)
Grassley	Agriculture, Nutrition, and Forestry. Budget. Finance. Judiciary. Joint Committee on Taxation.
Hagan	Armed Services. Banking, Housing, and Urban Affairs. Health, Education, Labor, and Pensions. Small Business and Entrepreneurship.
Harkin	Health, Education, Labor, and Pensions, *chair.* Agriculture, Nutrition, and Forestry. Appropriations. Small Business and Entrepreneurship.
Hatch	Finance. Health, Education, Labor, and Pensions. Judiciary. Joint Committee on Taxation. Special Committee on Aging.
Heller	Commerce, Science, and Transportation. Energy and Natural Resources. Special Committee on Aging.
Hoeven	Indian Affairs. Agriculture, Nutrition, and Forestry. Appropriations. Energy and Natural Resources.
Hutchison	Appropriations. Commerce, Science, and Transportation. Rules and Administration.
Inhofe	Armed Services. Environment and Public Works. Foreign Relations.
Inouye	Appropriations, *chair.* Indian Affairs. Commerce, Science, and Transportation. Rules and Administration.
Isakson	Commerce, Science, and Transportation. Foreign Relations. Health, Education, Labor, and Pensions. Veterans' Affairs. Select Committee on Ethics.
Johanns	Agriculture, Nutrition, and Forestry. Banking, Housing, and Urban Affairs. Environment and Public Works. Indian Affairs. Veterans' Affairs.
Johnson, Ron, of Wisconsin	Appropriations. Budget. Homeland Security and Governmental Affairs. Special Committee on Aging.
Johnson, Tim, of South Dakota	Banking, Housing, and Urban Affairs, *chair.* Appropriations. Energy and Natural Resources. Indian Affairs.

Senator	Committees (Standing, Joint, Special, Select)
Kerry	Foreign Relations, *chair.* Commerce, Science, and Transportation. Finance. Small Business and Entrepreneurship. Joint Select Committee on Deficit Reduction.
Kirk	Appropriations. Banking, Housing, and Urban Affairs. Health, Education, Labor, and Pensions. Special Committee on Aging.
Klobuchar	Agriculture, Nutrition, and Forestry. Commerce, Science, and Transportation. Judiciary. Joint Economic Committee.
Kohl	Special Committee on Aging, *chair.* Appropriations. Banking, Housing, and Urban Affairs. Judiciary.
Kyl	Finance. Judiciary. Joint Select Committee on Deficit Reduction.
Landrieu	Small Business and Entrepreneurship, *chair.* Appropriations. Energy and Natural Resources. Homeland Security and Governmental Affairs.
Lautenberg	Appropriations. Commerce, Science, and Transportation. Environment and Public Works.
Leahy	Judiciary, *chair.* Agriculture, Nutrition, and Forestry. Appropriations. Rules and Administration. Joint Committee on the Library.
Lee	Energy and Natural Resources. Foreign Relations. Judiciary. Joint Economic Committee.
Levin	Armed Services, *chair.* Homeland Security and Governmental Affairs. Small Business and Entrepreneurship. Select Committee on Intelligence.
LIEBERMAN	Homeland Security and Governmental Affairs, *chair.* Armed Services. Small Business and Entrepreneurship.
Lugar	Agriculture, Nutrition, and Forestry. Foreign Relations.
McCain	Armed Services. Homeland Security and Governmental Affairs. Health, Education, Labor, and Pensions. Indian Affairs. Select Committee on Intelligence.
McCaskill	Armed Services. Commerce, Science, and Transportation. Homeland Security and Governmental Affairs. Special Committee on Aging.

Senator	Committees (Standing, Joint, Special, Select)
McConnell	Agriculture, Nutrition, and Forestry. Appropriations. Rules and Administration. Select Committee on Intelligence.
Manchin	Armed Services. Energy and Natural Resources. Special Committee on Aging.
Menendez	Banking, Housing, and Urban Affairs. Finance. Foreign Relations.
Merkley	Banking, Housing, and Urban Affairs. Budget. Environment and Public Works. Health, Education, Labor, and Pensions.
Mikulski	Appropriations. Health, Education, Labor, and Pensions. Select Committee on Intelligence.
Moran	Appropriations. Banking, Housing, and Urban Affairs. Homeland Security and Governmental Affairs. Small Business and Entrepreneurship. Veterans' Affairs. Special Committee on Aging.
Murkowski	Appropriations. Energy and Natural Resources. Health, Education, Labor, and Pensions. Indian Affairs.
Murray	Veterans' Affairs, *chair.* Joint Select Committee on Deficit Reduction, *co-chair.* Appropriations. Budget. Health, Education, Labor, and Pensions. Rules and Administration. Joint Committee on the Printing.
Nelson, Ben, of Nebraska	Agriculture, Nutrition, and Forestry. Appropriations. Armed Services. Rules and Administration.
Nelson, Bill, of Florida	Budget. Commerce, Science, and Transportation. Finance. Select Committee on Intelligence. Special Committee on Aging.
Paul	Energy and Natural Resources. Homeland Security and Governmental Affairs. Health, Education, Labor, and Pensions. Small Business and Entrepreneurship.
Portman	Armed Services. Budget. Energy and Natural Resources. Homeland Security and Governmental Affairs. Joint Select Committee on Deficit Reduction.
Pryor	Appropriations. Commerce, Science, and Transportation. Homeland Security and Governmental Affairs. Rules and Administration. Small Business and Entrepreneurship. Select Committee on Ethics.

Senator	Committees (Standing, Joint, Special, Select)
Reed	Appropriations. Armed Services. Banking, Housing, and Urban Affairs.
Reid	Select Committee on Intelligence.
Risch	Energy and Natural Resources. Foreign Relations. Small Business and Entrepreneurship. Select Committee on Ethics. Select Committee on Intelligence.
Roberts	Agriculture, Nutrition, and Forestry. Finance. Health, Education, Labor, and Pensions. Rules and Administration. Select Committee on Ethics.
Rockefeller	Commerce, Science, and Transportation, *chair.* Finance. Veterans' Affairs. Joint Committee on Taxation. Select Committee on Intelligence.
Rubio	Commerce, Science, and Transportation. Foreign Relations. Small Business and Entrepreneurship. Select Committee on Intelligence.
SANDERS	Budget. Energy and Natural Resources. Environment and Public Works. Health, Education, Labor, and Pensions. Veterans' Affairs. Joint Economic Committee.
Schumer	Rules and Administration, *chair.* Joint Committee on the Library, *chair.* Joint Committee on Printing, *vice chair.* Banking, Housing, and Urban Affairs. Finance. Judiciary.
Sessions	Armed Services. Budget. Environment and Public Works. Judiciary.
Shaheen	Armed Services. Energy and Natural Resources. Foreign Relations. Small Business and Entrepreneurship.
Shelby	Appropriations. Banking, Housing, and Urban Affairs. Rules and Administration. Special Committee on Aging.
Snowe	Commerce, Science, and Transportation. Finance. Small Business and Entrepreneurship. Select Committee on Intelligence.
Stabenow	Agriculture, Nutrition, and Forestry, *chair.* Budget. Energy and Natural Resources. Finance.

Senator	Committees (Standing, Joint, Special, Select)
Tester	Appropriations. Banking, Housing, and Urban Affairs. Homeland Security and Governmental Affairs. Indian Affairs. Veterans' Affairs.
Thune	Agriculture, Nutrition, and Forestry. Budget. Commerce, Science, and Transportation. Finance.
Toomey	Banking, Housing, and Urban Affairs. Budget. Commerce, Science, and Transportation. Joint Economic Committee. Joint Select Committee on Deficit Reduction.
Udall, Mark, of Colorado	Armed Services. Energy and Natural Resources. Select Committee on Intelligence. Special Committee on Aging.
Udall, Tom, of New Mexico	Commerce, Science, and Transportation. Environment and Public Works. Foreign Relations. Indian Affairs. Rules and Administration. Joint Committee on Printing.
Vitter	Armed Services. Banking, Housing, and Urban Affairs. Environment and Public Works. Small Business and Entrepreneurship.
Warner	Banking, Housing, and Urban Affairs. Budget. Commerce, Science, and Transportation. Rules and Administration. Joint Economic Committee. Select Committee on Intelligence.
Webb	Armed Services. Foreign Relations. Veterans' Affairs. Joint Economic Committee.
Whitehouse	Budget. Environment and Public Works. Health, Education, Labor, and Pensions. Judiciary. Special Committee on Aging.
Wicker	Armed Services. Banking, Housing, and Urban Affairs. Commerce, Science, and Transportation. Veterans' Affairs.
Wyden	Energy and Natural Resources, *chair.* Budget. Finance. Select Committee on Intelligence. Special Committee on Aging.

ASSIGNMENTS OF REPRESENTATIVES, RESIDENT COMMISSIONER, AND DELEGATES TO COMMITTEES

[Republicans in roman (242); Democrats in *italic* (192); Vacancy (1); Resident Commissioner and Delegates in ***boldface italic*** (6); total, 441]

Representative	Committees (Standing, Joint, and Select)
Ackerman	Financial Services Foreign Affairs.
Adams	Judiciary. Science, Space, and Technology.
Aderholt	Appropriations.
Akin	Armed Services. Budget. Science, Space, and Technology.
Alexander	Appropriations.
Altmire	Education and the Workforce. Transportation and Infrastructure.
Amash	Budget. Oversight and Government Reform. Joint Economic Committee.
Amodei	Judiciary. Natural Resources. Veterans' Affairs.
Andrews	Armed Services. Education and the Workforce.
Austria	Appropriations.
Baca	Agriculture. Financial Services.
Bachmann	Financial Services. Permanent Select Committee on Intelligence.
Bachus	Financial Services, *chair*.
Baldwin	Energy and Commerce.
Barletta	Education and the Workforce. Small Business. Transportation and Infrastructure.
Barrow	Energy and Commerce. Veterans' Affairs.
Bartlett	Armed Services. Science, Space, and Technology. Small Business.
Barton, Joe, of Texas	Energy and Commerce.
Bass, Charles F., of New Hampshire	Energy and Commerce.
Bass, Karen, of California	Budget. Foreign Affairs.

Representative	Committees (Standing, Joint, and Select)
Becerra	Ways and Means. Joint Select Committee on Deficit Reduction.
Benishek	Natural Resources. Science, Space, and Technology. Veterans' Affairs.
Berg	Ways and Means.
Berkley	Ways and Means.
Berman	Foreign Affairs. Judiciary.
Biggert	Education and the Workforce. Financial Services. Science, Space, and Technology.
Bilbray	Energy and Commerce.
Bilirakis	Foreign Affairs. Homeland Security. Veterans' Affairs.
Bishop, Rob, of Utah	Natural Resources. Rules.
Bishop, Sanford D., Jr., of Georgia	Appropriations.
Bishop, Timothy H., of New York	Education and the Workforce. Transportation and Infrastructure.
Black	Budget. Ways and Means.
Blackburn	Energy and Commerce.
Blumenauer	Budget. Ways and Means.
Boehner	The Speaker.
Bonner	Ethics, *chair*. Appropriations.
Bono Mack	Energy and Commerce.
Bordallo	Armed Services. Natural Resources.
Boren	Natural Resources. Permanent Select Committee on Intelligence.
Boswell	Agriculture. Transportation and Infrastructure.
Boustany	Ways and Means.
Brady, Kevin, of Texas	Joint Economic Committee, *vice chair*. Ways and Means.
Brady, Robert A., of Pennsylvania	Armed Services. House Administration. Joint Committee on the Library. Joint Committee on Printing.
Braley, Bruce L., of Iowa	Oversight and Government Reform. Veterans' Affairs.

Representative	Committees (Standing, Joint, and Select)
Brooks	Armed Services. Science, Space, and Technology.
Broun, Paul C., Georgia of	Homeland Security. Natural Resources. Science, Space, and Technology.
Brown, Corrine of Florida	Transportation and Infrastructure. Veterans' Affairs.
Buchanan	Ways and Means.
Bucshon	Education and the Workforce. Science, Space, and Technology. Transportation and Infrastructure.
Buerkle	Foreign Affairs. Oversight and Government Reform. Veterans' Affairs.
Burgess	Energy and Commerce. Joint Economic Committee.
Burton, Dan, of Indiana	Foreign Affairs. Oversight and Government Reform.
Butterfield	Energy and Commerce.
Calvert	Appropriations. Budget.
Camp	Ways and Means, *chair*. Joint Committee on Taxation, *chair*. Joint Select Committee on Deficit Reduction.
Campbell	Budget. Financial Services. Joint Economic Committee.
Canseco	Financial Services.
Cantor	Majority Leader.
Capito	Financial Services. Transportation and Infrastructure.
Capps	Energy and Commerce.
Capuano	Financial Services. Transportation and Infrastructure.
Cardoza	Agriculture. Foreign Affairs.
Carnahan	Foreign Affairs. Transportation and Infrastructure. Veterans' Affairs.
Carney	Financial Services.
Carson, André, of Indiana	Financial Services.
Carter	Appropriations.
Cassidy	Energy and Commerce.
Castor, Kathy, of Florida	Budget. Energy and Commerce.
Chabot	Foreign Affairs. Judiciary. Small Business.

Representative	Committees (Standing, Joint, and Select)
Chaffetz	Budget. Judiciary. Oversight and Government Reform.
Chandler	Foreign Affairs. Permanent Select Committee on Intelligence.
Christensen	Energy and Commerce.
Chu	Judiciary. Small Business.
Cicilline	Foreign Affairs. Small Business.
Clarke, Hansen, of Michigan	Homeland Security. Science, Space, and Technology.
Clarke, Yvette D., of New York	Homeland Security. Small Business.
Clay	Financial Services. Oversight and Government Reform.
Cleaver	Financial Services.
Clyburn	Assistant Democratic Leader. Joint Select Committee on Deficit Reduction.
Coble	Judiciary. Transportation and Infrastructure.
Coffman, Mike, of Colorado	Armed Services. Natural Resources. Small Business.
Cohen	Judiciary. Transportation and Infrastructure.
Cole	Appropriations. Budget.
Conaway	Agriculture. Armed Services. Ethics. Permanent Select Committee on Intelligence.
Connolly, Gerald E., of Virginia	Foreign Affairs. Oversight and Government Reform.
Conyers	Judiciary.
Cooper	Armed Services. Oversight and Government Reform.
Costa	Agriculture. Natural Resources.
Costello	Science, Space, and Technology. Transportation and Infrastructure.
Courtney	Agriculture. Armed Services. Ethics.
Cravaack	Homeland Security. Science, Space, and Technology. Transportation and Infrastructure.
Crawford	Agriculture. Transportation and Infrastructure.

Representative	Committees (Standing, Joint, and Select)
Crenshaw	Appropriations. Joint Committee on the Library.
Critz	Armed Services. Small Business.
Crowley	Ways and Means.
Cuellar	Agriculture. Homeland Security.
Culberson	Appropriations.
Cummings	Oversight and Government Reform. Transportation and Infrastructure. Joint Economic Committee.
Davis, Danny K., of Illinois	Homeland Security. Oversight and Government Reform.
Davis, Geoff, of Kentucky	Ways and Means.
Davis, Susan A., of California	Armed Services. Education and the Workforce.
DeFazio	Natural Resources. Transportation and Infrastructure.
DeGette	Energy and Commerce.
DeLauro	Appropriations.
Denham	Natural Resources. Transportation and Infrastructure. Veterans' Affairs.
Dent	Appropriations. Ethics.
DesJarlais	Agriculture. Education and the Workforce. Oversight and Government Reform.
Deutch	Foreign Affairs. Judiciary.
Diaz-Balart	Appropriations.
Dicks	Appropriations.
Dingell	Energy and Commerce.
Doggett	Budget. Ways and Means.
Dold	Financial Services.
Donnelly, Joe, of Indiana	Financial Services. Veterans' Affairs.
Doyle	Energy and Commerce.
Dreier	Rules, *chair*.
Duffy	Financial Services. Joint Economic Committee.
Duncan, Jeff, of South Carolina	Foreign Affairs. Homeland Security. Natural Resources.

Representative	Committees (Standing, Joint, and Select)
Duncan, John J., Jr., of Tennessee	Natural Resources. Transportation and Infrastructure.
Edwards	Ethics. Science, Space, and Technology. Transportation and Infrastructure.
Ellison	Financial Services.
Ellmers	Agriculture. Foreign Affairs. Small Business.
Emerson	Appropriations.
Engel	Energy and Commerce. Foreign Affairs.
Eshoo	Energy and Commerce.
Faleomavaega	Foreign Affairs. Natural Resources.
Farenthold	Homeland Security. Oversight and Government Reform. Transportation and Infrastructure.
Farr	Appropriations.
Fattah	Appropriations.
Filner	Transportation and Infrastructure. Veterans' Affairs.
Fincher	Financial Services.
Fitzpatrick	Financial Services.
Flake	Appropriations.
Fleischmann	Natural Resources. Science, Space, and Technology. Transportation and Infrastructure.
Fleming	Armed Services. Natural Resources.
Flores	Budget. Natural Resources. Veterans' Affairs.
Forbes	Armed Services. Judiciary.
Fortenberry	Agriculture. Foreign Affairs.
Foxx	Education and the Workforce. Rules.
Frank, Barney, of Massachusetts	Financial Services.
Franks, Trent, of Arizona	Armed Services. Judiciary.
Frelinghuysen	Appropriations.
Fudge	Agriculture. Science, Space, and Technology.
Gallegly	Foreign Affairs. Judiciary.

Representative	Committees (Standing, Joint, and Select)
Garamendi	Armed Services. Natural Resources.
Gardner	Energy and Commerce.
Garrett	Budget. Financial Services.
Gerlach	Ways and Means.
Gibbs	Agriculture. Transportation and Infrastructure.
Gibson	Agriculture. Armed Services.
Giffords	Armed Services. Science, Space, and Technology.
Gingrey, Phil, of Georgia	Energy and Commerce. House Administration.
Gohmert	Judiciary. Natural Resources.
Gonzalez	Energy and Commerce. House Administration. Joint Committee on Printing.
Goodlatte	Agriculture. Education and the Workforce. Judiciary.
Gosar	Natural Resources. Oversight and Government Reform.
Gowdy	Education and the Workforce. Judiciary. Oversight and Government Reform.
Granger	Appropriations.
Graves, Sam, of Missouri	Small Business, *chair*. Transportation and Infrastructure.
Graves, Tom, of Georgia	Appropriations.
Green, Al, of Texas	Financial Services.
Green, Gene, of Texas	Energy and Commerce.
Griffin, Tim, of Arkansas	Armed Services. Foreign Affairs. Judiciary.
Griffith, H. Morgan, of Virginia	Energy and Commerce.
Grijalva	Education and the Workforce. Natural Resources.
Grimm	Financial Services.
Guinta	Budget. Oversight and Government Reform. Transportation and Infrastructure.
Guthrie	Energy and Commerce.
Gutierrez	Financial Services. Permanent Select Committee on Intelligence.
Hahn	Homeland Security. Small Business.

Representative	Committees (Standing, Joint, and Select)
Hall	Science, Space, and Technology, *chair.*
Hanabusa	Armed Services. Natural Resources.
Hanna	Education and the Workforce. Small Business. Transportation and Infrastructure.
Harper	Joint Committee on Printing, *chair.* Joint Committee on the Library, *vice chair.* Energy and Commerce. Ethics. House Administration.
Harris	Natural Resources. Science, Space, and Technology. Transportation and Infrastructure.
Hartzler	Agriculture. Armed Services.
Hastings, Alcee L., of Florida	Rules.
Hastings, Doc, of Washington	Natural Resources, *chair.*
Hayworth	Financial Services.
Heck	Armed Services. Education and the Workforce. Permanent Select Committee on Intelligence.
Heinrich	Armed Services. Natural Resources.
Hensarling	Joint Select Committee on Deficit Reduction, *co-chair.* Financial Services.
Herger	Ways and Means. Joint Committee on Taxation.
Herrera Beutler	Small Business. Transportation and Infrastructure.
Higgins	Foreign Affairs. Homeland Security.
Himes	Financial Services.
Hinchey	Appropriations. Joint Economic Committee.
Hinojosa	Education and the Workforce. Financial Services.
Hirono	Education and the Workforce. Transportation and Infrastructure.
Hochul	Armed Services. Homeland Security.
Holden	Agriculture. Transportation and Infrastructure.
Holt	Education and the Workforce. Natural Resources.
Honda	Appropriations. Budget.
Hoyer	Democratic Whip.
Huelskamp	Agriculture. Budget. Veterans' Affairs.

Representative	Committees (Standing, Joint, and Select)
Huizenga, Bill, of Michigan	Financial Services.
Hultgren	Agriculture. Science, Space, and Technology. Transportation and Infrastructure.
Hunter	Armed Services. Education and the Workforce. Transportation and Infrastructure.
Hurt	Financial Services.
Inslee	Energy and Commerce.
Israel	No committee assignments.
Issa	Oversight and Government Reform, *chair*. Judiciary.
Jackson, Jesse L., Jr., of Illinois ..	Appropriations.
Jackson Lee, Sheila, of Texas	Homeland Security. Judiciary.
Jenkins	Ways and Means.
Johnson, Bill, of Ohio	Foreign Affairs. Natural Resources. Veterans' Affairs.
Johnson, Eddie Bernice, of Texas	Science, Space, and Technology. Transportation and Infrastructure.
Johnson, Henry C. "Hank", Jr., of Georgia	Armed Services. Judiciary.
Johnson, Sam, of Texas	Ways and Means. Joint Committee on Taxation.
Johnson, Timothy V., of Illinois ...	Agriculture. Transportation and Infrastructure.
Jones	Armed Services. Financial Services.
Jordan	Judiciary. Oversight and Government Reform.
Kaptur	Appropriations. Budget.
Keating	Foreign Affairs. Homeland Security. Small Business.
Kelly	Education and the Workforce. Foreign Affairs. Oversight and Government Reform.
Kildee	Education and the Workforce. Natural Resources.
Kind	Ways and Means.
King, Peter T., of New York	Homeland Security, *chair*. Financial Services. Permanent Select Committee on Intelligence.
King, Steve, of Iowa	Agriculture. Judiciary. Small Business.

Representative	Committees (Standing, Joint, and Select)
Kingston	Appropriations.
Kinzinger, Adam, of Illinois	Energy and Commerce.
Kissell	Agriculture. Armed Services.
Kline	Education and the Workforce, *chair*. Armed Services.
Kucinich	Education and the Workforce. Oversight and Government Reform.
Labrador	Natural Resources. Oversight and Government Reform.
Lamborn	Armed Services. Natural Resources. Veterans' Affairs.
Lance	Energy and Commerce.
Landry	Natural Resources. Small Business. Transportation and Infrastructure.
Langevin	Armed Services. Permanent Select Committee on Intelligence.
Lankford	Budget. Oversight and Government Reform. Transportation and Infrastructure.
Larsen, Rick, of Washington	Armed Services. Transportation and Infrastructure.
Larson, John B., of Connecticut	Ways and Means.
Latham	Appropriations.
LaTourette	Appropriations.
Latta	Energy and Commerce.
Lee	Appropriations.
Levin	Ways and Means. Joint Committee on Taxation.
Lewis, Jerry, of California	Appropriations.
Lewis, John, of Georgia	Ways and Means.
Lipinski	Science, Space, and Technology. Transportation and Infrastructure.
LoBiondo	Armed Services. Transportation and Infrastructure. Permanent Select Committee on Intelligence.
Loebsack	Armed Services. Education and the Workforce.
Lofgren, Zoe, of California	House Administration. Judiciary. Science, Space, and Technology. Joint Committee on the Library.
Long	Homeland Security. Transportation and Infrastructure.

Representative	Committees (Standing, Joint, and Select)
Lowey	Appropriations.
Lucas	Agriculture, *chair*. Financial Services. Science, Space, and Technology.
Luetkemeyer	Financial Services.
Luján	Natural Resources. Science, Space, and Technology.
Lummis	Appropriations.
Lungren, Daniel E., of California	House Administration, *chair*. Homeland Security. Judiciary. Joint Committee on the Library. Joint Committee on Printing.
Lynch	Financial Services. Oversight and Government Reform.
McCarthy, Carolyn, of New York	Education and the Workforce. Financial Services.
McCarthy, Kevin, of California	Majority Whip. Financial Services.
McCaul	Ethics. Foreign Affairs. Homeland Security. Science, Space, and Technology.
McClintock	Budget. Natural Resources.
McCollum	Appropriations. Budget.
McCotter	Financial Services.
McDermott	Ways and Means.
McGovern	Agriculture. Rules.
McHenry	Financial Services. Oversight and Government Reform.
McIntyre	Agriculture. Armed Services.
McKeon	Armed Services, *chair*. Education and the Workforce.
McKinley	Energy and Commerce.
McMorris Rodgers	Energy and Commerce.
McNerney	Science, Space, and Technology. Veterans' Affairs.
Mack	Foreign Affairs. Oversight and Government Reform.
Maloney	Financial Services. Oversight and Government Reform. Joint Economic Committee.
Manzullo	Financial Services. Foreign Affairs.

Representative	Committees (Standing, Joint, and Select)
Marchant	Ways and Means.
Marino	Foreign Affairs. Homeland Security. Judiciary.
Markey	Energy and Commerce. Natural Resources.
Matheson	Energy and Commerce.
Matsui	Energy and Commerce.
Meehan	Homeland Security. Oversight and Government Reform. Transportation and Infrastructure.
Meeks	Financial Services. Foreign Affairs.
Mica	Transportation and Infrastructure, *chair.* Oversight and Government Reform.
Michaud	Transportation and Infrastructure. Veterans' Affairs.
Miller, Brad, of North Carolina	Financial Services. Science, Space, and Technology.
Miller, Candice S., of Michigan	Homeland Security. Transportation and Infrastructure.
Miller, Gary G., of California	Financial Services. Transportation and Infrastructure.
Miller, George, of California	Education and the Workforce.
Miller, Jeff, of Florida	Veterans' Affairs, *chair.* Armed Services. Permanent Select Committee on Intelligence.
Moore	Budget. Financial Services.
Moran	Appropriations.
Mulvaney	Budget. Small Business. Joint Economic Committee.
Murphy, Christopher S., of Connecticut	Foreign Affairs. Oversight and Government Reform.
Murphy, Tim, of Pennsylvania	Energy and Commerce.
Myrick	Energy and Commerce. Permanent Select Committee on Intelligence.
Nadler	Judiciary. Transportation and Infrastructure.
Napolitano	Natural Resources. Transportation and Infrastructure.
Neal	Ways and Means.
Neugebauer	Agriculture. Financial Services. Science, Space, and Technology.

Representative	Committees (Standing, Joint, and Select)
Noem	Agriculture. Education and the Workforce. Natural Resources.
Norton	Oversight and Government Reform. Transportation and Infrastructure.
Nugent	House Administration. Rules.
Nunes	Ways and Means. Permanent Select Committee on Intelligence.
Nunnelee	Appropriations.
Olson	Energy and Commerce.
Olver	Appropriations.
Owens	Agriculture. Armed Services. Small Business.
Palazzo	Armed Services. Science, Space, and Technology.
Pallone	Energy and Commerce. Natural Resources.
Pascrell	Budget. Ways and Means.
Pastor, Ed, of Arizona	Appropriations.
Paul	Financial Services. Foreign Affairs.
Paulsen	Ways and Means.
Payne	Education and the Workforce. Foreign Affairs.
Pearce	Financial Services.
Pelosi	Democratic Leader.
Pence	Foreign Affairs. Judiciary.
Perlmutter	Financial Services.
Peters	Financial Services. Small Business.
Peterson	Agriculture.
Petri	Education and the Workforce. Transportation and Infrastructure.
Pierluisi	Ethics. Judiciary. Natural Resources.
Pingree, Chellie, of Maine	Agriculture. Armed Services.
Pitts	Energy and Commerce.
Platts	Armed Services. Education and the Workforce. Oversight and Government Reform.

Representative	Committees (Standing, Joint, and Select)
Poe, Ted, of Texas	Foreign Affairs. Judiciary.
Polis	Rules.
Pompeo	Energy and Commerce.
Posey	Financial Services.
Price, David E., of North Carolina	Appropriations.
Price, Tom, of Georgia	Budget. Ways and Means.
Quayle	Homeland Security. Judiciary. Science, Space, and Technology.
Quigley	Judiciary. Oversight and Government Reform.
Rahall	Transportation and Infrastructure.
Rangel	Ways and Means. Joint Committee on Taxation.
Reed	Ways and Means.
Rehberg	Appropriations.
Reichert	Ways and Means.
Renacci	Financial Services.
Reyes	Armed Services. Veterans' Affairs.
Ribble	Agriculture. Budget. Transportation and Infrastructure.
Richardson	Homeland Security. Transportation and Infrastructure.
Richmond	Homeland Security. Small Business.
Rigell	Armed Services. Homeland Security. Science, Space, and Technology.
Rivera	Foreign Affairs. Natural Resources.
Roby	Agriculture. Armed Services. Education and the Workforce.
Roe, David P., of Tennessee	Education and the Workforce. Veterans' Affairs.
Rogers, Harold of Kentucky	Appropriations, *chair.*
Rogers, Mike, of Alabama	Armed Services. Homeland Security.
Rogers, Mike, of Michigan	Permanent Select Committee on Intelligence, *chair.* Energy and Commerce.
Rohrabacher	Foreign Affairs. Science, Space, and Technology.

Representative	Committees (Standing, Joint, and Select)
Rokita	Budget. Education and the Workforce. House Administration.
Rooney	Agriculture. Armed Services. Permanent Select Committee on Intelligence.
Roskam	Ways and Means.
Ros-Lehtinen	Foreign Affairs, *chair.*
Ross, Dennis A., of Florida	Education and the Workforce. Judiciary. Oversight and Government Reform.
Ross, Mike, of Arkansas	Energy and Commerce.
Rothman, Steven R., of New Jersey	Appropriations.
Roybal-Allard	Appropriations.
Royce	Financial Services. Foreign Affairs.
Runyan	Armed Services. Natural Resources. Veterans' Affairs.
Ruppersberger	Armed Services. Permanent Select Committee on Intelligence.
Rush	Energy and Commerce.
Ryan, Paul, of Wisconsin	Budget, *chair.* Ways and Means.
Ryan, Tim, of Ohio	Armed Services. Budget.
Sablan	Agriculture. Natural Resources.
Sánchez, Linda T., of California	Ethics. Judiciary. Veterans' Affairs.
Sanchez, Loretta, of California	Armed Services. Homeland Security. Joint Economic Committee.
Sarbanes	Natural Resources. Science, Space, and Technology.
Scalise	Energy and Commerce.
Schakowsky	Energy and Commerce. Permanent Select Committee on Intelligence.
Schiff	Appropriations. Permanent Select Committee on Intelligence.
Schilling	Agriculture. Armed Services. Small Business.
Schmidt	Agriculture. Foreign Affairs. Transportation and Infrastructure.
Schock	House Administration. Ways and Means. Joint Committee on Printing.

Representative	Committees (Standing, Joint, and Select)
Schrader	Agriculture. Small Business.
Schwartz	Budget. Foreign Affairs.
Schweikert	Financial Services.
Scott, Austin, of Georgia	Agriculture. Armed Services.
Scott, David, of Georgia	Agriculture. Financial Services.
Scott, Robert C. "Bobby", of Virginia	Education and the Workforce. Judiciary.
Scott, Tim, of South Carolina	Rules.
Sensenbrenner	Judiciary. Science, Space, and Technology.
Serrano	Appropriations.
Sessions	Rules.
Sewell	Agriculture. Science, Space, and Technology.
Sherman	Financial Services. Foreign Affairs.
Shimkus	Energy and Commerce.
Shuler	Budget. Transportation and Infrastructure.
Shuster	Armed Services. Transportation and Infrastructure.
Simpson	Appropriations. Budget.
Sires	Foreign Affairs. Transportation and Infrastructure.
Slaughter	Rules.
Smith, Adam, of Washington	Armed Services.
Smith, Adrian, of Nebraska	Ways and Means.
Smith, Christopher H., of New Jersey	Foreign Affairs.
Smith, Lamar, of Texas	Judiciary, *chair*. Homeland Security. Science, Space, and Technology.
Southerland	Agriculture. Natural Resources. Transportation and Infrastructure.
Speier	Homeland Security. Oversight and Government Reform.
Stark	Ways and Means.
Stearns	Energy and Commerce. Veterans' Affairs.
Stivers	Financial Services.

Representative	Committees (Standing, Joint, and Select)
Stutzman	Agriculture. Budget. Veterans' Affairs.
Sullivan	Energy and Commerce.
Sutton	Armed Services. Natural Resources.
Terry	Energy and Commerce.
Thompson, Bennie G., of Mississippi	Homeland Security.
Thompson, Glenn, of Pennsylvania	Agriculture. Education and the Workforce. Natural Resources.
Thompson, Mike, of California	Ways and Means. Permanent Select Committee on Intelligence.
Thornberry	Armed Services. Permanent Select Committee on Intelligence.
Tiberi	Ways and Means.
Tierney	Education and the Workforce. Oversight and Government Reform.
Tipton	Agriculture. Natural Resources. Small Business.
Tonko	Budget. Science, Space, and Technology.
Towns	Energy and Commerce. Oversight and Government Reform.
Tsongas	Armed Services. Natural Resources.
Turner, Michael R., of Ohio	Armed Services. Oversight and Government Reform.
Turner, Robert L., of New York	Foreign Affairs. Homeland Security. Veterans' Affairs.
Upton	Energy and Commerce, *chair*. Joint Select Committee on Deficit Reduction.
Van Hollen	Budget. Joint Select Committee on Deficit Reduction.
Velázquez	Financial Services. Small Business.
Visclosky	Appropriations.
Walberg	Education and the Workforce. Homeland Security. Oversight and Government Reform.
Walden	Energy and Commerce.
Walsh, Joe, of Illinois	Homeland Security. Oversight and Government Reform. Small Business.

Representative	Committees (Standing, Joint, and Select)
Walz, Timothy J., of Minnesota	Agriculture. Transportation and Infrastructure. Veterans' Affairs.
Wasserman Schultz	Budget.
Waters	Financial Services. Judiciary.
Watt	Financial Services. Judiciary.
Waxman	Energy and Commerce.
Webster	Rules.
Welch	Agriculture. Oversight and Government Reform.
West	Armed Services. Small Business.
Westmoreland	Financial Services. Permanent Select Committee on Intelligence.
Whitfield	Energy and Commerce.
Wilson, Frederica S., of Florida ...	Foreign Affairs. Science, Space, and Technology.
Wilson, Joe, of South Carolina	Armed Services. Education and the Workforce. Foreign Affairs.
Wittman	Armed Services. Natural Resources.
Wolf	Appropriations.
Womack	Appropriations.
Woodall	Budget. Rules.
Woolsey	Education and the Workforce. Science, Space, and Technology.
Yarmuth	Budget. Ethics. Oversight and Government Reform.
Yoder	Appropriations.
Young, C. W. Bill, of Florida	Appropriations.
Young, Don, of Alaska	Natural Resources. Transportation and Infrastructure.
Young, Todd C., of Indiana	Armed Services. Budget.

CONGRESSIONAL ADVISORY BOARDS, COMMISSIONS, AND GROUPS

UNITED STATES AIR FORCE ACADEMY BOARD OF VISITORS

[Title 10, U.S.C., Section 9355(a)]

Board Member	**Year Appointed**
Appointed by the President:	
Susan C. Schwab, (Chair)	2009
Robin Hayes	2009
Marcelite Harris	2010
Arlen Jameson	2010
Sue C. Ross	2008
Appointed by the Vice President or the Senate President Pro Tempore:	
Senator *Lindsey Graham,* of South Carolina	2011
Senator *John Hoeven,* of North Dakota	2011
Senator Ben Nelson, of Nebraska	2007
Appointed by the Speaker of the House of Representatives:	
Representative *Jared Polis,* of Colorado	2009
Representative Doug Lamborn, of Colorado	2007
Representative Loretta Sanchez, of California	2007
Alfredo Sandoval	2010
Appointed by the Chairman, Senate Armed Services Committee:	
Senator Michael F. Bennet, of Colorado	2011
Appointed by the Chairman, House Armed Services Committee:	
Representative *Niki Tsongas,* of Massachusetts	2008

UNITED STATES MILITARY ACADEMY BOARD OF VISITORS

[Title 10, U.S.C., Section 4355(a)]

Jack Reed, of Rhode Island.
Mary L. Landrieu, of Louisiana.
Kay Bailey Hutchison, of Texas.
Richard Burr, of North Carolina.
Maurice D. Hinchey, of New York.
Jerry Lewis, of California.
John Shimkus, of Illinois.

UNITED STATES NAVAL ACADEMY BOARD OF VISITORS

[Title 10, U.S.C., Section 6968(a)]

Appointed by the President:

Hon. Nancy Johnson, (Vice Chair) Senior Public Policy Advisor, Baker, Donelson, Bearman, Caldwell & Berkowitz, PC.
Albert Hawkins III, Former Executive Commissioner, Texas HHS Commission.
ADM John Nathman, USN (Ret.) Former Commander, U.S. Fleet Forces.
Lt. Gen. Frank Petersen, USMC (Ret.) Chairman Emeritus, National Marrow Donor Program.
RADM Michelle Howard, USN, Chief of Staff, J–5, Joint Staff.

Roland Garcia, Litigator, Office of Greenberg Tauring, LLP.

Appointed by the Vice President:

Senator Barbara A. Mikulski, of Maryland.
Senator Benjamin L. Cardin, of Maryland.
Senator *Mark Kirk,* of Illinois.

Designees of the Chairmen, SASC/HASC:

Senator *John McCain,* of Arizona.
Representative Robert J. Wittman, of Virginia, Chair.

Appointed by the Speaker of the House:

Representative *C.A. Dutch Ruppersberger,* of Maryland.
Representative *Elijah E. Cummings,* of Maryland.
Representative John Kline, of Minnesota.
Representative Rodney P. Frelinghuysen, of New Jersey.

UNITED STATES COAST GUARD ACADEMY BOARD OF VISITORS

[Title 14 U.S.C., Section 194(a)]

John D. Rockefeller IV, of West Virginia.
Mark Begich, of Alaska.
Roger F. Wicker, of Mississippi.
Patrick J. Toomey, of Pennsylvania.

John L. Mica, of Florida.
Howard Coble, of North Carolina.
Frank C. Guinta, of New Hampshire.
Andy Harris, of Maryland.
Joe Courtney, of Connecticut.
Rick Larsen, of Washington.

BRITISH–AMERICAN PARLIAMENTARY GROUP

Senate Hart Building, Room 808, phone 224–3047

[Created by Public Law 98–164]

Senate Delegation:
Chair.—Patrick J. Leahy, Senator from Vermont.
Vice Chair.—Thad Cochran, Senator from Mississippi.

CANADA–UNITED STATES INTERPARLIAMENTARY GROUP

Senate Hart Building, Room 808, 224–3047

[Created by Public Law 86–42, 22 U.S.C., 1928a–1928d, 276d–276g]

Senate Delegation:
Chair.—Amy Klobuchar, Senator from Minnesota.
Vice Chair.—Mike Crapo, Senator from Idaho.

House Delegation:
Chair.—Donald A. Manzullo, Representative of Illinois.
Vice Chair.—Brian Higgins, Representative of New York.

CHINA–UNITED STATES INTERPARLIAMENTARY GROUP

Senate Hart Building, Room 808, phone 224–3047

[Created by Public Law 108–199, Section 153]

Senate Delegation:
Chair.—Patty Murray, Senator from Washington.
Vice Chair.—Vacant.

JAPAN–INTERPARLIAMENTARY GROUP

Senate Delegation:
Chair.—Daniel K. Inouye, Senator from Hawaii.
Vice Chair.—Vacant.

KOREA–UNITED STATES INTERPARLIAMENTARY GROUP

House Delegation:
Chair.—Edward R. Royce, Representative of California.

MEXICO–UNITED STATES INTERPARLIAMENTARY GROUP

Senate Hart Building, Room 808, phone 224–3047

[Created by Public Law 82–420, 22 U.S.C. 276h–276k]

Senate Delegation:
Chair.—Tom Udall, Senator from New Mexico.
Vice Chair.—Kay Bailey Hutchison, Senator from Texas.

House Delegation:
Chair.—David Dreier, Representative of California.
Vice Chair.—Ed Pastor, Representative of Arizona.

NATO PARLIAMENTARY ASSEMBLY

Headquarters: Place du Petit Sablon 3, B–1000 Brussels, Belgium

[Created by Public Law 84–689, 22 U.S.C., 1928z]

Senate Delegation:
Chair.—Vacant.
Vice Chair.—Vacant.

House Delegation:
Chair.—Michael R. Turner, Representative of Ohio.
Vice Chair.—Mike Ross, Representative of Arkansas.

STAFF

Secretary, Senate Delegation.—Julia Hart Reed, Interparliamentary Services, SH–808, 224–3047.
Secretary, House Delegation.—Riley Moore.

RUSSIA–UNITED STATES INTERPARLIAMENTARY GROUP

Senate Hart Building, Room 808, phone 224–3047

[Created by Public Law 108–199, Section 154]

Senate Delegation:
Chair.—Ben Nelson, Senator from Nebraska.
Vice Chair.—Vacant.

COMMISSION ON CONGRESSIONAL MAILING STANDARDS

1313 Longworth House Office Building, phone 226–0647

[Created by Public Law 93–191]

Chairman.—Aaron Schock, of Illinois.
Tom Price, of Georgia.
Robert E. Latta, of Ohio.

Susan A. Davis, of California.
Brad Sherman, of California.
Cedric L. Richmond, of Louisiana.

STAFF

Majority Staff Director.—Jack Dail, 226–0647.
Professional Staff: Richard Cappetto, Sean C. Evins, George Hadjiski, Ryan Kelly, John Rich.
Counsel.—Peter Schalestock.
Minority Staff Director.—Connie Thomas, 225–9337.
Professional Staff: Gregory Abbott, Matthew A. DeFreitas, Kimberly Stevens.
Counsel.—Michael Harrison.

COMMISSION ON SECURITY AND COOPERATION IN EUROPE

234 Ford House Office Building, phone 225–1901, fax 226–4199

http://www.csce.gov

Christopher H. Smith, Representative from New Jersey, *Chair*
Benjamin L. Cardin, Senator from Maryland, *Co-Chair*

LEGISLATIVE BRANCH COMMISSIONERS

Senate

Sheldon Whitehouse, of Rhode Island.
Tom Udall, of New Mexico.
Jeanne Shaheen, of New Hampshire.
Richard Blumenthal, of Connecticut.
Roger F. Wicker, of Mississippi.
Saxby Chambliss, of Georgia.
Marco Rubio, of Florida.
Kelly Ayotte, of New Hampshire.

House

Joseph R. Pitts, of Pennsylvania.
Robert B. Aderholt, of Alabama.
Phil Gingrey, of Georgia.
Michael C. Burgess, of Texas.
Alcee L. Hastings, of Florida.
Louise McIntosh Slaughter, of New York.
Mike McIntyre, of North Carolina.
G. K. Butterfield, of North Carolina.
Steve Cohen, of Tennessee.

EXECUTIVE BRANCH COMMISSIONERS

Department of State.—Michael H. Posner.
Department of Commerce.—Michael C. Camuñez.
Department of Defense.—Alexander Vershbow.

COMMISSION STAFF

Chief of Staff.—Marak S. Milosch.
Deputy Chief of Staff.—Fred L. Turner.
Senior State Department Advisor.—Cynthia Efird.
Policy Advisors: Angel Colón-Rivera, Orest Deychakiwsky, Shelly Han, Robert Hand, Janice Helwig, Michael Ochs, Winsome Packer, Kyle Parker, Mischa E. Thompson.
Representative of the Helsinki Commission to the USOSCE.—Alex T. Johnson.
General Counsel.—Marlene Kaufmann.
Office Manager.—Daniel R. Redfield.
Counsel for International Law.—Erika B. Schlager.
Staff Associate.—Josh Shapiro.

CONGRESSIONAL AWARD FOUNDATION

379 Ford House Office Building, phone (202) 226–0130, fax 226–0131

[Created by Public Law 96–114]

Chair.—Paxton K. Baker, BET Networks.
Vice Chairs:
Linda Mitchell, Mississippi State University Extension Service (662) 534–7776.
Hon. Rodney E. Slater, Patton Boggs, LLP.
Secretary.—Mary Rogers, Pennsylvania.
Treasurer.—Lee Klumpp, BDO.
Chairman Emeritus.—John Falk, Firecreek Ltd.
Members:
Cliff Akiyama, Philadelphia College of Osteopathic Medicine.
Hon. Max Baucus, United States Senate.
Hon. Gus M. Bilirakis, United States Congress.
Ed Blansitt, Montgomery County Inspector General Office.
Hon. Kwame Brown, DC Council Chairman.
Laurel Call, National Association of Health Underwriters.
Michael Carozza, Maryland.
Edward Cohen, Lerner Enterprises.
Kathy Didawick, BlueCross BlueShield Association.
Dr. Wiley Dobbs, Idaho.
Mike Esser, Edward Jones.
David Falk, FAME.
Jeffrey S. Fried, Washington, DC.
Ron Gillyard, Los Angeles, CA.
George B. Gould, Washington, DC.
Dr. Lawrence Green, Maryland.
J. Steven Hart, Esq., Williams and Jensen, P.C.
Erica Wheelan Heyse, National Director.
David W. Hunt, Esq., Nexant.
Hon. Johnny Isakson, United States Senate.
Hon. Sheila Jackson-Lee, United States Congress.
Paul Kelly, National Association of Chain Drug Stores.
Conrad Lass, American Petroleum Institute.
Lynn Lyons, Florida.
Patrick McLain, Sanofi-Aventis, U.S.
Marc Monyek, McDonald's Corporation.
Patrick Murphy, 3 Click Solutions.
Major General Robert B. Newman, Jr., Virginia.
Amb. Roger F. Noriega, Vision Americas, LLC.
Kimberly Norman, Texas.
Andrew F. Ortiz, Ortiz Leadership Systems.
Jerry Prout, FMC Corporation.
Glenn Reynolds, USTelecom Association.
Adam Ruiz, Kentucky.
Dan Scherder, Scherder and Associates.
Jimmie Lee Solomon, Major League Baseball.
Jeffrey L. Thompson, California.
Hon. Jeri Thomson, Former Secretary of the United States Senate.
Joe Watson, Virginia.
Kathryn Weeden, United States Senate Page School.
Jon Wood, Alpha Natural Resources.

CONGRESSIONAL CLUB

2001 New Hampshire Avenue, NW., 20009, phone (202) 332–1155, fax 797–0698

President.—Vicki Miller.
Vice Presidents:
(1st) Carolina Reyes.
(2d) Julie Reichert.
(3d) Betty Ann Tanner.
(4th) Freda Manzullo.

(5th) Peggo Horstmann Hodes.
(6th) Virginia Pitts.
Treasurer.—Billie Gingrey.
Recording Secretary.—Peachy Melancon.
Corresponding Secretary.—Judy Istook.
Administrative Assistant.—Lydia de La Vina de Foley.

Executive Board
President.—Carolina Reyes.
Vice Presidents:
(1st) Julie Reichert.
(2d) Deborah Stark.
(3d) Billie Gingrey.
(4th) Jan English.
(5th) Katie Posey.
(6th) Betty Ann Tanner.
Treasurer.—Kay Ruppersberger.
Recording Secretary.—Jeanie Lamborn.
Corresponding Secretary.—Vera Davis.

CONGRESSIONAL EXECUTIVE COMMISSION ON CHINA

242 Ford House Office Building, phone 226–3766, fax 226–3804

[Created by Public Law 106–286]

Christopher H. Smith, Representative from New Jersey, *Chair.*

Sherrod Brown, Senator from Ohio, *Co-Chair.*

LEGISLATIVE BRANCH COMMISSIONERS

House

Christopher H. Smith, Representative of New Jersey.

Senate

Max Baucus, of Montana.
Carl Levin, of Michigan.
Dianne Feinstein, of California.
Jeff Merkley, of Oregon.
Susan M. Collins, of Maine.
James E. Risch, of Idaho.

EXECUTIVE BRANCH COMMISSIONERS

Seth David Harris, Department of Labor.
Maria Otero, Department of State.
Francisco J. Sanchez, Department of Commerce.
Kurt M. Campbell, Department of State.
Nisha Desai Biswal, U.S. Agency for International Development.

COMMISSION STAFF

Staff Director.—Paul B. Protic.
Deputy Staff Director.—Lawrence Liu.
Director of Administration.—Judy Wright.
Advocacy Director.—Kara Abramson.
Senior Advisors: Anna Brettell, Steve Marshall.
Senior Counsels: Sharon Mann, Eden Forsythe.
Senior Research Associates: Jesse Heatley, Anka Lee.
Senior Research Associate and Manager of Special Projects.—Abigail Story.
Printer and Outreach Associate.—Deidre Jackson.

HOUSE DEMOCRACY PARTNERSHIP

341 Ford House Office Building, phone 226–1641, fax 226–6062

democracy@mail.house.gov, http://democracy.house.gov

[Created by H. Res. 5, 112th Congress]

Chair.—David Dreier, of California.
Ranking Member.—David E. Price, of North Carolina.

COMMISSIONERS

Jeff Fortenberry, of Nebraska.
Judy Biggert, of Illinois.
Charles W. Boustany, Jr., of Louisiana.
K. Michael Conaway, of Texas.
Vern Buchanan, of Florida.
Ander Crenshaw, of Florida.
Joe Wilson, of South Carolina.
Mario Diaz-Balart, of Florida.
Peter J. Roskam, of Illlinois.
Lois Capps, of California.
Rush D. Holt, of New Jersey.
Sam Farr, of California.
Keith Ellison, of Minnesota.
Mazie K. Hirono, of Hawaii.
Lucille Roybal-Allard, of California.
Susan A. Davis, of California.
Gwen Moore, of Wisconsin.

Staff Director.—John J. Lis.
Professional Staff Member.—Robert B. Lawrence.

HOUSE OFFICE BUILDING COMMISSION

H–232 The Capitol, phone 225–0600

[Title 40, U.S.C. 175–176]

Chair.—John A. Boehner, Speaker of the House of Representatives.
Eric Cantor, House Majority Leader.
Nancy Pelosi, House Minority Leader.

JAPAN–UNITED STATES FRIENDSHIP COMMISSION

1201 15th Street, NW., Suite 330, phone (202) 653–9800, fax 653–9802

[Created by Public Law 94–118]

Chairman.—Thierry Porte, c / o JC Flowers.
Vice-Chairman.—Dr. Michael J. Green, Japan Chair and Senior Advisor, Center for Strategic and International Studies.
Executive Director.—Paige Cottingham-Streater.
Assistant Executive Director.—Margaret P. Mihori.
Assistant Executive Director, CULCON.—Pamela L. Fields.
Executive Assistant.—Sylvia L. Dandridge.

Members:
Hon. Kurt N. Campbell, Assistant Secretary of State for East Asian and Pacific Affairs, U.S. Department of State.
Dr. Robert A. Feldman, Managing Director, Morgan Stanley Japan Securities Co. Ltd.
Ellen H. Hammond, Curator, East Asian Library, Yale University.
Dr. Velina Hasu Hammond, Professor of Theater, School of Theater, University of Southern California.
Hon. Rocco Landesman, Chairman, National Endowment for the Arts.
Hon. James Leach, Chairman, National Endowment for the Humanities.
Hon. James McDermott, U.S. House of Representatives.
Dr. Anne Nishimura Morse, Curator of Japanese Art, Museum of Fine Arts, Boston.
Hon. Lisa Murkowski, U.S. Senate.
Hon. Eduardo M. Ochoa, Assistant Secretary of Education for Post-Secondary Education, U.S. Department of Education.
Dr. T.J. Pempel, Professor of Political Science, University of California, Berkeley.
Hon. Thomas E. Petri, U.S. House of Representatives.

Dr. Susan J. Pharr, Edwin O. Reischauer Professor of Japanese Politics, Harvard University.
Amelia Porges.
Hon. John D. Rockefeller IV, U.S. Senate.

MIGRATORY BIRD CONSERVATION COMMISSION

4401 North Fairfax Drive, Room 622, Arlington, VA 22203
phone (703) 358–1716, fax (703) 358–2223
[Created by act of February 18, 1929, 16 U.S.C. 715a]

Chair.—Ken Salazar, Secretary of the Interior.
Mark L. Pryor, Senator from Arkansas.
Thad Cochran, Senator from Mississippi.
John D. Dingell, Representative from Michigan.
Robert J. Wittman, Representative from Virginia.
Tom Vilsack, Secretary of Agriculture.
Lisa P. Jackson, Administrator of Environmental Protection Agency.
Secretary.—A. Eric Alvarez.

PERMANENT COMMITTEE FOR THE OLIVER WENDELL HOLMES DEVISE FUND

Library of Congress, 20540, phone 707–1082
[Created by act of Congress approved Aug. 5, 1955 (Public Law 246, 84th Congress), to administer Oliver Wendell Holmes Devise Fund, established by same act]

Chairman ex officio.—James H. Billington.
Administrative Officer for the Devise.—James H. Hutson.

UNITED STATES–CHINA ECONOMIC AND SECURITY REVIEW COMMISSION

444 North Capitol Street, NW., Suite 602, phone 624–1407, fax 624–1406
[Created by Public Law 106–398, 114 STAT]

COMMISSIONERS

Chair.—William A. Reinsch, President, National Foreign Trade Council.
Vice Chair.—Daniel M. Slane, Founder and co-owner of the Slane Company.

Members:
Carolyn Bartholomew.
Daniel A. Blumenthal, Resident Fellow in Asian Studies, American Enterprise Institute.
Peter Brookes, Senior Fellow for National Security Affairs, Heritage Foundation.
Robin Cleveland, Principal Olivet Consulting, LLC.
Hon. C. Richard D'Amato, Attorney, Advisor Climate Change.
Jeffrey L. Fiedler, Director, Special Projects and Initiatives, International Union of Operating Engineers.
Hon. Patrick A. Mulloy, Adjunct Professor of International Trade Law at Catholic University and George Mason University Law Schools.
Hon. Dennis C. Shea, Attorney, Government and Public Policy.
Michael R. Wessel, President, The Wessel Group, Inc.
Larry M. Wortzel, Ph.D.

COMMISSION STAFF

Executive Director.—Michael R. Danis.
Associate Director.—Kathleen J. Michels.
Senior Policy Analyst, Economics and Trade Issues.—Paul C. Magnusson.
Policy Analyst for Economics and Trade Issues.—Nargiza S. Salidjanova.
Senior Policy Analyst, Military-Security Issues.—Daniel M. Hartnett.
Policy Analyst for Military-Security Issues.—Robert G. Sheldon.
Policy Analyst, Energy and Foreign Affairs.—Caitlin E. Campbell.
Congressional and Public Affairs Coordinator.—Jonathan G. Weston.
Research Coordinator.—John D. Dotson.

Administrative-Program Specialist.—M.L. Faunce.
Administrative-Program Assistant.—Timothy L. Lipka.
Budget and Accounting Specialist.—Kathleen Wilson.
Human Resources Coordinator.—Douglas G. Fehrer.
Travel and Procurement Specialist.—Christopher P. Fioravante.

SENATE NATIONAL SECURITY WORKING GROUP

311 Hart Senate Office Building, 20510, phone 228–6425

Administrative Co-Chair.—John F. Kerry, Senator from Massachusetts.
Administrative Co-Chair.—*Jon Kyl,* Senator from Arizona.
Democratic Leader.—Harry Reid, Senator from Nevada.
Republican Leader.—*Mitch McConnell,* Senator from Kentucky.
Co-Chair.—Carl Levin, Senator from Michigan.
Co-Chair.—*Thad Cochran,* Senator from Mississippi.
Co-Chair.—Frank R. Lautenberg, Senator from New Jersey.
Co-Chair.—Daniel K. Inouye, Senator from Hawaii.
Co-Chair.—*Lindsey Graham,* Senator from South Carolina.

Members:
Richard J. Durbin, Senator from Illinois.
Robert P. Casey, Jr., Senator from Pennsylvania.
Bill Nelson, Senator from Florida.
JOSEPH I. LIEBERMAN, Senator from Connecticut.
Benjamin L. Cardin, Senator from Maryland.
Richard G. Lugar, Senator from Indiana.
Jeff Sessions, Senator from Alabama.
Bob Corker, Senator from Tennessee.
Roy Blunt, Senator from Missouri.
John McCain, Senator from Arizona.
James E. Risch, Senator from Idaho.

STAFF

Democratic Staff Director.—Anthony Wier, 224–4651.
Republican Staff Director.—Carolyn Leddy, 224–4521.

U.S. ASSOCIATION OF FORMER MEMBERS OF CONGRESS

1401 K Street, NW., Suite 503, 20005

phone (202) 222–0972, fax 222–0977

The nonpartisan United States Association of Former Members of Congress was founded in 1970 as a nonprofit, educational, research and social organization. It has been chartered by the United States Congress and has approximately 600 members who represented American citizens in both the U.S. Senate and the House of Representatives. The Association promotes improved public understanding of the role of Congress as a unique institution as well as the crucial importance of representative democracy as a system of government, both domestically and internationally.

President.—Dennis Hertel, of Michigan.
Vice President.—Constance A. ''Connie'' Morella, of Maryland.
Treasurer.—Barbara B. Kennelly, of Connecticut.
Secretary.—Jim Kolbe, of Arizona.
Immediate Past President.—Jim Slattery, of Kansas.
Honorary Co-Chair.—Dennis Hastert, of Illinois.
Honorary Co-Chair.—Tom Foley, of Washington.
Executive Director.—Peter M. Weichlein.
Counselors: Dan Glickman, of Kansas; Margaret M. Heckler, of Massachusetts; Matthew F. McHugh, of New York; Mike Parker, of Mississippi; Richard T. Schulze, of Pennsylvania; James W. Symington, of Missouri.

U.S. CAPITOL HISTORICAL SOCIETY

200 Maryland Avenue, NE., 20002, phone (202) 543–8919, fax 544–8244

[Congressional Charter, October 20, 1978, Public Law 95–493, 95th Congress, 92 Stat. 1643]

Chairman of the Board.—Hon. E. Thomas Coleman.
President.—Hon. Ron Sarasin.
Treasurer.—L. Neale Cosby.
General Secretary.—Suzanne C. Dicks.
Vice President of:
Finance and Administration.—Paul E. McGuire.
Membership and Development.—Rebecca A. Evans.
Merchandising.—Diana E. Wailes.
Scholarship and Education.—Donald R. Kennon, Ph.D.

EXECUTIVE COMMITTEE

Tamra Bentsen
Donald G. Carlson
Hon. E. Thomas Coleman
L. Neale Cosby
Suzanne C. Dicks
Fred Graefe
Bryce Larry Harlow
Bruce Heiman
Jim Longley
Tim Lynch
Dave Regan
Hon. Ron Sarasin

STAFF

Director of:
Historical Programs.—Lauren Borchard
Public Programs and Chief Guide.—Steve Livengood.
Manager of:
Accounting Department.—Sheri Williams.
Corporate Giving.—Marilyn Green.
Historical Programs.—Joanna L. Hallac.
Membership Programs.—Maggie Esteves.
Development Associate.—Allie Swislocki.
Development Coordinator.—Laurent Piereth.
Operations Manager.—Randy Groves.
Receptionist, Merchandise Clerk.—Ann McNeil.
Receiving Supervisor.—Vince Scott.
Fulfillment Clerk—Mike Lawson.

U.S. CAPITOL PRESERVATION COMMISSION

[Created pursuant to Public Law 100–696]

Co-Chairs:
John A. Boehner, Speaker of the House.
Daniel K. Inouye, Senate President Pro Tempore.

Senate Members:
Harry Reid, Majority Leader.
Mitch McConnell, Republican Leader.
Charles E. Schumer.
Lamar Alexander.
Vacant.
Ben Nelson.
Richard J. Durbin.
John Hoeven.

House Members:
Eric Cantor, Majority Leader.
Nancy Pelosi, Democratic Leader.
Daniel E. Lungren.
Robert A. Brady.
Gregg Harper.
Marcy Kaptur.
Vacant.
Vacant.

Ex-Officio Member-Architect of the Capitol.—Stephen T. Ayers, AIA, LEED AP.

U.S. HOUSE OF REPRESENTATIVES FINE ARTS BOARD

1309 Longworth House Office Building, phone 225–8281

[Created by Public Law 101–696]

Chair.—Daniel E. Lungren, of California.

Members:
Gregg Harper, of Mississippi.
Robert A. Brady, of Pennsylvania.
Zoe Lofgren, of California.
Ander Crenshaw, of Florida.

U.S. SENATE COMMISSION ON ART

S–411 The Capitol, phone 224–2955

[Created by Public Law 100–696]

Chair.—Harry Reid, of Nevada.
Vice Chair.—*Mitch McConnell,* of Kentucky.

Members:
Daniel K. Inouye, of Hawaii.
Charles E. Schumer, of New York.
Lamar Alexander, of Tennessee.

STAFF

Executive Secretary.—Nancy Erickson.
Curator.—Diane K. Skvarla.
Administrator.—Scott M. Strong.
Associate Curator.—Melinda K. Smith.
Historic Preservation Officer.—Kelly Steele.
Collections Manager.—Deborah Wood.
Registrar.—Courtney Morfeld.
Collections Specialist.—Theresa Malanum.
Museum Specialist.—Richard L. Doerner.
Curatorial Assistant.—Amy Burton.
Executive Assistant.—Bryant Stukes.

OTHER CONGRESSIONAL OFFICIALS AND SERVICES

ARCHITECT OF THE CAPITOL

ARCHITECT'S OFFICE

SB–15, U.S. Capitol, phone 228–1793, fax 228–1893, http://www.aoc.gov

Architect of the Capitol.—Stephen T. Ayers, AIA, LEED AP, 228–1793.
Assistant to the Architect of the Capitol.—Michael G. Turnbull, 228–1221.
Chief Operating Officer.—Christine Merdon, P.E., CMM, 228–1793.
Chief Executive Officer for Visitor Services.—Beth Plemmons, 593–1837.
Inspector General.—Carol Bates, 593–0260.
Director of:
Congressional and External Relations.—Mike Culver, 228–1701.
Safety, Fire and Environmental Programs.—Susan Adams, 226–0630.
Chief Administrative Officer.—David Ferguson, 228–1205.
Chief Financial Officer.—Tom Carroll (acting), 228–1819.
Budget Officer.—Lauri Smith, 228–1793.
Communications Officer.—Eva Malecki, 228–1793.
General Counsel.—Peter Kushner, 228–1793.
Executive Officer, U.S. Botanic Garden.—Holly Shimizu, 225–6670.
Curator.—Barbara Wolanin, 228–1222.

U.S. CAPITOL

HT–42, Capitol Superintendent's Service Center, phone 228–8800, fax 225–1957

Superintendent.—Carlos Elias.
Deputy Superintendent.—Larry Brown.
Assistant Superintendent.—Luis Rosario, 228–1875.

U.S. CAPITOL VISITOR CENTER

U.S. Capitol Visitor Center, Room SVC–101, 20515, phone 593–1816

Recorded Information 226–8000, Special Services 224–4048, TTY 224–4049

CEO for Visitor Services.—Beth Plemmons.
Director of:
Communications and Marketing.—Tom Fontana.
Exhibits and Education.—Rob Lukens.
Gift Shops.—Susan Sisk.
Restaurant/Special Events.—Miguel Lopez.
Visitor Services.—Tina Pearson.
Volunteer Coordinator.—Wayne Kehoe.

SENATE OFFICE BUILDINGS

G–45 Dirksen Senate Office Building, phone 224–3141, fax 224–0652

Superintendent.—Robin Morey, 224–6951.
Deputy Superintendent.—Takis Tzamaras, 224–2021.
Assistant Superintendents: Dennis Campbell, Jean Gilles, Michael Shirven, M. Trent Wolfersberger, 224–5023.

HOUSE OFFICE BUILDINGS

B–341 Rayburn House Office Building, phone 225–4141, fax 225–3003

Superintendent.—William M. Weidemeyer, P.E., CFM, 225–7012.
Deputy Superintendent.—Thomas J. Carroll, 225–4142.
Assistant Superintendents: Daniel Murphy, Mark Reed, Sterling Thomas, Bill Wood, 225–4142.

CAPITOL TELEPHONE EXCHANGE

6110 Postal Square Building, phone 224–3121

Supervisor.—Joan Sartori.

CHILD CARE CENTERS

HOUSE OF REPRESENTATIVES CHILD CARE CENTER

147 Ford House Office Building
Virginia Avenue and 3rd Street, SW., 20515
phone 226–9320, fax 225–6908

Director.—Monica Barnabae.
Program Director.—Paige Beatty.

SENATE EMPLOYEES' CHILD CARE CENTER

United States Senate, 20510
phone 224–1461, fax 228–3686

Director.—Christine Schoppe Wauls.

COMBINED AIRLINES TICKET OFFICES (CATO)

1800 North Kent Street, Suite 950, Arlington, VA 22209
phone (703) 522–8664, fax 522–0616

General Manager.—Charles A. Dinardo.
Administrative Assistant.—Susan Willis.

B–222 Longworth House Office Building
phone (703) 522–2286, fax (202) 226–5992

Supervisor.—Misty Conner.

B–24 Russell Senate Office Building
phone (703) 522–2286, fax (202) 393–1981

Supervisor.—Cathy Barnhardt.

CONGRESSIONAL RECORD DAILY DIGEST

HOUSE SECTION

HT–13 The Capitol, phone 225–2868 (committees), 225–1501 (chamber)

Editors for—
Committee Meetings.—Allys Lasky.
Chamber Action.—Jenelle Pulis.

SENATE SECTION

S–421 The Capitol, phone 224–2658, fax 224–1220

Editor.—Elizabeth Brown.
Assistant Editor.—Joseph Johnston.

CONGRESSIONAL RECORD INDEX OFFICE

U.S. Government Printing Office, Room C–738

North Capitol and H Streets, NW., 20401, phone 512–0275

Director.—Marcia Thompson, 512–2010, ext. 3–1975.
Deputy Director.—Philip C. Hart, 512–2010, ext. 3–1973.
Historian of Bills.—Barbre A. Brunson, 512–2010, ext. 3–1957.
Editors: Grafton J. Daniels, Jason Parsons.
Indexers: Ytta B. Carr, Joel K. Church, Jennifer E. Jones, Jane M. Wallace.

OFFICE OF CONGRESSIONAL ACCESSIBILITY SERVICES

S–156 Crypt of the Capitol 20510, phone 224–4048, TTY 224–4049

Director.—David Hauck.

LIAISON OFFICES

AIR FORCE

B–322 Rayburn House Office Building

phone 225–6656, 685–4530, DSN 325–4530, fax 685–2592

Chief.—Col. Todd Harmer.
Deputy Chief.—Lt. Col. Todd Taylor.
Liaison Officers: Lt. Col. Renee Campbell, Lt. Col. James ''Jim'' Ward.
Budget and Appropriations Liaison Officer.—MAJ Michelle ''Shelli'' Brunswick.
Legislative Assistants: Alice Geishecker, MSgt Marvin Tasby.

182 Russell Senate Office Building, phone 224–2481, fax 685–2575

Chief.—Col. Brad Spacy.
Deputy Chief.—Lt. Col. Doug McCobb.
Liaison Officers: Maj. Tony Cianciolo, Lt. Col. Lori Largen, Maj. Keith McCormack.
Appropriations Liaison Officer.—Lt. Col. Sean Boles.

ARMY

B–325 Rayburn House Office Building, phone (202) 685–2676, fax 685–2674

Chief.—COL Wilson Shoffner.
Deputy Chief.—LTC Christopher Boyle.
Liaison Officers: SGM Tammy Coon, MAJ Alison Hamilton, MAJ Ed Kennedy, LTC Kevin Wallace, CPT Malcolm Warbrick.
Congressional Caseworkers: Samy Guy, Gail Warren.

183 Russell Senate Office Building, phone 224–2881, fax 685–2570

Chief.—Vacant.

Deputy Chief.—Larnell Exum.
Liaison Officers: MAJ Colin Brooks, MAJ James Kleager, LTC Ed Larkin, MAJ Jennifer McDonough, LTC Richard Root, MAJ Michael Stella, MSG Olivia Warner.
Congressional Caseworker.—Cynthia Gray.

COAST GUARD

B–320 Rayburn House Office Building, phone 225–4775, fax 426–6081

Director, House Liaison Officer.—CDR Bion Stewart.
Deputy, House Liaison Officer.—LCDR Stephanie Morrison.
Assistant House Liaison.—LT Walter Krolman.

183 Russell Senate Office Building, phone 224–2913, fax 755–1695

Liaison Officer.—CDR Michael ''Joe'' Raymond.
Liaison Assistant.—LCDR Thomas Shuler.

NAVY / MARINE CORPS

B–324 Rayburn House Office Building, phone: Navy 225–7126; Marine Corps 225–7124

Director.—CAPT Andy Whitson, USN.
Deputy Director.—CDR Brian Tanaka, USN.
USN Liaison Officers: LT Kacee Jossis, USN; LCDR Chester Morgan, USN (contracts); LT Jared Raftery, USN; LT Jonathan Wachtel, USN.
Director USMC.—COL Jason Bohm, USMC.
USMC Liaison Officers: MAJ Kaheem Jackson, USMC; CPT Kyleanne Hunter, USMC.
Office Manager / Administrative Clerk.—SSGT Charles Aaron, USMC.

182 Russell Senate Office Building, phone: Navy 685–6003; Marine Corps 685–6010

Director.—CAPT Jim Loeblein, USN.
Deputy Director.—CDR Mark Melson, USN.
USN Liaison Officers: LT Lawrie Heyworth, USN; LT Kari Szewczyk, USN; LCDR Jeremy Newton, USN.
Director, USMC.—COL Harold Van Opdorp, USMC.
USMC Liaison Officers.—MAJ Craig Abele, USMC; MAJ Myle Hammond, USMC.
Assistant Liaison Officers: GYSGT Enrique Alaniz, USMC; SGT Megan Cavanaugh, USMC.

GOVERNMENT ACCOUNTABILITY OFFICE

Room 7125, 441 G Street, 20548, phone 512–4400, fax 512–7919 or 512–4641

Managing Director, Congressional Relations.—Ralph Dawn, 512–4544.
Director.—Anne-Marie Fennell, 512–4146.
Executive Assistant.—Jane Lusby, 512–4378.
Legislative Advisers: Blake Ainsworth, 512–4609; Sato Bagdoyan, 512–4749; Carlos Diz, 512–8256; Rosa Harris, 512–9492; Carolyn Kirby, 512–9843; Paul Thompson, 512–9867; Mary Frances Widner, 512–3804.
Associate Legislative Adviser.—Preston Heard, 512–9367.
Congressional Information Systems Specialist.—Ellen Wedge, 512–6817.
Congressional Correspondence Assistant.—Hazel Baker, 512–5326.
Engagement and Administrative Operations Assistant.—Theodora Guardado-Gallegos, 512–6224.

OFFICE OF PERSONNEL MANAGEMENT

B–332 Rayburn House Office Building, phone 225–4955

Chief.—Charlene E. Luskey.
Senior Civil Service Officer.—Carlos Tingle.
Administrative Assistant.—Kirk H. Brightman.

SOCIAL SECURITY ADMINISTRATION

G3, L1, Rayburn House Office Building, phone 225–3133, fax 225–3144

Director.—Sharon Wilson.
Congressional Relations Liaisons: Sylvia Taylor-Mackey, Latrice Wingo.

STATE DEPARTMENT LIAISON OFFICE

B–330 Rayburn House Office Building, phone 226–4640, fax 226–4643

Office Director.—Brian Anselman.
Consular Officer.—Paul Schultz.
Congressional Relations Specialist.—Stephanie Hoostal.

VETERANS' AFFAIRS

B–328 Rayburn House Office Building, phone 225–2280, fax 453–5225

Director.—Dr. Ron Maurer.
Assistant Director.—Adam Anicich.
Liaison Assistants: Frank Morgan, Elaine Waldrop.
Representatives: Tasha Adams, Richard Armstrong, Jr., Gloria Galloway.
Outreach: Brian McGough, Mandy Martin.

189 Russell Senate Office Building, phone 224–5351, fax 453–5218

Director.—Dr. Ron Maurer.
Assistant Director.—Adam Anicich.
Senior Liaison Assistant.—Runako N. Dade.
Representative.—Stuart A. Weiner.
Outreach.—Margo Ellis.

UNITED STATES SENATE PAGE SCHOOL

United States Senate, Washington, 20510–7248, fax 224–1838

Principal.—Kathryn S. Weeden, 224–3926.
English.—Frances Owens, 228–1024.
Mathematics.—Raymond Cwalina, 228–1018.
Science.—John Malek, 228–1025.
Social Studies.—Michael Bowers, 228–1012.
Secretary.—Kathleen Martin, 224–3927.

U.S. CAPITOL POLICE

119 D Street, NE., 20510–7218

Office of the Chief 224–9806, Command Center 224–0908
Communications 224–5151, Emergency 224–0911

U.S. CAPITOL POLICE BOARD

Sergeant at Arms, U.S. Senate.—Terrance W. ''Terry'' Gainer.
Sergeant at Arms, U.S. House of Representatives.—Wilson ''Bill'' Livingood.
Architect of the Capitol.—Stephen T. Ayers, AIA, LEED AP.

OFFICE OF THE CHIEF

Chief of Police.—Phillip D. Morse, Sr.
Executive Officer.—Carol A. Absher.
General Counsel.—Gretchen DeMar.
Deputy Counsel.—Thomas DiBiase.
Office of:
Policy and Management Systems.—Jan E. Jones.
Professional Responsibility.—Capt. George Hawco.
Public Information.—Sgt. Kimberly A. Schneider.
Chief of Staff.—Vacant.

CHIEF OF OPERATIONS

Assistant Chief.—Daniel R. Nichols.
Executive Officer.—Vacant.

MISSION ASSURANCE BUREAU

Bureau Commander.—Robert Young.
Executive Officer.—Robin Annison.
Command Center: Capt. William Hanny, Capt. Elizabeth Dodgson, Insp. Matthew K. Perkins, Capt. Jeff Wills.
Emergency Management Division.—Director Scott Linsky.
Special Events.—Lt. Stefanie Bloxson.

OPERATIONAL SERVICES BUREAU

Bureau Commander.—Deputy Chief Thomas Reynolds.
Hazardous Incident Response Division.—Insp. Jeffrey Pickett.
Patrol/Mobile Response Division.—Insp. Lawrence Loughery.

PROTECTIVE SERVICES BUREAU

Bureau Commander.—Insp. Daniel Malloy, Jr. (acting).
Investigations Division.—Capt. Eric Waldow.
Dignitary Protection Division.—Capt. Sean Gallagher (acting).

UNIFORM SERVICES BUREAU

Bureau Commander.—Deputy Chief Fredinal Rogers.
Executive Officer.—Lt. Debbie Proctor.
Capitol Division Commander.—Insp. Donald Rouiller.
Senate Division Commander.—Insp. Wesley Mahr.

House Division Commander.—Insp. Alan Morris.
Library Division Commander.—Insp. Debra Reynolds.

CHIEF ADMINISTRATIVE OFFICER

Chief Administrative Officer.—Richard Braddock.
Deputy Chief Administrative Officer.—Deputy Chief Matthew Verderosa.
Director, Office of:
Financial Management.—Jay Miller.
Human Resources.—Thomas Madigan.
Information Systems.—Norm Farley.
Logistics.—Cathleen English.
Commander, Training Services Bureau.—Deputy Chief Yancey Garner, Jr.

STATISTICAL INFORMATION

VOTES CAST FOR SENATORS IN 2006, 2008, and 2010

[Compiled from official statistics obtained by the Clerk of the House. Figures in the last column, for the 2010 election, may include totals for more candidates than the ones shown.]

State	Vote						Total vote cast in 2010
	2006		2008		2010		
	Democrat	Republican	Democrat	Republican	Democrat	Republican	
Alabama	....	....	752,391	1,305,383	515,619	968,181	1,485,499
Alaska	....	....	1,51,767	147,814	60,045	90,839	255,503
Arizona	664,141	814,398	....	....	592,011	1,005,615	1,708,484
Arkansas	....	....	804,678	....	288,156	451,618	779,957
California	5,076,289	2,990,822	....	....	5,218,441	4,217,366	10,000,160
Colorado	....	....	1,230,994	990,755	851,590	822,731	1,772,286
Connecticut	450,844 [1]	109,198	....	....	605,204	498,341	1,153,115
Delaware	170,567	69,734	257,539	140,595	174,012	123,053	307,402
Florida	2,890,548	1,826,127	....	....	1,092,936	2,645,743	5,411,106
Georgia	....	....	909,923	1,228,033	996,516	1,489,904	2,555,258
Hawaii	210,330	126,097	....	....	277,228	79,939	370,583
Idaho	....	....	219,903	371,744	112,057	319,953	449,530
Illinois	....	....	3,615,844	1,520,621	1,719,478	1,778,698	3,704,473
Indiana	....	1,171,553	....	....	697,775	952,116	1,744,481
Iowa	....	....	941,665	560,006	371,686	718,215	1,116,063
Kansas	....	....	441,399	727,121	220,971	587,175	837,692
Kentucky	....	....	847,005	953,816	600,052	755,706	1,356,096
Louisiana	....	....	988,298	867,177	476,572	715,415	1,264,994
Maine	113,131	405,596	279,510	444,300	....	....	....
Maryland	965,477	787,182	....	....	1,140,531	655,666	1,833,858
Massachusetts	1,500,738	661,532	1,971,974	926,044	....	....	....
Michigan	2,151,278	1,559,597	3,038,386	1,641,070	....	....	....
Minnesota	1,278,849	835,653	1,212,629	1,212,317	....	....	....
Mississippi	213,000	388,399	480,915	1,449,520	....	....	....
Missouri	1,055,255	1,006,941	....	....	789,736	1,054,160	1,943,899
Montana	199,845	196,283	348,289	129,369	....	....	....
Nebraska	378,388	213,928	317,456	455,854	....	....	....
Nevada	238,796	322,501	....	....	362,785	321,361	721,404
New Hampshire	....	....	358,438	314,403	167,545	273,218	454,710
New Jersey	58,333	41,998	1,951,218	1,461,025	....	....	....
New Mexico	394,365	163,826	505,128	318,522	....	....	....
New York	2,698,931	1,212,902	....	....	3,047,880	1,239,605	4,763,899
North Carolina	....	....	2,249,311	1,887,510	1,145,074	1,458,046	2,660,079
North Dakota	150,146	64,417	....	....	52,955	181,689	238,534
Ohio	2,257,369	1,761,037	....	....	1,503,297	2,168,742	3,815,098
Oklahoma	....	....	527,736	763,375	265,814	718,482	1,017,151
Oregon	....	....	864,392	805,159	825,507	566,199	1,442,588
Pennsylvania	2,392,984	1,684,778	....	....	1,948,716	2,028,945	3,977,661
Rhode Island	206,043	178,950	320,644	116,174	....	....	....
South Carolina	....	....	790,621	1,076,534	364,598	810,771	1,318,794
South Dakota	....	....	237,889	142,784	....	227,947	227,947
Tennessee	879,976	929,911	767,236	1,579,477	....	....	....
Texas	1,555,202	2,661,789	3,389,365	4,337,469	....	....	....
Utah	177,459	356,238	....	....	191,732	360,403	585,230
Vermont	........(2)	84,924	....	....	151,281	72,699	235,178
Virginia	1,175,606	1,166,277	2,369,327	1,228,830	....	....	....
Washington	1,184,659	832,106	....	....	1,314,930	1,196,164	2,511,094
West Virginia	159,154	47,408	447,560	254,629	283,358	230,013	529,948
Wisconsin	1,439,214	630,299	....	....	1,020,958	1,125,999	2,171,331
Wyoming	57,671	135,174	126,833	372,109	....	....	....

[1] Independent Democrat Joseph I. Lieberman was elected on November 7, 2006 with 564,095 votes.
[2] Independent Bernard Sanders was elected on November 7, 2006 with 171,638 votes.

VOTES CAST FOR REPRESENTATIVES, RESIDENT COMMISSIONER, AND DELEGATES IN 2006, 2008, and 2010

[The figures, compiled from official statistics obtained by the Clerk of the House, show the votes for the Republican and Democratic nominees, except as otherwise indicated. Figures in the last column, for the 2010 election, may include totals for more candidates than the ones shown.]

State and district	Vote cast in 2006		State and district	Vote cast in 2008		State and district	Vote cast in 2010		Total vote cast in 2010
	Demo-crat	Repub-lican		Demo-crat	Repub-lican		Repub-lican	Demo-crat	
AL:			AL:			AL:			
1st	52,770	112,944	1st	....	210,660	1st	129,063	....	156,281
2d	54,450	124,302	2d	144,368	142,578	2d	111,645	106,865	219,028
3d	63,559	98,257	3d	121,080	142,708	3d	117,736	80,204	198,139
4th	54,382	128,484	4th	66,077	196,741	4th	167,714	....	169,721
5th	143,015	....	5th	158,324	147,314	5th	131,109	95,192	226,490
6th	....	163,514	6th	....	280,902	6th	205,288	....	209,364
7th	133,870	....	7th	228,518	....	7th	51,890	136,696	188,724
AK:			AK:			AK:			
At large	93,879	132,743	At large	142,560	158,939	At large	175,384	77,606	254,335
AZ:			AZ:			AZ:			
1st	88,691	105,646	1st	155,791	109,924	1st	112,816	99,233	226,918
2d	89,671	135,150	2d	125,611	200,914	2d	173,173	82,891	266,894
3d	72,586	112,519	3d	115,759	148,800	3d	108,689	85,610	208,071
4th	56,464	18,627	4th	89,721	26,435	4th	25,300	61,524	91,907
5th	101,838	93,815	5th	149,033	122,165	5th	110,374	91,749	212,250
6th	....	152,201	6th	115,457	208,582	6th	165,649	72,615	249,383
7th	80,354	46,498	7th	124,304	64,425	7th	70,385	79,935	159,144
8th	137,655	106,790	8th	179,629	140,553	8th	134,124	138,280	283,578
AR:			AR:			AR:			
1st	127,577	56,611	1st	[1]	....	1st	93,224	78,267	180,016
2d	124,871	81,432	2d	212,303	....	2d	122,091	80,687	210,852
3d	75,885	125,039	3d	....	215,196	3d	148,581	56,542	205,123
4th	128,236	43,360	4th	203,178	....	4th	71,526	102,479	178,134
CA:			CA:			CA:			
1st	144,409	63,194	1st	197,812	67,853	1st	72,803	147,307	234,592
2d	68,234	134,911	2d	118,878	163,459	2d	130,837	98,092	228,940
3d	86,318	135,709	3d	137,971	155,424	3d	131,169	113,128	261,938
4th	126,999	135,818	4th	183,990	185,790	4th	186,397	95,653	304,229
5th	105,676	35,106	5th	164,242	46,002	5th	43,577	124,220	172,410
6th	173,190	64,405	6th	229,672	77,073	6th	77,361	172,216	261,152
7th	118,000	....	7th	170,962	51,166	7th	56,764	122,435	179,199
8th	148,435	19,800	8th	204,996	27,614	8th	31,711	167,957	209,696
9th	167,245	20,786	9th	238,915	26,917	9th	23,054	180,400	214,085
10th	130,859	66,069	10th	192,226	91,877	10th	88,512	137,578	233,806
11th	109,868	96,396	11th	164,500	133,104	11th	112,703	115,361	240,503
12th	138,650	43,674	12th	200,442	49,258	12th	44,475	152,044	201,162
13th	110,756	37,141	13th	166,829	51,447	13th	45,575	118,278	164,378
14th	141,153	48,097	14th	190,301	60,610	14th	60,917	151,217	218,869
15th	115,532	44,186	15th	170,977	55,489	15th	60,468	126,147	186,615
16th	98,929	37,130	16th	146,481	49,399	16th	37,913	105,841	156,058
17th	120,750	35,932	17th	168,907	59,037	17th	53,176	118,734	178,139
18th	71,182	37,531	18th	130,192	....	18th	51,716	72,853	124,569
19th	71,748	110,246	19th	....	179,245	19th	128,394	69,912	198,902
20th	61,120	....	20th	93,023	32,118	20th	43,197	46,247	89,444
21st	42,718	95,214	21st	66,317	143,498	21st	135,979	....	135,979
22d	55,226	133,278	22d	....	224,549	22d	173,490	....	175,663
23d	114,661	61,272	23d	171,403	80,385	23d	72,744	111,768	193,463
24th	79,461	129,812	24th	125,560	174,492	24th	144,055	96,279	240,334
25th	55,913	93,987	25th	105,929	144,660	25th	118,308	73,028	191,336
26th	67,878	102,028	26th	108,039	140,615	26th	112,774	76,093	208,347
27th	92,650	42,074	27th	145,812	52,852	27th	55,056	102,927	157,983
28th	79,866	20,629	28th	137,471	....	28th	28,493	88,385	127,107
29th	91,014	39,321	29th	146,198	56,727	29th	51,534	104,374	161,126
30th	151,284	55,904	30th	242,792	....	30th	75,948	153,663	237,747
31st	64,952	....	31st	110,955	....	31st	14,740	76,363	91,106
32d	76,059	....	32d	130,142	....	32d	31,697	77,759	109,456
33d	113,715	....	33d	186,924	26,536	33d	21,342	131,990	153,333
34th	57,459	17,359	34th	98,503	29,266	34th	20,457	69,382	89,839
35th	82,498	....	35th	150,778	24,169	35th	25,561	98,131	123,694
36th	105,323	53,068	36th	171,948	78,543	36th	66,706	114,489	192,035
37th	80,716	....	37th	131,342	....	37th	29,159	85,799	125,518
38th	75,181	24,620	38th	130,211	....	38th	30,883	85,459	116,342
39th	72,149	37,384	39th	125,289	54,533	39th	42,037	81,590	128,961
40th	46,418	100,995	40th	86,772	144,923	40th	119,455	59,400	178,855
41st	54,235	109,761	41st	99,214	159,486	41st	127,857	74,394	202,286
42d	....	129,720	42d	104,909	158,404	42d	127,161	65,122	204,398
43d	52,791	29,069	43d	108,259	48,312	43d	36,890	70,026	106,916
44th	55,275	89,555	44th	123,890	129,937	44th	107,482	85,784	193,266
45th	64,613	99,638	45th	111,026	155,166	45th	106,472	87,141	206,801
46th	71,573	116,176	46th	122,891	149,818	46th	139,822	84,940	224,782
47th	47,134	28,485	47th	85,878	31,432	47th	37,679	50,832	95,954
48th	74,647	120,130	48th	125,537	171,658	48th	145,481	88,465	242,719
49th	52,227	98,831	49th	90,138	140,300	49th	119,088	59,714	189,677
50th	96,612	118,018	50th	141,635	157,502	50th	142,247	97,818	251,081
51st	78,114	34,931	51st	148,281	49,345	51st	57,488	86,423	143,916

VOTES CAST FOR REPRESENTATIVES, RESIDENT COMMISSIONER, AND DELEGATES IN 2006, 2008, and 2010—CONTINUED

[The figures, compiled from official statistics obtained by the Clerk of the House, show the votes for the Republican and Democratic nominees, except as otherwise indicated. Figures in the last column, for the 2010 election, may include totals for more candidates than the ones shown.]

State and district	Vote cast in 2006		State and district	Vote cast in 2008		State and district	Vote cast in 2010		Total vote cast in 2010
	Demo-crat	Repub-lican		Demo-crat	Repub-lican		Repub-lican	Demo-crat	
52d	61,208	123,696	52d	111,051	160,724	52d	139,460	70,870	221,062
53d	97,541	43,312	53d	161,315	64,658	53d	57,230	104,800	168,328
CO:			CO:			CO:			
1st	129,446	....	1st	203,755	67,345	1st	59,747	140,073	207,751
2d	157,850	65,481	2d	215,571	116,591	2d	98,171	148,720	259,034
3d	146,488	86,930	3d	203,455	126,762	3d	129,257	118,048	257,999
4th	103,748	109,732	4th	187,347	146,028	4th	138,634	109,249	264,181
5th	83,431	123,264	5th	113,025	183,178	5th	152,829	68,039	232,434
6th	108,007	158,806	6th	162,639	250,877	6th	217,368	104,104	330,943
7th	103,918	79,571	7th	173,931	100,055	7th	88,026	112,667	210,810
CT:			CT:			CT:			
1st	154,539	53,010	1st	194,493	76,860	1st	84,076	130,538	226,038
2d	121,248	121,165	2d	198,984	104,574	2d	95,671	140,888	246,809
3d	150,436	44,386	3d	204,761	58,583	3d	74,107	134,544	220,661
4th	99,450	106,510	4th	149,345	146,854	4th	102,030	110,746	217,391
5th	....	94,824	5th	161,178	117,914	5th	102,092	118,231	227,303
DE:			DE:			DE:			
At large	97,565	143,897	At large	146,434	235,437	At large	125,442	173,543	305,636
FL:			FL:			FL:			
1st	62,340	135,786	1st	98,797	232,559	1st	170,821	....	213,526
2d	(2)	....	2d	216,804	133,404	2d	136,371	105,211	254,438
3d	(2)	....	3d	(2)	....	3d	50,932	94,744	150,301
4th	61,704	141,759	4th	119,330	224,112	4th	178,238	....	230,845
5th	108,959	162,421	5th	168,446	265,186	5th	208,815	100,858	309,673
6th	91,528	136,601	6th	146,655	228,302	6th	179,349	....	250,981
7th	87,584	149,656	7th	146,292	238,721	7th	185,470	83,206	268,676
8th	82,526	95,258	8th	172,854	159,490	8th	123,586	84,167	220,244
9th	96,978	123,016	9th	126,346	216,591	9th	165,433	66,158	231,591
10th	67,950	131,488	10th	118,430	182,781	10th	137,943	71,313	209,256
11th	97,470	42,454	11th	184,106	72,825	11th	61,817	91,328	153,145
12th	....	124,452	12th	137,465	185,698	12th	102,704	87,769	213,330
13th	118,940	119,309	13th	137,967	204,382	13th	183,811	83,123	266,934
14th	83,920	151,615	14th	93,590	224,602	14th	188,341	74,525	274,691
15th	97,834	125,965	15th	151,951	192,151	15th	157,079	85,595	242,674
16th	115,832	111,415	16th	139,373	209,874	16th	162,285	80,327	242,763
17th	90,663	....	17th	(2)	....	17th	....	106,361	123,370
18th	48,499	79,631	18th	102,372	140,617	18th	102,360	46,235	148,595
19th	(2)	....	19th	202,465	83,357	19th	78,733	132,098	211,059
20th	(2)	....	20th	202,832	....	20th	63,845	100,787	167,570
21st	45,522	66,784	21st	99,776	137,226	21st	(2)	....	(2)
22d	108,688	100,663	22d	169,041	140,104	22d	118,890	99,804	218,694
23d	(2)	....	23d	172,835	37,431	23d	26,414	100,066	126,480
24th	89,863	123,795	24th	211,284	151,863	24th	146,129	98,787	245,031
25th	43,168	60,765	25th	115,820	130,891	25th	74,859	61,138	143,553
GA:			GA:			GA:			
1st	43,668	94,961	1st	83,444	165,890	1st	117,270	46,449	163,719
2d	88,662	41,967	2d	158,435	71,351	2d	81,673	86,520	168,193
3d	62,371	130,428	3d	117,522	225,055	3d	168,304	73,932	242,239
4th	106,352	34,778	4th	224,494	....	4th	44,707	131,760	176,467
5th	122,380	....	5th	231,368	....	5th	46,622	130,782	177,404
6th	55,294	144,958	6th	106,551	231,520	6th	198,100	....	198,288
7th	53,553	130,561	7th	128,159	209,354	7th	160,898	78,996	239,894
8th	80,660	78,908	8th	157,241	117,446	8th	102,770	92,250	195,020
9th	39,240	128,685	9th	70,537	217,493	9th	173,512	....	173,512
10th	57,032	117,721	10th	114,638	177,265	10th	138,062	66,905	204,967
11th	48,261	118,524	11th	95,220	204,082	11th	163,515	....	163,515
12th	71,651	70,787	12th	164,562	84,773	12th	70,938	92,459	163,397
13th	103,019	45,770	13th	205,919	92,320	13th	61,771	140,294	202,065
HI:			HI:			HI:			
1st	112,904	49,890	1st	154,208	38,115	1st	82,723	94,140	176,863
2d	106,906	68,244	2d	165,748	44,425	2d	46,404	132,290	183,258
ID:			ID:			ID:			
1st	103,935	115,843	1st	175,898	171,687	1st	126,231	102,135	247,427
2d	73,441	132,262	2d	83,878	205,777	2d	137,468	48,749	199,717
IL:			IL:			IL:			
1st	146,623	27,804	1st	233,036	38,361	1st	29,253	148,170	184,386
2d	146,347	20,395	2d	251,052	29,721	2d	25,883	150,666	187,113
3d	127,768	37,954	3d	172,581	50,336	3d	40,479	116,120	166,627
4th	69,910	11,532	4th	112,529	16,024	4th	11,711	63,273	81,792
5th	114,319	32,250	5th	170,728	50,881	5th	38,935	108,360	153,435
6th	86,572	91,382	6th	109,007	147,906	6th	114,456	65,379	179,835
7th	143,071	21,939	7th	235,343	41,474	7th	29,575	149,846	183,849
8th	93,355	80,720	8th	179,444	116,081	8th	98,115	97,825	202,435
9th	122,852	41,858	9th	181,948	53,593	9th	55,182	117,553	177,207
10th	94,278	107,929	10th	138,176	153,082	10th	109,941	105,290	215,232
11th	88,846	109,009	11th	185,652	109,608	11th	129,108	96,019	225,127

VOTES CAST FOR REPRESENTATIVES, RESIDENT COMMISSIONER, AND DELEGATES IN 2006, 2008, and 2010—CONTINUED

[The figures, compiled from official statistics obtained by the Clerk of the House, show the votes for the Republican and Democratic nominees, except as otherwise indicated. Figures in the last column, for the 2010 election, may include totals for more candidates than the ones shown.]

State and district	Vote cast in 2006		State and district	Vote cast in 2008		State and district	Vote cast in 2010		Total vote cast in 2010
	Demo-crat	Repub-lican		Demo-crat	Repub-lican		Repub-lican	Demo-crat	
12th	157,284	....	12th	212,891	74,382	12th	74,046	121,272	202,705
13th	85,507	119,720	13th	147,430	180,888	13th	152,132	86,281	238,413
14th	79,274	117,870	14th	185,404	135,653	14th	112,369	98,645	219,013
15th	86,025	116,810	15th	104,393	187,121	15th	136,915	75,948	212,863
16th	63,462	125,508	16th	112,648	190,039	16th	138,299	66,037	212,761
17th	115,025	86,161	17th	220,961	....	17th	104,583	85,454	198,898
18th	73,052	150,194	18th	117,642	182,589	18th	152,868	57,046	221,170
19th	92,861	143,491	19th	105,338	203,434	19th	166,166	67,132	233,298
IN:			IN:			IN:			
1st	104,195	40,146	1st	199,954	76,647	1st	65,558	99,387	169,707
2d	103,561	88,300	2d	187,416	84,455	2d	88,803	91,341	189,591
3d	80,357	95,421	3d	112,309	155,693	3d	116,140	61,267	185,049
4th	66,986	111,057	4th	129,038	192,526	4th	138,732	53,167	202,322
5th	64,362	133,118	5th	123,357	234,705	5th	146,899	60,024	236,407
6th	76,812	115,266	6th	94,265	180,608	6th	126,027	56,647	189,309
7th	74,750	64,304	7th	172,650	92,645	7th	55,213	86,011	146,039
8th	131,019	83,704	8th	188,693	102,769	8th	117,259	76,265	203,764
9th	110,454	100,469	9th	181,281	120,529	9th	118,040	95,353	225,532
IA:			IA:			IA:			
1st	114,322	89,729	1st	186,991	102,439	1st	100,219	104,428	210,902
2d	107,683	101,707	2d	175,218	118,778	2d	104,319	115,839	227,175
3d	115,769	103,722	3d	176,904	132,136	3d	111,925	122,147	240,756
4th	90,982	121,650	4th	120,746	185,458	4th	152,588	74,300	232,519
5th	64,181	105,580	5th	99,601	159,430	5th	128,363	63,160	195,239
KS:			KS:			KS:			
1st	39,781	156,728	1st	34,771	214,549	1st	142,281	44,068	192,886
2d	114,139	106,329	2d	142,013	155,532	2d	130,034	66,588	205,975
3d	153,105	79,824	3d	202,541	142,307	3d	136,246	90,193	233,285
4th	62,166	116,386	4th	90,706	177,617	4th	119,575	74,143	203,383
KY:			KY:			KY:			
1st	83,865	123,618	1st	98,674	178,107	1st	153,840	62,090	215,930
2d	95,415	118,548	2d	143,379	158,936	2d	155,906	73,749	229,655
3d	122,489	116,568	3d	203,843	139,527	3d	112,627	139,940	255,930
4th	88,822	105,845	4th	111,549	190,210	4th	151,813	66,694	218,507
5th	52,367	147,201	5th	....	177,024	5th	151,019	44,034	195,053
6th	158,765	....	6th	203,764	111,378	6th	119,164	119,812	239,223
LA:			LA:			LA:			
1st	15,944	130,508	1st	98,839	189,168	1st	157,182	38,416	200,176
2d	93,211	13,928	2d	31,318	33,132	2d	43,378	83,705	129,604
3d	79,213	54,950	3d	([3])	....	3d	108,963	61,914	170,877
4th	40,545	93,727	4th	44,151	44,501	4th	105,223	54,609	168,794
5th	33,233	78,211	5th	....	([3])	5th	122,033	....	155,312
6th	....	94,658	6th	125,886	150,332	6th	138,607	72,577	211,184
7th	47,133	113,720	7th	98,280	177,173	7th	([3])	....	([3])
ME:			ME:			ME:			
1st	170,949	88,009	1st	205,629	168,930	1st	128,501	169,114	297,657
2d	179,772	75,156	2d	226,274	109,268	2d	119,669	147,042	266,711
MD:			MD:			MD:			
1st	83,738	185,177	1st	177,065	174,213	1st	155,118	120,400	286,812
2d	135,818	60,195	2d	198,578	68,561	2d	69,523	134,133	208,904
3d	150,142	79,174	3d	203,711	87,971	3d	86,947	147,448	241,429
4th	141,897	32,792	4th	258,704	38,739	4th	31,467	160,228	192,020
5th	168,114	....	5th	253,854	82,631	5th	83,575	155,110	241,383
6th	92,030	141,200	6th	128,207	190,926	6th	148,820	80,455	242,189
7th	158,830	....	7th	227,379	53,147	7th	46,375	152,669	203,068
8th	168,872	48,324	8th	229,740	66,351	8th	52,421	153,613	209,667
MA:			MA:			MA:			
1st	158,057	....	1st	215,696	80,067	1st	74,418	128,011	213,364
2d	164,939	....	2d	234,369	....	2d	91,209	122,751	214,124
3d	166,973	....	3d	227,619	....	3d	85,124	122,708	217,352
4th	176,513	....	4th	203,032	75,571	4th	101,517	126,194	234,127
5th	159,120	....	5th	225,947	....	5th	94,646	122,858	224,029
6th	168,056	72,997	6th	226,216	94,845	6th	107,930	142,732	251,081
7th	171,902	....	7th	212,304	67,978	7th	73,467	145,696	219,357
8th	125,515	....	8th	185,530	....	8th	....	134,974	137,660
9th	169,420	47,114	9th	242,166	....	9th	59,965	157,071	229,964
10th	171,812	78,439	10th	272,899	....	10th	120,029	132,743	283,197
MI:			MI:			MI:			
1st	180,448	72,753	1st	213,216	107,340	1st	120,523	94,824	232,037
2d	86,950	183,006	2d	119,506	214,100	2d	148,864	72,118	228,078
3d	93,846	171,212	3d	117,961	203,799	3d	133,714	83,953	224,063
4th	100,260	160,041	4th	117,665	204,259	4th	148,531	68,458	224,354
5th	176,171	60,967	5th	221,841	85,017	5th	89,680	107,286	202,263
6th	88,978	142,125	6th	123,257	188,157	6th	123,142	66,729	198,696
7th	112,665	122,348	7th	157,213	149,781	7th	113,185	102,402	225,669
8th	122,107	157,237	8th	145,491	204,408	8th	156,931	84,069	244,894

VOTES CAST FOR REPRESENTATIVES, RESIDENT COMMISSIONER, AND DELEGATES IN 2006, 2008, and 2010—CONTINUED

[The figures, compiled from official statistics obtained by the Clerk of the House, show the votes for the Republican and Democratic nominees, except as otherwise indicated. Figures in the last column, for the 2010 election, may include totals for more candidates than the ones shown.]

State and district	Vote cast in 2006		State and district	Vote cast in 2008		State and district	Vote cast in 2010		Total vote cast in 2010
	Democrat	Republican		Democrat	Republican		Republican	Democrat	
9th	127,620	142,390	9th	183,311	150,035	9th	119,325	125,730	252,650
10th	84,689	179,072	10th	108,354	230,471	10th	168,364	58,530	233,930
11th	114,248	143,658	11th	156,625	177,461	11th	141,224	91,710	238,287
12th	168,494	62,689	12th	225,094	74,565	12th	71,372	124,671	204,117
13th	126,308	....	13th	167,481	43,098	13th	23,462	100,885	127,076
14th	158,755	27,367	14th	227,841	....	14th	29,902	115,511	150,478
15th	181,946	....	15th	231,784	81,802	15th	83,488	118,336	208,309
MN:			MN:			MN:			
1st	141,556	126,486	1st	207,753	109,453	1st	109,242	122,365	248,005
2d	116,343	163,269	2d	164,093	220,924	2d	181,341	104,809	286,453
3d	99,588	184,333	3d	150,787	178,932	3d	161,177	100,240	274,092
4th	172,096	74,797	4th	216,267	98,936	4th	80,141	136,746	231,426
5th	136,060	52,263	5th	228,776	71,020	5th	55,222	154,833	228,746
6th	127,144	151,248	6th	175,786	187,817	6th	159,476	120,846	303,691
7th	179,164	74,557	7th	227,187	87,062	7th	90,652	133,096	241,097
8th	180,670	97,683	8th	241,831	114,871	8th	133,490	129,091	277,081
MS:			MS:			MS:			
1st	49,174	95,098	1st	185,959	149,818	1st	121,074	89,388	219,093
2d	100,160	55,672	2d	201,606	90,364	2d	64,499	105,327	171,356
3d	....	125,421	3d	127,698	213,171	3d	132,393	60,737	194,716
4th	110,996	28,117	4th	216,542	73,977	4th	105,613	95,243	203,384
MO:			MO:			MO:			
1st	141,574	47,893	1st	242,570	....	1st	43,649	135,907	184,779
2d	105,242	176,452	2d	132,068	232,276	2d	180,481	77,467	265,632
3d	145,219	70,189	3d	202,470	92,759	3d	94,757	99,398	203,085
4th	159,303	69,254	4th	200,009	103,446	4th	113,489	101,532	225,056
5th	136,149	68,456	5th	197,249	109,166	5th	84,578	102,076	191,423
6th	87,477	150,882	6th	121,894	196,526	6th	154,103	67,762	221,912
7th	72,592	160,942	7th	91,010	219,016	7th	141,010	67,545	222,431
8th	57,557	156,164	8th	72,790	198,798	8th	128,499	56,377	195,999
9th	87,145	149,114	9th	152,956	161,031	9th	162,724	46,817	210,358
MT:			MT:			MT:			
At large ..	158,916	239,124	At large ..	155,930	308,470	At large ..	217,696	121,954	360,341
NE:			NE:			NE:			
1st	86,360	121,015	1st	77,897	184,923	1st	116,871	47,106	163,977
2d	82,504	99,475	2d	131,901	142,473	2d	93,840	60,486	154,326
3d	93,046	113,687	3d	55,087	183,117	3d	117,275	29,932	167,243
NV:			NV:			NV:			
1st	85,025	40,917	1st	154,860	64,837	1st	58,995	103,246	167,206
2d	104,593	117,168	2d	136,548	170,771	2d	169,458	87,421	267,708
3d	98,261	102,232	3d	165,912	147,940	3d	128,916	127,168	267,874
NH:			NH:			NH:			
1st	100,691	95,527	1st	176,435	156,338	1st	121,655	95,503	225,124
2d	108,743	94,088	2d	188,332	138,222	2d	108,610	105,060	224,663
NJ:			NJ:			NJ:			
1st	140,110	....	1st	206,453	74,001	1st	58,562	106,334	168,267
2d	64,277	111,245	2d	110,990	167,701	2d	109,460	51,690	167,120
3d	86,113	122,559	3d	166,390	153,122	3d	110,215	104,252	220,309
4th	62,905	124,482	4th	100,036	202,972	4th	129,752	52,118	186,938
5th	89,503	112,142	5th	131,033	172,653	5th	124,030	62,634	190,993
6th	98,615	43,539	6th	164,077	77,469	6th	65,413	81,933	149,662
7th	95,454	98,399	7th	124,818	148,461	7th	105,084	71,902	176,986
8th	97,568	39,053	8th	159,279	63,107	8th	51,023	88,478	141,208
9th	105,853	40,879	9th	151,182	69,503	9th	52,082	83,564	137,626
10th	90,264	....	10th	169,945	....	10th	14,357	95,299	111,877
11th	74,414	126,085	11th	113,510	189,696	11th	122,149	55,472	181,800
12th	125,468	65,509	12th	193,732	108,400	12th	93,634	108,214	204,002
13th	77,238	19,284	13th	120,382	34,735	13th	19,538	62,840	84,796
NM:			NM:			NM:			
1st	105,125	105,986	1st	166,271	132,485	1st	104,215	112,010	216,225
2d	63,119	92,620	2d	129,572	101,980	2d	94,053	75,708	169,761
3d	144,880	49,219	3d	161,292	86,618	3d	90,617	120,048	210,665
NY:			NY:			NY:			
1st	92,546	54,044	1st	141,727	100,036	1st	78,300	98,316	202,007
2d	94,100	37,671	2d	143,759	70,145	2d	58,525	94,594	174,490
3d	76,169	86,918	3d	93,481	149,344	3d	131,674	51,346	185,768
4th	93,041	48,121	4th	151,792	84,444	4th	69,323	94,483	176,253
5th	70,033	....	5th	105,836	43,039	5th	36,861	72,239	120,926
6th	69,405	....	6th	141,180	....	6th	10,057	85,096	111,573
7th	60,266	10,402	7th	113,988	19,373	7th	13,751	71,247	97,971
8th	96,115	17,413	8th	152,153	36,897	8th	29,514	98,839	143,126
9th	67,040	....	9th	106,097	....	9th	37,750	67,011	117,613
10th	72,171	4,666	10th	155,090	8,204	10th	7,419	95,485	119,872
11th	75,520	6,776	11th	158,235	11,644	11th	9,119	104,297	124,914
12th	55,674	6,143	12th	115,633	12,486	12th	....	68,624	86,753
13th	42,229	49,818	13th	107,640	62,441	13th	55,821	60,773	131,426

VOTES CAST FOR REPRESENTATIVES, RESIDENT COMMISSIONER, AND DELEGATES IN 2006, 2008, and 2010—CONTINUED

[The figures, compiled from official statistics obtained by the Clerk of the House, show the votes for the Republican and Democratic nominees, except as otherwise indicated. Figures in the last column, for the 2010 election, may include totals for more candidates than the ones shown.]

State and district	Vote cast in 2006		State and district	Vote cast in 2008		State and district	Vote cast in 2010		Total vote cast in 2010
	Democrat	Republican		Democrat	Republican		Republican	Democrat	
14th	107,095	....	14th	176,426	43,385	14th	32,065	107,327	150,481
15th	93,857	6,592	15th	170,372	15,676	15th	10,678	91,225	127,046
16th	53,179	2,045	16th	123,312	3,941	16th	2,257	61,642	71,349
17th	88,714	22,608	17th	149,676	35,994	17th	29,792	95,346	139,126
18th	119,041	45,472	18th	167,365	73,237	18th	60,513	115,619	187,364
19th	100,119	79,545	19th	141,173	103,813	19th	88,734	98,766	215,738
20th	116,416	94,093	20th	178,996	99,930	20th	110,813	107,075	244,768
21st	139,997	46,752	21st	159,849	85,267	21st	70,211	124,889	219,425
22d	104,423	....	22d	147,238	76,569	22d	75,558	98,661	193,358
23d	58,859	89,482	23d	70,037	120,778	23d	73,646	82,232	182,510
24th	96,093	83,228	24th	121,345	103,379	24th	85,702	89,809	198,453
25th	100,605	[4]91,187	25th	148,290	106,653	25th	81,380	103,954	215,613
26th	85,145	94,157	26th	109,615	124,845	26th	151,449	54,307	221,763
27th	116,935	36,614	27th	169,196	50,420	27th	63,015	119,085	205,897
28th	98,382	33,361	28th	155,409	42,016	28th	45,630	102,514	168,055
29th	94,609	[4]91,383	29th	131,526	116,137	29th	93,167	....	210,145
NC:			NC:			NC:			
1st	82,510	....	1st	192,765	81,506	1st	70,867	103,294	174,161
2d	85,993	43,271	2d	199,730	93,323	2d	93,876	92,393	189,774
3d	45,458	99,519	3d	104,364	201,686	3d	143,225	51,317	199,304
4th	127,340	68,599	4th	265,751	153,947	4th	116,448	155,384	271,832
5th	72,061	96,138	5th	136,103	190,820	5th	140,525	72,762	213,287
6th	44,661	108,433	6th	108,873	221,018	6th	156,252	51,507	207,759
7th	101,787	38,033	7th	215,383	97,472	7th	98,328	113,957	212,285
8th	60,597	60,926	8th	157,185	126,634	8th	73,129	88,776	167,442
9th	53,437	106,206	9th	138,719	241,053	9th	158,790	71,450	230,240
10th	58,214	94,179	10th	126,699	171,774	10th	130,813	52,972	183,785
11th	124,972	107,342	11th	211,112	122,087	11th	110,246	131,225	241,471
12th	71,345	35,127	12th	215,908	85,814	12th	55,315	103,495	162,007
13th	98,540	56,120	13th	221,379	114,383	13th	93,099	116,103	209,202
ND:			ND:			ND:			
At large	142,934	74,687	At large	194,577	119,388	At large	129,802	106,542	236,344
OH:			OH:			OH:			
1st	96,584	105,680	1st	155,455	140,683	1st	103,770	92,672	201,518
2d	117,595	120,112	2d	124,213	148,671	2d	139,027	82,431	237,845
3d	90,650	127,978	3d	115,976	200,204	3d	152,629	71,455	224,084
4th	86,678	129,958	4th	99,499	186,154	4th	146,029	50,533	204,270
5th	98,544	129,813	5th	105,840	188,905	5th	140,703	54,919	207,453
6th	135,628	82,848	6th	176,330	92,968	6th	103,170	92,823	205,575
7th	89,579	137,899	7th	125,547	174,915	7th	135,721	70,400	218,313
8th	77,640	136,863	8th	95,510	202,063	8th	142,731	65,883	217,436
9th	153,880	55,119	9th	222,054	76,512	9th	83,423	121,819	205,242
10th	138,393	69,996	10th	157,268	107,918	10th	83,809	101,343	191,026
11th	146,799	29,125	11th	212,667	36,708	11th	28,754	139,693	168,447
12th	108,746	145,943	12th	152,234	197,447	12th	150,163	110,307	269,180
13th	135,639	85,922	13th	192,593	105,050	13th	94,367	118,806	213,173
14th	97,753	144,069	14th	125,214	188,488	14th	149,878	72,604	230,865
15th	109,659	110,714	15th	139,584	137,272	15th	119,471	91,077	220,596
16th	97,955	137,167	16th	169,044	136,293	16th	114,652	90,833	220,137
17th	170,369	41,925	17th	218,896	61,216	17th	57,352	102,758	190,666
18th	129,646	79,259	18th	164,187	110,031	18th	107,426	80,756	199,448
OK:			OK:			OK:			
1st	56,724	116,920	1st	98,890	193,404	1st	151,173	45,656	196,829
2d	122,347	45,861	2d	173,757	72,815	2d	83,226	108,203	191,429
3d	61,749	128,042	3d	62,297	184,306	3d	161,927	45,689	207,616
4th	64,775	118,266	4th	79,674	180,080	4th	([4])	....	([4])
5th	67,293	108,936	5th	88,996	171,925	5th	123,236	68,074	197,105
OR:			OR:			OR:			
1st	169,409	90,904	1st	237,567	....	1st	122,858	160,357	292,909
2d	82,484	181,529	2d	87,649	236,560	2d	206,245	72,173	279,037
3d	186,380	59,529	3d	254,235	71,063	3d	67,714	193,104	275,802
4th	180,607	109,105	4th	275,143	....	4th	129,877	162,416	298,052
5th	146,973	116,424	5th	181,577	128,297	5th	130,313	145,319	283,556
PA:			PA:			PA:			
1st	137,987	....	1st	242,799	24,714	1st	....	149,944	149,944
2d	165,867	17,291	2d	276,870	34,466	2d	21,907	182,800	204,707
3d	85,110	108,525	3d	146,846	139,707	3d	111,909	88,924	200,833
4th	131,847	122,049	4th	186,536	147,411	4th	116,958	120,827	237,785
5th	76,456	115,126	5th	112,509	155,513	5th	127,427	52,375	185,512
6th	117,892	121,047	6th	164,952	179,423	6th	133,770	100,493	234,263
7th	147,898	114,426	7th	209,955	142,362	7th	137,825	110,314	250,847
8th	125,656	124,138	8th	197,869	145,103	8th	130,759	113,547	244,306
9th	79,610	121,069	9th	98,735	174,951	9th	141,904	52,322	194,226
10th	110,115	97,862	10th	160,837	124,681	10th	110,599	89,846	200,445
11th	134,340	51,033	11th	146,379	137,151	11th	102,179	84,618	186,797

VOTES CAST FOR REPRESENTATIVES, RESIDENT COMMISSIONER, AND DELEGATES IN 2006, 2008, and 2010—CONTINUED

[The figures, compiled from official statistics obtained by the Clerk of the House, show the votes for the Republican and Democratic nominees, except as otherwise indicated. Figures in the last column, for the 2010 election, may include totals for more candidates than the ones shown.]

State and district	Vote cast in 2006		State and district	Vote cast in 2008		State and district	Vote cast in 2010		Total vote cast in 2010
	Democrat	Republican		Democrat	Republican		Republican	Democrat	
12th	123,472	79,612	12th	155,268	113,120	12th	91,170	94,056	185,226
13th	147,368	75,492	13th	196,868	108,271	13th	91,987	118,710	210,697
14th	161,075	....	14th	242,326	....	14th	49,997	122,073	177,470
15th	86,186	106,153	15th	128,333	181,433	15th	109,534	79,766	204,548
16th	80,915	115,741	16th	120,193	170,329	16th	134,113	70,994	205,107
17th	137,253	75,455	17th	192,699	109,909	17th	95,000	118,486	213,486
18th	105,419	144,632	18th	119,661	213,349	18th	161,888	78,558	240,446
19th	74,625	142,512	19th	109,533	218,862	19th	165,219	53,549	229,756
RI:			RI:			RI:			
1st	124,634	41,836	1st	145,254	51,340	1st	71,542	81,269	160,814
2d	140,315	....	2d	158,416	67,433	2d	55,409	104,442	174,670
SC:			SC:			SC:			
1st	....	115,766	1st	163,724	177,540	1st	152,755	67,008	233,695
2d	76,090	127,811	2d	158,627	184,583	2d	138,861	113,625	259,672
3d	....	111,882	3d	101,724	186,799	3d	126,235	66,497	202,108
4th	57,490	115,553	4th	113,291	184,440	4th	137,586	62,438	216,838
5th	99,669	75,422	5th	188,785	113,282	5th	125,834	102,296	228,286
6th	100,213	53,181	6th	193,378	93,059	6th	72,661	125,459	199,590
SD:			SD:			SD:			
At large	230,468	97,864	At large	256,041	122,966	At large	153,703	146,589	319,426
TN:			TN:			TN:			
1st	65,538	108,336	1st	57,525	168,343	1st	123,006	26,045	152,161
2d	45,025	157,095	2d	63,639	227,120	2d	141,796	25,400	173,380
3d	68,324	130,791	3d	73,059	184,964	3d	92,032	45,387	162,056
4th	123,666	62,449	4th	146,776	94,447	4th	103,969	70,254	182,191
5th	122,919	49,702	5th	181,467	85,471	5th	74,204	99,162	176,362
6th	129,069	60,392	6th	194,264	....	6th	128,517	56,145	191,084
7th	73,369	152,288	7th	99,549	217,332	7th	158,916	54,347	219,583
8th	129,610	47,492	8th	180,465	....	8th	98,759	64,960	167,405
9th	103,341	31,002	9th	198,798	....	9th	33,879	99,827	134,907
TX:			TX:			TX:			
1st	46,303	104,099	1st	....	189,012	1st	129,398	....	144,209
2d	45,080	90,490	2d	....	175,101	2d	130,020	....	146,731
3d	49,529	88,690	3d	108,693	170,742	3d	101,180	47,848	152,652
4th	55,278	106,495	4th	88,067	206,906	4th	136,338	40,975	186,286
5th	50,983	88,478	5th	....	162,894	5th	106,742	41,649	151,349
6th	56,369	91,927	6th	99,919	174,008	6th	107,140	50,717	162,557
7th	64,514	99,318	7th	123,242	162,635	7th	143,655	....	176,378
8th	51,393	105,665	8th	70,758	207,128	8th	161,417	34,694	201,099
9th	60,253	....	9th	143,868	....	9th	24,201	80,107	105,767
10th	71,415	97,726	10th	143,719	179,493	10th	144,980	74,086	224,171
11th	....	107,268	11th	....	189,625	11th	125,581	23,989	155,340
12th	45,676	98,371	12th	82,250	181,662	12th	109,882	38,434	152,917
13th	33,460	10,107	13th	51,841	180,078	13th	113,201	....	130,043
14th	62,429	94,380	14th	....	191,293	14th	140,623	44,431	185,054
15th	43,236	26,751	15th	107,578	52,303	15th	39,964	53,546	96,080
16th	61,116	....	16th	130,375	16,348	16th	31,051	49,301	84,892
17th	92,478	64,142	17th	134,592	115,581	17th	106,696	63,138	172,642
18th	65,936	16,448	18th	148,617	39,095	18th	33,067	85,108	121,321
19th	41,676	94,785	19th	58,030	168,501	19th	106,059	25,984	136,358
20th	68,348	....	20th	127,298	44,585	20th	31,757	58,645	92,185
21st	68,312	122,486	21st	....	243,471	21st	162,924	65,927	236,545
22d	76,775	....	22d	140,160	161,996	22d	140,537	62,082	208,223
23d	38,256	32,217	23d	134,090	100,799	23d	74,853	67,348	151,534
24th	52,075	83,835	24th	111,089	151,434	24th	100,078	....	122,687
25th	109,911	42,975	25th	191,755	88,693	25th	84,849	99,967	189,247
26th	58,271	94,219	26th	118,167	195,181	26th	120,984	55,385	180,431
27th	62,058	42,538	27th	104,864	69,458	27th	50,976	50,179	106,531
28th	68,372	....	28th	123,494	52,524	28th	46,740	62,773	111,402
29th	37,174	12,347	29th	79,718	25,512	29th	22,825	43,257	66,948
30th	81,348	17,850	30th	168,249	32,361	30th	24,668	86,322	113,978
31st	60,293	90,869	31st	106,559	175,563	31st	126,384	....	153,119
32d	52,269	71,461	32d	82,406	116,283	32d	79,433	44,258	126,869
UT:			UT:			UT:			
1st	57,922	112,546	1st	92,469	196,799	1st	135,247	46,765	195,462
2d	133,231	84,234	2d	220,666	120,083	2d	116,001	127,151	251,847
3d	53,330	95,455	3d	80,626	187,035	3d	139,721	44,320	193,186
VT:			VT:			VT:			
At large	139,815	117,023	At large	248,203	....	At large	76,403	154,006	238,521
VA:			VA:			VA:			
1st	81,083	143,889	1st	150,432	203,839	1st	135,564	73,824	212,236
2d	83,901	88,777	2d	141,857	128,486	2d	88,340	70,591	166,289
3d	133,546	....	3d	239,911	....	3d	44,553	114,754	163,900
4th	....	150,967	4th	135,041	199,075	4th	123,659	74,298	198,389
5th	84,682	125,370	5th	158,810	158,083	5th	119,560	110,562	235,299
6th	....	153,187	6th	114,367	192,350	6th	127,487	....	167,154

VOTES CAST FOR REPRESENTATIVES, RESIDENT COMMISSIONER, AND DELEGATES IN 2006, 2008, and 2010—CONTINUED

[The figures, compiled from official statistics obtained by the Clerk of the House, show the votes for the Republican and Democratic nominees, except as otherwise indicated. Figures in the last column, for the 2010 election, may include totals for more candidates than the ones shown.]

State and district	Vote cast in 2006		State and district	Vote cast in 2008		State and district	Vote cast in 2010		Total vote cast in 2010
	Demo-crat	Repub-lican		Demo-crat	Repub-lican		Repub-lican	Demo-crat	
7th	88,206	163,706	7th	138,123	233,531	7th	138,209	79,616	233,402
8th	144,700	66,639	8th	222,986	97,425	8th	71,145	116,404	190,748
9th	129,705	61,574	9th	207,306	....	9th	95,726	86,743	186,917
10th	98,769	138,213	10th	147,357	223,140	10th	131,116	72,604	208,556
11th	102,511	130,468	11th	196,598	154,758	11th	110,739	111,720	226,951
WA:			WA:			WA:			
1st	163,832	78,105	1st	233,780	111,240	1st	126,737	172,642	299,379
2d	157,064	87,730	2d	217,416	131,051	2d	148,722	155,241	303,963
3d	147,065	85,915	3d	216,701	121,828	3d	152,799	135,654	288,453
4th	77,054	115,246	4th	99,430	169,940	4th	156,726	74,973	231,699
5th	104,357	134,967	5th	112,382	211,305	5th	177,235	101,146	278,381
6th	158,202	65,883	6th	205,991	102,081	6th	109,800	151,873	261,673
7th	195,462	38,715	7th	291,963	57,054	7th	....	232,649	280,390
8th	122,021	129,362	8th	171,358	191,568	8th	161,296	148,581	309,877
9th	119,038	62,082	9th	176,295	93,080	9th	101,851	123,743	225,594
WV:			WV:			WV:			
1st	100,939	55,963	1st	187,734	....	1st	90,660	89,220	179,880
2d	70,470	94,110	2d	110,819	147,334	2d	126,814	55,001	185,246
3d	92,413	40,820	3d	133,522	66,005	3d	65,611	83,636	149,247
WI:			WI:			WI:			
1st	95,761	161,320	1st	125,268	231,009	1st	179,819	79,363	263,627
2d	191,414	113,015	2d	277,914	122,513	2d	118,099	191,164	309,460
3d	163,322	88,523	3d	225,208	122,760	3d	116,838	126,380	251,340
4th	136,735	54,486	4th	222,728	....	4th	61,543	143,559	208,103
5th	112,451	194,669	5th	....	275,271	5th	229,642	90,634	331,258
6th	....	201,367	6th	126,090	221,875	6th	183,271	75,926	259,367
7th	161,903	91,069	7th	212,666	136,938	7th	132,551	113,018	254,389
8th	141,570	135,622	8th	193,662	164,621	8th	143,998	118,646	262,938
WY:			WY:			WY:			
At large ..	92,324	93,336	At large ..	106,758	131,244	At large ..	131,661	45,768	190,822

[Table continues on next page]

VOTES CAST FOR REPRESENTATIVES, RESIDENT COMMISSIONER, AND DELEGATES IN 2006, 2008, and 2010—CONTINUED

[The figures, compiled from official statistics obtained by the Clerk of the House, show the votes for the Republican and Democratic nominees, except as otherwise indicated. Figures in the last column, for the 2010 election, may include totals for more candidates than the ones shown.]

Commonwealth of Puerto Rico	Vote						Total vote cast in 2010
	2006		2008		2010		
	Popular Democrat	New Progressive	Popular Democrat	New Progressive	New Progressive	Popular Democrat	
Resident Commissioner (4-year term)	....	....	810,093	1,010,285	....	....	....

District of Columbia	Vote						Total vote cast in 2010
	2006		2008		2010		
	Democrat	Republican	Democrat	Republican	Republican	Democrat	
Delegate	111,726	....	245,800	17,367	8,109	117,990	126,099

Guam	Vote						Total vote cast in 2010
	2006		2008		2010		
	Democrat	Republican	Democrat	Write-in	Write-in	Democrat	
Delegate	32,677	....	28,247	1,617	1,502	35,919	37,421

Virgin Islands	Vote						Total vote cast in 2010
	2006		2008		2010		
	Democrat	Republican	Democrat	Write-in	Republican	Democrat	
Delegate	19,593	4,447	19,286	69	2,329	19,844	22,173

American Samoa	Vote						Total vote cast in 2010
	2006		2008		2010		
	Democrat	Republican	Democrat	Republican	Republican	Democrat	
Delegate	5,195	4,493	7,499	4,350	4,422	6,182	10,604

Northern Mariana Islands	Vote				Total vote cast in 2010
	2008		2010		
	Independent	Republican	Republican	Democrat	
Delegate	2,474	2,117	2,049	4,852	6,901

[1] According to Arkansas law, it is not required to tabulate votes for unopposed candidates.
[2] According to Florida law, the names of those with no opposition are not printed on the ballot.
[3] According to Louisiana law, the names of those with no opposition are not printed on the ballot.
[4] According to Oklahoma law, the names of those with no opposition are not printed on the ballot.

SESSIONS OF CONGRESS, 1st–112th CONGRESSES, 1789–2011

[Closing date for this table was September 15, 2011.]

MEETING DATES OF CONGRESS: Pursuant to a resolution of the Confederation Congress in 1788, the Constitution went into effect on March 4, 1789. From then until the 20th amendment took effect in January 1934, the term of each Congress began on March 4th of each odd-numbered year; however, Article I, section 4, of the Constitution provided that ''The Congress shall assemble at least once in every Year, and such Meeting shall be on the first Monday in December, unless they shall by law appoint a different day.'' The Congress therefore convened regularly on the first Monday in December until the 20th amendment became effective, which changed the beginning of Congress's term as well as its convening date to January 3rd. So prior to 1934, a new Congress typically would not convene for regular business until 13 months after being elected. One effect of this was that the last session of each Congress was a ''lame duck'' session. After the 20th amendment, the time from the election to the beginning of Congress's term as well as when it convened was reduced to two months. Recognizing that the need might exist for Congress to meet at times other than the regularly scheduled convening date, Article II, section 3 of the Constitution provides that the President ''may, on extraordinary occasions, convene both Houses, or either of them''; hence these sessions occur only if convened by Presidential proclamation. Except as noted, these are separately numbered sessions of a Congress, and are marked by an E in the session column of the table. Until the 20th amendment was adopted, there were also times when special sessions of the Senate were convened, principally for confirming Cabinet and other executive nominations, and occasionally for the ratification of treaties or other executive business. These Senate sessions were also called by Presidential proclamation (typically by the outgoing President, although on occasion by incumbents as well) and are marked by an S in the session column. MEETING PLACES OF CONGRESS: Congress met for the first and second sessions of the First Congress (1789 and 1790) in New York City. From the third session of the First Congress through the first session of the Sixth Congress (1790 to 1800), Philadelphia was the meeting place. Congress has convened in Washington since the second session of the Sixth Congress (1800).

Congress	Session	Convening Date	Adjournment Date	Length in days[1]	Recesses[2]		President pro tempore of the Senate[3]	Speaker of the House of Representatives
					Senate	House of Representatives		
1st	1	Mar. 4, 1789	Sept. 29, 1789	210			John Langdon, of New Hampshire	Frederick A.C. Muhlenberg, of Pennsylvania.
	2	Jan. 4, 1790	Aug. 12, 1790	221			...do.	
	3	Dec. 6, 1790	Mar. 3, 1791	88			...do.	
2d	S	Mar. 4, 1791	Mar. 4, 1791	1			...do.	
	1	Oct. 24, 1791	May 8, 1792	197			Richard Henry Lee, of Virginia	Jonathan Trumbull, of Connecticut.
	2	Nov. 5, 1792	Mar. 2, 1793	119			John Langdon, of New Hampshire.	
3d	S	Mar. 4, 1793	Mar. 4, 1793	1			...do.	
	1	Dec. 2, 1793	June 9, 1794	190			John Langdon, of New Hampshire; Ralph Izard, of South Carolina.	Frederick A.C. Muhlenberg, of Pennsylvania.
	2	Nov. 3, 1794	Mar. 3, 1795	121			Henry Tazewell, of Virginia.	
4th	S	June 8, 1795	June 26, 1795	19			...do.	
	1	Dec. 7, 1795	June 1, 1796	177			Henry Tazewell, of Virginia; Samuel Livermore, of New Hampshire.	Jonathan Dayton, of New Jersey.
	2	Dec. 5, 1796	Mar. 3, 1797	89			William Bingham, of Pennsylvania.	
5th	S	Mar. 4, 1797	Mar. 4, 1797	1				
	1–E	May 15, 1797	July 10, 1797	57			William Bradford, of Rhode Island	Do.
	S	July 17, 1798	July 19, 1798	3				
	2	Nov. 13, 1797	July 16, 1798	246			Jacob Read, of South Carolina; Theodore Sedgwick, of Massachusetts.	
	3	Dec. 3, 1798	Mar. 3, 1799	91			John Laurance, of New York; James Ross, of Pennsylvania.	
6th	1	Dec. 2, 1799	May 14, 1800	164			Samuel Livermore, of New Hampshire; Uriah Tracy, of Connecticut.	Theodore Sedgwick, of Massachusetts.
	2	Nov. 17, 1800	Mar. 3, 1801	107	Dec. 23–Dec. 30, 1800	Dec. 23–Dec. 30, 1800	John E. Howard, of Maryland; James Hillhouse, of Connecticut.	
7th	S	Mar. 4, 1801	Mar. 5, 1801	2				
	1	Dec. 7, 1801	May 3, 1802	148			Abraham Baldwin, of Georgia	Nathaniel Macon, of North Carolina.

	2	Dec. 6, 1802	Mar. 3, 1803	88			Stephen R. Bradley, of Vermont.	
8th	1–E	Oct. 17, 1803	Mar. 27, 1804	163			John Brown, of Kentucky; Jesse Franklin, of North Carolina.	Do.
	2	Nov. 5, 1804	Mar. 3, 1805	119			Joseph Anderson, of Tennessee.	
9th	1	Dec. 2, 1805	Apr. 21, 1806	141			Samuel Smith, of Maryland	Do.
	2	Dec. 1, 1806	Mar. 3, 1807	93			...do.	
10th	1–E	Oct. 26, 1807	Apr. 25, 1808	182			...do	Joseph B. Varnum, of Massachusetts.
	2	Nov. 7, 1808	Mar. 3, 1809	117			Stephen R. Bradley, of Vermont; John Milledge, of Georgia.	
11th	S	Mar. 4, 1809	Mar. 7, 1809	4				
	1	May 22, 1809	June 28, 1809	38			Andrew Gregg, of Pennsylvania	Do.
	2	Nov. 27, 1809	May 1, 1810	156			John Gaillard, of South Carolina.	
	3	Dec. 3, 1810	Mar. 3, 1811	91			John Pope, of Kentucky.	
12th	1–E	Nov. 4, 1811	July 6, 1812	245			William H. Crawford, of Georgia	Henry Clay, of Kentucky.
	2	Nov. 2, 1812	Mar. 3, 1813	122			...do.	
13th	1	May 24, 1813	Aug. 2, 1813	71			...do	Do.[4]
	2	Dec. 6, 1813	Apr. 18, 1814	134			Joseph B. Varnum, of Massachusetts; John Gaillard, of South Carolina.	Langdon Cheves, of South Carolina.[4]
	3–E	Sept. 19, 1814	Mar. 3, 1815	166			John Gaillard, of South Carolina.	
14th	1	Dec. 4, 1815	Apr. 30, 1816	148			...do	Henry Clay, of Kentucky.
	2	Dec. 2, 1816	Mar. 3, 1817	92			...do.	
15th	S	Mar. 4, 1817	Mar. 6, 1817	3			...do.	
	1	Dec. 1, 1817	Apr. 20, 1818	141	Dec. 24–Dec. 29, 1817	Dec. 24–Dec. 29, 1817	...do	Do.
	2	Nov. 16, 1818	Mar. 3, 1819	108			James Barbour, of Virginia.	
16th	1	Dec. 6, 1819	May 15, 1820	162			James Barbour, of Virginia; John Gaillard, of South Carolina.	Do.[5]
	2	Nov. 13, 1820	Mar. 3, 1821	111			John Gaillard, of South Carolina	John W. Taylor, of New York.[5]
17th	1	Dec. 3, 1821	May 8, 1822	157			...do	Philip P. Barbour, of Virginia.
	2	Dec. 2, 1822	Mar. 3, 1823	92			...do.	
18th	1	Dec. 1, 1823	May 27, 1824	178			...do	Henry Clay, of Kentucky.
	2	Dec. 6, 1824	Mar. 3, 1825	88			...do.	
19th	S	Mar. 4, 1825	Mar, 9, 1825	6			...do.	
	1	Dec. 5, 1825	May 22, 1826	169			Nathaniel Macon, of North Carolina	John W. Taylor, of New York.
	2	Dec. 4, 1826	Mar. 3, 1827	90			...do.	
20th	1	Dec. 3, 1827	May 26, 1828	175			Samuel Smith, of Maryland	Andrew Stevenson, of Virginia.
	2	Dec. 1, 1828	Mar. 3, 1829	93	Dec. 24–Dec. 29, 1828	Dec. 24–Dec. 29, 1828	...do.	
21st	S	Mar. 4, 1829	Mar. 17, 1829	14			...do.	
	1	Dec. 7, 1829	May 31, 1830	176			...do	Do.
	2	Dec. 6, 1830	Mar. 3, 1831	88			...do.	
22d	1	Dec. 5, 1831	July 16, 1832	225			Littleton Waller Tazewell, of Virginia	Do.
	2	Dec. 3, 1832	Mar. 2, 1833	91			Hugh Lawson White, of Tennessee.	
23d	1	Dec. 2, 1833	June 30, 1834	211			Hugh Lawson White, of Tennessee; George Poindexter, of Mississippi.	Do.[6]
	2	Dec. 1, 1834	Mar. 3, 1835	93			John Tyler, of Virginia	John Bell, of Tennessee.[6]
24th	1	Dec. 7, 1835	July 4, 1836	211			William R. King, of Alabama	James K. Polk, of Tennessee.
	2	Dec. 5, 1836	Mar. 3, 1837	89			...do.	
25th	S	Mar. 4, 1837	Mar. 10, 1837	7			...do.	
	1–E	Sept. 4, 1837	Oct. 16, 1837	43			...do	Do.
	2	Dec. 4, 1837	July 9, 1838	218			...do.	
	3	Dec. 3, 1838	Mar. 3, 1839	91			...do.	
26th	1	Dec. 2, 1839	July 21, 1840	233			...do	Robert M.T. Hunter, of Virginia.
	2	Dec. 7, 1840	Mar. 3, 1841	87			...do.	
27th	S	Mar. 4, 1841	Mar. 15, 1841	12			William R. King, of Alabama; Samuel L. Southard, of New Jersey.	

SESSIONS OF CONGRESS, 1st–112th CONGRESSES, 1789–2011—CONTINUED

[Closing date for this table was September 15, 2011.]

MEETING DATES OF CONGRESS: Pursuant to a resolution of the Confederation Congress in 1788, the Constitution went into effect on March 4, 1789. From then until the 20th amendment took effect in January 1934, the term of each Congress began on March 4th of each odd-numbered year; however, Article I, section 4, of the Constitution provided that ''The Congress shall assemble at least once in every Year, and such Meeting shall be on the first Monday in December, unless they shall by law appoint a different day.'' The Congress therefore convened regularly on the first Monday in December until the 20th amendment became effective, which changed the beginning of Congress's term as well as its convening date to January 3rd. So prior to 1934, a new Congress typically would not convene for regular business until 13 months after being elected. One effect of this was that the last session of each Congress was a ''lame duck'' session. After the 20th amendment, the time from the election to the beginning of Congress's term as well as when it convened was reduced to two months. Recognizing that the need might exist for Congress to meet at times other than the regularly scheduled convening date, Article II, section 3 of the Constitution provides that the President ''may, on extraordinary occasions, convene both Houses, or either of them''; hence these sessions occur only if convened by Presidential proclamation. Except as noted, these are separately numbered sessions of a Congress, and are marked by an E in the session column of the table. Until the 20th amendment was adopted, there were also times when special sessions of the Senate were convened, principally for confirming Cabinet and other executive nominations, and occasionally for the ratification of treaties or other executive business. These Senate sessions were also called by Presidential proclamation (typically by the outgoing President, although on occasion by incumbents as well) and are marked by an S in the session column. MEETING PLACES OF CONGRESS: Congress met for the first and second sessions of the First Congress (1789 and 1790) in New York City. From the third session of the First Congress through the first session of the Sixth Congress (1790 to 1800), Philadelphia was the meeting place. Congress has convened in Washington since the second session of the Sixth Congress (1800).

Congress	Session	Convening Date	Adjournment Date	Length in days [1]	Recesses [2]		President pro tempore of the Senate [3]	Speaker of the House of Representatives
					Senate	House of Representatives		
	1–E	May 31, 1841	Sept. 13, 1841	106			Samuel L. Southard, of New Jersey	John White, of Kentucky.
	2	Dec. 6, 1841	Aug. 31, 1842	269			Willie P. Mangum, of North Carolina.	
	3	Dec. 5, 1842	Mar. 3, 1843	89			...do.	
28th	1	Dec. 4, 1843	June 17, 1844	196			...do	John W. Jones, of Virginia.
	2	Dec. 2, 1844	Mar. 3, 1845	92			...do.	
29th	S	Mar. 4, 1845	Mar. 20, 1845	17				
	1	Dec. 1, 1845	Aug. 10, 1846	253			Ambrose H. Sevier; David R. Atchison, of Missouri.	John W. Davis, of Indiana.
	2	Dec. 7, 1846	Mar. 3, 1847	87			David R. Atchison, of Missouri.	
30th	1	Dec. 6, 1847	Aug. 14, 1848	254			...do	Robert C. Winthrop, of Massachusetts.
	2	Dec. 4, 1848	Mar. 3, 1849	90			...do.	
31st	S	Mar. 5, 1849	Mar. 23, 1849	19			...do.	
	1	Dec. 3, 1849	Sept. 30, 1850	302			William R. King, of Alabama	Howell Cobb, of Georgia.
	2	Dec. 2, 1850	Mar. 3, 1851	92			...do.	
32d	S	Mar. 4, 1851	Mar. 13, 1851	10				
	1	Dec. 1, 1851	Aug. 31, 1852	275			...do	Linn Boyd, of Kentucky.
	2	Dec. 6, 1852	Mar. 3, 1853	88			David R. Atchison, of Missouri.	
33d	S	Mar. 4, 1853	Apr. 11, 1853	39			...do.	
	1	Dec. 5, 1853	Aug. 7, 1854	246			...do	Do.
	2	Dec. 4, 1854	Mar. 3, 1855	90			Lewis Cass, of Michigan; Jesse D. Bright, of Indiana.	
34th	1	Dec. 3, 1855	Aug. 18, 1856	260			Charles E. Stuart, of Michigan; Jesse D. Bright, of Indiana.	Nathaniel P. Banks, of Massachusetts.
	2–E	Aug. 21, 1856	Aug. 30, 1856	10			Jesse D. Bright, of Indiana.	
	3	Dec. 1, 1856	Mar. 3, 1857	93			James M. Mason, of Virginia.	
35th	S	Mar. 4, 1857	Mar. 14, 1857	11			James M. Mason, of Virginia; Thomas J. Rusk, of Texas.	
	1	Dec. 7, 1857	June 14, 1858	189	Dec. 23, 1857–Jan. 4, 1858	Dec. 23, 1857–Jan. 4, 1858	Benjamin Fitzpatrick, of Alabama	James L. Orr, of South Carolina.

	S	June 15, 1858	June 16, 1858	2				
	2	Dec. 6, 1858	Mar. 3, 1859	88	Dec. 23, 1858–Jan. 4, 1859	Dec. 23, 1858–Jan. 4, 1859	...do.	
36th	S	Mar. 4, 1859	Mar. 10, 1859	7			...do.	
	1	Dec. 5, 1859	June 25, 1860	202			Benjamin Fitzpatrick, of Alabama; Jesse D. Bright, of Indiana.	William Pennington, of New Jersey.
	S	June 26, 1860	June 28, 1860	3			Benjamin Fitzpatrick, of Alabama.	
	2	Dec. 3, 1860	Mar. 3, 1861	93			Solomon Foot, of Vermont.	
37th	S	Mar. 4, 1861	Mar. 28, 1861	25			...do.	
	1–E	July 4, 1861	Aug. 6, 1861	34			...do	Galusha A. Grow, of Pennsylvania.
	2	Dec. 2, 1861	July 17, 1862	228			...do.	
	3	Dec. 1, 1862	Mar. 3, 1863	93	Dec. 23, 1862–Jan. 5, 1863	Dec. 23, 1862–Jan. 5, 1863	...do.	
38th	S	Mar. 4, 1863	Mar. 14, 1863	11			...do.	
	1	Dec. 7, 1863	July 4, 1864	209	Dec. 23, 1863–Jan. 5, 1864	Dec. 23, 1863–Jan. 5, 1864	Solomon Foot, of Vermont; Daniel Clark, of New Hampshire.	Schuyler Colfax, of Indiana.
	2	Dec. 5, 1864	Mar. 3, 1865	89	Dec. 22, 1864–Jan. 5, 1865	Dec. 22, 1864–Jan. 5, 1865	Daniel Clark, of New Hampshire.	
39th	S	Mar. 4, 1865	Mar. 11, 1865	8			Lafayette S. Foster, of Connecticut.	
	1	Dec. 4, 1865	July 28, 1866	237	Dec. 6–Dec. 11, 1865 Dec. 21, 1865–Jan. 5, 1866	Dec. 6–Dec. 11, 1865 Dec. 21, 1865–Jan. 5, 1866	...do	Do.
	2	Dec. 3, 1866	Mar. 3, 1867	91	Dec. 20, 1866–Jan. 3, 1867	Dec. 20, 1866–Jan. 3, 1867	Benjamin F. Wade, of Ohio.	
40th	1	Mar. 4, 1867	Dec. 1, 1867	273	Mar. 30–July 3, 1867 July 20–Nov. 21, 1867	Mar. 30–July 3, 1867 July 20–Nov. 21, 1867	...do	Do.[7]
	S	Apr. 1, 1867	Apr. 20, 1867	20				
	2	Dec. 2, 1867	Nov. 10, 1868	345	Dec. 20, 1867–Jan. 6, 1868 July 27–Sept. 21, 1868 Sept. 21–Oct. 16, 1868 Oct. 16–Nov. 10, 1868	Dec. 20, 1867–Jan. 6, 1868 July 27–Sept. 21, 1868 Sept. 21–Oct. 16, 1868 Oct. 16–Nov. 10, 1868		
	3	Dec. 7, 1868	Mar. 3, 1869	87	Dec. 21, 1868–Jan. 5, 1869	Dec. 21, 1868–Jan. 5, 1869	...do	Theodore M. Pomeroy, of New York.[7]
41st	1	Mar. 4, 1869	Apr. 10, 1869	38			Henry B. Anthony, of Rhode Island	James G. Blaine, of Maine.
	S	Apr. 12, 1869	Apr. 22, 1869	11				
	2	Dec. 6, 1869	July 15, 1870	222	Dec. 22, 1869–Jan. 10, 1870	Dec. 22, 1869–Jan. 10, 1870	...do.	
	3	Dec. 5, 1870	Mar. 3, 1871	89	Dec. 23, 1870–Jan. 4, 1871	Dec. 22, 1870–Jan. 4, 1871	...do.	
42d	1	Mar. 4, 1871	Apr. 20, 1871	48			...do	Do.
	S	May 10, 1871	May 27, 1871	18			...do.	
	2	Dec. 4, 1871	June 10, 1872	190	Dec. 21, 1871–Jan. 8, 1872	Dec. 21, 1871–Jan. 8, 1872	...do.	
	3	Dec. 2, 1872	Mar. 3, 1873	92	Dec. 20, 1872–Jan. 6, 1873	Dec. 20, 1872–Jan. 6, 1873	...do.	
43d	S	Mar. 4, 1873	Mar. 26, 1873	23			Matthew H. Carpenter, of Wisconsin.	
	1	Dec. 1, 1873	June 23, 1874	204	Dec. 19, 1873–Jan. 5, 1874	Dec. 19, 1873–Jan. 5, 1874	...do	Do.
	2	Dec. 7, 1874	Mar. 3, 1875	87	Dec. 23, 1874–Jan. 5, 1875	Dec. 23, 1874–Jan. 5, 1875	Matthew H. Carpenter, of Wisconsin; Henry B. Anthony, of Rhode Island.	
44th	S	Mar. 5, 1875	Mar. 24, 1875	20			Thomas W. Ferry, of Michigan.	
	1	Dec. 6, 1875	Aug. 15, 1876	254	Dec. 20, 1875–Jan. 5, 1876	Dec. 21, 1875–Jan. 5, 1876	...do	Michael C. Kerr, of Indiana.[8]
	2	Dec. 4, 1876	Mar. 3, 1877	90			...do	Samuel J. Randall, of Pennsylvania.[8]
45th	S	Mar. 5, 1877	Mar. 17, 1877	13			...do.	
	1–E	Oct. 15, 1877	Dec. 3, 1877	50			...do	Do.
	2	Dec. 3, 1877	June 20, 1878	200	Dec. 15, 1877–Jan. 10, 1878	Dec. 15, 1877–Jan. 10, 1878	...do.	
	3	Dec. 2, 1878	Mar. 3, 1879	92	Dec. 20, 1878–Jan. 7, 1879	Dec. 20, 1878–Jan. 7, 1879	...do.	
46th	1–E	Mar. 18, 1879	July 1, 1879	106			Allen G. Thurman, of Ohio	Do.
	2	Dec. 1, 1879	June 16, 1880	199	Dec. 19, 1879–Jan. 6, 1880	Dec. 19, 1879–Jan. 6, 1880	...do.	
	3	Dec. 6, 1880	Mar. 3, 1881	88	Dec. 23, 1880–Jan. 5, 1881	Dec. 23, 1880–Jan. 5, 1881	...do.	
47th	S	Mar. 4, 1881	May. 20, 1881	78				
	S	Oct. 10, 1881	Oct. 29, 1881	20			Thomas F. Bayard, of Delaware; David Davis, of Illinois.	
	1	Dec. 5, 1881	Aug. 8, 1882	247	Dec. 22, 1881–Jan. 5, 1882	Dec. 22, 1881–Jan. 5, 1882	David Davis, of Illinois	J. Warren Keifer, of Ohio.

SESSIONS OF CONGRESS, 1st–112th CONGRESSES, 1789–2011—CONTINUED

[Closing date for this table was September 15, 2011.]

MEETING DATES OF CONGRESS: Pursuant to a resolution of the Confederation Congress in 1788, the Constitution went into effect on March 4, 1789. From then until the 20th amendment took effect in January 1934, the term of each Congress began on March 4th of each odd-numbered year; however, Article I, section 4, of the Constitution provided that ''The Congress shall assemble at least once in every Year, and such Meeting shall be on the first Monday in December, unless they shall by law appoint a different day.'' The Congress therefore convened regularly on the first Monday in December until the 20th amendment became effective, which changed the beginning of Congress's term as well as its convening date to January 3rd. So prior to 1934, a new Congress typically would not convene for regular business until 13 months after being elected. One effect of this was that the last session of each Congress was a ''lame duck'' session. After the 20th amendment, the time from the election to the beginning of Congress's term as well as when it convened was reduced to two months. Recognizing that the need might exist for Congress to meet at times other than the regularly scheduled convening date, Article II, section 3 of the Constitution provides that the President ''may, on extraordinary occasions, convene both Houses, or either of them''; hence these sessions occur only if convened by Presidential proclamation. Except as noted, these are separately numbered sessions of a Congress, and are marked by an E in the session column of the table. Until the 20th amendment was adopted, there were also times when special sessions of the Senate were convened, principally for confirming Cabinet and other executive nominations, and occasionally for the ratification of treaties or other executive business. These Senate sessions were also called by Presidential proclamation (typically by the outgoing President, although on occasion by incumbents as well) and are marked by an S in the session column. MEETING PLACES OF CONGRESS: Congress met for the first and second sessions of the First Congress (1789 and 1790) in New York City. From the third session of the First Congress through the first session of the Sixth Congress (1790 to 1800), Philadelphia was the meeting place. Congress has convened in Washington since the second session of the Sixth Congress (1800).

Congress	Session	Convening Date	Adjournment Date	Length in days [1]	Recesses [2]		President pro tempore of the Senate [3]	Speaker of the House of Representatives
					Senate	House of Representatives		
	2	Dec. 4, 1882	Mar. 3, 1883	90			George F. Edmunds, of Vermont.	J. Warren Keifer, of Ohio.
48th	1	Dec. 3, 1883	July 7, 1884	218	Dec. 24, 1883–Jan. 7, 1884	Dec. 24, 1883–Jan. 7, 1884	...do	John G. Carlisle, of Kentucky.
	2	Dec. 1, 1884	Mar. 3, 1885	93	Dec. 24, 1884–Jan. 5, 1885	Dec. 24, 1884–Jan. 5, 1885	...do.	
49th	S	Mar. 4, 1885	Apr. 2, 1885	30				
	1	Dec. 7, 1885	Aug. 5, 1886	242	Dec. 21, 1885–Jan. 5, 1886	Dec. 21, 1885–Jan. 5, 1886	John Sherman, of Ohio	Do.
	2	Dec. 6, 1886	Mar. 3, 1887	88	Dec. 22, 1886–Jan. 4, 1887	Dec. 22, 1886–Jan. 4, 1887	John J. Ingalls, of Kansas.	
50th	1	Dec. 5, 1887	Oct. 20, 1888	321	Dec. 22, 1887–Jan. 4, 1888	Dec. 22, 1887–Jan. 4, 1888	...do	Do.
	2	Dec. 3, 1888	Mar. 3, 1889	91	Dec. 21, 1888–Jan. 2, 1889	Dec. 21, 1888–Jan. 2, 1889	...do.	
51st	S	Mar. 4, 1889	Apr. 2, 1889	30			...do.	
	1	Dec. 2, 1889	Oct. 1, 1890	304	Dec. 21, 1889–Jan. 6, 1890	Dec. 21, 1889–Jan. 6, 1890	...do	Thomas B. Reed, of Maine.
	2	Dec. 1, 1890	Mar. 3, 1891	93			Charles F. Manderson, of Nebraska.	
52d	1	Dec. 7, 1891	Aug. 5, 1892	251			...do	Charles F. Crisp, of Georgia.
	2	Dec. 5, 1892	Mar. 3, 1893	89	Dec. 22, 1892–Jan. 4, 1893	Dec. 22, 1892–Jan. 4, 1893	...do.	
53d	S	Mar. 4, 1893	Apr. 15, 1893	43			Charles F. Manderson, of Nebraska; Isham G. Harris, of Tennessee.	
	1–E	Aug. 7, 1893	Nov. 3, 1893	89			Isham G. Harris, of Tennessee	Do.
	2	Dec. 4, 1893	Aug. 28, 1894	268		Dec. 21, 1893–Jan. 3, 1894	...do.	
	3	Dec. 3, 1894	Mar. 3, 1895	97		Dec. 23, 1894–Jan. 3, 1895	Matt W. Ransom, of North Carolina; Isham G. Harris, of Tennessee.	
54th	1	Dec. 2, 1895	June 11, 1896	193			William P. Frye, of Maine	Thomas B. Reed, of Maine.
	2	Dec. 7, 1896	Mar. 3, 1897	87	Dec. 22, 1896–Jan. 5, 1897	Dec. 22, 1896–Jan. 5, 1897	...do.	
55th	S	Mar. 4, 1897	Mar. 10, 1897	11			...do.	
	1–E	Mar. 15, 1897	July 24, 1897	131			...do	Do.
	2	Dec. 6, 1897	July 8, 1898	215	Dec. 18, 1897–Jan. 5, 1898	Dec. 18, 1897–Jan. 5, 1898	...do.	
	3	Dec. 5, 1898	Mar. 3, 1899	89	Dec. 21, 1898–Jan. 4, 1899	Dec. 21, 1898–Jan. 4, 1899	...do.	
56th	1	Dec. 4, 1899	June 7, 1900	186	Dec. 20, 1899–Jan. 3, 1900	Dec. 20, 1899–Jan. 3, 1900	...do	David B. Henderson, of Iowa.
	2	Dec. 3, 1900	Mar. 3, 1901	91	Dec. 20, 1900–Jan. 3, 1901	Dec. 21, 1900–Jan. 3, 1901	...do.	
57th	S	Mar. 4, 1901	Mar. 9, 1901	6			...do.	

	1	Dec. 2, 1901	July 1, 1902	212	Dec. 19, 1901–Jan. 6, 1902	Dec. 19, 1901–Jan. 6, 1902	...do	Do.
	2	Dec. 1, 1902	Mar. 3, 1903	93	Dec. 20, 1902–Jan. 5, 1903	Dec. 20, 1902–Jan. 5, 1903	...do.	
58th	S	Mar. 5, 1903	Mar. 19, 1903	15			...do.	
	1–E	Nov. 9, 1903	Dec. 7, 1903	29			...do	Joseph G. Cannon, of Illinois.
	2	Dec. 7, 1903	Apr. 28, 1904	144	Dec. 19, 1903–Jan. 4, 1904	Dec. 19, 1903–Jan. 4, 1904	...do.	
	3	Dec. 5, 1904	Mar. 3, 1905	89	Dec. 21, 1904–Jan. 4, 1905	Dec. 21, 1904–Jan. 4, 1905	...do.	
59th	S	Mar. 4, 1905	Mar. 18, 1905	15			...do.	
	1	Dec. 4, 1905	June 30, 1906	209	Dec. 21, 1905–Jan. 4, 1906	Dec. 21, 1905–Jan. 4, 1906	...do	Do.
	2	Dec. 3, 1906	Mar. 3, 1907	91	Dec. 20, 1906–Jan. 3, 1907	Dec. 20, 1906–Jan. 3, 1907	...do.	
60th	1	Dec. 2, 1907	May 30, 1908	181	Dec. 21, 1907–Jan. 6, 1908	Dec. 21, 1907–Jan. 6, 1908	...do	Do.
	2	Dec. 7, 1908	Mar. 3, 1909	87	Dec. 19, 1908–Jan. 4, 1909	Dec. 19, 1908–Jan. 4, 1909	...do.	
61st	S	Mar. 4, 1909	Mar. 6, 1909	3			...do.	
	1–E	Mar. 15, 1909	Aug. 5, 1909	144			...do	Do.
	2	Dec. 6, 1909	June 25, 1910	202	Dec. 21, 1909–Jan. 4, 1910	Dec. 21, 1909–Jan. 4, 1910	...do.	
	3	Dec. 5, 1910	Mar. 3, 1911	89	Dec. 21, 1910–Jan. 5, 1911	Dec. 21, 1910–Jan. 5, 1911	...do.	
62d	1–E	Apr. 4, 1911	Aug. 22, 1911	141			...do.[9]	Champ Clark, of Missouri.
	2	Dec. 4, 1911	Aug. 26, 1912	267	Dec. 21, 1911–Jan. 3, 1912	Dec. 21, 1911–Jan. 3, 1912	Charles Curtis, of Kansas; Augustus O. Bacon, of Georgia; Jacob H. Gallinger, of New Hampshire; Henry Cabot Lodge, of Massachusetts; Frank B. Brandegee, of Connecticut.	
	3	Dec. 2, 1912	Mar. 3, 1913	92	Dec. 19, 1912–Jan. 2, 1913	Dec. 19, 1912–Jan. 2, 1913	Augustus O. Bacon, of Georgia; Jacob H. Gallinger, of New Hampshire.	
63d	S	Mar. 4, 1913	Mar. 17, 1913	14			James P. Clarke, of Arkansas.	
	1–E	Apr. 7, 1913	Dec. 1, 1913	239			...do	Do.
	2	Dec. 1, 1913	Oct. 24, 1914	328	Dec. 23, 1913–Jan. 12, 1914	Dec. 23, 1913–Jan. 12, 1914	...do.	
	3	Dec. 7, 1914	Mar. 3, 1915	87	Dec. 23–Dec. 28, 1914	Dec. 23–Dec. 28, 1914	...do.	
64th	1	Dec. 6, 1915	Sept. 8, 1916	278	Dec. 17, 1915–Jan. 4, 1916	Dec. 17, 1915–Jan. 4, 1916	...do[10]	Do.
	2	Dec. 4, 1916	Mar. 3, 1917	90	Dec. 22, 1916–Jan. 2, 1917	Dec. 22, 1916–Jan. 2, 1917	Willard Saulsbury, of Delaware[10]	
65th	S	Mar. 5, 1917	Mar. 16, 1917	12			...do.	
	1–E	Apr. 2, 1917	Oct. 6, 1917	188			...do	Do.
	2	Dec. 3, 1917	Nov. 21, 1918	354	Dec. 18, 1917–Jan. 3, 1918	Dec. 18, 1917–Jan. 3, 1918	...do.	
	3	Dec. 2, 1918	Mar. 3, 1919	92			...do.	
66th	1–E	May 19, 1919	Nov. 19, 1919	185	July 1–July 8, 1919	July 1–July 8, 1919	Albert B. Cummins, of Iowa	Frederick H. Gillett, of Massachusetts.
	2	Dec. 1, 1919	June 5, 1920	188	Dec. 20, 1919–Jan. 5, 1920	Dec. 20, 1919–Jan. 5, 1920	...do.	
	3	Dec. 6, 1920	Mar. 3, 1921	88			...do.	
67th	S	Mar. 4, 1921	Mar. 15, 1921	12			...do.	
	1–E	Apr. 11, 1921	Nov. 23, 1921	227	Aug. 24–Sept. 21, 1921	Aug. 24–Sept. 21, 1921	...do	Do.
	2	Dec. 5, 1921	Sept. 22, 1922	292	Dec. 22, 1921–Jan. 3, 1922	Dec. 22, 1921–Jan. 3, 1922	...do.	
	3–E	Nov. 20, 1922	Dec. 4, 1922	15			...do.	
	4	Dec. 4, 1922	Mar. 3, 1923	90			...do.	
68th	1	Dec. 3, 1923	June 7, 1924	188	Dec. 20, 1923–Jan. 3, 1924	Dec. 20, 1923–Jan. 3, 1924	...do	Do.
	2	Dec. 1, 1924	Mar. 3, 1925	93	Dec. 20–Dec. 29, 1924	Dec. 20–Dec. 29, 1924	...do.	
69th	S	Mar. 4, 1925	Mar. 18, 1925	15			Albert B. Cummins, of Iowa; George H. Moses, of New Hampshire.	
	1	Dec. 7, 1925	July 3, 1926	209	Dec. 22, 1925–Jan. 4, 1926	Dec. 22, 1925–Jan. 4, 1926	...do	Nicholas Longworth, of Ohio.
	2	Dec. 6, 1926	Mar. 4, 1927	88	Dec. 22, 1926–Jan. 3, 1927	Dec. 22, 1926–Jan. 3, 1927	...do.	
70th	1	Dec. 5, 1927	May 29, 1928	177	Dec. 21, 1927–Jan. 4, 1928	Dec. 21, 1927–Jan. 4, 1928	...do	Do.
	2	Dec. 3, 1928	Mar. 3, 1929	91	Dec. 22, 1928–Jan. 3, 1929	Dec. 22, 1928–Jan. 3, 1929	...do.	
71st	S	Mar. 4, 1929	Mar. 5, 1929	2			...do.	
	1–E	Apr. 15, 1929	Nov. 22, 1929	222	June 19–Aug. 19, 1929	June 19–Sept. 23, 1929	...do	Do.
	2	Dec. 2, 1929	July 3, 1930	214	Dec. 21, 1929–Jan. 6, 1930	Dec. 21, 1929–Jan. 6, 1930	...do.	
	S	July 7, 1930	July 21, 1930	15			...do.	

SESSIONS OF CONGRESS, 1st–112th CONGRESSES, 1789–2011—CONTINUED

[Closing date for this table was September 15, 2011.]

MEETING DATES OF CONGRESS: Pursuant to a resolution of the Confederation Congress in 1788, the Constitution went into effect on March 4, 1789. From then until the 20th amendment took effect in January 1934, the term of each Congress began on March 4th of each odd-numbered year; however, Article I, section 4, of the Constitution provided that ''The Congress shall assemble at least once in every Year, and such Meeting shall be on the first Monday in December, unless they shall by law appoint a different day.'' The Congress therefore convened regularly on the first Monday in December until the 20th amendment became effective, which changed the beginning of Congress's term as well as its convening date to January 3rd. So prior to 1934, a new Congress typically would not convene for regular business until 13 months after being elected. One effect of this was that the last session of each Congress was a ''lame duck'' session. After the 20th amendment, the time from the election to the beginning of Congress's term as well as when it convened was reduced to two months. Recognizing that the need might exist for Congress to meet at times other than the regularly scheduled convening date, Article II, section 3 of the Constitution provides that the President ''may, on extraordinary occasions, convene both Houses, or either of them''; hence these sessions occur only if convened by Presidential proclamation. Except as noted, these are separately numbered sessions of a Congress, and are marked by an E in the session column of the table. Until the 20th amendment was adopted, there were also times when special sessions of the Senate were convened, principally for confirming Cabinet and other executive nominations, and occasionally for the ratification of treaties or other executive business. These Senate sessions were also called by Presidential proclamation (typically by the outgoing President, although on occasion by incumbents as well) and are marked by an S in the session column. MEETING PLACES OF CONGRESS: Congress met for the first and second sessions of the First Congress (1789 and 1790) in New York City. From the third session of the First Congress through the first session of the Sixth Congress (1790 to 1800), Philadelphia was the meeting place. Congress has convened in Washington since the second session of the Sixth Congress (1800).

Congress	Session	Convening Date	Adjournment Date	Length in days [1]	Recesses [2]		President pro tempore of the Senate [3]	Speaker of the House of Representatives
					Senate	House of Representatives		
	3	Dec. 1, 1930	Mar. 3, 1931	93	Dec. 20, 1930–Jan. 5, 1931	Dec. 20, 1930–Jan. 5, 1931	George H. Moses, of New Hampshire	Nicholas Longworth, of Ohio.
72d	1	Dec. 7, 1931	July 16, 1932	223	Dec. 22, 1931–Jan. 4, 1932	Dec. 22, 1931–Jan. 4, 1932	...do	John N. Garner, of Texas.
	2	Dec. 5, 1932	Mar. 3, 1933	89			...do.	
73d	S	Mar. 4, 1933	Mar. 6, 1933	3			...do.	
	1–E	Mar. 9, 1933	June 15, 1933	99			Key Pittman, of Nevada	Henry T. Rainey, of Illinois.
	2	Jan. 3, 1934	June 18, 1934	167			...do.	
74th	1	Jan. 3, 1935	Aug. 26, 1935	236			...do	Joseph W. Byrns, of Tennessee.[11]
	2	Jan. 3, 1936	June 20, 1936	170	June 8–June 15, 1936	June 8–June 15, 1936	...do	William B. Bankhead, of Alabama.[11]
75th	1	Jan. 5, 1937	Aug. 21, 1937	229			...do	Do.
	2–E	Nov. 15, 1937	Dec. 21, 1937	37			...do.	
	3	Jan. 3, 1938	June 16, 1938	165			...do.	
76th	1	Jan. 3, 1939	Aug. 5, 1939	215			...do	Do.[12]
	2–E	Sept. 21, 1939	Nov. 3, 1939	44			...do.	
	3	Jan. 3, 1940	Jan. 3, 1941	366	July 11–July 22, 1940	July 11–July 22, 1940	Key Pittman, of Nevada;[13] William H. King, of Utah.[13]	Sam Rayburn, of Texas.[12]
77th	1	Jan. 3, 1941	Jan. 2, 1942	365			Pat Harrison, of Mississippi;[14] Carter Glass, of Virginia.[14]	Do.
	2	Jan. 5, 1942	Dec. 16, 1942	346			Carter Glass, of Virginia.	
78th	1	Jan. 6, 1943	Dec. 21, 1943	350	July 8–Sept. 14, 1943	July 8–Sept. 14, 1943	...do	Do.
	2	Jan. 10, 1944	Dec. 19, 1944	345	Apr. 1–Apr. 12, 1944 June 23–Aug. 1, 1944 Sept. 21–Nov. 14, 1944	Apr. 1–Apr. 12, 1944 June 23–Aug. 1, 1944 Sept. 21–Nov. 14, 1944	...do.	
79th	1	Jan. 3, 1945	Dec. 21, 1945	353	Aug. 1–Sept. 5, 1945	July 21–Sept. 5, 1945	Kenneth McKellar, of Tennessee	Do.
	2	Jan. 14, 1946	Aug. 2, 1946	201		Apr. 18–Apr. 30, 1946	...do.	
80th	[15] 1	Jan. 3, 1947	Dec. 19, 1947	351	July 27–Nov. 17, 1947	July 27–Nov. 17, 1947	Arthur H. Vandenberg, of Michigan	Joseph W. Martin, Jr., of Massachusetts.
	[15] 2	Jan. 6, 1948	Dec. 31, 1948	361	June 20–July 26, 1948 Aug. 7–Dec. 31, 1948	June 20–July 26, 1948 Aug. 7–Dec. 31, 1948	...do.	

81st	1	Jan. 3, 1949	Oct. 19, 1949	290			Kenneth McKellar, of Tennessee	Sam Rayburn, of Texas.
	2	Jan. 3, 1950	Jan. 2, 1951	365	Sept. 23–Nov. 27, 1950[p]	Apr. 6–Apr. 18, 1950 Sept. 23–Nov. 27, 1950	...do.	
82d	1	Jan. 3, 1951	Oct. 20, 1951	291		Mar. 22–Apr. 2, 1951 Aug. 23–Sept. 12, 1951	...do	Do.
	2	Jan. 8, 1952	July 7, 1952	182		Apr. 10–Apr. 22, 1952	...do.	
83d	1	Jan. 3, 1953	Aug. 3, 1953	213		Apr. 2–Apr. 13, 1953	Styles Bridges, of New Hampshire	Joseph W. Martin, Jr., of Massachusetts.
	2	Jan. 6, 1954	Dec. 2, 1954	331	Aug. 20–Nov. 8, 1954 Nov. 18–Nov. 29, 1954	Apr. 15–Apr. 22, 1954 Adjourned sine die Aug. 20, 1954	...do.	
84th	1	Jan. 5, 1955	Aug. 2, 1955	210	Apr. 4–Apr. 13, 1955	Apr. 4–Apr. 13, 1955	Walter F. George, of Georgia	Sam Rayburn, of Texas.
	2	Jan. 3, 1956	July 27, 1956	207	Mar. 29–Apr. 9, 1956	Mar. 29–Apr. 9, 1956	...do.	
85th	1	Jan. 3, 1957	Aug. 30, 1957	239	Apr. 18–Apr. 29, 1957	Apr. 18–Apr. 29, 1957	Carl Hayden, of Arizona	Do.
	2	Jan. 7, 1958	Aug. 24, 1958	230	Apr. 3–Apr. 14, 1958	Apr. 3–Apr. 14, 1958	...do.	
86th	1	Jan. 7, 1959	Sept. 15, 1959	252	Mar. 26–Apr. 7, 1959	Mar. 26–Apr. 7, 1959	...do	Do.
	2	Jan. 6, 1960	Sept. 1, 1960	240	Apr. 14–Apr. 18, 1960 May 27–May 31, 1960 July 3–Aug. 8, 1960	Apr. 14–Apr. 18, 1960 May 27–May 31, 1960 July 3–Aug. 15, 1960	...do.	
87th	1	Jan. 3, 1961	Sept. 27, 1961	268		Mar. 30–Apr. 10, 1961	...do	Do.[16]
	2	Jan. 10, 1962	Oct. 13, 1962	277		Apr. 19–Apr. 30, 1962	...do	John W. McCormack, of Massachusetts.[16]
88th	1	Jan. 9, 1963	Dec. 30, 1963	356		Apr. 11–Apr. 22, 1963	...do	Do.
	2	Jan. 7, 1964	Oct. 3, 1964	270	July 10–July 20, 1964 Aug. 21–Aug. 31, 1964	Mar. 26–Apr. 6, 1964 July 2–July 20, 1964 Aug. 21–Aug. 31, 1964	...do.	
89th	1	Jan. 4, 1965	Oct. 23, 1965	293			...do	Do.
	2	Jan. 10, 1966	Oct. 22, 1966	286	Apr. 7–Apr. 13, 1966 June 30–July 11, 1966	Apr. 7–Apr. 18, 1966 June 30–July 11, 1966	...do.	
90th	1	Jan. 10, 1967	Dec. 15, 1967	340	Mar. 23–Apr. 3, 1967 June 29–July 10, 1967 Aug. 31–Sept. 11, 1967 Nov. 22–Nov. 27, 1967	Mar. 23–Apr. 3, 1967 June 29–July 10, 1967 Aug. 31–Sept. 11, 1967 Nov. 22–Nov. 27, 1967	...do	Do.
	2	Jan. 15, 1968	Oct. 14, 1968	274	Apr. 11–Apr. 17, 1968 May 29–June 3, 1968 June 3–July 8, 1968 Aug. 2–Sept. 4, 1968	Apr. 11–Apr. 22, 1968 May 29–June 3, 1968 June 3–July 8, 1968 Aug. 2–Sept. 4, 1968	...do.	
91st	1	Jan. 3, 1969	Dec. 23, 1969	355	Feb. 7–Feb. 17, 1969 Apr. 3–Apr. 14, 1969 July 2–July 7, 1969 Aug. 13–Sept. 3, 1969 Nov. 26–Dec. 1, 1969	Feb. 7–Feb. 17, 1969 Apr. 3–Apr. 14, 1969 May 28–June 2, 1969 July 2–July 7, 1969 Aug. 13–Sept. 3, 1969 Nov. 6–Nov. 12, 1969 Nov. 26–Dec. 1, 1969	Richard B. Russell, of Georgia	Do.
	2	Jan. 19, 1970	Jan. 2, 1971	349	Feb. 10–Feb. 16, 1970 Mar. 26–Mar. 31, 1970 Sept. 2–Sept. 8, 1970 Oct. 14–Nov. 16, 1970 Nov. 25–Nov. 30, 1970 Dec. 22–Dec. 28, 1970	Feb. 10–Feb. 16, 1970 Mar. 26–Mar. 31, 1970 May 27–June 1, 1970 July 1–July 6, 1970 Aug. 14–Sept. 9, 1970 Oct. 14–Nov. 16, 1970 Nov. 25–Nov. 30, 1970 Dec. 22–Dec. 29, 1970	...do.	

SESSIONS OF CONGRESS, 1st–112th CONGRESSES, 1789–2011—CONTINUED

[Closing date for this table was September 15, 2011.]

MEETING DATES OF CONGRESS: Pursuant to a resolution of the Confederation Congress in 1788, the Constitution went into effect on March 4, 1789. From then until the 20th amendment took effect in January 1934, the term of each Congress began on March 4th of each odd-numbered year; however, Article I, section 4, of the Constitution provided that "The Congress shall assemble at least once in every Year, and such Meeting shall be on the first Monday in December, unless they shall by law appoint a different day." The Congress therefore convened regularly on the first Monday in December until the 20th amendment became effective, which changed the beginning of Congress's term as well as its convening date to January 3rd. So prior to 1934, a new Congress typically would not convene for regular business until 13 months after being elected. One effect of this was that the last session of each Congress was a "lame duck" session. After the 20th amendment, the time from the election to the beginning of Congress's term as well as when it convened was reduced to two months. Recognizing that the need might exist for Congress to meet at times other than the regularly scheduled convening date, Article II, section 3 of the Constitution provides that the President "may, on extraordinary occasions, convene both Houses, or either of them"; hence these sessions occur only if convened by Presidential proclamation. Except as noted, these are separately numbered sessions of a Congress, and are marked by an E in the session column of the table. Until the 20th amendment was adopted, there were also times when special sessions of the Senate were convened, principally for confirming Cabinet and other executive nominations, and occasionally for the ratification of treaties or other executive business. These Senate sessions were also called by Presidential proclamation (typically by the outgoing President, although on occasion by incumbents as well) and are marked by an S in the session column. MEETING PLACES OF CONGRESS: Congress met for the first and second sessions of the First Congress (1789 and 1790) in New York City. From the third session of the First Congress through the first session of the Sixth Congress (1790 to 1800), Philadelphia was the meeting place. Congress has convened in Washington since the second session of the Sixth Congress (1800).

Congress	Session	Convening Date	Adjournment Date	Length in days [1]	Recesses [2]		President pro tempore of the Senate [3]	Speaker of the House of Representatives
					Senate	House of Representatives		
92d	1	Jan. 21, 1971	Dec. 17, 1971 ...	331	Feb. 11–Feb. 17, 1971 .... Apr. 7–Apr. 14, 1971 May 26–June 1, 1971 June 30–July 6, 1971 Aug. 6–Sept. 8, 1971 Oct. 21–Oct. 26, 1971 Nov. 24–Nov. 29, 1971	Feb. 10–Feb. 17, 1971 .... Apr. 7–Apr. 19, 1971 May 27–June 1, 1971 July 1–July 6, 1971 Aug. 6–Sept. 8, 1971 Oct. 7–Oct. 12, 1971 Oct. 21–Oct. 26, 1971 Nov. 19–Nov. 29, 1971	Richard B. Russell, of Georgia;[17] Allen J. Ellender, of Louisiana.[17]	Carl B. Albert, of Oklahoma.
	2	Jan. 18, 1972	Oct. 18, 1972 ...	275	Feb. 9–Feb. 14, 1972 .... Mar. 30–Apr. 4, 1972 May 25–May 30, 1972 June 30–July 17, 1972 Aug. 18–Sept. 5, 1972	Feb. 9–Feb. 16, 1972 .... Mar. 29–Apr. 10, 1972 May 24–May 30, 1972 June 30–July 17, 1972 Aug. 18–Sept. 5, 1972	Allen J. Ellender, of Louisiana;[18] James O. Eastland, of Mississippi.[18]	
93d	1	Jan. 3, 1973	Dec. 22, 1973 ...	354	Feb. 8–Feb. 15, 1973 .... Apr. 18–Apr. 30, 1973 May 23–May 29, 1973 June 30–July 9, 1973 Aug. 3–Sept. 5, 1973 Oct. 18–Oct. 23, 1973 Nov. 21–Nov. 26, 1973	Feb. 8–Feb. 19, 1973 .... Apr. 19–Apr. 30, 1973 May 24–May 29, 1973 June 30–July 10, 1973 Aug. 3–Sept. 5, 1973 Oct. 4–Oct. 9, 1973 Oct. 18–Oct. 23, 1973 Nov. 15–Nov. 26, 1973	James O. Eastland, of Mississippi	Do.
	2	Jan. 21, 1974	Dec. 20, 1974 ...	334	Feb. 8–Feb. 18, 1974 .... Mar. 13–Mar. 19, 1974 Apr. 11–Apr. 22, 1974 May 23–May 28, 1974 Aug. 22–Sept. 4, 1974 Oct. 17–Nov. 18, 1974 Nov. 26–Dec. 2, 1974	Feb. 7–Feb. 13, 1974 .... Apr. 11–Apr. 22, 1974 May 23–May 28, 1974 Aug. 22–Sept. 11, 1974 Oct. 17–Nov. 18, 1974 Nov. 26–Dec. 3, 1974	...do.	

94th ...	1	Jan. 14, 1975	Dec. 19, 1975 ...	340	Mar. 26–Apr. 7, 1975 .... May 22–June 2, 1975 June 27–July 7, 1975 Aug. 1–Sept. 3, 1975 Oct. 9–Oct. 20, 1975 Oct. 23–Oct. 28, 1975 Nov. 20–Dec. 1, 1975	Mar. 26–Apr. 7, 1975 .... May 22–June 2, 1975 June 26–July 8, 1975 Aug. 1–Sept. 3, 1975 Oct. 9–Oct. 20, 1975 Oct. 23–Oct. 28, 1975 Nov. 20–Dec. 1, 1975	...do	Do.
	2	Jan. 19, 1976	Oct. 1, 1976	257	Feb. 6–Feb. 16, 1976 .... Apr. 14–Apr. 26, 1976 May 28–June 2, 1976 July 2–July 19, 1976 Aug. 10–Aug. 23, 1976 Sept. 1–Sept. 7, 1976	Feb. 11–Feb. 16, 1976 .... Apr. 14–Apr. 26, 1976 May 27–June 1, 1976 July 2–July 19, 1976 Aug. 10–Aug. 23, 1976 Sept. 2–Sept. 8, 1976	...do.	
95th ...	1	Jan. 4, 1977	Dec. 15, 1977 ...	346	Feb. 11–Feb. 21, 1977 .... Apr. 7–Apr. 18, 1977 May 27–June 6, 1977 July 1–July 11, 1977 Aug. 6–Sept. 7, 1977	Feb. 9–Feb. 16, 1977 .... Apr. 6–Apr. 18, 1977 May 26–June 1, 1977 June 30–July 11, 1977 Aug. 5–Sept. 7, 1977 Oct. 6–Oct. 11, 1977	...do	Thomas P. O'Neill, Jr., of Massachusetts.
	2	Jan. 19, 1978	Oct. 15, 1978 ...	270	Feb. 10–Feb. 20, 1978 .... Mar. 23–Apr. 3, 1978 May 26–June 5, 1978 June 29–July 10, 1978 Aug. 25–Sept. 6, 1978	Feb. 9–Feb. 14, 1978 .... Mar. 22–Apr. 3, 1978 May 25–May 31, 1978 June 29–July 10, 1978 Aug. 17–Sept. 6, 1978	...do.	
96th ...	1	Jan. 15, 1979	Jan. 3, 1980	354	Feb. 9–Feb. 19, 1979 .... Apr. 10–Apr. 23, 1979 May 24–June 4, 1979 June 27–July 9, 1979 Aug. 3–Sept. 5, 1979 Nov. 20–Nov. 26, 1979 Adjourned sine die, Dec. 20, 1979	Feb. 8–Feb. 13, 1979 .... Apr. 10–Apr. 23, 1979 May 24–May 30, 1979 June 29–July 9, 1979 Aug. 2–Sept. 5, 1979 Nov. 20–Nov. 26, 1979	Warren G. Magnuson, of Washington ...	Do.
	2	Jan. 3, 1980	Dec. 16, 1980 ...	349	Apr. 3–Apr. 15, 1980 .... May 22–May 28, 1980 July 2–July 21, 1980 Aug. 6–Aug. 18, 1980 Aug. 27–Sept. 3, 1980 Oct. 1–Nov. 12, 1980 Nov. 25–Dec. 1, 1980	Feb. 13–Feb. 19, 1980 .... Apr. 2–Apr. 15, 1980 May 22–May 28, 1980 July 2–July 21, 1980 Aug. 1–Aug. 18, 1980 Aug. 28–Sept. 3, 1980 Oct. 2–Nov. 12, 1980 Nov. 21–Dec. 1, 1980	Warren G. Magnuson, of Washington; Milton Young, of North Dakota;[19] Warren G. Magnuson, of Washington.[19]	
97th ...	1	Jan. 5, 1981	Dec. 16, 1981 ...	347	Feb. 6–Feb. 16, 1981 .... Apr. 10–Apr. 27, 1981 June 25–July 8, 1981 Aug. 3–Sept. 9, 1981 Oct. 7–Oct. 14, 1981 Nov. 24–Nov. 30, 1981	Feb. 6–Feb. 17, 1981 .... Apr. 10–Apr. 27, 1981 June 26–July 8, 1981 Aug. 4–Sept. 9, 1981 Oct. 7–Oct. 13, 1981 Nov. 23–Nov. 30, 1981	Strom Thurmond, of South Carolina	Do.
	2	Jan. 25, 1982	Dec. 23, 1982 ...	333	Feb. 11–Feb. 22, 1982 .... Apr. 1–Apr. 13, 1982 May 27–June 8, 1982 July 1–July 12, 1982 Aug. 20–Sept. 8, 1982 Oct. 1–Nov. 29, 1982	Feb. 10–Feb. 22, 1982 .... Apr. 6–Apr. 20, 1982 May 27–June 2, 1982 July 1–July 12, 1982 Aug. 20–Sept. 8, 1982 Oct. 1–Nov. 29, 1982	...do	

SESSIONS OF CONGRESS, 1st–112th CONGRESSES, 1789–2011—CONTINUED

[Closing date for this table was September 15, 2011.]

MEETING DATES OF CONGRESS: Pursuant to a resolution of the Confederation Congress in 1788, the Constitution went into effect on March 4, 1789. From then until the 20th amendment took effect in January 1934, the term of each Congress began on March 4th of each odd-numbered year; however, Article I, section 4, of the Constitution provided that ''The Congress shall assemble at least once in every Year, and such Meeting shall be on the first Monday in December, unless they shall by law appoint a different day.'' The Congress therefore convened regularly on the first Monday in December until the 20th amendment became effective, which changed the beginning of Congress's term as well as its convening date to January 3rd. So prior to 1934, a new Congress typically would not convene for regular business until 13 months after being elected. One effect of this was that the last session of each Congress was a ''lame duck'' session. After the 20th amendment, the time from the election to the beginning of Congress's term as well as when it convened was reduced to two months. Recognizing that the need might exist for Congress to meet at times other than the regularly scheduled convening date, Article II, section 3 of the Constitution provides that the President ''may, on extraordinary occasions, convene both Houses, or either of them''; hence these sessions occur only if convened by Presidential proclamation. Except as noted, these are separately numbered sessions of a Congress, and are marked by an E in the session column of the table. Until the 20th amendment was adopted, there were also times when special sessions of the Senate were convened, principally for confirming Cabinet and other executive nominations, and occasionally for the ratification of treaties or other executive business. These Senate sessions were also called by Presidential proclamation (typically by the outgoing President, although on occasion by incumbents as well) and are marked by an S in the session column. MEETING PLACES OF CONGRESS: Congress met for the first and second sessions of the First Congress (1789 and 1790) in New York City. From the third session of the First Congress through the first session of the Sixth Congress (1790 to 1800), Philadelphia was the meeting place. Congress has convened in Washington since the second session of the Sixth Congress (1800).

Congress	Session	Convening Date	Adjournment Date	Length in days [1]	Recesses [2]		President pro tempore of the Senate [3]	Speaker of the House of Representatives
					Senate	House of Representatives		
98th ...	1	Jan. 3, 1983	Nov. 18, 1983 ..	320	Jan. 3–Jan. 25, 1983 .... Feb. 3–Feb. 14, 1983 Mar. 24–Apr. 5, 1983 May 26–June 6, 1983 June 29–July 11, 1983 Aug. 4–Sept. 12, 1983 Oct. 7–Oct. 17, 1983	Jan. 6–Jan. 25, 1983 .... Feb. 17–Feb. 22, 1983 Mar. 24–Apr. 5, 1983 May 26–June 1, 1983 June 30–July 11, 1983 Aug. 4–Sept. 12, 1983 Oct. 6–Oct. 17, 1983	Strom Thurmond, of South Carolina	Thomas P. O'Neill, Jr., of Massachusetts.
	2	Jan. 23, 1984	Oct. 12, 1984 ...	264	Feb. 9–Feb. 20, 1984 .... Apr. 12–Apr. 24, 1984 May 24–May 31, 1984 June 29–July 23, 1984 Aug. 10–Sept. 5, 1984	Feb. 9–Feb. 21, 1984 .... Apr. 12–Apr. 24, 1984 May 24–May 30, 1984 June 29–July 23, 1984 Aug. 10–Sept. 5, 1984	...do.	
99th ...	1	Jan. 3, 1985	Dec. 20, 1985 ...	352	Jan. 7–Jan. 21, 1985 .... Feb. 7–Feb. 18, 1985 Apr. 4–Apr. 15, 1985 May 9–May 14, 1985 May 24–June 3, 1985 June 27–July 8, 1985 Aug. 1–Sept. 9, 1985 Nov. 23–Dec. 2, 1985	Jan. 3–Jan. 21, 1985 .... Feb. 7–Feb. 19, 1985 Mar. 7–Mar. 19, 1985 Apr. 4–Apr. 15, 1985 May 23–June 3, 1985 June 27–July 8, 1985 Aug. 1–Sept. 4, 1985 Nov. 21–Dec. 2, 1985	...do	Do.
	2	Jan. 21, 1986	Oct. 18, 1986 ...	278	Feb. 7–Feb. 17, 1986 .... Mar. 27–Apr. 8, 1986 May 21–June 2, 1986 June 26–July 7, 1986 Aug. 15–Sept. 8, 1986	Feb. 6–Feb. 18, 1986 .... Mar. 25–Apr. 8, 1986 May 22–June 3, 1986 June 26–July 14, 1986 Aug. 16–Sept. 8, 1986	...do.	

100th	1	Jan. 6, 1987	Dec. 22, 1987	351	Jan. 6–Jan. 12, 1987 Feb. 5–Feb. 16, 1987 Apr. 10–Apr. 21, 1987 May 21–May 27, 1987 July 1–July 7, 1987 Aug. 7–Sept. 9, 1987 Nov. 20–Nov. 30, 1987	Jan. 8–Jan. 20, 1987 Feb. 11–Feb. 18, 1987 Apr. 9–Apr. 21, 1987 May 21–May 27, 1987 July 1–July 7, 1987 July 15–July 20, 1987 Aug. 7–Sept. 9, 1987 Nov. 10–Nov. 16, 1987 Nov. 20–Nov. 30, 1987	John C. Stennis, of Mississippi	James C. Wright, Jr., of Texas.
	2	Jan. 25, 1988	Oct. 22, 1988	272	Feb. 4–Feb. 15, 1988 Mar. 4– Mar. 14, 1988 Mar. 31–Apr. 11, 1988 Apr. 29–May 9, 1988 May 27–June 6, 1988 June 29–July 6, 1988 July 14–July 25, 1988 Aug. 11–Sept. 7, 1988	Feb. 9–Feb. 16, 1988 Mar. 31–Apr. 11, 1988 May 26–June 1, 1988 June 30–July 7, 1988 July 14–July 26, 1988 Aug. 11–Sept. 7,1988	...do.	
101st	1	Jan. 3, 1989	Nov. 22, 1989	324	Jan. 4–Jan. 20, 1989 Jan. 20–Jan. 25, 1989 Feb. 9–Feb. 21, 1989 Mar. 17–Apr. 4, 1989 Apr. 19–May 1, 1989 May 18–May 31, 1989 June 23–July 11, 1989 Aug. 4–Sept. 6, 1989	Jan. 4–Jan. 19, 1989 Feb. 9–Feb. 21, 1989 Mar. 23–Apr. 3, 1989 Apr. 18–Apr. 25, 1989 May 25–May 31, 1989 June 29–July 10, 1989 Aug. 5–Sept. 6, 1989	Robert C. Byrd, of West Virginia	James C. Wright, Jr., of Texas;[20] Thomas S. Foley, of Washington.[20]
	2	Jan. 23, 1990	Oct. 28, 1990	260	Feb. 8–Feb. 20, 1990 Mar. 9–Mar. 20, 1990 Apr. 5–Apr. 18, 1990 May 24–June 5, 1990 June 28–July 10, 1990 Aug. 4–Sept. 10, 1990	Feb. 7–Feb. 20, 1990 Apr. 4–Apr. 18, 1990 May 25–June 5, 1990 June 28–July 10, 1990 Aug. 4–Sept. 5, 1990	...do.	
102d	1	Jan. 3, 1991	Jan. 3, 1992	366	Feb. 7–Feb. 19, 1991 Mar. 22–Apr. 9, 1991 Apr. 25–May 6, 1991 May 24–June 3, 1991 June 28–July 8, 1991 Aug. 2–Sept. 10, 1991 Nov. 27, 1991–Jan. 3, 1992	Feb. 6–Feb. 19, 1991 Mar. 22–Apr. 9, 1991 May 23–May 29, 1991 June 27–July 9, 1991 Aug. 2–Sept. 11, 1991 Nov. 27, 1991–Jan. 3, 1992	...do	Thomas S. Foley, of Washington.
	2	Jan. 3, 1992	Oct. 9, 1992	281	Jan. 3–Jan. 21, 1992 Feb. 7–Feb. 18, 1992 P Apr. 10–Apr. 28, 1992 May 21–June 1, 1992 July 2–July 20, 1992 Aug. 12–Sept. 8, 1992	Jan. 3–Jan. 22, 1992 Apr. 10–Apr. 28, 1992 May 21–May 26, 1992 July 2–July 7, 1992 July 9–July 21, 1992 Aug. 12–Sept. 9, 1992	...do.	

SESSIONS OF CONGRESS, 1st–112th CONGRESSES, 1789–2011—CONTINUED

[Closing date for this table was September 15, 2011.]

MEETING DATES OF CONGRESS: Pursuant to a resolution of the Confederation Congress in 1788, the Constitution went into effect on March 4, 1789. From then until the 20th amendment took effect in January 1934, the term of each Congress began on March 4th of each odd-numbered year; however, Article I, section 4, of the Constitution provided that ''The Congress shall assemble at least once in every Year, and such Meeting shall be on the first Monday in December, unless they shall by law appoint a different day.'' The Congress therefore convened regularly on the first Monday in December until the 20th amendment became effective, which changed the beginning of Congress's term as well as its convening date to January 3rd. So prior to 1934, a new Congress typically would not convene for regular business until 13 months after being elected. One effect of this was that the last session of each Congress was a ''lame duck'' session. After the 20th amendment, the time from the election to the beginning of Congress's term as well as when it convened was reduced to two months. Recognizing that the need might exist for Congress to meet at times other than the regularly scheduled convening date, Article II, section 3 of the Constitution provides that the President ''may, on extraordinary occasions, convene both Houses, or either of them''; hence these sessions occur only if convened by Presidential proclamation. Except as noted, these are separately numbered sessions of a Congress, and are marked by an E in the session column of the table. Until the 20th amendment was adopted, there were also times when special sessions of the Senate were convened, principally for confirming Cabinet and other executive nominations, and occasionally for the ratification of treaties or other executive business. These Senate sessions were also called by Presidential proclamation (typically by the outgoing President, although on occasion by incumbents as well) and are marked by an S in the session column. MEETING PLACES OF CONGRESS: Congress met for the first and second sessions of the First Congress (1789 and 1790) in New York City. From the third session of the First Congress through the first session of the Sixth Congress (1790 to 1800), Philadelphia was the meeting place. Congress has convened in Washington since the second session of the Sixth Congress (1800).

Congress	Session	Convening Date	Adjournment Date	Length in days[1]	Recesses[2]		President pro tempore of the Senate[3]	Speaker of the House of Representatives
					Senate	House of Representatives		
103d ...	1	Jan. 5, 1993	Nov. 26, 1993 ..	326	Jan. 7–Jan. 20, 1993 .... Feb. 4–Feb. 16, 1993 Feb. 18–Feb. 24, 1993 p Apr. 7–Apr. 19, 1993 May 28–June 7, 1993 July 1–July 13, 1993 Aug. 7–Sept. 7, 1993 Oct. 7–Oct. 13, 1993 Nov. 11–Nov. 16, 1993	Jan. 6–Jan. 20, 1993 .... Jan. 27–Feb. 2, 1993 Feb. 4–Feb. 16, 1993 Apr. 7–Apr. 19, 1993 May 27–June 8, 1993 July 1–July 13, 1993 Aug. 6–Sept. 8, 1993 Sept. 15–Sept. 21, 1993 Oct. 7–Oct. 12, 1993 Nov. 10–Nov. 15, 1993	Robert C. Byrd, of West Virginia	Thomas S. Foley, of Washington.
	2	Jan. 25, 1994	Dec. 1, 1994	311	Feb. 11–Feb. 22, 1994 .... Mar. 26–Apr. 11, 1994 May 25–June 7, 1994 July 1–July 11, 1994 Aug. 25–Sept. 12, 1994 Oct. 8–Nov. 30, 1994	Jan. 26–Feb. 1, 1994 .... Feb. 11–Feb. 22, 1994 Mar. 24–Apr. 12, 1994 May 26–June 8, 1994 June 30–July 12, 1994 Aug. 26–Sept. 12, 1994 Oct. 8–Nov. 29, 1994	...do.	
104th .	1	Jan. 4, 1995	Jan. 3, 1996	365	Feb. 16–Feb. 22, 1995 .... Apr. 7–Apr. 24, 1995 May 26–June 5, 1995 June 30–July 10, 1995 Aug. 11–Sept. 5, 1995 Sept. 29–Oct. 10, 1995 Nov. 20–Nov. 27, 1995	Feb. 16–Feb. 21, 1995 .... Mar. 16–Mar. 21, 1995 Apr. 7–May 1, 1995 May 3–May 9, 1995 May 25–June 6, 1995 June 30–July 10, 1995 Aug. 4–Sept. 6, 1995 Sept. 29–Oct. 6, 1995 Nov. 20–Nov. 28, 1995	Strom Thurmond, of South Carolina	Newt Gingrich, of Georgia.

	2	Jan. 3, 1996	Oct. 4, 1996	276	Jan. 10–Jan. 22, 1996 Feb. 1–Feb. 6, 1996 P Feb. 7–Feb. 20, 1996 P Feb. 29–Mar. 5, 1996 P Mar. 29–Apr. 15, 1996 May 24–June 3, 1996 June 28–July 8, 1996 Aug. 2–Sept. 3, 1996	Jan. 9–Jan. 22, 1996 Feb. 1–Feb. 27, 1996 P Mar. 29–Apr. 15, 1996 May 23–May 29, 1996 June 28–July 8, 1996 Aug. 2–Sept. 4, 1996	...do.	
105th.	1	Jan. 7, 1997	Nov. 13, 1997	311	Jan. 9–Jan. 21, 1997 Feb. 13–Feb. 24, 1997 Mar. 21–Apr. 7, 1997 May 23–June 2, 1997 P June 27–July 7, 1997 July 31–Sept. 2, 1997 Oct. 9–Oct. 20, 1997	Jan. 9–Jan. 20, 1997 Jan. 21–Feb. 4, 1997 Feb. 13–Feb. 25, 1997 Mar. 21–Apr. 8, 1997 June 26–July 8, 1997 Aug. 1–Sept. 3, 1997 Oct. 9–Oct. 21, 1997	...do	Do.
	2	Jan. 27, 1998	Dec. 19, 1998	327	Feb. 13–Feb. 23, 1998 Apr. 3–Apr. 20, 1998 May 22–June 1, 1998 June 26–July 6, 1998 July 31–Aug. 31, 1998 Adjourned sine die, Oct. 21, 1998.	Jan. 28–Feb. 3, 1998 Feb. 5–Feb. 11, 1998 Feb. 12–Feb. 24, 1998 Apr. 1–Apr. 21, 1998 May 22–June 3, 1998 June 25–July 14, 1998 Aug. 7–Sept. 9, 1998 Oct. 21–Dec. 17, 1998	...do.	
106th.	1	Jan. 6, 1999	Nov. 22, 1999	321	Feb. 12–Feb. 22, 1999 Mar. 25–Apr. 12, 1999 May 27–June 7, 1999 July 1–July 12, 1999 Aug. 5–Sept. 8, 1999	Jan. 6–Jan. 19, 1999 Jan. 19–Feb. 2, 1999 Feb. 12–Feb. 23, 1999 Mar. 25–Apr. 12, 1999 May 27–June 7, 1999 July 1–July 12, 1999 Aug. 6–Sept. 8, 1999	...do	J. Dennis Hastert, of Illinois.
	2	Jan. 24, 2000	Dec. 15, 2000	326	Feb. 10–Feb. 22, 2000 Mar. 9–Mar. 20, 2000 Apr. 13–Apr. 25, 2000 May 25–June 6, 2000 June 30–July 10, 2000 July 27–Sept. 5, 2000 Nov. 2–Nov. 14, 2000 Nov. 14–Dec. 5, 2000	Feb. 16–Feb. 29, 2000 Apr. 13–May 2, 2000 May 25–June 6, 2000 June 30–July 10, 2000 July 27–Sept. 6, 2000 Nov. 3–Nov. 13, 2000 Nov. 14–Dec. 4, 2000	...do.	
107th.	1	Jan. 3, 2001	Dec. 20, 2001	352	Jan. 8–Jan. 20, 2001 Feb. 15–Feb. 26, 2001 Apr. 6–Apr. 23, 2001 May 26–June 5, 2001 June 29–July 9, 2001 Aug. 3–Sept. 4, 2001 Oct. 18–Oct. 23, 2001 Nov. 16–Nov. 27, 2001	Jan. 6–Jan. 20, 2001 Jan. 20–Jan 30, 2001 Jan. 31–Feb. 6, 2001 Feb. 14–Feb. 26, 2001 Apr. 4–Apr. 24, 2001 May 26–June 5, 2001 June 28–July 10, 2001 Aug. 2–Sept. 5, 2001 Oct. 17–Oct. 23, 2001 Nov. 19–Nov. 27, 2001	Robert C. Byrd, of West Virginia;[21] Strom Thurmond, of South Carolina;[21] Robert C. Byrd, of West Virginia.[21]	Do.

SESSIONS OF CONGRESS, 1st–112th CONGRESSES, 1789–2011—CONTINUED

[Closing date for this table was September 15, 2011.]

MEETING DATES OF CONGRESS: Pursuant to a resolution of the Confederation Congress in 1788, the Constitution went into effect on March 4, 1789. From then until the 20th amendment took effect in January 1934, the term of each Congress began on March 4th of each odd-numbered year; however, Article I, section 4, of the Constitution provided that ''The Congress shall assemble at least once in every Year, and such Meeting shall be on the first Monday in December, unless they shall by law appoint a different day.'' The Congress therefore convened regularly on the first Monday in December until the 20th amendment became effective, which changed the beginning of Congress's term as well as its convening date to January 3rd. So prior to 1934, a new Congress typically would not convene for regular business until 13 months after being elected. One effect of this was that the last session of each Congress was a ''lame duck'' session. After the 20th amendment, the time from the election to the beginning of Congress's term as well as when it convened was reduced to two months. Recognizing that the need might exist for Congress to meet at times other than the regularly scheduled convening date, Article II, section 3 of the Constitution provides that the President ''may, on extraordinary occasions, convene both Houses, or either of them''; hence these sessions occur only if convened by Presidential proclamation. Except as noted, these are separately numbered sessions of a Congress, and are marked by an E in the session column of the table. Until the 20th amendment was adopted, there were also times when special sessions of the Senate were convened, principally for confirming Cabinet and other executive nominations, and occasionally for the ratification of treaties or other executive business. These Senate sessions were also called by Presidential proclamation (typically by the outgoing President, although on occasion by incumbents as well) and are marked by an S in the session column. MEETING PLACES OF CONGRESS: Congress met for the first and second sessions of the First Congress (1789 and 1790) in New York City. From the third session of the First Congress through the first session of the Sixth Congress (1790 to 1800), Philadelphia was the meeting place. Congress has convened in Washington since the second session of the Sixth Congress (1800).

Congress	Session	Convening Date	Adjournment Date	Length in days [1]	Recesses [2]		President pro tempore of the Senate [3]	Speaker of the House of Representatives
					Senate	House of Representatives		
	2	Jan. 23, 2002	Nov. 22, 2002	304	Jan. 29–Feb. 4, 2002 Feb. 15–Feb. 25, 2002 Mar. 22–Apr. 8, 2002 May 23–June 3, 2002 June 28–July 8, 2002 Aug. 1–Sept. 3, 2002 Oct. 17–Nov. 12, 2002 P	Jan. 29–Feb. 4, 2002 Feb. 14–Feb. 26, 2002 Mar. 20–Apr. 9, 2002 May 24–June 4, 2002 June 28–July 8, 2002 July 27–Sept. 4, 2002	Robert C. Byrd, of West Virginia.	
108th	1	Jan. 7, 2003	Dec. 9, 2003	337	Feb. 14–Feb. 24, 2003 Apr. 11–Apr. 28, 2003 May 23–June 2, 2003 June 27–July 7, 2003 Aug. 1–Sept 2, 2003 Oct. 3–Oct. 14, 2003 Nov. 25–Dec. 9, 2003	Jan. 8–Jan. 27, 2003 Feb. 13–Feb. 25, 2003 Apr. 12–Apr. 29, 2003 May 23–June 2, 2003 June 27–July 7, 2003 July 29–Sept. 3, 2003 Nov. 25–Dec. 8, 2003	Ted Stevens, of Alaska	J. Dennis Hastert, of Illinois.
	2	Jan. 20, 2004	Dec. 8, 2004	324	Feb. 12–Feb. 23, 2004 Mar. 12–Mar. 22, 2004 Apr. 8–Apr. 19, 2004 May 21–June 1, 2004 June 9–June 14, 2004 June 25–July 6, 2004 July 22–Sept. 7, 2004 Oct. 11–Nov. 16, 2004 Nov. 24–Dec. 7, 2004	Feb. 11–Feb. 24, 2004 Apr. 2–Apr. 20, 2004 May 20–June 1, 2004 June 9–June 14, 2004 June 25–July 6, 2004 July 22–Sept. 7, 2004 Oct. 9–Nov. 16, 2004 Nov. 24–Dec. 6, 2004	...do.	

109th	1	Jan. 4, 2005	Dec. 22, 2005	353	Jan. 6–Jan. 20, 2005 Jan. 26–Jan. 31, 2005 Feb. 18–Feb. 28, 2005 Mar. 20–Apr. 4, 2005 Apr. 29–May 9, 2005 May 26–June 6, 2005 July 1–July 11, 2005 July 29–Sept. 1, 2005 Sept. 1–Sept. 6, 2005 Oct. 7–Oct. 17, 2005 Nov. 18–Dec. 12, 2005	Jan. 6–Jan. 20, 2005 Jan. 20–Jan. 25, 2005 Jan. 26–Feb. 1, 2005 Feb. 2–Feb. 8, 2005 Feb. 17–Mar. 1, 2005 Mar. 21–Apr. 5, 2005 May 26–June 7, 2005 July 1–July 11, 2005 July 29–Sept. 2, 2005 Oct. 7–Oct. 17, 2005 Nov. 18–Dec. 6, 2005	...do	Do.
	2	Jan. 3, 2006	Dec. 9, 2006	341	Jan. 3–Jan. 18, 2006 Feb. 17–Feb. 27, 2006 Mar. 16–Mar. 27, 2006 Apr. 7–Apr. 24, 2006 May 26–June 5, 2006 June 29–July 10, 2006 Aug. 4–Sept. 5, 2006 Sept. 30–Nov. 9, 2006 Nov. 16–Dec. 4, 2006	Jan. 3–Jan. 31, 2006 Feb. 1–Feb. 7, 2006 Feb. 8–Feb. 14, 2006 Feb. 16–Feb. 28, 2006 Mar. 16–Mar. 28, 2006 Apr. 6–Apr. 25, 2006 May 25–June 6, 2006 June 29–July 10, 2006 Aug. 2–Sept. 6, 2006 Sept. 30–Nov. 9, 2006 Nov. 15–Dec. 5, 2006	...do.	
110th	1	Jan. 4, 2007	Dec. 31, 2007	362	Feb. 17–Feb. 26, 2007 Mar. 29–Apr. 10, 2007 May 25–June 4, 2007 June 29–July 9, 2007 Aug. 3–Sept. 4, 2007 Oct. 5–Oct. 15, 2007 Nov. 16–Dec. 3, 2007 P Dec. 19–Dec. 31, 2007 P	Jan. 24–Jan. 29, 2007 Feb. 16–Feb. 27, 2007 Mar. 30–Apr. 16, 2007 May 24–June 5, 2007 June 28–July 10, 2007 Aug. 4–Sept. 4, 2007 Nov. 15–Dec. 4, 2007	Robert C. Byrd, of West Virginia	Nancy Pelosi, of California.
	2	Jan. 3, 2008	Jan. 3, 2009	367	Jan. 3–Jan. 22, 2008 P Feb. 14–Feb. 26, 2008 P Mar. 13–Mar. 31, 2008 P May 22–June 2, 2008 P June 27–July 7, 2008 Aug. 1–Sept. 8, 2008 P Oct. 2–Nov. 17, 2008 P Nov. 20–Dec. 8, 2008 P Dec. 11–Jan. 2, 2009 P	Jan. 3–Jan. 15, 2008 Mar. 14–Mar. 31, 2008 May 22–June 3, 2008 June 26–July 8, 2008 Aug. 1–Sept. 8, 2008 Oct. 3–Nov. 19, 2008 Nov. 20–Dec. 9, 2008 Dec. 10–Jan. 3, 2009	...do	
111th	1	Jan. 6, 2009	Dec. 24, 2009	353	Feb. 13–Feb. 23, 2009 P Apr. 2–Apr. 20, 2009 May 21–June 1, 2009 June 25–July 6, 2009 Aug. 7–Sept. 8, 2009 P Oct. 8–Oct. 13, 2009 P Nov. 10–Nov. 16, 2009 Nov. 21–Nov. 30, 2009	Feb. 13–Feb. 23, 2009 Apr. 2–Apr. 21, 2009 May 21–June 2, 2009 June 26–July 7, 2009 July 31–Sept. 8, 2009 Nov. 6–Nov. 16, 2009 Nov. 19–Dec. 1, 2009	...do	Do.

SESSIONS OF CONGRESS, 1st–112th CONGRESSES, 1789–2011—CONTINUED

[Closing date for this table was September 15, 2011.]

MEETING DATES OF CONGRESS: Pursuant to a resolution of the Confederation Congress in 1788, the Constitution went into effect on March 4, 1789. From then until the 20th amendment took effect in January 1934, the term of each Congress began on March 4th of each odd-numbered year; however, Article I, section 4, of the Constitution provided that ''The Congress shall assemble at least once in every Year, and such Meeting shall be on the first Monday in December, unless they shall by law appoint a different day.'' The Congress therefore convened regularly on the first Monday in December until the 20th amendment became effective, which changed the beginning of Congress's term as well as its convening date to January 3rd. So prior to 1934, a new Congress typically would not convene for regular business until 13 months after being elected. One effect of this was that the last session of each Congress was a ''lame duck'' session. After the 20th amendment, the time from the election to the beginning of Congress's term as well as when it convened was reduced to two months. Recognizing that the need might exist for Congress to meet at times other than the regularly scheduled convening date, Article II, section 3 of the Constitution provides that the President ''may, on extraordinary occasions, convene both Houses, or either of them''; hence these sessions occur only if convened by Presidential proclamation. Except as noted, these are separately numbered sessions of a Congress, and are marked by an E in the session column of the table. Until the 20th amendment was adopted, there were also times when special sessions of the Senate were convened, principally for confirming Cabinet and other executive nominations, and occasionally for the ratification of treaties or other executive business. These Senate sessions were also called by Presidential proclamation (typically by the outgoing President, although on occasion by incumbents as well) and are marked by an S in the session column. MEETING PLACES OF CONGRESS: Congress met for the first and second sessions of the First Congress (1789 and 1790) in New York City. From the third session of the First Congress through the first session of the Sixth Congress (1790 to 1800), Philadelphia was the meeting place. Congress has convened in Washington since the second session of the Sixth Congress (1800).

Congress	Session	Convening Date	Adjournment Date	Length in days [1]	Recesses [2]		President pro tempore of the Senate [3]	Speaker of the House of Representatives
					Senate	House of Representatives		
	2	Jan. 5, 2010	Dec. 22, 2010	352	Jan. 5–Jan. 20, 2010 P Feb. 11–Feb. 23, 2010 Mar. 26–Apr. 12, 2010 May 28–June 7, 2010 June 30–July 12, 2010 Aug. 5–Aug. 12, 2010 Aug. 12–Sept. 13, 2010 Sept. 29–Nov. 15, 2010 P Nov. 19–Nov. 29, 2010	Jan. 5–Jan. 12, 2010 Feb. 9–Feb. 22, 2010 Mar. 25–Apr. 13, 2010 May 28–Une 8, 2010 July 1–July 13, 2010 July 30–Aug. 9, 2010 Aug. 10–Sept. 14, 2010 Sept. 29–Nov. 15, 2010 Nov. 18–Nov. 29, 2010	Robert C. Byrd, of West Virginia; [22] Daniel K. Inouye, of Hawaii.[22]	
112th.	1	Jan. 5, 2011	....	....	Jan. 5 –Jan. 25, 2011 Feb. 17–Feb. 28, 2011 Mar. 17–Mar. 28, 2011 Apr. 14–May 2, 2011 May 26–June 6, 2011 P Aug 2–Sept. 6, 2011 P	Jan. 26–Feb. 8, 2011 Feb. 18–Feb. 28, 2011 Mar. 17–Mar. 29, 2011 Apr. 15–May 2, 2011 May 13–May 23, 2011 June 24–July 5, 2011 P Aug. 1–Sept. 6, 2011 P	Daniel K. Inouye, of Hawaii	John A. Boehner, of Ohio.

[1] For the purposes of this table, a session's ''length in days'' is defined as the total number of calendar days from the convening date to the adjournment date, inclusive. It does not mean the actual number of days that Congress met during that session.

[2] For the purposes of this table, a ''recess'' is defined as a break in House or Senate proceedings of three or more days, excluding Sundays. According to Article I, section 5 of the U.S. Constitution, neither house may adjourn for more than three days without the consent of the other. On occasion, both chambers have held one or more pro forma sessions because of this constitutional obligation or for other purposes. Treated here as recesses, usually no business is conducted during these time periods. On this table, beginning in the 1990s, such pro forma sessions are indicated with a P.

[3] The election and role of the President pro tempore has evolved considerably over the Senate's history. ''*Pro tempore* is Latin for 'for the time being'; thus, the post was conceived as a temporary presiding officer. In the eighteenth and nineteenth centuries, the Senate frequently elected several Presidents pro tempore during a single session. Since Vice Presidents presided routinely, the Senate thought it necessary to choose a President pro tempore only for the limited periods when the Vice President might be ill or otherwise absent.'' Since no provision was in place (until the 25th amendment was adopted in 1967) for replacing the Vice President if he died or resigned from office, or if he assumed the Presidency, the President pro tempore would continue under such circumstances to fill the duties of the chair until the next Vice President was elected. Since Mar. 12, 1890, however, Presidents pro tempore have served until ''the Senate otherwise ordered.'' Since 1949, while still elected, the position has gone to the most senior member of the majority party (see footnote 19 for a minority party exception). To gain a more complete understanding of this position, see Robert C. Byrd's *The Senate 1789–1989: Addresses on the History of the United States Senate*, vol. 2, ch. 6 ''The President Pro Tempore,'' pp. 167–183, from which the quotes in this footnote are taken. Also, a complete listing of the dates of election of the Presidents pro tempore is in vol. 4 of the Byrd series (*The Senate 1789–1989: Historical Statistics, 1789–1992*), table 6–2, pp. 647–653.

[4] Henry Clay resigned as Speaker on Jan. 19, 1814. He was succeeded by Langdon Cheves who was elected on that same day.

[5] Henry Clay resigned as Speaker on Oct. 28, 1820, after the sine die adjournment of the first session of the 16th Congress. He was succeeded by John W. Taylor who was elected at the beginning of the second session.

[6] Andrew Stevenson resigned as Speaker on June 2, 1834. He was succeeded by John Bell who was elected on that same day.

[7] Speaker Schuyler Colfax resigned as Speaker on the last day of the 40th Congress, Mar. 3, 1869, in preparation for becoming Vice President of the United States on the following day. Theodore M. Pomeroy was elected Speaker on Mar. 3, and served for only that one day.

[8] Speaker Michael C. Kerr died on Aug. 19, 1876, after the sine die adjournment of the first session of the 44th Congress. Samuel J. Randall was elected Speaker at the beginning of the second session.

[9] William P. Frye resigned as President pro tempore on Apr. 27, 1911.

[10] President pro tempore James P. Clarke died on Oct. 1, 1916, after the sine die adjournment of the first session of the 64th Congress. Willard Saulsbury was elected President pro tempore during the second session.

[11] Speaker Joseph W. Byrns died on June 4, 1936. He was succeeded by William B. Bankhead who was elected Speaker on that same day.

[12] Speaker William B. Bankhead died on Sept. 15, 1940. He was succeeded by Sam Rayburn who was elected Speaker on that same day.

[13] President pro tempore Key Pittman died on Nov. 10, 1940. He was succeeded by William H. King who was elected President pro tempore on Nov. 19, 1940.

[14] President pro tempore Pat Harrison died on June 22, 1941. He was succeeded by Carter Glass who was elected President pro tempore on July 10, 1941.

[15] President Harry S. Truman called the Congress into extraordinary session twice, both times during the 80th Congress. Each time Congress had essentially wrapped up its business for the year, but for technical reasons had not adjourned sine die, so in each case the extraordinary session is considered an extension of the regularly numbered session rather than a separately numbered one. The dates of these extraordinary sessions were Nov. 17 to Dec. 19, 1947, and July 26 to Aug. 7, 1948.

[16] Speaker Sam Rayburn died on Nov. 16, 1961, after the sine die adjournment of the first session of the 87th Congress. John W. McCormack was elected Speaker at the beginning of the second session.

[17] President pro tempore Richard B. Russell died on Jan. 21, 1971. He was succeeded by Allen J. Ellender who was elected to that position on Jan. 22, 1971.

[18] President pro tempore Allen J. Ellender died on July 27, 1972. He was succeeded by James O. Eastland who was elected President pro tempore on July 28, 1972.

[19] Milton Young was elected President pro tempore for one day, Dec. 5, 1980, which was at the end of his 36-year career in the Senate. He was a Republican, which was the minority party at that time. Warren G. Magnuson resumed the position of President pro tempore on Dec. 6, 1980.

[20] James C. Wright, Jr., resigned as Speaker on June 6, 1989. He was succeeded by Thomas S. Foley who was elected on that same day.

[21] The 2000 election resulted in an even split in the Senate between Republicans and Democrats. From the date the 107th Congress convened on Jan. 3, 2001, until Inauguration Day on Jan. 20, 2001, Vice President Albert Gore's tie breaking vote resulted in a Democratic majority, hence Robert C. Byrd served as President pro tempore during this brief period. When Vice President Richard B. Cheney took office on Jan. 20, the Republicans became the majority party, and Strom Thurmond was elected President pro tempore. On June 6, 2001, Republican Senator James Jeffords became an Independent, creating a Democratic majority, and Robert C. Byrd was elected President pro tempore on that day.

[22] President pro tempore Robert C. Byrd died on June 28, 2010. He was succeeded by Daniel K. Inouye who was elected President pro tempore on that same day.

CEREMONIAL MEETINGS OF CONGRESS

The following ceremonial meetings of Congress occurred on the following dates, at the designated locations, and for the reasons indicated. Please note that Congress was not in session on these occasions.

-July 16, 1987, 100th Congress, Philadelphia, Pennsylvania, Independence Hall and Congress Hall—In honor of the bicentennial of the Constitution, and in commemoration of the Great Compromise of the Constitutional Convention which was agreed to on July 16, 1787.

-September 6, 2002, 107th Congress, New York City, New York, Federal Hall—In remembrance of the victims and heroes of September 11, 2001, and in recognition of the courage and spirit of the City of New York.

JOINT SESSIONS AND MEETINGS, ADDRESSES TO THE SENATE OR THE HOUSE, AND INAUGURATIONS

1st–112th CONGRESSES, 1789–2011[1]

The parliamentary difference between a joint session and a joint meeting has evolved over time. In recent years the distinctions have become clearer: a joint session is more formal, and occurs upon the adoption of a concurrent resolution; a joint meeting occurs when each body adopts a unanimous consent agreement to recess to meet with the other legislative body. Joint sessions typically are held to hear an address from the President of the United States or to count electoral votes. Joint meetings typically are held to hear an address from a foreign dignitary or visitors other than the President.

The Speaker of the House of Representatives usually presides over joint sessions and joint meetings; however, the President of the Senate does preside over joint sessions where the electoral votes are counted, as required by the Constitution.

In the earliest years of the Republic, 1789 and 1790, when the national legislature met in New York City, joint gatherings were held in the Senate Chamber in Federal Hall. In Philadelphia, when the legislature met in Congress Hall, such meetings were held in the Senate Chamber, 1790–1793, and in the Hall of the House of Representatives, 1794–1799. Once the Congress moved to the Capitol in Washington in 1800, the Senate Chamber again was used for joint gatherings through 1805. Since 1809, with few exceptions, joint sessions and joint meetings have occurred in the Hall of the House.

Presidential messages on the state of the Union were originally known as the "Annual Message," but since the 80th Congress, in 1947, have been called the "State of the Union Address." After President John Adams's Annual Message on November 22, 1800, these addresses were read by clerks to the individual bodies until President Woodrow Wilson resumed the practice of delivering them to joint sessions on December 2, 1913.

In some instances more than one joint gathering has occurred on the same day. For example, on January 6, 1941, Congress met in joint session to count electoral votes for President and Vice President, and then met again in joint session to receive President Franklin Delano Roosevelt's Annual Message.

Whereas in more recent decades, foreign dignitaries invited to speak before Congress have typically done so at joint meetings, in earlier times (and with several notable exceptions), such visitors were received by the Senate and the House separately, or by one or the other singly, a tradition begun with the visit of General Lafayette of France in 1824. At that time a joint committee decided that each body would honor Lafayette separately, establishing the precedent. (See footnote 7 for more details.) Not all such occasions included formal addresses by such dignitaries (e.g., Lafayette's reception by the Senate in their chamber, at which he did not speak before they adjourned to greet him), hence the "occasions" listed in the third column of the table include not only addresses, but also remarks (defined as brief greetings or off-the-cuff comments often requested of the visitor at the last minute) and receptions. Relatively few foreign dignitaries were received by Congress before World War I.

Congress has hosted inaugurations since the first occasion in 1789. They always have been formal joint gatherings, and sometimes they also were joint sessions. Inaugurations were joint sessions when both houses of Congress were in session, and they processed to the ceremony as part of the business of the day. In many cases, however, one or both houses were not in session or were in recess at the time of the ceremony. In this table, inaugurations that were not joint sessions are listed in the second column. Those that were joint sessions are so identified and described in the third column.

JOINT SESSIONS AND MEETINGS, ADDRESSES TO THE SENATE OR THE HOUSE, AND INAUGURATIONS

[See notes at end of table]

Congress & Date	Type	Occasion, topic, or inaugural location	Name and position of dignitary (where applicable)
		NEW YORK CITY	
1st CONGRESS			
Apr. 6, 1789	Joint session	Counting electoral votes	N.A.
Apr. 30, 1789	...do	Inauguration and church service [2]	President George Washington; Right Reverend Samuel Provoost, Senate-appointed Chaplain.
Jan. 8, 1790	...do	Annual Message	President George Washington.
		PHILADELPHIA	
Dec. 8, 1790	...do	...do	Do.
2d CONGRESS			
Oct. 25, 1791	...do	...do	Do.
Nov. 6, 1792	...do	...do	Do.
Feb. 13, 1793	...do	Counting electoral votes	N.A.
3d CONGRESS			
Mar. 4, 1793	Inauguration	Senate Chamber	President George Washington.
Dec. 3, 1793	Joint session	Annual Message	Do.
Nov. 19, 1794	...do	...do	Do.
4th CONGRESS			
Dec. 8, 1795	...do	...do	Do.
Dec. 7, 1796	...do	...do	Do.
Feb. 8, 1797	...do	Counting electoral votes	N.A.
5th CONGRESS			
Mar. 4, 1797	Inauguration	Hall of the House	President John Adams.
May 16, 1797	Joint session	Relations with France	Do.
Nov. 23, 1797	...do	Annual Message	Do.
Dec. 8, 1798	...do	...do	Do.
6th CONGRESS			
Dec. 3, 1799	...do	...do	Do.
Dec. 26, 1799	...do	Funeral procession and oration in memory of George Washington.[3]	Representative Henry Lee.
		WASHINGTON	
Nov. 22, 1800	...do	Annual Message	President John Adams.
Feb. 11, 1801	...do	Counting electoral votes [4]	N.A.
7th CONGRESS			
Mar. 4, 1801	Inauguration	Senate Chamber	President Thomas Jefferson.
8th CONGRESS			
Feb. 13, 1805	Joint session	Counting electoral votes	N.A.
9th CONGRESS			
Mar. 4, 1805	Inauguration	Senate Chamber	President Thomas Jefferson.
10th CONGRESS			
Feb. 8, 1809	Joint session	Counting electoral votes	N.A.
11th CONGRESS			
Mar. 4, 1809	Inauguration	Hall of the House	President James Madison.
12th CONGRESS			
Feb. 10, 1813	Joint session	Counting electoral votes	N.A.
13th CONGRESS			
Mar. 4, 1813	Inauguration	Hall of the House	President James Madison.
14th CONGRESS			
Feb. 12, 1817	Joint session	Counting electoral votes [5]	N.A.
15th CONGRESS			
Mar. 4, 1817	Inauguration	In front of Brick Capitol	President James Monroe.
16th CONGRESS			
Feb. 14, 1821	Joint session	Counting electoral votes [6]	N.A.
17th CONGRESS			
Mar. 5, 1821	Inauguration	Hall of the House	President James Monroe.
18th CONGRESS			
Dec. 9, 1824	Senate	Reception	General Gilbert du Motier, Marquis de Lafayette, of France.

JOINT SESSIONS AND MEETINGS, ADDRESSES TO THE SENATE OR THE HOUSE, AND INAUGURATIONS—CONTINUED

[See notes at end of table]

Congress & Date	Type	Occasion, topic, or inaugural location	Name and position of dignitary (where applicable)
Dec. 10, 1824	House [7]	Address	Speaker Henry Clay; General Gilbert du Motier, Marquis de Lafayette, of France.
Feb. 9, 1825	Joint session	Counting electoral votes [8]	N.A.
19th CONGRESS			
Mar. 4, 1825	Inauguration	Hall of the House	President John Quincy Adams.
20th CONGRESS			
Feb. 11, 1829	Joint session	Counting electoral votes	N.A.
21st CONGRESS			
Mar. 4, 1829	Inauguration	East Portico [9]	President Andrew Jackson.
22d CONGRESS			
Feb. 13, 1833	Joint session	Counting electoral votes	N.A.
23d CONGRESS			
Mar. 4, 1833	Inauguration	Hall of the House [10]	President Andrew Jackson.
Dec. 31, 1834	Joint session	Lafayette eulogy	Representative and former President John Quincy Adams; ceremony attended by President Andrew Jackson.
24th CONGRESS			
Feb. 8, 1837	...do	Counting electoral votes	N.A.
25th CONGRESS			
Mar. 4, 1837	Inauguration	East Portico	President Martin Van Buren.
26th CONGRESS			
Feb. 10, 1841	Joint session	Counting electoral votes	N.A.
27th CONGRESS			
Mar. 4, 1841	Inauguration	East Portico	President William Henry Harrison.
28th CONGRESS			
Feb. 12, 1845	Joint session	Counting electoral votes	N.A.
29th CONGRESS			
Mar. 4, 1845	Inauguration	East Portico	President James Knox Polk.
30th CONGRESS			
Feb. 14, 1849	Joint session	Counting electoral votes	N.A.
31st CONGRESS			
Mar. 5, 1849	Inauguration	East Portico	President Zachary Taylor.
July 10, 1850	Joint session	Oath of office to President Millard Fillmore.[11]	N.A.
32d CONGRESS			
Jan. 5, 1852	Senate	Reception	Louis Kossuth, exiled Governor of Hungary.
Jan. 7, 1852	House	Remarks and Reception	Do.
Feb. 9, 1853	Joint session	Counting electoral votes	N.A.
33d CONGRESS			
Mar. 4, 1853	Inauguration	East Portico	President Franklin Pierce.
34th CONGRESS			
Feb. 11, 1857	Joint session	Counting electoral votes	N.A.
35th CONGRESS			
Mar. 4, 1857	Inauguration	East Portico	President James Buchanan.
36th CONGRESS			
Feb. 13, 1861	Joint session	Counting electoral votes	N.A.
37th CONGRESS			
Mar. 4, 1861	Inauguration	East Portico	President Abraham Lincoln.
Feb. 22, 1862	Joint session	Reading of Washington's farewell address.	John W. Forney, Secretary of the Senate.
38th CONGRESS			
Feb. 8, 1865	...do	Counting electoral votes	N.A.
39th CONGRESS			
Mar. 4, 1865	Inauguration	East Portico	President Abraham Lincoln.
Feb. 12, 1866	Joint session	Memorial to Abraham Lincoln	George Bancroft, historian; ceremony attended by President Andrew Johnson.

JOINT SESSIONS AND MEETINGS, ADDRESSES TO THE SENATE OR THE HOUSE, AND INAUGURATIONS—CONTINUED

[See notes at end of table]

Congress & Date	Type	Occasion, topic, or inaugural location	Name and position of dignitary (where applicable)
40th CONGRESS			
June 9, 1868	House	Address	Anson Burlingame, Envoy to the U.S. from China, and former Representative.
Feb. 10, 1869	Joint session	Counting electoral votes	N.A.
41st CONGRESS			
Mar. 4, 1869	Inauguration	East Portico	President Ulysses S. Grant.
42d CONGRESS			
Mar. 6, 1872	House	Address	Tomomi Iwakura, Ambassador from Japan.
Feb. 12, 1873	Joint session	Counting electoral votes [12]	N.A.
43d CONGRESS			
Mar. 4, 1873	Inauguration	East Portico	President Ulysses S. Grant.
Dec. 18, 1874	Joint meeting	Reception and Remarks	Speaker James G. Blaine; David Kalakaua, King of the Hawaiian Islands.[13]
44th CONGRESS			
Feb. 1, 1877 Feb. 10, 1877 Feb. 12, 1877 Feb. 19, 1877 Feb. 20, 1877 Feb. 21, 1877 Feb. 24, 1877 Feb. 26, 1877 Feb. 28, 1877 Mar. 1, 1877 Mar. 2, 1877	Joint session	Counting electoral votes [14]	N.A.
45th CONGRESS			
Mar. 5, 1877	Inauguration	East Portico	President Rutherford B. Hayes.
46th CONGRESS			
Feb. 2, 1880	House	Address	Charles Stewart Parnell, member of Parliament from Ireland.
Feb. 9, 1881	Joint session	Counting electoral votes	N.A.
47th CONGRESS			
Mar. 4, 1881	Inauguration	East Portico	President James A. Garfield.
Feb. 27, 1882	Joint session	Memorial to James A. Garfield	James G. Blaine, former Speaker, Senator, and Secretary of State; ceremony attended by President Chester A. Arthur.
48th CONGRESS			
Feb. 11, 1885	...do	Counting electoral votes	N.A.
Feb. 21, 1885	...do	Completion of Washington Monument	Representative John D. Long; Representative-elect John W. Daniel,[15] ceremony attended by President Chester A. Arthur.
49th CONGRESS			
Mar. 4, 1885	Inauguration	East Portico	President Grover Cleveland.
50th CONGRESS			
Feb. 13, 1889	Joint session	Counting electoral votes	N.A.
51st CONGRESS			
Mar. 4, 1889	Inauguration	East Portico	President Benjamin Harrison.
Dec. 11, 1889	Joint session	Centennial of George Washington's first inauguration.	Melville W. Fuller, Chief Justice of the United States; ceremony attended by President Benjamin Harrison.
52d CONGRESS			
Feb. 8, 1893	...do	Counting electoral votes	N.A.
53d CONGRESS			
Mar. 4, 1893	Inauguration	East Portico	President Grover Cleveland.
54th CONGRESS			
Feb. 10, 1897	Joint session	Counting electoral votes	N.A.
55th CONGRESS			
Mar. 4, 1897	Inauguration	In front of original Senate Wing of Capitol.	President William McKinley.

JOINT SESSIONS AND MEETINGS, ADDRESSES TO THE SENATE OR THE HOUSE, AND INAUGURATIONS—CONTINUED

[See notes at end of table]

Congress & Date	Type	Occasion, topic, or inaugural location	Name and position of dignitary (where applicable)
56th CONGRESS			
Dec. 12, 1900	Joint meeting	Centennial of the Capital City	Representatives James D. Richardson and Sereno E. Payne, and Senator George F. Hoar; ceremony attended by President William McKinley.
Feb. 13, 1901	Joint session	Counting electoral votes	N.A.
57th CONGRESS			
Mar. 4, 1901	Inauguration	East Portico	President William McKinley.
Feb. 27, 1902	Joint session	Memorial to William McKinley	John Hay, Secretary of State; ceremony attended by President Theodore Roosevelt and Prince Henry of Prussia.
58th CONGRESS			
Feb. 8, 1905	...do	Counting electoral votes	N.A.
59th CONGRESS			
Mar. 4, 1905	Inauguration	East Portico	President Theodore Roosevelt.
60th CONGRESS			
Feb. 10, 1909	Joint session	Counting electoral votes	N.A.
61st CONGRESS			
Mar. 4, 1909	Inauguration	Senate Chamber [16]	President William Howard Taft.
Feb. 9, 1911	House	Address	Count Albert Apponyi, Minister of Education from Hungary.
62d CONGRESS			
Feb. 12, 1913	Joint session	Counting electoral votes	N.A.
Feb. 15, 1913	...do	Memorial for Vice President James S. Sherman.[17]	Senators Elihu Root, Thomas S. Martin, Jacob H. Gallinger, John R. Thornton, Henry Cabot Lodge, John W. Kern, Robert M. LaFollette, John Sharp Williams, Charles Curtis, Albert B. Cummins, George T. Oliver, James A. O'Gorman; Speaker Champ Clark; President William Howard Taft.
63d CONGRESS			
Mar. 4, 1913	Inauguration	East Portico	President Woodrow Wilson.
Apr. 8, 1913	Joint session	Tariff message	Do.
June 23, 1913	...do	Currency and bank reform message	Do.
Aug. 27, 1913	...do	Mexican affairs message	Do.
Dec. 2, 1913	...do	Annual Message	Do.
Jan. 20, 1914	...do	Trusts message	Do.
Mar. 5, 1914	...do	Panama Canal tolls	Do.
Apr. 20, 1914	...do	Mexico message	Do.
Sept. 4, 1914	...do	War tax message	Do.
Dec. 8, 1914	...do	Annual Message	Do.
64th CONGRESS			
Dec. 7, 1915	...do	...do	Do.
Aug. 29, 1916	...do	Railroad message (labor-management dispute).	Do.
Dec. 5, 1916	...do	Annual Message	Do.
Jan. 22, 1917	Senate	Planning ahead for peace	Do.
Feb. 3, 1917	Joint session	Severing diplomatic relations with Germany.	Do.
Feb. 14, 1917	...do	Counting electoral votes	N.A.
Feb. 26, 1917	...do	Arming of merchant ships	President Woodrow Wilson.
65th CONGRESS			
Mar. 5, 1917	Inauguration	East Portico	Do.
Apr. 2, 1917	Joint session	War with Germany	Do.
May 1, 1917	Senate	Address	René Raphaël Viviani, Minister of Justice from France; Jules Jusserand, Ambassador from France; address attended by Marshal Joseph Jacques Césaire Joffre, member of French Commission to U.S.
May 3, 1917	House	...do	Do.
May 5, 1917	...do	...do	Arthur James Balfour, British Secretary of State for Foreign Affairs.
May 8, 1917	Senate	...do	Do.
May 31, 1917	...do	...do	Ferdinando di'Savoia, Prince of Udine, Head of Italian Mission to U.S.
June 2, 1917	House	...do	Ferdinando di'Savoia, Prince of Udine, Head of Italian Mission to U.S.; Guglielmo Marconi, member of Italian Mission to U.S.

JOINT SESSIONS AND MEETINGS, ADDRESSES TO THE SENATE OR THE HOUSE, AND INAUGURATIONS—CONTINUED

[See notes at end of table]

Congress & Date	Type	Occasion, topic, or inaugural location	Name and position of dignitary (where applicable)
June 22, 1917	Senate	Address	Baron Moncheur, Chief of Political Bureau of Belgian Foreign Office at Havre.
June 23, 1917	House	...do	Boris Bakhmetieff, Ambassador from Russia.[18]
June 26, 1917	Senate	...do	Do.
June 27, 1917	House	...do	Baron Moncheur, Chief of Political Bureau of Belgian Foreign Office at Havre.
Aug. 30, 1917	Senate	...do	Kikujirō Ishii, Ambassador from Japan.
Sept. 5, 1917	House	...do	Do.
Dec. 4, 1917	Joint session	Annual Message/War with Austria-Hungary.	President Woodrow Wilson.
Jan. 4, 1918	...do	Federal operation of transportation systems.	Do.
Jan. 5, 1918	Senate	Address	Milenko Vesnic, Head of Serbian War Mission.
Jan. 8, 1918	House	...do	Do.
Do	Joint session	Program for world's peace	President Woodrow Wilson.
Feb. 11, 1918	...do	Peace message	Do.
May 27, 1918	...do	War finance message	Do.
Sept. 24, 1918	Senate	Address and Reception[19]	Jules Jusserand, Ambassador from France; Vice President Thomas R. Marshall.
Sept. 30 1918	...do	Support of woman suffrage	President Woodrow Wilson.
Nov. 11, 1918	Joint session	Terms of armistice signed by Germany	Do.
Dec. 2, 1918	...do	Annual Message	Do.
Feb. 9, 1919	...do	Memorial to Theodore Roosevelt	Senator Henry Cabot Lodge, Sr.; ceremony attended by former President William Howard Taft.
66th CONGRESS			
June 23, 1919	Senate	Address	Epitácio da Silva Pessoa, President-elect of Brazil.
July 10, 1919	...do	Versailles Treaty	President Woodrow Wilson.
Aug. 8, 1919	Joint session	Cost of living message	Do.
Sept. 18, 1919	...do	Address	President pro tempore Albert B. Cummins; Speaker Frederick H. Gillett; Representative and former Speaker Champ Clark; General John J. Pershing.
Oct. 28, 1919	Senate	...do	Albert I, King of the Belgians.
Do	House	...do	Do.
Feb. 9, 1921	Joint session	Counting electoral votes	N.A.
67th CONGRESS			
Mar. 4, 1921	Inauguration	East Portico	President Warren G. Harding.
Apr. 12, 1921	Joint session	Federal problem message	Do.
July 12, 1921	Senate	Adjusted compensation for veterans of the World War[20].	Do.
Dec. 6, 1921	Joint session	Annual Message	Do.
Feb. 28, 1922	...do	Maintenance of the merchant marine	Do.
Aug. 18, 1922	...do	Coal and railroad message	Do.
Nov. 21, 1922	...do	Promotion of the American merchant marine.	Do.
Dec. 8, 1922	...do	Annual Message[21]	Do.
Feb. 7, 1923	...do	British debt due to the United States	Do.
68th CONGRESS			
Dec. 6, 1923	...do	Annual Message	President Calvin Coolidge.
Feb. 27, 1924	...do	Memorial to Warren G. Harding	Charles Evans Hughes, Secretary of State; ceremony attended by President Calvin Coolidge.
Dec. 15, 1924	...do	Memorial to Woodrow Wilson	Dr. Edwin Anderson Alderman, President of the University of Virginia; ceremony attended by President Calvin Coolidge.
Feb. 11, 1925	...do	Counting electoral votes	N.A.
69th CONGRESS			
Mar. 4, 1925	Inauguration	East Portico	President Calvin Coolidge.
Feb. 22, 1927	Joint session	George Washington birthday message	Do.
70th CONGRESS			
Jan. 25, 1928	House	Reception and Address	William Thomas Cosgrave, President of Executive Council of Ireland.
Feb. 13, 1929	Joint session	Counting electoral votes	N.A.
71st CONGRESS			
Mar. 4, 1929	Inauguration	East Portico	President Herbert Hoover.

JOINT SESSIONS AND MEETINGS, ADDRESSES TO THE SENATE OR THE HOUSE, AND INAUGURATIONS—CONTINUED

[See notes at end of table]

Congress & Date	Type	Occasion, topic, or inaugural location	Name and position of dignitary (where applicable)
Oct. 7, 1929	Senate	Address	James Ramsay MacDonald, Prime Minister of the United Kingdom.
Jan. 13, 1930	...do	Reception	Jan Christiaan Smuts, former Prime Minister of South Africa.
72d CONGRESS			
Feb. 22, 1932	Joint session	Bicentennial of George Washington's birth.	President Herbert Hoover.
May 31, 1932	Senate	Emergency character of economic situation in U.S.	Do.
Feb. 6, 1933	Joint meeting	Memorial to Calvin Coolidge	Arthur Prentice Rugg, Chief Justice of the Supreme Judicial Court of Massachusetts; ceremony attended by President Herbert Hoover.
Feb. 8, 1933	Joint session	Counting electoral votes	N.A.
73d CONGRESS			
Mar. 4, 1933	Inauguration	East Portico	President Franklin Delano Roosevelt.
Jan. 3, 1934	Joint session	Annual Message	Do.
May 20, 1934	...do	100th anniversary, death of Lafayette	André de Laboulaye, Ambassador of France; President Franklin Delano Roosevelt; ceremony attended by Count de Chambrun, great-grandson of Lafayette.
74th CONGRESS			
Jan. 4, 1935	...do	Annual Message	President Franklin Delano Roosevelt.
May 22, 1935	...do	Veto message	Do.
Jan. 3, 1936	...do	Annual Message	Do.
75th CONGRESS			
Jan. 6, 1937	...do	Counting electoral votes	N.A.
Do	...do	Annual Message	President Franklin Delano Roosevelt.
Jan. 20, 1937	Inauguration	East Portico	President Franklin Delano Roosevelt; Vice President John Nance Garner.[22]
Apr. 1, 1937	Senate	Address	John Buchan, Lord Tweedsmuir, Governor General of Canada.
Do	House	...do	Do.
Jan. 3, 1938	Joint session	Annual Message	President Franklin Delano Roosevelt.
76th CONGRESS			
Jan. 4, 1939	...do	...do	Do.
Mar. 4, 1939	...do	Sesquicentennial of the 1st Congress	Do.
May 8, 1939	Senate	Address	Anastasio Somoza Garcia, President of Nicaragua.
Do	House	...do	Do.
June 9, 1939	Joint meeting	Reception[23]	George VI and Elizabeth, King and Queen of the United Kingdom.
Sept. 21, 1939	Joint session	Neutrality address	President Franklin Delano Roosevelt.
Jan. 3, 1940	...do	Annual Message	Do.
May 16, 1940	...do	National defense message	Do.
77th CONGRESS			
Jan. 6, 1941	...do	Counting electoral votes	N.A.
Do	...do	Annual Message	President Franklin Delano Roosevelt.
Jan. 20, 1941	...do	Inauguration, East Portico	President Franklin Delano Roosevelt; Vice President Henry A. Wallace.
Dec. 8, 1941	...do	War with Japan	President Franklin Delano Roosevelt.
Dec. 26, 1941	Joint meeting[24]	Address	Winston Churchill, Prime Minister of the United Kingdom.
Jan. 6, 1942	Joint session	Annual Message	President Franklin Delano Roosevelt.
May 11, 1942	Senate	Address	Manuel Prado, President of Peru.
Do	House	...do	Do.
June 2, 1942	...do	...do	Manuel Luis Quezon, President of the Philippines.[25]
June 4, 1942	Senate	...do	Do.
June 15, 1942	...do	...do	George II, King of Greece.[26]
Do	House	...do	Do.
June 25, 1942	Senate	...do	Peter II, King of Yugoslavia.[26]
Do	House	...do	Do.
Aug. 6, 1942	Senate[27]	...do	Wilhelmina, Queen of the Netherlands.[26]
Nov. 24, 1942	House	...do	Carlos Arroyo del Río, President of Ecuador.
Nov. 25, 1942	Senate	...do	Do.
Dec. 10, 1942	House	...do	Fulgencio Batista, President of Cuba.
78th CONGRESS			
Jan. 7, 1943	Joint session	Annual Message	President Franklin Delano Roosevelt.
Feb. 18, 1943	Senate	Remarks	Madame Chiang Kai-shek, of China.
Do	House	Address	Do.

JOINT SESSIONS AND MEETINGS, ADDRESSES TO THE SENATE OR THE HOUSE, AND INAUGURATIONS—CONTINUED

[See notes at end of table]

Congress & Date	Type	Occasion, topic, or inaugural location	Name and position of dignitary (where applicable)
May 6, 1943	Senate	Address	Enrique Peñaranda, President of Bolivia.
Do	House	...do	Do.
May 13, 1943	Senate	...do	Edvard Beneš, President of Czechoslovakia.[26]
Do	House	...do	Do.
May 19, 1943	Joint meeting	...do	Winston Churchill, Prime Minister of the United Kingdom.
May 27, 1943	Senate	Remarks	Edwin Barclay, President of Liberia.
Do	House	Address	Do.
June 10, 1943	Senate	...do	President Hininio Moriñigo M., President of Paraguay.
Do	House	...do	Do.
Oct. 15, 1943	Senate	...do	Elie Lescot, President of Haiti.
Nov. 18, 1943	Joint meeting	Moscow Conference	Cordell Hull, Secretary of State.
Jan. 20, 1944	Senate	Address	Isaías Medina Angarita, President of Venezuela.
Do	House	...do	Do.
79th CONGRESS			
Jan. 6, 1945	Joint session	Counting electoral votes	N.A.
Do	...do	Annual Message	President Roosevelt was not present. His message was read before the Joint Session of Congress.
Jan. 20, 1945	Inauguration	South Portico, The White House[28]	President Franklin Delano Roosevelt; Vice President Harry S. Truman.
Mar. 1, 1945	Joint session	Yalta Conference	President Franklin Delano Roosevelt.
Apr. 16, 1945	...do	Prosecution of the War	President Harry S. Truman.
May 21, 1945	...do	Bestowal of Congressional Medal of Honor on Tech. Sgt. Jake William Lindsey.	General George C. Marshall, Chief of Staff, U.S. Army; President Harry S. Truman.
June 18, 1945	Joint meeting	Address	General Dwight D. Eisenhower, Supreme Commander, Allied Expeditionary Force.
July 2, 1945	Senate	United Nations Charter	President Harry S. Truman.
Oct. 5, 1945	Joint meeting	Address	Admiral Chester W. Nimitz, Commander-in-Chief, Pacific Fleet.
Oct. 23, 1945	Joint session	Universal military training message	President Harry S. Truman.
Nov. 13, 1945	Joint meeting	Address	Clement R. Attlee, Prime Minister of the United Kingdom.
May 25, 1946	Joint session	Railroad strike message	President Harry S. Truman.
July 1, 1946	...do	Memorial to Franklin Delano Roosevelt	John Winant, U.S. Representative on the Economic and Social Council of the United Nations; ceremony attended by President Harry S. Truman and Mrs. Franklin Delano Roosevelt.
80th CONGRESS			
Jan. 6, 1947	...do	State of the Union Address[29]	President Harry S. Truman.
Mar. 12, 1947	...do	Greek-Turkish aid policy	Do.
May 1, 1947	Joint meeting	Address	Miguel Alemán, President of Mexico.
Nov. 17, 1947	Joint session	Aid to Europe message	President Harry S. Truman.
Jan. 7, 1948	...do	State of the Union Address	Do.
Mar. 17, 1948	...do	National security and conditions in Europe.	Do.
Apr. 19, 1948	...do	50th anniversary, liberation of Cuba	President Harry S. Truman; Guillermo Belt, Ambassador of Cuba.
July 27, 1948	...do	Inflation, housing, and civil rights	President Harry S. Truman.
81st CONGRESS			
Jan. 5, 1949	...do	State of the Union Address	Do.
Jan. 6, 1949	...do	Counting electoral votes	N.A.
Jan. 20, 1949	...do	Inauguration, East Portico	President Harry S. Truman; Vice President Alben W. Barkley.
May 17, 1949	House	Reception	General Lucius D. Clay.
Do	Senate	Address	Do.
May 19, 1949	Joint meeting	...do	Eurico Gaspar Dutra, President of Brazil.
Aug. 9, 1949	House	...do	Elpidio Quirino, President of the Philippines.
Do	Senate	...do	Do.
Oct. 13, 1949	...do	...do	Jawaharlal Nehru, Prime Minister of India.
Do	House	...do	Do.
Jan. 4, 1950	Joint session	State of the Union Address	President Harry S. Truman.
Apr. 13, 1950	Senate	Address	Gabriel González-Videla, President of Chile.
May 4, 1950	...do	...do	Liaquat Ali Khan, Prime Minister of Pakistan.
Do	House	...do	Do.
May 31, 1950	Joint meeting	...do	Dean Acheson, Secretary of State.

JOINT SESSIONS AND MEETINGS, ADDRESSES TO THE SENATE OR THE HOUSE, AND INAUGURATIONS—CONTINUED

[See notes at end of table]

Congress & Date	Type	Occasion, topic, or inaugural location	Name and position of dignitary (where applicable)
July 28, 1950	Senate	Address	Chōjirō Kuriyama, member of Japanese Diet.
July 31, 1950	House	...do	Tokutarō Kitamura, member of Japanese Diet.
Aug. 1, 1950	...do	...do	Robert Gordon Menzies, Prime Minister of Australia.
Do	Senate	...do	Do.
82d CONGRESS			
Jan. 8, 1951	Joint session	State of the Union Address	President Harry S. Truman.
Feb. 1, 1951	Joint meeting [30]	North Atlantic Treaty Organization	General Dwight D. Eisenhower.
Apr. 2, 1951	...do	Address	Vincent Auriol, President of France.
Apr. 19, 1951	...do	Return from Pacific Command	General Douglas MacArthur.
June 21, 1951	...do	Address	Galo Plaza, President of Ecuador.
July 2, 1951	Senate	Addresses	Tadao Kuraishi, and Aisuke Okamoto, members of Japanese Diet.
Aug. 23, 1951	...do	Address	Zentarō Kosaka, member of Japanese Diet.
Sept. 24, 1951	Joint meeting	...do	Alcide de Gasperi, Prime Minister of Italy.
Jan. 9, 1952	Joint session	State of the Union Address	President Harry S. Truman.
Jan. 17, 1952	Joint meeting	Address	Winston Churchill, Prime Minister of the United Kingdom.
Apr. 3, 1952	...do	...do	Juliana, Queen of the Netherlands.
May 22, 1952	...do	Korea	General Matthew B. Ridgway.
June 10, 1952	Joint session	Steel industry dispute	President Harry S. Truman.
83d CONGRESS			
Jan. 6, 1953	...do	Counting electoral votes	N.A.
Jan. 20, 1953	...do	Inauguration, East Portico	President Dwight D. Eisenhower; Vice President Richard M. Nixon.
Feb. 2, 1953	...do	State of the Union Address	President Dwight D. Eisenhower.
Jan. 7, 1954	...do	...do	Do.
Jan. 29, 1954	Joint meeting	Address	Celal Bayar, President of Turkey.
May 4, 1954	...do	...do	Vincent Massey, Governor General of Canada.
May 28, 1954	...do	...do	Haile Selassie I, Emperor of Ethiopia.
July 28, 1954	...do	...do	Syngman Rhee, President of South Korea.
Nov. 12, 1954	Senate	Remarks	Shigeru Yoshida, Prime Minister of Japan.
Nov. 17, 1954	...do	Address [31]	Sarvepalli Radhakrishnan, Vice President of India.
Nov. 18, 1954	...do	Remarks	Pierre Mendès-France, Premier of France.
84th CONGRESS			
Jan. 6, 1955	Joint session	State of the Union Address	President Dwight D. Eisenhower.
Jan. 27, 1955	Joint meeting	Address	Paul E. Magliore, President of Haiti.
Mar. 16, 1955	Senate	...do	Robert Gordon Menzies, Prime Minister of Australia.
Do	House	...do	Do.
Mar. 30, 1955	Senate	...do	Mario Scelba, Prime Minister of Italy.
Do	House	...do	Do.
May 4, 1955	Senate	...do	P. Phibunsongkhram, Prime Minister of Thailand.
Do	House	...do	Do.
June 30, 1955	Senate	...do	U Nu, Prime Minister of Burma.
Do	House	...do	Do.
Jan. 5, 1956	Senate	...do	Juscelino Kubitschek de Oliverira, President-elect of Brazil.
Feb. 2, 1956	...do	...do	Anthony Eden, Prime Minister of the United Kingdom.
Do	House	...do	Do.
Feb. 29, 1956	Joint meeting	...do	Giovanni Gronchi, President of Italy.
Mar. 15, 1956	Senate	...do	John Aloysius Costello, Prime Minister of Ireland.
Do	House	...do	Do.
Apr. 30, 1956	Senate	...do	João Goulart, Vice President of Brazil.
May 17, 1956	Joint meeting	...do	Sukarno, President of Indonesia.
85th CONGRESS			
Jan. 5, 1957	Joint session	Middle East message	President Dwight D. Eisenhower.
Jan. 7, 1957	...do	Counting electoral votes	N.A.
Jan. 10, 1957	...do	State of the Union Address	President Dwight D. Eisenhower.
Jan. 21, 1957	...do	Inauguration, East Portico	President Dwight D. Eisenhower; Vice President Richard M. Nixon.
Feb. 27, 1957	House	Address	Guy Mollet, Premier of France.
Do	Senate	...do	Do.
May 9, 1957	Joint meeting	...do	Ngo Dinh Diem, President of Vietnam.

JOINT SESSIONS AND MEETINGS, ADDRESSES TO THE SENATE OR THE HOUSE, AND INAUGURATIONS—CONTINUED

[See notes at end of table]

Congress & Date	Type	Occasion, topic, or inaugural location	Name and position of dignitary (where applicable)
May 28, 1957	House	Address	Konrad Adenauer, Chancellor of West Germany.
Do	Senate	...do	Do.
June 20, 1957	...do	...do	Nobusuke Kishi, Prime Minister of Japan.
Do	House	...do	Do.
July 11, 1957	Senate	...do	Husseyn Shaheed Suhrawardy, Prime Minister of Pakistan.
Jan. 9, 1958	Joint session	State of the Union Address	President Dwight D. Eisenhower.
June 5, 1958	Joint meeting	Address	Theodor Heuss, President of West Germany.
June 10, 1958	Senate	...do	Harold Macmillan, Prime Minister of the United Kingdom.
June 18, 1958	Joint meeting	...do	Carlos F. Garcia, President of the Philippines.
June 25, 1958	House	...do	Muhammad Daoud Khan, Prime Minister of Afghanistan.
Do	Senate	...do	Do.
July 24, 1958	...do	...do	Kwame Nkrumah, Prime Minister of Ghana.
July 25, 1958	House	...do	Do.
July 29, 1958	Senate	...do	Amintore Fanfani, Prime Minister of Italy.
Do	House	...do	Do.
86th CONGRESS			
Jan. 9, 1959	Joint session	State of the Union Address	President Dwight D. Eisenhower.
Jan. 21, 1959	Joint meeting	Address	Arturo Frondizi, President of Argentina.
Feb. 12, 1959	Joint session	Sesquicentennial of Abraham Lincoln's birth.	Fredric March, actor; Carl Sandburg, poet.
Mar. 11, 1959	Joint meeting	Address	Jose Maria Lemus, President of El Salvador.
Mar. 18, 1959	...do	...do	Sean T. O'Kelly, President of Ireland.
May 12, 1959	...do	...do	Baudouin, King of the Belgians.
Jan. 7, 1960	Joint session	State of the Union Address	President Dwight D. Eisenhower.
Mar. 30, 1960	Senate	Address	Harold Macmillan, Prime Minister of the United Kingdom.
Apr. 6, 1960	Joint meeting	...do	Alberto Lleras-Camargo, President of Colombia.
Apr. 25, 1960	...do	...do	Charles de Gaulle, President of France.
Apr. 28, 1960	...do	...do	Mahendra, King of Nepal.
June 29, 1960	...do	...do	Bhumibol Adulyadej, King of Thailand.
87th CONGRESS			
Jan. 6, 1961	Joint session	Counting electoral votes	N.A.
Jan. 20, 1961	...do	Inauguration, East Portico	President John F. Kennedy; Vice President Lyndon B. Johnson.
Jan. 30, 1961	...do	State of the Union Address	President John F. Kennedy.
Apr. 13, 1961	Senate	Remarks	Konrad Adenauer, Chancellor of West Germany.
Apr. 18, 1961	House	Address	Constantine Karamanlis, Prime Minister of Greece.
May 4, 1961	Joint meeting	...do	Habib Bourguiba, President of Tunisia.
May 25, 1961	Joint session	Urgent national needs: foreign aid, defense, civil defense, and outer space.	President John F. Kennedy.
June 22, 1961	Senate	Remarks	Hayato Ikeda, Prime Minister of Japan.
Do	House	Address	Do.
July 12, 1961	Joint meeting	...do	Mohammad Ayub Khan, President of Pakistan.
July 26, 1961	House	...do	Abubakar Tafawa Balewa, Prime Minister of Nigeria.
Sept. 21, 1961	Joint meeting	...do	Manuel Prado, President of Peru.
Jan. 11, 1962	Joint session	State of the Union Address	President John F. Kennedy.
Feb. 26, 1962	Joint meeting	Friendship 7: 1st United States orbital space flight.	Lt. Col. John H. Glenn, Jr., USMC; Friendship 7 astronaut.
Apr. 4, 1962	...do	Address	João Goulart, President of Brazil.
Apr. 12, 1962	...do	...do	Mohammad Reza Shah Pahlavi, Shahanshah of Iran.
88th CONGRESS			
Jan. 14, 1963	Joint session	State of the Union Address	President John F. Kennedy.
May 21, 1963	Joint meeting	Flight of Faith 7 Spacecraft	Maj. Gordon L. Cooper, Jr., USAF, Faith 7 astronaut.
Oct. 2, 1963	Senate	Address	Haile Selassie I, Emperor of Ethiopia.
Nov. 27, 1963	Joint session	Assumption of office	President Lyndon B. Johnson.
Jan. 8, 1964	...do	State of the Union Address	Do.
Jan. 15, 1964	Joint meeting	Address	Antonio Segni, President of Italy.
May 28, 1964	...do	...do	Eamon de Valera, President of Ireland.
89th CONGRESS			
Jan. 4, 1965	Joint session	State of the Union Address	President Lyndon B. Johnson.

JOINT SESSIONS AND MEETINGS, ADDRESSES TO THE SENATE OR THE HOUSE, AND INAUGURATIONS—CONTINUED

[See notes at end of table]

Congress & Date	Type	Occasion, topic, or inaugural location	Name and position of dignitary (where applicable)
Jan. 6, 1965	Joint session	Counting electoral votes	N.A.
Jan. 20, 1965	...do [32]	Inauguration, East Portico	President Lyndon B. Johnson; Vice President Hubert H. Humphrey.
Mar. 15, 1965	...do	Voting rights	President Lyndon B. Johnson.
Sept. 14, 1965	Joint meeting	Flight of Gemini 5 Spacecraft	Lt. Col. Gordon L. Cooper, Jr., USAF; and Charles Conrad, Jr., USN; Gemini 5 astronauts.
Jan. 12, 1966	Joint session	State of the Union Address	President Lyndon B. Johnson.
Sept. 15, 1966	Joint meeting	Address	Ferdinand E. Marcos, President of the Philippines.
90th CONGRESS			
Jan. 10, 1967	Joint session	State of the Union Address	President Lyndon B. Johnson.
Apr. 28, 1967	Joint meeting	Vietnam policy	General William C. Westmoreland.
Aug. 16, 1967	Senate	Address	Kurt George Kiesinger, Chancellor of West Germany.
Oct. 27, 1967	Joint meeting	...do	Gustavo Diaz Ordaz, President of Mexico.
Jan. 17, 1968	Joint session	State of the Union Address	President Lyndon B. Johnson.
91st CONGRESS			
Jan. 6, 1969	...do	Counting electoral votes [33]	N.A.
Jan. 9, 1969	Joint meeting	Apollo 8: 1st flight around the moon	Col. Frank Borman, USAF; Capt. James A. Lowell, Jr., USN; Lt. Col. William A. Anders, USAF; Apollo 8 astronauts.
Jan. 14, 1969	Joint session	State of the Union Address	President Lyndon B. Johnson.
Jan. 20, 1969	...do [32]	Inauguration, East Portico	President Richard M. Nixon; Vice President Spiro T. Agnew.
Sept. 16, 1969	Joint meeting	Apollo 11: 1st lunar landing	Neil A. Armstrong; Col. Edwin E. Aldrin, Jr., USAF; and Lt. Col. Michael Collins, USAF; Apollo 11 astronauts.
Nov. 13, 1969	House	Executive-Legislative branch relations and Vietnam policy.	President Richard M. Nixon.
Do	Senate	...do	Do.
Jan. 22, 1970	Joint session	State of the Union Address	Do.
Feb. 25, 1970	Joint meeting	Address	Georges Pompidou, President of France.
June 3, 1970	...do	...do	Rafael Caldera, President of Venezuela.
Sept. 22, 1970	...do	Report on prisoners of war	Col. Frank Borman, Representative to the President on Prisoners of War.
92d CONGRESS			
Jan. 22, 1971	Joint session	State of the Union Address	President Richard M. Nixon.
Sept. 9, 1971	...do	Economic policy	Do.
Do	Joint meeting	Apollo 15: lunar mission	Col. David R. Scott, USAF; Col. James B. Irwin, USAF; and Lt. Col. Alfred M. Worden, USAF; Apollo 15 astronauts.
Jan. 20, 1972	Joint session	State of the Union Address	President Richard M. Nixon.
June 1, 1972	...do	European trip report	Do.
June 15, 1972	Joint meeting	Address	Luis Echeverria Alvarez, President of Mexico.
93d CONGRESS			
Jan. 6, 1973	Joint session	Counting electoral votes	N.A.
Jan. 20, 1973	Inauguration	East Portico	President Richard M. Nixon; Vice President Spiro T. Agnew.
Dec. 6, 1973	Joint meeting	Oath of office to, and Address by Vice President Gerald R. Ford.	Vice President Gerald R. Ford; ceremony attended by President Richard M. Nixon.
Do	Senate	Remarks and Reception	Vice President Gerald R. Ford.
Jan. 30 1974	Joint session	State of the Union Address	President Richard M. Nixon.
Aug. 12, 1974	...do	Assumption of office	President Gerald R. Ford.
Oct. 8, 1974	...do	Economy	Do.
Dec. 19, 1974	Senate	Address [34]	Vice President Nelson A. Rockefeller.
94th CONGRESS			
Jan. 15, 1975	Joint session	State of the Union Address	President Gerald R. Ford.
Apr. 10, 1975	...do	State of the World message	Do.
June 17, 1975	Joint meeting	Address	Walter Scheel, President of West Germany.
Nov. 5, 1975	...do	...do	Anwar El Sadat, President of Egypt.
Jan. 19, 1976	Joint session	State of the Union Address	President Gerald R. Ford.
Jan. 28, 1976	Joint meeting	Address	Yitzhak Rabin, Prime Minister of Israel.
Mar. 17, 1976	...do	...do	Liam Cosgrave, Prime Minister of Ireland.
May 18, 1976	...do	...do	Valery Giscard d'Estaing, President of France.
June 2, 1976	...do	...do	Juan Carlos I, King of Spain.

JOINT SESSIONS AND MEETINGS, ADDRESSES TO THE SENATE OR THE HOUSE, AND INAUGURATIONS—CONTINUED

[See notes at end of table]

Congress & Date	Type	Occasion, topic, or inaugural location	Name and position of dignitary (where applicable)
Sept. 23, 1976	Joint meeting	Address	William R. Tolbert, Jr., President of Liberia.
95th CONGRESS			
Jan. 6, 1977	Joint session	Counting electoral votes	N.A.
Jan. 12, 1977	...do	State of the Union Address	President Gerald R. Ford.
Jan. 20, 1977	Inauguration	East Portico	President Jimmy Carter; Vice President Walter F. Mondale.
Feb. 17, 1977	House	Address	José López Portillo, President of Mexico.
Feb. 22, 1977	Joint meeting	...do	Pierre Elliot Trudeau, Prime Minister of Canada.
Apr. 20, 1977	Joint session	Energy	President Jimmy Carter.
Jan. 19, 1978	...do	State of the Union Address	Do.
Sept. 18, 1978	...do	Middle East Peace agreements	President Jimmy Carter; joint session attended by Anwar El Sadat, President of Egypt, and by Menachem Begin, Prime Minister of Israel.
96th CONGRESS			
Jan. 23, 1979	...do	State of the Union Address	Do.
June 18, 1979	...do	Salt II agreements	Do.
Jan. 23, 1980	...do	State of the Union Address	Do.
97th CONGRESS			
Jan. 6, 1981	...do	Counting electoral votes	N.A.
Jan. 20, 1981	...do [32]	Inauguration, West Front	President Ronald Reagan; Vice President George Bush.
Feb. 18, 1981	...do	Economic recovery	President Ronald Reagan.
Apr. 28, 1981	...do	Economic recovery—inflation	Do.
Jan. 26, 1982	...do	State of the Union Address	Do.
Jan. 28, 1982	Joint meeting	Centennial of birth of Franklin Delano Roosevelt.	Dr. Arthur Schlesinger, historian; Senator Jennings Randolph; Representative Claude Pepper; Averell Harriman, former Governor of New York [35]; former Representative James Roosevelt, son of President Roosevelt.
Apr. 21, 1982	...do	Address	Beatrix, Queen of the Netherlands.
98th CONGRESS			
Jan. 25, 1983	Joint session	State of the Union Address	President Ronald Reagan.
Apr. 27, 1983	...do	Central America	Do.
Oct. 5, 1983	Joint meeting	Address	Karl Carstens, President of West Germany.
Jan. 25, 1984	Joint session	State of the Union Address	President Ronald Reagan.
Mar. 15, 1984	Joint meeting	Address	Dr. Garett FitzGerald, Prime Minister of Ireland.
Mar. 22, 1984	...do	...do	François Mitterand, President of France.
May 8, 1984	...do	Centennial of birth of Harry S. Truman	Representatives Ike Skelton and Alan Wheat; former Senator Stuart Symington; Margaret Truman Daniel, daughter of President Truman; and Senator Mark Hatfield.
May 16, 1984	...do	Address	Miguel de la Madrid, President of Mexico.
99th CONGRESS			
Jan. 7, 1985	Joint session	Counting electoral votes	N.A.
Jan. 21, 1985	Inauguration	Rotunda [36]	President Ronald Reagan; Vice President George Bush.
Feb. 6, 1985	Joint session	State of the Union Address	President Ronald Reagan.
Feb. 20, 1985	Joint meeting	Address	Margaret Thatcher, Prime Minister of the United Kingdom.
Mar. 6, 1985	...do	...do	Bettino Craxi, President of the Council of Ministers of Italy.
Mar. 20, 1985	...do	...do	Raul Alfonsin, President of Argentina.
June 13, 1985	...do	...do	Rajiv Gandhi, Prime Minister of India.
Oct. 9, 1985	...do	...do	Lee Kuan Yew, Prime Minister of Singapore.
Nov. 21, 1985	Joint session	Geneva Summit	President Ronald Reagan.
Feb. 4, 1986	...do	State of the Union Address	Do.
Sept. 11, 1986	Joint meeting	Address	Jose Sarney, President of Brazil.
Sept. 18, 1986	...do	...do	Corazon C. Aquino, President of the Philippines.
100th CONGRESS			
Jan. 27, 1987	Joint session	State of the Union Address	President Ronald Reagan.
Nov. 10, 1987	Joint meeting	Address	Chaim Herzog, President of Israel.
Jan. 25, 1988	Joint session	State of the Union Address	President Ronald Reagan.
Apr. 27, 1988	Joint meeting	Address	Brian Mulroney, Prime Minister of Canada.

JOINT SESSIONS AND MEETINGS, ADDRESSES TO THE SENATE OR THE HOUSE, AND INAUGURATIONS—CONTINUED

[See notes at end of table]

Congress & Date	Type	Occasion, topic, or inaugural location	Name and position of dignitary (where applicable)
June 23, 1988	Joint meeting	Address	Robert Hawke, Prime Minister of Australia.
101st CONGRESS			
Jan. 4, 1989	Joint session	Counting electoral votes	N.A.
Jan. 20, 1989	Inauguration	West Front	President George Bush; Vice President Dan Quayle.
Feb. 9, 1989	Joint session	Building a Better America	President George Bush.
Mar. 2, 1989	Joint meeting	Bicentennial of the 1st Congress	President Pro Tempore Robert C. Byrd; Speaker James C. Wright, Jr.; Representatives Lindy Boggs, Thomas S. Foley, and Robert H. Michel; Senators George Mitchell and Robert Dole; Howard Nemerov, Poet Laureate of the United States; David McCullough, historian; Anthony M. Frank, Postmaster General; former Senator Nicholas Brady, Secretary of the Treasury.
Apr. 6, 1989	Senate [37]	Addresses on the 200th anniversary commemoration of Senate's first legislative session.	Former Senators Thomas F. Eagleton and Howard H. Baker, Jr.
June 7, 1989	Joint meeting	Address	Benazir Bhutto, Prime Minister of Pakistan.
Oct. 4, 1989	...do	...do	Carlos Salinas de Gortari, President of Mexico.
Oct. 18, 1989	...do	...do	Roh Tae Woo, President of South Korea.
Nov. 15, 1989	...do	...do	Lech Walesa, chairman of Solidarnośc labor union, Poland.
Jan. 31, 1990	Joint session	State of the Union Address	President George Bush.
Feb. 21, 1990	Joint meeting	Address	Vaclav Hável, President of Czechoslovakia.
Mar. 7, 1990	...do	...do	Giulio Andreotti, President of the Council of Ministers of Italy.
Mar. 27, 1990	...do	Centennial of birth of Dwight D. Eisenhower.	Senator Robert Dole; Walter Cronkite, television journalist; Winston S. Churchill, member of British Parliament and grandson of Prime Minister Churchill; Clark M. Clifford, former Secretary of Defense; James D. Robinson III, chairman of Eisenhower Centennial Foundation; Arnold Palmer, professional golfer; John S.D. Eisenhower, former Ambassador to Belgium and son of President Eisenhower; Representatives Beverly Byron, William F. Goodling, and Pat Roberts.
June 26, 1990	...do	Address	Nelson Mandela, Deputy President of the African National Congress, South Africa.
Sept. 11, 1990	Joint session	Invasion of Kuwait by Iraq	President George Bush.
102d CONGRESS			
Jan. 29, 1991	...do	State of the Union Address	Do.
Mar. 6, 1991	...do	Conclusion of Persian Gulf War	Do.
Apr. 16, 1991	Joint meeting	Address	Violeta B. de Chamorro, President of Nicaragua.
May 8, 1991	House [38]	...do	General H. Norman Schwarzkopf.
May 16, 1991	Joint meeting	...do	Elizabeth II, Queen of the United Kingdom; joint meeting also attended by Prince Philip.
Nov. 14, 1991	...do	...do	Carlos Saul Menem, President of Argentina.
Jan. 28, 1992	Joint session	State of the Union Address	President George Bush.
Apr. 30, 1992	Joint meeting	Address	Richard von Weizsäcker, President of Germany.
June 17, 1992	...do	...do	Boris Yeltsin, President of Russia.
103d CONGRESS			
Jan. 6, 1993	Joint session	Counting electoral votes	N.A.
Jan. 20, 1993	Inauguration	West Front	President William J. Clinton; Vice President Albert Gore.
Feb. 17, 1993	Joint session	Economic Address [39]	President William J. Clinton.
Sept. 22, 1993	...do	Health care reform	Do.
Jan. 25, 1994	...do	State of the Union Address	Do.
May 18, 1994	Joint meeting	Address	Narasimha Rao, Prime Minister of India.
July 26, 1994	...do	Addresses	Hussein I, King of Jordan; Yitzhak Rabin, Prime Minister of Israel.
Oct. 6, 1994	...do	Address	Nelson Mandela, President of South Africa.

JOINT SESSIONS AND MEETINGS, ADDRESSES TO THE SENATE OR THE HOUSE, AND INAUGURATIONS—CONTINUED

[See notes at end of table]

Congress & Date	Type	Occasion, topic, or inaugural location	Name and position of dignitary (where applicable)
104th CONGRESS			
Jan. 24, 1995	Joint session	State of the Union Address	President William J. Clinton.
July 26, 1995	Joint meeting	Address	Kim Yong-sam, President of South Korea.[40]
Oct. 11, 1995	...do	Close of the Commemoration of the 50th Anniversary of World War II.	Speaker Newt Gingrich; Vice President Albert Gore; President Pro Tempore Strom Thurmond; Representatives Henry J. Hyde and G.V. "Sonny" Montgomery; Senators Daniel K. Inouye and Robert Dole; former Representative Robert H. Michel; General Louis H. Wilson (ret.), former Commandant of the Marine Corps.
Dec. 12, 1995	...do	Address	Shimon Peres, Prime Minister of Israel.
Jan. 30, 1996	Joint session	State of the Union Address	President William J. Clinton.
Feb. 1, 1996	Joint meeting	Address	Jacques Chirac, President of France.
July 10, 1996	...do	...do	Binyamin Netanyahu, Prime Minister of Israel.
Sept. 11, 1996	...do	...do	John Bruton, Prime Minister of Ireland.
105th CONGRESS			
Jan. 9, 1997	Joint session	Counting electoral votes	N.A.
Jan. 20, 1997	Inauguration	West Front	President William J. Clinton; Vice President Albert Gore.
Feb. 4, 1997	Joint session	State of the Union Address[41]	President William J. Clinton.
Feb. 27, 1997	Joint meeting	Address	Eduardo Frei, President of Chile.
Jan. 27, 1998	Joint session	State of the Union Address	President William J. Clinton.
June 10, 1998	Joint meeting	Address	Kim Dae-jung, President of South Korea.
July 15, 1998	...do	...do	Emil Constantinescu, President of Romania.
106th CONGRESS			
Jan. 19, 1999	Joint session	State of the Union Address	President William J. Clinton.
Jan. 27, 2000	...do	...do	Do.
Sept. 14, 2000	Joint meeting	Address	Atal Bihari Vajpayee, Prime Minister of India.
107th CONGRESS			
Jan. 6, 2001	Joint session	Counting electoral votes	N.A.
Jan. 20, 2001	Inauguration	West Front	President George W. Bush; Vice President Richard B. Cheney.
Feb. 27, 2001	Joint session	Budget message[39]	President George W. Bush.
Sept. 6, 2001	Joint meeting	Address	Vicente Fox, President of Mexico.
Sept. 20, 2001	Joint session	War on terrorism	President George W. Bush; joint session attended by Tony Blair, Prime Minister of the United Kingdom, by Tom Ridge, Governor of Pennsylvania, by George Pataki, Governor of New York, and by Rudolph Giuliani, Mayor of New York City.
Jan. 29, 2002	...do	State of the Union Address	President George W. Bush; joint session attended by Hamid Karzai, Chairman of the Interim Authority of Afghanistan.
June 12, 2002	Joint meeting	Address[42]	John Howard, Prime Minister of Australia.
108th CONGRESS			
Jan. 28, 2003	Joint session	State of the Union Address	President George W. Bush.
July 17, 2003	Joint meeting	Address	Tony Blair, Prime Minister of the United Kingdom; joint meeting attended by Mrs. George W. Bush.
Jan. 20, 2004	Joint session	State of the Union Address	President George W. Bush.
Feb. 4, 2004	Joint meeting	Address	Jose Maria Aznar, President of the Government of Spain.
June 15, 2004	...do	...do	Hamid Karzai, President of Afghanistan.
Sept. 23, 2004	...do	...do	Ayad Allawi, Interim Prime Minister of Iraq.
109th CONGRESS			
Jan. 6, 2005	Joint session	Counting electoral votes[43]	N.A.
Jan. 20, 2005	Inauguration	West Front	President George W. Bush; Vice President Richard B. Cheney.
Feb. 2, 2005	Joint session	State of the Union Address	President George W. Bush.
Apr. 6, 2005	Joint meeting	Address	Viktor Yushchenko, President of Ukraine.
July 19, 2005	...do	...do	Dr. Manmohan Singh, Prime Minister of India.
Jan. 31, 2006	Joint session	State of the Union Address	President George W. Bush.
Mar. 1, 2006	Joint meeting	Address	Silvio Berlusconi, Prime Minister of Italy.

JOINT SESSIONS AND MEETINGS, ADDRESSES TO THE SENATE OR THE HOUSE, AND INAUGURATIONS—CONTINUED

[See notes at end of table]

Congress & Date	Type	Occasion, topic, or inaugural location	Name and position of dignitary (where applicable)
Mar. 15, 2006	Joint meeting	Address	Ellen Johnson Sirleaf, President of Liberia.
May 24, 2006	...do	...do	Ehud Olmert, Prime Minister of Israel.
June 7, 2006	...do	...do	Dr. Vaira Vike-Freiberga, President of Latvia.
July 26, 2006	...do	...do	Nouri Al-Maliki, Prime Minister of Iraq.
110th CONGRESS			
Jan. 23, 2007	Joint session	State of the Union Address	President George W. Bush.
Mar. 7, 2007	Joint meeting	Address	Abdullah II Ibn Al Hussein, King of Jordan.
Nov. 7, 2007	...do	...do	Nicolas Sarkozy, President of France.
Jan. 28, 2008	Joint session	State of the Union Address	President George W. Bush.
Apr. 30, 2008	Joint meeting	Address	Bertie Ahern, Prime Minister of Ireland.
111th CONGRESS			
Jan. 8, 2009	Joint session	Counting electoral votes	N.A.
Jan. 20, 2009	Inauguration	West Front	President Barack H. Obama; Vice President Joseph R. Biden, Jr.
Feb. 24, 2009	Joint session	Economic Address	President Barack H. Obama.
Mar. 4, 2009	Joint meeting	...do	Gordon Brown, Prime Minister of the United Kingdom.
Sept. 9, 2009	Joint session	Health care reform	President Barack H. Obama.
Nov. 2, 2009	Joint meeting	Address	Angela Merkel, Chancellor of Germany.
Jan. 27, 2010	Joint session	State of the Union Address	President Barack H. Obama.
May 20, 2010	Joint meeting	Address	Felipe Calderon Hinojosa, President of Mexico.
112th CONGRESS			
Jan. 25, 2011	Joint session	State of the Union Address	President Barack H. Obama.
Mar. 9, 2011	Joint meeting	Address	Julia Gillard, Prime Minister of Australia.
May 24, 2011	...do	...do	Binyamin Netanyahu, Prime Minister of Israel.
Sept. 8, 2011	Joint session	American Jobs Act	President Barack H. Obama.

[1] Closing date for this table was September 8, 2011.

[2] The oath of office was administered to George Washington outside on the gallery in front of the Senate Chamber, after which the Congress and the President returned to the chamber to hear the inaugural address. They then proceeded to St. Paul's Chapel for the "divine service" performed by the Chaplain of the Congress. Adjournment of the ceremony did not occur until the Congress returned to Federal Hall.

[3] Funeral oration was delivered at the German Lutheran Church in Philadelphia.

[4] Because of a tie in the electoral vote between Thomas Jefferson and Aaron Burr, the House of Representatives had to decide the election. Thirty-six ballots were required to break the deadlock, with Jefferson's election as President and Burr's as Vice President on February 17. The Twelfth Amendment was added to the Constitution to prevent the 1800 problem from recurring.

[5] During most of the period while the Capitol was being reconstructed following the fire of 1814, the Congress met in the "Brick Capitol," constructed on the site of the present Supreme Court building. This joint session took place in the Representatives' chamber on the 2d floor of the building.

[6] The joint session to count electoral votes was dissolved because the House and Senate disagreed on Missouri's status regarding statehood. The joint session was reconvened the same day and Missouri's votes were counted.

[7] While this occasion has historically been referred to as the first joint meeting of Congress, the Journals of the House and Senate indicate that Lafayette actually addressed the House of Representatives, with some of the Senators present as guests of the House (having been invited at the last minute to attend). Similar occasions, when members of the one body were invited as guests of the other, include the Senate address by Queen Wilhelmina of the Netherlands on Aug. 6, 1942, and the House address by General H. Norman Schwarzkopf on May 8, 1991.

[8] Although Andrew Jackson won the popular vote by a substantial amount and had the highest number of electoral votes from among the several candidates, he did not receive the required majority of the electoral votes. The responsibility for choosing the new President therefore devolved upon the House of Representatives. As soon as the Senators left the chamber, the balloting proceeded, and John Quincy Adams was elected on the first ballot.

[9] The ceremony was moved outside to accommodate the extraordinarily large crowd of people who had come to Washington to see the inauguration.

[10] The ceremony was moved inside because of cold weather.

[11] Following the death of President Zachary Taylor, Vice President Millard Fillmore took the Presidential oath of office in a special joint session in the Hall of the House.

[12] The joint session to count electoral votes was dissolved three times so that the House and Senate could resolve several electoral disputes.

[13] Because of a severe cold and hoarseness, the King could not deliver his speech, which was read by former Representative Elisha Hunt Allen, then serving as Chancellor and Chief Justice of the Hawaiian Islands.

[14] The contested election between Rutherford B. Hayes and Samuel J. Tilden created a constitutional crisis. Tilden won the popular vote by a close margin, but disputes concerning the electoral vote returns from four states deadlocked the proceedings of the joint session. Anticipating this development, the Congress had created a special commission of five Senators, five Representatives, and five Supreme Court Justices to resolve such disputes. The Commission met in the Supreme Court Chamber (the present Old Senate Chamber) as each problem arose. In each case, the Commission accepted the Hayes electors, securing his election by one electoral vote. The joint session was convened on 15 occasions, with the last on March 2, just three days before the inauguration.

[15] The speech was written by former Speaker and Senator Robert C. Winthrop, who could not attend the ceremony because of ill health.

[16] Because of a blizzard, the ceremony was moved inside, where it was held as part of the Senate's special session. President William Howard Taft took the oath of office and gave his inaugural address after Vice President James S. Sherman's inaugural address and the swearing-in of the new senators.

[17] Held in the Senate Chamber.

[18] Bakhmetieff represented the provisional government of Russia set up after the overthrow of the monarchy in March 1917 and recognized by the United States. The Bolsheviks took over in November 1917.

[19] The address and reception were in conjunction with the presentation to the Senate by France of two Sèvres vases in appreciation of the United States' involvement in World War I. The vases are today in the Senate lobby, just off the Senate floor. Two additional Sèvres vases were given without ceremony to the House of Representatives, which today are in the Rayburn Room, not far from the floor of the House.

[20] Senators later objected to President Harding's speech (given with no advance notice to most of the Senators) as an unconstitutional effort to interfere with the deliberations of the Senate, and Harding did not repeat visits of this kind.

[21] This was the first Annual Message broadcast live on radio.

[22] This was the first inauguration held pursuant to the Twentieth Amendment, which changed the date from March 4 to January 20. The Vice Presidential oath, which previously had been given earlier on the same day in the Senate Chamber, was added to the inaugural ceremony as well, but the Vice Presidential inaugural address was discontinued.

[23] A joint reception for the King and Queen of the United Kingdom was held in the Rotunda, authorized by Senate Concurrent Resolution 17, 76th Congress. Although the concurrent resolution was structured to establish a joint meeting, the Senate, in fact, adjourned rather than recessed as called for by the resolution.

[24] Held in the Senate Chamber.

[25] At this time, the Philippines was still a possession of the United States, although it had been made a self-governing commonwealth in 1935, in preparation for full independence in 1946. From 1909 to 1916, Quezon had served in the U.S. House of Representatives as the resident commissioner from the Philippines.

[26] In exile.

[27] For this Senate Address by Queen Wilhelmina, the members of the House of Representatives were invited as guests. This occasion has sometimes been mistakenly referred to as a joint meeting.

[28] The oaths of office were taken in simple ceremonies at the White House because the expense and festivity of a Capitol ceremony were thought inappropriate because of the war. The Joint Committee on Arrangements of the Congress was in charge, however, and both the Senate and the House of Representatives were present.

[29] This was the first time the term "State of the Union Address" was used for the President's Annual Message. Also, it was the first time the address was shown live on television.

[30] This was an informal meeting in the Coolidge Auditorium of the Library of Congress.

[31] Presentation of new ivory gavel to the Senate.

[32] According to the Congressional Record, the Senate adjourned prior to the inaugural ceremonies, even though the previously adopted resolution had stated the adjournment would come immediately following the inauguration. The Senate Journal records the adjournment as called for in the resolution, hence this listing as a joint session.

[33] The joint session to count electoral votes was dissolved so that the House and Senate could each resolve the dispute regarding a ballot from North Carolina. The joint session was reconvened the same day and the North Carolina vote was counted.

[34] Rockefeller was sworn in as Vice President by Chief Justice Warren E. Burger, after which, by unanimous consent, he was allowed to address the Senate.

[35] Because the Governor had laryngitis, his speech was read by his wife, Pamela.

[36] The ceremony was moved inside because of extremely cold weather.

[37] These commemorative addresses were given in the Old Senate Chamber during a regular legislative session.

[38] For this House Address by General Schwarzkopf, the members of the Senate were invited as guests.

[39] This speech was mislabeled in many sources as a State of the Union Address.

[40] President Kim Yong-sam was in Washington for the dedication of the Korean Veterans' Memorial, held the day after this joint meeting.

[41] This was the first State of the Union Address carried live on the Internet.

[42] Prime Minister Howard was originally scheduled to address a joint meeting on September 12, 2001, but because of the attack on the United States on September 11, 2001, the event was postponed until this occasion.

[43] The joint session to count electoral votes was dissolved so that the House and Senate could each discuss the dispute regarding the ballots from Ohio. The joint session was reconvened the same day and the Ohio votes were counted.

REPRESENTATIVES UNDER EACH APPORTIONMENT

The original apportionment of Representatives was assigned in 1787 in the Constitution and remained in effect for the 1st and 2d Congresses. Subsequent apportionments based on the censuses over the years have been figured using several different methods approved by Congress, all with the goal of dividing representation among the states as equally as possible. After each census up to and including the thirteenth in 1910, Congress would enact a law designating the specific changese in the actual number of Representatives as well as the increase in the ratio of persons-per-Representative. After having made no apportionment after the Fourteenth census in 1920, Congress by statute in 1929 fixed the total number of Representatives at 435 (the number attained with the apportionment after the 1910 census), and since that time, only the ratio of persons-per-Representative has continued to increase, in fact, significantly so. Since the total is now fixed, the specific number of Representatives per state is adjusted after each census to reflect its percentage of the entire population. Since the Sixteenth Census in 1940, the "equal proportions" method of apportioning Representatives within the 435 total has been employed. A detailed explanation of the entire apportionment process can be found in *The Historical Atlas of United States Congressional Districts, 1989–1983.* Kenneth C. Martis, The Free Press, New York, 1982.

State	Constitutional apportionment	First Census, 1790	Second Census, 1800	Third Census, 1810	Fourth Census, 1820	Fifth Census, 1830	Sixth Census, 1840	Seventh Census, 1850	Eighth Census, 1860	Ninth Census, 1870	Tenth Census, 1880	Eleventh Census, 1890	Twelfth Census, 1900	Thirteenth Census, 1910	Fifteenth Census, 1930[1]	Sixteenth Census, 1940	Seventeenth Census, 1950	Eighteenth Census, 1960	Nineteenth Census, 1970	Twentieth Census, 1980	Twenty-First Census, 1990	Twenty-Second Census, 2000	Twenty-Third Census, 2010
AL	......	......	......	[2]	3	5	7	7	6	8	8	9	9	10	9	9	9	8	7	7	7	7	7
AK	......	......	......	......	......	......	......	......	......	......	......	......	......	......	......	......	[2,3]	1	1	1	1	1	1
AZ	......	......	......	......	......	......	......	......	......	......	......	......	[2]	[4]1	1	2	2	3	4	5	6	8	9
AR	......	......	......	......	......	[2]	1	2	3	4	5	6	7	7	7	7	6	4	4	4	4	4	4
CA	......	......	......	......	......	......	[2]	[4]2	3	4	6	7	8	11	20	23	30	38	43	45	52	53	53
CO	......	......	......	......	......	......	......	......	......	[2]	1	2	3	4	4	4	4	4	5	6	6	7	7
CT	5	7	7	7	6	6	4	4	4	4	4	4	5	5	6	6	6	6	6	6	6	5	5
DE	1	1	1	2	1	1	1	1	1	1	1	1	1	1	1	1	1	1	1	1	1	1	1
FL	......	......	......	......	......	......	[2]	1	1	2	2	2	3	4	5	6	8	12	15	19	23	25	27
GA	3	2	4	6	7	9	8	8	7	9	10	11	11	12	10	10	10	10	10	10	11	13	14
HI	......	......	......	......	......	......	......	......	......	......	......	......	......	......	......	......	[2,3]	2	2	2	2	2	2
ID	......	......	......	......	......	......	......	......	......	......	[2]	1	1	2	2	2	2	2	2	2	2	2	2
IL	......	......	......	[2]	1	3	7	9	14	19	20	22	25	27	27	26	25	24	24	22	20	19	18
IN	......	......	......	[2]	3	7	10	11	11	13	13	13	13	13	12	11	11	11	11	10	10	9	9
IA	......	......	......	......	......	......	[2]	2	6	9	11	11	11	11	9	8	8	7	6	6	5	5	4
KS	......	......	......	......	......	......	......	[2]	[4]1	3	7	8	8	8	7	6	6	5	5	5	4	4	4
KY	[2]	[4]2	6	10	12	13	10	10	9	10	11	11	11	11	9	9	8	7	7	7	6	6	6
LA	......	......	......	[2]	3	3	4	4	5	6	6	6	7	8	8	8	8	8	8	8	7	7	6
ME	......	......	......	[5]	7	8	7	6	5	5	4	4	4	4	3	3	3	2	2	2	2	2	2
MD	6	8	9	9	9	8	6	6	5	6	6	6	6	6	6	6	7	8	8	8	8	8	8
MA	8	14	17	[5]20	13	12	10	11	10	11	12	13	14	16	15	14	14	12	12	11	10	10	9
MI	......	......	......	......	......	[2]	3	4	6	9	11	12	12	13	17	17	18	19	19	18	16	15	14
MN	......	......	......	......	......	......	......	[2]	2	3	5	7	9	10	9	9	9	8	8	8	8	8	8
MS	......	......	......	[2]	1	2	4	5	5	6	7	7	8	8	7	7	6	5	5	5	5	4	4
MO	......	......	......	[2]	[4]1	2	5	7	9	13	14	15	16	16	13	13	11	10	10	9	9	9	8
MT	......	......	......	......	......	......	......	......	......	......	[2]	1	1	2	2	2	2	2	2	2	1	1	1
NE	......	......	......	......	......	......	......	......	[2]	1	3	6	6	6	5	4	4	3	3	3	3	3	3
NV	......	......	......	......	......	......	......	......	[2]	1	1	1	1	1	1	1	1	1	1	2	2	3	4
NH	3	4	5	6	6	5	4	3	3	3	2	2	2	2	2	2	2	2	2	2	2	2	2
NJ	4	5	6	6	6	6	5	5	5	7	7	8	10	12	14	14	14	15	15	14	13	13	12
NM	......	......	......	......	......	......	......	......	......	......	......	......	[2]	[4]1	1	2	2	2	2	3	3	3	3
NY	6	10	17	27	34	40	34	33	31	33	34	34	37	43	45	45	43	41	39	34	31	29	27
NC	5	10	12	13	13	13	9	8	7	8	9	9	10	10	11	12	12	11	11	11	12	13	13
ND	......	......	......	......	......	......	......	......	......	......	[2]	1	2	3	2	2	2	2	1	1	1	1	1
OH	......	......	[2]	6	14	19	21	21	19	20	21	21	21	22	24	23	23	24	23	21	19	18	16
OK	......	......	......	......	......	......	......	......	......	......	......	......	[2]	8	9	8	6	6	6	6	6	5	5
OR	......	......	......	......	......	......	......	[2]	1	1	1	2	2	3	3	4	4	4	4	5	5	5	5
PA	8	13	18	23	26	28	24	25	24	27	28	30	32	36	34	33	30	27	25	23	21	19	18
RI	1	2	2	2	2	2	2	2	2	2	2	2	2	3	2	2	2	2	2	2	2	2	2
SC	5	6	8	9	9	9	7	6	4	5	7	7	7	7	6	6	6	6	6	6	6	6	7
SD	......	......	......	......	......	......	......	......	......	......	[2]	2	2	3	2	2	2	2	2	1	1	1	1
TN	......	[2]	3	6	9	13	11	10	8	10	10	10	10	10	9	10	9	9	8	9	9	9	9
TX	......	......	......	......	......	......	[2]	2	4	6	11	13	16	18	21	21	22	23	24	27	30	32	36
UT	......	......	......	......	......	......	......	......	......	......	......	[2]	1	2	2	2	2	2	2	3	3	3	4
VT	[2]	[4]2	4	6	5	5	4	3	3	3	2	2	2	2	1	1	1	1	1	1	1	1	1
VA	10	19	22	23	22	21	15	13	[6]11	9	10	10	10	10	9	9	10	10	10	10	11	11	11
WA	......	......	......	......	......	......	......	......	......	......	[2]	2	3	5	6	6	7	7	7	8	9	9	10
WV	......	......	......	......	......	......	......	......	[6]	3	4	4	5	6	6	6	6	5	4	4	3	3	3
WI	......	......	......	......	......	......	[2]	3	6	8	9	10	11	11	10	10	10	10	9	9	9	8	8
WY	......	......	......	......	......	......	......	......	......	......	[2]	1	1	1	1	1	1	1	1	1	1	1	1
Total	65	105	141	181	213	240	223	234	241	292	325	356	386	435	435	435	435	435	435	435	435	435	435

NOTE: Information for table obtained from the U.S. Census Bureau.

[1] No apportionment was made after the 1920 census.

[2] The following Representatives were added after the indicated apportionments when these states were admitted in the years listed. The number of these additional Representatives for each state remained in effect until the next census's apportionment (with the exceptions of California and New Mexico, as explained in footnote 4). They are not included in the total for each column. In reading this table, please remember that the apportionments made after each census took effect with the election two years after the census date. As a result, in the table footnote 2 is placed for several states under the decade preceding the one in which it entered the Union, since the previous decade's apportionment was still in effect at the time of statehood. *Constitutional:* Vermont (1791), 2; Kentucky (1792), 2; *First:* Tennessee (1796), 1; *Second:* Ohio (1803), 1; *Third:* Louisiana (1812), 1; Indiana (1816), 1; Mississippi (1817), 1; Illinois (1818), 1; Alabama (1819), 1; Missouri (1821), 1; *Fifth:* Arkansas (1836), 1; Michigan (1837), 1; *Sixth:* Florida (1845), 1; Texas (1845), 2; Iowa (1846), 2; Wisconsin (1848), 2; California (1850), 2; *Seventh:* Minnesota (1858), 2; Oregon (1859), 1; Kansas (1861), 1; *Eighth:* Nevada (1864), 1; Nebraska (1867), 1; *Ninth:* Colorado (1876), 1; *Tenth:* North Dakota (1889), 1; South Dakota (1889), 2; Montana (1889), 1; Washington (1889), 1; Idaho (1890), 1; Wyoming (1890), 1; *Eleventh:* Utah (1896), 1; *Twelth:* Oklahoma (1907), 5; New Mexico (1912), 2; Arizona (1912), 1; *Seventeenth:* Alaska (1959), 1; Hawaii (1959), 1.

[3] When Alaska and then Hawaii joined the Union in 1959, the law was changed to allow the total membership of the House of Representatives to increase to 436 and then to 437, apportioning one new Representative for each of those states. The total returned to 435 in 1963, when the 1960 census apportionment took effect.

[4] Even though the respective censuses were taken before the following states joined the Union, Representatives for them were apportioned either because of anticipation of statehood or because they had become states in the period between the census and the apportionment, hence they are included in the totals of the respective columns. *First:* Vermont (1791); Kentucky (1792); *Fourth:* Missouri (1821); *Seventh:* California (1850); *Eighth:* Kansas (1861); *Thirteenth:* New Mexico (1912); Arizona (1912). (Please note: These seven states are also included in footnote 2 because they became states while the previous decade's apportionment was still in effect for the House of Representatives.) California's situation was unusual. It was scheduled for inclusion in the figures for the 1850 census apportionment; however, when the apportionment law was passed in 1852, California's census returns were still incomplete so Congress made special provision that the state would retain "the number of Representatives [two] prescribed by the act of admission * * * into the Union until a new apportionment [i.e., after the 1860 census]" would be made. The number of Representatives from California actually increased before the next apportionment to three when Congress gave the state an extra Representative during part of the 37th Congress, from 1862 to 1863. Regarding New Mexico, the 1911 apportionment law, passed by the 62d Congress in response to the 1910 census and effective with the 63d Congress in 1913, stated that "if the Territor[y] of * * * New Mexico shall become [a State] in the Union before the apportionment of Representatives under the next decennial census [it] shall have one Representative * * *." When New Mexico became a state in 1912 during the 62d Congress, it was given two Representatives. The number was decreased to one beginning the next year in the 63d.

[5] The "Maine District" of Massachusetts became a separate state during the term of the 16th Congress, in 1820. For the remainder of that Congress, Maine was assigned one "at large" Representative while Massachusetts continued to have 20 Representatives, the number apportioned to it after the 1810 census. For the 17th Congress (the last before the 1820 census apportionment took effect), seven of Massachusetts's Representatives were reassigned to Maine, leaving Massachusetts with 13.

[6] Of the 11 Representatives apportioned to Virginia after the 1860 census, three were reassigned to West Virginia when that part of Virginia became a separate state in 1863. Since the Virginia seats in the House were vacant at that time because of the Civil War, all of the new Representatives from West Virginia were able to take their seats at once. When Representatives from Virginia reentered the House in 1870, only eight members represented it.

IMPEACHMENT PROCEEDINGS

The provisions of the United States Constitution which apply specifically to impeachments are as follows: Article I, section 2, clause 5; Article I, section 3, clauses 6 and 7; Article II, section 2, clause 1; Article II, section 4; and Article III, section 2, clause 3.

For the officials listed below, the date of impeachment by the House of Representatives is followed by the dates of the Senate trial, with the result of each listed at the end of the entry.

WILLIAM BLOUNT, a Senator of the United States from Tennessee; impeached July 7, 1797; tried Monday, December 17, 1798, to Monday, January 14, 1799; charges dismissed for want of jurisdiction.

JOHN PICKERING, judge of the United States District Court for the District of New Hampshire; impeached March 2, 1803; tried Thursday, March 3, 1803, to Monday, March 12, 1804; removed from office.

SAMUEL CHASE, Associate Justice of the Supreme Court of the United States; impeached March 12, 1804; tried Friday, November 30, 1804, to Friday, March 1, 1805; acquitted.

JAMES H. PECK, judge of the United States District Court for the District of Missouri; impeached April 24, 1830; tried Monday, April 26, 1830, to Monday, January 31, 1831; acquitted.

WEST H. HUMPHREYS, judge of the United States District Court for the Middle, Eastern, and Western Districts of Tennessee; impeached May 6, 1862; tried Wednesday, May 7, 1862, to Thursday, June 26, 1862; removed from office and disqualified from future office.

ANDREW JOHNSON, President of the United States; impeached February 24, 1868; tried Tuesday, February 25, 1868, to Tuesday, May 26, 1868; acquitted.

MARK DELAHAY, judge of the United States District Court of Kansas; impeached February 28, 1873; resigned office Friday, December 12, 1873, before the Senate trial was held, with no further action taken by the Senate.

WILLIAM W. BELKNAP, Secretary of War; impeached March 2, 1876; tried Friday, March 3, 1876, to Tuesday, August 1, 1876; acquitted.

CHARLES SWAYNE, judge of the United States District Court for the Northern District of Florida; impeached December 13, 1904; tried Wednesday, December 14, 1904, to Monday, February 27, 1905; acquitted.

ROBERT W. ARCHBALD, associate judge, United States Commerce Court; impeached July 11, 1912; tried Saturday, July 13, 1912, to Monday, January 13, 1913; removed from office and disqualified from future office.

GEORGE W. ENGLISH, judge of the United States District Court for the Eastern District of Illinois; impeached April 1, 1926; tried Friday, April 23, 1926, to Monday, December 13, 1926; resigned office Thursday, November 4, 1926; Court of Impeachment adjourned to December 13, 1926, when, on request of House managers, the proceedings were dismissed.

HAROLD LOUDERBACK, judge of the United States District Court for the Northern District of California; impeached February 24, 1933; tried Monday, May 15, 1933, to Wednesday, May 24, 1933; acquitted.

HALSTED L. RITTER, judge of the United States District Court for the Southern District of Florida; impeached March 2, 1936; tried Monday, April 6, 1936, to Friday, April 17, 1936; removed from office.

HARRY E. CLAIBORNE, judge of the United States District Court of Nevada; impeached July 22, 1986; tried Tuesday, October 7, 1986, to Thursday, October 9, 1986; removed from office.

ALCEE L. HASTINGS, judge of the United States District Court for the Southern District of Florida; impeached August 3, 1988; tried Wednesday, October 18, 1989, to Friday, October 20, 1989; removed from office.

WALTER L. NIXON, judge of the United States District Court for the Southern District of Mississippi; impeached May 10, 1989; tried Wednesday, November 1, 1989, to Friday, November 3, 1989; removed from office.

WILLIAM JEFFERSON CLINTON, President of the United States; impeached December 19, 1998; tried Thursday, January 7, 1999, to Friday, February 12, 1999; acquitted.

SAMUEL B. KENT, judge of the United States District Court for the Southern District of Texas; impeached June 19, 2009; resigned office effective Tuesday, June 30, 2009; Court of Impeachment convened on Wednesday, July 22, 2009, when, on request of House managers, proceedings were dismissed.

G. THOMAS PORTEOUS, JR., judge of the United States District Court for the Eastern District of Louisiana; impeached March 11, 2010; tried Tuesday, December 7, 2010, to Wednesday, December 8, 2010; removed from office and disqualified from future office.

REPRESENTATIVES, SENATORS, DELEGATES, AND RESIDENT COMMISSIONERS SERVING IN THE 1st–112th CONGRESSES *

Since the U.S. Congress convened on March 4, 1789, 12,014 individuals have served as Representatives, Senators, or in both capacities. There have been 10,083 Members who served only as Representatives, 1,277 Members who served only in the Senate, and 654 Members with service in both chambers. The total number of Representatives (including individuals serving in both bodies) is 10,737.

These numbers do not include statutory representatives: Resident Commissioners and Delegates. An additional 143 people have served only as Territorial Delegates in the House and 32 people have served only as Resident Commissioners from Puerto Rico or the Philippines.

State/Territory	Date Became a U.S. Territory	Date Entered the Union	Delegates/ Resident Commissioners (Only) [1]	Representatives (Only) [2]	Representatives and Delegates	Senators (Only) [3]	Senators and Representatives [4]	Senators and Delegates	Senators, Representatives, and Delegates	Total House Members
Alabama	Mar. 3, 1817	Dec. 14, 1819 (22d)	0	167	1	27	13	0	0	181
Alaska	Aug. 24, 1912	Jan. 3, 1959 (49th)	7	4	0	6	0	1	0	12
American Samoa	Apr. 17, 1900		2	0	0	0	0	0	0	2
Arizona	Feb. 24, 1863	Feb. 14, 1912 (48th)	10	31	0	5	3	2	0	46
Arkansas	Mar. 2, 1819	June 15, 1836 (25th)	2	85	0	22	11	1	0	99
California		Sept. 9, 1850 (31st)	0	335	0	34	9	0	0	344
Colorado	Feb. 28, 1861	Aug. 1, 1876 (38th)	2	59	0	23	9	2	1	73
Connecticut		Jan. 9, 1788 (5th)	0	209	0	29	25	0	0	235
Delaware		Dec. 7, 1787 (1st)	0	62	0	37	14	0	0	76
District of Columbia	July 16, 1790		3	0	0	0	0	0	0	3
Florida	Mar. 20, 1822	Mar. 3, 1845 (27th)	4	121	0	27	6	1	0	132
Georgia		Jan. 2, 1788 (4th)	0	279	0	38	22	0	0	301
Guam	Apr. 11, 1899		4	0	0	0	0	0	0	4
Hawaii	June 14, 1900	Aug. 21, 1959 (50th)	10	9	0	2	3	0	0	22
Idaho	Mar. 3, 1863	July 3, 1890 (43d)	8	27	0	19	6	1	0	42
Illinois	Feb. 3, 1809	Dec. 3, 1818 (21st)	3	443	0	31	19	0	0	464
Indiana	May 7, 1800	Dec. 11, 1816 (19th)	2	299	1	27	17	0	0	319
Iowa	June 12, 1838	Dec. 28, 1846 (29th)	1	169	0	21	11	1	0	182
Kansas	May 30, 1854	Jan. 29, 1861 (34th)	2	108	0	24	9	0	0	119
Kentucky		June 1, 1792 (15th)	0	309	0	38	28	0	0	337
Louisiana [5]	Mar. 4, 1804	Apr. 30, 1812 (18th)	2	147	0	35	13	0	0	162
Maine		Mar. 15, 1820 (23d)	0	134	0	21	15	0	0	149
Mariana Islands	Apr. 11, 1899		1	0	0	0	0	0	0	1
Maryland		Apr. 28, 1788 (7th)	0	279	0	29	27	0	0	306
Massachusetts		Feb. 6, 1788 (6th)	0	402	0	22	28	0	0	430
Michigan	Jan. 11, 1805	Jan. 26, 1837 (26th)	5	253	0	23	13	1	1	273
Minnesota	Mar. 3, 1849	May 11, 1858 (32d)	2	121	0	28	10	1	0	134
Mississippi	Apr. 17, 1798	Dec. 10, 1817 (20th)	3	110	0	29	14	0	1	128
Missouri	June 4, 1812	Aug. 10, 1821 (24th)	2	291	1	35	10	0	0	304
Montana	May 26, 1864	Nov. 8, 1889 (41st)	5	25	0	14	5	0	1	36
Nebraska	May 30, 1854	Mar. 1, 1867 (37th)	5	86	0	29	6	1	0	98

Nevada	Mar. 2, 1861	Oct. 31, 1864 (36th)	2	28	0	19	6	0	0	36
New Hampshire		June 21, 1788 (9th)	0	134	0	37	26	0	0	160
New Jersey		Dec. 18, 1787 (3d)	0	319	0	49	15	0	0	334
New Mexico	Sept. 9, 1850	Jan. 6, 1912 (47th)	16	23	1	11	4	1	0	45
New York		July 26, 1788 (11th)	0	1,439	0	36	23	0	0	1,462
North Carolina		Nov. 21, 1789 (12th)	0	326	0	36	18	0	0	344
North Dakota [6]	Mar. 2, 1861	Nov. 2, 1889 (39th)	9	13	0	16	6	0	0	28
Ohio		Mar. 1, 1803 (17th)	2	630	0	36	19	0	1	652
Oklahoma	May 2, 1890	Nov. 16, 1907 (46th)	3	73	1	11	6	0	0	83
Oregon	Aug. 14, 1848	Feb. 14, 1859 (33d)	1	56	0	32	4	1	0	62
Pennsylvania		Dec. 12, 1787 (2d)	0	1,049	0	33	21	0	0	1,069
Philippines [7]	Apr. 11, 1899		13	0	0	0	0	0	0	13
Puerto Rico [7]	Apr. 11, 1899		19	0	0	0	0	0	0	19
Rhode Island		May 29, 1790 (13th)	0	78	0	38	10	0	0	88
South Carolina		May 23, 1788 (8th)	0	225	0	37	16	0	0	241
South Dakota [6]	Mar. 2, 1861	Nov. 2, 1889 (40th)	9	14	1	15	10	1	0	35
Tennessee		June 1, 1796 (16th)	1	246	0	40	18	0	0	265
Texas		Dec. 29, 1845 (28th)	0	240	0	22	9	0	0	249
Utah	Sept. 9, 1850	Jan. 4, 1896 (45th)	5	33	0	11	3	2	0	43
Vermont		Mar. 4, 1791 (14th)	0	80	0	24	16	0	0	96
Virgin Islands	Mar. 31, 1917		4	0	0	0	0	0	0	4
Virginia		June 25, 1788 (10th)	0	413	0	26	27	0	0	439
Washington	Mar. 2, 1853	Nov. 11, 1889 (42d)	12	69	0	12	10	1	0	92
West Virginia		June 20, 1863 (35th)	0	86	0	24	8	0	0	94
Wisconsin	Apr. 20, 1836	May 29, 1848 (30th)	4	171	1	19	7	1	0	184
Wyoming	July 25, 1868	July 10, 1890 (44th)	6	15	0	17	3	1	0	25

* State Representation March 4, 1789 to July 13, 2011.

[1] Includes 3 members who served as Representatives and 2 members who served as Senators from a different state.

[2] Includes 3 members who served as Delegates and 18 members who served as Senators from a different state.

[3] Includes 18 members who served as Representatives from a different state. One Senator served from two states and one Senator served from three states.

[4] Includes only those members who served as both a Representative and a Senator from the same state. Eighteen members served as a Senator from one state and a Representative from a different state.

[5] Designated Orleans Territory before attaining statehood in 1812.

[6] Dakota Territory became North and South Dakota in 1889. The nine Delegates from this territory are included in counts for both states. The two Delegates who became Representatives from South Dakota are included only in that state's count.

[7] Resident Commissioners served the Philippines (1902–1946) and continue to serve Puerto Rico (1900 to present). Floor and committee privileges granted to statutory representatives (Territorial Delegates and Resident Commissioners) have changed over time; however, they have never been permitted to vote on the final passage of a bill. The Resident Commissioner's duties vary from that of a Delegate in that he has diplomatic privileges as well as most of those of a Member of Congress. The Puerto Rican Resident Commissioner has served a four-year term since 1917. For more information, see "Status of Delegates and Resident Commissioner," Deschler's Precedents, H.Doc. 94–661, Volume 2, Chapter 7, Section 3.

SOURCE: Biographical Directory of the United States Congress.

POLITICAL DIVISIONS OF THE SENATE AND HOUSE FROM 1855 TO 2011

[All Figures Reflect Immediate Result of Elections. Figures Supplied by the Clerk of the House]

Congress	Years	SENATE					HOUSE OF REPRESENTATIVES				
		No. of Senators	Democrats	Republicans	Other parties	Vacancies	No. of Representatives	Democrats	Republicans	Other parties	Vacancies
34th	1855–1857	62	42	15	5	....	234	83	108	43	....
35th	1857–1859	64	39	20	5	....	237	131	92	14	....
36th	1859–1861	66	38	26	2	....	237	101	113	23	....
37th	1861–1863	50	11	31	7	1	178	42	106	28	2
38th	1863–1865	51	12	39	....	....	183	80	103	....	....
39th	1865–1867	52	10	42	....	....	191	46	145	....	....
40th	1867–1869	53	11	42	....	....	193	49	143	....	1
41st	1869–1871	74	11	61	....	2	243	73	170	....	....
42d	1871–1873	74	17	57	....	....	243	104	139	....	....
43d	1873–1875	74	19	54	....	1	293	88	203	....	2
44th	1875–1877	76	29	46	....	1	293	181	107	3	2
45th	1877–1879	76	36	39	1	....	293	156	137	....	....
46th	1879–1881	76	43	33	....	....	293	150	128	14	1
47th	1881–1883	76	37	37	2	....	293	130	152	11	....
48th	1883–1885	76	36	40	....	....	325	200	119	6	....
49th	1885–1887	76	34	41	....	1	325	182	140	2	1
50th	1887–1889	76	37	39	....	....	325	170	151	4	....
51st	1889–1891	84	37	47	....	....	330	156	173	1	....
52d	1891–1893	88	39	47	2	....	333	231	88	14	....
53d	1893–1895	88	44	38	3	3	356	220	126	10	....
54th	1895–1897	88	39	44	5	....	357	104	246	7	....
55th	1897–1899	90	34	46	10	....	357	134	206	16	1
56th	1899–1901	90	26	53	11	....	357	163	185	9	....
57th	1901–1903	90	29	56	3	2	357	153	198	5	1
58th	1903–1905	90	32	58	....	....	386	178	207	....	1
59th	1905–1907	90	32	58	....	....	386	136	250	....	....
60th	1907–1909	92	29	61	....	2	386	164	222	....	....
61st	1909–1911	92	32	59	....	1	391	172	219	....	....
62d	1911–1913	92	42	49	....	1	391	228	162	1	....
63d	1913–1915	96	51	44	1	....	435	290	127	18	....
64th	1915–1917	96	56	39	1	....	435	231	193	8	3
65th	1917–1919	96	42	53	1	....	435	[1] 210	216	9	....
66th	1919–1921	96	47	48	1	....	435	191	237	7	....
67th	1921–1923	96	37	59	....	....	435	132	300	1	2
68th	1923–1925	96	43	51	2	....	435	207	225	3	....
69th	1925–1927	96	40	54	1	1	435	183	247	5	....
70th	1927–1929	96	47	48	1	....	435	195	237	3	....
71st	1929–1931	96	39	56	1	....	435	163	267	1	4
72d	1931–1933	96	47	48	1	....	435	[2] 216	218	1	....
73d	1933–1935	96	59	36	1	....	435	313	117	5	....
74th	1935–1937	96	69	25	2	....	435	322	103	10	....
75th	1937–1939	96	75	17	4	....	435	333	89	13	....
76th	1939–1941	96	69	23	4	....	435	262	169	4	....
77th	1941–1943	96	66	28	2	....	435	267	162	6	....
78th	1943–1945	96	57	38	1	....	435	222	209	4	....
79th	1945–1947	96	57	38	1	....	435	243	190	2	....
80th	1947–1949	96	45	51	....	....	435	188	246	1	....
81st	1949–1951	96	54	42	....	....	435	263	171	1	....
82d	1951–1953	96	48	47	1	....	435	234	199	2	....
83d	1953–1955	96	46	48	2	....	435	213	221	1	....
84th	1955–1957	96	48	47	1	....	435	232	203	....	....
85th	1957–1959	96	49	47	....	....	435	234	201	....	....
86th	1959–1961	98	64	34	....	....	[3] 436	283	153	....	....
87th	1961–1963	100	64	36	....	....	[4] 437	262	175	....	....
88th	1963–1965	100	67	33	....	....	435	258	176	....	1
89th	1965–1967	100	68	32	....	....	435	295	140	....	....
90th	1967–1969	100	64	36	....	....	435	248	187	....	....
91st	1969–1971	100	58	42	....	....	435	243	192	....	....
92d	1971–1973	100	54	44	2	....	435	255	180	....	....
93d	1973–1975	100	56	42	2	....	435	242	192	1	....
94th	1975–1977	100	60	37	2	....	435	291	144	1	....
95th	1977–1979	100	61	38	1	....	435	292	143	....	....
96th	1979–1981	100	58	41	1	....	435	277	158	....	....
97th	1981–1983	100	46	53	1	....	435	242	192	1	....
98th	1983–1985	100	46	54	....	....	435	269	166	....	....
99th	1985–1987	100	47	53	....	....	435	253	182	....	....
100th	1987–1989	100	55	45	....	....	435	258	177	....	....
101st	1989–1991	100	55	45	....	....	435	260	175	....	....
102d	1991–1993	100	56	44	....	....	435	267	167	1	....
103d	1993–1995	100	57	43	....	....	435	258	176	1	....
104th	1995–1997	100	48	52	....	....	435	204	230	1	....
105th	1997–1999	100	45	55	....	....	435	207	226	2	....
106th	1999–2001	100	45	55	....	....	435	211	223	1	....
107th	2001–2003	100	50	50	....	....	435	212	221	2	....
108th	2003–2005	100	48	51	1	....	435	204	229	1	1
109th	2005–2007	100	44	55	1	....	435	202	232	1	....
110th	2007–2009	100	49	49	2	....	435	233	202	....	....
111th	2009–2011	100	55	41	2	2	435	256	178	....	1
112th	2011–2013	100	51	47	2	....	435	193	242	....	....

[1] Democrats organized House with help of other parties.

[2] Democrats organized House because of Republican deaths.

[3] Proclamation declaring Alaska a State issued January 3, 1959.

[4] Proclamation declaring Hawaii a State issued August 21, 1959.

GOVERNORS OF THE STATES, COMMONWEALTH, AND TERRITORIES—2011

State, Commonwealth, or Territory	Capital	Governor	Party	Term of service	Expiration of term
STATE				*Years*	
Alabama	Montgomery	Robert Bentley	Republican	[c] 4	Jan. 2015
Alaska	Juneau	Sean Parnell	Republican	[f] 4	Dec. 2014
Arizona	Phoenix	Jan Brewer	Republican	[f] 4	Jan. 2015
Arkansas	Little Rock	Mike Beebe	Democrat	[c] 4	Jan. 2015
California	Sacramento	Jerry Brown	Democrat	[c] 4	Jan. 2015
Colorado	Denver	John Hickenlooper	Democratic	[c] 4	Jan. 2015
Connecticut	Hartford	Dan Malloy	Democrat	[b] 4	Jan. 2015
Delaware	Dover	Jack Markell	Democrat	[c] 4	Jan. 2013
Florida	Tallahassee	Rick Scott	Republican	[f] 4	Jan. 2015
Georgia	Atlanta	Nathan Deal	Republican	[f] 4	Jan. 2015
Hawaii	Honolulu	Neil Abercrombie	Democrat	[c] 4	Dec. 2014
Idaho	Boise	C.L. "Butch" Otter	Republican	[b] 4	Jan. 2015
Illinois	Springfield	Pat Quinn	Democrat	[b] 4	Jan. 2015
Indiana	Indianapolis	Mitch Daniels	Republican	[f] 4	Jan. 2013
Iowa	Des Moines	Terry Branstad	Republican	[b] 4	Jan. 2015
Kansas	Topeka	Sam Brownback	Republican	[c] 4	Jan. 2015
Kentucky	Frankfort	Steven L. Beshear	Democrat	[c] 4	Dec. 2011
Louisiana	Baton Rouge	Bobby Jindal	Republican	[f] 4	Jan. 2012
Maine	Augusta	Paul LePage	Republican	[f] 4	Jan. 2015
Maryland	Annapolis	Martin O'Malley	Democrat	[f] 4	Jan. 2015
Massachusetts	Boston	Deval Patrick	Democrat	[b] 4	Jan. 2015
Michigan	Lansing	Rick Snyder	Republican	[b] 4	Jan. 2015
Minnesota	St. Paul	Mark Dayton	Democrat	[b] 4	Jan. 2015
Mississippi	Jackson	Haley Barbour	Republican	[c] 4	Jan. 2012
Missouri	Jefferson City	Jay Nixon	Democrat	[c] 4	Jan. 2013
Montana	Helena	Brian Schweitzer	Democrat	[g] 4	Jan. 2013
Nebraska	Lincoln	Dave Heineman	Republican	[c] 4	Jan. 2015
Nevada	Carson City	Brian Sandoval	Republican	[c] 4	Jan. 2015
New Hampshire	Concord	John Lynch	Democrat	[b] 2	Jan. 2013
New Jersey	Trenton	Chris Christie	Republican	[c] 4	Jan. 2014
New Mexico	Santa Fe	Susana Martinez	Republican	[c] 4	Jan. 2015
New York	Albany	Andrew Cuomo	Democratic	[b] 4	Jan. 2015
North Carolina	Raleigh	Beverly Perdue	Democrat	[c] 4	Jan. 2013
North Dakota	Bismarck	Jack Dalrymple	Republican	[b] 4	Dec. 2014
Ohio	Columbus	John Kasich	Republican	[c] 4	Jan. 2015
Oklahoma	Oklahoma City	Mary Fallin	Republican	[c] 4	Jan. 2015
Oregon	Salem	John Kitzhaber	Democrat	[f] 4	Jan. 2015
Pennsylvania	Harrisburg	Tom Corbett	Republican	[c] 4	Jan. 2015
Rhode Island	Providence	Lincoln Chafee	Independent	[c] 4	Jan. 2015
South Carolina	Columbia	Nikki R. Haley	Republican	[c] 4	Jan. 2015
South Dakota	Pierre	Dennis Daugaard	Republican	[c] 4	Jan. 2015
Tennessee	Nashville	Bill Haslam	Republican	[c] 4	Jan. 2015
Texas	Austin	Rick Perry	Republican	[b] 4	Jan. 2015
Utah	Salt Lake City	Gary R. Herbert	Republican	[b] 4	Jan. 2013
Vermont	Montpelier	Peter Shumlin	Democrat	[b] 2	Jan. 2013
Virginia	Richmond	Bob McDonnell	Republican	[a] 4	Jan. 2014
Washington	Olympia	Chris Gregoire	Democrat	[d] 4	Jan. 2013
West Virginia	Charleston	Earl Ray Tomblin	Democrat	[c] 4	Jan. 2013
Wisconsin	Madison	Scott Walker	Republican	[b] 4	Jan. 2015
Wyoming	Cheyenne	Matthew Mead	Republican	[c] 4	Jan. 2015
COMMONWEALTH OF					
Puerto Rico	San Juan	Luis G. Fortuño	Republican	[b] 4	Jan. 2013
TERRITORIES					
Guam	Agana	Eddie Calvo	Republican	[c] 4	Jan. 2015
Virgin Islands	Charlotte Amalie	John deJongh, Jr.	Democrat	[c] 4	Jan. 2014
American Samoa	Pago Pago	Togiola T.A. Tulafono	Democrat	[c] 4	Jan. 2013
Northern Mariana Islands.	Saipan	Benigno Fitial	Republican	[h] 5	Jan. 2015

[a] Cannot succeed himself. [b] No limit. [c] Can serve 2 consecutive terms. [d] Can serve 3 consecutive terms. [e] Can serve 4 consecutive terms. [f] Can serve no more than 8 years in a 12-year period. [g] Can serve no more than 8 years in a 16-year period. [h] The dates for gubernatorial elections in the Northern Mariana Islands are being changed from odd-numbered years to even-numbered ones, beginning in November 2014 (rather than November 2013); therefore, for the current term only, the governor is serving a 5-year term rather than a 4-year term.

NOTE: Information for table obtained from the National Governors Association.

PRESIDENTS AND VICE PRESIDENTS AND THE CONGRESSES COINCIDENT WITH THEIR TERMS [1]

President	Vice President	Service	Congresses
George Washington	John Adams	Apr. 30, 1789–Mar. 3, 1797	1, 2, 3, 4.
John Adams	Thomas Jefferson	Mar. 4, 1797–Mar. 3, 1801	5, 6.
Thomas Jefferson	Aaron Burr	Mar. 4, 1801–Mar. 3, 1805	7, 8.
Do	George Clinton	Mar. 4, 1805–Mar. 3, 1809	9, 10.
James Madison	...do. [2]	Mar. 4, 1809–Mar. 3, 1813	11, 12.
Do	Elbridge Gerry [3]	Mar. 4, 1813–Mar. 3, 1817	13, 14.
James Monroe	Daniel D. Tompkins	Mar. 4, 1817–Mar. 3, 1825	15, 16, 17, 18, 19
John Quincy Adams	John C. Calhoun	Mar. 4, 1825–Mar. 3, 1829	19, 20.
Andrew Jackson	...do. [4]	Mar. 4, 1829–Mar. 3, 1833	21, 22.
Do	Martin Van Buren	Mar. 4, 1833–Mar. 3, 1837	23, 24.
Martin Van Buren	Richard M. Johnson	Mar. 4, 1837–Mar. 3, 1841	25, 26.
William Henry Harrison [5]	John Tyler	Mar. 4, 1841–Apr. 4, 1841	27.
John Tyler		Apr. 6, 1841 –Mar. 3, 1845	27, 28.
James K. Polk	George M. Dallas	Mar. 4, 1845–Mar. 3, 1849	29, 30.
Zachary Taylor [5]	Millard Fillmore	Mar. 5, 1849–July 9, 1850	31.
Millard Fillmore		July 10, 1850–Mar. 3, 1853	31, 32.
Franklin Pierce	William R. King [6]	Mar. 4, 1853–Mar. 3, 1857	33, 34.
James Buchanan	John C. Breckinridge	Mar. 4, 1857–Mar. 3, 1861	35, 36.
Abraham Lincoln	Hannibal Hamlin	Mar. 4, 1861–Mar. 3, 1865	37, 38.
Do.[5]	Andrew Johnson	Mar. 4, 1865–Apr. 15, 1865	39.
Andrew Johnson		Apr. 15, 1865–Mar. 3, 1869	39, 40.
Ulysses S. Grant	Schuyler Colfax	Mar. 4, 1869–Mar. 3, 1873	41, 42.
Do	Henry Wilson [7]	Mar. 4, 1873–Mar. 3, 1877	43, 44.
Rutherford B. Hayes	William A. Wheeler	Mar. 4, 1877–Mar. 3, 1881	45, 46.
James A. Garfield [5]	Chester A. Arthur	Mar. 4, 1881–Sept. 19, 1881	47.
Chester A. Arthur		Sept. 20, 1881–Mar. 3, 1885	47, 48.
Grover Cleveland	Thomas A. Hendricks [8]	Mar. 4, 1885–Mar. 3, 1889	49, 50.
Benjamin Harrison	Levi P. Morton	Mar. 4, 1889–Mar. 3, 1893	51, 52.
Grover Cleveland	Adlai E. Stevenson	Mar. 4, 1893–Mar. 3, 1897	53, 54.
William McKinley	Garret A. Hobart [9]	Mar. 4, 1897–Mar. 3, 1901	55, 56.
Do.[5]	Theodore Roosevelt	Mar. 4, 1901–Sept. 14, 1901	57.
Theodore Roosevelt		Sept. 14, 1901–Mar. 3, 1905	57, 58.
Do	Charles W. Fairbanks	Mar. 4, 1905–Mar. 3, 1909	59, 60.
William H. Taft	James S. Sherman [10]	Mar. 4, 1909–Mar. 3, 1913	61, 62.
Woodrow Wilson	Thomas R. Marshall	Mar. 4, 1913–Mar. 3, 1921	63, 64, 65, 66, 67.
Warren G. Harding [5]	Calvin Coolidge	Mar. 4, 1921–Aug. 2, 1923	67.
Calvin Coolidge		Aug. 3, 1923–Mar. 3, 1925	68.
Do	Charles G. Dawes	Mar. 4, 1925–Mar. 3, 1929	69, 70.
Herbert C. Hoover	Charles Curtis	Mar. 4, 1929–Mar. 3, 1933	71, 72.
Franklin D. Roosevelt	John N. Garner	Mar. 4, 1933–Jan. 20, 1941	73, 74, 75, 76, 77.
Do	Henry A. Wallace	Jan. 20, 1941–Jan. 20, 1945	77, 78, 79.
Do.[5]	Harry S. Truman	Jan. 20, 1945–Apr. 12, 1945	79.
Harry S. Truman		Apr. 12, 1945–Jan. 20, 1949	79, 80, 81.
Do	Alben W. Barkley	Jan. 20, 1949–Jan. 20, 1953	81, 82, 83.
Dwight D. Eisenhower	Richard M. Nixon	Jan. 20, 1953–Jan. 20, 1961	83, 84, 85, 86, 87.
John F. Kennedy [5]	Lyndon B. Johnson	Jan. 20, 1961–Nov. 22, 1963	87, 88, 89.
Lyndon B. Johnson		Nov. 22, 1963–Jan. 20, 1965	88, 89.
Do	Hubert H. Humphrey	Jan. 20, 1965–Jan. 20, 1969	89, 90, 91.
Richard M. Nixon	Spiro T. Agnew [11]	Jan. 20, 1969–Dec. 6, 1973	91, 92, 93.
Do. [13]	Gerald R. Ford [12]	Dec. 6, 1973–Aug. 9, 1974	93.
Gerald R. Ford		Aug. 9, 1974–Dec. 19, 1974	93.
Do	Nelson A. Rockefeller [14]	Dec. 19, 1974–Jan. 20, 1977	93, 94, 95.
James Earl "Jimmy" Carter	Walter F. Mondale	Jan. 20, 1977–Jan. 20, 1981	95, 96, 97.
Ronald Reagan	George Bush	Jan. 20, 1981–Jan. 20, 1989	97, 98, 99, 100, 101.
George Bush	Dan Quayle	Jan. 20, 1989–Jan. 20, 1993	101, 102, 103.
William J. Clinton	Albert Gore	Jan. 20, 1993–Jan. 20, 2001	103, 104, 105, 106, 107.
George W. Bush	Richard B. Cheney	Jan. 20, 2001–Jan. 20, 2009	107, 108, 109, 110, 111.
Barack H. Obama	Joseph R. Biden, Jr.	Jan. 20, 2009–	111, 112.

[1] From 1789 until 1933, the terms of the President and Vice President and the term of the Congress coincided, beginning on March 4 and ending on March 3. This changed when the 20th amendment to the Constitution was adopted in 1933. Beginning in 1934 the convening date for Congress became January 3, and beginning in 1937 the starting date for the Presidential term became January 20. Because of this change, the number of Congresses overlapping with a Presidential term increased from two to three, although the third only overlaps by a few weeks.

[2] Died Apr. 20, 1812.

[3] Died Nov. 23, 1814.

[4] Resigned Dec. 28, 1832, to become a United States Senator from South Carolina.

[5] Died in office.

[6] Died Apr. 18, 1853.

[7] Died Nov. 22, 1875.

[8] Died Nov. 25, 1885.

[9] Died Nov. 21, 1899.

[10] Died Oct. 30, 1912.

[11] Resigned Oct. 10, 1973.

[12] Nominated to be Vice President by President Richard M. Nixon on Oct. 12, 1973; confirmed by the Senate on Nov. 27, 1973; confirmed by the House of Representatives on Dec. 6, 1973; took the oath of office on Dec. 6, 1973 in the Hall of the House of Representatives. This was the first time a Vice President was nominated by the President and confirmed by the Congress pursuant to the 25th amendment to the Constitution.

[13] Resigned from office.

[14] Nominated to be Vice President by President Gerald R. Ford on Aug. 20, 1974; confirmed by the Senate on Dec. 10, 1974; confirmed by the House of Representatives on Dec. 19, 1974; took the oath of office on Dec. 19, 1974, in the Senate Chamber.

CAPITOL BUILDINGS AND GROUNDS

UNITED STATES CAPITOL

OVERVIEW OF THE BUILDING AND ITS FUNCTION

The United States Capitol is among the most architecturally impressive and symbolically important buildings in the world. It has housed the chambers of the Senate and the House of Representatives for more than two centuries. Begun in 1793, the Capitol has been built, burnt, rebuilt, extended, and restored; today, it stands as a monument not only to its builders but also to the American people and their government.

As the focal point of the government's legislative branch, the Capitol is the centerpiece of the Capitol complex, which includes the six principal congressional office buildings and three Library of Congress buildings constructed on Capitol Hill in the 19th and 20th centuries.

In addition to its active use by Congress, the Capitol is a museum of American art and history. Each year, it is visited by millions of people from around the world.

A fine example of 19th-century neoclassical architecture, the Capitol combines function with aesthetics. Its design was derived from ancient Greece and Rome and evokes the ideals that guided the nation's founders as they framed their new republic. As the building was expanded from its original design, harmony with the existing portions was carefully maintained.

Today, the Capitol covers a ground area of 175,170 square feet, or about 4 acres, and has a floor area of approximately 16½ acres. Its length, from north to south, is 751 feet 4 inches; its greatest width, including approaches, is 350 feet. Its height above the base line on the east front to the top of the Statue of Freedom is 288 feet; from the basement floor to the top of the dome is an ascent of 365 steps.

The building is divided into five levels. The first, or ground, floor is occupied chiefly by committee rooms and the spaces allocated to various congressional officers. The areas accessible to visitors on this level include the Hall of Columns, the restored Old Supreme Court Chamber, and the Crypt beneath the Rotunda.

The second floor holds the chambers of the House of Representatives (in the south wing) and the Senate (in the north wing). This floor also contains three major public areas. In the center under the dome is the Rotunda, a circular ceremonial space that also serves as a gallery of paintings and sculpture depicting significant people and events in the nation's history. The Rotunda is 96 feet in diameter and rises 180 feet 3 inches to the canopy. The semicircular chamber south of the Rotunda served as the Hall of the House until 1857; now designated National Statuary Hall, it houses part of the Capitol's collection of statues donated by the states in commemoration of notable citizens. The Old Senate Chamber northeast of the Rotunda, which was used by the Senate until 1859, has been returned to its mid-19th-century appearance.

The third floor allows access to the galleries from which visitors to the Capitol may watch the proceedings of the House and the Senate when Congress is in session. The rest of this floor is occupied by offices, committee rooms, and press galleries.

The fourth floor and the basement/terrace level of the Capitol are occupied by offices, machinery rooms, workshops, and other support areas.

Located beneath the East Front plaza, the newest addition to the Capitol is the Capitol Visitor Center (CVC). Preparatory construction activities began in 2002, and the CVC was opened to the public on December 2, 2008. This date was chosen for its significance in the Capitol's history: it was on December 2, 1863, that the Statue of Freedom was placed atop the Capitol to signify completion of the construction of the new dome. The CVC occupies 580,000 square feet of space on three levels and includes an Exhibition Hall, a restaurant, orientation theaters, gift shops, and other visitor amenities as well as office and meeting space for the House and Senate.

LOCATION OF THE CAPITOL

The Capitol is located at the eastern end of the Mall on a plateau 88 feet above the level of the Potomac River, commanding a westward view across the Capitol Reflecting Pool to the Washington Monument 1.4 miles away and the Lincoln Memorial 2.2 miles away.

Before 1791, the Federal Government had no permanent site. The early Congresses met in eight different cities: Philadelphia, Baltimore, Lancaster, York, Princeton, Annapolis, Trenton, and New York City. The subject of a permanent capital for the Government of the United States was first raised by Congress in 1783; it was ultimately addressed in Article I, Section 8 of the Constitution (1787), which gave the Congress legislative authority over ''such District (not exceeding ten Miles square) as may, by Cession of Particular States, and the Acceptance of Congress, become the Seat of the Government of the United States. . . .''

In 1788, the State of Maryland ceded to Congress ''any district in this State, not exceeding ten miles square,'' and in 1789 the State of Virginia ceded an equivalent amount of land. In accordance with the ''Residence Act'' passed by Congress in 1790, President Washington in 1791 selected the area that is now the District of Columbia from the land ceded by Maryland (private landowners whose property fell within this area were compensated by a payment of £25 per acre); that ceded by Virginia was not used for the capital and was returned to Virginia in 1846. Also under the provisions of that Act, he selected three commissioners to survey the site and oversee the design and construction of the capital city and its government buildings. The commissioners, in turn, selected the French-American engineer Pierre Charles L'Enfant to plan the new city of Washington. L'Enfant's plan, which was influenced by the gardens at Versailles, arranged the city's streets and avenues in a grid overlaid with baroque diagonals; the result is a functional and aesthetic whole in which government buildings are balanced against public lawns, gardens, squares, and paths. The Capitol itself was located at the elevated east end of the Mall, on the brow of what was then called Jenkins' Hill. The site was, in L'Enfant's words, ''a pedestal waiting for a monument.''

SELECTION OF A PLAN

L'Enfant was expected to design the Capitol and to supervise its construction. However, he refused to produce any drawings for the building, claiming that he carried the design ''in his head''; this fact and his refusal to consider himself subject to the commissioners' authority led to his dismissal in 1792. In March of that year the commissioners announced a competition, suggested by Secretary of State Thomas Jefferson, that would award $500 and a city lot to whoever produced ''the most approved plan'' for the Capitol by mid-July. None of the 17 plans submitted, however, was wholly satisfactory. In October, a letter arrived from Dr. William Thornton, a Scottish-trained physician living in Tortola, British West Indies, requesting an opportunity to present a plan even though the competition had closed. The commissioners granted this request.

Thornton's plan depicted a building composed of three sections. The central section, which was topped by a low dome, was to be flanked on the north and south by two rectangular wings (one for the Senate and one for the House of Representatives). President Washington commended the plan for its ''grandeur, simplicity and convenience,'' and on April 5, 1793, it was accepted by the commissioners; Washington gave his formal approval on July 25.

BRIEF CONSTRUCTION HISTORY

1793–1829

The cornerstone was laid by President Washington in the building's southeast corner on September 18, 1793, with Masonic ceremonies. Work progressed under the direction of three architects in succession. Stephen H. Hallet (an entrant in the earlier competition) and George Hadfield were eventually dismissed by the commissioners because of inappropriate design changes that they tried to impose; James Hoban, the architect of the White House, saw the first phase of the project through to completion.

Construction was a laborious and time-consuming process: the sandstone used for the building had to be ferried on boats from the quarries at Aquia, Virginia; workers had to be induced to leave their homes to come to the relative wilderness of Capitol Hill; and funding was inadequate. By August 1796 the commissioners were forced to focus the entire work effort on the building's north wing so that it at least could be ready for government occupancy as scheduled. Even so, some third-floor rooms were still unfinished when the Congress, the Supreme Court, the Library of Congress, and the courts of the District of Columbia occupied the Capitol in late 1800.

In 1803, Congress allocated funds to resume construction. A year earlier, the office of the Commissioners had been abolished and replaced by a superintendent of the city of Washington. To oversee the renewed construction effort, Benjamin Henry Latrobe was appointed surveyor of public buildings. The first professional architect and engineer to work in America, Latrobe modified Thornton's plan for the south wing to include space for offices and committee rooms; he also introduced alterations to simplify the construction work. Latrobe began work by removing a squat, oval, temporary building known as "the Oven," which had been erected in 1801 as a meeting place for the House of Representatives. By 1807 construction on the south wing was sufficiently advanced that the House was able to occupy its new legislative chamber, and the wing was completed in 1811.

In 1808, as work on the south wing progressed, Latrobe began the rebuilding of the north wing, which had fallen into disrepair. Rather than simply repair the wing, he redesigned the interior of the building to increase its usefulness and durability; among his changes was the addition of a chamber for the Supreme Court. By 1811, he had completed the eastern half of this wing, but funding was being increasingly diverted to preparations for a second war with Great Britain. By 1813, Latrobe had no further work in Washington and so he departed, leaving the north and south wings of the Capitol connected only by a temporary wooden passageway.

The War of 1812 left the Capitol, in Latrobe's later words, "a most magnificent ruin": on August 24, 1814, British troops set fire to the building, and only a sudden rainstorm prevented its complete destruction. Immediately after the fire, Congress met for one session in Blodget's Hotel, which was at Seventh and E Streets, NW. From 1815 to 1819, Congress occupied a building erected for it on First Street, NE., on part of the site now occupied by the Supreme Court Building. This building later came to be known as the Old Brick Capitol.

Latrobe returned to Washington in 1815, when he was rehired to restore the Capitol. In addition to making repairs, he took advantage of this opportunity to make further changes in the building's interior design (for example, an enlargement of the Senate Chamber) and introduce new materials (for example, marble discovered along the upper Potomac). However, he came under increasing pressure because of construction delays (most of which were beyond his control) and cost overruns; finally, he resigned his post in November 1817.

On January 8, 1818, Charles Bulfinch, a prominent Boston architect, was appointed Latrobe's successor. Continuing the restoration of the north and south wings, he was able to make the chambers for the Supreme Court, the House, and the Senate ready for use by 1819. Bulfinch also redesigned and supervised the construction of the Capitol's central section. The copper-covered wooden dome that topped this section was made higher than Bulfinch considered appropriate to the building's size (at the direction of President James Monroe and Secretary of State John Quincy Adams). After completing the last part of the building in 1826, Bulfinch spent the next few years on the Capitol's decoration and landscaping. In 1829, his work was done and his position with the government was terminated. In the 38 years following Bulfinch's tenure, the Capitol was entrusted to the care of the commissioner of public buildings.

1830–1868

The Capitol was by this point already an impressive structure. At ground level, its length was 351 feet 7½ inches and its width was 282 feet 10½ inches. Up to the year 1827—records from later years being incomplete—the project cost was $2,432,851.34. Improvements to the building continued in the years to come (running water in 1832, gas lighting in the 1840s), but by 1850 its size could no longer accommodate the increasing numbers of Senators and Representatives from newly admitted states. The Senate therefore voted to hold another competition, offering a prize of $500 for the best plan to extend the Capitol. Several suitable plans were submitted, some proposing an eastward extension of the building and others proposing the addition of large north and south wings. However, Congress was unable to decide between these two approaches, and the prize money was divided among five architects. Thus, the tasks of selecting a plan and appointing an architect fell to President Millard Fillmore.

Fillmore's choice was Thomas U. Walter, a Philadelphia architect who had entered the competition. On July 4, 1851, in a ceremony whose principal oration was delivered by Secretary of State Daniel Webster, the president laid the cornerstone in the northeast corner of the House wing. Over the next 14 years, Walter supervised the construction of the extension, ensuring their compatibility with the architectural style of the existing building. However, because the Aquia Creek sandstone used earlier had deteriorated noticeably, he chose to use marble for the exterior. For the veneer, Walter selected marble quarried at Lee, Massachusetts, and for the columns he used marble from Cockeysville, Maryland.

Walter faced several significant challenges during the course of construction. Chief among these was the steady imposition by the government of additional tasks without additional pay. Aside from his work on the Capitol extension, Walter designed the wings of the Patent Office building, extensions to the Treasury and Post Office buildings, and the Marine barracks in Pensacola and Brooklyn. When the Library of Congress in the Capitol's west central section was gutted by a fire in 1851, Walter was commissioned to restore it. He also encountered obstacles in his work on the Capitol extensions. His location of the legislative chambers was changed in 1853 at the direction of President Franklin Pierce, based on the suggestions of the newly appointed supervising engineer, Captain Montgomery C. Meigs. In general, however, the project progressed rapidly: the House of Representatives was able to meet in its new chamber on December 16, 1857, and the Senate first met in its present chamber on January 4, 1859. The old House chamber was later designated National Statuary Hall. In 1861 most construction was suspended because of the Civil War, and the Capitol was used briefly as a military barracks, hospital, and bakery. In 1862 work on the entire building was resumed.

As the new wings were constructed, more than doubling the length of the Capitol, it became apparent that the dome erected by Bulfinch no longer suited the building's proportions. In 1855 Congress voted for its replacement based on Walter's design for a new, fireproof cast-iron dome. The old dome was removed in 1856 and 5,000,000 pounds of new masonry was placed on the existing rotunda walls. Iron used in the dome construction had an aggregate weight of 8,909,200 pounds and was lifted into place by steam-powered derricks.

In 1859, Thomas Crawford's plaster model for the Statue of Freedom, designed for the top of the dome, arrived from the sculptor's studio in Rome. With a height of 19 feet 6 inches, the statue was almost 3 feet taller than specified, and Walter was compelled to make revisions to his design for the dome. When cast in bronze by Clark Mills at his foundry on the outskirts of Washington, it weighed 14,985 pounds. The statue was lifted into place atop the dome in 1863, its final section being installed on December 2 to the accompaniment of gun salutes from the forts around the city.

The work on the dome and the extension was completed under the direction of Edward Clark, who had served as Walter's assistant and was appointed Architect of the Capitol in 1865 after Walter's resignation. In 1866, the Italian-born artist Constantino Brumidi finished the canopy fresco, a monumental painting entitled *The Apotheosis of George Washington.* The Capitol extension was completed in 1868.

1869–1902

Clark continued to hold the post of Architect of the Capitol until his death in 1902. During his tenure, the Capitol underwent considerable modernization. Steam heat was gradually installed in the old Capitol. In 1874 the first elevator was installed, and in the 1880s electric lighting began to replace gas lights.

Between 1884 and 1891, the marble terraces on the north, west, and south sides of the Capitol were constructed. As part of the landscape plan devised by Frederick Law Olmsted, these terraces not only added over 100 rooms to the Capitol but also provided a broader, more substantial visual base for the building.

On November 6, 1898, a gas explosion and fire in the original north wing dramatically illustrated the need for fireproofing. The roofs over the Statuary Hall wing and the original north wing were reconstructed and fireproofed, the work being completed in 1902 by Clark's successor, Elliott Woods. In 1901, the space in the west central front vacated by the Library of Congress was converted to committee rooms.

1903–1970

During the remainder of Woods's service, which ended with his death in 1923, no major structural work was required on the Capitol. The activities performed in the building were limited chiefly to cleaning and refurbishing the interior. David Lynn, the Architect of the Capitol from 1923 until his retirement in 1954, continued these tasks. Between July 1949 and January 1951, the corroded roofs and skylights of both wings and the connecting corridors were replaced with new roofs of concrete and steel, covered with copper. The cast-iron and glass ceilings of the House and Senate chambers were replaced with ceilings of stainless steel and plaster, with a laylight of carved glass and bronze in the middle of each. The House and Senate chambers were completely redecorated, modern lighting was added, and acoustical problems were solved. During this renovation program, the House and Senate vacated their chambers on several occasions so that the work could progress.

The next significant modification made to the Capitol was the east front extension. This project was carried out under the supervision of Architect of the Capitol J. George Stewart, who served from 1954 until his death in 1970. Begun in 1958, it involved the construction of a new east front 32 feet 6 inches east of the old front, faithfully reproducing the sandstone structure in marble. The old sandstone walls were not destroyed; rather, they were left in place to become a part of the interior wall and are now buttressed by the addition. The marble columns of the connecting corridors were also moved and reused. Other elements of this project included repairing the dome, constructing a subway terminal under the Senate steps, reconstructing those steps, cleaning both wings, birdproofing the building, providing furniture and furnishings for 90 new rooms created by the extension, and improving the lighting throughout the building. The project was completed in 1962.

1971–Present

During the nearly 25-year tenure (1971–1995) of Architect of the Capitol George M. White, FAIA, the building was both modernized and restored. Electronic voting equipment was installed in the House chamber in 1973; facilities were added to allow television coverage of the House and Senate debates in 1979 and 1986, respectively; and improved climate control, electronic surveillance systems, and new computer and communications facilities have been added to bring the Capitol up-to-date. The Old Senate Chamber, National Statuary Hall, and the Old Supreme Court Chamber, on the other hand, were restored to their mid-19th-century appearance in the 1970s.

In 1983, work began on the strengthening, renovation, and preservation of the west front of the Capitol. Structural problems had developed over the years because of defects in the original foundations, deterioration of the sandstone facing material, alterations to the basic building fabric (a fourth-floor addition and channeling of the walls to install interior utilities), and damage from the fires of 1814 and 1851 and the 1898 gas explosion.

To strengthen the structure, over 1,000 stainless steel tie rods were set into the building's masonry. More than 30 layers of paint were removed, and damaged stonework was repaired or replicated. Ultimately, 40 percent of the sandstone blocks were replaced with limestone. The walls were treated with a special consolidant and then painted to match the marble wings. The entire project was completed in 1987.

A related project, completed in January 1993, effected the repair of the Olmsted terraces, which had been subject to damage from settling, and converted the terrace courtyards into several thousand square feet of meeting space.

As the Capitol enters its third century, restoration and modernization work continues. Alan M. Hantman, FAIA, was appointed in February 1997 to a 10-year term as Architect of the Capitol. Projects under his direction included rehabilitation of the Capitol dome; conservation of murals; improvement of speech-reinforcement, electrical, and fire-protection systems in the Capitol and the Congressional office buildings; work on security improvements within the Capitol complex; restoration of the U.S. Botanic Garden Conservatory; the design and construction of the National Garden adjacent to the Botanic Garden Conservatory; renovation of the building systems in the Dirksen Senate Office Building; publication of the first comprehensive history of the Capitol to appear in a century; and construction of the Capitol Visitor Center. At the end of Mr. Hantman's term in February 2007, Mr. Stephen T. Ayers, AIA, LEED AP, assumed the position of Acting Architect of the Capitol. On February 24, 2010, President Barack Obama nominated Mr. Ayers to serve as the 11th Architect of the Capitol. On May 12, 2010, the United States Senate, by unanimous consent, confirmed Mr. Ayers, and on May 13, 2010, the President officially appointed Mr. Ayers to a 10-year term as Architect of the Capitol.

HOUSE OFFICE BUILDINGS

Cannon House Office Building

An increased membership of the Senate and House resulted in a demand for additional rooms for the accommodations of the Senators and Representatives. On March 3, 1903, the Congress authorized the erection of a fireproofed office building for the use of the House. It was designed by the firm of Carrere & Hastings of New York City in the Beaux Arts style. The first brick was laid July 5, 1905, in square No. 690, and formal exercises were held at the laying of the cornerstone on April 14, 1906, in which President Theodore Roosevelt participated. The building was completed and occupied January 10, 1908. A subsequent change in the basis of congressional representation made necessary the building of an additional story in 1913–1914. The total cost of the building, including site, furnishings, equipment, and the subway connecting it with the U.S. Capitol, amounted to $4,860,155. This office building contains about 500 rooms, and was considered at the time of its completion fully equipped for all the needs of a modern building for office purposes. A garage was added in the building's courtyard in the 1960s.

Pursuant to authority in the Second Supplemental Appropriations Act, 1955, and subsequent action of the House Office Building Commission, remodeling of the Cannon Building began in 1966. The estimated cost of this work was $5,200,000. Pursuant to the provisions of Public Law 87–453, approved May 21, 1962, the building was named in honor of Joseph G. Cannon of Illinois, who was Speaker at the time the building was constructed.

Longworth House Office Building

Under legislation contained in the Authorization Act of January 10, 1929, and in the urgent deficiency bill of March 4, 1929, provisions were made for an additional House office building, to be located on the west side of New Jersey Avenue (opposite the first House office building). The building was designed by the Allied Architects of Washington in the Neoclassical Revival style.

The cornerstone was laid June 24, 1932, and the building was completed on April 20, 1933. It contains 251 two-room suites and 16 committee rooms. Each suite and committee room is provided with a storeroom. Eight floors are occupied by members. The basement and subbasement contain shops and mechanical areas needed for the maintenance of the building. A cafeteria was added in the building's courtyard in the 1960s. The cost of this building, including site, furnishings, and equipment, was $7,805,705. Pursuant to the provisions of Public Law 87–453, approved May 21, 1962, the building was named in honor of Nicholas Longworth of Ohio, who was Speaker when the second House office building was constructed.

Rayburn House Office Building and Other Related Changes and Improvements

Under legislation contained in the Second Supplemental Appropriations Act, 1955, provision was made for construction of a fireproof office building for the House of Representatives.

All work was carried forward by the Architect of the Capitol under the direction of the House Office Building Commission at a cost totaling $135,279,000.

The Rayburn Building is connected to the Capitol by a subway. Designs for the building were prepared by the firm of Harbeson, Hough, Livingston & Larson of Philadelphia, Associate Architects. The building contains 169 congressional suites; full-committee hearing rooms for 9 standing committees, 16 subcommittee hearing rooms, committee staff rooms and other committee facilities; a large cafeteria and other restaurant facilities; an underground garage; and a variety of liaison offices, press and television facilities, maintenance and equipment shops or rooms, and storage areas. This building has nine stories and a penthouse for machinery.

The cornerstone was laid May 24, 1962, by John W. McCormack, Speaker of the House of Representatives. President John F. Kennedy participated in the cornerstone laying and delivered the address.

A portion of the basement floor was occupied beginning March 12, 1964, by House of Representatives personnel moved from the George Washington Inn property. Full occupancy of the Rayburn Building, under the room-filing regulations, was begun February 23, 1965, and completed April 2, 1965. Pursuant to the provisions of Public Law 87–453, approved May 21, 1962, the building was named in honor of Sam Rayburn of Texas.

House Office Building Annex No. 2, named the "Gerald R. Ford House of Representatives Office Building," was acquired in 1975 from the General Services Administration. The structure, located at Second and D Streets, SW., was built in 1939 for the Federal Bureau of Investigation as a fingerprint file archives. This building has approximately 432,000 square feet of space.

SENATE OFFICE BUILDINGS

RICHARD BREVARD RUSSELL SENATE OFFICE BUILDING

In 1891 the Senate provided itself with office space by the purchase of the Maltby Building, then located on the northwest corner of B Street (now Constitution Avenue) and New Jersey Avenue, NW. When it was condemned as an unsafe structure, Senators needed safer and more commodious office space. Under authorization of the Act of April 28, 1904, square 686 on the northeast corner of Delaware Avenue and B Street, NE. was purchased as a site for the Senate Office Building. The plans for the House Office Building were adapted for the Senate Office Building by the firm of Carrere & Hastings, with the exception that the side of the building fronting on First Street, NE. was temporarily omitted. The cornerstone was laid without special exercises on July 31, 1906, and the building was occupied March 5, 1909. In 1931, the completion of the fourth side of the building was commenced. In 1933 it was completed, together with alterations to the C Street facade, and the construction of terraces, balustrades, and approaches. The cost of the completed building, including the site, furnishings, equipment and the subway connecting it with the United States Capitol, was $8,390,892.

The building was named the ''Richard Brevard Russell Senate Office Building'' by Senate Resolution 296, 92nd Congress, agreed to October 11, 1972, as amended by Senate Resolution 295, 96th Congress, agreed to December 3, 1979.

EVERETT MCKINLEY DIRKSEN SENATE OFFICE BUILDING

Under legislation contained in the Second Deficiency Appropriations Act, 1948, Public Law 80–785, provision was made for an additional office building for the United States Senate with limits of cost of $1,100,000 for acquisition of the site and $20,600,000 for constructing and equipping the building.

The construction cost limit was subsequently increased to $24,196,000. All work was carried forward by the Architect of the Capitol under the direction of the Senate Office Building Commission. The New York firm of Eggers & Higgins served as the consulting architect.

The site was acquired and cleared in 1948–49 at a total cost of $1,011,492.

A contract for excavation, concrete footings, and mats for the new building was awarded in January 1955, in the amount of $747,200. Groundbreaking ceremonies were held January 26, 1955.

A contract for the superstructure of the new building was awarded September 9, 1955, in the amount of $17,200,000. The cornerstone was laid July 13, 1956.

As a part of this project, a new underground subway system was installed from the Capitol to both the Old and New Senate Office Buildings.

An appropriation of $1,000,000 for furniture and furnishings for the new building was provided in 1958. The building was accepted for beneficial occupancy on October 15, 1958.

The building was named the ''Everett McKinley Dirksen Senate Office Building'' by Senate Resolution 296, 92nd Congress, agreed to October 11, 1972, and Senate Resolution 295, 96th Congress, agreed to December 3, 1979.

PHILIP A. HART SENATE OFFICE BUILDING

Construction as an extension to the Dirksen Senate Office Building was authorized on October 31, 1972; legislation enacted in subsequent years increased the scope of the project and established a total cost ceiling of $137,700,400. The firm of John Carl Warnecke & Associates served as Associate Architect for the project.

Senate Resolution 525, passed August 30, 1976, amended by Senate Resolution 295, 96th Congress, agreed to December 3, 1979, provided that upon completion of the extension it would be named the ''Philip A. Hart Senate Office Building'' to honor the Senator from Michigan.

The contract for clearing of the site, piping for utilities, excavation, and construction of foundation was awarded in December 1975. Groundbreaking took place January 5, 1976. The contract for furnishing and delivery of the exterior stone was awarded in February 1977, and the contract for the superstructure, which included wall and roof systems and the erection of all exterior stonework, was awarded in October 1977. The contract for the first portion of the interior and related work was awarded in December 1978. A contract for interior finishing was awarded in July 1980. The first suite was occupied on November 22, 1982. Alexander Calder's mobile/stabile *Mountains and Clouds* was installed in the building's atrium in November 1986.

CAPITOL POWER PLANT

During the development of the plans for the Cannon and Russell Buildings, the question of heat, light, and power was considered. The Senate and House wings of the Capitol were heated by separate heating plants. The Library of Congress also had a heating plant for that building. It was determined that needs for heating and lighting and electrical power could be met by a central power plant.

A site was selected in Garfield Park. Since this park was a Government reservation, an appropriation was not required to secure title. The determining factors leading to the selection of this site were its proximity to the tracks of what is now the Penn Central Railroad and to the buildings to be served.

The dimensions of the Capitol Power Plant, which was authorized on April 28, 1904, and completed in 1910, were 244 feet 8 inches by 117 feet.

The buildings originally served by the Capitol Power Plant were connected to it by a reinforced-concrete steam tunnel.

In September 1951, when the demand for electrical energy was reaching the maximum capacity of the Capitol Power Plant, arrangements were made to purchase electrical service from the local public utility company and to discontinue electrical generation. The heating and cooling functions of the Capitol Power Plant were expanded in 1935, 1939, 1958, 1973, and 1980. A new refrigeration plant modernization and expansion project was completed in 2007.

U.S. CAPITOL GROUNDS

A Description of the Grounds

Originally a wooded wilderness, the U.S. Capitol Grounds today provide a park-like setting for the Nation's Capitol, offering a picturesque counterpoint to the building's formal architecture. The grounds immediately surrounding the Capitol are bordered by a stone wall and cover an area of 58.8 acres. Their boundaries are Independence Avenue on the south, Constitution Avenue on the north, First Street, NE./SE. on the east, and First Street, NW./SW. on the west. Over 100 varieties of trees and bushes are planted around the Capitol, and thousands of flowers are used in seasonal displays. In contrast to the building's straight, neoclassical lines, most of the walkways in the grounds are curved. Benches along the paths offer pleasant spots for visitors to appreciate the building, its landscape, and the surrounding areas, most notably the Mall to the west.

The grounds were designed by Frederick Law Olmsted (1822–1903), who planned the landscaping of the area that was performed from 1874 to 1892. Olmsted, who also designed New York's Central Park, is considered the greatest American landscape architect of his day. He was a pioneer in the development of public parks in America, and many of his designs were influenced by his studies of European parks, gardens, and estates. In describing his plan for the Capitol Grounds, Olmsted noted that, ''The ground is in design part of the Capitol, but in all respects subsidiary to the central structure.'' Therefore, he was careful not to group trees or other landscape features in any way that would distract the viewer from the Capitol. The use of sculpture and other ornamentation has also been kept to a minimum.

Many of the trees on the Capitol Grounds have historic or memorial associations. Over 30 states have made symbolic gifts of their state trees to the Capitol Grounds. Many of the trees on the grounds bear plaques that identify their species and their historic significance.

At the East Capitol Street entrance to the Capitol plaza are two large rectangular stone fountains. Six massive red granite lamp piers topped with light fixtures in wrought-iron cages, and 16 smaller bronze light fixtures, line the paved plaza. Three sets of benches are enclosed with wrought-iron railings and grilles; the roofed bench was originally a shelter for streetcar passengers.

The northern part of the grounds offers a shaded walk among trees, flowers, and shrubbery. A small, hexagonal brick structure named the Summer House may be found in the northwest corner of the grounds. This structure contains shaded benches, a central ornamental fountain, and three public drinking fountains. In a small grotto on the eastern side of the Summer House, a stream of water flows and splashes over rocks to create a pleasing sound and cool the summer breezes.

A Brief History of the Grounds Before Olmsted

The land on which the Capitol stands was first occupied by the Manahoacs and the Monacans, who were subtribes of the Algonquin Indians. Early settlers reported that these tribes occasionally held councils not far from the foot of the hill. This land eventually became a part of Cerne Abbey Manor, and at the time of its acquisition by the Federal Government it was owned by Daniel Carroll of Duddington.

The ''Residence Act'' of 1790 provided that the Federal Government should be established in a permanent location by the year 1800. In early March 1791, the commissioners of the city of Washington, who had been appointed by President George Washington, selected the French engineer Pierre Charles L'Enfant to plan the new federal city. L'Enfant decided to locate the Capitol at the elevated east end of the Mall (on what was then called Jenkins' Hill); he described the site as ''a pedestal waiting for a monument.''

At this time the site of the Capitol was a relative wilderness partly overgrown with scrub oak. Oliver Wolcott, a signer of the Declaration of Independence, described the soil as an ''*exceedingly stiff* clay, becoming dust in dry and mortar in rainy weather.''

In 1825, a plan was devised for imposing order on the Capitol Grounds, and it was carried out for almost 15 years. The plan divided the area into flat, rectangular grassy areas bordered by trees, flower beds, and gravel walks. The growth of the trees, however, soon deprived the other plantings of nourishment, and the design became increasingly difficult to maintain in light of sporadic and small appropriations. John Foy, who had charge of the grounds during most of this period, was ''superseded for political reasons,'' and the area was then maintained with little care or forethought. Many rapidly growing but short-lived trees were introduced and soon depleted the soil; a lack of proper pruning and thinning left the majority of the area's vegetation ill-grown, feeble, or dead. Virtually all was removed by the early 1870s, either to make way for building operations during Thomas U. Walter's enlargement of the Capitol or as required by changes in grading to accommodate the new work on the building or the alterations to surrounding streets.

The Olmsted Plan

The mid-19th-century extension of the Capitol, in which the House and Senate wings and the new dome were added, also required that the Capitol Grounds be enlarged, and in 1874 Frederick Law Olmsted was commissioned to plan and oversee the project. As noted above, Olmsted was determined that the grounds should complement the building. In addition, he addressed an architectural problem that had persisted for some years: from the west (the growth of the city had nothing to do with the terraces)—the earthen terraces at the building's base made it seem inadequately supported at the top of the hill. The solution, Olmsted believed, was to construct marble terraces on the north, west, and south sides of the building, thereby causing it to ''gain greatly in the supreme qualities of stability, endurance, and repose.'' He submitted his design for these features in 1875, and after extensive study it was approved.

Work on the grounds began in 1874, concentrating first on the east side and then progressing to the west, north, and south sides. First, the ground was reduced in elevation. Almost 300,000 cubic yards of earth and other material were eventually removed, and over 200 trees were removed. New sewer, gas, and water lines were installed. The soil was then enriched with fertilizers to provide a suitable growth medium for new plantings. Paths and roadways were graded and laid.

By 1876, gas and water service was completed for the entire grounds, and electrical lamp-lighting apparatuses had been installed. Stables and workshops had been removed from the northwest and southwest corners. A streetcar system north and south of the west grounds had been relocated farther from the Capitol, and ornamental shelters were in place at the north and south car-track termini. The granite and bronze lamp piers and ornamental bronze lamps for the east plaza area were completed.

Work accelerated in 1877. By this time, according to Olmsted's report, ''altogether 7,837 plants and trees [had] been set out.'' However, not all had survived: hundreds were stolen or destroyed by vandals, and, as Olmsted explained, ''a large number of cattle [had] been caught trespassing.'' Other work met with less difficulty. Foot-walks were laid with artificial stone, a mixture of cement and sand, and approaches were paved with concrete. An ornamental iron trellis had been installed on the northern east-side walk, and another was under way on the southern walk.

The 1878 appointment of watchmen to patrol the grounds was quite effective in preventing further vandalism, allowing the lawns to be completed and much shrubbery to be added. Also in that year, the roads throughout the grounds were paved.

Most of the work required on the east side of the grounds was completed by 1879, and effort thus shifted largely to the west side. The Pennsylvania Avenue approach was virtually finished, and work on the Maryland Avenue approach had begun. The stone walls on the west side of the grounds were almost finished, and the red granite lamp piers were placed at the eastward entrance from Pennsylvania Avenue.

In the years 1880–1882, many features of the grounds were completed. These included the walls and coping around the entire perimeter, the approaches and entrances, and the Summer House. Work on the terraces began in 1882, and most work from this point until 1892 was concentrated on these structures.

In 1885, Olmsted retired from superintendency of the terrace project; he continued to direct the work on the grounds until 1889. Landscaping work was performed to adapt the surrounding areas to the new construction, grading the ground and planting shrubs at the bases of the walls, as the progress of the masonry work allowed. Some trees and other types of vegetation were removed, either because they had decayed or as part of a careful thinning-out process.

In 1888, the wrought-iron lamp frames and railings were placed at the Maryland Avenue entrance, making it the last to be completed. In 1892, the streetcar track that had extended into grounds from Independence Avenue was removed.

The Grounds After Olmsted

In the last years of the 19th century, work on the grounds consisted chiefly of maintenance and repairs as needed. Trees, lawns, and plantings were tended, pruned, and thinned to allow their best growth. This work was quite successful: by 1894, the grounds were so deeply shaded by trees and shrubs that Architect of the Capitol Edward Clark recommended an all-night patrol by watchmen to ensure public safety. A hurricane in September 1896 damaged or destroyed a number of trees, requiring extensive removals in the following year. Also in 1897, electric lighting replaced gas lighting in the grounds.

Between 1910 and 1935, 61.4 acres north of Constitution Avenue were added to the grounds. Approximately 100 acres was added in subsequent years, bringing the total area to 274 acres.

Since 1983, increased security measures have been put into effect, however, the area still functions in many ways as a public park, and visitors are welcome to use the walks to tour the grounds. Demonstrations and ceremonies are often held on the grounds. In the summer, a series of evening concerts by the bands of the Armed Forces is offered free of charge on the west front plaza. On various holidays, concerts by the National Symphony Orchestra are held on the west front lawn.

LEGISLATIVE BRANCH AGENCIES

CONGRESSIONAL BUDGET OFFICE

H2–405 Ford House Office Building, Second and D Streets, SW., 20515
phone (202) 226–2600, http://www.cbo.gov

[Created by Public Law 93–344]

Director.—Douglas W. Elmendorf, 6–2700.
Deputy Director.—Robert A. Sunshine, 6–2700.
General Counsel.—Mark P. Hadley, 6–2633.
Assistant Director for—
Budget Analysis.—Peter H. Fontaine, 6–2800.
Health and Human Resources.—Bruce Vavrichek, 6–2666.
Macroeconomic Analysis.—Robert A. Dennis, 6–2750.
Management, Business and Information Services.—Rod Goodwin, 6–2600.
Microeconomic Studies.—Joseph Kile, 6–2940.
National Security.—David E. Mosher, 6–2900.
Tax Analysis.—Frank J. Sammartino, 6–2680.

GOVERNMENT ACCOUNTABILITY OFFICE

441 G Street, NW., 20548, phone (202) 512–3000
http://www.gao.gov

Comptroller General of the United States.—Gene L. Dodaro, 512–5500, fax 512–5507.
Chief Operating Officer.—Patricia Dalton, 512–5600.
Chief Administrative Officer.—David Fisher, 512–5800.
General Counsel and Ethics Counselor.—Lynn Gibson, 512–5207.
Deputy Ethics Counselor.—James Lager, 512–8170.

TEAMS

Acquisition and Sourcing Management.—Paul Francis, 512–2811.
Applied Research and Methods.—Nancy Kingsbury, 512–2700.
Defense Capabilities and Management.—Janet St. Laurent, 512–4300.
Education Workforce and Income Security.—Barbara D. Bovbjerg, 512–7215.
Financial Management and Assurance.—Jeanette M. Franzel, 512–2600.
Financial Markets and Community Investments.—Rick Hillman, 512–8678.
Forensic Audits and Special Investigations.—Gregory D. Kutz, 512–6722.
Health Care.—Cynthia A. Bascetta, 512–7207.
Homeland Security and Justice.—Cathleen Berrick, 512–3404.
Information Technology.—Joel Willemssen, 512–6408.
International Affairs and Trade.—Jacquie Williams-Bridgers, 512–3101.
Natural Resources and Environment.—Mark Gaffigan, 512–3841.
Physical Infrastructure.—Katherine Siggerud, 512–2834.
Strategic Issues.—J. Christopher Mihm, 512–6806.

SUPPORT FUNCTIONS

Congressional Relations.—Ralph Dawn, 512–4400.
Legislative Advisers: Blake Ainsworth, 512–4609; Carlos Diz, 512–8256; Rosa Harris, 512–9492; Elizabeth Johnston, 512–6345; Casey Keplinger, 512–9323; Carolyn Kirby, 512–9843; Mary Frances Widner, 512–3804.
Associate Legislative Adviser.—Preston Heart, Jr., 512–9367.

Field Operations.—Denise Hunter (617) 788–0575.
Inspector General.—Frances Garcia, 512–5748.
Opportunity and Inclusiveness.—Reginld E. Jones, 512–8401.
Personnel Appeals Board.—Stuart Melnick, 512–3836.
Public Affairs.—Charles ''Chuck'' Young, 512–3823.
Quality and Continuous Improvement.—Tim Bowling, 512–6100.
Strategic Planning and External Liaison.—Helen Hsing, 512–2639.

MISSION SUPPORT OFFICES

Chief Information Officer.—Howard Williams, Jr., 512–5589.
Controller.—Cheryl Whitaker (acting), 512–5800.
Human Capital Officer.—Patrina M. Clark, 512–6620.
Knowledge Services Officer.—Catherine Teti, 512–9255.
Professional Development Program.—Dave Clark, 512–4126.

U.S. GOVERNMENT PRINTING OFFICE

732 North Capitol Street, NW., 20401

Phone (202) 512–0000, http://www.gpo.gov

Public Printer of the United States.—William J. Boarman, 512–1000, wboarman@gpo.gov.
Deputy Public Printer.—Vacant, 512–1000.
Assistant Public Printer, Operations.—Jim Bradley, 512–0111, jbradley@gpo.gov.
Assistant Public Printer, Superintendent of Documents.—Mary Alice Baish, 512–1313, mabaish@gpo.gov.
Chief of Staff.—Davita Vance-Cooks, 512–0014, dvance-cooks@gpo.gov.
Chief Financial Officer.—Steven T. Shedd, 512–2073, sshedd@gpo.gov.
Chief Communications Officer.—Andrew M. Sherman, 512–1991, fax 512–1293, asherman @gpo.gov.
Director, Equal Employment Opportunity.—Nadine L. Elzy, 512–2014, nelzy@gpo.gov.
General Counsel.—Drew Spalding, 512–0033, dspalding@gpo.gov.
Inspector General.—Michael A. Raponi, 512–0039, mraponi@gpo.gov.

GENERAL COUNSEL

General Counsel.—Drew Spalding, 512–0033, dspalding@gpo.gov.
Deputy General Counsel.—Jennifer Seifert, 512–0033, jseifert@gpo.gov.
Director, Labor Relations.—Neal Fine, 512–1336, nfine@gpo.gov.

CONGRESSIONAL, PUBLIC, AND EMPLOYEE COMMUNICATIONS

Chief Communications Officer.—Andrew M. Sherman, 512–1991, fax 512–1293, asherman @gpo.gov.
Director—
Congressional Relations.—Andrew M. Sherman, 512–1991, asherman@gpo.gov.
Media and Public Relations Manager.—Gary Somerset, 512–1957, gsomerset@gpo.gov.

FINANCE AND ADMINISTRATION

Chief Financial Officer.—Steve Shedd, 512–2073, sshedd@gpo.gov.
Deputy Chief Financial Officer—William L. Boesch, Jr., 512–2073, wboesch@gpo.gov.
Controller, Plant.—June Vance (acting), 512–2073, jvance@gpo.gov.
Controller, Information Dissemination.—William J. Grennon III, 512–2010, wgrennon @gpo.gov.
Directors of—
Accounts Receivable and Collections.—Donald Bartolomei, 512–1078, dbartolomei@gpo.gov.
Financial Planning and Control.—Frank McCraw, 512–0832, fmccraw@gpo.gov.

CHIEF OF STAFF

Chief of Staff.—Davita Vance-Cooks, 512–0014, dvance-cooks@gpo.gov.

HUMAN CAPITAL

Chief Human Capital Officer.—William T. Harris, 512–1111, wtharris@gpo.gov.
Directors of—
GPO University.—Eve L. Princler, 512–1144, eprincler@gpo.gov
Human Capital Operations.—Ginger Thomas, 512–2010, gthomas@gpo.gov.
Human Capital Shared Services.—Stephanie Smith (acting), 512–0874, ssmith@gpo.gov.
Strategic Policy.—Vacant.
Workforce Development, Education and Training.—Eve L. Princler, 512–1144, eprincler@gpo.gov.
Occupational Health Programs.—Al Troupe, 512–1267, atroupe@gpo.gov.
Chief Medical Officer.—Sheridan B. Easterling, MD, 512–2061, seasterling@gpo.gov.
Safety and Environment.—Reginal N. Johnson, 512–1036, rnjohnson@gpo.gov.

ACQUISITION SERVICES

Director, Acquisition Operations.—Sheree Young, 512–2022, syoung@gpo.gov.
Chief of—
Specialized Procurements.—Larry R. Ferezan, 512–0937, lferezan@gpo.gov.
Complex Acquisitions.—Vacant.
Paper and General Procurements.—Vacant.

INFORMATION TECHNOLOGY AND SYSTEMS

Chief Information Officer.—Charles Riddle, 512–2001, criddle@gpo.gov.
Director of—
Systems Development.—Richard G. Leeds, Jr, 512–0029, rleeds@gpo.gov.
Application Support.—Layton F. Clay, 512–2001, lclay@gpo.gov.
End User Support.—Melvin C. Eley, 512–0737, meley@gpo.gov.
Enterprise Architecture.—Vacant.
Information Security.—John L. Hannan, 512–1021, jhannan@gpo.gov.
Systems Integration.—Byron C. Blocker, 512–2198, bcblocker@gpo.gov.
IT Operations.—Vacant.

SECURITY SERVICES

Director, Security Services.—LaMont R. Vernon, 512–1103, lvernon@gpo.gov.
Deputy Director.—Gresham Harkless, 512–1367, gharkless@gpo.gov.
Commander, Uniformed Police.—Paul Eply, 512–1084, peply@gpo.gov.
Product Security.—Jeffrey Dorn, 512–0708, jdorn@gpo.gov.

ASSISTANT PUBLIC PRINTER OF OPERATIONS

Assistant Public Printer, Operations.—Jim Bradley, 512–0111, jbradley@gpo.gov.

OFFICIAL JOURNALS OF GOVERNMENT

Director of—
Congressional Publishing Services.—Lyle L. Green, 512–0224, llgreen@gpo.gov.
Congressional Record Index Office.—Marcia Thompson, 512–0275, mthompson2@gpo.gov.
Office of Federal Register Publishing Services.—Jeffrey D. MacAfee, 512–2100, jmacafee@gpo.gov.

PLANT OPERATIONS

Managing Director.—Olivier A. Girod, 512–0707, ogirod@gpo.gov.
Chief Engineering Officer.—Dennis J. Carey, 512–1018, dcarey@gpo.gov.
Director, Operations Support.—Gary B. Englehart, 512–1042, genglehart@gpo.gov.

Manager, Quality Control and Technical Department.—Michael P. Mooney, 512–0766, mmooney@gpo.gov.

Technical Manager, Strategic Planning and Analysis.—Sylvia S.Y. Subt, 512–0707, ssubt@gpo.gov.

Production Manager.—John W. Crawford, 512–0707, jcrawford@gpo.gov.

Assistant Production Manager (shift 1).—Shelley N. Welcher, 512–0589, swelcher@gpo.gov.

Assistant Production Manager (shift 2).—Richard C. Lewis, 512–0688, rclewis@gpo.gov.

Assistant Production Manager (shift 3).—Dannie E. Young, 512–0688, dyoung@gpo.gov.

Manager, Production Engineering.—David J. Robare, 512–1370, drobare@gpo.gov.

Superintendents of—

Pre-Press.—David Camp, 512–0625, dcamp@gpo.gov.

Press.—Greg Estep, 512–0673, gestep@gpo.gov.

Binding.—Walter Wingo, 512–0593, wwingo@gpo.gov.

Production Planning and Control.—Philip J. Markett, Jr., 512–0233, pmarkett@gpo.gov.

SECURITY AND INTELLIGENT DOCUMENTS

Managing Director.—Stephen G. LeBlanc, 512–2285, sleblanc@gpo.gov.

Operations Manager.—David H. Ford, 512–1194, dford@gpo.gov.

Director of—

Business Development.—Gerald Egan, 512–2010, gegan@gpo.gov.

Secure Production Manager.—Robert H. Allegar, 512–1485, rallegar@gpo.gov.

SALES AND MARKETING

Director.—Bruce A. Seger, 512–2213, bseger@gpo.gov.

Directors of—

Institute for Federal Printing and Electronic Publishing.—Bruce A. Seger, 512–2213, bseger@gpo.gov.

Program Analysis and Research.—Paul J. Giannini, 512–2270, pgiannini@gpo.gov.

CUSTOMER SERVICES

Director.—Raymond T. Sullivan (acting), 512–2374, rsullivan@gpo.gov.

Directors of—

Agency Publishing Services, Regional Operations.—Sandra K. MacAfee, 512–0320, smacafee@gpo.gov.

Agency Publishing Services, Central Office.—Julie A. Hasenfus, 512–0655, jhasenfus@gpo.gov.

Procurement Policy and Planning.—Jeffrey R. Dulberg, 512–0376, jdulberg@gpo.gov.

Printing Support Operations.—Larry P. Vines, 512–0485, lvines@gpo.gov.

GPO REGIONAL PRINTING PROCUREMENT OFFICES

Atlanta.—Gary C. Bush, Manager, 1888 Emery Street, Suite 110, Atlanta, GA 30318–2542 (404) 605–9160, fax 605–9185, gbush@gpo.gov.

Boston.—Catherine M. Miller, Manager, John F. Kennedy Federal Building, 15 New Sudbury Street E270, Boston, MA 02203–0002 (617) 565–1370, fax 565–1385, cmiller@gpo.gov.

Charleston Satellite Office.—J. Robert Mann, Manager, 2825 Noisette Boulevard, Charleston, SC 29405–1819 (843) 743–2036, fax 743–2068, jmann@gpo.gov.

Chicago.—Clint J. Mixon, Manager, 200 North La Salle Street, Suite 810, Chicago, IL 60601–1055 (312) 353–3916, fax 886–3163, cmixon@gpo.gov.

Columbus.—Steven A. Boortz, Manager, 1335 Dublin Road, Suite 112–B, Columbus, OH 43215–7034 (614) 488–4616, fax 488-4577, sboortz@gpo.gov.

Dallas.—Kelle J. Chatham, Manager, Federal Office Building, 1100 Commerce Street, Room 731, Dallas, TX 75242–1027 (214) 767–0451, fax 767–4101, kchatham@gpo.gov.

Denver.—Diane Abeyta, Manager, 12345 West Alameda Parkway, Suite 208, Lakewood, CO 80228–2824 (303) 236–5292, fax 236–5304, dabeyta@gpo.gov.

Hampton, VA.—J. Robert Mann, Manager, 11836 Canon Boulevard, Suite 400, Newport News, VA 23606–2591 (757) 873–2800, fax 873-2805, jmann@gpo.gov.

New York.—Catherine M. Miller, Manager, 26 Federal Plaza Room 2930, New York, NY 10278–0004 (212) 264–2252, fax 264–2413, cmiller@gpo.gov

Oklahoma City Satellite Office.—Diane Abeyta, Manager, 3420 D Avenue, Suite 100, Tinker AFB, OK 73145–9188 (405) 610–4146, fax 610–4125, dabeyta@gpo.gov.

Philadelphia.—Catherine M. Miller, Manager, 928 Jaymore Road, Suite A190, Southampton, PA 18966–3820 (215) 364–6465, fax 364–6479, cmiller@gpo.gov.
San Antonio Satellite Office.—Kelle J. Chatham, Manager, 1531 Connally Street, Suite 2, Lackland AFB, TX 78236–5515 (210) 675–1480, fax 675–2429, kchatham@gpo.gov.
San Diego Satellite Office.—Michael A. Barnes, Manager, 8880 Rio San Diego Drive, 8th Floor, San Diego, CA 92108–3609 (619) 209–6178, fax 209–6179, mbarnes@gpo.gov.
San Francisco.—Michael A. Barnes, Manager, 536 Stone Road, Suite 1, Benicia, CA 94510–1170 (707) 748–1970, fax 748–1980, mbarnes@gpo.gov.
Seattle.—David S. Goldberg, Manager, Federal Center South, 4735 East Marginal Way South, Seattle, WA 98134–2397 (206) 764–3726, fax 764–3301, dgoldberg@gpo.gov.

BUSINESS PRODUCTS AND SERVICES

Managing Director.—Herbert H. Jackson, Jr., 512–0952, hjackson@gpo.gov.
Directors of—
Creative Services.—Janice E. Sterling, 512–2012, jsterling@gpo.gov.

PROGRAMS, STRATEGY, AND TECHNOLOGY

Chief Technology Officer.—Richard G. Davis, 512–1622, rdavis@gpo.gov.
Director, Technology Development and Management/Chief FDsys Architect.—Deng Wu, 512–2107, dwu@gpo.gov.
FDsys Program Manager.—Selene T. Knoll, 512–0108, sknoll@gpo.gov.

ASSISTANT PUBLIC PRINTER, SUPERINTENDENT OF DOCUMENTS

Assistant Public Printer, Superintendent of Documents.—Mary Alice Baish, 512–1313, mabaish@gpo.gov.

LIBRARY SERVICES AND CONTENT MANAGEMENT

Managing Director.—Laurie Beyer Hall (acting), 512–1622, lhall@gpo.gov.
Directors of—
Collection Management and Preservation.—Robin L. Haun-Mohamed, 512–0052, rhaun-mohamad@gpo.gov.
Library Planning and Development.—Vacant.
Library Technical Information Services.—Laurie Beyer Hall, 512–1114, lhall@gpo.gov.

PUBLICATION AND INFORMATION SALES

Managing Director.—Herbert H. Jackson, Jr., 512–0952.
Directors of—
Distribution.—Lisa L. Williams, 512–1065, llwilliams@gpo.gov.
Sales Planning and Development.—Jeffrey Turner, 512–1055, jturner@gpo.gov.
Assistant Directors of—
Contact Center.—Esther Edmonds, 512–1694, eedmonds@gpo.gov.
Inventory Acquisition and Analysis.—Alan E. Ptak, 512–2010, aptak@gpo.gov.

GPO BOOKSTORE

Manager.—Donna Harding, 512–2214, dharding@gpo.gov.
Washington, DC, Metropolitan Area: GPO Bookstore, 710 North Capitol Street, NW., Washington, DC 20401, 512–0132.

TO ORDER PUBLICATIONS

Phone toll free (866) 512–1800 [DC area: (202) 512–1800, fax (202) 512–2104]. Mail orders to Superintendent of Documents, P.O. Box 371954, Pittsburgh, PA 15250–7954, or order online from http://bookstore.gpo.gov. GPO Access technical support: contactcenter@gpo.gov, or toll free (888) 293–6498, [DC area (202) 512–1530].

LAUREL FACILITY

Operations Manager.—Robert E. Mitchell, 8660 Cherry Lane, Mail Stop: SSR, Room 236D1, Laurel, MD 20707–4982 (301) 953–9751, remitchell@gpo.gov.

PUEBLO PUBLIC DOCUMENTS DISTRIBUTION CENTER

Operations Manager.—Michael C. Alston, P.O. Box 4007, Pueblo, CO 81003 (719) 948–2240, fax 948–9320, malston@gpo.gov.

LIBRARY OF CONGRESS

101 Independence Avenue, SE., 20540, phone (202) 707–5000, fax 707–5844

http://www.loc.gov

OFFICE OF THE LIBRARIAN, LM 608

The Librarian of Congress.—James H. Billington, 707–5205.
Confidential Assistant to the Librarian.—Timothy L. Robbins, 707–8174.
Chief of Staff.—Robert Dizard, Jr., 707–0351.
Liaison Specialist.—Alana Calfee, 707–5216.
Director, Office of:
Communications.—Matt Raymond, LM 105, 707–2905.
Editor for—
Calendar of Events.—Erin Allen Sanchez, 707–7302.
Library of Congress Information Bulletin.—Audrey Fischer, 707–0022.
The Gazette.—Mark Hartsell, 707–9194.
Congressional Relations.—Kathleen Ott, LM 611, 707–3217.
Development.—Susan Siegel, LM 605, 707–1447.
Special Events and Public Programs.—Larry Stafford, LM 612, 707–5218.
General Counsel.—Elizabeth Pugh, LM 601, 707–6316.

OFFICE OF INSPECTOR GENERAL, LM 630

Inspector General.—Karl W. Schornagel, 707–6314.
Director, Office of Investigations.—Kenneth R. Keeler, LA 319, 707–3423.

OFFICE OF THE CHIEF FINANCIAL OFFICER, LM 613

Chief Financial Officer.—Jeffrey Page, LM 613, 707–7350.
Budget Officer.—Mary Klutts, 707–2418.
Disbursing Officer.—Melissa LaDieu, 707–9726.
Deputy Chief Financial Officer.—Jay Miller, 707–3548.
Accouting Operations Officer.—Nicole Broadus, 707–5547.
Director, Strategic Planning Office.—Karen Lloyd, LM 603, 707–6074.

OFFICE OF STRATEGIC INITIATIVES, LM 637

Associate Librarian for Strategic Initiatives/Chief Information Officer.—Laura E. Campbell, 707–3300.
Deputy Associate Librarian for Strategic Initiatives.—James M. Gallagher, 707–5563.
Executive Program Officer.—George Coulbourne, 707–7856.
Director, Digital Resource Management and Planning.—Molly H. Johnson, 707–0809.
Director, Integration Management.—Elizabeth S. Dulabahn, 707–2369.
Director, National Digital Information Infrastructure and Preservaton Program.—Martha Anderson, LM 630, 707–2598.
Director for Information Technology Services.—Al Banks, LM G51, 707–9562.
Executive Management Assistant.—Michael Pippin, 707–6695.

LAW LIBRARY, OFFICE OF THE LAW LIBRARIAN, LM 240

Law Librarian.—Roberta I. Shaffer, 707–9825.
Deputy Law Librarian.—David Mao, 707–4839.
Assistant Law Librarians for—
Collections, Outreach and Services.—Robert R. Newlen, 707–4313.
Operations and Planning.—Donald Simon, 707–4884.
Chief of:
Collections Services.—Mark Strattner, LM 232, 707–9863.
Eastern Law Division.—Peter Roudik, LM 235, 707–9861.
Public Services.—Robert N. Gee, LM 201, 707–0638.
Western Law Division.—Vacant.

LIBRARY SERVICES, OFFICE OF THE ASSOCIATE LIBRARIAN FOR LIBRARY SERVICES, LM 642

Associate Librarian.—Deanna Marcum, 707–5325.
Deputy Associate Librarian/Programs.—Michael Handy, 707–8338.
Deputy Associate Librarian/Administrative Services.—Sandra Lawson, 707–3332.
Director of:
American Folklife Center.—Peggy Bulger, LJ G59, 707–1745.
Veterans History Project.—Robert W. Patrick, LA 143, 707–7308.
Director for Acquisitions and Bibliographic Access.—Beacher Wiggins, 707–5137.
Chief of:
African, Latin American and Western European Division.—Angela Kinney, LM 543, 707–5572.
Asian and Middle Eastern Division.—Philip A. Melzer, LM 535, 707–7961.
Cooperative and Instructional Programs Division.—Judith Cannan, LA 140, 707–2031.
Germanic and Slavic Division.—Linda T. Stubbs, LM 527, 707–7108.
Overseas Operations Division.—Vacant, LM 642, 707–5325.
Policy and Standards Division.—Barbara Tillett, LA 305, 707–4714.
Special Materials Cataloging Division.—Vacant, LM 547, 707–5260.
U.S. and Publisher Liaison Division.—LM 547, 707–6428.
U.S. General Division.—Karl Edward Debus-Lopez, LM 515, 707–6641.
Director, Office for Collections and Services.—Jeremy Adamson, LM 642, 707–7789.
Chief of:
African and Middle Eastern Division.—Mary Jane Deeb, LJ 220, 707–7937.
Asian Division.—Anchi Hoh (acting), LJ 149, 707–5673.
Children's Literature Center.—Sybille A. Jagusch, LJ 100, 707–5535.
Collections Access, Loan and Management.—Steven J. Herman, LJ G02, 707–7400.
European Division.—Georgette M. Dorn (acting), LJ 250, 707–5414.
Federal Research Division.—David Osborne, LA 5282, 707–3919.
Geography and Map Division.—John R. Hébert, LM B02, 707–8530.
Hispanic Division.—Georgette M. Dorn, LJ 240, 707–5400.
Humanities and Social Sciences Division.—Vacant, LJ 139A, 707–5530.
Manuscript Division.—James H. Hutson, LM 102, 707–5383.
Music Division.—Susan H. Vita, LM 113, 707–5503.
Packard Campus of the National Audio-Visual Conservation Center.—Patrick Loughney, 707–7064.
Prints and Photographs Division.—Helena Zinkham, LM 339, 707–2922.
Rare Book and Special Collections Division.—Mark G. Dimunation, LJ Dk A, 707–5434.
Science Technology and Business Division.—Ronald S. Bluestone, LA 5203, 707–0948.
Director, Partnerships and Outreach Programs.—Kathryn Mendenhall, LM 642, 707–5572.
Director, Center for the Book.—John Y. Cole, Jr., LM 650, 707–5221.
Executive Director, Federal Library and Information Center Committee.—Blane K. Dessy, 707–4801.
Interpretive Programs Officer.—William Jacobs, LA G25, 707–3689.
Director, Office of National Library Service for the Blind and Physically Handicapped, TSA.—Frank K. Cylke, 707–5104.
Director, Office of Scholarly Programs.—Carolyn Brown, LJ 120, 707–3302.
Director, Publishing Office.—W. Ralph Eubanks, LM 602, 707–3892.
Visitor Services Officer.—Guilia Adelfio, LJ G59, 707–9779.
Business Enterprises Officer.—Eugene Flanagan, LA 206, 707–8203.
Director for Preservation.—Dianne van der Reyden, LM 642, 707–7423.
Director for Technology Policy.—Ruth Scovill, LM 642, 707–0076.

CONGRESSIONAL RESEARCH SERVICE, LM 203

Director.—Mary B. Mazanec (acting), 707–7375.
Deputy Director.—Vacant.
Chief Information Officer.—Lisa M. Hoppis, LM 413, 707–2559.
Associate Director, Office of:
Congressional Affairs and Counselor to the Director.—Lizanne Dinoto Kelley, LM 203, 707–8833.
Finance and Administration.—Edward Jablonski, LM 209, 707–8397.
Legislative Information.—Clifford Cohen, LM 215, 707–1858.
Workforce Development.—Bessie E.H. Alkisswani, LM 208, 707–8835.
Assistant Director of:
American Law Division.—Karen L. Lewis, LM 227, 707–7460.
Domestic Social Policy Division.—Laura B. Shrestha, LM 323, 707–7046.
Foreign Affairs, Defense and Trade Division.—Michael L. Moodie, LM 315, 707–8470.
Government and Finance Division.—Collen J. Shogan, LM 303, 707–8321.
Knowledge Services Group.—Lisa B. Dove (acting), LM 215, 707–5007.
Resources, Science and Industry Division.—John L. Moore, LM 423, 707–7232.

U.S. COPYRIGHT OFFICE, LM 403

Associate Librarian for Copyright Services and Register of Copyrights.—Maria A. Pallante (acting), 707–8350.
General Counsel.—David Carson, 707–8353.
Deputy General Counsel.—Robert J. Kasunic, 707–0229.
Chief Operating Officer.—Elizabeth Scheffler, 707–6042.
Chief of:
Administrative Services.—Bruce McCubbin, LM 458, 707–8395.
Copyright Technology Office.—Douglas Ament, LM 560, 707–5440.
Associate Register for International Affairs and Policy.—Michele J. Woods, 707–5613.
Associate Register for Registration and Recordation.—Nanette Petruzzelli, 707–8350.
Registration and Recordation Program Manager.—Susan Harley Todd, LM 443, 707–8299.
Chief of:
Copyright Acquisitions Division.—Jewel Player, LM 438C, 707–7125.
Information and Records Division.—David Christopher (acting), LM 453, 707–6800.
Licensing Division.—James B. Enzinna, LM 504, 707–6801.
Literary Division.—Ted Hirakawa, LM 444, 707–6181.
Performing Arts Division.—Melissa Dadant, LM 422, 707–8211.
Receipt Analysis and Control Division.—Victor A. Holmes, LM 422, 707–8244.
Visual Arts and Recordation Division.—John Ashley, LM 433, 707–8223.

OFFICE OF SUPPORT OPERATIONS, LM 624

Chief of Office of Support Operations.—Lucy D. Suddreth, 707–2758.
Director for Integrated Support Services.—Mary Berghaus Levering, LM 327, 707–1393.
Chief of:
Contracts.—Robert Williams (acting), LM G23, 707–2871.
Facility Services Office.—Neal Graham, 707–7512.
Grants.—George Daves, LA 322, 707–6975.
Health Services Office.—Sandra Charles, LM G40, 707–8035.
Safety Services Officer.—Robert Browne, LM B28, 707–6204.
Director of Office of Security and Emergency Preparedness.—Kenneth Lopez, LM G03, 707–8708.
Director of Office of Opportunity, Inclusiveness and Compliance.—Naomi Earp, LM 623, 707–6024.
Alternative Dispute Resolution and EEO Complaints.—707–6024.
ADA.—707–6024.
Interpreting Services.—707–6024.
Director of Human Resources Services.—Dennis Hanratty, LM 645, 707–5659.
Director, Office of:
HRS Customer Service Center.—LM 207, 7–5627.
Strategic Planning and Automation.—John Sigmon, LM 626, 707–6544.
Workforce Acquisitions.—Susan Frieswyk (acting), 707–6959.
Workforce Management.—Charles Carron, LM 653, 707–6637.
Workforce Performance and Development.—Kimberly Powell, LM 646, 707–8976.

Worklife Services.—Susan Frieswyk, 707–6959.

UNITED STATES BOTANIC GARDEN

245 First Street, SW., Washington, DC 20024

(202) 225–8333 (information); (202) 226–8333 (receptionist)

http://www.usbg.gov

Director.—Stephen T. Ayers (acting), Architect of the Capitol, 228–1204.
Executive Director.—Holly H. Shimizu, 225–6670.
Administrative Officer.—Tonda S. Cave, 225–5002.
Public Programs Manager.—Christine A. Flanagan, 225–1269.
Horticulture Division Manager.—James T. Kaufmann, 225–6647.
Facility Manager.—John M. Gallagher, 225–6646.

THE CABINET

Vice President of the United States	JOSEPH R. BIDEN, JR.
Secretary of State	HILLARY RODHAM CLINTON.
Secretary of the Treasury	TIMOTHY F. GEITHNER.
Secretary of Defense	LEON E. PANETTA.
Attorney General	ERIC H. HOLDER, JR.
Secretary of the Interior	KENNETH L. SALAZAR.
Secretary of Agriculture	THOMAS J. VILSACK.
Secretary of Commerce	JOHN E. BRYSON.
Secretary of Labor	HILDA L. SOLIS.
Secretary of Health and Human Services	KATHLEEN SEBELIUS.
Secretary of Housing and Urban Development	SHAUN L.S. DONOVAN.
Secretary of Transportation	RAYMOND H. LAHOOD.
Secretary of Energy	STEVEN CHU.
Secretary of Education	ARNE DUNCAN.
Secretary of Veterans Affairs	ERIC K. SHINSEKI.
Secretary of Homeland Security	JANET A. NAPOLITANO.
Chief of Staff	BILL DALEY.
Director, Office of Management and Budget	JACOB J. LEW.
U.S. Trade Representative	RONALD KIRK.
Administrator, Environmental Protection Agency	LISA P. JACKSON.
Chair, Council of Economic Advisers	VACANT.
Ambassador, United States Ambassador to the United Nations	SUSAN RICE.

EXECUTIVE BRANCH

THE PRESIDENT

BARACK H. OBAMA, Senator from Illinois and 44th President of the United States; born in Honolulu, Hawaii, August 4, 1961; received a B.A. in 1983 from Columbia University, New York City; worked as a community organizer in Chicago, IL; studied law at Harvard University, where he became the first African American president of the *Harvard Law Review,* and received a J.D. in 1991; practiced law in Chicago, IL; lecturer on constitutional law, University of Chicago; member, Illinois State Senate, 1997–2004; elected as a Democrat to the U.S. Senate in 2004; and served from January 3, 2005, to November 16, 2008, when he resigned from office, having been elected President; family: married to Michelle; two children: Malia and Sasha; elected as President of the United States on November 4, 2008, and took the oath of office on January 20, 2009.

EXECUTIVE OFFICE OF THE PRESIDENT

1600 Pennsylvania Avenue, NW., 20500

Eisenhower Executive Office Building (EEOB), 17th Street and Pennsylvania Avenue, NW., 20500, phone (202) 456–1414, http://www.whitehouse.gov

The President of the United States.—Barack H. Obama.
Personal Aide to the President.—Katherine Johnson.
Special Assistant to the President and Personal Aide.—Reginald Love.

OFFICE OF THE VICE PRESIDENT

phone (202) 456–1414

The Vice President.—Joseph R. Biden, Jr.
Chief of Staff to the Vice President.—Bruce Reed, EEOB, room 202, 456–9000.
Deputy Chief of Staff to the Vice President.—Alan Hoffman, EEOB, room 202, 456–9000.
Counsel to the Vice President.—Cynthia Hogan, EEOB, room 246, 456–3241.
Director of Communications to the Vice President.—Shailagh Murray, EEOB, room 284, 456–5249.
Press Secretary to the Vice President.—Kendra Barkoff, EEOB, room 284, 456–5249.
Assistant to the Vice President for—
Domestic Policy.—Terrell McSweeny, EEOB, room 222, 456–3071.
Economic Policy.—Sarah Bianchi, EEOB, room 222, 456–3071.
National Security Advisor.—Tony Blinken, EEOB, room 246, 456–2646.
Chief of Staff to Dr. Jill Biden.—Cathy Russell, EEOB, room 200, 456–6773.
Director of Scheduling to the Vice President.—Elisabeth Hire, EEOB, room 239, 456–6773.
Director of Advance to the Vice President.—Sam Myers, EEOB, room 241, 456–6773.
Executive Assistants to the Vice President: Michele Smith, Kellen Suber, West Wing.
Director of Correspondence.—Jillian Doody, EEOB, room 233, 456–6770.

COUNCIL OF ECONOMIC ADVISERS

725 Seventeenth Street, NW., 20006, phone (202) 395–5084
http://www.whitehouse.gov/cea

Chair.—Vacant.
Executive Director.—Nan Gibson.

Member.—Cecilia Elena Rouse.

COUNCIL ON ENVIRONMENTAL QUALITY

730 Jackson Place, NW., 20503, phone (202) 456–6224
http://www.whitehouse.gov/ceq

Chair.—Nancy Sutley.
Special Assistants to the Chair: Kira Mesdag, Ming Yuan Zhou.
Scheduler to the Chair.—Paola Ramos.
Chief of Staff.—Michael ''Mike'' Boots (acting).
Deputy Chief of Staff.—Christine Glunz.
Deputy Director and General Counsel.—Gary Guzy.
Senior Counsel.—Ellen Athas.
Deputy General Counsel.—Katherine ''Katie'' Scharf.
Deputy Associate Director for—
International Affairs.—Megan Samenfeld-Specht.
Regulatory Policy.—Manisha Patel.
Records and Information Specialist.—William ''Bill'' Bullman.
Administrative Officer.—Angela Stewart.
Administrative Services Specialist.—Essence Washington.
Administrative Assistant.—Brenda Butler.
Federal Environmental Executive.—Michelle Moore.
Deputy Associate Director for OFEE.—William Garvey.
OFEE Senior Program Manager for Federal Outreach: Victoria Cummiskey.
OFEE Senior Program Managers: Allison Dennis, Leslie Gillespie-Marthaler, Juan Lopez, Alexandra Pressman.
Deputy Associate Director for GreenGov.—Matthew Kasdan.
Associate Director for Energy and Climate Change.—Jason Bordoff.
Special Assistant to the Associate Director for Energy and Climate Change.—Daniel Kilduff.
Deputy Associate Directors for Energy and Climate Change: Mikhail ''Misha'' Adamantiades, Allen Fawcett, Ann Ferris, Anhar Karimjee.
Deputy Associate Director for Climate Change Adaptation.—Cathleen Kelly.
Climate Change Adaptation Analyst.—Judsen Bruzgul.
Climate Adaptation Analyst.—Allison Castellan.
Deputy Associate Director for Transmission and Renewable Energy Siting.—Thomas ''Tom'' Darin.
Deputy Associate Director for Electricity and Consumer Policy.—Robert Letzler.
Policy Advisor.—Andrew ''Drew'' McConville.
Associate Director for Communities, Environmental Protection and Green Jobs.—Nicole ''Nikki'' Buffa.
Special Assistant to the Associate Director for Communities, Environmental Protection and Green Jobs.—Lindsay Randall.
Deputy Associate Directors for—
Chemical Regulations.—Jamie Strong.
Communities.—Toni Morales.
Energy Efficiency.—Jennifer Krajewski.
Environmental Protection.—Warren Friedman.
Deputy Associate Directors for—
Ecosystems.—Erika Feller.
Natural Resources.—Robyn Colosimo.
Ocean and Coastal Policy.—Michael Weiss.
Ocean Policy Advisors: Mary Boatman, Andrew Lipsky, Jeffrey Luster, Roxanne Nikolaus, Alisa Praskovich.
Senior Policy Analyst.—Franklin ''Frank'' Schwing.
Asian Carp Director.—John Goss.
Special Assistant to the Asian Carp Director.—Paul Angelone.
Deputy Asian Carp Director.—James Bredin.
Special Assistant to the Associate Director for Land and Water Ecosystems.—Margrette Thompson.
Deputy Associate Director for Water Policy.—Jeff Peterson.
Presidential Management Fellows for Land and Water: Lauren Leuck, Thomas Liu.
Fellow.—Jason Brodsky.
Ecosystem Policy Advisor.—Scott Nuzum.
Associate Director for Communications.—Sahar Wali.
Deputy Associate Director for Communications.—Taryn Tuss.

Associate Director for NEPA Oversight.—Horst Greczmiel.
Deputy Associate Director for NEPA Oversight.—Kimberley DePaul.
Assistant to the Associate Director for NEPA Oversight.—Lauren Cusick.
Associate Director for Legislative Affairs.—Jessica Maher.
Special Assistant to the Associate Director for Legislative Affairs.—Gregory Degen.
Deputy Associate Director for Legislative Affairs.—Amy Sharp.
Associate Director for Policy Outreach.—Amelia ''Amy'' Salzman.
Deputy Associate Directors for Policy Outreach: Raymond ''Ray'' Rivera, Kenli Schaaf, Jonathan ''Jack'' Shapiro.
Deputy Associate Director for Let's Move Outside!.—Ali Kelley.

PRESIDENT'S INTELLIGENCE ADVISORY BOARD

phone (202) 456–2352

Executive Director.—Stefanie Osburn.
General Counsel.—Ray Heddings.

NATIONAL SECURITY COUNCIL

phone (202) 456–9491

MEMBERS

The President.—Barack H. Obama.
The Vice President.—Joseph R. Biden, Jr.
The Secretary of State.—Hillary Rodham Clinton.
The Secretary of Defense.—Leon Panetta.
The Secretary of Energy.—Steven Chu.
The Secretary of Treasury.—Timothy F. Geithner.
The Attorney General.—Eric H. Holder, Jr.
The Secretary of Homeland Security.—Janet Napolitano.
The Representative of the United States of America to the United Nations.—Amb. Susan Rice.
The Assistant to the President and Chief of Staff (Chief of Staff to the President).—William Daley.
The Assistant to the President for National Security Affairs.—Tom Donilon.

STATUTORY ADVISERS

Director of National Intelligence.—James R. Clapper, Jr.
Chairman, Joint Chiefs of Staff.—Gen. Martin E. Dempsey.

OFFICE OF ADMINISTRATION

Eisenhower Executive Office Building, phone (202) 456–2861

Director of the Office of Administration.—Cameron Moody.
Deputy Director.—Vacant.
Chief, Office of:
Equal Employment Opportunity.—Clara Patterson.
Finance.—Allyson Laackman.
General Counsel.—Angela Ohm.
Information.—Brook Colangelo.
Operations.—Zoe Garmendia.
Security.—Leonard Cooke.

OFFICE OF MANAGEMENT AND BUDGET

Eisenhower Executive Office Building, phone (202) 395–4840

Director.—Jacob J. Lew.
Deputy Director.—Vacant.

Deputy Director for Management.—Jeffrey Zients.
Executive Associate Director.—Robert Gordon.
Administrator, Office of:
Federal Procurement Policy.—Lesley Field (acting).
Information and Regulatory Affairs.—Cass Sunstein.
Assistant Director for—
Budget.—Courtney Timberlake (acting).
Legislative Reference.—James J. Jukes.
Associate Director for—
Communications.—Kenneth Baer.
Economic Policy.—Michael Falkenheim (acting).
Education, Income Maintenance and Labor Programs.—Martha Coven.
General Government Programs.—Xavier Briggs.
Health Programs.—Keith Fontenot.
Legislative Affairs.—Alyssa Fisher (acting).
National Security Programs.—Steve Kosiak.
Natural Resources, Energy and Science Programs.—Sally Ericsson.
General Counsel.—Preeta Bansal.

OFFICE OF NATIONAL DRUG CONTROL POLICY

750 17th Street, NW., phone (202) 395–6700, fax 395–6711

Director.—R. Gil Kerlikowske, room 810, 395–6700.
Deputy Director.—Vacant, room 803, 395–6700.
Chief of Staff.—Timothy J. Quinn, room 809, 395–6762.
Deputy Chief of Staff.—Jennifer L. deVallance, room 805, 395–6762.
Deputy Director, Office of:
Demand Reduction.—David K. Mineta, room 609, 395–6751.
State and Local Affairs.—Benjamin B. Tucker, room 661, 395–7252.
Supply Reduction.—Vacant, room 713, 395–7225.
Assistant Deputy Director, Office of:
Demand Reduction.—Martha M. Gagné, room 610, 395–4622.
Supply Reduction.—Patrick M. Ward, room 712, 395–5535.
General Counsel.—Jeffrey J. Teitz, room 518, 395–6601.
Associate Director, Office of:
Legislative Affairs.—Christine M. Leonard, room 825, 395–7225.
Management and Administration.—Michele C. Marx, room 326, 395–6883.
Performance and Budget.—Jon E. Rice, room 535, 395–6791.
Public Affairs.—Rafael E. Lemaitre, room 846, 395–6649.
Research/Data Analysis.—Terry W. Zobeck, room 836, 395–5503.
Intergovernmental Public Liaison.—Tony Martinez, room 845, 395–5758.

OFFICE OF SCIENCE AND TECHNOLOGY POLICY

Eisenhower Executive Office Building, phone (202) 456–7116, fax 456–6021
http://www.ostp.gov

Director.—John P. Holdren.
Associate Director for—
Energy and Environment.—Shere Abbott.
National Security and International Affairs.—Philip Coyle.
Science.—Carl Wieman.
Technology and Chief Technology Officer.—Aneesh Chopra.
Chief of Staff.—Jim Kohlenberger.
Executive Director for National Science and Technology Council.—Pedro Espina.
Executive Director for President's Council of Advisors on Science and Technology.—Deborah D. Stine.

OFFICE OF THE UNITED STATES TRADE REPRESENTATIVE

600 17th Street, NW., 20508, phone (202) 395–6890
http://www.ustr.gov

United States Trade Representative.—Ronald Kirk.

Deputy United States Trade Representative.—Demetrios Marantis.
Deputy U.S. Trade Representative, Geneva.—Michael Punke.
Associate U.S. Trade Representative.—Vacant.
Special Textile Negotiator.—Gail Strickler.
Chief Agricultural Negotiator.—Isi Siddiqui.
General Counsel.—Timothy Reif.
Assistant U.S. Trade Representative for—
Administration.—Fred Ames.
Africa.—Florie Liser.
Agricultural Affairs.—Vacant.
China Affairs.—Claire Reade.
Congressional Affairs.—Luis Jimenez.
Economic Affairs.—William Shpiece.
Environment and Natural Resources.—Mark Linscott.
Europe and the Mediterranean.—Dan Mullaney.
Industry.—Jim Sanford.
Intergovernmental Affairs and Public Liaison.—Lisa Garcia.
Japan, Korea and APEC Affairs.—Wendy Cutler.
Monitoring and Enforcement.—Dan Brinza.
Office of the Americas.—Vacant.
Policy Coordination.—Carmen Suro-Bredie.
Public/Media Affairs.—Carol Guthrie.
Services, Investment and Intellectual Property.—Christine Bliss.
South Asian Affairs.—Douglas Hartwick.
Southeast Asia, Pacific and Pharmaceutical Policy.—Barbara Weisel.
Trade and Labor.—Lewis Karesh.
World Trade Organization (WTO) and Multilateral Affairs.—Chris Wilson.

THE WHITE HOUSE OFFICE

CABINET AFFAIRS

Assistant to the President and Cabinet Secretary.—Christopher Lu.
Deputy Assistant to the President and Deputy Cabinet Secretary.—Elizabeth Sears Smith.

CHIEF OF STAFF

Assistant to the President and Chief of Staff.—William Daley.
Counselor to the President.—Peter Rouse.
Assistant to the President and Deputy Chief of Staff for Operations.—Alyssa Mastromonaco.
Assistant to the President and Deputy Chief of Staff for Policy.—Nancy-Ann DeParle.
Assistant to the President and Senior Advisor.—David Plouffe.
Assistant to the President and Deputy Senior Advisor.—Philip Schiliro.

COMMUNICATIONS

Assistant to the President and Director of Communications.—Dan Pfeiffer.
Assistant to the President and Deputy Senior Advisor.—Stephanie Cutter.
Assistant to the President and Director of Speechwriting.—Jonathan Favreau.
Assistant to the President and Press Secretary.—James Carney.
Deputy Assistant to the President and Deputy Director of Communications.—Jennifer Psaki.

OFFICE OF DIGITAL STRATEGY

Special Assistant to the President and Director of Digital Strategy.—Macon Phillips.

DOMESTIC POLICY COUNCIL

Assistant to the President and Director of the Domestic Policy Council.—Melody C. Barnes.

Deputy Assistant to the President and Deputy Director of the Domestic Policy Council.—Mark Zuckerman.

Deputy Assistant to the President for Health Policy.—Jeanne Lambrew.

Deputy Assistant to the President for Energy and Climate Change.—Heather R. Zichal.

Deputy Assistant to the President and Director, Office of Social Innovation and Civic Participation.—Sonal Shah.

Special Assistant to the President for Education Policy.—Roberto Rodriguez.

Special Assistant to the President and Executive Director of the White House Office of Faith-Based and Neighborhood Partnerships.—Joshua DuBois.

Special Assistant to the President for Justice and Regulatory Policy.—Steven Croley.

Special Assistant to the President for Urban Affairs.—Derek Douglas.

Special Assistant to the President for Mobility and Opportunity Policy.—Martha Coven.

Director of the Office of National AIDS Policy and Senior Advisor on Disability Policy.—Jeffrey Crowley.

OFFICE OF THE FIRST LADY

Assistant to the President, Chief of Staff to the First Lady and Counsel.—Tina Tchen.

Deputy Assistant to the President and Director of Policy and Projects for the First Lady.—Jocelyn Frye.

Special Assistant to the President and White House Social Secretary.—Jeremy Bernard.

OFFICE OF LEGISLATIVE AFFAIRS

Assistant to the President and Director, Office of Legislative Affairs.—Rob Nabors.

Deputy Assistant to the President for Legislative Affairs.—Lisa M. Konwinski.

Deputy Assistant to the President for Legislative Affairs and Senate Liaison.—Shawn P. Maher.

OFFICE OF MANAGEMENT AND ADMINISTRATION

Assistant to the President for Management and Administration.—Bradley J. Kiley.

Deputy Assistant to the President for Management and Administration.—Henry F. DeSio.

Special Assistant to the President and Director of White House Operations.—Katy A. Kale.

NATIONAL ECONOMIC COUNCIL

Assistant to the President for Economic Policy and Director of the National Economic Council.—Gene Sperling.

Assistant to the President and Principal Deputy Director of the National Economic Council.—Jason Furman.

Assistant to the President for Manufacturing Policy.—Ron Bloom.

OFFICE OF THE NATIONAL SECURITY ADVISOR

Assistant to the President and National Security Advisor.—Thomas Donilon.

Assistant to the President and Deputy National Security Advisor.—Denis McDonough.

Assistant to the President for Homeland Security and Counterterrorism.—John O. Brennan.

Deputy Assistant to the President and Chief of Staff for National Security Operations.—Mark Lippert.

Deputy Assistant to the President and National Security Staff Chief of Staff and Counselor.—Brooke Anderson.

OFFICE OF PRESIDENTIAL PERSONNEL

Deputy Assistant to the President and Director of Presidential Personnel.—Nancy Hogan.

Special Assistant to the President and Deputy Director of Presidential Personnel.—Jonathan McBride.

Special Assistant to the President and Chief of Staff for Presidential Personnel.—Margaret McLaughlin.

OFFICE OF PUBLIC ENGAGEMENT AND INTERGOVERNMENTAL AFFAIRS

Senior Advisor and Assistant to the President for Intergovernmental Affairs and Public Engagement.—Valerie Jarrett.

Deputy Assistant to the President and Counselor to the Senior Advisor for Strategic Engagement.—Michael Strautmanis.

Deputy Assistant to the President and Director of the Office of Public Engagement.—Jonathan Carson.

Deputy Assistant to the President and Director of Intergovernmental Affairs.—Cecelia Muñoz.

OFFICE OF SCHEDULING AND ADVANCE

Deputy Assistant to the President and Director of Scheduling and Advance.—Danielle Crutchfield.

Deputy Assistant to the President and Director of Scheduling.—Jessica Wright.

Deputy Assistant to the President and Director of Advance and Operations.—David Cusack.

OFFICE OF THE STAFF SECRETARY

Deputy Assistant to the President and Deputy Staff Secretary.—Raj De.

Special Assistant to the President and Director of Presidential Correspondence.—Elizabeth Olson.

WHITE HOUSE COUNSEL

Assistant to the President and Counsel to the President.—Kathryn Ruemmler.

Deputy Assistant to the President and Principal Deputy Counsel to the President.—Vacant.

Deputy Assistants to the President and Deputy Counsel to the President: Susan Davies, Donald Verrilli.

PRESIDENT'S COMMISSION ON WHITE HOUSE FELLOWSHIPS

Director.—Cindy Moelis.

WHITE HOUSE MILITARY OFFICE

Director.—George Mulligan (acting).

DEPARTMENT OF STATE

2201 C Street, NW., 20520, phone (202) 647–4000

HILLARY RODHAM CLINTON, Secretary of State; born in Chicago, IL, October 26, 1947; education: B.A., Wellesley College, 1969; J.D., Yale Law School, 1973; professional: Assistant Professor, University of Arkansas School of Law, 1975; Attorney and Partner, Rose Law Firm, 1976–92; board member, Legal Services Corporation Board, 1978–81; First Lady of Arkansas, 1979–81 and 1983–92; board member, Children's Defense Fund, 1986–92; First Lady of the United States, 1993–2001; author, *It Takes A Village,* 1996; *Living History,* 2000; Senator from New York, 2001–09; committees: Armed Services; Budget; Environment and Public Works; Health, Education, Labor and Pensions; Select Committee on Aging; candidate for president, 2007–08; nominated by President Barack Obama to become the 67th Secretary of State, and was confirmed by the U.S. Senate on January 21, 2009.

OFFICE OF THE SECRETARY

Secretary of State.—Hillary Rodham Clinton, room 7226, 647–9572.
Deputy Secretary.—James B. Steinberg.
Deputy Secretary for Management and Resources.—Thomas Nides.
Executive Assistant.—Joseph E. Macmanus, 647–9572.
Chief of Staff.—Cheryl Mills, 647–5548.

AMBASSADOR-AT-LARGE FOR WAR CRIMES ISSUES

Ambassador-at-Large.—Stephen J. Rapp, room 7419A, 647–8218.
Deputy.—Diane F. Orentlicher, 647–9880.

OFFICE OF THE CHIEF OF PROTOCOL

Chief of Protocol.—Capricia Penavic Marshall, room 1232, 647–4543.
Deputy Chief.—Lee Satterfield, 647–4120.
Deputy Chief.—Dennis Cheng, 647–4616.

OFFICE OF CIVIL RIGHTS

Director.—John M. Robinson, room 7428, 647–9295.
Deputy Director.—Gregory B. Smith.

OFFICE OF COORDINATOR FOR COUNTERTERRORISM

Coordinator/Ambassador–at–Large.—Amb. Daniel S. Benjamin, room 2509, 647–9892.
Principal Deputy Coordinator.—Robert Godec, Jr., 647–8949.

COORDINATOR FOR RECONSTRUCTION AND STABILIZATION

Coordinator.—Amb. Robert Loftin, 663–0307.
Principal Deputy Coordinator.—John F. McNamara (acting), 663–0803.
Deputy Coordinator.—Bill Jeffers, 663–0856.

EXECUTIVE SECRETARIAT

Special Assistant and Executive Secretary.—Stephen Mull, room 7224, 647–5301.
Deputy Executive Secretaries: Virginia Bennett, 647–5302; Kin Moy, 647–8448; Paul D. Wohlers, 647–5302.

OFFICE OF THE INSPECTOR GENERAL

2121 Virginia Avenue, NW., 20037

Inspector General.—Vacant, room 8100, 663–0361.
Deputy Inspector General.—Harold W. Geisel, 663–0361.

BUREAU OF INTELLIGENCE AND RESEARCH

Assistant Secretary.—Philip S. Goldberg, room 6468, 647–9177.
Principal Deputy Assistant Secretary.—John R. Dinger, 647–7826.
Deputy Assistant Secretaries: Catherine Brown, 647–7754; James Buchanan, 647–9633.

OFFICE OF LEGAL ADVISER

The Legal Advisor.—Harold Hongju Koh, room 6421, 647–9598.
Principal Deputy Legal Adviser.—Mary McLeod, 647–5036.
Deputy Legal Advisers: Susan Biniaz, 647–8461; Jonathan B. Schwartz, 647–5036; James Thessin, 647–8460.

BUREAU OF LEGISLATIVE AFFAIRS

Assistant Secretary.—Richard R. Verma, room 7325, 647–4204.
Deputy Assistant Secretary (Global, Regional and Functional).—David Turk, 647–1656.
Deputy Assistant Secretary (Senate).—Miguel Rodriguez, 647–2645.
Deputy Assistant Secretary (House).—David Adams, 647–2623.

POLICY PLANNING STAFF

Director.—Jacob Sullivan, room 7311, 647–2972.
Principal Deputy Director.—Vacant.

BUREAU OF RESOURCE MANAGEMENT

Assistant Secretary/Chief Financial Officer.—Vacant, room 7427, 647–7490.
Deputy Chief Financial Officer.—Christopher Flaggs, 261–8620.

OFFICE OF THE U.S. GLOBAL AIDS COORDINATOR

Coordinator.—Amb. Eric Goosby, room SA–29, 663–2304.
Deputy U.S. Global Aids Coordinator/Chief of Staff.—Ann Gavaghan, 663–2639.
Assistant Coordinator.—Michele Moloney-Kitts, 663–2704.
Director of Multilateral Outreach.—Margaret Lidstone, 663–2586.

UNDER SECRETARY FOR POLITICAL AFFAIRS

Under Secretary.—Amb. William J. Burns, room 7240, 647–2471.
Executive Assistant.—Alice Wells, 647–1598.

AFRICAN AFFAIRS

Assistant Secretary.—Johnnie Carson, room 6234A, 647–4440.
Principal Deputy Assistant Secretary.—Donald Yamamoto, 647–4485.

EAST ASIAN AND PACIFIC AFFAIRS

Assistant Secretary.—Kurt Campbell, 647–9596.
Principal Deputy Assistant Secretary.—Joseph R. Donovan, 736–4393.
Deputy Assistant Secretaries: Alex Arvizu, 647–8929; Scott Marciel, 647–6904; John Norris, 647–6910.

EUROPEAN AND EURASIAN AFFAIRS

Assistant Secretary.—Kurt Campbell, room 6205, 647–7161.
Principal Deputy Assistant Secretary.—Joseph Donovan, 647–6321.
Deputy Assistant Secretaries: Frankie Reed, 647–6601; David Shear, 647–7156; Jennifer Park Stout, 647–3653; Joseph Y. Yun, 647–6595.

NEAR EASTERN AFFAIRS

Assistant Secretary.—Jeffrey Feltman, room 6242, 647–7209.
Principal Deputy Assistant Secretary.—Ronald Schlicher, 647–7207.
Deputy Assistant Secretaries: Michael Corbin, 647–0554; Janet Sanderson, 647–7166; Jacob Walles, 647–7170; Tamara Wittes, 647–7168.

SOUTH AND CENTRAL ASIAN AFFAIRS

Assistant Secretary.—Robert Blake, room 6254, 736–4325.
Principal Deputy Assistant Secretary.—Geoffrey Pyatt, 736–4331.
Deputy Assistant Secretaries: Alyssa Ayres, 736–4328; Susan Elliott, 736–4328; James Moore, 736–4331.

WESTERN HEMISPHERE AFFAIRS

Assistant Secretary.—Arturo Valenzuela, room 6262, 647–5780.
Principal Deputy Assistant Secretary.—Roberta Jacobson, 647–8387.
Principal Deputy Assistant Secretary.—Fabiola Rodriguez-Ciampoli, 647–1313.
Deputy Assistant Secretaries: Jeff Delaurentis, 647–8563; Julissa Reynoso, 647–7337; Matthew Rooney, 647–6755.

INTERNATIONAL NARCOTICS AND LAW ENFORCEMENT AFFAIRS

Assistant Secretary.—William Brownfield, room 7333, 647–8464.
Principal Deputy Assistant Secretary.—William J. McGlynn, 647–6642.
Deputy Assistant Secretaries: Charles Snyder, Elizabeth Verville, 647–9822.

INTERNATIONAL ORGANIZATION AFFAIRS

Assistant Secretary.—Esther Brimmer, room 6323, 647–9600.
Principal Deputy Assistant Secretary.—H. Dean Pittman, 647–9602.
Deputy Assistant Secretaries: Nerissa J. Cook, 647–5798; Victoria K. Holt, 647–9604; Suzanne F. Nossel, 647–9431.

UNDER SECRETARY FOR ECONOMIC, ENERGY, AND AGRICULTURAL AFFAIRS

Under Secretary.—Robert Hormats, room 7256, 647–7575.
Executive Assistant.—Tom Smitham, 647–7674.

ECONOMIC, ENERGY, AND BUSINESS AFFAIRS

Assistant Secretary.—Jose W. Fernandez, room 4932/4934, 647–7971.
Principal Deputy Assistant Secretary.—Deborah A. McCarthy, 647–9496.
Deputy Assistant Secretaries: William Craft, 647–5968; Krishna Urs, 647–4045.

UNDER SECRETARY FOR ARMS CONTROL AND INTERNATIONAL SECURITY

Under Secretary.—Ellen Tauscher, room 7208, 647–1049.
Executive Assistant.—Wade Boese, 647–6634.

INTERNATIONAL SECURITY AND NONPROLIFERATION

Principal Deputy Assistant Secretary.—Eliott Kang, room 3932, 647–5999.

Deputy Assistant Secretary for Nonproliferation Programs.—Simon Limage (acting), 647–9612.

POLITICAL-MILITARY AFFAIRS

Assistant Secretary.—Andrew J. Shapiro, room 6212, 647–9022.
Principal Deputy Assistant Secretary.—Kurt Amend, 647–9023.
Deputy Assistant Secretaries: BG Thomas Masciell, 647–9023, Beth McCormick, 647–0337.

ARMS CONTROL, VERIFICATION AND COMPLIANCE

Assistant Secretary.—Rose Gottemoeller, room 5950, 647–5315.
Principal Deputy Assistant Secretary.—Karin Look, 647–6830.
Deputy Assistant Secretaries: Marcie Ries, 647–5553; Frank Rose, 647–7821.

UNDER SECRETARY FOR PUBLIC DIPLOMACY AND PUBLIC AFFAIRS

Under Secretary.—Judith A. McHale, room 5932, 647–9199.
Chief of Staff.—Kitty DiMartino.
Executive Assistant.—Maureen McCormack.

EDUCATIONAL AND CULTURAL AFFAIRS

Assistant Secretary.—Ann Stock, 632–6445.
Principal Deputy Assistant Secretary.—Adam Ereli, 632–9444.
Deputy Assistant Secretaries: Stanley Colvin, 632–9288; Alina Romanowski, 632–9331.

INTERNATIONAL INFORMATION PROGRAMS

Coordinator.—Dawn McCall, 632–2942.

PUBLIC AFFAIRS

Assistant Secretary.—Philip Crowley, room 6800, 647–6607.
Deputy Assistant Secretaries: Cheryl Benton, Dana Smith.
Deputy Spokesman.—Mark Toner, 647–9606.

UNDER SECRETARY FOR MANAGEMENT

Under Secretary.—Patrick F. Kennedy, room 7207, 647–1500.
Executive Assistant.—Kathleeen Austin-Ferguson, 647–1501.

ADMINISTRATION

Assistant Secretary.—Steven Rodriguez, room 6330, 647–1492.
Deputy Assistant Secretaries: Margaret Grafeld, 621–8300; William Moser (703) 857–6956; Steven Rodriguez, 647–1492.

CONSULAR AFFAIRS

Assistant Secretary.—Janice L. Jacobs, room 6811, 647–9576.
Principal Deputy Assistant Secretary.—Michael D. Kirby, 647–9577.
Deputy Assistant Secretaries: David Donahue, 647–6541; James Pettit, 647–6541; Brenda Sprague, 647–5366.

DIPLOMATIC SECURITY AND OFFICE OF FOREIGN MISSIONS

Assistant Secretary.—Eric J. Boswell, room 6316, 647–6290.

Principal Deputy Assistant Secretary.—Jeffrey Culver (571) 345–3815.
Deputy Assistant Secretaries: Charlene R. Lamb, 345–3841; Justine Sincavage, 647–3417; Gentry Smith (571) 345–3836.

DIRECTOR GENERAL OF THE FOREIGN SERVICE AND DIRECTOR OF HUMAN RESOURCES

Director General.—Nancy J. Powell, room 6218, 647–9898.
Principal Deputy Assistant Secretary.—Amb. Steve Browning, 647–9438.
Deputy Assistant Secretaries: Robert Manzanares, 647–9438; Linda Taglialatela, 647–5152.

FOREIGN SERVICE INSTITUTE

Director.—Ruth Whiteside, room F2102 (703) 302–6703.
Deputy Director.—Tracey Jacobson (703) 302–6707.

INFORMATION RESOURCE MANAGEMENT

Assistant Secretary.—Vacant, 647–2889.
Chief Technology Officer of Operations.—Charlie Wisecarver, 634–3084.
Chief Knowledge Officer of Business Management and Planning.—Janice Fedak, 634–3083.
Chief Information Security Officer of Information Assurance.—John Streufert (703) 812–2555.

MEDICAL SERVICES

Assistant Secretary.—Thomas W. Yun, 663–1649.
Deputy Assistant Secretary.—Brooks Taylor, 663–1641.

OVERSEAS BUILDINGS OPERATIONS

Assistant Secretary.—Adam Namm (acting), (703) 875–4114.
Deputy Director.—Lydia Muniz (703) 875–7493.
Executive Assistant.—Nicholas Giacobbe (703) 875–5036.

UNDER SECRETARY FOR DEMOCRACY AND GLOBAL AFFAIRS

Under Secretary.—Maria Otero, room 7261, 647–6240.
Executive Assistant.—David J. Young, 647–7609.

DEMOCRACY, HUMAN RIGHTS AND LABOR

Assistant Secretary.—Michael H. Posner, room 7802, 647–2126.
Principal Deputy Assistant Secretary.—Deborah Graze, 647–2590.

OCEANS AND INTERNATIONAL ENVIRONMENTAL AND SCIENTIFIC AFFAIRS

Assistant Secretary.—Dr. Kerri-Ann Jones, room 3880, 647–1554.
Principal Deputy Assistant Secretary.—Daniel Clune, 647–6950.
Deputy Assistant Secretaries: David A. Balton, 647–1561; Larry Gumbiner, 647–1561; Daniel Reifsnyder, 647–2232.

POPULATION, REFUGEES AND MIGRATION

Assistant Secretary.—Eric Schwartz, room 5805, 647–7360.
Principal Deputy Assistant Secretary.—David Robinson, 647–5982.
Deputy Assistant Secretaries: Reuben Brigety, 647–5822; Kelly Clements, 647–5822.

UNITED STATES PERMANENT REPRESENTATIVE TO THE UNITED NATIONS

U.S. Permanent Representative.—Susan E. Rice, room 6333, 736–7555.

Deputy to the Ambassador.—Rexon Y. Ryu.

DIRECTOR OF FOREIGN ASSISTANCE

Deputy Director.—Robert Goldberg, room 5923, 647–2527.
Chief of Staff.—Khushali Shah, 647–2877.

UNITED STATES DIPLOMATIC OFFICES—FOREIGN SERVICE

(C= Consular Office, N= No Embassy or Consular Office)

http://usembassy.state.gov

LIST OF CHIEFS OF MISSION

AFGHANISTAN, ISLAMIC REPUBLIC OF (Kabul).
Hon. Karl W. Eikenberry.
ALBANIA, REPUBLIC OF (Tirana).
Hon. Alexander A. Arvizu.
ALGERIA, DEMOCRATIC AND POPULAR REPUBLIC OF (Algiers).
Hon. David D. Pearce.
ANDORRA (Andorra La Vella) (N)
Hon. Alan D. Solomont.
ANGOLA, REPUBLIC OF (Luanda).
Hon. Christopher J. McMullen.
ANTIGUA AND BARBUDA (St. John's) (N).
Vacant.
ARGENTINA (Buenos Aires).
Hon. Vilma Martinez.
ARMENIA, REPUBLIC OF (Yerevan).
Hon. Marie L. Yovanovitch.
AUSTRALIA (Canberra).
Hon. Jeffrey L. Bleich.
AUSTRIA, REPUBLIC OF (Vienna).
Hon. William Carlton Eacho III.
AZERBAIJAN, REPUBLIC OF (Baku).
Hon. Matthew J. Bryza.
BAHAMAS, THE COMMONWEALTH OF THE (Nassau).
Nicole Avant.
BAHRAIN, STATE OF (Manama).
Hon. Joseph Adam Ereli.
BANGLADESH, PEOPLE'S REPUBLIC OF (Dhaka).
Hon. James Francis Moriarty.
BARBADOS (Bridgetown).
Charge' d' Affaires D. Brent Hardt.
BELARUS, REPUBLIC OF (Minsk).
Vacant.
BELGIUM (Brussels).
Howard G. Gutman.
BELIZE (Belmopan).
Hon. Vinai Thummalapally.
BENIN, REPUBLIC OF (Cotonou).
Hon. James Knight.
BOLIVIA, REPUBLIC OF (La Paz).
Charge' d' Affaires John Creamer.
BOSNIA–HERZEGOVINA (Sarajevo).
Hon. Patrick S. Moon.
BOTSWANA, REPUBLIC OF (Gaborone).
Hon. Stephen James Nolan.
BRAZIL, FEDERATIVE REPUBLIC OF (Brasilia).
Hon. Thomas Alfred Shannon, Jr.
BRUNEI DARUSSALAM (Bandar Seri Begawan).
Vacant.
BULGARIA, REPUBLIC OF (Sofia).
Hon. James B. Warlick, Jr.
BURKINA FASO (Ouagadougou).
Hon. J. Thomas Dougherty.
BURMA, UNION OF (Rangoon).
Mr. Larry M. Dinger.
BURUNDI, REPUBLIC OF (Bujumbura).
Hon. Pamela Jo Howell Slutz.
CAMBODIA, KINGDOM OF (Phnom Penh).
Hon. Carol Ann Rodley.
CAMEROON, REPUBLIC OF (Yaounde).
Hon. Robert Porter Jackson.
CANADA (Ottawa).
Amb. David Jacobson.
CAPE VERDE, REPUBLIC OF (Praia).
Charge' d' Affaires Dana M. Brown.
CENTRAL AFRICAN REPUBLIC (Bangui).
Hon. Laurence D. Wohlers.
CHAD, REPUBLIC OF (N'Djamena).
Hon. Mark M. Boulware.
CHILE, REPUBLIC OF (Santiago).
Hon. Alexandro Daniel Wolff.
CHINA, PEOPLE'S REPUBLIC OF (Beijing).
Jon M. Huntsman, Jr.
COLOMBIA, REPUBLIC OF (Bogota).
Hon. Peter Michael McKinley.
COMOROS, UNION OF (Moroni) (N).
Hon. R. Niels Marquardt.
CONGO, REPUBLIC OF THE (Brazzaville).
Hon. Christopher W. Murray.
CONGO, DEMOCRATIC REPUBLIC OF THE (Kinshasa).
Hon. James Frederick Entwistle.
COSTA RICA, REPUBLIC OF (San Jose).
Hon. Anne Slaughter Andrew.
COTE D'IVOIRE, REPUBLIC OF (Abidjan).
Hon. Phillip Carter III.
CROATIA, REPUBLIC OF (Zagreb).
Hon. James B. Foley.
CUBA (Havana).
Principal Officer Mr. Jonathan Farrar.
CURACAO and ST. MAARTEN
Chief of Mission Valerie Belon.
CYPRUS, REPUBLIC OF (Nicosia).

Hon. Frank Charles Urbancic, Jr.
CZECH REPUBLIC (Prague).
Hon. Norman L. Eisen.
DENMARK (Copenhagen).
Hon. Laurie Susan Fulton.
DJIBOUTI, REPUBLIC OF (Djibouti).
Hon. James Christopher Swan.
DOMINICAN REPUBLIC (Santo Domingo).
Hon. Raul Yzaguirre.
EAST TIMOR, DEMOCRATIC REPUBLIC OF (Dili).
Hon. Judith R. Fergin.
ECUADOR, REPUBLIC OF (Quito).
Hon. Heather M. Hodges.
EGYPT, ARAB REPUBLIC OF (Cairo).
Hon. Margaret Scobey.
EL SALVADOR, REPUBLIC OF (San Salvador).
Hon. MarCarmen Aponte.
EQUATORIAL GUINEA, REPUBLIC OF (Malabo) (N).
Alberto M. Fernandez.
ERITREA, STATE OF (Asmara).
Deputy in Charge of Mission Joel R. Reifman.
ESTONIA, REPUBLIC OF (Tallinn).
Hon. Michael C. Polt.
ETHIOPIA, FEDERAL DEMOCRATIC REPUBLIC OF (Addis Ababa).
Hon. Donald E. Booth.
FIJI ISLANDS, REPUBLIC OF THE (Suva).
Hon. C. Steven McGann.
FINLAND, REPUBLIC OF (Helsinki).
Hon. Bruce J. Oreck.
FRANCE (Paris).
Hon. Charles H. Rivkin.
GABONESE REPUBLIC (Libreville).
Hon. Eric D. Benjaminson.
GAMBIA, REPUBLIC OF THE (Banjul).
Hon. Pamela Ann White.
GEORGIA (Tbilisi).
Hon. John R. Bass.
GERMANY, FEDERAL REPUBLIC OF (Berlin).
Hon. Philip D. Murphy.
GHANA, REPUBLIC OF (Accra).
Hon. Donald Gene Teitelbaum.
GREECE (Athens).
Hon. Daniel Bennett Smith.
GRENADA (St. George) (N).
Charge' d' Affaires Bernard Link.
GUATEMALA, REPUBLIC OF (Guatemala).
Hon. Stephen George McFarland.
GUINEA, REPUBLIC OF (Conakry).
Patricia Newton Moller.
GUINEA-BISSAU, REPUBLIC OF (Bissau) (N).
Hon. Marcia Stephens Bloom Bernicat.
GUYANA, CO-OPERATIVE REPUBLIC OF (Georgetown).
Charge' d' Affaires Tom Pierce.
HAITI, REPUBLIC OF (Port-au-Prince).
Hon. Kenneth Merten.
HOLY SEE (Vatican City).
Hon. Miguel Humberto Diaz.
HONDURAS, REPUBLIC OF (Tegucigalpa).
Hon. Hugo Llorens.
HONG KONG (Hong Kong) (C).
Principal Officer Stephen M. Young.
HUNGARY, REPUBLIC OF (Budapest).
Hon. Eleni Tsakopoulos Kounalakis.
ICELAND, REPUBLIC OF (Reykjavik).
Hon. Luis E. Arreaga-Rodas.
INDIA (New Delhi).
Hon. Timothy J. Roemer.
INDONESIA, REPUBLIC OF (Jakarta).
Hon. Scot Alan Marciel.
IRAQ, REPUBLIC OF (Baghdad).
Hon. James Franklin Jeffrey.
IRELAND (Dublin).
Hon. Daniel M. Rooney.
ISRAEL, STATE OF (Tel Aviv).
Hon. James B. Cunningham.
ITALY (Rome).
Hon. David H. Thorne.
JAMAICA (Kingston).
Hon. Pamela Bridgewater Awkard.
JAPAN (Tokyo).
Hon. John Victor Roos.
JERUSALEM
Consul General Daniel Rubinstein.
JORDAN, HASHEMITE KINGDOM OF (Amman).
Hon. Robert Stephen Beecroft.
KAZAKHSTAN, REPUBLIC OF (Almaty).
Hon. Richard E. Hoagland.
KENYA, REPUBLIC OF (Nairobi).
Hon. Michael E. Ranneberger.
KIRIBATI, REPUBLIC OF (Tarawa) (N).
Hon. C. Steven McGann.
KOREA, REPUBLIC OF (Seoul).
Hon. D. Kathleen Stephens.
KOSOVO (Pristina).
Hon. Christopher William Dell.
KYRGYZ REPUBLIC (Bishkek).
Hon. Tatiana C. Gfoeller-Volkoff.
KUWAIT, STATE OF (Kuwait City).
Hon. Deborah K. Jones.
LAO PEOPLE'S DEMOCRATIC REPUBLIC (Vientiane).
Hon. Karen Brevard Stewart.
LATVIA, REPUBLIC OF (Riga).
Judith Gail Garber.
LEBANON, REPUBLIC OF (Beirut).
Hon. Maura Connelly.
LESOTHO, KINGDOM OF (Maseru).
Hon. Michele Thoren Bond.
LIBERIA, REPUBLIC OF (Monrovia).
Hon. Linda Thomas-Greenfield.
LIBYA (Tripoli).
Hon. Gene Allen Cretz.
LIECHTENSTEIN, PRINCIPALITY OF (Vaduz) (N).
Hon. Donald Sternoff Beyer, Jr.
LITHUANIA, REPUBLIC OF (Vilnius).
Hon. Anne Elizabeth Derse.
LUXEMBOURG, GRAND DUCHY OF (Luxembourg).
Hon. Cynthia Stroum.
MACEDONIA, REPUBLIC OF (Skopje).
Hon. Philip Thomas Reeker.
MADAGASCAR, REPUBLIC OF (Antananarivo).

Hon. R. Niels Marquardt.
MALAWI, REPUBLIC OF (Lilongwe).
Deputy Chief of Mission Lisa A. Vickers.
MALAYSIA (Kuala Lumpur).
Hon. Paul W. Jones.
MALDIVES, REPUBLIC OF (Male) (N).
Hon. Patricia A. Butenis.
MALI, REPUBLIC OF (Bamako).
Hon. Gillian Arlette Milovanovic.
MALTA, REPUBLIC OF (Valletta).
Douglas W. Kmiec.
MARSHALL ISLANDS, REPUBLIC OF THE (Majuro).
Hon. Martha Larzelere Campbell.
MAURITANIA, ISLAMIC REPUBLIC OF (Nouakchott).
Hon. Jo Ellen Powell.
MAURITIUS, REPUBLIC OF (Port Louis).
Hon. Mary Jo Wills.
MEXICO (Mexico City).
Hon. Carlos Pascual.
MICRONESIA, FEDERATED STATES OF (Kolonia).
Hon. Peter Alan Prahar.
MOLDOVA, REPUBLIC OF (Chisinau).
Hon. Asif Chaudhry.
MONACO (Monaco).
Hon. Charles H. Rivkin.
MONGOLIA (Ulaanbaatar).
Hon. Jonathan S. Addleton.
MONTENEGRO, REPUBLIC OF (Podgorica).
Vacant.
MOROCCO, KINGDOM OF (Rabat).
Samuel Louis Kaplan.
MOZAMBIQUE, REPUBLIC OF (Maputo).
Leslie V. Rowe.
NAMIBIA, REPUBLIC OF (Windhoek).
Hon. Wanda L. Nesbitt.
NAURU, REPUBLIC OF (Yaren) (N).
Hon. C. Steven McGann.
NEPAL, KINGDOM OF (Kathmandu).
Hon. Scott H. DeLisi.
NETHERLANDS, KINGDOM OF THE (The Hague).
Hon. Fay Hartog-Levin.
NEW ZEALAND (Wellington).
David Huebner.
NICARAGUA, REPUBLIC OF (Managua).
Hon. Robert J. Callahan.
NIGER, REPUBLIC OF (Niamey).
Hon. Bisa Williams.
NIGERIA, FEDERAL REPUBLIC OF (Abuja).
Hon. Terence Patrick McCulley.
NORWAY (Oslo).
Hon. Barry B. White.
OMAN, SULTANATE OF (Muscat).
Hon. Richard J. Schmierer.
PAKISTAN, ISLAMIC REPUBLIC OF (Islamabad).
Hon. Cameron Munter.
PALAU, REPUBLIC OF (Koror).
Hon. Helen Patricia Reed-Rowe.
PANAMA, REPUBLIC OF (Panama).
Hon. Phyllis Marie Powers.
PAPUA NEW GUINEA (Port Moresby).
Hon. Teddy Bernard Taylor.
PARAGUAY, REPUBLIC OF (Asuncion)
Hon. Liliana Ayalde.
PERU, REPUBLIC OF (Lima).
Hon. Rose Likins.
PHILIPPINES, REPUBLIC OF THE (Manila).
Hon. Harry K. Thomas, Jr.
POLAND, REPUBLIC OF (Warsaw).
Hon. Lee Andrew Feinstein.
PORTUGAL, REPUBLIC OF (Lisbon).
Allan J. Katz.
QATAR, STATE OF (Doha).
Hon. Joseph Evan LeBaron.
ROMANIA (Bucharest).
Mark Henry Gitenstein.
RUSSIAN FEDERATION (Moscow).
Hon. John R. Beyrle.
RWANDA, REPUBLIC OF (Kigali).
Hon. W. Stuart Symington.
SAINT KITTS AND NEVIS (Basseterre) (N).
Vacant.
SAINT LUCIA (Castries) (N).
Vacant.
SAINT VINCENT AND THE GRENADINES (Kingstown) (N).
Vacant.
SAMOA (Apia) (N).
Hon. David Huebner.
SAN MARINO, REPUBLIC OF (San Marino) (N).
Hon. David H. Thorne.
SAO TOME AND PRINCIPE, DEMOCRATIC REPUBLIC OF (Sao Tome) (N).
Hon. Eric D. Benjaminson.
SAUDI ARABIA, KINGDOM OF (Riyadh).
Hon. James B. Smith.
SENEGAL, REPUBLIC OF (Dakar).
Hon. Marcia Stephens Bloom Bernicat.
SERBIA (Belgrade)
Hon. Mary Burce Warlick.
SEYCHELLES, REPUBLIC OF (Victoria) (N).
Hon. Mary Jo Willis.
SIERRA LEONE, REPUBLIC OF (Freetown).
Hon. Michael S. Owen.
SINGAPORE, REPUBLIC OF (Singapore).
Hon. David Adelman.
SLOVAK REPUBLIC (Bratislava).
Hon. Theodore Sedgwick.
SLOVENIA, REPUBLIC OF (Ljubljana).
Hon. Joseph A. Mussomeli.
SOLOMON ISLANDS (Honiara) (N).
Hon. Teddy Bernard Taylor.
SOUTH AFRICA, REPUBLIC OF (Pretoria).
Donald Henry Gips.
SPAIN (Madrid).
Hon. Alan D. Solomont.
SRI LANKA, DEMOCRATIC SOCIALIST REPUBLIC OF (Colombo).
Hon. Patricia A. Butenis.
SUDAN, REPUBLIC OF THE (Khartoum).
Charge d' Affaires Robert E. Whitehead.
SURINAME, REPUBLIC OF (Paramaribo).
Hon. John Nay.
SWAZILAND, KINGDOM OF (Mbabane).

Hon. Earl Michael Irving.
SWEDEN (Stockholm).
Hon. Matthew Winthrop Barzun.
SWITZERLAND (Bern).
Hon. Donald Sternoff Beyer, Jr.
SYRIAN ARAB REPUBLIC (Damascus).
Robert Stephen Ford.
TAJIKISTAN, REPUBLIC OF (Dushanbe).
Hon. Kenneth E. Gross, Jr.
TANZANIA, UNITED REPUBLIC OF (Dar es Salaam).
Alfonso E. Lenhardt.
THAILAND, KINGDOM OF (Bangkok).
Hon. Kristie Anne Kenney.
TOGOLESE REPUBLIC (Lome).
Hon. Patricia McMahon Hawkins.
TONGA, KINGDOM OF (Nuku'alofe) (N).
Hon. C. Steven McGann.
TRINIDAD AND TOBAGO, REPUBLIC OF (Port-of-Spain).
Hon. Beatrice Weltere.
TUNISIA, REPUBLIC OF (Tunis).
Hon. Gordon Gray.
TURKEY, REPUBLIC OF (Ankara).
Hon. Francis Joseph Ricciardone, Jr.
TURKMENISTAN (Ashgabat).
Vacant.
TUVALU (Funafuti) (N).
Hon. C. Steven McGann.
UGANDA, REPUBLIC OF (Kampala).
Hon. Jerry P. Lanier.
UKRAINE (Kyiv).
Hon. John F. Tefft.
UNITED ARAB EMIRATES (Abu Dhabi).
Hon. Richard G. Olson.
UNITED KINGDOM OF GREAT BRITAIN AND NORTHERN IRELAND (London).
Hon. Louis B. Susman.
URUGUAY, ORIENTAL REPUBLIC OF (Montevideo).
Hon. David Daniel Nelson.
UZBEKISTAN, REPUBLIC OF (Tashkent).
Vacant.
VANUATU, REPUBLIC OF (Port Vila) (N).
Hon. Teddy Bernard Taylor.
VENEZUELA, BOLIVARIAN REPUBLIC OF (Caracas).
Charge' d' Affaires John Caulfield.
VIETNAM, SOCIALIST REPUBLIC OF (Hanoi).
Hon. Michael W. Michalak.
YEMEN, REPUBLIC OF (Sanaa).
Hon. Gerald M. Feierstein.
ZAMBIA, REPUBLIC OF (Lusaka).
Hon. Mark Charles Storella.
ZIMBABWE, REPUBLIC OF (Harare).
Hon. Charles Aaron Ray.

UNITED STATES PERMANENT DIPLOMATIC MISSIONS TO INTERNATIONAL ORGANIZATIONS

AFRICAN UNION (Addis Ababa).
Hon. Michael Anthony Battle, Sr.
EUROPEAN UNION (Brussels).
Amb. William E. Kennard.
NORTH ATLANTIC TREATY ORGANIZATION (Brussels).
Hon. Ivo Daadlder.
ORGANIZATION FOR ECONOMIC COOPERATION AND DEVELOPMENT (Paris).
Hon. Karen Kornbluh.
ORGANIZATION FOR SECURITY AND COOPERATION IN EUROPE (Vienna).
Hon. Ian C. Kelly.
ORGANIZATION OF AMERICAN STATES (Washington, DC).
Hon. Carmen Lomellin.
UNITED NATIONS (Geneva).
Hon. Betty E. King.
UNITED NATIONS (New York).
Hon. Susan E. Rice.
UNITED NATIONS (Vienna).
Hon. Glyn T. Davies.

DEPARTMENT OF THE TREASURY

1500 Pennsylvania Avenue, NW., 20220, phone (202) 622–2000, http://www.ustreas.gov

TIMOTHY F. GEITHNER, Secretary of the Treasury; born in New York, NY, August 18, 1961; education: B.A., Dartmouth College, 1983; M.A. in International Economics and East Asian Studies, Johns Hopkins School for Advanced International Studies, 1985; professional: International Economist, Overseas Private Investment Corporation, 1984–85; Research Associate, Kissinger Associates, 1985–88; International Economist, Treasury, 1988–89; Assistant to the U.S. Financial Services Negotiator, Treasury, 1989–90; Assistant Financial Attaché, Treasury, 1990–91; Special Assistant to the Assistant Secretary for International Affairs, Treasury, 1991–92; Special Assistant to the Under Secretary for International Affairs, Treasury, 1992–94; Deputy Assistant Secretary for International Monetary and Financial Policy, Treasury, 1994–97; Senior Deputy Assistant Secretary, International Monetary and Financial Policy, Treasury 1997; Assistant Secretary for International Affairs, Treasury, 1997–98; Under Secretary for International Affairs, Treasury, 1998-2001; Senior Fellow, Council on Foreign Relations, 2001; Director, Policy Development and Review, International Monetary Fund, 2001–03; President and CEO, Federal Reserve Bank of New York, 2003–09; married: Carole; children: Elise and Benjamin; nominated by President Barack Obama to become the 75th Secretary of the Treasury and confirmed by the U.S. Senate on January 26, 2009.

OFFICE OF THE SECRETARY

Secretary of the Treasury.—Timothy F. Geithner, room 3330 (202) 622–1100.
Executive Assistant.—Shirley E. Gathers, 622–5377.
Confidential Assistant.—Cheryl L. Matera, 622–1100.

OFFICE OF THE DEPUTY SECRETARY

Deputy Secretary.—Neal S. Wolin, room 3326 (202) 622–1080.
Special Assistant.—Lauren Mandelker, 622–1080.
Review Analyst.—Hanna Slomianyj, 622–1080.

OFFICE OF THE CHIEF OF STAFF

Chief of Staff.—Mark Patterson, room 3408 (202) 622–1906.
Deputy Chief of Staff and Executive Secretary.—Alastair Fitzpayne, room 3414, 622–5780.
Review Analyst.—Reavie Harvey, 622–0626.
White House Liaison.—Patrick Maloney, room 3420, 622–9469.

OFFICE OF THE GENERAL COUNSEL

General Counsel.—George W. Madison, room 3000 (202) 622–0283.
Principal Deputy General Counsel.—Christopher Meade (202) 622–6105.
Deputy General Counsel.—Christian Weideman, 622–1135.
Staff Assistants: Aloma A. Shaw, Kim Wilson, 622–0283.
Senior Advisor to the General Counsel.—Alexander Krulic, room 3006, 622–1223.
Assistant General Counsel for—
Banking and Finance.—Laurie Schaffer, room 2312, 622–1988.
Enforcement and Intelligence.—Mark Monborne, room 2304, 622–1286.
General Law and Ethics.—Rochelle Granat, room 3020, 622–6052.
International Affairs.—Himamauli ''Him'' Das, room 2308, 622–1147.
Legislation and Litigation.—Tom McGivern, room 2312, 622–2317.
Deputy Assistant General Counsel for—
Banking and Finance.—Peter Bieger, room 2020, 622–1975.
Enforcement and Intelligence.—Mike Maher, room 2301, 622–3654.

General Law and Ethics.—Brian Sonfield, room 2023, 622–9804.
International Affairs.—Rupa Bhattacharyya, room 2306, 622–2122.
Chief Counsel, Foreign Assets Control.—Sean Thorton, Annex 3123, 622–9880.
Deputy Chief Counsel.—Matthew Tuchband, Annex 3121, 622–1654.

OFFICE OF THE INSPECTOR GENERAL

Inspector General.—Eric Thorson, room 4436 (202) 622–1090.
Deputy Inspector General.—Dennis S. Schindel.
Counsel to the Inspector General.—Richard Delmar, suite 510, 927–0650.
Assistant Inspector General for—
Audit.—Marla Freedman, suite 600, 927–5400.
Investigations.—P. Brian Crane, 799 9th Street, NW., 8th floor, 927–5260.
Management Services.—Patricia Hollis (acting), suite 510, 927–5200.
Deputy Assistant Inspector General for—
Audit.—Robert Taylor, suite 600, 927–5400.
Investigations.—Vacant.
Management.—Debra McGruder, suite 510, 927–5229.

OFFICE OF THE UNDER SECRETARY FOR DOMESTIC FINANCE

Under Secretary.—Jeffrey Goldstein, room 3312 (202) 622–1703.
Senior Advisors to the Under Secretary: Christopher D'Angelo, room 3024, 611–2483; Sarah Miller, room 3024, 622–4231.

OFFICE OF THE ASSISTANT SECRETARY FOR FINANCIAL INSTITUTIONS

Assistant Secretary.—Vacant, room 2326 (202) 622–2610.
Senior Advisor.—Amias Gerety, 622–8716.
Deputy Assistant Secretary, Office of:
Consumer Protection.—Vacant, 622–0488.
Financial Education.—Vacant.
Director, Office of:
Community Adjustment and Investment Program (CAIP).—Louisa Quittman, room 1414, 622–8103.
Financial Institutions Policy.—Lance Auer, room 1418, 622–1262.
Financial Education.—Dubis Correal, room 1413, 622–4848.
Outreach.—Vacant.
Executive Director, Office of:
Community Development Financial Institutions Fund.—Donna Gambrell, 601 13th Street, 2nd floor, 622–4203.
Terrorism Risk Insurance Program.—Jeffrey S. Bragg, 1425 New York Avenue, NW., room 2114, 622–6770.

OFFICE OF THE ASSISTANT SECRETARY FOR FINANCIAL MARKETS

Assistant Secretary.—Mary Miller, room 2324 (202) 622–5571.
Deputy Assistant Secretary, Office of:
Federal Finance.—Matthew Rutherford, room 2418, 622–4995.
Government Financial Policy.—Vacant.
Director, Office of:
Debt Management.—Colin Kim, room 2414, 622–7087.
Federal Lending.—Gary Burner, National Press Building, suite 228, 622–2470.
Financial Market Policy.—Heidilynne Schultheiss, room 1404, 622–2692.
Policy and Legislative Review.—Paula Farrell, National Press Building, suite 1148, 622–2450.

OFFICE OF THE FISCAL ASSISTANT SECRETARY

Assistant Secretary.—Richard Gregg, room 2118 (202) 622–0560.
Deputy Assistant Secretary for—
Accounting Policy.—Mark Reger, room 2104, 622–6943.
Fiscal Operations and Policy.—Gary Grippo, room 2108, 622–0570.
Director, Office of Fiscal Projections.—David Monroe, room 2040, 622–0580.

Director, Office of Financial Innovation and Transformation.—Adam Goldberg, room 200P, 927–0638.
Director, Financial Services and Operations.—John Hill, room 2313, 622–8516.

OFFICE OF RESEARCH AND QUANTITATIVE STUDIES

Director.—Lewis Alexander, room 1334 (202) 622–7955.

OFFICE OF THE ASSISTANT SECRETARY FOR FINANCIAL STABILITY

Assistant Secretary.—Vacant.
Senior Advisor.—Rawan Abdelrazek, 622–0240.
Chief Office of:
Compliance Officer.—Paul Wolfteich, 622–6338.
Counsel.—Duane Morse, 622–1192.
Financial Officer.—Jennifer Main, 927–9458.
Investment Officer.—Vacant.
Operating Officer.—Howard Schweitzer, 622–6963.
Risk Officer.—Vacant, 622–8722.
Capital Purchase Program.—Ted Schaffner, 622–6872.
Financial Agent Management.—Gary Grippo (acting), 622–0570.
Homeownership Preservation.—Nancy Fleetwood (acting), 927–4000.

FINANCIAL MANAGEMENT SERVICE

401 14th Street, SW., 20227, phone (202) 874–6740, fax 874–7016

Commissioner.—David A. Lebryk.
Deputy Commissioner.—Wanda Rogers.
Assistant Commissioner for—
Business Architecture.—John Kopec.
Debt Management Services.—Scott Johnson.
Federal Finance.—Kristine Conrath.
Government-wide Accounting.—David Rebich.
Information Resources (Chief Information Officer).—John Kopec (acting).
Management (Chief Financial Officer).—Linda Kimberling.
Payments Management.—Sheryl Morrow.
Chief Counsel.—Margaret Marquette.
Director for Legislative and Public Affairs.—Melody Barrett.

BUREAU OF THE PUBLIC DEBT

799 9th Street, NW., 20239, phone (202) 504–3500, fax 504–3630

[Codified under U.S.C. 31, section 306]

Commissioner.—Van Zeck.
Deputy Commissioner.—Anita Shandor.
Executive Director for—
Administrative Resource Center.—Cynthia Springer (304) 480–7227.
Government Securities Regulations Staff.—Lori Santamorena, 504–3632.
Public and Legislative Affairs Staff.—Kim B. Treat, 504–3535.
Assistant Commissioner, Office of:
Financing.—Dara Seaman, 504–3550.
Management Services.—Fred Pyatt (304) 480–8101.
Office of Information Technology.—Kim McCoy (304) 480–6988.
Public Debt Accounting.—Debra Hines (304) 480–5101.
Retail Securities.—Paul Crowe (304) 480–6516.

OFFICE OF THE UNDER SECRETARY FOR INTERNATIONAL AFFAIRS

Under Secretary.—Lael Brainard, room 3432 MT (202) 622–1270.
Senior Advisors.—Paige Gebhardt, room 3213 MT, 622–1193; Michael Pyle, room 3217, 622–6508.
Staff Assistant.—Karen DeLaBarre Chase, room 3213, 622–0060.
Executive Secretary and Senior Coordinator for China and the Strategic and Economic Dialogue.—David Loevinger, room 3224 MT, 622–1231.

Chief Economist.—Michael Klein, room 4464 MT, 622–2417.
Director, Strategic Initiatives.—Ann DeFabio-Doyle, room 3041B MT, 622–6427.
Senior Director, Business Operations.—Jennifer Beasley, room 5127 MT, 622–6843.

OFFICE OF THE ASSISTANT SECRETARY FOR INTERNATIONAL AFFAIRS

Assistant Secretary for International Finance.—Charles Collyns, room 3430 MT, 622–0656.
Senior Advisor.—Rory MacFarquhar, room 3041A MT, 622–7110.
Staff Assistant.—Pat Griffin, room 3430 MT, 622–7588.
Assistant Secretary for International Markets and Developments.—Marisa Lago, room 4138A MT, 622–0200.
Senior Advisor.—Peter Wisner, 4138C MT, 622–9066.
Staff Assistant.—Kimberly Richards, 4138B MT, 622–4826.
Deputy Assistant Secretary for—
Africa and the Middle East.—Andy Baukol, room 3218A MT, 622–2159.
Asian Nations.—Robert Dohner, room 3218B MT, 622–7222.
Environment and Energy.—William ''Billy'' Pizer, room 3221 MT, 622–0173.
Europe and Eurasia.—Christopher Smart, room 3213 MT, 622–0117.
International Development, Finance and Debt.—Scott Morris, room 3204A MT, 622–8125.
International Monetary and Financial Policy.—Mark Sobel, room 3034 MT, 622–0168.
Investment Security.—Mark Jaskowiak, room 3203 MT, 622–0478.
Technical Assistance Policy.—W. Larry McDonald, room 3037 MT, 622–5504.
Trade and Investment Policy.—Sharon Yuan, room 3205A MT, 622–6883.
Western Hemisphere.—Nancy Lee, room 3204B MT, 622–2916.
Directors for International Affairs:
Afghanistan (IEA).—Malachy Nugent, room 5028 MT, 622–3831.
Africa (INN).—Dan Peters, room 1064C MT, 622–5280.
East Asia (ISA).—Chris Winship, room 4462 MT, 622–0132.
Environment and Energy Policy.—Beth Urbanas, room 1024B MT, 622–2956.
Europe and Eurasia (ICN).—Jeff Baker, room 4122C MT, 622–4845.
Global Economics Group (IMG).—John Weeks, room 5422F MT, 622–9885.
International Banking and Securities Markets (IMB).—William Murden, room 5310 MT, 622–2775.
International Debt Policy (IDD).—John Hurley, room 5417B MT, 622–9124.
International Monetary Policy (IMF).—E. Clay Berry, room 5326 MT, 622–2156.
International Trade (ITT).—Whit Warthin, room 5204A MT, 622–1733.
Investment Security (IFI).—Aimen Mir, room 5211A MT, 622–0184.
Middle East and North Africa (INM).—Luyen Tran, room 5008 MT, 622–0763.
Multilateral Development Banks (IDB).—Karen Mathiasen, room 5313M MT, 622–0070.
South and Southeast Asia (ISS).—Michael Kaplan, room 4440 MT, 622–4262.
Technical Assistance.—Mike Ruffner, 740 15th Street, NW., 622–2886.
Trade Finance and Investment Negotiations (ITF).—David Drysdale, room 5419J MT, 622–1749.
Western Hemisphere (IWH).—Carrie McKellogg, room 1458A MT, 622–4072.

U.S. BANKS

U.S. Executive Director of:
Inter-American Development Bank.—Gustavo Arnavat (202) 623–1075.
International Monetary Fund.—Meg Lundsager, 623–7764.
World Bank.—Ian H. Solomon, 458–0115.

OVERSEAS

U.S. Executive Director of:
African Development Bank and Fund (Tunis, Tunisia).—Walter Jones, 011–216–71–102–010.
Asian Development Bank (Manila, Philippines).—Skipp Orr, 011–632–632–6050.
European Bank for Reconstruction and Development (London, England).—James L. Hudson, 011–44–207–338–6459.

UNDER SECRETARY FOR TERRORISM AND FINANCIAL INTELLIGENCE

Under Secretary.—Stuart Levey, room 4326 (202) 622–8260.

ASSISTANT SECRETARY FOR TERRORIST FINANCING

Assistant Secretary.—David S. Cohen.
Deputy Assistant Secretary for Terrorist Financing and Financial Crimes.—Daniel Glaser, room 4000-MT, 622–1943.
Director, Office of:
Global Affairs.—Brian Grant, room 4001-MT, 622–0769.
Strategic Policy.—Chip Poncy, room 4308-MT, 622–9761.

ASSISTANT SECRETARY FOR INTELLIGENCE AND ANALYSIS

Assistant Secretary.—S. Leslie Ireland, room 4332 (202) 622–1835.
Deputy Assistant Secretary.—Howard Mendelsohn, room 2441, 622–1841.
Deputy Assistant Secretary for Security.—Charles Cavella, room 2523, 622–2585.
Director, Emergency Programs.—Kelly Wolslayer, room 1020, 622–2195.

OFFICE OF FOREIGN ASSETS CONTROL

Director.—Adam J. Szubin, room 2240 (202) 622–2510.

EXECUTIVE OFFICE FOR ASSET FORFEITURE

1341 G Street, NW., Suite 900, 20005, phone (202) 622–9600

Director.—Eric Hampl.

FINANCIAL CRIMES ENFORCEMENT NETWORK (FINCEN)

P.O. Box 39, Vienna, VA 22183, phone (703) 905–3591

Director.—James H. Freis, Jr.

OFFICE OF THE ASSISTANT SECRETARY FOR ECONOMIC POLICY

Assistant Secretary.—Vacant, room 3454, (202) 622–2200.
Senior Advisor to the Assistant Secretary.—Vacant, room 3445D.
Deputy Assistant Secretary for Policy Coordination.—Aaron Klein, room 3449, 622–2220.
Deputy Assistant Secretary for Macroeconomic Analysis.—John Shea, room 3450, 622–2734.
Director, Office of Macroeconomic Analysis.—Vacant, room 2449, 622–2293.
Deputy Assistant Secretary for Microeconomic Analysis.—John Bellows, room 3439, 622–1513.
Director, Office of Microeconomic Analysis.—Vacant, room 4426, 622–2683.

OFFICE OF THE ASSISTANT SECRETARY FOR LEGISLATIVE AFFAIRS

Assistant Secretary.—Kim N. Wallace, room 3134 (202) 622–1900.
Deputy to the Assistant Secretary.—Sandra Y. Namoos, room 3464, 622–1900.
Executive Assistant to the Assistant Secretary.—Betty Ann Hunt, room 3134, 622–1900.
Staff Assistant to the Assistant Secretary.—Menno Goedman, room 3134, 622–1900.
Deputy Assistant Secretary for—
Appropriations and Management.—Lisa L. Pena, room 3132, 622–1900.
Banking and Finance.—Charles C. Yi, room 3124–B, 622–1900.
Special Assistant.—Megan O. Moore, room 3124–A, 622–1900.
Housing, Insurance and Terrorist Finance.—Kathleen L. Mellody, room 3124–C, 622–1900.
International Affairs.—Stephane J. LeBouder, room 3127, 622–1900.
Special Assistant.—Roberto Rodriguez, room 3128–B, 622–1900.
Tax and Budget.—David P. Vandivier, room 3462, 622–1900.
Special Assistant.—Kristin M. Eagan, room 3128–A, 622–1900.
Administrative Specialist to the Assistant Secretary.—Linda L. Powell, room 3453–D, 622–0535.
Congressional Inquiries Analyst.—Ora D. Starks, room 3453–B, 622–0576.
Legislative Research Analyst.—Gail Harris-Berry, room 3453–C, 622–4401.

OFFICE OF THE ASSISTANT SECRETARY FOR MANAGEMENT / CHIEF FINANCIAL OFFICER

Assistant Secretary for Management, Chief Financial Officer and Chief Performance Officer.—Dan Tangherlini, room 2438 (202) 622–0410.

Deputy Assistant Secretary for Management and Budget.—Nani Coloretti, 622–0016.

Deputy Assistant Secretary for Human Resources and Chief Human Capital Officer.—Anita Blair, 1801 L Street, NW., 927–0341.

Deputy Chief Financial Officer.—Al Runnels, room 6253, 622–0750.

Director of:

Accounting and Internal Control.—Carole Banks, room 6263, 927–5281.

Asset Management.—Charles Ingram, room 6179, 622–2178.

Budget Officer.—Robert Mahaffie, room 6118, 622–1471.

Conference Events and Meeting Services.—Lucinda Gooch, room 1128, 622–2071.

Disclosure Services.—Dale Underwood, room 6200, Annex, 622–0874.

Environmental Safety and Health.—Eric Bradley, 622–0728.

Equal Opportunity and Diversity.—Mariam Harvey, 1801 L Street, NW., 622–1160.

Facilities Management.—Polly Dietz, room 1155, 622–7067.

Facilities Support Services.—James Thomas, room 6100, Annex, 622–4080.

Financial Management.—Dorrice Roth, Met Square, room 6W549, 622–1693.

Human Resource Strategy and Solutions.—Nicole Johnson, 1801 L Street, NW., room 6120, 622–4822.

Human Resources Operations.—Kristy Kaptur, 1801 L Street, NW., room 6626, 927–4919.

Information Services.—Veronica Marco, room 6904, 622–2477.

Printing and Graphics.—Craig Larsen, room 6100, Annex, 622–1409.

Procurement Services.—Kevin Youel-Page, room 6B513, Met Square, 622–0651.

Small and Disadvantaged Business Utilization.—Teresa Lewis, room 6099, Met Square, 622–2826.

Strategic Planning and Performance Management.—Martin Melone, room 6133, Met Square, 622–9316.

Senior Procurement Executive.—Thomas Sharpe, room 6111, Met Square, 622–1039.

Accounting Officer.—David Legge, room 6070, Met Square, 622–1167.

Facilities Support Services DD.—Sharon Kershbaum, Annex 6129, 622–0323.

OFFICE OF THE ASSISTANT SECRETARY FOR PUBLIC AFFAIRS

Assistant Secretary.—Vacant, room 3438 MT (202) 622–2910.

Deputy Assistant Secretary, Public Affairs Operations.—Jenni LeCompte, room 3446 MT, 622–2910.

Deputy Assistant Secretary, Public Affairs.—Steve Adamske, room 3438 MT, 622–2920.

Senior Advisor, Public Affairs.—Molly Buford, room 2126 MT, 622–3431.

Deputy Assistant Secretary/Public Liaison.—Gabrielle Trebat, room 3122 MT, 622–2792.

Review Analyst and Scheduling Coordinator.—Carmen Alvarado, room 3442 MT, 622–7483.

Spokesperson for—

Domestic Finance.—Colleen Murray, room 2124 MT, 622–2960.

Enforcement Specialist.—Marti Adams, room 2124 MT, 622–2960.

International Affairs.—Natalie Wyeth, room 2124 MT, 622–2960.

MHA & HHF.—Andrea Risotto, 1801 L St., room 817 MT, 927–8726.

OFS.—Mark Paustenbach, room 2124 MT, 622–2960.

Tax, Budget, Economic Policy.—Sandra Salstrom, room 2124 MT, 622–2960.

Speechwriter to the Secretary.—Mark Cohen, room 3111 MT, 622–5176.

Media Coordinator.—Erika Gudmundson, room 2124 MT, 622–0470.

Media Affairs Specialist.—Matt Anderson, room 2124 MT, 622–0631.

Senior Advisor (Public Liaison).—Victoria Suarez-Palomo, room 3111 MT, 622–9245.

Press Assistant.—Lacey Rose, room 2124 MT, 622–2960.

OFFICE OF THE ASSISTANT SECRETARY FOR TAX POLICY

Assistant Secretary.—Michael F. Mundaca, room 3120 MT (202) 622–0050.

Deputy Assistant Secretary for—

International Tax Affairs.—Stephen Shay, room 3045 MT, 622–9525.

Tax Analysis.—Mark Mazur, room 3064 MT, 622–0120.

Tax Policy.—Emily McMahon, room 3112 MT, 622–0140.

Tax, Trade and Tariff Policy.—Timothy Skud, room 3104 MT, 622–0220.
Retirement and Health Policy and Senior Advisor to the Secretary—J. Mark Iwry, room 3063 MT, 622–7827.
Tax Legislative Counsel.—Jeffrey Van Hove, room 3048 MT, 622–0835.
Deputy Tax Legislative Counsel.—John Parcell, room 4224 MT, 622–2578.
International Tax Counsel.—Manal Corwin, room 3054 MT, 622–1317.
Deputy International Tax Counsel: Michael Caballero, room 4043 MT, 622–1788; Henry Louis, room 5064 MT, 622–1791.
Benefits Tax Counsel.—George Bostick, room 3050 MT, 622–1341.
Deputy Benefits Tax Counsel.—Helen Morrison, room 4028 MT, 622–1357.
Director, Office of Tax Analysis.—James Mackie, room 4116 MT, 622–1326.
Director, Division of:
Business and International Taxation.—Geraldine A. Gerardi, room 4221 MT, 622–1782.
Economic Modeling and Computer Applications.—Robert Gillette, room 4039 MT, 622–0852.
Individual Taxation.—Janet McCubbin, room 4043 MT, 622–0589.
Receipts Forecasting.—Scott Jaquette, room 4064 MT, 622–1319.
Revenue Estimating.—John McClelland, room 4112 MT, 622–1129.

BUREAU OF ENGRAVING AND PRINTING

14th and C Streets, NW., 20228, phone (202) 874–2000

[Created by act of July 11, 1862; codified under U.S.C. 31, section 303]

Director.—Larry R. Felix.
Deputy Director.—Pamela J. Gardiner, 874–2016.
Chief Counsel.—Kevin Rice, 874–2306.
Associate Directors:
Chief Financial Officer (CFO).—Leonard R. Olijar, 874–2020.
Chief Information Officer (CIO).—Peter O. Johnson, 874–3000.
Associate Director for—
Eastern Currency Facility.—Jon J. Cameron, 874–2032.
Western Currency Facility.—Charlene Williams (817) 847–3802.
Management.—Scott Wilson, 874–2040.
Product and Technology Development.—Judith Diaz-Myers, 874–2008.
Corporate Planning and Strategic Analysis.—Andrew Brunhart, 874–4340.

OFFICE OF THE COMPTROLLER OF THE CURRENCY

250 E Street, SW., 20219, phone (202) 874–5000

Comptroller.—John Walsh (acting), 874–4900.
Chief of Staff and Public Affairs.—William A. Rowe (acting), 874–4880.
Chief Counsel.—Julie L. Williams, 874–5200.
Senior Deputy Comptroller for—
Bank Supervision Policy and Chief National Bank Examiner.—Timothy W. Long, 874–2870.
Chief Financial Officer.—Thomas R. Bloom, 874–5080.
Economics.—Mark Levonian, 874–5010.
Large Bank Supervision.—Michael L. Brosnan, 874–4610.
Midsize and Community Bank Supervision.—Jennifer C. Kelly, 874–5020.
Director for Congressional Liaison.—John Hardage, 874–4840.
Ombudsman.—Larry Hattix, 874–1530.
Chief Information Officer.—Edward J. Dorris, 874–4480.

INTERNAL REVENUE SERVICE

1111 Constitution Avenue, NW., 20224, phone (202) 622–5000

[Created by act of July 1, 1862; codified under U.S.C. 26, section 7802]

Commissioner.—Douglas H. Shulman, 622–9511.
Chief of Staff.—Jonathan Davis, 622–9511.
Deputy Commissioner, Services and Enforcement.—Steven Miller, 622–6860.

Commissioner of:

Large Business and International Division.—Heather Maloy, 283–8710.

Small Business / Self-Employed.—Chris Wagner, 622–0600.

Tax Exempt and Government Entities.—Sarah Hall Ingram, 283–2500.

Wage and Investment.—Richard Byrd (404) 338–7060.

Chief, Criminal Investigation.—Victor S.O. Song, 622–3200.

Directors:

Office of Professional Responsibility.—Karen Hawkins, 927–3812.

Whistleblower Office.—Steve Whitlock, 622–0351.

Deputy Commissioner, Operations Support.—Beth Tucker, 622–4255.

Chief:

Agency-Wide Shared Services.—Dave Grant, 622–7500.

Appeals.—Diane Ryan, 435–5600.

Communications and Liaison.—Frank Keith, 622–5440.

Equity, Diversity and Inclusion.—Debra Chew, 622–5400.

Financial Officer.—Pamela LaRue, 622–6400.

IRS Human Capital Officer.—James Falcone, 622–7676.

Office of Privacy, Information Protection and Data Security.—Rebecca A. Chiaramida, 622–2988.

Technology Officer.—Terence Milholland, 622–6800.

Chief Counsel.—William J. Wilkins, 622–3300.

National Taxpayer Advocate.—Nina E. Olson, 622–6100.

Director, Office of Research, Analysis and Statistics.—Rosemary Marcuss, 874–0100.

Office of Legislative Affairs.—Floyd Williams, 622–3720.

OFFICE OF THRIFT SUPERVISION

1700 G Street, NW., 20552, phone (202) 906–6000, fax 906–5660

[Codified in U.S.C. 12, section 1462a]

Director.—John E. Bowman (acting), 906–6372.

Deputy Director.—Thomas A. Barnes, 906–5650.

Chief Counsel.—Deborah Dakin, 906–6445.

Assistant Deputy Director, Examinations, Supervision and Consumer Protection.—Lori J. Quigley, 906–6265.

Managing Director, External Affairs.—Barbara Shycoff, 906–6288.

Chief Information Officer.—James J. Vercellone, 906–6714.

INSPECTOR GENERAL FOR TAX ADMINISTRATION (TIGTA)

1125 15th Street, NW., Room 700A, 20005

phone (202) 622–6500, fax 927–0001

Inspector General.—J. Russell George.

Principal Deputy Inspector General.—Joseph Hungate.

Congressional Liaison.—Judith M. Grady, 927–7164.

Chief Counsel.—Margaret Martin (acting), 622–3139.

Deputy Inspector General for Audit.—Michael R. Phillips, 927–7085.

Assistant Inspector General for—

Compliance and Enforcement Operations.—Margaret Begg, 622–8510.

Management Services and Organizations.—Nancy Nakamura, 622–8500.

Returns Processing and Accounts Services.—Michael McKenney, 622–5916.

Deputy Inspector General for Investigations.—Timothy P. Camus, 927–7160.

Assistant Inspectors General for Investigations: Michael A. Delgado, Terry Peacock.

Deputy Assistant Inspector General for Investigations.—John S. Fowler.

Associate Inspector General for Mission Support.—Larry Koskinen, 622–8482.

Chief of Operations.—Jennifer Donnan, (404) 274–8258.

Deputy Inspector General for Inspections and Evaluations.—David Holmgren, 927–7048.

OFFICE OF THE TREASURER OF THE UNITED STATES

Treasurer.—Rosie Rios (202) 622–0100.

Special Assistant.—Kristin Ward.

Executive Assistant.—Vacant.

Director, Advanced Counterfeit Deterrence.—Reese Fuller.

ACD Program Analyst.—Idalia Smith.

UNITED STATES MINT

801 9th Street, NW., 20002, phone (202) 354–7200, fax 756–6160

Director.—Richard Peterson (acting).
Executive Assistant to the Director.—Arnetta Cain.
Deputy Director.—Richard Peterson.
Executive Assistant to the Deputy Director.—Trena Jones.
Chief Counsel.—Dan Shaver (202) 354–7280.
Director, Legislative and Intergovernmental Affairs.—Vacant (202) 354–6700.
Director, Public Affairs.—Tom Jurkowsky (202) 354–7720.
Associate Director for Protection.—Dennis O'Connor (202) 354–7300.
Deputy Associate Director.—Bill R. Bailey (202) 354–7300.
Associate Director/Chief Information Officer.—Vacant.
Deputy Associate Director.—Goutam Kundu (202) 354–7700.
Associate Director/Chief Financial Officer.—Patricia M. Greiner (202) 354–7800.
Deputy Associate Director.—David Motl (202) 354–7800.
Associate Director, Sales and Marketing.—B.B. Craig (202) 354–7500.
Deputy Associate Director.—Sherry Suggs (202) 354–7800.
Associate Director, Manufacturing.—Vacant.
Deputy Associate Director.—Vacant.

DEPARTMENT OF DEFENSE

The Pentagon 20301–1155, phone (703) 545–6700
fax 695–3362/693–2161, http://www.defenselink.mil

LEON E. PANETTA, Secretary of Defense; born in Monterey, CA, June 28, 1938, where his Italian immigrant parents operated a restaurant; education: B.A., *magna cum laude,* political science, Santa Clara University, 1960; J.D., Santa Clara University School of Law, 1963; military service: U.S. Army, 1964–66; served as an Army Intelligence Officer and First Lieutenant; professional: ten years co-directing with his wife, the Leon & Sylvia Panetta Institute for Public Policy at California State University. The Institute is a nonpartisan, not-for-profit center that seeks to instill in young men and women the virtues and values of public service, he also spent five years in private law practice; member of the U.S. House of Representatives, 1977–93; chair, Budget Committee, 1989–93; director of the Office of Management and Budget, 1993–94; White House Chief of Staff to President Bill Clinton, 1994–97; member of the Iraq Study Group, a bipartisan committee established at the urging of Congress to conduct an independent assessment of the war in Iraq, 2006; director of the Central Intelligence Agency (CIA), 2009–11; he also served as legislative assistant to Senator Thomas H. Kuchel of California, special assistant to the Secretary of Health, Education and Welfare, director of the U.S. Office for Civil Rights, and executive assistant to Mayor John Lindsay of New York; award: received Army Commendation Medal, 1966; family: married to Sylvia; three sons and six grandchildren; nominated by President Barack Obama to become the 23rd Secretary of Defense, and was confirmed by the U.S. Senate on July 1, 2011.

OFFICE OF THE SECRETARY

1000 Defense Pentagon, Room 3E880, 20301–1000
phone (703) 692–7100, fax (703) 571–8951

Secretary of Defense.—Leon E. Panetta.

OFFICE OF THE DEPUTY SECRETARY

1010 Defense Pentagon, Room 3E944, 20301–1010, phone (703) 692–7150

Deputy Secretary of Defense.—William J. Lynn.

EXECUTIVE SECRETARIAT

Pentagon, Room 3E718, 20301–1000, phone (703) 692–7120, fax 571–8951

Executive Secretary.—Michael Bruhn.

GENERAL COUNSEL

Pentagon, Room 3E788, 20301–1600, phone (703) 695–3341, fax 693–7278

General Counsel.—Jeh Charles Johnson.
Principal Deputy.—Robert S. Taylor (703) 697–7248.

OPERATIONAL TEST AND EVALUATION

Pentagon, Room 3E1088, 20301–1700, phone (703) 697–4813, fax 614–9103

Director.—Dr. J. Michael Gilmore.

INSPECTOR GENERAL

400 Army Navy Drive, Suite 1000, Arlington, VA 22202–4704, phone (703) 604–8300 fax 604–8310, hotline 1–800–424–9098, hotline

fax 604–8567

Inspector General.—Hon. Gordon S. Heddell.

UNDER SECRETARY OF DEFENSE FOR ACQUISITION, TECHNOLOGY AND LOGISTICS

Pentagon, Room 3E1010, phone (703) 697–7021

Under Secretary.—Dr. Ashton B. Carter.
Principal Deputy Under Secretary.—Frank Kendall.
Deputy Under Secretary for—
Industrial Policy.—Brett Lambert.
Installations and Environment.—Dr. Dorothy Robyn.
Logistics and Materiel Readiness.—Alan Estevez (acting).
Director, Office of Small Business Program.—Linda Oliver (acting).
Director, Defense Research and Engineering.—Zachary Lemnios.
Assistant to the Secretary of Defense for Nuclear and Chemical and Biological Defense Programs.—Andrew Weber.

JOINT STRIKE FIGHTER PROGRAM OFFICE

200 12th Street South, Suite 600, Arlington, VA 22202–5402, phone (703) 602–7640, fax 602–7649

Program Executive Officer.—VADM David Venlet.

UNDER SECRETARY OF DEFENSE (COMPTROLLER) AND CHIEF FINANCIAL OFFICER

Pentagon, Room 3E770, 20301–1100, phone (703) 695–3237

Under Secretary/Chief Financial Officer.—Robert F. Hale.
Principal Deputy Under Secretary.—Michael J. McCord.

UNDER SECRETARY OF DEFENSE FOR PERSONNEL AND READINESS

Pentagon, Room 3E764, 20301–4000, phone (703) 695–5254

Under Secretary.—Dr. Clifford L. Stanley.
Principal Deputy Under Secretary (performing the duties of).—Lynn C. Simpson, 697–2121.
Assistant Secretary for—
Health Affairs.—Dr. Jonathan Woodson, 697–2113.
Reserve Affairs.—Dennis McCarthy, 697–6631.
Deputy Under Secretary for—
Civilian Personnel Policy.—Pat Tamburrino, 614–9487.
Military Community and Family Policy.—Robert Gordon, 697–7220.
Military Personnel Policy.—Virginia Penrod, 571–0116.
Readiness.—Dr. Samuel Kleinman, 693–0466.
Requirements and Strategic Integration.—Dr. Laura Stubbs, 571–0094.

UNDER SECRETARY OF DEFENSE FOR POLICY

Pentagon, Room 3E806, 20301–2000, phone (703) 697–7200

Under Secretary.—Hon. Michèle A. Flournoy.
Principal Deputy.—Hon. James N. Miller.
Assistant Secretary of Defense for—
Homeland Defense and America's Security Affairs.—Hon. Paul Stockton.

International Security Affairs.—Hon. Alexander R. Vershbow.
Special Operations/Low-Intensity Conflict and Interdependent Capabilities.—Hon. Michael G. Vickers.
Global Strategic Affairs.—Kenneth B. Handelman (acting).
Asian and Pacific Security Affairs.—Hon. Wallace C. Gregson.

ASSISTANT SECRETARY FOR NETWORKS AND INFORMATION INTEGRATION/CHIEF INFORMATION OFFICER

Pentagon, Room 3E1030, 20301–6000, phone (703) 695–0348

Assistant Secretary.—Teri Takai (acting).
Deputy Assistant Secretary.—Rob Carey.

ASSISTANT SECRETARY FOR LEGISLATIVE AFFAIRS

Pentagon, Room 3E970, 20301–1300, phone (703) 697–6210, fax 695–5860

Assistant Secretary.—Elizabeth King.
Principal Deputy.—Marcel Lettre.

ASSISTANT TO THE SECRETARY OF DEFENSE FOR INTELLIGENCE OVERSIGHT

Pentagon, Room 2E1052, 20301–7200, phone (703) 697–1346

Assistant to the Secretary.—Michael H. Decker.

ASSISTANT SECRETARY FOR PUBLIC AFFAIRS

Pentagon, Room 2E694, 20301–1400, phone (703) 697–9312, fax 695–4299
public inquiries 571–3343

Assistant Secretary.—Douglas B. Wilson.
Principal Deputy.—Bryan G. Whitman.

ADMINISTRATION AND MANAGEMENT

Pentagon, Room 3E971, 20301–1950, phone (703) 692–7138

Director.—Michael L. Rhodes, room 3E971, 692–7138.
Deputy Director.—William E. Brazis, room 3E971, 693–7906.

DEPARTMENT OF DEFENSE FIELD ACTIVITIES

DEFENSE MEDIA ACTIVITY

EFC Plaza, 601 North Fairfax Street, Suite 250, Alexandria, VA 22314

phone (703) 428–1200

Director.—Melvin W. Russell (acting).
Director for American Forces Radio and Television Services.—Melvin W. Russell.
Executive Officer.—Roger L. King.

DEPARTMENT OF DEFENSE EDUCATION ACTIVITY

4040 North Fairfax Drive, Arlington, VA 22203

School Information (703) 588–3030

Director.—Marilee Fitzgerald (acting), 588–3200.
Principal Deputy Director and Associate Director for Education.—Charlie Toth, 588–3105.
Associate Director for Finance and Business Operations.—Kevin Kelly, 588–3305.
General Counsel.—Karen Grosso Lambert, 588–3064.

DEPARTMENT OF DEFENSE HUMAN RESOURCES ACTIVITY

4040 Fairfax Drive, Arlington, VA 22209, phone (703) 696–1036

Director.—Vacant.
Deputy Director.—Vacant.
Executive Director.—Sharon Cooper, 696–0909.

TRICARE MANAGEMENT ACTIVITY

5111 Leesburg Pike, Suite 810, Falls Church, VA 22041, phone (703) 681–8707

Director.—Dr. Jonathan Woodson.
Deputy Director.—RADM Christine Hunter.

DEFENSE PRISONER OF WAR / MISSING PERSONNEL OFFICE

241 18th Street South, Suite 800, Arlington, VA 22202, phone (703) 699–1102, fax 602–1890

Director.—Robert Newberry.

OFFICE OF ECONOMIC ADJUSTMENT

400 Army Navy Drive, Suite 200, Arlington, VA 22202, phone (703) 604–6020

Director.—Patrick J. O'Brien.
Deputy Director of:
Operations.—Ronald Adkins, 604–5141.
Programs.—Dave Larson, 604–5148.
Sacramento Regional Manager.—Gary Kuwabara (acting), (916) 557–7365.

WASHINGTON HEADQUARTERS SERVICES

Pentagon, phone (703) 693–7906

Director.—William ''Bill'' Brazis.
Deputy Director.—Mary R. George
Directors for—
Acquisition and Procurement Office.—Linda Allen, 696–4030.
Administrative and Program Support.—Frank Wilson, 601–6100.
Defense Facilities.—Sajeel Ahmed (acting), 697–7241.
Executive Services.—Craig Glassner, 693–7965.
Financial Management.—Roberta Lowe, 699–3350.
Human Resources.—Chris Koehle (571) 256–4505.
Information Technology Management.—Lytwaive Hutchinson, 604–4569.
OSD Networks Directorate.—Ron Bechtold, 692–7453.
Pentagon Renovation Program Office.—Sajeel Ahmed, 614–5129.
Planning and Evaluation.—Anne O'Connor, 588–8140.
Raven Rock Mountain Complex.—COL Jeffrey Brlecic (717) 878–3343.
WHS General Counsel.—Don Perkal, 693–7374.

JOINT CHIEFS OF STAFF

OFFICE OF THE CHAIRMAN

Pentagon, Room 2E872, 20318–0001, phone (703) 697–9121

Chairman.—ADM Michael G. Mullen, USN.
Vice Chairman.—GEN James E. Cartwright, USMC, room 2E724, 614–8948.
Assistant to the Chairman, Joint Chiefs of Staff.—Lt. Gen. Paul J. Selva, USAF, room 2E868, 695–4605.

JOINT STAFF

Director.—VADM William Gortney, USN, room 2E936, 614–5221.
Vice Director.—Maj. Gen. Craig A. Franklin, USAF, room 2E936, 614–5223.
Director for—

Manpower and Personnel, J–1.—BG Walter M. Golden, Jr., USA, room 1E948, 697–6098.
Joint Staff Intelligence, J–2.—RADM Michael Rogers, USN, room 1E880, 697–9773.
Operations, J–3.—LTG Robert B. Neller, USMC, room 2D874, 697–3702.
Logistics, J–4.—LTG Kathleen M. Gainey, USA, room 2E828, 697–7000.
Strategic Plans and Policy, J–5.—LTG Charles H. Jacoby, USN, room 2E996, 695–5618.
Command, Control, Communications and Computer Systems, J–6.—LTG Dennis L. Via, USA, room 2D860, 695–6478.
Operational Plans and Joint Force Development, J–7.—BG Ralph O. Baker, USA, room 2B865, 697–9031.
Force Structure, Resources, and Assessment, J–8.—Lt. Gen. Larry O. Spencer, USAF, room 1E962, 697–8853.

DEFENSE AGENCIES

BALLISTIC MISSILE DEFENSE AGENCY

7100 Defense Pentagon, 20301–7100

phone (703) 695–6344

Director.—LTG Patrick O'Reilly, USA, 695–6344.
Deputy Director.—RDML Randall Hendrickson, USN, 695–6330.
Director, Public Affairs.—Richard Lehner, 697–8997.
Director, Legislative Affairs.—Kimo Hollingsworth, 693–9117.

DEFENSE ADVANCED RESEARCH PROJECTS AGENCY

3701 North Fairfax Drive, Arlington, VA 22203, phone (703) 696–2444

Director.—Dr. Regina Dugan, 696–2400.
Deputy Director.—Dr. Kaigham Gabriel, 696–2402.

DEFENSE COMMISSARY AGENCY

1300 E Avenue, Fort Lee, VA 23801–1800, phone (804) 734–8718 / 8330

Director.—Joseph H. Jeu, 734–8720.
Chief Operating Officer.—Thomas E. Milks, 734–8330.

WASHINGTON OFFICE

241 18th Street, Suite 302, Arlington, VA 22202–3405, phone (703) 602–0157 / 2297

Chief.—Daniel W. Sclater.

DEFENSE CONTRACT AUDIT AGENCY

8725 John J. Kingman Road, Suite 2135, Fort Belvoir, VA 22060

phone (703) 767–3200

Director.—Patrick J. Fitzgerald, 767–3200
Deputy Director.—Vacant.

DEFENSE FINANCE AND ACCOUNTING SERVICE

1851 South Bell Street, Room 920, Arlington, VA 22240
phone (703) 607–2616

Director.—Teresa A. McKay.
Deputy Director.—Richard P. Gustafson.

DEFENSE INFORMATION SYSTEMS AGENCY

P.O. Box 549, Fort Meade, MD 20755

Director.—LTG Carroll Pollett, USA, room C6D16B (301) 225–6042.
Vice Director.—Maj. Gen. Ronnie Hawkins, USAF, room C6D16D (301) 225–6021.

DEFENSE INTELLIGENCE AGENCY

200 MacDill Boulevard, Washington, DC 20340, phone (703) 695–0071

Director.—LTG Ronald L. Burgess, USA.
Deputy Director.—David R. Shedd.

DEFENSE LEGAL SERVICES AGENCY

Pentagon, Room 3E788, 20301–1600, phone (703) 695–3341, fax 693–7278

Director/General Counsel.—Jeh C. Johnson.
Principal Deputy Director.—Robert S. Taylor, 697–7248.

DEFENSE LOGISTICS AGENCY

8725 John J. Kingman Road, Suite 2533, Ft. Belvoir, VA 22060
phone (703) 767–5264

Director.—VADM Alan S. Thompson, SC, USN.
Vice Director.—Mae De Vincentis.

DEFENSE SECURITY COOPERATION AGENCY

201 12th Street South, Suite 203, Arlington, VA 22202–5408, phone (703) 604–6605

Director.—VADM William E. Landay III, USN.
Deputy Director.—Richard Genaille, 604–6606.

DEFENSE SECURITY SERVICE

1340 Braddock Place, Alexandria, VA 22314–1651, phone (703) 325–5310

Director.—Stanley L. Sims.

DEFENSE THREAT REDUCTION AGENCY

8725 John J. Kingman Road, Stop 6201, Ft. Belvoir, VA 22060–6201
phone (703) 767–7594

Director.—Kenneth A. Myers III.
Deputy Director.—RADM Garland P. Wright, Jr., USN.
Chief, Legislative and Governmental Affairs.—Don Minner.

NATIONAL GEOSPATIAL—INTELLIGENCE AGENCY

4600 Sangamore Road, Bethesda, MD 20816, phone (301) 227–7400

Director.—Letitia A. Long.
Deputy Director.—Lloyd B. Rowland.

NATIONAL SECURITY AGENCY/CENTRAL SECURITY SERVICE

Ft. George G. Meade, MD 20755, phone (301) 688–6524

Director, NSA/Chief, CSS.—GEN Keith B. Alexander, USA.

Deputy Director, NSA.—John C. Inglis.
Deputy Chief, CSS.—Brig. Gen. Jim Keffer, USAF.

JOINT SERVICE SCHOOLS

9820 Belvoir Road, Ft. Belvoir, VA 22060, phone (800) 845–7606

DEFENSE ACQUISITION UNIVERSITY

President.—Katharina G. McFarland (703) 805–3360.
Vice President.—James McMichael (703) 805–4592.
Chief of Staff.—Joseph Johnson (703) 805–2828.

NATIONAL DEFENSE INTELLIGENCE COLLEGE

President.—David R. Ellison (202) 231–3344.

NATIONAL DEFENSE UNIVERSITY

Fort McNair, Building 62, 300 Fifth Avenue, 20319
phone (202) 685–3912

President.—VADM Ann E. Rondeau, USN, room 307, 685–3936.
Senior Vice President.—Amb. Thomas C. Krajeski, room 307A, 685–3923.

INFORMATION RESOURCES MANAGEMENT COLLEGE

Chancellor.— Dr. Robert D. Childs (202) 685–3886.

JOINT FORCES STAFF COLLEGE

7800 Hampton Boulevard, Norfolk, VA 23511–1702, phone (757) 443–6200

Commandant.—Brig. Gen. Marvin T. Smoot, Jr., USAF, room A202.

INDUSTRIAL COLLEGE OF THE ARMED FORCES

Commandant.—Maj. Gen. Joseph D. Brown, IV, USAF, room 200 (202) 685–4337.

NATIONAL WAR COLLEGE

Commandant.—RADM Douglas J. McAneny, USN, room 124 (202) 685–4341.

UNIFORMED SERVICES UNIVERSITY OF THE HEALTH SCIENCES

4301 Jones Bridge Road, Bethesda, MD 20814

President.—Charles L. Rice, M.D., room A1019 (301) 295–3013.

DEPARTMENT OF THE AIR FORCE

Pentagon, 1670 Air Force, Washington, DC 20330–1670

phone (703) 697–7376, fax 695–8809

SECRETARY OF THE AIR FORCE

Secretary of the Air Force.—Michael B. Donley, room 4E878.
Confidential Assistant.—Becky Gorman.
Senior Military Assistant.—Col. Peggy Poore.
Deputy Military Assistant.—Lt. Col. David Graff.
Military Aid.—Maj. Thad Middleton.

SECAF / CSAF EXECUTIVE ACTION GROUP

Chief.—Col. Mark Hicks (703) 697–5540.
Deputy Chief.—Col. Darryle J. Grimes.

UNDER SECRETARY OF THE AIR FORCE

Pentagon, 1670 Air Force, Room 4E858, 20330–1670, phone (703) 697–1361

Under Secretary.—Hon. Erin C. Conaton.
Confidential Assistant.—Ms. Kimberly Bender.
Senior Military Assistant.—Col. Peter Bloom.
Military Assistant.—Lt. Col. Wendy Wasik.
Executive Assistant.—MSgt John Aegerter.

CHIEF OF STAFF

Pentagon, 1670 Air Force, Room 4E924, 20330

phone (703) 697–9225

Chief of Staff.—Gen. Norton A. Schwartz.
Executive Officer.—Col. Dean Clemons.
Vice Chief of Staff.—Gen. Philip Breedlove, room 4E938, 695–7911.
Assistant Vice Chief of Staff.—Lt. Gen. Dick Newton, room 4E944, 695–7913.
Director, Operations Group.—Col. Mark Hicks, room 4D919, 697–5540.
Chief Master Sergeant of the Air Force.—CMSAF James Roy, room 4E941, 695–0498.

DEPUTY UNDER SECRETARY FOR INTERNATIONAL AFFAIRS

Pentagon, 1080 Air Force Pentagon, Room 4E192, 20330–1080

Rosslyn, 1500 Wilson Boulevard, 8th Floor, Arlington, VA 22209

Deputy Under Secretary.—Heidi H. Grant (703) 695–7262.
Assistant Deputy.—Maj. Gen. Michael A. Snodgrass, 695–7261.
Senior Executive Officer.—Lt. Col. Monica Partridge, 695–7262.
Executive Officers: Lt. Col. Darrell Smith, 693–1941; Maj. Christopher Nemeth, 695–7261.
Non-Commissioned Officer in Charge, Executive Assistant.—SSgt. Alexandria Florig, 695–7263.
Executive Officers: Lt. Col. Craig Lucey, 588–8828; Maj. Angel Santiago, 588–8833.
Executive Assistant.—Lindsey Heil, 588–8800.
Director of Policy.—Gerald R. Hust, 588–5560.
Director of Regional Affairs.—Brig. Gen. Lyn D. Sherlock, 588–8820.

Director of Strategy, Operations and Resources.—Kelli Seybolt, 588–8800.

ASSISTANT SECRETARY FOR ACQUISITION

Pentagon, 1060 Air Force, 20330

1500 Wilson Boulevard, Arlington, VA 22209

1745 Jefferson Davis Highway, Suite 307, Arlington, VA 22202

110 Luke Avenue, Suite 200, Bolling AFB, DC 20032–6400

Assistant Secretary.—Vacant (703) 697–6361.
Air Force Service Acquisition Executive.—David M. Van Buren, 693–9373.
Senior Military Assistant.—Col. Tim Freeman, 697–6990.
Military Assistant.—Vacant, 697–6362.

Principal Deputy.—David M. Van Buren, 697–9373.
Military Assistant.—Lt. Col. Sean Jackson, 693–9350.

Military Deputy.—Lt. Gen. Mark Shackelford, 697–6363.
Executive Officer.—Maj. Erik Quigley, 695–7311.

DEPUTY ASSISTANT SECRETARY FOR ACQUISITION INTEGRATION

Deputy Assistant Secretary.—Blaise J. Durante (571) 256–0355.
Associate Deputy Assistant Secretary.—Vacant, 256–0351.
Executive Officer.—Maj. Deven Lowman, 256–0356.

DEPUTY ASSISTANT SECRETARY FOR CONTRACTING

Deputy Assistant Secretary.—Roger S. Correll (571) 256–2397.
Associate Deputy Assistant Secretary.—Pamela C. Schwenke, 256–2397.
Executive Officer.—Maj. Larry Mercier, 256–2397.

DEPUTY ASSISTANT SECRETARY FOR SCIENCE, TECHNOLOGY AND ENGINEERING

Deputy Assistant Secretary.—Dr. Steven Walker (571) 256–0303.
Associate Deputy Assistant Secretary.—Col. Mark Koch, 256–0303.
Executive Officer.—Maj. Dan Richards, 256–0294.

CAPABILITY DIRECTORATE FOR GLOBAL POWER PROGRAMS

Director.—Maj. Gen. Jay H. Lindell (571) 256–0191.
Deputy Director.—Col. James Lovell, 256–0192.
Executive Officer.—Maj. Eric Morgan, 256–0196.

CAPABILITY DIRECTORATE FOR GLOBAL REACH PROGRAMS

Director.—Maj. Gen. Randal D. Fullhart (571) 256–0489.
Deputy Director.—Col. Janet Kasmer, 256–0497.
Executive Officer.—Maj. Aaron Taylor, 256–0522.

CAPABILITY DIRECTORATE FOR INFORMATION DOMINANCE

Director.—Randall Walden (571) 256–0081.
Deputy Director.—Col. Greg Gutterman, 256–0082.
Executive Officer.—Maj. Steve Grace, 256–0083.

CAPABILITY DIRECTORATE FOR SPACE PROGRAMS

Director.—Maj. Gen. John Hyten (703) 588–7350.
Deputy Director.—Col. Michael Taylor, 588–7331.

Executive Officer.—Lt. Col. David Menke, 588–7333.

DIRECTORATE FOR SPECIAL PROGRAMS

Director.—Col. Tim Woods (202) 767–3890.
Deputy Director.—Col. Chris DiNenna (571) 256–0005.
Associate Director.—Ryan Dow (202) 767–3939.
Executive Assistant.—Roxanne Ramnauth 767–3890.

DIRECTORATE FOR AIR FORCE RAPID CAPABILITIES

Director.—David E. Hamilton (202) 767–1800.
Deputy and Technical Director.—Deven Cate, 767–1800.
Executive Officer.—David Wrazen, 767–3203.

ASSISTANT SECRETARY FOR FINANCIAL MANAGEMENT AND COMPTROLLER OF THE AIR FORCE

Pentagon, 1130 Air Force, 20330

CGN, Air Force Cost Analysis Agency, Crystal Gateway North

1111 Jefferson Davis Highway, Suite 403, Arlington, VA 22202

Assistant Secretary.—Dr. Jamie M. Morin, room 4E978 (703) 697–1974.
Military Assistant.—Col. Samuel Grable, 695–0837.
Chief, Enlisted Matters.—CMSgt Jesse Stirling, 614–5437.

PRINCIPAL DEPUTY ASSISTANT SECRETARY FOR FINANCIAL MANAGEMENT

Principal Deputy Assistant Secretary.—Patricia J. Zarodkiewicz (703) 697–4464.
Military Assistant.—Capt. Latonya Kelly, 695–0829.

DEPUTY ASSISTANT SECRETARY FOR BUDGET

Deputy Assistant Secretary.—Maj. Gen. Alfred Flowers, room 5D912 (703) 695–1875.
Executive Officer.—Lt. Col. Terry Jones, 695–1876.
Deputy.—Marilyn Thomas, 695–1875.
Director of:
Budget and Appropriations Liaison.—Col. Tracey Watkins, room 5C949, 614–8114.
Budget Investment.—Vacant, room 5D912, 697–1220.
Budget Management and Execution.—Judith Oliva, room 5D912, 695–9737.
Budget Operations and Personnel.—Brig. Gen. Joseph Ward, room 5D912, 697–0627.
Budget Programs.—Col. Charles Fulghum, room 5C950, 614–7883.

DEPUTY ASSISTANT SECRETARY FOR COST AND ECONOMICS

Deputy Assistant Secretary.—Richard K. Hartley, room 5E975 (703) 697–5311.
Associate Deputy Assistant Secretary.—Kathy Watern, 697–5313.
Executive Officer.—Lt. Col. Christopher Crane, 697–5312.
Technical Director for Cost and Economics.—Ranae Woods, room 403, 604–0400.
Director, Economics and Business Management.—Stephen M. Connair, room 4C843, 693–9347.

DEPUTY ASSISTANT SECRETARY FOR FINANCIAL OPERATIONS

Deputy Assistant Secretary.—Joan Causey, Pentagon, room 5D739.
Associate Deputy Assistant Secretary.—Douglas Bennett, room 5D739 (703) 614–4180.
Military Assistant.—Lt. Col. Andy Gwinupp, Pentagon, room 5D739 614–4180.
Director for—
Accounting Policy and Reporting.—Fred Carr, Andrews AFB, MD (301) 981–9222.

AF Financial Systems Organization.—Rick Staley, Wright-Patterson AFB, OH (937) 257–8447.
Financial Services.—Vacant, Ellsworth AFB, SD (605) 385–8696.
Information Systems and Technology.—Vacant.

ASSISTANT SECRETARY FOR INSTALLATIONS, ENVIRONMENT AND LOGISTICS

Assistant Secretary.—The Honorable Terry A. Yonkers, room 4E996 (703) 697–4936.
Principal Deputy Assistant Secretary.—Debra K. Tune, 697–4936.
Executive Officer.—Lt. Col. Benjamin Spencer, 697–4219.
Military Assistant.—Col. Calvin Williams, 697–5023.
Special Assistant.—Dr. Camron Gourguinpour, 697–6300.
Confidential Assistant.—Cathy Hudock, 697–4936.
Resource Manager.—Everette Dewaine Longus, 697–4391.

DEPUTY ASSISTANT SECRETARY FOR INSTALLATIONS (SAF/IEI)

Deputy Assistant Secretary.—Kathleen I. Ferguson, room 4B941 (703) 695–3592.
Deputy for Installation Policy.—James P. Holland, 614–6232.
Administrative Support Specialist/Secretary.—Pamela L. Coghill, 695–3592.
Executive Officer.—Lt. Col. Susan Riordan-Smith, 695–6456.
Director, Planning and Strategic Development.—Col. Lowell Nelson, 697–7003.
Director, Installation Management.—Lt. Col. Tony Davit, 694–4638.
Director, Installation Programs.—Major Jason Loschinskey, 695–5730.
Legislative/Public Affairs Manager.—Frank Smolinsky, 697–1980.
Air Force Real Property Agency Liaison.—Robert McCann, 697–7244.
Director, Air National Guard and Reserve Affairs.—Lt. Col. Russ Ponder, 697–0997.
Director, Asset Management.—Edward Pokora, 693–9328.
Asset Management.—Marriane Serrano, 614–6230.
Installation Programs.—Steve Zander, 571–3325.
Workflow Manager.—Alma Schaffer, 697–6492.

BRAC PROGRAM MANAGEMENT OFFICE (SAF/IEI–PMO)

Director.—Col. Joseph Morganti, Crystal Gateway 1, suite 1000, (703) 604–5276.
Director Resources Division.—Wellington Selden, 604–5295.
Resources.—Paul Freund, 604–5298; Helen Griffith, 604–5210.
Information Management.—JJ Cook, 604–5273.
Program Managers: Tim Brennan, 604–5253; Steve Cornish, 604–5256; Greg Keysor, 604–5288; Ray Neall, 604–5359; Robert Niswonger, 601–0181; Donna Oscepinski, 602–5438; George "Stu" Pugh, 604–5272.

AIR FORCE REAL PROPERTY AGENCY

2261 Hughes Avenue, Suite 121, San Antonio, TX 78236–9821

Director.—Robert "Bob" Moore, (210) 395–9501.
Deputy Director.—Jeffrey Domm, 395–9502.
Secretary to the Director.—Linda Cosper, 395–9503.
Secretary to the Deputy Director.—Vacant.

DEPUTY ASSISTANT SECRETARY FOR ENVIRONMENT, SAFETY AND OCCUPATIONAL HEALTH (SAF/IEE)

Deputy Assistant Secretary.—Timothy K. Bridges, room 4B941, (703) 697–9297.
Deputy for ESOH Policy.—Michael McGhee, 697–1019.
Executive Secretary.—Sheenia Williams, 697–9297.
Executive Officer.—Maj. David Pugh, 693–3254.
Director for—
Safety Policy.—Vance Lineberger, 693–7706.
Environment Policy.—Michele Indermark, 614–8458.
ESOH Integration Policy.—Lt. Col. Jeffrey Gillen, 692–9515.
Occupational Health Policy.—Maj. Elisa Hammer, 571–5771.
ESOH Policy Support.—Daniel Kowalczyk, 697–1198.

DEPUTY ASSISTANT SECRETARY FOR LOGISTICS (SAF/IEL)

Deputy Assistant Secretary.—S. Mark Reynolds, room 4B941, 697–7070.
Director, Logistics and Transformation.—Mark Van Gilst, 692–9090.
Executive Secretary.—Jayne Wright, 571–5774.
Chief, Depot Operations and Strategic Planning/Executive Officer.—Lt. Col. Henry Myers, 693–2185.
Chief, Strategic Resources.—Candy Jones, 695–6716.
Director, Life Cycle Management.—Al Bello, 697–1641.
Chief, Life Cycle Integration.—Doug Dynes, 697–1016.
Chief, Weapon System Integration.—Rita Dixon, 614–6240.

DEPUTY ASSISTANT SECRETARY FOR ENERGY (SAF/IEN)

Deputy Assistant Secretary.—Kevin T. Geiss, room 5E1000, 256–4711.
Deputy for Energy Policy.—Carol Ann Beda, 697–1207.
Executive Officer.—Cameron Stanley, 256–4711.
Logistics Energy Management Specialist.—Chris Ferris, 697–1098.
Energy Facilities Engineer.—Vickie Davis, 697–1113.
Acquisition Energy Program Manager.—Omar Mendoza, 256–1809.
Energy Integration Program Manager.—RuthAnne Darling, 697–0785.
Aviation Energy Program Analyst.—Raul Bennett, 571–5773.

ASSISTANT SECRETARY FOR MANPOWER AND RESERVE AFFAIRS

1660 Air Force Pentagon, Room 4E1010, 20330–1660

Assistant Secretary.—Daniel B. Ginsberg (703) 697–2302.
Principal Deputy Assistant.—Sheila M. Earle (703) 697–1258.
Mobilization Assistant.—Brig. Gen. Kevin Pottinger, 604–8136.
Confidential Assistant.—Ruth N. Thornton, 695–6677.
Military Assistant.—Lt. Col. David DuHadway, 697–2303.
Executive Officer.—Lt. Col. Amy Johnson, 697–1258.
Superintendent.—Jamie Robinson, 614–5654.

DEPUTY ASSISTANT SECRETARY FOR FORCE MANAGEMENT INTEGRATION

Deputy Assistant Secretary.—William H. Booth (703) 614–4751.
Executive Secretary.—Dottie A. Baltimore, 614–4751.
Assistant Deputy for—
Family Programs.—Linda Stephens-Jones, 693–9574.
Force Management and Development.—Lt. Col. Donna M. Pike, 695–2459.
Force Management Integration.—Charlene M. Bradley, 614–4753.
Force Support Services.—Maj. Shawn W. Campbell, 693–9765.
Health Policy.—Carol J. Thompson, 693–9764.
Military Force Management.—Thomas E. Booth, 697–7783.
Officer Accessions and Programs.—David A. French, 693–9333.
Plans and Legislative Integration.—Lt. Col. Justin W. Hall, 697–7058.

DEPUTY ASSISTANT SECRETARY FOR RESERVE AFFAIRS

Deputy Assistant Secretary.—R. Philip Deavel, room 5D742 (703) 697–6376.
Executive Secretary.—Stephanie Parry, 697–6375.
Assistant for—
Air Force Reserve Matters.—Col. Michelle Ryan, 697–6431.
ANG Matters.—Col. Elizabeth Hill, 693–9512.
Career Broadner.—Kathy Simonton (571) 256–4044.
Chief RC Business Integration.—Col. Cathy Haverstock (703) 697–6429.
Director, AF Auxiliary Programs.—R. Brian Arnold, 697–9504.
Enlisted Matters.—CMSgt. Malinda Price, 693–9505.
Executive Director for Air Reserve Forces Policy Committee.—Lt. Col. Douglas Hill, 697–6430.
IMA to SAF/MRR.—Col. Sharon Olbeter, 693–9511.

DEPUTY ASSISTANT SECRETARY FOR STRATEGIC DIVERSITY INTEGRATION

Deputy Assistant Secretary.—Dr. Jarris L. Taylor, Jr., room 5E783 (703) 697–6586.
Assistant Deputy.—Kathleen Ryan (703) 697–6583.
Executive Secretary.—Karen Sauls (703) 697–6586.

AIR FORCE REVIEW BOARDS AGENCY (SAF/MRB)

1500 West Perimeter Road, Suite 3700, Joint Base Andrews NAF, MD 20762

Director.—Joe G. Lineberger (240) 612–5400.
Legal Advisor.—Victor Donovan, 612–5404.
Medical Advisor.—Horace Carson, 612–5405.
Chief, Review Boards.—CMSgt Valerie Barnes, 612–5402.
Confidential Assistant.—Marilyn Redmond, 612–5400.

AIR FORCE BOARD FOR CORRECTION OF MILITARY RECORDS (AFBCMR) SAF/MRBC

Executive Director.—Al Walker (240) 612–5371.
Deputy.—Phillip Horton, 612–5372.
Chief Examiners: Janet Hutson, 612–5373; Daryl Lawrence, 612–5381.
Chief, AFBCMR Operations.—Charles Hollings, 612–5387.

AIR FORCE CIVILIAN APPELLATE REVIEW OFFICE (AFCARO), SAF/MRBA

Director.—Rita S. Looney (240) 612–5331.
Assistant Director.—Sharon E. Hanlon, 612–5330.

SECRETARY OF THE AIR FORCE PERSONNEL COUNCIL (SAFPC), SAF/MRBP

Director.—Col. Kenneth Klein (240) 612–5353.
Deputy Director.—Col. Scott Blum, 612–5369.
Senior Legal Advisor.—Col. Lou Cherry, 612–5358.
Senior Medical Advisor.—Col. Richard Stahlman, 612–5360.
Chief, Air Force Discharge Review Board.—Col. Steven Wright, 612–5365.
Chief, Awards/Decorations/Air Force Reserve Advisor.—Col. Beth Mann, 612–5355.
Executive Secretary/Attorney Advisor on Clemency/Parole Board.—James Johnston, 612–5364.
Executive Secretary, DoD Civilian/Military Service Review Board.—James Johnston, 612–5364.

AIR FORCE PERSONNEL SECURITY APPEAL BOARD (PSAB), SAF/MRBS

President.—Richard Mazza (240) 612–5349.
Deputy.—Joseph Schott, 612–5350.

DoD PHYSICAL DISABILITY BOARD OF REVIEW (PDBR), SAF/MRBD

Crystal City, VA

President.—Michael LoGrande (703) 601–0199.
Deputy.—Christopher Honeycutt, 607–0120.

CHIEF OF WARFIGHTING INTEGRATION AND CHIEF INFORMATION OFFICER

1800 Air Force Pentagon, Room 4E1050, 20330

Chief of Warfighting Integration and Chief Information Officer.—Lt. Gen. William T. Lord (703) 695–6829.
Deputy Chief of Warfighting Integration and Deputy Chief Information Officer.—Daniel F. McMillin, 697–1605.

Director of:
Warfighter Systems Integration and Deployment.—Brig. Gen. William Ranck, room 1D857, 695–1835.
Infrastructure Delivery.—Maj. Gen. Paul Capasso, room 1D857, 692–4584.
Policy and Resources.—Bobby Smart, room 1D857, 695–1839.

DEPUTY CHIEF OF STAFF FOR INTELLIGENCE, SURVEILLANCE AND RECONNAISSANCE (ISR)

Deputy Chief of Staff.—Lt. Gen. Larry James (703) 695–5613.
Assistant Deputy Chief of Staff.—Maj. Gen. James Poss.
Executive Officer.—Lt. Col. Craig Perry.
Director of:
ISR Capabilities.—Brig. Gen. Robert Otto, 695–5818.
ISR Innovations.—James Clark, 693–3377.
ISR Resources.—Kenneth Dumm, 614–2144.
ISR Strategy, Plans, Doctrine and Force Development.—Brig. Gen. (Select) Mark Westergren, 614–3478.
Special Program Integration.—Dean Yount, 693–5201.

DEPUTY CHIEF OF STAFF FOR LOGISTICS, INSTALLATIONS AND MISSION SUPPORT

Pentagon, 1030 Air Force, 20330

Deputy Chief of Staff.—Lt. Gen. Loren M. Reno, Pentagon, room 4E154 (703) 695–5590.
Assistant Deputy.—Patricia M. Young, Pentagon, room 4E260, 695–6236.
Director of:
Global Combat Support.—David Beecroft, Pentagon, room 1E718A, 697–8860.
Transformation.—Grover L. Dunn, Pentagon, room 5E768, 697–6559.
Logistics.—Maj. Gen. Judith Fedder, Pentagon, room 4E278, 695–4900.
Resources Integration.—Maj. Gen. Duane Jones, Pentagon, room 4A272, 697–2822.
Security Forces.—Brig. Gen. Jimmy McMillian, Pentagon, room 5E1040, 693–5401.
The Civil Engineer.—Maj. Gen. Timothy Byers, Pentagon, room 4C1057, 693–4301.

DEPUTY CHIEF OF STAFF FOR MANPOWER, PERSONNEL AND SERVICES

Pentagon, 1040 Air Force, Room 4E168, 20330

Deputy Chief of Staff.—Lt. Gen. Darrell D. Jones (703) 697–6088.
Assistant Deputy Chief of Staff.—Tim Beyland.
Chief, Personnel Issues Team.—Lt. Col. Drysdale Hernandez, room 4E169, 695–4212.
Director of:
Air Force General Officer Management.—Col. Thomas Sharpy, room 4D1066, 697–1181.
Executive Services.—MSgt. Philip Eckenrod, room 4D1089, 697–1125.
Force Development.—Daniel Sitterly, room 4D950, 695–2144.
Force Management Policy.—Brig. Gen. Sharon Dunbar, room 4D950A, 695–6770.
Manpower, Organization, and Resources.—Brig. Gen. Philip Ruhlman, room 5A328, 692–1601.
Plans and Integration.—Mark Doboga, room 4D1054A, 697–5222.

DEPUTY CHIEF OF STAFF FOR OPERATIONS, PLANS AND REQUIREMENTS

Pentagon, 1630 Air Force, Room 4E1024, 20330

Deputy Chief of Staff.—Lt. Gen. Hawk Carlisle (703) 697–9991.
Assistant Deputy.—Maj. Gen. Johnny Weida, 697–9881.
Mobility Assistant.—Maj. Gen. Michael N. Wilson, 697–3087.
Director of:
Operational Capability Requirements.—Maj. Gen. David Scott, room 5C889A, 695–3018.
Operational Planning, Policy and Strategy.—Maj. Gen. Richard Devereaux, room 5E857, 614–2711.
Operations.—Maj. Gen. Brett Williams, room 5D756, 695–7602.
Resource Integration.—Mark Budgeon, room 5E873, 697–7833.
Space and Cyber Operations.—Maj. Gen. Edward Bolton, room 5D756, 697–6745.

DEPUTY CHIEF OF STAFF FOR STRATEGIC PLANS AND PROGRAMS

Pentagon, 1070 Air Force, Room 4E1082, 20330–1070

Deputy Chief of Staff.—Lt. Gen. Christopher D. Miller (703) 697–9472.
Assistant Deputy Chief of Staff.—Barbara Westgate, 692–9944.
Military Assistant Deputy Chief of Staff.—Brig. Gen. James D. Demeritt.
Directorate of Programs.—Maj. Gen. Robert Worley, room 5D1088, 697–2038.
Director for Strategic Planning.—Maj. Gen. Richard C. Johnston, room 5D1050, 697–3117.

DIRECTORATE OF STUDIES AND ANALYSIS ASSESSMENTS AND LESSONS LEARNED

Pentagon, 1570 Air Force, Room 4E214

Washington, DC 20330–1570

Director.—Dr. Jacqueline R. Henningsen, Ph.D., SES (571) 256–2015.
Principal Deputy Director.—Mr. Kevin E. Williams, SES.
Military Deputy Director.—Brig. Gen. Joseph T. Callahan III.
Senior Advisor.—Vacant.
Technical Director.—Dr. Mark A. Gallagher, Ph.D., SL.
Chief Analyst.—Col. Jeffrey W. Lanning.

STRATEGIC DETERRENCE AND NUCLEAR INTEGRATION (A10)

Pentagon, 1488 Air Force, Suite 4E240, 20330

Assistant Chief of Staff.—Maj. Gen. William Chambers (703) 693–9747.
Deputy Assistant Chief of Staff.—Maj. Gen. (Ret.) Ron Henderson, SES, 693–9747.
Associate Assistant Chief of Staff.—Dr. Billy Mullins, Ph.D., SES, 693–9747.
HQE.—Dr. Jim Blackwell, Ph.D., 695–1365.
MA.—Col. Tal Angelosante, 697–0808.
Director of Staff.—Mike Shoults, 693–9748.
Senior Executive.—Lt. Col. Rob Pedersen, 693–9747.
Junior Executive.—Maj. Frank Landry, 693–9747.
Administrative Assistant.—Diane Berger, 693–9747.
Division Chiefs:
Executive Services.—Lt. Col. Curt McGiffin, 697–7734.
Assessments.—Lt. Col. Jeff Neischel (202) 767–7420.
Operations.—Col. George Farfour, 767–4259.
Planning, Policy and Strategy.—Col. Norm Worthen (703) 697–4098.
Capabilities.—Mike Hargrove, 588–0904.
Strategic Implementation.—Mike Loughran (202) 767–5337.

ADMINISTRATIVE ASSISTANT TO THE SECRETARY

Pentagon, 1720 Air Force, 20330

2221 South Clark Street, Arlington, VA 22202 (CP6)

229 Brookley Avenue, Bolling AFB, Washington, DC 20032 (BAFB1)

3 Brookley Avenue, Box 94, Bolling AFB, Washington, DC 20032 (BAFB2)

Administrative Assistant.—William A. Davidson, Pentagon, room 4E824 (703) 695–9492.
Deputy Administrative Assistant.—Robert E. Corsi, Jr., 695–9492.
Senior Executive Assistant.—Maj. Tara Valentine, 695–9492.
Junior Executive Assistant.—Capt. Kelli Kinley, 695–9492.
Executive Administrator.—SSgt. Clarice Mack.
General Manager, Executive Dining Facility.—Alfonso Sisneros, room 4D869, 697–1112.
Director of:
Art Program Office.—Russell Kirk, room 5E271, 697–2858.
Central Adjudication Facility.—Col. Laura Hickman, BAFB1 (202) 767–9236.
Declassification Office.—Linda Smith, CP6, Suite 600, 604–4665.
Departmental Publishing Office.—Jessica Spencer-Gallucci, BAFB2 (202) 404–2380.
Facilities Support Division.—Susan Bench-Snow, room 5D855, 697–8222.

Human Resources and Manpower Division.—Ed Bezdziecki, room 4D828, 697–5895.
Policy, Plans and Resources Division.—Carolyn Lunsford, room 5D883, 695–4007.
Security, Counterintelligence and Special Programs Oversight Division.—Scott Deacon, room MD779, 693–2013.
Information Protection Division.—Daniel McGarvey, room MC832, 693–0614.

AUDITOR GENERAL

Pentagon, 1120 Air Force, 20330

4170 Hebble Creek Road, Building 280, Room 1
Wright-Patterson AFB, OH 45433 (WPAFB)

5023 Fourth Street, March ARB, CA 95218 (MARB)

1101 Wilson Boulevard, Suite 1010, Arlington, VA 22201 (Rosslyn)

4701 I Street East, Randolph AFB, TX 78150–4332

Auditor General.—Theodore J. Williams, room 4E204 (703) 614–5626.

AIR FORCE AUDIT AGENCY

Assistant Deputy Auditor General.—Michael V. Barbino, Rosslyn (703) 696–7764.
Assistant Auditor General for—
Acquisition and Logistics Audits.—Sharon Puschmann, WPAFB (937) 257–7473.
Financial and Systems Audits.—Alfred Massey (acting), MAFB (951) 655–7011.
Support and Personnel Audits.—James W. Salter, Jr., Randolph AFB (210) 536–1999.

CHIEF OF CHAPLAINS

1380 AF Pentagon, Room 4E260, Washington, DC 20330

Chief.—Chaplain (Maj. Gen.) Cecil R. Richardson (571) 256–7729.
Deputy Chief.—Chaplain (Brig. Gen.) Howard Stendahl, 256–7729.

AIR FORCE CHIEF OF SAFETY

Pentagon, 1400 Air Force Pentagon, Room 4E252, 20330–1400

Chief of Air Force Safety/Commander, Air Force Safety Center.—Maj. Gen. Gregory Feest, (703) 693–7281.
Deputy Chief of Air Force Safety/Executive Director, Air Force Safety Center.—Roberto Guerrero (505) 846–2372.
Executive Officer.—Lt. Col. Brian Musselman (703) 614–3389.
Director, Safety Issues Division.—Col. Lesley Spraker, 693–3333.

GENERAL COUNSEL

Pentagon, 1740 Air Force, 20330

General Counsel.—Charles A. Blanchard (703) 697–0941.
Principal Deputy.—Vacant.
Military Assistant.—Col. Patricia A. McHugh, 693–7304.
Executive Assistant.—Rudy A. Sheffer, 697–8418.
Deputy General Counsel for—
Acquisition.—James A. Hughes, room 5B914, 693–7284.
Contractor Responsibility.—Steven A. Shaw, Ballston, 588–0057.
Dispute Resolution.—Lynda O'Sullivan, room 4E836, 693–7305.
Environment and Installations.—Gordon O. Tanner, room 4C755A, 614–8253.
Fiscal, Ethics and Administrative Law.—Cheri Cannon, room 4C934, 693–9291.
International Affairs.—Michael W. Zehner, room 4C756, 697–5196.
National Security and Military Affairs.—W. Kipling AtLee, room 4C756, 695–5663.

AIR FORCE HISTORIAN

1190 Air Force Pentagon, Room 4E284, Washington, DC 20330–1190

Director.—C.R. ''Dick'' Anderegg (703) 697–5600.

Executive Officer.—Lt. Col. Steven Heinlein, 697–2289.
Director, Air Force Historical Research Agency, Maxwell AFB, AL.—Dr. Charles O'Connell (334) 953–5342.

INSPECTOR GENERAL

Pentagon, 1140 Air Force, Room 4E1040, 20330–1140

Inspector General.—Lt. Gen. Marc E. Rogers (703) 697–6733.
Deputy Inspector General.—Maj. Gen. Harold L. Mitchell, 697–4351.
Executive Officer.—Lt. Col. Edward Wold, 697–4787.
Advisor for—
Air National Guard Matters.—Col. Steven Ver Helst, room 5B937, 697–0339.
Reserve Matters.—Col. Michael Shieh, room 5B937 (571) 256–4758.
Director of:
Complaints Resolution Directorate.—Col. Richard Leatherman, room 110 (703) 588–1558.
Inspections.—Col. Robert Hyde, room 110, 696–0027.
Senior Officials Inquiries.—Col. Robert McCormick, room 5B937, 693–3579.
Special Investigations.—Col. James Hudson, room 5B919, 697–0411.

JUDGE ADVOCATE GENERAL

Pentagon, 1420 Air Force, 20330

1501 West Perimeter Road, Joint Base Andrews Naval Air Facility Washington, MD 20762

The Judge Advocate General.—Lt. Gen. Richard C. Harding, room 4E180 (703) 614–5732.
Deputy Judge Advocate General.—Maj. Gen. Steven J. Lepper, room 4E180, 614–5732.
Senior Paralegal Manager.—CMSgt John P. Vassallo, room 5D116, 614–9003.
Director for—
Acquisition Law and Litigation.—Col. Mark Teskey, JBANAFW, suite 1780 (240) 612–6620.
Administrative Law.—Conrad Von Wald, room 5D116 (703) 614–4075.
Civil Law and Litigation.—Col. Thomas Zimmerman, JBNAFW, suite 1530 (240) 612–4610.
Operations and International Law.—Col. Craig Miller, room 5D116 (703) 695–9633.
Plans and Programs.—David Sprowls, room 5D116, 692–2828.
Professional Development.—Col. Peter Marksteiner, room 5D116, 614–3021.
USAF Court of Criminal Appeals.—Col. Barbara Brand, JBANAFW, suite 1900 (240) 612–5070.
USAF Judiciary.—Col. Gordon Hammock, JBANAFW, suite 1310, 612–4760.
USAF Trial Judiciary.—Col. Mark Allred, JBANAFW, suite 1150, 612–4570.

LEGAL OPERATIONS

Commander, Air Force Legal Operations Agency.—Brig. Gen. Dixie A. Morrow, JBANAFW, suite 1320 (240) 612–4590.

DIRECTORATE OF LEGISLATIVE LIAISON

Pentagon, 1160 Air Force, 20330

Rayburn House Office Building, Room B–322, 20515 (RHOB)

Russell Senate Office Building, Room SR–182, 20510 (RSOB)

Director.—Maj. Gen. Lori Robinson, room 4E812 (703) 697–8153.
Deputy Director.—Brig. Gen. (sel) John Dolan, 697–2650.
Director of Staff.—Anthony Reardon, 4B852, 693–0315.
Mobilization Assistant to the Director.—Col. Michael LoGrande, 695–2650.
Executive Officer to the Director.—Maj. Megan Kinne, 697–4142.
Chief of:
Air Operations.—Vacant, room 4B852, 697–1500.
Congressional Action Group.—Tom Lawhead, room 4B852, 695–0182.
Congressional Inquiries.—Col. Kelly Goggin, room 4B852, 697–3783.
House Liaison Office.—Col. Todd Harmer, RHOB (202) 685–4531.

Programs and Legislation.—Col. Jeff Morgan, room 4B852 (703) 697–7950.
Senate Liaison Office.—Col. Brad Spacy, RSOB (202) 685–2573.
Weapons Systems.—Col. Patrick McKenzie, room 4B852 (703) 697–3376.

NATIONAL GUARD BUREAU

1411 Jefferson Davis Highway, Arlington, VA 22202

Chief.—GEN Craig R. McKinley, Pentagon, room 1E169 (703) 614–3087.
Legislative Liaison.—BG Sandra Dittig, Pentagon, room 1E157 (571) 256–7339.
Director for—
Air National Guard.—LTG Harry M. Wyatt, Pentagon, room 4E126 (703) 614–8033.
Army National Guard.—MG Raymond Carpenter (acting), Readiness Center, Arlington, VA, 607–7002.
Joint Staff.—MG Randy E. Manner, Pentagon, room 1E159 (703) 614–3088.

OFFICE OF PUBLIC AFFAIRS

Director.—Brig. Gen. Les Kodlick (703) 967–6061.
Executive Officer.—Maj. John Sheets.
Chief of:
Current Operations.—Lt. Col. Todd Vician, 695–0640.
Engagement.—Wendy Varhegyi, 695–9664.
Requirements and Development.—Sherry Medders, 697–6701.
Strategy and Assessment.—Col. Steven Marsman.

AIR FORCE RESERVE

Pentagon, 1150 Air Force, Room 4E138, 20330

Chief, Air Force Reserve/Commander, Air Force Reserve Command.—Lt. Gen. Charles E. Stenner, Jr. (703) 695–9225.
Deputy to Chief of Air Force Reserve.—Maj. Gen. James F. Jackson, 695–5528.
Deputy Executive Officer.—Lt. Col. Shelly Kavlick, 695–5528.
Executive NCO.—MSgt Edna Gardner, 614–7307.

SCIENTIFIC ADVISORY BOARD

1500 West Perimeter Road, Suite 3300, Joint Base Andrews, MD 20762

Chair.—John Betz (240) 612–5500.
Vice Chair.—Rami Razouk, 612–5500.
Military Director.—Lt. Gen. Mark Shackelford (Pentagon 4E962), (703) 695–7311.
Executive Director.—Lt. Col. Matthew Zuber, 612–5502.
Administration.—TSgt Cindy Winterton, 612–5500.

AIR FORCE SCIENTIST

Pentagon, 1075 Air Force, Room 4E288, 20330

Chief Scientist.—Dr. Mark Maybury (703) 697–7842.
Military Assistant.—Col. Eric Silkowkski.

AIR FORCE OFFICE OF SMALL BUSINESS PROGRAMS

1060 Air Force Pentagon, Room 4E268, Washington, DC 20330–1060

Director.—Ronald A. Poussard (571) 256–8052.

SURGEON GENERAL

Pentagon, 1780 Air Force, Room 4E1084, 20330–1780

Bolling AFB, 110 Luke Avenue, Building 5681, Suite 400, Washington, DC 20332–7050

Surgeon General.—Lt. Gen. C. Bruce Green (703) 692–6800.

Executive Officer.—Col. Chuck Potter, 692–6990.
Deputy Surgeon General.—Maj. Gen. Thomas W. Travis, 588–7210.
Executive Officer.—Maj. Joe Dell, 588–7217.
Director for—
Congressional and Public Affairs.—Donna Tinsley, 588–7124.
Financial Management.—Col. Billy Cecil, 588–6510.
Force Development.—Maj. Gen. Kimberly Siniscalchi, 588–7700.
Medical Operations.—Col. James Collier, 588–6346.
Modernization.—Brig. Gen. James Carroll, 588–6208.
Strategic Plans and Programs.—Brig. Gen. Michael Miller, 588–0009.
Corps Directors for—
Biomedical Sciences.—Col. Bonnie Johnson, 588–7740.
Dental Corps.—Col. Roosevelt Allen, 588–7757.
Medical.—Col. Dominic DeFrancis, 588–7766.
Medical Services.—Col. Perry Cooper, 588–7755.
Nursing.—Col. Rose Layman, 588–7756.

DIRECTORATE OF TEST AND EVALUATION

Pentagon, 1650 Air Force, Room 4E276, 20330

Director.—John Manclark (703) 697–4774.
Deputy Director.—Ricky Peters.
Executive Assistant.—Ruby Chason Jones.

ARMY AND AIR FORCE EXCHANGE SERVICE

3911 S. Walton Walker Boulevard, Dallas, TX 75236, phone 1–800–527–6790

Commander.—MG Bruce A. Casella, USA.
Chief Operating Officer.—Michael P. Howard.

WASHINGTON OFFICE / OFFICE OF THE BOARD OF DIRECTORS

2530 Crystal Drive, Suite 4158

Arlington, VA 22202, phone (703) 604–7523, DSN 664–7523

Director / Executive Secretary.—Gregg Cox.
Deputy Director / Executive Assistant.—Rick Struss.

DEPARTMENT OF THE ARMY

The Pentagon, Washington, DC 20310, phone (703) 695–2442

OFFICE OF THE SECRETARY

Pentagon, Room 3E700, 20310–0101, phone (703) 695–1717, fax 697–8036

Secretary of the Army.—John M. McHugh.
Executive Officer.—COL Peter Jones, 695–1717.

OFFICE OF THE UNDER SECRETARY

Pentagon, Room 3E700, 20310–0102, phone (703) 695–4311

Under Secretary of the Army.—Hon. Joseph W. Westphal.
Executive Officer.—COL Burdett K. Thompson.

CHIEF OF STAFF

Pentagon, Room 3E672, 20310–0200, phone (703) 697–0900

Chief of Staff, Army.—GEN Martin E. Dempsey.
Vice Chief of Staff, Army.—GEN Peter W. Chiarelli, 695–4371.
Director, CSA Staff Group.—COL Bruce Crawford, room 3D654, 693–8371.
Director of the Army Staff.—LTG William J. Troy, room 3E663, 695–3542.
Sergeant Major of the Army.—SMA Raymond F. Chandler III, room 3E677, 695–2150.
Director, Office of:
Army Protocol.—Linda Jacobs, room 3A532, 697–0692.
Executive Communications and Control.—Thea Harvell III, room 3D664, 695–7552.
Joint and Defense Affairs.—COL Katherine Cook, room 3D644, 614–8217.

DEPUTY UNDER SECRETARY OF THE ARMY

101 Army Pentagon, Room 3E650, 20310–0001, phone (703) 697–5075

Deputy Under Secretary.—Thomas E. Hawley.
Executive Officer.—Mark Von Heeringen.
Administrative Assistant.—Carol Hopper.
Deputy.—Jeffrey White.
Executive Officer.—Mark Von Heeringen.
Executive Assistant.—Carol Hopper.

ASSISTANT SECRETARY FOR ACQUISITION, LOGISTICS AND TECHNOLOGY

103 Army Pentagon, Room 2E532, 20310–0103, phone (703) 693–6154

Assistant Secretary.—Malcolm R. O'Neill.
Confidential Assistant.—Anita J. Odom, 695–6154.
Chief of Staff.—COL Neil Thurgood, 695–5749.
Executive Officer.—LTC Gordon T. Wallace, 695–6742.
Principal Deputy.—Heidi Shyu, 614–5372.
Secretary to the Principal Deputy.—Joyce Marshall, 614–4818.
Executive Officer to the Principal Deputy.—LTC Johnnie Edmonds, 614–5358.
Principal Military Deputy.—LTG William Phillips, 697–0356.
Secretary to the Military Deputy.—Patty Laws, 693–3927.
Executive Officer to the Military Deputy.—MAJ Bradley Bruce, 697–0356.

DASA Acquisition and Systems Management.—BG Mark Brown, 695–3115.
DASA Defense Export and Cooperation.—Keith Webster, 588–8070.
DASA Elimination of Chemical Weapons.—Carmen Spencer, 604–2303.
DASA Plans, Programs and Resources.—Tom Mullins, 697–0387.
DASA Policy and Logistics.—Wimpy Pybus, 697–5050.
DASA Procurement.—Vacant, 695–2488.
DASA Science and Technology.—Dr. Marilyn Freeman, 692–1830.
DASA Strategic Communications and Business Transformation.—Lee Thompson, 693–7050.

ASSISTANT SECRETARY FOR CIVIL WORKS

Pentagon, Room 3E446, 20310–0108, phone (703) 697–4672, fax 697–7401

Assistant Secretary.—Hon. Jo-Ellen Darcy.
Deputy Assistant Secretary.—Terrence C. Salt, 695–1370.
Executive Officer.—COL Byron G. Jorns, 697–9809.
Military Assistant.—LTC Thomas J. Tickner, 695–0482.
Deputy Assistant Secretary for—
Management and Budget.—Claudia L. Tornblom, 695–1376.
Policy and Legislation.—Lee Mon Lee, 695–1370.
Policy, Planning and Review.—Douglas Lamont (202) 761–0016.

ASSISTANT SECRETARY FOR FINANCIAL MANAGEMENT AND COMPTROLLER

109 Army Pentagon, Room 3E324, 20310–0109, phone (703) 614–1506

Assistant Secretary.—Hon. Mary Sally Matiella.
Military Deputy for Budget.—LTG Edgar E. Stanton, room 3E320, 614–4034.
Military Assistant.—MAJ Noah Cloud, room 3E320, 614–5548.
Executive Officer.—COL Paul Chamberlain, room 3E320, 614–4292.
Executive Assistant.—Deborah Glembocki, room 3E320, 614–1506.
Deputy Assistant Secretary for—
Army Budget.—MG Phillip McGhee, room 3E336, 614–1595.
Cost and Economics.—Steve Bagby, room 3E352, 692–1722.
Financial Operations.—John Argodale, room 3A320, 692–7294.

ASSISTANT SECRETARY FOR INSTALLATIONS, ENERGY AND ENVIRONMENT

Pentagon, Room 3E464, 20310–0110, phone (703) 692–9800

Assistant Secretary.—Katherine G. Hammack.
Executive Officer.—COL Tracey Nicholson, 692–9804.
Military Assistant.—COL Anthony Haager, 692–9805.
Executive Assistant / Scheduler.—Phyllis Owens, 692–9800.
Principal Deputy Assistant Secretary.—L. Jerry Hansen, 692–9802.
Executive Assistant.—Margo Brown, 692–9802.
Deputy Assistant Secretary for—
Energy and Sustainability.—Richard Kidd, room 3D453, 692–9890.
Executive Assistant.—Yongsun McCarley, 692–9892.
Environment, Safety and Occupational Health.—Hershel ''Hew'' Wolfe, room 3D453, 697–1913.
Executive Assistant.—Irene Chamberlain, 697–2014.
Installations, Housing, and Partnerships.—Joseph F. Calcara, room 3E475, 697–8161.
Executive Assistant.—Sharon Parker, 697–0654.
Strategic Initiatives.—Mark Rocke, room 3D453, 692–9817.
Executive Assistant.—Viola Cash, 614–6713.

ASSISTANT SECRETARY OF THE ARMY (MANPOWER AND RESERVE AFFAIRS)

Pentagon, Room 2E460, 20310–0111, phone (703) 697–9253

Assistant Secretary.—Hon. Thomas R. Lamont.
Principal Deputy Assistant Secretary.—Karl F. Schneider, room 2E460.
Executive Officer.—COL Jason T. Evans, 614–2850.
Army Review Boards Agency.—Catherine C. Mitrano, Crystal City, 607–1438.

Civilian Personnel/Quality of Life.—Anthony J. Stamilio, room 2D484, 614–1648.
Civilian Senior Leader Management Office.—Gwendolyn R. DeFilippi, room 1D755, 693–1125.
Diversity and Leadership.—Larry Stubblefield, Crystal City, 604–0582.
Force Management, Manpower and Resources.—Jay Aronowitz, room 2E485, 614–8143.
Military Personnel.—Samuel B. Retherford, room 2E469, 697–2044.
Strategic Initiatives.—Mark S. Davis, room 2E460, 695–2455.
Training, Readiness and Mobilization.—John W. Newman, room 2E482, 697–2631.

ASSISTANT CHIEF OF STAFF FOR INSTALLATION MANAGEMENT

Pentagon, Room 3E474, 20310–0600, phone (703) 693–3233, fax 693–3507

Assistant Chief of Staff.—LTG Rick Lynch.
Deputy Assistant.—Dr. Craig College.

OFFICE OF THE ADMINISTRATIVE ASSISTANT TO THE SECRETARY OF THE ARMY (OAA)

Pentagon, room 3E733, phone (703) 695–2442, fax 697–6194

www.oaa.army.mil

Administrative Assistant to the Secretary of the Army.—Joyce E. Morrow.
Deputy Administrative Assistant.—Gerald B. O'Keefe, room 3E733, 697–7741.
Executive Officer.—Karan Reidenbach, room 3E733, 695–7444.
Civilian Aides to the Secretary of the Army (CASA).—Laura DeFrancisco, room 3D742, 697–2639.
Chief, Resource Operations Center.—Mary Fletcher, Taylor Building, room 13094, 545–0636.
U.S. Army Center of Military History.—Rob Dalessandro, Ft. McNair Building, room 35 (202) 685–2704.
U.S. Army Resources and Programs Agency.—Gerald B. O'Keefe, Taylor Building, room 13116, 545–0561.
U.S. Army Headquarters Services.—Steve Redmann, Taylor Building, room 13178, 602–6269.
U.S. Army Information Technology Agency.—Donald E. Adcock, Pentagon, room ME882, (571) 256–1660.

ARMY RESERVE

Pentagon, Room 3E562, 20310–2400, phone (703) 695–0031

Chief.—LTG Jack C. Stultz.
Assistant Chief.—James L. Snyder, 697–1260.
Deputy Chief.—BG Leslie Purser (571) 256–4483/85.
Chief of Staff.—BG William Gothard (910) 570–8026.

AUDITOR GENERAL

3101 Park Center Drive, Alexandria, VA 22302–1596

phone (703) 681–9809, fax 681–4602

Auditor General.—Randall L. Exley.
Principal Deputy Auditor General.—Benjamin J. Piccolo, 681–9881.
Executive Officer.—COL Sheila C. Denham, 681–9812.
Chief of Staff.—David H. Branham, 681–9810.
General Counsel.—William J. Guinan, 681–9893.
Director, Policy and Operations Management.—Kevin F. Kelly, 681–1288.
Deputy Auditor General for—
Acquisition and Logistics Audits.—Joseph P. Mizzoni, 681–5752.
Forces and Financial Audits.—Felix Strelsky (acting), 681–6046.
Installations, Energy and Environment Audits.—Joseph P. Bentz, 681–9841.

CHIEF INFORMATION OFFICER / G–6

Pentagon, Room 3E608, 20310–0107, phone (703) 695–4366, fax 695–3091

Chief Information Officer.—LTG Susan S. Lawrence.
Deputy Chief Information Officer.—Michael Krieger, 695–6604.
Executive Officer.—COL Jacinto Santiago, Jr., 697–5503.
Director of:
Architecture, Operations, Network and Space.—MG Mark Bowman, room 1E1629, 602–3842.
Governance, Acquisition and Chief Knowledge Office.—Greta Lehman (acting), room 7178, Taylor Building, Arlington, VA, 545–1525.
Chief Integration Office.—BG James T. Walton, Taylor Building, room 7154, Arlington, VA (571) 256–8989.
Chief of Cyber Operations.—MG Steven Smith, Taylor Building, room 6016, Arlington, VA (571) 256–8989.
Commander, NETCOM.—MG Jennifer Napper, Ft. Huachuca, AZ (502) 538–6161.

CHIEF OF CHAPLAINS

Pentagon, Room 3E524, 20310–2700, phone (703) 695–1133, fax 695–9834

Chief of Chaplain.—Chaplain (MG) Douglas L. Carver.
Deputy Chief of Chaplains.—Chaplain (BG) Donald L. Rutherford, 695–1135.

CHIEF OF ENGINEERS

GAO Building, 441 G Street, NW., 20314, phone (202) 761–0001
fax 761–4463

Chief of Engineers/Commanding General for U.S. Army Corps of Engineers.—LTG Robert L. Van Antwerp.
Deputy Commander.—MG Merdith ''Bo'' Temple, 761–0002.
Deputy Commanding General for Civil and Emergency Operations.—MG William ''Bill'' Grisoli, 761–0099.
Director of Civil Works.—Steve Stockton, 761–0100.
Deputy Commanding General for Military and International Operations.—MG Jeffrey ''Jeff'' Dorko, 761–0379.
Director of Military Programs.—Robert ''Bob'' Slockbower, 761–0382.
Chief of Staff.—COL Dionysios ''Dan'' Anninos, 761–0761.

GENERAL COUNSEL

Pentagon, Room 2E724, 20310–0104, phone (703) 693–9235, fax 693–9254

General Counsel.—Vacant.
Principal Deputy General Counsel.—Levator Norsworthy, Jr. (acting).
Executive Officer/Special Counsel.—COL Gregory B. Coe.
Deputy General Counsel for—
Acquisition.—Levator Norsworthy, Jr., room 3C546, 697–5120.
Civil Works and Environment.—Craig R. Schmauder, room 3C546, 695–3024.
Ethics and Fiscal Law.—Brent Green, room 3C546, 695–4296.
Operations and Personnel.—Stephanie Barna, room 3C546, 695–0562.

INSPECTOR GENERAL

Pentagon, Room 3E588, 20310–1700, phone (703) 695–1500, fax 614–5628

Inspector General.—Vacant.
Deputy Inspector General.—MG William McCoy (acting).
Executive Officer.—COL Clyde Moore, 695–1502.

INTELLIGENCE / G–2

Pentagon, Room 2E408, 20310–1000, phone (703) 695–3033

Deputy Chief of Staff.—LTG Richard Zahner.

Executive Officer.—LTC Ruth Bellerive (acting).
Assistant Deputy Chief.—James Faust.
Director, Office of:
Counterintelligence/HUMINT.—Gerry Turnbow, 695–2374.
Foreign Intelligence.—COL Dave Clark, 695–2186.
Foreign Liaison.—COL Jose Smith, 692–1467.
Information Management.—Lynn Schnurr, 693–7019.
Intelligence Futures.—Terry Mitchell, 695–4158.
Operations and Plans.—COL Jamie MacDonald, 695–1623.
Resource Integration.—Roxanne Hammond, 695–1233.

THE JUDGE ADVOCATE GENERAL

Pentagon, Room 3E542, 20310–2200, phone (703) 697–5151, fax 693–0600

The Judge Advocate General.—LTG Dana K. Chipman.
Deputy Judge Advocate General.—MG Clyde J. Tate II, 693–5112.
Assistant Judge Advocate General for Military Law and Operations.—BG Thomas E. Ayres (571) 256–2865.
Commander, United States Army Legal Services Agency.—BG Flora D. Darpino, Ballston, VA, 588–6269.
Commander/Commandant, USA The Judge Advocate General's Legal Center and School.—BG John W. Miller II, Charlottesville, VA (434) 971–3301.

LEGISLATIVE LIAISON

Pentagon, Room 1E416, 20310–1600, phone (703) 697–6767, fax 614–7599

Chief.—MG Frederick B. Hodges.
Deputy Chief.—COL Timothy McGuire, 695–1235.
Principal Deputy.—Bernard P. Ingold, 697–0278.
Executive Officer.—COL Kyle McClelland, 695–3524.
Chief of:
Congressional Inquiry.—Harry Williams, room 1E423, 697–8381.
Congressional Operations Division.—COL Linda Jantzen, room 1D437, 697–3206.
House Liaison Division.—COL Shoffner, room B325, Rayburn House Office Building, Washington, DC (202) 685–2676.
Investigations and Legislative Division.—COL Tania Martin, room 1E433, 697–0276.
Programs Division.—COL T.C. Williams, room 1E385, 693–8766.
Senate Liaison Division.—COL Paul Bricker, room SR183, Senate Russell Office Building, Washington, DC (202) 685–3682.
Support Operations Division.—Debra Billington, room 1E423, 693–9910.

LIAISON OFFICES

Pentagon, Room 2A474, 20310–2200

U.S. Army, Europe (USAREUR): David Dull, Dr. Bryan T. van Sweringen, SFC Ralf S. Vogt (703) 692–6886, fax 614–9714.
U.S. Army Accessions Command.—LTG Benjamin C. Freakley (757) 788–4859.
U.S. Army Forces Command (FORSCOM)/U.S. Army Training and Doctrine Command (TRADOC): MAJ Leevaine Williams, Jr., Laverne De Sett, SSG Catherine Dankwart, 697–2591/2552, Celeste Johnson, SSG Frederick Wright, 697–2588, fax 697–5725.
U.S. Army, Pacific (USARPAC).—Robert Ralston, 693–4032, fax 693–4036.
U.S. Forces Korea (USFK): Cathy Abell, Harrison J. Parker III, Ronald R. Rollison, Sharon L. Smith, 693–4038, fax 695–4576.

LOGISTICS/G–4

Pentagon, Room 1E394, 20310–0500, phone (703) 695–4102, fax 692–0759

Deputy Chief of Staff.—LTG Mitchell H. Stevenson.
Assistant Deputy Chief of Staff.—Kathleen S. Miller.
Director of:
Corporate Information Office.—Carlos D. Morrison.
Force Projection and Distribution.—Mark F. Averill.

Logistics Integration Agency.—Vic S. Ramdass.
Maintenance.—Christopher J. Lowman.
Operations and Logistics Readiness.—BG John R. O'Connor, room 1E367.
Resource Integration.—Robert J. Turzak.
Strategy and Integration.—COL(P) Susan A. Davidson.
Supply.—Michael W. Brown.

NATIONAL GUARD BUREAU

1636 Defense Pentagon, Washington, DC 20301–1636

phone (703) 614–3087, fax 614–0274

Chief.—GEN Craig R. McKinley.
Directors:
Air National Guard.—Lt. Gen. Harry M. Wyatt III, 614–8033.
Army National Guard.—MG Raymond Carpenter (acting), 607–7001.
Joint Staff.—MG Randy Manner, 614–8033.

OPERATIONS AND PLANS / G–3/5/7

Pentagon, Room 2E670, 20310–0400, phone (703) 695–2904

Deputy Chief of Staff.—LTG Daniel P. Bolger.
Assistant Deputy Chiefs of Staff: James Gunlicks, 695–0728; MG James O. Barclay, 697–5180.

PERSONNEL / G–1

Pentagon, Room 2E446, 20310–0300, phone (703) 697–8060

Deputy Chief of Staff.—LTG Thomas P. Bostick.
Assistant Deputy Chief of Staff.—Joseph M. McDade, 692–1585.
Assistant Deputy Chief of Staff for Mobilization and Reserve Affairs.—MG Jeffrey L. Arnold, room 1C449, 695–7693.
Director, Office of:
Army Research Institute.—Dr. Michelle Sams, 602–7766.
Civilian Personnel.—Dr. Susan L. Duncan, room 2C453, 695–5701.
Human Resources.—MG Jeffrey L. Arnold, room 2C453, 695–5418.
MANPRINT.—Dr. Michael Drillings, room 2C485, 695–6761.
Military Personnel Management.—BG Gary H. Cheeks, room 1D429, 695–5871.
Plans, Resources and Operations.—Roy Wallace, room 2B453, 697–5263.

PROGRAMS / G–8

Pentagon, Room 3E406, 20310–0700, phone (703) 697–8232

Deputy Chief of Staff.—LTG Robert P. Lennox, 697–8232.
Executive Officer.—COL John George, 697–8232.
Assistant Deputy Chief.—Donald Tison, 692–9099.
Special Assistant to the G–8.—BG Leodis Jennings, 614–0942.
Directors:
Concepts Analysis Agency.—Edgar Vandiver, 806–5510.
Force Development.—MG Thomas Spoehr, 692–5695.
Program Analysis and Evaluation.—MG Joseph Martz, 695–4694.
Quadrennial Defense Review.—Timothy Muchmore, 614–5591.

PUBLIC AFFAIRS

Pentagon, Room 1E484, 20310–1500, phone (703) 695–5135, fax 693–8362

Chief.—MG Steve Lanza.
Deputy Chief.—BG Lew Boone.
Principal Deputy Chief.—Stephanie Hoehne.
Chief of Staff.—COL Ken Boehme.
Executive Officer.—LTC Steve Stover.
Chief of:

Community Relations and Outreach Division.—COL Virginia Zoller.
Media Relations Division.—COL Tom Collins.
Plans.—COL James Hutton.
Strategic Communications.—COL Bob Henstrand.
Resource Management Division.—Tina Kitts.

SMALL BUSINESS PROGRAMS

Pentagon, Room 3B514, 20310–0106, phone (703) 697–2868, fax 693–3898

Director.—Tracey L. Pinson.
Deputy Director.—Suellen Jeffress.

MAJOR ARMY COMMANDS

U.S. ARMY CRIMINAL INVESTIGATION COMMAND (USACIDC)

Quantico, VA 22134–2253, phone (571) 305–4009

Commanding General.—BG Colleen McGuire.
Executive Officer.—LTC Duane Miller.
Deputy Commanding General.—COL Joe E. Ethridge.
Chief of Staff.—Daniel M. Quinn, 305–4004.
Command Chief Warrant Officer.—CW5 T.L. Williams, 305–4007.
Command Sergeant Major.—CSM Thomas Seaman, 305–4006.
Secretary of the General Staff.—Jennifer Gray, 305–4008.
Operations Center.—Guy Surian, 305–4302.

U.S. ARMY FORCES COMMAND (FORSCOM)

Fort Bragg, NC 28307, phone (910) 570–5000

Commanding General.—GEN David M. Rodriguez.
Executive Officer.—COL James Blackburn.
Deputy Commanding General for—
Chief of Staff.—LTG Howard B. Bromberg, 570–5001.
U.S. Army Reserve.—LTG Jack C. Stultz, Jr., 464–8002.
Command Sergeant Major.—Vacant, 570–5002.
Secretary of the General Staff.—COL John Pollock, 570–5004.
Operations Center.—COL William Hardy (800) 974–8480.
Liaison Office (Washington, DC).—LTC Wayne Cherry (703) 697–2591.

U.S. ARMY MATERIEL COMMAND (AMC)

4400 Martin Road, Redstone Arsenal, AL 35898–5000

Commanding General.—GEN Ann Dunwoody (256) 450–6000.
Executive Officer.—COL John Haley, 450–6005.
Deputy Commanding General.—LTG Dennis Via, 450–6100.
Executive Officer.—COL David Luders, 450–6105.
Executive Deputy Commanding General.—John Nerger, 450–6206.
Executive Officer.—LTC Richard Hall, 450–8026.
Chief of Staff.—BG John Wharton, 450–6020.
Command Sergeant Major.—CSM Jeffrey Mellinger, 450–6300.
Secretary of the General Staff.—MAJ Karl Linderman, 450–6440.
Director of Operations/G3.—MG Larry Wyche, 450–6400.
Legislative Liaison.—COL Henry Huntley (703) 806–8120.

U.S ARMY SPECIAL FORCES COMMAND

Fort Bragg, NC 28310

Commanding General.—BG Edward M. Reeder, Jr.
Deputy Commanding General.—BG Steven W. Duff.
Command Sergeant Major.—CSM William W. Zaiser.

U.S. ARMY SPECIAL OPERATIONS COMMAND

Fort Bragg, NC 28310

Commanding General.—LTG John F. Mulholland.
Command Sergeant Major.—CSM Parry Baer.
Deputy Commanding General.—MG Kurt Fuller.
Chief of Staff.—COL (P) James B. Linder.
Executive Officer.—LTC Mitchell Franks.
Assistant Chief of Staff.—Mark Phillips.
Secretary of the General Staff.—Charles Pimble.

U.S. ARMY TRAINING AND DOCTRINE COMMAND (TRADOC)

Fort Eustis, VA 23604–5700

Commanding General.—GEN Robert W. Cone (757) 501–6474.
Executive Officer.—COL Christopher Queen, 501–6472.
Deputy Commanding General/Chief of Staff.—LTG John E. Sterling, 501–6478.
Executive Officer.—LTC Hubert Davis, 501–6466.
Assistant Chief of Staff.—COL David McCauley, 501–6480.
Deputy Commanding General, Initial Military Training.—MG Richard Longo, 501–7079.
Executive Officer.—Paul Reoyo, 501–7106.
Command Sergeant Major.—CSM David Bruner, 501–6464.
Staff Actions Division Chief.—Radames Cornier, 501–5204.
Operations Center.—James Lynch, 501–5094.
Liaison Office (Washington, DC).—MAJ William McKannay (703) 697–2591.

JOINT FORCE HEADQUARTERS–NATIONAL CAPITAL REGION AND MILITARY DISTRICT OF WASHINGTON (JFHQ-NCR/MDW)

Fort Lesley J. McNair, 20319

Commanding General.—MG Michael S. Linnington (202) 685–2807.
Executive Officer.—LTC Michael J. Snipes, 685–2817.
Aide de Camp.—MAJ Timothy R. Garland, 685–2807.
Secretary.—Kai Brown, 685–2808.
Deputy Commander.—Egon F. Hawrylak (SES), 685–0641.
Executive Officer.—Bill Hegedusich, 685–1949.
Secretary.—Kai Brown, 685–2808.
Congressional Liaison.—Darrell E. Adams, 685–4940.
Interagency Officer.—Arnaldo Claudio, 685–4928.
Strategic Planning Officer.—Lee C. Campbell, 685–2933.
Chief of Staff.—COL Jerry L. Blixt, 685–2812.
Executive Assistant.—Sherri Williams, 685–4926.
Secretary of the General Staff.—Corey Langenwalter, 685–0640.
Protocol Officer.—Susan Jones, 685–2803.
Command Sergeant Major.—Michael W. Williams, 685–2923.
Administration NCO.—SGT Twanica Nelson, 685–2923.

SURGEON GENERAL/U.S. ARMY MEDICAL COMMAND (MEDCOM)

5109 Leesburg Pike, Skyline 6, Suite 672, Falls Church, VA 22041–3258

phone (703) 681–3000

Surgeon General/Commanding General.—LTG Eric B. Schoomaker.
Chief of Staff.—Herbert A. Coley (210) 221–6411.
Executive Officer.—COL Patrick O. Wilson (703) 681–3004.

DEPARTMENT OF THE NAVY

Pentagon 20350–1000, phone (703) 695–3131

OFFICE OF THE SECRETARY OF THE NAVY

Pentagon, Room 4E686, phone (703) 695–3131

Secretary of the Navy.—Ray Mabus.
Confidential Assistant.—J. Scarbrough.
Executive Assistant.—CAPT D. Shepherd, USN.
Special Assistant.—T. Oppel.
Administrative Aide.—CDR D. Gordon, USN, 695–5410.
Personal Aide.—LCDR P. Halvorsen, USN.
Special Assistant for Public Affairs.—CAPT P. Kunze, 697–7491.
Senior Military Assistant.—COL E. Banta, USMC.

OFFICE OF THE UNDER SECRETARY OF THE NAVY

Pentagon, Room 4E720, phone (703) 695–3141

Under Secretary of the Navy.—Robert O. Work.
Executive Assistant and Naval Aide.—CAPT David Emich.
Military Assistant and Marine Aide.—COL Pete Keating.
Special Assistant.—Caroline Wilson.
Administrative Assistants: YN1 Granville ''Jason'' Johns, SSgt Nickolas Smith.

GENERAL COUNSEL

Pentagon, Room 4E782
Washington Navy Yard, Building 36, 720 Kennon Street, SE., 20374
phone (703) 614–1994

General Counsel.—Hon. Paul Oostburg Sanz.
Principal Deputy General Counsel.—Anne Brennan, 614–8733.
Executive Assistant and Special Counsel.—CAPT Anne Fischer, JAGC, USN.
Associate General Counsel for—
Litigation.—R. Borro, building 36, 685–6989.
Management.—T. Ledvina, room 4E635, 614–6870.
Assistant General Counsel for—
Ethics.—D. LaCroix, room 4D641, 614–7425.
Manpower and Reserve Affairs.—R. Woods, room 4D548, 614–1377.
Research, Development and Acquisition.—Tom Frankfurt, room 4C682, 614–6985.
Military Assistant.—LTC William Ferrell, USMC, room 4E782, 692–6164.
Administrative Assistant.—LT Mitchell Fury, USN, room 4E782, 693–7813.

NAVAL INSPECTOR GENERAL

Washington Navy Yard, 1254 9th Street, SE., Building 172, 20374, phone (202) 433–2000

Inspector General.—VADM James P. Wisecup.
Deputy Naval Inspector General.—Andrea Brotherton.

OFFICE OF INFORMATION

Pentagon, Room 4B463, phone (703) 697–7391

Chief of Information.—RDML Dennis Moynihan.
Deputy Chief of Information.—CAPT Anthony Cooper.
Executive Assistant.—CDR Scott Miller.
Flag Aide.—LT Nathan Christensen.
Assistant Chief for—

Administration and Resource Management.—William Mason, 692–4747.
Community Outreach.—Rob Newell, 614–1879.
Media Operations.—CDR Danny Hernandez, 697–5342.
Requirements and Policy.—Bruce Cole, 695–0911.
Strategic Plans.—CAPT Dave Werner, 692–4728.
Visual Information.—Chris Madden, 614–9154.

JUDGE ADVOCATE GENERAL

Pentagon, Room 4C 642

Washington Navy Yard, 1322 Patterson Avenue, Suite 3000, 20374–5066

phone (703) 614–7420, fax (703) 697–4610

Judge Advocate General.—VADM James W. Houck.
Executive Assistant.—CAPT Erin E. Stone.
Deputy Judge Advocate General.—RADM Nanette M. DeRenzi.
Executive Assistant to the Deputy Judge Advocate General.—CDR Justin B. Clancy.
Assistant Judge Advocate General for Civil Law.—CAPT Michael Quinn, Pentagon, Room 4D640, 614–7415, fax 614–9400.
Deputy Assistant Judge Advocate General for—
Administrative Law.—CAPT Mary Horrigan, 614–7415.
Admiralty.—CDR Robert Hyde (202) 685–5075.
Claims, Investigations and Tort Litigation.—Patricia A. Leonard (202) 685–4600, fax 685–5484.
General Litigation.—Grant Lattin (202) 685–5450, fax 685–5472.
International and Operational Law.—CAPT James R. Crisfield, 697–9161.
Legal Assistance.—CDR Andrew Smith (202) 685–4642, fax 685–5486.
National Security Litigation and Intelligence Law.—CDR Jane Brill (202) 685–5464, fax 685–5467.
Assistant Judge Advocate General for Military Justice.—COL John Ewers, USMC, Building 58, 3rd Floor, Washington Navy Yard, 20374–1111 (202) 685–7053, fax 685–7084.
Deputy Assistant Judge Advocate General for Criminal Law.—CAPT Dave Harrison, USN (202) 685–7060, fax 685–7687.
Assistant Judge Advocate General for Operations and Management.—CAPT John Hannink (202) 685–5190, fax 685–8510.
Deputy Assistant Judge Advocate General for—
Management and Plans.—CAPT Joel Doolin (202) 685–8372, fax 685–5479.
Military Personnel.—CDR Scott Thompson (202) 685–7254, fax 685–5489.
Reserve and Retired Personnel Programs.—LCDR Liam Connel (202) 685–5397, fax 685–8510.
Special Assistants to the Judge Advocate General—
Command Master Chief.—LNCM Chris Browning (202) 685–5194, fax 685–8510.
Comptroller.—Dennis J. Oppman (202) 685–5274, fax 685–5455.
Inspector General.—Joseph Scranton (202) 685–5192, fax 685–5461.

LEGISLATIVE AFFAIRS

Room 4C549, phone (703) 697–7146, fax 697–1009

Chief.—RADM Thomas H. Copeman III.
Deputy Chief.—CAPT Chip Jaenichen.
Executive Assistant.—LCDR Walt Mainor.
Congressional Information and Public Affairs.—CDR Katherine Goode, 695–0395.
Congressional Operations.—Dee Wingfield, 693–5764.
Director for—
House Liaison.—CAPT Andy Whitson (202) 225–7808.
Assistant House Liaison.—LCDR Brian Tanaka (202) 225–3075.
Legislation.—CAPT Don Martin, 697–2851.
Naval Programs.—Tom Crowley, 693–2919.
Senate Liaison.—CAPT James Loeblein (202) 685–6006.
Assistant Senate Liaison.—CAPT C.J. Cassidy (202) 685–6007.

ASSISTANT SECRETARY FOR FINANCIAL MANAGEMENT AND COMPTROLLER

Pentagon, Room 4E618, phone (703) 697–2325

Executive Assistant and Naval Aide.—CAPT Daniel H. Fillion, USN.
Military Assistant and Marine Aide.—MAJ Christopher W. Huff, USMC.
Director, Office of:
Budget.—RADM Joseph R. Mulloy, USN, room 4E348, 697–7105.
Financial Operations.—D. Taitano, WNY (202) 685–6701.

ASSISTANT SECRETARY FOR ENERGY, INSTALLATIONS AND ENVIRONMENT

Pentagon, Room 4E739, phone (703) 693–4530

Assistant Secretary.—Hon. Jackalyne Pfannenstiel.
Executive Assistant and Naval Aide.—CAPT John Scorby.
Confidential Assistant.—SSgt Lauren M. Ferrell.
Military Aide.—LCDR Michael James.
Principal Deputy for Energy, Installations and Environment.—Roger Natsuhara, room 4E731, 693–4527.
Assistant General Counsel.—Craig Jensen, 614–1090.
Deputy of:
Energy.—Tom Hicks (571) 256–7877.
Environment.—D. Schregardus, 614–5080.
Safety.—Tom Rollow, 614–5179.

ASSISTANT SECRETARY FOR MANPOWER AND RESERVE AFFAIRS

Pentagon, Room 4E598, phone (703) 695–4333

Assistant Secretary.—Hon. Juan M. Garcia, room 4E598, 695–4333.
Principal Deputy.—Robert Cali, room 4E598, 692–6162.
Executive Assistant and Naval Aide.—CAPT Rich Brown, room 4E598, 695–4537.
Military Assistant and Marine Aide.—COL Emily Swain, room 4E598, 697–0975.
Secretary.—Antonio Sturgis, room 4E598, 695–4333.
Administrative Officer.—Maj Laurie Gillespie, room 4E590, 614–8288.
Administrative Chief.—YNC Tyrone Pierce, room 4E590, 695–6472.
Assistant Administrative Officer.—Michael Stokes, room 4E590, 697–2179.
Deputy Assistant Secretary of:
Civilian Human Resources.—Patricia C. Adams, room 4D548, 695–2633.
Manpower Personnel Policy.—Dr. Russell W. Beland, room 4D548, 693–1213.
Reserve Affairs.—Dennis Biddick, room 4D548, 614–1327.

SECRETARY OF THE NAVY COUNCIL OF REVIEW BOARDS

Washington Navy Yard, 720 Kennon Street, SE., Room 309, 20374–5023
phone (202) 685–6408, fax 685–6610

Director.—Jeffrey Riehl.
Counsel.—Roger R. Claussen.
Staff Assistant to Director.—LaVerne C. Queen.
Physical Evaluation Board.—Robert Powers.
Naval Clemency and Parole Board.—Randall Lamoureux.
Naval Discharge Review Board.—CAPT John D. Reeser, USN.
Combat-Related Special Compensation Board.—Leif Larsen.
Board of Decorations and Medals.—James Nierle.

ASSISTANT SECRETARY FOR RESEARCH, DEVELOPMENT AND ACQUISITION

Pentagon, Room 4E665, phone (703) 695–6315

Assistant Secretary.—Hon. Sean J. Stackley.
Special Assistant.—Candy R. Hearn.
Executive Assistant and Naval Aide.—CAPT Brian Antonio.
Military Assistant and Marine Aide.—COL John Albers.

Principal Military Deputy.—VADM Walter Skinner.
Executive Assistant and Naval Aide.—CAPT Eric Hendrickson.
Principal Civilian Deputy.—James Thomsen, 614–6430.
Executive Assistant and Naval Aide.—CDR Dave Norley.
Deputy Assistant Secretary of the Navy for—
Acquisition and Logistics Management.—Elliott Branch, BF992, 614–9445.
Air Programs.—Richard Gilpin, room 4C712, 614–7794.
C4I and Space Programs.—Dr. John Zangardi, room BF963, 914–6589.
Expeditionary Warfare Programs.—Brian Detter, room 4C712, 614–4794.
International Programs.—RDML Joseph Rixey, WNY (202) 433–5900.
Management and Budget.—BJ White-Olson, room 4C656, 695–6370.
Ship/Integrated Warfare Systems Programs.—Allison Stiller, room 4C712, 697–1710.

CHIEF INFORMATION OFFICER

Chief Information Officer.—Terry A. Halvorsen, Pentagon, room 4A268 (703) 695–1840.

CHIEF OF NAVAL OPERATIONS

Pentagon, Room 4E662, phone (703) 695–0532, fax 693–9408

Chief of Naval Operations.—ADM Gary Roughead.
Vice Chief of Naval Operations.—ADM Jonathan Greenert.
Judge Advocate General of the Navy.—VADM James Houck.
President, Board of Inspection and Survey.—RADM Robert Wray.
Director, Office of:
Naval Criminal Investigative Service.—Mark Clookie.
Naval Intelligence. —VADM Kendall Card.
Naval Nuclear Propulsion Program.—ADM Kirkland Donald.
Navy Staff.—VADM John Bird.
Chief of:
Chaplains.—RADM Mark Tidd.
Information.—RDML Dennis Moynihan.
Legislative Affairs.—RADM Thomas Copeman.
Naval Education Training.—RADM Joseph Kilkenny.
Naval Reserve.—RDML Bryan Cutchen.
Commander, Naval Safety Center.—RADM Brian Prindle.
Deputy for—
Fleet Readiness and Logistics.—RDML Timothy Matthews.
Information, Plans, and Strategy.—VADM Bruce Clingan.
Integration of Capabilities and Resources.—VADM John Blake.
Manpower, Personnel, Education, and Training.—VADM Mark Ferguson.
Surgeon General of the Navy.—VADM Adam Robinson.
Oceanographer of the Navy.—RADM David Titley.

BUREAU OF MEDICINE AND SURGERY

2300 E Street, NW., 20372–5300, phone (202) 762–3701
fax 762–3750

Chief.—VADM Adam M. Robinson, Jr., MC, USN.

MILITARY SEALIFT COMMAND

914 Charles Morris Court, SE., Washington Navy Yard, 20398–5540
phone (202) 685–5001, fax 685–5020

Commander.—RADM Mark H. Buzby.

WALTER REED NATIONAL MILITARY MEDICAL CENTER

8901 Wisconsin Avenue, Bethesda, MD 20889–5600, phone (301) 295–5800/5802, fax 295–5336.

Commander.—RADM Matthew L. Nathan, MC, USN.

NAVAL AIR SYSTEMS COMMAND
47123 Buse Road, Building 2272, Patuxent River, MD 20670
phone (301) 757–1487

Commander.—VADM David Architzel.

NAVAL CRIMINAL INVESTIGATIVE SERVICE COMMAND
27130 Telegraph Road, Quantico, VA 22134, phone (571) 305–9000

Director.—Mark D. Clookie.

NAVAL DISTRICT OF WASHINGTON
1343 Dahlgren Avenue, SE., 20374–5001, phone (202) 433–2777, fax 433–2207

Commandant.—RDML Patrick J. Lorge.
Chief of Staff.—CAPT Mark J. Olson.

NAVAL FACILITIES ENGINEERING COMMAND
1322 Patterson Avenue, SE., Washington Navy Yard, 20374–5065
phone (202) 685–9499, fax 685–1463

Commander.—RADM Christopher J. Mossey, CEC, USN.

OFFICE OF NAVAL INTELLIGENCE
4251 Suitland Road, 20395, phone (301) 669–3001, fax 669–3509

Commander.—CAPT Robert Rupp.

NAVAL SEA SYSTEMS COMMAND
Washington Navy Yard, 1333 Isaac Hull Avenue, SE., Stop 1010, 20376–1010
phone (202) 781–0100

Commander.—VADM Kevin M. McCoy.

NAVAL SUPPLY SYSTEMS COMMAND
Mechanicsburg, PA, phone (717) 605–3433

Commander.—RADM Mark Heinrich.

SPACE AND NAVAL WARFARE SYSTEMS COMMAND SPACE FIELD ACTIVITY
14675 Lee Road, Chantilly, VA 20151, phone (703) 808–4317
fax 808–1448

Commander.—CAPT Boris Becker.

U.S. NAVAL ACADEMY
Annapolis, MD 21402, phone (410) 293–1000

Superintendent.—VADM Michael H. Miller, USN, 293–1500.

U.S. MARINE CORPS HEADQUARTERS
Pentagon, Room 4E734, phone (703) 614–2500

Commandant.—Gen. J.F. Amos.

Assistant Commandant.—Gen. J.F. Dunford, 614–1201.
Aide-de-Camp.—Lt. Col. C.F. Wortman.
Chaplain.—RADM M.G. Kibben, 614–4627.
Dental Officer.—CAPT J.L. Haun.
Fiscal Director of the Marine Corps.—SES C.E. Spangler.
Inspector General of the Marine Corps.—Maj. Gen. D.C. Garza, 614–1533.
Judge Advocate.—Maj. Gen. V.A. Ary, 614–8661.
Legislative Assistant.—Brig. Gen. S.R. Rudder, 614–1686.
Medical Officer.—RADM (UH) R.R. Jeffries.
Military Secretary.—Col. J.W. Bierman.
Sergeant Major of the Marine Corps.—Sgt. Maj. M.P. Barrett, 614–8762.
Deputy Commandant of Marine Corps for—
Aviation.—Lt. Gen. T.G. Robling, 614–1010.
Installations and Logistics.—Lt. Gen. F.A. Panter, 695–8572.
Manpower and Reserve Affairs.—Lt. Gen. R.E. Milstead, 695–1929.
Plans, Policies, and Operations.—Lt. Gen. R.T. Tryon, 614–8521.
Public Affairs.—Col. B.F. Salas.
Programs and Resources.—Lt. Gen. J.E. Wissler, 614–3435.
Director of:
Intelligence.—Brig. Gen. V.R. Stewart.
Marine Corps History and Museums.—Dr. C.P. Neimeyer.

MARINE BARRACKS

Eighth and I Streets, SE., 20390, phone (202) 433–4094

Commanding Officer.—Col. P.A. Montanus.

TRAINING AND EDUCATION COMMAND

3300 Russell Road, Quantico, VA 22134, phone (703) 784–3730, fax 784–3724

Commanding General.—Maj. Gen. R.C. Fox.

DEPARTMENT OF JUSTICE

Robert F. Kennedy Department of Justice Building

950 Pennsylvania Avenue, NW., 20530, phone (202) 514–2000

http://www.usdoj.gov

ERIC H. HOLDER, JR., Attorney General; born in New York City, NY, education: Columbia College, 1973; Columbia Law School, 1976; professional: Department of Justice Criminal Division, 1976–88; Associate Judge of the Superior Court of the District of Columbia, 1988–93; United States Attorney for the District of Columbia, 1993–97; Deputy Attorney General, 1997–2001; partner with law firm of Covington & Burling L.L.P., 2001–09; nominated by President Barack Obama to become the Attorney General of the United States on December 1, 2008 and was confirmed by the U.S. Senate on February 2, 2009.

OFFICE OF THE ATTORNEY GENERAL

RFK Main Justice Building, Room 5111, phone (202) 514–2001

Attorney General.—Eric H. Holder, Jr.

Chief of Staff and Counselor to the Attorney General.—Gary G. Grindler, room 5115, 514–3892.

Deputy Chief of Staff and Counselor.—Monty Wilkinson, room 5112, 514–9798.

Counselors to the Attorney General: Denise Cheung, room 5116, 305–7378; Stuart Delery, room 5110, 616–7740; Molly Moran, room 5134, 305–8674; Margaret Richardson, room 5119, 514–9665.

Counsels to the Attorney General: Aaron Lewis, room 5214, 616–2372; Jenny Mosier, room 5230, 514–9797.

Director of Advance.—Vincent Fazzio, room 5131, 514–4195.

Director of Scheduling.—Linda Long, room 5127, 514–4195.

Confidential Assistant.—Annie Bradley, room 5111, 514–2001.

OFFICE OF THE DEPUTY ATTORNEY GENERAL

RFK Main Justice Building, Room 4111, phone (202) 514–2101

Deputy Attorney General.—James M. Cole, room 4111.

Principal Associate Deputy Attorney General.—Lisa O. Monaco, room 4208, 514–2105.

Chief of Staff and Counselor.—Stuart M. Goldberg, room 4210, 305–8878.

Associate Deputy Attorneys General: James A. Baker, room 4311, 514–6907; Charlotte A. Burrows, room 4129, 514–6753; Deborah A. Johnston, room 4116, 305–3481; David Margolis, room 4113, 514–4945; David O'Neil, room 4218, 514–3712; Scott N. Schools, room 4119, 305–7848; Robert N. Weiner, room 4216, 305–4127.

Associate Deputy Attorney General and Director, OCDETF.—James H. Dinan, room 4115, 514–0049.

Senior Counsels to the Deputy Attorney General: Armando O. Bonilla, room 4313, 616–1621; Jason C. Chipman, room 4220, 353–3030; Karyn Temple Claggett, room 4214, 514–5705; Eric R. Columbus, room 4131, 307–2510; Bradley T. Smith, room 4315, 305–9886; Miriam Vogel, room 4215, 514–7473.

Counsel to the Deputy Attorney General.—Jessica Hertz, room 4409, 307–1045.

Special Assistant to the Deputy Attorney General.—Mark E. Michalic, room 4112, 514–0438.

Confidential Assistant to the Deputy Attorney General.—Melanie L. Dix, room 4111, 514–1904.

Chief Privacy and Civil Liberties Officer.—Nancy C. Libin, room 4222, 307–0697.

Director, Financial Fraud Enforcement Task Forces.—Robb C. Adkins, room 4114, 514–4680.

National Coordinator for Child Exploitation Prevention and Interdiction.—Francey Hakes, room 4415, 305–0620.

Senior Counsel for Rule of Law.—Joseph Jones, room 4317, 514–9340.

Counsel for Rule of Law–Iraq.—Douglas A. Allen, room 4411, 514–3853.

Counsel for Rule of Law–Afghanistan.—Brian Tomney, room 4413, 305–8657.

OFFICE OF THE ASSOCIATE ATTORNEY GENERAL

RFK Main Justice Building, Room 5706, phone (202) 514–9500

Associate Attorney General.—Thomas J. Perrelli.

Principal Deputy Associate Attorney General.—Elizabeth G. Taylor.

Deputy Associate Attorneys General: Helaine Greenfeld, room 5722, 616–0038; Samuel Hirsch, room 5732, 616–2728; Karol V. Mason, room 5726, 514–0624; A. Marisa Chun, room 5724, 305–1777.

Senior Counsel to the Associate Attorney General.—Brian Hauck, room 5730, 353–2811.

Counsel to the Associate Attorney General.—Mala Adiga, 307–5803.

Confidential Assistant.—Currie Gunn, room 5708, 305–2636.

Staff Assistant.—Nathaniel Gamble, room 5706, 514–5732.

OFFICE OF THE SOLICITOR GENERAL

RFK Main Justice Building, Room 5143, phone (202) 514–2201

http://www.usdoj.gov/osg

Solicitor General.—Neal Kumar Katyal (acting), room 5143, 514–2201.

Principal Deputy Solicitor General.—Leondra R. Kruger (acting), room 5143, 514–4038.

Deputy Solicitors General: Michael R. Dreeben, room 5623, 514–2255; Edwin S. Kneedler, room 5137, 514–3261; Malcolm L. Stewart, room 5137, 514–4218.

Executive Officer.—Valerie H. Hall, room 5142, 514–3957.

Supervisory Case Management Specialist.—Emily C. Spadoni, room 5608, 514–2218.

Chief, Research and Publications Section.—Vacant, room 6634, 514–4459.

ANTITRUST DIVISION

RFK Main Justice Building, 950 Pennsylvania Avenue, NW., 20530

Liberty Square Building, 450 5th Street, NW., 20530 (LSB)

Assistant Attorney General.—Christine A. Varney, room 3109 (202) 514–2401.

Deputy Assistant Attorneys General: Katherine Forrest, room 3214, 353–1535; Scott M. Hammond, room 3214, 514–3543; Sharis A. Pozen, room 3113, 514–0497; Joseph Wayland, room 3121, 514–1157;.

Director of:

Civil Enforcement.—Patricia A. Brink, room 3213, 514–2562.

Criminal Enforcement.—Marc Siegel, room 3214, 353–1535.

Economics Enforcement.—W. Robert Majure, room 3416.

Operations.—Katherine Forrest, room 3214, 514–3544.

Freedom of Information Act Officer.—SueAnn Slates (LSB), room 1040, 307–1398.

Executive Officer.—Thomas D. King (LSB), room 10150, 514–4005.

Section Chiefs:

Appellate.—Catherine G. O'Sullivan, room 3222, 514–2413.

Competition Policy.—W. Robert Majure, room 3416, 9400, 307–6341.

Economic Litigation.—Norman Familant (LSB), room 9912, 307–6323.

Economic Regulatory.—Beth Armington (LSB), room 3700, 307–6332.

Foreign Commerce.—Edward T. Hand (LSB), room 11000, 514–2464.

Legal Policy.—Robert A. Potter (LSB), room 11700, 514–2512.

Litigation I.—Joshua H. Soven (LSB), room 4700, 307–0001.

Litigation II.—Maribeth Petrizzi (LSB), room 8700, 307–0924.

Litigation III.—John R. Read (LPB), room 300, 616–5935.

National Criminal Enforcement.—Lisa M. Phelan (LSB), room 11400, 307–6694.

Networks and Technology.—James Tierney (LSB), room 7700, 307–6640.

Telecommunications and Media.—Nancy M. Goodman (LSB), room 7000, 514–5621.

Transportation, Energy, and Agriculture.—Donna Kooperstein (LSB), room 8000, 307–6349.

FIELD OFFICES

California: Phillip H. Warren, 450 Golden Gate Avenue, Room 10–0101, Box 36046, San Francisco, CA 94102 (415) 436–6660.

Georgia: Nezida S. Davis, Richard B. Russell Building, 75 Spring Street, SW., Suite 1176, Atlanta, GA 30303 (404) 331–7100.

Illinois: Marvin N. Price, Jr., Rookery Building, 209 South LaSalle Street, Suite 600, Chicago, IL 60604 (312) 353–7530.

New York: Ralph T. Giordano, 26 Federal Plaza, Room 3630, New York, NY 10278 (212) 264–0391.

New York: Deirdre A. McEvoy, 26 Federal Plaza, Room 3630, New York, NY 10278–1040, (212) 264–0391.

Ohio: Scott M. Watson, Plaza 9 Building, 55 Erieview Plaza, Suite 700, Cleveland, OH 44114 (216) 522–4070.

Pennsylvania: Robert E. Connolly, Curtis Center, One Independence Square West, 7th and Walnut Streets, Suite 650, Philadelphia, PA 19106 (215) 597–7405.

Texas: Duncan S. Currie, Thanksgiving Tower, 1601 Elm Street, Suite 4950, Dallas, TX 75201 (214) 880–9401.

CIVIL DIVISION

RFK Main Justice Building, 950 Pennsylvania Avenue, NW., 20530

20 Massachusetts Avenue, NW., 20530 (20MASS)

1100 L Street, NW., 20530 (L ST)

National Place Building, 1331 Pennsylvania Avenue, NW., 20530 (NATP)

1425 New York Avenue, NW., 20530 (NYAV)

Patrick Henry Building, 601 D Street, NW., 20530 (PHB)

Assistant Attorney General.—Tony West, room 3601 (202) 514–3301.

Chief of Staff.—Brian Martinez, room 3605, 353–2793.

APPELLATE STAFF

Deputy Assistant Attorney General.—Beth Brinkmann, room 3135, 353–8679.

Director.—Robert E. Kopp, room 7519, 514–3311.

Deputy Director.—William Kanter, room 7517, 514–4575.

COMMERCIAL LITIGATION BRANCH

Deputy Assistant Attorney General.—Michael F. Hertz, room 3607, 514–7179.

Directors: David M. Cohen (L ST), room 12124, 514–7300; John N. Fargo (L ST), room 11116, 514–7223; J. Christopher Kohn (L ST), room 10036, 514–7450.

Office of Foreign Litigation.—Robert Hollis (L ST), room 11006, 514–7455.

Deputy Directors: Joyce R. Branda (PHB), room 9904, 307–0231; Jeanne Davidson (L ST), room 12132, 307–0290.

Legal Officer.—Donna C. Maizel, Esq., U.S. Department of Justice, Civil Division European Office, The American Embassy, London, England, PSC 801, Box 42, FPO AE, 09498–4042, 9+011–44–20–7894–0840.

Attorney-in-Charge.—Barbara Williams, Suite 359, 26 Federal Plaza, New York, NY 10278 (212) 264–9240.

CONSUMER LITIGATION

Deputy Assistant Attorney General.—Ann Ravel, room 3127, 514–0441.

Director.—Eugene M. Thirolf (NATP), room 950N, 307–3009.

FEDERAL PROGRAMS BRANCH

Deputy Assistant Attorney General.—Ian Gershengorn, room 3137, 514–2331.

Directors: Felix Baxter (20MASS), room 7100, 514–4651; Joseph H. Hunt, room 7348, 514–1259; Jennifer D. Richetts (20MASS), room 6100, 514–3671.

Deputy Directors: Vincent M. Garvey (20MASS), room 7346, 514–3449; Sheila M. Lieber (20MASS), room 7102, 514–3786.

IMMIGRATION LITIGATION

Deputy Assistant Attorney General.—William H. Orrick III, room 3131, 353–7958.

Director.—Thomas W. Hussey (NATP), room 7026S, 616–4852.

Deputy Directors: Donald E. Keener (NATP), room 7022S, 616–4878; David J. Kline (NATP), room 7006N, 616–4856; David M. McConnell (NATP), room 7260N, 616–4881.

MANAGEMENT PROGRAMS

Director.—Kenneth L. Zwick, room 3140, 514–4552.
Directors, Office of:
Administration.—Donna Cornett (L ST), room 9018, 307–0261.
Planning, Budget, and Evaluation.—Linda S. Liner (L ST), room 9042, 307–0034.
Management Information.—Dorothy Bahr (L ST), room 8044, 616–8026.
Litigation Support.—Vacant, (L ST), room 9126, 616–5014.
Policy and Management Operations.—Vacant, (L ST), room 8128, 616–8073.

TORTS BRANCH

Deputy Assistant Attorney General.—Ann Ravel, room 3127, 514–0441.
Directors: Peter Frost (NYAV), room 10122, 616–4000; Timothy P. Garren (NYAV), room 8122, 616–4171; J. Patrick Glynn (NATP), room 8028S, 616–4200; Phyllis J. Pyles (NATP), room 8098N, 616–4252.
Deputy Directors: JoAnn J. Bordeaux (NATP), room 8024S, 616–4204; Paul F. Figley (NATP), room 8096N, 616–4248.
Attorneys-in-Charge: Robert Underhill, 450 Golden Gate Avenue, 10/6610, Box 36028, San Francisco, CA 94102–3463, FTS: (415) 436–6630; Vacant, Suite 320, 26 Federal Plaza, New York, NY 10278–0140, FTS: (212) 264–0480.

CIVIL RIGHTS DIVISION

RFK Main Justice Building, 950 Pennsylvania Avenue, NW., 20530

1425 New York Avenue, NW., 20035 (NYAV)

601 D Street, NW., 20004 (PHB)

100 Indiana Avenue, NW., 20004 (NALC)

1800 G Street, NW., 20004 (NWB)

http://www.usdoj.gov/crt

Assistant Attorney General.—Thomas Perez, room 5643 (202) 514–2151.
Principal Deputy Assistant Attorney General.—Sam Bagenstos, room 5744, 353–9065.
Deputy Assistant Attorneys General: Roy Austin, room 5531, 514–3845; Julie Fernandes, room 5637, 514–2337; Loretta King, room 5748, 616–1278; Leon Rodriguez, room 5541, 307–2563.
Counsels to the Assistant Attorney General: Mazen Basrawi, room 5742, 305–1876; Matthew Colangelo, room 5646, 514–5441; Eric Halperin, room 5533, 532–5099; Emily Loeb, room 5746, 307–2502; Joan Magagna, room 5644, 514–7741; Matt Nosanchuk, room 5535, 305–0864; Monica Ramirez, room 5539, 514–8390; Jocelyn Samuels, room 5529, 307–6639; Vicki Schultz, room 5537, 353–2816.
Chief of Staff.—Leon Rodriguez, room 5541, 307–2563.
Section Chiefs:
Appellate.—David K. Flynn, room 3704, 514–2195.
Criminal.—Mark Kappelhoff (PHB), room 5102, 514–3204.
Disability Rights.—John Wodatch, (NYAV), room 4055, 307–2227.
Educational Opportunities.—Anurima Bhargava (PHB), room 4002, 514–4092.
Employment Litigation.—Loretta King (acting), (PHB), room 4040, 514–3831.
Housing and Civil Enforcement.—Steven Rosenbaum, (NWB), room 7036, 514–4713.
Policy and Strategy Section.—Karen Stevens (acting), (PHB), room 5006, 514–4734.
Special Litigation.—Jonathan Smith (PHB), room 5034, 514–5393.
Voting.—Chris Herren (NWB), room 7254, 307–2767.
Office Special Counsel.—Katherine Baldwin (acting), room 9030, 514–3896.

OFFICE OF COMMUNITY ORIENTED POLICING SERVICES

145 N Street, NE., 20530

DIRECTOR'S OFFICE

Director.—Bernard K. Melekian, 11th floor (202) 616–2888.
Principal Deputy Director.—Joshua Ederheimer, 11th floor, 616–2888.

Chiefs of Staff.—Timothy Quinn; Rebekah Whiteaker, 11th floor.
Office Manager.—Kimberly Brummett, 11th floor, 353–9769.
Deputy Director for—
Management Services.—Dave Buchanan, 616–9416.
Community Policing Advancement.—Matthew Scheider (acting), 514–8289.
Grant Operations.—Sandra Webb (acting), 616–3256.

ADMINISTRATIVE DIVISION

Assistant Director.—Wayne Henry, 514–3973.
Human Capital Manager.—Debbie Brown, 514–8956.

EXTERNAL AFFAIRS

Assistant Director.—Dean Kueter, 11th floor, 353–9961.

AUDIT DIVISION

Assistant Director.—Cynthia Bowie, 11th floor, 616–3645.

GRANTS ADMINISTRATION DIVISION

Assistant Director.—Andy Dorr, 353–9736.
Grant Regional Supervisors:
Linda Gist, 11th floor, 514–8091.
Scott McNichol, 11th floor, 616–9266.
John Oliphant, 11th floor, 307–3411.
Keesha Thompson, 11th floor, 616–1902.

GRANT MONITORING DIVISION

Assistant Director.—Marcia Samuels, 11th floor, 514–8507.

LEGAL DIVISION

General Counsel.—Lani Lee, 11th floor, 514–3750.
Deputy General Counsel.—Charlotte C. Grzebien, 616–2899.
Associate General Counsel.—Jenny Wu, 514–9424.

PROGRAM / POLICY SUPPORT AND EVALUATION

Assistant Director.—Matthew Scheider, 11th floor, 514–8289.

TECHNICAL ASSISTANCE AND TRAINING DIVISION

Assistant Director.—Beverly Alford, 11th floor, 514–5775.

COMMUNITY RELATIONS SERVICE

600 E Street, NW., Suite 6000, 20530, phone (202) 305–2935
fax 305–3009 (BICN)

Director.—Becky Monroe (acting).
Deputy Director.—Diane Mitchum.
Attorney Advisor.—George Henderson, 305–2964.
Media Affairs Officer.—Vacant, 305–2966.

REGIONAL DIRECTORS

New England.—Francis Amoroso, 408 Atlantic Avenue, Suite 222, Boston, MA 02110–1032 (617) 424–5715.

Northeast Region.—Reinaldo Rivera, 26 Federal Plaza, Suite 36–118, New York, NY 10278 (212) 264–0700.

Mid-Atlantic Region.—Harpreet Singh Mokha, Customs House, Second and Chestnut Streets, Suite 208, Philadelphia, PA 19106 (215) 597–2344.

Southeast Region.—Thomas Battles, Citizens Trust Company Bank Building, Suite 900, 75 Piedmont Avenue NE., Atlanta, GA 30303 (404) 331–6883.

Midwest Region.—Mary Gorecki, 230 South Dearborn Street, Suite 2130, Chicago, IL 60604.

Southwest Region.—Carmelita P. Freeman, Hardwood Center, 1999 Bryan Street, Suite 2050, Dallas, TX 75201 (214) 655–8175.

Central Region.—Pascual Marquez, 601 East 12th Street, Suite 0802, Kansas City, MO 64106.

Rocky Mountain Region.—Philip Arreola, 1244 Speer Boulevard, Suite 650, Denver, CO 80204–3584 (303) 844–2973.

Western Region.—Ronald Wakabayashi, 888 South Figueroa Street, Suite 1880, Los Angeles, CA 90017 (213) 894–2941.

Northwest Region.—Rosa Melendez, Federal Office Building, 915 Second Avenue, Suite 1808, Seattle, WA 98174 (206) 220–6700.

CRIMINAL DIVISION

RFK Main Justice Building, 950 Pennsylvania Avenue, NW., 20530

phone (202) 514–2601

Bond Building, 1400 New York Avenue, NW., 20005 (Bond)

1331 F Street, NW., 20004 (F Street)

John C. Keeney Building, 1301 New York Avenue, NW., 20530 (1301 NY)

Patrick Henry Building, 601 D Street, NW., 20530 (PHB)

Assistant Attorney General.—Lanny A. Breuer, room 2107, 514–7200.

Chief of Staff and Principal Deputy Assistant Attorney General.—Mythili Raman, room 2206, 514–2601.

Deputy Assistant Attorneys General: Greg D. Andres, room 2212, 514–0762; Kenneth A. Blanco, room 2121, 514–3027; Mary Patrice Brown, room 2115, 514–9085; Bruce C. Swartz, room 2119, 514–2333; Jason M. Weinstein, room 2113, 305–9827.

Deputy Chief of Staff.—Amy E. Pope, room 2208, 514–0770.

Counselor to the Assistant Attorney General.—Jonathan Wroblewski, room 2218, 514–4730.

Senior Counsels to the Assistant Attorney General: Matthew S. Axelrod, room 2226, 353–4660; Adam S. Lurie, room 2220, 307–0412; Richard M. Rogers, room 2110, 307–0030; Daniel M. Suleiman, room 2224, 514–9724.

Executive Officer.—Karl Maschino (Bond), room 5100, 514–2641.

Section Chiefs/Office Directors:

Appellate.—Patty M. Stemler, room 1264, 514–2611.

Asset Forfeiture and Money Laundering.—Jennifer Shasky (Bond), suite 10100, 514–1263.

Capital Case Unit.—Kevin Carwile (1301 NY), room 6140, 353–7172.

Child Exploitation and Obscenity.—Andrew G. Oosterbaan (Bond), suite 6000, 514–5780.

Computer Crime and Intellectual Property.—Michael DuBose (1301 NY), suite 600, 514–1026.

Enforcement Operations.—Paul O'Brien (1301 NY), suite 1200, 514–6809.

Fraud.—Denis McInerney (Bond), room 4100, 514–7023.

Human Rights and Special Prosecution.—Teresa McHenry (1301 NY), room 112, 616–5731.

International Affairs.—Mary Ellen Warlow (1301 NY), suite 900, 514–0000.

International Criminal Investigative Training Assistant Program.—Carr Trevillian IV (F Street), suite 500, 305–8190.

Narcotics and Dangerous Drugs.—Arthur Wyatt (Bond), room 11100, 514–0917.

Organized Crime and Racketeering.—Bruce G. Ohr (1301 NY), suite 700, 514–3595.

Overseas Prosecutorial Development, Assistance and Training.—Carl Alexandre (F Street), room 400, 514–1323.

Policy and Legislation.—Jonathan Wroblewski, room 7730, 514–4194.

Public Integrity.—Jack Smith (Bond), suite 12100, 514–1412.

OFFICE OF DISPUTE RESOLUTION

RFK Main Justice Building, Room 4531, phone (202) 616–9471 / 616–9472

http://www.usdoj.gov/odr

Director / Senior Counsel.—Joanna M. Jacobs (acting), room 4529, 305–4439.

DRUG ENFORCEMENT ADMINISTRATION

Lincoln Place-1 (East), 600 Army-Navy Drive, Arlington, VA 22202 (LP–1)

Lincoln Place-2 (West), 700 Army-Navy Drive, Arlington, VA 22202 (LP–2)

Administrator.—Michele M. Leonhart, room W–12060 (202) 307–8000.
Chief of Staff.—Vacant, room 12060, 307–8003.
Deputy Administrator.—Vacant, room W–12058–F, 307–7345.
Equal Employment Opportunity Officer.—Oliver C. Allen, room E–11275, 307–8888.
Executive Assistants: Scott Masumoto, room W–12058–E, 353–1250; Gary Tuggle, room W–12058–C, 307–7348; Vacant, room 12060, 307–8003.
Chief, Congressional and Public Affairs.—Mary Irene Cooper, room W–12228, 307–7363.
Chief, Executive Policy and Strategic Planning.—Kevin D. Whaley, room W–11100, 307–7420.
Section Chiefs:
Congressional Affairs.—Sheldon Shoemaker, room W–12104, 307–4461.
Demand Reduction.—Eric Akers, room W–9049–E, 307–7988.
Information Services.—Vacant, room W–12232, 307–7967.
Public Affairs.—Dawn Dearden, 307–2402.
Chief Counsel.—Wendy H. Goggin, room W–12142–C, 307–7322.
Deputy Chief Counsel.—Robert C. Gleason, room E–12375, 307–8020.
Chief, Office of Administrative Law Judges.—Vacant, room E–2129, 307–8188.

FINANCIAL MANAGEMENT DIVISION

Chief Financial Officer.—Frank M. Kalder, room W–12138, 307–7330.
Deputy Assistant Administrators for—
Acquisition Management.—Christinia K. Sisk, room W–5100, 307–7888.
Finance.—Daniel Gillette, room E–7397, 307–7002.
Resource Management.—Brian Horn, room E–5102, 307–4800.
Section Chiefs:
Acquisition Management.—Nancy Costello, room E–8281, 307–5364.
Controls and Coordination.—Brian Parks, room E–5384, 307–5276.
Evaluations and Planning.—Donna Lipsmeyer, room E–5334, 307–7463.
Financial Integrity.—Bradley J. Honkus, room E–7331, 307–7082.
Financial Operations.—Tammy Balas, room E–7165, 307–9933.
Financial Reports.—Sherri Woodle, room E–7297, 307–7040.
Financial Systems.—Renaldo Prillman (acting), room E–8001, 307–7043.
Organization and Staffing Management.—Donna Ciccolella, room E–5284, 307–7077.
Policy and Transportation.—Vacant, room W–5018, 307–7808.
Program Liaison and Analysis.—James Evans, room E–5104, 353–9545.
Statistical Services.—Gamaliel Rose, room E–5332, 307–8276.

HUMAN RESOURCES DIVISION

Assistant Administrator.—Raymond Pagliarini, room W–12020, 307–4177.
Section Chiefs:
Administrative Management.—Glenda A. Rollins, room E–9355, 307–4701.
Recruitment and Placement.—Jodi Johnson, room W–3242, 307–4251.
Career Board Executive Secretary.—Karen Marrero, room W–2268, 307–7349.
Chairman, Board of Professional Conduct.—Patrick T. Dunn, room E–9333, 307–8980.
Special Agent-in-Charge, Office of Training.—Jeffrey Sweetin, 2500 Investigation Parkway, DEA Academy, Quantico, VA 22135 (703) 632–5010.
Assistant Special Agents-in-Charge:
Domestic Training Section 1.—William Faiella (703) 632–5110.
Domestic Training Section 2.—Michael Blackwood (703) 632–5310.
International Training Section.—James T. Farnsworth (703) 632–5330.

INSPECTIONS DIVISION

Chief Inspector.—James Kasson, room W–12042A, 307–7358.
Deputy Chief Inspector, Office of:
Inspections.—Kevin M. Foley (acting), room W–4348, 307–4866.
Professional Responsibility.—Karl C. Colder, room W–4176, 307–8235.
Security Programs.—Barbara M. Roach, room W–2340, 307–3465.

INTELLIGENCE DIVISION

Assistant Administrator.—Rodney Benson, room W–12020A, 307–3607.
Special Agent in Charge, El Paso Intelligence Center.—Arthur Doty, Building 11339, SSG Sims Street, El Paso, TX 79908–8098 (915) 760–2011.
Deputy Assistant Administrator, Office of Intelligence.—Douglas Poole, room W–12020C, 307–3607.
Executive Assistant.—Marilyn Wankel, 307–3607.
Deputy Assistant Administrator, Office of:
Fusion Center.—John Riley (703) 561–7117.
National Security Intelligence.—Doug Poole, 307–7600.
Special Intelligence.—Stephen Murphy, Merrifield, VA, 561–7467.
Section Chiefs:
Associate National Security.—Barry Zulauf, 307–7769.
Data Management.—Scott Linn (acting), (703) 561–7437.
Indications/Warnings.—Cheryl Hooper, 307–4358.
Investigative Intelligence.—Lourdes Border, 307–9284.
Investigative Support.—Vacant (703) 488–4246.
Management and Production Section.—James A. Curtin, room W–7174, 307–7534.
Operational Support.—Benjamin J. Sanborn, room E–5015, 307–3645.
Policy Liaison.—Pat Lowery, 307–8541.
Requirements/Production.—Thomas Neal, (202) 307–4825.
Strategic Intelligence.—Sallie Castro, 353–9581.
Technical Support.—Gisele Gatjanis (703) 561–7107.

OPERATIONS DIVISION

Chief of Operations.—Thomas G. Harrigan, room W–12050, 307–7340.
Chiefs of:
Enforcement/Administrative Support.—Vacant.
Financial Operations.—John Arvanitis, room W–10190, 307–4379.
Global Enforcement Operations.—Vacant, room W–11070, 307–7927.
International Programs.—Vacant, room W–11024, 307–4233.
Operations Management.—David Dongilli, room W–11148, 307–4200.
Special Projects.—Curt Clements, 307–4233.
Deputy Assistant Administrator, Office of Diversion Control.—Joseph T. Rannazzisi, room E–6295, 307–7165.
Special Agent in Charge, Aviation Division.—Gary Olenkiewicz, Ft. Worth, TX (817) 837–2004.
Special Agent in Charge, Special Operations Division.—Derek S. Maltz, Chantilly, VA (703) 488–4205.

OPERATIONAL SUPPORT DIVISION

Assistant Administrator.—Preston Grubbs, room W–12142, 307–4730.
Deputy Assistant Administrator, Office of:
Administration.—Mary E. Colarusso, room W–9088, 307–7708.
Forensic Sciences.—Nelson Santos, room W–7342, 307–8866.
Information Systems.—Dennis R. McCrary, room E–3105, 307–7454.
Investigative Technology.—Vacant, Lorton, VA (703) 495–6500.
Section Chiefs:
Administrative Operations.—Janet Gates, room W–5100–A, 307–7868.
Concord Program Management.—Millie Tyler, room E–3007, 307–9895.
Facilities and Finance.—Valerie McDonald, room W–5244, 307–7792.
Hazardous Waste Disposal.—Betty Myers (acting), room W–7310, 307–8872.
Integration and Management.—Venita Phillips, room E–4063, 307–9892.

Laboratory Operations.—Bradley Campbell, room W–7310, 307–8880.
Laboratory Support.—Richard P. Meyers, room W–7348, 307–8785.
Operations and Support.—Barry Smallwood, room E–4111, 307–9896.
Program Planning and Control Staff.—Maria Hughes, room E–3163, 307–9885.
Software Development.—Ruth Torres, room E–3285, 307–9883.
Surveillance Support.—Albert Laurita, Lorton, VA (703) 495–6736.
Technology Officer.—Mark Shafernich.
Telecommunications/Intercept Support.—Earl W. Hewitt, Lorton, VA (703) 495–6676.

Associate Deputy Assistant Administrator, Office of:
Information Systems.—Julie Jones, room E–3005, 307–5269.
Forensic Sciences: Nelson A. Santos, room W–7344, 307–8866; Steven M. Sottolano, room W–7346, 307–8868.

FIELD OFFICES

Special Agent-in-Charge:

Atlanta Division.—Rodney Benson, Room 800, 75 Spring Street, SW., Atlanta, GA 30303 (404) 893–7100.

Boston Division.—Steven W. Derr, JFK Federal Building, Room E–400, 15 New Sudbury Street, Boston, MA 02203–0402 (617) 557–2100.

Caribbean Division.—Javier Pena, Metro Office Park, Millennium Park Plaza #15, 2nd Street, Suite 710, Guaynabo, PR 00968 (787) 277–4700.

Chicago Division.—John J. Riley, Suite 1200, John C. Kluczynski Federal Building, 230 South Dearborn Street, Chicago, IL 60604 (312) 353–7875.

Dallas Division.—James L. Capra, 10160 Technology Boulevard East, Dallas, TX 75220 (214) 366–6900.

Denver Division.—Kevin R. Merrill (acting), 115 Inverness Drive East, Englewood, CO 80112–5116 (303) 705–7300.

Detroit Division.—Robert L. Corso, 431 Howard Street, Detroit, MI 48226 (313) 234–4000.

El Paso Division.—Joseph Arabit, 660 Mesa Hills Drive, Suite 2000, El Paso, TX 79912 (915) 832–6000.

Houston Division.—Thomas Hinojosa (acting), 1433 West Loop South, Suite 600, Houston, TX 77027–9506 (713) 693–3000.

Los Angeles Division.—Timothy J. Landrum, 255 East Temple Street, 20th Floor, Los Angeles, CA 90012 (213) 621–6700.

Miami Division.—Mark Trouville, Phoenix Building, 8400 NW. 53rd Street, Miami, FL 33166 (305) 994–4870.

Newark Division.—John McCabe (acting), 80 Mulberry Street, 2nd Floor, Newark, NJ 07102–4206 (973) 776–1100.

New Orleans Division.—Jimmy S. Fox III, 3838 North Causeway Boulevard, Suite 1800, 3 Lakeway Center, Metaire, LA 70002 (504) 840–1100.

New York Division.—John P. Gilbride, 99 10th Avenue, New York, NY 10011 (212) 337–3900.

Philadelphia Division.—Joseph Bryfonski, William J. Green Federal Building, 600 Arch Street, Room 10224, Philadelphia, PA 19106 (215) 861–3474.

Phoenix Division.—Douglas W. Coleman (acting), 3010 North Second Street, Suite 301, Phoenix, AZ 85012 (602) 664–5600.

San Diego Division.—William R. Sherman (acting), 4560 Viewridge Avenue, San Diego, CA 92123–1672 (858) 616–4100.

San Francisco Division.—Anthony D. Williams, 450 Golden Gate Avenue, 14th Floor, San Francisco, CA 94102 (415) 436–7900.

Seattle Division.—Mark C. Thomas (acting), 400 Second Avenue West, Seattle, WA 98119 (206) 553–5443.

St. Louis Division.—Harry Sommers, 317 South 16th Street, St. Louis, MO 63103 (314) 538–4600.

Washington, DC Division.—Ava Cooper-Davis, 800 K Street, NW., Suite 500, Washington, DC 20001 (202) 305–8500.

OTHER DEA OFFICES

Special Agents-in-Charge:

Arthur A. Doty, El Paso Intelligence Center, Building 11339, SSG Sims Street, El Paso, TX 79908 (915) 760–2000.

Gary G. Olenkiewicz, Aviation Operations Division, 2300 Horizon Drive, Fort Worth, TX 76177 (817) 837–2000.

Derek S. Maltz, Special Operations Division, 14560 Avion Parkway, Chantilly, VA 20151 (703) 488–4200.

William Faiella (acting), Office of Training, P.O. Box 1475, Quantico, VA 22134 (703) 632–5000.

FOREIGN OFFICES

Ankara, Turkey: American Embassy Ankara, DEA / Justice, PSC 93, Box 5000, APO AE 09823–5000, 9–011–90–312–468–6136.

Asuncion, Paraguay: DEA / Justice, American Embassy Asuncion, Unit 4740, APO AA 34036, 9–011–595–21–210–738.

Athens, Greece: American Embassy Athens, DEA / Justice, PSC 108, Box 14, APO AE 09842, 9–011–30–210–643–4328.

Bangkok, Thailand: American Embassy, DEA / Justice, Box 49, APO AP 96546–0001, 9–011–662–205–4984.

Beijing, China: American Embassy Beijing, DEA / Justice, PSC 461, Box 50, FPO AP 96521–0002, 9–011–8610–8529–6880.

Belmopan, Belize: American Embassy Belmopan, DEA / Justice, PSC 120, Unit 7405, APO AA 34025, 301–985–9387.

Bern, Switzerland: Department of State, DEA / Justice, 5110 Bern Place, Washington, DC 20521–5110, 9–011–41–31–357–7367.

Bogota, Colombia: American Embassy Bogota, DEA / Justice, Unit 5116, APO AA 34038, 9–011–571–315–2121.

Brasilia, Brazil: DEA / Justice, American Embassy Brasilia, Unit 3500, APO AA 34030, 9–011–55–61–3312–7122.

Bridgetown, Barbados: American Embassy Bridgetown, CMR 1014, DEA / Justice, FPO AA 34055, 9–1–246–227–4171.

Brussels, Belgium: American Embassy Brussels, DEA / Justice, PSC 82, Box 137, APO AE 09710, 9–011–32–2–508–2420.

Buenos Aires, Argentina: DEA / Justice, American Embassy Buenos Aires, Unit 4309, APO AA 34034, 9–011–5411–5777–4696.

Cairo, Egypt: American Embassy Cairo, DEA / Justice, Unit 64900, Box 25, APO AE 09839–4900, 9–011–20–2–2797–2461.

Canberra, Australia: American Embassy Canberra, DEA / Justice, APO AP 96549, 9–011–61–2–6214–5903.

Caracas, Venezuela: American Embassy Caracas, DEA / Justice, Unit 4962, APO AA 34037, 9–011–582–212–975–8380 / 8443 / 8407.

Cartagena, Resident Office: American Embassy, DEA Cartagena, Unit 5141, APO AA 34038, 9–011–575–664–9369.

Chiang-Mai, Resident Office: American Embassy Chiang-Mai, Box C, APO AP 96546, 9–011–66–53–217–285.

Ciudad, Resident Office: U.S. Consulate / Ciudad Juarez Resident Office, P.O. Box 10545, El Paso, TX 79925 9–011–52–656–611–1179.

Cochabamba, Resident Office: Unit 3220, Box 211, APO AA 34032, 9–011–591–4–429–3320.

Copenhagen, Denmark: American Embassy Copenhagen, DEA / Justice, PSC 73, APO AE 09716, 9–011–45–35–42–2680.

Curacao, Netherlands Antilles: American Consulate Curacao, DEA / Justice, Washington, DC 20521, 9–011–5999–461–6985.

Dubai, United Arab Emirates: U.S. Consulate General, DEA / Justice, 6020 Dubai Place, Dulles, VA 20189–6020, 9–011–971–4–311–6220.

Dushanbe, Tajikistan: American Embassy Dushanbe, DEA / Justice, Drug Enforcement Administration, 7090 Dushanbe Place, Dulles, VA 20189–7090, 9–011–992–37–229–2807.

Frankfurt, Resident Office: American Consulate General Frankfurt, DEA / Justice, PSC 115, Box 1017, APO AE 09213–0115, 9–011–49–69–7535–3770.

Freeport, Bahamas Resident Office: GPS, c/o U.S. Embassy, DEA, 5115 Northwest 17th Terrace, Hanger #39A, Ft. Lauderdale, FL 33309, 9–1–242–352–5353 / 5354.

Guadalajara, Resident Office: DEA, Guadalajara Resident Office, P.O. Box 9001, Brownsville, TX 78520, 9–011–52–33–3268–2191.

Guatemala City, Guatemala: American Embassy Guatemala City, DEA / Justice, Unit 3311, APO AA 34024, 9–011–502–331–4389.

Guayaquil, Resident Office: DEA / Justice, American Embassy Guayaquil, Unit 5350, APO AA, 34039, 9–011–593–42–32–3715.

The Hague, Netherlands: American Embassy The Hague, DEA / Justice, Unit 6707, Box 8, APO AE 09715, 9–011–31–70–310–2327.

Hanoi, Vietnam: American Embassy Hanoi, DEA / Justice, PSC 461, Box 400, FPO AP 96521–0002, 9–011–844–850–5011.

Hermosillo, Resident Office: U.S. Consulate—Hermosillo, P.O. Box 1689, Nogales, AZ 85628–1689, 9–011–52–662–289–3550.

Hong Kong, Resident Office: U.S. Consulate General Hong Kong, DEA / Justice, PSC 461, Box 16, FPO AP 96521–0006, 9–011–852–2521–4536.

Islamabad, Pakistan Country Office: DEA / Justice, American Embassy Islamabad, DEA / Justice, Unit 62215, APO AE 09812–2215, 9–011–92–51–208–2918.

Istanbul, Turkey Resident Office: American Consulate General, DEA / Justice, PSC 97, Box 0002, APO AE 09827, 9–011–90–212–335–9179.

Kabul, Afghanistan Country Office: DEA / Justice, American Embassy Kabul, 8160 Kabul Place, Washington, DC 20521–6180, 301–490–1042.

Kingston, Jamaica Country Office: U.S. Embassy Kingston, 142 Old Hope Road, Kingston 6, Jamaica 9–1–876–702–6004.

Kuala Lumpur, Malaysia Country Office: American Embassy Kuala Lumpur, DEA / Justice, APO AP 96535–8152, 9–011–603–2142–1779.

Lagos, Nigeria: Department of State, DEA / Justice, 8300 Lagos Place, Washington, DC 20521–8300, 9–011–234–1–261–9837.

La Paz, Bolivia: American Embassy La Paz, DEA / Justice, Unit 3220, DPO AA 34032, 9–011–591–2–216–8313.

Lima, Peru: American Embassy Lima, DEA / Justice, Unit 3810, APO AA 34031, 9–011–511–618–2475.

London, England: American Embassy London, DEA / Justice, Unit 8400, Box 0008, FPO AE 09498–4008, 9–011–44–207–894–0826.

Madrid, Spain: American Embassy Madrid, DEA / Justice, PSC 61, Box 0014, APO AE 09642, 9–011–34–91–587–2280.

Managua, Nicaragua: DEA, American Embassy Nicaragua, Unit 2700, Box 21, APO AA 34021, 9–011–505–252–7738.

Manila, Philippines: American Embassy Manila, DEA / Justice, PSC 500, Box 11, FPO AP 96515, 9–011–632–301–2084.

Matamoros, Mexico Resident Office: Matamoros DEA, P.O. Box 9004, Brownsville, TX 78501, 9–011–52–868–149–1285.

Mazatlan, Resident Office: DEA, Mazatlan Resident Office, P.O. Box 9006, Brownsville, TX 78520–0906, 9–011–669–982–1775.

Merida, Mexico: U.S. Consulate—Merida, P.O. Box 9003, Brownsville, TX 78520–0903, 9–011–52–999–942–5738.

Mexico City, Mexico: DEA / Justice, U.S. Embassy Mexico City, P.O. Box 9000, Brownsville, TX 78520, 9–011–52–55–5080–2600.

Milan, Resident Office: American Consulate Milan, DEA / Justice, PSC 833, Box 60–M, FPO AE 09624, 9–011–39–02–2903–5422.

Monterrey, Resident Office: U.S. Consulate General, Monterrey Resident Office, P.O. Box 9002, Brownsville, TX 78520–0902, 9–011–5281–8340–1299.

Moscow, Russia: American Embassy Moscow, DEA / Justice, PSC 77, APO AE 09721, 9–011–7–495–728–5218.

Nassau: Nassau Country Office, DEA / Justice, American Embassy Nassau, 3370 Nassau Place, Washington, DC 20520, 9–1–242–322–1700.

New Delhi, India: American Embassy New Delhi, Department of State, 9000 New Delhi Place, Washington, DC 20521, 9–011–91–11–2419–8495.

Nicosia, Cyprus: American Embassy Nicosia, DEA / Justice, PSC 815, Box 1, FPO AE 09836–0001, 9–011–357–22–393–302.

Nuevo Laredo, Mexico: DEA, Nuevo Laredo Resident Office, P.O. Box 3089, Laredo, TX 78044–3089, 9–011–52–867–714–0512.

Ottawa, Canada: American Embassy Ottawa, DEA / Justice, P.O. Box 35, Ogdensburg, New York 13669, 9–1–613–238–5633.

Panama City, Panama: American Embassy Panama, DEA / Justice, Unit 0945, APO AA 34002, 9–011–507–317–5541.

Paramaribo, Suriname: American Embassy Paramaribo, DEA / Justice, 3390 Paramaribo Place, Dulles, VA 20189–3390, 301–985–8693.

Paris, France: American Embassy Paris, DEA / Justice, PSC 116, Box A–224, APO AE 09777, 9–011–33–1–4312–2732.

Peshawar, Pakistan: American Consulate Peshawar, DEA / Justice, Unit 62217, APO AE 09812–2217, 9–011–92–91–584–0424 / 0425.

Port–Au–Prince, Haiti: U.S. Department of State, 3400 Port-au-Prince, DEA, Washington, DC 20521, 9–011–509–2–229–8413.

Port of Spain, Trinidad and Tobago: Department of State DEA / Justice, Port of Spain Country Office, 3410 Port of Spain Place, Washington, DC 20537, 9–1–868–628–8136.

Pretoria, South Africa: American Embassy Pretoria, Department of State, DEA / Justice, Washington, DC 20521-9300, 9–011–2712–362–5008.

Quito, Ecuador: DEA / Justice, American Embassy Quito, Unit 5338, APO AA 34039, 9–011–593–22–231–547.

Rangoon, Burma: American Embassy Rangoon, DEA / Justice, Box B, APO AP 96546, 9–011–95–1–536–509.

Rome, Italy: American Embassy Rome, DEA / Justice, PSC 833, Box 22, FPO AE 09624, 9–011–39–06–4674–2319.

San Jose, Costa Rica: American Embassy San Jose, DEA / Justice, Unit 3440, Box 376, APO AA 34020–0376, 9–011–506–22–20–2433.

San Salvador, El Salvador: American Embassy San Salvador, DEA / Justice, Unit 3130, APO AA 34023, 9–011–503–2278–6005.

Santa Cruz, Resident Office: DEA / Justice, American Embassy, Unit 3913 (Santa Cruz), APO AA 34032, 9–011–591–332–7153.

Santiago, Chile: DEA / Justice, American Embassy Santiago, Unit 3460, Box 136, APO AA 34033–0136, 9–011–56–2–330–3401.

Santo Domingo, Dominican Republic: American Embassy Santo Domingo, DEA / Justice, Unit 3470, APO AA 34041, 9–1–809–687–3754.

Sao Paulo, Resident Office: DEA / Justice, American Embassy Sao Paulo, Unit 3502, APO AA 34030, 301–985–9364.

Seoul, Korea: American Embassy Seoul, DEA / Justice, Unit 15550, APO AP 96205–0001, 9–011–82–2–397–4260.

Singapore: American Embassy Singapore, Unit 4280 Box #30, FPO AP 96507–0030, 9–011–65–6476–9021.

Tashkent: Uzbekistan Country Office, DEA / Justice, 7110 Tashkent Place, Washington, DC 20521, 9–011–998–371–120–8924.

Tegucigalpa, Honduras: American Embassy Tegucigalpa, Tegucigalpa Country Office, Unit 3480, Box 212, APO AA 34022, 301–985–9321.

Tijuana, Resident Office: DEA, Tijuana Resident Office, P.O. 439039, San Diego, CA 92143–9039, 9–011–526–646–22–7452.

Tokyo, Japan: American Embassy Tokyo, DEA / Justice, Unit 45004, Box 224, APO AP 96337–5004, 9–011–81–3–3224–5452.

Trinidad, Bolivia Resident Office: American Embassy La Paz, DEA / Justice, Unit 3220 TRO, DPO AA 34032, 301–985–9398.

Udorn, Thailand Resident Office: American Embassy (Udorn), Box UD, APO AP 96546, 9–011–66–42–247–636.

Vancouver Resident Office: DEA Vancouver, 1574 Gulf Road #1509, Point Roberts, WA 98281, 9–1–604–694–7710.

Vienna, Austria: Vienna Country Office, DEA / Justice, American Embassy, 9900 Vienna Place, Dulles, VA 20189–9900, 9–011–43–1–31339–7551.

Vientiane, Laos: American Embassy Vientiane, DEA / Justice, Unit 8165, Box V, APO AP 96546, 9–011–856–21–219–565.

Warsaw, Poland Country Office: DEA / Justice, American Embassy Warsaw, Unit 5010, Box 27, DPO AE 09730–5010, 9–011–48–22–504–2000.

ENVIRONMENT AND NATURAL RESOURCES DIVISION

RFK Main Justice Building, 950 Pennsylvania Avenue, NW., 20530

601 D Street, NW., 20004 (PHB)

Assistant Attorney General.—Ignacia S. Moreno, room 2143 (202) 514–2701.

Principal Deputy Assistant Attorney General.—Robert G. Dreher, room 2141, 514–3370.

Deputy Assistant Attorneys General: John C. Cruden, room 2611, 514–2718; Ethan Shenkman, room 2135, 616–7349; Patrice L. Simms, room 2607, 514–0943; Jean Williams, room 2129, 305–0228.

Counsels to the Assistant Attorney General: Crystal Brown, room 2133, 514–4760; Jeffrey M. Prieto, room 2610, 307–9950.

Executive Officer.—Andrew Collier (PHB), room 2038, 616–3147.

Section Chiefs:

Appellate.—James C. Kilbourne (PHB), room 8046, 514–2748.

Environmental Crimes.—Stacey H. Mitchell (PHB), room 2102, 305–0363.
Environmental Defense.—Letitia J. Grishaw (PHB), room 8002, 514–2219.
Environmental Enforcement.—Bruce Gelber (NYAV), room 13063, 514–4624.
General Litigation.—Tom Clark (acting), (PHB), room 3102, 305–0438.
Indian Resources.—Craig Alexander (PHB), room 3016, 514–9080.
Land Acquisition.—Andrew Goldfrank (PHB), room 3638, 305–0316.
Policy, Legislation, and Special Litigation.—Pauline M. Milius (PHB), room 8022, 514–2586.
Wildlife and Marine Resources.—Seth Barsky (PHB), room 3902, 305–0210.

FIELD OFFICES

801 B Street, Suite 504, Anchorage, AK 99501–3657

Trial Attorneys: Regina Belt (907) 271–3456; Dean Dunsmore (907) 271–5452.

501 I Street, Suite 9–700, Sacramento, CA 95814–2322

Trial Attorneys: Stephen Macfarlane (916) 930–2204; Charles Shockey (916) 930–2203.

301 Howard Street, Suite 1050, San Francisco, CA 94105–2001

Trial Attorneys: David Glazer (415) 744–6477; Robert Mullaney (415) 744–6483; Bradley O'Brien (415) 744–6484; Judith Rabinowitz (415) 744–6486; Mark Rigau (415) 744–6487.

999 18th Street, Suite 945, North Tower, Denver, CO 80202

Trial Attorneys: David Askman (303) 844–1381; Bruce Bernard (303) 844–1361; Bradley Bridgewater (303) 844–1359; Dave Carson (303) 844–1349; Jerry Ellington (303) 844–1363; Robert Foster (303) 844–1362; Jim Freeman (303) 844–1489; Dave Gehlert (303) 844–1386; Alan Greenberg (303) 844–1366; David Harder (303) 844–1372; Robert Homiak (303) 844–1391; Lee Leininger (303) 844–1364; John Moscato (303) 844–1380; Mark Nitcynski (303) 844–1498; Terry Petrie (303) 844–1369; Daniel Pinkston (303) 844–1804; Susan Schneider (303) 844–1348.
Administrative Officer.—David Jones (303) 844–1807.

161 East Mallard Drive, Suite A, Boise, ID 83706

Trial Attorneys: David Negri (208) 334–1936; Ronald Sutcliffe (208) 334–9124.

One Gateway Center, Suite 6116, Newton Corner, MA 02158

Trial Attorneys: Catherine Fiske (617) 450–0444; Donald Frankel (617) 450–0442.

c/o U.S. Attorney's Office, 105 East Pine Street, 2nd Floor, Missoula, MT 59802

Trial Attorney.—Robert Anderson (406) 829–3322.

c/o U.S. Attorney's Office, 555 Pleasant Street, Suite 352, Concord, NH 03301

Trial Attorney.— Kristine Tardiff (603) 225–1562, ext. 283.

c/o U.S. Attorney's Office, 201 Third Street, NW., Suite 900, Albuquerque, NM 87102

Trial Attorney.—Andrew Smith (505) 224–1468.

c/o NOAA / DARCNW, 7600 San Point Way, NE., Seattle, WA 98115–0070

Trial Attorneys: Brian McLachlan (206) 526–6681; Mike Zevenbergen (206) 526–6607.

EXECUTIVE OFFICE FOR IMMIGRATION REVIEW (EOIR)

5107 Leesburg Pike, Suite 2600, Falls Church, VA 22041

Director.—Juan P. Osuna (acting), 2600 SKYT (703) 305–0169.
Deputy Director.—Vacant.
Associate Director/Chief of Staff.—Paula Nasca.
Executive Secretariat.—Rhonda Caldwell.
Assistant Director/General Counsel.—Robin Stutman, 2600 SKYT, 305–0470.
Deputy General Counsel.—Juan Carlos Hunt.
Assistant Director of:
Administration.—Lawrence M. D'Elia, 2300 SKYT, 305–1171.
Management Programs.—Frances A. Mooney, 2600 SKYT, 305–0289.
Planning, Analysis and Technology.—Amy Dale, 2600 SKYT, 605–0445.
Chairman, Board of Immigration Appeals.—David L. Neal (acting), 2400 SKYT, 305–1194.
Chief, Office of the Chief Administrative Hearing Officer.—Michael J. Creppy, 2500 SKYT, 305–0864.
Chief Judge, Office of the Chief Immigration Judge.—Brian M. O'Leary, 2500 SKYT, 305–1247.
Deputy Chief Immigration Judge.—Michael C. McGoings.
Telephone Directory Coordinator.—Annette Thomas, 2300 SKYT, 605–1336.

EXECUTIVE OFFICE FOR UNITED STATES ATTORNEYS (EOUSA)

RFK Main Justice Building, Room 2245, phone (202) 252–1300

Director.—H. Marshall Jarrett, room 2243.
Principal Deputy Director/Chief of Staff.—Terry L. Derden, room 2244.
Deputy Director and Counsel to the Director.—Norman Wong, room 2246.
Deputy Director for Administration and Management.—Katherine C. Gugulis, room 2247.
Deputy Director for Legal Management.—Suzanne L. Bell, room 2242.
Special Counsel to Principal Deputy Director.—Judith Wish, room 2515, 252–1324.
Administrative Officer.—Patricia Mallette, room 8011, BICN, 252–5555.
Executive Assistant/Attorney Generals Advisory Committee Liaison.—Judith Beeman, room 2335, RFK, 252–1374.
Director, Office of Legal Education.—Michael Bailie, National Advocacy Center, 1620 Pendleton Street, Columbia, SC 29201 (803) 705–5100.
Palmetto Project Manager Staff.—Paul Suddes, (803) 705–5678.
General Counsel.—Jay Macklin, room 5500, 501 3rd Street, NW., (202) 252–1600.
Chief, Planning, Evaluation and Performance (PEP) Staff.—Wayne Gibson, room 8108, BICN, 252–5802.
Assistant Directors:
Communication and Law Enforcement Coordinator Staff.—Tammy Reno (acting), room 2523, RFK, 252–5493.
Data Analysis Staff.—Michelle Slusher, room 2000, BICN, 252–5571.
Detailee Management Staff.—Carrie Mudd, room 8107, BICN, 252–1014.
District Management and Assistance Program.—David Downs, room 5700, BICN, 252–5777.
Evaluation and Review Staff.—Virginia Howard, room 8500, BICN, 252–5909.
Equal Employment Opportunity Staff.—Jason Osborne, Suite 106, National Place Building, NPB, 252–1460.
FOIA and Privacy Act Staff.—Garry Stewart, room 7300, BICN, 252–6058.
Planning and Performance Staff.—Robert "Rob" Carr, room 8110, BICN, 252–5909.
Counsel for Legal Initiatives.—David Smith, room 2256, RFK, 252–1326.
Counsel for Crisis Management and Resource.—Brit Featherston, room 2257, 252–1323.
Legislative Counsel.—Anne Pings, room 2509, 252–1435.
Counsel for Legal and Victim Programs.—Dan Villegas, room 7600, BICN, 252–58.
Victim Witness Staff.—Kristina Neal, room 7600, BICN, 252–5833 88.
Indian Violent and Cyber Crimes Staff.—Gretchen C. Shappert, room 7622, BICN, 252–5841.
White Collar and Civil Ligitagion Staff.—Vacant.
Asset Recovery Staff.—Vacant.
Chief Financial Officer.—Lisa Bevels, room 2200, BICN, 252–5605.
Assistant Director of:
Audit and Review.—Louisa McCarter Dadzie, room 2200, BICN, 252–5624.

Budget Execution.—Mary Ellen Kline, room 2200, BICN, 252–5607.
Budget Formulation.—Kevin Fick, room 2200, BICN.
Financial Systems Staff.—Christopher Kraft, room 2213, BICN, 252–5610.
Chief Information Officer.—Mark Fleshman, room 9078, BICN, 252–6246.
Assistant Director of:
Case Management Staff.—Joe Welsh, room 9125, BICN, 252–6120.
EVOIP Program Staff.—Burke Daidy, room 9012, BICN, 272–4462.
Information Security Staff.—Ted Shelkey, room 9074, BICN, 252–6090.
Office Automation Staff.—Ram Murthy, room 9208A, BICN, 252–6270.
Records and Information Management Staff (RIM).—Gail Ratliffe, room 9080, BICN, 252–6488.
Telecommunications and Technology Development Staff.—Denny Ko, room 9136, BICN, 252–6430.
Assistant Director of:
Acquisitions Staff.—Janis Harrington, room 5200, BICN, 252–5405.
Employee Assistance Staff.—Ed Neunlist, room 6800, BICN, 252–5455.
Facilities/Support Services Staff.—Ana Indovina, room 5200, BICN, 252–5964.
HR Operations Staff.—Mike Smith, room 8426, BICN, 252–5353.
HR Policy Staff.—Pete McSwain, room 8401, BICN, 252–5315.
Personnel Staff.—Jean Dunn, room 8430, BICN, 252–5310.
Litigation Technology Service Center.—Sarah Montgomery, room 5738, 514–9500.
Security Programs Staff.—Tim George, room 2600, BICN, 252–5694.
Victims Rights Ombudsman.—Marie O'Rourke, room 2600, BICN, 252–1317.
Office of Tribal Justice.—Tracy Toulou, room 2310, Main, 514–5994.

EXECUTIVE OFFICE FOR UNITED STATES TRUSTEES

20 Massachusetts Avenue, NW., 20530, phone (202) 307–1391

http://www.usdoj.gov/ust

Director.—Clifford J. White III, room 8000.
Deputy Director Field Operations.—Mark A. Redmiles.
Deputy Director General Counsel.—Ramona Elliott, room 8100, 307–1399.
Deputy Director Management.—Phillip Crewson.
Chief Information Officer.—Monique K. Bourque, 353–3548.
Assistant Director, Office of:
Administration.—Monique K. Bourque, room 8200, 353–3548.
Oversight.—Doreen Solomon, room 8338, 305–0222.
Planning and Evaluation.—Thomas Kearns, room 8308, 305–7827.

U.S. TRUSTEES

Region I:
Room 1000, 5 Post Office Square, Boston, MA 02109 (617) 788–0440.
Suite 303, 537 Congress Street, Portland, ME 04101 (207) 780–3564.
14th Floor, Sovereign Tower Bldg., 446 Main, Worchester, MA 01608 (508) 793–0555.
Suite 605, 1000 Elm Street, Manchester, NH 03101 (603) 666–7908.
Suite 910, 10 Dorrance Street, Providence, RI 02903 (401) 528–5551.
Region II:
21st floor, 33 Whitehall Street, New York, NY 10004 (212) 510–0500.
Suite 200, 74 Chapel Street, Albany, NY 12207 (518) 434–4553.
Suite 401, 300 Pearl Street, Buffalo, NY 14202 (716) 551–5541.
Long Island Federal Courthouse, 560 Federal Plaza, Central Islip, NY 11722–4456 (631) 715–7800.
Suite 302, 150 Court Street, New Haven, CT 06510 (203) 773–2210.
Room 609, 100 State Street, Rochester, NY 14614 (716) 263–5812.
Room 105, 10 Broad Street, Utica, NY 13501 (315) 793–8191.
Suite 4529, 271 Cadman Plaza East, Brooklyn, NY 11201 (718) 422–4960
Region III:
Suite 500, 833 Chestnut Street, Philadelphia, PA 19107 (215) 597–4411.
Suite 2100, One Newark Center, Newark, NJ 07102 (973) 645–3014.
Suite 970, 1001 Liberty Avenue, Pittsburgh, PA 15222 (412) 644–4756.
Suite 1190, 228 Walnut Street, Harrisburg, PA 17101 or P.O. Box 969, Harrisburg, PA 17108 (717) 221–4533.

Suite 2207, 844 King Street, Wilmington, DE 19801 (302) 573–6491.

Region IV:

Suite 953, 1835 Assembly Street, Columbia, SC 29201 (803) 765–5235.
Room 210, 115 S. Union Street, Alexandria, VA 22314 (703) 557–7274.
Room 625, 200 Granby Street, Norfolk, VA 23510 (757) 441–6012.
Room 2025, 300 Virginia Street East, Charleston, WV 25301 (304) 347–3400.
First Campbell Square Building, 210 First Street, SW., Suite 505, Roanoke, VA 24011 (540) 857–2838.
Suite 4304, U.S. Courthouse, 701 East Broad Street, Richmond, VA 23219 (804) 771–2310.
Suite 600, 6305 Ivy Lane, Greenbelt, MD 20770 (301) 344–6220.
Suite 2625, 101 West Lombard Street, Baltimore, MD 21201 (410) 962–4300.

Region V:

Suite 2110, 400 Poydras Street, New Orleans, LA 70130 (504) 589–4018.
Suite 3196, 300 Fannin Street, Shreveport, LA 71101–3099 (318) 676–3456.
Suite 6–430, 501 East Court Street, Jackson, MS 32901 (601) 965–5241.

Region VI:

Room 976, 1100 Commerce Street, Dallas, TX 75242 (214) 767–1070.
Room 300, 110 North College Avenue, Tyler, TX 75702 (903) 965–5241.

Region VII:

Suite 3516, 515 Rusk Avenue, Houston, TX 77002 (713) 718–4650.
Room 230, 903 San Jacinto, Austin, TX 78701 (512) 916–5328.
Suite 533, 615 East Houston Street, San Antonio, TX 78205 (210) 472–4640.
Suite 1107, 606 North Carancahua Street, Corpus Christi, TX 78476 (361) 888–3261.

Region VIII:

Suite 400, 200 Jefferson Avenue, Memphis, TN 38103 (901) 544–3322.
Suite 512, 601 West Broadway, Louisville, KY 40202 (502) 582–6000.
Fourth floor, 31 East 11th Street, Chattanooga, TN 37402 (423) 752–5156.
Room 318, 701 Broadway, Nashville, TN 37203 (615) 736–2258.
Suite 500, 100 East Vine Street, Lexington, KY 40507 (859) 233–2822.

Region IX:

Suite 441, BP Building, 201 Superior Avenue East, Cleveland, OH 44114 (216) 522–7800.
Suite 200, Schaff Building, 170 North High Street, Columbus, OH 43215–2403 (614) 469–7411.
Suite 2030, 36 East Seventh Street, Cincinnati, OH 45202 (513) 684–6988.
Suite 700, 211 West Fort Street, Detroit, MI 48226 (313) 226–7934.
Suite 200R, 125 Ottawa Street, Grand Rapids, MI 49503 (616) 456–2002.

Region X:

Room 1000, 101 West Ohio Street, Indianapolis, IN 46204 (317) 226–6370.
Suite 1100, 401 Main Street, Peoria, IL 61602 (309) 671–7854.
Suite 555, 100 East Wayne Street, South Bend, IN 46601 (219) 236–8105.

Region XI:

Suite 873, 219 S. Dearborn Street, Chicago, IL 60606 (312) 353–9297.
Room 430, 517 East Wisconsin Avenue, Milwaukee, WI 53202 (414) 297–4499.
Suite 304, 780 Regent Street, Madison, WI 53715 (608) 264–5522.

Region XII:

Suite 400, 225 Second Street, SE., Cedar Rapids, IA 52401 (319) 364–2211.
Suite 1015, U.S. Courthouse, 300 S. Fourth Street, Minneapolis, MN 55415 (612) 334–1353.
Room 793, 210 Walnut Street, Des Moines, IA 50309–2108 (515) 284–4982.
Suite 303, 314 South Main Street, Sioux Falls, SD 57102–6321 (605) 330–4450.

Region XIII:

Suite 3440, 400 East 9th Street, Kansas City, MO 64106–1910 (816) 512–1940.
Suite 6353, 111 South 10th Street, St. Louis, MO 63102 (314) 539–2976.
Suite 1200, 200 West Capital Avenue, Little Rock, AR 72201–3344 (501) 324–7357.
Suite 1148, 111 South 18th Plaza, Omaha, NE 68102 (402) 221–4304.

Region XIV:

Suite 204, 230 North First Avenue, Phoenix, AZ 85003 or P.O. Box 36170, Phoenix, AZ 85067 (602) 682–2600.

Region XV:

Suite 600, 402 West Broadway Street, San Diego, CA 92101–8511 (619) 557–5013.
Suite 602, 1132 Bishop Street, Honolulu, HI 96813–2836 (808) 522–8154.

Region XVI:

725 South Figueroa, Suite 2600, Los Angeles, CA 90017 (213) 894–6811.
Suite 9041, 411 West Fourth Street, Santa Ana, CA 92701–8000 (714) 338–3405.
Suite 300, 3685 Main Street, Riverside, CA 92501 (951) 276–6975.
Suite 115, 21051 Warner Center Lane, Woodland Hills, CA 91367 (818) 716–8800.

Region XVII:
Suite 700, 235 Pine Street, San Francisco, CA 94104–3401 (415) 705–3300.
Suite 7–500, U.S. Courthouse, 501 I Street, Sacramento, CA 95814–2322 (916) 930–2099.
Suite 1401, 2500 Tulare Street, Fresno, CA 93721 (559) 487–5002.
Suite 690N, 1301 Clay Street, Oakland, CA 94612–5217 (510) 637–3206.
Room 4300, 300 Las Vegas Boulevard South, Las Vegas, NV 89101 (702) 388–6600.
Suite 3009, 300 Booth Street, Reno, NV 89502 (775) 784–5335.
Room 268, 280 South First Street, San Jose, CA 95113 (408) 535–5525.

Region XVIII:
Suite 5103, 700 Stewart Street, Seattle, WA 98101 (206) 553–2000.
Suite 213, 620 Southwest Main Street, Portland, OR 97205 (503) 326–4000.
Suite 220, 720 Park Boulevard, Boise, ID 83712 (208) 334–1300.
Room 593, 920 West Riverside, Spokane, WA 99201 (509) 353–2999.
Suite 204, 301 Central Avenue, Great Falls, MT 59401 (406) 761–8777.
Suite 258, 605 West Fourth Avenue, Anchorage, AK 99501 (907) 271–2604.
Suite 1100, 405 East Eighth Avenue, Eugene, OR 97401 (541) 465–6331.

Region XIX:
Suite 1551, 999 Eighteenth Street, Denver, CO 80202 (303) 312–7230.
Suite 203, 308 West 21st Street, Cheyenne, WY 82001 (307) 772–2790.
Suite 300, 405 South Main Street, Salt Lake City, UT 84111 (801) 524–5734.

Region XX:
Room 500, Epic Center, 301 North Main Street, Wichita, KS 67202 (316) 269–6161.
Suite 112, 421 Gold Street, SW., Albuquerque, NM 87102 (505) 248–6544.
Suite 408, 215 Northwest Dean A. McGee Avenue, Oklahoma City, OK 73102 (405) 231–5950.
Suite 225, 224 South Boulder Avenue, Tulsa, OK 74103 (918) 581–6670.

Region XXI:
Room 362, 75 Spring Street, SW., Atlanta, GA 30303 (404) 331–4437.
Suite 301, EDIFICIO OCHOA, 500 Tanca Street, San Juan, PR 00901 (787) 729–7444.
Room 1204, 51 Southwest First Avenue, Miami, FL 33130 (305) 536–7285.
Suite 302, 222 West Oglethorpe Avenue, Savannah, GA 31401 (912) 652–4112.
Suite 1200, 501 East Polk Street, Tampa, FL 33602 (813) 228–2000.
Suite 302, 440 Martin Luther King Boulevard, Macon, GA 31201 (478) 752–3401.
Suite 128, 110 East Park Avenue, Tallahassee, FL 32301 (850) 521–5050.
Suite 620, 135 West Central Boulevard, Orlando, FL 32801 (407) 648–6301.

BUREAU OF ALCOHOL, TOBACCO, FIREARMS, AND EXPLOSIVES (ATF)

99 New York Avenue, NE., 20226

OFFICE OF THE DIRECTOR

Director.—Kenneth Melson (acting), (202) 648–8700.
Deputy Director.—William J. Hoover, 648–8710.

OFFICE OF CHIEF COUNSEL

Chief Counsel.—Stephen R. Rubenstein, 648–7000.
Deputy Chief Counsel.—Vacant.

OFFICE OF ENFORCEMENT PROGRAMS AND SERVICES

Assistant Director.—Arthur Herbert, 648–7080.
Deputy Assistant Director.—Teresa Ficaretta.

OFFICE OF EQUAL OPPORTUNITY

Executive Assistant.—Stacie Brockman, 648–7597.

Deputy Executive Assistant.—Dora Silas, 648–7393.

OFFICE OF FIELD OPERATIONS

Assistant Director.—Mark R. Chait, 648–8410.
Deputy Assistant Director for—
Central.—Mike Boxler.
East.—Julie Torres.
West.—William McMahon.
Industry Operations.—Harry McCabe.

OFFICE OF MANAGEMENT/CFO

Assistant Director/Chief Financial Officer.—Vivian Michalic, 648–7800.
Deputy Assistant Director.—Robert Edgeton.

OFFICE OF OMBUDSMAN

Ombudsman.—Marianne Ketels, 648–8750.

OFFICE OF PROFESSIONAL RESPONSIBILITY AND SECURITY OPERATIONS

Assistant Director.—Melanie Stinnett, 648–7500.
Deputy Assistant Director.—Vacant.

OFFICE OF PUBLIC AND GOVERNMENTAL AFFAIRS

Assistant Director.—James E. McDermond, 648–8500.
Deputy Assistant Director.—Vacant.
Chief of:
Legislative Affairs Division.—Greg Rasnake, 648–8510.
Public Affairs Division.—Scott Thomasson, 648–8500.

OFFICE OF SCIENCE AND TECHNOLOGY/CIO

Assistant Director/Chief Information Officer.—H. Richard Holgate, 648–8390.
Deputy Assistant Director for—
Forensic Services.—Greg Czarnopys.
Information Technology.—Francis Frande (acting).

OFFICE OF STRATEGIC INTELLIGENCE AND INFORMATION

Assistant Director.—W. Larry Ford, 648–7600.
Deputy Assistant Director.—Steve Martin.

OFFICE OF HUMAN RESOURCES AND PROFESSIONAL DEVELOPMENT

Assistant Director.—Vacant, 648–8416.
Deputy Assistant Director.—Audrey Stucko.

FEDERAL BUREAU OF INVESTIGATION

J. Edgar Hoover Building, 935 Pennsylvania Avenue, NW., 20535–0001

phone (202) 324–3000, http://www.fbi.gov

Director.—Robert S. Mueller III, 324–3444.
Deputy Director.—Timothy Murphy, 324–3315.
Associate Deputy Director.—Thomas Harrington, 324–4180.
Chief of Staff.—John Carlin, 324–3444.

OFFICE OF THE DIRECTOR / DEPUTY DIRECTOR / ASSOCIATE DEPUTY DIRECTOR

Office of the General Counsel.—Valerie E. Caproni, 324–6829.
Office of Public Affairs.—Michael Kortan, 324–5352.
Office of Congressional Affairs.—Stephen Kelly, 324–5051.
Office of Professional Responsibility.—Candice M. Will, 324–8284.
Office of Equal Employment Opportunity Affairs.—Veronica Venture, 324–4128.
Office of the Ombudsman.—Monique Bookstein, 324–2156.
Inspection Division.—Amy Jo Lyons, 324–2901.
Facilities and Logistics Services Division.—Patrick G. Findlay, 324–2875.
Finance Division.—Richard Haley II, 324–4104.
Records Management Division.—Richard Klein (acting), 324–7141.
Security Division.—Michael J. Folmar, Jr., 324–7112.

OFFICE OF THE CHIEF INFORMATION OFFICER

Executive Assistant Director / Chief Information Officer.—Chad Fulgham, 324–6165.
Assistant Director of:
Information Technology Management Division.—John Hope (703) 872–5050.
Information Technology Engineering Division.—Jeffery Johnson, 324–2559.
Office of the Chief Technology Officer.—Clayton Grigg (703) 872–5270.

CRIMINAL INVESTIGATIONS BRANCH

Executive Assistant Director.—Shawn Henry, 324–4880.
Assistant Director of:
Criminal Investigative Division.—Kevin Perkins, Jr., 324–4260.
Critical Incident Response Group.—Robert Blecksmith (703) 632–4100.
Cyber Division.—Gordon Snow, 651–3044.
International Operations Division.—Joseph Dermarest, Jr., 324–5904.
Law Enforcement Coordination Office.—Ronald Ruecker, 324–7126.

HUMAN RESOURCES BRANCH

Executive Assistant Director.—Janet Kamerman, 324–3000.
Assistant Director of:
Human Resources Division.—Anthony Bladen, 324–3514.
Training and Development Division.—Thomas Browne (703) 632–1100.

NATIONAL SECURITY BRANCH

Executive Assistant Director.—Sean Joyce, 324–7045.
Assistant Director of:
Counterintelligence Division.—Frank Figliuzzi, 324–4614.
Counterterrorism Division.—Mark Giuliano, Jr., 324–2771.
Directorate of Intelligence.—Tracy Reinhold, 324–7605.
Weapons of Mass Destruction Directorate.—Dr. Vahid Majidi, 324–4965.

SCIENCE AND TECHNOLOGY BRANCH

Executive Assistant Director.—Louis Grever (202) 324–0805.
Assistant Director of:
Criminal Justice Information Services Division.—Dan Roberts III (304) 625–2700.
Laboratory Division.—D. Christian Hassell (703) 632–7001.
Operational Technology Division.—Marcus C. Thomas (703) 632–6100.

FIELD DIVISIONS

Albany: 200 McCarty Avenue, Albany, NY 12209 (518) 465–7551.
Albuquerque: 4200 Luecking Park Avenue NE., Albuquerque, NM 87107 (505) 224–2000.
Anchorage: 101 East Sixth Avenue, Anchorage, AK 99501 (907) 258–5322.
Atlanta: 2635 Century Center Parkway, NE., Suite 400, Atlanta, GA 30345 (404) 679–9000.
Baltimore: 2600 Lord Baltimore Avenue, Baltimore, MD 21244 (410) 265–8080.
Birmingham: 1000 18th Street North, Birmingham, AL 35203 (205) 326–6166.
Boston: One Center Plaza, Suite 600, Boston, MA 02108 (617) 742–5533.
Buffalo: One FBI Plaza, Buffalo, NY 14202 (716) 856–7800.
Charlotte: Wachovia Building, 400 South Tryon Street, Suite 900, Charlotte, NC 28285 (704) 377–9200.
Chicago: 2111 West Roosevelt Road, Chicago, IL 60608–1128 (312) 431–1333.
Cincinnati: Federal Office Building, 550 Main Street, Room 9000, Cincinnati, OH 45202 (513) 421–4310.
Cleveland: 1501 Lakeside Avenue, Cleveland, OH 44114 (216) 522–1400.
Columbia: 151 Westpark Boulevard, Columbia, SC 29210 (803) 551–4200.
Dallas: J. Gordon Shanklin Building, One Justice Way, Dallas, TX 75220 (972) 559–5000.
Denver: Federal Office Building, 1961 Stout Street, Room 1823, Denver, CO 80294 (303) 629–7171.
Detroit: P.V. McNamara Federal Office Building, 477 Michigan Avenue, 26th Floor, Detroit, MI 48226 (313) 965–2323.
El Paso: 660 South Mesa Hills Drive, Suite 3000, El Paso, TX 79912 (915) 832–5000.
Honolulu: Kalanianaole Federal Office Building, 300 Ala Moana Boulevard, Room 4–230, Honolulu, HI 96850 (808) 566–4300.
Houston: 2500 East T.C. Jester, Suite 200, Houston, TX 77008 (713) 693–5000.
Indianapolis: Federal Office Building, 575 North Pennsylvania Street, Room 679, Indianapolis, IN 46204 (371) 639–3301.
Jackson: Federal Office Building, 100 West Capitol Street, Suite 1553, Jackson, MS 39269 (601) 948–5000.
Jacksonville: 7820 Arlington Expressway, Suite 200, Jacksonville, FL 32211 (904) 721–1211.
Kansas City: 1300 Summit, Kansas City, MO 64105 (816) 512–8200.
Knoxville: John J. Duncan Federal Office Building, 710 Locust Street, Room 600, Knoxville, TN 37902 (423) 544–0751.
Las Vegas: John Lawrence Bailey Building, 1787 West Lake Mead Boulevard, Las Vegas, NV 89106–2135 (702) 385–1281.
Little Rock: #24 Shackleford West Boulevard, Little Rock, AR 72211 (501) 221–9100.
Los Angeles: Federal Office Building, 11000 Wilshire Boulevard, Suite 1700, Los Angeles, CA 90024 (310) 477–6565.
Louisville: 600 Martin Luther King, Jr. Place, Room 500, Louisville, KY 40202 (502) 583–2941.
Memphis: Eagle Crest Building, 225 North Humphreys Boulevard, Suite 3000, Memphis, TN 38120 (901) 747–4300.
Miami: 16320 Northwest Second Avenue, Miami, FL 33169 (305) 944–9101.
Milwaukee: 330 East Kilbourn Avenue, Suite 600, Milwaukee, WI 53202 (414) 276–4684.
Minneapolis: 111 Washington Avenue South, Suite 100, Minneapolis, MN 55401 (612) 376–3200.
Mobile: 200 North Royal Street, Mobile, AL 36602 (334) 438–3674.
New Haven: 600 State Street, New Haven, CT 06511 (203) 777–6311.
New Orleans: 2901 Leon C. Simon Boulevard, New Orleans, LA 70126 (504) 816–3122.
New York: 26 Federal Plaza, 23rd Floor, New York, NY 10278 (212) 384–1000.
Newark: Claremont Tower Building, 11 Centre Place, Newark, NJ 07102 (973) 792–3000.
Norfolk: 150 Corporate Boulevard, Norfolk, VA 23502 (757) 455–0100.
Oklahoma City: 3301 West Memorial, Oklahoma City, OK 73134 (405) 290–7770.
Omaha: 10755 Burt Street, Omaha, NE 68114 (402) 493–8688.
Philadelphia: William J. Green, Jr., Federal Office Building, 600 Arch Street, Eighth Floor, Philadelphia, PA 19106 (215) 418–4000.
Phoenix: 201 East Indianola Avenue, Suite 400, Phoenix, AZ 85012 (602) 279–5511.
Pittsburgh: Martha Dixon Building, 3311 East Carson Street, Pittsburgh, PA 15203 (412) 432–4000.
Portland: Crown Plaza Building, 1500 Southwest First Avenue, Suite 401, Portland, OR 97201 (503) 224–4181.
Richmond: 1970 East Parham Road, Richmond, VA 23228 (804) 261–1044.
Sacramento: 4500 Orange Grove Avenue, Sacramento, CA 95841 (916) 481–9110.
Salt Lake City: 257 Towers Building, 257 East, 200 South, Suite 1200, Salt Lake City, UT 84111 (801) 579–1400.

San Antonio: 5740 University Heights Boulevard, San Antonio, TX 78249 (210) 225–6741.
San Diego: Federal Office Building, 9797 Aero Drive, San Diego, CA 92123 (858) 565–1255.
San Francisco: 450 Golden Gate Avenue, 13th Floor, San Francisco, CA 64102 (415) 553–7400.
San Juan: U.S. Federal Office Building, 150 Chardon Avenue, Room 526, Hato Rey, PR 00918 (787) 754–6000.
Seattle: 1110 Third Avenue, Seattle, WA 98101 (206) 622–0460.
Springfield: 900 East Linton Avenue, Springfield, IL 62703 (217) 522–9675.
St. Louis: 2222 Market Street, St. Louis, MO 63103 (314) 241–5357.
Tampa: 5525 West Gray Street, Tampa, FL 33609 (813) 273–4566.
Washington, DC: 601 Fourth Street, NW., Washington, DC 20535 (202) 278–3400.

FEDERAL BUREAU OF PRISONS (BOP)

320 First Street, NW., 20534

General Information Number (202) 307–3198

Director.—Harley G. Lappin, room 654, HOLC, 307–3250.
Director, National Institute of Corrections.—Morris L. Thigpen, Sr., 7th floor, 500 FRST, 307–3106.
Assistant Director of:
Administration.—William Dalius, 9th floor, 500 FRST, 307–3230.
Correctional Programs.—Charles E. Samuels, Jr., room 554, HOLC, 307–3226.
General Counsel.—Kathleen M. Kenney, room 958C, HOLC, 307–3062.
Health Services.—Newton Kendig, M.D., room 1054, HOLC, 307–3055.
Human Resources Management.—Kim M. White, room 754, HOLC, 307–3082.
Industries, Education, and Vocational Training.—Paul Laird, 8th floor, 400 FRST, 305–3501.
Information, Policy and Public Affairs.—Thomas R. Kane, Ph.D., room 641, HOLC, 514–6537.
Regional Director for—
Mid-Atlantic.—Louis Eichenlaub (301) 317–3101.
North Central.—Michael K. Nalley (913) 621–3939.
Northeast.—Joseph Norwood (215) 521–7300.
South Central.—Gerardo Maldonado (214) 224–3389.
Southeast.—Ray Holt (678) 686–1200.
Western.—Robert McFadden (209) 956–9700.
Telephone Directory Coordinator.—Marla Clayton, 307–3250.

OFFICE OF THE FEDERAL DETENTION TRUSTEE

4601 N. Fairfax Drive, Suite 9110, Arlington, VA 22203, phone (202) 353–4601

Trustee.—Michael A. Pearson.
Deputy Trustee.—Vacant.

FOREIGN CLAIMS SETTLEMENT COMMISSION

Bicentennial Building (BICN), 600 E Street, NW., Suite 6002, 20579

phone (202) 616–6986

Chair.—Vacant.
Commissioner.—Rafael E. Martinez.
Chief Counsel.—Jaleh F. Barrett.
Executive Officer.—Judith H. Lock.

OFFICE OF INFORMATION POLICY

1425 New York Avenue, NW., 20530, phone (202) 514–3642

Director.—Melanie Ann Pustay.
Chief of Staff.—Carmen L. Mallon.
Associate Director.—Janice Galli McLeod.

OFFICE OF THE INSPECTOR GENERAL

RFK Main Justice Building, Room 4706, phone (202) 514–3435

950 Pennsylvania Avenue, NW., 20530

Inspector General.—Cynthia A. Schnedar (acting).
Deputy Inspector General.—Vacant.
Senior Counsel.—Jay Lerner.
General Counsel.—William Blier, RFK, Suite 4726, 616–0646.
Assistant Inspectors General:
Audit.—Caryn Marske (NYAV), Suite 13000, 616–1697.
Evaluations and Inspections.—Mike Gulledge (NYAV), Suite 6100, 616–4620.
Investigations.—Thomas F. McLaughlin (NYAV), Suite 7100, 616–4760.
Management and Planning.—Gregory T. Peters (NYAV), Suite 7000, 616–4550.
Oversight and Review.—Carol F. Ochoa (NYAV), Suite 13000, 616–0645.

REGIONAL AUDIT OFFICES

Atlanta: Ferris B. Polk, Suite 1130, 75 Spring Street, Atlanta, GA 30303 (404) 331–5928.

Chicago: Carol S. Taraszka, Suite 3510, Citicorp Center, 500 West Madison Street, Chicago, IL 60661 (312) 353–1203.

Dallas: Robert J. Kaufman, Room 575, Box 4, 207 South Houston Street, Dallas, TX 75202–4724 (214) 655–5000.

Denver: David M. Sheeren, Suite 1500, Chancery Building, 1120 Lincoln Street, Denver, CO 80203 (303) 864–2000.

Philadelphia: Thomas O. Puerzer, Suite 201, 701 Market Street, Philadelphia, PA 19106 (215) 580–2111.

San Francisco: David J. Gaschke, Suite 201, 1200 Bayhill Drive, San Bruno, CA 94066 (650) 876–9220.

Washington: Troy M. Meyer, 1300 North 17th Street, Suite 3400, Arlington, VA 22209 (202) 616–4688.

Computer Security and Information Technology Audit Office: Reginald Allen, room 5000 (202) 616–3801.

Financial Statement Audit Office: Mark L. Hayes, 1425 New York Avenue, NW., #13000, Washington, DC 20530 (202) 616–4660.

REGIONAL INVESTIGATIONS OFFICES

Atlanta: Eddie D. Davis, 60 Forsyth Street, SW., Room 8M45, Atlanta, GA 30303 (404) 562–1980.

Boston: Thomas M. Hopkins, U.S. Courthouse, 1 Courthouse Way, Room 9200, Boston, MA 02210 (617) 748–3218.

Chicago: John F. Oleskowicz, P.O. Box 1802, Chicago, IL 60690 (312) 886–7050.

Denver: Norman K. Lau, Suite 1501, 1120 Lincoln Street, Denver, CO 80203 (303) 335–4201.

Dallas: James H. Mahon, 2505 State Highway 360, Room 410, Grand Prairie, TX 75050 (817) 385–5200.

Detroit: Nicholas V. Candela, Suite 1402, 211 West Fort Street, Detroit, MI 48226 (313) 226–4005.

El Paso: Eric Benn, Suite 135, 4050 Rio Bravo, El Paso, TX 79902 (915) 577–0102.

Houston: Carlos Capano, P.O. Box 53509, Houston, TX 77052 (713) 718–4888.

Los Angeles: Kenneth R. Strange, Jr., Suite 655, 330 North Brand Street, Glendale, CA 91203 (818) 543–1172.

Miami: Teresa M. Gulotta Powers, Suite 200, 510 Shotgun Road, Sunrise, FL 33326 (954) 370–8300.

New York: Eric J. Blachman, One Battery Park Plaza, 29th floor, New York, NY 10004 (212) 824–3650.

New Jersey: Kenneth R. Connaughton, Jr., 361 Scotch Road, West Trenton, NJ 08628 (609) 883–5423.

San Francisco: Michael Barranti, Suite 220, 1200 Bayhill Drive, San Bruno, CA 94066 (650) 876–9058.

Seattle: Wayne Hawney, Suite 104, 620 Kirkland Way, Kirkland, WA 98033 (253) 852–0194.

Tucson: Joseph V. Cuffari, 405 West Congress, Room 3600, Tucson, AZ 85701 (520) 620–7389.

Washington: Scott Barden, 1425 New York Avenue, NW., Suite 7100, Washington, DC 20530 (202) 616–4760.
Fraud Detection Office.—Joseph Barlow, room 7100 (202) 353–2975.

INTERPOL—U.S. NATIONAL CENTRAL BUREAU
phone (202) 616–9000

Director.—Timothy A. Williams, 616–9700.
Deputy Director.—Shawn A. Bray, 616–9700.
Executive Office.—Warren A. Lewis, 616–8810.
General Counsel.—Kevin Smith, 616–4103.
Assistant Director, Division of:
Alien/Fugitive.—Sean P. Fahey, 616–0310.
Drug.—William M. Simons, 616–3379.
Economic Crimes.—Robert Montemorra, 616–5466.
Human Trafficking and Child Protection.—George Guzman, 616–1753.
INTERPOL Operations and Command Center.—Patrick P. Ott, 616–3459, (24/7 Command Center).
State and Local Liaison.—Michael D. Muth, 616–8272.
Terrorism and Violent Crimes.—David Roth, 616–7258.

OFFICE OF INTERGOVERNMENTAL AND PUBLIC LIAISON
RFK Main Justice Building, Room 1629, phone (202) 514–3465

Director.—Portia Roberson.
Deputy Director.—Vacant.
Associate Director.—Alexa Chappell.

JUSTICE MANAGEMENT DIVISION
RFK Main Justice Building, 950 Pennsylvania Avenue, NW., 20530
2CON—145 N Street, NE., 20530
LSB—Liberty Square Building, 450 5th Street, NW., 20530

Assistant Attorney General for Administration.—Lee J. Lofthus, room 1111 (202) 514–3101.
Deputy Assistant Attorney General/Policy, Management and Planning.—Michael H. Allen, room 1111 (202) 514–3101.
Staff Directors for—
Department Ethics Office.—Janice Rodgers (2CON), room 8E310, 514–8196.
General Counsel Office.—Stuart Frisch, General Counsel (2CON), room 8E528, 514–3452.
Internal Review and Evaluation Office.—Neil Ryder, (2CON), room 8W1419, 616–5499.
Management and Planning.—Lou Santone (acting), (2CON), room 8W300, 307–1800.
Procurement Executive.—Michael H. Allen, room 1111, 514–3101.
Records Management Policy Office.—Jeanette Plante (2CON), room 8W1401, 514–3528.
Small and Disadvantaged Business Utilization Office.—David Sutton (2CON), room 8E1009, 616–0521.
Deputy Assistant Attorney General/Controller.—Jolene Lauria-Sullens, room 1117, 514–1843.
Staff Directors for—
Asset Forfeiture Management.—Candace Olds (2CON), room 5W725, 616–8000.
Budget.—Karin O'Leary, room 7601, 514–4082.
Debt Collection Management.—Holley O'Brien (2CON), room 5E103, 514–5343.
Finance.—Melinda Morgan (2CON), room 7E202, 616–5800.
Procurement Services.—James Johnston (2CON), room 8E202, 307–2000.
Unified Financial System Project Management Office.—Kay Clarey (2CON), room 6W102, 305–3651.
Deputy Assistant Attorney General, Human Resources/Administration.—Mari Santangelo, room 1112, 514–5501.
Staff Directors for—
Attorney Recruitment and Management Office.—Louis DeFalaise, Suite 10200, 450 5th Street, NW. (Liberty Square), 514–8900.

Consolidated Executive Office.—Cyntoria Carter, room 7113, 514–5537.
DOJ Executive Secretariat.—Dana Paige, room 4412, 514–2063.
Equal Employment Opportunity.—Richard Toscano (2CON), room 1W102, 616–4800.
Facilities and Administrative Services.—Edward A. Hamilton (2CON), room 9E206, 616–2995.
Library.—Dennis Feldt, room 7535, 514–2133.
Personnel.—Rodney Markham (2CON), room 9W102, 514–6788.
Security and Emergency Planning.—James Dunlap, room 6217, 514–2094.

Deputy Assistant Attorney General/Information Resources Management and CIO.—Vance Hitch, room 1310–A, 514–0507.

Staff Directors for—
E-Government Services.—Eric Olson (2CON), room 3W701, 353–2355.
Enterprise Solutions.—John Murray (2CON), room 3E202, 305–9635.
IT Security.—Kevin Deeley (2CON), room 4E1407, 353–2421.
Operation Services.—Roger Beasley (2CON), room 4W701, 514–0778.
Policy and Planning.—Kent Holgrewe (2CON), room 2E202, 305–3154.

OFFICE OF JUSTICE PROGRAMS (OJP)

810 7th Street, NW., 20531

OFFICE OF THE ASSISTANT ATTORNEY GENERAL

Assistant Attorney General.—Laurie O. Robinson (acting), (202) 307–5933.
Principal Deputy Assistant General.—Mary Lou Leary, 307–1006
Deputy Assistant Attorney General.—Phillip Merkle (acting), 307–5933.
Manager, Equal Employment Opportunity.—Carl Lucas, 307–3355.

BUREAU OF JUSTICE ASSISTANCE

Director.—James Burch III (acting), 616–6500.
Deputy Directors of:
Policy.—Pamela Cammarata (acting), 514–9193.
Planning.—Eileen Garry, 307–6226.
Programs.—Tracey Trautman, 305–1491.

BUREAU OF JUSTICE STATISTICS

Director.—James P. Lynch, 307–2900.
Deputy Directors of:
Statistical Collections and Analysis: Victimization, Corrections, and Special Projects Division.—William Sabol, 514–1062.
Statistical Collections and Analysis: Law Enforcement, Prosecution, and Courts Division.—Vacant, 307–0765.
Statistical Planning, Policy and Operations.—Gerard Ramker, 307–0759.

NATIONAL INSTITUTE OF JUSTICE

Director.—John Laub, 307–2942.
Deputy Directors: Kristina Rose, 307–0466; Ellen Scrivner, 514–4693.
Investigative and Forensic Sciences.—Michael Sheppo, 353–3756.
Research and Evaluation.—Phyllis Newton, 305–2457.
Science and Technology.—George Tillery, 305–9829.

OFFICE OF JUVENILE JUSTICE AND DELINQUENCY PREVENTION

Administrator.—Jeff Slowikowski (acting), 307–5911.
Deputy Administrator of:
Policy.—Melodee Hanes (acting), 305–1973.
Programs.—Marilyn Roberts, 616–9055.

OFFICE FOR VICTIMS OF CRIME

Director.—Joye E. Frost (acting), 307–5983.

Deputy Director.—Barbara Walker, 305–2172.

COMMUNITY CAPACITY DEVELOPMENT OFFICE

Director.—Dennis Greenhouse, 616–1152.
Deputy Director, Policy.—Denise Viera, 616–1152
Associate Director, Programs.—Faith Baker, 305–2586

OFFICE OF ADMINISTRATION

Director.—Phillip K. Merkle, 307–0087.
Deputy Director, Division of:
Acquisition Management.—Nichele C. Robinson, 514–9497.
Human Resources.—Jennifer McCarthy, 616–0389.
Support Services.—Larry A. Sotomayor, 514–8446

OFFICE OF THE CHIEF FINANCIAL OFFICER

Chief Financial Officer.—Leigh Benda, 353–8153.
Deputy Chief Financial Officer.—Ralph Martin, 305–1802.

OFFICE OF THE CHIEF INFORMATION OFFICER

Chief Information Officer.—Walter Iwanow, 305–9071.
Deputy Chief Information Officer.—Angel Santa, 514–9089.

OFFICE FOR CIVIL RIGHTS

Director.—Michael Alston, 307–0690.

OFFICE OF COMMUNICATION

Director.—Sabra Horne, 353–0798.
Deputy Director.—Vacant

OFFICE OF THE GENERAL COUNSEL

General Counsel.—Rafael A. Madan, 307–6235.

OFFICE OF SEX OFFENDER SENTENCING, MONITORING, APPREHENDING, REGISTERING, AND TRACKING

Director.—Linda M. Baldwin, 305–2463.
Deputy Director.—Dawn Doran, 353–3040.

OFFICE OF LEGAL COUNSEL

RFK Main Justice Building, Room 5218, phone (202) 514–2051

Assistant Attorney General.—Vacant.
Deputy Assistant Attorneys General: Daniel Koffsky, room 5238, 514–2030, Cristina Rodriguez, room 5231, 514–9700.
Principal Deputy Assistant Attorney General.—Caroline D. Krass, room 5218, 514–4132.
Special Counsels: Paul P. Colborn, room 5240, 514–2048; Rosemary Hart, room 5242, 514–2027.
Senior Counsel.—Jeffrey Singdahlsen, room 5262, 514–4174.

OFFICE OF LEGAL POLICY

RFK Main Justice Building, Room 4234, phone (202) 514–4601

Assistant Attorney General.—Christopher H. Schroeder, room 4236.

Principal Deputy Assistant Attorney General.—Pamela Harris, room 4238, 353–7206.
Deputy Assistant Attorneys General: Kevin Jones, room 4248, 514–4604; Robyn Thiemann, room 4237, 514–8356; Elana Tyrangiel, room 4228, 514–5651; Michael Zubrensky, room 4229, 514–4606.
Chief of Staff.—Lamar Baker, room 4240, 305–4870.
Executive Officer.—Matrina Matthews, room 4517, 616–0040.

OFFICE OF LEGISLATIVE AFFAIRS

RFK Main Justice Building, Room 1145, phone (202) 514–2141

Assistant Attorney General.—Ronald Weich.
Deputy Assistant Attorneys General: Mark D. Agrast, Judith C. ''Judy'' Appelbaum.

NATIONAL DRUG INTELLIGENCE CENTER (NDIC)

319 Washington Street, Johnstown, PA 15901–1622, phone (814) 532–4601

RFK Main Justice Building, Room 3341, 20530, phone (202) 532–4040

Director.—Michael F. Walther (814) 532–4607.
Deputy Director.—Tony Tomlinson (814) 532–4669.
Chief of Staff.—Steven R. Frank (814) 532–4728.
Chief Counsel.—Kevin M. Walker (814) 532–4660.
Assistant Director for—
Intelligence Division.—Vacant.
Intelligence Support Division.—David J. Mrozowski (814) 532–4926.
Policy and Interagency Affairs.—Joseph E. Donovan (202) 532–4036.
Telephone Directory Coordinator.—Pamela F. Warchola (814) 532–4607.

NATIONAL SECURITY DIVISION

RFK Main Justice Building, Room 7339, phone (202) 514–1057

Assistant Attorney General.—David S. Kris.
Principal Deputy Assistant Attorney General.—Brad Wiegmann.
Deputy Assistant Attorneys General: Tashina Gauhar, Todd Hinnen, George Toscas.
Chief of Staff.—Donald Vieira.
Deputy Chief of Staff.—Brian Nelson.
Counsels to the Assistant Attorney General: Joanna Baltes, Jennifer Daskal, Tom Reilly, James Rybicki.
Special Assistant to the Assistant Attorney General.—Paula Wright.

COUNTERESPIONAGE SECTION

600 E Street, NW., Suite 10606, phone (202) 233–0963

Chief.—John Dion, room 10800.
Deputy Chief.—Steve Pelak.

COUNTERTERRORISM SECTION

Chief.—Michael J. Mullaney, room 2643, 514–0849.
Deputy Chief for—
International Terrorism Unit I.—Sharon Lever.
International Terrorism Unit II.—Jennifer Smith.
Policy, Legislation, and Planning Unit.—Scott Glick.
Terrorist Financing Unit.—Michael Taxay.

OFFICE OF INTELLIGENCE

Counsel for Intelligence Policy.—James A. Baker, room 6150, 514–5600.

Section Chief for—
Litigation.—Nancy Newcomb.
Operations.—Gabriel Sanz-Rexach.
Oversight.—Kevin O'Connor.

OFFICE OF JUSTICE FOR VICTIMS OF OVERSEAS TERRORISM

600 E Street, NW., Suite 10606, 20004

Director.—Mara Kohn (acting), 233–0719.

OFFICE OF THE PARDON ATTORNEY

1425 New York Avenue, NW., 20530, phone (202) 616–6070

Pardon Attorney.—Ronald L. Rodgers.
Deputy Pardon Attorney.—Helen M. Bollwerk.

OFFICE OF PROFESSIONAL RESPONSIBILITY

RFK Main Justice Building, Room 3266, phone (202) 514–3365

Counsel.—Robin C. Ashton.
Deputy Counsel.—Vacant.
Associate Counsels: William J. Birney, Raymond C. "Neil" Hurley, Ruth Plagenhoef (acting).
Senior Assistant Counsel.— Paul Colby.
Assistant Counsels: Mary Aubry, Kathleen Brandon, William Causey, Suzanne Drouet, Mark G. Fraase, Amy Goldfrank, Gregory Gonzalez, Lyn Hardy, Lisa Howard, Frederick Leiner, Cathleen Mahoney, Mark Masling, Noreen McCarthy, Margaret McCarty, Oliver McDaniel, John Tavana, James Vargason, Marlene Wahowiak, Barbara Ward.

PROFESSIONAL RESPONSIBILITY ADVISORY OFFICE

1425 New York Avenue, NW., 20530, phone (202) 514–0458

Director.—Jerri Dunston.
Deputy Director.—Stacy Ludwig.

OFFICE OF PUBLIC AFFAIRS

RFK Main Justice Building, Room 1220, phone (202) 514–2007

Director.—Matthew A. Miller.
Deputy Directors: Tracy Schmaler, Gina M. Talamona.

TAX DIVISION

RFK Main Justice Building, 950 Pennsylvania Avenue, NW., 20530

Judiciary Center Building, 555 Fourth Street, NW., 20001 (JCB)

Maxus Energy Tower, 7717 North Harwood Street, Suite 400, Dallas, TX 75242 (MAX)

Patrick Henry Building, 601 D Street, NW., 20004 (PHB)

Assistant Attorney General.—John A. DiCicco (acting), room 4141 (202) 514–2901.
Deputy Assistant Attorneys General: Ronald A. Cimino, room 4613 (Main) 514–2915 (Criminal Matters); D. Patrick Mullarkey (acting), room 4609 (Main), 307–6533 (Civil Trial Matters); Gilbert S. Rothenberg (acting), room 4333 (Main), 514–3361 (Appellate and Review). Vacant, room 4607 (Main) (Policy and Planning).
Senior Legislative Counsel.—Eileen M. Shatz, room 4134 (Main), 307–6419.
Chief of Staff.—Noreene C. Stehlik, room 4140 (Main), 514–6489.
Civil Trial Section Chiefs:
Central Region.—Seth Heald (JCB), room 8921–B, 514–6502.
Eastern Region.—David A. Hubbert (JCB) room 6126, 307–6426.

Northern Region.—Gerald C. Miller (acting), (JCB), room 7804–A, 307–6490.
Southern Region.—Michael Kearns (JCB), room 6243–A, 514–5905.
Southwestern Region.—Louise P. Hytken (MAX), room 4100 (214) 880–9725.
Western Region.—Richard R. Ward (JCB), room 7907–B, 307–6413.
Criminal Enforcement Section Chiefs:
Northern Region.—Rosemary E. Paguni (PHB), room 7334, 514–2323.
Southern Region.—Bruce Salad (PHB), room 7640, 514–5112.
Western Region.—Mitchell J. Ballweg (acting), (PHB), room 7038, 514–5072.
Section Chiefs:
Appellate.—Gilbert S. Rothenberg, room 4333, 514–3361.
Court of Federal Claims.—Steven I. Frahm (JCB), room 8804–A, 307–6440.
Criminal Appeals and Tax Enforcement Policy.—Frank Cihlar (PHB), room 7101, 514–2839.
Office of Review.—Deborah Meland (JCB), room 6846, 307–6567.
Executive Officer.—Joseph E. Young (PHB), room 7802, 616–0010.

UNITED STATES MARSHALS SERVICE (USMS)

Washington, DC 20530–1000

[Use (202) for 307 exchange and (703) for 557, 603, 416 and 285 exchanges]

fax (202) 307–5040

Director.—Stacia A. Hylton (202) 307–9000.
Deputy Director.—Chris Dudley, 307–9000.
Chief of Staff.—David Anderson (acting), 307–9841.
Associate Director for Administration.—Don Donovan, 307–9028.
Associate Director for Operations.—Robert J. Finan II, 307–9136.
Chief, Congressional Affairs.—Doug Disrud, 307–9220, fax 307–5228.
Deputy Chief, Congressional Affairs.—Jennifer Eskra, 307–9220.
Chief, Public Affairs.—Jeff Carter, 353–1469, fax 307–8729.
Deputy Chief, Public Affairs.—Steve Blando, 307–9344.

EQUAL EMPLOYMENT OPPORTUNITY (EEO)

Chief.—Marcus Williams, 307–9048, fax 307–8765.

OFFICE OF THE GENERAL COUNSEL (OGC)

Chief.—Gerald M. Auerbach, 307–9054, fax 307–9456.
Principal Deputy General Counsel.—Lisa Dickinson, 307–9054.

OFFICE OF INSPECTION (OI)

Chief.—Herman Brewer, Jr., 307–9155.

ASSET FORFEITURE DIVISION (AFD)

Assistant Director.—Eben Morales, 307–9221, fax 307–5020.

FINANCIAL SERVICES DIVISION (FSD)

Assistant Director.—Albert Hemphill, 307–9027, fax 353–8340.
Deputy Assistant Director.—Jim Murphy, 307–8711.

HUMAN RESOURCES DIVISION (HRD)

Assistant Director.—Darla K. Callaghan, 307–9871, fax 307–9461.
Deputy Assistant Director.—Cheryl Jacobs, 307–9423.

INFORMATION TECHNOLOGY DIVISION (ITD)

Assistant Director.—Lisa Davis, (703) 604–2296, fax 307–5130.

Deputy Assistant Director.—Judd Nicholson. 604–2054.

MANAGEMENT SUPPORT DIVISION (MSD)

Assistant Director.—Shannon Brown, 307–9307, fax 353–7827.

TRAINING DIVISION

Assistant Director.—Bill Fallon, (912) 267–2505, fax 267–2882.

INVESTIGATIVE OPERATIONS DIVISION (IOD)

Assistant Director.—T. Michael Earp, 307–9195, fax 307–9299.
Deputy Assistant Director.—Geoff Shank, 307–9043.

JUSTICE PRISONER AND ALIEN TRANSPORTATION SYSTEM (JPATS)

Assistant Director.—Scott C. Rolstad, Kansas City, MO (816) 467–1900, fax 467–1980.

JUDICIAL SECURITY DIVISION (JSD)

Assistant Director.—Michael J. Prout, 307–9500, fax 307–5206.
Judicial Operations, Deputy Assistant Director.—Carl Caulk, 353–5257.
Judicial Services, Deputy Assistant Director.—Steven Conboy, 307–4987.

PRISONER OPERATIONS DIVISION (POD)

Assistant Director.—Candra S. Symonds, 307–5100, fax 307–9234.

TACTICAL OPERATIONS DIVISION (TOD)

Assistant Director.—William Snelson, 307–3437, fax 307–3446.

WITNESS SECURITY DIVISION (WSD)

Assistant Director.—Sylvester E. Jones, 307–9862, fax 353–8327.
Deputy Assistant Director.—Tom Wight, 307–9862.

U.S. PAROLE COMMISSION

5550 Friendship Boulevard, Suite 420, Chevy Chase, MD 20815, phone (301) 492–5990 fax 492–6694

Chairman.—Isaac Fulwood, Jr.
Vice Chairman.—Cranston J. Mitchell.
Commissioners: Patricia A. Cushwa, J. Patricia Wilson Smoot.
Special Assistant to the Chairman.—Albert H. Herring.
Case Operations Administrator.—Stephen J. Husk.
Case Service Administrator.—Deirdre M. Jackson.
General Counsel.—Rockne J. Chickinell.
Chief Information Officer.—Jonathan H. Pinkerton.
Executive Officer.—Judy I. Carter.
Staff Assistant to the Chairman.—Patricia W. Moore.

OFFICE ON VIOLENCE AGAINST WOMEN

145 N Street, NE., Suites 10W & 10E, 20530

Director.—Hon. Susan B. Carbon (202) 307–3876.
Deputy Director for Tribal Affairs.—Lorraine Edmo, 514–8804.
Senior Policy Advisor.—Anna Martinez, 514–6975.
Deputy Director for Policy Development.—Virginia Davis, 305–9660.

Associate Directors: Michelle Brickley, 514–3590; Darlene Johnson, 307–6795; Lauren Nassikas, 305–1792; Nadine Neufville, 305–2590; Donna Simmons, 514–1015; Susan Williams, 616–3851.

DEPARTMENT OF THE INTERIOR

Interior Building, 1849 C Street, NW., 20240, phone (202) 208–3100, http://www.doi.gov

KEN SALAZAR, Secretary of the Interior; born in Alamosa, CO, March 2, 1955; education: J.D., University of Michigan Law School; B.A., Colorado College; professional: United States Senator from Colorado, 2005–09; Attorney General of Colorado, 1999–2005; Executive Director, Colorado Department of Natural Resources, 1990–94; chief legal counsel to Governor Roy Romer, 1987–90; Natural Resources Lawyer, Small Business Owner, Farmer; member, Colorado College Board of Trustees; chair, Conference of Western Attorneys General; chair, National Association of Attorneys General Environment Committee; chair, Colorado Peace Officers Standards and Training Board; chair, Rio Grande Compact Commission; chair, Sangre de Cristo Land Grant Commission; chair, Great Outdoors Colorado; religion: Roman Catholic; married: Hope; children: Melinda and Andrea; granddaughter: Mireya; nominated by President Barack Obama to become the 50th Secretary of the Interior, and was confirmed by the U.S. Senate on January 20, 2009.

OFFICE OF THE SECRETARY

Secretary of the Interior.—Ken Salazar, room 6156, 208–7351.
Special Assistant/Director, Scheduling and Advance.—Joan Padilla, room 6043.
Special Assistant.—Terri Johnson.
Chief of Staff.—Laura Davis, room 6144.
Deputy Chief of Staff.—Matt Lee-Ashley, room 6140.
Senior Advisor for Economic Recovery.—Chris Henderson, room 6122, 208–7471.
Senior Advisor to the Secretary.—Kenneth ''Ken'' Lane, room 6142.
Director of External and Intergovernmental Affairs.—Gail Adams, room 6311, 208–1923.
Senior Advisor for Alaska Affairs.—Kim Elton, room 6325, 208–4177.
Counselor to the Secretary.—Steve Black, room 6130, 208–4123.

EXECUTIVE SECRETARIAT

Director.—Fay Iudicello, room 7314, 208–3181.

CONGRESSIONAL AND LEGISLATIVE AFFAIRS

Director.—Christopher Mansour, room 6358, 208–7264.
Deputy Directors: Lara Levison, room 6346; Heather Urban, room 6344.
Legislative Counsel.—Chris Salotti, room 6357.

OFFICE OF COMMUNICATIONS

Director.—Matt Lee-Ashley, room 6140, 208–6415.
Deputy Director.—Kendra Barkoff.
Press Secretary.—Kendra Barkoff.
New Media Director.—Tim Fullerton.
Information Officers: Joan Moody, Frank Quimby, Hugh Vickery.

OFFICE OF THE DEPUTY SECRETARY

Deputy Secretary.—David Hayes, room 6117, 208–6291.
Special Assistant to the Deputy Secretary.—Courtenay Lewis, room 6125, 208–3744.
Associate Deputy Secretary.—Meghan Conklin, room 6117, 208–6291.
Science Advisor to the Deputy Secretary.—Vacant.

ASSISTANT SECRETARY FOR FISH AND WILDLIFE AND PARKS

Assistant Secretary.—Will Shafroth (acting), room 3160 (202) 208–5347.
Principal Deputy Assistant Secretary.—Will Shafroth, room 3159, 208–5347.
Deputy Assistant Secretaries: Jane Lyder, room 3144, 208–4416; Eileen Sobeck, room 3151, 208–4416.
Chief of Staff.—Melissa Koenigsberg, room 3140, 208–4416.
Counsel to Assistant Secretary.—Michael Bean, room 3152, 508–4416.

U.S. FISH AND WILDLIFE SERVICE

Director.—Vacant (202) 208–4717.
Deputy Director.—Dan Ashe, 208–4545.
Acting Deputy Directors: Rowan Gould, 208–4545; Greg Siekaniec, 208–4545.
Chief, Office of Law Enforcement.—William Woody, 208–3809.
Assistant Director for External Affairs.—Elizabeth H. Stevens, 208–6541.
Chief, Division of:
Congressional and Legislative Affairs.—Matt Auggler (703) 358–2243.
Public Affairs.—Chris Tollefson (703) 358–2222.
Assistant Director for—
Migratory Birds.—Paul Schmidt, 208–1050.
Budget, Planning, and Human Capital.—Denise Sheehan (703) 358–2400.
Business Management and Operations.—Paul Henne (703) 358–1822.
Endangered Species.—Gary Frazer, 208–4646.
Fisheries and Habitat Conservation.—Brian Arroyo, 208–6394.
Information Resources and Technology Management.—Kenneth Taylor (703) 358–1729.
International Affairs.—Teiko Saito, 208–6393.
Wildlife and Sport Fish Restoration.—Hannibal Bolton, 208–7337.
Chief, National Wildlife Refuge System.—Gregory Siekaniec, 208–5333.
Regional Directors:
Region 1.—Robyn Thorson, Eastside Federal Complex, 911 Northeast 11th Avenue, Portland, OR 97232 (503) 231–6118, fax 872–2716.
Region 2.—Benjamin Tuggle, Room 1306, 500 Gold Avenue, SW., Albuquerque, NM 87103 (505) 248–6845, fax (503) 872–2716.
Region 3.—Thomas Melius, Federal Building, Fort Snelling, Twin Cities, MN 55111 (612) 713–5301, fax 713–5284.
Region 4.—Cynthia Dohner, 1875 Century Boulevard, Atlanta, GA 30345 (404) 679–4000, fax 679–4006.
Region 5.—Marvin Moriarty, 300 Westgate Center Drive, Hadley, MA 01035 (413) 253–8300, fax 253–8308.
Region 6.—Stephen Guertin, 134 Union Boulevard, #400, Lakewood, CO 80228 (303) 236–7920, fax 236–8295.
Region 7.—Geoff Hasketts, 1011 East Tudor Road, Anchorage, AK 99503 (907) 786–3542, fax 786–3306.
Region 8.—Renne Lohoefener, 2800 Cottage Way, #W2606, Sacramento, CA 95825 (916) 414–6464, fax 414–6484.

NATIONAL PARK SERVICE

Director.—Jon Jarvis, room 3112 (202) 208–4621.
Deputy Director, Operations.—Peggy O'Dell, room 3113, 208–3818.
Deputy Director, Communications and Community Assistance.—Mickey Fearn, room 3116, 208–4621.
Chief of Staff.—Maureen Foster, room 3114, 208–3818.
Associate Director for—
Business Services.—Kate Stevenson, room 2274, 208–5651.
Cultural Resources.—Stephanie Toothman, room 3128, 208–7625.
Interpretation and Education.—Julia Washburn, room 3129, 208–4829.
Natural Resource Stewardship and Science.—Bert Frost, room 3130, 208–3884.
Park Planning, Facilities and Lands.—Steve Whitesell, room 3124, 208–3264.
Partnerships and Civic Engagement.—Rich Weideman (acting), room 3129, 208–4829.
Visitor and Resource Protection.—Steve Shackelton, room 3120, 565–1020.
Workforce Management.—Jerry Simpson, room 3129, 208–5587.
Comptroller.—Bruce Sheaffer, room 2280, 208–4566.
Assistant Director, Legislative and Congressional Affairs.—Don Hellman, room 3309, 208–5656.

Assistant Director, Office of Communications.—Sue Waldron, room 3320, 208–3046.

Regional Directors:

Alaska.—Sue Masica, 240 West Fifth Avenue, Room 114, Anchorage, AK 99501 (907) 644–3510, fax 644–3816.

Intermountain.—John Wessels, P.O. Box 25287, 12795 West Alameda Parkway, Denver, CO 80225 (303) 969–2500, fax 969–2785.

Midwest.—Michael Reynolds, 601 Riverfront Drive, Omaha, NE 68102 (402) 661–1736, fax 661–1737.

National Capital.—Woody Smeck (acting), 1100 Ohio Drive, SW., Washington, DC 20242 (202) 619–7000, fax 619–7220.

Northeast.—Dennis Reidenbach, U.S. Custom House, 200 Chestnut Street, Suite 306, Philadelphia, PA 19106 (215) 597–7013, fax 597–0815.

Southeast.—David Vela, 100 Alabama Street, NW., 1924 Building, Atlanta, GA 30303 (404) 562–3327, fax 562–3216.

Pacific West.—Christine Lehnertz, 1111 Jackson Street, Suite 700, Oakland, CA 94607 (510) 817–1304, fax 817–1485.

ASSISTANT SECRETARY FOR INDIAN AFFAIRS

Assistant Secretary.—Larry Echo Hawk, room 4160, 208–7163.

Principal Deputy Assistant Secretary.—Del Laverdure, room 4151, 208–7163.

Deputy Assistant Secretary for—

Management.—George Skibine, 208–7163.

Policy and Economic Development.—Jodi Gillette, 208–7163.

Director of:

Congressional Affairs.—Darren Pete, 208–5610.

Public Affairs.—Nedra Darling, 219–4150.

BUREAU OF INDIAN AFFAIRS

Director.—Mike Black (202) 208–5116.

Deputy Director of:

Field Operations.—Michael Smith, 208–5116.

Justice Services.—Darren Cruzan, 208–5787.

Tribal Services.—Kevin Bearquiver, 208–2874.

Trust Services.—Darryl LaCounte, 208–7513.

BUREAU OF INDIAN EDUCATION

Director.—Keith Moore (202) 208–6123.

ASSISTANT SECRETARY FOR LAND AND MINERALS MANAGEMENT

Assistant Secretary.—Wilma Lewis, room 6612 (202) 208–6734.

Deputy Assistant Secretaries: Sylvia Baca, room 6625; Ned Farquhar, room 6614.

BUREAU OF LAND MANAGEMENT

Director.—Robert V. Abbey, room 5661 (202) 208–3801.

Deputy Director of:

Operations.—Mike Pool.

Programs and Policy.—Marcilynn Burke.

Division Chief, Legislative Affairs and Correspondence.—Patrick Wilkerson, 452–5010.

Deputy Division Chief.—Andrea Nelson.

State Directors:

Alaska.—Bud Cribley, 222 West Seventh Avenue, No. 13, Anchorage, AK 99513 (907) 271–5080, fax 271–4596.

Arizona.—Jim Kenna, One North Central Avenue, Phoenix, AZ 85004 (602) 417–9500, fax 417–9398.

California.—Jim Abbott (acting), 2800 Cottage Way, Suite W1834, Sacramento, CA 95825 (916) 978–4600, fax 978–4699.

Colorado.—Helen Hankins, 2850 Youngfield Street, Lakewood, CO 80215 (303) 239–3700, fax 239–3934.

Eastern States.—Tim Spisak (acting), 7450 Boston Boulevard, Springfield, VA 22153 (703) 440–1700, fax 440–1701.
Idaho.—Steven Ellis, 1387 South Vinnell Way, Boise, ID 83709 (208) 373–4000, fax 373–3919.
Montana.—Jamie Connell, 5001 Southgate Drive, Billings, MT 59101 (406) 896–5012, fax 896–5004.
Nevada.—Amy Lueders (acting), 1340 Financial Boulevard, Reno, NV 89502 (775) 861–6590, fax 861–6601.
New Mexico.—Linda S.C. Rundell, 1474 Rodeo Road, P.O. Box 27115, Sante Fe, NM 87505 (505) 438–7501, fax 438–7452.
Oregon.—Ed Shepard, 333 Southwest 1st Avenue, P.O. Box 2965, Portland, OR 97204 (503) 808–6024, fax 808–6308.
Utah.—Juan Palma, 440 West 200 South, Suite 500, P.O. Box 45155, Salt Lake City, UT 84101 (801) 539–4010, fax 539–4013.
Wyoming.—Don Simpson, 5353 Yellowstone Road, P.O. Box 1828, Cheyenne, WY 82003 (307) 775–6001, fax 775–6028.

BUREAU OF OCEAN ENERGY MANAGEMENT, REGULATION AND ENFORCEMENT

Director.—Michael E. Bromwich (202) 208–3500.
Deputy Director.—Walter D. Cruickshank.
Associate Director for—
Administration and Budget.—Robert E. Brown, 208–3220.
Offshore Energy and Minerals Management.—Bob LaBelle, 208–3530.
Policy and Management Improvement.—George F. Triebsch, 208–3398.
Congressional Affairs:
Director.—M. Lyn Herdt, 208–3502, fax 208–3918.
Outer Continental Shelf Regional Directors:
Alaska.—James Kendall (acting), 949 East 36th Avenue, Suite 300, Anchorage, AK 99508 (907) 334–5200.
Gulf of Mexico.—Lars T. Herbst, 1201 Elmwood Park Boulevard, New Orleans, LA 70123 (504) 736–2589.
Pacific.—Ellen G. Aronson, 770 Paseo Camarillo, Camarillo, CA 93010 (805) 389–7502.

OFFICE OF SURFACE MINING RECLAMATION AND ENFORCEMENT

Director.—Joseph G. Pizerchik, room 233 (202) 208–4006.
Deputy Director.—Glenda Owens, 208–4006.
Assistant Director for Finance and Administration.—Ted Woronka, 208–2546.
Congressional Contact.—Peter Mali, 208–2566.
Regional Director for—
Appalachian Coordinating Center.—Thomas D. Shope, Three Parkway Center, Pittsburgh, PA 15220 (412) 937–2828, fax 937–2903.
Mid-Continent Coordinating Center.—Ervin Barchenger, 501 Belle Street, Room 216, Alton, IL 62002 (618) 463–6463, fax 463–6470.
Western Coordinating Center.—Allen Klein, 1999 Broadway, Suite 3320, Denver, CO 80202 (303) 844–1401, fax 844–1522.

ASSISTANT SECRETARY FOR POLICY, MANAGEMENT AND BUDGET

Assistant Secretary.—Rhea Suh, room 5110 (202) 208–1927.
Deputy Assistant Secretary for—
Budget, Finance, Performance and Acquisition.—Pam Haze, 208–4775.
Human Capital and Diversity.—Pam Malam, 208–1738.
Law Enforcement, Security and Emergency Management.—Kim Thorsen, 208–5773.
Natural Resources Revenue.—Greg Gould (acting), 208–3096.
Office of Youth in the Great Outdoors.—Julie Rodriguez, 208–1508.
Policy and International Affairs.—Lori Faeth, 208–4852.
Technology, Information and Business Services.—Andrew Jackson, 208–7966.
Youth, Partnership and Service.—Vacant, 208–1508.

ASSISTANT SECRETARY FOR WATER AND SCIENCE

Assistant Secretary.—Anne J. Castle, room 6657 (202) 208–3186.

Principal Deputy Assistant Secretary.—John Tubbs.
Deputy Assistant Secretary.—Lori Caramanian (acting).
Chief of Staff.—Kerry Rae, room 6645, 513–0535.

U.S. GEOLOGICAL SURVEY

The National Center, 12201 Sunrise Valley Drive, Reston, VA 20192

phone (703) 648–7411, fax 648–4454

Director.—Marsha McNutt.
Deputy Director.—Suzette M. Kimball, 648–7412.
Chief of Staff.—Judy Nowakowski (703) 648–4411.
Office of:
Administrative Policy and Services.—Karen Baker, 648–7200.
Budget and Performance.—Carla Burzyk, 648–4443.
Communications and Outreach.—Barbara Wainman, 648–5750.
Congressional Liaison Officer.—Timothy J. West, 648–4300.
Human Capital.—Ralph Charlip, 648–7414.
Public Affairs Officer.—Anne-Berry Wade, 648–4483.
Associate Directors for—
Climate and Land Use Change.—Matthew Larsen (703) 648–5212.
Core Science Systems.—Kevin Gallagher, 648–5747.
Ecosystems.—Anne Kinsinger, 648–4050.
Energy and Minerals, and Environmental Health.—Ione Taylor, 648–6403.
Natural Hazards.—William Leith (acting), 648–6600.
Water Resources.—William Werkheiser, 648–4557.
Regional Executives for—
Northeast Area.—David Russ (703) 648–6600.
Southeast Area.—Jess Weaver, USGS Southeast Regional Office, 3850 Holcomb Bridge Road, Suite 160, Norcross, GA 30092, (770) 409–7701.
Midwest Area.—Leon Carl, USGS Midwest Regional Office, 1451 Green Road, Anne Arbor, MI 48105, (734) 214–7201.
South Central Area.—Max Ethridge, USGS South Central Regional Office, 4200 New Haven Road, Columbia, MO 65201, (573) 777–1661.
Rocky Mountain Area.—Randall Updike, P.O. Box 25046, Denver Federal Center, Building 810, Denver, CO 80225, (303) 236–5438.
Pacific Northwest Area.—Leslie Dierauf, USGS Pacific Northwest Regional Office, Federal Office Building, 909 First Avenue, 8th Floor, Seattle, WA 98104, (206) 220–4600.
Pacific Southwest Area.—Michael Shulters, USGS Pacific Southwest Regional Office, Menlo Park Campus, Building 3, 345 Middlefield Road, Menlo Park, CA 94025, (916) 278–9551.
Alaska.—Leslie Holland-Bartels, USGS Alaska Regional Office, 4230 University Drive, Suite 201, Anchorage, AK 99508, (907) 786–7055.

BUREAU OF RECLAMATION

Commissioner.—Michael Connor, room 7657 (202) 513–0501.
Deputy Commissioner for—
External and Intergovernmental Affairs.—Kira Finkler, room 7645, 513–0615.
Operations.—David Murillo, room 7653, 513–0617.
Policy, Administration, and Budget.—Grayford Payne, room 7650, 513–0542.
Chief of Staff.—Robert Quint, room 7641.
Chief of:
Congressional and Legislative Affairs.—Dionne Thompson, room 7643, 513–0570.
Public Affairs.—Daniel J. DuBray, room 7644, 513–0574.
Regional Directors:
Great Plains.—Michael J. Ryan, P.O. Box 36900, Billings, MT 59107 (406) 247–7795, fax 247–7793.
Lower Colorado.—Lorri Gray-Lee, P.O. Box 61470, Boulder City, NV 89006 (702) 293–8000, fax 293–8614.
Mid-Pacific.—Donald Glaser, 2800 Cottage Way, Sacramento, CA 95825 (916) 978–5580, fax 978–5599.
Pacific Northwest.—Karl Wirkus, 1150 North Curtis Road, Suite 100, Boise, ID 83706 (208) 378–5127, fax 378–5129.
Upper Colorado.—Larry Walkoviak, 125 South State Street, room 6107, Salt Lake City, UT 84138 (801) 524–3785, fax 524–5499.

OFFICE OF INSPECTOR GENERAL

Inspector General.—Mary Kendall (acting), room 4410 (202) 208–5745.
Deputy Inspector General.—Vacant, room 4420.
Associate Inspector General for Whistleblower Protection.—Laurie Larson-Jackson, room 4416.
Associate Inspector General for External Affairs.—Kris Kolesnik, room 4445.

OFFICE OF THE SOLICITOR

Solicitor.—Hilary C. Tompkins, room 6415 (202) 208–4423.
Principal Deputy Solicitor.—Rachel Jacobson.
Deputy Solicitors: Arthur E. Gary, Jack Haugrud, Patrice Kunesh.
Associate Solicitor for—
General Law.—Ed Keable.
Indian Affairs.—Edith Blackwell.
Land and Water.—Laura Brown.
Mineral Resources.—Karen Hawbecker.
Parks and Wildlife.—Barry Roth.
Counselor to Solicitor for Indian Trust Litigation.—Sarah Greenberger.
Senior Counsel CADR.—Shayla Simmons.
Designated Agency Ethics Official.—Melinda Loftin, 208–5295.

OFFICE OF THE SPECIAL TRUSTEE FOR AMERICAN INDIANS

Principal Deputy Special Trustee.—Ray Joseph, room 2611 (202) 208–4866.

DEPARTMENT OF AGRICULTURE

Jamie L. Whitten Building, 1400 Independence Avenue, SW., 20250
phone (202) 720–3631, http://www.usda.gov

TOM VILSACK, Secretary of Agriculture; education: B.A., Hamilton College; J.D., Albany Law School; professional: Governor, Iowa, 1999–2007; nominated by President Barack Obama to become the 30th Secretary of Agriculture, and was confirmed by the U.S. Senate on January 20, 2009.

OFFICE OF THE SECRETARY

Secretary of Agriculture.—Tom Vilsack, room 200–A (202) 720–3631.
Deputy Secretary.—Kathleen Merrigan.
Chief of Staff.—Krysta Harden.
Deputy Chief of Staff.—Carole Jett.

ASSISTANT SECRETARY FOR ADMINISTRATION

Jamie L. Whitten Building, Room 240–W, phone (202) 720–3291

Assistant Secretary.—Pearlie S. Reed.
Deputy Assistant Secretaries: Robin Heard, Dr. Alma C. Hobbs.
Executive Assistants: Tiffany Brooks, Shirley Hill, Francesca Yabraian.
Chief of Staff.—Roberta S. Jeanquart.
Special Assistant.—James Gore.

OFFICE OF ADMINISTRATIVE LAW JUDGES

South Agriculture Building, Room 1070–S, phone (202) 720–6383

Chief Administrative Law Judge.—Peter Davenport.
Secretary to the Chief Administrative Law Judge.—Diane Green.
Administrative Law Judges: Jill S. Clifton, Victor W. Palmer, 720–8161.
Hearing Clerk.—Leslie E. Whitfield, 720–4443.

OFFICE OF HUMAN RESOURCES MANAGEMENT

Jamie L. Whitten Building, Room 302–W, phone (202) 720–3585

Director.—Karen Messmore.
Secretary.—Melanie Clemons.
Deputy Director.—William Milton.
Division Director for—
Departmental Human Resources and Executive Resources.—Rhonda Carr, 720–2101.
Employee Recruitment/Development.—Monshi Radass, 720–5618.

OFFICE OF THE JUDICIAL OFFICER

South Agriculture Building, Room 1449–S, phone (202) 720–4764

Judicial Officer.—William G. Jenson.
Attorney.—Stephen Reilly.
Legal Technician.—Gloria Derobertis.

OFFICE OF MANAGEMENT SERVICES

Office of Management Services.—Rick Swenson (202) 720–9824.

Secretary.—Nanette McGraw.
Director of:
Budget Formulation Division.—Telora Dean, 690–1331.

OFFICE OF OPERATIONS

South Agriculture Building, Room 1456–S, phone (202) 720–3937

Director.—John Crew.
Director, Office of:
Facilities.—Valencia Winstead, 720–2804.
Management Services.—Morris Tate.
Director for—
Beltsville Service Center.—Randall Carter, (301) 394–0410.
Mail and Reproduction.—Michele Lambert, 720–8393.
Washington Area Service Center.—Steve Law, 720–2777.

OFFICE OF PROCUREMENT AND PROPERTY MANAGEMENT

Reporters Building, Room 302, phone (202) 720–9448

Director.—Lisa Wilusz.
Division Director for—
Procurement Operations.—Shawn Kerkes, 690–0142.
Procurement Policy.—Dorothy Lilly, 690–1060.
Procurement Systems.—Vacant, 401–1023.
Property Management.—Vacant, 720–7283.
Radiation Safety.—Vacant (301) 504–2440.

OFFICE OF HOMELAND SECURITY

Director.—Todd Repass, room S–310 (202) 720–0272.
Division Chief for—
Continuity of Operations Planning.—Jessica Fantinato, 720–2667.
Personnel and Document Security.—Richard Coleman, 720–7373.
Physical Security.—Richard Holman, 720–3901.
Director, Office of:
Emergency Programs.—James Redington, 690–3191.
Protective Operations.—John Stroud, 720–6270.

OFFICE OF SMALL AND DISADVANTAGED BUSINESS UTILIZATION

South Agriculture Building, Room 1085–S, phone (202) 720–7117

Director.—Quinton Robinson.

ASSISTANT SECRETARY FOR CIVIL RIGHTS

Jamie L. Whitten Building, Room 240–W, phone (202) 720–3808

Assistant Secretary.—Joe Leonard, Jr., Ph.D.
Deputy Assistant Secretary.—Fred Pfaeffle.

OFFICE OF BUDGET AND PROGRAM ANALYSIS

Jamie L. Whitten Building, Room 101–A, phone (202) 720–3323

Director.—Michael L. Young.
Associate Director.—Don Bice, 720–5303.
Deputy Director for—
Budget, Legislative and Regulatory Systems.—Diem-Linh Jones, room 102–E, 720–6667.
Program Analysis.—Christopher Zehren, room 126–W, 720–3396.

OFFICE OF THE CHIEF ECONOMIST

Jamie L. Whitten Building, Room 112–A, phone (202) 720–4164

Chief Economist.—Joseph W. Glauber.
Deputy Chief Economist.—James Hrubovcak, room 112–A, 720–4737.
Chairperson, World Agricultural Outlook Board.—Gerald A. Bange, room 4419–S, 720–6030.
Chief Meteorologist.—Ray Motha, room 4441–S, 720–8651.
Global Change Program Office.—William Hohenstein, room 4407–S, 720–6698.
Office of Energy Policy and New Uses.—Harry Baumes, room 4059–S, 401–0461.
Office of Risk Assessment and Cost Benefit Analysis.—James D. Schaub, room 4032–S, 720–8022.
Office of Sustainable Development.—Carol Kramer-LeBlanc, room 112–A, 720–2456.
Supervisory Meteorologist, National Weather Service.—Brad Pugh, room 4443–S, 720–6030.

OFFICE OF THE CHIEF FINANCIAL OFFICER

Jamie L. Whitten Building, Room 143–W, phone (202) 720–5539

Chief Financial Officer.—Vacant.
Deputy Chief Financial Officer.—Jon M. Holladay, room 143–W, 720–0727.
Associate Chief Financial Officers for—
Financial Operations.—John Brewer, room 3053–S, 720–9427.
Financial Policy and Planning.—Vacant.
Financial Systems.—Michael Clanton, room 3057–S, 690–3068.
Director, National Finance Center.—John White, P.O. Box 60000, New Orleans, LA 70160 (504) 426–0120.

OFFICE OF THE CHIEF INFORMATION OFFICER

Jamie L. Whitten Building, Room 414–W, phone (202) 720–8833

Chief Information Officer.—Chris L. Smith (acting).
Deputy Chief Information Officer for Cyber Security and Privacy Information Operations.—Chris L. Smith.
Deputy Chief Information Officer for Policy and Architecture.—Charles McClam, 690–3361.
Associate Chief Information Officer for—
Cyber and Privacy Policy and Oversight.—Richard Coffee (acting), 690–0048.
Data Center Operations (National Information Technology Center).—Kent Armstrong, 8930 Ward Parkway, Kansas City, MO 64114, (816) 926–6501.
International Security Operations Center.—Chris Lowe (acting), 720–5939.
International Technology Services.—David Shearer, 2150 Centre Avenue, Building A, Fort Collins, CO 80526 (970) 295–5020.
Director for—
E-Learning-AgLearn.—Jerome Davin, 694–0006.
Innovations and Operational Architecture.—Owen Unangst, 2150 Centre Avenue, Building A, Fort Collins, CO 80526, (970) 295–5538.
Resource Management.—Lisa Keeter, 720–4109.
Telecommunications Services and Operations.—John Donovan, 720–8695.

OFFICE OF COMMUNICATIONS

Jamie L. Whitten Building, Room 402–A, phone (202) 720–4623

Director.—Chris Mather.
Deputy Directors: David Black, Justin DeJong.
Press Secretaries: Tom Fazzini, Courtney Rowe.
Center Director for—
Broadcast Media and Technology.—Garth Clark.
Constituent Affairs.—Vacant.
Creative Services.—Carolyn O'Connor.
Information Technology.—Wayne Moore.
Web Communication.—Amanda Eamich (acting).

OFFICE OF CONGRESSIONAL RELATIONS

Jamie L. Whitten Building, Room 212–A, phone (202) 720–7095

Assistant Secretary.—John Berge (acting).
Deputy Assistant Secretary.—John Berge.
Congressional Liaison for—
Farm and Foreign Agricultural Service.—Lilia McFarland.
Food Safety and Food, Nutrition and Consumer Services.—Erin Hannigan.
Marketing and Regulatory Programs/Rural Development.—Rebecca Blue.
Natural Resources and Environment.—Lilia McFarland.
Research, Economics and Education.—Franz Hochstrasser.

EXTERNAL AND INTERGOVERNMENTAL AFFAIRS

Room 216–A, phone (202) 720–6643

Director.—Jennifer Yezak.
Deputy Director.—Oscar Gonzales.

OFFICE OF TRIBAL AFFAIRS

Room 544–A, phone (202) 690–1615

Director.—Janie Hipp.

OFFICE OF THE EXECUTIVE SECRETARIAT

Jamie L. Whitten Building, Room 116–A, phone (202) 720–7100

Director.—Greg Diephouse.
Deputy Director.—David Aten.

GENERAL COUNSEL

Jamie L. Whitten Building, Room 107–W, phone (202) 720–3351

General Counsel.—Ramona Romero.
Deputy General Counsel.—Steve Silverman.
Associate General Counsel for—
Civil Rights.—Arlean Leland, 720–1760.
International Affairs, Commodity Programs and Food Assistance Programs.—Ralph Linden, 720–6883.
Legislation, Litigation, General Law.—James Michael Kelly, 720–3351.
Marketing, Regulatory and Food Safety Programs.—John Golden, 720–3155.
Natural Resources.—Thomas Millett, 720–9311.
Rural Development.—David P. Grahn, 720–6187.
Assistant General Counsel, Division of:
Community Development.—Vacant, 720–4591.
Conservation and Environment.—Stuart L. Shelton, 720–7121.
Food and Nutrition.—Kevin Meckus (acting), 720–6181.
General Law.—L. Benjamin Young, Jr., 720–5565.
International Affairs and Commodity Programs Division.—Peter Bonner, 720–9246.
Legislation.—Michael J. Knipe, 720–5354.
Litigation.—Leslie Lagomarcino, 720–4733.
Marketing.—Kenneth H. Vail, 720–5935.
Natural Resources.—Thomas Millet, 720–7121.
Regulatory.—Thomas M. Walsh, 720–5550.
Rural Utilities.—Terence M. Brady, 720–2764.
Trade Practices.—Vacant, 720–5293.
Director, Administration and Resource Management.—Charlene Buckner, 720–6324.
Resource Management Specialist.—Robyn Davis, 720–4861.

INSPECTOR GENERAL

Jamie L. Whitten Building, Room 117–W, phone (202) 720–8001, fax 690–1278

Inspector General.—Phyllis K. Fong.
Deputy Inspector General.—David Gray.
Assistant Inspector General for—
Audit.—Gil Harden, room 403–E, 720–6945.
Investigations.—Karen Ellis, room 507–A, 720–3306.
Management.—Suzanne Murrin, room 5–E, 720–6979.

NATIONAL APPEALS DIVISION

3101 Park Center Drive, Suite 1100, Alexandria, VA 22302

Director.—Roger J. Klurfeld (703) 305–2708.

UNDER SECRETARY FOR NATURAL RESOURCES AND ENVIRONMENT

Jamie L. Whitten Building, Room 217–E, phone (202) 720–7173

Deputy Under Secretaries: Jay Jensen, Ann Mills.

FOREST SERVICE

Sydney R. Yates Building, 201 14th Street, SW., 20250, phone (202) 205–1661

Chief.—Thomas Tidwell.
Associate Chief.—Mary Wagner, 205–1779.
Director for—
International Programs.—Valdis E. Mezainis, 205–1650.
Law Enforcement and Investigations.—David Ferrell (acting), (703) 605–4690.
Legislative Affairs.—Douglas Crandall, 205–1637.

BUSINESS OPERATIONS

Sydney R. Yates Building, Fifth Floor, phone (202) 205–1707.

Deputy Chief.—Charles L. Myers.
Associate Deputy Chiefs: Barbara Cooper, Jacqueline Myers, 205–1709.
Senior Staff Assistant.—Vacant, 401–4470.
Director for—
Acquisition Management.—Melissa Dyniec (703) 605–4744.
Budget and Financial Management.—Michael Clonts (505) 563–7103.
Civil Rights.—Debra Muse, 205–0827.
Freedom of Information/Privacy Act.—George Vargas (acting), 205–0444.
Homeland Security.—Arthur Bryant, 205–0942.
Human Resources Management.—Robin Bailey (503) 563–9700.
Information Resources Management.—Douglas Nash (505) 563–7978.
Job Corps.—Larry Dawson (303) 236–9939.
Regulatory and Management Services.—Thelma Strong, 205–5102.
Safety and Occupational Health.—Gary Helmer (703) 605–4482.
Strategic Program and Budget Analysis.—Kathleen Atkinson, 205–1088.

NATIONAL FOREST SYSTEM

Sydney R. Yates Building, Third Floor, phone (202) 205–1523

Deputy Chief.—Joel Holtrop.
Associate Deputy Chief.—Joe Mead (acting).
Staff Director of:
Ecosystem Management Coordination.—Tony Tooke, 205–0895.
Engineering.—Lou Leibbrand (703) 605–4646.
Forest Management.—Nora Rasure, 205–0893.

Lands and Realty Staff.—Greg Smith, 205–1248.
Minerals and Geology Management.—Tony Ferguson (703) 605–4545.
Range Management.—Janette Kaiser, 205–0893.
Recreation and Heritage Resources.—Jim Bedwell, 205–0900.
Watershed, Fish, Wildlife, Air and Rare Plants.—Anne Zimmermann, 205–1671.
Wilderness, Wild and Scenic Resources.—Jeff Vail, 205–0925.

RESEARCH AND DEVELOPMENT

Sydney R. Yates Building, First Floor, phone (202) 205–1665

Deputy Chief.—Dr. Jim Reapes, 205–1665.
Associate Deputy Chief.—Angela Coleman, 205–1702.
Staff Assistants: Daina Apple, 205–1452; John Kusano, 205–1105.
Staff Director of:
Environmental Sciences.—Vacant (703) 605–5277.
Forest Management Sciences.—Carlos Rodriguez-Franco (703) 605–5252.
Policy Analysis.—William Lange, 205–1775.
Quantitative Sciences.—Richard W. Guldin (703) 605–4177.
Resource Use Sciences.—Vacant (703) 605–4880.
Science Quality Services.—John Sebelius (703) 605–5294.

STATE AND PRIVATE FORESTRY

Sydney R. Yates Building, Second Floor, phone (202) 205–1657

Deputy Chief.—James E. Hubbard, 205–1606.
Associate Deputy Chiefs: John Phipps, Robin Thompson.
Staff Assistants: Jaelith Hall-Rivera, Debbie Pressman.
Director of:
Conservation Education.—Safiya Samman, 205–5681.
Cooperative Forestry.—Paul Ries, 205–1389.
Fire and Aviation Management.—Tom Harbour, 205–1483.
Forest Health Protection.—Rob Mangold (703) 605–5334.
Office of Tribal Relations.—Fred Clark, 205–1514.

NATURAL RESOURCES CONSERVATION SERVICE

South Building, Room 5105–A, phone (202) 720–7246

Chief.—Dave White.
Associate Chiefs: Virginia "Ginger" Murphy, Homer Wilkes (acting) 720–4531.
Director, Division of:
Civil Rights.—Gregory Singleton (301) 504–2181.
Legislative.—Keira Franz, 720–3210.
Public Affairs.—Patty Lawrence, 720–3210.

DEPUTY CHIEF FOR FINANCIAL MANAGEMENT

Deputy Chief.—David Morris, 720–5904, 720–4251.
Director Civil Rights.—Gregory Singleton.
Director Outreach.—Frank Clearfield.
Team Leaders:
Accounting Team.—Robin Aldridge, 205–5415.
Budget Team.—Selena Miller, 205–6134.
Fiscal Team.—Robin Kelly, 205–0113.

DEPUTY CHIEF OF MANAGEMENT

Deputy Chief.—Eloris Speight (acting), (202) 720–7847.
Associate Deputy Chief.—Curtis Wilburn.
Ethics Officer.—Ellen Pearson (301) 205–1826.
Director, Division of:
Human Resources Management.—Yvette Gray, 720–2227.

Management Services.—Tim Beard, 720–4102.
National Employee Development Center.—Sandra Detter (817) 509–3242.
Chief Information Officer.—Gary Washington (970) 217–8185.
Supervisory Agency Representative.—Lauren Ruby (301) 504–2176.

DEPUTY CHIEF OF PROGRAMS

Deputy Chiefs: Anthony Kramer (202) 720–4527; Diane Gilbert 205–7704.
Director, Division of:
Easement Programs.—Andree DuVarney, 720–1854.
Financial Assistance Programs.—Gregory Johnson, 720–1845.
Watershed.—Keith Admire, 720–1510.

DEPUTY CHIEF OF SCIENCE AND TECHNOLOGY

Deputy Chief.—C. Wayne Honeycutt (202) 720–4630.
Director, Division of:
Conservation Engineering.—Noller Herbert, 720–2520.
Ecological Sciences.—Terrell Erickson, 720–2587.

DEPUTY CHIEF OF SOIL SURVEY AND RESOURCE ASSESSMENT

Deputy Chief.—Doug Lawrence (202) 690–4616.
Director, Division of:
International Programs.—Melvin Westbrook (301) 504–2271.
Resources Assessment.—Michele Laur.
Resources Inventory and Assessment.—Jeff Gobel (acting), (301) 504–2300.
Soil Survey.—Michael L. Golden, 720–1820.

DEPUTY CHIEF OF STRATEGIC PLANNING AND ACCOUNTABILITY

Deputy Chief.—Lesia Reed (acting), (202) 720–6297.
Director, Division of:
Budget Planning and Analysis.—Mary Koskinen, 720–4533.
Strategic and Performance Planning—Craig Aiello, 720–8388.

UNDER SECRETARY FOR FARM AND FOREIGN AGRICULTURAL SERVICES

Under Secretary.—Michael Scuse.
Deputy Under Secretaries: Karis Gutter, 720–7107; Darci Vetter (202) 720–3111.

FARM SERVICE AGENCY

South Building, Room 3086–S, phone (202) 720–3467

Administrator.—Val Dolcini (acting).
Associate Administrator for Operations and Management.—Carolyn Cooksie.
Civil Rights.—Johnny Toles, 410–7197.
Economic and Policy Analysis Staff.—Joy Harwood (acting), room 3741–S, 720–3451.
Deputy Administrator for Farm Programs.—Brandon Willis, room 3612–S, 720–3175.
Assistant Deputy Administrator.—Vacant, 720–2070.
Conservation and Environmental Programs Division.—Robert Stephenson, room 4714–S, 720–6221.
Price Support Division.—Soloman Whitfield, room 4095–S, 720–7901.
Production, Emergencies and Compliance Division.—Candice Thompson, room 4754, 720–7641.
Deputy Administrator for Farm Loan Programs.—Chris Beyerhelm, 720–4671.
Program Development and Economic Enhancement Division.—Nancy New, room 4919–S, 720–3647.
Loan Making Division.—Vacant, room 5438–S, 720–1632.
Loan Servicing and Property Management Division.—Michael Hinton, room 5449–S, 720–4572.

Deputy Administrator for Field Operations.—Michael Wooden, room 3092, 690–2807.
Assistant Deputy Administrator.—John W. Chott, Jr., room 8092, 690–2807.
Operations Review and Analysis Staff.—Phillip Sharp, room 2720–S, 690–2532.
Deputy Administrator for Commodity Operations.—James Monahan, room 3080–S, 720–3217.
Kansas City Commodity Office.—Vacant (816) 926–6301.
Deputy Administrator for Management.—Phil Short, room 3095–S, 720–3438.
Budget Division.—Ricky Valentine, room 4720–S.
Human Resources Division.—Jacqueline Whitaker, room 5200 (L–St), 418–8950.
Information Technology Services Division.—Jim Gwinn, room 5768–S, 720–5320.
Management Services Division.—Ezekiel Dennison, room 520–PRTL, 720–3438.

FOREIGN AGRICULTURAL SERVICE

South Building, Room 5071, phone (202) 720–3935, fax 690–2159

Administrator.—John Brewer.
Senior Advisors to the Administrator: Christine Turner, 690–4267.
Associate Administrator.—Janet Nuzum, 690–8108.
General Sales Manager.—Suzanne Heinen, 720–4055.
Director of:
Civil Rights Staff.—Debra Lewis, 720–7061.
Legislative and Public Affairs.—Christopher Church, 720–6830.
Public Affairs and Executive Correspondence.—Sally Klusaritz, 720–4064.

OFFICE OF ADMINISTRATIVE OPERATIONS

Deputy Administrator.—Larry Bevan (202) 720–0690.
Senior Advisor.—David Pendlum, 720–1293.
Director, Division of:
Budget.—Scott Redman, 690–4052.
Information Technology.—Swarnali Haldar, 690–2936.
Program Management.—Ted Goldammer, 720–3241.

OFFICE OF CAPACITY BUILDING AND DEVELOPMENT

Deputy Administrator.—Patricia R. Sheikh (202) 720–6887.
Assistant Deputy Administrators: Gary Groves, 690–4056; Roger Mireles, 690–1791.
Policy Coordination and Planning Staff.—Vacant, 720–1314.
Director, Division of:
Development Resources and Disaster Assistance.—Robert Curtis, 690–1924.
Food Assistance.—Ronald Croushorn, 720–4221.
Trade and Scientific Capacity Building.—Vacant, 690–4872.
Trade and Scientific Exchanges.—Ali Abdi, 690–1821.

OFFICE OF COUNTRY AND REGIONAL AFFAIRS

Deputy Administrator.—Lloyd Harbert (202) 720–7562.
Assistant Deputy Administrators: Jocelyn Brown, 690–1779; Mark Dries, 720–1134.
Director, Division of:
Africa and Middle East.—Stan Phillips, 720–1326.
Asia.—Cina Radler, 720–3403.
Europe.—Sharynne Nenon, 720–1330.
Western Hemisphere.—John Passino, 720–5219.

OFFICE OF FOREIGN SERVICE OPERATIONS

Deputy Administrator.—James Higgiston (202) 720–8322.
Assistant Deputy Administrator.—Bonnie Boris, 690–4062.
Director for—
Africa and Middle East Area.—Kim Svec, 690–4066.
Asia Area.—Kathleen Wainio, 690–4053.
Europe Area.—Michael Conlon, 690–4057.

Planning and Global Resources Staff.—Pamela Sherard, 720–1346.
Western Hemisphere Area.—Hugh Maginnis, 720–3223.

OFFICE OF GLOBAL ANALYSIS

Deputy Administrator.—Robert Riemenschneider (202) 720–6301.
Assistant Deputy Administrators: Ralph Gifford, 690–1198; Patrick Packnett, 720–1590.
Director, Division of:
Industry and Sector Analysis Division.—Tim Rocke, 690–0292.
International Production Assessment Division.—Derrick Williams, 720–2974.
Trade and Biofuels Analysis Division.—Mike Dwyer, 720–3124.

OFFICE OF AGREEMENTS AND SCIENTIFIC AFFAIRS

Assistant Deputy Administrators: Brian Grunenfelder, Robert Macke, Christine Sloop, 720–4434.
Policy Formulation Staff:
Senior Policy Advisor.—Gary Meyer, 720–1286.
Senior Trade Negotiator.—David Miller, 720–1324.
Planning and Operations Group:
Assistant to the Deputy Administrators: Lore Fitzsimmons, Jim Warden, Barbara Wolff.
Animal Division:
Division Director.—Casey Bean, 720–1353.
Deputy Director.—Catherine Fulton, 720–2461.
Multilateral Affairs:
Division Director.—Andrew Burst, 720–9519.
Bilateral Agreements and Enforcement Division:
Division Director.—Charles Bertsch, 720–6278.
International Regulations and Standards Division:
Division Director.—Cathy McKinnell, 690–0929.
New Technologies and Production Methods Division:
Director.—Ed Porter, 720–2502.
Plant Division:
Division Director.—Peter Tabor, 720–0765.
Processed Products and Technical Regulations Division:
Division Director.—Marianne McElroy, 720–7227.

OFFICE OF TRADE PROGRAMS

Deputy Administrator.—Christian Foster (202) 401–0015.
Assistant Deputy Administrators: Marcus Lower, 720–2705; Lynne Reich, 401–0023.
Director, Division of:
Cooperator Programs Division.—Eric Wenberg, 690–0159.
Credit Programs.—Mark Rowse, 720–0624.
Import Policies and Export Reporting Division.—Elizabeth Berry, 720–0638.
Program Operations Division.—Mark Slupek, 720–4327.

RISK MANAGEMENT AGENCY

South Building, Room 6092–S, phone (202) 690–2803

Administrator.—William J. Murphy (acting).
Associate Administrator.—Barbara Leach.
Deputy Administrator for—
Compliance.—Michael Hand, room 4619–S, 720–0642.
Insurance Services.—Michael Ofton, room 6709–S, 690–4494.
Product Management.—Timothy Witt, Kansas City (816) 926–7394 / 7822.

UNDER SECRETARY FOR RURAL DEVELOPMENT

Jamie L. Whitten Building, phone (202) 720–4581

Under Secretary.—Dallas Tonsager.

Deputy Under Secretaries: Cheryl L. Coak, Doug O'Brien.
Chief of Staff.—John Padalino.
Deputy Chief of Staff.—Vacant.
Director, Legislative and Public Affairs.—Timothy McNeilly, 720–1019.

BUSINESS AND COOPERATIVE PROGRAMS

South Building, Room 5801–S, phone (202) 690–4730

Administrator.—Judith A. Canales.
Associate Administrator.—Curtis A. Wiley, 720–6165.
Oversight/Resource Coordination Staff (OCS).—Nannie Hill-Midgett, 690–4100.
Deputy Administrator for Business Programs.—Pandor H. Hadjy, 720–7287.
Director of:
Business and Industry Division.—Vacant, 690–4103.
Specialty Lenders Division.—Mark Brodzinski, 720–1400.
Deputy Administrator for Cooperative Programs.—Andrew Jermolowizc (acting), 720–7558.
Assistant Deputy Administrator.—Andy Jermolowizc, 720–8460.
Director of:
Cooperative Development Division.—John H. Wells, 720–3350.
Cooperative Marketing Division.—David Sears, 690–0368.
Cooperative Resources Management Division.—Bruce Reynolds (acting), 690–1374.

RURAL HOUSING SERVICE

South Building, Room 5014–S, phone (202) 690–1533

Administrator.—Tammye Trevino.
Director, Program Support Staff.—Richard A. Davis, 720–9619.
Deputy Administrator for Single Family.—Chadwick Parker (acting), 720–5177.
Director of:
Family Housing Direct Loan Division.—George Irvin, 720–1474.
Family Housing Guaranteed Loan Division.—Joaquin Tremols, 720–1452.
Deputy Administrator for Multi-Family Housing.—Bryan Hooper, 720–3773.
Deputy Director.—Sue Harris-Green, 720–1606.
Director of:
Direct Loan and Grant Processing Division.—Chadwick Parker, 720–1502.
Multi-Family Housing Portfolio Management Division, Direct Housing.—Stephanie White, 720–1600.

RURAL UTILITIES SERVICE

South Building, Room 5135, phone (202) 720–9540

Administrator.—Jonathan Adelstein.
Deputy Administrator.—Jessica Zufolo.
Assistant Administrator for—
Electric Division.—Nivin Elgohary (acting), room 5165, 720–9505.
Program Accounting and Regulatory Analysis.—Kenneth M. Ackerman, room 5159, 720–9450.
Telecommunications.—David Villano, room 5151, 720–9554.
Water and Environmental Programs.—Jacqueline Ponti-Lazaruk, room 5145, 690–2670.
Director of:
Advanced Services Division.—Vacant, room 2845–S, 690–4493.
Broadband Division.—Kenneth Kuchno, room 2846–S, 690–4673.
Electric Staff Division.—George Shultz, room 1246–S, 720–1900.
Northern Regional Electric Division.—Joseph Badin, room 0243–S, 720–1420.
Northern Area, Telecommunications Program.—Shawn Arner (acting), room 2835–S, 720–1025.
Power Supply Division.—Victor T. Vu, room 270–S, 720–6436.
Southern Regional Electric Division.—Doris Nolte, room 221–S, 720–0848.
Southern Area, Telecommunications Program.—Ken B. Chandler, room 2808–S, 720–0800.
Telecommunications Standards Division.—John Schnell (acting), room 2868–S, 720–8663.
Chief, Portfolio Management Branch.—Steve Saulnier, room 2231–S, 720–9631.

Engineering and Environmental Staff.—Mark Plank, room 2237, 720–1649.

FOOD, NUTRITION, AND CONSUMER SERVICES

1400 Independence Avenue, SW., Room 216–E, Whitten Building, 20250

Under Secretary.—Kevin Concannon, (202) 720–7711.
Deputy Under Secretary.—Janey Thornton.

FOOD AND NUTRITION SERVICE

3101 Park Center Drive, Room 906, Alexandria, VA 22302, (703) 305–2062

OFFICE OF THE ADMINISTRATOR

Administrator.—Julia Paradis.
Deputy Administrator, Supplemental Nutrition Assistance Program.—Lisa Pino (703) 305–2064.
Deputy Administrator, Special Nutrition Programs.—Audrey Rowe, 305–2060.

OFFICE OF RESEARCH AND ANALYSIS

Association Administration (ORA) Communication and Strategic.—Steven Carlson, room 1014 (703) 305–2017.
Assistant Director.—Rich Lucas, room 1002, 605–0707.
Division, Director of:
Family Program Staff.—Carol Olander, room 1030, 305–2134.
Special Nutrition Staff.—Jay Hirschman, room 1010, 305–2117.

OFFICE OF COMMUNICATIONS AND GOVERNMENTAL AFFAIRS

Director.—Bruce C. Alexander, room 926–A (703) 305–2281.
Deputy Director.—Susan Siemietkowski, room 926–B, 305–2281.
Division, Director of:
Controlled Correspondence Officer.—Twanda Rodgers, room 918, 305–2066.
Governmental Affairs.—Scott A. Carter, room 918, 305–2010.
Public Affairs.—Jean Daniel, room 912, 305–2286.

OFFICE OF MANAGEMENT TECHNOLOGY AND FINANCE

Associate Administrator.—Jeffery Tribiano, room 906 (703) 305–2064.
Director of Civil Rights.—Deborah Minor, room 942, 305–2195.

MANAGEMENT

Deputy Administrator.—Mark Rucker, room 400 (703) 305–2030.
Division, Director of:
Contracts Management.—Lance Patterway (acting), room 220, 305–2251.
Human Resources.—Frank McDonna, room 404, 305–2326.
Logistics and Facility Management.—Mark Rucker, room 222, 305–2220.

FINANCIAL MANAGEMENT

Deputy Administrator (CFO).—Steven Butler, room 712 (703) 305–2046.
Division, Director of:
Accounting.—Linda Washington, room 724, 305–2850.
Administrative Operations.—Larry Blim, room 716, 305–2240.
Budget.—Lisa Greenwood, room 708, 305–2172.
Grants and Fiscal Policy.—Lael Lubing, room 732, 305–2048.
Internal Controls, Audits, and Investigations Liaison.—Katherine Day, room 732, 305–2493.

INFORMATION TECHNOLOGY

Deputy Administrator.—Jonathan Alboum, room 314 (703) 605–4318.
Information Security Officer.—Brad Nix, room 314, 305–2242.
Division, Director of:
Financial Systems.—Rich Platt, room 314, 305–2346.
Portfolio Management.—Jacquie Butler, room 314, 605–4318.
Technology.—Rory Schultz, room 316, 305–2244.

REGIONAL OPERATIONS AND SUPPORT

Associate Administrator.—Yvette Jackson, room 906 (703) 305–2060.
Division, Director of:
Office of Emergency Management and Food Safety.—Brenda Lisi, room 1441, 305–1504.
Office of Strategic Initiatives Partnership and Outreach.—Duke Storen, room 1441, 305–1504.

OFFICE OF SUPPLEMENTAL NUTRITION ASSISTANCE PROGRAM

Associate Administrator.—Jessica Shahin, room 808 (703) 305–2026.
Division, Director of:
Benefit Redemption.—Andrea Gold, room 408, 305–2434.
Program Accountability and Administration.—David Burr, room 816, 305–2413.
Program Development.—Liz Beth Silbernan, room 814, 305–2494.

OFFICE OF SPECIAL NUTRITION PROGRAMS

Associate Administrator.—Tim O'Connor, room 628 (703) 305–2052.
Division, Director of:
Child Nutrition.—Cindy Long, room 640, 305–2590.
Food Distribution.—Cathie McCullough (acting), room 500, 305–2680.
Supplemental Food Program.—Debra Whitford, room 520, 305–2746.

CENTER FOR NUTRITION POLICY AND PROMOTION

Executive Director.—Dr. Raj Anand, room 1034 (703) 305–7600.
Deputy Director.—Robert Post, room 1034, 305–7600.
Division, Director of:
Evidence Analysis Library.—Joanne Spahn, room 1034, 305–2870.
Nutrition Guidance and Analysis.—Carole Davis, room 1034, 605–4265.
Nutrition Marketing and Communication Division.—Jackie Haven, room 1034, 605–4434.
Public Affairs and FNS Liaison.—John Webster, room 1034, 605–4270.

UNDER SECRETARY FOR FOOD SAFETY

Under Secretary.—Elisabeth Hagen (202) 720–0350.
Deputy Under Secretary.—Jerold Mande.
Confidential Assistant to the Under Secretary.—Fahad Faruqi.

FOOD SAFETY AND INSPECTION SERVICE

Jamie L. Whitten Building, Room 331–E, phone (202) 720–7025, fax 690–0550

Administrator.—Alfred V. Almanza.
Deputy Administrator.—Bryce Quick, 720–7900.
U.S. Manager for Codex.—Karen Stuck, room 4861–S, 720–2057.

OFFICE OF FIELD OPERATIONS (OFO)

Assistant Administrator.—Dr. Kenneth E. Petersen, room 344–E (202) 720–8803.

Deputy Assistant Administrator.—Judy Riggins, 720–5190.
Executive Associates, Regulatory Operations: Cheryl Hicks, room 3159–S, 690–2709; Dr. William James, room 3153–S, 720–9521; Dr. Armia Tawadrous, room 3161–S, 720–5714.
Director of:
Recall Management Staff.—Dr. Lisa Volk, room 0010–S, 690–6536.

OFFICE OF DATA INTEGRATION AND FOOD PROTECTION (ODIFP)

Assistant Administrator.—Terri Nintemann (acting), room 3130–S (202) 720–5643.
Deputy Assistant Administrator.—Christopher Alvares (acting), 205–0452.
Director of:
Biosurveillance and Emergency Response Staff.—Mary K. Cutshall, 414 Aero Building, 690–6523.

OFFICE OF INTERNATIONAL AFFAIRS (OIA)

Assistant Administrator.—Dr. Ronald Jones, room 3143–S (202) 720–3473.
Deputy Assistant Administrator.—Vacant, 720–5362.
Director, Import Inspection Division.—Jerry Elliott, room 1–2288B (301) 504–2153.

OFFICE OF MANAGEMENT (OM)

Assistant Administrator.—Anthony Thompson, room 347–E (202) 720–4425.
Deputy Assistant Administrator.—Lorrena Carraco, 720–4744.

OFFICE OF POLICY AND PROGRAM DEVELOPMENT (OPPD)

Assistant Administrator.—Daniel Engeljohn, room 350–E (202) 720–2709.
Deputy Assistant Administrator.—Vacant, 205–0495.

OFFICE OF PROGRAM EVALUATION, ENFORCEMENT AND REVIEW (OPEER)

Assistant Administrator.—William C. ''Bill'' Smith, room 3133–S (202) 720–8609.
Deputy Assistant Administrator.—Dr. Jane Roth, room 3133–S, 720–8609.
Director of:
Compliance and Investigations Division.—Randy Robertson, room 300B–CQ, WEC, 418–8874.
Program Evaluation and Improvement Staff.—Matthew Michael, room 3831–S, 720–6735.

OFFICE OF PUBLIC AFFAIRS AND CONSUMER EDUCATION (OPACE)

Assistant Administrator.—Lisa Picard, room 339–E (202) 720–8217.
Deputy Assistant Administrator.—Vacant, room 3137–S, 720–3884.
Director of:
Congressional and Public Affairs Staff.—Carol Blake, room 1175–S, 720–9891 or 9113.
Executive Correspondence and Issues Management Staff.—Alicemary Leach, room 1167–S, 690–3882.

OFFICE OF PUBLIC HEALTH SCIENCE (OPHS)

Assistant Administrator.—Dr. David Goldman, room 341–E (202) 720–2644.
Deputy Assistant Administrator.—Dr. Vivian Chen, room 341–E, 205–0293.

OFFICE OF OUTREACH, EMPLOYEE EDUCATION AND TRAINING (OOEET)

Assistant Administrator.—Lisa Picard, room 4862–S, 205–0194.

UNDER SECRETARY FOR RESEARCH, EDUCATION, AND ECONOMICS

Under Secretary.—Dr. Kathy Woteki (202) 720–5923.
Deputy Under Secretary.—Ann Bartuska.

AGRICULTURAL RESEARCH SERVICE

Administration Building, Room 302–A, phone (202) 720–3656, fax 720–5427

Administrator.—Edward B. Knipling.
Associate Administrator for—
Research Operations.—Dr. Caird E. Rexroad, 720–3658.
Research Programs.—Judy St. John (301) 504–5084.
Director of:
Budget and Program Management Staff.—Michael Arnold, room 358–A, 720–4421.
Legislative Affairs.—David Kelly, 720–3173.
Information Staff.—Sandy Miller-Hays (301) 504–1638.
Assistant Administrator, Research Operations and Management, Office of Technology Transfer.—Richard J. Brenner (301) 504–6905.
Deputy Administrator, Administrative and Financial Management.—James H. Bradley, 690–2575.
National Agricultural Library.—Vacant (301) 504–5248.

AREA OFFICES

Director of:
Beltsville Area.—Joseph Spence, 10300 Baltimore Boulevard, Building 003, Room 223, BARC–West, Beltsville, MD 20705 (301) 504–6078.
Mid South Area.—Edgar King, Jr., 141 Experiment Station Road, Stoneville, MS 38776 (662) 686–5265.
Midwest Area.—Larry Chandler, 1815 North University Street, Room 2004, Peoria, IL 61604–0000 (309) 681–6602.
North Atlantic Area.—Dariusz Swietlik, 600 East Mermaid Lane, Room 2031, Wyndmoor, PA 19038 (215) 233–6593.
Northern Plains Area.—Wilbert H. Blackburn, 2150 Centre Avenue, Building D, Ft. Collins, CO 80525–8119 (970) 492–7057.
Pacific West Area.—Andrew Hammond, 800 Buchanan Street, Room 2030, Albany, CA 94710 (510) 559–6060.
South Atlantic Area.—Deborah Brennan, P.O. Box 5677, College Station Road, Room 201, Athens, GA 30605 (706) 546–3311.
Southern Plains Area.—Dan Upchurch, 1001 Holleman Drive East, College Station, TX 77845 (979) 260–9346.

COOPERATIVE STATE RESEARCH, EDUCATION AND EXTENSION SERVICE

Jamie L. Whitten Building, Room 305–A, phone (202) 720–4423, fax 720–8987

Administrator.—Roger N. Beachy.
Deputy Director.—Meryl Broussard, 720–7441.
Assistant Administrator/Legislative Liaison.—Betty Lou Gilliland, room 305–A, 720–8187.
Directors, Office of:
Budget.—Vacant, room 332–A, 720–2675.
Communications.—Ellen Frank, room 4231, 720–2677.
Equal Opportunity Staff.—Curt DeVille, room 1230, 720–2700.
Planning and Accountability.—Bart Hewitt (acting), room 1315, 720–5623.
Deputy Administrator for—
Bioenergy, Climate, Environment/Science and Education Resources Development.—Frank Boteler, room 4343, 720–7947.
Extramural Programs.—Andrea Brandon, room 2256, 401–6021.
Information Systems and Technology Management.—Michel Desbois, room 4122, 401–0117.
Institute of Food/Production and Sustainability.—Deborah Sheely (acting), room 2334, 401–5024.
Youth Families Community.—Vacant, room 3231, 401–4555.

ECONOMIC RESEARCH SERVICE

1800 M Street, NW., 20036–5831, phone (202) 694–5000

Administrator.—Katherine R. Smith (acting), room N4145.
Associate Administrators: John Kort, room N4150; Stephen Crutchfield, room N4149.
Special Assistant to Administrator.—Leslee Lowstutter, room N4151.
Civil Rights Director.—Vacant, room N4152.
Division Directors:
Food Economics.—Laurian Unnevehr, room N2168, 694–5400.
Information Services.—Ron Bianchi, room S2032, 694–5100.
Market Trade and Economics.—Sally Thompson, room N5119, 694–5200.
Resource and Rural Economics.—Mary Bohman, room S4182, 694–5500.

NATIONAL AGRICULTURAL STATISTICS SERVICE

South Agriculture Building, Room 5041A–S, phone (202) 720–2707, fax 720–9013

Administrator.—Cynthia Clark.
Associate Administrator.—Joseph T. Reilly, 720–4333.
Deputy Administrator for—
Eastern Field Operations.—Norman Bennett, room 5053, 720–3638.
Programs and Products.—Hubert Hamer, room 5029, 690–8141.
Division Directors for—
Census and Survey.—Renee Picanso, room 6306, 720–4557.
Information Technology.—Michael Valivullah, room 5847, 720–2984.
Research and Development.—James M. Harris, Fairfax, (703) 877–8000, ext. 100.
Statistics.—Joseph Prusacki, room 5433, 720–3896.

UNDER SECRETARY FOR MARKETING AND REGULATORY PROGRAMS

Jamie L. Whitten Building, Room 228–W, phone (202) 720–4256, fax 720–5775

Under Secretary.—Edward Avalos.
Deputy Under Secretary.—Ann Wright.
Special Assistant to the Under Secretary.—Katie Naessens.
Confidential Assistant to the Under Secretary.—Lucas Knowles, 690–2832.

AGRICULTURAL MARKETING SERVICE

South Agriculture Building, Room 3064–S, phone (202) 720–5115, fax 720–8477

Administrator.—Rayne Pegg.
Associate Administrator.—David R. Shipman, 720–4276.
Deputy Associate Administrator.—Erin Morris, 720–4024.
Deputy Administrator for—
Compliance and Analysis Programs.—Ellen King, room 3507–S, 720–6766.
Cotton and Tobacco Programs.—Darryl Earnest, room 2639–S, 720–3193.
Dairy Programs.—Dana Cole, room 2968–S, 720–4392.
Fruit and Vegetable Programs.—Robert C. Keeney, room 2077–S, 720–4722.
Poultry Programs.—Craig Morse, room 2902–S, 720–5705.
Science and Technology.—Robert L. Epstein, room 1090–S, 720–5231.
Transportation and Marketing.—Barbara C. Robinson, room 1098, 690–1300.
Director, Legislative and Review Staff.—Chris Sarcone, room 2625–S, 720–3203.

ANIMAL AND PLANT HEALTH INSPECTION SERVICE (APHIS)

Jamie L. Whitten Building, Room 312–E, phone (202) 720–3668, fax 720–3054

OFFICE OF THE ADMINISTRATOR

Administrator.—Cindy J. Smith.
Associate Administrator.—Kevin Shea.

Director of Civil Rights Enforcement and Compliance.—Myra Young, room 1137–S, 720–6312, fax 720–2365.

ANIMAL CARE

4700 River Road, Riverdale, MD 20737, phone (301) 734–4980, fax 734–4328

Deputy Administrator.—Chester Gipson.
Associate Deputy Administrator.—Andrea Morgan.

BIOTECHNOLOGY REGULATORY SERVICES

4700 River Road, Riverdale, MD 20737, phone (301) 734–7324, fax 734–8724

Deputy Administrator.—Michael Gregoire.
Assistant Deputy Administrator.—Sidney Abel, 734–5716.

INTERNATIONAL SERVICES

Jamie L. Whitten Building, Room 324–E, phone (202) 720–7593, fax 690–1484

Deputy Administrator.—Ronald Hicks.
Active Deputy Administrator.—Karen Sliter, 720–7021.
Division Directors: Freida Skaggs (301) 734–5214; John Wyss, 734–3779.
Trade Support Team.—John Greifer, room 1128, 720–7677.

LEGISLATIVE AND PUBLIC AFFAIRS

South Building, Room 1147–S, phone (202) 720–2511, fax 720–3982

Deputy Administrator.—Bethany Jones.
Associate Deputy Administrator.—James Ivy.
Assistant Director of:
Executive Correspondence.—Christina Myers (301) 734–7776.
Freedom of Information.—Tonya Woods (301) 734–8296.
Public Affairs.—Ed Curlett (301) 734–7799.

MARKETING AND REGULATORY PROGRAMS BUSINESS SERVICES

Jamie L. Whitten Building, Room 308–E, phone (202) 720–5213, fax 690–0686

Deputy Administrator.—Joanne Munno, 720–5214, (301) 734–3768.
Associate Deputy Administrator.—Vacant.

PLANT PROTECTION AND QUARANTINE

Jamie L. Whitten Building, Room 302–E, phone (202) 720–5601, fax 690–0472

Deputy Administrator.—Rebecca Bech.
Associate Deputy Administrator.—Paul Eggert, 720–4441.
Assistant to the Deputy Administrator.—John H. Payne, 720–5601.
Director of:
Biocontrol.—Dr. Alan Dowdy (301) 734–5667.
Center for Plant Health Science and Technology.—Gordon Gordh (919) 513–2400.
Resource Management Support.—Terri Burrell (301) 734–7764.
Technical Information Systems.—Allison Young (301) 734–5518.

POLICY AND PROGRAM DEVELOPMENT

4700 River Road, Riverdale, MD 20737, phone (301) 734–5136, fax 734–5899

Deputy Administrator.—Christine Zakarka.
Associate Deputy Administrator.—Shannon Hamm.

Unit Chiefs:
Environmental and Risk Analysis Service.—Ken Seeley, 734–3634.
Planning, Evaluation and Monitoring.—Connie Williams, 734–8512.
Policy Analysis and Development.—Parveen Sepia, 734–8667.
Regulatory Analysis and Development.—Stephen O'Neil, 734–0682.

VETERINARY SERVICES

Jamie L. Whitten Building, Room 317–E, phone (202) 720–5193, fax 690–4171

Deputy Administrator.—John Clifford.
Administrative Assistant.—Paula Lee, 720–5793.
Associate Deputy Administrator for Regional Operations.—Jere Dick, 720–5193.
Assistant Deputy Administrators: India Wilson, David Zimmerman (301) 734–3754.
Director for—
Emergency Programs.—Jose Diez (301) 734–8073.
Inspection and Compliance.—Steven A. "Ames" Karli (515) 232–5785.
National Center of Import and Export.—Gary S. Colgrave (301) 734–4356.
Outreach Liaison.—Joseph Annelli (301) 794–8073.
Policy, Evaluation and Licensing.—Richard E. Hill, Jr. (515) 232–5785.

WILDLIFE SERVICES

South Building, Room 1624, phone (202) 720–2054, fax 690–0053

Deputy Administrator.—William H. Clay.
Assistant Deputy Administrator.—Vacant.
Director for Operational Support.—Joanne Garrett (301) 734–7921.

GRAIN INSPECTION, PACKERS AND STOCKYARDS ADMINISTRATION

South Building, Room 2055, phone (202) 720–0219, fax 205–9237

Administrator.—J. Dudley Butler.
Director of:
Budget and Planning Staff.—MaryAnn Plaus, room 2045–S, 720–0231.
Civil Rights Staff.—Eugene Bass, room 0623–S, 720–0218.
Management and Budget Services.—Frieda Achtentuch, Albert Conerly, room 2446–S, 720–1741.
Deputy Administrator for Federal Grain Inspection Service.—Randall Jones, room 2063–S, 720–9170.
Director of:
Compliance.—Thomas O'Connor, room 1647–S, 720–8262.
Departmental and International Affairs.—John Pitchford, room 1629–S, 720–0226.
Field Management Division.—Robert Lijewski, room 2409–S, 720–0228.
Technical Services Division.—Donald Kendall (acting), Kansas City, MO (816) 891–0463.
Deputy Administrator for Packers and Stockyards Programs.—Alan Christian, room 2055–S, 25–8281.
Director of:
Business and Economic Analysis Division.—Gary McBryde, room 2430–S, 720–7455.
Regional Supervisors:
Atlanta, GA.—Elkin Parker (404) 562–5840.
Aurora, CO.—John Barthel (303) 375–4240.
Des Moines, IA.—Jay Johnson (515) 323–2579.

DEPARTMENT OF COMMERCE

Herbert C. Hoover Building

14th Street between Pennsylvania and Constitution Avenues, NW., 20230

phone (202) 482–2000, http://www.doc.gov

JOHN E. BRYSON, Secretary of Commerce; born in New York, NY, July 24, 1943; education: graduated, Cleveland High School, Portland, OR, 1961; B.A., history, Stanford University, 1965; J.D., Yale University School of Law, 1969; professional: co-founder and attorney at the Natural Resources Defense Council, 1970–74; attorney at Davies, Biggs, Strayer, Stoel & Boley, 1975–76; visiting faculty at Stanford Law School; 1977–79; Chairman of the California State Water Resources Control Board, 1976–79; President of the California Public Utilities Commission, 1979–82; partner in the San Francisco Office of Morrison & Foerster, 1982–84; Southern California Edison, Executive Vice President and Chief Financial Officer, 1984-1990; Chairman and Chief Executive Officer of Edison International, the parent company of Southern California Edison and Edison Mission Group, 1990–2008; retired Chairman and CEO of Edison International, 2008–11; married: Louise Henry Bryson; four children: Julia Easton, Jane Templeton, Ruth Randall, and Kathleen Louise; nominated by President Barack Obama to become the 37th Secretary of Commerce, and was confirmed by the U.S. Senate on October 20, 2011.

OFFICE OF THE SECRETARY

Secretary of Commerce.—John E. Bryson, room 5858 (202) 482–2112.
Deputy Secretary.—Vacant, room 5838, 482–8376.
Chief of Staff.—Ellen Moran, room 5858, 482–4246.
Senior Advisor and Deputy Chief of Staff.—Rick Wade, room 5862, 482–4246.
Deputy Chief of Staff.—Jay Reich.
Chief Protocol Officer.—Vacant, room 5847, 482–8011.
Director, Office of:
Business Liaison.—Vacant, room 5062, 482–1360.
Executive Secretariat.—Latoya Murphy, room 5516, 482–3934.
Policy and Strategic Planning.—Vacant, room 5865, 482–4127.
Public Affairs.—Kevin Griffis, room 5413, 482–4883.
Scheduling and Advance.—Roger Fisk, room 5883, 482–5129.
White House Liaison.—Rick Siger, room 5835, 482–1684.

GENERAL COUNSEL

General Counsel.—Cameron F. Kerry, room 5870 (202) 482–4772.
Deputy General Counsel.—Geovette Washington.

ASSISTANT SECRETARY FOR LEGISLATIVE AND INTERGOVERNMENTAL AFFAIRS

Assistant Secretary.—April Boyd, room 5421 (202) 482–3663, fax 482–4420.
Deputy Assistant Secretary.—Daraka Satcher, room 5421, 482–3663.
Director for—
Intergovernmental Affairs.—William Ramos, room 5422, 482–3663, fax 482–4420.
Legislative Affairs.—Jim Stowers, room 5422, 482–3663, fax 482–4420.

CHIEF FINANCIAL OFFICER (CFO) AND ASSISTANT SECRETARY FOR ADMINISTRATION

Chief Financial Officer and Assistant Secretary.—Scott Quehl, room 5830 (202) 482–4951, fax 482–3592.
Deputy Assistant Secretary for Administration.—Fred Stephens, room 5830.
Deputy Chief Financial Officer/Director for Financial Management.—Lisa Casias, room 6827, 482–1207, fax 482–5070.

Director for—

Acquisition Management.—Helen M. Hurcombe, room 6422, 482–4248, fax 482–1711.

Administrative Services.—Mary Pleffner, room 6316, 482–1200, fax 482–8890.

Budget.—Vacant, room 5820, 482–5969, fax 482–3361.

Civil Rights.—Suzan J. Aramaki, room 6010, 482–0625, fax 482–3364.

Human Resources Management.—William Fleming, room 5001, 482–4807, fax 482–0249.

Program Evaluation and Risk Management.—Vacant, room 5327, 482–3707, fax 482–1423.

Security.—Alfred Broadbent, room 1069, 482–4371, fax 501–6355.

Small and Disadvantaged Business Utilization.—LaJuene Desmukes, room 6411, 482–1472, fax 482–0501.

CHIEF INFORMATION OFFICER

Chief Information Officer.—Simon Szykman, room 5029B, (202) 482–4797.

Deputy Chief Information Officer.—Izella Dornell, room 5027.

Office of:

IT Policy and Planning.—Diana Hynek, room 6612, 482–0266.

IT Security, Infrastructure and Technology.—Earl Neal, room 6895, 482–4708.

Networking and Telecommunications Operations.—Wayne Blackwood, room 6078, 482–3175.

INSPECTOR GENERAL

Inspector General.—Todd J. Zinser, room 7898C, (202) 482–4661.

Deputy Inspector General.—Scott S. Dahl, room 7898C, 482–3516.

Chief of Staff.—Rick Dubik, room 7898C, 482–5422.

Counsel to Inspector General.—Wade Green, Jr., room 7892, 482–1577.

Principal Assistant Inspector General Audit and Evaluation.—Anne Eilers, room 7886B, 482–2754.

Assistant Inspector General, Office of:

Auditing.—Andrew Katsaros, room 7886B, 482–2600.

Economic and Statistical Program Assessment.—Ron Prevost, room 7520, 482–3052.

Investigations.—Scott Berenberg, room 7087, 482–3860.

Systems Acquisition and IT Security.—Allen Crawley, room 7876, 482–1855.

ECONOMICS AND STATISTICS ADMINISTRATION

Under Secretary for Economic Affairs.—Rebecca Blank, room 4848, (202) 482–3727.

Deputy Under Secretary for Economic Affairs.—Nancy Potok, room 4848, 482–3727.

Chief Counsel.—Roxie Jamison Jones, room 4868A, 482–5394.

Chief Economist.—Mark Doms, room 4842, 482–3523.

Deputy Chief Economist.—Rob Rubinovitz, room 4861, 482–4871.

Associate Under Secretary for—

Communications.—Joanne Caldwell, room 4836, 482–2760.

Management.—James K. White, room 4834, 482–2405.

Chief Financial Officer.—Joanne Buenzli-Crane, room 4842, 482–3038.

BUREAU OF ECONOMIC ANALYSIS

1441 L Street, NW., 20230, phone (202) 606–9900

Director.—J. Steven Landefeld, room 6006, 606–9600.

Deputy Director.—Brian Moyer, room 6005, 606–9602.

Chief Economist.—Ana Aizcorbe, room 6060, 606–9985.

Chief Information Officer.—Brian Callahan, room 6052, 606–9906.

Chief Statistician.—Dennis J. Fixler, room 6060, 606–9607.

Associate Director for—

Industry Economics.—Brian Moyer (acting), room 6004, 606–9612.

International Economics.—Robert Yuskavage (acting), room 6062, 606–9604.

National Economic Accounts.—Brent R. Moulton, room 6064, 606–9606.

Regional Economics.—Joel Platt, room 6065, 606–9605.

Chief Administrative Officer.—Kurt S. Bersani, room 6027, 606–9325.

Division Chiefs:

Administrative Services.—C. Brian Grove, room 3003, 606–9624.
Balance of Payments.—Robert Yuskavage, room 8024, 606–9672.
Communications.—H. Lucas Hitt, room 3029, 606–9223.
Direct Investment Division.—David Galler, room 7005, 606–9835.
Government.—Pamela Kelly, room 4067, 606–9781.
Industry Applications Division.—Erich Strassner, room 4006, 606–9539.
Industry Sector Division.—Nicole Mayerhauser, room 4028, 606–9742.
National Income and Wealth.—Carol E. Moylan, room 5006, 606–9711.
Regional Income Division.—Sharon C. Carnevale (acting), room 8065a, 606–9247.
Regional Product Division.—C. Ian Mead, room 9018, 606–9661.

THE BUREAU OF THE CENSUS

4600 Silver Hill Road, Suitland, MD 20746

Director.—Robert M. Groves, room 8H002, (301) 763–2135.
Deputy Director and Chief Operating Officer.—Thomas Mesenbourg, room 8H006, 763–2138.
Associate Director for—
Administration and Chief Financial Officer.—Ted A. Johnson, room 8H144, 763–3464.
Communications.—Steven Jost, room 8H138, 763–2512.
Comptroller.—Ted A. Johnson, room 8H144, 763–3464.
Decennial Census.—Arnold Jackson, room 8H122, 763–8626.
Demographic Programs.—Howard Hogan, room 8H134, 763–2160.
Economic Programs.—William G. Bostic, Jr., room 8K108, 763–8842.
Field Operations.—Marilia Matos, room 8H126, 763–2072.
Information Technology and CIO.—Brian McGrath, room 8H140, 763–2117.
Strategic Planning and Innovation.—Nancy M. Gordon, room 8H128, 763–2126.
Assistant Director for Communications.—Burton Reist, room 8H062, 763–3949.
Chief Technology Officer.—Avi Bender, room 5K030, 763–7807.
Assistant Director for—
Acquisition Division.—Michael L. Palensky, room 3J438, 763–1818.
Decennial (Census) Management and American Community Survey.—Daniel Weinberg, room 3H162, 763–5791.
Economic Programs.—Vacant, room 8K108, 763–2932.
Division and Office Chiefs for—
Administrative and Customer Services.—F. Grailand Hall, room 3J436, 763–1629.
Administrative and Management Systems Division.—James Aikman, room 3K138, 763–3149.
Advisory Committee Office.—Jeri Green, room 8H153, 763–6590.
American Community Survey Office.—James B. Treat, room 3K276, 763–3609.
Analysis and Executive Support.—Kathleen Styles, room 8H028, 763–3460.
Budget Division.—Carol Rose, room 2K122, 763–5818.
Census 2010 Publicity Office.—Stephen L. Buckner (acting), room 8H484, 763–3586.
Center for Economic Studies.—Ron Jarmin, room 2K124, 763–1858.
Company Statistics Division.—Jeffrey L. Mayer, room 6K064, 763–2905.
Computer Services Division.—Thomas J. Berti, Bowie 28, 763–4341.
Congressional Affairs Office.—Angela M. Manso, room 8H166, 763–6100.
Customer Liaison and Marketing Services Office.—Kendall B. Johnson (acting), room 8H180, 763–1911.
Decennial Automation Contract Management Office.—Vacant.
Decennial Management Division.—Frank Vitrano, room 3H174, 763–3691.
Decennial Statistical Studies Division.—David Whitford, room 4K276, 763–4035.
Decennial Systems and Contract Management Office.—Michael T. Thieme (acting), room 2H174, 763–9062.
Demographic Statistical Methods Division.—Ruth Ann Killion, room 7H162, 763–2048.
Demographic Surveys Division.—Cheryl Landman, room 7H128, 763–3773.
Economic Planning and Coordination Division.—Shirin A. Ahmed, room 8K122, 763–2558.
Economic Statistical Methods and Programming Division.—Samuel Jones, room 7K108, 763–7600.
Equal Employment Opportunity Office.—Roy P. Castro, room 3K106, 763–5120.
Field Division.—Brian Monaghan, room 5H128, 763–2011.
Finance Division.—Joan Simms, room 2K106, 763–6803.
Foreign Trade Division.—Nick Orsini, room 6K032, 763–2255.
Geography Division.—Timothy Trainor, room 4H174, 763–2131.

Governments Division.—Lisa Blumerman, room 5K156, 763–8050.
Housing and Household Economic Statistics.—David S. Johnson, room 7H174, 763–6443.
Human Resources Division.—Ted A. Johnson (acting), room 2J436, 763–3721.
Information Systems Support and Review Office.—John Leidich (acting), room 4K020, 763–5740.
Information Technology Security Office.—Timothy P. Ruland, room 5K124, 763–2869.
International Relations Office.—Carole Popoff, room 8H017, 763–3222.
Manufacturing and Construction.—Thomas Zabelsky, Jr., room 7K154, 763–4593.
National Processing Center.—David Hackbarth (812) 218–3344.
Population.—Enrique Lamas, room 5H174, 763–2071.
Privacy Office.—Mary Frazier, room 8H168, 763–2906.
Public Information Office.—Kenneth C. Meyer, room 8H160, 763–3100.
Security Office.—Harold L. Washington, Jr., room 2J438, 763–1716.
Service Sector Statistics.—Mark E. Wallace, room 2J438, 763–2683.
Statistical Research Division.—Tommy Wright, room 5K108, 763–1702.
Systems Support.—Nora Bea Parker, room 5K032, 763–2999.
Technologies Management Office.—Barbara M. LoPresti, room 5H160, 763–7765.
Telecommunications Office.—Scott Williams, room 4K032, 763–1793.

BUREAU OF INDUSTRY AND SECURITY

Under Secretary.—Eric L. Hirschhorn, room 3898B, (202) 482–1455.
Deputy Under Secretary.—Daniel O. Hill, room 3892, 482–1427.
Chief Counsel.—John Masterson, room 3839, 482–2315.
Office of Congressional and Public Affairs.—Sean Foertsch, room 3897, 482–0097.
Director, Office of Administration.—Gay Shrum, room 6622, 482–1900.
Chief Information Officer.—Eddie Donnell, room 6092, 482–4848.
Assistant Secretary for Export Administration.—Kevin Wolf, room 3886c, 482–5491.
Deputy Assistant Secretary.—Matthew Borman, room 3886c, 482–5711.
Operating Committee Chair.—Dennis Krepp (acting), room 3889, 482–5863 / 5864.
End-User Review Committee Chair.—Karen Nies-Vogel, room 2625, 482–5991.
Office of:
Exporter Services.—Bernard Kritzer, room 1093, 482–0436.
National Security and Technology Transfer Controls.—Eileen M. Albanese, room 2616, 482–4196.
Nonproliferation and Treaty Compliance.—Alexander Lopes, room 2093, 482–3825.
Strategic Industries and Economic Security.—Michael Vaccaro, room 3878, 482–4506.
Technology Evaluation.—Kevin Kurland, room 3886, 482–2385.
Assistant Secretary for Export Enforcement.—Kevin Delli-Colli (acting), room 3730, 482–3618.
Deputy Assistant Secretary.—David Mills, room 3723, 482–3618.
Office of:
Antiboycott Compliance.—Edward Weant, room 6098, 482–5914.
Enforcement Analysis.—Glenn Krizay, room 4065, 482–4255.
Export Enforcement.—Douglas Hassebrock, room 4508, 482–5079.

ECONOMIC DEVELOPMENT ADMINISTRATION

Assistant Secretary.—John R. Fernandez, room 7300, (202) 482–5081.
Deputy Assistant Secretary for—
EDA and Chief Operating Officer.—Brian McGowan, room 7300, 482–5081.
Regional Affairs.—Thomas Guevara, room 7800, 482–5891.
Chief Counsel.—Barry Bird, room D–100, 482–4687.
Chief Information Officer.—Brian McGowan (acting), room 7300, 482–5081.
Chief Financial Officer and Chief Administrative Officer.—Sandra R. Walters, room 7231, 482–5892.
Director, Office of:
Budget and Finance Division.—James LeDuc, room 7217, 482–0547.
External Affairs.—Angela Martinez, room 7814, 482–2900.
Innovation and Entrepreneurship.—Esther Lee, room 7019, 482–2042.
Legislative Affairs.—Angela Ewell-Madison (acting), room 7816, 482–2900.
Public Affairs.—Cleve Mesidor, room 7814, 482–4085.
Trade Adjustment Assistance.—Bryan Borlik, room D–100, 482–0556.

INTERNATIONAL TRADE ADMINISTRATION

Under Secretary.—Francisco Sanchez, room 3850, (202) 482–2867.
Deputy Under Secretary.—Michelle O'Neill, room 3842, 482–3917.
Chief of Staff.—Vacant, room 3850, 482–2867.
Legislative and Intergovernmental Affairs.—Peter Kaldes, room 3424, 482–3015.
Public Affairs.—Mary Trupo, room 3416, 482–3809.
Chief Counsel for International Commerce.—John Cobau, room 5624, 482–0937.

ADMINISTRATION

Director and Chief Financial Officer.—Patricia M. Sefcik, room 3827, (202) 482–5855.
Deputy Chief Financial Officer and Director, Office of Financial Management.—Jim Donahue, FL A, Suite 300, 482–0210.
Chief Information Officer.—Renee Macklin, room 4800, 482–3801.
Director, Office of:
Management and Operations.—Victor E. Powers, FL A, Suite 300, 482–5436.
Strategic Resources.—Ronald Glaser, room 2006, 482–3505.

TRADE PROMOTION AND U.S. AND FOREIGN COMMERCIAL SERVICE

Assistant Secretary for Trade Promotion and Director General of the U.S. and Foreign Commercial Service.—Suresh Kumar, room 7313, (202) 482–5777.
Deputy Director General.—Charles Ford, room 7313, 482–5777.
Deputy Assistant Secretary for—
Domestic Operations.—Romit Khanna, RRB, 482–4767.
Trade Promotion Programs Executive Director.—Pat Kirwan, RRB, 482–9093.
National Director.—Anne Grey, room 3813, 482–5927.
International Operations.—Karen Zens, room 3013, 482–6228.
Regional Director for—
Africa, Near East and South Asia.—Christian Reed, room 2011, 482–1209.
East Asia and Pacific.—Patrick Santillo, room 3009, 482–0423.
Europe.—Reginald Miller, room 1227, 482–5402.
Western Hemisphere.—James Koloditch, room 1223, 482–3913.
Trade Promotion Coordinating Committee.—Pat Kirwan, room 3051, 482–5455.
Director, Office of Professional Development.—Vacant, room 1222, 482–2286.

ASSISTANT SECRETARY FOR IMPORT ADMINISTRATION

Assistant Secretary.—Vacant, room 3099, (202) 482–1780.
Deputy Assistant Secretary.—Ronald Lorentzen, room 3099B, 482–1780.
Chief Counsel.—John D. McInerney, room 3622, 482–5589.
Director for—
Office of Accounting.—Neal Halper, room 3087B, 482–2210.
Office of Policy.—Carole Showers, room 3713, 482–4412.
Deputy Assistant Secretary for—
Antidumping Countervailing Duty Operations.—Christian Marsh, room 3095, 482–5497.
Antidumping Countervailing Duty Policy and Negotiations.—Paul Piquado, room 3089, 482–6199.
Textiles and Apparel.—Kimberly Thompson Glas, room 3001A, 482–3737.

ASSISTANT SECRETARY FOR MARKET ACCESS AND COMPLIANCE

Assistant Secretary.—Michael C. Camunez, room 3868A, (202) 482–3022.
Deputy Assistant Secretary.—John Andersen (acting), room 3868A, 482–3022.
Deputy Assistant Secretary for—
Asia.—Craig Allen, room 2038, 482–4527.
Trade Agreements Compliance.—Skip Jones, room 3043, 482–5767.
Europe.—Juan Verde, room 3863, 482–5638.
Africa, the Middle East and South Asia.—Holly Vineyard, room 2329, 482–4651.
Western Hemisphere.—Walter Bastian, room 3826, 482–5324.
Director, Office of:
Africa.—Kevin Boyd, room 2037, 482–4227.
China Economic Area.—Nicole Melcher, room 3204, 428–2515.

European Country Affairs.—Jay Burgess, room 3319, 482–4915.
European Union.—David DeFalco, room 3513, 482–2178.
Intellectual Property Rights.—Susan Wilson, room 3043, 482–6097.
Japan.—Keith Roth, room 2320, 482–5012.
Latin America and the Caribbean.—John Anderson, room 3203, 482–2436.
Middle East.—Cherie Loustanau, room 2031, 482–4442.
Multilateral Affairs.—Christopher Rosettie, room 3033, 482–3227.
North and Central America and the Caribbean.—Geri Word, room 3024, 482–6452.
Pacific Basin.—Jeffrey Dutton, room 2319, 482–0358.
Russia, Ukraine, and Eurasia.—Jack Brougher, room 3318, 482–0998.
South Asia and Oceania.—Linda Droker, room 2312, 482–2955.
South America.—Anne Driscoll, room 3203, 482–1648.
Trade Compliance Center.—Beverly Vaughan, room 3043, 482–1191.

ASSISTANT SECRETARY FOR MANUFACTURING AND SERVICES

Assistant Secretary.—Nicole Y. Lamb-Hale, room 3832, (202) 482–1461.
Deputy Assistant Secretary.—Mary Saunders, room 3832.
Deputy Assistant Secretary for—
Industry Analysis.—Praveen Dixit, room 2814B, 482–3177.
Manufacturing.—Peter Perez, room 2800A, 482–1872.
Services.—Joel Secundy, room 1128, 482–5261.

PRESIDENT'S EXPORT COUNCIL

[Authorized by Executive Orders 12131, 12534, 12551, 12610, 12692, 12774, 12869, and 12974 (May through September 1995)]

Executive Director, Under Secretary of International Trade.—Francisco Sanchez, room 3850, (202) 482–1124.
Executive Secretary and Staff Director.—Mark Chittum, room 4043.

MINORITY BUSINESS DEVELOPMENT AGENCY

Director.—David Hinson, room 5051, (202) 482–2332.
National Deputy Director.—Alejandra Castillo, room 5051, 482–2332.
Associate Directors for—
Business Development.—Alex Done, room 5079, 482–6045.
Management.—Edith McCloud, room 5092, 482–6224.
Senior Advisor on Native American Affairs.—Donald Chapman, room 5093, 482–5644.
Chief Counsel.—Jedd Vertman, room 5069, 482–5045.
Chief Financial Officer.—Ronald Marin, room 5089, 482–1621.
Chief Information Officer.—Yolanda Whitley, room 5082, 482–3831.
Chief of Legislative, Educational and Intergovernmental Affairs.—Bridget Gonzales, room 5069A, 482–3774.

NATIONAL OCEANIC AND ATMOSPHERIC ADMINISTRATION

Under Secretary of Commerce for Oceans and Atmosphere.—Jane Lubchenco, Ph.D., room 7316 (202) 482–3436.
Assistant Secretary for Conservation and Management/Deputy Administrator.—Dr. Larry Robinson, room 6054, 482–6255.
Assistant Secretary Environmental Observation and Prediction/Deputy Administrator.—Vacant.
Chief Scientist.—Dr. Paul Sandifer (acting), room 6807, 482–9049.
Principal Deputy Under Secretary for Oceans and Atmosphere.—Monica Medina, room 7324, 482–3567.
Deputy Under Secretary for Operations.—Mary M. Glackin, room 5810, 482–4569.
Chief of Staff.—Margaret Spring, room 7316, 482–3436.
Deputy Assistant Secretary for International Fisheries.—Russell Smith, room 6224, 482–5682.
Senior Advisor for International Affairs.—Dr. James Turner, room 6224, 482–6076.
Director, Office of:
General Counsel.—Lois Schiffer, room 5814, 482–4080.

Policy and Senior Advisor to Under Secretary.—Sally Yozell, room 7324, 482–3567.
Communications and External Affairs.—Justin Kenney, room 6217, 482–6090.
Education.—Louisa Koch, room 6869, 482–3384.
Federal Coordinator for Meteorology.—Samuel P. Williamson, SSMC1, room 1500, (301) 427–2002.
Legislative and Intergovernmental Affairs.—John Gray, room 5221, 482–4981.
Marine and Aviation Operations.—RADM Jonathan W. Bailey, Jr., 8403 Colesville Road, Suite 500, Silver Spring, MD 20910 (301) 713–7600.
Strategic Initiatives and Partnerships.—Vacant.
Chief Financial Officer.—Maureen Wylie, room D200, 482–0917.
Chief Administrative Officer.—Vacant, SSMC4, room 8431, 713–0836, ext. 105.
Chief Information Officer/High Performance Computing and Communications.—Joseph Klimavicz, SSMC3, room 9651, 713–9600.
Acquisition and Grants.—Mitchell Ross, SSMC1, room 6300, 713–0325.
Decision Coordination and Executive Secretariat.—Kelly Quickle, room 5230, 482–2985.
Workforce Management.—Sandra Manning, SSMC4, room 12520, 713–6300.

NATIONAL MARINE FISHERIES SERVICE

1315 East-West Highway, Silver Spring, MD 20910

Assistant Administrator.—Eric Schwaab, room 14636, (301) 713–2239.
Deputy Assistant Administrator for—
Operations.—John Oliver, room 14743, 713–2239.
Regulatory Programs.—Samuel Rauch, room 14657, 713–2239.
Director, Office of:
Habitat Conservation.—Patricia Montanio, room 14828, 713–2325.
International Affairs.—Rebecca Lent, Ph.D., room 12659, 713–9090.
Law Enforcement.—Alan Risenhoover (acting), room 415, 427–2300.
Management and Budget.—Gary Reisner, room 14450, 713–2259.
Protected Resources.—Jim Lecky, room 13821, 713–2332.
Science and Technology.—Ned Cyr, Ph.D., room 12450, 713–2367.
Scientific Programs and Chief Science Advisor.—Doug DeMaster, Ph.D. (acting) room 14659, 713–2239.
Seafood Inspection Program.—Tim Hansen, room 10837, 713–2351.
Sustainable Fisheries.—Emily Menashes (acting), room 13362, 713–2334.
Chief Information Officer.—Larry Tyminski, room 3657, 713–2372.
Aquaculture Program.—Michael Rubino, room 13117, 713–9079.
Policy.—Mark Holliday, Ph.D., room 14451, 713–9070.

NATIONAL OCEAN SERVICE

Assistant Administrator.—David Kennedy, room 13632 (301) 713–3074.
Deputy Assistant Administrator.—Holly Bamford, room 13635, 713–3074.
Director, Center for Operational Oceanographic Products and Services.—Richard Edwing, room 6650, 713–2981.
Deputy Director.—Ellen Clark, room 6633, 713–2981.
Chief Financial Officer.—Christopher Cartwright, room 13442, 713–3056.
Director, Office of:
Coast Survey.—CAPT John Lowell, room 6147, 713–2770.
International Programs.—Clement Lewsey, room 10414, 713–3078.
National Centers for Coastal Ocean Science.—Russell Callender (acting), room 8211, 713–3020.
National Geodetic Survey.—Juliana Blackwell, room 8657, 713–3222.
National Marine Sanctuaries.—Daniel Basta, room 11523, 713–7235.
NOAA Coastal Services.—Margaret A. Davidson (843) 740–1220.
Ocean and Coastal Resource Management.—Donna Wieting (acting), room 10413, 713–3155.
Response and Restoration.—Dave Westerholm, room 10102, 713–2989.
Special Projects.—Vacant, room 9515, 713–3000.

NATIONAL ENVIRONMENTAL SATELLITE, DATA AND INFORMATION SERVICE

1315 East-West Highway, Silver Spring, MD 20910

Assistant Administrator.—Mary E. Kicza, room 8268 (301) 713–3578.
Deputy Assistant Administrator.—Charles S. Baker, room 8300, 713–2010.
Deputy Assistant Administrator, Systems.—Abigail Harper, room 8338, 713–2005.
Chief Information Officer.—Catrinia Purvis (acting), room 7103, 713–1283.
Chief Financial Officer.—Michael H. Abreu, room 8338, 713–9476.
Deputy Chief Financial Officer.—Cherish Johnson, room 8340, 713–9228.
International and Interagency Affairs Chief.—D. Brent Smith, room 7315, 713–2024.
Director, Office of:
Coastal Ocean Laboratory.—Wayne Wilmot, room 4651, 713–3272.
Commercial Remote Sensing Regulatory Affairs.—Al Robinson (acting), room 8260, 713–3385.
Environmental Information Services.—Darrah Bailey-Armstrong, room 7214, 713–1260.
GOES–R Program.—Gregory A. Mandt, NASA GSFC, room C100D, 286–1355.
Joint Polar Satellite System.—Gary Davis (acting), room 3301, 286–1355.
National Climatic Data Center.—Scott Hausman (acting), room 557–C (828) 271–4476.
National Geophysical Data Center.—Christopher Fox, room 1B148 (303) 497–6215.
National Oceanographic Data Center.—Margarita Gregg, room 4820, 713–3270.
Satellite and Product Operations.—Kathleen Kelly, room 1605, 817–4000.
Satellite Applications and Research.—Al Powell, room 701, 763–8127.
Space Commercialization.—Charles S. Baker (acting), room 8300, 713–2010.
Systems Development.—Gary K. Davis, room 6234, 713–0100.

NATIONAL WEATHER SERVICE

1315 East-West Highway, Silver Spring, MD 20910

Assistant Administrator.—John ''Jack'' Hayes, Ph.D., room 18150 (301) 713–9095.
Deputy Assistant Administrator.—Laura Furgione, room 18130, 713–0711.
Chief Financial Officer.—Robert J. Byrd, room 18176, 713–0397.
Deputy Chief Financial Officer.—Barbara MacNeill, room 18212, 713–0718.
Chief Information Officer.—Iftikhar Jamil, room 17424, 713–1360.
Director, Office of:
Climate, Water and Weather Services.—David Caldwell, room 14348, 713–0700.
Hydrologic Development.—Gary M. Carter, room 8212, 713–1658.
National Centers for Environmental Prediction.—Louis W. Uccellini, room 101, 763–8016.
Operational Systems.—Mark Paese, room 16212, 713–0165.
Science and Technology.—Donald Berchoff, room 15146, 713–1746.

OCEANIC AND ATMOSPHERIC RESEARCH

1315 East-West Highway, Silver Spring, MD 20910

Assistant Administrator.—Craig McLean (acting), (301) 713–2458.
Deputy Assistant Administrator for—
Labs and Cooperative Institutes.—Alexander MacDonald, Ph.D., (303) 497–6005.
Programs and Administration.—Steven Fine, Ph.D. (acting).
Director of:
Earth System Research Laboratory.—Alexander MacDonald, Ph.D. (303) 497–6005.
Division of:
Chemical Sciences.—A.R. ''Ravi'' Ravishankara, Ph.D. (303) 497–5821.
Global Monitoring.—Jim Butler, Ph.D. (303) 497–6898.
Global Systems.—Vacant.
Physical Science.—William Neff, Ph.D. (303) 497–6265.
Air Resources Laboratory.—Michael Uhart, Ph.D. (301) 734–1177.
Atlantic Oceanographic and Meteorological Laboratory.—Robert Atlas (305) 361–4300.
Geophysical Fluid Dynamics Laboratory.—Ram Ramaswamy, Ph.D. (609) 452–6510.
Great Lakes Environmental Research Laboratory.—Mare Colton, Ph.D. (734) 741–2254.
National Sea Grant College Program.—Leon Cammen, room 11716, 713–1088.
National Severe Storms Laboratory.—Steve Koch, Ph.D. (405) 325–6900.
Pacific Marine Environmental Laboratory.—Mark Koehn, (206) 526–6810.
Director, Office of:
Arctic Research.—John Calder (301) 427–2470.

Climate Program.—Chester Koblinsky, 427–1263.
Oceanic Exploration and Research.—William Corso, 734–1145.

PROGRAM PLANNING AND INTEGRATION

Assistant Administrator.—Laura K. Furgione, room 15628 (301) 713–1632.
Deputy Assistant Administrator.—Paul N. Doremus, room 15629, 713–3318.

UNITED STATES PATENT AND TRADEMARK OFFICE

P.O. Box 1450, 600 Dulany Street, Arlington, VA 22313–1450

phone (571) 272–8600

Under Secretary of Commerce for Intellectual Property and Director of U.S. Patent and Trademark Office.—David J. Kappos.
Deputy Under Secretary of Commerce for Intellectual Property and Deputy Director of the U.S. Patent and Trademark Office.—Teresa Stanek Rea.
Chief of Staff.—Andrew Hirshfield, 272–8600.
Deputy Chief of Staff.—Toni Hickey, 272–8600.
Director of Public Affairs.—Peter Pappas, 272–3500.

COMMISSIONER FOR PATENTS

Commissioner.—Robert Stoll (571) 272–8800.
Deputy Commissioner for Patent Examination Policy.—Peggy A. Focarino.
Associate Commissioner for—
Patent Information Management.—Fred Schmidt.
Patent Resources and Planning.—Bo Bounkong.
Director, Office of:
Patent Cooperation Treaty Legal Administration.—Charles A. Pearson, 272–3224.
Patent Legal Administration.—Brian Hanlon, 272–7735.
Assistant Deputy Commissioner for Patent Operations:
Chemical Discipline.—Bob Oberleitner (TC 1600, 1700, and 2900).
Electrical I Discipline.—Andrew Faile (TC 2100 and 2400).
Electrical II Discipline.—James Dwyer (TC 2600 and 2800).
Mechanical Discipline.—Bruce Kisliuk (TC 3600 and 3700).
Patent Examining Group Directors:
Technology Center 1600 (biotechnology and organic chemistry): George Elliott, 272–0600; Jacqueline Stone, 272–0500; Irem Yucel, 272–0700.
Technology Center 1700/2900 (chemical and materials engineering/design): Yvonne Eyler, 272–1200; Sharon Gibson, 272–1100; Gary Jones, 272–1300.
Technology Center 2100 (computer architecture and software): Wendy Garber, 272–1400; Jackie Harvey, 272–2168; Nestor Ramirez, 272–4150.
Technology Center 2400 (networking, multiplexing, cable, and security): Timothy Callahan, 272–1740; Nancy Lee, 272–4056; Valencia Martin-Wallace 272–4020.
Technology Center 2600 (communications): Mark R. Powell, 272–4550; Wanda Walker, 272–4750; John LeGuyader, 272–4650.
Technology Center 2800 (semiconductor, electrical mechanical and physics/optics): John Cabeca, 272–8004; Richard Seidel, 272–2950.
Technology Center 3600 (transportation, construction, electronic commerce, agriculture, national security, and license and review): Wynn Coggins, 272–5350; Katherine Matecki, 272–5250; Dave Talbot, 272–5150.
Technology Center 3700 (mechanical engineering, manufacturing, and products): Donald Hajec, 272–2975; Angela Sykes, 272–6788; Karen Young, 272–3750.
Director, Office of:
Central Reexamination Unit.—Vacant, 272–3838.
Data Management (PUBS).—Deborah Stephens (703) 756–1492.
Legal Administration and Petitions (PCT).—Charles Pearson, 272–3224.
Oversees South Tower Operations.—Robert Olszewski (703) 756–1491.
Patent Application Processing (PCT Operations): Kevin Little, (703) 756–1451.
Patent Classification.—Olik Chaudhuri (acting), 272–1855.
Patent Financial Management.—John Buie, 272–6283.
Patent Legal Administration.—Brian Hanlon, 272–7735.
Patent Processing Services (OIPE).—Thomas Koontz (703) 756–1490.
Patent Quality Assurance.—Paula Hutzell, 272–0531.

Patent Training.—Jin Ng, 272–7400.
Administrator, Office of:
Patent Resources Administration.—John Mielcarek, 272–8110.
Search and Information Resources Administration.—Vacant, 272–1934.

COMMISSIONER FOR TRADEMARKS

Commissioner.—Deborah Cohn (571) 272–8901.
Deputy Commissioner for Trademark Operations.—Vacant.
Trademark Examination Law Office Managing Attorneys:
Law Office 101.—Ron Sussman, 272–9696.
Law Office 102.—Karen Strzyz, 272–9419.
Law Office 103.—Michael Hamilton, 272–9278.
Law Office 104.—Chris Doninger, 272–9297.
Law Office 105.—Thomas G. Howell, 272–9302.
Law Office 106.—Mary Sparrow, 272–9332.
Law Office 107.—Leslie Bishop, 272–9445.
Law Office 108.—Andrew Lawrence, 272–9342.
Law Office 109.—Dan Vavonese, 272–9288.
Law Office 110.—Chris Pedersen, 272–9371.
Law Office 111.—Craig Taylor, 272–9395.
Law Office 112.—Angela Wilson, 272–9443.
Law Office 113.—Odette Bonnet, 272–9426.
Law Office 114.—Margaret Le, 272–9456.
Law Office 115.—Thomas Vlcek, 272–9485.
Law Office 116.—Michael Baird, 272–9487.
Law Office 117.—Loretta Beck, 272–9245.
Director, Office of Trademark Program Control.—Betty Andrews, 272–9666.
Deputy Commissioner for Trademark Examination Policy.—Sharon Marsh, 272–8901.
Director, Office of Trademark Quality Review.—Kevin Peska, 272–9658.

POLICY AND EXTERNAL AFFAIRS

Administrator.—Albert Tramposch.
Deputy Administrator for External Affairs.—Jasmine Chambers (571) 272–9300.
Director, Office of:
Copyright.—Michael Shapiro, 272–9300.
Enforcement.—Peter Fowler, 272–9300.
Governmental Affairs.—Dana Colarulli, 272–7300.
International Trade.—Paul Salmon, 272–9300.
Patents.—Mary Critharis, 272–9300.
Trademark.—Amy Cotton, 272–9300.
Director of Global Intellectual Property Academy.—James Housel, 272–1500.

CHIEF FINANCIAL OFFICER

Chief Financial Officer.—Anothy Scardino (571) 272–9200.
Deputy Chief Financial Officer.—Mark Olechowski.
Senior Financial Manager.—Michelle Picard.
Director of:
Corporate Planning.—Brendan Hourigan (acting), 272–6295.
Finance.—Mark Krieger, 272–6339.
Financial Management Systems.—Gita Zoks, 272–6363.
Procurement.—Katherine Kudrewicz, 272–6575.

CHIEF ADMINISTRATIVE OFFICER

Chief Administrative Officer.—Patricia Ritchter (571) 272–9600.
Director of:
Corporate Services.—John Hassett, 272–6250.
Civil Rights.—Bismarck Myrick, 272–6315.
Human Resources.—Karen Karlinchak, 272–6200.

OFFICE OF GENERAL COUNSEL

General Counsel.—Bernard J. Knight, Jr. (571) 272–7000.
Deputy General Counsel for—
General Law.—William Covey, 272–3000.
Intellectual Property Law and Solicitor.—Raymond Chen, 272–9035.
Chief Administrative Patent Judge, Board of Patent Appeals and Interferences.—Michael R. Fleming, 272–9797.
Vice Chief Administrative Patent Judge.—James T. Moore, 272–9797.
Chief Administrative Trademark Judge, Trademark Trial and Appeal Board.—J. David Sams, 272–4304.
Director, Office of Enrollment and Discipline.—Harry I. Moatz, 272–4097.

CHIEF INFORMATION OFFICER

Chief Information Officer.—John B. Owens II (571) 272–9400.
Chief of Staff.—John S. ''Scott'' Williams, 272–5664.
Deputy Chief Information Officer.—Kevin Smith, 272–9410.
Chief Technology Officer/Director of Infrastructure Engineering and Operations.—James P. ''Jim'' Flanagan, 272–6908.
Director of:
Administrative Management.—Toby D. Bennett, 272–6205.
Budget and Finance.—Keith M. Vanderbrink, 272–5662.
Program Administration Organization.—Kay Melvin, 272–9025.
Customer Information Services.—Ted L. Parr (703) 756–1267.
Manager, Office of:
Electronic Information Products.—Lyn Donaldson (703) 756–1222.
Public Information Services.—Martha Sneed (703) 756–1236.
Public Records Division.—Ted L. Parr (acting), (703) 756–1267.
Customer Support Services.—Pam H. Kitchens, 272–8987.
Enterprise Systems Services.—Carol R. Eakins, 272–5426.
Director of IT and Security Management.—Rod W. Turk, 272–1975.
Network and Telecommunications.—Vacant.
Director of Information Management Services.—Holly Higgins (acting), 272–4877.
Quality Management.—Brain R. Jones, 272–1659.
Systems Development and Maintenance.—David C. Conley, 272–8783.

CHIEF PERFORMANCE IMPROVEMENT OFFICER

Chief Performance Improvement Officer.—Vacant (571) 272–9200.

NATIONAL INSTITUTE OF STANDARDS AND TECHNOLOGY

Director.—Dr. Patrick Gallagher (acting), (301) 975–2300.
Deputy Director.—Dr. Patrick Gallagher.
Chief Scientist.—Dr. Richard Kayser, 975–2300.
Baldrige National Quality Program.—Dr. Harry S. Hertz, 975–2360.
International and Academic Affairs.—Dr. Claire M. Saundry, 975–2386.
NIST/Boulder Laboratories.—Dr. Kent Rochford (303) 497–5285.
Chief of Staff.—Kevin Kimball (acting), 975–3070.
Congressional and Legislative Affairs.—Jim Schufreider, 975–5675.
Program Office.—Dr. Jason Boehm, 975–8678.
Public and Business Affairs.—Gail J. Porter, 975–3392.
Chief Financial Officer.—Todd Grams, 975–5000.
Budget.—Thomas P. Klausing, 975–2669.
Business Systems.—Fred Lehnhoff, 975–2290.
Finance.—Marvin Washington, 975–6897.
Grants and Agreements Management.—Laura Cesario, 975–8006.
Chief Human Capital Officer.—Essex Brown (acting), 975–3002.
Human Resources Management.—Essex Brown, 975–3801.
Management and Organization.—Catherine S. Fletcher, 975–4054.
Safety, Health and Environment.—Rosamond A. Rutledge-Burns, 975–5818.
Civil Rights and Diversity Office.—Mirta-Marie M. Keys, 975–2042.
Chief Information Officer.—Dr. Simon Szykman, 975–6500.
Applications Systems.—L. Dale Little, 975–8982.

Customer Access and Support.—Tim Halton, 975–8920.
Enterprise Systems.—James E. Fowler, 975–6888.
Information Technology Security and Networking.—Robert Glenn, 975–3667.
Telecommunications and CIO Support.—Bruce Rosen, 975–3299.
Chief Facilities Management Officer.—Stella Fiotes, 975–8836.
Administrative Services.—David T. Henry, 975–8994.
Emergency Services.—Dr. Benjamin Overbey, 975–8247.
Engineering, Maintenance and Support Services.—Stephen S. Salber (303) 497–5680.
Plant.—John Bollinger, 975–6900.
Director, Technology Services.—Dr. Belinda L. Collins, 975–4500.
Deputy Director.—Vacant, 975–4510.
Information Services.—Mary-Deirdre Coraggio, 975–5158.
Measurement Services.—Robert L. Watters, Jr., 975–4122.
Standards Services.—Dave Alderman, 975–2396.
Weights and Measures.—Carol Hockert, 975–5507.
Director, Technology Innovation Program.—Marc G. Stanley, 975–2162.
Deputy Director.—Dr. Lorel Wisniewski, 975–5232.
Project Management Office.—Linda Beth Schilling, 975–2887.
Selection Management Office.—Thomas Wiggins, 975–5416.
Director, Hollings Manufacturing Extension Partnership Program.—Roger D. Kilmer, 975–4676.
Deputy Director.—Aimee Dobrzeniecki, 975–8322.
Program Development Office.—Stephen J. Thompson, 975–5042.
Systems Operations Office.—Michael J. Simpson, 975–6147.
Director, Electronics and Electrical Engineering Laboratory.—Dr. Kent Rochford (acting), (303) 497–5285.
Deputy Director.—Dr. James Otthoff, 975–2220.
Electromagnetics.—Dr. Peter Wilson (acting), (303) 497–3406.
Optoelectronics.—Dr. Robert Hickernell (acting), (303) 497–3455.
Quantum Electrical Metrology.—Dr. Michael Kelley (303) 497–4736.
Semiconductor Electronics.—Dr. David G. Seiler, 975–2054.
Director, Center for Nanoscale Science and Technology.—Dr. Robert Celotta, 975–8001.
Director, Manufacturing Engineering Laboratory.—Dr. Howard Harary (acting), 975–3400.
Deputy Director.—Dr. Al Wavering, 975–3401.
Fabrication Technology.—Mark E. Luce, 975–2159.
Intelligent Systems.—Elena Messina, 975–3510.
Manufacturing Metrology.—Kevin K. Jurrens (acting), 975–5486.
Manufacturing Systems Integration.—Vacant, 975–3508.
Precision Engineering.—Dr. Michael Postek, 975–2299.
Director, Chemical Science and Technology Laboratory.—Dr. Willie E. May, 975–8300.
Deputy Director.—Dr. Richard Cavanagh, 975–8301.
Analytical Chemistry.—Dr. Stephen A. Wise, 975–3108.
Biochemical Science.—Dr. Laurie E. Locascio, 975–3130.
Process Measurements.—Dr. James R. Whetstone, 975–2609.
Surface and Microanalysis Science.—Dr. John Small, 975–3900.
Thermophysical Properties.—Dr. Daniel G. Friend (303) 497–5424.
Director, Physical Laboratory.—Dr. Katharine B. Gebbie, 975–4201.
Deputy Director.—Dr. William R. Ott, 975–4202.
Atomic Physics.—Dr. Carl J. Williams, 975–3531.
Electron and Optical Physics.—Dr. Charles W. Clark, 975–3709.
Ionizing Radiation.—Dr. Lisa R. Karam, 975–5561.
Optical Technology.—Dr. Gerald Fraser, 975–3797.
Quantum Physics.—Dr. Steven T. Cundiff (303) 497–7858.
Time and Frequency.—Dr. Thomas R. O'Brian (303) 497–4570.
Director, Materials Science and Engineering Laboratory.—Dr. Eric J. Amis (acting), 975–5658.
Deputy Director.—Dr. Eric J. Amis, 975–6681.
Ceramics.—Dr. Debra L. Kaiser, 975–6119.
Materials Reliability.—Dr. Stephanie Hooker (303) 497–4326.
Metallurgy.—Dr. Frank W. Gayle, 975–6161.
Polymers.—Dr. Eric Lin (acting), 975–6743.
Director, NIST Center for Neutron Research.—Dr. Robert Dimeo (acting), 975–6210.
Director, Building and Fire Research Laboratory.—Dr. S. Shyam-Sunder, 975–5900.
Deputy Director.—Dr. William L. Grosshandler, 975–6850.
Building Environment.—Dr. Hunter Fanney, 975–5864.
Fire Research.—Dr. Anthony Hamins, 975–6598.

Materials and Construction Research.—Dr. Jonathan W. Martin, 975–6707.
Director, Information Technology Laboratory.—Cita M. Furlani, 975–2900.
Deputy Director.—James A. St. Pierre, 975–2900.
Advanced Network Technologies.—Dr. David Su, 975–6194.
Computer Security.—William Curt Barker, 975–8443.
Information Access.—Dr. Martin Herman, 975–4495.
Mathematical and Computational Sciences.—Dr. Ronald F. Boisvert, 975–3800.
Software Diagnostics and Conformance Testing.—Kathleen Roberts, 975–2144.
Statistical Engineering.—Dr. Antonio Possolo (acting), 975–2853.

NATIONAL TECHNICAL INFORMATION SERVICE

5285 Port Royal Road, Springfield, VA 22161

Director.—Bruce Borzino (703) 605–6400.
Deputy Director.—Vacant, 605–6405.
Chief Financial Officer.—Mary Houff, 605–6611.
Chief Information Officer.—Keith Sinner, 605–6310.
Congressional Affairs and Policy.—Steve Needle, 605–6404.
Federal Services.—Liz Shaw, 605–6351.
Product Management and Acquisitions.—Don Hagen, 605–6142.
Production Services.—Vacant.

NATIONAL TELECOMMUNICATIONS AND INFORMATION ADMINISTRATION

1401 Constitution Avenue, NW., 20230

Assistant Secretary and Administrator.—Lawrence E. Stickling, room 4898 (202) 482–1840.
Deputy Assistant Secretary.—Anna M. Gomez, 482–1840.
Chief of Staff.—Thomas Power, 482–1840.
Deputy Chief of Staff and Congressional Affairs Director.—James Wasilewski.
Senior Advisors: Larry Atlas, Marsha MacBride.
Advisor.—Angela Simpson.
Chief Counsel.—Kathy Smith.
Director, Office of:
Communications and Information Infrastructure Assurance.—Daniel Hurley.
Institute for Telecommunication Sciences.—Al Vincent (303) 497–3500.
International Affairs.—Fiona Alexander.
Policy Analysis and Development.—Daniel J. Weitzner.
Public Affairs Director.—Rochelle Cohen.
Spectrum Management.—Karl Nebbia.
Telecommunications and Information Applications.—Bernadette McGuire-Rivera.

DEPARTMENT OF LABOR

Frances Perkins Building, Third Street and Constitution Avenue, NW., 20210
phone (202) 693–5000, http://www.dol.gov

HILDA L. SOLIS, Secretary of Labor; education: B.A., California State Polytechnic University, Pomona, 1979; M.P.A., University of Southern California, 1981; professional: White House Office of Hispanic Affairs, 1980–81; Management Analyst, Office of Management and Budget, 1981; California State Assembly, 1992–94; California State Senate, 1994–2000; member of 32nd Congressional District in California, 2001–09; member of Rio Hondo Community College Board of Trustees, 1985; member of California Senate Industrial Relations Committee, 1996; vice chair, of the Helsinki Commission's General Committee on Democracy, Human Rights and Humanitarian Questions, 2007; married: Sam H. Sayyad; recipient of John F. Kennedy Profile in Courage Award, 2000; and other awards for professional accomplishments; nominated by President Barack Obama to become the 25th Secretary of Labor, and was confirmed by the U.S. Senate on February 24, 2009.

OFFICE OF THE SECRETARY

phone (202) 693–6000

Secretary of Labor.—Hilda L. Solis.
Deputy Secretary.—Seth Harris.
Associate Deputy Secretary.—Laura McClintock.
Executive Secretariat Director.—Elizabeth Kim.
Chief of Staff.—Katherine Archuleta.
Director of Advance and Scheduling.—Carolyn Mosley.

OFFICE OF PUBLIC ENGAGEMENT

Senior Advisor and Director.—Dr. Gabriela Lemus (202) 693–6000, fax (202) 693–6145.

ADMINISTRATIVE LAW JUDGES

Techworld, 800 K Street, NW., Suite 400–N, 20001–8002

Chief Administrative Law Judge.—Stephen L. Purcell (202) 693–7542.
Associate Chief Judges: William S. Colwell, Paul C. Johnson, Jr. (acting).

ADMINISTRATIVE REVIEW BOARD

Chief and Chair.—Paul M. Igasaki, room N–5404 (202) 693–6200.
Vice Chair.—E. Cooper Brown, room N–5404, 693–6200.

ASSISTANT SECRETARY FOR ADMINISTRATION AND MANAGEMENT

Assistant Secretary.—T. Michael Kerr, room S–2203 (202) 693–4040.
Deputy Assistant Secretary for—
Budget and Performance Planning.—Vacant.
Operations.—Edward C. Hugler.
Policy.—Charlotte Hayes.
Security and Emergency Management.—Kenneth McCreless, room S–1229G, 693–7990.
Special Assistant.—M. Lucero Ortiz.
Administrative Officer.—Christopher Yerxa.
Staff Assistants: Kamilia Epps, Douglas Robins.

BUSINESS OPERATIONS CENTER

Director.—Al Stewart, room S–1524 (202) 693–4028.
Deputy Director.—John Saracco.
Office of:
Acquisition Management Services.—Carol Jenkins, room S–1513–C, 693–7246.
Administrative Services.—Phil Puckett, room S–1521, 693–6650.
Competitive Sourcing.—William Keisler, room S–1519A, 693–4020.
Management Support Services.—Vacant, room S–1519B, 693–7272.
Procurement Services.—Sandra Foster, room S–4307, 693–4570.
Worker Safety and Health Services.—Stephanie Semmer, room S–1321, 693–6670.

CENTER FOR PROGRAM PLANNING AND RESULTS

Director.—Vacant.
Director.—David Frederickson (acting), room S–3317 (202) 693–7123.
Office of:
DOL Historian.—Linda Stinson, room N–2445, 693–4085.
Planning.—Karen Gever, 693–7126.
Wirtz Labor Library.—Vacant, room N–2445, 693–6600.

CIVIL RIGHTS CENTER

Director.—Ramos Suris Fernandez, room N–4123 (202) 693–6500.
Staff Assistant.—Katrina Creek.
Office of:
Compliance Assistance and Planning.—Kevin Malone, 693–6531.
EEO Coordinator of Counselors.—Lillian Winstead, 693–6504.
Enforcement/External.—Julia Mankata Tamakloe (acting), 693–6502.
Enforcement/Internal.—Naomi Berry Perez, 693–6503.
Reasonable Accommodation Hotline.—Dawn Johnson, room N–4123, 693–6569.

DEPARTMENTAL BUDGET CENTER

Director.—Geoff Kenyon, room S–4020 (202) 693–4090.
Deputy Director.—Mark P. Wichlin.
Staff Assistant.—Patricia Smith.
Office of:
Agency Budget Programs.—James Martin, 693–4077.
Budget Policy and Systems.—Sandra Mulcahy, 693–4078.
Financial Management Operations.—Chris Calogero (acting), room S–5526, 693–4087.

EMERGENCY MANAGEMENT CENTER

Director.—Greg Rize, 800 K Street, NW., Suite 450 North, 20001–8002 (202) 693–7555.
Deputy Director.—Mary Jo Hogan.
Staff Assistant.—Brenda Vaughn.

GOVBENEFITS.GOV

Program Manager.—Curtis Turner, room N–4309 (202) 693–4025.

HUMAN RESOURCES CENTER

Director.—Eugenio Sexton, room C–5526 (202) 693–7600.
Deputy Director.—Vacant.
Office of:
Administration and Management Services.—Tracey Schaeffer, C–5517, 693–7773.
Continuous Learning and Career Management.—Kim Green, room N–5464, 693–7630.
Employee and Labor Management Relations.—Sydney Rose, room N–5464, 693–7670.
Executive Resources.—Crystal Scott, room C–5508, 693–7800.
Human Resources Consulting and Operations.—Maria McAplin, room C–5516, 693–7690.
Human Resources Policy and Accountability.—Jerome Bonner, room 5464, 693–7720.

Personnel Security.—Lillie Hughes, room N–2453, 693–0004.
Workforce Planning and e-Innovations.—Alvin Black, room S–3314, 693–7740.
Worklife and Benefits Programs.—Deborah Dudley, room N–5454, 693–7610.

INFORMATION TECHNOLOGY CENTER

Director.—Thomas Wiesner, room N–1301 (202) 693–4567.
Staff Assistant.—Rosita Blyden.
Deputy Director.—Vacant.
Administrative Officer.—Kathy Fox, 693–4215.
Director, Office of:
Chief Information Officer Programs.—Peter Sullivan, 693–4211.
Systems Development and Integration.—Richard Lewis, 693–4149.
Technical Services.—Louis Charlier, 693–4147.
IT Help Desk.—8 a.m. to 6:30 p.m., room N–1505, 693–4444.

SECURITY CENTER

Director.—Tom Holman, room S–1229G (202) 693–7200.
Deputy Director.—Stacey Thompson.
Staff Assistant.—Claudette Brito.

ASSISTANT SECRETARY FOR POLICY

Assistant Secretary.—William E. Spriggs, room S–2312 (202) 693–5959.
Deputy Assistant Secretary.—Megan Uzzell.
Chief of Staff.—Vacant.
Staff Assistant.—Vacant.
Director, Office of:
Compliance Assistance Policy.—Vacant.
Economic Policy and Analysis.—Vacant.
Regulatory and Programmatic Policy.—Kathleen Franks, 693–5072.

BENEFITS REVIEW BOARD

Chair.—Nancy S. Dolder, room N5101 (202) 693–6300.

BUREAU OF LABOR STATISTICS

Postal Square Building, Suite 4040, 2 Massachusetts Avenue, NE., 20212

phone (202) 691–7800

Commissioner.—Keith Hall.
Deputy Commissioner.—Philip L. Rones, 691–7802.
Associate Commissioner, Office of:
Administration.—Daniel J. Lacey, suite 4060, 691–7777.
Compensation and Working Conditions.—William Wiatrowski, suite 4130, 691–6300.
Employment and Unemployment Statistics.—John M. Galvin, suite 4945, 691–6400.
Field Operations.—Jay Mousa, suite 2935, 691–5800.
Prices and Living Conditions.—Michael Horrigan, suite 3120, 691–6960.
Productivity and Technology.—Michael Harper, suite 2150, 691–5600.
Publications and Special Studies.—Michael Levi, suite 4110, 691–5900.
Survey Methods Research.—John Eltinge, suite 1950, 691–7404.
Technology and Survey Processing.—Fernando Burbano, suite 5025, 691–7600.
Assistant Commissioner, Office of:
Compensation Levels and Trends.—Phil Doyle, suite 4130, 691–6200.
Consumer Prices and Price Indexes.—John Layng, suite 3130, 691–6955.
Current Employment Analysis.—Thomas Nardone, suite 4675, 691–6379.
Industrial Prices and Price Indexes.—David Friedman, suite 4170, 691–6307.
Industry Employment Statistics.—Patricia Getz, suite 4840, 691–6521.
Occupational Statistics and Employment Projections.—Dixie Sommers, suite 2135, 691–5701.
Director of:

Survey Processing.—Richard L. Schroeder, suite 5025, 691–6730.
Technology and Computing Services.—Rick Kryger, suite 5025, 691–7562.

BUREAU OF INTERNATIONAL LABOR AFFAIRS

Deputy Under Secretary.—Sandra Polaski, room S–2235 (202) 693–4770.
Associate Deputy Under Secretary.—Carol Pier, room S–2235, 693–4770.
Special Assistants: Thomas Heckroth, Kathleen Schalch, room S–2235, 693–4770.
Chief of Staff.—Amit Pandya, room S–2235, 693–4770.
Director of Policy, Planning and Implementation.—Timothy Wedding, room S–2235, 693–4871.
Administrative Officer.—Vacant.
Executive Assistants: Alfreda Johnson, Diane Ward, room S–2235, 693–4770.

OFFICE OF TRADE AND LABOR AFFAIRS

Director.—Gregory Schoepfle, room S–5303 (202) 693–4887.
Deputy Director.—Sueryun Hahn (acting), room S–5303, 693–4800.

OFFICE OF CHILD LABOR, FORCED LABOR, AND HUMAN TRAFFICKING

Director.—Marcia Eugenio, room S–5317, (202) 693–4849.
Deputy Director.—Kevin Willcutts, room S–5317 693–4832.

OFFICE OF INTERNATIONAL RELATIONS

Director.—Robert B. Shepard, room S–5317, (202) 693–4808
Deputy Director.—James Shea, room S–5317, 693–4912.
Deputy Director for Management and Foreign Relations.—Zhao Li, room S–5207, 693–4803.

OFFICE OF THE CHIEF FINANCIAL OFFICER

Chief Financial Officer.—James Taylor, room S–4030 (202) 693–6800.
Deputy Chief Financial Officer.—Karen Tekleberhan.
Associate Deputy CFO for—
Financial Systems.—Ken Bode (acting), room N–2719.
Fiscal Integrity.—Yoko Albayrak.
Administrative Officer.—Marella Turner (acting).

OFFICE OF FISCAL INTEGRITY

Division of:
Central Accounting Operations.—Sahra Torres-Rivera, room S–4502.
Client Accounting Services.—Shelia Alexander, room N–5526.
E Travel.—Cynthia Jones, room N–2719, 693–6829.
Financial Compliance.—Ellen Waterhouse, room S–4502.
Financial Policy and Analysis.—Stan Karczewski (acting), room S–4030.
Financial Reporting.—Miguel Reyes, room S–4502, 693–6800.

OFFICE OF FINANCIAL SYSTEMS

Division of:
Systems Architecture and Development.—Kenneth Bode, room N–2719, 693–6844.
Quality Assurance and Security.—Vacant, room N–2719, 693–6919.
Payroll Systems Support.—Roy Abreu, room S–4214, 693–4324.
Production Support and System Administration.—Richard Westmark, room N–2719, 693–6900.

OFFICE OF CONGRESSIONAL AND INTERGOVERNMENTAL AFFAIRS

Assistant Secretary.—Brian Kennedy, room S–2006 (202) 693–4601.
Chief of Staff.—Laura MacDonald, room S–2006, 693–4601.

Staff Assistant.—Glenda Manning, room S–2006, 693–4601.
Deputy Assistant Secretary, Congressional and Intergovernmental Affairs.—Sharon Block, room S–2220, 693–4600.
Director for Intergovernmental Affairs.—Elmy A. Bermejo, S–2220, 693–6400.
Deputy Director for Intergovernmental Affairs.—Livia Y. Lam, S–2220.
Associate Assistant Secretary/Budget and Appropriations.—Teri Bergman, room S–2220, 693–4600.
Senior Legislative Officers:
Employee Benefits.—Ben Gruenbaum, room S–2220, 693–4600.
Employment and Training.—Adri Jayaratne, room S–2220, 693–4600.
VETS/Employment and Training/Foreign Labor Certification.—Tony Zaffirini, room S–2220, 693–4600.
Wage and Hour Division and ILAB/International Affairs.—Nikki McKinney, room S–2220, 693–4600.
Senior Legislative Counsel for Oversight/Investigation and Labor Management Standards.—Patrick Findlay, room S–1318, 693–4600.
Legislative Officers: Brittany Diegel, Sara Kinsley, Andria Oliver, Michelle Rose, Carrianna Suiter, Laura de la Torre, room S–2220, 693–4600.
Congressional Research Assistant.—Vacant.
Senior Intergovernmental Officer.—Vacant.
Administrative Officer.—Joycelyn Daniels, room S–1318, 693–4600.

SECRETARY'S REPRESENTATIVES IN THE REGIONAL OFFICES

Region II, New York.—Robert Angelo, Connecticut, Delaware, District of Columbia, New Hampshire, New Jersey, New York, Pennsylvania, Vermont, Virginia, West Virginia.
Region V, Chicago.—Ken Williams-Bennett, Illinois, Indiana, Iowa, Kentucky, Michigan, Minnesota, Missouri, Ohio, Wisconsin.
Region VIII, Denver.—Dusti Gurule, Colorado, Kansas, Nebraska, New Mexico, Oklahoma, Texas.
Region IX, Los Angeles.—Alicia Villarreal, Arizona, California, Hawaii, Nevada, Utah.
Region X, Seattle.—Vacant, Alaska, Idaho, Montana, North Dakota, Oregon, South Dakota, Washington, Wyoming.

OFFICE OF DISABILITY EMPLOYMENT POLICY

Assistant Secretary.—Kathleen Martinez, room S–1303, (202) 693–7880, TTY 693–7881.
Deputy Assistant Secretary.—John R. Beverly III.
Chief of Staff.—Vacant.
Special Assistant.—Dylan Orr.
Director of Policy Development.—Susan Parker.

EMPLOYEE BENEFITS SECURITY ADMINISTRATION

Assistant Secretary.—Phyllis C. Borzi, room S–2524 (202) 693–8300.
Deputy Assistant Secretary.—Michael L. Davis (202) 693–8300.
Special Assistants: Ali Khawar, Nicole Price, 693–8300.
Confidential Assistant.—Michelle S. Brown.
Deputy Assistant Secretary for Program Operations.—Alan D. Lebowitz, room N–5677, 693–8315.
Executive Assistant.—Becki Marchand, 693–8315.
Director of:
Program, Planning, Evaluation and Management.—Brian C. McDonnell, room N–5668, 693–8480.
Chief Accountant.—Ian Dingwall, room N–5459, 693–8360.
Enforcement.—Virginia Smith, room N–5702, 693–8440.
Exemption Determinations.—Ivan L. Strasfeld, room N–5649, 693–8540.
Technology and Information Services.—Diane Schweizer, room N–5459, 693–8600.
Particiapnt Assistance.—Sharon Watson, room N–5625, 693–8630.
Regulations and Interpretations.—Robert Doyle, room N–5669, 693–8500.
Policy and Research.—Joseph Piacentini, room N–5718, 693–8410.
Health Plan Standards and Compliance Assistance.—Daniel Maguire, room 5653, 693–8335.

EMPLOYEES' COMPENSATION APPEALS BOARD

Chairman and Chief Judge.—Alec J. Koromilas, room N–5416 (202) 693–6420.

EMPLOYMENT AND TRAINING ADMINISTRATION

Assistant Secretary.—Jane Oates, room S–2307 (202) 693–2700.
Deputy Assistant Secretary.—Gerri Fiala, room S–2307, 693–2700.
Administrator, Office of:
Apprenticeship.—John Ladd, room N–5311, 693–2796.
Contracts Management.—Linda Heartley, room N–4702, 693–2800.
Financial and Administrative Management.—Daphne Jefferson, room N–4653, 693–2800.
Foreign Labor Certification.—William Carlson, room C–4312, 693–3010.
Information System and Technology.—Curtis Turner (acting), room S–5206, 693–3334.
Job Corps.—Edna Primrose, room N–4463, 693–3000.
National Response.—Erica Cantor, room C–5321, 693–3500.
Policy Development and Research.—Mike Jones (acting), room N–5637, 693–3700.
Regional Operations.—Jacqui Shoholm, room C–4517, 693–3690.
Trade Adjustment Assistance.—Erin Fitzgerald, room C–5321, 693–3560.
Unemployment Insurance.—Gay Gilbert, room S–4231, 693–3029.
Workforce Investment.—Grace Kilbane, room S–4231, 693–3980.

DOL CENTER FOR FAITH-BASED AND NEIGHBORHOOD PARTNERSHIPS

Director.—Philip Tom (202) 693–6030.
Deputy Director.—Benjamin Seigel, 693–6032.

OFFICE OF THE INSPECTOR GENERAL

Inspector General.—Vacant, room S–5502 (202) 693–5100.
Deputy Inspector General.—Daniel R. Petrole (acting).
Chief of Staff.—Dale F. Wilson.
Assistant Inspector General for—
Audit.—Elliot P. Lewis, room S–5518, 693–5168.
Inspection and Special Investigation.—Asa ''Gene'' Cunningham, room S–5021.
Labor Racketeering and Fraud Investigations.—Thomas F. Farrell, room S–5014, 693–7034.
Legal Services.—Howard L. Shapiro, room S–5506, 693–5116.
Management and Policy.—Nancy Ruiz de Gamboa, room S–5028, 693–5191.

MINE SAFETY AND HEALTH ADMINISTRATION

1100 Wilson Boulevard, Arlington, VA 22209–3939, phone (202) 693–9414

fax 693–9401, http://www.msha.gov

Assistant Secretary.—Joseph A. Main, room 2322, 693–9414.
Deputy Assistant Secretary for Policy.—Dr. Gregory Wagner, room 2321.
Deputy Assistant Secretary for Operations.—Patricia W. Silvey, room 2324.
Director, Office of:
Accountability.—Pete Montali (acting), room 2326, 693–9604.
Assessments.—Jay P. Mattos, room 2518, 693–9702.
Diversity and Equal Opportunity.—Darlene Farrar-Warren, room 2407, 693–9885.
Employee Safety and Health.—Richard D. Feehan, room 2434, 693–9586.
Program Education and Outreach Services.—Layne Lathram, room 2317, 693–9422.
Program Evaluation and Information Resources.—George M. Fesak, Jr., room 2300, 693–9750.
Standards, Regulations and Variances.—April Nelson (acting), room 2313, 693–9440.
Technical Support.—Linda Zeiler (acting), room 2330, 693–9470.

COAL MINE SAFETY AND HEALTH

Administrator.—Kevin Stricklin, room 2424, 693–9500.
Deputy Administrator.—Charles J. Thomas (acting), room 2426, 693–9503

METAL AND NONMETAL MINE SAFETY AND HEALTH

Administrator.—Neal H. Merrifield, room 2436, 693–9600.
Deputy Administrator.—Don Foster (acting), room 2437, 693–9645.

EDUCATIONAL POLICY AND DEVELOPMENT

Director.—Jeffrey A. Duncan, room 2100, 693–9570.
Deputy Director.—Thomas Kesslar, room 2148, 693–9570.

OCCUPATIONAL SAFETY AND HEALTH ADMINISTRATION

Assistant Secretary.—David Michaels, room S–2315 (202) 693–2000.
Deputy Assistant Secretaries: Jordan Barab, Richard Fairfax, 693–2000.
Chief of Staff.—Deborah Berkowitz, 693–2000.
Director, Office of:
Equal Employment Opportunity.—Catherine Fortune, 693–2150.
Communications.—Deborah Berkowitz, 693–1999.
Director of:
Administrative Programs.—Kimberly A. Locey, 693–1600.
Construction.—Jim Maddux, 693–2100.
Cooperative and State Programs.—Greg Baxter (acting), 693–2200.
Enforcement Programs.—Thomas Galassi, 693–2100.
Evaluation and Analysis.—Keith Goddard, 693–2400.
Information Technology.—Cheryle Greenaugh, 693–1818.
Technology Support and Emergency Management.—Tom Galassi (acting), 693–2300.
Standards and Guidance.—Dorothy Dougherty, 693–1950.

OFFICE OF PUBLIC AFFAIRS

Senior Advisor for Communications and Public Affairs.—Carl Fillichio, room S–2514 (202) 693–4676.
Senior Managing Director.—Jaime Zapata.

REGIONAL OFFICES

Region I.—Connecticut, Maine, Massachusetts, New Hampshire, Rhode Island, Vermont.
Public Affairs Director.—John Chavez, JFK Federal Building, Government Center, 25 New Sudbury Street, Room 525–A, Boston, MA 02203 (617) 565–2075.
Region IIA.—New York, Puerto Rico, Virgin Islands.
Public Affairs Director.—John Chavez, JFK Federal Building, Government Center, 25 New Sudbury Street, Room 525–A, Boston, Massachusetts 02203 (617) 565–2075.
Region IIB.—New Jersey.
Public Affairs Director.—Leni Uddyback-Fortson, Curtis Center, 170 S. Independence Mall West, Suite 633-East, Philadelphia, PA 19106–3306 (215) 861–5102.
Region III.—Delaware, District of Columbia, Maryland, Pennsylvania, Virginia, West Virginia.
Public Affairs Director.—Leni Uddyback-Fortson, Curtis Center, 170 S. Independence Mall West, Suite 633-East, Philadelphia, PA 19106–3306 (215) 861–5102.
Region IV.—Alabama, Florida, Georgia, Kentucky, Mississippi, North Carolina, South Carolina, Tennessee.
Public Affairs Director.—Mike Wald, Atlanta Federal Center, 61 Forsyth, SW., Suite 6B75, Atlanta, GA 30303 (404) 562–2078.
Region V.—Illinois, Indiana, Michigan, Minnesota, Ohio, Wisconsin.
Public Affairs Director.—Scott Allen, Room 3194, 230 South Dearborn Street, Room 3192, Chicago, IL 60604 (312) 353–4727.
Region VI.—Arkansas, Louisiana, New Mexico, Oklahoma, Texas.
Public Affairs Director.—Elizabeth Todd (acting), Room 734, 525 Griffin Street, Dallas, TX 75202 (972) 850–4710.
Region VII.—Iowa, Kansas, Missouri, Nebraska.
Public Affairs Specialist.—Rich Kulczewski, 1999 Broadway, Suite 1640, Denver, CO 80202 (303) 844–1302.
Region VIII.—Colorado, Montana, North Dakota, South Dakota, Utah, Wyoming.
Public Affairs Director.—Rich Kulczewski, 1999 Broadway, Suite 1640, Denver, CO 80202 (303) 844–1302.
Region IX.—Arizona, California, Guam, Hawaii, Nevada.

Public Affairs Director.—Deanne Amaden, Suite 2–650, 90 7th Street, San Francisco, CA 94103–1516 (415) 625–2630.

Region X.—Alaska, Idaho, Oregon, Washington.

Public Affairs Director.—Mike Shimizu, room 930, 1111 Third Avenue, Seattle, WA 98101 (206) 553–7620.

OFFICE OF SMALL AND DISADVANTAGED BUSINESS UTILIZATION

Director.—Sonya Carrion, N–6432 (202) 693–7299.

OFFICE OF THE SOLICITOR

Solicitor.—M. Patricia Smith, room S–2002 (202) 693–5260.
Deputy Solicitor.—Deborah Greenfield.
Staff Assistant.—Gail Swann.
Special Assistant.—Rajesh Nayak.
Deputy Solicitor for—
National Operations.—Steven J. Mandel, 693–5260.
Regional Operations.—Katherine Bissell, 693–5260.

DIVISION OF BLACK LUNG AND LONGSHORE LEGAL SERVICES

Associate Solicitor.—Rae Ellen James, room N–2117 (202) 693–5660.
Deputy Associate Solicitor.—M. Elizebeth Medaglia.
Counsel for—
Administrative Litigation and Legal Advice.—Michael J. Rutledge.
Appellate Litigation.—Patricia M. Nece.
Longshore.—Mark A. Reinhalter.

DIVISION OF CIVIL RIGHTS AND LABOR-MANAGEMENT

Associate Solicitor.—Vacant, room N–2474 (202) 693–5740.
Deputy Associate Solicitor.—Beverly Dankowitz.
Counsel for—
Advice and Statutory Programs.—Mark S. Flynn.
Interpretation and Advice.—Suzan Chastain.
Litigation and Regional Coordination.—Beverly I. Dankowitz.
LMRDA Programs.—Sharon E. Hanley.

DIVISION OF EMPLOYMENT AND TRAINING LEGAL SERVICES

Associate Solicitor.—Gary M. Buff, room N–2101 (202) 693–5710.
Deputy Associate Solicitor.—Jonathan H. Waxman, 693–5730.
Counsel for—
Employment and Training Advise.—Robert P. Hines, Michael N. Apfelbaum.
Immigration Programs.—Vacant.
International Affairs and USERRA.—Donald D. Carter, Jr.
Litigation.—Harry L. Sheinfeld.

DIVISION OF FAIR LABOR STANDARDS

Associate Solicitor.—Jennifer Brand, room N–2716 (202) 693–5555.
Deputy Associate Solicitor.—William C. Lesser.
Counsel for—
Appellate Litigation.—Paul L. Frieden.
Legal Advice.—Lynn McIntosh.
Trial Litigation.—Jonathan M. Kronheim.
Whistleblower Programs.—Ellen R. Edmond.

DIVISION OF FEDERAL EMPLOYEE AND ENERGY WORKERS COMPENSATION

Associate Solicitor.—Jeffrey L. Nesvet, room S–4325 (202) 693–5320.

Deputy Associate Solicitor.—Thomas G. Giblin.
Counsel for—
Claims and Compensation.—Catherine P. Carter.
Energy Employees Compensation.—Sheldon O. Turley, Jr.
Chief, FECA Subrogation Unit.—Gertrude B. Gordon.

DIVISION OF MINE SAFETY AND HEALTH

1100 Wilson Boulevard, 22nd Floor, Arlington, VA 22209

Associate Solicitor.—Heidi W. Strassler, room 2222 (202) 693–9333.
Deputy Associate Solicitor.—Thomas Paige.
Counsel for—
Appellate Litigation.—W. Christian Schumann, room 2220.
Standards and Legal Advice.—April E. Nelson, room 2224.
Trial Litigation.—Mark K. Malecki, room 2226.

DIVISION OF OCCUPATIONAL SAFETY AND HEALTH

Associate Solicitor.—Joseph M. Woodward, room S–4004 (202) 693–5452.
Deputy Associate Solicitor.—Ann S. Rosenthal.
Counsel for—
Appellate Litigation: Michael P. Doyle, Charles F. James.
Health Standards.—Ian J. Moar.
Regional Litigation and Legal Advice: Orlando J. Pannocchia, Robert W. Swain.
Safety Standards.—Robert J. Biersner.
Special Litigation.—Kenneth A. Hellman.

DIVISION OF PLAN BENEFITS SECURITY

Associate Solicitor.—Timothy D. Hauser, room N–4611 (202) 693–5600.
Deputy Associate Solicitor.—William Scott.
Counsel for—
Appellate and Special Litigation: Elizabeth Hopkins, Nathaniel I. Spiller.
Fiduciary Litigation.—Risa D. Sandler.
General Litigation.—Leslie Canfield Perlman.
Regulation.—William White Taylor.

HONORS PROGRAM

Director.—Nancy M. Rooney, room N–2700 (202) 693–5260.

OFFICE OF LEGAL COUNSEL

Associate Solicitor.—Robert A. Shapiro, room N–2700 (202) 693–5500.
Counsel for—
Ethics.—Robert M. Sadler, 693–5528.
Legislative Affairs.—Jill M. Otte, 693–5525.

MANAGEMENT AND ADMINISTRATIVE LEGAL SERVICES

Associate Solicitor.—William W. Thompson II, room N–2428 (202) 693–5405.
Counsel for—
Administrative Law.—Ray Mitten, Jr., 693–5405.
Appropriations and Contracts.—Ginger Ackerman, 693–5378.
FOIA/FACA.—Joseph J. Plick, 693–5527.
Chief, Human Resources.—Matthew Green, 693–5324.
Financial Manager.—James Taylor, room N–2427, 693–5412.
IT/IRM Manager.—Cheryl C. Hogans, room N–2414, 693–5368.

VETERANS' EMPLOYMENT AND TRAINING SERVICE

Assistant Secretary.—Raymond M. Jefferson, room S–1312 (202) 693–4700.

Deputy Assistant Secretary for Operations and Management.—John McWilliam.
Chief of Staff.—Amit Magdieli.
Special Assistant.—Vacant.
Director for—
Agency Management and Budget.—Vacant.
Compliance, Investigations, and Research.—Ruth Samardick, 693–4706.
Government and Legislative Affairs.—Nancy Hogan, 693–4708.
Grants and Transition Programs.—Gordon Burke, 693–4707.

REGIONAL OFFICES

Atlanta:
Administrator.—William J. Bolls, Jr. (404) 562–2305.
Boston:
Administrator.—David W. Houle (617) 565–2080.
Chicago / Kansas City:
Administrator.—Heather Higgins (312) 353–0970.
Dallas / Denver:
Administrator.—Lester L. Williams, Jr. (972) 850–4718.
Philadelphia:
Administrator.—Joseph W. Hortiz, Jr. (215) 861–5390.
Seattle / San Francisco:
Administrator.—Christopher D. Still (415) 625–7670.

WOMEN'S BUREAU

Director.—Sara Manzano-Diaz, room S–3002 (202) 693–6730.
Chief of Staff.—Sandra Vega.
National Office Coordinator.—Karen Furia.
Field Coordinator.—Latifa Lyles (972) 850–4700.
Chief, Office of:
Information and Support Services.—Catherine Breitenbach.
Policy and Programs.—Karen Furia (acting).

DEPARTMENT OF HEALTH AND HUMAN SERVICES

200 Independence Avenue, SW., 20201, http://www.hhs.gov

KATHLEEN G. SEBELIUS, Secretary of Health and Human Services; born in Cincinnati, OH, May 15, 1948; education: B.S., Trinity University, 1970; M.P.A., University of Kansas, 1977; professional: elected Governor of Kansas, 2002 and re-elected, 2006; before tenure as Governor, served as the Kansas State Insurance Commissioner for 8 years; served as a member of the Kansas House of Representatives, 1986–94; married: Gary, a federal magistrate judge; children: two sons, Ned and John; nominated by President Barack Obama to become the 21st Secretary of Health and Human Services, confirmed by the U.S. Senate and sworn in, both on April 28, 2009.

OFFICE OF THE SECRETARY

Secretary of Health and Human Services.—Kathleen G. Sebelius (202) 690–7000.
  Executive Assistant to the Secretary.—Lynda M. Gyles.

OFFICE OF THE DEPUTY SECRETARY

Chief of Staff.—William V. Corr (202) 690–6133.
  Deputy Chief of Staff.—Laura Petrou, 690–8157.
  Executive Secretary.—Dawn Small, 690–5627.
  Deputy Executive Secretary.—Barbara Holland, 690–5627.
  Director, Intergovernmental Affairs.—Vacant, 690–6060.
  Chair, Departmental Appeals Board.—Constance Tobias, 565–0220.

ASSISTANT SECRETARY FOR ADMINISTRATION AND MANAGEMENT

Assistant Secretary.—E.J. ''Ned'' Holland (acting), (202) 690–7431.
  Deputy Assistant Secretary.—Denise Wells, 690–6191.
  Associate Deputy Assistant Secretary.—Antonia Harris, 690–6191.
  Deputy Assistant Secretary for—
    Acquisition Management and Policy.—Nancy Gunderson (acting), 205–9452.
    Business Transformation.—Robert Noonan, 690–5803.
    Facilities Management and Policy.—Howard Kelsey, 401–1437.
  Director, Office of:
    Diversity Management and Equal Employment Opportunity.—Vacant, 205–2821.
    Program Support Center.—Paul Bartley, (301) 492–4600.
    Small and Disadvantaged Business Utilization.—Debbie Ridgely, 690–7235.

PROGRAM SUPPORT CENTER

5600 Fishers Lane, Rockville, MD 20857

Director.—Paul S. Bartley (301) 492–4600.
  Deputy Director.—Terry Hurst, 443–2365.
  Federal Operational Health.—Gene Migliaccio, Ph.D., (301) 594–0245.
  Financial Management Service.—William McCabe, 443–1478.
  Administrative Operations Service.—Michael Tyllas, Ph.D., 443–2516.
  Strategic Acquisitions Service.—Christie Goodman, 443–6557.
  Information and Systems Management Service.—Terry Hurst, 443–2365.

ASSISTANT SECRETARY FOR LEGISLATION

Assistant Secretary.—Jim Esquea (202) 690–7627.
  Deputy Assistant Secretary for—
    Congressional Liaison.—Fatima Cuevas, 690–6786.
    Discretionary Health Programs.—Jeremy Sharp, 690–7450.
    Human Services Programs.—Doug Steiger, 690–6311.
    Mandatory Health Programs.—Vacant, 690–6311.

ASSISTANT SECRETARY FOR PLANNING AND EVALUATION

Assistant Secretary for Planning and Evaluation.—Sherry Glied (202) 690–7858.
Principal Deputy Assistant Secretary.—Donald Moulds, 690–7858.
Deputy Assistant Secretary for—
Disability and Long Term Care.—Richard Frank, 690–6443.
Health Policy.—Richard Kronick, 690–6870.
Human Services Policy.—David Harris, 690–7409.
Science and Data Policy.—Jim Scanlon, 690–7100.

ASSISTANT SECRETARY FOR PUBLIC AFFAIRS

Assistant Secretary.—Vacant (202) 690–7850.
Deputy Assistant Secretary for Media.—Richard Sorian, 690–7850, fax 690–6247.
Director, Division of Freedom of Information/Privacy.—Robert Eckert, 690–7453.

ASSISTANT SECRETARY FOR PREPAREDNESS AND RESPONSE

Assistant Secretary.—RADM Nicole Lurie (202) 260–1158.
Principal Deputy Assistant Secretary.—Dr. Gerald Parker.
Principal Deputy Director and Director for the Office Biomedical Advanced Research and Development Authority.—Dr. Robin Robinson, 260–1200.
Deputy Assistant Secretary and Director, Office for—
Medicine, Science, and Public Health.—Dr. Kevin Yeskey, 205–8387.
Preparedness and Emergency Operations.—Dr. Kevin Yeskey, 205–0872.
Director for the Office of Resource Planning and Evaluation.—Lisa Kaplowitz, 260–8519.

ASSISTANT SECRETARY FOR FINANCIAL RESOURCES

Assistant Secretary.—Ellen G. Murray (202) 690–6396.
Principal Deputy Assistant Secretary.—Richard Turman, 690–6061.
Deputy Assistant Secretary for—
Budget.—Norris Cochran, 690–7393.
Finance.—Shelia Conley, 690–7084.
Grants.—Nancy Gunderson, 690–6617.
Chief, Information Office.—Michael Carleton, 690–6162.

OFFICE FOR CIVIL RIGHTS

Director.—Georgina Verdugo (202) 619–0403.
Principal Deputy Director.—Robinsue Frohboese.
Deputy Directors for—
Civil Rights Division.—Gary Steinberg, J.D., 619–0403.
Health Information Privacy.—Susan McAndrew, J.D., 619–0403.
Management Operations.—Vacant, 619–0403.
Toll Free Voice Number (Nationwide).—1–800–368–1019.
Toll Free TDD Number (Nationwide).—1–800–527–7697.

OFFICE OF THE GENERAL COUNSEL

fax [Immediate Office] 690–7998, fax [Admin. Office] 690–5452

General Counsel.—William B. Schultz (acting).
Deputy General Counsels: David S. Cade, Ken Choe, David Horowitz, Sally A. Howard, 690–7741.
Senior Advisor to the General Counsel.—Elizabeth Gianturco (202) 690–7741.
Associate General Counsel for:
Centers for Medicare and Medicaid Division.—Janice Hoffman, 619–0150.
Children, Family and Aging Division.—Robert Keith, 690–8005.
Civil Rights Division.—Edwin Woo, 619–0900.
Ethics Division/Special Counsel for Ethics.—Edgar Swindell, 690–7258.
Food and Drug Division.—Ralph Tyler (301) 827–1137.
General Law Division.—Jeffrey Davis, 619–0150.
Legislation Division.—Sondra Steigen Wallace, 690–7773.
Public Health Division.—David Benor (301) 443–2644.

OFFICE OF GLOBAL HEALTH AFFAIRS

Director.—Nils Daulaire, (202) 690–6174.

OFFICE OF THE INSPECTOR GENERAL
330 Independence Avenue, SW., 20201

Inspector General.—Daniel R. Levinson (202) 619–3148.
Principal Deputy Inspector General.—Larry J. Goldberg, 619–3148.
Chief Counsel to the Inspector General.—Lewis Morris, 619–0335.
Deputy Inspector General for—
Audit Services.—Joseph Vengrin, 619–3155.
Evaluation and Inspections.—Stuart Wright, 619–0480.
Investigations.—Tim Menke, 619–3210.
Management and Policy.—JoAnne Chiedi, 205–5154.
Director, External Affairs.—Claire Barnard, 619–1343.

OFFICE OF MEDICARE HEARINGS AND APPEALS

Chief Administrative Law Judge.—Nancy Griswold (703) 235–0141.
Executive Director.—Vacant (703) 265–0689.
Director, Management Operations.—Robert Velasco, 235–0141.

OFFICE OF THE NATIONAL COORDINATOR FOR HEALTH INFORMATION TECHNOLOGY

National Coordinator for Health Information Technology.—David Blumenthal, M.D., M.P.P. (202) 690–7151.

OFFICE OF PUBLIC HEALTH AND SCIENCE

Assistant Secretary for Health.—Howard K. Koh, M.D., M.P.H. (202) 690–7694.
Assistant to the Assistant Secretary for Health.—Howard Koh, 401–8034.
Principal Deputy Assistant Secretary for Health.—Wanda Jones, M.D., M.P.H., 401–8034.
The Surgeon General.—Vacant (301) 443–4000.
Deputy Assistant Secretary, Office of:
Disease Prevention and Health Promotion.—Penelope Royall, P.T., M.S.W. (240) 453–8279.
HIV/AIDS Policy.—Christopher Bates, (202) 690–5560.
Minority Health.—Garth Graham, M.D., M.P.H. (240) 453–6179.
Population Affairs.—Evelyn Kappeler (acting), (240) 453–2805.
President's Council on Physical Fitness and Sports.—Sergio Rojas (202) 690–5187.
Research Integrity.—Donald Wright, M.D., M.P.H. (acting), (301) 443–4000.
Women's Health.—Francis Ashe-Goins (202) 401–9583.
Acting Deputy Assistant Secretary for
Commissioned Corps Force Management.—Denise Canton (240) 453–6083.
Human Research Protections.—Jerry Menikoff, M.D., J.D. (240) 453–6900.
National Vaccine Programs.—Bruce Gellin, M.D., M.P.H. (202) 205–5294.
Regional Administrators for—
Region I: CT, ME, MA, NH, RI, VT.—Michael Milner, PA–C (617) 565–4999.
Region II: NJ, NY, PR, VI.—Robert L. Davidson, MSW, M.D., M.S. (212) 742–7036.
Region III: DE, DC, MD, PA, VA, WV.—Dalton G. Paxman, Ph.D. (215) 861–4631.
Region IV: AL, FL, GA, KY, MS, NC, SC, TN.—Clara H. Cobb, M.S., R.N. (404) 562–7894.
Region V: IL, IN, MI, MN, OH, WI.—James Galloway, M.D., FACP, FACC (312) 353–1385.
Region VI: AR, LA, NM, OK, TX.—Epi Elizondo, Ph.D., PA–C (214) 767–3879.
Region VII: IA, KS, MO, NE.—John Babb, R.P.H., M.P.A. (816) 426–3291.
Region VIII: CO, MT, ND, SD, UT, WY.—Zachery Taylor, M.D., M.S. (303) 844–7680.
Region IX: AZ, CA, HI, NV, Guam, American Samoa, CNMI, FSMI, RMI, Palau.—Ronald Banks, M.D., M.P.H. (415) 437–8096.
Region X: AK, ID, OR, WA.—Patrick O'Carroll, M.D., M.P.H., FACPM (206) 615–2469.

ADMINISTRATION ON AGING

1 Massachusetts Avenue, NW., 20001

Assistant Secretaries.—Kathy Greenlee (202) 401–4541; Edwin L. Walker (acting), 401–4634.
Deputy Assistant Secretary for Policy and Management.—Cindy Greenlee, 401–4634.
Director for—
Communications.—Edwin L. Walker, 357–3590.
Executive Secretariat.—Harry Posman, 357–3540.
Evaluation.—Saadia Greenberg, 357–3554.
Planning and Policy Development.—Lori Gerhard, 357–3443.

ADMINISTRATION FOR CHILDREN AND FAMILIES

370 L'Enfant Promenade, SW., 20447

Assistant Secretary.—David Hansell (acting), (202) 401–5180.
Principal Deputy Assistant Secretary.—Mark Greenberg.
Deputy Assistant Secretary for Policy and External Affairs.—Joan Lombardi, 401–6781.
Deputy Assistant Secretary for Administration.—Tony Hardy, 401–9238.
Senior Advisor to the Assistant Secretary.—Vacant, 401–6947.
Director, Regional Operations Staff.—Diann Dawson, 401–4802.
Commissioner for Administration on:
Children, Youth and Families.—Maiso Bryant (acting), 205–8347.
Developmental Disabilities.—Patricia Morrissey (acting), 690–6590.
Deputy Commissioner, Administration for Native Americans.—Lillian Sparks.
Commissioner, Office of Child Support Enforcement.—Vicki Turteski, 401–9369.
Associate Commissioner for—
Children's Bureau.—Shannon Rudisill, 690–5780.
Family and Youth Services Bureau.—Vacant, 205–8102.
Director, Office of:
Community Services.—Yolanda Butler (acting), 401–9333.
Family Assistance.—Vacant, 401–9275.
Head Start.—Patricia Brown (acting), 205–8573.
Legislative Affairs and Budget.—Madeline Mocko (acting), 401–9223.
Planning, Research and Evaluation.—Noami Goldstein (acting), 401–9220.
Public Affairs.—Pamela Carter (acting), 401–9215.
Refugee Resettlement.—Martha Newton (acting), 401–9246.
Regional Operations.—Diann Dawson (acting), 401–4802.

AGENCY FOR HEALTHCARE RESEARCH AND QUALITY (AHRQ)

Director.—Carolyn Clancy, M.D. (301) 427–1200.
Deputy Director.—Kathleen Kendrick, R.N.

AGENCY FOR TOXIC SUBSTANCES AND DISEASE REGISTRY

1600 Clifton Road, NE., Atlanta, GA 30333

Administrator.—Richard E. Besser, M.D. (acting), (404) 639–7000.
Deputy Administrator.—Anne Schuchat, M.D. (acting).
Assistant Administrator.—Howard Frumkin, M.D., Ph.D., 498–0004.

CENTER FOR DISEASE CONTROL AND PREVENTION

1600 Clifton Road, NE., Atlanta, GA 30333, phone (404) 639–7000

Director.—Richard E. Besser, M.D. (acting).
Deputy Director for—
Policy, Legislation and Communication.—Donald Shriber, J.D., M.P.H. (acting).
Management and Budget.—Bill Nichols, M.P.A. (acting).
Science and Public Health Program.—Anne Schuchat, M.D. (acting).
Chief of:
Operating Officer.—William P. Nichols, M.P.A. (acting).
Public Health Practice.—Dr. Stephanie B. Bailey, M.D., Ph.D.
Science Office.—Dr. Tanja Popovic, M.D., Ph.D.

Chief of Staff.—Joe Henderson (acting).
Staff Offices—
CDC Washington.—Edward L. Hunter, M.A. (acting), (202) 245–0600.
Enterprise Communication.—Donna Garland, B.A., 639–7540.
Dispute Resolution Equal Employment Opportunity.—Gilbert Camacho, M.S. (770) 488–3227.
Strategy and Innovation.—Brad Perkins, M.D., M.B.A., 639–7000.
Workforce and Career Development.—Stephen B. Thacker, M.D., 639–6010.
Coordinating Office for:
Global Health.—Steven Blount, M.P.H., 639–7429.
Terrorism Preparedness and Response.—Daniel M. Sosin, M.D., M.P.H. (acting), 639–3057.
Coordinating Center for Environmental Health and Injury Prevention.—Henry Falk, M.D. (770) 488–0608.
National Center for Environmental Health/Agency for Toxic Substances and Disease Registry.—Howard Frumkin, M.D. (770) 488–0604.
National Center for Injury Prevention and Control.—Ileana Arias, Ph.D. (770) 488–4696.
Coordinating Center for Health Information and Services.—Steve Solomon, M.D., 498–0123.
National Center for Health Marketing.—Jay Bernhardt, Ph.D., 498–0990.
National Center for Health Statistics.—Edward J. Sondik, Ph.D. (301) 458–4500.
National Center for Public Health Informatics.—Leslie Lenert, M.D., M.S., 498–2475.
Coordinating Center for Health Promotion.—Kathleen Toomey, M.D., M.P.H., 498–6700.
National Center for Birth Defects and Developmental Disabilities.—Edwin Trevathan, M.D., M.P.H., 498–3800.
National Center for Chronic Disease Prevention and Health Promotion.—Janet Collins, Ph.D. (770) 488–5401.
Coordinating Center for Infectious Diseases.—Mitch Cohen, M.D., 639–2100.
National Center for Immunization and Respiratory Diseases.—Beth Bell, M.D., M.P.H. (acting), 639–8200.
National Center for Zoonotic, Vector-Borne and Enteric Diseases.—Lonnie King, D.V.M., 639–7380.
National Center for HIV/AIDS, Viral Hepatitis, STD, and TB Prevention.—Kevin Fenton, M.D., 639–8000.
National Center for Preparedness, Detection and Control of Infectious Diseases.—Rima Khabbaz, M.D., 639–3967.
National Institute for Occupational Safety and Health.—Christine Branche, Ph.D. (acting), (202) 245–0625.

CENTER FOR FAITH BASED AND COMMUNITY INITIATIVES

Director.—Alexia Kelley, (202) 401–2956.

CENTERS FOR MEDICARE AND MEDICAID SERVICES

200 Independence Avenue, SW., 20201, phone (202) 690–6726

Administrator.—Donald M. Berwick, M.D.
Principal Deputy Administrator and Chief Operating Officer.—Marilyn Tavenner.
Deputy Chief Operating Officer.—Michelle Snyder (410) 786–3151.
Chief Actuary, Office of the Actuary.—Rick Foster (410) 786–6374.
Deputy Administrator and Director, Center for:
Consumer Information and Insurance Oversight.—Steve Larsen (301) 492–4124.
Medicaid, CHIP, Survey and Certification.—Cindy Mann (202) 690–7428.
Medicare.—Jonathan Blum (202) 690–6301.
Strategic Planning.—Anthony Rodgers (410) 786–2151.
Program Integrity.—Peter Budetti (410) 786–2140.
Director, Center for Medicare and Medicaid Innovation.—Richard Gilfillan (acting), (410) 786–3316.
Director, Office of:
Acquisitions and Grants Management.—Daniel Kane (acting), (410) 786–1391.
Clinical Standards and Quality.—Dennis Wagner (acting), (410) 786–6841.
E-Health Standards and Services.—Karen Trudel (acting), (410) 786–9937.
Equal Opportunity and Civil Rights.—Arlene Austin (410) 786–5110.

External Affairs and Beneficiary Services.—Teresa Nino (202) 401–3135.
Federal Coordinated Health Care.—Melanie Bella (202) 260–1291.
Financial Management.—Deborah Taylor (410) 786–5448.
Information Services.—Tony Trenkle (acting), (410) 786–1800.
Legislation.—Amy Hall (202) 690–5960.
Operations Management.—James Weber (410) 786–1051.
Policy.—Karen Milgate (202) 690–0630.
Research, Development, and Information.—Tom Reilly (acting), (410) 786–0631.
Strategic Operations and Regulatory Support.—Jacqueline White (202) 690–8390.
Regional Administrator for:
Atlanta.—Renard Murray (404) 562–7150.
Boston.—Jaye Weisman (617) 565–1188.
Chicago.—Jackie Garner (312) 886–6432.
Dallas.—James Farris, M.D. (214) 767–6427.
Denver.—Jeff Hinson (303) 844–2111.
Kansas City.—Nanette Foster Reilly (816) 426–5233.
New York.—James T. Kerr (212) 616–2205.
Philadelphia.—Nancy O'Connor (215) 861–4140.
San Francisco.—David Sayen (415) 744–3501.
Seattle.—John Hammarlund (206) 615–2306.

FOOD AND DRUG ADMINISTRATION

10903 New Hampshire Avenue, Silver Spring, MD 20993

Commissioner.—Margaret A. Hamburg, M.D., (301) 796–5000.
Deputy Commissioner for International and Special Programs.—Murray M. Lumpkin, M.D., 796–8400.
Deputy Commissioner for Operations.—Curtis Coy (acting), 796–4700.
Deputy Commissioner for Policy.—David Dorsey (acting), 796–4800.
Chief Counsel.—Ralph Tyler, 796–8450.
Associate Commissioner for—
External Relations.—Lawrence Bachorik, 827–3330.
Operations.—Robert Miller, 796–4578.
Planning.—Malcolm Bertoni, 796–4850.
Regulatory Affairs.—Dara Corrigan, 796–8800.
Assistant Commissioner for—
International Programs.—Mary Lou Valdez, 796–8400.
Legislation.—Jeanne Ireland, 796–8900.
Planning.—Malcolm Bertoni, 796–4850.
Policy.—David Dorsey (acting), 796–4800.
Public Affairs.—Bethany Martino, 796–4540.
Special Health Issues.—Theresa A. Toigo, 796–8473.
Women's Health.—Michelle Yeboah, 796–4649.
Director, Center for—
Biologics Evaluation and Research.—Karen Midthun, 827–0372.
Devices and Radiological Health.—Jeffrey Shuren, 796–5900.
Drug Evaluation and Research.—Janet Woodcock, M.D., 796–5400.
Food Safety and Applied Nutrition.—Michael Landa, 436–1600.
Veterinary Medicine.—Bernadette Dunham, D.V.M., Ph.D., (240) 276–9000.
National Center for Toxicological Research.—William Slikker, Jr., Ph.D., (870) 543–7517.
Director, Office of:
Executive Secretariat.—Martina Varnado, 796–4520.
Executive Operations.—L'Tonya Davis, 796–4557.
Equal Opportunity and Diversity Management.—LaJuana Caldwell, 796–9400.
Financial Management.—William Collinson, 796–7183.
Orphan Products Development.—Tim Cote, 796–8662.

HEALTH RESOURCES AND SERVICES ADMINISTRATION

5600 Fishers Lane, Rockville, MD 20857

Administrator.—Mary K. Wakefield, Ph.D., RN (301) 443–2216.
Deputy Administrator.—Marcia K. Brand, Ph.D., 443–2194.
Senior Advisor.—Tina M. Cheatham, 443–2216.

Chief Public Health Officer.—Sarah Linde-Feucht, M.D. (acting), 443–2216.
Chief Operating Officer.—Thomas G. Morford, 443–4244.
Associate Administrator for—
Clinician Recruitment and Service.—Rebecca Spitzgo, 594–4130.
Federal Assistance Management.—Michael Nelson, 443–3524.
Health Professions.—Janet Heinrich, Ph.D., RN, 443–5794.
Healthcare Systems.—Joyce Somsak, 443–3300.
HIV/AIDS.—RADM Deborah Parham-Hopson, 443–1993.
Maternal and Child Health.—Peter C. van Dyck, M.D., 443–2170.
Primary Health Care.—James Macrae, 594–4110.
Regional Operations.—Dennis Malcomson (acting), 594–4130.
Rural Health Policy.—Tom Morris, 443–0835.
Director, Office of:
Communications.—Martin Kramer, 443–3376.
Equal Opportunity, Civil Rights and Diversity Management.—M. June Horner, 443–5636.
Legislation.—Leslie Atkinson, 443–1890.
Planning, Evaluation and Analysis.—Rebecca Slifkin, Ph.D., 443–3983.
Special Health Affairs.—Terry Adirim, M.D., 443–2825.

INDIAN HEALTH SERVICE

801 Thompson Avenue, Rockville, MD 20852

Director.—Yvette Roubideaux, M.D., M.P.H. (301) 443–1083.
Deputy Director.—Randy Grinnell.
Deputy Director for:
Field Operations.—Kathleen Annette, M.D. (acting).
Intergovernmental Affairs.—Sandra Pattea.
Management Operations.—Robert McSwain.
Chief Medical Officer.—Susan V. Karol, M.D.
Senior Advisor.—Geoffrey Roth.
Director of:
Direct Service and Contracting Tribes.—Roselyn Tso (acting), 443–1104.
Equal Employment Opportunity.—Pauline Bruce, 443–1108.
Legislative and Congressional Affairs.—Michael Mahsetky, 443–7261.
Public Affairs.—Thomas W. Sweeney, 443–3593.
Tribal Self-Governance.—Hankie Ortiz, 443–7821.
Urban Indian Health Programs.—Phyllis Wolfe, 443–4680.

NATIONAL INSTITUTES OF HEALTH

9000 Rockville Pike, Bethesda, MD 20892

Director.—Francis Collins (301) 496–2433.
Deputy Director.—Raynard S. Kington, 496–7322.
Assistant Director for OD Coordination.—Susan Persons, 496–2433.
Director, Executive Secretariat.—Ann Brewer, R.N., 496–1461.
Director, Office of Federal Adivsory Committee Policy.—Jennifer Spaeth, 496–2123.
Executive Officer, Office of the Director.—LaVerne Y. Stringfield, 594–8231.
Chief Information Officer.—John F. ''Jack'' Jones, Ph.D., 496–5703.
Legal Advisor, Office of the General Counsel.—Barbara M. McGarey, J.D., 496–6043.
Deputy Director for—
Extramural Research.—Sally J. Rockey (acting), Ph.D., 496–1096.
Intramural Research.—Michael M. Gottesman, M.D., 496–1921.
Management.—Colleen Barros, 496–3271.
Director, Division of Program Coordination, Planning, and Strategic Initiatives.—Lana S. Skirboll (acting), 402–9852.
Associate Director for—
Administration.—Diane Frasier (acting), 496–4422.
AIDS Research.—Jack E. Whitescarver, Ph.D., 496–0357.
Behavioral and Social Sciences Research.—Christine Bachrach (acting), Ph.D., 496–9485.
Budget.—John Bartrum, 496–4477.
Communications and Public Liaison.—John T. Burklow, 496–4461.
Disease Prevention.—Barnett S. Kramer, M.D., M.P.H., 496–1508.
Research on Women's Health.—Vivian W. Pinn, M.D., 402–1770.

Research Services.—Alfred C. Johnson, Ph.D., 496–2215.
Science Policy.—Amy Patterson (acting), M.D., 496–2122.
Director, Office of:
Ethics.—Raynard S. Kington, M.D., Ph.D. (acting), 402–6628.
Equal Opportunity and Diversity Management.—Lawrence N. Self, 496–6301.
Financial Management.—Kenneth Stith, 402–8831.
Human Resources.—Chris Major, 496–3592.
Legislative Policy and Analysis.—Roz Gray (acting), 496–3471.
Management Assessment.—Suzanne J. Servis, 496–1873.
Research Facilities Development and Operations.—Daniel Wheeland, 594–0999.
Technology Transfer.—Mark L. Rohrbaugh, Ph.D., J.D., 594–7700.
Directors:
Eunice Kennedy Shriver National Institute of Child Health and Human Development.—Duane F. Alexander, M.D., 496–3454.
Fogarty International Center.—Roger I. Glass, M.D., Ph.D., 496–1415.
National Center on Minority Health and Health Disparities.—John Ruffin, Ph.D., 402–1366.
National Library of Medicine.—Donald A. B. Lindberg, M.D., 496–6221.
Warren Grant Magnuson Clinical Center.—John I. Gallin, M.D., 496–4114.
Director, Center for—
Information Technology.—John F. ''Jack'' Jones, Ph.D (acting), 496–5703.
Scientific Review.—Antonio Scarpa, M.D., Ph.D., 435–1114.
Director, National Center for—
Complementary and Alternative Medicine.—Josephine P. Briggs, M.D., 435–6826.
Research Resources.—Barbara Alving, M.D., 496–5793.
Director, National Institute on:
Aging.—Richard J. Hodes, M.D., 496–9265.
Alcohol Abuse and Alcoholism.—Kenneth R. Warren, Ph.D. (acting), 443–3885.
Drug Abuse.—Nora D. Volkow, M.D., 443–6480.
Deafness and Other Communication Disorders.—James F. Battey, Jr., M.D., Ph.D., 402–0900.
Director, National Institute of:
Allergy and Infectious Diseases.—Anthony S. Fauci, M.D., 496–2263.
Arthritis and Musculoskeletal and Skin Diseases.—Stephen I. Katz, M.D., Ph.D., 496–4353.
Biomedical Imaging and Bioengineering.—Roderic I. Pettigrew, Ph.D., M.D., 496–8859.
Dental and Craniofacial Research.—Lawrence Tabak, D.D.S., Ph.D., 496–3571.
Diabetes and Digestive and Kidney Diseases.—Griffin P. Rodgers, M.D., M.A.C.P., 496–5877.
Environmental Health Sciences.—Linda S. Birnbaum, Ph.D., D.A.B.T., A.T.S. (919) 541–3201.
General Medical Sciences.—Jeremy M. Berg, Ph.D., 594–2172.
Mental Health.—Thomas Insel, M.D., 443–3673.
Neurological Disorders and Stroke.—Story C. Landis, Ph.D., 496–9746.
Nursing Research.—Patricia A. Grady, Ph.D., R.N., 496–8230.
Director, National:
Cancer Institute.—John E. Niederhuber, M.D., 496–5615.
Eye Institute.—Paul A. Sieving, M.D., Ph.D., 496–2234.
Heart, Lung and Blood Institute.—Elizabeth G. Nabel, M.D., 496–5166.
Human Genome Research Institute.—Alan E. Guttmacher, M.D. (acting), 496–0844.

SUBSTANCE ABUSE AND MENTAL HEALTH SERVICES ADMINISTRATION

1 Choke Cherry Road, Rockville, MD 20857

Administrator.—Pamela Hyde, room 8–1061 (240) 276–2000.
Deputy Administrator.—Eric Broderick, room 8–1059, 276–2000.
Principal Advisor to the Administrator.—Kana Enomoto, room 8–1076, 276–2001.
Policy Planning and Budget.—Daryl Kade, 276–2200.
Director, Center for—
Mental Health Services.—A. Kathryn Power, M.Ed., room 6–1057, 276–1310.
Substance Abuse Prevention.—Frances M. Harding, room 4–1057, 276–2420.
Substance Abuse Treatment.—H. Westley Clark, M.D., J.D., M.P.H., CAS, FASAM, room 5–1015, 276–1660.
Director, Office of:
Applied Studies.—Peter Delany, Ph.D., LCSW–C, room 7–1047, 276–1250.

Communications.—Bradford Stone (acting), room 8–1031, 276–2130.
Policy, Planning and Budget.—Daryl W. Kade, room 8–1083, 276–2200.
Program Services.—Elaine Parry, M.S., room 7–1073, 276–1110.

DEPARTMENT OF HOUSING AND URBAN DEVELOPMENT

Robert C. Weaver Federal Building, 451 Seventh Street, SW., 20410
phone (202) 708–1112, http://www.hud.gov

SHAUN DONOVAN, Democrat, of Washington, DC; born in New York, NY, January 24, 1966; undergraduate and graduate degrees from Harvard University, graduating from Harvard College in 1987, Master of Public Administration from the John F. Kennedy School of Government and a master's in architecture at the Graduate School of Design in 1995. Commissioner of the New York City Department of Housing Preservation and Development (HPD); visiting scholar, New York University; consultant to the Millennial Housing Commission; Deputy Assistant Secretary for Multifamily Housing and acting FHA commissioner (HUD); Community Preservation Corporation (CPC), a non-profit lender and developer of affordable housing. Married to Liza Gilbert; two sons; nominated by President-elect Barack Obama on December 13, 2008; confirmed by the U.S. Senate through unanimous consent on January 22, 2009; sworn-in on January 26.

OFFICE OF THE SECRETARY

Secretary of Housing and Urban Development.—Shaun Donovan, room 10000 (202) 708–0417.
Chief of Staff.—Laurel A. Blatchford, 708–2713.
Deputy Chief of Staff.—Christopher Murphy, 708–1781.
Executive Operations Officer.—Tawanna Preston, 708–3750.
Administrative Officer.—Karen Lake, 708–3750.

OFFICE OF THE DEPUTY SECRETARY

Deputy Secretary.—Ron C. Sims, room 10100 (202) 708–0123.
Chief of Staff for the Deputy Secretary.—Jim Lopez, room 10100, 708–0123.

ASSISTANT SECRETARY FOR COMMUNITY PLANNING AND DEVELOPMENT

Assistant Secretary.—Mercedes Márquez, room 7100 (202) 708–2690.
General Deputy Assistant Secretary.—Clifford Taffet, room 7100, 708–2690.
Deputy Assistant Secretary for—
Grant Programs.—Yolanda Chavez.
Operations.—Ronald Herbert (acting).
Special Needs.—Mark Johnston, 708–1590.

ASSISTANT SECRETARY FOR CONGRESSIONAL AND INTERGOVERNMENTAL RELATIONS

Assistant Secretary.—Peter Kovar, room 10120 (202) 708–0005.
General Deputy Assistant Secretary.—Mark A. Linton, room 10120, 708–0005.
Deputy Assistant Secretary for—
Congressional Relations.—Bernard Fulton, room 10120, 708–0005.
Intergovernmental Relations.—Francey Youngberg, room 10148, 708–0005.

ASSISTANT SECRETARY FOR FAIR HOUSING AND EQUAL OPPORTUNITY

Assistant Secretary.—John Trasviña, room 5100 (202) 708–4252.
General Deputy Assistant Secretary.—Bryan Greene, 708–4211.
Deputy Assistant Secretary for—

Enforcement and Programs.—Sara Pratt, 619–8046.
Operations and Management.—David Ziaya, 708–0768.

ASSISTANT SECRETARY FOR HOUSING

Assistant Secretary/Federal Housing Commissioner.—David H. Stevens, room 9100 (202) 708–2601.
General Deputy Assistant Secretary.—Joseph F. Smith.
Associated General Deputy Assistant Secretary.—Ronald Y. Spraker (acting).
Deputy Assistant Secretary for—
Finance and Budget.—George Tomchick, 401–8975.
Healthcare Programs.—Roger Miller, 708–0599.
Housing Operations.—Lori Michalski, 708–1104.
Multifamily Housing.—Carol Galante, 708–2495.
Risk Management and Regulatory Affairs and Manufactured Housing.—Robert Ryan.
Single Family Housing.—Vicki Bott, 708–3175.

ASSISTANT SECRETARY FOR POLICY DEVELOPMENT AND RESEARCH

Assistant Secretary.—Raphael W. Bostic, room 8100 (202) 708–1600.
General Deputy Assistant Secretary.—Jean Lin Pao, room 8100, 708–1600.
Deputy Assistant Secretary for the Office of:
Economic Affairs.—Kurt G. Usowski, room 8204, 708–3080.
International and Philanthropic Innovation.—Ana Marie Argilagos, room 8138, 708–0770.
Policy Development.—Erika Poethig, room 8106, 708–1537.
Research, Evaluation, and Monitoring.—Kevin J. Neary, room 8124, 708–4230.

ASSISTANT SECRETARY FOR PUBLIC AFFAIRS

General Deputy Assistant Secretary.—Neill Coleman, room 10132 (202) 708–0980.
Deputy Assistant Secretary.—Jereon M. Brown.
Press Secretary.—Melanie Roussell.

ASSISTANT SECRETARY FOR PUBLIC AND INDIAN HOUSING

Assistant Secretary.—Sandra B. Henriquez, room 4100 (202) 708–0950.
General Deputy Assistant Secretary.—Deborah Hernandez.
Office of Field Operations.—Donald Lavy, 708–4016.
Policy, Programs and Legislative Initiatives.—Debra Gross, 708–0713.
Real Estate Assessment Center.—David A. Vargas, 475–8906.

OFFICE OF FIELD POLICY AND MANAGEMENT

Director.—Patricia A. Hoban-Moore, room 7106 (202) 708–2426.

GOVERNMENT NATIONAL MORTGAGE ASSOCIATION

President.—Theodore W. Tozer (202) 708–0926.
Executive Vice President.—Mary K. Kinney, 708–0926.
Senior Vice President, Office of:
Capital Markets.—Kirk D. Freeman, 401–8970.
Finance.—Michael J. Najjum, 401–2064.
Mortgage-Backed Securities.—Stephen L. Ledbetter, 708–4141.
Program Operations.—Thomas R. Weakland, 708–2884.
Senior Vice President and Chief Risk Officer.—Gregory A. Keith, 708–0926.

CHIEF FINANCIAL OFFICER

Chief Financial Officer.—Douglas A. Criscitello, room 3126 (202) 708–6399.
Deputy Chief Financial Officer.—David P. Sadari, room 3126, 708–6526.
Assistant Chief Financial Officer for—

Accounting.—Nita Nigam, 708–6850.
Budget.—Frank J. Murphy (acting), 708–6630.
Financial Management.—Jerome A. Vaiana (acting), 708–8106.
Systems.—Gail B. Dise, 708–1757.

CHIEF INFORMATION OFFICER

Chief Information Officer.—Jerry E. Williams, room 4160 (202) 708–0306.
Deputy Chief Information Officer.—Kevin R. Cooke, Jr., room 4160, 708–0306.
Deputy Chief Information Officer for—
IT Operations.—Mike Milazzo, room 4258, 708–4562, ext. 6098.
Chief Information Security Officer.—Marion Cody, room 4156, 619–9057, ext. 3108.

CHIEF PROCUREMENT OFFICER

Chief Procurement Officer.—Jemine A. Bryon, room 5280 (202) 708–0600.
Deputy Chief Procurement Officer.—Keith Surber, room 5256, 708–1290.
Associate Chief Procurement Officer.—Vacant.

GENERAL COUNSEL

General Counsel.—Helen R. Kanovsky, room 10110 (202) 708–2244.
Principal Deputy General Counsel.—Kevin M. Simpson.
Deputy General Counsel for—
Housing Programs.—Elton Lester, room 10238, 402–5280.
Operations.—Linda M. Cruciani, room 10240, 402–5108.
Associate General Counsel for—
Assisted Housing and Community Development.—Althea Forrester, room 8166, 708–0470.
Ethics.—Peter J. Constantine, room 10164, 708–2864.
Fair Housing.—Kathleen Pennington, room 10270, 708–2787.
Finance and Regulatory Compliance.—John P. Opitz, room 8150, 708–2203.
Insured Housing.—John J. Daly, room 9226, 708–1274.
Legislation and Regulations.—Camille E. Acevedo, room 10282, 708–1793.
Litigation.—Nancy Christopher, room 10258, 708–0300.
Program Enforcement.—Dane M. Narode, PORTALS, 245–4141.
Deputy Director, Departmental Enforcement Center.—Craig Clemmensen, PORTALS, 245–4195.

INSPECTOR GENERAL

Inspector General.—Michael P. Stephens (acting), room 8256 (202) 708–0430.
Deputy Inspector General.—Michael P. Stephens.
Counsel to the Inspector General, Office of Legal Counsel.—J. Bryan Howell, 708–1613.
Assistant Inspector General, Office of:
Audit.—James Heist, 708–0364.
Investigation.—John McCarty, 708–0390.
Management and Policy.—Helen Albert, 708–0006.

OFFICE OF DEPARTMENTAL EQUAL EMPLOYMENT OPPORTUNITY

Director.—Michelle A. Cottom (acting), room 2134 (202) 708–3362.

OFFICE OF THE HUMAN CAPITAL OFFICER

Chief Human Capital Officer.—Janie L. Payne, room 6100 (202) 708–0940.
Deputy Chief Human Capital Officer.—Karen S. Jackson.
Executive Secretariat.—Dr. Delores Cole, 708–3054.
Director of Budget and Services.—Wandra Simmons, 402–6577.
Office of Human Capital Services.—Allison Hopkins, 708–2000.

OFFICE OF DEPARTMENTAL OPERATIONS AND COORDINATION

Director.—Inez Banks-Dubose, room 2124 (202) 708–2806.
Deputy Director.—Joseph F. Smith.

OFFICE OF HEALTHY HOMES AND LEAD HAZARD CONTROL

Director.—Jon L. Gant, room 8236 (202) 708–0310.
Deputy Director.—Matthew Ammon.

SMALL AND DISADVANTAGED BUSINESS UTILIZATION

Director.—Sharman Lancefield, room 2200 (202) 708–1428.

HUD REGIONAL DIRECTORS

Region I.—Connecticut, Maine, Massachusetts, New Hampshire, Rhode Island, Vermont.
Regional Administrator.—Barbara G. Fields, Federal Building, 10 Causeway Street, Room 301, Boston, MA 02222–1092 (617) 994–8200.
Region II.—New Jersey, New York.
Regional Administrator.—Adolfo Carrion, Jr., 26 Federal Plaza, Suite 3541, New York, NY 10278–0068 (212) 264–8000, ext. 7109.
Region III.—Delaware, District of Columbia, Maryland, Pennsylvania, Virginia, West Virginia.
Regional Administrator.—Jane C.W. Vincent, The Wanamaker Building, 100 Penn Square East, Philadelphia, PA 19107–3380 (215) 656–0600.
Region IV.—Alabama, Florida, Georgia, Kentucky, Mississippi, North Carolina, Puerto Rico, South Carolina, Tennessee.
Regional Administrator.—Edward Jennings, Jr., Five Points Plaza, 40 Marietta Street, NW., 2nd Floor, Atlanta, GA 30303–2806 (404) 331–5001.
Region V.—Illinois, Indiana, Michigan, Minnesota, Ohio, Wisconsin.
Regional Administrator.—Antonio Riley, Ralph Metcalfe Federal Building, 77 West Jackson Boulevard, Chicago, IL 60604–3507 (312) 353–5680.
Region VI.—Arkansas, Louisiana, New Mexico, Oklahoma, Texas.
Regional Administrator.—C. Donald Babers, 801 Cherry Street, Fort Worth, TX 76113–2905 (817) 978–5540.
Region VII.—Iowa, Kansas, Missouri, Nebraska.
Regional Administrator.—Derrith R. Watchman-Moore, Gateway Tower II, 400 State Avenue, Room 200, Kansas City, KS 66101–2406 (913) 551–5462.
Region VIII.—Colorado, Montana, North Dakota, South Dakota, Utah, Wyoming.
Regional Administrator.—Rick M. Garcia, 1670 Broadway, Denver, CO 80202–4801 (303) 672–5440.
Region IX.—Arizona, California, Hawaii, Nevada.
Regional Administrator.—Ophelia Basgal, 600 Harrison Street, 3rd Floor, San Francisco, CA 94107–1300 (415) 489–6400.
Region X.—Alaska, Idaho, Oregon, Washington.
Regional Administrator.—Mary McBride, Seattle Federal Office Building, 909 First Avenue, Suite 200, Seattle, WA 98104–1000 (206) 220–5101.

DEPARTMENT OF TRANSPORTATION

1200 New Jersey Avenue, SE., Washington, DC 20590

phone (202) 366–4000, http://www.dot.gov

RAY LAHOOD, Secretary of Transportation; born in Peoria, IL, December 6, 1945; education: B.A., Bradley University, Peoria, IL; professional: United States Congressman from 1995–2009; member of the House Committees on Transportation and Infrastructure; Veterans' Affairs; Agriculture; Intelligence; and Appropriations; chairman of four Bipartisan Congressional retreats; Chief of Staff to U.S. Congressman Robert Michel, 1983–94; Illinois State Representative from 1982–83; District Administrative Assistant to Congressman Thomas Rails, 1977–82; Bi-State Metropolitan Planning Commission, 1974–77; teacher; director, Rock Island County Youth Services Bureau, 1972–74; family: married to Kathy LaHood; four children: Darin, Amy, Sam, and Sara; nine grandchildren; nominated by President Barack H. Obama to become the 16th Secretary of Transportation, and was confirmed by the U.S. Senate on January 23, 2009.

OFFICE OF THE SECRETARY

[Created by the act of October 15, 1966; codified under U.S.C. 49]

Secretary of Transportation.—Ray LaHood, room W93–317 (202) 366–1111.
Deputy Secretary.—John D. Porcari, 366–2222.
Chief of Staff.—Joan DeBoer, 366–1103.
Deputy Chief of Staff.—Marlise Streitmatter, 366–6800.
Under Secretary of Transportation for Policy.—Roy Kienitz, 366–1815.
Director, Office of:
Civil Rights.—Mary N. Jones (acting), room W78–318, 366–4648.
Executive Secretariat.—Carol C. Darr, room W93–324, 366–4277.
Intelligence and Security.—Michael Lowder, room W56–302, 366–6525.
Small and Disadvantaged Business Utilization.—Brandon Neal, room W56–308, 366–1930.

ASSISTANT SECRETARY FOR ADMINISTRATION

Assistant Secretary.—Vacant, room W80–322 (202) 366–2332.
Deputy Assistant Secretary.—Brodi Fontenot, W80–320, 366–2332.
Director, Office of:
Facilities, Information and Asset Management.—George Fields, room W58–334, 366–9756.
Financial Management.—Marie Petrosino, room W81–306, 366–3967.
Hearings, Chief Administrative Law Judge.—Judge Ronnie A. Yoder, room E12–356, 366–2142.
Human Resource Management.—Nancy Mowry, room W81–302, 366–4088.
Security.—Rob Lee (acting), room W54–336, 366–4677.
Senior Procurement Executive.—Willie Smith, room W83–306, 366–4212.

ASSISTANT SECRETARY FOR AVIATION AND INTERNATIONAL AFFAIRS

Assistant Secretary.—Susan Kurland, room W88–314 (202) 366–8822.
Deputy Assistant Secretaries: Robert Letteney, room W88–324; Susan McDermott, room W88–326, 366–4551.
Director, Office of:

Aviation Analysis.—Todd Homan, room W86–481, 366–5903.
International Aviation.—Paul Gretch, room W86–406, 366–2423.
International Transportation and Trade.—David DeCarme, room W88–306, 366–4398.

ASSISTANT SECRETARY FOR BUDGET AND PROGRAMS

Assistant Secretary/Chief Financial Officer.—Chris Bertram, room W95–330 (202) 366–9191.
Deputy Assistant Secretary.—Lana Hurdle, room W95–316, 366–9192.
Deputy Chief Financial Officer.—Vacant, room W95–302, 366–9192.
Director, Office of:
Budget and Program Performance.—Ellen Heup, room W93–308, 366–4594.
Financial Management.—Laurie Howard, room W93–322, 366–1306.

ASSISTANT SECRETARY FOR GOVERNMENTAL AFFAIRS

Assistant Secretary.—Dana Gresham, room W85–326 (202) 366–4573.
Deputy Assistant Secretaries: Robert Letteney, Joanna Turner.
Associate Directors: Curtis Johnson, Yasmin Yaver.

ASSISTANT SECRETARY FOR TRANSPORTATION POLICY

Assistant Secretary.—Polly Trottenberg, room 10228 (202) 366–0582.
Deputy Assistant Secretaries: Elizabeth Osborne, room W82–314, 366–8979; Joel Szabat, room W82–308, 493–2208.

GENERAL COUNSEL

General Counsel.—Robert Rivkin, room W92–300, 366–4702.
Deputy General Counsel.—Rosalind A. Knapp.
Assistant General Counsel for—
Aviation Enforcement and Proceedings.—Samuel Podberesky, room W96–322, 366–9342.
International Law.—Donald H. Horn, room W98–324, 366–2972.
Legislation.—Thomas W. Herlihy, room W96–326, 366–4687.
Litigation.—Paul M. Geier, room W94–310, 366–4731.
Regulation and Enforcement.—Neil K. Eisner, room W96–302, 366–4723.
Operatoins.—Ronald Jackson, room W96–304, 366–4710.

INSPECTOR GENERAL

Inspector General.—Calvin L. Scovel III, room W70–300 (202) 366–1959.
Deputy Inspector General.—David A. Dobbs, 366–6767.
Principal Assistant Inspector General for Auditing and Evaluation.—Ann Calvaresi Barr, room 9217, 366–0500.
Assistant Inspector General for—
Acquisition and Procurement Audits.—Mark Zabarsky, room 9228, 366–1496.
Aviation and Special Program Audits.—Lou Dixon, 366–0500.
Competition and Economic Analysis.—David Tornquist, 366–9682.
Financial and Information Technology Audits.—Rebecca Leng, 366–1496.
Investigations.—Tim Barry, 366–1967.
Legal, Legislative and External Affairs.—Brian A. Dettelbach, 366–8751.
Surface and Maritime Program Audits.—Joe Come, 366–5630.
Deputy Assistant Inspector General for—
Aviation and Special Program Audits.—Matthew Hamption, 366–0500.
Surface and Maritime Program Audits.—Rosalyn Millman, 366–5630.

REGIONAL AUDIT OFFICES

Regional Program Directors:
Tina Nysted, 61 Forsyth Street, SW., Suite 17T60, Atlanta, GA 30303 (404) 562–3854.
Scott Macey, 201 Mission Street, Suite 1750, San Francisco, CA 94105 (415) 744–3090.
Darren Murphy, 915 Second Avenue, Room 644, Seattle, WA 98174 (206) 220–7754.

Earl Hedges, 10 South Howard Street, Suite 4500, Baltimore, MD 21201 (410) 962–3612.

REGIONAL INVESTIGATIONS OFFICES

Special Agents-In-Charge:

Region I.—Ted Doherty, 55 Broadway, Room 1055, Cambridge, MA 02142 (617) 494–2701.

Region II.—Ned E. Schwartz, 201 Varick Street, Room 1161, New York, NY 10014 (212) 337–1250.

Region III.—Kathryn Jones, 409 3rd Street, SW., Room 301, Washington, DC 20024 (202) 260–8580.

Region IV.—John Long, 61 Forsythe Street, SW., Suite 17T60, Atlanta, GA 30303 (404) 562–3850.

Region V.—Michelle McVicker, 200 West Adams Street, Suite 300, Chicago, IL 60606 (312) 353–0106.

Region VI.—Max Smith, 819 Taylor Street, Room 13A42, Fort Worth, TX 76102 (817) 978–3236.

Region IX.—Hank W. Smedley, 201 Mission Street, Suite 1750, San Francisco, CA 94105 (415) 744–3090.

OFFICE OF PUBLIC AFFAIRS

Assistant to the Secretary and Director of Public Affairs.—Jill Zuckman, room W93–310 (202) 366–4570.

Deputy Director.—Maureen Knightly.

Associate Director of Media Relation.—William S. ''Bill'' Adams, 366–5580.

Speech Writing and Research Division.—Amy Bernsteen, room 10413, 366–5580.

FEDERAL AVIATION ADMINISTRATION

800 Independence Avenue, SW., 20591 (202) 267–3484

Administrator.—Randy Babbitt, 267–3111.

Chief of Staff.—David Weingart, 267–7416.

Senior Advisor to the Administrator.—Darlene Freeman, 267–3574.

Executive Assistant to the Administrator.—Sharon Harrison, 267–3111.

Deputy Administrator.—Michael Huerta, 267–8111.

Senior Advisor to the Deputy Administrator.—Chris Rocheleau, 267–3180.

Assistant Administrator for Financial Services.—Ramesh Punwani, 267–9105.

Deputy Assistant Administrator.—Vacant, 267–3882.

Director of Budget.—Carl Burrus, 267–8010.

Deputy Directors of Budget: Wayne Hiebeck, 267–4029; Bob Schramm, 493–4673.

Director of:

Financial Controls.—David Rickard (acting), 267–7140.

Financial Management.—Allison Ritman, 267–3018.

Financial Operations.—Peter Basso, 267–8242.

Assistant Administrator for Civil Rights.—Fanny Rivera, 267–3254.

Deputy Assistant Administrator.—Vacant, 267–3254.

Assistant Administrator for Policy, International Affairs and Environment.—Julie Oettinger, 267–3927.

Deputy Assistant Administrator.—Carl Burleson (acting), 267–7954.

Executive Director of:

Aviation Policy and Plans.—Nan Shellabarger, 267–3274.

Environment and Energy.—Carl Burleson, 267–7954.

International Affairs.—Carey Fagan (acting), 385–8900.

Director of:

Asia-Pacific.—Jeri Alles, 011–65–6543–1952.

Europe, Africa, and Middle East.—Steve Creamer, 011–322–508–2700.

Western Hemisphere.—Dawn Veatch, 385–8900.

Chief Counsel.—Marc Warren (acting), 267–3222.

Deputy Chief Counsel.—Marc Warren, 267–3773.

Director of Audit and Evaluation.—H. Clayton Foushee, 267–9440.

Assistant Administrator for Government and Industry Affairs.—Roderick Hall, 267–3277.
Deputy Assistant Administrator.—Molly Harris, 267–8211.
Assistant Administrator for Human Resource Management.—Catherine Emerson, 267–3456.
Deputy Assistant Administrator.—Angela Porter (acting), 267–3850.
Executive Director of:
Accountability Board.—Maria Fernandez-Greczmiel, 267–3065.
Corporate Learning.—Jana Murphy, 493–4507.
HR Field Operations.—Ken Nephew (817) 222–5809.
Human Resources Management Programs and Policies.—Jay Aul (acting), 267–3850.
Labor Management Relations.—Kimberly Moseley, 267–7306.
Assistant Administrator for Information Services.—David Bowen (CIO), 493–4570.
Director of:
Information Systems Security.—Christopher Garcia (acting), 267–7104.
Information Technology Enterprise Services.—Robert Rovinsky, 493–4019.
Information Technology Optimization.—Cheryl Rogers, 267–9477.
Information Technology Research and Development.—Doug Roseboro, 385–8054.
Assistant Administrator for Communications.—Sasha J. Johnson, 267–3883.
Deputy Assistant Administrator for Corporate Communications.—Carmen Marco, 267–8859.
Deputy Assistant Administrator for Public Affairs.—Laura J. Brown, 267–3883.
Assistant Administrator for Regions and Center Operations.—Paula Lewis, 267–7369.
Deputy Assistant Administrator.—Michael A. Cirillo, 267–7369.
Director of Aviation Logistics Organization.—Mamie Malory, 267–7369.
Regional Administrator for—
Alaskan.—Robert N. Lewis (907) 271–5645.
Central.—Joseph N. Miniace (816) 329–3050.
Eastern.—Carmine Gallo (718) 553–3000.
Great Lakes.—Barry D. Cooper (847) 294–7294.
New England.—Amy Lind Corbett (781) 238–7020.
Northwest Mountain.—Kathryn Vernon (425) 227–2001.
Southern.—Douglas Murphy (404) 305–5000.
Southwest.—Teresa Bruner (817) 222–5001.
Western-Pacific.—William C. Withycombe (310) 725–3550.
Director, Mike Monroney Aeronautical Center.—Lindy Ritz (405) 954–4521.
Assistant Administrator for Security and Hazardous Materials.—Claudio Manno, 267–7211.
Deputy Assistant Administrator.—Thomas D. Ryan, 267–7211.
Director of:
Office of Emergency Operations, Communications, and Investigations.—Angela Stubblefield, 267–7576.
Office of Executive and Center Operations.—Victor Kemens, 267–3538.
Office of Hazardous Materials Safety.—Chris Glasow, 385–4904.
Director of:
Joint Security and Hazardous Materials Safety, Central.—Marty Alford (817) 222–5700.
Joint Security and Hazardous Materials Safety, East.—Willie J. Gripper (404) 305–6750.
Joint Security and Hazardous Materials Safety, West.—Patricia Pausch (425) 227–2705.
Office of Security.—Bruce Herron, 493–5405.
Chief Operating Officer for Air Traffic Services.—J. David Grizzle (acting), 493–5602.
Senior Vice President for—
Finance.—Mark House, 267–3022.
NextGen and Operations Planning.—Victoria Cox, 267–7111.
Operations.—Rick Ducharme, 267–7224.
Strategy and Performance.—John Pipes, 267–5724.
Vice President for—
Acquisition and Business.—Patricia McNall, 267–7222.
En Route and Oceanic Services.—Greg Burke, 385–8501.
Mission Support Services.—Elizabeth Ray, 267–8261.
Safety.—Joseph Teixeira, 267–3341.
Technical Operations Service Unit.—Teri Bristol, 267–3366.
Technical Training.—Robert Tartar, 267–8311.
Terminal Service Unit.—Steve Osterdahl, 385–8801.
Associate Administrator for Airports.—Catherine Lang, 267–9471.
Deputy Associate Administrator.—Benito DeLeon (acting), 267–9471.

Director of:
Airport Compliance and Field Operations.—Randall Fiertz, 267–3085.
Airport Planning and Programming.—Elliott Black (acting), 267–8775.
Airport Safety and Standards.—Michael J. O'Donnell, 267–3053.
Associate Administrator for Commercial Space Transportation.—Dr. George C. Nield, 267–7793.
Deputy Associate Administrator.—James E. VanLaak, 267–7848.
Associate Administrator for Aviation Safety.—Peggy Gilligan, 267–3131.
Deputy Associate Administrator.—John J. Hickey, 267–7804.
Federal Air Surgeon.—Dr. Fred Tilton, 267–3535.
Director of:
Accident Investigation and Prevention.—Tony Fazio, 267–9612.
Aircraft Certification Service.—Dorenda Baker, 267–8235.
Flight Standards Service.—John Allen, 267–8237.
Office of Air Traffic Oversight.—Anthony Ferrante, 267–5202.
Quality, Integration and Executive Service.—Tina Amereihn, 493–5717.
Rulemaking.—Pamela Hamilton, 267–9677.

FEDERAL HIGHWAY ADMINISTRATION

Washington Headquarters, 1200 New Jersey Avenue, SE., 20590–9898

Turner-Fairbank Highway Research Center (TFHRC)

6300 Georgetown Pike, McLean, VA 22201

Administrator.—Victor Mendez (202) 366–0650.
Deputy Administrator.—Greg Nadeau, 366–0650.
Associate Administrator/Director of TFHRC.—Michael F. Trentacoste, 493–3259.
Associate Administrator for Administration.—Patricia A. Prosperi, 366–0604.
Executive Director.—Jeffrey F. Paniati, 366–2242.
Chief Counsel.—Fred Wagner, 366–0740.
Chief Financial Officer.—Elissa K. Konove, 366–0622.
Associate Administrator for—
Civil Rights.—Vacant, 366–0752.
Federal Lands.—John R. Baxter, 366–9472.
Infrastructure.—King W. Gee, 366–0371.
Operations.—Jeffrey A. Lindley, 366–9210.
Planning, Environment, and Realty.—Gloria M. Shepherd, 366–0116.
Policy.—Shailen P. Bhatt, 366–0585.
Public Affairs.—Cathy St. Denis, 366–0660.
Safety.—Joseph S. Toole, 366–2288.

FIELD SERVICES

Organizationally report to Executive Director (HOA–3), Washington, DC

Director of Technical Services.—Amy Lucero, 12300 West Dakota Avenue, Suite 340, Lakewood, CO 80228 (720) 963–3246.
Director of:
Field Services—North.—Joyce A. Curtis, 10 South Howard Street, Baltimore, MD 21201–2819 (410) 962–0739.
Field Services—South.—David C. Gibbs, 61 Forsyth Street, SW., Suite 17T26, Atlanta, GA 30303–3104 (404) 562–3573.
Field Services—West.—Walter Waidelich, 2520 West 4700 South, Suite 9C, Salt Lake City, UT 84118–1847 (801) 955–3530.

FEDERAL MOTOR CARRIER SAFETY ADMINISTRATION

Administrator.—Anne S. Ferro, room W60–308 (202) 366–1927.
Deputy Administrator.—William A. Bronrott.
Chief Safety Officer.—John Van Steenburg.
Chief Counsel.—Alais Griffin, 493–0349.
Associate Administrator for Field Operation.—Anne L. Collins, 366–2027.
Director, Office of Communications.—Candice Tolliver, 366–8810.

FIELD OFFICES

Eastern Service Center (CT, DC, DE, MA, MD, ME, NJ, NH, NY, PA, PR, RI, VA, VT, WV).—802 Cromwell Park Drive, Suite N, Glen Burnie, MD 21061 (443) 703–2240.

Midwestern Service Center (IA, IL, IN, KS, MI, MO, MN, NE, OH, WI).—4749 Lincoln Mall Drive, Suite 300A, Matteson, IL 60443 (708) 283–3577.

Southern Service Center (AL, AR, FL, GA, KY, LA, MS, NC, NM, OK, SC, TN, TX).—1800 Century Boulevard, Suite 1700, Atlanta, GA 30345 (404) 327–7400.

Western Service Center (American Samoa, AK, AZ, CA, CO, Guam, HI, ID, Mariana Islands, MT, ND, NV, NM, OR, SD, UT, WA, WY).—Golden Hills Office Centre, 12600 W. Colfax Avenue, Suite B–300, Lakewood, CO 80215 (303) 407–2350.

FEDERAL RAILROAD ADMINISTRATION

1200 New Jersey Avenue, SE., Washington, DC 20590

http://www.fra.dot.gov

Administrator.—Joseph C. Szabo, room W30–308, 493–6014.
Associate Administrator for—
Finance Management and Administration.—Kimberly Coronel, room W36–306, 493–6454.
Policy and Program Development.—Timothy Barkley, room W33–320, 493–1305.
Railroad Development.—Mark E. Yachmetz, room W38–316, 493–6484.
Safety.—Jo Strang, room W35–328, 493–6304.
Chief Counsel.—Mark Lindsey, room W31–320, 493–6048.
Director of:
Budget.—Donna Alwine, room W36–308, 493–6455.
Civil Rights.—Calvin Gibson, room W33–316, 493–6010.
Financial Management.—Kimberly Orben, room W36–306, 493–6454.
Public Affairs.—Brie Sachse, room W31–324, 366–1299.

REGIONAL OFFICES (RAILROAD SAFETY)

Region 1 (Northeastern).—Connecticut, Maine, Massachusetts, New Hampshire, New Jersey, New York, Rhode Island, Vermont.
Regional Administrator.—Les Fiorenzo, Room 1077, 55 Broadway, Cambridge, MA 02142 (617) 494–2302.

Region 2 (Eastern).—Delaware, District of Columbia, Maryland, Pennsylvania, Virginia, West Virginia, Ohio.
Regional Administrator.—Les Fiorenzo (acting), 1510 Chester Pike, Baldwin Tower, Suite 660, Crum Lynne, PA 19022 (610) 521–8200.

Region 3 (Southern).—Kentucky, Tennessee, Mississippi, North Carolina, South Carolina, Georgia, Alabama, Florida.
Regional Administrator.—Bonnie Murphy (acting), 61 Forsyth Street, NW., Suite 16T20, Atlanta, GA 30303 (404) 562–3800.

Region 4 (Central).—Minnesota, Illinois, Indiana, Michigan, Wisconsin.
Regional Administrator.—Lawrence Hasvold, 200 W. Adams Street, Chicago, IL 60606 (312) 353–6203.

Region 5 (Southwestern).—Arkansas, Louisiana, New Mexico, Oklahoma, Texas.
Regional Administrator.—Bonnie Murphy, 4100 International Plaza, Suite 450, Ft. Worth, TX 96109 (817) 862–2200.

Region 6 (Midwestern).—Iowa, Missouri, Kansas, Nebraska, Colorado.
Regional Administrator.—Darrell J. Tisor, DOT Building, 901 Locust Street, Suite 464, Kansas City, MO 64106 (816) 329–3840.

Region 7 (Western).—Arizona, California, Nevada, Utah.
Regional Administrator.—Alvin L. Settle, 801 I Street, Suite 466, Sacramento, CA 95814 (916) 498–6540.

Region 8 (Northwestern).—Idaho, Oregon, Wyoming, Montana, North Dakota, South Dakota, Washington, Alaska.
Regional Administrator.—Dave Brooks, 500 Broadway, Murdock Executive Plaza, Suite 240, Vancouver, WA 98660 (360) 696–7536.

FEDERAL TRANSIT ADMINISTRATION

Administrator.—Peter Rogoff.
Deputy Administrator.—Therese McMillan.
Chief Counsel.—Dorval Carter, 366–4011.
Director, Office of Civil Rights.—Linda C. Ford (acting), 366–6161.
Director, Planning and Environment.—Sherry Riklin (acting), 366–4033.
Associate Administrator for—
Administration.—Ann Linnertz, 366–4018.
Budget and Policy.—Robert Tuccillo, 366–1691.
Communications and Congressional Affairs.—Brian Farber, 366–4043.
Program Management.—Henrika Buchanan-Smith, 366–4020.
Research, Demonstration and Innovation.—Vincent Valdes, 366–3052.

MARITIME ADMINISTRATION

Administrator and Chairman, Maritime Subsidy Board.—David T. Matsuda, room W22–318 (202) 366–1719.
Deputy Administrator.—Orlando Gotay, room W22–314, 366–5823.
Secretary, Maritime Administration and Maritime Subsidy Board.—Vacant, 366–5746.
Chief Counsel and Member, Maritime Subsidy Board.—Kathryn Denise Rucker Krepp, room W24–310, 366–0709.
Director, Office of Congressional and Public Affairs.—Cheron Victoria Wicker, room W22–324, 366–5067.
Public Affairs Officer.—Kim Riddle, room W22–323, 366–5747.
Office of Assistant Administrator.—James E. Caponiti, room W28–316, 366–5772.
Director of:
International Activities.—Gregory Hall, room W28–314, 366–2765.
Policy and Plans.—Janice G. Weaver, room W28–310, 366–5482.
Associate Administrator for Budget and Programs / Chief Financial Officer.—Lydia Moschkin, room W21–334, 366–3071.
Director, Office of:
Accounting.—Jim Chen, room W26–307, 366–5103.
Budget.—James Lampert, room W26–310, 366–1369.
National Security Resource Management.—Jennifer Fallis, room W25–1947, 366–1947.
Resources.—Vacant, room W26–309, 366–5110.
Associate Administrator for Administration.—Paula Ewen, room W26–321, 366–2181.
Director, Office of:
Acquisition.—Wayne Leon, room W26–324, 366–5620.
Information Technology.—Robert Ellington, room W26–320, 366–2531.
Management and Information Services.—Carol Bowling, room W26–302, 366–2811.
Personnel.—Kim Norris, room W28–304, 366–4141.
Associate Administrator for Environment and Compliance.—Joseph A. Byrne, room W21–326, 366–1931.
Director, Office of:
Environment.—Michael C. Carter, room W28–313, 366–9431.
Safety.—Christopher McMahon, room W28–312, 366–7018.
Security.—Owen Doherty, room W23–312, 366–1883.
Associate Administrator for Intermodal System Development.—Keith Lesnick, room W21–320, 366–1624.
Deputy.—Roger V. Bohnert, room W21–324, 366–0720.
Director, Office of:
Deepwater Ports and Offshore Activities.—Yvette Fields, room W21–309, 366–0926.
Gateway Offices.—Christopher Moore, room W21–312, 366–5005.
Infrastructure Development and Congestion Mitigation.—Robert Bouchard, room W21–308, 366–5076.
Marine Highways and Passenger Services.—Lauren Brand, room W23–311, 366–7057.
Shipper and Carrier Outreach.—Richard J. Lolich, room W21–310, 366–0704.
Associate Administrator for National Security.—Kevin M. Tokarski, room W25–330, 366–5400.
Director, Office of:
Emergency Preparedness.—Thomas M.P. Christensen, room W23–304, 366–5909.
Sealift Support.—Jerome D. Davis, room W25–310, 366–0688.
Ship Disposal.—Curt J. Michanczyk, room W23–312, 366–6467.
Ship Operations.—William H. Cahill, room W25–336, 366–1875.
Associate Administrator for Business and Workforce Development.—Vacant, room W21–318, 366–5737.

Director, Office of:
Cargo Preference and Domestic Trade.—Vacant, room W23–314, 366–5515.
Financial Approvals and Marine Insurance.—Edmond J. Fitzgerald, room W23–322, 366–2279.
Chief, Division of:
Business Finance.—Gregory V. Sparkman, room W23–321, 366–1908.
Director, Office of:
Maritime Workforce Development.—Anne Wehde, room W23–314, 366–5469.
Shipyards and Marine Finance.—Vacant, room W21–318, 366–5737.

FIELD ACTIVITIES

Director for:
Great Lakes and Upper Inland Waterways Region.—Floyd Miras, Suite 185, 2860 South River Road, Des Plaines, IL 60018 (847) 905–0122.
North Atlantic Region.—Jeffrey Flumignan, 1 Bowling Green, Room 418, New York, NY 10004 (212) 668–2064.
Northern California/Hawaii Region.—John Hummer, Suite 2200, 201 Mission Street, San Francisco, CA 94105 (415) 744–3125.
South Atlantic Region.—Frances Bohnsack, Building 4D, Room 211, 7737 Hampton Boulevard, Norfolk, VA 23505 (757) 441–6393.

U.S. MERCHANT MARINE ACADEMY

Superintendent.—RADM Philip H. Greene, Jr., Kings Point, NY 11024 (516) 773–5000.
Assistant Superintendent for Academic Affairs (Academic Dean).—Shashi N. Kumar.

NATIONAL HIGHWAY TRAFFIC SAFETY ADMINISTRATION

Administrator.—David Strickland, room W42–302 (202) 366–1836.
Deputy Administrator.—Ronald L. Medford, 366–1836.
Director, Communications.—Vacant.
Director, Governmental Affairs, Policy and Strategic Planning.—Chan Lieu, 366–1836.
Senior Associate Administrator for—
Policy and Operation.—Gregory Walter, 366–2330.
Traffic Injury Control.—Brian McLaughlin, 366–1755.
Vehicle Safety.—Daniel Smith, 366–9700.
Associate Administrator for—
Communications and Consumer Information.—Susan Gorcowski, 366–9550.
Enforcement.—Claude Harris (acting), 366–2669.
National Center for Statistics and Analysis.—Jeff Michael (acting), 366–1503.
Planning, Administrative and Financial Management.—Rebecca Pennington, 366–2550.
Regional Operations and Program Delivery.—Maggi Gunnels, 366–2121.
Research and Program Development.—Michael Brown (acting), 366–1755.
Rulemaking.—Chris Bonanati, 366–1810.
Vehicle Safety Research Program.—John Maddox, 366–4862.
Chief Information Officer.—Colleen Coggins, 366–4878.
Director, Office of Civil Rights.—Philip Newby, 366–0972.
Chief Counsel.—O. Kevin Vincent, 366–9511.
Director, Executive Correspondence.—Gregory Walter, 366–2330.
Supervisor, Executive Correspondence.—Bernadette Millings, 366–5470.

REGIONAL OFFICES

Region 1.—Connecticut, Maine, Massachusetts, New Hampshire, Rhode Island, Vermont.
Regional Administrator.—Philip J. Weiser, Volpe National Transportation Center, 55 Broadway, Kendall Square, Code RTV–8E, Cambridge, MA 02142 (617) 494–3427.
Region 2.—Pennsylvania, New York, New Jersey, Puerto Rico, Virgin Islands.
Regional Administrator.—Thomas M. Louizou, 222 Mamaroneck Avenue, Suite 204, White Plains, NY 10605 (914) 682–6162.
Region 3.—Delaware, District of Columbia, Maryland, Kentucky, North Carolina, Virginia, West Virginia.
Regional Administrator.—Elizabeth Baker, 10 South Howard Street, Suite 6700, Baltimore, MD 21201 (410) 962–0090.

Region 4.—Alabama, Florida, Georgia, South Carolina, Tennessee.
Regional Administrator.—Terrance D. Schiavone, Atlanta Federal Center, 61 Forsyth Street, SW., Suite 17T30, Atlanta, GA 30303–3106 (404) 562–3739.
Region 5.—Illinois, Indiana, Michigan, Minnesota, Ohio, Wisconsin.
Regional Administrator.—Michael Witter, 19900 Governors Drive, Suite 201, Olympia Fields, IL 60461 (708) 503–8892.
Region 6.—Louisiana, Mississippi, New Mexico, Oklahoma, Texas, Indian Nations.
Regional Administrator.—George S. Chakiris, 819 Taylor Street, Room 8A38, Fort Worth, TX 76102–6177 (817) 978–3653.
Region 7.—Arkansas, Iowa, Kansas, Missouri, Nebraska.
Regional Administrator.—Romell Cooks, 901 Locust Street, Room 466, Kansas City, MO 64106 (816) 329–3900.
Region 8.—Colorado, North Dakota, Nevada, South Dakota, Utah, Wyoming.
Regional Administrator.—Bill Watada, 12300 West Dakota Avenue, Suite 140, Lakewood, CO 80228–2583 (720) 963–3100.
Region 9.—American Samoa, Arizona, California, Guam, Mariana Islands, Hawaii.
Regional Administrator.—David Manning, 201 Mission Street, Suite 1600, San Francisco, CA 94105 (415) 744–3089.
Region 10.—Alaska, Idaho, Montana, Oregon, Washington.
Regional Administrator.—John Moffat, Federal Building, 915 Second Avenue, Suite 3140, Seattle, WA 98174 (206) 220–7640.

PIPELINE AND HAZARDOUS MATERIALS SAFETY ADMINISTRATION

Administrator.—Cynthia Quarterman, room E27–300 (202) 366–4433.
Deputy Administrator.—Timothy Butters, room E27–300, 366–4461.
Assistant Administrator / Chief Safety Officer.—Vacant.
Chief Counsel.—Bizunesh Scott, room E26–320 366–4400.
Director, Office of Civil Rights.—Helen E. Hagin, room E27–334, 366–9638.
Chief Financial Officer.—Monica Summitt, room E32–330, 366–5608.
Associate Administrator for—
Governmental, International and Public Affairs.—Julia Valentine, room E27–300, 366–4831.
Hazardous Materials Safety.—Dr. Magdy El-Sibaie, room E21–316, 366–0656.
Management and Administration.—Scott Poyer, room E22–312, 366–5608.
Pipeline Safety.—Jeffrey Wiese, room E22–321, 366–4595.

HAZARDOUS MATERIALS SAFETY OFFICES

Chief of:
Eastern Region.—Colleen D. Abbenhaus, 820 Bear Tavern Road, Suite 306, West Trenton, NJ 08628 (609) 989–2256.
Central Region.—Kevin Boehne, Suite 478, 2350 East Devon Avenue, Des Plaines, IL 60018 (847) 294–8580.
Western Region.—Shelly Negrete, 3401 Centre Lake Drive, Suite 550–B, Ontario, CA 91761 (909) 937–3279.
Southern Region.—John Heneghan, 233 Peachtree Street, NE., Suite 602, Atlanta, GA 30303 (404) 832–1140.
Southwest Region.—Robert Strollo, 8701 South Gessner Road, Suite 1110, Houston, TX 77004 (713) 272–2820.

PIPELINE SAFETY OFFICES

Director of:
Eastern Region.—Byron Coy, 820 Bear Tavern Road, Suite 103, West Trenton, NJ 08628 (609) 989–2171.
Central Region.—David Barrett, 901 Locust Street, Room 462, Kansas City, MO 64106 (816) 329–3800.
Western Region.—Chris Hoidal, 12300 West Dakota Avenue, Suite 110, Lakewood, CO 80228 (720) 963–3160.
Southwest Region.—Rodrick M. Seeley, 8701 South Gessner, Suite 1110, Houston, TX 77074 (713) 272–2859.
Southern Region.—Wayne Lemoi, 233 Peachtree Street, NE., Suite 600, Atlanta, GA 30303 (404) 832–1140.

RESEARCH AND INNOVATIVE TECHNOLOGY ADMINISTRATION (RITA)

http://www.rita.dot.gov

Deputy Administrator.—Dr. Robert Bertini, room E37–312 (202) 366–3833.
Chief Counsel.—Gregory Winfree, room E35–330, 366–4412.
Chief Financial Officer.—Katherine Montgomery, room E33–310, 366–2577.
Public Affairs Contact, Bureau of Transportation Statistics.—David Smallen, room E36–328, 366–5568.
Director for—
Governmental, International and Public Affairs.—Jane Mellow, room E36–334, 366–4792.
Intelligent Transportation Systems.—Shelly Row, 366–5719.
Transportation Safety Institute.—Dr. Steve Dillingham, room MPB 348B, 6500 South MacArthur Boulevard, Oklahoma City, OK 73169 (405) 954–3153.
Volpe National Transportation Systems Center.—Robert Johns, room 1240, 55 Broadway, Kendall Square, Cambridge, MA 02142 (617) 494–2222.

SAINT LAWRENCE SEAWAY DEVELOPMENT CORPORATION-U.S. DOT

Administrator.—Collister Johnson, Jr., room W32–300 (202) 366–0091, fax 366–7147.
Deputy Administrator.—Craig H. Middlebrook, room W32–300 (202) 366–0105.
Chief of Staff.—Anita K. Blackman, room W32–300, 366–0107.
Director, Office of:
Budget and Programs.—Kevin P. O'Malley.
Congressional and Public Relations.—Nancy T. Alcalde.
Trade Development.—Rebecca McGill.

SEAWAY OPERATIONS

180 Andrews Street, P.O. Box 520, Massena, NY 13662–0520

phone (315) 764–3200, fax (315) 764–3235

Associate Administrator.—Salvatore Pisani.
Deputy Associate Administrator.—Carol A. Fenton.
Assistant.—Mary C. Fregoe.
Chief Counsel.—Carrie Mann Lavigne.
Director, Office of:
Engineering and Maintenance.—Thomas A. Lavigne.
Financial Management and Administration and CFO.—Marsha Sienkiewicz.
Lock Operations and Marine Services.—Lori K. Curran.

SURFACE TRANSPORTATION BOARD

395 E Street, SW., 20423–0001, phone (202) 245–0245

http://www.stb.dot.gov

Chairman.—Daniel R. Elliott III, 245–0220.
Vice Chairman.—Ann Begeman, 245–0203.
Commissioner.—Francis P. Mulvey, 245–0213.
Office of:
Economics, Environmental Analysis, and Administration.—Leland L. Gardner, 245–0291.
General Counsel.—Ray Atkins, 245–0261.
Director, Office of:
Proceedings.—Rachel D. Campbell, 245–0352.
Public Assistance, Governmental Affairs, and Compliance.—Matthew T. Wallen, 245–0238.

DEPARTMENT OF ENERGY

James Forrestal Building, 1000 Independence Avenue, SW., 20585

phone (202) 586–5000, http://www.energy.gov

STEVEN CHU, Secretary of Energy; born on February 28, 1948, in St. Louis, MO; education: A.B., mathematics; B.S., physics, the University of Rochester, 1970; Ph.D., physics, University of California, Berkeley, 1976; honorary degrees from 10 universities; professional: 1997 Nobel Prize in Physics; Director, Lawrence Berkeley National Laboratory; professor, University of California, Berkley; professor, Stanford; Bell Labs; organizations: National Academy of Sciences; American Philosophical Society; Chinese Academy of Sciences; Academia Sinica; Korean Academy of Sciences; Technology and numerous other civic and professional organizations; married: Dr. Jean Chu; two children, two stepchildren, and six grandchildren; nominated by President Barack Obama to become the 12th Secretary of Energy, and was confirmed by the U.S. Senate on January 20, 2009.

OFFICE OF THE SECRETARY

Secretary of Energy.—Steven Chu (202) 586–6210.
Deputy Secretary.—Daniel B. Poneman, 586–5500.
Associate Deputy Secretary.—Melvin G. Williams, Jr., 586–7131.
Chief of Staff.—Brandon Hurlbut, 586–9712.
Inspector General.—Gregory H. Friedman, 586–4393.
Assistant Secretary for—
Congressional and Intergovernmental Affairs.—Jeffrey Lane, 586–5450.
Policy and International Affairs.—David Sandalow, 586–5800.
General Counsel.—Sean Lev (acting), 586–5281.
Chief Information Officer.—Michael Locatis, 586–0166.
Chief Human Capital Officer.—Michael Kane, 586–5610.
Chief Financial Officer.—Steve Isakowitz, 586–4171.
Chief Health Safety and Security Officer.—Glenn Podonsky, 586–9275.
Executive Director of the Loan Programs Office.—Jonathan Silver, 287–5900.
Director, Office of:
Economic Impact and Diversity.—William Valdez (acting), 586–8383.
Hearings and Appeals.—Poli Marmolejos, 287–1566.
Intelligence and Counterintelligence.—Edward ''Bruce'' Held, 586–2610.
Management.—Ingrid Kolb, 586–2550.
Public Affairs.—Dan Leistikow, 586–4940.
Director for Advanced Research Projects Agency-Energy.—Arun Majumdar, 287–1004.
Administrator for Energy Information Administration.—Richard Newell, 586–4361.

UNDER SECRETARY OF ENERGY

Under Secretary of Energy.—Arun Majumdar (acting), (202) 586–7700.
Assistant Secretary for—
Electricity Delivery and Energy Reliability.—Patricia Hoffman, 586–1411.
Energy Efficiency and Renewable Energy.—Henry Kelly (acting), 586–9220.
Environmental Management.—Inés Triay, 586–7709.
Fossil Energy.—Vic Der (acting), 586–6660.
Nuclear Energy.—Peter Lyons (acting), 586–6630.
Director, Office of:
Legacy Management.—David Geiser, 586–7550.

UNDER SECRETARY FOR SCIENCE

Under Secretary for Science.—Steven Koonin (202) 586–0505.

Director, Office of Science.—William Brinkman, 586–0505.

NATIONAL NUCLEAR SECURITY ADMINISTRATION

Administrator for National Nuclear Security Administration/Under Secretary for Nuclear Security.—Thomas D'Agostino (202) 586–5555.
Principal Deputy Administrator.—Neile Miller, 586–5555.
Deputy Administrator for—
Defense Programs.—Donald Cook, 586–2179.
Defense Nuclear Nonproliferation.—Anne Harrington, 586–0645.
Naval Reactors.—Admiral Kirtland Donald, USN, 781–6174.
Deputy Under Secretary for Counterterrorism.—Dr. Steven Aoki, 586–1734.
Associate Administrator for—
Defense Nuclear Security.—Bradley Peterson, 586–8900.
Emergency Operations.—Rear Admiral Joseph Krol, USN (Ret.), 586–9892.
Infrastructure and Environment.—Kenneth Powers, 586–8115.

MAJOR FIELD ORGANIZATIONS

OPERATIONS OFFICES

Managers:
Idaho.—Richard Provencher (208) 526–7300, fax (208) 526–0542.
Oak Ridge.—Gerald Boyd (865) 576–4444, fax (865) 576–0006.
Richland.—Mat McCormick (509) 376–7395, fax (509) 376–4789.
Savannah River.—David Moody (803) 952–8725, fax (803) 952–8144.

INTEGRATED SUPPORT/BUSINESS CENTERS

Managers:
Chicago Office.—Roxanne E. Purucker (630) 252–2110.
EM Consolidated Business Center.—Jack Craig (513) 246–0460.
NNSA Service Center.—Karen Boardman (505) 845–6050.

POWER MARKETING ADMINISTRATIONS

Administrator, Power Administration:
Bonneville.—Stephen J. Wright (503) 230–5101, fax (503) 230–4018.
Southeastern Area.—Kenneth Legg (706) 213–3800, fax (706) 213–3884.
Southwestern Area.—Jon C. Worthington (918) 595–6601, fax (918) 595–6755.
Western Area.—Timothy J. Meeks (720) 962–7077, fax (720) 962–7083.

PETROLEUM RESERVES

Deputy Assistant Secretary for Petroleum Reserves.—David Johnson (202) 586–4733.

FEDERAL ENERGY REGULATORY COMMISSION

888 First Street, NE., 20426

Chair.—Jon Wellinghoff (202) 502–6580.
Commissioners:
Cheryl A. LaFleur, 502–8961.
Philip D. Moeller, 502–8852.
John R. Norris, 502–6530.
Marc Spitzer, 502–8366.
Chief Administrative Law Judge.—Curtis L. Wagner, Jr., 502–8500.
Executive Director.—Charles H. Schneider, 502–8916.
General Counsel.—Michael A. Bardee, 502–6000.
Director, Office of:
Administrative Litigation.—Ted Gerarden, 502–8700.

Electric Reliability.—Joseph McClelland, 502–8600.
Energy Market Regulation.—Michael McLaughlin, 502–6700.
Energy Policy and Innovation.—Jamie L. Simler, 502–8934.
Energy Projects.—Jeff Wright, 502–8700.
Enforcement.—Norman Bay, 502–8100.
External Affairs.—Leonard Tao, 502–8004.

DEPARTMENT OF EDUCATION

400 Maryland Avenue, SW., 20202

phone (202) 401–3000, fax 401–0596, http://www.ed.gov

ARNE DUNCAN, Secretary of Education; born in Chicago, IL, November 6, 1964; children: Clare and Ryan; education: B.A., Harvard University, *magna cum laude*, 1987; professional: professional basketball player in Australia, 1987–91; Director of Ariel Education Initiative, 1992–98; Deputy Chief of Staff to the Chief Executive Officer of the Chicago Public Schools, 1999–2001; Chief Executive Officer of the Chicago Public Schools, 2001–09; nominated by President Barack Obama to become the 9th Secretary of Education on December 16, 2008; confirmed on January 20, 2009.

OFFICE OF THE SECRETARY

Room 7W301, phone (202) 401–3000, fax 260–7867

Secretary of Education.—Arne Duncan.
Chief of Staff.—Joanne Weiss.
Deputy Chief of Staff.—Eric Waldo.

OFFICE OF THE DEPUTY SECRETARY

Room 7W308, phone 401–1000

Deputy Secretary.—Anthony Miller.
Chief of Staff.—Jason Snyder.

OFFICE OF THE UNDER SECRETARY

Room 7E307, phone (202) 401–0429

Under Secretary.—Martha J. Kanter.
Deputy Under Secretary.—James Kvaal.
Chief of Staff.—Alejandra Ceja.

OFFICE OF THE CHIEF FINANCIAL OFFICER

PCP 550 12th Street, SW., phone (202) 245–8144, fax 485–0162

Chief Financial Officer.—Thomas Skelly (acting), LBJ, 400 Maryland Avenue, SW., room 4E313, 401–0287.
Deputy Chief Financial Officer.—Hugh Hurwitz, PCP, room 6124, 245–6555.
Executive Officer.—Michael Holloway, PCP, room 6090, 245–8150.
Director of:
Contracts and Acquisitions Management.—James Ropelewski, PCP, room 7153, 245–6221.
Financial Improvement and Post Audit Operations.—Craig Stanton, PCP, room 6056, 245–8102.
Financial Management Operations.—Gary Wood, PCP, room 6089, 245–8118.

OFFICE OF THE CHIEF INFORMATION OFFICER

PCP 550 12th Street, SW., phone (202) 245–6400, fax 245–6621

Chief Information Officer.—Danny Harris, PCP, room 9112, 245–6252.
Deputy Chief Information Officer.—Shawn Wang, PCP, room 9149, 245–6338.
Executive Officer.—Michael Holloway, PCP, room 6090, 245–8150.
Director of:
Financial Systems Services.—Constance Davis, PCP, room 9150, 245–7173.
Information Assurance Services.—Michele Iversen, PCP, room 10057, 245–8287.
Information Technology Program Services.—Ken Moore, PCP, room 9109, 245–6908.
Information Technology Services.—Tony Wood, PCP, room 9151, 245–7214.

OFFICE OF MANAGEMENT

Room 2W301, phone (202) 401–5848, fax 260–3761

Assistant Secretary.—Winona H. Varnon (acting), room 2W311, 401–1583, fax 260–3761.
Principal Deputy Assistant Secretary.—Winona H. Varnon, room 2W311, 401–1583, fax 260–3761.
Chief of Staff.—Donna Butler, room 2W309, 401–8530.
Executive Officer.—David Cogdill, room 2W227, 401–0695, fax 401–3513.
Service Director of:
Equal Employment Opportunity Services.—Selina Lee, room 2W240, 205–0518, fax 205–5760.
Facilities Services.—Scott Taylor, room 2E315, 401–9496, fax 453–5579.
Human Capital and Client Services.—Robert Buggs, room 2E314, fax 401–0520.
Management Services.—Wanda Davis, room 2E315, 401–5931, fax 205–1866.
Office of Hearings and Appeals.—Frank J. Furey, L'Enfant Plaza–2134, 619–9701, fax 619–9726.
Privacy, Information and Records Management Services.—Kathleen Styles, room 6W247, 453–5587, fax 401–0920.
Security Services.—Ronald Luczak (acting), room 2W251, 260–7727, fax 260–3761.

OFFICE FOR CIVIL RIGHTS

400 Maryland Avenue, SW., Room 4E319, 20202–1100, phone (202) 423–5900, fax 423–6010

Assistant Secretary.—Russlynn Ali, room 4E313, 453–5900.
Principal Deputy Assistant Secretary.—Ricardo Soto, room 4E329, 453–5954.
Deputy Assistant Secretary for—
Enforcement.—Sandra Battle, room 4E314, 453–5958.
Policy.—Sunil Mansukhani, room 4E348, 453–5959.
Resource Management Group.—Lester Slayton, room 4E305, 453–5966.
Chief of Staff.—Sandra Matthews, room 4E311, 453–6594.
Senior Counsel.—Gabriel Sandoval, room 4E309, 401–8586.
Confidential Assistant.—Andrew Amore, room 4E319, 453–6359.
Special Assistant.—Michael Lamb, room 4E327, 453–5955.
Director of Enforcement.—Randolph Wills, room 4E332, 453–5956.

OFFICE OF COMMUNICATIONS AND OUTREACH

Room 5E300, phone (202) 401–0404, fax 401–8607

Assistant Secretary.—Peter Cunningham, room 7W101, LBJ, 401–2563.
Press Secretary.—John White, room 7E203, LBJ, 401–8459.
Deputy Assistant Secretaries:
Communication Development.—David Hoff, room 7W103, LBJ, 401–6359.
Communication Services.—John McGrath, room 5E231, LBJ, 401–1309.
External Affairs / Outreach.—Massie Ritsch, room 5E330, LBJ, 260–2671.

OFFICE OF ELEMENTARY AND SECONDARY EDUCATION

Room 3W300, phone (202) 401–0113, fax 205–0303

Assistant Secretary.—Thelma Melendez de Santa Ana, room 3W315, 401–0113.
Deputy Assistant Secretary.—Carl Harris, room 3W305, 453–5549.
Chief of Staff.—Carolyn Webb de Macias, room 3W311, 453–6585.
Deputy Assistant Secretary for—
Management.—Alex Goniprow, room 3W314, 401–9090.
Policy and Strategic Initiatives.—Michael Yudin, room 3W309, 453–6050.
Director of:
Academic Improvement and Teacher Quality Programs.—Sylvia Lyles (acting), room 3E314, 260–8228, fax 260–8969.
Impact Aid Programs.—Alfred Lott, room 3E105, 260–3858, fax 205–0088.
Office of Indian Education.—Jenelle Leonard (acting), room 3E121, 205–0687.
Office of Migrant Education.—Lisa Ramirez, room 3E317, 260–1127, fax 205–0089.
School Support and Technology Programs.—Jenelle Leonard, room 3W203, 401–3641.
Student Achievement and School Accountability Programs.—Patricia McKee (acting), room 3W230, 206–0826.

OFFICE OF ENGLISH LANGUAGE ACQUISITION

400 Maryland Avenue, SW., 5C–132, 20202, phone (202) 401–4300, fax 401–8452

Assistant Deputy Secretary and Director.—Rosalinda B. Barrera.
Deputy Director.—Joanne Urrutia.

OFFICE OF FEDERAL STUDENT AID

830 First Street, NE., 20202, phone (202) 377–3000, fax 275–5000

Chief Operating Officer.—Bill Taggart.
Deputy Chief Operating Officer.—Jim Runcie.
Chief of Staff.—Jim Manning, 377–3007.
Ombudsman.—Mike Turpenoff (acting), room 41F3, 377–3477.
Chief:
Business Operations Officer.—Sue Szabo, room 83E3, 377–3437.
Communications Officer.—Christopher B. Greene, room 22C7, 377–4003.
Compliance Officer.—Robin Minor, room 81K2, 377–4273.
Financial Officer.—Jay Hurt, room 54E1, 377–3453.
Information Officer.—Richard Gordon, room 102E3, 377–3707.
Director, Policy Liaison and Implementation Staff.—Jeff Baker, room 113C1, 377–4009.
Chief of Administration Services.—Irma Blanchett, room 21A5, 377–4165.
Chief Customer Experience Officer.—Brenda Wensil, room 114F1, 377–4671.

OFFICE OF THE GENERAL COUNSEL

Room 6E313, phone (202) 401–6000, fax 205–2689

General Counsel.—Charles P. Rose.
Senior Counsel.—Robert Wexler.
Chief of Staff and Special Counsel.—Julie Miceli.
Executive Officer.—LaVerne Chester, 401–5937.
Deputy General Counsel for—
Departmental Law and Postsecondary Education.—Georgia Yuan.
Ethics, Legislative Counsel and Regulatory Service.—Elizabeth McFadden.
Program Services.—Philip Rosenfelt.

OFFICE OF INNOVATION AND IMPROVEMENT

phone (202) 205–4500

Assistant Deputy Secretary.—James Shelton, 401–0479.
Associate Assistant Deputy Secretary.—Margo Anderson.

Chief of Staff.—Nia Phillips.

OFFICE OF INSPECTOR GENERAL

Potomac Center Plaza (PCP), 8th Floor, 20024, phone (202) 245–6900, fax 245–6993

Inspector General.—Kathleen Tighe.
Deputy Inspector General.—Mary Mitchelson.
Counsel to the Inspector General.—Marta Erceg, 245–7015.
Assistant Inspector General for—
Audit Services.—Keith West, 245–7041.
Evaluation, Inspection and Management Services.—Wanda Scott, 245–6065.
Investigations.—William Hamel, 245–6922.
IT Audit and Computer Crimes Investigations.—Charles Coe, 245–7034.

INTERNATIONAL AFFAIRS OFFICE

Room 1W112, phone (202) 401–0430, fax 401–2508

Director.—Maureen McLaughlin.
Deputy Director.—JoAnne Livingston.
Office Administrator.—Mone't Peterson-Cox.

INSTITUTE OF EDUCATION SCIENCES

555 New Jersey Avenue, NW., Room 600, 20208, phone (202) 219–1385, fax 219–1466

Director.—John Q. Easton, 219–1385.
Deputy Director for—
Administration and Policy.—Sue Betka, 219–1385.
Science.—Anne Riccuiti, 219–2247.
National Center for Education Evaluation and Regional Assistance.—Rebecca Maynard, 208–1289.
National Center for Education Research.—Lynn Okagaki, 219–2006.
National Center for Education Statistics.—Jack Buckley, 219–7001.
National Center for Special Education Research.—Lynn Okagaki (acting), 219–2006.

OFFICE OF LEGISLATION AND CONGRESSIONAL AFFAIRS

Room 6W301, phone (202) 401–0020, fax 401–1438

Assistant Secretary.—Gabriella Gomez, 401–0020.
Deputy Assistant Secretary.—J. Lloyd Horwich, 205–0490.
Chief of Staff.—Jodie Fingland, 401–1043.

OFFICE OF PLANNING, EVALUATION AND POLICY DEVELOPMENT

Room 5E301, phone (202) 401–0831, fax 401–8607

Assistant Secretary.—Carmel Martin, room 5E313.
Deputy Assistant Secretaries: Denise Forte, room 5E311; Emma Vadehra, room 5E309.
Executive Officer.—Brenda Long, room 7E201.
Director of:
Budget Service.—Thomas Skelly, room 5W313, 401–7888.
Performance Information Management Service.—Ross C. Santy, room 6W231, 401–1959.
Policy and Program Studies Service.—Stuart Kerachsky, room 6W230, 401–3132.

OFFICE OF POSTSECONDARY EDUCATION

1990 K Street, NW., 20006, phone (202) 502–7750, fax 502–7677

Assistant Secretary.—Eduardo M. Ochoa.
Chief of Staff.—Francine Picoult.

Deputy Assistant Secretary for Higher Education Programs.—Lynn Mahaffie (acting interim), 502–7903.

Deputy Assistant Secretary for Policy, Planning and Innovation.—David Bergeron, 502–7950.

Deputy Assistant Secretary for International and Foreign Language Education.—Andre Lewis, 502–7317.

OFFICE OF SAFE AND DRUG-FREE SCHOOLS

550 12th Street, SW., 20202, phone (202) 245–7895

Assistant Deputy Secretary.—Kevin Jennings, room 10087, 245–7830.
Associate Assistant Deputy Secretary.—Bill Modzeleski.

OFFICE OF SPECIAL EDUCATION AND REHABILITATIVE SERVICES

Potomac Center Plaza (PCP), 550 12th Street, SW., 5th Floor, 20202

phone (202) 245–7468, fax 245–7638

Assistant Secretary.—Alexa E. Posny, room 5107, 245–6496.
Executive Administrator.—Andrew J. Pepin, room 5106, 245–7632.
Deputy Assistant Secretary.—Sue Swenson, room 5138, 245–8021.
Director of:
National Institute on Disability and Rehabilitation Research.—Sue Swenson (acting).
Office of Special Education Programs.—Melody Musgrove.
Commissioner of the Rehabilitation Services Administration.—Lynnae Ruttledge.

OFFICE OF VOCATIONAL AND ADULT EDUCATION

550 12th Street, SW., Room 1100, 20202, phone (202) 245–7700, fax 245–7171

Assistant Secretary.—Brenda Dann-Messier, brenda.dann-messier@ed.gov.
Chief of Staff.—George Smith, george.smith@ed.gov.
Deputy Assistant Secretary.—Frank Chong, frank.chong@ed.gov.
Staff Assistants: Russella Davis-Rogers, russella.davis@ed.gov; Francine Sinclair, francine.sinclair@ed.gov.

DEPARTMENT OF VETERANS AFFAIRS

Mail should be addressed to 810 Vermont Avenue, NW., Washington, DC 20420
http://www.va.gov

ERIC K. SHINSEKI, Secretary of Veterans Affairs; education: graduated, U.S. Military Academy, West Point, NY, 1965; M.A., Duke University; graduated, National War College; military service: Chief of Staff, U.S. Army, 1999–2003; Vice Chief of Staff, U.S. Army, 1998–99; Commanding General, United States Army, Europe and Seventh Army; Commanding General NATO Land Forces, Central Europe; Commander NATO-led Stabilization Force, Bosnia-Herzegovina; Vietnam War Veteran; military awards: Defense Distinguished Service Medal, Distinguished Service Medal, Legion of Merit (with Oak Leaf Clusters), Bronze Star Medal with ''V'' Device (with 2 Oak Leaf Clusters), Purple Heart (with Oak Leaf Cluster), Defense Meritorious Service Medal, Meritorious Service Medal (with 2 Oak Leaf Clusters), Air Medal, Parachutist Badge, Ranger Tab, Joint Chiefs of Staff Identification Badge, and Army Staff Identification Badge; married: Patricia; two children; nominated by President Barack Obama to become 7th Secretary of Veterans Affairs, and was confirmed by the U.S. Senate on January 21, 2009.

OFFICE OF THE SECRETARY

Secretary of Veterans Affairs.—Eric K. Shinseki (202) 461–4800.
Deputy Secretary of Veterans Affairs.—W. Scott Gould, 461–4817.
Chief of Staff.—John R. Gingrich, 461–4808.
Deputy Chief of Staff.—Michael Galloucis, 461–4808.
Senior Advisor to the Secretary.—John Spinelli, 461–4874.
Special Assistant for Veterans Service Organizations Liaison.—Kevin S. Secor, 461–4835.
Executive Secretary.—Kenneth Greenberg, 461–4869.
Director, Center for—
Faith-Based Community Initiative.—Rev. E. Terri LaVelle, 461–7611.
Minority Veterans.—Lucretia McClenney, 461–6191.
Women Veterans.—Irene Trowell-Harris, Ed.D., RN, 461–6193.
Employment Discrimination Complaint Adjudication.—Maxanne R. Witkin, 1722 I Street, NW., 461–1650.
Small and Disadvantaged Business Utilization.—Tom Leney, 801 I Street, NW., 461–4300.

BOARD OF VETERANS' APPEALS

Chairman.—Steve Keller (acting), 811 Vermont Avenue, NW. (202) 461–8001.
Vice Chairman.—Steve Keller.

OFFICE OF GENERAL COUNSEL

General Counsel.—Will A. Gunn (202) 461–4995.
Deputy General Counsel.—John ''Jack'' Thompson, 461–4995.

OFFICE OF INSPECTOR GENERAL

Inspector General.—George J. Opfer, 801 I Street, NW. (202) 461–4720.
Deputy Inspector General.—Richard J. Griffin.

OFFICE OF ACQUISITIONS, LOGISTICS, AND CONSTRUCTION

Executive Director.—Glenn D. Haggstrom, 425 I Street, NW. (202) 461–8007.
Deputy Assistant Secretary. Office of Acquisition and Logistics.—Jan R. Frye, 810 Vermont Avenue, NW., 461–6920.

Director, Office of Construction and Facilities Management.—Robert L. Neary (acting), 425 I Street, NW., 461–8197.

ASSISTANT SECRETARY FOR CONGRESSIONAL AND LEGISLATIVE AFFAIRS

Assistant Secretary.—Joan M. Evans (202) 461–6619.
Director of Operations.—Terrence Stinson, 461–6490.
Deputy Assistant Secretary.—Emory Ray Helton.
Associate Deputy Assistant Secretary.—Christopher E. O'Connor, 461–6490.
Legislative Advisor.—David Ballenger, 461–6492.
Health Benefits.—Vacant.
Director for—
Congressional and Legislative Affairs.—Len Sistek, 461–6492.
Congressional Liaison.—Ronald Maurer, 224–5351.
Corporate Enterprise Service.—Mary K. Stack, 461–6453.
Legislative Affairs Service.—John Kruse, 461–6492.

ASSISTANT SECRETARY FOR PUBLIC AND INTERGOVERNMENTAL AFFAIRS

Assistant Secretary.—L. Tammy Duckworth (202) 461–7500.
Deputy Assistant Secretary for—
Intergovernmental and International Affairs.—John Garcia, 461–7400.
Public Affairs.—Nathan Naylor.

ASSISTANT SECRETARY FOR POLICY AND PLANNING

Assistant Secretary.—Dr. Raul Perea-Henze, M.D., 461–5800.
Principal Deputy Assistant Secretary.—Robert Snyder, 461–5800.
Deputy Assistant Secretary for—
Data Governance and Analysis.—Dat Tran, 461–5788.
Policy.—Nancy Dolan, 461–5663.
Executive Director for—
Corporate Analysis and Evaluation.—Albert J. Starnes, 461–5752.
Enterprise Program Management Office.—Greg L. Giddens, 461–6986.
VA/DoD Collaboration.—John P. Medve, 461–5626.

ASSISTANT SECRETARY FOR OPERATIONS, SECURITY AND PREPAREDNESS

Assistant Secretary.—Jose D. Riojas (202) 461–4980.
Deputy Assistant Secretary for—
Emergency Management.—Kevin Hanretta, 461–4985.
Security and Law Enforcement.—Frederick R. Jackson, 461–6920.

ASSISTANT SECRETARY FOR MANAGEMENT

Assistant Secretary/Chief Financial Officer.—W. Todd Grams (acting), (202) 461–6600.
Principal Deputy Assistant Secretary.—W. Todd Grams 461–6703.
Executive Director of Operations.—Helen Tierney 461–6703.
Deputy Assistant Secretary for—
Budget.—Daniel A. Tucker, 461–6630.
Finance.—Edward J. Murray, 461–6180.

ASSISTANT SECRETARY FOR INFORMATION AND TECHNOLOGY

Assistant Secretary.—Roger W. Baker (202) 461–6911.
Principal Deputy Assistant Secretary.—Stephen W. Warren, 461–6910.

ASSISTANT SECRETARY FOR HUMAN RESOURCES AND ADMINISTRATION

Assistant Secretary.—John U. Sepulveda (202) 461–7750.
Principal Deputy Assistant Secretary.—Rafael Torres (acting), 501–2662.
Deputy Assistant Secretary for—

Administration.—Catherine Biggs-Silvers, 461–5000.
Diversity Management and Inclusion.—Georgia Coffey, 1575 I Street, NW., 461–4131.
Human Resources Management.—Tonya Deanes, 461–7765.
Labor-Management Relations.—Leslie Wiggins, 461–4119.
Resolution Management.—Rafael Torres, 1575 I Street, NW., 501–280.

NATIONAL CEMETERY ADMINISTRATION

Under Secretary for Memorial Affairs.—Steve L. Muro (acting), (202) 461–6112.
Executive Assistants: Beth Beardsley, 461–6242; George D. Eisenbach, Jr., 461–6014.
Deputy Under Secretary.—Ron Walters (acting), 461–6510.
Executive Assistant.—Sharon Stevens, 461–6740.
Deputy Under Secretary for Management.—Dave Schettler, 461–6234.
Associate Director for Field Programs.—Glenn Powers (acting), 461–6071.
Deputy Under Secretary for Finance and Planning/CFO.—Ron Walters, 461–6738.
Director of:
Budget Service.—Joan Jefferies, 461–6742.
Design and Construction.—Fred Neun, 461–8919.
Field Programs.—Kimberly Wright, 461–6748.
Information Technology and Business Requirements.—Joe Nosari, 461–8975.
Management Support and Communication Service.—Deanna Wilson (acting), 461–6232.
Memorial Programs Service.—Anita Hanson, 501–3060.
Veterans Cemetery Grants Service.—Frank Salvas, 249–7396.

VETERANS BENEFITS ADMINISTRATION

Under Secretary.—Michael Walcoff (acting), 1800 G Street, NW. (202) 461–9300.
Principal Deputy Under Secretary.—Michael Cardarelli.
Chief of Staff.—Lois Mittelstaedt.
Deputy Under Secretary for—
Disability Assistance.—Thomas Pamperin, 461–9320.
Economic Opportunity.—Vacant, 461–9320.
Field Operations.—Diana Rubens, 461–9340.
Chief Financial Officer.—Jamie Manker, 461–9900.
Director of:
Business Process Integration.—Brad Houston, 215–2588.
Compensation.—Thomas Murphy, 461–9700.
Education.—Keith M. Wilson, 461–9800.
Employee Development and Training.—Terrence Meehan, 461–9860.
Insurance.—Thomas Lastowka (215) 381–3100.
Loan Guaranty.—Richard Fyne (acting), (571) 272–0001.
Management.—Bonnie Miranda, 461–9412.
Pension and Fiduciary.—Vacant, 461–9700.
Performance Analysis and Integrity.—William Kane, 461–9040.
Strategic Planning.—Vacant, 461–9222.
Veterans Benefits Management System.—Mark Bologna (acting), 461–9640.
Veterans Relationship Management.—Leo Phelan,
Vocational Rehabilitation and Employment.—Ruth Fanning, 461–9333.

VETERANS HEALTH ADMINISTRATION

Under Secretary.—Robert A. Petzel, M.D. (202) 461–7000.
Principal Deputy Under Secretary for Health.—Robert L. Jesse, M.D., Ph.D., 461–7008.
Deputy Under Secretary for Health for Operations and Management.—William C. Schoenhard, FACHE, 461–7026.
Chief of Staff.—Lisa Thomas, Ph.D. (acting), 461–7016.
Deputy Chief of Staff.—Ann C. Patterson, 461–7016.
Deputy Under Secretary for Health for Policy and Services.—Madhulika Agarwal, M.D., M.P.H., 461–7590.
Assistant Deputy Under Secretary for—
Health for Clinical and Organizational Support.—Laura O'Grady, RN, M.S.N., 461–7008.
Health for Policy and Planning.—Patricia Vandenberg, M.H.A., B.S.N., 461–7100.
Associate Deputy Under Secretary for Health for Quality and Safety.—William E. Duncan, M.D., Ph.D., M.A.C.P., 461–7254.

Medical Inspector.—John Pierce, M.D., 1575 I Street, NW., 501–2000.
Executive Director, Federal Recovery Program.—Karen Guice, M.D., M.P.P., 461–4839.
Chief Officer for—
Academic Affiliations.—Malcolm Cox, M.D., 461–9490.
Business.—Gary M. Baker, 461–1600.
Communications.—John S. Hale, 461–7070.
Compliance and Business Integrity.—Caitlin O'Brien, 1575 I Street, NW., 501–0364.
Employee Education System.—Louise R. Van Diepen, M.S., C.G.P., (acting), 461–4076.
Ethics in Health Care.—Ellen Fox, M.D., 1575 I Street, NW., 501–0364.
Financial.—W. Paul Kearns III, FACHE, FHFMA, CPA, 461–6666.
Health Information.—Craig B. Luigart, 461–5848.
Nursing.—Cathy Rick, RN, CNAA, FACHE, 461–6962.
Patient Care Services.—Margaret Hammond, M.D. (acting), 461–7590.
Patient Safety.—James P. Bagian, M.D., PE (734) 930–5920.
Procurement and Logistics.—Frederick Downs, Jr., 461–1770.
Public Health and Environmental Hazards.—Victoria Davey, Ph.D., 461–1000.
Quality and Performance.—Joseph Francis, M.D., M.P.H. (acting), 1717 H Street, NW., 266–4533.
Readjustment Counseling.—Alfonso R. Batres, Ph.D., M.S.S.W., 461–6525.
Research and Development.—Joel Kupersmith, M.D., 461–1700.
Research Oversight.—J. Thomas Puglisi, Ph.D., CIP, 1717 H Street, NW., 266–4580.

DEPARTMENT OF HOMELAND SECURITY

U.S. Naval Security Station, 3801 Nebraska Avenue, NW., 20393

phone (202) 282–8000

JANET NAPOLITANO, Secretary of Homeland Security; born on November 29, 1957, in New York City, NY; education: graduated from Santa Clara University in 1979, where she won a Truman Scholarship and received her Juris Doctor (J.D.) in 1983 from the University of Virginia School of Law; public service: Prior to joining the Obama Administration, Napolitano was mid-way through her second term as Governor of the State of Arizona. While Governor, Napolitano was the first woman to chair the National Governors Association where she was instrumental in creating the Public Safety Task Force and the Homeland Security Advisors Council. She also chaired the Western Governors Association. Napolitano previously served as the Attorney General of Arizona and the U.S. Attorney for the District of Arizona; nominated by President Barak Obama to become the 3rd Secretary of Homeland Security on December 1, 2008, and was confirmed by the U.S. Senate on January 20, 2009. Janet Napolitano was sworn in January 21, 2009, as the 3rd Secretary of the Department of Homeland Security.

OFFICE OF THE SECRETARY

Secretary of Homeland Security.—Janet Napolitano.
Deputy Secretary of Homeland Security.—Jane Holl Lute.
Chief of Staff.—Noah Kroloff.

CITIZENSHIP AND IMMIGRATION SERVICES OMBUDSMAN

Ombudsman.—January Contreras.

CIVIL RIGHTS AND CIVIL LIBERTIES

phone (202) 401–1474, Toll Free: 1–866–644–8360

Officer for Civil Rights and Civil Liberties.—Margo Schlanger.

OFFICE OF COUNTERNARCOTICS ENFORCEMENT

Director.—Grayling Williams.

EXECUTIVE SECRETARIAT

Executive Secretary.—Philip McNamara.

OFFICE OF THE GENERAL COUNSEL

General Counsel.—Ivan K. Fong.

OFFICE OF INSPECTOR GENERAL

phone (202) 254–4100

Inspector General.—Charles K. Edwards (acting).
Deputy Inspector General.—Charles K. Edwards.

General Counsel to the Inspector General.—Richard N. Reback.
Assistant Inspector General for—
Audits.—Anne L. Richards.
Emergency Management Oversight.—Matthew A. Jadacki.
Information Technology.—Frank Deffer.
Inspections.—Carlton I. Mann.
Investigations.—Thomas Frost.
Management.—Louise McGlathery (acting).
Director, Governmental and Public Affairs.—Rene Rocque Lee (acting).
Director, Legislative Affairs.—Marta Metelko.
Chief of Staff.—Yvonne Manino (acting).

OFFICE OF INTELLIGENCE AND ANALYSIS

phone (202) 282–8353

Under Secretary and Chief Intelligence Officer.—Caryn A. Wagner.
Principal Deputy Under Secretary.—Bart R. Johnson.
Chief of Staff.—Christopher Button.
State and Local Program Office Director.—Christopher Button (acting).
Deputy Under Secretaries for—
Analysis.—Dawn Scalici.
Enterprise and Mission Support.—Michael Potts.
Plans, Policy, and Performance Management.—Todd Rosenblum.

OFFICE OF INTERGOVERNMENTAL AFFAIRS

phone (202) 282–9310

Assistant Secretary.—Betsy Markey.
Principal Deputy Assistant Secretary.—Jarrod Bernstein.
Deputy Assistant Secretary.—Stephanie Tennyson.

OFFICE OF LEGISLATIVE AFFAIRS

phone (202) 447–5890

Assistant Secretary.—Nelson Peacock.
Deputy Assistant Secretaries: Leslie Gross-Davis, Michael Stroud.

MILITARY ADVISOR'S OFFICE

phone (202) 282–8239

Military Advisor to the Secretary.—RDML Fred Midgette.

PRIVACY OFFICE

phone (703) 235–0780

Chief Privacy Officer.—Mary Ellen Challahan.

OFFICE OF PUBLIC AFFAIRS

Assistant Secretary.—Brent Colburn.
Deputy Assistant Secretaries: Jennifer Friedman, Amy Kudwa.

NATIONAL PROTECTION AND PROGRAMS DIRECTORATE

phone (202) 282–8400

Under Secretary.—Rand Beers.
Deputy Under Secretary.—Philip Reitinger.
Chief of Staff.—Caitlin Durkovich.

Assistant Secretary for—
Cybersecurity and Communications.—Gregory Schaffer.
Infrastructure Protection.—Todd Keil.
Director for—
Federal Protective Service.—L. Eric Patterson.
Risk Management and Analysis.—Tina Gabbrielli.
United States Visitor and Immigrant Status Indicator Technology.—Robert Mocny.

SCIENCE AND TECHNOLOGY DIRECTORATE

Under Secretary.—Tara O'Toole.
Deputy Under Secretary.—Paul Benda (acting).
Chief of Staff.—Paul Benda.
Deputy Chief of Staff.—Christina Murata.
Director of:
Acquisition Support and Operations Analysis.—Henry Gonzalez.
Homeland Security Advanced Research Projects Agency.—Christopher Doyle (acting).
Research and Development Partnerships.—Tom Cellucci (acting).
Support to the Homeland Security Enterprise and First Responders.—Robert Griffin.

MANAGEMENT DIRECTORATE

Under Secretary.—Elaine C. Duke.
Deputy Under Secretary.—Sharie Bourbeau.
Chief Administrative Services Officer.—Donald Bathurst.
Chief Financial Officer.—Vacant.
Chief Human Capital Officer.—Jeff Neal.
Chief Information Officer.—Margie Graves (acting).
Chief Procurement Officer.—Richard Gunderson (acting).
Chief Security Officer.—Jerry Williams.

OFFICE OF POLICY DIRECTORATE

Assistant Secretary.—David Heyman.
Chief of Staff.—Leonard Joseph.
Deputy Chief of Staff.—Gail Kaufman.
Deputy Assistant Secretary, Office of:
Immigration and Border Security.—Kelly Ryan (acting).
International Affairs: Mark Koumans, Mariko Silver.
Policy Development.—Vacant.
Private Sector.—Douglas A. Smith.
Screening Coordination.—Patricia Cogswell (acting).
Strategic Plans.—Alan Cohn.
State and Local Law Enforcement.—Vacant.
Director Office of:
Immigration Statistics.—Michael Hoefer.
Operations and Resource Management.—Jeffrey Paul Johnson.
Chair, Homeland Security Advisory Council.—Becca Sharp.

FEDERAL EMERGENCY MANAGEMENT AGENCY (FEMA) DIRECTORATE

500 C Street, SW., 20472, phone (202) 646–2500

Administrator.—W. Craig Fugate.
Deputy Administrator.—Richard Serino.
Chief of Staff.—Jason McNamara.
Director, Office of:
Executive Secretariat.—Alyson Price.
National Advisory Council.—Patricia A. Kalla.
Chief Counsel.—Brad Kieserman.
Deputy Administrator, Protection and National Preparedness.—Timothy W. Manning.
Assistant Administrators:
Grant Programs.—Elizabeth M. Harman.
National Continuity Programs.—Damon Penn.

National Preparedness.—Corey Gruber.
Director, Office of National Capital Region Coordination.—Steward D. Beckham.
Administrator, U.S. Fire Administration.—Glenn A. Gaines (acting).
Associate Administrator, Mission Support Bureau.—David Garratt.
Deputy Associate Administrator, Mission Support Bureau.—Albert B. Sligh, Jr.
Chief Administrative Officer, Mission Support Bureau.—Delia Davis.
Chief Procurement Officer, Mission Support Bureau.—Anthony Martoccia (acting).
Chief Information Officer, Mission Support Bureau.—Jeanne Etzel.
Chief Component Human Capital Officer, Mission Support Bureau.—Sheila Clark.
Chief Security Officer, Mission Support Bureau.—Burt Thomas.
Associate Administrator, Response and Recovery.—William ''Bill'' L. Carwile III.
Deputy Associate Administrator, Response and Recovery.—Elizabeth Zimmerman.
Assistant Administrators:
Logistics.—Eric Smith.
Recovery.—Deborah Ingram.
Response.—Robert J. Fenton, Jr.
Director, Office of Federal Coordinating Officer Operations.—Theodore A. ''Ted'' Monette, Jr.
Administrator, Federal Insurance and Mitigation Administration.—Edward Connor (acting).
Deputy Federal Insurance and Mitigation Administrator, Insurance.—Edward Connor.
Deputy Federal Insurance and Mitigation Administrator, Mitigation.—Sandra Knight.
Chief Financial Officer.—Norman S. Dong.
Director, Office of:
Equal Rights.—Pauline Campbell.
External Affairs.—Pat Hart (acting).
Law Enforcement Advisor to the Administrator.—James Hagy (acting).
Directors, Office of:
Disability Integration and Coordination.—Marcie Roth.
Policy and Program Analysis.—David J. Kaufman.
Regional Operations.—Elizabeth Edge.
Director, Center for Faith-Based and Neighborhood Partnerships.—David L. Myers.

OFFICE OF OPERATIONS COORDINATION AND PLANNING

phone (202) 282–9580

Director.—Richard Chávez (acting).
Deputy Director.—Frank DiFalco (acting).
Chief of Staff.—Mary Kruger.

DOMESTIC NUCLEAR DETECTION OFFICE

phone (202) 254–7300

Director.—Warren M. Stern.
Deputy Director.—Dr. Huban Gowadia.
Chief of Staff.—Patrick Philbin.
Assistant Director, Office of:
Mission Management.—Matthew Barton (acting).
National Technical Nuclear Forensics Center.—William Daitch.
Operations Support.—Ernest Muenchau.
Product Acquisition and Deployment.—Brucy Rayno (acting).
Red Team/Net Assessments.—Kevin McCarthy.
Systems Architecture.—John Zabko (acting).
Systems Engineering and Evaluation.—Julian Hill.
Transformational Research and Development.—Joel Rynes.

TRANSPORTATION SECURITY ADMINISTRATION (TSA)

601 South 12th Street, Arlington, VA 20598–6001

Administrator/Assistant Secretary.—John S. Pistole.
Deputy Administrator.—Gale D. Rossides.
Chief of Staff.—Art Macias.

UNITED STATES CUSTOMS AND BORDER PROTECTION (CBP)

1300 Pennsylvania Avenue, NW., 20229

Commissioner.—Alan D. Bersin, (202) 344–1010 / 344–2001.
Deputy Commissioner.—David V. Aguilar, 344–1010 / 2001.
Chief of Staff.—Marco A. Lopez, 344–1080 / 1001.
Deputy Chief of Staff.—Luke Lopez, 344–2568.
Chief Counsel.—Alfonso Robles, 344–2990.
Assistant Commissioner, Office of:
Administration.—Eugene H. Schied, 344–2300.
Air and Marine.—Michael C. Kostelnik, 344–3950.
Congressional Affairs.—Michael Yeager, 344–1760.
Field Operations.—Tom S. Winkowski, 344–1620.
Human Resources Management.—Christine E. Gaugler, 863–6100.
Information and Technology.—Charles R. Armstrong, 344–1680.
Intelligence and Operations Coordination.—Donna Bucella, 344–1150.
Internal Affairs.—James F. Tomsheck, 344–1800.
International Affairs and Trade Relations.—Charles Stallworth (acting), 344–3000.
International Trade.—Allen Gina, 863–6000.
Public Affairs.—Tom Walters (acting), 344–1700.
Technology Innovation and Acquisition.—Mark Borkowski, 344–2450.
Training and Development.—Patricia Duffy, 344–1130.
Chief, Office of Border Patrol.—Michael Fisher, 344–2050.
Executive Director, Office of:
Diversity and Civil Rights.—Franklin C. Jones, 344–1610.
Policy and Planning.—Mark Dolan (acting), 344–2700.
Director, State, Local and Tribal Governments.—Carry Huffman (acting), 344–1619.
Director, Executive Secretariat.—Joseph E. Tezak, 344–1040.
Senior Advisor Trade Relations.—Maria Luisa O'Connell, 325–4290.

UNITED STATES IMMIGRATION AND CUSTOMS ENFORCEMENT (ICE)

Director.—John Morton (202) 732–3000.
Chief of Staff.—Suzie Barr, 732–3011.
Deputy Chief of Staff.—Edward Dolan, 732–3016.
Executive Secretariat.—Cynthia O'Connor, 732–5580.
Deputy Director.—Kumar Kibble, 732–3000.
Assistant Deputy Director.—Beth Gibson, 732–3000.
Assistant Deputy Director.—Erik Barnett, 732–3318.
Assistant Director, Office of:
Detention Policy and Planning.—Kevin Landy.
Professional Responsibility.—Timothy Moynihan, 732–8339.
Principal Legal Advisor.—Peter S. Vincent, 732–5000.
Assistant Director, Office of:
Congressional Relations.—Elliot Williams, 732–6171.
Public Affairs.—Brian P. Hale, 732–4250.
State, Local and Tribal Coordination.—Harold Hurtt, 732–5060.
Executive Associate Director, Enforcement and Removal Operations.—Gary Mead, 732–5958.
Deputy Executive Associate Director of Enforcement and Removal Operations.—Thomas Homan, 732–5545.
Assistant Director of:
Detention Management.—Tae Johnson, 732–3110.
Enforcement.—Gregory Archambeault (acting), 732–5959.
Field Operations.—David Venturella, 732–3941.
ICE Health Service Corps.—Dr. John Krohmer, 732–3915.
Mission Support.—Linda Pena, 732–3090.
Removal.—Robert Helwig, 732–4511.
Secure Communities.—Marc Rapp (acting), 732–3915.
Executive Associate Director, Homeland Security Investigations.—James Dinkins, 732–5100.
Deputy Associate Director, Homeland Security Investigations.—Peter Edge, 732–5100.
Assistant Director of:
Intelligence.—James Chaparro, 732–3101.
International Affairs.—Luis Alvarez, 732–0375.
Mission Support.—Staci Barrera, 732–5702.

National IPR Coordination Center.—Vacant.
Operations.—Janice Ayala, 732–5849.
Programs.—Michael Holt, 732–5116.
Executive Associate Director, Management and Administration.—Daniel Ragsdale, 732–3000.
Acquisition Management.—William Randolph, 732–2600.
Diversity Officer and Civil Rights.—Scott Lanum, 732–0190.
Financial Officer.—Radha Sekar, 732–3077.
Freedom of Information Act.—Catrina Pavlik Keenan, 732–0300.
Human Capital Officer.—Kimberlyn Bauhs, 732–7770.
Information Officer.—Luke McCormack, 732–2000.
National Firearms and Tactical Training Unit.—Humberto Medina, 732–3937.
Office of Policy.—Rachel Canty, 732–5904.
Privacy Officer.—Lyn Rahilly, 732–3301.
Training and Development.—Charles DeVita, 732–7800.

FEDERAL LAW ENFORCEMENT TRAINING CENTER

1131 Chapel Crossing Road, Glynco, GA 31524

Director.—Connie L. Patrick (912) 267–2070.
Deputy Director.—Ken Keene, 267–2680.
Chief of Staff.—Brenda Lloyd, 267–2070.
Assistant Director for—
Administration.—Marcus Hill, 267–2231.
Artesia Operations.—Woody Wright (575) 748–8178.
Washington Operations.—Brian Beckwith (202) 233–0260.
Assistant Director/Chief Financial Officer.—Don Lewis, 267–2999.
Assistant Director/Chief Information Officer.—Sandy Peavy, 267–2014.
Assistant Director for—
Field Training.—Cindy Atwood, 267–2445.
Glynco Training.—Dominick Braccio, 267–3373.
Training Innovation and Management.—Mike Hanneld, 267–2934.
Chief Counsel.—Dave Brunjes, 267–2441.

UNITED STATES CITIZENSHIP AND IMMIGRATION SERVICES

20 Massachusetts Avenue, NW., Washington, DC 20529, phone (202) 272–1000

Director.—Alejandro Mayorkas.
Deputy Director.—Lori Scialabba.
Chief of Staff.—Lauren Kielsmeier.
Chief Information Officer.—Mark Schwartz.
Associate Director for—
Fraud Detection and National Security Directorate.—Don Crocetti.
Refugee, Asylum and International Operations Directorate.—Steve Bucher.
Service Center Operations Directorate.—Donald Neufeld.
Chief, Office of:
Administration.—Nancy Guilliams.
Administrative Appeals.—Perry Rhew.
Chief Counsel.—Dea Carpenter (acting).
Chief Financial Officer.—David Garner.
Citizenship.—Rebecca Carson.
Communications.—Angie Alfonso-Royals (acting).
Legislative Affairs.—James McCament.
Policy and Strategy.—Denise Vanison.

UNITED STATES COAST GUARD

2100 Second Street, SW., 20593, phone (202) 372–4400

Commandant.—ADM Robert J. Papp, Jr.
Vice Commandant.—VADM Sally Brice-O'Hara.
Deputy Commandant for—
Mission Support.—VADM John Currier.
Operations.—VADM Brian Salerno.

Chief Administrative Law Judge.—Hon. Joseph N. Ingolia.
Judge Advocate General/Chief Counsel.—RDML Fred Kenney.
Deputy Judge Advocate General/Deputy Chief Counsel.—Calvin Lederer.
Director of Governmental and Public Affairs.—RDML Karl Schultz.
Senior Military Advisor to the Secretary of Homeland Security.—RDML Fred Midgette.

UNITED STATES SECRET SERVICE

245 Murray Drive, SW., Building 410, 20223

Director.—Mark Sullivan.
Deputy Director.—Keith Prewitt.
Deputy Assistant Director, Congressional Affairs Program.—Faron Paramore (202) 406–5676, fax 406–5740.

INDEPENDENT AGENCIES, COMMISSIONS, BOARDS

ADVISORY COUNCIL ON HISTORIC PRESERVATION

1100 Pennsylvania Avenue, NW., Suite 803, 20004

phone (202) 606–8503, http://www.achp.gov

[Created by Public Law 89–665, as amended]

Executive Director.—John M. Fowler.
Chairman.—Milford Wayne Donaldson, Sacramento, California.
Vice Chairman.—Vacant.
Directors for:
Office of Administration.—Ralston Cox.
Office of Communications, Education, and Outreach.—Susan A. Glimcher.
Office of Federal Agency Programs.—Reid J. Nelson.
Office of Native American Affairs.—Valerie Hauser.
Office of Preservation Initiatives.—Ronald D. Anzalone.
Expert Members:
Jack Williams, Seattle, Washington.
Ann Alexander Pritzlaff, Denver, Colorado.
Julia A. King, St. Leonard, Maryland.
Horace H. Foxall, Jr., Seattle, Washington.
Citizen Members:
Bradford J. White, Evanston, Illinois.
John A. Garcia, Albuquerque, New Mexico.
Mark A. Sadd, Esq., Charleston, West Virginia.
Native American Member.—John L. Berrey, Quapaw, Oklahoma.
Governor.—Vacant.
Mayor.—Hon. Michael B. Coleman, Columbus, Ohio.
Architect of the Capitol.—Stephen T. Ayers, AIA.
Secretary, Department of:
Agriculture.—Hon. Thomas J. Vilsack.
Commerce.—Hon. John E. Bryson.
Defense.—Dr. Robert Gates.
Education.—Hon. Arne Duncan.
Housing and Urban Development.—Hon. Shaun Donovan.
Interior.—Hon. Kenneth L. Salazar.
Transportation.—Hon. Ray LaHood.
Veterans' Affairs.—Hon. Eric K. Shinseki.
Administrator of General Services Administration.—Martha Johnson.
National Conference of State Historic Preservation Officer.—Ruth Pierpont, President, Waterford, New York.
National Trust for Historic Preservation.—Carolyn Brody, Chairman, Washington, DC.

AMERICAN BATTLE MONUMENTS COMMISSION

Courthouse Plaza II, Suite 500, 2300 Clarendon Boulevard, Arlington, VA 22201–3367

phone (703) 696–6902

[Created by Public Law 105–225]

Chairman.—Merrill A. McPeak appointed as of 6/3/11.
Commissioners:
Hon. Barbaralee Diamonstein-Spielvogel.
Hon. Darrell Dorgan.
Hon. John Estrada.
Hon. Evelyn Foote.
Hon. Rolland Kidder.
Hon. Richard Klass.
Hon. Constance Morella.
Hon. Maura Sullivan.
Secretary.—Joseph Maxwell Cleland.

Deputy Secretary.—Raymond J. Wollman.
Director for—
Finance.—Christine Fant.
Human Resources and Administration.—Frank Manies.
Public Affairs.—Michael G. Conley.
U.S. Memorials.—Thomas R. Sole.

(Note: Public law changed to 105–225, August 1998; H.R. 1085).

AMERICAN NATIONAL RED CROSS

National Headquarters, 430 17th Street, 20006, phone (202) 303–5000

Government Relations and Strategic Partnerships, phone (202) 303–4371, fax 638–3960

HONORARY OFFICERS

Honorary Chair.—Barack H. Obama, President of the United States.

CORPORATE OFFICERS

Chairman.—Bonnie McElveen-Hunter.
President/CEO.—Gail J. McGovern.
Chief Audit Executive.—Dale P. Bateman.
General Counsel/Secretary.—Mary S. Elcano.
Chief Financial Officer.—Brian Rhoa.

BOARD OF GOVERNORS

Cesar A. Aristeiguieta
Paula E. Boggs
Richard K. Davis
Richard M. Fountain
Allan I. Goldberg
Ann F. Kaplan
James W. Keyes
Bonnie McElveen-Hunter
Gail J. McGovern
Judith A. McGrath
Youngme E. Moon
Suzanne Nora Johnson
Richard C. Patton
Laurence E. Paul
Joseph B. Pereles
Josue Robles, Jr.
Melanie R. Sabelhaus
H. Marshall Schwarz
William S. Simon
Steven H. Wunning

ADMINISTRATIVE OFFICERS

President of Humanitarian Services.—Gerald DeFrancisco.
President of Biomedical Services.—Shaun P. Gilmore.
Chief Public Affairs Officer.—Suzanne DeFrancis.
Corporate Ombudsman.—Kevin Jessar.
Chief Information Officer.—John Crary.
Chief Marketing Officer.—Peggy Dyer.
National Chair of Volunteers.—Pam Farr.
Senior Vice President-Human Resources.—Melissa Hurst.
Chief Development Officer.—Neal Litvack.
President-Preparedness and Health and Safety Services.—Jack McMaster.
Chief Diversity Officer.—Floyd Pitts.

GOVERNMENTAL RELATIONS AND STRATEGIC PARTNERSHIPS

Senior Vice President for Government Relations and Strategic Partnerships.—Neal Denton.
Senior Policy Advisor.—Dawn P. Latham.
Congressional Liason.—Marin Reynes.

APPALACHIAN REGIONAL COMMISSION

1666 Connecticut Avenue, NW., 20009, phone (202) 884–7660, fax 884–7693

Federal Co-Chair.—Earl F. Gohl.
Alternate Federal Co-Chair.—Vacant.
States' Washington Representative.—Cameron Whitman.
Executive Director.—Thomas M. Hunter.
Chief of Staff.—Guy Land.

ARMED FORCES RETIREMENT HOME

3700 North Capitol Street, NW., Box 1303, Washington, DC 20011–8400

phone (202) 541–7535, fax 541–7506

Chief Operating Officer.—Steven G. McManus (acting).
Deputy Chief Operating Officer/Chief Financial Officer.—Steven G. McManus.
Chief Information Officer.—Maurice Swinton.

ARMED FORCES RETIREMENT HOME—WASHINGTON

phone (202) 541–7537, fax 541–7509

Director.—David Watkins.

ARMED FORCES RETIREMENT HOME—GULFPORT

1800 Beach Drive, Gulfport, MS 39507

phone (202) 897–4408, fax 897–4488

Director.—Richard Heath.

BOARD OF GOVERNORS OF THE FEDERAL RESERVE SYSTEM

Constitution Avenue and 20th Street, NW., 20551, phone (202) 452–3000

Chairman.—Ben S. Bernanke.
Vice Chair.—Janet L. Yellen.
Members: Elizabeth A. Duke, Daniel K. Tarullo, Sarah Bloom Raskin.
Assistant to the Board and Division Director.—Michelle A. Smith.
Assistants to the Board: Linda L. Robertson, Rosanna Pianalto Cameron, David W. Skidmore.
Special Assistants to the Board: Brian J. Gross, Lucretia M. Boyer, Winthrop P. Hambley.

DIVISION OF BANKING SUPERVISION AND REGULATION

Director.—Patrick M. Parkinson.
Deputy Director.—Maryann F. Hunter.
Senior Associate Directors: Barbara J. Bouchard, Michael R. Foley, Jack P. Jennings, Arthur W. Lindo, Peter J. Purcell, William G. Spaniel, Mark E. Van Der Weide.
Associate Directors: Kevin M. Bertsch, Betsy Cross, Nida Davis, Gerald A. Edwards, Jr., David S. Jones.
Assistant Directors: Robert T. Ashman, Kevin J. Clarke, Lisa M. DeFerrari, Adrienne T. Haden, Anna Lee Hewko, Michael J. Kraemer, Robert T. Maahs, Steven P. Merriett, Richard Naylor II, Dana E. Payne, Nancy J. Perkins, Lisa H. Ryu, Sarkis D. Yoghourtdjian.
Senior Advisers: Norah M. Barger, Timothy P. Clark, Charles H. Holm.
Adviser.—William F. Treacy.

DIVISION OF CONSUMER AND COMMUNITY AFFAIRS

Director.—Sandra F. Braunstein.
Deputy Director.—Leonard Chanin.
Senior Associate Directors: Timothy R. Burniston, Anna Alvarez Boyd, Tonda E. Price.

Assistant Directors: Joseph Firschein, Allen J. Fishbein, Suzanne G. Killian, James A. Michaels.

DIVISION OF FEDERAL RESERVE BANK OPERATIONS AND PAYMENT SYSTEMS

Director.—Louise L. Roseman.
Deputy Directors: Donald V. Hammond, Jeffrey C. Marquardt.
Senior Associate Director.—Jeff J. Stehm.
Associate Directors: Kenneth D. Buckley, Susan V. Foley, Dorothy B. LaChapelle.
Deputy Associate Directors: Gregory L. Evans, Lisa K. Hoskins, Michael J. Lambert.
Assistant Directors: Jennifer A. Lucier, Stuart E. Sperry, Michael J. Stan, Leonard J. Tanis.
Senior Adviser.—Paul W. Bettge.

DIVISION OF INFORMATION TECHNOLOGY

Director.—Maureen T. Hannan.
Deputy Directors: Geary L. Cunningham, Wayne A. Edmondson, Sharon L. Mowry.
Deputy Associate Directors: Lisa M. Bell, Susan F. Marycz, Raymond Romero, Kofi A. Sapong.
Assistant Directors: Lisa Bell, Glenn Eskow, Kofi Sapong, Raj Yelisetty.

DIVISION OF INTERNATIONAL FINANCE

Director.—Nathan Sheets.
Deputy Directors: Thomas A. Connors, Steven B. Kamin.
Senior Associate Director.—Michael Leahy.
Associate Directors: Trevor A. Reeve, Ralph W. Tryon.
Deputy Associate Director.—Christopher J. Erceg.
Assistant Directors: David H. Bowman, Charles P. Thomas, Beth Anne Wilson.
Senior Advisers: Mark S. Carey, John H. Rogers, Jane Haltmaier.
Adviser.—Sally M. Davies.

DIVISION OF MONETARY AFFAIRS

Director.—William B. English.
Deputy Directors: James A. Clouse, Deborah J. Danker, William R. Nelson.
Senior Associate Director.—Seth B. Carpenter.
Deputy Associate Directors: Gretchen C. Weinbach, Egon Zakrajsek.
Assistant Directors: William F. Bassett, Margaret DeBoer, Jane E. Ihrig, J. David Lopez-Salido, Matthew M. Luecke, Fabio M. Natalucci.
Senior Advisers: Andrew T. Levin, Stephen A. Meyer.
Adviser.—Mary T. Hoffman.

DIVISION OF RESEARCH AND STATISTICS

Director.—David J. Stockton.
Deputy Director.—David Wilcox.
Senior Associate Directors: Michael S. Gibson, David L. Reifschneider, Janice Shack-Marquez, Daniel E. Sichel, Lawrence Slifman, William L. Wascher III, Alice Patricia White.
Associate Directors: Daniel M. Covitz, Matthew J. Eichner, Eric M. Engen, Michael T. Kiley, David E. Lebow, Michael G. Palumbo, S. Wayne Passmore.
Deputy Associate Directors: Sean D. Campbell, Michael S. Cringoli, Joshua H. Gallin, Diana Hancock, Robin A. Prager, Joyce K. Zickler.
Assistant Directors: Jeffrey C. Campione, Sandra A. Cannon, Arthur Kennickell, Elizabeth K. Kiser, Karen M. Pence, John M. Roberts, Steven A. Sharpe, John J. Stevens, Stacey M. Tevlin, Mary M. West.
Senior Adviser.—Glenn B. Canner.

INSPECTOR GENERAL

Inspector General.—Mark Bialek.
Associate Inspector Generals: Jacqueline M. Becker, Anthony J. Castaldo, Elise M. Ennis, Andrew Patchan, Jr., Harvey Witherspoon.

LEGAL DIVISION

General Counsel.—Scott G. Alvarez.
Deputy General Counsels: Richard M. Ashton, Kathleen M. O'Day.
Associate General Counsels: Stephanie Martin, Ann E. Misback, Katherine H. Wheatley.
Assistant General Counsels: Stephen Horace Meyer, Cary K. Williams.

MANAGEMENT DIVISION

Director.—Richard A. Anderson.
Deputy Directors: Michell C. Clark, Donald A. Spicer.
Senior Associate Director.—William L. Mitchell.
Associate Directors: Christine M. Fields, Brender L. Gregory, Charles F. O'Malley, James R. Riesz, Marie S. Savoy.
Deputy Associate Directors: Elaine M. Boutilier, Tara Tinsley Pelitere.
Assistant Directors: Keith F. Bates, Jeffrey R. Peirce, Theresa A. Trimble, Karen Vassallo.
Special Advisers: Todd A. Glissman, Carol A. Sanders, Christopher J. Suma.

OFFICE OF THE SECRETARY

Secretary.—Jennifer J. Johnson.
Deputy Secretary.—Robert deV. Frierson.
Associate Secretary.—Margaret M. Shanks.

OFFICE OF STAFF DIRECTOR

Staff Director.—Stephen R. Malphrus.
Deputy Staff Director.—Charles S. Struckmeyer.
Program Director, Office of Diversity and Inclusion.—Sheila Clark.
Senior Adviser.—Lynn S. Fox.
Adviser.—Adrienne D. Hurt.

OFFICE OF FINANCIAL STABILITY POLICY AND RESEARCH

Director.—J. Nellie Liang.
Deputy Director.—Andreas W. Lehnert.
Chief of Staff.—Seth F. Wheeler.

BROADCASTING BOARD OF GOVERNORS

330 Independence Avenue, SW., Suite 3360, 20237
phone (202) 203–4545, fax 203–4568

The Broadcasting Board of Governors oversees the operation of the IBB and provides yearly funding grants approved by Congress to three non-profit grantee corporations, Radio Free Europe/Radio Liberty, Radio Free Asia, and the Middle East Broadcasting Networks.

Chairman.—Walter Isaacson.

INTERNATIONAL BROADCASTING BUREAU
[Created by Public Law 103–236]

The International Broadcasting Bureau (IBB) is composed of the Voice of America, and Radio and TV Marti.

International Broadcasting Bureau.—Richard M. Lobo, (202) 203–4515, fax 203–4587.
Director of:
Cuba Broadcasting.—Carlos Garcia-Perez (305) 437–7012, fax 437–7016.
Voice of America.—David B. Ensor (202) 203–4500, fax 203–4513.
President, Radio Free Asia.—Libby Liu (202) 530–4900, fax 530–7795.
President, Radio Free Europe.—Steven W. Korn, (202) 457–6900, fax 457–6933.
President, Middle East Broadcasting Networks.—Brian Conniff (703) 852–9000, fax 991–1250.

GOVERNORS

Victor Ashe
Michael Lynton
Susan McCue
Michael Meehan
Dennis Mulhaupt
Dana Perino
S. Enders Wimbush
Hillary Rodham Clinton (ex officio)

STAFF

Executive Director.—Jeffrey Trimble.
Director of Strategic Planning.—Bruce Sherman.
Chief Financial Officer.—Maryjean Buhler.
Congressional Coordinator.—Susan Andross.
Executive Assistant.—Armanda Matthews.
Deputy General Counsel.—Paul Kollmer-Dorsey.
Special Projects Officer.—Oanh Tran.

CENTRAL INTELLIGENCE AGENCY

phone (703) 482–1100

Director.—David H. Petraeus.
Deputy Director.—Michael J. Morell.
Associate Deputy Director.—V. Sue Bromley.
General Counsel.—Stephen W. Preston.
Director of:
Intelligence.—Fran Moore.
Public Affairs.—Cynthia L. "Didi" Rapp.
Science and Technology.—Glenn Gaffney.
Support.—John E. Pereira.
Congressional Affairs.—George "Chip" Walter.

COMMISSION OF FINE ARTS

National Building Museum, 401 F Street, NW., Suite 312, 20001–2728

phone (202) 504–2200, fax 504–2195, http://www.cfa.gov

Commissioners:
Earl A. Powell III, Washington, DC, Chair.
Pamela Nelson, Dallas, TX, Vice-Chair.
Diana Balmori, New York, NY.
Edwin Schlossberg, New York, NY.
N. Michael McKinnell, Boston, MA.
Witold Rybczynski, Philadelphia, PA.
Elizabeth Plater-Zyberk, Miami, FL.

Secretary.—Thomas Luebke, FAIA.
Assistant Secretary.—Frederick J. Lindstrom.

BOARD OF ARCHITECTURAL CONSULTANTS FOR THE OLD GEORGETOWN ACT

Stephen Vanze, AIA, Chair.
David Cox, FAIA.
Anne Lewis, FAIA.

COMMITTEE FOR PURCHASE FROM PEOPLE WHO ARE BLIND OR SEVERELY DISABLED

1421 Jefferson Davis Highway, Jefferson Plaza 2, Suite 10800

Arlington, VA 22202–3259, phone (703) 603–7740, fax 603–0655

Chairperson.—J. Anthony ''Tony'' Poleo.
Vice Chairperson.—James M. Kesteloot.
Executive Director.—Tina Ballard.
Members:
Perry Edward ''Ed'' Anthony, Department of Education.
Paul Laird, Department of Justice.
Pamela C. Schwenke, Department of the Air Force.
J. Anthony ''Tony'' Poleo, Department of Defense.
Kathleen Martinez, Department of Labor.
James M. Kesteloot, Private Citizen (Obstacles to Employment of People Who Are Blind).
James H. Omvig, Private Citizen (Nonprofit Agency Employees Who Are Blind).
Andrew D. Houghton, Private Citizen (Nonprofit Agency Employees with Other Severe Disabilities).
Robert T. Kelly, Jr., Private Citizen (Obstacles to Employment of People with Other Severe Disabilities).
Vacant, Department of Commerce.
Vacant, Department of the Army.
Vacant, Department of the Navy.
Vacant, Department of Agriculture.
Vacant, General Services Administration.
Vacant, Department of Veterans Affairs.

COMMODITY FUTURES TRADING COMMISSION

Three Lafayette Centre, 1155 21st Street, NW., 20581, phone (202) 418–5000

fax 418–5521, http://www.cftc.gov

Chairman.—Gary Gensler, 418–5150.
Senior Counsel to the Chairman.—Eric Juzenas, 418–5050.
Commissioners:
Michael V. Dunn, 418–5070.
Jill Sommers, 418–5030.
Bart Chilton, 418–5060.
Scott O'Malia, 418–5870.
Executive Director.—Tony Thompson, 418–5160.
General Counsel.—Dan Berkovitz, 418–5120.
Chief Economist.—Andrei Kirilenko, 418–5000.
Director, Division of:
Clearing and Intermediary Oversight.—Ananda Radhakrishnan, 418–5430.
Enforcement.—David Meister, 418–5000.
Market Oversight.—Rick Shilts, 418–5260.
Director, Office of:
Equal Employment Opportunity.—Pam Gibbs, 418–5400.
Inspector General.—A. Roy Lavik, 418–5110.
International Affairs.—Jacqueline H. Mesa, 418–5645.
Legislative Affairs.—John Riley, 418–5075.
Secretary.—David Stawick, 418–5100.

REGIONAL OFFICES

Chicago: 525 West Monroe Street, Suite 1100, Chicago, IL 60601 (312) 596–0700, fax 596–0716.
Kansas City: Two Emanuel Cleaver II Boulevard, Suite 300, Kansas City, MO 64112, (816) 960–7700, fax 960–7750.
New York: 140 Broadway, Nineteenth floor, New York, NY 10005 (646) 746–9700, fax 746–9938.

CONSUMER PRODUCT SAFETY COMMISSION

4330 East West Highway, Bethesda, MD 20814, phone (301) 504–7923

fax 504–0124, http://www.cpsc.gov

[Created by Public Law 92–573]

Chairperson.—Inez Tenenbaum, 504–7900.
Commissioners:
Robert ''Bob'' Adler, 504–7731.
Thomas H. Moore, 504–7902.
Nancy Nord, 504–7901.
Ann Northup, 504–7780.
Executive Director.—Kenneth R. Hinson, 504–7625.
Deputy Executive Director.—Jacqueline Elder, 504–7625.
Director, Office of:
The Secretary.—Todd A. Stevenson, 504–7923.
Congressional Relations.—Christopher Day, 504–7853.
General Counsel.—Cheryl A. Falvey, 504–7642.

CORPORATION FOR NATIONAL AND COMMUNITY SERVICE

1201 New York Avenue, NW., 20525, phone (202) 606–5000
http://www.cns.gov

[Executive Order 11603, June 30, 1971; codified in 42 U.S.C., section 4951]

Chief Executive Officer.—Robert Velasco II (acting).
Chief of Staff.—James Siegal.
Chief Financial Officer.—Bill Anderson, 606–6980.
Inspector General.—Kenneth Bach (acting).
Director of:
AmeriCorps/National Civilian Community Corps.—Kate Raftery, 606–6706.
AmeriCorps/State and National.—John Gomperts, 606–6790.
AmeriCorps/VISTA.—Mary Strasser, 606–6943.
Learn and Serve America.—Nicole Gallant, 606–6927.
National Senior Service Corps.—Erwin Tan, 606–3237.
Office of Government Relations.—Rhoda Glickman, 606–6731.
General Counsel.—Valerie Green, 606–6677.

DEFENSE NUCLEAR FACILITIES SAFETY BOARD

625 Indiana Avenue, NW., Suite 700, 20004, phone (202) 694–7000

fax 208–6518, http://www.dnfsb.gov

Chairman.—Peter S. Winokur.
Vice Chairman.—Jessie Hill-Roberson.
Members: Joseph F. Bader, John E. Mansfield.
General Counsel.—Richard A. Azzaro.
General Manager.—Brian Grosner.
Technical Director.—Timothy J. Dwyer.

DELAWARE RIVER BASIN COMMISSION

25 State Police Drive, P.O. Box 7360, West Trenton, NJ 08628–0360

phone (609) 883–9500, fax 883–9522, http://www.drbc.net

[Created by Public Law 87–328]

FEDERAL REPRESENTATIVES

Federal Commissioner.—COL Peter A. DeLuca, Commander, U.S. Army Corps of Engineers, North Atlantic Division (718) 765–7000.
First Alternate.—LTC Philip M. Secrist, District Engineer, U.S. Army Corps of Engineers, Philadelphia (215) 656–6502.
Second Alternate.—David J. Leach (acting) Director of Programs, U.S. Army Corps of Engineers, North Atlantic Division (718) 765–7129.

STAFF

Executive Director.—Carol R. Collier, ext. 200.
Deputy Executive Director.—Robert Tudor, ext. 208.
Commission Secretary/Assistant General Counsel.—Pamela M. Bush, Esq., ext. 203.
Communications Manager.—Clarke Rupert, ext. 260.

DELAWARE REPRESENTATIVES

State Commissioner.—Jack A. Markell, Governor (302) 577–3210.
First Alternate.—Collin P. O'Mara, Secretary, Delaware Department of Natural Resources and Environmental Control (DNREC), (302) 739–9000.
Second Alternate.—Kathleen M. Stiller, Director, Division of Water Resources (DNREC), (302) 739–9949.

NEW JERSEY REPRESENTATIVES

State Commissioner.—Chris Christie, Governor (609) 292–6000.
First Alternate.—Bob Martin, Commissioner, New Jersey Department of Environmental Protection (NJDEP), (609) 292–2885.
Second Alternate.—John Plonski, Assistant Commissioner, Water Resource Management, (NJDEP), (609) 292–4543.
Third Alternate.—Michele Putman, Director, Division of Water Quality (NJDEP), (609) 292–9977.
Fourth Alternate.—Fred Sickels, Assistant Director of Water Supply Permitting Element (NJDEP), (609) 292–2957.
Pending Fifth Alternate.—Dr. Karl W. Muessig, State Geologist, New Jersey Geological Survey, (609) 292–1185.

NEW YORK REPRESENTATIVES

State Commissioner.—Andrew M. Cuomo, Governor (518) 474–8390.
First Alternate.—Joe Martens, Commissioner, New York State Department of Environmental Conservation (NYSDEC), (518) 402–8545.
Second Alternate.—Mark Klotz, P.E., Director, Division of Water (NYSDEC), (518) 402–8233.
Third Alternate.—Tom Cullen, Assistant Director, Division of Water (NYSDEC), (518) 402–8233.
Fourth Alternate.—Angus Eaton (NYSDEC), (518) 402–8132.

PENNSYLVANIA REPRESENTATIVES

State Commissioner.—Thomas W. Corbett, Governor (717) 787–2500.
First Alternate.—Michael L. Krancer, Secretary, Pennsylvania Department of Environmental Protection (PADEP), (717) 787–2814.
Second Alternate.—John T. Hines (acting) Executive Deputy Secretary for Programs, (PADEP), (717) 787–2814.
Third Alternate.—Kelly Jean Heffner (acting) Deputy Secretary for Water Management (PADEP), (717) 783–4693.
Fourth Alternate.—Charles W. Kirkwood (570) 421–6513.

ENVIRONMENTAL PROTECTION AGENCY

1200 Pennsylvania Avenue, NW., 20460, phone (202) 564–4700, http://www.epa.gov

Administrator.—Lisa P. Jackson.
Deputy Administrator.—Bob Perciasepa, 564–4711.
Chief of Staff.—Diane Thompson, 564–6999.
Deputy Chief of Staff.—John Reeder, 564–4715.
Agriculture Counsel.—Larry Elworth, 564–7719.
White House Liaison.—Dan Kanninen, 564–7960.
Environmental Appeals Board: Charles Sheehan, Edward Reich, Kathie Stein, Anna Wolgast, 233–0122.
Associate Administrator for—
Congressional and Intergovernmental Relations.—Arvin Ganesan, 564–5200.
Homeland Security.—Debbie Dietrich, 564–6978.
Policy, Economics, and Innovation.—Michael Goo, 564–4332.

Public Affairs.—Brendan Gilfillan, 564–8368.
Director, Office of:
Children's Health Protection.—Peter Grevatt, 564–2188.
Civil Rights.—Rafael DeLeon, 564–7272.
Cooperative Environmental Management.—Vacant, 233–0090.
Executive Secretariat.—Eric Wachter, 564–7311.
Executive Services.—Diane Bazzle, 564–0444.
Science Advisory Board.—Vanessa Vu, 343–9999.
Small and Disadvantaged Business Utilization.—Jeanette L. Brown, 564–4100.
Director of Management, Office of Administrative Law Judges.—Susan Biro, 564–6255.

ADMINISTRATION AND RESOURCES MANAGEMENT

Assistant Administrator.—Craig Hooks, 564–4600.
Deputy Assistant Administrator.—Nancy Gelb (acting), 564–4600.

AIR AND RADIATION

Assistant Administrator.—Gina McCarthy, 564–7404.
Principle Deputy Assistant Administrator.—Janet McCabe, 564–7400.

ENFORCEMENT AND COMPLIANCE ASSURANCE

Assistant Administrator.—Cynthia Giles, 564–2440.
Principal Deputy Assistant Administrator.—Catherine McCabe.

OFFICE OF ENVIRONMENTAL INFORMATION

Assistant Administrator.—Malcom Jackson, 564–6665.
Deputy Assistant Administrator.—Renee Wynn.

CHIEF FINANCIAL OFFICER

Chief Financial Officer.—Barbara Bennett, 564–1151.
Deputy Chief Financial Officer.—Maryann Froehlich.

GENERAL COUNSEL

General Counsel.—Scott Fulton, 564–8040.
Principal Deputy General Counsel.—Brenda Mallory, 564–8064.
Deputy General Counsels: Avi Garbow, Tseming Yang, 564–8040.

INSPECTOR GENERAL

Inspector General.—Arthur Elkins, Jr., 566–0847.
Deputy Inspector General.—Mark Bialek.

INTERNATIONAL AFFAIRS

Assistant Administrator.—Michelle DePass, 564–6600.
Deputy Assistant Administrators: Michael Stahl, Shalini Vajjhala.

CHEMICAL SAFETY AND POLLUTION PREVENTION

Assistant Administrator.—Steve Owens, 564–2902.
Principal Deputy Assistant Administrator.—William Diamond.

RESEARCH AND DEVELOPMENT

Assistant Administrator.—Paul Anastas, 564–6620.
Deputy Assistant Administrator of:
Management.—Lek Kadelis.
Science.—Kevin Teichman.

SOLID WASTE AND EMERGENCY RESPONSE

Assistant Administrator.—Mathy Stanislaus, 566–0200.
Principal Deputy Assistant Administrator.—Barry Breen.

WATER

Assistant Administrator.—Nancy Stoner (acting), 564–5700.
Director of Emergency Management.—Jim Wheeler.

REGIONAL ADMINISTRATION

Region I, Boston.—Connecticut, Maine, New Hampshire, Rhode Island, Vermont.
Regional Administrator.—Curt Spalding, One Congress Street, Suite 1100, Boston, MA 02114 (617) 918–1010.
Public Affairs.—Nancy Grantham.
Region II, New York City.—New Jersey, New York, Puerto Rico, Virgin Islands.
Regional Administrator.—Judith Enck, 290 Broadway, New York, NY 10007 (212) 637–5000.
Public Affairs.—Bonnie Bellow (212) 637–3660.
Region III, Philadelphia.—Delaware, Washington, DC, Maryland, Pennsylvania, Virginia, West Virginia.
Regional Administrator.—Shawn Garvin, 1650 Arch Street, Philadelphia, PA 19103–2029 (215) 814–2900.
Public Affairs.—Michael Kulik (acting), (215) 814–5100.
Region IV, Atlanta.—Alabama, Florida, Georgia, Kentucky, Mississippi, North Carolina, South Carolina, Tennessee.
Regional Administrator.—Gwendolyn Keyes-Fleming, 61 Forsyth Street, SW., Atlanta, GA 30303–8960 (404) 562–8357.
Public Affairs.—Allison Wise (404) 562–8327.
Region V, Chicago.—Illinois, Indiana, Michigan, Minnesota, Ohio, Wisconsin.
Regional Administrator.—Susan Hedman, 77 West Jackson Boulevard, Chicago, IL 60604–3507 (312) 886–3000.
Public Affairs.—Anne Rowan.
Region VI, Dallas.—Arkansas, Louisiana, New Mexico, Oklahoma, Texas.
Regional Administrator.—Alfredo Armendariz, Fountain Place, 1445 Ross Avenue, 12th Floor, Suite 1200, Dallas, TX 75202–2733 (214) 665–2100.
Public Affairs.—David W. Gray.
Region VII, Kansas City.—Iowa, Kansas, Missouri, Nebraska.
Regional Administrator.—Karl Brooks, 901 North 5th Street, Kansas City, MO 66101 (913) 551–7006.
Public Affairs.—Rich Hood (913) 551–7305.
Region VIII, Denver.—Colorado, Montana, North Dakota, South Dakota, Utah, Wyoming.
Regional Administrator.—James Martin, 999 18th Street, Suite 300, Denver, CO 80202–2466 (303) 312–6308.
Public Affairs.—Larry Grandison (303) 312–6599.
Region IX, San Francisco.—Arizona, California, Hawaii, Nevada, American Samoa, Guam.
Regional Administrator.—Jared Blumenfeld, 75 Hawthorne Street, San Francisco, CA 94105 (415) 947–8702.
Public Affairs.—Kathleen Johnson.
Region X, Seattle.—Alaska, Idaho, Oregon, Washington.
Regional Administrator.—Dennis McLerran, 1200 Sixth Avenue, Seattle, WA 98101 (206) 553–1234.
Public Affairs.—Marianne Holsman (206) 553–1234.

EQUAL EMPLOYMENT OPPORTUNITY COMMISSION

131 M Street, NE., 20507, phone (202) 663–4900

Chairman.—Jacqueline A. Berrien, suite 6NW08F, 663–4001, fax 663–4110.
Chief Operating Officer.—Claudia Withers, suite 6NW08F.
Deputy Chief Operating Officer.—Vacant.
Confidential Assistant.—Michelle Waldron Patterson, suite 6NW08F, 663–4002.
Commissioners: Constance Barker, suite 6NE25F, 663–4027, fax 663–7121; Chai R. Feldblum, suite 6NE07F, 663–4090, fax 663–7101; Stuart J. Ishimaru, suite 6NE37F, 663–4052, fax 663–4108; Victoria Lipnic, suite 6NE19F, 663–4099, fax 663–7086.

General Counsel.—P. David Lopez, 5th floor, 663–7034, fax 663–4196.
Legal Counsel.—Peggy Mastroianni, 5th floor, 663–4327, fax 663–4639.
Director, Office of:
Chief Financial Officer.—Jeffrey Smith, 4th floor, 663–4200, fax 663–7068.
Communications and Legislative Affairs.—Todd A. Cox, 6th floor, 663–4191, fax 663–4912.
Equal Opportunity.—Matthew Murphy (acting), 6th floor, 663–7081, fax 663–7003.
Executive Secretariat/Executive Secretary.—Stephen Llewellyn, 6th floor, 663–4070, fax 663–4114.
Field Operations.—Carlton Hadden, 5th floor, 663–4599, fax 633–7022.
Field Programs.—Nicholas Inzeo, 5th floor, 663–4801, fax 663–7190.
Human Resources.—Lisa Williams, 4th floor, 663–4306, fax 663–4324.
Information Technology.—Kimberly Hancher, 4th floor, 663–4447, fax 663–4451.
Inspector General.—Milton Mayo, 6th floor, 663–4327, fax 663–7204.
Research, Information and Planning.—Deidre Flippen, 4th floor, 663–4853, fax 663–4093.

EXPORT-IMPORT BANK OF THE UNITED STATES

811 Vermont Avenue, NW., 20571, phone (800) 565–EXIM, fax 565–3380

President and Chairman.—Fred Hochberg, room 1215, 565–3500.
First Vice President and Vice Chair.—Wanda Felton, room 1229, 565–3546.
Director.—Sean Mulvaney, room 1241, 565–3530.
General Counsel.—Angela Freye, room 947, 565–3430.
Chief Financial Officer.—John Simonson, room 1054, 565–3952.
Chief Information Officer.—Fernanda Young, room 1045, 565–3798.
Senior Vice President of:
Communications.—Maura Policelli, room 1267, 565–3200.
Congressional Affairs.—Scott Schloegel, room 1261, 565–3230.
Credit Risk Management.—Kenneth Tinsley, room 919, 565–3222.
Export Finance.—John McAdams, room 1115, 565–3222.
Policy and Planning.—James C. Cruse, room 1243, 565–3761.
Resource Management.—Michael Cushing, room 1017, 565–3561.
Small Business.—Charles Tansey, room 1115, 565–3701.
Vice President of:
Business Credit.—Pamela Bowers, room 1129, 565–3792.
Communications.—Phil Cogan, room 1264, 565–3203.
Congressional Affairs.—William Hellert, room 1261–A, 565–3233.
Controller.—Joseph Sorbera, room 1053, 565–3241.
Country Risk and Economic Analysis.—William Marsteller, room 701, 565–3739.
Credit Review and Compliance.—Walter Hill, Jr., room 915, 565–3672.
Credit Underwriting.—David Carter, room 919, 565–3667.
Domestic Business Development.—Wayne L. Gardella, room 1137, 565–3787.
Engineering and Environment.—James Mahoney, room 1169, 565–3573.
Office of Industry Sector Development.—C. Michael Forgione, room 1107, 565–3224.
Operation and Data Quality.—Michele Kuester, room 719, 565–3221.
Policy Analysis.—Helene Walsh, room 1238, 565–3768.
Project and Corporate Portfolio Management.—Richard Park, room 1068, 565–3631.
Short-Term Trade Finance.—Walter Kosciow, room 1176, 565–3649.
Structured Finance.—John Schuster, room 1005, 565–3691.
Strategic Initiatives.—Raymond Ellis, room 1123, 565–3674.
Trade Finance and Insurance.—Jeffrey Abramson, room 931, 565–3633.
Transportation.—Robert A. Morin, room 1035, 565–3453.
Transportation Portfolio Management.—Michele Dixey, room 1059, 565–3554.
Treasurer.—David Sena, room 1051, 565–3272.
Directors of:
Contracting Services.—Mark Pitra, room 1023, 565–3388.
Human Resources.—Natasha McCarthy, room 771, 565–3592.
Inspector General.—Osvaldo Gratacos, room 975, 565–3923.
Security.—William Barboza, room 1021, 565–3313.

FARM CREDIT ADMINISTRATION

1501 Farm Credit Drive, McLean, VA 22102–5090

phone (703) 883–4000, fax 734–5784

[Reorganization pursuant to Public Law 99–205, December 23, 1985]

Chairman and Chief Executive Officer.—Leland A. Strom.
Board Members:
Kenneth A. Spearman.
Jill Long Thompson.
Secretary to the Board.—Dale L. Aultman, 883–4009, fax 790–5241.
Chief Operating Officer.—William J. Hoffman, 883–4340, fax 790–5241.
Director, Office of:
Congressional and Public Affairs.—Michael A. Stokke, 883–4056, fax 790–3260.
Examination.—S. Robert Coleman, 883–4160, fax 893–2978.
General Counsel.—Charles R. Rawls, 883–4020, fax 790–0052.
Inspector General.—Carl A. Clinefelter, 883–4030, fax 883–4059.
Management Services.—Stephen G. Smith, 883–4200, fax 883–4151.
Regulatory Policy.—Gary K. Van Meter, 883–4414, fax 883–4477.
Secondary Market Oversight.—Laurie Rea, 883–4280, fax 883–4478.
Chief Human Capital Officer.—Philip Shebest, 883–4200, fax 893–2608.
Chief Information Officer.—Doug Valcour, 883–4200, fax 883–4151.
Director, Equal Employment Opportunity.—Jeff McGiboney, 883–4353, fax 883–4151.

FEDERAL COMMUNICATIONS COMMISSION

445 12th Street, SW., 20554, phone (202) 418–0200, http://www.fcc.gov

FCC National Consumer Center: 1–888–225–5322 / 1–888–835–5322 (TTY)

Chairman.—Julius Genachowski, room 8–B201, 418–1000.
Confidential Assistant.—Maria Gaglio.
Chief of Staff.—Edward Lazarus.
Chief Counsel and Senior Legal Advisor.—Zachary Katz.
Senior Counselor.—Josh Gottheimer.
Senior Counsel and Legal Advisor.—Sherrese Smith.
Special Counsel and Legal Advisor.—Amy Levine.
Special Assistant.—Daniel Ornstein.
Commissioner.—Michael J. Copps, room 8–B115, 418–2000
Confidential Assistant.—Carolyn Conyers.
Chief of Staff.—Mark Stone.
Legal Advisors: Joshua Cinelli, Margaret McCarthy.
Commissioner.—Robert McDowell, room 8–C302, 418–2200.
Confidential Advisor.—Brigid Calamis.
Chief of Staff/Senior Legal Advisor.—Angela Giancarlo.
Legal Advisor.—Rosemary Harold.
Media Advisor.—Erin A. McGrath.
Wireline Advisor.—Christine Kurth.
Commissioner.—Mignon Clyburn, room 8–A302, 418–2100.
Chief of Staff / Media Legal Advisor.—Dave Grimaldi.
Deputy Chief of Staff.—Drema Johnson.
Legal Advisor (Wireline).—Angela Kronenberg.
Legal Advisor (Wireless).—Louis Peraertz.

OFFICE OF ADMINISTRATIVE LAW JUDGES

Administrative Law Judge.—Richard L. Sipple, room 1–C768, 418–2280.

OFFICE OF COMMUNICATIONS BUSINESS OPPORTUNITIES

Director.—Thomas Reed, room 4–A760.

CONSUMER AND GOVERNMENTAL AFFAIRS BUREAU

Chief.—Joel Gurin, room 5–C758, 418–1400.

Chief of Staff.—Rachel Kazan, room 5–C739, 418–0651.
Associate Bureau Chief of:
Administrative and Management.—Tamika Jackson, room 5–A847, 418–0159.
Consumer Information.—Bill Cline, room 5–A729, 418–0267.
Education and Outreach.—Roger Goldblatt, room 5–A848, 418–1035.
Division Chief of:
Consumer Affairs and Outreach.—Susan McLean, room 3–A644, 418–7868.
Consumer Inquiries and Complaints.—Sharon Bowers (Gettysburg), (717) 338–2533.
Consumer Policy.—Colleen Heitkam, room 5–A844, 418–0974.
Web and Print Publishing.—Howard Parnell, room 1–B115, 418–7280.
Office Chief of:
Disability Rights.—Gregory Hlibok, room 3–C341, 559–5158.
Intergovernmental Affairs.—Gregory Vadas, room 5–A660, 418–1798.
Office of Native Affairs and Policy.—Gregory Blackwell, room 4–C763, 418–3629.
Reference Information Center.—Charles Alston (acting), room CY–B516, 418–0283.

ENFORCEMENT BUREAU

Chief.—P. Michelle Ellison, room 3–C252, 418–7450.
Deputy Bureau Chiefs: William Davenport (acting), room 3C255, 418–7450; Suzanne Tetreault, room 3–C250, 418–7450.
Chief, Division of:
Investigations and Hearings.—Theresa Cavanaugh (acting), room 4–C322, 418–1573.
Market Disputes Resolutions.—Alexander Starr, room 4–C342, 418–7284.
Spectrum Enforcement.—John Poutasse (acting), room 3–C366, 418–2172.
Telecommunications.—Richard Hindman, room 4–C224, 418–3613.
Director of:
North East Region: Chicago, IL.—Michael Moffitt.
South Central Region: Kansas City, MO.—Denny Carlton.
Western Region: San Diego, CA.—Rebecca Dorch.

OFFICE OF ENGINEERING AND TECHNOLOGY

Chief.—Julius P. Knapp, room 7–C155, 418–2470.

OFFICE OF GENERAL COUNSEL

General Counsel.—Austin Schlick, room 8–C750, 418–1700.
Deputy General Counsels: Peter Karanjia, room 8–C758, 418–1700, Julie Veach, room 8–C758, 418–1700.
Associate General Counsel and Chief Diversity Officer.—Mark Lloyd, room 8–C860, 418–7390.
Associate General Counsel.—Jennifer Tatel, room 8–C833, 418–1700.

OFFICE OF INSPECTOR GENERAL

Inspector General.—David L. Hunt, room 2–C327, 418–0470.

INTERNATIONAL BUREAU

Chief.—Mindel De La Torre, room 6–C750, 418–0437.
Deputy Chiefs: Roderick Porter, room 6–C752, 418–0423; Troy Tanner, room 6–C475, 418–1475.
Chief, Division of:
Policy.—James Ball, room 7–A760, 418–0427.
Satellite.—Robert Nelson, room 6–A665, 418–0719.
Strategic Analysis and Negotiations.—Narda Jones, room 6–A763, 418–2489.

OFFICE OF LEGISLATIVE AFFAIRS

Director.—Greg Guice, room 8–C464, 418–0095.
Deputy Director.—Christopher Lewis, room 8–C457, 418–7285.

OFFICE OF MANAGING DIRECTOR

Managing Director.—Vacant.

Deputy Managing Directors: Mindy Ginsburg, room 1–C154, 418–0983; Joseph Hall, room 1–C150, 216–4024; Dana Shaffer, room 1–C155, 418–0832.

Secretary.—Marlene Dortch, room TW–B204, 418–0300.

Chief Human Capital Office.—Bonita Tinley, room 1–A100, 418–0293, TTY 481–0150 (employment verification).

Associate Managing Directors:

Administrative Operations.—Wanda Sims, room 1–C402, 418–2990.

Financial Operations.—Mark Stephens, 418–0817.

Information Technology.—Robert Naylor, room 1–C264, 218–2020.

Performance Evaluations and Records Management.—Walter Boswell, room 1–A105, 418–2178.

Assistant Chief for Management.—Eileen Devan, room CY–B523, 418–1927.

MEDIA BUREAU

Chief.—Williams Lake, room 3–C740, 418–7200.

Deputy Bureau Chiefs: Michelle Carey, room 3–C830, 418–7200; Kris Monteith, room 3–C486, 418–7200; Robert Ratcliffe, room 3–C742, 418–7200; Sarah Whitesell, room 3–C458, 418–7200.

Chief of Staff.—Thomas Horan, room 3–C478, 418–7200.

Chief, Division of:

Audio Division.—Peter Doyle, room 2–A360, 418–2700.

Engineering Division.—John Wong, room 4–A838, 418–7012.

Industry Analysis Division.—Hillary DeNigro, room 2–C360, 418–2330.

Policy Division.—Mary Beth Murphy, room 4–A766, 418–2120.

Video Division.—Barbara A. Kreisman, room 2–A666, 418–1600.

OFFICE OF MEDIA RELATIONS

Director.—Tammy Sun, room CY–C314B, 418–0505.

Deputy Director.—David Fiske, room CY–C314C, 418–0513.

OFFICE OF STRATEGIC PLANNING AND POLICY ANALYSIS

Chief.—Paul de Sa, room 7C357, 418–2030.

Deputy Chief.—Elizabeth Andrion, room 7C450, 418–2030.

Chief Economist.—Marius Schwartz, room 7–C452, 418–2039.

Chief Technologist.—Douglas Sicker, room 7–C252, 418–1544.

WIRELESS TELECOMMUNICATIONS BUREAU

Chief.—Rick Kaplan, room 6411, 418–0600.

Deputy Bureau Chiefs: John Liebovitz, room 6417, 418–0600; Jim Schlichting, room 6413, 418–0600.

Assistant Bureau Chief for Management.—Carlette Smith, room 6442, 418–2466.

Chiefs, Division of:

Action and Spectrum Access.—Margaret Wiener, room 6419, 418–0660.

Broadband.—Blaise Scinto, room 3–C124, 418–BITS.

Mobility.—Roger Noel, room 6411, 418–0620.

Spectrum and Competition Policy.—Nese Guendelsberger, room 6405, 418–0634.

Technology, Systems and Innovation.—Mary Bucher (Gettysburg), (717) 338–2656.

WIRELINE COMPETITION BUREAU

Chief.—Sharon Gillett, room 5–C354, 418–1500.

Chief Economist.—Eric Ralph, room 5–C450, 418–1500.

OFFICE WORKPLACE DIVERSITY

Director.—Thomas Wyatt, room 5–C750. 418–1799.

REGIONAL AND FIELD OFFICES

NORTHEAST REGION

Regional Director of:

Chicago: G. Michael Moffitt, Park Ridge Office Center, Room 306, 1550 Northwest Highway, Park Ridge, IL 60068 (847) 813–4671.

FIELD OFFICES—NORTHEAST REGION

Director of:

Boston: Dennis V. Loria, One Batterymarch Park, Quincy, MA 02169 (617) 786–1154.

Columbia: James T. Higgins, 9200 Farm House Lane, Columbia, MD 21046 (301) 725–0019.

Detroit: James A. Bridgewater, 24897 Hathaway Street, Farmington Hills, MI 48335 (248) 471–5661.

New York: Dan Noel, 201 Varick Street, Room 1151, New York, NY 10014 (212) 337–1865.

Philadelphia: Gene J. Stanbro, One Oxford Valley Office Building, Room 404, 2300 East Lincoln Highway, Langhorne, PA 19047 (215) 741–3022.

SOUTH CENTRAL REGION

Regional Director of:

Kansas City: Ronald Ramage, 520 NE Colbern Road, Second Floor, Lee's Summit, MO 64086 (816) 316–1243.

FIELD OFFICES—SOUTH CENTRAL REGION

Director of:

Atlanta: Doug Miller, Koger Center, 3575 Koger Boulevard, Suite 320, Duluth, GA 30096 (770) 935–3372.

Dallas: James D. Wells, 9330 LBJ Freeway, Room 1170, Dallas, TX 75243 (214) 575–6361.

Kansas City: Robert C. McKinney, 520 Northeast Colbern Road, Second Floor, Lee's Summit, MO 64086 (816) 316–1248.

New Orleans: Walter Gernon, 2424 Edenborn Avenue, Room 460, Metarie, LA 70001 (504) 219–8989.

Tampa: Ralph M. Barlow, 4010 W. Boy Scout Boulevard, Suite 425, Tampa, FL 33607 (813) 348–1741.

WESTERN REGION

Regional Director of:

Denver: Rebecca Dorch, 215 South Wadsworth Boulevard, Suite 303, Lakewood, CO 80226 (303) 407–8708.

FIELD OFFICES—WESTERN REGION

Director of:

Denver: Nikki Shears, 215 South Wadsworth Boulevard, Suite 303, Lakewood, CO 80226 (303) 231–5212.

Los Angeles: Nader Haghighat, Cerritos Corporate Towers, 18000 Studebaker Road, Room 660, Cerritos, CA 90701 (562) 865–0235.

San Diego: James Lyons, Interstate Office Park, 4542 Ruffner Street, Room 370, San Diego, CA 92111 (858) 496–5125.

San Francisco: Thomas N. Van Stavern, 5653 Stoneridge Drive, Suite 105, Pleasanton, CA 94588 (925) 416–9777.

Seattle: Kris McGowan, 11410 Northeast 122nd Way, Room 312, Kirkland, WA 98034 (425) 820–6271.

FEDERAL DEPOSIT INSURANCE CORPORATION

550 17th Street, NW., 20429

phone (877) 275–3342, http://www.fdic.gov

Chairman.—Martin J. Gruenberg (acting), 898–3888.
Chief of Staff to the Acting Chairman.—Barbara Ryan, 898–3841.
Deputy to the Chairman for External Affairs.—Paul Nash, 898–6962.
Deputy to the Chairman and Chief Financial Officer.—Steve App, 898–8732.
Vice Chairman.—Martin J. Gruenberg, 898–3888.
Deputy to the Vice Chairman.—Barbara Ryan, 898–3841.
Director.—Thomas J. Curry, 898–3957.
Special Assistant to the Director.—Kenyon Kilber, 898–8935.
Director (OCC).—John Walsh (acting), 874–4900.
Deputy.—William Rowe, 898–6960.
Deputy Director, Office of Legislative Affairs.—Alice Goodman, 898–8730, fax 898–3745.

FEDERAL ELECTION COMMISSION

999 E Street, NW., 20463

phone (202) 694–1000, Toll Free (800) 424–9530, fax 219–3880, http://www.fec.gov

Chair.—Cynthia L. Bauerly, 694–1020.
Vice Chair.—Caroline C. Hunter, 694–1045.
Commissioners:
Donald F. McGahn II, 694–1050.
Matthew S. Petersen, 694–1011.
Steven T. Walther, 694–1055.
Ellen L. Weintraub, 694–1035.
Staff Director.—D. Alec Palmer, 694–1007, fax 219–2338.
Deputy Staff Director for—
Compliance/Chief Compliance Officer.—Patricia Carmona, 694–1150.
Information Technology/Chief Information Officer.—D. Alec Palmer, 694–1250.
Assistant Staff Director for—
Information Division.—Greg Scott, 694–1100.
Disclosure.—Patricia Klein Young, 694–1120.
Director for Congressional Affairs.—J. Duane Pugh, 694–1006.
Press Officer.—Judith Ingram, 694–1220.
Director Human Resources.—Judy McLaughlin, 694–1080.
Administrative Officer.—India K. Robinson, 694–1240.
EEO Director.—Kevin Salley, 694–1229.
General Counsel.—P. Christopher Hughey (acting), 694–1650.
Deputy General Counsel.—P. Christopher Hughey.
Associate General Counsel for—
Enforcement.—Kathleen Guith (acting).
General Law and Advice.—Lawrence Calvert.
Litigation.—David Kolker.
Policy.—Rosemary C. Smith.
Library Director (Law).—Leta L. Holley.
Chief Financial Officer.—Mary Sprague, 694–1217.
Deputy Chief Financial Officer/Budget Director.—Gilbert Ford, 694–1216.
Director of Accounting.—Judy Berning, 694–1230.
Inspector General.—Lynne A. McFarland, 694–1015.
Deputy Inspector General.—Jonathon A. Hatfield.

FEDERAL HOUSING FINANCE AGENCY *

1700 G Street, NW., 4th Floor, 20552

phone (202) 414–3800, fax 414–3823, and

1625 Eye Street, NW., 4th Floor, 20006

phone (202) 408–2500, fax 408–1435, http://www.fhfa.gov

[Created by Housing and Economic Recovery Act of 2008, 122 Stat. 2654, Public Law 110–289—July 30, 2008]

Director.—Edward J. DeMarco (acting), 414–6923.

Deputy Director, Division of:
Federal Home Loan Bank Regulation.—Stephen Cross, 408–2500.
Enterprise Regulation.—Christopher Dickerson (acting), 414–6923.
Examination Programs and Support.—Wanda DeLeo, 343–1830.
Housing, Mission and Goals.—Edward J. DeMarco, 414–6923.
General Counsel.—Alfred Pollard, 414–6924.
Senior Deputy General Counsel.—Christopher T. Curtis, 414–6924.

OFFICE OF CONGRESSIONAL AFFAIRS AND COMMUNICATIONS

Senior Associate Director.—Meg Burn (acting), 414–6923.
Associate Director for Congressional Affairs.—Peter Brereton, 414–6922.
Congressional Affairs Staff: Jennifer Cowell, 414–3767; Patricia Driver, 343–1337; Jeannine Schroeder, 414–8881.
Associate Director for Agency Communications.—Mary Ellen Taylor, 414–6922.
Public Affairs Staff: Stefanie Johnson, 414–6376; Corinne Russell, 414–6921.
Executive Advisor for Consumer Communications.—Christine Eldarrat, 414–6922.
Senior Associate Director for Conservatorship.—Jeff Spohn, 414–6923.
Ombudsman.—Michael Powers, 408–2500.
Associate Director for the Office of Minority and Women Inclusion.—Lee Bowman, 408–2500.
Chief Operating Officer.—Stephen Cross (acting), 408–2500.
Deputy Chief Operating Officer.—Paula Hayes, 408–2500.
Chief Information Officer.—Kevin Winkler, 414–6923.
Associate Director for the Office of Quality Assurance.—Lou Scalza, 408–2500.
Inspector General.—Steve Linick (800) 793–7724.

FEDERAL LABOR RELATIONS AUTHORITY

1400 K Street, NW., 20424–0001, phone (202) 218–7770, fax 482–6635

FLRA Agency Head.—Carol Waller Pope, 218–7900.
Executive Director.—Sonna Stampone, 218–7941.
Counsel for Regulatory and External Affairs.—Sarah Whittle Spooner, 218–7791.
Solicitor.—Rosa Koppel, 218–7999.
Inspector General.—Dana Rooney-Fisher, 218–7744.
Collaboration and Alternative Dispute Resolution Program.—Michael Wolf, 218–7933.
Foreign Service Impasse Disputes Panel.—Chairman Mary Jacksteit, 218–7790.
Foreign Service Labor Relations Board.—Carol Waller Pope, 218–7900.

AUTHORITY

Chairman.—Carol Waller Pope, 218–7900.
Chief Counsel.—Susan D. McCluskey, 218–7900.
Member.—Thomas M. Beck, 218–7930.
Chief Counsel.—James Abbott, 218–7930.
Member.—Ernest DuBester, 218–7920.
Chief Counsel.—William Tobey, 218–7920.
Chief, Case Intake and Publication.—Gina Grippando, 218–7740.

GENERAL COUNSEL OF THE FLRA

General Counsel.—Julia A. Clark, 218–7910.
Deputy General Counsel.—Dennis Walsh, 218–7910
Assistant General Counsel for Appeals.—Richard Zorn, 218–7910.

OFFICE OF ADMINISTRATIVE LAW JUDGES

Chief Judge.—Charles Center, 218–7950.

---

*The Federal Housing Finance Agency (FHFA) was created on July 30, 2008, when President Bush signed into law the Housing and Economic Recovery Act of 2008. The Act created a world-class, empowered regulator with all of the authorities necessary to oversee vital components of our country's secondary mortgage markets—Fannie Mae, Freddie Mac, and the Federal Home Loan Banks. In addition, this law combined the staffs of the Office of Federal Housing Enterprise Oversight (OFHEO), the Federal Housing Finance Board (FHFB), and the GSE mission office at the Department of Housing and Urban Development (HUD).

FEDERAL SERVICE IMPASSES PANEL (FSIP)

FSIP Chairman.—Mary Jacksteit, 218–7790.
Executive Director.—H. Joseph Schimansky, 218–7790.

REGIONAL OFFICES

Regional Directors:
Atlanta.—Richard S. Jones (acting), Marquis Two Tower, Suite 701, 285 Peachtree Center Avenue, Atlanta, GA 30303 (404) 331–5300, fax (404) 331–5280.
Boston.—Philip T. Roberts (acting), 10 Causeway Street, Suite 472, Boston, MA 02222 (617) 565–5100, fax 565–6262.
Chicago.—Peter A. Sutton, 55 West Monroe, Suite 1150, Chicago, IL 60603 (312) 886–3465, fax 886–5977.
Dallas.—James E. Petrucci, 525 Griffin Street, Suite 926, LB 107, Dallas, TX 75202 (214) 767–6266, fax 767–0156.
Denver.—Matthew Jarvinen, 1244 Speer Boulevard, Suite 100, Denver, CO 80204 (303) 844–5224, fax 844–2774.
San Francisco.—Gerald M. Cole, 901 Market Street, Suite 220, San Francisco, CA 94103 (415) 356–5000, fax 356–5017.
Washington, DC.—Barbara Kraft, 1400 K Street, NW., Suite 200, Washington, DC 20005 (202) 357–6029, fax (202) 482–6724.

FEDERAL MARITIME COMMISSION

800 North Capitol Street, NW., 20573

phone (202) 523–5725, fax 523–0014

OFFICE OF THE CHAIRMAN

Chairman.—Richard A. Lidinsky, room 1000, 523–5911.
Counsel.—Lowry A. Crook.
Commissioner.—Joseph E. Brennan, room 1026, 523–5723.
Counsel.—Steven D. Najarian.
Commissioner.—Rebecca F. Dye, room 1038, 523–5715.
Counsel.—Edward L. Lee, Jr.
Commissioner.—Michael A. Khouri, room 1044, 523–5712.
Counsel.—John A. Moran.
Commissioner.—Mario Cordero, room 1032, 523–5721.
Counsel.—Vacant.

OFFICE OF THE SECRETARY

Secretary.—Karen V. Gregory, room 1046, 523–5725.
Assistant Secretary.—Rachel E. Dickon.
Librarian.—Charlotte C. White, room 1085, 523–5762.

OFFICE OF EQUAL EMPLOYMENT OPPORTUNITY

Director.—Keith I. Gilmore, room 1052, 523–5859.

OFFICE OF THE GENERAL COUNSEL

General Counsel.—Rebecca A. Fenneman, room 1018, 523–5740.
Deputy General Counsel.—Vacant.

OFFICE OF CONSUMER AFFAIRS AND DISPUTE RESOLUTION

Director.—Vern W. Hill, room 932, 523–5807.
Deputy Director.—Vacant.

OFFICE OF ADMINISTRATIVE LAW JUDGES

Chief Judge.—Clay G. Guthridge, room 1088, 523–5750.
Administrative Law Judge.—Erin M. Wirth, room 1088, 523–5750.

OFFICE OF THE INSPECTOR GENERAL

Inspector General.—Adam R. Trzeciak, room 1054, 523–5863.

OFFICE OF THE MANAGING DIRECTOR

Director.—Ronald D. Murphy, room 1082, 523–5800.
Deputy Director.—Florence A. Carr.
Area Representatives:
Houston.—Debra A. Zezima (281) 591–6088.
Los Angeles.—Oliver E. Clark (310) 514–4905.
New Orleans.—Bruce N. Johnson, Sr. (504) 589–6662.
New York: Emanuel J. Mingione (718) 553–2228; Joseph A. Castellano (718) 553–2223.
Seattle.—Michael A. Moneck (206) 553–0221.
South Florida.—Andrew Margolis (954) 963–5362; Eric O. Mintz (954) 963–5284.
Director, Office of:
Budget and Finance.—Karon E. Douglass, room 916, 523–5770.
Human Resources.—Hatsie H. Charbonneau, room 924, 523–5773.
Information Technology.—Anthony Haywood, room 904, 523–5835.
Management Services.—Michael H. Kilby, room 924, 523–5900.

BUREAU OF CERTIFICATION AND LICENSING

Director.—Sandra L. Kusumoto, room 970, 523–5787.
Deputy Director.—Tanga S. FitzGibbon.
Director, Office of:
Passenger Vessels and Information Processing.—James A. Nussbaumer, 523–5818.
Transportation Intermediaries.—Ronald Podlaskowich, 523–5843.

BUREAU OF ENFORCEMENT

Director.—Peter J. King, room 900, 523–5783 or 523–5860.
Deputy Director.—Vacant.

BUREAU OF TRADE ANALYSIS

Director.—Austin L. Schmitt, room 940, 523–5796.
Deputy Director.—Roy J. Pearson.
Director, Office of:
Agreements.—Jeremiah D. Hospital, 523–5793.
Economics and Competition Analysis.—Vacant, 523–5845.
Service Contracts and Tariffs.—F. Gary Kardian, room 940, 523–5856.

FEDERAL MEDIATION AND CONCILIATION SERVICE

2100 K Street, NW., 20427, phone (202) 606–8100, fax 606–4251

[Codified under 29 U.S.C. 172]

Director.—George Cohen.
Deputy Director.—Scot L. Beckenbaugh.
Chief of Staff.—Fran L. Leonard, 606–3661.
General Counsel.—Dawn Starr, 606–8090.
Director for—
ADR/International/FMCS Institute.—Allison Beck, 606–8100.
Arbitration Services.—Vella M. Traynham, 606–5111.
Budget and Finance.—Fran L. Leonard, 606–3661.

Grants.—Linda Gray-Broughton, 606–8181.
Human Resources.—Adam Ramsey, 606–5460.
Information Systems.—Doug Jones, 606–5483.
Administrative Services.—Berkina Porter, 606–5477.
Regional Director (Eastern/Western).—John F. Buettner (216) 520–4805.

FEDERAL MINE SAFETY AND HEALTH REVIEW COMMISSION

601 New Jersey Avenue, NW., Suite 9500, 20001

phone (202) 434–9900, fax 434–9944

[Created by Public Law 95–164]

Chairperson.—Mary Lu Jordan, room 9527, 434–9900.
Commissioners: Robert F. Cohen, Jr., room 9527; Michael F. Duffy, room 9515; Patrick K. Nakamura, room 9525; Michael G. Young, room 9517, 434–9900.
Executive Director.—Lisa M. Boyd, room 9509, 434–9905.
Chief Administrative Law Judge.—Robert J. Lesnick, room 8515, 434–9958.
General Counsel.—Michael McCord, room 9547, 434–9935.

FEDERAL RETIREMENT THRIFT INVESTMENT BOARD

1250 H Street, NW., 20005, phone (202) 942–1600, fax 942–1676

[Authorized by 5 U.S.C. 8472]

Executive Director.—Gregory T. Long, 942–1601.
General Counsel.—Thomas K. Emswiler, 942–1660.
Director, Office of:
Automated Systems.—Mark Hagerty, 942–1610.
External Affairs.—Thomas J. Trabucco, 942–1640.
Finance.—James B. Petrick, 942–1630.
Investments.—Theresa Ray, 942–1630.
Participant Services.—Pamela-Jeanne Moran, 942–1450.
Research and Strategic Planning.—Renee Wilder, 942–1630.

Chairman.—Andrew M. Saul, 942–1660.
Board Members:
Alejandro M. Sanchez.
Terrence A. Duffy.
Michael Kennedy.
Dana K. Bilyeu.

FEDERAL TRADE COMMISSION

600 Pennsylvania Avenue, NW., 20580

phone (202) 326–2222, http://www.ftc.gov

Chairman.—Jonathan Leibowitz, room 338, 326–3400.
Staff Assistant.—June Young, room 340, 326–2105.
Chief of Staff.—Joni Lupovitz, room 346, 326–3743.
Commissioners: Julie Brill, room 328, 326–2626; William E. Kovacic, room 538, 326–3661; Edith Ramirez, room 438, 326–2856; J. Thomas Rosch, room 528, 326–3651.
Director, Office of:
Competition.—Richard A. Feinstein, room 370, 326–3658.
Congressional Relations.—Jeanne Bumpus, room 408, 326–2946.
Consumer Protection.—David Vladeck, room 470, 326–2234.
Economics.—Joseph Farrell, room 270, 326–2888.
Policy Planning.—Susan S. DeSanti, room 392, 326–2210.
Public Affairs.—Cecelia Prewett, room 421, 326–3220.
Executive Director.—Eileen Harrington, room 426, 326–3127.
General Counsel.—Willard K. Tom, room 570, 326–3020.
Secretary.—Donald S. Clark, room 172, 326–2514.

Inspector General.—John Seeba, room 1119NJ, 326–2800.
Chief Administrative Law Judge.—D. Michael Chappell, room 106, 326–3637.

REGIONAL DIRECTORS

East Central Region: Jonathan M. Steiger, Eaton Center, Suite 200, 1111 Superior Avenue, Cleveland, OH 44114 (216) 263–3455.
Midwest Region: C. Steve Baker, 55 East Monroe Street, Suite 1825, Chicago, IL 60603 (312) 960–5634.
Northeast Region: Leonard Gordon, One Bowling Green, Suite 318, New York, NY 10004 (212) 607–2829.
Northwest Region: Robert J. Schroeder, 915 Second Avenue, Suite 2896, Seattle, WA 98174 (206) 220–6350.
Southeast Region: Cindy A. Liebes, 225 Peachtree Street, NE., Suite 1500, Atlanta, GA 30303 (404) 656–1390.
Southwest Region: Deanya T. Kueckelhan, 1999 Bryan Street, Suite 2150, Dallas, TX 75201 (214) 979–9350.
Western Region—Los Angeles: Jeffrey Klurfeld, 18077 Wilshire Boulevard, Suite 700, Los Angeles, CA 90024–3679 (310) 824–4343.
Western Region—San Francisco: Jeffrey Klurfeld, 901 Market Street, Suite 570, San Francisco, CA 94103 (415) 848–5100.

FOREIGN–TRADE ZONES BOARD

1401 Constitution Avenue, NW., Room 2111, 20230

phone (202) 482–2862, fax 482–0002

Chairman.—John E. Bryson, Secretary of Commerce.
Member.—Timothy F. Geithner, Secretary of the Treasury.
Executive Secretary.—Andrew McGilvray.

GENERAL SERVICES ADMINISTRATION

1275 F Street, NW., 20417, phone (202) 501–0800, http://www.gsa.gov

OFFICE OF THE ADMINISTRATOR

Administrator.—Martha N. Johnson.
Deputy Administrator.—Susan F. Brita.
Chief of Staff.—Michael J. Robertson.
Senior Counsel to the Administrator.—Stephen R. Leeds.
Chief Leadership Officer.—Gail Lovelace.
White House Liaison.—Greg Mecher.

CENTRAL OFFICE

OFFICE OF CONGRESSIONAL AND INTERGOVERNMENTAL AFFAIRS

Associate Administrator.—Rodney P. Emery, 501–0563.
Deputy Associate Administrators: Lisa Austin, Jeanne ''Patrice'' Willoughby.
Director of:
Congressional Operations.—Erin Mewhirter.
Congressional Support Services.—Marcia Herzog.
Senior Advisor for Appropriations.—Michael Gurgo.

OFFICE OF THE CHIEF FINANCIAL OFFICER

Chief Financial Officer.—Alison L. Doone, 501–1721.
Director of:
Budget.—Craig Hull (acting).
Controller.—Faye Basden.
Finance.—Douglas Glenn.
Financial Management Systems.—Lynne E. Johnson (acting).

OFFICE OF THE CHIEF PEOPLE OFFICER

Chief People Officer.—Anthony ''Tony'' Costa, 501–0398.
Chief of Staff.—Peter Russelburg.

OFFICE OF THE GENERAL COUNSEL

General Counsel.—Kris Durmer, 501–2200
Deputy General Counsel.—Lennard S. Loewentritt.
Associate General Counsel for—
General Law.—Eugenia D. Ellison, 501–1460.
Personal Property.—Janet Harney, 501–1156.
Real Property.—Barry Segal, 501–0430.

OFFICE OF THE CHIEF INFORMATION OFFICER

Chief Information Officer.—Casey Coleman, 501–1000.
Director, Office of:
Enterprise Infrastructure.—Kurt Garbars (acting).
Enterprise Management Service.—Daryle ''Mike'' Seckar.
Enterprise Solutions.—Sonny Hashmi (acting).

OFFICE OF GOVERNMENTWIDE POLICY

Associate Administrator.—Kathleen Turco, 501–8880.
Chief Acquisition Officer.—Mindy Connolly.
Chief of Staff.—Stephanie Rivera.
Executive Officer.—Teresa Tippins.
Executive Director, Office of Policy Initiatives.—James L. Dean, 273–3563.
Deputy Associate Administrator, Office of:
Real Property Management.—Carolyn Austin-Diggs, 501–0856.
Travel, Transportation, and Asset Management.—Janet Dobbs, 501–1777.
Assistant Deputy Associate Administrator, Office of Technology Strategy.—Angela Smith (acting) 501–0202.

OFFICE OF CITIZEN SERVICES AND INNOVATIVE TECHNOLOGIES

Associate Administrator.—David L. McClure, 501–0705.
Deputy Associate Administrator.—Kathy Conrad.

OFFICE OF CIVIL RIGHTS

Associate Administrator.—Madeline Caliendo, 501–0767.

OFFICE OF SMALL BUSINESS UTILIZATION

Associate Administrator.—Jiyoung Park, 501–1021.
Deputy Associate Administrator.—Thomas Green.

OFFICE OF THE INSPECTOR GENERAL

Inspector General.—Brian D. Miller, 501–0450.
Deputy Inspector General.—Robert C. Erickson, Jr., 501–3105.
Director of Communications and Congressional Affairs.—Dave Farley, 219–1062.
Director, Office of Internal Evaluation and Analysis.—Patricia Sheenan, 273–4989.
Counsel to the Inspector General.—Richard Levi, 501–1932.
Assistant Inspector General for—
Administration.—Larry Gregg, 219–1041.
Auditing.—Theodore R. Stehney, 501–0374.
Investigations.—Jeff Scherrington, 501–0035.

CIVILIAN BOARD OF CONTRACT APPEALS

Chairman.—Stephen M. Daniels (202) 606–8820.

Vice Chairman.—Jeri K. Somers, 606–8831.
Chief Counsel.—James G. Parks, 606–8787.
Clerk.—Cheryl L. Hilton, 606–8800.
Board Judges, 606–8820: Anthony S. Borwick, Stephen M. Daniels, Jerome Drummond, Beryl Gilmore, Catherine B. Hyatt, H. Chuck Kullberg, R. Anthony McCann, Howard Pollack, Patricia Sheridan, Jeri Somers, Candida Steel, James Stern, Joseph Vergilio, Richard Walters.

NATIONAL SERVICES

FEDERAL ACQUISITION SERVICE

Commissioner.—Stephen Kempf (703) 605–5400.
Deputy Commissioner.—Jon A. Jordan.
Chief of Staff.—Betty Feit, 605–2578.
Controller.—Agnes W. Leung.
Chief Information Officer.—Elizabeth F. DelNegro.
Assistant Commissioner for Office of:
Administration.—Karen Hampel, 605–5574.
Acquisition Management.—Houston W. Taylor.
Assisted Acquisition Services.—Timothy E. Fleming (acting).
Customer Accounts and Research.—Tamela L. Riggs.
General Supplies and Services.—William Sisk.
Integrated Technology Services.—Mary Davie.
Strategic Business Planning and Process Improvement.—Amanda Fredriksen (acting), (703) 605–5513.
Travel, Motor Vehicle and Card Services.—Bill Webster (703) 605–5500.

PUBLIC BUILDINGS SERVICE

Commissioner.—Robert Peck (202) 501–1100.
Deputy Commissioner.—David Foley.
Chief of Staff.—Linda Osgood (acting).
Associate Commissioner.—Desa Sealy.
Chief Architect.—Leslie Shepherd, 501–1888.
PBS Assistant Commissioner for—
Budget and Financial Management.—Sean Mildrew, 501–4433.
Organizational Resources.—Erika Dinnie (acting) 501–0971.

REGIONAL OFFICES

National Capital Region (NCR 11): 7th and D Streets, SW., Washington, DC 20407 (202) 708–9100.
Regional Administrator.—Julia E. Hudson.
Regional Commissioner for Federal Acquisition Service.—Alfonso Finley.
Regional Commissioner for Public Buildings Service.—Cathy Kronopolus.
Regional Counsel.—Paula DeMuth.
New England Region 1: Thomas P. O'Neill Federal Building, 10 Causeway Street, Boston, MA 02222 (617) 565–5860.
Regional Administrator.—Robert Zartneske.
Regional Commissioner for Federal Acquisition Service.—Sharon A. Wall.
Regional Commissioner for Public Buildings Service.—Glenn Rotondo.
Northeast and Caribbean Region 2: 26 Federal Plaza, New York, NY 10278 (212) 264–2600.
Regional Administrator.—Denise L. Pease.
Regional Commissioner for Federal Acquisition Service.—Paul J. McDermott.
Regional Commissioner for Public Buildings Service.—Joanna Rosato (acting).
Mid-Atlantic Region 3: The Strawbridge's Building, 20 North Eighth Street, Philadelphia, PA 19107 (215) 446–4900.
Regional Administrator.—David H. Ehrenwerth.
Regional Commissioner for Federal Acquisition Service.—Linda C. Chero.
Regional Commissioner for Public Buildings Service.—Robert Hewell.
Regional Counsel.—Robert J. McCall.
Southeast Sunbelt Region 4: 77 Forsyth Street, Suite 600, Atlanta, GA 30303 (404) 331–3200.

Regional Administrator.—Shyam K. Reddy.
Regional Commissioner for Federal Acquisition Service.—Kelley Holcombe, Jr.
Regional Commissioner for Public Buildings Service.—James Weller (acting).
Great Lakes Region 5: 230 South Dearborn Street, Chicago, IL 60604 (312) 353–5395.
Regional Administrator.—Ann P. Kalayil.
Regional Commissioner for Federal Acquisition Service.—Micael A. Tyllas.
Regional Commissioner for Public Buildings Service.—David Hood.
Heartland Region 6: 1500 East Bannister Road, Kansas City, MO 64131 (816) 926–7201.
Regional Administrator.—Jason O. Klumb.
Regional Commissioner for Federal Acquisition Service.—Michael T. Brincks.
Regional Commissioner for Public Buildings Service.—Mary Ruwwe.
Greater Southwest Region 7: 819 Taylor Street, Fort Worth, TX 76102 (817) 978–2321.
Regional Administrator.—Juan ''J.D.'' Salinas.
Regional Commissioner for Federal Acquisition Service.—Kathy E. Colomo (acting).
Regional Commissioner for Public Buildings Service.—Jim Weller.
Rocky Mountain Region 8: Building 41, Denver Federal Center, Denver, CO 80225 (303) 236–7329.
Regional Administrator.—Susan B. Damour.
Regional Commissioner for Federal Acquisition Service.—Timothy O. Horne.
Regional Commissioner for Public Buildings Service.—Paul Prouty.
Pacific Rim Region 9: 450 Golden Gate Avenue, room 5–2690, San Francisco, CA 94102 (415) 522–3001.
Regional Administrator.—Ruth Cox.
Regional Commissioner for Federal Acquisition Service.—Michael S. Gelber.
Regional Commissioner for Public Buildings Service.—Jeff Neely.
Northwest/Arctic Region 10: GSA Center, 400 15th Street, SW., Auburn, WA 98001 (253) 931–7000.
Regional Administrator .—George E. Northcroft.
Regional Commissioner for Federal Acquisition Service.—James L. Hamilton (acting).
Regional Commissioner for Public Buildings Service.—Rob Graf.

HARRY S. TRUMAN SCHOLARSHIP FOUNDATION

712 Jackson Place, NW., 20006

phone (202) 395–4831, fax 395–6995

[Created by Public Law 93–642]

BOARD OF TRUSTEES

President.—Madeleine K. Albright.
Chairman Emeritus.—Elmer B. Staats.
Vice President.—Max Sherman.
General Counsel.—C. Westbrook Murphy.
Members:
W. Todd Akin, Representative from Missouri.
Mark Begich, Senator from Alaska.
Javaid Anwar, CEO, Quality Care Consultants, LLC.
Hon. Arne Duncan, Secretary of Education.
Hon. Dave Heineman, Governor, State of Nebraska.
Roger Hunt, U.S. District Judge.
John Kidde, Vice President, Ventura Foods.
Hon. John Peyton, Mayor, City of Jacksonville, Florida.
Sharon ''Nyota'' Tucker, Assistant Professor, Albany State University.
Juanita Vasquez-Gardner, Judge, 399th District Court of Texas.
Executive Secretary.—Andrew Rich.
Deputy Executive Secretary.—Tara Yglesias.
Chief Information Officer.—Tonji Wade.
Education Officer.—Ruth Keen.
Program Manager.—Andrew Kirk.

JAMES MADISON MEMORIAL FELLOWSHIP FOUNDATION

2000 K Street, Suite 303, NW., 20006–1809

phone (202) 653–8700, fax 653–6045

[Created by Public Law 99–591]

BOARD OF TRUSTEES

Members Appointed by the President of the United States:

John Cornyn, Senator from Texas, *Chairman.*
Benjamin L. Cardin, Senator from Maryland.
Steven M. Colloton, U.S. Circuit Judge, U.S. Court of Appeals 8th Circuit, Des Moines, Iowa.
John J. Faso, Attorney, Manatt, Phelps and Phillips, Albany, New York.
William Terrell Hodges, Senior U.S. District Judge, Middle District, Florida.
Drew R. McCoy, Department of History, Clark University.
J.C.A. Stagg, Editor, *The Papers of James Madison,* University of Virginia, Charlottesville, Virginia.
Harvey M. Tettlebaum, Partner, Husch Blackwell Sanders LLP, Jefferson City, Missouri.
Arne Duncan, U.S. Secretary of Education (ex officio).

Foundation Staff:

President Emeritus.—Admiral Paul A. Yost, Jr.
President.—Lewis F. Larsen.
Academic Advisor to the President.—Herman Belz.
Director of Special Programs.—Claire Griffin.
Special Assistant / Office Manager.—Anne Marie Kanakkanatt.
Academic Assistant.—Sheila Osbourne.
Management and Program Analysis Officer.—Elizabeth G. Ray.

INTER-AMERICAN FOUNDATION

901 North Stuart Street, 10th Floor, Arlington, VA 22203, phone (703) 306–4301

Chair, Board of Directors.—John P. Salazar (acting).
Vice Chair, Board of Directors.—Thomas J. Dodd (acting).
President.—Robert N. Kaplan.
General Counsel and Senior Vice President.—Jennifer Hodges Reynolds.
Vice President of Operations.—Linda Kolko.
Vice President for Programs.—Stephen Cox.

JOHN F. KENNEDY CENTER FOR THE PERFORMING ARTS

2700 F Street, NW., 20566, phone (202) 416–8000, fax 416–8205

BOARD OF TRUSTEES

Honorary Chairs:

Mrs. Michelle Obama
Mrs. Laura Bush
Secretary Hillary Rodham Clinton
Mrs. George Bush
Mrs. Ronald Reagan
Mrs. Jimmy Carter
Mrs. Gerald R. Ford (deceased)

Officers:

Chairman.—David M. Rubenstein.
President.—Michael M. Kaiser.
Secretary.—Jean Kennedy Smith.
Treasurer.—Adrienne Arsht.
General Counsel.—Maria C. Kersten.
Assistant Secretary.—Kathy Kruse.

Members Appointed by the President of the United States:

Wilma E. Bernstein
Nancy Goodman Brinker
Gordon J. Davis
Edward W. Easton
Judith Ann Eisenberg
Emilio Estefan, Jr.
Fred Eychaner
Giselle Fernandez
Norma Lee Funger
Donald J. Hall, Jr.
James A. Haslam II
Joan E. Hotchkis
Sheldon B. Kamins
Victoria Reggie Kennedy
James V. Kimsey
Herbert V. Kohler, Jr.
C. Michael Kojaian
Carl H. Lindner III

Ex Officio Members Designated by Act of Congress
(Note: The names of Senators and Representatives appear in order of their years of service)

Hillary Rodham Clinton, Secretary of State.
Arne Duncan, Secretary of Education.
Kathleen Sebelius, Secretary of Health and Human Services.
James Inhofe, Senator from Oklahoma.
Harry Reid, Senator Majority Leader from Nevada.
Thad Cochran, Senator from Mississippi.
Mitch McConnell, Senate Republican Leader from Kentucky.
Barbara Boxer, Senator from California.
Dianne Feinstein, Senator from California.
Kent Conrad, Senator from North Dakota.
Nancy Pelosi, Democratic Leader of the House of Representatives from California.
John A. Boehner, Speaker of the House of Representatives from Ohio.
John L. Mica, Representative from Florida.
Rosa L. DeLauro, Representative from Connecticut.
Nick J. Rahall II, Representative from West Virginia.
Vincent C. Gray, Mayor, District of Columbia.
Dr. G. Wayne Clough, Secretary, Smithsonian Institution.
James H. Billington, Librarian of Congress.
Earl A. Powell III, Chairman of the Commission of Fine Arts.
Jonathan Jarvis, Director, National Park Service.
Kaya Henderson, Chancellor, DC Public Schools.

Senior Counsel.—Robert Barnett.
Founding Chairman.—Roger L. Stevens (deceased).
Chairmen Emeriti: James A. Johnson, Stephen A. Schwarzman, James D. Wolfensohn.
Honorary Trustees:

Buffy Cafritz
Kenneth M. Duberstein
James H. Evans
Alma Gildenhorn
Melvin R. Laird
Leonard L. Silverstein

LEGAL SERVICES CORPORATION

3333 K Street, NW., 3rd Floor, 20007–3522
phone (202) 295–1500, fax 337–6797

BOARD OF DIRECTORS

John G. Levi, Board *Chair*
Martha L. Minow, Board *Vice Chair*
Sharon L. Browne
Robert J. Grey, Jr.
Charles N.W. Keckler
Harry Korrell
Victor B. Maddox
Laurie I. Mikva
Rev. Joseph Pius Pietrzyk
Julie A. Reiskin
Gloria Valencia-Weber

President.—James J. Sandman.
Vice President, Legal Affairs, General Counsel and Corporate Secretary.—Victor M. Fortuno.
Comptroller and Treasurer.—David L. Richardson.
Inspector General.—Jeffrey E. Schanz.
Director, Government Relations and Public Affairs.—John Constance.
Media Director.—Stephen Barr.

NATIONAL AERONAUTICS AND SPACE ADMINISTRATION

300 E Street, SW., 20546, phone (202) 358–0000, http://www.nasa.gov

OFFICE OF THE ADMINISTRATOR

Code AA000, Room 9F44, phone 358–1010

Administrator.—Charles F. Bolden, Jr.

Deputy Administrator.—Lori Garver, 358–1020.
Executive Assistant.—Kathryn Manuel, 358–1020.
Chief of Staff.—David Radzanowski, 358–1827.
White House Liaison.—David Noble, 358–2198.
Chief Health and Medical Officer.—Dr. Richard S. Williams, room 7P13, 358–2390.

AERONAUTICS RESEARCH MISSION DIRECTORATE

Code EA000, Room 6J39–A, phone 358–4700

Associate Administrator.—Jaiwon Shin.
Deputy Associate Administrator.—Thomas B. Irvine.

OFFICE OF THE CHIEF FINANCIAL OFFICER (CFO)

Code 1A000, Room 8E39–A, phone 358–0978

Chief Financial Officer/Chief Acquisition Officer.—Elizabeth Robinson.
Deputy Chief Financial Officer.—Terry Bowie, 358–1135.

OFFICE OF DIVERSITY AND EQUAL OPPORTUNITY PROGRAMS

Code YA000, Room 4Y23, phone 358–2167

Associate Administrator for Equal Opportunity Programs.—Brenda R. Manuel.

OFFICE OF INTERNATIONAL AND INTERAGENCY RELATIONS

Code TA000, Room 7V39, phone 358–0450

Assistant Administrator.—Michael F. O'Brien.
Deputy Assistant Administrator.—Al Condes.

OFFICE OF THE GENERAL COUNSEL

Code MA000, Room 9V39, phone 358–2450

General Counsel.—Michael Wholley.
Deputy General Counsel.—Richard W. Sherman.

OFFICE OF HUMAN CAPITAL MANAGEMENT

Code LE000–A, Room 4V84, phone 358–0520

Assistant Administrator.—Jeri Buchholz.

MISSION SUPPORT DIRECTORATE

Code LA000, Room 4K39, phone 358–0227

Associate Administrator.—Woodrow Whitlow, Jr.
Deputy Associate Administrator.—Lewis S.G. Braxton III.
Executive Director Headquarters Operations.—Jay Henn.

OFFICE OF INSPECTOR GENERAL

Code WAH10, Room 8U79, phone 358–1220

Inspector General.—Paul K. Martin.
Deputy Inspector General.—Gail A. Robinson.

OFFICE OF LEGISLATIVE AFFAIRS

Code VA000, Room 9K39, phone 358–1948

Associate Administrator.—Seth Statler.
Deputy Assistant Administrator.—Mary D. Kerwin.

OFFICE OF PROCUREMENT

Code LP010, Room 5G70, phone 358–2090

Assistant Administrator.—Bill McNally.

OFFICE OF COMMUNICATIONS

Code NB000, Room 9P39, phone 358–1600

Associate Administrator.—David Weaver.

SAFETY AND MISSION ASSURANCE

Code GA000, Room 5W21, phone 358–2406

Chief Officer.—Bryan D. O'Connor.
Deputy Chief Officer.—Wilson B. Harkins.

SCIENCE MISSION DIRECTORATE

Code DA000, room 3C26, phone 358–3889

Associate Administrator.—Edward Weiler.
Deputy Associate Administrator.—Michael Luther, 358–2165.
Deputy Associate Administrator for Programs.—Michael R. Luther, 358–0260.
NASA Chiefs:
Engineer.—Dr. Mike Ryschkewitsch, 358–1823.
Scientist.—Dr. Waleed Abdalati, 358–1163.
Technologist.—Joseph Parrish (acting), 358–3000.

OFFICE OF PROTECTIVE SERVICES

Code LP020, Room 9U70, phone 358–2010

Associate Administrator.—Jack Forsythe.
Deputy Associate Administrator.—Charles Lombard.

OFFICE OF SMALL BUSINESS PROGRAMS

Code ZA000, Room 2K39, phone 358–2088

Assistant Administrator.—Glenn A. Delgado.

HUMAN EXPLORATION AND OPERATIONS MISSION DIRECTORATE

Code CA000, Room 7K39, phone 358–2015

Associate Administrator.—William H. Gerstenmaier.
Deputy Associate Administrator.—Lynn F.H. Cline.

NASA NATIONAL OFFICES

Air Force Space Command / XPX (NASA): Peterson Air Force Base, CO 80914.
NASA Senior Representative.—Jeffrey Ashby (719) 554–4900.
Ames Research Center: Moffett Field, CA 94035.
Director.—Simon P. Worden (650) 604–5000.
Dryden Flight Research Center: P.O. Box 273, Edwards, CA 93523.
Director.—David McBride (661) 276–3449
Glenn Research Center at Lewisfield: 21000 Brookpark Road, Cleveland, OH 44135.
Director.—Ramon Lugo (216) 433–4000.
Goddard Institute for Space Studies: Goddard Space Flight Center, 2880 Broadway, New York, NY 10025.
Head.—Dr. James E. Hansen (212) 678–5500.
Goddard Space Flight Center: 8800 Greenbelt Road, Greenbelt, MD 20771.
Director.—Robert Strain (301) 286–2000.
Jet Propulsion Laboratory: 4800 Oak Grove Drive, Pasadena, CA 91109.
Director.—Dr. Charles Elachi (818) 354–4321.
Lyndon B. Johnson Space Center: 2101 NASA Parkway Houston, TX 77058–3696.
Director.—Michael L. Coats (281) 483–0123.
John F. Kennedy Space Center: Kennedy Space Center, FL 32899.
Director.—Robert Cabana (321) 867–5000.
Langley Research Center: Hampton, VA 23681.
Director.—Lesa Roe (757) 864–1000.
George C. Marshall Space Flight Center: Marshall Space Flight Center, AL 35812.

Director.—Robert Lightfoot (256) 544–2121.

Michoud Assembly Facility: P.O. Box 29300, New Orleans, LA 70189.

Manager.—Stephen C. Doering (504) 257–3311.

NASA IV and V Facility: NASA Independent Verification and Validation Facility, 100 University Drive, Fairmont, WV 26554.

Director.—Gregory D. Blaney (304) 367–8200.

NASA Management Office: Jet Propulsion Laboratory, 4800 Oak Grove Drive, Pasadena, CA 91109.

Director.—Eugene Trinh (818) 354–5359.

John C. Stennis Space Center: Stennis Space Center, MS 39529.

Director.—Patrick Scheuermann (228) 688–2211.

Vandenberg AFB: P.O. Box 425, Lompoc, CA 93438.

Manager.—Ted L. Oglesby (805) 866–5859.

Wallops Flight Facility: Goddard Space Flight Center, Wallops Island, VA 23337.

Director.—William Wrobel (757) 824–1000.

White Sands Test Facility: Johnson Space Center, P.O. Drawer MM, Las Cruces, NM 88004.

Manager.—Frank J. Benz (505) 524–5771.

NASA OVERSEAS REPRESENTATIVES

Europe: U.S. Embassy-Paris, Unit 9200, Box 1653, DPO, AE 09777, 011–33–1–4312–7070.

NASA Representative.—Gilbert Kirkham.

Japan: U.S. Embassy, Tokyo, Unit 9800, Box 544, DPO 96303–0554, 011–81–3–3224–5827.

NASA Representative.—Justin Tilman.

Russia: U.S. Embassy, Moscow, NASA, DPO AE 09721, (256) 961–6333.

NASA Representative.—Thomas Plumb.

NATIONAL ARCHIVES AND RECORDS ADMINISTRATION

700 Pennsylvania Avenue, NW., 20408–0001

8601 Adelphi Road, College Park, MD 20740–6001

http://www.nara.gov

[Created by Public Law 98–497]

Archivist of the United States.—David S. Ferriero (202) 357–5900, fax 357–5901.

Deputy Archivist of the United States.—Debra S. Wall (202) 357–5900; 837–1600, fax 837–3218.

Chief of Staff.—Vacant (301) 837–1600, fax 837–3218.

Assistant Archivist, Office of:

Administration.—Charles Piercy (301) 837–3050, fax 837–3217.

Federal Register.—Raymond A. Mosely (202) 741–6010, fax 741–6012.

Information Services.—Michael Wash (301) 837–3670, fax 837–3213.

Presidential Libraries.—Jim Gardner (301) 837–3250, fax 837–3199.

Records Services, Washington, DC.—Vacant (301) 837–3110, fax 837–1617.

Regional Records Services.—William Bosanko (301) 837–2950, fax 837–1617.

Executive Director, National Historical Publications and Records Commission.—Kathleen Williams (202) 501–5010, fax 357–5914.

Director for—

Congressional Affairs Staff.—John O. Hamilton (202) 357–5100, fax 357–5959.

Public and Media Communications.—Susan Cooper (202) 357–5300 fax 357–5999.

Strategy and Communications.—Donna Garland.

Equal Employment Opportunity and Diversity Programs.—Robert Jew (301) 837–1849, fax 837–0869.

Information Security Oversight Office.—John Fitzpatrick (202) 357–5250, fax 357–5907.

Policy and Planning Staff.—Maryann Hadyka (acting), (301) 837–1850, fax 837–0319.

General Counsel.—Gary M. Stern (301) 837–1750, fax 837–0293.

Inspector General.—Paul Brachfeld (301) 837–3000, fax 837–3197.

ADMINISTRATIVE COMMITTEE OF THE FEDERAL REGISTER

800 North Capitol Street, NW., Suite 700, 20002, phone (202) 741–6071

Mailing Address: 8601 Adelphi Road, College Park, MD 20740

Members:
David Ferriero, Archivist of the United States, *Chair.*
William Boarman, Public Printer of the United States.
Rosemary Hart, Senior Counsel, Department of Justice.
Secretary.—Raymond A. Mosley, Director of the Federal Register, National Archives and Records Administration.

NATIONAL ARCHIVES TRUST FUND BOARD

phone (301) 837–3550, fax 837–3191

Members:
David Ferriero, Archivist of the United States, *Chair.*
Jim Leach, Chairman, National Endowment for the Humanities.
Richard Gregg, Fiscal Assistant Secretary, Department of the Treasury.
Secretary.—Lawrence Post.

NATIONAL HISTORICAL PUBLICATIONS AND RECORDS COMMISSION

700 Pennsylvania Avenue, NW., 20408

phone (202) 357–5010, fax 357–5914

http://www.archives.gov/nhprc

Members:
David S. Ferriero Chairman, Archivist of the United States, National Archives and Records Administration.
Barbara Jacobs Rothstein, Director, Federal Judicial Center, Judicial Branch.
Benjamin L. Cardin, Senator of Maryland.
Vacant, Representative of Congress.
James W. Ceaser, Department of Politics, University of Virginia, Presidential Appointee.
Nancy Davenport, President, Nancy Davenport and Associates, LLC, Presidential Appointee.
Erin Mahan, Chief Historian, Office of the Secretary, Department of Defense.
Deanna Marcum, Associate Librarian for Library Services, Library of Congress.
Edward Brynn, Office of the Historian, Department of State.
Raymond Smock, Director, Robert C. Byrd Center for Legislative Studies, Association for Documentary Editing.
Rodger E. Stroup, Curator, South Carolina Railroad Museum, American Association for State and Local History.
Stanley N. Katz, Lecturer with the rank of Professor, Director, Center for Arts and Cultural Policy Studies, Woodrow Wilson School, Princeton University, American Historical Association.
F. Gerald Handfield, State Archivist, Washington State Archives, National Association of Government Archives and Records Administrators.
Julie Saville, Professor of History, University of Chicago, Organization of American Historians.
Timothy L. Ericson, Senior Lecturer Emeritus, University of Wisconsin-Milwaukee, Society of American Archivists.
Executive Director.—Kathleen Williams (202) 357–5010.

REGIONAL LIAISONS

Central Plains Region: *Regional Liaison.*—Diane Cejka (816) 268–8031.
Central Plains Region.—400 West Pershing Road, Kansas City, MO 64108 (816) 268–8026.
Great Lakes Region: *Regional Liaison.*—Denis Paskaukas (acting), (773) 948–9012.
Chicago.—7358 South Pulaski Road, Chicago, IL 60629 (773) 948–9007.
Dayton.—3150 Springboro Road, Dayton, OH 45439 (937) 425–0605.
Mid Atlantic Region: *Regional Liaison.*—V. Chapman Smith (215) 606–0102.
Center City Philadelphia.—900 Market Street, Philadelphia, PA 19107 (215) 606–2100.
Northeast Philadelphia.—14700 Townsend Road, Philadelphia, PA 19154 (215) 305–2000.

Northeast Region: *Regional Liaison.*—Diane LeBlanc (781) 663–0133.
Boston.—380 Trapelo Road, Waltham, MA 02452–6399 (781) 663–0130.
Pittsfield.—10 Conte Drive, Pittsfield, MA 01201–8230 (413) 236–3600.
New York City.—201 Varick St., New York, NY 10014–4811 (212) 401–1620.
Pacific Alaska Region: *Regional Liaison.*—Candance Lein Hayes (206) 336–5142.
Seattle.—6125 Sand Point Way NE, Seattle, WA 98115 (206) 336–5143.
Anchorage.—654 West Third Avenue, Anchorage, AK 99501 (907) 261–7810.
Pacific Region: *Regional Liaison.*—David Drake (650) 238–3477.
San Francisco.—1000 Commodore Drive, San Bruno, CA 94066 (650) 238–2471.
Rocky Mountain Region: *Regional Liaison.*—Barbara Voss (303) 407–5701.
Rocky Mountain Region.—Building 48, Denver Federal Center, Denver, CO 80225 (303) 407–5703.
Southeast Region: *Regional Liaison.*—James McSweeney (770) 968–2505.
Southeast Region.—4712 Southpark Boulevard, Ellenwood, GA 30294.
Southwest Region: *Regional Liaison.*—Preston Huff (817) 551–2001.
Southwest Region.—501 W. Felix Street, Ft. Worth, TX 76115 (817) 831–5904.
National Personnel Records Center: *Regional Liaison.*—Scott Levins (314) 801–0587.
National Personnel Records Center.—9700 Page Avenue, St. Louis, MO 63132 (314) 801–9221.

Presidential Libraries.—Susan Donius (acting), (301) 837–3250, fax (301) 837–3199.
Director for—
Herbert Hoover Library.—Thomas Schwartz, West Branch, IA 52358–0488 (319) 643–5301.
Franklin D. Roosevelt Library.—Lynn Bassanese (acting), Hyde Park, NY 12538–1999 (845) 486–7770.
Harry S. Truman Library.—Michael Devine, Independence, MO 64050–1798 (816) 268–8200.
Dwight D. Eisenhower Library.—Karl Weissenbach, Abilene, KS 67410–2900 (785) 263–6700.
John F. Kennedy Library.—Thomas Putnam, Boston, MA 02125–3398 (617) 514–1600.
Lyndon Baines Johnson Library.—Mark Updegrove, Austin, TX 78705–5702 (512) 721–0200.
Richard Nixon Library.—Timothy Naftali, Yorba Linda, CA 92886 (714) 983–9121.
Gerald R. Ford Library.—Elaine K. Didier, Ann Arbor, MI 48109–2114 (734) 205–0555.
Gerald R. Ford Museum.—Elaine K. Didier, Grand Rapids, MI 49504–5353 (616) 254–0400.
Jimmy Carter Library.—Jay E. Hakes, Atlanta, GA 30307–1498 (404) 865–7100.
Ronald Reagan Library.—R. Duke Blackwood, Simi Valley, CA 93065–0699 (800) 410–8354.
George Bush Library.—Warren Finch, College Station, TX 77845 (979) 691–4000.
William J. Clinton Library.—Terri Garner, Little Rock, AR 72201 (501) 244–2887.
George W. Bush Library.—Alan Lowe, Lewisville, TX 75057 (972) 353–0500.

NATIONAL CAPITAL PLANNING COMMISSION

401 9th Street, NW., North Lobby, Suite 500, 20004, phone (202) 482–7200

fax 482–7272, info@ncpc.gov, http://www.ncpc.gov

APPOINTIVE MEMBERS

Presidential Appointees:
L. Preston Bryant, Jr., *Chair.*
Vacant
John M. Hart.
Mayoral Appointees:
Arrington Dixon.
Robert E. Miller, NCPC Vice Chairman.
Ex Officio Members:
Leon E. Panetta, Secretary of Defense.
First Alternate.—Michael L. Rhodes.
Second Alternate.—Bradley Provancha.
Ken Salazar, Secretary of the Interior.
First Alternate.—Jonathan B. Jarvis.
Second Alternate.—Vacant.

Third Alternate.—Woody Smeck.
Fourth Alternate.—Peter May.
Martha Johnson, Administrator of General Services.
First Alternate.—Julia E. Hudson.
Second Alternate.—Cathleen Kronopolus.
Third Alternate.—Mina Wright.
Fourth Alternate.—Michael S. McGill.
Joseph I. Lieberman, Chairman, Senate Committee on Homeland Security and Governmental Affairs.
Alternate.—Elyse Greenwald.
Darrell E. Issa, Chairman, House Committee on Oversight and Government Reform.
First Alternate.—John Cuaderes.
Second Alternate.—Peter Warren.
Third Alternate.—Howard A. Denis.
Vincent C. Gray, Mayor of the District of Columbia.
First Alternate.—Harriet Tregoning.
Second Alternate.—Jennifer Steingasser.
Kwame R. Brown, Chairman, Council of the District of Columbia.
First Alternate.—Megan Vahey.

EXECUTIVE STAFF

Executive Director.—Marcel C. Acosta, 482–7221.
Chief Operating Officer.—Barry S. Socks, 482–7209.
Chief Urban Designer.—Christine Saum, 482–7245.
Secretariat.—Deborah B. Young, 482–7228.
General Counsel.—Anne R. Schuyler, 482–7223.
Director, Office of:
Administration.—Charles J. ''Jody'' Rieder, 482–7255.
Intergovernmental Affairs.—Julia A. Koster, 482–7211.
Physical Planning.—William G. Dowd, 482–7240.
Policy and Research.—Michael A. Sherman, 482–7254.
Public Affairs.—Lisa N. MacSpadden, 482–7263.
Urban Design and Plan Review.—David W. Levy, 482–7247.

NATIONAL COUNCIL ON DISABILITY

1331 F Street, NW., Suite 850, 20004, phone (202) 272–2004, TTY (202) 272–2074, fax 272–2022

Chairman.—Jonathan Young, Bethesda, MD.
Vice Chair.—Fernando Torres-Gil, Los Angeles, CA.
Members:
Gary Blumenthal, Sudbury, MA.
Chester Finn, Albany, NY.
Sara Gelser, Corvalis, OR.
Marylyn Howe, Savannah, GA.
Janice Lehrer-Stein, San Francisco, CA.
Lonnie Moore, Chula Vista, CA.
Ari Ne'eman, Silver Spring, MD.
Dongwoo Joseph ''Joe'' Pak, Garden Grove, CA.
Carol Jean Reynolds, Evergreen, CO.
Clyde Terry, Concord, NH.
Linda Wetters, Columbus, OH.
Pamela Young-Holmes, Madison, WI.

NATIONAL CREDIT UNION ADMINISTRATION

1775 Duke Street, Alexandria, VA 22314–3428, phone (703) 518–6300, fax 518–6319

Chairman.—Debbie Matz.
Board Members: Michael E. Fryzel, Christiane Gigi Hyland.
Secretary to the Board.—Mary Rupp.
Executive Director.—David Marquis, 518–6320, fax 518–6661.
Deputy Executive Director.—Melinda Love, 518–6320.
Deputy Director Inspector General.—William DeSarno, 518–6350.
Director, Office of:
Capital Markets.—Owen Cole, 518–6620, fax 518–6663.
Chief Financial Officer.—Mary Ann Woodson, 518–6570, fax 518–6664.
Chief Information Officer.—Doug Verner, 518–6440, fax 518–6669.

Corporate Credit Unions.—Scott Hunt, 518–6640, fax 518–6665.
EEO.—S. Denise Hendricks, 518–6325.
Examination and Insurance.—Larry Fazio, 518–6360, fax 518–6666.
General Counsel.—Michael McKenna, 518–6540, fax 518–6667.
Deputy General Counsel.—Vacant.
Human Resources.—Lorraine Phillips, 518–6510, fax 518–6668.
Public and Congressional Affairs.—Todd M. Harper, 518–6330.
Small Credit Union Initiatives.—William Myers, 518–6610.

REGIONAL OFFICES

Director, Office of:

Region I (Albany).—Mark Treichel, 9 Washington Square, Washington Avenue Extension, Albany, NY 12205 (518) 862–7400, fax 862–7420.

Region II (National Capital Region).—Jane A. Walters, 1775 Duke Street, Suite 4206, Alexandria, VA 22314 (703) 519–4600, fax 519–4620.

Region III (Atlanta).—Herbert Yolles, 7000 Central Parkway, Suite 1600, Atlanta, GA 30328 (678) 443–3000, fax 443–3020.

Region IV (Austin).—Keith Morton, 4807 Spicewood Springs Road, Suite 5200, Austin, TX 78759–8490 (512) 342–5600, fax 342–5620.

Region V (Tempe).—Elizabeth Whitehead, 1230 West Washington Street, Suite 301, Tempe, AZ 85281 (602) 302–6000, fax 302–6024.

President, Asset Management and Assistance Center (Austin).—Mike Barton, 4807 Spicewood Springs Road, Suite 5100, Austin, TX 78759–8490 (512) 231–7900, fax 231–7920.

NATIONAL FOUNDATION ON THE ARTS AND THE HUMANITIES
Old Post Office Building, 1100 Pennsylvania Avenue, NW., 20506

NATIONAL ENDOWMENT FOR THE ARTS
http://www.arts.gov

Chairman.—Rocco Landesman (202) 682–5414.
Senior Deputy Chairman.—Joan Shigekawa, 682–5415.
Deputy Chairman for Management and Budget.—Laurence Baden, 682–5408.
Chief of Staff.—Jamie Bennett, 682–5434.
Congressional Liaison.—Mike Griffin, 682–5773.
Senior Adviser for Program Innovation.—Bill O'Brien, 682–5550.
Director of Research and Analysis.—Sunil Iyengar, 682–5424.
General Counsel.—Karen Elias, 682–5418.
Inspector General.—Toni Jones, 682–5402.

THE NATIONAL COUNCIL ON THE ARTS

Chairman.—Rocco Landesman.

Members:

James K. Ballinger
Miguel Campaneria
Ben Donenberg
JoAnn Falletta
Lee Greenwood
Joan Israelite
Charlotte Kessler
Bret Lott
Irvin Mayfield
Barbara Ernst Prey
Frank Price
Terry Teachout
Karen Lias Wolff

Ex Officio Members:

Claire McCaskill, Senator
Sheldon Whitehouse, Senator
Betty McCollum, Representative
Patrick J. Tiberi, Representative

NATIONAL ENDOWMENT FOR THE HUMANITIES
phone 1–800–NEH–1121, or (202) 606–8400, info@neh.gov, http://www.neh.gov

Chairman.—James A. Leach, 606–8310.

Deputy Chairman.—Carole Watson, 606–8572.
Director, Communications.—Judy Havemann, 606–8446.
Director, White House and Congressional Affairs.—Courtney Chapin, 606–8298.
General Counsel.—Michael McDonald, 606–8322.
Inspector General.—Laura M.H. Davis, 606–8574.
Public Information Officer.—Christopher Flynn, 606–8446.
Director, Planning and Budget.—Larry Myers, 606–8428.

NATIONAL COUNCIL ON THE HUMANITIES

Members:

Rolena K. Adorno
Adele L. Alexander
Albert J. Beveridge III
Allison Blakely
Constance M. Carroll
Jamsheed K. Choksy
Cathy N. Davidson
Dawn H. Delbanco
Jane M. Doggett
Paula B. Duffy
Jean B. Elshtain
Gary D. Glenn
Allen C. Guelzo
Mary Habeck
David M. Hertz
Marvin Krislov
Iris C. Love
Robert S. Martin
Wilfred M. McClay
Richard J. Quinones
Carol M. Swain
Martha W. Weinberg
Kenneth R. Weinstein
Jay Winik

FEDERAL COUNCIL ON THE ARTS AND THE HUMANITIES

Federal Council Members:

Rocco Landesman, Chairman, National Endowment for the Arts.
James A. Leach, Chairman, National Endowment for the Humanities.
Arne Duncan, Secretary, Department of Education.
G. Wayne Clough, Secretary, Smithsonian Institution.
Subra Suresh, Director, National Science Foundation.
James H. Billington, Librarian of Congress, Library of Congress.
Earl A. Powell III, Director, National Gallery of Art, Chairman, Commission of Fine Arts.
David S. Ferriero, Archivist of the United States, National Archives and Records Administration.
Robert M. Peck, Commissioner, Public Building Service General Services Administration.
J. Adam Ereli, Assistant Secretary of State, Bureau of Educational and Cultural Affairs.
Ken Salazar, Secretary, Department of the Interior.
Nancy Erickson, Secretary, United States Senate.
Fortney Pete Stark, Jr., Member, United States House of Representatives.
John E. Bryson, Secretary, Department of Commerce.
Ray H. LaHood, Secretary, Department of Transportation.
Susan Hildreth, Chairperson, National Museum and Library Services Board, Director, Institute of Museum and Library Services.
Shaun Donovan, Secretary, Department of Housing and Urban Development.
Martha N. Johnson, Administrator, General Services Administration.
Hilda L. Solis, Secretary, Department of Labor.
Eric K. Shinseki, Secretary, Department of Veteran's Affairs.
Kathy Greenlee, Assistant Secretary for Aging, Department of Health and Human Services.

INSTITUTE OF MUSEUM AND LIBRARY SERVICES

phone (202) 653–4657, fax 653–4625, http://www.imls.gov

[The Institute of Museum and Library Services was created by the Museum and Library Services Act of 1996, Public Law 104–208]

Director.—Susan Hildreth, 653–4659.
Director of Operations.—Madeline McCain, 653–4659.
Deputy Director for Library Services.—Mary Chute, 653–4700.
Deputy Director for Museum Services.—Claudia French, 653–4789.
Director of Strategic Partnerships.—Marsha Semmel, 653–4692.
Director, Office of:
Communications and Government Affairs.—Mamie Bittner, 653–4757.
Planning, Research and Evaluation.—A. Carlos Manjarrez, 653–4759.
Associate Deputy Director for—
Library Services.—Joyce Ray, Ph.D., 653–4700.
Museum Services.—Christopher Reich, 653–4789.

State Programs.—Laurie Brooks, 653–4650.
Chief Financial Officer.—Michael Jerger, 653–4737.
General Counsel.—Nancy Weiss, 653–4787.

NATIONAL MUSEUM AND LIBRARY SERVICES BOARD

Members:

Katherine M. B. Berger	Carla Hayden	Lotsee Patterson
Julia W. Bland	Mark Y. Herring	Sandra Pickett
Karen Brosius	Ioannis N. Miaoulis	Lawrence J. Pijeaux, Jr.
Jan Cellucci	Mary Minow	Harry Robinson, Jr.
Mary L. Chute	Douglas G. Myers	Katina Strauch
John Coppola	Christina Orr-Cahall	Winston Tabb
William J. Hagenah	Jeffrey H. Patchen	Robert Wedgeworth

NATIONAL GALLERY OF ART

Sixth Street and Constitution Avenue, NW., 20565

phone (202) 737–4215, http://www.nga.gov

[Under the direction of the Board of Trustees of the National Gallery of Art]

BOARD OF TRUSTEES

General Trustees:
John Wilmerding, Chairman.
Victoria P. Sant, President.
Frederick W. Beinecke.
Mitchell P. Rales.
Sharon Percy Rockefeller.
Trustees Emeriti:
Robert F. Erburu.
Julian Ganz, Jr.
Alexander M. Laughlin.
David O. Maxwell.
Ruth Carter Stevenson.
Ex Officio Trustees:
John G. Roberts, Jr., Chief Justice of the United States.
Hillary Rodham Clinton, Secretary of State.
Timothy F. Geithner, Secretary of the Treasury.
G. Wayne Clough, Secretary of the Smithsonian Institution.
Director.—Earl A. Powell III.
Deputy Director.—Franklin Kelly.
Dean, Center for Advanced Study in the Visual Arts.—Elizabeth Cropper.
Administrator.—Darrell Willson.
Treasurer.—William W. McClure.
Secretary-General Counsel.—Elizabeth A. Croog.
Executive Officer, Development and External Affairs.—Joseph J. Krakora.

NATIONAL LABOR RELATIONS BOARD

1099 14th Street, NW., 20570–0001

Personnel Locator (202) 273–1000

Chairman.—Wilma B. Liebman, 273–1770, fax 273–4270. (Term expires August 27, 2011)
Chief Counsel.—John Colwell.
Deputy Chief Counsel.—Andrew Krafts.
Members:
Board Member.—Vacant, 273–1790.
Chief Counsel.—Terence Flynn.
Deputy Chief Counsel.—Robert F. Kane.
Board Member.—Craig Becker, 273–1740.
Chief Counsel.—Pete Winkler.
Deputy Chief Counsel.—Rachel G. Lennie.
Board Member.—Mark Gaston Pearce, 273–1070.
Chief Counsel.—Kent Y. Hirozawa.

Deputy Chief Counsel.—Kathleen Nixon.
Board Member.—Brian E. Hayes, 273–1770.
Chief Counsel.—James R. Murphy.
Deputy Chief Counsel.—David P. Martin.
Executive Secretary.—Lester A. Heltzer, 273–1940, fax 273–4270.
Deputy Executive Secretary.—Gary W. Shinners, 272–3737.
Associate Executive Secretaries: Henry S. Breiteneicher, 273–2917; Vacant, 273–1935; Vacant, 273–1937.
Solicitor.—William B. Cowen, 273–2914, fax 273–1962.
Inspector General.—David P. Berry, 273–1960, fax 273–2344.
Director, Representation Appeals.—Vacant, 273–1975, fax 273–1962.
Director, Office of Public Affairs.—Nancy Cleeland, 273–1991, fax 273–1789.
General Counsel.—Lafe E. Solomon (acting), 273–3700, fax 273–4483.
Deputy General Counsel.—Celeste Mattina (acting).

DIVISION OF JUDGES

Chief Administrative Law Judge.—Robert A. Giannasi, 501–8800, fax 501–8686.
Deputy Chief Administrative Law Judge.—Vacant, 501–8800.
Associate Chief Administrative Law Judge.—Arthur Amchan.
Associate Chief Administrative Law Judges:
Joel P. Biblowitz, 120 West 45th Street, 11th Floor, New York, NY 10036–5503 (212) 944–2943, fax 944–4904.
William N. Cates, 401 West Peachtree Street, NW., Suite 1708, Atlanta, GA 30308–3510 (404) 331–6654, fax 331–2061.
Mary Miller Cracraft, 901 Market Street, Suite 300, San Francisco, CA 94103–1779 (415) 356–5255, fax 356–5254.
Director, Office of Appeals.—Yvonne T. Dixon, 273–3760, 273–4283.
Deputy Director.—Deborah M.P. Yaffe.
Director, Division of Administration.—Gloria J. Joseph, 273–3890, fax 273–2928.
Deputy Director.—Kathleen James.

DIVISION OF OPERATIONS MANAGEMENT

Associate General Counsel.—Anne G. Purcell, 273–2900, fax 273–4274.
Deputy Associate General Counsel.—Nelson Levin.
Assistant General Counsels: Charles Posner, 273–2885; Shelley S. Korch, 273–2885; Vacant, 273–2893; James G. Paulsen, 273–2881.
Special Counsels: Elizabeth Bach, Joseph M. Davis, Jennifer Kovachich, Barry F. Smith, 273–2918, fax 273–0864.

DIVISION OF ADVICE

Associate General Counsel.—Barry J. Kearney, 273–3800, fax 273–4275.
Deputy Associate General Counsel.—Ellen A. Farrell.
Assistant General Counsels:
Injunction Litigation Branch.—Judith I. Katz, 273–3812.
Regional Advice Branch.—Jayme Sophir, 273–3837.
Research and Policy Planning Branch.—Jacqueline A. Young, 273–3825.

DIVISION OF ENFORCEMENT LITIGATION

Associate General Counsel.—John H. Ferguson, 273–2950, fax 273–4244.
Deputy Associate General Counsel.—Margery E. Lieber, 273–2950.
Appellate and Supreme Court Litigation Branch:
Deputy Associate General Counsel.—Linda J. Dreeben, 273–2960.
Assistant General Counsel.—David Haberistreit, 273–0979.
Deputy Assistant General Counsels: Fred Jacob, 273–2971; Margaret Gaines, 273–2984; Meredith Jason, 273–2945.
Special Litigation Branch:
Assistant General Counsel.—Eric G. Moskowitz, 273–2930, fax 273–1799.
Deputy Assistant General Counsel.—Abby P. Simms, 273–2934.
Contempt Litigation and Compliance Branch:
Assistant General Counsel.—Stanley R. Zirkin, 273–3739, fax 273–4244.
Deputy Assistant General Counsels: Daniel F. Collopy, 273–3745; Kenneth J. Shapiro, 273–3741.

NATIONAL MEDIATION BOARD

1301 K Street, NW., Suite 250 East, 20005, phone (202) 692–5000, fax 692–5080

Chairman.—Linda Puchala, 692–5016.
Board Members: Elizabeth Dougherty, 692–5022; Harry Hoglander, 692–5021.
Director, Office of:
Administration.—June D.W. King, 692–5010.
Chief of Staff.—Daniel Rainey, 692–5051.
Arbitration Services.—Roland Watkins, 692–5055.
Legal Affairs.—Mary L. Johnson, 692–5040.
Mediation Services.—Larry Gibbons, 692–5040.

NATIONAL RESEARCH COUNCIL—NATIONAL ACADEMY OF SCIENCES NATIONAL ACADEMY OF ENGINEERING—INSTITUTE OF MEDICINE

2101 Constitution Avenue, NW., 20418, phone (202) 334–2000

(Mailing address: 500 Fifth Street, NW., 20001)

The National Research Council, National Academy of Sciences, National Academy of Engineering, and Institute of Medicine, serves as an independent adviser to the Federal Government on scientific and technical questions of national importance. Although operating under a congressional charter granted the National Academy of Sciences in 1863, the National Research Council and its three parent organizations are private organizations, not agencies of the Federal Government, and receive no appropriations from Congress.

NATIONAL RESEARCH COUNCIL

Chairman.—Ralph Cicerone, President, National Academy of Sciences, 334–2100.
Vice Chairman.—Charles Vest, President, National Academy of Engineering, 334–3200.
Executive Officer.—Vacant.
Director, Office of Congressional and Government Affairs.—James E. Jensen, 334–1601.

NATIONAL ACADEMY OF SCIENCES

President.—Ralph Cicerone, 334–2100.
Vice President.—Barbara Schaal, Washington University, St. Louis.
Home Secretary.—Susan R. Wessler, University of California, Riverside.
Foreign Secretary.—M.T. Clegg, University of California, Irvine.
Treasurer.—Jeremiah P. Ostriker, Princeton University.
Executive Officer.—Vacant, 334–3000.

NATIONAL ACADEMY OF ENGINEERING

President.—Charles Vest, 334–3200.
Chairman.—Irwin M. Jacobs, Qualcomm, Inc.
Vice President.—Maxine Savitz (Ret.), Honeywell, Inc.
Home Secretary.—Thomas Budinger, Lawrence Berkeley National Laboratory.
Foreign Secretary.—Venkatesh Narayanamurti, Harvard University.
Executive Officer.—Lance Davis, 334–3677.
Treasurer.—C. Dan Mote, Jr., University of Maryland, Regents Professor and Glenn L. Martin Institute Professor of Engineering.

INSTITUTE OF MEDICINE

President.—Harvey V. Fineberg, M.D., 334–3300.
Executive Officer.—Judith A. Salerno, 334–2177.

NATIONAL SCIENCE FOUNDATION

4201 Wilson Boulevard, Suite 1245, Arlington, VA 22230

phone (703) 292–5111, http://www.nsf.gov

Director.—Subra Suresh, 292–8000.

Deputy Director.—Cora Marrett, 292–8001.
Inspector General.—Allison C. Lerner, 292–7100.
Equal Opportunity Programs.—Claudia Postell, 292–8020.
Director, Office of:
General Counsel.—Lawrence Rudolph, 292–8060.
Integrative Activities.—Clifford J. Gabriel (acting), 292–8040.
Legislative and Public Affairs.—Vacant, 292–8070.
Polar Programs.—Karl Erb, 292–8030.
Assistant Director for—
Biological Sciences.—Joann P. Roskoski (acting), 292–8400.
Computer and Information Science and Engineering.—Farnam Jahanian, 292–8900.
Education and Human Resources.—Joan Ferrini-Mundy, 292–8300.
Engineering.—Thomas W. Peterson, 292–8300.
Geosciences.—Tim Killeen, 292–8500.
Mathematical and Physical Sciences.—Edward Seidel, 292–8800.
Social, Behavorial, and Economic Sciences.—Myron Gutmann, 292–8700.
Director, Office of:
Budget, Finance, and Award Management.—Martha Rubenstein, 292–8200.
Information and Resource Management.—Amy Northcutt (acting), 292–8100.

NATIONAL SCIENCE BOARD

Chairman.—Steven C. Beering (703) 292–7000.
Vice Chairman.—Patricia D. Galloway.
Executive Officer.—Crai R. Robinson.

MEMBERS

Mark Abbott
Dan E. Arvizu
Camilla Benbow
Ray M. Bowen
John Bruer
France A. Cordova
Kelvin K. Droegemier
Patricia D. Galloway
Jose-Marie Griffiths
Esin Gulari
Louis J. Lanzerotti
Alan I. Leshner
G.P Peterson
Douglas D. Randall
Arthur K. Reilly
Annelia Sargent*
Diane L Souvaine
Arnold F. Stancell*
Claude M. Steele*
Robert J. Zimmer*

*consultants

NATIONAL TRANSPORTATION SAFETY BOARD

490 L'Enfant Plaza, SW., 20594, phone (202) 314–6000

Chairman.—Deborah A.P. Hersman, 314–6660.
Vice Chairman.—Christopher A. Hart, 314–6149.
Member.—Robert L. Sumwalt III, 314–6021.
Managing Director.—David Mayer (acting), 314–6318.
General Counsel.—David Tochen, 314–6616.
Chief Administrative Law Judge.—William W. Fowler, Jr., 314–6150.
Chief Financial Officer.—Steven Goldberg, 314–6212.
Director, Office of:
Aviation Safety.—Thomas Haueter, 314–6302.
Communications.—Sharon Bryson (acting), 314–6188.
Government Affairs.—Vacant.
Highway Safety.—Donald Karol, 314–6419.
Marine Safety.—Vacant.
Public Affairs.—Kelly Nantel, 314–6100.
Railroad, Pipeline and Hazardous Materials Investigations.—Stephen Klejst, 314–6098.
Research and Engineering.—Joseph Kolly, 314–6501.
Safety Advocacy.—Danielle Roeber, 314–6436.
Transportation Disaster Assistance.—Paul Sledzik, 314–6134.

NEIGHBORHOOD REINVESTMENT CORPORATION

(Doing business as NeighborWorks America)

1325 G Street, NW., Suite 800, 20005, phone (202) 220–2300, fax 376–2600

BOARD OF DIRECTORS

Chair.—Thomas J. Curry, Director, Federal Deposit Insurance Corporation.
Vice Chair.—Julie L. Williams, First Senior Deputy Comptroller and Chief Counsel, Office of the Comptroller of the Currency.
Members:
Hon. Raphael Bostic, U.S. Department of Housing and Urban Development.
Hon. Sarah Bloom Raskin, Member, Board of Governors, Federal Reserve System.
Hon. John E. Bowman (acting), Member, Director, Office of Thrift Supervision.
Hon. Christiane Gigi Hyland, Member, National Credit Union Administration.
Chief Executive Director.—Eileen Fitzgerald, 220–2452.
General Counsel / Secretary.—Jeffrey T. Bryson, 220–2372.
Chief Operating Officer.—Paul Kealey (acting), 220–2375.
Chief Financial Officer.—Michael Forster, 220–2374.
Director for—
Development and Communications.—Christine Poward (acting), 220–7076.
Field Operations.—Robert Burns, 220–2313.
Finance and Administration.—Michael Forster, 220–2374.
Internal Audit.—Frederick Udochi, 220–2409.
Public Policy and Legislative Affairs.—Steven J. Tuminaro, 220–2415.
Training.—John McCloskey (acting), 220–2398.

NUCLEAR REGULATORY COMMISSION

Washington, DC 20555–0001, phone (301) 415–7000, http//www.nrc.gov

[Authorized by 42 U.S.C. 5801 and U.S.C. 1201]

OFFICE OF THE CHAIRMAN

Chairman.—Gregory B. Jaczko, 415–1820.
Chief of Staff.—Josh Batkin, 415–1750.
Administrative Assistant.—Patti Pace, 415–1820.

COMMISSIONERS

Kristine L. Svinicki—415–1855.
Chief of Staff.—Jeffry Sharkey.
Administrative Assistant.—Janet L. Lepre.

William D. Magwood IV—415–8430.
Chief of Staff.—Patrice Bubar.
Administrative Assistant—Carrie Crawford.

George Apostolakis—415–1810.
Chief of Staff.—Belkys Sosa.
Administrative Assistant.—Kathleen Blake.

William C. Ostendorff—415–1759.
Chief of Staff.—Ho Nieh.
Administrative Assistant.—Linda S. Herr.

STAFF OFFICES OF THE COMMISSION

Secretary.—Annette L. Vietti-Cook, 415–1969, fax 415–1672.
Chief Financial Officer.—James E. Dyer, 415–7322, fax 415–4236.
Commission Appellate Adjudication.—Brooke D. Poole, 415–2653, fax 415–3200.
Congressional Affairs.—Rebecca L. Schmidt, 415–1776, fax 415–8571.
General Counsel.—Stephen G. Burns, 415–1743, fax 415–3086.
Inspector General.—Hubert T. Bell, 415–5930, fax 415–5091.
International Programs.—Margaret M. Doane, 415–1780, fax 415–2400.

Public Affairs.—Eliot B. Brenner, 415–8200, fax 415–2234.

ADVISORY COMMITTEE ON MEDICAL USES OF ISOTOPES

Chariman.—Said Abdel-Khalik.
Committee Coordinator.—Ashley Cockerham, (240) 888–7129.

ADVISORY COMMITTEE ON REACTOR SAFEGUARDS

Chairman.—Said Abdel-Khalik.
Executive Director.—Edwin M. Hackett, 415–7360, fax 415–5589.

ATOMIC SAFETY AND LICENSING BOARD PANEL

Chief Administrative Judge.—E. Roy Hawkens, 415–7454, fax 415–5599.

OFFICE OF THE EXECUTIVE DIRECTOR FOR OPERATIONS

Executive Director for Operations.—R. William Borchardt, 415–1700, fax 415–2700.
Deputy Executive Director for—
Corporate Management.—Darren Ash, 415–7443, fax 415–2700.
Materials, Waste, Research, State, Tribal and Compliance Programs.—Michael F. Weber, 415–1705, fax 415–2700.
Reactor and Preparedness Programs.—Martin J. Virgilio, 415–1713, fax 415–2700.
Director, Office of:
Administration.—Kathryn O. Greene, 492–3500, fax 492–5400.
Enforcement.—Roy Zimmerman, 415–2741, fax 415–3431.
Federal and State Materials and Environmental Management Programs.—Cynthia Carpenter (acting), 415–7197, fax 415–6680.
Human Resources.—Miriam L. Cohen, 492–2076, fax 492–2247.
Information Services.—Thomas M. Boyce, 415–8700, fax 415–4246.
Investigations.—Cheryl L. McCrary, 415–2373, fax 415–2370.
New Reactors.—Michael R. Johnson, 415–1897, fax 415–2700.
Nuclear Material Safety and Safeguards.—Catherine Haney, 492–3557, fax 492–3360.
Nuclear Reactor Regulation.—Eric J. Leeds, 415–1270, fax 415–8333.
Nuclear Regulatory Research.—Brian W. Sheron, 251–7400, fax 251–7426.
Nuclear Security and Incident Response.—James Wiggins, 415–8003, fax 415–6382.
Small Business and Civil Rights.—Corenthis B. Kelley, 415–7380, fax 415–5953.

REGIONAL OFFICES

Region I: Bill Dean, 475 Allendale Road, King of Prussia, PA 19406 (610) 337–5299, fax 337–5241.
Region II: Victor McCree, 61 Forsyth Street SE, Atlanta, GA 30303 (404) 562–4410, fax 562–4766.
Region III: Mark A. Satorius, 2443 Warrensville Road, Suite 210, Lisle, IL 60532 (630) 829–9657, fax 515–1096.
Region IV: Elmo E. Collins, Suite 400, 611 Ryan Plaza Drive, Arlington, TX 76011 (817) 860–8225, fax 860–8122.

OCCUPATIONAL SAFETY AND HEALTH REVIEW COMMISSION

1120 20th Street, NW., 20036–3457, phone (202) 606–5100

[Created by Public Law 91–596]

Chairman.—Thomasina V. Rogers, 606–5370.
Chief of Staff and Legal Counsel to the Chairman.—Richard L. Huberman, 606–5723.
Confidential Assistant to the Chairman (Public Affairs Officer).—Melik Ahmir-abdul.
Commissioner.—Cynthia L. Attwood,—606–5377.
Chief Counsel to the Commissioner.—Janice L. Glick, 606–5703.
Administrative Law Judges:
Patrick B. Augustine, U.S. Customs House, 721 19th Street, Room 407, Denver, CO 80202–2517.

Carol A. Baumerich, 1120 20th Street, NW., 9th Floor, Washington, DC 20036–3457.
G. Marvin Bober, 1120 20th Street, NW., 9th Floor, Washington, DC 20036–3457.
Sharon D. Calhoun, 100 Alabama Street, SW., Building 1924, Room 2R90, Atlanta, GA 30303–3104.
Sidney J. Goldstein, U.S. Customs House, 721 19th Street, Room 407, Denver, CO 80202–2517.
Dennis L. Phillips, 1120 20th Street, NW., 9th Floor, Washington, DC 20036–3457.
Covette Rooney, 1120 20th Street, NW., 9th Floor, Washington, DC 20036–3457.
James R. Rucker, Jr., U.S. Customs House, 721 19th Street, Room 407, Denver, CO 80202–2517.
John H. Schumacher, U.S. Customs House, 721 19th Street, Room 407, Denver, CO 80202–2517.
Stephen J. Simko, 100 Alabama Street, SW., Building 1924, Room 2R90, Atlanta, GA 30303–3104.
Ken S. Welsch, 100 Alabama Street, SW., Building 1924, Room 2R90, Atlanta, GA 30303–3104.

General Counsel.—Nadine N. Mancini.
Executive Secretary.—Ray H. Darling, Jr.
Executive Director.—Debra A. Hall (acting).

OFFICE OF GOVERNMENT ETHICS

1201 New York Avenue, NW., Suite 500, 20005, phone (202) 482–9300, fax 482–9238

[Created by Act of October 1, 1989; codified in 5 U.S.C. app., section 401]

Director.—Don W. Fox (acting).
Confidential Assistant.—Vacant.
General Counsel.—Don W. Fox.
Deputy General Counsel.—Walter M. Shaub, Jr.
Deputy Director for—
Administration and Information Management.—Barbara A. Mullen-Roth.
Agency Programs.—Joseph E. Gangloff.
International Assistant and Governance Initiatives.—Jane S. Ley.
Associate Director for—
Education Division.—Matthew S. Cross.
Information Resources Management (CIO).—James T. ''Ty'' Cooper.
Program Review Division.—Rashmi Bartlett.
Program Services Division.—Dale A. ''Chip'' Christopher.
Operations and Special Projects.—Patricia C. Zemple.

OFFICE OF PERSONNEL MANAGEMENT

Theodore Roosevelt Building, 1900 E Street, NW., 20415–0001

phone (202) 606–1800, http://www.opm.gov

OFFICE OF THE DIRECTOR

Director.—John Berry, 606–1000.
Executive Assistant.—Demetriss Williams.
Deputy Director.—Vacant.
Executive Assistant.—Vacant.
Senior Advisor.—Vacant.
Chief of Staff.—Elizabeth Montoya.
Deputy Chiefs of Staff: Justin Johnson, Jennifer I. Mason.
Senior Executive Assistant.—Blondell Darby-Boone.
Counselors to the Director: Vic Basile, Michael A. Grant.
Executive Assistant.—Torlanda Young.
Chief Operating Officer.—Chuck Grimes.
Executive Secretariat and Ombudsman, Director.—Richard B. Lowe.
Special Assistant to the Director.—Matthew W. Collier.
White House Fellow.—Vacant.
CHCO Executive Director.—Kathryn M. Medina.

CHIEF FINANCIAL OFFICER

Chief Financial Officer.—Stephen J. Agostini, 606–1918.
Deputy Chief Financial Officer.—Daniel K. Marella, 606–2638.
Executive Officer/Resource Management.—Katina P. Cotton, 606–4725.
OPM Initiatives Project Management.—Vacant.
Policy and Internal Control.—Robert T. Wurster, 606–1102.
Associate CFO, Budget and Performance.—Margaret Ponds, 606–1491.
Associate CFO, Financial Services.—Emily Dean, 606–6423.
Associate CFO, Financial Systems Management.—Rochelle S. Bayard, 606–4366.

COMMUNICATIONS AND PUBLIC LIAISON

Director.—Rosemary J. Williams, 606–2402.
Deputy Director.—Catherine Hand.
Press Secretary.—Sedelta Verble.
Director, External Communications.—Edmund D. Byrnes.
Web Presence.—Vivian Mackey.
Speechwriting and Editorial.—Harry J. Kruglik.
Administrative Assistant.—Jean A. Smith.

CONGRESSIONAL AND LEGISLATIVE AFFAIRS

Director.—Tania A. Shand, 606–1300.
Executive Assistant.—Julia F. Brown.
Deputy Director.—Thomas Richards.
Congressional and Operations Officer.—Donna G. Lease.
Congressional Relations Officers: Jill L. Crissman, Katie M. Pennell, N. Malik Walker.
Chief, Legislative Analysis.—Crystal D. Ford, 606–1424.
Legislative Analysts: Lena C. Chang, Steven J. Driscoll, Christopher M. Wallace.
Administrative Assistant.—Randle T. Logan.
Chief, Constituent Services, Capitol Hill.—Charlene E. Luskey, B332 Rayburn House Office Building, 225–4955, fax 225–4974.
Constituent Services Representative.—Carlos E. Tingle.
Administrative Assistant.—Kirk H. Brightman.

FEDERAL INVESTIGATIVE SERVICES

Associate Director.—Merton Miller (724) 794–5612.
Deputy Associate Director.—Vacant.
Executive Assistant.—Jody L. Montgomery.
Deputy Associate Directors:
Administrative Services.—Thomas L. Forman, 606–1042.
External Affairs.—M. Colleen Crowley, 606–1042.
Operations.—Mark P. Sherwin (acting), (724) 794–5612.
Technical Services.—Joy S. Fairtile, 606–1042.

MERIT SYSTEM AUDIT AND COMPLIANCE

Associate Director.—Jeffrey E. Sumberg, 606–2980.
Deputy Associate Director.—Ana Mazzi.
Director, CFC Operations.—Keith Willingham, 606–2564.
Operations Officer/Resource Management.—Judith A. Davis, 606–2327.

CHIEF INFORMATION OFFICER

Chief Information Officer.—Matthew E. Perry, 606–2150.
Deputy Chief Information Officer.—Chris G. Willey.
Executive Assistant.—Linda A. Vera.
Operations Technology Management.—Vacant.
Information Management.—Vacant.

HUMAN RESOURCES SOLUTIONS

Associate Director.—Nancy H. Kichak, 606–0900.
Deputy Associate Director.—Kathleen McGettigan.
Executive Assistant.—Makaela T. Bratcher.
Administrative Law Judge.—Juanita Howard Love, 606–3822.
Deputy Associate Directors:
Emerging Solutions/HR Innovations.—Reginald M. Brown, 606–1332.
Leadership and Talent Management Solutions.—Frank Esquivel, 606–1029.
HR Strategy and Evaluation Solutions.—Leslie Pollack, 606–1426.
HR Management Solutions.—Joseph J. Donald, 606–1105.
Leadership and HR Development Solutions.—Sydney Smith-Heimbrock, 606–2762.
Federal Executive Institute Director.—Joseph Kraemer (acting).
Management Development Center, East.—Charles W. Cranford (304) 870–8000.
Management Development Center, West.—Myhre ''Bud'' Paulson (303) 671–1010.

RETIREMENT SERVICES

Associate Director.—Kenneth Zawodny, Jr. (724) 794–2005.
Deputy Associate Directors.—Linda Bradford (acting), Nicholas Ashenden, 606–4168.
Deputy Associate Director for Retirement Operations.—Vacant.

OFFICE OF THE GENERAL COUNSEL

General Counsel.—Elaine Kaplan, 606–1700.
Deputy General Counsel.—Kathie Ann Whipple.
Senior Policy Counsel.—Robert H. Shriver.
Associate General Counsel (Compensation, Benefits, Products and Services).—R. Alan Miller.
Assistant General Counsel (Merit Systems and Accountability).—Steven E. Abow.
Chief, Administration (Administrative Officer).—Gloria V. Clark.

OFFICE OF THE INSPECTOR GENERAL

Inspector General.—Patrick E. McFarland, 606–1200.
Deputy Inspector General.—Norbert E. Vint.
Executive Assistant.—A. Paulette Berry.
Assistant Inspector General for Legal Affairs.—J. David Cope.
Counsel to the Inspector General.—Timothy C. Watkins, 606–2030.
Assistant Inspector General for Management.—Terri H. Fazio, 606–0846.
Deputy Assistant Inspector General for Management.—Jill S. Henderson, 606–4722.
Assistant Inspector General for Audits.—Michael R. Esser, 606–1200.
Deputy Assistant Inspector General for Audits.—Jeffrey E. Cole.
Chief, Community-Rated Audits Group.—Melissa D. Brown, 606–4714.
Assistant Inspector General for Investigations.—Michelle B. Schmitz, 606–1200.
Deputy Assistant Inspector General for Investigations/Field Operations.—Kimberly A. McKinley.

FACILITIES, SECURITY, AND CONTRACTING

Director.—Tina B. McGuire, 606–2200.
Deputy Director.—Dean Hunter, 606–3130.
Resource Management.—James S. Connors, 606–1047.
Small and Disadvantaged Business Utilization and Policy.—George W. Leininger, 606–1598.
Contracting.—W. Neal Patterson, 606–1984.
Facilities Management.—Mariano S. Aquino, 606–4590.
Publications Management.—Ray J. Theirault, 606–1822.
Security Services.—Richard S. Eligan, Jr., 606–1496.
Personnel Security.—Melinda M. Davis, (724) 794–7112.
Emergency Actions.—Sandra L. Hawthorne, 606–5068.

EQUAL EMPLOYMENT OPPORTUNITY

Director.—Lorna Lewis, 606–2460.

DIVERSITY AND INCLUSION

Director.—Veronica E. Villalobos, 606–1000.
Special Assistant.—Edgar Gonzales, 606–2984.

INTERNAL OVERSIGHT AND COMPLIANCE

Director.—Mark W. Lambert, 606–3207.
Deputy Director.—Janet L. Barnes.
Administrative Assistant.—Kimberlin C. Clark.

EXECUTIVE SECRETARIAT AND OMBUDSMAN

Director.—Richard B. Lowe, 606–1100.
Ombudsman.—Barbara Malebranche, 606–3132.
Resource Management.—Jozetta R. Robinson, 606–9166.
Administrative Officer.—Anne M. Schamel, 606–1000.
Correspondence.—Joann C. Rockwell.

HEALTHCARE AND INSURANCE

Director.—John O'Brien, 606–1000.
Deputy Director.—Daniel A. Green, 606–1051.
Resource Management.—Danny A. Cieslicki, 606–0067.
Assistant Director for Federal Employee Insurance Operations.—Shirley Patterson.
Assistant Director for National Healthcare Operations.—Susan V. McNally, 606–1234.

EMPLOYEE SERVICES

Associate Director and Chief Human Capital Officer.—Angela Bailey, 606–0388.
Principal Deputy Associate Director.—Joseph S. Kennedy, 606–1575.
Deputy Associate Directors:
Agency and Veterans Support.—Ray Decker, 606–5090.
Executive Resources and Employee Development.—Stephen T. Shih.
Pay and Leave.—Jerome D. Mikowicz, 606–2858.
Partnership and Labor Relations.—Tim F. Curry, 606–2584.
Recruitment and Hiring.—Andrea J. Bright, 606–8087.
Recruitment and USAJOBS.—Kim Bauhs, 606–1386.
Veterans Services.—Ray Decker (acting).
Program Assessment and Special Programs.—Patsy Stevens (acting), 606–1574.
Agency Support and Technical Assistance.—Maureen B. Higgins, 606–2855.
Human Resources Services.—Gordon J. Kato, 606–1255.
Work/Life/Wellness.—Marie C. L'Etoile, 606–4901.
Deputy Associate Director, OPM Human Resources and Deputy Chief Human Capital Officer.—Mark D. Reinhold, 606–2310.
Senior Advisor.—Janet T. Cope, 606–1402.

OFFICE OF THE SPECIAL COUNSEL

1730 M Street, NW., Suite 300, 20036–4505, phone (202) 254–2000

[Authorized by 5 U.S.C 1101 and 5 U.S.C 1211]

Special Counsel.—Carolyn Lerner.
Deputy Special Counsel.—Mark Cohen.
Policy and Congressional Affairs Division.—Adam Miles.
Senior Legal Counsel.—Jason Zuckerman.

THE PEACE CORPS

1111 20th Street, NW., 20526, phone (202) 692–2000

Phone (202) 692–2000, Toll-Free Number (800) 424–8580, http://www.peacecorps.gov

[Created by Public Law 97–113]

OFFICE OF THE DIRECTOR

phone (202) 962–2100, fax 692–2101

Director.—Aaron Williams.

Deputy Director.—Carrie Hessler-Radelet.
Chief of Staff/Chief of Operations.—W. Stacy Rhodes.
Senior Advisor to the Chief of Staff.—Kathy Rulon.
White House Liaison/Senior Advisor to the Director.—Elisa Montoya.
Senior Advisor to the Director.—Carl Sosebee.
Senior Advisor to the Deputy Director.—Maryann Minutillo.
Expert Consultant.—James Cuffe.
Administrative Officer.—Nina Basiliko.
American Diversity Program Manager.—Grace Ross.
Director, Office of:
Communications.—Allison Price.
Deputy Director of Communications.—Kristina Edmunson.
Congressional Relations.—Paul Weinberger.
Deputy Director of Congressional Relations.—Suzie Carroll.
Press Relations.—Janice Laurente.
Private Sector Initiatives.—Jennifer Chavez-Rubio.
General Counsel for Strategic Information, Research and Planning.—Bill Rubin.
AIDS Relief.—Buck Buckingham.
Regional Directors of:
Africa Operations.—Dick Day.
Europe, Mediterranean and Asia Operations.—Helen Lowman.
Inter-America and Pacific Operations.—Carlos Torres.
Chief Acquisitions and Contract Management.—Lisa Bilder.
Chief Financial Officer.—Joe Hepp.
Deputy Chief Financial Officer.—Charles Kemp.
Chief Information Officer.—Dorine Andrews.
Directors, Office of:
Accounting and Financial Reporting.—Richard Lubarski.
Accounts Receivable and Cash Management.—Alcindor Rosier.
Budget and Analysis Officer.—Samuel Taylor.
Global Accounts Payable.—Paul Shea.
Volunteer and PSC Financial Services.—Sandra Hahn.
Application Systems.—Terry Keyfauver.
IT Planning and Strategy/CISO.—El-Farouk Umar.
Operations and Infrastructure.—Steve Moore.
Inspector General.—Kathy Buller.
Management Associate.—Earl Yates.
Administrative Services Chief.—James Pimpedly.
Human Resource Management.—Pat Connelly.
Overseas Building Operations Manager.—Vacant.
Overseas Executive Selection and Support Manager.—Peter Loan.
Peace Corps Response.—Sarah Morgenthau.
Overseas Programming and Training Support.—Sonia Derenoncourt.
Field Assistance Support Division Chief.—Howard Anderson.
Knowledge Exchange and Professional Development Chief.—Scott Wilson.
Safety and Security Associate.—Ed Hobson.
Volunteer Recruitment and Selection Associate.—Rosie Mauk.
Chief of Operations.—Michael McKay.
Director of Recruitment.—Shari Hubert.
Director of Placement and Staging.—Andrej Kolaja.
Director of Office of Public Engagement.—David Medina.
University Programs, Office of:
Fellows/USA Program Manager.—Debra Timmons (acting).
Master's International Program Manager.—Eric Goldman.
Coverdell World Wise Schools.—Marjorie Anctil.
Operations, Office of:
Volunteer Support Associate.—Jules Delaune.
Volunteer Support Deputy Associate Director.—Brenda Goodman.
Medical Services.—Barry Simon.
Counseling and Outreach.—Tim Lawler.

REGIONAL OFFICES

Atlanta (FL, GA, TN, MS, AL, SC, PR): 60 Forsyth Street, Suite 3M40, Atlanta, GA 30303 (404) 562–3451, fax 562–3455.
Manager.—Kenton Ayers.
Public Affairs Specialist.—Vacant.

Boston (MA, VT, NH, RI, ME): Tip O'Neill Federal Building, 10 Causeway Street, Suite 450, Boston, MA 02222–1099 (617) 565–5555, fax 565–5539.
Manager.—Erin Mone.
Public Affairs Specialist.—Elizabeth Chamberlain.
Chicago (IL, IN, KY, MI, MO, OH, IA, MN, ND, SD, WI): 55 West Monroe Street, Suite 450, Chicago, IL 60603 (312) 353–4990, fax 353–4192.
Manager.—Kathryn O'Connor (acting).
Public Affairs Specialist.—Christine Torres.
Dallas (AR, LA, NM, OK, TX, CO, KS, NE, UT, WY): 1100 Commerce Street, Suite 427, Dallas, TX 75242 (214) 253–5400, fax 253–5401.
Manager.—Vacant.
Public Affairs Specialist.—LaShonda Walker.
Los Angeles (Southern CA, AZ): 2361 Rosecrans Avenue, Suite 155, El Segundo, CA 90245–0916 (310) 356–1100, fax 356–1125.
Manager.—Robert Robinson.
Public Affairs Specialist.—Kate Kuykendall.
New York (NY, NJ, CT, PA): 201 Varick Street, Suite 1025, New York, NY 10014 (212) 352–5440, fax 352–5442.
Manager.—Vincent Wickes.
Public Affairs Specialist.—Molly Jennings Levine.
San Francisco (Northern CA, NV, HI): 1301 Clay Street, Suite 620N, Oakland, CA 94612; (510) 452–8444, fax 452–8441.
Manager.—Janet Allen.
Public Affairs Specialist.—Nathan Sargent.
Seattle (WA, OR, ID, AK, MT): Westlake Building, 1601 5th Avenue, Suite 605, Seattle, WA 98101 (206) 553–5490, fax 553–2343.
Manager.—Erin Carlson.
Public Affairs Specialist.—Melanie Forthun.
Washington, DC (DC, MD, NC, WV, DE, VA): 1111 20th Street, NW., Washington, DC 20526 (202) 692–1040, fax 692–1041.
Manager.—Christopher Gilson.
Public Affairs Specialist.—Stephen Chapman.

PENSION BENEFIT GUARANTY CORPORATION

1200 K Street, 20005–4026, (202) 326–4000

BOARD OF DIRECTORS

Chairman.—Hilda L. Solis, Secretary of Labor.
Members:
Timothy F. Geithner, Secretary of the Treasury.
John Bryson (nominee), Secretary of Commerce.

OFFICIALS

Director.—Josh Gotbaum, 326–4010.
Deputy Director.—Vincent Snowbarger.
Chief Officer for—
Finance.—Patricia Kelly, 326–4060.
Information.—Richard Macy, 326–4000.
Insurance Program.—Michael Rae (acting), 326–4000.
Management.—Alice Maroni, 326–4000.
Department Director for—
Benefits Administration and Payment.—Bennie Hagans, 326–4050.
Budget and Organizational Performance.—Edgar Bennett, 326–4120.
Communications and Public Affairs.—Jioni Palmer, 326–4040.
Contracts and Controls Review.—Martin Boehm, 326–4161.
Facilities and Services.—Patricia Davis, 326–4150.
Financial Operations.—Theodore Winter, 326–4060.
General Counsel.—Judith Starr, 326–4020.
Human Resources.—Arrie Etheridge, 326–4110.
Information Technology Infrastructure Operations.—Deborah Herald, 326–4130.
Information Technology and Business Modernization.—Srividhya Shyamsunder, 326–4000.
Insurance Supervision and Compliance.—Robert Bacon (acting), 326–4070.
Legislative and Regulatory Affairs.—John Hanley, 326–4000.
Policy, Research and Analysis.—David Gustafson, 326–4080.

Procurement.—Arthur Block, 326–4160.
Chief Counsel.—Israel Goldowitz, 326–4020.
Inspector General.—Rebecca Batts, 326–4030.

POSTAL REGULATORY COMMISSION

901 New York Avenue, NW., Suite 200, 20268–0001
phone (202) 789–6800, fax 789–6886

Chairman.—Ruth Y. Goldway, 789–6810.
Vice Chairman.—Mark Acton, 789–6866.
Commissioners:
Tony Hammond, 789–6805.
Nanci Langley, 789–6887.
Chief Administrative Officer and Secretary.—Shoshana Grove, 789–6842.
Director, Public Affairs and Government Relations.—Ann Fisher, 789–6803.
General Counsel.—Stephen L. Sharfman, 789–6818.
Director, Office of Accountability and Compliance.—Margaret Cigno, 789–6855.

SECURITIES AND EXCHANGE COMMISSION

100 F Street, NE., 20549, phone (202) 551–7500
TTY Relay Service 1–800–877–8339 http://www.sec.gov

THE COMMISSION

Chairman.—Mary L. Schapiro, 551–2100, fax 772–9200.
Chief of Staff.—Didem A. Nisanci.
Deputy Chief of Staff.—James Burns.
Special Counsel.—Ricardo Delfin.
Senior Advisors to the Chairman: Stephen Devine, Jennifer McHugh.
Counsels: Timothy Hensler, Cristie Marsh, Matthew Strada, Erica Williams.
Commissioners:
Elisse Walter, 551–2800, fax 772–9340.
Counsels to the Commissioner: Christian Broadbent, Brian Murphy, Lesli Sheppard.
Luis A. Aguilar, 551–2500, fax 772–9335.
Counsels to the Commissioner: Michael Coe, Liban Jama, Marc Leaf, Smeeta Ramarathnam.
Troy A. Paredes, 551–2700, fax 772–9330.
Counsels to the Commissioner: Dawn Jessen, Gena Lai, Scott Kimpel, Saurabh Shah.

OFFICE OF THE SECRETARY

Secretary.—Elizabeth Murphy, 551–5400, fax 772–9324.
Deputy Secretary.—Kevin O'Neill, 551–5472; Lynn Powalski, 551–4927.
Assistant Secretary.—Jill Peterson, 551–5458.

OFFICE OF LEGISLATIVE AND INTERGOVERNMENTAL AFFAIRS

Director.—Eric J. Spitler, 551–2010, fax 772–9250.
Deputy Directors: Julie Z. Davis, Timothy Henseler.

OFFICE OF THE CHIEF OPERATING OFFICER

Chief Operating Officer.—Jeff Heslop, 551–2200.

OFFICE OF INVESTOR EDUCATION AND ADVOCACY

Director.—Lori J. Schock, 551–6500, fax 772–9295.
Deputy Director.—Mary S. Head, 551–6351.

OFFICE OF FOIA, RECORDS MANAGEMENT AND SECURITY

Director/Chief FOIA Officer.—Barry Walters, 551–8400.

FOIA and Privacy Act Officer.—M. Celia Winter, 551–8400, fax 772–9336.
FOIA/PA Branch Chiefs: David Henshall, 551–8316; Lizzette Katilius, 551–7910; John Livornese, 551–3831; Jeff Ovall, 551–6376.

OFFICE OF EQUAL EMPLOYMENT OPPORTUNITY

Director.—Alta Rodriguez, 551–6040, fax 772–9316.

OFFICE OF THE CHIEF ACCOUNTANT

Chief Accountant.—James Kroeker, 551–5300, fax 772–9253.
Deputy Chief Accountant:
Accounting.—Paul Beswick, 551–5364.
International.—Julie Erhardt, 551–5344.
Policy.—James "Mike" Starr, 551–5649.
Professional Practice.—Brian Croteau, 551–5880.
Senior Associate Chief Accountants: Edmund Bailey, 551–5339; Shelly Luisi, 551–5350; Jenifer Minke-Girard, 551–5351; John Offenbacher, 551–5329.
Chief Counsel.—Jeff Minton, 551–5342.

OFFICE OF COMPLIANCE INSPECTIONS AND EXAMINATIONS

Director.—Carlo V. di Florio, 551–6200, fax 772–9179.
Senior Counsel to the Director.—George Kramer.
Deputy Director.—Norman Champ.
Managing Executive Chief Operating Officer.—Robert Fishman, 551–6280.
Associate Director/Chief Counsel.—Vacant, 551–6460.
Associate Directors: Julius Leiman-Carbia (Broker/Dealer), (212) 336–0970, 551–6400; Dawn Patterson (Clearance and Settlement), (212) 336–0047; John Polise (Market Oversight), 551–4981; Vacant (Investment Adviser/Investment Company), 551–6300.
Assistant Directors: Marita Bartolini (Investment Adviser/Investment Company), 551–6378; Tina Barry (Self-Regulatory Organization), 551–6210; Mark Donohue (Self-Regulatory Organization), 551–6210; James Giles (Large Firm Monitoring), 551–5536; Richard Hannibal (Broker/Dealer), 551–6400; Rina Hussain (Self-Regulatory Organization), 5516219; Mavis Kelly (Investment Adviser/Investment Company), 551–6300; Abraham Losice (Credit Rating), 551–6422; Helene McGee (Self-Regulatory Organization), 551–6270; Suzanne McGovern (Broker/Dealer), 551–6459.

DIVISION OF RISK, STRATEGY, AND FINANCIAL INNOVATION

Director and Chief Economist.—Craig Lewis, 551–6646, fax 756–0505.
Deputy Director.—Kathleen Hanley, 551–6255.
Associate Managing Director.—Paul Knight, 551–3334.
Head of Policy and Development.—Richard Bookstaber, 551–3539.
Co-Chief Counsels: Adam Glass, 551–3551; Bruce Kraus, 551–3522.
Assistant Director Office of:
Buy-Side.—Harvey Westbrook, 551–6609.
Disclosure and Governance.—Scott Bauguess (acting), 551–6660.
Litigation Support.—Chyhe Becker, 551–6654.
Markets.—Amy Edwards, 551–6663.
Sell-Side.—Jennifer Marietta-Westberg, 551–6659.
Associate Director, Office of Data and Data Analytics.—David Blaszkowsky (acting), 551–5359.
Inactive Data.—Vacant.

OFFICE OF THE GENERAL COUNSEL

General Counsel.—Mark D. Cahn, 551–5100, fax 772–9260.
Deputy General Counsels: Meridith Mitchell, 551–5184; Anne Small, 551–5100.
Ethics Counsel.—Shira Minton, 551–5170.
Associate General Counsel for Litigation and Adjudication.—Joan Loizeaux, 551–5169.
Assistant General Counsels for Adjudication: Kermit Kennedy, 551–5164; Joan McCarthy, 551–5150; David Tess, 551–5025.
Solicitor, Appellate Litigation and Bankruptcy.—Jacob Stillman, 551–5130.

Deputy Solicitor.—Michael Conley, 551–5127.
Special Counsel to the Solicitor.—Allan Capute, 551–5122.
Assistant General Counsels for Appellate Litigation and Bankruptcy: John Avery, 551–5107; Mark Pennington, 551–5189; Randall Quinn, 551–5198.
Associate General Counsel for Legal Policy 1.—Vacant.
Associate General Counsel for Legal Policy 2.—Richard Levine, 551–5168.
Assistant General Counsels for Legal Policy: David Frederickson, 551–5144; Laura Jarsulic, 551–4873; Paula Jenson, 551–5554; Lori Price, 551–5184.
Assistant General Counsel for Legislation and Financial Services.—Stephen Jung, 551–5162.
Associate General Counsel for Litigation and Administrative Practice.—Richard M. Humes, 551–5140.
Assistant General Counsels for Litigation and Administrative Practice: George Brown, 551–5121; Samuel Forstein, 551–5139; Melinda Hardy, 551–5149; Thomas Karr, 551–5163.

DIVISION OF INVESTMENT MANAGEMENT

Director.—Eileen Rominger, 551–6720, fax 772–9288.
Deputy Director.—Robert Plaze, 551–6780.
Senior Advisor to the Director.—Vacant, 551–6720.
Associate Director, Chief Counsel.—Douglas J. Scheidt, 551–6701.
Assistant Chief Counsels: David W. Grim (International Issues), 551–6825; Nadya B. Roytblat (Financial Institutions), 551–6825.
Enforcement Liaison.—Barbara Chretien-Dar, 551–6785.
Associate Director, Office of:
Disclosure and Insurance Product Regulation.—Susan Nash, 551–6742.
Exemptive Applications and Special Projects.—Elizabeth G. Osterman, 551–6746.
Legal and Disclosure.—Barry D. Miller, 551–6725.
Regulatory Policy and Investment Adviser Regulation.—Vacant.
Assistant Director, Office of:
Disclosure and Review No. 1.—Brent J. Fields, 551–6921.
Disclosure and Review No. 2.—Frank J. Donaty, 551–6925.
Disclosure Regulation.—Mark T. Uyeda, 551–6784.
Enforcement Liaison.—Barbara Chretien-Dar, 551–6785.
Financial Analysis.—Paul B. Goldman, 551–6715.
Insurance Products.—William J. Kotapish, 551–6795.
Investment Adviser Regulation.—Daniel Kahl, 551–6730.
Investment Company Regulation No. 1.—Janet M. Grossnickle, 551–6821.
Investment Company Regulation No. 2.—Vacant.
Regulatory Policy: C. Hunter Jones, Penelope W. Saltzman, 551–6792.
Chief Accountant, Office of Chief Accountant.—Jaime Eichen, 551–6918.

DIVISION OF CORPORATION FINANCE

Director.—Meredith Cross, 551–3100, fax 772–9215.
Deputy Director of:
Disclosure Operations.—Shelley E. Parratt, 551–3130.
Legal and Regulatory.—Lona Nallengara, 551–3120.
Policy and Capital Markets.—Paula Dubberly, 551–3180.
Associate Director, Regulatory Policy.—Mauri L. Osheroff, 551–3190.
Chief Accountant.—Vacant, 551–3400.
Disclosure Operations: Paul Belvin, 551–3150; James Daly, 551–3140; Karen Garnett, 551–3780; Mark Kronforst, 551–3870; Barry Summer, 551–3160.
Chief Counsel.—Thomas Kim, 551–3520.
Chief, Office of:
CF Information Technology.—Cecile Peters, 551–3610.
Disclosure Support.—Patti Dennis, 551–3610.
Enforcement Liaison.—Mary Kosterlitz, 551–3420.
International Corporate Finance.—Paul Dudek, 551–3450.
Mergers and Acquisitions.—Michele Anderson, 551–3440.
Rulemaking.—Felicia Kung, 551–3430.
Small Business Policy.—Gerald Laporte, 551–3460.
Assistant Directors: Suzanne Hayes, 551–3675; Barbara Jacobs, 551–3730; Pamela Long, 551–3760; Mike McTiernan, 551–3780; Amanda Ravitz, 551–3412; Jeffrey Reidler, 551–3710; John Reynolds, 551–3790; Todd Schiffman, 551–3770; H. Roger Schwall, 551–3740; Larry Spirgel, 551–3810; Max Webb, 551–3750.

DIVISION OF ENFORCEMENT

Director.—Robert Khuzami, 551–4500, fax 772–9279.
Senior Counsel to Director, Margaret McGuire.—Suzanne Ashley.
Counsel to the Director, Stephen Jones.—Sarit Klein.
Deputy Director.—Lorin Reisner, 551–4787.
Managing Executive.—Adam Storch, 551–4625.
Associate Directors: Gerald Hodgkins, 551–4719; Thomas Sporkin, 551–4892.
Assistant Directors: Conway Dodge, 551–4748; Gregory Faragasso, 551–4734; Douglas McAllister, 551–4939; Moira Roberts, 551–4714; Andrew Sporkin, 551–4940; Jeffrey Weiss, 551–4825.
Associate Director.—Vacant.
Assistant Directors: Charles Cain, 551–4911; Tracy Price, 551–4490.
Associate Director.—Stephen Cohen, 551–4834.
Assistant Directors: James Lee Buck, 551–4598; Timothy England, 551–4959; Josh Felker, 551–4960; Jennifer Leete, 551–4971; Melissa Robertson, 551–4926; Rami Sibay, 551–4815; Ivonia Slade, 551–4771; David Wiederkehr, 551–4628.
Associate Director.—Scott Friestad, 551–4962.
Assistant Directors: Nina Finston, 551–4961; David Frohlich, 551–4963; Laura Josephs, 551–5117; Linda Moran, 551–4975; Brian Quinn, 551–4982; Julie Riewe, 551–4546; Scott Weisman, 551–4763.
Chief, Market Surveillance.—Mark Lineberry, 551–4549.
Associate Director.—Antonia Chion, 551–4842.
Assistant Directors: Kara Brockmeyer, 551–4829; Robert Cohen, 551–4869; Lisa Deitch, 551–4999; Alec Koch, 551–4762; Deborah Tarasevich, 551–4726; Yuri Zelinsky, 551–4769.
Associate Directors: Robert Kaplan, 551–4969; Kenneth Lench, 551–4938; Reid Muoio, 551–4488.
Chief Counsel.—Joseph Brenner, 551–4933.
Assistant Chief Counsels: Charlotte L. Buford, Samuel Waldon, 551–4843.
Chief Litigation Counsel.—Matthew Martens, 551–4481.
Deputy Chief Litigation Counsel.—Vacant.
Chief Accountant.—Howard Scheck.
Deputy Chief Accountant.—Jason Flemmons.
Associate Chief Accountants: Regina M. Barrett, 551–4615; Dwayne Brown, 551–4616; David M. Estabrook, 551–4621; Pierron Leef, 551–4620.
Office of Collections: Gordon Brumback, 551–4424; Marsha Massey, 551–4452.
Distributions.—Jennifer Matheison, 551–4541.
Office of Whistleblower, Chief.—Sean McKessey, 551–4786.

DIVISION OF TRADING AND MARKETS

Director.—Robert Cook, 551–5500, fax 772–9273.
Deputy Directors: John Ramsay, Vacant, 551–5733.
Associate Director, Chief Counsel.—David Blass, 551–5165.
Assistant Chief Counsels: Joe Furey, 551–5760; Lourdes Gonzalez, 551–5580.
Associate Directors:
Broker Dealer Finances.—Michael Macchiaroli, 551–5525.
Clearance and Settlement.—Peter Curley, 551–5696.
Trading Practices.—Brian Bussey, 551–5571.
Market Supervision: Heather Seidel, 551–5608; David Shillman, 551–5685.
Assistant Directors (Market Supervision): Victoria Crane, 551–5744; Katherine England, 551–5611; Michael Gaw, 551–5602; Richard Holley, 551–5614; David Hsu, 551–5664; Kelly Riley, 551–5661; John Roeser, 551–5631; Nancy Sanow, 551–5621.
Assistant Directors:
Broker Dealer Risk Management Practices.—Ray Doherty (212) 336–0445.
Clearance and Settlement (Equities and Fixed Income).—Jerry Carpenter, 551–5710.
Clearance and Settlement (International and Derivatives).—Jeff Mooney, 551–5712.
Clearing Agency Monitoring.—Marta Chaffee, 551–5661.
Enforcement Liaison and Institutional Trading.—Jo Anne Swindler, 551–5750.
Financial Responsibility.—Randall Roy, 551–5522.
Market Operations.—Herb Brooks, 551–5670.
Market Watch.—Alton Harvey, 551–5691.
Trading Practices.—Josephine Tao, 551–5799.

OFFICE OF ADMINISTRATIVE LAW JUDGES

Chief Administrative Law Judge.—Brenda Murray, 551–6030, fax 777–1031.
Administrative Law Judges: Cameron Elliot, Carol Fox Foelak, Robert Mahony.

OFFICE OF INTERNATIONAL AFFAIRS

Director.—Ethiopis Tafara, 551–6690, fax 772–9280.
Deputy Director.—Elizabeth Jacobs, 551–6676.
Assistant Directors: Alberto Arevalo, 551–6697; Sherman Boone, 551–6686; Robert Fisher, 551–6652; Robert Peterson, 551–6696.

OFFICE OF THE INSPECTOR GENERAL

Inspector General.—David Kotz, 551–6060, fax 772–9265.
Deputy Inspector General.—Noelle Frangipane, 551–6035.

OFFICE OF PUBLIC AFFAIRS

Director.—John Nester, 551–4120, fax 777–1026.
Deputy Director.—Florence Harmon, 551–5604.

OFFICE OF FINANCIAL MANAGEMENT

Chief Financial Officer.—Kenneth Johnson, 551–7840, fax 756–0473.
Chief Accounting Officer.—Caryn Kauffman, 551–8834.
Assistant Director for Finance and Accounting.—Zayra Okrak, 551–7856.
Assistant Director for Planning and Budget.—Diane Galvin, 551–7853.

OFFICE OF INFORMATION TECHNOLOGY

Director/Chief Information Officer.—Thomas A. Bayer, 551–8800, fax (703) 914–2621.

OFFICE OF ADMINISTRATIVE SERVICES

Associate Executive Director.—Jayne Seidman (acting), 551–7400, fax (703) 914–4459.
Assistant Directors:
Acquisition Services.—Juliana Basile, 551–8699.
Real Property and Facilities Support.—John Branch, 551–8344.
Security and Publishing.—Beth Blackwood, 551–7408.

OFFICE OF HUMAN RESOURCES

Associate Executive Director.—Cristin Fair (acting), 551–7500, fax 777–1028.
Assistant Directors: Timothy Buckley (Center for Strategy, Policy and Learning), 551–7902; Teri Ellison (Center for Talent Management and Employee Programs), 551–4105.

REGIONAL OFFICES

Atlanta Regional Office: 3475 Lenox Road, NE., Suite 1000, Atlanta, GA 30326 (404) 842–7600, fax (404) 842–7633.
Regional Director.—Rhea Kemble Dignam, 842–7610.
Associate Regional Director.—William P. Hicks, 842–7675.
Assistant Regional Directors, Enforcement: Peter Diskin, 842–7631; Stephen Donahue, 842–7618; Aaron Lipson, 842–7694; Matt McNamara, 842–7688.
Associate Director, Examinations.—Askari J. Foy, 842–7623.
Assistant Regional Director, Broker/Dealer Examinations.—Howard Dennis, 842–7643.
Associate Regional Directors, Investment Company/Investment Adviser Examinations: Herbert Campbell, 842–7677; Askari Foy, 842–7623.
Regional Trail Counsel.—Madison Loomis, 842–7622.
Boston Regional Office: 33 Arch Street, 23rd Floor, Boston, MA 02110 (617) 573–8900, fax (617) 573–4590.
Regional Director.—David Bergers, 573–8927.

Associate District Director, Enforcement.—John Dugan, 573–8936.

Assistant District Director, Enforcement: Sandra Bailey, 573–8976; Lee Ann Gaunt, 573–8945; Philip Koski, 573–8964.

Supervisory Regional Trial Counsel.—Martin Healey, 573–8952.

Associate Regional Director, Examinations.—Lucile Corkery, 573–8932.

Assistant District Administrators, Investment Adviser/Investment Company Examinations: Andrew Caverly, (Broker/Dealer), 573–8922; Michael Garrity (Investment Adviser/Investment Company), 573–8944; Joseph Mick (Investment Adviser/Investment Company), 573–8975; Elizabeth Salini, 573–8931.

Chicago Regional Office: 175 West Jackson Boulevard, Suite 900, Chicago, IL 60604 (312) 353–7390, fax 353–7398.

Regional Director.—Merri Jo Gillette, 353–9338.

Senior Associate Regional Director, Enforcement.—Robert J. Burson, 353–7428.

Associate Regional Director, Enforcement.—Timothy L. Warren, 353–7394.

Associate Regional Directors, Examinations: Jane E. Jarcho, 353–5479; Barbara S. Lorenzen, 353–7436.

Assistant Regional Directors, Enforcement: Peter Chan, 353–7410; James A. Davidson, 353–5712; Scott J. Hlavacek, 353–1679; Barry Isenman, 886–8515; Charles J. Kerstetter, 353–7435; Steven L. Klawans, 886–1738; Anne C. McKinley, 886–1588; Paul A. Montoya, 353–7429; Kathryn A. Pyszka, 353–7416; John J. Sikora, 353–7418; Thomas E. Vincus, 353–7216.

Assistant Regional Directors, Examinations: Doug R. Adams, 353–7402; George Buhai-Jacobus, 886–8507; Maureen Dempsey, 886–1496; Peter B. Driscoll, 886–1715; Lewis A. Garcia, 353–6888; Daniel R. Gregus, 353–7423; Thomas N. Kirk, 886–3956; David J. Mueller, 353–7404; Thomas Murphy, 886–8513; Larry P. Perdue, 353–7219.

Denver Regional Office: 1801 California Street, Suite 1500, Denver, CO 80202 (303) 844–1000, fax (303) 844–1010.

Regional Director.—Donald M. Hoerl, 844–1060.

Associate Regional Director.—Julie K. Lutz, 844–1056.

Assistant Regional Directors, Enforcement: Mary S. Brady, 844–1023; Kurt L. Gottschall, 844–1119; Ian S. Karpel, 844–1017; Laura Metcalfe, 844–1092; James A. Scoggins, 844–1105.

Supervisory Trial Counsel.—Thomas J. Krysa, 844–1118.

Associate Regional Director, Office of the Regulator.—Kevin Goodman, 844–1040.

Assistant Regional Director, Broker/Dealer and Transfer Agent Examinations.—Denise S. Saxon, 844–1061.

Assistant Regional Director, Investment Adviser and Company Examinations.—Thomas Piccone, 844–1016.

Fort Worth Regional Office: 801 Cherry Street, Unit #18, Fort Worth, TX 76102 (817) 978–3821, fax 978–2700.

Regional Director.—David Woodcock (300) 844–1060.

Associate Regional Director, Enforcement.—Stephen Korotash, 978–6490.

Regional Trial Counsel.—Toby Galloway, 978–6447.

Assistant Regional Directors, Enforcement: Kevin Edmundson, 978–1411; Barbara L. Gunn, 978–6467; Michael D. King, 978–1405; David Peavler, 978–6459; Jonathan P. Scott, 978–0581; Stephen Webster, 978–6459; Eric R. Werner, 978–2654.

Associate Regional Director, Examinations.—Kimberly Garber, 900–2622.

Assistant Regional Director, Broker/Dealer Examinations.—Donna Esau, 900–2612.

Assistant Regional Directors, Investment Company/Investment Adviser Examinations: David Taylor, 978–1414; Mary Walters, 978–6487.

Assistant Regional Director, Investor Services.—Julie A. Preuitt, 978–6428.

Los Angeles Regional Office: 5670 Wilshire Boulevard, 11th Floor, Los Angeles, CA 90036 (323) 965–3998, fax 965–3816.

Regional Director.—Rosalind R. Tyson, 965–3893.

Associate Regional Directors, Enforcement: John McCoy III, 965–3864; Michele Wein Layne, 965–3850.

Senior Regional Trial Counsel, Enforcement.—Kelly C. Bowers, 965–3924.

Assistant Regional Directors, Enforcement: Marc Blau, 965–3975; Kelly C. Bowers, 965–3924; Lorraine Echavarria, 695–3914; Finola Halloran Manvelian, 965–3980; Victoria A. Levin, 965–3872; Alka Patel, 965–2627; Marshall Sprung, 965–3320; Diana Tani, 965–3991.

Associate Regional Director, Regulation.—Martin J. Murphy, 965–3859.

Assistant Regional Directors, Investment Company/Investment Adviser Examinations: Charles T. Liao, 965–2688; Thomas J. Mackin, 965–3940.

Assistant Regional Directors, Broker/Dealer Examinations: Karol L.K. Pollock, 965–3861; Cindy S. Wong, 965–3927.

Miami Regional Office: 801 Brickell Avenue, Suite 1800, Miami, FL 33131 (305) 982–6300, fax (305) 536–4120.

Regional Director.—Eric Bustillo, 982–6332.

Associate Regional Directors:

Enforcement.—Glenn S. Gordon, 536–6360.

Examination.—John C. Mattimore, 982–6357.

Assistant Regional Directors:

Enforcement: Eric R. Busto, 982–6362; Chedly C. Dumomay, 982–6377; Thierry O. Desmet, 982–6374; Chad A. Earnst, 982–6355; Elisha L. Frank, 982–6392; Teresa Verges, 982–6384.

Examination: Faye A. Chin, 982–6305; Nicholas A. Monaco, 982–6310.

New York Regional Office: 3 World Financial Center, Suite 400, New York, NY 10281–1022, (212) 336–1100, fax (212) 336–1323.

Regional Director.—George S. Canellos, 336–1020.

Associate Regional Directors, Enforcement: Robert B. Blackburn, 336–1050; Andrew Calamari, 336–0042; David Rosenfeld, 336–0153; Sanjay Wadhwa, 336–0181.

Assistant Regional Directors, Enforcement: Alistaire Bambach, 336–0027; Celeste Chase, 336–0049; Alison Conn, 336–0052; Amelia Cottrell, 336–1056; Robert DeLeonardis (Investigations), 336–0056; Joseph Dever, Jr.; 336–0058; Gerald Gross, 336–0085; Ken Joseph, 336–0097; Bruce Karpati, 336–0104; Leslie Kazon, 336–0107; Robert Keyes, 336–0109; Maureen Lewis, 336–0125; James McGovern, 336–0134; David Markowitz, 336–0128; Michael Osnato, 336–0156; Michael Paley, 336–0145; Stephanie Shuler, 336–0166; George Stepaniuk, 336–0173; Steven Rawlings, 336–0149; Alex Vasilescu, 336–0178; Scott York, 336–0188.

Associate Regional Director, Investment Adviser/Investment Company Examinations.—James A. Capezzuto, 336–0590.

Assistant Regional Directors: Dawn Blankenship, 336–0197; William Delmage, 336–0495; Joseph Di Maria, 336–0497; Dorothy Eschwie, 336–0502; Anthony P. Fiduccia, 336–0505.

Associate Regional Directors, Broker/Dealer: Richard D. Lee, 336–1010; Robert A. Sollazzo, 336–1070.

Assistant Regional Directors, Broker/Dealer Examinations: Richard A. Heapy, 336–0464; Linda Lettieri, 336–0474; John M. Nee, 336–0484; Rosanne R. Smith, 336–0928; Steven Vitulano, 336–0936.

Philadelphia Regional Office: Mellon Independence Center, 701 Market Street, Suite 2000, Philadelphia, PA 19106 (215) 597–3100, fax 597–3194.

Regional Director.—Daniel Hawke, 597–3191.

Associate Regional Director, Regulation.—Joy G. Thompson, 597–6135.

Associate Regional Directors, Enforcement.—Elaine C. Greenberg, 597–3107.

Salt Lake Regional Office: 15 West South Temple Street, Suite 1800, Salt Lake City, UT 84101 (801) 524–5796, fax 524–3558.

Regional Director.—Kenneth D. Israel, 524–6745.

San Francisco Regional Office: 44 Montgomery Street, Suite 2600, San Francisco, CA 94104 (415) 705–2500, fax 705–2501.

Regional Director.—Marc J. Fagel, 705–2449.

Associate Regional Director.—Michael S. Dicke, 705–2458.

Assistant Regional Directors, Enforcement: Jina L. Choi, 705–2372; Tracy Davis, 705–2318; Robert S. Leach, 705–2353; Cary Robnett, 705–2335.

Associate Regional Director, Regulation.—Vacant.

Assistant Regional Directors: Carla Carriveau (Broker/Dealer), 705–2482; Edward Haddad (Investment Adviser/Investment Company), 705–2344; Matthew O'Toole (Investment Adviser/Investment Company), 705–2477.

SELECTIVE SERVICE SYSTEM

1515 Wilson Boulevard, 5th Floor, Arlington, VA 22209–2425

phone (703) 605–4100, fax 605–4106, http://www.sss.gov

Director.—Lawrence G. Romo, 605–4010.

Inspector General.—Carlo Verdino, 605–4022.

Director for—

Operations.—Mariano Campos, 605–4110.

Resource Management.—Vacant, 605–4032.

Public and Intergovernmental Affairs.—Richard S. Flahavan, 605–4017, fax 605–4106.

Financial Management.—Carlo Verdino, 605–4022.

Registration Information Office, P.O. Box 94638, Palatine, IL 60094–4638, phone (847) 688–6888, fax (847) 688–2860.

SMALL BUSINESS ADMINISTRATION

409 Third Street, SW., 20416

phone (202) 205–6600, fax 205–7064, http://www.sbaonline.sba.gov

Administrator.—Karen Mills, 205–6605.
Deputy Administrator.—Marie Johns, 205–6605.
Chief of Staff (A).—Jonathan Swain, 205–6605
Director of Executive Secretariat.—Kim Bradley, 205–6608.
General Counsel.—Sara Lipscomb, 205–6642.
Chief Counsel for Advocacy.—Winslow Sargeant, 205–6533.
Inspector General.—Peg Gustafson, 205–6580.
Chief Financial Officer.—Jonathan Carver, 205–6449.
Associate Administrator for—
Disaster Assistant.—James Rivera, 205–6734.
Field Operations.—Robert Hill, 205–6808.
Assistant Administrator for—
Communications and Public Liason.—Fred Baldassaro, 205–6740.
Associate Administrator for—
Congressional and Legislative Affairs.—Jordan Haas, 205–6700.
Equal Employment Opportunity and Civil Rights Compliance.—Vacant, 205–6750.
Hearings and Appeals.—Delorice Ford, 205–7340.
Associate Administrator for Management and Administration.—Vacant, 205–6610.
Chief Information Officer.—Paul Christy, 205–6706.
Chief, Human Capital Management.—Kevin Mahoney, 205–6784.
Associate Administrator for Capital Access.—Sean J. Greene, 205–2227.
Associate Administrator for Business and Community Initiatives.—Ellen Thrasher, 205–6665.
Director, Financial Assistance.—Grady Hedgespeth, 205–6490.
Director, Investment.—Tom Morris, 205–6510.
Technology.—Edsel Brown, 205–6450.
Director (A), Credit Risk Management.—Eugene Stewman, 205–3049.
Associate Administrator for Small Business Development Centers.—Vacant, 205–6766.
Director, Surety Guarantees.—Frank Lalumiere, 205–6540.
Associate Administrator for International Trade.—Dario Gomez, 205–6720.
Assistant Administrator for Veterans' Affairs.—William Elmore, 205–6773.
Assistant Administrator (A), Women's Business Ownership.—Ana Harvey, 205–6673.
Associate Administrator for Government Contracting and Business Development.—Joe Jordan, 205–6459.
Assistant Administrator for——
Business Development.—Darryl Hairston, 205–5852.
Government Contracting (A).—John Klein, 205–6460.
Size Standard.—Khem Sharma, 205–6618.

SMITHSONIAN INSTITUTION

Smithsonian Institution Building—The Castle (SIB), 1000 Jefferson Drive, SW., 20560

phone (202) 633–1000, http://www.smithsonian.org

The Smithsonian Institution is an independent trust instrumentality created in accordance with the terms of the will of James Smithson of England who in 1826 bequeathed his property to the United States of America "to found at Washington under the name of the Smithsonian Institution an establishment for the increase and diffusion of knowledge among men." Congress pledged the faith of the United States to carry out the trust in 1836 (Act of July 1, 1836, C. 252, 5 Stat. 64), and established the Institution in its present form in 1846 (August 10, 1846, C. 178, 9 Stat. 102), entrusting the management of the institution to its independent Board of Regents.

THE BOARD OF REGENTS

ex officio

Chief Justice of the United States.—John G. Roberts, Jr., Chancellor.
Vice President of the United States.—Joseph R. Biden, Jr.

Appointed by the President of the Senate
Hon. Thad Cochran
Hon. Jack Reed
Hon. Patrick J. Leahy

Appointed by the Speaker of the House
Hon. Sam Johnson
Hon. Steven C. LaTourette
Hon. Xavier Becerra

Appointed by Joint Resolution of Congress

France Córdova
Shirley Ann Jackson
Robert Kogod
David Rubenstein
Dr. Patty Stonesifer
Alan G. Spoon
Roger Sant
John McCarter
Steve Case

Chief of Staff to the Regents.—John K. Lapiana, 633–5230.

OFFICE OF THE SECRETARY

Secretary.—G. Wayne Clough, 633–1846.
Chief of Staff.—Patricia Bartlett, 633–1869.
Inspector General.—Sprightley Ryan, 633–7050.
General Counsel.—Judith Leonard, 633–5099.
Director of:
Communications and Public Affairs.—Evelyn Lieberman, 633–5190.
External Affairs.—Virginia Clark, 633–5021.
Government Relations.—Nell Payne, 633–5125.
Policy and Analysis.—Carole M.P. Neves, 633–5585.

OFFICE OF THE UNDER SECRETARY FOR FINANCE AND ADMINISTRATION

Under Secretary.—Alison McNally, 633–5240.
Director of:
Accessibility Program.—Elizabeth Ziebarth, 633–2946.
Exhibits, The Arts and Industries Building and the International Gallery.—Ellen Dorn, 633–7421.
Special Events and Protocol.—Karen Keller, 633–2020.
Director, Office of:
Equal Employment and Minority Affairs.—Era Marshall, 633–6414.
Exhibits Central.—Vacant, 633–4514.
Facilities Engineering and Operations.—Bruce Kendall, 633–1873.
Human Resources.—James Douglas, 633–6301.
Chief, Office of:
Finance.—Vacant, 633–7120.
Information Technology.—Vacant, 633–1688.
Ombudsman.—Chandra Heilman, 633–2010.

OFFICE OF THE UNDER SECRETARY FOR HISTORY, ART, AND CULTURE

Under Secretary.—Dr. Richard Kurin, 633–5240.
Assistant Secretary for Education and Access.—Claudine Brown, 633–0077.
Director of:
Anacostia Community Museum.—Camille Akeju, 633–4839.
Archives of American Art.—Vacant, 275–1874.
Asian Pacific American Program.—Conrad Ng, 786–2963.
Center for Folklife and Cultural Heritage.—Dan Sheehy, 633–6440.
Cooper Hewitt, National Design Museum.—Bill Moggridge, (212) 849–8370.
Freer and Sackler Galleries.—Julian Raby, 633–0456.
Hirshhorn Museum and Sculpture Garden.—Richard Koshalek, 633–2824.
National Museum of African American History and Culture.—Lonnie Bunch, 633–4751.
National Museum of African Art.—Dr. Johnnetta Cole, 633–4610.
National Museum of American History.—Marc Pachter (Interim), 633–3435.
National Museum of the American Indian.—Kevin Gover, 633–6700.
National Portrait Gallery.—Martin Sullivan, 275–1740.
National Postal Museum.—Allen Kane, 633–5500.
Smithsonian Affiliations Program.—Harold Closter, 633–5321.
Smithsonian American Art Museum.—Elizabeth Broun, 275–1515.
Smithsonian Associates Program.—Barbara Tuceling, 633–8880.

Smithsonian Center for Education and Museum Studies.—Stephanie L. Norby, 633–5297.
Smithsonian Latino Center.—Eduardo Diaz, 633–1240.
Smithsonian Institution Archives.—Anne Van Camp, 633–5908.
Smithsonian Institution Libraries.—Nancy Gwinn, 633–2240.
Smithsonian Institution Traveling Exhibition Service.—Anna Cohn, 633–3136.
Smithsonian Photography Initiative.—Merry Foresta, 633–2928.

OFFICE OF THE UNDER SECRETARY FOR SCIENCE

Under Secretary.—Dr. Eva Pell, 633–5127.
Director of:
International Relations.—Francine Berkowitz, 633–4795.
National Air and Space Museum.—Jack Dailey, 633–2350.
National Museum of Natural History.—Dr. Cristián Samper, 633–2664.
National Science Resources Center.—Sally Goetz Shuler, 633–2972.
National Zoological Park.—Dennis Kelly, 633–4442.
Office of Research and Training Services.—Catherine Harris, 633–7070.
Smithsonian Astrophysical Observatory.—Charles Alcock (617) 495–7100.
Smithsonian Environmental Research Center.—Anson Hines (443) 482–2208.
Smithsonian Museum Conservation Institute.—Robert Koestler (301) 238–1205.
Smithsonian Tropical Research Institute.—Eldredge Bermingham, 011–507–212–8110.

SMITHSONIAN ENTERPRISES

President.—Tom Ott, 633–5169.
Publisher, Smithsonian Magazine.—Kerry Bianchi, 633–6090.
Editor, Smithsonian Magazine.—Vacant, 633–6072.

SOCIAL SECURITY ADMINISTRATION

Altmeyer Building, 6401 Security Boulevard, Baltimore, MD 21235 (ALTMB)

Annex Building, 6401 Security Boulevard, Baltimore, MD 21235 (ANXB)

East High Rise Building, 6401 Security Boulevard, Baltimore, MD 21235 (EHRB)

Gwynn Oak Building, 1710 Gwynn Oak Avenue, Baltimore, MD 21207 (GWOB)

International Trade Commission Building, 500 E Street, SW., Washington, DC 20254 (ITCB)

Meadows East Building, 6401 Security Boulevard, Baltimore, MD 21235 (ME)

Metro West Tower Building, 300 North Greene Street, Baltimore, MD 21201 (MWTB)

National Computer Center, 6201 Security Boulevard, Baltimore, MD 21235 (NCC)

One Skyline Tower, 5107 Leesburg Pike, Falls Church, VA 22041 (SKY)

Robert M. Ball Building, 6401 Security Boulevard, Baltimore, MD 21235 (RMBB)

Rolling Road Commerce Center, 2709 Rolling Road, Baltimore, MD 21244 (RRCC)

Security West Tower, 1500 Woodlawn Drive, Baltimore, MD 21241 (SWTB)

West High Rise Building, 6401 Security Boulevard, Baltimore, MD 21235 (WHRB)

http://www.socialsecurity.gov

OFFICE OF THE COMMISSIONER

Commissioner.—Michael J. Astrue, ALTMB, suite 900 (410) 965–3120 or ITCB, room 850 (202) 358–6000.
Deputy Commissioner.—Carolyn W. Colvin, ALTMB, suite 960 (410) 965–9000 or ITCB, room 874 (202) 358–6064.
Chief of Staff.—Margaret J. Tittel, ALTMB, suite 900 (410) 965–9050 or ITCB, room 858 (202) 358–6000.

Deputy Chief of Staff.—Dean S. Landis, ALTMB, suite 900 (410) 965–0520.
Executive Counselor to the Commissioner.—Vacant.
Executive Secretary.—Tiffany Flick (acting), ALTMB, suite 900 (410) 965–3500.
Associate Commissioner, Office of International Programs.—Diane K. Braunstein, RMBB, room 3700 (410) 597–1649 or ITCB, room 869 (202) 358–6177.

OFFICE OF THE CHIEF ACTUARY

Chief Actuary.—Stephen C. Goss, ALTMB, room 700 (410) 965–3000.
Deputy Chief Actuary for—
Long Range.—Alice H. Wade, ALTMB, room 700 (410) 965–3002.
Short Range.—Eli N. Donkar, ALTMB, room 760 (410) 965–3004.

OFFICE OF COMMUNICATIONS

Deputy Commissioner.—James Courtney, ALTMB, room 460 (410) 965–1720, or ITCB, room 866 (202) 358–6131.
Assistant Deputy Commissioner.—Philip A. Gambino, ALTMB, room 460 (410) 965–1720.
Associate Commissioner, Office of:
Communication, Planning, and Technology.—Jeffrey Buckner, (acting), ANXB, room 3165 (410) 965–4029.
External Affairs.—Kojuan Almond, (acting), ANXB, room 3505 (410) 965–1804.
Open Government.—Alan Lane, 1126 WHRB, (410) 965–4331.
Public Inquiries.—Betsy Bake, Windsor Park (410) 965–5330.
Press Officer.—Vacant, ALTMB, room 440 (410) 965–8904.

OFFICE OF DISABILITY ADJUDICATION AND REVIEW

Deputy Commissioner.—Glenn E. Sklar, SKY, suite 1600 (703) 605–8200, or ALTMB, room 560 (410) 965–6006.
Assistant Deputy Commissioner.—James Borland, SKY, suite 1600 (703) 605–8200, or ALTMB, room 560 (410) 965–5200.
Executive Director, Office of Appellate Operations.—Patricia A. Jonas, SKY, suite 1400 (703) 605–7100.
Chief Administrative Law Judge.—Debra Bice, SKY, suite 1608 (703) 605–8500.
Associate Commissioner, Office of Executive Operations and Human Resources.—James ''Jim'' Julian (acting), SKY, suite 1700 (703) 605–8700.
Associate Commissioner, Budget, Facilities and Security.—Frank Biro (acting), SKY, suite 1604 (703) 605–8910.
Associate Commissioner, Electronic Services and Strategic Information.—Natalie Lu (acting), SKY, suite 1600 (703) 605–8396.
Regional Chief Administrative Law Judges:
Atlanta.—Ollie L. Garmon, 61 Forsyth Street, SW., Suite 20T10, Atlanta, GA 30303 (404) 562–1182.
Boston.—Carol Sax, One Bowdoin Square, 10th Floor, Boston, MA 02114 (617) 720–0438.
Chicago.—Sherry Thompson (acting), 200 West Adams Street, Suite 2901, Chicago, IL 60606 (312) 886–5252.
Dallas.—Joan Parks Saunders, 1301 Young Street, Suite 460, Dallas, TX 75202 (214) 767–9401.
Denver.—Marsha R. Stroup, 1244 North Speer Boulevard, Suite 600, Denver, CO 80204 (303) 844–6100.
Kansas City.—John H. Fraze, 1100 Main Street, Suite 1700, Kansas City, MO 64105 (888) 238–7975.
New York.—Mark Sochaczewsky, 26 Federal Plaza, Room 34–116, New York, NY 10278 (212) 264–4036.
Philadelphia.—Jasper J. Bede, 300 Spring Garden Street, 4th Floor, Philadelphia, PA 19123 (215) 597–4100.
San Francisco.—William J. King, 555 Battery Street, 5th Floor, San Francisco, CA 94111 (415) 705–2000.
Seattle.—David J. DeLaittre, 701 5th Avenue, Suite 2900 M/S 904, Seattle, WA 98104 (206) 615–2236.

OFFICE OF RETIREMENT AND DISABILITY POLICY

Deputy Commissioner.—David A. Rust, ALTMB, room 100 (410) 965–0100.
Assistant Deputy Commissioner.—LaTina Burse Greene, ALTMB, room 100 (410) 965–4507.
Associate Commissioner, Office of:
Income Security Programs.—Michelle King, ALTMB, room 250 (410) 965–7748.
Disability Programs.—Art Spencer, Annex, room 4555 (410) 966–5766.
Employment Support Programs.—Bob Williams, OPRB, room 2607 (410) 597–1352. ITC, room 830 (202) 358–6921.
Medical and Vocational Expertise.—Robert E. Emrich, Jr., Oak Meadows, room 120 (410) 966–4800.
Program Development and Research.—Richard Balkus, ALTMB, room 128 (410) 966–7918.
Research, Evaluation and Statistics.—Manuel de la Puente, ITCB, room 828 (202) 358–6020.
Retirement Policy.—Vacant, ITCB, room 819 (202) 358–6053.
Director, PolicyNet and Program Support.—Stephen Evangelista (acting), RRCC, room 1910 (410) 965–6522.
Director, Office of Regulations.—Paul Kryglik, WHRB, room 4400 (410) 965–3735.

OFFICE OF BUDGET, FINANCE AND MANAGEMENT

Deputy Commissioner.—Michael G. Gallagher, ALTMB, room 800 (410) 965–3148.
Assistant Deputy Commissioner.—Stephanie Hall, ALTMB, room 800 (410) 965–9704.
Associate Commissioner, Office of:
Acquisition and Grants.—Dianne L. Rose, 7111 Security Boulevard (rear entrance), room 120 (410) 965–9455.
Budget.—Bonnie Kind, WHRB, room 2126 (410) 965–3501.
Facilities and Supply Management.—Michael Keegan, ANXB, room 1540 (410) 965–4272.
Financial Policy and Operations.—Carla Krabbe, EHRB, room 200 (410) 965–3403.
Security and Emergency Preparedness.—James Bentley, RMBB, room 1540 (410) 966–7444.
Director, Records Management and Audit Liaison Staff.—Teresa Rojas, ALTMB, room 807 (410) 966–7284.

OFFICE OF THE GENERAL COUNSEL

General Counsel.—David F. Black, ALTMB, room 600 (410) 965–0600.
Deputy General Counsel.—Thomas W. Crawley, ALTMB, room 600 (410) 966–3414.
Associate General Counsel for—
General Law.—Tina M. Waddell, room G300c (410) 965–5288.
Program Law.—Gwen Jones Kelley, ALTMB, room 624 (410) 965–0495.
Public Disclosure.—Dan Callahan, G400–F (410) 965–0644.
Regional Chief Counsel for—
Atlanta.—Mary Ann Sloan, Atlanta Federal Center, 61 Forsyth Street, SW., Suite 20T45, Atlanta, GA 30303 (404) 562–1010.
Boston.—Robert J. Triba, JFK Federal Building, Room 625, Boston, MA 02203 (617) 565–2380.
Chicago.—Grace Kim (acting), 200 West Adams Street, 30th Floor, Chicago, IL 60606, 1–877–800–7578, ext. 19138.
Dallas.—Mike McGaughran, 1301 Young Street, Room A–702, Dallas, TX 75202–5433 (214) 767–4660.
Denver.—John J. Lee, 1001 17th Street, Denver, CO 80202 (303) 844–0013.
Kansas City.—Kristi A. Schmidt, Federal Office Building, 601 East 12th Street, Room 965, Kansas City, MO 64106 (816) 936–5756.
New York.—Stephen P. Conte, 26 Federal Plaza, Suite 3904, New York, NY 12078 (212) 264–2216.
Philadelphia.—Eric P. Kressman, 300 Spring Garden Street, 6th Floor, Philadelphia, PA 19123 (215) 597–1847.
San Francisco.—Donna Calvert (acting), 333 Market Street, Suite 1500, San Francisco, CA 94105 (415) 977–8971.
Seattle.—David Morado, 701 Fifth Avenue, Suite 2900, M/S 901, Seattle, WA 98104 (206) 615–2662.

OFFICE OF HUMAN RESOURCES

Deputy Commissioner.—Dr. Reginald F. Wells, ALTMB, room 200 (410) 965–1900.
Assistant Deputy Commissioner.—Donna L. Siegel, ALTMB, room 200 (410) 965–7642.
Associate Commissioner for—
Civil Rights and Equal Opportunity.—A. Jacy Thurmond, ANXB, room 2571 (410) 965–3318.
Labor Management and Employee Relations.—Milton R. Beever, ANXB, room 2170 (410) 965–5772.
Office of:
Learning.—Steven Patrick, EHRB, room 100 (410) 965–0709.
Personnel.—Bonnie L. Doyle, ANXB, room 2510 (410) 965–4463.
Director of:
Executive and Special Services.—Bonnie L. Doyle, ANXB, room 2510 (410) 965–4463.
Human Capital Planning.—Linda Walk, EHRB, room GD5 (410) 965–8171.

OFFICE OF THE INSPECTOR GENERAL

Inspector General.—Patrick P. O'Carroll, ALTMB, suite 300 (410) 966–8385.
Deputy Inspector General.—James A. Kissko, ALTMB, suite 300 (410) 966–8385.
Counsel to the Inspector General.—B. Chad Bungard, 3–ME–1 (410) 966–2323.
Assistant Inspector General for—
Audit.—Steven L. Schaeffer, 3–ME–2 (410) 965–9701.
External Relations.—Jonathan L. Lasher, 3–ME–4 (410) 965–7178.
Investigations.—Richard A. Rohde, 3–ME–3 (410) 966–2436.
Technology and Resource Management.—Michael D. Robinson, 2–ME–4 (410) 965–8240.

OFFICE OF LEGISLATION AND CONGRESSIONAL AFFAIRS

Deputy Commissioner.—Scott Frey, ITCB, room 816 (202) 358–6030, or ALTMB, room 152 (410) 966–8088.
Assistant Deputy Commissioner.—Angela Jones Arnett, ITCB, room 818 (202) 358–6030 or ALTMB, room 144 (410) 965–1651.
Associate Commissioner for—
Legislative Development.—Thomas M. Parrott, ALTMB, room 146 (410) 965–3737.
Legislative Operations.—Vacant, ALTMB, room 150 (410) 966–8088.
Director for—
Congressional Constituent Relations.—Sharon A. Wilson, WHRB, room 3202 (410) 965–3531.
Disability Insurance.—John Brzostowski, WHRB, room 3216 (410) 965–1472.
Immigration, Data Exchange and Enumeration.—Kitty Chilcoat, WHRB, room 3223 (410) 966–5482.
Retirement and Survivors Insurance Benefits.—Timothy J. Kelley, WHRB, room 3210 (410) 965–3293.
Supplemental Security Income and Health.—Erik Hansen, WHRB, room 3227 (410) 965–3112.

OFFICE OF OPERATIONS

Deputy Commissioner.—Mary Glenn-Croft, WHRB, room 1204 (410) 965–3143.
Assistant Deputy Commissioners: Roger P. McDonnell, WHRB, room 1204 (410) 965–4292; Theresa Gruber, WHRB, room 1204 (410) 965–7842.
Associate Commissioner, Office of:
Automation Support.—Jo Armstrong, ANXB, room 4705 (410) 965–7166.
Central Operations.—Terry Stradtman, SWTB, room 7000 (410) 966–7000.
Disability Determinations.—Linda Dorn, ANXB, room 3570 (410) 594–0125.
Electronic Services.—Sylviane Haldiman, ANXB, room 3840 (410) 966–8040.
Public Service and Operations Support.—Marianna LaCanfora, WHRB, room 1224 (410) 965–5514.
Telephone Services.—Roy Snyder, ANXB, room 4845 (410) 965–1111.
Regional Commissioner for—
Atlanta.—Michael Grochowski, 61 Forsyth Street, Suite 23T30, Atlanta, GA 30303 (404) 562–5600.
Boston.—Susan Harding, JFK Federal Building, Room 1900, Boston, MA 02203 (617) 565–2870.

Chicago.—Nancy A. Berryhill, Harold Washington Social Security Center, 600 West Madison Street, Chicago, IL 60661 (312) 575–4000.

Dallas.—Martha Lambie, 1301 Young Street, Suite 130, Dallas, TX 75202–5433 (214) 767–4207.

Denver.—Sean Brune, Federal Office Building, 1961 Stout Street, Room 325, Denver, CO 80294 (303) 844–2388.

Kansas City.—Carolyn Simmons, Federal Office Building, 601 East 12th Street, Room 436, Kansas City, MO 64106 (816) 936–5700.

New York.—Beatrice Disman, 26 Federal Plaza, Room 40–102, New York, NY 10278 (212) 264–3915.

Philadelphia.—Laurie Watkins, P.O. Box 8788, 300 Spring Garden Street, Philadelphia, PA 19123 (215) 597–5157.

San Francisco.—Bill Zielinski, 1221 Nevin Avenue, Richmond, CA 94801 (510) 970–8400.

Seattle.—Stanley Friendship, 701 5th Avenue, Seattle, WA 98104–7075 (206) 615–3762.

OFFICE OF SYSTEMS/OFFICE OF THE CHIEF INFORMATION OFFICER

Deputy Commissioner and Chief Information Officer.—Kelly Croft, ALTMB, room 400 (410) 965–7481.

Assistant Deputy Commissioner and Deputy Chief Information Officer.—Debbi Russell, ALTMB, room 400 (410) 965–1345.

Associate Commissioner, Office of:

Applications and Supplemental Security Income Systems.—Debby Ellis, RMBB, room 2100 (410) 965–3072.

Disability Systems.—Roderick Hairston, RMBB, room 3606 (410) 965–8227.

Earnings, Enumeration and Administrative Systems.—Karen Martin, RMBB, room 3100 (410) 965–5069.

Enterprise Support, Architecture and Engineering.—Ron Burdinski, RMBB, room 4100 (410) 965–1233.

Retirement and Survivors Insurance Systems.—John W. Simermeyer, RMBB, room 4700 (410) 965–5789.

Systems Electronic Services.—Diana Andrews, RMBB, room 3003 (410) 965–7641.

Telecommunications and Systems Operations.—Thomas G. Grzymski, NCC, room 550 (410) 965–7626.

Office of Information Security, Chief Information Security Officer.—Brad A. Flick, Annex Building, suite 3840 (410) 966–4297.

OFFICE OF QUALITY PERFORMANCE

Deputy Commissioner.—Ronald T. Raborg, ALTMB, room 860 (410) 965–5200.

Assistant Deputy Commissioner.—David V. Foster, ALTMB, room 860 (410) 965–8804.

Associate Commissioner, Office of:

Quality Data Management.—Robin Sabatino, EHRB, room 5141 (410) 965–9885.

Quality Improvement.—Daryl X. Wise, EHRB, room 4138 (410) 965–4557.

Quality Review.—Martin Hansen, EHRB, room 6145 (410) 965–5328.

Field Directors—

Atlanta.—Robert L. Raines, 61 Forsyth Street, SW., Suite 21T60, Atlanta, GA 30303 (404) 562–5676.

Baltimore.—Patricia A. Biggers, Oak Meadows, Room 261 (410) 966–9230.

Boston.—Christine D. Tebbetts, 99 High Street, Suite 400, Boston, MA 02110 (617) 695–6631.

Chicago.—Mary T. Byrns, 600 West Madison Street, 5th Floor, Chicago, IL 60661 (312) 575–6002.

Dallas.—Sheena Hayes, 1301 Young Street, Room 300, Dallas, TX 75202 (214) 767–3164.

Denver.—Ronald R. Miller, 1961 Stout Street, FOB Room 126, Denver, CO 80294 (303) 844–2601.

Kansas City.—Carrie Taber, 601 East 12th Street, Room 1200 South, Kansas City, MO 64106 (816) 936–5151.

New York.—Darryl Donaldson, 26 Federal Plaza, Room 4128, New York, NY 10278 (212) 264–4055.

Philadelphia.—Diane Graboyes, 300 Spring Garden, 2nd Floor East, Philadelphia, PA 19123 (215) 597–1188.

San Francisco.—Darryl Moore, 1301 Clay Street, Suite 900 North, Oakland, CA 94612 (877) 700–4841.

Seattle.—Rubie J. Toney, 701 5th Avenue, Suite 2900, Seattle, WA 98104 (206) 615–2146.

STATE JUSTICE INSTITUTE

11951 Freedom Drive, Suite 1020, Reston, VA 20190, phone (571) 313–8843

http://www.sji.gov

BOARD OF DIRECTORS

Chairman.—James R. Hannah.
Vice Chairman.—Daniel J. Becker.
Secretary.—Gayle A. Nachtigal.
Treasurer.—Hernan D. Vera.

Members:

Robert A. Miller
Chase T. Rogers
Wilfredo Martinez
Marsha J. Rabiteau
John B. Nalbandian
Isabel Framer

Officer:

Executive Director.—Jonathan D. Mattiello.

SUSQUEHANNA RIVER BASIN COMMISSION

COMMISSIONERS AND ALTERNATES

Federal Government.—COL Christopher J. Larsen (Commissioner); COL David E. Anderson (Alternate); David J. Leach (2nd Alternate).
New York.—James M. Tierney (Commissioner); Kenneth P. Lynch (Alternate); Peter Freehafer (2nd Alternate).
Pennsylvania.—Michael L. Krancer (Commissioner); John T. Hines (Alternate); Kelly J. Heffner (2nd Alternate).
Maryland.—Dr. Robert Summers (Commissioner); Herbert Sachs (Alternate).

STAFF

1721 North Front Street, Harrisburg, PA 17102, phone (717) 238–0423

srbc@srbc.net, http://www.srbc.net

Executive Director.—Paul O. Swartz.
Deputy Executive Director.—Thomas W. Beauduy.
Director of Administration and Finance.—Marcia E. Rynearson.
Director of Technical Programs.—Dr. James Richenderfer.
Secretary to the Commission.—Stephanie L. Richardson.
Director of Communications.—Susan S. Obleski.

TENNESSEE VALLEY AUTHORITY

One Massachusetts Avenue, NW., Suite 300, 20444, phone (202) 898–2999

Knoxville, TN 37902, phone (865) 632–2101

Chattanooga, TN 37401, phone (423) 751–0011

BOARD OF DIRECTORS

Chairman: Dennis C. Bottorff (865) 632–4000 (Knoxville).
Directors: Marilyn A. Brown (Knoxville), Robert M. Duncan (Knoxville), Thomas C. Gilliland (Knoxville), William H. Graves (Knoxville), Barbara S. Haskew (Knoxville), Richard C. Howorth (Knoxville), Neil G. McBride (Knoxville), William B. Sansom (Knoxville).

EXECUTIVE OFFICERS

President and Chief Executive Officer.—Tom Kilgore (865) 632–2366 (Knoxville).
Group President, Strategy and External Relations.—Kimberly S. Greene (865) 632–4049 (Knoxville).
Chief Operating Officer.—William R. McCollum, Jr. (423) 751–6016 (Chattanooga).

Executive Vice President, People and Performance.—Janet C. Herrin (865) 632–6770 (Knoxville).
Chief Financial Officer.—John M. Thomas, III (423) 751–8919 (Chattanooga).
General Counsel.—Ralph E. Rodgers (865) 632–4131 (Knoxville).
Vice President and Chief Information Officer.—Daniel Traynor (423) 751–4793 (Chattanooga).

WASHINGTON OFFICE

Government Relations Director.—Justin Maierhofer (202) 898–2999, fax: 898–2998.

U.S. ADVISORY COMMISSION ON PUBLIC DIPLOMACY

2200 C Street, NW., SA–5, C2E15, 20520–0582

phone (202) 203–7880, fax 203–7886

[Created by Executive Order 12048 and Public Law 96–60]

Chair.—William J. Hybl.
Members: Vice-Chairman, Amb. Lyndon Olson, Jr., Amb. Penne K. Peacock, Sim Farar, Lezlee Westine.
Executive Director.—Matthew Armstrong.
Administrative Specialist.—Jamice Clayton.

U.S. AGENCY FOR INTERNATIONAL DEVELOPMENT

1300 Pennsylvania Avenue, NW., 20523, phone (202) 712–0000

http://www.usaid.gov

Administrator.—Rajiv Shah, room 6.09, 712–4040, fax 216–3445.
Deputy Administrator.—Donald Steinberg, room 6.09, 712–4040, fax 216–3445.
Counselor.—Hilda Arellano, room 6.08, 712–5010.
Chief Operating Officer.—Sean Carroll, room 6.09–042, 712–1200.
Executive Secretary.—Christa White, room 6.08–032, 712–0700.
Assistant Administrator for—
Africa.—Vacant, room 4.08–031, 712–0500.
Asia.—Nisha Biswal, room 4.09, 712–0200.
Democracy, Conflict and Humanitarian Assistance.—Nancy Lindborg, room 8.06–084, 712–0100.
Economic Growth, Agriculture, and Trade.—Eric Postel, room 3.09–008, 712–0670.
Europe and Eurasia.—Paige Alexander, room 5.06, 567–4001.
Global Health.—Ariel Pablos-Mendez, room 3.06, 712–4120.
Latin America and the Caribbean.—Mark Feierstein, room 5.09–012, 712–4800.
Legislative and Public Affairs.—Barbara Larkin (acting), room 6.10–107, 712–4300.
Management.—Sean Carroll (acting), room 6.08, 712–1200.
Middle East.—Mara Rudman, room 4.09–005, 712–0300.
Director, Office of:
Senior Counselor to the Administrator and Chief Innovation Officer.—Maura O'Neill, room 6.08–025, 712–4190.
Office of Civil Rights and Diversity.—Ambassador Barry Wells, room 4.06–143, 712–1110.
Security.—Randy Streufert, room 2.06, 712–0990.
Small and Disadvantaged Business Utilization.—Mauricio Vera, room 848–E, 567–4735, SA–44.
General Counsel.—Lisa Gomer, room 6.06–125, 712–0900.
Inspector General.—Donald Gambatesa, room 6.06D, 712–1150.

U.S. COMMISSION ON CIVIL RIGHTS

624 Ninth Street, NW., 20425, phone (202) 376–7700, fax 376–7672

(Codified in 42 U.S.C., section 1975)

Chairperson.—Martin Casttro.
Vice Chairperson.—Abigail Thernstrom.
Commissioners: Roberta Achtenberg, Todd Gaziano, Gail Heriot, Peter N. Kirsanow, David Kladney, Michael Yaki.

Staff Director.—Kimberly Tolhurst, Delegated the Authority of the Staff Director.

U.S. ELECTION ASSISTANCE COMMISSION

1201 New York Avenue, NW., Suite 300, Washington, DC 20005

phone (202) 566–3100, (866) 747–1471, fax 566–3127, http://www.eac.gov

[Created by Public Law 107–252]

Commissioner.—Donetta L. Davidson.
Commissioner.—Gineen Bresso.
Commissioner.—Vacant.
Commissioner.—Vacant.

OFFICE OF THE EXECUTIVE DIRECTOR

Executive Director.—Thomas R. ''Tom'' Wilkey (202) 566–3100.
Chief Operating Officer.—Alice P. Miller.
Chief Financial Officer.—Annette Lafferty.

OFFICE OF COMMUNICATIONS AND CONGRESSIONAL AFFAIRS

Director of Communications.—Jeannie Layson (202) 566–3103.

OFFICE OF THE GENERAL COUNSEL

General Counsel.—Mark Robbins (202) 566–3100.

OFFICE OF THE INSPECTOR GENERAL

Inspector General.—Curtis Crider (202) 566–3125.

U.S. HOLOCAUST MEMORIAL COUNCIL

The United States Holocaust Memorial Museum

100 Raoul Wallenberg Place, SW., 20024, phones (202) 488–0400 / (202) 314–7881
fax 488–2690

Officials:
Chair.—Tom A. Bernstein, New York, NY.
Vice Chair.—Joshua B. Bolten, Washington, DC.
Director.—Sara J. Bloomfield, Washington, DC.

Members:
Debra Abrams, Boca Raton, FL.
Elliott Abrams, Great Falls, VA.
Miriam Adelson, Las Vegas, NV.
Matthew L. Adler, Miami, FL.
Norman R. Bobins, Chicago, IL.
Joseph M. Brodecki, Washington, DC.
Alan I. Casden, Beverly Hills, CA.
Michael Chertoff, Potomac, MD.
Carol B. Cohen, Highland Park, IL.
William J. Danhof, Lansing, MI.
Kitty Dukakis, Brookline, MA.
Michael David Epstein, Rockville, MD.
Donald Etra, Los Angeles, CA.
David M. Flaum, Rochester, NY.
Marilyn R. Fox, Clayton, MO.
K. Chaya Friedman, Baltimore, MD.
Joel M. Geiderman, Los Angeles, CA.
Michael J. Gerson, Alexandria, VA.
Nancy B. Gilbert, Boca Raton, FL.
Constance B. Girard-diCarlo, Philadelphia, PA.
Zvi Y. Gitelman, Ann Arbor, MI.
Marc Goldman, Boca Raton, FL.
Mark D. Goodman, Cambridge, MA.
Sanford L. Gottesman, Austin, TX.
Cheryl F. Halpern, Livingston, NJ.
J. David Heller, Cleveland, OH.
Andrew S. Hochberg, Northbrook, IL.
Amy Kaslow, Potomac, MD.
Ezra Katz, Coconut Grove, FL.
Edward I. Koch, New York, NY.
Howard Konar, West Henrietta, NY.
Douglas R. Korn, New York, NY.
M. Ronald Krongold, Miami, FL.

Norma Lerner, Hunting Valley, OH.
William S. Levine, Phoenix, AZ.
Hadassah F. Lieberman, New Haven, CT.
Deborah E. Lipstadt, Atlanta, GA.
Kenneth B. Mehlman, Washington, DC.
Michael B. Mukasey, New York, NY.
Dennis Prager, Glendale, CA.
Pierre-Richard Prosper, Salt Lake City, UT.
Ronald Ratner, Cleveland, OH.
Alan N. Rechtschaffen, New York, NY.
J. Philip Rosen, New York, NY.
Menachem Z. Rosensaft, New York, NY.
Kirk A. Rudy, Austin, TX.
Daniel J. Silva, Washington, DC.
Marc R. Stanley, Dallas, TX.
Elie Wiesel, Boston, MA.
Jeffrey S. Wilpon, Flushing, NY.
Bradley D. Wine, Washington, DC.
Judith Yudof, Lafayette, CA.
Fred S. Zeidman, Houston, TX.

Former Chairs:
Fred S. Zeidman, 2002–2010.
Irving Greenberg, 2000–2002.
*Miles Lerman, 1993–2000.
Harvey M. Meyerhoff, 1987–1993.
Elie Wiesel, 1980–1986.

Fomer Vice Chairs:
Joel M. Geiderman, 2005–2010.
Ruth B. Mandel, 1993–2005.
*William J. Lowenberg, 1986–1993.
Mark E. Talisman, 1980–1986.

Congressional Members:

U.S. House of Representatives:
Gabrielle Giffords, from Arizona.
Michael G. Grimm, from New York.
Nan A.S. Hayworth, from New York.
Patrick Meehan, from Pennsylvania.
Henry A. Waxman, from California.

U.S. Senate:
Richard J. Durbin, from Illinois.
Orrin G. Hatch, from Utah.
Frank R. Lautenberg, from New Jersey.
BERNARD SANDERS, from Vermont.

Ex Officio Members:
U.S. Department of:
Education.—Philip H. Rosenfelt.
Interior.—Jane M. Lyder.
State.—Douglas A. Davidson.

Council Staff:
General Counsel.—Gerard Leval.
Secretary of the Council.—Jane M. Miller.

**Deceased*

U.S. INSTITUTE OF PEACE

2301 Constitution Avenue, NW., 20037
phone (202) 457–1700, fax 429–6063

BOARD OF DIRECTORS

Public Members:
Chairman.—J. Robinson West.
Vice Chairman.—George E. Moose.
Members:
Judith A. Ansley
Eric Edelman
Kerry Kennedy
Ikram U. Khan
Stephen D. Krasner
John A. Lancaster
Jeremy A. Rabkin
Judy Van Rest
Nancy Zirkin
Ex Officio:
Department of Defense.—Leon Panetta (Dr. James N. Miller: Secretary's Designate).
Department of State.—Hillary Rodham Clinton (Michael H. Posner: Secretary's Designate).
National Defense University.—Vice Admiral Ann E. Rondeau.
United States Institute of Peace.—Richard H. Solomon.
Officials:
President.—Richard H. Solomon.
Executive Vice President.—Tara Sonenshine.
Chief Financial Officer.—Michael Graham.
Chief of Staff.—Paul D. Hughes.
Senior Vice President for—
Academy for International Conflict Management and Peacebuilding.—Pamela A. Aall.
Center for Conflict Management.—Dr. Abioudun Williams (acting).
Centers of Innovation.—David R. Smock.
Vice President for—
Operations and Chief Human Resources Officer.—Paula B. King.
Outreach and Communications.—Stephanie S. Fouch.

Director of:
Afghanistan and Pakistan Programs.—Andrew R. Wilder.
Gender and Peacebuilding Center.—Kathleen R. Kuehnast.
Global Peace Building Center.—Ann-Louise D. Colgan.
Iraq, Iran and North Africa Programs.—Manal M. Omar.
Media, Science and Technology.—Sheldon J. Himelfarb.
Religion and Peacemaking.—David R. Smock.
Rule of Law Center.—Colette L Rausch.
Security Sector Governance Center.—Robert M. Perito.
Sudan Program.—Jonathan H. Temin.
Sustainable Economies Center.—Raymond Gilpin.
Dean of:
Curriculum.—Jeffrey W. Helsing.
Students.—Theodore Feifer.
Director, Office of:
Administration.—Christopher M. de Paola.
Budget.—Joseph R. Lataille.
Conferences, Meetings and Events.—Lisa D. Frazier.
Congressional Relations.—Laurie Schultz Heim.
Grants Administration.—April R. Hall.
Human Resources.—Paula B. King.
Information Services.—Vacant.
Intergovernmental Affairs.—Beth C. Cole.
Procurement.—Francis E. Sullivan.
Public Affairs and Communication.—P. David Early.
Publications.—Valerie Norville.
Security.—William F. Rothenbecker.

U.S. INTERNATIONAL TRADE COMMISSION

500 E Street, SW., 20436

phone (202) 205–2000, fax 205–2798, http://www.usitc.gov

COMMISSIONERS

Chairman.—Deanna Tanner Okun.
Vice Chairman.—Irving A. Williamson.
Commissioners:
Charlotte R. Lane.
Daniel R. Pearson.
Shara L. Aranoff.
Dean A. Pinkert.
Congressional Relations Officer.—Joshua Levy, 205–3151.
External Relations.—Lyn M. Schlitt, 205–3141.
General Counsel.—James M. Lyons.
Secretary.—James Holbein.
Inspector General.—Philip M. Heneghan.
Director, Office of:
Economics.—Robert B. Koopman.
Industries.—Karen Laney.
Tariff Affairs and Trade Agreements.—David Beck.

U.S. MERIT SYSTEMS PROTECTION BOARD

1615 M Street, NW., 20419

phone (202) 653–7200, toll-free (800) 209–8960, fax 653–7130

[Created by Public Law 95–454]

Chairman.—Susan Tsui Grundmann.
Vice Chairman.—Anne M. Wagner.
Member.—Mary M. Rose.
Executive Director.—Steve Lenkart.
General Counsel.—James Eisenmann.
Appeals Counsel.—Lynore Carnes.

REGIONAL OFFICES

Regional Directors:

Atlanta Regional Office: Covering Alabama, Florida, Georgia, Mississippi, South Carolina, Tennessee.—Thomas J. Lanphear, 10th Floor, 401 West Peachtree Street, NW., Atlanta, GA 30308–3519 (404) 730–2751, fax 730–2767.

Central Regional Office: Covering Illinois, Iowa, Kansas City, Kansas, Kentucky, Indiana, Michigan, Minnesota, Missouri, Ohio, Wisconsin.—Martin Baumgaertner, 31st Floor, 230 South Dearborn Street, Chicago, IL 60604–1669 (312) 353–2923, fax 886–4231.

Dallas Regional Office: Covering Arkansas, Louisiana, Oklahoma, Texas.—Sharon F. Jackson, Room 620, 1100 Commerce Street, Dallas, TX 75242–9979 (214) 767–0555, fax 767–0102.

Northeastern Regional Office: Covering Connecticut, Delaware, Maine Maryland (except Montgomery and Prince Georges counties), Massachusetts, New Hampshire, New Jersey (except the counties of Bergen, Essex, Hudson, and Union), Pennsylvania, Rhode Island, Vermont, West Virginia.—William L. Boulden, 1601 Market Street, Suite 1700, Philadelphia, PA 19103–2310 (215) 597–9960, fax 597–3456.

Western Regional Office: Covering Alaska, California, Hawaii, Idaho, Nevada, Oregon, Washington, and Pacific Overseas.—Amy Dunning, 201 Mission Street, Suite 2310, San Francisco, CA 94105–1831 (415) 904–6772, fax 904–0580.

Washington Regional Office: Covering Washington, DC; Maryland (counties of Montgomery and Prince Georges), North Carolina; Virginia; all overseas areas not otherwise covered.—Jeremiah Cassidy, 1811 Diagonal Road, Suite 205, Alexandria, VA 22314–2840 (703) 756–6250, fax 756–7112.

New York Field Office: Covering New York, Puerto Rico, Virgin Islands, the following counties in New Jersey: Bergen, Essex, Hudson, Union.—Arthur Joseph, Chief Administrative Judge, Room 3137–A, 26 Federal Plaza, New York, NY 10278–0022 (212) 264–9372, fax 264–1417.

Denver Field Office: Covering Arizona, Colorado, Kansas (except Kansas City), Montana, Nebraska, New Mexico, North Dakota, South Dakota, Utah, Wyoming.—Laura M. Albornoz, Chief Administrative Judge, 165 South Union Boulevard, Suite 318, Lakewood, CO 80228–2211 (303) 969–5101, fax 969–5109.

U.S. OVERSEAS PRIVATE INVESTMENT CORPORATION

1100 New York Avenue, NW., 20527, phone (202) 336–8400

President and CEO.—Elizabeth L. Littlefield.

Executive Vice President.—Mimi Alemayehou.

Chief of Staff.—Matthew Schneider.

Vice President and General Counsel.—Deborah Burand.

Head of Investment Funds and Chief Investment Strategist.—Jay L. Koh.

Vice President for Investment Policy.—John Morton.

Deputy Chief of Staff and Senior Advisor to the President.—Jacqueline Strasser.

Managing Director Investment Development and Coordination.—John Moran.

Vice President for—

External Affairs.—Judith Pryor.

Insurance.—Rod Morris.

Investment Policy.—John Morton.

Small and Medium Enterprise Finance.—James Polan.

Structured Finance.—Robert B. Drumheller.

Chief Financial Officer (Acting).—Allan Villabroza.

Special Assistant for Congressional and Intergovernmental Affairs.—James W. Morrison, 336–8417.

BOARD OF DIRECTORS

Government Directors:

Dr. Rajiv Shah, Administrator, U.S. Agency for International Development.

Demetrios Marantis, Deputy U.S. Trade Representative.

Elizabeth L. Littlefield, President and Chief Executive Officer, OPIC.

Francisco J. Sánchez, U.S. Department of Commerce.

Seth D. Harris, Deputy Secretary, U.S. Department of Labor.

Robert Hormats, Under Secretary for Economic, Energy and Agricultural Affairs, U.S. Department of State.

Lael Brainard, Under Secretary for International Affairs, U.S. Department of the Treasury.

Private Sector Directors:

Samuel E. Ebbesen (General, USA, Ret.), Chief Executive Officer, Omni Systems, Inc., Vienna, Virginia.

Michael J. Warren, Principal, Albright Stonebridge Group, LLC.

Kevin G. Nealer, Principal and Partner, The Scowcroft Group, Washington, DC.

Diane Ingels Moss, President and Owner, Cartera Investment Corporation, Dallas, Texas.

C. William Swank, Retired Executive Vice President, Ohio Farm Bureau Federation, Westerville, Ohio.

Patrick J. Durkin, Managing Director, Barclays Capital, New York, New York.

U.S. POSTAL SERVICE

475 L'Enfant Plaza, SW., 20260–0010, phone (202) 268–2000

BOARD OF GOVERNORS

Chairman.—Louis J. Giuliano.

Vice Chairman.—Thurgood Marshall, Jr.

Postmaster General/CEO.—Patrick R. Donahoe.

Deputy Postmaster General.—Ronald A. Stroman.

MEMBERS

Mickey D. Barnett
James C. Miller III
Dennis J. Toner
Ellen C. Williams
James H. Bilbray

OFFICERS OF THE BOARD OF GOVERNORS

Secretary to the Board of Governors.—Julie S. Moore.

OFFICERS OF THE POSTAL SERVICE

Postmaster General, Chief Executive Officer.—Patrick R. Donahoe, 268–2550.

Deputy Postmaster General.—Ronald A. Stroman, 268–4290.

Chief Postal Inspector.—Guy J. Cottrell, 268–5615.

Judicial Officer.—William A. Campbell, 703–812–1902, 2101 Wilson Boulevard, Suite 600, Arlington, VA 22201–3078.

Vice President of:

Consumer and Industry Affairs.—Susan M. LaChance, 268–8877.

Corporate Communications.—Samuel M. Pulcrano, 268–2143.

Government Relations and Public Policy.—Marie Therese Dominguez, 268–2506.

Chief Operating Officer and Executive Vice President.—Megan J. Brennan, 268–4842.

Vice President of:

Delivery and Post Office Operations.—Dean J. Granholm, 268–6500.

Facilities.—Tom A. Samra, 268–3389.

Network Operations.—David E. Williams, 268–4305.

Chief Information Officer and Executive Vice President.—Ellis A. Burgoyne, 268–6900.

Vice President of:

Engineering Systems.—Michael J. Amato (703) 280–7001, 8403 Lee Highway, 4th Floor, Merrifield, VA 22082–8101.

Information Technology.—John T. Edgar, 268–3977.

Mail Entry and Payment Technology.—Pritha Mehra, 268–8049.

Product Information.—James P. Cochrane, 268–7536.

Chief Financial Officer and Executive Vice President.—Joseph Corbett, 268–5272.

Vice President of:

Controller.—Timothy F. O'Reilly, 268–5521.

Finance and Planning.—Stephen J. Masse, 268–7645.

Supply Management.—Susan M. Brownell, 268–4040.

General Counsel and Executive Vice President.—Mary Anne Gibbons, 268–2950.

Chief Human Resources Officer and Executive Vice President.—Anthony J. Vegliante, 268–7852.

Vice President of:

Employee Resource Management.—Deborah Giannoni-Jackson, 268–3783.

Labor Relations.—Douglas A. Tulino, 268–7447.
President and Chief Marketing/Sales Officer.—Paul Vogel, 268–7666.
Vice President of:
Channel Access.—Kelly M. Sigmon, 268–2252.
Domestic Products.—Gary C. Reblin, 268–6078.
Global Business.—Giselle E. Valera, 268–2131.
Pricing.—Maura Robinson, 268–7319.
Sales.—Cliff Rucker, 268–8800.

U.S. RAILROAD RETIREMENT BOARD

844 North Rush Street, Chicago, IL 60611, phone (312) 751–4777, fax 751–7154
Office of Legislative Affairs, 1310 G Street, NW., Suite 500, 20005
phone (202) 272–7742, fax 272–7728, e-mail: ola@rrb.gov
http://www.rrb.gov

Chairman.—Michael S. Schwartz (312) 751–4900, fax 751–7193.
Assistant to the Chairman.—Nancy S. Pittman.
Counsel to the Chairman.—Stephen W. Seiple.
Labor Member.—V.M. Speakman, Jr., 751–4905, fax 751–7194.
Assistants to the Labor Members: James C. Boehner, Geraldine L. Clark, Michael J. Collins.
Counsel to the Labor Member.—Thomas W. Sadler.
Management Member.—Jerome F. Kever, 751–4910, fax 751–7189.
Assistant to the Management Member.—Joseph M. Waechter.
Counsel to the Management Member.—Robert M. Perbohner.
Attorney-Advisor to the Management Member.—Ann L. Chaney.
Inspector General.—Martin J. Dickman, 751–4690, fax 751–4342.
General Counsel.—Steven A. Bartholow, 751–4935, fax 751–7102.
Assistant General Counsel.—Marguerite P. Dadabo, 751–4945, fax 751–7102.
Secretary to the Board.—Martha P. ''Pat'' Rico, 751–4920, fax 751–4923.
Director of:
Equal Opportunity.—Lynn E. Cousins, 751–4942, fax 751–7179.
Field Service.—Martha M. Barringer, 751–4515, fax 751–3360.
Hearings and Appeals.—Karl T. Blank, 751–4941, fax 751–7159.
Human Resources.—Keith B. Earley, 751–4392, fax 751–7164.
Legislative Affairs.—Margaret A. Lindsley (202) 272–7742, fax 272–7728.
Operations.—Robert J. Duda, 751–4698, fax 751–7157.
Policy and Systems.—Ronald Russo, 751–4984, fax 751–4650.
Program Evaluation and Management Services.—Janet M. Hallman, 751–4543, fax 751–7190.
Programs.—Dorothy A. Isherwood, 751–4860, fax 751–4333.
Supervisor of:
Acquisition Management.—Paul T. Ahern, 751–7130, fax 751–4923.
Congressional Inquiry.—Carl D. Mende, 751–4970, fax 751–7154.
Public Affairs.—Anita J. Rogers, 751–4777, fax 751–7154.
Chief of:
Actuary.—Frank J. Buzzi, 751–4915, fax 751–7129.
Benefit and Employment Analysis.—Marla L. Huddleston, 751–4779, fax 751–7129.
Finance.—George V. Govan, 751–4930, fax 751–4931.
Information.—Terri S. Morgan, 751–4851, fax 751–7169.
Librarian.—Katherine Tsang, 751–4926, fax 751–4926.
SEO/Director of Administration.—Henry M. Valiulis, 751–4990, fax 751–7197.

U.S. SENTENCING COMMISSION

One Columbus Circle, NE., Suite 2–500, South Lobby, 20002–8002

phone (202) 502–4500, fax 502–4699

Chair.—Patti B. Saris.
Vice Chairs: William B. Carr, Jr., Ketanji B. Jackson.
Commissioners: Ricardo H. Hinojosa, Dabney L. Friedrich, Beryl A. Howell.
Commissioners, ex officio: Isaac Fulwood, Jr., Jonathan J. Wroblewski.
Staff Director.—Judith W. Sheon, 502–4510.
General Counsel.—Kenneth P. Cohen, 502–4520.

Director of:
Administration.—Susan Brazel, 502–4610.
Research and Data Collection.—Glenn R. Schmitt, 502–4530.
Director and Chief Counsel of Office of Training.—Pamela G. Montgomery, 502–4540.
Public Affairs Officer.—Jeanne Doherty (acting), 502–4502.
Legislative and Governmental Affairs.—Lisa A. Rich, 502–4519.

U.S. TRADE AND DEVELOPMENT AGENCY

1000 Wilson Boulevard, Suite 1600, Arlington, VA 22209, phone (703) 875–4357

Director.—Leocadia I. Zak.
Deputy Director.—Peggy Philbin.
Chief of Staff.—Christopher Wyant.
Administrative Officer.—Carolyn Hum.
Director for Congressional Affairs and Public Relations.—Thomas R. Hardy.
Director for Export Promotion.—Leila Afas.
Contracting Officer.—Vacant.
Evaluations Officer.—Diana Rossiter.
Financial Manager.—Vacant.
General Counsel.—James A. Wilderotter.
Grants Administrator.—Patricia Daughetee.
Director for Policy and Program.—Geoffrey Jackson.
Resource Advisor.—Micheal Hillier.
Regional Director for—
East Asia and Eurasia.—Geoffrey Jackson.
Latin America and the Caribbean.—Nathan Younge.
Middle East, North Africa and Europe.—Carl B. Kress.
South and Southeast Asia.—Henry Steingass.
Sub-Saharan Africa.—Paul Marin.

WASHINGTON METROPOLITAN AREA TRANSIT AUTHORITY

600 Fifth Street, NW., 20001, phone (202) 637–1234

General Manager and Chief Executive Officer.—Richard Sarles.
General Counsel.—Carol A. O'Keeffe.
Deputy General Manager Administration/Chief Financial Officer.—Carol D. Kissal.
Assistant General Manager for—
Bus Service.—Jack Requa.
Customer Service, Communications and Marketing.—Barbara Richardson.
Deputy General Manager, Operations.—Dave Kubicek.
Chief Safety Officer.—James Dougherty.
Director, Office of Government Relations.—Regina Sullivan.
Managing Director, Public Relations.—Lynn Bowersox.
Chief, Metro Transit Police Department.—Michael Taborn.

WASHINGTON NATIONAL MONUMENT SOCIETY

[Organized 1833; chartered 1859; amended by Acts of August 2, 1876, October, 1888]

President Ex Officio.—Barack H. Obama, President of the United States.
First Vice President.—James W. Symington, 1666 K Street, NW., Suite 500, Washington, DC 20006–2107 (202) 778–2107.
Treasurer.—Henry Ravenel, Jr.
Secretary.—Robert Vogel, Superintendent, National Mall and Memorial Parks, 900 Ohio Drive, SW., Washington, DC 20024–2000, 485–9875.

Members:
Christopher Addison
Vincent C. Burke, Jr.
Robert W. Duemling
Gilbert M. Grosvenor
C. Boyden Gray
John D.H. Kane
John A. Washington

Member Emeritus:
Harry F. Byrd, Jr.

WOODROW WILSON INTERNATIONAL CENTER FOR SCHOLARS

One Woodrow Wilson Plaza, 1300 Pennsylvania Avenue, NW., 20004–3027

phone (202) 691–4000, fax 691–4001

(Under the direction of the Board of Trustees of
Woodrow Wilson International Center for Scholars)

Director/President/CEO.—Jane Harman, 691–4202.
Executive Vice President.—Michael Van Dusen, 691–4055.
Vice President for—
Administration and Resource Management.—Leslie Johnson, 691–4103.
Communications and Media Relations.—Peter Reid, 691–4122.
Development.—Barbara Hall, 691–4168.
Programs.—Robert Litwak, 691–4179.
Public Education and Outreach.—Sharon McCarter, 691–4016.
Chief Financial Officer.—John Dysland, 691–4096.

Board of Trustees:
Chairman.—Joseph B. Gildenhorn.
Vice Chairman.—Sander R. Gerber.

Private Members:
Timothy Broas
John T. Casteen III
Charles E. Cobb, Jr.
Thelma Duggin
Carlos M. Gutierrez
Susan Hutchison
Barry S. Jackson

Public Members:
James H. Billington, Librarian of Congress.
Hillary Rodham Clinton, Secretary of State.
G. Wayne Clough, Secretary of the Smithsonian Institution.
Arne Duncan, Secretary of Education.
David Ferriero, Archivist of the United States.
James Leach, Chairman of the National Endowment for the Humanities.
Kathleen Sebelius, Secretary of Health and Human Services.
Designated Appointee of the President of the United States from within the Federal Government:
Melody Barnes, Director, Domestic Policy Council, The White House.

JUDICIARY

SUPREME COURT OF THE UNITED STATES

One First Street, NE., 20543, phone (202) 479–3000

JOHN G. ROBERTS, JR., Chief Justice of the United States, was born in Buffalo, NY, January 27, 1955. He married Jane Marie Sullivan in 1996 and they have two children, Josephine and John. He received an A.B. from Harvard College in 1976 and a J.D. from Harvard Law School in 1979. He served as a law clerk for Judge Henry J. Friendly of the United States Court of Appeals for the Second Circuit from 1979–80 and as a law clerk for then Associate Justice William H. Rehnquist of the Supreme Court of the United States during the 1980 term. He was Special Assistant to the Attorney General, U.S. Department of Justice from 1981–82, Associate Counsel to President Ronald Reagan, White House Counsel's Office from 1982–86, and Principal Deputy Solicitor General, U.S. Department of Justice from 1989–93. From 1986–89 and 1993–2003, he practiced law in Washington, DC. He was appointed to the United States Court of Appeals for the District of Columbia Circuit in 2003. President George W. Bush nominated him as Chief Justice of the United States, and he took his seat September 29, 2005.

ANTONIN SCALIA, Associate Justice, was born in Trenton, NJ, March 11, 1936. He married Maureen McCarthy and has nine children, Ann Forrest, Eugene, John Francis, Catherine Elisabeth, Mary Clare, Paul David, Matthew, Christopher James, and Margaret Jane. He received his A.B. from Georgetown University and the University of Fribourg, Switzerland, and his LL.B. from Harvard Law School, and was a Sheldon Fellow of Harvard University from 1960–61. He was in private practice in Cleveland, OH from 1961–67, a Professor of Law at the University of Virginia from 1967–71, and a Professor of Law at the University of Chicago from 1977–82, and a Visiting Professor of Law at Georgetown University and Stanford University. He was chairman of the American Bar Association's Section of Administrative Law, 1981–82, and its Conference of Section Chairmen, 1982–83. He served the Federal Government as General Counsel of the Office of Telecommunications Policy from 1971–72, Chairman of the Administrative Conference of the United States from 1972–74, and Assistant Attorney General for the Office of Legal Counsel from 1974–77. He was appointed Judge of the United States Court of Appeals for the District of Columbia Circuit in 1982. President Reagan nominated him as an Associate Justice of the Supreme Court, and he took his seat September 26, 1986.

ANTHONY M. KENNEDY, Associate Justice, was born in Sacramento, CA, July 23, 1936. He married Mary Davis and has three children. He received his B.A. from Stanford University and the London School of Economics, and his LL.B. from Harvard Law School. He was in private practice in San Francisco, CA from 1961–63, as well as in Sacramento, CA from 1963–75. From 1965 to 1988, he was a Professor of Constitutional Law at the McGeorge School of Law, University of the Pacific. He has served in numerous positions during his career, including a member of the California Army National Guard in 1961, the board of the Federal Judicial Center from 1987–88, and two committees of the Judicial Conference of the United States: the Advisory Panel on Financial Disclosure Reports and Judicial Activities, subsequently renamed the Advisory Committee on Codes of Conduct, from 1979–87, and the Committee on Pacific Territories from 1979–90, which he chaired from 1982–90. He was appointed to the United States Court of Appeals for the Ninth Circuit in 1975. President Reagan nominated him as an Associate Justice of the Supreme Court, and he took his seat February 18, 1988.

CLARENCE THOMAS, Associate Justice, was born in the Pin Point community of Georgia near Savannah June 23, 1948. He married Virginia Lamp in 1987 and has one child, Jamal

Adeen, by a previous marriage. He attended Conception Seminary and received an A.B., *cum laude,* from Holy Cross College, and a J.D. from Yale Law School in 1974. He was admitted to law practice in Missouri in 1974, and served as an Assistant Attorney General of Missouri from 1974–77, an attorney with the Monsanto Company from 1977–79, and Legislative Assistant to Senator John Danforth from 1979–81. From 1981–82, he served as Assistant Secretary for Civil Rights, U.S. Department of Education, and as Chairman of the U.S. Equal Employment Opportunity Commission from 1982–90. He became a Judge of the United States Court of Appeals for the District of Columbia Circuit in 1990. President George W. Bush nominated him as an Associate Justice of the Supreme Court, and he took his seat October 23, 1991.

RUTH BADER GINSBURG, Associate Justice, was born in Brooklyn, NY, March 15, 1933. She married Martin D. Ginsburg in 1954, and has a daughter, Jane, and a son, James. She received her B.A. from Cornell University, attended Harvard Law School, and received her LL.B. from Columbia Law School. She served as a law clerk to the Honorable Edmund L. Palmieri, Judge of the United States District Court for the Southern District of New York, from 1959–61. From 1961–63, she was a research associate and then associate director of the Columbia Law School Project on International Procedure. She was a Professor of Law at Rutgers University School of Law from 1963–72, and Columbia Law School from 1972–80, and a fellow at the Center for Advanced Study in the Behavioral Sciences in Stanford, CA from 1977–78. In 1971, she was instrumental in launching the Women's Rights Project of the American Civil Liberties Union, and served as the ACLU's General Counsel from 1973–80, and on the National Board of Directors from 1974–80. She was appointed a Judge of the United States Court of Appeals for the District of Columbia Circuit in 1980. President Clinton nominated her as an Associate Justice of the Supreme Court, and she took her seat August 10, 1993.

STEPHEN G. BREYER, Associate Justice, was born in San Francisco, CA, August 15, 1938. He married Joanna Hare in 1967, and has three children, Chloe, Nell, and Michael. He received an A.B. from Stanford University, a B.A. from Magdalen College, Oxford, and an LL.B. from Harvard Law School. He served as a law clerk to Justice Arthur Goldberg of the Supreme Court of the United States during the 1964 term, as a Special Assistant to the Assistant U.S. Attorney General for Antitrust, 1965–67, as an Assistant Special Prosecutor of the Watergate Special Prosecution Force, 1973, as Special Counsel of the U.S. Senate Judiciary Committee, 1974–75, and as Chief Counsel of the committee, 1979–80. He was an Assistant Professor, Professor of Law, and Lecturer at Harvard Law School, 1967–94, a Professor at the Harvard University Kennedy School of Government, 1977–80, and a Visiting Professor at the College of Law, Sydney, Australia and at the University of Rome. From 1980–90, he served as a Judge of the United States Court of Appeals for the First Circuit, and as its Chief Judge, 1990–94. He also served as a member of the Judicial Conference of the United States, 1990–94, and of the United States Sentencing Commission, 1985–89. President Clinton nominated him as an Associate Justice of the Supreme Court, and he took his seat August 3, 1994.

SAMUEL ANTHONY ALITO, JR., Associate Justice, was born in Trenton, NJ, April 1, 1950. He married Martha-Ann Bomgardner in 1985, and has two children, Philip and Laura. He served as a law clerk for Leonard I. Garth of the United States Court of Appeals for the Third Circuit from 1976–77. He was Assistant U.S. Attorney, District of New Jersey, 1977–81, Assistant to the Solicitor General, U.S. Department of Justice, 1981–85, Deputy Assistant Attorney General, U.S. Department of Justice, 1985–87, and U.S. Attorney, District of New Jersey, 1987–90. He was appointed to the United States Court of Appeals for the Third Circuit in 1990. President George W. Bush nominated him as an Associate Justice of the Supreme Court, and he took his seat January 31, 2006.

SONIA SOTOMAYOR, Associate Justice of the United States Supreme Court, was born in Bronx, NY, June 25, 1954. She earned a B.A. in 1976 from Princeton University, graduating *summa cum laude* and receiving the university's highest academic honor. In 1979, she earned a J.D. from Yale Law School where she served as an editor of the *Yale Law Journal.* She served as Assistant District Attorney in the New York County District Attorney's Office from 1979–84. She then litigated international commercial matters in New York City at Pavia & Harcourt, where she served as an associate and then partner from 1984–92. In 1991, President George H.W. Bush nominated her to the U.S. District Court Southern District of New York, and she served in that role from 1992–98. She served as a judge on the United States Court of Appeals for the Second Circuit from 1998–2009. President Barack Obama nominated her as an Associate Justice of the Supreme Court on May 26, 2009, and she assumed this role August 8, 2009.

ELENA KAGAN, Associate Justice, was born in New York, NY, on April 28, 1960. She received an A.B., *summa cum laude,* in 1981 from Princeton University. She attended Worcester College, Oxford University, as Princeton's Daniel M. Sachs Graduating Fellow, and received an M.Phil. in 1983. In 1986, she earned a J.D. from Harvard Law School, graduating *magna cum laude,* where she was supervising editor of the *Harvard Law Review.* She served as a law clerk to Judge Abner Mikva of the U.S. Court of Appeals for the District of Columbia Circuit from 1986–87. She served as a law clerk to Justice Thurgood Marshall of the Supreme Court of the United States during the 1987 term. She worked as an associate in the Washington, DC, law firm of Williams & Connolly, LLP, from 1989–91. She became an assistant professor at the University of Chicago Law School in 1991 and a tenured professor of law in 1995. From 1995–99, she was associate counsel to President Clinton and then served as deputy assistant to the President for Domestic Policy and Deputy Director of the Domestic Policy Council. She joined Harvard Law School as a visiting professor in 1999 and became professor of law in 2001. She was the Charles Hamilton Houston Professor of Law and was appointed the 11th Dean of Harvard Law School in 2003. President Obama nominated her to serve as the 45th Solicitor General of the United States and she was confirmed on March 19, 2009. President Obama nominated her as an Associate Justice of the Supreme Court on May 10, 2010, and she assumed this role on August 7, 2010.

RETIRED ASSOCIATE JUSTICE

SANDRA DAY O'CONNOR (Retired), Associate Justice, was born in El Paso, TX, March 26, 1930. She married John Jay O'Connor III in 1952 and has three sons, Scott, Brian, and Jay. She received her B.A. and LL.B. from Stanford University. She served as Deputy County Attorney of San Mateo County, CA from 1952–53 and as a civilian attorney for Quartermaster Market Center, Frankfurt, Germany from 1954–57. From 1958–60, she practiced law in Maryvale, AZ, and served as Assistant Attorney General of Arizona from 1965–69. She was appointed to the Arizona State Senate in 1969 and was subsequently reelected to two two-year terms. In 1975 she was elected Judge of the Maricopa County Superior Court and served until 1979, when she was appointed to the Arizona Court of Appeals. President Reagan nominated her as an Associate Justice of the Supreme Court, and she took her seat September 25, 1981. Justice O'Connor retired from the Supreme Court on January 31, 2006.

DAVID H. SOUTER (Retired), Associate Justice, was born in Melrose, MA, September 17, 1939. He graduated from Harvard College, from which he received his A.B. After two years as a Rhodes Scholar at Magdalen College, Oxford, he received an A.B. in Jurisprudence from Oxford University and an M.A. in 1989. After receiving an LL.B. from Harvard Law School, he was an associate at Orr and Reno in Concord, NH from 1966 to 1968, when he became an Assistant Attorney General of New Hampshire. In 1971 he became Deputy Attorney General and in 1976, Attorney General of New Hampshire. In 1978 he was named an Associate Justice of the Superior Court of New Hampshire, and was appointed to the Supreme Court of New Hampshire as an Associate Justice in 1983. He became a Judge of the United States Court of Appeals for the First Circuit on May 25, 1990. President Bush nominated him as an Associate Justice of the Supreme Court, and he took his seat October 9, 1990. Justice Souter retired from the Supreme Court on June 29, 2009.

JOHN PAUL STEVENS (Retired), Associate Justice, was born in Chicago, IL, April 20, 1920. He married Maryan Mulholland, and has four children, John Joseph (deceased), Kathryn, Elizabeth Jane, and Susan Roberta. He received an A.B. from the University of Chicago, and a J.D. from Northwestern University School of Law. He served in the United States Navy from 1942–45, and was a law clerk to Justice Wiley Rutledge of the Supreme Court of the United States during the 1947 term. He was admitted to law practice in Illinois in 1949. He was Associate Counsel to the Subcommittee on the Study of Monopoly Power of the Judiciary Committee of the U.S. House of Representatives, 1951–52, and a member of the Attorney General's National Committee to Study Antitrust Law, 1953–55. He was Second Vice President of the Chicago Bar Association in 1970. From 1970–75, he served as a Judge of the United States Court of Appeals for the Seventh Circuit. President Ford nominated him as an Associate Justice of the Supreme Court, and he took his seat December 19, 1975. Justice Stevens retired from the Supreme Court on June 29, 2010.

Officers of the Supreme Court

Counselor to the Chief Justice.—Jeffrey P. Minear.

Clerk.—William K. Suter.
Librarian.—Judith A. Gaskell.
Marshal.—Pamela Talkin.
Reporter of Decisions.—Christine L. Fallon.
Court Counsel.—Scott Harris.
Curator.—Catherine E. Fitts.
Director of Information Technology.—Robert J. Hawkins.
Public Information Officer.—Kathleen L. Arberg.

UNITED STATES COURTS OF APPEALS

First Judicial Circuit (Districts of Maine, Massachusetts, New Hampshire, Puerto Rico, and Rhode Island).—*Chief Judge:* Sandra L. Lynch. *Circuit Judges:* Michael Boudin; Juan R. Torruella; Kermit V. Lipez; Jeffrey R. Howard; O. Rogeriee Thompson. *Senior Circuit Judges:* Bruce M. Selya; Norman H. Stahl. *Circuit Executive:* Gary H. Wente (617) 748–9613. *Clerk:* Margaret Carter (617) 748–9057, John Joseph Moakley U.S. Courthouse, One Courthouse Way, Suite 2500, Boston, MA 02210.

Second Judicial Circuit (Districts of Connecticut, New York, and Vermont).—*Chief Judge:* Dennis Jacobs; José A. Cabranes; Susan L. Carney; Denny Chin; Peter W. Hall; Robert A. Katzmann; Debra A. Livingston; Raymond J. Lohier; Gerard E. Lynch; Rosemary S. Pooler; Reena Raggi; Richard C. Wesley. *Senior Judges:* Giudo Calabresi; Wilfred Feinberg; Amalya L. Kearse; Pierre N. Leval; Joseph M. McLaughlin; Roger J. Miner; Jon O. Newman; Barrington D. Parker, Jr.; Robert D. Sack; Chester J. Straub; John M. Walker, Jr.; Ralph K. Winter. *Circuit Executive:* Karen Greve Milton. *Clerk:* Catherine O'Hagan Wolfe (212) 857–8700, Thurgood Marshall United States Courthouse, 40 Foley Square, New York, NY 10007–1581.

Third Judicial Circuit (Districts of Delaware, New Jersey, Pennsylvania, and Virgin Islands).—*Chief Judge:* Theodore A. McKee. *Circuit Judges:* Anthony J. Scirica; Dolores K. Sloviter; Marjorie O. Rendell; Thomas L. Ambro; Julio M. Fuentes; D. Brooks Smith; D. Michael Fisher; Michael A. Chagares; Kent A. Jordan; Thomas M. Hardiman; Joseph A. Greenaway, Jr.; Thomas I. Vanaskie. *Senior Circuit Judges:* Ruggero J. Aldisert; Maryanne Trump Barry; Joseph F. Weis, Jr.; Leonard I. Garth; Walter K. Stapleton; Morton I. Greenberg; Robert E. Cowen; Richard L. Nygaard; Jane R. Roth; Franklin S. VanAntwerpen. *Circuit Executive:* Toby D. Slawsky (215) 597–0718. *Clerk:* Marcia M. Waldron (215) 597–2995, U.S. Courthouse, 601 Market Street, Philadelphia, PA 19106.

Fourth Judicial Circuit (Districts of Maryland, North Carolina, South Carolina, Virginia, and West Virginia).—*Chief Judge:* William B. Traxler, Jr. *Circuit Judges:* J. Harvie Wilkinson III; Paul V. Niemeyer; Diana Gribbon Motz; Robert B. King; Roger L. Gregory; Dennis W. Shedd; Allyson K. Duncan; G. Steven Agee; Andre M. Davis; Barbara Milano Keenan; James A. Wynn, Jr.; Albert Diaz. *Senior Circuit Judge:* Clyde H. Hamilton. *Circuit Executive:* Samuel W. Phillips (804) 916–2184. *Clerk:* Patricia S. Connor (804) 916–2700, Lewis F. Powell, Jr. U.S. Courthouse Annex, 1100 E. Main Street, Richmond, VA 23219.

Fifth Judicial Circuit (Districts of Louisiana, Mississippi, and Texas).—*Chief Judge:* Edith H. Jones. *Circuit Judges:* Carolyn Dineen King; E. Grady Jolly; W. Eugene Davis; Jerry E. Smith; Emilio M. Garza; Fortunato P. Benavides; Carl E. Stewart; James L. Dennis; Edith Brown Clement; Edward C. Prado; Priscilla R. Owen; Jennifer Walker Elrod; Leslie H. Southwick; Catharina Haynes; James E. Graves, Jr. *Senior Circuit Judges:* Thomas M. Reavley; Will Garwood; Patrick E. Higginbotham; John M. Duhé, Jr; Jacques L. Wiener, Jr.; Rhesa H. Barksdale; Harold R. DeMoss, Jr. *Circuit Executive:* Gregory A. Nussel (504) 310–7777. *Clerk:* Lyle W. Cayce (504) 310–7700, John Minor Wisdom, U.S. Court of Appeals Building, 600 Camp Street, New Orleans, LA 70130–3425.

Sixth Judicial Circuit (Districts of Kentucky, Michigan, Ohio, and Tennessee).—*Chief Judge:* Alice M. Batchelder. *Circuit Judges:* Boyce F. Martin, Jr.; Danny J. Boggs; Karen Nelson Moore; R. Guy Cole, Jr.; Eric Lee Clay; Julie Smith Gibbons; John M. Rogers; Jeffrey S. Sutton; Deborah L. Cook; David McKeague; Richard Allen Griffin; Raymond M. Kethledge; Helene N. White; Jane B. Stranch. *Senior Circuit Judges:* Damon J. Keith; Gilbert S. Merritt; Cornelius G. Kennedy; Ralph B. Guy; Alan E. Norris; Richard F. Suhrheinrich; Eugene E. Siler, Jr.; Martha Craig Daughtrey; Ronald Lee Gilman. *Circuit Executive:* Clarence Maddox (513) 564–7200. *Clerk:* Leonard Green (513) 564–7000, Potter Stewart U.S. Courthouse, 100 E. Fifth Street, Cincinnati, OH 45202.

Seventh Judicial Circuit (Districts of Illinois, Indiana, and Wisconsin).—*Chief Judge:* Frank H. Easterbrook. *Circuit Judges:* Richard A. Posner; Joel M. Flaum; Michael S. Kanne; Ilana Diamond Rovner; Diane P. Wood; Ann Claire Williams; Diane S. Sykes; John Daniel Tinder; David F. Hamilton. *Senior Circuit Judges:* William J. Bauer; Richard D. Cudahy; John L. Coffey; Kenneth F. Ripple; Daniel A. Manion; Terence T. Evans. *Circuit Executive:*

Collins T. Fitzpatrick (312) 435–5803. *Clerk:* Gino J. Agnello (312) 435–5850, 2722 U.S. Courthouse, 219 S. Dearborn Street, Chicago, IL 60604.

Eighth Judicial Circuit (Districts of Arkansas, Iowa, Minnesota, Missouri, Nebraska, North Dakota, and South Dakota).—*Chief Judge:* William Jay Riley. *Circuit Judges:* Roger L. Wollman; James B. Loken; Diana E. Murphy; Kermit E. Bye; Michael J. Melloy; Lavenski R. Smith; Steven M. Colloton; Raymond W. Gruender; Duane Benton; Bobby E. Shepherd. *Senior Circuit Judges:* Myron H. Bright; Pasco M. Bowman II; C. Arlen Beam; Morris S. Arnold. *Circuit Executive:* Millie Adams (314) 244–2600. *Clerk:* Michael E. Gans (314) 244–2400, 111 S. Tenth Street, Suite 24.327, St. Louis, MO 63102.

Ninth Judicial Circuit (Districts of Alaska, Arizona, Central California, Eastern California, Northern California, Southern California, Guam, Hawaii, Idaho, Montana, Nevada, Northern Mariana Islands, Oregon, Eastern Washington, Western Washington).—*Chief Judge:* Alex Kozinski. *Circuit Judges:* Mary M. Schroeder; Harry Pregerson; Stephen R. Reinhardt; Diarmuid F. O'Scannlain; Pamela A. Rymer; Sidney R. Thomas; Barry G. Silverman; Susan P. Graber; M. Margaret McKeown; Kim McLane Wardlaw; William A. Fletcher; Raymond C. Fisher; Ronald M. Gould; Richard A. Paez; Marsha L. Berzon; Richard C. Tallman; Johnnie B. Rawlinson; Richard R. Clifton; Consuelo M. Callahan; Carlos T. Bea; Milan D. Smith, Jr.; Sandra S. Ikuta; N. Randy Smith. *Senior Circuit Judges:* James R. Browning; Alfred T. Goodwin; J. Clifford Wallace; Procter R. Hug, Jr.; Otto R. Skopil, Jr.; Betty B. Fletcher; J. Jerome Farris; Arthur L. Alarcón; Dorothy W. Nelson; William C. Canby, Jr.; Robert Boochever; Robert R. Beezer; John T. Noonan, Jr.; Edward Leavy; Stephen S. Trott; Ferdinand F. Fernandez; Andrew J. Kleinfeld; Michael D. Hawkins; A. Wallace Tashima. *Circuit and Court of Appeals Executive:* Cathy A. Catterson (415) 355–8800. *Clerk:* Molly C. Dwyer (415) 355–8000. P.O. Box 193939, San Francisco, CA 94119–3939.

Tenth Judicial Circuit (Districts of Colorado, Kansas, New Mexico, Oklahoma, Utah, and Wyoming).—*Chief Judge:* Mary Beck Briscoe. *Circuit Judges:* Paul J. Kelly, Jr.; Carlos F. Lucero; Michael R. Murphy; Harris L Hartz; Terrence L. O'Brien; Timothy M. Tymkovich; Neil M. Gorsuch; Jerome A. Holmes; Scott M. Matheson, Jr. *Senior Circuit Judges:* William J. Holloway, Jr.; Robert H. McWilliams; Monroe G. McKay; Stephanie K. Seymour; John C. Porfilio; Stephen H. Anderson; Bobby R. Baldock; Wade Brorby; David M. Ebel. *Circuit Executive:* David Tighe (303) 844–2067. *Clerk:* Betsy Shumaker (303) 844–3157, Byron White United States Courthouse, 1823 Stout Street, Denver, CO 80257.

Eleventh Judicial Circuit (Districts of Alabama, Florida, and Georgia).—*Chief Judge:* Joel F. Dubina. *Circuit Judges:* Gerald Bard Tjoflat; J. L. Edmondson; Ed Carnes; Rosemary Barkett; Frank M. Hull; Stanley Marcus; Charles R. Wilson; William H. Pryor, Jr; Beverly B. Martin. *Senior Circuit Judges:* James C. Hill; Peter T. Fay; Phyllis A. Kravitch; Emmett R. Cox; R. Lanier Anderson III; Susan H. Black. *Circuit Executive:* James P. Gerstenlauer (404) 335–6535. Clerk: John P. Ley (404) 335–6100, 56 Forsyth Street, NW., Atlanta, GA 30303.

UNITED STATES COURT OF APPEALS

FOR THE DISTRICT OF COLUMBIA CIRCUIT

333 Constitution Avenue, NW., 20001, phone (202) 216–7300

DAVID BRYAN SENTELLE, chief circuit judge, born in Canton, NC, February 12, 1943; son of Horace and Maude Sentelle; married to Jane LaRue Oldham; three daughters and four granddaughters; B.A., University of North Carolina at Chapel Hill, 1965; J.D. with honors, University of North Carolina School of Law, 1968; associate, Uzzell and Dumont, Charlotte, 1968–79; Assistant U.S. Attorney, Charlotte, 1970–74; North Carolina State District Judge, 1974–77; partner, Tucker, Hicks, Sentelle, Moon and Hodge, Charlotte, 1977–85; U.S. District Judge for the Western District of North Carolina, 1985–87; appointed to the U.S. Court of Appeals by President Reagan in October 1987; assumed the position of Chief Judge on February 11, 2008.

DOUGLAS HOWARD GINSBURG, circuit judge; born in Chicago, IL, May 25, 1946; diploma, Latin School of Chicago, 1963; B.S., Cornell University, 1970 (Phi Kappa Phi, Ives Award); J.D., University of Chicago, 1973 (Mecham Prize Scholarship 1970–73, Casper Platt Award, 1973, Order of Coif, Articles and Book Rev. Ed., 40 U. Chi. L. Rev.); bar admissions: Illinois (1973), Massachusetts (1982), U.S. Supreme Court (1984), U.S. Court of Appeals for the Ninth Circuit (1986); member: Mont Pelerin Society, American Economic Association, American Law and Economics Association, Honor Society of Phi Kappa Phi, American Bar Association, Antitrust Section, Council, 1985–86 (ex officio), judicial liaison (2000–03 and 2009–12); advisory boards: Competition Policy International; Harvard Journal of Law and Public Policy; Journal of Competition Law and Economics; Law and Economics Center, George Mason University School of Law; Supreme Court Economic Review; University of Chicago Law Review; Board of Directors: Foundation for Research in Economics and the Environment, 1991–2004; Rappahannock County Conservation Alliance, 1998–2004; Rappahannock Association for Arts and Community, 1997–99; Committees: Judicial Conference of the United States, 2002–08, Budget Committee, 1997–2001, Committee on Judicial Resources, 1987–96; Boston University Law School, Visiting Committee, 1994–97; University of Chicago Law School, Visiting Committee, 1985–88; law clerk to: Judge Carl McGowan, U.S. Court of Appeals for the District of Columbia Circuit, 1973–74; Associate Justice Thurgood Marshall, U.S. Supreme Court, 1974–75; previous positions: assistant professor, Harvard University Law School, 1975–81; Professor 1981–83; Deputy Assistant Attorney General, Antitrust Division, U.S. Department of Justice, 1983–84; Administrator for Information and Regulatory Affairs, Executive Office of the President, Office of Management and Budget, 1984–85; Assistant Attorney General, Antitrust Division, U.S. Department of Justice, 1985–86; lecturer in law, Columbia University, New York City, 1987–88, 2009–11; lecturer in law, Harvard University, Cambridge, MA, 1988–89; distinguished professor of law, George Mason University, Arlington, VA, 1988–present; senior lecturer, University of Chicago Law School, 1990–present; lecturer on law, New York Law School, 2005–09; Visiting Professor, Faculty of Laws, University College, London, 2010–15; appointed to U.S. Court of Appeals for the District of Columbia Circuit by President Reagan on October 14, 1986, taking the oath of office on November 10, 1986, Chief Judge, 2001–08.

KAREN LeCRAFT HENDERSON, circuit judge. [Biographical information not supplied, per Judge Henderson's request.]

JUDITH W. ROGERS, circuit judge; born in New York, NY; A.B. (with honors), Radcliffe College, 1961; Phi Beta Kappa honors member; LL.B., Harvard Law School, 1964; LL.M., University of Virginia School of Law, 1988; law clerk, D.C. Juvenile Court, 1964–65; assistant U.S. Attorney for the District of Columbia, 1965–68; trial attorney, San Francisco Neighborhood Legal Assistance Foundation, 1968–69; Attorney, U.S. Department of Justice, Office of the Associate Deputy Attorney General and Criminal Division, 1969–71; General Counsel, Congressional Commission on the Organization of the D.C. Government, 1971–72; legislative assistant to D.C. Mayor Walter E. Washington, 1972–79; Corporation Counsel for the District of Columbia, 1979–83; trustee, Radcliffe College, 1982–90; member of Visiting Committee to Harvard Law School, 1984–90 and 2006–11; appointed by President Reagan to the District of Columbia Court of Appeals as an Associate Judge on September 15, 1983; served as Chief Judge, November 1, 1988 to March 17, 1994; appointed by President Clinton to the U.S. Court of Appeals for the District of Columbia Circuit on March 18, 1994, and entered on duty March 21, 1994; member of Executive Committee, Conference of Chief Justices, 1993–94; member, U.S. Judicial Conference Committee on the Codes of Conduct, 1998–2004.

DAVID S. TATEL, circuit judge; born in Washington, DC, March 16, 1942; son of Molly and Dr. Howard Tatel (deceased); married to the former Edith Bassichis, 1965; children: Rebecca, Stephanie, Joshua, and Emily; grandchildren: Olivia, Maya, Olin, Reuben, Rae, Cameron, and Ozzie; B.A., University of Michigan, 1963; J.D., University of Chicago Law School, 1966; instructor, University of Michigan Law School, 1966–67; associate, Sidley and Austin, 1967–69, 1970–72; director, Chicago Lawyers' Committee for Civil Rights Under Law, 1969–70; director, National Lawyers' Committee for Civil Rights Under Law, 1972–74; director, Office for Civil Rights, U.S. Department of Health, Education and Welfare, 1977–79; associate and partner, Hogan and Hartson, 1974–77, 1979–94; lecturer, Stanford University Law School, 1991–92; board of directors, Spencer Foundation, 1987–97 (chair, 1990–97); board of directors, National Board for Professional Teaching Standards, 1997–2000; National Lawyers' Committee for Civil Rights Under Law, co-chair, 1989–91; board of directors, Carnegie Foundation for the Advancement of Teaching, (chair, 2005–09); board of directors, Equal Justice Works; member of the American Philosophical Society, the National Academy of Education, and the National Academy of Sciences Committee on Science, Technology and Law; admitted to practice law in Illinois in 1966 and the District Columbia in 1970; appointed to the U.S. Court of Appeals for the District of Columbia Circuit by President Clinton on October 7, 1994, and entered on duty October 11, 1994.

MERRICK BRIAN GARLAND, circuit judge; born in Chicago, IL, 1952; A.B., Harvard University, 1974, *summa cum laude,* Phi Beta Kappa, Paul Revere Frothingham and Richard Perkins Parker Award; J.D., Harvard Law School, 1977, *magna cum laude,* articles editor, Harvard Law Review; law clerk to Judge Henry J. Friendly, U.S. Court of Appeals for the 2d Circuit, 1977–78; law clerk to Justice William J. Brennan, Jr., U.S. Supreme Court, 1978–79; Special Assistant to the Attorney General, 1979–81; associate then partner, Arnold and Porter, Washington, DC, 1981–89; Assistant U.S. Attorney, Washington, DC, 1989–92; partner, Arnold and Porter, 1992–93; Deputy Assistant Attorney General, Criminal Division, U.S. Department of Justice, 1993–94; Principal Associate Deputy Attorney General, 1994–97; Lecturer on Law, Harvard Law School, 1985–86; Associate Independent Counsel, 1987–88. Edmund J. Randolph Award, U.S. Department of Justice, 1997. Admitted to the bars of the District of Columbia; U.S. District Court; Court of Appeals, District of Columbia Circuit; U.S. Courts of Appeals for the 4th, 9th, and 10th Circuits; and U.S. Supreme Court. Author: *Antitrust and State Action,* 96 Yale Law Journal 486 (1987); *Antitrust and Federalism,* 96 Yale Law Journal 1291 (1987); *Deregulation and Judicial Review,* 98 Harvard Law Review 505 (1985); co-chair, Administrative Law Section, District of Columbia Bar, 1991–94; President, Board of Overseers, Harvard University, 2009–10, member, 2003–09; American Law Institute; U.S. Judiciary Conference Committee on Judicial Security, 2008–present, Committee on the Judicial Branch, 2001–05; appointed to the U.S. Court of Appeals for the District of Columbia Circuit on April 9, 1997.

JANICE ROGERS BROWN, circuit judge; born in Greenville, AL; B.A., California State University, 1974; J.D., University of California School of Law, 1977; LL.M., University of Virginia School of Law, 2004; Deputy Legislative Counsel, Legislative Counsel Bureau, 1977–79; Deputy Attorney General, California Department of Justice, 1979–87; Deputy Secretary and General Counsel, California Business, Transportation, and Housing Agency, 1987–90; Senior Associate, Nielsen, Merksamer, Parinello, Mueller and Naylor, 1990–91; Legal Affairs Secretary for Governor Pete Wilson, 1991–94; Associate Justice, California Court of Appeals for the Third District, 1994–96; Associate Justice, California Supreme Court, 1996–2005; appointed to the U.S. Court of Appeals for the District of Columbia Circuit by President George W. Bush on June 10, 2005 and sworn in on July 1, 2005.

THOMAS B. GRIFFITH, circuit judge; born in Yokohama, Japan, July 5, 1954; B.A., Brigham Young University, 1978; J.D., University of Virginia School of Law, 1985; editor, Virginia Law Review; associate, Robinson, Bradshaw and Hinson, Charlotte, NC, 1985–89; associate and then a partner, Wiley, Rein and Fielding, Washington, DC, 1989–95 and 1999–2000; Senate Legal Counsel of the United States, 1995–99; Assistant to the President and General Counsel, Brigham Young University, Provo, UT, 2000–05; member, Executive Committee of the American Bar Association's Central European and Eurasian Law Initiative;

appointed to the United States Court of Appeals for the District of Columbia Circuit on June 14, 2005 and sworn in on June 29, 2005.

BRETT M. KAVANAUGH, circuit judge; born in Washington, DC, February 12, 1965; son of Edward and Martha Kavanaugh; married to Ashley Estes; two daughters; B.A., *cum laude*, Yale College, 1987; J.D., Yale Law School, 1990; law clerk to Judge Walter Stapleton of the U.S. Court of Appeals for the Third Circuit, 1990–91; law clerk for Judge Alex Kozinski of the U.S. Court of Appeals for the Ninth Circuit, 1991–92; attorney, Office of the Solicitor General of the United States, 1992–93; law clerk to Associate Justice Anthony Kennedy of the U.S. Supreme Court, 1993–94; Associate Counsel, Office of Independent Counsel, 1994–97; partner, Kirkland & Ellis LLP, 1997–98, 1999–2001; Associate Counsel and then Senior Associate Counsel to President George W. Bush, 2001–03; Assistant to the President and Staff Secretary to President Bush, 2003–06; Adjunct Professor of Law, Georgetown University Law Center, 2007; Lecturer on Law, Harvard Law School, 2008–12; appointed to the U.S. Court of Appeals for the District of Columbia Circuit on May 30, 2006.

SENIOR CIRCUIT JUDGES

HARRY T. EDWARDS, senior circuit judge; born in New York, NY, November 3, 1940; son of George H. Edwards and Arline (Ross) Lyle; married to Pamela Carrington Edwards; children: Brent and Michelle; B.S., Cornell University, 1962; J.D. (with distinction), University of Michigan Law School, 1965; associate with Seyfarth, Shaw, Fairweather and Geraldson, 1965–70; professor of law, University of Michigan, 1970–75 and 1977–80; professor of law, Harvard University, 1975–77; visiting professor of law, Free University of Brussels, 1974; arbitrator of labor/management disputes, 1970–80; vice president, National.Academy of Arbitrators, 1978–80; member (1977–79) and chairman (1979–80), National Railroad Passenger Corporation (Amtrak); Executive Committee of the Association of American Law Schools, 1979–80; public member of the Administrative Conference of the United States, 1976–80; International Women's Year Commission, 1976–77; American Bar Association Commission of Law and the Economy; co-author of five books: *Labor Relations Law in the Public Sector, The Lawyer as a Negotiator, Higher Education and the Law*, and *Collective Bargaining and Labor Arbitration*; and, most recently, Edwards & Ellliot, *Federal Standards of Review*, recipient of the Judge William B. Groat Alumni Award, 1978, given by Cornell University; the Society of American Law Teachers Award (for "distinguished contributions to teaching and public service"); the Whitney North Seymour Medal presented by the American Arbitration Association for outstanding contributions to the use of arbitration; Recipient of the 2004 Robert J. Kutak Award, presented by the American Bar Association Selection of Legal Education and Admission to the Bar "to a person who meets the highest standards of professional responsibility and demonstrates substantial achievement toward increased understanding between legal education and the active practice of law", and several Honorary Doctor of Laws degrees; has been a Visiting Professor of Law at NYU School of Law since 1990; has also taught part-time at Duke, Georgetown, Michigan, and Harvard Law Schools; co-chair of the Forensics Science Committee established by the National Academy of Sciences, 2006–09; appointed to the U.S. Court of Appeals, February 20, 1980; served as chief judge September 15, 1994 to July 16, 2001.

LAURENCE HIRSCH SILBERMAN, senior circuit judge; recipient of the Presidential Medal of Freedom, June 19, 2008; born in York, PA, October 12, 1935; son of William Silberman and Anna (Hirsch); married to Rosalie G. Gaull on April 28, 1957 (deceased), married Patricia Winn on January 5, 2008; children: Robert Stephen Silberman, Katherine DeBoer Balaban, and Anne Gaull Otis; B.A., Dartmouth College, 1957; LL.B., Harvard Law School, 1961; admitted to Hawaii Bar, 1962; District of Columbia Bar, 1973; associate, Moore, Torkildson and Rice, 1961–64; partner (Moore, Silberman and Schulze), Honolulu, 1964–67; attorney, National Labor Relations Board, Office of General Counsel, Appellate Division, 1967–69; Solicitor, Department of Labor, 1969–70; Under Secretary of Labor, 1970–73; partner, Steptoe and Johnson, 1973–74; Deputy Attorney General of the United States, 1974–75; Ambassador to Yugoslavia, 1975–77; President's Special Envoy on ILO Affairs, 1976; senior fellow, American Enterprise Institute, 1977–78; visiting fellow, 1978–85; managing partner, Morrison and Foerster, 1978–79 and 1983–85; executive vice president, Crocker National Bank, 1979–83; lecturer, University of Hawaii, 1962–63; board of directors, Commission on Present Danger, 1978–85, Institute for Educational Affairs, New York, NY, 1981–85, member: General Advisory Committee on Arms Control and Disarmament, 1981–85; Defense Policy Board, 1981–85; vice chairman, State Department's Commission on Security and Economic Assistance, 1983–84; American Bar Association (Labor Law Committee, 1965–72,

Corporations and Banking Committee, 1973, Law and National Security Advisory Committee, 1981–85); Hawaii Bar Association Ethics Committee, 1965–67; Council on Foreign Relations, 1977–present; Judicial Conference Committee on Court Administration and Case Management, 1994; member, U.S. Foreign Intelligence Surveillance Act Court of Review, 1996–2003; Adjunct Professor of Law (Administrative Law and Labor Law) Georgetown Law Center, 1987–94; 1997; Adjunct Professor of Law, New York University Law School, 1995–96; Distinguished Visitor from the Judiciary, Georgetown Law Center, 2003–present; co-chairman of the President's Commission on The Intelligence Capabilities of the United States Regarding Weapons of Mass Destruction, 2004–05; appointed to the U.S. Court of Appeals for the District of Columbia Circuit by President Reagan on October 28, 1985.

STEPHEN F. WILLIAMS, senior circuit judge; born in New York, NY, September 23, 1936; son of Charles Dickerman Williams and Virginia (Fain); married to Faith Morrow, 1966; children: Susan, Geoffrey, Sarah, Timothy, and Nicholas; B.A., Yale, 1958, J.D., Harvard Law School, 1961; U.S. Army Reserves, 1961–62; associate, Debevoise, Plimpton, Lyons and Gates, 1962–66; Assistant U.S. Attorney, Southern District of New York, 1966–69; associate professor and professor of law, University of Colorado School of Law, 1969–86; visiting professor of law, UCLA, 1975–76; visiting professor of law and fellow in law and economics, University Chicago Law School, 1979–80; visiting George W. Hutchison Professor of Energy Law, SMU, 1983–84; consultant to: Administrative Conference of the United States, 1974–76; Federal Trade Commission on energy-related issues, 1983–85; member, American Law Institute; appointed to the U.S. Court of Appeals for the District of Columbia Circuit by President Reagan, June 16, 1986.

A. RAYMOND RANDOLPH, senior circuit judge; born in Riverside, NJ, November 1, 1943; son of Arthur Raymond Randolph, Sr. and Marile (Kelly); two children: John Trevor and Cynthia Lee Randolph; married to Eileen Janette O'Connor, May 18, 1984. B.S., Drexel University, 1966; J.D., University of Pennsylvania Law School, 1969, *summa cum laude;* managing editor, University of Pennsylvania Law Review; Order of the Coif. Admitted to Supreme Court of the United States; Supreme Court of California; District of Columbia Court of Appeals; U.S. Courts of Appeals for the First, Second, Fourth, Fifth, Sixth, Seventh, Ninth, Eleventh, and District of Columbia Circuits. Memberships: American Law Institute. Law clerk to Judge Henry J. Friendly, U.S. Court of Appeals for the Second Circuit, 1969–70; Assistant to the Solicitor General, 1970–73; adjunct professor of law, Georgetown University Law Center, 1974–78; George Mason School of Law, 1992; Deputy Solicitor General, 1975–77; Special Counsel, Committee on Standards of Official Conduct, House of Representatives, 1979–80; special assistant attorney general, State of Montana (honorary), 1983–July 1990; special assistant attorney general, State of New Mexico, 1985–July 1990; special assistant attorney general, State of Utah, 1986–July 1990; advisory panel, Federal Courts Study Committee, 1989–July 1990; partner, Pepper, Hamilton and Scheetz, 1987–July 1990; chairman, Committee on Codes of Conduct, U.S. Judicial Conference, 1995–98; distinguished professor of law, George Mason Law School, 1999–present; recipient, Distinguished Alumnus Award, University of Pennsylvania Law School, 2002; appointed to the U.S. Court of Appeals for the District of Columbia Circuit by President George H.W. Bush on July 16, 1990, and took oath of office on July 20, 1990.

OFFICERS OF THE UNITED STATES COURT OF APPEALS FOR THE DISTRICT OF COLUMBIA CIRCUIT

Circuit Executive.—Betsy Paret (202) 216–7340.
Clerk.—Mark J. Langer, 216–7000.
Chief Deputy Clerk.—Marilyn R. Sargent, 216–7000.
Chief, Legal Division.—Martha Tomich, 216–7500.

UNITED STATES COURT OF APPEALS

FEDERAL CIRCUIT

717 Madison Place, NW., 20439, phone (202) 633–6550

RANDALL R. RADER, cheif circuit judge; born in Hastings, NE, April 21, 1949; son of Raymond A. and Gloria R. Rader; B.A., Brigham Young University, 1971–74, (*magna cum laude*), Phi Beta Kappa; J.D., George Washington University Law Center, 1974–78; legislative assistant to Representative Virginia Smith; legislative director, counsel, House Committee on Ways and Means to Representative Philip M. Crane, 1978–81; General Counsel, Chief Counsel, Subcommittee on the Constitution, 1981–86; Minority Chief Counsel, Staff Director, Subcommittee on Patents, Trademarks and Copyrights, Senate Committee on Judiciary, 1987–88; Judge, U.S. Claims Court, 1988–90, nominated by President Ronald Reagan; recipient: Outstanding Young Federal Lawyer Award by Federal Bar Association, 1983; Jefferson Medal Award, 2003; bar member: District of Columbia, 1978; Supreme Court of the United States, 1984; nominated to the U.S Court of Appeals for the Federal Circuit by President George H.W. Bush on June 12, 1990; confirmed by Senate August 3, 1990, sworn in August 14, 1990.

PAULINE NEWMAN, circuit judge; born in New York, NY, June 20, 1927; daughter of Maxwell H. and Rosella G. Newman; B.A., Vassar College, 1947; M.A. in pure science, Columbia University, 1948; Ph.D. degree in chemistry, Yale University, 1952; LL.B., New York University School of Law, 1958; Doctor of Laws (honorary), Franklin Pierce School of Law, 1991; admitted to the New York bar in 1958 and to the Pennsylvania bar in 1979; worked as research scientist for the American Cyanamid Co. from 1951–54; worked for the FMC Corp. from 1954–84 as patent attorney and house counsel and, since 1969, as director of the Patent, Trademark, and Licensing Department; on leave from FMC Corp. worked for the United Nations Educational, Scientific and Cultural Organization as a science policy specialist in the Department of Natural Sciences, 1961–62; offices in scientific and professional organizations include: member of Council of the Patent, Trademark and Copyright Section of the American Bar Association, 1982–84; board of directors of the American Patent Law Association, 1981–84; vice president of the United States Trademark Association, 1978–79, and member of the board of directors, 1975–76, 1977–79; board of governors of the New York Patent Law Association, 1970–74; president of the Pacific Industrial Property Association, 1978–80; executive committee of the International Patent and Trademark Association, 1982–84; board of directors: the American Chemical Society, 1973–75, 1976–78, 1979–81; American Institute of Chemists, 1960–66, 1970–76; Research Corp., 1982–84; member: board of trustees of Philadelphia College of Pharmacy and Science, 1983–84; patent policy board of State University of New York, 1983–84; national board of Medical College of Pennsylvania, 1975–84; governmental committees include: State Department Advisory Committee on International Intellectual Property, 1974–84; advisory committee to the Domestic Policy Review of Industrial Innovation, 1978–79; special advisory committee on Patent Office Procedure and Practice, 1972–74; member of the U.S. Delegation to the Diplomatic Conference on the Revision of the Paris Convention for the Protection of Industrial Property, 1982–84; awarded Wilbur Cross Medal of Yale University Graduate School, 1989, the Jefferson Medal of the New Jersey Intellectual Property Law Association, 1988; the Eli Whitney Award of the Connecticut Patent Law Association, 1999; Lifetime Achievement Award; Managing Intellectual Property, 2008; AIPLA Present's Outstanding Service Award, 2007; Outstanding Public Service Award; New York Intellectual Property Law Association, 2005; Lifetime Achievement Award; Sedona Conference, 2006; the Award for Outstanding Contributions in the Intellectual Property Field of the Pacific Industrial Property Association, 1987; Vanderbilt Medal of New York University School of Law, 1995; Vasser College Distinguished Achievement Award, 2002; Distinguished Professor of Law, George Mason University School of Law (adjunct faculty); Council on Foreign Relations; appointed judge of the U.S. Court of Appeals for the Federal Circuit by President Reagan and entered upon duties of that office on May 7, 1984.

ALAN D. LOURIE, circuit judge; born in Boston, MA, January 13, 1935; son of Joseph Lourie and Rose; educated in public schools in Brookline, MA; A.B., Harvard University, 1956; M.S., University of Wisconsin, 1958; Ph.D., University of Pennsylvania, 1965; J.D., Temple University, 1970; married; two children; four grandchildren; employed at Monsanto Company (chemist, 1957–59); Wyeth Laboratories (chemist, literature scientist, patent liaison specialist, 1959–64); SmithKline Beecham Corporation, (Patent Agent, 1964–70; assistant director, Corporate Patents, 1970–76; director, Corporate Patents, 1976–77; vice president, Corporate Patents and Trademarks and Associate General Counsel, 1977–90); vice chairman of the Industry Functional Advisory Committee on Intellectual Property Rights for Trade Policy Matters (IFAC 3) for the Department of Commerce and the Office of the U.S. Trade Representative, 1987–90; Treasurer of the Association of Corporate Patent Counsel, 1987–89; President of the Philadelphia Patent Law Association, 1984–85; member of the board of directors of the American Intellectual Property Law Association (formerly American Patent Law Association), 1982–85; member of the U.S. delegation to the Diplomatic Conference on the Revision of the Paris Convention for the Protection of Industrial Property, October–November 1982, March 1984; chairman of the Patent Committee of the Law Section of the Pharmaceutical Manufacturers Association, 1980–85; member of the Judicial Conference Committee on Financial Disclosure, 1990–98; member of the Judicial Conference Committee on Codes of Conduct, 2005; member of the American Bar Association, the American Chemical Society, the Cosmos Club, and the Harvard Club of Washington; recipient of the Jefferson Medal of the New Jersey Intellectual Property Law Association for outstanding contributions to intellectual property law, 1998; recipient of the first Distinguished Intellectual Property Professional Award of the Intellectual Property Owners Education Foundation, 2008; admitted to: Supreme Court of Pennsylvania, U.S. District Court for the Eastern District of Pennsylvania, U.S. Court of Appeals for the Third Circuit, U.S. Court of Appeals for the Federal Circuit, U.S. Supreme Court; nominated January 25, 1990, by President George H.W. Bush to be circuit judge, U.S. Court of Appeals for the Federal Circuit, confirmed by the Senate on April 5, 1990, and assumed duties of the office on April 11, 1990.

WILLIAM CURTIS BRYSON, circuit judge; born in Houston, TX, August 19, 1945; A.B., Harvard University, 1969; J.D., University of Texas School of Law, 1973; married with two children; law clerk to Hon. Henry J. Friendly, circuit judge, U.S. Court of Appeals for the Second Circuit, 1973–74, and Hon. Thurgood Marshall, associate justice, U.S. Supreme Court, 1974–75; associate, Miller, Cassidy, Larroca and Lewin, Washington, DC, 1975–78; Department of Justice, Criminal Division, 1979–86, Office of Solicitor General, 1978–79 and 1986–94; Office of the Associate Attorney General, 1994; nominated in June 1994 by President Clinton to be circuit judge, U.S. Court of Appeals for the Federal Circuit, and assumed duties of the office on October 7, 1994.

ARTHUR J. GAJARSA, circuit judge; born in Norcia (Pro. Perugia), Italy, March 1, 1941; married to Melanie Gajarsa; five children; Rensselaer Polytechnic Institute, Troy, NY, 1958–62, B.S.E.E., Bausch and Lomb Medal, 1958, Benjamin Franklin Award, 1958; Catholic University of America, Washington, DC, 1968; M.A. in economics, graduate studies; J.D., Georgetown University Law Center, Washington, DC, 1967; patent examiner, U.S. Patent Office, Department of Commerce, 1962–63; patent adviser, U.S. Air Force, Department of Defense, 1963–64; patent adviser, Cushman, Darby and Cushman, 1964–67; law clerk to Judge Joseph McGarraghy, U.S. District Court for the District of Columbia, Washington, DC, 1967–68; attorney, Office of General Counsel, Aetna Life and Casualty Co., 1968–69; special counsel and assistant to the Commissioner of Indian Affairs, Bureau of Indian Affairs, Department of Interior, 1969–71; associate, Duncan and Brown, 1971–72; partner, Gajarsa, Liss and Sterenbuch, 1972–78; partner, Garjarsa, Liss and Conroy, 1978–80; partner, Wender, Murase and White, 1980–86; partner and officer, Joseph Gajarsa, McDermott and Reiner, P.C., 1987–97; registered patent agent, registered patent attorney, 1963; admitted to the D.C. bar, U.S. District Court for the District of Columbia, and U.S. Court of Appeals for the District of Columbia, 1968; Connecticut State Bar, 1969; U.S. Supreme Court, 1971; Superior Court for D.C., Court of Appeals for D.C., 1972; U.S. Courts of Appeals for the Ninth and Federal Circuits, 1974; U.S. District Court for the Northern District of New York, 1980; awards: Sun and Balance Medal, Rensselaer Polytechnic Institute, 1990; Gigi Pieri Award, Camp Hale Association, Boston, MA, 1992; Rensselaer Key Alumni Award, 1992; 125th Anniversary Medal, Georgetown University Law Center, 1995; Order of Commendatore, Republic of Italy, 1995; Alumni Fellow Award, Rensselaer Alumni Association, 1996; Board of Directors, National Italian American Foundation, 1976–97, serving as general counsel, 1976–89, president, 1989–92, and vice chair, 1993–96; Rensselaer Neuman Foundation, trustee, 1973–present; Foundation for Improving Understanding of the Arts, trustee, 1982–96; Outward Bound, U.S.A., trustee, 1987–2002; John Carroll Society, Board of Governors, 1992–96; Rensselaer Polytechnic Institute, trustee, 1994–present; Georgetown University, regent,

1995–2001; Georgetown University Board of Directors, 2001–present; member: Federal, American, Federal Circuit, and D.C. Bar Associations; American Judicature Association; nominated for appointment to the U.S. Court of Appeals for the Federal Circuit on April 18, 1996 by President Clinton; confirmed by the Senate on July 31, 1997; entered service September 12, 1997.

RICHARD LINN, circuit judge; Polytechnic Preparatory County Day School, Brooklyn, NY, Bachelor of Electrical Engineering degree, Rensselaer Polytechnic Institute; J.D., Georgetown University Law Center; served as patent examiner at the U.S. Patent and Trademark Office, 1965–68; member of the founding Board of Governors of the Virginia State Bar Section on Patent, Trademark and Copyright Law, chairman, 1975; member of the American Intellectual Property Law Association; the Virginia Bar Intellectual Property Law Section; and the Federal Circuit Bar Association; admitted to the Virginia bar in 1969, the District of Columbia bar in 1970, and the New York bar in 1994; admitted to practice before the U.S. Supreme Court, the U.S. Courts of Appeals for the Fourth, Sixth, District of Columbia, and Federal Circuits, and the U.S. District Courts for the Eastern District of Virginia and the District of Columbia; partner, Marks and Murase, L.L.P., 1977–97, and member of the Executive Committee, 1987–97; partner, Foley and Lardner, 1997–99, Practice Group Leader, Electronics Practice Group, and Intellectual Property Department, 1997–99; recipient, Rensselaer Alumni Association Fellows Award for 2000; adjunct professor of law and professional lecturer, George Washington University Law School, 2001–03; member, Advisory Board of the George Washington University Law School, 2001–present; Master, Giles S. Rich American Inn of Court, 2000–present, president, 2004–05; member, Richard Linn American Inn of Court, 2007–present; visiting member, Hon. William C. Conner American Inn of Court, 2008–present; nominated to be Circuit Judge by President Clinton on September 28, 1999, and confirmed by the Senate on November 19, 1999; assumed duties of the office on January 1, 2000.

TIMOTHY B. DYK, circuit judge; A.B., Harvard College (*cum laude*), 1958; LL.B. (*magna cum laude*), Harvard Law School, 1961; law clerk to Justices Reed and Burton (retired), 1961–62; law clerk to Chief Justice Warren, 1962–63; special assistant to Assistant Attorney General, Louis F. Oberdorfer, 1963–64; associate and partner, Wilmer, Cutler & Pickering, 1964–90; partner, and chair, of Issues & Appeals Practice area (until nomination) with Jones, Day, Reavis and Pogue, 1990–2000; and Adjunct Professor at Yale, University of Virginia and Georgetown Law Schools; nominated for appointment to the U.S. Court of Appeals for the Federal Circuit on April 1, 1998 by President Clinton; confirmed by the Senate on May 24, 2000; entered on duty June 9, 2000.

SHARON PROST, circuit judge; born in Newburyport, MA; daughter of Zyskind and Ester Prost; two sons, Matthew and Jeffrey; educated in Hartford, CT; B.S., Cornell University, 1973; M.B.A., George Washington University, 1975; J.D., Washington College of Law, American University, 1979; admitted to practice in Washington, DC, 1979; LL.M., George Washington University School of Law, 1984; Labor Relations Specialist, U.S. Civil Service Commission, 1973–76; Labor Relations Specialist / Auditor, U.S. General Accounting Office, 1976–79; Trial Attorney, Federal Labor Relations Authority, 1979–82; Chief Counsel's Office, Department of Treasury, 1982–84; Assistant Solicitor, Associate Solicitor, and then Acting Solicitor, National Labor Relations Board, 1984–89; Adjunct Professor of Labor Law, George Mason University School of Law, 1986–87; Chief Labor Counsel, Senate Labor Committee—minority, 1989–93; Chief Counsel, Senate Judiciary Committee—minority, 1993–95; Deputy Chief Counsel, Senate Judiciary Committee—majority, 1995–2001; Chief Counsel, Senate Judiciary Committee—majority, 2001; appointed by President George W. Bush to the U.S. Court of Appeals for the Federal Circuit, September 21, 2001; assumed duties of the office on October 3, 2001.

KIMBERLY H. MOORE, circuit judge; born in Baltimore, MD; married to Matthew J. Moore; four children; B.S.E.E., Massachusetts Institute of Technology, 1990; M.S., Massachusetts Institute of Technology, 1991; J.D. (*cum laude*), Georgetown University Law Center, 1994; Electrical Engineer, Naval Surface Warfare Center, 1988–92; Associate, Kirkland & Ellis, 1994–95; Judicial Clerk, Hon. Glenn L. Archer, Jr., Chief Judge, United States Court of Appeals for the Federal Circuit, 1995–97; Assistant Professor of Law, Chicago-Kent College of Law, 1997–99; Associate Director of the Intellectual Property Law Program, Chicago-Kent College of Law, 1998–99; Assistant Professor of Law, University of Maryland School of Law, 1999–2000; Associate Professor of Law, George Mason University School of Law, 2000–04; Professor of Law, George Mason University School of Law, 2004–06; nominated to the United States Court of Appeals for the Federal Circuit by President George W. Bush on May 18, 2006; confirmed by the Senate on September 5, 2006 and assumed the duties of office on September 8, 2006.

SENIOR CIRCUIT JUDGES

GLENN LEROY ARCHER, JR., senior circuit judge; born in Densmore, KS, March 21, 1929; son of Glenn L. and Ruth Agnes Archer; educated in Kansas public schools; B.A., Yale University, 1951; J.D., with honors, George Washington University Law School, 1954; married to Carole Joan Thomas; children: Susan, Sharon, Glenn III, and Thomas; First Lieutenant, Judge Advocate General's Office, U.S. Air Force, 1954–56; associate (1956–60) and partner (1960–81), Hamel, Park, McCabe and Saunders, Washington, DC; nominated in 1981 by President Ronald Reagan to be Assistant Attorney General for the Tax Division, U.S. Department of Justice, and served in that position from December 1981 to December 1985; nominated in October 1985 by President Reagan to be circuit judge, U.S. Court of Appeals for the Federal Circuit; took the oath of office as a Circuit Judge in December 1985; elevated to the position of Chief Judge on March 18, 1994, served in that capacity until December 24, 1997; took senior status beginning December 25, 1997.

S. JAY PLAGER, senior circuit judge; born May 16, 1931; son of A.L. and Clara Plager; three children; educated public schools, Long Branch, NJ; A.B., University of North Carolina, 1952; J.D., University of Florida, with high honors, 1958; LL.M., Columbia University, 1961; Phi Beta Kappa, Phi Kappa Phi, Order of the Coif, Holloway Fellow, University of North Carolina; Editor-in-Chief, University of Florida Law Review; Charles Evans Hughes Fellow, Columbia University; commissioned, Ensign U.S. Navy, 1952; active duty Korean conflict; honorable discharge as Commander, USNR, 1971; professor, Faculty of Law, University of Florida, 1958–64; University of Illinois, 1964–77; Indiana University School of Law, Bloomington, 1977–89; visiting research professor of law, University of Wisconsin, 1967–68; visiting fellow, Trinity College and visiting professor, Cambridge University, 1980; visiting scholar, Stanford University Law School, 1984–85; dean, Indiana University School of Law, Bloomington, 1977–84; counselor to the Under Secretary, U.S. Department of Health and Human Services, 1986–87; Associate Director, Office of Management and Budget; Executive Office of the President of the United States, 1987–88; Administrator, Office of Information and Regulatory Affairs; Office of Management and Budget; Executive Office of the President of the United States, 1988–89; appointed by President George H.W. Bush to the U.S. Court of Appeals for the Federal Circuit in November 1989; assumed senior status November 2000.

RAYMOND C. CLEVENGER III, senior circuit judge; born in Topeka, KS, August 27, 1937; son of R. Charles and Mary Margaret Clevenger; educated in the public schools in Topeka, Kansas, and at Phillips Academy, Andover, MA; B.A., Yale University, 1959; LL.B., Yale University, 1966; law clerk to Justice White, October term, 1966; practice of law at Wilmer, Cutler and Pickering, Washington, DC, 1967–90; nominated to the U.S. Court of Appeals for the Federal Circuit by President George H.W. Bush on January 24, 1990, confirmed on April 27, 1990 and assumed duties on May 3, 1990.

HALDANE ROBERT MAYER, senior circuit judge; born in Buffalo, NY, February 21, 1941; educated in the public schools of Lockport, NY; B.S., U.S. Military Academy, West Point, NY, 1963; J.D., Marshall-Wythe School of Law, The College of William and Mary in Virginia, 1971; editor-in-chief, *William and Mary Law Review,* Omicron Delta Kappa; admitted to practice in Virginia and the District of Columbia; board of directors, William and Mary Law School Association, 1979–85; served in the U.S. Army, 1963–75, in the Infantry and the Judge Advocate General's Corps; awarded the Bronze Star Medal, Meritorious Service Medal, Army Commendation Medal with Oak Leaf Cluster, Combat Infantryman Badge, Parachutist Badge, Ranger Tab, Ranger Combat Badge (RVN), Campaign and Service Ribbons; resigned from Regular Army and was commissioned in the U.S. Army Reserve, currently Lieutenant Colonel, retired; law clerk for Judge John D. Butzner, Jr., U.S. Court of Appeals for the Fourth Circuit, 1971–72; private practice with McGuire, Woods and Battle in Charlottesville, VA, 1975–77; adjunct professor, University of Virginia School of Law, 1975–77, 1992–94, George Washington University National Law Center, 1992–96; Special Assistant to the Chief Justice of the United States, Warren E. Burger, 1977–80; private practice with Baker and McKenzie in Washington, DC, 1980–81; Deputy and Acting Special Counsel (by designation of the President), 1981–82; appointed by President Reagan to the U.S. Claims Court, 1982; appointed by President Reagan to the U.S. Court of Appeals for the Federal Circuit, June 15, 1987; assumed duties of the office, June 19, 1987; elevated to the position of Chief Judge on December 25, 1997; relinquished that position on December 24, 2004, after having held it for seven years; Judicial Conference of the U.S. Committee on the International Appellate Judges Conference, 1988–91, Committee on Judicial Resources,

1990–97 and 2007–present; member of the Judicial Conference of the United States, 1997–2004.

ALVIN A. SCHALL, senior circuit judge; born in New York City, NY, April 4, 1944; son of Gordon W. Schall and Helen D. Schall; preparatory education: St. Paul's School, Concord, NH, 1956–62, graduated *cum laude*; higher education: B.A., Princeton University, 1962–66; J.D., Tulane Law School, 1966–69; married to the former Sharon Frances LeBlanc, children: Amanda and Anthony; associate with the law firm of Shearman and Sterling in New York City, 1969–73; Assistant United States Attorney, Office of the United States Attorney for the Eastern District of New York, 1973–78; Chief of the Appeals Division, 1977–78; Trial Attorney, Senior Trial Counsel, Civil Division, United States Department of Justice, Washington, DC, 1978–87; member of the Washington, DC law firm of Perlman and Partners, 1987–88; Assistant to the Attorney General of the United States, 1988–92; author, *Federal Contract Disputes and Forums, Chapter 9 in Construction Litigation: Strategies and Techniques,* published by John Wiley and Sons (Wiley Law Publications), 1989; bar memberships: State of New York (1970), U.S. District Courts for the Eastern and Southern Districts of New York (1973), U.S. Court of Appeals for the Second Circuit (1974), U.S. Court of Federal Claims, formerly the U.S. Claims Court (1978), District of Columbia (1980), U.S. Court of Appeals for the Federal Circuit (1982), Supreme Court of the United States (1989), U.S. Court of Appeals for the District of Columbia Circuit (1991), and United States District Court for the District of Columbia (1991); appointed U.S. Court of Appeals for the Federal Circuit by President George H.W. Bush on August 17, 1992, sworn in on August 19, 1992.

OFFICERS OF THE UNITED STATES COURT OF APPEALS FOR THE FEDERAL CIRCUIT

Circuit Executive and Clerk of Court.—Jan Horbaly (202) 275–8020.
Senior Staff Attorney.—J. Douglas Steere, 275–8061.
Circuit Librarian.—Patricia M. McDermott, 275–8400.
Information Technology Office.—Mona Harrington, 275–8422.
Administrative Services Office.—Dale Bosley, 275–8141.
Chief Deputy Clerk for Operations.—Pamela Twiford, 275–8021.

UNITED STATES DISTRICT COURT FOR THE DISTRICT OF COLUMBIA

E. Barrett Prettyman U.S. Courthouse, 333 Constitution Avenue, NW., Room 2002, 20001 phone (202) 354–3320, fax 354–3412

ROYCE C. LAMBERTH, chief judge; born in San Antonio, TX, July 16, 1943; son of Nell Elizabeth Synder and Larimore S. Lamberth, Sr.; South San Antonio High School, 1961; B.A., University of Texas at Austin, 1966; LL.B., University of Texas School of Law, 1967; permanent president, class of 1967, University of Texas School of Law; U.S. Army (Captain, Judge Advocate General's Corps, 1968–74; Vietnam Service Medal, Air Medal, Bronze Star with Oak Leaf Cluster, Meritorious Service Medal with Oak Leaf Cluster); assistant U.S. attorney, District of Columbia, 1974–87 (chief, civil division, 1978–87); President's Reorganization Project, Federal Legal Representation Study, 1978–79; honorary faculty, Army Judge Advocate General's School, 1976; Attorney General's Special Commendation Award; Attorney General's John Marshall Award, 1982; vice chairman, Armed Services and Veterans Affairs Committee, Section on Administrative Law, American Bar Association, 1979–82, chairman, 1983–84; chairman, Professional Ethics Committee, 1989–91; co-chairman, Committee of Article III Judges, Judiciary Section 1989–present; chairman, Federal Litigation Section, 1986–87; chairman, Federal Rules Committee, 1985–86; deputy chairman, Council of the Federal Lawyer, 1980–83; chairman, Career Service Committee, Federal Bar Association, 1978–80; appointed judge, U.S. District Court for the District of Columbia by President Reagan, November 16, 1987; appointed by Chief Justice Rehnquist to be presiding judge of the United States Foreign Intelligence Surveillance Court, May 1995–2002.

EMMET G. SULLIVAN, judge; born in Washington, DC; graduated McKinley High School, 1964; B.A., Howard University, 1968; J.D., Howard University Law School, 1971; law clerk to Judge James A. Washington, Jr.; joined the law firm of Houston and Gardner, 1973–80, became a partner; thereafter was a partner with Houston, Sullivan and Gardner; board of directors of the D.C. Law Students in Court Program; D.C. Judicial Conference Voluntary Arbitration Committee; Nominating Committee of the Bar Association of the District of Columbia; U.S. District Court Committee on Grievances; adjunct professor at Howard University School of Law; member: National Bar Association, Washington Bar Association, Bar Association of the District of Columbia; appointed by President Reagan to the Superior Court of the District of Columbia as an associate judge, 1984; deputy presiding judge and presiding judge of the probate and tax division; chairperson of the rules committees for the probate and tax divisions; member: Court Rules Committee and the Jury Plan Committee; appointed by President George H.W. Bush to serve as an associate judge of the District of Columbia Court of Appeals, 1991; chairperson for the nineteenth annual judicial conference of the District of Columbia, 1994 (the Conference theme was ''Rejuvenating Juvenile Justice—Responses to the Problems of Juvenile Violence in the District of Columbia''); appointed by chief judge Wagner to chair the ''Task Force on Families and Violence for the District of Columbia Courts''; nominated to the U.S. District Court by President Clinton on March 22, 1994; and confirmed by the U.S. Senate on June 15, 1994; appointed by Chief Justice Rehnquist to serve on the Federal Judicial Conference Committee on Criminal Law, 1998; District of Columbia Judicial Disabilities and Tenure Commission, 1996–2001; presently serving on the District of Columbia Judicial Nomination Commission; first person in the District of Columbia to have been appointed to three judicial positions by three different U.S. Presidents.

COLLEEN KOLLAR-KOTELLY, judge; born in New York, NY; daughter of Konstantine and Irene Kollar; attended bilingual schools in Mexico, Ecuador and Venezuela, and Georgetown Visitation Preparatory School in Washington, DC; received B.A. degree in English at Catholic University (Delta Epsilon Honor Society); received J.D. at Catholic University's Columbus School of Law (Moot Court Board of Governors); law clerk to Hon. Catherine B. Kelly, District of Columbia Court of Appeals, 1968–69; attorney, United States Department of Justice, Criminal Division, Appellate Section, 1969–72; chief legal counsel, Saint Elizabeths Hospital, Department of Health and Human Services, 1972–84; received Saint Elizabeths Hospital Certificate of Appreciation, 1981; Meritorious Achievement Award from Alcohol, Drug Abuse and Mental Health Administration (ADAMHA), Department of Health and Human Services, 1981; appointed judge, Superior Court of the District of Columbia by President

Reagan, October 3, 1984, took oath of office October 21, 1984; served as Deputy Presiding Judge, Criminal Division, January 1996–April 1997; received Achievement Recognition Award, Hispanic Heritage CORO Awards Celebration, 1996; appointed judge, U.S. District Court for the District of Columbia by President Clinton on March 26, 1997, took oath of office May 12, 1997; appointed by Chief Justice Rehnquist to serve on the Financial Disclosure Committee, 2000–02; presiding judge of the United States Foreign Intelligence Surveillance Court, 2002–09.

HENRY H. KENNEDY, Jr., judge; born in Columbia, SC, February 22, 1948; son of Henry and Rachel Kennedy; A.B., Princeton University, 1970; J.D., Harvard University, 1973; admitted to the Bar of the District of Columbia, 1973; Reavis, Pogue, Neal and Rose, 1972 and 1973; Assistant United States Attorney for the District of Columbia, 1973–76; United States Magistrate for the District of Columbia, April 1976–79; appointed judge, Superior Court of the District of Columbia, by President Carter, December 17, 1979; member: American Bar Foundation; District of Columbia Bar; Washington Bar Association; Bar Association of the District of Columbia; American Law Institute; member: The Barristers; Sigma Pi Phi; Epsilon Boule; Trustee, Princeton University; appointed judge, United States District Court for the District of Columbia, by President Clinton on September 18, 1997.

RICHARD W. ROBERTS, judge; born in New York, NY; son of Beverly N. Roberts and Angeline T. Roberts; graduate of the High School of Music and Art, 1970; A.B. Vassar College, 1974; M.I.A. School for International Training, 1978; J.D., Columbia Law School, 1978; Honors Program Trial Attorney, Criminal Section, Civil Rights Division, U.S. Department of Justice, Washington, DC, 1978–82; Associate, Covington and Burling, Washington, DC, 1982–86; Assistant U.S. Attorney, Southern District of NY, 1986–88; Assistant U.S. Attorney, 1988–93, then Principal Assistant U.S. Attorney, District of Columbia, 1993–95; Chief, Criminal Section, Civil Rights Division, U.S. Department of Justice, Washington, DC, 1995–98; adjunct professor of trial practice, Georgetown University Law Center, Washington, DC, 1983–84; Guest faculty, Harvard Law School, Trial Advocacy Workshop, 1984–present; admitted to bars of NY (1979) and DC (1983); U.S. District Court for District of Columbia, 1983; U.S. Court of Appeals for the D.C. Circuit, 1984; U.S. Supreme Court, 1985; U.S. District Court for the Southern District of NY and U.S. Court of Appeals for the Second Circuit, 1986; past or present member or officer of National Black Prosecutors Association; Washington Bar Association; National Conference of Black Lawyers; Department of Justice Association of Black Attorneys; Department of Justice Association of Hispanic Employees for Advancement and Development; DC Bar, Committee on Professionalism and Public Understanding About the Law; American Bar Association Criminal Justice Section Committees on Continuing Legal Education, and Race and Racism in the Criminal Justice System; ABA Task Force on the Judiciary; DC Circuit Judicial Conference Arrangements Committee; D.C. Judicial Conference Planning Committee; Edward Bennett Williams Inn of Court, Washington, DC, master; board of directors, Alumnae and Alumni of Vassar College; African American Alumni of Vassar College; Vassar Club of Washington, DC; Concerned Black Men, Inc., Washington, DC Chapter; Sigma Pi Phi, Epsilon Boule; Council on Foreign Relations; DC Coalition Against Drugs and Violence; Murch Elementary School Restructuring Team; nominated as U.S. District Judge for the District of Columbia by President Clinton on January 27, 1998 and confirmed by the Senate on June 5, 1998; took oath of office on July 31, 1998.

ELLEN SEGAL HUVELLE, judge; born in Boston, MA, June 3, 1948; daughter of Robert M. Segal, Esq. and Sharlee Segal; B.A., Wellesley College, 1970; Masters in City Planning, Yale University, 1972; J.D., *magna cum laude*, Boston College Law School, 1975 (Order of the Coif; Articles Editor of the law review); law clerk to Chief Justice Edward F. Hennessey, Massachusetts Supreme Judicial Court, 1975–76; associate, Williams & Connolly, 1976–84; partner, Williams & Connolly, 1984–90; associate judge, Superior Court of the District of Columbia, 1990–99; member: American Bar Association, District of Columbia Bar, Women's Bar Association; Fellow of the American Bar Foundation; Master in the Edward Bennett Williams Inn of Court and member of the Inn's Executive Committee; instructor of Trial Advocacy at the University of Virginia Law School; member of Visiting Faculty at Harvard Law School's Trial Advocacy Workshop; Boston College Law School Board of Overseers; appointed judge, U.S. District Court for the District of Columbia by President Clinton in October 1999, and took oath of office on February 25, 2000.

REGGIE B. WALTON, judge; born in Donora, PA, February 8, 1949; son of the late Theodore and Ruth (Garard) Walton; B.A., West Virginia State College, 1971; J.D., American University, Washington College of Law, 1974; admitted to the bars of the Supreme Court of Pennsylvania, 1974; United States District Court for the Eastern District of Pennsylvania, 1975; District of Columbia Court of Appeals, 1976; United States Court of Appeals for the District of Columbia Circuit, 1977; Supreme Court of the United States, 1980; United States District Court for the District of Columbia; Staff Attorney, Defender Association of Philadelphia, 1974–76; Assistant United States Attorney for the District of Columbia, 1976–80; Chief, Career Criminal Unit, Assistant United States Attorney for the District of Columbia, 1979–80; Executive Assistant United States Attorney for the District of Columbia, 1980–81; Associate Judge, Superior Court of the District of Columbia, 1981–89; deputy presiding judge of the Criminal Division, Superior Court of the District of Columbia, 1986–89; Associate Director, Office of National Drug Control Policy, Executive Office of the President, 1989–91; Senior White House Advisor for Crime, The White House, 1991; Associate Judge, Superior Court of the District of Columbia, 1991–2001; Presiding Judge of the Domestic Violence Unit, Superior Court of the District of Columbia, 2000; Presiding Judge of the Family Division, Superior Court of the District of Columbia, 2001; Instructor: National Judicial College, Reno, Nevada, 1999–present; Harvard University Law School, Trial Advocacy Workshop, 1994–present; National Institute of Trial Advocacy, Georgetown University Law School, 1983–present; Co-author, Pretrial Drug Testing—An Essential Component of the National Drug Control Strategy, Brigham Young University Law Journal of Public Law (1991); Distinguished Alumnus Award, American University, Washington College of Law (1991); The William H. Hastie Award, The Judicial Council of the National Bar Association (1993); Commissioned as a Kentucky Colonel by the Governor (1990, 1991); Governor's Proclamation declaring April 9, 1991, Judge Reggie B. Walton Day in the State of Louisiana; The West Virginia State College National Alumni Association James R. Waddy Meritorious Service Award (1990); Secretary's Award, United States Department of Veterans Affairs (1990); Outstanding Alumnus Award, Ringgold High School (1987); Director's Award for Superior Performance as an Assistant United States Attorney (1980); Profiled in book entitled ''Black Judges on Justice: Prospectives From The Bench'' by Linn Washington (1995); appointed district judge, United States District Court for the District of Columbia by President George W. Bush, September 24, 2001, and took oath of office October 29, 2001; appointed by President Bush in June of 2004 to serve as the Chairperson of the National Prison Rape Reduction Commission, a two-year commission created by the United States Congress that is tasked with the mission of identifying methods to curb the incidents of prison rape; member, Foreign Intelligence Surveillance Court, 2007–present.

JOHN D. BATES, judge; born in Elizabeth, NJ, October 11, 1946; son of Richard D. and Sarah (Deacon) Bates; B.A., Wesleyan University, 1968; J.D., University of Maryland School of Law, 1976; U.S. Army (1968–71, 1st Lt., Vietnam Service Medal, Bronze Star); law clerk to Hon. Roszel Thomsen, U.S. District Court for the District of Maryland, 1976–77; Assistant U.S. Attorney, District of Columbia, 1980–97 (Chief, Civil Division, 1987–97); Director's Award for Superior Performance (1983); Attorney General's Special commendation Award (1986); Deputy Independent Counsel, Whitewater Investigation, 1995–97; private practice of law, Miller & Chevalier (partner, 1998–2001), Chair of Government Contracts Litigation Department and member of Executive Committee), Steptoe & Johnson (associate, 1977–80); District of Columbia Circuit Advisory Committee for Procedures, 1989–93; Civil Justice Reform Committee of the U.S. District Court for the District of Columbia, 1996–2001; Treasurer, D.C. Bar, 1992–93; Publications Committee, D.C. Bar (1991–97, Chair 1994–97); D.C. Bar Special Committee on Government Lawyers, 1990–91; D.C. Bar Task Force on Civility in the Profession, 1994–96; D.C. Bar Committee on Examination of Rule 49, 1995–96; Chairman, Litigation Section, Federal Bar Association, 1986–89; Board of Directors, Washington Lawyers Committee for Civil Rights and Urban Affairs, 1999–2001; appointed to the U.S. District Court for the District of Columbia in December, 2001; presiding judge, Foreign Intelligence Surveillance Court, 2009–present.

RICHARD J. LEON, judge; born in South Natick, MA, December 3, 1949; son of Silvano B. Leon and Rita (O'Rorke) Leon; A.B., Holy Cross College, 1971, J.D., *cum laude,* Suffolk Law School, 1974; LL.M. Harvard Law School, 1981; Law Clerk to Chief Justice McLaughlin and the Associate Justices, Superior Court of Massachusetts, 1974–75; Law Clerk to Hon. Thomas F. Kelleher, Supreme Court of Rhode Island, 1975–76; admitted to bar, Rhode Island, 1975 and District of Columbia, 1991; Special Assistant U.S. Attorney, Southern District of New York, 1977–78; Assistant Professor of Law, St. John's Law School, New York, 1979–83; Senior Trial Attorney, Criminal Section, Tax Division, U.S. Department of Justice, 1983–87; Deputy Chief Minority Counsel, U.S. House Select ''Iran-Contra'' Committee, 1987–88; Deputy Assistant U.S. Attorney General, Environment Division, 1988–89; Partner, Baker & Hostetler, Washington, DC, 1989–99; Commissioner, The White House Fellows Commission, 1990–92; Chief Minority Counsel, U.S. House Foreign Affairs Committee ''October Suprise'' Task Force, 1992–93; Special Counsel, U.S. House Banking Committee ''Whitewater'' Investigation, 1994; Special Counsel, U.S. House Ethics Reform Task Force, 1997; Adjunct Professor, Georgetown University Law Center, 1997–present; Partner, Vorys, Sater, Seymour and Pease, Washington, DC, 1999–2002; Commissioner, Judicial Review Commission on Foreign Asset Control, 2000–01; Master, Edward Bennett Williams Inn of Court; appointed U.S. District Judge for the District of Columbia by President George W. Bush on February 19, 2002; took oath of office on March 20, 2002.

ROSEMARY M. COLLYER, judge; born in White Plains, NY, November 19, 1945; daughter of Thomas C. and Alice Henry Mayers; educated in parochial and public schools in Stamford, Connecticut; B.A., Trinity College, Washington, DC, 1968; J.D., University of Denver College of Law, 1977; practiced with Sherman & Howard, Denver, Colorado, 1977–81; Chairman, Federal Mine Safety and Health Review Commission, 1981–84 by appointment of President Reagan with Senate confirmation; General Counsel, National Labor Relations Board, 1984–89 by appointment of President Reagan with Senate confirmation; private practice with Crowell & Moring LLP, Washington, DC 1989–2003; member and chairman of the firm's Management Committee; appointed U.S. District Judge for the District of Columbia by President George W. Bush and took oath of office on January 2, 2003.

BERYL A. HOWELL, judge; born in Fort Benning, GA; daughter of Col. (Ret.) Leamon and Ruth Howell; Killeen High School, 1974; B.A. with honors in philosophy, Bryn Mawr College (President and Member, Honor Board, 1976–78); J.D., Columbia University School of Law, 1983 (Harlan Fiske Stone Scholar, 1981–82; International Fellows Program, 1982–83, Transnational Law Journal, Notes Editor); law clerk to Hon. Dickinson R. Debevoise, District of New Jersey, 1983–84; litigation associate, Schulte, Roth & Zabel, 1985–87; Assistant United States Attorney, United States District Court for the Eastern District of New York, 1987–93; Deputy Chief, Narcotics Section, 1987–93; Senior Counsel, U.S. Senate Committee on the Judiciary Subcommittee on Technology and the Law, 1993–94; Senior Counsel, U.S Senate Committee on the Judiciary Subcommittee on Antitrust, Business Rights and Competition, 1995–96; General Counsel, U.S. Senate Committee on the Judiciary, 1997–2003; Executive Managing Director and General Counsel, Stroz Friedberg, 2003–09; Member, Commission on Cyber Security for the 44th Presidency, 2008; Adjunct Professor of Law, American University's Washington College of Law, 2010; Awards include U.S. Attorney's Special Achievement Award for Sustained Superior Performance, 1990, 1991; Drug Enforcement Administration Commendations, 1990, 1992, 1993; Attorney General's Director's Award for Superior Performance, 1991; Federal Bureau of Investigation Award and New York City Department of Investigation Award for public corruption investigation and prosecution, 1992; Freedom of Information Hall of Fame, 2001; First Amendment Award, Society of Professional Journalists, 2004; Federal Bureau of Investigation Director's Award, 2006; Book chapters and law review article publications include *Seven Weeks: The Making of the USA PATRIOT Act, The George Washington Law Review,* 2004; *FISA's Fruits in Criminal Cases: An Opportunity for Improved Accountability, UCLA Journal of International Law and Foreign Affairs,* 2007; Book Chapters include: *Real World Problems of Virtual Crime,* in Cybercrime: Digital Cops in a Networked Environment, 2007; Foreign Intelligence Surveillance Act: *Has the Solution Become the Problem,* in Protecting What Matters: *Technology, Security, and Liberty Since 9/11, 2006* and articles in the *New York Law Journal, Journal of Internet Law,* the *Vermont Bar Journal,* and *Yale Journal of Law and Technology;* Appointed Commissioner, United States Sentencing Commission, 2004–11; appointed judge, U.S. District Court for the District of Columbia by President Obama on December 27, 2010, took oath of office on January 21, 2011.

ROBERT L. WILKINS, judge; born Muncie, Indiana; graduated *cum laude* from Rose-Hulman Institute of Technology in 1986 with a B.S. in chemical engineering; received J.D. from Harvard Law School in 1989 (Executive Editor and Comments Editor of the *Civil Rights-Civil Liberties Law Review*); law clerk to the Honorable Earl B. Gilliam of the United States District Court for the Southern District of California 1989–90; Staff Attorney for the District of Columbia Public Defender Service (PDS) 1990–95; PDS Chief of Special Litigation and Programs Division 1995–99; PDS Staff Attorney for special litigation and projects 1999–2000; President National African American Museum & Cultural Complex, Inc. (played key role in congressional legislation which authorized creation of the Smithsonian's National Museum of African American History and Culture slated to open on the National Mall in 2015) 2000–02; private law practice-partner, Venable LLP 2002–11; lead plaintiff in *Wilkins, et al.* v. *State of Maryland,* a civil rights lawsuit against the Maryland State Police which resulted in two landmark settlements that were the first to require statewide systematic compilation and publication by a police agency of data for all highway drug and weapons searches, including data regarding the race of the motorist involved, the justification for the search and the outcome of the search—these settlements inspired a June 1999 Executive Order by President Clinton, Congressional hearings and legislation that has been enacted in over half of the fifty states; named one of the *40 Under 40 Most Successful Young Litigators in America* by the *National Law Journal,* 2002; Named one of the *90 Greatest Washington Lawyers of the Last 30 Years* by the *Legal Times,* 2008; appointed judge, United States District Court for the District of Columbia by President Barack Obama December 27, 2010; took oath of office March 1, 2011.

JAMES E. BOASBERG, judge; born San Francisco, CA, 1963; son of Emanuel Boasberg III and Sarah Szold Boasberg; graduated St. Albans School, Washington, DC, 1981; B.A., *magna cum laude* in history from Yale College, 1985; M.St. in modern European history from Oxford University, 1986; J.D. from Yale Law School, 1990; law clerk to Judge Dorothy W. Nelson on the U.S. Court of Appeals for the Ninth Circuit, 1990–91; associate, Keker & Van Nest in San Francisco, CA, 1991–94; associate, Kellogg, Huber, Hansen, Todd & Evans in Washington, DC, 1995–96; Assistant United States Attorney for the District of Columbia, 1996–2002; visiting lecturer, George Washington Law School, 2003; Associate Judge, District of Columbia Superior Court, 2002–11; United States District Judge for the District of Columbia, 2011–present.

AMY BERMAN JACKSON, judge; appointed March of 2011; prior to joining the Court, engaged in private practice in Washington, DC as a member of Trout Cacheris, specializing in complex criminal and civil trials and appeals; earlier, partner at Venable, Baetjer, Howard, and Civiletti; Assistant United States Attorney for the District of Columbia, 1880–86; received Department of Justice Special Achievement Awards for work on murder and sexual assault cases; J.D., *cum laude,* Harvard Law School, 1979; A.B. cum laude, Harvard College, 1976; law clerk to the Honorable Harrison L. Winter of the United States Court of Appeals for the Fourth Circuit; lectured on corporate criminal investigations and has been a regular teacher at the National Institute of Trial Advocacy, the Georgetown University Law Center CLE Intensive Session in Trial Advocacy Skills, and the Harvard Law School Trial Advocacy workshop; while in private practice, was elected to serve as a DC Bar delegate to the ABA House of Delegates; active in the ABA Litigation Section, the ABA Criminal Justice Section White Collar Crime Committee, and DC Bar and Women's Bar Association committee activities; member of the Parent Steering Committee of the Interdisciplinary Council on Developmental and Learning Disorders; served on the Board of the DC Rape Crisis Center and other educational and community organizations.

SENIOR JUDGES

LOUIS FALK OBERDORFER, senior judge; born in Birmingham, AL, February 21, 1919; son of A. Leo and Stella Falk Oberdorfer; A.B., Dartmouth College, 1939; LL.B., *Yale Law School,* 1946 (editor in chief, *Yale Law Journal,* 1941); admitted to the Bar of Alabama, 1947, District of Columbia, 1949; U.S. Army, rising from private to captain, 1941–45; law clerk to Justice Hugo L. Black, 1946–47; attorney, Paul Weiss, Wharton, Garrison, 1947–51; partner, Wilmer, Cutler and Pickering, and predecessor firms, 1951–61 and 1965–77; Assistant Attorney General, Tax Division, U.S. Department of Justice, 1961–65; president, District of Columbia Bar, 1977; transition chief executive officer, Legal Services Corp., 1975; co-chairman, Lawyers' Committee for Civil Rights Under Law, 1967–69; member, Advisory Committee on Federal Rules of Civil Procedure, 1963–84; visiting lecturer, Yale Law School, 1966, 1971; adjunct professor, Georgetown Law Center, 1993–present; appointed judge of the U.S. District Court for the District of Columbia by President Carter on October 11, 1977, and took oath of office on November 1, 1977; senior status July 31, 1992.

THOMAS F. HOGAN, senior judge; born in Washington, DC, May 31, 1938; son of Adm. Bartholomew W. (MC) (USN) Surgeon Gen., USN, 1956–62, and Grace (Gloninger) Hogan; Georgetown Preparatory School, 1956; A.B., Georgetown University (classical), 1960; master's program, American and English literature, George Washington University, 1960–62; J.D., Georgetown University, 1965–66; Honorary Degree, Doctor of Laws, Georgetown University Law Center, May 1999; St. Thomas More Fellow, Georgetown University Law Center, 1965–66; American Jurisprudence Award: Corporation Law; member, bars of the District of Columbia and Maryland; law clerk to Hon. William B. Jones, U.S. District Court for the District of Columbia, 1966–67; counsel, Federal Commission on Reform of Federal Criminal Laws, 1967–68; private practice of law in the District of Columbia and Maryland, 1968–82; adjunct professor of law, Potomac School of Law, 1977–79; adjunct professor of law, Georgetown University Law Center, 1986–88; public member, officer evaluation board, U.S. Foreign Service, 1973; member: American Bar Association, State Chairman, Maryland Drug Abuse Education Program, Young Lawyers Section (1970–73), District of Columbia Bar Association, Bar Association of the District of Columbia, Maryland State Bar Association, Montgomery County Bar Association, National Institute for Trial Advocacy, Defense Research Institute, The Barristers, The Lawyers Club; chairman, board of directors, Christ Child Institute for Emotionally Ill Children, 1971–74; served on many committees; USDC Executive Committee; Conference Committee on Administration of Federal Magistrates System, 1988–91; chairman, Inter-Circuit Assignment Committee, 1990–present; appointed judge of the U.S. District Court for the District of Columbia by President Reagan on October 4, 1982; chief judge, June 19, 2001; member: Judicial Conference of the United States 2001–present; Executive Committee of the Judicial Conference, July 2001–08; member, Foreign Intelligence Surveillance Court, 2009–present.

GLADYS KESSLER, senior judge; born in New York, NY, January 22, 1938; B.A., Cornell University, 1959; LL.B. Harvard Law School, 1962; member: American Judicature Society (board of directors, 1985–89); National Center for State Courts (board of directors, 1984–87); National Association of Women Judges (president, 1983–84); Women Judges' Fund for Justice, (president, 1980–82); Fellows of the American Bar Foundation; President's Council of Cornell Women; American Law Institute; American Bar Association—committees: Alternative Dispute Resolution, Bioethics and AIDS; Executive Committee, Conference of Federal Trial Judges; private law practice—partner, Roisman, Kessler and Cashdan, 1969–77; associate judge, Superior Court of the District of Columbia, 1977–94; court administrative activities: District of Columbia Courts Joint Committee on Judicial Administration, 1989–94; Domestic Violence Coordinating Council (chairperson, 1993–94); Multi-Door Dispute Resolution Program (supervising judge, 1985–90); family division, D.C. Superior Court (presiding judge, 1981–85); Einshac Institute Board of Directors; U.S. Judicial Conference Committee on Court Administration and Court Management; Frederick B. Abramson Memorial Foundation Board of Directors; Our Place Board of Directors; Vice Chair, District of Columbia Judicial Disabilities and Tenure Commission; appointed judge, U.S. District Court for the District of Columbia by President Clinton, June 16, 1994, and took oath of office, July 18, 1994.

PAUL L. FRIEDMAN, senior judge; born in Buffalo, NY, February 20, 1944; son of Cecil A. and Charlotte Wagner Friedman; B.A. (political science), Cornell University, 1965; J.D., *cum laude,* School of Law, State University of New York at Buffalo, 1968; admitted to the bars of the District of Columbia, New York, U.S. Supreme Court, and U.S. Courts of Appeals for the D.C., Federal, Fourth, Fifth, Sixth, Seventh, Ninth and Eleventh Circuits; Law Clerk to Judge Aubrey E. Robinson, Jr., U.S. district court for the District of Columbia, 1968–69; Law Clerk to Judge Roger Robb, U.S. Court of Appeals for the District of Columbia Circuit, 1969–70; Assistant U.S. Attorney for the District of Columbia, 1970–74; assistant to the Solicitor General of the United States, 1974–76; associate independent counsel, Iran-Contra investigation, 1987–88, private law practice, White and Case (partner, 1979–94; associate, 1976–79); member: American Bar Association, Commission on Multidisciplinary Practice (1998–2000), District of Columbia Bar (president, 1986–87), American Law Institute (1984) and ALI Council, 1998, American Academy of Appellate Lawyers, Bar Association of the District of Columbia, Women's Bar Association of the District of Columbia, Washington Bar Association, Hispanic Bar Association, Assistant United States Attorneys Association of the District of Columbia (president, 1976–77), Civil Justice Reform Act Advisory Group (chair, 1991–94), District of Columbia Judicial Nomination Commission (member, 1990–94; chair, 1992–94), Advisory Committee on Procedures, U.S. Court of Appeals for the D.C. Circuit (1982–88), Grievance Committee; U.S. District Court for the District of Columbia (member, 1981–87; chair, 1983–85); fellow, American College of Trial Lawyers; fellow, American Bar Foundation; board of directors: Frederick B. Abramson Memorial Foundation (president, 1991–94), Washington Area Lawyers for the Arts (1988–92), Washington Legal Clinic for the Homeless (member, 1987–92; vice-president 1988–91), Stuart Stiller Memorial Foundation (1980–94), American Judicature Society (1990–94), District of Columbia Public Defender Service (1989–92); member: Cosmos Club, Lawyers Club of Washington; appointed judge, U.S. District Court for the District of Columbia by President Clinton, June 16, 1994, and took oath of office August 1, 1994; U.S. Judicial Conference Advisory Committee on Federal Criminal Rules.

RICARDO M. URBINA, senior judge; born of an Honduran father and Puerto Rican mother in Manhattan, NY; B.A., Georgetown University, 1967; J.D., Georgetown Law Center, 1970; staff attorney, D.C. Public Defender Service, 1970–72; after a period of private practice with an emphasis on commercial litigation, joined the faculty of Howard University School of Law, during which time he maintained a private practice; directed the university's criminal justice clinic and taught criminal law, criminal procedure and torts, 1974–81; voted Professor of the Year by the Howard Law School student body, 1978; nominated to the D.C. Superior Court by President Carter, 1980; appointed to the bench as President Reagan's first presidential judicial appointment and the first Hispanic judge in the history of the District of Columbia, 1981; during his thirteen years on the Superior Court, Judge Urbina served as Chief Presiding Judge of the Family Division for three years and chaired the committee that drafted the Child Support Guidelines later adopted as the District of Columbia's child support law;

managed a criminal calendar (1989–90) that consisted exclusively of first degree murder, rape and child molestation cases; designated by the chief judge to handle a special calendar consisting of complex civil litigation; twice recognized by the United States Department of Health and Human Services for his work with children and families; selected one of the Washingtonians of the Year by *Washington Magazine,* 1986; received Hugh Johnson Memorial Award for his many contributions to ''. . . the creation of harmony among diverse elements of the community and the bar by D.C. Hispanic Bar Association;'' received the Hispanic National Bar Association's 1993 award for demonstrated commitment to the ''Preservation of Civil and Constitutional Rights of All Americans'', and the 1995 NBC-Hispanic Magazine National VIDA Award in recognition of lifetime community service; adjunct professor at the George Washington University Law School since 1993; served as a visiting instructor of trial advocacy at the Harvard Law School, 1996–97; Latino Civil Rights Center presented him with the Justice Award in 1999; conferred Distinguished Adjunct Teacher Award by George Washington University Law School in 2001 and in 2005 has been awarded the David Seidlson Chair for Trial Advocacy; appointment by President Clinton to the U.S. District Court for the District of Columbia in 1994 made him the first Latino ever appointed to the federal bench in Washington, DC.

OFFICERS OF THE UNITED STATES DISTRICT COURT FOR THE DISTRICT OF COLUMBIA

Bankruptcy Judge.—S. Martin Teel, Jr.
United States Magistrate Judges: Deborah A. Robinson; Alan Kay; John M. Facciola.
Clerk of Court.—Angela Caesar.
Administrative Assistant to the Chief Judge.—Sheldon L. Snook.

UNITED STATES COURT OF INTERNATIONAL TRADE

One Federal Plaza, New York, NY 10278–0001, phone (212) 264–2800

DONALD C. POGUE, chief judge; graduated *magna cum laude,* Phi Beta Kappa from Dartmouth College; did graduate work at the University of Essex, England; J.D., Yale Law School and a Masters of Philosophy, Yale University; married 1971; served as judge in Connecticut's Superior Court; appointed to the bench in 1994; served as chairman of Connecticut's Commission on Hospitals and Health Care; practiced law in Hartford for 15 years; lectured on labor law at the University of Connecticut School of Law; assisted in teaching the Harvard Law School's program on negotiations and dispute resolution for lawyers; chaired the Connecticut Bar Association's Labor and Employment Law Section; appointed a judge of the United States Court of International Trade in 1995; prior to becoming chief judge, he chaired the Court's Long Range Planning Committee and Budget Committee; he also chaired the Judicial Conference's Committee on the Administrative Office; service by designation in the 2d, 3d, 5th, 9th, 11th and Federal Circuits and in the D.C. and New York Southern district courts.

GREGORY W. CARMAN, judge; born in Farmingdale, Long Island, NY; son of Nassau County District Court Judge Willis B. and Marjorie Sosa Carman; B.A., St. Lawrence University, Canton, NY, 1958; J.D., St. John's University School of Law (honors program), 1961; University of Virginia Law School, JAG (with honors), 1962; admitted to New York Bar, 1961; practiced law with firm of Carman, Callahan and Sabino, Farmingdale, NY; admitted to practice: U.S. Court of Military Appeals 1962, U.S. District Courts, Eastern and Southern Districts of New York 1965, Second Circuit Court of Appeals 1966, Supreme Court of the United States 1967, U.S. Court of Appeals, District of Columbia 1982; Councilman Town of Oyster Bay 1972–80; member U.S. House of Representatives, 97th Congress; member Banking, Finance and Urban Affairs Committee and Select Committee on Aging; member International Trade, Investment, and Monetary Policy Subcommittee; U.S. Congressional Delegate to International I.M.F. Conference; nominated by President Reagan, confirmed and appointed Judge of the U.S. Court of International Trade, March 2, 1983; Acting Chief Judge 1991; Chief Judge 1996–2003; Statutory Member, Judicial Conference of United States; member Executive Committee, Judicial Branch Committee, and Subcommittees on Long Range Planning, Benefits, Civic Education, and Seminars; Captain, U.S. Army, 1958–64; awarded Army Commendation Medal for Meritorious Service 1964; Member Rotary International 1964–present; named Paul Harris Fellow of the Rotary Foundation of Rotary International; member Holland Society, and recipient of its 1999 Gold Medal for Distinguished Achievement in Jurisprudence; member Federal Bar Association, American Bar Association, Fellow of American Bar Foundation, member New York State Bar Association, member and former chair New York State Bar Association's Committee on Courts and the Community, and recipient of its 1996 Special Recognition Award; Doctor of Laws, *honoris causa,* Nova Southeastern University, 1999; Distinguished Jurist in Residence, Touro College Law Center, 2000; Doctor of Laws, *honoris causa,* St. John's University, 2002; Inaugural Lecturer, DiCarlo U.S. Court of International Trade Lecture, John Marshall Law School 2003; Distinguished Alumni Citation, St. Lawrence University 2003; Italian Board of Guardians Public Service Award 2003; director and member Respect For Law Alliance, Inc.; Executive Committee member and past president Theodore Roosevelt American Inn of Court; past president Protestant Lawyers Association of Long Island; member Vestry, St. Thomas's Episcopal Church, Farmingdale, NY; married to Nancy Endruschat (deceased); children: Gregory Wright, Jr., John Frederick, James Matthew, and Mira Catherine; married to Judith L. Dennehy.

JANE A. RESTANI, judge; born in San Francisco, CA, 1948; parents: Emilia C. and Roy J. Restani; husband: Ira Bloom; B.A., University of California at Berkeley, 1969; J.D., University of California at Davis, 1973; law review staff writer, 1971–72; articles editor, 1972–73; member, Order of the Coif; elected to Phi Kappa Phi Honor Society; admitted to the bar of the Supreme Court of the State of California, 1973; joined the civil division of the Department of Justice under the Attorney General's Honor Program in 1973 as a trial attorney; assistant chief commercial litigation section, civil division, 1976–80; director, commercial litigation branch, civil division, 1980–83; recipient of the John Marshall Award of outstanding legal achievement in 1983; Judicial Improvements Committee (now Committee on Court Administration and Case Management) of the Judicial Conference of the United States, 1987–94; Judicial Conference Advisory Committee on the Federal Rules of Bankruptcy Procedure, and liaison to the Advisory Committee on the Federal Rules of Civil Procedure, 1994–96; member Judicial Conference of the United States, 2003–10; Executive Committee of the Judicial Conference, 2010; ABA Standing Committee on Customs Laws, 1990–93; and the Board of Directors, New York State Association of Women Judges, 1992–present; nominated to the United States Court of International Trade on November 2, 1983 by President Reagan; entered upon the duties of that office on November 25, 1983; Chief Judge, 2003–10.

EVAN J. WALLACH, judge; born in Superior, AZ, November 11, 1949; son of Albert A. and Sara F. Wallach; married to Katherine Colleen Tobin, 1992; graduate of Acalanes High School, Lafayette, CA, 1967; attended Diablo Valley Junior College, Pleasant Hill, CA, 1967–68; news editor, *Viking Reporter;* member, Alfa Gamma Sigma, National Junior College Honor Society, member, Junior Varsity Wrestling Team; enlisted United States Army, January, 1969, PVT–SGT, served as Reconnaissance Sergeant 8th Engineer Bn., 1st Calvary Division (Air Mobile), Republic of Vietnam, 1970–71, Bronze Star Medal, Air Medal, Valorous Unit Citation, Good Conduct Medal; attended University of Arizona, 1971–73, graduated B.A., journalism (high honors), Phi Beta Kappa, Phi Kappa Phi, Kappa Tau Alfa, Rufenacht French Language Prize, Douglas Martin Journalism Scholarship; attended University of California, Berkeley, 1973–76, graduated J.D., 1976, research assistant to Prof. Melvin Eisenberg, member of University of California Honor Society; Associate (1976–82) and Partner (1983–95) Lionel Sawyer and Collins, Las Vegas, NV with emphasis on media representation; attended Cambridge University, Cambridge, England, LL.B. (international law) (honors), 1981, member Hughes Hall College Rowing Club, Cambridge University Tennis Club; elected, Honorary Fellow Hughes Hall College, 2008–present; General Counsel and Public Policy Advisor to U.S. Senator Harry Reid (D) of Nevada, 1987–88; served CAPT–MAJ Nevada Army National Guard, 1989–95; served as Attorney / Advisor, International Affairs Division; Office of the Judge Advocate General of the Army, February-June, 1991–92; Meritorious Service Medal (oak leaf cluster); Nevada Medal of Merit; General Counsel, Nevada Democratic Party, 1978–80, 1982–86; General Counsel, Reid for Congress campaign, 1982, 1984; Reid for Senate campaign, 1986, 1992; General Counsel, Bryan for Senate campaign, 1988; Nevada State Director, Mondale for President campaign, 1984; State Director, Nevada and Arizona, Gore for President campaign, 1988; General Counsel Nevada Assembly Democratic Caucus, 1990–95; General Counsel, Society for Professional Journalists, 1988–95; General Counsel, Nevada Press Association, 1989–95; awarded American Bar Association Liberty Bell Award, 1993; Nevada State Press Association President's Award, 1994; Clark County School Librarians Intellectual Freedom Award, 1995; Law of War, Adjunct Professor, New York Law School, 1997–present; Brooklyn Law School, 2000–present; member, Nevada Bar Association, 1977; U.S. District Court, District of Nevada, 1977; District of Columbia, 1988; Ninth Circuit Court of Appeals, 1989; American Law Institute and ALI Adviser on Principles of World Trade Law: National Treatment; author, Legal Handbook for Nevada Reporters (1994); Comparison of British and American Defense Based Prior Restraint, ICLQ (1984); Treatment of Crude Oil as a War Munition, ICLQ (1992); Three Ways Nevada Unconstitutionally Chills the Media; Nevada Lawyer (1994); Co-Editor, Nevada Civil Practice Handbook (1993); Extradition to the Rwandan War Crimes Tribunal: Is Another Treaty Required, USCLA Journal of International Law and Foreign Affairs (Spring / Summer, 1998); The Procedural and Evidentiary Rules of the Post World War II War Crimes Trials: Did They Provide an Outline for International Criminal Procedure? Columbia Journal of Translational Law (Spring, 1999); Webmaster, International Law of War Association, lawofwar.org; Afghanistan, Yamashita and Uchiyama: Does the Sauce Suit the Gander? *The Army Lawyer* (June 2003); The Logical Nexus Between the Decision to Deny Application of the Third Geneva Convention to the Taliban and Al Queda and the Mistreatment of Prisoners of War in Abu Ghraib, Case *Western Reserve Journal of International Law* 541 (2004); Drop by Drop: Forgetting the History of Water Torture in U.S. Courts, *Columbia Journal of Transnational Law* (2007). Command Responsibility, co-author of Chapter in Bassouni, *International Criminal Law* (3rd Ed.) (2008). A Tiny Problem with Huge Implications-Nanotech Agents as Enablers or Substitutes for Banned Chemical Weapons: Is a New Treaty Needed?, *Fordham International Law Journal* (2010); Pirates, Partisans, and Pancho Villa: How International and National Law Handled Non-State Fighters in the ''Good Old Days'' Before 1949 and That Approach's Applicability to the ''War on Terror'', *Emory International Law Journal* (2010).

DELISSA A. RIDGWAY, judge; born in Kirksville, MO, June 28, 1955; B.A. (honors), University of Missouri-Columbia, 1975; graduate work, University of Missouri-Columbia, 1975–76; J.D., Northeastern University School of Law, 1979; Shaw Pittman Potts and Trowbridge (Washington, DC), 1979–94; Chair, Foreign Claims Settlement Commission of the

U.S., 1994–98; Adjunct Professor of Law, Cornell Law School, 1999–present; Adjunct Professor of Law/Lecturer, Washington College of Law / The American University, 1992–94; District of Columbia Bar, Secretary, 1991–92; Board of Governors, 1992–98; President, Women's Bar Association, 1992–93; American Bar Association, Standing Committee on Federal Judicial Improvements (2008–present); Co-Chair, Section of Litigation Task Force on Implicit Bias (2010–12); Commission on Women in the Profession, 2002–05; Federal Bar Association, National Council, 1993–2002, 2003–present; Government Relations Committee, 1996–2008, Public Relations Committee Chair, 1998–99; Board of Directors, Federal Bar Building Corporation; Executive Committee, National Conference of Federal Trial Judges, 2004–present; chair, National Conference of Federal Trial Judges, 2009–10; Board of Directors, American Judicature Society (2010–present); Founding Member of Board, D.C. Conference on Opportunities for Minorities in the Legal Profession, 1992–93; Chair, D.C. Bar Summit on Women in the Legal Profession, 1995–98; Fellow, American Bar Foundation; Member, American Law Institute; Fellow, Federal Bar Foundation; Earl W. Kintner Award of the Federal Bar Association (2000); Woman Lawyer of the Year, Washington, DC (2001); Distinguished Visiting Scholar-in-Residence, University of Missouri-Columbia (2003); sworn in as a judge to the U.S. Court of International Trade in May 1998.

RICHARD K. EATON, judge; born in Walton, NY; married to Susan Henshaw Jones; two children: Alice and Elizabeth; attended Walton public schools; B.A., Ithaca College, J.D., Union University Albany Law School, 1974; professional experience: Eaton & Eaton, partner; Mudge Rose Guthrie Alexander & Ferdon, New York, NY, associate and partner; Stroock & Stroock & Lavan, partner served on the staff of Senator Daniel Patrick Moynihan; confirmed by the United States Senate to the U.S. Court of International Trade on October 22, 1999.

TIMOTHY C. STANCEU, judge; born in Canton, OH; A.B., Colgate University, 1973; J.D., Georgetown University Law Center, 1979; appointed to the U.S. Court of International Trade by President George W. Bush and began serving on April 15, 2003; prior to appointment, private practice for 13 years in Washington, DC, with the law firm Hogan & Hartson, L.L.P., during which he represented clients in a variety of matters involving customs and international trade law; Deputy Director, Office of Trade and Tariff Affairs, U.S. Department of the Treasury; where his responsibilities involved the regulatory and enforcement matters of the U.S. Customs Service and other agencies; Special Assistant to the Assistant Secretary of the Office of Enforcement, U.S. Department of the Treasury; Program Analyst and Environmental Protection Specialist, U.S. Environmental Protection Agency, where he concentrated on the development and review of regulations on various environmental subjects.

LEO M. GORDON, judge; graduate of Newark Academy in Livingston, NJ; University of North Carolina–Chapel Hill, Phi Beta Kappa, 1973; J.D., Emory University School of Law, 1977; member of the Bars of New Jersey, Georgia and the District of Columbia; Assistant Counsel at the Subcommittee on Monopolies and Commercial Law, Committee on the Judiciary, U.S. House of Representatives, 1977–81; in that capacity, Judge Gordon was the principal attorney responsible for the Customs Courts Act of 1980 that created the U.S. Court of International Trade; for 25 years, Judge Gordon was on the staff at the Court, serving first as Assistant Clerk from 1981–99, and then Clerk of the Court from 1999–2006; appointed to the U.S. Court of International Trade in March 2006.

SENIOR JUDGES

THOMAS J. AQUILINO, JR., senior judge; born in Mount Kisco, NY, December 7, 1939; son of Thomas J. and Virginia B. (Doughty) Aquilino; married to Edith Berndt Aquilino; children: Christopher Thomas, Philip Andrew, Alexander Berndt; attended Cornell University, 1957–59; B.A., Drew University, 1959–60, 1961–62; University of Munich, Germany, 1960–61; Free University of Berlin, Germany, 1965–66; J.D., Rutgers University School of Law, 1966–69; research assistant, Prof. L.F.E. Goldie (Resources for the Future-Ford Foundation), 1967–69; administrator, Northern Region, 1969 Jessup International Law Moot Court Competition; served in the U.S. Army, 1962–65; law clerk, Hon. John M. Cannella, U.S. District Court for the Southern District of New York, 1969–71; attorney with Davis Polk and Wardwell, New York, NY, 1971–85; admitted to practice New York, U.S. Supreme Court, U.S. Court of Appeals for Second and Third Circuits, U.S. Court of International Trade, U.S. Court of Claims, U.S. District Courts for Eastern, Southern and Northern Districts of New York, Interstate Commerce Commission; adjunct professor of law, Benjamin N. Cardozo School of Law, 1984–95; Mem., Drew University Board of Visitors, 1997–present; appointed to the U.S. Court of International Trade by President Reagan on February 22, 1985; confirmed by U.S. Senate, April 3, 1985.

NICHOLAS TSOUCALAS, senior judge; born in New York, NY, August 24, 1926; one of five children of George M. and Maria (Monogenis) Tsoucalas; married to Catherine Aravantinos; two daughters: Stephanie and Georgia; five grandchildren; B.S., Kent State University, 1949; LL.B., New York Law School, 1951; attended New York University Law School; entered U.S. Navy, 1944–46; served in the American and European Theaters of War on board the USS *Oden*, the USS *Monticello* and USS *Europa;* reentered Navy, 1951–52 and served on the carrier, USS *Wasp;* admitted to New York Bar, 1953; appointed Assistant U.S. Attorney for the Southern District of New York, 1955–59; appointed in 1959 as supervisor of 1960 census for the 17th and 18th Congressional Districts; appointed chairman, Board of Commissioners of Appraisal; appointed judge of Criminal Court of the City of New York, 1968; designated acting Supreme Court Justice, Kings and Queens Counties, 1975–82; resumed service as judge of the Criminal Court of the City of New York until June 1986; former chairman: Committee on Juvenile Delinquency, Federal Bar Association, and the Subcommittee on Public Order and Responsibility of the American Citizenship Committee of the New York County Lawyers' Association; member of the American Bar Association, New York State Bar Association; founder of Eastern Orthodox Lawyers' Association; former president: Greek-American Lawyers' Association, and Board of Directors of Greek Orthodox Church of ''Evangelismos'', St. John's Theologos Society, and Parthenon Foundation; member, Order of Ahepa, Parthenon Lodge, F.A.M.; appointed judge of the U.S. Court of International Trade by President Reagan on September 9, 1985, and confirmed by U.S. Senate on June 6, 1986; assumed senior status on September 30, 1996.

R. KENTON MUSGRAVE, senior judge; born in Clearwater, FL, September 7, 1927; married May 7, 1949 to former Ruth Shippen Hoppe, of Atlanta, GA; three children: Laura Marie Musgrave (deceased), Ruth Shippen Musgrave, Esq., and Forest Kenton Musgrave; attended Augusta Academy (Virginia); B.A., University of Washington, 1948; editorial staff, Journal of International Law, Emory University; J.D., with distinction, Emory University, 1953; assistant general counsel, Lockheed Aircraft and Lockheed International, 1953–62; vice president and general counsel, Mattel, Inc., 1963–71; director, Ringling Bros. and Barnum and Bailey Combined Shows, Inc., 1968–72; commissioner, BSA (Atlanta), 1952–55; partner, Musgrave, Welbourn and Fertman, 1972–75; assistant general counsel, Pacific Enterprises, 1975–81; vice president, general counsel and secretary, Vivitar Corporation, 1981–85; vice president and director, Santa Barbara Applied Research Corp., 1982–87; trustee, Morris Animal Foundation, 1981–94; director Emeritus, Pet Protection Society, 1981–present; director, Dolphins of Shark Bay (Australia) Foundation, 1985–present; trustee, The Dian Fossey Gorilla Fund, 1987–present; trustee, The Ocean Conservancy, 2000–present; vice president and director, South Bay Social Services Group, 1963–70; director, Palos Verdes Community Arts Association, 1973–79; member, Governor of Florida's Council of 100, 1970–73; director, Orlando Bank and Trust, 1970–73; counsel, League of Women Voters, 1964–66; member, State Bar of Georgia, 1953–present; State Bar of California, 1962–present; Los Angeles County Bar Association, 1962–87 and chairman, Corporate Law Departments Section, 1965–66; admitted to practice before the U.S. Supreme Court, 1962; Supreme Court of Georgia, 1953; California Supreme Court, 1962; U.S. Customs Court, 1967; U.S. Court of International Trade, 1980; nominated to the U.S. Court of International Trade by President Reagan on July 1, 1987; confirmed by the Senate on November 9, and took oath of office on November 13, 1987.

RICHARD W. GOLDBERG, senior judge; born in Fargo, ND, September 23, 1927; married; two children, a daughter and a son; J.D., University of Miami, 1952; served on active duty as an Air Force Judge Advocate, 1953–56; admitted to Washington, DC Bar, Florida Bar and North Dakota Bar; from 1959 to 1983, owned and operated a regional grain processing firm in North Dakota; served as State Senator from North Dakota for eight years; taught military law for the Army and Air Force ROTC at North Dakota State University; was vice-chairman of the board of Minneapolis Grain Exchange; joined the Reagan Administration in 1983 in Washington at the U.S. Department of Agriculture; served as Deputy Under Secretary for International Affairs and Commodity Programs and later as Acting Under Secretary; in 1990 joined the Washington, DC law firm of Anderson, Hibey and Blair; appointed judge of the U.S. Court of International Trade in 1991; assumed senior status in 2001.

JUDITH M. BARZILAY, senior judge; born in Russell, KS, January 3, 1944; husband, Sal (Doron) Barzilay; children, Ilan and Michael; parents, Arthur and Hilda Morgenstern; B.A., Wichita State University, 1965; M.L.S., Rutgers University School of Library and Information Science, 1971; J.D., Rutgers University School of Law, 1981, Moot Court Board, 1980–81; trial attorney, U.S. Department of Justice (International Trade Field Office), 1983–86; litigation associate, Siegel, Mandell and Davidson, New York, NY, 1986–88; Sony Corporation of America, 1988–98; customs and international trade counsel, 1988–89; vice-president for import and export operations, 1989–96; vice-president for government affairs, 1996–98; executive board of the American Association of Exporters and Importers, 1993–98; appointed by Treasury Secretary Robert Rubin to the Advisory Committee on Commercial Operations of the United States Customs Service, 1995–98; nominated for appointment on January 27, 1998 by President Clinton; sworn in as judge June 3, 1998.

Officers of the United States Court of International Trade

Clerk.—Tina Potuto Kimble (212) 264–2814.

UNITED STATES COURT OF FEDERAL CLAIMS

Lafayette Square, 717 Madison Place, NW., 20005, phone (202) 219–9657

EDWARD J. DAMICH, chief judge; born in Pittsburgh, PA, June 19, 1948; son of John and Josephine (Lovrencic) Damich; A.B., St. Stephen's College, 1970; J.D., Catholic University, 1976; professor of law at Delaware School of Law of Widener University, 1976–84; served as a Law and Economics Fellow at Columbia University School of Law, where he earned his L.L.M. in 1983 and his J.S.D. in 1991; professor of law at George Mason University, 1984–98; appointed by President George H.W. Bush to be a Commissioner of the Copyright Royalty Tribunal, 1992–93; Chief Intellectual Property Counsel for the Senate Judiciary Committee, 1995–98; admitted to the Bars of the District of Columbia and Pennsylvania; member of the District of Columbia Bar Association, Pennsylvania Bar Association, American Bar Association, Supreme Court of the United States, the Federal Circuit and *Association litteraire et artistique internationale;* president of the National Federation of Croatian Americans, 1994–95; appointed by President Clinton as judge, U.S. Court of Federal Claims, October 22, 1998; appointed by President George W. Bush as chief judge, U.S. Court of Federal Claims, May 13, 2002; at present Judge Damich is an adjunct professor of law at the Georgetown University Law Center.

LAWRENCE M. BASKIR, judge; born in Brooklyn, NY, January 10, 1938; married to Marna Tucker, two children; A.B., *magna cum laude*, Princeton University; Woodrow Wilson School of Public and International Affairs, 1959; LL.B., Harvard Law School, 1962; Principal Deputy General Counsel, Department of the Army, 1994–98; private practice and Editor-In-Chief, Military Law Reporter, 1981–94; Legislative Director to Senator Bill Bradley, 1979–81; Deputy Assistant Secretary (Legislation), Office of the Secretary, Department of the Treasury, 1977–79; Director, Vietnam Offender Study; Faculty Fellow, University of Notre Dame Law School, 1975–77; Director, Presidential (Ford) Clemancy Board, White House, 1974–75; Chief Counsel, Subcommittees on Constitutional Rights and Separation of Powers, Senate Judiciary Committee, Senator Sam J. Ervin, Chairman, 1967–74; publications include *Chance and Circumstances: The Draft, the War and the Vietnam Generation*; consultant to Information Intelligence Committees, U.S. Congress; Adjunct Professor and Lecturer, Georgetown, Notre Dame, Catholic Law Schools, and American University; appointed judge of the U.S. Court of Federal Claims on October 22, 1998; chief judge, July 11, 2000 to May 10, 2002.

CHRISTINE ODELL COOK "O.C." MILLER, judge; born in Oakland, CA, August 26, 1944; married to Dennis F. Miller; B.A., Stanford University, 1966; J.D., University of Utah College of Law, 1969; Comment Editor, Utah Law Review; member, Utah Chapter Order of the Coif; clerk to Chief Judge David T. Lewis, U.S. Court of Appeals for the 10th Circuit; trial attorney, Civil Division, U.S. Department of Justice; trial attorney, Federal Trade Commission, Bureau of Consumer Protection; Hogan and Hartson, litigation section; Pension Benefit Guaranty Corporation, Special Counsel; U.S. Railway Association, Assistant General Counsel; Shack and Kimball P.C., litigation; member of the Bars of the State of California and District of Columbia; member of the University Club and the Cosmos Club; appointed to the U.S. Court of Federal Claims by President Reagan on December 10, 1982, and confirmed as Christine Cook Nettsheim; reappointed by President Clinton on February 4, 1998.

MARIAN BLANK HORN, judge; born in New York, NY, 1943; daughter of Werner P. and Mady R. Blank; married to Robert Jack Horn; three daughters; attended Fieldston School, New York, NY, Barnard College, Columbia University and Fordham University School of Law; admitted to practice U.S. Supreme Court, 1973, Federal and State courts in New York, 1970, and Washington, DC, 1973; assistant district attorney, Deputy Chief Appeals Bureau, Bronx County, NY, 1969–72; attorney, Arent, Fox, Kintner, Plotkin and Kahn, 1972–73; adjunct professor of law, Washington College of Law, American University, 1973–76; litigation attorney, Federal Energy Administration, 1975–76; senior attorney, Office of General

Counsel, Strategic Petroleum Reserve Branch, Department of Energy, 1976–79; deputy assistant general counsel for procurement and financial incentives, Department of Energy, 1979–81; deputy associate solicitor, Division of Surface Mining, Department of the Interior, 1981–83; associate solicitor, Division of General Law, Department of the Interior, 1983–85; principal deputy solicitor and acting solicitor, Department of Interior, 1985–86; adjunct professor of law, George Washington University National Law Center, 1991–present; Woodrow Wilson Visiting Fellow, 1994; assumed duties of judge, U.S. Court of Federal Claims in 1986 and confirmed for a second term in 2003.

LYNN J. BUSH, judge; born in Little Rock, AR, December 30, 1948; daughter of John E. Bush III and Alice (Saville) Bush; one son, Brian Bush Ferguson; B.A., Antioch College, 1970, Thomas J. Watson Fellow; J.D., Georgetown University Law Center, 1976; admitted to the Arkansas Bar in 1976 and to the District of Columbia Bar in 1977; trial attorney, Commercial Litigation Branch, Civil Division, U.S. Department of Justice, 1976–87; senior trial attorney, Naval Facilities Engineering Command, Department of the Navy, 1987–89; counsel, Engineering Field Activity Chesapeake, Naval Facilities Engineering Command, Department of the Navy, 1989–96; administrative judge, U.S. Department of Housing and Urban Development Board of Contract Appeals, 1996–98; nominated by President Clinton to the U.S. Court of Federal Claims, June 22, 1998; and assumed duties of the office on October 26, 1998.

NANCY B. FIRESTONE, judge; born in Manchester, NH, October 17, 1951; B.A., Washington University, 1973; J.D., University of Missouri, Kansas City, 1977; one child: Amanda Leigh; attorney, Appellate Section and Environmental Enforcement Section, U.S. Department of Justice, Washington, DC, 1977–84; assistant chief, Policy Legislation and Special Litigation, Environment and Natural Resources Division, Department of Justice, Washington, DC, 1984–85; Deputy Chief, Environmental Enforcement Section, Department of Justice, Washington, DC, 1985–89; associate deputy administrator, Environmental Protection Agency, Washington, DC, 1989–92; judge, Environmental Appeals Board, Environmental Protection Agency, Washington, DC, 1992–95; Deputy Assistant Attorney General, Environment and Natural Resources Division, Department of Justice, Washington, DC, 1995–98; adjunct professor, Georgetown University Law Center, 1985–present; appointed to the U.S. Court of Federal Claims by President Clinton on October 22, 1998.

EMILY CLARK HEWITT, judge; born in Baltimore, MD, May 26, 1944; educated at the Roland Park Country School, Baltimore, MD, 1949–62; A.B., Cornell University, 1966; M. Phil., Union Theological Seminary, 1975; J.D. c.l., Harvard Law School, 1978; ordained minister in the Episcopal Church (diaconate, 1972; priesthood, 1974); member, Bar of the Supreme Judicial Court of The Commonwealth of Massachusetts, 1978; administrator, Cornell / Hofstra Upward Bound Program, 1967–69; lecturer, Union Theological Seminary, 1972–73 and 1974–75; assistant professor, Andover Newton Theological School, 1973–75; private practice of law, Hill & Barlow, 1978–93; council member, Real Property Section, Massachusetts Bar Association, 1983–86; member, Executive Committee and chair, Practice Standards Committee, Massachusetts Conveyancers Association, 1990–92; General Counsel, U.S. General Services Administration, 1993–98; member, Administrative Conference of the United States, 1993–95; member, President's Interagency Council on Women, 1995–98; appointed to the U.S. Court of Federal Claims on October 22, 1998; entered duty on November 10, 1998.

FRANCIS M. ALLEGRA, judge; born in Cleveland, OH, October 14, 1957; married to Regina Allegra; one child (Domenic); B.A., Borromeo College of Ohio, 1978; J.D., Cleveland State University, 1981; judicial clerk to Chief Trial Judge Philip R. Miller, U.S. Court of Claims, 1981–82; associate, Squire, Sanders & Dempsey (Cleveland), 1982–84; line attorney, Appellate Section, then 1984–89, Counselor to the Assistant Attorney General, both with Tax Division, U.S. Department of Justice; Counselor to the Associate Attorney General (1994) then Deputy Associate Attorney General (1994–98), U.S. Department of Justice; appointed to the U.S. Court of Federal Claims on October 22, 1998.

LAWRENCE J. BLOCK, judge, born in New York City, March 15, 1951; son of Jerome Block and Eve Silver; B.A., *magna cum laude,* New York University, 1973; J.D., The John Marshall Law School, 1981; law clerk for Hon. Roger J. Miner, United States District Court Judge for Northern District of New York, 1981–83; associate, New York office of Skadden, Arps, Slate, Meagher and Flom, 1983–86; attorney, Commercial Litigation Branch, U.S. Department of Justice, 1986; senior attorney-advisor, Office of Legal Policy and Policy Development, U.S. Department of Justice, 1987–90; adjunct professor, George Mason University School of Law, 1990–91; acting general counsel for legal policy and deputy assistant general counsel for legal policy, U.S. Department of Energy, 1990–94; senior counsel, Senate Judiciary Committee, 1994–02; admitted to the bar of Connecticut; admitted to practice in the U.S. Supreme Court, 1982, the United States District Court for the northern district of New York, 1982, the U.S. Court of Appeals for the Eleventh Circuit, 1985, the United States District Court for the Eastern District of New York, 1985; appointed by President George W. Bush on October 3, 2002, to a 15-years term as judge, U.S. Court of Federal Claims.

SUSAN G. BRADEN, judge, born in Youngstown, OH, November 8, 1948; married to Thomas M. Susman; daughter (Daily); B.A., Case Western Reserve University, 1970; J.D., Case Western Reserve University School of Law, 1973; post graduate study Harvard Law School, Summer, 1979; private practice, 1985–2003 (1997–2003 Baker & McKenzie); Federal Trade Commission: special counsel to Chairman, 1984–85, senior attorney advisor to Commissioner and Acting Chairman, 1980–83; U.S. Department of Justice, Antitrust Division, Senior Trial Attorney, Energy Section, 1978–80; Cleveland Field Office, 1973–78; Special Assistant Attorney General for the State of Alabama, 1990; Consultant to the Administrative Conference of the United States, 1984–85; 2000 co-chair, Lawyers for Bush-Cheney; General Counsel Presidential Debate for Dole-Kemp Campaign, 1996; counsel to RNC Platform, 1996; coordinator for Regulatory Reform and Antitrust Policy, Dole Presidential Campaign, 1995–96; National Steering Committee, Lawyers for Bush-Quayle, 1992; Assistant General Counsel, Republican National Convention, 1988, 1992, 1996, 2000; elected At-Large Member, D.C. Republican National Committee, 2000–02; member of the American Bar Association (Council Member, Section on Administrative Law and Regulatory Practice, 1996–99), Federal Circuit Bar Association, District of Columbia Bar Association, Computer Law Bar Association; admitted to the Supreme Court of Ohio, 1973, U.S. District Court for the District of Columbia, 1980, U.S. Supreme Court, 1980; U.S. Court of Appeals for the District of Columbia, 1992; U.S. Court of Appeals for the Second Circuit, 1993, U.S. Court of Appeals for the Federal Circuit, 2001; appointed to the U.S. Court of Federal Claims by President George W. Bush on July 14, 2003.

CHARLES F. LETTOW, judge, born in Iowa Falls, IA, February 10, 1941; son of Carl F. and Catherine Lettow; B.S.Ch.E., Iowa State University, 1962; LL.B., Stanford University, 1968, Order of the Coif; M.A., Brown University, 2001; Note Editor, *Stanford Law Review;* married to B. Sue Lettow; children: Renee Burnett, Carl Frederick II, John Stangland, and Paul Vorbeck; served U.S. Army, 1963–65; law clerk to Judge Ben C. Duniway, U.S. Court of Appeals for the Ninth Circuit, 1968–69, and Chief Justice Warren E. Burger, Supreme Court of the United States, 1969–70; counsel, Council on Environmental Quality, Executive Office of the President, 1970–73; associate (1973–76) and partner (1976–2003), Cleary, Gottlieb, Steen & Hamilton, Washington, DC; admitted to practice before the U.S. Supreme Court, the U.S. Courts of Appeals for the D.C., Second, Third, Fourth, Fifth, Sixth, Eighth, Ninth, Tenth, and Federal Circuits, the U.S. District Courts for the District of Columbia, the Northern District of California, and the District of Maryland, and the U.S. Court of Federal Claims; member: American Law Institute, the American Bar Association, the D.C. Bar, the California State Bar, the Iowa State Bar Association, and the Maryland State Bar; nominated by President George W. Bush to the U.S. Court of Federal Claims in 2001 and confirmed and took office in 2003.

MARY ELLEN COSTER WILLIAMS, judge; born in Flushing, NY, April 3, 1953; married to Mark Calhoun Williams; son: Justin; daughter: Jacquelyn; B.A. *summa cum laude* (Greek and Latin); M.A. (Latin), Catholic University, 1974; J.D. Duke University; Editorial Board, *Duke Law Journal,* 1976–77; admitted to the District of Columbia Bar; associate, Fulbright and Jaworski, 1977–79; associate, Schnader, Harrison, Segal and Lewis, 1979–83; Assistant U.S. Attorney, Civil Division, District of Columbia, 1983–87; partner—Janis, Schuelke, and Wechsler, 1987–89; administrative judge, General Services Board of Contract Appeals March 1989–July 2003; secretary, District of Columbia Bar, 1988–89; Fellow, American Bar Foundation, elected, 1985; Board of Directors, Bar Association of District of Columbia, 1985–88; Chairman, Young Lawyers Section, Bar Association of District of Columbia, 1985–86; Chair, Public Contract Law Section of American Bar Association, 2002–03, Chair-Elect, Vice-Chair, Secretary, Council, 1995–2002; Delegate, Section of Public Contract Law, ABA House of Delegates 2003–04; Lecturer, Government Contract Law, 1989–present; appointed to the U.S. Court of Federal Claims on July 21, 2003.

VICTOR JOHN WOLSKI, judge; born in New Brunswick, NJ, November 14, 1962; son of Vito and Eugenia Wolski; B.A., B.S., University of Pennsylvania, 1984; J.D., University of Virginia School of Law, 1991; married to Lisa Wolski, June 3, 2000; admitted to Supreme Court of the United States, 1995; California Supreme Court, 1992; Washington Supreme Court, 1994; Oregon Supreme Court, 1996; District of Columbia Court of Appeals, 2001; U.S. Court of Appeals for the Ninth Circuit, 1993; U.S. Court of Appeals for the Federal

Circuit, 2001; U.S. District Court for the Eastern District of California, 1993; U.S. District Court for the Northern District of California, 1995; U.S. Court of Federal Claims, 2001; U.S. District Court for the District of Columbia, 2002; research assistant, Center for Strategic and International Studies, 1984–85; research associate, Institute for Political Economy, 1985–88; confidential assistant and speechwriter to the Secretary, U.S. Department of Agriculture, 1988; paralegal specialist, Office of the general counsel, U.S. Department of Energy, 1989; law clerk to Judge Vaughn R. Walker, U.S. District Court for the Northern District of California, 1991–92; attorney, Pacific Legal Foundation, 1992–97; general counsel, Sacramento County Republican Central Committee, 1995–97; counsel to Senator Connie Mack, Vice-Chairman of the Joint Economic Committee, U.S. Congress, 1997–98; general counsel and chief tax adviser, Joint Economic Committee, U.S. Congress, 1999–2000; associate, Cooper, Carvin & Rosenthal, 2000–01; associate, Cooper & Kirk, 2001–03; nominated by President George W. Bush to the U.S. Court of Federal Claims on September 12, 2002, renominated January 7, 2003, and confirmed by U.S. Senate on July 9, 2003.

THOMAS C. WHEELER, judge; born in Chicago, IL, March 18, 1948; married; two grown children; B.A., Gettysburg College, 1970; J.D., Georgetown University Law School, 1973; private practice in Washington, DC, 1973–2005; associate and partner, Pettit & Martin until 1995; partner, Piper & Marbury (later Piper Marbury Rudnick & Wolfe, and then DLA Piper Rudnick Gray Cary); member of the District of Columbia Bar; American Bar Association's Public Contracts and Litigation Sections; appointed to the U.S. Court of Federal Claims on October 24, 2005.

MARGARET M. SWEENEY, judge; born in Baltimore, MD; B.A. in history, Notre Dame of Maryland, 1977; J.D., Delaware Law School, 1981; Delaware Family Court Master, 1981–83; litigation associate, Fedorko, Gilbert, & Lanctot, Morrisville, PA, 1983–85; law clerk to Hon. Loren A. Smith, Chief Judge of the U.S. Court of Federal Claims, 1985–87; trial attorney in the General Litigation Section of the Environment and Natural Resources Division of the United States Department of Justice, 1987–99; president, U.S. Court of Federal Claims Bar Association, 1999; attorney advisor, United States Department of Justice Office of Intelligence Policy and Review, 1999–2003; special master, U.S. Court of Federal Claims, 2003–05; member of the Bars of the Supreme Court of Pennsylvania and the District of Columbia Court of Appeals; appointed to the U.S. Court of Federal Claims by President George W. Bush on October 24, 2005, and entered duty on December 14, 2005.

GEORGE W. MILLER, judge, born in Schenectady, NY; married to Mary Katherine ''Kay'' Miller, three children; A.B., *magna cum laude,* Princeton University, 1963; J.D., Harvard Law School, 1966; L.L.M. in taxation, George Washington University Law School, 1968; law clerk to the late Judge Bruce M. Forrester of the United States Tax Court, 1966–67; officer, U.S. Navy Judge Advocate General Corps, 1967–70; trial attorney and partner at Hogan & Hartson (now Hogan Lovells), 1970–2004; District of Columbia Court of Appeals Board of Professional Responsibility, 1985 (Vice Chairman 1988–89, Chairman 1989–91); D.C. Court of Appeals Task Force on Racial and Ethnic Bias in the D.C. Courts, 1990–92; United States Court of Appeals for the District of Columbia Advisory Committee on Admissions and Grievances, 2002–04; United States Court of Federal Claims Advisory Council, 1994–2004; United States Court of Federal Claims Litigation Practice Task Force, 1995; member United States Court of Federal Claims Bar Association Board of Governors, 2004; admitted to the Bars of Virginia, District of Columbia, and New York; appointed to the United States Court of Federal Claims by President George W. Bush, 2004.

SENIOR JUDGES

JAMES F. MEROW, senior judge; born in Salamanca, NY, March 16, 1932; educated in the public schools of Little Valley, NY and Alexandria, VA; A.B. (with distinction), George Washington University, 1953; J.D. (with distinction), George Washington University Law School, 1956; member: Phi Beta Kappa, Order of the Coif, Omicron Delta Kappa; married; officer, U.S. Army Judge Advocate General's Corps, 1956–59; trial attorney-branch director, Civil Division, U.S. Department of Justice, 1959–78; trial judge, U.S. Court of Claims, 1978–82; member of Virginia State Bar, District of Columbia Bar, American Bar Association, and Federal Bar Association; judge, U.S. Court of Federal Claims since October 1, 1982 and reappointed by President Reagan to a 15-year term commencing August 5, 1983.

JOHN PAUL WIESE, senior judge; born in Brooklyn, NY, April 19, 1934; son of Gustav and Margaret Wiese; B.A., *cum laude*, Hobart College, 1962, Phi Beta Kappa; LL.B., University of Virginia School of Law, 1965; married to Alice Mary Donoghue, June, 1961; one son,

John Patrick; served U.S. Army, 1957–59; law clerk: U.S. Court of Claims, trial division, 1965–66, and Judge Linton M. Collins, U.S. Court of Claims, appellate division, 1966–67; private practice in District of Columbia, 1967–74 (specializing in government contract litigation); trial judge, U.S. Court of Claims, 1974–82; admitted to Bar of the District of Columbia, 1966; admitted to practice in the U.S. Supreme Court, the U.S. Court of Appeals for the Federal Circuit, the U.S. Court of Federal Claims; member: District of Columbia Bar Association and American Bar Association; designated in Federal Courts Improvement Act of 1982 as judge, U.S. Court of Federal Claims and reappointed by President Reagan to 15-year term on October 14, 1986.

ROBERT J. YOCK, senior judge; born in St. James, MN, January 11, 1938; son of Dr. William J. and Erma Yock; B.A. St. Olaf College, 1959; J.D., University of Michigan Law School, 1962; married to Carla M. Moen, June 13, 1964; children: Signe Kara and Torunn Ingrid; admitted to the Minnesota Supreme Court in 1962; Court of Military Appeals, 1964; U.S. Supreme Court, 1965; U.S. District Court for the District of Minnesota, 1966; U.S. District Court for the District of Columbia, 1972; U.S. Court of Claims, 1979; and U.S. Court of Federal Claims, 1982; member: Minnesota State Bar Association, and District of Columbia Bar Association; served in the U.S. Navy, Judge Advocate General's Corps, 1962–66; private practice, St. Paul, MN, 1966–69; entered Government service as chief counsel to the National Archives and Record Services of the General Services Administration, 1969–70; executive assistant and legal advisor to the Administrator of General Services, 1970–72; assistant general counsel at GSA, 1972–77; trial judge, U.S. Court of Claims, 1977–82; designated by Public Law 97–164 as judge, U.S. Court of Federal Claims, 1982–83; renominated by President Reagan as judge, U.S. Court of Federal Claims, June 20, 1983, confirmed by U.S. Senate, August 4, 1983, reappointed to 15-year term, August 5, 1983.

LAWRENCE S. MARGOLIS, senior judge; born in Philadelphia, PA, March 13, 1935; son of Reuben and Mollie Margolis; B.A., Central High School, Philadelphia, PA; B.S. in mechanical engineering from the Drexel Institute of Technology (now Drexel University), 1957; J.D., George Washington University Law School, 1961; married to Doris May Rosenberg, January 30, 1960; children: Mary Aleta and Paul Oliver; admitted to the District of Columbia Bar; patent examiner, U.S. Patent Office, 1957–62; patent counsel, Naval Ordnance Laboratory, White Oak, MD, 1962–63; assistant corporation counsel for the District of Columbia, 1963–66; attorney, criminal division, U.S. Department of Justice and special assistant U.S. attorney for District of Columbia, 1966–68; assistant U.S. attorney for the District of Columbia, 1968–71; appointed U.S. magistrate for District of Columbia in 1971; reappointed for a second 8-year term in 1979 and served until December, 1982 when appointed a judge, U.S. Court of Federal Claims; chairman, U.S. Court of Federal Claims: Security Committee, Building Committee, and Alternative Dispute Resolution Committee; chairman, American Bar Association, judicial administration division, 1980–81; chairman, National Conference of Special Court Judges, 1977–78; board of directors, Bar Association of the District of Columbia, 1970–72; editor: DC Bar Journal, 1966–73, Young Lawyers Newspaper editor, 1965–66; executive council, Young Lawyers Section, 1968–69; board of editors, The Judges' Journal and The District Lawyer; president, George Washington University National Law Association, 1983–84; president, George Washington Law Association, District of Columbia Chapter, 1975–76; board of governors, George Washington University General Alumni Association, 1978–85; fellow, Institute of Judicial Administration, 1993–present; member, District of Columbia Judicial Conference; former member, board of directors, National Council of U.S. Magistrates; former president, Federal Bar Toastmasters; former technical editor, Federal Bar Journal; faculty, Federal Judicial Center; trustee, Drexel University, 1983–91; member, Rotary Club; Board of Managers, Central High (Philadelphia, PA); president, Washington, DC, Rotary Club, 1988–89, District governor, 1991–92; American Bar Association Judicial Administration Division Award for distinguished service as chairman for 1980–81; Drexel University and George Washington University Distinguished Alumni Achievement Awards; Drexel University 100 (one of top 100 graduates); Center for Public Resources Alternative Dispute Resolution Achievement Award, 1987; George Washington University Community Service Award; nominated by President Ronald Reagan as a judge on the U.S. Court of Federal Claims on September 27, 1982, confirmed by the Senate and received Commission on December 10, 1982, took oath of office on December 15, 1982.

LOREN ALLAN SMITH, senior judge; born in Chicago, IL, December 22, 1944; son of Alvin D. and Selma (Halpern) Smith; B.A., Northwestern University, 1966; J.D., Northwestern University School of Law, 1969; married; admitted to the Bars of the Illinois Supreme Court; the Court of Military Appeals; the U.S. Court of Appeals, District of Columbia Circuit; the U.S. Court of Appeals for the Federal Circuit; the U.S. Supreme Court; the U.S. Court of Federal Claims; honorary member: The University Club; consultant, Sidley and Austin Chicago, 1972–73; general attorney, Federal Communications Commission, 1973; assistant to the Special Counsel to the President, 1973–74; Special Assistant U.S. Attorney, District of Columbia, 1974–75; chief counsel, Reagan for President campaigns, 1976 and 1980; professor, Delaware Law School, 1976–84; distinguished lecturer at Columbus School of Law, The Catholic University of America and distinguished adjunct professor at George Mason University School of Law; deputy director, Executive Branch Management Office of Presidential Transition, 1980–81; Chairman, Administrative Conference of the Unites States, 1981–85; served as a member of the President's Cabinet Councils on Legal Policy and on Management and Administration; appointed to the U.S. Court of Federal Claims on July 11, 1985; entered on duty September 12, 1985; served as chief judge from January 14, 1986, until July 11, 2000.

ERIC G. BRUGGINK, senior judge; born in Kalidjati, Indonesia, September 11, 1949; naturalized U.S. citizen, 1961; married to Melinda Harris Bruggink; sons: John and David; B.A., *cum laude* (sociology), Auburn University, AL, 1971; M.A. (speech), 1972; J.D., University of Alabama, 1975; Hugo Black Scholar and Note and Comments Editor of Alabama Law Review; member, Alabama State Bar and District of Columbia Bar; served as law clerk to chief judge Frank H. McFadden, Northern District of Alabama, 1975–76; associate, Hardwick, Hause and Segrest, Dothan, AL, 1976–77; assistant director, Alabama Law Institute, 1977–79; director, Office of Energy and Environmental Law, 1977–79; associate, Steiner, Crum and Baker, Montgomery, AL, 1979–82; Director, Office of Appeals Counsel, Merit Systems Protection Board, 1982–86; appointed to the U.S. Court of Federal Claims on April 15, 1986.

BOHDAN A. FUTEY, senior judge; born in Ukraine, June 28, 1939; B.A., Western Reserve University, 1962; M.A., 1964; J.D., Cleveland Marshall Law School, 1968; married to the former Myra Fur; three children: Andrew, Lidia, and Daria; partner, Futey and Rakowsky, 1968–72; chief assistant police prosecutor, city of Cleveland, 1972–74; executive assistant to the mayor of Cleveland, 1974–75; partner, Bazarko, Futey and Oryshkewych, 1975–84; chairman, U.S. Foreign Claims Settlement Commission, May 1984–87; member: District of Columbia Bar Association, the Ukrainian American Bar Association; actively involved with Democratization and Rule of Law programs organized by the Judicial Conference of the United States, the Department of State, and the American Bar Association in Ukraine and Russia; has participated in judicial exchange programs, seminars, and workshops and has been a consultant to the working group on Ukraine's Constitution and Ukrainian Parliament; advisor to the International Foundation for Election Systems (IFES) and the International Republican Institutes (IRI) democracy programs for Ukraine; served as an official observer during the parliamentary and presidential elections in 1994 and 1998 and conducted briefings on Ukraine's election law for international observers; has lectured on Constitutional Law at the Ukrainian Free University in Munich and Passau University, Germany; also at Kyiv State University and Lviv University in Ukraine; nominated judge of the U.S. Court of Federal Claims on January 30, 1987, and entered on duty, May 29, 1987.

ROBERT HAYNE HODGES, Jr., senior judge; born in Columbia, SC, September 11, 1944, son of Robert Hayne and Mary (Lawton) Hodges; educated in the public schools of Columbia, SC; attended Wofford College, Spartanburg, SC; B.S., University of South Carolina, 1966; J.D., University of South Carolina Law School, 1969; married to Ruth Nicholson (Lady) Hodges, August 23, 1963; three children; appointed to the U.S. Court of Federal Claims on March 12, 1990.

UNITED STATES TAX COURT

400 Second Street, NW., 20217, phone (202) 521–0700

JOHN O. COLVIN, chief judge; born in Ohio, 1946; A.B., University of Missouri, 1968; J.D., 1971; LL.M., Taxation, Georgetown University Law Center, 1978; admitted to practice law in Missouri (1971) and District of Columbia (1974); Office of the Chief Counsel, U.S. Coast Guard, Washington, DC, 1971–75; served as Tax Counsel, Senator Bob Packwood, 1975–84; Chief Counsel (1985–87), and Chief Minority Counsel (1987–88), U.S. Senate Finance Committee; past Chair, Tax Section, Federal Bar Association and recipient of the FBA Tax Section's Liles Award; Adjunct Professor of Law, Georgetown University Law Center and recipient of Charles Fahy Distinguished Adjunct Professor Award; appointed by President Reagan as Judge, United States Tax Court, on September 1, 1988, for a term ending August 31, 2003; reappointed on August. 12, 2004, for a term ending August 11, 2019; elected as Chief Judge for two-year terms beginning June 1, 2006, June 1, 2008, and June 1, 2010.

MARY ANN COHEN, judge; born in New Mexico, 1943; attended public schools in Los Angeles, CA; B.S., University of California, at Los Angeles, 1964; J.D., University of Southern California School of Law, 1967; practiced law in Los Angeles, member in law firm of Abbott and Cohen; American Bar Association, Section of Taxation, and Continuing Legal Education activities; received Dana Latham Memorial Award from Los Angeles County Bar Association Taxation Section, 1997; Jules Ritholz Memorial Merit Award from ABA Tax Section Committee on Civil and Criminal Tax Penalties, 1999; Bruce I. Hochman Award from the UCLA Tax Controversy program, 2007; and Joanne M. Garvey Award from California Bar Taxation Section, 2008; appointed by President Reagan as Judge, United States Tax Court, on September 24, 1982, for a term ending September 23, 1997; served as Chief Judge from June 1, 1996 to September 23, 1997; reappointed on November 7, 1997, for a term ending November 6, 2012, and served again as Chief Judge from November 7, 1997 to May 31, 2000.

JAMES S. HALPERN, judge; born in New York, 1945; Hackley School, Terrytown, NY, 1963; B.S., Wharton School, University of Pennsylvania, 1967; J.D., University of Pennsylvania Law School, 1972; LL.M., Taxation, New York University Law School, 1975; Associate Attorney, Mudge, Rose, Guthrie and Alexander, New York City, 1972–74; assistant professor of law, Washington and Lee University, 1975–76; assistant professor of law, St. John's University, New York City, 1976–78; visiting professor, Law School, New York University, 1978–79; associate attorney, Roberts and Holland, New York City, 1979–80; Principal Technical Advisor, Assistant Commissioner (Technical) and Associate Chief Counsel (Technical), Internal Revenue Service, Washington, DC, 1980–83; partner, Baker and Hostetler, Washington, DC, 1983–90; Adjunct Professor, Law School, George Washington University, Washington, DC, 1984–present; Colonel, U.S. Army Reserve (retired); appointed by President George H.W. Bush as Judge, United States Tax Court, on July 3, 1990, for a term ending July 2, 2005; reappointed on November 2, 2005, for a term ending November 1, 2020.

MAURICE B. FOLEY, judge; born in Illinois, 1960; B.A., Swarthmore College; J.D., Boalt Hall School of Law at the University of California at Berkeley; LL.M., Georgetown University Law Center; attorney for the Legislation and Regulations Division of the Internal Revenue Service, Tax Counsel for the United States Senate Committee on Finance; Deputy Tax Legislative Counsel in the U.S. Treasury's Office of Tax Policy; appointed by President Clinton as Judge, United States Tax Court, on April 9, 1995, for a term ending April 8, 2010.

JUAN F. VASQUEZ, judge; born in San Antonio, Texas, 1948; attended Fox Tech High School; A.D. (Data Processing), San Antonio Junior College; B.B.A. (Accounting), University of Texas, Austin, 1972; attended State University of New York, Buffalo in 1st year law school, 1975; J.D., University of Houston Law Center, 1977; LL.M., Taxation, New York University Law School of Law, 1978; Certified Public Accountant, Certificate from Texas, 1976; admitted to State Bar of Texas, 1977; admitted to the United States Tax Court, 1978; certified in tax law by Texas Board of Legal Specialization, 1984; admitted to the United States District Court, Southern District of Texas, 1982, Western District of Texas, 1985 and United States Court of Appeals for the Fifth Circuit, 1982; and the Supreme Court of the United States of America, 1996; private practice of tax law, in San Antonio, TX, 1987–April 1995; partner, Leighton, Hood and Vasquez, in San Antonio, TX, 1982–87; Trial Attorney, Office of Chief Counsel, Internal Revenue Service, Houston, TX, 1978–82; accountant, Coopers and Lybrand, Los Angeles, CA, 1972–74; member of American Bar Association, Tax Section; Texas State Bar, Tax Section; Fellow of Texas and San Antonio Bar Foundations; College of State Bar of Texas; National Hispanic Bar Association and Hispanic Bar Association of the District of Columbia; Mexican American Bar Association (MABA) of San Antonio 1982–95; Houston MABA 1978–82; Texas MABA 1986–88; National Association of Hispanic CPA's San Antonio Chapter (founding member) 1983–88; member of Greater Austin Tax Litigation Association 1989–95; served on Austin Internal Revenue Service District Director's Practitioner Liaison Committee, 1990–91 (chairman, 1991); appointed by President Clinton as Judge, United States Tax Court, on May 1, 1995, for a term ending April 30, 2010.

JOSEPH H. GALE, judge; born in Virginia, 1953; A.B., Philosophy, Princeton University, 1976; J.D., University of Virginia School of Law, Dillard Fellow, 1980; practiced law as an Associate Attorney, Dewey Ballantine, Washington, DC, and New York, 1980–83; Dickstein, Shapiro and Morin, Washington, DC, 1983–85; served as Tax Legislative Counsel for Senator Daniel Patrick Moynihan (D–NY), 1985–88; Administrative Assistant and Tax Legislative Counsel, 1989; Chief Counsel, 1990–93; Chief Tax Counsel, Committee on Finance, U.S. Senate, 1993–95; minority Chief Tax Counsel, Senate Finance Committee, January 1995–July 1995; minority Staff Director and Chief Counsel, Senate Finance Committee, July 1995–January 1996; admitted to District of Columbia Bar; member of American Bar Association, Section of Taxation; appointed by President Clinton as Judge, United States Tax Court, February 6, 1996, for a term ending February 5, 2011.

MICHAEL B. THORNTON, judge; born in Mississippi, 1954; B.S. in Accounting, *summa cum laude,* University of Southern Mississippi, 1976; M.S. in Accounting, 1997; M.A. in English Literature, University of Tennessee, 1979; J.D. (with distinction), Duke University School of Law, 1982; Order of the Coif, Duke Law Journal Editorial Board; admitted to District of Columbia Bar, 1982; served as Law Clerk to the Honorable Charles Clark, Chief Judge, U.S. Court of Appeals for the Fifth Circuit, 1983–84; practiced law as an Associate Attorney, Sutherland, Asbill and Brennan, Washington, DC, 1982–83 and summer 1981; Miller and Chevalier, Chartered, Washington, DC, 1985–88; served as Tax Counsel, U.S. House Committee on Ways and Means, 1988–93; Chief Minority Tax Counsel, U.S. House Committee on Ways and Means, January 1995; Attorney-Adviser, U.S. Treasury Department, February–April 1995; Deputy Tax Legislative Counsel in the Office of Tax Policy, United States Treasury Department, April 1995–February 1998; recipient of Treasury Secretary's Annual Award, U.S. Department of the Treasury, 1997; Meritorious Service Award, U.S. Department of the Treasury, 1998; appointed by President Clinton as Judge, United States Tax Court, on March 8, 1998, for a term ending March 7, 2013.

L. PAIGE MARVEL, judge; born in Maryland, 1949; B.A., *magna cum laude,* College of Notre Dame, 1971; J.D. with honors, University of Maryland School of Law, Baltimore, MD, 1974; Order of the Coif; member, Maryland Law Review and Moot Court Board; Garbis and Schwait, P.A., associate (1974–76) and shareholder (1976–85); shareholder, Garbis, Marvel and Junghans, P.A., 1985–86; shareholder, Melnicove, Kaufman, Weiner, Smouse and Garbis, P.A., 1986–88; partner, Venabel, Baetjer and Howard LLP, 1988–98; member, American Bar Association, Section of Taxation, Vice-Chair, Committee Operations, 1993–95; Council Director 1989–92; Chair, Court Procedure Committee, 1985–87; Maryland State Bar Association, Board of Governors, 1988–90, and 1996–98; Chair, Taxation Section 1982–83; Federal Bar Association, Section of Taxation, Section Council, 1984–90; Fellow, American Bar Foundation; Fellow, Maryland Bar Foundation; fellow and former Regent, American College of Tax Counsel, 1996–98; member, American Law Institute; advisor, ALI *Restatement of Law, Third, The Law Governing Lawyers* 1988–98; University of Maryland Law School Board of Visitors, 1995–2001; Loyola/Notre Dame Library, Inc. Board of Trustees, 1996–2003; Advisory Committee, University of Baltimore Graduate Tax Program, 1986–present; Co-editor, Procedure Department, The Journal of Taxation, 1990–98; member, Commissioner's Review Panel on IRS Integrity, 1989–91; member and Chair, Procedure Subcommittee, Commission to Revise the Annotated Code of Maryland (Tax Provisions), 1981–87; member,

Advisory Commission to the Maryland State Department of Economic and Community Development, 1978–81; recipient, President's Medal, College of Notre Dame, 2006; Jules Ritholz award, ABA Tax Section's Civil and Criminal Tax Penalties Comm., 2004; First Annual Tax Excellence Award, Maryland State Bar Association Tax Section, 2002; named one of Maryland's Top 100 Women, 1998; recipient, ABA Tax Section's Distinguished Service Award, 1995; MSBA Distinguished Service Award, 1982–83; listed in Best Lawyers in America, 1991–98, *Who's Who in America, Who's Who in American Law, Who's Who in the East;* author of various articles and book chapters on tax and tax litigation topics; appointed by President Clinton as Judge, United States Tax Court, on April 6, 1998, for a term ending April 5, 2013.

JOSEPH ROBERT GOEKE, judge; born in Kentucky, 1950; B.S., *cum laude,* Xavier University, 1972; J.D., University of Kentucky College of Law, 1975 (Order of the Coif); admitted to Illinois and Kentucky Bar, U.S. District Court for the Northern District of Illinois (Trial Bar), U.S. Court of Federal Claims; Trial Attorney, Chief Counsel's Office, Internal Revenue Service, New Orleans, LA, 1975–80; Senior Trial Attorney, Chief Counsel's Office, Internal Revenue Service, Cincinnati, OH, 1980–85; Special International Trial Attorney, Chief Counsel's Office, Internal Revenue Service, Cincinnati, OH, 1985–88; partner, Law Firm of Mayer, Brown, Rowe and Maw, Chicago, IL, 1988–2003; appointed by President George W. Bush as Judge, United States Tax Court, on April 22, 2003, for a term ending April 21, 2018.

ROBERT A. WHERRY, Jr., judge; born in Virginia, 1944; B.S., and J.D., University of Colorado; LL.M., Taxation, New York University Law School; fellow and former Regent of the American College of Tax Counsel and former chairman of the Taxation Section of the Colorado Bar Association; served as chairman of the Small-Business Tax Committee of the Colorado Association of Commerce and Industry, as president of the Greater Denver Tax Counsel Association, is a past chairman of the Administrative Practice Committee of the American Bar Association Tax Section, a member of the Council, and a member of the Advisory Committee of the American Bar Association Section of Dispute Resolution; listed in *The Best Lawyers in America* (in tax litigation); his articles have appeared in ALI–ABA publications, *The Colorado Lawyer, Tax Notes, and State Tax Notes;* former Colorado correspondent for *State Tax Notes* and has spoken at numerous tax institutes, including the University of Denver Tax Institute, Tulane University Tax Institute, and American Bar Association Tax Section programs; was an instructor in Tax Court litigation for the National Institute for Trial Advocacy; appointed by President George W. Bush as Judge, United States Tax Court, on April 23, 2003, for a term ending April 22, 2018.

DIANE L. KROUPA, judge; born in South Dakota, 1955; B.S.F.S., Georgetown University School of Foreign Service, 1978; J.D., University of South Dakota Law School, 1981; practiced tax law at Faegre and Benson, LLP in Minneapolis, MN; Minnesota Tax Court Judge, 1995–2001 (Chief Judge, 1998–2001); attorney-advisor, Legislation and Regulations Division, Office of Chief Counsel (1981–84) and served as attorney-advisor to Judge Joel Gerber, United States Tax Court, 1984–85; admitted to practice law in South Dakota (1981), District of Columbia (1985) and Minnesota (1986); member: American Bar Association (Tax Section), Minnesota State Bar Association (Tax Section), National Association of Women Judges (1995–present), American Judicature Society (1995–present); Distinguished Service Award Recipient (2001), Minnesota State Bar Association (Tax Section); Volunteer of the Year Award, Junior League of Minneapolis (1993); Community Volunteer of the Year, Minnesota State Bar Association (1998); appointed by President George W. Bush as Judge, United States Tax Court, on June 13, 2003, for a term ending June 12, 2018.

MARK V. HOLMES, judge; born in New York, 1960; B.A., Harvard College, 1979; J.D., University of Chicago Law School, 1983; admitted to New York and District of Columbia Bars; U.S. Supreme Court; DC, Second, Fifth and Ninth Circuits; Southern and Eastern Districts of New York, Court of Federal Claims; practiced in New York as an Associate, Cahill Gordon and Reindel, 1983–85; Sullivan and Cromwell, 1987–91; served as clerk to the Hon. Alex Kozinski, Ninth Circuit, 1985–87; and in Washington as Counsel to Commissioners, United States International Trade Commission, 1991–96; Counsel, Miller and Chevalier, 1996–2001; Deputy Assistant Attorney General, Tax Division, 2001–03; member, American Bar Association (Litigation and Tax Sections); appointed by President George W. Bush as Judge, United States Tax Court, on June 30, 2003, for a term ending June 29, 2018.

DAVID GUSTAFSON, judge; born in Greenville, South Carolina, in 1956. Bob Jones University, B.A. *summa cum laude,* 1978. Duke University School of Law, J.D. with distinction, 1981. Order of the Coif (1981). Executive Editor of the *Duke Law Journal* (1980–81). Admitted to the District of Columbia Bar, 1981. Associate at the law firm of Sutherland, Asbill and Brennan, in Washington, DC, 1981–83. Trial Attorney (1983–89), Assistant Chief (1989–2005), and Chief (2005–08) in the Court of Federal Claims Section of the Tax Division in the U.S. Department of Justice; and Coordinator of Tax Shelter Litigation for the entire Tax Division (2002–06). Tax Division Outstanding Attorney Awards, 1985, 1989, 1997, 2001–05. Federal Bar Association's Younger Attorney Award, 1991. President of the Court of Federal Claims Bar Association (2001). Appointed by President George W. Bush as Judge, United States Tax Court, on July 29, 2008, for a term ending July 29, 2023.

RICHARD T. MORRISON, judge; born in Hutchinson, Kansas 1967. B.A., B.S., University of Kansas, 1989; visiting student at Mansfield College, Oxford University, 1987–88; J.D., University of Chicago Law School, 1993; M.A., University of Chicago, 1994. Clerk to Judge Jerry E. Smith, United States Court of Appeals for the Fifth Circuit, 1993–94. Associate, Baker and McKenzie, Chicago, Illinois, 1994–96. Associate, Mayer Brown and Platt, Chicago, Illinois 1996–2001. Deputy Assistant Attorney General for Review and Appellate Matters, Tax Division, United States Department of Justice, from 2001 to 2008 (except for term as Acting Assistant Attorney General, from July 2007 to January 2008). Nominated by President George W. Bush as Judge, United States Tax Court, on November 15, 2007; confirmed by Senate, July 7, 2008.

ELIZABETH CREWSON PARIS, judge; born in Oklahoma, 1958; B.S., University of Tulsa, 1980; J.D., University of Tulsa College of Law, 1987; LL.M., Taxation, University of Denver College of Law, 1993. Admitted to the Supreme Court of Oklahoma and U.S. District Court for the District of Oklahoma, 1988; U.S. Tax Court, U.S. Court of Federal Claims, U.S. Court of Appeals for the Tenth Circuit, 1993; Supreme Court of Colorado, 1994. Former partner, Brumley Bishop and Paris, 1992; Senior Associate, McKenna and Cueno, 1994; Tax Partner, Reinhart, Boerner, Van Deuren, Norris and Rieselbach, 1998. Tax Counsel to the United States Senate Finance Committee, 2000–08. Member of the American Bar Association, Section of Taxation and Real Property and Probate Sections, formerly served as Vice Chair to both Agriculture and Entity Selection Committees. Member of Colorado and Oklahoma Bar Associations. Recognized as Distinguished Alumnus by the University of Tulsa School of law. Author of numerous tax, estate planning, real property, agriculture articles and chapters. Former adjunct professor, Georgetown University Law Center, LL.M. Taxation Program, and University of Tulsa College of Law. Appointed by President George W. Bush as Judge, United States Tax Court, on July 30, 2008, for a term ending July 29, 2023.

SENIOR JUDGES

HOWARD A. DAWSON, Jr., senior judge; born in Arkansas, 1922; Woodrow Wilson High School, Washington, DC, 1940; B.S. in Commerce, University of North Carolina, 1946; J.D. with honors, George Washington University School of Law, 1949; President, Case Club; Secretary-Treasurer, Student Bar Association; private practice of law, Washington, DC, 1949–50; served with the United States Treasury Department, Internal Revenue Service, as follows: Attorney, Civil Division, Office of Chief Counsel, 1950–53; Civil Advisory Counsel, Atlanta Region, 1953–57; Regional Counsel, Atlanta Region, 1958; Personal Assistant to Chief Counsel, 1958–59, Assistant Chief Counsel (Administration), 1959–62; U.S. Army Finance Corps, 1943–45; two years in European Theater; Captain, Finance Corps, U.S. Army Reserve (Retired); member of District of Columbia Bar (1949), Georgia Bar (1958), American Bar Association (Section of Taxation), Federal Bar Association, Chi Psi, Delta Theta Phi, George Washington University Law Alumni Association; appointed by President Kennedy as Judge, Tax Court of the United States, on August 21, 1962, for a term ending June 1, 1970; reappointed by President Nixon on June 2, 1970, for a term ending June 1, 1985; served as Chief Judge from July 1, 1973 to June 30, 1977, during which time the United States Tax Court's Courthouse was built and dedicated; and served again as Chief Judge from July 1, 1983 to June 1, 1985; retired on June 2, 1985; David Brennan Distinguished Professor of Law, University of Akron Law School, Spring Term, 1986; Professor and Director, Graduate Tax Program, University of Baltimore Law School, 1986–89; Distinguished Visiting Professor of Law, University of San Diego, Winter 1991. Recalled as Senior Judge to perform judicial duties 1990–to–present. In 2009, the Court established the Howard A. Dawson, Jr. Award to honor exemplary service by Tax Court employees. On January 18, 2011, became the then longest serving judge in Tax Court history.

HERBERT L. CHABOT, senior judge; born in New York, 1931; Stuyvesant High School, 1948; B.A., *cum laude,* C.C.N.Y., 1952; LL.B., Columbia University, 1957; LL.M. in Taxation, Georgetown University, 1964; served in United States Army, 2 years, and Army Reserves (civil affairs units), for 8 years; served on legal staff, American Jewish Congress, 1957–61; attorney-adviser to Judge Russell E. Train, 1961–65; Congressional Joint Committee on Taxation, 1965–78; elected Delegate, Maryland Constitutional Convention, 1967–68; adjunct professor, National Law Center, George Washington University, 1974–83; member of American Bar Association, Tax Section, and Federal Bar Association; appointed by President Carter as Judge, United States Tax Court, on April 3, 1978, for a term ending April 2, 1993; served as Senior Judge on recall performing judicial duties until reappointed on October 20, 1993, for a term ending October 19, 2008; retired on June 30, 2001, but recalled on July 1, 2001, as Senior Judge to perform judicial duties to the present time.

ARTHUR L. NIMS III, senior judge; born in Oklahoma, 1923; attended public schools, Macon, GA, and Deerfield Academy, Deerfield, MA; B.A., Williams College; LL.B., University of Georgia Law School; LL.M., Taxation, New York University Law School; served as an officer, lieutenant (jg.), U.S. Naval Reserve, on active duty in the Pacific Theater during World War II; admitted to Georgia Bar, 1949; practiced law in Macon, GA, 1949–51; Special Attorney, Office of the District Counsel, Internal Revenue Service, New York, 1951–54; attorney, Legislation and Regulations Division, Chief Counsel's Office, Washington, DC, 1954–55; admitted to New Jersey Bar, 1955; partner in the law firm of McCarter and English, Newark, NJ, 1961–79; Secretary, Section of Taxation, American Bar Association, 1977–79; Chairman, Section of Taxation, New Jersey State Bar Association, 1969–71; member, American Law Institute; American College of Tax Counsel; received Kellogg Award for Lifetime Achievement from Williams College; received Tax Society of New York University Award for lifetime achievement; received award for lifetime achievement from American College of Tax Counsel; appointed by President Carter as Judge, United States Tax Court, on June 29, 1979, for a term ending June 28, 1994; served as Chief Judge of the Tax Court from June 1, 1988 to May 31, 1992; recalled on June 1, 1992, as Senior Judge to perform judicial duties from that date to the present.

JULIAN I. JACOBS, senior judge; born in Maryland, 1937; B.A., University of Maryland, 1958; LL.B., University of Maryland Law School, 1960; LL.M., Taxation, Georgetown Law Center, 1965; admitted to Maryland Bar, 1960; attorney, Internal Revenue Service, Washington, DC, 1961–65, and Buffalo, NY, in Regional Counsel's Office, 1965–67; entered private practice of law in Baltimore, MD, 1967; associate (1972–74) and partner (1974–84) in the Law Firm of Gordon, Feinblatt, Rothman, Hoffberger and Hollander; Chairman, study commission to improve the quality of the Maryland Tax Court, 1978; member, study groups to consider changes in the Maryland tax laws; Commissioner on a commission to reorganize and recodify article of Maryland law dealing with taxation, 1980; Lecturer, tax seminars and professional programs; Chairman, Section of Taxation, Maryland State Bar Association; adjunct professor of Law, Graduate Tax Program, University of Baltimore School of Law, 1991–93; Adjunct Professor of Law, Graduate Tax Program, University of San Diego School of Law, 2001; Adjunct Professor of Law, Graduate Tax Program, University of Denver School of Law, 2001–04; appointed by President Reagan as Judge, United States Tax Court, on March 30, 1984, for a term ending March 29, 1999; recalled on March 30, 1999, as Senior Judge to perform judicial duties from that date to the present.

JOEL GERBER, senior judge; born in Illinois, 1940; B.S., business administration, Roosevelt University, 1962; J.D., DePaul University, 1965; LL.M., Taxation, Boston University Law School, 1968; admitted to the Illinois Bar, 1965; Georgia Bar, 1974; Tennessee Bar, 1978; served with U.S. Treasury Department, Internal Revenue Service, as trial attorney, Boston, MA, 1965–72; senior trial attorney, Atlanta, GA, 1972–76; District Counsel, Nashville, TN, 1976–80; Deputy Chief Counsel, Washington, DC, 1980–84; Acting Chief Counsel, May 1983–March 1984; recipient of a Presidential Meritorious Rank Award, 1983; Secretary of the Treasury's Exceptional Service Award, 1984; Lecturer in Law, Vanderbilt University, 1976–80; appointed by President Reagan as Judge, United States Tax Court, on June 18, 1984, for a term ending June 17, 1999; served as Senior Judge on recall performing judicial duties until reappointed on December 15, 2000, for a term ending December 14, 2015; served as Chief Judge from June 1, 2004, to May 31, 2006; assumed senior status on June 1, 2006.

ROBERT PAUL RUWE, senior judge; born in Ohio, 1941; Roger Bacon High School, St. Bernard, OH, 1959; Xavier University, Cincinnati, OH, 1963; J.D., Salmon P. Chase College of Law (graduated first in class), 1970; admitted to Ohio Bar, 1970; Special Agent, Intelligence Division, Internal Revenue Service, 1963–70; joined Office of Chief Counsel, Internal Revenue Service in 1970, and held the following positions: Trial Attorney (Indianapolis), Director, Criminal Tax Division, Deputy Associate Chief Counsel (Litigation), and Director, Tax Litigation Division; appointed by President Reagan as Judge, United States Tax Court, on November 20, 1987, for a term ending November 19, 2002; recalled on November 20, 2002, as Senior Judge to perform judicial duties from that date to the present.

LAURENCE J. WHALEN, senior judge; born in Pennsylvania, 1944; A.B., Georgetown University, 1967; J.D., Georgetown University Law Center, 1970; LL.M., 1971; admitted to District of Columbia and Oklahoma Bars; Special Assistant to the Assistant Attorney General, Tax Division, Department of Justice, 1971–72; trial attorney, Tax Division, 1971–75; private law practice in Washington, DC, with Hamel and Park (now Hopkins, Sutter, Hamel and Park), 1977–84; also in Oklahoma City, OK, with Crowe and Dunlevy, 1984–87; member of Oklahoma Bar Association, District of Columbia Bar Association, and American Bar Association, appointed by President Reagan as Judge, United States Tax Court, on November 23, 1987, for a term ending November 22, 2002; recalled on November 23, 2002, as Senior Judge to perform judicial duties from that date to the present.

RENATO BEGHE, senior judge; born in Illinois, 1933; A.B., University of Chicago, 1951; J.D., University of Chicago, 1954; Phi Beta Kappa, Order of the Coif, co-managing editor of *Law Review, Phi Gamma Delta;* admitted New York Bar, 1955; practiced law with Carter, Ledyard and Milburn, New York City (associate 1954–65, partner 1965–83) and Morgan, Lewis and Bockius, New York City, partner 1983–89; bar associations: Association of the Bar of City of New York, nonresident member, Taxation Committee (1962–65), Art Law Committee (1979–83), Chairman (1980–83), Special Committee on Lawyer's Role in Tax Practice (1981–83), Committee on Taxation of International Transactions (1990); New York State Bar Association, nonresident member, Tax Section Chairman (1977–78), Co-Chairman, Joint Practice Committee of Lawyers and Accountants (1989–90); American Bar Association, Tax Section; former member, International Bar Association, Business Section Committee on (Taxation), Judge's Forum, Human Rights Institute; former member, International Fiscal Association; life member, American Law Institute, Income Tax Advisory Group (1981–89); American College of Tax Counsel (since 1981); former member, America-Italy Society, Inc; member, Honorable Order of Kentucky Colonels; appointed by President George H.W. Bush as Judge, United States Tax Court, on March 26, 1991, for a term ending March 25, 2006; retired on February 28, 2003, but continues to perform judicial duties as a Senior Judge on recall.

CAROLYN P. CHIECHI, senior judge; born in New Jersey, 1943; B.S. (*magna cum laude,* Class Rank: 1), Georgetown University, 1965; J.D., 1969 (Class Rank: 9); LL.M., Taxation, 1971; Doctor of Laws, Honoris Causa, 2000; practiced with law firm of Sutherland, Asbill and Brennan, Washington, DC and Atlanta, GA (partner, 1976–92; associate, 1971–76); served as attorney-adviser to Judge Leo H. Irwin, United States Tax Court, 1969–71; member, District of Columbia Bar, 1969–present (member, Taxation Section, 1973–99; member, Taxation Section Steering Committee, 1980–82, Chairperson, 1981–82; member, Tax Audits and Litigation Committee, 1986–92, Chairperson, 1987–88); member, American Bar Association, 1969–present (member, Section of Taxation, 1969–present; member, Committee on Court Procedure, 1991–present; member, Litigation Section, 1995–2000; member, Judicial Division, 1997–2000); Federal Bar Association, 1969–present (member, Section of Taxation, 1969–present; member, Judiciary Division, 1992–present); Fellow, American College of Tax Counsel; Fellow, American Bar Foundation; member, Women's Bar Association of the District of Columbia, 1992–present; Board of Governors, Georgetown University Alumni Association, 1994–97, 1997–2000; Board of Regents, Georgetown University, 1988–94, 1995–2001; National Law Alumni Board, Georgetown University, 1986–93; Board of Directors, Stuart Stiller Memorial Foundation, 1986–99; American Judicature Society, 1994–present; one of several recipients of the first Georgetown University Law Alumni Awards (1994); one of several recipients of the first Georgetown University Law Center Alumnae Achievement Awards (1998); admitted to *Who's Who in American Law, Who's Who of American Women, Who's Who in America,* and *Who's Who in the East;* appointed by President George H.W. Bush as Judge, United States Tax Court, on October 1, 1992, for a term ending September 30, 2007; serving as Senior Judge, United States Tax Court, October 1, 2007–present.

DAVID LARO, senior judge; born in Michigan, 1942; appointed by President Bush to the U.S. Tax Court in November, 1992. Formerly practiced tax law in Flint and Ann Arbor

Michigan for 24 years. Graduate of New York University Law School (LL.M. in Taxation 1970), the University of Illinois Law School (J.D. 1967) and the University of Michigan (B.A. 1964). Regent of the University of Michigan, a member of the State Board of Education in Michigan, and Chairman of the State Tenure Commission in Michigan. Teaches corporate tax and business planning at Georgetown Law school, and the University of San Diego Law School. Co-Author of *Business Valuation and Taxes: Procedure, Law and Perspective* (Second edition, 2011), a 500 page text on tax valuation. At the request of the American Bar Association (CEELI), contributed written comments on the Draft Laws of Ukraine and Uzbekistan. As a consultant for Harvard University (Harvard Institute for International Development) and Georgia State University, lectured in Moscow on the subjects of tax reform and litigation. Consultant on Russian Tax Reform under a project through USAID. At the invitation of the Supreme Court of Kazakhstan in 2007, lectured to members of the Kazakhstan Judiciary, and lectured to members of the Russian Judiciary in Moscow in 2007–10. In May 2006, and June 2007, at the invitation of the State Tax Administration and other government officials, lectured in Beijing, China on economic substance. Serving as senior judge, U.S. Tax Court November 2007 to present.

HARRY A. HAINES, senior judge; born in Montana, 1939; B.A., St. Olaf College, 1961; J.D., University of Montana Law School, 1964; LL.M., Taxation, New York University Law School, 1966; admitted to Montana Bar and U.S. District Court, Montana, 1964; practiced law in Missoula, MT, as a partner, Law Firm of Worden, Thane and Haines, 1966–2003; adjunct professor, Law School, University of Montana, 1967–91; appointed by President George W. Bush as Judge, United States Tax Court, on April 22, 2003 for a term ending April 21, 2018. Recalled on May 30, 2009, as Senior Judge to perform judicial duties from that date to the present.

THOMAS B. WELLS, senior judge; born in Ohio, 1945; B.S., Miami University, Oxford, OH, 1967; J.D., Emory University Law School, Atlanta, GA, 1973; LL.M., Taxation, New York University Law School, New York, 1978; Supply Corps Officer, U.S. Naval Reserve, active duty 1967–70, Morocco and Vietnam, received Joint Service Commendation Medal; admitted to practice law in Georgia; member of law firm of Graham and Wells, P.C.; County Attorney for Toombs County, GA; City Attorney, Vidalia, GA, until 1977; law firm of Hurt, Richardson, Garner, Todd and Cadenhead, Atlanta, until 1981; law firm of Shearer and Wells, P.C. until 1986; member of American Bar Association, Section of Taxation; State Bar of Georgia, member of Board of Governors; Board of Editors, Georgia State Bar Journal; member, Atlanta Bar Association; Editor of the *Atlanta Lawyer;* active in various tax organizations, such as Atlanta Tax Forum (presently, Honorary Member); Director, Atlanta Estate Planning Council; Director, North Atlanta Tax Council; American College of Tax Counsel, Honorary Fellow; Emory Law Alumni Association's Distinguished Alumnus Award, 2001; Life Member, National Eagle Scout Association, Eagle Scout, 1960; member: Vidalia Kiwanis Club (President); recipient, Distinguished President Award; appointed by President Reagan as Judge, United States Tax Court, on October 13, 1986, for a term ending October 12, 2001; reappointed by President Bush on October 10, 2001, for a term ending October 9, 2016; served as Chief Judge from September 24, 1997 to November 6, 1997, and from June 1, 2000 to May 31, 2004. Recalled on January 1, 2011, as Senior Judge to perform judicial duties from that date to the present.

SPECIAL TRIAL JUDGES OF THE COURT

Robert N. Armen, Jr.; Lewis R. Carluzzo; John F. Dean; Peter J. Panuthos (chief special trial judge).

COURT STAFF

Clerk.—Robert R. Di Trolio, 521–4600.
Counsel for Court Services.—Janet L. Wilson, 521–4600.
General Counsel.—Daniel A. Guy, 521–3390.
Deputy General Counsel.—Fig Ruggieri, 521–3390.
Director of Human Resources.—Ellene P. Footer, 521–4700.
Reporter of Decisions.—Sheila A. Murphy, 521–4577.
Librarian.—Tania V. Andreeff, 521–4585.

UNITED STATES COURT OF APPEALS FOR THE ARMED FORCES[1]

450 E Street, NW., 20442–0001, phone 761–1448, fax 761–4672

ANDREW S. EFFRON, chief judge; born in Stamford, CT, September 18, 1948; A.B., Harvard College, 1970; J.D., Harvard Law School, 1975; The Judge Advocate General's School, U.S. Army, 1976, 1983; legislative aide to the late Representative William A. Steiger, 1970–76 (two years full-time, the balance between school semesters); judge advocate, Office of the Staff Judge Advocate, Fort McClellan, Alabama, 1976–77; attorney-adviser, Office of the General Counsel, Department of Defense, 1977–87; Counsel, General Counsel, and Minority Counsel, Committee on Armed Services, U.S. Senate, 1987–96; nominated by President Clinton to serve on the U.S. Court of Appeals for the Armed Forces, June 21, 1996; confirmed by the Senate, July 12, 1996; took office on August 1, 1996.

JAMES E. BAKER, associate judge; born in New Haven, CT, March 25, 1960; education: BA., Yale University, 1982; J.D., Yale Law School, 1990; Attorney, Department of State, 1990–93; Counsel, President's Foreign Intelligence Advisory Board / Intelligence Oversight Board, 1993–94; Deputy Legal Advisor, National Security Counsel, 1994–97; Special Assistant to the President and Legal Advisor, National Security Counsel, 1997–2000; military service: U.S. Marine Corps and U.S. Marine Corp Reserve; nominated by President Clinton to serve on the U.S. Court of Appeals for the Armed Forces; began service on September 19, 2000.

CHARLES E. ERDMANN, associate judge; born in Great Falls, MT, June 26, 1946; B.A., Montana State University, 1972; J.D., University of Montana Law School, 1975; Air Force Judge Advocate Staff Officers Course, 1981; Air Command and Staff College, 1992; Air War College, 1994; Military Service: U.S. Marine Corps, 1967–70; Air National Guard, 1981–2002 (retired as a Colonel); Assistant Montana Attorney General, 1975–76; Chief Counsel, Montana State Auditor's Office, 1976–78; Chief Staff Attorney, Montana Attorney General's Office, Antitrust Bureau; Bureau Chief, Montana Medicaid Fraud Bureau, 1980–82; General Counsel, Montana School Boards Association, 1982–86; private practice of law, 1986–95; Associate Justice, Montana Supreme Court, 1995–97; Office of High Representative of Bosnia and Herzegovina, Judicial Reform Coordinator, 1998–99; Office of High Representative of Bosnia and Herzegovina, Head of Human Rights and Rule of Law Department, 1999; Chairman and Chief Judge, Bosnian Election Court, 2000–01; Judicial Reform and International Law Consultant, 2001–2002; appointed by President George W. Bush to serve on the U.S. Court of Appeals for the Armed Forces on October 9, 2002, commenced service on October 15, 2002.

SCOTT W. STUCKY, associate judge; born in Hutchinson, KS, January 11, 1948; B.A. (*summa cum laude*), Wichita State University, 1970; J.D., Harvard Law School, 1973; M.A., Trinity University, 1980; LL.M. with highest honors, George Washington University, 1983; Federal Executive Institute, 1988; Harvard Program for Senior Officials in National Security, 1990; National War College, 1993; admitted to bar, Kansas and District of Columbia; U.S. Air Force, judge advocate, 1973–78; U.S. Air Force Reserve, 1982–2003 (retired as colonel); married to Jean Elsie Seibert of Oxon Hill, MD, August 18, 1973; children: Mary-Clare, Joseph; private law practice, Washington, DC, 1978–82; branch chief, U.S. Nuclear Regulatory Commission, 1982–83; legislative counsel and principal legislative counsel, U.S. Air Force, 1983–96; General Counsel, Committee on Armed Services, U.S. Senate, 1996–2001 and 2003–06; Minority Counsel, 2001–03; National Commander-in-Chief, Military Order of the Loyal Legion of the United States, 1993–95; Board of Directors, Adoption Service Information Agency, 1998–2002 and 2004–07; Board of Directors, Omicron Delta Kappa Society, 2006–present; member, Federal Bar Association (Pentagon Chapter), Judge Advocates Association,

[1] Prior to October 5, 1994, United States Court of Military Appeals.

The District of Columbia Bar; OPM LEGIS Fellow, office of Senator John Warner (R–VA), 1986–87; member and panel chairman, Air Force Board for Correction of Military records, 1989–96; nominated by President George W. Bush to serve on the U.S. Court of Appeals for the Armed Forces on November 15, 2006; confirmed by the Senate, December 9, 2006; began service on December 20, 2006.

MARGARET A. RYAN, associate judge; born in Chicago, IL, May 23, 1964; B.A. (*cum laude*), Knox College; J.D. (*summa cum laude*), University of Notre Dame Law School; recipient of the William T. Kirby Legal Writing Award and the Colonel William J. Hoynes Award for Outstanding Scholarship; active duty in the U.S. Marine Corps, 1986–99, serving as a communications officer, staff officer, company commander, platoon commander and operations officer in units within the II and III Marine Expeditionary Forces and as a judge advocate in Okinawa, Japan, and Quantico, VA; also served as Aide de Camp to General Charles C. Krulak, the 31st Commandant of the Marine Corps; law clerk to the Honorable J. Michael Luttig, U.S. Court of Appeals for the Fourth Circuit, and law clerk to the Honorable Clarence Thomas, Associate Justice of the Supreme Court of the United States; litigation partner at the law firm of Bartlik Beck Herman Palenchar & Scott LLP and partner in litigation and appellate practices at the law firm Wiley Rein Fielding LLP; nominated by President George W. Bush to serve on the U.S. Court of Appeals for the Armed Forces on November 15, 2006; confirmed by the Senate on December 9, 2006; began service on December 20, 2006.

SENIOR JUDGES

WILLIAM HORACE DARDEN, senior judge; born in Union Point, GA, May 16, 1923; son of William W. and Sara (Newsom) Darden; B.B.A., University of Georgia, 1946; LL.B., University of Georgia, 1948; admitted to bar of Georgia and to practice before the Georgia Supreme Court, 1948; active duty in U.S. Navy from July 1, 1943 to July 3, 1946, when released to inactive duty as lieutenant (jg.); married to Mary Parrish Viccellio of Chatham, VA, December 31, 1949; children: Sara Newsom, Martha Hardy, William H., Jr., Daniel Hobson; secretary to U.S. Senator Richard B. Russell, 1948–51; chief clerk of U.S. Senate Committee on Armed Services, 1951–53; professional staff member and later chief of staff, U.S. Senate Committee on Armed Services, February 1953 to November 1968; received recess appointment as judge of the U.S. Court of Military Appeals from President Johnson on November 5, 1968, to succeed the late Judge Paul J. Kilday; took oath of office on November 13, 1968; nominated by President Johnson for the unexpired part of the term of the late Judge Paul J. Kilday ending May 1, 1976; confirmed by Senate on January 14, 1969; designated chief judge by President Nixon on June 23, 1971; resigned December 29, 1973; elected to become senior judge on February 11, 1974.

WALTER THOMPSON COX III, senior judge; born in Anderson, SC, August 13, 1942; son of Walter T. Cox and Mary Johnson Cox; married to Vicki Grubbs of Anderson, SC, February 8, 1963; children: Lisa and Walter; B.S., Clemson University, 1964; J.D. (*cum laude*), University of South Carolina School of Law, 1967; graduated Defense Language Institute (German), 1969; graduated basic course, the Judge Advocate General's School, Charlottesville, VA, 1967; studied procurement law at that same school, 1968; active duty, U.S. Army judge advocate general's corps, 1964–72 (1964–67, excess leave to U.S.C. Law School); private law practice, 1973–78; elected resident judge, 10th Judicial Circuit, South Carolina, 1978–84; also served as acting associate justice of South Carolina supreme court, on the judicial council, on the circuit court advisory committee, and as a hearing officer of the judicial standards commission; member: bar of the Supreme Court of the United States; bar of the U.S. Court of Military Appeals; South Carolina Bar Association; Anderson County Bar Association; the American Bar Association; the South Carolina Trial Lawyers Association; the Federal Bar Association; and the Bar Association of the District of Columbia; has served as a member of the House of Delegates of the South Carolina Bar, and the Board of Commissioners on Grievances and Discipline; nominated by President Reagan, as judge of U.S. Court of Military Appeals, June 28, 1984, for a term of 15 years; confirmed by the Senate, July 26, 1984; sworn-in and officially assumed his duties on September 6, 1984; retired on September 30, 1999 and immediately assumed status of senior judge on October 1, 1999 and returned to full active service until September 19, 2000.

EUGENE R. SULLIVAN, senior judge; born in St. Louis, MO, August 2, 1941; son of Raymond V. and Rosemary K. Sullivan; married to Lis U. Johansen of Ribe, Denmark, June 18, 1966; children: Kim A. and Eugene R. II; B.S., U.S. Military Academy, West Point, 1964; J.D., Georgetown Law Center, Washington, DC, 1971; active duty with the

U.S. Army, 1964–69; service included duty with the 3rd Armored Division in Germany, and the 4th Infantry Division in Vietnam; R&D assignments with the Army Aviation Systems Command; one year as an instructor at the Army Ranger School, Ft. Benning, GA; decorations include: Bronze Star, Air Medal, Army Commendation Medal, Ranger and Parachutist Badges, Air Force Exceptional Civilian Service Medal; following graduation from law school, clerked with U.S. Court of Appeals (8th Circuit), St. Louis, 1971–72; private law practice, Washington, DC, 1972–74; assistant special counsel, White House, 1974; trial attorney, U.S. Department of Justice, 1974–82; deputy general counsel, Department of the Air Force, 1982–84; general counsel of the Department of Air Force, 1984–86; Governor of Wake Island, 1984–86; presently serves on the Board of Governors for the West Point Society of the District of Columbia; the American Cancer Society (Montgomery County Chapter); nominated by President Reagan, as judge, U.S. Court of Military Appeals on February 25, 1986, and confirmed by the Senate on May 20, 1986, and assumed his office on May 27, 1986; President George H.W. Bush named him the chief judge of the U.S. Court of Military Appeals, effective October 1, 1990, a position he held for five years; he retired on September 30, 2001 and immediately assumed status of senior judge and returned to full active service until Sept. 30, 2002.

H.F. ''SPARKY'' GIERKE, senior judge; born in Williston, ND, March 13, 1943; son of Herman F. Gierke, Jr., and Mary Kelly Gierke; children: Todd, Scott, Craig, and Michelle; B.A., University of North Dakota, 1964; J.D., University of North Dakota, 1966; graduated basic course, the Judge Advocate General's School, Charlottesville, VA, 1967; graduated military judge course, the Judge Advocate General's School, Charlottesville, VA, 1969; active duty, U.S. Army judge advocate general's corps, 1967–71; private practice of law, 1971–83; served as a justice of the North Dakota supreme court from October 1, 1983 until appointment to U.S. Court of Military Appeals; admitted to the North Dakota Bar, 1966; admitted to practice law before all North Dakota Courts, U.S. District Court for the District of North Dakota, U.S. District Court for the Southern District of Georgia, U.S. Court of Military Appeals, and U.S. Supreme Court; served as president of the State Bar Association of North Dakota in 1982–83; served as president of the North Dakota State's Attorneys Association in 1979–80; served on the board of governors of the North Dakota Trial Lawyers Association from 1977–83; served on the board of governors of the North Dakota State Bar Association from 1977–79 and from 1981–84; served as vice chairman and later chairman of the North Dakota Judicial Conference from June 1989 until November 1991; fellow of the American Bar Foundation and the American College of Probate Counsel; member of the American Bar Association, American Judicature Society, Association of Trial Lawyers of America, Blue Key National Honor Fraternity, Kappa Sigma Social Fraternity, University of North Dakota President's Club; in 1984, received the Governor's Award from Governor Allen I. Olson for outstanding service to the State of North Dakota; in 1988 and again in 1991, awarded the North Dakota National Leadership Award of Excellence by Governor George A. Sinner; in 1989, selected as the Man of the Year by the Delta Mu Chapter of the Kappa Sigma Fraternity and as Outstanding Greek Alumnus of the University of North Dakota; also awarded the University of North Dakota Sioux Award (UND's alumni association's highest honor); in 1983–84, served as the first Vietnam era state commander of the North Dakota American Legion; in 1988–89, served as the first Vietnam era national commander of the American Legion; nominated by President George H.W. Bush, October 1, 1991; confirmed by the Senate, November 14, 1991; sworn-in and assumed office on the U.S. Court of Military Appeals, November 20, 1991; on October 1, 2004, he became the Chief Judge until his retirement on September 30, 2006.

SUSAN J. CRAWFORD, senior judge; born in Pittsburgh, PA, April 22, 1947; daughter of William E. and Joan B. Crawford; married to Roger W. Higgins of Geneva, NY, September 8, 1979; one child, Kelley S. Higgins; B.A., Bucknell University, Pennsylvania, 1969; J.D. (*cum laude*), Dean's Award, Arthur McClean Founder's Award, New England School of Law, Boston, MA, 1977; history teacher and coach of women's athletics, Radnor High School, Pennsylvania, 1969–74; associate, Burnett and Eiswert, Oakland, MD, 1977–79; Assistant State's Attorney, Garrett County, Maryland, 1978–80; partner, Burnett, Eiswert and Crasford, 1979–81; instructor, Garrett County Community College, 1979–81; deputy general counsel, 1981–83, and general counsel, Department of the Army, 1983–89; special counsel to Secretary of Defense, 1989; inspector general, Department of Defense, 1989–91; member: bar of the Supreme Court of the United States; bar of the U.S. Court of Military Appeals, Maryland Bar Association, District of Columbia Bar Association, American Bar Association, Federal Bar Association, and the Edward Bennett Williams American Inn of Court; member: board of trustees, 1989–present, and Corporation, 1992–present, of New England School of Law; board of trustees, 1988–present, Bucknell University; nominated by President Bush as judge, U.S. Court of Military Appeals, February 19, 1991, for a term of 15 years; confirmed by the Senate on November 14, 1991, sworn in and officially assumed her duties on November 19, 1991; on October 1, 1999, she became the Chief Judge for a term of five years.

OFFICERS OF THE U.S. COURT OF APPEALS FOR THE ARMED FORCES

Clerk of the Court.—William A. DeCicco.
Chief Deputy Clerk of the Court.—David A. Anderson.
Deputy Clerk for Opinions.—Patricia Mariani.
Court Executive.—Keith Roberts.
Librarian.—Agnes Kiang.

UNITED STATES COURT OF APPEALS FOR VETERANS CLAIMS

625 Indiana Avenue, NW., Suite 900, 20004, phone (202) 501–5970

BRUCE E. KASOLD, chief judge; born in New York, 1951; B.S., United States Military Academy, 1973; J.D., *cum laude*, University of Florida, 1979; LL.M., Georgetown University, 1982; Honors Graduate, the Judge Advocate General's School Graduate Program, 1984; admitted to the bars of the U.S. Supreme Court, the Florida Supreme Court, the District of Columbia Court of Appeals; member: Florida Bar, District of Columbia Bar, the Federal Bar Association, Order of the Coif; retired from the U.S. Army, Lieutenant Colonel, Air Defense Artillery and Judge Advocate General's Corp, 1994; commercial litigation attorney, Holland & Knight Law Firm, 1994–95; Chief Counsel, U.S. Senate Committee on Rules and Administration, 1995–98; Chief Counsel, Secretary of the Senate and Senate Sergeant at Arms, 1998–2003; appointed by President George W. Bush to the U.S. Court of Appeals for Veterans Claims on December 13, 2003; sworn in December 31, 2003.

LAWRENCE B. HAGEL, judge; born in Washington, IN, 1947; B.S., United States Naval Academy, 1969; J.D., University of the Pacific McGeorge School of Law, 1976; LL.M. (Labor Law, with highest honors) The National Law Center, George Washington University, 1983; admitted to the bars of the U.S. Supreme Court, the United States Court of Appeals for the Fourth, Ninth, Tenth, D.C. and Federal Circuits, U.S. Court of Appeals for the Armed Forces, U.S. Court of Appeals for Veterans Claims, Supreme Court of the States of Iowa and California and the District of Columbia; commissioned in the U.S. Marine Corps, second lieutenant, infantry officer 1969–72 service in Vietnam and Puerto Rico; Marine Corps Judge Advocate 1973–90, assignments concentrated in criminal and civil litigation; Deputy General Counsel and General Counsel, Paralyzed Veterans of America, 1990–2003; appointed by President George W. Bush in December 2003, to the U.S. Court of Appeals for Veterans Claims; confirmed by the U.S. Senate to the Court of Appeals on December 9, 2003; sworn in January 2, 2004.

WILLIAM A. MOORMAN, judge; born in Chicago, IL, January 23, 1945; B.A., University of Illinois at Champaign-Urbana, 1967; J.D., University of Illinois College of Law, 1970; commissioned in the United States Air Force, second lieutenant, Reserve Officers Training Corps, 1970; entered active duty, 1971; Judge Advocate General's Corps, 1972–2002, serving as the senior attorney at every level of command, culminating his active military service with his appointment as the Judge Advocate General of the United States Air Force; military decorations include the Superior Service Medal with oak leaf cluster, the Legion of Merit with oak leaf cluster, the Joint Meritorious Service Medal, and the Meritorious Service Medal with four oak leaf clusters; retired from the Air Force in April 2002, in the grade of Major General; Counselor to the General Counsel, Department of Veterans Affairs, 2002; Assistant to the Secretary for Regulation Policy and Management, Department of Veterans Affairs, 2003; appointed by President George W. Bush as Acting Assistant Secretary of Management for the Department of Veterans Affairs, August 2004; author: ''Executive Privilege and the Freedom of Information Act: Sufficient Protection for Aircraft Mishap Reports?'', 21 *Air Force Law Review* 581 (1979); ''Cross-Examination Techniques,'' 27 *Air Force Law Review* 105 (1987); ''Fifty Years of Military Justice: Does the UCMJ Need To Be Changed?'', 48 *Air Force Law Review* 185 (2000); ''Humanitarian Intervention and International Law in the Case of Kosovo,'' 36 *New England Law Review* 775 (2002); ''Serving Our Veterans Through Clearer Rules,'' 56 *Administrative Law Review* 207 (2004); recipient: Albert M. Kuhfeld Outstanding Young Judge Advocate of the Air Force Award 1979, Stuart R. Reichart Outstanding Senior Attorney of the Air Force Award 1992, University of Illinois College of Law Distinguished Alumnus Award 2001, Department of Veterans Affairs Exceptional Service Award 2004; nominated for appointment to the U.S. Court of Appeals for Veterans Claims on September 21, 2004, by President George W. Bush; confirmed by the U.S. Senate November 20, 2004; sworn in December 16, 2004.

ALAN G. LANCE, Sr., judge; born in McComb, OH, April 27, 1949; B.A. in english and history, distinguished military graduate, South Dakota State University, 1971; commissioned U.S. Army, June 1971; graduated University of Toledo School of Law and Law Review, 1973; admitted to the U.S. Supreme Court, U.S. Court of Military Appeals, State of Ohio, State of Idaho; commissioned U.S. Army, Judge Advocate Generals Corps, 1974 and served as Claims Officer, defense counsel, Chief of Defense Counsel, Legal Assistance Officer, Administrative Law Officer and in the absence of a military Judge, military Magistrate for the 172nd Infantry Brigade (Alaska) 1974–77; Army Commendation Medal 1977; served as the Command Judge Advocate, Corpus Christi Army Depot, 1977–78; engaged in private practice of law, Ada County, Idaho, 1978–94; elected to the Idaho House of Representatives, 1990, and served as Majority Caucus chairman, 1992–94; elected as Idaho Attorney General (31st) in 1994 and 1998; Distinguished Alumnus Award, University of Toledo School of Law, 2002; inducted into the Ohio Veterans Hall of Fame, November 2004; nominated as a Judge of the United States Court of Appeals for Veterans Claims by President George W. Bush; confirmed by the U.S. Senate to the Court of Appeals for Veterans Claims, November 2004 and sworn in on December 17, 2004.

ROBERT N. DAVIS, judge; born in Kewanee, IL, September 20, 1953; graduated from Davenport Central High School, Davenport, IA, 1971; B.A., University of Hartford, 1975; J.D. Georgetown University Law Center, 1978; admitted to the bars of the U.S. Supreme Court, the Ninth Circuit Court of Appeals; the State of Virginia; and the State of Iowa; career record 1978–83 appellate attorney with the Commodity Futures Trading Commission; 1983–88 attorney with the United States Department of Education, Business and Administrative Law Division of the Office of General Counsel; 1983 Governmental exchange program with the United States Attorneys office, District of Columbia; Special Assistant United States Attorney; 1988–2001 Professor of Law, University of Mississippi School of Law; 2001–05 Professor of Law, Stetson University College of Law; Published extensively in the areas of constitutional law, administrative law, national security law and sports law. Founder and Faculty Editor-in-Chief, Journal of National Security Law, arbitrator/mediator with the American Arbitration Association and the United States Postal Service. Gubernatorial appointment to the National Conference of Commissioners on Uniform State Laws 1993–2000. Joined the United States Navy Reserve Intelligence Program in 1988. Presidential recall to active duty in 1999, Bosnia and 2001 for the Global War on Terrorism. Military decorations include Joint Service Commendation Medal, Joint Service Achievement Medal, Navy Achievement Medal, NATO Medal, Armed Forces Expeditionary Medal, Armed Forces Reserve Medal with ''M'' device, Overseas Service Ribbon, National Defense Ribbon, Joint Meritorious Unit Award, and Global War on Terrorism Medal. Nominated for appointment by President George W. Bush on March 23, 2003; confirmed by the United States Senate on November 21, 2004; Commissioned on December 4, 2004 as a Judge, United States Court of Appeals for Veterans Claims.

MARY J. SCHOELEN, judge; born in Rota, Spain; B.A., political science, University of California at Irvine, 1990; J.D., George Washington University Law School, 1993; admitted to the State Bar of California; law clerk for the National Veterans Legal Services Project, 1992–93; legal intern to the U.S. Senate Committee on Veterans' Affairs, 1994; staff attorney for Vietnam Veterans of America's Veterans Benefits Program, 1994–97; Minority Counsel, U.S. Senate Committee on Veterans' Affairs, 1997–2001; Minority General Counsel, March 2001–June 2001; Deputy Staff Director, Benefits Programs/General Counsel, June 2001–03; Minority Deputy Staff Director, Benefits Programs/General Counsel, 2003–04; nominated by President George W. Bush; appointed a Judge of the United States Court of Appeals for Veterans Claims; confirmed by the U.S. Senate to the United States Court of Appeals for Veterans Claims on November 20, 2004; sworn in December 20, 2004.

Officers of the U.S. Court of Veterans Appeals

Clerk of the Court.—Gregory O. Block, 501–5970.
Chief Deputy Clerk Operations Manager.—Anne P. Stygles.
Counsel to the Clerk.—Cary P. Sklar.
Senior Staff Attorney (Central Legal Staff).—Cynthia Brandon-Arnold.
Deputy Executive Officer.—Robert J. Bieber.
Librarian.—Allison Fentress.

UNITED STATES JUDICIAL PANEL ON MULTIDISTRICT LITIGATION

Thurgood Marshall Federal Judiciary Building, Room G–255, North Lobby, One Columbus Circle, NE., 20002, phone (202) 502–2800, fax 502–2888

(National jurisdiction to centralize related cases pending in multiple circuits and districts under 28 U.S.C. §§ 1407 & 2112)

Chairman.—John G. Heyburn II, U.S. District Judge, Western District of Kentucky.
Judges:
Robert L. Miller, Jr., Chief Judge, U.S. District Court, Northern District of Indiana.
Kathryn H. Vratil, Chief Judge, U.S. District Court, District of Kansas.
David R. Hansen, Senior U.S. Court of Appeals Judge, Eighth Circuit.
W. Royal Furgeson, Jr., U.S. District Judge, Northern District of Texas.
Frank C. Damrell, Jr., Senior U.S. District Judge, Eastern District of California.
Barbara S. Jones, U.S. District Judge, Southern District of New York.
Paul J. Barbadoro, U.S. District Judge, District of New Hampshire.
Executive Attorney.—Robert A. Cahn.
Panel Executive.—Thomasenia P. Duncan.
Clerk.—Jeffery N. Lüthi.

ADMINISTRATIVE OFFICE OF THE UNITED STATES COURTS

Thurgood Marshall Federal Judiciary Building

One Columbus Circle, NE., 20544, phone (202) 502–2600

Director.—James C. Duff, 502–3000.
Deputy Director.—Jill C. Sayenga, 502–3015.
Chief, Office of:
Audit.—Rick Lewis, 502–1000.
Long-Range Planning.—Brian Lynch, 502–1300.
Management, Planning and Assessment.—Cathy A. McCarthy, 502–1300.
Associate Director and General Counsel.—William R. Burchill, Jr., 502–1100.
Deputy General Counsel.—Robert K. Loesche.
Assistant Director, Judicial Conference Executive Secretariat.—Laura C. Minor, 502–2400.
Deputy Assistant Directors: Jeffrey A. Hennemuth, Wendy Jennis.
Assistant Director, Legislative Affairs.—Cordia A. Strom, 502–1700.
Deputy Assistant Director.—Daniel A. Cunningham.
Chief, Judicial Impact Office.—Richard A. Jaffe.
Assistant Director, Public Affairs.—David A. Sellers, 502–2600.
Assistant Director, Office of Court Administration.—Noel J. Augustyn, 502–1500.
Deputy Assistant Director.—Glen K. Palman.
Chief of:
Appellate Court and Circuit Administration Division.—Gary Bowden, 502–1520.
Bankruptcy Court Administration Division.—Glen K. Palman, 502–1540.
Court Administration Policy Staff.—Abel J. Mattos, 502–1560.
District Court Administration Division.—Robert Lowney, 502–1570.
Public Access and Records Management Division.—Michel M. Ishakian, 502–1500.
Technology Division.—Gary L. Bockweg, 502–2500.
Assistant Director, Office of Defender Services.—Ted Lidz, 502–3030.
Deputy Assistant Director.—Steven G. Asin.
Chief of:
Information Technology Division.—George M. Drakulich.
Legal, Policy and Training Division.—Richard A. Wolff.
Program Budget, Operations and Assessment Division.—Steven G. Asin (acting).
Assistant Director, Office of Facilities and Security.—Ross Eisenman, 502–1200.
Deputy Assistant Director.—William J. Lehman.
Office of Court Security Office.—Edward M. Templeman, 502–1280.
Chief of:
Judiciary Emergency Preparedness Office.—William J. Lehman.
Security and Facilities Policy Staff.—Melanie F. Gilbert.
Space and Facilities Division.—John D. Casey, 502–1340.
Assistant Director, Office of Finance and Budget.—George H. Schafer, 502–2000.
Deputy Assistant Director.—Michael N. Milby.
Chief of:
Accounting and Financial Systems Division.—Charles S. Glenn, 502–2200.
Budget Division.—James R. Baugher, 502–2100.
Financial Liaison and Analysis Office.—Penny Jacobs Fleming, 502–2028.
Assistant Director, Office of Human Resources.—Patricia J. Fitzgibbons, 502–1170.
Deputy Assistant Director.—Nancy E. Ward.
Chief of:
Benefits Division.—Cynthia Roth, 502–1160.
Business Technology Optimization Division.—Christopher D. Mays, 502–3210.
Court Personnel Management Division.—Patricia E. Tuccio, 502–3100.
Fair Employment Practices Office.—Trudi M. Morrison, 502–1380.
Judges Compensation and Retirement Services Office.—Carol S. Sefren, 502–1380.

Policy and Strategic Initiatives Office.—Harvey L. Jones, 502–3185.
Assistant Director, Office of Information Technology.—Joseph R. Peters, 502–2300.
Deputy Assistant Director.—Vacant.
Chief Technology Officer.—Richard D. Fennell.
Chief of:
IT Infrastructure Management Division.—Timothy Hanlon, 502–2640.
IT Policy and Resource Management Office.—Terry A. Cain, 502–3300.
IT Technology Management Services Division.—Robert D. Morse, 502–2377.
IT Security Office.—Bethany DeLude, 502–2350.
IT Systems Deployment and Support Division.—Ronald E. Blankenship, 502–2700.
Assistant Director for Internal Services.—Doreen Bydume, 502–4200.
Chief of:
AO Administrative Services Division.—Iris Guerra, 502–1220.
AO Information and Technology Services Division.—John C. Chang, 502–2830.
AO Personnel Division.—Cheri Thompson Reid, 502–3800.
AO Procurement Management Division.—William Roeder, 502–1330.
Assistant Director for Judges Programs.—Peter G. McCabe, 502–1800.
Deputy Assistant Director.—R. Townsend Robinson, 502–1800.
Chief of:
Article III Judges Division.—Michele E. Reed (acting), 502–1860.
Bankruptcy Judges Division.—Amanda Anderson, 502–1900.
Magistrate Judges Division.—Thomas C. Hnatowski, 502–1830.
Rules Committee Support Office.—Peter G. McCabe, 502–1820.
Statistics Division.—Steven R. Schlesinger, 502–1440.
Assistant Director, Office of Probation and Pretrial Services.—John M. Hughes, 502–1600.
Deputy Assistant Director.—Matthew G. Rowland.
Chief of:
Criminal Law Policy Staff.—John Fitzgerald.
Programs Administration Division.—Nancy Beatty Gregoire.
Special Projects Office.—Nancy Lee Bradshaw.
Technology Division.—Nicholas B. DiSabatino.

FEDERAL JUDICIAL CENTER

One Columbus Circle, NE., 20002–8003, phone (202) 502–4000

Director.—Judge Barbara J. Rothstein, 502–4160, fax 502–4099.
Deputy Director.—John S. Cooke, 502–4060, fax 502–4099.
Director of:
Communications Policy and Design Office.—Sylvan A. Sobel, 502–4250, fax 502–4077.
Education Division.—Bruce M. Clarke, 502–4257, fax 502–4299.
Federal Judicial History Office.—Bruce A. Ragsdale, 502–4181, fax 502–4077.
International Judicial Relations Office.—Mira Gur-Arie, 502–4191, fax 502–4099.
Research Division.—James B. Eaglin, 502–4070, fax 502–4199.
Systems Innovation and Development Office.—Ted Coleman, 502–4223, fax 502–4288.

DISTRICT OF COLUMBIA COURTS

H. Carl Moultrie I Courthouse, 500 Indiana Avenue, NW., 20001
phone (202) 879–1010

Executive Officer.—Anne B. Wicks, 879–1700.
Deputy Executive Officer.—Cheryl R. Bailey, 879–1700; fax 879–4829.
Director, Legislative, Intergovernmental and Public Affairs.—Leah Gurowitz, 879–1700.

DISTRICT OF COLUMBIA COURT OF APPEALS

phone (202) 879–1010

Chief Judge.—Eric T. Washington.

Associate Judges:
Kathryn A. Oberly.
Vanessa Ruiz.
Inez Smith Reid.
Stephen H. Glickman.
John R. Fisher.
Anna Blackburne-Rigsby.
Phyllis D. Thompson.

Senior Judges:
Theodore R. Newman.
William C. Pryor.
Annice M. Wagner.
John W. Kern III.
James A. Belson.
Warren R. King.
John M. Ferren.
Frank Q. Nebeker.
John M. Steadman.
John A. Terry.
Frank E. Schwelb.
Michael W. Farrell.

Clerk.—Julio Castillo, 879–2725.
Chief Deputy Clerk.—Tracy Nutall (acting), 879–2773.
Administration Director.—Reginald Turner, 879–2755.
Admissions Director.—Jacqueline Smith, 879–2714.
Public Office Operations Director.—Terry Lambert, 879–2702.
Senior Staff Attorney.—Rosanna M. Mason, 879–2718.

SUPERIOR COURT OF THE DISTRICT OF COLUMBIA

phone (202) 879–1010

Chief Judge.—Lee F. Satterfield.
Associate Judges:
Jennifer Anderson.
Judith Bartnoff.
Ronna L. Beck.
Patricia A. Broderick.
A. Franklin Burgess, Jr.
Zoe Bush.
Jerry S. Byrd.
John M. Campbell.
Russell F. Canan.
Erik P. Christian.
Jeanette Clark.
Natalia M. Combs Greene.
Laura A. Cordero.
Harold L. Cushenberry, Jr.
Carol Dalton
Linda Kay Davis.
Marisa Demeo.
Herbert B. Dixon, Jr.
Todd E. Edelman.
Anthony Epstein.
Gerald I. Fisher.
Wendell P. Gardner, Jr.
Brian Holeman.
Alfred S. Irving.
Craig Iscoe.
Gregory Jackson.
William M. Jackson.
John Ramsey Johnson.
Anita Josey-Herring.
Ann O'Regan Keary.
Neal E. Kravitz.
Milton C. Lee
Lynn Leibowitz.
Cheryl M. Long.
José M. López.
Judith N. Macaluso.
Juliet McKenna.
Zinora Mitchell-Rankin.
Robert E. Morin.
Thomas J. Motley.
John M. Mott.
Stuart G. Nash.
Florence Y. Pan.
Heidi Pasichow.
Hiram E. Puig-Lugo.
Yaribeth Raffinan.
Michael L. Rankin.
Robert I. Richter.
Robert R. Rigsby.
Maurice A. Ross.
Michael Ryan.
Fern Flanagan Saddler.
Judith Smith.
Frederick H. Weisberg.
Rhonda Reid-Winston.
Melvin R. Wright.
Joan Zeldon.

Magistrate Judges:
Janet Albert.
Errol Arthur.
Joseph E. Beshouri.
Diane Brenneman.
Julie Breslow.
J. Dennis Doyle.
Diana Harris Epps.
Tara Fentress.
Joan Goldfrank.
S. Pamela Gray.
Andrea L. Harnett.
Karen Howze.

Noel Johnson.
Kimberly Knowles.
John McCabe.
Michael McCarthy.
Aida L. Melendez.
Lloyd U. Nolan.
William W. Nooter.
Lori Parker.
Richard H. Ringell.
Mary Grace Rook.
Frederick J. Sullivan.
Elizabeth Carroll Wingo.

Senior Judges:

Mary Ellen Abrecht.
Geoffrey M. Alprin.
John H. Bayly, Jr.
Bruce D. Beaudin.
Leonard Braman.
Arthur L. Burnett, Sr.
Kayek Christian.
Frederick D. Dorsey.
Stephanie Duncan-Peters.
Stephen F. Eilperin.
George Herbert Goodrich.
Henry F. Greene.
Eugene N. Hamilton.
Brook Hedge.
John R. Hess.
Rufus G. King III
Richard A. Levie.
Cheryl M. Long.
Bruce S. Mencher.
Stephen G. Milliken.
J. Gregory Mize.
Truman A. Morrison III.
Tim Murphy.
Judith E. Retchin.
Nan R. Shuker.
Robert S. Tignor.
Linda D. Turner.
Fred B. Ugast.
Paul R. Webber III.
Ronald P. Wertheim.
Susan R. Winfield.
Peter H. Wolf.
Patricia A. Wynn.

Clerk of the Court.—Duane B. Delaney, 879–1400.

GOVERNMENT OF THE DISTRICT OF COLUMBIA

John A. Wilson Building, 1350 Pennsylvania Avenue, NW., 20004

phone (202) 724–8000

[All area codes within this section are (202)]

COUNCIL OF THE DISTRICT OF COLUMBIA

Council Chairman (at Large).—Kwame R. Brown, Suite 504, 724–8032.
Chairman Pro Tempore.—Mary Cheh.
Council Members (at Large):
David A. Catania, Suite 404, 724–7772.
Phil Mendelson, Suite 402, 724–8064.
Vincent Orange, Sr., Suite 410, 724–8174.
Michael A. Brown, Suite 406, 724–8105.
Council Members:
Jim Graham, Ward 1, Suite 105, 724–8181.
Jack Evans, Ward 2, Suite 106, 724–8058.
Mary M. Cheh, Ward 3, Suite 108, 724–8062.
Muriel Bowser, Ward 4, Suite 110, 724–8052.
Harry Thomas, Jr., Ward 5, Suite 107, 724–8028.
Thomas Wells, Ward 6, Suite 408, 724–8072.
Yvette M. Alexander, Ward 7, Suite 400, 724–8068.
Marion Barry, Ward 8, Suite 102, 724–8045.
Council Officers:
Secretary to the Council.—Nyasha Smith, Suite 5, 724–8080.
Budget Director.—Jennifer Budoff, Suite 506, 724–8139.
General Counsel.—David Zvenyach, Suite 4, 724–8026.
Policy Analysis Director.—Vacant, Suite 11, 654–6183.
D.C. Auditor.—Vacant, 717 14th Street, NW., 727–3600.

EXECUTIVE OFFICE OF THE MAYOR

6th Floor, phone (202) 727–6263, fax 727–6561

Mayor of the District of Columbia.—Hon. Vincent C. Gray.
Confidential Assistant to the Mayor.—Jason Cross.
Chief of Staff.—Paul Quander, Jr. (acting).
Special Assistant to the Chief of Staff.—Erin Meadors, 6th Floor, 727–6300, fax 727–6561.
Deputy Chief of Staff.—Vacant.
Deputy Mayor for—
Education.—De'Shawn Wright, Suite 307, 727–3636, fax 727–8198.
Human Services.—Beatriz ''BB'' Otero.
Planning and Economic Development.—Victor Hoskins, Suite 317, 727–6365, fax 727–6703.
Public Safety and Justice.—Paul Quander, Jr.
Attorney General.—Irvin B. Nathan, 441 4th Street, NW., Suite 1100 South, 727–3400, fax 347–8922.
Inspector General.—Charles Willoughby, Esq., 717 14th Street, NW., 5th Floor, 727–2540, fax 727–9846.
General Counsel.—Brian K. Flowers, Suite 300, 724–7681, fax 724–7743.
Secretary of the District of Columbia.—Cynthia Brock-Smith, Suite 419, 727–6306, fax 727–3582.
Director of:
Budget.—Eric Goulet, Suite 211, 727–3380, fax 727–5931.
Communications.—Linda Wharton Boyd, Suite 311, 727–5011, fax 727–8527.

Office of Community Relations and Services.—Steve Glaude, Suite 327, 442–8150, fax 727–2357.

Office of Policy and Legislative Affairs.—Janene Jackson, Suite 531, 727–6979, fax 727–3765.

OFFICE OF THE CITY ADMINISTRATOR

Suite 513, phone (202) 478–9200, fax (202) 727–9878

City Administrator.—Allen Y. Lew.

Executive Assistant to City Administrator.—J. Laverne Moss.

COMMISSIONS

Arts and Humanities, 1371 Harvard Street, NW., 20004, 724–5613, fax 727–4135.
Executive Director.—Ayris Scales.
Chairperson.—Anne Ashmore-Hudson, Ph.D.

Judicial Disabilities and Tenure, 515 5th Street, NW., Suite 312, 20001, 727–1363, fax 727–9718.
Executive Director.—Cathaee Hudgins.
Chairperson.—Hon. Gladys Kessler.

Judicial Nominations, 616 H Street, NW., Suite 623, 20001, 879–0478, fax 737–9126.
Executive Director.—Kim M. Whatley.

Serve DC, 441 4th Street, NW., Suite 1140 North, 20001, 727–7925, fax 727–9198.
Executive Director.—Patricia L. Evans.

Washington Metropolitan Area Transit, 8701 Georgia Avenue, Suite 808, Silver Spring, MD 20910–3700, (301) 588–5260, fax 588–5262.
Executive Director.—Bill Morrow.

DEPARTMENTS

Child and Family Services Agency, 400 6th Street, SW., 5th Floor, 20024, 442–6100, fax 727–6505.
Director.—Dr. Roque Gerald.

Consumer and Regulatory Affairs, 941 North Capitol Street, NE., 20002, 442–4400, fax 442–9445.
Director.—Nicholas A. Majett.

Corrections, 1923 Vermont Avenue, NW., Room 207 North, 20001, 673–7316, fax 671–2043.
Director.—Thomas P. Hoey.

Environment, 1200 First Street, NE., 5th Floor, 20002, 535–2600, fax 673–6993.
Director.—Christophe A. G. Tulou.

Employment Services, 4058 Minnesota Avenue, NE., 20019, 724–7000, fax 673–6993.
Director.—Dr. Lisa Maria Mallory.

Fire and Emergency Medical Services, 1923 Vermont Avenue, NW., Suite 201, 20001, 673–3320, fax 462–0807.
Fire Chief.—Kenneth B. Ellerbe.

Health, 899 North Capitol Street, NE., 5th Floor, 20002, 442–5955, fax 442–4795.
Director.—Dr. Mohammad N. Akhter.

Housing and Community Development, 1800 Martin Luther King, Jr. Avenue, SE., 20020, 442–7200, fax 645–6730.
Director.—John Hall.

Human Services, 64 New York Avenue, NE., 6th Floor, 20002, 671–4200, fax 671–4325.
Director.—David A. Berns.

Insurance, Securities and Banking, 810 1st Street, NE., Suite 701, 20002, 727–8000, fax 535–1196.
Commissioner.—William P. White.

Mental Health, 64 New York Avenue, NE., 4th Floor, 20002, 673–7440, fax 673–3433.
Director.—Stephen T. Baron.

Metropolitan Police, 300 Indiana Avenue, NW., 20001, phone 311 or (202) 737–4404 if calling from outside DC, fax 727–9524.
Police Chief.—Cathy L. Lanier.

Motor Vehicles, 301 C Street, NW., 20001, 727–5000, fax 727–4653.
Director.—Lucinda M. Babers.

Parks and Recreation, 3149 16th Street, NW., 20010, 673–7647, fax 673–2087.
Director.—Jésus Aguirre.

Public Works, 2000 14th Street, NW., 6th Floor, 20009, 673–6833, fax 671–0642.
Director.—William O. Howland, Jr.

Small and Local Business Development, 441 4th Street, NW., Suite 970 North, 20001, 727–3900, fax 724–3786.
Director.—Antonio Hunter.

Transportation, 55 M Street, SE., Suite 400, 20003, 673–6813, fax 671–0650.
Director.—Terry Bellamy.

Youth Rehabilitation Services, 450 H Street, NW., 10th Floor, 20001, 576–8175, fax 727–4434.
Director.—Neil Stanley.

OFFICES

Administrative Hearings, One Judiciary Square, 441 4th Street, NW., 20001, 442–9091, fax 442–9451.
Chief Judge.—Mary Oates Walker.

Aging, 441 4th Street, NW., Suite 900 South, 20001, 724–5622, fax 724–4979.
Director.—John M. Thompson, Ph.D.

Asian and Pacific Islander Affairs, 441 4th Street, NW., Suite 721 North, 20001, 727–3120, fax 727–9655.
Executive Director.—Soohyun ''Julie'' Koo.

Attorney General, 441 4th Street, NW., Suite 400 South, 20001, 727–3400, fax 347–8922.
Attorney General.—Irvin B. Nathan.

Boards and Commissions, 1350 Pennsylvania Avenue, NW., Suite 302, 20004, 727–1372, fax 727–2359.
Director.—Ronald R. Collins.

Cable Television and Telecommunications, 3007 Tilden Street, NW., Pod P, 20008, 671–0066, fax 332–7020.
Acting Director.—Eric E. Richardson.

Chief Financial Officer, 1350 Pennsylvania Avenue, NW., Suite 203, 20004, 727–2476, fax 727–1643.
Chief Financial Officer.—Natwar M. Gandhi.

Chief Medical Examiner, 1910 Massachusetts Avenue, SE., Building 27, 20003, 698–9000, fax 698–9100.
Chief Medical Examiner.—Dr. Marie-Lydie Pierre-Louis.

Chief Technology Officer, 441 4th Street, NW., Suite 930 South, 20001, 727–2277, fax 727–6857.
Chief Technology Officer.—Rob Mancini.

Communications Office, 1350 Pennsylvania Avenue, NW., Suite 310, 20004, 727–5011, fax 727–8527.
Director.—Linda Wharton Boyd.

Office of Community Affairs, 1350 Pennsylvania Avenue, NW., Suite 327, 20004, 442–8150, fax 727–5931.
Director.—Stephen Glaude.

Contracting and Procurement, 441 4th Street, NW., Suite 700 South, 20001, 727–0252, fax 727–0245.
Chief Procurement Officer.—James D. Staton.

Emergency Management Agency, 2720 Martin Luther King, Jr. Avenue, SE., 20032, 727–6161, fax 715–7288.
Director.—Millicent W. West.

Employee Appeals, 1100 4th Street, SW., Suite 620 East, 20024, 727–0004, fax 727–5631.
Executive Director.—Sheila Barfield, Esq.

Finance and Resource Management, 441 4th Street, NW., Suite 890 North, 20001, 727–0333, fax 727–0659.
Director of Finance Operations.—Mohamed Mohamed.

Human Resources, 441 4th Street, NW., Suite 330 South, 20001, 442–9600, fax 727–6827.
Director.—Shawn Stokes.

Human Rights, 441 4th Street, NW., Suite 570 North, 20001, 727–4559, fax 727–9589.
Director.—Gustavo F. Velasquez.

Labor Relations and Collective Bargaining, 441 4th Street, NW., Suite 820 North, 20001, 724–4953, fax 727–6887.
Director.—Natasha Campbell.

Latino Affairs, 2000 14th Street, NW., 2nd Floor, 20009, 671–2825, fax 673–4557.
Director.—Roxana Olivas.

Lesbian, Gay, Bisexual and Transgender Affairs, 1350 Pennsylvania Avenue, NW., Suite 327, 20004, 727–9493, fax 727–5931.
Director.—Jeffrey Richardson.

Motion Picture and Television Development, 3007 Tilden Street, NW., 4th Floor, 20008, 727–6608, fax 727–3246.
Director.—Crystal Palmer.

Office of Planning, 1100 4th Street, SW., Suite E650, 20024, 442–7600, fax 442–7638.
Director.—Harriet Tregoning.

Policy and Legislative Affairs, 1350 Pennsylvania Avenue, NW., Suite 533, 20004, 727–6979, fax 727–3765.
Director.—Janene Jackson.

Department of Real Estate Services, 2000 14th Street, NW., 8th Floor, 20009, 724–4400, fax 727–9877.
Director.—Brian J. Hanlon.

Risk Management, 441 4th Street, NW., Suite 800 South, 20001, 727–8600, fax 727–8319.
Director.—Phillip A. Lattimore.

Office of the State Superintendent of Education, 810 First Street, NE., 9th Floor, 20002, 727–6436, fax 727–2019.
Superintendent.—Hosanna Mahaley.

Unified Communications, 2720 Martin Luther King Jr. Avenue, SE., 20032, 730–0524, fax 730–1425.
Interim Director.—Teddy Kavaleri.

Veterans Affairs, 441 4th Street, NW., Suite 570 South, 20001, 724–5454, fax 727–7117.
Interim Director.—Matthew J. Cary.

Victim Services, 1350 Pennsylvania Avenue, NW., Suite 407, 20004, 727–3934, fax 727–1617.
Director.—Melissa Hook.

Zoning, 441 4th Street, NW., Suite 200 South, 20001, 727–6311, fax 727–6072.
Director.—Jamison L. Weinbaum.

INDEPENDENT AGENCIES

Advisory Neighborhood Commissions, 1350 Pennsylvania Avenue, NW., Room 8, 20004, 727–9945, fax 727–0289.
Executive Director.—Gottlieb Simon.

Alcoholic Beverage Regulation Administration, 2000 14th Street, NW., Suite 400 South, 20009, 442–4423, fax 442–9563.
Director.—Fred Moosally.

Board of Elections and Ethics, 441 4th Street, NW., Suite 250 North, 20001, 727–2525, fax 347–2648.
Chairperson of the Board.—Togo D. West, Jr.

Criminal Justice Coordinating Council, 441 4th Street, NW., Suite 727 North, 20001, 442–9283, fax 724–3691.
Executive Director.—Mannone Butler.

District of Columbia Court of Appeals, 430 E Street, Room 115, 20001, 879–2701, fax 626–8840.
Chief Judge.—Eric T. Washington.

District of Columbia Housing Authority, 1133 North Capitol Street, NE., 20001, 535–1500, fax 535–1740.
Executive Director.—Adrianne Todman.

District of Columbia Public Defender Service, 633 Indiana Avenue, NW., 20001, 628–1200, fax 824–2784.
Director.—Avis Buchanan.

District of Columbia Public Library, 901 G Street, NW., Suite 400, 20001, 727–1101, fax 727–1129.
Director.—Ginnie Cooper.

District of Columbia Public Schools, 825 North Capitol Street, NW., Suite 9026, 20002, 442–4226, fax 442–5026.
Chancellor.—Kaya Henderson.

District of Columbia Retirement Board, 900 7th Street, NW., 2nd Floor, 20001, 343–3200, fax 566–5000.
Executive Director.—Eric Stanchfield.

District of Columbia Sentencing and Criminal Code Revision Commission, 441 4th Street, NW., Suite 830 South, 20001, 727–8822, fax 727–7929.
Executive Director.—Barbara Tombs-Souvey.

District Lottery and Charitable Games Control Board, 2101 Martin Luther King Jr. Avenue, SE., 20020, 645–8000, fax 645–7914.
Executive Director.—Buddy Roogow.

Housing Finance Agency, 815 Florida Avenue, NW., 20001, 777–1600, fax 986–6705.
Executive Director.—Harry D. Sewell.

Metropolitan Washington Council of Governments, 777 North Capitol Street, NE., 20002, 962–3200, fax 962–3201.
Executive Director.—Dave Robertson.

People's Counsel, 1133 15th Street, NW., Suite 500, 20005, 727–3071, fax 727–1014.
People's Counsel.—Sandra Mattavous-Frye, Esq.

Police Complaints, 1400 I Street, NW., Suite 700, 20005, 727–3838, fax 727–9182.
Executive Director.—Philip K. Eure.

Public Charter School Board, 3333 14th Street, NW., Suite 210, 20010, 328–2660, fax 328–2661.
Interim Executive Director.—Jeremy Williams.

Public Employee Relations Board, 1100 4th Street, SW., Suite E630, 20024, 727–1822, fax 727–9116.
Executive Director.—Ondray Harris.

Public Service Commission, 1333 H Street, NW., Suite 200 West Tower, 20005, 626–5100, fax 393–1389.
Chairperson.—Betty Ann Kane.

Superior Court of the District of Columbia, H. Carl Moultrie I Courthouse, 500 Indiana Avenue, NW., 20001, 879–1010.
Chief Judge.—Lee F. Satterfield.

Taxicab Commission, 2041 Martin Luther King Jr. Avenue, SE., Suite 204, 20020, 645–6018, fax 889–3604.
Chairperson.—Dena C. Reed.

Washington Convention Center Authority, 801 Mount Vernon Place, NW., 20001, 249–3012, fax 249–3133.
President and CEO.—Greg O'Dell.

Destination DC, 1212 New York Avenue, NW., Suite 600, 20005, 904–0616 or 249–3012, fax 789–7037.
President and CEO.—Elliot Ferguson.

Water and Sewer Authority, 5000 Overlook Avenue, SW., 20032, 787–2000, fax 787–2210.
Chairman.—William M. Walker.
General Manager.—George S. Hawkins.

Workforce Investment Council, 4058 Minnesota Avenue, NE., 20009, 671–1900, fax 673–6993.
Chairperson.—Vacant.

OTHER

Board of Real Property Assessments and Appeals, 441 4th Street, NW., Suite 430, 20001, 727–6860, fax 727–0392.
Chairperson.—Towanda Paul-Bryant.

Contract Appeals Board, 441 4th Street, NW., Suite N350, 727–6597, fax 727–3993.
Chief Administrative Judge.—Marc D. Loud, Sr.

Justice Grants Administration, 1350 Pennsylvania Avenue, NW., Suite 327A, 20004, 727–6239, fax 727–1617.
Director.—Josh Weber.

Rehabilitation Services Administration, 1125 15th Street, NW., 20005, 730–1700, fax 730–1516.
Administrator.—Vacant.

DISTRICT OF COLUMBIA POST OFFICE LOCATIONS

900 Brentwood Road, NE., 20066–9998, General Information (202) 636–1200

Postmaster.—Gerald A. Roane.

CLASSIFIED STATIONS

Station	Phone	Location / Zip Code
Anacostia	(301) 423–9091/9092	3719 Branch Ave., Temple Hills, MD 20748
Ben Franklin	523–2386	1200 Pennsylvania Ave., NW., 20044
B.F. Carriers	636–2289	900 Brentwood Rd., NE., 20004
Benning	523–2391	3937–½ Minnesota Ave., NE., 20029
Bolling AFB	767–4419	Bldg. 10, Brookley Ave., 20332
Brightwood	726–8119	6323 Georgia Ave., NW., 20
Brookland	523–2126	3401 12th St., NE., 20017
Calvert	523–2908	2336 Wisconsin Ave., NW., 20007
Cleveland Park	523–2396	3430 Connecticut Ave., NW., 20008
Columbia Heights	523–2192	6510 Chillum Pl., NW., 20010
Congress Heights	523–2112	400 Southern Ave., SE., 20032
Customs House	523–2195	3178 Bladensburg Rd., NE., 20018
Dulles	(703) 471–9497	Dulles International Airport, 20041
Farragut	523–2507	1145 19th St., NW., 20033
Fort Davis	842–4964	3843 Pennsylvania Ave., SE., 20020
Fort McNair	523–2144	300 A. St., SW., 20319
Frederick Douglass	842–4959	Alabama Ave., SE., 20020
Friendship	523–2130	4005 Wisconsin Ave., NW., 20016
Georgetown	523–2406	1215 31st St., NW., 20007
Government Mail	523–2138 / 2139	3300 V Street, NE., 20018–9998

CLASSIFIED STATIONS—CONTINUED

Station	Phone	Location / Zip Code
Headsville	357–3029	Smithsonian Institute, 20560
Kalorama	523–2906	2300 18th St., NW., 20009
Lamond Riggs	523–2041	6200 North Capitol St., NW., 20011
LeDroit Park	483–0973	416 Florida Ave., NW., 20001
L'Enfant Plaza	523–2014	458 L'Enfant Plaza, SW., 20026
Main Office Window	636–2130	Curseen / Morris P&DC, 900 Brentwood Rd., NE., 20066–9998
Martin L. King, Jr	523–2001	1400 L St., NW., 20043
McPherson	523–2394	1750 Pennsylvania Ave., NW., 20038
Mid City	....	Temporarily Closed
NASA	358–0235	600 Independence Ave., SW., 20546
National Capitol	523–2368	2 Massachusetts Ave., NE., 20002
Naval Research Lab	767–3426	4565 Overlook Ave., 20390
Navy Annex	(703) 920–0815	1668 D Street, 20335
Northeast	388–5216	1563 Maryland Ave., NE., 20002
Northwest	523–2570	5632 Connecticut Ave., NW., 20015
Palisades	842–2291	5136 MacArthur Blvd., NW., 20016
Pavilion Postique	523–2571	1100 Pennsylvania Ave., NW., 20004
Pentagon	(703) 695–6835	Concourse Pentagon (Army-20301 / 20310; Air Force-20330; Navy-20350)
Petworth	523–2681	4211 9th St., NW., 20011
Postal Square	523–2022	2 Massachusetts Ave., NW., 20002
Randle	584–6807	2341 Pennsylvania Ave., SE., 20023
River Terrace	523–2988	3621 Benning Rd., NE., 20019
Southeast	523–2174	327 7th St., SE., 20003
Southwest	523–2597	45 L St., SW., 20024
State Department	523–2574	2201 C St., NW., 20520
T Street	232–6301	1915 14th St., NW., 20009
Tech World	523–2019	800 K St., NW., 20001
Temple Heights	523–2563	1921 Florida Ave., NW., 20009
Twentieth Street	523–2411	2001 M St., NW., 20036
U.S. Naval	433–2216	940 M St., SE., 20374
V Street	636–2272 / 2273	Section 2, Curseen / Morris P&DC, 900 Brentwood Rd., NE., 20002–9998
Walter Reed	782–3768	6800 Georgia Ave., NW., 20012
Ward Place	523–2109	2121 Ward Pl., NW., 20037
Washington Square	523–2632	1050 Connecticut Ave., NW., 20035
Watergate	965–4598	2512 Virginia Ave., NW., 20037
Woodridge	523–2195	2211 Rhode Island Ave., NE., 20018

INTERNATIONAL ORGANIZATIONS

EUROPEAN SPACE AGENCY (E.S.A.)

Headquarters: 8–10 Rue Mario Nikis, 75738 Paris Cedex 15, France
phone 011–33–1–5369–7654, fax 011–33–1–5369–7560

Chairman of the Council.—David Williams.
Director General.—Jean-Jacques Dordain.

Member Countries:

Austria	Ireland	Spain
Belgium	Italy	Sweden
Denmark	Luxembourg	Switzerland
Finland	Netherlands	United Kingdom
France	Norway	Czech Republic
Germany	Portugal	
Greece	Romania	

Cooperative Agreement.—Canada.

European Space Operations Center (E.S.O.C.), Robert-Bosch-Str. 5, D–64293 Darmstadt, Germany, phone 011–49–6151–900, fax 011–49–6151–90495.

European Space Research and Technology Center (E.S.T.E.C.), Keplerlaan 1, NL–2201, AZ Noordwijk, ZH, The Netherlands, phone 011–31–71–565–6565, Telex: 844–39098, fax 011–31–71–565–6040.

European Space Research Institute (E.S.R.I.N.), Via Galileo Galilei, Casella Postale 64, 00044 Frascati, Italy, phone 011–39–6–94–18–01, fax 011–39–6–9418–0280.

Washington Office (E.S.A.), 955 L'Enfant Plaza, SW., Suite 7800, 20024.
Head of Office.—Dieckmann Andreas (202) 488–4158, fax 488–4930, *Diekmann.andreas@esa.int.*

INTER-AMERICAN DEFENSE BOARD

2600 16th Street, NW., 20441, phone (202) 939–6041, fax 387–2880

Chairman.—Lt. Gen. Guy Thibault, Canadian Forces.
Vice Chairman.—GD Omar Vaquerano, Army, El Salvador.
Chairman's Executive Officer.—Lt. Col. Denis Giguere, Canada.
Director General.—LTG Juarez Aparecido de Paula Cunha, Army, Brazil.
Deputy Secretary for—
Administration.—COL Matthew Anderson, USA.
Conference.—LTC Carlos Gamarra, Peru.

CHIEFS OF DELEGATION

Antigua and Barbuda.—COL Trevor Thomas, Defense Forces.
Argentina.—Minister Francisco Julian Licastro, Civilian.
Barbados.—LTC Clyde Parris, Army.
Belize.—COL Stephen Heusner, Defense Forces.
Boliva.—Vacant.
Brazil.—Maj. Gen. Átila Maia da Rocha, Air Force.
Canada.—MG Doug Langton, Canadian Forces.
Chile.—GB Juan Biskupovic Moya, Army.
Colombia.—Maj. Gen. Eduardo Behar Benitez, Air Force.
Dominican Republic.—MG Andres Apolinar Disla, Army.

Ecuador.—COL Juan Villegas Aldaz, Army.
El Salvador.—COL Victor Manuel Bolaños, Army.
Guatemala.—Col. Julio Cesar Lopez, Air Force.
Guyana.—COL Mark Anthony Philips, Army.
Haiti.—Minister Counselor Charles Leon, Civilian.
Honduras.—Contalmirante Jose Eduardo Espinal (suspended), Navy.
Jamaica.—COL Anthony Anderson, Defense Forces.
Mexico.—GB Juan A. Cordero, Army.
Nicaragua.—COL Ronald Torres, Army.
Panama.—Comisionado Jaime Ruiz, Civilian.
Paraguay.—COL Adalberto Garcete, Army.
Peru.—Almirante Carlos Gamarra, Navy.
Suriname.—COL Glenn Sedney, Army.
Trinidad and Tobago.—COL Ronald Maunday, Army.
United States.—Maj. Gen. Darren McDew, Air Force.
Uruguay.—Contralmirante Federico Lebel, Navy.
Venezuela.—Primer Secretario Carlos Alberto Rodriguez Torrealba, Civilian.

INTER-AMERICAN DEFENSE COLLEGE

Director.—RADM Moira Flanders, Navy, USA.
Vice Director.—Maj. Gen. Ivan Rosas, Brazil.
Chief of Studies.—GB Roberto Efrain Rodriguez, Army, Guatemala.

INTER-AMERICAN DEVELOPMENT BANK

1300 New York Avenue, NW., 20577, phone (202) 623–1000

http://www.iadb.org

OFFICERS

President.—Luis Alberto Moreno (Colombia).
Chief, Office of the President.—Luis Alberto Giorgio.
Executive Vice President.—Julie T. Katzman (United States).
Chief Advisor.—Juan Pablo Bonilla.
Director, Office of Evaluation and Oversight.—Cheryl Gray.
Manager of the Research Department and Chief Economist.—Eduardo Lora.
Executive Auditor.—Alan N. Siegfried.
Advisor, Office of External Relations.—George de Lama.
Ombudsperson.—Doris Campos-Infantino.
Secretary.—German Quintana.
Advisor, Office of Outreach and Partnerships.—Bernardo Guillamón.
Advisor, Office of Risk Management.—Gustavo De Rosa.
Manager, Office of Strategic Planning and Development Effectiveness.—Luis Estanislao Echebarria.
Chief, Office of Institutional Integrity.—Brígida Benítez.
Vice-President for Countries.—Roberto Vellutini.
Country Manager, Office of:
Department Andean Group.—Verónica Zavala Lombardi.
Department Caribbea.—Gerard S. Johnson.
Department Central America, Mexico, Panama and Dominican Republic.—Gina Montiel.
Department Southern Cone.—Carlos Hurtado López.
Vice President for Sectors and Knowledge.—Santiago Levy.
Manager of:
Infrastructure and Environment Sector.—Alexandre Meira da Rosa.
Institutional Capacity and Finance Sector.—Ana María Rodríguez-Ortiz.
Knowledge and Learning.—Graciela Schamis.
Social Sector.—Kei Kawabata.
Trade and Integration.—Antoni Estevadeorval.
Vice President for Finance and Administration.—Jaime Sujoy.
Manager of:
Budget and Administrative Services.—Yeshvanth Edwin.
Finance Department.—Edward Bartholomew.

Human Resources.—Claudia Bock-Valotta.
Information Technology.—Simon Gauthier.
Legal Department.—James Spinner.
Vice President for Private Sector and Non-Sovereign Guaranteed Operations.—Steven Puig.
Manager of:
Office of the Multilateral Investment Fund.—Nancy Lee.
Opportunities for the Majority Sector.—Luiz Ros.
Structured and Corporate Financing Department.—Hans Schulz.

BOARD OF EXECUTIVE DIRECTORS

Argentina and Haiti.—Eugenio Diaz-Bonilla.
Alternate.—Martin Bes.
Austria, Denmark, Finland, France, Norway, Spain, and Sweden.—Marc Olivier Strauss-Kahn.
Alternate.—Marita Olson.
Bahamas, Barbados, Guyana, Jamaica, Trinidad and Tobago.—Richard Bernal.
Alternate.—Kurt Mukesh Anthony Kisto.
Belgium, Germany, Israel, Italy, The Netherlands, and Switzerland.—Mattia Adani.
Alternate.—Ulrike Metzger.
Belize, Costa Rica, El Salvador, Guatemala, Honduras and Nicaragua.—Carmen Maria Madriz.
Alternate.—Tomas Rosada.
Bolivia, Paraguay and Uruguay.—Hugo Rafael Cáceres Aguero.
Alternate.—Luis Hernando Larrazabal.
Brazil and Suriname.—Jose Carlos Miranda.
Alternate.—Sergio Portugal.
Canada.—Vinita Watson.
Alternate.—Peter Cameron.
Chile and Ecuador.—Alejandro Foxley.
Alternate.—Eduardo Santillan.
Colombia and Peru.—Juan Valdivia.
Alternate.—Roberto Prieto Uribe.
Croatia, Japan, Korea, Portugal, Slovenia and United Kingdom.—Yasusuke Tsukagoshi.
Alternate.—Gerald Duffy.
Dominican Republic and Mexico.—Cecilia Ramos Avila.
Alternate.—Muriel A. Alfonseca.
Panama and Venezuela.—Adina Mercedes Bastidas Castillo.
Alternate.—Antonio De Roux.
United States of America.—Gustavo Arnavat.

INTER-AMERICAN TROPICAL TUNA COMMISSION

8604 La Jolla, Shores Drive, La Jolla, CA 92037–1508
phone (858) 546–7100, fax (858) 546–7133, http://www.iattc.org

Director.—Guillermo A. Compeán.

Commissioners:
Belize:
Abilio Dominguez, IMMARBE / International Merchant Marine Registry of Belize, Marina Towers, Suite 204, Newtown Barracks, Belize City, Belize, phone (501) 223–5026, fax (501) 223–5070; e-mail: abilio@immarbe.com.
James Azueta, Belize Fisheries, Department, C/O Marine Towers, Suite 204, Newtown Barracks, Belize City, Belize, phone (501) 223–2187, fax (501) 223–5070; e-mail: jamesazueta_bz@yahoo.com.
Valerie Lanza, IMMARBE / International Merchant Marine Registry of Belize, Marina Towers, Suite 204, Newtown Barracks, Belize City, Belize, phone (501) 223–5026, fax (501) 223–5070; e-mail: valerie@immarbe.com, immarbe@btl.net.
Wilfredo Pott, Ministry of Agriculture, and Fisheries, C/O Marine Towers, Suite 204, Newtown Barracks, Belize City, Belize, phone (501) 223–2187; e-mail: wilpott@gmail.com.
Canada:
Larry Teague, Bristish Columbia Tuna Fishermen's Association (BCTFA), Box 372, Shawnigan Lake, Bristish Columbia V0R 2W0, Canada, phone (250) 743–5002; e-mail: bctfa@shaw.ca.

Patrice Laquerre, Oceans and Environmental Law Division, 125 promenade Sussex Drive, Ottawa, ON K1A 0G2 Canada, phone (613) 944–3077, fax (613) 992–6483; e-mail: patrice.laquerre@international.gc.ca.

Steves Neves, Oceans and Environmental Law Division, 125 Sussex Drive, Lester B. Pearson Building, Otawa, K1A 0G2, Canada, phone (613) 996–2643, fax (613) 992–6483; e-mail: steve.neves@international.gc.ca.

Sylvie Lapointe, Fisheries, and Oceans Canada/Peches et Océans Canada, 200 Kent Street, Station 8E240, Ottawa, ONT K1A 0E6, Canada, phone (613) 993–6853, fax (613) 993–5995; e-mail: sylvie.lapointe@dfo-mpo.gc.ca.

China:

Gang Zhao, Ministry of Agriculture, Room 1216 Jingchao Mansion, No. 5, Nongzhanguan Nanlu, Chaoyang District, Beijing 100125, People's Republic of China, phone (86–10) 6585–4085, fax (86–10) 6585–0551; e-mail: admin@tuna.org.cn.

Hai Yan Zhou, Ministry of Foreign Affairs, No. 2 Chao Yang Men Nan Da Jie, Beijing, 100701, People's Republic of China, phone (86–10) 6596–3266, fax (86–10) 6596–3276; e-mail: zhou_haiyan@mfa.gov.cn.

Xiaobing, Liu, Bureau of Fisheries of the Ministry of Agriculture, No. 11 Nong Zhan Guan Nan Li, Beijing, 100026 People's Republic of China, phone (86–10) 6419–2928, (86–10) 6419–2974, fax (86–10) 6419–2951; e-mail: inter-coop@agri.gov.cn.

Colombia:

Carlos Alberto Robles Cocuyame, Ministerio de Agricultura y Desarrollo Rural, Avenida Jiménez 7–65, Bogotá, D.C 001, Colombia, phone (57–1) 334–1199 ext. 310 (57–1) 283–3977, fax (57–1) 334–1199; e-mail: carlos.robles@minagricultura.gov.co.

José Alfredo Ramos González, Ministerio de Comercio Industria y Turismo, Calle 28 No. 13A–15 piso 6, Bogotá, Colombia, phone (57–1) 606–7530, fax (57–1) 606–7534; e-mail: aramos@mincomercio.gov.co.

Paula Caballero Gómez, Ministerio de Relaciones Exteriores, Calle 10 No. 5–51 Palacio de San Carlos, Bogotá, DC, Colombia, phone (57–1) 381–4265, fax (57–1) 381–4747; e-mail: paula.caballero@cancilleria.gov.co.

Xiomara Sanclemente, Ministerio de Ambiente, Vivienda y Desarrollo Territorial, Calle 37 No. 8–40, Bogota, Colombia, phone (57–1) 332–3434, (57–1) 332–3400; e-mail: xsanclemente@minambiente.gov.co.

Costa Rica:

Asdrúbal Vásquez, Ministerio de Agricultura y Ganadería, Oriental del TEC, 300 mts. Sur. Oeste, Cartago, 549–7050, Costa Rica, phone (506) 2234–1498, fax (506) 2253–4321; e-mail: vazqueza1@ice.co.cr, vasqueza@sardimar.com.

Lic. Bernal A. Chavarría V., Ministerio de Agricultura y Ganadería, Sabana Sur, 400 Sur, 25 Este de la Contraloría General de la República San José, San José 1000 Costa Rica, phone (506) 2290–8868 (506) 8822–4709, fax (506) 2232–4651; e-mail: bchavarria@lsg-cr.com, bchavarria@bcvabogados.com.

Lic. Luís Dobles Ramírez, INCOPESCA / Instituto Costarricense de Pesca y Acuicultura Contiguo a Consejo Nacional de Producción Yamuni Avenida 10 San José, San José 1000 Costa Rica, phone (506) 2248–1130, fax (506) 2248–1196; e-mail: ludora@ice.co.cr, rocioperezp@yahoo.es.

Ecuador:

Ing. Luís Torres Navarrete, Subsecretaría de Recursos Pesqueros, Víctor Manuel Rendón 1006 y Lorenzo de Garaicoa, Guayaquil, Guayas, Ecuador, phone (593–4) 256–0993 (593–4) 256–4300 ext. 103, fax (593–4) 230–0636; e-mail: luis.torres@pesca.gov.ec, probecuador@gye.satnet.net.

Iván Prieto, Ministerio de Agricultura Ganadería, Acuacultura y Pesca, Av. 3 y Calle 12, Manta, Manabí, Ecuador, phone (593–5) 262–7930; e-mail: stephanie.zambrano@pesca.gov.ec.

Leonardo Maridueña, Ministerio de Agricultura, Ganadería, Acuacultura y Pesca, Av. Fco. De Orellana, Ed. Ministerio del Litoral, Piso 12 Guayaquil, Ecuador, phone: (593–4) 268–1005; e-mail: viceministroap@magap.gob.ec.

Erika Pazmiño, Subsecretaría de Recursos Pesqueros, Av. 3 y Calle 12 Manta Ecuador, phone (593–5) 262 7930, fax (593–5) 262–7911; e-mail: rmontaño@pesca.gov.ec.

El Salvador:

Alejandro Flores, CENDEPESCA, Final 1a. Avenida Norte y Avenida Manuel Gallardo, Santa Tecla. El Salvador, phone (503) 2534–9882, (503) 7820–4560, fax (503) 2534–9885; e-mail: alejandro.flores@mag.gob.sv.

Hugo Alexander Flores, Ministerio De Agricultura y Ganadería Final 1a. Av. Norte y Av. Manuel Gallardo, Santa Tecla El Salvador.

Manuel Calvo García-Benavides, Calvopesca / Grupo Calvo, Plaza de Carlos Trías Bertrán, no. 7, 6a. Planta, Madrid, 28020, Spain, phone (34–91) 782–3300, fax (34–91) 561–5304; e-mail: mane.calvo@calvo.es.

María Cristina Herrera Gómez, DGPA (CENDEPESCA)-MAG, Final 1a. Ave. Norte y Ave. Manuel Gallardo, Santa Tecla La Libertad, El Salvador, phone (503) 2534–9880, fax (503) 2534–9885; e-mail: maria.herrera@mag.gob.sv.

European Union:

Marco D'Ambrosio, European Commission, Rue Joseph II, 99, Brussels, 1049, Belgium, phone (32–2) 299–3765, fax (32–2) 299–5570; e-mail: marco.dambrosio@ec.europa.eu.

Roberto Cesari, European Commission, Rue Joseph II, 99, Brussels, 1049, Belgium, phone (32–2) 299–4276, fax (32–2) 299–5570; e-mail: roberto.cesari@ec.europa.eu.

France:

Christiane Laurent-Monpetit, Ministere de l' Intérieur, de l' Outre-Mer et des Collectivites T., 27, rue Oudinot, Paris, 75358 F SPO7, France, phone (33–1) 5369–2466, fax (33–1) 5369–2065; e-mail: christiane.laurent-monpetit@outre-mer.gouv.fr.

Jonathan Lemeunier, Minitere de l' Agriculture et de la Peche, Direction des Peches Maritimes, Secretariat d'Etat a la Mer, 3 Place Fontenoy, Paris, 75700, France, phone (33–1) 4955–4390, fax (33–1) 4955–8200; e-mail: jonathan.lemeunieer@agriculture.gouv.fr.

Marie-Sophie Dufau-Richet, Secretariat d'etat a la Mer, 16 Boulevard Raspail, Paris, 75700, France, phone (33–1) 5363–4153, fax (33–1) 5363–4178; e-mail: Amarie.sophie.dufau-richet@pm.gouv.fr.

Michel Sallenave, Haut Commissariat de la République Française en Polynésie, 43 Avenue Bruat. BP 115, Papeete, 98713, French Polynesia, phone (689) 468–517, fax (689) 468–600; e-mail: michel.sallenave@polynesie-francaise.pref.gouv.fr.

Guatemala:

Dr. Fraterno Díaz Monge, Ministerio de Agricultura, Ganadería y Alimentación, Km. 22 Carretera al Pacífico, Ed.La Ceiba, 3er. Nivel. Guatemala, Guatemala, phone (502) 6640–9320, fax (502) 6640–9321; e-mail: diaz.monge@hotmail.com, unipesca04@yahoo.com.mx.

Hugo Alsina Lagos, Ministerio de Agricultura, Ganadería y Alimentación, 3er. Nivel, Edificio la Ceiba, Carretera al Pacífico, Km 22 B. Villanueva Guatemala, phone (502) 6640–9320 (502) 6630–5883, fax (502) 6640–9321; e-mail: hugo@alsina-et-al.org, hugo.alsina@maga.gob.gt.

Ing. Alfredo de Jesús Orellana Mejía, Ministerio de Agricultura, Ganadería y Alimentación, Km.22 Carretera al Pacífico, Edif. La Ceiba, 3er. Nivel, Villa Nueva, Guatemala, phone (502) 6640 9320, fax (502) 6640–9321; e-mail: alfredo.orellana@maga.gob.gt.

Lic. Bryslie Siomara Cifuentes Velasco, Ministerio de Agricultura, Ganadería y Alimentación, Km. 22 Carretera al Pacífico, Edificio La Ceiba, 3er. Nivel, Guatemala, Guatemala, phone (502) 6640–9320, fax (502) 6640–9321; e-mail: brysliec@hotmail.com, bcifuentes@maga.gob.gt.

Japan:

Masahiro Ishikawa, Federation of Japan Tuna Fisheries Cooperative Associations, 2–3–22 Kudankita Chiyoda-Ku, Tokyo, Japan, phone (81–3) 3264–6167 (81–3) 3264–6161, fax (81–3) 3234–7455; e-mail: section1@intldiv.japantuna.or.jp.

Shingo Ota, Fisheries Agency of Japan, 1–2–1 Kasumigaseki, Chiyoda-ku, Chiyoda-Ku, Tokyo, 100–8907, Japan, phone (81–3) 3591–1086, fax (81–3) 3502–0571; e-mail: shingo_oota@nm.maff.go.jp.

Yutaka Aoki, Ministry of Foreign Affairs, 2–2–1 Kasumigaseki, Tokyo, 100–8919, Japan, phone (81–3) 5501–8000, fax (81–3) 5501–8332; e-mail: yutaka.aoki@mofa.go.jp.

Korea:

Dr. Il Jeong Jeong, Ministry of Food, Agriculture, Forestry and Fisheries, 88, Gwanmun-do, Gwacheon-si, Gyeonggi-do, 427–719, Republic of Korea, phone (82–2) 500–2422, fax (82–2) 503–9174; e-mail: ijeong@korea.kr, icdmomaf@chol.com.

Hyun Wook Kwon, Ministry of Agriculture and Fisheries, Government Complex Bldg., #2, Gwacheon, Gyeonggi-do, 427–719 Republic of Korea, phone (82–2) 500–2414, fax (82–2) 503–9174; e-mail: 6103kwon@naver.com, hwkwonsh@yahoo.com.

Jeongseok Park, Ministry of Food, Agriculture, Forestry and Fisheries, Government Complex Gwacheon, Jungang-dong 1, Gwacheon, Gyeonggi-do, Republic of Korea, phone (82–2) 500–2426, fax (82–2) 503–9174; e-mail: jspark2@mifaff.go.kr.

México:

Dr. Ramón Corral Avila, CONAPESCA / Comisión Nacional de Pesca y Acuacultura Av. Camarón Sábalo S/N, 6to. Piso, Mazatlán, Sin 82100, México, phone (52–669) 915–6900, fax (52–669) 915–6904; e-mail: rcorrala@conapesca.sagarpa.gob.mx.

Mario Aguilar, CONAPESCA / Comisión Nacional de Acuicultura y Pesca, 1666 K Street, NW., 12th floor, Washington, DC 20006, USA, phone (202) 333–8266, fax (202) 887–6970; e-mail: mariogaguilars@aol.com.

Michel Dreyfus, Instituto Nacional de la Pesca, Km 97.5 carretera Tijuana-Ensenada Ensenada, B.C. 22890, México, phone (52–646) 174–6085, fax (52–646) 174–6135; e-mail: dreyfus@cicese.mx.

Miguel A. Cisneros, Instituto Nacional de la Pesca, Pitágoras #1320, Piso 8vo. Col. Sta Cruz Atoyac, México, D.F. 03310 México, phone (52–55) 3781–9501 (52–55) 3871 9502, fax (52–55) 3626–8421; e-mail: miguel.cisneros@inapesca.sagarpa.gob.mx.

Nicaragua:

Armando Segura, Cámara de la Pesca de Nicaragua / CAPENIC, Av. 27 de Mayo, Managua, Nicaragua, phone (505) 2266–6704, fax (505) 2222–5818; e-mail: capenic@ibw.com.ni.

Danilo Rosales Pichardo, INPESCA / Instituto Nicaragüense de la Pesca y Acuicultura, Del Busto José Martí 5c al Este Barrio Largaespada, Managua, Nicaragua, phone (505) 2251–0487, fax (505) 2248–7149; e-mail: drosales@inpesca.gob.ni.

Julio César Guevara Q, INATUN / Industrial Atunera de Nicaragua, Balboa Ancón, Panamá City, 0843–02264, Panamá, phone (507) 6400 3849, fax (507) 204–4651; e-mail: juliocgq@gmail.com, cpesca@g-elysium.com.

Steadman Fagoth, INPESCA / Instituto Nicaragüense de la Pesca y Acuicultura, Del Busto Jose Marti, 5 cuadras al Este, Bo. Largaespada Managua, Nicaragua, phone (505) 248–7149 (505) 248–7851 ext. 109; e-mail: cpaiz@inpesca.gob.ni, sfagoth@mific.gob.ni.

Panamá:

Giovanni Lauri, ARAP / Autoridad de los Recursos Acuáticos de Panamá, Altos de Curundu, C. Manuel Melo, Edificio 571 Panamá City 0819–05850, Panamá, phone (507) 511–6015 (507) 511 6000 ext. 304 / 303, fax (507) 511 6071; e-mail: glauri@arap.gob.pa, giovanni.lauri@gmail.com.

José Antonio Isaza, Asociación Panameña de la Industria del Atún (APIA), Calle 50 con vía Brasil, Edif. Plaza 50, Piso 2, Of.1 Panamá City, Panamá, phone (507) 393 0600, fax (507) 393–0601; e-mail: apiapanama@cableonda.net.

María Patricia Díaz, FIPESCA, Corozal, Zona Libre de Proceso, Edif. 319, Panamá City, Panamá, phone (507) 317–3861, fax (507) 317–3862; e-mail: latintuna@yahoo.com, pinky_diaz@hotmail.com.

Maricel Morales, ARAP / Autoridad de los Recursos Acuáticos de Panamá Edif. El Paso Elevado, frente a la intersección de Vía Transístmica, Panamá City, Panamá, phone (507) 511–6015, fax (507) 511–6071; e-mail: mmorales@arap.gob.pa.

Perú:

Alberto Valencia Carlo, Ministerio de Relaciones Exteriores, Jr. Lampa 545, Cercado de Lima, Perú, phone (51–1) 204–2400; e-mail: avalencia@rree.gob.pe.

Gladys Cárdenas, Instituto del Mar del Perú, Esquina de Gamarra y General Valle s/n Chucuito-Callao Lima, Perú, phone (51–1) 420–0144 (51–1) 4297–630, fax (51–1) 420–0144; e-mail: gcardenas@imarpe.gob.pe.

Jorge Vértiz Calderón, Ministerio de Producción (Pesquería), Calle 1 Oeste #60, Urb. Córpac, San Isidro, Lima 27, Perú, phone (51–1) 224–3423, fax (51–1) 224–2381; e-mail: jvertiz@produce.gob.pe.

María Isabel Talledo, Ministerio de la Producción, Calle Uno Oeste No. 060 Urb. Corpac, San Isidro, Lima, Lima 27, Perú, phone (51–1) 616–2208 (51–1) 224–3334; e-mail: mtalledo@produce.gob.pe.

Taipei Chino:

Chung-Hai Kwoh, Fisheries Agency, Council of Agriculture, No. 2 Chaochow Street, Taipei, 100, Taiwan, phone (886–2) 3343–6114, fax (886–2) 3343–6268; e-mail: chunghai@fa.gov.tw, chunghai@ms1.fa.gov.tw.

Hong-Yen Huang, Fisheries Agency, No. 1 Fishing Harbor North 1st. Rd., Kaohsiung, Taiwan, 80672, Taiwan, phone (886–7) 823–9828, fax (886–7) 815 8278; e-mail: hangyen@ms1.fa.gov.tw, chiennan@ms1.fa.gov.tw.

USA:

Donald Hansen, Pacific Fishery Management Council, 79 Marbell, San Clemente, CA 92673, USA, phone (949) 240–8892; e-mail: don@danawharfsportfishing.com.

Ed Stockwell, U.S. Commissioner-IATTC, 14 Fescue Ct., Florence, KY 41042, USA, phone (859) 384–4720, fax (859) 384–7433; e-mail: ed.stockwell@insightbb.com, kittyfescue@prodigy.net.

Rodney McInnis, NOAA / National Marine Fisheries Service, 501 West Ocean Blvd., Suite 4200, Long Beach, CA 90802–4213, USA, phone (562) 980–4005, fax (562) 980–4018; e-mail: rod.mcinnis@noaa.gov, miki.hirano@noaa.gov.

William Fox, U.S. Commissioner, P.O. Box 60633, San Diego, CA 92166, USA, phone (202) 495–4397, fax (619) 222–2489; e-mail: bill.fox@wwfus.org.

Vanuatu:

Christophe Emelee, Vanuatu Government Agent, P.O. Box 1640, Club Hippique Vanuatu, Port Vila, Sheffa 1640, Vanuatu, phone (678) 774–0219, fax (678) 29012; e-mail: tunafishing@vanuatu.com.vu.

Dimitri Malvirlani, Vanuatu IATTC Commissioner, Marine Quay, P.O. Box 320, Port-Vila, Vanuatu, phone (678) 23128, fax (678) 22949; e-mail: vma@vanuatu.com.vn.

Laurent Parente, Vanuatu IATTC Commissioner, P.O. Box 1435, Port Vila Vanuatu, phone (336) 9951–1207; e-mail: laurentparente-vanuatu-imo@hotmail.com.

Roy M. Joy, Embassy of Vanuatu, Avenue de Tervueren 380 Chemin de Ronde, Brussels 1150, Belgium, phone (32–2) 771–7494, fax (32–2) 771–7494; e-mail: rjoy@vanuatuembassy.net, joyroymickey@gmail.com.

Venezuela:

Alvin Delgado Martínez, FUNDATUN-PNOV, Av. Ppal. EL dique Edf. San Pablo, PH Cumaná, Sucre, 6101, Venezuela, phone (58–293) 433–0431, fax (58–293) 433–0431; e-mail: adelgadopnov@cantv.net, fundatunpnov@yahoo.com.

Gilberto Giménez, INSOPESCA / Instituto Socialista de la Pesca y Acuacultura Av. Principal El Bosque, entre Avds. Sta. Isabel y Sta. Lucía, Torre Credicard, piso 9, Caracas, Venezuela, phone (58–212) 461–9225 (58–212) 509–0384, fax (58–212) 574 3587; e-mail: ori@insopesca.gob.ve, presidencia@inapesca.gob.ve.

Nancy Tablante, INSOPESCA / Instituto Socialista de la Pesca y Acuicultura, Av. Principal El Bosque, entre Avds. Sta. Isabel y Sta. Lucía, Torre Credicard, piso 9, Caracas, DC Venezuela, phone (58–212) 953–9972, fax (58–212) 952–0707; e-mail: ntablante@hotmail.com.

INTERNATIONAL BOUNDARY AND WATER COMMISSION, UNITED STATES AND MEXICO

UNITED STATES SECTION

The Commons, Building C, Suite 100, 4171 North Mesa, El Paso, TX 79902–1441

phone (915) 832–4100, fax 832–4190, http://www.ibwc.gov

Commissioner.—Edward Drusina, 832–4101.
Foreign Affairs Secretary.—Adolfo Mata, 832–4105.
Principal Engineers: John Merino, 832–4749; Carlos Peña, 832–4160.
Human Resources Director.—Kevin Petz, 832–4114.
General Counsel / Legal Advisor.—Steven Fitten, 832–4109.

MEXICAN SECTION

Avenida Universidad, No. 2180, Zona de El Chamizal, A.P. 1612–D, C.P. 32310,

Ciudad Juarez, Chihuahua, Mexico

P.O. Box 10525, El Paso, TX 79995.

phone 011–52–16–13–7311 or 011–52–16–13–7363 (Mexico)

Commissioner.—Roberto F. Salmon Castello.
Foreign Affairs Secretary.—Jose de Jesus Luevano Grano.
Principal Engineers: Gilberto Elizalde Hernandez, L. Antonio Rascon Mendoza.

INTERNATIONAL BOUNDARY COMMISSION, UNITED STATES AND CANADA

UNITED STATES SECTION

2000 L Street, NW., Suite 615, 20036, phone (202) 736–9100

Commissioner.—Kyle Hipsley (acting).
Deputy Commissioner.—Kyle Hipsley.
Administrative Officer.—Tracy Morris.

CANADIAN SECTION

615 Booth Street, Room 555, Ottawa, ON, Canada K1A 0E9, phone (613) 944–4515

Commissioner.—Peter Sullivan.
Deputy Commissioner.—Daniel Fortin.

INTERNATIONAL COTTON ADVISORY COMMITTEE

Headquarters: 1629 K Street, NW., Suite 702, 20006, secretariat@icac.org
phone (202) 463–6660, fax 463–6950

(Permanent Secretariat of the Organization)

MEMBER COUNTRIES

Argentina
Australia
Belgium
Brazil
Burkina Faso
Cameroon
Chad
China (Taiwan)
Colombia
Côte d'Ivoire
Egypt
Finland
France
Germany
Greece
India
Iran
Israel
Italy
Kazakhstan
Kenya
Korea, Republic of
Mali
Mozambique
Netherlands
Nigeria
Pakistan
Poland
Russia
South Africa
Spain
Sudan
Switzerland
Syria
Tanzania
Togo
Turkey
Uganda
United States
Uzbekistan
Zambia
Zimbabwe

Executive Director.—Terry P. Townsend.
Statistician.—Armelle Gruere.
Economists: Andrei Guitchounts, Alejandro Plastina.
Head of Technical Information Section.—M. Rafiq Chaudhry.

INTERNATIONAL JOINT COMMISSION, UNITED STATES AND CANADA

UNITED STATES SECTION

2000 L Street, NW., Suite 615, 20440

phone (202) 736–9000, fax 632–2006, http://www.ijc.org

Chair.—Lana B. Pollack.
Commissioners: Irene B. Brooks, Sam Speck.
Secretary.—Charles A. Lawson.
Legal Advisor.—Susan Daniel.
Engineering Advisor.—Mark Colosimo.
Public Information Officer.—Frank Bevacqua.
Ecologist.—Victor Serveiss.
GIS Coordinator.—Michael Laitta.
Policy Advisor.—David Dempsey.
Senior Advisor.—Anne L. Chick.

CANADIAN SECTION

234 Laurier Avenue West, Ottawa, Ontario Canada K1P 6K6
phone (613) 995–2984, fax 993–5583

Chairman.—Hon. Joe Comuzzi.
Commissioners: Pierre Trépanier, Lyle Knott.
Secretary.—Paul Pilon (acting).
Legal Advisor.—Gavin Murphy.
Public Affairs Adviser.—Bernard Beckhoff.

Engineering Advisers: Tom McAuley, Paul Pilon, Cindy Warwick.
Senior Advisers: Nick Heisler, Joel Weiner.
Senior Science Adviser.—Ted Yuzyk.

GREAT LAKES REGIONAL OFFICE

Eighth Floor, 100 Ouellette Avenue, Windsor, Ontario Canada N9A 6T3
phone (519) 257–6700 (Canada), (313) 226–2170 (U.S.)

Director.—Saad Y. Jasim.
Public Affairs Officer.—John Nevin.
Physical Scientist.—Mark Burrows.
Environmental Scientist.—Bruce Kirschner.
Physical Scientists: Antonette Arvai, Raj Bejankiwar, John E. Wilson.

INTERNATIONAL LABOR ORGANIZATION

Headquarters: 4, route des Morillons, CH-1211, Geneva 22, Switzerland

phone 41–22–799–6111, http://www.ilo.org

Washington Office, 1808 I Street, NW., Suite 900, 20006

phone (202) 617–3952, fax 617–3960, http://www.ilo.org/washington

Liaison Office with the United Nations

220 East 42nd Street, Suite 3101, New York, NY 10017–5806

phone (212) 697–0150, fax 647–5218

International Labor Office (Permanent Secretariat of the Organization)
Headquarters Geneva:
Director-General.—Juan Somavia.
Washington:
Director.—Nancy Donaldson.
New York:
Director.—Jane Stewart.

INTERNATIONAL MONETARY FUND

700 19th Street, NW., 20431, phone (202) 623–7000

http://www.imf.org

MANAGEMENT AND SENIOR OFFICERS

Managing Director.—Christine Lagarde.
First Deputy Managing Director.—John Lipsky.
Deputy Managing Directors: Naoyuki Shinohara, Nemat Shafik.
Special Advisor to the Managing Director.—Min Zhu.
Economic Counselor.—Olivier Blanchard.
IMF Institute Director.—Leslie Lipschitz.
Legal Department General Counsel.—Sean Hagan.
Departmental Directors:
African.—Antoinette Sayeh.
Asia and Pacific.—Anoop Singh.
Budget and Planning.—Siddharth Tiwari.
European.—Antonio Borges.
External Relations.—Caroline Atkinson.
Finance.—Andrew Tweedie.
Fiscal Affairs.—Carlo Cottarelli.
Internal Audit and Inspection.—G. Russell Kincaid.
Middle East and Central Asia.—Masood Ahmed.
Monetary and Capital Markets.—Jose Vinals.
Policy Development and Review.—Reza Moghadam.
Research.—Olivier Blanchard.

Secretary.—Siddharth Tiwari.
Statistics.—Adelheid Burgi-Schmelz.
Technology and General Services.—Frank Harnischfeger.
Western Hemisphere.—Nicolas Eyzaguirre.
Director, Regional Office for Asia and the Pacific.—Shogo Ishii.
Director, Europe Offices.—Emmanuel van der Meensbrugghe.
Director and Special Representative to the United Nations.—Elliott Harris.

EXECUTIVE DIRECTORS AND ALTERNATES

Executive Directors:
Ahmed Abdulkarim Alkholifey, represents Saudi Arabia.
Alternate.—Ahmed Al Nassar.
Ambroise Fayolle, represents France.
Alternate.—Aymeric Ducrocq.
Benny Andersen, represents Denmark, Estonia, Finland, Iceland, Latvia, Lithuania, Norway, Sweden.
Alternate.—Audun Gronn.
Carlos Perez-Verdia, represents Costa Rica, El Salvador, Guatemala, Honduras, Mexico, Nicaragua, Spain, Venezuela (Republica Bolivariana de).
Alternate.—Jose Alejandro Rojas Ramirez.
Thomas Hockin, represents Antigua and Barbuda, the Bahamas, Barbados, Belize, Canada, Dominica, Grenada, Ireland, Jamaica, St. Kitts and Nevis, St. Lucia, St. Vincent and the Grenadines.
Alternate.—Stephen O'Sullivan.
Moeketsi Majoro, represents Angola, Botswana, Burundi, Eritrea, Ethiopia, Gambia, Kenya, Lesotho, Malawi, Mozambique, Namibia, Nigeria, Sierra Leone, South Africa, Sudan, Swaziland, Tanzania, Uganda, Zambia, Zimbabwe.
Alternate.—Momodou Bamba Saho.
Arvind Virmani, represents Bangladesh, Bhutan, India, Sri Lanka.
Alternate.—P. Nandalal Weerasinghe.
Der Jiun Chia, represents Brunei Darussalam, Cambodia, Fiji, Indonesia, Lao People's Democratic Republic, Malaysia, Myanmar, Nepal, Singapore, Thailand, Tonga, Vietnam.
Alternate.—Aida S. Budiman.
Rene Weber, represents Azerbaijan, Kyrgyz Republic, Poland, Switzerland, Tajikistan, Turkmenistan, Uzbekistan, Serbia.
Alternate.—Katarzyna Zajdel-Kurowska.
Paulo Nogueira Batista, Jr., represents Brazil, Colombia, Dominican Republic, Ecuador, Guyana, Haiti, Panama, Suriname, Trinidad and Tobago.
Alternate.—Maria Angelica Arbelaez.
Willy Kiekens, represents Austria, Belarus, Belgium, Czech Republic, Hungary, Kazakhstan, Luxembourg, Slovak Republic, Slovenia, Turkey.
Alternate.—Johann Prader.
Kossi Assimaidou, represents Benin, Burkina Faso, Cameroon, Cape Verde, Central African Republic, Chad, Comoros, Congo (Democratic Republic of), Congo (Republic of), Côte d'Ivoire, Djibouti, Equatorial Guinea, Gabon, Guinea, Guinea-Bissau, Madagascar, Mali, Mauritania, Mauritius, Niger, Rwanda, São Tomé and Principe, Senegal, Togo.
Alternate.—Ngueto Tiraina Yambaye.
Arrigo Sadun, represents Albania, Greece, Italy, Malta, Portugal, San Marino.
Alternate.—Panagiotis Roumeliotis.
Meg Lundsager, represents United States.
Alternate.—Douglas A. Rediker.
Mitsuhiro Furusawa, represents Japan.
Alternate.—Tomoyuki Shimoda.
Jafar Mojarrad, represents Afghanistan (Islamic Republic of), Algeria, Ghana, Iran (Islamic Republic of), Morocco, Pakistan, Tunisia.
Alternate.—Mohammed Daïri.
Alfredo Mac Laughlin, represents Argentina, Bolivia, Chile, Paraguay, Peru, Uruguay.
Alternate.—Pablo Garcia-Silva.
Hubert Temmeyer, represents Germany.
Alternate.—Steffen Meyer.
A. Shakour Shaalan, represents Bahrain, Egypt, Iraq, Jordan, Kuwait, Lebanon, Libya Arab, Jamahiriya, Maldives, Oman, Qatar, Syrian Arab Republic, United Arab Emirates, Yemen (Republic of).
Alternate.—Sami Geadah.
Aleksei V. Mozhin, represents Russian Federation.

Alternate.—Andrei Lushin.

Christopher Y. Legg, represents Australia, Kiribati, Korea, Marshall Islands, Micronesia (Federated States of), Mongolia, New Zealand, Palau, Papua New Guinea, Philippines, Samoa, Seychelles, Solomon Islands, Vanuatu.

Alternate.—Heenam Choi.

Age F.P. Bakker, represents Armenia, Bosnia and Herzegovina, Bulgaria, Croatia, Cyprus, Georgia, Israel, Macedonia (former Yugoslav Republic of), Moldova, Montenegro Republic, Netherlands, Romania, Ukraine.

Alternate.—Yuriy G. Yakusha.

Jianxiong He, represents China.

Alternate.—Yang Luo.

Alexander Gibbs, represents United Kingdom.

Alternate.—Robert James Elder.

INTERNATIONAL ORGANIZATION FOR MIGRATION

Headquarters: 17 Route Des Morillons (P.O. Box 71), CH1211, Geneva 19, Switzerland, phone +41.22.798.61.50

Washington Mission: 1752 N Street, NW., Suite 700, 20036, phone (202) 862–1826

New York Mission: 122 East 42nd Street, 48th Floor, New York, NY 10168–1610 phone (212) 681–7000

HEADQUARTERS

Director General.—William Lacy Swing (United States).

Deputy Director General.—Laura Thompson (Costa Rica).

Washington Regional Representative.—Richard E. Scott (United States).

New York Chief of Mission.—Michel Tonneau (Belgian).

Permanent Observer to the United Nations.—Michele Klein Solomon (United States).

MEMBER STATES

Afghanistan
Albania
Algeria
Angola
Argentina
Armenia
Australia
Austria
Azerbaijan
Bahamas
Bangladesh
Belarus
Belgium
Belize
Benin
Bolivia
Bosnia and Herzegovina
Brazil
Bulgaria
Burkina Faso
Burundi
Cambodia
Cameroon
Canada
Cape Verde
Chile
Colombia
Congo
Costa Rica
Côte d'Ivoire
Croatia
Cyprus
Czech Republic
Democratic Republic of the Congo
Denmark
Dominican Republic
Ecuador
Egypt
El Salvador
Estonia
Finland
France
Gabon
Gambia
Georgia
Germany
Ghana
Greece
Guatemala
Guinea
Guinea-Bissau
Haiti
Honduras
Hungary
India
Iran, Islamic Republic of
Ireland
Israel
Italy
Jamaica
Japan
Jordan
Kazakhstan
Kenya
Kyrgyzstan
Latvia
Liberia
Libyan Arab Jamahiriya
Lithuania
Luxembourg
Madagascar
Mali
Malta
Mauritania
Mexico
Mongolia
Montenegro
Morocco
Namibia
Nepal
Netherlands
New Zealand

Nicaragua
Nigeria
Niger (the)
Norway
Pakistan
Panama
Paraguay
Peru
Philippines
Poland
Portugal
Republic of Korea
Republic of Mauritius
Republic of Moldova
Romania
Rwanda
Senegal
Serbia
Sierra Leone
Slovakia
Slovenia
Somalia
South Africa
Spain
Sri Lanka
Sudan
Sweden
Switzerland
Tajikistan
Thailand
Togo
Trinidad and Tobago
Tunisia
Turkey
Uganda
Ukraine
United Kingdom of Great Britain and Northern Ireland
United Republic of Tanzania
United States of America
Uruguay
Venezuela, Bolivarian Republic of
Vietnam
Yemen
Zambia
Zimbabwe

STATES WITH OBSERVER STATUS

Bahrain
Bhutan
China
Cuba
Ethiopia
Guyana
Holy See
Indonesia
Mozambique
Namibia
Papua New Guinea
Qatar
Russian Federation
San Marino
Sao Tomé and Principe
The former Yugoslav Republic of Macedonia
Turkmenistan

IOM OVERSEAS LIAISON AND OPERATIONAL OFFICES

Afghanistan, Herat, Kabul
Albania, Tirana
Angola, Luanda
Argentina, Buenos Aires *
Armenia, Yerevan
Australia, Canberra *
Austria, Wien *
Azerbaijan, Baku
Bangladesh, Dhaka *
Belarus, Minsk
Belgium / Luxembourg, Bruxelles *
Bolivia, La Paz
Bosnia and Herzegovina, Sarajevo
Bulgaria, Sofia
Cambodia, Phnom Penh
Cameroun, Yaoundé
Canada, Ottawa, Ontario
Chile, Santiago de Chile
China, Hong Kong
Colombia, Santafé de Bogotá
Congo, Brazzaville
Congo, (Democratic Republic of), Gombe, Kinshasa
Costa Rica, San José *
Cote D'Ivoire, Abidjan
Croatia, Zagreb
Czech Republic, Praha
Dominican Republic, Santo Domingo
Ecuador, Quito
Egypt, Cairo *
El Salvador, San Salvador
Estonia, Tallinn
Ethiopia, Addis Ababa
Finland, Helsinki *
France, Paris
Gambia, Banjul
Georgia, Tbilisi
Germany, Berlin, Nuremberg
Ghana, Accra North
Greece, Athens
Guatemala, Ciudad de Guatemala
Guinea, Conakry
Guinea-Bissau, Guinea Bissau
Haita, Port au Prince
Honduras, Tegucigalpa
Hungary, Budapest *
India, Hyderabad
Indonesia, Jakarta, Banda Aceh, Mataram Kupang, Situbondo, Yogkakarta, Nias
Iran, Tehran
Iraq, Amman
Ireland, Dublin
Italy, Roma *
Jamaica, Kingston
Japan, Tokyo
Jordan, Amman
Kazakhstan, Almaty
Kenya, Nairobi *
Korea (Republic of), Seoul
Kosovo, Pristina
Kuwait, Kuwait City
Kyrgyzstan, Bishkek City
Lao, Vientiane
Latvia, Riga
Lebanon, Beirut
Liberia, Monrovia
Libya Arab Jamhiriya, Tripoli
Lithuania, Vilnius
Mali, Bamako
Malta, Valletta
Mauritania, Nouakchott
Mauritius, Port Louis
Mexico, Mexico DF
Moldova, (Republic of) Chisinau
Montenegro, Podgorica
Morocco, Rabat
Mozambique, Maputo
Myanmar, Yangon
Nauru (Republic of), Central Pacific
Nepal, Kathmandu
Netherlands, Den Haag
Nicaragua, Managua
Niger, Niamey
Nigeria, Abuja
Norway, Oslo
Pakistan, Islamabad *
Panama, Panama
Papua New Guinea, Manus
Peru, Lima *
Philippines, Metro Manila *
Poland, Warszawa
Portugal, Lisboa
Romania, Bucharest
Russia, Moscow
Saudi Arabia, Riyadh
Senegal, Dakar *
Serbia, Belgrade
Sierra Leone, Freetown

Slovak Republic, Bratislava
Slovenia, Ljubljana
Somalia, Somaliland
South Africa, Pretoria *
Spain, Madrid
Sri Lanka, Colombo
Sudan, Khartoum
Switzerland, Bern
Syrian Arab Republic, Damascus
Tajikistan, Dushanbe
Tanzania, Dar es Salaam
Thailand, Bangkok *
The Former Yogoslav Republic of Macedonia, Skopje
Timor Leste, Dili
Trinidad and Tobago, Port of Spain
Tunisia, Tunis
Turkey, Ankara
Turkmenistan, Ashgabad
Uganda, Kampala
Ukraine, Kyiv
United Kingdom, London
United States of America, Washington *, New York *, Los Angeles, Miami,
Uruguay, Montevideo
Uzbekistan, Tashkent
Venezuela, Caracas
Vietnam, Hanoi, Ho Chi Minh City
Yemen, Yemen
Zambia, Lusaka
Zimbabwe, Harare

INTERNATIONAL PACIFIC HALIBUT COMMISSION, UNITED STATES AND CANADA

Headquarters: University of Washington, Seattle, WA 98199

phone (206) 634–1838, fax 632–2983

Mailing address: 2320 West Commodore Way, Suite 300, Seattle, WA 98199–1287

American Commissioners:

Ralph G. Hoard, 4019 21st Avenue W., Seattle, WA 98199, (206) 282–0988, fax 281–0329.

Phillip Lestenkof, P.O. Box 288, St. Paul Island, AK 99660, (907) 546–2597.

Dr. Jim Balsiger, National Marine Fisheries Service, P.O. Box 21668, Juneau, AK 99802, (907) 586–7221, fax 586–7249.

Canadian Commissioners:

Dr. Laura Richards, Pacific Biological Station, 3190 Hammond Bay Road, Nanaimo, B.C., Canada V9T 6N7, (250) 729–8369, fax 756–7053.

Larry Johnson, Huu-ay-aht First Nations, 3483 3rd Avenue, Port Alberni, B.C., Canada V9Y 4E4 (250) 723–0100.

Gary Robinson, 7055 Vivian Drive, Vancouver, B.C., Canada V5S 2V2 (604) 321–8244, fax 321–8264.

Director and Secretary (ex officio).—Dr. Bruce M. Leaman, 2320 West Commodore Way, Suite 300, Seattle, WA 98199–1287.

ORGANIZATION OF AMERICAN STATES

17th Street and Constitution Avenue, NW., 20006

phone (202) 458–3000, fax 458–3967

PERMANENT MISSIONS TO THE OAS

Antigua and Barbuda.—Ambassador Deborah Mae-Lovell, Permanent Representative, 3216 New Mexico Avenue, NW., 20016, phone 362–5122 / 5166 / 5211, fax 362–5225.

Argentina.—Martin Gomez Bustillo, Interim Representative, 1816 Corcoran Street, NW., 20009, phone 387–4142 / 4146 / 4170, fax 328–1591.

The Bahamas.—Ambassador Cornelius A. Smith, Permanent Representative, 2220 Massachusetts Avenue, NW., 20008, phone 319–2660 to 2667, fax 319–2668.

Barbados.—Ambassador John E. Beale, Permanent Representative, 2144 Wyoming Avenue, NW., 20008, phone 939–9200 / 9201 / 9202, fax 332–7467.

Belize.—Ambassador Nestor Mendez, Permanent Representative, 2535 Massachusetts Avenue, NW., 20008–3098, phone 332–9636, ext. 228, fax 332–6888.

Bolivia.—Ambassador Diego Pary, Permanent Representative, 1929 19th Street, NW., 20009, phone 785–0218 / 0219 / 0224, fax 296–0563.

Brazil.—Ambassador Ruy Casaes, Permanent Representative, 2600 Virginia Avenue, NW., Suite 412, 20037, phone 333–4224 / 4225 / 4226, fax 333–6610.

Canada.—Ambassador Allan Culham, Permanent Representative, 501 Pennsylvania Avenue, NW., 20001, phone 682–1768, Ext. 7724, fax 682–7624.

* Mission with Regional Functions.

Chile.—Ambassador Dario Paya, Permanent Representative, 2000 L Street, NW., Suite 720, 20036, phone 887–5475 / 5476 / 5477, fax 775–0713.

Colombia.—Ambassador Luis Alfonso Hoyos, Permanent Representative, 1609 22nd Street, NW., 20008, phone 332–8003 / 8004, fax 234–9781.

Costa Rica.—Ambassador Rita Maria Hernandez Bolaños, Interim Representative, 2112 S Street, NW., Suite 300, 20008, phone 234–9280 / 9281, fax 986–2274.

Dominica.—Ambassador Hubert J. Charles, Permanent Representative, 3216 New Mexico Avenue, NW., 20016, phone 364–6781, fax 364–6791.

Dominican Republic.—Ambassador Roberto Bernardo Saladin, Permanent Representative, 1715 22nd Street, NW., 20008, phone 332–9142 / 0616 / 0772, fax 232–5038.

Ecuador.—Ambassador Maria Isabel Salvador, Permanent Representative, 2535 15th Street, NW., 20009, phone 234–1494 / 1692 / 8053, fax 667–3482.

El Salvador.—Ambassador Luis Menendez, Interim Representative, 1400 16th Street, NW., 20036, phone 595–7546 / 7545, fax 232–4806.

Grenada.—Ambassador Gilliam M.S. Bristol, Permanent Representative, 1701 New Hampshire Avenue, NW., 20009, phone 265–2561, fax 265–2468.

Guatemala.—Ambassador Jorge Skinner-Klee, Permanent Representative, 1507 22nd Street, NW., 20037, phone 833–4015 / 4016 / 4017, fax 833–4011.

Guyana.—Ambassador Bayney R. Karran, Permanent Representative, 2490 Tracy Place, NW., 20008, phone 265–6900 / 6901, fax 232–1297.

Haiti.—Ambassador Duly Brutus, Permanent Representative, 2311 Massachusetts Avenue, NW., 20008, phone 332–4090 / 4096, fax 518–8742.

Jamaica.—Ambassador Audrey Marks, Permanent Representative, 1520 New Hampshire Avenue, NW., 20036, phone 986–0121 / 0123 / 452–0660, fax 452–9395.

Mexico.—Ambassador Joel Antonio Hernandez Garcia, Permanent Representative, 2440 Massachusetts Avenue, NW., 20008, phone 332–3663 / 3664 / 3984, fax 234–0602.

Nicaragua.— Ambassador Denis Ronaldo Moncada Colindres, Permanent Representative, 1627 New Hampshire Avenue, NW., 20009, phone 332–1643 / 1644 / 939–6536, fax 745–0710.

Panama.—Ambassador Guillermo Cochez, Permanent Representative, 2201 Wisconsin Avenue, NW., Suite 240, 20007, phone 965–4826 / 4819, fax 965–4836.

Paraguay.—Ambassador Bernardino Hugo Saguier, Permanent Representative, 2022 Connecticut Avenue, NW., 20008, phone 232–8020 / 8021 / 8022, fax 244–3005.

Peru.—Ambassador Hugo de Zela, Permanent Representative, 1901 Pennsylvania Avenue, NW., Suite 402, 20006, phone 232–2281 / 2282 / 1973, fax 466–3068.

Saint Kitts and Nevis.—Ambassador Jacinth Lorna Henry-Martin, Permanent Representative, 3216 New Mexico Avenue, NW., 20016, phone 686–2636, fax 686–5740.

Saint Lucia.—Ambassador Michael Louis, Permanent Representative, 3216 New Mexico Avenue, NW., 20016, phone 364–6792 to 6795, fax 364–6723.

Saint Vincent and The Grenadines.— Ambassador La Celia A. Prince, Permanent Representative, 3216 New Mexico Avenue, NW., 20016, phone 364–6730, fax 364–6736.

Suriname.—Ambassador Jacques R.C. Kross, Permanent Representative, 4301 Connecticut Avenue, NW., Suite 462, 20008, phone 244–7488 / 7590 / 7591 / 7592, fax 244–5878.

Trinidad and Tobago.—Ambassador Neil Parsan, Permanent Representative, 1708 Massachusetts Avenue, NW., 20036–1903, phone 467–6490, fax 785–3130.

United States of America.—Ambassador Carmen Lomellin, Permanent Representative, WHA / USOAS Bureau of Western Hemisphere Affairs, Department of State, Room 5914, 20520–6258, phone 647–9376, fax 647–0911 / 6973.

Uruguay.—Olga Graziella Reyes Marfetan, Interim Representative, 2801 New Mexico Avenue, NW., Suite 1210, 20007, phone 333–0588 / 0687, fax 337–3758.

Venezuela.—Ambassador Roy Chaderton Matos, Permanent Representative, 1099 30th Street, NW., Second Floor, 20007, phone 342–5837 / 5838 / 5839 / 5840 / 5841, fax 625–5657.

GENERAL SECRETARIAT

Secretary General.—José Miguel Insulza, 458–3000.
  Chief of Staff to the Secretary General.—Ricardo Domínguez, 458–3705.
Assistant Secretary General.—Albert R. Ramdin, 458–6046, fax 458–3011.
  Chief of Staff to the Assistant Secretary General.—Carmen de la Pava, 458–6871.
Executive Secretary for—
  Integral Development.—Jorge Saggiante (acting), 458–3181.
  Inter-American Commission on Human Rights.—Santiago A. Canton, 458–6002.
Secretary for—
  Administration and Finance.—Gerald Anderson, 458–3437.
  Multidimensional Security.—Adam Blackwell, 458–6010.
  Political Affairs.—Victor Rico, 458–3589.

External Relations.—Alfonso Quiñonez, 458–3151.
Legal Services.—Jean Michel Arrighi, 458–3407.
Director for—
Summits Secretariat.—Sherry Tross, 458–3127.
Press and Communications.—Patricia Esquenazi, 458–6829.

ORGANIZATION FOR ECONOMIC CO-OPERATION AND DEVELOPMENT

Headquarters: 2 rue André-Pascal, 75775 Paris CEDEX 16, France

phone (331) 4524–8200, fax 4524–8500

Secretary-General.—Angel Gurria.
Deputy Secretaries General: Mario Amano, Richard Boucher, Aart Jan de Geus, Pier Carlo Padoan.
Member Countries:

Australia
Austria
Belgium
Canada
Chile
Czech Republic
Denmark
Estonia
Finland
France
Germany
Greece
Hungary
Iceland
Ireland
Israel
Italy
Japan
Korea
Luxembourg
Mexico
Netherlands
New Zealand
Norway
Poland
Portugal
Slovak Republic
Slovenia
Spain
Sweden
Switzerland
Turkey
United Kingdom
United States

OECD WASHINGTON CENTER

2001 L Street, NW., Suite 650, 20036, phone (202) 785–6323, fax 785–0350

http://www.oecd.org/washington

Head of Center.—Jill A. Schuker.

PAN AMERICAN HEALTH ORGANIZATION (PAHO)

REGIONAL OFFICE OF THE WORLD HEALTH ORGANIZATION

525 23rd Street, NW., 20037, phone (202) 974–3000

fax 974–3663

Director.—Dr. Mirta Roses Periago, 974–3408.
Deputy Director.—Dr. Jon Andrus, 974–3178.
Assistant Director.—Dr. Socorro Gross-Galiano, 974–3404.
Director of Administration.—Guillermo Birmingham, 974–3412.

PAHO / WHO FIELD OFFICES

OPS / WHO OFICINAS DE LOS REPRESENTANTES EN LOS PAISES

Barbados and Eastern Caribbean Countries (OECC serves the following countries, territories and departments: Antigua and Barbuda, Barbados, Dominica, Grenada, St. Kitts and Nevis, Saint Lucia, St. Vincent and the Grenadines. Overseas Territories (Anguilla, British Virgin Islands, Montserrat).—Dr. Gina Watson, Dayralls and Navy Garden Roads, Christ Church, (P.O. Box 508), Bridgetown, Barbados, phone (246) 426–3860 / 435–9263, fax 228–5402, email: ECC@ecc.paho.org, http://www.cpc.paho.org.
Caribbean Program Coordination, CPC.—Dr. Ernest Pate, Caribbean Program Coordinator, Dayralls and Navy Garden Roads, Christ Church, Bridgetown, Barbados (P.O. Box 508), (French Antilles: Guadaloupe, Martinique, St. Martin and St. Bartholomew, French Guiana), phone (246) 426–3860 / 3865 / 427–9434, fax 436–9779, email: email@cpc.paho.org, http://www.cpc.paho.org.
PAHO / WHO Representatives:

Argentina.—Dr. Pier Paolo Balladelli, Marcelo T. de Alvear 684, 4o. piso, 1058 Buenos Aires, Argentina, phone (54–11) 4319–4200, fax 4319–4201, e-mail: info@ops.org.ar, http://www.ops.org.ar.

Bahamas (Turks and Caicos).—Dr. Merle Lewis, Union Court, Elizabeth Avenue, P.O. Box N 4833, Nassau, Bahamas, phone (242) 326–7299 / 356–4730, fax 326–7012, e-mail: email@bah.paho.org.

Belize.—Dr. Gerardo de Cosio, 4792 Coney Drive, Coney Drive Business Plaza, 3rd Floor, P.O. Box 1834, Belize City, Belize, phone (501–2) 2448–85 / 2339–46, fax 2309–17, e-mail: admin@blz.paho.org, http://www.blz.paho.org.

Bolivia.—Dr. Fernando J. Amado, a.i., Calle Víctor Sanjines 2678, Edificio Torre Barcelona, pisos 1, 6 y 7, Zona Sopocachi, Casillas Postales 9790 y 2504, La Paz, Bolivia, phone (591–2) 2412–465 / 313, fax 2412–598, e-mail: pwrbol@bol.ops-oms.org, http://www.ops.org.bo.

Brazil.—Mr. Diego Victoria, Setor de Embaixadas Norte, Lote 19, 70800–400, Brasília, Caixa Postal 08–729, 70312–970, Brasilia, D.F., Brasil, phone (55–61)3251–9595 / 9549 / 9500, fax 3251–9591, e-mail: email@bra.ops–oms.org, http://www.opas.org.br/.

Chile.—Dr. José Antonio Pages, Av. Dag Hammarskjold 3269, Vitacura, Santiago, Chile. (Casilla No. 177, CP 7630412), phone (56–2) 437–4600 / 4605, fax 264–9311, e-mail: email@chi.ops–oms.org, http://www.chi.ops-oms.org.

Colombia.—Dr. Ana Cristina Nogueira, Carrera 7 No. 74–21, Piso 9, Edificio Seguros Aurora, Apartado Aéreo 253367, Santa Fe de Bogotá, D.C., Colombia, phone (57–1) 314–4141 / 254–7050, fax 254–7070, e-mail: ops–col@latino.net.co, http://www.col.ops-oms.org/.

Costa Rica.—Dr. Federico Hernández Pimentel, a.i., Calle 16, Avenida 6 y 8, Distrito Hospital, Apartado 3745, San Jose, Costa Rica, phone (506) 2258–5810 / 257–6034, fax 2258–5830, e-mail: email@cor.ops–oms.org, http://www.cor.ops–oms.org.

Cuba.—Dra. Lea Guido, Calle 4 No. 407, entre 17 y 19 Vedado, Apartado Postal 68, La Habana, Cuba C.P. 10400, phone (53–7) 831–8944 / 837–5808, fax 833–2075 / 866–2075, e-mail: pwr@cub.ops–oms.org or cruzmari@cub.ops–oms.org, http://www.cub.ops–oms.org.

Dominican Republic.—Dr. Lilian Reneau-Vernon, Edificio OPS / OMS, y Defensa Civil, Calle Pepillo Salcedo–Recta Final, Plaza de la Salud, Ensanche La Fe, Apartado Postal 1464, Santo Domingo, Republica Dominicana, phone (809) 562–1519 / 544–3241, fax 544–0322, e-mail: email@dor.ops–oms.org, http://www.dor.ops–oms.org.

Ecuador.—Dr. Celia Riera a.i., Av. Amazonas 2889 y Mariana de Jesus, Quito, Ecuador, phone (593–2) 2460–330 / 296 / 215, fax 2460–325, e-mail: email@ecu.ops-oms.org, http://www.opsecu.org.ec.

El Salvador.—Dr. José Ruales, 73 Avenida Sur No. 135, Colonia Escalón, Apartado Postal 1072, Sucursal Centro, San Salvador, El Salvador, phone (503) 2298–3491 / 0021 / 2279–1650, fax 2298–1168, e-mail: email@els.ops-oms.org, http://www.ops.org.sv/.

Guatemala.—Dr. Juan Guillermo Orozco, a.i., Edificio Etisa, Plaza España, 7ª Avenida 12–23, Zona 9, Apartado Postal 383, Guatemala, Guatemala, phone (011–502) 2332–2032 / 2334–3803 / 2331–0583, fax 2334–3804, http://www.ops.org.gt.

Guyana.—Dr. Beverly Barnett, Lot 8 Brickdam Stabroek, P.O. Box 10969, Georgetown, Guyana, phone (592) 225–3000 / 227–5150 / 5158 / 5159 / 6371 / 223–6372, fax 226–6654 / 227–4205, e-mail: email@guy.paho.org.

Haiti.—Dr. Peter Jan Graaff, No. 295 Avenue John Brown, Boite Postale 1330, Port-au-Prince, Haiti, phone (509) 2245–7675, fax 245–6917, e-mail: email@hai.ops-oms.org.

Honduras.—Dr. Gina E. Watson, Edificio Imperial, 6o.y 7o.piso, Avenida Republica de Panama, Frente a la Casa de Naciones Unidas, Apartado Postal 728, Tegucigalpa MDC, Honduras, phone (504) 221–6091 / 6102, fax 221–6103, e-mail: pwr@hon.ops–oms.org, http://www.paho-who.hn.

Jamaica (Bermuda and Cayman).—Dr. Hugo Prado Monje, a.i., Old Oceana Building, 7th Floor, 2–4 King Street, P.O. Box 384, Cross Roads, Kingston 5, Jamaica, phone (876) 967–4626 / 4691 / 5198 / 922–4630 / 4424, fax 967–5189, e-mail: email@jam.ops-oms.org.

México.—Dr. Philippe Lamy, Edificio Torre Prisma, Horacio Nº 1855, 3er. Piso, Of. 305, (Blvd. Manuel Avila Camacho No. 191), Colonia Los Morales, Polanco, Apartado Postal 06–601, México D.F., 11510, México, phone (52–55) 5089–0880 / 0870, fax 5395–5681, e-mail: e-mail@mex.ops-oms.org, http://www.mex.ops–oms.org.

Nicaragua.—Dr. Jorge Luis Prosperi, Complejo Nacional de Salud, Camino a la Sabana, Apartado Postal 1309, Managua, Nicaragua, phone (505) 2289–4200 / 4800, fax 2289–4999, e-mail: email@nic.ops-oms.org, http://www.ops.org.ni.

Panamá.—Dr. Joaquín Molina Leza, Ministerio de Salud de Panamá, Ancon, Avenida Gorgas, Edificio 261, 2o piso, Apartado Postal 0843–3441, Panamá, Republica de Panamá, phone (507) 262–0030 / 1996, fax 262–4052, e-mail: email@pan.ops–oms.org, http://ops-oms.org.pa.

Paraguay.—Dr. Rubén Figueroa, Edificio ''Faro del Rio'' Mcal Lopez 957 Esq. Estados Unidos, Casilla de Correo 839, Asunción, Paraguay, phone (595–21) 450–495 / 496 / 497 / 499 / 499–864, fax 450–498, e-mail: email@par.ops–oms.org, http://www.par.ops-oms.org.

Perú.—Dr. Luis Fernando Leanes, Los Pinos 251, Urbanizacĩon Camacho, La Molina, Lima 27, Perú, phone (51–1) 319–5700 / 5781, fax 437–3640, e-mail: email@per.ops-oms.org, http://www.per.ops.oms.org.

Puerto Rico.—Dr. Raúl Castellanos Bran, P.O. Box 70184, San Juan, Puerto Rico 00936, phone (787) 274–7608, fax 250–6547 / 767–8341.

Suriname.—Dr. Stephen Simon, Burenstraat #33 (PPS Building), P.O. Box 1863, Paramaribo, Suriname, phone (597) 471–676 / 425–355, fax 471–568, e-mail: email@sur.paho.org.

Trinidad and Tobago.—Dr. Bernadette Theodore-Gandi, Sweet Briar Place, First Floor, 10–12 Sweet Briar Road, St. Clair, Trinidad, phone (868) 624–7524 / 4376 / 5642 / 5928 / 625–4492, fax 624–5643, email: email@trt.paho.org.

Uruguay.—Dr. Eduardo Levcovitz, Ave. Brasil 2697, Aptos. 5, 6 y 8, 2do. Piso, Casilla de Correo 1821, 11300, Montevideo, Uruguay, phone (598–2) 707–3589 / 3590, fax 707–3530, e-mail: pwr@uru.ops-oms.org, http://www.ops.org.uy/.

Venezuela (Netherlands Antilles).—Dr. Jorge Jenkins, Avenida Sexta entre 5a y 6a, Apartado 6722, Carmelitas, Transversal, Altamira, Caracas 1010, Venezuela, phone (58–212) 206–5022 / 5000 / 0403, fax 261–6069, e-mail: email@ven.ops-oms.org, http://www.ops-oms.org.ve/.

CENTERS

Caribbean Epidemiology Center (CAREC).—Dr. Beryl Irons, 16–18 Jamaica Boulevard, Federation Park, P.O. Box 164, Port–of–Spain, Trinidad, phone (1–868) 622–4261 / 4262 / 3168 / 3277, fax 622–2792, e-mail: email@carec.ops-oms.org.

Caribbean Food and Nutrition Institute (CFNI).—Dr. Fitzroy J. Henry, University of the West Indies, P.O. Box 140–Mona, Kingston 7, Jamaica, phone (1–876), 927–1540 / 1541 / 1927, fax 927–2657, e-mail: e-mail@cfni.paho.org.

Institute of Nutrition of Central America and Panama (INCAP).—Dr. Jose Adan Montes, Carretera Roosevelt, Zona 11, Apartado Postal 1188, Guatemala, Guatemala, phone (502) 2471–5655 / 0148 / 2473–6518, fax 2473–6529, e-mail: email@incap.ops-oms.org, Biblioteca Virtual en Salud: http://www.incap.bvssan.org.gt.

Latin American and Caribbean Center on Health Sciences Information (BIREME).—Dr. Pedro Urra González, Rua Botucatu 862, Vila Clementino, Caixa Postal 20381, CEP.04023–062, Sao Paulo, SP, Brasil, phone (55–11) 5576–9800 / 5572–3226, fax 575–8868 / 5549–2590, e-mail: email@bireme.ops-oms.org.

Latin American Center for Perinatology and Human Development (CLAP).—Dr. Ricardo Fescina, Hospital de Clinicas, Piso 16, Casilla de Correo 627, Montevideo, Uruguay, phone (598–2) 487–2929 / 2930 / 2931 / 2933, fax 487–2593, e-mail: postmaster@clap.ops–oms.org.

Pan American Center for Sanitary Engineering and Environmental Sciences (CEPIS).—Dr. Mauricio Pardon Ojeda, Calle Los Pinos 251, Urbanizacion Camacho, Casilla Postal 4337, Lima 100, Peru, phone (51–1) 319–5700 / 5785, fax 437–3640, e-mail: cepis@cepis.ops-oms.org.

Pan American Foot-and-Mouth Disease Center (PANAFTOSA).—Dr. Ottorino Cosivi, Avenida Presidente Kennedy 7778, (Antiga Estrada Rio-Petropolis), São Bento, Duque de Caxias, CEP 25040–000, Caixa Postal 589, 20001 Rio de Janeiro, Brasil, phone (55–21) 3661–9000 / 9005 / 9002, fax 3661–9001, e-mail: panaftosa@panaftosa.pos-oms.org.

Pan American Health and Education Foundation (PAHEF).—Mr. Edward L. Kadunc, 525 Twenty-Third St., NW., Washington, DC 20037, phone (202) 974–3416, fax 974–3636.

Regional Program on Bioethics.—Dr. Julio Suarez, Programa Regional de Bioética, Providencia 1017, Piso 7, Providencia, Santiago, Chile, phone (56–2) 437–4600, fax 346–7219.

PAHO HIV Caribbean Office.—112–114 Duke Street, Port-of-Spain, Trinidad W.I., phone (868) 624–0400 / 623–9417, fax 974–8001.

United States-Mexico Border.—Dr. Maria Teresa Cerqueira, 5400 Suncrest Drive, Suite C–4, El Paso, TX 79912, United States of America, phone (915) 845–5950, fax 845–4361, email: email@fep.paho.org, http://www.fep.paho.org/.

PERMANENT JOINT BOARD ON DEFENSE, CANADA–UNITED STATES

CANADIAN SECTION

National Defence Headquarters, MG George R. Pearkes Building, Ottawa, ON Canada K1A OK2, phone (613) 992–4423

Members:

Canadian Co-Chairman.—Hon. Laurie Hawn, P.C., C.D., M.P.

Military Policy.—BG Michael Hood, Deputy Director, International Security Policy.

Defence Policy.—Jill Sinclair, Assistant Deputy, Minister Policy.

Foreign Affairs.—Don Sinclair, DFAIT Director General, International Security Bureau.

Privy Council Office.—BG David Millar, Director of Operations.

CANADACOM.—BG Richard Foster, Chief of Staff, Canada Command.

NORAD.—LTG Thomas Lawson, Deputy Commander NORAD.

Public Safety.—Barbara Motzeny, Director General, Border Policy and International Affairs.

Military Secretary.—CDR Daniel Stovel, Directorate of Western Hemisphere Policy.

Political Secretary.—Jordon Zed, DFAIT Directorate of International Defence Relations.

UNITED STATES SECTION

JCS, J–5, Western Hemisphere Directorate, Pentagon, Room 2E773, 20318

phone (703) 695–4955

Members:

Military Policy (Joint Staff).—BG Randy Kee, room 2E773, 695–4955.

Defense Policy (OSD).—Dr. Frank Mora, room 5D435, 697–3915.

State Department.—Ned Nolan, room 3917, State Department (202) 647–2273.

National Security Council.—Kevin O'Reilly (202) 456–9139.

USNORTHCOM.—Maj. Gen. Chris Miller (719) 554–1429.

NORAD.—Vacant.

DHS.—RDML Charlie Ray (202) 282–8155.

Military Secretary.—CDR Larry Kistler, 695–4477.

Political Secretary.—Eric Lundberg, room 3917, State Department (202) 647–2475.

SECRETARIAT OF THE PACIFIC COMMUNITY

B.P. D5, 98848 Noumea Cedex, New Caledonia, phone (687) 26.20.00, fax 26.38.18

E-mail: spc@spc.int, http://www.spc.int

Director-General.—Dr. Jimmie Rodgers.

Senior Deputy Director General, Suva.—Fekitamoeloa Utoikamanu.

Deputy Director General, Noumea.—Richard Mann.

Director of Corporate Services.—Leslie Walker.

Director of Programme Support Services.—Richard Mann.

Director of Public Health Division.—William Parr.

Director of Fisheries, Aquaculture and Marine Ecosystems Division.—Michael Batty.

Director of Land Resources Division.—Inoke Ratukalou (acting).

Director of Economic Development Division.—John Hogan.

Director of the Applied Geoscience and Technology (SOPAC) Division.—Dr. Russell Howorth.

Director Education, Training and Human Development Division.—Fekitamoeloa Utoikamanu.

Head Strategic Engagement, Policy and Planning Facility.—Patricia Sachs-Cornish (acting).

Head Statistics for Development Programme.—Gerald Haberkorn.

U.S. Contact: Bureau of East Asian and Pacific Affairs, Office of Australia, New Zealand and Pacific Island Affairs, Department of State, Washington, DC 20520, phone (202) 736–4741, fax 647–0118

Member Countries and Territories of the SPC:

- American Samoa
- Australia
- Cook Islands
- Federated States of Micronesia
- Fiji
- France
- French Polynesia
- Guam
- Kiribati
- Marshall Islands
- Nauru
- New Caledonia
- New Zealand
- Northern Mariana Islands
- Palau
- Papua New Guinea
- Pitcairn Islands
- Samoa
- Solomon Islands
- Tokelau
- Tonga
- Tuvalu
- United States
- Vanuatu
- Wallis and Futuna

SECRETARIAT OF THE PACIFIC REGIONAL ENVIRONMENTAL PROGRAMME

P.O. Box 240, Apia, Samoa, phone (685) 21929, fax (685) 20231

E-mail: sprep@sprep.org, http://www.sprep.org

Director.—David Sheppard.
Deputy Director.—Kosi Latu.
Director of Island Ecosystems Programme.—Stuart Chape.
Director of Pacific Futures Programme.—Netatua Pelesikoti.

U.S. Contact: Bureau of Oceans, Evironment and Science, Office of Ocean and Polar Affairs, Department of State, Washington, DC 20520, phone (202) 647–3262

Member Countries and Territories of SPREP:

- American Samoa
- Australia
- Cook Islands
- Federated States of Micronesia
- Fiji
- France
- French Polynesia
- Guam
- Kiribati
- Marshall Islands
- Nauru
- New Caledonia
- New Zealand
- Niue
- Northern Mariana Islands
- Palau
- Papua New Guinea
- Samoa
- Solomon Islands
- Tokelau
- Tonga
- Tuvalu
- United States
- Vanuatu
- Wallis and Futuna

UNITED NATIONS

GENERAL ASSEMBLY

The General Assembly is composed of all 193 United Nations Member States.

SECURITY COUNCIL

The Security Council has 15 members. The United Nations Charter designates five States as permanent members, and the General Assembly elects 10 other members for two-year terms. The term of office for each non-permanent member of the Council ends on 31 December of the year indicated in parentheses next to its name.

The five permanent members of the Security Council are China, France, Russian Federation, United Kingdom and the United States.

The 10 non-permanent members of the Council in 2011 are Bosnia and Herzegovina (2011), Brazil (2011), Colombia (2012), Gabon (2011), Germany (2012), India (2012), Lebanon (2011), Nigeria (2011), Portugal (2012), South Africa (2012).

ECONOMIC AND SOCIAL COUNCIL

The Economic and Social Council has 54 members, elected for three-year terms by the General Assembly. The term of office for each member expires on 31 December of the year indicated in parentheses next to its name. Voting in the Council is by simple majority; each member has one vote. In 2011, the Council is composed of the following 54 States:

Argentina (2012)
Australia (2013)
Bahamas (2012)
Bangladesh (2012)
Belgium (2012)
Cameroon (2013)
Canada (2012)
Chile (2012)
China (2013)
Comoros (2012)
Cote d'Ivoire (2011)
Ecuador (2013)
Egypt (2012)
Estonia (2011)
Finland (2013)
France (2011)
Gabon (2013)
Germany (2011)
Ghana (2012)
Guatemala (2011)
Guinea-Bissau (2011)
Hungary (2013)
India (2011)
Iraq (2012)
Italy (2012)
Japan (2011)
Latvia (2013)
Malawi (2013)
Malta (2011)
Mauritius (2011)
Mexico (2013)
Mongolia (2012)
Morocco (2011)
Namibia (2011)
Nicaragua (2013)
Norway (2013)
Pakistan (2013)
Peru (2011)
Philippines (2012)
Qatar (2013)
Republic of Korea (2013)
Russian Federation (2013)
Rwanda (2012)
Saint Kitts and Nevis (2011)
Saudi Arabia (2011)
Senegal (2013)
Slovakia (2012)
Spain (2011)
Switzerland (2011)
Ukraine (2012)
United Kingdom of Great Britain and Northern Ireland (2013)
United States of America (2012)
Venezuela (Bolivarian Republic of) (2011)
Zambia (2012)

TRUSTEESHIP COUNCIL

The Trusteeship Council has five members: China, France, Russian Federation, United Kingdom and the United States. With the independence of Palau, the last remaining United Nations trust territory, the Council formally suspended operation on 1 November 1994. By a resolution adopted on that day, the Council amended its rules of procedure to drop the obligation to meet annually and agreed to meet as occasion required—by its decision or the decision of its President, or at the request of a majority of its members or the General Assembly or the Security Council.

INTERNATIONAL COURT OF JUSTICE

The International Court of Justice has 15 members, elected by both the General Assembly and the Security Council. Judges hold nine-year terms.

The current composition of the court is as follows: President Hisashi Owada (Japan); Vice-President Peter Tomka (Slovakia). Judges: Abdul G. Koroma (Sierra Leone), Awn Shawkat Al-Khasawneh (Jordan), Bruno Simma (Germany), Ronny Abraham (France), Kenneth Keith (New Zealand), Bernardo Sepulveda-Amor (Mexico), Mohamed Bennouna (Morocco), Leonid Skotnikov (Russian Federation), Antonio A. Cancado Trindade (Brazil), Abdulqawi Ahmed Yusuf (Somalia), Christopher Greenwood (United Kingdom of Great Britain and Northern Ireland), Xue Hanqin (China), Joan E. Donoghue (United States of America).

The Registrar of the Court is Mr. Philippe Couvreur (Belgium).

UNITED NATIONS SECRETARIAT

One United Nations Plaza, New York, NY 10017, (212) 963–1234, http://www.un.org.

Secretary General.—Ban Ki-moon (Republic of Korea).

Deputy Secretary.—Dr. Asha Rose Migiro (Tanzania).

EXECUTIVE OFFICE OF THE SECRETARY-GENERAL

Chief of Staff.—Vijay Nambiar (India).
Assistant Secretary-General for Policy Planning.—Robert C. Orr (United States).
Spokesman.—Martin Nesirky.

OFFICE OF INTERNAL OVERSIGHT SERVICES

Under-Secretary-General.—Carman Louise Lapointe (Canada).

OFFICE OF LEGAL AFFAIRS

Under-Secretary-General and Legal Counsel.—Patricia O'Brien.
Assistant Secretary General.—Stephen Mathias.

DEPARTMENT OF POLITICAL AFFAIRS

Under-Secretary-General.—B. Lynn Pascoe (United States).
Assistant Secretary-General.—Oscar Fernandez-Taranco.
Assistant Secretary-General.—Taye-Brook Zerihoun.

DEPARTMENT FOR DISARMAMENT AFFAIRS

Under-Secretary-General.—Sergio de Queiroz Duarte.

DEPARTMENT OF PEACE-KEEPING OPERATIONS

Under-Secretary-General.—Alain Le Roy.
Assistant Secretary-General.—Edmond Mulet.
Assistant Secretary-General.—Dimitry Titov.
Military Adviser.—Gaye Babacar.

OFFICE FOR THE COORDINATION OF HUMANITARIAN AFFAIRS

Under-Secretary-General, Emergency Relief Coordinator.—Valerie Amos (United Kingdom).
Assistant Secretary General/Deputy Emergency Relief Coordinator.—Catherine Bragg.

DEPARTMENT OF ECONOMIC AND SOCIAL AFFAIRS

Under-Secretary-General.—Zukang Sha.
Assistant Secretary-General.—Kwame Sundaram Jomo.
Assistant Secretary-General.—Thomas Stelzer.

DEPARTMENT OF GENERAL ASSEMBLY AND CONFERENCE MANAGEMENT

Under-Secretary-General.—Shaaban M. Shaaban.
Assistant Secretary-General.—Franz Baumann.

DEPARTMENT OF PUBLIC INFORMATION

Under-Secretary-General.—Kiyotaka Akasaka (Japan).

DEPARTMENT OF MANAGEMENT

Under-Secretary-General.—Angela Kane.
Assistant Secretary-General, Controller.—Jun Yamazaki.
Assistant Secretary-General, Human Resources Management.—Catherine Pollard.

Assistant Secretary-General, Central Support Services.—Warren Sach.
Assistant Secretary-General, Capital Master Plan.—Michael Adlerstein.

OFFICE OF THE SPECIAL REPRESENTATIVE OF THE SECRETARY-GENERAL FOR CHILDREN AND ARMED CONFLICT

Under-Secretary-General.—Radhika Coomaraswamy (Sri Lanka).

UNITED NATIONS FUND FOR INTERNATIONAL PARTNERSHIPS

Executive Director.—Amir A. Dossal (United Kingdom).

UNITED NATIONS AT GENEVA (UNOG)

Palais des Nations, 1211 Geneva 10, Switzerland, phone (41–22) 917–1234.
Director-General of UNOG/Assistant Secretary-General.—Sergei A. Ordzhonikidze (Russian Federation).

UNITED NATIONS AT VIENNA (UNOV)

Vienna International Centre, P.O. Box 500, A–1400 Vienna, Austria, phone (43–1) 21345.
Director-General.—Yury Fedotov (Russian Federation).

UNITED NATIONS INFORMATION CENTRE

1775 K Street, NW., Suite 400, Washington, DC 20006

phone: (202) 331–8670, fax: (202) 331–9191, email: unicdc@unicwash.org

http://www.unicwash.org

Director.—William Davis (United States).

REGIONAL ECONOMIC COMMISSIONS

Economic Commission for Africa (ECA), Africa Hall, P.O. Box 3001, Addis Ababa Ethiopia, phone (251–1) 51–72–00, fax (251–1) 51–44–16.
Executive Secretary.—Abdoulie Jannah (Gambia).

Economic Commission for Europe (ECE) Palais des Nations, 1211 Geneva 10, Switzerland, phone (41–22) 917–2893.
Executive Secretary.—Jan Kubis.

Economic Commission for Latin America and the Caribbean (ECLAC), Casilla 179–D, Santiago, Chile, phone (56–2) 210–2000, fax (56–2) 208–0252.
Executive Secretary.—Alicia Barcena.

Economic and Social Commission for Asia and the Pacific (ESCAP), United Nations Building, Rejdamnern Avenue, Bangkok, Thailand, phone (66–2) 288–1234, fax (66–2) 288–1000.
Executive Secretary.—Noeleen Heyzer.

Economic and Social Commission for Western Asia (ESCWA), P.O. Box 11–8575, Riad El-Solh Square, Beirut, Lebanon, phone 9611–981301, fax 9611–981510.
Executive Secretary.—Rima Khalaf.

Regional Commissions, New York Office, (ECE, ESCAP, ECLAC, ECA, ESCWA), fax 963–1500, phone 212 963–8088.
Director.—Amr Nour.
Social Affairs Officer.—Daniela Simioni.
Documentation.—Vacant.
Staff Assistant.—Yesenia Copperman.

FUNDS, PROGRAMMES, AND BODIES OF THE UNITED NATIONS

Advisory Committee on Administrative and Budgetary Questions (ACABQ), One United Nations Plaza, New York, NY 10017, phone (212) 963–7456.
Executive Secretary.—Shari Klugman.
Chairman.—Collen Kelapile.

Office of the High Commissioner for Human Rights, Palais des Nations, 8–14 Avenue de la Paix, 1211 Geneva 10, Switzerland, phone (41–22) 917–1234.

High Commissioner for Human Rights.—Navanethem Pillay.

International Civil Service Commission (ICSC), One United Nations Plaza, New York, NY 10017, phone (212) 963–8464.

Chairman.—Kingston Rhodes (Sierra Leone).

Joint Inspection Unit (JIU), Palais des Nations, 1211 Geneva 10, Switzerland, phone (41–22) 917–1234.

Chairman.—Gerard Biraud (France).

Panel of External Auditors of the UN, Specialized Agencies and International Atomic Energy Agency, One United Nations Plaza, New York, NY 10017, phone (212) 963–5623.

Executive Secretary to the Board.—Swatantra Anand Goolsarran.

Chairman of the Board.—Liu Jiayi.

United Nations Human Settlements Programme (UN–HABITAT), UN Office at Nairobi, P.O. Box 30030, Nairobi, Kenya, phone (254–2) 621–1234.

Executive Director.—Joan Clos (Spain).

United Nations Children's Fund (UNICEF), UNICEF House, 3 UN Plaza, New York, NY 10017, phone (212) 326–7000.

Executive Director.—Anthony Lake (USA).

United Nations Conference on Trade and Development (UNCTAD), Palais des Nations, 8–14 Avenue de la Paix, 1211 Geneva 10, Switzerland, phone (41–22) 917–1234.

Secretary General.—Supachai Panitchpakdi.

United Nations Development Fund for Women (UNIFEM), 304 East 45th Street, Sixth Floor, New York, NY 10017, phone (212) 906–6400.

Director.—Michelle Bachelet.

United Nations Development Programme (UNDP), 1 United Nations Plaza, New York, NY 10017, phone (212) 906–5000.

Administrator.—Helen Clark (New Zealand).

United Nations Development Programme (UNDP), Liaison Office, 1775 K Street, NW., Suite 420, Washington, DC 20006, phone (202) 331–9130.

Director.—Paolo Galli (acting), (Italy).

United Nations Environment Programme (UNEP), P.O. Box 30552, Nairobi, Kenya, phone (254–2) 621–1234.

Executive Director.—Achim Steiner.

United Nations High Commissioner for Refugees (UNHCR), Case Postale 2500, CH–1211 Geneve 2 Depot, Switzerland, phone (41–22) 739–8111.

High Commissioner.—Antonio Guterres (Portugal).

United Nations High Commissioner for Refugees (UNHCR), Regional Office for the United States and the Caribbean, 1775 K Street, NW., Third Floor, Washington, DC 20006, phone (202) 296–5191.

Regional Representative.—Vincent Cochetel.

United Nations Institute for Disarmament Research (UNIDIR), Palais des Nations, 1211 Geneva 10, Switzerland, phone (41–22) 917–4292.

Director.—Theresa Hitchens (United Kingdom).

United Nations Institute for Training and Research (UNITAR), Palais des Nations, 1211 Geneva 10, Switzerland, phone (41–22) 798–5850.

Executive Director.—Carlos Lopes (Guinea Bissau).

United Nations International Drug Control Programme (UNODC), P.O. Box 500, A–1400 Vienna, Austria, phone (43–1) 21345, ext. 4251.

Executive Director.—Yury Fedotov (Russian Federation).

United Nations International Research and Training Institute for the Advancement of Women (INSTRAW), P.O. Box 21747, Santo Domingo, Dominican Republic, phone (1–809) 685–2111.

Director.—Michelle Bachelet (Chili).

United Nations Interregional Crime and Justice Research Institute (UNICRI), Viale Maestri del Lavoro, 10, 10127 Turin, Italy, phone (39–11) 6537–111.

Director.—Jonathan Lucas (Seychelles).

United Nations Office for Project Services (UNOPS), P.O. Box 2695, 2100 Copenhagen, Denmark, phone (45–3) 546–7500.

Executive Director.—Jan Mattsson (Sweden).

United Nations Population Fund (UNFPA), 220 East 42nd Street, New York, NY 10017, phone (212) 297–5000.
Executive Director.—Babatunde Osotimehin (Nigeria).

United Nations Relief and Works Agency for Palestine Refugees in the Near East (UNRWA), Headquarters Amman, P.O. Box 140157, Amman 11814, Jordan, phone (+ 962 6) 580–8100. Headquarters Gaza, P.O. Box 61, Gaza City, or P.O. Box 338, Ashqelon, phone (+ 972 8) 288–7333.
Commissioner-General.—Filippo Grandi (Italy).

United Nations Research Institute for Social Development (UNRISD), Palais des Nations, 1211 Geneva 10, Switzerland, phone (41–22) 917–3020.
Deputy Director (Officer in Charge).—Sarah Cook (United Kingdom).

United Nations Volunteers Programme (UNV), Postfach 260111, D–53153 Bonn, Germany, phone (49–228) 815–2000.
Executive Coordinator.—Flavia Pansieri (Italy).

World Food Programme (WFP), Via C.G.Viola 68, Parco dei Medici, 00148 Rome, Italy, phone (39–6) 65131.
Executive Director.—Josette Sheeran (USA).

United Nations University (UNU), 5–53–70 Jingumae, Shibuya-ku, Tokyo 150–8925, Japan, phone (81–3) 5467–1212.
Rector.—Konrad Osterwalder (Switzerland).

SPECIALIZED AGENCIES

Food and Agriculture Organization (FAO), Viale delle Terme di Caracalla, 00153 Rome, Italy, phone (39–6) 57051.
Director-General.—Jacques Diouf (Senegal).

Food and Agriculture Organization, Liaison Office for North America, Suite 500, 2175 K Street, NW., Washington, DC 20037, phone (1–202) 653–2400.
Director.—Daniel J. Gustafson.

International Civil Aviation Organization (ICAO), 999 University Street, Montreal, Quebec H3C 5H7, Canada, phone (1–514) 954–8219.
Secretary-General.—Raymond Benjamin (France).

International Fund for Agricultural Development (IFAD), Via Paolo di Dono, 44, 00142 Rome, Italy, phone (39–6) 54591.
President.—Kanayo F. Nwanze (Nigeria).

External Affairs Department, IFAD North American Liaison Office, 1775 K Street, NW., Suite 410, Washington, DC 20006, phone (1–202) 331–9099.
Director.—Cheryl Morden (USA).

International Labour Organization (ILO), 4, Routes des Morillons, CH–1211 Geneva 22, Switzerland, phone (41–22) 799–6111.
Director-General.—Juan Somavia (Chile).

ILO Washington Branch Office, 1828 L Street, NW., Suite 600, Washington, DC 20036, phone (1–202) 653–7652.
Director.—Nancy Donaldson.

International Maritime Organization (IMO), 4 Albert Embankment, London SE1 7SR, United Kingdom, phone (44–20) 7735–7611.
Secretary-General.—Koji Sekimizu (Japan).

International Monetary Fund (IMF), 700 19th Street, NW., Washington, DC20431, phone (1–202) 623–7000.

Managing Director.—Christine Lagarde (France).

International Telecommunications Union (ITU), Palais des Nations, 1211 Geneva 20, Switzerland, phone (41–22) 730–5111.
Secretary-General.—Hamadoun Toure (Mali).

United Nations Educational, Scientific and Cultural Organization (UNESCO), 7 Place de Fontenoy, 75732 Paris 07 SP, France, phone (33–1) 4568–1000.
Director-General.—Irina Bokova (Bulgaria).

United Nations Industrial Development Organization (UNIDO), Vienna International Centre, Wagramerstr. 5, P.O. Box 300, A–1400 Vienna, Austria, phone (43–1) 26026–0.

Director-General.—Kandeh Yumkella (Sierra Leone).

Universal Postal Union (UPU), International Bureau, Case Postale, 3000 Berne 15, Switzerland, phone (41–31) 350–3111.
Director-General.—Edouard Dayan (France).

World Bank Group, 1818 H Street, NW., Washington, DC 20433, phone (1–202) 473–1000.
President.—Robert B. Zoellick (USA).

World Health Organization (WHO), 20 Avenue Appia, 1211 Geneva 27, Switzerland, phone (41–22) 791–2111.
Director-General.—Margaret Chan (China).

World Health Organization Liaison Office, 1 Dag Hammarskjold Plaza, 26th Floor New York, NY 10017, Washington, DC 20006, phone 646 626–6060.
Special Adviser to the Director-General.—Ian Smith (USA).

World Intellectual Property Organization (WIPO), 34, chemin des Colombettes, CH–1211 Geneva 20, Switzerland, phone (41–22) 338–9111.
Director General.—Francis Gurry (Australia).

World Meteorological Organization (WMO), 7bis, avenue de la Paix, Case Postale 2300, CH–1211 Geneva 2, Switzerland, phone (41–22) 730–8111.
Secretary-General.—Michel Jarraud (France).

RELATED BODY

International Atomic Energy Agency (IAEA), P.O. Box 100, Wagramer Strasse 5, A–1400 Vienna, Austria, phone (431) 2600–0.
Director General.—Yukiya Amano (Japan).

(The IAEA is an independent intergovernmental organization under the aegis of the UN).

SPECIAL AND PERSONAL REPRESENTATIVES AND ENVOYS OF THE SECRETARY-GENERAL

AFRICA

African Region:
Special Adviser to the Secretary-General on Africa and High Representative for the Least Developed Countries, Landlocked Developing Countries and Small Island Developing States.—Cheick Sidi Diarra (Mali).

Burundi:
Executive Representative of the Secretary-General for Burundi and Head of the UN Integrated Office in Burundi.—Karin Landgren (Sweden).

Central African Republic:
Special Representative of the Secretary-General and Head of the United Nations Peacebuilding Office in the Central African Republic.—Margaret Vogt (Nigeria).

Central Africa and Chad:
Special Representative of the Secretary-General and Head of the United Nations Mission in Central Africa and Chad Principal.—Abou Moussa (Chad).

Cote d'Ivoire:
Special Representative of the Secretary-General for Cote d'Ivoire.—Albert Gerard Koenders (Netherlands).
Principal Deputy Special Representative of the Secretary-General.—Arnauld Antone Akodjenou (Benin).
Deputy Special Representative of the Secretary-General for Humanitarian Coordination, Recovery and Reconstruction.—Ndolamb Ngokwey (DRC).

Democratic Republic of the Congo:
Special Representative of the Secretary-General for the Democratic Republic of the Congo.—Roger Meece (USA).
Deputy Special Representative of the Secretary-General for the Democratic Republic of the Congo.—Fidele Sarassoro (Cote d'Ivoire).
Deputy Special Representative of the Secretary-General for the Democratic Republic of the Congo.—Leila Zerrougui (Algeria)

Equatorial Guinea and Gabon:
Special Adviser to the Secretary-General and Mediator in the border dispute between Equatorial Guinea and Gabon.—Nicolas Michel (Switzerland).

Great Lakes Region:
Special Representative of the Secretary-General for the Great Lakes Region.—Olusegun Obasanjo (Nigeria).

Guinea-Bissau:
Representative of the Secretary-General and Head of UNOGBIS.—Joseph Mutaboba (Rwanda).

Horn of Africa:
Special Envoy.—Kjell Magne Bondevik (Norway).

Liberia:
Special Representative.—Ellen Margareth Loj (Denmark).
Deputy Special Representative for Recover and Good Governance.—Moustapha Soumare (Mali).
Deputy Special Representative for Rule of Law.—Henrietta Joy Abena Nyarko Mensa-Bonsu (Ghana).

Sierra Leone:
Executive Representative for United Nations Integrated Peacebuilding Office in Sierra Leone (UNIPSIL).—Michael von der Schulenburg (Germany).

Somalia:
Special Representative.—Augustine Mahiga (Tanzania).

Sudan:
Special Representative.—Haili Menkerios (South Africa).

Sudan / Darfur:
Joint Special Representative for the African Union and the United Nations Hybrid Operations in Darfur.—Vacant.
Deputy Joint AU–UN Special Representative for Operations and Management.—Mohamed Yonis (Somalia).

West Africa:
Special Representative.—Said Djinnit (Algeria).

Western Sahara:
Special Representative.—Hany Abdel-Aziz (Egypt).
Personal Envoy.—Christopher Ross (United States).

THE AMERICAS

Latin American Region:
Special Adviser.—Diego Cordovez (Ecuador).

Haiti:
Special Representative.—Mariano Fernandez (Chili).
Principal Deputy Special Representative.—Kevin Kennedy (USA)
Deputy Special Representative and Humanitarian Coordinator, Resident Coordinator and Resident Representative for UNDP.—Nigel Fisher (Canada).
Special Envoy.—William J. Clinton (United States).
Deputy Special Envoy.—Paul Farmer (United States).

ASIA AND THE PACIFIC

Afghanistan:
Special Representative.—Staffan de Mistura (Sweden).
Deputy Special Representative for Relief, Recovery and Reconstruction; UN Resident Coordinator and the UN Humanitarian Coordinator in Afghanistan.—Michael Keating (United Kingdom).
Deputy Special Representative for Political Issues.—Martin Kobler (Germany).

Central Asia:
Special Representative and Head of the UN Regional Centre for Preventive Diplomacy for Central Asia.—Miroslav Jenca (Slovakia).

Nepal:
Representative.—Karin Landgren (Sweden).

Pakistan:
Special Envoy for Assistance.—Rauf Engin Soysal (Turkey).

Timor Leste:
Special Representative.—Ameerah Haq (Bangladesh).
Deputy Special Representative for Governance Support, Development and Humanitarian Coordination.—Finn Reske-Nielsen (Denmark).

Deputy Special Representative for Security Sector Support and Rule of Law.—Shigeru Mochida (Japan).

EUROPE

Cyprus:
Special Representative.—Lisa Buttenheim (USA).

Former Yugoslav Republic of Macedonia-Greece:
Personal Envoy.—Matthew Nimetz (United States).

Georgia:
Special Representative.—Antti Turunen (Finland).

Kosovo:
Special Representative.—Farid Zarif (Afghanistan).

MIDDLE EAST

Middle East:
Special Coordinator for the Middle East Peace Process.—Robert H. Serry (Netherlands).
Deputy Special Coordinator for the Middle East Peace Process.—Max Gaylard (Australia).
Special Envoy for the Implementation of Security Council Resolution 1559.—Terje Roed-Larsen (Norway).

Iraq:
Special Representative.—Ad Melkert (Netherlands).
Deputy Special Representative for the Political, Electoral and Constitutional Support.—Jerzy Skuratowicz (Poland).
Deputy Special Representative for Humanitarian, Reconstruction and Development Affairs.—Christine McNab (Sweden).

Iraq (International Compact):
Special Adviser on the International Compact with Iraq and Other Issues.—Ibrahim Gambari (Nigeria).

Iraq / Kuwait:
Secretary-General's High-level Coordinator for compliance by Iraq with its obligations regarding the repatriation or return of all Kuwaiti and third country nationals or their remains, as well as the return of all Kuwaiti property, including archives seized by Iraq.—Gennady P. Tarasov (Russian Federation).

Lebanon:
Special Coordinator of the Secretary-General for Lebanon.—Michael C. Williams (United Kingdom).

OTHER HIGH LEVEL APPOINTMENTS

Alliance of Civilizations:
High Representative.—Jorge Sampaio (Portugal).

Children and Armed Conflict:
Special Representative.—Radhika Coomaraswamy (Sri Lanka).

Climate Change:
Special Envoys on Climate Change.—Gro Harlem Brundtland (Norway), Ricardo Lagos Escobar (Chile), Festus Mogae (Botswana), Srgjan Kerim (former Yugoslav Republic of Macedonia).

Disaster Reduction:
Special Representative.—Margareta Wahlstrom (Sweden).

Financing for Development:
Special Adviser.—Phillipe Douste-Blazy (France).

Gender Issues and Advancement of Women:
Special Adviser.—Rachel N. Mayanja (Uganda).

Global Compact:
Special Adviser.—Klaus M. Leisinger (United States).

HIV / AIDS in Africa:
Special Envoy.—Elizabeth Mataka (Botswana).

HIV / AIDS in Asia:
Special Envoy.—Nafis Sadik (Pakistan).

HIV / AIDS in the Caribbean Region:
Special Envoy.—George Alleyne (Barbados).

HIV / AIDS in Eastern Europe:
Vacant.

Human Rights:
Special Representative.—Margaret Sekaggya (Uganda).

Human Rights and the Business Community:
Special Representative.—John Ruggie (United States).

Human Rights in Cambodia:
Special Representative.—Yash Ghai (Kenya).

Malaria:
Special Envoy.—Ray Chambers (United States).

Migration:
Special Representative.—Peter Sutherland (Ireland).

Internally Displaced Persons:
Representative.—Walter Kalin (Switzerland).

Least Developed Countries, Landlocked Developing Countries, and Small Island Developing States:
Special Adviser.—Cheick Sidi Diarra (Mali), (Also Special Adviser to the Secretary General on Africa).

Millennium Development Goals:
Special Adviser.—Jeffrey D. Sachs (United States).
Executive Coordinator.—Eveline Herfkens (Netherlands).

Prevention of Genocide:
Special Advisor.—Francis Deng (Sudan).

Sport for Development and Peace:
Special Adviser.—Wilfried Lemke (Germany).

Tuberculosis:
Special Representative.—Jorge Sampaio (Portugal).

United Nations International School (UNIS):
Special Representative.—Silvia Fuhrman (United States).

Violence Against Children:
Special Representative.—Marta Santos Pais (Portugal).

World Summit on Information Society:
Special Adviser.—Nitin Desai (India).

WORLD BANK GROUP

The World Bank Group comprises five organizations: the International Bank for Reconstruction and Development (IBRD), the International Development Association (IDA), the International Finance Corporation (IFC), the Multilateral Investment Guarantee Agency (MIGA) and the International Centre for the Settlement of Investment Disputes (ICSID).

Headquarters: 1818 H Street, NW., 20433, (202) 473–1000

INTERNATIONAL BANK FOR RECONSTRUCTION AND DEVELOPMENT

President.—Robert Zoellick.
Managing Directors: Mahmoud Mohieldin, Sri Mulyani, Ngozi N. Okonjo-Iweala.
Senior Vice President and General Counsel.—Anne-Marie Leroy.
Senior Vice President, Development Economics, and Chief Economist.—Justin Yifu Lin.
Vice President and Head, Human Development Network.—Tamar Manuelyan Atinc.
Chief Financial Officer.—Vincenzo La Via.
Vice President and Chief Information Officer and Head, Information Solutions Network.—Shelley B. Leibowitz.
Vice President and Controller.—Charles McDonough.
Vice President and Corporate Secretary.—Jorge F. Calderon.
Vice President and Treasurer.—Madelyn Antoncic.
Vice President of:
Africa.—Obiageli Katryn Ezekwesili.

East Asia and Pacific.—James W. Adams.
South Asia.—Isabel Guerrero.
Vice President and Network Head Sustainable Development Network.—Inger Andersen.
Vice President External Affairs.—Caroline Anstey.
North American Affairs (External Affairs) Special Representative.—Craig M. Albright.
Europe (External Affairs) Special Representative.—Carlos Braga.
UN External Affairs, Special Representative.—Dominique Bichara.
Japan-External Affairs, Special Representative.—Kazu Tanigushi.
Human Resources.—Hasan A. Tuluy.
Latin America and the Caribbean.—Pamela Cox.
Middle East and North Africa.—Shamshad Akhtar.
Europe and Central Asia.—Philippe Le Houerou.
Vice President and Network Head, Operations Policy and Country Services.—Joachim von Amsberg.
Vice President and Network Head Poverty Reduction and Economic Management Network.—Otaviano Canuto.
Vice President and Network Head Financial and Private Sector Development (World Bank and IFC).—Janamitra Devan.
Resource Mobilization and Cofinancing.—Axel Van Trotsenburg.
Vice President and Bank Group Risk Officer.—Robert Kopech.
Vice President, World Bank Institute.—Sanjay Pradhan.
Director-General, Independent Evaluation.—Vinod Thomas.
Vice President, Corporate Finance and Risk Management.—Van Pulley.
Vice President, Concessional Finance and Global Partnerships.—Axel Van Trotsenburg.
Vice President and Auditor-General.—Clare Brady.
Vice President, Institutional Integrity.—Leonard McCarthy.

OTHER WORLD BANK OFFICES

London: New Zealand House, 15th Floor, Haymarket, London SW1Y 4TE, England.
Geneva: 3, Chemin Louis Dunant, CP 66, CH 1211, Geneva 10, Switzerland.
Paris: 66, Avenue d'Iena, 75116 Paris, France.
Brussels: 10, rue Montoyer, B–1000 Brussels, Belgium.
Tokyo: Fukoku Seimei Building, 10th Floor, 2–2–2 Uchisawai-cho, Chiyoda-Ku, Tokyo 100, Japan.
Sydney: c/o South Pacific Project Facility, 89 York Street, Level 8, GPO Box 1612, Sydney, NSW 2000, Australia.
Frankfurt: Bockenheimer Landstrasse 109, 60325 Frankfurt am Main, Germany.

BOARD OF EXECUTIVE DIRECTORS

Bahrain, Egypt (Arab Republic of), Iraq, Jordan, Kuwait, Lebanon, Libya, Maldives, Oman, Qatar, Syrian Arab Republic, United Arab Emirates, Yemen (Republic of).
Executive Director.—Merza H. Hasan.
Alternate.—Ayman Alkaffas.
Saudi Arabia.
Executive Director.—Abdulrahman M. Almofadhi.
Alternate.—Ibrahim M. I. Alturki.
Austria, Belarus, Belgium, Czech Republic, Hungary, Kazakhstan, Luxembourg, Slovak Republic, Slovenia, Turkey.
Executive Director.—Konstantin Huber (Austria).
Alternate.—Gino Alzetta (Belgium).
Australia, Cambodia, Kiribati, Korea (Republic of), Marshall Islands, Micronesia (Federated States of), Mongolia, New Zealand, Palau, Papua New Guinea, Samoa, Solomon Islands, Vanuatu.
Executive Director.—James Hagan.
Alternate.—In-Khan Cho.
Albania, Greece, Italy, Malta, Portugal, San Marino, Timor-Leste.
Executive Director.—Piero Cipollone.
Alternate.—Nuno Mota Pinto.
United States.
Executive Director.—Ian H. Solomon.
Brazil, Colombia, Dominican Republic, Ecuador, Haiti, Panama, Philippines, Suriname, Trinidad and Tobago.

Executive Director.—Studart Rogerio.
Alternate.—Dhanpaul Vishnu.
Germany.
Executive Director.—Ingrid Hoven.
Alternate.—Dr. Ruediger von Kleist.
Afghanistan, Algeria, Ghana, Iran (Islamic Republic of), Morocco, Pakistan, Tunisia.
Executive Director.—Javed Talat.
Alternate.—Sid Ahmed Dib.
France.
Executive Director.—Ambroise Fayolle.
Alternate.—Anne Cindy Touret.
Benin, Burkina Faso, Cameroon, Cape Verde, Central African Republic, Chad, Comoros, Congo (Democratic Republic of), Congo (Republic of), Cote d'lvoire, Djibouti, Equatorial Guinea, Gabon, Guinea, Guinea-Bissau, Madagascar, Mali, Mauritania, Mauritius, Niger, Rwanda, Sao Tome and Principe, Senegal, Togo.
Executive Director.—Agapito Mendes Dias.
Alternate.—Mohamed Sikieh Kayad.
Brunei Darussalam, Fiji, Indonesia, Lao People's Democratic Republic, Malaysia, Myanmar, Nepal, Singapore, Thailand, Tonga, Vietnam.
Executive Director.—Hekinus Manao.
Alternate.—Irfa Ampri.
Denmark, Estonia, Finland, Iceland, Latvia, Lithuania, Norway, Sweden.
Executive Director.—Anna Brandt.
Alternate.—Jens Haarlov.
Russian Federation.
Executive Director.—Vadim Nikolaevich Grishin.
Alternate.—Eugene Miagkov.
Costa Rica, El Salvador, Guatemala, Honduras, Mexico, Nicaragua, Spain, Venezuela (Republica Bolivariana de).
Executive Director.—Marta Garcia Jauregui.
Antigua and Barbuda, Bahamas (The), Barbados, Belize, Canada, Dominica, Grenada, Guyana, Ireland, Jamaica, St. Kitts and Nevis, St. Lucia, St. Vincent and the Grenadines.
Executive Director.—Marie-Lucie Morin.
Alternate.—Kelvin Dalrymple.
Armenia, Bosnia and Herzegovina, Bulgaria, Croatia, Cyprus, Georgia, Israel, Macedonia (former Yugoslav Republic of), Moldova, Netherlands, Romania, Ukraine.
Executive Director.—Rudolf Treffers.
Alternate.—Tamara Solyanyk.
Japan.
Executive Director.—Nobumitsu Hayashi.
Alternate.—Yasuo Takamura.
Argentina, Bolivia, Chile, Paraguay, Peru, Uruguay.
Executive Director.—Felix Alberto Camarasa.
Alternate.—Varinia Daza Foronda.
United Kingdom.
Executive Director.—Susanna Moorehead.
Alternate.—Stewart Simon James.
Angola, Nigeria, South Africa.
Executive Director.—Renosi Mokate.
Alternate.—Mansur Muhtar.
Botswana, Burundi, Eritrea, Ethiopia, Gambia (The), Kenya, Lesotho, Liberia, Malawi, Mozambique, Namibia, Seychelles, Sierra Leone, Sudan, Swaziland, Tanzania, Uganda, Zambia, Zimbabwe.
Executive Director.—Hassan A. Taha.
Alternate.—Denny H. Kalyalya.
Bangladesh, Bhutan, India, Sri Lanka.
Executive Director.—Pulok Chatterji.
Alternate.—Kazi M. Aminul Islam.
Azerbaijan, Serbia and Montenegro, Kyrgyz Republic, Poland, Switzerland, Tajikistan, Turkmenistan, Uzbekistan, Yugoslavia (Fed. Rep. of), Switzerland, Yemen, Republic of.
Executive Director.—Jorg Frieden.
Alternate.—Michal Krupinski.
China.
Executive Director.—Shaolin Yang.
Alternate.—Ciyong Zou.

INTERNATIONAL DEVELOPMENT ASSOCIATION

[The officers, executive directors, and alternates are the same as those of the International Bank for Reconstruction and Development.]

INTERNATIONAL FINANCE CORPORATION

President.—Robert Zoellick.
Executive Vice President.—Lars Thunell.
Vice President and Corporate Secretary.—Jorge Familiar Calderon.
Vice President:
Human Resources, Communication and Administration.—Dorothy H. Berry.
Financial and Private Sector Development.—Janamitra Devan.
Risk Finance and Strategy.—Saadia Khairi.
Director-General, Independent Evaluation.—Vinod Thomas.
Vice President, Treasury and Information Technology.—Jingdong Hua.
Compliance Advisor/Ombudsman (IFC/MIGA).—Meg Taylor.
Vice President and General Counsel.—Rachel Robbins.
Vice President, Business Advisory Services.—Rachel Kyte.
Vice President, East Asia and Pacific.—Karin Finkelston.
Vice President, Sub-Saharan Africa, Latin America and the Caribbean, and Western Europe.—Thierry Tandoh.
Vice President, Eastern and Southern Europe, Central Asia, Middle East and North Africa.—Dimitris Tsitsiragos.
Vice President, Global Industries.—Rashad Kaldany.
CEO, IFC Asset Management Company.—Gavin Wilson.
Director, Corporate Relations Unit Manager.—Bruce Moats.
Chief Information Officer and Director, Corporate Business Technologies.—Stephanie von Friedeburg.
Director, Office of:
Accounting and Financial Operations.—Bernard Lauwers.
Advisory Services and Operations.—Anita Bhatia.
Business Risk.—Alzbeta Klein.
Corporate Strategy.—Christian Grossman.
Credit Review.—Vivek Pathak.
Development Impact.—Nigel Twose.
East and Southern Africa.—Jean Philippe Prosper.
Environment, Social and Governance.—William Bulmer.
Equity Department.—Sakdiyiam Kupasrimonkol.
Financial Markets.—James Peter Srciven.
Financial Markets Asia.—Serge Devieux.
Human Resources.—Cheikh O. Seydi.
Inclusive Business Models.—Toshiya Masuoka.
Indicators and Analysis.—Augusto Lopez Claros.
Infrastructure and Natural Resources.—Vincent Gouarne.
Integrated Risk Management.—Avi Hofman.
Investment Climate.—Pierre Guislain.
Manufacturing, Agribusiness and Services.—Atul Mehta.
Manufacturing, Agribusiness and Services, Asia.—Sergio Pimenta.
Manufacturing, Agribusiness and Services, Middle East and North Africa.—Guy M. Ellena.
Risk Management.—Maria da Graca Domingues.
Short-Term Finance.—Georgina Baker.
Special Operations.—Saran G. Kebet-Koulibaly.
Structured and Securitized Products.—Lee Meddin.
Syndicated Loans and Management.—Ritva Laukkanen.
West and Central Africa.—Yolande Duhem.

MULTILATERAL INVESTMENT GUARANTEE AGENCY

President.—Robert Zoellick.
Executive Vice President.—Izumi Kobayashi.
Vice President and General Counsel, Legal Affairs and Claims Group.—Ana-Mita Betancourt.
Compliance Advisor/Ombudsman (IFC/ICC AND MIGA).—Meg Taylor.

Chief Operating Officer.—James P. Bond.
Operations Group.—Edith Quintrell.
Director and Chief Economist, Economics and Policy Group.—Ravi Vish.
Director and Chief Financial Officer, Finance and Risk Management Group.—Lakshmi Shyam-Sunder.

FOREIGN DIPLOMATIC OFFICES IN THE UNITED STATES

AFGHANISTAN

Embassy of Afghanistan
2341 Wyoming Avenue, NW., Washington, DC 20008
phone (202) 483–6410, fax 483–6488
His Excellency Eklil Ahmad Hakimi
Ambassador E. and P.
Consular Offices:
California, Los Angeles
New York, New York

AFRICAN UNION

Delegaton of the African Union Mission
1919 Pennsylvania Avenue, NW., Suite 7001, Washington, DC 20006
Embassy of the African Union
phone (202) 293–8006, fax 429–7130
Her Excellency Amina Salum Ali
Ambassador (Head of Delegation)

ALBANIA

Embassy of the Republic of Albania
1312 18th Street, NW., Washington, DC 20036
phone (202) 223–4942, fax 628–7342
His Excellency Gilbert Galanxhi
Ambassador E. and P.
Consular Offices:
Connecticut, Greenwich
Georgia, Avondale Estates
Louisiana, New Orleans
Massachusetts, Boston
Michigan, West Bloomfield
Missouri, Blue Springs
New York, New York
North Carolina, Pinehurst
Ohio, Cleveland
Texas, Houston

ALGERIA

Embassy of the Democratic Republic of Algeria
2118 Kalorama Road, NW., Washington, DC 20008
phone (202) 265–2800, fax 667–2174
His Excellency Abdallah Baali
Ambassador E. and P.

ANDORRA

Embassy of Andorra
Two United Nations Plaza, 27th Floor, New York, NY 10017
phone (212) 750–8064, fax 750–6630
Mr. Andreu Jordi Tomas
First Secretary (Charge D'Affaires, A.I.)

ANGOLA

Embassy of the Republic of Angola
2100–2108 16th Street, NW., Washington, DC 20009
phone (202) 785–1156, fax 785–1258
Her Excellency Josefina Pitra Diakité
Ambassador E. and P.
Consular Offices:
New York, New York
Texas, Houston

ANTIGUA AND BARBUDA

Embassy of Antigua and Barbuda
3216 New Mexico Avenue, NW., Washington, DC 20016
phone (202) 362–5122, fax 362–5225
Her Excellency Deborah Mae Lovell
Ambassador E. and P. / Consul General
Consular Offices:
District of Columbia, Washington
Florida, Miami
New York, New York
Puerto Rico, Guaynabo

ARGENTINA

Embassy of the Argentine Republic
1600 New Hampshire Avenue, NW., Washington, DC 20009
phone (202) 238–6400, fax 332–3171
His Excellency Alfredo Vicente Chiaradia
Ambassador E. and P.
Consular Offices:
California, Los Angeles
Florida, Miami
Georgia, Atlanta
Illinois, Chicago
New York, New York
Texas, Houston

ARMENIA

Embassy of the Republic of Armenia
2225 R Street, NW., Washington, DC 20008
phone (202) 319–1976, fax 319–2982
His Excellency Tatoul Markarian
Ambassador E. and P.
Consular Offices:
California, Los Angeles

District of Columbia, Washington

AUSTRALIA

Embassy of Australia
1601 Massachusetts Avenue, NW., Washington, DC 20036
phone (202) 797–3000, fax 797–3168
His Excellency Kim Christian Beazley
Ambassador E. and P.
Consular Offices:
California:
Los Angeles
San Francisco
Colorado, Denver
District of Columbia, Washington
Georgia, Atlanta
Hawaii, Honolulu
Illinois, Chicago
New York, New York
Texas, Houston
Trust Territories of the Pacific Islands:
Kolonia, Micronesia
Pago Pago
Washington, Seattle

AUSTRIA

Embassy of Austria
3524 International Court, NW., Washington, DC 20008–3035
phone (202) 895–6700, fax 895–6773
Her Excellency Dr. Christian Prosl
Ambassador E. and P.
Consular Offices:
Alaska, Anchorage
Arizona, Scottsdale
California:
Los Angeles
San Francisco
District of Columbia, Washington
Florida:
Estero
Hollywood
Orlando
Georgia, Atlanta
Hawaii, Honolulu
Illinois, Chicago
Louisiana, New Orleans
Massachusetts, Boston
Michigan, Detroit
Minnesota, St. Paul
Missouri:
Kansas City
St. Louis
Nevada, Las Vegas
New York:
Buffalo
New York
Ohio, Columbus
Oregon, Portland
Pennsylvania, Pittsburgh
Puerto Rico, San Juan
South Carolina, Cowpens
Texas, Houston
Utah, Salt Lake City
Virgin Islands, St. Thomas
Virginia, Richmond
Washington, Seattle

AZERBAIJAN

Embassy of the Republic of Azerbaijan
2741 34th Street, NW., Washington, DC 20008
phone (202) 337–3500, fax 337–5911
His Excellency Yashar Aliyev
Ambassador E. and P.
Consular Offices:
California, Los Angeles
District of Columbia, Washington
New Mexico, Santa Fe

BAHAMAS

Embassy of the Commonwealth of The Bahamas
2220 Massachusetts Avenue, NW., Washington, DC 20008
phone (202) 319–2660, fax 319–2668
His Excellency Cornelius Alvin Smith
Ambassador E. and P.
Consular Offices:
District of Columbia, Washington
Florida, Miami
Georgia, Atlanta
New York, New York

BAHRAIN

Embassy of the Kingdom of Bahrain
3502 International Drive, NW., Washington, DC 20008
phone (202) 342–0741, fax 362–2192
Her Excellency Huda Ezra Ebrahim Nonoo
Ambassador E. and P.
Consular Offices:
California, San Diego
New York, New York

BANGLADESH

Embassy of the People's Republic of Bangladesh
3510 International Drive, NW., Washington, DC 20008
phone (202) 244–0183, fax 244–5366
His Excellency Akramul Gader
Ambassador E. and P.
Consular Offices:
California, Los Angeles
Hawaii, Honolulu
Louisiana, New Orleans
New York, New York
Texas, Houston

BARBADOS

Embassy of Barbados
2144 Wyoming Avenue, NW., Washington, DC 20008
phone (202) 939–9200, fax 332–7467
His Excellency John Ernest Beale
Ambassador E. and P.
Consular Offices:
- California:
  - Los Angeles
  - San Francisco
- Colorado, Denver
- District of Columbia, Washington
- Florida, Miami
- Georgia, Atlanta
- Illinois, Chicago
- Kentucky, Louisville
- Louisiana, New Orleans
- Michigan, Detroit
- New York, New York
- Oregon, Portland
- South Carolina, Charleston
- Texas, Sugar Land

BELARUS

Embassy of the Republic of Belarus
1619 New Hampshire Avenue, NW., Washington, DC 20009
phone (202) 986–1604, fax 986–1805
Mr. Oleg Kravchenko
Counselor (Charge D'Affaires Ad Interim)
Consular Offices:
- District of Columbia, Washington
- New York, New York

BELGIUM

Embassy of Belgium
3330 Garfield Street, NW., Washington, DC 20008
phone (202) 333–6900, fax 333–3079
His Excellency Jan Jozef Matthysen
Ambassador E. and P. / Consul General
Consular Offices:
- Alaska, Anchorage
- Arizona, Phoenix
- California:
  - Los Angeles
  - San Diego
  - San Francisco
- Colorado, Denver
- Connecticut, Greenwich
- District of Columbia, Washington
- Florida, Miami
- Georgia, Atlanta
- Hawaii, Honolulu
- Illinois:
  - Chicago
  - Moline
- Kansas, Kansas City
- Kentucky, Louisville
- Louisiana, New Orleans
- Maryland, Baltimore
- Massachusetts, Boston
- Michigan, Bloomfield
- Minnesota, St. Paul
- Missouri, St. Louis
- New York, New York
- Ohio, Cincinnati
- Oregon, Portland
- Pennsylvania:
  - Philadelphia
  - Pittsburgh
- Puerto Rico, San Juan
- Texas:
  - Fort Worth
  - Houston
  - San Antonio
- Utah, Salt Lake City
- Virginia, Norfolk
- Washington, Seattle
- Wisconsin, Milwaukee

BELIZE

Embassy of Belize
2535 Massachusetts Avenue, NW., Washington, DC 20008
phone (202) 332–9636, fax 332–6888
His Excellency Nestor E. Mendez
Ambassador E. and P.
Consular Offices:
- California:
  - Los Angeles
  - San Francisco
- District of Columbia, Washington
- Florida, Miami
- Georgia, Atlanta
- Illinois:
  - Belleville
  - Des Plaines
- Louisiana, New Orleans
- Michigan, Detroit
- Nevada, Las Vegas
- North Carolina, Wilmington
- Ohio, Dayton
- Puerto Rico, San Juan
- Texas:
  - Dallas
  - Houston
  - San Antonio

BENIN

Embassy of the Republic of Benin
2124 Kalorama Road, NW., Washington, DC 20008
phone (202) 232–6656, fax 265–1996
His Excellency Segbe Cyrille Oguin
Ambassador E. and P.
Consular Office: California, Los Angeles

BHUTAN

Consular Offices:
- District of Columbia, Washington
- New York, New York

BOLIVIA

Embassy of the Republic of Bolivia
3014 Massachusetts Avenue, NW., Washington, DC 20008
phone (202) 483–4410, fax 328–3712
Ms. Erika Angela Duenas Loayza
Minister / Counselor (Charge D'Affaires, A.I.)
Consular Offices:
- California, Los Angeles
- District of Columbia, Washington
- Florida, Miami
- Minnesota, Maple Grove
- New York, New York
- Puerto Rico, San Juan
- Texas, Houston

BOSNIA AND HERZEGOVINA

Embassy of Bosnia and Herzegovina
2109 E Street, NW., Washington, DC 20037
phone (202) 337–1500, fax 337–1502
Her Excellency Mitar Kujundzic
Ambassador E. and P.
Consular Offices:
- District of Columbia, Washington
- Illinois, Chicago
- New York, New York

BOTSWANA

Embassy of the Republic of Botswana
1531–1533 New Hampshire Avenue, NW., Washington, DC 20036
phone (202) 244–4990, fax 244–4164
His Excellency Tebelelo Seretse
Ambassador E. and P.
Consular Offices:
- California, San Francisco
- Georgia, Atlanta
- Texas, Houston

BRAZIL

Brazilian Embassy
3006 Massachusetts Avenue, NW., Washington, DC 20008
phone (202) 238–2700, fax 238–2827
His Excellency Mauro Vieira
Ambassador E. and P.
Consular Offices:
- Alabama, Birmingham
- California:
  - La Jolla
  - Los Angeles
  - San Francisco
- Connecticut, Hartford
- District of Columbia, Washington
- Florida:
  - Boca Raton
  - Miami
- Georgia:
  - Atlanta
  - Savannah
- Hawaii, Honolulu
- Illinois, Chicago
- Louisiana, New Orleans
- Massachusetts, Boston
- Nevada, Las Vegas
- New York, New York
- Pennsylvania, Philadelphia
- Tennessee, Memphis
- Texas, Houston
- Trust Territories of the Pacific Islands:
  - Hong Kong
- Utah, Salt Lake City
- Virginia, Norfolk
- Washington, Seattle

BRUNEI

Embassy of the State of Brunei Darussalam
3520 International Court, NW., Washington, DC 20008
phone (202) 237–1838, fax 885–0560
His Excellency Dato Yusoff Abd Hamid
Ambassador E. and P.

BULGARIA

Embassy of the Republic of Bulgaria
1621 22nd Street, NW., Washington, DC 20008
phone (202) 387–0174, fax 234–7973
His Excellency Elena Poptodorova Petrova
Ambassador E. and P.
Consular Offices:
- California:
  - Los Angeles
  - Palm Springs
  - Sacramento
- District of Columbia, Washington
- Florida, Boca Raton
- Illinois, Chicago
- Maine, Portland
- Massachusetts, Newton
- Nevada, Las Vegas
- New York, New York
- Pennsylvania, Media
- South Carolina, Columbia

BURKINA FASO

Embassy of Burkina Faso
2340 Massachusetts Avenue, NW., Washington, DC 20008
phone (202) 332–5577, fax 667–1882
His Excellency Paramanga Ernest Yonli
Ambassador E. and P.
Consular Offices:

California, Los Angeles
Louisiana, New Orleans

BURMA

Embassy of the Union of Burma
2300 S Street, NW., Washington, DC 20008
phone (202) 332–3344, fax 332–4351
Mr. Soe Paing
Minister / Counselor (Charge D'Affaires, Ad Interim)
Consular Office: New York, New York

BURUNDI

Embassy of the Republic of Burundi
2233 Wisconsin Avenue, NW., Suite 212, Washington, DC 20007
phone (202) 342–2574, fax 342–2578
Her Excellency Angele Niyuhire
Ambassador E. and P.
Consular Office: California, Los Angeles

CAMBODIA

Royal Embassy of Cambodia
4530 16th Street, NW., Washington, DC 20011
phone (202) 726–7742, fax 726–8381
His Excellency Heng Hem
Ambassador E. and P.
Consular Offices:
Massachusetts, Lowell
Pennsylvania, Philadelphia
Washington, Seattle

CAMEROON

Embassy of the Republic of Cameroon
2349 Massachusetts Avenue, NW., Washington, DC 20008
phone (202) 265–8790, fax 387–3826
His Excellency Bienvenu Joseph C. Foe Atangana
Ambassador E. and P.
Consular Offices:
California, San Francisco
Texas, Houston

CANADA

Embassy of Canada
501 Pennsylvania Avenue, NW., Washington, DC 20001
phone (202) 682–1740, fax 682–7726
His Excellency Gary Albert Doer
Ambassador E. and P.
Consular Offices:
Alaska, Anchorage
Arizona:
Phoenix
Tucson
California:
Los Angeles
Palo Alto
San Diego
San Francisco
Colorado, Denver
District of Columbia, Washington
Florida:
Miami
Tampa
Georgia, Atlanta
Hawaii, Honolulu
Illinois, Chicago
Louisiana, New Orleans
Maine, Portland
Massachusetts, Boston
Michigan, Detroit
Minnesota, Minneapolis
Missouri, St. Louis
Montana, Nashua
New Jersey, Princeton
New York:
Buffalo
New York
North Carolina:
Huntersville
Raleigh
North Dakota, Bismarck
Oregon, Portland
Pennsylvania:
Philadelphia
Pittsburgh
Puerto Rico, San Juan
Tennessee, Memphis
Texas:
Dallas
Houston
San Antonio
Utah, Bountiful
Virginia, Richmond
Washington, Seattle

CAPE VERDE

Embassy of the Republic of Cape Verde
3415 Massachusetts Avenue, NW., Washington, DC 20007
phone (202) 965–6820, fax 965–1207
Her Excellency Maria De Fatima Da Veiga
Ambassador E. and P.
Consular Office: Massachusetts, Boston

CENTRAL AFRICAN REPUBLIC

Embassy of Central African Republic
1618 22nd Street, NW., Washington, DC 20008
phone (202) 483–7800, fax 332–9893
His Excellency Stanislas Moussa Kembe
Ambassador E. and P.
Consular Offices:
California, Los Angeles
New York, New York

CHAD

Embassy of the Republic of Chad
2401 Massachusetts Avenue, NW., Washington, DC 20008
phone (202) 462–4009, fax 265–1937
His Excellency Bechir Mahamoud Adam
Ambassador E. and P.

CHILE

Embassy of the Republic of Chile
1732 Massachusetts Avenue, NW., Washington, DC 20036
phone (202) 785–1746, fax 887–5579
His Excellency Arturo I. Fermandois Vohringer
Ambassador E. and P.
Consular Offices:
California:
Los Angeles
San Diego
San Francisco
Santa Clara
District of Columbia, Washington
Florida:
Miami
Orlando
Georgia, Atlanta
Hawaii, Honolulu
Illinois, Chicago
Louisiana, New Orleans
Massachusetts, Boston
Michigan, Grosse Pointe Park
Missouri, Kansas City
Nevada, Las Vegas
New York, New York
Pennsylvania, Philadelphia
Puerto Rico, San Juan
South Carolina, Charleston
Texas:
Dallas
Houston
Washington, Olympia

CHINA

Embassy of the People's Republic of China
3505 International Place, NW., Washington, DC 20008
phone (202) 495–2000, fax 495–2138
His Excellency Yesui Zhang
Ambassador E. and P.
Consular Offices:
California:
Los Angeles
San Francisco
District of Columbia, Washington
Illinois, Chicago
New York, New York
Texas, Houston

COLOMBIA

Embassy of Colombia
2118 Leroy Place, NW., Washington, DC 20008
phone (202) 387–8338, fax 232–8643
His Excellency Gabriel Silva Lujan
Ambassador E. and P.
Consular Offices:
California:
Beverly Hills
San Francisco
District of Columbia, Washington
Florida, Miami
Georgia, Atlanta
Illinois, Chicago
Massachusetts, Boston
New York, New York
Puerto Rico, San Juan
Texas, Houston

COMOROS

Embassy of the Union of Comoros
866 United Nations Plaza, Suite 418, New York, NY 10017
phone (212) 750–1637, fax 750–1657
His Excellency Mohamed Toihiri
Ambassador E. and P.

CONGO, DEMOCRATIC REPUBLIC OF

Embassy of the Democratic Republic of Congo
1726 M Street, NW., Suite 601, Washington, DC 20036
phone (202) 234–7690, fax 234–2609
Her Excellency Faida Mitifu
Ambassador E. and P.
Consular Office: New York, New York

CONGO, REPUBLIC OF

Embassy of the Republic of the Congo
4891 Colorado Avenue, NW., Washington, DC 20011
phone (202) 726–5500, fax 726–1860
His Excellency Serge Mombouli
Ambassador E. and P.
Consular Office: Louisiana, New Orleans

COOK ISLANDS

Consular Office: California, Los Angeles

COSTA RICA

Embassy of Costa Rica
2114 S Street, NW., Washington, DC 20008
phone (202) 234–2945, fax 265–4795
Her Excellency Meta Shanon Figueres Boggs
Ambassador E. and P.
Consular Offices:
Arizona, Tucson
California, Los Angeles

Colorado, Denver
District of Columbia, Washington
Florida, Miami
Georgia, Atlanta
Illinois, Chicago
Massachusetts, Boston
Minnesota, Minneapolis
New York, New York
Puerto Rico, San Juan
Texas:
Austin
Dallas
Houston

CÔTE D'IVOIRE

Embassy of the Republic of Côte d'Ivoire
2424 Massachusetts Avenue, NW., Washington, DC 20008
phone (202) 797–0300, fax 462–9444
His Excellency Daouda Diabate
Ambassador E. and P.
Consular Offices:
California:
Los Angeles
San Francisco
Connecticut, Stamford
Florida, Orlando
Michigan, Detroit
Texas, Houston

CROATIA

Embassy of the Republic of Croatia
2343 Massachusetts Avenue, NW., Washington, DC 20008
phone (202) 588–5899, fax 588–8936
Her Excellency Kolinda Grabar Kitarovic
Ambassador E. and P.
Consular Offices:
California, Los Angeles
Illinois, Chicago
Kansas, Kansas City
Louisiana, New Orleans
New York, New York
Pennsylvania, Pittsburgh
Washington, Seattle

CYPRUS

Embassy of the Republic of Cyprus
2211 R Street, NW., Washington, DC 20008
phone (202) 462–5772, fax 483–6710
His Excellency Pavlos Anastasiades
Ambassador E. and P.
Consular Offices:
Arizona, Phoenix
California:
Los Angeles
San Francisco
District of Columbia, Washington
Georgia, Atlanta
Illinois, Chicago
Louisiana, New Orleans
Massachusetts, Boston
Michigan, Detroit
New York, New York
North Carolina, Jacksonville
Oregon, Portland
Texas, Houston
Washington, Seattle

CZECH REPUBLIC

Embassy of the Czech Republic
3900 Spring of Freedom Street, NW., Washington, DC 20008
phone (202) 274–9100, fax 966–8540
Mr. Daniel Kostoval
Minister/Counselor (Charge D'Affaires Ad Interim)
Consular Offices:
Alaska, Anchorage
California:
Los Angeles
San Francisco
Florida:
Ft. Lauderdale
Orlando
Georgia, Atlanta
Hawaii, Honolulu
Illinois, Chicago
Louisiana, New Orleans
Massachusetts, Wellesley
Minnesota, St. Paul
Missouri, Kansas City
Montana, Livington
New York:
Buffalo
New York
Oregon, Portland
Pennsylvania:
Philadelphia
Pittsburgh
Puerto Rico, San Juan
Texas, Houston
Utah, Salt Lake City

DENMARK

Royal Danish Embassy
3200 Whitehaven Street, NW., Washington, DC 20008
phone (202) 234–4300, fax 328–1470
His Excellency Peter Taksoe Jensen
Ambassador E. and P.
Consular Offices:
Alabama, Mobile
Alaska, Anchorage
Arizona, Scottsdale
California:
San Diego

San Francisco
Studio City
Colorado, Denver
Florida:
Hollywood
Jacksonville
Tampa
Georgia:
Atlanta
Macon
Illinois, Chicago
Indiana, Indianapolis
Iowa, Des Moines
Louisiana, New Orleans
Maryland, Baltimore
Massachusetts, Boston
Michigan, Detroit
Minnesota, Minneapolis
Missouri:
Kansas City
St. Louis
Nebraska, Omaha
New York, New York
Ohio, Cleveland
Oregon, Portland
Pennsylvania:
Philadelphia
Pittsburgh
Puerto Rico, San Juan
South Carolina, Charleston
Tennessee, Nashville
Texas:
Dallas
Houston
Utah, Salt Lake City
Virgin Islands, St. Thomas
Virginia, Virginia Beach
Washington, Seattle
Wisconsin, Milwaukee

DJIBOUTI

Embassy of the Republic of Djibouti
1156 15th Street, NW., Suite 515, Washington, DC 20005
phone (202) 331–0270, fax 331–0302
His Excellency Roble Olhaye
Ambassador E. and P.

DOMINICA

Embassy of the Commonwealth of Dominica
3216 New Mexico Avenue, NW., Washington, DC 20016
phone (202) 364–6781, fax 364–6791
His Excellency Hubert John Charles
Ambassador E. and P.
Consular Offices:
New York, New York
Puerto Rico, Guaynabo

DOMINICAN REPUBLIC

Embassy of the Dominican Republic
1715 22nd Street, NW., Washington, DC 20008
phone (202) 332–6280, fax 265–8057
His Excellency Roberto Bernardo Saladin Selin
Ambassador E. and P.
Consular Offices:
California, Sun Valley
Florida, Miami
Illinois, Chicago
Louisiana, New Orleans
Massachusetts, Boston
New York, New York
Puerto Rico:
Mayaguez
San Juan

ECUADOR

Embassy of Ecuador
2535 15th Street, NW., Washington, DC 20009
phone (202) 234–7200, fax 667–3482
Mr. Mauricio Efrain Baus Palacios
Minister (Charge D'Affaires A.I.)
Consular Offices:
Arizona, Phoenix
California:
Los Angeles
San Francisco
Connecticut, New Haven
District of Columbia, Washington
Florida:
Miami
West Palm Beach
Georgia, Atlanta
Illinois, Chicago
Louisiana, New Orleans
Massachusetts, Boston
Minnesota, Minneapolis
Nevada, Las Vegas
New Jersey, Newark
New York:
New York
Woodside
Puerto Rico, San Juan
Texas:
Dallas
Houston

EGYPT

Embassy of the Arab Republic of Egypt
3521 International Court, NW., Washington, DC 20008
phone (202) 895–5400, fax 244–4319
His Excellency Sameh Hassan Shoukry
Ambassador E. and P.
Consular Offices:
California, Los Angeles

Illinois, Chicago
New York, New York
Texas, Houston

EL SALVADOR

Embassy of El Salvador
1400 16th Street, NW., Suite 100, Washington, DC 20036
phone (202) 265–9671, fax 232–3763
His Excellency Francisco R. Altschul Fuentes
Ambassador E. and P.
Consular Offices:
- Arizona:
  - Fountain Hills
  - Tucson
- California:
  - Chula Vista
  - Costa Mesa
  - Los Angeles
  - Oakland
  - San Francisco
  - Santa Ana
- District of Columbia, Washington
- Florida, Coral Gables
- Georgia, Woodstock
- Illinois, Chicago
- Indiana, Indianapolis
- Louisiana, New Orleans
- Massachusetts, Boston
- Missouri:
  - Kansas City
  - St. Louis
- Nevada, Las Vegas
- New Jersey, Elizabeth
- New York:
  - Brentwood
  - New York
- Pennsylvania, Philadelphia
- Puerto Rico, Bayamon
- Texas:
  - Dallas
  - Houston
- Utah, Salt Lake City
- Virginia, Woodbridge

EQUATORIAL GUINEA

Embassy of the Republic of Equatorial Guinea
2020 16th Street, NW., Washington, DC 20009
phone (202) 518–5700, fax 518–5252
Her Excellency Purificacion Angue Ondo
Ambassador E. and P.
Consular Office: Texas, Houston

ERITREA

Embassy of the State of Eritrea
1708 New Hampshire Avenue, NW., Washington, DC 20009
phone (202) 319–1991, fax 319–1304
His Excellency Ghirmai Ghebremariam
Ambassador E. and P.
Consular Office: District of Columbia, Washington

ESTONIA

Embassy of Estonia
2131 Massachusetts Avenue, NW., Washington, DC 20008
phone (202) 588–0101, fax 588–0108
His Excellency Vaino Reinart
Ambassador E. and P.
Consular Offices:
- Arizona, Scottsdale
- California:
  - Los Angeles
  - San Francisco
- Illinois, Chicago
- Louisiana, New Orleans
- Nebraska, Lincoln
- New Hampshire, Portsmouth
- New York, New York
- South Carolina, Charleston
- Texas, Houston
- Washington, Seattle

ETHIOPIA

Embassy of Ethiopia
3506 International Drive, NW., Washington, DC 20008
phone (202) 364–1200, fax 686–9551
His Excellency Girma Birru Geda
Ambassador E. and P.
Consular Offices:
- California, Los Angeles
- New York, New York
- Texas, Houston
- Washington, Seattle

EUROPEAN UNION

Delegation of the European Commission
2175 K Street, NW., Washington, DC 20037
phone (202) 862–9500, fax 429–1766
His Excellency Joao Vale De Almeida
Ambassador (Head of Delegation)

FIJI

Embassy of the Republic of the Fiji Islands
2000 M Street, NW., Suite 710, Washington, DC 20036
phone (202) 466–8320, fax 466–8325
His Excellency Winston Thompson
Ambassador E. and P.
Consular Offices:
- California:
  - El Segundo
  - San Francisco
- Oregon, Portland
- Texas, Dallas

FINLAND

Embassy of Finland
3301 Massachusetts Avenue, NW., Washington, DC 20008
phone (202) 298–5800, fax 298–6030
His Excellency Pekka Lintu
Ambassador E. and P.
Consular Offices:
- Alabama, Birmingham
- Arizona, Phoenix
- California:
  - Los Angeles
  - San Diego
  - San Francisco
- Colorado, Highlands Ranch
- Connecticut, Norwich
- Florida:
  - Lake Worth
  - Miami
- Georgia, Atlanta
- Hawaii, Honolulu
- Illinois, Chicago
- Louisiana, New Orleans
- Maryland, Baltimore
- Massachusetts, Boston
- Michigan:
  - Farmington
  - Hancock
- Minnesota:
  - Minneapolis
  - Virginia
- New Jersey, Newark
- New York, New York
- Pennsylvania, Philadelphia
- Puerto Rico, San Juan
- Texas:
  - Dallas
  - Houston
- Utah, Salt Lake City
- Virginia, Norfolk
- Washington, Seattle

FRANCE

Embassy of France
4101 Reservoir Road, NW., Washington, DC 20007
phone (202) 944–6000, fax 944–6166
His Excellency Francois Marie Delattre
Ambassador E. and P.
Consular Offices:
- Alabama, Auburn University
- Alaska, Anchorage
- Arizona, Phoenix
- Arkansas, Little Rock
- California:
  - Los Angeles
  - Los Gatos
  - Sacramento
  - San Diego
  - San Francisco
- Colorado, Denver
- Connecticut, Hartford
- District of Columbia, Washington
- Florida:
  - Clearwater
  - Jacksonville
  - Miami
  - Orlando
- Georgia:
  - Atlanta
  - Savannah
- Guam, Tamuning
- Hawaii, Honolulu
- Idaho, Boise
- Illinois, Chicago
- Indiana, Indianapolis
- Iowa, Indianola
- Kentucky, Louisville
- Louisiana:
  - Lafayette
  - New Orleans
  - Shreveport
- Maine, Portland
- Massachusetts, Boston
- Michigan, Detroit
- Minnesota, Minneapolis
- Mississippi, Hattiesburg
- Missouri:
  - Kansas City
  - Saint Louis
- Montana, Hamilton
- Nebraska, Omaha
- Nevada:
  - Las Vegas
  - Reno
- New Hampshire, Manchester
- New Jersey, Princeton
- New Mexico, Albuquerque
- New York:
  - Buffalo
  - New York
- North Carolina:
  - Charlotte
  - Raleigh
- Ohio:
  - Cincinnati
  - Cleveland
- Oklahoma, Oklahoma City
- Oregon, Portland
- Pennsylvania:
  - Philadelphia
  - Pittsburgh
- Rhode Island, Providence
- South Carolina:
  - Greenville

Mount Pleasant
Tennessee:
Memphis
Nashville
Texas:
Austin
Dallas
Houston
San Antonio
Utah, Salt Lake City
Vermont, Burlington
Virgin Islands, St. Thomas
Virginia, Norfolk
Washington, Seattle
Wyoming, Dubois

GABON

Embassy of the Gabonese Republic
2034 20th Street, NW., Suite 200, Washington, DC 20009
phone (202) 797–1000, fax 332–0668
His Excellency Carlos Victor Boungou
Ambassador E. and P.
Consular Office: New York, New York

GAMBIA

Embassy of The Gambia
1424 K Street, NW., Suite 600, Washington, DC 20005
phone (202) 785–1379, fax 785–1430
His Excellency Alieu Momodou Ngum
Ambassador E. and P.
Consular Office: Florida, Miami

GEORGIA

Embassy of the Republic of Georgia
2209 Massachusetts Avenue, NW., Washington, DC 20008
phone (202) 387–2390, fax 393–4537
His Excellency Temuri Yakobashvili
Ambassador E. and P.
Consular Offices:
Alabama, Mobile
California, Orange
District of Columbia, Washington
Georgia, Atlanta
Massachusetts, Boston
New Jersey, Jersey City
New York, New York
Pennsylvania, Pittsburgh
Texas, Houston

GERMANY, FEDERAL REPUBLIC OF

Embassy of the Federal Republic of Germany
4645 Reservoir Road, NW., Washington, DC 20007
phone (202) 298–4000, fax 298–4249
His Excellency Dr. Klaus Scharioth
Ambassador E. and P.
Consular Offices:
Alabama, Birmingham
Alaska, Anchorage
Arizona, Phoenix
California:
Los Angeles
San Diego
San Francisco
Colorado, Denver
District of Columbia, Washington
Florida:
Miami
Naples
Orlando
Georgia:
Atlanta
Savannah
Illinois, Chicago
Indiana, Indianapolis
Iowa, Indianola
Kansas, Leawood
Kentucky, Louisville
Louisiana, New Orleans
Maine, Portland
Massachusetts, Boston
Michigan, Auburn Hills
Minnesota, Minneapolis
Nevada, Las Vegas
Mississippi, Jackson
Missouri, St. Louis
New Mexico, Albuquerque
New York:
Buffalo
New York
Deutsche Bundesbank
North Carolina, Charlotte
Ohio:
Cincinnati
Cleveland
Oklahoma, Oklahoma City
Oregon, Portland
Pennsylvania:
Philadelphia
Pittsburgh
Puerto Rico, San Juan
South Carolina, Greer
Tennessee, Nashville
Texas:
Dallas
Houston
San Antonio
Trust Territories of the Pacific Islands:
Manila, Philippines
Wellington, New Zealand
Utah, Salt Lake City

Virginia, Virginia Beach
Washington, Mercer Island

GHANA

Embassy of Ghana
3512 International Drive, NW., Washington, DC 20008
phone (202) 686–4520, fax 686–4527
His Excellency Daniel Ohene Agyekum
Ambassador E. and P.
Consular Offices:
District of Columbia, Washington
New York, New York
Texas, Houston

GREECE

Embassy of Greece
2217 Massachusetts Avenue, NW., Washington, DC 20008
phone (202) 939–1300, fax 939–1324
His Excellency Vassilis Kaskarelis
Ambassador E. and P.
Consular Offices:
California:
Los Angeles
San Francisco
District of Columbia, Washington
Florida, Tampa
Georgia, Atlanta
Illinois, Chicago
Louisiana, New Orleans
Massachusetts, Boston
New York, New York
Texas, Houston

GRENADA

Embassy of Grenada
1701 New Hampshire Avenue, NW., Washington, DC 20009
phone (202) 265–2561, fax 265–2468
Her Excellency Gillian Margaret Susan Bristol
Ambassador E. and P.
Consular Offices:
Florida, Ft. Lauderdale
Illinois, Chicago
Michigan, Northville
New York, New York
Puerto Rico, Guaynabo

GUATEMALA

Embassy of Guatemala
2220 R Street, NW., Washington, DC 20008
phone (202) 745–4952, fax 745–1908
His Excellency Francisco Villagran De Leon
Ambassador E. and P.
Consular Offices:
Alabama, Montgomery
Arizona, Phoenix
California:
Los Angeles
San Diego
San Francisco
Colorado, Denver
District of Columbia, Washington
Florida:
Ft. Lauderdale
Jupiter
Miami
Georgia, Atlanta
Illinois, Chicago
Louisiana:
Lafayette
New Orleans
Maryland, Silver Spring
Massachusetts, Newton
Missouri, Kansas City
Nevada, North Las Vegas
New York, New York
North Carolina, Charlotte
Oklahoma, Oklahoma City
Oregon, Portland
Pennsylvania, Philadelphia
Puerto Rico, San Juan
Rhode Island, Providence
South Carolina, Columbia
Tennessee, Memphis
Texas:
Houston
San Antonio
Washington, Seattle
Wisconsin, Madison

GUINEA

Embassy of the Republic of Guinea
2112 Leroy Place, NW., Washington, DC 20008
phone (202) 986–4300, fax 986–3800
His Excellency Mory Karamoko Kaba
Ambassador E. and P.
Consular Offices:
District of Columbia, Washington
Florida, Jacksonville
Ohio, Cleveland
Pennsylvania, Philadelphia

GUINEA-BISSAU

Embassy of the Republic of Guinea-Bissau
P.O. Box 33813, Washington, DC 20033
phone (301) 947–3958
Mr. Henrique Adriano Da Silva
Minister-Counselor

GUYANA

Embassy of Guyana
2490 Tracy Place, NW., Washington, DC 20008
phone (202) 265–6900, fax 232–1297

His Excellency Bayney Karran
Ambassador E. and P.
Consular Offices:
- Florida, Miami
- New York, New York
- Texas, Houston

HAITI

Embassy of the Republic of Haiti
2311 Massachusetts Avenue, NW., Washington, DC 20008
phone (202) 332–4090, fax 745–7215
His Excellency Louis Harold Joseph
Ambassador E. and P.
Consular Offices:
- California, San Francisco
- Florida:
  - Miami
  - Orlando
- Georgia, Atlanta
- Illinois, Chicago
- Louisiana, New Orleans
- Massachusetts, Boston
- New Jersey, Trenton
- New York, New York
- Pennsylvania:
  - Philadelphia
  - Pottsville
- Puerto Rico, San Juan
- Texas, Houston

HOLY SEE

Apostolic Nunciature
3339 Massachusetts Avenue, NW., Washington, DC 20008
phone (202) 333–7121, fax 337–4036
His Excellency Pietro Sambi
Apostolic Nuncio

HONDURAS

Embassy of Honduras
3007 Tilden Street, NW., Suite 4–M, Washington, DC 20008
phone (202) 966–2604, fax 966–9751
His Excellency Jorge Ramon Hernandez Alcerro
Ambassador E. and P.
Consular Offices:
- Arizona, Phoenix
- California:
  - Los Angeles
  - San Diego
  - San Francisco
- Florida:
  - Miami
  - Tampa
- Georgia, Atlanta
- Hawaii, Honolulu
- Illinois, Chicago
- Louisiana:
  - Baton Rouge
  - New Orleans
- Maryland, Baltimore
- Massachusetts, Belmont
- Missouri, St. Louis
- Nevada, Reno
- New York, New York
- Texas, Houston

HUNGARY

Embassy of the Republic of Hungary
3910 Shoemaker Street, NW., Washington, DC 20008
phone (202) 362–6730, fax 966–8135
His Excellency Gyoergy Szapary
Ambassador E. and P.
Consular Offices:
- California:
  - Los Angeles
  - Sacramento
  - San Francisco
- Colorado, Denver
- District of Columbia, Washington
- Florida, Miami
- Georgia, Morrow
- Illinois, Chicago
- Louisiana, New Orleans
- Massachusetts, Boston
- Missouri, St. Louis
- New York, New York
- Ohio, Cleveland
- Puerto Rico, Mayaguez
- Texas, Houston
- Utah, Sandy
- Washington, Seattle

ICELAND

Embassy of Iceland
1156 15th Street, NW., Suite 1200, Washington, DC 20005
phone (202) 265–6653, fax 265–6656
His Excellency Hjalmar W. Hannesson
Ambassador E. and P.
Consular Offices:
- Alaska, Anchorage
- Arizona, Phoenix
- California:
  - Los Angeles
  - San Diego
  - San Francisco
- Colorado, Englewood
- Florida:
  - Orlando
  - Plantation
- Georgia, Atlanta
- Illinois, Chicago

Kentucky, Louisville
Louisiana, New Orleans
Massachusetts, Boston
Michigan, Detroit
Minnesota, Minneapolis
Missouri, Grandview
New York, New York
North Dakota, Grand Fork
Oregon, Portland
Pennsylvania, Harrisburg
Puerto Rico, Guaynabo
South Carolina, Charleston
Texas:
Dallas
Houston
Utah, Salt Lake City
Virginia, Norfolk
Washington, Seattle
Wisconsin, Madison

INDIA

Embassy of India
2107 Massachusetts Avenue, NW., Washington, DC 20008
phone (202) 939–7000, fax 483–3972
Her Excellency Meera Shankar
Ambassador E. and P.
Consular Offices:
California, San Francisco
Illinois, Chicago
New York, New York
Texas, Houston

INDONESIA

Embassy of the Republic of Indonesia
2020 Massachusetts Avenue, NW., Washington, DC 20036
phone (202) 775–5200, fax 775–5365
His Excellency Dino Patti Djalal
Ambassador E. and P.
Consular Offices:
California:
Los Angeles
San Francisco
Hawaii, Honolulu
Illinois, Chicago
New York, New York
Texas, Houston

IRAN

See Pakistan

IRAQ

Embassy of the Republic of Iraq
3421 Massachusetts Avenue, NW., Washington, DC 20007
phone (202) 742–1600, fax 462–5066
His Excellency Samir Shakir Mahmood Sumaida'ie
Ambassador E. and P.
Consular Offices:
California, Los Angeles
Michigan, Southfield

IRELAND

Embassy of Ireland
2234 Massachusetts Avenue, NW., Washington, DC 20008
phone (202) 462–3939, fax 232–5993
His Excellency Michael Collins
Ambassador E. and P.
Consular Offices:
California:
Los Angeles
San Francisco
Colorado, Denver
Florida, Naples
Georgia, Atlanta
Illinois, Chicago
Louisiana, New Orleans
Massachusetts, Boston
Missouri, St. Louis
New York, New York
Pennsylvania, Pittsburgh
Texas, Houston
Washington, Seattle

ISRAEL

Embassy of Israel
3514 International Drive, NW., Washington, DC 20008
phone (202) 364–5500, fax 364–5607
His Excellency Michael Scott Oren
Ambassador E. and P.
Consular Offices:
California:
Los Angeles
San Francisco
District of Columbia, Washington
Florida, Miami
Georgia, Atlanta
Illinois, Chicago
Massachusetts, Boston
New York, New York
Pennsylvania, Philadelphia
Texas, Houston

ITALY

Embassy of Italy
3000 Whitehaven Street, NW., Washington, DC 20008
phone (202) 612–4400, fax 518–2151
His Excellency Giuliomaria Terzi Di Sant'Agata
Ambassador E. and P.
Consular Offices:
Alaska, Anchorage

Arizona, Scottsdale
California:
  Fresno
  Los Angeles
  Sacramento
  San Diego
  San Francisco
  San Jose
Colorado, Denver
Connecticut, Hartford
Florida:
  Miami
  Orlando
Georgia:
  Atlanta
  Savannah
Hawaii, Honolulu
Illinois, Chicago
Indiana, Indianapolis
Kansas, Leawood
Louisiana, New Orleans
Maryland, Baltimore
Massachusetts:
  Boston
  Worcester
Michigan, Detroit
Missouri, St. Louis
Nevada, Las Vegas
New Jersey:
  Newark
  Trenton
New York:
  Buffalo
  Mineola
  Mt. Vernon
  New York
  Rochester
North Carolina, Charlotte
Ohio, Cleveland
Oregon, Portland
Pennsylvania:
  Philadelphia
  Pittsburgh
Puerto Rico, San Juan
Rhode Island, Providence
South Carolina, Charleston
Tennessee, Nashville
Texas, Houston
Utah, Salt Lake City
Virginia, Norfolk
Washington, Seattle

JAMAICA

Embassy of Jamaica
1520 New Hampshire Avenue, NW., Washington, DC 20036
phone (202) 452–0660, fax 452–0081
Her Excellency Audrey Patrice Marks
Ambassador E. and P.
Consular Offices:
  California, San Francisco
  District of Columbia, Washington
  Florida, Miami
  Georgia, Atlanta
  Illinois, Chicago
  Massachusetts, Boston
  New Hampshire, Concord
  New York, New York
  Pennsylvania, Philadelphia
  Texas:
    Dallas
    Houston
  Virginia, Richmond
  Washington, Seattle

JAPAN

Embassy of Japan
2520 Massachusetts Avenue, NW., Washington, DC 20008
phone (202) 238–6700, fax 328–2187
His Excellency Ichiro Fujisaki
Ambassador E. and P.
Consular Offices:
  Alabama, Birmingham
  Alaska, Anchorage
  Arizona, Tempe
  California:
    Los Angeles
    San Diego
    San Francisco
  Colorado, Denver
  Connecticut, Simsbury
  District of Columbia, Washington
  Florida:
    Miami
    Orlando
  Georgia, Atlanta
  Guam, Agana
  Hawaii:
    Hilo
    Honolulu
  Idaho, Boise
  Illinois, Chicago
  Indiana, Indianapolis
  Kansas, Prairie Village
  Kentucky, Lexington
  Louisiana, New Orleans
  Massachusetts, Boston
  Michigan, Detroit
  Minnesota, Minneapolis
  Missouri, St. Louis
  Nebraska, Omaha
  Nevada, Las Vegas
  New Mexico, Albuquerque

New York:
Buffalo
New York
North Carolina, Durham
Northern Mariana Islands, Mariana Islands
Ohio, Dublin
Oklahoma, Oklahoma City
Oregon, Portland
Pennsylvania, Philadelphia
Puerto Rico, San Juan
Tennessee, Nashville
Texas:
Dallas
Houston
Trust Territories of the Pacific Islands: Pago Pago
Washington, Seattle
Wyoming, Casper

JORDAN

Embassy of the Hashemite Kingdom of Jordan
3504 International Drive, NW., Washington, DC 20008
phone (202) 966–2664, fax 966–3110
Her Excellency Dr. Alia Mohamad Ali Hatough Bouran
Ambassador E. and P.
Consular Offices:
California, San Francisco
Illinois, Chicago
Michigan, Detroit

KAZAKHSTAN

Embassy of the Republic of Kazakhstan
1401 16th Street, NW., Washington, DC 20036
phone (202) 232–5488, fax 232–5845
His Excellency Erlan A. Idrissov
Ambassador E. and P.
Consular Offices:
California:
San Francisco
Santa Monica
District of Columbia, Washington
Louisiana, Baton Rouge
New York, New York
Texas, Katy

KENYA

Embassy of the Republic of Kenya
2249 R Street, NW., Washington, DC 20008
phone (202) 387–6101, fax 462–3829
His Excellency Elkanah Odembo Absalom
Ambassador E. and P.
Consular Offices:
California, Los Angeles
New York, New York

KIRIBATI

Consular Office: Hawaii, Honolulu

KOREA

Embassy of the Republic of Korea
2450 Massachusetts Avenue, NW., Washington, DC 20008
phone (202) 939–5600, fax 387–0250
His Excellency Duck Soo Han
Ambassador E. and P.
Consular Offices:
Alaska, Anchorage
California:
Los Angeles
San Francisco
District of Columbia, Washington
Florida, Miami
Georgia, Atlanta
Guam, Agana
Hawaii, Honolulu
Illinois, Chicago
Louisiana, New Orleans
Massachusetts, Boston
Michigan, Southfield
New York, New York
Oklahoma, Oklahoma City
Oregon, Portland
Pennsylvania, Philadelphia
Puerto Rico, San Juan
Texas:
Dallas
Houston
Washington, Seattle

KOSOVO REPUBLIC

Embassy of the Republic of Kosovo
900 19th Street, NW., Suite 400, Washington, DC 20006
phone (202) 380–3581, fax 380–3628
Mr. Avni Spahiu
Charge D'Affaires Ad Interim
Consular Office: New York, New York

KUWAIT

Embassy of the State of Kuwait
2940 Tilden Street, NW., Washington, DC 20008
phone (202) 966–0702, fax 966–0517
His Excellency Sheikh Salem Abdullah Al Jaber Al-Sabah
Ambassador E. and P.
Consular Office: California, Los Angeles

KYRGYZSTAN

Embassy of the Kyrgyz Republic
2360 Massachusetts Avenue, NW., Suite 600, Washington, DC 20008
phone (202) 449–9823, fax 386–7550
His Excellency Muktar Djumaliev
Ambassador E. and P.
Consular Offices:
District of Columbia, Washington

Montana, Helena
New Jersey, South Plainfield
New York, New York
Texas, Houston

LAOS

Embassy of the Lao People's Democratic Republic
2222 S Street, NW., Washington, DC 20008
phone (202) 332–6416, fax 332–4923
His Excellency Seng Soukhathivong
Ambassador E. and P.

LATVIA

Embassy of Latvia
2306 Massachusetts Avenue, NW., Washington, DC 20008
phone (202) 328–2840, fax 328–2860
His Excellency Andrejs Pildegovics
Ambassador E. and P.
Consular Offices:
Connecticut, Greenwich
Florida, Ft. Lauderdale
Illinois, Chicago
Massachusetts, Needham
Michigan, West Bloomfield
Minnesota, Minneapolis
New York:
Buffalo
New York
Ohio, Cincinnati
Pennsylvania, Philadelphia
Rhode Island, North Kingstown
Texas, Houston
Washington, Snohomish

LEBANON

Embassy of Lebanon
2560 28th Street, NW., Washington, DC 20008
phone (202) 939–6300, fax 939–6324
His Excellency Antoine Chedid
Ambassador E. and P.
Consular Offices:
California, Los Angeles
Florida, Miami
Massachusetts, Boston
Michigan, Detroit
New York, New York
North Carolina, Raleigh
Texas, Houston

LESOTHO

Embassy of the Kingdom of Lesotho
2511 Massachusetts Avenue, NW., Washington, DC 20008
phone (202) 797–5533, fax 234–6815
His Excellency David Mohlomi Rantekoa
Ambassador E. and P.
Consular Offices:
Louisiana, New Orleans
Texas, Austin

LIBERIA

Embassy of the Republic of Liberia
5201 16th Street, NW., Washington, DC 20011
phone (202) 723–0437, fax 723–0436
Mr. William V.S. Bull
Minister (Charge D'Affaires Ad Interim)
Consular Offices:
California:
Los Angeles
San Francisco
District of Columbia, Washington
Florida, Tampa
Georgia, Atlanta
Illinois, Chicago
Michigan, Detroit
New York, New York
Pennsylvania, Philadelphia

LIBYA

Embassy of the Libyan Arab Jamahiriya
2600 Virginia Avenue, NW., Suite 705, Washington, DC 20037
phone (202) 944–9601, fax 944–9606
His Excellency Ali Suleiman Aujali
Ambassador E. and P.

LIECHTENSTEIN

Embassy of the Principality of Liechtenstein
2900 K Street, NW., Suite 602B, Washington, DC 20007
phone (202) 331–0590, fax 331–3221
Her Excellency Claudia Fritsche
Ambassador E. and P.
Consular Offices:
California, Los Angeles
Georgia, Macon
Illinois, Chicago
Oregon, Portland

LITHUANIA

Embassy of the Republic of Lithuania
2622 16th Street, NW., Washington, DC 20009
phone (202) 234–5860, fax 328–0466
His Excellency Zygimantas Pavilionis
Ambassador E. and P.
Consular Offices:
Arizona, Phoenix
California:
Lafayette
Santa Monica
Florida:
Palm Beach
St. Petersburg
Georgia, Marietta
Illinois, Chicago

Michigan:
Farmington
Lansing
Minnesota, Stillwater
Nevada, Las Vegas
New Hampshire, Manchester
New York:
New York
Webster
Ohio, Cleveland
Oregon, Portland
Pennsylvania, Philadelphia
Texas, Houston
Washington, Seattle

LUXEMBOURG

Embassy of Grand Duchy of Luxembourg
2200 Massachusetts Avenue, NW., Washington, DC 20008
phone (202) 265–4171, fax 328–8270
His Excellency Jean Paul Ernest Senninger
Ambassador E. and P.
Consular Offices:
Arizona, Scottsdale
California:
San Francisco
Woodland Hills
Colorado, Louisville
District of Columbia, Washington
Florida, Estero
Georgia, Atlanta
Hawaii, Kapolei
Illinois, Elburn
Indiana, Indianapolis
Louisiana, New Orleans
Massachusetts, Boston
Michigan, Auburn Hills
Minnesota, Edina
Missouri, Kansas City
New York, New York
Ohio, Cleveland
Oregon, Portland
Texas, Ft. Worth
Washington, Seattle

MACEDONIA

Embassy of the Republic of Macedonia
2129 Wyoming Avenue, NW., Washington, DC 20008
phone (202) 667–0501, fax 667–2131
His Excellency Zoran Jolevski
Ambassador E. and P.
Consular Offices:
California, San Diego
Florida:
Hollywood
Naples
Illinois, Chicago
Michigan, Southfield
New Jersey, Clifton
New York, New York
Ohio, Columbus

MADAGASCAR

Embassy of the Republic of Madagascar
2374 Massachusetts Avenue, NW., Washington, DC 20008
phone (202) 265–5525, fax 265–3034
His Excellency Jocelyn Bertin Radifera
Ambassador E. and P.
Consular Offices:
California, San Diego
New York, New York

MALAWI

Embassy of Malawi
2408 Massachusetts Avenue, NW., Washington, DC 20008
phone (202) 721–0270, fax 721–0288
His Excellency Stephen Dick Tennyson Matenje
Ambassador E. and P.

MALAYSIA

Embassy of Malaysia
3516 International Court, NW., Washington, DC 20008
phone (202) 572–9700, fax 572–9882
His Excellency Dr. Jamaludin Bin Jarjis
Ambassador E. and P.
Consular Offices:
California, Los Angeles
New York, New York
Oregon, Portland
Texas, Houston

MALDIVES

Embassy of the Republic of Maldives
800 2nd Avenue, Suite 400E, New York, NY 10017
phone (212) 599–6195, fax 661–6405
His Excellency Abdul Ghafoor Mohamed
Ambassador E. and P.

MALI

Embassy of the Republic of Mali
2130 R Street, NW., Washington, DC 20008
phone (202) 332–2249, fax 332–6603
His Excellency Mamadou Traore
Ambassador E. and P.
Consular Offices:
California, Cupertino
Florida, Ft. Lauderdale
Georgia, Atlanta
Louisiana, New Orleans

MALTA

Embassy of Malta

2017 Connecticut Avenue, NW., Washington, DC 20008
phone (202) 462–3611, fax 387–5470
His Excellency Mark Anthony Miceli Farrugia
Ambassador E. and P.
Consular Offices:
- California:
  - Los Angeles
  - San Francisco
- District of Columbia, Washington
- Florida:
  - Ft. Lauderdale
  - Miami
- Illinois, Barrington
- Louisiana, Metairie
- Massachusetts, Bellmont
- Michigan:
  - Detroit
  - Taylor
- Minnesota, St. Paul
- New York, New York
- Pennsylvania, Philadelphia
- Tennessee, Kingsport
- Texas:
  - Dallas
  - Houston
- Washington, Seattle

MARSHALL ISLANDS

Embassy of the Republic of the Marshall Islands
2433 Massachusetts Avenue, NW., 1st Floor, Washington, DC 20008
phone (202) 234–5414, fax 232–3236
Mr. Charles Rudolph Page
First Secretary (Charge D'Affaires Ad Interim)
Consular Offices:
- Arkansas, Springdale
- Guam, Agana
- Hawaii, Honolulu

MAURITANIA

Embassy of the Islamic Republic of Mauritania
2129 Leroy Place, NW., Washington, DC 20008
phone (202) 232–5700, fax 319–2623
His Excellency Mohamed Lemine El Haycen
Ambassador E. and P.
Consular Office: Pennsylvania, Newtown Square

MAURITIUS

Embassy of the Republic of Mauritius
4301 Connecticut Avenue, NW., Suite 441, Washington, DC 20008
phone (202) 244–1491, fax 966–0983
His Excellency Somduth Soborun
Ambassador E. and P.
Consular Offices:
- Arizona, Sun City
- California:
  - Los Angeles
  - San Francisco
- Illinois, Aurora

MEXICO

Embassy of Mexico
1911 Pennsylvania Avenue, NW., Washington, DC 20006
phone (202) 728–1600, fax 728–1698
His Excellency Arturo Sarukhan Casamitjana
Ambassador E. and P.
Consular Offices:
- Alaska, Anchorage
- Arizona:
  - Douglas
  - Nogales
  - Phoenix
  - Tucson
  - Yuma
- Arkansas, Little Rock
- California:
  - Calexico
  - Fresno
  - Los Angeles
  - Oxnard
  - Sacramento
  - Salinas
  - San Bernardino
  - San Diego
  - San Francisco
  - San Jose
  - Santa Ana
- Colorado, Denver
- District of Columbia, Washington
- Florida:
  - Jacksonville
  - Miami
  - Orlando
- Georgia, Atlanta
- Idaho, Boise
- Illinois, Chicago
- Indiana, Indianapolis
- Louisiana, New Orleans
- Massachusetts, Boston
- Michigan, Detroit
- Minnesota, St. Paul
- Missouri, Kansas City
- Nebraska, Omaha
- Nevada, Las Vegas
- New Mexico, Albuquerque
- New York, New York
- North Carolina:
  - Charlotte
  - Raleigh
- Oregon, Portland
- Pennsylvania, Philadelphia
- Puerto Rico, San Juan
- Texas:

Austin
Brownsville
Dallas
Del Rio
Eagle Pass
El Paso
Houston
Laredo
McAllen
Midland
San Antonio
Utah, Salt Lake City
Virginia, Richmond
Washington, Seattle
Wisconsin, Madison

MICRONESIA

Embassy of the Federated States of Micronesia
1725 N Street, NW., Washington, DC 20036
phone (202) 223–4383, fax 223–4391
His Excellency Yosiwo P. George
Ambassador E. and P.
Consular Offices:
Guam, Tamuning
Hawaii, Honolulu

MOLDOVA

Embassy of the Republic of Moldova
2101 S Street, NW., Washington, DC 20008
phone (202) 667–1130, fax 667–1204
His Excellency Nicolae Chirtoaca
Ambassador E. and P.
Consular Offices:
District of Columbia, Washington
North Carolina, Hickory

MONACO

Embassy of Monoco
3400 International Drive, NW., Suite 2K–100, Washington, DC 20008
phone (202) 234–1530, fax 244–7656
His Excellency Gilles Alexandre Noghes
Ambassador E. and P.
Consular Offices:
California:
Los Angeles
San Francisco
Florida, Miami
Georgia, Atlanta
Illinois, Chicago
Massachusetts, Boston
Nevada, Las Vegas
New York, New York
Texas, Dallas

MONGOLIA

Embassy of Mongolia
2833 M Street, NW., Washington, DC 20007
phone (202) 333–7117, fax 298–9227
His Excellency Bekhbat Khasbazar
Ambassador E. and P.
Consular Offices:
California, San Francisco
Colorado, Denver
District of Columbia, Washington
Georgia, Atlanta
Illinois, Chicago
Montana, Bozeman
New York, New York
Texas, Houston
Utah, Springville

MONTENEGRO

Embassy of the Republic of Montenegro
1610 New Hampshire Avenue, NW., Washington, DC 20009
phone (202) 234–6108, fax 234–6109
His Excellency Professor Srdan Darmanovic
Ambassador E. and P.
Consular Offices:
Colorado, Denver
New York, New York

MOROCCO

Embassy of the Kingdom of Morocco
1601 21st Street, NW., Washington, DC 20009
phone (202) 462–7980, fax 265–0161
His Excellency Aziz Mekouar
Ambassador E. and P.
Consular Offices:
California, Los Angeles
Colorado, Denver
Hawaii, Honolulu
Illinois, Chicago
Kansas, Kansas City
Massachusetts, Cambridge
New York, New York
Utah, Bountiful

MOZAMBIQUE

Embassy of the Republic of Mozambique
1525 New Hampshire Avenue, NW., Washington, DC 20036
phone (202) 293–7146, fax 835–0245
Her Excellency Amelia Narciso Matos Sumbana
Ambassador E. and P.

NAMIBIA

Embassy of the Republic of Namibia
1605 New Hampshire Avenue, NW., Washington, DC 20009
phone (202) 986–0540, fax 986–0443
His Excellency Martin Andjaba
Ambassador E. and P.
Consular Offices:
California, San Jose

Florida, Orlando
Michigan, Detroit
Nevada, Las Vegas
North Carolina, Greenville
Texas, Houston

NAURU

Embassy of the Republic of Nauru
800 Second Avenue, New York, NY 10017
phone (212) 937–0074, fax 937–0079
Her Excellency Marlene Inemwin Moses
Ambassador E. and P.
Consular Offices:
Guam, Agana
Hawaii, Honolulu
Trust Territories of the Pacific Islands:
Pago Pago

NEPAL

Embassy of Nepal
2131 Leroy Place, NW., Washington, DC 20008
phone (202) 667–4550, fax 667–5534
His Excellency Shankar Prasad Sharma
Ambassador E. and P.
Consular Offices:
California:
Auburn
Los Angeles
San Francisco
Colorado, Boulder
Hawaii, Naalehu
Illinois, Chicago
Maryland, Baltimore
Massachusetts, Boston
New York, New York

NETHERLANDS

Royal Netherlands Embassy
4200 Linnean Avenue, NW., Washington, DC 20008
phone (202) 244–5300, fax 362–3430
His Excellency Regina Veronica Maria Bos Jones
Ambassador E. and P.
Consular Offices:
Arizona, Phoenix
California:
Los Angeles
San Francisco
Colorado, Denver
District of Columbia, Washington
Florida:
Jacksonville
Miami
Orlando
Georgia, Atlanta
Hawaii, Honolulu
Illinois, Chicago
Louisiana, New Orleans
Massachusetts, Boston
Michigan:
Detroit
Grand Rapids
Minnesota, Minneapolis
Missouri, St. Louis
New York, New York
North Carolina, Raleigh
Ohio, Cleveland
Oregon, Portland
Puerto Rico, Guaynabo
Texas, Houston
Trust Territories of the Pacific Islands:
Manila, Phillipines
Utah, Salt Lake City
Washington, Bellevue

NEW ZEALAND

Embassy of New Zealand
37 Observatory Circle, NW., Washington, DC 20008
phone (202) 328–4800, fax 667–5227
His Excellency Michael Kenneth Moore
Ambassador E. and P.
Consular Offices:
California:
El Macero
Sacramento
San Diego
San Francisco
Santa Monica
District of Columbia, Washington
Georgia, Atlanta
Guam, Tamuning
Hawaii, Honolulu
Illinois, Chicago
New Hampshire, Boston
New York, New York
Texas, Houston
Trust Territories of the Pacific Islands:
Pago Pago
Utah, Salt Lake City
Washington, Seattle

NICARAGUA

Embassy of the Republic of Nicaragua
1627 New Hampshire Avenue, NW., Washington, DC 20009
phone (202) 939–6570, fax 939–6545
His Excellency Francisco Obadiah Campbell Hooker
Ambassador E. and P.
Consular Offices:
California:
Los Angeles
San Francisco
Colorado, Denver
District of Columbia, Washington
Florida, Miami

Georgia, Atlanta
Louisiana, Baton Rouge
Massachusetts, Springfield
New York, New York
North Carolina, Charlotte
Oklahoma, Tulsa
Pennsylvania:
Philadelphia
Pittsburgh
Puerto Rico, San Juan
Texas, Houston

NIGER

Embassy of the Republic of Niger
2204 R Street, NW., Washington, DC 20008
phone (202) 483–4224, fax 483–3169
Her Excellency Aminata Maiga Djibrilla
Ambassador E. and P.

NIGERIA

Embassy of the Federal Republic of Nigeria
3519 International Court, NW., Washington, DC 20008
phone (202) 986–8400, fax 362–6541
Mr. Baba Gana Wakil
Minister (Charge D'Affaires, A.I.)
Consular Offices:
Georgia, Atlanta
New York, New York

NORWAY

Royal Norwegian Embassy
2720 34th Street, NW., Washington, DC 20008
phone (202) 333–6000, fax 337–0870
His Excellency Wegger Christian Strommen
Ambassador E. and P.
Consular Offices:
Alabama, Mobile
Alaska, Anchorage
Arizona, Glendale
California:
Los Angeles
San Diego
San Francisco
Colorado, Denver
District of Columbia, Washington
Florida:
Jacksonville
Miami
Pensacola
Tampa
Georgia, Atlanta
Hawaii, Honolulu
Illinois, Chicago
Iowa, Des Moines
Louisiana, New Orleans
Massachusetts, Boston
Michigan, Detroit
Minnesota, Minneapolis
Montana, Billings
Nebraska, Omaha
New York, New York
North Dakota, Fargo
Oklahoma, Tulsa
Oregon, Portland
Pennsylvania, Philadelphia
Puerto Rico:
Ponce
San Juan
South Carolina, Charleston
South Dakota, Sioux Falls
Texas:
Dallas
Houston
Utah, Salt Lake City
Virginia, Norfolk
Washington, Seattle
Wisconsin, Madison

OMAN

Embassy of the Sultanate of Oman
2535 Belmont Road, NW., Washington, DC 20008
phone (202) 387–1980, fax 745–4933
Her Excellency Hunaina Sultan Ahmed al-Mughairy
Ambassador E. and P.
Consular Offices:
California, Los Angeles
Pennsylvania, Pittsburgh

PAKISTAN

Embassy of Pakistan
3517 International Court, NW., Washington, DC 20008
phone (202) 243–6500, fax 686–1544
His Excellency Husain Haqqani
Ambassador E. and P.
Consular Offices:
California:
Los Angeles
Sunnyvale
Connecticut, Rocky Hill
Illinois, Chicago
Maine, Portland
Massachusetts, Boston
Missouri, St. Louis
New York, New York
Texas, Houston

PALAU

Embassy of the Republic of Palau
1700 Pennsylvania Avenue, NW., Suite 400, Washington, DC 20006
phone (202) 452–6814, fax 452–6281
His Excellency Hersey Kyota
Ambassador E. and P.
Consular Offices:

California, La Canada Flintridge
Guam, Tamuning
Hawaii, Honolulu

PANAMA

Embassy of the Republic of Panama
2862 McGill Terrace, NW., Washington, DC 20008
phone (202) 483–1407, fax 483–8416
His Excellency Mario Ernesto Jaramillo Castillo
Ambassador E. and P.
Consular Offices:
California, San Diego
District of Columbia, Washington
Florida:
Miami
Tampa
Hawaii, Honolulu
Louisiana, New Orleans
New York, New York
Pennsylvania, Philadelphia
Puerto Rico, San Juan
Texas, Houston

PAPUA NEW GUINEA

Embassy of Papua New Guinea
1779 Massachusetts Avenue, NW., Suite 805, Washington, DC 20036
phone (202) 745–3680, fax 745–3679
His Excellency Evan Jeremy Paki
Ambassador E. and P.
Consular Offices:
California, Los Angeles
Texas, Houston

PARAGUAY

Embassy of Paraguay
2400 Massachusetts Avenue, NW., Washington, DC 20008
phone (202) 483–6960, fax 234–4508
His Excellency Rigoberto Gauto Vielman
Ambassador E. and P.
Consular Offices:
Arizona, Tucson
California, Los Angeles
Florida, Miami
Michigan, Detroit
New York, New York
Puerto Rico, San Juan
Texas:
Bellaire
Fort Worth

PERU

Embassy of Peru
1700 Massachusetts Avenue, NW., Washington, DC 20036
phone (202) 833–9860, fax 659–8124
His Excellency Luis Miguel Valdivieso Montano
Ambassador E. and P.
Consular Offices:
Arizona, Mesa
California:
Los Angeles
Sacramento
San Francisco
Colorado, Denver
Connecticut, Hartford
District of Columbia, Washington
Florida:
Miami
Tampa
Georgia, Atlanta
Hawaii, Honolulu
Illinois, Chicago
Louisiana, Gretna
Massachusetts, Boston
Missouri, St. Louis
New Jersey, Paterson
New York, New York
Oklahoma, Tulsa
Puerto Rico, San Juan
Texas:
Dallas
Houston
Utah, Salt Lake City
Washington, Seattle

PHILIPPINES

Embassy of the Republic of the Philippines
1600 Massachusetts Avenue, NW., Washington, DC 20036
phone (202) 467–9300, fax 467–9417
His Excellency Jose Lampa Cuisia, Jr.
Ambassador E. and P.
Consular Offices:
California:
Los Angeles
San Francisco
District of Columbia, Washington
Florida, North Miami
Georgia, Atlanta
Guam, Tamuning
Hawaii, Honolulu
Illinois, Chicago
Louisiana, New Orleans
Michigan, Livonia
New York, New York
Northern Mariana Islands, Saipan
Oregon, Portland
Trust Territories of the Pacific Islands:
Mariana Islands
Virgin Islands, St. Thomas

POLAND

Embassy of the Republic of Poland

2640 16th Street, NW., Washington, DC 20009
phone (202) 234–3800, fax 328–6271
His Excellency Robert Ryszard Kupiecki
Ambassador E. and P.
Consular Offices:
- Alaska, Anchorage
- California:
  - Belmont
  - Los Angeles
  - San Francisco
- Colorado, Longmont
- District of Columbia, Washington
- Florida, Miami
- Georgia, Atlanta
- Hawaii, Honolulu
- Idaho, Ketchum
- Illinois, Chicago
- Massachusetts, Boston
- Missouri, St. Louis
- Nevada, Las Vegas
- New York, New York
- North Carolina, Raleigh
- Ohio, Oxford
- Pennsylvania, Pittsburgh
- Puerto Rico, Catano
- Texas, Houston

PORTUGAL

Embassy of Portugal
2012 Massachusetts Avenue, NW., Washington, DC 20036
phone (202) 328–8610, fax 462–3726
His Excellency Nuno F. Alves Salvador E Brito
Ambassador E. and P.
Consular Offices:
- California:
  - Los Angeles
  - San Francisco
  - Tulare
- Connecticut, Waterbury
- Florida:
  - Miami
  - Orlando
- Hawaii, Honolulu
- Illinois, Chicago
- Louisiana, New Orleans
- Massachusetts:
  - Boston
  - New Bedford
- New Jersey, Newark
- New York, New York
- Puerto Rico, San Juan
- Rhode Island, Providence
- Texas, Houston

QATAR

Embassy of the State of Qatar
2555 M Street, NW., Suite 200, Washington, DC 20037
phone (202) 274–1600, fax 237–0061
His Excellency Ali Bin Fahad Faleh Al-Hajri
Ambassador E. and P.
Consular Office: Texas, Houston

ROMANIA

Embassy of Romania
1607 23rd Street, NW., Washington, DC 20008
phone (202) 332–4846, fax 232–4748
His Excellency Adrian Cosmin Vierita
Ambassador E. and P.
Consular Offices:
- Arizona, Temple
- California:
  - Los Angeles
  - San Francisco
- District of Columbia, Washington
- Florida, Hollywood
- Georgia, Atlanta
- Illinois, Chicago
- Indiana, Indianapolis
- Louisiana, New Orleans
- Massachusetts, Boston
- Michigan, Detroit
- Minnesota, Minneapolis
- Nevada, Las Vegas
- New York, New York
- Ohio, Cleveland
- Oklahoma, Norman
- Oregon, Portland
- Pennsylvania, Philadelphia
- Texas:
  - Dallas
  - Houston
- Utah, Salt Lake City
- Virginia, Norfolk

RUSSIA

Embassy of the Russian Federation
2650 Wisconsin Avenue, NW., Washington, DC 20007
phone (202) 298–5700, fax 298–5735
His Excellency Sergey Ivanovich Kislyak
Ambassador E. and P.
Consular Offices:
- Alaska, Anchorage
- California, San Francisco
- Colorado, Denver
- District of Columbia, Washington
- Florida, Pinellas Park
- Hawaii, Honolulu
- Minnesota, Minneapolis
- New York, New York
- Puerto Rico, San Juan
- Texas, Houston
- Utah, Salt Lake City

Washington, Seattle

RWANDA

Embassy of the Republic of Rwanda
1714 New Hampshire Avenue, NW., Washington, DC 20009
phone (202) 232–2882, fax 232–4544
His Excellency James Kimonyo
Ambassador E. and P.
Consular Offices:
California, San Francisco
Illinois, Geneva
Massachusetts, Boston
Texas, Houston

SAMOA

Embassy of the Independent State of Samoa
800 2nd Avenue, 4th Floor, New York, NY 10017
phone (212) 599–6196, fax 599–0797
His Excellency Ali'ioaiga Feturi Elisaia
Ambassador E. and P.
Consular Offices:
American Samoa, Pago Pago
California, Torrance

SAN MARINO

Embassy of Republic of San Marino
2650 Virginia Avenue, NW., Washington, DC 20037
phone (202) 250–1535
His Excellency Paolo Rondelli
Ambassador E. and P.
Consular Offices:
District of Columbia, Washington
Hawaii, Honolulu
Michigan, Troy
New York, New York

SAO TOME AND PRINCIPE

Embassy of Sao Tome and Principe
1211 Connecticut Avenue, NW., Suite 300, Washington, DC 20036
phone (202) 775–2075, fax 775–2077
His Excellency Ovidio Pequeno
Ambassador E. and P.
Consular Offices:
Georgia, Atlanta
Illinois, Chicago

SAUDI ARABIA

Royal Embassy of Saudi Arabia
601 New Hampshire Avenue, NW., Washington, DC 20037
phone (202) 342–3800, fax 944–3113
His Excellency Adel bin Ahmed Al-Jubeir
Ambassador E. and P.
Consular Offices:
California, Los Angeles
District of Columbia, Washington
New York, New York
Texas, Houston

SENEGAL

Embassy of the Republic of Senegal
2112 Wyoming Avenue, NW., Washington, DC 20008
phone (202) 234–0540, fax 332–6315
Her Excellency Fatou Danielle Diagne
Ambassador E. and P.
Consular Offices:
Florida, Miami
Georgia, Atlanta
Louisiana, Baton Rouge
Massachusetts, Boston
Missouri, Clayton
New York, New York
Rhode Island, Providence
Texas, Houston

SERBIA

Embassy of the Republic of Serbia
2134 Kalorama Road, NW., Washington, DC 20008
phone (202) 332–0333, fax 332–3933
His Excellency Vladimir Petrovic
Ambassador E. and P.
Consular Offices:
Colorado, Denver
Illinois, Chicago
Louisiana, Metairie
New York, New York
Ohio, Cleveland
Wyoming, Cheyenne

SEYCHELLES

Embassy of the Republic of Seychelles
800 2nd Avenue, Suite 400C, New York, NY 10017
phone (212) 972–1785, fax 972–1786
His Excellency Ronald Jean Jumeau
Ambassador E. and P.
Consular Offices:
Alaska, Anchorage
Arizona, Sun City
California, Los Angeles
Washington, Seattle

SIERRA LEONE

Embassy of Sierra Leone
1701 19th Street, NW., Washington, DC 20009
phone (202) 939–9261, fax 483–1793
His Excellency Bockari Kortu Stevens
Ambassador E. and P.
Consular Office: Texas, Houston

SINGAPORE

Embassy of the Republic of Singapore
3501 International Place, NW., Washington, DC 20008

phone (202) 537–3100, fax 537–0876
Her Excellency Heng Chee Chan
Ambassador E. and P.
Consular Offices:
- California, San Francisco
- Florida, Miami
- Illinois, Chicago
- New York, New York

SLOVAK REPUBLIC

Embassy of the Slovak Republic
3523 International Court, NW., Washington, DC 20008
phone (202) 237–1054, fax 237–6438
His Excellency Peter Burian
Ambassador E. and P.
Consular Offices:
- California:
  - Los Angeles
  - San Francisco
- Colorado, Denver
- District of Columbia, Washington
- Florida, Miami
- Indiana, Indianapolis
- Massachusetts, Weston
- Michigan, Detroit
- Minnesota, Bloomington
- Missouri, Kansas City
- New York, New York
- Pennsylvania, Pittsburgh
- Texas, Dallas
- Washington, Bainbridge Island

SLOVENIA

Embassy of the Republic of Slovenia
1525 New Hampshire Avenue, NW., Washington, DC 20036
phone (202) 332–9332, fax 667–4563
His Excellency Roman Kirn
Ambassador E. and P.
Consular Offices:
- California, San Francisco
- Colorado, Denver
- Florida, Miami Beach
- Georgia, Atlanta
- Hawaii, Honolulu
- Illinois, Chicago
- Kansas, Mission Hills
- New York, New York
- Ohio, Cleveland
- Tennessee, Knoxville
- Texas, Houston

SOLOMON ISLANDS

Embassy of the Solomon Islands
800 2nd Avenue, Suite 400L, New York, NY 10017
phone (212) 599–6192, fax 661–8925
His Excellency Collin D. Beck
Ambassador E. and P.

SOUTH AFRICA

Embassy of the Republic of South Africa
3051 Massachusetts Avenue, NW., Washington, DC 20008
phone (202) 232–4400, fax 265–1607
His Excellency Ebrahim Rasool
Ambassador E. and P.
Consular Offices:
- Alabama, Mobile
- California, Los Angeles
- Illinois, Chicago
- Kansas, Kansas City
- Minnesota, Minneapolis
- New York, New York
- Texas, Dallas
- Utah, Salt Lake City
- Wisconsin, Milwaukee

SPAIN

Embassy of Spain
2375 Pennsylvania Avenue, NW., Washington, DC 20037
phone (202) 452–0100, fax 833–5670
His Excellency Jorge Dezcallar De Mazarredo
Ambassador E. and P.
Consular Offices:
- Alabama, Birmingham
- Alaska, Anchorage
- Arizona, Phoenix
- California:
  - Los Angeles
  - San Diego
  - San Francisco
- Colorado, Englewood
- District of Columbia, Washington
- Florida:
  - Miami
  - Orlando
  - Pensacola
  - Tampa
- Georgia, Atlanta
- Hawaii, Honolulu
- Idaho, Boise
- Illinois, Chicago
- Louisiana, New Orleans
- Massachusetts, Boston
- Michigan, Ann Arbor
- Minnesota, St. Paul
- Missouri:
  - Kansas City
  - St. Louis
- New Jersey, Newark
- New Mexico:
  - Albuquerque
  - Santa Fe
- New York, New York

North Carolina, Durham
Ohio:
Cincinnati
Cleveland
Oklahoma, Oklahoma City
Pennsylvania, Philadelphia
Puerto Rico, San Juan
Texas:
Corpus Christi
Dallas
El Paso
Houston
San Antonio
Utah, Salt Lake City
Washington, Seattle

SRI LANKA

Embassy of the Democratic Socialist Republic of Sri Lanka
2148 Wyoming Avenue, NW., Washington, DC 20008
phone (202) 483–4025, fax 232–7181
His Excellency Jaliya Chitran Wickramasuriya
Ambassador E. and P.
Consular Offices:
Arizona, Phoenix
California, Los Angeles
Georgia, Atlanta
Hawaii, Honolulu
Illinois, Chicago
Louisiana, New Orleans
Massachusetts, Boston
New Jersey, Newark
New Mexico, Santa Fe
New York, New York
Texas, Houston

ST. KITTS AND NEVIS

Embassy of St. Kitts and Nevis
3216 New Mexico Avenue, NW., Washington, DC 20016
phone (202) 686–2636, fax 686–5740
Her Excellency Jacinth Henry Martin
Ambassador E. and P.
Consular Offices:
California, Los Angeles
District of Columbia, Washington
Florida, Miami
Georgia, Atlanta
New York, New York
Pennsylvania, Philadelphia
Puerto Rico, Guaynabo
Texas, Dallas
Virgin Islands, St. Thomas

ST. LUCIA

Embassy of St. Lucia
3216 New Mexico Avenue, NW., Washington, DC 20016
phone (202) 364–6792, fax 364–6723
His Excellency Dr. Michael Louis
Ambassador E. and P.
Consular Offices:
California, Los Angeles
Florida, Miami
New York, New York
Puerto Rico, Guaynabo
Virgin Islands, St. Croix

ST. VINCENT AND THE GRENADINES

Embassy of St. Vincent and the Grenadines
3216 New Mexico Avenue, NW., Washington, DC 20016
phone (202) 364–6730, fax 364–6736
Her Excellency La Celia A. Prince
Ambassador E. and P.
Consular Offices:
California, Los Angeles
Florida, Groveland
Louisiana, New Orleans
New York, New York
Puerto Rico, Guaynabo

SUDAN

Embassy of the Republic of the Sudan
2210 Massachusetts Avenue, NW., Washington, DC 20008
phone (202) 338–8565, fax 667–2406
Mr. Fatahel Rahman Ali Mohamed
Minister (Charge D'Affaires Ad Interim)

SURINAME

Embassy of the Republic of Suriname
4301 Connecticut Avenue, NW., Suite 460, Washington, DC 20008
phone (202) 244–7488, fax 244–5878
His Excellency Subhas Chandra Mungra
Ambassador E. and P.
Consular Offices:
Florida, Miami
Louisiana, New Orleans

SWAZILAND

Embassy of the Kingdom of Swaziland
1712 New Hampshire Avenue, NW., Washington, DC 20009
phone (202) 234–5002, fax 234–8254
His Excellency Reverend Abednego Mandla Ntshangase
Ambassador E. and P.

SWEDEN

Embassy of Sweden
2900 K Street, NW., Washington, DC 20007

phone (202) 467–2600, fax 467–2699
His Excellency Sven Jonas Hafstroem
Ambassador E. and P.
Consular Offices:
- Alaska, Anchorage
- Arizona, Scottsdale
- California:
  - San Diego
  - San Francisco
- Colorado, Denver
- District of Columbia, Washington
- Florida:
  - Ft. Lauderdale
  - Tampa
- Georgia, Atlanta
- Hawaii, Honolulu
- Illinois, Chicago
- Kansas, Merriam
- Louisiana, New Orleans
- Massachusetts, Boston
- Michigan, Ann Arbor
- Minnesota, Minneapolis
- Missouri, St. Louis
- Nebraska, Omaha
- Nevada, Las Vegas
- New York:
  - Jamestown
  - New York
- North Carolina, Raleigh
- Ohio, Cleveland
- Pennsylvania, Ardmore
- Puerto Rico, San Juan
- Texas:
  - Dallas
  - Houston
- Utah, Salt Lake City
- Virgin Islands, St. Thomas
- Virginia, Norfolk
- Washington, Seattle
- Wisconsin, Milwaukee

SWITZERLAND

Embassy of Switzerland
2900 Cathedral Avenue, NW., Washington, DC 20008
phone (202) 745–7900, fax 387–2564
His Excellency Manuel Sager
Ambassador E. and P.
Consular Offices:
- Arizona, Scottsdale
- California:
  - Los Angeles
  - San Francisco
- Colorado, Boulder
- District of Columbia, Washington
- Florida:
  - Miami
  - Orlando
- Georgia, Atlanta
- Hawaii, Honolulu
- Illinois, Chicago
- Indiana, Indianapolis
- Louisiana, New Orleans
- Massachusetts, Boston
- Michigan, Dearborn
- Minnesota, Minneapollis
- Missouri, Kansas City
- Nevada, Las Vegas
- New York:
  - New York
  - Williamsville
- North Carolina, Charlotte
- Ohio, Cleveland
- Oklahoma, Edmond
- Pennsylvnaia:
  - Philadelphia
  - Pittsburgh
- Puerto Rico, San Juan
- Texas:
  - Dallas
  - Houston
- Trust Territories of the Pacific Islands:
  - Pago Pago
- Utah, Salt Lake City
- Washington, Mercer Island

SYRIA

Embassy of the Syrian Arab Republic
2215 Wyoming Avenue, NW., Washington, DC 20008
phone (202) 232–6313, fax 234–9548
His Excellency Dr. Imad Moustapha
Ambassador E. and P.
Consular Offices:
- California, Los Angeles
- District of Columbia, Washington
- Michigan, Detroit
- Texas, Houston

TAJIKISTAN

Embassy of the Republic of Tajikistan
1005 New Hampshire Avenue, NW., Washington, DC 20037
phone (202) 223–6090, fax 223–6091
His Excellency Abdujabbor Shirinov
Ambassador E. and P.
Consular Office: District of Columbia, Washington

TANZANIA

Embassy of the United Republic of Tanzania
2139 R Street, NW., Washington, DC 20008
phone (202) 939–6125, fax 797–7408
Her Excellency Mwanaidi Sinare Maajar
Ambassador E. and P.
Consular Offices:

Georgia, Atlanta
Illinois, St. Louis
Minnesota, Minneapolis

THAILAND

Embassy of Thailand
1024 Wisconsin Avenue, NW., Washington, DC 20007
phone (202) 944–3600, fax 944–3611
His Excellency Kittiphong Na Ranong
Ambassador E. and P.
Consular Offices:
Alabama, Montgomery
California, Los Angeles
Colorado, Denver
Florida, Coral Gables
Georgia, Atlanta
Hawaii, Honolulu
Illinois, Chicago
Kansas, Kansas City
Louisiana, New Orleans
Massachusetts, Boston
New York, New York
Oklahoma, Broken Arrow
Oregon, Portland
Puerto Rico, Hato Rey
Texas:
Dallas
Houston
Utah, Salt Lake City

TIMOR LESTE

Embassy of the Democratic Republic of Timor Leste
4201 Connecticut Avenue, NW., Suite 504, Washington, DC 20008
phone (202) 966–3202, fax 966–3205
His Excellency Constancio Da Conceicao Pinto
Ambassador E. and P.

TOGO

Embassy of the Republic of Togo
2208 Massachusetts Avenue, NW., Washington, DC 20008
phone (202) 234–4212, fax 232–3190
His Excellency Edawe Limbiye Kadangha Bariki
Ambassador E. and P.
Consular Offices:
California, Chatsworth
Florida, Miami

TONGA

Embassy of the Kingdom of Tonga
250 East 51st Street, New York, NY 10022
phone (917) 369–1025, fax 369–1024
His Excellency Sonatane Tua Taumoepeau Tupou
Ambassador E. and P.
Consular Offices:
California, San Francisco
Hawaii, Honolulu

TRINIDAD AND TOBAGO

Embassy of the Republic of Trinidad and Tobago
1708 Massachusetts Avenue, NW., Washington, DC 20036
phone (202) 467–6490, fax 785–3130
His Excellency Dr. Neil Nadesh Parsan
Ambassador E. and P.
Consular Offices:
Florida, Miami
New York, New York
Puerto Rico, San Juan
Texas, Houston

TUNISIA

Embassy of Tunisia
1515 Massachusetts Avenue, NW., Washington, DC 20005
phone (202) 862–1850, fax 862–1858
His Excellency Mohamed Salah Tekaya
Ambassador E. and P.
Consular Offices:
California, San Francisco
Florida, Miami
New York, New York
Texas:
Dallas
Houston

TURKEY

Embassy of the Republic of Turkey
2525 Massachusetts Avenue, NW., Washington, DC 20008
phone (202) 612–6700, fax 612–6744
His Excellency Namik Tan
Ambassador E. and P.
Consular Offices:
California:
Fair Oaks
Los Angeles
Oakland
Georgia, Atlanta
Illinois, Chicago
Maryland, Baltimore
Michigan, Farmington
Mississippi, Jackson
Missouri, Kansas City
New York, New York
Texas, Houston
Washington, Seattle

TURKMENISTAN

Embassy of Turkmenistan
2207 Massachusetts Avenue, NW., Washington, DC 20008
phone (202) 588–1500, fax 588–0697
His Excellency Meret Bairamovich Orazov
Ambassador E. and P.

TUVALU

Embassy of Tuvalu
800 Second Avenue, Suite 400D, New York, NY 10017
phone (212) 490–0534
His Excellency Afelee Falema Pita
Ambassador E. and P.

UGANDA

Embassy of the Republic of Uganda
5911 16th Street, NW., Washington, DC 20011
phone (202) 726–0416, fax 726–1727
His Excellency Perezi Karukubiro Kamunanwire
Ambassador E. and P.
Consular Offices:
California:
Los Angeles
San Diego
Colorado, Aurora
Florida, Jupiter
Georgia, Macon
Illinois, Chicago
New York, New York
Pennsylvania, Harrisburg
Texas, Dallas
Washington, Gig Harbor

UKRAINE

Embassy of Ukraine
3350 M Street, NW., Washington, DC 20007
phone (202) 349–2920, fax 333–0817
His Excellency Olexander Motsyk
Ambassador E. and P.
Consular Offices:
Alabama, Birmingham
Arizona, Tucson
California, San Francisco
District of Columbia, Washington
Georgia, Alpharetta
Illinois, Chicago
Michigan, Detroit
New York, New York
Ohio, Cleveland
Texas, Houston
Utah, Salt Lake City

UNITED ARAB EMIRATES

Embassy of the United Arab Emirates
3522 International Court, NW., Washington, DC 20008
phone (202) 243–2400, fax 243–2432
His Excellency Yousif Mana Saeed Alotaiba
Ambassador E. and P.

UNITED KINGDOM

British Embassy
3100 Massachusetts Avenue, NW., Washington, DC 20008
phone (202) 588–6500, fax 588–7870
His Excellency Sir Nigel Elton Sheinwald
Ambassador E. and P.
Consular Offices:
Alaska, Anchorage
Arizona, Phoenix
California:
Los Angeles
San Diego
San Francisco
San Jose
Colorado, Denver
District of Columbia, Washington
Florida:
Miami
Orlando
Tallahassee
Georgia, Atlanta
Illinois, Chicago
Massachusetts, Boston
Michigan, Detroit
Minnesota, Minneapolis
Nevada, Las Vegas
New York, New York
North Carolina, Charlotte
Ohio, Cleveland
Oklahoma, Tulsa
Oregon, Portland
Pennsylvania:
Philadelphia
Pittsburgh
Puerto Rico, San Juan
Tennessee, Nashville
Texas:
Dallas
Houston
San Antonio
Trust Territories of the Pacific Islands:
Nuku'alofa, Tonga
Utah, Salt Lake City
Washington, Bellevue
Wisconsin, Madison

URUGUAY

Embassy of Uruguay
1913 I Street, NW., Washington, DC 20006
phone (202) 331–1313, fax 331–8142
His Excellency Carlos Alberto Gianelli
Ambassador E. and P.
Consular Offices:
California:
Los Angeles
Sacramento
San Francisco
District of Columbia, Washington
Florida, Miami
Illinois, Chicago
Louisiana, New Orleans

Nevada, Reno
New York, New York
Puerto Rico, San Juan
Texas, Houston
Utah, Salt Lake City

UZBEKISTAN

Embassy of the Republic of Uzbekistan
1746 Massachusetts Avenue, NW., Washington, DC 20036
phone (202) 293–6803, fax 293–6804
His Excellency Ilhomjon Tuychievich Nematov
Ambassador E. and P.
Consular Offices:
District of Columbia, Washington
Georgia, Greensboro
New York, New York
Washington, Seattle

VANUATU

Consular Office: Northern Mariana Islands, Saipan

VENEZUELA

Embassy of the Bolivarian Republic of Venezuela
1099 30th Street, NW., Washington, DC 20007
phone (202) 342–2214, fax 342–6820
His Excellency Bernardo Alvarez Herrera
Ambassador E. and P.
Consular Offices:
California, San Francisco
Florida, Miami
Illinois, Chicago
Louisiana, New Orleans
Massachusetts, Boston
New York, New York
Puerto Rico, San Juan
Texas, Houston

VIETNAM

Embassy of Vietnam
1233 20th Street, NW., Suite 400, Washington, DC 20036
phone (202) 861–0737, fax 861–0917
His Excellency Phung Cong Le
Ambassador E. and P.
Consular Offices:
California, San Francisco
New York, New York
Texas, Houston

YEMEN

Embassy of the Republic of Yemen
2319 Wyoming Avenue, NW., Washington, DC 20008
phone (202) 965–4760, fax 337–2017
His Excellency Abdulwahab A. Al-Hajjri
Ambassador E. and P.
Consular Offices:
California, San Francisco
District of Columbia, Washington
Michigan, Dearborn

ZAMBIA

Embassy of the Republic of Zambia
2419 Massachusetts Avenue, NW., Washington, DC 20008
phone (202) 265–9717, fax 332–0826
Her Excellency Sheila Zimba Siwela
Ambassador E. and P.

ZIMBABWE

Embassy of the Republic of Zimbabwe
1608 New Hampshire Avenue, NW., Washington, DC 20009
phone (202) 332–7100, fax 483–9326
His Excellency Dr. Machivenyika T. Mapuranga
Ambassador E. and P.

The following is a list of countries with which diplomatic relations have been severed:

After each country, in parenthesis, is the name of the country's protecting power in the United States.

CUBA (Switzerland)
IRAN (Pakistan)

PRESS GALLERIES *

SENATE PRESS GALLERY

The Capitol, Room S–316, phone 224–0241

Director.—S. Joseph Keenan
Deputy Director.—Joan McKinney

Senior Media Coordinators:
Amy H. Gross
Kristyn K. Socknat
Media Coordinators:
James D. Saris
Wendy A. Oscarson-Kirchner
Elizabeth B. Crowley

HOUSE PRESS GALLERY

The Capitol, Room H–315, phone 225–3945

Superintendent.—Jerry L. Gallegos
Deputy Superintendent.—Justin J. Supon
Assistant Superintendents:
Ric Anderson
Laura Reed
Drew Cannon
Molly Cain

STANDING COMMITTEE OF CORRESPONDENTS

Thomas Burr, The Salt Lake Tribune, Chair
Joseph Morton, Omaha World-Herald, Secretary
Jim Rowley, Bloomberg News
Laurie Kellman, Associated Press
Brian Friel, Bloomberg News

RULES GOVERNING PRESS GALLERIES

1. Administration of the press galleries shall be vested in a Standing Committee of Correspondents elected by accredited members of the galleries. The Committee shall consist of five persons elected to serve for terms of two years. Provided, however, that at the election in January 1951, the three candidates receiving the highest number of votes shall serve for two years and the remaining two for one year. Thereafter, three members shall be elected in odd-numbered years and two in even-numbered years. Elections shall be held in January. The Committee shall elect its own chairman and secretary. Vacancies on the Committee shall be filled by special election to be called by the Standing Committee.

2. Persons desiring admission to the press galleries of Congress shall make application in accordance with Rule VI of the House of Representatives, subject to the direction and control of the Speaker and Rule 33 of the Senate, which rules shall be interpreted and administered by the Standing Committee of Correspondents, subject to the review and an approval by the Senate Committee on Rules and Administration.

*Information is based on data furnished and edited by each respective gallery.

3. The Standing Committee of Correspondents shall limit membership in the press galleries to bone fide correspondents of repute in their profession, under such rules as the Standing Committee of Correspondents shall prescribe.

4. An applicant for press credentials through the Daily Press Galleries must establish to the satisfaction of the Standing Committee of Correspondents that he or she is a full-time, paid correspondent who requires on-site access to congressional members and staff. Correspondents must be employed by a news organization:

(a) with General Publication periodicals mailing privileges under U.S. Postal Service rules, and which publishes daily; or

(b) whose principal business is the daily dissemination of original news and opinion of interest to a broad segment of the public, and which has published continuously for 18 months.

The applicant must reside in the Washington, D.C. area, and must not be engaged in any lobbying or paid advocacy, advertising, publicity or promotion work for any individual, political party, corporation, organization, or agency of the U.S. government, or in prosecuting any claim before Congress or any federal government department, and will not do so while a member of the Daily Press Galleries.

Applicants' publications must be editorially independent of any institution, foundation or interest group that lobbies the federal government, or that is not principally a general news organization.

Failure to provide information to the Standing Committee for this determination, or misrepresenting information, can result in the denial or revocation of credentials.

5. Members of the families of correspondents are not entitled to the privileges of the galleries.

6. The Standing Committee of Correspondents shall propose no changes in these rules except upon petition in writing signed by not less than 100 accredited members of the galleries. The above rules have been approved by the Committee on Rules and Administration.

JOHN A. BOEHNER,
Speaker of the House of Representatives.

CHARLES E. SCHUMER,
Chair, Senate Committee on Rules and Administration.

MEMBERS ENTITLED TO ADMISSION

PRESS GALLERIES

Abbott, Charles: Thomson Reuters
Abdullah, Halimah: McClatchy Newspapers
Abel, Allen: Postmedia News
Abrams, James: Associated Press
Ackerman, Andrew: Dow Jones / Wall Street Journal
Adair, William: St. Petersburg Times
Adams, Christopher: McClatchy Newspapers
Adams, Katy: Washington Examiner
Adams, Laurel: Center for Public Integrity
Adams, Rebecca: Congressional Quarterly
Adams, Richard: London Guardian
Adamy, Janet: Wall Street Journal
Adcock, Beryl: McClatchy Newspapers
Adler, Joseph: American Banker
Aemisegger, Celine: EFE News Services
Agiesta, Jennifer: Associated Press
Ahmann, Timothy: Thomson Reuters
Ahn, Sung Joong: Korea Times
Aizenman, Nurith: Washington Post
Al-Mubarak, Haifa: Saudi Press Agency
Alamiri, Yasmeen: Saudi Press Agency
Alandete, David: El Pais
Alberts, Sheldon: Postmedia News
Alexander, Charles: Thomson Reuters
Alexander, Keith: Washington Post
Alexandrov, Alexander: Argus Media
Alfaro, Xeyli: La Prensa Grafica of El Salvador
Ali, Syed: Bloomberg News
Allen, Amanda: Congressional Quarterly
Allen, JoAnne: Thomson Reuters
Allen, Kent: Congressional Quarterly
Allen, Ross: Argus Media
Allen, Victoria: Thomson Reuters
Alonso, Luis: Associated Press
Alonso-Zaldivar, Ricardo: Associated Press
Alpert, Bruce: New Orleans Times-Picayune
Altman, George: Press Register (Alabama)
Alvarez, Maria: ANSA Italian News Agency
Anderson, Andre: McClatchy Newspapers
Anderson, Joanna: Congressional Quarterly
Anderson, Mark: Dow Jones / Wall Street Journal
Anderson, Nick: Washington Post
Anderson, Stacy: Associated Press
Aparicio, Melissa: Bloomberg News
Apcar, Leonard: New York Times
Appelbaum, Binyamin: New York Times
Appleby, Julie: Kaiser Health News
Apuzzo, Matt: Associated Press
Aratani, Lori: Washington Post
Argetsinger, Amy: Washington Post
Armao, JoAnn: Washington Post
Armour, Stephanie: Bloomberg News
Armstrong, Andrew: Bloomberg News
Arndt, Dennis: Congressional Quarterly
Arnold, John Jay: Associated Press
Arnold, Laurence: Bloomberg News
Arsenault, Mark: Boston Globe
Arvelo, Jason: Bloomberg News
Asher, James: McClatchy Newspapers
Ashizuka, Tomoko: Nikkei
Asseo, Laurie: Bloomberg News
Atlas, Terry: Bloomberg News
Attias, Melissa: Congressional Quarterly
Aukofer, Frank: Artists & Writers Syndicate
Austin, Janet: Congressional Quarterly
Aversa, Jeannine: Bloomberg News
Awaji, Ai: Jiji Press
Ayuso Determeyer, Sylvia: German Press Agency-DPA
Azuma, Yasushi: Kyodo News
Babcock, Charles: Bloomberg News
Babington, Charles: Associated Press
Bacon, Jr., Perry: Washington Post
Baert, Patrick: Agence France-Presse
Baker, Peter: New York Times
Baldor, Lolita: Associated Press
Ball, Michael: Argus Media
Balz, Daniel: Washington Post
Banales, Jorge: EFE News Services
Banerjee, Neela: Los Angeles Times
Banks, Adelle: Religion News Service
Banks, David: Bloomberg News
Baquet, Dean: New York Times
Barakat, Matthew: Associated Press
Barbara, Philip: Thomson Reuters
Barbash, Fred: Congressional Quarterly
Barker, Jeffrey: Baltimore Sun
Barkley, Tom: Dow Jones / Wall Street Journal
Barnard, Katherine: Washington Post
Barnes, Julian: Wall Street Journal
Barnes, Robert: Washington Post
Barone, Michael: Washington Examiner
Barrera, Ruben: Notimex Mexican News Agency
Barrett, Barbara: McClatchy Newspapers
Barrett, Devlin: Wall Street Journal
Barrett, Jason: Congressional Quarterly
Barrett, Terrence: Bloomberg News
Barry, Matthew: Bloomberg News
Bartash, Jeffry: MarketWatch
Barton, Paul: Gannett Washington Bureau
Bartscht, Jill: Washington Post

MEMBERS ENTITLED TO ADMISSION—Continued

Bartz, Diane: Thomson Reuters
Baschuk, Bryce: Washington Internet Daily
Bashir, Mustafa: Saudi Press Agency
Bass, Frank: Bloomberg News
Bassett, Laura: Huffington Post
Bater, Jeffrey: Dow Jones / Wall Street Journal
Baygents, Ronald: Kuwait News Agency
Baylis, Jamie: Congressional Quarterly
Beary, Brian: Europolitics
Beattie, Jeff: Energy Daily
Beatty, Andrew: Agence France-Presse
Beckner, Steven: Market News International
Beckwith, Ryan: Congressional Quarterly
Beech, Eric: Thomson Reuters
Bell, Alistair: Thomson Reuters
Bell, Jarrett: USA Today
Bell, Peter: National Journal Daily
Bello, Marisol: USA Today
Bendavid, Naftali: Wall Street Journal
Bender, Adam: Communications Daily
Bender, Bryan: Boston Globe
Bendery, Jennifer: Huffington Post
Benenson, Robert: Congressional Quarterly
Benesova, Dagmar: World Business Press
Bengali, Shashank: McClatchy Newspapers
Benjaminson, Wendy: Associated Press
Benkelman, Susan: Congressional Quarterly
Bennett, Brian: Tribune Company
Benson, Clea: Bloomberg News
Benson, Ted: Congressional Quarterly
Berley, Max: Bloomberg News
Berrett, Dan: Inside Higher Ed
Berry, Deborah: Gannett Washington Bureau
Bettelheim, Adriel: Bloomberg News
Bewley, Elizabeth: Gannett Washington Bureau
Bicknell, Arwen Adams: Congressional Quarterly
Bicknell, John: Congressional Quarterly
Biddle, Joanna: Agence France-Presse
Biegelsen, Amy: Center for Public Integrity
Bilski, Christina: Nikkei
Birch, Douglas: Associated Press
Birnbaum, Ben: Washington Times
Biskupic, Joan: USA Today
Bivins, Larry: Gannett Washington Bureau
Bjerga, Alan: Bloomberg News
Blackledge, Brett: Associated Press
Blake, Aaron: Washington Post News Service with Bloomberg News
Bland, Melissa: Thomson Reuters
Blasco, Emilio: ABC Newspaper
Blinch, Russell: Thomson Reuters
Bliss, Jeffrey: Bloomberg News
Bloom, Michelle: National Journal Daily
Blum, Justin: Bloomberg News
Blumenthal, Mark: Huffington Post
Bohan, Caren: Thomson Reuters
Bok, Matt: Bloomberg News
Bolden, Michael: Washington Post
Boles, Corey: Dow Jones / Wall Street Journal
Bolstad, Erika: McClatchy Newspapers
Borak, Donna: American Banker
Borden, Jeremy: Center for Public Integrity
Borenstein, Seth: Associated Press
Bostick, Romaine: Bloomberg News
Bouza, Teresa: EFE News Services
Bowen, Joel: Congressional Quarterly
Bowers, Rebecca: St. Petersburg Times
Bowman, Curtis Lee: Scripps Howard News Service
Boyd, Robert: McClatchy Newspapers
Boyer, David: Washington Times
Boyle, Matthew: Daily Caller
Brady, Erik: USA Today
Braithwaite, Tom: Financial Times
Brancato, Kevin: Bloomberg News
Brand, Chad: Congressional Quarterly
Brandmaier, Frank: German Press Agency-DPA
Brandt, Martin: Thomson Reuters
Brasher, Philip: Des Moines Register
Brauchli, Marcus: Washington Post
Braun, Stephen: Associated Press
Bravin, Jess: Wall Street Journal
Bridis, Ted: Associated Press
Broder, John: New York Times
Broder, Jonathan: Congressional Quarterly
Brodmann, Ronald: Congressional Quarterly
Brooks, David: La Jornada
Broughton, Kristin: Congressional Quarterly
Brower, Kate: Bloomberg News
Brown, DeNeen: Washington Post
Brown, Emily: LRP Publications
Brown, Emily: USA Today
Brumfield, Sarah: Associated Press
Brune, Brett: Smartgrid Today
Brune, Thomas: Newsday
Brush, Silla: Bloomberg News
Buckley, Edward: Bloomberg News
Bumiller, Elisabeth: New York Times
Bunis, Dena: Congressional Quarterly
Burgess, Jeff: New York Times
Burke, Daniel: Religion News Service
Burns, Robert: Associated Press
Burr, Thomas: Salt Lake Tribune
Buskirk, Howard: Communications Daily
Butler, Desmond: Associated Press
Buzbee, Sally: Associated Press
Cadei, Emily: Congressional Quarterly
Cadiz, Antonieta: La Opinion
Cahlink, George: Congressional Quarterly
Caño, Antonio: El Pais
Caldwell, Alicia: Associated Press
Calmes, Jackie: New York Times
Camia, Catalina: USA Today
Caminiti, Matthew: Bloomberg News
Campbell, Scott: Congressional Quarterly
Campo, Marcello: ANSA Italian News Agency

MEMBERS ENTITLED TO ADMISSION—Continued

Canham, Matt: Salt Lake Tribune
Capaccio, Anthony: Bloomberg News
Caplan, Abby: Argus Media
Cappiello, Dina: Associated Press
Carey, Amanda: Daily Caller
Carey, Mary Agnes: Kaiser Health News
Carliner, Leah: Congressional Quarterly
Carlson, Tucker: Daily Caller
Carmichael, Lachlan: Agence France-Presse
Carnevale, MaryLu: Wall Street Journal
Carney, Dan: USA Today
Carney, David: Tech Law Journal
Carney, Timothy: Washington Examiner
Carroll, James: Louisville Courier Journal
Carroll, Rory: Thomson Reuters
Carter, Charlene: Congressional Quarterly
Carter, Sara: Washington Times
Carter, Zachary: Huffington Post
Caruso, Lisa: Bloomberg News
Cass, Connie: Associated Press
Cassata, Donna: Associated Press
Casteel, Chris: Oklahoman
Catan, Thomas: Wall Street Journal
Cauvin, Henri: Washington Post
Cermak, Christopher: German Press Agency-DPA
Chadbourn, Margaret: Thomson Reuters
Chaddock, Gail: Christian Science Monitor
Chan, Megan: USA Today
Chan, Sammie: Gannett Washington Bureau
Chandra, Shobhana: Bloomberg News
Charles, Deborah: Thomson Reuters
Chase, Randall: Associated Press
Chebium, Raju: Gannett Washington Bureau
Chiacu, Doina: Thomson Reuters
Chiantaretto, Mariuccia: Il Giornale
Chikazawa, Moriyasu: Kyodo News
Chipman, Kimberly: Bloomberg News
Choate, Patricia: Scripps Howard News Service
Choi, Young Hae: Korea Dong-A Ilbo
Chong, Christina Young: Korea Times
Chou, Yung-Chieh: Central News Agency
Christensen, Mike: Congressional Quarterly
Christian, Molly: Argus Media
Christie, Rebecca: Bloomberg News
Chua, Chin: Singapore Straits Times
Chun, Youngsik: Munwha Ilbo
Chwallek, Gabriele: German Press Agency-DPA
Ciaramella, C.J.: Daily Caller
Cillizza, Chris: Washington Post
Clark, Colin: Huffington Post
Clark, Lesley: Miami Herald
Clarke, David: Thomson Reuters
Clearwater, Cindy: Thomson Reuters
Clevenger, Andrew: Western Communications
Cloud, David: Chicago Tribune
Clymer, Adam: New York Times
Codrea, George: Congressional Quarterly
Cohen, Kristin: Bloomberg News
Cohen, Pninit: Scripps Howard News Service
Cohen, Richard: Congressional Quarterly
Coleman, Michael: Albuquerque Journal
Collins, Michael: Scripps Howard News Service
Collinson, Stephen: Agence France-Presse
Colman, Zachary: Smartgrid Today
Colvin, Ross: Thomson Reuters
Condon, Jr., George: National Journal Daily
Conery, Ben: Washington Times
Conlon, Charles: Congressional Quarterly
Conway, Neal: Congressional Quarterly
Conyer, Kristen: Congressional Quarterly
Cook, David: Christian Science Monitor
Cooper, Helene: New York Times
Cooper, Lauren: Associated Press
Cooper, Richard: Los Angeles Times
Corbett Dooren, Jennifer: Dow Jones / Wall Street Journal
Corbett, Rebecca: New York Times
Corbin, Kenneth: Internetnews.com
Corchado, Alfredo: Dallas Morning News
Cornwell, Susan: Thomson Reuters
Costelloe, Kevin: Bloomberg News
Cottle, Michelle: Daily Beast
Cowan, Richard: Thomson Reuters
Coyner, Kristin: Congressional Quarterly
Craig, Tim: Washington Post
Crane, Stephen: Cronkite News Service
Cranford, John: Congressional Quarterly
Crawley, John: Thomson Reuters
Crittenden, Michael: Dow Jones / Wall Street Journal
Crutsinger, Martin: Associated Press
Cuellar, Jessica: Congressional Quarterly
Cunningham, Paige: Washington Times
Curran, Timothy: Washington Post
Cushman, Jr., John: New York Times
da Costa, Mario Navarro: ABIM
da Costa, Pedro: Thomson Reuters
Dagony, Ron: Tel Aviv Globes
Daly, Corbett: Thomson Reuters
Daly, Dan: Washington Times
Daly, Matthew: Associated Press
Daniel, Douglass: Associated Press
Daniels, Alex: Arkansas Democrat-Gazette
Davidson, Joe: Washington Post
Davidson, Julie: LRP Publications
Davidson, Paul: USA Today
Davis, Aaron: Washington Post
Davis, David: Congressional Quarterly
Davis, Julie Hirschfeld: Bloomberg News
Davis, Robert: Wall Street Journal
De Francia, Ricardo: El Periodico
de Montvalon, Martin: Agence France-Presse
DeBonis, Mike: Washington Post
Debusmann, Bernd: Thomson Reuters
Decamme, Guillaume: Agence France-Presse
Decker, Brett: Washington Times

MEMBERS ENTITLED TO ADMISSION—Continued

Decker, Jonathan: Thomson Reuters
Decker, Susan: Bloomberg News
DeFrank, Thomas: New York Daily News
Del Giudice, Vincent: Bloomberg News
Del Riccio, Cristiano: ANSA Italian News Agency
Delaney, Arthur: Huffington Post
Delgado, Jose: El Nuevo Dia
DeLuce, Daniel: Agence France-Presse
Demirjian, Karoun: Las Vegas Sun
Dennis, Brady: Washington Post
Deparle, Jason: New York Times
Dermody, William: USA Today
Dessouky, Dean: Saudi Press Agency
Devaney, Tim: Washington Times
deVise, Daniel: Washington Post
Di Leo, Luca: Dow Jones / Wall Street Journal
Diamond, Richard: Washington Times
Diaz, Kevin: Minneapolis Star Tribune
Diaz-Briseno, Jose: Reforma Newspaper
Dick, Jason: National Journal Daily
Dilanian, Ken: Los Angeles Times
Dinan, Stephen: Washington Times
Dineen, John: Congressional Quarterly
DiNovi, William: Yomiuri Shimbun
Dishneau, David: Associated Press
Divis, Dee Ann: Washington Examiner
Dixon, Kim: Thomson Reuters
Dlouhy, Jennifer: Hearst Newspapers
Dobbyn, Timothy: Thomson Reuters
Dodge, Catherine: Bloomberg News
Doering, Christopher: Thomson Reuters
Doggett, Tom: Thomson Reuters
Doherty, Robert: Thomson Reuters
Dolan, Christopher: Washington Times
Dolge, Adam: LRP Publications
Dolinger, David: Dow Jones / Wall Street Journal
Dombey, Daniel: Financial Times
Dominguez, Alex: Associated Press
Donald, David: Center for Public Integrity
Dong, Lee Chi: Yonhap News Agency
Donmoyer, Ryan: Bloomberg News
Donnelly, John: Congressional Quarterly
Donovan, Laura: Daily Caller
Dooley, Benjamin: Kyodo News
Dorell, Oren: USA Today
Dorning, Mike: Bloomberg News
Dougherty, Carter: Bloomberg News
Douglas, William: McClatchy Newspapers
Dowd, Maureen: New York Times
Downing, James: Restructuring Today
Doyle, Michael: McClatchy Newspapers
Dozier, Kimberly: Associated Press
Drajem, Mark: Bloomberg News
Drawbaugh, Kevin: Thomson Reuters
Drinkard, Jim: Associated Press
Drogin, Robert: Los Angeles Times
Drummond, Bob: Bloomberg News
Du, Jing: Xinhua News Agency
Duggan, Loren: Bloomberg News
Duggan, Paul: Washington Post
duLac, Joshua Freedom: Washington Post
Dumain, Emma: Congressional Quarterly
Dunham, Richard: Houston Chronicle
Dunham, Will: Thomson Reuters
Dunkum, Johnnie: Wall Street Journal
Dunphy, Harry: Associated Press
Duran, Nicole: Daily Deal
Duszak, Alexandra: Center for Public Integrity
Dwyer, Paula: Bloomberg News
Earle, Geoff: New York Post
Eaton, Joseph: Center for Public Integrity
Eaton, Sabrina: Cleveland Plain Dealer
Ebitty-Doro, Estelle: Associated Press
Eckert, Paul: Thomson Reuters
Eckert, Toby: Congressional Quarterly
Eckstrom, Kevin: Religion News Service
Edney, Anna: Bloomberg News
Edsall, Thomas: Huffington Post
Eggen, Daniel: Washington Post
Eichelberger, Curtis: Bloomberg News
Eichenberg, Fernando: O Globo
Eilperin, Juliet: Washington Post
Eisenberg, Carol: Congressional Quarterly
Eisler, Peter: USA Today
El Hamti, Maribel: EFE News Services
El Nasser, Haya: USA Today
Elboghdady, Dina: Washington Post
Eldridge, David: Washington Times
Eliassen, Ingeborg: Stavanger Aftenblad
Elkins, Donald: Associated Press
Ellicott, Val: Gannett Washington Bureau
Elliott, Philip: Associated Press
Ellis, David: Bloomberg News
Ellis, Kristi: Fairchild Publications
Emery, Theo: Boston Globe
Engleman, Eric: Bloomberg News
Enoch, Daniel: Bloomberg News
Entous, Adam: Wall Street Journal
Epstein, Edward: Argus Media
Epstein, Keith: Center for Public Integrity
Espo, David: Associated Press
Ethridge, Emily: Congressional Quarterly
Evans, Michael: London Times
Ewing, Philip: Military.com
Fabel, Leah: Washington Examiner
Fahrenthold, David: Washington Post
Fairhall, John: Kaiser Health News
Faler, Brian: Bloomberg News
Fallis, David: Washington Post
Farha, Samer: Thomson Reuters
Farhi, Paul: Washington Post
Farnam, Timothy: Washington Post
Farrell, John: Center for Public Integrity
Faur, Fabienne: Agence France-Presse

MEMBERS ENTITLED TO ADMISSION—Continued

Favole, Jared: Dow Jones / Wall Street Journal
Fears, Darryl: Washington Post
Feldhaus, Katelyn: National Journal Daily
Feldman, Carole: Associated Press
Feldmann, Linda: Christian Science Monitor
Felker, Edward: Energy Guardian
Feller, Ben: Associated Press
Felsenthal, Mark: Thomson Reuters
Fendrich, Howard: Associated Press
Ferguson, Ellyn: Congressional Quarterly
Fernandez, Alfonso: EFE News Services
Fernandez, Christina: El Pais
Ferragutcasas, Nuria: Ara
Ferraro, Thomas: Thomson Reuters
Ferrechio, Susan: Washington Examiner
Ferrer, Sandra: Agence France-Presse
Fields, Gary: Wall Street Journal
Fifield, Anna: Financial Times
Fineman, Howard: Huffington Post
Finn, Peter: Washington Post
Fireman, Ken: Bloomberg News
Fisher, Marc: Washington Post
Fitzgerald, Alison: Bloomberg News
Fitzsimons, Thomas: Sunday Times of London
Flaherty, Anne: Associated Press
Flaherty, Mary Pat: Washington Post
Flanders, Gwen: USA Today
Flattau, Edward: Global Horizons Syndicate
Flavelle, Christopher: Bloomberg News
Fletcher, Michael: Washington Post
Foley, Elise: Huffington Post
Forden, Sara: Bloomberg News
Fox, Michael: National Journal Daily
Fram, Alan: Associated Press
Francis, Juliann: Bloomberg News
Frank, Jacqueline: Thomson Reuters
Frank, Thomas: USA Today
Freddoso, David: Washington Examiner
Freedman, Dan: Hearst Newspapers
Freking, Kevin: Associated Press
Frieden, Joyce: medpagetoday.com
Friedman, Daniel: National Journal Daily
Friedman, Robert: Scripps Howard News Service
Friel, Brian: Bloomberg News
Fritze, John: Baltimore Sun
Frommer, Frederic: Associated Press
Froomkin, Daniel: Huffington Post
Fry, Jamey: Congressional Quarterly
Fudo, Takashi: Jiji Press
Fuhrig, Frank: German Press Agency-DPA
Fuller, Matthew: Congressional Quarterly
Fullerton, Jane: Arkansas Democrat-Gazette
Fuog, Karin: Congressional Quarterly
Furlow, Robert: Associated Press
Furumoto, Yoso: Mainichi Shimbun
Galewitz, Phil: Kaiser Health News
Gallagher, Brian: USA Today
Gallu, Joshua: Bloomberg News
Gamboa, Suzanne: Associated Press
Gaouette, Nicole: Bloomberg News
Garcia, Jose: El Universal
Garcia, Maria: Notimex Mexican News Agency
Garcia, Sandra: Kyodo News
Gardiner, Andrew: USA Today
Gardner, Amy: Washington Post
Gardner, Lauren: Congressional Quarterly
Gardner, Tim: Thomson Reuters
Gaudiano Albright, Nicole: Gannett Washington Bureau
Ge, Xiangwen: Xinhua News Agency
Gearan, Anne: Associated Press
Gehrke, Joel: Washington Examiner
Geiger, Kim: Los Angeles Times
Geimann, Stephen: Bloomberg News
Geldner, Andreas: Stuttgarter Zeitung
Gendar, Alison: New York Daily News
Gentile, Gary: Platts News Service
Gerhart, Ann: Washington Post
Germain, Dan: Congressional Quarterly
Gertz, William: Washington Times
Gettinger, Steve: Congressional Quarterly
Gibson, William: Sun-Sentinel
Gienger, Viola: Bloomberg News
Gilbert, Craig: Milwaukee Journal Sentinel
Gilchrist, Diane: London Guardian
Giles, Ben: Washington Examiner
Gillman, Todd: Dallas Morning News
Gillum, Jack: Associated Press
Ginley, Caitlin: Center for Public Integrity
Giroux, Gregory: Bloomberg News
Girshman, Peggy: Kaiser Health News
Givens, David: Argus Media
Glass, Pamela: Le Mauricien
Glass, Robert: Associated Press
Glod, Maria: Washington Post
Gnoffo, Anthony: Bloomberg News
Goad, Ben: Riverside Press-Enterprise
Goins, Cole: Center for Public Integrity
Gold, Jenny: Kaiser Health News
Gold, Matea: Los Angeles Times
Goldbacher, Raymond: USA Today
Goldberg, Jonathan: Congressional Quarterly
Golden, Rodrek: Thomson Reuters
Goldenberg, Suzanne: London Guardian
Goldfarb, Sam: Congressional Quarterly
Goldfarb, Zachary: Washington Post
Goldman, Adam: Associated Press
Goldman, Julianna: Bloomberg News
Goldschmidt, Jim: McClatchy Newspapers
Goldstein, Amy: Washington Post
Goldstein, David: Kansas City Star
Goldstein, Steven: MarketWatch
Golle, Vince: Bloomberg News
Goller, Howard Scot: Thomson Reuters
Gomez, Alan: USA Today

MEMBERS ENTITLED TO ADMISSION—Continued

Gomez, Sergio: El Tiempo
Gomez, Shawn: Associated Press
Gomi, Lisa: Yomiuri Shimbun
Goodridge, Elizabeth: New York Times
Gordon, Greg: McClatchy Newspapers
Gordon, Marcy: Associated Press
Gordon, Michael: New York Times
Gorman, Siobhan: Wall Street Journal
Gossman, Jean: LRP Publications
Grant, David: Christian Science Monitor
Grasgreen, Allie: Inside Higher Ed
Graves, Lucia: Huffington Post
Greeley, Brendan: Bloomberg News
Green, Andrew: Center for Public Integrity
Green, Anneke: Washington Times
Green, Laura: The Palm Beach Post
Greenberg, Brigitte: Bloomberg News
Greene, Robert: Bloomberg News
Greene, Ronnie: Center for Public Integrity
Greiling Keane, Angela: Bloomberg News
Gresko, Jessica: Associated Press
Grier, Peter: Christian Science Monitor
Griesemer, Becca: Scripps Howard News Service
Griffith, Stephanie: Agence France-Presse
Grim, Ryan: Huffington Post
Grimaldi, James: Washington Post
Grishman, Peggy: Kaiser Health News
Groer, Anne: Freelance
Groppe, Maureen: Gannett Washington Bureau
Grossman, Elaine: National Journal Group's Global Security Newswire
Gruenwald, Juliana: National Journal Daily
Guensburg, Carol: Scripps Howard News Service
Guevara, Marina: Center for Public Integrity
Guevara, Tomas: El Diario de Hoy
Gugarats, Haik: Argus Media
Guggenheim, Ken: Associated Press
Guihaire, Edouard: Agence France-Presse
Gulino, Denny: Market News International
Gully, Andrew: Agence France-Presse
Gutman, Roy: McClatchy Newspapers
Gyllenhaal, Anders: McClatchy Newspapers
Ha, Taewon: Korea Dong-A Ilbo
Hackett, Laurie: Scripps Howard News Service
Hager, George: USA Today
Hall, Kevin: McClatchy Newspapers
Hall, Mimi: USA Today
Hallock, Kimberly: Bloomberg News
Hallow, Ralph: Washington Times
Halsey, Ashley: Washington Post
Hamann, Carlos: Agence France-Presse
Hamburger, Thomas: Los Angeles Times
Hamby, Chris: Center for Public Integrity
Hamilton, Jesse: Bloomberg News
Hamilton, Martha: St. Petersburg Times
Hampton, Olivia: Agence France-Presse
Hananel, Sam: Associated Press
Handley, Paul: Agence France-Presse
Hanson, Clayton: Congressional Quarterly
Haque, Fahima: Main Justice
Harder, Amy: National Journal Daily
Harding, Robin: Financial Times
Hargrove, Thomas: Scripps Howard News Service
Harnden, Toby: London Daily Telegraph
Harper, Jennifer: Washington Times
Harper, Jonathan: Asahi Shimbun
Harris, Gardiner: New York Times
Harris, Mike: Washington Times
Harrison, David: Congressional Quarterly
Hart, Alexander: Congressional Quarterly
Hart, Dan: Bloomberg News
Hartson, Merrill: Associated Press
Haruki, Kazuhiro: Kyodo News
Hathaway, Ian: Bloomberg News
Hattem, Julian: Yomiuri Shimbun
Hawkings, David: Congressional Quarterly
Hayakawa, Toshiyuki: Sekai Nippo
Hayashi, Hiromasa: Kyodo News
Hayden, Kathleen: Bloomberg News
Hazar, Hasan: Turkiye Daily
Healy, James: USA Today
Healy, Robert: Congressional Quarterly
Heath, Brad: USA Today
Heath, David: Center for Public Integrity
Heavey, Susan: Thomson Reuters
Hedgpeth, Dana: Washington Post
Hefling, Kimberly: Associated Press
Helderman, Rosalind: Washington Post
Heller, Marc: Watertown Daily Times
Hendel, Caitlin: Congressional Quarterly
Henderson, Celia Nell: Wall Street Journal
Henderson, Gregory: Associated Press
Henderson, Nia-Malika: Washington Post
Hendrie, Paul: Congressional Quarterly
Hennessey, Kathleen: Los Angeles Times
Henriksson, Karin: Svenska Dagbladet
Henry, Devin: MinnPost
Henry, Kellen: Bloomberg News
Herb, Jeremy: Minneapolis Star Tribune
Hernandez, Jose: El Universal
Hernandez, Raymond: New York Times
Herrmann, Frank: Rheinische Post
Hersh, Joshua: Daily (The)
Herszenhorn, David: New York Times
Hesse, Monica: Washington Post
Hetherington, Kells: Daily Caller
Hiar, Corbin: Center for Public Integrity
Hicken, Jospeh: Bloomberg News
Hickey, Neil: Wall Street Journal
Hicks, Amanda: Congressional Quarterly
Higgins, Sean: Investor's Business Daily
Higham, Scott: Washington Post
Hill, Patrice: Washington Times
Hill, Robb: Congressional Quarterly
Hilsenrath, David: Washington Post

MEMBERS ENTITLED TO ADMISSION—Continued

Hilsenrath, Jon: Wall Street Journal
Hines, Nico: London Times
Hinton, Christopher: MarketWatch
Hinton, Earl: Associated Press
Hisadome, Shinichi: Tokyo Chunichi Shimbun
Ho, William: Dow Jones / Wall Street Journal
Hobson, Margaret: Congressional Quarterly
Hodge, Nathan: Wall Street Journal
Hoffecker, Leslie: Bloomberg News
Hoffman, Brian: Associated Press
Hoffman, Lisa: Scripps Howard News Service
Hogberg, David: Investor's Business Daily
Holland, Jesse: Associated Press
Holland, Steve: Thomson Reuters
Holly, Christopher: Energy Daily
Holmes, Allan: Bloomberg News
Holzer, Jessica: Dow Jones / Wall Street Journal
Holzer, Linda: Gannett Washington Bureau
Homan, Timothy: Bloomberg News
Honore, Hugues: Agence France-Presse
Hook, Janet: Wall Street Journal
Hopkins, Cheyenne: American Banker
Horowitz, Jason: Washington Post
Hortobagyi, Monica: USA Today
Horwich, Lee: USA Today
Horwitz, Sari: Washington Post
Hosenball, Mark: Thomson Reuters
Hotakainen, Rob: McClatchy Newspapers
House, Billy: National Journal Daily
Hoy, Anne: Congressional Quarterly
Hoyt, Clark: Bloomberg News
Hsu, Spencer: Washington Post
Hu, Zep: Central News Agency
Huetteman, Emmarie: New York Times
Huey-Burns, Caitlin: Real Clear Politics
Hughes, Brian: Washington Examiner
Hughes, John: Bloomberg News
Hughes, Paul: Bloomberg News
Hughes, Siobhan: Dow Jones / Wall Street Journal
Hughey, Ann: Bloomberg News
Hulse, Carl: New York Times
Hultman, Tamela: AllAfrica.com
Hume, Lynn: Bond Buyer
Hummer, Matthew: Bloomberg News
Hunley, Johnathan: News and Messenger
Hunt, Albert: Bloomberg News
Hunt, Terence: Associated Press
Hunter, Kathleen: Bloomberg News
Hurst, Nathan: Congressional Quarterly
Hurst, Steven: Associated Press
Huttinger, Robert: Congressional Quarterly
Hwang, Jae Hoon: Yonhap News Agency
Hyong, Hwang Doo: Yonhap News Agency
Iafolla, Robert: Los Angeles Daily Journal
Ignatiou, Michail: Ethnos Greece
Ikeuchi, Takao: Kyodo News
Ilustre, Josefina: Malaya
Im, Hyuk: Chosun Ilbo
Ingram, Ronnell: Bloomberg News
Insinna, Valerie: Tokyo Chunichi Shimbun
Inuzuka, Yosuke: Sankei Shimbun
Irons, John: Congressional Quarterly
Ishikawa, Junko: Jiji Press
Israel, Joashua: Center for Public Integrity
Issenberg, Sasha: Boston Globe
Itkowitz, Colby: Allentown Morning Call
Ito, Hiroshi: Asahi Shimbun
Ito, Kosuke: Jiji Press
Ivanovich, David: Argus Media
Ives-Halperin, Benton: Congressional Quarterly
Ivory, Danielle: Bloomberg News
Iwamoto, Masako: Nikkei
Iwata, Nakahiro: Tokyo Chunichi Shimbun
Jackler, Rosalind: USA Today
Jackson, David: USA Today
Jackson, Flavia: Bloomberg News
Jackson, Henry: Associated Press
Jackson, Herbert: Record (Bergen County, NJ)
Jackson-Randall, Maya: Dow Jones / Wall Street Journal
Jacobson, Louis: St. Petersburg Times
Jacoby, Mary: Main Justice
Jalonick, Mary Clare: Associated Press
Jamieson, Dave: Huffington Post
Jamrisko, Michelle: Bloomberg News
Jan, Tracy: Boston Globe
Jang, Gwang Ik: Maeil Business Newspaper
Jansen, Bart: Gannett Washington Bureau
Jelinek, Pauline: Associated Press
Jenks, Paul: Congressional Quarterly
Jennings, Angel: Wall Street Journal
Jha, Lalit: India Press Trust
Joachim, David: New York Times
Johnson, Amanda: Congressional Quarterly
Johnson, Glen: Boston Globe
Johnson, Keith: Wall Street Journal
Johnson, Kendra: Scripps Howard News Service
Johnson, Kevin: USA Today
Johnson, Robert: Thomson Reuters
Johnson, Sandy: Center for Public Integrity
Johnston, Nicholas: Bloomberg News
Jones, Kasey: Associated Press
Jordan, Alethea: Gannett Washington Bureau
Jordan, Bryant: Military.com
Jourdain, Stephane: Agence France-Presse
Jourdier, Marc: Agence France-Presse
Joy, Patricia: Congressional Quarterly
Joyce, Daniel: Bloomberg News
Ju, Hui: China Youth Daily
Juarex, Berenice: Bloomberg News
Junius, Dennis: Associated Press
Kaiho, Masato: Mainichi Shimbun
Kaiser, Robert: Washington Post
Kakiuchi, Kosuke: Sankei Shimbun
Kaldunski, Benjamin: Argus Media

MEMBERS ENTITLED TO ADMISSION—Continued

Kamalick, Joseph: ICIS News
Kamen, Al: Washington Post
Kampeas, Ron: Jewish Telegraphic Agency
Kane, Paul: Washington Post
Kaper, Stacy Lynn: National Journal Daily
Karam, Joyce: Al-Hayat
Karasmeighan, Elizabeth: Bloomberg News
Kash, Wyatt: AOL Government
Kastner, Kevin: Market News International
Kasuya, Jacquelyn: Mainichi Shimbun
Kato, Takefumi: Jiji Press
Katsuda, Toshihiko: Asahi Shimbun
Katz, Ian: Bloomberg News
Keefe, Stephen: Nikkei
Kell, Amanda: Associated Press
Kellman Blazar, Laurie: Associated Press
Kelly, Dennis: USA Today
Kelly, Erin: Gannett Washington Bureau
Kemper, Bob: Washington Examiner
Kendall, Brent: Dow Jones / Wall Street Journal
Kenen, Joanne: Congressional Quarterly
Kennard, Matthew: Financial Times
Kennedy, Kelly: USA Today
Kercheval, Nancy: Bloomberg News
Kerr, Jennifer: Associated Press
Kertes, Noella: Congressional Quarterly
Kessler, Aaron: Detroit Free Press
Kessler, Glenn: Washington Post
Khaledi, Kayvon: Congressional Quarterly
Khatami, Elham: Congressional Quarterly
Kiefer, Francine: Christian Science Monitor
Kiely, Kathy: National Journal Daily
Kildea, Joseph: Daily Caller
Kilian, Martin: Tages Anzeiger
Kim, Angela: Congressional Quarterly
Kim, Anne: Congressional Quarterly
Kim, Hong Yeol: Korea Economic Daily
Kim, Jungwook: Joongang Ilbo
Kim, Myung Ho: Kukmin Daily
Kim, Sang-Yeon: Seoul Shimbun
Kimura, Kazuhiro: Kyodo News
King, Ledyard: Gannett Washington Bureau
King, Neil: Wall Street Journal
King, Peter: Congressional Quarterly
Kingery, Allison: Tokyo Chunichi Shimbun
Kipling, Bogdan: Kipling News Service
Kirchgaessner, Stephanie: Financial Times
Kirsanov, Dmitry: Itar-Tass News Agency
Kishi, Masayuki: Hokkaido Shimbun
Kishida, Yoshi: Jiji Press
Kittross, David: LRP Publications
Klapper, Bradley: Associated Press
Klein, Allison: Washington Post
Klein, Philip: Washington Examiner
Klimasinska, Katarzyna: Bloomberg News
Klimek, Eric: Associated Press
Kluever, Reymer: Sueddeutsche Zeitung
Kniazkov, Maxim: Agence France-Presse
Knott, Alex: Congressional Quarterly
Knowlton, Brian: International Herald Tribune
Knox, Olivier: Agence France-Presse
Kobayashi, Toshiya: Akahata
Koconis, Benjamin: Merger Market of Financial Times
Koenig, Robert: St. Louis Beacon
Koff, Stephen: Cleveland Plain Dealer
Kolowich, Steve: Inside Higher Ed
Komarow, Steven: Bloomberg News
Komori, Yoshihisa: Sankei Shimbun
Konjevoda, Jerry: Thomson Financial News
Korade, Matthew: Congressional Quarterly
Koring, Paul: Globe and Mail
Kornblut, Anne: Washington Post
Korte, Gregory: USA Today
Kosova, Weston: Washington Post
Koss, Geof: Congressional Quarterly
Kovach, Kaitlin: Congressional Quarterly
Kowalski, Alexander: Bloomberg News
Kramer, Reed: AllAfrica.com
Kranish, Michael: Boston Globe
Krauss, Joseph: Agence France-Presse
Kravitz, Derek: Associated Press
Krawzak, Paul: Congressional Quarterly
Kredo, Adam: Jewish Telegraphic Agency
Kreisher, Otto: National Journal Daily
Krieger, Hilary: Jerusalem Post
Krieger, Kim: Argus Media
Kucinich, Jacqueline: USA Today
Kuhnhenn, Jim: Associated Press
Kulkarni, Shefali: Kaiser Health News
Kumar, Arun: Indo-Asian News Service
Kumar, Dinesh: Communications Daily
Kummer, Luke: Daily (The)
Kurose, Yoshinari: Yomiuri Shimbun
Kwon, Taeho: Hankyoreh Daily
Labbe, Theola: Washington Post
Labriny, Azeddine: Saudi Press Agency
LaFranchi, Howard: Christian Science Monitor
Lakashmanan, Indira: Bloomberg News
Lake, Eli: Washington Times
Lamb, Celia: Argus Media
Lamb, Christina: Sunday Times of London
Lambert, Lisa: Thomson Reuters
Lambrecht, William: St. Louis Post-Dispatch
Lancaster, Marc: Washington Times
Landay, Jonathan: McClatchy Newspapers
Landers, James: Dallas Morning News
Landers, Peter: Wall Street Journal
Landler, Mark: New York Times
Lane, Kamala: Communications Daily
Langan, Michael: Agence France-Presse
Lange, Jason: Thomson Reuters
Lanman, Scott: Bloomberg News
Lanteaume, Sylvie: Agence France-Presse
Lardner, Richard: Associated Press

MEMBERS ENTITLED TO ADMISSION—Continued

Laris, Michael: Washington Post
Larkin, Catherine: Bloomberg News
Laurent, Anne: Bloomberg News
Lauter, David: Los Angeles Times
Lawder, David: Thomson Reuters
Lawrence, Jill: Daily Beast
Lawrence, Sarah: Congressional Quarterly
Layton, Lyndsey: Washington Post
Leahy, Michael: Washington Post
Leal, Lucia: EFE News Services
Leary, Alex: St. Petersburg Times
Lebling, Madonna: Washington Post
Lederman, Douglas: Inside Higher Ed
Lee, Byonghan: Korea Times
Lee, Carol: Wall Street Journal
Lee, Chang-Yul: Korea Times
Lee, Don: Los Angeles Times
Lee, Hae Young: Yonhap News Agency
Lee, Jong: Korea Times
Lee, Matthew: Associated Press
Lee, Sung Eun (Grace): Korea Daily
Lee, Yong: Korea Daily
Leeds, Charles: Washington Post News Service with Bloomberg News
Lefkow, David: Agence France-Presse
Leger, Donna: USA Today
Leiby, Richard: Washington Post
Lengell, Sean: Washington Times
Leonard, Kimberly: Center for Public Integrity
Leonatti, Andrew: National Journal Daily
Lerer, Lisa: Bloomberg News
Lerman, David: Bloomberg News
Lesnes, Corine: Le Monde
Lesniewski, Niels: Congressional Quarterly
Lesparre, Michael: Voterama in Congress
Lester, William: Associated Press
Leubsdorf, Carl: Dallas Morning News
Lever, Robert: Agence France-Presse
Levey, Noam: Los Angeles Times
Levin, Adam: Congressional Quarterly
Levin, Alan: USA Today
Levinson, Alexis: Daily Caller
Levinson, Robert: Bloomberg News
Levitz, Jennifer: Wall Street Journal
Lewis, Charles: Hearst Newspapers
Lewis, Finlay: Congressional Quarterly
Lewis, Katherine: Freelance
Lewis, Matthew: Daily Caller
Li, Zhengxin: China Economic Daily
Liao Han Yuan, Tony: Taiwan Central News Agency
Lichtblau, Eric: New York Times
Liebert, Larry: Bloomberg News
Lightman, David: McClatchy Newspapers
Lin, Betty: World Journal
Lin, Yu: Xinhua News Agency
Lincoln, Erik: Center for Public Integrity
Lindeman, Eric: Energy Daily
Linnane, Jacqueline: Congressional Quarterly
Lipari, James: Associated Press
Liptak, Adam: New York Times
Lipton, Eric: New York Times
Little, Walter: Bloomberg News
Litvan, Laura: Bloomberg News
Liu, Kuen-Yuan: Taiwan Central News Agency
Liu, Lina: Xinhua News Agency
Liu, Yung-Hsiang: United Daily News
Lobe, James: Inter Press Service
Lobsenz, George: Energy Daily
Lochhead, Carolyn: San Francisco Chronicle
Lomax, Simon: Bloomberg News
Londres, Eduardo: Bloomberg News
Longo, Daniel: Asahi Shimbun
Lopez Zamorano, Jose: Notimex Mexican News Agency
Loubette, Celine: Agence France-Presse
Louis, Meera: Bloomberg News
Lowe, Christian: Military.com
Lowy, Joan: Associated Press
Lucas, Elizabeth: Center for Public Integrity
Lucas, Tammy: Congressional Quarterly
Lynch, David: Bloomberg News
Lynch, Sarah: Thomson Reuters
Lytle, Tamara: Freelance
Macaron, Joe: Kuwait News Agency
Macaskill, Ewen: London Guardian
MacInnis, Laura: Thomson Reuters
MacPherson, John: Bloomberg News
MacPherson, Robert: Agence France-Presse
Madden, Ruth: MarketWatch
Magner, Mike: National Journal Daily
Mahabir, Karen: Associated Press
Maher, Aya: Asahi Shimbun
Majmudar, Nishad: Bloomberg News
Make, Jonathan: Communications Daily
Malandain, Lucile: Agence France-Presse
Malenic, Maria: Defense Daily
Maler, Sandra: Thomson Reuters
Malhotra, Sunil: Associated Press
Malloy, Daniel: Atlanta Journal Constitution
Mandel, Kristin: Thomson Reuters
Mann, Simon: Sydney Morning Herald
Mann, William: Associated Press
Mannion, James: Agence France-Presse
Marcus, Ruth: Washington Post
Marcy, Jessica: Kaiser Health News
Marfil, Jude: Wall Street Journal
Margasak, Lawrence: Associated Press
Margetta, Robert: Congressional Quarterly
Marimow, Ann: Washington Post
Marino-Nachison, David: Washington Post
Marklein, Mary Beth: USA Today
Markoe, Lauren: Religion News Service
Markon, Jerome: Washington Post
Marlowe, Lara: Irish Times
Marschall, Christophe: Der Tagesspiegel

MEMBERS ENTITLED TO ADMISSION—Continued

Marsh, Joanna: Argus Media
Marsh, Wendell: Thomson Reuters
Marshall, Stephen: USA Today
Martel, Ned: Washington Post
Martin, Eric: Bloomberg News
Martin, Gary: San Antonio Express-News
Mascaro, Lisa: Los Angeles Times
Mason, Jeff: Thomson Reuters
Mason, Melanie: Los Angeles Times
Masterson, Lauren: Argus Media
Mathes, Michael: Agence France-Presse
Matthews, Christopher: Main Justice
Matthews, Mark: Orlando Sentinel
Mattingly, Philip: Bloomberg News
Mauriello, Tracie: Pittsburgh Post-Gazette
May, Caroline: Daily Caller
Maynard, Michael: MarketWatch
Mazyck, Jamal: Bloomberg News
Mazzetti, Mark: New York Times
McAuliff, Michael: New York Daily News
McCabe, Scott: Washington Examiner
McCalmont, Lucy: Sunday Times of London
McCarthy, Meghan: National Journal Daily
McCarthy, Mike: German Press Agency-DPA
McConnell, William: Daily Deal
McFeatters, Dale: Scripps Howard News Service
McGarry, Brendan: Bloomberg News
McGaughy, Lauren: Asahi Shimbun
McGeehan, Anna: Congressional Quarterly
McGinley, Laurie: Kaiser Health News
McGough, Michael: Los Angeles Times
McGrane, Victoria: Wall Street Journal
McGreal, Chris: London Guardian
McGregor, Richard: Financial Times
McKendry, Ian: Market News International
McKenna, Brendan: RTT News
McKinnon, John: Wall Street Journal
McLaughlin, Seth: Washington Times
McManus, Doyle: Los Angeles Times
McMillan, Traci: Bloomberg News
McNeil, Margaret: MarketWatch
McPike, Erin: Real Clear Politics
McQuillan, Mark: Bloomberg News
McQuillen, William: Bloomberg News
Meadows, Clifton: New York Times
Meckler, Laura: Wall Street Journal
Meehan, Brian: Bloomberg News
Meeks, David: Los Angeles Times
Mehta, Aaron: Center for Public Integrity
Meinert, Peer: German Press Agency-DPA
Melvin, Jasmin: Thomson Reuters
Memoli, Michael: Tribune Company
Mercer, Marsha: Mercer Media
Merida, Kevin: Washington Post
Mertens, Margaret: Bloomberg News
Meszoly, Robin: Bloomberg News
Meyers, David: Congressional Quarterly
Michaels, David: Dallas Morning News
Michaels, Jim: USA Today
Middleton, Chris: Bloomberg News
Mierke, Marco: German Press Agency-DPA
Miga, Andrew: Associated Press
Mikes, Zoltan: World Business Press
Milbank, Dana: Washington Post
Militana, Tait: Congressional Quarterly
Miller, Emily: Washington Times
Miller, Greg: Los Angeles Times
Miller, Kathleen: Bloomberg News
Miller, Reuben: Merger Market of Financial Times
Miller, Richard: Bloomberg News
Miller, Steven: New York Post
Millikin, David: Agence France-Presse
Mills, Betty: Griffin-Larrabee News Service
Mills, Michael: Congressional Quarterly
Min, Xiong: 21st Century Business Herald
Mingote, Jose Manuel: EFE News Services
Mitchell, Joshua: Dow Jones / Wall Street Journal
Miyazaki, Masaharu: Nishi-Nippon Shimbun
Miyazawa, Kaoru: Jiji Press
Mochizuki, Hirotsugu: Asahi Shimbun
Mohammed, Arshad: Thomson Reuters
Molotsky, Irvin: National Journal Daily
Moltz, Andrew: Inside Higher Ed
Monahan, Kenneth: Bloomberg News
Monge, Yolanda: El Pais
Montet, Virginie: Agence France-Presse
Montgomery, David: Washington Post
Montgomery, Lori: Washington Post
Moody, Chris: Daily Caller
Moore, Dennis: Bond Buyer
Morello, Carol: Washington Post
Morgan, David: Thomson Reuters
Morgan, Jon: Bloomberg News
Morris, James: Center for Public Integrity
Morrison, James: Washington Times
Morton, Joseph: Omaha World-Herald
Moss, Daniel: Bloomberg News
Mott, Gregory: Bloomberg News
Mozgovaya, Natasha: Haaretz Daily
Mufson, Steven: Washington Post
Mulero, Eugene: Congressional Quarterly
Mullen, Kent: Asahi Shimbun
Mulligan, John: Providence Journal
Mulligan, Megan: Daily Caller
Mullins, Brody: Wall Street Journal
Mulrine, Anna: Christian Science Monitor
Mundy, Alicia: Wall Street Journal
Munoz, Carlo: Defense Daily
Munro, Neil: Daily Caller
Murayama, Yusuke: Asahi Shimbun
Murphy, Kathleen: Congressional Quarterly
Murphy, Patricia: Daily Beast
Murray, Sara: Wall Street Journal
Murray, William: Oil Daily

MEMBERS ENTITLED TO ADMISSION—Continued

Mutikani, Lucia: Thomson Reuters
Myers, Bill: Communications Daily
Myers, Jim: Tulsa World
Myers, Michael: Myers News Service
Myers, Steven: New York Times
N'Diaye, Yali: Market News International
Nafzlger, Kevin: Merger Market of Financial Times
Nahmias, Melinda: Congressional Quarterly
Nail, Dawson: Communications Daily
Naing, Eric: Congressional Quarterly
Nakajima, Kentaro: Yomiuri Shimbun
Nakamura, David: Washington Post
Nakashima, Ellen: Washington Post
Nakaya, Yuji: Kyodo News
Nakayama, Shin: Nikkei
Namekata, Shiko: Asahi Shimbun
Nasiripour, Shahien: Huffington Post
Nayak, Malathi: Thomson Reuters
Nayar, Krishnan: Calcutta Telegraph
Neergaard, Lauran: Associated Press
Nelson, Eliot: Huffington Post
Nelson, Libby: Inside Higher Ed
Nelson, Steven: Daily Caller
Neubauer, Chuck: Washington Times
Newman, Christopher: Argus Media
Nguyen, Tina: Daily Caller
Nicholas, Peter: Los Angeles Times
Nichols, Hans: Bloomberg News
Nielsen, David: Scripps Howard News Service
Nishimura, Hiroshi: Akahata
Niskakangas, Tuomas: Helsingin Sanomat
Nixon, Ron: New York Times
Njuguna, Wangui: LRP Publications
Nkansah, E. Roy: Congressional Quarterly
Noel, Essex: Thomson Reuters
Noone, Dennis: Gannett Washington Bureau
Norington, Brad: Australian
Norman, Jane: Congressional Quarterly
Norton, C. JoAnne: Bloomberg News
Nshom, Vimombi: IFR Markets
Nuckols, Ben: Associated Press
Nutting, Rex: MarketWatch
Nylen, Leah: Bloomberg News
O'Callaghan, John: Thomson Reuters
O'Connor, Patrick: Wall Street Journal
O'Harrow, Robert: Washington Post
O'Keefe, Edward: Washington Post
O'Neal, Glenn: USA Today
O'Reilly, II, Joseph: Bloomberg News
O'Sullivan, James: National Journal Daily
O'Toole, Molly: Thomson Reuters
Odion-Esene, Braimoh: Market News International
Ogata, Toshihiko: Asahi Shimbun
Ogawa, Satoshi: Yomiuri Shimbun
Ogle, Alexander: Agence France-Presse
Ohlemacher, Stephen: Associated Press
Oishi, Itaru: Nikkei
Okada, Akihiro: Yomiuri Shimbun
Okamoto, Michiro: Yomiuri Shimbun
Olchowy, Mark: Associated Press
Oliphant, James: Los Angeles Times
Oliveri, Frank: Congressional Quarterly
Omdal, Sven: Stavanger Aftenblad
Orndorff Troyan, Mary: Birmingham News
Orol, Ronald: MarketWatch
Oshirabe, Masakuni: Nikkei
Ostermann, Dietmar: Frankfurter Rundschau
Ota, Alan: Congressional Quarterly
Ourlian, Robert: Wall Street Journal
Overberg, Paul: USA Today
Pace, David: Associated Press
Pagan, Louis: Associated Press
Page, Clarence: Chicago Tribune
Page, Susan: USA Today
Pain, John: Associated Press
Pakhomov, Alexander: Itar-Tass News Agency
Palacios, Albert: Bloomberg News
Paletta, Damian: Wall Street Journal
Palmer, Doug: Thomson Reuters
Palomo, Elvira: EFE News Services
Paltrow, Scot: Thomson Reuters
Pandi, Nicolas: Jiji Press
Pappas, Alex: Daily Caller
Parisi, Christina: Congressional Quarterly
Parisse, Emmanuel: Agence France-Presse
Park, Jungbin: Yonhap News Agency
Park, Kwang Duk: Korea Times
Park, Sang Hyun: Yonhap News Agency
Parks, Daniel: Bloomberg News
Parsons, Christi: Chicago Tribune
Patel, Anjali: LRP Publications
Patel, Julie: Sun-Sentinel
Patrick, Jarondakie: McClatchy Newspapers
Patterson, Scott: Wall Street Journal
Peake, Daniel: Congressional Quarterly
Pear, Robert: New York Times
Pelofsky, Jeremy: Thomson Reuters
Pena, Maria: EFE News Services
Penjarla, Nadikant: Center for Public Integrity
Pennington, Matthew: Associated Press
Pennix, Timothy: Bloomberg News
Perez, Evan: Wall Street Journal
Perine, Keith: Congressional Quarterly
Perrone, Matthew: Associated Press
Pershing, Ben: Washington Post
Petak, Lisa: New York Times
Peters, William: Argus Media
Peterson, Hayley: Washington Examiner
Peterson, Kristina: Dow Jones / Wall Street Journal
Peterson, Molly: Bloomberg News
Phelps, Timothy: Los Angeles Times
Philip, Catherine: London Times
Phillips, Michael: Wall Street Journal
Philpott, Thomas: Military Update

MEMBERS ENTITLED TO ADMISSION—Continued

Pickard-Cambridge, Claire: Argus Media
Picket, Kerry: Washington Times
Pickler, Nedra: Associated Press
Pincus, Walter: Washington Post
Pingolt, Margaret: Cronkite News Service
Pisani, Silvia: La Nacion
Plocek, Joseph: Market News International
Plungis, Jeff: Bloomberg News
Poe, Emily: Congressional Quarterly
Politi, James: Financial Times
Pollard, Sonya: Bloomberg News
Poor, Robert: Daily Caller
Pope, Charles: Oregonian
Potter, Ben: Austrailian Financial Review
Powell, Stewart: Hearst Newspapers
Power, Stephen: Wall Street Journal
Poyrazlar, Elcin: Cumhuriyet
Preciphs, Joi: Bloomberg News
Price, Deborah: Detroit News
Przybyla, Heidi: Bloomberg News
Puente, Maria: USA Today
Pugh, Anthony: McClatchy Newspapers
Purce, Melinda: Associated Press
Purdy, Jamisha: Congressional Quarterly
Putman, Eileen: Associated Press
Puzzanghera, James: Los Angeles Times
Qiang, Zou: China Legal Daily
Quek, Tracy: Singapore Straits Times
Quemener, Tangi: Agence France-Presse
Quigley, Joan: Bond Buyer
Quinn, Andrew: Thomson Reuters
Quintanilla, Eloise: Christian Science Monitor
Raasch, Charles: Gannett Washington Bureau
Rabechault, Matthieu: Agence France-Presse
Radnofsky, Louise: Wall Street Journal
Raimon, Marcelo: ANSA Italian News Agency
Rajagopalan, Sethuraman: Pioneer (India)
Rajghatta, Chidanand: Times of India
Ramadan, Wafik: L'Orient-Le Jour
Ramonas, Andrew: Main Justice
Rampton, Roberta: Thomson Reuters
Ran, Jordan: Kaiser Health News
Ran, Wei: Xinhua News Agency
Rankin, Robert: McClatchy Newspapers
Raphaelle, Picard: Agence France-Presse
Rapp, David: Bloomberg News
Rascoe, Ayesha: Thomson Reuters
Rastello, Sandrine: Bloomberg News
Ratnam, Gopal: Bloomberg News
Raum, Thomas: Associated Press
Ray, Eric: Congressional Quarterly
Reback, Sanford: Bloomberg News
Reber, Paticia: German Press Agency-DPA
Recio, Maria: Fort Worth Star-Telegram
Reddy, Sudeep: Wall Street Journal
Reed, John: Military.com
Rehrmann, Laura: Gannett Washington Bureau
Reichard, John: Congressional Quarterly
Rein, Lisa: Washington Post
Ren, Haijun: Xinhua News Agency
Reyes, Eli: Washington Post
Reynolds, Maura: Bloomberg News
Ricci, Andrea: Thomson Reuters
Richardson, Betty: Congressional Quarterly
Richey, Warren: Christian Science Monitor
Richter, Joseph: Bloomberg News
Richter, Paul: Los Angeles Times
Richwine, Lisa: Thomson Reuters
Rickett, Keith: Associated Press
Rickman, Jonathan: Energy Daily
Riddell, Kelly: Bloomberg News
Riggs, Michael: Daily Caller
Riley, Kim: LRP Publications
Riley, Lauren: Saudi Press Agency
Riley, Michael: Bloomberg News
Riskind, Jonathan: Portland Press Herald
Rizzo, Katherine: Bloomberg News
Roarty, Alex: National Journal Daily
Robb, Gregory: MarketWatch
Roberts, James: Congressional Quarterly
Roberts, Roxanne: Washington Post
Robertson, Reiko: Kumamoto Nichinichi Shimbun
Robinson, Eugene: Washington Post
Robinson, James: Los Angeles Times
Robinson, John: Defense Daily
Rocco, Peter: Congressional Quarterly
Rogge, Joachim: Westdeutsche Allgemeine
Rohner, Mark: Bloomberg News
Roig-Franzia, Manuel: Washington Post
Romano, Lois: Washington Post
Roosevelt, Ann: Defense Daily
Rose, Matthew: Wall Street Journal
Rose, Stephen: Bloomberg News
Rosen, James: McClatchy Newspapers
Rosenberg, Carol: McClatchy Newspapers
Rosenkrantz, Holly: Bloomberg News
Ross, Sonya: Associated Press
Roth, Bennett: Bloomberg News
Rowland, Christopher: Boston Globe
Rowland, Kara: Washington Times
Rowley, James: Bloomberg News
Roy, Debarati: Bloomberg News
Ruane, Michael: Washington Post
Rubin, Richard: Bloomberg News
Rubio, Jennifer: Congressional Quarterly
Rucker, Philip: Washington Post
Ruf, Renzo: Aargauer Zeitung
Rulon Herman, Malia: Gannett Washington Bureau
Runningen, Roger: Bloomberg News
Rutherford, Emelie: Defense Daily
Ryan, Timothy: Thomson Reuters
Rye, Brian: Bloomberg News
Sacks, Michael: Huffington Post
Sadeqi, Sherouq: Kuwait News Agency

MEMBERS ENTITLED TO ADMISSION—Continued

Saito, Mari: Thomson Reuters
Saito, Nobuhiro: Mainichi Shimbun
Salant, Jonathan: Bloomberg News
Salcedo, Michele: Associated Press
Salmeron, Marvin: Bloomberg News
Samukawa, Akira: Kyodo News
Sanchez, Humberto: National Journal Daily
Sandler, Michael: Associated Press
Sandoval Palos, Ricardo: Center for Public Integrity
Sands, David: Washington Times
Sands, Kenneth: Bloomberg News
Sanger, David: New York Times
Santini, Jean-Louis: Agence France-Presse
Sasaki, Rui: Sankei Shimbun
Savage, Charlie: New York Times
Savage, David: Los Angeles Times
Scally, William: William Scally Reports
Schank, Adam: Congressional Quarterly
Schatz, Amy: Wall Street Journal
Schatz, Joseph: Congressional Quarterly
Scheuble, Kristy: Bloomberg News
Schmid, Randolph: Associated Press
Schmidt, Christophe: Agence France-Presse
Schmidt, Robert: Bloomberg News
Schmitt, Eric: New York Times
Schneider, Jodi: Bloomberg News
Schoenberg, Tom: Bloomberg News
Scholtes, Jennifer: Congressional Quarterly
Schoof, Renee: McClatchy Newspapers
Schouten, Fredreka: USA Today
Schram, Martin: Scripps Howard News Service
Schroeder, Robert: MarketWatch
Schulte, Brigid: Washington Post
Schulte, Fred: Center for Public Integrity
Schultz, Marisa: Detroit News
Schwab, Nicole: Washington Examiner
Schwed, Craig: Gannett Washington Bureau
Schweid, Barry: Associated Press
Scott, Heather: Market News International
Scully, Megan: National Journal Daily
Seib, Gerald: Wall Street Journal
Seibel, Mark: McClatchy Newspapers
Seligman, Lara: National Journal Daily
Selway, William: Bloomberg News
Selyukh, Alina: Thomson Reuters
Semler, Peter: Merger Market of Financial Times
Seong, Ghihong: Yonhap News Agency
Seper, Jerry: Washington Times
Serafini, Marilyn: Kaiser Health News
Serita, Shinichiro: Kyodo News
Serrano, Richard: Los Angeles Times
Seung-Gwon, Lee: Yonhap News Agency
Shah, Nikhil: Thomson Reuters
Shah, Sopen: Bloomberg News
Shalal-Esa, Andrea: Thomson Reuters
Shane, Scott: New York Times
Shanker, Thomas: New York Times
Shaw, John: Market News International
Shear, Michael: New York Times
Sheikh, Nezar: Saudi Press Agency
Shepard, Michael: Bloomberg News
Shepardson, David: Detroit News
Sherfinski, David: Washington Examiner
Sheridan, Kerry Colleen: Agence France-Presse
Sheridan, Mary Beth: Washington Post
Sherman, Mark: Associated Press
Sherry, Allison: Denver Post
Sherzai, Magan: Agence France-Presse
Shesgreen, Dierdre: Connecticut Mirror
Shields, Gerard: Baton Rouge Advocate
Shields, Mark: Creators Syndicate
Shields, Todd: Bloomberg News
Shiffman, John: Philadelphia Inquirer
Shimada, Akihiro: Tokyo Chunichi Shimbun
Shimada, Yuko: Kyodo News
Shirato, Keiichi: Mainichi Shimbun
Shuppy, Anne: Congressional Quarterly
Sichelman, Lew: United Media
Sidoti, Elizabeth: Associated Press
Silva, Mark: Bloomberg News
Simendinger, Alexis: Real Clear Politics
Simmons, Deborah: Washington Times
Simon, Richard: Los Angeles Times
Sippen, Anya: Scripps Howard News Service
Sisk, Richard: New York Daily News
Sisto, Carrie: Argus Media
Sitov, Andrei: Itar-Tass News Agency
Skarzenski, Ronald: New York Times
Skiba, Katherine: Chicago Tribune
Skotzko, Stacey: Congressional Quarterly
Slack, Donovan: Boston Globe
Slater, James: Agence France-Presse
Sloan, David: IFR Markets
Sloan, Steven: Bloomberg News
Smith, Donna: Thomson Reuters
Smith, Elliot: Bloomberg News
Smith, Jada: New York Times
Smith, Jeffrey: Washington Post
Smith, Josh: National Journal Daily
Smith, Lauren: Congressional Quarterly
Smith, Peter: Center for Public Integrity
Smith, Veronica: Agence France-Presse
Smith-Parker, Jennifer: Merger Market of Financial Times
Smolkin, Rachel: USA Today
Snell, Kelsey: National Journal Daily
Snider, Michael: USA Today
Sniffen, Michael: Associated Press
Snyder, Andrea: Bloomberg News
Snyder, Anne: New York Times
Snyder, Jim: Bloomberg News
Sobczyk, Joseph: Bloomberg News
Solomon, Deborah: Wall Street Journal
Solomon, John: Center for Public Integrity
Somashekhar, Sandhya: Washington Post

MEMBERS ENTITLED TO ADMISSION—Continued

Somerville, Glenn: Thomson Reuters
Song, Kyung: Seattle Times
Sonmez, Felicia: Washington Post
Southall, Ashley: New York Times
Sowdwer-Staley, Megan: Congressional Quarterly
Spang, Thomas: US-Report (Germany)
Spangler, Todd: Detroit Free Press
Sparshott, Jeffrey: Dow Jones / Wall Street Journal
Spence, Matthew: London Times
Spencer, Jim: Minneapolis Star Tribune
Spencer, Samuel: Smartgrid Today
Spillius, Alexander: London Daily Telegraph
Spivack, Miranda: Washington Post
Spolar, Christine: Bloomberg News
Stapleton, Stephanie: Kaiser Health News
Starks, Tim: Congressional Quarterly
Stech, Katherine: Dow Jones / Wall Street Journal
Stein, Robert: Washington Post
Stein, Sam: Huffington Post
Steinhauer, Jennifer: New York Times
Stempleman, Neil: Thomson Reuters
Stephens, Joe: Washington Post
Stephenson, Emily: Thomson Reuters
Stern, Linda: Thomson Reuters
Stern, Seth: Bloomberg News
Sternberg, Steve: USA Today
Sternberg, William: USA Today
Stevens, Patrick: Washington Times
Stevenson, Richard: New York Times
Stewart, Bruce: Sankei Shimbun
Stewart, Ian: Argus Media
Stewart, Nikita: Washington Post
Stewart, Phillip: Thomson Reuters
Stockman, Farah: Boston Globe
Stohr, Greg: Bloomberg News
Stolberg, Sheryl: New York Times
Stone, Andrea: AOL Government
Stone, Andrea: Huffington Post
Stone, Peter: Center for Public Integrity
Storey, William: New York Times
Stoughton, Stephenie: Bloomberg News
Stout, David: Main Justice
Strass, Nina: Associated Press
Strasser, Fred: Bloomberg News
Straw, Joseph: New York Daily News
Strobel, Warren: McClatchy Newspapers
Strohm, Chris: National Journal Daily
Stromberg, Stephen: Washington Post
Strong, Jonathan: Daily Caller
Strong, Thomas: Associated Press
Stuever, Hank: Washington Post
Stumme, Susan: Agence France-Presse
Sugimoto, Ichiro: Kyodo News
Sugita, Yushin: Kyodo News
Suhail, Adrienne: Asahi Shimbun
Sullivan, Andy: Thomson Reuters
Sullivan, Bartholomew: Scripps Howard News Service
Sullivan, Eileen: Associated Press
Sullivan, Gail: Congressional Quarterly
Sun, Lena: Washington Post
Supervielle, Ana Baron: Clarin
Superville, Darlene: Associated Press
Surniak, Greg: Congressional Quarterly
Surzhanskiy, Andrey: Itar-Tass News Agency
Sutherland, Tracy: Argus Media
Sweeney, Jeanne: LRP Publications
Sweet, Lynn: Chicago Sun-Times
Symes, Frances: Congressional Quarterly
Taborek, Nick: Bloomberg News
Tachino, Junji: Asahi Shimbun
Tackett, Michael: Bloomberg News
Taegyu, Lee: Hankook Ilbo
Takei, Toru: Kyodo News
Talev, Margaret: McClatchy Newspapers
Talley, Ian: Dow Jones / Wall Street Journal
Tandon, Shaun: Agence France-Presse
Tanis, Tolga: Hurriyet
Tanzi, Alex: Bloomberg News
Tate, Curtis: McClatchy Newspapers
Tavara, Santiago: Notimex Mexican News Agency
Taylor, Andrew: Associated Press
Taylor, Marisa: McClatchy Newspapers
Teinowitz, Ira: Daily Deal
Teitelbaum, Michael: Congressional Quarterly
Temple-West, Patrick: Bond Buyer
Terkel, Amanda: Huffington Post
Tessler, Joelle: Associated Press
Tetreault, Stephan: Stephens Media Group
Theobald, William: Gannett Washington Bureau
Theranger, Katherine: Bloomberg News
Thomas, Ken: Associated Press
Thomas, Richard: Voterama in Congress
Thomma, Steven: McClatchy Newspapers
Thompson, Cheryl: Washington Post
Thompson, Ginger: New York Times
Thompson, Krissah: Washington Post
Thompson, Marilyn: Washington Post
Tilove, Jonathan: New Orleans Times-Picayune
Timberg, Craig: Washington Post
Tiron, Roxana: Bloomberg News
Tokito, Mineko: Yomiuri Shimbun
Toloui-Semnani, Neda: Congressional Quarterly
Tomkin, Robert: Congressional Quarterly
Tompson, Trevor: Associated Press
Tomson, Bill: Dow Jones / Wall Street Journal
Toppo, Gregory: USA Today
Toroglu, Bariskan: Anatolia News Agency
Toroglu, Ozkul: Anatolia News Agency
Torres, Carlos: Bloomberg News
Torres, Craig: Bloomberg News
Torry, Jack: Columbus Dispatch
Tracy, Ryan: Dow Jones / Wall Street Journal
Tracy, Tennile: Dow Jones / Wall Street Journal
Tranausky, Todd: Argus Media

MEMBERS ENTITLED TO ADMISSION—Continued

Trescott, Jacqueline: Washington Post
Trindle, Jamila: Dow Jones / Wall Street Journal
Trottman, Melanie: Wall Street Journal
Tsao, Nadia: Liberty Times
Tsiatsiorkin, Kiryl: Associated Press
Tucker, Cynthia: Atlanta Journal Constitution
Tucker, Eric: Associated Press
Tucker, Geraldine: USA Today
Tucker, Neely: Washington Post
Tumulty, Brian: Gannett Washington Bureau
Tumulty, Karen: Washington Post
Turque, Bill: Washington Post
Tyson, Ann: Washington Post
Tyson, James: Bloomberg News
Ukman, Jason: Washington Post
Ullerup, Jorgen: Jyllands-Posten
Urano, Eri: Tokyo Chunichi Shimbun
Urban, Peter: Connecticut Post
Urdaneta, Diego: Agence France-Presse
Vadala, Gregory: Congressional Quarterly
Vaida, Bara: Kaiser Health News
Valery, Chantal: Agence France-Presse
Vallejo, Stephanie: Boston Globe
Van Nostrand, Jim: McClatchy Newspapers
Vanden Brook, Tom: USA Today
Vanderbilt, Sarah: Congressional Quarterly
Vedantam, Shankar: Washington Post
Vergano, Dan: USA Today
Vicini, James: Thomson Reuters
Vidal-Ly, Macarena: EFE News Services
Villegas, Andrew: Kaiser Health News
Vineys, Kevin: Associated Press
Viser, Matthew: Boston Globe
Viswanatha, Aruna: Main Justice
Vogel, Stephen: Washington Post
Vogt, Christophe: Agence France-Presse
Volcovici, Valerie: Thomson Reuters
Volpe, Paul: New York Times
Von Marschall, Christoph: Der Tagesspiegel
Vorman, Julie: Center for Public Integrity
Wack, Kevin: American Banker
Wagman, Robert: Newspaper Enterprise
Walcott, John: Bloomberg News
Wald, Matthew: New York Times
Walerius, Randolph: Bloomberg News
Walker, Emily: medpagetoday.com
Wallbank, Derek: Bloomberg News
Waller, Douglas: Bloomberg News
Wallsten, Peter: Washington Post
Walsh, Stephen: Bloomberg News
Walters, Anne: German Press Agency-DPA
Wan, William: Washington Post
Wang, Fengfeng: Xinhua News Agency
Wang, Yu-Ting: Communications Daily
Ward, Jon: Huffington Post
Warmbrodt, Zachary: Argus Media
Warminsky, Joseph: Congressional Quarterly
Warren, Timothy: Warren Communications News
Warrick, Joby: Washington Post
Waschinski, Gregor: Agence France-Presse
Waterman, Shaun: Washington Times
Watters, Susan: Fairchild Publications
Wayne, Alexander: Bloomberg News
Webber, Caitlin: Bloomberg News
Weber, Joseph: Washington Times
Weekes, Jr., Michael: Thomson Reuters
Wehrman, Jessica: Columbus Dispatch
Wei, Wang: Xinhua News Agency
Weiner, Joann: Bloomberg News
Weiner, Mark: Syracuse Post-Standard
Weiner, Rachel: Washington Post
Weinstein, Jamie: Daily Caller
Weir, Kytja: Washington Examiner
Weisman, Jonathan: Wall Street Journal
Weiss, Brian: Bloomberg News
Weiss, Miles: Bloomberg News
Welch, James: USA Today
Wellisz, Chris: Bloomberg News
Wells, Letitia: McClatchy Newspapers
Wells, Robert: Dow Jones / Wall Street Journal
Welter, Patrick: Frankfurter Allgemeine Zeitung
Werner, Erica: Associated Press
Wessel, David: Wall Street Journal
West, Paul: Los Angeles Times
Wetzstein, Cheryl: Washington Times
Weyl, Ben: Congressional Quarterly
White, Christian: Congressional Quarterly
White, Dina: Chicago Tribune
White, Gordon: Washington Telecommunications Services
White, Joseph: Wall Street Journal
White, Jr., Joseph: Associated Press
Whitelaw, Kevin: Congressional Quarterly
Whitesides, John: Thomson Reuters
Whitlock, Craig: Washington Post
Whitmire, Guy: Congressional Quarterly
Whittell, Giles: London Times
Whoriskey, Peter: Washington Post
Wiggins, Ovetta: Washington Post
Wilber, Del Quentin: Washington Post
Wilburn, Thomas: Congressional Quarterly
Williamson, Elizabeth: Wall Street Journal
Willis, Derek: New York Times
Willis, Robert: Bloomberg News
Wilson, George: National Journal Daily
Wilson, Scott: Washington Post
Wingfield, Brian: Bloomberg News
Winkler, Jeffrey: Daily Caller
Winski, Joe: Bloomberg News
Witcover, Jules: Tribune Media Services
Witkin, Gordon: Center for Public Integrity
Witkowski, Nancy: Associated Press
Witte, Brian: Associated Press
Woellert, Lorraine: Bloomberg News
Wolf, Carol: Bloomberg News

MEMBERS ENTITLED TO ADMISSION—Continued

Wolf, Daniel: Scripps Howard News Service
Wolf, Jim: Thomson Reuters
Wolf, Richard: USA Today
Wolfe, Frank: LRP Publications
Wolfe, Kathryn: Congressional Quarterly
Wolfgang, Benjamin: Washington Times
Woo, Yee: Congressional Quarterly
Wood, David: Huffington Post
Woodward, Bob: Washington Post
Woodward, Calvin: Associated Press
Wright, Christopher: Congressional Quarterly
Wroughton, Lesley: Thomson Reuters
Wu, Qingcai: China News Service
Wutkowski, Karey: Thomson Reuters
Wyatt, Edward: New York Times
Wynn, Randall: Congressional Quarterly
Xia, Xiaoyang: Wen Hui Daily
Xian, Wen: China People's Daily
Xiong, Min: 21st Century Business Herald
Xufeng, Jiang: Xinhua News Agency
Yadron, Daniel: Wall Street Journal
Yakabuski, Konrad: Globe and Mail
Yamada, Tetsuro: Yomiuri Shimbun
Yamaguchi, Kyoko: Yomiuri Shimbun
Yamahiro, Tsaneo: Bloomberg News
Yamour, Heather: Kuwait News Agency
Yan, Feng: Xinhua News Agency
Yan, Sophia: Bloomberg News
Yancey, Matthew: Associated Press
Yang, Jian: Xinhua News Agency
Yang, Julie: Asahi Shimbun
Yazawa, Toshiki: Nikkei
Yen, Hope: Associated Press
Yerkey, Gary: Svenska Dagbladet
Yi, Aijun: Xinhua News Agency
Yoder, Eric: Washington Post
Yoder, Tim: Congressional Quarterly
York, Byron: Washington Examiner
Yoshio, Nami: Kyodo News
Yost, Pete: Associated Press
You, Seng Lim: Korea Daily
Young, Alison: USA Today
Young, Donna: Scrip
Young, Jeffrey: Bloomberg News
Young, Kerry: Congressional Quarterly
Younglai, Rachelle: Thomson Reuters
Yourish, Karen: Washington Post
Youssef, Nancy: McClatchy Newspapers
Yu, Donghui: China Press
Yu, Lily: Bloomberg News
Yukhananov, Anna: Thomson Reuters
Zabarenko, Deborah: Thomson Reuters
Zahler, Andrew: Bloomberg News
Zajac, Andrew: Bloomberg News
Zak, Dan: Washington Post
Zakaria, Tabassum: Thomson Reuters
Zamora Barcelo, Jordi: Agence France-Presse
Zapotosky, Matt: Washington Post
Zeitvogel, Karin: Agence France-Presse
Zeleny, Jeff: New York Times
Zeller, Shawn: Congressional Quarterly
Zengerle, Patricia: Thomson Reuters
Zibel, Alan: Dow Jones / Wall Street Journal
Ziener, Markus: Handelsblatt
Zisman, Matthew: Bloomberg News
Zitner, Aaron: Wall Street Journal
Zlodorev, Dmitri: Itar-Tass News Agency
Zongker, Brett: Associated Press
Zoroya, Gregg: USA Today
Zoupaniotis, Apostolos: Cyprus News Agency
Zremski, Jerry: Buffalo News
Zumbrun, Joshua: Bloomberg News
Zwelling, Michael: Restructuring Today

NEWSPAPERS REPRESENTED IN PRESS GALLERIES

House Gallery 225–3945, 225–6722 Senate Gallery 224–0241

21ST CENTURY BUSINESS HERALD—(202) 431–2606; 1706 Euclid Street, NW., Washington, DC 20002: Xiong Min.

AARGAUER ZEITUNG—(202) 403–7115; 31 Kennedy Street, NW., Suite 202, Washington, DC 20011: Renzo Ruf.

ABC NEWSPAPER—(202) 588–0207; 1750 P Street, NW., Suite 306, Washington, DC 20036: Emilio Blasco.

ABIM—(703) 243–2104; 1344 Merrie Ridge Road, McLean, VA 22101: Mario Navarro da Costa.

AGENCE FRANCE-PRESSE—(202) 414–0541; 1500 K Street, NW., Suite 600, Washington, DC 20005: Patrick Baert, Andrew Beatty, Joanna Biddle, Lachlan Carmichael, Stephen Collinson, Martin de Montvalon, Guillaume Decamme, Daniel DeLuce, Fabienne Faur, Sandra Ferrer, Stephanie Griffith, Edouard Guihaire, Andrew Gully, Carlos Hamann, Olivia Hampton, Paul Handley, Hugues Honore, Stephane Jourdain, Marc Jourdier, Maxim Kniazkov, Olivier Knox, Joseph Krauss, Michael Langan, Sylvie Lanteaume, David Christopher Lefkow, Robert Lever, Celine Loubette, Robert MacPherson, Lucile Malandain, James Mannion, Michael Mathes, David Millikin, Virginie Montet, Alexander Ogle, Emmanuel Parisse, Tangi Quemener, Matthieu Rabechault, Picard Raphaelle, Jean-Louis Santini, Christophe Schmidt, Kerry Colleen Sheridan, Magan Sherzai, James Slater, Veronica Smith, Susan Stumme, Shaun Tandon, Diego Urdaneta, Chantal Valery, Christophe Vogt, Gregor Waschinski, Jordi Zamora Barcelo, Karin Zeitvogel.

AKAHATA—(202) 393–5238; 978 National Press Building, 529 14th Street, NW., Washington, DC 20045: Toshiya Kobayashi, Hiroshi Nishimura.

ALBUQUERQUE JOURNAL—(202) 329–4743; 116 6th Street, SE., Apartment 3, Washington, DC 20003: Michael T. Coleman.

AL-HAYAT—(202) 783–5544; 1185 National Press Building, 529 14th Street, NW., Washington, DC 20045: Joyce Karam.

ALLAFRICA.COM—(202) 546–0777; 922 M Street, SE., Washington, DC 20003: Tamela Hultman, Reed Kramer.

ALLENTOWN MORNING CALL—(202) 824–8216; 1090 Vermont Avenue, NW., Suite 1000, Washington, DC 20005: Colby Itkowitz.

AMERICAN BANKER—(571) 403–3832; 4401 Wilson Boulevard, Suite 910, Arlington, VA 22209: Joseph Adler, Donna Borak, Cheyenne Hopkins, Kevin Wack.

ANATOLIA NEWS AGENCY—(202) 550–0904; Bariskan Unal Toroglu, Ozkul Mehmet Toroglu.

ANSA ITALIAN NEWS AGENCY—(202) 628–3317; 1285 National Press Building, 529 14th Street, NW., Washington, DC 20045: Maria Alvarez, Marcello Campo, Cristiano Del Riccio, Marcelo Raimon.

AOL GOVERNMENT—(703) 265–8074; 22070 Broderick Drive, Dulles, VA 20166: Wyatt Kash, Andrea Stone.

ARA—(516) 653–1501; 410 Cedar Street, NW., Apartment 6, Washington, DC 20012: Nuria Ferragutcasas.

ARGUS MEDIA—(202) 349–2887; 1012 14th Street, NW., Suite 1500, Washington, DC 20005: Alexander Alexandrov, Ross Allen, Michael Ball, Abby Caplan, Molly Christian, Edward Epstein, David Givens, Haik Gugarats, David Ivanovich, Benjamin Gregory Kaldunski, Kim Krieger, Celia Lamb, Joanna Franco Marsh, Lauren Masterson, Christopher Newman, William Peters, Claire Pickard-Cambridge, Carrie Sisto, Ian Stewart, Tracy Sutherland, Todd Tranausky, Zachary Warmbrodt.

ARKANSAS DEMOCRAT-GAZETTE—(202) 662–7690; 1190 National Press Building, 529 14th Street, NW., Washington, DC 20045: Alex Daniels, Jane Fullerton.

ARTISTS & WRITERS SYNDICATE—(703) 820–4232; 6325 Beachway Drive, Falls Church, VA 22044: Frank A. Aukofer.

ASAHI SHIMBUN—(202) 783–1000; 1022 National Press Building, 529 14th Street, NW., Washington, DC 20045: Jonathan Harper, Hiroshi Ito, Toshihiko Katsuda, Daniel Longo, Aya Lee Maher, Lauren McGaughy, Hirotsugu Mochizuki, Kent Mullen, Yusuke Murayama, Shiko Namekata, Toshihiko Ogata, Adrienne Renee Atkinson Suhail, Junji Tachino, Julie Yang.

ASSOCIATED PRESS—(202) 641–9400; 1100 13th Street, NW., Suite 700, Washington, DC 20005: James R. Abrams, Jennifer Agiesta, Luis Alonso, Ricardo Alonso-Zaldivar, Stacy Anderson, Matt Apuzzo, John Jay Arnold, Charles Babington, Lolita Baldor, Matthew Barakat, Wendy Benjaminson, Douglas Birch, Brett J. Blackledge, Seth Borenstein, Stephen Braun, Ted Bridis, Sarah Brumfield, Robert Burns, Desmond Butler, Sally Buzbee, Alicia Caldwell, Dina Cappiello, Connie Cass, Donna Cassata, Randall Chase, Lauren Cooper, Martin S. Crutsinger, Matthew Daly, Douglass K. Daniel, David Dishneau, Alex Dominguez, Kimberly Dozier, Jim Drinkard, Harry Dunphy, Estelle Ebitty-

NEWSPAPERS REPRESENTED—Continued

Doro, Donald Elkins, Philip Elliott, David M. Espo, Carole Feldman, Ben Feller, Howard Fendrich, Anne Flaherty, Alan Fram, Kevin Freking, Frederic Frommer, Robert S. Furlow, Suzanne Gamboa, Anne R. Gearan, Jack Gillum, Robert Glass, Adam Michael Goldman, Shawn Gomez, Marcy G. Gordon, Jessica Gresko, Ken Guggenheim, Sam Hananel, Merrill Hartson, Kimberly Hefling, Gregory Henderson, Earl Hinton, Brian Scott Hoffman, Jesse J. Holland, Terence Hunt, Steven R. Hurst, Henry Jackson, Mary Clare Jalonick, Pauline V. Jelinek, Kasey Jones, Dennis Junius, Amanda Kell, Laurie Kellman Blazar, Jennifer Kerr, Bradley Klapper, Eric Klimek, Derek Kravitz, Jim Kuhnhenn, Richard Lardner, Matthew Lee, William J. Lester, James Lipari, Joan Lowy, Karen Mahabir, Sunil Malhotra, William C. Mann, Lawrence N. Margasak, Andrew Miga, Lauran Neergaard, Ben Nuckols, Stephen Ohlemacher, Mark Olchowy, David H. Pace, Louis Pagan, John Pain, Matthew Pennington, Matthew Perrone, Nedra Pickler, Melinda Purce, Eileen Putman, Thomas Raum, Keith Rickett, Sonya Ross, Michele Salcedo, Michael Sandler, Randolph E. Schmid, Barry Schweid, Mark J. Sherman, Elizabeth Sidoti, Michael Sniffen, Nina Strass, Thomas J. Strong, Eileen Sullivan, Darlene E. Superville, Andrew Taylor, Joelle Tessler, Ken Thomas, Trevor Tompson, Kiryl Tsiatsiorkin, Eric Tucker, Kevin S. Vineys, Erica Werner, Joseph Gatlin White, Jr., Nancy Benac Witkowski, Brian Witte, Calvin Woodward, Matthew L. Yancey, Hope Yen, Pete Yost, Brett Zongker.

ATLANTA JOURNAL CONSTITUTION—(202) 777–7033; 400 North Capitol Street, NW., Suite 750, Washington, DC 20001: Daniel Malloy, Cynthia Tucker.

AUSTRALIAN FINANCIAL REVIEW—(202) 716–1971; 1310 G Street, NW., Washington, DC 20005: Ben Potter.

AUSTRALIAN—(202) 628–7079; 446 National Press Building, 529 14th Street, NW., Washington, DC 20045: Brad Norington.

BALTIMORE SUN—(410) 979–2052; 1090 Vermont Avenue, NW., Suite 1000, Washington, DC 20005: Jeffrey Barker, John Fritze.

BATON ROUGE ADVOCATE—(202) 254–0458; 22 Finale Drive, Silver Spring, MD 20901: Gerard Shields.

BIRMINGHAM NEWS—(202) 744–5574; 700 12th Street, NW., Suite 1000, Washington, DC 20005: Mary Orndorff Troyan.

BLOOMBERG NEWS—(202) 624–1800; 1399 New York Avenue, NW., 11th Floor, Washington, DC 20005: Mary Orndorff Troyan,Bloomberg News: Syed Ali, Melissa Eduviges Aparicio, Stephanie Armour, Andrew Armstrong, Laurence Arnold, Jason Arvelo, Laurie Asseo, Terry Atlas, Jeannine Aversa, Charles Babcock, David Banks, Terrence Barrett, Matthew Barry, Frank Bass, Clea Benson, Max Berley, Adriel Bettelheim, Alan Bjerga, Jeffrey Bliss, Justin Blum, Matt Bok, Romaine Bostick, Kevin Brancato, Kate Anderson Brower, Silla Brush, Edward F. Buckley, Matthew Caminiti, Anthony W. Capaccio, Lisa Caruso, Shobhana Chandra, Kimberly Chipman, Rebecca Christie, Kristin Jensen Cohen, Kevin Costelloe, Julie Hirschfeld Davis, Susan Decker, Vincent A. Del Giudice, Catherine Dodge, Ryan Donmoyer, Mike Dorning, Carter Dougherty, Mark Drajem, Bob Drummond, Loren Duggan, Paula Dwyer, Anna Edney, Curtis Eichelberger, David Ellis, Eric Engleman, Daniel Enoch, Brian Faler, Ken Fireman, Alison Fitzgerald, Christopher Flavelle, Sara Gay Forden, Juliann Neher Francis, Brian Friel, Joshua Gallu, Nicole Gaouette, Stephen Geimann, Viola Gienger, Gregory L. Giroux, Anthony Gnoffo, Julianna Goldman, Vince Golle, Brendan Greeley, Brigitte Greenberg, Robert T. Greene, Angela Greiling Keane, Kimberly Hallock, Jesse Hamilton, Dan Hart, Ian Hathaway, Kathleen Janet Hayden, Kellen M. Henry, Jospeh Hicken, Leslie Hoffecker, Allan Holmes, Timothy Homan, Clark Hoyt, Paul Hughes, John Hughes, Ann Hughey, Matthew Hummer, Albert Hunt, Kathleen Hunter, Ronnell Ingram, Danielle Ivory, Flavia Jackson, Michelle Jamrisko, Nicholas Johnston, Daniel Joyce, Berenice Juarex, Elizabeth Karasmeighan, Ian Katz, Nancy Kercheval, Katarzyna Klimasinska, Steven Komarow, Alexander Kowalski, Indira Lakashmanan, Scott Lanman, Catherine Larkin, Anne Laurent, Lisa Lerer, David Lerman, Robert Levinson, Larry Liebert, Walter Little, Laura Litvan, Simon Lomax, Eduardo Londres, Meera Louis, David Lynch, John Muir Macpherson, Nishad Majmudar, Eric Martin, Philip Mattingly, Jamal E. Mazyck, Brendan McGarry, Traci Lynn McMillan, Mark McQuillan, William McQuillen, Brian Meehan, Margaret Mertens, Robin D. Meszoly, Chris Middleton, Richard Miller, Kathleen Miller, Kenneth Monahan, Jon Morgan, Daniel Moss, Gregory Mott, Hans Nichols, C. JoAnne Norton, Leah Nylen, Joseph O'Reilly II, Albert Palacios, Daniel J. Parks, Timothy Pennix, Molly Peterson, Jeff Plungis, Sonya Cooper Pollard, Joi Preciphs, Heidi Przybyla, David Rapp, Sandrine Rastello, Gopal Ratnam, Sanford Reback, Maura Reynolds, Joseph Richter, Kelly Riddell, Michael A. Riley, Michael George Riley, Katherine Rizzo, Mark Rohner, Stephen Rose, Holly Rosenkrantz, Bennett Roth, James C. Rowley, Debarati Roy, Richard Rubin, Roger D. Runningen, Brian Rye, Jonathan D. Salant, Marvin Salmeron, Kenneth Sands, Kristy Scheuble, Robert Schmidt, Jodi Schneider, Tom Schoenberg, William Selway, Sopen Shah, Michael Shepard, Todd Shields, Mark Silva, Steven Sloan, Elliot Blair Smith, Jim Snyder, Andrea Snyder, Joseph A. Sobczyk, Christine Spolar, Seth Stern, Greg Stohr, Stephenie Stoughton, Fred Strasser, Nick Taborek, Michael Tackett, Alex Tanzi, Katherine Theranger, Roxana Tiron, Carlos Torres, Craig R. Torres, James Tyson, John Walcott, Randolph Walerius, Derek Wallbank, Douglas Carlyle Waller, Stephen Walsh, Alexander Wayne, Caitlin Webber, Joann Weiner, Miles Geoffrey Weiss, Brian Weiss, Chris Wellisz, Robert

NEWSPAPERS REPRESENTED—Continued

Willis, Brian Wingfield, Joe Winski, Lorraine Woellert, Carol Wolf, Tsaneo Yamahiro, Sophia Chien-Chun Yan, Jeffrey Young, Lily Yu, Andrew Zahler, Andrew Zajac, Matthew Zisman, Joshua H. Zumbrun.

BOND BUYER—(571) 403–3843; 4401 Wilson Boulevard, Suite 910, Arlington, VA 22203: Lynn S. Hume, Dennis Moore, Joan Quigley, Patrick Temple-West.

BOSTON GLOBE—(202) 857–5050; 1130 Connecticut Avenue, NW., Suite 520, Washington, DC 20036: Mark Arsenault, Bryan Bender, Theo Emery, Sasha Issenberg, Tracy Jan, Glen Johnson, Michael A. Kranish, Christopher Rowland, Donovan Slack, Farah Stockman, Stephanie Vallejo, Matthew Viser.

BUFFALO NEWS—(202) 234–3188; 1715 15th Street, NW., #24, Washington, DC 20009: Jerry Zremski.

CALCUTTA TELEGRAPH—(301) 654–6008; 5500 Friendship Boulevard, Suite 1217, Chevy Chase, MD 20815: Krishnan Parameswaran Nayar.

CENTER FOR PUBLIC INTEGRITY—(202) 461–1300; 910 17th Street, NW., 7th Floor, Washington, DC 20006: Laurel Adams, Amy Biegelsen, Jeremy Borden, David Donald, Alexandra Duszak, Joseph Eaton, Keith C. Epstein, John Aloysius Farrell, Caitlin Ginley, Cole Goins, Andrew Green, Ronnie Greene, Marina Walker Guevara, Chris Hamby, David Heath, Corbin Hiar, Joshua Israel, Sandy K. Johnson, Kimberly Leonard, Erik Lincoln, Elizabeth Lucas, Aaron Mehta, James G. Morris, Nadikant Penjarla, Ricardo Sandoval Palos, Fred Schulte, Peter Smith, John Solomon, Peter Stone, Julie Vorman, Gordon Witkin.

CENTRAL NEWS AGENCY—(202) 550–7953; 1173 National Press Building, 529 14th Street, NW., Washington, DC 20045: Yung-Chieh Chou, Zep Hu.

CHICAGO SUN-TIMES—(202) 244–5522; 3831 Windom Place, NW., Washington, DC 20016: Lynn Sweet.

CHICAGO TRIBUNE—(202) 824–8376; 1090 Vermont Avenue, NW., Suite 1000, Washington, DC 20005: David Cloud, Clarence Page, Christi Parsons, Katherine Skiba, Dina White.

CHINA ECONOMIC DAILY—(703) 698–8579; 3305 Crest Haven Court, Falls Church, VA 22042: Zhengxin Li.

CHINA LEGAL DAILY—(703) 237–4635; 5601 26th Street, North Arlington, VA 22207: Zou Qiang.

CHINA NEWS SERVICE—(703) 527–1409; 1020 North Stafford Street, Apartment 100, Arlington, VA 22201: Qingcai Wu.

CHINA PEOPLE'S DAILY—(703) 698–1298; 2506 Fallsmere Court, Falls Church, VA 22043: Wen Xian.

CHINA PRESS—(703) 725–0720; 2021 Brooks Square Place, Falls Church, VA 22043: Donghui Yu.

CHINA YOUTH DAILY—(703) 956–1933; 2816 North Jefferson Street, Arlington, VA 22207: Hui Ju.

CHOSUN ILBO—(202) 783–4236; 1291 National Press Building, 529 14th Street, NW., Washington, DC 20045: Hyuk Min Im.

CHRISTIAN SCIENCE MONITOR—(202) 481–6642; 910 16th Street, NW., Suite 200, Washington, DC 20006: Gail R. Chaddock, David T. Cook, Linda Feldmann, David Grant, Peter Grier, Francine Kiefer, Howard LaFranchi, Anna Mulrine, Eloise Quintanilla, Warren Richey.

CLARIN—(202) 737–4850; 1271 National Press Building, 529 14th Street, NW., Washington, DC 20045: Ana Baron Supervielle.

CLEVELAND PLAIN DEALER—(202) 638–1366; 930 National Press Building, 529 14th Street, NW., Washington, DC 20045: Sabrina Eaton, Stephen Koff.

COLUMBUS DISPATCH—(202) 824–6765; 400 North Capitol Street, Suite 850, Washington, DC 20001: Jack Torry, Jessica Wehrman.

COMMUNICATIONS DAILY—(202) 872–9202; 2115 Ward Court, NW., Washington, DC 20037: Adam Bender, Howard Buskirk, Dinesh Kumar, Kamala Lane, Jonathan Make, Bill Myers, Dawson Nail, Yu-Ting Wang.

CONGRESSIONAL QUARTERLY—(202) 650–6500; 77 K Street, NE., Washington, DC 20002: Rebecca Adams, Amanda Allen, Kent Allen, Joanna Anderson, Dennis Arndt, Melissa Attias, Janet R. Austin, Fred Barbash, Jason Barrett, Jamie Baylis, Ryan Teague Beckwith, Robert A. Benenson, Susan Benkelman, Ted Benson, John Bicknell, Arwen Adams Bicknell, Joel Bowen, Chad Brand, Jonathan Broder, Ronald Brodmann, Kristin Broughton, Dena Bunis, Emily Cadei, George Cahlink, Scott Benjamin Campbell, Leah Carliner, Charlene Carter, Mike Christensen, George Codrea, Richard E. Cohen, Charles Conlon, Neal Conway, Kristen Conyer, Kristin Coyner, John R. Cranford, Jessica Cuellar, David Davis, John Dineen, John Donnelly, Emma Dumain, Toby Eckert, Carol Eisenberg, Emily Ethridge, Ellyn Ferguson, Jamey Fry, Matthew Fuller, Karin Fuog, Lauren Gardner, Dan Germain, Steve Gettinger, Jonathan Goldberg, Sam Goldfarb, Clayton Hanson, David Harrison, Alexander Hart, David Hawkings, Robert E. Healy, Caitlin Hendel, Paul Hendrie, Amanda Hicks, Robb Hill, Margaret Hobson, Anne Q. Hoy, Nathan Hurst, Robert Huttinger, John A. Irons, Benton Ives-Halperin, Paul Jenks, Amanda Grace Johnson, Patricia Joy, Joanne Kenen, Noella Kertes, Kayvon Khaledi, Elham Khatami, Anne Kim, Angela Kim, Peter King, Alex Knott, Matthew Korade, Geof Koss, Kaitlin Kovach, Paul M. Krawzak, Sarah Lawrence, Niels Lesniewski, Adam Levin, Finlay Lewis, Jacqueline Linnane, Tammy Lucas, Robert James Margetta, Anna McGeehan, David Meyers, Tait Militana, Michael Mills, Eugene Mulero, Kathleen Murphy, Melinda Nahmias, Eric Naing, E. Roy Nkansah, Jane Norman, Frank Oliveri, Alan K. Ota, Christina C. Parisi, Daniel Peake, Keith Perine, Emily Poe, Jamisha Purdy, Eric Ray, John Reichard, Betty Richardson, James A. Roberts, Peter Rocco, Jennifer Rubio, Adam

NEWSPAPERS REPRESENTED—Continued

Schank, Joseph J. Schatz, Jennifer Scholtes, Anne Shuppy, Stacey Skotzko, Lauren Smith, Megan Sowdwer-Staley, Tim Starks, Gail Sullivan, Greg Surniak, Frances Symes, Michael Teitelbaum, Neda Toloui-Semnani, Robert Tomkin, Gregory Vadala, Sarah Vanderbilt, Joseph Warminsky, Ben Weyl, Christian White, Kevin Whitelaw, Guy Whitmire, Thomas Wilburn, Kathryn A. Wolfe, Yee Ling Woo, Christopher Wright, Randall L. Wynn, Tim Yoder, Kerry Young, Shawn Zeller.

CONNECTICUT MIRROR—(202) 330–3890: Dierdre Shesgreen.

CONNECTICUT POST—(202) 783–1760; 1255 National Press Building, 529 14th Street, NW., Washington, DC 20045: Peter H. Urban.

CREATORS SYNDICATE—(202) 662–1255; 5777 West Century Boulevard, Suite 700, Los Angeles, CA 90045: Mark Shields.

CUMHURIYET—(202) 360–3883; 603 A Street, SE., Washington, DC 20003: Elcin Poyrazlar.

CYPRUS NEWS AGENCY—(202) 462–5772; 2211 R Street, NW., Washington, DC 20008: Apostolos Zoupaniotis.

DAILY (THE)—(212) 462–5403: Joshua Hersh, Luke Jerod Kummer (202) 870–8910.

DAILY BEAST—(202) 257–5988; 7950 Jones Branch Road, McLean, VA 22108: Michelle Cottle, Jill D. Lawrence, Patricia Murphy.

DAILY CALLER—(202) 506–2027; 1050 17th Street, Suite 900, Washington, DC 20036: Matthew Boyle, Amanda Carey, Tucker Carlson, C.J. Ciaramella, Laura Donovan, Kells Hetherington, Joseph Patrick Kildea, Alexis Levinson, Matthew Kenneth Lewis, Caroline May, Chris Moody, Megan Mulligan, Neil Pat Munro, Steven Nelson, Tina Thien-Nga Nguyen, Alex Pappas, Robert Jeffrey Poor, Michael Riggs, Jonathan Strong, Jamie Weinstein, Jeffrey Winkler.

DAILY DEAL—(202) 429–2994; 236 Massachusetts Avenue, NE., Washington, DC 20002: Nicole Duran, William McConnell, Ira Teinowitz.

DALLAS MORNING NEWS—(202) 661–8410; 1252 National Press Building, 529 14th Street, NW., Washington, DC 20045: Alfredo Corchado, Todd Gillman, James M. Landers, Carl P. Leubsdorf, David Michaels.

DEFENSE DAILY—(703) 785–5261; 1500 Wilson Boulevard, Suite 1500, Arlington, VA 22209: Maria Malenic, Carlo Munoz, John A. Robinson, Ann Roosevelt, Emelie Rutherford.

DENVER POST—(202) 662–8907; 969 National Press Building, 529 14th Street, NW., Washington, DC 20045: Allison Sherry.

DER TAGESSPIEGEL—(202) 686–3947; 3200 Patterson Street, NW., Washington, DC 20015: Christophe V. Marschall, Christoph Von Marschall.

DES MOINES REGISTER—(202) 906–8138; 1100 New York Avenue, Washington, DC 20005: Philip Brasher.

DETROIT FREE PRESS—(202) 906–8204; 1100 New York Avenue, Suite 200E, Washington, DC 20005: Aaron Kessler, Todd Spangler.

DETROIT NEWS—(202) 906–8205; 969 National Press Building, 529 14th Street, NW., Washington, DC 20045: Deborah J. Price, Marisa Schultz, David Shepardson.

DOW JONES / WALL STREET JOURNAL—(202) 862–9200; 1025 Connecticut Avenue, NW., Suite 800, Washington, DC 20036: Andrew Ackerman, Mark Anderson, Tom Barkley, Jeffrey P. Bater, Corey Boles, Jennifer Corbett Dooren, Michael Crittenden, Luca Di Leo, David Dolinger, Jared A. Favole, William Ho, Jessica Holzer, Siobhan Hughes, Maya Jackson-Randall, Brent Kendall, Joshua Mitchell, Kristina Peterson, Jeffrey Sparshott, Katherine Stech, Ian Talley, Bill Tomson, Ryan Tracy, Tennile Tracy, Jamila Trindle, Robert Wells, Alan Zibel.

EFE NEWS SERVICES—(202) 745–7692; 1220 National Press Building, 529 14th Street, NW., Washington DC 20045: Celine Aemisegger, Jorge E. Banales, Teresa Bouza, Maribel El Hamti, Alfonso Fernandez, Lucia Leal, Jose Manuel Sanz Mingote, Elvira Palomo, Maria Pena, Macarena Vidal-Ly.

EL DIARIO DE HOY—(703) 845–4962; 4600 South Four Mile Run Drive, Arlington, VA 22204: Tomas Guevara.

EL NUEVO DIA—(202) 662–7360; 960d National Press Building, 529 14th Street, NW., Washington, DC 20045: Jose Delgado.

EL PAIS—(202) 638–1533; 1134 National Press Building, 529 14th Street, NW., Washington, DC 20045: David Alandete, Antonio Caño, Christina Fernandez, Yolanda Monge.

EL PERIODICO; 4801 Hampden Lane, Bethesda, MD 20814: Ricardo Mir De Francia.

EL TIEMPO—(202) 607–5929; 5597 Seminary Road, Apartment 714 South, Washington, DC 20041: Sergio Gomez.

EL UNIVERSAL—(202) 662–7190; 1193 National Press Building, 529 14th Street, NW., Washington, DC 20045: Jose Jaime Hernandez Garcia, Jose Hernandez.

ENERGY DAILY—(703) 358–9295; 1500 Wilson Boulevard, Suite 515, Arlington, VA 22209: Jeff Beattie, Christopher P. Holly, Eric Lindeman, George Lobsenz, Jonathan Rickman.

ENERGY GUARDIAN—(202) 277–2487: Edward R. Felker.

ETHNOS GREECE—(202) 361–7843; 1133 14th Street, NW., Washington, DC 20005: Michail Ignatiou.

EUROPOLITICS—(202) 758–8462; 1403 12th Street, NW., #4, Washington, DC 20005: Brian Beary.

FAIRCHILD PUBLICATIONS—(202) 955–0966; 1730 Rhode Island Avenue, Suite 603, Washington, DC 20036: Kristi Ellis, Susan W. Watters.

NEWSPAPERS REPRESENTED—Continued

FINANCIAL TIMES—(202) 434–0972; 1023 15th Street, NW., Suite 700, Washington, DC 20005: Tom Braithwaite, Daniel Dombey, Anna Fifield, Robin Harding, Matthew Kennard, Stephanie Kirchgaessner, Richard McGregor, James Politi.

FORT WORTH STAR-TELEGRAM—(202) 383–6103; 700 12th Street, NW., Suite 1000, Washington, DC 20005: Maria E. Recio.

FRANKFURTER ALLGEMEINE ZEITUNG—(202) 986–0965; 2100 Connecticut Avenue, NW., Suite 502, Washington, DC: Patrick Welter.

FRANKFURTER RUNDSCHAU—(301) 762–9661; 1717 Sunrise Drive, Rockville, MD 20854: Dietmar Ostermann.

FREELANCE—Anne Groer (202) 338–8581, Katherine Reynolds Lewis (301) 375–0675, Tamara Lytle (202) 277–5931.

GANNETT WASHINGTON BUREAU—(703) 854–8900; 1575 I Street, NW., Suite 350, Washington, DC 20005: Paul Barton, Deborah Berry, Elizabeth Bewley, Larry Bivins, Sammie Chan, Raju Chebium, Val Ellicott, Nicole Gaudiano Albright, Maureen Groppe, Linda R. Holzer, Bart Jansen, Alethea Jordan, Erin Kelly, Ledyard King, Dennis Noone, Charles Raasch, Laura Rehrmann, Malia Rulon Herman, Craig Schwed, William Theobald, Brian J. Tumulty.

GERMAN PRESS AGENCY-DPA—(202) 662–1220; 1112 National Press Building, 529 14th Street, NW., Washington, DC 20045: Sylvia Ayuso Determeyer, Frank Brandmaier, Christopher Cermak, Gabriele Chwallek, Frank Fuhrig, Mike McCarthy, Peer Meinert, Marco Mierke, Paticia Reber, Anne Walters.

GLOBAL HORIZONS SYNDICATE—(202) 966–8636; 1330 New Hampshire Avenue, NW., Washington, DC 20036: Edward Flattau.

GLOBE AND MAIL—(202) 662–7167; 2000 M Street, NW., Suite 330, Washington, DC 20036: Paul Koring, Konrad Yakabuski.

GRIFFIN-LARRABEE NEWS SERVICE—(703) 548–6343; 2404 Davis Avenue, Alexandria, VA 22302: Betty Mills.

HAARETZ DAILY—(240) 274–9100; 718 Market Street East, Gaithersburg, MD 20878: Natasha Mozgovaya.

HANDELSBLATT—(202) 244–0238; 3823 Fessenden Street, NW., Washington, DC 20016: Markus Ziener.

HANKOOK ILBO—(202) 783–2674; 986 National Press Building, 529 14th Street, NW., Washington, DC 20045: Lee Taegyu.

HANKYOREH DAILY—(202) 341–9411; 821 National Press Building, 529 14th Street, NW., Washington, DC 20045: Taeho Kwon.

HEARST NEWSPAPERS—(202) 263–6400; 700 12th Street, NW., Suite 1000, Washington, DC 20005: Jennifer Dlouhy, Dan Freedman, Charles J. Lewis, Stewart M. Powell.

HELSINGIN SANOMAT—(301) 907–0080; 1726 M Street, NW., Suite 700, Washington, DC 20036: Tuomas Niskakangas.

HOKKAIDO SHIMBUN—(202) 783–6033; 1012 National Press Building, 529 14th Street, NW., Washington, DC 20045: Masayuki Kishi.

HOUSTON CHRONICLE—(202) 263–6511; 700 12th Street, NW., Suite 1000, Washington, DC 20005: Richard Dunham.

HUFFINGTON POST—(202) 567–2634; 1730 Pennsylvania Avenue, NW., #825, Washington, DC 20006: Laura Bassett, Jennifer Bendery, Mark Blumenthal, Zachary Carter, Colin Clark, Arthur Delaney, Thomas Edsall, Howard Fineman, Elise Foley, Daniel Froomkin, Lucia Graves, Ryan Grim, Dave Jamieson, Shahien Nasiripour, Eliot Nelson, Michael Sacks, Sam Stein, Andrea Stone, Amanda Terkel, Jon Ward, David Wood.

HURRIYET—(917) 340–2466; 16 Grove Ridge Court, Rockville, MD 20852: Tolga Tanis.

ICIS NEWS—(202) 836–3448; 333 North Fairfax Street, Suite 301, Alexandria, VA 22314: Joseph Kamalick.

IFR MARKETS—(202) 904–0959: Vimombi Nshom, David Sloan.

IL GIORNALE—(202) 237–1019; 2841 Arizona Terrace, Washington, DC 20016: Mariuccia Chiantaretto.

INDIA PRESS TRUST—(301) 564–2963; 10500 Rockville Pike, North Bethesda, MD 20852: Lalit K. Jha.

INDO-ASIAN NEWS SERVICE—(301) 412–9234; 4801 Kenmore Avene, Apartment 910, Alexandria, VA 22304: Arun Kumar.

INSIDE HIGHER ED—(202) 659–9208; 1015 18th Street, NW., Suite 1100, Washington, DC 20036: Dan Berrett, Allie Grasgreen, Steve Kolowich, Douglas Lederman, Andrew David Moltz, Libby Nelson.

INTER PRESS SERVICE—(202) 662–7160; 1293 National Press Building, 529 14th Street, NW., Washington, DC 20045: James Lobe.

INTERNATIONAL HERALD TRIBUNE—(202) 862–0357; 1627 I Street, NW., Suite 700, Washington, DC 20006: Brian B. Knowlton.

INTERNETNEWS.COM—(202) 506–7743; 2800 Quebec Street, NW., Apartment 823, Washington, DC 20001: Kenneth Corbin.

INVESTOR'S BUSINESS DAILY—(202) 728–2152; 1001 Connecticut Avenue, Suite 415, Washington, DC 20036: Sean Geary Higgins, David Hogberg.

IRISH TIMES—(202) 525–5140: Lara Marlowe.

NEWSPAPERS REPRESENTED—Continued

ITAR-TASS NEWS AGENCY—(202) 662–7080; 1004 National Press Building, 529 14th Street, NW., Washington, DC 20045: Dmitry Kirsanov, Alexander Pakhomov, Andrei K. Sitov, Andrey A. Surzhanskiy, Dmitri Zlodorev.

JERUSALEM POST—(202) 758–0862; 1508 17th Street, NW., Apartment 3, Washington, DC 20036: Hilary Leila Krieger.

JEWISH TELEGRAPHIC AGENCY—(202) 737–0935; 1025 Vermont Avenue, NW., #504, Washington, DC 20005: Ron Kampeas.

JIJI PRESS—(202) 783–4330; 550 National Press Building, NW., 529 14th Street, NW., Washington, DC 20045: Ai Awaji, Takashi Fudo, Junko Ishikawa, Kosuke Ito, Takefumi Kato, Yoshi Kishida, Kaoru Miyazawa, Nicolas Pandi.

JOONGANG ILBO—(202) 347–0122: Jungwook Kim.

JYLLANDS-POSTEN—(202) 450–5552; 1700 Lanier Place, NW., Washington, DC 20009: Jorgen Ullerup.

KAISER HEALTH NEWS—(202) 654–1353; 1330 G Street, NW., Washington, DC 20005: Julie Appleby, Mary Agnes Carey, John Fairhall, Phil Galewitz, Peggy Girshman, Jenny Gold, Peggy Grishman, Shefali S. Kulkarni, Jessica Marcy, Laurie McGinley, Jordan Ran, Marilyn Werber Serafini, Stephanie Stapleton, Bara Vaida, Andrew Villegas.

KANSAS CITY STAR—(202) 383–6105; 700 12th Street, NW., Suite 1000, Washington, DC 20005: David Goldstein.

KIPLING NEWS SERVICE—(301) 929–0760; 12611 Farnell Drive, Silver Spring, MD 20906: Bogdan Kipling.

KOREA DAILY—(703) 819–2030; 7023 Little River Turnpike, Suite 300, Annandale, VA 22003: Yong Sung Lee, Sung Eun ''Grace'' Lee, Seng Lim You.

KOREA DONG-A ILBO—(202) 347–4097; 974 National Press Building, 529 14th Street, NW., Washington, DC 20045: Young Hae Choi, Taewon Ha.

KOREA ECONOMIC DAILY—(703) 850–3396; 821 National Press Building, 529 14th Street, NW., Washington, DC 20045: Hong Yeol Kim.

KOREA TIMES—(703) 941–8002; 7601 Little River Turnpike, Annandale, VA 22003: Sung Joong Ahn, Christina Young Chong, Jong Kook Lee, Chang-Yul Lee, Byonghan Lee, Kwang Duk Park.

KUKMIN DAILY—(202) 637–0567; 909 National Press Building, 529 14th Street, NW., Washington, DC 20045: Myung Ho Kim.

KUMAMOTO NICHINICHI SHIMBUN—(301) 299–3775; 10625 Rock Run Drive, Potomac, MD 20854: Reiko Kamata Robertson.

KUWAIT NEWS AGENCY—(202) 347–5554; 906 National Press Building, 529 14th Street, NW., Washington, DC 20045: Ronald Baygents, Joe Macaron, Sherouq Sadeqi, Heather Yamour.

KYODO NEWS—(202) 347–5767; 400 National Press Building, 529 14th Street, NW., Washington, DC 20045: Yasushi Azuma, Moriyasu Chikazawa, Benjamin Dooley, Sandra Garcia, Kazuhiro Haruki, Hiromasa Hayashi, Takao Ikeuchi, Kazuhiro Kimura, Yuji Nakaya, Akira Samukawa, Shinichiro Serita, Yuko Shimada, Ichiro Sugimoto, Yushin Sugita, Toru Takei, Nami Yoshio.

LA JORNADA—(202) 669–7760; 2708 Fourth Street, NE., Washington, DC 20002: David Brooks.

LA NACION—(202) 628–7907; 1193 National Press Building, 529 14th Street, NW., Washington, DC 20045: Silvia Pisani.

LA OPINION—(213) 369–8006; 110 West 39th Street, Apartment 616, Baltimore, MD 21210: Antonieta Cadiz.

LA—PRENSA GRAFICA OF EL SALVADOR; 5635 Fillmore Avenue, Alexandria, VA 22377: Xeyli Alfaro.

LAS VEGAS SUN—(202) 662–7436; 1290 National Press Building, 529 14th Street, NW., Washington, DC 20045: Karoun Demirjian.

LE MAURICIEN—(301) 728–7442; 1084 Pipestem Place, Potomac, MD 20854: Pamela Glass.

LE MONDE—(202) 248–9075; 3841 Harrison Street, NW., Washington, DC 20015: Corine Lesnes.

LIBERTY TIMES—(202) 879–6765; 1294 National Press Building, 529 14th Street, NW., Washington, DC 20045: Nadia Yu-Fen Tsao.

LONDON DAILY TELEGRAPH—(202) 393–5195; 1310 G Street, NW., Suite 750, Washington, DC 20005: Toby Harnden, Alexander Spillius.

LONDON GUARDIAN—(202) 785–8275; 900 17th Street, NW., Suite 250, Washington, DC 20006: Richard Adams, Diane Gilchrist, Suzanne Goldenberg, Ewen Macaskill, Chris McGreal.

LONDON TIMES—(202) 347–7659; 446 National Press Building, 529 14th Street, NW., Washington, DC 20045: Michael Evans, Nico Hines, Catherine Philip, Matthew Spence, Giles Whittell.

L'ORIENT-LE JOUR—(202) 342–1213; 1045 31st Street, #404, Washington, DC 20007: Wafik Ramadan.

LOS ANGELES DAILY JOURNAL—(202) 484–8255; 963 National Press Building, 529 14th Street, NW., Washington, DC 20045: Robert Iafolla.

LOS ANGELES TIMES—(202) 824–8259; 1090 Vermont Avenue, NW., Suite 1000, Washington, DC 20005: Neela Banerjee, Richard Cooper, Ken Dilanian, Robert Drogin, Kim Geiger, Matea Gold, Thomas Hamburger, Kathleen Hennessey, David Lauter, Don Lee, Noam Levey, Lisa Mascaro, Melanie Mason, Michael McGough, Doyle McManus, David Meeks, Greg Miller, Peter Nicholas, James Oliphant,

NEWSPAPERS REPRESENTED—Continued

Timothy Phelps, James Puzzanghera, Paul Richter, James Robinson, David G. Savage, Richard A. Serrano, Richard J. Simon, Paul West.

LOUISVILLE COURIER JOURNAL—(202) 906–8141; 1100 New York Avenue, NW., Washington, DC 20005: James Carroll.

LRP PUBLICATIONS—(202) 294–6357; 1901 North Moore Street, Suite 1106, Arlington, VA 22209: Emily Ann Brown, Julie Davidson, Adam Dolge, Jean Gossman, David Kittross, Wangui Njuguna, Anjali Patel, Kim Riley, Jeanne Sweeney, Frank Wolfe.

MAEIL BUSINESS NEWSPAPER—(202) 637–0567; 909 National Press Building, 529 14th Street, NW., Washington, DC 20045: Gwang Ik Jang.

MAIN JUSTICE—(202) 654–7051: Fahima Haque, Mary Jacoby, Christopher Murray Matthews, Andrew Ramonas, David Stout, Aruna Viswanatha.

MAINICHI SHIMBUN—(202) 737–2817; 340 National Press Building, 529 14th Street, NW., Washington, DC 20045: Yoso Furumoto, Masato Kaiho, Jacquelyn Kasuya, Nobuhiro Saito, Keiichi Shirato.

MALAYA—(703) 715–8879; 10724 Midsummer Drive, Reston, VA 20191: Josefina Ilustre.

MARKET NEWS INTERNATIONAL—(202) 371–2121; 1100 National Press Building, 529 14th Street, NW., Washington, DC 20045: Steven K. Beckner, Denny Gulino, Kevin P. Kastner, Ian McKendry, Yali N'Diaye, Braimoh Odion-Esene, Joseph E. Plocek, Heather Scott, John Shaw.

MARKETWATCH—(202) 824–0548; 1025 Connecticut Avenue, NW., Washington, DC 20036: Jeffry Bartash, Steven Goldstein, Christopher Hinton, Ruth Mantell Madden, Michael Maynard, Margaret McNeil, Rex Nutting, Ronald Orol, Gregory Robb, Robert Schroeder.

MCCLATCHY NEWSPAPERS—(202) 383–6004; 700 12th Street, NW., Suite 1000, Washington, DC 20005: Halimah Abdullah, Christopher Adams, Beryl Adcock, Andre Anderson, James Asher, Barbara Barrett, Shashank Bengali, Erika Bolstad, Robert Boyd, William Douglas, Michael Doyle, Jim Goldschmidt, Greg Gordon, Roy Gutman, Anders Gyllenhaal, Kevin Hall, Rob Hotakainen, Jonathan Landay, David Lightman, Jarondakie Patrick, Anthony Pugh, Robert Rankin, James M. Rosen, Carol Rosenberg, Renee Schoof, Mark Seibel, Warren Strobel, Margaret Talev, Curtis Tate, Marisa Taylor, Steven Thomma, Jim Van Nostrand, Letitia Wells, Nancy Youssef.

MEDPAGETODAY.COM—(202) 230–6628; 2101 16th Street, NW., Apartment 816, Washington, DC 20009: Joyce Frieden, Emily Walker.

MERCER MEDIA—(202) 834–1261: Marsha D. Mercer.

MERGER MARKET OF FINANCIAL TIMES—(202) 434–1075; 1012 K Street, NW., Suite 915, Washington, DC 20005: Benjamin J. Koconis, Reuben Miller, Kevin Nafzlger, Jennifer Smith-Parker.

MIAMI HERALD—(202) 383–6054; 700 12th Street, NW., Suite 1000, Washington, DC 20005: Lesley Clark.

MILITARY UPDATE—(703) 830–6863; P.O. Box 231111, Centreville, VA 20120: Thomas R. Philpott.

MILITARY.COM—(202) 441–7218: Philip Ewing, Bryant Jordan, Christian Lowe, John Reed.

MILWAUKEE JOURNAL SENTINEL—(202) 662–2291; 940 National Press Building, 529 14th Street, NW., Washington, DC 20045: Craig Gilbert.

MINNEAPOLIS STAR TRIBUNE—(202) 408–2753; 1090 Vermont Avenue, NW., Suite 1000, Washington, DC 20005: Kevin Diaz, Jeremy Herb, Jim Spencer.

MINNPOST—(612) 455–6950; 6809 Beacon Place, Riverdale, MD 20737: Devin Kendrick Henry.

MUNWHA ILBO—(202) 662–7342; 1149 National Press Building, 529 14th Street, NW., Washington, DC 20045: Youngsik Chun.

MYERS NEWS SERVICE—(703) 451–9044; 8213 Taunton Place, Springfield, VA 22152: Michael Myers.

NATIONAL JOURNAL DAILY—(202) 739–8400; 600 New Hampshire Avenue, NW., Washington, DC 20037: Peter Bell, Michelle Bloom, George Condon, Jr., Jason Dick, Katelyn Feldhaus, Michael Fox, Daniel Friedman, Juliana Gruenwald, Amy Harder, Billy House, Stacy Lynn Kaper, Kathy Kiely, Otto Kreisher, Andrew Leonatti, Mike Magner, Meghan McCarthy, Irvin Molotsky, James O'Sullivan, Alex Roarty, Humberto Sanchez, Megan Scully, Lara Seligman, Josh Smith, Kelsey Snell, Chris Strohm, George Wilson.

NATIONAL JOURNAL GROUP'S GLOBAL SECURITY NEWSWIRE—(202) 266–7248; 600 New Hampshire Avenue, NW., Washington, DC 20037: Elaine Grossman.

NEW ORLEANS TIMES-PICAYUNE—(202) 383–7861; 700 12th Street, NW., Suite 1000, Washington, DC 20005: Bruce S. Alpert, Jonathan Tilove.

NEW YORK DAILY NEWS—(202) 467–6670; 1050 Thomas Jefferson Street, Second Floor, Washington, DC 20007: Thomas M. DeFrank, Alison Gendar, Michael McAuliff, Richard P. Sisk, Joseph Straw.

NEW YORK POST—(202) 393–1787; 1114 National Press Building, 529 14th Street, NW., Washington, DC 20045: Geoff Earle, Steven A. Miller.

NEW YORK TIMES—(202) 862–0300; 1627 I Street, NW., Suite 700, Washington, DC 20006: Leonard Apcar, Binyamin Appelbaum, Peter Baker, Dean Baquet, John Broder, Elisabeth Bumiller, Jeff Burgess, Jackie Calmes, Adam Clymer, Helene Cooper, Rebecca Corbett, John H. Cushman, Jr., Jason Deparle, Maureen Dowd, Elizabeth Goodridge, Michael Gordon, Gardiner Harris, Raymond Hernandez, David Herszenhorn, Emmarie Huetteman, Carl Hulse, David S. Joachim, Mark Landler, Eric Lichtblau, Adam Liptak, Eric Lipton, Mark Mazzetti, Clifton E. Meadows, Steven Lee Myers, Ron Nixon, Robert

NEWSPAPERS REPRESENTED—Continued

L. Pear, Lisa Faye Petak, David E. Sanger, Charlie Savage, Eric Schmitt, Scott Shane, Thomas D. Shanker, Michael Shear, Ronald Skarzenski, Jada F. Smith, Anne Snyder, Ashley Southall, Jennifer Steinhauer, Richard W. Stevenson, Sheryl Gay Stolberg, William Storey, Ginger Thompson, Paul Volpe, Matthew L. Wald, Derek Willis, Edward Wyatt, Jeff Zeleny.

NEWS AND MESSENGER—(703) 369–5738: Johnathan Hunley.

NEWSDAY—(202) 408–2715; 1090 Vermont Avenue, NW., Washington, DC 20005: Thomas F. Brune.

NEWSPAPER ENTERPRISE—(301) 320–5559; 6008 Osceola Road, Bethesda, MD 20816: Robert Wagman.

NIKKEI—(202) 393–1388; 815 Connecticut Avenue, NW., Suite 310, Washington, DC 20006: Tomoko Ashizuka, Christina Bilski, Masako Iwamoto, Stephen R. Keefe, Shin Nakayama, Itaru Oishi, Masakuni Oshirabe, Toshiki Yazawa.

NISHI-NIPPON SHIMBUN—(202) 393–5812; 1012 National Press Building, 529 14th Street, NW., Washington, DC 20045: Masaharu Miyazaki.

NOTIMEX MEXICAN NEWS AGENCY—(202) 347–5227; 975 National Press Building, 529 14th Street, NW., Washington, DC 20045: Ruben Barrera, Maria Garcia, Jose G. Lopez Zamorano, Santiago Tavara.

O GLOBO—(202) 885–8694: Fernando Eichenberg.

OIL DAILY—(202) 662–0723; 1411 K Street, NW., Suite 602, Washington, DC 20005: William Murray.

OKLAHOMAN—(202) 662–7543; 914 National Press Building, 529 14th Street, NW., Washington, DC 20045: Chris Casteel.

OMAHA WORLD-HERALD—(202) 997–9787; 836 National Press Building, 529 14th Street, NW., Washington, DC 20045: Joseph Morton.

OREGONIAN—(202) 731–5152; 18923 Impulse Lane, Gaithersburg, MD 20879: Charles Pope.

ORLANDO SENTINEL—(202) 824–8222; 1025 F Street, NW., Suite 700, Washington, DC 20004: Mark Matthews.

PALM BEACH POST —(202) 777–7090; 400 North Capitol Street, #750, Washington, DC 20001: Laura Green.

PHILADELPHIA INQUIRER—(301) 320–6655; Box 577, Glen Echo, MD 20812: John Shiffman.

PIONEER-INDIA—(703) 876–6149; 2731 Pleasantdale Road, #203, Vienna, VA 22180: Sethuraman Rajagopalan.

PITTSBURGH POST-GAZETTE—(717) 787–2141; 2000 North Adams Street, Apartment 510, Arlington, VA 22201: Tracie Mauriello.

PLATTS NEWS SERVICE—(202) 383–2251; 1200 G Street, Suite 1100, Washington, DC 20005: Gary Gentile.

PORTLAND PRESS HERALD—(202) 697–0741; 5008 Rodman Road, Bethesda, MD 20816: Jonathan Riskind.

POSTMEDIA NEWS—(301) 233–8479; 1206 National Press Building, 529 14th Street, NW., Washington, DC 20045: Allen Abel, Sheldon Alberts.

PRESS REGISTER—(202) 360–8458: George Altman.

PROVIDENCE JOURNAL—(202) 661–8423; 1252 National Press Building, 529 14th Street, NW., Washington, DC 20045: John Mulligan.

REAL CLEAR POLITICS—(301) 412–9639; 1500 Massachusetts Avenue, NW., Washington, DC 20005: Caitlin Huey-Burns, Erin McPike, Alexis Simendinger.

RECORD (BERGEN COUNTY, NJ)—(202) 249–2160; 1701 16th Street, Apartment 615, Washington, DC 20009: Herbert Jackson.

REFORMA NEWSPAPER—(202) 341–3255; 1009 New Hampshire Avenue, NW., Apartment 7, Washington, DC 20037: Jose Diaz-Briseno.

RELIGION NEWS SERVICE—(202) 463–8777; 1930 18th Street, NW., Suite B2, Washington, DC 20009: Adelle M. Banks, Daniel Burke, Kevin Eckstrom, Lauren Markoe.

RESTRUCTURING TODAY—(202) 384–4833; 4908 Hornbeam Drive, Rockville, MD 20853: James Downing, Michael Zwelling.

RHEINISCHE POST—(202) 966–2303; 5810 Chevy Chase Parkway, NW., Washington, DC 20015: Frank Herrmann.

RIVERSIDE PRESS-ENTERPRISE—(202) 661–8422; 1252 National Press Building, 529 14th Street, NW., Washington, DC 20045: Ben Goad.

RTT NEWS—(202) 349–4091: Brendan McKenna.

SALT LAKE TRIBUNE—(202) 662–8732; 1255 National Press Building, 529 14th Street, NW., Washington, DC 20045: Thomas Burr, Matt Canham.

SAN ANTONIO EXPRESS-NEWS—(202) 263–6451; 700 12th Street, NW., Suite 1000, Washington, DC 20005: Gary R. Martin.

SAN FRANCISCO CHRONICLE—(202) 263–6573; 700 12th Street, NW., Suite 1000, Washington, DC 20005: Carolyn Lochhead.

SANKEI SHIMBUN—(202) 347–2015; 330 National Press Building, 529 14th Street, NW., Washington, DC 20045: Yosuke Inuzuka, Kosuke Kakiuchi, Yoshihisa Komori, Rui Sasaki, Bruce Scott Stewart.

NEWSPAPERS REPRESENTED—Continued

SAUDI PRESS AGENCY—(202) 944–3890; 601 New Hampshire Avenue, NW., Washington, DC 20037: Yasmeen Alamiri, Haifa Al-Mubarak, Mustafa A. Bashir, Dean Dessouky, Azeddine Labriny, Lauren Riley, Nezar Sheikh.

SCRIP—(301) 216–2433; 13109 Millhaven Place, Germantown, MD 20874: Donna Young.

SCRIPPS HOWARD NEWS SERVICE—(202) 408–1484; 1090 Vermont Avenue, Suite 1000, Washington, DC 20005: Curtis Lee Bowman, Patricia Choate, Pninit Cohen, Michael Collins, Robert Friedman, Becca Jane Griesemer, Carol Guensburg, Laurie Hackett, Thomas K. Hargrove, Lisa Hoffman, Kendra DeNise Johnson, Dale B. McFeatters, David Nielsen, Martin Schram, Anya Hope Sippen, Bartholomew Sullivan, Daniel Isaac Wolf, Seattle Times: Kyung Song, Sekai Nippo: Toshiyuki Hayakawa, Seoul Shimbun: Sang-Yeon Kim, Singapore Straits Times: Chin Hon Chua, Tracy Quek.

SEATTLE TIMES—(202) 662–7455; 920 National Press Building, 529 14th Street, NW., Washington, DC 20045: Kyung Song.

SEKAI NIPPO—(202) 898–8292; 1133 19th Street, NW., 8th Floor, Washington, DC 20036: Toshiyuki Hayakawa.

SEOUL SHIMBUN—(202) 393–4061; 905 National Press Building, 529 14th Street, NW., Washington, DC 20045: Sang-Yeon Kim.

SINGAPORE STRAITS TIMES—(202) 662–8728; 916 National Press Building, 529 14th Street, NW., Washington, DC 20045: Chin Hon Chua, Tracy Quek.

SMARTGRID TODAY—(213) 505–7503; 4908 Hornbeam Drive, Rockville, MD 20853: Brett Brune, Zachary Colman, Samuel Spencer.

ST. LOUIS BEACON—(301) 538–8644: Robert L. Koenig.

ST. LOUIS POST-DISPATCH—(202) 298–6880; 1025 Connecticut Avenue, Suite 1102, Washington, DC 20036: William Lambrecht.

ST. PETERSBURG TIMES—(202) 463–0575; 1100 Connecticut Avenue, 4th Floor, Washington, DC 20036: William R. Adair, Rebecca Anderson Bowers, Martha Hamilton, Louis Jacobson, Alex Leary.

STAVANGER AFTENBLAD—(703) 385–6905: Ingeborg Eliassen, Sven Egil Omdal.

STEPHENS MEDIA GROUP—(202) 783–1760; 666 11th Street, Suite 535, Washington, DC 20001: Stephan R. Tetreault.

STUTTGARTER ZEITUNG—(240) 743–4041; 6520 Lone Oak Court, Bethesda, MD 20817: Andreas Geldner.

SUEDDEUTSCHE ZEITUNG—(301) 229–3736; 7017 Hopewood Street, Bethesda, MD 20817: Reymer Kluever.

SUNDAY TIMES OF LONDON—(202) 316–3002; 1025 Connecticut Avenue, NW., Suite 800, Washington, DC 20036: Thomas Timothy Fitzsimons, Christina Lamb, Lucy McCalmont.

SUN-SENTINEL—(202) 824–8256; 1090 Vermont Avenue, NW., Suite 1000, Washington, DC 20005: William Gibson, Julie Patel.

SVENSKA DAGBLADET—(202) 362–8253; 3601 Connecticut Avenue, #622, Washington, DC 20008: Karin Henriksson, Gary Yerkey.

SYDNEY MORNING HERALD—(202) 737–6360; 1310 G Street, #750, Washington, DC 20005: Simon Mann.

SYRACUSE POST-STANDARD—(571) 970–3751; 3900 Fairfax Drive, Suite 1321, Arlington, VA 22203: Mark Weiner.

TAGES ANZEIGER—(202) 332–8575; 2026 16th Street, NW., #5, Washington, DC 20009: Martin Kilian.

TAIWAN CENTRAL NEWS AGENCY—(202) 628–2378; 1173 National Press Building, 529 14th Street, NW., Washington, DC 20045: Tony Liao Han Yuan, Kuen-Yuan Liu.

TECH LAW JOURNAL—(202) 364–8882; 3034 Newark Street, NW., Washington, DC 20008: David Carney.

TEL AVIV GLOBES—(301) 217–9278; 23 Chantilly Court, Rockville, MD 20850: Ron Dagony.

THOMSON FINANCIAL NEWS—(202) 777–8507; 1100 13th Street, NW., Suite 200, Washington, DC 20005: Jerry Konjevoda.

THOMSON REUTERS—(202) 898–8300; 1333 H Street, Suite 500, Washington, DC 20005: Charles J. Abbott, Timothy D. Ahmann, Charles David Alexander, Victoria L. Allen, JoAnne Allen, Philip Barbara, Diane Bartz, Eric Beech, Alistair Bell, Melissa R. Bland, Russell Blinch, Caren Bohan, Martin Brandt, Rory Carroll, Margaret Lynn Chadbourn, Deborah Charles, Doina Chiacu, David Clarke, Cindy Clearwater, Ross Colvin, Susan Cornwell, Richard Cowan, John Crawley, Pedro da Costa, Corbett B. Daly, Bernd Debusmann, Jonathan Decker, Kim Dixon, Timothy H. Dobbyn, Christopher Doering, Tom Doggett, Robert Doherty, Kevin Drawbaugh, Will Dunham, Paul Eckert, Samer Farha, Mark Felsenthal, Thomas M. Ferraro, Jacqueline Frank, Tim Gardner, Rodrek A. Golden, Howard Scot Goller, Susan Heavey, Steve Holland, Mark Hosenball, Robert Johnson, Lisa Lambert, Jason Lange, David Lawder, Sarah Lynch, Laura MacInnis, Sandra Maler, Kristin Roberts Mandel, Wendell Marsh, Jeff Mason, Jasmin Melvin, Arshad Mohammed, David Morgan, Lucia Mutikani, Malathi K. Nayak, Malathi Nayak, Essex Noel, John O'Callaghan, Molly O'Toole, Molly O'Toole, Doug Palmer, Scot Paltrow, Jeremy Pelofsky, Andrew Quinn, Roberta Rampton, Ayesha Rascoe, Andrea Ricci, Lisa Richwine, Timothy F. Ryan, Mari Saito, Alina Selyukh, Alina Selyukh, Nikhil Shah, Andrea Shalal-Esa, Donna M. Smith, Glenn F. Somerville, Neil Stempleman, Emily Stephenson, Linda

NEWSPAPERS REPRESENTED—Continued

Stern, Phillip Stewart, Andy Sullivan, James Vicini, Valerie Volcovici, Michael Weekes, Jr., John L. Whitesides, Jim H. Wolf, Lesley Wroughton, Karey Wutkowski, Rachelle Younglai, Anna Yukhananov, Deborah Zabarenko, Tabassum Zakaria, Patricia Zengerle.

TIMES OF INDIA—(301) 695–9348; 7505 Akfred Drive, Silver Spring, MD 20910: Chidanand Rajghatta.

TOKYO CHUNICHI SHIMBUN—(202) 550–4103; 1012 National Press Building, 529 14th Street, NW., Washington, DC 20045: Shinichi Hisadome, Valerie Insinna, Nakahiro Iwata, Allison Kingery, Akihiro Shimada, Eri Urano.

TRIBUNE COMPANY—(202) 824–8368; 2911 Tilden Street, NW., Washington, DC 20008: Brian Bennett, Michael Memoli.

TRIBUNE MEDIA SERVICES—(202) 298–8359; 3042 Q Street, NW., Washington, DC 20007: Jules Witcover.

TULSA WORLD—(202) 484–1424; 1417 North Inglewood Street, Arlington, VA 22205: Jim Myers.

TURKIYE DAILY—(202) 253–3289; 12704 Hallman Court, North Potomac, MD 20878: Hasan M. Hazar.

UNITED DAILY NEWS—(240) 619–0256; 954 National Press Building, 529 14th Street, NW., Washington, DC 20045: Yung-Hsiang Liu.

UNITED MEDIA—(301) 494–0430; 3330 Blue Heron Drive North, Chesapeake Beach, MD 20732: Lew Sichelman.

USA TODAY—(703) 854–8900; 1575 I Street, NW., Suite 350, Washington, DC 20005: Jarrett Bell, Marisol Bello, Joan Biskupic, Erik Brady, Emily G. Brown, Catalina Camia, Dan Carney, Megan Chan, Paul Davidson, William Dermody, Oren Dorell, Peter R. Eisler, Haya El Nasser, Gwen Flanders, Thomas Frank, Brian Gallagher, Andrew Gardiner, Raymond Goldbacher, Alan Gomez, George Hager, Mimi Hall, James Healy, Brad Heath, Monica Hortobagyi, Lee Horwich, Rosalind Jackler, David Jackson, Kevin Johnson, Dennis Kelly, Kelly Kennedy, Gregory Korte, Jacqueline Kucinich, Donna Leinwand Leger, Alan Levin, Mary Beth Marklein, Stephen B. Marshall, Jim Michaels, Glenn O'Neal, Paul Overberg, Susan L. Page, Maria Puente, Fredreka Schouten, Rachel Smolkin, Michael Snider, Steve Sternberg, William Sternberg, Gregory Toppo, Geraldine Coleman Tucker, Tom Vanden Brook, Dan Vergano, James E. Welch, Richard J. Wolf, Alison Young, Gregg Zoroya.

US-REPORT (GERMANY)—(301) 299–5777; 10201 Windsor View Drive, Potomac, MD 20854: Thomas Spang.

VOTERAMA IN CONGRESS—(202) 667–9760; 1822 Corcoran Street, NW., Washington, DC 20009: Michael Lesparre, Richard Thomas.

WALL STREET JOURNAL—(202) 862–9200; 1025 Connecticut Avenue, NW., Suite 800, Washington, DC 20036: Janet Adamy, Julian Barnes, Devlin Barrett, Naftali Bendavid, Jess Bravin, MaryLu Carnevale, Thomas Catan, Robert Davis, Johnnie Dunkum, Adam Entous, Gary Fields, Siobhan Gorman, Celia Nell Henderson, Neil Hickey, Jon Hilsenrath, Jon Hilsenrath, Nathan Hodge, Janet Hook, Angel Jennings, Keith Johnson, Neil King, Peter Landers, Carol Lee, Jennifer Levitz, Jude O. Marfil, Victoria McGrane, John D. McKinnon, Laura Meckler, Brody Mullins, Alicia Mundy, Sara Murray, Patrick O'Connor, Robert Ourlian, Damian Paletta, Scott Patterson, Evan Perez, Michael M. Phillips, Stephen Lynch Power, Louise Radnofsky, Sudeep Reddy, Matthew Rose, Amy Schatz, Gerald F. Seib, Deborah Solomon, Melanie Trottman, Jonathan Weisman, David Wessel, Joseph B. White, Elizabeth Williamson, Daniel Yadron, Aaron Zitner.

WARREN COMMUNICATIONS NEWS—(202) 872–9202; 2115 Ward Court, Washington, DC 20037: Timothy Warren.

WASHINGTON EXAMINER—(202) 903–2000; 1015 15th Street, NW., Suite 500, Washington, DC 20005: Katy Adams, Michael Barone, Timothy Carney, Dee Ann Divis, Leah Fabel, Susan Ferrechio, David Freddoso, Joel S. Gehrke, Ben Giles, Brian Hughes, Bob Kemper, Philip Klein, Scott McCabe, Hayley Peterson, Nicole Schwab, David Sherfinski, Kytja Weir, Byron York.

WASHINGTON INTERNET DAILY—(202) 872–9200; 2115 Ward Court, Washington, DC 20037: Bryce Baschuk.

WASHINGTON POST—(202) 334–4121; 1150 15th Street, NW., Washington, DC 20071: Nurith Celina Aizenman, Keith Alexander, Nick Anderson, Lori Aratani, Amy Argetsinger, JoAnn Armao, Perry Bacon, Jr., Daniel J. Balz, Katherine Shaver Barnard, Robert Barnes, Jill Bartscht, Michael Bolden, Marcus Brauchli, DeNeen Brown, Henri Cauvin, Chris Cillizza, Tim Craig, Timothy Curran, Joe Davidson, Aaron Davis, Mike DeBonis, Brady Dennis, Daniel deVise, Paul Duggan, Joshua Freedom duLac, Daniel Eggen, Juliet Eilperin, Dina Elboghdady, David Fahrenthold, David Fallis, Paul Farhi, Timothy W. Farnam, Darryl Fears, Peter Finn, Marc Fisher, Mary Pat Flaherty, Michael Fletcher, Amy Gardner, Ann Gerhart, Maria Glod, Zachary Goldfarb, Amy Goldstein, James V. Grimaldi, Ashley Halsey, Dana Hedgpeth, Rosalind Heiderman, Rosalind Helderman, Nia-Malika Henderson, Monica Hesse, Scott Higham, David Hilsenrath, Jason Horowitz, Sari Horwitz, Spencer S. Hsu, Robert Kaiser, Al Kamen, Paul Kane, Glenn Kessler, Allison Klein, Anne Kornblut, Weston Kosova, Theola Labbe, Michael Laris, Lyndsey Layton, Michael Leahy, Madonna Lebling, Richard N. Leiby, Ruth Marcus, Ann Marimow, David Marino-Nachison, Jerome Markon, Ned Martel, Kevin Merida, Dana Milbank, Lori Montgomery, David Montgomery, Carol Morello, Steven Mufson, David Nakamura, Ellen Nakashima, Robert O'Harrow, Edward O'Keefe, Ben Pershing, Walter Pincus, Lisa Rein, Eli

NEWSPAPERS REPRESENTED—Continued

Reyes, Roxanne Roberts, Eugene H. Robinson, Manuel Roig-Franzia, Lois Romano, Michael Ruane, Philip Rucker, Brigid Schulte, Mary Beth Sheridan, Jeffrey Smith, Sandhya Somashekhar, Felicia Sonmez, Miranda Spivack, Miranda Spivack, Robert Stein, Joe Stephens, Nikita Stewart, Stephen Stromberg, Hank Stuever, Lena Sun, Krissah Thompson, Cheryl Thompson, Marilyn Thompson, Craig Timberg, Jacqueline E. Trescott, Neely Tucker, Karen Tumulty, Bill Turque, Ann Scott Tyson, Jason Ukman, Shankar Vedantam, Stephen Vogel, Peter Wallsten, William Wan, Joby Warrick, Rachel Weiner, Craig Whitlock, Peter Whoriskey, Ovetta Wiggins, Del Quentin Wilber, Scott Wilson, Bob Woodward, Eric Yoder, Karen Yourish, Dan Zak, Matt Zapotosky.

WASHINGTON POST NEWS SERVICE WITH BLOOMBERG NEWS—(202) 503–4669; 1150 15th Street, NW., Washington, DC 20071: Aaron Blake, Charles Leeds.

WASHINGTON TELECOMMUNICATIONS SERVICES—(804) 695–4648; 1006 Harrison Circle, Alexandria, VA 22304: Gordon E. White.

WASHINGTON TIMES—(202) 636–3000; 3600 New York Avenue, NE., Washington, DC 20002: Ben Birnbaum, David Boyer, Sara Carter, Ben Conery, Paige Winfield Cunningham, Dan Daly, Brett Decker, Tim Devaney, Richard Diamond, Stephen Dinan, Christopher Dolan, David Eldridge, William Gertz, Anneke E. Green, Ralph Hallow, Jennifer Harper, Mike Harris, Patrice Hill, Eli Lake, Marc Lancaster, Sean Lengell, Seth McLaughlin, Emily Miller, James Morrison, Chuck Neubauer, Kerry Picket, Kara Rowland, David Sands, Jerry Seper, Deborah Simmons, Patrick Stevens, Shaun Waterman, Joseph Weber, Cheryl Wetzstein, Benjamin Wolfgang.

WATERTOWN DAILY TIMES—(202) 662–7085; 1001 National Press Building, 529 14th Street, NW., Washington, DC 20045: Marc R. Heller.

WEN HUI DAILY—(202) 262–6781; 1600 South Eads Street, Suite 1134 North, Arlington, VA 22202: Xiaoyang Xia.

WESTDEUTSCHE ALLGEMEINE—(301) 530–2360; 6901 Marbury Road, Bethesda, MD 20817: Joachim Rogge.

WESTERN COMMUNICATIONS—(202) 662–7456; 920 National Press Building, 529 14th Street, NW., Washington, DC 20045: Andrew W. Clevenger.

WILLIAM SCALLY REPORTS—(202) 362–2382; 2918 Legation Street, NW., Washington, DC 20015: William F. Scally.

WORLD BUSINESS PRESS—(703) 942–8318; 4706 Commons Drive, A–303, Annandale, VA 22003: Dagmar Benesova, Zoltan Mikes.

WORLD JOURNAL—(202) 737–6426; 954 National Press Building, 529 14th Street, NW., Washington, DC 20045: Betty Lin.

XINHUA NEWS AGENCY—(703) 647–1598; 1201 National Press Building, Washington, DC 20045: Jing Du, Xiangwen Ge, Yu Lin, Lina Liu, Wei Ran, Haijun Ren, Fengfeng Wang, Wang Wei, Jiang Xufeng, Feng Yan, Jian Yang, Aijun Yi.

YOMIURI SHIMBUN—(202) 783–0363; 802 National Press Building, 529 14th Street, NW., Washington, DC 20045: William DiNovi, Lisa Gomi, Julian Hattem, Yoshinari Kurose, Kentaro Nakajima, Satoshi Ogawa, Akihiro Okada, Michiro Okamoto, Mineko Tokito, Tetsuro Yamada, Kyoko Yamaguchi.

YONHAP NEWS AGENCY—(202) 783–5539; 914 National Press Building, 529 14th Street, NW., Washington, DC 20045: Lee Chi Dong, Jae Hoon Hwang, Hwang Doo Hyong, Hae Young Lee, Jungbin Park, Sang Hyun Park, Ghihong Seong, Lee Seung-Gwon.

PRESS PHOTOGRAPHERS' GALLERY*

The Capitol, Room S–317, 224–6548

www.senate.gov/galleries/photo

Director.—Jeffrey S. Kent.
Deputy Director.—Mark A. Abraham.
Assistant Director.—Tricia Munro.

STANDING COMMITTEE OF PRESS PHOTOGRAPHERS

Scott Applewhite, Associated Press, *Chair*
Win McNamee, Getty Images, *Secretary-Treasurer*
Jim Bourg, Reuters
Khue Bui, Newsweek
Stephen Crowley, New York Times
Ronald Sachs, Consolidated News Pictures

RULES GOVERNING PRESS PHOTOGRAPHERS' GALLERY

1. (a) Administration of the Press Photographers' Gallery is vested in a Standing Committee of Press Photographers consisting of six persons elected by accredited members of the Gallery. The Committee shall be composed of one member each from Associated Press Photos; Reuters News Pictures or AFP Photos; magazine media; local newspapers; agency or freelance member; and one at-large member. The at-large member may be, but need not be, selected from media otherwise represented on the Committee; however no organization may have more than one representative on the Committee.

(b) Elections shall be held as early as practicable in each year, and in no case later than March 31. A vacancy in the membership of the Committee occurring prior to the expiration of a term shall be filled by a special election called for that purpose by the Committee.

(c) The Standing Committee of the Press Photographers' Gallery shall propose no change or changes in these rules except upon petition in writing signed by not less than 25 accredited members of the gallery.

2. Persons desiring admission to the Press Photographers' Gallery of the Senate shall make application in accordance with Rule 33 of the Senate, which rule shall be interpreted and administered by the Standing Committee of Press Photographers subject to the review and approval of the Senate Committee on Rules and Administration.

3. The Standing Committee of Press photographers shall limit membership in the photographers' gallery to bona fide news photographers of repute in their profession and Heads of Photographic Bureaus under such rules as the Standing Committee of Press Photographers shall prescribe.

4. Provided, however, that the Standing Committee of Press Photographers shall admit to the gallery no person who does not establish to the satisfaction of the Committee all of the following:

(a) That any member is not engaged in paid publicity or promotion work or in prosecuting any claim before Congress or before any department of the Government, and will not become so engaged while a member of the gallery.

*Information is based on data furnished and edited by each respective gallery.

(b) That he or she is not engaged in any lobbying activity and will not become so engaged while a member of the gallery.

The above rules have been approved by the Committee on Rules and Administration.

JOHN A. BOEHNER,
Speaker, House of Representatives.

CHARLES E. SCHUMER,
Chair, Senate Committee on Rules and Administration.

MEMBERS ENTITLED FOR ADMISSION

PRESS PHOTOGRAPHERS' GALLERY

Ake, David : Associated Press Photos
Alvarez, Luis M.: Freelance
Alvarez, Miguel: Freelance
Almalvy, Vincent: Agence France-Presse
Angerer, Drew: Washington Times
Applewhite, J. Scott: Associated Press Photos
Archambault, Charlie; Freelance
Ashley, Douglas G.: Suburban Communications Corp.
Augustino, Jocelyn: Freelance
Auth, Bill: Freelance
Barouh, Stan: 1105 Media
Barrett, Stephen E.: Freelance
Barrick, Matthew: Freelance
Bartz, Jason: Scripps Howard News Service
Beiser, H. Darr: USA / Today
Benic, Patrick T.: United Press International
Berg, Lisa: Freelance
Biddle, Susan: Washington Post
Bingham, Mary (Molly): Freelance
Binks, Porter L.: Sports Illustrated
Bivera, Johnny: Freelance
Blass, Eileen M.: USA/Today
Bleier-Schmeets, Karen: Agence France-Presse
Bloom, Richard: Freelance
Bochatey, Terry F.: Reuters News Pictures
Boitano, Stephen J.: Freelance
Bourg, Jim: Reuters News Pictures
Bowe, Christy: ImageCatcher News
Bowler, Dana Rene: Freelance
Brack, William D.: Black Star
Brandon, James Alex: Associated Press Photos
Brier, Joe: Freelance
Brown, Robert A.: Richmond Times Dispatch
Brown, Thomas: Gannett Government Media
Bui, Khue: Newsweek
Cabrera, Mario Baudilio: Freelance
Calvert, Mary F.: Freelance
Cameron, Gary A.: Reuters News Pictures
Carioti, Richard A.: Washington Post
Carroll, Lauren: National Journal
Castoro, Susan: Associated Press Photos
Cedeno, Ken: Freelance
Ceneta, Manuel B.: Associated Press Photos
Chikwendiu, Jahi: Washington Post
Clark, Bill: Roll Call
Clark, Kevin: Washington Post
Clement, Richard: Bloomberg Government
Cochran, Mick: USA/Today
Cohen, Marshall H.: Bigmarsh News Photos
Connor, Kristopher Cory: Freelance
Conrad, Fred: The New York Times
Coppage, Gary R.: Photo Press International
Councill, Andrew: Freelance
Crowley, Stephen: The New York Times
Curtis, Rob: Gannett Government Media
Cutraro, Andrew: Freelance
Davidson, Linda: Washington Post
Deutsh, Robert: USA/Today
Devorah, Carrie: Freelance
Dharapak, Charles: Associated Press Photos
Dietsch, Kevin: United Press International
Dietz, James: Associated Press Photos
Doctorian, Sonya: Washington Post
Dougherty, Sean: USA/Today
Douliery, Olivier: Abaca
Downing, Lawrence S.: Reuters News Pictures
Drenner, Dennis: Freelance
Du Cille, Michel: Washington Post
Eddins, Jr., Joseph M.: Washington Times
Edmonds, Ronald: Associated Press Photos
Eile, Evan: USA/Today
Ellis, Richard: Getty Images
Elswick, Jon: Associated Press Photos
Ernst, Jonathan: Freelance
Esquivel, Robert: Herald Standard
Fabiano, Gary: Sipa Press
Falk, Steven M.: The Philadelphia Daily News
Ferrell, Scott: CQ Weekly
Franko, Jeff: Gannett
Fremson, Ruth: The New York Times
Frey, Katherine: Washington Post
Gail, Carl Mark: Washington Post
Gainer, Denny: USA/Today
Gamarra, Ruben F.: Notimex
Gandhi, Pareshkumar A.: Rediff.com/ India Abroad Pub.
Garcia, Mannie: Freelance
Ghanbari, Haraz: Associated Press Photos
Golden, Melissa : Redux
Graham, Douglas: Roll Call
Gripas, Yuri: Freelance
Gruber, Jack: USA/Today
Guerrucci, Aude: Polaris Images
Gupta, Avijit: U.S. News & World Report
Guzy, Carol: Washington Post
Hambach, Eva: Agence France-Presse
Hamburg, Harry: Freelance
Harnik, Andrew: The Washington Examiner
Harrer, Andrew: Bloomberg
Harrington, John H.: Black Star
Heisenfelt, Ann: Freelance

MEMBERS ENTITLED FOR ADMISSION—Continued

Heisler, Todd: The New York Times
Helber, Stephen: Associated Press Photos
Henry, Dennis: European Pressphoto Agency
Hershorn, Gary: Reuters News Pictures
Hill, Robb: Freelance
Hockstein, Evelyn: Freelance
Hoffman, Brendan W.: Freelance
Holt, Victor: Washington Informer
Hubbard, Garrett: USA / Today
Jones, Leah: Freelance
Jorrin, Alexander Toby: Freelance
Joseph, Marvin: Washington Post
Kahn, Nikki: Washington Post
Kamm, Nicholas: Agence France-Presse
Kang, Hyungwon: Reuters News Pictures
Kaster, Carolyn: Associated Press Photos
Katz, Martin I.: Chesapeake News Service
Kelly, Ryan: CQ Weekly
Kennerly, David H.: Freelance
Key, Michael Patrick: Washington Blade
Kim, Hyunsoo Lee: Virginia Pilot
Kirkpatrick, T.J.: Freelance
Kittner, Sam: Freelance
Kleponis, Chris: Freelance
Konishi, Taro: Yomiuri Shimbun
Kraft, Brooks: Time Magazine
Lamarque, Kevin: Reuters News Pictures
Lamkey, Jr., Rod A.: Washington Times
Lane, Keith: Freelance
Lanham, Yuko: Asahi Shimbun
LaVor, Martin L.: Freelance
Lawidjaja, Rudy: Freelance
Lee, David Y.: Freelance
Lee, James J.: Gannett Government Media
Lee, James Jason: Gannett Government Media
Lessig, Alan: Gannett Government Media
Levine, Lewis: Freelance
Lewis, Roy: Washington Informer
Lindsey, Debra: Washington Post
Lipski, Richard A.: Washington Post
Lizik, Ron: Associated Press Photos
Lockley, Peter: Freelance
Loeb, Saul: Agence France-Presse
LoScalzo, Jim: European Pressphoto Agency
Lynch, Liz: National Journal
Lynch, M. Patricia: Frontiers News Magazine
Maddaloni, Chris: Gannett Government Media
Madrid, Michael: USA / Today
Magana, Jose Luis: Freelance
Mahaskey, M. Scott: Gannett Government Media
Malet, Jeffrey: Freelance
Mallin, Jay: Freelance
Malonson, Jacqueline: Freelance
Maltby, Melissa: Washington Post
Mara, Melina: Washington Post
Markel, Brad: Capri
Marks, Donovan: Freelance
Marovich, Jr., Pete: Zuma Press
Martin, Jacquelyn: Associated Press Photos
Martineau, Gerald: Washington Post
Martinez Monsivais, Pablo: Associated Press Photos
Matatquin, Oscar: Freelance
Mathieson, Greg E.: MAI Photo Agency
McCrehin, Jud: USA / Today
McDonnell, John: Washington Post
McNamee, Win: Getty Images
Miller, Elisa: New York Daily News
Miller, Mark: Washington Post
Miller, Robert: Washington Post
Mills, Douglas: The New York Times
Mock-Bunning, Logan: Freelance
Morigi, Paul: Freelance
Morones, Mike: Gannett Government Media
Morse, Paul: Freelance
Mount, Bonnie Jo: Washington Post
Muhammad, Ozier: The New York Times
Myers, Benjamin: Freelance
Naji-Allah, Khalid: Freelance
Nash, Greg: The Hill
Newton, Jonathan: Washington Post
Ngan, Mandel: Agence France-Presse
Nipp, Lisa: Freelance
Nordby, Leslie: Freelance
O'Leary, William P: Washington Post
Palu, Louie: Zuma Press
Panagos, Dimitrios: Greek American News Agency
Parcell, James A.: Washington Post
Park, Maxine: USA / Today
Partlow, Wayne: Associated Press Photos
Patterson, Kathryn B.: USA / Today
Perkins, Lucian: Washington Post
Petros, Bill: Freelance
Pfueller, Jenna Isackson: Freelance
Piggott, Rhyne: USA / Today
Poleski, David: Freelance
Powers, Carol T: Freelance
Powers, Christopher: Bloomberg Government
Premack, Jay: Freelance
Purcell, Steven: Freelance
Raab, Susana A: Freelance
Radzinschi, Diego: National Law Journal
Raedle, Joe: Getty Images
Reed, Jason: Reuters News Pictures
Reicken, Astrid: Freelance
Reinhard, Rick: Impact Digitals
Reynolds, Michael: European Pressphoto Agency
Richards, Paul J.: Agence France-Presse
Richardson, Joey M.: McClatchy Tribune
Riley, Molly: Reuters News Pictures
Roberts, Joshua: Freelance
Robinson, Scott: Freelance
Rogowski, David: Bloomberg Government
Rolfe, Judy: Freelance
Rubenstein, Larry: Reuters News Pictures

MEMBERS ENTITLED FOR ADMISSION—Continued

Ryan, Patrick: Freelance
Sachs, Ronald M.: Consolidated News Pictures
Salisbury, Barbara L.: Washington Times
Samad, Jewel: Agence France-Presse
Samperton, Kyle: Freelance
Sandys, Toni L.: Washington Post
Saunders, Ray K.: Washington Post
Savoia, Stephon: Associated Press Photos
Schaeffer, Sandra L.: MAI Photo Agency
Schmallz, Julia: Bloomberg Government
Schwartz, Michael: The Politico
Scott, Andrew: USA/Today
Semiatin, Morris: Freelance
Shelley, Allison: Freelance
Shinkle, John: The Politico
Silverman, Joseph A.: Freelance
Simon, Martin: Corbis
Smialowski, Brendan: Freelance
Somodevilla, Kenneth: Getty Images
Squires, Derek: Tax Analysts
Susslin, Chet: National Journal
Sweets, Fredric F.: St. Louis American
Sykes, Jack W.: Professional Pilot Magazine
Temchine, Michael: Freelance
Theiler, Michael: Freelance
Thew, Shawn: European Pressphoto Agency
Thomas, Ricardo: The Detroit News
Thomas, Ron: Freelance
Thresher, James M.: Washington Post
Trippett, Robert: Freelance
Turner, Tyrone: Freelance
Usher, Chris: Freelance
Varias, Stelios A.: Reuters News Pictures
Vick, Vanessa: Freelance
Voisin, Sarah L.: Washington Post
Voss, Stephen: Freelance
Vucci, Evan: Associated Press Photos
Walker, Harry E.: McClatchy Tribune
Walsh, Susan: Associated Press Photos
Watkins, Jr., Frederick L.: Freelance
Watson, James H.: Agence France-Presse
Wells, Jonathan: Sipa Press
Westcott, Jay: The Politico
Whitesell, Gregory: Freelance
Williams, Tom: Roll Call
Williamson, Michael: Washington Post
Wilson, Mark L.: Getty Images
Winter, Damon: The New York Times
Wolf, Kevin: Freelance
Wolf, Lloyd: Freelance
Wollenberg, Roger L.: United Press International
Wong, Alex: Getty Images
Woodward, Tracy A.: Washington Post
Yim, Heesoon: Hana
Young, Jim: Reuters News Pictures
Zhang, Jun: Xinhua News Agency
Ziegler, Brett Thomas: U.S. News & World Report
Ziffer, Steve: Freelance

SERVICES REPRESENTED

(Service and telephone number, office address, and name of representative)

ABACA—1203 South Buchanan Street, Arlington, VA 22204: Douliery, Olivier.

AGENCE FRANCE PRESSE—(202) 414–0521; 1500 K Street, NW., Suite 600, Washington, DC 20005: Amalvy, Vincent; Bleier-Schmeets, Karen; Hambach, Eva; Kamm, Nicholas; Loeb, Saul; Ngan, Mandel; Richards, Paul J.; Samad, Jewel; Watson, James H.

ASAHI SHIMBUN—(202) 783–1000; 1022 National Press Building, 529 14th Street, NW., Washington, DC 20045: Lanham, Yuko

ASSOCIATED PRESS PHOTOS—(202) 776–9510; 1100 13th Street, Suite 700, Washington, DC 20005: Ake, David; Applewhite, J. Scott; Brandon, James Alex; Castoro, Susan; Ceneta, Manuel B.; Dharapak, Charles; Dietz, James; Edmonds, Ronald; Elswick, Jon; Ghanbari, Haraz; Helber, Stephen; Kaster, Carolyn; Lizik, Ron; Martin, Jacquelyn; Martinez Monsivais, Pablo; Partlow, Wayne; Savoia, Stephon; Vucci, Evan; Walsh, Susan

BIGMARSH NEWS PHOTOS—(202) 364–8332; 5131 52nd Street, NW., Washington, DC 20016: Cohen, Marshall.

BLACK STAR—(703) 547–1176; 7704 Tauxemont Road, Alexandria, VA 22308: Brack, William; Harrington, John.

BLOOMBERG—(202) 654–7300; 1399 New York Avenue, Washington, DC 20005; Harrer, Andrew.

BLOOMBERG GOVERNMENT—(202) 624–1820; 1399 New York Avenue, 11th Floor Washington, DC 20005: Clement, Richard; Powers, Christopher; Rogowski, David; Schmallz, Julia.

CAPRI—(717) 757–2962; 485 Sundale Drive, York, PA 17402: Markel, Brad.

CHESAPEAKE NEWS SERVICE—(410) 484–3500; P.O. Box 141, Brooklandville, MD 21022: Katz, Martin.

CONSOLIDATED NEWS PICTURES—(202) 543–3203; 10305 Leslie Street, Silver Spring, MD 20902–4857: Sachs, Ronald.

CORBIS—902 Broadway, 4th Floor, New York, NY 10010: Simon, Martin.

CQ WEEKLY—(202) 650–6844; 77 K Street, NE., Washington, DC 20004: Ferrell, Scott; Kelly, Ryan.

EUROPEAN PRESS PHOTO—(202) 347–4694; 1252 National Press Building, 529 14th Street, NW., Washington, DC 20045: Henry, Dennis; LoScalzo, Jim; Reynolds, Michael; Thew, Shawn.

FRONTIERS NEWS MAGAZINE—(301) 229–0635; P.O. Box 634, Glen Echo, MD 20812: Lynch, M., Patricia.

GANNETT—(703) 854–5800; 7950 Jones Branch Drive, McLean, VA 22107: Franko, Jeff.

GANNET GOVERNMENT MEDIA—(703) 750–8196: Brown, Thomas; Curtis, Rob; Lee, James; J.; Lee, James Jason; Lessig, Alan; Maddaloni, Chris; Mahaskey, M. Scott Scott; Morones, Mike.

GETTY IMAGES—(202) 347–2050; National Press Building, 529 14th Street, NW., Suite 1125, Washington, DC 20045: Ellis, Richard; McNamee, Win; Raedle, Joe; Somodevilla, Kenneth; Wilson, Mark L.; Wong, Alex.

GREEK AMERICAN NEWS AGENCY—(516) 931–2333; 107 Frederick Avenue, Babylon, NY 11702: Panagos, Dimitrios.

HANA—(202) 262–4541; 11311 Park Drive, Fairfax, VA 22030: Yim, Heesoon.

IMAGECATCHER NEWS—4911 Hampden Lane, Apt. #3, Bethesda, MD 20814: Bowe, Christy.

IMPACT DIGITALS—(212) 614–8406; 171 Thompson Street, #9, New York, NY 10012: Reinhard, Rick.

KNIGHT RIDDER TRIBUNE NEWS SERVICE—(202) 383–6142; 700 12th Street, NW., Suite 1000, Washington, DC 20005: Bridges, George; Walker, Harry.

LA PRENSA GRAFICA OF EL SALVADOR—(503) 2241–2670; Boulevard Santa Elena, Antiguo Casadian: Alvarez, Miguel Angel.

MAI PHOTO AGENCY—(703) 968–0030; 6601 Ashmere Lane, Centreville, VA 20120: Mathieson, Greg; Schaeffer, Sandra.

NATIONAL JOURNAL—(202) 739–8400; 600 New Hampshire Avenue, NW., Washington, DC 20037: Bloom, Richard; Carroll, Lauren.

NATIONAL LAW JOURNAL—6516 Gardenwick Road, Baltimore, MD 21209: Radzinschi, Diego.

NEW YORK DAILY NEWS—(212) 210–1511; 450 West 33rd Street, New York, NY 10001: Miller, Elisa.

NEWSWEEK—(202) 626–2085; 1750 Pennsylvania Avenue, NW., Washington, DC 20006: Bui, Khue.

NOTIMEX—(202) 347–5227; 529 14th Street, NW., Suite 425, Washington, DC 20045–1401: Gamarra, Ruben.

PHOTO PRESS INTERNATIONAL—(540) 286–1045; P.O. Box 190, Goldvein, VA 22720: Coppage, Gary.

SERVICES REPRESENTED—Continued

POLARIS IMAGES—259 West 30th Street, 13th Floor, New York, NY 10001: Guerrucci, Aude.

PROFESSIONAL PILOT MAGAZINE—3014 Colvin Street, Alexandria, VA 22314: Sykes, Jack.

REDIFF.COM/INDIA ABROAD PUB.—(646) 432–6054; 43 West 24th Street, 2nd Floor, New York, NY 10010: Gandhi, Pareshkumar.

REUTERS NEWS PICTURES—(202) 898–8333; 1333 H Street, NW., Suite 500, Washington, DC 20005: Bochatey, Terry F.; Bourg, Jim; Cameron, Gary A.; Downing, Lawrence S.; Hershorn, Gary; Kang, Hyungwon; Lamarque, Kevin; Reed, Jason; Riley, Molly; Rubenstein, Larry, Varias, Stelios A.; Young, Jim.

REDUX—(212) 253–0399; 11 Hanover Square, 26th Floor, New York, NY 10005: Golden, Melissa.

ROLL CALL—(202) 650–6844; 77 K Street, NE., Washington, DC 20002: Clark, Bill; Graham, Douglas; Williams, Tom.

SCRIPPS HOWARD NEWS SERVICE—(202) 408–2723; 1090 Vermont Avenue, NW., Washington, DC 20005: Bartz, Jason.

SIPA PRESS—(212) 463–0150; 307 7th Avenue, Suite 807, New York, NY 10001: Fabiano, Gary.

SPORTS ILLUSTRATED—(212) 522–3325; 1271 Avenue of the Americas, Room 31–306, New York, NY 10020: Binks, Porter.

ST. LOUIS AMERICAN—(314) 533–8000; 4242 Lindell Boulevard, St. Louis, MO 63108: Sweets, Fredric F.

SUBURBAN COMMUNICATIONS CORP.—(248) 568–0006; 872 Dursley Road, Bloomfield Hills, ME 48304: Ashley, Douglas.

TAX ANALYSTS—(703) 533–4400; 400 South Maple Avenue, Suite 400, Falls Church, VA 22046: Squires, Derek.

THE DETROIT NEWS—(312) 222–2030; 615 West Lafayette Avenue, Photo Department, Detroit, MI 48226: Thomas, Ricardo.

THE HILL—(202) 628–8525; 1625 K Street, Washington, DC 20006: Nash, Greg.

THE NEW YORK TIMES—(202) 862–0300; 1627 Eye Street, NW., Washington, DC 20006: Conrad, Fred; Crowley, Stephen; Fremson, Ruth; Heisler, Todd; Mills, Douglas; Muhammad, Ozier; Winter, Damon.

THE PHILADELPHIA DAILY NEWS—(215) 854–2000; 400 North Broad Street, Philadelphia, PA 19130: Falk, Steven.

THE POLITICO—(703) 647–7694; 1100 Wilson Boulevard, 6th Floor, Arlington, VA 22209: Schwartz, Michael; Shinkle, John; Westcott, Jay.

THE RICHMOND TIMES DISPATCH—(804) 649–6486; 300 East Franklin Street, Richmond, VA 23219: Brown, Robert.

THE WASHINGTON BLADE—1712 14th Street, NW., Washington, DC 20009: Key, Michael Patrick.

THE WASHINGTON INFORMER—(202) 561–4100; 3117 Martin L. King Avenue, SE, Washington, DC 20032: Holt, Victor; Lewis, Roy.

THE WASHINGTON EXAMINER—(202) 903–2000; 1015 15th Street, NW., Suite 500, Washington, DC 20005: Harnik, Andrew.

THE WASHINGTON POST—(202) 334–7380; 1150 15th Street, NW., Washington, DC 20071: Clark, Kevin; Davidson, Linda; Doctorian, Sonya; Du Cille, Michel; Frey, Katherine; Gail, Carl Mark; Guzy, Carol; Joseph, Marvin; Kahn, Nikki; Lindsey, Debra; Lipski, Richard A.; Maltby, Melissa; Mara, Melina; Martineau, Gerald; McDonnell, John; Miller, Mark; Miller, Robert; Mount, Bonnie Jo; Newton, Jonathan; O'Leary, William P.; Parcell, James A.; Perkins, Lucian; Sandys, Toni L.; Saunders, Ray K.; Thresher, James M.; Voisin, Sarah L.; Williamson, Michael; Woodward, Tracy A.

THE WASHINGTON TIMES—(202) 636–3000; 3600 New York Avenue, NE., Washington, DC 20002: Angerer, Drew; Eddins, Jr., Joseph M.; Lamkey, Jr., Rod A.; Salisbury, Barbara L.

THE YOMIURI SHIMBUN—Room 208, National Press Building, Washington, DC 20045: Konishi, Taro.

TIME MAGAZINE—(202) 861–4062; 1130 Conneticut Avenue, Suite 900, Washington, DC 20036: Kraft, Brooks.

UNITED PRESS INTERNATIONAL—(202) 898–8071; 1133 19th Street, Suite 800, Washington, DC 20036: Benic, Patrick T.; Dietsch, Kevin; Wollenberg, Roger L.

USA/TODAY—(703) 854–5216; 7950 Jones Branch Road, McLean, VA 22107: Beiser, H. Darr; Blass, Eileen M.; Cochran, Mick; Deutsh, Robert; Dougherty, Sean; Eile, Evan; Gainer, Denny; Gruber, Jack; Hubbard, Garrett; Madrid, Michael; McCrehin, Jud; Park, Maxine; Patterson, Kathryn B.; Piggott, Rhyne; Scott, Andrew.

VIRGINIAN PILOT—(757) 446–2000; 150 West Brambleton Avenue, Norfolk, VA 23510: Kim, Hyunsoo Lee.

XINHUA NEWS AGENCY—(703) 875–0082; 1740 North 14th Street, Arlington, VA 22209: Zhang, Jun.

ZUMA PRESS—34189 Pacific Coast Highway, Dana Point, CA 92629: Marovich, Jr., Pete; Palu, Louie.

SERVICES REPRESENTED—Continued

FREELANCE

Freelance—Alvarez, Luis M.; Archambault, Charlie; Augustino, Jocelyn, Auth, Bill, Barrett, Stephen E.; Barrick, Matthew; Berg, Lisa; Bingham, Mary (Molly); Bivera, Johnny F.; Boitano, Stephen J.; Bowler, Dana Rene; Brier, Joe; Cabrera, Mario; Calvert, Mary F.; Cedeno, Ken; Connor, Kristopher Cory; Councill, Andrew; Cutraro, Andrew; Devorah, Carrie; Drenner, Dennis; Ernst, Jonathan; Garcia, Mannie; Gripas, Yuri; Hamburg, Harry; Heisenfelt, Ann; Hill, Robb; Hockstein, Evelyn; Hoffman, Brendan W.; Jones, Leah; Jorrin, Alexander "Toby" Jorrin ; Kennerly, David H.; Kirkpatrick, T.J.; Kittner, Sam; Kleponis, Chris; Lane, Keith; LaVor, Martin L.; Lawidjaja, Rudy; Lee, David Y.; Levine, Lewis; Lockley, Peter; Magana, Jose Luis; Malet, Jeffrey; Mallin, Jay; Malonson, Jacqueline; Marks, Donovan; Matatquin, Oscar, Mock–Bunning, Logan, Morigi, Paul, Morse, Paul, Myers, Benjamin; Naji–Allah, Khalid; Nipp, Lisa; Nordby, Leslie; Petros, Bill; Pfueller, Jenna Isackson; Poleski, David, Powers, Carol T.; Premack, Jay; Purcell, Steven; Raab, Susana A.; Reicken, Astrid; Roberts, Joshua; Robinson, Scott; Rolfe, Judy; Ryan, Patrick; Samperton, Kyle; Semiatin, Morris; Shelley, Allison; Silverman, Joseph A.; Smialowski, Brendan; Temchine, Michael; Theiler, Michael; Thomas, Ron; Trippett, Robert; Turner, Tyrone; Usher, Chris; Vick, Vanessa; Voss, Stephen; Watkins, Jr., Frederick L.; Whitesell, Gregory; Wolf, Kevin; Wolf, Lloyd; Ziffer, Steve.

WHITE HOUSE NEWS PHOTOGRAPHERS' ASSOCIATION

P.O. Box 7119 Ben Franklin Station, Washington, DC 20044–7119

www.whnpa.org

OFFICERS

Ronald Sachs, Consolidated News, *President*
Douglas Wilkes, WTTG–TV, *Vice President*
Elisa Miller, Freelance, *Secretary*
Jonathan Elswick, Associated Press, *Treasurer*

EXECUTIVE BOARD

Toni Sandys (Washington Post)
Alex Wong (Getty Images)
Charles Dharapak (Associated Press)
Ed Eaves (NBC News)
Charles MacDonald (National Geographic Channel)
Chip Somodevilla, Contest Chair (Getty Images)
Pege Gilgannon, Contest Chair, Television (WJLA–TV)
Pierre Kattar, Contest Chair, New Media
Jamie Rose, Contest Chair, Student (Freelance)
Pablo Monsivais, Education Chair (Associated Press)

MEMBERS REPRESENTED

Abdallah, Khalil: CNN
Adlerblum, Robin: CBS News
Ake, J. David: Associated Press
Albert, Christopher: CBS News
Alberter, Jr., William: CNN
Allard, Marc: Freelance
Allen, Tom: Washington Post (Ret.)
Andrews, Scott: Canon Rep
Angerer, Drew: Washington Times
Applewhite, J. Scott: Associated Press
Apt Johnson, Roslyn: CBS News
Arias, Juana:
Arrington, Clyde: ABC News
Asenbrennerova, Jana:
Ashley, Douglas: Surburban Newspapers & ABC TV
Assaf, Christopher: Baltimore Sun
Atherton, James:
Aubry, Timothy: Greenpeace Magazine
Auth, William: Freelance
Bacheler, Peter: Freelance
Bahler, Barry: Department of Homeland Security
Bahruth, William:
Baker, David: ITN
Barrick, Matthew: Caring Magazine
Baysden, III, Earl: WTTG–TV
Beiser, H. Darr: USA Today
Benic, Patrick: UPI
Bennett, Ronald T.: Executive Branch
Bennett, Brian: Freelance
Berglie, James: Zuma Press
Berkman, Eliezer: Freelance
Biddle, Susan: Washington Post
Bindelgalss, Perry: Freelance
Binks, Porter: Sports Illustrated
Bivera, Johnny: Freelance
Blaylock, Kenneth:
Bodnar, John: CNN
Bourg, James: Reuters
Bowe, Christy: ImageCatcher News
Bowler, Dana: Freelance
Bracco, II, Dominic: Freelance
Brack, Dennis: Black Star
Brandon, Alex: Associated Press
Brantley, James: Freelance
Bridgham, Kenneth:
Brier, Joseph: Freelance
Brown, Stephen:

MEMBERS REPRESENTED—Continued

Brown, Sr., Henry: ABC
Bruce, Andrea: Washington Post
Bryan, Beverly:
Bui, Khue: Freelance
Burgess, Robert: Freelance
Burke, Jr., William C.: Page One Photography
Burnett, David: Contact Press Images
Burns, David: New York Daily News
Cairns, Taylor: Student
Calvert, Mary: Washington Times
Cannarozzi, Melissa: Washington Times
Carioti, Ricky: Washington Post
Carlson, David: Canon
Cassetta, Guido: Freelance
Castoro, Susan: Associated Press
Cedeno, Ken: Freelance
Ceneta, Manuel: Associated Press
Chikwendiu, Jahi: Washington Post
Cirace, Robert: CNN (Ret.)
Cirone, Jopseph: Responsive Media
Clark, Bill: Roll Call
Clark, Kevin: Washington Post
Clarkson, Rich: Rich Clarkson & Associates
Cochran, Michael: USA Today
Cohen, Marshall: Big Marsh News Photos
Cohen, Stuart: Freelance
Colburn, James: Freelance
Collins, Maxine: BBC TV
Conger, Dean:
Connor, Kristopher: Freelance
Connor, Michael:
Cook, Dennis:
Costello, II, Thomas: Asbury Park Press
Couig, Caroline: Freelance
Craighead, Shealah: Freelance
Crane, Arnold: The LaVor Group
Crowley, Stephen: The New York Times
Curran, Patrick: WTTG–TV
Curtiss, Cathaleen: AOL
D'Angelo, Rebecca: Freelance
Daniell, Parker: Freelance
Daugherty, Bob:
Davidson, Linda: Washington Post
Davis, Amy: Baltimore Sun
de la Cruz, Benedict: Washingtonpost.com
Delaney, Danita: The Washington Afro
Dennehey, Paul:
Desfor, Max:
Devorah, Carrie: Freelance
Dharapak, Charles: Associated Press
Dietsch, Kevin: UPI
Dillon, Tim:
Doane, Martin: WJLA–TV
Dorwin, Harold: Smithsonian Institution
Douliery, Oliver: Abaca Press
Downing, Larry: Reuters
Drapkin, Arnold: TIME Magazine
Dryden, Valerie: Freelance
duCille, Michel: Washington Post
Dukehart, Coburn: NPR Digital News
Dukehart, Jr., Thomas: WUSA–TV (Ret.)
Dunmire, John: WTTG–TV (Ret.)
Eaves, Ed: NBC News
Eddins, Joseph: Washington Times
Edmonds, Ron: Associated Press
Edrington, Michael: DMIOC
Eisert, Sandra: Consultant
Elbert, II, Joseph: Bus Run Productions
Elswick, Jonathan: Associated Press
Ernst, Jonathan: Freelance
Eroglu, Levent: Australian Broadcasting Corp.
Ewan, Julia: Washington Post
Ewing, David: Freelance
Falk, Steven: Philadelphia Daily News
Falkenberg, Katie: LA Times
Farmer, Sharon: Freelance
Feld, Ric: Associated Press
Feldman, Randy: Viewpoint Communications, Inc.
Feldman, Roy: Freelance
Fielman, Sheldon: NBC News
Fine, Paul: Fine Films
Fine, Holly: Fine Films
Fisher, Gail: National Geographic
Fitz-Patrick, Bill: Freelance
Folwell, Frank: Freelance
Fookes, Gary: Freelance (Ret.)
Ford, Nancy: IFPO / American International News
Ford, Matt: Associated Press
Forrest, James: (Ret.) WRC–TV News
Forte, B.J.: WTTG–TV
Foss, Philip: Speed Graphic
Foster, H. William: Freelance
Foy, Mary Lou: Washington Post
Frame, John: WTTG–TV
Freeman, Roland: Freelance
Freeman, Barry: ABC News
Frey, Katherine: Washington Post
Fridrich, George: Brighter Images Productions LLC
Fuchs, Christian: Jesuit Refugee Service
Gail, C. Mark: Washington Post
Gainer, Dennis: USA Today
Garcia, Mannie: Freelance
Garcia, Alexandra: WPNI
Geiger, Ken: National Geographic
Geissinger, Michael: Freelance
Geraci, Andrew: Washington Times
Ghanbari, Haraz: Associated Press
Giebel, Edward: ABC News Freelance
Gilgannon, Pege: WJLA
Gilkey, David: NPR
Glenn, Alexis: UPI
Gmiter, Bernard: Freelance
Golden, Melissa: Freelance
Goodman, Jeffrey: NBC / Freelance

MEMBERS REPRESENTED—Continued

Goulait, Bert: Freelance
Gould-Phillips, Carol: Current Viewpoint
Goyal, Raghubir: Asia Today & India Globe / ATN News
Graham, Douglas: Roll Call
Grant, Kelli: Pixways, Inc.
Green, Barnaby: Sky News
Greenblatt, William: UPI
Gripas, Yuri: Reuters
Guerrucci, Aude: Polaris
Gundy, Dorry: BBC News
Guzy, Carol: Washington Post
Hakuta, Michael: Wash. Post Newsweek Interactive
Halstead, Dirck: The Digital Journalist
Hamburg, Harry: (Ret.)
Harnik, Andrew: Washington Times
Harrer, Andrew: Bloomberg
Harrington, John: Freelance
Harrity, Chick: Whimsy Works
Heikes, Darryl: Freelance
Heilemann, Tami: Department of Interior
Heiner, Steve: Nikon
Henderson, Gregory: Associated Press
Herbert, Gerald: Associated Press
Hershorn, Gary: Reuters
Hill, Robb: Freelance
Hillian, Vanessa: Washington Post (Ret.)
Hinds, Hugh: WRC / NBC
Hoffman, Brendan: Freelance
Hoiland, Harald:
Holloway, David: Freelance
Holt, Victor: Washington Informer
Hopkins, Brian: WJLA–TV
Hopkins, Gary: AOL
Horan, Michael: WTTG–TV
Hoyt, Michael: Catholic Standard
Hubbard, Garrett: USA Today
Huling, Pam: Gaslight Media Consulting
Hutchens, Jeff: Freelance
Imai, Kesaharu: World Photo Press
Ing, Lance: WTTG–TV
Irby, Kenneth: Poynter Institute
Isaacson-Pfueller, Jenna: Freelance
Jenkins, David: CNN
Johnson, Kenneth: ABC–TV
Johnston, Frank: Washington Post
Jones, Nelson: WTTG–TV
Joseph, Marvin: Washington Post
Kahn, Nikki: Washington Post
Kang, Hyungwon: Reuters News Pictures
Kapustin, Doug: Baltimore Sun
Kaster, Carolyn: Associated Press
Kattar, Pierre:
Katz, Marty: Chesapeake News Service
Kawajiri, Chiaki: Baltimore Sun
Kennedy, Thomas: Kennedy Multimedia
Kennerly, David: Eagles Roar Inc.
Kent, Jeffrey: Press Photographers' Gallery
Kieffer, Gary: The Outlook
Kittner, Sam: Freelance
Kleber, David:
Koppelman, Mitch: Reuters Television
Kossoff, Leslie: LK Photos
Kraft, Brooks: Time Magazine
Lamarque, Kevin: Reuters
Lambert, H.M.:
Lamkey, Jr., Rod:
Langer, Christopher: Student
Larsen, Gregory: Freelance
Lavies, Bianca: Freelance
LaVor, Marty: Freelance
Lawrence, Jeffrey:
Lessig, Alan: Army Times
Levine, Lewis: Costal News Service
Levy, Glenn Ann: Freelance
Levy, John:
Lipski, Richard: Washington Post
Lizik, Ronald: Associated Press
Lockhart, June:
Lockley, Peter: Washington Times
Loeb, Saul: AFP
LoScalzo, James: U.S. News & World Report
Love, Diane: Tribal Cultures Productions
Lucidon, Amanda: Freelance
Lynaugh, Mike: Freelance
Lynch, Elizabeth: National Journal
Lyons, Paul: NET (Ret.)
MacDonald, Charles: National Geographic Channel
MacDonald, Jim: Canadian TV Network
Maddaloni, Christopher: Roll Call
Magana, Jose Luis: Freelance / AP
Maggiolo, Vito: CNN
Mallin, Jay: Freelance
Mann, Donna:
Mara, Melina: Washington Post
Mark, Leighton: Associated Press
Marks, Donovan: Freelance
Marovich, Jr., Peter: Zuma Press
Martin, Jacquelin: AP
Martin Jr., James: ABC News
Martineau, Gerald: Washington Post
Martinez Monsivais, Pablo: Associated Press
Mason, Thomas: WTTG–TV
Mathieson, Greg: MAI Photo News Agency, Inc.
Mazariegos, Mark: CBS News
Maze, Stephanie: Maze Productions, Inc. / Moonstone Press LLC
Mazer Field, Joni: Freelance
Mazzatenta, O.: Freelance
McCarthy, III, Edward: Freelance
McDermott, Richard: NBC Universal
McDonnell, John: Washington Post
McGinnis, Lowell: Roll Call / Contract
McGreevy, Allen: Freelance
McKee, Staci: Freelance
McKenna, William: BBC World News America

MEMBERS REPRESENTED—Continued

McKiernan, Scott: Zuma Press
McNamee, Win: Getty Images
McNamee, Wallace: Freelance
McNay, James: Editor
Miller, Elisa: Freelance
Mills, Doug: New York Times
Mock-Brunting, Logan: Freelance
Mole, Robert: NBC (Ret.)
Morris, Larry: Washington Post (Ret.)
Morris, Peter: CNN
Morse, Paul: Freelance
Moulton, Paul:
Murphy, John: Freelance
Murphy, Heather: NPR
Murtaugh, Peter: Murtaugh Productions, LLC
Nakashima, Giuliana: Washington Post
Natoli, Sharon: Freelance
Newton, Jonathan: Washington Post
Nguyen, Phi: U.S. House of Representatives
Nighswander, Marcia: Ohio University
Nikpour, Javad: Ace Photo / Freelance / Metropole photo, LLC
Nolan, David: Nolan & Company
Norling, Richard: Freelance
O'Leary, William: Washington Post
O'Neill, Claire: NPR
Oates, Walter:
Ortez, George: (Ret.) since 1980
Owen, Cliff: Freelance
Palu, Louie: Zuma Press
Panzer, Chester: NBC–WRC
Parcell, James: Washington Post (Ret.)
Partlow, Wayne: Associated Press
Pekala, Bill: Nikon
Pergola, Nichoals:
Perkins, Lucian: Freelance
Petros, Bill: Freelance
Pinczuk, Murray: Freelance
Polich, John: (Ret.)
Poole, John: NPR
Popper, Andrew: Business Week
Potasznik, David: Point of View Production Services, Inc.
Powell, Jr., William: NBC (Ret.)
Powers, Carol: Freelance
Premack, Jay: Freelance
Raab, Susana: Freelance
Rabbage, Mark: BBC TV
Raker, Lester: ABC News
Reed, Jason: Reuters
Reeder, Robert:
Rensberger, Scott: Freelance
Reynolds, Michael: European Pressphoto Agency
Ribeiro, Luiz: The New York Post
Richards, Paul: AFP
Richards, Roger: The Digital Filmmaker
Richardson, Charlotte: Freelance
Riecken, Astrid: Washington Times
Riley, Molly: Reuters
Roberts, Joshua: Freelance
Robinson, Sr., Clyde:
Robles, Diego: Student / Denver Post new hire
Ronay, Vivian: Freelance
Rose, Jamie: Freelance
Rossman, Megan: WPNI
Roth, Jr., Johnie: NBC (Ret.)
Russek, II, Ronald: UPI
Sachs, Ronald: Consolidated News Photos
Salisbury, Barbara:
Samad, Jewel: AFP
Sandys, Toni: Washington Post
Sanfuentes, Jose ''Antoine'': NBC News
Santos, Jerry: CNN
Sardari, Kaveh: Sadari Group, Inc.
Satter, Andrew: Roll Call
Saunders, Ray: Washington Post
Schlegel, Barry: Team Video Services Inc. / CNN
Schmick, Paul: Freelance (Ret.)
Schneider, Jack: NBC–TV
Schwartz, Erin: Student
Schwartz, Herb: CBS News
Scicchitano, Carmine: NBC
Semiatin, Morris: Morris Semiatin-Photographer
Shaffir, Kimberlee: CBS News
Shannon, Dennis: CBS News
Sharrett, Luke: Student / NYT Intern
Shefte, Whitney: Washingtonpost.com
Shelley, Allison: Washington Times
Sheras, Michael: Canon USA, Inc.
Shinkle, John: Politico
Shirmohammadi, Abbas: Panoramic Visions
Shlemon, Christopher: Independent TV News
Shoemaker, Charles: Corbis Contributor
Sikes, Laura: Freelance
Simons, Beth: ABC News
Sisco, Paul: (Ret.)
Skeans, Jr., Ronald: BBC
Sloan, Tim: AFP
Smialowski, Brendan: Freelance
Smith, Dayna:
Smith, Jason: WTTG–TV
Sommer, Emilie: Freelance
Somodevilla, Kenneth: Getty Images
Stearns, Stan: Freelance
Stein, Norman: Ascent Media Systems and Technology Services
Stein, III, Arthur: Freelance
Stephenson, Al: Freelance
Stoddard, Mark: Freelance
Suban, Mark: NIKON
Suddeth, Rick: Freelance
Swain, Bethany Anne: CNN
Sweetapple, Daniel: Australian Broadcasting Corp.
Swenson, Gordon: ABC (Ret.)
Swiatkowski, Edward:
Sykes, Jack: Professional Pilot Magazine

MEMBERS REPRESENTED—Continued

Temchine, Michael: Freelance
Tessmer, Joseph: Freelance
Thalman, Mark: Across the Pond Productions
Thew, Shawn: European Pressphoto Agency
Thomas, Ronald: Office Cable Television & Telecommunications
Thomas, Margaret:
Tiffen, Steve: The Tiffen Company
Tinsley, Jeff: Smithsonian Institution (Ret.)
Tolbert, IV, George Dalton: Freelance (Ret.) U.S. Senate
Trippett, Robert: Freelance
Tripplaar, Kristoffer: Freelance
Tsuboi, Kazuo: World Photo Press
Usher, Chris: Freelance
Valentine, Vikki: NPR
Valeri, Charlene: National Geographic
Van Riper, Frank: Goodman / Van Riper Photography
Vicario, Virginia: ABC News
Vineys, Kevin: Associated Press
Voisin, Sarah: Washington Post
Vorndran, James: NBC News
Voss, Stephen: Freelance
Vucci, Evan: Associated Press
Walker, Diana: Freelance
Wallace, Jim: Smithsonian Institution
Walsh, Susan: Associated Press
Walz, Mark: CNN
Ward, Fred: Black Star
Watrud, Donald: WTTG–TV
Watson, James: AFP
Weik, David: ABC Television News (Ret.)
Wells, Jim: Freelance
Wiegman, Jr., Dave: (Ret.) NBC
Wilkes, Douglas: WTTG–TV
Williams, Milton: Freelance (Ret.)
Williams, Robert: NBC News
Williams, Thomas: Roll Call Newspaper
Williamson, Michael: Washington Post
Wilson, Jim: New York Times Photo
Wilson, Mark: Getty Images
Wolf, Kevin: Freelance
Wollenberg, Roger: United Press International
Wong, Alex: Getty Images
Woodward, Tracy: Washington Post
Wu, Enoch: Student
Yokota, Victoria: Freelance
Young, Jim: Reuters
Zervos, Stratis: Freelance-Zervos Video Productions, LLC
Ziccardi, Marc: PNY Technologies, Inc.

RADIO AND TELEVISION CORRESPONDENTS' GALLERIES*

SENATE RADIO AND TELEVISION GALLERY

The Capitol, Room S–325, 224–6421

Director.—Michael J. Mastrian
Deputy Director.—Ellen Eckert
Senior Media Relations Coordinators: Michael Lawrence, Erin Yeatman
Media Coordinator.—Chris Bois

HOUSE RADIO AND TELEVISION GALLERY

The Capitol, Room H–320, 225–5214

Director.—Olga Ramirez Kornacki
Deputy Director.—Andy Elias
Administrative Operations Manager.—Gail Davis
Media Logistics Coordinators: Kinsey Harvey, Anthony Kellaher, Kim Oates

EXECUTIVE COMMITTEE OF THE RADIO AND TELEVISION CORRESPONDENTS' GALLERIES

Jay McMichael, CNN, *Chair*
John Wallace, Fox News, *Vice Chair*
Leigh Ann Caldwell, C–SPAN, *Treasurer*
Jeffrey Ballou, Aljazeera
Libby Casey, Alaska Public Radio
Jill Jackson, CBS News
Andrea Seabrook, NPR

RULES GOVERNING RADIO AND TELEVISION CORRESPONDENTS' GALLERIES

1. Persons desiring admission to the Radio and Television Galleries of Congress shall make application to the Speaker, as required by Rule 34 of the House of Representatives, as amended, and to the Committee on Rules and Administration of the Senate, as required by Rule 33, as amended, for the regulation of the Senate wing of the Capitol. Applicants shall state in writing the names of all radio stations, television stations, systems, or news-gathering organizations by which they are employed and what other occupation or employment they may have, if any. Applicants shall further declare that they are not engaged in the prosecution of claims or the promotion of legislation pending before Congress, the Departments, or the independent agencies, and that they will not become so employed without resigning from the galleries. They shall further declare that they are not employed in any legislative or executive department or independent agency of the Government, or by any foreign govern-

*Information is based on data furnished and edited by each respective gallery.

ment or representative thereof; that they are not engaged in any lobbying activities; that they do not and will not, directly or indirectly, furnish special information to any organization, individual, or group of individuals for the influencing of prices on any commodity or stock exchange; that they will not do so during the time they retain membership in the galleries. Holders of visitors' cards who may be allowed temporary admission to the galleries must conform to all the restrictions of this paragraph.

2. It shall be a prerequisite to membership that the radio station, television station, system, or news-gathering agency which the applicant represents shall certify in writing to the Radio and Television Correspondents' Galleries that the applicant conforms to the foregoing regulations.

3. The applications required by the above rule shall be authenticated in a manner that shall be satisfactory to the Executive Committee of the Radio and Television Correspondents' Galleries who shall see that the occupation of the galleries is confined to bona fide news gatherers and/or reporters of reputable standing in their business who represent radio stations, television stations, systems, or news-gathering agencies engaged primarily in serving radio stations, television stations, or systems. It shall be the duty of the Executive Committee of the Radio and Television Correspondents' Galleries to report, at its discretion, violation of the privileges of the galleries to the Speaker or to the Senate Committee on Rules and Administration, and pending action thereon, the offending individual may be suspended.

4. Persons engaged in other occupations, whose chief attention is not given to—or more than one-half of their earned income is not derived from—the gathering or reporting of news for radio stations, television stations, systems, or news-gathering agencies primarily serving radio stations or systems, shall not be entitled to admission to the Radio and Television Galleries. The Radio and Television Correspondents' List in the Congressional Directory shall be a list only of persons whose chief attention is given to or more than one-half of their earned income is derived from the gathering and reporting of news for radio stations, television stations, and systems engaged in the daily dissemination of news, and of representatives of news-gathering agencies engaged in the daily service of news to such radio stations, television stations, or systems.

5. Members of the families of correspondents are not entitled to the privileges of the galleries.

6. The Radio and Television Galleries shall be under the control of the Executive Committee of the Radio and Television Correspondents' Galleries, subject to the approval and supervision of the Speaker of the House of Representatives and the Senate Committee on Rules and Administration.

Approved.

JOHN A. BOEHNER,
Speaker, House of Representatives.

CHARLES E. SCHUMER,
Chair, Senate Committee on Rules and Administration.

MEMBERS ENTITLED TO ADMISSION

RADIO AND TELEVISION CORRESPONDENTS' GALLERIES

Abbott, Stacey: National Public Radio
Abdalla, Hebah: Aljazeera International
Abdallah, Khalil: CNN
Abdalwahab, Yamen: Al Arabiya TV
Abdulkareem, Akram: ABS Network
Abe, Takaaki: Nippon TV Network
Abernethy, Robert G.: Religion & Ethics Newsweekly
Abeshouse, Bob: Aljazeera International
Aboud, Abdushakur: Voice of America
Abramson, Larry: National Public Radio
Abtar, Rana: Middle East Television Network (Alhurra)
Abu-Hamdyia, Reema: Russia Today Television
Aburahma, Eyad: Aljazeera Satellite Channel (Peninsula)
Acevedo, Juan Antonio: WFDC–TV Univision
Acharya, Niharika: Bloomberg Radio & TV
Ackerman, Tom: Aljazeera International
Acosta, Jim: CNN
Adams, Angelyn: Al Arabiya TV
Adams, Douglas A.: NBC News
Adams, Kim: National Public Radio
Adams, Marc: BBC
Adams, Paul: BBC
Adkinson, Jeff: AP–Broadcast
Adler, Shannan: CNN
Advani, Reena: National Public Radio
Ahlers, Mike: CNN
Ahlquist, Greg: Fox News
Ahmadi, Mohammad: Voice of America
Ahmadyar, Najibullah: Voice of America
Ahmed, Ali: Middle East Television Network (Alhurra)
Ahmed, Aziz: America Abroad Media
Ahmed, Lukman: BBC
Ahmed, M. Anis: Voice of America
Aich, Atirath: Aljazeera International
Aiello, Jr., Augustine ''Bud'': National Public Radio
Akahori, Yuichi: Nippon TV Network
Akey, Zachary: CBS News
Akhavi, Khodayar: Aljazeera International
Akkad, Reem: Aljazeera International
Al-Karkhi, Mohammed: ABS Network
Alajlouni, Mohammed: ABS Network
Alam, Farhan: America Abroad Media
Alami, Mohammed: Aljazeera Satellite Channel (Peninsula)
Alarian, Laila: Aljazeera International
Albano, Thomas: CBS News
Albert, Christopher: CBS News
Alberter, William: CNN
Alcazar, Carlos: Hispanic Communications Network
Alcazar, Obdulia: Hispanic Communications Network
Aldag, Jason: Washington Post
Alegret, Gustau: RAC1
Alexander, Clinton N.: CBS News
Alexander, Kenneth: C–SPAN
Alexander, Robert: WJLA–TV / Newschannel 8
Alfa, Nadine: Reuters Radio & TV
Alfaro, Jorge Andres: WZDC–TV
Alford, Kelly: Middle East Television Network (Alhurra)
Alger, Jack Mayo: CNN
Ali, Omar: ABS Network
Ali, Raad: ABS Network
Ali, Saad: ABS Network
Aliaga, Julio: WZDC–TV
Alikozai, Hasib: Voice of America
Allahyari, Gholamreza: Voice of America
Allard, John William: ABC News
Allbritton, Robert: WJLA–TV / Newschannel 8
Alldredge, Thomas: C–SPAN
Allen, Brian: Voice of America
Allen, Darrell: Voice of America
Allen, Keith: Reuters Radio & TV
Allison, Lynn Quarles: WETA
Alnwick, Melanie: WTTG–Fox Television
Alqadiree, Faisal: ABC News
Alrawi, Khaldoun: AP–Broadcast
Altman, Joshua: The Hill
Alves, Jevan: Energy Now
Alvey, Jay: WRC–TV / NBC–4
Amara, Kate: Hearst–Argyle Television
Amirault-Michel, Theresa: C–SPAN
Amparo, Raquel Divina: WTTG–Fox Television
Anderson, Charles: WETA
Anderson, Chinita: National Public Radio
Andree, Eric: AP–Broadcast
Andrews, Wyatt: CBS News
Aneiva, Roberto: NBC News
Ang, Sarita: Voice of America
Angelini, Mark Lloyd: Russia Today Television
Angle, James L.: Fox News
Anthony, Tony: Morningside Partners, LLC
Anyse, Alana: CBS News
Aoyama, Kazuhiro: Nippon TV Network
Apsell, Natalie: CNN
Aragon, Carlos O.: WPWC–AM (Radio Fiesta)
Archer, Nelson: CNN
Arenas, Andrea: Telesur

MEMBERS ENTITLED TO ADMISSION—Continued

Arensberg, Chloe: CBS News
Arenstein, Howard: CBS News
Armfield, Robert: Fox News
Arrasmith, Christine: National Public Radio
Arreaga, Marco Vinicio: CNN
Art, Jeremy: C–SPAN
Artesona, Eva: TV3–Televisio De Catalunya
Arthy, Sally: SKY News
Aryankalavil, Babu: Middle East Television Network (Alhurra)
Asante, John: National Public Radio
Asberg, Stefan Rolf: Swedish Broadcasting
Asher, Julie: TF1–French TV
Ashong, Derrick: Aljazeera International
Asprilla, Yeferson: RCN–TV (Colombia)
Assmann, Karin: Spiegel German TV
Assuras, Thalia: Energy Now
Atai, Shahin: C–SPAN
Atif, Muhammad: Voice of America
Atkinson, Emily: CNN
Attawia, Moaz: American Press and TV Services (APTVS)
Attkisson, Sharyl: CBS News
Auerbach, Jonathan: CNN
Augenstein, Neal: WTOP Radio
Auger, Michel C.: Canadian Broadcasting Corporation (CBC)
Augustus, Shannon: C–SPAN
Aung, Kyaw Kyaw: Radio Free Asia
Auster, Bruce: National Public Radio
Austin, Jonathan: CTV Canadian TV
Austin, Kenneth: NBC News
Avila, Martha Lucia: RCN–TV (Colombia)
Avrutine, Matthew: CNN
Awad, Zeina: Aljazeera International
Ayala, Jorge Armando: Televisa News Network (ECO)
Azizova, Naida: Russia Today Television
Azizzada, Abdul Ahad: Voice of America
Azzam, Heni: Aljazeera Satellite Channel (Peninsula)
Babich, Jennifer Rowena: Time Warner Cable Washington Bureau
Bacha, Haroon: Radio Free Europe
Bacheler, David: CNN
Baghi, Baubak: Aljazeera Satellite Channel (Peninsula)
Bagnall, Thomas: Voice of America
Bagnato, Barry: CBS News
Baier, Bret: Fox News
Baik, Sungwon: Voice of America
Bailey, John: NBC News
Bailor, Michelle: C–SPAN
Baker, Dai: Independent Television News (ITN)
Baker, Les: Fox News
Baker, Ray Linton: Whur
Baker, Sarah E.: CNN
Balcomb, Theo: National Public Radio
Ballou, Jeff: Aljazeera International
Banaszak, Brendan: National Public Radio
Banhawy, Fahd: American Press and TV Services (APTVS)
Banks, Erik: CNN
Banks, James: Eurovision Americas, Inc.
Banks, Josh: Fox News
Banks, Laquasha: CNN
Banks, Morris: CBS News
Bannigan, Mike: Fox Business Network
Banning, Holger: N–TV German News Channel
Bannon, Chris: FEDNET
Banville, David Joseph: CNN
Baragona, Steve: Voice of America
Barnard, Bob: WTTG–Fox Television
Barnes, David: Community TV of PG's
Barnes, Peter: Fox Business Network
Barnett, James: CNN
Barr, Bruce: CBS News
Barrera, Javier: America Abroad Media
Barrett, Calvin Wesley: Fox News
Barrett, Natasha: WJLA–TV / Newschannel 8
Barrett, Ted: CNN
Bartlett, Sandra: National Public Radio
Barton, Tomoko: Fuji TV Japan
Basch, Michelle: WTOP Radio
Bash, Dana: CNN
Basinger, Stuart: Fox News
Baskerville, Kia: CBS News
Bass, Tyler: Federal News Service
Bassas, Antoni: TV3–Televisio De Catalunya
Batten, Rodney: NBC News
Baumel, Susan: Voyage Productions
Bautista, Mark: CBN News
Bazinet, Kenneth: Talk Radio News Service
Beahn, James: WTTG–Fox Television
Beall, Gary: NBC News
Beard, Elisha: ABC News
Becker, Bruce: Fox Business Network
Becker, Chris: Fox News
Becker, Farrel: CBS News
Becker, Frank: WJLA–TV / Newschannel 8
Bediako, Regina: NHK–Japan Broadcasting Corporation
Bee, Angelita: Aljazeera International
Beemsterboer, Nicole: National Public Radio
Behringer, Charles Andrew: Aljazeera Satellite Channel (Peninsula)
Behrouznami, Malak: Real News Network
Bejarano, Mark: National Public Radio
Bell, Brad: WJLA–TV / Newschannel 8
Bellard, Joseph: Bloomberg Radio & TV
Belter, Stephen Lowell: C–SPAN
Bena, John: CNN
Bender, Jason: C–SPAN
Benetato, Michael: NBC News
Benincasa, Robert: National Public Radio
Benitez, Barbara: Aljazeera International

MEMBERS ENTITLED TO ADMISSION—Continued

Bennett, Geoffrey: National Public Radio
Bennett, Josh: National Public Radio
Bennett, Justin: NBC News
Bennett, Mark R.: CBS News
Bennett, Shepard: SRN News (SALEM)
Bensen, Jackie: WRC–TV / NBC–4
Benson, Miles: Link TV
Benson, Pamela S.: CNN
Bentz, Leslie Ann: CNN
Bentz, Thomas: CNN
Berger, Judson: Fox News
Bergmann, Christina: Deutsche Welle TV
Berko, Art: Viewpoint Communications
Berman, David: CNN
Bernal, Richard: CNN
Bernardi, Ashley: Energy Now
Bernardini, Laura: CNN
Bernier, Marc: Talk Radio News Service
Bernius, Andrew: C–SPAN
Betsill, Brett: C–SPAN
Bevington, Ben: BBC
Beyer Kelly, Sarah: National Public Radio
Beyer, William: WTTG–Fox Television
Bezdrob, Shayla: Fox News
Bharania, Anoopam: Reuters Radio & TV
Bhatia, Varuna: Fox News
Biat, Clement: TF1–French TV
Biddle, Michael: C–SPAN
Bilbassy-Charters, Nadia: MBC–Dubai
Billups, Erin Evelyne: Time Warner Cable Washington Bureau
Binswanger, Joshua: Morningside Partners, LLC
Bishara, Marwan: Aljazeera International
Bisson, Jean-Francois: Canadian Broadcasting Corporation (CBC)
Bistis, George: Voice of America
Black, Phillip M.: ABC News
Blackburn, Regina: NBC News
Blackman, Jay: NBC News
Blackman, John: NBC News
Blackwill, Sarah: NBC News
Blair, Adam: Independent Television News (ITN)
Blake, Andrew: Russia Today Television
Blakley, Jonathan: National Public Radio
Blanco, Hugo: AP–Broadcast
Blanco, Jamie: Federal News Radio AM 1050
Blitzer, Wolf: CNN
Block, Melissa: CNN
Block, Melissa: National Public Radio
Blooston, Victoria: NBC News
Blount, Jeffrey: NBC News
Blyden, Rudolph: WTTG–Fox Television
Blythe, Andrew: Eurovision Americas, Inc.
Bock, Nicolas: Canadian Broadcasting Corporation (CBC)
Bodlander, Gerald: AP–Broadcast
Bodnar, John: CNN
Boghosian, Kristen: Washington Post
Bohannon, Garrett: Eurovision Americas, Inc.
Bohannon, Joseph: NBC News
Bohn, Kevin: CNN
Bolduan, Katherine: CNN
Bolter, Brian: WTTG–Fox Television
Bonds, Howard: Aljazeera International
Bonner, Susan: Canadian Broadcasting Corporation (CBC)
Booker, Brakkton: National Public Radio
Bookhultz, Bruce: WJLA–TV / Newschannel 8
Boone, Dannie: C–SPAN
Borger, Gloria: CNN
Borniger, Herta: German TV ARD
Bortner, Christopher: CNN
Bosch van Rosenthal, Eelco: Nos Dutch Public Radio & TV (VRT)
Bosland, Katie MacLean: ABC News
Bost, Mark: WUSA–TV
Boswell, Craig: Fox News
Boughton, Bryan: Fox News
Bouleau, Gilles: TF1–French TV
Bowen, Timothy: WETA
Bowman, Michael: Voice of America
Bowman, Quinn: The Newshour with Jim Lehrer
Bowman, Tom: National Public Radio
Bowser, Betty Ann: The Newshour with Jim Lehrer
Brablec, Radek: National Public Radio
Braddel, Andrew: AP–Broadcast
Bradley Hagerty, Barbara: National Public Radio
Bradley, Emily: CBS News
Bradley, Tahman: ABC News
Bragale, Charles: WRC–TV / NBC–4
Bramson, Robert E.: ABC News
Branche, Glennwood: ABC News
Brandt, John: Fox News
Brandus, Paul: WTOP Radio
Bransford, Fletcher: Fox News
Brasch, Darci: WTOP Radio
Braun, Joshua: CNN
Brawner, Donald: WETA
Brawner, Greta: C–SPAN
Bream, Shannon: Fox News
Breese, Shiny Li: Radio Free Asia
Breijo, Stephanie: Energy Now
Breiterman, Charles: ABC News
Breitner, Stephan: France 2 Television
Breslow, Peter: National Public Radio
Brevner, Michael: CNN
Bright, Whitney: WJLA–TV / Newschannel 8
Brissenden, Michael Piercy: Australian Broadcasting Corporation
Britch, Ray: CNN
Britt, Lanna: Fox News
Brittain, Becky: CNN
Brockman, Joshua: National Public Radio
Brody, David: CBN News
Broffman, Craig A.: CNN
Bronstein, Scott: CNN

MEMBERS ENTITLED TO ADMISSION—Continued

Brooks, Kurt: WUSA–TV
Brooks, Sam: ABC News
Broom, Jr., William Wescott: WUSA–TV
Brower, Brooke: NBC News
Brown, Daniel: WTTG–Fox Television
Brown, Daryl: WTTG–Fox Television
Brown, Edgar: Fox News
Brown, Gail: WJLA–TV / Newschannel 8
Brown, Henry M.: ABC News
Brown, Jeffrey: The Newshour with Jim Lehrer
Brown, Jerome: Voice of America
Brown, Joel L.: CBS News
Brown, Kristin: Fox News
Brown, Malcolm: Feature Story News
Brown, Pamela: WJLA–TV / Newschannel 8
Brown, Paul: C–SPAN
Brown, Paul: National Public Radio
Brown, Randall: NBC News
Brown, Tracy Ann: AP–Broadcast
Browning, Robert: C–SPAN
Bruce, Mary: ABC News
Bruns, David: AP–Broadcast
Brusk, Steven: CNN
Bryant, Aubrey: WUSA–TV
Brzezinski, Mika: NBC News
Bsharah, Jacquelyn: AP–Broadcast
Bua, Jon-Christopher: SKY News
Buchanan, Marisa: NBC News
Buck, Melanie: CNN
Buckhorn, Burke: CNN
Buckley, Julia Redpath: National Public Radio
Buddenhagen, Kristina: C–SPAN
Buehler, Paul: WTTG–Fox Television
Buel, Meredith: Voice of America
Bulla, Mark: Russia Today Television
Bullard Harmon, Susan: CBS News
Bullard, Larry: WRC–TV / NBC–4
Bullock, Peter: Reuters Radio & TV
Bullock, Tom: National Public Radio
Bundock, Susan J.: C–SPAN
Burch, Brian: CNN
Burdick, Leslie: C–SPAN
Burgarella, Hunter: CNN
Burgdorf, Louis: NBC News
Burgot, Maryse: France 2 Television
Burke, James: C–SPAN
Burke, Michael C.: Voice of America
Burketh, Ivan: National Public Radio
Burlij, Terence: The Newshour with Jim Lehrer
Burnett, Gordon: Radio Free Asia
Burns, Alison: Cox Broadcasting
Buse, Askan: German TV ZDF
Buse, Gabriele: German TV ZDF
Bushman, Monica: America Abroad Media
Bustamante, Antonio: RCN–TV (Colombia)
Butcher, Robert E.: National Public Radio
Butler, Joan: Voice of America
Butler, Norman Anthony: NBC News
Byrne, Joseph: Talk Radio News Service
Byrnes, Dennis: National Public Radio
C.W. Hsu, Roger: Voice of America
Cabral, Juan E.: CNN
Cahill Murphy, Kathy: C–SPAN
Caifa, Karin: CNN
Cajee, Muhammad: Aljazeera International
Calfat, Marcel: Canadian Broadcasting Corporation (CBC)
Callahan, Michael: Bloomberg Radio & TV
Calo-Christian, Nancy: C–SPAN
Cameron, Carl: Fox News
Cameron, Scott: National Public Radio
Campbell, Barbara: National Public Radio
Campbell, Christopher: Aljazeera Satellite Channel (Peninsula)
Campbell, Colin: American Press And TV Services (APTVS)
Candia, Kirsten: German TV ZDF
Canizales, Cesar: Fox Business Network
Cannon, Catherine: CBS News
Caperton, Katherine: Siriusxm Satellite Radio
Caplan, Craig: C–SPAN
Capra, Anthony: NBC News
Carberry, Sean: America Abroad Media
Carberry, Sean: National Public Radio
Carey, Julie: WRC–TV / NBC–4
Carlson, Christopher: ABC News
Carlson, Steve: Fox News
Carlsson, Leif: Swedish Broadcasting
Carlsson, Lisa: Swedish Broadcasting
Carner, John: Eurovision Americas, Inc.
Carney, Greg: Energy Now
Carney, Keith: FEDNET
Carpeaux, Emily: Feature Story News
Carpel, Michael: Fox News
Carr, Martin: WETA
Carrick, Kenneth: C–SPAN
Carroll, Patricia: CNN
Carruth, Neal: National Public Radio
Carson, Charles: WTTG–Fox Television
Carter, Brianne: WJLA–TV / Newschannel 8
Carter, Christopher: CNN
Carter, Jr., Walter: Fox News
Caryl, Christian: Radio Free Europe
Casanas, Juan: Fox News
Casey, Libby: Alaska Public Radio Network
Casey, Sean: WRC–TV / NBC–4
Cassidy, David: Belo Capital Bureau
Castaneda, Diana Carolina: RCN–TV (Colombia)
Castiel, Carol: Voice of America
Castro, Pablo: Hispanic Communications Network
Cater, Franklyn: National Public Radio
Catrett, David Keith: CNN
Causey, Mike: Federal News Radio AM 1050
Cavin, Anthony: CBS News
Centanni, Steve: Fox News

MEMBERS ENTITLED TO ADMISSION—Continued

Cermak, Chris: Need To Know News
Cerpa, Hector: Voice of America
Cetta, Denise: CBS News
Chace, Zoe: National Public Radio
Chalian, David: The Newshour with Jim Lehrer
Chalupa, Irena: Radio Free Europe
Chamberlain, Richard: WJLA–TV / Newschannel 8
Chandler, Matthew: Aljazeera International
Chang, Ching-Yi: Hong Kong Phoenix Satellite Television
Chang, Darzen: WETA
Chang, Peggy: Voice of America
Chang, Wen-Hsiang: ETTV
Changuris, Zeke: WJLA–TV / Newschannel 8
Chapin, Edith: CNN
Chapman, Irwin: Bloomberg Radio & TV
Chapman, Karolina: Aljazeera International
Chapman, Michael W.: CNSnews.com
Chappell, Jill: CNN
Charpa, Silvia: German Broadcasting Systems-ARD
Chase, David: Cox Broadcasting
Chattman, Tanya: C–SPAN
Chavar, AJ: Washington Post
Chekuru, Kavitha: Aljazeera International
Chen, Yen Ying: Hong Kong Phoenix Satellite Television
Chen, Yi Qiu: Hong Kong Phoenix Satellite Television
Chenevey, Steve: WTTG–Fox Television
Cherkaoui, Adil: Middle East Television Network (Alhurra)
Cherkasov, Andrey: Channel One Russian TV
Chernenkoff, Kelly: Fox News
Chevez, Carlos: National Public Radio
Chiba, Yuko: NHK–Japan Broadcasting Corporation
Chicca, Trish: CNN
Chichakyan, Gayane: Russia Today Television
Chick, Jane S.: CBS News
Ching, Nike: Voice of America
Chinn Lucie, Surae: WUSA–TV
Choi, Kyoosik: Korean Broadcasting Systems
Chomiak, Catherine: NBC News
Christian, George: CBS News
Christy, Andrew Chapman: National Public Radio
Chung, E-Ting: CTI–TV (Taiwan)
Cinque, Vicente: TV Globo International
Claar, Matthew: C–SPAN
Clark, Grant: National Public Radio
Clark, James: C–SPAN
Clark, Stephen: Fox News
Clarke, John: Reuters Radio & TV
Clemann, William: WUSA–TV
Clemons, Bobby: CNN
Cline, Betsy: NBC News
Cloherty, Jack: ABC News
Clugston, Gregory: SRN News (SALEM)
Cockerham, Richard: Fox News
Cofske, Harvey: Irish Radio & TV (RTE)
Cohen, Josh: C–SPAN
Cohen, Thomas S.: CNN
Cohencious, Rebecca: Native American Television
Cohencious, Robert: Native American Television
Colak, Umut: American Press And TV Services (APTVS)
Cole, Bryan: Fox News
Coleman, Steven: AP–Broadcast
Coles, David: The Newshour with Jim Lehrer
Colimore, Eric: Fox News
Coll, Dennis: National Public Radio
Collender, Howard: Mobile Video Services, LTD.
Collins, Bruce D.: C–SPAN
Collins, Pat: WRC–TV / NBC–4
Colombant, Nico: Voice of America
Colton, Michael: Canadian Broadcasting Corporation (CBC)
Combs, Cody: CNN
Compton, Mary Webster: ABC News
Compton, Woodrow: CNN
Conan, Neal: National Public Radio
Concaugh Jr., Joseph: Diversified Communications, Inc. (DCI)
Condon, Stephanie: CBS News
Conlin, Sheila: NBC Newschannel
Conneen, Mike: WJLA–TV / Newschannel 8
Conner, Eric: Fox News
Connors, Ben: Aljazeera International
Conroy, Margaret: NBC News
Contreras, Evelio: Washington Post
Contreras, Felix: National Public Radio
Contreras, Glenda: Telemundo Network
Contreras, Jorge: Univision
Conway, Jon Robert: Russia Today Television
Cook, James L.: C–SPAN
Cook, Peter: Bloomberg Radio & TV
Cooke, David M.: Diversified Communications, Inc. (DCI)
Coolidge, Richard L.: ABC News
Cooper, Rebecca J.: WJLA–TV / Newschannel 8
Corcoran, Patricia: WTTG–Fox Television
Cordes, Nancy: CBS News
Corner, Cleve: C–SPAN
Cornish-Emery, Audie: National Public Radio
Correa, Alessandra: BBC
Correa, Lina: Voice of America
Costantini, Bob: CNN
Costello, Amanda Elizabeth: CNN
Costello, Thomas: NBC News
Coudoux, Sylvain: NHK–Japan Broadcasting Corporation
Couronne, Ivan: Agence France Presse (AFP–TV)
Courson, Paul: CNN
Courtney, Sarah: Fox News
Cousins, Bria C.: CNBC
Cover, Matthew: CNSnews.com
Cowan, Jane: Australian Broadcasting Corporation
Cox, Jerry: This Is America With Dennis Wholey

MEMBERS ENTITLED TO ADMISSION—Continued

Coyte, Benjamin: CNN
Craig, John: Diversified Communications, Inc. (DCI)
Crane, Stephen: Cronkite News Service
Cratty, Carol A.: CNN
Cravedi, Dennis: C–SPAN
Craven, William C.: National Public Radio
Crawford, James: CNN
Crawford, Jan: CBS News
Crawford, Woody: Voice of America
Crawley, Plummer: CNBC
Cridland, Jeffrey: WUSA–TV
Cronkite, IV, Walter: CBS News
Crosswhite-Chigbue, Karla: CNN
Crowley, Candy: CNN
Crowley, Dennis: United News And Information
Crum, John: CBS News
Crupi, Nick: Voice of America
Crutchfield, Curtis: Community TV of PG's
Cucchiara, Natalie: NBC News
Cuddy, Matthew: CNBC
Cullen, Michael: National Public Radio
Cullum, James W.: Talk Radio News Service
Cunha, John: CNN
Cupal, Tim: ORF (Osterreichischer Rundfunk)
Currier, Liam: C–SPAN
Curtis, Alexander: C–SPAN
Curtis, Jodie: Fox News
Cypress, Alicia F.: National Public Radio
Czaplinski, Michael: National Public Radio
Czzowitz, Greg: C–SPAN
D'Annibale, Thomas J.: ABC News
D'Elia IV, Bartholomew J.: CBS News
Dade, Corey: National Public Radio
Dahl, Heather: Feature Story News
Dahlgren, Kristen Ann: NBC Newschannel
Dalbah, Mohammad: Aljazeera Satellite Channel (Peninsula)
Dalmasy, Patricia: Voice of America
Dalton, Benjamin Eric: TV Tokyo
Daly, John: CBS News
Dambach, Jessica: FEDNET
Daniels, Pete: C–SPAN
Danilko, Derek: AP–Broadcast
Dann, Caroline: NBC News
Dargakis, Minas: Voice of America
Daschle, Kelly: AP–Broadcast
Date, Shirish V.: National Public Radio
Dauchess, Matthew: C–SPAN
Daugherty, Jeffery: Voice of America
Davalos, Anna: Energy Now
Davie, Bianca: AP–Broadcast
Davieaud, Helene: TF1–French TV
Davis, Mitch: Fox News Radio
Davis, Patrick A.: CNN
Davis, Tanya: C–SPAN
Davoudi, Rima: Aljazeera International
Davydov, Allan: Radio Free Europe
Dawkins, Julian: The Newshour with Jim Lehrer
Day, Kara: CNN
de Franceschi, Jela: Voice of America
de Guise, Louis: Canadian Broadcasting Corporation (CBC)
De La Cruz, Benedict: Washington Post
de Schaetzen, Emilie: Eurovision Americas, Inc.
Debre, Guillaume: TF1–French TV
DeChagas, Bridget: National Public Radio
Decker, Jonathan: Reuters Radio & TV
Decker, Jonathan: Siriusxm Satellite Radio
Deen, Azfar: ABC News
DeFrank, Debra: Fox News
DeFrank, Joe: Fox News
Dehghanpour, Siamak: Voice of America
DeJean, Charlotte: Bloomberg Radio & TV
Delargy, Christine: CBS News
Delmore, Erin: NBC News
Deluca, Joan: Voice of America
DeManche, Heather: C–SPAN
DeMar, Brian: National Public Radio
DeMarco, Lauren: WTTG–Fox Television
DeMark, Michael: Fox News
Demir, Ercan: Turkish Radio Television (TRT)
Dennert, Mary Pat: Fox News
Densmore, Steven: Voice of America
DePuyt, Bruce: WJLA–TV / Newschannel 8
Deroche, Sylvie: Swiss Broadcasting
Desbois, Laurent: France 2 Television
Deshishku, Stacia Phillips: CNN
Desjardins, Lisa: CNN
Detrow, Jon: AP–Broadcast
DeVito, Andrea: Fox News
Dhaliwal, Daljit: Aljazeera International
Dhue, Stephanie Woods: CNBC
Diakides, Anastasia: CNN
Diamond, Aaron: France 2 Television
DiBella, Rick: CNN
DiCarlo, Patricia: CNN
DiCaro, Martin: WMAL Radio
Dickenson, Alex: C–SPAN
Diggs, Bridget: C–SPAN
Dimmler, Erika: CNN
Dimsdale, Alexandra: AP–Broadcast
Dimsdale, John: Marketplace Radio
Dirner, Elizabeth Cullen: ABC News
Disselkamp, Henry: ABC News
Divaris, Oliver: German TV ZDF
Dixon, Greg: National Public Radio
Dixson, Charles H.: CBS News
Doane, Martin C.: WJLA–TV / Newschannel 8
Doebele, Constance: C–SPAN
Doherty, Brian: Fox News
Doherty, Peter M.: ABC News
Dolce, Stephen: CNN
Dolinh, Dzung: Radio Free Asia
Dolma, Rigdhen: Radio Free Asia
Donahue, Edward: AP–Broadcast

MEMBERS ENTITLED TO ADMISSION—Continued

Donelan, Jennifer: WJLA–TV / Newschannel 8
Donner, Jason: Fox News
Donovan, Beth: National Public Radio
Donovan, Christopher: NBC News
Doocy, Peter: Fox News
Doren, Jennifer: WRC–TV / NBC–4
Dorn, Jason: AP–Broadcast
Dougherty, David: Real News Network
Dougherty, Jill: CNN
Dougherty, Martin: CNN
Dougherty, Megan Marie: CNN
Dowlatshahi, Tala: Talk Radio News Service
Downer, Carlton L.: CNN
Downes, Richard: Irish Radio & TV (RTE)
Downs, RaKenya: CBS News
Doyle Belvedere, Jessica: WUSA–TV
Doyle, Brian James: Talk Radio News Service
Dreisbach, Thomas: National Public Radio
Dubroff, Richard: C–SPAN
Duckham, Justin: Talk Radio News Service
Dukehart, Coburn: National Public Radio
Dukeman, Paige: Fox News
Dumpe, Megan: Fox News
Dunaway, John: CNN
Duncan, Victoria: NBC News
Dunlap-Elkins, Brenda: Aljazeera International
Dunlavey, Dennis: ABC News
Dunlavey, Thomas: CNN
Dunlop, William: Eurovision Americas, Inc.
Dunn, Lauren: WRC–TV / NBC–4
Dupree, Jamie: Cox Broadcasting
Durand, Lucho: Aljazeera International
Durham, Deborah: Univision
Durham, Timothy: Aljazeera International
Durkin, Edward: WRC–TV / NBC–4
Durnin, Gordon: Aljazeera International
Dwyer, Devin Patrick: ABC News
Dyer, Lois: CBS News
Dymond, Jonny: BBC
Eades, Jr, Paul: C–SPAN
Eaton, Hugh: National Public Radio
Eaves, James: NBC News
Eborn, Katrice: C–SPAN
Echevarria, Pedro L.: C–SPAN
Echols, Jerry: Fox News
Eck, Christina: German Press Agency
Eckenrode, Kaelyn Forde: Russia Today Television
Eckert, Jessica: Gannett Government Media Corp
Eckmann, Jacqueline Maria: Nos Dutch Public Radio & TV (VRT)
Edmondson, William: Fox News
Edoro, Jesse: NBC News
Edson, Rich: Fox Business Network
Edwards, Bruce: Canadian Broadcasting Corporation (CBC)
Ehrenberg, Richard: ABC News
Eisenbarth, Ronald: C–SPAN
Eisler, Ben: WJLA–TV / Newschannel 8
Eizeldin, Sam T.: American Press And TV Services (APTVS)
El Murr, Jessy: BBC
El-Hamalawy, Mahmoud: Aljazeera Satellite Channel (Peninsula)
Eldridge, James W.: Fox News
Eldridge, Michael: Washington Bureau News Service
Elgin, John: Middle East Television Network (Alhurra)
Elhassani, Camille: Aljazeera International
Ellard, Nancy: NBC Newschannel
Ellena, Peter: National Public Radio
Ellenwood, Gary: C–SPAN
Elliott-Taylor, Debbie: National Public Radio
Elving, Ronald: National Public Radio
Elvington, Daniel Glenn: ABC News
Emanuel, Mike: Fox News
Emerling, Gary: WTOP Radio
Emery, Edie: CNN
Endo, Sandra: CNN
Engel, Seth: C–SPAN
Engelke, Anja: German TV ARD
Ensign, Ernie: WJLA–TV / Newschannel 8
Epatko, Larisa: The Newshour with Jim Lehrer
Epstein, Simon: WETA
Erbe, Bonnie: To The Contrary (Persephone Productions)
Eroglu, Levent: Australian Broadcasting Corporation
Esfandiari, Golnaz: Radio Free Europe
Espinoza, Cholene: Talk Radio News Service
Esquivel, Patricia: C–SPAN
Estefan, Felipe: CNN
Evans, Laura: WTTG–Fox Television
Evans, Tyler: Fox News
Evstatieva, Monika: National Public Radio
Fabian, Jordan Harris: Univision
Fabian, Kathleen: CNN
Fabic, Greg: C–SPAN
Fagen, Joel: Fox News
Fahrendorff, Claus: Danish Broadcasting Corporation
Falvella-Garraty, Susan: Fox Business Network
Fancher, Diane: Stateline.org
Fant, Barbara: NBC News
Fantacone, John L.: CBS News
Fantis, Manny: WUSA–TV
Farhoodi, Ali: Voice of America
Farkas, Daniel: Middle East Television Network (Alhurra)
Farkas, Mark: C–SPAN
Farley, Tim: Siriusxm Satellite Radio
Farmer, Christopher: Environment & Energy Publishing, LLC
Fattahi, Kambiz: BBC
Feeney, Joesph: C–SPAN
Fehr, Stephen C.: Stateline.org
Feist, Sam: CNN

MEMBERS ENTITLED TO ADMISSION—Continued

Felde, Kitty: KPCC
Feldman, Randy: Viewpoint Communications
Fendley, Gail: Religion & Ethics Newsweekly
Fenston, Jacob: Free Speech Radio News
Ferder, Bruce: Voice of America
Ferdinando, Lisa: Voice of America
Ferguson, Patrick: Canadian Broadcasting Corporation (CBC)
Ferrigno, Tony: WJLA–TV / Newschannel 8
Ferrise, Patrick William: Siriusxm Satellite Radio
Fessler, Pam: National Public Radio
Fetzer, Robert: Diversified Communications, Inc. (DCI)
Fiegel, Eric James: CNN
Fielman, Sheldon: NBC News
Fierro, Juan Martinez: Cope Radio (Spain)
Filburn, Sean: Russia Today Television
Fils, Dyane: Eurovision Americas, Inc.
Finamore, Charles: ABC News
Finch, Mark: Fox News
Fingar, Craig: CNN
Finkel, Ben: Viewpoint Communications
Finland, Alexander: Fox News
Finnerty, Robert: Fox News Radio
Finney, Richard: Radio Free Asia
Fischer, Elizabeth: NBC News
Fishel, Justin: Fox News
Fisher, Harold Thomas: Whur
Fisher, Kristin Anne: WUSA–TV
Fisher, Siobhan N.: ABC News
Fitzgerald, Andrew: Aljazeera International
Fitzgerald, Tom: WTTG–Fox Television
Fixel, Taryn: CNN
Flaherty, Lindsay: Mobile Video Services, LTD.
Flanagan, Danielle: WUSA–TV
Fleeson, Richard: C–SPAN
Flood, Randolph G.: Native American Television
Floquet, Michel: TF1–French TV
Flores, Cesar: BT Video Productions
Floyd, Kent: NBC News
Flynn, Michael: WUSA–TV
Fodrea, Linda: Fox News
Fogarty, Kevin: Reuters Radio & TV
Fogarty, Patrick: AP–Broadcast
Forcucci, Michael: WJLA–TV / Newschannel 8
Ford, Christopher Abram: CNN
Ford, Sam: WJLA–TV / Newschannel 8
Foreman, Thomas: CNN
Forman, David: NBC News
Forsythe, Jonathan Putnam: Washington Post
Forte, B.J.: WTTG–Fox Television
Foster Mathewson, Lesli: WUSA–TV
Foster, Carl: C–SPAN
Foster, Scott: NBC News
Foti, Tim: Energy Now
Foukara, Abderrahim: Aljazeera Satellite Channel (Peninsula)
Foundas, John: WTTG–Fox Television
Fournelis, Yianis: WTTG–Fox Television
Fowler, Maria: Gannett News Service
Fowler, Marlo: CNN
Fowlin, Joy: To The Contrary (Persephone Productions)
Fox, Michael: Aljazeera Satellite Channel (Peninsula)
Fox, Peggy: WUSA–TV
Frado, John: CBS News
Frail, Marie: Reuters Radio & TV
Frame, John: WTTG–Fox Television
Frank, Jocelyn: BBC
Frankel, Bruce: TF1–French TV
Frazao, Kristin: Russia Today Television
Frazier, William: C–SPAN
Fredrickson, Drew: NBC News
Frei, Matt: Independent Television News (ITN)
Frieden, Terry: CNN
Friedman, Matthew: AP–Broadcast
Friend-Daniel, Kenya: CNN
Fritz, Sabrina: German Public Radio (ARD)
Frost, Adrian Lee: Talk Radio News Service
Frost, Lovisa: Talk Radio News Service
Fu, Peng: China Central TV Bureau
Fuhr, Michael: WUSA–TV
Fullwood, Adrian: AP–Broadcast
Fulton, April: National Public Radio
Fulton, Bradley: CTV Canadian TV
Fung, Kenneth Chee Yang: Need To Know News
Fuquen, Luis: C–SPAN
Furlow, Tony: CBS News
Furman, Hal E.: CBS News
Fuss, Brian: CBS News
Fuss, Robert J.: CBS News
Futrowsky, David: Voice of America
Gabriel, III, Oscar W.: AP–Broadcast
Gacka, Monica: Fox News
Gaetano, Lawrence: NBC News
Gaffney, Dennis: NBC News
Gaffney, Matthew: WTTG–Fox Television
Gallagher, John: C–SPAN
Gallagher, Joseph: Voice of America
Gallasch, Hillery D.: German TV ARD
Gallo, Dan: Fox News
Gangel, Jamie: NBC News
Gao, Qi: China Central TV Bureau
Garber, Scott: CNN
Garcia, Alexandra: Washington Post
Garcia, Gina: CBS News
Garcia, Guillermo: Reuters Radio & TV
Garcia, Jon D.: ABC News
Garda, Imran: Aljazeera International
Gardella, Richard: NBC News
Garfield, Lindsay Meghan: Russia Today Television
Gargagliano, Richard: Native American Television
Garifo, Stephen: WUSA–TV
Garlock, John: C–SPAN
Garner, Dave: WTOP Radio

MEMBERS ENTITLED TO ADMISSION—Continued

Garner, Jean: Aljazeera International
Garraty, Timothy C.: CNN
Garrison, Stanley Martin: National Public Radio
Gary, Garney: C–SPAN
Gaskin, Keith: NBC News
Gasparello, Linda: White House Chronicle
Gassot, Philippe: Arte TV
Gastelum, Juan: Univision
Gaudino, Ralph: NBC News
Gauthier, Arthur R.: ABC News
Gavasheli, Mindia Mikhailovich: Russia Today Television
Geewax, Marilyn: National Public Radio
Geier, Wolfgang: ORF (Osterreichischer Rundfunk)
Geldon, Ben: Bloomberg Radio & TV
Gelius, Jon: Norwegian Broadcasting
Gelman, Micah: AP–Broadcast
Gembara, Deborah: Reuters Radio & TV
Gentilo, Richard: AP–Broadcast
Gentry, Pamela: BET Nightly News
Gentry, Robert: TV Asahi
George, John: WETA
George, Maurice: CNN
George, Pavithra: Reuters Radio & TV
George, Susannah: National Public Radio
Gergely, Valer: Voice of America
Gerien, Matthew: Hearst–Argyle Television
Gersh, Darren: Nightly Business Report
Getter, Thomas: Radio One
Ghanem, Pierre: Al Arabiya TV
Giammetta, Max: WTTG–Fox Television
Gibbons, Sarah: Eurovision Americas, Inc.
Gibson, Jake: Fox News
Gibson, Jenna: Fox News
Gibson, Sheri Lynn: NBC Newschannel
Gibson, Teneille: WRC–TV / NBC–4
Gieras, Cladia Melissa: WPWC–AM (Radio Fiesta)
Gilardoni, Diego: Swiss Broadcasting
Gilchrist, Aaron: WRC–TV / NBC–4
Gilgannon, Pege: WJLA–TV / Newschannel 8
Gilkey, David: National Public Radio
Gillis, Gary: Fox News
Gilman, Jeff: WTTG–Fox Television
Gimbel, Tara: ABC News
Ginsburg, Benson: CBS News
Girouard, April: Fox News
Giusto, Thomas M.: ABC News
Gjelten, Tom: National Public Radio
Gjoni, Nikoletta: Fox News
Glassman, Matt: WRC–TV / NBC–4
Globensky, Manon: Canadian Broadcasting Corporation (CBC)
Goddard, Andre: CNN
Godfrey, Autria: WJLA–TV / Newschannel 8
Godsick, Andrew L.: NBC Newschannel
Goff, Angie Renee: WUSA–TV
Goggans, Stephanie: CNN
Gold, Lawrence: AP–Broadcast
Gold, Peter: Fuji TV Japan
Goldman, David: Community TV of PG's
Goldman, Jeff Scott: CBS News
Goldstein, Daniel: Energy Now
Goldstein, Tom: National Public Radio
Goler, Wendell: Fox News
Gomes, Karina: Aljazeera International
Gomez, Ruben: Federal News Radio AM 1050
Goncalves Perry, Delia Neves: WUSA–TV
Gongadze, Myroslava: Voice of America
Gonsar, Dhondup: Radio Free Asia
Gonyea, Don: National Public Radio
Gonzalez, Antonio: German TV ARD
Gonzalez, John: WJLA–TV / Newschannel 8
Gonzalez, Julio: Hispanic Communications Network
Goodknight, Charles A.: WRC–TV / NBC–4
Goodman, Jeffrey: NBC News
Goodman, Josh: Stateline.org
Gorap, Pema: Voice of America
Gorbutt, Richard: WUSA–TV
Gordemer, Barry: National Public Radio
Gordon, Herbert: WRC–TV / NBC–4
Gorman, James W.: AP–Broadcast
Gottlieb, Brian: BBC
Gould, Robert: C–SPAN
Gracey, Allison: CNN
Gracey, David: CNN
Gradison, Robin: ABC News
Gram, Steffen William: Danish Broadcasting Corporation
Gramlich, John P.: Stateline.org
Grams, Michael Warren: Diversified Communications, Inc. (DCI)
Granda, Marco: RCN–TV (Colombia)
Granitz, Peter: National Public Radio
Grant, Megan Elizabeth: CNN
Grasso, Neil: CBS News
Gray, Bill: C–SPAN
Gray, James: CNN
Gray, Tim: C–SPAN
Graydon, James: CNN
Grayson, Gisele: National Public Radio
Green, Barnaby: SKY News
Green, Jessie J.: WTOP Radio
Green, Molette Eileen: Whur
Green, Richard: Voice of America
Greenback, William: Voice of America
Greenbaum, Adam: Voice of America
Greenberg, Sarah: NBC News
Greenblatt, Larry: Viewpoint Communications
Greene, James M.: NBC News
Greene, Thomas: CNN
Greenfieldboyce, Nell: National Public Radio
Greenwood, John K.: Danish Broadcasting Corporation
Gregory, David: NBC News
Greisiger, Jan: ORF (Osterreichischer Rundfunk)
Grether, Nicole: AP–Broadcast

MEMBERS ENTITLED TO ADMISSION—Continued

Griffin, Jennifer: Fox News
Griffin, Regina Doreen: WUSA–TV
Griffith, Brandis: WJLA–TV / Newschannel 8
Griffitts, William: Mobile Video Services, LTD.
Griggs, Kendall: WJLA–TV / Newschannel 8
Grigsby, Lee: Eurovision Americas, Inc.
Groome, Marsha: NBC News
Gross, Andrew F.: NBC News
Gross, David: CBS News
Gross, Josh: CBS News
Gross, Jr., Eddie S.: CNN
Groussain, Caroline: Agence France Presse (AFP–TV)
Grzech, Cherie: Fox News
Guastadisegni, Richard: WJLA–TV / Newschannel 8
Guest, Frank: Federal News Service
Guevara.Frey, Eric: Swiss Broadcasting
Guez, Bertrand: TF1–French TV
Guise, Gregory: WUSA–TV
Gupta, Brendan: C–SPAN
Gura, David: Marketplace Radio
Gursky, Gregg L.: Fox News
Gustafson, Jordana: America Abroad Media
Guthrie, Savannah: NBC News
Gutmann, Hanna Ida: Washington Radio and Press Service
Guttman, Nathan: Israel Television And Radio
Guzman, Armando: Azteca America
Gyldensted, Cathrine: Danish Broadcasting Corporation
Gypson, Katherine: America Abroad Media
Ha, Gwen: Radio Free Asia
Haan, Mike: CNN
Haberstick, Fred: Fox News
Habib, Elias: Al Arabiya TV
Habibzada, Mohammad: Voice of America
Hackel, Clifford: CNN
Hackett, Steve: WJLA–TV / Newschannel 8
Hadad, Norman: Hearst–Argyle Television
Hadad, Norman: WJLA–TV / Newschannel 8
Haddad, Karim: Aljazeera International
Haefeli, Brian: Fox News
Hafiz, Jihan: Real News Network
Hage, Jesse Mesner: Aljazeera International
Hager, Mary: CBS News
Hager, Nathan: WTOP Radio
Haggerty, Patrick: This Week In Agribusiness (RFD–TV)
Hahn, Jay: Eurovision Americas, Inc.
Hahn, Stephen: ABC News
Haidari, Mohamed-Ali: Middle East Television Network (Alhurra)
Haider, Roquia: Voice of America
Haim, Laura.: Canal Plus French TV
Haj, Affra: Atlantic Television News
Hakamada, Ken: TV Tokyo
Hakel, Peter: WJLA–TV / Newschannel 8
Hakuta, Michael Akira: Washington Post
Halik, Ozana: WTTG–Fox Television
Halkett, Kimberly: Aljazeera International
Hall, Kata: Fox News
Hall, Richard: C–SPAN
Hall, Sylvia: Nightly Business Report
Haller, Sylvia: NBC News
Halloran, Liz: National Public Radio
Halpern, Jared Daniel: Fox News Radio
Halpern, Lacey: Fox News
Ham, MaryKatharine: WMAL Radio
Hamberg, Steven: Viewpoint Communications
Hamby, Peter: CNN
Hamilton, Christopher: Middle East Television Network (Alhurra)
Hamilton, James: Aljazeera International
Hamilton, Jon: National Public Radio
Hamrick, Mark: AP–Broadcast
Han, Carol: Cox Broadcasting
Hanazawa, Yuichiro: NHK–Japan Broadcasting Corporation
Handel, Sarah: National Public Radio
Handelsman, Steve: NBC Newschannel
Handleman, Michelle: CBS News
Haning, Evan: WTOP Radio
Hanley, Patricia: Religion & Ethics Newsweekly
Hanneman, Kirk: Federal News Service
Hanner, Mark: Energy Now
Hannon, Tom: Medill News Service
Hansen, Eric: C–SPAN
Hanson, Chris: C–SPAN
Hanson, David: NBC News
Harding, Alison: CNN
Hardymon, Barrie: National Public Radio
Harima, Takushi: Tokyo Broadcasting System
Harkness, Stephen: C–SPAN
Harlan, Jeremy: CNN
Harleston, Robb: C–SPAN
Harper, Steve: Eurovision Americas, Inc.
Harrell, Phil: National Public Radio
Harrington, Candice: NBC News
Harris, Lanese: CNN
Harris, Leon: WJLA–TV / Newschannel 8
Harris, Richard: National Public Radio
Harrison, David: Stateline.org
Harrison, Haley: WJLA–TV / Newschannel 8
Hartman, Brian Robert: ABC News
Hartung, Kaylee: CBS News
Harvey, Alan: NBC News
Harwood, John: CNBC
Haselton, Brennan: WTOP Radio
Hash, James: WUSA–TV
Hashemi, Sayed: Voice of America
Hass, Thomas: Eurovision Americas, Inc.
Hassan, Alegra: CBN News
Hassanein, Gamal: American Press and TV Services (APTVS)
Hasselmann, Silke: German Public Radio (ARD)

MEMBERS ENTITLED TO ADMISSION—Continued

Hastings Wotring, Melanie: WJLA–TV / Newschannel 8
Hatton, Laura: New Tang Dynasty TV
Hatuqa, Dalia: Aljazeera Satellite Channel (Peninsula)
Hawa, Daoud Abu: MBC–Dubai
Hawke, Anne: National Public Radio
Hawkins, Nyia: AP–Broadcast
Hawkins, Shonty: WUSA–TV
Hayes, Drew: WMAL Radio
Hayes, John: C–SPAN
Hayes, Samantha: CNN
Haynes, Maurice: C–SPAN
Hazelton, Jennifer: Fox News
He, Yun: China Central TV Bureau
Heath, Kendall A.: ABC News
Hebert, Casey: CNN
Heffley, William: C–SPAN
Heidarpour, Sarah: NBC News
Heiner, Stephen: Middle East Television Network (Alhurra)
Heinzman, Elaine: National Public Radio
Helgason, Sveinn: Icelandic National Broadcasting Service
Helm, Ronald G.: CNN
Helman, Jonathan: CNN
Henderson, Susan: AP–Broadcast
Hendin, Robert: CBS News
Hendren, John Edward: ABC News
Henneberg, Mary Janne: Fox News
Henrehan, John: WTTG–Fox Television
Henry, Ed: CNN
Henry, Jonelle P.: C–SPAN
Henry, Shirley: CNN
Hensley, Scott: National Public Radio
Herald, Vernon: Middle East Television Network (Alhurra)
Herbas, Francis: Fox News
Hernandez-Arthur, Simon: CNN
Herrera, Angelica Maria: WZDC–TV
Herrera, Esequiel: ABC News
Herrera, Ruben: German TV ZDF
Herridge, Catherine: Fox News
Herrod, Michael: Independent Television News (ITN)
Hess, Bill: WMAL Radio
Hibbitts, Mi Jeong Y.: Voice of America
Hickman, Stacy: Fox News
Hidaka, Masano: Diversified Communications, Inc. (DCI)
Hidaka, Yoshiki: Diversified Communications, Inc. (DCI)
Highland, Dan: Hearst–Argyle Television
Hilgen, Jim: Capitol News Connection (CNC)
Hill, Dallas: C–SPAN
Hill, Lee: National Public Radio
Hill, Martin: Fox News
Hilleary, Cecily: Voice of America
Hindes, Walter R.: SRN News (SALEM)
Hirano, Ayuko: Nippon TV Network
Hirzel, Conrad: CNN
Ho, King Man: Radio Free Asia
Hochman, Jordana: National Public Radio
Hoese, Christine: Mobile Video Services, LTD.
Hoffman, Michelle: Agence France Presse (AFP–TV)
Hofmann, Maximillian: Deutsche Welle TV
Holden, Michael: C–SPAN
Holland, John: NBC News
Holland, Sarah B.: CNN
Holland, TaShick: National Public Radio
Hollenbeck, Paul: Bt Video Productions
Holman, Kwame: The Newshour with Jim Lehrer
Holmes, Gerry: National Public Radio
Holmes, Horace: WJLA–TV / Newschannel 8
Holmes, LA.: Fox News
Holtzman, Geoff: Talk Radio News Service
Hommel, Roger William: CNN
Hong, Albert: Radio Free Asia
Hong, Kisub: Korean Broadcasting Systems
Hooley, Gemma: National Public Radio
Hopkins, Adrienne Moira: Fox News
Hopkins, Brian: WJLA–TV / Newschannel 8
Hopper, Dave: BBC
Horan, Michael: WTTG–Fox Television
Horie, Tomoko: Nippon TV Network
Hormuth, Tom: WJLA–TV / Newschannel 8
Horn, Caroline: CBS News
Horn, Charles: Viewpoint Communications
Hornick, Jr., Edward: CNN
Horsley, Scott William: National Public Radio
Hosford, Matthew Alan: ABC News
Hou, Lijun: China Central TV Bureau
Houston, Karen Gray: WTTG–Fox Television
Hovell, Bret: ABC News
Hovell, Brett: CBS News
Howard, Cory R.: Fox News
Howard, Kate Tamba: McClatchy Company
Howell, George: C–SPAN
Hoye, Matthew: CNN
Hristova, Rozalia: BBC
Hsieh, Yi-Pe: C–SPAN
Hssani, Nasser: Aljazeera Satellite Channel (Peninsula)
Hsu, Andrea: National Public Radio
Htike Oo, Thein: Voice of America
Hubert-Hogg, Aja: Energy Now
Huckeby, Paul: Fox News
Huebler, Ryan: WTTG–Fox Television
Huesch, Johanna: German TV ARD
Huff, Dan: AP–Broadcast
Huff, Priscilla: Feature Story News
Hugel, David: CNN
Hughes, James: NBC News
Hughes, Katherine: C–SPAN
Hume, Brit: Fox News

MEMBERS ENTITLED TO ADMISSION—Continued

Humeau, Thierry: Aljazeera International
Hummelsiep, Julia: German Broadcasting Systems-ARD
Hunn, Johney Burke: National Public Radio
Hunter, Paul: Canadian Broadcasting Corporation (CBC)
Hunter, Tracy: C–SPAN
Hurley, Charles: CNN
Hurt, James: NBC Newschannel
Hussain, Iftikhar: Voice of America
Hussein, Mohammed: BBC
Hussin, Utami: Voice of America
Hutchins, Argin: National Public Radio
Hutchins, Davin: Voice of America
Hydeck, Michael Edward: WUSA–TV
Hylton, Winston: WJLA–TV / Newschannel 8
Hyman, Mark: Sinclair Broadcast Group
Iadarola, Lea: CNN
Ibrahim, Lila: AP–Broadcast
Ibrahim, Mohammad: Voice of America
Ide, Charles: WETA
Ide, William: Voice of America
Ifill, Gwen: The Newshour with Jim Lehrer
Illenseer, Erik: German TV ZDF
Imtiaz, Huma: America Abroad Media
Ing, Lance: WTTG–Fox Television
Ingle, Cynthia: C–SPAN
Ingle, Julian: Aljazeera International
Ingram, Julian: Community TV of PG's
Inoue, Yusuke: TV Asahi
Inskeep, Steve: National Public Radio
Irwin, Sarah: Reuters Radio & TV
Isella, Elena: Fox News
Isham, Christopher: CBS News
Isikoff, Michael: NBC News
Italiano, Michael: AP–Broadcast
Izumitani, Kaho Ogawa: NHK–Japan Broadcasting Corporation
Jaakson, Uelle-Mall: ORF (Osterreichischer Rundfunk)
Jablow, Matthew J.: WUSA–TV
Jackson, Craig: CNN
Jackson, Jill: CBS News
Jackson, Katharine: Reuters Radio & TV
Jackson, Lesley: Voice of America
Jackson, Robert: National Public Radio
Jackson, Roberta: C–SPAN
Jackson, Samuel: WJLA–TV / Newschannel 8
Jacobi, Steve: CBN News
Jacobs, Adia: CNN
Jaconi, Michelle: CNN
Jaeger, Kevin: WJLA–TV / Newschannel 8
Jaffe, Gary: Voice of America
Jaffe, Matthew: ABC News
Jafri, Syed: Voice of America
James, Frank: National Public Radio
James, Karen: CNBC
James, Thomas: WUSA–TV
Jamison, Dennis: CBS News
Jamshidi, Kaveh: Voice of America
Janney, Oliver: CNN
Jansen, Lesa: CNN
Japaridze, NuNu: CNN
Jarrett, Rick: National Public Radio
Jarvis, Emily: Federal News Radio AM 1050
Jarvis, Julie: NBC Newschannel
Jaskot, Sheila: C–SPAN
Javers, Eamon: CNBC
Jay, Courtney: CBS News
Jay, Paul: Real News Network
Jazzaa, Ziad Turkey: Al Arabiya TV
Jeannet, Francois: Swiss Broadcasting
Jeffrey, Terence: CNSNEWS.COM
Jenkins, David: CNN
Jenkins, Gene: CBN News
Jenkins, Keith: National Public Radio
Jenkins, William G.: Fox News
Jennings, Alicia: NBC News
Jennings, Lori: Bloomberg Radio & TV
Jensen, Heidi: ABC News
Jermin, Ede: WRC–TV / NBC–4
Jesenicnik, Vlasta: Rtv Slovenija
Jessup, John: CBN News
Jewsevskyj, George: Fox News
Jia, Elizabeth Yi Chao: WUSA–TV
Jia, Jian: China Central TV Bureau
Jiang, Xin: China Central TV Bureau
Jibai, Wafaa: BBC
Jimenez, Martin: Fox Business Network
Jing, Hui: New Tang Dynasty TV
Joehnk, Astrid: German Public Radio (ARD)
John, Joseph: Aljazeera International
Johns, Joseph: CNN
Johnson, Bruce: WUSA–TV
Johnson, Carrie: National Public Radio
Johnson, Douglas: Voice of America
Johnson, Helena D.: National Public Radio
Johnson, Irene: WJLA–TV / Newschannel 8
Johnson, Jennifer: NBC Newschannel
Johnson, Kevin: Cox Broadcasting
Johnson, Kia: Reuters Radio & TV
Johnson, Rich: Fox News Radio
Johnson, Stephanie: WTTG–Fox Television
Johnson, Stephen Whitney: CBS News
Johnson, Tiane: To The Contrary (Persephone Productions)
Johnson-Wilson, Latraniecesa: C–SPAN
Johnston, Cindy: National Public Radio
Johnston, Derek Leon: ABC News
Johnston, Jeffrey: CBS News
Joho, Haruka: Fuji TV Japan
Joneidi, Majid: BBC
Jones, Andrew McFerren: BBC
Jones, Andrew: C–SPAN
Jones, Athena: NBC News
Jones, Gwyneth: NBC News

MEMBERS ENTITLED TO ADMISSION—Continued

Jones, Jenine: Aljazeera International
Jones, Lyrone Steven: WTTG–Fox Television
Jones, Morris: WJLA–TV / Newschannel 8
Jones, Nelson: WTTG–Fox Television
Jones, Shawn: Energy Now
Jones, Tara: BET Nightly News
Jones, Torrance: Fox News
Jones, Victoria: Talk Radio News Service
Jong, de Wessel: Nos Dutch Public Radio & TV (VRT)
Joo, Mae: Fox News
Joost, Nathalie: Fox News
Joslyn, James: WJLA–TV / Newschannel 8
Joy, Richard: Ventana Productions
Joyce, Christopher: National Public Radio
Joyner, Arcelious: Middle East Television Network (Alhurra)
Joyner, Shannon: NBC News
Ju, YoungJin: Seoul Broadcasting System (Sbs)
Jubar, Muriel: Aljazeera International
Juma, Mamatjan: Radio Free Asia
Jung, Ahreum: Radio Free Asia
Jung, Mark: Seoul Broadcasting System (Sbs)
Kabasawa, Ichiro: NHK–Japan Broadcasting Corporation
Kafanov, Lucy: Russia Today Television
Kajiwara, Takamoto: NHK–Japan Broadcasting Corporation
Kamilindi, Thomas: Voice of America
Kane, James F.: ABC News
Kang, Kang: China Central TV Bureau
Kangerloo, Kasra N.: Need To Know News
Kanneth, Polson: ABC News
Kanzler, Sheila Joan: CNN
Kapp, Bonney Lea: CNN
Kapp, Bonney: CBS News
Kara-Murza, Vladimir: Rtvi / Echo–TV
Karl, Jonathan: ABC News
Kasloff, Stewart: Energy Now
Kastan, Klaus: German Public Radio (ARD)
Kato, Atsushi: NHK–Japan Broadcasting Corporation
Katz, Amy: Voice of America
Katz, Barry: C–SPAN
Katz, Craig: CBS News
Kaye, Matthew: The Berns Bureau, Inc.
Kaye, Stephanie: C–SPAN
Kearns, Kara: NBC News
Keator, John C.: National Public Radio
Keedy, Matthew: CBN News
Kehnemui, Sharon: Fox News
Kehoe, Steve: C–SPAN
Keilar, Brianna: CNN
Keith, Tamara: National Public Radio
Kelbling, Julia U.: Story House Productions
Kelemen, Michele: National Public Radio
Kell, Laura: Voice of America
Kellerman, Mike: American Press and TV Services (APTVS)
Kelley, Alice: German TV ZDF
Kelley, Bridget: National Public Radio
Kelley, Colleen: Fox News
Kelley, Jon: C–SPAN
Kelley, Pamela: CNN
Kellogg, Alex: National Public Radio
Kelly, Colin Francis: Gannett Government Media Corp
Kelly, Terence: NBC News
Kennedy, Robert: C–SPAN
Kennedy, Suzanne: WJLA–TV / Newschannel 8
Kenney, Colleen: WTTG–Fox Television
Kenny, Justin: Reuters Radio & TV
Kenworthy, Alison: WJLA–TV / Newschannel 8
Kenworthy, Zachary: Fox News
Kenyon, Linda: SRN News (SALEM)
Kerley, David P.: ABC News
Kerr, Roxane: C–SPAN
Kerr, Ryan: Bloomberg Radio & TV
Ketcham, Lew: C–SPAN
Kettlewell, Christian: AP–Broadcast
Keuper, Dirk: German TV ARD
Keyes, Allison: National Public Radio
Keyes, Charley: CNN
Khalaf, Lina: Aljazeera Satellite Channel (Peninsula)
Khalaf, Mysa: Aljazeera Satellite Channel (Peninsula)
Khalid, Asma: National Public Radio
Khallash, Jonas: Atlantic Television News
Khallash, Taleb: Atlantic Television News
Khallash, Zina: Atlantic Television News
Khan, Huma: ABC News
Khan, Riz: Aljazeera International
Khananayev, Grigory: Fox News
Kharel, Ram C.: Sagarmatha Television
Khedrup, Tsewang: Voice of America
Khyzhnyak, Nataliya: BBC
Kiang, Kylene: Aljazeera International
Kianpour, Suzanne: NBC News
Kidd, Sally F.: Hearst–Argyle Television
Kieffer, Vivian: Radio Free Asia
Kiernan, Ryan: NBC News
Kiesch, Zachary: WRC–TV / NBC–4
Kill, Adrian: Diversified Communications, Inc. (DCI)
Killion, Nikole: Hearst–Argyle Television
Kim, Chulho: Korean Broadcasting Systems
Kim, JaeEun: Korean Broadcasting Systems
Kim, Jin Kuk: Radio Free Asia
Kim, Keunsam: Voice of America
Kim, Sang Jin: MBC–TV Korea (Munhwa)
Kim, Youllee: Korean Broadcasting Systems
Kimani, Julia: CBS News
King Lilleston, Kristi: WTOP Radio
King, John: CNN

MEMBERS ENTITLED TO ADMISSION—Continued

King, Kevin G.: WUSA–TV
King, Kevin: C–SPAN
King, Letitia: Voice of America
King, Llewellyn: White House Chronicle
King, Steven: Washington Post
Kingstone, Steve: BBC
Kinlaw, Worth: CNN
Kinney, George P.: CNN
Kinney, Jeff: CNN
Kirby, Michael: FEDNET
Kirkland, Pamela: Siriusxm Satellite Radio
Kiyasu, Adilson: CNN
Klayman, Elliot: Eye-To-Eye Video
Klein, Stacey: NBC News
Klein, Kent: Voice of America
Klein, Markus: German TV ZDF
Klein, Richard G.: ABC News
Klenk, Ann: NBC News
Kline, Deirdre: Middle East Television Network (Alhurra)
Klinger, Carol: National Public Radio
Klopp, Felicitas: German TV ARD
Klos, Daniel Sakae: CBS News
Knapp, Timothy: Mobile Video Services, LTD.
Knezek, Paul: Eurovision Americas, Inc.
Knighton, David: C–SPAN
Knoller, Mark: CBS News
Knott, John: ABC News
Koh, Thomas Hyunseung: Seoul Broadcasting System (Sbs)
Kokufuda, Kaoru: Tokyo Broadcasting System
Kono, Torao: NHK–Japan Broadcasting Corporation
Koolhof, Vanessa M.: WJLA–TV / Newschannel 8
Kopp, Emily: Federal News Radio AM 1050
Korff, Jay: WJLA–TV / Newschannel 8
Kornely, Michael: Voice of America
Kos, Martin: Bt Video Productions
Koslow, Marc: NBC News
Kosnar, Michael: NBC News
Kotuby, Stephanie: CNN
Kovach, Robert S.: CNN
Kozel, Sandy: AP–Broadcast
Krantz, Laura: National Public Radio
Kraus, Melissa: Fox News Radio
Kreinbihl, Mary: Fox Business Network
Kreindler, Virginia Coyne: NBC Newschannel
Kreuz, Greta: WJLA–TV / Newschannel 8
Krichevsky, Aliza: CNN
Krohn, Tina- Jane: Story House Productions
Kroll, Donald Eugene: ABC News
Ksiazek, Whitney: Fox News
Ku, Nancy H.: Fuji TV Japan
Kube, Courtney: NBC News
Kubota, Suzanne: Federal News Radio AM 1050
Kuczynski, Ronald: CNN·
Kunitz, Dan: Capitol News Connection (CNC)
Labaton, Arnolds: Religion & Ethics Newsweekly
LaBella, Michael: Hearst–Argyle Television
Labott, Elise: CNN
Laboy, Felix: C–SPAN
Lacey, Donna: Fox News
Lai, Daniel: Hong Kong Phoenix Satellite Television
Lai, Mai: Radio Free Asia
Lamb, Brian: C–SPAN
Lambidakis, Stephanie: CBS News
Lamonica, Ely: Voyage Productions
LaMonica, Gabe: CNN
Landay, Woodrow: Australian Broadcasting Corporation
Landy, John: BBC
Lane, Christopher: WETA
Langley, Kevin: National Public Radio
Lanier, Peter Andrew: CNN
Lanningham, Kyle: Swedish Broadcasting
Lanzara, Catherine: WJLA–TV / Newschannel 8
Larade, Darren: C–SPAN
Larchuck, Travis: National Public Radio
Laslo, Matt: Free Speech Radio News
Latendresse, Richard: Groupe TVa
Laughlin, Ara: Community TV of PG's
Laurin, Caroline: Canadian Broadcasting Corporation (CBC)
Laville, Molly: C–SPAN
Law, Katharine: BBC
Lawrence, Chris: CNN
Lawrence, John: Ventana Productions
Lawsen, Michael: Free Speech Radio News
Lawton, Kim: Religion & Ethics Newsweekly
Layne, B Christopher: WRC–TV / NBC–4
Lazar, Robert: C–SPAN
Lazo, Larry: CNN
Le, Viet: National Public Radio
Leamy, Elisabeth: ABC News
Lebedeva, Natasha: NBC News
LeCroy, Philip: Fox News
Leddon, Jerome: C–SPAN
Lee, Choonho: Korean Broadcasting Systems
Lee, Donald A.: CBS News
Lee, Edward: WETA
Lee, Erik: WTTG–Fox Television
Lee, Eunmi: Environment & Energy Publishing, LLC
Lee, Hun-Min: Hong Kong Phoenix Satellite Television
Lee, Jaehoon: MBC–TV Korea (Munhwa)
Lee, Jolie: Federal News Radio AM 1050
Lee, Kenneth Lawrence: CNN
Lehrer, Jim: The Newshour with Jim Lehrer
Leidelmeyer, Ronald: WRC–TV / NBC–4
Leiner, Jonathon Moses: CNN
Leist, Elizabeth: NBC News
Leister, Meaghan: Fox News
Leone, Amy Patricia: WUSA–TV
Leong, Ming: WJLA–TV / Newschannel 8
Leroy, Jean-Pierre: Voice of America
Leshan, Bruce: WUSA–TV

MEMBERS ENTITLED TO ADMISSION—Continued

Lesser, Howard M.: Washington Radio and Press Service
Lester, Paul: WUSA–TV
Lestina, Fred: Federal News Service
Levin, Adam: NBC News
Levine, Adam: CNN
Levine, Matthew: Washington Post
Levine, Michael: Fox News
Lewis, Dorothy Elizabeth: CNN
Lewis, Edward: Fox News
Lewis, Jerry S.: WETA
Lewis, John B.: WJLA–TV / Newschannel 8
Lewis, Kim: Voice of America
Lewis, Victoria: NBC News
Lewnes, Pericles: Middle East Television Network (Alhurra)
Lhundup, Tenzin: Voice of America
Liasson, Mara: National Public Radio
Liberto, Jennifer: CNN
Libretto, John: NBC News
Licht, Christopher: NBC News
Lielischkies, Udo: German TV ARD
Lien, Arthur: NBC News
Lien, Jonathan: CBS News
Likowski, Alex: WJLA–TV / Newschannel 8
Lilling, Dave: Metro Teleproductions
Lim, Jae-Hak: Radio Free Asia
Lim, Lister: Aljazeera International
Lin, Chuan: New Tang Dynasty TV
Lin, Dongwei: China Central TV Bureau
Lin, Joy: Fox News
Lindberg, Lyle: Voice of America
Lindblom, Mark: C–SPAN
Lindsay, Reed: Real News Network
Lingner, Tilman: Swiss Broadcasting
Lipes, Joshua: Radio Free Asia
Lipson, David: SKY News
Liptak, Kevin: CNN
Little, Craig: WTTG–Fox Television
Littleton, Philip: CNN
Litzinger, Sam: CBS News
Liu, Enming: Voice of America
Liu, Zhengzhu: Hong Kong Phoenix Satellite Television
Liu, Zhuoye: China Central TV Bureau
Livingston, Rebecca: CNN
Lloyd, Brian: C–SPAN
Lockhart, Kathleen: NBC News
Lockwood, Erin: Fox News
Lodoe, Kalden: Radio Free Asia
Loebach, Joseph W.: NBC News
Loeschke, Paul: C–SPAN
Loffman, Matt: NBC News
Logan, Lara: CBS News
Logan, Russell: C–SPAN
Logreira, Diana: Voice of America
Lomax, Simon: Energy Now
Long, James V.: NBC News
Loper, Catherine: Fox News
Lopez, Edwing: Azteca America
Lopez, Juan Carlos: CNN
Lopez-Isa, Anthony: WTTG–Fox Television
Lora, Edwin: CNN
Lora, Willie A.: CNN
Lord, Bill: WJLA–TV / Newschannel 8
Losey, Andrew: CNN
Lovelace, Jr., Anthony Lee: Native American Television
Lowman, Wayne: Fox News
Lucas, Dave: WJLA–TV / Newschannel 8
Lucas, Fred: CNSnews.com
Lucas, Mary Grace: CNN
Lucchini, Maria Rosa: WFDC–TV Univision
Ludden, Jennifer: National Public Radio
Luhn, Laurie: Fox News
Lule, Julie: Talk Radio News Service
Lutterbeck, Deborah: Reuters Radio & TV
Luzader, Doug: Fox News
Ly, Sherri: WTTG–Fox Television
Lyders, Caroline: WJLA–TV / Newschannel 8
Lynds, Stacia: Fox News
Lynn, Gary: NBC News
Lyon, Danny: Energy Now
Lyon, Michael: Fox News
Lyster, Lauren: Russia Today Television
Mabry, Krystal Michelle: CNN
MacAdam, Alison: National Public Radio
MacDonald, James: CTV Canadian TV
MacDonald, Neil: Canadian Broadcasting Corporation (CBC)
MacFarlane, Scott: Cox Broadcasting
Macholz, Wolfgang: German TV ZDF
Mack-Fitzhugh, Mark: NBC News
MacNeil, Lachlan Murdoch: ABC News
MacQuarrie, Joseph: German TV ARD
Maer, Peter: CBS News
Magaziner, Paris: CBS News
Mager, Dickon: SKY News
Maher, Heather: Radio Free Europe
Majchrowitz, Mike: Fox News Radio
Makori, Vincent: Voice of America
Malayang, Nathie: CNN
Malbon, Joy: CTV Canadian TV
Malone, Freddie: NBC News
Malone, James: Voice of America
Maltas, Michael: CNN
Manby, Mary: NBC News
Mandelson, Adam: Eurovision Americas, Inc.
Mankey Hidem, Emma: Religion & Ethics Newsweekly
Mann, Jon: WJLA–TV / Newschannel 8
Mansour, Fadi: Aljazeera Satellite Channel (Peninsula)
Manuel, Melissa: Fox News
Marantz, Michael: WTTG–Fox Television
Marcacci, Silvio: Energy Now

MEMBERS ENTITLED TO ADMISSION—Continued

Marcano, Antonio: National Public Radio
Marchione, Mark Anthony: CNN
Marchitto, Tom: National Public Radio
Marcus, Gale: ABC News
Mardell, Mark: BBC
Marder, Jennifer: The Newshour with Jim Lehrer
Marenco, Julio Ernesto: RCN–TV (Colombia)
Marks, Carole: Talk Radio News Service
Marks, Simon: Feature Story News
Markwald, Nicole: German Broadcasting Systems-ARD
Marno, Joseph: Aljazeera International
Marno, Mike: Aljazeera International
Marquis, Melissa: National Public Radio
Marrapodi, Eric Christian: CNN
Marshall, Amanda: Fox News
Marshall, Steve: CBS News
Marshall-Genzer, Nancy: Marketplace Radio
Martin Ewing, Samara: WUSA–TV
Martin, David: CBS News
Martin, Joseph Eugene: WUSA–TV
Martin, Jr., James: ABC News
Martin, Lori: Fox News
Martin, Michel: National Public Radio
Martin, Rachel: National Public Radio
Martin, Wisdom: WTTG–Fox Television
Martinez, Benny: Talk Radio News Service
Martinez, Luis: ABC News
Martinez, Matt: National Public Radio
Mashack, Julie Ann: Religion & Ethics Newsweekly
Mastis, Lindsey Janiece: WUSA–TV
Matera, Kevin: National Public Radio
Mathews, Molly: Fox News
Mathias, Joseph: NBC News
Mathieu, Joe: Siriusxm Satellite Radio
Matsuo, Eriko: Nippon TV Network
Matthews, Chris: NBC News
Matthews, Lisa N.: AP–Broadcast
Matthews, Paul: CNN
Matthews, Valerie: C–SPAN
Matzka, Jeffrey Alan: SRN News (SALEM)
Maurer, Pola: German TV ARD
May, Tim: Fox News
Mayer, Charles: National Public Radio
Mayer, Petra: National Public Radio
Mayes, Leslie A.: Time Warner Cable Washington Bureau
Maynard, Melissa: Stateline.org
Mazariegos, Mark: CBS News
Mazrieva, Eva: Voice of America
Mazyck, Robin: CBN News
McAllister, Ian: Energy Now
McAndrew, Ken: C–SPAN
McCabe, Valerie: France 2 Television
McCann, Michael: C–SPAN
McCann, Sean: C–SPAN
McCarren, Andrea Austin: WUSA–TV
McCarty, D. Page: CBS News
McCaughan, Timothy: CNN
McClam, Kevin: Fox News
McClellan, Max: CBS News
McCloskey, George: Fox News
McConnell, Alison: Need To Know News
McConnell, Dave: WTOP Radio
McConnell, Dugald: CNN
McCrary, Scott: CBS News
McDermott, Michele Marie: ABC News
McDevitt, Lauren: Hearst–Argyle Television
McDevitt, Rebecca: WJLA–TV / Newschannel 8
McDonald, Mark: Capitol News Connection (CNC)
McFadden, Kerith: CNN
McFadden, Samuel James: WTTG–Fox Television
McGarrity, Gerard: C–SPAN
McGarvy, Sean: WTTG–Fox Television
McGinn, Anne: Fox News
McGinty, Derek: WUSA–TV
McGlinchy, Jim: CBS News
McGrath, Megan: WRC–TV / NBC–4
McGrath, Patrick: WTTG–Fox Television
McGreevy, Allen: BBC
McGuire, Gitte Gustavsen: Danish Broadcasting Corporation
McGuire, Lorna: WTTG–Fox Television
McGuire, Michael: CBS News
McHenry, Brittany: WJLA–TV / Newschannel 8
McIntosh, Denise: CNN
McKelway, Doug: Fox News
McKinley, Robert: CBS News
McKinnon, Kyle: National Public Radio
McKnight, William Charles: CNN
McManamon, Erin T.: Hearst–Argyle Television
McManus, Nicole: NBC Newschannel
McMichael, IV, Samuel J.: CNN
McMinn, Nan Hee: AP–Broadcast
McMullan, Michael: CNN
McMurtrie, Craig: Australian Broadcasting Corporation
McNair, Erik T.: ABC News
McNair, Romaine Desaree: Whur
McNary, Kirstin: Fox News Radio
McWhinney, David: Aljazeera International
Means, Jeffrey: Voice of America
Mears, Carroll Ann: NBC News
Mears, William: CNN
Medina, Christie Corologos: CNN
Medvee, Dennis: National Public Radio
Meech, James: CNN
Meghani, Sagar: AP–Broadcast
Meier, Markus: ORF (Osterreichischer Rundfunk)
Mejia, Douglas: WZDC–TV
Melhem, Omar: Al Arabiya TV
Melhem, Richard: Al Arabiya TV
Melia, Natalia: Energy Now
Melick, Rob: NBC News
Mellio, Lisa: Cn8 The Comcast Network
Meluza, Lourdes: Univision

MEMBERS ENTITLED TO ADMISSION—Continued

Melvin, Craig: WRC–TV / NBC–4
Memmott, Mark: National Public Radio
Men, Kimseng: Voice of America
Mena, Alexia V.: CNN
Mendoza, Jose Lixander: WZDC–TV
Mendoza, Natalia: TF1–French TV
Meraji, Shereen: National Public Radio
Meraz, Gregorio: Televisa News Network (ECO)
Merena, Michael: National Public Radio
Merobshoev, Seeno: C–SPAN
Meserve, Jeanne: CNN
Meshkinpour, Sanaz: National Public Radio
Messer, Christopher: Aljazeera Satellite Channel (Peninsula)
Metherell, John: Aljazeera International
Metlin, Philip: WTTG–Fox Television
Metzger, Edward Robert: CNN
Metzger, Justin: C–SPAN
Metzger, Rochelle: Community TV of PG's
Michaud, Robert: Aljazeera International
Miklaszewski, James: NBC News
Mila, Lorenzo: TVe - Spanish Public Television
Milam, Greg: SKY News
Milenic, Alexander: WTTG–Fox Television
Milford, Robert H.: Mobile Video Services, LTD.
Millar, Christopher: NBC News
Millar, Lisa Joy: Australian Broadcasting Corporation
Miller, Andrew Peter: C–SPAN
Miller, Avery: ABC News
Miller, Jason: Federal News Radio AM 1050
Miller, Josh: WJLA–TV / Newschannel 8
Miller, Mitchell: WTOP Radio
Miller, Paul Keith: CNN
Miller, Richard F.: Talk Radio News Service
Miller, Sunlen Mari: ABC News
Miller, Tim: Middle East Television Network (Alhurra)
Miller, Veronica: National Public Radio
Mills, Chris: Fox Business Network
Mills, Joe: National Public Radio
Mills, Kate: C–SPAN
Milstead, Jr., William H.: Diversified Communications, Inc. (DCI)
Minhas, Osmaan: Aljazeera International
Minkovski, Alyona: Russia Today Television
Minner, Richard: NBC News
Minoso, Guillermo: National Public Radio
Minott, Gloria: WPFW–FM
Mintz, Elianna Sara: Talk Radio News Service
Mir, Laura: Radio Free Europe
Mirsaeedi, Guita: Voice of America
Mitchell, Andrea: NBC News
Mitchell, Carrie: Federal News Service
Mitnick, Steven: NBC News
Miyake, Yuko: TV Tokyo
Moday, Todd: Bloomberg Radio & TV
Moe, Alexandra: NBC News
Mohen, Peter: CNN
Mok, Joseph: Voice of America
Mokhtari, Mohamed: Middle East Television Network (Alhurra)
Molestina, Kenny Charles: WUSA–TV
Molinares-Hess, Ione Indira: CNN
Molineaux, Diana: Radio Marti
Mollenbeck, Andrew: WTOP Radio
Monack, David: C–SPAN
Monange, Arielle: France 2 Television
Monosso, Jeff: Fox News Radio
Monsalve, Lizeth Juliana: WZDC–TV
Montanaro, Domenico: NBC News
Montenegro, Lori: Telemundo Network
Montero, Luisa Fernanda: Hispanic Communications Network
Montgomery, Alicia: National Public Radio
Montoro, Victor R: C–SPAN
Mooar, Brian: NBC Newschannel
Moody, Kate: Feature Story News
Moon, Cedric: Russia Today Television
Mooney, Alex: CNN
Moore, Garrette: C–SPAN
Moore, Jacob: CBN News
Moore, Linwood: C–SPAN
Moore, Robert: Independent Television News (ITN)
Moore, Terrence: Metro Networks
Moore, W. Harrison: Middle East Television Network (Alhurra)
Moorhead, Jeremy: CNN
Mora, Edwin: CNSnews.com
Morada, Ray: NBC News
Morales, Isabel: CNN
Morehouse, Brittany Catherine: WUSA–TV
Morgan, Donald: CBS News
Morgan, Keith B.: ABC News
Morgan, Marcia: National Public Radio
Morgan, Nancy Gerstman: WETA
Mori, Sumiko: Fuji TV Japan
Morris, Amy: Federal News Radio AM 1050
Morris, Holly: WTTG–Fox Television
Morris, Peter: CNN
Morrisette, Roland: Bloomberg Radio & TV
Morrissey, John: AP–Broadcast
Morse, Richard: Fox News
Mortman, Howard: C–SPAN
Morton, Dan: C–SPAN
Mortreux, Vincent: TF1–French TV
Mosk, Matthew: ABC News
Mosley, Matthew: Fuji TV Japan
Mouangkham, Bounchanh: Radio Free Asia
Mozaffari, Shaheen: NBC News
Mueller, John: Middle East Television Network (Alhurra)
Mueller-Thum, Sabine: German Broadcasting Systems-ARD
Muhammad, Alverda: National Scene News
Muhammad, Askia: National Scene News

MEMBERS ENTITLED TO ADMISSION—Continued

Muhammad, Seleena M.: Fox News
Muir, Robert: Reuters Radio & TV
Munford, Corey: Radio Free Asia
Munoz, Luis: Middle East Television Network (Alhurra)
Munoz, Luis: Radio Marti
Muratani, Tateki: Nippon TV Network
Murno, Steve: National Public Radio
Murphy, Heather: National Public Radio
Murphy, Richard: WTTG–Fox Television
Murphy, Rick: Aljazeera International
Murphy, Terry: C–SPAN
Murray, Mark: NBC News
Murray, Timothy K.: Ventana Productions
Mursa, Alexander: Russia Today Television
Murtaugh, Peter: BBC
Musha, Jilili: Radio Free Asia
Muskat, Steven Charles: NBC Newschannel
Muturi, Muthoni: National Public Radio
Myers, Lisa: NBC News
Myrick, Yetta: C–SPAN
Nadar, Danya: Real News Network
Naidoo, Anand: Aljazeera International
Naing, Ingjin: Radio Free Asia
Naing, Thet Su: Voice of America
Nannes, Steven: CNN
Napier, Joyce: Canadian Broadcasting Corporation (CBC)
Narahari, Priya: Eurovision Americas, Inc.
Nardi, William: WRC–TV / NBC–4
Nash, Renee Jacqueline: WHUR
Nason, Andrew: C–SPAN
Nasr, Sarah: Aljazeera International
Nassar, Mohamed El Hussin: Middle East Television Network (Alhurra)
Nathan, Nancy: NBC News
Nawaz, Amna: NBC News
Naylor, Brian: National Public Radio
Naylor, Robert: Voice of America
Neal, Jason: NBC News
Neal, Michelle: NBC News
Neel, Joe R.: National Public Radio
Neely, Brett: Minnesota Public Radio News
Nehman, Bryan: WMAL Radio
Nelson, Christopher: National Public Radio
Nelson, Donna: NBC News
Nelson, Graham: Tokyo Broadcasting System
Nelson, James: Fox News
Nelson, Joseph: Washington Bureau News Service
Nerman, Anneli: Russia Today Television
Neubauer, Kristin: Reuters Radio & TV
Neuman, Scott L.: National Public Radio
Nevins, Elizabeth: NBC News
Newberry, Tom: NBC Newschannel
Newell, Joshua: Need To Know News
Nha, Kevin: Korean Broadcasting Systems
Ni, Chia-Hui: TVBS
Nicci, Nicholette: CNN
Nicholas, Eric: FEDNET
Nichter, Luke: C–SPAN
Nicolaidis, Virginia: CNN
Nikuradze, David: Rustavi 2 Broadcasting Company
Niland, Martin: Energy Now
Ninh, Trang: WJLA–TV / Newschannel 8
Nisbet-Smith, Robert: SKY News
Niu, Haifeng: China Central TV Bureau
Nixon, Adam: Middle East Television Network (Alhurra)
Nocciolo, Ernest G.: CNN
Nogel, Randy: Aljazeera International
Noguchi, Yuki: National Public Radio
Noh, Jung Min: Radio Free Asia
Nolen, John: CBS News
Noor, Matiullah Abid: Voice of America
Noorzai, Roshan: Voice of America
Norins, Jamie: Diversified Communications, Inc. (DCI)
Norris, Donna: C–SPAN
Norris, James: Middle East Television Network (Alhurra)
Norris, Michele: National Public Radio
Northam, Jackie: National Public Radio
Nowak, Christopher: CNN
Noye, Kelvin: NBC News
Nozoe, Kaisei: TV Asahi
Nurre, Bridget: NBC News
Nyane, Khin Maung: Radio Free Asia
Nyrop, Siri E.: Voice of America
Nyunt Oo, Thar: Voice of America
O'Banion, Beverly: CNN
O'Brien, David: NBC News
O'Connell, Benjamin: C–SPAN
O'Connell, Mike: NBC Newschannel
O'Connell, Rosalie: Voice of America
O'Connor, Gabe: National Public Radio
O'Connor, Kerry: Fox News
O'Donnell, Kelly: NBC News
O'Donnell, Norah: NBC News
O'Donnell, Patrick: Eye-To-Eye Video
O'Gara, Patrick M.: Hearst–Argyle Television
O'Leary, Lizzie: Bloomberg Radio & TV
O'Neill, Emily: Independent Television News (ITN)
O'Regan, Michael: WRC–TV / NBC–4
Oakley, Angela Ann: WTTG–Fox Television
Oblaender, Carsten: Story House Productions
Ochenschlager, Emily: National Public Radio
Odom, Quillie: Fox News
Oduro, Angela: Fox News
Offermann, Claudia: German TV ZDF
Oinounou, Mosheh: CBS News
Oko, Jennifer: Energy Now
Olabanji, Jummy: WJLA–TV / Newschannel 8
Olick, Diana: CNBC
Oliger, Brian: WTOP Radio
Oliver, Sarah: National Public Radio
Ollstein, Alice: Free Speech Radio News

MEMBERS ENTITLED TO ADMISSION—Continued

Olmsted, Alan: C–SPAN
Olson, Anna: Nightly Business Report
Oo, Aung Lwin: Voice of America
Orchard, Mark: Aljazeera International
Orgel, Paul: C–SPAN
Orr, Bob: CBS News
Ortiz, Fabien: TF1–French TV
Ortiz, Felix Junior: WUSA–TV
Osinski, Krystyna: AP–Broadcast
Oszancak, Hakan: AP–Broadcast
Ota, Kanako: TV Tokyo
Otth, John: CNN
Overby, Peter: National Public Radio
Owen, Andrea: ABC News
Oyebanjo, Nike: C–SPAN
Ozug, Matt: America Abroad Media
Pace, Julie: AP–Broadcast
Pacheco, Antonio: WETA
Padilla-Cirino, Mercy: Hispanic Communications Network
Pagan, Louis: AP–Broadcast
Page, David: CBN News
Paggini, Thomas: Swiss Broadcasting
Palacio, Zulima: Voice of America
Palca, Joe: National Public Radio
Pang, Jin: New Tang Dynasty TV
Panov, Alexander: Rtvi / Echo–TV
Panzer, Chester: WRC–TV / NBC–4
Papadeas, Tamatha: CBN News
Papinashvili, Aleksandre: Rustavi 2 Broadcasting Company
Parabaniuk, Julia: Voice of America
Paris, Brian: Medill News Service
Park, Jung-Woo: Radio Free Asia
Park, Kathy: WJLA–TV / Newschannel 8
Parker, Andre: CNN
Parker, Beth: WTTG–Fox Television
Parker, Eric: Federal News Service
Parker, Julie: WJLA–TV / Newschannel 8
Parker, Robert Geoffrey: CNN
Parkinson, John R.: ABC News
Parkinson, Malik C.: Atlantic Television News
Parks, Chris: CNN
Parrott, Katherine: CNN
Parsell, Robert: Voice of America
Paterson, Leigh Sclater: CTV Canadian TV
Patrick, Dan: WJLA–TV / Newschannel 8
Patruznick, Michael: C–SPAN
Patsalos, Connie: NBC News
Patterson, Jacob: Talk Radio News Service
Patterson, Jay E.: ABC News
Paulert, Ruediger: German TV ARD
Paxton, Bradford S.: Fox News
Payne, Aaron C.: CNN
Payne, Ebony: Living on Earth
Payne, Nathan: CNN
Payton, Strader: TV Tokyo
Peaches, Sandra: Community TV of PG's
Peaks, Gershon: Reuters Radio & TV
Pearson, Hampton: CNBC
Pearson, Mark Graham: WUSA–TV
Pearson, Vincent: National Public Radio
Peltier, Yves: Canadian Broadcasting Corporation (CBC)
Penaloza, Marisa: National Public Radio
Pennell, Elizabeth: Morningside Partners, LLC
Pennybacker, Gail: WJLA–TV / Newschannel 8
Peppers, Greg: AP–Broadcast
Perez, Simone: CNN
Pergram, Chad: Fox News
Peries, Sharmini: Real News Network
Perkins, Anthony D.: WTTG–Fox Television
Perkins, Vernon: C–SPAN
Perl, Drora S.: Galei-Tzahal (Israel Army Radio)
Perry, Christina: C–SPAN
Perry, Jr., Timothy: The Newshour with Jim Lehrer
Peslis, Chris: Fox News
Pessin, Don: Reuters Radio & TV
Peterson, Gordon: WJLA–TV / Newschannel 8
Peterson, Karen: WUSA–TV
Peterson, Rebecca: CBS News
Petraitis, Gerald: AP–Broadcast
Petrucci, Michael: Energy Now
Pettit, Debra: NBC News
Peyton, Michael: CBS News
Pflugh, Chelsea: C–SPAN
Pham, Jacqueline: Fox News
Philippe, Jean: Voice of America
Philippon, Alan: CNN
Phillips, Sean: National Public Radio
Phillips, Steven: Reuters Radio & TV
Pick, Lauren: Fox News
Pigott, III, Bernard: Fox News Radio
Pimble, William: CBS News
Pineda, Juan: Ventana Productions
Piper, Jeff: WRC–TV / NBC–4
Pitocco, Nickolas: C–SPAN
Pitts, Eritria: Aljazeera International
Pizarro, Fernando: Univision
Placie, Jordan: CNN
Plante, William: CBS News
Plater, Sean Dwayne: Whur
Pliszak, Richard K.: ABC News
Plotkin, Mark: WTOP Radio
Poch, Reasey: Voice of America
Poduch, Shelby: NBC News
Polanski, Roman: N–TV German News Channel
Poley, Michelle: CNN
Polmer, Brendan: CNN
Ponnudurai, Parameswaran: Radio Free Asia
Poole, John: National Public Radio
Popovici, Andrei: Rtvi / Echo–TV
Popp, Chris: CNN
Porsella, Claude L.: Radio France Internationale
Port, Carrie: CNN
Porter, Almon: C–SPAN

MEMBERS ENTITLED TO ADMISSION—Continued

Porter, Taylor: C–SPAN
Portnoy, Ellen: Morningside Partners, LLC
Portnoy, Steven A.: ABC News
Posley, Aaron Lamont: CNN
Postovit, David: Hearst–Argyle Television
Potts, Tracie: NBC Newschannel
Pourziaiee, Mehrnoosh: BBC
Powell, Brian William: Radio Free Asia
Powell, Lee: AP–Broadcast
Pozniak, Stephen: WJLA–TV / Newschannel 8
Prah, Pamela M.: STATELINE.ORG
Prasad, Tara: Cn8 The Comcast Network
Pratz, Megan: To The Contrary (Persephone Productions)
Preloh, Anne: C–SPAN
Presto, Suzanne: Voice of America
Preston, Mark: CNN
Presutti, Carolyn: Voice of America
Privitera, Alessandro: N24 German TV
Pronko, Tony: C–SPAN
Publicover, Robert: WTOP Radio
Pugliese, Pat: CNBC
Pulido, Hector: TVe - Spanish Public Television
Pulte, Lauren: C–SPAN
Qudah, Mohammad: ABS Network
Queen, Shegoftah: Voice of America
Quinn, Diana: CBS News
Quinn, John: Voice of America
Quinn, Mary: ABC News
Quinnette, John: NBC News
Rabin, Carrie: CBS News
Rachou, Jr., Carol J.: CNN
Radia, Kirit M.: ABC News
Radu, Bogdan: CNN
Rady, Meaghan: NBC News
Ragle, Brian: The Newshour with Jim Lehrer
Rakes, Allison: CBS News
Rama, Padmananda: CNN
Ramchandani, Lavina: Hearst–Argyle Television
Ramirez, Roselena: Russia Today Television
Ramos, Raul: WFDC–TV Univision
Randev, Sonia: Community TV of PG's
Raney, Adam: Aljazeera International
Rapalo, Manuel: Atlantic Television News
Raphel, Paul: WTTG–Fox Television
Rathner, Jeffrey: WETA
Ratner, Ellen: Talk Radio News Service
Ratner, Victor: ABC News
Rattansi, Shihab: Aljazeera International
Raval, Nikhil: C–SPAN
Raviv, Daniel: CBS News
Ray, Alonzo: NBC News
Raz, Guy: National Public Radio
Reap, Patrick Thomas: Bloomberg Radio & TV
Reber, Susanne: National Public Radio
Redding, William: ABC News
Redman, Justine: CNN
Reeve, Richard: WJLA–TV / Newschannel 8
Reeves, Alea: Aljazeera International
Reeves, Austin: WTTG–Fox Television
Reeves, TraLanenia Nicole: Hearst–Argyle Television
Reid, Charles: CBS News
Reid, Johnathan: CBN News
Reilly, Robert: C–SPAN
Reiss, Katie: Energy Now
Remillard, Michelle: C–SPAN
Remme, Klaus: Deutscheland Radio
Ren, Meixing: Hong Kong Phoenix Satellite Television
Renaud, Jean: CNN
Renken, David: Fox News
Rensberger, Scott: Nos Dutch Public Radio & TV (VRT)
Resnick, Jon: AP–Broadcast
Reuter, Cynthia: C–SPAN
Rex, Andy: Independent Television News (ITN)
Reyes, Malissa: WJLA–TV / Newschannel 8
Reyes, Victor: Telemundo Network
Reynes, Raphael: Radio France Internationale
Reynolds, Andrew: National Public Radio
Reynolds, Catherine C.: Cox Broadcasting
Reynolds, Judy: Religion & Ethics Newsweekly
Reynolds, Robert: Aljazeera International
Reynolds, Talesha: ABC News
Rhee, Hanjun: MBC–TV Korea (Munhwa)
Rhee, Hoin: MBC–TV Korea (Munhwa)
Rhodes Glinton, Sonari: National Public Radio
Rhodes, Elizabeth: Fox News
Ricalde, Katheryn C.: Fox News
Rice, Ben: WJLA–TV / Newschannel 8
Rice, Eric: Talk Radio News Service
Richard, Emmanuelle: France 2 Television
Richard, Sylvain: Canadian Broadcasting Corporation (CBC)
Rickard, Michael: WTTG–Fox Television
Ridolfi, Sarah Santer: Fox News
Riggs, James: CNN
Rigney, Paul: C–SPAN
Riha, Anne Marie: Fox News
Ringe, Linda: Voice of America
Rios, Delia: C–SPAN
Rios-Hernandez, Raul: CNN
Ritchie, Thomas: AP–Broadcast
Ritter, Dana Brown: CBN News
Rizzi, Jared: Siriusxm Satellite Radio
Rizzo, Jennifer: CNN
Roach, Kevin: AP–Broadcast
Roane Skehan, Andrea: WUSA–TV
Robbins, Christina: Fox News
Robbins, Diana Claudia: German TV ARD
Robbins, Francisco: CBS News
Robbins, Michael: Fox News
Roberts, Corinne: ABC News
Roberts, Jean Pierre: Eurovision Americas, Inc.
Robertson Migas, Portia: National Public Radio

MEMBERS ENTITLED TO ADMISSION—Continued

Robertson, Greg: CNN
Robertson, Tamara: Fox News
Robinson, Courtney: WJLA–TV / Newschannel 8
Robinson, Daniel: Voice of America
Robinson, David: CNN
Robinson, Margaret: The Newshour with Jim Lehrer
Robinson, Querry: NBC News
Robinson, Tamara: C–SPAN
Robinson, Veronica: WTOP Radio
Roca, Xavier: TV3–Televisio De Catalunya
Rocha, Juan: Ventana Productions
Rocque, Tiffany: C–SPAN
Rodeffer, Mark: C–SPAN
Rodriguez, Janet: CNN
Rodriguez, Martine: C–SPAN
Rodriguez, Susan: CNN
Roeckerath, Christoph: German TV ZDF
Roeller, Ulf-Jensen: German TV ZDF
Rogers, Richelle: CNN
Rohrbeck, Douglas: Fox News
Rojas, Carlos A.: ABC News
Rokus, Brian: CNN
Roller, Richard L.: ABC News
Rollins, Bonnie: NBC Newschannel
Rose, Art: WTOP Radio
Rose, Francis: Federal News Radio AM 1050
Rose, Jeff: WJLA–TV / Newschannel 8
Rose, Joe: WJLA–TV / Newschannel 8
Roselli, H. Michael: CNN
Rosen, James: Fox News
Rosen, Nancy: To The Contrary (Persephone Productions)
Rosen, Rachel: CNN
Rosen, Shari: CNBC
Rosenberg, Gary: ABC News
Rosenberg, Howard: CBS News
Rosenberg, Jeffrey: National Public Radio
Rosetti, Jeff: CNN
Rosewicz, Barbara: Stateline.org
Rosgaard, Jessica: CNN
Ross Taylor, Allyson: CBS News
Ross, Jane: Reuters Radio & TV
Ross, Lee: Fox News
Ross, Mary Katherine: CNN
Roth, Linda: CNN
Rovner, Julie: National Public Radio
Rowe, Hildrun: German TV ZDF
Rowe, Tom: Reuters Radio & TV
Royce, Lindy: CNN
Roycraft, David: WUSA–TV
Royster, Meredith: WTTG–Fox Television
Rudd, Michael: WJLA–TV / Newschannel 8
Rudin, Ken: National Public Radio
Ruff, David: CNN
Ruff, Jennifer: C–SPAN
Ruffini, Christina: CBS News
Ruggiero, Diane: CNN
Rushing, Ian William: CBN News
Rushing, J. Taylor: Capitol News Connection (CNC)
Rushing, Joshua: Aljazeera International
Russell, Eugene: WTTG–Fox Television
Russert, Luke: NBC News
Rust, Emily: CNN
Ryan, Fred: WJLA–TV / Newschannel 8
Ryan, Jason: ABC News
Ryan, Kate: WTOP Radio
Rydell, Kate: CBS News
Ryntjes, Daniel: Feature Story News
Rysak, F. David: WTTG–Fox Television
Sababa, Ghassan: Aljazeera Satellite Channel (Peninsula)
Sacks, Howard: NBC News
Sadighi, Nader: Radio Free Europe
Sadighi, Shahla: Voice of America
Saenz, Katherine Arlette: ABC News
Sagalyn, Daniel: The Newshour with Jim Lehrer
Saine-Spang, Cynthia: Voice of America
Sainsbury, Peter: Radio Free Asia
Saito, Mari: Reuters Radio & TV
Sakurai, Reiko: NHK–Japan Broadcasting Corporation
Salahuddin, Aliya: America Abroad Media
Salan, Jennifer: Aljazeera International
Salas, Pedro: CNN
Salazar, Jose: Atlantic Television News
Salazar, Marcela: CNN
Saleem, Awais: America Abroad Media
Sali, Sanil: Aljazeera International
Salim, Yuni: Voice of America
Sallstrom, Royce: CBN News
Saloomey, Kristen: Aljazeera International
Salzman, Eric: CBS News
Samimi, Mehrnaz: Voice of America
Sammon, Bill: Fox News
Sampaio, Frederico: C–SPAN
Samperio, Aurora: Telesur
Sampy, David: Independent Television News (ITN)
Sanchez, George D.: ABC News
Sanchez, Pablo: Univision
Sanders, Molly: C–SPAN
Sanders, Sam: National Public Radio
Sanders-Smith, Sherry: C–SPAN
Sandiford, Michelle: C–SPAN
Sands-Sadowitz, Geneva: The Hill
Sanfuentes, Jose ''Antoine'': NBC News
Santa-Rita, Joad Jose: Voice of America
Santos, Jose G.: CNN
Sanvido, Colleen: NBC News
Sarfo-Kantanka, Johnson: C–SPAN
Sargent, Mark: WTTG–Fox Television
Sargent, Thayer Anne: CNN
Sarkar, Kabiruddin: Voice of America
Sassenberg, Thomas M.: Story House Productions
Satchell, David: WUSA–TV
Satter, Andrew: Congressional Quarterly
Satterfield, John Thomas: WETA

MEMBERS ENTITLED TO ADMISSION—Continued

Savage, Craig: Fox News
Sawera, Thomas: German TV ARD
Sayegh, Jr., Tony Elias Elias: Talk Radio News Service
Scalise, Michelle: CBS News
Scanlan, William: C–SPAN
Scanlon, Jason: Fox News
Scarpelli, Leah: National Public Radio
Schall, Fred: WTTG–Fox Television
Schank, Lindsey Arent: Bloomberg Radio & TV
Schantz, Douglas N.: CNN
Scharf, Jason: Eurovision Americas, Inc.
Scheid, Harry: FEDNET
Scheiner, Eric: CNSnews.com
Scherer, Klaus: German TV ARD
Scheuer, John: C–SPAN
Schieffer, Bob: CBS News
Schiff, Brian: Voice of America
Schiffman, Keren: Aljazeera International
Schindler, Max: Aljazeera International
Schlegel, Barry C.: CNN
Schlenker, Aungthu: Radio Free Asia
Schmickler, Marion: German TV ARD
Schmidt, Andrea: Aljazeera International
Schneider, Jr., Edward: Voice of America
Schneider, Fred: CBS News
Schneider, James: WETA
Schnurre, Laura: Story House Productions
Schoenholtz, Howard David: ABC News
Scholl, Christopher: CBS News
Schott, Sonia: Radio Valera Venezuela
Schrier, Daniela: Voice of America
Schulter, Jonathan M.: CNSnews.com
Schultze, Emily: CNN
Schuster, Henry: CBS News
Schwandt, Kimberly: Fox News
Schwarz, Gabriella: CNN
Schweiger, Ellen: C–SPAN
Scicchitano, Carmine: NBC News
Scott, Beth: NBC News
Scott, Harry: Radio Free Asia
Scott, Heather M.: CBS News
Scott, James: WJLA–TV / Newschannel 8
Scott, Linda: The Newshour with Jim Lehrer
Scott, Raquel: CNN
Scriabine, Raisa: Link TV
Scritchfield, Andrew: NBC News
Scruggs, Wesley: NBC News
Scully, Steven: C–SPAN
Seabrook, Andrea: National Public Radio
Seabrook, Willliam: WETA
Seaby, Gregory: WJLA–TV / Newschannel 8
Sealock, Danella: WRC–TV / NBC–4
Sears, Abby: Fox News
Sears, Carl: NBC News
Seem, Thomas H.: CBS News
Segraves, Mark: WTOP Radio
Seidman, Joel: NBC News
Seifert, Lauren: CBS News
Selma, Reginald G.: CNN
Selsky, Lauren: NBC News
Seo, Ja Ryen: Korean Broadcasting Systems
Serbu, Jared: Federal News Radio AM 1050
Serper, Noelle: Religion & Ethics Newsweekly
Settele, Hanno: ORF (Osterreichischer Rundfunk)
Seymour, Allison: WTTG–Fox Television
Seymour, William Nicoll: WJLA–TV / Newschannel 8
Shackelford, Rachael Louise: CNN
Shaffir, Gregory: CBS News
Shakhov, Dmytro: Rtvi / Echo–TV
Shalhoup, Joseph: NBC News
Shan, Zijun: Radio Free Asia
Shannon, Dennis: CBS News
Shannon, Holly: WJLA–TV / Newschannel 8
Shapiro, Adam: Fox Business Network
Shapiro, Ari: National Public Radio
Shapiro, Joseph: National Public Radio
Sharma, B. K.: WJLA–TV / Newschannel 8
Sharp, Cynthia: AP–Broadcast
Shastri, Namgyal: Voice of America
Shaughnessy, Lawrence: CNN
Shaw, Cathy: National Public Radio
Shaw, Joseph: NHK–Japan Broadcasting Corporation
Shefte, Whitney: Washington Post
Shekinskaya, Nargiz: Rtvi / Echo–TV
Shelton, Steve: Fox News
Shen, Chen: China Central TV Bureau
Sheng, Qing: China Central TV Bureau
Shepherd, Shawna: CNN
Sherwood, Ian: BBC
Sherwood, Tom: WRC–TV / NBC–4
Shields, Daniel: Fox News Radio
Shihab-Eldin, Ahmed: Aljazeera International
Shikaki, Muna: Al Arabiya TV
Shimana) Shimbori, Satoko: TV Asahi
Shinkman, Paul: WTOP Radio
Shipman, Claire: ABC News
Shlemon, Chris: Independent Television News (ITN)
Shoffner, Harry: BBC
Shogren, Elizabeth: National Public Radio
Shoji, Shin: NHK–Japan Broadcasting Corporation
Shon, Robert: WTTG–Fox Television
Shott, Dave: Fox News
Showell, Andre Duane: BET Nightly News
Shukhin, Daniel: National Public Radio
Shull, Roger: Reuters Radio & TV
Siddiqui, Imran: Voice of America
Siegel, Robert C.: National Public Radio
Siegfriedt, Anita: Fox News
Sierra, Joann Lucia: CNN
Siff, Dawn: Fox News Radio
Sills, Cecil John: NBC Newschannel
Silman, III, Jimmie: WUSA–TV

MEMBERS ENTITLED TO ADMISSION—Continued

Silva-Pinto, Lauren: ORF (Osterreichischer Rundfunk)
Silva-Pinto, Luis Fernando: TV Globo International
Silver, David: NBC News
Silver, Diane: The Newshour with Jim Lehrer
Silver, Janet E.: Australian Broadcasting Corporation
Silverberg, Hank: WTOP Radio
Silverleib, Alan Jay: CNN
Silverman, Art: National Public Radio
Silverman, Rachel: Feature Story News
Simaan, Angela: Al Arabiya TV
Simeone, Ron: NBC News
Simmons, Gregory Catherine: ABC News
Simmons, Sarah: WTTG–Fox Television
Simms, Jeffery: CNN
Simon, Jeff: CNN
Simon, Scott: National Public Radio
Simons, John: Aljazeera International
Simpson, Cynne: WJLA–TV / Newschannel 8
Simpson, Shelley: Energy Now
Sims, LaToya: NBC News
Sina, Ralph: German TV ARD
Sinderbrand, Rebecca: CNN
Sisco, Paul: Voice of America
Skeans, Ron: BBC
Skene, Mathieu: Aljazeera International
Skopek, Aaron Robert: NBC News
Slack, Mary Beth: Need To Know News
Slafka, Kristi: CNN
Slansky, Heike: German TV ZDF
Slattery, Julie: Bloomberg Radio & TV
Slen, Peter: C–SPAN
Sloane, Ward C.: CBS News
Slobogin, Kathy: CNN
Smith, Andrew: Russia Today Television
Smith, Cindy: ABC News
Smith, Graham: National Public Radio
Smith, Heather: WMAL Radio
Smith, James E.: ABC News
Smith, Jason H.: WTTG–Fox Television
Smith, Lauren: NBC News
Smith, Lindley: C–SPAN
Smith, Mark S.: AP–Broadcast
Smith, Michael: WETA
Smith, Phillip: Aljazeera International
Smith, Robert: National Public Radio
Smith, Sarah: Independent Television News (ITN)
Smith, William: Belo Capital Bureau
Smoot, Kelly: CNN
Smyth, Chris: Hearst–Argyle Television
Sneed, Kimberly: NBC News
Snyder, Rebecca: Federal News Service
Socolovsky, Jerome: Voice of America
Soe, Khin Maung: Radio Free Asia
Sok, Pov: Voice of America
Sokolova, Elena: Russian State TV And Radio (RTR)
Solash, Richard: Radio Free Europe
Soley, Joan: BBC
Solimani-Lezhnev, Andrey: Russian State TV And Radio (RTR)
Solodovnikov, Mikhail: Russian State TV And Radio (RTR)
Solorzano, Gilbert: NBC News
Sonnheim, Jon: Cox Broadcasting
Sorensen, Eric D.: Global TV Canada
Sorenson, Ben: C–SPAN
Sorge, Kristina: BBC
Soric, Miodrag: Deutsche Welle TV
Soucy, Peggy: Eurovision Americas, Inc.
Spear, Anita Brikmanis: WUSA–TV
Speck, Alan: C–SPAN
Spector, Teresa: Fox News
Speiser, Matthew: CNN
Spencer, Darcy: WRC–TV / NBC–4
Spevak, Joe: WTTG–Fox Television
Spinelli, Paul: Russia Today Television
Spire, Hardy: Energy Now
Spoerry, Philip Scott: CNN
Sponder, Myron: Talk Radio News Service
Sprankle, James: Fox News
Springer, Drake: Fox News
Springer, Steven: Voice of America
Sproul, David: Wmal Radio
Sproul, Robin: ABC News
Sreenivasan, Hari: The Newshour with Jim Lehrer
Sridhar, Priya: Russia Today Television
Srivastava, Amish: Voice of America
St. Jean, Johnny: C–SPAN
St. John, Jonathan: Fox Business Network
Stahl, Steven: CNN
Stakelbeck, Erick: CBN News
Stalnaker, Kurt: National Public Radio
Stamberg, Susan: National Public Radio
Staniar, Britton: Bloomberg Radio & TV
Stanitz, Emily: ABC News
Stanke, Donald E.: WTTG–Fox Television
Starikoff, Gary: C–SPAN
Stark, Lisa: ABC News
Starling, Alison: WJLA–TV / Newschannel 8
Starnes, Todd: Fox News Radio
Starr, Barbara: CNN
Starr, Penny: CNSNEWS.COM
Stay, Daniel J.: Fox News
Stead, Scott: CNN
Stefany, Steve: ABC News
Stein, Cari Weiss: To The Contrary (Persephone Productions)
Steinberger, Daniel: ABC News
Steinhauser, Paul: CNN
Steinman, Mindy: C–SPAN
Stemple, Lexi: Fox News
Stennett, Stephen George: NBC News
Sterling, Vaughn: CNN
Steven, Norma: C–SPAN

MEMBERS ENTITLED TO ADMISSION—Continued

Stevens, Seneca: Fox News
Stevenson, Louis: WTTG–Fox Television
Stewart, Andrew: SRN News (SALEM)
Stewart, Philip: WJLA–TV / Newschannel 8
Stewart, Rebecca Joy: CNN
Stewart, Robin Anthony: Ventana Productions
Stirewalt, Chris: Fox News
Stix, Gabriel: CBS News
Stockman, Michelle: Agence France Presse (AFP–TV)
Stoddard, Rick: C–SPAN
Stodder, Mark: Federal News Service
Stok, Silvester: Rtv Slovenija
Stone, Evie: National Public Radio
Stout, Matthew: Fox News
Stoutzenberger, Timothy: CNN
Strand, Paul: CBN News
Strasser, Franz: BBC
Straub, Terry: Diversified Communications, Inc. (DCI)
Streitfeld, Rachel: CNN
Strickland, Kenneth: NBC News
Strickler, Laura: CBS News
Stringer, Ashley: CNBC
Strothe, Stephen: N24 German TV
Styles, Julian: CNN
Suarez, Fernando: CBS News
Suarez, Rafael: The Newshour with Jim Lehrer
Suda, Masaki: NHK–Japan Broadcasting Corporation
Sughroue, Jon: NBC News
Suiters, Tyler: Energy Now
Sullivan, Beth: Fox News
Sullivan, Laura: National Public Radio
Sullivan, Lee Patrick: Energy Now
Sullivan, Robert: NBC News
Sullivan, Sarah: America Abroad Media
Sullivan, Virginia L.: National Public Radio
Sum, Sok Ry: Radio Free Asia
Summers, Elizabeth: The Newshour with Jim Lehrer
Summers, Patrick: Fox News
Sumrel, John: Fox News
Sun, Ping: China Central TV Bureau
Surles, Ashlea: NBC News
Suto, Ena: TV Asahi
Suyat, Julius: Voice of America
Suzara, Jennifer: Fox News
Svahn, Nina Ann-Mari: Finnish Broadcasting Company (YLE)
Swagler, Craig: CBS News
Swain, Bethany: CNN
Swain, Susan: C–SPAN
Swain, Todd: Mobile Video Services, LTD.
Swanier, Sherrell: CNN
Swanson, Carl: Voice of America
Sweeney, Robert: WRC–TV / NBC–4
Sweetapple, Dan: Australian Broadcasting Corporation
Swicord, Jeffrey: Voice of America
Swope, Christopher: Stateline.org
Sylvester, John: Fox News Radio
Sylvester, Lisa: CNN
Symanski, Mary: C–SPAN
Syrjanen, Janne: Aljazeera International
Szematowicz, Daniel A.: CNN
Szoboszlay, Orsolya: BBC
Szypulski, Tom: Aljazeera International
Tabaar, Mohammed: BBC
Tahir, Muhammad: Radio Free Europe
Taing, Sarada: Radio Free Asia
Taj, Mitra: Living on Earth
Takagane, Yuka: NHK–Japan Broadcasting Corporation
Takagi, Yosuke: NHK–Japan Broadcasting Corporation
Takao, Jun: NHK–Japan Broadcasting Corporation
Takezaki, Tomoyasu: Nippon TV Network
Takruri, Dena: Aljazeera Satellite Channel (Peninsula)
Tamboli, Jay: Talk Radio News Service
Tamerlani, George: Reuters Radio & TV
Tang, Shiding: China Central TV Bureau
Tanner, Scott Kenneth: Whur
Tapper, Jake: ABC News
Tashi, Yeshi: Radio Free Asia
Tasillo, Mary Ellen: Fox News
Tate, Lauren: Fox News
Tate, Simon: Aljazeera International
Tate, Tiffany: BET Nightly News
Tavangar, Sayeh: WUSA–TV
Taylor, Audrey: ABC News
Taylor, Christina: C–SPAN
Taylor, John: WRC–TV / NBC–4
Taylor, Russell J.: C–SPAN
Teboe, Mark: Aljazeera International
Teeples, Joseph: C–SPAN
Tejerina, Pilar: Aljazeera International
Temin, Thomas R: Federal News Radio AM 1050
Tennent, Gerald W.: National Public Radio
Terpstra, Patrick: Capitol News Connection (CNC)
Terrett, John: Aljazeera International
Terry, Janet: WUSA–TV
Tevault, Neil David: National Public Radio
Tha, Kyaw Zan: Voice of America
Thai, Xuan: CNN
Thalman, Mark: Ventana Productions
Thein, Kyaw K.: Voice of America
Thelin, David: NBC News
Thoman, Eric: C–SPAN
Thomas, III, James B.: CNN
Thomas, Amy Jo: ABC News
Thomas, Christopher: Community TV of PG's
Thomas, Pierre: ABC News
Thomas, Sharahn: National Public Radio
Thomas, Shawna: NBC News
Thomas, Will: WTTG–Fox Television

MEMBERS ENTITLED TO ADMISSION—Continued

Thompson Anderson, Laetitia: WTTG–Fox Television
Thompson, Ron: Radio One
Thomson, Sylvia: Canadian Broadcasting Corporation (CBC)
Thorne, C. Patrick: Washington Bureau News Service
Thornton, Ronald: NBC News
Thuman, Scott: WJLA–TV / Newschannel 8
Tiller, Arthur: C–SPAN
Tillman, Thomas E.: CBS News
Tilman, Brandon: C–SPAN
Tin, Annie: C–SPAN
Tobianski, Sarah: C–SPAN
Todd, Brian: CNN
Todd, Chuck: NBC News
Todt, Jacqueline: WETA
Toksvig, Nick: Aljazeera International
Tolk, Matthew A.: Russia Today Television
Tomlinson, Blair: Gannett Government Media Corp
Tong, Scott: Marketplace Radio
Torlone, Lauren: C–SPAN
Torpey, Robert: Fox News
Toso, Nicolas: CNN
Totenberg, Nina: National Public Radio
Totty, Lindsay: National Public Radio
Tovarek, Steve: CNN
Toya, Mitsuhiro: Tokyo Broadcasting System
Tracey, Bree: Fox News
Trainor, Thomas: Eurovision Americas, Inc.
Trammell, Michael: WUSA–TV
Trauzzi, Monica: Environment & Energy Publishing, LLC
Travers, Karen Lynn: ABC News
Travis, Shannon: CNN
Traynham, Peter C.: CBS News
Traynham, Robert: Cn8 The Comcast Network
Triay, Andres P.: CBS News
Trosclair, Clayton: Eurovision Americas, Inc.
Trunov, Denis Mikhaylovich: Russia Today Television
Tschida, Stephen: WJLA–TV / Newschannel 8
Tserenbaljid, Uyanga: German TV ZDF
Tsugawa, Takafumi: Tokyo Broadcasting System
Tuan, Shih-Yuan: TVBS
Tucker, Elke: German TV ZDF
Tuman, Anna: NBC News
Tuohey, Kenneth: CNN
Turner, Carla: Canadian Broadcasting Corporation (CBC)
Turner, Catherine: Aljazeera International
Turner, Chris: CNN
Turner, Cory: National Public Radio
Turner, Patricia: Fox News
Turner, Sue: Belo Capital Bureau
Turnham, Steve: CNN
Turpin, Christopher: National Public Radio
Tuss, Adam: WTOP Radio
Tuszynski, Tom: Al Arabiya TV
Tutman, Dan D.: CBS News
TVegard, Anders: Norwegian Broadcasting
Tyler, Brett: CNN
Tyler, Lamonte Bryant: Fox News
Ubeda, Anna: TVe - Spanish Public Television
Uceda, Claudia: WFDC–TV Univision
Uchimiya, Ellen: Bloomberg Radio & TV
Udo, Justin: Federal News Radio AM 1050
Uhl, Kim: CNN
Ulbrich-Strothe, Sabine: N24 German TV
Ulloa, Victor: CBS News
Ulmer, Kenya Sheri: CNN
Umeh, Maureen: WTTG–Fox Television
Umrani, Anthony R.: CNN
Uprety, Sharmila: Sagarmatha Television
Urbanski, Tina: NBC News
Ure, Laurie: CNN
Ureta, Juan: NBC News
Uribe, Juvenal: Morningside Partners, LLC
Vail, Patrick: Washington Bureau News Service
Valentine, Natlie: Cn8 The Comcast Network
Van Cleave, Kristopher: WJLA–TV / Newschannel 8
Van de Mark, Ellen: CNN
Van Nostrand, Jim: McClatchy Company
Van Susteren, Greta: Fox News
Van Vleet, Peter: AP–Broadcast
Vance, Denise: AP–Broadcast
Vandendolder, Tess: FEDNET
VanderVeen, Jacob: Mobile Video Services, LTD.
VanderVeen, Lawrence: Mobile Video Services, LTD.
Vasa, Sampath: WETA
Vaughan, Scott: Reuters Radio & TV
Vaughn, Mike: WJLA–TV / Newschannel 8
Vennell, Vicki A.: ABC News
Verdugo, Adam: NBC News
Vestal, Christine: Stateline.org
Vicario, Virginia A.: ABC News
Viers, Dana: CNN
Vila, Xavier: Catalunya Radio
Vilen, Paula Hannele: Finnish Broadcasting Company (YLE)
Villamizar, Jecsy Carolina: WZDC–TV
Villamizar, Monica: Aljazeera International
Villone Garcia, Patricia: Community TV of PG's
Vinson, Bryce: Fox News
Viqueira, Michael: NBC News
Visioli, Todd: Fox News
Visley, Andrew G.: AP–Broadcast
Vitorovich, Susan: NBC News
Vizcarra, Mario: Univision
Vock, Daniel: Stateline.org
Voegeli, Peter: Swiss Broadcasting
Vogel, Erin: Fox News
Vogel, Phil: Fox News
Vohar, Den: AP–Broadcast

MEMBERS ENTITLED TO ADMISSION—Continued

Volk Harper, Kristin: Scripps Howard News Service
Volkov, Dimitri: Channel One Russian TV
Volokhonovich, Vera: Russia Today Television
von Bonsdorff, Juri Tomas: Finnish Broadcasting Company (YLE)
Von Kanel, Joseph Charles: CNN
Vorus, Jr., Jerome: CNSnews.com
Voth, Charles: WETA
Vu, Tu H.: CNN
Vukmer, David: NBC News
Wafa, Mohamed: Middle East Television Network (Alhurra)
Waghorn, Dominic: SKY News
Waghorn, Noel: AP–Broadcast
Wagner, Paul: WTTG–Fox Television
Wait, Kevin: National Public Radio
Waite, Cynthia Sharon: TV Asahi
Walker, James: WJLA–TV / Newschannel 8
Walker, John: Voice of America
Walker, Sebastian: Aljazeera International
Walker, Teshima: National Public Radio
Walker, William: CBS News
Wallace, Chris: Fox News
Wallace, John L.: Fox News
Wallace, Keith: Voice of America
Wallace, Roger: Fox Business Network
Walsh, Carly: Aljazeera International
Walsh, Deirdre: CNN
Walsh, Mary: CBS News
Walter, Amy: ABC News
Walter, Christopher: CNN
Walton-James, Vickie: National Public Radio
Walz, Mark: CNN
Wang, Bingru: Hong Kong Phoenix Satellite Television
Wang, Fenghua: China Central TV Bureau
Wang, Jin: Aljazeera International
Wang, Taofeng: Hong Kong Phoenix Satellite Television
Wang, Yang: New Tang Dynasty TV
Waqfi, Wajd: Aljazeera Satellite Channel (Peninsula)
Warner, Craig: CBS News
Warner, Margaret: The Newshour with Jim Lehrer
Warren, Thomas: WTOP Radio
Warrick, David: Fox News
Warzel, Charles: NBC News
Wasgien, Sonja: German TV ARD
Washburn, Kevin: C–SPAN
Washington, III, Richard: WTTG–Fox Television
Washington Anderson, Robert: WJLA–TV / Newschannel 8
Washington, Erick: CBS News
Washington, Ervin: Nightly Business Report
Watkins, Duane: WTTG–Fox Television
Watrel, Jane: WRC–TV / NBC–4
Watrud, Don: WTTG–Fox Television
Watson, Carline: National Public Radio
Watson, Walter: National Public Radio
Watts, Andrew: National Public Radio
Weakly, David: NBC News
Webb, David: WJLA–TV / Newschannel 8
Webb, Haley: Capitol News Connection (CNC)
Webb, Tracey: CNN
Webster, Marquida: CNN
Weeks, Linton: National Public Radio
Wegmann, Christopher: Radio One
Wehinger, Amy: Fox News
Weinberg, Ali: NBC News
Weinberg, Ilana: America Abroad Media
Weinbloom, Hank: Fox News Radio
Weiner, Eric: Tokyo Broadcasting System
Weinfeld, Michael: AP–Broadcast
Weinstein, Richard: C–SPAN
Weinstock, Roy: WRC–TV / NBC–4
Weisbrod, Eric: CNN
Weiss, Brian: Bloomberg Radio & TV
Weiss, Jessica Elizabeth: CNN
Wells, Letitia: McClatchy Company
Welna, David: National Public Radio
Welter, Juergen: German TV ARD
Wertheimer, Linda: National Public Radio
Westerwelle, Fabian: ABC News
Westpheling, Paul: Voice of America
Wharton, Ned: National Public Radio
Wheeler, Brian: Aljazeera International
White, Amanda Gail: CNN
White, Douglas: ABC News
White, Edward: CNN
White, Jordan: Federal News Service
White, Kevin: Bloomberg Radio & TV
White, Mark: CBS News
Whitehurst, Maurice: NBC News
Whitfield, Jr., Christopher Levon: Radio One
Whitley, John H.: CBS News
Whitley, Walter: Fox News
Whitney, Michael: Washington Bureau News Service
Whitsett, Kyrie Lauren: Nippon TV Network
Whittington, Christopher: NBC News
Wholey, Dennis: This Is America With Dennis Wholey
Wiedenbauer, Heidi: Cox Broadcasting
Wiggins, Christopher: NBC Newschannel
Wiggins, Dion Antwan: WUSA–TV
Wik, Snorre: Aljazeera International
Wildman, Jim: National Public Radio
Wilk, Wendy: Hearst–Argyle Television
Wilkes, Douglas H.: WTTG–Fox Television
Williams, Abigail: NBC News
Williams, Colleen: Fox News
Williams, Jeffrey L.: Cox Broadcasting
Williams, John: Fox News
Williams, Keith: WUSA–TV
Williams, Kenneth E.: CBS News
Williams, Louis "Pete": NBC News

MEMBERS ENTITLED TO ADMISSION—Continued

Williams, Margot: National Public Radio
Williams, Robert T.: NBC News
Williams, Steven: WTTG–Fox Television
Williamson, Christopher: NBC News
Willingham, Val: CNN
Willis, Anne Marie: Fox News
Wilp, Christian: N–TV German News Channel
Wilson, Brian: Wmal Radio
Wilson, George: Whur
Wilson, Natalie: Community TV of PG's
Wilson, Stephanie: WUSA–TV
Wims, Jeffrey Anthony: Whur
Windham, Ron: WJLA–TV / Newschannel 8
Winerman, Lea: The Newshour with Jim Lehrer
Winn, Thomas ''Pete'': CNSnews.com
Winterhalter, Ruthann: C–SPAN
Wishon, Jennifer Ann: CBN News
Wisniewski, Erica: The Hill
Witte, Joel: WTTG–Fox Television
Witten, Robert: NBC News
Wittstock, Melinda: Capitol News Connection (CNC)
Wlach, Jennifer Lauren: ABC News
Wolf, Zachary B.: ABC News
Wolfe, Lisa: Federal News Radio AM 1050
Wood, Christopher: C–SPAN
Wood, Winston: Voice of America
Woodall, Crystal: CBN News
Woodruff, Judy: The Newshour with Jim Lehrer
Wordock, Colleen: Bloomberg Radio & TV
Workman, Paul: CTV Canadian TV
Wright, Dale: WJLA–TV / Newschannel 8
Wright, James: Aljazeera International
Wright, Kelly: Fox News
Wrona, Marcin Wojciech: TVN Poland
Wu, Hanying: China Central TV Bureau
Wu, Wei: New Tang Dynasty TV
Wynne Johnson, Elizabeth: Capitol News Connection (CNC)
Wyszogrodzki, Marcin: TVN Poland
Xavier, Wilkins: Aljazeera International
Xiang, Dong: New Tang Dynasty TV
Xu, Jinglu: New Tang Dynasty TV
Xu, Susie: CNN
Xue, Bin: New Tang Dynasty TV
Yaffe, Ethan: NBC News
Yager, Joshua: CBS News
Yaklyvich, Brian: CNN
Yam, Raymond: Voice of America
Yamaguchi, Daisuke: NHK–Japan Broadcasting Corporation
Yancy, Shawn: WTTG–Fox Television
Yang, Carter: CBS News
Yang, Chunfang: New Tang Dynasty TV
Yang, Eun: WRC–TV / NBC–4
Yang, Hee Jung: Radio Free Asia
Yang, Sungwon: Radio Free Asia
Yang, Yang: Bloomberg Radio & TV
Yarborough, Rick: WTTG–Fox Television
Yarmuth, Floyd: CNN
Yates, H. William: CBS News
Yates, Mark P.: Australian Broadcasting Corporation
Yazaki, Anthony: NHK–Japan Broadcasting Corporation
Ydstie, John: National Public Radio
Yellin, Jessica: CNN
Yeshi, Lobsang: Radio Free Asia
Yianopoulos, Karen: Middle East Television Network (Alhurra)
Yin, Chunsheng: China Central TV Bureau
Yoon, Robert: CNN
Young, Jr., Jerome: CBN News
Young, Jeremy: Aljazeera International
Young, Melissa A.: ABC News
Young, Robert Latimer: C–SPAN
Young, Saundra: CNN
Younis, Omar: Reuters Radio & TV
Yousef, Dania: Aljazeera International
Yu, Annie: WTTG–Fox Television
Yu, John: New Tang Dynasty TV
Yun, Samean: Radio Free Asia
Yun, Taeho: Korean Broadcasting Systems
Zahora, Jack: Aljazeera International
Zairi, Said: ABS Network
Zajko, Robert: Diversified Communications, Inc. (DCI)
Zanatta, Dennis: TV Globo International
Zang, Guohua: CTI–TV (Taiwan)
Zariquiey, Juan Pablo: WZDC–TV
Zayed, Nahedah: Aljazeera International
Zderic, Srdjan: Aljazeera International
Zechar, David: ABC News
Zeledon, Franklin: Morningside Partners, LLC
Zeliger, Robert: The Newshour with Jim Lehrer
Zhang, Xiaoyan: Voice of America
Zhao, Peng: China Central TV Bureau
Zheng, Haoran: New Tang Dynasty TV
Zhodzishsky, Ilya: Russia Today Television
Zhu, Haiqing: China Central TV Bureau
Zhu, Hua: China Central TV Bureau
Zibel, Eve: Fox News
Ziegenbein, Darren: WRC–TV / NBC–4
Ziegler, Julia: Federal News Radio AM 1050
Zimerman, Ariel: RCN–TV (Colombia)
Zimmerman, Douglas: Environment & Energy Publishing, LLC
Zmidzinski, Andy: WJLA–TV / Newschannel 8
Zoldan, Ari: Talk Radio News Service
Zosso, Elizabeth: Middle East Television Network (Alhurra)
Zwerdling, Daniel: National Public Radio
Zwillich, Todd: WNYC

NETWORKS, STATIONS, AND SERVICES REPRESENTED

Senate Gallery 224–6421 House Gallery 225–5214

ABC NEWS—(202) 222–7212; 1717 DeSales Street, NW., Washington, DC 20036: John William Allard, Faisal Alqadiree, Jane Aylor, Elisha Beard, Phillip M. Black, Katie MacLean Bosland, Tahman Bradley, Robert E. Bramson, Glennwood Branche, Charles Breiterman, Sam Brooks, Henry M. Brown, Mary Bruce, Christopher Carlson, Jack Cloherty, Mary Webster Compton, Richard L. Coolidge, Thomas J. d'Annibale, Azfar Deen, Elizabeth Cullen Dirner, Henry Disselkamp, Peter M. Doherty, Dennis Dunlavey, Devin Patrick Dwyer, Richard Ehrenberg, Daniel Glenn Elvington, Charles Finamore, Siobhan N. Fisher, Jon D. Garcia, Arthur R. Gauthier, Tara Gimbel, Thomas M. Giusto, Robin Gradison, Stephen Hahn, Brian Robert Hartman, Kendall A. Heath, John Edward Hendren, Esequiel Herrera, Matthew Alan Hosford, Bret Hovell, Matthew Jaffe, Heidi Jensen, Derek Leon Johnston, James F. Kane, Polson Kanneth, Jonathan Karl, David P. Kerley, Huma Khan, Richard G. Klein, John Knott, Donald Eugene Kroll, Elisabeth Leamy, Lachlan Murdoch MacNeil, Gale Marcus, James Martin, Jr., Luis Martinez, Michele Marie McDermott, Erik T. McNair, Sunlen Mari Miller, Avery Miller, Keith B. Morgan, Matthew Mosk, Meredith Nettles, Andrea Owen, John R. Parkinson, Jay E. Patterson, Richard K. Pliszak, Steven A. Portnoy, Mary Quinn, Kirit M. Radia, Victor Ratner, William Redding, Talesha Reynolds, Corinne Roberts, Carlos A. Rojas, Richard L. Roller, Gary Rosenberg, Jason Ryan, Katherine Arlette Saenz, George D. Sanchez, Howard David Schoenholtz, Claire Shipman, Gregory Catherine Simmons, James E. Smith, Cindy Smith, Robin Sproul, Emily Stanitz, Lisa Stark, Steve Stefany, Daniel Steinberger, Jake Tapper, Audrey Taylor, Amy Jo Thomas, Pierre Thomas, Karen Lynn Travers, Vicki A. Vennell, Virginia A. Vicario, Amy Walter, Fabian Westerwelle, Douglas White, Jennifer Lauren Wlach, Zachary B. Wolf, Melissa A. Young, David Zechar.

ABS NETWORK—(917) 836–6844; 50 F. Street, NW., Suite 1–C, Washington, DC 20001: Akram Abdulkareem, Mohammed Alajlouni, Raad Ali, Omar Ali, Saad Ali, Mohammed Al-Karkhi, Mohammad Qudah, Said Zairi.

ADVENTURE HILL ENG—(703) 644–6909; 9216 Capricorn Court, Burke, VA 22015: Michael Angelo DeMark.

AGENCE FRANCE PRESSE (AFP–TV)—(202) 414–0602; 1500 K. Street, NW., Washington, DC 20005: Mary Ann Campagna, Ivan Couronne, Caroline Groussain, Michelle Hoffman, Michelle Stockman.

AL ARABIYA TV—(202) 288–6095; National Press Building, 529 14th Street, NW., Suite 530 Washington, DC 20045: Yamen Abdalwahab, Angelyn Adams, Pierre Ghanem, Elias Habib, Ziad Turkey Jazzaa, Omar Melhem, Richard Melhem, Muna Shikaki, Angela Simaan, Tom Tuszynski.

ALASKA PUBLIC RADIO NETWORK—(202) 488–1961; 810 East Ninth Avenue, Anchorage, AL 99501: Libby Casey.

ALJAZEERA INTERNATIONAL—(202) 397–2469; 1627 K. Street, NW., Suite 4006, Washington, DC 20006: Hebah Abdalla, Bob Abeshouse, Tom Ackerman, Atirath Aich, Khodayar Akhavi, Reem Akkad, Laila Alarian, Derrick Ashong, Zeina Awad, Jeff Ballou, Angelita Bee, Barbara Benitez, Marwan Bishara, Howard Bonds, Muhammad Cajee, Matthew Chandler, Karolina Chapman, Kavitha Chekuru, Ben Connors, Rima Davoudi, Daljit Dhaliwal, Brenda Dunlap-Elkins, Lucho Durand, Timothy Durham, Gordon Durnin, Camille Elhassani, Andrew Fitzgerald, Imran Garda, Jean Garner, Karina Gomes, Karim Haddad, Jesse Mesner Hage, Kimberly Halkett, James Hamilton, Thierry Humeau, Julian Ingle, Joseph John, Jenine Jones, Muriel Jubar, Riz Khan, Kylene Kiang, Lister Lim, Mike Marno, Joseph Marno, David McWhinney, John Metherell, Robert Michaud, Osmaan Minhas, Rick Murphy, Anand Naidoo, Sarah Nasr, Randy Nogel, Mark Orchard, Eritria Pitts, Adam Raney, Shihab Rattansi, Alea Reeves, Robert Reynolds, Joshua Rushing, Jennifer Salan, Sanil Sali, Kristen Saloomey, Keren Schiffman, Max Schindler, Andrea Schmidt, Ahmed Shihab-Eldin, John Simons, Mathieu Skene, Phillip Smith, Janne Syrjanen, Tom Szypulski, Simon Tate, Mark Teboe, Pilar Tejerina, John Terrett, Nick Toksvig, Catherine Turner, Monica Villamizar, Sebastian Walker, Carly Walsh, Jin Wang, Brian Wheeler, Snorre Wik, James Wright, Wilkins Xavier, Jeremy Young, Dania Yousef, Jack Zahora, Nahedah Zayed, Srdjan Zderic.

ALJAZEERA SATELLITE CHANNEL (PENINSULA)—(202) 327–8200; 1627 K. Street, NW., Suite 200, Washington, DC 20006: Eyad Aburahma, Mohammed Alami, Heni Azzam, Baubak Baghi, Charles Andrew Behringer, Christopher Campbell, Mohammad Dalbah, Mahmoud El-Hamalawy, Abderrahim Foukara, Michael Fox, Dalia Hatuqa, Nasser Hssani, Mysa Khalaf, Lina Khalaf, Fadi Mansour, Christopher Messer, Dianne McNair, Ghassan Sababa, Dena Takruri, Wajd Waqfi.

AMERICA ABROAD MEDIA—(202) 457–8050; 1020 19th Street, NW., Suite 650, Washington, DC 20036: Aziz Ahmed, Farhan Alam, Javier Barrera, Monica Bushman, Sean Carberry, Jordana Gustafson,

NETWORKS, STATIONS, AND SERVICES REPRESENTED—Continued

Katherine Gypson, Huma Imtiaz, Matt Ozug, Aliya Salahuddin, Awais Saleem, Sarah Sullivan, Ilana Weinberg.

AMERICAN PRESS AND TV SERVICES (APTVS)—(202) 903–0271; 1919 M. Street, NW., Washington, DC 20036: Moaz Attawia, Fahd Banhawy, Colin Campbell, Umut Colak, Sam T. Eizeldin, Gamal Hassanein, Mike Kellerman.

AP–BROADCAST—(202) 736–1172; 1100 13th St, NW., Suite 700, Washington, DC 20005: Jeff Adkinson, Khaldoun Alrawi, Eric Andree, Hugo Blanco, Gerald Bodlander, Andrew Braddel, Tracy Ann Brown, David Bruns, Jacquelyn Bsharah, Steven Coleman, Derek Danilko, Kelly Daschle, Bianca Davie, Jon Detrow, Alexandra Dimsdale, Edward Donahue, Jason Dorn, Patrick Fogarty, Matthew Friedman, Adrian Fullwood, Oscar W. Gabriel III, Micah Gelman, Richard Gentilo, Lawrence Gold, James W. Gorman, Nicole Grether, Mark Hamrick, Nyia Hawkins, Susan Henderson, Dan Huff, Lila Ibrahim, Michael Italiano, Christian Kettlewell, Sandy Kozel, Lisa N. Matthews, Nan Hee McMinn, Sagar Meghani, John Morrissey, Mellanie Ng, Krystyna Osinski, Hakan Oszancak, Julie Pace, Louis Pagan, Greg Peppers, Gerald Petraitis, Lee Powell, Jon Resnick, Thomas Ritchie, Kevin Roach, Cynthia Sharp, Mark S. Smith, Peter Van Vleet, Denise Vance, Andrew G. Visley, Den Vohar, Noel Waghorn, Michael Weinfeld.

ARTE TV—(202) 297–3651; 2000 M. Street, NW., Washington, DC 20036: Philippe Gassot.

ATLANTIC TELEVISION NEWS—(202) 223–1709; 1990 K. Street, Washington, DC 20006: Affra Haj, Jonas Khallash, Taleb Khallash, Zina Khallash, Malik C. Parkinson, Manuel Rapalo, Jose Salazar.

AUSTRALIAN BROADCASTING CORPORATION—(202) 626–5161; 2000 M. Street, NW., Suite 660, Washington, DC 20036: Michael Piercy Brissenden, Jane Cowan, Levent Eroglu, Woodrow Landay, Craig McMurtrie, Lisa Joy Millar, Janet E. Silver, Dan Sweetapple, Mark P. Yates.

AZTECA AMERICA—(202) 419–6134; 400 North Capitol, NW., Suite 361, Washington, DC 20001: Armando Guzman, Edwing Lopez.

BBC—(917) 494–9749; 2000 M. Street, NW., #800, Washington, DC 20009: Marc Adams, Paul Adams, Lukman Ahmed, Ben Bevington, Alessandra Correa, Jonny Dymond, Jessy El Murr, Kambiz Fattahi, Jocelyn Frank, Brian Gottlieb, Dave Hopper, Rozalia Hristova, Mohammed Hussein, Wafaa Jibai, Majid Joneidi, Andrew McFerren Jones, Nataliya Khyzhnyak, Steve Kingstone, John Landy, Katharine Law, Mark Mardell, Allen McGreevy, Laura Murcia, Peter Murtaugh, Mehrnoosh Pourziaiee, Ian Sherwood, Harry Shoffner, Ron Skeans, Joan Soley, Kristina Sorge, Franz Strasser, Orsolya Szoboszlay, Mohammed Tabaar.

BELO CAPITAL BUREAU—(202) 661–8471; 1325 C. Street, NW., Suite 250, Washington, DC 20005: Al Banegas, David Cassidy, Wayne Lynch, Ashley Patterson, William Smith, Sue Turner.

BET NIGHTLY NEWS—(202) 841–5435; 400 North Capitol Street, NW., Suite 361, Washington, DC 20001: Pamela Gentry, Tara Jones, Andre Duane Showell, Tiffany Tate.

BLOOMBERG RADIO & TV—(202) 624–1933; 1399 New York Avenue, NW., 11th Floor, Washington, DC 20005: Niharika Acharya, Joseph Bellard, Michael Callahan, Irwin Chapman, Peter Cook, Sonya Cooper, Charlotte DeJean, Ben Geldon, Lori Jennings, Ryan Kerr, Todd Moday, Roland Morrisette, Lizzie O'Leary, Patrick Thomas Reap, Lindsey Arent Schank, Julie Slattery, Britton Staniar, Ellen Uchimiya, Brian Weiss, Kevin White, Joe Winski, Colleen Wordock, Yang Yang.

BT VIDEO PRODUCTIONS—(301) 370–0808; 7117 Wolftree Lane, Rockville, MD 20852: Cesar Flores, Paul Hollenbeck, Martin Kos.

CANADIAN BROADCASTING CORPORATION (CBC)—(202) 383–2965; National Press Building, 529 14th Street, NW., Suite 500, Washington, DC 20045: Michel C. Auger, Jean-Francois Bisson, Nicolas Bock, Susan Bonner, Marcel Calfat, Michael Colton, Louis de Guise, Bruce Edwards, Patrick Ferguson, Manon Globensky, Paul Hunter, Caroline Laurin, Neil MacDonald, Joyce Napier, Yves Peltier, Sylvain Richard, Sylvia Thomson, Carla Turner.

CANAL PLUS FRENCH TV—(202) 641–9289; 1100 13th Street, NW., Suite 400, Washington, DC 20001: Laura Haim.

CAPITOL NEWS CONNECTION (CNC)—(202) 546–8650; 110 Maryland Avenue, NE., Washington, DC 20002: Jim Hilgen, Dan Kunitz, Mark McDonald, J. Taylor Rushing, Patrick Terpstra, Haley Webb, Melinda Wittstock, Elizabeth Wynne Johnson.

CATALUNYA RADIO—(301) 845–2358; 311 Fallsworth Place, Walkersville, MD 21793: Xavier Vila.

CBN NEWS—(202) 467–2526; 1919 M. Street, NW., Suite 100, Washington, DC 20036: Mark Bautista, David Brody, Alegra Hassan, Steve Jacobi, Gene Jenkins, John Jessup, Matthew Keedy, Robin Mazyck, Jacob Moore, David Page, Tamatha Papadeas, Johnathan Reid, Dana Brown Ritter, Ian William Rushing, Royce Sallstrom, Erick Stakelbeck, Paul Strand, Jennifer Ann Wishon, Crystal Woodall, Jerome Young, Jr.

CBS NEWS—(202) 457–1548; 2020 M. Street, NW., Washington, DC 20036: Zachary Akey, Thomas Albano, Christopher Albert, Clinton N. Alexander, Wyatt Andrews, Alana Anyse, Chloe Arensberg, Howard Arenstein, Sharyl Attkisson, Barry Bagnato, Morris Banks, Bruce Barr, Kia Baskerville, Farrel Becker, Mark R. Bennett, Emily Bradley, Joel L. Brown, Susan Bullard Harmon, Catherine Cannon, Anthony Cavin, Denise Cetta, Jane S. Chick, George Christian, Stephanie Condon, Nancy Cordes, Jan Crawford, Walter Cronkite IV, John Crum, John Daly, Christine Delargy, Bartholomew J. D'Elia

NETWORKS, STATIONS, AND SERVICES REPRESENTED—Continued

IV, Charles H. Dixson, RaKenya Downs, Lois Dyer, John L. Fantacone, John Frado, Tony Furlow, Hal E. Furman, Brian Fuss, Robert J. Fuss, Gina Garcia, Benson Ginsburg, Jeff Scott Goldman, Neil Grasso, Josh Gross, David Gross, Mary Hager, Michelle Handleman, Susan Harmon, Kaylee Hartung, Robert Hendin, Caroline Horn, Brett Hovell, Christopher Isham, Jill Jackson, Dennis Jamison, Courtney Jay, Stephen Whitney Johnson, Jeffrey Johnston, Bonney Kapp, Craig Katz, Julia Kimani, Daniel Sakae Klos, Mark Knoller, Stephanie Lambidakis, Donald A. Lee, Jonathan Lien, Sam Litzinger, Lara Logan, Peter Maer, Paris Magaziner, Steve Marshall, David Martin, Mark Mazariegos, D. Page McCarty, Max McClellan, Scott McCrary, Jim McGlinchy, Michael McGuire, Robert McKinley, Donald Morgan, John Nolen, Mosheh Oinounou, Bob Orr, Rebecca Peterson, Michael Peyton, William Pimble, William Plante, Diana Quinn, Carrie Rabin, Allison Rakes, Daniel Raviv, Charles Reid, Francisco Robbins, Howard Rosenberg, Allyson Ross Taylor, Christina Ruffini, Kate Rydell, Eric Salzman, Michelle Scalise, Bob Schieffer, Fred Schneider, Christopher Scholl, Henry Schuster, Heather M. Scott, Thomas H. Seem, Lauren Seifert, Gregory Shaffir, Dennis Shannon, Ward C. Sloane, Gabriel Stix, Laura Strickler, Fernando Suarez, Craig Swagler, Thomas E. Tillman, Peter C. Traynham, Andres P. Triay, Dan D. Tutman, Victor Ulloa, William Walker, Mary Walsh, Craig Warner, Erick Washington, Mark White, John H. Whitley, Kenneth E. Williams, Joshua Yager, Carter Yang, H. William Yates.

CHANNEL ONE RUSSIAN TV—(202) 320–1001; 1100 13th Street, NW., Suite 400, Washington, DC 20005: Andrey Cherkasov, Dimitri Volkov.

CHINA CENTRAL TV BUREAU—(301) 530–2932; 2000 M. Street, NW., Suite 880, Washington, DC 20036: Peng Fu, Qi Gao, Yun He, Lijun Hou, Jian Jia, Xin Jiang, Kang Kang, Dongwei Lin, Zhuoye Liu, Haifeng Niu, Chen Shen, Qing Sheng, Ping Sun, Shiding Tang, Fenghua Wang, Hanying Wu, Chunsheng Yin, Peng Zhao, Haiqing Zhu, Hua Zhu.

CN8 THE COMCAST NETWORK—(202) 719–9201; 101 Constitution Avenue, NW., Suite L–150, Washington, DC 20001: Lisa Mellio, Tara Prasad, Robert Traynham, Natlie Valentine.

CNBC—(202) 776–7405; 1025 Conneticut Avenue, NW., Washington, DC 20836: Bria C. Cousins, Plummer Crawley, Matthew Cuddy, Stephanie Woods Dhue, John Harwood, Karen James, Eamon Javers, Diana Olick, Hampton Pearson, Pat Pugliese, Shari Rosen, Ashley Stringer.

CNN—(202) 898–7911; 820 1st Street, NE., Washington, DC 20002: Khalil Abdallah, Jim Acosta, Shannan Adler, Mike Ahlers, William Alberter, Jack Mayo Alger, Natalie Apsell, Nelson Archer, Marco Vinicio Arreaga, Emily Atkinson, Jonathan Auerbach, Matthew Avrutine, David Bacheler, Sarah E. Baker, Laquasha Banks, Erik Banks, David Joseph Banville, James Barnett, Ted Barrett, Dana Bash, John Bena, Pamela S. Benson, Thomas Bentz, Leslie Ann Bentz, David Berman, Richard Bernal, Laura Bernardini, Wolf Blitzer, Melissa Block, John Bodnar, Kevin Bohn, Katherine Bolduan, Gloria Borger, Christopher Bortner, Joshua Braun, Michael Brevner, Ray Britch, Becky Brittain, Craig A. Broffman, Scott Bronstein, Steven Brusk, Melanie Buck, Burke Buckhorn, Brian Burch, Hunter Burgarella, Juan E. Cabral, Karin Caifa, Patricia Carroll, Christopher Carter, David Keith Catrett, Edith Chapin, Jill Chappell, Trish Chicca, Bobby Clemons, Thomas S. Cohen, Cody Combs, Woodrow Compton, Bob Costantini, Amanda Elizabeth Costello, Paul Courson, Benjamin Coyte, Carol A. Cratty, James Crawford, Karla Crosswhite-Chigbue, Candy Crowley, John Cunha, Patrick A. Davis, Kara Day, Stacia Phillips Deshishku, Lisa Desjardins, Anastasia Diakides, Rick DiBella, Patricia DiCarlo, Erika Dimmler, Stephen Dolce, Jill Dougherty, Martin Dougherty, Megan Marie Dougherty, Carlton L. Downer, John Dunaway, Thomas Dunlavey, Edie Emery, Sandra Endo, Felipe Estefan, Kathleen Fabian, Sam Feist, Eric James Fiegel, Craig Fingar, Taryn Fixel, Christopher Abram Ford, Thomas Foreman, Marlo Fowler, Terry Frieden, Kenya Friend-Daniel, Scott Garber, Timothy C. Garraty, Maurice George, Andre Goddard, Stephanie Goggans, David Gracey, Allison Gracey, Megan Elizabeth Grant, James Gray, James Graydon, Thomas Greene, Eddie S. Gross, Jr., Mike Haan, Clifford Hackel, Peter Hamby, Alison Harding, Jeremy Harlan, Lanese Harris, Samantha Hayes, Casey Hebert, Ronald G. Helm, Jonathan Helman, Shirley Henry, Ed Henry, Simon Hernandez-Arthur, Conrad Hirzel, Sarah B. Holland, Roger William Hommel, Edward Hornick, Jr., Matthew Hoye, David Hugel, Charles Hurley, Lea Iadarola, Craig Jackson, Adia Jacobs, Michelle Jaconi, Oliver Janney, Lesa Jansen, NuNu Japaridze, David Jenkins, Joseph Johns, Sheila Joan Kanzler, Bonney Lea Kapp, Brianna Keilar, Pamela Kelley, Charley Keyes, John King, Worth Kinlaw, George P. Kinney, Jeff Kinney, Adilson Kiyasu, Stephanie Kotuby, Robert S. Kovach, Aliza Krichevsky, Ronald Kuczynski, Elise Labott, Gabe LaMonica, Peter Andrew Lanier, Chris Lawrence, Larry Lazo, Kenneth Lawrence Lee, Jonathon Moses Leiner, Adam Levine, Dorothy Elizabeth Lewis, Jennifer Liberto, Kevin Liptak, Philip Littleton, Rebecca Livingston, Juan Carlos Lopez, Edwin Lora, Willie A. Lora, Andrew Losey, Mary Grace Lucas, Krystal Michelle Mabry, Nathie Malayang, Michael Maltas, Mark Anthony Marchione, Eric Christian Marrapodi, Paul Matthews, Timothy McCaughan, Dugald McConnell, Kerith McFadden, Denise McIntosh, William Charles McKnight, Samuel J. McMichael IV, Michael McMullan, William Mears, Christie Corologos Medina, James Meech, Alexia V. Mena, Jeanne Meserve, Edward Robert Metzger, Paul Keith Miller, Peter Mohen, Ione Indira Molinares-Hess, Alex Mooney, Jeremy Moorhead, Isabel Morales, Peter Morris, Steven Nannes, Nicholette Nicci, Virginia Nicolaidis, Ernest G. Nocciolo, Christopher Nowak, Beverly O'Banion, John Otth, Andre Parker, Robert Geoffrey Parker, Chris Parks, Katherine Parrott, Nathan Payne, Aaron C. Payne, Simone Perez, Alan Philippon, Jordan Placie, Michelle Poley, Brendan Polmer,

NETWORKS, STATIONS, AND SERVICES REPRESENTED—Continued

Chris Popp, Carrie Port, Aaron Lamont Posley, Mark Preston, Carol J. Rachou, Jr., Bogdan Radu, Padmananda Rama, Justine Redman, Jean Renaud, James Riggs, Raul Rios-Hernandez, Jennifer Rizzo, Greg Robertson, David Robinson, Janet Rodriguez, Susan Rodriguez, Richelle Rogers, Brian Rokus, H. Michael Roselli, Rachel Rosen, Jeff Rosetti, Jessica Rosgaard, Mary Katherine Ross, Linda Roth, Lindy Royce, David Ruff, Diane Ruggiero, Emily Rust, Pedro Salas, Marcela Salazar, Jose G. Santos, Thayer Anne Sargent, Douglas N. Schantz, Barry C. Schlegel, Emily Schultze, Gabriella Schwarz, Raquel Scott, Reginald G. Selma, Rachael Louise Shackelford, Lawrence Shaughnessy, Shawna Shepherd, Joann Lucia Sierra, Alan Jay Silverleib, Jeffery Simms, Jeff Simon, Rebecca Sinderbrand, Kristi Slafka, Kathy Slobogin, Kelly Smoot, Matthew Speiser, Philip Scott Spoerry, Steven Stahl, Barbara Starr, Scott Stead, Paul Steinhauser, Vaughn Sterling, Rebecca Joy Stewart, Timothy Stoutzenberger, Rachel Streitfeld, Julian Styles, Bethany Swain, Sherrell Swanier, Lisa Sylvester, Daniel A. Szematowicz, Xuan Thai, James B. Thomas III, Brian Todd, Nicolas Toso, Steve Tovarek, Shannon Travis, Kenneth Tuohey, Chris Turner, Steve Turnham, Brett Tyler, Kim Uhl, Kenya Sheri Ulmer, Anthony R. Umrani, Laurie Ure, Ellen Van de Mark, Dana Viers, Joseph Charles Von Kanel, Tu H. Vu, Deirdre Walsh, Christopher Walter, Mark Walz, Tracey Webb, Marquida Webster, Eric Weisbrod, Jessica Elizabeth Weiss, Edward White, Amanda Gail White, Val Willingham, Susie Xu, Brian Yaklyvich, Floyd Yarmuth, Jessica Yellin, Robert Yoon, Saundra Young,

CNSNEWS.COM—(703) 683–7045; 325 South Patrick Street, Alexandria, VA 22314: Michael W. Chapman, Matthew Cover, Terence Jeffrey, Fred Lucas, Edwin Mora, Eric Scheiner, Jonathan M. Schulter, Penny Starr, Jerome Vorus, Jr., Thomas ''Pete'' Winn.

COMMUNITY TV OF PG'S—(301) 464–4560; 9475 Lottsford Road, Largo, MD 20774: David Barnes, Curtis Crutchfield, David Goldman, Julian Ingram, Ara Laughlin, Rochelle Metzger, Sandra Peaches, Sonia Randev, Christopher Thomas, Patricia Villone Garcia, Natalie Wilson.

CONGRESSIONAL QUARTERLY—(202) 419–8640; 1255 22nd Street, NW., Suite 200, Washington, DC 20037: Andrew Satter.

COPE RADIO (SPAIN)—(202) 686–1982; 4904 Bett Road, NW., Washington, DC 20016: Juan Martinez Fierro.

COX BROADCASTING—(202) 777–7000; 400 North Capitol Street, NW., #750, Washington, DC 20001: Alison Burns, David Chase, Jamie Dupree, Carol Han, Kevin Johnson, Scott MacFarlane, Catherine C. Reynolds, Jon Sonnheim, Heidi Wiedenbauer, Jeffrey L. Williams.

CRONKITE NEWS SERVICE—(202) 684–2400; 1834 Connecticut Avenue, NW., Washington, DC 20009: Steve Crane.

C–SPAN—(202) 737–3220; 400 North Capitol Street, NW., #650, Washington, DC 20001: Kenneth Alexander, Thomas Alldredge, Theresa Amirault-Michel, Jeremy Art, Shahin Atai, Shannon Augustus, Michelle Bailor, Stephen Lowell Belter, Jason Bender, Andrew Bernius, Brett Betsill, Michael Biddle, Dannie Boone, Greta Brawner, Paul Brown, Robert Browning, Kristina Buddenhagen, Susan J. Bundock, Leslie Burdick, James Burke, Kathy Cahill Murphy, Nancy Calo-Christian, Craig Caplan, Kenneth Carrick, Tanya Chattman, Matthew Claar, James Clark, Josh Cohen, Bruce D. Collins, James L. Cook, Cleve Corner, Dennis Cravedi, Liam Currier, Alexander Curtis, Greg Czzowitz, Pete Daniels, Matthew Dauchess, Tanya Davis, Heather DeManche, Alex Dickenson, Bridget Diggs, Constance Doebele, Michelle Doell, Richard Dubroff, Paul Eades, Jr., Katrice Eborn, Pedro L. Echevarria, Ronald Eisenbarth, Gary Ellenwood, Seth Engel, Patricia Esquivel, Greg Fabic, Mark Farkas, Joesph Feeney, Richard Fleeson, Carl Foster, William Frazier, Luis Fuquen, John Gallagher, John Garlock, Garney Gary, Robert Gould, Tim Gray, Bill Gray, Brendan Gupta, Richard Hall, Eric Hansen, Chris Hanson, Stephen Harkness, Robb Harleston, John Hayes, Maurice Haynes, William Heffley, Jonelle P. Henry, Dallas Hill, Michael Holden, George Howell, Yi-Pe Hsieh, Katherine Hughes, Tracy Hunter, Cynthia Ingle, Roberta Jackson, Sheila Jaskot, Latraniecesa Johnson-Wilson, Andrew Jones, Barry Katz, Stephanie Kaye, Steve Kehoe, Jon Kelley, Robert Kennedy, Roxane Kerr, Lew Ketcham, Kevin King, David Knighton, Felix Laboy, Brian Lamb, Darren Larade, Molly Laville, Robert Lazar, Jerome Leddon, Mark Lindblom, Brian Lloyd, Paul Loeschke, Russell Logan, Valerie Matthews, Ken McAndrew, Sean McCann, Michael McCann, Gerard McGarrity, Seeno Merobshoev, Justin Metzger, Andrew Peter Miller, Kate Mills, David Monack, Victor R. Montoro, Garrette Moore, Linwood Moore, Howard Mortman, Dan Morton, Terry Murphy, Yetta Myrick, Andrew Nason, Luke Nichter, Donna Norris, Benjamin O'Connell, Alan Olmsted, Paul Orgel, Nike Oyebanjo, Michael Patruznick, Vernon Perkins, Christina Perry, Chelsea Pflugh, Nickolas Pitocco, Taylor Porter, Almon Porter, Anne Preloh, Tony Pronko, Lauren Pulte, Nikhil Raval, Robert Reilly, Michelle Remillard, Cynthia Reuter, Paul Rigney, Delia Rios, Tamara Robinson, Tiffany Rocque, Mark Rodeffer, Martine Rodriguez, Jennifer Ruff, Frederico Sampaio, Molly Sanders, Sherry Sanders-Smith, Michelle Sandiford, Johnson Sarfo-Kantanka, William Scanlan, John Scheuer, Ellen Schweiger, Steven Scully, Peter Slen, Lindley Smith, Ben Sorenson, Alan Speck, Johnny St. Jean, Gary Starikoff, Mindy Steinman, Norma Steven, Rick Stoddard, Susan Swain, Mary Symanski, Russell J. Taylor, Christina Taylor, Joseph Teeples, Eric Thoman, Arthur Tiller, Brandon Tilman, Annie Tin, Sarah Tobianski, Lauren Torlone, Kevin Washburn, Richard Weinstein, Ruthann Winterhalter, Christopher Wood, Robert Latimer Young.

NETWORKS, STATIONS, AND SERVICES REPRESENTED—Continued

CTI–TV (TAIWAN)—(301) 792–8888; 7 Monona Court, Derwood, MD 20855: E-Ting Chung, Guohua Zang.

CTV CANADIAN TV—(202) 466–3595; 2000 M. Street, NW., Suite #330, Washington, DC 20036: Jonathan Austin, Thomas Clark, Bradley Fulton, Denise Kimmel, James MacDonald, Joy Malbon, Leigh Sclater Paterson, Paul Workman.

DANISH BROADCASTING CORPORATION—(202) 785–1460; 3643 Jenifer Street, NW., Washington, DC 20015: Claus Fahrendorff, Steffen William Gram, John K. Greenwood, Cathrine Gyldensted, Gitte Gustavsen McGuire, Grethe Winther.

DEUTSCHE WELLE TV—(202) 785–5730; 2000 M. Street, NW., Suite 335, Washington, DC 20036: Christina Bergmann, Lori Hannan, Maximillian Hofmann, Miodrag Soric.

DEUTSCHELAND RADIO—(301) 765–0211: Klaus Remme.

DIVERSIFIED COMMUNICATIONS, INC. (DCI)—(202) 775–4300; 2000 M. Street, NW., 3rd Floor, Washington, DC 20036: Joseph Concaugh, Jr., David M. Cooke, John Craig, Robert Fetzer, Michael Warren Grams, Masano Hidaka, Yoshiki Hidaka, Adrian Kill, William H. Milstead, Jr., Jamie Norins, Terry Straub, Robert Zajko,

ENERGY NOW—(202) 621–2916; 750 1st Street, NE., Suite 1115, Washington, DC 20002: Jevan Alves, Thalia Assuras, Ashley Bernardi, Stephanie Breijo, Greg Carney, Anna Davalos, Tim Foti, Daniel Goldstein, Mark Hanner, Aja Hubert-Hogg, Shawn Jones, Stewart Kasloff, Simon Lomax, Danny Lyon, Silvio Marcacci, Ian McAllister, Natalia Melia, Martin Niland, Jennifer Oko, Michael Petrucci, Katie Reiss, Shelley Simpson, Hardy Spire, Tyler Suiters, Lee Patrick Sullivan.

ENVIRONMENT & ENERGY PUBLISHING, LLC—(202) 446–0445; 122 C. Street, NW., Suite 722, Washington, DC 20001: Christopher Farmer, Eunmi Lee, Monica Trauzzi, Douglas Zimmerman.

ETTV—(202) 659–3592; 1825 K. Street, NW., Washington, DC 20036: Wen-Hsiang Chang.

EUROVISION AMERICAS, INC.—(202) 293–9371; 2000 M. Street, NW., Suite 300, Washington, DC 20036: James Banks, Andrew Blythe, Garrett Bohannon, John Carner, Emilie de Schaetzen, William Dunlop, Dyane Fils, Sarah Gibbons, Lee Grigsby, Jay Hahn, Steve Harper, Thomas Hass, Paul Knezek, Adam Mandelson, Priya Narahari, Jean Pierre Roberts, Jason Scharf, Peggy Soucy, Thomas Trainor, Clayton Trosclair.

EYE–TO–EYE VIDEO—(301) 907–7464; 4614 Chevy Chase Boulevard, Chevy Chase, MD 20815: Elliot Klayman, Patrick O'Donnell.

FEATURE STORY NEWS—(202) 296–9012; 1730 Rhode Island Avenue, Suite 405, Washington, DC 20036: Malcolm Brown, Emily Carpeaux, Heather Dahl, Priscilla Huff, Simon Marks, Kate Moody, Daniel Ryntjes, Rachel Silverman.

FEDERAL NEWS RADIO AM 1050—(202) 895–5137: Jamie Blanco, Mike Causey, Ruben Gomez, Emily Jarvis, Emily Kopp, Suzanne Kubota, Jolie Lee, Jason Miller, Amy Morris, Francis Rose, Jared Serbu, Thomas R. Temin, Justin Udo, Lisa Wolfe, Julia Ziegler.

FEDERAL NEWS SERVICE—(202) 216–2807; 1000 Vermont Avenue, NW., Washington, DC 20005: Tyler Bass, Frank Guest, Kirk Hanneman, Fred Lestina, Carrie Mitchell, Eric Parker, Rebecca Snyder, Mark Stodder, Jordan White.

FEDNET—(202) 393–7300; 50 F. Street, NW., Suite 1C, Washington, DC 20001: Chris Bannon, Keith Carney, Jessica Dambach, Michael Kirby, Eric Nicholas, Harry Scheid, Tess Vandendolder.

FINNISH BROADCASTING COMPANY (YLE)—(202) 785–1460: Nina Ann-Mari Svahn, Paula Hannele Vilen, Juri Tomas von Bonsdorff, Grethe Winther.

FOX BUSINESS NETWORK—(202) 715–1687; 400 North Capitol, Street, NW., Washington, DC 20001: Mike Bannigan, Peter Barnes, Bruce Becker, Cesar Canizales, Rich Edson, Susan Falvella-Garraty, Martin Jimenez, Mary Kreinbihl, Chris Mills, Adam Shapiro, Jonathan St. John, Roger Wallace.

FOX NEWS—(202) 824–6345; 400 North Capitol Street, NW., Washington, DC 20001: Greg Ahlquist, James L. Angle, Robert Armfield, Bret Baier, Les Baker, Josh Banks, Calvin Wesley Barrett, Stuart Basinger, Chris Becker, Judson Berger, Shayla Bezdrob, Varuna Bhatia, Craig Boswell, Bryan Boughton, John Brandt, Fletcher Bransford, Shannon Bream, Lanna Britt, Kristin Brown, Edgar Brown, Carl Cameron, Steve Carlson, Michael Carpel, Walter Carter, Jr., Juan Casanas, Steve Centanni, Kelly Chernenkoff, Stephen Clark, Richard Cockerham, Bryan Cole, Eric Colimore, Eric Conner, Sarah Courtney, Jodie Curtis, Debra DeFrank, Joe DeFrank, Michael DeMark, Mary Pat Dennert, Andrea DeVito, Brian Doherty, Jason Donner, Peter Doocy, Paige Dukeman, Megan Dumpe, Jerry Echols, William Edmondson, James W. Eldridge, Mike Emanuel, Tyler Evans, Joel Fagen, Mark Finch, Alexander Finland, Justin Fishel, Linda Fodrea, Monica Gacka, Dan Gallo, Jake Gibson, Jenna Gibson, Gary Gillis, April Girouard, Nikoletta Gjoni, Wendell Goler, Jennifer Griffin, Cherie Grzech, Gregg L. Gursky, Fred Haberstick, Brian Haefeli, Kata Hall, Lacey Halpern, Jennifer Hazelton, Mary Janne Henneberg, Francis Herbas, Catherine Herridge, Stacy Hickman, Martin Hill, LA Holmes, Adrienne Moira Hopkins, Cory R. Howard, Paul Huckeby, Brit Hume, Elena Isella, William G. Jenkins, George Jewsevskyj, Torrance Jones, Mae Joo, Nathalie Joost, Sharon Kehnemui, Colleen Kelley, Zachary Kenworthy, Grigory Khananayev, Whitney Ksiazek, Donna Lacey, Philip LeCroy, Meaghan Leister, Michael Levine, Edward Lewis, Joy Lin, Erin Lockwood, Catherine Loper, Wayne Lowman, Laurie Luhn, Doug Luzader, Stacia Lynds, Michael Lyon, Melissa Manuel, Amanda Marshall, Lori Martin,

NETWORKS, STATIONS, AND SERVICES REPRESENTED—Continued

Molly Mathews, Tim May, Kevin McClam, George McCloskey, Anne McGinn, Doug McKelway, Richard Morse, Seleena M. Muhammad, James Nelson, Kerry O'Connor, Quillie Odom, Angela Oduro, Bradford S. Paxton, Chad Pergram, Chris Peslis, Jacqueline Pham, Lauren Pick, David Renken, Elizabeth Rhodes, Katheryn C. Ricalde, Sarah Santer Ridolfi, Anne Marie Riha, Michael Robbins, Christina Robbins, Tamara Robertson, Douglas Rohrbeck, James Rosen, Lee Ross, Bill Sammon, Craig Savage, Jason Scanlon, Kimberly Schwandt, Abby Sears, Steve Shelton, Dave Shott, Anita Siegfriedt, Teresa Spector, James Sprankle, Drake Springer, Daniel J. Stay, Lexi Stemple, Seneca Stevens, Chris Stirewalt, Matthew Stout, Beth Sullivan, Patrick Summers, John Sumrel, Jennifer Suzara, Mary Ellen Tasillo, Lauren Tate, Robert Torpey, Bree Tracey, Patricia Turner, Lamonte Bryant Tyler, Greta Van Susteren, Bryce Vinson, Todd Visioli, Erin Vogel, Phil Vogel, John L. Wallace, Chris Wallace, David Warrick, Amy Wehinger, Walter Whitley, Colleen Williams, John Williams, Anne Marie Willis, Kelly Wright, Eve Zibel.

FOX NEWS RADIO—(917) 846–5533; 5353 Cassons Neck Road, Cambridge, MD 21613: Mitch Davis, Robert Finnerty, Jared Daniel Halpern, Rich Johnson, Melissa Kraus, Mike Majchrowitz, Kirstin McNary, Jeff Monosso, Bernard Pigott III, Daniel Shields, Dawn Siff, Todd Starnes, John Sylvester, Hank Weinbloom, Dawn Weiner.

FRANCE 2 TELEVISION—(202) 833–1818; 2000 M. Street, NW., Suite 320, Washington, DC 20036: Stephan Breitner, Maryse Burgot, Laurent Desbois, Aaron Diamond, Valerie McCabe, Arielle Monange, Emmanuelle Richard.

FREE SPEECH RADIO NEWS—(804) 222–7945; 2390 Champlain Street, NW., Washington, DC 20009: Catherine Comp, Jacob Fenston, Matt Laslo, Michael Lawsen, Alice Ollstein, Alan Searle.

FUJI TV JAPAN—(202) 347–1600; 529 14th Street, NW., Suite 330, Washington, DC 20045: Tomoko Barton, Peter Gold, Haruka Joho, Nancy H. Ku, Sumiko Mori, Matthew Mosley.

GALEI–TZAHAL (ISRAEL ARMY RADIO)—(301) 520–2503; 112 Shaw Avenue, Silver Spring, MD 20904: Drora S. Perl.

GANNETT GOVERNMENT MEDIA CORP—(703) 750–8196; 6883 Commercial Drive, Springfield, VA 22159: Jessica Eckert, Colin Francis Kelly, Alan Lessig, Scott Mahaskey, Blair Tomlinson.

GANNETT NEWS SERVICE—(202) 906–8125; 1100 New York Avenue, Washington, DC 20005: Maria Fowler.

GERMAN BROADCASTING SYSTEMS-ARD—(202) 944–5290: Jens Borchers, Silvia Charpa, Julia Hummelsiep, Nicole Markwald, Sabine Mueller-Thum.

GERMAN PRESS AGENCY—(202) 662–1277; 1112 National Press Building, Washington, DC 20045: Christina Eck, Peer Meinert, Gertraud Zangl.

GERMAN PUBLIC RADIO (ARD)—(202) 625–2503; 1200 Eton Court, NW., Washington, DC 20007: Sabrina Fritz, Silke Hasselmann, Astrid Joehnk, Klaus Kastan.

GERMAN TV ARD—(202) 298–6535; 3132 M. Street, NW., Washington, DC 20007: Herta Borniger, Gabriela Eaglesome, Anja Engelke, Hillery D. Gallasch, Antonio Gonzalez, Johanna Huesch, Dirk Keuper, Felicitas Klopp, Udo Lielischkies, Joseph MacQuarrie, Pola Maurer, Ruediger Paulert, Diana Claudia Robbins, Thomas Sawera, Klaus Scherer, Marion Schmickler, Ralph Sina, Sonja Wasgien, Juergen Welter.

GERMAN TV ZDF—(202) 333–3909; 1077 31st Street, NW., Washington, DC 20007: Gabriele Buse, Askan Buse, Kirsten Candia, Oliver Divaris, Ruben Herrera, Erik Illenseer, Alice Kelley, Markus Klein, Wolfgang Macholz, Claudia Offermann, Christoph Roeckerath, Ulf-Jensen Roeller, Hildrun Rowe, Heike Slansky, Uyanga Tserenbaljid, Elke Tucker.

GLOBAL TV CANADA—(202) 824–0426; 400 North Capitol Street, NW., #850, Washington, DC 20001: Eric D. Sorensen.

GROUPE TVA—(202) 822–4588; 820 1st Street, NE., Washington, DC 20002: Richard Latendresse.

HEARST-ARGYLE TELEVISION—(202) 457–0220; 1825 K. Street, NW., #720, Washington, DC 20006: Kate Amara, Matthew Gerien, Norman Hadad, Dan Highland, Sally F. Kidd, Nikole Killion, Michael LaBella, Lauren McDevitt, Erin T. McManamon, Shaun Neville, Patrick M. O'Gara, David Postovit, Lavina Ramchandani, TraLanenia Nicole Reeves, Chris Smyth, Wendy Wilk.

HISPANIC COMMUNICATIONS NETWORK—(202) 360–4112; 1126 16th Street, NW., 3rd Floor, Washington, DC 20036: Carlos Alcazar, Obdulia Alcazar, Pablo Castro, Julio Gonzalez, Luisa Fernanda Montero, Mercy Padilla-Cirino.

HONG KONG PHOENIX SATELLITE TELEVISION—(202) 420–5510; 1100 13th Street, NW., Suite 400, Washington, DC 20005: Ching-Yi Chang, Yen Ying Chen, Yi Qiu Chen, Daniel Lai, Hun-Min Lee, Zhengzhu Liu, Meixing Ren, Bingru Wang, Taofeng Wang.

ICELANDIC NATIONAL BROADCASTING SERVICE—(203) 517–8079: Sveinn Helgason.

INDEPENDENT TELEVISION NEWS (ITN)—(202) 429–9080; 400 North Capitol Street, NW., #899, Washington, DC 20008: Dai Baker, Adam Blair, Matt Frei, Ian Glover-James, Michael Herrod, Robert Moore, Emily O'Neill, Andy Rex, David Sampy, Chris Shlemon, Sarah Smith.

IRISH RADIO & TV (RTE)—(202) 467–5933; 1750 16th Street, NW., #53, Washington, DC 20009: Harvey Cofske, Richard Downes, Robert Shortt, Lesley Steinhauser.

ISRAEL TELEVISION AND RADIO—(202) 271–8192: Nathan Guttman.

NETWORKS, STATIONS, AND SERVICES REPRESENTED—Continued

KOREAN BROADCASTING SYSTEMS—(202) 662–7345; 529 14th Street, NW., Suite 1055, Washington, DC 20045: Kyoosik Choi, Kisub Hong, Chulho Kim, Youllee Kim, JaeEun Kim, Choonho Lee, Kevin Nha, Ja Ryen Seo, Taeho Yun.

KPCC—(202) 713–0947: Kitty Felde.

LINK TV—(202) 255–5594: Miles Benson, Raisa Scriabine.

LIVING ON EARTH—(202) 554–0644: Eileen Bolinsky, Ebony Payne, Mitra Taj, Jeff Young.

MARKETPLACE RADIO—(202) 223–6699; 1750 K. Street, NW., Suite 300, Washington, DC 20006: John Dimsdale, David Gura, Nancy Marshall-Genzer, Scott Tong.

MBC–DUBAI—(202) 294–8013; 529 14th Street, NW., Suite 530, Washington, DC 20045: Nadia Bilbassy-Charters, Daoud Abu Hawa.

MBC–TV KOREA (MUNHWA)—(202) 349-0078; 529 14th Street, NW., #1131, Washington, DC 20045: Sang Jin Kim, Jaihong Kwon, Jaehoon Lee, Hanjun Rhee, Hoin Rhee.

MCCLATCHY COMPANY—(831) 601–6110; 700 12th Street, NW., Suite 1000, Washington, DC 20005: Kate Tamba Howard, Jim Van Nostrand, Letitia Wells.

MEDILL NEWS SERVICE—(202) 661–0144; 1325 G. Street, NW., #730, Washington, DC 20005: Tom Hannon, Brian Paris, Ellen Shearer.

METRO NETWORKS—(301) 628–2766; 8403 Colesville Road, #1500, Silver Spring, MD 20910: Terrence Moore, Rachel Roberts-Crowson.

METRO TELEPRODUCTIONS—(301) 608–9077; 1400 East West Highway, Suite 628, Silver Spring, MD 20910: Dave Lilling.

MIDDLE EAST TELEVISION NETWORK (ALHURRA)—(202) 852–9338; 7600–D, Boston Boulevard, Springfield, VA 22153: Rana Abtar, Ali Ahmed, Kelly Alford, Babu Aryankalavil, Adil Cherkaoui, John Elgin, Daniel Farkas, Mohamed-Ali Haidari, Christopher Hamilton, Stephen Heiner, Vernon Herald, Arcelious Joyner, Deirdre Kline, Pericles Lewnes, Tim Miller, Mohamed Mokhtari, W. Harrison Moore, John Mueller, Luis Munoz, Mohamed El Hussin Nassar, Adam Nixon, James Norris, Mohamed Wafa, Karen Yianopoulos, Elizabeth Zosso.

MINNESOTA PUBLIC RADIO NEWS—(202) 596–5414; 1750 K. Street, NW., Suite 300, Washington, DC 20006: Brett Neely.

MOBILE VIDEO SERVICES, LTD.—(202) 331–8882; 1620 I. Street, NW., #1000, Washington, DC 20006: Howard Collender, Lindsay Flaherty, William Griffitts, Christine Hoese, Timothy Knapp, Robert H. Milford, Todd Swain, Lawrence VanderVeen, Jacob VanderVeen.

MORNINGSIDE PARTNERS, LLC—(410) 694–9333; 4200 Forbes Road, Suite 200, Lanham, MD 20706: Tony Anthony, Joshua Binswanger, Elizabeth Pennell, Ellen Portnoy, Juvenal Uribe, Franklin Zeledon.

N24 GERMAN TV—(202) 331–9400: Alessandro Privitera, Stephen Strothe, Sabine Ulbrich-Strothe.

NATIONAL PUBLIC RADIO—(202) 513–2000; 635 Massachussetts Avenue, NW., Washington, DC 20001: Stacey Abbott, Larry Abramson, Kim Adams, Reena Advani, Augustine ''Bud'' Aiello, Jr., Chinita Anderson, Christine Arrasmith, John Asante, Bruce Auster, Theo Balcomb, Brendan Banaszak, Sandra Bartlett, Nicole Beemsterboer, Mark Bejarano, Robert Benincasa, Geoffrey Bennett, Josh Bennett, Sarah Beyer Kelly, Jonathan Blakley, Melissa Block, Brakkton Booker, Tom Bowman, Radek Brablec, Barbara Bradley Hagerty, Peter Breslow, Joshua Brockman, Paul Brown, Julia Redpath Buckley, Tom Bullock, Ivan Burketh, Robert E. Butcher, Dennis Byrnes, Scott Cameron, Barbara Campbell, Sean Carberry, Neal Carruth, Franklyn Cater, Zoe Chace, Carlos Chevez, Andrew Chapman Christy, Grant Clark, Dennis Coll, Neal Conan, Felix Contreras, Audie Cornish-Emery, William C. Craven, Michael Cullen, Alicia F. Cypress, Michael Czaplinski, Corey Dade, Shirish V. Date, Bridget DeChagas, Brian DeMar, Greg Dixon, Beth Donovan, Thomas Dreisbach, Coburn Dukehart, Hugh Eaton, Peter Ellena, Debbie Elliott-Taylor, Ronald Elving, Monika Evstatieva, Pam Fessler, April Fulton, Stanley Martin Garrison, Marilyn Geewax, Susannah George, David Gilkey, Tom Gjelten, Tom Goldstein, Don Gonyea, Barry Gordemer, Peter Granitz, Gisele Grayson, Nell Greenfieldboyce, Liz Halloran, Jon Hamilton, Sarah Handel, Barrie Hardymon, Phil Harrell, Richard Harris, Anne Hawke, Elaine Heinzman, Scott Hensley, Lee Hill, Jordana Hochman, TaShick Holland, Gerry Holmes, Gemma Hooley, Scott William Horsley, Andrea Hsu, Johney Burke Hunn, Argin Hutchins, Steve Inskeep, Robert Jackson, Frank James, Rick Jarrett, Keith Jenkins, Carrie Johnson, Helena D. Johnson, Cindy Johnston, Christopher Joyce, John C. Keator, Tamara Keith, Michele Kelemen, Bridget Kelley, Alex Kellogg, Allison Keyes, Asma Khalid, Carol Klinger, Laura Krantz, Kevin Langley, Travis Larchuck, Viet Le, Mara Liasson, Jennifer Ludden, Alison MacAdam, Antonio Marcano, Tom Marchitto, Melissa Marquis, Michel Martin, Rachel Martin, Matt Martinez, Kevin Matera, Charles Mayer, Petra Mayer, Kyle McKinnon, Dennis Medvee, Mark Memmott, Shereen Meraji, Michael Merena, Sanaz Meshkinpour, Veronica Miller, Joe Mills, Guillermo Minoso, Alicia Montgomery, Marcia Morgan, Steve Murno, Heather Murphy, Muthoni Muturi, Brian Naylor, Joe R. Neel, Christopher Nelson, Scott L. Neuman, Yuki Noguchi, Michele Norris, Jackie Northam, Emily Ochenschlager, Gabe O'Connor, Sarah Oliver, Peter Overby, Joe Palca, Vincent Pearson, Marisa Penaloza, Sean Phillips, John Poole, Guy Raz, Susanne Reber, Andrew Reynolds, Sonari Rhodes Glinton, Portia Robertson Migas, Jeffrey Rosenberg, Julie Rovner, Ken Rudin, Sam Sanders, Leah Scarpelli, Andrea Seabrook, Joseph Shapiro, Ari Shapiro, Cathy Shaw, Elizabeth Shogren, Daniel Shukhin, Robert C. Siegel, Art Silverman, Scott Simon, Graham

NETWORKS, STATIONS, AND SERVICES REPRESENTED—Continued

Smith, Robert Smith, Kurt Stalnaker, Susan Stamberg, Evie Stone, Laura Sullivan, Virginia L. Sullivan, Gerald W. Tennent, Neil David Tevault, Sharahn Thomas, Nina Totenberg, Lindsay Totty, Cory Turner, Christopher Turpin, Kevin Wait, Teshima Walker, Vickie Walton-James, Carline Watson, Walter Watson, Andrew Watts, Linton Weeks, David Welna, Linda Wertheimer, Ned Wharton, Jim Wildman, Margot Williams, John Ydstie, Daniel Zwerdling.

NATIONAL SCENE NEWS—(202) 298–9519; 1718 M. Street, NW., #333, Washington, DC 20036: Alverda Muhammad, Askia Muhammad.

NATIVE AMERICAN TELEVISION—(202) 347–9713; 444 North Capitol Street, NW., Suite 524, Washington, DC 20001: Rebecca Cohencious, Robert Cohencious, Randolph G. Flood, Richard Gargagliano, Anthony Lee Lovelace, Jr.

NBC NEWS—(202) 885–4200; 4001 Nebraska Avenue, NW., Washington, DC 20016: Douglas A. Adams, Roberto Aneiva, Kenneth Austin, John Bailey, Rodney Batten, Gary Beall, Michael Benetato, Justin Bennett, Regina Blackburn, John Blackman, Jay Blackman, Sarah Blackwill, Victoria Blooston, Jeffrey Blount, Joseph Bohannon, Brooke Brower, Randall Brown, Mika Brzezinski, Marisa Buchanan, Louis Burgdorf, Norman Anthony Butler, Anthony Capra, Catherine Chomiak, Betsy Cline, Margaret Conroy, Thomas Costello, Natalie Cucchiara, Caroline Dann, Erin Delmore, Christopher Donovan, Victoria Duncan, James Eaves, Jesse Edoro, Barbara Fant, Sheldon Fielman, Elizabeth Fischer, Kent Floyd, David Forman, Scott Foster, Drew Fredrickson, Lawrence Gaetano, Dennis Gaffney, Jamie Gangel, Richard Gardella, Keith Gaskin, Ralph Gaudino, Jeffrey Goodman, Sarah Greenberg, James M. Greene, David Gregory, Marsha Groome, Andrew F. Gross, Savannah Guthrie, Sylvia Haller, David Hanson, Candice Harrington, Alan Harvey, Sarah Heidarpour, John Holland, James Hughes, Michael Isikoff, Alicia Jennings, Athena Jones, Gwyneth Jones, Shannon Joyner, Kara Kearns, Terence Kelly, Suzanne Kianpour, Ryan Kiernan, Stacey Klein, Ann Klenk, Marc Koslow, Michael Kosnar, Courtney Kube, Natasha Lebedeva, Elizabeth Leist, Adam Levin, Victoria Lewis, John Libretto, Christopher Licht, Arthur Lien, Kathleen Lockhart, Joseph W. Loebach, Matt Loffman, James V. Long, Gary Lynn, Mark Mack-Fitzhugh, Freddie Malone, Mary Manby, Joseph Mathias, Chris Matthews, Carroll Ann Mears, Rob Melick, James Miklaszewski, Christopher Millar, Richard Minner, Andrea Mitchell, Steven Mitnick, Alexandra Moe, Domenico Montanaro, Ray Morada, Shaheen Mozaffari, Mark Murray, Lisa Myers, Nancy Nathan, Amna Nawaz, Michelle Neal, Jason Neal, Donna Nelson, Elizabeth Nevins, Kelvin Noye, Bridget Nurre, David O'Brien, Kelly O'Donnell, Norah O'Donnell, Connie Patsalos, Debra Pettit, Shelby Poduch, John Quinnette, Meaghan Rady, Alonzo Ray, Querry Robinson, Luke Russert, Howard Sacks, Jose ''Antoine'' Sanfuentes, Colleen Sanvido, Carmine Scicchitano, Beth Scott, Andrew Scritchfield, Wesley Scruggs, Carl Sears, Joel Seidman, Lauren Selsky, Joseph Shalhoup, David Silver, Ron Simeone, LaToya Sims, Aaron Robert Skopek, Lauren Smith, Kimberly Sneed, Gilbert Solorzano, Sharon Spurrier, Stephen George Stennett, Kenneth Strickland, Jon Sughroue, Robert Sullivan, Ashlea Surles, David Thelin, Shawna Thomas, Ronald Thornton, Chuck Todd, Anna Tuman, Tina Urbanski, Juan Ureta, Adam Verdugo, Michael Viqueira, Susan Vitorovich, David Vukmer, Charles Warzel, David Weakly, Ali Weinberg, Maurice Whitehurst, Christopher Whittington, Abigail Williams, Robert T. Williams, Louis ''Pete'' Williams, Christopher Williamson, Robert Witten, Ethan Yaffe.

NBC NEWSCHANNEL—(202) 783–2615; 400 North Capitol Street, Suite 850, Washington, DC 20001: Sheila Conlin, Kristen Ann Dahlgren, Nancy Ellard, Sheri Lynn Gibson, Andrew L. Godsick, Steve Handelsman, James Hurt, Julie Jarvis, Jennifer Johnson, Virginia Coyne Kreindler, Nicole McManus, Brian Mooar, Steven Charles Muskat, Tom Newberry, Mike O'Connell, Tracie Potts, Bonnie Rollins, Cecil John Sills, Christopher Wiggins.

NEED TO KNOW NEWS—(202) 506–1705; 440 South LaSalle Street, #1208, Chicago, IL 60605: Chris Cermak, Kenneth Chee Yang Fung, Kasra N. Kangerloo, Alison McConnell, Noel Nedli, Joshua Newell, Mary Beth Slack.

NEW TANG DYNASTY TV—(301) 515–5422; 229 West 28th Street, Suite 1200, New York, NY 10001: Laura Hatton, Hui Jing, Chuan Lin, Jin Pang, Yang Wang, Wei Wu, Dong Xiang, Jinglu Xu, Bin Xue, Chunfang Yang, John Yu, Haoran Zheng.

NHK–JAPAN BROADCASTING CORPORATION—(202) 828–5180; 2030 M. Street, NW., Suite 706, Washington, DC 20036: Regina Bediako, Yuko Chiba, Sylvain Coudoux, Yuichiro Hanazawa, Kaho Ogawa Izumitani, Ichiro Kabasawa, Takamoto Kajiwara, Atsushi Kato, Torao Kono, Reiko Sakurai, Joseph Shaw, Shin Shoji, Masaki Suda, Yuka Takagane, Yosuke Takagi, Jun Takao, Daisuke Yamaguchi, Anthony Yazaki.

NIGHTLY BUSINESS REPORT—(202) 682–9029; 1325 G. Street, NW., #1005, Washington, DC 20005: Darren Gersh, Sylvia Hall, Anna Olson, Ervin Washington.

NIPPON TV NETWORK—(202) 638–0890; 529 14th Street, NW., #1036, Washington, DC 20045: Takaaki Abe, Yuichi Akahori, Kazuhiro Aoyama, Ayuko Hirano, Tomoko Horie, Eriko Matsuo, Tateki Muratani, Tomoyasu Takezaki, Kyrie Lauren Whitsett.

NORWEGIAN BROADCASTING—(202) 785–1460; 2000 M. Street, NW., #890, Washington, DC 20036: Jon Gelius, Anders Tvegard, Grethe Winther.

NETWORKS, STATIONS, AND SERVICES REPRESENTED—Continued

NOS DUTCH PUBLIC RADIO & TV (VRT)—(202) 466–8793; 2000 M. Street, NW., #365, Washington, DC 20036: Wessel de Jong, Jacqueline Maria Eckmann, Scott Rensberger, Eelco Bosch van Rosenthal.

N–TV GERMAN NEWS CHANNEL—(202) 420–5530; 1100 13th Street, NW., Suite 400, Washington, DC 20005: Holger Banning, Roman Polanski, Christian Wilp.

ORF (OSTERREICHISCHER RUNDFUNK)—(703) 821–9682; 1206 Eton Court, NW., Washington, DC 20007: Tim Cupal, Wolfgang Geier, Jan Greisiger, Uelle-Mall Jaakson, Markus Meier, Hanno Settele, Lauren Silva-Pinto.

RAC1—(202) 286–4878; 1545 18 Street, NW., Suite 102, Washington, DC 20036: Gustau Alegret.

RADIO FRANCE INTERNATIONALE—(202) 714–9816; 3700 Massachusetts Avenue, NW., #538 Washington, DC 20016: Donaig Le Du, Claude L. Porsella, Raphael Reynes, Anne Toulouse.

RADIO FREE ASIA—(202) 721–7443; 2025 M. Street, NW., Sutie 300, Washington, DC 20036: Kyaw Kyaw Aung, Shiny Li Breese, Gordon Burnett, Dzung Dolinh, Rigdhen Dolma, Richard Finney, Dhondup Gonsar, Gwen Ha, King Man Ho, Albert Hong, Mamatjan Juma, Ahreum Jung, Vivian Kieffer, Jin Kuk Kim, Mai Lai, Jae-Hak Lim, Joshua Lipes, Kalden Lodoe, Bounchanh Mouangkham, Corey Munford, Jilili Musha, Ingjin Naing, Jung Min Noh, Khin Maung Nyane, Jung-Woo Park, Parameswaran Ponnudurai, Brian William Powell, Peter Sainsbury, Aungthu Schlenker, Harry Scott, Zijun Shan, Khin Maung Soe, Sok Ry Sum, Sarada Taing, Yeshi Tashi, Sungwon Yang, Hee Jung Yang, Lobsang Yeshi, Samean Yun.

RADIO FREE EUROPE—(202) 457–6950; 1201 Connecticut Avenue, NW., Washington, DC 20036: Haroon Bacha, Christian Caryl, Irena Chalupa, Allan Davydov, Golnaz Esfandiari, Heather Maher, Laura Mir, Nader Sadighi, Richard Solash, Muhammad Tahir, Andrew Tully.

RADIO MARTI—(305) 437–7185; 4201 Northwest 77th Avenue, Miami, FL 33166: Godofredo Granados, Diana Molineaux, Luis Munoz, Elena Rodrigues, Gilberto Rosal.

RADIO ONE—(301) 429–2673; 5900 Princess Garden Parkway, 7th Floor, Lanham, MD 20706: Thomas Getter, Ronald Thompson, Christopher Wegmann, Christopher Levon Whitfield, Jr.

RADIO VALERA VENEZUELA—(202) 528–6540; 529 14th Street, NW., 8th Floor, Washington, DC 20045: Sonia Schott.

RCN–TV (COLOMBIA)—(202) 415–3162; 1333 H. Street, NW., Washington, DC 20005: Yeferson Asprilla, Martha Lucia Avila, Antonio Bustamante, Diana Carolina Castaneda, Marco Granda, Julio Ernesto Marenco, Ariel Zimerman.

REAL NEWS NETWORK—(310) 990–6408; 700 12th Street, NW., Suite 1000, Washington, DC 20005: Malak Behrouznami, David Dougherty, Jihan Hafiz, Paul Jay, Reed Lindsay, Danya Nadar, Sharmini Peries.

RELIGION & ETHICS NEWSWEEKLY—(202) 216–4400; 1333 H. Street, NW., 6th Floor, Washington, DC 20005: Robert G. Abernethy, Gail Fendley, Patricia Hanley, Arnolds Labaton, Kim Lawton, Emma Mankey Hidem, Julie Ann Mashack, Judy Reynolds, Noelle Serper.

REUTERS RADIO & TV—(202) 310–6475; 1333 H. Street, NW., 6th Floor, Washington, DC 20005: Nadine Alfa, Keith Allen, Anoopam Bharania, Peter Bullock, John Clarke, Jonathan Decker, Kevin Fogarty, Marie Frail, Guillermo Garcia, Deborah Gembara, Pavithra George, Sarah Irwin, Katharine Jackson, Kia Johnson, Justin Kenny, Deborah Lutterbeck, Robert Muir, Kristin Neubauer, Gershon Peaks, Don Pessin, Steven Phillips, Jane Ross, Tom Rowe, Mari Saito, Roger Shull, George Tamerlani, Scott Vaughan, Omar Younis.

RTV SLOVENIJA—(202) 364–2624: Vlasta Jesenicnik, Silvester Stok.

RTVI/ECHO–TV—(202) 742–6576; 1001 Pennsylvania Avenue, NW., Suite #6310, Washington, DC 20004: Vladimir Kara-Murza, Alexander Panov, Andrei Popovici, Dmytro Shakhov, Nargiz Shekinskaya.

RUSSIA TODAY TELEVISION—(202) 942–7447; 1325 G. Street, NW., Suite 250, Washington, DC 20005: Reema Abu-Hamdyia, Mark Lloyd Angelini, Naida Azizova, Andrew Blake, Mark Bulla, Gayane Chichakyan, Jon Robert Conway, Kaelyn Forde Eckenrode, Sean Filburn, Kristin Frazao, Lindsay Meghan Garfield, Mindia Mikhailovich Gavasheli, Lucy Kafanov, Lauren Lyster, Alyona Minkovski, Cedric Moon, Alexander Mursa, Anneli Nerman, Roselena Ramirez, Andrew Smith, Paul Spinelli, Priya Sridhar, Matthew A. Tolk, Denis Mikhaylovich Trunov, Vera Volokhonovich, Ilya Zhodzishsky.

RUSSIAN STATE TV AND RADIO (RTR)—(202) 460–6830; 2000 N. Street, NW., Suite 810, Washington, DC 20007: Elena Sokolova, Andrey Solimani-Lezhnev, Mikhail Solodovnikov.

RUSTAVI 2 BROADCASTING COMPANY—(202) 957–4496; 1111 Army Navy Drive, Unit 127, Arlington, VA 22202: David Nikuradze, Aleksandre Papinashvili.

SAGARMATHA TELEVISION—(703) 646–5110; 9655 Hawkshead Drive, Lorton, VA 22079: Ram C. Kharel, Sharmila Uprety.

SCRIPPS HOWARD NEWS SERVICE—(202) 408–2730; 1090 Vermont Avenue, NW., Washington, DC 20005: Kristin Volk Harper.

SEOUL BROADCASTING SYSTEM (SBS)—(202) 637–9850; 529 14th Street, NW., #979, Washington, DC 20045: Young Jin Ju, Mark Jung, Thomas Hyunseung Koh, Kyung Youl Shin.

SINCLAIR BROADCAST GROUP—(410) 568–1565; 10706 Beaver Dam Road, Cockeysville, MD 21030: Mark Hyman.

NETWORKS, STATIONS, AND SERVICES REPRESENTED—Continued

SIRIUSXM SATELLITE RADIO—(202) 412–9430; 1500 Eckington Place, NE., Washington, DC 20002: Katherine Caperton, Jonathan Decker, Tim Farley, Patrick William Ferrise, Pamela Kirkland, Joe Mathieu, Joe Mathews, Jared Rizzi.

SKY NEWS—(202) 824–6580; 400 North Capitol Street, NW., #550, Washington, DC 20001: Sally Arthy, Jon-Christopher Bua, Barnaby Green, David Lipson, Dickon Mager, Greg Milam, Robert Nisbet-Smith, Dominic Waghorn, Andoun Wilson.

SPIEGEL GERMAN TV—(202) 347–1735; 1202 National Press Building, Washington, DC 20045: Karin Assman.

SRN NEWS (SALEM)—(703) 528–6213; 1901 North Moore Street, #201, Arlington, VA 22209: Shepard Bennett, Gregory Clugston, Walter R. Hindes, Linda Kenyon, Ken Lormand, Jeffrey Alan Matzka, Andrew Stewart.

STATELINE.ORG—(202) 419–4464; 1615 L. Street, NW., Washington, DC 20016: Joshua Brockman, Diane Fancher, Stephen C. Fehr, Gene Gibbons, Josh Goodman, John P. Gramlich, David Harrison, Melissa Maynard, Pamela M. Prah, Barbara Rosewicz, Christopher Swope, Christine Vestal, Daniel Vock.

STORY HOUSE PRODUCTIONS—(202) 464–7211; 2233 Wisconsin Avenue, NW., #420, Washington, DC 20007: Julia U. Kelbling, Tina- Jane Krohn, Carsten Oblaender, Thomas M. Sassenberg, Laura Schnurre.

SWEDISH BROADCASTING—(202) 785–1460; 2000 M. Street, NW., Suite 890, Washington, DC 20036: Stefan Rolf Asberg, Lisa Carlsson, Leif Carlsson, Kyle Lanningham, Grethe Winther.

SWISS BROADCASTING—(202) 429–9668; 2000 M. Street, NW., Suite 370, Washington, DC 20036: Sylvie Deroche, Diego Gilardoni, Eric Guevara.Frey, Francois Jeannet, Tilman Lingner, Thomas Paggini, Peter Voegeli.

TALK RADIO NEWS SERVICE—(202) 337–5322; 236 Massachusetts Avenue, NE., Suite 306, Washington, DC 20002: Kenneth Bazinet, Marc Bernier, Joseph Byrne, James W. Cullum, Tala Dowlatshahi, Brian James Doyle, Justin Duckham, Cholene Espinoza, Adrian Lee Frost, Lovisa Frost, Geoff Holtzman, Victoria Jones, Julie Lule, Carole Marks, Benny Martinez, Richard F. Miller, Elianna Sara Mintz, Jacob Patterson, Ellen Ratner, Eric Rice, Tony Elias Elias Sayegh, Jr., Myron Sponder, Jay Tamboli, Ari Zoldan.

TELEMUNDO NETWORK—(202) 737–7830; 400 North Capitol Street, NW., Suite 850, Washington, DC 20001: Glenda Contreras, Guillermo Martinez, Lori Montenegro, Victor Reyes.

TELESUR—(202) 316–1212; 1825 K. Street, NW., Suite 710, Washington, DC 20006: Andrea Arenas, Aurora Samperio.

TELEVISA NEWS NETWORK (ECO)—(202) 347–0407; 1825 K. Street, NW., Suite 710–G, Washington, DC 20006: Jorge Armando Ayala, Gregorio Meraz.

TF1–FRENCH TV—(202) 223–3642; 2000 M. Street, NW., Suite 870, Washington, DC 20036: Julie Asher, Clement Biat, Gilles Bouleau, Helene Davieaud, Guillaume Debre, Michel Floquet, Bruce Frankel, Bertrand Guez, Natalia Mendoza, Vincent Mortreux, Fabien Ortiz.

THE BERNS BUREAU, INC.—(202) 314–5165: Matthew Kaye.

THE HILL—(202) 628–8510; 1625 K. Street, NE., Suite 900, Washington, DC 20006: Joshua Altman, Sheila Casey, Geneva Sands-Sadowitz, Erica Wisniewski.

THE NEWSHOUR WITH JIM LEHRER—(703) 998–2137; 3620 South 27th Street, Arlington, VA 22206: Quinn Bowman, Betty Ann Bowser, Jeffrey Brown, Terence Burlij, David Chalian, David Coles, Julian Dawkins, Larisa Epatko, Kwame Holman, Gwen Ifill, Jim Lehrer, Jennifer Marder, Timothy Perry, Jr., Brian Ragle, Margaret Robinson, Daniel Sagalyn, Linda Scott, Diane Silver, Hari Sreenivasan, Rafael Suarez, Elizabeth Summers, Margaret Warner, Judy Willis, Lea Winerman, Judy Woodruff, Daniel Yang, Robert Zeliger.

THIS IS AMERICA WITH DENNIS WHOLEY—(703) 757–5866; 1333 H. Street, NW., Washington, DC 20005: Jerry Cox, Dennis Wholey.

THIS WEEK IN AGRIBUSINESS (RFD–TV)—(301) 942–1996; 9915 Hillridge Drive, Kensington, MD 20895: Patrick Haggerty, Orion Samuelson.

TIME WARNER CABLE WASHINGTON BUREAU—(202) 500–2778; 400 North Capitol, NW., Suite G–95, Washington, DC 20001: Jennifer Rowena Babich, Erin Evelyne Billups, Leslie A. Mayes.

TO THE CONTRARY (PERSEPHONE PRODUCTIONS)—(202) 973–2066; 1819 L. Street, NW., 7th Floor, Washington, DC 20036: Bonnie Erbe, Joy Fowlin, Tiane Johnson, Megan Pratz, Nancy Rosen, Cari Weiss Stein.

TOKYO BROADCASTING SYSTEM—(202) 288–1333; 1088 National Press Building, Washington, DC 20045: Takushi Harima, Kaoru Kokufuda, Graham Nelson, Mitsuhiro Toya, Takafumi Tsugawa, Eric Weiner.

TURKISH RADIO TELEVISION (TRT)—(202) 494–0709; 529 14th Street, NW., #1273 Washington, DC 20045: Ercan Demir.

TV ASAHI—(202) 347–2933; 529 14th Street, NW., #1280, Washington, DC 20045: Robert Gentry, Yusuke Inoue, Kaisei Nozoe, Satoko Shimana-Shimbori, Ena Suto, Cynthia Sharon Waite.

TV GLOBO INTERNATIONAL—(202) 429–2525; 2141 Wisconsin Avenue, NW., Suite L, Washington, DC 20007: Vicente Cinque, Luis Fernando Silva-Pinto, Dennis Zanatta.

NETWORKS, STATIONS, AND SERVICES REPRESENTED—Continued

TV TOKYO—(202) 638–0441; 1333 H. Street, NW., 5th Floor, Washington, DC 20005: Motoyasu Asaoka, Benjamin Eric Dalton, Ken Hakamada, Yuko Miyake, Kanako Ota, Strader Payton.

TV3–TELEVISIO DE CATALUNYA—(202) 785–0580; 2000 M. Street, NW., Suite 830, Washington, DC 20036: Eva Artesona, Antoni Bassas, Albert Elfa, Xavier Roca.

TVBS—(202) 812–2821: Chia-Hui Ni, Jessica Ni, Shih-Yuan Tuan.

TVE–SPANISH PUBLIC TELEVISION—(202) 785–1813; 2000 M. Street, NW., #325, Washington, DC 20036: Lorenzo Mila, Hector Pulido, Anna Ubeda.

TVN POLAND—(202) 215–5052; 7429 Chummley Court, Falls Church, VA 22043: Marcin Wojciech Wrona, Marcin Wyszogrodzki.

UNITED NEWS AND INFORMATION—(202) 783–2002; 529 14th Street, NW., Suite 1057D, Washington, DC 20045: Dennis Crowley, Sharon Gotkin.

UNIVISION—(202) 682–6160; 101 Constitution Avenue, NW., Suite 810E, Washington, DC 20001: Jorge Contreras, Deborah Durham, Jordan Harris Fabian, Juan Gastelum, Lourdes Meluza, Fernando Pizarro, Pablo Sanchez, Mario Vizcarra.

VENTANA PRODUCTIONS—(202) 785–5112; 1825 K. Street, NW., #501, Washington, DC 20006: Armando Almanza, Grace I-Tang, Richard Joy, John Lawrence, Timothy K. Murray, Juan Pineda, Juan Rocha, Robin Anthony Stewart, Mark Thalman.

VIEWPOINT COMMUNICATIONS—(301) 565–1650; 8607 2nd Avenue, Suite 400, Silver Spring, MD 20910: Art Berko, Randy Feldman, Ben Finkel, Larry Greenblatt, Steven Hamberg, Charles Horn.

VOICE OF AMERICA—(202) 382–5130; 330 Independence Avenue, SW., Washington, DC 20237: Abdushakur Aboud, Mohammad Ahmadi, Najibullah Ahmadyar, M. Anis Ahmed, Hasib Alikozai, Gholamreza Allahyari, Darrell Allen, Brian Allen, Sarita Ang, Muhammad Atif, Abdul Ahad Azizzada, Thomas Bagnall, Sungwon Baik, Steve Baragona, George Bistis, Michael Bowman, Jerome Brown, Meredith Buel, Michael C. Burke, Joan Butler, Roger C. W. Hsu, Carol Castiel, Hector Cerpa, Peggy Chang, Nike Ching, Nico Colombant, Lina Correa, Woody Crawford, Nick Crupi, Patricia Dalmasy, Minas Dargakis, Jeffery Daugherty, Jela de Franceschi, Siamak Dehghanpour, Joan Deluca, Steven Densmore, Ali Farhoodi, Bruce Ferder, Lisa Ferdinando, David Futrowsky, Joseph Gallagher, Valer Gergely, Myroslava Gongadze, Pema Gorap, Richard Green, William Greenback, Adam Greenbaum, Mohammad Habibzada, Roquia Haider, Sayed Hashemi, Mi Jeong Y. Hibbitts, Cecily Hilleary, Thein Htike Oo, Iftikhar Hussain, Utami Hussin, Davin Hutchins, Mohammad Ibrahim, William Ide, Lesley Jackson, Gary Jaffe, Syed Jafri, Kaveh Jamshidi, Douglas Johnson, Thomas Kamilindi, Amy Katz, Laura Kell, Tsewang Khedrup, Keunsam Kim, Letitia King, Kent Klein, Michael Kornely, Jean-Pierre Leroy, Kim Lewis, Tenzin Lhundup, Lyle Lindberg, Enming Liu, Diana Logreira, Vincent Makori, James Malone, Eva Mazrieva, Jeffrey Means, Kimseng Men, Guita Mirsaeedi, Joseph Mok, Thet Su Naing, Robert Naylor, Matiullah Abid Noor, Roshan Noorzai, Siri E. Nyrop, Thar Nyunt Oo, Rosalie O'Connell, Aung Lwin Oo, Zulima Palacio, Julia Parabaniuk, Robert Parsell, Jean Philippe, Reasey Poch, Suzanne Presto, Carolyn Presutti, Shegoftah Queen, John Quinn, Linda Ringe, Daniel Robinson, Shahla Sadighi, Cynthia Saine-Spang, Yuni Salim, Mehrnaz Samimi, Joad Jose Santa-Rita, Kabiruddin Sarkar, Brian Schiff, Edward Schneider, Jr., Daniela Schrier, Namgyal Shastri, Imran Siddiqui, Paul Sisco, Jerome Socolovsky, Pov Sok, Steven Springer, Amish Srivastava, Julius Suyat, Carl Swanson, Jeffrey Swicord, Kyaw Zan Tha, Kyaw K. Thein, John Walker, Keith Wallace, Paul Westpheling, Winston Wood, Raymond Yam, Xiaoyan Zhang.

VOYAGE PRODUCTIONS—(202) 296–2389; 565 Pennsylvania Avenue, NW., #302, Washington, DC 20001: Susan Baumel, Ely Lamonica.

WASHINGTON BUREAU NEWS SERVICE—(202) 255–8685; 7425 Savan Point Way, Columbia, MD 21045: Michael Eldridge, Joseph Nelson, C. Patrick Thorne, Patrick Vail, Michael Whitney.

WASHINGTON POST—(202) 334–7431; 1150 15th Street, NW., Washington, DC 20071: Jason Aldag, Kristen Boghosian, Jill Bartscht, AJ Chavar, Evelio Contreras, Benedict De La Cruz, Jonathan Putnam Forsythe, Alexandra Garcia, Michael Akira Hakuta, Steven King, Matthew Levine, Whitney Shefte.

WASHINGTON RADIO AND PRESS SERVICE—(301) 580–9134; 6702 Pawtucket Road, Bethesda, MD 20817: Hanna Ida Gutmann, Howard M. Lesser.

WETA—(703) 998–2660; 2775 South Quincy Street, Arlington, VA 22206: Megan Adair, Lynn Quarles Allison, Charles Anderson, Timothy Bowen, Donald Brawner, Martin Carr, Darzen Chang, Simon Epstein, John George, Charles Ide, Christopher Lane, Edward Lee, Jerry S. Lewis, Nancy Gerstman Morgan, Antonio Pacheco, Jeffrey Rathner, John Thomas Satterfield, James Schneider, Willliam Seabrook, Michael Smith, Jacqueline Todt, Sampath Vasa, Charles Voth.

WFDC–TV UNIVISION—(202) 522–8643; 101 Constitution Avenue, NW., Suite L–100, Washington, DC 20001: Juan Antonio Acevedo, Ernesto Clavijo, Maria Rosa Lucchini, Norma Montenegro, Raul Ramos, Claudia Uceda.

WHITE HOUSE CHRONICLE—(202) 662–9745; 1042 Wisconsin Avenue, NW., Washington, DC 20007: Linda Gasparello, Llewellyn King.

WHUR—(202) 253–4331; 529 Bryant Street, NW., Washington, DC 20059: Ray Linton Baker, Harold Thomas Fisher, Molette Eileen Green, Romaine Desaree McNair, Renee Jacqueline Nash, Sean Dwayne Plater, Scott Kenneth Tanner, George Wilson, Jeffrey Anthony Wims.

NETWORKS, STATIONS, AND SERVICES REPRESENTED—Continued

WJLA–TV/NEWSCHANNEL 8—(703) 236–9480; 1100 Wilson Boulevard, Arlington, VA 22209: Robert Alexander, Robert Allbritton, Natasha Barrett, Frank Becker, Brad Bell, Bruce Bookhultz, Whitney Bright, Gail Brown, Pamela Brown, Brianne Carter, Richard Chamberlain, Zeke Changuris, Mike Conneen, Rebecca J. Cooper, Bruce DePuyt, Martin C. Doane, Jennifer Donelan, Ben Eisler, Ernie Ensign, Tony Ferrigno, Michael Forcucci, Sam Ford, Pege Gilgannon, Autria Godfrey, John Gonzalez, Brandis Griffith, Kendall Griggs, Richard Guastadisegni, Steve Hackett, Norman Hadad, Peter Hakel, Leon Harris, Haley Harrison, Melanie Hastings Wotring, Horace Holmes, Brian Hopkins, Tom Hormuth, Winston Hylton, Samuel Jackson, Kevin Jaeger, Irene Johnson, Morris Jones, James Joslyn, Suzanne Kennedy, Alison Kenworthy, Vanessa M. Koolhof, Jay Korff, Greta Kreuz, Catherine Lanzara, Ming Leong, John B. Lewis, Alex Likowski, Bill Lord, Dave Lucas, Caroline Lyders, Jon Mann, Rebecca McDevitt, Brittany McHenry, Josh Miller, Trang Ninh, Jummy Olabanji, Kathy Park, Julie Parker, Dan Patrick, Gail Pennybacker, Gordon Peterson, Stephen Pozniak, Richard Reeve, Malissa Reyes, Ben Rice, Courtney Robinson, Joe Rose, Jeff Rose, Michael Rudd, Fred Ryan, James Scott, Gregory Seaby, William Nicoll Seymour, Holly Shannon, B. K. Sharma, Cynne Simpson, Alison Starling, Philip Stewart, Scott Thuman, Stephen Tschida, Kristopher Van Cleave, Mike Vaughn, James Walker, Robert Washington Anderson, David Webb, Ron Windham, Dale Wright, Andy Zmidzinski.

WMAL RADIO—(202) 895–2358: Martin DiCaro, MaryKatharine Ham, Drew Hayes, Bill Hess, Bryan Nehman, Heather Smith, David Sproul, Brian Wilson.

WNYC—(202) 277–5529: Todd Zwillich.

WPFW–FM—(202) 588–0999; 2390 Champlain Street, NW., Washington, DC 20009: Gloria Minott, Robert West.

WPWC–AM (RADIO FIESTA)—(703) 494–0100: Carlos O. Aragon, Cladia Melissa Gieras.

WRC–TV/NBC–4—(202) 885–4111; 4001 Nebraska Avenue, NW., Suite 6, Washington, DC 20016: Jay Alvey, Jackie Bensen, Charles Bragale, Larry Bullard, Vickie Burns, Julie Carey, Sean Casey, Pat Collins, Jennifer Doren, Lauren Dunn, Edward Durkin, Teneille Gibson, Aaron Gilchrist, Matt Glassman, Charles A. Goodknight, Herbert Gordon, Ede Jermin, Zachary Kiesch, B. Christopher Layne, Ronald Leidelmeyer, Megan McGrath, Craig Melvin, William Nardi, Michael O'Regan, Chester Panzer, Jeff Piper, Danella Sealock, Tom Sherwood, Darcy Spencer, Robert Sweeney, John Taylor, Jane Watrel, Roy Weinstock, Eun Yang, Darren Ziegenbein.

WTOP RADIO—(202) 895–5060; 3400 Idaho Avenue, NW., Washington, DC 20016: Neal Augenstein, Michelle Basch, Paul Brandus, Darci Brasch, Gary Emerling, Dave Garner, Jessie J. Green, Nathan Hager, Evan Haning, Brennan Haselton, Kristi King Lilleston, Dave McConnell, Mike McMearty, Mitchell Miller, Andrew Mollenbeck, Brian Oliger, Mark Plotkin, Robert Publicover, Veronica Robinson, Art Rose, Kate Ryan, Mark Segraves, Paul Shinkman, Hank Silverberg, Adam Tuss, Thomas Warren.

WTTG–FOX TELEVISION—(202) 895–3130; 5151 Wisconsin Avenue, NW., Washington, DC 20016: Melanie Alnwick, Raquel Divina Amparo, Bob Barnard, James Beahn, William Beyer, Rudolph Blyden, Brian Bolter, Daniel Brown, Daryl Brown, Paul Buehler, Charles Carson, Steve Chenevey, Patricia Corcoran, Lauren DeMarco, Laura Evans, Tom Fitzgerald, B.J. Forte, John Foundas, Yianis Fournelis, John Frame, Matthew Gaffney, Max Giammetta, Jeff Gilman, Ozana Halik, John Henrehan, Michael Horan, Karen Gray Houston, Ryan Huebler, Lance Ing, Stephanie Johnson, Lyrone Steven Jones, Nelson Jones, Colleen Kenney, Erik Lee, Craig Little, Anthony Lopez-Isa, Sherri Ly, Michael Marantz, Wisdom Martin, Samuel James McFadden, Sean McGarvy, Patrick McGrath, Lorna McGuire, Philip Metlin, Alexander Milenic, Holly Morris, Richard Murphy, Angela Ann Oakley, Beth Parker, Anthony D. Perkins, Paul Raphel, Austin Reeves, Michael Rickard, Meredith Royster, Eugene Russell, F. David Rysak, Mark Sargent, Fred Schall, Allison Seymour, Robert Shon, Sarah Simmons, Jason H. Smith, Joe Spevak, Donald E. Stanke, Louis Stevenson, Will Thomas, Laetitia Thompson Anderson, Maureen Umeh, Paul Wagner, Richard Washington III, Duane Watkins, Don Watrud, Douglas H. Wilkes, Steven Williams, Joel Witte, Shawn Yancy, Rick Yarborough, Annie Yu.

WUSA–TV—(202) 895–5551; 4100 Wisconsin Avenue, NW., Washington, DC 20016: Mark Bost, Kurt Brooks, William Wescott Broom, Jr., Aubrey Bryant, Surae Chinn Lucie, William Clemann, Jeffrey Cridland, Jessica Doyle Belvedere, Manny Fantis, Kristin Anne Fisher, Danielle Flanagan, Michael Flynn, Lesli Foster Mathewson, Peggy Fox, Michael Fuhr, Stephen Garifo, Angie Renee Goff, Delia Neves Goncalves Perry, Richard Gorbutt, Regina Doreen Griffin, Gregory Guise, James Hash, Shonty Hawkins, Michael Edward Hydeck, Matthew J. Jablow, Thomas James, Elizabeth Yi Chao Jia, Bruce Johnson, Kevin G. King, Amy Patricia Leone, Bruce Leshan, Paul Lester, Joseph Eugene Martin, Samara Martin Ewing, Lindsey Janiece Mastis, Andrea Austin McCarren, Derek McGinty, Kenny Charles Molestina, Brittany Catherine Morehouse, Felix Junior Ortiz, Mark Graham Pearson, Karen Peterson, Andrea Roane Skehan, David Roycraft, David Satchell, Jimmie Silman III, Anita Brikmanis Spear, Sayeh Tavangar, Janet Terry, Michael Trammell, Dion Antwan Wiggins, Keith Williams, Stephanie Wilson.

NETWORKS, STATIONS, AND SERVICES REPRESENTED—Continued

WZDC–TV—(703) 820–8333: Jorge Andres Alfaro, Julio Aliaga, Jamillah Echeverria, Angelica Maria Herrera, Douglas Mejia, Jose Lixander Mendoza, Lizeth Juliana Monsalve, Jecsy Carolina Villamizar, Juan Pablo Zariquiey.

FREELANCE

Freelancers: Francis Manuel Abbey, Atef Abdulgawad, Matthew Ackland, Robin Adlerblum, Nihad Ali Akbar, Sameen Amin, Stuart Ammerman, Patrick Anastasi, Angela Andersen, Patrick Anderson, Lorraine Aprile-Holtzman, Arash Arabasadi, Bruno Arena, Patricia M. Armstrong, Thomas Ayres Armstrong, Adrian Armwood, Mohamed H. Awada, Jean-Pascal Azais, Travis Renee Baldwin, Daniel Balinovic, Sreya Banerjee, Mark Banks, Anthony Barber, Lantz Barbour, Audrey Barnes, Emile Baroody, Eric Barreda, Stephen Bartlett, Marilisa Battistella, William Baty, Earl T. Baysden III, Ingo Roman Becker, Michael Bellis, Brian Benjamin, Catherine Berger, Michael P. Berry, Kevin Beyer, Marcia Biggs, Tim R. Bintrim, Warren Bolden, Arlene Borenstein, Richard Calhoun Bortz, Laurel Bowman, Wayne F. Boyd, Robert Brewster, Annette Brieger, Michael Broleman, Kristi Brown, Matthew Wilson Burton, Tim Camarda, James Canty, David Caravello, Brett Carlson, Dave Carter, Carl Cyril Catherine, Margaret Chadbourn, Andrew Chappelle, David Chaytor, Robert Cherouny, David C. Cilberti, Gregory Clary, Megan Cloherty, Anne Cocklin, Stephen Cocklin, Stacey Lynn Cohan, Thomas Coleman, Nicole Kristine Collins, Carol Coney, Camille Connolly, Joe Cooke, Andrew Coombes, John Cooper, Pedro Correa, William Fernando Pinzon Cortez, Timothy Cote, Christina Cotterman, Thomas Craca, Bethany Crudele, Patricia Culhane, Maurice Curran, Patrick J. Curran, Joseph Arthur Danielewicz, Clinton Davis, Jennifer Davis, Michael Angelo DeMark, Joey Deveaux, Mirona Diaaeldein, Juan Carlos Diaz, Juanita Dillard, Daniela Doan, Bill Donald, Brian Donovan, Margaret Dore, Paul G. Dougherty, Geoffrey Doyle, John Dunkin, Barton Eckert, Brian Edwards, Richard Ehrenberg, Arlene Eiras, Alfred Scott Eisenhuth, Ibrahim El Gendy, Hosny Elgazar, Dina Elshinnawi, Matthew Engel, Manuel Ernst, Robert Mosley Eustis, Fritz Faerber, John Falls, Mahtab Farid, Anne-Marie Fendrick, Andy Field, John Figura, Lisa Fletcher, Kristin Foellmer, Laura Foran, Michael Ford, Thomas Forty, Tom Foster, Hida Fouladvand, David Fox, Michael A. French, Patrick French, Dave Friedman, Jo Ann Marie Fyanes, Randy Gafner, Christian Galdabini, Nicole Garner, Phil Geyelin, Nelson Ginebra, David Girard, John Glennon, Sam Goodall, Lindsay Graves, Nicholas P. Greiner, Kevin R. Griffin, David Alan Grip, Fayrouz Guerouani, Michael Hagerty, Tom Haller, Daniel Hallstead, Bill Harding, Claus L. Harding, Jillian Harding, Arthur Hardy, Kenneth Harris, Roy Harris, Dustin Harrison-Atlas, Oscar Haynes, Barry Haywood, Sean Healey, Barry Hecht, Martin Heina, Liliana Henao, Karen Hendren, Sarah Herndon, Louise Marie Hernon, Ricardo Higgins, Hugh Hinds, Andrea Hines, James M. Hishchynsky, Darnley Hodge, Michael Hok, Toni Hoover, Dean Hovell, Jason Hubert, Megan Hughes, Trudy Hutcherson, Heather Hutchinson, Yasmeen Ibrahim, Zena Ibrahim, Donna Inserra, William Iversen, Ryan Jackson, Elmira Jafari, Tristan Jermann, Peder Jessen, Aaron Johnson, Fletcher Johnson, Paul Johnson, Rolanda Johnson, Rosiland Jordan, Steve E. Joya, Hans Juergens, Hakim Kabbaj, Magda Kamal, Bill Kaplan, John M. Kavanaugh, Kathleen Keller, Eric C. Kerchner, Jonathan L. Kessler, Noorulain Khawaja, Mike Klein, Rob Klein, Wolfgang Kotke, Laura Kraus, Carmen Kupper, Marianna LaFollette, Greg Larsen, France Latremoliere, James Laughlin, Sam Lawson, Myron A. Leake, George Leidsmar, Katherine Leiken, Paul Lenihan, David Lent, Dexter Leong, Lisa Lewnes, Bruce Liffiton, Louis Linden, Melvin A. Lindsey, Stanley Lorek, Judy Lyons, Eric Magnuson, Mansoor Malik, Mary Kay Mallonee, Mai Marriott, Marc Marriott, Michael Marriott, Mercedes Lugo Martinez, Jeffrey Martino, Tim Matkosky, Ronald H. Matthews, Mathieu Mazza, Donald Jay McCarty, Douglas McCash, Daniel McClellan, Tipp K. McClure, Christopher Colin McCullough, Rich McDermott, Ian McDougall, Patty McFarland, Robert McHenry, Jr., Kevin Anthony McManus, Chris McMorrow, Tara Mergener, Kerry Meyer, David Mikutsky, Jon Miles, Eric Miller, Mike Mock, Melissa Mollet, William Montague, John Monte, Donald Morrison, Marcia Morrow, Martin P. Moser, Jr., John Murphy, Matthew Murray, Megan Murray, Rosetta Murry, Ruqaiyah Najjar, Stephen Narisi, Todd Nash, Mohamed Nasser, Michael Neapolitan, Anh Nguyen, Richard A. Norling, Christopher Charles Norris, Danielle Nottingham, James Novosel, Gary Keith Nurenberg, D. Kerry O'Berry, Daniel J. O'Shea, Jr., Timothy O'Toole, Ralf Oberti, Andrew Och, Mohamed Said Ouafi, Dominique Pastre, Daniel Patsko, Scott Payne, Grant Peacock, Douglas W. Perkins, Robert Peterson, Jeniece Pettitt, Murray Pinczuk, Wingel Pinzon, Christopher Plater, Michael Poole, Michael J. Purbaugh, Omar A. Quinonez, Mana Rabiee, Mark Rabin, Ali Rad, Ana Radelat, Bryan Rager, Wafik Ramadan, Edwin Ramirez, Douglas Ray, Ed Reinsel, Elaine Reyes, Douglas Reynolds, LaVenia Rice, Steffanie Riess, Olivier Robert, Eugene W. Roberts, Samuel Rocha, Eduardo Rodriguez, Abu Bakr Roland, George Romilly, Peter Roof, Adrienne Ross, Misa Rossetti-Meyer, Theodore Roth, Nicky Russell-Smith, Jeffery Lynn Saffelle, Samuel Santamaria, Dinah De Saracho, Andrea Sarralde, Tomoaki Sasaki, Gregory Savoy, Arwa Sawan, Catherine Schell, Peter Schloemer, Emily Schmidt, Donald Schoenmann, John Schriffen, Chris Sciannela, Christopher Eric Scott, Ali Serhan, Jacob Serwer, Michael Patrick Shannon, Timothy Shipman, Robert Shire, Caroline Shively, Daniela Sicuranza ''Kelley'', James Sides, Juan Silva Llancaleo, Mariam Simpson, Paul Skomal, Stephanie Slewka, Charles Slie, Anthony Grey Smith, Brian Smith, Christie Smith,

NETWORKS, STATIONS, AND SERVICES REPRESENTED—Continued

Cynthia Smith, John Cannon Smith, Randall Sorenson, Gus Soudah, George A. Sozio, Theodore Spiegler, Thomas M. Staton, Mark S. Stoddard, Jessica Stone, James Suddeth, Rick Suddeth, Kimberly Suiters, Kevork Tashdjian, Krista Talvikki Taubert, Jacqueline Taylor, Ramon Taylor, Editha Tendencia, Shari Thomas, Joseph Thompson, Jr., Shaleem Thompson, Frank Thorp, George Toman, Sarah Fiona Toms, Armando Ernesto Trull, Ted Tuel, Thomas Joseph Tyler, Wade Tyree, Brad Ulery, Dick Uliano, Melinda Ulloa, Paul Vanderveen, Ilona Viczian, Marcos Vigil, Anar Virji, Kelley Vlahos, Ambrose Vurnis, Jackie Lyn Walker, Douglas Wallick, Derrick Ward, Tarik Warner, Aaron Webster, George D. Weller, James White, John P. Whiteside, Chris Widmer, Stefan Wiesen, Tracee Wilkins, Roger Wilkison, Armstrong Williams, Austen Williams, Mark Wilson, Ronald Winters, Tracey Marie Wright, John W. Wulff, Markus Zeffler, Stratis Zervos.

PERIODICAL PRESS GALLERIES*

HOUSE PERIODICAL PRESS GALLERY

The Capitol, H–304, 225–2941

Director.—Robert M. Zatkowski
Deputy Director.—Gerald Rupert
Assistant Directors: Laura Eckart, Jenn Walters

SENATE PERIODICAL PRESS GALLERY

The Capitol, S–320, 224–0265

Director.—Edward V. Pesce
Deputy Director.—Justin Wilson
Assistant Director.—Shawna Blair

EXECUTIVE COMMITTEE OF CORRESPONDENTS

Heather Rothman, BNA News, *Chairman*
Jay Newton-Small, Time Magazine, *Secretary*
Meg Shreve, Tax Notes, *Treasurer*
Lauren Whittington, Roll Call
Paul Bedard, U.S. News & World Report
Stephen K. Cooper, CCH, Inc.
Manu Raju, Politico

RULES GOVERNING PERIODICAL PRESS GALLERIES

1. Persons eligible for admission to the Periodical Press Galleries must be bona fide resident correspondents of reputable standing, giving their chief attention to the gathering and reporting of news. They shall state in writing the names of their employers and their additional sources of earned income; and they shall declare that, while a member of the Galleries, they will not act as an agent in the prosecution of claims, and will not become engaged or assist, directly or indirectly, in any lobbying, promotion, advertising, or publicity activity intended to influence legislation or any other action of the Congress, nor any matter before any independent agency, or any department or other instrumentality of the Executive Branch; and that they will not act as an agent for, or be employed by the Federal, or any State, local or foreign government or representatives thereof; and that they will not, directly or indirectly, furnish special or ''insider'' information intended to influence prices or for the purpose of trading on any commodity or stock exchange; and that they will not become employed, directly or indirectly, by any stock exchange, board of trade or other organization or member thereof, or brokerage house or broker engaged in the buying and selling of any security or commodity. Applications shall be submitted to the Executive Committee of the Periodical Correspondents' Association and shall be authenticated in a manner satisfactory to the Executive Committee.

2. Applicants must be employed by periodicals that regularly publish a substantial volume of news material of either general, economic, industrial, technical, cultural, or trade character. The periodical must require such Washington coverage on a continuing basis and must be owned and operated independently of any government, industry, institution, association, or lobbying organization. Applicants must also be employed by a periodical that is published for profit and is supported chiefly by advertising or by subscription, or by a periodical meeting the conditions in this paragraph but published by a nonprofit organization that, first, operates independently of any government, industry, or institution and, second, does

*Information is based on data furnished and edited by each respective gallery.

not engage, directly or indirectly, in any lobbying or other activity intended to influence any matter before Congress or before any independent agency or any department or other instrumentality of the Executive Branch. House organs are not eligible.

3. Members of the families of correspondents are not entitled to the privileges of the galleries.

4. The Executive Committee may issue temporary credentials permitting the privileges of the galleries to individuals who meet the rules of eligibility but who may be on short-term assignment or temporarily residing in Washington.

5. Under the authority of Rule 6 of the House of Representatives and of Rule 33 of the Senate, the Periodical Galleries shall be under the control of the Executive Committee, subject to the approval and supervision of the Speaker of the House of Representatives and the Senate Committee on Rules and Administration. It shall be the duty of the Executive Committee, at its discretion, to report violations of the privileges of the galleries to the Speaker or the Senate Committee on Rules and Administration, and pending action thereon, the offending correspondent may be suspended. The committee shall be elected at the start of each Congress by members of the Periodical Correspondents' Association and shall consist of seven members with no more than one member from any one publishing organization. The committee shall elect its own officers and a majority of the committee may fill vacancies on the committee. The list in the Congressional Directory shall be a list only of members of the Periodical Correspondents' Association.

JOHN A. BOEHNER,
Speaker, House of Representatives.

CHARLES E. SCHUMER,
Chair, Senate Committee on Rules and Administration.

MEMBERS ENTITLED TO ADMISSION

PERIODICAL PRESS GALLERIES

Abbott, Ryan M.: Courthouse News Service
Abrahamson, Zachary G.: Politico
Abramson, Julie L.: National Journal
Abruzzese, Sarah M.: Environment & Energy Publishing
Abse, Nathan: Federal Employees News Digest
Ackerman, Spencer J.: Wired.com
Ackley, Kate: Roll Call
Aftab, Mirza Z.: BNA News
Albergo, Paul F.: BNA News
Alberta, Timothy: Hotline
Alexis, Alexei: BNA News
Ali, Ambreen E.: Roll Call
Allen, Jonathan J.: Politico
Allen, Michael P.: Politico
Altman, Alex: Time Magazine
Altscher, Judy K.: The Hill
Amber, Michelle L.: BNA News
Ambinder, Marc: National Journal
Ambrosio, Patrick: BNA News
Anderson, Karen A.: UCG
Anderson, Sarah E.: Exchange Monitor Publications
Anselmo, Joseph C.: Aviation Week
Antle, W. James: American Spectator
Antonides, David Scott S.: Tax Notes
Aplin, Donald G.: BNA News
Aquino, John T.: BNA News
Ashton, Jerome C.: BNA News
Ashworth, Jerry: Thompson Publishing Group
Asker, James R.: Aviation Week
Assam, Cecelia M.: BNA News
Atkins, Pamela S.: BNA News
Atwood, John Filar: CCH, Inc.
August, Melissa A.: Time Magazine
Aulino, Margaret: BNA News
Ault, Alicia: International Medical News Group
Ayers, Cameron S.: Thompson Publishing Group
Ayers, Carl A.: UCG
Bachman, Kathryn M.: Adweek
Bade, Rachael M.: Roll Call
Baker, Samuel U.: The Hill
Ball, Molly: Politico
Baltazar, Gemma L.: Inside Mortgage Finance
Bancroft, John R.: Inside Mortgage Finance
Barash, Martina S.: BNA News
Barbagallo, Paul: BNA News
Barbic, Kari J.: Weekly Standard
Bardwell, Brian D.: Tax Notes
Barnes, Fred W.: Weekly Standard
Barnes, James A.: National Journal
Barr, Andrew T.: Politico
Barr, Sarah M.: BNA News
Barry, Theresa A.: BNA News
Basken, Paul A.: Chronicle of Higher Education
Bason, Tamlin H.: BNA News
Basu, Sandra L.: U.S. Medicine
Baumann, Jeannie: BNA News
Beam, Christopher: Slate
Beard, David: National Journal
Beaven, Lara W.: Inside Washington Publishers
Becker, Amanda M.: Roll Call
Becker, Bernard A.: The Hill
Bedard, Paul: U.S. News & World Report
Behr, Peter B.: Environment & Energy Publishing
Behsudi, Adam: Inside Washington Publishers
Bellantoni, Christina M.: Roll Call
Beller, Michael J.: Tax Notes
Belogolova, Olga: National Journal
Belz, Emily C.: World Magazine
Bennett, Alison E.: BNA News
Bennett, John T.: The Hill
Benson, Guy: Townhall
Benton, Nicholas F.: Falls Church News Press
Ben-Yosef, Andrea L.: BNA News
Berger, James R.: Washington Trade Daily
Berger, Mary L.: Washington Trade Daily
Bergin, Ulrike M.: Tax Notes
Berke, Kenneth H.: Government Contractor
Berlin, Joshua L.: Elsevier Business Intelligence
Berman, Dan: Politico
Berman, Russell L.: The Hill
Berman-Gorvine, Martin J.: Elsevier Business Intelligence
Bernstein, Rachel: Space News
Berrong, Stephanie J.: Tax Notes
Bertuca, Anthony F.: Inside Washington Publishers
Besser, James David: New York Jewish Week
Beutler, Brian A.: Talking Points Memo
Biggs, Alicia E.: BNA News
Billings, Deborah D.: BNA News
Bivins, Amy E.: BNA News
Blank, Peter L.: Kiplinger Washington Editors
Blumenstyk, Goldie: Chronicle of Higher Education
Boak, Josh: Politico
Bobic, Igor: Talking Points Memo
Boerma, Lindsey: National Journal
Bogardus, Kevin J.: The Hill
Boliek, Brooks: Politico
Bolton, Alexander: The Hill
Bompey, Nanci B.: Inside Washington Publishers
Bomster, Mark W.: Education Week
Bondioli, Sara E.: Roll Call

MEMBERS ENTITLED TO ADMISSION, PERIODICAL PRESS GALLERIES—Continued

Borchersen-Keto, Sarah A.: CCH, Inc.
Bouve, Andrew: Slate
Boyd, John D.: Journal of Commerce
Boyles, William R.: Health Market Survey
Bracken, Leonard A.: BNA News
Bradford, Hazel M.: Crain Communications
Brady, Jessica L.: Roll Call
Brandolph, David B.: BNA News
Brannen, Kate O.: Gannett Government Media Corp.
Braun, Kevin D.: Environment & Energy Publishing
Bravender, Robin L.: Politico
Breech, Laura E.: Tax Notes
Breen, Timothy: Agri-Pulse
Breger, Esther M.: New Republic
Brennan, Kevin: Hotline
Bresnahan, John: Politico
Brevetti, Rossella E.: BNA News
Bridgeford, Lydell C.: BNA News
Brinton, S. Turner: Space News
Broderick, Brian J.: BNA News
Brodsky, Robert G.: Government Executive
Brooks, George A.: Inside Mortgage Finance
Brown, Janet M.: Press Associates
Brown, Jill: Atlantic Information Services
Brown, Simon A.: Tax Notes
Brownstein, Andrew D.: Thompson Publishing Group
Brownstein, Ronald J.: National Journal
Bruce, R. Christian: BNA News
Bruninga, Susan E.: BNA News
Bruno, Michael: Aviation Week
Buckley, Elizabeth J.: Food Chemical News
Budoff Brown, Carrie D.: Politico
Buford, Talia N.: Politico
Buhl, John M.: Tax Notes
Bullock, Lorinda M.: International Medical News Group
Burns, Alexander I.: Politico
Burt, Andrew O.: Inside Washington Publishers
Busch, Alaina V.: Inside Washington Publishers
Busetti, Max S.: Thompson Publishing Group
Butler, Amy: Aviation Week
Bylander, Jessica E.: Elsevier Business Intelligence
Cain, Derrick: BNA News
Calabresi, Massimo T.: Time Magazine
Caldwell, Christopher S.: Weekly Standard
Callahan, Madelyn R.: BNA News
Carey, William J.: Aviation International News
Carlile, Amy V.: Environment & Energy Publishing
Carlozzo, Anntherese: BNA News
Carlson, Jeffrey E.: CCH, Inc.
Carneal, Jeffrey: Human Events
Carney, Eliza Newlin: Roll Call
Carpenter, John: CCH, Inc.
Carr, Jennifer: Tax Notes
Casabona, Elizabeth M.: Thompson Publishing Group
Cash, Catherine: McGraw-Hill Co.
Cassidy, William B.: Journal of Commerce
Castelli, Christopher: Inside Washington Publishers
Casuga, Jay-Anne B.: BNA News
Catalini, Michael: National Journal
Catanese, David P.: Politico
Cavallaro, Gina: Gannett Government Media Corp.
Cavanagh, Sean M.: Education Week
Cavas, Christopher P.: Gannett Government Media Corp.
Caygle, Heather N.: BNA News
Cecala, Guy David: Inside Mortgage Finance
Chacko, Sarah E.: Gannett Government Media Corp.
Chamberlain, Kenneth: National Journal
Chappell, Kevin U.: Jet/Ebony
Charnitski, Jonathan W.: Broadband Census
Chemnick, Jean M.: Environment & Energy Publishing
Chew, Cassie M.: The Wrap
Chi, Tina M.: BNA News
Chibbaro, Jr., Louis M.: Washington Blade
Childers, Andrew J.: BNA News
Chiu, Lisa S.: Chronicle of Higher Education
Chokshi, Niraj: National Journal
Chronister, Gregory: Education Week
Chu, Keith T.: McGraw-Hill Co.
Ciampoli, Paul G.: McGraw-Hill Co.
Cinquegrani, Gayle C.: BNA News
Clapp, Stephen C.: Food Chemical News
Clark, Charles S.: Government Executive
Clark, Timothy: Government Executive
Clarke, David Paul: Inside Washington Publishers
Clemmitt, Marcia A.: CQ Researcher
Clift, Eleanor: Newsweek
Coder, Jeremiah G.: Tax Notes
Coffin, James B.: Public Lands News
Cofield, Gwendolyn: Thompson Publishing Group
Cogan, Marin: Politico
Cohen, Janey: BNA News
Cohen, Michelle M.: Falls Church News Press
Colarusso, Laura M.: Newsweek
Cole, Christopher M.: Inside Washington Publishers
Collins, Brian: National Mortgage News
Collins, Evelyn: Atlantic Information Services
Comer, John Matthew: Environment & Energy Publishing
Compart, Andrew W.: Aviation Week
Conant, Eve K.: Newsweek
Connolly, Paul C.: BNA News
Conroy, Declan A.: Food Protection Report
Continetti, Matthew J.: Weekly Standard
Cook, Jr., Charles E.: Cook Political Report
Cook, Robert C.: BNA News
Cook, Steven: BNA News
Coomes, Jessica M.: BNA News
Cooper, Matthew: National Journal
Cooper, Stephen K.: CCH, Inc.
Corbett, Warren P.: Set-Aside Alert
Corley, Matilda M.: BNA News

MEMBERS ENTITLED TO ADMISSION, PERIODICAL PRESS GALLERIES—Continued

Correa, Frances: International Medical News Group
Corrin, Amber: Defense Systems
Costa, Hilary C.: McGraw-Hill Co.
Costa, Robert V.: National Review
Coughlin, Brett G.: Politico
Cowden, Richard H.: BNA News
Cox, Bowman D.: Elsevier Business Intelligence
Cox, Ramsey C.: The Hill
Coyle, Marcia: National Law Journal
Coyne, Martin J.: McGraw-Hill Co.
Crabtree, Susan J.: Talking Points Memo
Craig, Geoffrey W.: McGraw-Hill Co.
Craver, Martha L.: Kiplinger Washington Editors
Crawford, Elizabeth R.: Elsevier Business Intelligence
Crider, Richie A.: Thompson Publishing Group
Crook, Clive: National Journal
Crowley, Michael: Time Magazine
Cruickshank, Paula L.: CCH, Inc.
Cummings, Jeanne M.: Politico
Curran, John P.: Telecommunications Reports
Cusack, Robert: The Hill
D'Aprile, Shane T.: The Hill
Daly, Richard F.: Crain Communications
Darcey, Susan W.: Elsevier Business Intelligence
Davenport, Coral: National Journal
David, Peter H.: Economist
Davis, Jeffrey J.: Transportation Weekly
Davis, S. Diane: BNA News
Davis, Steve W.: Atlantic Information Services
Davis, Susan J.: National Journal
Davolt, Steve: Atlantic Information Services
Day, Jeff: BNA News
Deigh, Gloria: BNA News
Dela Rosa, Darrell D.: CQ Researcher
DeLeon, Carrie R.: Telecommunications Reports
Dennis, Steven T.: Roll Call
Dettmer, Jamie W.: The Hill
Diamond, Phyllis: BNA News
Dick, Jason J.: Roll Call
Dickerson, John F.: Slate
Dickson, Virgil T.: Washington Business Information
DiCosmo, Bridget: Inside Washington Publishers
Diegmueller, Karen: Education Week
DiMascio, Jennifer: Aviation Week
DiPietro, Leah N.: Thompson Publishing Group
DiSciullo, Joseph: Tax Notes
Ditta, Sara A.: Inside Washington Publishers
Dixit, Rachana: Inside Washington Publishers
Dixon, Darius A.: Politico
DoBias, Matthew: Politico
Dobson, Jon: Elsevier Business Intelligence
Dolley, Steven D.: McGraw-Hill Co.
Dombrowski, Cathy H.: Elsevier Business Intelligence
Domone, Dana J.: BNA News
Donlan, Thomas G.: Barron's
Douglas, Genevievé: BNA News
Dovere, Edward-Isaac: Politico
Downey, Kirstin E.: FTC: Watch
Doyle, Kenneth P.: BNA News
Doyle, Susan: BNA News
Draper, Robert L.: GQ Magazine
Dreazen, Yochi: National Journal
Drucker, David M.: Roll Call
Duarte, Nicole A.: Tax Notes
Dube, Jr., Lawrence E.: BNA News
Duffy, Jennifer E.: Cook Political Report
Duffy, Michael W.: Time Magazine
Dumain, Emma: Roll Call
Durrett, LaTasha S.: Research Institute of America Group
Dutra, Antonio: BNA News
Dwoskin, Elizabeth S.: Businessweek
Eastland, Terry: Weekly Standard
Easton, Nina J.: Fortune Magazine
Eckstein, Megan A.: Inside Washington Publishers
Edmondson, Thomas: BNA News
Edmonson, Robert G.: Journal of Commerce
Edwards, Charles J.: Thompson Publishing Group
Edwards, Jewel W.: BNA News
Edwards, Julia L.: National Journal
Edwards, Thomas J.: CD Publications
Ege, Konrad: Freitag
Eggerton, John S.: Broadcasting & Cable
Eglovitch, Joanne S.: Elsevier Business Intelligence
Eisele, Albert: The Hill
Eisenstein, Michael: BNA News
Elfin, Dana A.: BNA News
Elliott, Amy S.: Tax Notes
Ellis, Isobel: National Journal
Elmore, Wesley A.: Tax Notes
Epstein, Jennifer: Politico
Epstein, Reid: Politico
Ericksen, Charlie: Hispanic Link News Service
Esquivel, J. Jesus: Proceso
Estepa, Jessica M.: Roll Call
Evans, Jeffrey: International Medical News Group
Everstine, Brian W.: Inside Washington Publishers
Ezzard, Catherine S.: BNA News
Fabey, Michael J.: Aviation Week
Fabian, Jordan: The Hill
Fabian, Thecla R.: BNA News
Falk, Leora M.: BNA News
Falvella-Garraty, Susan M.: Irish Echo
Fath, Meredith: Tax Notes
Feder, Joseph L.: Politico
Fellow, Avery: BNA News
Fellows, Jody C.: Falls Church News Press
Ferguson, Andrew: Weekly Standard
Ferguson, Brett A.: BNA News
Fernholz, Tim: National Journal
Ferullo, Michael A.: BNA News
Fialka, John J.: Environment & Energy Publishing
Fickling, Amy: McGraw-Hill Co.

MEMBERS ENTITLED TO ADMISSION, PERIODICAL PRESS GALLERIES—Continued

Field, Kelly E.: Chronicle of Higher Education
Field, Matthew G.: Inside Washington Publishers
Fielding, Adrianne: Thompson Publishing Group
Finet, J.P.: BNA News
Finkle, Victoria J.: Inside Washington Publishers
Fischer, Karin E.: Chronicle of Higher Education
Fitzpatrick, Erika: Thompson Publishing Group
Fleet, Leslie G.: BNA News
Fletcher, Kenneth R.: Exchange Monitor Publications
Flynn, Joan Marie: Thompson Publishing Group
Fontaine, Scott A.: Gannett Government Media Corp.
Forbes, Sean I.: BNA News
Fordney, Jason L.: McGraw-Hill Co.
Fourney, Susan: Government Executive
Fournier, Ronald: National Journal
Fox, Maggie: National Journal
France, Stephen: BNA News
Francis, Laura: BNA News
Frank, Patrick J.: Human Events
Franke-Ruta, Garance R.: Atlantic Monthly
Franklin, Mary Beth: Kiplinger Washington Editors
Frates, Chris: Politico
Freda, Diane: BNA News
Freebairn, William A.: McGraw-Hill Co.
Freedberg, Jr., Sydney J.: National Journal
Frerking, Elizabeth M.: Politico
Fried, Lissa: Tax Notes
Friedman, Lisa F.: Environment & Energy Publishing
Fryer-Biggs, Zachary: Gannett Government Media Corp.
Fulghum, David A.: Aviation Week
Fung, Althea: National Journal
Gaitonde, Rahul V.: Broadband Census
Galentine, Elizabeth R.: Employee Benefit Adviser
Galloway, Brit: UCG
Gamber, Chelsea M.: Thompson Publishing Group
Gannon, John: BNA News
Gantz, Rachel: UCG
Garland, Susan B.: Kiplinger Washington Editors
Garner, W. Lynn: BNA News
Garrett, Major: National Journal
Gartrell, Peter T.: McGraw-Hill Co.
Gates-Davis, Marilyn: Roll Call
Gatz, Nicholas T.: Falls Church News Press
Geidner, Chris R.: Metro Weekly
Geisel, Jerome M.: Crain Communications
Geman, Ben A.: The Hill
Gerecht, Michael S.: CD Publications
Gerstein, Joshua A.: Politico
Gerstner, Lisa A.: Kiplinger Washington Editors
Gewertz, Catherine: Education Week
Gilbert, Lorraine S.: BNA News
Gilcrest, Laura H.: McGraw-Hill Co.
Gilmer, Ellen M.: Environment & Energy Publishing
Gilston, Meredith L.: Gilston-Kalin Communications
Gilston, Samuel M.: Gilston-Kalin Communications
Gingery, Derrick J.: Elsevier Business Intelligence
Givhan, Robin: Newsweek
Gizzi, John M.: Human Events
Glass, Andrew J.: Politico
Glass, Kevin W.: Townhall
Gleeson, Michael: Tax Notes
Gnezditskaia, Anastasia: McGraw-Hill Co.
Goehausen, Hilary A.: CCH, Inc.
Goindi, Geeta: Express India
Goldberg, Jeffrey M.: Atlantic Monthly
Goldwyn, Brant: CCH Inc.
Golub, Barbra: Atlantic Information Services
Gonzales, Nathan: Rothenberg Political Report
Gonzalez, Jennifer: Chronicle of Higher Education
Gonzalez, Sarah S.: Agri-Pulse
Good, Christopher E.: Atlantic Monthly
Goode, Darren T.: Politico
Goodin, Emily L.: The Hill
Goodwine, Velma: Research Institute of America Group
Gordon, D. Craig: Politico
Gordon, Meghan: McGraw-Hill Co.
Gordon, Meryl: Elle
Gotsch, Ted: Telecommunications Reports
Gough, Robert: UCG
Gould, Joseph M.: Gannett Government Media Corp.
Goulder, Robert: Tax Notes
Goyal, Raghubir: Asia Today
Gray, Melanie J.: Gannett Government Media Corp.
Gray, Steven M.: Time Magazine
Green, Charles A.: National Journal
Green, Joshua: Atlantic Monthly
Greene, Virginia W.: National Law Journal
Greenhalgh, Keiron: McGraw-Hill Co.
Gregg, Diana I.: BNA News
Greive, Timothy P.: Politico
Grena Manley, Mary Ann: BNA News
Grimaldi, Christine H.: BNA News
Gross, Grant J.: IDG News Service
Gruber, Amelia M.: Government Executive
Gruenberg, Mark J.: Press Associates
Guarino, Douglas: Inside Washington Publishers
Guay, Thomas A.: Progressive Business Publications
Guerriero, Joseph A.: Human Events
Guillen, Alexander C.: Politico
Gutman, James H.: Atlantic Information Services
Haas, Joseph A.: Elsevier Business Intelligence
Haberkorn, Jennifer A.: Politico
Hagstrom, Jerry: National Journal
Hallerman, Tamar: Exchange Monitor Publications
Halper, Daniel M.: Weekly Standard
Hamilton, Amy L.: Tax Notes
Hamilton, Bill B.: Politico
Hancock, Benjamin: Inside Washington Publishers
Handley, Megan M.: U.S. News & World Report
Haniffa, Aziz A.: India Abroad

MEMBERS ENTITLED TO ADMISSION, PERIODICAL PRESS GALLERIES—Continued

Hansard, Sara E.: BNA News
Hansen, Brian: McGraw-Hill Co.
Hansen, Dave A.: Politico
Harbrecht, Douglas A.: Kiplinger Washington Editors
Hardy, Michael: Federal Computer Week
Harman, Thomas H.: CD Publications
Harmon, Andrew: Advocate
Harris, Joann Christine: Tax Notes
Harris, John F.: Politico
Harrison, David: BNA News
Harrison, Tom: McGraw-Hill Co.
Harsch, Jonathan H.: Agri-Pulse
Hart, Alexander C.: New Republic
Hartman, Rachel R.: Yahoo! News
Haseley, Donna L.: Inside Washington Publishers
Hatch, David M.: National Journal
Hayes, Christopher L.: Nation
Hayes, Peter S.: BNA News
Hayes, Stephen F.: Weekly Standard
Healy, Amber M.: Food Chemical News
Hebel, Sara: Chronicle of Higher Education
Hegstad, Maria A.: Inside Washington Publishers
Heil, Emily A.: Roll Call
Heinze, Christian P.: The Hill
Helbling, Laura A.: Elsevier Business Intelligence
Heller, Christopher: National Journal
Hellman, Gregory S.: BNA News
Helminski, Edward L.: Exchange Monitor Publications
Heltman, John H.: Inside Washington Publishers
Hemingway, Mark W.: Weekly Standard
Hennig, Jutta: Inside Washington Publishers
Henry, Patricia M.: BNA News
Hess, Ryan E.: MII Publications
Heydt, Marci K.: UCG
Hicks, Travis: Thompson Publishing Group
Hill, Kashmir M.: Forbes
Hill, Keith M.: BNA News
Hill, Richard: BNA News
Hillman, G. Robert: Politico
Hirschhorn, Dan: Politico
Hiruo, Elaine: McGraw-Hill Co.
Ho, Soyoung: Research Institute of America Group
Hobbs, M. Nielsen: Elsevier Business Intelligence
Hobbs, Susan R.: BNA News
Hodes, David H.: Gulfshore Business Magazine
Hoffman, Michael R.: Gannett Government Media Corp.
Hoffman, Rebecca E.: BNA News
Hoffman, III, William S.: Thompson Publishing Group
Hofmann, Mark A.: Crain Communications
Hogan, Monica J.: Elsevier Business Intelligence
Hohmann, James P.: Politico
Holeywell, Ryan M.: Governing
Holland, Rita: BNA News
Holland, William: McGraw-Hill Co.
Hollander, Catherine: National Journal
Hollmer, Mark H.: Elsevier Business Intelligence
Holmes, Gwendolyn C.: BNA News
Hooper, Molly K.: The Hill
Hoover, Kent D.: Washington Business Journal
Hopkinson, Jenny A.: Inside Washington Publishers
Horowitz, Jay: BNA News
Horwood, Rachel J.: Economist
Hoskinson, Charles E.: Politico
Host, Patrick K.: Inside Washington Publishers
Houghton, Mary J.: Elsevier Business Intelligence
Howell, Katie J.: Environment & Energy Publishing
Huang, Grant G.: UCG
Hudnall, Chad E.: Thompson Publishing Group
Hudson, Audrey: Human Events
Hudson, Elizabeth L.: Inside Washington Publishers
Huffman, Jason A.: Food Chemical News
Huisman, Matthew L.: National Law Journal
Hujer, Marc A.: Der Spiegel
Humes, James E.: National Journal
Humphrey, Shonda: Tax Notes
Hunt, Kasie: Politico
Hunter, Pamela E.: McGraw-Hill Co.
Hurley, Lawrence: Environment & Energy Publishing
Hyland, Kristyn J.: BNA News
Hyland, Terence: BNA News
Iannotta, Benjamin J.: Gannett Government Media Corp.
Ichniowski, Thomas F.: McGraw-Hill Co.
Idaszak, Jerome: Kiplinger Washington Editors
Iekel, John F.: Thompson Publishing Group
Ingram, David H.: National Law Journal
Ip, Gregory W.: Economist
Irgang, Anke B.: UCG
Isenstadt, Alex: Politico
Jackman, Francis L.: Aviation Week
Jackson, Jr., David Randall: Tax Notes
Jackson, II, James E.: BNA News
Jackson, Valarie N.: McGraw-Hill Co.
Jackson, William: Government Computer News
Jacobs, Jeremy P.: Environment & Energy Publishing
Jacobson, Todd K.: Exchange Monitor Publications
James, Betty W.: Government Contractor
Jaworski, Thomas: Tax Notes
Jerome, Sara M.: The Hill
Johnson, Alisa A.: BNA News
Johnson, Chris: Washington Blade
Johnson, Fawn: National Journal
Johnson, Katie: BNA News
Johnson, Nicole: Gannett Government Media Corp.
Johnson, Regina: McGraw-Hill Co.
Jones, Danielle D.: Politico
Jones, George G.: CCH, Inc.
Jones, Joyce: Black Enterprise
Jonson, Kimberly Hart: Politico
Jonson, Nick G.: McGraw-Hill Co.

MEMBERS ENTITLED TO ADMISSION, PERIODICAL PRESS GALLERIES—Continued

Joseph, Andrew: National Journal
Joseph, Cameron E.: The Hill
Jost, Kenneth W.: CQ Researcher
Jowers, Karen G.: Gannett Government Media Corp.
Judis, John B.: New Republic
Judson, Jennifer A.: Inside Washington Publishers
Juliano, Nicholas P.: McGraw-Hill Co.
Kady, II, Martin J.: Politico
Kalb, Claudia: Newsweek
Kalish, Brian M.: Employee Benefit News
Kamen, Jess M.: Politico
Kamens, Jessie K.: BNA News
Kaplan, Hugh B.: BNA News
Kaplan, Karen H.: Nature
Kaplan, Rebecca: National Journal
Kapur, Sahil: Inside Washington Publishers
Kasperowicz, Peter I.: The Hill
Katel, Peter A.: CQ Researcher
Kaufman, Bruce S.: BNA News
Kaufmann, Gregory R.: Nation
Kavruck, Deborah A.: Washington Counseletter
Kelly, Catherine A.: Elsevier Business Intelligence
Kelman, Alison: Broadband Census
Kennedy, Laura W.: Kiplinger Washington Editors
Kenyon, Henry: Defense Systems
Kern, Rebecca M.: Elsevier Business Intelligence
Kessler, Ronald B.: Newsmax
Khan, Altaf U.: BNA News
Khan, Alyah: Federal Computer Week
Khan, Naureen: National Journal
Kim, Mallie J.: U.S. News & World Report
Kim, Seung Min: Politico
Kime, Patricia N.: Gannett Government Media Corp.
King, Robert P.: Politico
Kingsbury, Alex P.: U.S. News & World Report
Kingsley-McMearty, Kim: Politico
Kirby, Paul S.: Telecommunications Reports
Kirkland, Joel G.: Environment & Energy Publishing
Kirkland, John R.: BNA News
Kitfield, James: National Journal
Kitto, Kristofer E.: The Hill
Klamper, Amy E.: Space News
Klapper, Ethan: National Journal
Klein, Alyson: Education Week
Kliff, Sarah L.: Politico
Klimko, Frank J.: CD Publications
Klingst, Martin E.: Die Zeit
Knobbe, Martin: Stern
Kondracke, Morton M.: Roll Call
Koster, Kathleen R.: Employee Benefit News
Koszczuk, Jaculine M.: National Journal
Kovski, Alan D.: BNA News
Kraft, Scott G.: UCG
Kramer, Linda: Glamour Magazine
Kraushaar, Josh: Hotline
Krigman, Eliza V.: Politico
Kroh, Eric L.: Tax Notes
Kubetin, Sally: International Medical News Group
Kubetin, W. Randy: BNA News
Kuckro, Rod W.: McGraw-Hill Co.
Kukuk, Brad A.: Mine Safety and Health News
Kurtz, David M.: Talking Points Memo
Kurtz, Howard: Newsweek
Kurtz, Josh: Environment & Energy Publishing
Kurtzleben, Danielle J.: U.S. News & World Report
Kushin, Philip H.: BNA News
Kushner, Adam: National Journal
LaBrecque, Louis C.: BNA News
Lacey, Anthony: Inside Washington Publishers
Laffler, Mary Jo: Elsevier Business Intelligence
Laing, Keith A.: The Hill
Lake, Eli: Newsweek
Lambert, Kevin C.: BNA News
Lamothe, Daniel G.: Gannett Government Media Corp.
Lankford, Kimberly E.: Kiplinger Washington Editors
Larsen, Kathy Carolin C.: McGraw-Hill Co.
Larson, Cathleen R.: BNA News
Larter, David B.: Gannett Government Media Corp.
Last, Jonathan V.: Weekly Standard
Laster, Jillian E.: Gannett Government Media Corp.
Lawson, Alex R.: Inside Washington Publishers
Leatherman, Jacquelyn D.: CCH, Inc.
Ledbetter, Titus: Inside Washington Publishers
Lederman, Joshua: The Hill
Lee, Anthony J.: Human Events
Lee, Min Jung: Politico
Lee, Steve K.: BNA News
Leeuwenburgh, Todd H.: Thompson Publishing Group
Lehmann, Evan W.: Environment & Energy Publishing
Leone, Daniel M.: Space News
Leopold, George H.: EE Times
Lesesne, William: Research Institute of America Group
Leven, Rachel P.: The Hill
Levin, Joshua: Slate
Levinthal, David: Politico
Liang, John: Inside Washington Publishers
Libby, Sara D.: Politico
Lillis, Michael P.: The Hill
Lindeman, Ralph: BNA News
Lipowicz, Alice: Federal Computer Week
Lithwick, Dahlia Hannah: Slate
Littleton, Julia A.: Environment & Energy Publishing
Lizza, Ryan C.: New Yorker
Loatman, Michael O.: BNA News
Loeb, Matthew: Hotline
Lokshin, Maria L.: BNA News
Long, Emily A.: Government Executive
Long Rayburn, Karen S.: UCG
Lopez, Kathryn J.: National Review

MEMBERS ENTITLED TO ADMISSION, PERIODICAL PRESS GALLERIES—Continued

Lorber, Sarah Jane M.: Roll Call
Lorenzo, Aaron E.: BNA News
Losey, Stephen: Gannett Government Media Corp.
Lotven, Amy L.: Inside Washington Publishers
Loveless, William E.: McGraw-Hill Co.
Lovell, Aaron J.: Inside Washington Publishers
Lovley, Erika M.: Politico
Lowe, Paul D.: Aviation International News
Lowther, William A.: Mail on Sunday
Lubell, Jennifer G.: Atlantic Information Services
Luccioli, Colleen M.: Environment & Energy Publishing
Lundell, Drake: Kiplinger Washington Editors
Lunney, Kellie: Government Executive
Lustig, Joe: BNA News
Maas, Angela K.: Atlantic Information Services
MacDonald, Neil A.: Technology Commercialization
Macy, Daniel J.: Thompson Publishing Group
Madhani, Aamer: National Journal
Mahtesian, Charles G.: Politico
Maine, Amanda: CCH, Inc.
Maixner, Edward: Kiplinger Washington Editors
Majcher, Kristin M.: Aviation Week
Majumdar, Dave: Gannett Government Media Corp.
Malloy, Eileen: BNA News
Mandel, Jennifer A.: Environment & Energy Publishing
Mandell, Dara: Jewish Press
Mann, Jason: National Journal
Marcucci, Carl A.: Radio Business Report
Mark, David F.: Politico
Marks, Clifford: National Journal
Marks, Joseph H.: Government Executive
Maron, Dina F.: Environment & Energy Publishing
Marron, Jessica: McGraw-Hill Co.
Marshall, Christa: Environment & Energy Publishing
Martin, Jonathan L.: Politico
Martinez, Jennifer M.: Politico
Martinson, Erica L.: Inside Washington Publishers
Mattera, Jason J.: Human Events
Matus, Victorino L.: Weekly Standard
Mauro, Antony E.: National Law Journal
Maze, Richard: Gannett Government Media Corp.
Mazumdar, Anandashankar: BNA News
McAllister, III, William H.: Linn's Stamp News & Coin World
McArdle, John E.: Environment & Energy Publishing
McAuley, David: BNA News
McBeth Laping, Karen: McGraw-Hill Co.
McBride, Edward P.: Economist
McCaffery, Gregory: BNA News
McCalmont, Lucy: Politico
McCaney, Kevin: Government Computer News
McCarter, Mickey: HS Today
McCarthy, Elizabeth W.: BNA News
McClamb, Chantelle D.: BNA News
McCleskey, Ellen E.: BNA News
McCord, Quinn T.: Hotline
McCormack, John M.: Weekly Standard
McCormack, Richard A.: Manufacturing & Technology News
McCormally, Kevin: Kiplinger Washington Editors
McCracken, Rebecca P.: BNA News
McCutcheon, Chuck A.: National Journal
McElwaine, Sandra: Newsweek
McGann, Laura K.: Politico
McGill, Brian: National Journal
McGolrick, Susan J.: BNA News
McGowan, Kevin P.: BNA News
McInerney, Susan M.: BNA News
McIntosh, Toby: BNA News
McKinney, Amber: BNA News
McLeary, Paul J.: Aviation Week
McMahon, Francine M.: The Hill
McMahon, Robert F.: Inside Washington Publishers
McMorris-Santoro, Evan: Talking Points Memo
McNeil, Michele: Education Week
McSherry, Alison B.: Roll Call
McTague, James A.: Barron's
McWilliams, Rita M.: BNA News
Mechcatie, Elizabeth: International Medical News Group
Medici, Andrew S.: Gannett Government Media Corp.
Meinecke, Elisabeth C.: Townhall
Merrion, Paul Robert: Crain Communications
Mihalcik, Carrie: National Journal
Milhiser, Ellen B.: Synopsis
Miller, Joshua: Roll Call
Miller, Margaret H.: Thompson Publishing Group
Miller, Naseem S.: International Medical News Group
Miller, Sean: The Hill
Millman, Jason: Politico
Milone, Tiffany F.: BNA News
Mimms, Sarah: Hotline
Miners, Zach A.: Elsevier Business Intelligence
Mishory, Jordana L.: Inside Washington Publishers
Mixter, Bronwyn: BNA News
Mokhiber, Russell J.: Corporate Crime Reporter
Mola, Roger A.: Aviation International News
Monastersky, Richard A.: Nature
Montgomery, Scott R.: Roll Call
Moody, Brittany Elyse: Aviation Week
Moody, Christopher S.: Yahoo! News
Moody, Erica L.: CD Publications
Moore, Michael D.: BNA News
Moore, Miles David: Crain Communications
Moragne, Lenora: Black Congressional Monitor
Morales, Cecilio: MII Publications
Morello, Lauren: Environment & Energy Publishing
Morford, Stacy L.: Education Week
Morley, Jefferson: Salon.com

MEMBERS ENTITLED TO ADMISSION, PERIODICAL PRESS GALLERIES—Continued

Morring, Jr., Frank: Aviation Week
Morris, David J.: Kiplinger Washington Editors
Morris, Jefferson F.: Aviation Week
Morris, Ryan: National Journal
Morton, Peter G.: Financial Post
Moscovitch, Ben: Inside Washington Publishers
Mracek, Karen L.: Kiplinger Washington Editors
Mulkern, Anne C.: Environment & Energy Publishing
Mullins, Richard A.: Aviation Week
Munoz, German: News Bites
Munoz-Temple, Amanda: Hotline
Muolo, Paul A.: National Mortgage News
Muradian, Vardges: Gannett Government Media Corp.
Murphy, Joan F.: Food Chemical News
Mutcherson-Ridley, Joyce: CCH Inc.
Nagelis, Anita I.: Tax Notes
Nagesh, Gautham V.: The Hill
Nardella Botterbusch, Lauren: Elsevier Business Intelligence
Nartker, Michael: Exchange Monitor Publications
Naseef, Kate M.: BNA News
Nather, David R.: Politico
Natter, Aryeh J.: BNA News
Naylor, Sean D.: Gannett Government Media Corp.
Needham, Vicki: The Hill
Nelson, Gabriel K.: Environment & Energy Publishing
Newell, Ashley C.: Tax Notes
Newhauser, Daniel J.: Roll Call
Newkumet, Christopher J.: McGraw-Hill Co.
Newman, Michael: Slate
Newmyer, Tory G.: Fortune Magazine
Newton-Small, Jay: Time Magazine
Nichols, William D.: Politico
Nicholson, Jonathan: BNA News
Noah, Timothy Robert: Slate
Nocera, Katherine R.: Politico
Noh, Chang: McGraw-Hill Co.
Norman, Brett: Politico
Northey, Hannah M.: Environment & Energy Publishing
Norton, Christopher J.: Law360
Novack, Janet E.: Forbes
O'Brien, Michael P.: The Hill
O'Donnell, Katy: National Journal
O'Shea, Brian E.: UCG
O'Toole, Charles C.: Tax Notes
O'Toole, Thomas: BNA News
Oakley, Daniel: UCG
Oberdorfer, Carol: BNA News
Oberle, Sean F.: Product Safety Letter
Obey, Douglas: Inside Washington Publishers
Oczypok, Katherine M.: The Hill
Odom, Che L.: BNA News
Ognanovich, Nancy: BNA News
Olsen, Florence E.: BNA News
Onley, Gloria R.: BNA News
Orchowski, Margaret: Hispanic Outlook in Higher Education
Orth, Maureen: Vanity Fair
Ortman, Emily M.: Roll Call
Ostroff, James J.: McGraw-Hill Co.
Otteman, Scott A.: Inside Washington Publishers
Page, Paul B.: Journal of Commerce
Pak, Janne Kum Cha: USA Journal
Palla, Stephanie: Hotline
Palleschi, Amanda S.: Inside Washington Publishers
Palmer, Anna A.: Politico
Parillo, Kristen A.: Tax Notes
Parker, Alexander M.: U.S. News & World Report
Parker, Stuart H.: Inside Washington Publishers
Parnes, Amie M.: Politico
Paschal, Mack Arthur: BNA News
Patterson, James B.: Kiplinger Washington Editors
Patton, Oliver B.: Heavy Duty Trucking
Pavlich, Catherine: Townhall
Pazanowski, Bernard J.: BNA News
Pazanowski, Mary Anne: BNA News
Pearl, Larry: Food Chemical News
Peck, Louis: National Journal
Pecquet, Julian J.: The Hill
Pekow, Charles W.: Community College Week
Peleo-Lazar, Chris: Hotline
Peoples, Stephen P.: Roll Call
Perelman, Isabella O.: BNA News
Perriello, Anthony M.: BNA News
Perry, Suzanne: Chronicle of Higher Education
Peterka, Amanda E.: Environment & Energy Publishing
Peters, Katherine M.: Government Executive
Petersen, Laura A.: Environment & Energy Publishing
Peterson, Denise: Elsevier Business Intelligence
Pettingell, Dolia E.: Poder
Phenicie, Carolyn B.: Elsevier Business Intelligence
Phillip, Abigail D.: Politico
Phillips, Bergrek: Tax Notes
Piegari, Nick: International Medical News Group
Piemonte, Philip M.: Federal Employees News Digest
Pierce, Emily K.: Roll Call
Pierson, Drew M.: Tax Notes
Pimley, Ward: BNA News
Pippenger, Nathan M.: New Republic
Pittman, David L.: Washington Business Information
Pitts, Edward L.: World Magazine
Plank, Kendra Casey: BNA News
Plautz, Jason T.: Environment & Energy Publishing
Plotz, David: Slate
Plumer, Bradford T.: New Republic
Pollard, Nathan A.: BNA News
Ponnuru, Ramesh: National Review
Postal, Arthur D.: National Underwriter

MEMBERS ENTITLED TO ADMISSION, PERIODICAL PRESS GALLERIES—Continued

Poulson, Theresa: National Journal
Powers, Martha C.: Mid-Atlantic Research
Preston, Caroline S.: Chronicle of Higher Education
Prochnau, William W.: Vanity Fair
Proescholdt, James C.: Thompson Publishing Group
Pruitt, Claude P.: Yahoo! News
Purdum, Todd S.: Vanity Fair
Quillen, Ian N.: Education Week
Quinlan, Paul R.: Environment & Energy Publishing
Quinn, Kristin M.: Gannett Government Media Corp.
Quinn, Peter C.: BNA News
Quinones, Manuel G.: Environment & Energy Publishing
Quinton, Sophie A.: National Journal
Radford, Bruce W.: Public Utilities Fortnightly
Rahim, Saqib: Environment & Energy Publishing
Rajala, Liisa N.: Kiplinger Washington Editors
Raju, Manu K.: Politico
Ramonas, Andrew D.: National Law Journal
Ransom, Alexia: Tax Notes
Rauf, David S.: Politico
Ravani, Sarah: CD Publications
Rees, John: Mid-Atlantic Research
Reeves, Dawn L.: Inside Washington Publishers
Reilly, Ryan: Talking Points Memo
Reilly, Sean C.: Gannett Government Media Corp.
Reinhard, Beth: National Journal
Reis, Patrick C.: Politico
Reishus, Mark: Thompson Publishing Group
Ressler, Thomas S.: Inside Mortgage Finance
Restuccia, Andrew M.: The Hill
Rettig, Jessica L.: U.S. News & World Report
Ricaurte, Kristen C.: BNA News
Richardson, Nathaline: BNA News
Richman, Sheldon B.: BNA News
Riggs, Marli D.: Employee Benefit Adviser
Ritter, Kera: BNA News
Rizzuto, Pat: BNA News
Robelen, Erik: Education Week
Roberts, Edward S.: Credit Union Journal
Roberts, Victoria: BNA News
Robillard, Kevin P.: Politico
Robinson, Thomas S.: Mass Transit Lawyer
Rockelli, Lisa A.: BNA News
Roeder, Linda: BNA News
Roem, Dan: Hotline
Rogers, David E.: Politico
Rogin, Joshua: Foreign Policy Magazine
Rohrer, S. Scott: National Journal
Rojas, Warren: Roll Call
Roland, Neil D.: Crain Communications
Rolfsen, Bruce R.: BNA News
Romano, Lois: Newsweek
Romm, Tony: Politico
Rose, Michael F.: BNA News
Rose, Phil: Professional Pilot Magazine
Rosen, Jeffrey M.: New Republic
Roshania, Neema P.: Kiplinger Washington Editors
Ross, Patrick: Managing IP Magazine
Roth, Bennett: Roll Call
Rothenberg, Stuart: Rothenberg Political Report
Rothman, Heather M.: BNA News
Rowinski, Dan M.: Government Computer News
Roy, Daniel J.: BNA News
Rudd, Jr., Terrence: International Medical News Group
Rudnick, Sarah E.: Inside Mortgage Finance
Russo, Eugene I.: Nature
Ryan, Jr., Frederick J.: Politico
Ryan, John J.: National Journal
Ryan, Josiah D.: The Hill
Saenz, Cheryl L.: BNA News
Saiyid, Amena H.: BNA News
Saletan, William B.: Slate
Salvemini, Grazia M.: Hispanic Link News Service
Salzano, Carlo J.: Waterways Journal
Sami, Tamra S.: Elsevier Business Intelligence
Sammon, Richard: Kiplinger Washington Editors
Samuel, Terence: National Journal
Samuels, Christina: Education Week
Samuelsohn, Darren: Politico
Samuelson, Robert J.: Newsweek
Sanborn, James K.: Gannett Government Media Corp.
Sanchez, Humberto: Roll Call
Sander, Libby C.: Chronicle of Higher Education
Sands, Derek O.: McGraw-Hill Co.
Sandza, Richard W.: Gannett Government Media Corp.
Sanger-Katz, Margot: National Journal
Sangillo, Gregg Thomas: National Journal
Sarlin, Benjamin V.: Talking Points Memo
Sasso, Brendan S.: The Hill
Saunders, Karen J.: BNA News
Savage, Luiza C.: Maclean's
Savoie, Andy: Aviation Week
Sawchuk, Stephen A.: Education Week
Scarcella, Michael A.: National Law Journal
Scheiber, Noam J.: New Republic
Scheid, Brian J.: McGraw-Hill Co.
Scherer, Michael B.: Time Magazine
Scherman, Bob: Satellite Business News
Schewel, Matthew A.: Inside Washington Publishers
Schieken, William: Government Contractor
Schiff, Daniel A.: Elsevier Business Intelligence
Schlesinger, Robert: U.S. News & World Report
Schneider, Martin A.: Exchange Monitor Publications
Schoeff, Jr., Mark: Crain Communications
Schomisch, Jeffrey W.: Thompson Publishing Group
Schonberger, Jennifer A.: Kiplinger Washington Editors
Schor, Elana A.: Environment & Energy Publishing
Schroeder, Peter C.: The Hill
Schultheis, Emily: Politico

MEMBERS ENTITLED TO ADMISSION, PERIODICAL PRESS GALLERIES—Continued

Schwartz, David H.: BNA News
Scott, Dean T.: BNA News
Selingo, Jeffrey: Chronicle of Higher Education
Semeniuk, Ivan: Nature
Sen, Ashish K.: Outlook Magazine
Setze, Karen Jeanne: Tax Notes
Sevidal, Jay A.: Journal of Commerce
Sfiligoj, Mark L.: Kiplinger Washington Editors
Shafer, Jack: Slate
Shah, Nirvi H.: Education Week
Shannon, Darren J.: Aviation Week
Shapiro, Walter E.: New Republic
Sharpe, Stephanie: McGraw-Hill Co.
Sheedy, Rachel L.: Kiplinger Washington Editors
Sheets, Scott Andrew: Tax Notes
Shepard, Steven G.: Hotline
Sheppard, Doug: Tax Notes
Sherman, Jake S.: Politico
Shiner, Meredith H.: Roll Call
Shreve, Margaret: Tax Notes
Siciliano, John: Inside Washington Publishers
Siegelbaum, Deborah J.: The Hill
Silva, Christopher D.: Atlantic Information Services
Simmons, Quintin: Tax Notes
Simon, Roger M.: Politico
Singer, Paul B.: Roll Call
Skinner, Liz: Crain Communications
Slaughter, David A.: Thompson Publishing Group
Smee, Bill D.: Slate
Smelson, Cheryl: BNA News
Smith, Jasper B.: Tax Notes
Smith, Joseph J.: NewBay Media
Smith, Katie: Roll Call
Smith, Lee H.: Weekly Standard
Smith, Sarah C.: McGraw-Hill Co.
Smolkin, Rachel: Politico
Snider, Adam: BNA News
Snider, Ann E.: Environment & Energy Publishing
Snow, Nicholas J.: Oil & Gas Journal
Snyder, Katharine: Mine Safety and Health News
Sobel, Julie: Hotline
Sobieraj Westfall, Sandra J.: People Magazine
Solomon, Goody L.: News Bites
Soraghan, Michael: Environment & Energy Publishing
Sorcher, Sara: National Journal
Southern, E. Richard: Government Contractor
Sparks, Sarah D.: Education Week
Spence, Charles F.: General Aviation News
Spicer, Malcolm E.: Elsevier Business Intelligence
Splete, Heidi: International Medical News Group
Spotswood, Stephen: U.S. Medicine
Sprenger, Sebastian: Inside Washington Publishers
Squire, Matthew R.: Telecommunications Reports
Stam, John H.: BNA News
Stanage, Niall G.: The Hill
Standifer, Lauren M.: Inside Washington Publishers
Stanley, Tiffany L.: New Republic
Stanton, John: Roll Call
Stanton, Lynn E.: Telecommunications Reports
Starkey, Melanie R.: Roll Call
Starosta, Gabriel: Inside Washington Publishers
Stecker, Tiffany A.: Environment & Energy Publishing
Steinberg, Julie A.: BNA News
Steinke, Scott A.: Elsevier Business Intelligence
Stepman, Jarrett L.: Human Events
Sternstein, Aliya E.: Government Executive
Stewart, David D.: Tax Notes
Stewart, Joshua P.: Gannett Government Media Corp.
Stiles, Andrew J.: National Review
Stimson, James A.: BNA News
Stimson, Leslie P.: NewBay Media
Stoddard, Alexandra B.: The Hill
Stokeld, Frederick W.: Tax Notes
Stone, Daniel E.: Newsweek
Straub, Noelle C.: Environment & Energy Publishing
Strauss, Daniel L.: The Hill
Strawbridge, James: Inside Washington Publishers
Strong, Jonathan: Roll Call
Sturges, Peyton Mackay: BNA News
Sullivan, Andrew: Newsweek
Sullivan, John H.: BNA News
Sullivan, Monica C.: National Journal
Sullivan, Sean: Hotline
Summers, Juana: Politico
Supiano, Beckie: Chronicle of Higher Education
Sutter, Susan M.: Elsevier Business Intelligence
Sutton, Eileen C.: BNA News
Swango, Alissa: National Journal
Swann, James L.: BNA News
Sweeney, Ray F.: CD Publications
Sweetman, Bill A.: Aviation Week
Swisher, Larry: BNA News
Szakonyi, Mark: Journal of Commerce
Tanabe, Karin E.: Politico
Tankersley, Jim: National Journal
Tau, Byron C.: Politico
Tavangar, Sayeh: McGraw-Hill Co.
Taylor, II, B.J.: Atlantic Information Services
Taylor, Dan: Inside Washington Publishers
Taylor, Jessica: Hotline
Taylor, Joy M.: Kiplinger Washington Editors
Taylor, Philip A.: Environment & Energy Publishing
Taylor, Ronald A.: BNA News
Taylor, Jr., Stuart: National Journal
Taylor, Thomas P.: BNA News
Taylor, Vincent E.: UCG
Taylor, William G.: Roll Call
Tegtmeier, Lee Ann: Aviation Week
Terris, Ben: National Journal
Terzian, Philip: Weekly Standard
Teske, Steve J.: BNA News
Thibodeau, Patrick: IDG Communications

MEMBERS ENTITLED TO ADMISSION, PERIODICAL PRESS GALLERIES—Continued

Thomas, Helen A.: Falls Church News Press
Thomas, Kevin: CCH, Inc.
Thompson, Derek K.: Atlantic Monthly
Thompson, Mark J.: Time Magazine
Thompson, Wenoka S.: DC Spotlight Newspaper
Thrush, Glenn H.: Politico
Tice, James S.: Gannett Government Media Corp.
Tiernan, Tom: McGraw-Hill Co.
Tilghman, Andrew S.: Gannett Government Media Corp.
Tillman, Zoe M.: National Law Journal
Timmerman, Kenneth R.: Newsmax
Tinkelman, Joseph A.: BNA News
Toeplitz, Shira: Roll Call
Tollefson, Jeffrey S.: Nature
Tomasky, Michael J.: Newsweek
Topor, Eric D.: BNA News
Torrance, Kelly J.: Weekly Standard
Tosh, Dennis A.: Thompson Publishing Group
Touhey, Noel Emmanuel: The Hill
Tragone, Adam J.: Human Events
Tranum, Samuel R.: Nuclear Intelligence Weekly
Travis, Jesse T.: BNA News
Trenkner, Christina M.: Governing
Trilling, Stefanie S.: BNA News
Triplett, Michael R.: BNA News
Trivedi, Shamik N.: Tax Notes
Trowbridge, Alexander: Politico
Trygstad, Kyle K.: Roll Call
Tsui, Amy: BNA News
Tucker, Miriam E.: International Medical News Group
Tummarello, Kate A.: Roll Call
Twachtman, Gregory: Elsevier Business Intelligence
Unnikrishnan, Madhu: Aviation Week
van den Berg, David T.: Tax Notes
van Zuylen-Wood, Simon: New Republic
Vandehei, James: Politico
Verespej, Michael: Crain Communications
Viadero-Rogers, Debra: Education Week
Victor, Kirk: National Journal
Viebeck, Elise J.: The Hill
Vissiere, Helene A.: Le Point
Vogel, Kenneth P.: Politico
Voosen, Paul E.: Environment & Energy Publishing
Wachter, Kerri: International Medical News Group
Waddell, Melanie L.: Investment Advisor Magazine
Wadman, Meredith K.: Nature
Walker, Karen J.: Gannett Government Media Corp.
Walsh, Kenneth T.: U.S. News & World Report
Walsh, Mark F.: Education Week
Wang, Herman D.: McGraw-Hill Co.
Ward, Mary E.: McGraw-Hill Co.
Ware, Patricia A.: BNA News
Warren, Michael R.: Weekly Standard
Warwick, Allan G.: Aviation Week
Wasserman, David N.: Cook Political Report
Wasserman, Elizabeth A.: Politico
Wasson, Erik L.: The Hill
Watkins, Steven M.: Gannett Government Media Corp.
Weaver, Dustin A.: The Hill
Webber, Diane: Politico
Weber, Rick: Inside Washington Publishers
Webster, Henry C.: McGraw-Hill Co.
Webster, James C.: Webster Communications
Wechsler, Jill: Pharmaceutical Executive
Weigel, David A.: Slate
Weigelt, Matthew: Federal Computer Week
Weisgerber, Marcus A.: Gannett Government Media Corp.
Weixel, Nathaniel L.: BNA News
Whieldon, Esther: McGraw-Hill Co.
Whitaker, Joel: Whitaker Newsletters
White, III, Frank: BNA News
White, Keith P.: The Hill
White, Nicola M.: Tax Notes
White, Rodney A.: McGraw-Hill Co.
Whitney, Blake K.: Roll Call
Whittington, Lauren: Roll Call
Wiener, Aaron M.: Talking Points Memo
Wieser, Eric M.: McGraw-Hill Co.
Wilczek, Yin: BNA News
Wilhelm, Ian L.: Chronicle of Higher Education
Wilkerson, John S.: Inside Washington Publishers
Wilkie, Christina W.: The Hill
Williams, Jeffrey: Satellite Business News
Williams, Joseph: Politico
Williams, Lauren C.: UCG
Williams, Mark A.: BNA News
Williams, Risa D.: Tax Notes
Wilson, Benet J.: Aviation Week
Wilson, Chris E.: Slate
Wilson, Patsy: National Journal
Wilson, Reid: Hotline
Wilson, Stanley E.: Institutional Investor
Windsor, Joseph K.: Government Contractor
Winebrenner, Jane A.: BNA News
Winston, Kate: McGraw-Hill Co.
Winter, Allison A.: Environment & Energy Publishing
Wisniowski, Charles M.: Inside Mortgage Finance
Wong, Scott B.: Politico
Wood, Graeme C.: Atlantic Monthly
Xie, Yanmei: McGraw-Hill Co.
Yager, Christopher J.: The Hill
Yaksick, Jr., George L.: CCH, Inc.
Yamazaki, Kazutami: Washington Watch
Yasin, Rutrell: Government Computer News
Ybarra, Margaret A.: Inside Washington Publishers
Yehle, Emily J.: Environment & Energy Publishing
Yingling, Jennifer S.: The Hill
Yochelson, Mindy: BNA News
Yohannan, Suzanne M.: Inside Washington Publishers
Yordanova-Kline, Milena: McGraw-Hill Co.

MEMBERS ENTITLED TO ADMISSION, PERIODICAL PRESS GALLERIES—Continued

Young, Sam: Tax Notes
Youngman, Sam A.: The Hill
Yuill, Barbara: BNA News
Zalan, Kira: U.S. News & World Report
Zaman, Gulnar: Tax Notes
Zaneski, Cyril T.: Environment & Energy Publishing
Zapler, Michael: Politico
Zehr, Mary Ann: Education Week
Zigmond, Jessica A.: Crain Communications
Zornick, George L.: Nation
Zung, Robert Te-Kang: BNA News
Zurcher, Anthony W.: Congressional Digest

PERIODICALS REPRESENTED IN PRESS GALLERIES

House Gallery 225–2941, Senate Gallery 224–0265

ADVOCATE—(310) 943–5858; 130 M Street, NE., #1021, Washington, DC 20002: Andrew Harmon.

ADWEEK—(703) 212–0540; 31 Arell Court, Alexandria, VA 22304: Kathryn M. Bachman.

AGRI-PULSE—(202) 470–0960; 635 Maryland Avenue, NE., Washington, DC 20002: Timothy Breen, Sarah S. Gonzalez, Jonathan H. Harsch.

AMERICAN SPECTATOR—(703) 807–2011; 1611 North Kent Street, Arlington, VA 22209: W. James Antle.

ASIA TODAY—(202) 271–1100; 27025 McPherson Square Street, Washington, DC 20038: Raghubir Goyal.

ATLANTIC INFORMATION SERVICES—(202) 775–9008; 1100 17th Street, NW., Suite 300, Washington, DC 20036: Jill Brown, Evelyn Collins, Steve W. Davis, Steve Davolt, Barbra Golub, James H. Gutman, Jennifer G. Lubell, Angela K. Maas, Christopher D. Silva, B.J. Taylor II.

ATLANTIC MONTHLY—(202) 266–7000; 600 New Hampshire Avenue, NW., Washington, DC 20037: Garance R. Franke-Ruta, Jeffrey M. Goldberg, Christopher E. Good, Joshua Green, Derek K. Thompson, Graeme C. Wood.

AVIATION INTERNATIONAL NEWS—(301) 230–4520; 5605 Alderbrook Court, #T6, Rockville, MD 20851: William J. Carey, Paul D. Lowe, Roger A. Mola.

AVIATION WEEK—(202) 383–2300; 1200 G Street, NW., Suite 900, Washington, DC 20005: Joseph C. Anselmo, James R. Asker, Michael Bruno, Amy Butler, Andrew W. Compart, Jennifer DiMascio, Michael J. Fabey, David A. Fulghum, Francis L. Jackman, Kristin M. Majcher, Paul J. McLeary, Brittany Elyse Moody, Frank Morring, Jr., Jefferson F. Morris, Richard A. Mullins, Andy Savoie, Darren J. Shannon, Bill A. Sweetman, Lee Ann Tegtmeier, Madhu Unnikrishnan, Allan G. Warwick, Benet J. Wilson.

BARRON'S—(202) 862–6606; 1025 Connecticut Avenue, NW., Suite 800, Washington, DC 20036: Thomas G. Donlan, James A. McTague.

BLACK CONGRESSIONAL MONITOR—(202) 488–8879; 607 4th Street, SW., Washington, DC 20024: Lenora Moragne.

BLACK ENTERPRISE—(202) 544–3143; 1220 Orren Street, NE., Washington, DC 20002: Joyce Jones.

BNA NEWS—(703) 341–3000; 1801 South Bell Street, Arlington, VA 22202: Mirza Z. Aftab, Paul F. Albergo, Alexei Alexis, Michelle L. Amber, Patrick Ambrosio, Donald G. Aplin, John T. Aquino, Jerome C. Ashton, Cecelia M. Assam, Pamela S. Atkins, Margaret Aulino, Martina S. Barash, Paul Barbagallo, Sarah M. Barr, Theresa A. Barry, Tamlin H. Bason, Jeannie Baumann, Alison E. Bennett, Andrea L. Ben-Yosef, Alicia E. Biggs, Deborah D. Billings, Amy E. Bivins, Leonard A. Bracken, David B. Brandolph, Rossella E. Brevetti, Lydell C. Bridgeford, Brian J. Broderick, R. Christian Bruce, Susan E. Bruninga, Derrick Cain, Madelyn R. Callahan, Anntherese Carlozzo, Jay-Anne B. Casuga, Heather N. Caygle, Tina M. Chi, Andrew J. Childers, Gayle C. Cinquegrani, Janey Cohen, Paul C. Connolly, Robert C. Cook, Steven Cook, Jessica M. Coomes, Matilda M. Corley, Richard H. Cowden, S. Diane Davis, Jeff Day, Gloria Deigh, Phyllis Diamond, Dana J. Domone, Genevieve Douglas, Kenneth P. Doyle, Susan Doyle, Lawrence E. Dube, Jr., Antonio Dutra, Thomas Edmondson, Jewel W. Edwards, Michael Eisenstein, Dana A. Elfin, Catherine S. Ezzard, Thecla R. Fabian, Leora M. Falk, Avery Fellow, Brett A. Ferguson, Michael A. Ferullo, J.P. Finet, Leslie G. Fleet, Sean I. Forbes, Stephen France, Laura Francis, Diane Freda, John Gannon, W. Lynn Garner, Lorraine S. Gilbert, Diana I. Gregg, Mary Ann Grena Manley, Christine H. Grimaldi, Sara E. Hansard, David Harrison, Peter S. Hayes, Gregory S. Hellman, Patricia M. Henry, Keith M. Hill, Richard Hill, Susan R. Hobbs, Rebecca E. Hoffman, Rita Holland, Gwendolyn C. Holmes, Jay Horowitz, Kristyn J. Hyland, Terence Hyland, James E. Jackson II, Alisa A. Johnson, Katie Johnson, Jessie K. Kamens, Hugh B. Kaplan, Bruce S. Kaufman, Altaf U. Khan, John R. Kirkland, Alan D. Kovski, W. Randy Kubetin, Philip H. Kushin, Louis C. LaBrecque, Kevin C. Lambert, Cathleen R. Larson, Steve K. Lee, Ralph Lindeman, Michael O. Loatman, Maria L. Lokshin, Aaron E. Lorenzo, Joe Lustig, Eileen Malloy, Anandashankar Mazumdar, David McAuley, Gregory McCaffery, Elizabeth W. McCarthy, Chantelle D. McClamb, Ellen E. McCleskey, Rebecca P. McCracken, Susan J. McGolrick, Kevin P. McGowan, Susan M. McInerney, Toby McIntosh, Amber McKinney, Rita M. McWilliams, Tiffany F. Milone, Bronwyn Mixter, Michael D. Moore, Kate M. Naseef, Aryeh J. Natter, Jonathan Nicholson, Carol Oberdorfer, Che L. Odom, Nancy Ognanovich, Florence E. Olsen, Gloria R. Onley, Thomas O'Toole, Mack Arthur Paschal, Bernard J. Pazanowski, Mary Anne Pazanowski, Isabella O. Perelman, Anthony M. Perriello, Ward Pimley, Kendra Casey Plank, Nathan A. Pollard, Peter C. Quinn, Kristen C. Ricaurte, Nathaline Richardson, Sheldon B. Richman, Kera Ritter, Pat Rizzuto, Victoria Roberts, Lisa A. Rockelli, Linda Roeder, Bruce R. Rolfsen, Michael F. Rose, Heather M. Rothman, Daniel J. Roy, Cheryl L. Saenz, Amena H. Saiyid, Karen J. Saunders, David H. Schwartz, Dean T. Scott, Cheryl Smelson, Adam Snider, John H. Stam, Julie A. Steinberg, James A. Stimson, Peyton Mackay Sturges, John H. Sullivan, Eileen C. Sutton, James L. Swann, Larry Swisher, Ronald A. Taylor, Thomas P. Taylor, Steve J. Teske, Joseph A. Tinkelman, Eric D. Topor, Jesse T. Travis, Stefanie S. Trilling, Michael R. Triplett, Amy Tsui, Patricia A. Ware, Nathaniel L. Weixel, Frank White III, Yin Wilczek, Mark A. Williams, Jane A. Winebrenner, Mindy Yochelson, Barbara Yuill, Robert Te-Kang Zung.

PERIODICALS REPRESENTED IN PRESS GALLERIES—Continued

BROADBAND CENSUS—(202) 580–8196; 1705 Warner Avenue, McLean, VA 22101: Jonathan W. Charnitski, Rahul V. Gaitonde, Alison Kelman.

BROADCASTING & CABLE—(571) 830–6440; 8015 Hatteras Lane, Springfield, VA 22151: John S. Eggerton.

BUSINESSWEEK—(202) 624–1800; 1399 New York Avenue, NW., 11th Floor, Washington, DC 20005: Elizabeth S. Dwoskin.

CCH, INC.—(202) 842–7355; 1015 15th Street, NW., 10th Floor, Washington, DC 20005: John Filar Atwood, Sarah A. Borchersen-Keto, Jeffrey E. Carlson, John Carpenter, Stephen K. Cooper, Paula L. Cruickshank, Hilary A. Goehausen, Brant Goldwyn, George G. Jones, Jacquelyn D. Leatherman, Amanda Maine, Joyce Mutcherson-Ridley, Kevin Thomas, George L. Yaksick, Jr.

CD PUBLICATIONS—(301) 588–6380; 8204 Fenton Street, Silver Spring, MD 20910: Thomas J. Edwards, Michael S. Gerecht, Thomas H. Harman, Frank J. Klimko, Erica L. Moody, Sarah Ravani, Ray F. Sweeney.

CHRONICLE OF HIGHER EDUCATION—(202) 466–1000; 1255 23rd Street, NW., Suite 700, Washington, DC 20037: Paul A. Basken, Goldie Blumenstyk, Lisa S. Chiu, Kelly E. Field, Karin E. Fischer, Jennifer Gonzalez, Sara Hebel, Suzanne Perry, Caroline S. Preston, Libby C. Sander, Jeffrey Selingo, Beckie Supiano, Ian L. Wilhelm.

COMMUNITY COLLEGE WEEK—(301) 493–6926; 5225 Pooks Hill Road, #1118 N, Bethesda, MD 20814: Charles W. Pekow.

CONGRESSIONAL DIGEST—(202) 258–7586; 3307 M Street, NW., Suite 301, Washington, DC 20007: Anthony W. Zurcher.

COOK POLITICAL REPORT—(202) 739–8525; 600 New Hampshire Avenue, NW., Washington, DC 20037: Charles E. Cook, Jr., Jennifer E. Duffy, David N. Wasserman.

CORPORATE CRIME REPORTER—(202) 737–1680; 1209 National Press Building, Washington, DC 20045: Russell J. Mokhiber.

COURTHOUSE NEWS SERVICE—(443) 783–1463; 530 First Street, Annapolis, MD 21403: Ryan M. Abbott.

CQ RESEARCHER—(202) 729–1900; 2300 N Street, NW., Suite 800, Washington, DC 20037: Marcia A. Clemmitt, Darrell D. Dela Rosa, Kenneth W. Jost, Peter A. Katel.

CRAIN COMMUNICATIONS—(202) 662–7200; 814 National Press Building, Washington, DC 20045: Hazel M. Bradford, Richard F. Daly, Jerome M. Geisel, Mark A. Hofmann, Paul Robert Merrion, Miles David Moore, Neil D. Roland, Mark Schoeff, Jr., Liz Skinner, Michael Verespej, Jessica A. Zigmond.

CREDIT UNION JOURNAL—(240) 631–9872; 4401 Wilson Boulevard, Arlington, VA 22203: Edward S. Roberts.

DC SPOTLIGHT NEWSPAPER—(301) 288–7997; 13903 Castle Boulevard, Suite 14, Silver Spring, MD 20904: Wenoka S. Thompson.

DEFENSE SYSTEMS—(703) 876–5100; 3141 Fairview Park Drive, Suite 777, Falls Church, VA 22042: Amber Corrin, Henry Kenyon.

DER SPIEGEL—(202) 347–5222; 1202 National Press Building, Washington, DC 20045: Marc A. Hujer.

DIE ZEIT—(301) 312–8453; 7303 Maple Avenue, Chevy Chase, MD 20815: Martin E. Klingst.

ECONOMIST—(202) 429–0890; 1730 Rhode Island Avenue, NW., Suite 1210, Washington, DC 20036: Peter H. David, Rachel J. Horwood, Gregory W. Ip, Edward P. McBride.

EDUCATION WEEK—(301) 280–3100; 6935 Arlington Road, Suite 100, Bethesda, MD 20814: Mark W. Bomster, Sean M. Cavanagh, Gregory Chronister, Karen Diegmueller, Catherine Gewertz, Alyson Klein, Michele McNeil, Stacy L. Morford, Ian N. Quillen, Erik Robelen, Christina Samuels, Stephen A. Sawchuk, Nirvi H. Shah, Sarah D. Sparks, Debra Viadero-Rogers, Mark F. Walsh, Mary Ann Zehr.

EE TIMES—(202) 746–0611; 1639 York Mills Lane, Reston, VA 20194: George H. Leopold.

ELLE—(202) 462–2957; 3133 Connecticut Avenue, NW., #315, Washington, DC 20008: Meryl Gordon.

ELSEVIER BUSINESS INTELLIGENCE—(240) 221–4500; 5635 Fishers Lane, Suite 6000, Rockville, MD 20852: Joshua L. Berlin, Martin J. Berman-Gorvine, Jessica E. Bylander, Bowman D. Cox, Elizabeth R. Crawford, Susan W. Darcey, Jon Dobson, Cathy H. Dombrowski, Joanne S. Eglovitch, Derrick J. Gingery, Joseph A. Haas, Laura A. Helbling, M. Nielsen Hobbs, Monica J. Hogan, Mark H. Hollmer, Mary J. Houghton, Catherine A. Kelly, Rebecca M. Kern, Mary Jo Laffler, Zach A. Miners, Lauren Nardella Botterbusch, Denise Peterson, Carolyn B. Phenicie, Tamra S. Sami, Daniel A. Schiff, Malcolm E. Spicer, Scott A. Steinke, Susan M. Sutter, Gregory Twachtman.

EMPLOYEE BENEFIT ADVISER—(571) 403–3840; 4401 Wilson Boulevard, Suite 910, Arlington, VA 22203: Elizabeth R. Galentine, Marli D. Riggs.

EMPLOYEE BENEFIT NEWS—(571) 403–3847; 4401 Wilson Boulevard, Suite 910, Arlington, VA 22203: Brian M. Kalish, Kathleen R. Koster.

ENVIRONMENT & ENERGY PUBLISHING—(202) 628–6500; 122 C Street, NW., Suite 722, Washington, DC 20001: Sarah M. Abruzzese, Peter B. Behr, Kevin D. Braun, Amy V. Carlile, Jean M. Chemnick, John Matthew Comer, John J. Fialka, Lisa F. Friedman, Ellen M. Gilmer, Katie J. Howell, Lawrence

PERIODICALS REPRESENTED IN PRESS GALLERIES—Continued

Hurley, Jeremy P. Jacobs, Joel G. Kirkland, Josh Kurtz, Evan W. Lehmann, Julia A. Littleton, Colleen M. Luccioli, Jennifer A. Mandel, Dina F. Maron, Christa Marshall, John E. McArdle, Lauren Morello, Anne C. Mulkern, Gabriel K. Nelson, Hannah M. Northey, Amanda E. Peterka, Laura A. Petersen, Jason T. Plautz, Paul R. Quinlan, Manuel G. Quinones, Saqib Rahim, Elana A. Schor, Ann E. Snider, Michael Soraghan, Tiffany A. Stecker, Noelle C. Straub, Philip A. Taylor, Paul E. Voosen, Allison A. Winter, Emily J. Yehle, Cyril T Zaneski.

EXCHANGE MONITOR PUBLICATIONS—(202) 296–2814; 4455 Connecticut Avenue, NW., Suite A–700, Washington, DC 20008: Sarah E. Anderson, Kenneth R. Fletcher, Tamar Hallerman, Edward L. Helminski, Todd K. Jacobson, Michael Nartker, Martin A. Schneider.

EXPRESS INDIA—(703) 599–6623; 1541 Wellingham Court, Vienna, VA 22182: Geeta Goindi.

FALLS CHURCH NEWS PRESS—(703) 532–3267; 450 West Broad Street, Suite 321, Falls Church, VA 22046: Nicholas F. Benton, Michelle M. Cohen, Jody C. Fellows, Nicholas T. Gatz, Helen A. Thomas.

FEDERAL COMPUTER WEEK—(703) 876–5100; 3141 Fairview Park Drive, Suite 777, Falls Church, VA 22042: Michael Hardy, Alyah Khan, Alice Lipowicz, Matthew Weigelt.

FEDERAL EMPLOYEES NEWS DIGEST—(703) 891–8554; 3141 Fairview Park Drive, Suite 777, Falls Church, VA 22042: Nathan Abse, Philip M. Piemonte.

FINANCIAL POST—(202) 842–1190; 6300 Dahlonega Road, Bethesda, MD 20816: Peter G. Morton.

FOOD CHEMICAL NEWS—(703) 527–1680; 2200 Clarendon Boulevard, Suite 1401, Arlington, VA 22201: Elizabeth J. Buckley, Stephen C. Clapp, Amber M. Healy, Jason A. Huffman, Joan F. Murphy, Larry Pearl.

FOOD PROTECTION REPORT—(703) 548–3146; P.O. Box 25277, Alexandria, VA 22313: Declan A. Conroy.

FORBES—(202) 785–1470; 1101 17th Street, NW., Suite 409, Washington, DC 20036: Kashmir M. Hill, Janet E. Novack.

FOREIGN POLICY MAGAZINE—(202) 728–7300; 1899 L Street, NW., Suite 500, Washington, DC 20036: Joshua Rogin.

FORTUNE MAGAZINE—(202) 861–4000; 1130 Connecticut Avenue, NW., Suite 900, Washington, DC 20036: Nina J. Easton, Tory G. Newmyer.

FREITAG—(301) 699–3908; 4506 32nd Street, Mt. Rainier, MD 20712: Konrad Ege.

FTC: WATCH—(703) 684–7171; 604 Cameron Street, Alexandria, VA 22314: Kirstin E. Downey.

GANNETT GOVERNMENT MEDIA CORP.—(703) 750–9000; 6883 Commercial Drive, Springfield, VA 22159: Kate O. Brannen, Gina Cavallaro, Christopher P. Cavas, Sarah E. Chacko, Scott A. Fontaine, Zachary Fryer-Biggs, Joseph M. Gould, Melanie J. Gray, Michael R. Hoffman, Benjamin J. Iannotta, Nicole Johnson, Karen G. Jowers, Patricia N. Kime, Daniel G. Lamothe, David B. Larter, Jillian E. Laster, Stephen Losey, Dave Majumdar, Richard Maze, Andrew S. Medici, Vardges Muradian, Sean D. Naylor, Kristin M. Quinn, Sean C. Reilly, James K. Sanborn, Richard W. Sandza, Joshua P. Stewart, James S. Tice, Andrew S. Tilghman, Karen J. Walker, Steven M. Watkins, Marcus A. Weisgerber.

GENERAL AVIATION NEWS—(301) 330–2715; 1915 Windjammer Way, Gaithersburg, MD 20879: Charles F. Spence.

GILSTON-KALIN COMMUNICATIONS—(301) 570–4544; 4816 Sweetbirch Drive, Rockville, MD 20853: Meredith L. Gilston, Samuel M. Gilston.

GLAMOUR MAGAZINE—(703) 317–4949; 6100 Edgewood Terrace, Alexandria, VA 22307: Linda Kramer.

GOVERNING—(202) 862–8802; 1100 Connecticut Avenue, NW., #1300, Washington, DC 20036: Ryan M. Holeywell, Christina M. Trenkner.

GOVERNMENT COMPUTER NEWS—(703) 876–5100; 3141 Fairview Park Drive, Suite 777, Falls Church, VA 22042: William Jackson, Kevin McCaney, Dan M. Rowinski, Rutrell Yasin.

GOVERNMENT CONTRACTOR—(202) 772–8295; 1100 13th Street, NW., Suite 200, Washington, DC 20005: Kenneth H. Berke, Betty W. James, William Schieken, E. Richard Southern, Joseph K. Windsor.

GOVERNMENT EXECUTIVE—(202) 739–8501; 600 New Hampshire Avenue, NW., Washington, DC 20037: Robert G. Brodsky, Charles S. Clark, Timothy Clark, Susan Fourney, Amelia M. Gruber, Emily A. Long, Kellie Lunney, Joseph H. Marks, Katherine M. Peters, Aliya E. Sternstein.

GQ MAGAZINE—(202) 615–5003; 1420 K Street, SE., Washington, DC 20003: Robert L. Draper.

GULFSHORE BUSINESS MAGAZINE—(202) 596–5037; 816 North Oakland, #802, Arlington, VA 22203: David H. Hodes.

HEALTH MARKET SURVEY—(202) 277–1994; 3767 Oliver Street, NW., Washington, DC 20015: William R. Boyles.

HEAVY DUTY TRUCKING—(703) 683–9935; 320 Mansion Drive, Alexandria, VA 22302: Oliver B. Patton.

THE HILL—(202) 628–8500; 1625 K Street, NW., Suite 900, Washington, DC 20006: Judy K. Altscher, Samuel U. Baker, Bernard A. Becker, John T. Bennett, Russell L. Berman, Kevin J. Bogardus, Alexander Bolton, Ramsey C. Cox, Robert Cusack, Shane T. D'Aprile, Jamie W. Dettmer, Albert Eisele, Jordan Fabian, Ben A. Geman, Emily L. Goodin, Christian P. Heinze, Molly K. Hooper,

PERIODICALS REPRESENTED IN PRESS GALLERIES—Continued

Sara M. Jerome, Cameron E. Joseph, Peter I. Kasperowicz, Kristofer E. Kitto, Keith A. Laing, Joshua Lederman, Rachel P. Leven, Michael P. Lillis, Francine M. McMahon, Sean Miller, Gautham V. Nagesh, Vicki Needham, Michael P. O'Brien, Katherine M. Oczypok, Julian J. Pecquet, Andrew M. Restuccia, Josiah D. Ryan, Brendan S. Sasso, Peter C. Schroeder, Deborah J. Siegelbaum, Niall G. Stanage, Alexandra B. Stoddard, Daniel L. Strauss, Noel Emmanuel Touhey, Elise J. Viebeck, Erik L. Wasson, Dustin A. Weaver, Keith P. White, Christina W. Wilkie, Christopher J. Yager, Jennifer S. Yingling, Sam A. Youngman.

HISPANIC LINK NEWS SERVICE—(202) 234–0280; 1420 N Street, NW., Suite 101, Washington, DC 20005: Charlie Ericksen, Grazia M. Salvemini.

HISPANIC OUTLOOK IN HIGHER EDUCATION—(202) 236–5595; 2627 O Street, NW., Washington, DC 20007: Margaret Orchowski.

HOTLINE—(202) 739–8400; 600 New Hampshire Avenue, NW., Washington, DC 20037: Timothy Alberta, Kevin Brennan, Josh Kraushaar, Matthew Loeb, Quinn T. McCord, Sarah Mimms, Amanda Munoz-Temple, Stephanie Palla, Chris Peleo-Lazar, Dan Roem, Steven G. Shepard, Julie Sobel, Sean Sullivan, Jessica Taylor, Reid Wilson.

HS TODAY—(202) 427–8780; P.O. Box 5843, Washington, DC 20016: Mickey McCarter.

HUMAN EVENTS—(202) 216–0600; One Massachusetts Avenue, NW., Washington, DC 20001: Jeffrey Carneal, Patrick J. Frank, John M. Gizzi, Joseph A. Guerriero, Audrey Hudson, Anthony J. Lee, Jason J. Mattera, Jarrett L. Stepman, Adam J. Tragone.

IDG COMMUNICATIONS—(202) 333–2448; 2630 Adams Mill Road, NW., Apt. #304, Washington, DC 20009: Patrick Thibodeau.

IDG NEWS SERVICE—(202) 595–9882; 906 Phillip Powers Drive, Laurel, MD 20707: Grant J. Gross.

INDIA ABROAD—(703) 218–0790; 5026 Huntwood Manor Drive, Fairfax, VA 22030: Aziz A. Haniffa.

INSIDE MORTGAGE FINANCE—(301) 951–1240; 7910 Woodmont Avenue, Suite 1000, Bethesda, MD 20814: Gemma L. Baltazar, John R. Bancroft, George A. Brooks, Guy David Cecala, Thomas S. Ressler, Sarah E. Rudnick, Charles M. Wisniowski.

INSIDE WASHINGTON PUBLISHERS—(703) 416–8500; 1919 South Eads Street, #201, Arlington, VA 22202: Lara W. Beaven, Adam Behsudi, Anthony F. Bertuca, Nanci B. Bompey, Andrew O. Burt, Alaina V. Busch, Christopher Castelli, David Paul Clarke, Christopher M. Cole, Bridget DiCosmo, Sara A. Ditta, Rachana Dixit, Megan A. Eckstein, Brian W. Everstine, Matthew G. Field, Victoria J. Finkle, Douglas Guarino, Benjamin Hancock, Donna L. Haseley, Maria A. Hegstad, John H. Heltman, Jutta Hennig, Jenny A. Hopkinson, Patrick K. Host, Elizabeth L. Hudson, Jennifer A. Judson, Sahil Kapur, Anthony Lacey, Alex R. Lawson, Titus Ledbetter, John Liang, Amy L. Lotven, Aaron J. Lovell, Erica L. Martinson, Robert F. McMahon, Jordana L. Mishory, Ben Moscovitch, Douglas Obey, Scott A. Otteman, Amanda S. Palleschi, Stuart H. Parker, Dawn L. Reeves, Matthew A. Schewel, John Siciliano, Sebastian Sprenger, Lauren M. Standifer, Gabriel Starosta, James Strawbridge, Dan Taylor, Rick Weber, John S. Wilkerson, Margaret A. Ybarra, Suzanne M. Yohannan.

INSTITUTIONAL INVESTOR—(202) 393–0728; 1319 F Street, NW., Suite 805, Washington, DC 20004: Stanley E. Wilson.

INTERNATIONAL MEDICAL NEWS GROUP—(240) 221–4500; 5635 Fishers Lane, Suite 6000, Rockville, MD 20852: Alicia Ault, Lorinda M. Bullock, Frances Correa, Jeffrey Evans, Sally Kubetin, Elizabeth Mechcatie, Naseem S. Miller, Nick Piegari, Terrence Rudd, Jr., Heidi Splete, Miriam E. Tucker, Kerri Wachter.

INVESTMENT ADVISOR MAGAZINE—(202) 370–4810; 1301 Connecticut Avenue, NW., Washington, DC 20036: Melanie L. Waddell.

IRISH ECHO—(202) 870–7404; 9534 Fernwood Road, Bethesda, MD 20817: Susan M. Falvella-Garraty.

JET/EBONY—(202) 321–4282; 16115 Eckhart Road, Bowie, MD 20716: Kevin U. Chappell.

JEWISH PRESS—(718) 330–1100; 1725 20th Street, NW., Fl, Washington, DC 20009: Dara Mandell.

JOURNAL OF COMMERCE—(202) 355–1170; 1270 National Press Building, Washington, DC 20045: John D. Boyd, William B. Cassidy, Robert G. Edmonson, Paul B. Page, Jay A. Sevidal, Mark Szakonyi.

KIPLINGER WASHINGTON EDITORS—(202) 887–6400; 1729 H Street, NW., Washington, DC 20006: Peter L. Blank, Martha L. Craver, Mary Beth Franklin, Susan B. Garland, Lisa A. Gerstner, Douglas A. Harbrecht, Jerome Idaszak, Laura W. Kennedy, Kimberly E. Lankford, Drake Lundell, Edward Maixner, Kevin McCormally, David J. Morris, Karen L. Mracek, James B. Patterson, Liisa N. Rajala, Neema P. Roshania, Richard Sammon, Jennifer A. Schonberger, Mark L. Sfiligoj, Rachel L. Sheedy, Joy M. Taylor.

LAW360—(201) 803–4091; 740 Rock Creek Church Road, NW., Washington, DC 20010: Christopher J. Norton.

LE POINT—(202) 244–6656; 3234 McKinley Street, NW., Washington, DC 20015: Helene A. Vissiere.

LINN'S STAMP NEWS & COIN WORLD—(703) 385–6996; 10121 Ratcliffe Manor Drive Fairfax, VA 22030: William H. McAllister III.

MACLEAN'S—(703) 534–1283; 6316 24th Street N, Arlington, VA22207: Luiza C. Savage.

MAIL ON SUNDAY—(202) 547–7980; 510 Constitution Avenue, NE., Washington, DC 20002: William A. Lowther.

PERIODICALS REPRESENTED IN PRESS GALLERIES—Continued

MANAGING IP MAGAZINE—(202) 246–6631; 5815 Colfax Avenue, Alexandria, VA 22311: Patrick Ross.

MANUFACTURING & TECHNOLOGY NEWS—(703) 750–2664; P.O. Box 36, Annandale, VA 22003: Richard A. McCormack.

MASS TRANSIT LAWYER—(703) 548–5177; P.O. Box 320308, Alexandria, VA 22320: Thomas S. Robinson.

MCGRAW-HILL CO.—(202) 383–2000; 1200 G Street, NW., Suite 1000, Washington, DC 20005: Catherine Cash, Keith T. Chu, Paul G. Ciampoli, Hilary C. Costa, Martin J. Coyne, Geoffrey W. Craig, Steven D. Dolley, Amy Fickling, Jason L. Fordney, William A. Freebairn, Peter T. Gartrell, Laura H. Gilcrest, Anastasia Gnezditskaia, Meghan Gordon, Keiron Greenhalgh, Brian Hansen, Tom Harrison, Elaine Hiruo, William Holland, Pamela E. Hunter, Thomas F. Ichniowski, Valarie N. Jackson, Regina Johnson, Nick G. Jonson, Nicholas P. Juliano, Rod W. Kuckro, Kathy Carolin C. Larsen, William E. Loveless, Jessica Marron, Karen McBeth Laping, Christopher J. Newkumet, Chang Noh, James J. Ostroff, Derek O. Sands, Brian J. Scheid, Stephanie Sharpe, Sarah C. Smith, Sayeh Tavangar, Tom Tiernan, Herman D. Wang, Mary E. Ward, Henry C. Webster, Esther Whieldon, Rodney A. White, Eric M. Wieser, Kate Winston, Yanmei Xie, Milena Yordanova-Kline.

METRO WEEKLY—(202) 638–6830; 1012 14th Street, NW., Suite 209, Washington, DC 20005: Chris R. Geidner.

MID-ATLANTIC RESEARCH—(800) 227–7140; 2805 St. Paul Street, Baltimore, MD 21218: Martha C. Powers, John Rees.

MII PUBLICATIONS—(202) 347–4822; 1800 I Street, NW., Suite 301, Washington, DC 20006: Ryan E. Hess, Cecilio Morales.

MINE SAFETY AND HEALTH NEWS—(703) 217–8270; 5935 4th Street, North Arlington, VA 22203: Brad A. Kukuk, Katharine Snyder.

NATION—(202) 546–2239; 110 Maryland Avenue, NE., Suite 308, Washington, DC 20002: Christopher L. Hayes, Gregory R. Kaufmann, George L. Zornick.

NATIONAL JOURNAL—(202) 739–8400; 600 New Hampshire Avenue, NW., Washington, DC 20037: Julie L. Abramson, Marc Ambinder, James A. Barnes, David Beard, Olga Belogolova, Lindsey Boerma, Ronald J. Brownstein, Michael Catalini, Kenneth Chamberlain, Niraj Chokshi, Matthew Cooper, Clive Crook, Coral Davenport, Susan J. Davis, Yochi Dreazen, Julia L. Edwards, Isobel Ellis, Tim Fernholz, Ronald Fournier, Maggie Fox, Sydney J. Freedberg, Jr., Althea Fung, Major Garrett, Charles A. Green, Jerry Hagstrom, David M. Hatch, Christopher Heller, Catherine Hollander, James E. Humes, Fawn Johnson, Andrew Joseph, Rebecca Kaplan, Naureen Khan, James Kitfield, Ethan Klapper, Jaculine M. Koszczuk, Adam Kushner, Aamer Madhani, Jason Mann, Clifford Marks, Chuck A. McCutcheon, Brian McGill, Carrie Mihalcik, Ryan Morris, Katy O'Donnell, Louis Peck, Theresa Poulson, Sophie A. Quinton, Beth Reinhard, S. Scott Rohrer, John J. Ryan, Terence Samuel, Margot Sanger-Katz, Gregg Thomas Sangillo, Sara Sorcher, Monica C. Sullivan, Alissa Swango, Jim Tankersley, Stuart Taylor, Jr., Ben Terris, Kirk Victor, Patsy Wilson.

NATIONAL LAW JOURNAL—(202) 457–0686; 1730 M Street, NW., Suite 802, Washington, DC 20036: Marcia Coyle, Virginia W. Greene, Matthew L. Huisman, David H. Ingram, Antony E. Mauro, Andrew D. Ramonas, Michael A. Scarcella, Zoe M. Tillman.

NATIONAL MORTGAGE NEWS—(571) 403–3837; 4401 Wilson Boulevard, Suite 910, Arlington, VA 22203: Brian Collins, Paul A. Muolo.

NATIONAL REVIEW—(202) 543–9226; 233 Pennsylvania Avenue, SE., 3rd Floor, Washington, DC 20003: Robert V. Costa, Kathryn J. Lopez, Ramesh Ponnuru, Andrew J. Stiles.

NATIONAL UNDERWRITER—(202) 370–4819; 1301 Connecticut Avenue, NW., Washington, DC 20036: Arthur D. Postal.

NATURE—(202) 737–2355; 968 National Press Building, Washington, DC 20045: Karen H. Kaplan, Richard A. Monastersky, Eugene I. Russo, Ivan Semeniuk, Jeffrey S. Tollefson, Meredith K. Wadman.

NEW REPUBLIC—(202) 508–4444; 1331 H Street, NW., Suite 700, Washington, DC 20005: Esther M. Breger, Alexander C. Hart, John B. Judis, Nathan M. Pippenger, Bradford T. Plumer, Jeffrey M. Rosen, Noam J. Scheiber, Walter E. Shapiro, Tiffany L. Stanley, Simon van Zuylen-Wood.

NEW YORK JEWISH WEEK—(703) 978–4724; 8713 Braeburn Drive, Annandale, VA 22003: James David Besser.

NEW YORKER—(202) 955–0960; 1730 Rhode Island Avenue, NW., Suite 603, Washington, DC 20036: Ryan C. Lizza.

NEWBAY MEDIA—(703) 852–4600; 5285 Shawnee Road, Suite 100, Alexandria, VA 22312: Joseph J. Smith, Leslie P. Stimson.

NEWS BITES—(202) 723–2477; 1712 Taylor Street, NW., Washington, DC 20011: German Munoz, Goody L. Solomon.

NEWSMAX—(301) 279–5818; 2516 Stratton Drive, Potomac, MD 20854: Ronald B. Kessler, Kenneth R. Timmerman.

NEWSWEEK—(202) 626–2000; 1750 Pennsylvania Avenue, NW., Suite 1220, Washington, DC 20006: Eleanor Clift, Laura M. Colarusso, Eve K. Conant, Robin Givhan, Claudia Kalb, Howard Kurtz,

PERIODICALS REPRESENTED IN PRESS GALLERIES—Continued

Eli Lake, Sandra McElwaine, Lois Romano, Robert J. Samuelson, Daniel E. Stone, Andrew Sullivan, Michael J. Tomasky.

NUCLEAR INTELLIGENCE WEEKLY—(202) 662–0706; 1411 K Street, NW., Suite 602, Washington, DC 20005: Samuel R. Tranum.

OIL & GAS JOURNAL—(703) 533–1552; 7013 Jefferson Avenue, Falls Church, VA 22042: Nicholas J. Snow.

OUTLOOK MAGAZINE—(202) 629–4321; 1419 R Street, NW., #41, Washington, DC 20009: Ashish K. Sen.

PEOPLE MAGAZINE—(202) 861–4000; 1130 Connecticut Avenue, NW., Suite 900, Washington, DC 20036: Sandra J. Sobieraj Westfall.

PHARMACEUTICAL EXECUTIVE—(301) 656–4634; 7715 Rocton Avenue, Chevy Chase, MD 20815: Jill Wechsler.

PODER—(703) 707–0236; 230 Darius Lane, Reston, VA 20191: Dolia E. Pettingell.

POLITICO—(703) 647–8700; 1100 Wilson Boulevard, 6th Floor, Arlington, VA 22209: Zachary G. Abrahamson, Jonathan J. Allen, Michael P. Allen, Molly Ball, Andrew T. Barr, Dan Berman, Josh Boak, Brooks Boliek, Robin L. Bravender, John Bresnahan, Carrie D. Budoff Brown, Talia N. Buford, Alexander I. Burns, David P. Catanese, Marin Cogan, Brett G. Coughlin, Jeanne M. Cummings, Darius A. Dixon, Matthew DoBias, Edward-Isaac Dovere, Jennifer Epstein, Reid Epstein, Joseph L. Feder, Chris Frates, Elizabeth M. Frerking, Joshua A. Gerstein, Andrew J. Glass, Darren T. Goode, D. Craig Gordon, Timothy P. Greive, Alexander C. Guillen, Jennifer A. Haberkorn, Bill B. Hamilton, Dave A. Hansen, John F. Harris, G. Robert Hillman, Dan Hirschhorn, James P. Hohmann, Charles E. Hoskinson, Kasie Hunt, Alex Isenstadt, Danielle D. Jones, Martin J. Kady II, Jess M. Kamen, Seung Min Kim, Robert P. King, Kim Kingsley-McMearty, Sarah L. Kliff, Eliza V. Krigman, Min Jung Lee, David Levinthal, Sara D. Libby, Erika M. Lovley, Charles G. Mahtesian, David F. Mark, Jonathan L. Martin, Jennifer M. Martinez, Lucy McCalmont, Laura K. McGann, Jason Millman, David R. Nather, William D. Nichols, Katherine R. Nocera, Brett Norman, Anna A. Palmer, Amie M. Parnes, Abigail D. Phillip, Manu K. Raju, David S. Rauf, Patrick C. Reis, Kevin P. Robillard, David E. Rogers, Tony Romm, Frederick J. Ryan, Jr., Darren Samuelsohn, Emily Schultheis, Jake S. Sherman, Roger M. Simon, Rachel Smolkin, Juana Summers, Karin E. Tanabe, Byron C. Tau, Glenn H. Thrush, Alexander Trowbridge, James Vandehei, Kenneth P. Vogel, Elizabeth A. Wasserman, Diane Webber, Joseph Williams, Scott B. Wong, Michael Zapler.

PRESS ASSOCIATES—(202) 898–4825; 2605 P Street, NW., Suite A, Washington, DC 20007: Janet M. Brown, Mark J. Gruenberg.

PROCESO—(202) 737–1538; 529 14th Street, NW., Suite 1117, Washington, DC 20045: J. Jesus Esquivel.

PRODUCT SAFETY LETTER—(301) 229–1027; 4907 Bayard Boulevard, Bethesda, MD 20816: Sean F. Oberle.

PROFESSIONAL PILOT MAGAZINE—(703) 370–0606; 30 South Quaker Lane, Suite 300, Alexandria, VA 22314: Phil Rose.

PROGRESSIVE BUSINESS PUBLICATIONS—(410) 349–8200; 1528 Circle Drive, Annapolis, MD 21409: Thomas A. Guay.

PUBLIC LANDS NEWS—(703) 553–0552; 133 South Buchanan Street, Arlington, VA 22204: James B. Coffin.

PUBLIC UTILITIES FORTNIGHTLY—(703) 847–7720; 8229 Boone Boulevard, Suite 400, Vienna, VA 22182: Bruce W. Radford.

RADIO BUSINESS REPORT—(703) 670–2860; 4402 Boxwood Drive, Montclair, VA 22025: Carl A. Marcucci.

RESEARCH INSTITUTE OF AMERICA GROUP—(202) 842–1546; 1275 K Street, NW., Suite 875, Washington, DC 20005: LaTasha S. Durrett, Velma Goodwine, Soyoung Ho, William Lesesne.

ROLL CALL—(202) 824–6800; 77 K Street, NE., 8th Floor, Washington, DC 20002: Kate Ackley, Ambreen E. Ali, Rachael M. Bade, Amanda M. Becker, Christina M. Bellantoni, Sara E. Bondioli, Jessica L. Brady, Eliza Newlin Carney, Steven T. Dennis, Jason J. Dick, Emma Dumain, David M. Drucker, Jessica M. Estepa, Marilyn Gates-Davis, Emily A. Heil, Morton M. Kondracke, Sarah Jane M. Lorber, Alison B. McSherry, Joshua Miller, Scott R. Montgomery, Daniel J. Newhauser, Emily M. Ortman, Stephen P. Peoples, Emily K. Pierce, Warren Rojas, Bennett Roth, Humberto Sanchez, Meredith H. Shiner, Paul B. Singer, Katie Smith, John Stanton, Melanie R. Starkey, Jonathan Strong, William G. Taylor, Shira Toeplitz, Kyle K. Trygstad, Kate A. Tummarello, Blake K. Whitney, Lauren Whittington.

ROTHENBERG POLITICAL REPORT—(202) 546–2822; 77 K Street, NE., 8th Floor, Washington, DC 20002: Nathan Gonzales, Stuart Rothenberg.

SALON.COM—(202) 413–7841; 1804 Kenyon Street, NW., Washington, DC 20010: Jefferson Morley.

SATELLITE BUSINESS NEWS—(202) 785–0505; 5505 Connecticut Avenue, NW., #281, Washington, DC 20015: Bob Scherman, Jeffrey Williams.

SET-ASIDE ALERT—(301) 229–5561; 7720 Wisconsin Avenue, Suite 213, Bethesda, MD 20814: Warren P. Corbett.

SLATE—(202) 261–1393; 1350 Connecticut Avenue, Suite 400, Washington, DC 20036: Christopher Beam, Andrew Bouve, John F. Dickerson, Joshua Levin, Dahlia Hannah Lithwick, Michael Newman, Timothy

PERIODICALS REPRESENTED IN PRESS GALLERIES—Continued

Robert Noah, David Plotz, William B. Saletan, Jack Shafer, Bill D. Smee, David A. Weigel, Chris E. Wilson.

SPACE NEWS—(703) 658–8400; 6883 Commercial Drive, Springfield, VA 22159: Rachel Bernstein, S. Turner Brinton, Amy E. Klamper, Daniel M. Leone.

STERN—(646) 546–8458; 2480 16th Street, NW., #719, Washington, DC 20009: Martin Knobbe.

SYNOPSIS—(703) 498–7959; 20312 Aspenwood Lane, Montgomery Village, MD 20886: Ellen B. Milhiser.

TALKING POINTS MEMO—(202) 758–3048; 236 Massachusetts Avenue, NE., Suite 610, Washington, DC 20002: Brian A. Beutler, Igor Bobic, Susan J. Crabtree, David M. Kurtz, Evan McMorris-Santoro, Ryan Reilly, Benjamin V. Sarlin, Aaron M. Wiener.

TAX NOTES—(703) 533–4400; 400 South Maple Avenue, Suite 400, Falls Church, VA 22046: David Scott S. Antonides, Brian D. Bardwell, Michael J. Beller, Ulrike M. Bergin, Stephanie J. Berrong, Laura E. Breech, Simon A. Brown, John M. Buhl, Jennifer Carr, Jeremiah G. Coder, Joseph DiSciullo, Nicole A. Duarte, Amy S. Elliott, Wesley A. Elmore, Meredith Fath, Lissa Fried, Michael Gleeson, Robert Goulder, Amy L. Hamilton, Joann Christine Harris, Shonda Humphrey, David Randall Jackson, Jr., Thomas Jaworski, Eric L. Kroh, Anita I. Nagelis, Ashley C. Newell, Charles C. O'Toole, Kristen A. Parillo, Bergrek Phillips, Drew M. Pierson, Alexia Ransom, Karen Jeanne Setze, Scott Andrew Sheets, Doug Sheppard, Margaret Shreve, Quintin Simmons, Jasper B. Smith, David D. Stewart, Frederick W. Stokeld, Shamik N. Trivedi, David T. van den Berg, Nicola M. White, Risa D. Williams, Sam Young, Gulnar Zaman.

TECHNOLOGY COMMERCIALIZATION—(703) 522–6648; P.O. Box 100595, Arlington, VA 22210: Neil A. MacDonald.

TELECOMMUNICATIONS REPORTS—(202) 842–8923; 1015 15th Street, NW., 10th Floor, Washington, DC 20005: John P. Curran, Carrie R. DeLeon, Ted Gotsch, Paul S. Kirby, Matthew R. Squire, Lynn E. Stanton.

THOMPSON PUBLISHING GROUP—(202) 872–4000; 805 15th Street, NW., 3rd Floor, Washington, DC 20005: Jerry Ashworth, Cameron S. Ayers, Andrew D. Brownstein, Max S. Busetti, Elizabeth M. Casabona, Gwendolyn Cofield, Richie A. Crider, Leah N. DiPietro, Charles J. Edwards, Adrianne Fielding, Erika Fitzpatrick, Joan Marie Flynn, Chelsea M. Gamber, Travis Hicks, William S. Hoffman III, Chad E. Hudnall, John F. Iekel, Todd H. Leeuwenburgh, Daniel J. Macy, Margaret H. Miller, James C. Proescholdt, Mark Reishus, Jeffrey W. Schomisch, David A. Slaughter, Dennis A. Tosh.

TIME MAGAZINE—(202) 861–4000; 1130 Connecticut Avenue, NW., Suite 900, Washington, DC 20036: Alex Altman, Melissa A. August, Massimo T. Calabresi, Michael Crowley, Michael W. Duffy, Steven M. Gray, Jay Newton-Small, Michael B. Scherer, Mark J. Thompson.

TOWNHALL—(703) 247–1251; 1901 North Moore Street, Suite 701, Arlington, VA 22209: Guy Benson, Kevin W. Glass, Elisabeth C. Meinecke, Catherine Pavlich.

TRANSPORTATION WEEKLY—(703) 371–1226; 2301 North Stafford Street, Arlington, VA 22207: Jeffrey J. Davis.

U.S. MEDICINE—(202) 488–0611; 350 G Street, SW., #N215, Washington, DC 20024: Sandra L. Basu, Stephen Spotswood.

U.S. NEWS & WORLD REPORT—(202) 955–2000; 1050 Thomas Jefferson Street, NW., Washington, DC 20007: Paul Bedard, Megan M. Handley, Mallie J. Kim, Alex P. Kingsbury, Danielle J. Kurtzleben, Alexander M. Parker, Jessica L. Rettig, Robert Schlesinger, Kenneth T. Walsh, Kira Zalan.

UCG—(301) 287–2700; 9737 Washingtonian Boulevard, Suite 100, Gaithersburg, MD 20878: Karen A. Anderson, Carl A. Ayers, Brit Galloway, Rachel Gantz, Robert Gough, Marci K. Heydt, Grant G. Huang, Anke B. Irgang, Scott G. Kraft, Karen S. Long Rayburn, Brian E. O'Shea, Daniel Oakley, Vincent E. Taylor, Lauren C. Williams.

USA JOURNAL—(202) 714–7330; P.O. Box 714, Washington, DC 20044: Janne Kum Cha Pak.

VANITY FAIR—(202) 244–3424; 5146 Klingle Street, NW., Washington, DC 20016: Maureen Orth, William W. Prochnau, Todd S. Purdum.

WASHINGTON BLADE—(202) 747–2077; 516 A Street, NE., #102, Washington, DC 20002: Louis M. Chibbaro, Jr., Chris Johnson.

WASHINGTON BUSINESS INFORMATION—(703) 538–7600; 300 North Washington Street, Falls Church, VA 22046: Virgil T. Dickson, David L. Pittman.

WASHINGTON BUSINESS JOURNAL—(703) 258–0845; 1555 Wilson Boulevard, Suite 400, Arlington, VA 22204: Kent D. Hoover.

WASHINGTON COUNSELETTER—(202) 244–6709; 5712 26th Street, NW., Washington, DC 20015: Deborah A. Kavruck.

WASHINGTON TRADE DAILY—(301) 946–0817; P.O. Box 1802, Wheaton, MD 20915: James R. Berger, Mary L. Berger.

WASHINGTON WATCH—(301) 263–9023; 5923 Onondaga Road, Bethesda, MD 20816: Kazutami Yamazaki.

WATERWAYS JOURNAL—(703) 524–2490; 5220 North Carlin Springs Road, Arlington, VA 22203: Carlo J. Salzano.

WEBSTER COMMUNICATIONS—(703) 525–4013; 3835 9th Street North, #401W, Arlington, VA 22203: James C. Webster.

PERIODICALS REPRESENTED IN PRESS GALLERIES—Continued

WEEKLY STANDARD—(202) 293–4900; 1150 17th Street, NW., Suite 505, Washington, DC 20036: Kari J. Barbic, Fred W. Barnes, Christopher S. Caldwell, Matthew J. Continetti, Terry Eastland, Andrew Ferguson, Daniel M. Halper, Stephen F. Hayes, Mark W. Hemingway, Jonathan V. Last, Victorino L. Matus, John M. McCormack, Lee H. Smith, Philip Terzian, Kelly J. Torrance, Michael R. Warren.

WHITAKER NEWSLETTERS—(240) 583–0280; P.O. Box 224, Spencerville, MD 20868: Joel Whitaker.

WIRED.COM—(202) 294–9523; 1816 New Hampshire Avenue, #908, Washington, DC 20009: Spencer J. Ackerman.

THE WRAP—(301) 585–0275; 1215 East-West Highway, #503, Silver Spring, MD 20910: Cassie M. Chew.

WORLD MAGAZINE—(202) 445–0454; 603 3rd Street, NE., Washington, DC 20002: Emily C. Belz, Edward L. Pitts.

YAHOO! NEWS—(202) 777–0017; 101 Constitution Avenue, NW., Suite 800W, Washington, DC 20001: Rachel R. Hartman, Christopher S. Moody, Claude P. Pruitt.

CONGRESSIONAL DISTRICT MAPS

ALABAMA—Congressional Districts—(7 Districts)

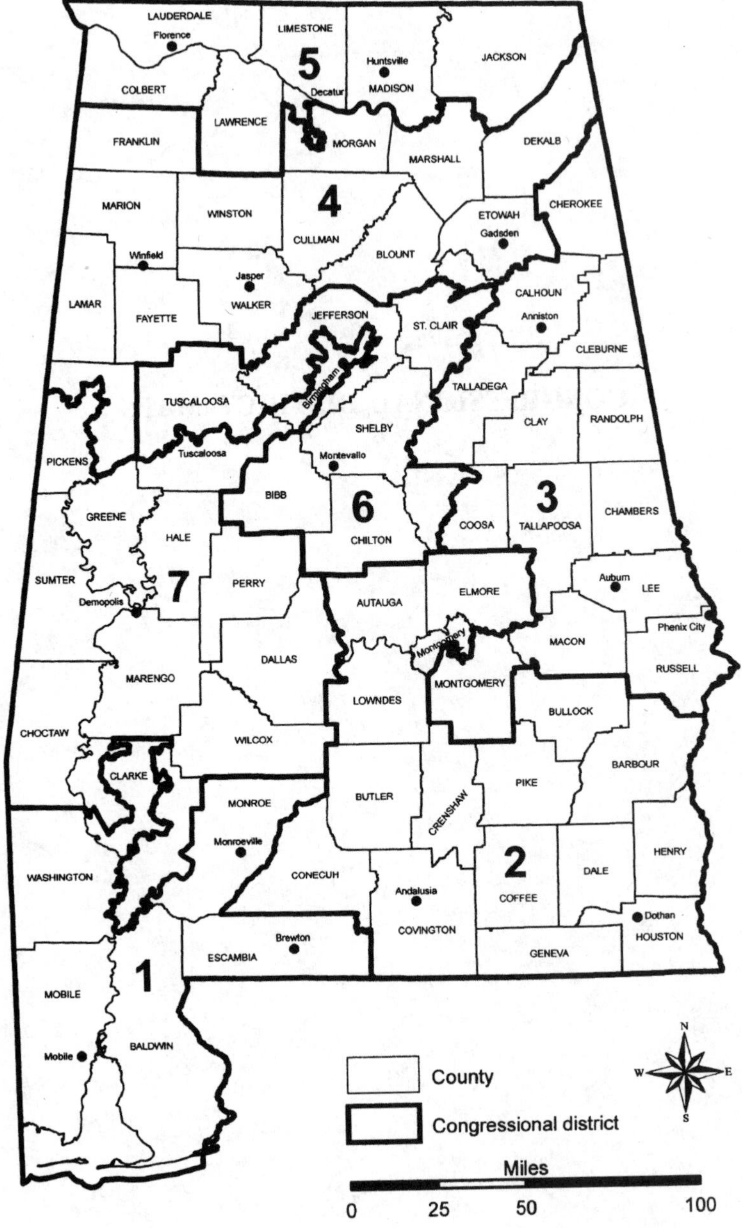

ALASKA—Congressional District—(1 District At Large)

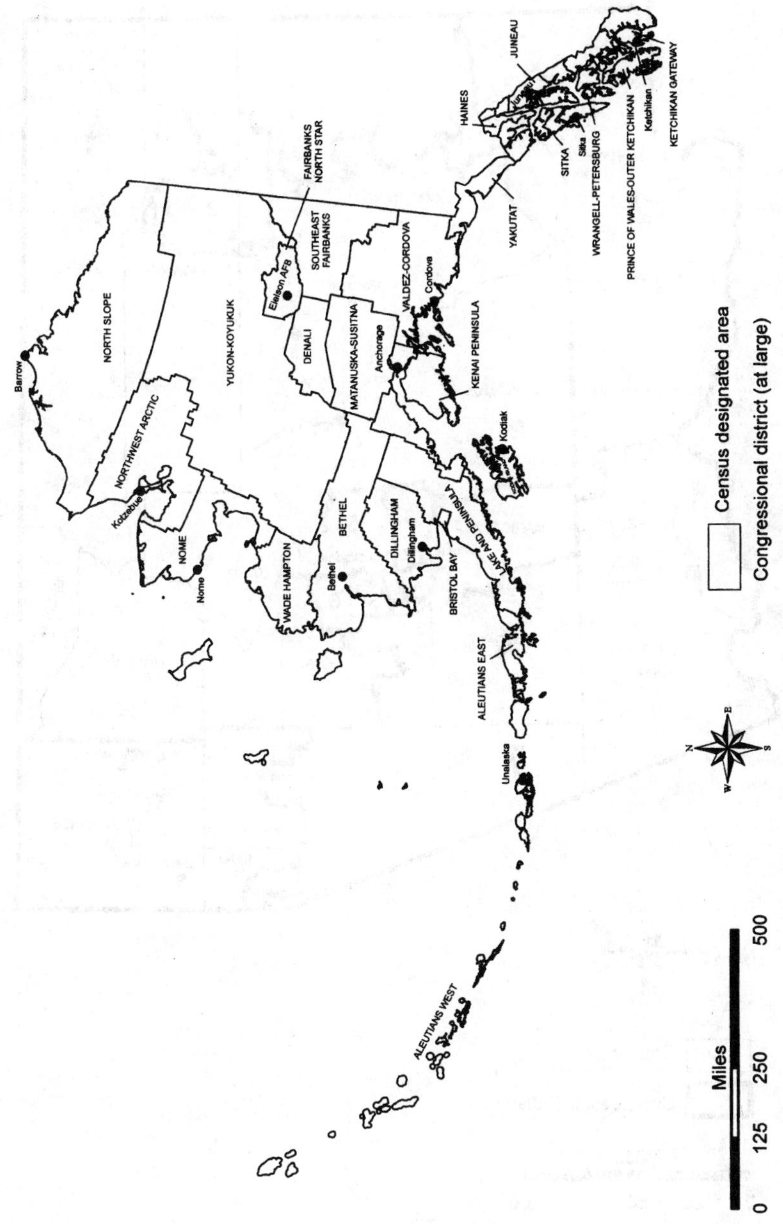

ARIZONA—Congressional Districts—(8 Districts)

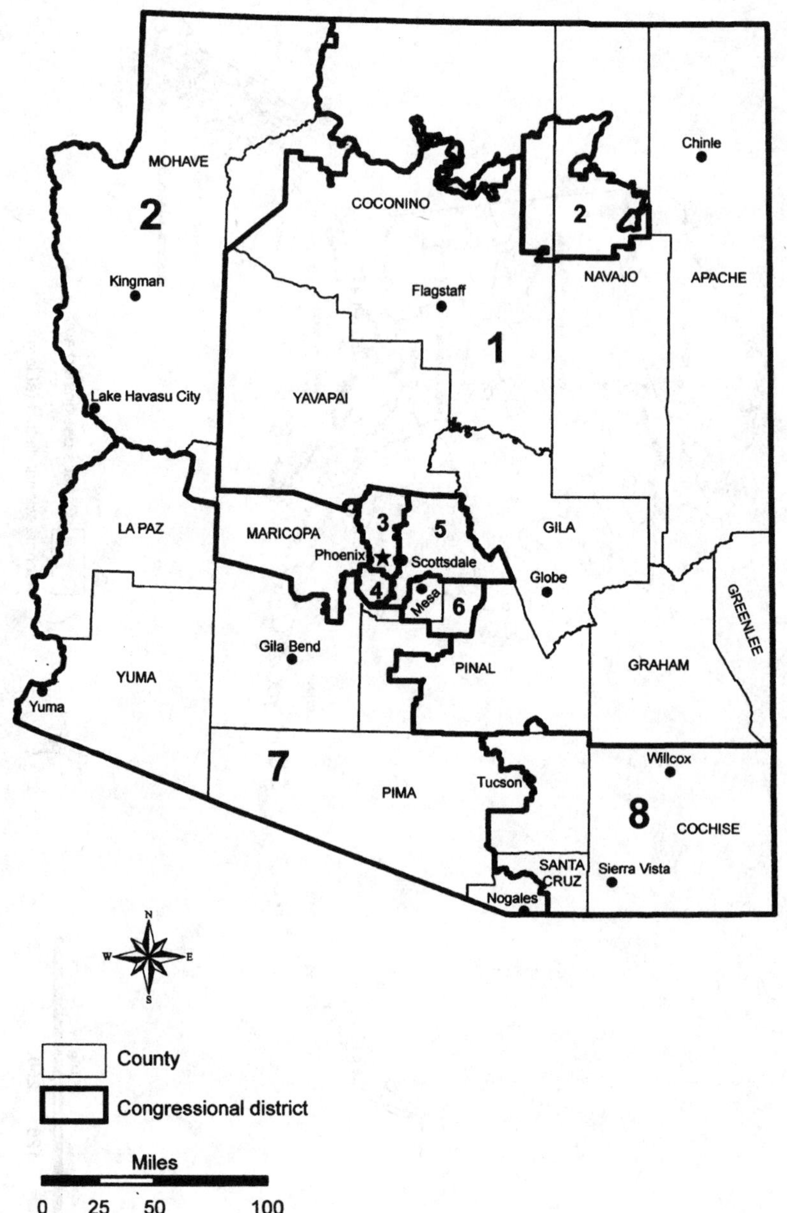

ARKANSAS—Congressional Districts—(4 Districts)

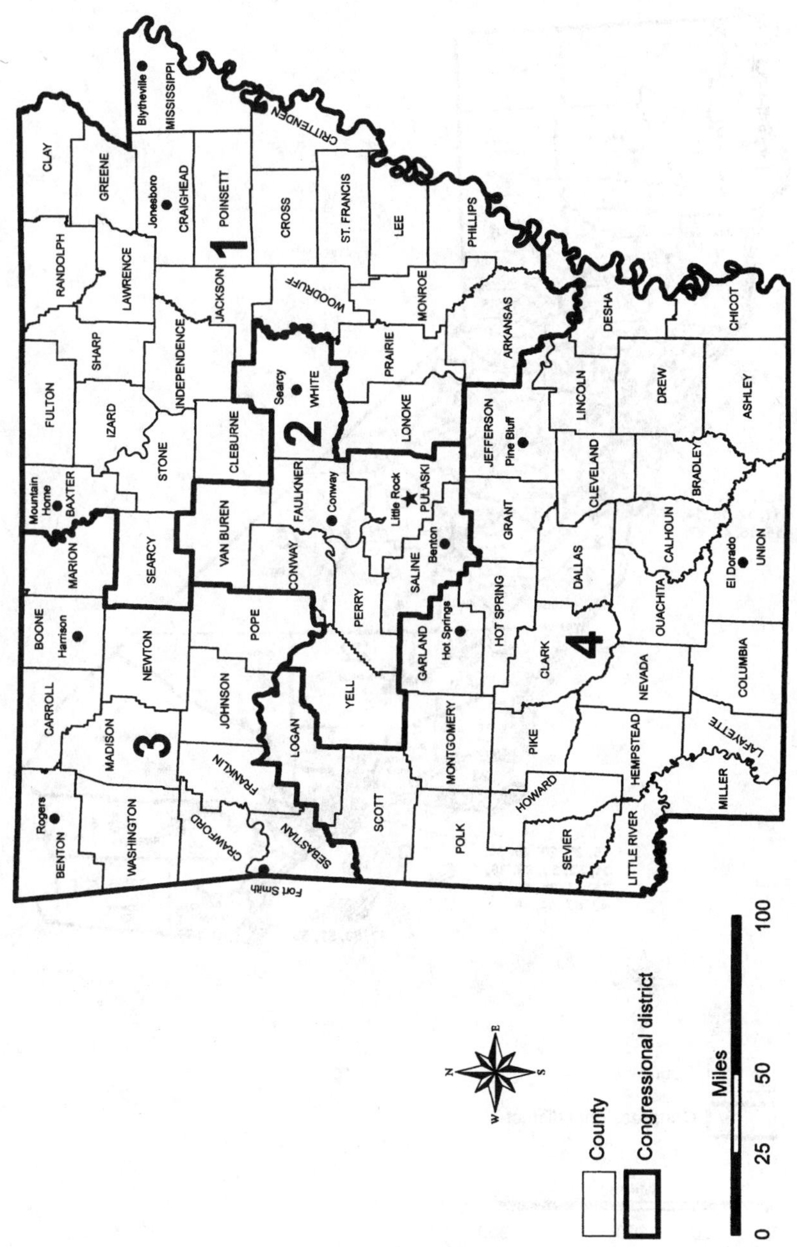

CALIFORNIA—Congressional Districts—(53 Districts)

COLORADO—Congressional Districts—(7 Districts)

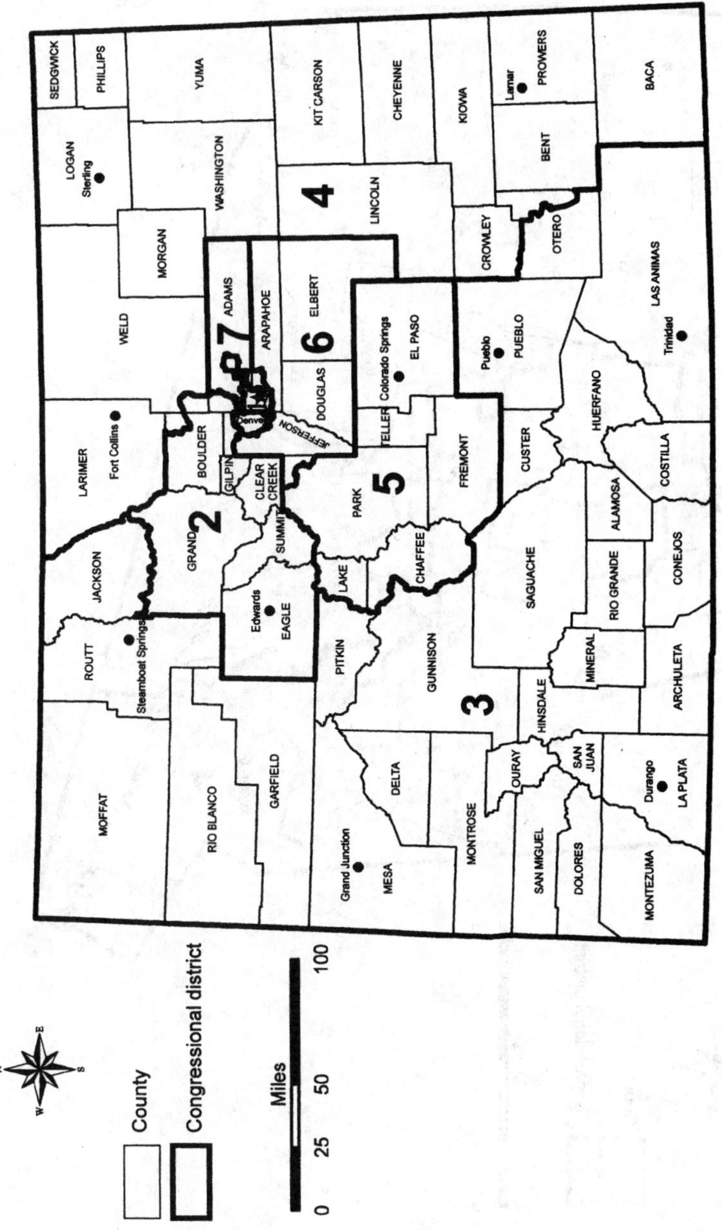

CONNECTICUT—Congressional Districts—(5 Districts)

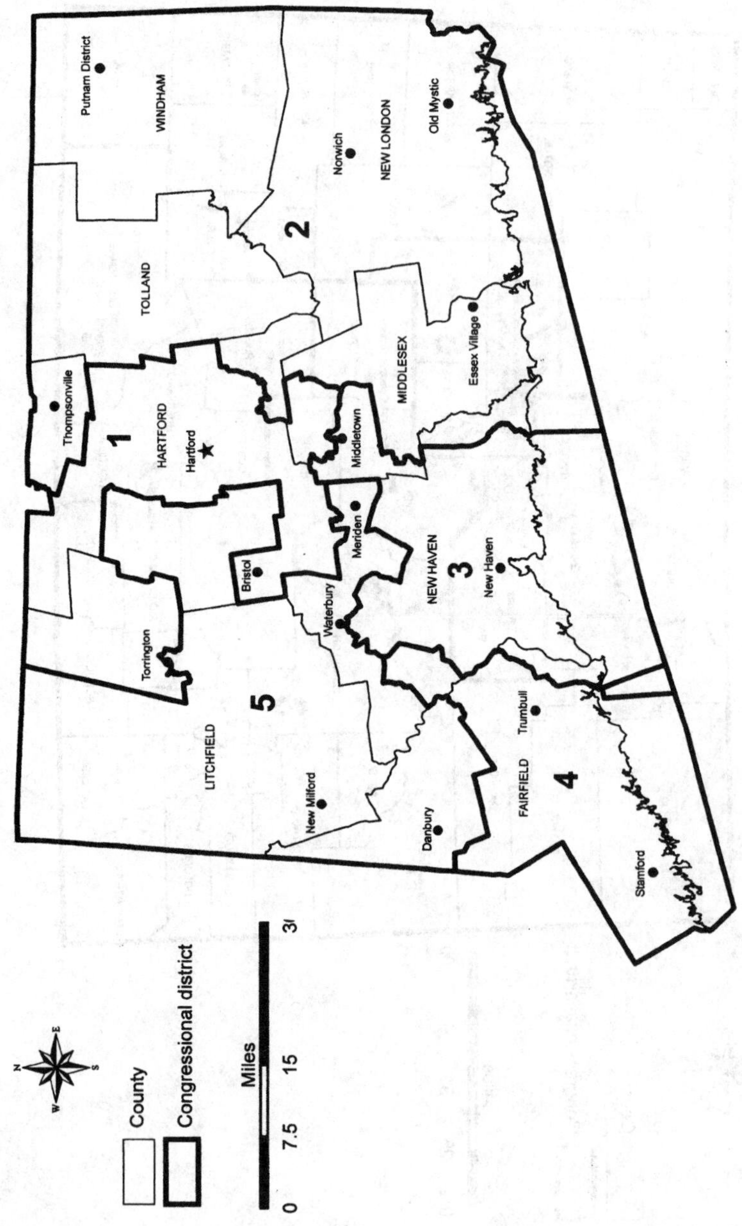

DELAWARE—Congressional District—(1 District At Large)

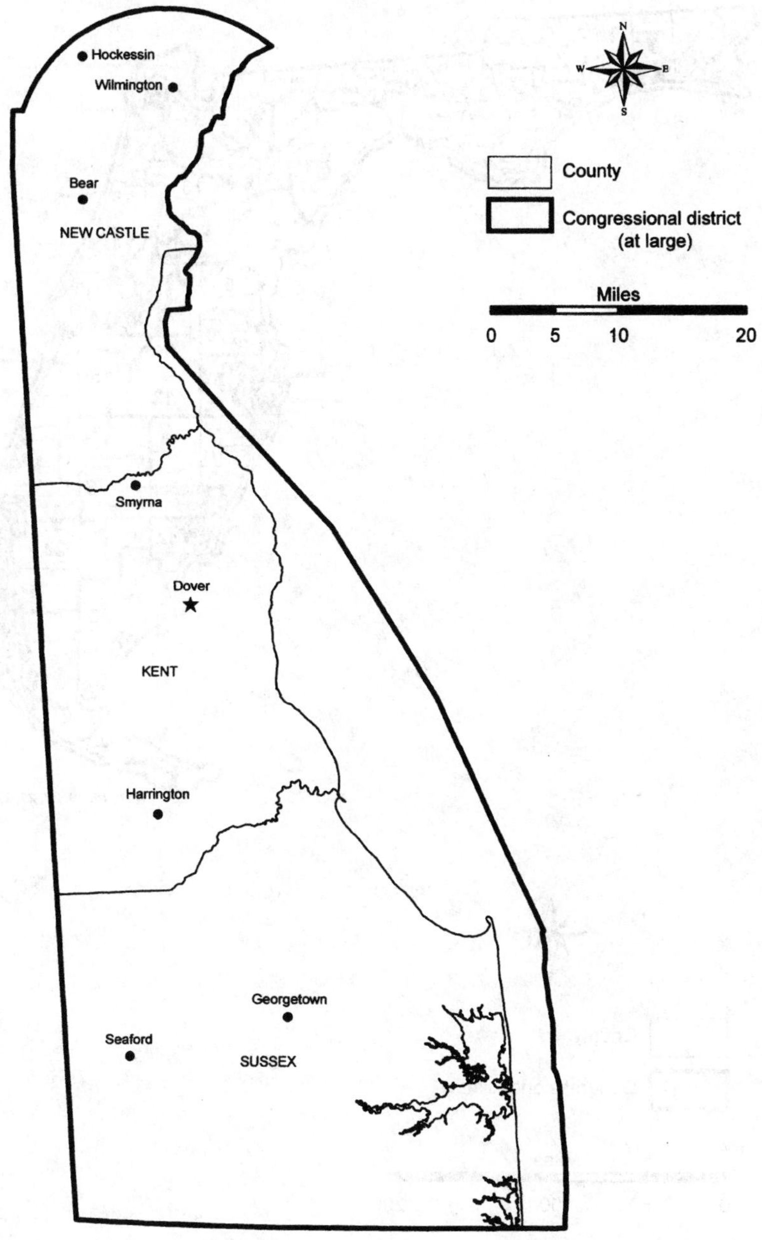

FLORIDA—Congressional Districts—(25 Districts)

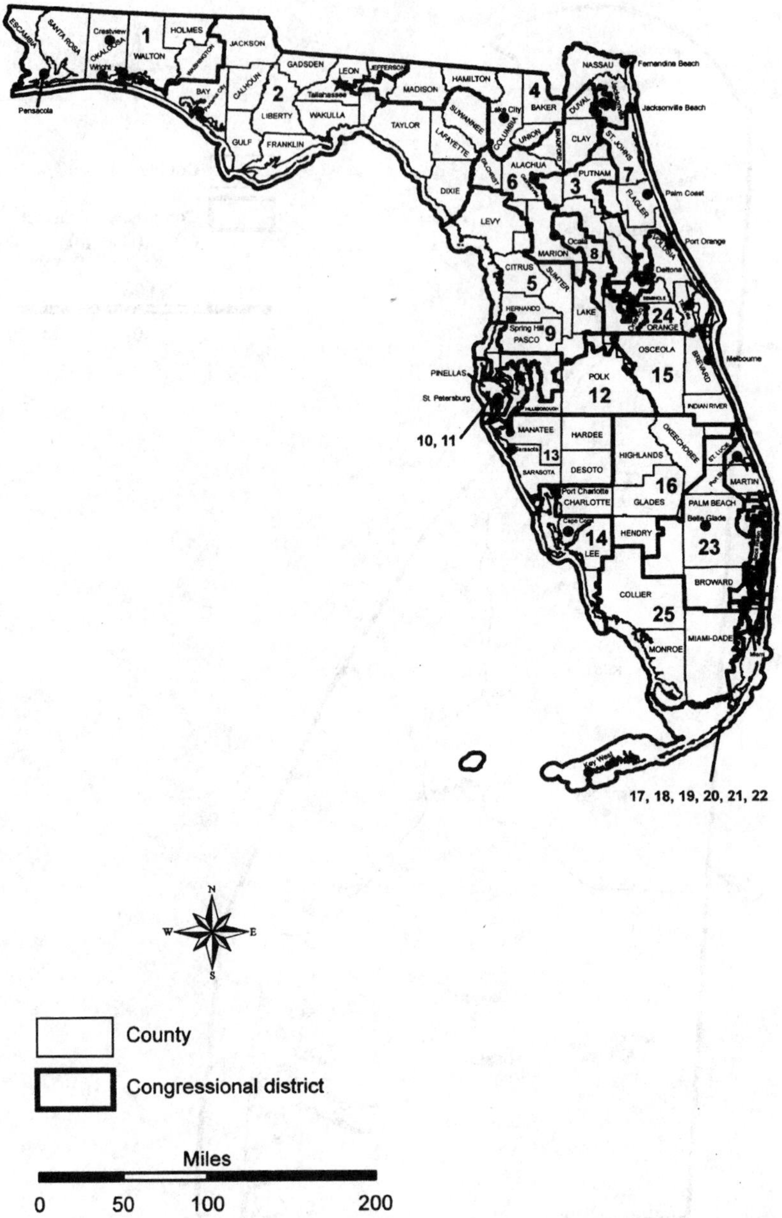

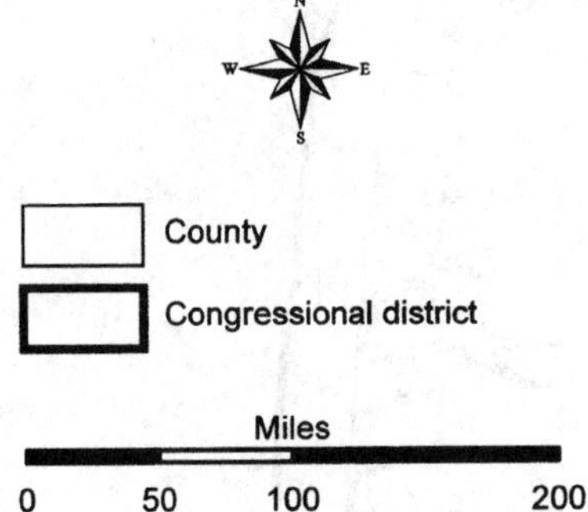

GEORGIA—Congressional Districts—(13 Districts)

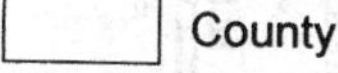

County

Congressional district
Effective May 06, 2005

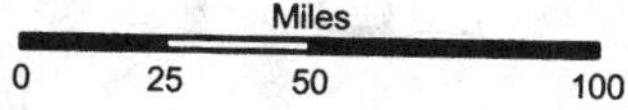

HAWAII—Congressional Districts—(2 Districts)

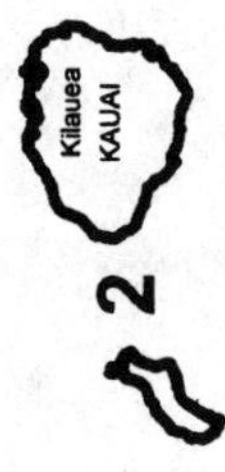

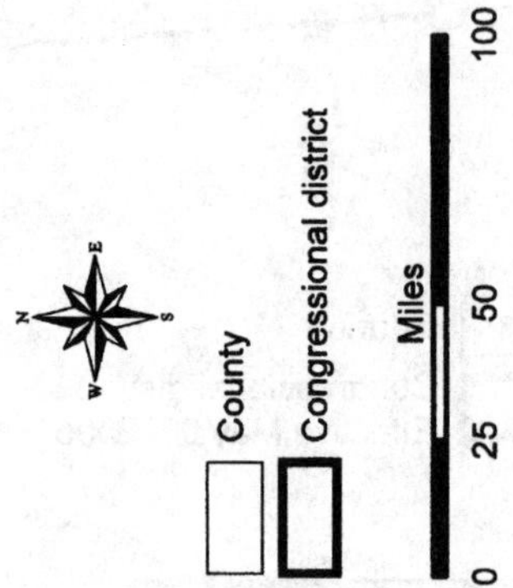

IDAHO—Congressional Districts—(2 Districts)

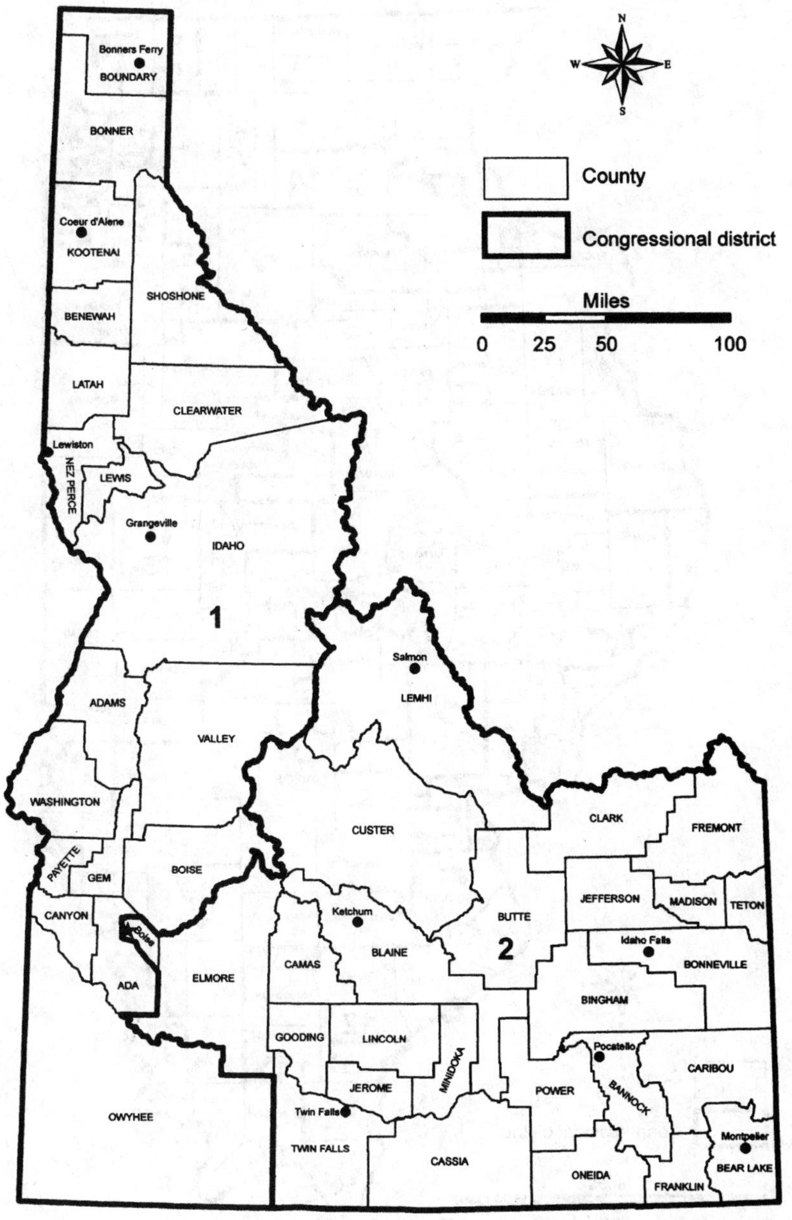

ILLINOIS—Congressional Districts—(19 Districts)

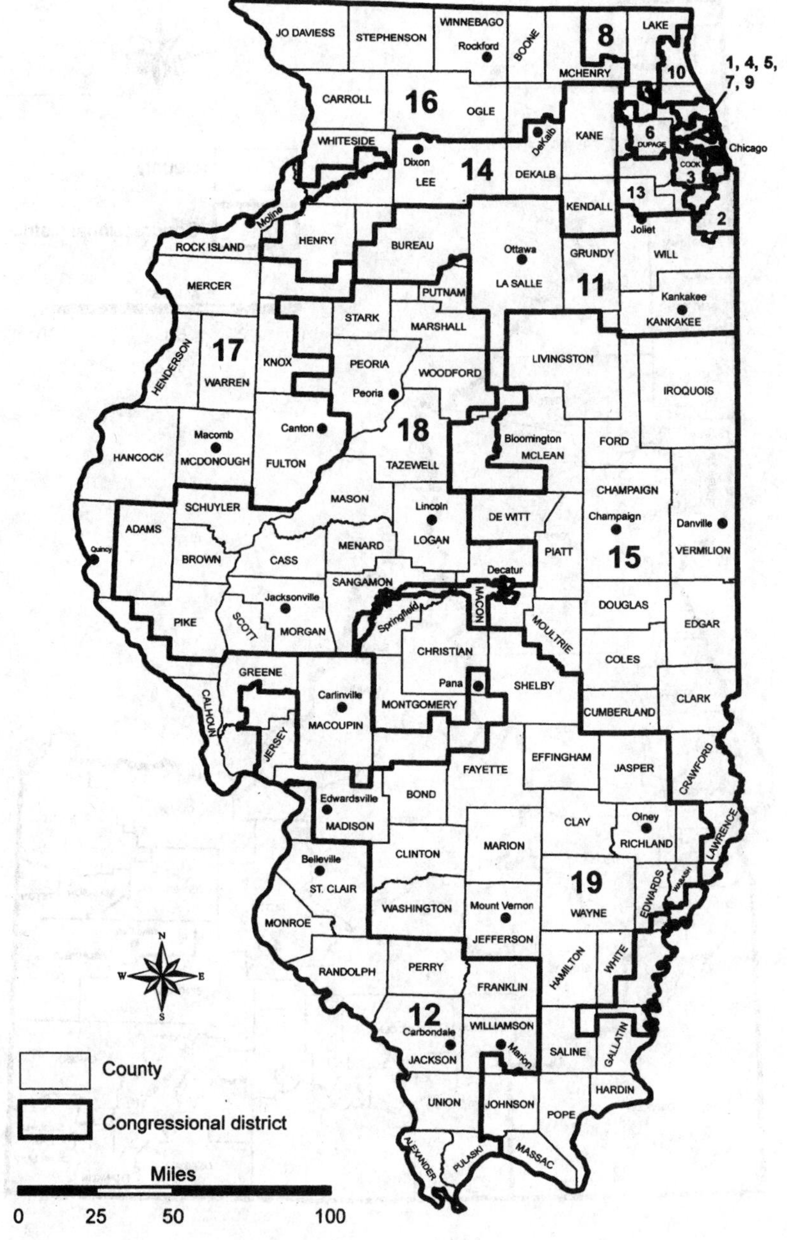

INDIANA—Congressional Districts—(9 Districts)

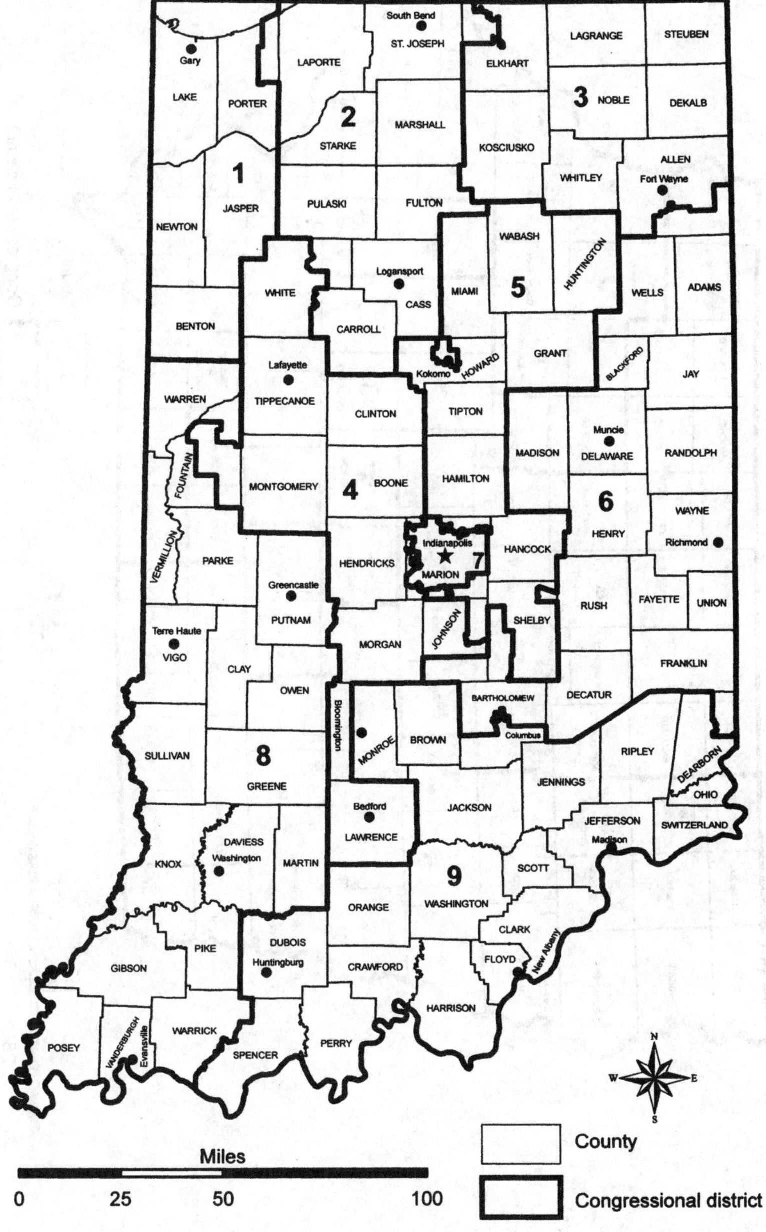

IOWA—Congressional Districts—(5 Districts)

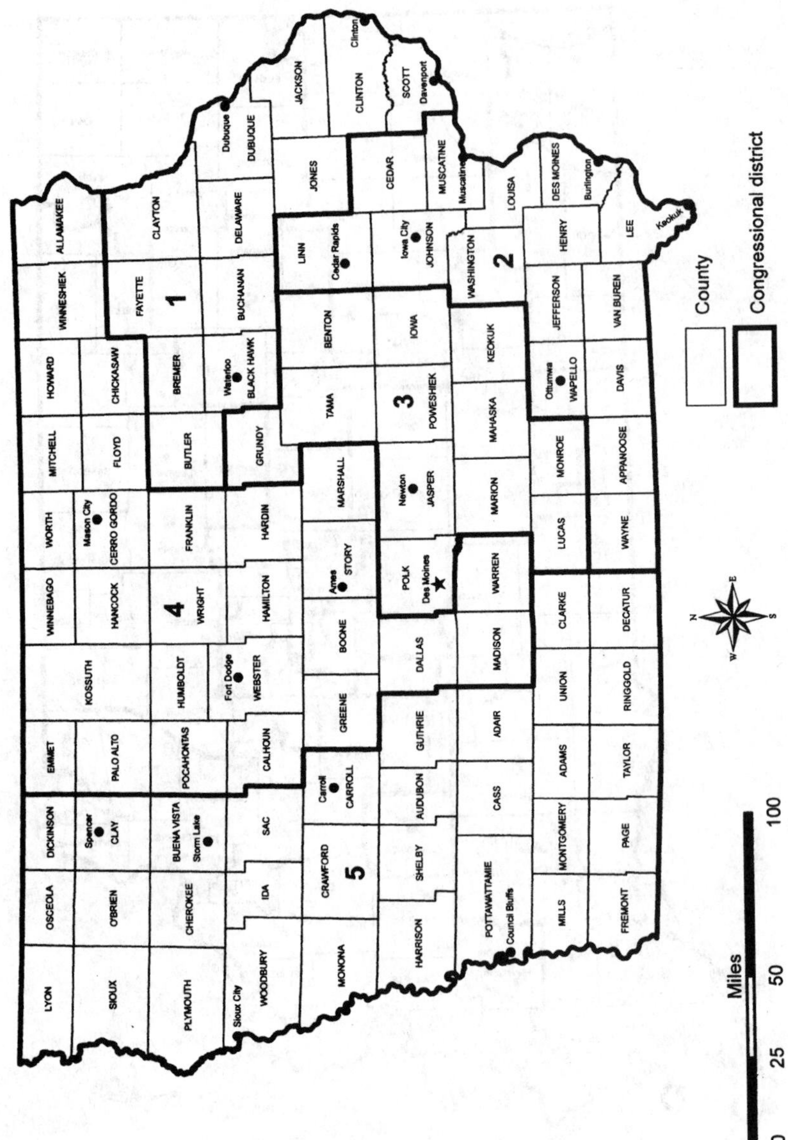

KANSAS—Congressional Districts—(4 Districts)

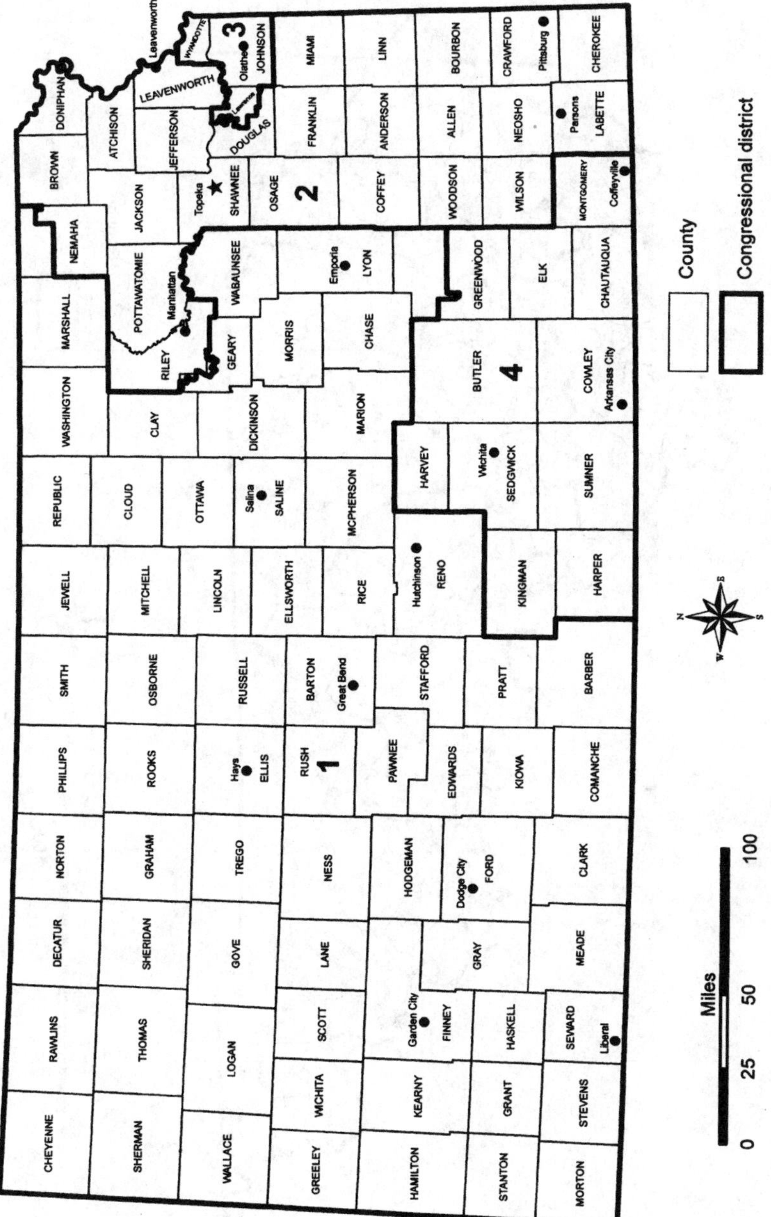

KENTUCKY—Congressional Districts—(6 Districts)

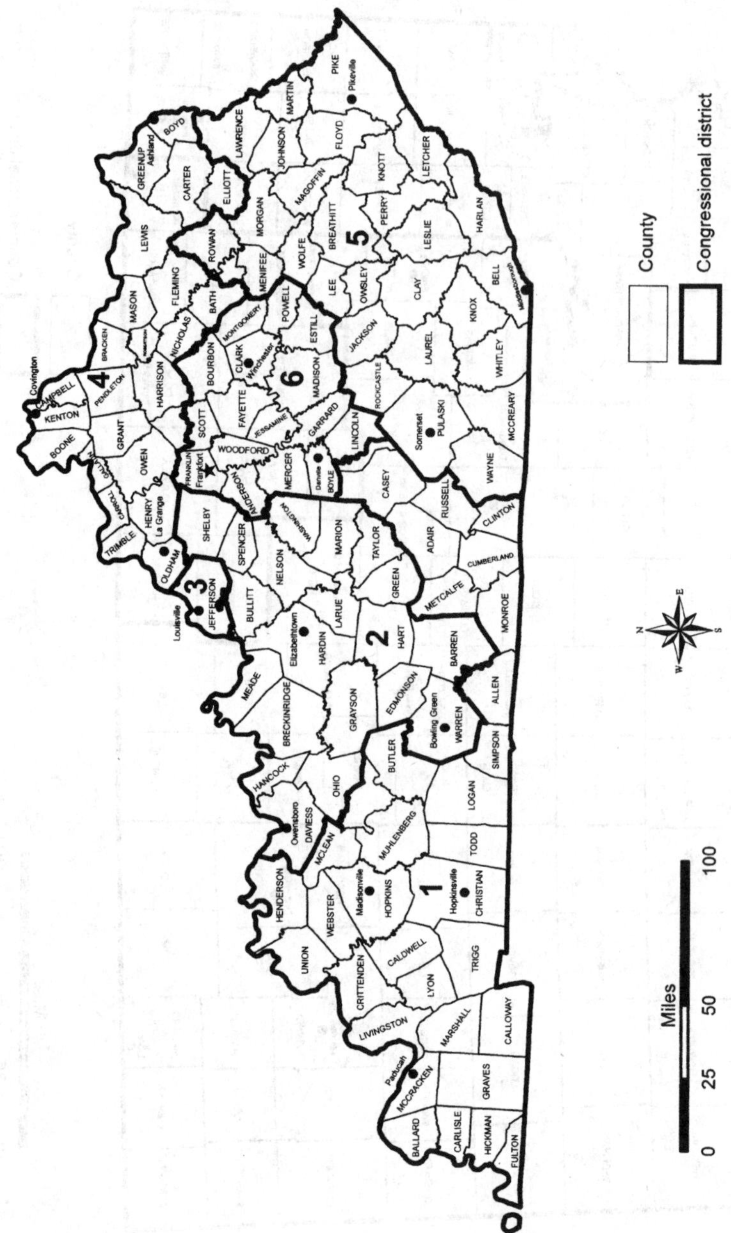

LOUISIANA—Congressional Districts—(7 Districts)

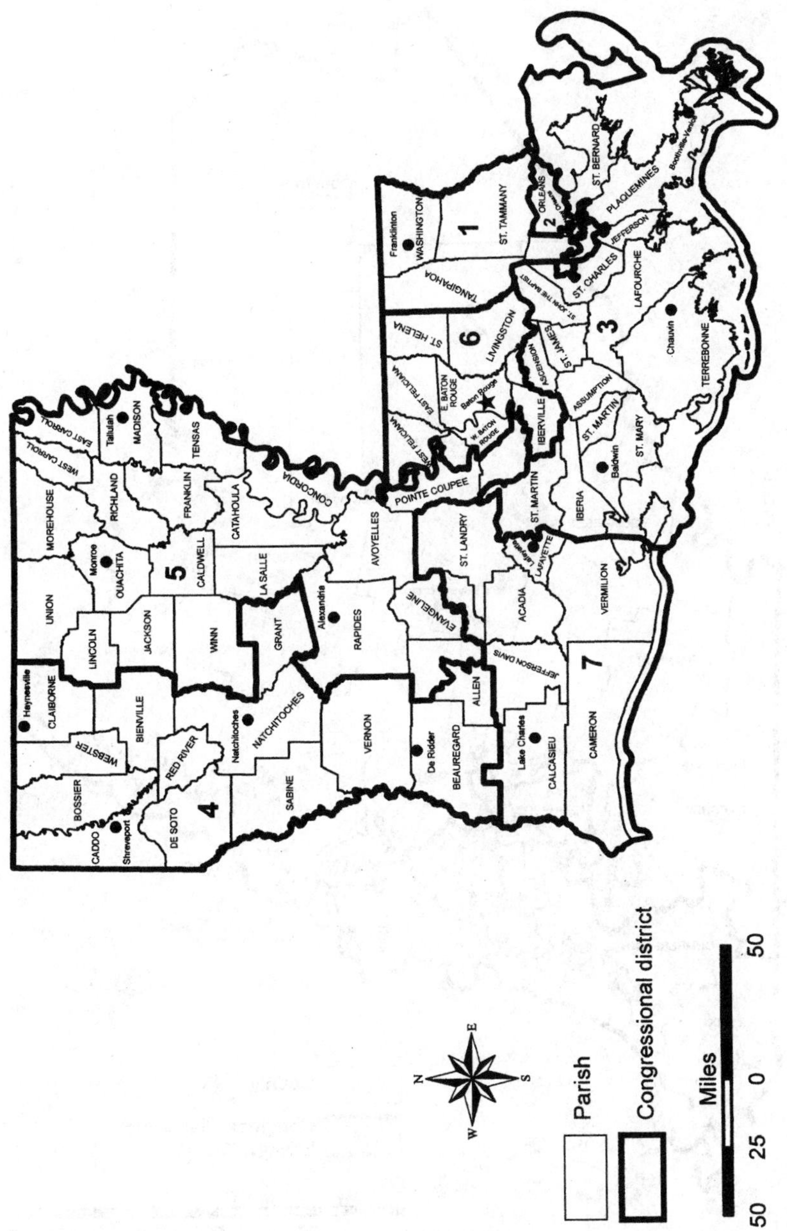

MAINE—Congressional Districts—(2 Districts)

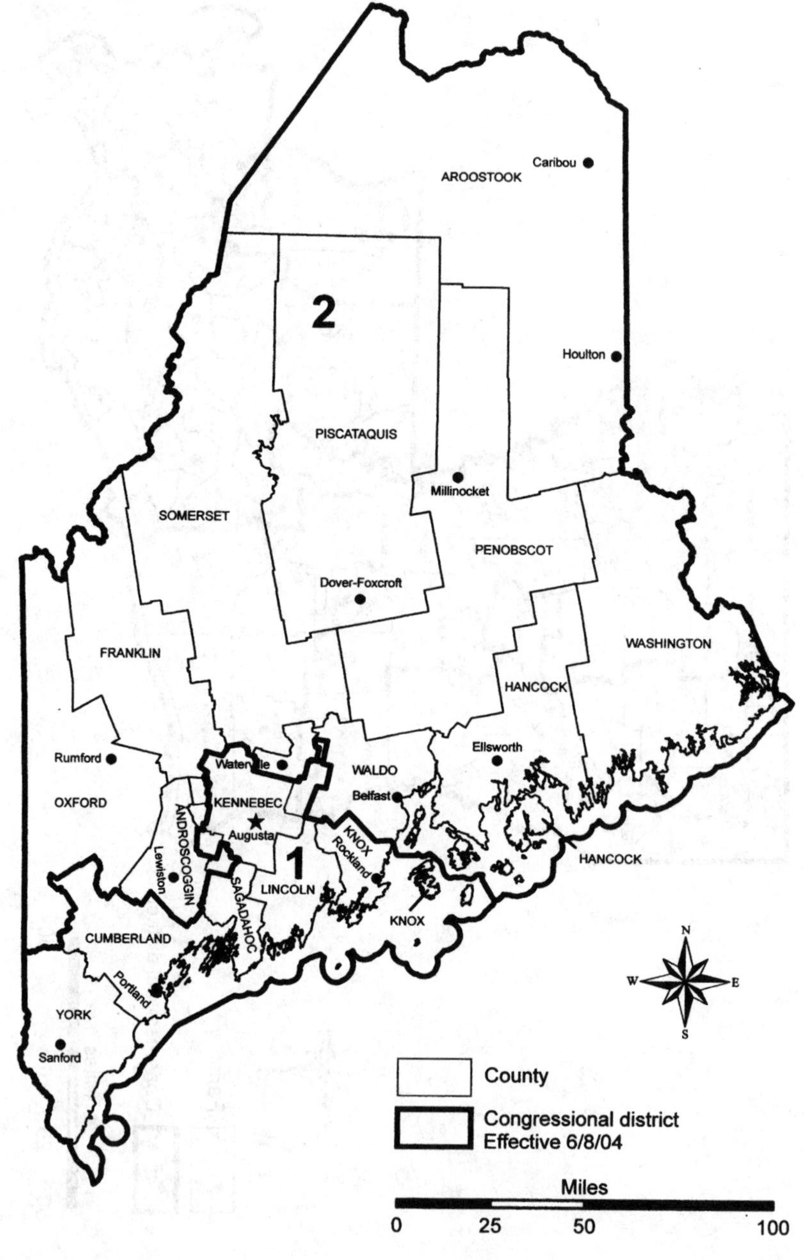

MARYLAND—Congressional Districts—(8 Districts)

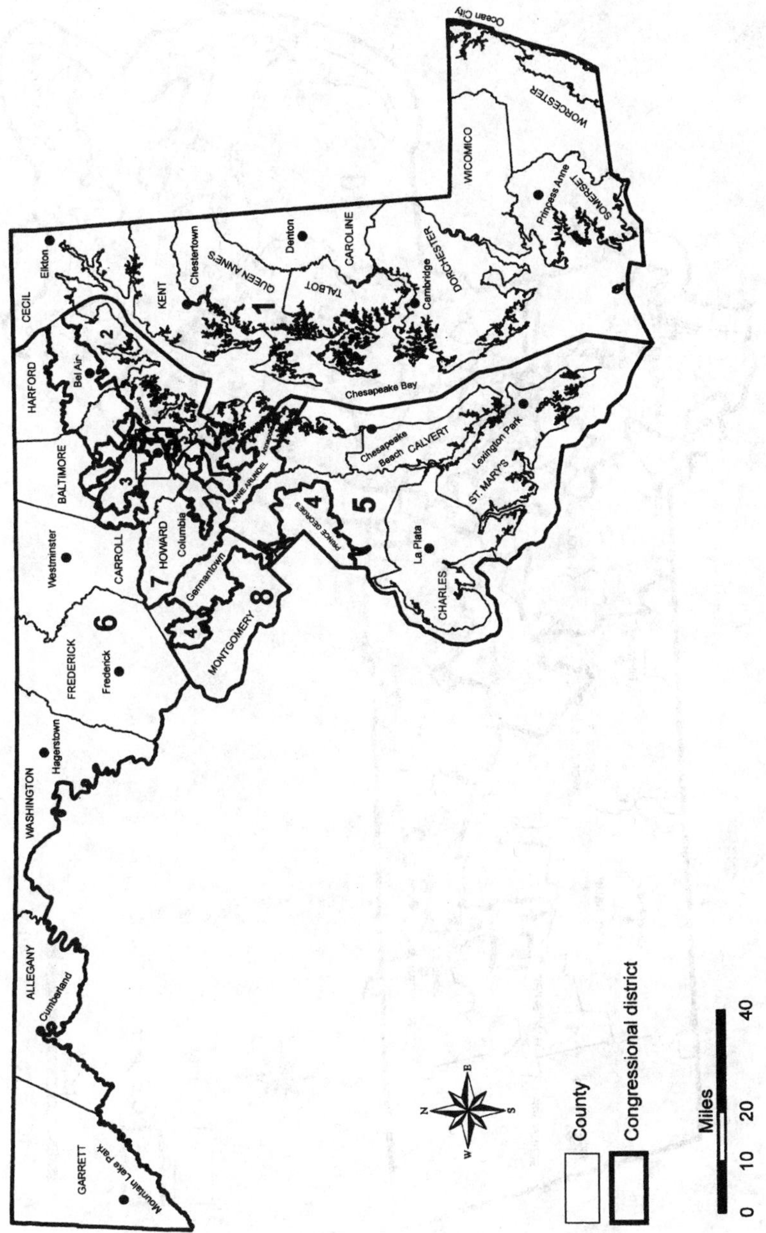

MASSACHUSETTS—Congressional Districts—(10 Districts)

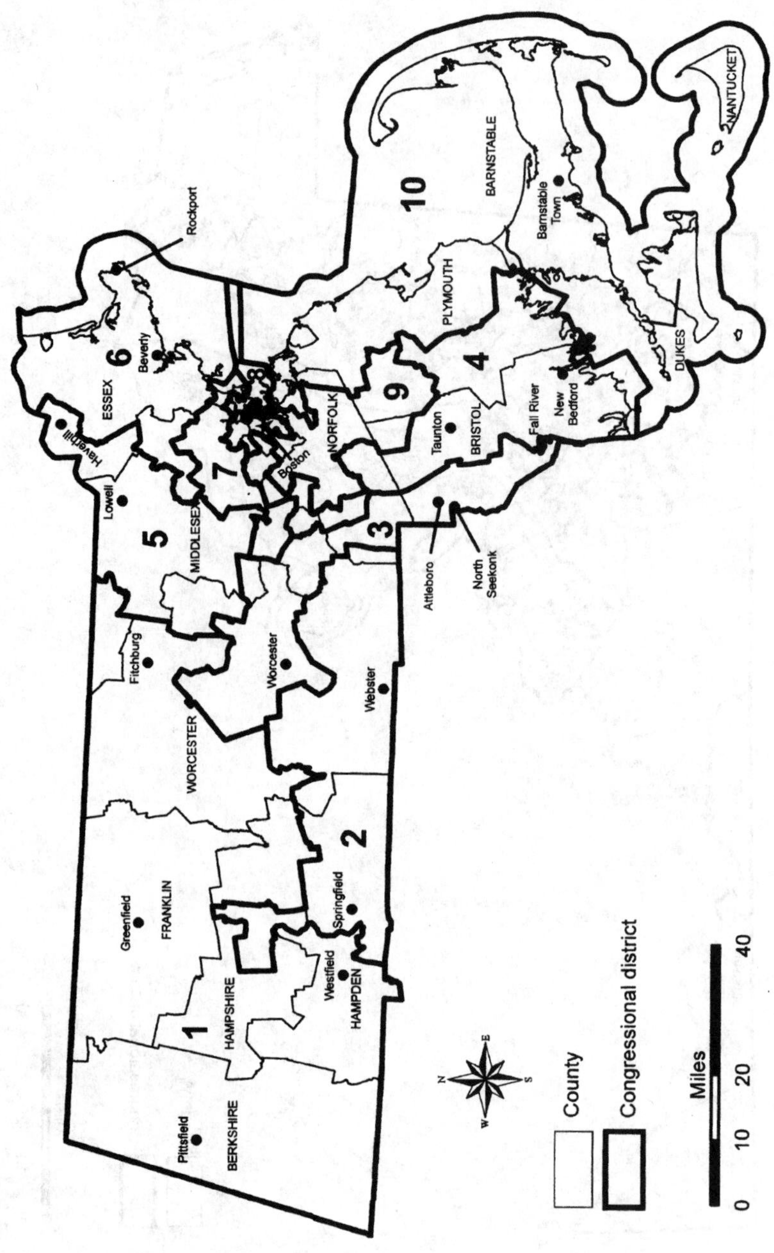

MICHIGAN—Congressional Districts—(15 Districts)

MINNESOTA—Congressional Districts—(8 Districts)

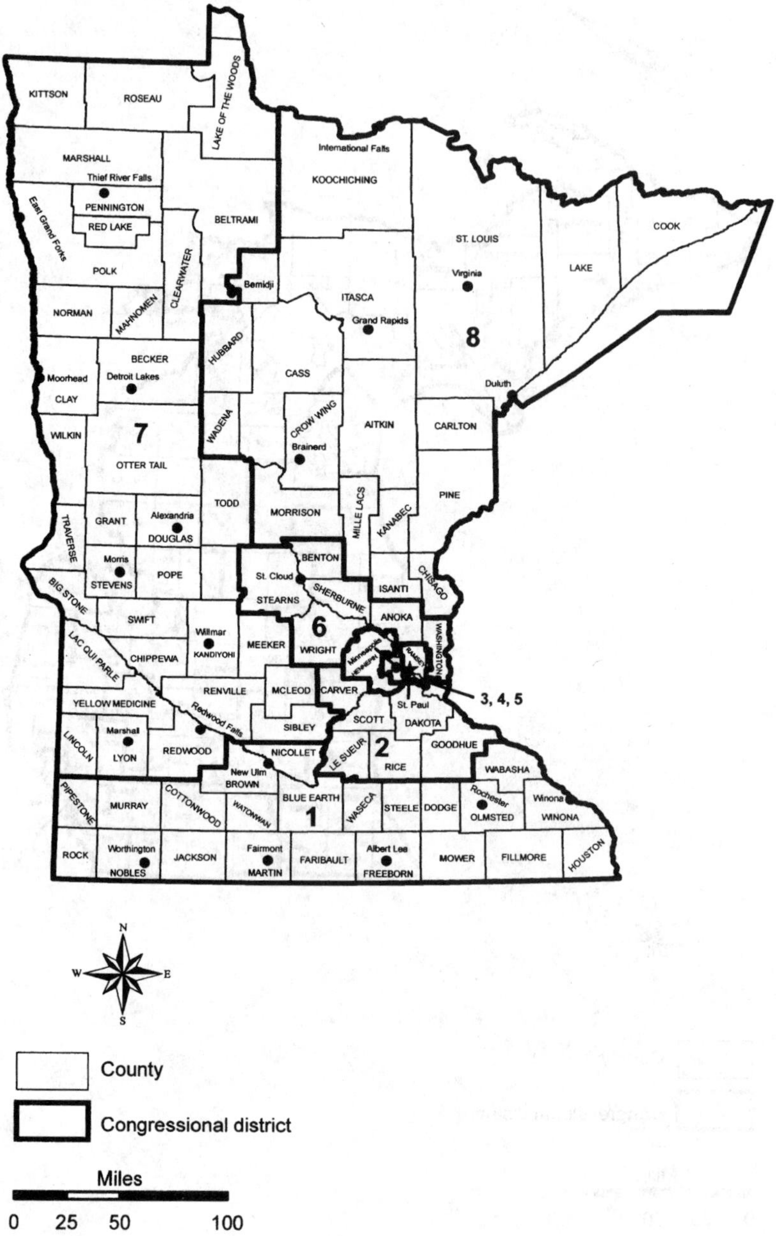

KITTSON
ROSEAU
LAKE OF THE WOODS
International Falls
KOOCHICHING
MARSHALL
Thief River Falls
PENNINGTON
RED LAKE
East Grand Forks
BELTRAMI
COOK
ST. LOUIS
POLK
CLEARWATER
Bemidji
Virginia
LAKE
NORMAN
MAHNOMEN
ITASCA
Grand Rapids
8
HUBBARD
BECKER
Moorhead
Detroit Lakes
CASS
Duluth
CLAY
WADENA
CROW WING
AITKIN
CARLTON
WILKIN
7
Brainerd
OTTER TAIL
PINE
TODD
MORRISON
MILLE LACS
KANABEC
GRANT
Alexandria
DOUGLAS
TRAVERSE
BENTON
Morris
STEVENS
POPE
St. Cloud
CHISAGO
BIG STONE
STEARNS
SHERBURNE
ISANTI
ANOKA
SWIFT
6
WASHINGTON
Willmar
KANDIYOHI
MEEKER
LAC QUI PARLE
CHIPPEWA
WRIGHT
Minneapolis
HENNEPIN
RAMSEY
RENVILLE
MCLEOD
CARVER
3, 4, 5
YELLOW MEDICINE
St. Paul
Redwood Falls
SCOTT
SIBLEY
DAKOTA
LINCOLN
Marshall
LYON
REDWOOD
2
GOODHUE
NICOLLET
LE SUEUR
RICE
WABASHA
New Ulm
BROWN
PIPESTONE
MURRAY
COTTONWOOD
WATONWAN
BLUE EARTH
1
WASECA
STEELE
DODGE
Rochester
OLMSTED
Winona
WINONA
ROCK
Worthington
NOBLES
JACKSON
Fairmont
MARTIN
FARIBAULT
Albert Lea
FREEBORN
MOWER
FILLMORE
HOUSTON

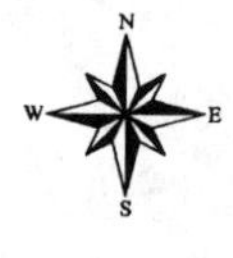

County

Congressional district

Miles

0 25 50 100

MISSISSIPPI—Congressional Districts—(4 Districts)

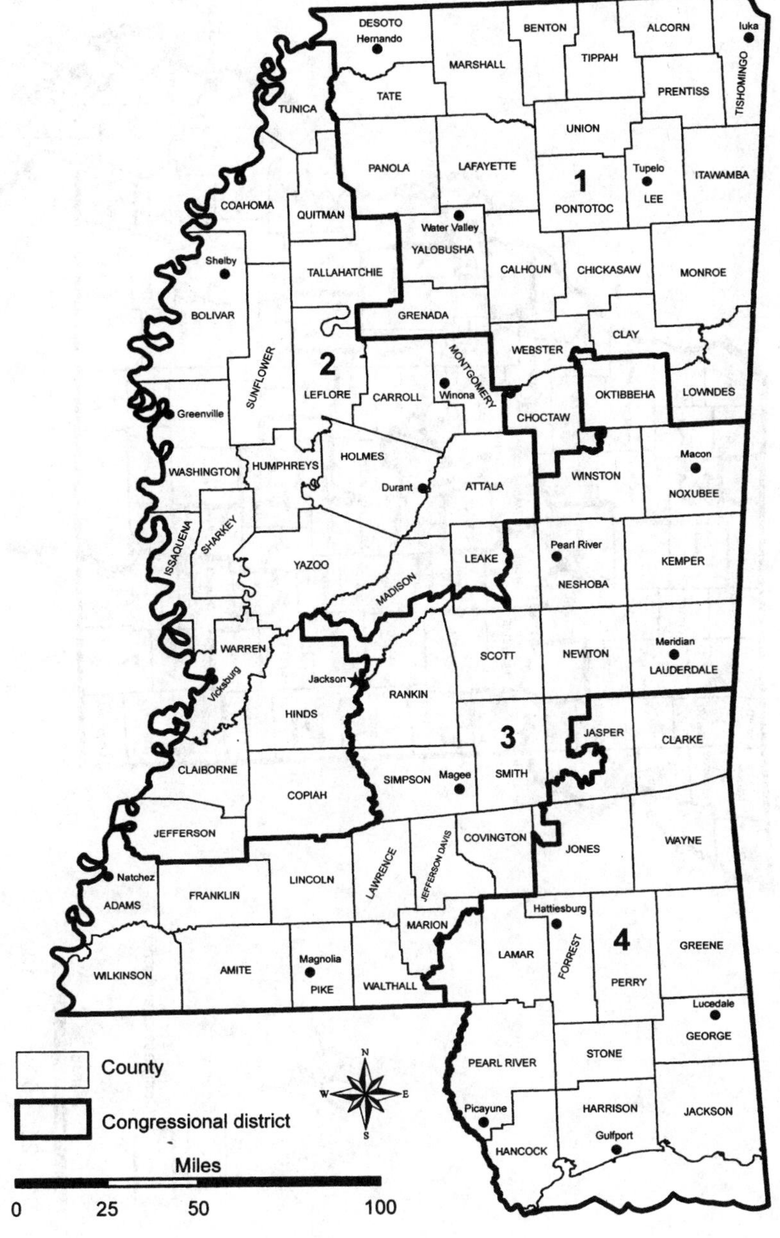

MISSOURI—Congressional Districts—(9 Districts)

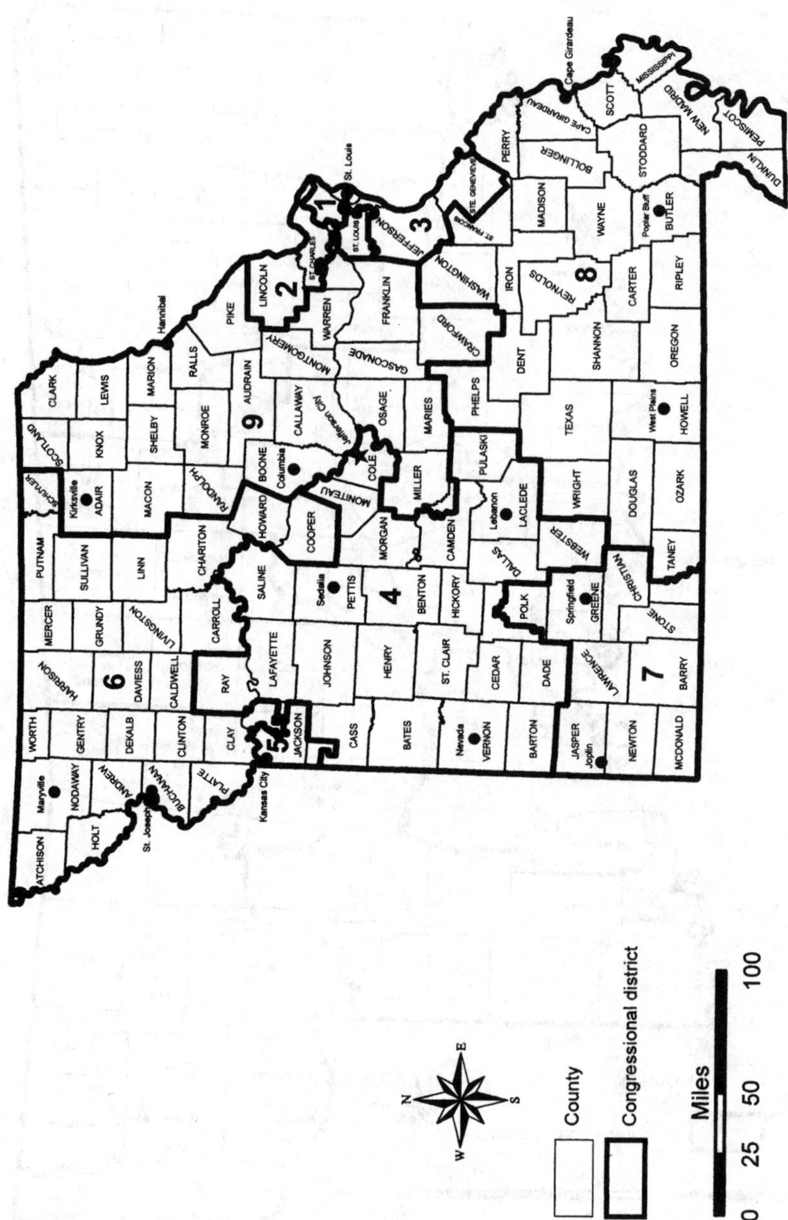

MONTANA—Congressional District—(1 District At Large)

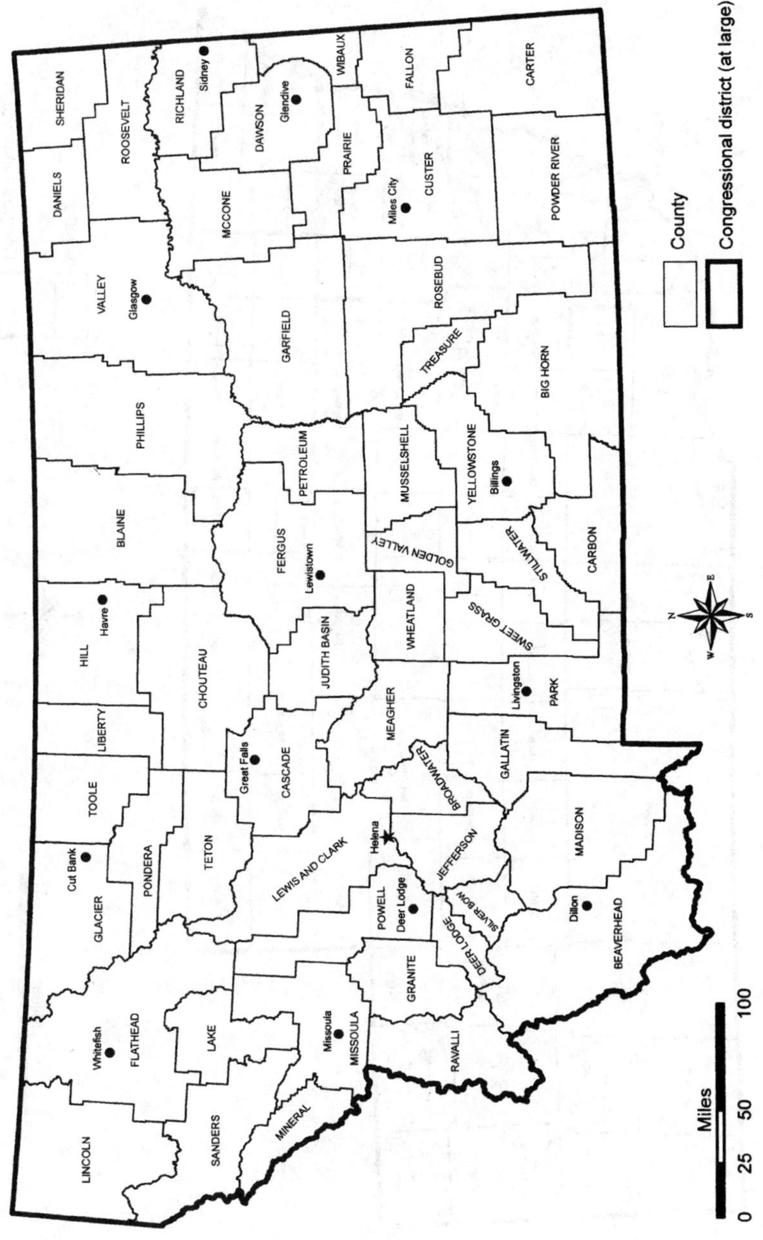

NEBRASKA—Congressional Districts—(3 Districts)

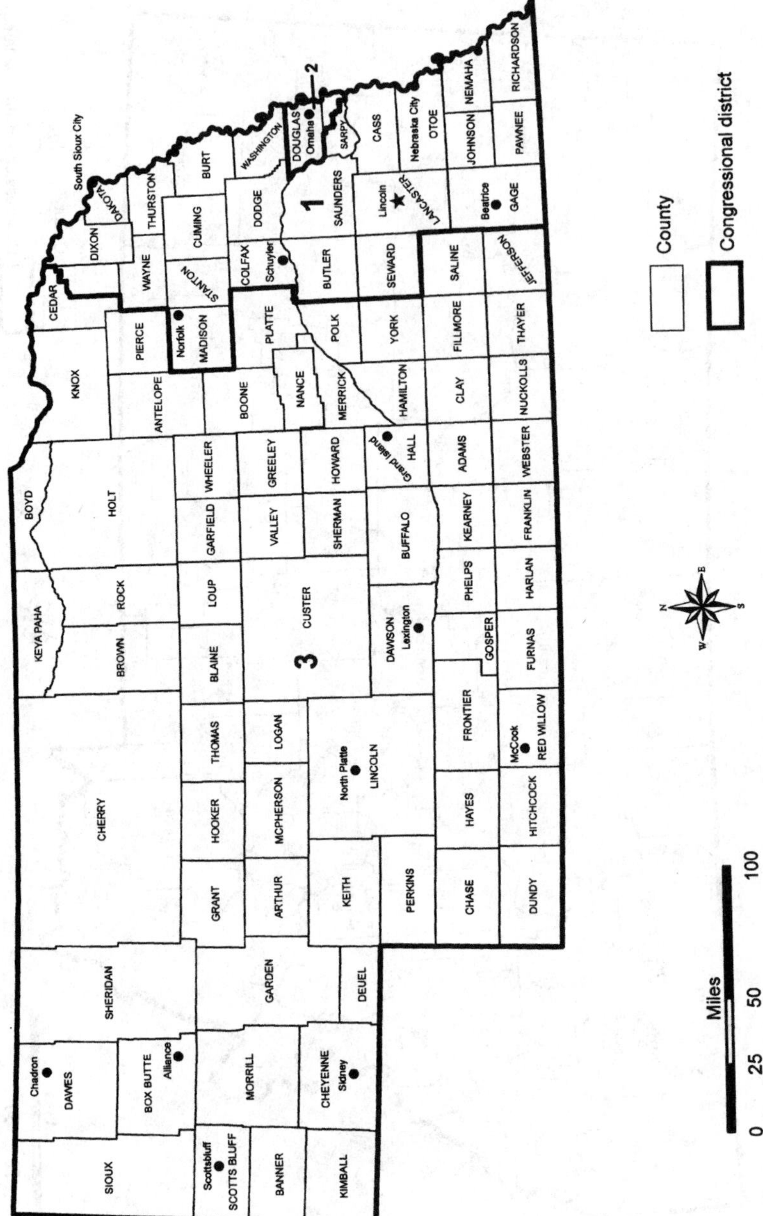

NEVADA—Congressional Districts—(3 Districts)

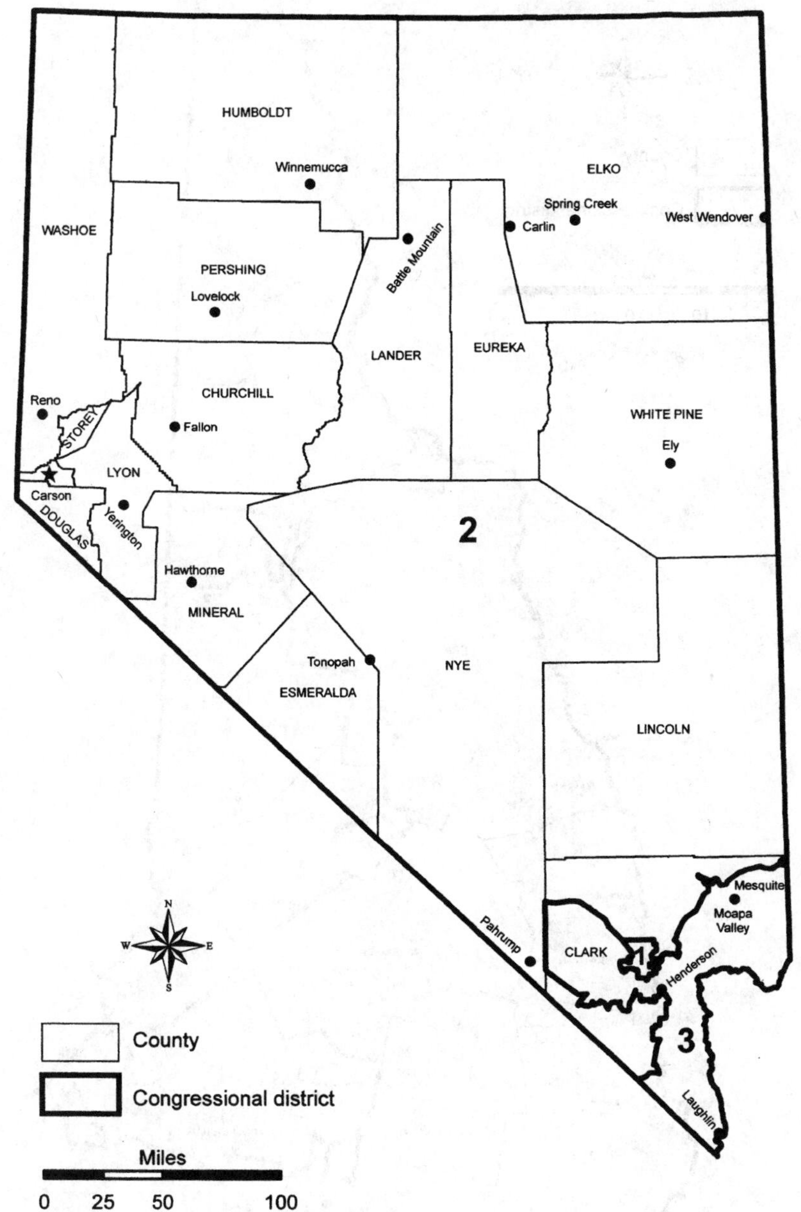

NEW HAMPSHIRE—Congressional Districts—(2 Districts)

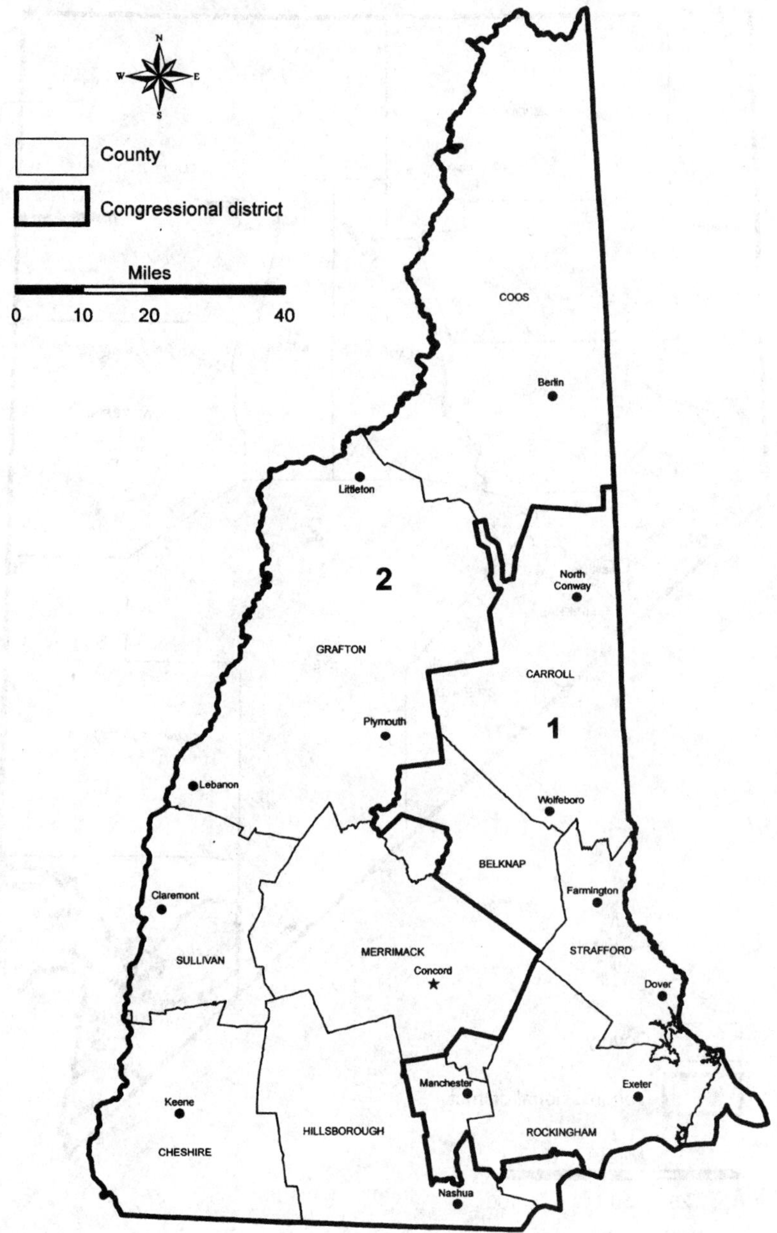

NEW JERSEY—Congressional Districts—(13 Districts)

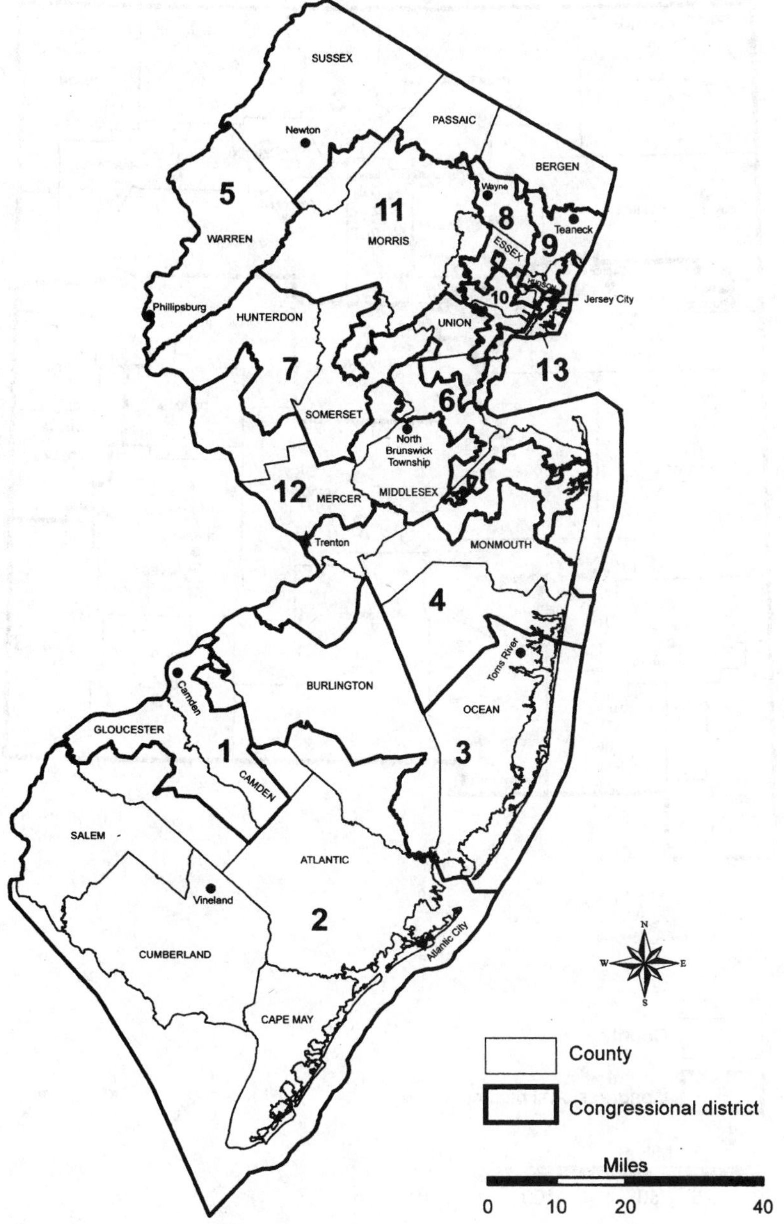

NEW MEXICO—Congressional Districts—(3 Districts)

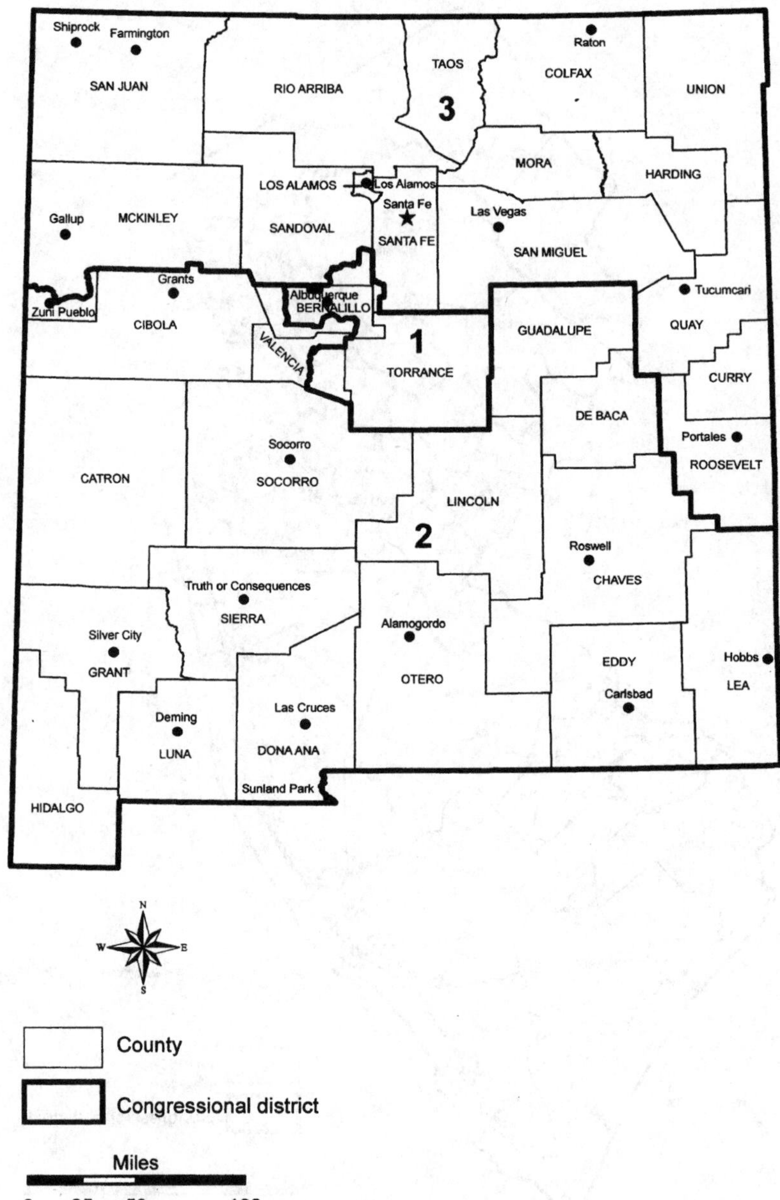

NEW YORK—Congressional Districts—(29 Districts)

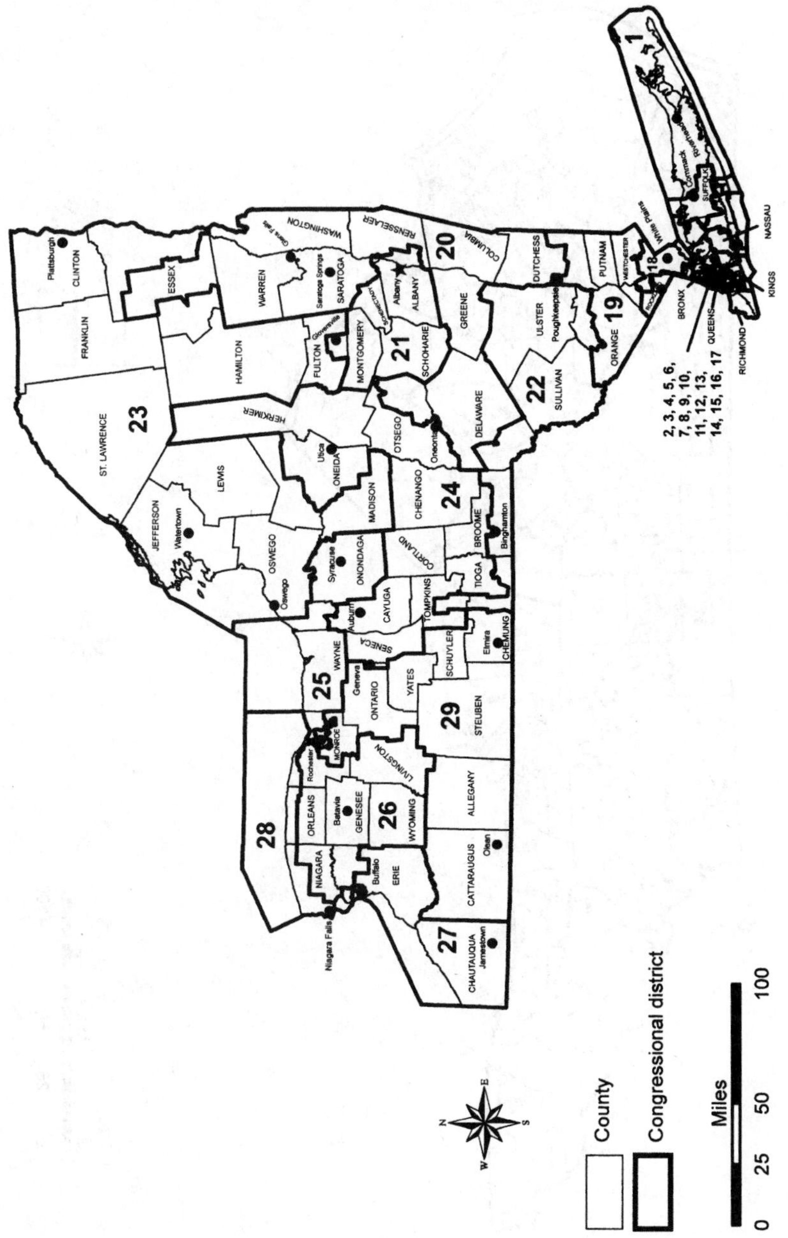

NORTH CAROLINA—Congressional Districts—(13 Districts)

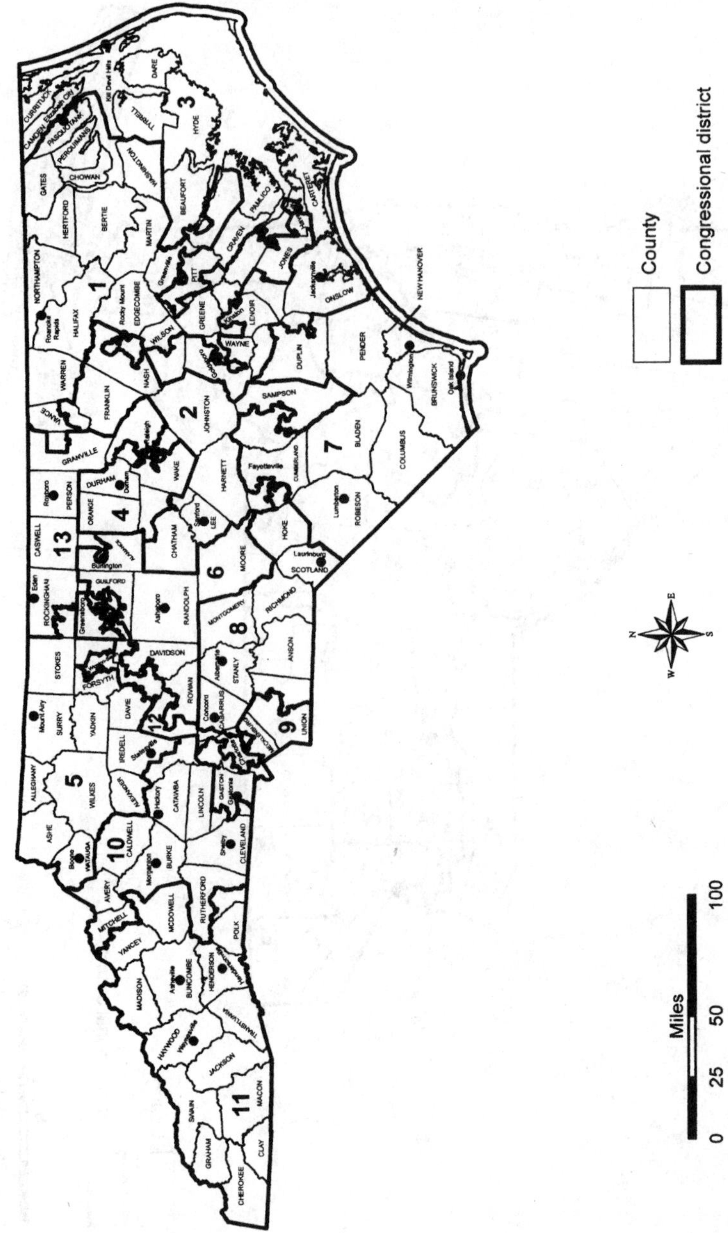

NORTH DAKOTA—Congressional District—(1 District At Large)

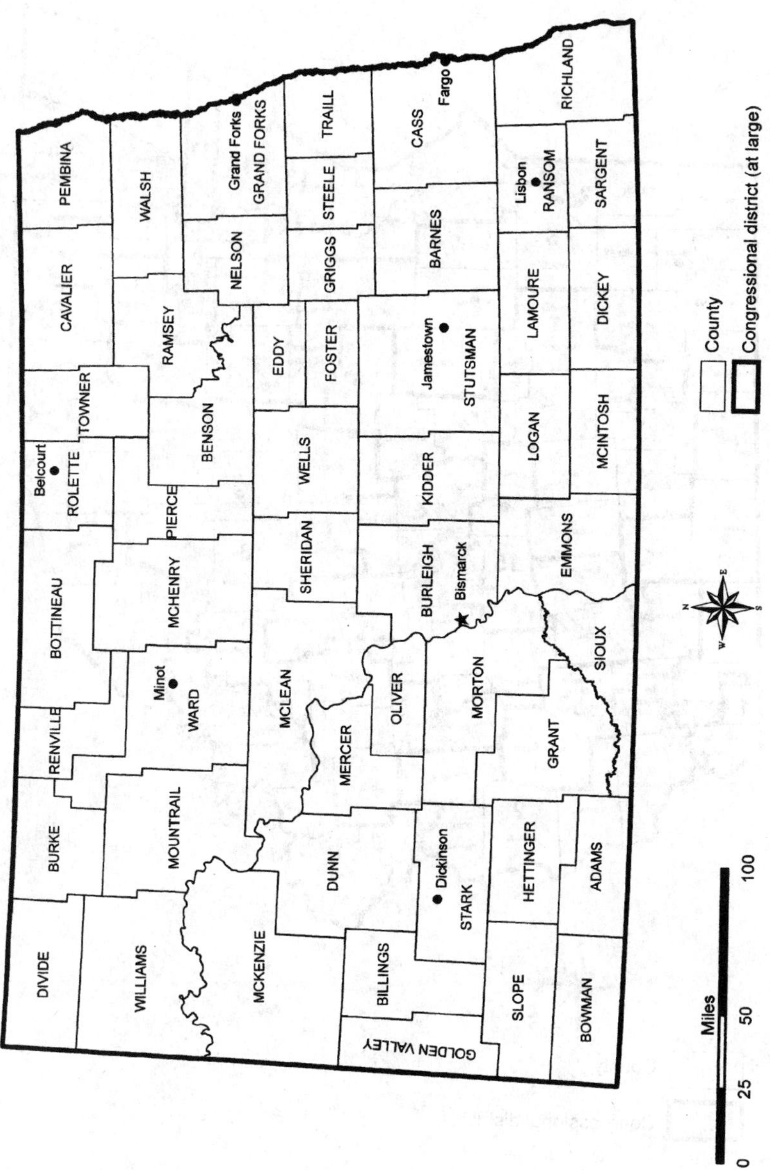

OHIO—Congressional Districts—(18 Districts)

OKLAHOMA—Congressional Districts—(5 Districts)

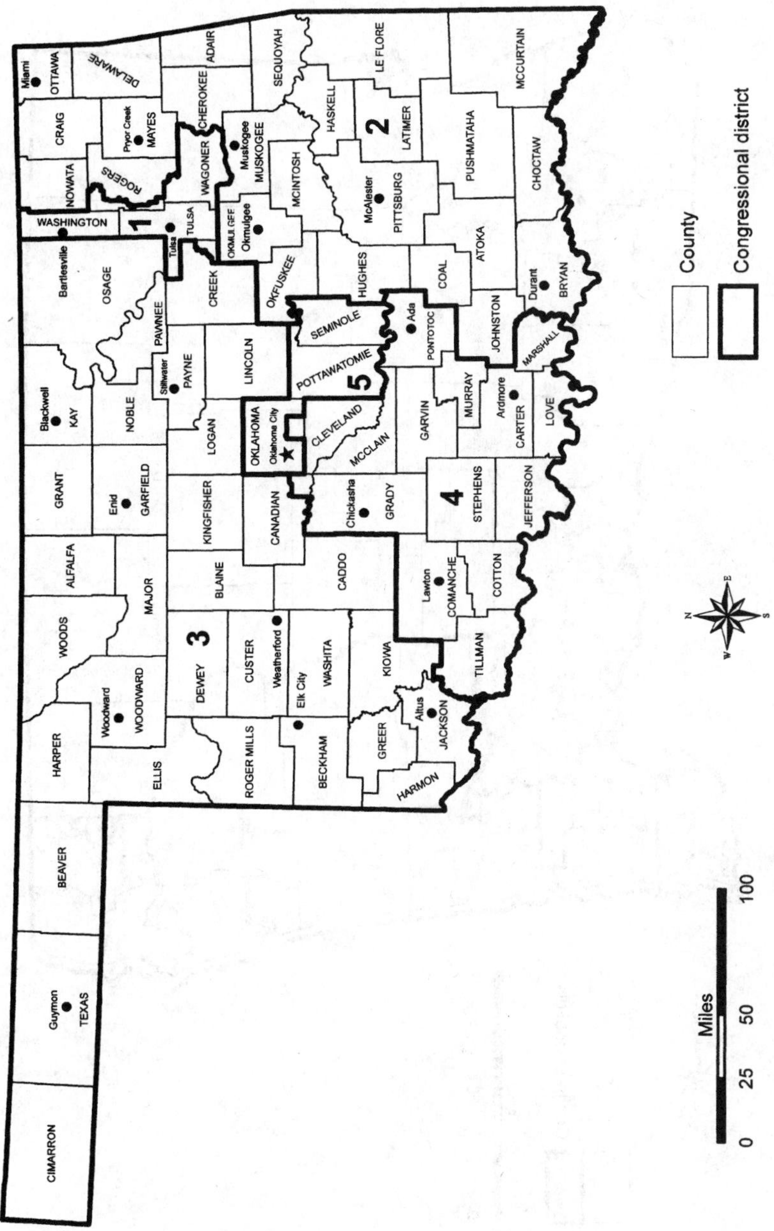

OREGON—Congressional Districts—(5 Districts)

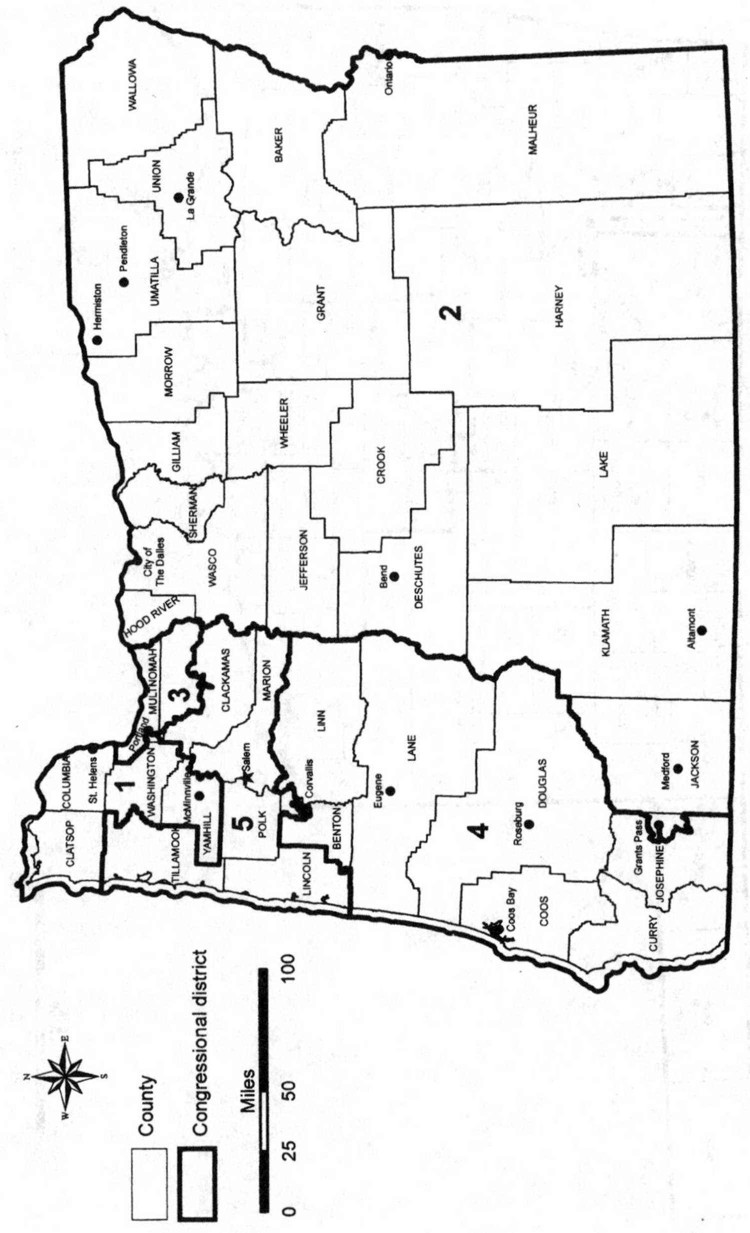

PENNSYLVANIA—Congressional Districts—(19 Districts)

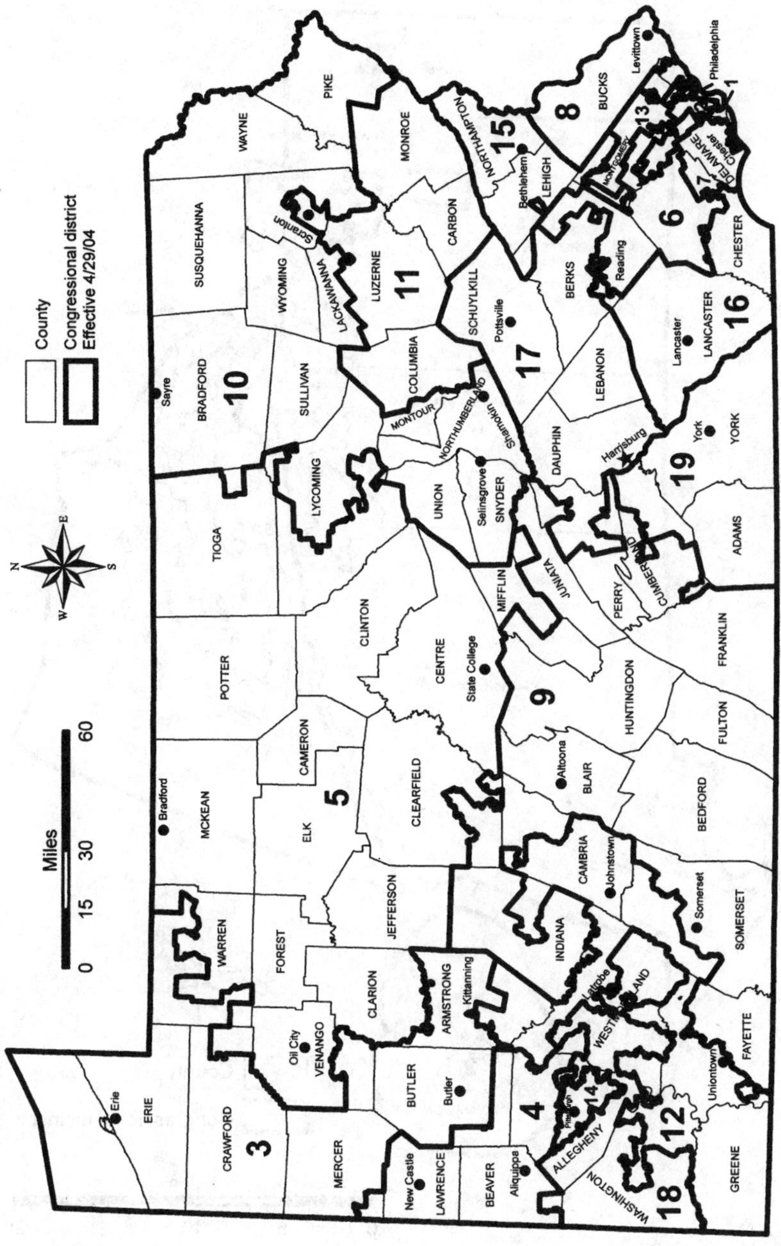

RHODE ISLAND—Congressional Districts—(2 Districts)

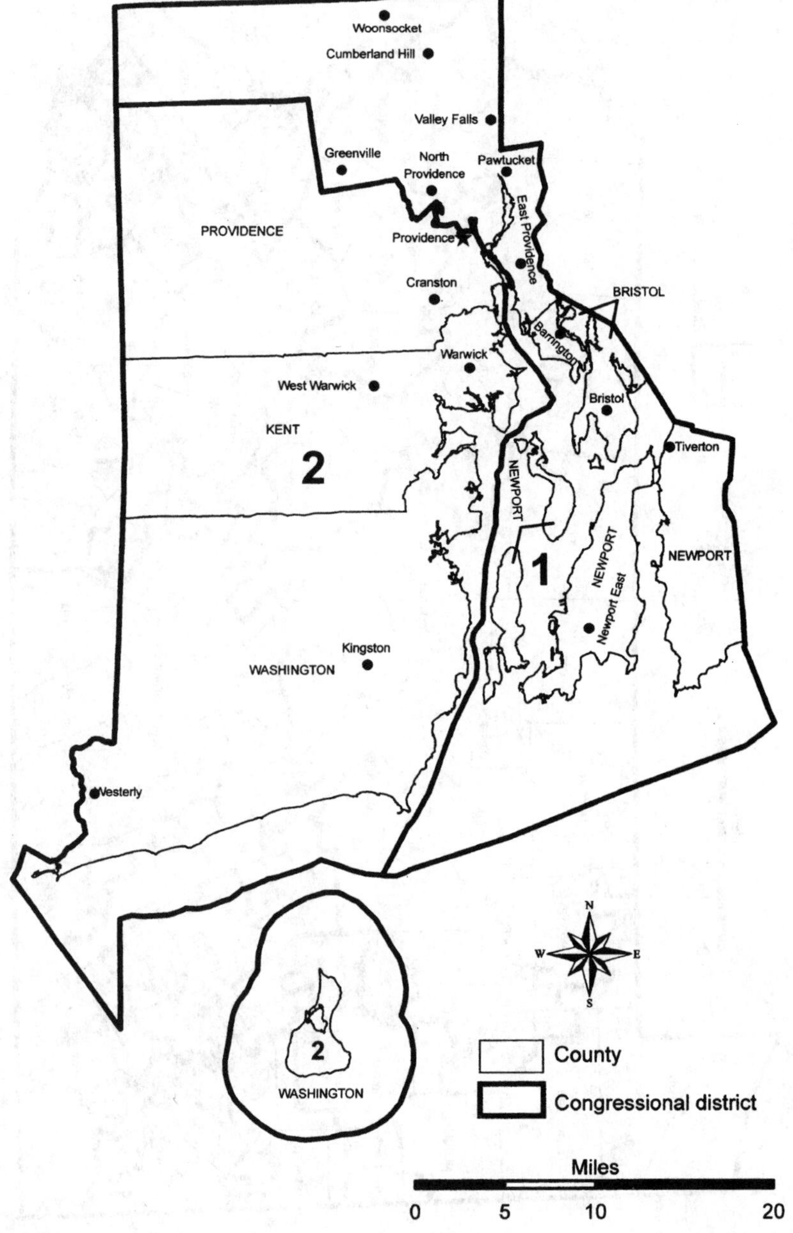

SOUTH CAROLINA—Congressional Districts—(6 Districts)

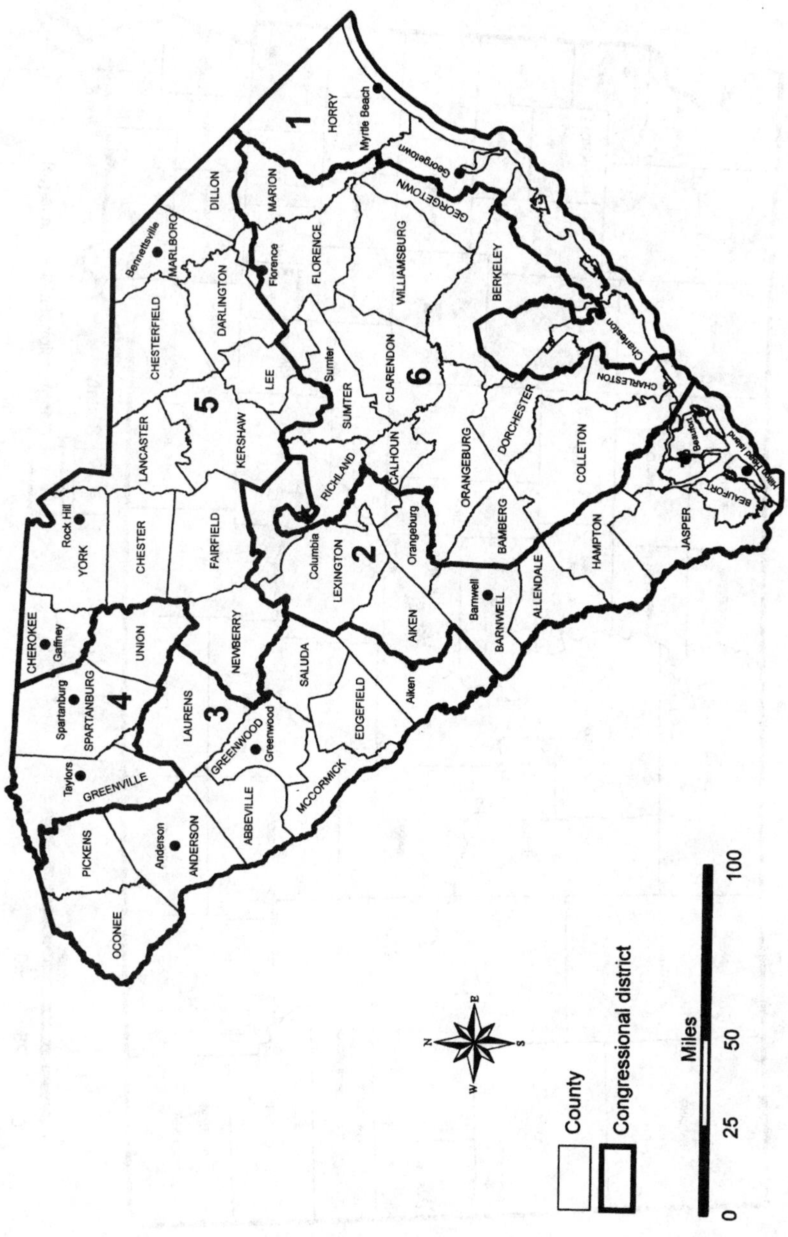

SOUTH DAKOTA—Congressional District—(1 District At Large)

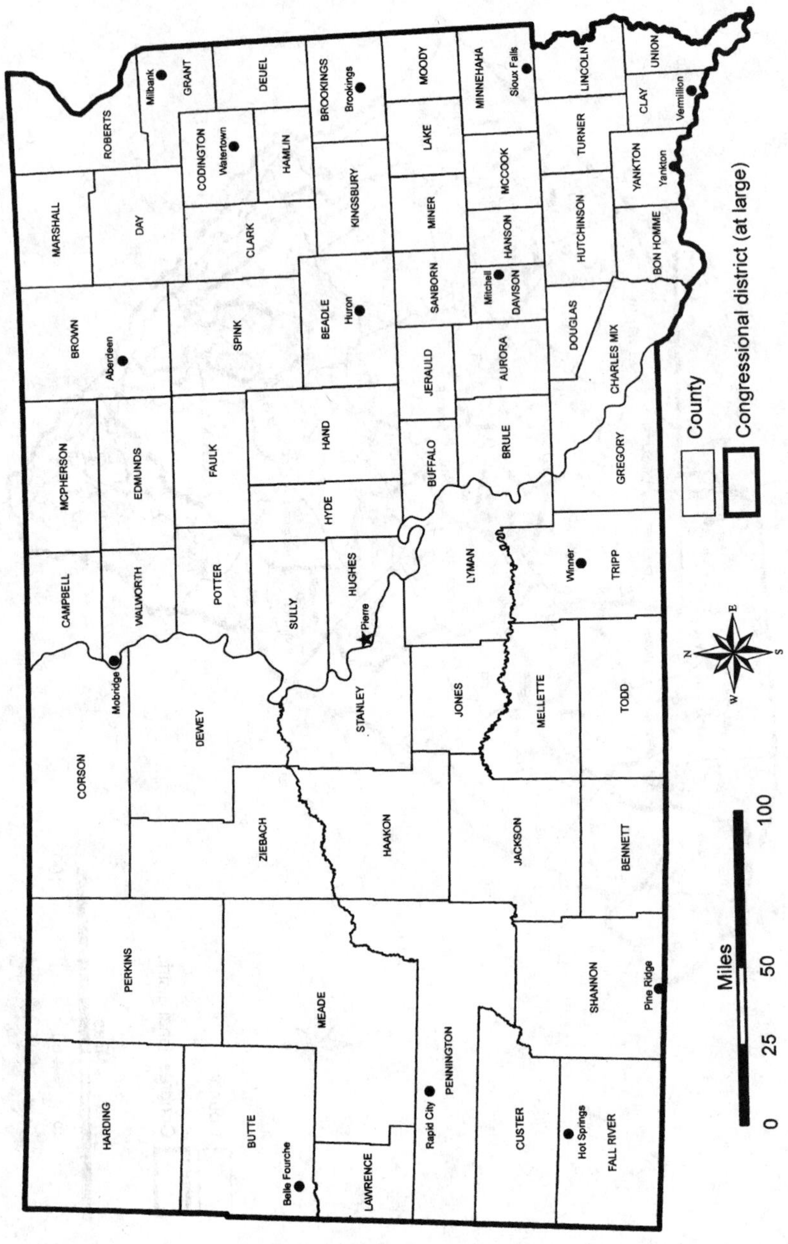

TENNESSEE—Congressional Districts—(9 Districts)

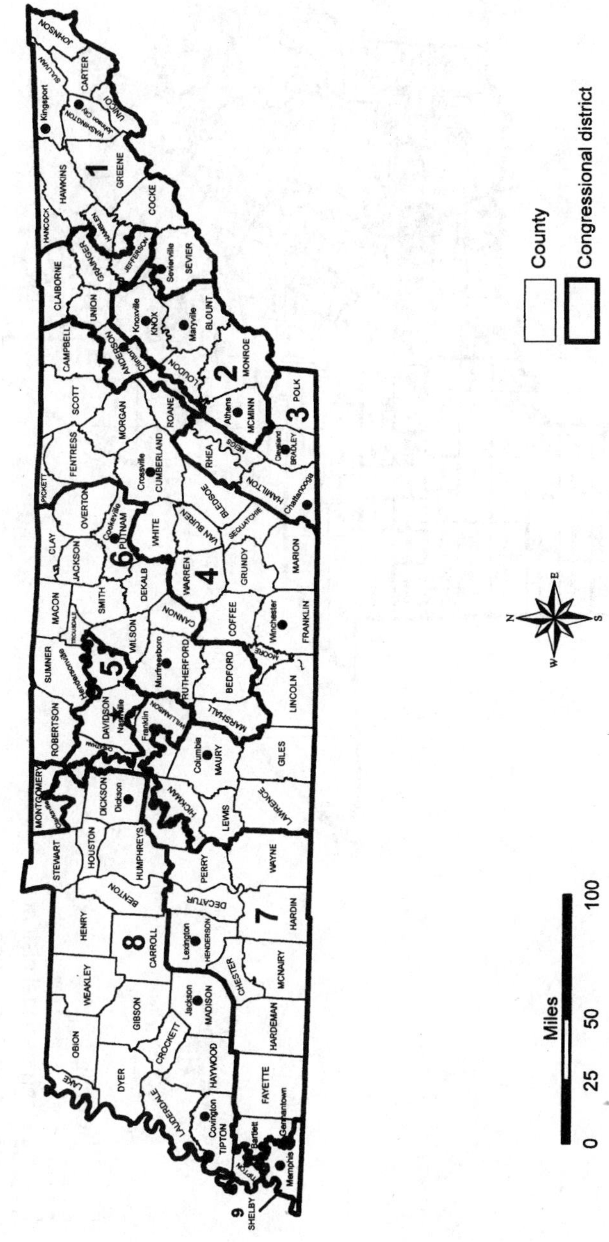

TEXAS—Congressional Districts—(32 Districts)

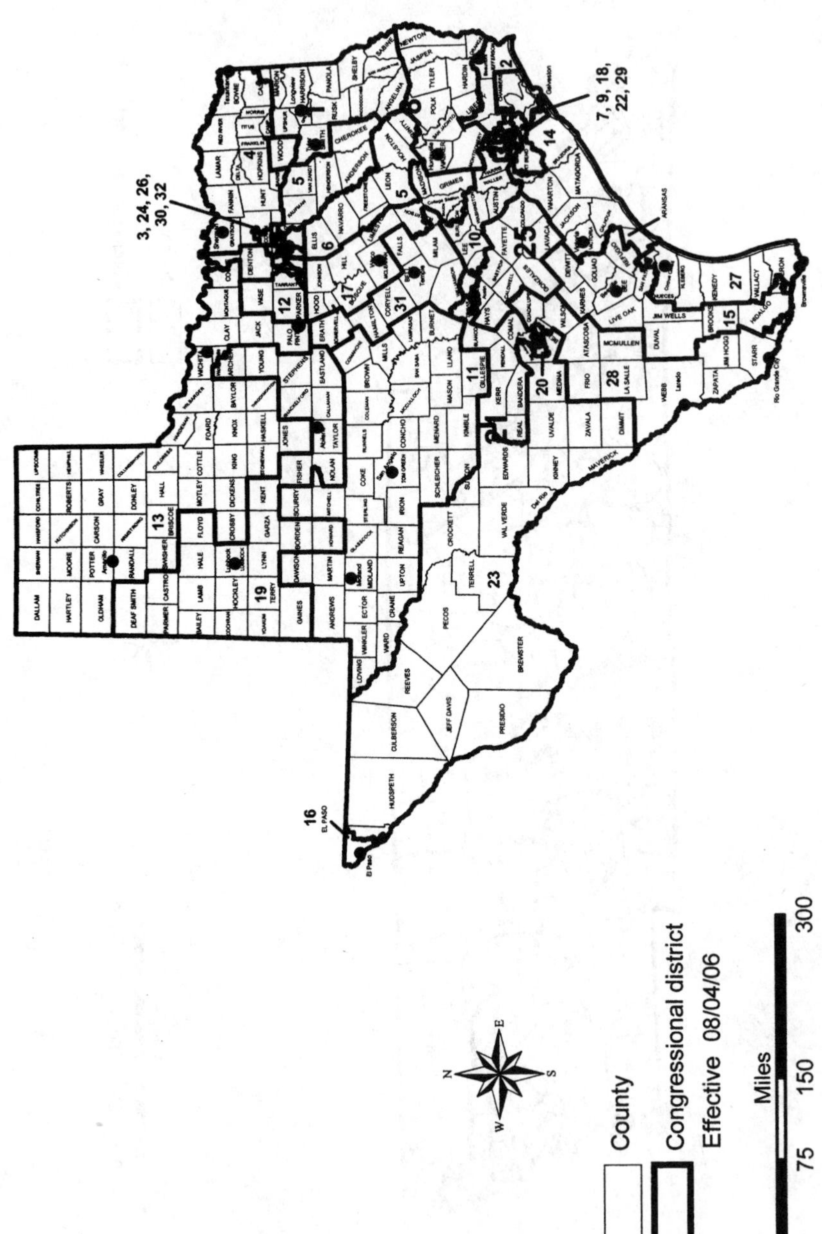

UTAH—Congressional Districts—(3 Districts)

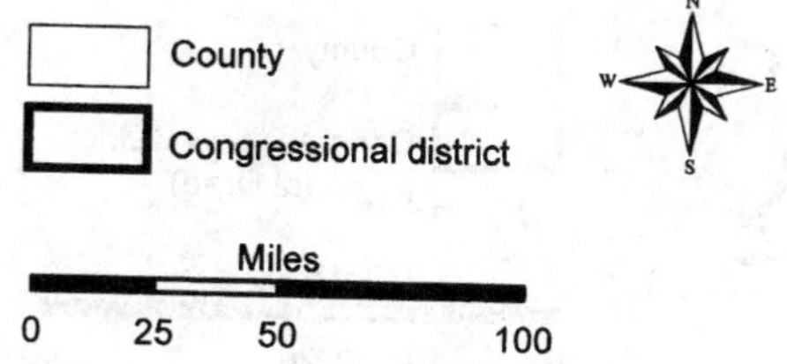

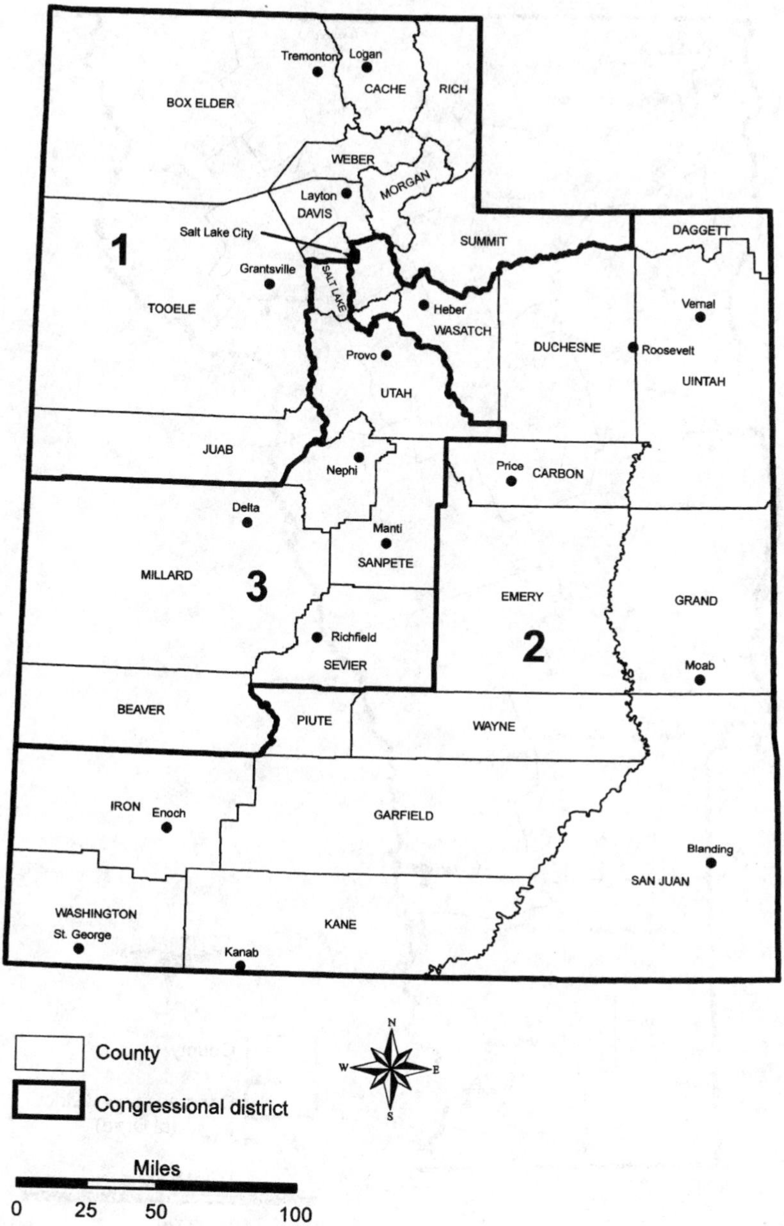

VERMONT—Congressional District—(1 District At Large)

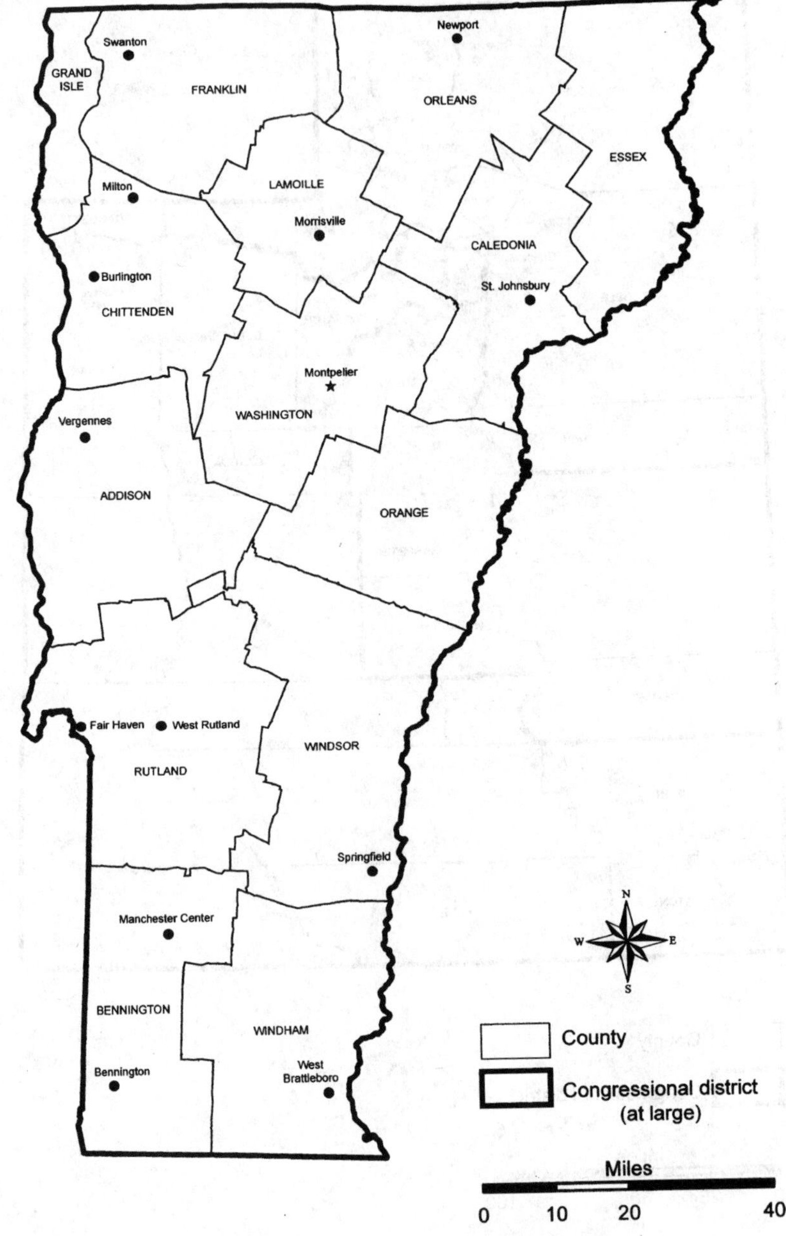

VIRGINIA—Congressional Districts—(11 Districts)

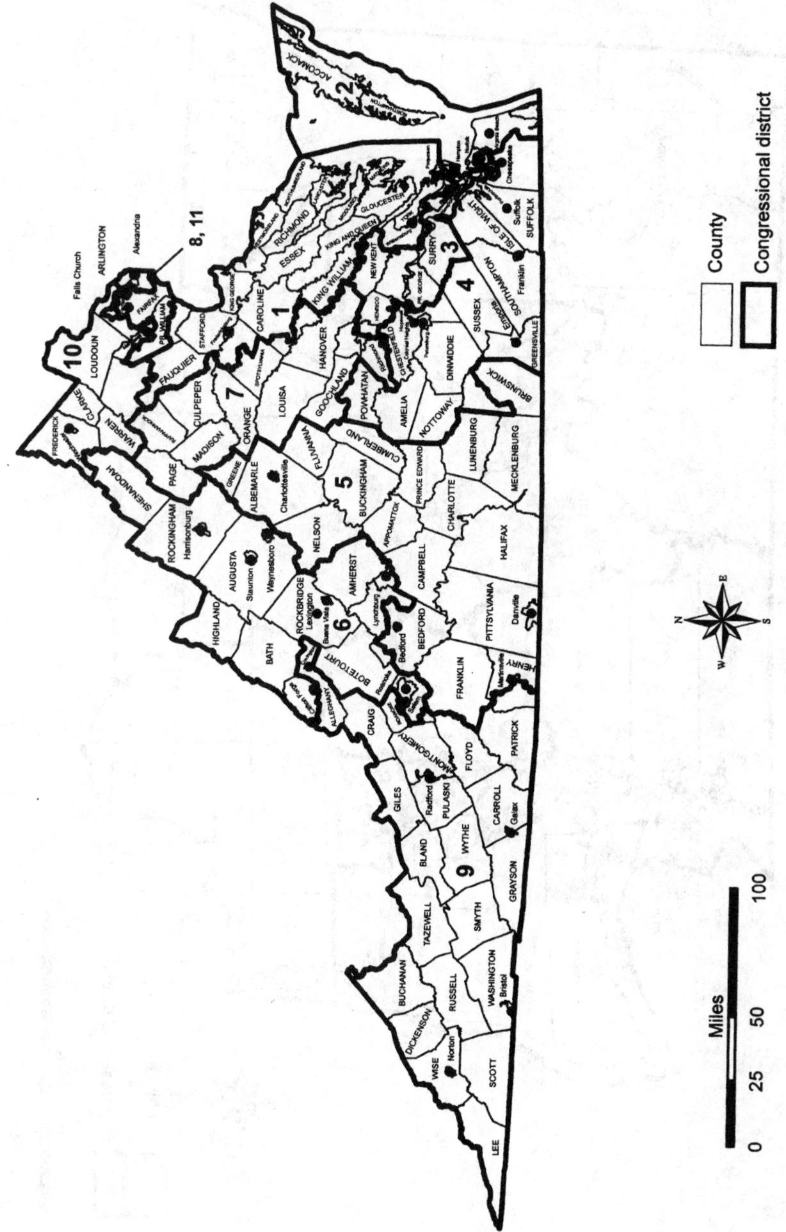

WASHINGTON—Congressional Districts—(9 Districts)

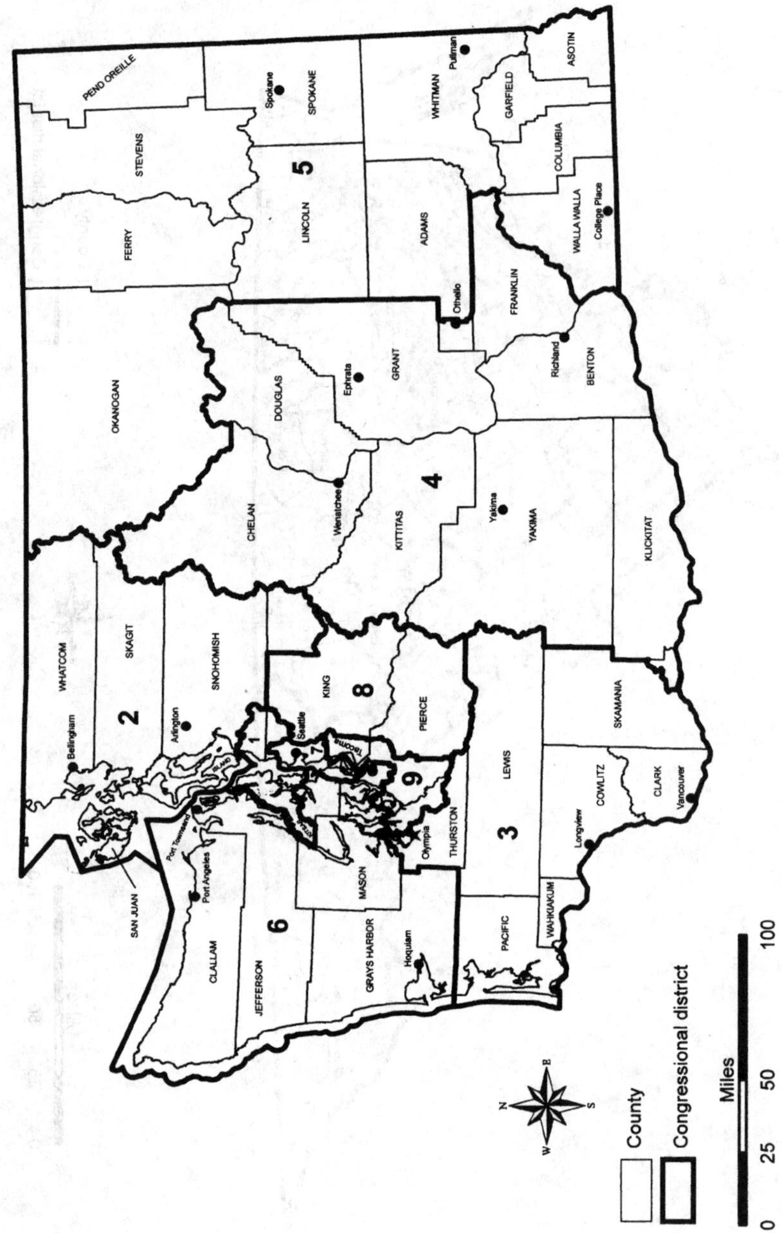

WEST VIRGINIA—Congressional Districts—(3 Districts)

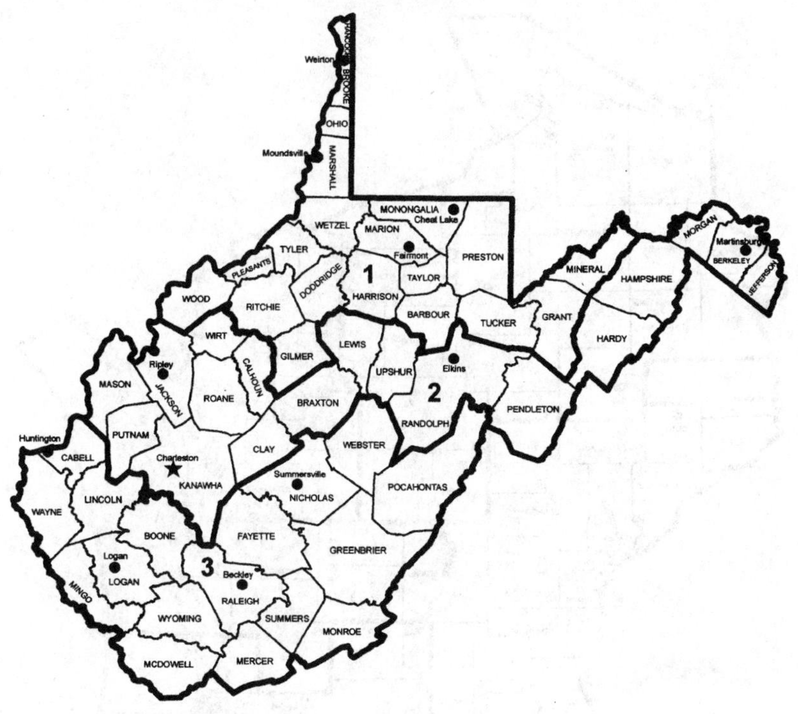

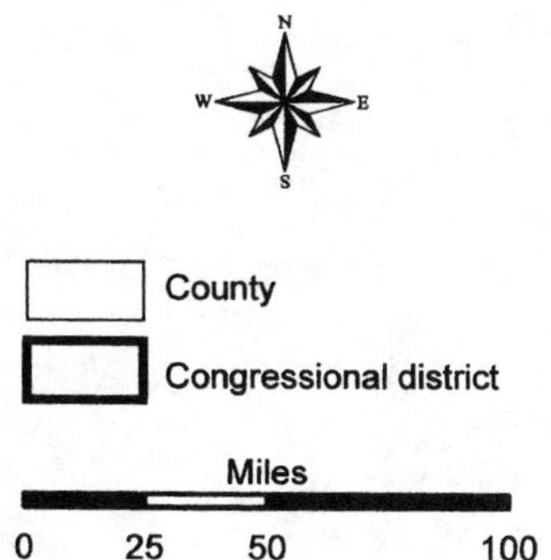

WISCONSIN—Congressional Districts—(8 Districts)

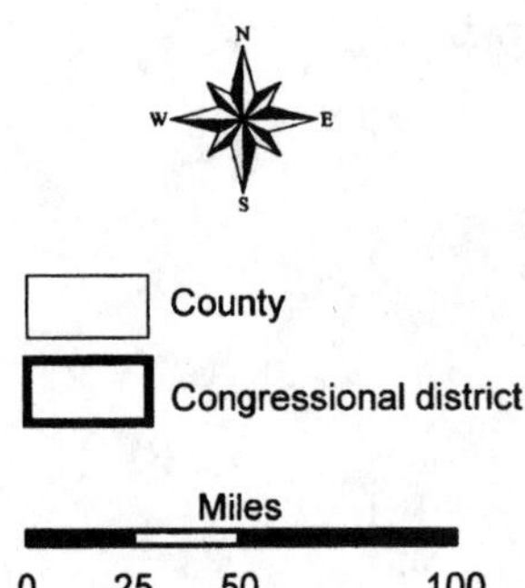

WYOMING—Congressional District—(1 District At Large)

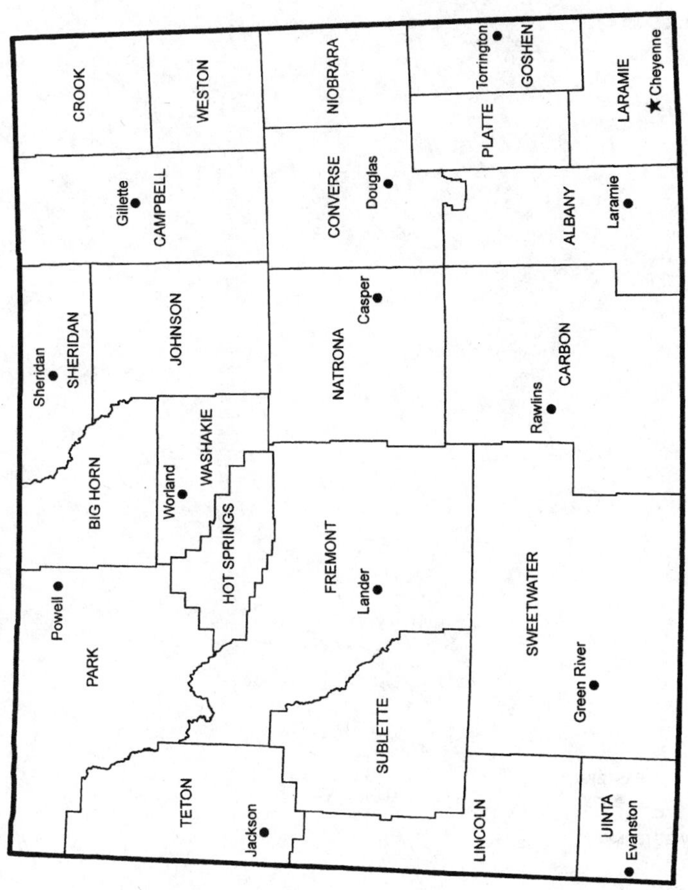

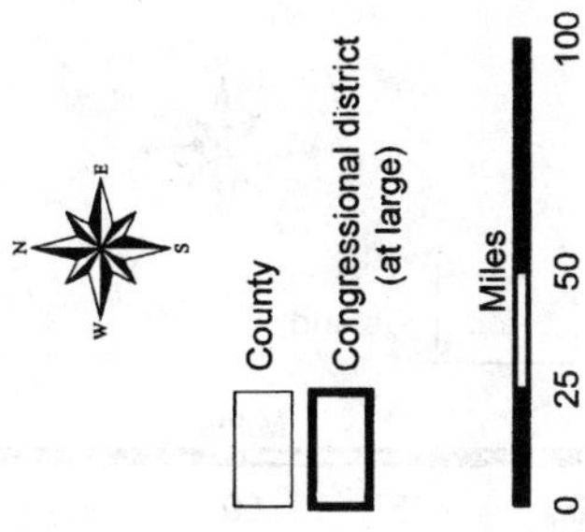

AMERICAN SAMOA—(1 Delegate At Large)

SWAINS ISLAND

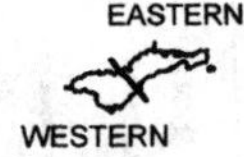

MANU'A

ROSE ISLAND

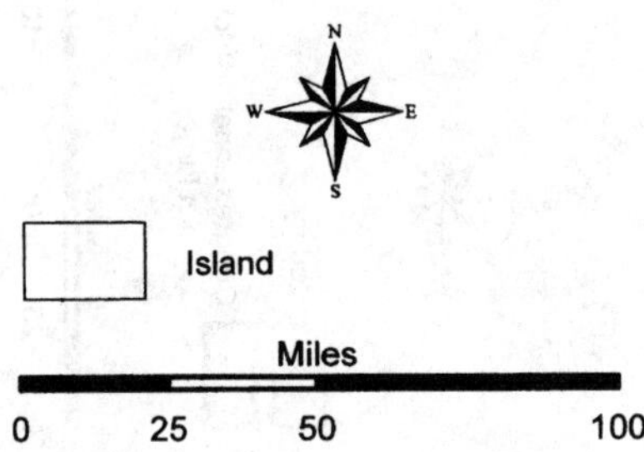

DISTRICT OF COLUMBIA—(1 Delegate At Large)

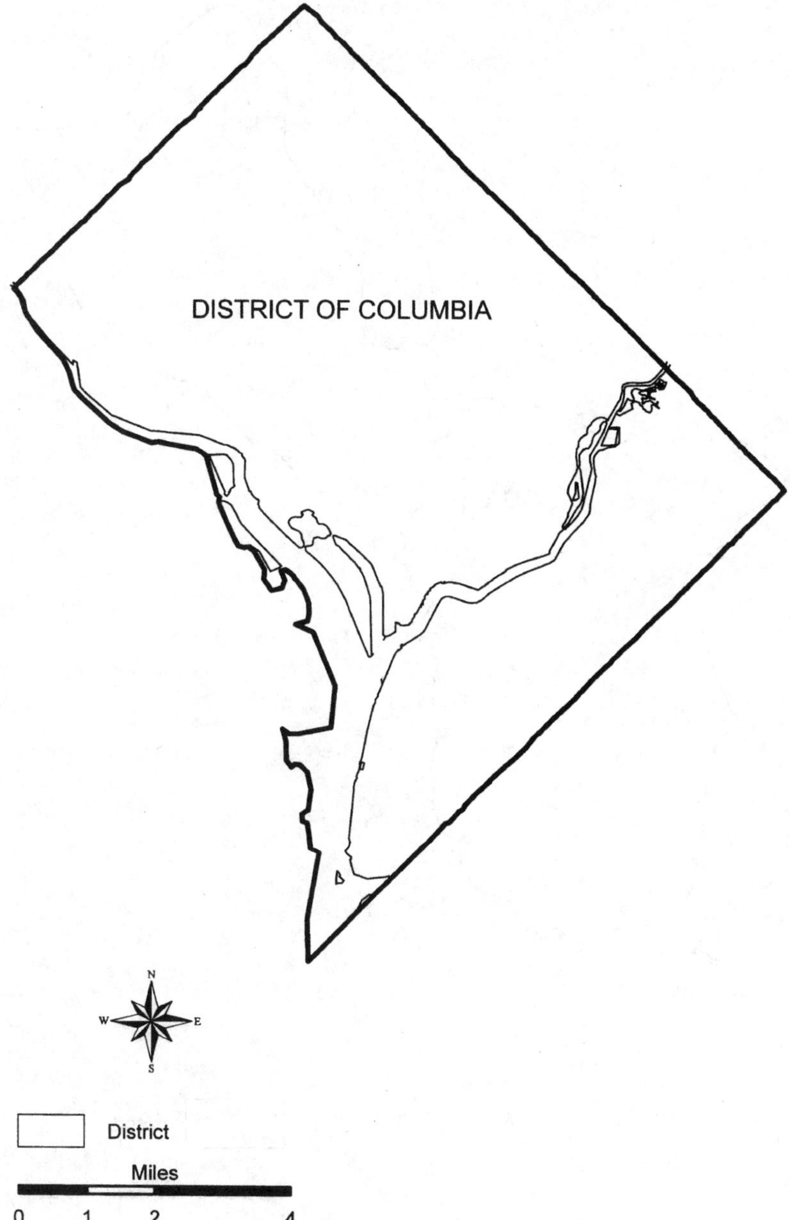

GUAM—(1 Delegate At Large)

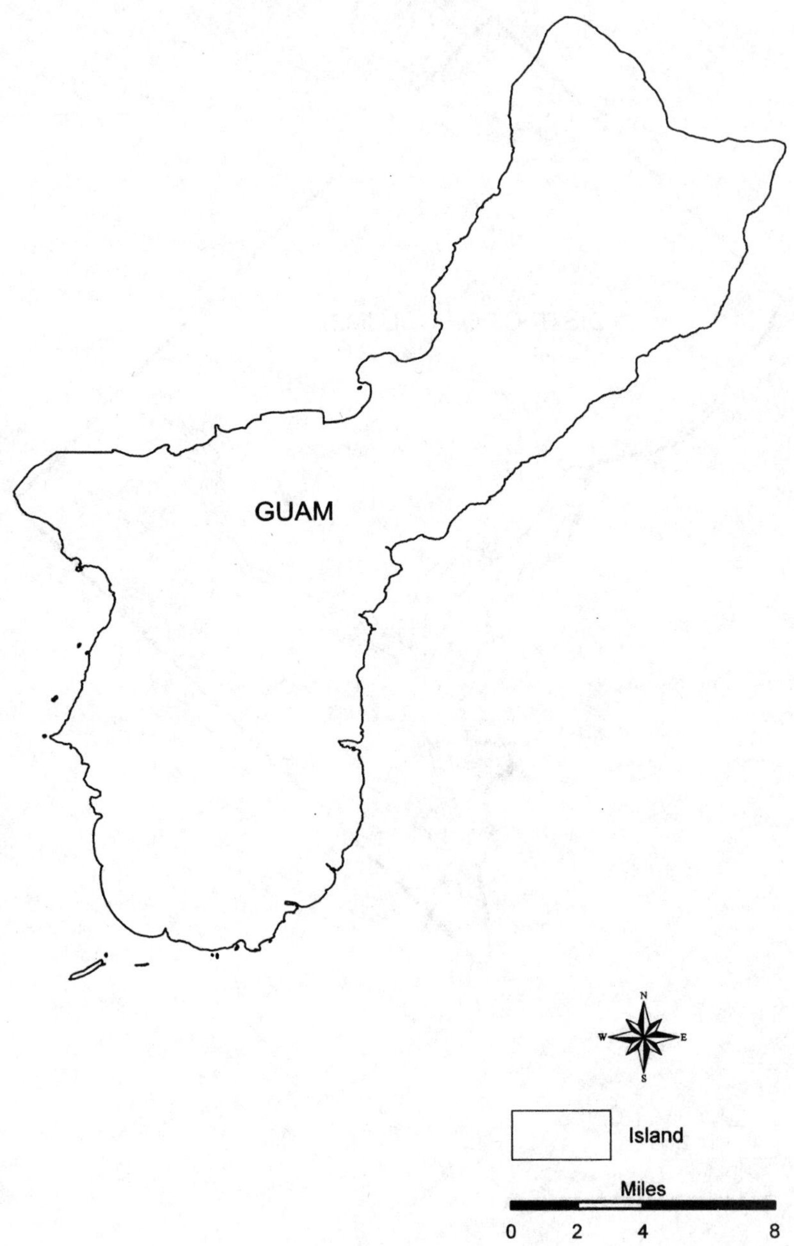

PUERTO RICO—(1 Resident Commissioner At Large)

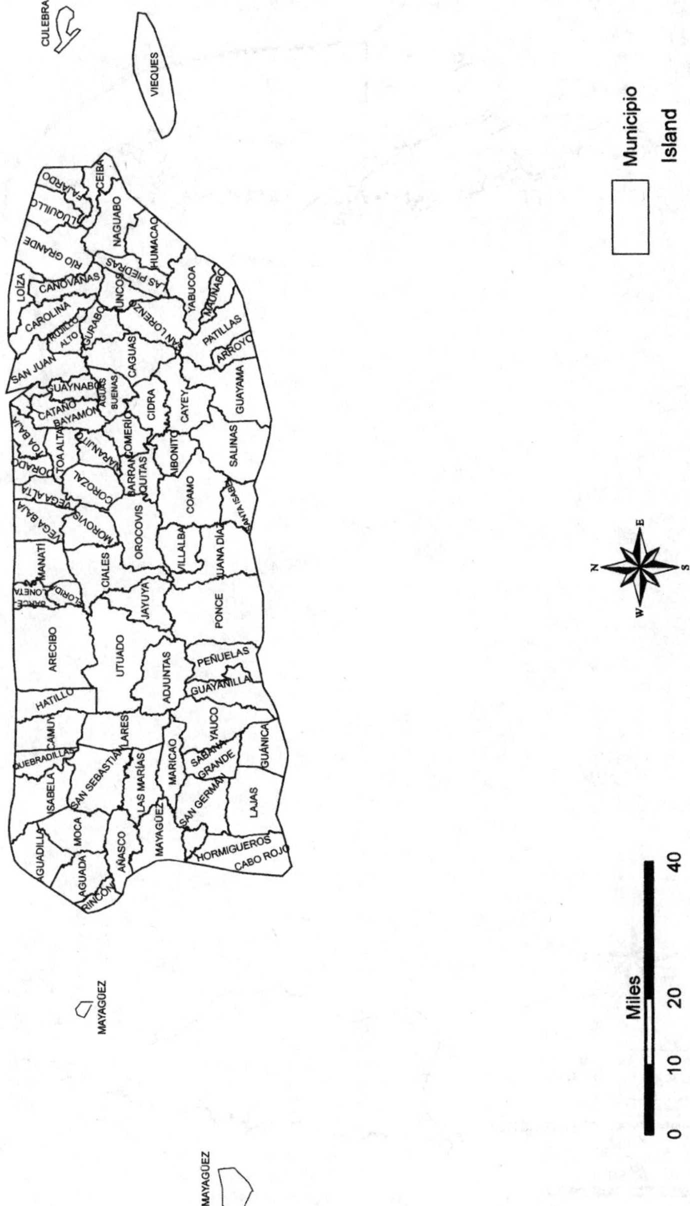

THE VIRGIN ISLANDS OF THE UNITED STATES—(1 Delegate At Large)

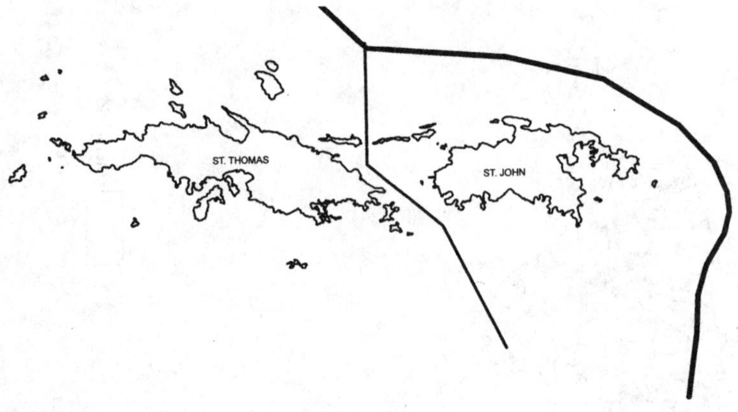

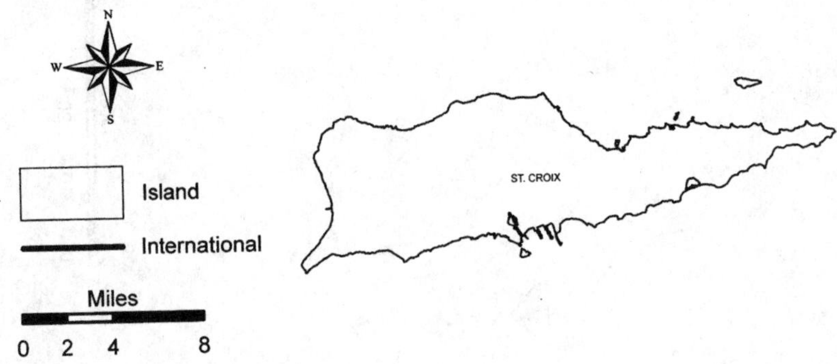

NAME INDEX

Page

A

Aall, Pamela A ... 837
Aaron, Charles ... 508
Abate, Tony ... 434
Abbenhaus, Colleen D ... 749
Abbey, Robert V ... 681
Abbott, Gregory ... 496
Abbott, James ... 790
Abbott, Jim ... 681
Abbott, Mark ... 811
Abbott, Shere ... 590
Abboud, Khalil ... 424
Abdalati, Waleed ... 801
Abdel-Aziz, Hany ... 930
Abdel-Khalik, Said ... 813
Abdelrazek, Rawan ... 607
Abdi, Ali ... 692
Abegg, John ... 388
Abel, Sidney ... 700
Abele, Craig ... 508
Abell, Cathy ... 639
Abernathy, Charles "Chip" ... 385
Abernathy, Sarah ... 405
Abeyta, Diane ... 578
Abney, Allison ... 6
Abouchar, Keith ... 458
Abow, Steven E ... 816
Abraham, Nicholas ... 412
Abraham, Ronny ... 924
Abraham, Ryan ... 364
Abram, Anna ... 370
Abram, Elijah ... 379
Abrams, Allie ... 372
Abrams, Debra ... 836
Abrams, Elliott ... 836
Abrams, Mark ... 163
Abramson, Jeffrey ... 784
Abramson, Kara ... 498
Abrecht, Mary Ellen ... 896
Abreu, Michael H ... 710
Abreu, Roy ... 720
Absher, Carol A ... 510
Abshire, Laura ... 16
Acevedo, Camille E ... 739
Acevedo, Eddy ... 420
Acevedo, Elaine ... 196
Achtenberg, Roberta ... 835
Achtentuch, Frieda ... 701
Ackerman, Gary L ... 182, 306, 327, 414, 415, 418, 419, 475
Ackerman, Ginger ... 725
Ackerman, Kenneth M ... 694
Acocella, Bart ... 22
Acosta, Marcel C ... 805
Acton, Betty ... 367
Acton, Mark ... 820
Acuna, Jennifer ... 449
Adamantiades, Mikhail "Misha" ... 588
Adami, Blake ... 265
Adamo, Chris ... 340
Adams, Darrell E ... 642
Adams, David ... 596
Adams, Doug R ... 825
Adams, Emily ... 97
Adams, Gail ... 679
Adams, James W ... 933
Adams, Jane ... 130
Adams, Julie ... 388
Adams, Katie ... 370
Adams, Laramie ... 217
Adams, Marti ... 610

Page

Adams, Millie ... 850
Adams, Patricia C ... 645
Adams, Sandy ... 70, 303, 335, 425, 426, 435, 436, 475
Adams, Susan ... 401, 505
Adams, Tasha ... 509
Adams, Will ... 135
Adams, William S. "Bill" ... 743
Adamske, Steve ... 610
Adamson, Jeremy ... 581
Adani, Mattia ... 907
Adcock, Donald E ... 637
Addison, Christopher ... 842
Addleton, Jonathan S ... 602
Adelfio, Guilia ... 581
Adelman, David ... 602
Adelson, Beth ... 274
Adelson, Miriam ... 836
Adelstein, Jonathan ... 694
Aden-Wansbury, Casey ... 142
Aderholt, Robert B ... 4, 330, 301, 398, 399, 496, 475
Adiga, Mala ... 650
Adirim, Terry ... 733
Adkins, Rick ... 239
Adkins, Robb C ... 649
Adkins, Ronald ... 618
Adler, Ann ... 443
Adler, Gabby ... 33, 420
Adler, Gabriel ... 364
Adler, Matthew L ... 836
Adler, Robert "Bob" ... 780
Adlerstein, Michael ... 926
Admire, Keith ... 691
Adorno, Rolena K ... 807
Aegerter, John ... 623
Afas, Leila ... 842
Agarwal, Madhulika ... 763
Agee, G. Steven ... 849
Aglieco, Elisa ... 459
Agnello, Gino J ... 850
Agostini, Stephen J ... 815
Agosto, Frances ... 299
Agrast, Mark D ... 674
Aguero, Hugo Rafael Caceres ... 907
Aguilar, David V ... 769
Aguilar, Luis A ... 820
Aguilar, Mario ... 909
Aguirre, Jesus ... 899
Agurkis, George ... 434
Ahern, Michael ... 38
Ahern, Paul T ... 841
Ahlberg, Brian ... 101
Ahlgren, Kate ... 408
Ahmad, Ali ... 433
Ahmed, Masood ... 913
Ahmed, Sajeel ... 618
Ahmed, Shirin A ... 705
Ahmir-abdul, Melik ... 813
Ahn, Justin ... 42
Aiello, Craig ... 691
Aiken, Tim ... 279
Aikman, James ... 705
Ainsworth, Blake ... 508, 575
Aitchison, Brandon ... 373
Aizcorbe, Ana ... 704
Aja, Rachel ... 10
Akai, Joan Ohashi ... 80
Akaka, Daniel K ... 80,303, 321, 324, 346, 347, 351, 352, 371, 379, 381, 384, 467
Akasaka, Kiyotaka ... 925
Akeju, Camille ... 828
Akers, Eric ... 655
Akhtar, Shamshad ... 933
Akhter, Assad ... 172

	Page
Akhter, Mohammad N	898
Akin, W. Todd	153, 305, 331, 402, 403, 404, 405, 435, 436, 475, 797
Akiyama, Cliff	497
Akodjenou, Arnauld Antone	929
Akpofure, Apps	205
Al-Khasawneh, Awn Shawkat	924
Alaniz, Enrique	508
Alarcon, Arthur L	850
Alaverdian, Yelena	21
Alaya, Sergio	376
Albanese, Eileen M	706
Albayrak, Yoko	720
Albee, Luke S	274
Albers, John	645
Albert, Helen	739
Albert, Janet	895
Albornoz, Laura M	839
Alboum, Jonathan	696
Albrecht-Taylor, Kimberly D	393
Albright, Aaron	408
Albright, Craig M	933
Albright, Leslie	401
Albright, Madeleine K	797
Albritton, Jason	362
Alcala, Caitlin	261
Alcalde, Nancy T	750
Alcock, Charles	829
Aldaz, Juan Villegas	906
Alderman, Dave	714
Aldisert, Ruggero J	849
Aldridge, Aaricka	437
Aldridge, Meghan	131
Aldridge, Robin	690
Alemayehou, Mimi	839
Alexander, Adele L	807
Alexander, Bruce C	695
Alexander, Craig	661
Alexander, Doug	427
Alexander, Duane F	734
Alexander, Fiona	715
Alexander, Keith B	620
Alexander, Lamar	244, 308, 322, 324, 341, 342, 343, 361, 362, 368, 377, 386, 464, 467, 502, 503
Alexander, LaVerne	173
Alexander, Lewis	607
Alexander, Michael	372
Alexander, Nicole	262
Alexander, Paige	835
Alexander, Rodney	116, 304, 331, 398, 399, 400, 475
Alexander, Shelia	720
Alexander, Shirley Y	420
Alexander, Thomas	433
Alexander, Yvette M	897
Alexandre, Carl	654
Alfonseca, Muriel A	907
Alfonso-Royals, Angie	770
Alford, Beverly	653
Alford, Latressa	23
Alford, Marty	744
Ali, Russlynn	756
Alioto, Nicole Damasco	25
Alito, Samuel Anthony, Jr	846
Alkaffas, Ayman	933
Alkholifey, Ahmed Abdulkarim	914
Alkisswani, Bessie E.H	582
Allegar, Robert H	578
Allegra, Francis M	873
Allem, Barbara	367
Allen, Bill	391
Allen, Craig	707
Allen, Douglas A	649
Allen, James	56
Allen, Janet	819
Allen, John	745
Allen, Laura	211
Allen, Linda	618
Allen, Michael	452
Allen, Michael H	671
Allen, Oliver C	655
Allen, Reginald	670
Allen, Ronald	433
Allen, Roosevelt	634
Allen, Sarah	426
Allen, Scott	723
Alles, Jeri	743
Alleyne, George	932
Alli, Tylease	407
Allison, Terisa L	417
Allison, William	218
Allred, Mark	632
Almanza, Alfred V	696
Almanza, Margie	93
Almofadhi, Abdulrahman M	933
Almond, Kojuan	830
Aloi, Liz	375
Alonso, Andrew	420
Alprin, Geoffrey M	896
Alspach, Clayton	411
Alston, Charles	786
Alston, Michael	673
Alston, Michael C	580
Altenburg, Alice	385
Altman, Michelle	218
Altmire, Jason	225, 308, 333, 406, 407, 440, 442, 443, 475
Alton, Kim	376
Alturki, Ibrahim M. I	933
Alvarado, Carmen	610
Alvarado, Clelia	401
Alvares, Christopher	697
Alvarez, A. Eric	500
Alvarez, Kathleen	389
Alvarez, Luis	769
Alvarez, Scott G	777
Alving, Barbara	734
Alwine, Donna	746
Alwood, Leann	377
Alzetta, Gino	933
Amaden, Deanne	724
Amado, Fernando J	920
Amano, Mario	919
Amano, Yukiya	929
Amaral, Johnny	29
Amarosa, Kristen	461
Amash, Justin	134, 305, 335, 405, 431, 432, 463, 475
Amato, Michael	404
Amato, Michael J	840
Amaya, John	375
Ambro, Thomas L	849
Ambrogi, Adam	377
Amchan, Arthur	809
Amend, Kurt	598
Ament, Douglas	582
Amereihn, Tina	745
Amerling, Kristin	412
Ames, Fred	591
Amin, Vishal	427
Amis, Eric J	714
Ammon, Matthew	740
Amodei, Mark E	164, 306, 335, 425, 445, 475
Amore, Andrew	756
Amoroso, Francis	654
Amos, J.F	647
Amos, Valerie	925
Ampri, Irfa	934
Anand, Raj	696
Anastas, Paul	782
Anctil, Marjorie	818
Andel, Michael	79
Anderegg, C.R. "Dick"	631
Andersen, Benny	914
Andersen, Ericka	97
Andersen, Inger	933
Andersen, John	707
Anderson, Allyson	360
Anderson, Amanda	894
Anderson, Anjulen	41
Anderson, Anthony	906
Anderson, Ashley	461
Anderson, Bill	780
Anderson, Brooke	592
Anderson, Carl	411
Anderson, David	293, 676
Anderson, David A	888
Anderson, David E	834
Anderson, Debra	224
Anderson, Douglas	419
Anderson, E.R	372
Anderson, Gerald	918
Anderson, Howard	818
Anderson, Jennifer	895
Anderson, John	444, 708
Anderson, Kris	456
Anderson, Margo	757
Anderson, Mark	162

Page

Anderson, Martha 580
Anderson, Matt 610
Anderson, Matthew 905
Anderson, Michele 822
Anderson, R. Lanier, III 850
Anderson, Richard A 777
Anderson, Robert 661
Anderson, Stephen H 850
Anderson-Flynn, Tiffany 136
Andreas, Dieckmann 905
Andreeff, Tania V 884
Andres, Betsy 455
Andres, Gary 411
Andres, Greg D 654
Andrew, Anne Slaughter 600
Andrews, Betty 712
Andrews, Bruce 357
Andrews, Diana 833
Andrews, Dorine 818
Andrews, Robert E 168, 306, 328, 402, 403, 406, 407, 475
Andrews, Tom 455
Andringa, Tara 133
Andrion, Elizabeth 787
Androff, Blake 443
Andross, Susan 778
Andrus, Jon 919
Angell, John 364
Angelo, Robert 721
Angelone, Paul 588
Angelosante, Tal 630
Angrisani, Chris 386
Anicich, Adam 509
Annelli, Joseph 701
Annette, Kathleen 733
Anninos, Dionysios "Dan" 638
Annison, Robin 510
Anselman, Brian 509
Ansley, Judith A 837
Anstey, Caroline 933
Anstine, Paul 422
Antell, Geoffrey 449
Anthony, Perry Edward "Ed" 779
Antoncic, Madelyn 932
Antonello, Kristin 170
Antonio, Brian 645
Anwar, Javaid 797
Anzalone, Ronald D 773
Aoki, Lenna 381
Aoki, Steven 752
Aoki, Yutaka 909
Apelbaum, Perry 427
Apfelbaum, Michael N 724
Aponte, MarCarmen 601
Apostolakis, George 812
Apostolou, Carolyn E 344
App, Steve 789
Appelbaum, Judith C. "Judy" 674
Apple, Daina 690
Appleton, Seth 157
Aquilino, Thomas J., Jr 869
Aquino, Mariano S 816
Arabit, Joseph 657
Aramaki, Suzan J 704
Aranegui, Monica 71
Arangio, Jennifer 422
Aranoff, Shara L 838
Arauz, Steve F 417
Arbelaez, Maria Angelica 914
Arberg, Kathleen L 848
Arcangeli, Paul 404
Archambeault, Gregory 769
Archer, Glenn LeRoy, Jr 858
Architzel, David 647
Archuleta, Katherine 717
Ardolina, Alexia 433
Arellano, Hilda 835
Arevalo, Alberto 824
Argilagos, Ana Marie 738
Argodale, John 636
Arguello, Hector 71
Ariale, John 59
Arias, Ileana 731
Aristeiguieta, Cesar A 774
Arlia, Eva 376
Armen, Robert N., Jr 884
Armendariz, Alfredo 783
Armenteros, Marilu 71

Page

Armington, Beth 650
Armstrong, Charles E 392
Armstrong, Charles R 769
Armstrong, Chris 449
Armstrong, Deirdre 373
Armstrong, Fulton 367
Armstrong, Jo 832
Armstrong, Kent 687
Armstrong, Lynden 377
Armstrong, Matthew 835
Armstrong, Richard, Jr 509
Armstrong, Sarah 172
Arnavat, Gustavo 608, 907
Arner, Shawn 694
Arnett, Angela Jones 832
Arnold, Jeffrey L 640
Arnold, Michael 698
Arnold, Morris S 850
Arnold, R. Brian 627
Aronchick, Jonathan 362
Aronowitz, Jay 637
Aronson, Ellen G 682
Arreaga-Rodas, Luis E 601
Arredondo, Brenda 463
Arreola, Philip 654
Arrighi, Jean Michel 919
Arrington, Sheryl 352
Arriola, Nathaly 384
Arroyo, Brian 680
Arsht, Adrienne 798
Arthur, Errol 895
Arvai, Antonette 913
Arvanitis, John 656
Arvizu, Alex 596
Arvizu, Alexander A 600
Arvizu, Dan E 811
Ary, V.A 648
Ascik, Mary Katherine 386
Ash, Darren 813
Ash, Michelle 412
Ashbrook, John 388
Ashby, Jeffrey 801
Ashby, Pizza 423
Ashdown, Keith 372
Ashe, Dan 680
Ashe, Victor 778
Ashe-Goins, Francis 729
Ashenden, Nicholas 816
Ashford, Jeff 401
Ashley, Brandon 430
Ashley, James 11
Ashley, John 582
Ashley, Michael T 67
Ashley, Patricia 74
Ashley, Suzanne 823
Ashman, Robert T 775
Ashmore-Hudson, Anne 898
Ashton, Richard M 777
Ashton, Robin C 675
Ashwal, Maya 7
Asin, Steven G 893
Askman, David 661
Asmus, Mike 262
Assimaidou, Kossi 914
Astrue, Michael J 829
Aten, David 688
Ates, Kerry 287
Athas, Ellen 588
Atinc, Tamar Manuelyan 932
Atkins, Ray 750
Atkinson, Caroline 913
Atkinson, Kathleen 689
Atkinson, Leslie 733
Atlas, Larry 715
Atlas, Robert 710
AtLee, W. Kipling 631
Atterbury, Kezmiche 298
Attridge, Dick 391
Attwood, Cynthia L 813
Atuatasi, Hana 297
Atwood, Cindy 770
Aubry, Mary 675
Auer, Lance 606
Auerbach, Gerald M 676
Auggler, Matt 680
Augustine, Patrick B 813
Augustyn, Noel J 893
Aul, Jay 744

Page

Aullman, Pat 296
Aultman, Dale L 785
Aumann, Mark 292
Austin, Arlene 731
Austin, Chris 24
Austin, Daysha 37
Austin, Keenan 67
Austin, Lisa 794
Austin, Nicole C 416
Austin, Roy 652
Austin-Diggs, Carolyn 795
Austin-Ferguson, Kathleeen 598
Austria, Steve 209, 307, 334, 398, 400, 475
Avalos, Edward 699
Avant, I. Lanier 423
Avant, Lanier 149
Avant, Nicole 600
Averill, Christopher 378
Averill, Mark F 639
Avery, John 822
Avila, Cecilia Ramos 907
Avila, Ramon Corral 909
Aviles, Danielle 458
Avondoglio, Bryant 455
Awkard, Pamela Bridgewater 601
Axelrod, Matthew S 654
Axthelm, Rick 296
Ayala, Janice 770
Ayalde, Liliana 602
Ayers, Kenton 818
Ayers, Stephen T 502, 505, 510, 583, 773
Ayotte, Kelly 166, 306, 323, 325, 346, 347, 354, 356, 357, 378, 496, 467
Ayoud, Laura M 392
Ayres, Alyssa 597
Ayres, Thomas E 639
Azueta, James 907
Azzaro, Richard A 780

B

Baack, Korry 96
Babacar, Gaye 925
Babb, Alison 11
Babb, John 729
Babbitt, Randy 743
Babcock, Sarah 364
Babers, C. Donald 740
Babers, Lucinda M 899
Babyak, Michael 200
Baca, Joe 40, 302, 330, 395, 396, 397, 414, 415, 416, 475
Baca, Sylvia 681
Bach, Elizabeth 809
Bach, Kenneth 780
Bachelet, Michelle 927
Bachmann, Michele 145, 305, 333, 415, 416, 451, 475
Bachorik, Lawrence 732
Bachrach, Christine 733
Bachus, Spencer 5, 301, 328, 415, 475
Bacon, Robert 819
Baden, Laurence 806
Bader, Chris 16
Bader, Joseph F 780
Badin, Joseph 694
Baer, Kenneth 590
Baer, Parry 642
Bagby, David 67
Bagby, Steve 636
Bagdoyan, Sato 508
Bagenstos, Sam 652
Baggaley, John W 392
Bagian, James P 764
Bagley, Moira 109
Bagramian, Levon 352
Bahr, Dorothy 652
Bailey, Angela 817
Bailey, Bill R 613
Bailey, Cheryl R 894
Bailey, Edmund 821
Bailey, Jen 48
Bailey, Jonathan W., Jr 709
Bailey, Nicholas 443
Bailey, Robin 689
Bailey, Ronnette 460
Bailey, Sandra 825
Bailey, Stephanie B 730
Bailey, Steve 354

Page

Bailey-Armstrong, Darrah 710
Bailie, Michael 662
Bain, Brittney 426
Bain, Michael 343, 344
Bain, Patsy 256
Baird, Michael 712
Baird, William R 392
Baish, Mary Alice 576, 579
Bake, Betsy 830
Baker, Andy 397
Baker, Arthur 426
Baker, Brett 449
Baker, C. Steve 794
Baker, Charles S 710
Baker, Charlotte 412
Baker, David 391
Baker, Dorenda 745
Baker, Elizabeth 748
Baker, Faith 673
Baker, Gary M 764
Baker, Georgina 935
Baker, Hazel 508
Baker, James A 649, 674
Baker, James E 885
Baker, Jeff 608, 757
Baker, Jesse 365
Baker, Jessica 426
Baker, Karen 683
Baker, Lamar 674
Baker, Michael 448
Baker, Paxton K 497
Baker, Ralph O 619
Baker, Roger W 762
Baker, Tim 77
Bakker, Age F.P 915
Balas, Tammy 655
Baldassaro, Fred 827
Baldauf, Sarah 88
Baldock, Bobby R 850
Baldwin, Katherine 652
Baldwin, Linda M 673
Baldwin, Monya 73
Baldwin, Tammy 291, 310, 330, 409, 410, 411, 475
Balis, Ellen J 405
Balkham, Dennis 345
Balkus, Richard 831
Ball, James 786
Balladelli, Pier Paolo 920
Ballard, Matthew 99
Ballard, Tina 779
Ballenger, David 762
Ballinger, James K 806
Ballman, Karin 46
Ballou, Wade 461
Ballweg, Mitchell J 676
Balmori, Diana 778
Balsiger, Jim 917
Baltes, Joanna 674
Baltimore, Dottie A 627
Balton, David A 599
Bambach, Alistaire 826
Bamford, Holly 709
Banas, JoBeth 69
Banducci, Andrew 407
Bange, Gerald A 687
Banjac, Srdan 454
Banks, Al 580
Banks, Alvin 412
Banks, Carole 610
Banks, George David 362
Banks, Katie 277
Banks, Ronald 729
Banks-Dubose, Inez 740
Bansal, Preeta 590
Bansemer, Kristi 340
Banta, E 643
Barab, Jordan 723
Barackman, Molly 344
Barackman-Eder, Molly 344
Baran, Jeff 412
Barash, Yael 424
Barbadoro, Paul J 891
Barber, Ron 13
Barbino, Michael V 631
Barboza, William 784
Barcena, Alicia 926
Barchenger, Ervin 682
Barclay, James O 640

Page

Bardee, Michael A 752
Barden, Scott 671
Barelli, Tim 358
Barfield, Sheila 900
Barger, Norah M 775
Barinbaum, Rachel 7
Barkeloo, Sharon 443
Barker, Adam J 347, 348, 350
Barker, Constance 783
Barker, William Curt 715
Barkett, Rosemary 850
Barkley, Chris 372
Barkley, Timothy 746
Barkoff, Kendra 1, 587, 679
Barksdale, Marshall 461
Barksdale, Rhesa H 849
Barletta, Lou 229, 308, 335, 406, 407, 438, 440, 441, 442, 475
Barlow, Joseph 671
Barlow, Kate 20
Barlow, Michelle 148
Barlow, Ralph M 788
Barna, Stephanie 638
Barnabae, Monica 506
Barnard, Brian 401
Barnard, Claire 729
Barnes, David 420
Barnes, Freddy 456
Barnes, Janet L 817
Barnes, Melody 843
Barnes, Melody C 591
Barnes, Michael A 579
Barnes, Thomas A 612
Barnes, Valerie 628
Barnett, Beverly 920
Barnett, Chelsea 217
Barnett, Erik 769
Barnett, Mickey D 840
Barnett, Phil 412
Barnett, Robert 799
Barnette, James 411
Barnhardt, Cathy 506
Barnosky, Jason 372
Baron, Dena 401
Baron, Stephen T 899
Barr, Ann Calvaresi 742
Barr, Delia 420
Barr, Patricia 397
Barr, Stephen 799
Barr, Suzie 769
Barranti, Michael 670
Barrasso, John 295, 310, 321, 325, 359, 361, 362, 366, 367, 381, 386, 467
Barrera, Amy 456
Barrera, Rosalinda B 757
Barrera, Staci 769
Barrett, Betsy 141
Barrett, David 749
Barrett, Gary 130
Barrett, Jaleh F 669
Barrett, M.P 648
Barrett, Melody 607
Barrett, Murphie 362
Barrett, Regina M 823
Barrick, Carl 345
Barringer, Martha M 841
Barron, Dan 362
Barros, Colleen 733
Barrow, John 78, 303, 332, 409, 410, 445, 475
Barry, Erin 352
Barry, Marion 897
Barry, Mary-Kate 457
Barry, Maryanne Trump 849
Barry, Tim 742
Barry, Tina 821
Bars, Michael 139
Barsky, Seth 661
Barthel, John 701
Bartheld, Elizabeth 216
Barthold, Thomas A 465
Bartholomew, Carolyn 500
Bartholomew, Edward 906
Bartholow, Steven A 841
Bartlett, Blaire 185
Bartlett, Liz 95
Bartlett, Patricia 828
Bartlett, Rashmi 814
Bartlett, Roscoe G 125, 304, 328, 402, 403, 404, 435, 436, 438, 475

Page

Bartley, Paul S 727
Bartling, John R 416
Bartnoff, Judith 895
Bartolini, Marita 821
Bartolomei, Donald 576
Bartolomei, Jason 376
Barton, Joe 253, 309, 327, 409, 410, 411, 475
Barton, Matthew 768
Barton, Mike 806
Barton, Stacy 170
Bartrum, John 401, 733
Bartuska, Ann 698
Barzilay, Judith M 870
Barzun, Matthew Winthrop 603
Bascetta, Cynthia A 575
Basden, Faye 794
Basgal, Ophelia 740
Bashford, Janice 260
Basile, Caroline 412
Basile, Juliana 824
Basile, Vic 814
Basiliko, Nina 818
Baskir, Lawrence M 872
Basrawi, Mazen 652
Bass, Charles F 167, 306, 331, 409, 410, 475
Bass, Dave 392
Bass, Eugene 701
Bass, John R 601
Bass, Karen 35, 302, 335, 405, 418, 419, 475
Bassanese, Lynn 804
Bassett, Cheryl 372
Bassett, Michael 383
Bassett, William F 776
Basso, Peter 743
Basta, Daniel 709
Bastian, Walter 707
Batchelder, Alice M 849
Batchelder, Lily 364
Bateman, Dale P 774
Bates, Carol 505
Bates, Christopher 729
Bates, John D 862
Bates, Keith F 777
Bath, George 424
Bath, Nick 369
Bathgate, Katherine 407
Bathurst, Donald 767
Batista, Paulo Nogueira, Jr 914
Batkin, Gabrielle 344
Batkin, Josh 812
Batres, Alfonso R 764
Batte, Katie 344, 345
Battey, James F., Jr 734
Battle, Michael Anthony, Sr 603
Battle, Sandra 756
Battles, Caroline Pelot 154
Battles, Thomas 654
Batts, Rebecca 820
Batty, Michael 922
Baucus, Max 158, 305, 322, 324, 339, 340, 361, 362, 363, 364, 384, 464, 466, 467, 497, 498
Bauer, William J 849
Bauerly, Cynthia L 789
Baugher, James R 893
Bauguess, Scott 821
Bauhs, Kim 817
Bauhs, Kimberlyn 770
Baukol, Andy 608
Bauld, Denise 237
Bauld, Laura 237
Baum, Ray 220, 411
Baumann, Franz 925
Baumann, Jeremiah 219
Baumann, Rose 142
Baumerich, Carol A 814
Baumes, Harry 687
Baumgaertner, Martin 839
Baxter, Felix 651
Baxter, Greg 723
Baxter, John R 745
Bay, Norman 753
Bayard, Rochelle S 815
Bayer, Mark 131
Bayer, Philip 461
Bayer, Thomas A 824
Baylor, Elizabeth 369
Bayly, John H., Jr 896
Bazemore, Bruce 73

Page

Bazzle, Diane ... 782
Bea, Carlos T ... 850
Beach, Maureen ... 458
Beachy, Roger N ... 698
Beale, John E ... 917
Beam, C. Arlen ... 850
Bean, Brian ... 391
Bean, Casey ... 693
Bean, Elise ... 372
Bean, Michael ... 680
Beard, Jean-Louise ... 197
Beard, Tim ... 691
Beardslee, Keith ... 157
Beardsley, Beth ... 763
Beares, Ellen ... 344
Bearquiver, Kevin ... 681
Beasley, Jennifer ... 608
Beasley, Roger ... 672
Beattie, Brien ... 433
Beatty, Paige ... 506
Beatty, Sarah ... 227
Beaubian, Traci ... 459
Beaudin, Bruce D ... 896
Beauduy, Thomas W ... 834
Beaulieu, Curt ... 365
Beavin, Mike ... 437
Bebeau, Michael ... 433
Becerra, Xavier ... 34, 302, 329, 447, 448, 454, 466, 476, 828
Bech, Rebecca ... 700
Bechtold, Ron ... 618
Beck, Allison ... 792
Beck, David ... 838
Beck, Loretta ... 712
Beck, Ronna L ... 895
Beck, Thomas M ... 790
Beckenbaugh, Scot L ... 792
Becker, Alex ... 455
Becker, Ben ... 340
Becker, Boris ... 647
Becker, Chyhe ... 821
Becker, Craig ... 808
Becker, Daniel J ... 834
Becker, Jacqueline M ... 777
Becker, Jonathan ... 142
Becker, Lynn ... 290
Becker, Tim ... 160
Beckerman, Michel ... 411
Beckford, Veronica ... 182
Beckham, Steward D ... 768
Beckhoff, Bernard ... 912
Beckner, Christian ... 372
Beckwith, Brian ... 770
Beda, Carol Ann ... 627
Bede, Jasper J ... 830
Bedingfield, Eric ... 240
Bedoya, Alvaro ... 376
Bedwell, Jim ... 690
Beecroft, David ... 629
Beecroft, Robert Stephen ... 601
Beeman, Judith ... 662
Beeman, Ray ... 448
Beering, Steven C ... 811
Beers, Rand ... 766
Beeton, Jonathon ... 68
Beever, Milton R ... 832
Beezer, Robert R ... 850
Begeman, Ann ... 750
Begg, Margaret ... 612
Beghe, Renato ... 883
Begich, Mark ... 7, 301, 322, 325, 346, 347, 354, 356, 357, 371, 372, 379, 384, 467, 494, 797
Behan, George ... 284
Behan, Michael ... 272
Beil, Jennifer ... 110
Beinecke, Frederick W ... 808
Beirne, Katie ... 383, 385
Bejankiwar, Raj ... 913
Bel, Megan ... 115
Belair, Brendan ... 267
Beland, Russell W ... 645
Belardo-Webster, Luz ... 300
Belcher, Robert E ... 460
Belden, Craig ... 191
Bell, Alison ... 461
Bell, Allyson ... 269
Bell, Beth ... 731
Bell, Hubert T ... 812
Bell, Jacqueline ... 228
Bell, Lisa ... 776
Bell, Lisa M ... 776
Bell, Mark ... 211
Bell, Stephen ... 115
Bell, Suzanne L ... 662
Bella, Melanie ... 732
Bellamy, Terry ... 899
Belland, Janelle ... 143
Bellerive, Ruth ... 639
Bellis, Douglass ... 461
Bello, Al ... 627
Bellow, Bonnie ... 783
Bellows, John ... 609
Belon, Valerie ... 600
Belson, James A ... 895
Belt, Brittany ... 184
Belt, Regina ... 661
Beltran, David ... 27
Belvin, Paul ... 822
Belz, Herman ... 798
Benavides, Fortunato P ... 849
Benbow, Camilla ... 811
Bench-Snow, Susan ... 630
Benda, Leigh ... 673
Benda, Paul ... 767
Bender, Avi ... 705
Bender, Kimberly ... 623
Benedetto, Kathy ... 430
Beneke, Patty ... 360
Benishek, Dan ... 133, 305, 335, 428, 429, 435, 436, 445, 476
Benitez, Brigida ... 906
Benitez, Eduardo Behar ... 905
Benjamin, Billy ... 455
Benjamin, Claire ... 120
Benjamin, Daniel S ... 595
Benjamin, Darlynn ... 145
Benjamin, Darren ... 401
Benjamin, Raymond ... 928
Benjamin, Tiffany ... 412
Benjaminson, Eric D ... 601, 602
Benn, Eric ... 670
Benn, Rebecca ... 344
Benner, Janine ... 221
Bennet, Michael F ... 46, 302, 323, 325, 339, 340, 351, 352, 368, 382, 467, 493
Bennett, A. Brooke ... 15
Bennett, Barbara ... 782
Bennett, Cheryl ... 245
Bennett, Douglas ... 625
Bennett, Edgar ... 819
Bennett, Jamie ... 806
Bennett, Mia ... 360
Bennett, Michael W ... 367
Bennett, Nathan ... 99
Bennett, Norman ... 699
Bennett, Raul ... 627
Bennett, Toby D ... 713
Bennett, Virginia ... 595
Bennion, Emily ... 269
Bennot, Adam ... 407
Bennouna, Mohamed ... 924
Benor, David ... 728
Benson, Rodney ... 656, 657
Benson-Walker, Gwen ... 298
Bentley, James ... 831
Benton, Brad ... 155
Benton, Cheryl ... 598
Benton, Duane ... 850
Bentsen, Tamra ... 502
Bentz, Joseph P ... 637
Benz, Frank J ... 802
Berardini, Chris ... 185
Berchoff, Donald ... 710
Berenberg, Scott ... 704
Berenholz, Jennifer ... 412
Berens, Kelly ... 457
Beresik, Michael T ... 417
Berg, Adam ... 434
Berg, Jeremy M ... 734
Berg, Nadine ... 187
Berg, Rick ... 203, 307, 335, 447, 448, 476
Berge, John ... 688
Berger, Diane ... 630
Berger, Katherine M. B ... 808
Berger, Ryan ... 244
Bergeron, David ... 759

	Page
Bergeron, James	407
Bergers, David	824
Bergman, Teri	721
Bergreen, Timothy	33
Bergren, Eric	110
Bergwin, Diana	422
Berkhahn, Jocelyn	293
Berkley, Shelley	164, 306, 330, 447, 448, 476
Berkovitz, Dan	779
Berkowitz, Deborah	723
Berkowitz, Francine	829
Berkowitz, Paul	420
Berlin, Jennifer	367
Berman, Howard L	32, 302, 327, 418, 425, 426, 476
Bermejo, Elmy A	721
Bermingham, Eldredge	829
Bern, Jaryd	216
Bernal, Dan	23
Bernal, Richard	907
Bernanke, Ben S	775
Bernard, Bruce	661
Bernard, Jeremy	592
Bernards, Stacey	458
Bernhardt, Bret	237
Bernhardt, Jay	731
Bernhardt, Lisa	344
Bernicat, Marcia Stephens Bloom	601, 602
Berning, Judy	789
Berns, David A	898
Bernsteen, Amy	743
Bernstein, Jarrod	766
Bernstein, Ryan	203
Bernstein, Tom A	836
Bernstein, Wilma E	798
Berquam, Taunja	401
Berrey, John L	773
Berrick, Cathleen	575
Berrien, Jacqueline A	783
Berry, A. Paulette	816
Berry, Ann	272
Berry, David P	809
Berry, Diane	422
Berry, Dorothy H	935
Berry, E. Clay	608
Berry, Elizabeth	693
Berry, Gregory	37
Berry, Jessica M	344
Berry, John	814
Berry, Moya	182
Berry, Tim	456
Berryhill, Nancy A	833
Bersani, Kurt S	704
Bersin, Alan D	769
Berti, Thomas J	705
Bertini, Robert	750
Bertoni, Malcolm	732
Bertoson, Todd	357
Bertram, Chris	742
Bertsch, Charles	693
Bertsch, Kevin M	775
Berwick, Donald M	731
Berzon, Marsha L	850
Bes, Martin	907
Beshouri, Joseph E	895
Besser, Richard E	730
Bessey, Kaylyn	83
Best, B. Jean	465
Best, David	375
Beswick, Paul	821
Betancourt, Ana-Mita	935
Betka, Sue	758
Better, Kate	189
Bettge, Paul W	776
Betz, John	633
Betz, Kim	284
Beutel, Richard	433
Bevacqua, Frank	912
Bevan, Larry	692
Bevels, Lisa	662
Beveridge, Albert J., III	807
Beverly, John R., III	721
Beyer, Donald Sternoff, Jr	601, 603
Beyerhelm, Chris	691
Beyland, Tim	629
Beyrle, John R	602
Bezdziecki, Ed	631
Bhargava, Anurima	652
Bharwani, Raj	437
Bhatia, Anita	935
Bhatt, Shailen P	745
Bhattacharyya, Rupa	606
Bialek, Mark	777, 782
Bialke, Brooke	145
Bianchi, Kerry	829
Bianchi, Ron	699
Bianchi, Sarah	1, 587
Bias, Lori	401
Bibbee, Alison	288
Biblowitz, Joel P	809
Bice, Debra	830
Bice, Don	686
Bichara, Dominique	933
Biddick, Dennis	645
Biden, Joseph R., Jr	1, 387, 585, 587, 589, 827
Bieber, Robert J	890
Bieger, Peter	605
Bieret, Stefan J	461
Bierman, J.W	648
Biersner, Robert J	725
Bigelow, Chris	188
Bigelow, Lelaine	35
Biggers, Patricia A	833
Biggert, Judy	90, 303, 330, 406, 414, 415, 416, 435, 436, 499, 476
Biggs-Silvers, Catherine	763
Bilbray, Ashlyn	384
Bilbray, Brian P	43, 302, 331, 409, 410, 411, 476
Bilbray, James H	840
Bilder, Lisa	818
Bilirakis, Gus M	62, 302, 418, 419, 421, 422, 445, 476, 497
Billimoria, Jim	448
Billings, John	167
Billingsley, Tara	360
Billington, Debra	639
Billington, James H	500, 580, 799, 807, 843
Billups, Karen	360
Bilyeu, Dana K	793
Bina, Betsy	401
Bingaman, Jeff	176, 306, 321, 324, 359, 363, 368, 384, 463, 467
Bingen, Kari	404
Bingham, Jeff	358
Biniaz, Susan	596
Biniek, Jean	354
Binkley, Wayne	219
Binsted, Anne	424
Biraud, Gerard	927
Birch, Debra	461
Bird, Barry	706
Bird, John	646
Birman, Igor	21
Birmingham, Guillermo	919
Birnbaum, Linda S	734
Birney, William J	675
Biro, Frank	830
Biro, Susan	782
Bishop, Cameron	4
Bishop, Leslie	712
Bishop, Norman R	417
Bishop, Rob	270, 309, 331, 428, 429, 434, 476
Bishop, Sanford D., Jr	73, 303, 329, 398, 400, 476
Bishop, Timothy H	180, 306, 331, 406, 407, 440, 441, 442, 443, 476
Bissell, Katherine	724
Biswal, Nisha	835
Biswal, Nisha Desai	498
Bitter, Sandra	39
Bittner, Emily	287
Bittner, Mamie	807
Bizzacco, Christopher	236
Bjorklund, Cybele	449
Blachman, Eric J	670
Black, Alvin	719
Black, Barry C	390
Black, Carol	459
Black, David	687
Black, David F	831
Black, Diane	247, 308, 335, 405, 447, 448, 476
Black, Elliott	745
Black, Heidi	221
Black, Jonathan	73, 360
Black, June	130
Black, Mike	681
Black, Steve	679
Black, Susan H	850

Page

Blackburn, James 641
Blackburn, Marsha 248, 308, 332, 409, 410, 411, 476
Blackburn, Robert B 826
Blackburn, Wilbert H 698
Blackburne-Rigsby, Anna 895
Blackman, Anita K 750
Blackwell, Adam 918
Blackwell, Edith 684
Blackwell, Gregory 786
Blackwell, Jim 630
Blackwell, Juliana 709
Blackwood, Beth 824
Blackwood, Michael 655
Blackwood, R. Duke 804
Blackwood, Sarah 90, 443
Blackwood, Wayne 704
Bladen, Anthony 667
Blair, Anita 610
Blair, John 177
Blair, Rob 401
Blake, Carol 697
Blake, Ike 385
Blake, John 646
Blake, Kathleen 812
Blake, Kristene 455
Blake, Robert 597
Blakely, Allison 807
Blanchard, Charles A 631
Blanchard, Olivier 913
Blanchett, Irma 757
Blanco, Kenneth A 654
Blanco, Marie 80
Bland, Julia W 808
Blando, Steve 676
Blando, Tony 290
Blaney, Gregory D 802
Blank, Jonah 367
Blank, Karl T 841
Blank, Rebecca 704
Blankenship, Dawn 826
Blankenship, Ronald E 894
Blansitt, Ed 497
Blase, Brian 433
Blass, David 823
Blaszkowsky, David 821
Blatchford, Laurel A 737
Blau, Marc 825
Blau, Zach 375
Blavin, Susan Mitchell 416
Blecksmith, Robert 667
Bleiberg, Paul 294
Bleich, Jeffrey L 600
Blessington, Carole 377
Blessum, Kale 369
Blevins, R. Brent 397
Blewett, Judson 385
Blier, William 670
Blim, Larry 695
Blinken, Tony 1, 387, 587
Bliss, Christine 591
Blixt, Jerry L 642
Blocher, Paul 146
Blocher, Sarah 420
Block, Arthur 820
Block, Gregory O 890
Block, Lawrence J 873
Block, Sharon 721
Blocker, Byron C 577
Blodgett, Timothy 461
Blom, Bryan 293
Bloom, Michael 457
Bloom, Peter 623
Bloom, Ron 592
Bloom, Seth 376
Bloom, Thomas R 611
Bloomberg, Lauren 449
Bloomfield, Sara J 836
Bloomquist, Michael 411
Blount, Elonda 461
Blount, Steven 731
Blount, Willie 461
Bloxson, Stefanie 510
Bloyer, John H 465
Blue, Rebecca 688
Bluestone, Ronald S 581
Blum, Jonathan 731
Blum, Scott 628
Blumenauer, Earl 220, 308, 329, 405, 447, 476
Blumenfeld, Jared 783
Blumenthal, Daniel A 500
Blumenthal, David 729
Blumenthal, Gary 805
Blumenthal, Richard 51, 302, 323, 325, 346, 347, 368, 374, 375, 382, 467, 496
Blumenthal, Rob 343
Blumerman, Lisa 706
Blunt, Roy 152, 305, 323, 325, 341, 342, 343, 356, 357, 377, 382, 467, 501
Blyden, Rosita 719
Blyth, Jonathan 69
Boardman, Karen 752
Boarman, Larry 401
Boarman, William 576, 803
Boasberg, James E 864
Boatman, Mary 588
Bober, G. Marvin 814
Bobins, Norman R 836
Bock-Valotta, Claudia 907
Bockenstedt, Jason 373
Bockweg, Gary L 893
Bode, Kenneth 720
Boeckel, Marty 203
Boehm, Jason 713
Boehm, Martin 819
Boehme, Ken 640
Boehne, Kevin 749
Boehner, James C 841
Boehner, John A 209, 307, 328, 452, 455, 476, 499, 502, 799
Boesch, William L., Jr 576
Boese, Wade 597
Boggs, Danny J 849
Boggs, Paula E 774
Bognanno, Chris 43
Bohl, Eric 154
Bohm, Jason 508
Bohman, Mary 699
Bohnert, Roger V 747
Bohnsack, Frances 748
Bohren, Brittany 413
Bohrer, Jason 83
Boisvert, Ronald F 715
Bokova, Irina 928
Boland, Robert 145
Bolanos, Rita Maria Hernandez 918
Bolanos, Victor Manuel 906
Bolden, Charles F., Jr 799
Boles, Sean 507
Bolger, Daniel P 640
Boll, Ted 463
Bolling, Patrice 14
Bollinger, John 714
Bolls, William J., Jr 726
Bollwerk, Helen M 675
Bologna, Mark 763
Bolten, Joshua B 836
Bolton, Edward 629
Bolton, Hannibal 680
Bolz, Leslie 49
Bomba, Margaret A 393
Bomberg, Jared 358
Bonaiuto, Dominic 280
Bonanati, Chris 748
Bond, James P 936
Bond, Michele Thoren 601
Bondevik, Kjell Magne 930
Bondi, Peter 352
Bonilla, Armando O 649
Bonilla, Juan Pablo 906
Bonine, David 274
Bonini, Kyle 134
Bonlender, Brian 282
Bonner, Bob 401
Bonner, Jerome 718
Bonner, Jo 3, 301, 332, 398, 399, 413, 476
Bonner, Peter 688
Bonnet, Odette 712
Bono Mack, Mary 330, 476
Bonvechio, Kate 422
Bonyun, Sean 411
Boochever, Robert 850
Bookbinder, Noah 375
Bookstaber, Richard 821
Bookstein, Monique 667
Boone, Lew 640
Boone, Sherman 824

Page

Boortz, Steven A 578
Booth, Donald E 601
Booth, Linda 430
Booth, Thomas E 627
Booth, William H 627
Boothe, Lisa 70
Boots, Michael "Mike" 588
Boozman, John 14, 301, 323, 325, 339, 340, 356, 357, 361, 362, 379, 468
Bope, Heath R 404
Borawski, June M 347
Borchard, Lauren 502
Borchardt, R. William 813
Bordallo, Madeleine Z 298, 310, 337, 402, 403, 428, 429, 476
Bordeaux, JoAnn J 652
Borden, Michael 416
Borden, Robert 433
Border, Lourdes 656
Bordewich, Jean Parvin 377
Bordoff, Jason 588
Boren, Dan 216, 307, 332, 428, 429, 451, 476
Borg, Stephen 91
Borges, Antonio 913
Boris, Bonnie 692
Borja, Angie 79
Borkowski, Mark 769
Borland, James 830
Borlik, Bryan 706
Borman, Matthew 706
Bornstein, Rachel 236
Borro, R 643
Borwick, Anthony S 796
Borzi, Phyllis C 721
Borzino, Bruce 715
Bosanko, William 802
Bosley, Dale 859
Bosse, Philip 120
Bossenmeyer, Jim 365
Bossi, Kristen 53
Bostic, Raphael 812
Bostic, Raphael W 738
Bostic, William G., Jr 705
Bostick, George 611
Bostick, Rayanne 51
Bostick, Thomas P 640
Bostrom, Lloyd 10
Boswell, Eric J 598
Boswell, Leonard L 102, 304, 330, 395, 396, 440, 441, 442, 476
Boswell, Walter 787
Boteler, Frank 698
Botelho, Jason 385
Bott, Vicki 738
Bottorff, Dennis C 834
Bouchard, Barbara J 775
Bouchard, Robert 747
Boucher, Richard 919
Boudin, Michael 849
Boulden, William L 839
Boulware, Mark M 600
Bounds, Lorissa 44
Bounkong, Bo 711
Bourbeau, Sharie 767
Bourke, Jaron 433
Bourne-Goldring, Kimberly 393
Bourque, Monique K 663
Boustany, Charles W., Jr 117, 304, 332, 447, 448, 476, 499
Bousum, Scott 404
Boutilier, Elaine M 777
Bovbjerg, Barbara D 575
Bowden, Gary 893
Bowen, David 744
Bowen, Jonathan 358
Bowen, Melanie 269
Bowen, Ray M 811
Bowers, Kelly C 825
Bowers, Mandy L 422
Bowers, Michael 509
Bowers, Pamela 784
Bowers, Sharon 786
Bowersox, Lynn 842
Bowie, Cynthia 653
Bowie, Maria 41
Bowie, Terry 800
Bowling, Carol 747
Bowling, Tim 576

Page

Bowman, Bertie H 367
Bowman, Casey 283
Bowman, David H 776
Bowman, Geoff 444
Bowman, John E 612, 812
Bowman, Kim 140
Bowman, Lee 790
Bowman, Mark 638
Bowman, Pasco M., II 850
Bowman, Sheilah 58
Bowser, David 77
Bowser, Muriel 897
Box, Courtney 217
Boxer, Barbara 18, 301, 323, 324, 356, 357, 361, 366, 367, 381, 384, 799, 468
Boxer, Rachel 48
Boxler, Mike 666
Boyce, Thomas M 813
Boyd, Anna Alvarez 775
Boyd, April 703
Boyd, Eric 37
Boyd, Gerald 752
Boyd, Judith 452
Boyd, Katie 455
Boyd, Kevin 707
Boyd, Krista 433
Boyd, Lisa M 793
Boyd, Stephen 3
Boyer, Brooke 401
Boyer, Kelly 19
Boyer, Lucretia M 775
Boyijian, Shant 443
Boyington, Will 433
Boykin, Lori 157
Boyl, Molly 433
Boyle, Christopher 507
Boyle, Erin 455
Boysen, Sharon 242
Bozell, Laura 449
Bozzi, Adam 46
Braccio, Dominick 770
Brachfeld, Paul 802
Brachman, Ellis 52
Brachman, Ellis Andrew 454
Braddock, Richard 511
Braden, Parish 226
Braden, Susan G 874
Bradford, Linda 816
Bradford, Martina L 390
Bradley, Anita 411
Bradley, Annie 649
Bradley, Charlene M 627
Bradley, Eric 610
Bradley, James H 698
Bradley, Jim 576, 577
Bradley, Kim 827
Bradley, Neil 278, 455
Bradley, Robert 372
Bradshaw, Nancy Lee 894
Bradshaw, Wayne 270
Brady, Brian 405
Brady, Clare 933
Brady, Gordon 463
Brady, Jenae 340
Brady, Kevin 254, 309, 330, 447, 448, 463, 476
Brady, Lawrence J 432
Brady, Mary S 825
Brady, Robert A 224, 308, 330, 402, 403, 424, 464, 476, 502, 503
Brady, Terence M 688
Braga, Carlos 933
Bragg, Catherine 925
Bragg, Jeffrey S 606
Brainard, Lael 607, 839
Braley, Bruce L 101, 304, 333, 431, 432, 445, 476
Braman, Leonard 896
Bramell, Brittany 209
Bramwell, Adam 389
Bran, Raul Castellanos 921
Branca, Arlene 290
Branch, Doug 463
Branch, Elliott 646
Branch, John 824
Branche, Christine 731
Brand, Adam 38
Brand, Barbara 632
Brand, Jennifer 724
Brand, Lauren 747

	Page
Brand, Marcia K	732
Brand, Norman J	465
Branda, Joyce R	651
Brandell, Jim	135
Brandon, Andrea	698
Brandon, Kathleen	675
Brandon-Arnold, Cynthia	890
Brandt, Andrew	261
Brandt, Anna	934
Brandt, Daniel	354
Brandt, Kim	365
Branegan, Jay	367
Branham, David H	637
Branscome, John	358
Branson, Cherri L	423
Brant, Marianne	31
Branton, Brian	47
Brasher, Traci L	462
Bratcher, Makaela T	816
Bratt, Jeremy	51
Braunstein, Diane K	830
Braunstein, Sandra F	775
Bravo, Matt	455
Braxton, Lewis S.G., III	800
Bray, Chara R	416
Bray, John	343
Bray, Shawn A	671
Bray, Vaughn	387
Brayton, Kathy	433
Brazauskas, Joseph	433
Brazel, Susan	842
Brazelton, Hallet	461
Brazis, William "Bill"	618
Brazis, William E	617
Bredin, James	588
Breeding, Beth	279
Breedlove, Philip	623
Breen, Barry	783
Breene, Samuel	225
Breidenbach, Carrie	449
Breitenbach, Catherine	726
Breiteneicher, Henry S	809
Brekenfeld, Joshua	377
Brenckle, Joe	369
Brennan, Anne	643
Brennan, Deborah	698
Brennan, John O	592
Brennan, Joseph E	791
Brennan, Kevin	462
Brennan, Matthew	226
Brennan, Megan J	840
Brennan, Tim	626
Brenneman, Diane	895
Brenner, Eliot B	813
Brenner, Joseph	823
Brenner, Richard J	698
Brereton, Peter	790
Breslow, Julie	895
Bressler, Shellie	367
Bresso, Gineen	836
Brettell, Anna	498
Breuer, Lanny A	654
Brewer, Ann	733
Brewer, David	433
Brewer, Herman, Jr	676
Brewer, John	687, 692
Brewer, Leah C	347
Breyer, Stephen G	846
Brice-O'Hara, Sally	770
Bricker, Paul	639
Brickley, Michelle	678
Bridgeman, Crystal	369
Bridges, Timothy K	626
Bridgewater, Bradley	661
Bridgewater, James A	788
Brigety, Reuben	599
Briggs, Colleen	340
Briggs, Josephine P	734
Briggs, Kelli	211
Briggs, Michael	272
Briggs, Xavier	590
Bright, Andrea J	817
Bright, Michael	352
Bright, Myron H	850
Brightman, Kirk H	509, 815
Briles, Rebecca	198
Brill, Jane	644
Brill, Julie	793
Brimmer, Esther	597
Brinck, Mike	446
Brincks, Michael T	797
Brink, Patricia A	650
Brinker, Barry	424
Brinker, Nancy Goodman	798
Brinker, Susan	214
Brinkman, William	752
Brinkmann, Beth	651
Brinson, Chris	4
Brinza, Dan	591
Briscoe, Mary Beck	850
Bristol, Gilliam M.S	918
Bristol, Teri	744
Brita, Susan F	794
Brito, Claudette	719
Britton, Joseph	46
Britton, Karl	90
Brlecic, Jeffrey	618
Broadbent, Alfred	704
Broadbent, Christian	820
Broadus, Nicole	580
Broas, Timothy	843
Brock-Smith, Cynthia	897
Brockman, Clay	383
Brockman, Stacie	665
Brockmeyer, Kara	823
Brodecki, Joseph M	836
Broderick, Eric	734
Broderick, Patricia A	895
Brodsky, Jason	588
Brody, Carolyn	773
Brody, Jennifer	376
Brody, Perry Finney	259
Brodzinski, Mark	694
Bromagen, Ashley	111
Bromberg, Howard B	641
Bromley, V. Sue	778
Bromwich, Michael E	682
Bronrott, William A	745
Bronson, Karen	459
Brookens, Katie	91
Brookes, Peter	500
Brooks, Catherine Modeste	391
Brooks, Colin	508
Brooks, Dave	746
Brooks, David	360
Brooks, Herb	823
Brooks, Irene B	912
Brooks, Karl	783
Brooks, Laurie	808
Brooks, Mo	5, 301, 335, 402, 403, 435, 436, 477
Brooks, Tiffany	685
Brorby, Wade	850
Brose, Christian D	347, 348, 350
Brosius, Karen	808
Brosnan, Michael L	611
Brotherton, Andrea	643
Brougher, Jack	708
Broun, Elizabeth	828
Broun, Paul C	77, 303, 333, 421, 428, 429, 435, 477
Broussard, Meryl	698
Brown, Ariella	211
Brown, Barry	264
Brown, Carolyn	581
Brown, Catherine	596
Brown, Chelsea	452
Brown, Chris	157
Brown, Claudine	828
Brown, Corrine	58, 302, 329, 440, 441, 442, 443, 445, 477
Brown, Crystal	660
Brown, Curtis	423
Brown, Dana M	600
Brown, Danielle	427
Brown, Danny	408
Brown, Dave	379
Brown, Debbie	653
Brown, Dwayne	823
Brown, E. Cooper	717
Brown, Edsel	827
Brown, Elizabeth	389, 507
Brown, Essex	713
Brown, George	205, 822
Brown, Isaac	88
Brown, James W	223
Brown, Jamie	437
Brown, Janice Rogers	852

Page

Brown, Jason 376
Brown, Jeanette L 782
Brown, Jennifer 262
Brown, Jereon M 738
Brown, Jocelyn 692
Brown, Julia F 815
Brown, Kai 642
Brown, Katie 362
Brown, Kwame R 497, 805, 897
Brown, Larry 505
Brown, Laura 684
Brown, Laura J 744
Brown, Margo 636
Brown, Marilyn A 834
Brown, Mark 636
Brown, Mary Patrice 654
Brown, Maryam 411
Brown, Melissa D 816
Brown, Michael 748
Brown, Michael A 897
Brown, Michael W 640
Brown, Michelle S 721
Brown, Mike 391
Brown, Neil 367
Brown, Patricia 730
Brown, Reginald M 816
Brown, Rich 645
Brown, Robert E 682
Brown, Roger 389
Brown, Scott P 127, 305, 321, 325, 346, 371, 378, 379, 468
Brown, Sean 254
Brown, Shannon 677
Brown, Sherrod 205, 307, 321, 325, 339, 340, 341, 342, 343, 351, 352, 379, 381, 383, 468, 498
Brown, Sherry 51
Brown, Timothy 461
Brown, Tom 155, 439
Brown, Joseph D., IV 621
Brown-Shaklee, Sally 388
Browne, Robert 582
Browne, Sharon L 799
Browne, Thomas 667
Brownell, Reb 109
Brownell, Susan M 840
Brownfield, William 597
Browning, Allyson 251
Browning, Chris 644
Browning, James R 850
Browning, Steve 599
Brubaker, Joel 288
Brubaker, Marcus 65
Brubaker, Paul 172
Bruce, Bonnie 430
Bruce, Bradley 635
Bruce, Marilyn 381
Bruce, Pauline 733
Bruckner, Caroline 378
Bruder, Jason 367
Bruer, John 811
Bruggink, Eric G 877
Bruhn, Michael 615
Brumas, Michael 388
Brumback, Gordon 823
Brumfield, Krystal 378
Brummett, Kimberly 653
Brundtland, Gro Harlem 931
Brune, Sean 833
Bruner, David 642
Bruner, Teresa 744
Brunhart, Andrew 611
Brunjes, Dave 770
Brunner, Ilana 276
Bruno, Liza 166
Bruns, Melissa 274
Brunson, Barbre A 507
Brunswick, Michelle "Shelli" 507
Brutus, Duly 918
Bruzgul, Judsen 588
Bryan, Joseph M 347, 349
Bryan, Patricia Mack 393
Bryant, Arthur 689
Bryant, Errical 3
Bryant, L. Preston, Jr 804
Bryant, Maiso 730
Bryant, Rick 85
Bryfonski, Joseph 657
Brynn, Edward 803

Page

Bryon, Jemine A 739
Bryson, Jeffrey T 812
Bryson, John 819
Bryson, John E 585, 703, 773, 794, 807
Bryson, Sharon 811
Bryson, William Curtis 856
Bryza, Matthew J 600
Brzostowski, John 832
Bubar, Patrice 812
Bucella, Donna 769
Buchanan, Avis 901
Buchanan, Brooke 9
Buchanan, Dave 653
Buchanan, Dee 452
Buchanan, James 596
Buchanan, Melissa 110
Buchanan, Natalie 456
Buchanan, Vern 64, 303, 333, 447, 448, 499, 477
Buchanan-Smith, Henrika 747
Bucher, Mary 787
Bucher, Steve 770
Buchholz, Jeri 800
Buck, Brendan 455
Buck, James Lee 823
Buck, Kelly 257
Buckalew, Adam 150
Buckingham, Buck 818
Buckles, Tony 44, 446
Buckley, Jack 758
Buckley, Kenneth D 776
Buckley, Timothy 824
Buckner, Charlene 688
Buckner, Jason 216
Buckner, Jeffrey 830
Buckner, Stephen L 705
Bucshon, Larry 99, 303, 335, 406, 407, 435, 436, 440, 442, 443, 477
Budetti, Peter 731
Budgeon, Mark 629
Budiman, Aida S 914
Budinger, Thomas 810
Budoff, Jennifer 897
Buehlmann, Beth 370
Buenzli-Crane, Joanne 704
Buerkle, Ann Marie 191, 307, 335, 418, 419, 431, 432, 445, 477
Buettner, John F 793
Buff, Gary M 724
Buffa, Nicole "Nikki" 588
Buford, Charlotte L 823
Buford, Molly 610
Buggs, Robert 756
Buhai-Jacobus, George 825
Buhl, Cindy 129
Buhler, Maryjean 778
Buie, John 711
Bulbotz, Casey 407
Bulger, Peggy 581
Bulger, Steve 189
Bull, Nicholas 465
Buller, Kathy 818
Bullman, William "Bill" 588
Bullock, Jed 299
Bulmer, William 935
Bumpus, Jeanne 793
Bums, Andrew 462
Bunaugh, Tremayne 382
Bunch, Lonnie 828
Bundy, Keith 283
Bungard, B. Chad 832
Bunn, Sheila 298
Burand, Deborah 839
Burbano, Fernando 719
Burch, James, III 672
Burcham, Jeanne 391
Burchill, William R., Jr 893
Burdinski, Ron 833
Burgeson, Eric 89
Burgess, A. Franklin, Jr 895
Burgess, E. Chase 417
Burgess, Jay 708
Burgess, Michael C 264, 309, 332, 409, 410, 411, 463, 477, 496
Burgess, Ronald L 620
Burgi-Schmelz, Adelheid 914
Burgoyne, Ellis A 840
Burhop, Anna 362
Burke, George 280

	Page
Burke, Gordon	726
Burke, Greg	744
Burke, Luke	422
Burke, Marcilynn	681
Burke, Vincent C., Jr	842
Burke, Warren	461
Burkett, Alex	443
Burkhardt, Justin	166
Burklow, John T	733
Burks, Jon	405
Burleson, Carl	743
Burleson, Kyle	138
Burn, Meg	790
Burner, Gary	606
Burnes, Austin	458
Burnett, Arthur L., Sr	896
Burnham, Heather L	392
Burnham-Snyder, Eben	430
Burnison, Melissa	429
Burniston, Timothy R	775
Burns, James	820
Burns, Robert	812
Burns, Stephen G	812
Burns, Stuart	65
Burns, William J	596
Burr, David	696
Burr, Matt	383
Burr, Richard	195, 307, 323, 324, 363, 368, 379, 382, 468, 493
Burrell, Janet	372
Burrell, Terri	700
Burrier, Ed	420
Burroughs, Harry	430
Burrows, Charlotte A	649
Burrows, Mark	913
Burrus, Carl	743
Burson, Robert J	825
Burst, Andrew	693
Burt, David	365
Burton, Amy	503
Burton, Dan	98, 303, 327, 418, 419, 431, 432, 477
Burton, Johnnie	296
Burzyk, Carla	683
Busbee, Allison	412
Busching, Mark	4
Buse, Mark	9
Bush, Douglas	404
Bush, Gary C	578
Bush, George	798
Bush, Jordan	135
Bush, Laura	798
Bush, Lynn J	873
Bush, Pamela M	781
Bush, Zoe	895
Bussey, Brian	823
Bustillo, Eric	826
Bustillo, Martin Gomez	917
Busto, Eric R	826
Butenis, Patricia A	602
Butler, Brenda	588
Butler, Donna	756
Butler, J. Dudley	701
Butler, Jacquie	696
Butler, Jim	710
Butler, Mannone	901
Butler, Robin	433
Butler, Sarah	430
Butler, Steven	695
Butler, Tanya	465
Butler, Yolanda	730
Buttarazzi, Ann	192
Buttarazzi, John	192
Buttenheim, Lisa	931
Butterfield, G. K	195, 307, 332, 409, 410, 477, 496
Butters, Timothy	749
Button, Christopher	766
Buzby, Mark H	646
Buzzi, Frank J	841
Bybee, Stewart	163
Bydume, Doreen	894
Bye, Kermit E	850
Byers, Dan	436
Byers, Timothy	629
Byrd, Cassandra	389
Byrd, Curtis	277
Byrd, Harry F., Jr	842
Byrd, Jerry S	895
Byrd, Richard	612
Byrd, Robert J	710
Byrne, Joseph A	747
Byrnes, Edmund D	815
Byrns, Mary T	833

C

	Page
Caballero, Michael	611
Caballero, Thomas E	393
Cabana, Robert	801
Cabeca, John	711
Cabranes, Jose A	849
Cade, David S	728
Caesar, Angela	866
Cafritz, Buffy	799
Cahill, Ellen	9
Cahill, James	460
Cahill, Tom	229
Cahill, William H	747
Cahn, Mark D	821
Cahn, Robert A	891
Cain, Arnetta	613
Cain, Charles	823
Cain, Eric	252
Cain, Hilary	437
Cain, Terry A	894
Cairncross, Sean	385
Calabresi, Giudo	849
Calabro, Rosemarie	360
Calamari, Andrew	826
Calamis, Brigid	785
Calcara, Joseph F	636
Calder, John	710
Calderon, Jorge Familiar	932, 935
Calderon, Jorge Vertiz	910
Calderon, Kathy	106
Calderon, Layla	420
Caldwell, Anne	2
Caldwell, David	710
Caldwell, Joanne	704
Caldwell, LaJuana	732
Caldwell, Rhonda	662
Calemine, Jody	407
Calfee, Alana	580
Calhoun, Larry	217
Calhoun, Sharon D	814
Cali, Robert	645
Caliendo, Madeline	795
Califf, Caroline	443
Calio, Lydia	434
Calixte, Katrina	372
Call, Laurel	497
Callaghan, Darla K	676
Callahan, Brian	704
Callahan, Caitlin	165
Callahan, Consuelo M	850
Callahan, Dan	831
Callahan, Joseph T., III	630
Callahan, Robert J	602
Callahan, Timothy	711
Callanan, Brian	373
Callas, George	448
Callen, Ashley	433
Callen, Paul	461
Callender, Russell	709
Calligan, Barb	125
Calogero, Chris	718
Calvert, Donna	831
Calvert, Ken	40, 302, 329, 398, 399, 400, 405, 477
Calvert, Lawrence	789
Calvo, Michael	78, 424
Camacho, Gilbert	731
Camarasa, Felix Alberto	934
Cameron, Jessica	449
Cameron, Jon J	611
Cameron, Peter	907
Cameron, Rosanna Pianalto	775
Cammack, Perry	367
Cammarata, Pamela	672
Cammen, Leon	710
Camp, Dave	135, 305, 328, 447, 464, 466, 477
Campaneria, Miguel	806
Campbell, Abigail	360
Campbell, Bradley	657
Campbell, Caitlin E	500
Campbell, Chelsey	452
Campbell, Chris	365
Campbell, Dennis	505

Page
Campbell, Douglas J ... 420
Campbell, Herbert ... 824
Campbell, Jane ... 114
Campbell, John ... 42, 205, 302, 332, 405, 414, 415, 416, 463, 477
Campbell, John M ... 895
Campbell, Kurt ... 596, 597
Campbell, Kurt M ... 498
Campbell, Kurt N ... 499
Campbell, Laura E ... 580
Campbell, Lee C ... 642
Campbell, Mac ... 281
Campbell, Martha Larzelere ... 602
Campbell, McKie ... 360
Campbell, Natasha ... 900
Campbell, Neil ... 235
Campbell, Pauline ... 768
Campbell, Rachel D ... 750
Campbell, Renee ... 507
Campbell, Scott ... 372
Campbell, Sean D ... 776
Campbell, Sharon ... 119
Campbell, Shawn W ... 627
Campbell, Stephanie ... 5
Campbell, William A ... 840
Campione, Jeffrey C ... 776
Campos, Laura ... 11
Campos, Mariano ... 826
Campos-Infantino, Doris ... 906
Camunez, Michael C ... 496, 707
Camus, Timothy P ... 612
Canada, Amanda ... 263
Canales, Judith A ... 694
Canan, Russell F ... 895
Canby, William C., Jr ... 850
Cancienne, Paul ... 41, 412
Candela, Nicholas V ... 670
Candisky, Caryn ... 205
Canellos, George S ... 826
Canfield, Neil ... 437
Canfield, Sally ... 57
Canipe, LuAnn ... 202
Cannan, Judith ... 581
Canner, Glenn B ... 776
Cannon, Angelique ... 383
Cannon, Bonnie ... 296
Cannon, Cheri ... 631
Cannon, Courtney ... 70
Cannon, Debbie ... 72
Cannon, Sandra A ... 776
Canseco, Francisco ''Quico'' ... 262, 309, 335, 414, 415, 416, 477
Canter, Matt ... 383
Canton, Denise ... 729
Canton, Don ... 203
Canton, Santiago A ... 918
Cantor, Eric ... 278, 309, 331, 452, 455, 499, 477, 502
Cantor, Erica ... 722
Cantu, Mario ... 423
Cantwell, Maria ... 281, 309, 321, 324, 356, 357, 359, 360, 363, 364, 378, 381, 468
Cantwell, Mike ... 206
Canty, Rachel ... 770
Canuto, Otaviano ... 933
Capano, Carlos ... 670
Capasso, Paul ... 629
Cape, Dave ... 391
Capezzuto, James A ... 826
Capito, Shelley Moore ... 288, 310, 331, 414, 415, 416, 440, 442, 443, 477
Capobianco, Mike ... 373
Caponiti, James E ... 747
Cappetto, Richard ... 424, 496
Capps, Lois ... 30, 302, 330, 409, 410, 411, 477, 499
Capra, James L ... 657
Capron, Margaret ... 457
Caproni, Valerie E ... 667
Capuano, Michael E ... 131, 305, 330, 415, 416, 440, 441, 442, 443, 477
Capute, Allan ... 822
Caputo, Annie ... 362
Caramanian, Lori ... 683
Carasso, Adam ... 405
Caravelli, Margaret ... 436
Carbon, Susan B ... 677
Carbullido, Adam ... 298
Card, Kati ... 384
Card, Kendall ... 646
Cardarelli, Michael ... 763
Cardenas, Ben ... 38
Cardenas, Gladys ... 910
Cardille, Stacia ... 412
Cardin, Benjamin L ... 122, 304, 321, 325, 354, 361, 362, 363, 364, 366, 367, 378, 477, 494, 496, 501, 798, 803
Cardona, Mario ... 369
Cardoza, Christiane ... 381
Cardoza, Dennis A ... 28, 302, 332, 395, 396, 418, 419, 477
Carey, Brittany ... 456
Carey, Dennis J ... 577
Carey, Mark S ... 776
Carey, Michelle ... 787
Carey, Rob ... 617
Carey, Ryan ... 364
Carl, Leon ... 683
Carle, David ... 272
Carleton, Michael ... 728
Carlile, Joe ... 401
Carlin, David ... 88
Carlin, Ellen ... 422
Carlin, John ... 666
Carlisle, Hawk ... 629
Carlisle, Homer ... 352
Carlo, Alberto Valencia ... 910
Carlson, Donald G ... 502
Carlson, Erin ... 819
Carlson, Stacy ... 459
Carlson, Steven ... 695
Carlson, William ... 722
Carlton, Denny ... 786
Carlton, Stephanie ... 365
Carluzzo, Lewis R ... 884
Carmack, Terry ... 109
Carman, Gregory W ... 867
Carmona, Patricia ... 789
Carnahan, Russ ... 153, 305, 332, 418, 419, 440, 441, 443, 445, 477
Carnegie, Ruth ... 38
Carnes, Ben ... 10
Carnes, Ed ... 850
Carnes, Lynore ... 838
Carnevale, Sharon C ... 705
Carney, Douglas ... 460
Carney, James ... 591
Carney, John C., Jr ... 55, 335, 302, 414, 415, 416, 477
Carney, Susan L ... 849
Carnucci, Joe ... 364
Caron, Chris ... 217
Carozza, Mary Beth ... 213
Carozza, Michael ... 497
Carpenter, Cherri ... 161
Carpenter, Cynthia ... 813
Carpenter, Dea ... 770
Carpenter, Jerry ... 823
Carpenter, Mary Randolph ... 137
Carpenter, Raymond ... 633, 640
Carpenter, Seth B ... 776
Carper, Thomas R ... 55, 302, 321, 324, 361, 362, 363, 364, 371, 372, 383, 468
Carr, Chris ... 72
Carr, Florence A ... 792
Carr, Fred ... 625
Carr, Julie ... 111
Carr, Karla ... 254
Carr, Michael ... 360
Carr, Rachel ... 444
Carr, Rhonda ... 685
Carr, Robert ''Rob'' ... 662
Carr, William B., Jr ... 841
Carr, Ytta B ... 507
Carraco, Lorrena ... 697
Carren, Turko ... 448
Carrillo, Pablo E ... 347, 348, 350
Carrion, Adolfo, Jr ... 740
Carrion, Sonya ... 724
Carriveau, Carla ... 826
Carro, Maria Teresa ... 300
Carroll, Alan ... 422
Carroll, Constance M ... 807
Carroll, Dominick ... 444
Carroll, James ... 634
Carroll, Jean ... 420
Carroll, Jeff ... 171
Carroll, Kevin ... 422
Carroll, Sean ... 835
Carroll, Suzie ... 818
Carroll, Thomas J ... 506

Page

Carroll, Tom ... 505
Carron, Charles ... 582
Carson, Andre ... 99, 303, 333, 414, 415, 416, 477
Carson, Dave ... 661
Carson, David ... 582
Carson, Horace ... 628
Carson, Johnnie ... 596
Carson, Jonathan ... 593
Carson, Rebecca ... 770
Carstensen, James ... 103
Carter, Ashton B ... 616
Carter, Catherine P ... 725
Carter, Cyntoria ... 672
Carter, David ... 784
Carter, Donald D., Jr ... 724
Carter, Dorval ... 747
Carter, Gary M ... 710
Carter, Genny ... 259
Carter, Hall ... 148
Carter, James ... 367
Carter, Jeff ... 676
Carter, Jessica ... 248
Carter, Jimmy ... 798
Carter, John R ... 267, 309, 332, 398, 399, 400, 452, 477
Carter, Judy I ... 677
Carter, Margaret ... 849
Carter, Michael C ... 747
Carter, Pamela ... 730
Carter, Phillip, III ... 600
Carter, Randall ... 686
Carter, Rich ... 92
Carter, Sandy ... 103
Carter, Scott A ... 695
Cartwright, Christopher ... 709
Cartwright, James E ... 618
Carty, Will ... 358
Caruso, Amanda ... 169
Carusone, Pia ... 13
Carvalho, George ... 235
Carver, Douglas L ... 638
Carver, Jonathan ... 827
Carwile, Kevin ... 654
Carwile, William "Bill" L., III ... 768
Cary, Matthew J ... 900
Casaes, Ruy ... 917
Cascio, Tricia ... 225
Casden, Alan I ... 836
Case, Steve ... 828
Casella, Bruce A ... 634
Casey, Gregory ... 127
Casey, John D ... 893
Casey, Julia ... 401
Casey, Michael ... 404
Casey, Robert P., Jr ... 223, 308, 321, 325, 339, 340, 366, 367, 368, 382, 463, 468, 501
Casey, Sharon ... 433
Cash, Evan ... 373
Cash, Viola ... 636
Cashman, Christopher ... 78
Cashman, Declan ... 457
Casias, Lisa ... 703
Casper, Jonathan ... 204
Cassady, Alison ... 412
Cassels, Fess ... 42
Cassidy, Bill ... 117, 304, 334, 409, 410, 411, 477
Cassidy, C.J ... 644
Cassidy, Ed ... 455
Cassidy, Jeremiah ... 839
Cassidy, Thomas ... 461
Castagna, Jennifer ... 344
Castaldo, Anthony J ... 777
Castaldo, Keith ... 172
Casteen, John T., III ... 843
Castellan, Allison ... 588
Castellano, Joseph A ... 792
Castello, Roberto F. Salmon ... 911
Castilla, Carla ... 30
Castillo, Adina Mercedes Bastidas ... 907
Castillo, Alejandra ... 708
Castillo, Andeliz ... 419
Castillo, Julio ... 895
Castillo, Sylvia ... 35
Castillo, Victor G ... 36
Castle, Anne J ... 682
Castle, Jason ... 376
Casto, Dan ... 288
Castor, Kathy ... 63, 303, 333, 405, 409, 410, 411, 477
Castor, Steve ... 433

Page

Castro, George ... 345
Castro, Roy P ... 705
Castro, Sallie ... 656
Casttro, Martin ... 835
Caswell, Michael ... 416
Catala, Carlos ... 300
Catalan, Sara ... 39
Catania, David A ... 897
Catanzaro, Mike ... 455
Cate, Deven ... 625
Catechis, Jennifer ... 178
Cates, William N ... 809
Cato, Van ... 237
Catterson, Cathy A ... 850
Caughran, Bess ... 437
Caulfield, John ... 603
Caulk, Carl ... 677
Causey, Joan ... 625
Causey, Jon ... 99
Causey, William ... 675
Cavanagh, Richard ... 714
Cavanaugh, Megan ... 508
Cavanaugh, Theresa ... 786
Cave, Tonda S ... 583
Cavella, Charles ... 609
Caverly, Andrew ... 825
Caviness, Stephen ... 211
Cayce, Lyle W ... 849
Cazenave, Jo ... 26
Ceaser, James W ... 803
Cecil, Billy ... 634
Cecil, Guy ... 383
Ceja, Alejandra ... 755
Cejka, Diane ... 803
Celebrezze, Rachelle E ... 393
Cellucci, Jan ... 808
Cellucci, Tom ... 767
Celotta, Robert ... 714
Center, Charles ... 790
Centilli, Doug ... 255
Cerga, Vladimir ... 420
Cerqueira, Maria Teresa ... 921
Cesari, Roberto ... 909
Cesario, Laura ... 713
Cevasco, Marc ... 173
Cha, Stephen ... 412
Chabot, Erica ... 375
Chabot, Herbert L ... 882
Chabot, Steve ... 205, 307, 330, 418, 419, 425, 426, 438, 477
Chaffee, Christopher ... 181
Chaffee, Marta ... 823
Chaffetz, Jason ... 270, 309, 334, 405, 425, 426, 431, 432, 478
Chagares, Michael A ... 849
Chait, Mark R ... 666
Chakiris, George S ... 749
Challahan, Mary Ellen ... 766
Chamberlain, Elizabeth ... 819
Chamberlain, Irene ... 636
Chamberlain, Paul ... 636
Chambers, Glen ... 152
Chambers, Hilarie ... 139
Chambers, Jasmine ... 712
Chambers, Ray ... 932
Chambers, Te-Reika ... 96
Chambers, William ... 630
Chambliss, Saxby ... 72, 303, 322, 324, 339, 340, 346, 347, 377, 382, 464, 468, 496
Champ, Norman ... 821
Chan, Darcie E ... 392
Chan, Margaret ... 929
Chan, Peter ... 825
Chandler, Ben ... 112, 304, 332, 418, 419, 451, 478
Chandler, Ken B ... 694
Chandler, Larry ... 698
Chandler, Marjorie ... 252
Chandler, Melissa ... 238
Chandler, Michael ... 391
Chandler, Peter ... 120
Chandler, Raymond F., III ... 635
Chandler, Shana ... 286
Chaney, Ann L ... 841
Chaney, Jacob ... 340
Chaney, Leslie ... 460
Chang, John C ... 894
Chang, Lena C ... 815
Chang, Shawn ... 412

	Page
Chang, Winnie	401
Chanin, Leonard	775
Chao, Daniel	38
Chaparro, James	769
Chape, Stuart	923
Chapin, Courtney	807
Chapla, John D	404
Chaplin, Kristen	455
Chapman, Donald	708
Chapman, Karen	26
Chapman, Stephen	362, 819
Chapman, Stuart	181
Chappell, Alexa	671
Chappell, D. Michael	794
Charbonneau, Hatsie H	792
Charles, Beverly R	211
Charles, Hubert J	918
Charles, Sandra	582
Charlier, Louis	719
Charlip, Ralph	683
Charters, Tim	430
Charville, Bridget Fallon	457
Chase, Celeste	826
Chase, Karen DeLaBarre	607
Chastain, Suzan	724
Chatham, Kelle J	578, 579
Chatterjee, Neil	388
Chatterji, Pulok	934
Chaudhry, Asif	602
Chaudhry, M. Rafiq	912
Chaudhuri, Olik	711
Chavarria, Bernal A	908
Chavez, John	723
Chavez, Mayra	24
Chavez, Richard	768
Chavez, Yolanda	737
Chavez-Rubio, Jennifer	818
Cheatham, Tina M	732
Cheeks, Gary H	640
Cheh, Mary M	897
Chen, Jim	747
Chen, Paul	463
Chen, Raymond	713
Chen, Vivian	697
Chenault, Jacqueline	430
Cheney, Craig	385
Cheney, Scott	369
Cheng, Becky	35
Cheng, Dennis	595
Chenoweth, Mark	107
Chero, Linda C	796
Cherry, David	164
Cherry, Lou	628
Cherry, Stephanie	457
Cherry, Wayne	641
Chertoff, Michael	836
Cheshire, Jaime	404
Chester, Bronwyn Lance	72
Chester, LaVerne	757
Chestnut, Monica	360
Cheung, Denise	649
Chevat, Ben	186
Chew, Debra	612
Chia, Der Jiun	914
Chiappardi, Frances	458
Chiaramida, Rebecca A	612
Chiarelli, Peter W	635
Chick, Anne L	912
Chickinell, Rockne J	677
Chiechi, Carolyn P	883
Chiedi, JoAnne	729
Chilcoat, Kitty	832
Childs, Robert D	621
Chilton, Bart	779
Chin, Denny	849
Chin, Faye A	826
Chinn, Monica	434
Chion, Antonia	823
Chipman, Dana K	639
Chipman, Jason C	649
Chittum, Mark	708
Cho, In-Khan	933
Chodroff, Carol	427
Choe, Ken	728
Choi, Heenam	915
Choi, Jina L	826
Choksy, Jamsheed K	807
Chong, Frank	759
Chopra, Aneesh	590
Chott, John W., Jr	692
Chotvacs, Anne Marie	401
Chretien-Dar, Barbara	822
Chriss, Sherry	461
Christ, Katelyn	433
Christensen	478
Christensen, Carlie	257
Christensen, Donna M	300, 310, 337, 409, 410, 411
Christensen, Nathan	643
Christensen, Thomas M.P	747
Christian, Adrienne	124
Christian, Alan	701
Christian, Erik P	895
Christian, Karen E	411
Christian, Kayek	896
Christian, Lisa	439
Christianson, Andrew	243
Christie, Chris	781
Christoferson, James	344
Christopher, Dale A. "Chip"	814
Christopher, David	582
Christopher, Nancy	739
Christopherson, Sarah	130
Christrup, Henry	461
Christy, Paul	827
Chrobocinski, Roy	124
Chrzaszcz, Monica	139
Chu, Judy	34, 302, 334, 425, 426, 438, 478
Chu, Steven	585, 589, 751
Chucovich, Emily	382
Chun, A. Marisa	650
Chung, Ed	375
Chung, Kathy	46
Church, A.J	82
Church, Christopher	692
Church, Joel K	507
Churchill, Adrielle	16
Chute, Mary	807
Chute, Mary L	808
Cianciolo, Tony	507
Ciarcia, Ray	373
Ciccolella, Donna	655
Cicerone, Ralph	810
Cicilline, David N	235, 308, 335, 418, 419, 438, 478
Cieslicki, Danny A	817
Cigno, Margaret	820
Cihlar, Frank	676
Cihota, Diane	58
Cikanek, Zachary	90
Cilke, James	465
Cimino, Anthony J	416
Cimino, Ronald A	675
Cinelli, Joshua	785
Cipollone, Piero	933
Cirillo, Michael A	744
Cirks, Jeremy	91
Cisneros, Miguel A	910
Claeys, Stephen	449
Claggett, Karyn Temple	649
Clancy, Carolyn	730
Clancy, Justin B	644
Clanton, Michael	687
Clapp, Doug	344
Clapper, James R., Jr	589
Clapsis, Tony	364
Clapton, Chuck	369
Clarey, Kay	671
Clark, Anthony	153
Clark, Bob	209
Clark, Charles W	714
Clark, Christie	296
Clark, Cindy	128
Clark, Cynthia	699
Clark, Dave	576, 639
Clark, Donald S	793
Clark, Ellen	709
Clark, Fred	690
Clark, Garth	687
Clark, Geraldine L	841
Clark, Gloria V	816
Clark, H. Westley	734
Clark, Helen	927
Clark, James	629
Clark, Jeanette	895
Clark, Johnathan D	347, 348, 349
Clark, Jon	446
Clark, Jordan	226

Page
Clark, Julia A........ 790
Clark, Kent........ 62
Clark, Kimberlin C........ 817
Clark, Michell C........ 777
Clark, Oliver E........ 792
Clark, Patrina M........ 576
Clark, Sheila........ 768, 777
Clark, Ted........ 448
Clark, Timothy P........ 775
Clark, Tom........ 661
Clark, Virginia........ 828
Clarke, Bruce M........ 894
Clarke, Hansen........ 140, 305, 335, 421, 422, 435, 436, 478
Clarke, Jerry........ 91
Clarke, Kevin J........ 775
Clarke, Sheria........ 413
Clarke, Tara........ 39
Clarke, Yvette D........ 184, 306, 333, 421, 422, 438, 478
Clarkson, Mary Anne........ 389
Claros, Augusto Lopez........ 935
Claudio, Arnaldo........ 642
Clauson, Ilene........ 283
Claussen, Cory........ 340
Claussen, Roger R........ 645
Clay, Eric Lee........ 849
Clay, Gordon M........ 465
Clay, Layton F........ 577
Clay, William H........ 701
Clay, Wm. Lacy........ 153, 305, 331, 414, 415, 416, 431, 432, 478
Clayton, Jamice........ 835
Clayton, Marla........ 669
Clearfield, Frank........ 690
Cleary, David........ 244
Cleaver, Emanuel........ 155, 305, 332, 414, 415, 416, 478
Cleeland, Nancy........ 809
Clegg, M.T........ 810
Cleland, Joseph Maxwell........ 773
Clement, Edith Brown........ 849
Clements, Curt........ 656
Clements, Kelly........ 599
Clemmensen, Craig........ 739
Clemons, Dean........ 623
Clemons, Melanie........ 685
Cleveland, Robin........ 500
Cleveland, Sally-Anne........ 460
Clevenger, Raymond C., III........ 858
Click, Molly........ 369
Clifford, John........ 701
Clifton, Jill S........ 685
Clifton, Richard R........ 850
Cline, Bill........ 786
Cline, Lynn F.H........ 801
Clinefelter, Carl A........ 785
Clingan, Bruce........ 646
Clinger, James H........ 416
Clinton, Hillary Rodham........ 585, 589, 595, 778, 798, 799, 808, 837, 843
Clinton, William J........ 930
Clonts, Michael........ 689
Clookie, Mark D........ 646, 647
Clos, Joan........ 927
Closter, Harold........ 828
Cloud, Noah........ 636
Clough, Andrew........ 357
Clough, G. Wayne........ 799, 807, 808, 828, 843
Clouse, James A........ 776
Clune, Daniel........ 599
Clurman, Cade........ 90
Clyburn, James E........ 240, 308, 329, 458, 466, 478
Clyburn, Mignon........ 785
Coady, Laurie A........ 465
Coak, Cheryl L........ 694
Coates, Patricia........ 273
Coats, Daniel........ 95, 303, 323, 325, 341, 342, 343, 359, 360, 382, 463, 468
Coats, Derek........ 152
Coats, Michael L........ 801
Cobau, John........ 707
Cobb, Charles E., Jr........ 843
Cobb, Clara H........ 729
Coble, Howard........ 198, 307, 327, 425, 426, 440, 441, 442, 478, 494
Coburn, Tom........ 215, 307, 323, 324, 363, 364, 371, 374, 375, 468
Cochetel, Vincent........ 927
Cochez, Guillermo........ 918
Cochran, Bob........ 31
Page
Cochran, Norris........ 728
Cochran, Thad........ 148, 305, 322, 324, 339, 340, 341, 342, 377, 464, 468, 494, 500, 501, 799, 828
Cochrane, James P........ 840
Cockerham, Ashley........ 813
Cockrell, Roger........ 344
Cocuyame, Carlos Alberto Robles........ 908
Cody, Lisa........ 433
Cody, Marion........ 739
Coe, Anthony C........ 392
Coe, Charles........ 758
Coe, Gregory B........ 638
Coe, Michael........ 820
Coffee, Richard........ 687
Coffey, Georgia........ 763
Coffey, John L........ 849
Coffman, Callie........ 136
Coffman, Mike........ 49, 302, 334, 402, 403, 428, 429, 438, 439, 478
Cogan, Phil........ 784
Cogdill, David........ 756
Coggins, Colleen........ 748
Coggins, Wynn........ 711
Coghill, Pamela L........ 626
Cogliani, Leland........ 344
Cogswell, Patricia........ 767
Cohen, Alan........ 364
Cohen, Ana Unruh........ 430
Cohen, Brian........ 412
Cohen, Bruce........ 375
Cohen, Carol B........ 836
Cohen, Clifford........ 582
Cohen, David........ 461
Cohen, David M........ 651
Cohen, David S........ 609
Cohen, Edward........ 497
Cohen, George........ 792
Cohen, Howard........ 411
Cohen, Ilona R........ 347, 349
Cohen, Ira........ 88
Cohen, Jacqueline........ 412
Cohen, Kenneth P........ 841
Cohen, Linda........ 452
Cohen, Lisa B........ 47
Cohen, Mark........ 610
Cohen, Mary Ann........ 878
Cohen, Miriam L........ 813
Cohen, Mitch........ 731
Cohen, Robert........ 823
Cohen, Robert F., Jr........ 793
Cohen, Rochelle........ 715
Cohen, Rosaline........ 423
Cohen, Stephen........ 823
Cohen, Steve........ 249, 308, 333, 425, 426, 440, 441, 442, 443, 478, 496
Cohn, Alan........ 767
Cohn, Anna........ 829
Cohn, Deborah........ 712
Coile, Zachary........ 19
Colangelo, Brook........ 589
Colangelo, Matthew........ 652
Colarulli, Dana........ 712
Colarusso, Mary E........ 656
Colbert, Drew........ 352
Colborn, Paul P........ 673
Colburn, Brent........ 766
Colby, Paul........ 675
Colder, Karl C........ 656
Cole, Beth C........ 838
Cole, Bruce........ 644
Cole, Dana........ 699
Cole, David........ 372
Cole, Delores........ 739
Cole, Gerald M........ 791
Cole, James M........ 649
Cole, Jason........ 53
Cole, Jeffrey E........ 816
Cole, John W........ 416
Cole, John Y., Jr........ 581
Cole, Johnnetta........ 828
Cole, Owen........ 805
Cole, R. Guy, Jr........ 849
Cole, Tasha........ 67
Cole, Thomas E........ 393
Cole, Tom........ 217, 307, 398, 399, 400, 405, 478
Coleman, Andy........ 358
Coleman, Angela........ 690
Coleman, Casey........ 795

Page
Coleman, Claire 433
Coleman, Douglas W 657
Coleman, E. Thomas 502
Coleman, Everett 404
Coleman, Joycelyn 430
Coleman, Michael B 773
Coleman, Neill 738
Coleman, Richard 686
Coleman, S. Robert 785
Coleman, Soncia 369
Coleman, Ted 894
Coles, Fabrice 115
Coley, Carla 187
Coley, Herbert A 642
Colgan, Ann-Louise D 838
Colgrave, Gary S 701
Colindres, Denis Ronaldo Moncada 918
College, Craig 637
Collentine, Caherine 173
Colliatie, Drew 433
Collier, Andrew 660
Collier, Carol R 781
Collier, James 634
Collier, Matthew W 814
Collier, Pat 384
Colligan, Dylan 452
Collins, Anne L 745
Collins, Belinda L 714
Collins, Bill 446
Collins, Conner 388
Collins, Elmo E 813
Collins, Francis 733
Collins, Janet 731
Collins, Joe 392
Collins, John 373
Collins, Kristin 360
Collins, Michael 75, 176
Collins, Michael J 841
Collins, Ronald R 899
Collins, Susan 86
Collins, Susan M 119, 304, 322, 324, 341, 342, 343, 346, 347, 371, 372, 382, 469
Collins, Tom 641
Collinson, William 732
Collis, Kristin 64
Collopy, Daniel F 809
Colloton, Steven M 798, 850
Collyer, Rosemary M 863
Collyns, Charles 608
Colomo, Kathy E 797
Colon-Rivera, Angel 496
Coloretti, Nani 610
Colosimo, Mark 912
Colosimo, Robyn 588
Colton, Mare 710
Columbus, Eric R 649
Colvin, Carolyn W 829
Colvin, John O 878
Colvin, Stanley 598
Colwell, John 808
Colwell, William S 717
Combs, Leslie 88
Come, Joe 742
Comer, Katie 436
Comis, Adam 423
Compean, Guillermo A 907
Comuzzi, Joe 912
Conaton, Erin C 623
Conaway, K. Michael 256, 309, 332, 395, 396, 402, 403, 413, 451, 478, 499
Conboy, Steven 677
Concannon, Kevin 695
Conda, Cesar 57
Condes, Al 800
Condon, David 284
Condon, Joan O 419
Cone, Robert W 642
Conelly, Mary 163
Conerly, Albert 701
Coney, Chloe 63
Conklin, Meghan 679
Conley, David C 713
Conley, Michael 822
Conley, Michael G 774
Conley, Shawn 461
Conley, Shelia 728
Conlin, Chris 375
Conlon, Michael 692

Page
Conn, Alison 826
Connair, Stephen M 625
Connaughton, Kenneth R., Jr 670
Connel, Liam 644
Connell, Jamie 682
Connell, John 100
Connelly, Chris 276
Connelly, Maura 601
Connelly, Meredith 417
Connelly, Pat 818
Conner, Misty 506
Conniff, Brian 778
Connolly, Brenda 182
Connolly, Doug 384
Connolly, Gerald E 280, 309, 334, 418, 419, 431, 432, 478
Connolly, Michael 464
Connolly, Mindy 795
Connolly, Robert E 651
Connor, Anne 437
Connor, Edward 768
Connor, Jeffrey 156
Connor, Michael 683
Connor, Patricia S 849
Connors, James S 816
Connors, Thomas A 776
Conrad, Kathy 795
Conrad, Kent 203, 307, 321, 324, 339, 340, 354, 363, 364, 381, 382, 384, 465, 469, 799
Conran, Brent 460
Conrath, Kristine 607
Conroy, Kevin 434
Conroy, Patrick J 459
Considine, Travis 44
Constance, John 799
Constantine, Peter J 739
Conston, Dan 87
Conte, Stephen P 831
Contois, Jenny 52
Contreras, January 765
Contreras, Tomas 461
Conway, John J 343
Conyers, Carolyn 785
Conyers, John, Jr 140, 305, 327, 425, 426, 478
Cook, Beth 388
Cook, Deborah L 849
Cook, Donald 752
Cook, Jim 375
Cook, JJ 626
Cook, Katherine 635
Cook, Nerissa J 597
Cook, Robert 823
Cook, Sarah 928
Cooke, Alyson 362
Cooke, John S 894
Cooke, Kevin R., Jr 739
Cooke, Leonard 589
Cooks, Romell 749
Cooks, Shirley 37
Cooksie, Carolyn 691
Coomaraswamy, Radhika 926, 931
Coon, James W 443
Coon, Tammy 507
Coons, Christopher A 55, 302, 322, 325, 354, 359, 366, 367, 374, 469
Cooper, Aaron 375
Cooper, Andrew 401
Cooper, Anthony 643
Cooper, Barbara 689
Cooper, Barry D 744
Cooper, Beth 352
Cooper, Brian C 461
Cooper, Ginnie 901
Cooper, James T. "Ty" 814
Cooper, Jim 247, 308, 328, 402, 403, 404, 431, 432, 478
Cooper, Mary Irene 655
Cooper, Perry 634
Cooper, Sharon 618
Cooper, Sophie 6
Cooper, Susan 802
Cooper-Davis, Ava 657
Cope, Grant 362
Cope, J. David 816
Cope, Janet T 817
Copeland, Mark 180
Copeman, Thomas H., III 644, 646
Coppage, Gail 367
Copperman, Yesenia 926

Page

Coppess, Jonathan ... 340
Coppler, Leslie ... 436
Coppola, John ... 808
Copps, Michael J ... 785
Coraggio, Mary-Deirdre ... 714
Corbett, Amy Lind ... 744
Corbett, April ... 422
Corbett, Joseph ... 840
Corbett, Thomas W ... 781
Corbin, Kevin ... 433
Corbin, Michael ... 597
Corcoran, Christine ... 212
Corcoran, Sean ... 412
Corcoran, Tom ... 452
Corcoran, William ... 382
Cordero, Juan A ... 906
Cordero, Laura A ... 895
Cordero, Mario ... 791
Cordova, France A ... 811, 828
Cordovez, Diego ... 930
Coriell, Scott ... 273
Corker, Bob ... 244, 308, 321, 325, 351, 352, 359, 360, 366, 367, 382, 469, 501
Corker, Julia ... 369
Corkery, Lucile ... 825
Cornell, Kevin ... 460
Cornett, Bobby ... 10
Cornett, Donna ... 652
Cornier, Radames ... 642
Cornish, Steve ... 626
Cornyn, John ... 250, 309, 322, 324, 346, 347, 354, 363, 364, 374, 385, 469, 798
Coronado, Liliana ... 427
Coronel, Kimberly ... 746
Corr, Allison ... 412
Corr, William V ... 727
Correal, Dubis ... 606
Correll, Roger S ... 624
Correoso, Javier ... 71
Corrigan, Dara ... 732
Corsi, Robert E., Jr ... 630
Corso, Robert L ... 657
Corso, William ... 711
Corwin, Manal ... 611
Cosby, L. Neale ... 502
Cosivi, Ottorino ... 921
Cosper, Linda ... 626
Costa, Anthony "Tony" ... 795
Costa, Jim ... 28, 302, 332, 395, 396, 397, 428, 429, 478
Costello, Jerry F ... 89, 303, 328, 435, 436, 440, 441, 442, 443, 478
Costello, Nancy ... 655
Costello, Yvonne ... 360
Cote, Blaise ... 364
Cote, Stephen ... 434
Cote, Tim ... 732
Cottarelli, Carlo ... 913
Cottingham, Ashley Carson ... 369
Cottingham, Lara ... 47
Cottingham-Streater, Paige ... 499
Cottle, Amber ... 364
Cotto, Anthony ... 372
Cottom, Michelle A ... 739
Cotton, Amy ... 712
Cotton, Katina P ... 815
Cottrell, Amelia ... 826
Cottrell, Guy J ... 840
Cottrell, Jackie ... 105
Coughin, Curt ... 461
Coughlan, Tony ... 365
Coulbourne, George ... 580
Coulter, Margaret ... 370
Couri, Gerald S., II ... 411
Couri, Heather ... 407
Courtney, James ... 830
Courtney, Joe ... 52, 302, 333, 395, 396, 402, 403, 413, 478, 494
Courtois, Kevin ... 375
Cousins, Lynn E ... 841
Couvreur, Philippe ... 924
Coven, Martha ... 590, 592
Covey, William ... 713
Covey-Brandt, Alexis ... 458
Covitz, Daniel M ... 776
Coward, Dorian ... 462
Cowart, Christine E ... 347
Cowell, Jennifer ... 790
Cowen, Robert E ... 849

Page

Cowen, William B ... 809
Cox, David ... 778
Cox, Emmett R ... 850
Cox, Gregg ... 634
Cox, Jennifer ... 13
Cox, Jordan ... 376
Cox, Malcolm ... 764
Cox, Pamela ... 933
Cox, Ralston ... 773
Cox, Ruth ... 797
Cox, Stephen ... 798
Cox, Todd A ... 784
Cox, Victoria ... 744
Cox, Walter Thompson, III ... 886
Coy, Byron ... 749
Coy, Curtis ... 732
Coyle, Philip ... 590
Cracraft, Mary Miller ... 809
Craft, William ... 597
Craig, B.B ... 613
Craig, Brynne ... 453
Craig, Dena ... 267
Craig, Jack ... 752
Craig, Tom ... 344
Craighill, Polly W ... 392
Cramer, Katie ... 358
Crandall, Douglas ... 689
Crane, Christopher ... 625
Crane, P. Brian ... 606
Crane, Steve ... 401
Crane, Victoria ... 823
Cranford, Charles W ... 816
Crapo, Mike ... 82, 303, 323, 324, 351, 352, 354, 361, 362, 363, 364, 381, 469, 494
Crary, John ... 774
Cravaack, Chip ... 146, 305, 335, 421, 422, 435, 436, 440, 441, 443, 478
Cravens, Michael ... 150
Cravins, Donald, Jr ... 378
Cravins, Yvette ... 433
Crawford, Brian ... 65
Crawford, Bruce ... 635
Crawford, Carrie ... 812
Crawford, Chris ... 73
Crawford, Eric A. "Rick" ... 14, 301, 335, 395, 396, 397, 440, 441, 442, 443, 478
Crawford, Harry ... 74
Crawford, John W ... 578
Crawford, Susan J ... 887
Crawley, Allen ... 704
Crawley, Thomas W ... 831
Creamer, John ... 600
Creamer, Steve ... 743
Crebo-Rediker, Heidi ... 367
Creedon, Madelyn R ... 347, 348, 349, 350
Creek, Katrina ... 718
Creighton, Francis ... 53
Crenshaw, Ander ... 59, 302, 331, 398, 399, 400, 464, 479, 499, 503
Crenshaw, Laurent ... 43
Creppy, Michael J ... 662
Cretz, Gene Allen ... 601
Creviston, Rachel ... 377
Crew, John ... 686
Crewson, Phillip ... 663
Cribb, Troy ... 372
Cribbs, Carol ... 344
Cribley, Bud ... 681
Crick, Cindy ... 239
Crider, Curtis ... 836
Crider, Jennifer ... 453
Cringoli, Michael S ... 776
Criscitello, Douglas A ... 738
Crisfield, James R ... 644
Crissman, Jill L ... 815
Criste, Dawn M ... 423
Cristinzio, Dayle ... 163, 387
Critharis, Mary ... 712
Critz, Mark S ... 229, 308, 334, 402, 403, 404, 438, 479
Crocetti, Don ... 770
Croft, Kelly ... 833
Croley, Steven ... 592
Cromer, Danny ... 401
Cronin, Meaghan ... 372
Croog, Elizabeth A ... 808
Crook, Lowry A ... 791
Crooks, Katy ... 436
Cropper, Elizabeth ... 808

Page
Cross, Betsy 775
Cross, Jason 897
Cross, Matthew S 814
Cross, Meredith 822
Cross, Stephen 790
Croteau, Brian 821
Crouch, Drew 449
Croushorn, Ronald 692
Crow, Matt 261
Crowe, Paul 607
Crowell, Heather 423
Crowell, Jim 352
Crowell, Michaeleen 75
Crowley, Jeffrey 592
Crowley, Joseph 183, 306, 330, 447, 448, 453, 479
Crowley, M. Colleen 815
Crowley, Philip 598
Crowley, Shannon 365
Crowley, Tom 644
Crozier, James 74
Cruciani, Linda M 739
Cruden, John C 660
Cruickshank, Walter D 682
Crumb, Tara 378
Crumpler, Ryan 404
Cruse, James C 784
Crutchfield, Danielle 593
Crutchfield, Stephen 699
Cruz, Alejandro 419
Cruz, Alex 67
Cruz, Chai 299
Cruzan, Darren 681
Cuaderes, John 433, 805
Cudahy, Richard D 849
Cuellar, Henry 265, 309, 332, 395, 397, 421, 479
Cueva-Flores, Sergio 281
Cuevas, Fatima 727
Cuffari, Joseph V 670
Cuffe, James 818
Culberson, John Abney 254, 309, 331, 398, 399, 400, 479
Culham, Allan 917
Cullen, Frank 41
Cullen, Jeff 404
Cullen, Richard 11
Cullen, Tom 781
Cullinane, Scott 420
Culver, Jeffrey 599
Culver, Mike 505
Cumming, Al 372
Cummings, Elijah E 126, 304, 329, 431, 440, 441, 442, 463, 479, 494
Cummins, John 117
Cummiskey, Victoria 588
Cummisky, Margaret 343
Cundiff, Steven T 714
Cunningham, Allison 177
Cunningham, Asa "Gene" 722
Cunningham, Cheryl 4
Cunningham, Daniel A 893
Cunningham, Geary L 776
Cunningham, James B 601
Cunningham, Mary Kate 404
Cunningham, Paul 36
Cunningham, Peter 756
Cunningham, Scott 263
Cunnington, Mike 83
Cuomo, Andrew M 781
Curlett, Ed 700
Curley, Peter 823
Curran, Lori K 750
Curran, Nick 185
Currie, Duncan S 651
Currie, Rachel 388
Currier, John 770
Currier, Patrick 411
Curry, Thomas J 789, 812
Curry, Tim F 817
Curtin, James A 656
Curtin, Teri 344
Curtis, Christopher T 790
Curtis, Debbie 26, 449
Curtis, Joyce A 745
Curtis, Margarida 389
Curtis, Robert 692
Curtis, Sarah 112
Curtsinger, Rick 148
Cusack, David 593
Cushenberry, Harold L., Jr 895
Cushing, Michael 784
Cushwa, Patricia A 677
Cusick, Lauren 589
Custer, Veronica 266
Cutchen, Bryan 646
Cutler, Aaron 411
Cutler, Allen 344
Cutler, Wendy 591
Cutrona, Danielle 375
Cutshall, Mary K 697
Cutter, Stephanie 591
Cwalina, Raymond 509
Cylke, Frank K 581
Cyr, Ned 709
Cyrul, Kate 101
Czarnecki, Karen 225
Czarniecki, Lani 99
Czarnopys, Greg 666

D

D'Agostino, Thomas 752
D'Alesandro, Paul 231
D'Amato, C. Richard 500
D'Ambrosio, Marco 909
D'Angelo, Christopher 606
D'Angelo, Gregory 355
D'Elia, John 408
D'Elia, Lawrence M 662
D'Luzansky, Gwen 433
da Graca Domingues, Maria 935
da Rocha, Atila Maia 905
da Rosa, Alexandre Meira 906
Daadlder, Ivo 603
Dababneh, Matthew 32
Dadabo, Marguerite P 841
Dadant, Melissa 582
Dade, Runako N 509
Dadzie, Louisa McCarter 662
Dagadakis, Stephen 454
Dahl, Scott S 704
Daidy, Burke 663
Dail, Jack 424, 496
Dailey, David 276
Dailey, Jack 829
Daimler-Nothdurft, Kristen 7
Dairi, Mohammed 914
Daitch, William 768
Dakin, Deborah 612
Dalal, Milan 182
Dale, Amy 662
Dalessandro, Rob 637
Daley, Bill 585
Daley, William 589, 591
Dalius, William 669
Dalrymple, Kelvin 934
Dalton, Carol 895
Dalton, Patricia 575
Daly, Erin 283
Daly, Jack 139
Daly, James 822
Daly, John J 739
Daly, Lisa 461
Daly, Mike 84
Dambach, Charles "Chic" 24
Damelin, Harold 426
Damich, Edward J 872
Damour, Susan B 797
Damrell, Frank C., Jr 891
Dancy, Kevin 255
Dandridge, Sylvia L 499
Daneshforouz, Danica 387
Danforth, Linda 286
Danhof, William J 836
Daniel, Jean 695
Daniel, Susan 912
Daniel, Ted 461
Daniels, Grafton J 507
Daniels, Jerica 211
Daniels, Joycelyn 721
Daniels, Madeline 369
Daniels, McKay 294
Daniels, Stephen M 795, 796
Danielson, Jack 133
Danis, Michael R 500
Danker, Deborah J 776
Dankler, Mike 87
Danko, Carol 185

	Page
Dankowitz, Beverly I	724
Dankwart, Catherine	639
Dann-Messier, Brenda	759
Dannenfelser, Marty	411
Danner, Jade	381
Danon, Steve	44
Darby, Reginald	69
Darby-Boone, Blondell	814
Darcy, Jo-Ellen	636
Darden, William Horace	886
Darin, Thomas "Tom"	588
Darling, Nedra	681
Darling, Ray H., Jr	814
Darling, RuthAnne	627
Darpino, Flora D	639
Darr, Carol C	741
Darrell, Nona	397
Das, Himamauli "Him"	605
Daskal, Jennifer	674
Dater, Keith	107
Daugherty, Becky	390
Daughetee, Patricia	842
Daughtrey, Erica	175
Daughtrey, Martha Craig	849
Daulaire, Nils	729
Daum, Margaret	373
Dauster, Bill	387
Davenport, Colin	280
Davenport, Karin	213
Davenport, Nancy	803
Davenport, Peter	685
Davenport, William	786
Daves, George	582
Davey, Victoria	764
David, Claudette	372
Davidson, Cathy N	807
Davidson, Donetta L	836
Davidson, Douglas A	837
Davidson, James A	825
Davidson, Jeanne	651
Davidson, Jonathan	46
Davidson, Margaret A	709
Davidson, Robert L	729
Davidson, Susan A	640
Davidson, William A	630
Davie, Mary	796
Davies, Frank	413
Davies, Glyn T	603
Davies, Rebecca	344
Davies, Sally M	776
Davies, Susan	593
Davin, Jerome	687
Davis, Aaron	230
Davis, Alec	228
Davis, Andre M	849
Davis, Carlton	433
Davis, Carole	696
Davis, Chad	352
Davis, Constance	756
Davis, Danny K	87, 303, 330, 421, 422, 431, 432, 479
Davis, David W	250
Davis, Delia	768
Davis, Eddie D	670
Davis, Eric	405
Davis, Gary K	710
Davis, Geoff	111, 304, 332, 447, 448, 479
Davis, Gordon J	798
Davis, Greg	258
Davis, Hubert	642
Davis, J.R	16
Davis, Jeffrey	728
Davis, Jerome D	747
Davis, John	102
Davis, Jonathan	611
Davis, Joseph M	809
Davis, Judith A	815
Davis, Julie Z	820
Davis, Karlos	392
Davis, Kathleen	92
Davis, Kevin M	392
Davis, Kolan	101, 375
Davis, L'Tonya	732
Davis, Lance	810
Davis, Laura	679
Davis, Laura M.H	807
Davis, Linda Kay	895
Davis, Lindsay	2
Davis, Lisa	676
Davis, Marilyn	35
Davis, Mark S	637
Davis, Melinda M	816
Davis, Michael L	721
Davis, Nezida S	650
Davis, Nida	775
Davis, Patricia	819
Davis, Raymond	389
Davis, Richard A	694
Davis, Richard K	774
Davis, Robert N	890
Davis, Robyn	688
Davis, Shelley	185
Davis, Susan A	45, 302, 331, 402, 403, 406, 479, 496, 499
Davis, Tracy	826
Davis, Vera	498
Davis, Vickie	627
Davis, Virginia	677
Davis, W. Eugene	849
Davis, Wanda	756
Davis, William	926
Davis-Rogers, Russella	759
Davit, Tony	626
Dawn, Ralph	508, 575
Dawson, Diann	730
Dawson, Howard A., Jr	881
Dawson, Larry	689
Dawson, Liz	401
Dawson, Mark	4
Day, Christopher	780
Day, Dick	818
Day, Jonathan	188
Day, Katherine	695
Day, Michael	185, 439
Day, Pamela	8
Day, Tamika	458
Day, Valerie	3
Day, Vanessa	405
Dayan, Edouard	929
Dayspring, Brad	456
de Cosio, Gerardo	920
de Gamboa, Nancy Ruiz	722
de Geus, Aart Jan	919
de Jesus Luevano Grano, Jose	911
de Jesus Orellana Mejia, Alfredo	909
de la Pava, Carmen	918
de la Puente, Manuel	831
De La Rosa, Omar	370
de la Torre, Laura	721
De La Torre, Mindel	786
de la Vara, Elisa	11
de La Vina de Foley, Lydia	498
de Lama, George	906
de Macias, Carolyn Webb	757
de Marty, Idalia Dominguez	187
de Mistura, Staffan	930
de Paola, Christopher M	838
de Paula Cunha, Juarez Aparecido	905
De Puy, Geraldine	454
de Queiroz Duarte, Sergio	925
De Rosa, Gustavo	906
De Roux, Antonio	907
de Sa, Paul	787
de Santa Ana, Thelma Melendez	757
De Sett, Laverne	639
De Vincentis, Mae	620
de Zela, Hugo	918
De, Raj	593
Deacon, Scott	631
Deal, Rocky	21
Dean, Bill	813
Dean, Emily	815
Dean, Greg	369
Dean, James L	795
Dean, John F	884
Dean, Laura	367
Dean, Telora	686
Dean, Tim	391
Deanes, Tonya	763
Dearborn, Rick	2
Dearden, Dawn	655
Deavel, R. Philip	627
DeBobes, Richard D	347
DeBoer, Joan	741
DeBoer, Margaret	776
DeBosier, Chris	458
Debus-Lopez, Karl Edward	581

Page

DeCarme, David 742
DeCasper, Jennifer 238, 434
DeCesaro, Anne 449
DeCicco, William A 888
Deck, Wiley 61
Deckard, Nancy 97
Decker, Elizabeth 38
Decker, Michael H 617
Decker, Ray 817
DeDona, John 373
Dedrick, Katherine 362
Deeb, Mary Jane 581
Deeley, Kevin 672
Dees, Karena 413
DeFabio-Doyle, Ann 608
DeFalaise, Louis 671
DeFalco, David 708
DeFazio, Peter A 221, 308, 328, 428, 429, 440, 441, 442, 479
DeFerrari, Lisa M 775
Deffer, Frank 766
DeFilippi, Gwendolyn R 637
DeFrancis, Dominic 634
DeFrancis, Suzanne 774
DeFrancisco, Gerald 774
DeFrancisco, Laura 637
DeFreitas, Matthew A 424, 496
Degen, Gregory 589
Degenfelder, Ken 381
DeGette, Diana 47, 302, 330, 409, 410, 411, 479
DeGraff, Kenneth 457
Dehmlow, Marta 400
Deist, Jeff 258
Deitch, Lisa 823
DeJong, Hillary 135
DeJong, Justin 687
DeKock, Pete 102
Delacenserie, Katie 372
DeLaCruz, Lauren M 393
DeLaittre, David J 830
Delaney, Deb 434
Delaney, Duane B 896
Delaney, Eric Louis 454
Delaney, Paul 365
Delany, Peter 734
DeLatte, Kim 114
Delaune, Jules 818
Delaurentis, Jeff 597
DeLauro, Rosa L 52, 302, 328, 398, 400, 453, 479, 799
Delbanco, Dawn H 807
Delcambre, Paula 423
DeLeo, Wanda 790
DeLeon, Benito 744
DeLeon, Patrick H 80
DeLeon, Rafael 782
DeLeonardis, Robert 826
Delery, Stuart 649
Delfin, Ricardo 820
Delgado, Glenn A 801
Delgado, Jose 38
Delgado, Martin 401
Delgado, Michael A 612
Delgado, Pat 34
Delgado, Tequia 392
DeLisi, Scott H 602
Dell, Christopher William 601
Dell, Eric 238
Dell, Joe 634
Delli-Colli, Kevin 706
Delmage, William 826
Delmar, Richard 606
DelNegro, Elizabeth F 796
DeLuca, Peter A 780
DeLude, Bethany 894
DeMar, Gretchen 510
DeMarco, Edward J 789, 790
DeMaster, Doug 709
Demeo, Marisa 895
Demeritt, James D 630
DeMint, Jim 237, 308, 323, 325, 351, 352, 356, 357, 366, 367, 463, 469
DeMoss, Harold R., Jr 849
Dempsey, David 912
Dempsey, Martin E 589, 635
Dempsey, Matt 362
Dempsey, Maureen 825
Dempsey, Robert 369
DeMuth, Paula 796

Page

Deng, Francis 932
Deng, Zhongrui 412
Denham, Jeff 28, 302, 335, 428, 429, 440, 441, 442, 443, 445, 479
Denham, Sheila C 637
DeNigro, Hillary 787
Denis, Cathy St 745
Denis, Howard 433
Denis, Howard A 805
Denis, Steve 206
Denkmann, Libby 286
Denmen, Kate 289
Dennis, Allison 588
Dennis, Howard 824
Dennis, Jakki 37
Dennis, James L 849
Dennis, Lisa 375
Dennis, Matt 188
Dennis, Patti 822
Dennis, Robert A 575
Dennison, Ezekiel 692
Dent, Charles W 231, 308, 332, 398, 399, 400, 413, 479
Denton, Neal 774
Denton, Wesley 237
DeParle, Nancy-Ann 591
DePass, Michelle 782
DePaul, Kimberley 589
DePriest, Trish 73
Der, Vic 751
Derden, Terry L 662
Derenoncourt, Sonia 818
DeRenzi, Nanette M 644
Dermarest, Joseph, Jr 667
Derobertis, Gloria 685
Derr, Sallie 219
Derr, Steven W 657
Derse, Anne Elizabeth 601
Desai, Nitin 932
Desai, Priyanka 420
DeSanti, Susan S 793
DeSarno, William 805
Desbois, Michel 698
Desiderio, Denise 381
DeSio, Henry F 592
DesJarlais, Scott 246, 308, 335, 395, 396, 406, 407, 431, 432, 479
Desmet, Thierry O 826
Desmukes, LaJuene 704
Dessy, Blane K 581
DeStefano, Johnny 455
Destro, Brenda 411
Dethloff, Lisa 105
Detmers, Deb 94
Dettelbach, Brian A 742
Detter, Brian 646
Detter, Sandra 691
Deutch, Theodore E 67, 303, 334, 418, 419, 425, 426, 479
Deutsch, Jeremy 284
Deutschmann, Sarah 373
deVallance, Jennifer L 590
Devan, Eileen 787
Devan, Janamitra 933, 935
Dever, Joseph, Jr 826
Devereaux, Richard 629
Devieux, Serge 935
DeVille, Curt 698
Devine, Ellen 378
Devine, Michael 804
Devine, Stephen 820
DeVita, Charles 770
Devlin, Patrick 458
DeVooght, Joe 96
Dewhirst, Diane 457
DeWitt, Brett 422
DeWitte, Jon 134
Dexter, Barry 463
Dey, Christopher 391
Deychakiwsky, Orest 496
di Florio, Carlo V 821
Diamond, Howard 420
Diamond, William 782
Diamonstein-Spielvogel, Barbaralee 773
Diarra, Cheick Sidi 929, 932
Dias, Agapito Mendes 934
Diaz, Albert 849
Diaz, Eduardo 829
Diaz, Maria Patricia 910

Page

Diaz, Miguel Humberto 601
Diaz-Balart, Mario 68, 303, 332, 398, 399, 400, 479, 499
Diaz-Bonilla, Eugenio 907
Diaz-Myers, Judith 611
Dib, Sid Ahmed 934
DiBiase, Thomas 510
DiCicco, John A 675
Dick, Darren 452
Dick, Jere 701
Dicke, Michael S 826
Dicken, JoEllen R 389
Dickens, Kate 84
Dickerman, Jamie 177
Dickerson, Christopher 790
Dickhut, Claire 84
Dickinson, Lisa 676
Dickman, Martin J 841
Dickon, Rachel E 791
Dicks, Norman D 284, 309, 327, 398, 399, 479
Dicks, Suzanne C 502
Didawick, Kathy 497
Didier, Elaine K 804
Diegel, Brittany 721
Diehl, Denise 10
Diephouse, Greg 688
Dierauf, Leslie 683
Dietrich, Debbie 781
Dietrich, Mary 119
Dietrich, Nathan 22
Dietz, Diane 378
Dietz, Lonnie 204
Dietz, Polly 610
Diez, Jose 701
DiFalco, Frank 768
Diffell, Brian 152
Dignam, Rhea Kemble 824
DiIorgi, Michele 173
DiJulio, Tara 95
Diller, Daniel C 367
Dillihay, Marilyn 249
Dillingham, Steve 750
Dillon, Corey 152
Dillon, Robert 360
Dillon, Thomas 461
Dillon, Victoria 193
Dilts, Barbara 296
Dimarob, Michelle 448
DiMartino, Kitty 598
Dimeo, Robert 714
Dimunation, Mark G 581
Dinan, James H 649
Dinardo, Charles A 506
DiNenna, Chris 625
Dingell, John D 140, 305, 327, 409, 410, 411, 479, 500
Dinger, John R 596
Dinger, Larry M 600
Dingmann, Daniel J 50
Dingwall, Ian 721
Dini, Kristin 231
Dinkins, James 769
Dinneen, Tiffany 10
Dinnie, Erika 796
Dion, John 674
Diorio, Gina 171
Diouf, Jacques 928
DiSabatino, Nicholas B 894
DiSanto, Dino 212
Dise, Gail B 739
Dishman, Lake 375
DiSilvestro, Michael P 389
Diskin, Peter 824
Disla, Andres Apolinar 905
Disman, Beatrice 833
Disrud, Doug 676
DiTraglia, Elena 199
Dittemore, Nicki 377
Dittig, Sandra 633
Dix, Melanie L 649
Dixey, Michele 784
Dixit, Praveen 708
Dixon, Arrington 804
Dixon, Carol 413
Dixon, Debra 34
Dixon, Herbert B., Jr 895
Dixon, Kelly 456
Dixon, Lou 742
Dixon, Rita 627
Dixon, Yvonne T 809

Page

Diz, Carlos 508, 575
Dizard, Robert, Jr 580
Djinnit, Said 930
Do, Alisa 32
Doane, Margaret M 812
Dobbs, David A 742
Dobbs, Janet 795
Dobbs, Wiley 497
Doboga, Mark 629
Dobrozsi, Jeff 118
Dobrzeniecki, Aimee 714
Doby, Chris J 389
Dockham, Andrew 372
Dodaro, Gene L 575
Dodd, Thomas J 798
Dodge, Candace 31
Dodge, Conway 823
Dodge, Penny 221
Dodgson, Elizabeth 510
Dodin, Reema 388
Doering, Stephen C 802
Doerner, Richard L 503
Doggett, Jane M 807
Doggett, Lloyd 263, 309, 329, 405, 447, 448, 479
Doheny, Tom 196
Doherty, Jeanne 842
Doherty, Mary 131
Doherty, Owen 747
Doherty, Ray 823
Doherty, Ted 743
Dohl, Sarah 264
Dohner, Cynthia 680
Dohner, Robert 608
Dohrmann, Andrew 362
Dolan, Coby 68
Dolan, Edward 769
Dolan, John 632
Dolan, Mark 769
Dolan, Nancy 762
Dolbow, Bill 455
Dolbow, Jim 76
Dolcini, Val 691
Dold, Robert J 89, 303, 335, 414, 415, 416, 479
Dolder, Nancy S 719
Dominguez, Abilio 907
Dominguez, Marie Therese 840
Dominguez, Ricardo 918
Domino, Karen 115
Domm, Jeffrey 626
Doms, Mark 704
Donaghue, Michael 375
Donahoe, Patrick R 840
Donahue, David 598
Donahue, Jim 707
Donahue, Stephen 824
Donald, Joseph J 816
Donald, Kirkland 646, 752
Donald, Whitney 151
Donaldson, Darryl 833
Donaldson, Lyn 713
Donaldson, Milford Wayne 773
Donaldson, Nancy 913, 928
Donaty, Frank J 822
Done, Alex 708
Donenberg, Ben 806
Donenberg, Jon 376
Donesa, Chris 452
Doneski, Ellen 357
Dong, Norman S 768
Dongilli, David 656
Donilon, Thomas 592
Donilon, Tom 589
Doninger, Chris 712
Donius, Susan 804
Donkar, Eli N 830
Donley, Michael B 623
Donnal, Mike 73
Donnan, Jennifer 612
Donnell, Eddie 706
Donnelly, Joe 96, 303, 333, 414, 415, 416, 445, 479
Donnelly, John 77
Donnelly, Kellie 360
Donoghue, Joan E 924
Donoghue, Joseph 9
Donohue, Caitlin 53
Donohue, Jennifer 158
Donohue, Mark 821
Donovan, Don 676

Page

Donovan, Elizabeth 369
Donovan, Garrett 132
Donovan, John 687
Donovan, Joseph 597
Donovan, Joseph E 674
Donovan, Joseph R 596
Donovan, Robert 375
Donovan, Shaun 737, 773, 807
Donovan, Shaun L.S 585
Donovan, Victor 628
Doody, Jillian 1, 587
Doolin, Joel 644
Doomes, Elliot 444
Doone, Alison L 794
Doran, Dawn 673
Doran, Kevin 74
Dorch, Rebecca 786, 788
Dordain, Jean-Jacques 905
Doremus, Paul N 711
Dorfman, Taryn 69
Dorgan, Darrell 773
Dorko, Jeffrey "Jeff" 638
Dorn, Ellen 828
Dorn, Georgette M 581
Dorn, Jeffrey 577
Dorn, Linda 832
Dorn, Teri 294
Dornatt, Rochelle 27
Dornell, Izella 704
Dornette, Marjorie 262
Dorobiala, Brooke 143
Dorothy, Michelle 225
Dorr, Andy 653
Dorrer, Jennifer 358
Dorris, Edward J 611
Dorsey, David 732
Dorsey, Frederick D 896
Dortch, Marlene 787
Dossal, Amir A 926
Dotson, Bernadine 446
Dotson, Greg 412
Dotson, John D 500
Doty, Arthur 656
Doty, Arthur A 658
Doty, John 183
Doud, Greg 340
Dougherty, Dorothy 723
Dougherty, Elizabeth 810
Dougherty, J. Thomas 600
Dougherty, James 842
Douglas, Derek 592
Douglas, James 828
Douglas, Marsha 405
Douglass, Karon E 792
Douste-Blazy, Phillipe 931
Dove, Laura 392
Dove, Lisa B 582
Dow, Ryan 625
Dowd, John P 272
Dowd, Kristin 154
Dowd, Timothy 465
Dowd, William G 805
Dowdy, Alan 700
Dower, Tom 357
Downey, Brian 375
Downey, Kyle 385
Downs, David 662
Downs, Frederick, Jr 764
Downs, Glen 197
Doyle, Bonnie L 832
Doyle, Christopher 767
Doyle, J. Dennis 895
Doyle, Jean 122
Doyle, Michael F 231, 308, 329, 409, 410, 479
Doyle, Michael P 725
Doyle, Peter 787
Doyle, Phil 719
Doyle, Robert 721
Drake, Celeste 38
Drake, David 804
Drake, John 358
Drakulich, George M 893
Drane, LaDavia 211
Dreeben, Linda J 809
Dreeben, Michael R 650
Dreher, Robert G 660
Dreier, David 32, 302, 327, 434, 495, 479, 499
Dresen, Rachel 11

Page

Dreyfus, Michel 910
Dries, Mark 692
Driessen, Patrick 465
Drillings, Michael 640
Driscoll, Anne 708
Driscoll, Peter B 825
Driscoll, Steven J 815
Driver, Patricia 790
Droegemier, Kelvin K 811
Droker, Linda 708
Drost, Julia 273
Drouet, Suzanne 675
Drumheller, Robert B 839
Drummond, Jerome 796
Drusina, Edward 911
Drysdale, David 608
Drzewicki, John 209
Duarte, Anthony 35
Dubberly, Paula 822
Duberstein, Andrew 412
Duberstein, Kenneth M 799
DuBester, Ernest 790
Dubik, Rick 704
Dubina, Joel F 850
DuBois, Joshua 592
DuBois, Stephanie 167
DuBose, Michael 654
DuBray, Daniel J 683
Dubyak, Meghan 205
Ducharme, Rick 744
Duckworth, L. Tammy 762
Ducrocq, Aymeric 914
Duda, Robert J 841
Dudek, Ben 444
Dudek, Paul 822
Dudley, Chris 676
Dudley, Deborah 719
Dudley, Drenan A 344
Duecker, Jonathan A 422
Duemling, Robert W 842
Dufau-Richet, Marie-Sophie 909
Duff, James C 893
Duff, Steven W 641
Duffy, Adam 358
Duffy, Beau 189
Duffy, Gerald 907
Duffy, Mary 465
Duffy, Michael F 793
Duffy, Patricia 769
Duffy, Paula B 807
Duffy, Sean P 293, 310, 335, 414, 415, 416, 463, 479
Duffy, Terrence A 793
Dugan, Cathey 355
Dugan, John 825
Dugan, Regina 619
Duggin, Thelma 843
Duggins, Cori 123
DuHadway, David 627
Duhe, John M., Jr 849
Duhem, Yolande 935
Duhnke, Bill 352
Dujon, Charles 85
Dukakis, Kitty 836
Duke, Andrew 253, 416
Duke, Elaine C 767
Duke, Elizabeth A 775
Dulabahn, Elizabeth S 580
Dulberg, Jeffrey R 578
Dull, David 639
Dulniak, Craig 249
Dumm, Kenneth 629
Dumomay, Chedly C 826
Dunahoo, Heather 373
Dunbar, Kate 433
Dunbar, Sharon 629
Duncan, Allyson K 849
Duncan, Arne 585, 755, 773, 797, 798, 799, 807, 843
Duncan, Jeff 239, 308, 335, 418, 419, 421, 422, 428, 429, 479
Duncan, Jeffrey 430
Duncan, Jeffrey A 723
Duncan, John J., Jr 245, 308, 328, 428, 429, 440, 441, 442, 443, 480
Duncan, Kirsten 437
Duncan, Robert 290
Duncan, Robert M 834
Duncan, Russell 449
Duncan, Susan L 640

Page

Duncan, Thomasenia P 891
Duncan, William E 763
Duncan-Peters, Stephanie 896
Dunford, J.F 648
Dungan, Hilary 439
Dunham, Bernadette 732
Dunham, Will 21
Dunlap, James 672
Dunlap, Mike 397
Dunn, Brendan 365
Dunn, Dolores 446
Dunn, Grover L 629
Dunn, Jean 663
Dunn, Michael V 779
Dunn, Nathan 61
Dunn, Patrick T 655
Dunn, Rich 385
Dunning, Amy 839
Dunsmore, Dean 661
Dunston, Jerri 675
Dunwoody, Ann 641
Duran, Gil 18
Durante, Blaise J 624
Durbin, Richard J 84, 303, 322, 324, 341, 342, 343, 366, 367, 374, 377, 383, 384, 388, 464, 469, 501, 502, 837
Durkin, Patrick J 840
Durkovich, Caitlin 766
Durmer, Kris 795
Durrer, Austin 279
Durrett, Jim 205
Dutcher, Jay 194
Dutton, Jeffrey 708
Dutton, John 123
Dutton, Steve 93
DuVarney, Andree 691
Dwyer, James 711
Dwyer, Julie 152
Dwyer, Mike 693
Dwyer, Molly C 850
Dwyer, Ryan P 207
Dwyer, Sheila M 389
Dwyer, Steve 458
Dwyer, Timothy J 780
Dye, Rebecca F 791
Dyer, James E 812
Dyer, Peggy 774
Dyk, Timothy B 857
Dykema, Rick 42
Dynes, Doug 627
Dyniec, Melissa 689
Dysland, John 843

E

Eacho, William Carlton, III 600
Eagan, Kristin M 609
Eaglin, James B 894
Eakins, Carol R 713
Ealman, Emily 354
Eamich, Amanda 687
Earle, Sheila M 627
Earley, Keith B 841
Early, P. David 838
Earnest, Darryl 699
Earnst, Chad A 826
Earp, Naomi 582
Earp, T. Michael 677
Easley, Dan 358
Easley, Stephanie 392
Easter, Alberta 375
Easterbrook, Frank H 849
Easterling, Sheridan B 577
Eastman, Sage 448
Easton, Edward W 798
Easton, John 166
Easton, John Q 758
Eaton, Angus 781
Eaton, Richard K 869
Eaves, Joseph 189
Ebbesen, Samuel E 840
Ebel, David M 850
Eberhard, Tony 203
Ebersole, Atalie 156
Echavarria, Lorraine 825
Echebarria, Luis Estanislao 906
Echols, Debi 5
Eckel, Scott 416
Eckenrod, Philip 629

Page

Eckert, Joe 392
Eckert, Robert 728
Eckstein, Mathew 461
Edattel, Paul 411
Eddings, Richard 152
Eddington, Mark 269
Eddy, Julie 21
Edelman, Eric 837
Edelman, Todd E 895
Eden, Ashley 369
Ederheimer, Joshua 652
Edgar, Jason 285
Edgar, John T 840
Edgar, Kevin R 416
Edge, Elizabeth 768
Edge, Peter 769
Edgerton, Vic 210
Edgeton, Robert 666
Edmo, Lorraine 677
Edmond, Ellen R 724
Edmonds, Esther 579
Edmonds, Johnnie 635
Edmondson, J. L 850
Edmondson, Laurel 223
Edmondson, Wayne A 776
Edmundson, Kevin 825
Edmunson, Kristina 818
Edwards, Amy 354, 821
Edwards, Bailey 443
Edwards, Cathy 401
Edwards, Charles K 765
Edwards, Donna F 124, 304, 333, 413, 435, 436, 440, 441, 442, 443, 480
Edwards, Gerald A., Jr 775
Edwards, Harry T 853
Edwards, Isaac 360
Edwards, Julie 219
Edwards, Rick 390
Edwards, Trent 246
Edwards, Yul 88
Edwin, Yeshvanth 906
Edwing, Richard 709
Effron, Andrew S 885
Efird, Cynthia 496
Egan, Gerald 578
Eggert, Paul 700
Ehrenwerth, David H 796
Eichen, Jaime 822
Eichenlaub, Louis 669
Eichhorn, Jared 455
Eichner, Matthew J 776
Eide, Kathy 29
Eikenberry, Karl W 600
Eilers, Anne 704
Eilperin, Stephen F 896
Eisele, Brooke 452
Eisen, Jean Toal 344
Eisen, Norman L 601
Eisenbach, George D., Jr 763
Eisenberg, Judith Ann 798
Eisenberg, Michael 458
Eisenberger, Hershel 461
Eisenman, Ross 893
Eisenmann, James 838
Eismeier, Jim 381
Eisner, Neil K 742
Eissenstat, Everett 365
El-Sibaie, Magdy 749
Elachi, Charles 801
Elam, Erik 8
Elcano, Mary S 774
Eldarrat, Christine 790
Elder, Jacqueline 780
Elder, Kathryn 378
Elder, Robert James 915
Eley, Melvin C 577
Elgohary, Nivin 694
Elhassani, Layth 46
Elias, Carlos 505
Elias, Karen 806
Elias, Mark 383
Elieson, Dayle 375
Eligan, Richard S., Jr 816
Eligan, Veronica 427
Elizondo, Epi 729
Elkins, Arthur, Jr 782
Ellard, Angela 449
Elledge, Jessica 53

Page

Ellena, Guy M 935
Ellerbe, Kenneth B 898
Elling, Dan 449
Ellington, Jerry 661
Ellington, Robert 747
Elliot, Cameron 824
Elliott, Cary 463
Elliott, Daniel R., III 750
Elliott, Erica 456
Elliott, Farar 458
Elliott, George 711
Elliott, Jerry 697
Elliott, Joel 96
Elliott, Ramona 663
Elliott, Rob 163
Elliott, Shiela 73
Elliott, Susan 597
Ellis, Debby 833
Ellis, Jacqueline 255
Ellis, Karen 689
Ellis, Kimberly 255
Ellis, Lauren 153
Ellis, Margo 509
Ellis, Raymond 784
Ellis, Steven 682
Ellison, David R 621
Ellison, Eugenia D 795
Ellison, Keith 145, 305, 333, 414, 415, 416, 453, 480, 499
Ellison, Matthew 458
Ellison, P. Michelle 786
Ellison, Teri 824
Ellmers, Renee L 196, 307, 335, 395, 396, 418, 419, 438, 439, 480
Elmendorf, Douglas W 575
Elmore, Stephen G 405
Elmore, William 827
Elrod, Adrienne 42
Elrod, Jennifer Walker 849
Elshami, Nadeam 457
Elshtain, Jean B 807
Eltinge, John 719
Elton, Kim 679
Elworth, Larry 781
Elzy, Nadine L 576
Emelee, Christophe 911
Emerick, Amy 12
Emerson, Catherine 744
Emerson, Jeffrey W 416
Emerson, Jo Ann 156, 305, 329, 398, 399, 400, 480
Emery, Rodney P 794
Emich, David 643
Emmans, Gene 354
Emrich, Robert E., Jr 831
Emswiler, Thomas K 793
Enck, Judith 783
Endicott, Gary L 392
Eng, Catherine 65
Engel, Eliot L 187, 307, 328, 409, 410, 411, 418, 419, 480
Engelhardt, Steven 153
Engeljohn, Daniel 697
Engemann, Dan 157
Engen, Eric M 776
England, Katherine 823
England, Timothy 823
Englehart, Gary B 577
Engling, Maximilian 424
English, Brystol 436
English, Cachavious 6
English, Cathleen 511
English, Jan 498
English, William B 776
Englund, Mary Sue 424
Ennis, Elise M 777
Enomoto, Kana 734
Enos, Katie 130
Ensor, David B 778
Entwistle, James Frederick 600
Enzi, Michael B 295, 310, 322, 324, 354, 363, 364, 368, 378, 469
Enzinna, James B 582
Eoyang, Mieke 26
Eply, Paul 577
Epley, Mark D 416
Epplin, Rob 119
Epps, Diana Harris 895
Epps, Kamilia 717

Page

Epstein, Anthony 895
Epstein, Michael David 836
Epstein, Robert L 699
Erb, Karl 811
Erburu, Robert F 808
Erceg, Christopher J 776
Erceg, Marta 758
Erdel, Grant 167
Erdmann, Charles E 885
Ereli, Adam 598
Ereli, J. Adam 807
Ereli, Joseph Adam 600
Erhardt, Julie 821
Erickson, Janet 444
Erickson, Kristofor S 417
Erickson, Nancy 389, 503, 807
Erickson, Robert C., Jr 795
Erickson, Terrell 691
Ericson, Timothy L 803
Ericsson, Sally 590
Ernst, Ruth A 393
Ertel, Elizabeth B 412
Ervin, Teresa 72
Esau, Donna 825
Esau, Laurie 144
Eschwie, Dorothy 826
Escoto, Carla 300
Eshoo, Anna G 26, 302, 329, 409, 410, 480
Eskeland, Phil 92
Eskow, Glenn 776
Eskra, Jennifer 676
Eskridge, Robert 413
Espina, Pedro 590
Espinal, Jose Eduardo 906
Espinosa, Sergio 266
Esposito, Jennifer 444
Esq, Charles Willoughby, 897
Esquea, Jim 727
Esquenazi, Patricia 919
Esquivel, Frank 816
Essalih, Tony 254
Esser, Michael R 816
Esser, Mike 497
Essig, Alisia 271
Estabrook, David M 823
Estefan, Emilio, Jr 798
Estep, Greg 578
Estes, Deborah 360
Estevadeorval, Antoni 906
Esteves, Maggie 502
Estevez, Alan 616
Estler, Heather 187
Estopinan, Arthur 67
Estrada, John 773
Etchart, Jeannie 93
Etheridge, Arrie 819
Ethridge, Joe E 641
Ethridge, Max 683
Etienne, Ashley 433
Etra, Donald 836
Etter, Robert 436
Etzel, Jeanne 768
Eubanks, W. Ralph 581
Eugene, Theresa 358
Eugenio, Marcia 720
Eure, Philip K 901
Evangelista, Stephen 831
Evans, Bruce 344
Evans, Christina 345, 369
Evans, Gregory L 776
Evans, Jack 897
Evans, James 655
Evans, James H 799
Evans, Jason T 636
Evans, Joan 378
Evans, Joan M 762
Evans, Melissa 207
Evans, Michelle 460
Evans, Patricia L 898
Evans, Rebecca A 502
Evans, Terence T 849
Evans, Tracee 255
Everett, Janece 110
Everett, Jason 427
Everly, George 355
Evich, Jordon 283
Evins, Sean 424
Evins, Sean C 496

Page

Ewell-Madison, Angela 706
Ewen, Paula 747
Ewers, John 644
Exley, Randall L 637
Exum, Larnell 508
Eychaner, Fred 798
Eyler, Christopher 370
Eyler, Yvonne 711
Eyzaguirre, Nicolas 914
Ezekwesili, Obiageli Katryn 932
Ezzell, Elizabeth 78

F

Fabrega, Laure 70
Facchiano, Greg 165
Facchiano, Kathee 14
Facciola, John M 866
Facey, Nathan 210
Fado, Kelly 377
Faeth, Lori 682
Fagan, Carey 743
Fagan, Tucker 296
Fagel, Marc J 826
Fagoth, Steadman 910
Fahey, Sean P 671
Fahrbach, Wes 205
Fahrer, Gabriella E 347, 348, 349
Faiella, William 655, 658
Faile, Andrew 711
Fair, Cristin 824
Fairfax, Richard 723
Fairtile, Joy S 815
Falcone, James 612
Faleomavaega, Eni F. H 297, 310, 337, 418, 419, 428, 429, 480
Falk, David 497
Falk, Henry 731
Falk, John 497
Falkenheim, Michael 590
Falletta, JoAnn 806
Fallis, Jennifer 747
Fallon, Bill 677
Fallon, Brian 383
Fallon, Christine L 848
Fallon, Laena 456
Falvey, Cheryl A 780
Familant, Norman 650
Fanney, Hunter 714
Fanning, Ruth 763
Fant, Christine 774
Fantinato, Jessica 686
Faragasso, Gregory 823
Farar, Sim 835
Farber, Brian 747
Farenthold, Blake 264, 309, 335, 421, 422, 431, 432, 440, 441, 442, 480
Farfour, George 630
Fargo, John N 651
Farley, Dave 795
Farley, Norm 511
Farmer, Paul 930
Farnsworth, James T 655
Farooq, Madge 55
Farquhar, Ned 681
Farr, Natalie 48
Farr, Pam 774
Farr, Sam 27, 302, 329, 398, 400, 480, 499
Farrar, Jonathan 600
Farrar-Warren, Darlene 722
Farrauto, Matt 32
Farrell, Alycia 344
Farrell, Ellen A 809
Farrell, Joseph 793
Farrell, Michael W 895
Farrell, Paula 606
Farrell, Thomas F 722
Farrington, Shari 10
Farris, J. Jerome 850
Farris, James 732
Farrow, Sandy 400
Faruqi, Fahad 696
Faso, John J 798
Fassler, Jess 179
Fasteau, Jamie P 408
Fatemi, Erik 344
Fattah, Chaka 224, 308, 329, 398, 399, 480
Fauci, Anthony S 734

Page

Faunce, M.L 501
Faust, James 639
Faust, Leona 389
Favreau, Jonathan 591
Fawcett, Allen 588
Fay, C. Scott 236
Fay, Peter T 850
Fayolle, Ambroise 914, 934
Fazio, Larry 806
Fazio, Terri H 816
Fazio, Tony 745
Fazzini, Tom 687
Fazzio, Vincent 649
Feagan, Sarah 448
Fearn, Mickey 680
Featherston, Brit 662
Fedak, Janice 599
Feddeman, Ed 437
Fedder, Judith 629
Fedotov, Yury 926, 927
Feehan, Richard D 722
Feeney, Anne Marie 221
Feest, Gregory 631
Fehrer, Douglas G 501
Feierstein, Gerald M 603
Feierstein, Mark 835
Feifer, Theodore 838
Feinberg, Evan 370
Feinberg, Wilfred 849
Feinstein, Dianne 18, 301, 321, 324, 341, 342, 343, 374, 377, 382, 383, 469, 498, 799
Feinstein, Lee Andrew 602
Feinstein, Richard A 793
Feit, Betty 796
Feldblum, Bryan J 461
Feldblum, Chai R 783
Feldman, Crystal 430
Feldman, Eric 138
Feldman, Robert A 499
Feldstein, Steven 367
Feldt, Dennis 672
Feliciano, Carmen M 299
Felix, Larry R 611
Felker, Josh 823
Feller, Erika 588
Feltman, Jeffrey 597
Felton, Wanda 784
Fennell, Anne-Marie 508
Fennell, Richard D 894
Fenneman, Rebecca A 791
Fennick, Renita 229
Fenstermacher, Nathan 96
Fenton, Carol A 750
Fenton, Kevin 731
Fenton, Robert J., Jr 768
Fentress, Allison 890
Fentress, Tara 895
Ference, Mike 455
Ferezan, Larry R 577
Fergin, Judith R 601
Ferguson, Carolyn 245
Ferguson, David 505
Ferguson, Elliot 902
Ferguson, Fred 271
Ferguson, Jesse 453
Ferguson, John H 809
Ferguson, Kathleen I 626
Ferguson, Mark 646
Ferguson, Russ 376
Ferguson, Tony 690
Fernandes, Julie 652
Fernandez, Alberto M 601
Fernandez, Angela 187
Fernandez, Ariel 71
Fernandez, Bruce 131
Fernandez, Ferdinand F 850
Fernandez, Giselle 798
Fernandez, John R 706
Fernandez, Jose W 597
Fernandez, Mariano 930
Fernandez, Ramos Suris 718
Fernandez-Greczmiel, Maria 744
Fernandez-Taranco, Oscar 925
Fernendez, Jessica 42
Ferrante, Anthony 745
Ferrell, David 689
Ferrell, Lauren M 645
Ferrell, William 643

Page

Ferren, John M 895
Ferrier, Antonia 365
Ferriero, David S 802, 803, 807, 843
Ferrini-Mundy, Joan 811
Ferris, Ann 588
Ferris, Chris 627
Ferro, Anne S 745
Fesak, George M., Jr 722
Fescina, Ricardo 921
Fetherston, Andrea 143
Fettig, Dwight 352
Feyerherm, Alan 161
Fiala, Gerri 722
Ficaretta, Teresa 665
Fick, Kevin 663
Fidler, Danielle 364
Fiduccia, Anthony P 826
Fiedler, Jeffrey L 500
Field, Lesley 590
Field, Matthew 424
Fieldhouse, Richard W 347, 348, 349
Fields, Barbara G 740
Fields, Brent J 822
Fields, Christine M 777
Fields, George 741
Fields, Pamela L 499
Fields, William 352
Fields, Yvette 747
Fierro, Jennifer 243
Fiertz, Randall 745
Figel, Kimberly 460
Figley, Paul F 652
Figliuzzi, Frank 667
Figueroa, Ana 36
Figueroa, Cristina 300
Figueroa, Ruben 921
Filipowich, Brian 352
Fillichio, Carl 723
Fillion, Daniel H 645
Filner, Bob 44, 302, 329, 440, 441, 442, 443, 445, 480
Finan, Robert J., II 676
Finch, Laura 91
Finch, Warren 804
Fincher, Stephen Lee 248, 308, 335, 414, 415, 416, 480
Findlay, Patrick 721
Findlay, Patrick G 667
Fine, Bailey 122
Fine, Neal 576
Fine, Steven 710
Fineberg, Harvey V 810
Finestone, Alexander 149
Finestone, Josh 77
Fingland, Jodie 758
Finkelmeyer, Curt 291
Finkelston, Karin 935
Finkler, Kira 683
Finks, LaVern 362
Finley, Alfonso 796
Finn, Chester 805
Finnegan, Patrick 455
Finston, Nina 823
Fioravante, Christopher P 501
Fiorenzo, Les 746
Fiotes, Stella 714
Firestone, Nancy B 873
Firoved, Aaron 372
Firschein, Joseph 776
Fischer, Anne 643
Fischer, Audrey 580
Fischer, Peter 82
Fish, Terry 118
Fishbein, Allen J 776
Fisher, Alyssa 590
Fisher, Andrew J 367
Fisher, Ann 820
Fisher, Bart 397
Fisher, D. Michael 849
Fisher, David 575
Fisher, Gerald I 895
Fisher, John R 895
Fisher, Max 340
Fisher, Michael 769
Fisher, Mischa 91
Fisher, Nigel 930
Fisher, Raymond C 850
Fisher, Rebecca 358
Fisher, Robert 824
Fisher, Sarah 412

Page

Fishman, George 427
Fishman, Julie 201
Fishman, Robert 821
Fisk, Roger 703
Fiske, Catherine 661
Fiske, David 787
Fite, David P 420
Fitten, Steven 911
Fitts, Catherine E 848
Fitzgerald, Edmond J 748
Fitzgerald, Eileen 812
Fitzgerald, Erin 722
Fitzgerald, John 894
Fitzgerald, Marilee 617
Fitzgerald, Patrick J 619
FitzGibbon, Tanga S 792
Fitzgibbons, Patricia J 893
Fitzpatrick, Collins T 850
Fitzpatrick, John 802
Fitzpatrick, Kate 344
Fitzpatrick, Kevin 420
Fitzpatrick, Michael G 227, 308, 335, 414, 415, 416, 463, 480
Fitzpatrick, Robert 461
Fitzpatrick, Sean 106
Fitzpayne, Alastair 605
Fitzsimmons, Lore 693
Fixler, Dennis J 704
Fjeld, Christian 358
Flach, Andrew 91
Flaggs, Christopher 596
Flahavan, Richard S 826
Flaherty, Eddie 424
Flake, Jeff 12, 301, 331, 398, 399, 400, 480
Flanagan, Christine A 583
Flanagan, Eugene 581
Flanagan, James P. "Jim" 713
Flanagan, Keith 370
Flanders, Moira 906
Flanz, Ken 82
Flaum, David M 836
Flaum, Joel M 849
Fleet, James 424
Fleetwood, Nancy 607
Fleischmann, Charles J. "Chuck" 246, 308, 335, 428, 435, 436, 440, 441, 442, 480
Fleishman, Susan 461
Fleites, Carlos 71
Fleming, Denis, Jr 112
Fleming, John 116, 304, 334, 402, 403, 404, 428, 429, 480
Fleming, Marcus 384
Fleming, Michael R 713
Fleming, Myron J 390
Fleming, Penny Jacobs 893
Fleming, Timothy E 796
Fleming, William 704
Flemma, Jean 444
Flemmons, Jason 823
Fleshman, Mark 663
Fletcher, Betty B 850
Fletcher, Catherine S 713
Fletcher, Lee 116
Fletcher, Letitia 355
Fletcher, Mary 637
Fletcher, William A 850
Flick, Brad A 833
Flick, Tiffany 830
Flippen, Deidre 784
Flitton, Jennifer 200
Flood, Clare 385
Florence, Justin 376
Flores, Alejandro 908
Flores, Bill 259, 309, 335, 405, 428, 429, 445, 480
Flores, Daniel 427
Flores, Hugo Alexander 908
Florig, Alexandria 623
Flournoy, Michele A 616
Flowers, Alfred 625
Flowers, Brian K 897
Floyd, Brooke 73
Fluhr, Chris 430
Flumignan, Jeffrey 748
Flynn, Christopher 807
Flynn, David K 652
Flynn, Mark S 724
Flynn, Terence 808
Flynn, Timothy 405

	Page
Flynt, Clark	375
Foard, Dawson	360
Focarino, Peggy A	711
Fodor, Catherine	197
Foelak, Carol Fox	824
Foertsch, Sean	706
Fogarty, Kevin	181
Foldi, Paul	367
Foley, David	796
Foley, James B	600
Foley, Kevin M	656
Foley, Martha	401
Foley, Maurice B	878
Foley, Meghan	430
Foley, Michael R	775
Foley, Susan V	776
Foley, Tom	501
Folino, Kelley	89
Folmar, Michael J., Jr	667
Foltz, Nicole	405
Fong, Isaac	225
Fong, Ivan K	765
Fong, Phyllis K	689
Fonnesbeck, Leif	344
Fonokalafi-McMullen, Ana	430
Fontaine, Peter H	575
Fontana, Tom	505
Fontenot, Brodi	741
Fontenot, Keith	590
Fontenot, Stephanie	16
Foote, Evelyn	773
Footer, Ellene P	884
Foran, Brianna	73
Forbes, J. Randy	276, 309, 331, 402, 403, 425, 426, 480
Forbes, Matt	146
Force, Ashley	437
Ford, Charles	707
Ford, Crystal D	815
Ford, David H	578
Ford, Delorice	827
Ford, Gerald R	798
Ford, Gilbert	789
Ford, Linda C	747
Ford, Robert Stephen	603
Ford, Rochelle	382
Ford, Tim	449
Ford, W. Larry	666
Fore, Karmen	221
Foresta, Merry	829
Forester, Pam	16
Forgione, C. Michael	784
Forman, Alfred J., Jr	417
Forman, Thomas L	815
Foronda, Varinia Daza	934
Forrest, Katherine	650
Forrester, Althea	739
Forsberg, Christina	463
Forstater, Ira	461
Forstein, Samuel	822
Forster, Michael	812
Forsythe, Eden	498
Forsythe, Jack	801
Forte, Denise	758
Forte-Mackay, Jackie	453
Fortenberry, Jeff	161, 306, 332, 395, 397, 418, 419, 480, 499
Forthun, Melanie	819
Fortin, Daniel	912
Fortune, Catherine	723
Fortuno, Victor M	799
Foskett, Monica	87
Foss, Paul-Martin	416
Fossum, John	46
Foster, Bob	148
Foster, Brice	261
Foster, Christian	693
Foster, Connie	463
Foster, David V	833
Foster, Don	723
Foster, Janet	16
Foster, Jason	375
Foster, Maureen	680
Foster, Richard	922
Foster, Rick	731
Foster, Robert	661
Foster, Robin Lake	30
Foster, Roland	215
Foster, Sandra	718
Foster, Shawn	62
Foster, Wade	220
Fouberg, Andi	242
Fouch, Stephanie S	837
Foughty, Trevor	100
Fountain, Galen	344
Fountain, Richard M	774
Foushee, H. Clayton	743
Fowler, James E	714
Fowler, John M	773
Fowler, John S	612
Fowler, Peter	712
Fowler, Sam	360
Fowler, William W., Jr	811
Fox, Amanda	373
Fox, Christopher	710
Fox, Don W	814
Fox, Elizabeth	362
Fox, Ellen	764
Fox, Jimmy S., III	657
Fox, Kathy	719
Fox, Lynn S	777
Fox, Marilyn R	836
Fox, Nancy	174
Fox, R.C	648
Fox, Thomas	362
Fox, William	910
Foxall, Horace H., Jr	773
Foxley, Alejandro	907
Foxx, Virginia	197, 307, 332, 406, 434, 480
Foy, Askari J	824
Foy, Sue	286
Fraase, Mark G	675
Frahm, Steven I	676
Framer, Isabel	834
Franceschi, Alexandra	263
Francis, Joseph	764
Francis, Paul	575
Frande, Francis	666
Franger, Melissa K	462
Frangipane, Noelle	824
Frank, Barney	129, 305, 327, 415, 480
Frank, Elisha L	826
Frank, Ellen	698
Frank, Richard	728
Frank, Steven R	674
Frankel, Donald	661
Frankel, Morgan J	393
Franken, Al	142, 305, 322, 325, 359, 368, 374, 375, 381, 469
Frankfurt, Tom	643
Franklin, Craig A	618
Franklin, Rick	277
Franks, Kathleen	719
Franks, Mitchell	642
Franks, Trent	10, 301, 332, 402, 403, 425, 480
Fransen, James W	392
Franz, Keira	340, 690
Franzel, Jeanette M	575
Fraser, Beverly Britton	433
Fraser, Gerald	714
Frasier, Diane	733
Fraze, John H	830
Frazer, Gary	680
Frazier, Elizabeth	120
Frazier, Lisa D	838
Frazier, Mary	706
Freakley, Benjamin C	639
Frederick, Jessica Arden	344
Frederick, Robert	92
Frederickson, David	718, 822
Fredriksen, Amanda	796
Freedhoff, Michal	430
Freedman, Marla	606
Freehafer, Peter	834
Freeland, Mark	178
Freeman, Carmelita P	654
Freeman, Darlene	743
Freeman, Jim	661
Freeman, Kirk D	738
Freeman, Marilyn	636
Freeman, Tim	624
Fregoe, Mary C	750
Freis, James H., Jr	609
Freitas, Bruno	129, 417
Frelinghuysen, Rodney P	173, 306, 329, 398, 399, 480, 494
French, Claudia	807

Page

French, David A ... 627
French, Katy ... 372
French, Towner ... 422
Fresco, Leon ... 376
Fretz, Nathan ... 397
Freund, Paul ... 626
Frey, Bridgett ... 126
Frey, Scott ... 832
Freye, Angela ... 784
Fridman, Ari ... 420
Fried, Jeffrey S ... 497
Fried, Neil ... 411
Friedberg, Michael ... 401
Friedel, Laura A ... 344
Frieden, Jorg ... 934
Frieden, Paul L ... 724
Friedlander, Liz ... 397
Friedman, Aharon ... 448
Friedman, David ... 719
Friedman, Eric ... 135
Friedman, Gregory H ... 751
Friedman, Jennifer ... 449, 766
Friedman, Joel ... 354
Friedman, K. Chaya ... 836
Friedman, Paul L ... 865
Friedman, Ruth ... 408
Friedman, Warren ... 588
Friedrich, Dabney L ... 841
Friefeld, Wendy ... 22
Friend, Daniel G ... 714
Friendship, Stanley ... 833
Frierson, Robert deV ... 777
Friestad, Scott ... 823
Frieswyk, Susan ... 582, 583
Frifield, Julia ... 122
Frisch, Stuart ... 671
Frisk, Jim ... 364
Frison, Teresa ... 25
Fritter, Carl ... 389
Froehlich, Kaleb ... 360
Froehlich, Maryann ... 782
Frohboese, Robinsue ... 728
Frohlich, David ... 823
Fromm, Adam ... 433
Frosch, Elizabeth ... 375
Frosch, Peter ... 144
Frost, Bert ... 680
Frost, Jared ... 182
Frost, Joye E ... 672
Frost, Lana ... 436
Frost, Peter ... 652
Frost, Thomas ... 766
Frotman, Scott ... 86
Frumberg, Emily J ... 417
Frumin, Alan S ... 389
Frumin, Lisa ... 352
Frumkin, Howard ... 730, 731
Fry, Courtney ... 458
Frye, Jan R ... 761
Frye, Jocelyn ... 592
Fryer, Lindsay ... 407
Fryzel, Michael E ... 805
Fudge, Marcia L ... 211, 307, 333, 395, 396, 397, 435, 436, 480
Fuehermeyer, Matt ... 384
Fuentes, Jennice ... 86
Fuentes, Julio M ... 849
Fugate, W. Craig ... 767
Fuhrman, Silvia ... 932
Fulgham, Chad ... 667
Fulghum, Charles ... 625
Fulkerson, Emma ... 392
Fuller, Janice ... 171
Fuller, Jessica ... 3
Fuller, Kim ... 182
Fuller, Kurt ... 642
Fuller, Reese ... 612
Fuller, Stacy ... 144
Fullerton, Laura ... 422
Fullerton, Tim ... 679
Fullhart, Randal D ... 624
Fulmer, Jack ... 381
Fulton, Bernard ... 737
Fulton, Catherine ... 693
Fulton, Laurie Susan ... 601
Fulton, Scott ... 782
Fultz, Annie ... 227
Fulwood, Isaac, Jr ... 677, 841

Page

Funger, Norma Lee ... 798
Funk, Bret ... 156
Furey, Frank J ... 756
Furey, Joe ... 823
Furgeson, W. Royal, Jr ... 891
Furgione, Laura ... 710
Furgione, Laura K ... 711
Furia, Karen ... 726
Furlani, Cita M ... 715
Furman, Jason ... 592
Furusawa, Mitsuhiro ... 914
Fury, Mitchell ... 643
Futey, Bohdan A ... 877
Fyne, Richard ... 763

G

Gabbrielli, Tina ... 767
Gabel, Ali ... 157
Gabriel, Clifford J ... 811
Gabriel, Kaigham ... 619
Gaeta, Joe ... 354
Gaffigan, Mark ... 575
Gaffney, Glenn ... 778
Gage, Paul ... 221
Gaglio, Maria ... 785
Gagne, Martha M ... 590
Gagnon, Jason ... 41
Gahan, Christopher ... 223
Gahun, Jamie ... 254
Gaiani, Vincent J ... 393
Gainer, Terrance W. "Terry" ... 390, 510
Gaines, Glenn A ... 768
Gaines, Margaret ... 809
Gainey, Kathleen M ... 619
Gajarsa, Arthur J ... 856
Galante, Carol ... 738
Galassi, Thomas ... 723
Galassi, Tom ... 723
Gale, Joseph H ... 879
Galicia, Catherine ... 352
Gall, Matt ... 430
Gallacher, Petie ... 389
Gallagher, James M ... 580
Gallagher, John M ... 583
Gallagher, Kevin ... 683
Gallagher, Mark A ... 630
Gallagher, Michael G ... 831
Gallagher, Patrick ... 713
Gallagher, Rosemary ... 461
Gallagher, Sean ... 510
Gallant, Nicole ... 780
Gallegly, Elton ... 31, 302, 328, 418, 419, 425, 426, 480
Gallegos, Chris ... 148, 344
Galler, David ... 705
Galli, Paolo ... 927
Gallin, John I ... 734
Gallin, Joshua H ... 776
Gallo, Carmine ... 744
Gallo, Marcy ... 437
Galloucis, Michael ... 761
Galloway, Gloria ... 509
Galloway, James ... 729
Galloway, Patricia D ... 811
Galloway, Toby ... 825
Galvin, Diane ... 824
Galvin, John M ... 719
Gamarra, Carlos ... 905, 906
Gambari, Ibrahim ... 931
Gambatesa, Donald ... 835
Gambino, Philip A ... 830
Gamble, Hugh ... 72
Gamble, Nathaniel ... 650
Gambo, Angela S ... 416
Gambo, Theresa ... 407
Gamboa, Javier ... 362
Gambrell, Donna ... 606
Gamel-McCormick, Michael ... 369
Gandhi, Natwar M ... 899
Gandhi, Sajit ... 420
Ganesan, Arvin ... 781
Gangloff, Joseph E ... 814
Ganley, Caitlin ... 227
Gans, Jon ... 388
Gans, Michael E ... 850
Gant, Jon L ... 740
Ganz, Julian, Jr ... 808
Garamendi, John ... 24, 302, 334, 402, 403, 404, 428, 429, 481

	Page
Garbars, Kurt	795
Garber, Judith Gail	601
Garber, Kimberly	825
Garber, Wendy	711
Garbow, Avi	782
Garcete, Adalberto	906
Garcia, Alina	71
Garcia, Chris	178
Garcia, Christopher	744
Garcia, Daniela	407
Garcia, Frances	576
Garcia, Frank	452
Garcia, Guillermina	420
Garcia, Ileana	71
Garcia, Ileana M	389
Garcia, Joel Antonio Hernandez	918
Garcia, John	762
Garcia, John A	773
Garcia, Juan M	645
Garcia, Lewis A	825
Garcia, Lisa	591
Garcia, Mory	439
Garcia, Pamela	178
Garcia, Rick M	740
Garcia, Roland	494
Garcia, Sam	40
Garcia, Sarah	373
Garcia-Benavides, Manuel Calvo	908
Garcia-Perez, Carlos	778
Garcia-Silva, Pablo	914
Gardella, Wayne L	784
Gardiner, Pamela J	611
Gardner, Cory	48, 302, 335, 409, 410, 411, 481
Gardner, Edna	633
Gardner, Evan	150
Gardner, Jan	122
Gardner, Jim	802
Gardner, Leland L	750
Gardner, Wendell P., Jr	895
Gardner, Wes	392
Garibay, Marisol	416
Garland, Donna	731, 802
Garland, Margaret	389
Garland, Merrick Brian	852
Garland, Sara	203
Garland, Timothy R	642
Garlock, Amber	420
Garman, Cathy	404
Garmendia, Zoe	589
Garmisa, Ben	388
Garmon, Ollie L	830
Garner, David	770
Garner, Jackie	732
Garner, Terri	804
Garner, Yancey, Jr	511
Garnett, Karen	822
Garratt, David	768
Garren, Timothy P	652
Garrett, Brian	404
Garrett, Joanne	701
Garrett, Scott	170, 306, 332, 405, 414, 415, 416, 481
Garrett, Teri	16
Garrity, Michael	825
Garry, Eileen	672
Garth, Leonard I	849
Garver, Lori	800
Garvey, Patrick	367
Garvey, Sandy	5
Garvey, Vincent M	651
Garvey, William	588
Garvin, Shawn	783
Garvin, Tim	169
Garwood, Will	849
Gary, Arthur E	684
Garza, D.C	648
Garza, Emilio M	849
Gaschke, David J	670
Gaskell, Judith A	848
Gass, Cathy	59
Gaston, Christopher	174
Gately, Nathan	420
Gates, Janet	656
Gates, Kevin	404
Gates, Perisha	385
Gates, Robert	773
Gatewood, Catherine	214
Gathers, Shirley E	605
Gatjanis, Gisele	656

	Page
Gaugler, Christine E	769
Gauhar, Tashina	674
Gaunt, Lee Ann	825
Gauthier, Simon	907
Gavaghan, Ann	596
Gavin, Patrick	65
Gaw, Michael	823
Gaydos, Colleen	344
Gaylard, Max	931
Gayle, Frank W	714
Gaynor, Amy E	393
Gaziano, Todd	835
Geadah, Sami	914
Geale, Nick	369
Gebbie, Katharine B	714
Gebhardt, Debra	293
Gebhardt, Paige	607
Gedalius, Ellen	63
Gee, King W	745
Gee, Robert N	581
Geer, Harlan	373
Geeslin, Chris	95
Geffroy, Sarah	452
Gehlert, Dave	661
Gehlhausen, Whitney	99
Geiderman, Joel M	836, 837
Geier, Paul M	742
Geiger, Teri	205
Geisel, Harold W	596
Geiser, David	751
Geishecker, Alice	507
Geiss, Kevin T	627
Geithner, Timothy F	585, 589, 605, 794, 808, 819
Gelb, Nancy	782
Gelber, Bruce	661
Gelber, Michael S	797
Gelfland, James	378
Gellin, Bruce	729
Gelser, Sara	805
Genachowski, Julius	785
Genaille, Richard	620
Gennawey, Ray	42
Gensemer, Elliot	458
Gensler, Gary	779
Gentile, Brad	189
Gentile, Kristen	223
Gentile, Michael	344
George, Bryan	164
George, Evangeline	457
George, J. Russell	612
George, John	640
George, Mary R	618
George, Molly	287
George, Tim	663
George-Winkler, Nkechi	276
Gerald J. Leeling	349
Gerald, Roque	898
Gerarden, Ted	752
Gerardi, Geraldine A	611
Gerber, Joel	882
Gerber, Sander R	843
Gerety, Amias	606
Gerhard, Lori	730
Gerlach, Jim	226, 308, 332, 447, 448, 481
Gernon, Walter	788
Gershengorn, Ian	651
Gerson, Michael J	836
Gerstenlauer, James P	850
Gerstenmaier, William H	801
Getterman, Edward	259
Getz, Patricia	719
Gever, Karen	718
Gfoeller-Volkoff, Tatiana C	601
Ghai, Yash	932
Ghent, Bill	55
Ghosh, Apratim	458
Giacobbe, Nicholas	599
Giaìer, Steven	422
Giambastiani, Pete	58
Giancarlo, Angela	785
Giancarlo, Angie	401
Giannasi, Robert A	809
Giannini, Paul J	578
Giannoni-Jackson, Deborah	840
Gianturco, Elizabeth	728
Gibbons, Julie Smith	849
Gibbons, Larry	810
Gibbons, Mary Anne	840

	Page
Gibbons, Mary Pat	129
Gibbs, Alexander	915
Gibbs, Aviva	87
Gibbs, Bob	307, 335, 395, 396, 440, 441, 442, 443, 481
Gibbs, David C	745
Gibbs, Pam	779
Gibbs, Robert B	214
Giblin, Thomas G	725
Gibson, Beth	769
Gibson, Calvin	746
Gibson, Chase	465
Gibson, Christopher P	189, 307, 335, 395, 396, 402, 403, 481
Gibson, Lynn	575
Gibson, Michael S	776
Gibson, Nan	587
Gibson, Sara	358
Gibson, Sharon	711
Gibson, Wayne	662
Giddens, Greg L	762
Gierke, H.F. "Sparky"	887
Giesta, Maria	129
Giesta, Maria E	417
Gifford, Ralph	693
Giffords, Gabrielle	13, 301, 333, 402, 403, 404, 435, 436, 481, 837
Giguere, Denis	905
Gilbert, Diane	691
Gilbert, Gay	722
Gilbert, Leslee	436
Gilbert, Melanie F	893
Gilbert, Nancy B	836
Gilbride, John P	657
Gildenhorn, Alma	799
Gildenhorn, Joseph B	843
Giles, Cynthia	782
Giles, James	821
Gilfillan, Brendan	782
Gilfillan, Richard	731
Gilford, Sam	352
Gill, Cory	367
Gill, Laura	386
Gill, Sonia	377
Gilleland, Steven	209
Gillen, Jeffrey	626
Gillers, David	378
Gilles, Jean	505
Gillespie, Josh	98
Gillespie, Laurie	645
Gillespie, Linda	254
Gillespie, Maura	455
Gillespie, Pam	65
Gillespie, Veronica	377
Gillespie-Marthaler, Leslie	588
Gillett, Sharon	787
Gillette, Daniel	655
Gillette, Jodi	681
Gillette, Merri Jo	825
Gillette, Robert	611
Gilliam-Moore, Danielle	372
Gillibrand, Kirsten E	179, 306, 321, 325, 339, 340, 346, 347, 361, 362, 382, 384, 469
Gillies, David	90
Gilligan, Peggy	745
Gilliland, Betty Lou	698
Gilliland, Thomas C	834
Gillis, Annette	382
Gillison, Jacob	75
Gillogly, Chelsey	105
Gillyard, Ron	497
Gilman, Ed	120
Gilman, Kate	362
Gilman, Ronald Lee	849
Gilmore, Beryl	796
Gilmore, Dee	277
Gilmore, J. Michael	615
Gilmore, Keith I	791
Gilmore, Shaun P	774
Gilpin, Raymond	838
Gilpin, Richard	646
Gilroy, Ed	407
Gilson, Christopher	819
Gimenez, Gilberto	911
Gina, Allen	769
Gingrey, Billie	498
Gingrey, Phil	78, 303, 332, 409, 410, 411, 424, 481, 496
Gingrich, John R	761
Gins, Meagan	360
Ginsberg, Daniel B	627
Ginsburg, Douglas Howard	851
Ginsburg, Mindy	787
Ginsburg, Ruth Bader	846
Giordano, Ralph T	651
Giorgio, Luis Alberto	906
Giovinazzi, Giles	443
Gips, Donald Henry	602
Gipson, Chester	700
Girard-diCarlo, Constance B	836
Girod, Olivier A	577
Giroux, Matt	355
Gist, Linda	653
Gitelman, Zvi Y	836
Gitenstein, Mark Henry	602
Giuliani, Michael	184
Giuliano, Louis J	840
Giuliano, Mark, Jr	667
Givens, Alexandra	375
Givens, Rod	267
Glackin, Mary M	708
Gladics, Frank	360
Glas, Kimberly Thompson	707
Glaser, Daniel	609
Glaser, Donald	683
Glaser, Ronald	707
Glasow, Chris	744
Glass, Adam	821
Glass, Roger I	734
Glasscock, Stacey	217
Glassner, Craig	618
Glauber, Joseph W	687
Glaude, Stephen	899
Glaude, Steve	898
Glazer, David	661
Glazewski, Tim	9
Gleason, Christy	55
Gleason, Jason	124
Gleason, Jessica	283
Gleason, John	420
Gleason, Robert C	655
Gleeson, James Monroe	454
Gleischman, Max	388
Glembocki, Deborah	636
Glenn, Charles S	893
Glenn, Douglas	794
Glenn, Gary D	807
Glenn, Harry	62
Glenn, Kristen	21
Glenn, Robert	714
Glenn-Croft, Mary	832
Glick, Janice L	813
Glick, Scott	674
Glickman, Dan	501
Glickman, Rhoda	780
Glickman, Stephen H	895
Glidden, Elizabeth	143
Glied, Sherry	728
Glimcher, Susan A	773
Glissman, Todd A	777
Glover, Martha	252
Glunz, Christine	588
Glynn, J. Patrick	652
Gobel, Jeff	691
Goddard, Keith	723
Goddard, Rick	164
Godec, Robert, Jr	595
Godwin, Elby	446
Goedman, Menno	609
Goehner, Brad	419
Goeke, Joseph Robert	880
Goes, Kelley	287
Goetcheus, John A	393
Goettle, Shane	203
Goff, Shuwanza	458
Goggin, Kelly	632
Goggin, Wendy H	655
Goggins, Jason M	416
Gohl, Earl F	775
Gohmert, Louie	250, 309, 332, 425, 426, 428, 429, 481
Goins, Hope	423
Gokcigdem, Murat	267
Gold, Andrea	696
Gold, Celeste	9, 388
Goldammer, Ted	692
Goldberg, Adam	607
Goldberg, Allan I	774
Goldberg, David S	579

	Page
Goldberg, John	397
Goldberg, Larry J	729
Goldberg, Philip S	596
Goldberg, Richard	84
Goldberg, Richard W	870
Goldberg, Robert	600
Goldberg, Steven	811
Goldberg, Stuart M	649
Goldblatt, Roger	786
Golden, John	688
Golden, Michael L	691
Golden, Scott	248
Golden, Walter M., Jr	619
Goldes, Jordan	182
Goldfrank, Amy	675
Goldfrank, Andrew	661
Goldfrank, Joan	895
Golding, Garrett	411
Goldman, David	358, 697
Goldman, Eric	818
Goldman, Marc	836
Goldman, Paul B	822
Goldowitz, Israel	820
Goldrosen, Juliana	376
Goldsmith, Alan	420
Goldstein, Cara	383
Goldstein, Jeffrey	606
Goldstein, Noami	730
Goldstein, Samantha	420
Goldstein, Scott	75
Goldstein, Sidney J	814
Goldway, Ruth Y	820
Gomer, Lisa	835
Gomez, Anna M	715
Gomez, Dario	827
Gomez, Gabriella	758
Gomez, Maria Cristina Herrera	909
Gomez, Paula Caballero	908
Gomperts, John	780
Goncalves-Drolet, Ines	129
Goniprow, Alex	757
Gonzales, Bridget	708
Gonzales, Edgar	817
Gonzales, Melody Star	454
Gonzales, Oscar	688
Gonzales, Walter	123
Gonzalez, Anna	70
Gonzalez, Breann	211
Gonzalez, Carlos	386
Gonzalez, Cesar A	68
Gonzalez, Charles A	261, 309, 330, 409, 410, 411, 424, 464, 481
Gonzalez, Daniela A	393
Gonzalez, Gregory	675
Gonzalez, Henry	767
Gonzalez, Jose Alfredo Ramos	908
Gonzalez, Lourdes	823
Gonzalez, Pedro Urra	921
Gonzalez, Samantha	446
Goo, Michael	781
Gooch, Anne	461
Gooch, Lesli	416
Gooch, Lucinda	610
Good, Linda	433
Goode, Katherine	644
Goodlatte, Bob	278, 309, 329, 395, 396, 406, 407, 425, 426, 481
Goodman, Alice	789
Goodman, Brenda	818
Goodman, Christie	727
Goodman, Jerilyn	291
Goodman, Kevin	825
Goodman, Mark D	836
Goodman, Max	64
Goodman, Meghan	51
Goodman, Nancy M	650
Goodman, Rob	458
Goodrich, George Herbert	896
Goodstein, Sam	235
Goodwin, Alfred T	850
Goodwin, Cathy	119
Goodwin, John	83
Goodwin, Kasi	364
Goodwin, Rod	575
Goolsarran, Swatantra Anand	927
Goon, Julie	411
Goosby, Eric	596
Goracke, Robin	146
Gorcowski, Susan	748
Gordh, Gordon	700
Gordon, Alicia	362
Gordon, D	643
Gordon, Eden	104
Gordon, Gertrude B	725
Gordon, Glenn S	826
Gordon, Leo M	869
Gordon, Leonard	794
Gordon, Nancy M	705
Gordon, Richard	757
Gordon, Robert	590, 616
Gordon, Waverly	408
Gore, James	685
Gore, Jennifer	145
Gorecki, Mary	654
Gorman, Becky	623
Gorman, Tori	354
Gorski, Jenny	434
Gorsuch, Neil M	850
Gortney, William	618
Gosar, Paul	9, 301, 335, 428, 429, 431, 432, 481
Goshorn, Daniel	372
Goss, John	588
Goss, Stephen C	830
Gosselin, Geoff	444
Gotay, Orlando	747
Gotbaum, Josh	819
Gothard, William	637
Gottemoeller, Rose	598
Gottesman, Michael M	733
Gottesman, Sanford L	836
Gottheimer, Josh	785
Gottschall, Kurt L	825
Gotwald, Robert C	465
Gouarne, Vincent	935
Gould, George B	497
Gould, Greg	682
Gould, Jennifer	449
Gould, Ronald M	850
Gould, Rowan	680
Gould, W. Scott	761
Goulet, Eric	897
Gourguinpour, Camron	626
Govan, George V	841
Gover, Kevin	828
Gowadia, Huban	768
Gowdy, Trey	239, 308, 335, 406, 407, 425, 426, 431, 432, 481
Graaff, Peter Jan	920
Grabelle, Justin	60
Graber, Brion D	465
Graber, Susan P	850
Grable, Samuel	625
Grabow, Paul	392
Graboyes, Diane	833
Grace, Steve	624
Grady, Judith M	612
Grady, Katherine	454
Grady, Patricia A	734
Graefe, Fred	502
Graf, Rob	797
Grafeld, Margaret	598
Grafestine, Theresa M	460
Graff, David	623
Graffeo, Jonathan	2, 352
Graham, Carlissia	179
Graham, Garth	729
Graham, Jim	897
Graham, Lindsey	237, 308, 322, 324, 341, 342, 343, 346, 347, 354, 374, 375, 382, 469, 493, 501
Graham, Michael	837
Graham, Neal	582
Grahn, David P	688
Gramiak, Doug	56
Grams, Todd	713
Grams, W. Todd	762
Granat, Rochelle	605
Grandi, Filippo	928
Grandison, Larry	783
Granger, Kay	257, 309, 330, 398, 399, 400, 481
Granholm, Dean J	840
Grannis, David	382
Grant, Brian	609
Grant, Dave	612
Grant, Heidi H	623
Grant, Katie	458
Grant, Michael	364

Page

Grant, Michael A ... 814
Grant, Patrick ... 352
Grant, Robert A ... 393
Grantham, Nancy ... 783
Grantz, Brad ... 233
Grappone, Jeff ... 166
Grassie, Jason ... 217
Grassley, Chuck ... 101, 304, 323, 324, 339, 340, 354, 363, 364, 374, 465, 470
Grassmeyer, Tyler ... 209
Gratacos, Osvaldo ... 784
Graupensperger, Joe ... 427
Graves, Bentley ... 104
Graves, James E., Jr ... 849
Graves, Margie ... 767
Graves, Rob ... 372
Graves, Sam ... 155, 305, 331, 438, 440, 441, 442, 481
Graves, Scott ... 265
Graves, Scott C ... 256
Graves, Tom ... 77, 303, 334, 398, 399, 481
Graves, William H ... 834
Gravitt, Blaine ... 64
Gray, Anita ... 211
Gray, Betty B ... 404
Gray, C. Boyden ... 842
Gray, Caley ... 168
Gray, Cheryl ... 906
Gray, Cynthia ... 508
Gray, David ... 689
Gray, David W ... 783
Gray, Gordon ... 603
Gray, Jason ... 401
Gray, Jennifer ... 641
Gray, John ... 709
Gray, Morgan ... 430
Gray, Roz ... 734
Gray, S. Pamela ... 895
Gray, Vincent C ... 799, 805, 897
Gray, Yvette ... 690
Gray-Broughton, Linda ... 793
Gray-Lee, Lorri ... 683
Graybill, Barbara ... 391
Grayson, Win ... 391
Graze, Deborah ... 599
Greczmiel, Horst ... 589
Green, Al ... 255, 309, 332, 414, 415, 481
Green, Brent ... 638
Green, C. Bruce ... 633
Green, Claire ... 364
Green, Creighton ... 349
Green, Daniel A ... 817
Green, Diane ... 685
Green, Don ... 64
Green, Gene ... 266, 309, 329, 409, 410, 411, 481
Green, Jeri ... 705
Green, Katherine ... 375
Green, Kim ... 718
Green, Lawrence ... 497
Green, Leonard ... 849
Green, Linda ... 277
Green, Lyle L ... 577
Green, Marilyn ... 502
Green, Matthew ... 725
Green, Michael J ... 499
Green, Nate ... 386
Green, Rashage ... 276
Green, Symone ... 360
Green, Thomas ... 795
Green, Valerie ... 780
Green, Wade, Jr ... 704
Green, Wanda ... 360
Greenaugh, Cheryle ... 723
Greenaway, Joseph A., Jr ... 849
Greenberg, Alan ... 661
Greenberg, Elaine C ... 826
Greenberg, Irving ... 837
Greenberg, Kenneth ... 761
Greenberg, Mark ... 730
Greenberg, Morton I ... 849
Greenberg, Saadia ... 730
Greenberger, Sarah ... 684
Greene, Bill ... 455
Greene, Bryan ... 737
Greene, Christopher B ... 757
Greene, Craig ... 404
Greene, Creighton ... 347, 348, 349, 350
Greene, Henry F ... 896
Greene, Jeff ... 372
Greene, Kathryn O ... 813
Greene, Kimberly S ... 834
Greene, LaTina Burse ... 831
Greene, Natalia M. Combs ... 895
Greene, Philip H., Jr ... 748
Greene, Reggie ... 448
Greene, Sean J ... 827
Greener, April ... 457
Greenert, Jonathan ... 646
Greenfeld, Helaine ... 650
Greenfield, Deborah ... 724
Greenhouse, Dennis ... 673
Greenhow, KaSandra ... 461
Greenlaw, Ryan ... 461
Greenlee, Cindy ... 730
Greenlee, Kathy ... 730, 807
Greenwald, Elyse ... 372, 805
Greenwell, George ... 387
Greenwood, Christopher ... 924
Greenwood, Lee ... 806
Greenwood, Lisa ... 695
Gregg, Jessica ... 430
Gregg, Larry ... 795
Gregg, Margarita ... 710
Gregg, Richard ... 606, 803
Gregoire, Michael ... 700
Gregoire, Nancy Beatty ... 894
Gregory, Brender L ... 777
Gregory, Karen V ... 791
Gregory, Roger L ... 849
Gregson, Wallace C ... 617
Gregus, Daniel R ... 825
Greifer, John ... 700
Greiner, Patricia M ... 613
Grennon, William J., III ... 576
Gresham, Dana ... 742
Greszler, Rachel ... 464
Gretch, Paul ... 742
Grevatt, Peter ... 782
Grever, Louis ... 667
Grey, Anne ... 707
Grey, Robert J., Jr ... 799
Gribbin, Billy ... 464
Griffin, Alais ... 745
Griffin, Ayo ... 376
Griffin, Claire ... 798
Griffin, Lisa ... 63
Griffin, Mike ... 806
Griffin, Pat ... 608
Griffin, Richard Allen ... 849
Griffin, Richard J ... 761
Griffin, Robert ... 767
Griffin, Tim ... 15, 301, 335, 402, 403, 418, 419, 425, 426, 481
Griffis, Kevin ... 703
Griffith, Brian ... 206
Griffith, H. Morgan ... 279, 309, 335, 409, 410, 411, 481
Griffith, Helen ... 626
Griffith, Thomas B ... 852
Griffiths, Jose-Marie ... 811
Griffiths, Pamela ... 461
Griffitts, Bob ... 245
Grigg, Clayton ... 667
Griggsby, Lydia ... 375
Grijalva, Raul M ... 12, 301, 332, 406, 428, 429, 481
Grim, David W ... 822
Grimaldi, Dave ... 785
Grimes, Chuck ... 814
Grimes, Darryle J ... 623
Grimes, Ron ... 214
Grimm, Michael G ... 185, 307, 335, 414, 415, 481, 837
Grimm, Tyler ... 433
Grindler, Gary G ... 649
Grinnell, Randy ... 733
Grippando, Gina ... 790
Gripper, Willie J ... 744
Grippo, Gary ... 606, 607
Grishaw, Letitia J ... 661
Grishin, Vadim Nikolaevich ... 934
Grisoli, William "Bill" ... 638
Griswold, Nancy ... 729
Grizzle, J. David ... 744
Grochowski, Michael ... 832
Grodin, Josh ... 69
Groen, Aaron ... 198
Groenert, Justin ... 100
Gronberg, Kevin ... 422
Gronn, Audun ... 914

Page
Gronniger, Tim 412
Grooms, Susanne Sachsman 433
Gropper, Adam 465
Groshart, Sarah Beth 376
Grosner, Brian 780
Gross, Brian J 775
Gross, Debra 738
Gross, Gerald 826
Gross, Jason 52
Gross, Jena 26
Gross, Joshua 239
Gross, Justin 461
Gross, Kenneth E., Jr 603
Gross-Davis, Leslie 766
Gross-Galiano, Socorro 919
Grosshandler, William L 714
Grossman, Beth 372
Grossman, Christian 935
Grossman, Edward G 460
Grossman, James 461
Grossnickle, Janet M 822
Grosvenor, Gilbert M 842
Grote, Matt 372
Grove, C. Brian 705
Grove, Paul 345
Grove, Shoshana 820
Groves, Gary 692
Groves, Randy 502
Groves, Robert M 705
Grubbs, Preston 656
Gruber, Corey 768
Gruber, Michael 411
Gruber, Theresa 832
Gruenbaum, Ben 721
Gruenberg, Martin J 789
Gruender, Raymond W 850
Gruere, Armelle 912
Grundmann, Susan Tsui 838
Grunenfelder, Brian 693
Gruters, Sydney 64
Grzebien, Charlotte C 653
Grzymski, Thomas G 833
Guarascio, Tiffany 171
Guardado-Gallegos, Theodora 508
Gudmundson, Erika 610
Guelzo, Allen C 807
Guendelsberger, Nese 787
Guerra, Iris 894
Guerrero, Isabel 933
Guerrero, Roberto 631
Guertin, Stephen 680
Guevara, Julio Cesar 910
Guevara, Thomas 706
Guggenheim, Andy 439
Gugulis, Katherine C 662
Guice, Greg 786
Guice, Karen 764
Guido, Lea 920
Guido, Rob 135
Guillamon, Bernardo 906
Guillen, Jose 405
Guillermo, Patricia 258
Guilliams, Nancy 770
Guillory, Emmanual 254
Guinan, William J 637
Guinta, Frank C 166, 306, 335, 405, 431, 432, 440, 441, 442, 481, 494
Guislain, Pierre 935
Guitchounts, Andrei 912
Guith, Kathleen 789
Gulari, Esin 811
Guldin, Richard W 690
Gulledge, Mike 670
Gumbiner, Larry 599
Gunaratna, Mahen 67
Gundersen, Kevin 422
Gunderson, Nancy 727, 728
Gunderson, Richard 767
Gunlicks, James 640
Gunn, Barbara L 825
Gunn, Currie 650
Gunn, Will A 761
Gunnels, Maggi 748
Gupta, Stephanie 401
Gur-Arie, Mira 894
Gural, Harry 417
Gurgo, Michael 794
Gurin, Joel 785

Page
Gurowitz, Leah 894
Gurria, Angel 919
Gurry, Francis 929
Gurule, Dusti 721
Gustafson, Daniel J 928
Gustafson, David 819, 881
Gustafson, Nicole 455
Gustafson, Peg 827
Gustafson, Richard P 619
Guterres, Antonio 927
Gutfrucht, Karl 420
Guthridge, Clay G 792
Guthrie, Brett 110, 304, 334, 409, 410, 411, 481
Guthrie, Carol 591
Gutierrez, Carlos M 843
Gutierrez, Luis V 86, 303, 329, 414, 415, 416, 451, 481
Gutman, Howard G 600
Gutman, Stanley "Huck" 272
Gutmann, Myron 811
Gutter, Karis 691
Gutterman, Greg 624
Guttmacher, Alan E 734
Guy, Daniel A 884
Guy, Ralph B 849
Guy, Samy 507
Guzman, George 671
Guzy, Gary 588
Gwinn, Jim 692
Gwinn, Nancy 829
Gwinupp, Andy 625
Gwyn, Nick 449
Gyles, Lynda M 727

H

Haager, Anthony 636
Haarlov, Jens 934
Haas, Greg 30
Haas, Jordan 827
Haas, Karen L 458
Haase, Molly 107
Habeck, Mary 807
Haberistreit, David 809
Haberkorn, Gerald 922
Haberman, Caitlin 412
Hackbarth, David 706
Hackett, Edwin M 813
Hackett, Jonathan 362
Hacking, Rose 172
Haddad, Edward 826
Hadden, Carlton 784
Haden, Adrienne T 775
Hadijski, Catina 389
Hadijski, George 424, 496
Hadjy, Pandor H 694
Hadley, Mark P 575
Hadley, Nancy 281
Hadlock, John 271
Hadyka, Maryann 802
Haensel, Curt 461
Hagan, James 933
Hagan, Katy 344
Hagan, Kay R 195, 307, 322, 325, 346, 347, 351, 352, 368, 378, 470
Hagan, Kristen 130
Hagan, Sean 913
Hagans, Bennie 819
Hagar, Stefanie 109, 388
Hagel, Lawrence B 889
Hagen, Don 715
Hagen, Elisabeth 696
Hagenah, William J 808
Hagerman, Heather 209
Hagerty, Mark 793
Hagerty, Matt 167
Haggstrom, Glenn D 761
Haghighat, Nader 788
Hagin, Helen E 749
Hagy, James 768
Hahn, Janice 36, 302, 335, 421, 438, 481
Hahn, Sandra 818
Hahn, Sueryun 720
Hailey, Sean 448
Haines, Christian 276
Haines, Harry A 884
Hair, Connie 251
Hairston, Darryl 827
Hairston, Roderick 833

Page

Hajec, Donald ... 711
Hakes, Francey ... 649
Hakes, Jay E ... 804
Halataei, Allison ... 426
Haldar, Swarnali ... 692
Haldeman, Jeremy ... 420
Haldiman, Sylviane ... 832
Hale, Brian P ... 769
Hale, John S ... 764
Hale, Robert F ... 616
Hale, Sarah ... 200
Haley, Bethany ... 10
Haley, John ... 641
Haley, Katherine ... 455
Haley, Richard, II ... 667
Haley, Sarah ... 2
Hall, Amy ... 732
Hall, April R ... 838
Hall, Barbara ... 843
Hall, Chad ... 16
Hall, Cindy ... 152
Hall, Clayton ... 15
Hall, Debra A ... 814
Hall, Donald J., Jr ... 798
Hall, F. Grailand ... 705
Hall, Gregory ... 747
Hall, Jennifer ... 444
Hall, John ... 898
Hall, Joseph ... 787
Hall, Justin W ... 627
Hall, Kathleen ... 85
Hall, Katrina M ... 460
Hall, Keith ... 719
Hall, Kevin ... 274
Hall, Laurie Beyer ... 579
Hall, Peter W ... 849
Hall, Ralph M ... 252, 309, 327, 435, 481
Hall, Richard ... 641
Hall, Roderick ... 744
Hall, Stephanie ... 831
Hall, Trinity ... 55
Hall, Valerie H ... 650
Hall-Rivera, Jaelith ... 690
Hallac, Joanna L ... 502
Hallahan, Kate ... 401
Hallen, Paige ... 354
Haller, Peter ... 433
Hallett, Adrienne ... 344
Hallford, Nathan ... 375
Halliwell, Kelley ... 228
Hallman, Janet M ... 841
Halnon, Emily ... 282
Halper, Neal ... 707
Halperin, Eric ... 652
Halpern, Amanda ... 422
Halpern, Cheryl F ... 836
Halpern, Hugh ... 434
Halpern, James S ... 878
Halpern, Jonathan ... 73
Halpin, Dennis ... 419
Halpin, Michael ... 260
Haltmaier, Jane ... 776
Halton, Tim ... 714
Halvorsen, P ... 643
Halvorsen, Terry A ... 646
Hamadanchy, Keramin ... 369
Hambleton, Ryan ... 433
Hambley, Winthrop P ... 775
Hamburg, Margaret A ... 732
Hamel, William ... 758
Hamer, Hubert ... 699
Hamilton, Alison ... 507
Hamilton, Clyde H ... 849
Hamilton, David E ... 625
Hamilton, David F ... 849
Hamilton, Diana Gourlay ... 344
Hamilton, Edward A ... 672
Hamilton, Eugene N ... 896
Hamilton, James L ... 797
Hamilton, John O ... 802
Hamilton, Lindsay ... 180, 426
Hamilton, Michael ... 712
Hamilton, Pamela ... 745
Hamilton, Samantha ... 367
Hamins, Anthony ... 714
Hamlett, Joyce ... 461
Hamling, Jeff ... 76
Hamm, Shannon ... 700

Page

Hammack, Katherine G ... 636
Hamman, Tyler ... 430
Hammarlund, John ... 732
Hammer, Elisa ... 626
Hammes, Ben ... 103
Hammill, Drew ... 457
Hammock, Gordon ... 632
Hammond, Andrew ... 698
Hammond, Casey ... 430
Hammond, Donald V ... 776
Hammond, Ellen H ... 499
Hammond, Eric ... 267
Hammond, John, IV ... 97
Hammond, Margaret ... 764
Hammond, Myle ... 508
Hammond, Roxanne ... 639
Hammond, Scott M ... 650
Hammond, Stephanie ... 10
Hammond, Tom ... 437
Hammond, Tony ... 820
Hammond, Velina Hasu ... 499
Hampel, Karen ... 796
Hampl, Eric ... 609
Hamption, Matthew ... 742
Han, Shelly ... 496
Hanabusa, Colleen W ... 80, 303, 335, 402, 403, 428, 429, 482
Hancher, Kimberly ... 784
Hancock, Diana ... 776
Hancock, Harold ... 448
Hand, Catherine ... 815
Hand, Edward T ... 650
Hand, Kelli ... 74
Hand, Michael ... 693
Hand, Robert ... 496
Handelman, Kenneth B ... 617
Handfield, F. Gerald ... 803
Handy, Michael ... 581
Hanes, Melodee ... 672
Haney, Catherine ... 813
Hankins, Helen ... 681
Hanks, Jamie ... 116
Hanley, Bill ... 232
Hanley, John ... 819
Hanley, Kathleen ... 821
Hanley, Keni L ... 461
Hanley, Mary ... 195
Hanley, Sharon E ... 724
Hanline, John ... 430
Hanlon, Brian ... 711
Hanlon, Brian J ... 900
Hanlon, Sharon E ... 628
Hanlon, Timothy ... 894
Hanna, Christopher ... 365
Hanna, Richard L ... 191, 307, 335, 406, 407, 438, 439, 440, 441, 442, 482
Hannah, James R ... 834
Hannahs, Jeffrey ... 460
Hannan, John L ... 577
Hannan, Maureen T ... 776
Hannel, Eric ... 446
Hanneld, Mike ... 770
Hannibal, Richard ... 821
Hannigan, Erin ... 688
Hannink, John ... 644
Hanny, William ... 510
Hanonu, Tina ... 460
Hanqin, Xue ... 924
Hanrahan, Peggi ... 2
Hanratty, Dennis ... 582
Hanretta, Kevin ... 762
Hansell, David ... 730
Hansen, Chris ... 48
Hansen, David R ... 891
Hansen, Donald ... 910
Hansen, Erik ... 832
Hansen, James E ... 801
Hansen, L. Jerry ... 636
Hansen, Martin ... 833
Hansen, Tim ... 709
Hansen, Will ... 463
Hanson, Alan ... 2
Hanson, Anita ... 763
Hanson-Kilbride, Jennifer ... 354
Haq, Ameerah ... 930
Harary, Howard ... 714
Harbert, Lloyd ... 692
Harbour, Tom ... 690

	Page
Harclerode, Justin	443
Hardage, John	611
Hardecke, Laura	157
Hardee, Leilani	116
Harden, Gil	689
Harden, Krysta	685
Harder, David	661
Harder, Hilda	379
Hardiman, Thomas M	849
Harding, Donna	579
Harding, Frances M	734
Harding, Justin	271
Harding, Richard C	632
Harding, Susan	832
Hardt, D. Brent	600
Hardy, Johanna	444
Hardy, Lyn	675
Hardy, Melinda	822
Hardy, Thomas R	842
Hardy, Tony	730
Hardy, William	641
Haren, Eric	376
Hargrove, Mike	630
Harjo, Rhonda	381
Harkless, Gresham	577
Harkin, Tom	101, 304, 322, 324, 339, 340, 341, 342, 343, 368, 378, 384, 470
Harkins, Donna	433
Harkins, Wilson B	801
Harley, Derek	20
Harlow, Bryce Larry	502
Harman, Charlie	72
Harman, Daniel "Dan"	97
Harman, Elizabeth M	767
Harman, Jane	843
Harmann, Jean	461
Harmer, Todd	507, 632
Harmon, Florence	824
Harmon, Karen	71
Harnett, Andrea L	895
Harney, Janet	795
Harney, Mike	195
Harnischfeger, Frank	914
Haro, Steve	177
Harold, Rosemary	785
Harper, Abigail	710
Harper, Barbara	70
Harper, Bill	144
Harper, Chuck	383
Harper, Gregg	150, 305, 334, 409, 410, 413, 424, 464, 482, 502, 503
Harper, Jason	4
Harper, Mary Annie	169
Harper, Michael	719
Harper, Todd M	806
Harrell, Jamie	221
Harrigan, Thomas G	656
Harrington, Anne	752
Harrington, Eileen	793
Harrington, Janis	663
Harrington, Mona	859
Harrington, Thomas	666
Harris, Andrea	369
Harris, Andy	123, 304, 335, 428, 429, 435, 436, 440, 441, 442, 443, 482, 494
Harris, Antonia	727
Harris, Carl	757
Harris, Catherine	829
Harris, Claude	748
Harris, Danny	756
Harris, David	728
Harris, Elliott	914
Harris, James M	699
Harris, Jason	70
Harris, Lorinda	372
Harris, Marcelite	493
Harris, Molly	744
Harris, Ondray	901
Harris, Pamela	674
Harris, Rosa	508, 575
Harris, Scott	848
Harris, Seth	717
Harris, Seth D	839
Harris, Seth David	498
Harris, Timothy "Tim"	97
Harris, William T	577
Harris, Zach	422
Harris-Berry, Gail	609
Harris-Green, Sue	694
Harrison, Dave	644
Harrison, Michael	424, 496
Harrison, Randolph	30
Harrison, Sharon	743
Harrison, Todd	411
Harroun, Tim	455
Harsha, Daniel	420
Hart, Christopher A	811
Hart, Elizabeth	56
Hart, J. Steven	497
Hart, John	215
Hart, John M	804
Hart, Pat	768
Hart, Philip C	507
Hart, Rosemary	673, 803
Hart, Ryan	283
Hartley, Richard K	625
Hartmann, Christopher	174
Hartnett, Daniel M	500
Hartog-Levin, Fay	602
Hartsell, Mark	580
Hartwick, Douglas	591
Hartz, Harris L	850
Hartz, Jerry	457
Hartz, Joe	439
Hartzler, Vicky	154, 305, 336, 395, 396, 397, 402, 403, 404, 482
Harvell, Thea, III	635
Harvey, Alton	823
Harvey, Ana	827
Harvey, Jackie	711
Harvey, Jeff	285
Harvey, Mariam	610
Harvey, Reavie	605
Harvey, Robert P	465
Harwood, Joy	691
Hasan, Merza H	933
Hasenfus, Julie A	578
Hashemi, Cookab	25
Hashmi, Sonny	795
Hasketts, Geoff	680
Haskew, Barbara S	834
Haskins, Conaway	274
Haslam, James A., II	798
Hassebrock, Douglas	706
Hassell, D. Christian	667
Hassett, John	712
Hastert, Dennis	501
Hastings, Alcee L	69, 303, 329, 434, 482, 496
Hastings, Doc	283, 309, 329, 428, 482
Hastings, Kelly	370
Hasvold, Lawrence	746
Hatch, Orrin G	269, 309, 321, 324, 363, 364, 368, 374, 375, 382, 465, 470, 837
Hatfield, Jonathon A	789
Hattix, Larry	611
Hauck, Brian	650
Hauck, David	507
Haueter, Bob	31
Haueter, Thomas	811
Haugrud, Jack	684
Hauhn, Lauren	404
Haun, J.L	648
Haun-Mohamed, Robin L	579
Hauptmann, David	388
Haurek, Alex	185, 439
Hauser, Dan	269
Hauser, Nate	452
Hauser, Timothy D	725
Hauser, Valerie	773
Hausman, Scott	710
Hauswirth, Michael	449
Havemann, Judy	807
Haven, Jackie	696
Haverstock, Cathy	627
Hawbecker, Karen	684
Hawco, George	510
Hawk, Larry Echo	681
Hawke, Daniel	826
Hawkens, E. Roy	813
Hawkes, Harrison	376
Hawkins, Albert, III	493
Hawkins, Andrew	137
Hawkins, George S	902
Hawkins, Karen	612
Hawkins, Michael D	850
Hawkins, Patricia McMahon	603

Page

Hawkins, Robert J 848
Hawkins, Ronnie 620
Hawkins, Tom 388
Hawkins, William 420
Hawks, Ann Woods 239
Hawks, Diane 149
Hawks, T.A 148
Hawley, Thomas E 635
Hawn, Laurie 922
Hawney, Wayne 670
Hawrylak, Egon F 642
Hawthorne, Sandra L 816
Hay, Dan 10
Hayashi, Nobumitsu 934
Hayden, Carla 808
Hayes, Brian E 809
Hayes, Candance Lein 804
Hayes, Charlotte 717
Hayes, Colin 360
Hayes, David 679
Hayes, Donna 413
Hayes, Jim 154
Hayes, John ''Jack'' 710
Hayes, Jonathan 58
Hayes, Mark 365
Hayes, Mark L 670
Hayes, Paula 790
Hayes, Robin 493
Hayes, Sean 411
Hayes, Sheena 833
Hayes, Suzanne 822
Hayman, Toby 385
Haynes, Catharina 849
Haynes, Josh 156
Haynes, Michelle 389
Haynes, Wil 457
Hays, Elizabeth 376
Haywood, Anthony 792
Hayworth, Nan A.S 188, 307, 336, 414, 415, 416, 482, 837
Haze, Pam 682
Hazlett, Anne 340
Hazlett, Kathleen 174
Hazlewood, Catherine 358
He, Jianxiong 915
Head, Daniel 295
Head, Mary S 820
Heald, Seth 675
Healey, Martin 825
Healton, Kelly 188
Healy, Colleen 463
Healy, Rick 401
Heapy, Richard A 826
Heard, Preston 508
Heard, Robin 685
Hearn, Candy R 645
Hearn, Jim 354
Hearne, Walter 401
Heart, Preston, Jr 575
Heartley, Linda 722
Heath, Jay 347, 348, 350
Heath, Richard 775
Heatley, Jesse 498
Hebert, John R 581
Hechavarria, Adam 166
Heck, Joseph J 165, 306, 336, 402, 403, 406, 407, 451, 482
Heckenberg, Loraine 401
Heckenkamp, Mitch 92
Hecker, Nick 386
Heckler, Margaret M 501
Heckroth, Thomas 720
Heddell, Gordon S 616
Heddings, Ray 589
Hedge, Brook 896
Hedgecock, Richard 216
Hedgepeth, Ryan 202
Hedger, Stephen 152
Hedges, Earl 743
Hedgespeth, Grady 827
Hedman, Susan 783
Heffner, Kelly J 834
Heffner, Kelly Jean 781
Hegedusich, Bill 642
Hegg, Dabney 345
Heighberger, Eric 372
Heil, Dave 252
Heil, Lindsey 623

Page

Heilig, Rebecca 115
Heilman, Chandra 828
Heim, Laurie Schultz 838
Heiman, Bruce 502
Heineman, Dave 797
Heinen, Suzanne 692
Heinlein, Steven 632
Heinrich, Janet 733
Heinrich, Mark 647
Heinrich, Martin 176, 306, 334, 402, 403, 404, 428, 429, 482
Heisler, Nick 913
Heist, James 739
Heitkam, Colleen 786
Hekhuis, Jeremy 205
Hekmat, Maureen 291
Held, Edward ''Bruce'' 751
Helgemo, Wendy 381
Heller, Dean 163, 306, 321, 325, 356, 357, 359, 360, 382, 470
Heller, J. David 836
Hellert, William 784
Hellman, Don 680
Hellman, Kenneth A 725
Helmer, Gary 689
Helmke, Mark 95, 367
Helms, Lila 343, 345
Helsing, Jeffrey W 838
Helst, Steven Ver 632
Helton, Emory Ray 762
Heltzer, Lester A 809
Helwig, Janice 496
Helwig, Robert 769
Hemingway, Jennifer 433
Hemphill, Albert 676
Henderson, Adam 372
Henderson, Chris 679
Henderson, George 653
Henderson, Jay 420
Henderson, Jill S 816
Henderson, Joe 731
Henderson, John A 393
Henderson, Karen LeCraft 851
Henderson, Kaya 799, 901
Henderson, Ron 630
Henderson, William 109
Hendricks, S. Denise 806
Hendrickson, Eric 646
Hendrickson, Randall 619
Heneghan, John 749
Heneghan, Philip M 838
Henken, Matt 50
Henline, Robert 424
Henn, Jay 800
Henne, Paul 680
Henneberg, Amanda 277
Henneberg, William 362
Hennemuth, Jeffrey A 893
Hennie, Alicia 383
Hennigan, Jamie 429
Henningsen, Jacqueline R 630
Henriquez, Sandra B 738
Henry, Charles 115
Henry, David T 714
Henry, Fitzroy J 921
Henry, George 186
Henry, Shawn 667
Henry, Sudafi 387
Henry, Taylor 114
Henry, Wayne 653
Henry-Martin, Jacinth Lorna 918
Henry-Spires, Diedra 364
Hensarling, Jeb 253, 309, 332, 414, 415, 452, 466, 482
Henseler, Timothy 820
Henshall, David 821
Henshaw, Karilyn 271
Hensler, Timothy 820
Henson, Margaret E 417
Henstrand, Bob 641
Hepp, Joe 818
Herald, Deborah 819
Herbert, Arthur 665
Herbert, Jason 263
Herbert, Marty 446
Herbert, Noller 691
Herbert, Ronald 737
Herbst, Lars T 682
Herdt, M. Lyn 682

	Page
Herfkens, Eveline	932
Herger, Wally	20, 301, 328, 447, 448, 464, 482
Heriot, Gail	835
Herlihy, Thomas W	742
Herman, Martin	715
Herman, Steven J	581
Hermann, Alicia	369
Hermann, Megan	360
Hernandez, Cyndy	35
Hernandez, Danny	644
Hernandez, Deborah	738
Hernandez, Drysdale	629
Hernandez, Gilberto Elizalde	911
Hernandez, Vanessa	30
Herndon, Chris	358
Herr, Linda S	812
Herren, Chris	652
Herrera Beutler, Jaime	282, 309, 336, 438, 439, 440, 442, 443, 482
Herrin, Janet C	835
Herring, Albert H	677
Herring, Mark Y	808
Herring, Oneshia	70
Herrle, Cindy	455
Herrmann, Matthew	298
Herron, Bruce	744
Hersh, Sarah	25
Hersman, Deborah A.P	811
Hertel, Dennis	501
Herther, Andrew	362
Hertling, Richard	426
Hertz, David M	807
Hertz, Harry S	713
Hertz, Jessica	649
Hertz, Michael F	651
Hervitz, Jesse	463
Herz, Jim	405
Herzog, Laura	244
Herzog, Marcia	794
Heslop, Jeff	820
Hess, John R	896
Hesse, Mike	48
Hesselbrock, Emily	388
Hessler-Radelet, Carrie	818
Heup, Ellen	742
Heusner, Stephen	905
Hewell, Robert	796
Hewitt, Bart	698
Hewitt, Brett	352
Hewitt, Earl W	657
Hewitt, Emily Clark	873
Hewitt, Grant	165
Hewko, Anna Lee	775
Heyburn, John G., II	891
Heyman, David	767
Heyse, Erica Wheelan	497
Heyworth, Lawrie	508
Heyzer, Noeleen	926
Hibbert, Farhanna	82
Hickernell, Robert	714
Hickey, John J	745
Hickey, Lauren	124
Hickey, Toni	711
Hickman, Bryan	365
Hickman, Chelsey	257
Hickman, Laura	630
Hickman, Natasha	195
Hicks, Cheryl	697
Hicks, Chris	340
Hicks, Cory	110, 412
Hicks, Kyle	370
Hicks, Mark	623
Hicks, Ronald	700
Hicks, Thomas	424
Hicks, Tom	645
Hicks, Trey	372
Hicks, William P	824
Hiebeck, Wayne	743
Hiestand, Robyn	354
Higdon, Michael	112
Higginbotham, Patrick E	849
Higgins, Brian	192, 307, 332, 418, 419, 421, 482, 494
Higgins, Craig	401
Higgins, Heather	726
Higgins, Holly	713
Higgins, James T	788
Higgins, Maureen B	817
Higgins, Michael R	404

	Page
Higgins, Stefanie	72
Higgins, Stephen	376
Higgiston, James	692
High, Mark	465
Hild, Edward	7
Hildebrand, Asher	197
Hildebrand, Leigh	389
Hildred, Kim	449
Hildreth, Shari	283
Hildreth, Susan	807
Hiler, Jonathan	453
Hilera, Eduardo	299
Hill, Anne Willis	358
Hill, Bernard	461
Hill, Daniel O	706
Hill, Douglas	627
Hill, Elizabeth	627
Hill, Frederick	433
Hill, Greg	256
Hill, James C	850
Hill, John	607
Hill, Julian	768
Hill, Laura	370
Hill, Marcus	770
Hill, Patricia L	80
Hill, Richard E., Jr	701
Hill, Robert	827
Hill, Shirley	685
Hill, Vern W	791
Hill, Walter, Jr	784
Hill-Midgett, Nannie	694
Hill-Roberson, Jessie	780
Hillebrands, Joan	136
Hiller, Aaron	427
Hillier, Micheal	842
Hillman, Rick	575
Hilton, Cheryl L	796
Himelfarb, Sheldon J	838
Himes, James A	53, 302, 334, 414, 415, 416, 482
Hinchey, Maurice D	190, 307, 329, 398, 399, 463, 482, 493
Hinck, Kaaren	127
Hinckley, Linda	169
Hindle, Ron	369
Hindman, Richard	786
Hines, Anson	829
Hines, Clint	443
Hines, Debra	607
Hines, John T	781, 834
Hines, Robert P	724
Hines, Shannon	352
Hing, Jennifer	400
Hingson, Dean	95
Hinnen, Todd	674
Hinojosa, Ricardo H	841
Hinojosa, Ruben	258, 309, 330, 406, 407, 414, 415, 482
Hinojosa, Thomas	657
Hinson, David	708
Hinson, Jeff	732
Hinson, Kenneth R	780
Hinton, Michael	691
Hinton, Tamara	397
Hinz, Jean	143
Hipp, Janie	688
Hippe, Jim	246
Hipsley, Kyle	911
Hirabayashi, Kai	370
Hirakawa, Ted	582
Hiratsuka, Mary	8
Hire, Elisabeth	1, 387, 587
Hirono, Mazie K	81, 303, 333, 406, 407, 440, 441, 442, 443, 482, 499
Hirozawa, Kent Y	808
Hirsch, Harold E	465
Hirsch, Samuel	650
Hirschhorn, Eric L	706
Hirschman, Jay	695
Hirshfield, Andrew	711
Hitch, Vance	672
Hitchens, Theresa	927
Hite, Jason	459
Hite, Matthew	362
Hitt, Ginny Clair	150
Hitt, H. Lucas	705
Hittle, Matthew	448
Hixon, Christopher	433
Hlavacek, Scott J	825
Hlibok, Gregory	786

Page
Hnatowski, Thomas C 894
Hoagland, Richard E 601
Hoaglun, Brad 82
Hoard, Ralph G 917
Hoban-Moore, Patricia A 738
Hobbs, Alma C 685
Hobbs, Rebecca 111
Hobson, Ed 818
Hochberg, Andrew S 836
Hochberg, Fred 784
Hochstrasser, Franz 688
Hochul, Kathleen C 192, 307, 336, 402, 421, 422, 482
Hockert, Carol 714
Hockin, Brian 375
Hockin, Thomas 914
Hodas, Sam 56
Hodes, Peggo Horstmann 498
Hodes, Richard J 734
Hodgdon, Dave 386
Hodge, Adam 73
Hodges, Frederick B 639
Hodges, Heather M 601
Hodges, Robert Hayne, Jr 877
Hodges, William Terrell 798
Hodgkins, Gerald 823
Hodgman, Colleen 293
Hodson, Nate 162
Hoefer, Michael 767
Hoehne, Jena 162
Hoehne, John 82
Hoehne, Stephanie 640
Hoelzer, Jennifer 219
Hoerl, Donald M 825
Hoeven, John 203, 307, 323, 325, 339, 340, 341, 342, 343, 359, 360, 381, 470, 493, 502
Hoey, Thomas P 898
Hoff, David 756
Hoffman, Alan 1, 387, 587
Hoffman, Bill 376
Hoffman, Janice 728
Hoffman, Jennifer 433
Hoffman, Kathy 23
Hoffman, Marjorie 465
Hoffman, Mary T 776
Hoffman, Patricia 751
Hoffman, William J 785
Hoffmann, Matt 405
Hofman, Avi 935
Hogan, Caroline 19
Hogan, Cynthia 1, 387, 587
Hogan, Howard 705
Hogan, John 922
Hogan, Mary Jo 718
Hogan, Nancy 592, 726
Hogan, Pat 372
Hogan, Thomas F 864
Hogans, Alice 401
Hogans, Cheryl C 725
Hoglander, Harry 810
Hogshead, Laura 401
Hoh, Anchi 581
Hohenstein, William 687
Hoidal, Chris 749
Holbein, James 838
Holcombe, Kelley, Jr 797
Holden, Tim 232, 308, 329, 395, 396, 440, 441, 442, 482
Holder, Eric H., Jr 585, 589, 649
Holder, Nick 25
Holdren, John P 590
Holeman, Brian 895
Holgate, H. Richard 666
Holgrewe, Kent 672
Holladay, Jon M 687
Holland, Barbara 727
Holland, Caroline 376
Holland, E.J. "Ned" 727
Holland, James P 626
Holland-Bartels, Leslie 683
Hollatz, Beth 243
Holley, David 453
Holley, Leta L 789
Holley, Richard 823
Holliday, Mark 709
Hollings, Charles 628
Hollingsworth, Kimo 619
Hollis, Kate 2
Hollis, Liz 407
Hollis, Patricia 606

Page
Hollis, Robert 651
Hollister, Hudson 433
Holloway, Michael 755, 756
Holloway, William J., Jr 850
Holm, Charles H 775
Holman, Richard 686
Holman, Tom 719
Holmberg, Tracie 180
Holmes, Jerome A 850
Holmes, Josh 109
Holmes, Mark V 880
Holmes, Noel 230
Holmes, Stewart 344
Holmes, Victor A 582
Holmgren, David 612
Holsman, Marianne 783
Holt, Michael 770
Holt, Ray 669
Holt, Rush D 174, 306, 330, 406, 407, 428, 429, 482, 499
Holt, Victoria K 597
Holtmann, Thomas P 465
Holtrop, Joel 689
Homa, Cherie 229
Homan, Thomas 769
Homan, Todd 742
Homiak, Robert 661
Honda, Michael M 26, 302, 331, 398, 400, 405, 482
Honeycutt, C. Wayne 691
Honeycutt, Christopher 628
Honkus, Bradley J 655
Hood, David 797
Hood, Michael 922
Hood, Rich 783
Hoog, Ben 407
Hook, Melissa 900
Hook, Vicki 194
Hooker, Stephanie 714
Hooks, Becky 358
Hooks, Craig 782
Hooper, Bryan 694
Hooper, Cheryl 656
Hoopes, Nathaniel 127
Hooshangi, Ryika 365
Hoostal, Stephanie 509
Hoover, William J 665
Hope, John 667
Hopkins, Allison 739
Hopkins, Elizabeth 725
Hopkins, Lara 63
Hopkins, Thomas M 670
Hopper, Carol 635
Hoppis, Lisa M 582
Horan, Thomas 787
Horbaly, Jan 859
Horgan, Katie 166
Horhn, Charlie 149
Hormats, Robert 597, 839
Horn, Brian 655
Horn, Donald H 742
Horn, Marian Blank 872
Horne, Sabra 673
Horne, Timothy O 797
Horner, M. June 733
Horner, Terrance, Jr 362
Horowitz, Andrew 25
Horowitz, David 728
Horrigan, Mary 644
Horrigan, Michael 719
Hortiz, Joseph W., Jr 726
Horton, Cory 423
Horton, Phillip 628
Horwich, J. Lloyd 758
Hoskins, Lisa K 776
Hoskins, Victor 897
Hospital, Jeremiah D 792
Hostetler, Margret 449
Hotchkis, Joan E 798
Hotopp, Heidi 102
Houck, James 646
Houck, James W 644
Houck, Tierney 224
Houerou, Philippe Le 933
Houff, Mary 715
Hougesen, Brook 89
Houghton, Andrew D 779
Houle, David W 726
Houlihan, Bill 84

	Page
Hourigan, Brendan	712
House, Andrew	29
House, Mark	744
House, Matt	179
House, Missy	239
Housel, James	712
Housel, Paul	4
Houser, Melani M	465
Houser, Sheila	245
Houston, Brad	763
Houton, Sean	358
Houy, Charles J	343
Hoven, Christopher	33
Hoven, Ingrid	934
Howard, Ben	456
Howard, Brad	16
Howard, Brian	412
Howard, Cyndi	404
Howard, Gary J	347
Howard, Jeffrey R	849
Howard, Kate	160
Howard, Laurie	742
Howard, Lisa	675
Howard, Megan	404
Howard, Michael	460
Howard, Michael P	634
Howard, Michelle	493
Howard, Sally A	728
Howard, Sara	154
Howard, Virginia	662
Howe, Marylyn	805
Howell, Beryl A	841, 863
Howell, J. Bryan	739
Howell, Jenny	254
Howell, Ryan	453
Howell, Thomas G	712
Howland, William O., Jr	899
Howorth, Richard C	834
Howorth, Russell	922
Howze, Karen	895
Hoy, Serena	387
Hoyer, Steny H	125, 304, 327, 457, 482
Hoyos, Luis Alfonso	918
Hromada, Erin M	459
Hrubovcak, James	687
Hsing, Helen	576
Hsu, David	823
Hsueh, Wallace K	378
Hua, Jingdong	935
Huang, Hong-Yen	910
Hubbard, James E	690
Hubbard, Jim	154
Hubbert, David A	675
Huber, Konstantin	933
Huberman, Richard L	813
Hubert, Shari	818
Huckleberry, Chris	221
Huddleston, Leslie	82
Huddleston, Marla L	841
Hudgins, Cathaee	898
Hudock, Cathy	626
Hudson, Adam	38
Hudson, James	632
Hudson, James L	608
Hudson, Julia E	796, 805
Hudson, Renee	11
Hudson, Richard	256
Huebner, David	602
Hueckel, Monica	213
Huelskamp, Tim	106, 304, 336, 395, 396, 405, 445, 482
Huerta, Michael	743
Huff, Christopher W	645
Huff, Daniel	426
Huff, Preston	804
Huffaker, Chris	16
Huffine, Betsy	198
Huffman, Carry	769
Hug, Procter R., Jr	850
Hughes, Adam	354
Hughes, Carolyn	276
Hughes, David	364
Hughes, James A	631
Hughes, John	458
Hughes, John M	894
Hughes, Lillie	719
Hughes, Maria	657
Hughes, Meghan	237
Hughes, Paul D	837
Hughes, Robert	239
Hughes, Seamus	372
Hughes, Tammy	401
Hughes, Tom	252
Hughey, P. Christopher	789
Hugler, Edward C	717
Huizenga, Bill	134, 305, 336, 414, 415, 416, 483
Hulen, Anthony	248
Hull, Craig	794
Hull, Frank M	850
Hultberg, Carla	433
Hultgren, Randy	90, 303, 336, 395, 396, 397, 435, 436, 440, 441, 442, 483
Hum, Carolyn	842
Humbrecht, Jean	433
Humes, Richard M	822
Hummer, John	748
Humphrey, Connie	258
Hungate, Joseph	612
Hunsicker, Lindsay	370
Hunt, Betty Ann	609
Hunt, David L	786
Hunt, David W	497
Hunt, Joseph H	651
Hunt, Juan Carlos	662
Hunt, Roger	797
Hunt, Ryan	344
Hunt, Scott	806
Hunter, Aaron	45
Hunter, Antonio	899
Hunter, Caroline C	789
Hunter, Christine	618
Hunter, Dean	816
Hunter, Debbie B	460
Hunter, Denise	576
Hunter, Duncan	44, 302, 334, 402, 403, 406, 440, 443, 483
Hunter, Edward L	731
Hunter, Kyleanne	508
Hunter, Leah	291
Hunter, Maryann F	775
Hunter, Thomas M	775
Hunter-Williams, Jill	88
Huntley, Henry	641
Huntsman, Jon M., Jr	600
Hurcombe, Helen M	704
Hurdle, Lana	742
Hurlbut, Brandon	751
Hurley, Anna	10
Hurley, Daniel	715
Hurley, John	608
Hurley, Raymond C. ''Neil''	675
Hurst, Hallie	239
Hurst, Melissa	774
Hurst, Terry	727
Hurt, Adrienne D	777
Hurt, Jay	757
Hurt, Robert	277, 309, 336, 414, 415, 416, 483
Hurtt, Harold	769
Hurwit, Cathy	88
Hurwitz, Hugh	755
Husband, Shelley	278
Husk, Stephen J	677
Hussain, Rina	821
Hussey, Jim	72
Hussey, Thomas W	651
Hust, Gerald R	623
Hutcheson, Thane	455
Hutchinson, Lytwaive	618
Hutchinson, Steven	373
Hutchison, Kay Bailey	250, 309, 321, 324, 341, 342, 343, 356, 377, 470, 493, 495
Hutchison, Susan	843
Hutson, James H	500, 581
Hutson, Janet	628
Hutto, Lori	58
Hutton, James	641
Hutzell, Paula	711
Huus, Amber	392
Huvelle, Ellen Segal	861
Huxhold, Kristy	56
Hyatt, Catherine B	796
Hybl, William J	835
Hyde, Pamela	734
Hyde, Robert	632, 644
Hydle, Lars	184
Hyland, Christiane Gigi	805, 812
Hylton, Stacia A	676

Page
Hynek, Diana 704
Hynes, Shaylyn 251
Hyten, John 624
Hytken, Louise P 676
Hyun, Karen 430

I

Iacaruso, Chris 146
Iacomini, Nancy 392
Idelson, Holly 372
Igasaki, Paul M 717
Iger, Michael 190
Igleheart, Alexandra 257
Ihrig, Jane E 776
Ikuta, Sandra S 850
Illston, Ted 362
Imbergamo, Bill 340
Imbrie, Andrew 367
Imparato, Andrew 369
Inderforth, Alison 50
Indermark, Michele 626
Indovina, Ana 663
Infield, Amanda 292
Inglee, William 400
Inglis, John C 621
Ingold, Bernard P 639
Ingolia, Joseph N 771
Ingram, Charles 610
Ingram, Deborah 768
Ingram, Judith 789
Ingram, Sarah Hall 612
Inhofe, James M 215, 307, 322, 324, 346, 347, 361, 366, 367, 470, 799
Inman, Celina 345
Inouye, Daniel K 80, 501, 303, 323, 324, 341, 342, 343, 356, 357, 377, 381, 384, 387, 470, 495, 502, 503
Insel, Thomas 734
Inslee, Jay 282, 309, 330, 409, 410, 483
Insulza, Jose Miguel 918
Inzeo, Nicholas 784
Ireland, Jeanne 732
Ireland, S. Leslie 609
Irlanda, Aimee 300
Irons, Beryl 921
Irvin, George 694
Irvine, Thomas B 800
Irving, Alfred S 895
Irving, Earl Michael 603
Irving, Walker 274
Irwin, Caitlin 358
Isaacson, Orly 186
Isaacson, Walter 777
Isabelli, Kristin 449
Isakowitz, Steve 751
Isakson, Johnny 72, 303, 323, 325, 356, 357, 366, 367, 368, 379, 381, 470, 497
Isaza, Jose Antonio 910
Iscoe, Craig 895
Isenberg, Erin 214
Isenman, Barry 825
Ishakian, Michel M 893
Isherwood, Dorothy A 841
Ishii, Shogo 914
Ishikawa, Masahiro 909
Ishimaru, Stuart J 783
Islam, Kazi M. Aminul 934
Isom, Charles 162
Israel, Kenneth D 826
Israel, Steve 180, 306, 331, 453, 483
Israeli, Tali 230
Israelite, Joan 806
Issa, Darrell E 43, 302, 331, 425, 426, 431, 483, 805
Istook, Judy 498
Iudicello, Fay 679
Ivancic, Charlotte 405
Iversen, Michele 756
Ivey, Joni L 276
Ivy, James 700
Iwanow, Walter 673
Iwry, J. Mark 611
Iyengar, Sunil 806
Izon, Hannah 175

J

Jablon, Ann 128
Jablonski, Edward 582

Page
Jackson, Amy Berman 864
Jackson, Andrew 682
Jackson, Arnold 705
Jackson, Barry 455
Jackson, Barry S 843
Jackson, David 65
Jackson, Deidre 498
Jackson, Deirdre M 677
Jackson, Diane 119
Jackson, Eric 401
Jackson, Frederick R 762
Jackson, Geoffrey 842
Jackson, Gregory 895
Jackson, Herbert H., Jr 579
Jackson, James F 633
Jackson, Jamie 267
Jackson, Janene 898, 900
Jackson, Jesse L., Jr 85, 303, 329, 398, 400, 483
Jackson, Joyce 300
Jackson, Kaheem 508
Jackson, Karen S 739
Jackson, Ketanji B 841
Jackson, Kristin 420
Jackson, Kyle 263
Jackson, Lisa P 500, 585, 781
Jackson, Malcom 782
Jackson, Michael 132
Jackson, Rhonda 266
Jackson, Robert Porter 600
Jackson, Ronald 742
Jackson, Rosalind 427
Jackson, Ryan 215
Jackson, Sean 624
Jackson, Sharon F 839
Jackson, Shirley Ann 828
Jackson, Tamika 786
Jackson, Timothy 5
Jackson, William M 895
Jackson, Yvette 696
Jackson Lee, Sheila 260, 309, 329, 421, 422, 425, 426, 483, 497
Jacksteit, Mary 790, 791
Jacob, Fred 809
Jacobs, Ann 123
Jacobs, Barbara 822
Jacobs, Cheryl 676
Jacobs, Chris 385
Jacobs, Dennis 849
Jacobs, Elizabeth 824
Jacobs, Irwin M 810
Jacobs, Janice L 598
Jacobs, Joanna M 655
Jacobs, Joshua 379
Jacobs, Julian I 882
Jacobs, Linda 635
Jacobs, Whitney 73
Jacobs, William 581
Jacobson, David 600
Jacobson, Noah 144
Jacobson, Rachel 684
Jacobson, Roberta 597
Jacobson, Tracey 599
Jacoby, Charles H 619
Jaczko, Gregory B 812
Jadacki, Matthew A 766
Jadallah, Diala 210
Jaeger, Cheryl 455
Jaenichen, Chip 644
Jafari, Beth 250
Jaffe, Richard A 893
Jaffer, Jamil 452
Jagger, Craig 397
Jagusch, Sybille A 581
Jahanian, Farnam 811
Jama, Liban 820
James, Alice 237
James, Charles F 725
James, David 65
James, Deirdre 465
James, Ginny 344
James, Jeanette S 404
James, Kathleen 809
James, Kenya 384
James, Larry 629
James, Lisa 443
James, Melissa 261
James, Michael 645
James, Rae Ellen 724

	Page
James, Stewart Simon	934
James, William	697
Jameson, Arlen	493
Jameson, Michael	10
Jameson, Robert	246
Jamil, Iftikhar	710
Jamison, Brooke	179
Jamrock, Melissa	144
Jankus, Ed	392
Jannah, Abdoulie	926
Jannuzi, Frank	367
Jansen, Dave	444
Jansen, Joe	206
Jantzen, Linda	639
Jaquette, Scott	611
Jarcho, Jane E	825
Jarmin, Ron	705
Jaroma, Emily	464
Jarraud, Michel	929
Jarrett, Ben	93
Jarrett, Debra	166
Jarrett, H. Marshall	662
Jarrett, Valerie	593
Jarsulic, Laura	822
Jarsulic, Marc	352
Jarvinen, Matthew	791
Jarvis, Adam	434
Jarvis, Jon	680
Jarvis, Jonathan	799
Jarvis, Jonathan B	804
Jasim, Saad Y	913
Jaskierski, Laura	364
Jaskowiak, Mark	608
Jason, Meredith	809
Jauregui, Marta Garcia	934
Jawetz, Tom	427
Jaworski, Kimberly Hazel	454
Jayaratne, Adri	721
Jean-Simon, Vanessa	367
Jeanquart, Roberta S	685
Jefferies, Ian	358
Jefferies, Joan	763
Jeffers, Bill	595
Jeffers, Erika	417
Jefferson, Daphne	722
Jefferson, Raymond M	725
Jeffress, Suellen	641
Jeffrey, James Franklin	601
Jeffries, Jim	244
Jeffries, R.R	648
Jelgerhuis, Jessica	109
Jemilohun, Kemi	35
Jenca, Miroslav	930
Jenckes, Christina	420
Jenkins, Carol	718
Jenkins, Daniel	372
Jenkins, Jorge	921
Jenkins, Lloyd A	461
Jenkins, Lynn	106, 304, 334, 447, 448, 483
Jenkins, Michelle	279
Jenkins, Sharon	85
Jennings, Edward, Jr	740
Jennings, Jack P	775
Jennings, Kevin	759
Jennings, Leodis	640
Jennis, Wendy	893
Jensen, Austen	167
Jensen, Craig	645
Jensen, James E	810
Jensen, Jay	689
Jensen, William F., III	392
Jensen-Lachmann, Susan	427
Jenson, Paula	822
Jenson, William G	685
Jentleson, Adam	383, 387
Jeong, Il Jeong	909
Jepson, Kristin	452
Jerger, Michael	808
Jerman, Mike	271
Jermolowizc, Andrew	694
Jesmer, Rob	385
Jessar, Kevin	774
Jesse, Robert L	763
Jessen, Dawn	820
Jester, Julia	437
Jett, Brianna	217
Jett, Carole	685
Jeu, Joseph H	619
Jew, Robert	802
Jezierski, Crystal	426
Jezierski, J.T	151, 288
Jiayi, Liu	927
Jimenez, Blanca	36
Jimenez, Luis	591
Jiminez, Andy	439
Jipping, Tom	376
Jirik, Monica	162
Jochum, Rita Lari	375
Joffrion, Philip	116
Johanns, Mike	160, 306, 322, 325, 339, 340, 351, 352, 361, 362, 379, 381, 470
Johanson, David	365
John, Judy St	698
Johner, Nancy	161
Johns, David	369
Johns, Granville "Jason"	643
Johns, Marie	827
Johns, Robert	750
Johnson, Alex	378
Johnson, Alex T	496
Johnson, Alfred C	734
Johnson, Alfreda	720
Johnson, Amy	627
Johnson, Barbara	23
Johnson, Bart R	766
Johnson, Bill	208, 307, 336, 418, 419, 428, 429, 445, 483
Johnson, Bonnie	634
Johnson, Bruce N., Sr	792
Johnson, Bud	389
Johnson, Celeste	639
Johnson, Charles W., III	461
Johnson, Cherish	710
Johnson, Collister, Jr	750
Johnson, Curtis	742
Johnson, Darlene	678
Johnson, Dave	340
Johnson, David	752
Johnson, David S	706
Johnson, Dawn	718
Johnson, Drema	785
Johnson, Eddie Bernice	266, 309, 329, 435, 440, 441, 442, 443, 483
Johnson, Erik	261
Johnson, Gerard S	906
Johnson, Grace	246
Johnson, Gregory	691
Johnson, Henry C. "Hank", Jr	74, 303, 333, 402, 403, 425, 426, 483
Johnson, James A	799
Johnson, Jay	701
Johnson, Jeff	377
Johnson, Jeffery	667
Johnson, Jeffrey Paul	767
Johnson, Jeh Charles	615, 620
Johnson, Jennifer J	777
Johnson, Jodi	655
Johnson, John N	404
Johnson, John Ramsey	895
Johnson, Joseph	621
Johnson, Josh	360
Johnson, Julian	73
Johnson, Juliet	47
Johnson, Justin	814
Johnson, Katherine	587
Johnson, Kathleen	459, 783
Johnson, Kendall B	705
Johnson, Kenneth	824
Johnson, Kim	126
Johnson, Kimberly	391
Johnson, Kirt Charles	293
Johnson, Larry	917
Johnson, Leslie	843
Johnson, Lynne E	794
Johnson, Martha	773, 805
Johnson, Martha N	794, 807
Johnson, Mary L	810
Johnson, Matthew	376
Johnson, Melissa	439
Johnson, Michael R	813
Johnson, Molly	217
Johnson, Molly H	580
Johnson, Nancy	493
Johnson, Nicole	610
Johnson, Nicole Wade	423
Johnson, Noel	896

Page

Johnson, Paul C., Jr 717
Johnson, Peter 413
Johnson, Peter O 611
Johnson, Ralph 375
Johnson, Reginal N 577
Johnson, Ron 290, 310, 323, 325, 341, 342, 343, 354, 371, 382, 470
Johnson, Sam 251, 309, 328, 447, 448, 464, 483, 828
Johnson, Sasha J 744
Johnson, Scott 607
Johnson, Stefanie 790
Johnson, Steven 460
Johnson, Suzanne Nora 774
Johnson, Tae 769
Johnson, Tallman 416
Johnson, Tanner 114
Johnson, Ted A 705, 706
Johnson, Teresa 461
Johnson, Terri 679
Johnson, Tim 5, 242, 308, 322, 324, 341, 342, 343, 351, 352, 359, 360, 381, 383, 470
Johnson, Timothy V 91, 303, 331, 395, 397, 440, 441, 442, 443, 483
Johnson, Todd 362
Johnson, Travis 352
Johnson, Velvet 373
Johnson, William S 404
Johnson-Weider, Michelle L 393
Johnston, Deborah A 649
Johnston, Elizabeth 575
Johnston, James 628, 671
Johnston, Joseph 389, 507
Johnston, Kimberly 282
Johnston, Lawrence 461
Johnston, Mark 737
Johnston, Richard C 630
Johnston, Steve 456
Jolley, Geoff 155
Jolly, E. Grady 849
Jomo, Kwame Sundaram 925
Jonas, Patricia A 830
Jones, Amy 407
Jones, Andrew 178
Jones, Ashley 78
Jones, Barbara S 891
Jones, Bethany 700
Jones, Brain R 713
Jones, Brenda 75
Jones, Brian 385
Jones, C. Hunter 822
Jones, Candy 627
Jones, Cynthia 720
Jones, Darrell D 629
Jones, David 661
Jones, David S 775
Jones, Deborah E 460
Jones, Deborah K 601
Jones, Diem-Linh 686
Jones, Doug 793
Jones, Duane 629
Jones, Edith H 849
Jones, Edward 497
Jones, Erik 357
Jones, Franklin C 769
Jones, Gary 711
Jones, Harvey L 894
Jones, Heather 413
Jones, Jan E 510
Jones, Jennifer E 507
Jones, John F. "Jack" 733, 734
Jones, Joseph 649
Jones, Julie 657
Jones, Kathryn 743
Jones, Keith 397
Jones, Kerri-Ann 599
Jones, Kevin 401, 674
Jones, Mary N 741
Jones, Mary Suit 377
Jones, Matt 296
Jones, Mike 354, 722
Jones, Narda 786
Jones, Nikki 126
Jones, Paul W 602
Jones, Peter 635
Jones, Rachel 344
Jones, Randall 701
Jones, Reginld E 576
Jones, Richard S 791

Page

Jones, Ronald 697
Jones, Roxie Jamison 704
Jones, Ruby Chason 634
Jones, Samuel 705
Jones, Sara Fox 393
Jones, Skip 707
Jones, Stephanie 465
Jones, Susan 642
Jones, Sylvester E 677
Jones, Terri E 85
Jones, Terry 625
Jones, Ticora 211
Jones, Tom 464
Jones, Toni 806
Jones, Trena 613
Jones, Vanessa 357
Jones, Vivian E 186
Jones, Walter 608
Jones, Walter B 196, 307, 329, 402, 403, 404, 414, 415, 483
Jones, Wanda 729
Jones,, Clinton Columbus, III 416
Jordan, Darrell 4
Jordan, Jim 207, 307, 333, 425, 426, 431, 432, 483
Jordan, Joe 827
Jordan, Jon A 796
Jordan, Kent A 849
Jordan, Mary Lu 793
Jorns, Byron G 636
Joseph, Arthur 839
Joseph, Gloria J 809
Joseph, Ken 826
Joseph, Leonard 767
Joseph, Meg 270
Joseph, Ray 684
Josephs, Laura 823
Josephson, Martha 146
Josey-Herring, Anita 895
Jossis, Kacee 508
Jost, Steven 705
Joy, Roy M 911
Joyce, Kathleen 461
Joyce, Madi 463
Joyce, Sean 667
Joyner, Chris 195
Joyner, Miekl 461
Juarez, Maria Elena 185
Judge, Kit 457
Judson, Allie 135
Juhnke, Shannon 146
Jukes, James J 590
Julian, James "Jim" 830
Juliana, Robin 344
Juliano, Robin 369
Jung, Stephen 822
Jungman, Elizabeth 369
Juola, Paul 401
Juris, Krysta 387
Jurkowsky, Tom 613
Jurrens, Kevin K 714
Jusino, Bill 184
Juzenas, Eric 779

K

Kade, Daryl W 734, 735
Kadelis, Lek 782
Kadunc, Edward L 921
Kaelin, Jim 461
Kagan, Elena 847
Kaguyutan, Janice 420
Kahl, Daniel 822
Kahn, Alan 373
Kahn, Tom 405
Kaigle, Aaron 375
Kaiser, Debra L 714
Kaiser, Janette 690
Kaiser, Michael M 798
Kalayil, Ann P 797
Kalbaugh, Greg 365
Kaldahl, Ryan 372
Kaldany, Rashad 935
Kalder, Frank M 655
Kaldes, Peter 707
Kale, Katy A 592
Kalin, Walter 932
Kalinga, Tatyana 24
Kalkut, Craig 375

	Page
Kalla, Patricia A	767
Kalyalya, Denny H	934
Kalyanam, Aruna	449
Kamerman, Janet	667
Kamin, Steven B	776
Kamins, Sheldon B	798
Kanakkanatt, Anne Marie	798
Kane, Allen	828
Kane, Angela	925
Kane, Betty Ann	901
Kane, Daniel	731
Kane, John D.H	842
Kane, Michael	751
Kane, Peggy	128
Kane, Robert F	808
Kane, Thomas R	669
Kane, William	763
Kang, Eliott	597
Kanne, Michael S	849
Kannenberg, Loren	292
Kanninen, Dan	781
Kanovsky, Helen R	739
Kanter, Martha J	755
Kanter, William	651
Kaplan, Ann F	774
Kaplan, Elaine	816
Kaplan, Marvin	407
Kaplan, Michael	608
Kaplan, Rick	787
Kaplan, Robert	823
Kaplan, Robert N	798
Kaplan, Samuel Louis	602
Kaplowitz, Lisa	728
Kappeler, Evelyn	729
Kappelhoff, Mark	652
Kappos, David J	711
Kaptur, Kristy	610
Kaptur, Marcy	210, 307, 327, 398, 399, 400, 405, 483, 502
Karafotas, Peter	136
Karakitsos, Dimitri	362
Karam, Lisa R	714
Karanjia, Peter	786
Karczewski, Stan	720
Kardian, F. Gary	792
Karellas, Andy	439
Karesh, Lewis	591
Karimjee, Anhar	588
Karli, Steven A. "Ames"	701
Karlin, Marni	376
Karlinchak, Karen	712
Karol, Donald	811
Karol, Susan V	733
Karoutsos, Demetrios	233
Karpati, Bruce	826
Karpel, Ian S	825
Karr, Barrett	407
Karr, Thomas	822
Karran, Bayney R	918
Karsting, Phil	290
Karvelas, Dave	64
Kasarabada, Anu	352
Kasdan, Matthew	588
Kaselonis, Raymond	460
Kaslow, Amy	836
Kaslow, Lewis	16
Kasmer, Janet	624
Kasold, Bruce E	889
Kasper, Joe	44
Kassiday, Joel D	31
Kasson, James	656
Kastens, Royal	367
Kasunic, Robert J	582
Katich, Steve	210
Katilius, Lizzette	821
Katims, Casey	282
Kato, Gordon J	817
Kato, Kathy	212
Kato, Ken	459
Katsaros, Andrew	704
Katyal, Neal Kumar	650
Katz, Allan J	602
Katz, Brad	191
Katz, Dan	168
Katz, David	372
Katz, Ezra	836
Katz, Judith I	809
Katz, Ruth	412
Katz, Stanley N	803
Katz, Stephen I	734
Katz, Zachary	785
Katzman, Julie T	906
Katzmann, Robert A	849
Kaufer, Kate	344
Kauffman, Caryn	824
Kauffman, Rick	391
Kaufman, David J	768
Kaufman, Gail	767
Kaufman, Robert J	670
Kaufmann, James T	583
Kaufmann, Marlene	496
Kaumo, Chris	12
Kausner, Greg	367
Kavaleri, Teddy	900
Kavanaugh, Brett M	853
Kaveney, Brian	21
Kavlick, Shelly	633
Kawabata, Kei	906
Kawamura, Jessica	364
Kay, Alan	866
Kayad, Mohamed Sikieh	934
Kayser, Richard	713
Kazan, Matt	364
Kazan, Rachel	786
Kazmeraski, Ashleigh	233
Kazon, Leslie	826
Keable, Ed	684
Keach, Chris	372
Kealey, Paul	812
Kearney, Barry J	809
Kearney, Ryan	407
Kearns, Jason	449
Kearns, Michael	676
Kearns, Thomas	663
Kearns, W. Paul, III	764
Kearny, Mark	420
Kearse, Amalya L	849
Keary, Ann O'Regan	895
Keating, Michael	930
Keating, Pete	643
Keating, Ryan	214
Keating, William R	132, 305, 336, 418, 419, 421, 422, 438, 483
Keaton, Molly	436
Kebet-Koulibaly, Saran G	935
Keckler, Charles N.W	799
Kee, Randy	922
Keech, Emily	456
Keech, Rosemary E	417
Keefe, Maura	166
Keegan, Michael	831
Keegan, Patricia	188
Keele, Liz	97
Keeler, Kenneth R	580
Keeler, Margo	64
Keeley, Joe	437
Keen, Kristen	200
Keen, Ruth	797
Keen, Steve	378
Keenan, Alex	345
Keenan, Barbara Milano	849
Keenan, Catrina Pavlik	770
Keenan, S. Joseph	391
Keene, Ken	770
Keener, Donald E	651
Keeney, Robert C	699
Keeter, Lisa	687
Keffer, Jim	621
Kehoe, Wayne	505
Keifhaber, Peter	344
Keil, Todd	767
Keiran, Alan N	390
Keiser, Andy	137
Keisler, William	718
Keita, Kamilah	457
Keith, Damon J	849
Keith, Frank	612
Keith, Gregory A	738
Keith, Kenneth	924
Keith, Robert	728
Keivel, Meghan	214
Kelaher, Marjorie "Gigi"	458
Kelapile, Collen	926
Kellaher, Donald T	461
Kellar, Robert	282
Kelleher, Kevin	385

Page

Keller, Andrew 367
Keller, Charlie 70
Keller, Debbee 412
Keller, Karen 828
Keller, Keenan 427
Keller, Steve 761
Kelley, Alexia 731
Kelley, Ali 589
Kelley, Chris 267
Kelley, Corenthis B 813
Kelley, Gwen Jones 831
Kelley, Kevin 119
Kelley, Lizanne Dinoto 582
Kelley, Michael 714
Kelley, Timothy J 832
Kelly, Amanda 360
Kelly, Blake 384
Kelly, Cathleen 588
Kelly, David 698
Kelly, Dennis 829
Kelly, Franklin 808
Kelly, Gail 119
Kelly, Henry 751
Kelly, Ian C 603
Kelly, James Michael 688
Kelly, Jennifer C 611
Kelly, Kathleen 710
Kelly, Keith 201, 617
Kelly, Kevin F 637
Kelly, Latonya 625
Kelly, Mark 106
Kelly, Mavis 821
Kelly, Melissa 262
Kelly, Mike 225, 308, 336, 406, 407, 418, 419, 431, 432, 483
Kelly, Pamela 705
Kelly, Patricia 819
Kelly, Paul 497
Kelly, Paul J., Jr 850
Kelly, Rebecca 376
Kelly, Robert 168
Kelly, Robert T., Jr 779
Kelly, Robin 690
Kelly, Ryan 424, 496
Kelly, Shawn 229
Kelly, Stephen 667
Kelsey, Howard 727
Kemens, Victor 744
Kemp, Charles 818
Kemp, Colleen 228
Kempf, Bart 340
Kempf, Purvee 412
Kempf, Stephen 796
Kendall, Bruce 828
Kendall, Donald 701
Kendall, Frank 616
Kendall, James 682
Kendall, Mary 684
Kendig, Newton 669
Kendrick, Alexandra 73
Kendrick, Kasey 99
Kendrick, Kathleen 730
Kendrick, Shannon 276
Kenna, Jim 681
Kennard, William E 603
Kennedy, Anthony M 845
Kennedy, Arthur W 70
Kennedy, Brian 720
Kennedy, Cornelius G 849
Kennedy, David 709
Kennedy, Ed 507
Kennedy, Henry H., Jr 861
Kennedy, John 104
Kennedy, Joseph S 817
Kennedy, Kermit 821
Kennedy, Kerry 837
Kennedy, Kevin 930
Kennedy, Michael 269, 793
Kennedy, Patrick F 598
Kennedy, Sean 373
Kennedy, Theresa 193
Kennedy, Thomas 232
Kennedy, Victoria Reggie 798
Kennelly, Barbara B 501
Kenney, Fred 771
Kenney, Justin 709
Kenney, Kathleen M 669
Kenney, Kristie Anne 603

Page

Kenney, Matt 388
Kennickell, Arthur 776
Kennon, Donald R 502
Kent, Don, Jr 290
Kent, Drew 228
Kent, Jeff 391
Kent, Trish 377
Kenyon, Geoff 718
Keplinger, Casey 575
Kerachsky, Stuart 758
Kerkes, Shawn 686
Kerlikowske, R. Gil 590
Kermick, Vanessa 82
Kern, John W., III 895
Kern-Scheerer, Stacy E 393
Kerner, Henry 433
Kerr, James T 732
Kerr, Mary 362
Kerr, T. Michael 717
Kerrigan, Mike 212
Kerry, Cameron F 703
Kerry, John F 127, 305, 322, 324, 356, 357, 363, 364, 366, 378, 384, 466, 471, 501
Kersey, Allison 169
Kershaw, Jessica 236
Kershbaum, Sharon 610
Kersten, Maria C 798
Kerstetter, Charles J 825
Kerwin, Mary D 800
Kesslar, Thomas 723
Kessler, Charlotte 806
Kessler, Gladys 865, 898
Kessler, Richard J 420
Kesteloot, James M 779
Ketchel, Micah 446
Ketels, Marianne 666
Kethledge, Raymond M 849
Ketterer, Jeremy 157
Kever, Jerome F 841
Key, Kendra 6
Keyak, Aaron 173
Keyes, James W 774
Keyes, Robert 826
Keyes-Fleming, Gwendolyn 783
Keyfauver, Terry 818
Keys, Mirta-Marie M 713
Keysor, Greg 626
Khabbaz, Rima 731
Khaing, Myat 285
Khairi, Saadia 935
Khalaf, Rima 926
Khalili, Deborah W 461
Khan, Ikram U 837
Khan, Maryam 358
Khan, Sadaf 40
Khan, Sanaa 367
Khanna, Ayesha 364
Khanna, Romit 707
Khawar, Ali 721
Khim, Christine 373
Khosla, Jay 269
Khouri, Michael A 791
Khuzami, Robert 823
Ki-moon, Ban 924
Kiang, Agnes 888
Kibben, M.G 648
Kibbey, Philip 382
Kibble, Kumar 769
Kibria, Behnaz 449
Kichak, Nancy H 816
Kicza, Mary E 710
Kidd, Richard 636
Kidde, John 797
Kidder, Rolland 773
Kieffer, Charles 344
Kiekens, Willy 914
Kielsmeier, Lauren 770
Kielty, Peter 411
Kienitz, Roy 741
Kieserman, Brad 767
Kiko, Philip 424
Kilbane, Grace 722
Kilber, Kenyon 789
Kilbourne, James C 660
Kilbride, Laura 372
Kilby, Michael H 792
Kildee, Dale E 136, 305, 327, 406, 407, 428, 429, 483
Kilduff, Daniel 588

Page

Kile, Joseph ... 575
Kiley, Bradley J ... 592
Kiley, Michael T ... 776
Kilgore, Tom ... 834
Kilkenny, Joseph ... 646
Killeen, Tim ... 811
Killian, Suzanne G ... 776
Killion, Ruth Ann ... 705
Kilmer, Roger D ... 714
Kilpatrick, Kimberly ... 375
Kilvington, John ... 373
Kim, Colin ... 606
Kim, Elizabeth ... 717
Kim, Gene ... 35
Kim, Grace ... 831
Kim, Justin ... 433
Kim, Sery ... 433
Kim, Thomas ... 822
Kimball, Kevin ... 713
Kimball, Suzette M ... 683
Kimberling, Linda ... 607
Kimble, Tina Pototo ... 871
Kimpel, Scott ... 820
Kimsey, James V ... 798
Kincaid, G. Russell ... 913
Kincaid, Paul ... 433
Kincaid, Trevor ... 152
Kind, Bonnie ... 831
Kind, Ron ... 291, 310, 330, 447, 448, 483
King, Betty E ... 603
King, Carolyn Dineen ... 849
King, Chris ... 437
King, Crystal ... 383
King, Edgar, Jr ... 698
King, Elizabeth ... 617
King, Elizabeth Aldridge ... 393
King, Ellen ... 699
King, Garrett ... 217
King, Heidi ... 411
King, Jackie ... 296
King, Julia A ... 773
King, June D.W ... 810
King, Keidra ... 111
King, Lonnie ... 731
King, Loretta ... 652
King, Michael D ... 825
King, Michelle ... 831
King, Paula B ... 837, 838
King, Peter J ... 792
King, Peter T ... 180, 306, 329, 414, 415, 416, 421, 451, 483
King, Robert B ... 849
King, Roger L ... 617
King, Rufus G., III ... 896
King, Steve ... 104, 304, 332, 395, 396, 397, 425, 426, 438, 439, 483
King, Thomas D ... 650
King, Warren R ... 895
King, William J ... 830
Kingsbury, Nancy ... 575
Kingston, Jack ... 73, 303, 329, 398, 399, 400, 484
Kingston, Jessica L ... 347
Kington, Raynard S ... 733, 734
Kinirons, Kerry ... 422
Kinley, Kelli ... 630
Kinne, Megan ... 632
Kinney, Angela ... 581
Kinney, Mary K ... 738
Kinsinger, Anne ... 683
Kinsley, Sara ... 721
Kinzel, Will ... 455
Kinzinger, Adam ... 89, 303, 336, 409, 410, 484
Kirby, Carolyn ... 508, 575
Kirby, Michael D ... 598
Kirby, Neal ... 430
Kirchner, Joan ... 72
Kiriakos, Kinsey ... 285
Kirilenko, Andrei ... 779
Kirk, Andrew ... 797
Kirk, Mark ... 84, 303, 323, 325, 341, 342, 343, 351, 352, 368, 382, 471, 494
Kirk, Ronald ... 585, 590
Kirk, Russell ... 630
Kirk, Thomas N ... 825
Kirkham, Gilbert ... 802
Kirkland, Diane ... 446
Kirkland, Steve ... 375
Kirksey, Daphne ... 246
Kirkwood, Charles W ... 781
Kirlin, Emily ... 386
Kirsanow, Peter N ... 835
Kirschner, Bruce ... 913
Kirwan, Pat ... 707
Kiser, Elizabeth K ... 776
Kish, Sarah ... 426
Kisiah, Jennifer ... 401
Kisliuk, Bruce ... 711
Kissal, Carol D ... 842
Kissell, Larry ... 199, 307, 334, 395, 396, 397, 402, 403, 404, 484
Kissko, James A ... 832
Kistler, Larry ... 922
Kisto, Kurt Mukesh Anthony ... 907
Kitchens, Pam H ... 713
Kitts, Tina ... 641
Kladney, David ... 835
Klajn, Tamara ... 367
Klappa, Mary ... 61
Klass, Richard ... 773
Klausing, Thomas P ... 713
Klawans, Steven L ... 825
Kleager, James ... 508
Kleeschulte, Chuck ... 360
Klein, Aaron ... 609
Klein, Allen ... 682
Klein, Alzbeta ... 935
Klein, John ... 827
Klein, Julie ... 384
Klein, Kenneth ... 628
Klein, Kevin ... 452
Klein, Michael ... 608
Klein, Richard ... 667
Klein, Sarit ... 823
Kleinfeld, Andrew J ... 850
Kleinman, Joan ... 126
Kleinman, Samuel ... 616
Klejst, Stephen ... 811
Klimavicz, Joseph ... 709
Klindt, Jason ... 155
Kline, David J ... 651
Kline, John ... 143, 305, 332, 402, 406, 407, 484, 494
Kline, Mary Ellen ... 663
Klingler, Hans ... 65
Klink, Jason ... 443
Klobuchar, Amy ... 142, 305, 321, 325, 339, 340, 356, 357, 374, 383, 463, 471, 494
Klosterman, Margo ... 16
Klotz, Mark ... 781
Klouda, Tom ... 364
Klugman, Shari ... 926
Klumb, Jason O ... 797
Klumpp, Lee ... 497
Klurfeld, Jeffrey ... 794
Klurfeld, Roger J ... 689
Klusaritz, Sally ... 692
Klutts, Mary ... 580
Kmiec, Douglas W ... 602
Knapp, Hubbell ... 420
Knapp, Julius P ... 786
Knapp, Rosalind A ... 742
Knauer, Chris ... 433
Kneedler, Edwin S ... 650
Knese, Christy ... 157
Knigge, Mary ... 397
Knight, Bernard J., Jr ... 713
Knight, James ... 600
Knight, Paul ... 821
Knight, Sandra ... 768
Knightly, Maureen ... 743
Knipe, Michael J ... 688
Knipling, Edward B ... 698
Knoll, Selene T ... 579
Knott, Lyle ... 912
Knouse, Ruth ... 225
Knowles, Camila ... 72
Knowles, Jennifer R ... 347, 348
Knowles, Jessica ... 463
Knowles, Kimberly ... 896
Knowles, Lucas ... 699
Knox, Jason ... 355
Knox, Wendy ... 439
Knudsen, Pat ... 405
Knudson, Kate ... 457
Knutson, Karen Y ... 7
Ko, Denny ... 663
Ko, Linda ... 124

Page

Kobayashi, Izumi 935
Kobelt, Kelsey 375
Kobler, Martin 930
Koblinsky, Chester 711
Koch, Alec 823
Koch, Edward I 836
Koch, Louisa 709
Koch, Mark 624
Koch, Steve 710
Kodani, Susan 81
Kodlick, Les 633
Koeberlein, Teresa 247
Koed, Betty K 389
Koehle, Chris 618
Koehn, Mark 710
Koella, Will 452
Koenders, Albert Gerard 929
Koenig, Andy 452
Koenigsberg, Melissa 680
Koepke, Priscilla 420
Koestler, Robert 829
Koffsky, Daniel 673
Kofinis, Chris 287
Kogod, Robert 828
Koh, Harold Hongju 596
Koh, Howard K 729
Koh, Jay L 839
Kohl, Herb 290, 310, 321, 324, 341, 342, 343, 351, 352, 374, 382, 384, 471
Kohl, Jennifer 126
Kohlenberger, Jim 590
Kohler, Herbert V., Jr 798
Kohn, J. Christopher 651
Kohn, Mara 675
Kojaian, C. Michael 798
Kojm, Rebecca 358
Kolaja, Andrej 818
Kolb, Ingrid 751
Kolb, Jim 444
Kolbe, Jim 501
Kolego, Trevor 455
Kolesnik, Kris 684
Kolker, David 789
Kolko, Linda 798
Kollar-Kotelly, Colleen 860
Kollmer-Dorsey, Paul 778
Kolly, Joseph 811
Koloditch, James 707
Kolodjeski, Erin 401
Kolpien, Tim 194
Kominsky, Mitchell 433
Konar, Howard 836
Kondor, Rachel 30
Konkus, John 60
Konove, Elissa K 745
Konwinski, Lisa M 592
Konya, John 397
Koo, Soohyun "Julie" 899
Koonin, Steven 751
Koontz, Thomas 711
Kooperstein, Donna 650
Koopman, Robert B 838
Kopec, John 607
Kopech, Robert 933
Kopocis, Ken 444
Kopp, Robert E 651
Koppel, Rosa 790
Kopshever, Kristin 436
Korch, Shelley S 809
Korman, Rebecca 32
Korn, Douglas R 836
Korn, Steven W 778
Kornbluh, Karen 603
Koroma, Abdul G 924
Koromilas, Alec J 722
Korotash, Stephen 825
Korrell, Harry 799
Kort, John 699
Kortan, Michael 667
Kosciow, Walter 784
Koshalek, Richard 828
Kosiak, Steve 590
Koski, Ian 55
Koski, James 221
Koski, Philip 825
Koskinen, Larry 612
Koskinen, Mary 691
Kostelnik, Michael C 769

Page

Koster, Julia A 805
Kosterlitz, Mary 822
Kostka, Gregory M 461
Kotapish, William J 822
Kotschwar, Nichole 106
Kotz, David 824
Koumans, Mark 767
Kounalakis, Eleni Tsakopoulos 601
Kouters, Angela 212
Kovachich, Jennifer 809
Kovacic, William E 793
Kovar, Peter 737
Kovis, Tim 429
Kowalczyk, Daniel 626
Kowalski, Dan 354
Kozeny, Jill 101
Kozinski, Alex 850
Kozubski, Susan 460
Krabbe, Carla 831
Kraden, Jonathan 372
Kraemer, Joseph 816
Kraemer, Michael J 775
Kraft, Barbara 791
Kraft, Christopher 663
Kraft, Seamus 433
Krafts, Andrew 808
Krajeski, Thomas C 621
Krajewski, Jennifer 588
Krakora, Joseph J 808
Kramer, Anthony 691
Kramer, Barnett S 733
Kramer, George 821
Kramer, Martin 733
Kramer-LeBlanc, Carol 687
Kramp, Kevin 397
Krancer, Michael L 781, 834
Kraninger, Kathy 401
Krasner, Stephen D 837
Krass, Caroline D 673
Kratovil, Lindley 97
Kratz, Jeff 344
Kraus, Bruce 821
Kravitch, Phyllis A 850
Kravitz, Neal E 895
Krebs, Thomas L 416
Kreisman, Barbara A 787
Kreple, Kristen 376
Krepp, Dennis 706
Krepp, Kathryn Denise Rucker 747
Kress, Carl B 842
Kresse, Carol 28
Kressman, Eric P 831
Krieger, Mark 712
Krieger, Michael 638
Krieger, Mick 209
Krimm, Jennifer 112
Kris, David S 674
Krishnamoorthy, Jenelle 369
Krislov, Marvin 807
Kristjansson, Brian 281
Kritzer, Bernard 706
Krizay, Glenn 706
Kroeker, James 821
Krohmer, John 769
Krol, Joseph 752
Kroll, Juliet 48
Krolman, Walter 508
Kroloff, Noah 765
Krone, David 163, 387
Kronenberg, Angela 785
Kronforst, Mark 822
Krongold, M. Ronald 836
Kronheim, Jonathan M 724
Kronick, Richard 728
Kronopolus, Cathleen 805
Kronopolus, Cathy 796
Kross, Jacques R.C 918
Kroupa, Diane L 880
Kruger, Leondra R 650
Kruger, Mary 768
Kruglik, Harry J 815
Krulic, Alexander 605
Krupinski, Michal 934
Krupnick, Daniel 192
Kruse, John 762
Kruse, Kathy 798
Kryger, Rick 720
Kryglik, Paul 831

Page

Krysa, Thomas J 825
Kubicek, Dave 842
Kubis, Jan 926
Kuchno, Kenneth 694
Kucinich, Dennis J 210, 307, 330, 406, 407, 431, 432, 484
Kudrewicz, Katherine 712
Kudwa, Amy 766
Kueckelhan, Deanya T 794
Kuehl, Sarah 354
Kuehnast, Kathleen R 838
Kuester, Michele 784
Kueter, Dean 653
Kugajevsky, Alex 404
Kuhn, Walt 376
Kuiken, Michael J 347, 348, 349
Kulczewski, Rich 723
Kulenkampff, Kathleen A 347, 348
Kulik, Lauren 205
Kulik, Michael 783
Kulikowski, Jim 400
Kullberg, H. Chuck 796
Kulnis, Dan 389
Kumar, Rohit 388
Kumar, Rosalyn 47, 434
Kumar, Shashi N 748
Kumar, Suresh 707
Kundanis, George 453, 457
Kundu, Goutam 613
Kunesh, Patrice 684
Kung, Felicia 822
Kunse, Suzanne 222
Kunsman, Dan 295
Kunze, P 643
Kupasrimonkol, Sakdiyiam 935
Kupersmith, Joel 764
Kurek, Missy 453
Kurin, Richard 828
Kurland, Kevin 706
Kurland, Susan 741
Kurth, Christine 785
Kurz, Zachary 436
Kusano, John 690
Kushner, Peter 505
Kussin-Shoptaw, Sam 379
Kusumoto, Sandra L 792
Kutz, Catherine 10
Kutz, Gregory D 575
Kutz, Randy 10
Kuwabara, Gary 618
Kuykendall, Kate 819
Kvaal, James 755
Kwak, Sally 465
Kwoh, Chung-Hai 910
Kwon, Hyun Wook 909
Kyl, Jon 9, 301, 321, 324, 363, 364, 374, 388, 466, 471, 501
Kyle, Mary J 347
Kyte, Rachel 935

L

L'Etoile, Marie C 817
La Via, Vincenzo 932
Laackman, Allyson 589
LaBarre, Andy 141
LaBelle, Bob 682
Laborde, Kate 375
Labrador, Raul R 83, 303, 336, 428, 429, 431, 432, 484
LaCanfora, Marianna 832
Lacey, Daniel J 719
LaChance, Susan M 840
LaChapelle, Dorothy B 776
Lachmann, David 427
Lackey, Holt 427
Lackey, Jennifer 426
Lackey, Miles 434
LaCounte, Darryl 681
LaCroix, D 643
Ladd, John 722
Ladden-Stirling, Amanda 16
LaDieu, Melissa 580
Lafargue, Sophia 182
Lafferty, Annette 836
LaFleur, Cheryl A 752
Lagarde, Christine 913, 928
Lager, James 575
Lago, Marisa 608
Lagomarcino, Leslie 688
Lagos, Hugo Alsina 909
Lahasky, Rosemary 407
LaHood, Ray 585, 741, 773, 807
Lahr, Megan 142
Lai, Gena 820
Laird, Carolyn 385
Laird, Kathleen 369
Laird, Melvin R 799
Laird, Paul 669, 779
Laisch, Mark 344
Laitin, Anna 358
Laitta, Michael 912
Lake, Anthony 927
Lake, Chip 74
Lake, Karen 737
Lake, Williams 787
Lalumiere, Frank 827
Lam, Kristine 372
Lam, Livia Y 408, 741
Lamas, Enrique 706
Lamb, Charlene R 599
Lamb, Jennifer 53
Lamb, Michael 756
Lamb, Tom 73
Lamb-Hale, Nicole Y 708
Lambert, Brett 616
Lambert, Karen Grosso 617
Lambert, Mark W 817
Lambert, Michael J 776
Lambert, Michele 686
Lambert, Terry 895
Lamberth, Royce C 860
Lambie, Martha 833
Lamborn, Doug 48, 302, 333, 402, 403, 404, 428, 429, 445, 484, 493
Lamborn, Jeanie 498
Lambrew, Jeanne 592
Lamont, Douglas 636
Lamont, Thomas R 636
Lamoureux, Randall 645
Lampert, James 747
Lampert, Justin 455
Lamy, Philippe 920
Lancaster, John A 837
Lance, Alan G., Sr 890
Lance, Leonard 171, 306, 334, 409, 411, 484
Lance, Linda 360
Lancefield, Sharman 740
Land, Guy 775
Landa, Michael 732
Landay, William E., III 620
Landefeld, J. Steven 704
Landeros, Clarinda 185
Landers, Nathan 38
Landesman, Rocco 499, 806, 807
Landgren, Karin 929, 930
Landis, Dean S 830
Landis, Story C 734
Landman, Cheryl 705
Landrieu, Mary L 114, 304, 322, 324, 341, 342, 343, 359, 371, 378, 383, 471, 493
Landrum, Timothy J 657
Landry, Frank 630
Landry, Jeffrey M 115, 304, 336, 428, 429, 438, 439, 440, 441, 442, 443, 484
Landy, Kevin 769
Lane, Alan 830
Lane, Charlotte R 838
Lane, Jeffrey 751
Lane, Katherine L 460
Lane, Kenneth "Ken" 679
Laney, Karen 838
Lang, Catherine 744
Lang, Christine G 347
Lange, William 690
Langenwalter, Corey 642
Langer, Mark J 854
Langevin, James R 236, 308, 331, 402, 403, 451, 484
Langill, Scott 372
Langley, Nanci 820
Langton, Doug 905
Lanier, Cathy L 899
Lanier, Jerry P 603
Lankford, James 217, 307, 336, 405, 431, 432, 440, 441, 443, 484
Lanning, Jeffrey W 630
Lanphear, Thomas J 839

Page
Lansing, Garret 87
Lansing, Gerrit 405
Lanum, Scott 770
Lanza, Steve 640
Lanza, Valerie 907
Lanzerotti, Louis J 811
Lapiana, John K 828
Lapointe, Carman Louise 925
Lapointe, Sylvie 908
Laporte, Gerald 822
Lappin, Harley G 669
Laquerre, Patrice 908
Lara, Ashley 283
Lara, Juan 446
Larew, Rob 397
Large, Alex 245
Largen, Lori 507
Larkin, Barbara 835
Larkin, Ed 508
Larkin, Kellie 417
Larkin, Pete 278
Laro, David 883
Larrabee, Jason 28
Larrazabal, Luis Hernando 907
Larrimore, Jeff 465
Larsen, Christopher J 834
Larsen, Craig 610
Larsen, Leif 645
Larsen, Lewis F 798
Larsen, Matthew 683
Larsen, Rick 282, 309, 331, 402, 403, 440, 441, 442, 484, 494
Larsen, Steve 731
Larson, Dave 618
Larson, Don 203
Larson, John B 51, 302, 330, 447, 448, 454, 484
Larson, Richard L 345
Larson-Jackson, Laurie 684
LaRue, Pamela 612
Lashbrook, Emily 200, 256
Lasher, Jonathan L 832
Lasky, Allys 507
Lass, Conrad 497
Laster, Gail 417
Lastowka, Thomas 763
Lasure, Sara 14
Lataille, Joseph R 838
Latham, Dawn P 774
Latham, Lori 134
Latham, Tom 103, 304, 329, 398, 399, 400, 484
Lathbury, Donald 24
Lathram, Layne 722
LaTourette, Steven C 212, 307, 329, 398, 399, 400, 484, 828
Latta, Robert E 207, 307, 333, 409, 410, 411, 484, 495
Lattimore, Phillip A 900
Lattin, Grant 644
Latu, Kosi 923
Lau, Norman K 670
Laub, John 672
Lauer, Ethan B 461
Laufer, John 299
Laug, Connie 205
Laughlin, Alexander M 808
Laughlin, Alfredo Mac 914
Laukitis, R.J 137
Laukkanen, Ritva 935
Laur, Michele 691
Laurent, Janet St 575
Laurent-Monpetit, Christiane 909
Laurente, Janice 818
Lauri, Giovanni 910
Lauria-Sullens, Jolene 671
Laurita, Albert 657
Lausten, Eric 86
Lautenberg, Frank R 168, 306, 322, 324, 341, 342, 343, 356, 357, 361, 362, 383, 471, 501, 837
Lauwers, Bernard 935
Laux, Jessica 433
LaVelle, E. Terri 761
LaVelle, LaVenia 384
Lavender, Larry C 416
Laverdure, Del 681
Lavigne, Carrie Mann 750
Lavigne, Thomas A 750
Lavik, A. Roy 779
Lavoie, Matt 20
Lavy, Donald 738

Page
Law, Christopher 364
Law, Steve 686
Lawhead, Tom 632
Lawler, Tim 818
Lawless, Julia 365
Lawrence, Andrew 712
Lawrence, Daryl 628
Lawrence, Doug 691
Lawrence, John 453, 457
Lawrence, Matt 379
Lawrence, Patty 690
Lawrence, Robert B 499
Lawrence, Susan S 638
Lawrimore, Emily 295
Laws, Patty 635
Lawson, Charles A 912
Lawson, Mike 502
Lawson, Sandra 581
Lawson, Thomas 922
Layman, Rose 634
Layne, Michele Wein 825
Layng, John 719
Layson, Jeannie 836
Lazarus, Edward 785
Le, Kim 443
Le, Margaret 712
Le, Ricky 424
Lea, Robyn 457
Leach, Alicemary 697
Leach, Barbara 693
Leach, David J 780, 834
Leach, James 499, 843
Leach, James A 806, 807
Leach, Jim 803
Leach, Robert S 826
Leaf, Marc 820
Leahy, Michael 776
Leahy, Patrick J 272, 309, 323, 324, 339, 340, 341, 342, 343, 374, 377, 384, 464, 471, 494, 828
Leaman, Bruce M 917
Leaman, Welby 449
Leanes, Luis Fernando 921
Leary, Mary Lou 672
Lease, Donna G 815
Leatherman, Richard 632
Leavandosky, Stacey 27
Leavitt, Tristan 375
Leavy, Edward 850
LeBaron, Joseph Evan 602
Lebel, Federico 906
LeBlanc, Diane 804
LeBlanc, Stephen G 578
LeBouder, Stephane J 609
Lebow, David E 776
Lebowitz, Alan D 721
Lebryk, David A 607
Lecky, Jim 709
LeCompte, Jenni 610
Ledbetter, Stephen L 738
Leddy, Carolyn 501
Ledeen, Barbara 375
Lederer, Calvin 771
Lederman, Gordon 372
LeDuc, James 706
LeDuc, Mark 372
Ledvina, T 643
Lee, Amy 283
Lee, Andrea 149
Lee, Andrew 420
Lee, Anka 498
Lee, Barbara 23, 302, 330, 398, 399, 400, 471
Lee, Catie 340
Lee, Edward L., Jr 791
Lee, Esther 706
Lee, Jane 405
Lee, Jessica 80
Lee, Jinyoung 284
Lee, John J 831
Lee, Kathleen 362
Lee, Katie 367
Lee, Lani 653
Lee, Lee Mon 636
Lee, Mara 21
Lee, Mike 269, 309, 323, 325, 359, 360, 366, 367, 374, 463, 484
Lee, Milton C 895
Lee, Nancy 608, 711, 907
Lee, Olivia 427

	Page
Lee, Paula	701
Lee, Rene Rocque	766
Lee, Richard	146
Lee, Richard D	826
Lee, Rob	741
Lee, Selina	756
Lee, Victoria	379
Lee-Ashley, Matt	679
Leeds, Eric J	813
Leeds, Richard G., Jr	577
Leeds, Stephen R	794
Leef, Pierron	823
Leek, Maisha	224
Leeling, Gerald J	347, 348, 349
Leeman, Cheryl	119
Leete, Jennifer	823
Leffingwell, Matt	257
Leftwich, Joel	340
LeGeyt, Curtis	375
Legg, Christopher Y	915
Legg, Kenneth	752
Legge, David	610
Leggieri, Rebecca	401
LeGrand, Ron	427
LeGuyader, John	711
Lehman, Greta	638
Lehman, Rob	205
Lehman, Ted	375
Lehman, William J	893
Lehner, Richard	619
Lehnert, Andreas W	777
Lehnertz, Christine	681
Lehnhoff, Fred	713
Lehrer-Stein, Janice	805
Leibbrand, Lou	689
Leibowitz, Jonathan	793
Leibowitz, Lynn	895
Leibowitz, Shelley B	932
Leiby, Sarah Kiko	420
Leidich, John	706
Leieritz, Jeff	439
Leighton, Matt	90
Leiman-Carbia, Julius	821
Leiner, Frederick	675
Leininger, George W	816
Leininger, Lee	661
Leisinger, Klaus M	931
Leistikow, Dan	751
Leith, William	683
Leland, Arlean	688
Lemaitre, Rafael E	590
Leman, Rachael	434
Lemasters, Scott	372
Lemeunier, Jonathan	909
Lemke, Wilfried	932
Lemnios, Zachary	616
Lemoi, Wayne	749
Lemos, Jessica	236
Lemus, Gabriela	717
Lench, Kenneth	823
Lenert, Leslie	731
Leney, Tom	761
Leng, Rebecca	742
Lenhardt, Alfonso E	603
Lenicheck, Jon	131
Lenihan, Keagan	268, 434
Lenkart, Steve	838
Lenn, Mike	292
Lennie, Rachel G	808
Lennon, Jaime	123
Lennox, Robert P	640
Lent, Rebecca	709
Lenter, David L	465
Leon, Charles	906
Leon, Richard J	862
Leon, Wayne	747
Leonard, Christine M	590
Leonard, Fran L	792
Leonard, Jenelle	757
Leonard, Joe, Jr	686
Leonard, Judith	828
Leonard, Patricia A	644
Leonczyk, Kenneth G	416
Leong, Edward	461
Leonhart, Michele M	655
Leopold, Pat	106
Lepper, Steven J	632
Lepre, Janet L	812
Lerma, Eduardo	42
Lerman, Miles	837
Lerner, Allison C	811
Lerner, Daniel A	347, 348, 350
Lerner, Jay	670
Lerner, Norma	837
Lerner, Robin	367
Leroy, Anne-Marie	932
Lesesne, Audrey	199
Leshner, Alan I	811
Lesnick, Keith	747
Lesnick, Robert J	793
Lessen, Ramona	244
Lesser, Bethany	179
Lesser, William C	724
Lessley, Lucinda	126, 433
LesStrang, Dave	401
Lestenkof, Phillip	917
Lester, Elton	739
Lett, Gloria	458
Letteney, Robert	741, 742
Lettieri, D'Ann	345
Lettieri, Linda	826
Lettow, Charles F	874
Lettre, Marcel	617
Letzler, Robert	588
Leuck, Lauren	588
Leung, Agnes W	796
Leuschen, James	458
Lev, Sean	751
Leval, Gerard	837
Leval, Pierre N	849
Levcovitz, Eduardo	921
Levenshus, Jonathan	30
Lever, Sharon	674
Levering, Mary Berghaus	582
Levey, Stuart	608
Levi, John G	799
Levi, Michael	719
Levi, Richard	795
Levie, Richard A	896
Levin, Andrew T	776
Levin, Anna	119
Levin, Brian P	408
Levin, Carl	133, 305, 322, 324, 346, 371, 378, 382, 384, 471, 498, 501
Levin, Joseph	401
Levin, Nelson	809
Levin, Sander M	139, 305, 327, 447, 464, 484
Levin, Sarah	383
Levin, Victoria A	825
Levine, Amy	785
Levine, Beth	375
Levine, Martin	126
Levine, Molly Jennings	819
Levine, Peter K	347, 348, 349, 350
Levine, Richard	822
Levine, William S	837
Levins, Scott	804
Levinson, Daniel R	729
Levinson, Margy	154
Levison, Lara	679
Levonian, Mark	611
Levy, David W	805
Levy, Joshua	838
Levy, Matt	354
Levy, Rachel	465
Levy, Santiago	906
Lew, Allen Y	898
Lew, Jacob J	585, 589
Lewis, Aaron	649
Lewis, Alvin	4
Lewis, Andre	759
Lewis, Anne	778
Lewis, Ashley	427
Lewis, Brian	388
Lewis, Charles	184
Lewis, Christopher	786
Lewis, Courtenay	679
Lewis, Craig	821
Lewis, Debra	692
Lewis, Don	770
Lewis, Elliot P	722
Lewis, Harrison	60
Lewis, Jeff	358
Lewis, Jerry	39, 302, 327, 398, 399, 400, 484, 493
Lewis, Jim	433
Lewis, John	75, 158, 303, 328, 447, 448, 484

	Page
Lewis, Karen L	582
Lewis, Lorna	816
Lewis, Mark R	404
Lewis, Maureen	826
Lewis, Merle	920
Lewis, Muffy	43
Lewis, Paul	404
Lewis, Paula	744
Lewis, Richard	719
Lewis, Richard C	578
Lewis, Rick	893
Lewis, Robert N	744
Lewis, Teresa	610
Lewis, Warren A	671
Lewis, Wilma	681
Lewsey, Clement	709
Lewter, John	382
Ley, Jane S	814
Ley, John P	850
Leydon, James	128
Leza, Joaquin Molina	920
Li, Allen	437
Li, Zhao	720
Liang, J. Nellie	777
Liao, Charles T	825
Libin, Nancy C	649
Licastro, Francisco Julian	905
Lidinsky, Richard A	791
Lidstone, Margaret	596
Lidz, Ted	893
Lieber, Jon	388
Lieber, Margery E	809
Lieber, Sheila M	651
Lieberman, Ben	411
Lieberman, Evelyn	828
Lieberman, Hadassah F	837
Lieberman, Joseph I	51, 302, 321, 324, 346, 347, 371, 378, 383, 471, 501, 805
Lieberman, Shane	64
Lieberson, Jeff	190
Liebes, Cindy A	794
Liebman, Wilma B	808
Liebovitz, John	787
Lierman, Terry	125, 457
Lieu, Chan	748
Lieu, Stephanie	358
Lightfoot, Karen	412
Lightfoot, Robert	802
Lijewski, Robert	701
Likins, Rose	602
Liles, W. Walton	416
Lilley, Millicent A	197
Lilley, Stephen	376
Lillis, Joe	156
Lilly, Dorothy	686
Lilly, Greg R	347
Limage, Simon	598
Lin, Eric	714
Lin, Justin Yifu	932
Lin, Kakuti	461
Linda, Yorba	804
Lindberg, Donald A. B	734
Lindborg, Nancy	835
Linde, Jason	37
Linde-Feucht, Sarah	733
Lindell, Jay H	624
Linden, Ralph	688
Linder, James B	642
Linderman, Karl	641
Lindley, Jeffrey A	745
Lindner, Carl H., III	798
Lindo, Arthur W	775
Lindsay, Scott	433
Lindsey, Brian	460
Lindsey, Mark	746
Lindsley, Margaret A	841
Lindstrom, Frederick J	778
Lineberger, Joe G	628
Lineberger, Vance	626
Lineberry, Mark	823
Linell, Jerald D	389
Liner, Linda S	652
Linick, Steve	790
Link, Bernard	601
Link, Jed	159
Linn, Richard	857
Linn, Scott	656
Linnertz, Ann	747
Linnington, Michael S	642
Linscott, Mark	591
Linsky, Scott	510
Linton, Mark A	737
Lintz, Gilda	105
Lipez, Kermit V	849
Lipford, Vivian	199
Lipinski, Daniel	85, 303, 332, 435, 436, 440, 441, 442, 484
Lipka, Timothy L	501
Lipman, Jonathan	166
Lipnic, Victoria	783
Lippert, Mark	592
Lipps, Brandon	397
Lipschitz, Leslie	913
Lipscomb, Sara	827
Lipsey, Yolanda	140
Lipsich, Wendi	68
Lipsky, Andrew	588
Lipsky, John	913
Lipsky, Kim	379
Lipsmeyer, Donna	655
Lipson, Aaron	824
Lipstadt, Deborah E	837
LipsteinFristedt, Andi	369
Lira, Matt	456
Lis, John J	499
Liser, Florie	591
Lisi, Brenda	696
Lister, Katharine	281
Liszt, Michelle	376
LiTrenta, Simone	458
Litsey, Richard	364
Littell, Darren	165
Little, Amanda	245
Little, Bethany	369
Little, Cathy	401
Little, Kevin	711
Little, Kimani	424
Little, L. Dale	713
Little, Ryan	433
Little, Sarah	105, 340
Littlefield, Elizabeth L	839
Littlewood, Maggie	427
Littman, Drew	142
Litvack, Neal	774
Litwak, Robert	843
Liu, Lawrence	498
Liu, Libby	778
Liu, Thomas	588
Liu, Xiaobing	908
Livengood, Steve	502
Livingood, Wilson "Bill"	461, 510
Livingston, Debra A	849
Livingston, JoAnne	758
Livornese, John	821
Lizarraga, Jaime	457
Llewellyn, Stephen	784
Llewellyn-Butts, Kathleen	355
Llorens, Hugo	601
Lloyd, Brenda	770
Lloyd, David	340
Lloyd, Hannah I	347, 348
Lloyd, Karen	580
Lloyd, Mark	786
Lloyd, Matt	98
Loach, Eric	460
Loan, Peter	818
LoBiondo, Frank A	169, 306, 329, 402, 403, 404, 440, 441, 442, 451, 484
Lobo, Richard M	778
Locascio, Laurie E	714
Locatis, Michael	751
Locey, Kimberly A	723
Loch, Brittney	157
Lochridge, Kathleen	388
Lock, Judith H	669
Locke, Nancy	430
Locken, Carrie	286
Lockhart, Stephen	460
Lockman, Alee	204
Loden, Kathy	429
Loeb, Emily	652
Loeblein, James	644
Loeblein, Jim	508
Loebsack, David	102, 304, 333, 402, 403, 406, 407, 484
Loesche, Robert K	893
Loevinger, David	607

Page

Loewentritt, Lennard S 795
Lofgren, Mike 355
Lofgren, Zoe 27, 302, 329, 424, 425, 426, 435, 464, 484, 503
LoFranco, Justin 433
Lofthus, Lee J 671
Loftin, Melinda 684
Loftin, Robert 595
Logan, Andrew 354
Logan, Randle T 815
LoGrande, Michael 628, 632
Lohier, Raymond J 849
Lohoefener, Renne 680
Loizeaux, Joan 821
Loj, Ellen Margareth 930
Loken, James B 850
Lolich, Richard J 747
Lolli, Tim 455
Lombard, Charles 801
Lombardi, Bill 158
Lombardi, Joan 730
Lombardi, Kyle 30
Lombardi, Veronica Zavala 906
Lomellin, Carmen 603, 918
Lonardo, Sara 372
Long, Billy 156, 305, 336, 421, 422, 440, 441, 442, 484
Long, Brenda 758
Long, Cheryl M 895, 896
Long, Cindy 696
Long, Gregory T 793
Long, John 743
Long, Karyn 153
Long, Letitia A 620
Long, Linda 649
Long, Michael 457
Long, Mike 456
Long, Pamela 822
Long, Ryan 411
Long, Timothy W 611
Longley, Jim 502
Longo, Jena 357
Longo, Richard 642
Longus, Everette Dewaine 626
Look, Karin 598
Loomis, Madison 824
Looney, Jack 461
Looney, Rita S 628
Lopach, Tom 158
Loper, Brett 455
Lopes, Alexander 706
Lopes, Carlos 927
Lopez, Adelana 71
Lopez, Barbara 71
Lopez, Carlos Hurtado 906
Lopez, Jim 737
Lopez, Jose M 895
Lopez, Juan 29, 588
Lopez, Julio Cesar 906
Lopez, Kenneth 582
Lopez, Luis Miguel 299
Lopez, Luke 769
Lopez, Marco A 769
Lopez, Mark 96
Lopez, Miguel 505
Lopez, P. David 784
Lopez-Salido, J. David 776
LoPresti, Barbara M 706
Lora, Eduardo 906
Lord, Mark 110
Lord, Patricia 417
Lord, William T 628
Lorentzen, Ronald 707
Lorenzen, Barbara S 825
Lorge, Patrick J 647
Loria, Dennis V 788
Loschinskey, Jason 626
Losice, Abraham 821
Loskarn, Ryan 244, 386
Lothamer, Molly 461
Lott, Alfred 757
Lott, Bret 806
Loud, Marc D., Sr 902
Loughery, Lawrence 510
Loughney, Patrick 581
Loughran, Mike 630
Louis, Henry 611
Louis, Michael 918
Louizou, Thomas M 748

Page

Lourie, Alan D 856
Loustanau, Cherie 708
Love, Fred 103
Love, Iris C 807
Love, Juanita Howard 816
Love, Melinda 805
Love, Reginald 587
Lovelace, Gail 794
Lovell, James 624
Lovenheim, Sarah 385
Loving, Andrea 427
Lovinger, Dvora 124
Lowder, Michael 741
Lowe, Alan 804
Lowe, Chris 687
Lowe, Richard B 814, 817
Lowe, Roberta 618
Lowe, Travis 453
Lowell, Heather A 393
Lowell, John 709
Lowenberg, William J 837
Lowenstein, Frank 367
Lower, Marcus 693
Lowery, Leon 360
Lowery, Nancy 192
Lowery, Pat 656
Lowey, Nita M 187, 307, 328, 398, 399, 400, 485
Lowman, Christopher J 640
Lowman, Deven 624
Lowman, Helen 818
Lowney, Lisa 129
Lowney, Robert 893
Lowrey, John 40
Lowry, Ashley 452
Lowstutter, Leslee 699
Lozupone, Amy 455
Lu, Christopher 591
Lu, Natalie 830
Lubarski, Richard 818
Lubchenco, Jane 708
Lubing, Lael 695
Lucas, Carl 672
Lucas, Chris 375
Lucas, David 231
Lucas, Frank D 216, 307, 329, 395, 414, 415, 435, 436, 485
Lucas, Jonathan 927
Lucas, Rich 695
Luce, Mark E 714
Lucero, Amy 745
Lucero, Carlos F 850
Lucey, Craig 623
Lucier, Jennifer A 776
Lucius, Kristine 375
Luczak, Ronald 756
Luders, David 641
Ludwig, Stacy 675
Luebke, Thomas 778
Luecke, Matthew M 776
Lueders, Amy 682
Luensmann, Diane 289
Luetkemeyer, Blaine 157, 305, 414, 415, 485
Lugar, Richard G 95, 303, 321, 324, 339, 340, 366, 471, 501
Luginbill, Scott 91
Lugo, Ramon 801
Luigart, Craig B 764
Luisi, Shelly 821
Lujan, Ben Ray 177, 306, 334, 428, 429, 435, 436, 485
Lukeman, Kate 455
Lukens, Rob 505
Lumia, Jason 247
Lummis, Cynthia M 296, 310, 334, 398, 399, 400, 485
Lumpkin, Murray M 732
Lundberg, Angie 172
Lundberg, Eric 922
Lundberg, Ken 119
Lundsager, Meg 608, 914
Lungren, Daniel E 20, 301, 330, 421, 422, 424, 425, 426, 464, 485, 502, 503
Lungren, David 362
Lunsford, Carolyn 631
Luo, Yang 915
Lupovitz, Joni 793
Lurie, Adam S 654
Lurie, Mike 453
Lurie, Nicole 728
Lusby, Jane 508

Page

Luse, Keith 367
Lushin, Andrei 915
Lusk, Dean 391
Luskey, Charlene E 509, 815
Luster, Jeffrey 588
Lute, Jane Holl 765
Luth, Erika 209
Luther, Michael R 801
Luthi, Jeffery N 891
Lutz, Julie K 825
Lyden, Patrick 227
Lyder, Jane 680
Lyder, Jane M 837
Lydon, Kathy 90
Lyle, Ian 430
Lyles, David 133
Lyles, Latifa 726
Lyles, Sylvia 757
Lynch, Brian 893
Lynch, Caroline 426
Lynch, Chris 122
Lynch, Gerard E 849
Lynch, James 642
Lynch, James P 672
Lynch, Jamie R 404
Lynch, Kenneth P 834
Lynch, Liza 259
Lynch, Mary Ann 239
Lynch, Mike 179
Lynch, Rick 637
Lynch, Sandra L 849
Lynch, Stephen F 131, 305, 331, 414, 415, 416, 431, 432, 485
Lynch, Tim 502
Lynn, William J 615
Lynton, Michael 778
Lyons, Amy Jo 667
Lyons, Chris 439
Lyons, Holly E. Woodruff 443
Lyons, James 365, 788
Lyons, James M 838
Lyons, Lynn 497
Lyons, Peter 751
Lytton, Al 196
Lyzenga, Meggie 134

M

Maahs, Robert T 775
Maben, Meri 27
Mabus, Ray 643
MacAfee, Jeffrey D 577
MacAfee, Sandra K 578
Macaluso, Judith N 895
MacBride, Marsha 715
Macchiarola, Frank 369
Macchiaroli, Michael 823
MacDonald, Alexander 710
MacDonald, Beverly 80
MacDonald, Brian 220
MacDonald, Chris 372
MacDonald, Don 32, 420
MacDonald, Jamie 639
MacDonald, Laura 720
MacDonough, Elizabeth 389
Maceda, Nell 191
Macey, Scott 742
Macfarlane, Stephen 661
MacFarquhar, Rory 608
Macias, Art 768
Macias, Linda 40
Mack, Carolyn 362
Mack, Clarice 630
Mack, Connie 64, 303, 333, 418, 419, 431, 432, 485
Mack, Mary Bono 41, 302, 409, 410
Macke, Robert 693
MacKenzie, Thomas 404
Mackey, Vivian 815
Mackie, James 611
Mackin, Thomas J 825
Macklin, Jay 662
Macklin, Renee 707
MacLellan, Jennifer 166
Macmanus, Joseph E 595
MacNaughton, Phil 404
MacNeill, Barbara 710
Macomber, Marshall 4
Macrae, James 733

Page

MacSlarrow, Jasper 282
MacSpadden, Lisa N 805
Macy, Richard 819
Madan, Rafael A 673
Madden, Chris 644
Maddox, Clarence 849
Maddox, John 748
Maddox, Victor B 799
Maddux, Jim 723
Madigan, Thomas 511
Madison, George W 605
Madison, Jonathan E 417
Madriz, Carmen Maria 907
Madunic, Adrian 92
Mae-Lovell, Deborah 917
Magagna, Joan 652
Magary, Adam 92
Magdieli, Amit 726
Magee, Richard "Dick" 407
Magee, Richard E 405
Magers, Sean 191
Maginnis, Hugh 693
Magner, Tara 375
Magnotti, Louis 459
Magnuson, Patrick 84
Magnuson, Rachel 230
Magnusson, Paul C 500
Maguire, Daniel 721
Magwood, William D., IV 812
Mahaffey, Michael 65
Mahaffie, Lynn 759
Mahaffie, Robert 610
Mahaley, Hosanna 900
Mahan, Erin 803
Mahan, Rodger 455
Mahar-Piersma, Auke 221
Maher, Jessica 589
Maher, Mike 605
Maher, Shawn P 592
Mahiga, Augustine 930
Mahler, Samuel C 417
Mahon, James H 670
Mahoney, Cathleen 675
Mahoney, James 784
Mahoney, Kevin 827
Mahony, Robert 824
Mahr, Tom 203
Mahr, Wesley 510
Mahsetky, Michael 733
Maier, Elizabeth 9
Maierhofer, Justin 835
Main, Jennifer 607
Main, Joseph A 722
Maines, Dub 254
Mainor, Walt 644
Maizel, Donna C 651
Majauskas, Richard 390
Majett, Nicholas A 898
Majidi, Vahid 667
Major, Chris 734
Majoro, Moeketsi 914
Majors, Heather 362
Majumdar, Arun 751
Majure, W. Robert 650
Makin, Sarah 453
Makovsky, Alan 420
Malam, Pam 682
Malanum, Theresa 503
Malcomson, Dennis 733
Maldonado, Anna 12
Maldonado, Gerardo 669
Malebranche, Barbara 817
Malech, David 43
Malecki, Eva 505
Malecki, Mark K 725
Malek, John 509
Mali, Peter 682
Mallard, Kris 401
Mallette, Patricia 662
Mallon, Carmen L 669
Mallory, Brenda 782
Mallory, Lisa Maria 898
Malloy, Brian 389
Malloy, Daniel, Jr 510
Malone, Kelly J 393
Malone, Kevin 718
Maloney, Carolyn B 186, 307, 329, 414, 415, 431, 432, 463, 485

Page

Maloney, Patrick 605
Malory, Mamie 744
Maloy, Heather 612
Maloy, Katie 95
Malphrus, Stephen R 777
Maltz, Derek S 656, 658
Malvaney, Scot 150
Malvirlani, Dimitri 911
Mamaux, Lale 70, 434
Manao, Hekinus 934
Manatt, Claire 177
Manatt, Nikole 345
Mancari, Jessica 277
Manchin, Joe, III 287, 321, 325, 310, 346, 347, 359, 360, 382, 472
Mancini, Nadine N 814
Mancini, Rob 899
Manclark, John 634
Mande, Jerold 696
Mandel, Arthur 172
Mandel, Matt 60
Mandel, Ruth B 837
Mandel, Steven J 724
Mandelker, Lauren 605
Mandt, Gregory A 710
Maness, Ted 209
Maney, Jo 434
Mangold, Rob 690
Manies, Frank 774
Manino, Yvonne 766
Manion, Daniel A 849
Manjarrez, A. Carlos 807
Manker, Jamie 763
Mann, Beth 628
Mann, Carlton I 766
Mann, Cindy 731
Mann, J. Robert 578
Mann, Richard 922
Mann, Sharon 498
Manner, Randy 640
Manner, Randy E 633
Manning, Alex 256
Manning, David 749
Manning, Glenda 721
Manning, Jean 389
Manning, Jim 757
Manning, Sandra 709
Manning, Timothy W 767
Manno, Claudio 744
Manosalvas, Marcos 417
Mansfield, John E 780
Manso, Angela M 705
Mansour, Christopher 679
Mansukhani, Sunil 756
Manuel, Brenda R 800
Manuel, Kathryn 800
Manvelian, Finola Halloran 825
Manzanares, Robert 599
Manzano, Michelle 300
Manzano-Diaz, Sara 726
Manzullo, Donald A 92, 303, 329, 414, 415, 416, 418, 419, 485, 494
Manzullo, Freda 497
Mao, David 581
Maradian, Ross 103
Marantis, Demetrios 591, 839
Marble, Gary 157
Marca, Danny 420
Marchand, Amber 152
Marchand, Becki 721
Marchant, Kenny 263, 309, 333, 447, 448, 486
Marchese, Steve 401
Marchione, Kara Ann 408
Marciel, Scot Alan 601
Marciel, Scott 596
Marco, Carmen 744
Marco, Veronica 610
Marcum, Deanna 581, 803
Marcus, Robert 420
Marcus, Stanley 850
Marcuss, Rosemary 612
Marella, Daniel K 815
Marfetan, Olga Graziella Reyes 918
Margolis, Andrew 792
Margolis, David 649
Margolis, Lawrence S 876
Maria, Joseph Di 826
Mariani, Patricia 888
Mariduena, Leonardo 908
Marietta-Westberg, Jennifer 821
Marin, Mark 433
Marin, Paul 842
Marin, Ronald 708
Marino, Tom 228, 308, 336, 418, 419, 421, 422, 425, 426, 486
Mark, Kristie 453
Mark, Rebecca 255
Markell, Jack A 781
Markett, Philip J., Jr 578
Markey, Betsy 766
Markey, Edward J 130, 305, 327, 409, 410, 411, 428, 486
Markham, Rodney 672
Markowitz, David 826
Marks, Audrey 918
Marks, Kathryn J 417
Marksteiner, Peter 632
Marmolejos, Poli 751
Maroney, Jason W 347, 348, 349, 350
Maroni, Alice 819
Marquardt, Jeffrey C 776
Marquardt, R. Niels 600, 602
Marquette, Margaret 607
Marquez, Mercedes 737
Marquez, Pascual 654
Marquis, David 805
Marr, Betsy Arnold 130
Marrero, Alexa 411
Marrero, Karen 655
Marrett, Cora 811
Marriott, Donna G 799
Marsh, Christian 707
Marsh, Cristie 820
Marsh, Sharon 712
Marshall, Capricia Penavic 595
Marshall, Era 828
Marshall, Joyce 635
Marshall, Julie 465
Marshall, Lane 386
Marshall, Misty 386
Marshall, Steve 498
Marshall, Susan 12
Marshall, Thurgood, Jr 840
Marske, Caryn 670
Marsman, Steven 633
Marsteller, William 784
Martens, Joe 781
Martens, John 401
Martens, Matthew 823
Martin, Beverly B 850
Martin, Bob 781
Martin, Boyce F., Jr 849
Martin, Brian 130
Martin, Carmel 758
Martin, Christine 433
Martin, Cynthia 140
Martin, David P 809
Martin, Don 644
Martin, James 718, 783
Martin, Jay 159
Martin, Jo-Marie St 455
Martin, John 245
Martin, Jonathan W 715
Martin, Josh 257
Martin, Julicann 254
Martin, Karen 833
Martin, Kathleen 509
Martin, Katie 288
Martin, Mandy 509
Martin, Margaret 612
Martin, Nora 344
Martin, Paul K 800
Martin, Ralph 673
Martin, Robert S 807
Martin, Ryan 449
Martin, Stephanie 777
Martin, Steve 666
Martin, Tania 639
Martin, Tod 152
Martin-Wallace, Valencia 711
Martineau, Michael 372
Martinelli, Nick 59, 444
Martinez, Alvin Delgado 911
Martinez, Angela 706
Martinez, Anna 677
Martinez, Brian 651

Page

Martinez, Craig 369
Martinez, Eloy 384
Martinez, Kathleen 721, 779
Martinez, Nicole 372
Martinez, Rafael E 669
Martinez, Tony 590
Martinez, Vilma 600
Martinez, Wilfredo 834
Martinko, Stephen 228
Martinko, Steve 444
Martino, Bethany 732
Martino, Steve 69
Martoccia, Anthony 768
Martorony, Gene 175
Martz, Joseph 640
Martz, Stephanie 376
Marvel, L. Paige 879
Marx, Michele C 590
Maryahin, Rafael 433
Marycz, Susan F 776
Mas, Jorge 300
Maschino, Karl 654
Masciell, Thomas 598
Masica, Sue 681
Masling, Mark 675
Mason, Jennifer I 814
Mason, Karol V 650
Mason, Rosanna M 895
Mason, William 644
Massa, Brian 369
Masse, Stephen J 840
Massey, Alfred 631
Massey, Marsha 823
Massimino, Julia 33
Masterson, John 706
Mastrian, Michael 391
Mastroianni, Peggy 784
Mastromonaco, Alyssa 591
Masumoto, Scott 655
Masuoka, Toshiya 935
Mata, Adolfo 911
Mataka, Elizabeth 931
Matal, Joe 376
Matecki, Katherine 711
Matera, Cheryl L 605
Matese, Lindsey 87
Matheison, Jennifer 823
Mather, Chris 687
Mather, Clark 284
Matheson, Jim 270, 309, 331, 409, 411, 486
Matheson, Scott M., Jr 850
Mathews, Dan 444
Mathias, Stephen 925
Mathiasen, Karen 608
Mathiesen, Mark J 392
Mathis, Josh 397
Matiella, Mary Sally 636
Matos, Marilia 705
Matos, Roy Chaderton 918
Matsdorf, Ty 51
Matsuda, David T 747
Matsui, Doris O 21, 302, 333, 409, 410, 486
Mattavous-Frye, Sandra 901
Matthews, Alex 437
Matthews, Armanda 778
Matthews, Heidi 213
Matthews, Linda R 211
Matthews, Macey 270
Matthews, Matrina 674
Matthews, Sandra 756
Matthews, Timothy 646
Mattiello, Jonathan D 834
Mattimore, John C 826
Mattina, Celeste 809
Mattler, Michael 367
Mattos, Abel J 893
Mattos, Jay P 722
Mattos, Luis 385
Mattox, Pamela 89
Mattsson, Jan 927
Matus, Nora 22
Matz, Debbie 805
Mauk, Rosie 818
Maunday, Ronald 906
Maurer, Ron 509
Maurer, Ronald 762
Maxwell, David O 808
Maxwell, Josh 397

Page

May, Peter 805
May, Tina 340
May, Willie E 714
Mayanja, Rachel N 931
Maybury, Mark 633
Mayer, David 811
Mayer, Deborah 413
Mayer, Haldane Robert 858
Mayer, Jeffrey L 705
Mayerhauser, Nicole 705
Mayfield, Irvin 806
Maynard, Rebecca 758
Mayne, Kat 375
Mayo, Milton 784
Mayorkas, Alejandro 770
Mays, Christopher D 893
Mays, Janice 449
Mazanec, Mary B 582
Mazonkey, Matthew 230
Mazur, Mark 610
Mazza, Nancy 198
Mazza, Richard 628
Mazzi, Ana 815
Mbabazi, Natasha 358
McAdams, John 784
McAfee, Karen 449
McAlister, Robert J 404
McAllister, Douglas 823
McAlvanah, Matt 281
McAndrew, Susan 728
McAneny, Douglas J 621
McAplin, Maria 718
McAthey, Tammy 99
McAuley, Tom 913
McBride, Brandon 340
McBride, David 801
McBride, Jonathan 592
McBride, Mary 740
McBride, Neil G 834
McBride, Stacy 344
McBroom, Dianna 138
McBryde, Gary 701
McCabe, Catherine 782
McCabe, Harry 666
McCabe, Janet 782
McCabe, John 657, 896
McCabe, Matthew 422
McCabe, Peter G 894
McCabe, William 727
McCain, John 9, 301, 323, 324, 346, 368, 371, 372, 381, 382, 471, 494, 501
McCain, Madeline 807
McCall, Dawn 598
McCall, Robert J 796
McCallum, Dana 389
McCallum, David 163, 387
McCament, James 770
McCandless, Scott 378
McCann, R. Anthony 796
McCann, Robert 626
McCann, Ted 405
McCardle, Kylin B 416
McCardle, Matt 401
McCarley, Yongsun 636
McCarragher, Ward 443
McCarron, Barbie 245
McCarter, John 828
McCarter, Sharon 843
McCarthy, Andrea 30
McCarthy, Carolyn 181, 306, 330, 406, 407, 414, 415, 416, 485
McCarthy, Cathy A 893
McCarthy, David 411
McCarthy, Deborah A 597
McCarthy, Dennis 616
McCarthy, Gina 782
McCarthy, Gregory 419
McCarthy, Jennifer 673
McCarthy, Jenny 379
McCarthy, Joan 821
McCarthy, Kevin 29, 302, 333, 414, 415, 456, 485, 768
McCarthy, Leonard 933
McCarthy, Margaret 785
McCarthy, Mary Ellen 379
McCarthy, Meaghan L 345
McCarthy, Michael 896
McCarthy, Natasha 784
McCarthy, Noreen 675

	Page
McCartin, Jude	176
McCarty, John	739
McCarty, Margaret	675
McCary, Judy	280
McCaskill, Claire	152, 305, 321, 325, 346, 347, 356, 357, 371, 372, 382, 471, 806
McCaul, Michael T	256, 309, 332, 413, 418, 419, 421, 422, 435, 436, 485
McCauley, David	642
McClain, Lauren	373
McClam, Charles	687
McClay, Wilfred M	807
McCleary, Bill	228
McClees, Timothy	404
McClellan, Kathy	198
McClellan, Wes	456
McClelland, John	611
McClelland, Joseph	753
McClelland, Kyle	639
McClelland, Wes	456
McClenney, Lucretia	761
McClintock, Laura	717
McClintock, Tom	21, 301, 334, 405, 428, 429, 485
McCloskey, John	812
McCloud, Edith	708
McClure, David L	795
McClure, William W	808
McCluskey, Susan D	790
McCluskie, Sean	34
McCluskie, Sean Edward	454
McCobb, Doug	507
McCollum, Betty	144, 305, 331, 398, 399, 400, 405, 485, 806
McCollum, Kelly Lungren	279
McCollum, William R., Jr.	834
McConagha, William	369
McConnaughey, Flip	295
McConnaughey, Ryan	296
McConnell, David M	651
McConnell, Mitch	109, 304, 322, 324, 339, 340, 341, 342, 343, 377, 382, 388, 472, 501, 502, 503, 799
McConnell, Thomas K	347, 348, 349, 350
McConville, Andrew "Drew"	588
McCook, Jake	360
McCord, Michael	793
McCord, Michael J	616
McCord, Ryan	369
McCormack, Keith	507
McCormack, Luke	770
McCormack, Maureen	598
McCormick, Beth	598
McCormick, James W. "Jamie"	420
McCormick, Mat	752
McCormick, Nick	367
McCormick, Robert	632
McCotter, Thaddeus G	139, 305, 332, 414, 415, 416, 485
McCoy, Dominique M	417
McCoy, Drew R	798
McCoy, John, III	825
McCoy, Kevin M	647
McCoy, Kim	607
McCoy, Moyer	449
McCoy, Ryan	269
McCoy, William	638
McCrary, Cheryl L	813
McCrary, Dennis R	656
McCraven, Marsha G	149
McCraw, Frank	576
McCray, Nathan	362
McCree, Victor	813
McCreless, Kenneth	717
McCubbin, Bruce	582
McCubbin, Janet	611
McCue, Susan	778
McCulley, Terence Patrick	602
McCullough, Brian	411
McCullough, Cathie	696
McCullough, Matt	58
McCurley, Alissa	107
McDade, Joseph M	640
McDaniel, Oliver	675
McDaniels, Thomas	423
McDermond, James E	666
McDermott, James	499
McDermott, Jerry P	127
McDermott, Jim	285, 309, 328, 447, 448, 485
McDermott, Kevin	130
McDermott, Patricia M	859
McDermott, Paul J	796
McDermott, Susan	741
McDew, Darren	906
McDonald, Ed	198
McDonald, John	162, 379
McDonald, Michael	807
McDonald, Valerie	656
McDonald, W. Larry	608
McDonna, Frank	695
McDonnell, Amanda	103
McDonnell, Brian C	721
McDonnell, Roger P	832
McDonough, Charles	932
McDonough, Chris	375
McDonough, Denis	592
McDonough, Jennifer	508
McDowell, Robert	785
McDowell, Sheila A	405
McElroy, Catherine A	404
McElroy, Marianne	693
McElveen-Hunter, Bonnie	774
McElwain, Laura	156
McElwee, George	231
McElwee, Roy	391
McEvoy, Deirdre A	651
McEvoy, Trecia	158
McFadden, Elizabeth	757
McFadden, Robert	669
McFarland, Katharina G	621
McFarland, Lilia	688
McFarland, Lynne A	789
McFarland, Patrick E	816
McFarland, Stephen George	601
McFarland, William	461
McFaul, Dan	58
McGahn, Donald F., II	789
McGahn, Shannon	453
McGann, C. Steven	601, 602, 603
McGarey, Barbara M	733
McGarr, Cappy R	799
McGarry, Natalie N	416
McGarvey, Daniel	631
McGaughran, Mike	831
McGee, Helene	821
McGee, Jim	372
McGeorge, Audra	38
McGettigan, Kathleen	816
McGhee, Kathleen P	382
McGhee, Michael	626
McGhee, Phillip	636
McGhie, Matthew D	393
McGiboney, Jeff	785
McGiffin, Curt	630
McGill, Michael S	805
McGill, Rebecca	750
McGilvray, Andrew	794
McGinley, Matt	76
McGinnis, Colin	352
McGivern, Tom	605
McGlathery, Louise	766
McGlinchey, Daniel	417
McGlynn, William J	597
McGoings, Michael C	662
McGough, Brian	509
McGovern, Gail J	774
McGovern, James	826
McGovern, James P	128, 305, 330, 395, 396, 397, 434, 485
McGovern, Sara	260
McGovern, Suzanne	821
McGowan, Brian	706
McGowan, Ernest	260
McGowan, Kris	788
McGowan, Matthew	377
McGowan, Phillip	458
McGrath, Brian	705
McGrath, Erin A	785
McGrath, John	756
McGrath, Judith A	774
McGrath, Rich	171
McGraw, Nanette	686
McGruder, Debra	606
McGuire, Brian	388
McGuire, Colleen	641
McGuire, Denzel	388
McGuire, Jamie	465
McGuire, Paul E	502
McGuire, Timothy	639

Page

McGuire, Tina B 816
McGuire-Rivera, Bernadette 715
McGunagle, Mark M 393
McHale, Judith A 598
McHenry, Patrick T 200, 307, 332, 414, 415, 416, 431, 432, 485
McHenry, Teresa 654
McHugh, Jennifer 820
McHugh, John M 635
McHugh, Matthew F 501
McHugh, Patricia A 631
McInerney, Denis 654
McInerney, John D 707
McInnis, Rodney 910
McIntosh, Donald 407
McIntosh, Lynn 724
McIntyre, Mike 199, 307, 330, 395, 396, 402, 403, 404, 485, 496
McIntyre, Natalie 388
McKannay, William 642
McKay, Michael 818
McKay, Monroe G 850
McKay, Teresa A 619
McKeague, David 849
McKee, Kevin 39
McKee, Patricia 757
McKee, Ryan 397
McKee, Theodore A 849
McKellogg, Carrie 608
McKenna, Juliet 895
McKenna, Michael 806
McKenney, Michael 612
McKenzie, Patrick 633
McKenzie, Stephanie 116
McKeon, Howard P. "Buck" 31, 302, 329, 402, 406, 485
McKeon, Kevin 453
McKeown, M. Margaret 850
McKessey, Sean 823
McKiernan, Neil 52
McKinley, Anne C 825
McKinley, Craig R 633, 640
McKinley, David B 287, 310, 336, 409, 410, 485
McKinley, Kimberly A 816
McKinley, Peter Michael 600
McKinnell, Cathy 693
McKinnell, N. Michael 778
McKinney, Nikki 721
McKinney, Robert C 788
McKoy, Mary 372
McLachlan, Brian 661
McLain, Patrick 497
McLaren, Ellen 67
McLaughlin, Brian 748
McLaughlin, Dan 57
McLaughlin, Joseph M 849
McLaughlin, Judy 789
McLaughlin, Margaret 593
McLaughlin, Maureen 365, 758
McLaughlin, Michael 86, 753
McLaughlin, Michele 369
McLaughlin, Sean 426
McLaughlin, Thomas F 670
McLean, Craig 710
McLean, Susan 786
McLemore, Tom 401
McLeod, Janice Galli 669
McLeod, Mary 596
McLerran, Dennis 783
McMahon, Christopher 747
McMahon, Emily 610
McMahon, Kyle Andrew 454
McMahon, William 666
McManus, Steven G 775
McMaster, David 289
McMaster, Jack 774
McMaster, Sean 443
McMichael, James 621
McMillan, Therese 747
McMillian, Jimmy 629
McMillin, Daniel F 628
McMorris Rodgers, Cathy 284, 309, 333, 409, 410, 411, 452, 485
McMullen, Christopher J 600
McMullen, Debra L 465
McMullen, Neval E 465
McMullen, Patrick 413
McMurray, Anya 375
McNab, Christine 931

Page

McNall, Patricia 744
McNally, Alison 828
McNally, Bill 800
McNally, Matt 384
McNally, Susan V 817
McNamara, Ellen 181
McNamara, Jason 767
McNamara, John F 595
McNamara, Matt 824
McNamara, Philip 765
McNeil, Ann 502
McNeill, Greg 354
McNeillie, Nancy 461
McNeilly, Timothy 694
McNerney, Jerry 24, 302, 333, 435, 445, 485
McNichol, Scott 653
McNicholas, Celine 408
McNiece, Jessica 369
McNutt, Marsha 683
McPeak, Merrill A 773
McSwain, Pete 663
McSwain, Robert 733
McSweeney, James 804
McSweeny, Terrell 1, 387, 587
McTiernan, Ian 172
McTiernan, Mike 822
McVeigh, Mary 420
McVicker, Michelle 743
McWhorter, Elizabeth 404
McWilliam, John 726
McWilliams, Carlyle 412
McWilliams, Jelena 378
McWilliams, Robert H 850
Meacham, Carl 367
Mead, C. Ian 705
Mead, Gary 769
Mead, Joe 689
Meade, Christopher 605
Meade, Jordan 283
Meade, Shannon 257
Meadors, Erin 897
Means, Kris 465
Mecher, Greg 794
Meckus, Kevin 688
Medaglia, M. Elizebeth 724
Medders, Sherry 633
Meddin, Lee 935
Mederos, Leticia 53
Medford, Ronald L 748
Medina, David 818
Medina, Francisco A 416
Medina, Humberto 770
Medina, Kathryn M 814
Medina, Monica 708
Medina, Rita 35
Medina, Rob 65
Meditz, Greg 408
Medlin, Melinda 457
Medve, John P 762
Meece, Roger 929
Meehan, Michael 778
Meehan, Patrick 227, 308, 336, 421, 431, 432, 440, 441, 442, 486, 837
Meehan, Terrence 763
Meek, James 422
Meeker, Shelee 64
Meeks, Daris 452
Meeks, Gregory W 182, 306, 330, 414, 415, 418, 419, 486
Meeks, Timothy J 752
Meenan, Mike 358
Meenan, Tom 392
Mehan, Doug 168
Mehler, Paul 358
Mehlman, Kenneth B 837
Mehra, Pritha 840
Mehta, Atul 935
Meister, David 779
Melancon, Peachy 498
Meland, Deborah 676
Melander, Lindsey 453
Melcher, Nicole 707
Melekian, Bernard K 652
Melendez, Aida L 896
Melendez, Rosa 654
Melendrez, Dahlia 379
Melius, Thomas 680
Melkert, Ad 931

	Page
Mellinger, Jeffrey	641
Mellody, April	223
Mellody, Kathleen L	609
Mellow, Jane	750
Melloy, Michael J	850
Melnick, Stuart	576
Melnyk, Brian	407
Melone, Martin	610
Melsheimer, Catherine	177
Melson, Kenneth	665
Melson, Mark	508
Melton, Noelle	131
Meltzer, Dick	457
Meltzer, Richard	453
Melvin, Kay	713
Melzer, Philip A	581
Memmott, Justin	381
Menashes, Emily	709
Mencher, Bruce S	896
Mende, Carl D	841
Mendelsohn, Howard	609
Mendelson, Phil	897
Mendenhall, Kathryn	581
Mendez, Nestor	917
Mendez, Victor	745
Mendiola, Evita	136
Mendoza, Felipe	412
Mendoza, L. Antonio Rascon	911
Mendoza, Miguel	68
Mendoza, Omar	627
Mendrala, Emily	367
Menendez, Luis	918
Menendez, Robert	168, 306, 321, 325, 351, 352, 363, 364, 366, 367, 472
Menikoff, Jerry	729
Menke, David	625
Menke, Tim	729
Menkerios, Haili	930
Meno, Rosanne	298
Menorca, Diane	98
Mensa-Bonsu, Henrietta Joy Abena Nyarko	930
Mercer, Christy	152
Mercer, Megan	392
Mercier, Larry	624
Merdon, Christine	505
Meredith, Amanda	379
Meredith, Diana	405
Merino, John	911
Merkel, Carol	123
Merkle, Phillip	672
Merkle, Phillip K	673
Merkley, Jeff	219, 307, 322, 325, 351, 352, 354, 361, 368, 472, 498
Merlino, John	389
Merola, Tressa	153
Merow, James F	875
Merrell, Michael	377
Merriett, Steven P	775
Merrifield, Neal H	723
Merrigan, Kathleen	685
Merrill, Debbie	27
Merrill, Dylan	358
Merrill, Kevin R	657
Merritt, Blaine	427
Merritt, Gilbert S	849
Merritt, Tim	457
Mershon, Michael	129
Mersinger, Summer	242
Merten, Kenneth	601
Meryweather, Kelly	461
Meryweather, Tom	461
Mesa, Jacqueline H	779
Mesdag, Kira	588
Mesenbourg, Thomas	705
Mesidor, Cleve	706
Mesmer, Matthew	382
Messick, Ashley	392
Messina, Elena	714
Messineo, Kim	44
Messmore, Karen	685
Metcalfe, Laura	825
Metelko, Marta	766
Mettler, Ashley	456
Metzger, Ulrike	907
Metzler, Chad	290
Mewhirter, Erin	794
Meyer, Gary	693
Meyer, Joyce	291
Meyer, Kenneth C	706
Meyer, Matt	245
Meyer, Rachel	344, 345
Meyer, Steffen	914
Meyer, Stephen A	776
Meyer, Stephen Horace	777
Meyer, Troy M	670
Meyerhoff, Harvey M	837
Meyers, Lindsay	436
Meyers, Richard P	657
Meyers, Virginia	424
Mezainis, Valdis E	689
Miagkov, Eugene	934
Miaoulis, Ioannis N	808
Mica, John L	60, 302, 329, 431, 432, 440, 494, 486, 799
Miceli, Julie	757
Micetich, Mallory	430
Michael, Jeff	748
Michael, Matthew	697
Michaels, David	723
Michaels, James A	776
Michaelson, David	463
Michalak, Michael W	603
Michalek, E.H. "Ned"	187
Michalic, Mark E	649
Michalic, Vivian	666
Michalik, Robert	54
Michalski, Lori	738
Michanczyk, Curt J	747
Michaud, Michael H	120, 304, 332, 440, 441, 442, 445, 486
Michel, Nicolas	929
Michels, Jeff	219
Michels, Kathleen J	500
Mick, Joseph	825
Middlebrook, Craig H	750
Middleton, Kate	10
Middleton, Thad	623
Middleton, Victoria	44
Midgett, Melissa	195
Midgette, Fred	766, 771
Midthun, Karen	732
Mielcarek, John	712
Migiro, Asha Rose	925
Migliaccio, Gene	727
Mihalache, Val	389
Mihm, J. Christopher	575
Mihori, Margaret P	499
Mikowicz, Jerome D	817
Mikulski, Barbara A	122, 304, 323, 324, 341, 342, 343, 368, 382, 383, 472, 494
Mikva, Laurie I	799
Milazzo, Mike	739
Milberg, Rachel	345
Milby, Michael N	893
Mildrew, Sean	796
Miles, William	433
Milgate, Karen	732
Milholland, Terence	612
Miligan, Blair	199
Milius, Pauline M	661
Milks, Thomas E	619
Millar, David	922
Millar, Gail	405
Millben, Michelle	427
Miller, Alice P	836
Miller, Amy	433
Miller, Anthony	755
Miller, Barry D	822
Miller, Brad	202, 307, 332, 414, 415, 416, 435, 486
Miller, Brian	31
Miller, Brian D	795
Miller, Candice S	138, 305, 332, 421, 440, 442, 443, 486
Miller, Casey	211
Miller, Catherine M	578, 579
Miller, Chris	922
Miller, Christine Odell Cook "O.C."	872
Miller, Christopher D	630
Miller, Craig	632
Miller, Dan	463
Miller, David	693
Miller, Doug	788
Miller, Duane	641
Miller, Fred	444
Miller, Gary G	39, 302, 330, 415, 416, 440, 442, 443, 486
Miller, George	22, 302, 327, 406, 407, 453, 486
Miller, George W	875

Page
Miller, Gerald C ... 676
Miller, James C., III ... 840
Miller, James N ... 616
Miller, Jamie ... 275
Miller, Jamie M ... 151
Miller, Jane M ... 837
Miller, Jason ... 422
Miller, Jay ... 511, 580
Miller, Jeff ... 57, 302, 331, 402, 445, 451, 486
Miller, Jennifer ... 401
Miller, Jim ... 354
Miller, Jimmy ... 443
Miller, John W., II ... 639
Miller, Jonas ... 267
Miller, Kathleen S ... 639
Miller, Kathy ... 430
Miller, Kyle ... 362
Miller, Mary ... 606
Miller, Matthew A ... 675
Miller, Merton ... 815
Miller, Michael ... 634
Miller, Michael H ... 647
Miller, Morna ... 449
Miller, Neile ... 752
Miller, Pamilyn ... 397
Miller, R. Alan ... 816
Miller, Reginald ... 707
Miller, Richard D ... 408
Miller, Robert ... 732
Miller, Robert A ... 834
Miller, Robert E ... 804
Miller, Robert L., Jr ... 891
Miller, Roger ... 738
Miller, Ronald R ... 833
Miller, Sarah ... 606
Miller, Scott ... 360, 643
Miller, Scott E ... 234
Miller, Selena ... 690
Miller, Stephen ... 354
Miller, Steven ... 611
Miller, Torrie ... 268
Miller, Vicki ... 497
Miller, Virgil ... 115
Miller-Hays, Sandy ... 698
Millet, Thomas ... 688
Millett, Thomas ... 688
Milligan, Colin ... 384
Milliken, Stephen G ... 896
Milliman, Jim ... 109
Millings, Bernadette ... 748
Millman, Rosalyn ... 742
Mills, Ann ... 689
Mills, Beau ... 197
Mills, Cheryl ... 595
Mills, David ... 706
Mills, Karen ... 827
Mills, Rachel ... 258
Mills, Tish ... 47
Millspaw, Tegan ... 433
Milne, Stephanie ... 385
Milner, Michael ... 729
Milosch, Marak S ... 496
Milovanovic, Gillian Arlette ... 602
Milstead, Jimmy ... 263
Milstead, R.E ... 648
Milton, Karen Greve ... 849
Milton, William ... 685
Min, James ... 30, 456
Minardi, Philip ... 144
Mindnich, Chris ... 157
Minear, Jeffrey P ... 847
Minehardt, Adam ... 439
Minehart, Robert ... 452
Miner, Roger J ... 849
Mineta, David K ... 590
Mineta, Norman Y ... 799
Mingione, Emanuel J ... 792
Miniace, Joseph N ... 744
Minichino, Cate ... 60
Minke-Girard, Jenifer ... 821
Minkel, Sarah ... 434
Minkler, Annie ... 455
Minner, Don ... 620
Minor, Deborah ... 695
Minor, Laura C ... 893
Minor, Matt ... 228
Minor, Robin ... 757
Minow, Martha L ... 799

Page
Minow, Mary ... 808
Minthorn, Cisco ... 381
Minton, Jeff ... 821
Minton, Shira ... 821
Mintz, Eric O ... 792
Minutillo, Maryann ... 818
Mir, Aimen ... 608
Miranda, Bonnie ... 763
Miranda, Jose Carlos ... 907
Mirani, Viraj ... 95
Miras, Floyd ... 748
Mireles, Roger ... 692
Misback, Ann E ... 777
Misenhimer, Marsha ... 389
Mitchell, Amy ... 446
Mitchell, Cranston J ... 677
Mitchell, Dean ... 199
Mitchell, Harold L ... 632
Mitchell, Jack ... 383
Mitchell, John ... 385
Mitchell, Linda ... 497
Mitchell, Meridith ... 821
Mitchell, Pete ... 57
Mitchell, Rob ... 227
Mitchell, Robert E ... 580
Mitchell, Robert L ... 112
Mitchell, Stacey H ... 661
Mitchell, Terry ... 639
Mitchell, Tim ... 392
Mitchell, Todd ... 172
Mitchell, William L ... 777
Mitchell-Rankin, Zinora ... 895
Mitchelson, Mary ... 758
Mitchum, Diane ... 653
Mitrano, Catherine C ... 636
Mittelstaedt, Lois ... 763
Mitten, Ray, Jr ... 725
Mixon, Blair ... 58
Mixon, Clint J ... 578
Miyasato, Diane ... 387
Mize, J. Gregory ... 896
Mizzoni, Joseph P ... 637
Moar, Ian J ... 725
Moats, Bruce ... 935
Moatz, Harry I ... 713
Mochida, Shigeru ... 931
Mocko, Madeline ... 730
Mocny, Robert ... 767
Modaff, Pete ... 284
Modeste, Brian ... 430
Modzeleski, Bill ... 759
Moe, Kari ... 145
Moelis, Cindy ... 593
Moeller, Philip D ... 752
Moffat, John ... 749
Moffet, Erin ... 70
Moffitt, G. Michael ... 788
Moffitt, Michael ... 786
Moggridge, Bill ... 828
Moghadam, Reza ... 913
Mohamed, Mohamed ... 900
Mohieldin, Mahmoud ... 932
Mohler, Katie ... 388
Mohning, Matthew ... 354
Mojarrad, Jafar ... 914
Moje, Annika ... 460
Mokate, Renosi ... 934
Mokha, Harpreet Singh ... 654
Molino, Heather ... 452
Molinoff, Sarah ... 383
Moller, Patricia Newton ... 601
Molloy, Kristen ... 172
Molof, Doug ... 264
Moloney-Kitts, Michele ... 596
Molyneux, Lisa ... 401
Monaco, Lisa O ... 649
Monaco, Nicholas A ... 826
Monaghan, Brian ... 705
Monahan, Brian P ... 460
Monahan, James ... 692
Monahan, William G.P ... 347, 348, 349
Monborne, Mark ... 605
Mone, Erin ... 819
Moneck, Michael A ... 792
Monet, Kathryn ... 379
Monette, Theodore A. "Ted", Jr ... 768
Monge, Fraterno Diaz ... 909
Monje, Hugo Prado ... 920

Page

Monroe, Becky 653
Monroe, David 606
Monroe, Ken 437
Monsif, John 193
Montali, Pete 722
Montanio, Patricia 709
Montanus, P.A 648
Monteith, Kris 787
Montemorra, Robert 671
Montenegro, Steve 10
Montes, Jose Adan 921
Montgomery, Anne 383
Montgomery, Jody L 815
Montgomery, Katherine 750
Montgomery, Lisa 3
Montgomery, Pamela G 842
Montgomery, Sarah 663
Montiel, Gina 906
Montoya, Elisa 818
Montoya, Elizabeth 814
Montoya, Paul A 825
Montoya, Ruth 269
Monyek, Marc 497
Moodie, Michael L 582
Moody, Bob 16
Moody, Brandon 294
Moody, Cameron 589
Moody, David 752
Moody, Joan 679
Mook, Robby 453
Moomau, Pamela H 465
Moon, Patrick S 600
Moon, Youngme E 774
Mooney, Frances A 662
Mooney, Jeff 823
Mooney, Michael P 578
Moore, Allison 388
Moore, Brad 225
Moore, Caryn 444
Moore, Christopher 747
Moore, Clyde 638
Moore, Darryl 833
Moore, Fran 778
Moore, Gwen 292, 310, 333, 405, 414, 415, 416, 486, 499
Moore, James 597
Moore, James T 713
Moore, Jay 392
Moore, Jocelyn 287
Moore, John L 582
Moore, Julie S 840
Moore, Karen 389
Moore, Karen Nelson 849
Moore, Karin 424
Moore, Keith 681
Moore, Ken 756
Moore, Kimberly H 857
Moore, Kristina 433
Moore, Lisa Mantarro 28
Moore, Lonnie 805
Moore, Mark 345
Moore, Megan O 609
Moore, Michelle 588
Moore, Mikael 36
Moore, Patricia W 677
Moore, Riley 420, 495
Moore, Robert "Bob" 626
Moore, Sean 19
Moore, Shane 42
Moore, Steve 818
Moore, Steven 87, 456
Moore, Terri 161
Moore, Thomas 367
Moore, Thomas H 780
Moore, Wayne 687
Moorehead, Susanna 934
Moorman, William A 889
Moosally, Fred 901
Moose, George E 837
Mora, Frank 922
Mora, Jasmine 454
Morado, David 831
Morales, Eben 676
Morales, Maricel 910
Morales, Toni 588
Moran, Ellen 703
Moran, James P 279, 309, 328, 398, 399, 400, 486
Moran, Jerry 105, 304, 323, 325, 341, 342, 343, 351, 352, 371, 372, 378, 379, 382, 472

Page

Moran, John 839
Moran, John A 791
Moran, Linda 823
Moran, Molly 649
Moran, Pamela-Jeanne 793
Moran, Sean 138
Morcombe, Cecilia 375
Morden, Cheryl 928
Morehouse, Jeff 259
Morell, Michael J 778
Morella, Constance 773
Morella, Constance A. "Connie" 501
Moreno, Ignacia S 660
Moreno, Luis Alberto 906
Morey, Robin 505
Morfeld, Courtney 503
Morford, Thomas G 733
Morgan, Andrea 700
Morgan, Chester 508
Morgan, Donda 176
Morgan, Eric 624
Morgan, Frank 509
Morgan, Jeff 633
Morgan, Katie 248
Morgan, Matthew 427
Morgan, Melinda 671
Morgan, Tara 149
Morgan, Teri 424
Morgan, Terri S 841
Morgans, Gareth 260
Morganti, Joseph 626
Morgenthau, Sarah 818
Moriarty, James Francis 600
Moriarty, Marvin 680
Morin, Jamie M 625
Morin, Marie-Lucie 934
Morin, Peter 119
Morin, Robert A 784
Morin, Robert E 895
Mork, David 87
Mork, Kirsten 253
Morosi, Mike 190
Morris, Alan 511
Morris, David 690
Morris, Dena 84
Morris, Dylan 355
Morris, Erin 699
Morris, Judith 284
Morris, Lewis 729
Morris, Martin W 95
Morris, Rod 839
Morris, Scott 608
Morris, Tom 733, 827
Morris, Tracy 911
Morris, Vincent 287, 357
Morrison, Carlos D 639
Morrison, Helen 611
Morrison, James W 839
Morrison, Richard T 881
Morrison, Sean 364
Morrison, Stephanie 508
Morrison, Trudi M 893
Morrison, Truman A., III 896
Morriss, David M 347, 348, 350
Morrissey, Nancy 131
Morrissey, Patricia 730
Morrow, Bill 898
Morrow, Dixie A 632
Morrow, Jennifer 29
Morrow, Joyce E 637
Morrow, Sheryl 607
Morse, Anne Nishimura 499
Morse, Craig 699
Morse, Duane 607
Morse, Phillip D., Sr 510
Morse, Robert D 894
Mortensen, Catherine 49
Mortier, Jeffrey 411
Morton, Andy 405
Morton, John 769, 839
Morton, Keith 806
Moscato, John 661
Moschkin, Lydia 747
Mosebey, Tracy G 443
Moseley, Henry 150
Moseley, Kimberly 744
Mosely, Raymond A 802
Moser, William 598

Page

Moses, Katie 354
Mosher, David E 575
Mosier, Jenny 649
Moskowitz, Andy 388
Moskowitz, Eric G 809
Moskowitz, Jedd 182
Mosley, Carolyn 717
Mosley, Raymond A 803
Moss, Diane Ingels 840
Moss, Dorinda 385
Moss, J. Laverne 898
Mosser, Kim 276
Mossey, Christopher J 647
Mosshart, Lindsay 266
Mosychuk, Susan 233
Mote, C. Dan, Jr 810
Motha, Ray 687
Motl, David 613
Motley, Rebecca 401
Motley, Thomas J 895
Mott, John M 895
Motta, Fernanda 343
Motz, Diana Gribbon 849
Motzeny, Barbara 922
Moulds, Donald 728
Moulton, Brent R 704
Mounts, Katie 96
Mousa, Jay 719
Moussa, Abou 929
Mowry, Nancy 741
Mowry, Sharon L 776
Moy, Kin 595
Moy, Ryan 263
Moya, Juan Biskupovic 905
Moyer, Brian 704
Moyer, Jensine 105
Moyerman, Amber 295
Moyerman, Megan 367
Moylan, Carol E 705
Moynihan, Dennis 643, 646
Moynihan, Timothy 769
Mozden, Michael 384
Mozhin, Aleksei V 914
Mrozowski, David J 674
Mucchetti, Michael J 264
Muchmore, Timothy 640
Muchnok, Kristie 424
Muchow, Dan 372
Mucklo, Otto 430
Mudd, Carrie 662
Mueller, David J 825
Mueller, Robert S., III 666
Muenchau, Ernest 768
Muessig, Karl W 781
Muhammad, Gail 184
Muhtar, Mansur 934
Muir, Linda 401
Mukasey, Michael B 837
Mulcahy, Sandra 718
Mule, Millard 116
Mulet, Edmond 925
Mulhaupt, Dennis 778
Mulhauser, Scott 364
Mulholland, John F 642
Mulka, Christina 388
Mull, Stephen 595
Mullan, John "Gib" 411
Mullane, Patrick 355
Mullaney, Dan 591
Mullaney, Michael J 674
Mullaney, Robert 661
Mullarkey, D. Patrick 675
Mullen, Michael G 618
Mullen, Suzanne 443
Mullen-Roth, Barbara A 814
Mulligan, Edward T 460
Mulligan, George 593
Mullins, Billy 630
Mullins, Tom 636
Mullon, David A., Jr 381
Mulloy, Joseph R 645
Mulloy, Patrick A 500
Mulvaney, Mick 240, 308, 336, 405, 438, 439, 463, 486
Mulvaney, Sean 784
Mulvey, Francis P 750
Mulyani, Sri 932
Mundaca, Michael F 610
Munday, Merrick 397

Page

Muniz, Lydia 599
Munno, Joanne 700
Munoz, Cecelia 593
Munoz, Leo 261
Munoz, Rene 63
Munro, Kayla 426
Munson, Lester 84
Munter, Cameron 602
Muoio, Reid 823
Murat, Bill 291
Murata, Christina 767
Murch, Garrett 354
Murden, William 608
Murillo, David 683
Murkowski, Lisa 7, 301, 323, 324, 341, 342, 343, 359, 368, 381, 472, 499
Muro, Steve L 763
Murph, Kathryn 72
Murphy, Aaron 158
Murphy, Alison 372
Murphy, Bonnie 746
Murphy, Brian 820
Murphy, C. Westbrook 797
Murphy, Christopher 737
Murphy, Christopher S 53, 302, 333, 418, 419, 431, 432, 486
Murphy, Daniel 506
Murphy, Darren 742
Murphy, Diana E 850
Murphy, Douglas 744
Murphy, Elizabeth 128, 820
Murphy, Emily 439
Murphy, Frank J 739
Murphy, Gavin 912
Murphy, James 372
Murphy, James R 809
Murphy, Jana 744
Murphy, Jim 676
Murphy, John 102
Murphy, Jolyn 41
Murphy, Latoya 703
Murphy, Martin J 825
Murphy, Mary Beth 787
Murphy, Matthew 784
Murphy, Meg 367
Murphy, Michael R 850
Murphy, Patrick 391, 497
Murphy, Philip D 601
Murphy, Ronald D 792
Murphy, Rory 364
Murphy, Sean 217, 281
Murphy, Sheila A 884
Murphy, Stephen 656
Murphy, Thomas 763, 825
Murphy, Tim 233, 308, 332, 409, 410, 411, 486, 896
Murphy, Timothy 666
Murphy, Travis 379
Murphy, Virginia "Ginger" 690
Murphy, William J 693
Murray, Brenda 824
Murray, Carol 446
Murray, Christopher W 600
Murray, Colleen 610
Murray, DaNita 397
Murray, Edward J 762
Murray, Elizabeth 458
Murray, Ellen G 728
Murray, Jeff 352
Murray, John 455, 672
Murray, Kathy 5
Murray, Patty 281, 309, 323, 324, 341, 342, 343, 354, 368, 377, 379, 383, 384, 464, 466, 472, 494
Murray, Renard 732
Murray, Shailagh 1, 387, 587
Murrin, Suzanne 689
Murry, Emily 456
Murtha, Katie 141
Murthy, Ram 663
Muse, Debra 689
Musgrave, R. Kenton 870
Musgrove, Melody 759
Musgrove, Rebekah J 393
Mushnick, Ashley 67
Musselman, Brian 631
Mussomeli, Joseph A 602
Mutaboba, Joseph 930
Muth, Michael D 671
Muzeroll, Kim 88

Page

Muzin, Nick ... 238
Myers, Aaron ... 385
Myers, Betty ... 656
Myers, Charles L ... 689
Myers, Christina ... 700
Myers, Dave ... 355
Myers, David L ... 768
Myers, Dean ... 195
Myers, Douglas G ... 808
Myers, Henry ... 627
Myers, Jacqueline ... 689
Myers, Kenneth A., III ... 620
Myers, Kenneth A., Jr ... 367
Myers, Larry ... 807
Myers, Merritt ... 73
Myers, Mindy ... 235
Myers, N. Lenette ... 85
Myers, Rod ... 462
Myers, Sam ... 1, 587
Myers, Stephanie ... 401
Myers, William ... 806
Myrick, Bismarck ... 712
Myrick, Gary ... 392
Myrick, Sue Wilkins ... 200, 307, 329, 409, 411, 451, 486

N

Nabel, Elizabeth G ... 734
Nabors, Rob ... 592
Nachtigal, Gayle A ... 834
Nadeau, Brianne ... 124
Nadeau, Greg ... 745
Nadler, Jerrold ... 183, 306, 328, 425, 426, 440, 442, 486
Naessens, Katie ... 699
Naftali, Timothy ... 804
Nagaoka, Ashley ... 81
Nagasako, Jessica ... 373
Nagle, Cathy ... 235
Nagle, Tom ... 176
Nagurka, Stu ... 354
Najarian, Steven D ... 791
Najjar, Sharef Al ... 260
Najjum, Michael J ... 738
Nakagawa, Melanie ... 367
Nakamura, Nancy ... 612
Nakamura, Patrick K ... 793
Nalbandian, John B ... 834
Nallengara, Lona ... 822
Nalley, Michael K ... 669
Nambiar, Vijay ... 925
Namm, Adam ... 599
Namoos, Sandra Y ... 609
Nance, Robert ... 240
Nance, Scott ... 344
Nantel, Kelly ... 811
Napoliello, David ... 362
Napolitano, Grace F ... 37, 302, 331, 428, 429, 440, 442, 443, 486
Napolitano, Janet A ... 585, 589, 765
Napper, Jennifer ... 638
Narayanamurti, Venkatesh ... 810
Nardone, Thomas ... 719
Narode, Dane M ... 739
Nasca, Paula ... 662
Nasca, Rebecca ... 365
Nash, Douglas ... 689
Nash, Patrick ... 465
Nash, Paul ... 789
Nash, Stuart G ... 895
Nash, Susan ... 822
Nassar, Ahmed Al ... 914
Nassikas, Lauren ... 678
Natalucci, Fabio M ... 776
Nathan, Elizabeth ... 404
Nathan, Irvin B ... 897, 899
Nathan, Matthew L ... 646
Nathanson, Benjamin ... 384
Nathman, John ... 493
Natsuhara, Roger ... 645
Navarrete, Luis Torres ... 908
Navratil, John F ... 465
Nay, John ... 602
Nayak, Rajesh ... 724
Naylor, Mary ... 354
Naylor, Nathan ... 762
Naylor, Richard, II ... 775
Naylor, Robert ... 787
Ne'eman, Ari ... 805

Page

Neal, Andrew S ... 461
Neal, Brandon ... 741
Neal, David L ... 662
Neal, Earl ... 704
Neal, Jeff ... 767
Neal, Kristina ... 662
Neal, Michael ... 463
Neal, Richard E ... 128, 305, 328, 447, 448, 486
Neal, Thomas ... 656
Neale, Brian ... 98
Nealer, Kevin G ... 840
Neall, Ray ... 626
Neary, Kevin J ... 738
Neary, Robert L ... 762
Nebbia, Karl ... 715
Nebeker, Frank Q ... 895
Nece, Patricia M ... 724
Nedzar, Tamar ... 413
Nee, John M ... 826
Needle, Steve ... 715
Neely, Jeff ... 797
Neff, William ... 710
Nega, Joseph W ... 465
Negrete, Paula ... 42
Negrete, Shelly ... 749
Negri, David ... 661
Neimeyer, C.P ... 648
Neischel, Jeff ... 630
Neller, Robert B ... 619
Nellor, Dianne ... 344
Nelson, Andrea ... 681
Nelson, April E ... 722, 725
Nelson, Ben ... 160, 306, 321, 324, 339, 340, 341, 342, 343, 346, 347, 377, 472, 493, 495, 502
Nelson, Bill ... 57, 302, 321, 324, 354, 356, 357, 363, 364, 382, 383, 472, 501
Nelson, Brian ... 674
Nelson, Damon ... 29
Nelson, Darnise ... 196
Nelson, David Daniel ... 603
Nelson, Dorothy W ... 850
Nelson, Karen ... 412
Nelson, Kristin ... 433
Nelson, Lisa ... 129
Nelson, Lowell ... 626
Nelson, Marilyn Carlson ... 799
Nelson, Michael ... 733
Nelson, Pamela ... 778
Nelson, Reid J ... 773
Nelson, Robert ... 786
Nelson, Ryan ... 242
Nelson, Tom ... 204
Nelson, Twanica ... 642
Nelson, Tyler ... 262
Nelson, Valerie ... 456
Nelson, William R ... 776
Nemeth, Christopher ... 623
Nenon, Sharynne ... 692
Nephew, Ken ... 744
Nerger, John ... 641
Nesbit, Sonja ... 449
Nesbitt, Wanda L ... 602
Nesirky, Martin ... 925
Nesmeyer, Diane E ... 393
Nester, John ... 824
Nesvet, Jeffrey L ... 724
Neubauer, Alison ... 412
Neubauer, Chris ... 178
Neufeld, Donald ... 770
Neufville, Nadine ... 678
Neugebauer, Dale ... 43
Neugebauer, Randy ... 260, 309, 332, 395, 396, 414, 415, 416, 435, 436, 486
Neumann, Dan ... 358, 463
Neumann, Kevin ... 71
Neumayr, Mary ... 411
Neun, Fred ... 763
Neunlist, Ed ... 663
Neves, Carole M.P ... 828
Neves, Steves ... 908
Neville, Gabe ... 232
Nevin, John ... 913
Nevins, Kyle ... 455
New, Nancy ... 691
New, Shelley ... 378
Newberry, Robert ... 618
Newby, Darek ... 401
Newby, Philip ... 748

Page

Newcomb, Nancy ... 675
Newell, Brian ... 407
Newell, Richard ... 751
Newell, Rob ... 644
Newland, "Ned" D.E ... 465
Newlen, Robert R ... 581
Newman, John W ... 637
Newman, Jon O ... 849
Newman, Robert B., Jr ... 497
Newman, Pauline ... 855
Newman, Theodore R ... 895
Newton, Dick ... 623
Newton, Erin ... 49
Newton, Jeremy ... 508
Newton, Jonathan ... 465
Newton, Karina ... 457
Newton, Martha ... 730
Newton, Patrick ... 245
Newton, Phyllis ... 672
Ng, Conrad ... 828
Ng, Jin ... 712
Ng, Kristina ... 372
Ng, Lena ... 35
Ngokwey, Ndolamb ... 929
Nguyen, Casaday ... 104
Nguyen, Hong ... 344
Nguyen, Nhan ... 376
Nguyen, Tommy ... 370
Nicholas, Kathleen ... 382
Nichols, Bill ... 730
Nichols, Daniel R ... 510
Nichols, William P ... 730
Nicholson, Ben ... 401
Nicholson, Judd ... 677
Nicholson, Kristin ... 236
Nicholson, Tracey ... 636
Nickel, Ryan ... 401
Nickson, Julie ... 24
Nides, Thomas ... 595
Niederhuber, John E ... 734
Niedzielski, Jon ... 128
Nieh, Ho ... 812
Nield, George C ... 745
Nieman, Lisa ... 372
Niemeyer, Lucian L ... 347, 348, 350
Niemeyer, Paul V ... 849
Nierle, James ... 645
Nies-Vogel, Karen ... 706
Nigam, Nita ... 739
Nikolaus, Roxanne ... 588
Nimetz, Matthew ... 931
Nims, Arthur L., III ... 882
Nino, Teresa ... 732
Nintemann, Terri ... 697
Nisanci, Didem A ... 820
Nishioki, Scott ... 29
Nishiyama, Drew ... 10
Niswonger, Robert ... 626
Nitcynski, Mark ... 661
Nitsche, Rachel ... 372
Nix, Anna ... 15
Nix, Brad ... 696
Nixon, Kathleen ... 809
Nixon, Natalie ... 423
Noble, Carolyn ... 43
Noble, David ... 800
Noblet, Michael J ... 347, 348, 349
Noel, Dan ... 788
Noel, Kobye ... 354
Noel, Roger ... 787
Noel, Tiffany ... 4, 5
Noem, Kristi L ... 242, 308, 336, 395, 396, 397, 406, 407, 428, 429, 487
Nogueira, Ana Cristina ... 920
Nolan, Lloyd U ... 896
Nolan, Ned ... 922
Nolan, Stephen James ... 600
Noles, Holly ... 267
Noll, Jennifer ... 427
Nolte, Doris ... 694
Noonan, John ... 404
Noonan, John T., Jr ... 850
Noonan, Mary McDermott ... 170
Noonan, Robert ... 727
Nooter, William W ... 896
Norby, Stephanie L ... 829
Nord, Nancy ... 780
Noriega, Roger F ... 497

Page

Norley, Dave ... 646
Norman, Hal G ... 465
Norman, Kimberly ... 497
Norris, Alan E ... 849
Norris, Courtney Yopp ... 110
Norris, John ... 596
Norris, John R ... 752
Norris, Kim ... 747
Norsworthy, Levator, Jr ... 638
Northcroft, George E ... 797
Northcutt, Amy ... 811
Northcutt, Eminence ... 439
Northern, Jayne ... 465
Northrop, Alison ... 423
Northup, Ann ... 780
Norton, Eleanor Holmes ... 297, 310, 337, 431, 432, 440, 441, 443, 487
Norton, Jessica ... 211
Norton, Molly ... 197
Norton, Patrick ... 129
Norton, Teddie ... 77
Norton, Travis ... 427
Norville, Valerie ... 838
Norwood, Joseph ... 669
Nosanchuk, Matt ... 652
Nosari, Joe ... 763
Nossel, Suzanne F ... 597
Nothnagle, Darcy ... 285
Notter, Jim ... 124
Nour, Amr ... 926
Nour, Nika ... 412
Novaria, Kathryn ... 412
Novascone, Sarah ... 353
Novascone, Todd ... 105
Novey, Larry ... 372
Nowak, Mary ... 397
Nowakowski, Judy ... 683
Nuebel, Kathy ... 375
Nugent, Malachy ... 608
Nugent, Richard B ... 59, 302, 336, 424, 434, 487
Nunes, Devin ... 29, 302, 332, 447, 448, 451, 487
Nunez-Neto, Blas ... 372
Nunnelee, Alan ... 149, 305, 336, 398, 399, 400, 487
Nunziata, Gregg ... 385
Nussbaumer, James A ... 792
Nussel, Gregory A ... 849
Nutall, Tracy ... 895
Nuzum, Janet ... 692
Nuzum, Scott ... 588
Nwanze, Kanayo F ... 928
Nygaard, Richard L ... 849
Nysted, Tina ... 742

O

O'Brian, Thomas R ... 714
O'Brien, Bill ... 806
O'Brien, Bradley ... 661
O'Brien, Caitlin ... 764
O'Brien, Coley ... 422
O'Brien, Danny ... 168
O'Brien, Doug ... 694
O'Brien, Holley ... 671
O'Brien, John ... 817
O'Brien, Lauren ... 111
O'Brien, Megan ... 256
O'Brien, Melissa A ... 465
O'Brien, Michael F ... 800
O'Brien, Patricia ... 925
O'Brien, Patrick J ... 618
O'Brien, Paul ... 654
O'Brien, Sean ... 87
O'Brien, Terrence L ... 850
O'Brien, Tom ... 401
O'Carroll, Patrick ... 729
O'Carroll, Patrick P ... 832
O'Connell, Charles ... 632
O'Connell, Maria Luisa ... 769
O'Connor, Anne ... 618
O'Connor, Bryan D ... 801
O'Connor, Carolyn ... 687
O'Connor, Christopher E ... 762
O'Connor, Cynthia ... 769
O'Connor, Dennis ... 613
O'Connor, John R ... 640
O'Connor, Kathryn ... 819
O'Connor, Kevin ... 675
O'Connor, Nancy ... 732

	Page
O'Connor, Sandra Day	847
O'Connor, Thomas	701
O'Connor, Tim	696
O'Day, Kathleen M	777
O'Dell, Greg	902
O'Dell, Peggy	680
O'Donnell, Allison	352
O'Donnell, Michael	177
O'Donnell, Michael J	745
O'Donnell, Thomas P	195
O'Donnell, Tom	173
O'Grady, Laura	763
O'Hara, John	352
O'Keefe, Gerald B	637
O'Keefe, Lois	292
O'Keeffe, Carol A	842
O'Keeffe, James	362
O'Leary, Brian M	662
O'Leary, Karin	671
O'Malia, Scott	779
O'Malley, Charles F	777
O'Malley, Kevin P	750
O'Neil, David	649
O'Neil, Stephen	701
O'Neill, Catlin W	457
O'Neill, Emily	135
O'Neill, Kevin	820
O'Neill, Malcolm R	635
O'Neill, Maura	835
O'Neill, Maureen	379
O'Neill, Michelle	707
O'Quinn, Robert	463
O'Reilly, Kevin	922
O'Reilly, Lauren	107
O'Reilly, Patrick	619
O'Reilly, Timothy F	840
O'Reily, Megan	407
O'Rielly, Michael	388
O'Rourke, Marie	663
O'Rourke, Molly	344, 345
O'Scannlain, Diarmuid F	850
O'Shea, Brian	263
O'Shea, John	411
O'Sullivan, Catherine G	650
O'Sullivan, Dan	391
O'Sullivan, Lynda	631
O'Sullivan, Stephen	914
O'Toole, Allison	142
O'Toole, Matthew	826
O'Toole, Tara	767
Oak, Dale	400
Oates, Jane	722
Obama, Barack H	587, 589, 774, 842
Obasanjo, Olusegun	930
Obeiter, Michael	354
Oberdorfer, Louis Falk	864
Oberhelman, Jim	103
Oberleitner, Bob	711
Oberly, Kathryn A	895
Obermann, Dick	436
Oblack, Sean	352
Obleski, Susan S	834
Ocampo, Lizet	458
Ochoa, Carol F	670
Ochoa, Christine C	36
Ochoa, Eduardo M	499, 758
Ochs, Michael	496
Odom, Anita J	635
Oettinger, Julie	743
Offenbacher, John	821
Ofori, Nuku	224
Ofosu, Asi	185
Ofton, Michael	693
Ogden, Joy	390
Oglesby, Ted L	802
Ohlbaum, Diana L	420
Ohly, John	433
Ohm, Angela	589
Ohr, Bruce G	654
Ojeda, Mauricio Pardon	921
Okagaki, Lynn	758
Okamoto, Jeffery	369
Okonjo-Iweala, Ngozi N	932
Okrak, Zayra	824
Okun, Deanna Tanner	838
Okuyiga, Andrew	264
Olander, Carol	695
Olander, Dave	448
Olave, Nikki	12
Olbeter, Sharon	627
Olcott, Jake	358
Olds, Candace	671
Olechowski, Mark	712
Olenkiewicz, Gary G	656, 658
Oleskowicz, John F	670
Olgilvie, Clark	397
Olijar, Leonard R	611
Olinksy, Ben	142
Oliphant, John	653
Oliva, Judith	625
Olivas, Roxana	900
Oliver, Andria	721
Oliver, Jack L., III	799
Oliver, Jan	439
Oliver, John	709
Oliver, Kyle	252, 437
Oliver, Linda	616
Oliveto, Danielle	47
Olmem, Andrew	352
Olsavsky, Patricia H	393
Olsen, Norma	210
Olson, Elizabeth	593
Olson, Eric	672
Olson, Erik	291
Olson, Kathryn	449
Olson, Lyndon, Jr	835
Olson, Marita	907
Olson, Mark J	647
Olson, Nina E	612
Olson, Pete	262, 309, 334, 409, 410, 487
Olson, Richard G	603
Olson, Scott	417
Olszewski, Robert	711
Olver, John W	127, 305, 328, 398, 399, 400, 487
Omar, Manal M	838
Omorogieva, Erica	389
Omvig, James H	779
Oneto, Paige	424
Ong, Joo-Jin	420
Oosterbaan, Andrew G	654
Opacak, Brittney	367
Opfer, George J	761
Opitz, John P	739
Oppel, T	643
Oppman, Dennis J	644
Orange, Vincent, Sr	897
Orben, Kimberly	746
Ordal, Paul	362
Ordzhonikidze, Sergei A	926
Oreck, Bruce J	601
Orentlicher, Diane F	595
Orfield, Craig	369
Oritz, Alvaro	255
Orloff, Nancy	158
Ornstein, Daniel	785
Orozco, Juan Guillermo	920
Orr, Dylan	721
Orr, Robert C	925
Orr, Skipp	608
Orr-Cahall, Christina	808
Orrick, William H., III	651
Orsini, Nick	705
Ortega, Fred	35
Orth, Patrick	208
Ortiz, Alvaro	255
Ortiz, Andrew F	497
Ortiz, Hankie	733
Ortiz, Luis	300
Ortiz, M. Lucero	717
Ortner, Charles B	799
Orton, Gregg	255
Orza, Tony	376
Osborne, Beth	282
Osborne, Christopher	461
Osborne, David	581
Osborne, Elizabeth	742
Osborne, Janine	198
Osborne, Jason	662
Osborne, Kara	388
Osbourne, Sheila	798
Osburn, Stefanie	589
Oscepinski, Donna	626
Osgood, Linda	796
Osheroff, Mauri L	822
Osnato, Michael	826
Osotimehin, Babatunde	928

Page

Osowski, Debbie 293
Osskopp, Mike 143
Ostendorff, William C 812
Oster, Jake 273
Osterdahl, Steve 744
Osterman, Elizabeth G 822
Osterwalder, Konrad 928
Ostrander, Kate 212
Ostriker, Jeremiah P 810
Osuna, Juan P 662
Ota, Shingo 909
Otero, Beatriz ''BB'' 897
Otero, Maria 498, 599
Otero, Miguel 68
Otis, Bud 125
Ott, Kathleen 580
Ott, Patrick P 671
Ott, Tom 829
Ott, William R 714
Otte, Jill M 725
Otten, Brad 243
Otthoff, James 714
Otto, Allison M 393
Otto, Robert 629
Ouertatani, Charla 36
Ouiment, Claire 74
Oursler, Susan 367
Oursler, Tara 123
Ourso, Elle 378
Ovall, Jeff 821
Overbeek, Kimberly 405
Overbey, Benjamin 714
Overend, Christopher J 465
Overton, Sarah 381
Owen, Danielle 201
Owen, Michael S 602
Owen, Priscilla R 849
Owens, Frances 509
Owens, Glenda 682
Owens, Jessica 376
Owens, John B., II 713
Owens, Phyllis 636
Owens, Steve 782
Owens, Tyler 344
Owens, William L 190, 307, 334, 395, 396, 402, 403, 404, 438, 487

P

Pa, Meagan 459
Pablos-Mendez, Ariel 835
Pace, Patti 812
Pachter, Marc 828
Packer, Winsome 496
Packnett, Patrick 693
Padalino, John 694
Padilla, Joan 679
Padilla, Marissa 176
Padoan, Pier Carlo 919
Paese, Mark 710
Paez, Richard A 850
Paffenback, Jean 443
Pagan, Michael 249
Pagano, Ed 272
Page, Anne 354
Page, Jeffrey 580
Pages, Jose Antonio 920
Pagliarini, Raymond 655
Paguni, Rosemary E 676
Paige, Dana 672
Paige, Thomas 725
Paine, Stuart 375
Pais, Marta Santos 932
Paisley, Katie 56
Pajcic, Helen 408
Pak, Dongwoo Joseph ''Joe'' 805
Palarino, Nick 422
Palazzo, Steven M 150, 305, 336, 402, 403, 435, 436, 487
Palensky, Michael L 705
Paley, Michael 826
Palisi, Annie 247
Pallante, Maria A 582
Pallone, Frank, Jr 171, 306, 409, 410, 411, 428, 429, 487
Palma, Juan 682
Palman, Glen K 893
Palmer, Bryan 365
Palmer, Crystal 900

Page

Palmer, D. Alec 789
Palmer, Irma 384
Palmer, Jioni 819
Palmer, Victor W 685
Palumbo, Michael G 776
Paluskiewicz, James 264
Pamperin, Thomas 763
Pan, Florence Y 895
Pandya, Amit 720
Panetta, Leon 589, 837
Panetta, Leon E 585, 615, 804
Paniati, Jeffrey F 745
Panitchpakdi, Supachai 927
Pannocchia, Orlando J 725
Pansieri, Flavia 928
Panter, F.A 648
Panuthos, Peter J 884
Pao, Jean Lin 738
Pape, Michael 110
Papirmeister, Charles 375
Papp, Robert J., Jr 770
Pappas, George 452
Pappas, Peter 711
Paradis, Julia 695
Paramore, Faron 771
Parcell, John 611
Pardue, Liz 434
Paredes, Troy A 820
Parente, Laurent 911
Paret, Betsy 854
Paretzky, Kenneth I 460
Parham-Hopson, Deborah 733
Parinello, Chris 107
Paris, Elizabeth Crewson 881
Paris, Jeremy 375
Park, Chan 375
Park, James 427
Park, Jeongseok 909
Park, Jiyoung 795
Park, Richard 784
Parker, Barrington D., Jr 849
Parker, Bryan D 347, 350
Parker, Chadwick 694
Parker, Elkin 701
Parker, Gerald 728
Parker, Harrison J., III 639
Parker, Jason 352
Parker, Kate 77
Parker, Kathleen M 393
Parker, Kyle 496
Parker, Laura 390
Parker, Lesley 14
Parker, Lori 896
Parker, Mike 501
Parker, Nora Bea 706
Parker, Oriana 379
Parker, Scott 270
Parker, Sharon 636
Parker, Susan 721
Parker, Wyndee 457
Parkin, Shaun 377
Parkinson, Edward 422
Parkinson, Patrick M 775
Parks, Brian 655
Parks, James G 796
Parks, Stephanie 405
Parmar, Naveeen 439
Parnell, Howard 786
Parr, Ted L 713
Parr, William 922
Parra, Jose 383
Parratt, Shelley E 822
Parris, Clyde 905
Parrish, Joseph 801
Parrott, Thomas M 832
Parry, Elaine 735
Parry, Stephanie 627
Parsan, Neil 918
Parsons, Bill 126
Parsons, Heather 202
Parsons, Jason 507
Partridge, Monica 623
Pary, Diego 917
Pascoe, B. Lynn 925
Pascrell, Bill, Jr 172, 306, 330, 405, 447, 487
Pascual, Carlos 602
Pasichow, Heidi 895
Paskaukas, Denis 803

Page

Pasko, Mike ... 93
Pasqualino, Donna L ... 393
Passante, Michael ... 352
Passino, John ... 692
Passmore, S. Wayne ... 776
Pastarnack, Lauren ... 375
Pasternak, Doug ... 437
Pastor, Ed ... 11, 301, 328, 398, 399, 400, 487, 495
Pataki, Tim ... 456
Patchan, Andrew, Jr ... 777
Patchen, Jeffrey H ... 808
Pate, Ernest ... 919
Patel, Alka ... 825
Patel, Manisha ... 588
Patel, Neal ... 238
Patel, Saad M ... 460
Pathak, Vivek ... 935
Patrick, Brian ... 456
Patrick, Connie L ... 770
Patrick, Robert W ... 581
Patrick, Steven ... 832
Patridge, Bryan ... 240
Patridge, Rob ... 220
Patrie, Miles ... 354
Patru, Katie ... 452
Pattea, Sandra ... 733
Patterson, Amy ... 734
Patterson, Ann C ... 763
Patterson, Clara ... 589
Patterson, Dawn ... 821
Patterson, Garth ... 129
Patterson, L. Eric ... 767
Patterson, Lotsee ... 808
Patterson, Mark ... 605
Patterson, Michelle Waldron ... 783
Patterson, Nicholas ... 376
Patterson, Shirley ... 817
Patterson, W. Neal ... 816
Patterway, Lance ... 695
Pattison, Karas ... 426
Patton, Angelina ... 461
Patton, Cynthia ... 45
Patton, Richard C ... 774
Paul, Christopher J ... 347, 348, 350, 348
Paul, Laurence E ... 774
Paul, Rand ... 109, 304, 323, 325, 359, 368, 371, 378, 472
Paul, Ron ... 258, 309, 328, 414, 415, 416, 418, 419, 487
Paul-Bryant, Towanda ... 902
Paulsen, Erik ... 144, 305, 334, 447, 448, 487
Paulsen, James G ... 809
Paulson, Adam ... 181
Paulson, Karen ... 455
Paulson, Myhre "Bud" ... 816
Pausch, Patricia ... 744
Paustenbach, Mark ... 610
Pavlik, Jennifer ... 98
Pawlow, Jonathan ... 444
Paxman, Dalton G ... 729
Paxton, Robert W ... 389
Paya, Dario ... 918
Payan, Sal ... 259
Payne, Dana E ... 775
Payne, Donald M ... 173, 306, 328, 406, 407, 418, 419, 487
Payne, Grayford ... 683
Payne, Janie L ... 739
Payne, Joel ... 24
Payne, John H ... 700
Payne, Kip ... 42
Payne, Nell ... 828
Payne, Warren ... 448
Pazmino, Erika ... 908
Pea, Janna ... 6
Peace, Fran ... 20
Peacock, Marcus ... 354
Peacock, Nelson ... 766
Peacock, Penne K ... 835
Peacock, Terry ... 612
Pearce, David D ... 600
Pearce, Krisann ... 407
Pearce, Mark Gaston ... 808
Pearce, Michele ... 404
Pearce, Stevan ... 177, 306, 333, 414, 415, 416, 487
Pearson, Charles ... 711
Pearson, Charles A ... 711
Pearson, Cindy ... 347
Pearson, Cyrus ... 386
Pearson, Dan ... 437
Pearson, Daniel R ... 838

Page

Pearson, Ellen ... 690
Pearson, Michael A ... 669
Pearson, Roy J ... 792
Pearson, Tim ... 427
Pearson, Tina ... 505
Pease, Denise L ... 796
Peavler, David ... 825
Peavy, Sandy ... 770
Peay, Deborah ... 413
Pecantee, Richard ... 153
Peck, Robert ... 796
Peck, Robert M ... 807
Pedersen, Chris ... 712
Pedersen, Jesper ... 420
Pedersen, Rob ... 630
Pederson, Spencer ... 430
Peer, Sarah ... 291
Pegg, Rayne ... 699
Peifer, Ann ... 33
Peiper, Pam ... 283
Peirce, Hester ... 352
Peirce, Jeffrey R ... 777
Pelak, Steve ... 674
Pelesikoti, Netatua ... 923
Pelham, Rachel ... 375
Pelitere, Tara Tinsley ... 777
Pell, Eva ... 829
Peller, Julie R ... 407
Pelosi, Nancy ... 23, 302, 328, 453, 457, 487, 499, 502, 799
Peluso, David ... 62
Pempel, T.J ... 499
Pemrick, Keith ... 232
Pena, Carlos ... 911
Pena, Javier ... 657
Pena, Linda ... 769
Pena, Lisa L ... 609
Pence, Karen M ... 776
Pence, Mike ... 98, 303, 331, 418, 419, 425, 426, 487
Pence, Robert Frank ... 799
Pendlum, David ... 692
Penn, Damon ... 767
Penn, Stephanie ... 388
Penna, Jim ... 230
Pennell, Katie M ... 815
Pennington, Amy ... 283
Pennington, Kathleen ... 739
Pennington, Kelly ... 358
Pennington, Mark ... 822
Pennington, Pepper ... 61
Pennington, Rebecca ... 748
Penrod, Virginia ... 616
Pepin, Andrew J ... 759
Pepper, Lori ... 457
Peraertz, Louis ... 785
Perbohner, Robert M ... 841
Perciasepa, Bob ... 781
Perdue, Larry P ... 825
Perea-Henze, Raul ... 762
Pereira, Emily ... 352
Pereira, John E ... 778
Pereles, Joseph B ... 774
Perez, Dennise ... 299
Perez, Janelle ... 420
Perez, Naomi Berry ... 718
Perez, Peter ... 708
Perez, Simone ... 443
Perez, Thomas ... 652
Perez, Vincent ... 259
Perez-Verdia, Carlos ... 914
Periago, Mirta Roses ... 919
Perin, Matt ... 397
Perino, Dana ... 778
Perito, Robert M ... 838
Perkal, Don ... 618
Perkins, Alex ... 449
Perkins, Brad ... 731
Perkins, Kevin, Jr ... 667
Perkins, Matthew K ... 510
Perkins, Nancy J ... 775
Perkins, Wuan ... 448
Perlman, Leslie Canfield ... 725
Perlmutter, Ed ... 49, 302, 333, 414, 415, 416, 487
Peronace, Antonio ... 454
Perrelli, Thomas J ... 650
Perrotta, Steve ... 370
Perry, Craig ... 629
Perry, Leah ... 433
Perry, Matthew E ... 815

Page

Perry, Richard 237
Perryman, Cole 216
Perselay, Lee 369
Persons, Susan 733
Pesce, Edward V 391
Peska, Kevin 712
Pete, Darren 681
Peter K. Levine 348
Peterlin, Meghann 422
Peters, Cecile 822
Peters, Dan 608
Peters, Gary C 138, 305, 334, 414, 415, 438, 439, 487
Peters, Gregory T 670
Peters, Joseph R 894
Peters, Louanner 85
Peters, Ricky 634
Peters, Sara 401
Petersen, Alana 142
Petersen, Frank 493
Petersen, Kenneth E 696
Petersen, Matthew S 789
Petersen, Melissa Z 344
Petersen, Steve 270
Peterson, Alexandra 42
Peterson, Bradley 752
Peterson, Clark 215
Peterson, Collin C 146, 305, 328, 395, 487
Peterson, G.P 811
Peterson, Jeff 588
Peterson, Jill 820
Peterson, Richard 613
Peterson, Robert 824
Peterson, Steve 434
Peterson, Thomas W 811
Peterson, Tim 401
Peterson-Cox, Mone't 758
Petkanas, Zac 384
Petraeus, David H 778
Petri, Thomas E 293, 310, 327, 406, 440, 441, 442, 487, 499
Petrick, James B 793
Petrie, Terry 661
Petrizzi, Maribeth 650
Petrole, Daniel R 722
Petrosino, Marie 741
Petrou, Laura 727
Petrucci, James E 791
Petruzzelli, Nanette 582
Pettig, Clark 138
Pettigrew, Emily 214
Pettigrew, Roderic I 734
Pettis, Leigh 275
Pettit, James 598
Pettit, Ryan 379
Pettitt, Mark 5
Petty, Randi 276
Petz, Kevin 911
Petzel, Robert A 763
Pew, Penny 10
Peyton, John 797
Pfaeffle, Fred 686
Pfaff, Bruce 206
Pfaff, Jim 106
Pfaff, Melissa 370
Pfannenstiel, Jackalyne 645
Pfeifer, Tom 31
Pfeiffer, Dan 591
Pfister, Zach 199
Pfrang, Steve 194
Pharr, Susan J 500
Phelan, Leo 763
Phelan, Lisa M 650
Phelan, Matt 260
Phelan, Michael 367
Phelen, Chris 49
Philbin, Christopher 129
Philbin, Patrick 768
Philbin, Peggy 842
Philippe, Kerli 427
Philips, Mark Anthony 906
Phillips, Brian 269, 463
Phillips, Clay 63
Phillips, Dennis L 814
Phillips, John 127
Phillips, Jonathon 430
Phillips, Leslie 372
Phillips, Lorraine 806
Phillips, Macon 591
Phillips, Mark 642
Phillips, Michael R 612
Phillips, Nia 758
Phillips, Page 281
Phillips, Roy F 347, 348, 349
Phillips, Samuel W 849
Phillips, Stan 692
Phillips, Venita 656
Phillips, William 635
Phills, Reisha 249
Philp, Curtis 251
Phipps, Jane 230
Phipps, John 690
Phipps, Rae Ann 362
Piacentini, Joseph 721
Piazza, John 436
Picanso, Renee 699
Picard, Lisa 697
Picard, Michelle 712
Picaut, Christopher R 460
Piccolo, Benjamin J 637
Piccolo, Fred 63
Piccone, Thomas 825
Pichardo, Danilo Rosales 910
Pick, Jacki 10
Pickel, Toni 74
Pickels, Hunter 118
Pickett, Jeffrey 510
Pickett, Sandra 808
Picolla, Joseph C 460
Picoult, Francine 758
Pier, Carol 720
Pierce, John 764
Pierce, Michael 124
Pierce, Tom 601
Pierce, Tyrone 645
Piercy, Charles 802
Piereth, Laurent 502
Pierluisi, Pedro R 299, 453, 310, 337, 413, 425, 426, 428, 429, 487
Pierpont, Ruth 773
Pierre, James A. St 715
Pierre-Louis, Marie-Lydie 899
Pierson, Jay 455
Pietrzyk, Joseph Pius 799
Piggee, Darryl A 153
Pijeaux, Lawrence J., Jr 808
Pike, Donna M 627
Pillay, Navanethem 927
Pilon, Paul 912, 913
Pimble, Charles 642
Pimenta, Sergio 935
Pimentel, Federico Hernandez 920
Pimpedly, James 818
Pinder, Joe 416
Pinegar, Phillip 452
Pineles, Barry 439
Pingree, Chellie 120, 304, 334, 395, 396, 402, 403, 487
Pings, Anne 662
Pinkele, Abigail 266
Pinkert, Dean A 838
Pinkerton, Jonathan H 677
Pinkos, Steve 456
Pinkston, Daniel 661
Pinkus, Matt 424
Pinn, Vivian W 733
Pino, Lisa 695
Pinson, Tracey L 641
Pinto, Ashok 433
Pinto, Lisa 34
Pinto, Nuno Mota 933
Piorkowski, Jennifer 219
Piper, Danielle Radovich 50
Pipes, John 744
Pippin, Michael 580
Piquado, Paul 707
Pisani, Salvatore 750
Pistole, John S 768
Pitchford, John 701
Pitcock, Joshua 98
Pitra, Mark 784
Pitre, Josh 381
Pittman, H. Dean 597
Pittman, Lisa 429
Pittman, Nancy S 841
Pitts, Floyd 774
Pitts, Joseph R 232, 308, 330, 409, 410, 411, 487, 496
Pitts, Virginia 498

	Page
Piwowar, Megan	135
Piwowar, Mike	352
Pizer, William ''Billy''	608
Pizerchik, Joseph G	682
Plagenhoef, Ruth	675
Plager, S. Jay	858
Plake, Lindsay	35
Plank, Mark	695
Plante, Jeanette	671
Plastina, Alejandro	912
Plater-Zyberk, Elizabeth	778
Platt, Andrew Joseph	454
Platt, Joel	704
Platt, Rich	696
Platts, Todd Russell	233, 308, 331, 402, 403, 404, 406, 431, 432, 487
Plaus, MaryAnn	701
Player, Jewel	582
Plaze, Robert	822
Pleffner, Mary	704
Plemmons, Beth	505
Plick, Joseph J	725
Plonski, John	781
Plouffe, David	591
Plumart, Perry	242
Plumb, Thomas	802
Plunkett, Vickie	404
Poblete, Yleem	419
Podberesky, Samuel	742
Podlaskowich, Ronald	792
Podonsky, Glenn	751
Podsiadly, Nick	375
Poe, Ted	251, 309, 333, 418, 419, 425, 426, 488
Poethig, Erika	738
Pogue, Donald C	867
Poindexter, Martha Scott	382
Poirier, Bettina	362
Pokora, Edward	626
Polan, James	839
Polanowicz, Kathleen	129
Polaski, Sandra	720
Poleo, J. Anthony ''Tony''	779
Polewski, Alyssa	206
Policelli, Maura	784
Poling, Caitlin	107
Poling, Parker	200
Polis, Jared	47, 302, 334, 434, 488, 493
Polise, John	821
Polisuk, Bryan	373
Polk, Ferris B	670
Polk, Jennifer	44
Pollack, Howard	796
Pollack, Lana B	912
Pollack, Leslie	816
Pollard, Alfred	790
Pollard, Catherine	925
Pollard, Ruda	378
Pollard, Trey	111
Pollett, Carroll	620
Pollock, John	641
Pollock, Karol L.K	825
Polt, Michael C	601
Pomerantz, David	401
Pomeroy, Julia	221
Pompei, Sarah	456
Pompeo, Mike	107, 304, 336, 409, 410, 488
Poncy, Chip	609
Ponder, Jacque	49
Ponder, Russ	626
Ponds, Margaret	815
Poneman, Daniel B	751
Ponti-Lazaruk, Jacqueline	694
Pool, Mike	681
Poole, Brooke D	812
Poole, Douglas	656
Poole, Jessica	45
Poole, Julie	460
Poole, Todd	198
Pooler, Rosemary S	849
Poore, Peggy	623
Pope, Amy E	654
Pope, Carol Waller	790
Popelka, Brecke	3
Popoff, Carole	706
Popovic, Tanja	730
Popp, David	453
Popp, Monica	411
Poppleton, Janet	252, 436
Porcari, John D	741
Porfilio, John C	850
Porges, Amelia	500
Porte, Thierry	499
Porteous, Alec	120
Porter, Amy	38
Porter, Angela	744
Porter, Audrey	96
Porter, Berkina	793
Porter, Ed	693
Porter, Emily	455
Porter, Gail J	713
Porter, Holly	364
Porter, John	397
Porter, Melissa	358
Porter, Roderick	786
Portillo, Christine del	67
Portman, Rob	205, 307, 323, 325, 346, 347, 354, 359, 371, 372, 466, 472
Portugal, Sergio	907
Posey, Bill	65, 303, 334, 414, 415, 416, 488
Posey, DeBorah	85
Posey, Katie	498
Posman, Harry	730
Posner, Charles	809
Posner, Michael H	496, 599
Posner, Richard A	849
Posner, Steve	354
Posny, Alexa E	759
Poss, James	629
Possolo, Antonio	715
Post, Jeffrey	433
Post, Lawrence	803
Post, Robert	696
Postek, Michael	714
Postel, Eric	835
Postell, Claudia	811
Postell, Joyce	67
Potok, Nancy	704
Pott, Wilfredo	907
Potter, Chuck	634
Potter, Robert A	650
Pottinger, Kevin	627
Potts, Brian	344
Potts, Michael	766
Pough, Tracie	68
Poulios, George	207
Poussard, Ronald A	633
Poutasse, John	786
Powaleny, Andrew	412
Powalski, Lynn	820
Poward, Christine	812
Powden, Mark	205
Powell, Al	710
Powell, Chauncey	401
Powell, Courtney	208
Powell, Earl A., III	778, 799, 807, 808
Powell, Erica	99
Powell, J. Mark	167
Powell, Jason	433
Powell, Jo Ellen	602
Powell, Joanne	256
Powell, Jonathan	457
Powell, Kimberly	582
Powell, Leanne	199
Powell, Linda L	609
Powell, Lisa	373
Powell, Mark R	711
Powell, Nancy J	599
Power, A. Kathryn	734
Power, Thomas	715
Powers, Glenn	763
Powers, Kenneth	752
Powers, Krista	422
Powers, Michael	790
Powers, Phyllis Marie	602
Powers, Robert	645
Powers, Teresa M. Gulotta	670
Powers, Tim	180
Powers, Victor E	707
Powers, William Charles	799
Poyer, Scott	749
Pozen, Sharis A	650
Prader, Johann	914
Pradhan, Sanjay	933
Prado, Edward C	849
Prager, Dennis	837
Prager, Robin A	776

Page

Prahar, Peter Alan 602
Praskovich, Alisa 588
Pratapas, Lauren 456
Prater, Mark 365
Pratt, Jack 180
Pratt, Sara 738
Pray, Keith 460
Pregerson, Harry 850
Preiss, Allison 205
Pressman, Alexandra 588
Pressman, Debbie 690
Preston, Stephen W 778
Preston, Tawanna 737
Preuitt, Julie A 825
Prevost, Ron 704
Prewett, Cecelia 793
Prewitt, Keith 771
Prey, Barbara Ernst 806
Price, Allison 818
Price, Alyson 767
Price, David E 197, 307, 328, 398, 399, 400, 488, 499
Price, Frank 806
Price, Joe 214
Price, Kerri 161
Price, Lori 822
Price, Malinda 627
Price, Marvin N., Jr 651
Price, Morris 47
Price, Nicole 721
Price, Reva 457
Price, Tom 75, 303, 333, 405, 447, 452, 488, 495
Price, Tonda E 775
Price, Tracy 823
Price, Wendi 215
Priehs, Kayla 167
Prieto, Ivan 908
Prieto, Jeffrey M 660
Prietsch, Christy 390
Prillman, Renaldo 655
Primrose, Edna 722
Primus, Robert 131
Primus, Wendell 457
Prince, La Celia A 918
Prince, Princess 378
Prince, Tim 401
Princler, Eve L 577
Prindle, Brian 646
Prinz, Belinda 211
Pritchard, Aaron 289
Pritschau, Mary 43
Pritzker, Penny 799
Pritzlaff, Ann Alexander 773
Probst, Scott 461
Proctor, Aleysha 267
Proctor, Debbie 510
Proctor, Kimberly 354
Prokes, Brian 62
Propp, Rebeccah 453, 455
Prosienski, Lisa 120
Prosper, Jean Philippe 935
Prosper, Pierre-Richard 837
Prosperi, Jorge Luis 920
Prosperi, Patricia A 745
Prosser, Cristin Buckels 117
Prost, Sharon 857
Protic, Paul B 498
Protopsaltis, Spiros 369
Prout, Jerry 497
Prout, Michael J 677
Prouty, Paul 797
Provancha, Bradley 804
Provencher, Richard 752
Prusacki, Joseph 699
Pryor, Judith 839
Pryor, Mark L 14, 301, 322, 324, 341, 342, 343, 356, 357, 371, 372, 377, 378, 381, 384, 472, 500
Pryor, William C 895
Pryor, William H., Jr 850
Psaki, Jennifer 591
Ptak, Alan E 579
Ptasienski, Michael T 460
Puchala, Linda 810
Puckett, Phil 718
Puerzer, Thomas O 670
Pugh, Brad 687
Pugh, David 626
Pugh, Debbie 105
Pugh, Elizabeth 580

Page

Pugh, George "Stu" 626
Pugh, J. Duane 789
Puglisi, J. Thomas 764
Puig, Steven 907
Puig-Lugo, Hiram E 895
Pulcrano, Samuel M 840
Pulis, Jenelle 507
Pulizzi, Philip 228
Pulju, Thomas 385
Pulley, Van 933
Punek, Blake J 417
Punke, Michael 591
Punwani, Ramesh 743
Purcell, Anne G 809
Purcell, Peter J 775
Purcell, Stephen L 717
Purcell, Virginia 128
Purpuro, Lawrence 134
Purser, Leslie 637
Purucker, Roxanne E 752
Purvis, Catrinia 710
Puschmann, Sharon 631
Puskar, John 452
Pustay, Kat 384
Pustay, Melanie Ann 669
Putman, Michele 781
Putnam, Robert W 343
Putnam, Thomas 804
Putz, Scott 443
Pyatt, Fred 607
Pyatt, Geoffrey 597
Pybus, Wimpy 636
Pyle, Michael 607
Pyles, Phyllis J 652
Pyszka, Kathryn A 825

Q

Quach, Hun 364
Qualtere, Tom 453
Quander, Paul, Jr 897
Quantius, Sue 401
Quarker, Kristal 420
Quarles, Robert 262
Quarterman, Cynthia 749
Quayle, Benjamin 11, 301, 336, 421, 425, 426, 435, 436, 488
Queen, Christopher 642
Queen, LaVerne C 645
Quehl, Scott 703
Queja, Irvin 391
Quick, Bryce 696
Quickle, Kelly 709
Quigley, Erik 624
Quigley, Lisa 247
Quigley, Lori J 612
Quigley, Mike 86, 303, 334, 425, 426, 431, 432, 488
Quilter, Peter 420
Quimby, Frank 679
Quinalty, David 358
Quinn, Brian 433, 823
Quinn, Daniel M 641
Quinn, James 117
Quinn, Michael 644
Quinn, Randall 822
Quinn, Susie Perez 57
Quinn, Timothy 653
Quinn, Timothy J 590
Quinones, Jackie 420
Quinones, Richard J 807
Quinonez, Alfonso 919
Quint, Robert 683
Quintana, German 906
Quinter, Neil 376
Quintrell, Edith 936
Quirk, John H., V 347, 348, 349, 350
Quittman, Louisa 606

R

Ra'anan, Gabriella 420
Raab, Scott 388
Rabbitt, Caroline 439
Rabinowitz, Judith 661
Rabiteau, Marsha J 834
Rabkin, Jeremy A 837
Raborg, Ronald T 833
Raby, Julian 828

	Page
Radass, Monshi	685
Rademaker, Andrew	443
Rader, Randall R	855
Radhakrishnan, Ananda	779
Radler, Cina	692
Radogno, Lisa	84
Radzanowski, David	800
Rae, Kerry	683
Rae, Michael	819
Raffinan, Yaribeth	895
Raftery, Jared	508
Raftery, Kate	780
Raggi, Reena	849
Ragland, Barbara	257
Ragsdale, Bruce A	894
Ragsdale, Daniel	770
Rahall, Nick J., II	289, 310, 327, 440, 488, 799
Rahilly, Lyn	770
Raimo, Bernie	457
Raines, Robert L	833
Rainey, Daniel	810
Raiti, Heather	372
Rales, Mitchell P	808
Ralph, Eric	787
Ralston, Robert	639
Ramage, Ronald	788
Raman, Mythili	654
Ramarathnam, Smeeta	820
Ramaswamy, Ram	710
Ramdass, Vic S	640
Ramdin, Albert R	918
Ramer, Sam	426
Ramey, Chad	283
Ramey, Dave	41
Rami, Alastair	265
Ramirez, Angela	178
Ramirez, Edith	793
Ramirez, Jose Alejandro Rojas	914
Ramirez, Lisa	757
Ramirez, Luis Dobles	908
Ramirez, Monica	652
Ramirez, Nestor	711
Ramirez, Sylvia	258
Ramker, Gerard	672
Ramnauth, Roxanne	625
Ramos, Paola	588
Ramos, William	703
Ramsay, Adrienne	401
Ramsay, John	823
Ramseur, David	7
Ramsey, Adam	793
Ramsey, George	239
Ranck, William	629
Randall, Douglas D	811
Randall, Lindsay	588
Randolph, A. Raymond	854
Randolph, William	770
Rangaswami, Viji	449
Rangel, Charles B	186, 307, 327, 447, 464, 488
Rangel, Steven	433
Rankin, Michael L	895
Rannazzisi, Joseph T	656
Ranneberger, Michael E	601
Ranstrom, Tim	128
Raponi, Michael A	576
Rapallo, Dave	433
Rapp, Cynthia L. "Didi"	778
Rapp, Marc	769
Rapp, Stephen J	595
Raschid, Omar	63
Raskin, Sarah Bloom	775, 812
Rasnake, Greg	666
Rasure, Nora	689
Ratcliffe, Robert	787
Ratliff, Dawn	352
Ratliff, James Kimble V., III	416
Ratliffe, Gail	663
Ratner, Jeff	372
Ratner, Ronald	837
Ratto, Mark	439
Ratukalou, Inoke	922
Rauch, David	152
Rauch, Samuel	709
Rausch, Colette L	838
Raveica, Ariana	116
Ravel, Ann	651, 652
Raven, Erik	344
Ravenel, Henry, Jr	842
Ravishankara, A.R. "Ravi"	710
Ravitz, Amanda	822
Ravjani, Abbas	452
Rawlings, Love	344
Rawlings, Steven	826
Rawlinson, Johnnie B	850
Rawls, Charles R	785
Ray, Charles Aaron	603
Ray, Charlie	922
Ray, Elizabeth	744
Ray, Elizabeth G	798
Ray, John	225
Ray, Joyce	807
Ray, Lindsey	252
Ray, Theresa	793
Rayfield, John	444
Rayman, Erik	89
Raymond, Christopher	81
Raymond, Matt	580
Raymond, Michael "Joe"	508
Rayno, Brucy	768
Razouk, Rami	633
Rea, Laurie	785
Rea, Lynsey Graham	352
Rea, Teresa Stanek	711
Read, John R	650
Reade, Claire	591
Ready, Anna	239
Reagan, Paul	274
Reagan, Ronald	798
Reapes, Jim	690
Reardon, Anthony	632
Reardon, Judy	166
Reavley, Thomas M	849
Reback, Richard N	766
Reberg, Mike	270
Rebich, David	607
Reblin, Gary C	841
Rechtschaffen, Alan N	837
Reddy, Shyam K	797
Redfield, Daniel R	496
Rediker, Douglas A	914
Redington, James	686
Redl, David	411
Redman, Scott	692
Redmann, Steve	637
Redmiles, Mark A	663
Redmond, Marilyn	628
Reece, Adam	378
Reed, Bruce	1, 387, 587
Reed, Christian	707
Reed, Dena C	901
Reed, Frankie	597
Reed, Heather	455
Reed, Jack	235, 308, 322, 324, 341, 342, 343, 346, 347, 351, 352, 473, 493, 828
Reed, Julia Hart	495
Reed, Lesia	691
Reed, Mark	506
Reed, Michael	73
Reed, Michele E	894
Reed, Mike	385
Reed, Pearlie S	685
Reed, Thomas	785
Reed, Tom	193, 307, 334, 447, 448, 488
Reed-Rowe, Helen Patricia	602
Reeder, Edward M., Jr	641
Reeder, John	781
Reeder, Tom	364
Reeker, Philip Thomas	601
Reel, Matt	6
Rees, Harold	419
Reese, Ann	401
Reese, Gary	344
Reeser, John D	645
Reeve, Trevor A	776
Reeves, Kristine	281
Reeves, Robert F	458
Regan, Dave	502
Regan, Greg	193
Reger, Mark	606
Regine, Meredith	408
Register, Kathy	75
Rehberg, Denny	159, 305, 331, 398, 399, 400, 488
Reich, Christopher	807
Reich, David	401
Reich, Edward	781
Reich, Jay	703

Page
Reich, Lynne ... 693
Reichert, David G ... 285, 309, 333, 447, 448, 488
Reichert, Julie ... 497, 498
Reid, Alex ... 465
Reid, Cheri Thompson ... 894
Reid, Harry ... 163, 306, 323, 324, 382, 383, 384, 385, 387, 473, 501, 502, 503, 799
Reid, Inez Smith ... 895
Reid, James ... 357
Reid, Peter ... 843
Reid, Randi ... 295
Reid-Winston, Rhonda ... 895
Reidenbach, Dennis ... 681
Reidenbach, Karan ... 637
Reidler, Jeffrey ... 822
Reidy, Cheri ... 354
Reidy, Ken ... 154, 291
Reif, Timothy ... 591
Reifman, Joel R ... 601
Reifschneider, David L ... 776
Reifsnyder, Daniel ... 599
Reigrut, Kevin ... 123
Reilly, Arthur K ... 811
Reilly, Bob ... 234
Reilly, Dan ... 458
Reilly, Jim ... 55
Reilly, Joseph T ... 699
Reilly, Nanette Foster ... 732
Reilly, Stephen ... 685
Reilly, Tom ... 674, 732
Reilly, Trish ... 232
Reinhalter, Mark A ... 724
Reinhard, Courtney ... 405
Reinhardt, Stephen R ... 850
Reinhold, Mark D ... 817
Reinhold, Tracy ... 667
Reinsch, William A ... 500
Reising, Bart ... 76
Reiskin, Julie A ... 799
Reisner, Gary ... 709
Reisner, Lorin ... 823
Reist, Burton ... 705
Reitinger, Philip ... 766
Relfe, Mitch ... 386
Remington, Danny ... 382
Renacci, James B ... 213, 307, 336, 414, 415, 416, 488
Renaud, Robert ... 101
Rendell, Marjorie O ... 849
Reneau-Vernon, Lilian ... 920
Renfrew, Megan ... 461
Renjel, Alex ... 362
Rennert, Kevin ... 360
Reno, Loren M ... 629
Reno, Tammy ... 662
Renteria, Amanda ... 133
Renz, Brandon ... 198, 434
Reoyo, Paul ... 642
Repass, Claire ... 92
Repass, Todd ... 686
Repko, Mary Frances ... 458
Reppas, Maria ... 144
Requa, Jack ... 842
Resendez, Marvene ... 52
Reske-Nielsen, Finn ... 930
Resta, Nicole Di ... 344
Restani, Jane A ... 867
Restuccia, Paul ... 405
Retchin, Judith E ... 896
Retherford, Samuel B ... 637
Reuschel, Ann ... 245
Reuschel, Claire ... 388
Reuss, Theresa ... 375
Rexroad, Caird E ... 698
Rexrode, Kathryn ... 278
Reyes, Carolina ... 497, 498
Reyes, Miguel ... 720
Reyes, Silvestre ... 259, 309, 330, 402, 403, 404, 445, 488
Reynes, Marin ... 774
Reynolds, Bobby ... 119
Reynolds, Bruce ... 694
Reynolds, Carol Jean ... 805
Reynolds, Chip ... 150
Reynolds, Debra ... 511
Reynolds, Glenn ... 497
Reynolds, Jennifer Hodges ... 798
Reynolds, John ... 822
Reynolds, Michael ... 681
Reynolds, Nichole Francis ... 6

Page
Reynolds, S. Mark ... 627
Reynolds, Thomas ... 510
Reynoso, Julissa ... 597
Rhea, Daniel ... 437
Rhew, Perry ... 770
Rhinehart, Melanie ... 19
Rhoa, Brian ... 774
Rhoad, Erica ... 401
Rhodes, Kingston ... 927
Rhodes, Michael L ... 617, 804
Rhodes, W. Stacy ... 818
Ribble, Reid J ... 294, 310, 336, 395, 396, 405, 440, 441, 442, 443, 488
Ribeiro, Pedro ... 27
Ricci, Michael ... 455
Ricciardone, Francis Joseph, Jr ... 603
Riccio, Marlena ... 300
Riccuiti, Anne ... 758
Rice, Charles L ... 621
Rice, Condoleezza ... 799
Rice, Edmund ... 420
Rice, Jon E ... 590
Rice, Kelicia ... 9, 388
Rice, Kevin ... 611
Rice, Susan ... 585, 589
Rice, Susan E ... 599, 603
Rich, Andrew ... 797
Rich, Ben ... 172
Rich, John ... 424, 496
Rich, Lisa A ... 842
Rich, Stacy ... 384
Richard, Alex ... 105
Richard, Gregg ... 353
Richards, Anne L ... 766
Richards, Dan ... 624
Richards, John ... 7
Richards, Kimberly ... 608
Richards, Laura ... 917
Richards, Thomas ... 815
Richards, Tina ... 411
Richards, Zachary ... 465
Richardson, Barbara ... 842
Richardson, Cecil R ... 631
Richardson, David L ... 799
Richardson, Eric E ... 899
Richardson, Jeffrey ... 900
Richardson, Jim ... 107
Richardson, Jodi ... 100
Richardson, Julia ... 377
Richardson, Laura ... 37, 302, 333, 421, 422, 440, 442, 443, 488
Richardson, Margaret ... 649
Richardson, Stephanie L ... 834
Richenderfer, James ... 834
Richetts, Jennifer D ... 651
Richmond, Cedric L ... 115, 304, 336, 421, 422, 438, 439, 488, 496
Richmond, David ... 297
Richter, John ... 119
Richter, Robert I ... 895
Richter, Sharon ... 74
Rick, Cathy ... 764
Rickard, David ... 743
Rickert, Sheri ... 420
Rico, Martha P. "Pat" ... 841
Rico, Victor ... 918
Riddle, Charles ... 577
Riddle, Clarine Nardi ... 51
Riddle, Kim ... 747
Rideout, Precious ... 387
Rider, Joanne ... 164
Ridgely, Debbie ... 727
Ridgway, Delissa A ... 868
Ridgway, Hunter ... 128
Rieder, Charles J. "Jody" ... 805
Riehl, Jeffrey ... 645
Riemenschneider, Robert ... 693
Riera, Celia ... 920
Ries, Marcie ... 598
Ries, Paul ... 690
Rieser, Tim ... 345
Riesz, James R ... 777
Riewe, Julie ... 823
Rigau, Mark ... 661
Rigell, E. Scott ... 275, 309, 336, 402, 403, 421, 422, 435, 436, 488
Riggins, Judy ... 697
Riggs, Jennifer ... 123

Page

Riggs, Tamela L 796
Righter, John 354
Rigsby, Robert R 895
Riklin, Sherry 747
Riley, Antonio 740
Riley, Barbara 59
Riley, John 656, 779
Riley, John J 657
Riley, Kelly 823
Riley, William Jay 850
Rilling, Juanita 391
Rimkunas, Mathew 237
Ringel, Aaron 185
Ringel, Noelle Busk 392
Ringell, Richard H 896
Ringler, Mike 401
Riojas, Jose D 762
Riordan-Smith, Susan 626
Rios, Rosie 612
Ripp, Kelli 93
Ripple, Kenneth F 849
Risch, James E 82, 303, 322, 325, 359, 360, 366, 367, 378, 381, 382, 473, 498, 501
Risenhoover, Alan 709
Risotto, Andrea 610
Ritchey, George 420
Ritchie, Branden 278
Ritchie, Donald A 389
Ritchter, Patricia 712
Ritman, Allison 743
Ritsch, Massie 756
Ritz, Lindy 744
Ritz, Robert 257
Rivera, David 70, 303, 336, 418, 419, 428, 429, 488
Rivera, Fanny 743
Rivera, James 827
Rivera, Raymond "Ray" 589
Rivera, Reinaldo 654
Rivera, Stephanie 795
Rivkin, Charles H 601, 602
Rivkin, Robert 742
Rixen, Erica 216
Rixey, Joseph 646
Rize, Greg 718
Roach, Barbara M 656
Roach, Douglas C 404
Roach, Elizabeth 391
Roach, Robert 372
Roane, Gerald A 902
Robare, David J 578
Robb, Karen 405
Robben, Rachel 105
Robbins, Erin 21
Robbins, Mark 836
Robbins, Michael 141
Robbins, Rachel 935
Robbins, Timothy L 580
Roberson, Portia 671
Robert, Joseph E., Jr 799
Roberti, Clifford 416
Roberts, Amber 364
Roberts, Craig 94
Roberts, Dan, III 667
Roberts, Duane R 799
Roberts, Gregory 460
Roberts, John G., Jr 808, 827, 845
Roberts, John M 776
Roberts, Kathleen 715
Roberts, Keith 888
Roberts, Marilyn 672
Roberts, Moira 823
Roberts, Pat 105, 304, 322, 324, 339, 363, 364, 368, 377, 381, 473
Roberts, Philip T 791
Roberts, Richard W 861
Roberts, Tracey 52
Robertson, Brian 464
Robertson, Dave 901
Robertson, James 433
Robertson, Linda L 775
Robertson, Mary 372
Robertson, Melissa 823
Robertson, Michael J 794
Robertson, Randy 697
Robey, Travis 291
Robins, Douglas 717
Robinson, Adam 646
Robinson, Adam M., Jr 646

Page

Robinson, Al 710
Robinson, Armstrong 111
Robinson, Barbara C 699
Robinson, Ben 216
Robinson, Crai R 811
Robinson, David 599
Robinson, Deborah A 866
Robinson, Elizabeth 800
Robinson, Gail A 800
Robinson, Gary 917
Robinson, Harry, Jr 808
Robinson, India K 789
Robinson, Jamie 627
Robinson, Janice 460
Robinson, John M 595
Robinson, Jozetta R 817
Robinson, Larry 708
Robinson, Laurie O 672
Robinson, Lori 632
Robinson, Maura 841
Robinson, Michael D 832
Robinson, Mike 400
Robinson, Nichele C 673
Robinson, Quinton 686
Robinson, R. Townsend 894
Robinson, Rob 10
Robinson, Robert 819
Robinson, Robin 728
Robinson, Steve 463
Robinson, Timothy 85
Robison, Nichole 285
Robles, Alfonso 769
Robles, Josue, Jr 774
Robling, T.G 648
Robnett, Cary 826
Roby, Martha 3, 301, 336, 395, 396, 402, 403, 404, 406, 407, 488
Robyn, Dorothy 616
Rocheleau, Chris 743
Rochelle, Courtney 23, 408
Rochford, Kent 713, 714
Rock, Cecily W 465
Rocke, Mark 636
Rocke, Tim 693
Rockefeller, John D., IV 287, 322, 324, 310, 356, 363, 364, 379, 382, 384, 465, 473, 494, 500
Rockefeller, Sharon Percy 808
Rockey, Sally J 733
Rockwell, Joann C 817
Rodgers, Anthony 731
Rodgers, Griffin P 734
Rodgers, Janice 671
Rodgers, Jimmie 922
Rodgers, Ralph E 835
Rodgers, Ronald L 675
Rodgers, Twanda 695
Rodley, Carol Ann 600
Rodman, Nicholas 404
Rodriguera, Sergio 456
Rodriguez, Alta 821
Rodriguez, Cristina 673
Rodriguez, David M 641
Rodriguez, Julie 682
Rodriguez, Leon 652
Rodriguez, Miguel 596
Rodriguez, Monica 461
Rodriguez, Roberto 592, 609
Rodriguez, Roberto Efrain 906
Rodriguez, Steven 598
Rodriguez, Traci 429
Rodriguez-Ciampoli, Fabiola 597
Rodriguez-Franco, Carlos 690
Rodriguez-Olvera, Lorenzo Antonio 454
Rodriguez-Ortiz, Ana Maria 906
Roe, David P 245, 308, 334, 406, 407, 445, 488
Roe, Jamie 138
Roe, Lesa 801
Roeber, Danielle 811
Roed-Larsen, Terje 931
Roeder, William 894
Roehl, Galen 358
Roehrenbeck, Jean 231
Roemer, Timothy J 601
Roeser, John 823
Roetter, Karen 82
Rogan, Bob 273
Rogerio, Studart 934
Rogers, Anita J 841

Page

Rogers, Chase T 834
Rogers, Cheryl 744
Rogers, Fredinal 510
Rogers, George 455
Rogers, Harold 112, 304, 327, 398, 488
Rogers, Hayden 201
Rogers, Jocelyn 217
Rogers, John H 776
Rogers, John M 849
Rogers, Judith W 851
Rogers, Lucia J 465
Rogers, Marc E 632
Rogers, Mary 497
Rogers, Michael 619
Rogers, Mike 137, 301, 305, 331, 332
Rogers, Mike 4, 402, 403, 409, 410, 411, 421, 422, 451, 488
Rogers, Richard M 654
Rogers, Sara 228
Rogers, Thomasina V 813
Rogers, Wanda 607
Roget, Gisele G 416
Rogge, Melanie 160
Rogin, Joshua 67
Rogness, Becky 145
Rogoff, Peter 747
Rohde, Richard A 832
Rohol, Susan 376
Rohrabacher, Dana 41, 302, 328, 418, 419, 435, 436, 488
Rohrbaugh, Mark L 734
Rojas, Ericka 344
Rojas, Sergio 729
Rojas, Teresa 831
Rokala, Jennifer 46
Rokeach, David 261
Rokita, Todd 97, 303, 336, 405, 406, 407, 424, 489
Rolland, Stacey 457
Rollings, Deborah 254
Rollins, Glenda A 655
Rollins, Sheri 4
Rollison, Ronald R 639
Rollow, Tom 645
Rolstad, Scott C 677
Roman, Mark 93
Roman, Mike 92
Romaniello, Cathy 229
Romanowski, Alina 598
Romero, Jennifer 430
Romero, Kristin K 393
Romero, Ramona 688
Romero, Raymond 776
Romick, Brian 458
Rominger, Eileen 822
Romito, Jon 405
Romo, Lawrence G 826
Rondeau, Ann E 621, 837
Ronen, Amit 281
Rones, Philip L 719
Rood, Justin 372
Roogow, Buddy 901
Rook, Mary Grace 896
Rooney, Covette 814
Rooney, Daniel M 601
Rooney, Mary Rose 422
Rooney, Matthew 597
Rooney, Nancy M 725
Rooney, Thomas J 65, 303, 334, 395, 396, 402, 403, 404, 451, 489
Rooney-Fisher, Dana 790
Roos, John Victor 601
Root, Richard 508
Ropelewski, James 755
Ros, Luiz 907
Ros-Lehtinen, Ileana 67, 303, 328, 418, 489
Rosa, Jason W 443
Rosada, Tomas 907
Rosario, Luis 505
Rosas, Ivan 906
Rosato, Joanna 796
Rosch, J. Thomas 793
Rose, Allison 35, 427
Rose, Anna 202
Rose, Carol 705
Rose, Charles P 757
Rose, Dianne L 831
Rose, Frank 598
Rose, Gamaliel 655
Rose, Joyce 444
Rose, Kristina 672
Rose, Lacey 610
Rose, Mary M 838
Rose, Michelle 721
Rose, Stu 236
Rose, Sydney 718
Roseboro, Doug 744
Roseman, Louise L 776
Rosen, Bruce 714
Rosen, J. Philip 837
Rosen, Mike 256
Rosen, Perry 461
Rosenbaum, Jeff 277
Rosenbaum, Steven 652
Rosenblum, Todd 766
Rosenbusch, Megan 401
Rosenfeld, Anne 181
Rosenfeld, David 453, 826
Rosenfelt, Philip 757
Rosenfelt, Philip H 837
Rosenkoetter, Darlene 383
Rosenkranz, Taryn 453
Rosensaft, Menachem Z 837
Rosenthal, Ann S 725
Rosenthall, Krista 411
Rosenworcel, Jessica 358
Rosettie, Christopher 708
Rosier, Alcindor 818
Roskam, Peter J 87, 303, 333, 447, 448, 499, 489
Roskoski, Joann P 811
Roslanowick, Jeanne M 417
Ross, Christopher 930
Ross, Dennis A 63, 303, 336, 406, 407, 425, 426, 431, 432, 489
Ross, Grace 818
Ross, Hadley 461
Ross, Halley 375
Ross, Kimberly 446
Ross, Maurice A 895
Ross, Mike 16, 301, 331, 409, 411, 489, 495
Ross, Mitchell 709
Ross, Priscilla 122
Ross, Rachel 226
Ross, Rebecca A 404
Ross, Sue C 493
Ross, Susan 401
Rossi, Janet 76, 434
Rossi, Nick 372
Rossides, Gale D 768
Rossini, Alisa 146
Rossiter, Diana 842
Rotert, Danny 155
Roth, Barry 684
Roth, Cynthia 893
Roth, David 671
Roth, Dorrice 610
Roth, Geoffrey 733
Roth, Jane 697
Roth, Jane R 849
Roth, Justin 88
Roth, Keith 708
Roth, Kristine 465
Roth, Marcie 768
Roth, Tyler 357
Roth-Warren, Margaret A 393
Rothenbecker, William F 838
Rothenberg, Gilbert S 675, 676
Rothman, Steven R 172, 306, 330, 398, 399, 400, 489
Rothrock, John 39
Rothschild, Tara 437
Rothstein, Barbara J 894
Rothstein, Barbara Jacobs 803
Rothwell, Patrick 229
Rotondo, Glenn 796
Roubideaux, Yvette 733
Roudik, Peter 581
Roughead, Gary 646
Rouiller, Donald 510
Roumeliotis, Panagiotis 914
Rouse, Cecilia Elena 588
Rouse, Peter 591
Rouse, Skip 390
Roussell, Melanie 738
Rovinsky, Robert 744
Rovner, Ilana Diamond 849
Row, Shelly 750
Rowan, Anne 783
Rowe, Audrey 695

	Page
Rowe, Courtney	687
Rowe, Julia	443
Rowe, Leslie V	602
Rowe, Ron	376
Rowe, William	789
Rowe, William A	611
Rowland, Lloyd B	620
Rowland, Matthew G	894
Rowland, Yvette	237
Rowley, Lori	367
Rowley, Molly	388
Rowse, Mark	693
Rowton, Judy	252
Roy, Alain Le	925
Roy, James	623
Roy, Randall	823
Roy, Robie I. Samanta	347, 348, 349, 350
Royall, Penelope	729
Roybal-Allard, Lucille	35, 302, 329, 398, 399, 400, 489, 499
Royce, Edward R	38, 302, 329, 414, 415, 418, 419, 489, 495
Roytblat, Nadya B	822
Rozansky, Genevieve	12
Rozier, Sarah	253
Ruales, Jose	920
Rubens, Diana	763
Rubenstein, David	828
Rubenstein, David M	798, 799
Rubenstein, Martha	811
Rubenstein, Stephen R	665
Rubin, Bill	818
Rubin, Kim	145
Rubiner, Laurie	51
Rubinfield, Sarah	30
Rubino, Michael	709
Rubino, Shelley	52, 454
Rubinovitz, Rob	704
Rubinstein, Daniel	601
Rubio, Marco	57, 302, 323, 325, 356, 357, 366, 367, 378, 382, 473, 496
Ruby, Lauren	691
Rucker, Bob	28
Rucker, Cliff	841
Rucker, James R., Jr	814
Rucker, Mark	695
Ruckert, Kyle	114
Ruckert, Lynnel	115
Rudder, S.R	648
Rudisill, Shannon	730
Rudisill, Zach	449
Rudman, Mara	835
Rudman, Rebecca	41
Rudolfsky, Daniel	376
Rudolph, Kim	99
Rudolph, Lawrence	811
Rudy, Kirk A	837
Ruecker, Ronald	667
Ruemmler, Kathryn	593
Ruffin, Andrew	358
Ruffin, John	734
Ruffner, Mike	608
Ruggie, John	932
Ruggieri, Fig	884
Ruhlen, Steve	262
Ruhlman, Philip	629
Ruiz, Adam	497
Ruiz, Jaime	906
Ruiz, Vanessa	895
Ruland, Timothy P	706
Rulon, Kathy	818
Rumbaugh, Russell	354
Runcie, Jim	757
Rundell, Linda S.C	682
Rundlett, Josie	196
Runk, Michelle	213
Runkle, Ben	404
Runnels, Al	610
Runyan, Jon	170, 306, 336, 402, 403, 404, 428, 429, 445, 489
Rupert, Clarke	781
Rupp, Mary	805
Rupp, Robert	647
Rupp, Tad	134
Ruppersberger, C.A. Dutch	123, 494, 304, 332, 402, 403, 451, 489
Ruppersberger, Kay	498
Rush, Bobby L	84, 303, 329, 409, 410, 489
Rush, Laura	433
Rushforth, Tyler	362
Rushing, Glenn	260
Ruskowsky, Dianna	407
Russ, David	683
Russelburg, Peter	795
Russell, Alexandria	240
Russell, Cathy	1, 387, 587
Russell, Corinne	790
Russell, Debbi	833
Russell, Gisele	276
Russell, Melvin W	617
Russell, Michael J	422
Russell, Scott R	405
Russell, Tracey	401
Russell, Tricia	180
Russo, Karl E	465
Russo, Peter	365
Russo, Ronald	841
Rust, David A	831
Rust, Tom	413
Rutherford, Donald L	638
Rutherford, Matthew	606
Rutkin, Amy	183
Rutledge, Michael J	724
Rutledge, Preston	365
Rutledge-Burns, Rosamond A	713
Ruttledge, Lynnae	759
Ruwe, Robert Paul	883
Ruwwe, Mary	797
Ryan, Barbara	789
Ryan, Diane	612
Ryan, Erin	25
Ryan, John	205
Ryan, Josh	354
Ryan, Kathleen	628
Ryan, Katie	424
Ryan, Kelly	767
Ryan, Kevin	131
Ryan, Margaret A	886
Ryan, Michael	895
Ryan, Michael J	683
Ryan, Michelle	627
Ryan, Mike	453
Ryan, Paul	290, 310, 331, 405, 447, 489
Ryan, Robert	738
Ryan, Sean	463
Ryan, Shawn	146
Ryan, Shirley W	799
Ryan, Sprightley	828
Ryan, Thomas D	744
Ryan, Tim	213, 307, 332, 402, 403, 405, 489
Rybczynski, Witold	778
Rybicki, James	674
Ryder, Neil	671
Rymer, Pamela A	850
Rynearson, Marcia E	834
Rynes, Joel	768
Ryschkewitsch, Mike	801
Ryu, Lisa H	775
Ryu, Rexon Y	600
Rzeczkowski, Kristin	383

S

	Page
Saavedra, Susie	255
Sabag, Terra	124
Sabatino, Robin	833
Sabelhaus, Melanie R	774
Sablan, Gregorio Kilili Camacho	299, 310, 337, 395, 396, 428, 429, 489
Sabol, William	672
Sacgesser, Jodi	254
Sach, Warren	926
Sachitano, Angela	69
Sachs, Herbert	834
Sachs, Jeffrey D	932
Sachs-Cornish, Patricia	922
Sachse, Brie	746
Sack, Robert D	849
Sadari, David P	738
Sadd, Mark A	773
Saddler, Fern Flanagan	895
Sadik, Nafis	931
Sadler, Robert M	725
Sadler, Thomas W	841
Sadoian, Allison	44
Sadosky, Jeff	205

Page

Sadun, Arrigo 914
Saez, Mariel 458
Safavian, Jennifer 449
Sagely, C. Matthew 14
Sager, Mike 455
Saggiante, Jorge 918
Saguier, Bernardino Hugo 918
Sagul, Peggy 74
Saho, Momodou Bamba 914
Saito, Teiko 680
Sajery, Algene 420
Salaam, Amirah 173
Salad, Bruce 676
Saladin, Roberto Bernardo 918
Salas, B.F 648
Salay, Katie 340
Salayandia, Marisela 423
Salazar, John P 798
Salazar, Kenneth L 500, 585, 679, 773, 804, 807
Salber, Stephen S 714
Saldivar, Liz 34
Salem, David 391
Salerno, Brian 770
Salerno, Judith A 810
Salidjanova, Nargiza S 500
Salinas, Juan "J.D." 797
Salinas, Norberto 427
Salini, Elizabeth 825
Sallenave, Michel 909
Salley, Kevin 789
Salley, Lori 439
Salmanowitz, Melissa 408
Salmi, Molly 407
Salmon, Paul 712
Salomon, Matt 354, 463
Salotti, Chris 679
Salpeter, Joshua H 67
Salstrom, Sandra 610
Salt, Terrence C 636
Salter, James W., Jr 631
Saltsman, Chip 246
Saltzman, Josh 268
Saltzman, Penelope W 822
Salvador, Maria Isabel 918
Salvas, Frank 763
Salzman, Amelia "Amy" 589
Samantar, Deborah Emerson 436
Samardick, Ruth 726
Samenfeld-Specht, Megan 588
Samford, Jonathan 15
Samman, Safiya 690
Sammartino, Frank J 575
Sampaio, Jorge 931, 932
Samper, Cristian 829
Samples, Colin 401
Samra, Tom A 840
Sams, J. David 713
Sams, Michelle 640
Samuels, Brenda 362
Samuels, Charles E., Jr 669
Samuels, Deanne 33
Samuels, Jocelyn 652
Samuels, Marcia 653
Samuelson, Drey 242
Sanborn, Benjamin J 656
Sanborn, Scott 389
Sanchez, Alejandro M 793
Sanchez, Ami 378
Sanchez, Carlos 457
Sanchez, Erin Allen 580
Sanchez, Francisco 707, 708
Sanchez, Francisco J 498, 839
Sanchez, Linda T 38, 302, 332, 413, 425, 426, 445, 489
Sanchez, Loretta 42 , 302, 330, 402, 403, 421, 463, 489, 493
Sanclemente, Xiomara 908
Sandalow, David 751
Sanders, Albert 376
Sanders, Bernard 272, 309, 321, 325, 354, 359, 360, 361, 362, 368, 379, 473, 463, 837
Sanders, Carol A 777
Sanders, Christopher "Chris" 97
Sanders, Emily 427
Sanders, Monica 422
Sanderson, Janet 597
Sandgreen, Matt 376
Sandifer, Paul 708
Sandler, Risa D 725
Sandman, Dana 37
Sandman, James J 799
Sandoval, Alfredo 493
Sandoval, Gabriel 756
Sands, Leonard 799
Sandy, John 82
Sanford, Jessica 270
Sanford, Jim 591
Sanow, Nancy 823
Sansom, William B 834
Sansonetti, Bonnie 244
Sant, Roger 828
Sant, Victoria P 808
Santa, Angel 673
Santa, Izzy 208
Santamaria, Alfred 71
Santamorena, Lori 607
Santangelo, Mari 671
Santiago, Angel 623
Santiago, Jacinto, Jr 638
Santillan, Eduardo 907
Santillo, Patrick 707
Santone, Lou 671
Santos, Nelson 656
Santos, Nelson A 657
Santucci, Gina 251
Santy, Ross C 758
Sanz, Paul Oostburg 643
Sanz-Rexach, Gabriel 675
Sapong, Kofi 776
Sapong, Kofi A 776
Saracco, John 718
Sarar, Ariana 401
Sarasin, Ron 502
Sarassoro, Fidele 929
Sarbanes, John P 124, 304, 333, 428, 429, 435, 436, 489
Sarcone, Chris 699
Sard, Keven 443
Sargeant, Winslow 827
Sargent, Annelia 811
Sargent, Marilyn R 854
Sargent, Nathan 819
Saris, Patti B 841
Sarkisian-Tatarian, Alisa 236
Sarles, Richard 842
Sarley, Christopher 412
Sartori, Joan 506
Sarvana, Adam 12
Sass, Paul 439
Sassaman, John C 382
Satcher, Daraka 703
Satorius, Mark A 813
Satterfield, Lee 595
Satterfield, Lee F 895, 901
Saul, Andrew M 793
Saulnier, Steve 694
Sauls, Karen 628
Saum, Christine 805
Saunders, Grant 455
Saunders, Joan Parks 830
Saunders, Mary 708
Saunders, Teresa 197
Saundry, Claire M 713
Savage, Hank 461
Savercool, Charlotte 412
Saville, Julie 803
Savino, Robert 228
Savitz, Maxine 810
Savory, Lauren 449
Savoy, Marie S 777
Sawyer, Heather 427
Sax, Carol 830
Saxon, Denise S 825
Sayago, Erin 138
Sayeh, Antoinette 913
Sayen, David 732
Sayenga, Jill C 893
Scales, Ayris 898
Scalia, Antonin 845
Scalici, Dawn 766
Scalise, Steve 114, 304, 334, 409, 410, 411, 489
Scalza, Lou 790
Scandling, Dan 280
Scanlon, Clarke 103
Scanlon, Jim 728
Scanlon, Shane 385
Scarbrough, J 643
Scardino, Anothy 712

Page

Scarpa, Antonio 734
Schaaf, Kenli 589
Schaal, Barbara 810
Schaefer, Adam 408
Schaeffer, Steven L 832
Schaeffer, Tracey 718
Schafer, George H 893
Schaffer, Alma 626
Schaffer, Christine 456
Schaffer, Gregory 767
Schaffer, Laurie 605
Schaffner, Ted 607
Schafle, Matt 429
Schakowsky, Janice D 88, 303, 331, 409, 411, 451, 489
Schalch, Kathleen 720
Schalestock, Peter 424, 496
Schall, Alvin A 859
Schamel, Anne M 817
Schamis, Graciela 906
Schannep, Greg 267
Schanz, Jeffrey E 799
Schapiro, Mary L 820
Schapitl, Ashley 30
Scharf, Katherine "Katie" 588
Schatz, Evan 281
Schaub, James D 687
Schaumburg, Amanda 407
Scheck, Howard 823
Scheffler, Elizabeth 582
Scheider, Matthew 653
Scheidt, Douglas J 822
Schell, Ben 437
Schenck, Linda 252
Scherder, Dan 497
Scherrington, Jeff 795
Schertz, Matt 397
Schettler, Dave 763
Scheuermann, Patrick 802
Schiappa, David J 392
Schiavone, Terrance D 749
Schied, Eugene H 769
Schiff, Adam B 33, 302, 331, 398, 400, 451, 489
Schiffer, Lois 708
Schiffman, Todd 822
Schifter, Laura 408
Schiliro, Philip 591
Schiller, Laura 19
Schilling, Linda Beth 714
Schilling, Robert T 92, 303, 336, 395, 396, 397, 402, 403, 438, 439, 489
Schimansky, H. Joseph 791
Schindel, Dennis S 606
Schlagenhauf, Jeff 463
Schlager, Erika B 496
Schlanger, Margo 765
Schlesinger, Steven R 894
Schlicher, Ronald 597
Schlichting, Jim 787
Schlick, Austin 786
Schlickeisen, Derek 221
Schlitt, Lyn M 838
Schloegel, Scott 784
Schlossberg, Edwin 778
Schmaler, Tracy 675
Schmalz, Jill 449
Schmauder, Craig R 638
Schmid, Betsy 344
Schmidt, Fred 711
Schmidt, Jean 206, 307, 333, 395, 396, 418, 419, 440, 441, 442, 489
Schmidt, Kristi A 831
Schmidt, Paul 680
Schmidt, Rebecca L 812
Schmierer, Richard J 602
Schmitt, Austin L 792
Schmitt, Bernard A 465
Schmitt, Glenn R 842
Schmitz, Michelle B 816
Schmucker, Kate 177
Schmutz, Eric 106
Schnedar, Cynthia A 670
Schneider, Charles H 752
Schneider, Dan 388
Schneider, Jacqlyn 340
Schneider, Jon 180
Schneider, Karl F 636
Schneider, Kimberly A 510
Schneider, Matthew 839
Schneider, Susan 661
Schnell, John 694
Schnittger, Dave 455
Schnurr, Lynn 639
Schock, Aaron 93, 303, 334, 424, 447, 448, 464, 495, 489
Schock, Lori J 820
Schoeffling, Kara 58
Schoelen, Mary J 890
Schoenfeld, Elyse 53
Schoenhard, William C 763
Schoepfle, Gregory 720
Schools, Scott N 649
Schoomaker, Eric B 642
Schornagel, Karl W 580
Schothorst, Lauryn 227
Schott, Joseph 628
Schrader, Kurt 221, 308, 335, 395, 396, 438, 439, 490
Schram, Zachary 372
Schramm, Bob 743
Schregardus, D 645
Schreibel, Tom 292
Schritz, Athena 364
Schroeder, Christopher H 673
Schroeder, Jeannine 790
Schroeder, Mary M 850
Schroeder, Rachelle 344, 345
Schroeder, Richard L 720
Schroeder, Robert J 794
Schuchat, Anne 730
Schufreider, Jim 713
Schuh, Martin 383
Schuker, Jill A 919
Schuler, Christopher 199
Schuler, Jack 404
Schulken, Chad 345
Schultheiss, Heidilynne 606
Schultz, Ben 116
Schultz, Karl 771
Schultz, Lisa 390
Schultz, Mary Beth 372
Schultz, Paul 509
Schultz, Rory 696
Schultz, Vicki 652
Schultz, William B 728
Schulz, Hans 907
Schulze, Richard T 501
Schumacher, Joe 275
Schumacher, John H 814
Schumann, W. Christian 725
Schumer, Charles E 179, 306, 323, 324, 351, 352, 363, 364, 374, 375, 377, 383, 464, 473, 502, 503
Schussler, Rebecca 247
Schuster, John 784
Schuyler, Anne R 805
Schwaab, Eric 709
Schwab, Oliver 12
Schwab, Susan C 493
Schwager, Dan 413
Schwalbach, Robert J 299
Schwall, H. Roger 822
Schwartz, Allyson Y 230, 453, 308, 333, 405, 418, 419, 490
Schwartz, Dave 123
Schwartz, David 364
Schwartz, Doug 385
Schwartz, Eric 599
Schwartz, Jamie 206
Schwartz, Jonathan B 596
Schwartz, Mariel 225
Schwartz, Marius 787
Schwartz, Mark 770
Schwartz, Michael 215
Schwartz, Michael S 841
Schwartz, Michelle 168
Schwartz, Ned E 743
Schwartz, Norton A 623
Schwartz, Thomas 804
Schwarz, H. Marshall 774
Schwarzbach, Kirk 417
Schwarzman, Stephen A 799
Schweer, Brad 162
Schweickhardt, Reynold 424
Schweikert, David 11, 301, 336, 414, 415, 490
Schweitzer, Howard 607
Schweizer, Diane 721
Schwelb, Frank E 895
Schwenke, Pamela C 624, 779

Page
Schwietert, Dave 242
Schwing, Franklin "Frank" 588
Scialabba, Lori 770
Sciascia, Anthony 461
Scinto, Blaise 787
Scirica, Anthony J 849
Sclater, Daniel W 619
Scobey, Margaret 601
Scoblic, Peter 367
Scoggins, James A 825
Scoggins, Marcy 150
Scorby, John 645
Scott, Austin 76, 303, 336, 395, 396, 397, 402, 403, 490
Scott, Bizunesh 749
Scott, Brett 412
Scott, Carly 452
Scott, Crystal 718
Scott, David 79, 303, 332, 395, 396, 414, 415, 416, 490, 629
Scott, Don 188
Scott, Doyle 10
Scott, Greg 789
Scott, Jennifer 271
Scott, Jonathan P 825
Scott, Leah 104, 452
Scott, Matt 413
Scott, Nicole 397
Scott, Richard E 915
Scott, Riley 106
Scott, Robert C. "Bobby" 276, 309, 329, 406, 407, 425, 426, 490
Scott, Shawn 139
Scott, Tamla 423
Scott, Tim 238, 308, 336, 434, 490
Scott, Vince 502
Scott, Wanda 758
Scott, William 725
Scovel, Calvin L., III 742
Scovill, Ruth 581
Scovitch, Joseph 364
Scranton, Joseph 644
Scrivner, Ellen 672
Scuse, Michael 691
Seabury, Brittany 254
Sealy, Desa 796
Seaman, Dara 607
Seaman, Thomas 641
Sears, David 694
Sears, Glen 352
Seay, Doug 419
Sebelius, John 690
Sebelius, Kathleen G 585, 727, 799, 843
Sebold, Brian F 347, 348
Sechrist, Amber 105
Seckar, Daryle "Mike" 795
Secor, Kevin S 761
Secrist, Philip M 780
Secundy, Joel 708
Sedgwick, Theodore 602
Sedney, Glenn 906
Seeba, John 794
Seeley, Ken 701
Seeley, Rodrick M 749
Seep, Ralph V 460
Sefcik, Patricia M 707
Sefren, Carol S 893
Segal, Barry 795
Seger, Bruce A 578
Segura, Armando 910
Seidel, Edward 811
Seidel, Heather 823
Seidel, Rebecca 358
Seidel, Richard 711
Seidman, Jayne 824
Seifert, Jennifer 576
Seigel, Benjamin 722
Seiger, Ryan 444
Seiler, David G 714
Seiple, Stephen W 841
Sekaggya, Margaret 932
Sekar, Radha 770
Sekimizu, Koji 928
Selden, Wellington 626
Self, Lawrence N 734
Selib, Jon 158
Seligman, Meyer 149
Sellers, David A 893
Sellmyer, Charlotte 426
Page
Selva, Paul J 618
Selya, Bruce M 849
Semmel, Marsha 807
Semmel, Rachel 12
Semmer, Stephanie 718
Sempolinski, Joe 194
Sena, David 784
Sendak, Katie 404
Sendek, Sara 248
Senger, John 216
Sense, Rick 294
Sensenbrenner, Bob 424
Sensenbrenner, F. James, Jr 292, 310, 327, 425, 426, 435, 436, 490
Sentelle, David Bryan 851
Seoud, Hanna Abou El 340
Sepia, Parveen 701
Sepp, Stephen 400
Sepulveda, Estee 376
Sepulveda, John U 762
Sepulveda-Amor, Bernardo 924
Serchuk, Vance 372
Sere, Andy 288
Serino, Richard 767
Serrano, John 437
Serrano, Jose E 187, 307, 328, 398, 399, 490
Serrano, Marriane 626
Serry, Robert H 931
Serveiss, Victor 912
Servis, Suzanne J 734
Sessions, Jeff 2, 301, 322, 324, 346, 347, 354, 361, 362, 374, 473, 501
Sessions, Justine 369
Sessions, Pete 267, 309, 330, 434, 452, 490
Setliff, Deborah 212
Setmayer, Tara 42
Settle, Alvin L 746
Seum, Jack 60
Sewell, Harry D 901
Sewell, Terri A 6, 301, 336, 395, 396, 397, 435, 436, 490
Sexton, Eugenio 718
Sexton, Pam 92
Seybolt, Kelli 624
Seydi, Cheikh O 935
Seyfert, Mike 340
Seyferth, Allison 360
Seymour, Don 455
Seymour, Lynne 355
Seymour, Stephanie K 850
Sha, Zukang 925
Shaaban, Shaaban M 925
Shaalan, A. Shakour 914
Shack-Marquez, Janice 776
Shackelford, Lindsey 261
Shackelford, Mark 624, 633
Shackelton, Steve 680
Shadegg, Courtney 215
Shafer, Sara 60
Shafernich, Mark 657
Shaffer, Dana 787
Shaffer, Roberta I 581
Shaffer, Russell L 347, 348, 349
Shaffron, Janet 280
Shafik, Nemat 913
Shafroth, Will 680
Shah, Dimple 427
Shah, Khushali 600
Shah, Rajiv 835, 839
Shah, Saurabh 820
Shah, Sonal 592
Shahbaz, Donna 401
Shaheen, Jeanne 166, 306, 322, 325, 346, 347, 359, 360, 366, 367, 378, 473, 496
Shahin, Jessica 696
Shahinian, Dean V 352
Shahmoradi, Heideh 345
Shanahan, Maureen 33
Shand, Tania A 815
Shandor, Anita 607
Shank, Amy 369
Shank, Geoff 677
Shank, Michael 27
Shanks, Margaret M 777
Shannon, Cliff 250
Shannon, Thomas Alfred, Jr 600
Shapiro, Andrew J 598
Shapiro, Angelyn 407

	Page
Shapiro, Arin	389
Shapiro, Howard L	722
Shapiro, Jeff	162
Shapiro, Jessica	461
Shapiro, Jonathan "Jack"	589
Shapiro, Josh	496
Shapiro, Kenneth J	809
Shapiro, Lauren	186
Shapiro, Michael	712
Shapiro, Robert A	725
Shappell, Elizabeth	96
Shappert, Gretchen C	662
Sharfman, Stephen L	820
Sharkey, Jeffry	812
Sharma, Khem	827
Sharon, Adam	35
Sharp, Amy	589
Sharp, Becca	767
Sharp, Jeffrey	430
Sharp, Jeremy	727
Sharp, Josh	453
Sharp, Kristen	14
Sharp, Phillip	692
Sharpe, Steven A	776
Sharpe, Thomas	610
Sharpley, Terri	6
Sharpy, Thomas	629
Shasky, Jennifer	654
Shatfer, Russell L	348, 349
Shattuck, Andrea	376
Shatz, Eileen M	675
Shaub, Walter M., Jr	814
Shaver, Dan	613
Shaw, Aloma A	605
Shaw, Andrew	171
Shaw, Liz	715
Shaw, Steven A	631
Shay, Stephen	610
Shea, Dennis C	500
Shea, James	720
Shea, John	609
Shea, Kelly	401
Shea, Kevin	699
Shea, Paul	818
Sheaffer, Bruce	680
Sheahan, Patrick	375
Shear, David	597
Shearer, David	687
Shearer, Steven	93
Shears, Nikki	788
Sheasby, David	10
Shebest, Philip	785
Shedd, David R	620
Shedd, Dennis W	849
Shedd, Leslie	74
Shedd, Steve	576
Shedd, Steven T	576
Sheehan, Charles	781
Sheehan, Denise	680
Sheehan, Tim	434
Sheehy, Dan	828
Sheehy, Joe	38
Sheehy, Tom	420
Sheely, Deborah	698
Sheenan, Patricia	795
Sheeran, Josette	928
Sheeren, David M	670
Sheets, John	633
Sheets, Nathan	776
Sheetz, Patty	161
Sheffer, Rudy A	631
Sheikh, Patricia R	692
Sheinfeld, Harry L	724
Sheinkman, Joshua	219
Shelat, Nina	254
Shelby, Richard C	2, 301, 323, 324, 341, 342, 343, 351, 377, 382, 473
Shelby, Rinia	140
Sheldon, Mark	91
Sheldon, Robert G	500
Shelkey, Ted	663
Shellabarger, Nan	743
Shelleby, Ed	142
Shelton, James	757
Shelton, Janice	163, 387
Shelton, Lisa	397
Shelton, Stuart L	688
Shenai, Neena	449
Shenkman, Ethan	660
Sheon, Judith W	841
Shepard, Ed	682
Shepard, Robert B	720
Shepherd, Bobby E	850
Shepherd, D	643
Shepherd, Gloria M	745
Shepherd, Leslie	796
Sheppard, David	923
Sheppard, Lesli	820
Sheppo, Michael	672
Sher, Rachel	412
Sherard, Pamela	693
Sheridan, Patricia	796
Sherlock, Lyn D	623
Sherman, Andrew M	576
Sherman, Brad	32, 302, 330, 414, 415, 416, 418, 419, 490, 496
Sherman, Bruce	778
Sherman, Donald	433
Sherman, Lisa	45
Sherman, Max	797
Sherman, Michael A	805
Sherman, Richard W	800
Sherman, Roger	412
Sherman, William R	657
Sherod, Michelle	152
Sheron, Brian W	813
Sherwin, Mark P	815
Shevlin, George Felix, IV	454
Shieh, Michael	632
Shields, Brendan	372
Shields, Joshua	243
Shifrin, Ian	385
Shigekawa, Joan	806
Shih, Stephen T	817
Shiller, Scott	156
Shilling, Abbey	275
Shillman, David	823
Shilts, Rick	779
Shima, Frank J	465
Shimizu, Holly	505
Shimizu, Holly H	583
Shimizu, Mike	724
Shimkus, John	93, 303, 330, 409, 410, 411, 493, 490
Shimoda, Tomoyuki	914
Shin, Jaiwon	800
Shinners, Gary W	809
Shinohara, Naoyuki	913
Shinseki, Eric K	585, 761, 773, 807
Shipman, David R	699
Shipp, Becky	365
Shirven, Michael	505
Shockey, Charles	661
Shoemaker, Sheldon	655
Shoffner, Wilson	507, 639
Shogan, Collen J	582
Shoholm, Jacqui	722
Sholars, Kent	137
Shope, Thomas D	682
Short, Phil	692
Shorter, Malcom	446
Shorts, Dan	407
Shott, Daniel	458
Shoults, Mike	630
Showalter, Thomas	369
Showers, Carole	707
Shpak, Anna	461
Shpiece, William	591
Shrestha, Laura B	582
Shriber, Donald	730
Shriver, Robert H	816
Shroeder, Ted	376
Shrum, Gay	706
Shuart, Amy	449
Shuffield, Jonathan	177
Shuker, Nan R	896
Shuler, Heath	201, 307, 334, 405, 440, 441, 442, 490
Shuler, Sally Goetz	829
Shuler, Stephanie	826
Shuler, Thomas	508
Shulman, Douglas H	611
Shulters, Michael	683
Shultz, George	694
Shultz, Joe	340
Shumaker, Betsy	850
Shumate, Jonah	15
Shunk, Chris	377

Page
Shupe, Brooke 439
Shuren, Jeffrey 732
Shust, Diane 285
Shuster, Bill 228, 308, 331, 402, 404, 440, 442, 443, 490
Shyam-Sunder, Lakshmi 936
Shyam-Sunder, S 714
Shyamsunder, Srividhya 819
Shycoff, Barbara 612
Shyu, Heidi 635
Sibay, Rami 823
Sichel, Daniel E 776
Sickels, Fred 781
Sicker, Douglas 787
Siddiqui, Isi 591
Siddiqui, Maheen 211
Sidney, Arthur D 75
Siegal, James 780
Siegel, Donna L 832
Siegel, Jeff 352
Siegel, Marc 650
Siegel, Michael 446
Siegel, Sharon 30
Siegel, Susan 580
Siegel, Teddy 206
Siegfried, Alan N 906
Siekaniec, Greg 680
Siekaniec, Gregory 680
Siemietkowski, Susan 695
Sienicki, David 404
Sienkiewicz, Marsha 750
Sierra, Cristina 300
Sieving, Paul A 734
Siger, Rick 703
Siggerud, Katherine 575
Sigmon, John 582
Sigmon, Kelly M 841
Sikora, John J 825
Silas, Dora 666
Silberman, Laurence Hirsch 853
Silbernan, Liz Beth 696
Siler, Eugene E., Jr 849
Silkowkski, Eric 633
Silva, Daniel J 837
Silva-Banuelos, Jorge 360
Silver, Jonathan 751
Silver, Mara 376
Silver, Mariko 767
Silverberg, Daniel 420
Silverman, Barry G 850
Silverman, David 457
Silverman, Garrette 105
Silverman, Rachel 340
Silverman, Steve 688
Silverstein, Leonard L 799
Silvey, Patricia W 722
Simermeyer, John W 833
Simioni, Daniela 926
Simko, Stephen J 814
Simler, Jamie L 753
Simler, Jenness 404
Simma, Bruno 924
Simmons, Aketa Marie 115
Simmons, Anne 397
Simmons, Anthony 392
Simmons, Bob 404
Simmons, Carolyn 833
Simmons, Christine J 465
Simmons, Donna 678
Simmons, E. Ronnie 59
Simmons, Robert 182
Simmons, Shayla 684
Simmons, Shelvin 352
Simmons, Wandra 739
Simms, Abby P 809
Simms, Joan 705
Simms, Patrice L 660
Simms, Rob 228
Simms, Vernon 126
Simon, Barry 818
Simon, Bob 360
Simon, David 59
Simon, Donald 581
Simon, Gottlieb 900
Simon, Stephen 921
Simon, William S 774
Simone, Raymond 235
Simonin, Rachel 161
Simonovich, Chelsey 382

Page
Simons, William M 671
Simonson, John 784
Simonton, Kathy 627
Simpkins, Gregory 420
Simpson, Al 240
Simpson, Angela 715
Simpson, Diana 401
Simpson, Don 682
Simpson, Ebony Y 75
Simpson, Jerry 680
Simpson, Kelly 277
Simpson, Kevin 360
Simpson, Kevin M 739
Simpson, Lexi 367
Simpson, Lynn C 616
Simpson, Michael J 714
Simpson, Michael K 83, 303, 331, 398, 399, 400, 405, 490
Simpson, Nick 386
Simpson, Sandy 110
Simpson, Susan 460
Sims, Bill 462
Sims, Ron C 737
Sims, Stanley L 620
Sims, Wanda 787
Sincavage, Justine 599
Sinclair, Don 922
Sinclair, Francine 759
Sinclair, Jill 922
Sinders, Vanessa 127
Singdahlsen, Jeffrey 673
Singh, Anoop 913
Singh, Manisha 367
Singh, Sanjit 10
Singletary, Barvetta 240, 458
Singleton, Gregory 690
Singleton, Norman 258
Siniawsky, Beth 141
Siniscalchi, Kimberly 634
Sinner, Keith 715
Sinnet, Vicki 391
Sipple, Richard L 785
Sires, Albio 175, 306, 333, 418, 419, 440, 442, 490
Sisk, Christinia K 655
Sisk, Susan 505
Sisk, William 796
Sisneros, Alfonso 630
Sisson, Don 434
Sistak, Michael J 347, 348
Sistek, Len 762
Sitterly, Daniel 629
Sivulich, Jay 401
Sixkiller, Mariah 458
Skaggs, Freida 700
Skala, Edward G 416
Skarvelis, Michele K 460
Skelly, Thomas 755, 758
Skibine, George 681
Skidmore, David W 775
Skiles, Kathleen J 412
Skinner, Walter 646
Skinner-Klee, Jorge 918
Skirboll, Lana S 733
Skladany, Jonathan 433
Sklar, Cary P 890
Sklar, Glenn E 830
Skopil, Otto R., Jr 850
Skotnikov, Leonid 924
Skrzycki, Kris 452
Skud, Timothy 611
Skuratowicz, Jerzy 931
Skvarla, Diane K 389, 503
Slade, Ivonia 823
Slaiman, Charlotte 376
Slane, Daniel M 500
Slater, Lee 52
Slater, Lindsay 83
Slater, Rebecca 26
Slater, Rodney E 497
Slates, SueAnn 650
Slattery, Jim 501
Slaughter, Louise McIntosh 193, 307, 328, 434, 490, 496
Slawsky, Toby D 849
Slayton, Cherie 146
Slayton, Lester 756
Sledzik, Paul 811
Slepian, James 213
Slifkin, Rebecca 733

Page

Slifman, Lawrence 776
Sligh, Albert B., Jr 768
Slikker, William 732
Sliter, Karen 700
Sloan, Mary Ann 831
Slobodin, Alan M 411
Sloca, Paul 157
Slockbower, Robert "Bob" 638
Slomianyj, Hanna 605
Sloop, Christine 693
Sloviter, Dolores K 849
Slowikowski, Jeff 672
Slupek, Mark 693
Slusher, Michelle 662
Slutz, Pamela Jo Howell 600
Small, Anne 821
Small, Dawn 727
Small, John 714
Small, Malisah 83
Smallen, David 750
Smallwood, Barry 657
Smar, Larry 223
Smart, Bobby 629
Smart, Christopher 608
Smart, Mike 364
Smeck, Woody 681, 805
Smedile, Cassie 76
Smedile, Jack 358
Smedley, Hank W 743
Smiley, Mitch 412
Smith, Aaron 116
Smith, Adam 286, 309, 330, 402, 490
Smith, Adrian 162, 306, 334, 447, 448, 490
Smith, Amy 171
Smith, Amy B 443
Smith, Andrew 644, 661
Smith, Angela 795
Smith, Anthony 10
Smith, Barry F 809
Smith, Bill 98, 185
Smith, Brad 434
Smith, Bradley T 649
Smith, Bradley W 32
Smith, Brandon 452
Smith, Bryan 452
Smith, Caleb J 416
Smith, Callan 364
Smith, Carlette 787
Smith, Chandler 163
Smith, Charles 375
Smith, Chris L 687
Smith, Christopher H 170, 306, 327, 418, 419, 490, 496, 498
Smith, Cindy J 699
Smith, Cornelius A 917
Smith, D. Brent 710
Smith, D. Brooks 849
Smith, Dana 598
Smith, Daniel 369, 748
Smith, Daniel Bennett 601
Smith, Darrell 623
Smith, David 662
Smith, David A 417
Smith, Debbie 397, 446
Smith, Dell 271
Smith, Diane 120
Smith, Douglas A 767
Smith, Elizabeth Sears 591
Smith, Eric 768
Smith, Faye 397
Smith, Gene 33
Smith, Gentry 599
Smith, George 759
Smith, Greg 690
Smith, Gregory B 595
Smith, Ian 929
Smith, Idalia 613
Smith, Jack 654
Smith, Jacqueline 59, 895
Smith, James B 602
Smith, Jason A 461
Smith, Jean A 815
Smith, Jean Kennedy 798, 799
Smith, Jeffrey 784
Smith, Jennifer 674
Smith, Jerry E 849
Smith, Jessica 274
Smith, Jonathan 138, 652
Smith, Jordan 369
Smith, Jose 639
Smith, Joseph F 738, 740
Smith, Judith 895
Smith, Katherine R 699
Smith, Kathy 715
Smith, Kelsey 115
Smith, Kevin 91, 455, 671, 713
Smith, Kim 426
Smith, Lamar 261, 309, 328, 421, 425, 435, 436, 490
Smith, LaShawnda 344, 345
Smith, Lauri 505
Smith, Lavenski R 850
Smith, Linda 630
Smith, Loren Allan 876
Smith, M. Patricia 724
Smith, MacKenzie 35
Smith, Matthew 375, 401
Smith, Max 743
Smith, Meghan 364
Smith, Melinda K 503
Smith, Michael 681
Smith, Michele 1, 387, 587
Smith, Michelle A 775
Smith, Mike 663
Smith, Milan D., Jr 850
Smith, Monisha 378
Smith, N. Randy 850
Smith, Nickolas 643
Smith, Nicole 422
Smith, Nyasha 897
Smith, Pam 369
Smith, Patricia 718
Smith, Patricia C 465
Smith, Rosanne R 826
Smith, Rosemary C 789
Smith, Russell 708
Smith, Sean 238
Smith, Shannon 367
Smith, Sharon L 639
Smith, Sherrese 785
Smith, Stephanie 577
Smith, Stephen G 785
Smith, Steven 638
Smith, Tanner 157
Smith, Tara 340
Smith, Tiffany 364
Smith, Tonia 382
Smith, Travis 107
Smith, Travis E 347
Smith, Trent 358
Smith, V. Chapman 803
Smith, Virginia 721
Smith, Will 400
Smith, William 354
Smith, William C. "Bill" 697
Smith, Willie 741
Smith-Heimbrock, Sydney 816
Smitham, Tom 597
Smock, David R 837, 838
Smock, Raymond 803
Smolinsky, Frank 626
Smoot, J. Patricia Wilson 677
Smoot, Marvin T., Jr 621
Smullen, Mike 208
Smythe, Austin 405
Sneed, Martha 713
Snelson, William 677
Snider, Casey 430
Snider, Shea 4
Snipes, Michael J 642
Snodgrass, Bill 245
Snodgrass, Michael A 623
Snook, Sheldon L 866
Snow, Andi 424
Snow, Gordon 667
Snowbarger, Vincent 819
Snowe, Olympia J 119, 304, 321, 324, 356, 357, 363, 364, 378, 382, 473
Snyder, Amiee 229
Snyder, Burson 152
Snyder, Charles 423, 597
Snyder, James L 637
Snyder, Jason 755
Snyder, Michelle 731
Snyder, Robert 762
Snyder, Roy 832
Sobeck, Eileen 680

Page

Sobel, Mark ... 608
Sobel, Sylvan A ... 894
Socha, Chris ... 82
Sochaczewsky, Mark ... 830
Socks, Barry S ... 805
Soderstrom, Sharon ... 388
Sokolov, Dahlia ... 437
Sole, Thomas R ... 774
Solem, Rebekah ... 146
Solis, Hilda L ... 585, 717, 807, 819
Sollazzo, Robert A ... 826
Sollberger, Alex ... 407
Solomon, Doreen ... 663
Solomon, Ian H ... 608, 933
Solomon, Jimmie Lee ... 497
Solomon, Lafe E ... 809
Solomon, Michele Klein ... 915
Solomon, Richard H ... 837
Solomon, Steve ... 731
Solomont, Alan D ... 600, 602
Solow, Corey ... 140
Solsby, Jeff ... 433
Solyanyk, Tamara ... 934
Somavia, Juan ... 913, 928
Somers, Jeri ... 796
Somers, Jeri K ... 796
Somers, Zachary ... 427
Somerset, Gary ... 576
Sommers, Dixie ... 719
Sommers, Harry ... 657
Sommers, Jill ... 779
Sommers, Mike ... 455
Somsak, Joyce ... 733
Son, Daniel ... 293
Sondik, Edward J ... 731
Sonenshine, Tara ... 837
Sonfield, Brian ... 606
Song, Victor S.O ... 612
Sonksen, Stephanie ... 209
Sophir, Jayme ... 809
Sorbera, Joseph ... 784
Sorian, Richard ... 728
Sosa, Belkys ... 812
Sosebee, Carl ... 818
Sosin, Daniel M ... 731
Soskin, Ben ... 354
Soto, Ricardo ... 756
Soto, Sandra ... 27
Sotomayor, Larry A ... 673
Sotomayor, Sonia ... 846
Sottolano, Steven M ... 657
Souders, Pat ... 388
Souders, Patrick ... 84
Soults, Joann ... 391
Soumare, Moustapha ... 930
Sours, David ... 78
Souter, David H ... 847
Southerland, Steve, II ... 58, 302, 336, 395, 396, 428, 429, 440, 441, 442, 490
Southwick, Leslie H ... 849
Souvaine, Diane L ... 811
Soven, Joshua H ... 650
Soysal, Rauf Engin ... 930
Sozan, Michael ... 46
Spacy, Brad ... 507, 633
Spadoni, Emily C ... 650
Spaeth, Jennifer ... 733
Spahn, Joanne ... 696
Spahn, Mike ... 281, 384
Spalding, Curt ... 783
Spalding, Drew ... 576
Spangler, C.E ... 648
Spangler, Katy ... 369
Spangler, Todd ... 370
Spaniel, William G ... 775
Sparkman, Gregory V ... 748
Sparkman, John ... 110
Sparks, Lillian ... 730
Sparrow, Mary ... 712
Speakman, V.M., Jr ... 841
Spealman, Jenna ... 405
Spearman, Kenneth A ... 785
Specht, Brittan ... 21
Specht, Jim ... 39
Specht, Matthew ... 12
Speck, Sam ... 912
Spector, Samuel ... 411
Speier, Jackie ... 25, 302, 334, 421, 422, 431, 432, 490

Page

Speight, Eloris ... 690
Spence, Joseph ... 698
Spencer, Alan ... 3
Spencer, Art ... 831
Spencer, Benjamin ... 626
Spencer, Carmen ... 636
Spencer, Garth ... 373
Spencer, Larry O ... 619
Spencer, Nanette Ladell ... 267
Spencer, Peter ... 411
Spencer-Gallucci, Jessica ... 630
Sperling, Gene ... 592
Sperry, Stuart E ... 776
Spicer, Donald A ... 777
Spiegelman, Richard D ... 223
Spiller, Nathaniel I ... 725
Spindel, Megan ... 110
Spinelli, John ... 761
Spinner, James ... 907
Spirgel, Larry ... 822
Spiro, Pete ... 180
Spisak, Tim ... 682
Spitler, Eric J ... 820
Spitzer, Marc ... 752
Spitzer, Max A ... 461
Spitzgo, Rebecca ... 733
Spoehr, Thomas ... 640
Spohn, Jeff ... 790
Spoon, Alan G ... 828
Spooner, Sarah Whittle ... 790
Sporck, Aaron T ... 416
Sporkin, Andrew ... 823
Sporkin, Thomas ... 823
Spoutz, Teri ... 344
Spraggins-Scott, Jody ... 390
Sprague, Brenda ... 598
Sprague, Mary ... 789
Spraker, Lesley ... 631
Spraker, Ronald Y ... 738
Spriggs, Deborah ... 401
Spriggs, William E ... 719
Spring, Margaret ... 708
Springer, Cynthia ... 607
Springer, Mary ... 275
Sprowls, David ... 632
Spruiell, Stephen ... 405
Sprung, Marshall ... 825
Spurlock, Chuck ... 3
Srciven, James Peter ... 935
Staats, Elmer B ... 797
Stabenow, Debbie ... 133, 305, 321, 324, 339, 354, 359, 360, 363, 364, 383, 473
Stack, Mary K ... 762
Stackley, Sean J ... 645
Stafford, Doug ... 109
Stafford, Gaye ... 426
Stafford, Jacquelyn ... 177
Stafford, Larry ... 580
Stagg, J.C.A ... 798
Stahl, Michael ... 782
Stahl, Norman H ... 849
Stahler, Jonathan ... 55
Stahlman, Richard ... 628
Staley, Michael ... 5, 416
Staley, Rick ... 626
Stallbaumer, Kate ... 384
Stallings, Tom ... 58
Stallmer, Steve ... 189
Stallworth, Charles ... 769
Stalnaker, Ryan ... 254
Stamilio, Anthony J ... 637
Stampone, Sonna ... 790
Stan, Michael J ... 776
Stanbro, Gene J ... 788
Stancell, Arnold F ... 811
Stanceu, Timothy C ... 869
Stanchfield, Eric ... 901
Stanislaus, Mathy ... 783
Stanley, Cameron ... 627
Stanley, Clifford L ... 616
Stanley, Elizabeth ... 188
Stanley, Marc G ... 714
Stanley, Marc R ... 837
Stanley, Neil ... 899
Stanski, Anne ... 133
Stanton, Craig ... 755
Stanton, Edgar E ... 636
Stapleton, Walter K ... 849

	Page
Stark, Cate	107
Stark, Deborah	498
Stark, Fortney Pete	25, 302, 327, 447, 448, 490, 807
Stark, Sharon	280
Starks, Ora D	609
Starnes, Albert J	762
Starr, Alexander	786
Starr, Dawn	792
Starr, James "Mike"	821
Starr, Judith	819
Staszak, Chris	433
Statler, Seth	800
Staton, James D	900
Staub, Benjamin	427
Stauch, Julie	103
Staunton, Kathleen	42
Stawick, David	779
Stayman, Al	360
Steacy, Zach	404
Steadman, John M	895
Stearns, Cliff	60, 302, 328, 409, 410, 411, 445, 490
Steckel, Anne	19
Stecklow, Eric	35
Steel, Candida	796
Steel, Cheyenne	433
Steel, Michael	455
Steele, Claude M	811
Steele, Graham	352
Steele, Kelly	503
Steele, Marvin	153
Steere, J. Douglas	859
Stefani, Challee	364
Stefanski, Daniel	10
Steffan, Richard	25
Stegman, Erik	381
Stegner, Peter	82
Stehlik, Noreene C	675
Stehm, Jeff J	776
Stehney, Theodore R	795
Steier, Carly	372
Steiger, Doug	727
Steiger, Jonathan M	794
Steil, Allison	291
Stein, Beth	369
Stein, Ed	420
Stein, Kara	353
Stein, Kathie	781
Stein, Shimmy	455
Stein, Todd	51
Steinbaum, Jason	420
Steinberg, Donald	835
Steinberg, Gary	728
Steinberg, James B	595
Steiner, Achim	927
Steiner, Eric	340
Steingass, Henry	842
Steingasser, Jennifer	805
Steinwald, Nathan	353
Stella, Michael	508
Stelzer, Thomas	925
Stemler, Patty M	654
Stendahl, Howard	631
Stenger, Michael	390
Stenger, Ryan	214
Stenner, Charles E., Jr	633
Stepaniuk, George	826
Stephens, D. Kathleen	601
Stephens, Deborah	711
Stephens, Fred	703
Stephens, Hope	378
Stephens, Mark	787
Stephens, Michael P	739
Stephens, Sarah	255
Stephens-Jones, Linda	627
Stephenson, Beth	405
Stephenson, Mark	433
Stephenson, Robert	691
Sterkx, Craig	461
Sterling, Janice E	577, 579
Sterling, John E	642
Stern, Gary M	802
Stern, James	796
Stern, Keith	434
Stern, Marc I	799
Stern, Warren M	768
Steurer, Robert	109
Stevens, Amanda	264
Stevens, Andrew	292
Stevens, Courtney	344, 345
Stevens, David H	738
Stevens, Elizabeth H	680
Stevens, Gill	91
Stevens, John J	776
Stevens, John Paul	847
Stevens, Justin	373
Stevens, Karen	652
Stevens, Kim	424
Stevens, Kimberly	496
Stevens, Linda	407
Stevens, Patsy	817
Stevens, Roger L	799
Stevens, Sharon	763
Stevenson, Kate	680
Stevenson, Mitchell H	639
Stevenson, Ruth Carter	808
Stevenson, Todd A	780
Steward, Karen	106
Steward, Sarah	174
Stewart, Al	718
Stewart, Angela	588
Stewart, Anne	81
Stewart, Bion	508
Stewart, Bryn	295
Stewart, Carl E	849
Stewart, Charles	357
Stewart, Christopher	138
Stewart, Cody	270
Stewart, David	455
Stewart, Don	388
Stewart, Garry	662
Stewart, Jane	913
Stewart, Jen	455
Stewart, Karen Brevard	601
Stewart, Lawranne	417
Stewart, Malcolm L	650
Stewart, Reginald	345
Stewart, V.R	648
Stewart, Virginia	116
Stewman, Eugene	827
Stickley, Cam	389, 391
Stickling, Lawrence E	715
Stiddard, Jennifer	267
Stiles, Wilbur	116
Still, Christopher D	726
Stiller, Allison	646
Stiller, Kathleen M	781
Stillman, Jacob	821
Stine, Brad	62
Stine, Deborah D	590
Stinnett, Melanie	666
Stinson, Linda	718
Stinson, Terrence	762
Stinson, Terry	265
Stipicevic, John	456
Stirling, Jesse	625
Stirrup, Heidi	412
Stith, Kenneth	734
Stivers, Jonathan	453, 457
Stivers, Steve	213, 307, 336, 414, 415, 416, 490
Stober, Mike	448
Stock, Ann	598
Stock, Troy	271
Stockton, David J	776
Stockton, Paul	616
Stockton, Steve	638
Stockwell, Ed	910
Stockwell, Kerry	455
Stoddard, Alex	405
Stoddard, Andrew	178
Stoddard, Clifford	413
Stofferahn, Scott	203
Stoick, Jordan	243
Stoker, Jennifer L	347
Stokes, Justin	191
Stokes, Michael	645
Stokes, Shawn	900
Stokes, Spencer	269
Stokke, Michael A	785
Stoll, Robert	711
Stombres, Steve	278, 455
Stone, Bradford	735
Stone, Erin E	644
Stone, Jacqueline	711
Stone, John	267, 411
Stone, Mark	785
Stoner, Nancy	783

Page

Stonesifer, Patty 828
Storch, Adam 823
Storella, Mark Charles 603
Storelli, Dominic 424
Storen, Duke 696
Storhaug, Ronald 354
Stormes, Janet 345
Story, Abigail 498
Story, Tod 164
Stottmann, Chris 448
Stout, Jennifer Park 597
Stovel, Daniel 922
Stover, Ashely 463
Stover, Steve 640
Stower, Elizabeth 291
Stowers, Jim 703
Strada, Matthew 820
Stradtman, Terry 832
Strain, Robert 801
Strait, Jill 429
Straka, Joshua 144
Stranch, Jane B 849
Strang, Jo 746
Strange, Kenneth R., Jr 670
Stransky, Michael 385
Strasfeld, Ivan L 721
Strasser, Jacqueline 839
Strasser, Mary 780
Strassler, Heidi W 725
Strassner, Erich 705
Strathdee, Amy 453
Strattner, Mark 581
Straub, Chester J 849
Strauch, Katina 808
Straughn, Pelham 397
Straus, Jessica 456
Strauss-Kahn, Marc Olivier 907
Strautmanis, Michael 593
Strawcutter, Alissa 407
Street, Casey 446
Streeter, Jim 430
Streeter, Pamela 352
Streit, Scott 48
Streitmatter, Marlise 741
Strelsky, Felix 637
Streufert, John 599
Streufert, Randy 835
Strickland, Brenda 57
Strickland, David 748
Strickland, Joe 458
Strickland, Kelle 3, 413
Strickler, Gail 591
Stricklin, Kevin 722
Striebel, Erica 59
String, Marik 367
Stringer, Brooke Hayes 345
Stringfield, LaVerne Y 733
Strobeck, Geoff 444
Strodel, Daniel J 459
Stroia, Matthew 225
Strokoff, Sandra L 460
Strollo, Robert 749
Strom, Cordia A 893
Strom, Leland A 785
Stroman, Ronald A 840
Strong, Jamie 588
Strong, Scott M 503
Strong, Thelma 689
Stroud, John 686
Stroud, Kelsey 373
Stroud, Michael 766
Stroum, Cynthia 601
Stroup, Marsha R 830
Stroup, Rodger E 803
Struckmeyer, Charles S 777
Strunk, Jeff 455
Strupp, Hunter 420
Struss, Rick 634
Strzyz, Karen 712
Stuart, David 381
Stuart, Keri 157
Stubbendieck, Todd 242
Stubblefield, Angela 744
Stubblefield, Larry 637
Stubbs, Laura 616
Stubbs, Linda T 581
Stuber, Laura 372
Stuck, Karen 696

Page

Stucko, Audrey 666
Stucky, Scott W 885
Stueve, Lea 108
Stukes, Bryant 503
Stultz, Jack C 637
Stultz, Jack C., Jr 641
Stuntz, Lori 465
Sturgeon, Lauren 397
Sturgis, Antonio 645
Stutman, Robin 662
Stutzman, Marlin A 97, 303, 335, 395, 396, 397, 405, 445, 491
Stygles, Anne P 890
Styles, Kathleen 705, 756
Su, David 715
Su, Nien 420
Suarez, Julio 921
Suarez-Palomo, Victoria 610
Subbio, Richard 424
Suber, Kellen 1, 587
Subt, Sylvia S.Y 578
Suchorzewski, Artur 139
Suddes, Paul 662
Suddreth, Lucy D 582
Sueppel, Rob 102
Suggs, Sherry 613
Sugiyama, George 362
Suh, Rhea 682
Suhrheinrich, Richard F 849
Suiter, Carrianna 721
Sujoy, Jaime 906
Sukol, Robert M 460
Suleiman, Daniel M 654
Suleman, Younus 85
Sulfab, Elmamoun 388
Sulla, Erin 444
Sullivan, Adam 73
Sullivan, Dwight 427
Sullivan, Emmet G 860
Sullivan, Eugene R 886
Sullivan, Francis E 838
Sullivan, Frederick J 896
Sullivan, Gael 358
Sullivan, Jacob 596
Sullivan, John 215, 307, 331, 409, 410, 411, 491
Sullivan, John F 404
Sullivan, John V 461
Sullivan, Kerry 385
Sullivan, Mark 771
Sullivan, Martin 828
Sullivan, Maura 773
Sullivan, Peter 719, 912
Sullivan, Raymond T 578
Sullivan, Regina 842
Sullivan, Russ 364
Sullivan, Tom 142
Suma, Christopher J 777
Sumar, Fatema 367
Sumberg, Jeffrey E 815
Summer, Barry 822
Summers, Robert 834
Summitt, Monica 749
Sumwalt, Robert L., III 811
Sun, Tammy 787
Sunshine, Robert A 575
Sunstein, Cass 590
Super, Tony 389
Surber, Keith 739
Suresh, Subra 807, 810
Surgeon, Bina 457
Surian, Guy 641
Suro-Bredie, Carmen 591
Suruma, Askia 449
Susalla, Michael P 462
Susman, Louis B 603
Sussman, Ron 712
Sutcliffe, Ronald 661
Suter, William K 848
Sutey, William K 347, 348, 349
Sutherland, Ellen J 461
Sutherland, Paige 107
Sutherland, Peter 932
Sutley, Nancy 588
Sutter, Brian 449
Sutton, Betty 212, 307, 334, 402, 403, 428, 429, 491
Sutton, Clay 453
Sutton, David 671
Sutton, Goodloe 344

	Page
Sutton, Jeffrey S	849
Sutton, Peter A	791
Sutton, William T	465
Svec, Kim	692
Svinicki, Kristine L	812
Swain, Carol M	807
Swain, Emily	645
Swain, Jonathan	827
Swain, Robert W	725
Swan, James Christopher	601
Swank, C. William	840
Swann, Gail	724
Swann, Lanier	388
Swanson, Bret	390
Swanson, Daniel	376
Swanson, Dayna	158
Swanson, Laura	352
Swanson, Randy	218
Swarthout, Luke	369
Swartz, Bruce C	654
Swartz, Paul O	834
Swartzfager, Philip	5
Swayze, Rich	358
Sweatt, Loren	407
Sweeney, Conor	405
Sweeney, John	183
Sweeney, Margaret M	875
Sweeney, Thomas W	733
Sweet, Phoebe	383, 387
Sweetin, Jeffrey	655
Swenson, Rick	685
Swenson, Sharmila K	282
Swenson, Sue	759
Swietlik, Dariusz	698
Swift, Afton	283
Swindell, Edgar	728
Swindler, Jo Anne	823
Swinehard, Riley	370
Swinehart, Sarah	448
Swing, William Lacy	915
Swinton, Maurice	775
Swintz, Monica	27
Swislocki, Allie	502
Sy, Christian	70
Sybenga, Kata	373
Syed, Khizer	452
Sykes, Angela	711
Sykes, Diane S	849
Symington, James W	501, 842
Symington, W. Stuart	602
Symonds, Candra S	677
Synnes, Mark	461
Sypolt, Jennifer	86
Syrjamaki, Josh	143
Szabat, Joel	742
Szabo, Joseph C	746
Szabo, Sue	757
Szewczyk, Kari	508
Szubin, Adam J	609
Szwec, Peter	461
Szykman, Simon	704, 713

T

	Page
Ta, Minh	145
Tabak, Lawrence	734
Tabb, Winston	808
Taber, Carrie	833
Tablante, Nancy	911
Tabler, Diana G	347, 348, 350
Tabor, Peter	693
Taborn, Michael	842
Tadeo, Michael	116
Taets, Jon	172
Tafara, Ethiopis	824
Taffet, Clifford	737
Taggart, Bill	757
Taglialatela, Linda	599
Tagmire, Fran	169
Taha, Hassan A	934
Tahirkheli, Sylvia	460
Taitano, D	645
Takai, Teri	617
Takamura, Yasuo	934
Talamona, Gina M	675
Talat, Javed	934
Talbert, Jessica	209
Talbot, Dave	711
Taliaferro, Jennabeth	261
Talisman, Mark E	837
Talkin, Pamela	848
Talledo, Maria Isabel	910
Tallman, Richard C	850
Tallmer, Matthew	433
Talverdian, Laura	367
Tamakloe, Julia Mankata	718
Tamarkin, Eric	373
Tamber, Kimberly A	393
Tamburrino, Pat	616
Tamerjan, Annabelle	463
Tan, Erwin	780
Tanaka, Brian	508, 644
Tandoh, Thierry	935
Tandy, Carolyn	111
Tangherlini, Dan	610
Tani, Diana	825
Tanigushi, Kazu	933
Tanis, Leonard J	776
Tanner, Betty Ann	497, 498
Tanner, Gordon O	631
Tanner, Robert	362
Tanner, Troy	786
Tanonaka, Rod	81
Tansey, Charles	784
Tantillo, Andy	193
Tao, Josephine	823
Tao, Leonard	753
Tapia, Loida	388
Tarasevich, Deborah	823
Tarasov, Gennady P	931
Taraszka, Carol S	670
Tardiff, Kristine	661
Tarek, Shams	181
Tarr, Jen	372
Tartar, Robert	744
Tarullo, Daniel K	775
Tasby, Marvin	507
Tashima, A. Wallace	850
Tassell, Van	19
Tate, Christopher	413
Tate, Clyde J., II	639
Tate, Katharine	123
Tate, Morris	686
Tateishi, Peter	21
Tatel, David S	852
Tatel, Jennifer	786
Tatz, Nicole	377
Tauscher, Ellen	597
Tausend, Stephen	376
Tavana, John	675
Tavenner, Marilyn	731
Tawadrous, Armia	697
Taxay, Michael	674
Taylor, Aaron	365, 624
Taylor, Brooks	599
Taylor, Craig	712
Taylor, Dan	375, 413
Taylor, David	825
Taylor, Deborah	732
Taylor, Elizabeth G	650
Taylor, Houston W	796
Taylor, Ione	683
Taylor, James	720, 725
Taylor, Jarris L., Jr	628
Taylor, Jennifer	4
Taylor, Kenneth	680
Taylor, Mary Elizabeth	392
Taylor, Mary Ellen	790
Taylor, Meg	935
Taylor, Michael	254, 624
Taylor, Miles	401
Taylor, Mona	218
Taylor, Paul	427
Taylor, Rachael	344
Taylor, Rachel Bauer	107
Taylor, Robert	606
Taylor, Robert S	615, 620
Taylor, Ryan	296
Taylor, Samuel	818
Taylor, Scott	756
Taylor, Teddy Bernard	602, 603
Taylor, Todd	507
Taylor, William White	725
Taylor, Zachery	729
Taylor-Mackey, Sylvia	509
Tchen, Tina	592

Page

Teachout, Terry 806
Teague, Cornell 401
Teague, John Abe 245
Teague, Larry 907
Teague, Michael 14
Tebbetts, Christine D 833
Tecklenburg, Michael 457
Teel, Alexander H 416
Teel, S. Martin, Jr 866
Tefft, John F 603
Teichman, Kevin 782
Teitelbaum, Donald Gene 601
Teitz, Alexandra 412
Teitz, Jeffrey J 590
Teixeira, Joseph 744
Tekleberhan, Karen 720
Temin, Jonathan H 838
Temmeyer, Hubert 914
Temple, Courtney 165
Temple, Merdith "Bo" 638
Templeman, Edward M 893
Tenenbaum, Inez 780
Tennyson, Stephanie 766
Tenorio, Mike 299
Tenpenny, Chad 105
Terr, Paul 401
Terry, Adam 116
Terry, Anne 372
Terry, Clyde 805
Terry, John A 895
Terry, Lee 161, 306, 331, 409, 410, 411, 491
Teschler, Lisa 10
Teskey, Mark 632
Tess, David 821
Tessieri, Jeanne 391
Tester, Jon 158, 305, 321, 325, 341, 342, 343, 351, 371, 372, 379, 381, 474
Teti, Catherine 576
Teti, Dennis 405
Tetreault, Suzanne 786
Tettlebaum, Harvey M 798
Tevlin, Stacey M 776
Tewelde, Yodit 284
Tezak, Joseph E 769
Thacker, Darin 20
Thacker, Jeff 16
Thacker, Stephen B 731
Thacker, Thomas 199
Thames, Beth 205
Tharpe, Amanda 430
Theirault, Ray J 816
Theodore-Gandi, Bernadette 921
Thernstrom, Abigail 835
Thessin, James 596
Thessin, Jonathan 299
Thibault, Guy 905
Thieman, Karla 340
Thiemann, Robyn 674
Thieme, Michael T 705
Thiessen, Pam 205
Thigpen, Allison 73
Thigpen, Morris L., Sr 669
Thirolf, Eugene M 651
Thomas, Annette 662
Thomas, Benjamin 407
Thomas, Bits 136
Thomas, Brad 407
Thomas, Brian 263
Thomas, Burt 768
Thomas, Cecelia 433
Thomas, Charles J 722
Thomas, Charles P 776
Thomas, Chelsea 364
Thomas, Clarence 845
Thomas, Connie 496
Thomas, Constance 424
Thomas, Ginger 577
Thomas, Harry K., Jr 602
Thomas, Harry, Jr 897
Thomas, Hill 78
Thomas, James 412, 610
Thomas, John 276
Thomas, Joseph 375
Thomas, Lisa 763
Thomas, Marcus C 667
Thomas, Marilyn 625
Thomas, Mark C 657
Thomas, Ronald Dale 458

Page

Thomas, Shelley 300
Thomas, Sidney R 850
Thomas, Sterling 506
Thomas, Trevor 905
Thomas, Vinod 933, 935
Thomas, John M., III 835
Thomas-Greenfield, Linda 601
Thomasson, Kelly 274
Thomasson, Russ 250, 376
Thomasson, Scott 666
Thompson, Alan S 620
Thompson, Anthony 697
Thompson, Bennie G 149, 305, 329, 421, 491
Thompson, Burdett K 635
Thompson, Candice 691
Thompson, Carol J 627
Thompson, Chris 18
Thompson, Christen 295
Thompson, Dean 456
Thompson, Diane 781
Thompson, Dionne 683
Thompson, Gerald 389
Thompson, Glenn 226, 308, 335, 395, 396, 397, 406, 407, 428, 491
Thompson, Jake 160
Thompson, Jarrod 358
Thompson, Jeffrey L 497
Thompson, Jill Long 785
Thompson, John "Jack" 761
Thompson, John M 899
Thompson, Joy G 826
Thompson, Keesha 653
Thompson, Laura 915
Thompson, Lee 636
Thompson, Marcia 507, 577
Thompson, Margrette 588
Thompson, Marie 199
Thompson, Melissa 58
Thompson, Mike 19, 301, 331, 447, 448, 451, 491
Thompson, Mischa E 496
Thompson, Monica 460
Thompson, O. Rogeriee 849
Thompson, Paul 508
Thompson, Phyllis D 895
Thompson, Robin 690
Thompson, Ryan 254
Thompson, Sally 699
Thompson, Sarah 375
Thompson, Scott 644
Thompson, Sherry 830
Thompson, Stacey 719
Thompson, Stephen J 714
Thompson, Terrence 384
Thompson, Tony 779
Thompson, Whitney 264
Thompson, William W., II 725
Thomsen, James 646
Thomson, Jeri 497
Thomson, Kristin 30, 456
Thomson, Richard G 397
Thornberry, Mac 257, 309, 329, 402, 403, 451, 491
Thorne, David H 601, 602
Thorne, Dray 408
Thornton, Janey 695
Thornton, Julia 225
Thornton, Matthew 235
Thornton, Michael B 879
Thornton, Rebecca 281
Thornton, Ruth N 627
Thornton, Steven 39
Thornton, Tracey 73
Thorpe, Amanda Rogers 452
Thorsen, Anne 455
Thorsen, Kim 682
Thorson, Eric 606
Thorson, Robyn 680
Thorton, Sean 606
Thrasher, Ellen 827
Threatt, Adrianne G 417
Thummalapally, Vinai 600
Thune, John 242, 308, 323, 325, 339, 340, 354, 356, 357, 363, 364, 385, 474
Thunell, Lars 935
Thurgood, Neil 635
Thurmond, A. Jacy 832
Thurmond, Ashling 49
Tiano, Melanie 357
Tibbetts, Sally 64

	Page
Tiberi, Patrick J	211, 307, 331, 447, 448, 491, 806
Tickner, Thomas J	636
Tidd, Mark	646
Tidwell, Daniel	4
Tidwell, Thomas	689
Tierney, Helen	762
Tierney, James	650
Tierney, James M	834
Tierney, John F	130, 305, 330, 406, 407, 431, 432, 491
Tighe, Bill	228
Tighe, David	850
Tighe, Kathleen	758
Tignor, Robert S	896
Tillery, George	672
Tillett, Barbara	581
Tilman, Justin	802
Tilton, Fred	745
Timberlake, Courtney	590
Timmons, Debra	818
Timoney, Sarah	163
Tinch, Greg	211
Tindall, Anne	412
Tinder, John Daniel	849
Tingle, Carlos	509
Tingle, Carlos E	815
Tinley, Bonita	787
Tinsley, Dan	392
Tinsley, Donna	634
Tinsley, Kenneth	784
Tinsley, Mary	157
Tippens, Julie	81
Tippins, Teresa	795
Tippit, Sarah	41
Tipton, Nathaniel	266
Tipton, Scott R	47, 302, 336, 395, 396, 428, 429, 438, 439, 491
Tisdale, Nicole	423
Tison, Donald	640
Tisor, Darrell J	746
Titley, David	646
Titov, Dimitry	925
Tittel, Margaret J	829
Tiwari, Siddharth	913, 914
Tjoflat, Gerald Bard	850
Tobey, William	790
Tobias, Constance	727
Tochen, David	811
Tocknell, Emily	375
Todd, Dan	365
Todd, Dustin	189
Todd, Elizabeth	723
Todd, Nora	120
Todd, Susan Harley	582
Todman, Adrianne	901
Toigo, Theresa A	732
Tokarski, Kevin M	747
Tolar, Helen	446
Toles, Johnny	691
Tolhurst, Kimberly	836
Tollefson, Chris	680
Tolleson, Jesse D., Jr	404
Tolliver, Candice	745
Tom, Philip	722
Tom, Willard K	793
Toma, Kathleen	465
Toman, Cara	225
Tomberlin, Mike	146
Tombs-Souvey, Barbara	901
Tomchick, George	738
Tomcsi, Jason	99
Tomero, Leonor	404
Tomich, Martha	854
Tomlinson, Tony	674
Tomney, Brian	649
Tompkins, Hilary C	684
Tomsheck, James F	769
Toner, Dennis J	840
Toner, Mark	598
Toney, Rubie J	834
Tonko, Paul D	189, 307, 335, 405, 435, 436, 491
Tonneau, Michel	915
Tonsager, Dallas	693
Tooke, Tony	689
Toole, Joseph S	745
Toomey, Kathleen	731
Toomey, Patrick J	223, 308, 323, 325, 351, 352, 354, 356, 357, 463, 474, 494, 466
Toothman, Stephanie	680
Topper, David	461
Toppings, Christopher	370
Tornblom, Claudia L	636
Tornquist, David	742
Torrealba, Carlos Alberto Rodriguez	906
Torres, Carlos	818
Torres, Christine	819
Torres, Julie	666
Torres, Luis	259
Torres, Orfa	446
Torres, Rafael	762, 763
Torres, Ronald	906
Torres, Ruth	657
Torres, Salomon	258
Torres, Sophie	261
Torres, Tim	412
Torres, Zoraida	389
Torres-Gil, Fernando	805
Torres-Rivera, Sahra	720
Torruella, Juan R	849
Toruno, Tiguel	413
Toscano, Richard	672
Toscas, George	674
Toskey, Katie	134
Toth, Charlie	617
Toulou, Tracy	663
Toure, Hamadoun	928
Touret, Anne Cindy	934
Touton, Camille Calimlim	430
Towers, Jon	446
Towhey, Jessica	208
Towns, Edolphus	184, 306, 409, 410, 411, 431, 491
Townsend, Christi	254
Townsend, Terry P	912
Towse, Linda	293
Tozer, Theodore W	738
Trabucco, Thomas J	793
Tracy, John	272
Tracy, Ryan	94
Trainor, Timothy	705
Tramposch, Albert	712
Tran, Dat	762
Tran, Luyen	608
Tran, Lynn	382
Tran, Oanh	778
Tranghese, William	128
Tranter, Scott	92
Trantin, John	463
Trasvina, John	737
Tratos, Mark S	389
Traub, Jon	448
Trautman, Tracey	672
Travieso, Amy	265
Travis, Thomas W	634
Traxler, William B., Jr	849
Traynham, Vella M	792
Traynor, Daniel	835
Treacy, William F	775
Treat, James B	705
Treat, Kim B	607
Trebat, Gabrielle	610
Treffers, Rudolf	934
Tregoning, Harriet	805, 900
Treichel, Mark	806
Tremblay, Carlene	120
Tremols, Joaquin	694
Trenkle, Tony	732
Trentacoste, Michael F	745
Trepanier, Pierre	912
Trevathan, Edwin	731
Trevillian, Carr, IV	654
Trevino, Tammye	694
Triay, Ines	751
Triba, Robert J	831
Tribiano, Jeffery	695
Triebsch, George F	682
Trigg, Brent	465
Trilling, Jim	357
Trimble, Cameron	267
Trimble, Jeffrey	778
Trimble, Kim	417
Trimble, Theresa A	777
Trindade, Antonio A. Cancado	924
Trinh, Eugene	802
Trivedi, Atman	367
Troast, Marc	41
Troha-Thompson, Tess	193
Trolan, W. Lee	462

Page

Trolio, Robert R. Di 884
Troller, Katharine 60, 434
Tronti, Zach 444
Tross, Sherry 919
Trott, Stephen S 850
Trottenberg, Polly 742
Troupe, Al 577
Trouville, Mark 657
Trowell-Harris, Irene 761
Troy, William J 635
Trudel, Karen 731
Truding, Bradley 298
Trujillo, Tara 46
Trupo, Mary 707
Trushel, Timothy D 460
Tryon, R.T 648
Tryon, Ralph W 776
Tryon, Warren 416
Trzeciak, Adam R 792
Tsang, Katherine 841
Tsitsiragos, Dimitris 935
Tso, Roselyn 733
Tsongas, Niki 129, 305, 334, 402, 403, 404, 428, 429, 491, 493
Tsoucalas, Nicholas 870
Tsukagoshi, Yasusuke 907
Tubbs, John 683
Tuccillo, Robert 747
Tuccio, Patricia E 893
Tuceling, Barbara 828
Tuchband, Matthew 606
Tuck, Chris 392
Tucker, Benjamin B 590
Tucker, Beth 612
Tucker, Daniel A 762
Tucker, David 446
Tucker, Sara 360
Tucker, Sharon "Nyota" 797
Tudor, Chris 21
Tudor, Robert 781
Tuell, Austin 456
Tuell, Loretta A 381
Tufts, Jackson 197
Tuggle, Benjamin 680
Tuggle, Gary 655
Tulino, Douglas A 841
Tully, Matthew 12
Tully, Pat 214
Tulou, Christophe A. G 898
Tuluy, Hasan A 933
Tuminaro, Steven J 812
Tune, Debra K 626
Turbitt, Noelle 433
Turbyfill, Brian 423
Turco, Kathleen 795
Turk, David 596
Turk, Rod W 713
Turkstra, Matthew 188
Turley, Sheldon O., Jr 725
Turman, Richard 728
Turnbow, Gerry 639
Turnbull, Michael G 505
Turner, Christine 692
Turner, Curtis 718, 722
Turner, Fred L 496
Turner, James 708
Turner, Jeffrey 579
Turner, Joanna 742
Turner, Johnny 5
Turner, Lee 116
Turner, Lesley 401
Turner, Linda D 896
Turner, Marella 720
Turner, Michael R 206, 307, 332, 402, 403, 404, 431, 432, 491, 495
Turner, Reginald 895
Turner, Robert L 183, 306, 336, 418, 421, 445, 491
Turner, Roslyne 375
Turpenoff, Mike 757
Turteski, Vicki 730
Turunen, Antti 931
Turzak, Robert J 640
Tuss, Taryn 588
Tuten, Bill 237
Tuttle, Melissa 404
Tutton, Adria 246
Tweedie, Andrew 913
Twiford, Pamela 859
Twinchek, Michael S 423
Twose, Nigel 935
Tyler, Amanda 264
Tyler, Michael 373
Tyler, Millie 656
Tyler, Peter 373
Tyler, Ralph 728, 732
Tyllas, Micael A 797
Tyllas, Michael 727
Tyminski, Larry 709
Tymkovich, Timothy M 850
Tymon, Jim 444
Tyrangiel, Elana 674
Tyree, Jennifer L 80
Tyrer, Trina Driessnack 372
Tyson, Rosalind R 825
Tzamaras, Takis 505

U

Uccellini, Louis W 710
Udall, Mark 46, 302, 322, 325, 346, 347, 359, 382, 474
Udall, Tom 176, 306, 322, 325, 356, 357, 361, 362, 366, 367, 377, 381, 464, 474, 495, 496
Uddyback-Fortson, Leni 723
Udochi, Frederick 812
Uehlecke, Nick 449
Ueng, Stephanie 457
Ugast, Fred B 896
Uhart, Michael 710
Ulrich, Linda 424
Ulrich, Tom 434
Umar, El-Farouk 818
Umhofer, Betsy 30
Unangst, Owen 687
Underhill, Robert 652
Underwood, Dale 610
Ungerecht, Todd 429
Ungson, Justin 463
Unnevehr, Laurian 699
Unruh, Chip 235
Upchurch, Dan 698
Updegrove, Mark 804
Updike, Randall 683
Upshur, Terry 460
Upton, Fred 136, 305, 328, 409, 466, 491
Upton, Marianne 344
Urban, Heather 679
Urbanas, Beth 608
Urbancic, Frank Charles, Jr 601
Urbina, Ricardo M 865
Urey, Richard 164
Uriarte, Carlos 433
Urias, Bryan 35
Uribe, Roberto Prieto 907
Urquhart, Celia 237
Urrutia, Joanne 757
Urs, Krishna 597
Usowski, Kurt G 738
Utoikamanu, Fekitamoeloa 922
Utsey, Alexandra 367
Utz, Sharon Meredith 433
Uyeda, Mark T 822
Uzzell, Megan 719

V

Vaccaro, Matt 430
Vaccaro, Michael 706
Vadas, Gregory 786
Vadehra, Emma 758
Vahey, Megan 805
Vaiana, Jerome A 739
Vail, Jeff 690
Vail, Kenneth H 688
Vajjhala, Shalini 782
Valcour, Doug 785
Valdes, Vincent 747
Valdez, Margarita 265
Valdez, Mary Lou 732
Valdez, William 751
Valdivia, Juan 907
Valencia, Pete 178
Valencia-Weber, Gloria 799
Valent, Joseph 448
Valentine, Julia 749
Valentine, Ricky 692
Valentine, Tara 630

Page

Valenzuela, Arturo 597
Valenzuela, Elvin 379
Valera, Giselle E 841
Valiulis, Henry M 841
Valivullah, Michael 699
Valladares, Marisela 71
Valle, Stephanie 189
Van Antwerp, Robert L 638
Van Buren, David M 624
Van Camp, Anne 829
Van der Heide, Jennifer 27
van der Meensbrugghe, Emmanuel 914
van der Reyden, Dianne 581
Van Diepen, Louise R 764
Van Doren, Terry 161
Van Dusen, Michael 843
van Dyck, Peter C 733
Van Flein, Tom 10
Van Gilst, Mark 627
Van Hollen, Chris 126, 304, 332, 405, 466, 491
van Hook, Brian 378
Van Hove, Jeffrey 611
Van Hovel, Brian 10
Van Mark, Ruth 362
Van Meter, Gary K 785
Van Opdorp, Harold 508
Van Patton, Matthew 239
Van Rest, Judy 837
van Santen, John 577
Van Scoyoc, Ed 430
Van Stavern, Thomas N 788
Van Steenburg, John 745
van Sweringen, Bryan T 639
Van Trotsenburg, Axel 933
Van Woerkom, Greg 134
VanAntwerpen, Franklin S 849
Vanaskie, Thomas I 849
Vance, June 576
Vance, Sarah 427
Vance-Cooks, Davita 576, 577
Vandenberg, Patricia 763
Vanderbrink, Keith M 713
Vanderslice, Jeff 42
Vanderveen, Ben 135
VanderWolk, Jeff 364
Vandiver, Edgar 640
Vandivier, David P 609
Vanek, Michelle 461
Vanison, Denise 770
VanLaak, James E 745
Vanlandingham, Andrew 345
VanMeter, Rick 111
Vansant, Goldey 458
Vanze, Stephen 778
Vaquerano, Omar 905
Varallo, Danielle 167
Vargas, David A 738
Vargas, George 689
Vargason, James 675
Varhegyi, Wendy 633
Varnado, Martina 732
Varnasidis, Sophia 429
Varney, Christine A 650
Varnhagen, Michele 407
Varnon, Winona H 756
Vasilescu, Alex 826
Vasquez, Asdrubal 908
Vasquez, Juan F 878
Vasquez-Gardner, Juanita 797
Vassallo, John P 632
Vassallo, Karen 777
Vassar, Banyon 427
Vassar, Bobby 427
Vaughan, Beverly 708
Vaughan, Heather 397
Vaughn, Brenda 718
Vaughn, Richard 246
Vavonese, Dan 712
Vavrichek, Bruce 575
Vaynberg, Yelena 143
Veach, Julie 786
Veatch, Dawn 743
Veatch, John E 461
Veazey, Autumn 340
Veenis, Suzanne 243
Vega, Sandra 726
Veghte, Ben 171
Vegliante, Anthony J 840

Page

Veiga, Leslie 71
Veitch, Alexandra 457
Veklich, Maria 345
Vela, David 681
Velasco, Bryslie Siomara Cifuentes 909
Velasco, Robert 729
Velasco, Robert, II 780
Velasquez, Gustavo F 900
Velazquez, Nydia M 185, 306, 329, 414, 415, 416, 438, 491
Velez, Angelique 299
Vellutini, Roberto 906
Venegas, Stephanie 34
Vengrin, Joseph 729
Venlet, David 616
Venture, Veronica 667
Venturella, David 769
Veoni, Dan 444
Vera, Hernan D 834
Vera, Linda A 815
Vera, Mauricio 835
Verble, Sedelta 815
Vercellone, James J 612
Verde, Juan 707
Verderosa, Matthew 511
Verdino, Carlo 826
Verdugo, Georgina 728
Verett, Whitney 4
Verges, Teresa 826
Vergilio, Joseph 796
Verma, Richard R 596
Vermillion, Stephen 71
Verner, Doug 805
Vernon, Kathryn 744
Vernon, LaMont R 577
Verrill, Ted 15
Verrilli, Donald 593
Vershbow, Alexander 496
Vershbow, Alexander R 617
Vertman, Jedd 708
Verville, Elizabeth 597
Vest, Charles 810
Vest, Teresa 426
Vetter, Darci 691
Vevurka, Austin 35
Veysey, John 86
Via, Dennis 641
Via, Dennis L 619
Vician, Todd 633
Vick, Jane 388
Vickers, Kate 72
Vickers, Lisa A 602
Vickers, Michael G 617
Vickery, Colin 401
Vickery, Hugh 679
Victor, Alexandra 179
Victor, Kyle 21
Victoria, Diego 920
Vidal, Lindsay 412
Vidulovic, Irena 68
Vieira, Donald 674
Viera, Denise 673
Vieson, Chris 455
Vietti-Cook, Annette L 812
Villa, Rick 461
Villabroza, Allan 839
Villalobos, Veronica E 817
Villano, David 694
Villano, Peter 404
Villarreal, Alejandra 404
Villarreal, Alicia 721
Villasenor, Cielo 439
Villegas, Dan 662
Vilsack, Thomas J 500, 585, 685, 773
Vina, Stephen 423
Vinals, Jose 913
Vincent, Al 715
Vincent, Erin 281
Vincent, Jane C.W 740
Vincent, O. Kevin 748
Vincent, Peter S 769
Vincent, Trudy 176
Vincus, Thomas E 825
Vines, Larry P 578
Vineyard, Holly 707
Vinik, Grant R 393
Vinovich, Paul 377
Vint, Norbert E 816

Page
Vinyard, Ashlee 262
Virgilio, Carla 191
Virgilio, Martin J 813
Virkstis, Matthew 375
Virmani, Arvind 914
Visclosky, Peter J 96, 303, 328, 398, 399, 491
Vish, Ravi 936
Vishnu, Dhanpaul 934
Vita, Susan H 581
Vitrano, Frank 705
Vitter, David 114, 304, 323, 325, 346, 347, 351, 352, 361, 362, 378, 474
Vitulano, Steven 826
Vizcarrondo, Rosemarie ''Mai'' 300
Vlacich, Mike 166
Vladeck, David 793
Vlasaty, Andrew 340
Vlcek, Thomas 712
Vocino, John 373
Vogel, Miriam 649
Vogel, Paul 841
Vogel, Randy 159
Vogel, Robert 842
Vogelphol, Carl 15
Vogt, Kaitlin 413
Vogt, Margaret 929
Vogt, Ralf S 639
Vogtsberger, Lindsay 213
Volante, Monica 232
Volberding, Emily 461
Volk, Lisa 697
Volkow, Nora D 734
Vollor, Valera 376
von Amsberg, Joachim 933
von der Schulenburg, Michael 930
von Friedeburg, Stephanie 935
Von Heeringen, Mark 635
von Kleist, Ruediger 934
Von Wald, Conrad 632
Vorpagel, Tyler 293
Voss, Barbara 804
Vought, Mary 290
Vowell, John Scott 6
Vratil, Kathryn H 891
Vreeburg, Jake 422
Vu, Vanessa 782
Vu, Victor T 694

W

Wachtel, Jonathan 508
Wachter, Eric 782
Wada, Debra S 404
Waddell, Tina M 831
Wade, Alice H 830
Wade, Anne-Berry 683
Wade, David 127
Wade, Rick 703
Wade, Tonji 797
Wadhwa, Sanjay 826
Waechter, Joseph M 841
Wagener, Sharon 44
Wagley, Doris 148
Wagner, Anne M 838
Wagner, Annice M 895
Wagner, Caryn A 766
Wagner, Chris 612
Wagner, Christine 404
Wagner, Curtis L., Jr 752
Wagner, Dennis 731
Wagner, Fred 745
Wagner, Gregory 722
Wagner, John F., Jr 460
Wagner, Mary 689
Wahlstrom, Margareta 931
Wahowiak, Marlene 675
Waidelich, Walter 745
Wailes, Diana E 502
Wainio, Kathleen 692
Wainman, Barbara 683
Wakabayashi, Ronald 654
Wakefield, Mary K 732
Walberg, Tim 137, 305, 335, 406, 407, 421, 422, 431, 432, 491
Walcoff, Michael 763
Wald, Mike 723
Walden, Greg 220, 308, 331, 409, 410, 491
Walden, Randall 624

Page
Walden, Shae 73
Waldo, Eric 755
Waldock, Andrea 229
Waldon, Samuel 823
Waldow, Eric 510
Waldrip, Brian 61
Waldron, Marcia M 849
Waldron, Sue 681
Waldrop, Elaine 509
Walgren, Chip 344
Wali, Sahar 588
Walk, Linda 832
Walker, Al 628
Walker, Antoine 449
Walker, Barbara 673
Walker, Beau 16
Walker, Don 245
Walker, Dustin 404
Walker, Eddie 433
Walker, Edwin L 730
Walker, Frank 434
Walker, John 267
Walker, John M., Jr 849
Walker, Kevin M 674
Walker, LaShonda 819
Walker, Leslie 922
Walker, Linda L 412
Walker, Mark 98, 420
Walker, Mary Oates 899
Walker, Matthew 378
Walker, Mindi 439
Walker, N. Malik 815
Walker, Ryan 208
Walker, Sally 461
Walker, Steve 392
Walker, Steven 624
Walker, Wanda 711
Walker, William M 902
Walkinshaw, James 280
Walkoviak, Larry 683
Wall, Anne 388
Wall, Debra S 802
Wall, Erin 32
Wall, Sharon A 796
Wall, Steven 148
Wallace, Christopher M 815
Wallace, Gordon T 635
Wallace, J. Clifford 850
Wallace, Jane M 507
Wallace, Joe 424
Wallace, Kevin 507
Wallace, Kim N 609
Wallace, Mark E 706
Wallace, Roy 640
Wallace, Sondra Steigen 728
Wallace, Will 412
Wallach, Evan J 868
Wallen, Matthew T 750
Walles, Jacob 597
Wallner, James 223
Wallner, Judith 384
Wallner, Kimberly 237
Walls, Tom 274
Walsh, Bonnie 89
Walsh, Brian 385
Walsh, David 433
Walsh, Dennis 790
Walsh, Helene 784
Walsh, Jennifer 28
Walsh, Joe 88, 303, 336, 421, 422, 431, 432, 438, 439, 491
Walsh, John 611, 789
Walsh, Richard F 347, 348, 350
Walsh, Sally 389
Walsh, Steve 154
Walsh, Thomas M 688
Walter, Andrew T 404
Walter, Elisse 820
Walter, George ''Chip'' 778
Walter, Gregory 748
Walter, Kori 227
Walters, Barry 820
Walters, Jane A 806
Walters, Mary 825
Walters, Richard 796
Walters, Ron 763
Walters, Sandra R 706
Walters, Tom 769

Page

Walther, Michael F 674
Walther, Steven T 789
Walton, James T 638
Walton, Reggie B 861
Walton, Robert 370
Walz, Timothy J 142, 305, 334, 395, 396, 440, 441, 442, 445, 492
Wang, Amelia 35
Wang, Shawn 756
Wang, Theresa 70
Wankel, Marilyn 656
Wanko, Brian 420
Wapner, Robyn 419
Warbrick, Malcolm 507
Warchola, Pamela F 674
Ward, Aaron 75
Ward, Barbara 675
Ward, Diane 720
Ward, James "Jim" 507
Ward, Joseph 625
Ward, Joyce 372
Ward, Kelly 453
Ward, Kristin 612
Ward, Lindsey 377
Ward, Mike 97
Ward, Nancy E 893
Ward, Patrick M 590
Ward, Rich 388
Ward, Richard R 676
Ward, Stephen 176
Warden, Jim 693
Wardlaw, Kim McLane 850
Waring, Greg R 405
Waring, Katherine 444
Warlick, James B., Jr 600
Warlick, Mary Burce 602
Warlow, Mary Ellen 654
Warner, Alison 133
Warner, Kathleen 53
Warner, Mark R 274, 309, 322, 325, 351, 352, 354, 356, 357, 377, 382, 463, 474
Warner, Nancy M 404
Warner, Olivia 508
Warner, Susie 279
Warren, Gail 507
Warren, Jennifer 3
Warren, Kenneth R 734
Warren, Marc 743
Warren, Michael J 840
Warren, Peter 433, 805
Warren, Phillip H 650
Warren, Stephen W 762
Warren, Timothy L 825
Warrington, Karen 224
Warthin, Whit 608
Warwick, Cindy 913
Wascher, William L., III 776
Wash, Michael 802
Washam, Todd 292
Washburn, Julia 680
Washington, Eric T 894, 901
Washington, Essence 588
Washington, Gary 691
Washington, Geovette 703
Washington, Harold L., Jr 706
Washington, Jacqueline 358
Washington, John A 842
Washington, Linda 695
Washington, Marvin 713
Washington, Matt 401
Wasik, Wendy 623
Wasilewski, James 715
Waske, Michael 369
Wasniewski, Mathew 459
Wason, John 404
Wasserman Schultz, Debbie 68, 303, 333, 405, 492
Watada, Bill 749
Watchman-Moore, Derrith R 740
Waterhouse, Ellen 720
Watern, Kathy 625
Waters, Maxine 36, 302, 328, 414, 415, 416, 425, 426, 492
Watkins, Chris 345
Watkins, David 430, 775
Watkins, Kerry Ann 423
Watkins, Laurie 833
Watkins, Rebecca 433
Watkins, Roland 810
Watkins, Stanley 85
Watkins, Timothy C 816
Watkins, Toby 67
Watkins, Tracey 625
Watkins, Yelberton 240
Watkins, Yelberton R 458
Watson, Adrienne 42
Watson, Bradley S 347
Watson, Carole 807
Watson, Gina E 920
Watson, Harlan 436
Watson, Joe 497
Watson, Monique Clendinen 300
Watson, Scott M 651
Watson, Sharon 721
Watson, Vinita 907
Watt, Brad 392
Watt, Melvin L 201, 307, 329, 414, 415, 416, 425, 426, 492
Watters, Robert L., Jr 714
Watts, John 18
Watts, Nikki 83
Watts, Sharon 465
Wauls, Christine Schoppe 506
Wavering, Al 714
Waxman, Henry A 33, 302, 327, 409, 492, 837
Waxman, Jonathan H 724
Way, Kashi 465
Way, Kristi 278
Wayland, Joseph 650
Wayne, Spencer 385
Weakland, Thomas R 738
Weant, Edward 706
Wease, Jeff 433
Weathers, Andrea R 405
Weaver, Angela 208
Weaver, Christina 260
Weaver, David 801
Weaver, Ellen 237
Weaver, Janice 260
Weaver, Janice G 747
Weaver, Jeff 16
Weaver, Jess 683
Weaver, Kiel 430
Weaver, Kyle 16
Weaver, Rachel 373
Webb, Beth Davis 239
Webb, Jim 274, 309, 321, 325, 346, 347, 366, 367, 379, 463, 474
Webb, Laura 5
Webb, Max 822
Webb, Sandra 653
Webber, Paul R., III 896
Weber, Andrew 616
Weber, Dan 124
Weber, Dave 229
Weber, James 732
Weber, John 91
Weber, Josh 902
Weber, Michael F 813
Weber, Michelle 397
Weber, Rene 914
Webster, Bill 796
Webster, Crystal 255
Webster, Daniel 61, 302, 336, 434, 492
Webster, John 696
Webster, Keith 636
Webster, Stephen 825
Webster, Todd 55
Wedding, Timothy 720
Wedge, Ellen 508
Wedgeworth, Robert 808
Weeden, Kathryn 497
Weeden, Kathryn S 389, 509
Weeks, John 608
Weems, Michael 254
Weerasinghe, P. Nandalal 914
Weghorst, Dee 206
Wegner, David 444
Wehde, Anne 748
Weich, Ronald 674
Weichlein, Peter M 501
Weida, Johnny 629
Weide, Mark E. Van Der 775
Weideman, Christian 605
Weideman, Rich 680
Weidemeyer, William M 506
Weidinger, Matt 449

Page

Weil, Nicholas ... 460
Weiler, Edward ... 801
Weinbach, Gretchen C ... 776
Weinbaum, Jamison L ... 900
Weinberg, Daniel ... 705
Weinberg, Martha W ... 807
Weinberg, Shannon M ... 411
Weinberger, Paul ... 818
Weiner, Joel ... 913
Weiner, Robert N ... 649
Weiner, Stuart A ... 509
Weiner, Todd ... 284
Weingart, David ... 743
Weinhagen, Robert ... 461
Weinreich, David ... 140
Weinstein, Jason M ... 654
Weinstein, Kenneth R ... 807
Weintraub, Ellen L ... 789
Weirich, Jeremy ... 344
Weis, Joseph F., Jr ... 849
Weis, Valentina ... 263
Weisberg, Frederick H ... 895
Weisel, Barbara ... 591
Weiser, Dan ... 459
Weiser, Philip J ... 748
Weisman, Jaye ... 732
Weisman, Scott ... 823
Weiss, Daniel ... 23, 408
Weiss, Jeffrey ... 823
Weiss, Jim ... 404
Weiss, Joanne ... 755
Weiss, Katie ... 218
Weiss, Michael ... 588
Weiss, Nancy ... 808
Weissenbach, Karl ... 804
Weitz, William ... 187
Weitzner, Daniel J ... 715
Welch, Creighton ... 62
Welch, Peter ... 272, 309, 334, 395, 396, 397, 431, 432, 492
Welch, Terri ... 198
Welcher, Shelley N ... 578
Weller, James ... 797
Wellinghoff, Jon ... 752
Wells, Alice ... 596
Wells, Ambassador Barry ... 835
Wells, Breon N ... 347, 348
Wells, Denise ... 727
Wells, James D ... 788
Wells, John H ... 694
Wells, Reginald F ... 832
Wells, Thomas ... 897
Wells, Thomas B ... 884
Welsch, Ken S ... 814
Welsh, Joe ... 663
Welsh, Kristin ... 365
Welter, Tim ... 100
Weltere, Beatrice ... 603
Wenberg, Eric ... 693
Wenger, Lauren ... 422
Wensil, Brenda ... 757
Wente, Gary H ... 849
Werkheiser, William ... 683
Werner, Brian ... 146
Werner, Dave ... 644
Werner, Eric R ... 825
Werner, Patrick ... 153
Werner, Sharon ... 225
Werstler, Brian ... 213
Wertheim, Ronald P ... 896
Werwa, Eric ... 27
Wescott, Mark ... 189
Wesley, Richard C ... 849
Wesner, Kate ... 69
Wessel, Michael R ... 500
Wessels, John ... 681
Wessinger, Tim ... 73
Wessler, Susan R ... 810
West, Allen B ... 69, 303, 336, 402, 403, 438, 439, 492
West, Celeste ... 434
West, Ed ... 110
West, J. Robinson ... 837
West, Keith ... 758
West, Mary M ... 776
West, Millicent W ... 900
West, Timothy J ... 683
West, Togo D., Jr ... 901
West, Tony ... 651
Westbrook, Harvey ... 821

Page

Westbrook, Melvin ... 691
Westerfield, Sheila ... 288
Westergren, Mark ... 629
Westerholm, Dave ... 709
Westgate, Barbara ... 630
Westine, Lezlee ... 835
Westmark, Richard ... 720
Westmoreland, Lynn A ... 74, 303, 333, 414, 415, 416, 451, 492
Weston, Jonathan G ... 500
Westphal, Joseph W ... 635
Wetherald, Margaret ... 397
Wetherington, Rusty ... 74
Wetters, Linda ... 805
Wexler, Nu ... 405
Wexler, Robert ... 757
Weyer, Jamie J ... 397
Whalen, Andrew ... 201
Whalen, Laurence J ... 883
Whaley, Dave ... 430
Whaley, Kevin D ... 655
Wharton, John ... 641
Wharton Boyd, Linda ... 897, 899
Whatley, Kim M ... 898
Whatley, Kyle ... 227
Whatley, Michael ... 433
Wheatley, Katherine H ... 777
Wheeland, Daniel ... 734
Wheelbarger, Katie ... 452
Wheeler, Jim ... 783
Wheeler, Joe ... 407
Wheeler, Kevin ... 378
Wheeler, Seth F ... 777
Wheeler, Susan ... 82
Wheeler, Thomas C ... 875
Whelan, Andrew ... 220
Wherry, Robert A., Jr ... 880
Whetstone, Courtney ... 213
Whetstone, James R ... 714
Whipple, Kathie Ann ... 816
Whisenant, Addie ... 417
Whitaker, Cheryl ... 576
Whitaker, Gertrud ... 206
Whitaker, Jacqueline ... 692
White, Alice Patricia ... 776
White, Barry B ... 602
White, Bradford J ... 773
White, Brandi Wilson ... 388
White, Charlotte C ... 791
White, Christa ... 835
White, Clifford J., III ... 663
White, Dave ... 690
White, Helene N ... 849
White, Jacqueline ... 732
White, James K ... 704
White, Jeffrey ... 635
White, Jerry ... 422
White, Joanne ... 413
White, John ... 687, 756
White, Kim M ... 669
White, Marian ... 427
White, Pamela Ann ... 601
White, Ron ... 277
White, Stan ... 224
White, Stephanie ... 694
White, Tricia ... 426
White, Virginia ... 176
White, William P ... 899
White-Olson, BJ ... 646
Whiteaker, Rebekah ... 653
Whitehead, Elizabeth ... 806
Whitehead, Robert E ... 602
Whitehouse, Sheldon ... 235, 308, 321, 325, 354, 361, 362, 368, 374, 375, 382, 474, 496, 806
Whitener, Jeanette ... 261
Whitener, Kelly ... 364
Whitescarver, Jack E ... 733
Whitesell, Sarah ... 787
Whitesell, Steve ... 680
Whiteside, Ruth ... 599
Whitfield, Ed ... 109, 304, 329, 409, 410, 411, 492
Whitfield, Emily ... 105
Whitfield, Leslie E ... 685
Whitfield, Soloman ... 691
Whitford, David ... 705
Whitford, Debra ... 696
Whiting, Sarah ... 99
Whitley, Yolanda ... 708

Page

Whitlock, Kelsey 426
Whitlock, Steve 612
Whitlow, Woodrow, Jr 800
Whitman, Bryan G 617
Whitman, Cameron 775
Whitman, Debra 383
Whitney, Brian 119
Whitney, David 427
Whitney, Jim 463
Whitney, Margaret 375
Whitney, Pam 437
Whitney, Toby 285
Whitson, Andy 508, 644
Whitt, John 298
Whittaker, Larry 436
Whittemore, Megan 456
Wholley, Michael 800
Wiatrowski, William 719
Wiblemo, Cathy 446
Wiblemo, Tom 296
Wichlin, Mark P 718
Wicker, Bill 360
Wicker, Cheron Victoria 747
Wicker, Roger F 148, 305, 321, 325, 346, 347, 351, 352, 356, 357, 379, 474, 494, 496
Wickes, Vincent 819
Wickham, Thomas J 461
Wicks, Anne B 894
Wicks, Joe 137
Wider, Collenne 358
Widner, Mary Frances 508, 575
Wiederkehr, David 823
Wiegmann, Brad 674
Wiehl, Lisa 128
Wieman, Carl 590
Wiener, Jacques L., Jr 849
Wiener, Margaret 787
Wier, Anthony 367, 501
Wiese, Jeffrey 749
Wiese, John Paul 875
Wiesel, Elie 837
Wiesner, Thomas 719
Wieting, Donna 709
Wiggins, Beacher 581
Wiggins, James 813
Wiggins, Leslie 763
Wiggins, Thomas 714
Wight, Tom 677
Wilbur, Tom 412
Wilburn, Curtis 690
Wilcox, David 776
Wilcoxen, Devin 92
Wild, Ken 236
Wilder, Andrew R 838
Wilder, Renee 793
Wilderotter, James A 842
Wileden, Lydia 457
Wiles, Brent 344
Wiley, Curtis A 694
Wiley, Kenya 372
Wilkerson, Patrick 681
Wilkes, Emily 265
Wilkes, Homer 690
Wilkey, Thomas R. "Tom" 836
Wilkins, Paul 158
Wilkins, Robert L 863
Wilkins, William J 612
Wilkinson, J. Harvie, III 849
Wilkinson, Keri 16
Wilkinson, Molly 372
Wilkinson, Monty 649
Will, Candice M 667
Willcutts, Kevin 720
Willemssen, Joel 575
Willens, Todd 177
Willett, Mary 293
Willey, Chris G 815
Willhite, Karissa 168
Williams, Aaron 817
Williams, Abioudun 837
Williams, Ann Claire 849
Williams, Anthony D 657
Williams, Barbara 651
Williams, Bisa 602
Williams, Bob 831
Williams, Brett 5, 629
Williams, Calvin 626
Williams, Carl J 714

Page

Williams, Cary K 777
Williams, Charlene 611
Williams, Cheri 284
Williams, Clifton 211
Williams, Connie 701
Williams, David 905
Williams, David E 840
Williams, Demetriss 814
Williams, Derrick 693
Williams, Ellen C 840
Williams, Elliot 769
Williams, Erica 820
Williams, Floyd 612
Williams, Grayling 765
Williams, Harry 639
Williams, Howard, Jr 576
Williams, Ivy 16
Williams, Jack 773
Williams, James 67
Williams, Jean 660
Williams, Jeremy 901
Williams, Jerry 767
Williams, Jerry E 739
Williams, Jessie 340
Williams, John 357
Williams, John S. "Scott" 713
Williams, Julie L 611, 812
Williams, Karen 58
Williams, Kathleen 802, 803
Williams, Kevin E 630
Williams, Lance 239
Williams, Leevaine, Jr 639
Williams, Lester L., Jr 726
Williams, Lisa 297, 420, 784
Williams, Lisa L 579
Williams, Lynn M 404
Williams, Marcus 676
Williams, Mark 252
Williams, Mary Ellen Coster 874
Williams, Mele 437
Williams, Melvin G., Jr 751
Williams, Michael C 931
Williams, Michael W 642
Williams, Nicole 174
Williams, Pamela 465
Williams, Paul 365
Williams, Reginald 260
Williams, Richard S 800
Williams, Robert 582
Williams, Rosemary J 815
Williams, Scott 706
Williams, Sheenia 626
Williams, Sheri 502
Williams, Sherri 642
Williams, Shimere 437
Williams, Stephen F 854
Williams, Susan 678
Williams, T.C 639
Williams, T.L 641
Williams, Theodore J 631
Williams, Timothy A 671
Williams, Tonya 196, 260
Williams, Tracy 392
Williams-Bennett, Ken 721
Williams-Bridgers, Jacquie 575
Williamson, Irving A 838
Williamson, Samuel P 709
Willingham, Keith 815
Willingham, Kimberly 251
Willis, Arlene 39
Willis, Brandon 691
Willis, Ken 196, 383
Willis, Mary Jo 602
Willis, Susan 506
Willoughby, Jeanne "Patrice" 794
Wills, Jeff 510
Wills, Mary Jo 602
Wills, Randolph 756
Willson, Darrell 808
Wilmerding, John 808
Wilmot, Ron 178
Wilmot, Wayne 710
Wilpon, Jeffrey S 837
Wilson, Alex 129
Wilson, Andrew 463
Wilson, Angela 712
Wilson, Beth Anne 776
Wilson, Caroline 643

Page

Wilson, Charles 73
Wilson, Charles R 850
Wilson, Chris 591
Wilson, Dale F 722
Wilson, Deanna 763
Wilson, Dennis 423
Wilson, Douglas B 617
Wilson, Elaine 92
Wilson, Emily 283
Wilson, Frank 618
Wilson, Frederica S 66, 303, 336, 418, 435, 436, 492
Wilson, Gavin 935
Wilson, India 701
Wilson, Janet L 884
Wilson, Joe 238, 308, 331, 402, 403, 404, 406, 407, 418, 419, 492, 499
Wilson, John E 913
Wilson, Kathleen 501
Wilson, Keith M 763
Wilson, Kim 605
Wilson, Michael N 629
Wilson, Patrick O 642
Wilson, Peter 714
Wilson, Richard 462
Wilson, Rick 98
Wilson, Scott 375, 611, 818
Wilson, Sharon 509
Wilson, Sharon A 832
Wilson, Steve 174
Wilson, Susan 708
Wiltshire, Albert 184
Wilusz, Lisa 686
Wimbush, S. Enders 778
Wimer, Andrew 232
Win, Kimball 390
Wingo, Walter 578
Wine, Bradley D 837
Winfield, Susan R 896
Winfree, Gregory 750
Wingfield, Dee 644
Wingo, Elizabeth Carroll 896
Wingo, Latrice 509
Winik, Jay 807
Winkler, Kate 183
Winkler, Kevin 790
Winkler, Pete 808
Winkler, Peter 226
Winkowski, Tom S 769
Winnett, Rebecca 388
Winokur, Peter S 780
Winship, Chris 608
Winstead, Lillian 718
Winstead, Valencia 686
Winter, M. Celia 821
Winter, Ralph K 849
Winter, Theodore 819
Winters, Shanna A 420
Winterton, Cindy 633
Wirkus, Karl 683
Wirth, Erin M 792
Wisdom, Karin 105
Wise, Allison 783
Wise, Daryl X 833
Wise, James 158
Wise, Stephen A 714
Wisecarver, Charlie 599
Wisecup, James P 643
Wish, Judith 662
Wisner, Peter 608
Wisniewski, Lorel 714
Wissel, Lupe 379
Wissler, J.E 648
Withers, Claudia 783
Witherspoon, Harvey 777
Withycombe, William C 744
Witkin, Maxanne R 761
Witt, Allison 208
Witt, Kristeen 465
Witt, Timothy 693
Witte, Eric 102
Witter, Michael 749
Wittes, Tamara 597
Wittman, Robert J 275, 309, 334, 402, 403, 428, 429, 492, 494, 500
Wixson, Jessica 283
Wodatch, John 652
Wofford, Carrie 369
Wofsy, Noah 461
Wohlers, Laurence D 600
Wohlers, Paul D 595
Wojeciechowski, Adrienne 375
Wolanin, Barbara 505
Wold, Edward 632
Wolf, Adam 455
Wolf, Carrie E 461
Wolf, Frank R 279, 309, 327, 398, 400, 492
Wolf, Ian 70
Wolf, Kevin 706
Wolf, Michael 790
Wolf, Peter H 896
Wolf, Sarah 228
Wolfe, Catherine O'Hagan 849
Wolfe, Hershel "Hew" 636
Wolfe, Phyllis 733
Wolfe, Shane 422
Wolfensohn, James D 799
Wolfersberger, M. Trent 505
Wolff, Alexandro Daniel 600
Wolff, Barbara 693
Wolff, Karen Lias 806
Wolff, Richard A 893
Wolfgang, Donna 460
Wolford, Judi 175
Wolfteich, Paul 607
Wolgast, Anna 781
Wolin, Neal S 605
Wollman, Raymond J 774
Wollman, Roger L 850
Wolman, Lauren 32
Woloshen, Amanda 172
Wolski, Lisa 388
Wolski, Victor John 874
Wolslayer, Kelly 609
Womack, Gerald 260
Womack, Steve 15, 301, 336, 398, 399, 400, 492
Womack, Todd 244
Wong, Bryson 429
Wong, Cindy S 825
Wong, Jetta 437
Wong, John 787
Wong, Norman 662
Woo, Edwin 728
Wood, Amanda 372
Wood, Bill 506
Wood, Deborah 503
Wood, Diane P 849
Wood, Gary 755
Wood, Jim 125
Wood, Jon 497
Wood, Salley 424
Wood, Tony 756
Woodall, George 355
Woodall, Rob 76, 303, 336, 405, 434, 492
Woodcock, Carol 119
Woodcock, David 825
Woodcock, Janet 732
Wooden, Michael 692
Woodle, Sherri 655
Woodrow, Jean M 412
Woodrum, Jeremy 183
Woods, Bronson E 260
Woods, Clint 437
Woods, Michele J 582
Woods, R 643
Woods, Ranae 625
Woods, Taylor 358
Woods, Tim 625
Woods, Tonya 700
Woodson, Jonathan 616, 618
Woodson, Mary Ann 805
Woodward, Gary 79
Woodward, Joseph M 725
Woody, William 680
Woolf, Aaron 373
Woolfork, Brent 420
Woolley, Leslie 155
Woolsey, Lynn C 22, 302, 329, 406, 407, 435, 492
Wooten, Todd 340
Wooters, C.R 126
Word, Geri 708
Worden, Chris 99
Worden, Simon P 801
Work, Robert O 643
Worley, Cheyne 107
Worley, Robert 630
Woronka, Ted 682

Page

Worth, Brian 456
Wortham, Micah 340
Worthen, Maria 369
Worthen, Norm 630
Worthington, Jon C 752
Wortman, C.F 648
Wortzel, Larry M 500
Woteki, Kathy 698
Wouters, Alexandra 174
Wrase, Jeff 365
Wrasse, Ryan 386
Wrathall, James 362
Wray, Robert 646
Wrazen, David 625
Wright, Alison J 393
Wright, Ann 699
Wright, Anna Bartlett 416
Wright, B.G 401
Wright, Bill 373
Wright, Candice 373
Wright, De'Shawn 897
Wright, Donald 729
Wright, Frederick 639
Wright, Garland P., Jr 620
Wright, Jayne 627
Wright, Jeff 753
Wright, Jessica 593
Wright, Judy 498
Wright, Kimberly 763
Wright, Melvin R 895
Wright, Mina 805
Wright, Niel 293
Wright, Paula 674
Wright, Sangina 436
Wright, Stephen J 752
Wright, Steven 628
Wright, Stuart 729
Wright, Tommy 706
Wright, Woody 770
Wrobel, William 802
Wroblewski, Jonathan 654
Wroblewski, Jonathan J 841
Wu, Deng 579
Wu, Jenny 653
Wunning, Steven H 774
Wurster, Robert T 815
Wyant, Christopher 842
Wyatt, Arthur 654
Wyatt, Harry M 633
Wyatt, Harry M., III 640
Wyatt, Nick 365
Wyatt, Thomas 787
Wyche, Larry 641
Wyden, Ron 219, 307, 323, 324, 354, 359, 360, 363, 364, 382, 383, 474
Wyeth, Natalie 610
Wylie, Maureen 709
Wymer, Michele 345
Wymer, Steve 161
Wynn, Elaine 799
Wynn, James A., Jr 849
Wynn, Patricia A 896
Wynn, Renee 782
Wyss, John 700

Y

Yabraian, Francesca 685
Yachmetz, Mark E 746
Yadav, Sandeep 465
Yaffe, Deborah M.P 809
Yaki, Michael 835
Yakusha, Yuriy G 915
Yamada, Debbie 122
Yamamoto, Donald 596
Yamazaki, Jun 925
Yambaye, Ngueto Tiraina 914
Yang, Shaolin 934
Yang, Tseming 782
Yanussi, Jason 372
Yarmuth, John A 111, 304, 334, 405, 413, 431, 432, 492
Yates, Earl 818
Yates, Jarod 16
Yates, Perry 401
Yaver, Yasmin 742
Ybarra, Uriel 281
Yea, Annie 42
Yeager, Michael 769

Page

Yeboah, Michelle 732
Yee, Britton 372
Yeldell, Scott 263
Yeldell, Spencer 263
Yelisetty, Raj 776
Yellen, Janet L 775
Yergin, Alex 412
Yerxa, Christopher 717
Yeskey, Kevin 728
Yezak, Jennifer 688
Yglesias, Tara 797
Yi, Charles 352
Yi, Charles C 609
Yi, Joanne 377
Yi, Sang 433
Yingst, Bambi 130
Yock, Robert J 876
Yoder, Kevin 107, 304, 337, 398, 399, 400, 492
Yoder, Ronnie A 741
Yoghourtdjian, Sarkis D 775
Yoken, Dan 384
Yolles, Herbert 806
Yonis, Mohamed 930
Yonkers, Terry A 626
Yonkman, Dave 137
Yonkura, Ray 207
York, Andy 14
York, Scott 826
Yost, Admiral Paul A., Jr 798
Youel-Page, Kevin 610
Young, Allison 700
Young, Brady 461
Young, C. W. Bill 62, 302, 327, 398, 399, 400, 492
Young, Cassandra 155
Young, Charles "Chuck" 576
Young, Dannie E 578
Young, David 101
Young, David J 599
Young, Deborah B 805
Young, Don 7, 301, 327, 428, 429, 440, 441, 442, 443, 492
Young, Ellen 231
Young, Fernanda 784
Young, Jacqueline A 809
Young, Jared 215
Young, Joby 76
Young, John 449
Young, Jonathan 805
Young, Joseph E 676
Young, June 793
Young, Karen 711
Young, L. Benjamin, Jr 688
Young, Max 383
Young, Michael G 793
Young, Michael L 686
Young, Myra 700
Young, Patricia Klein 789
Young, Patricia M 629
Young, Robert 510
Young, Sarah 401
Young, Shalanda 401
Young, Sheree 577
Young, Sherry 401
Young, Stephen M 601
Young, Todd 429
Young, Todd C 100, 303, 337, 402, 403, 405, 492
Young, Torlanda 814
Young, Troy 143
Young-Holmes, Pamela 805
Youngberg, Francey 737
Younge, Nathan 842
Yount, Dean 629
Youson, Washington, Jr 140
Yovanovitch, Marie L 600
Yozell, Sally 709
Yuan, Georgia 757
Yuan, Sharon 608
Yucel, Irem 711
Yudin, Michael 757
Yudof, Judith 837
Yumkella, Kandeh 929
Yun, Joseph Y 597
Yun, Thomas W 599
Yurgin, Tara 142
Yuskavage, Robert 704, 705
Yusuf, Abdulqawi Ahmed 924
Yuzyk, Ted 913
Yzaguirre, Raul 601

Z — Page

Zabarsky, Mark 742
Zabelsky, Thomas, Jr 706
Zabko, John 768
Zaccaro, Ray 37, 43
Zach, Andy 437
Zackon, Matt 456
Zader, Joshua 460
Zadrozny, John 433
Zaffirini, Tony 721
Zahner, Richard 638
Zahran, Nadia 433
Zaiser, William W 641
Zajdel-Kurowska, Katarzyna 914
Zak, Leocadia I 842
Zakarka, Christine 700
Zakheim, Roger 404
Zakrajsek, Egon 776
Zakula, Linden 142
Zakzeski, Corrine 163
Zaman, Nida 99
Zamore, Michael 219
Zampella, Al 173
Zamrzia, Mike 106
Zander, Steve 626
Zangardi, John 646
Zapata, Jaime 723
Zapata, Jian 446
Zarate, Bridget 343, 344
Zarco, Alvaro 340
Zarif, Farid 931
Zarodkiewicz, Patricia J 625
Zartneske, Robert 796
Zawodny, Kenneth, Jr 816
Zaykowski, Walter 370
Zea, Tracy 443
Zeck, Van 607
Zed, Jordon 922
Zehner, Michael W 631
Zehren, Christopher 686
Zeidman, Fred S 837
Zeigler, Chris 211
Zeiler, Linda 722
Zeldon, Joan 895
Zelinsky, Yuri 823
Zembik, Josh 52
Zemple, Patricia C 814
Zeng, Maile 387
Zens, Karen 707
Zerihoun, Taye-Brook 925

Page

Zerrougui, Leila 929
Zevenbergen, Mike 661
Zezima, Debra A 792
Zhao, Gang 908
Zheng, Denise 372
Zhou, Hai Yan 908
Zhou, Ming Yuan 588
Zhu, Min 913
Ziaya, David 738
Zichal, Heather R 592
Zickler, Joyce K 776
Ziebarth, Elizabeth 828
Zielinski, Bill 833
Zients, Jeffrey 590
Zimmer, Robert J 811
Zimmerman, Ari 69
Zimmerman, David 701
Zimmerman, Elizabeth 768
Zimmerman, Roy 813
Zimmerman, Stefani 10
Zimmerman, Thomas 632
Zimmermann, Anne 690
Zinkham, Helena 581
Zinser, Todd J 704
Zirkin, Nancy 837
Zirkin, Stanley R 809
Zobeck, Terry W 590
Zoellick, Robert 932, 935
Zoellick, Robert B 929
Zogby, Joseph 376
Zoia, Jim 443
Zoks, Gita 712
Zoller, Virginia 641
Zorc, Beth 352
Zorfas, Ethan 167
Zorn, Richard 790
Zou, Ciyong 934
Zuber, Matthew 633
Zubrensky, Michael 674
Zubricki, Jeff 357
Zuckerman, Mark 592
Zuckman, Jill 743
Zufolo, Jessica 694
Zulauf, Barry 656
Zulkosky, Ann 358
Zupancic, Nicholas 48
Zvenyach, David 897
Zweig, Matthew 419
Zwick, Kenneth L 652
Zyblikewycz, Helena 444